1001   02 262917   01 S   (IC-2
                              08/08/8
CONTEMPORARY AUTHOR\ SERIES 1
(0) 1984 . R 928

Contemporary Authors
NEW REVISION SERIES

Contemporary Authors

A Bio-Bibliographical Guide to
Current Writers in Fiction, General Nonfiction,
Poetry, Journalism, Drama, Motion Pictures,
Television, and Other Fields

LINDA METZGER
Editor

PETER M. GAREFFA
DEBORAH A. STRAUB
Associate Editors

NEW REVISION SERIES
volume **12**

GALE RESEARCH COMPANY • BOOK TOWER • DETROIT, MICHIGAN 48226

EDITORIAL STAFF

Linda Metzger, *Editor, New Revision Series*

Peter M. Gareffa and Deborah A. Straub, *Associate Editors*

James G. Lesniak, Donna Olendorf, and Thomas Wiloch, *Senior Assistant Editors*

Candace Cloutier, Nancy Hebb, Kerry L. Lutz, Margaret Mazurkiewicz, Susan Salter, Heidi A. Tietjen, Michaela Swart Wilson, and Robert T. Wilson, *Assistant Editors*

Jean W. Ross, *Interviewer*

Melissa J. Gaiownik, Timothy Marshall, and Mary Alice Rattenbury, *Editorial Assistants*

Marian Walters, *Contributing Editor*

Frederick G. Ruffner, *Publisher*
James M. Ethridge, *Executive Vice President/Editorial*
Dedria Bryfonski, *Editorial Director*
Christine Nasso, *Director, Literature Division*
Ann Evory, *Senior Editor, Contemporary Authors*

Copyright © 1963, 1964, 1965, 1966, 1967, 1968, 1969, 1970, 1971, 1972, 1973, 1974, 1975, 1976, 1977, 1978, 1979, 1980, 1981, 1982, 1984 by
GALE RESEARCH COMPANY

Library of Congress Catalog Card Number 81-640179
ISBN 0-8103-1941-1
ISSN 0275-7176

No part of this book may be reproduced in any form without permission in writing from the publisher, except by a reviewer who wishes to quote brief passages or entries in connection with a review written for inclusion in a magazine or newspaper. Manufactured in the United States of America.

Contents

Authors and Media People
Featured in This Volume 7

Preface 9

Volume Update Chart 13

Author Listings 15

Authors and Media People
Featured in This Volume

Vassily Aksyonov—Russian novelist, playwright, and short story writer who immigrated to the United States in 1980; his unconventional novels and plays, many of which delve into the grotesque and the fantastic, have been praised for their innovative style and political daring; among his books translated into English are *A Ticket to the Stars, The Steel Bird, and Other Stories, The Island of Crimea,* and *The Burn.*

Lisa Alther—American novelist; *Kinflicks,* her bestselling first novel, was often compared favorably to J. D. Salinger's *Catcher in the Rye;* her second novel, *Original Sins,* has been praised for its intelligence, style, and characterizations.

Jonathan Baumbach—American professor, playwright, novelist, and short story writer; considered experimental, his novels often employ unusual narrative structures and examine the relationship between the imagination, dreams, and external reality; among his works are the play "The One-Eyed Man Is King" and the novels *A Man to Conjure With, Reruns,* and *Chez Charlotte and Emily.* (Sketch includes interview.)

Peter Benchley—Popular American novelist and screenwriter; best known for his suspense novels about the sea, notably *Jaws, The Deep, The Island,* and *The Girl of the Sea of Cortez;* also author of screenplays based on his novels; an entry for his father, Nathaniel Benchley, also appears in this volume.

Marylin Bender—American journalist and author of nonfiction books, many of which chronicle the world of the wealthy and the powerful; her works include *The Beautiful People* (a view of the fashion industry), *At the Top* (a study of American corporate leaders), and *The Chosen Instrument* (a history of Pan American World Airways).

Gregory Benford—American physicist and science fiction writer; highly regarded in the scientific community for his research on the dynamics of pulsars, violent extragalactic events, and quasars; his 1980 novel *Timescape* won the Nebula Award, British Science Fiction Association award, John W. Campbell Award, and Dilmar Award for International Novel; among his other novels are *In the Ocean of Night, Against Infinity,* and *The Sea of Suns.*

Alfred Bester—American magazine editor, science fiction writer, and author of nonfiction; described as a "science-fiction writer's writer" by Peter Nicholls in *Washington Post Book World;* two of Bester's novels are recognized as science fiction classics—*The Demolished Man,* which was the first novel to win the Hugo Award, and *The Stars My Destination.*

Erma Bombeck—American humorist, columnist, and lecturer; in her widely syndicated column, "At Wit's End," she satirizes the domestic crises of the average American household; among her books are *The Grass Is Always Greener over the Septic Tank, If Life Is a Bowl of Cherries, What Am I Doing in the Pits?,* and *Motherhood: The Second Oldest Profession.* (Sketch includes interview.)

Heywood Hale Broun—American sportswriter, columnist, actor, and television critic and broadcaster; his books include the autobiographical *Whose Little Boy Are You?,* which recounts the unconventional upbringing he received from his celebrated parents, journalists Heywood Campbell Broun and Ruth Hale.

Angela Carter—British novelist, short story writer, and author of nonfiction; Gothic themes, violence, and an undercurrent of eroticism run throughout her fiction; among her books are the novels *The Magic Toyshop, Love,* and *The Passion of New Eve* and the widely reviewed nonfiction work *The Sadeian Women and the Ideology of Pornography.*

Julio Cortazar—Belgian-born Argentinian novelist, short story writer, poet, and translator who died in 1984; a constant experimenter in his writing, he strove to startle the reader out of a complacent acceptance of traditional modes of thinking; his fictional works translated into English include the novels *Hopscotch,* described in *Times Literary Supplement* as "the first great novel of Spanish America," *Cronopios and Famas,* and *A Manual for Manuel,* as well as the short story collection *Blow-Up, and Other Stories.*

John Coyne—American author of popular horror novels, notably *The Piercing, Hobgoblin,* and *The Shroud;* also author of books on such diverse topics as crafts methods of the Penland School, golf techniques, and alternatives to attending college. (Sketch includes interview.)

Umberto Eco—Italian scholar specializing in semiotics, the study of how cultures communicate through signs, and author of the bestselling novel *The Name of the Rose;* a complex, philosophical murder mystery set in a medieval monastery, this novel has been translated into more than twenty languages, won several of Europe's most prestigious literary awards, and sold more than a million copies.

David Edgar—Prolific British playwright and scriptwriter; his play "The Life and Adventures of Nicholas Nickleby," based on Charles Dickens's novel of the same title, won a 1982 Tony Award and New York Drama Critics Circle Award and set records for its eight-and-one-half hour length; his other plays include "The Jail Diary of Albie Sachs," "Mary Barnes," and "Maydays."

Marian Engel—Canadian novelist, children's author, and short story writer; many of her protagonists are "more-than-ordinarily sensitive women," according to Joyce Carol Oates in *Canadian Forum;* among Engel's novels are *Bear,* which won the Governor General's Award, *The Glassy Sea,* and *Lunatic Villas.* (Sketch includes interview.)

Nora Ephron—American journalist, novelist, and co-author of the screenplay "Silkwood"; known for her thinly disguised autobiographical writing, she chronicles the breakup of her marriage to Watergate reporter Carl Bernstein in her bestselling novel, *Heartburn;* an entry for her sister, Delia Ephron, also appears in this volume.

R. Buckminster Fuller—American inventor, architect, engineer, philosopher, environmentalist, lecturer, and writer who died in 1983; best known for inventing the geodesic dome and coining the term "Spaceship Earth," he advocated the use of science and technology to improve human life; among his many books are *Synergetics, Critical Path,* and *Grunch of Giants.*

Haynes Bonner Johnson—American journalist, currently a columnist for the *Washington Post;* winner of a 1966 Pulitzer Prize for his coverage of the Selma, Alabama, civil rights demonstrations; author of books on national affairs, including *The Bay of Pigs, The Fall of a President,* and *In the Absence of Power.*

R. A. Lafferty—American author of science fiction, historical novels, and short stories; his nontraditional works combine a comic exuberance with a concern for the struggle between good and evil approached from a Roman Catholic perspective; *Past Master, Fourth Mansions,* and *The Devil Is Dead* were all nominated for Nebula Awards, and *Past Master* was nominated for a Hugo Award, an award Lafferty won for the short story "Eurema's Dam."

Elmore Leonard—Popular American novelist and screenwriter; his action-packed, suspenseful novels include *The Bounty Hunter, Hombre, City Primeval,* and *Stick;* also author of screenplays, many based on his own novels, including "Mr. Majestyk" and "La Brava."

Judith Martin—American journalist, columnist, social critic, and novelist; best known for her syndicated etiquette column, "Miss Manners," in which she combines humor and common sense; among her books are *Miss Manners' Guide to Excrutiatingly Correct Behavior, Miss Manners' Guide to Rearing Perfect Children,* and the satirical novel *Gilbert.* (Sketch includes interview.)

Marshall McLuhan—Canadian communications theorist and critic who died in 1980; his aphorism "the medium is the message" summarizes his belief that society is shaped more by the nature of the media than by the message being conveyed; author of numerous books, notably *The Gutenberg Galaxy,* which won a Governor General's Award, and *Understanding Media.* (Sketch includes interview with Donald F. Theall, McLuhan's former student.)

Julia O'Faolain—British-born author of histories, novels, and short stories, many set in Ireland or dealing with Irish themes; her novels include *Three Lovers, Women in the Wall,* and *No Country for Young Men;* an entry for her husband, Lauro Martines, also appears in this volume.

Sean O'Faolain—Irish author of novels, short stories, and nonfiction; once closely identified with the Irish Republican cause, O'Faolain chronicles in his novels and short stories modern Ireland's troubled history; among his fictional works are the novels *A Nest of Simple Folk, Bird Alone,* and *And Again?,* as well as the short story collections *Midsummer Night Madness and Other Stories* and *The Heat of the Sun.*

David Plante—American teacher, novelist, and author of nonfiction who has lived in England since 1966; his early, experimental novels force the reader to focus on the inner lives of the protagonists; his widely reviewed trilogy—*The Family, The Woods,* and *The Country*—relates the history of a large, working-class Roman Catholic family; also author of the nonfictional *Difficult Women.* (Sketch includes interview.)

Anne Rice—American novelist whose work concentrates on the problems of societal outcasts; author of *The Feast of All Saints, Cry to Heaven,* and the bestselling *Interview with the Vampire,* an innovative, revisionist treatment of the vampire legend.

Jonathan Schell—American nonfiction writer and contributing editor to *New Yorker;* his *The Fate of the Earth,* which graphically examines the consequences of nuclear war, won the *Los Angeles Times* Book Prize and was nominated for a National Book Critics Circle Award; his other writing includes *The Village of Ben Suc, The Military Half,* and *The Time of Illusion.*

Susan Sheehan—Austrian-born American journalist; her account of a schizophrenic woman, *Is There No Place on Earth for Me?,* received a 1982 Pulitzer Prize and was nominated for a 1983 American Book Award; also author of *A Welfare Mother* and *A Prison and a Prisoner.*

Charles Simic—Yugoslavian-born poet, translator, and professor; his poetry, which draws heavily on European folklore, employs a simple style and focuses on common objects; his poetry collections include *Dismantling the Silence, Classic Ballroom Dances,* and *Austerities.*

Muriel Spark—Scottish-born novelist, poet, short story writer, playwright, and critic who resides in Italy; highly respected for her acerbic wit, concise characterizations, and economical prose; among her novels, which have been called modern morality tales told from a Roman Catholic outlook, are *The Comforters, The Prime of Miss Jean Brodie, The Abbess of Crewe,* and *Loitering with Intent.* (Sketch includes interview.)

Whitley Strieber—American writer best known for his horror novels *The Wolfen* and *The Hunger,* both of which were made into popular films; also co-author of the 1984 book *Warday,* which deals with the subject of nuclear war. (Sketch includes interview.)

Richard Valeriani—American television journalist, currently a correspondent with the National Broadcasting Company; his book *Travels with Henry* chronicles the more than one-half million miles he and other journalists logged accompanying former Secretary of State Henry Kissinger on diplomatic missions.

Theodore Ziolkowski—American professor and literary critic; nominated for a National Book Award and recipient of the James Russell Lowell Prize in Criticism for his book *Fictional Transfigurations of Jesus,* which traces the development of Christ as a "mythic figure" and "culture hero" in a wide range of nineteenth- and twentieth-century novels.

Preface

The *Contemporary Authors New Revision Series* provides completely updated information on authors listed in earlier volumes of *Contemporary Authors* (*CA*). Entries for active individual authors from *any* volume of *CA* may be included in a volume of the *New Revision Series*. The sketches appearing in *New Revision Series* Volume 12, for example, were selected from more than ten previously published *CA* volumes.

As always, the most recent *Contemporary Authors* cumulative index continues to be the user's guide to the location of an individual author's listing.

Compilation Methods

The editors make every effort to secure information directly from the authors. Copies of all sketches in selected *CA* volumes published several years ago are routinely sent to the authors at their last-known addresses. Authors mark material to be deleted or changed and insert any new personal data, new affiliations, new writings, new work in progress, new sidelights, and new biographical/critical sources. All author returns are assessed, more comprehensive research is done, if necessary, and those sketches requiring significant change are completely updated and published in the *New Revision Series*.

If, however, authors fail to reply, or if authors are now deceased, biographical dictionaries are checked for new information (a task made easier through the use of Gale's *Biography and Genealogy Master Index* and other volumes in the "Gale Biographical Index Series"), as are bibliographical sources such as *Cumulative Book Index* and *The National Union Catalog*. Using data from such sources, revision editors select and revise nonrespondents' entries that need substantial updating. Sketches not personally reviewed by the authors are marked with a dagger (†) to indicate that these listings have been revised from secondary sources believed to be reliable, but they have not been personally reviewed for this edition by the authors sketched.

In addition, reviews and articles in major periodicals, lists of prestigious awards, and, particularly, requests from *CA* users are monitored so that authors on whom new information is in demand can be identified and revised listings prepared promptly.

Comprehensive Revision

All listings in this volume have been revised and/or augmented in various ways, though the amount and type of change vary with the author. In many instances, sketches are totally rewritten, and the resulting *New Revision Series* entries are often considerably longer than the authors' previous listings. Revised entries include additions of or changes in such information as degrees, mailing addresses, literary agents, career items, career-related and civic activities, memberships, work in progress, and biographical/critical sources. They may also include the following:

1) Major new awards—Gregory Benford, David Edgar, and Susan Sheehan are only three of the numerous award-winning authors with updated entries in this volume. Physicist and science fiction novelist Gregory Benford described himself to *CA* as "a resolutely amateur writer, preferring to follow my own interests rather than try to produce fiction for a living. And anyway, I'm a scientist by first choice and shall remain so." Yet to the revised entry for this "amateur writer," associate editor Peter M. Gareffa has added the Nebula Award, British Science Fiction Association award, and John W. Campbell Award, all for Benford's 1980 novel *Timescape*. In the updated entry for playwright David Edgar, assistant editor Susan Salter cites the Tony Award and New York Drama Critics Circle Award his "The Life and Adventures of Nicholas Nickleby" received in 1982 as well as the 1983 Emmy Award nomination granted the play's television adaptation, which was also written by Edgar. And nonfiction writer Susan Sheehan's revised sketch, prepared by assistant editor Heidi A. Tietjen, records the 1983 American Book Award nomination and 1982 Pulitzer Prize *Is There No Place on Earth for Me?* garnered.

2) Extensive bibliographical additions—Free-lance writer Mel Marshall, whose works include general nonfiction, Western and mystery novels, and cookbooks, has sixteen new titles and two additional pseudonyms listed in his updated sketch. Assistant editor Nancy Hebb relays Marshall's comments to *CA:* "The suggestion of some of my contemporaries that I'm either a syndicate or a book packager, with a lot of work by others published under my name or my pseudonyms is not true. While still in my teens,...I learned to write fast and use the correct words the first time; the habit still persists." Other prolific authors with updated entries in this volume include British mystery novelist Kenneth Royce Gandley, whose revised entry records twenty-three books not in his previous *CA* entry, and juvenile and young adult author Marjorie Weinman Sharmat, whose writings section has been augmented to include the forty-seven books she has written since her sketch last appeared in *CA*.

3) Informative new sidelights—Numerous *CA* sketches contain sidelights, which provide personal dimensions to the listings, supply information about the critical reception the authors' works have received, or both. For example, in sidelights for Russian novelist and short story writer Vassily Aksyonov, associate editor Deborah A. Straub discusses the years of harassment and censorship Aksyonov experienced in his native Soviet Union. Finally labelled a "parasite" by the Soviet government and therefore unable to get his writing published in his own country, he came to the United States in 1980 where he continues to be a productive writer, unlike some other expatriate authors who find themselves unable to write away from the sounds and sights of their native countries. Maintaining a hope for the future of Russian literature, Aksyonov told Michiko Kakutani in a *New York Times* interview: "There are many talented people inside Russia, and despite all the restrictions, this will never be emptied—from under the pavement, there is always green grass rising. Maybe some day I will be allowed to come back to see it."

"No one expected *The Name of the Rose* to become an internationally acclaimed bestseller, least of all Umberto Eco," senior assistant editor Donna Olendorf writes in sidelights about the Italian scholar. Nonetheless, Eco's complex, philosophical murder mystery, set in a fourteenth-century monastery, has sold over a million copies and has been translated into more than twenty languages. Acknowledging the influence that the kidnapping and murder of former Italian premier Aldo Moro had on *The Name of the Rose,* Eco wants people who read the work to see the parallels that exist between medieval and modern times. "I hope readers see the roots, that everything that existed then—from banks and the inflationary spiral to the burning of libraries—exists today," Eco says in the *New York Times Book Review*. "In the nuclear age, we are never far from the Dark Ages."

Called "a writer's writer" by *Harper's* critic James Wolcott, novelist David Plante firmly established his literary reputation with *The Family, The Woods,* and *The Country,* a trilogy that has been praised for its originality, naturalistic realism, and economical language. As assistant editor Candace Cloutier explains in sidelights, Plante's experimentation in earlier novels—the frequent use of deliberately vague details of characterization and setting that force readers to focus on the protagonists' inner, emotional lives—was helpful to him when writing his trilogy. "I always wanted to write [the trilogy]," Plante comments in *Publishers Weekly,* "and in a way all my earlier work was an attempt to prepare myself for it, trying to learn a craft."

These sketches, as well as others with sidelights compiled by *CA*'s editors, provide informative and enjoyable reading.

Writers of Special Interest

CA's editors make every effort to include in each *New Revision Series* volume a substantial number of revised entries on active authors and media people of special interest to *CA*'s readers. Since the *New Revision Series* also includes sketches on noteworthy deceased writers, a significant amount of work on the part of *CA*'s editors goes into the revision of entries on important deceased authors. Some of the prominent writers, both living and deceased, whose sketches are contained in this volume are noted in the list on page 7 headed "Authors and Media People Featured in This Volume."

Exclusive Interviews

CA provides exclusive, primary information on certain authors in the form of interviews. Prepared specifically for *CA,* the never-before-published conversations presented in the section of the sketch headed *CA INTERVIEW* give *CA* users the opportunity to learn the authors' thoughts, in depth, about their craft. Subjects chosen for interviews are, the editors feel, authors who hold special interest for *CA*'s readers.

Authors and journalists in this volume whose sketches include interviews are Jonathan Baumbach, Erma Bombeck, John Coyne, Marian Engel, Judith Martin, Marshall McLuhan, David Plante, Muriel Spark, and Whitley Strieber.

CA Numbering System

Occasionally questions arise about the *CA* numbering system. Despite numbers like "97-100" and "110," the entire *CA* series consists of only 49 physical volumes with the publication of *CA New Revision Series* Volume 12 in June, 1984. The following information notes changes in the numbering system, as well as in cover design, to help *CA* users better understand the organization of the entire *CA* series.

***CA* First Revisions**	• 1-4R through 41-44R (11 books) *Cover:* Brown with black and gold trim. There will be no further *First Revisions* because revised entries are now being handled exclusively through the more efficient *New Revision Series* mentioned below.
***CA* Original Volumes**	• 45-48 through 97-100 (14 books) *Cover:* Brown with black and gold trim. • 101 through 110 (10 books) *Cover:* Blue and black with orange bands. The same as previous *CA* original volumes but with a new, simplified numbering system and new cover design.
***CA* New Revision Series**	• *CANR*-1 through *CANR*-12 (12 books) *Cover:* Blue and black with green bands. Includes only sketches requiring extensive change; **sketches are taken from any previously published *CA* volume.**
***CA* Permanent Series**	• *CAP*-1 and *CAP*-2 (2 books) *Cover:* Brown with red and gold trim. There will be no further *Permanent Series* volumes because revised entries are now being handled exclusively through the more efficient *New Revision Series* mentioned above.

Retaining *CA* Volumes

As new volumes in the series are published, users often ask which *CA* volumes, if any, can be discarded. The Volume Update Chart on page 13 is designed to assist users in keeping their collections as complete as possible. All volumes in the left column of the chart should be retained to have the most complete, up-to-date coverage possible; volumes in the right column can be discarded if the appropriate replacements are held.

Cumulative Index Should Always Be Consulted

The key to locating an individual author's listing is the *CA* cumulative index bound into the back of alternate original volumes (and available separately as an offprint). Since the *CA* cumulative index provides access to *all* entries in the *CA* series, the latest cumulative index should always be consulted to find the specific volume containing an author's original or most recently revised sketch.

Those authors whose entries appear in the *New Revision Series* are listed in the *CA* cumulative index with the designation **CANR-** in front of the specific volume number. For the convenience of those who do not have *New Revision Series* volumes, the cumulative index also notes the specific earlier volumes of *CA* in which the sketch appeared. Below is a sample index citation for an author whose revised sketch appears in a *New Revision Series* volume.

>   Vonnegut, Kurt, Jr. 1922- CANR-1
>   Earlier sketch in CA 3R
>   See also CLC 1, 2, 3, 4, 5, 8, 12, 22
>   See also AITN 1

For the most recent information on Vonnegut, users should refer to Volume 1 of the *New Revision Series,* as designated by "CANR-1"; if that volume is unavailable, refer to *CA* 1-4 First Revision, as indicated by "Earlier sketch in CA 3R," for his 1968 listing. (And if *CA* 1-4 First Revision is unavailable, refer to *CA* 3, published in 1963, for Vonnegut's original listing.)

Sketches not eligible for inclusion in a *New Revision Series* volume because the author or a revision editor has verified that no significant change is required will, of course, be available in previously published *CA* volumes. Users should always consult the most recent *CA* cumulative index to determine the location of these authors' entries.

For the convenience of *CA* users, the *CA* cumulative index also includes references to all entries in three related Gale series—*Something About the Author* (*SATA*), a series of heavily illustrated sketches on juvenile and young adult authors and illustrators from all eras, *Contemporary Literary Criticism* (*CLC*), which presents lengthy excerpts from current criticism of today's novelists, poets, playwrights, short story writers, filmmakers, scriptwriters, and other creative writers, and *Authors in the News* (*AITN*), a compilation of news stories and feature articles from American periodicals covering writers and other members of the communications media.

As always, suggestions from users about any aspect of *CA* will be welcomed.

Volume Update Chart

IF YOU HAVE:	YOU MAY DISCARD:
1-4 First Revision (1967)	1 (1962) 2 (1963) 3 (1963) 4 (1963)
5-8 First Revision (1969)	5-6 (1963) 7-8 (1963)
Both 9-12 First Revision (1974) AND *Contemporary Authors Permanent Series*, Volume 1 (1975)	9-10 (1964) 11-12 (1965)
Both 13-16 First Revision (1975) AND *Contemporary Authors Permanent Series*, Volumes 1 and 2 (1975, 1978)	13-14 (1965) 15-16 (1966)
Both 17-20 First Revision (1976) AND *Contemporary Authors Permanent Series*, Volumes 1 and 2 (1975, 1978)	17-18 (1967) 19-20 (1968)
Both 21-24 First Revision (1977) AND *Contemporary Authors Permanent Series*, Volumes 1 and 2 (1975, 1978)	21-22 (1969) 23-24 (1970)
Both 25-28 First Revision (1977) AND *Contemporary Authors Permanent Series*, Volume 2 (1978)	25-28 (1971)
Both 29-32 First Revision (1978) AND *Contemporary Authors Permanent Series*, Volume 2 (1978)	29-32 (1972)
Both 33-36 First Revision (1978) AND *Contemporary Authors Permanent Series*, Volume 2 (1978)	33-36 (1973)
37-40 First Revision (1979)	37-40 (1973)
41-44 First Revision (1979)	41-44 (1974)
45-48 (1974) 49-52 (1975) 53-56 (1975) 57-60 (1976) ↓ ↓ 110 (1984)	NONE: These volumes will not be superseded by corresponding revised volumes. Individual entries from these and all other volumes appearing in the left column of this chart will be revised and included in the *New Revision Series*.
Volumes in the *Contemporary Authors New Revision Series*	NONE: The *New Revision Series* does not replace any single volume of *CA*. All volumes appearing in the left column of this chart must be retained to have information on all authors in the series.

Contemporary Authors

NEW REVISION SERIES

† *Indicates that a listing has been revised from secondary sources believed to be reliable, but has not been personally reviewed for this edition by the author sketched.*

ABEL, Alan (Irwin) 1928-
(Julius Bristol)

PERSONAL: Born August 2, 1928, in Zanesville, Ohio; son of Louis and Ida (Hamberger) Abel; married Jeanne Allgeier (a writer), September 11, 1959. *Education:* Ohio State University, B.S., 1950. *Home:* 1 Crow Hollow Lane, Westport, Conn. 06880. *Agent:* Bruce Spencer, Spencer Productions, Inc., 234 Fifth Ave., New York, N.Y. 10061.

CAREER: Writer; lecturer at 1,500 schools and colleges between 1950 and 1965; *San Francisco Chronicle,* San Francisco, Calif., weekly columnist, beginning 1965; author, director, and producer of, and occasional performer in, films and stage and television productions. *Military service:* U.S. Army Air Forces, 1943-46.

WRITINGS: The Crazy Ads, Citadel, 1960; *The Great American Hoax* (also serialized by the *New York Post*), Trident, 1966 (published in England as *Yours for Decency,* Elek, 1967); (compiler with wife, Jeanne A. Abel) *The Button Book,* Citadel, 1967; *Confessions of a Hoaxer,* Macmillan, 1971; (with J. A. Abel; also producer and director) "Is There Sex after Death?" (film; also see below), Abel-Child Productions, 1971; (with J. A. Abel) *Is There Sex after Death?* (screenplay), Bantam, 1975; (with J. A. Abel; also producer and director) "The Faking of the President" (film), Ivy Films, 1979; *Don't Get Mad, Get Even,* illustrated with drawings by Simon Bond, Norton, 1983; *How to Thrive on Rejection: A Manual for Survival,* illustrated with drawings by Bond, Norton, 1984. Also author of, and performer in, "Jester-at-Large" (one-man stage show) and "The Unstable Roundtable" (panel discussion for cable television), both 1981.

SIDELIGHTS: Writer, performer, and all-around prankster Alan Abel first came to public attention in 1959 with his SINA (Society for Indecency to Naked Animals), a fake organization dedicated to seeing that both household pets and farm livestock be clothed for decency's sake. "Members feel," explains Abel to William Raidy in the *San Francisco Examiner,* "that unclad animals are a public disgrace, especially to children, and that seeing them along a road may distract drivers and cause accidents." For nearly five years the organization fooled such staid sources as the *Los Angeles Times,* the *San Francisco Chronicle,* the *New York Times, Life* magazine, and all three major network news programs, which regularly reported on SINA's "progress." The story of SINA is chronicled in Abel's book *The Great American Hoax.*

Abel's penchant for practical jokes has not waned with the passing years. In 1980 the *New York Times* solemnly printed the obituary of Alan Abel, who apparently had succumbed to a heart attack at Robert Redford's Sundance Ski Resort in Utah while scouting locations for his new film, "Who's Going to Bite Your Neck, Dear, When All of My Teeth Are Gone?" The next day the paper informed its readers that the death notice was, in fact, a hoax—a stunt that did not endear Abel to the *Times* staff. (Raidy notes that when the prankster confessed to the hoax and then asked a *Times* reporter "What can I do for you?" the newsman replied, "Drop dead.") In another incident, a meeting of the New York City chapter of Mensa, the high-I.Q. organization, was once graced with a visit from His Excellence, the Prince Emir Assad, of Middle Eastern royalty. The Prince lectured to the assembled Mensans, according to *New York* magazine's Bruce Jacoby, about world politics: "Iran has the lowest crime rate in the world. The ayatollah has allowed the criminal element to perform crimes without punishment, that's why. . . . The people of Libya recently discovered that the seven-day week was ineffectual. So now they have a six-day calendar. . . . The Cubans under Castro have developed a technique for ending war. They're training their children to fight with toy guns." Diplomatic relations with the Middle East were only briefly strained when Prince Emir Assad turned out to be a burnoose-clad Alan Abel.

Turning his attention to domestic issues, Abel has participated in a panel discussion with such savants as Ralph Schoenstein, AC-DC, Don Erickson, WASP, and Charles Laiken, DOA, on "The Unstable Roundtable," which was broadcast in New York by Manhattan Cable television. This gathering saw the men solving various problems plaguing modern society, including taxes ("abolish the present unfair income tax system. Instead, each head of the family 'weighs in' on April 15th and pays $2.00 a pound to the IRS. State taxes would be based on your height, 75¢ per inch.") and unemployment ("Able-bodied people out of work would appear in public in the nude until somebody takes pity and hires them. Those employed only mornings would be bottomless, or topless for afternoons.").

Finally, a politically-aware Abel invited voters to consider the Committee to Elect Alan Abel Mayor of New York City. His platform, as reported by Raidy, consists of "raising subway and bus fares to $2.00 'to attract a better class of passenger,' low-cost life insurance for suicides, . . . and the ingenious idea of requiring all doctors to publish their medical school grade averages in the telephone book after their names." As yet Abel has not been elected.

MEDIA ADAPTATIONS: The Great American Hoax has been purchased for filming.

BIOGRAPHICAL/CRITICAL SOURCES: New Yorker, September 15, 1951; *Detroit Free Press,* July 3, 1966; *New York,* August 6, 1979; *New York Times,* January 2, 1980, January 4, 1980; *San Francisco Examiner,* December 15, 1981.

* * *

ABLEMAN, Paul 1927-

PERSONAL: Born June 13, 1927, in Leeds, Yorkshire, England; married; children: one son. *Education:* Attended King's College, London. *Home:* Flat No. 37, Duncan House, Fellows Rd., London N.W.3, England. *Agent:* Jonathan Clowes, 19 Jeffrey's Place, London NW1 9PP, England.

CAREER: Writer.

WRITINGS—Novels: *I Hear Voices,* Olympia Press, 1958; *As Near As I Can Get,* Spearman, 1962; *Vac,* Gollancz, 1968; *The Twilight of the Vilp,* Gollancz, 1969; (with others) *London Consequences,* Greater London Arts Association for the Festivals of London, 1972; *Tornado Pratt,* Gollancz, 1977; *Shoestring* (novelization of a television play), BBC Publications, 1979; *Porridge: The Inside Story* (novelization of a television play), Pan Books, 1979; *Shoestring's Finest Hour,* BBC Publications, 1980; *County Hall,* BBC Publications, 1982.

Published plays: (With Gertrude Macauley) *Even His Enemy* (produced in London as "Letters to a Lady," 1951), Samuel French, 1948; *Green Julia* (produced in Edinburgh, 1965, in New York, 1972), Grove, 1966, new edition, 1973; *Tests* (playlets), Methuen, 1966; *Blue Comedy* (includes "Madly in Love" and "Hank's Night"; produced in London, 1968), Methuen, 1968.

Unpublished plays: "Help!" (revue), produced in London, 1963; "One Hand Clapping" (revue), produced in Edinburgh, 1964; "Dialogues," produced in London, 1965; "Emily and Heathcliff," produced in London, 1967; "The Black General" (adapted from *Othello*), produced in London, 1969; "Little Hopping Robin," produced in New York, 1973; "And Hum Our Sword," produced in London, 1973; "The Visitor," produced in London, 1974; "Windsor All-Sorts," produced in London, 1977.

Television plays: "Barlowe of the Car Park," 1961; "That Woman Is Wrecking Our Marriage," 1969; "Visit from a Stranger," 1970; "The Catch in a Cold," 1970.

Other: (Translator with Veronica Hull) Simone Lacourture, *Egypt,* Viking, 1963; *Bits* (experimental prose written in verse form), Latimer Press, 1969; *The Mouth and Oral Sex,* Running Man Press, 1969, published as *The Sensuous Mouth,* Ace Books, 1972. Also author of radio play "The Infant," 1974. Contributor to anthologies, including *Modern Short Comedies from Broadway and London,* edited by Stanley Richards, Random House, 1969. Contributor to *Transatlantic Review* and *Men Only.*†

ABRAMS, George J(oseph) 1918-1978 (George Hipp)

PERSONAL: Born February 14, 1918, in Hoboken, N.J.; died February 7, 1978; son of Leo (a tax consultant) and May (Hipp) Abrams; married Mary Della Sablom, November 15, 1941; children: Adele Lois. *Education:* Attended Rutgers University, 1936, and Balliol College, Oxford, 1945; New York University, B.S. (magna cum laude), 1947, M.B.A., 1949. *Politics:* Independent. *Religion:* Roman Catholic. *Residence:* West Caldwell, N.J.

CAREER: Evening Transcript, Orange, N.J., staff writer, 1934-36; National Biscuit Co., New York City, assistant to advertising director, 1936-41; Whitehall Pharmacal Co., New York city, product advertising manager, 1941-46; Eversharp, Inc., New York City, director of marketing research, 1946-47; Block Drug Co., Jersey City, N.J., vice-president of sales and advertising, 1947-55; Revlon, Inc., New York City, vice-president in charge of advertising, 1955-59; president and chief executive officer of cosmetics and toiletries division, Warner-Lambert Pharmaceutical Co., 1959-60; vice-president of corporate development, J. B. Williams Corp., 1960-62; Del Laboratories, Inc., New York City, chairman and president, 1962-65; senior vice-president and marketing executive, William Esty Co., 1965-67; executive vice-president, Reach, McClinton & Co., 1967-69; Cole Fischer Rogow, New York City, president, 1969-71; George J. Abrams & Associates, New York City, president, 1971-75; senior vice-president, Keyes, Martin & Co., 1975-78.

Lecturer in advertising management, New York University Graduate School of Business Administration, 1951-54; professor of marketing, Pace University Graduate School of Business Administration, 1976-78; professor of administrative sciences, Montclair State College, 1977-78. Chairman of board, Profit Centers, Inc., beginning 1972; member of board of governors, United Service Organizations (USO). Trustee, East Orange (N.J.) General Hospital. *Military service:* U.S. Naval Reserve, 1941-45; served in European, Atlantic, and Pacific theaters; became lieutenant junior grade.

MEMBER: Association of National Advertisers, Advertising Club (N.J.; governor, 1955), Beta Gamma Sigma, Alpha Delta Sigma, Alpha Phi Sigma, Pinnacle Club (New York City), Curzon House (London). *Awards, honors:* Award from Association of Advertising Men and Women (N.Y.), 1954; achievement award from Advertising Club of Washington, 1958; Alpha Delta Sigma award, 1958; Free Enterprise Association award, 1964; Brooklyn Philharmonia award, 1970; Association of National Advertisers award, 1970.

WRITINGS: How I Made a Million Dollars with Ideas, Playboy Press, 1973; (under pseudonym George Hipp) *The Guilt of Michael Pagett* (novel), Manor Books, 1974; *That Man,* Woodhill, 1977. Also author of film, "The Smartest Man in the World," 1974. Contributor to *Encyclopedia Americana* and to professional journals.

WORK IN PROGRESS: Fiction and nonfiction novels; writing television situation series, motion pictures, and television game shows.

* * *

ACCOLA, Louis W(ayne) 1937-

PERSONAL: Born September 16, 1937; married Kathleen Mae McMullen, July 3, 1976; children: (previous marriage) Terence, Steven, Hans Louis; (current marriage) Katie, Kent. *Education:* Luther College, Decorah, Iowa, B.A., 1959; Luther Theological Seminary, St. Paul, B.D. (with highest honors), 1964; Princeton Theological Seminary, Th.M. (with honors), 1965. *Home:* 9017 48th Ave. N., Minneapolis, Minn. 55428. *Office:* Parish Development, American Lutheran Church, 422 South Fifth St., Minneapolis, Minn. 55415.

CAREER: Ordained a Lutheran minister, 1965; Our Savior's Lutheran Church, Waterloo, Iowa, associate pastor, 1965-66; Our Savior's Lutheran Church, Milwaukee, Wis., pastor, 1966-73; American Lutheran Church, Minneapolis, Minn., director of Parish Development, 1973—. Instructor for two years in Rhodesia (now Zimbabwe); frequent lecturer on comparative religions, contemporary theology, and church renewal movement; guest lecturer, Alverno College and Marquette University. Board member of Milwaukee Conference Council; adult education chairman, Metropolitan Lutheran Council. *Member:* Common Cause, Center for the Study of Democratic Institutions.

WRITINGS—Published by American Lutheran Church, except as indicated: *Personal Faith for Human Crises,* Augsburg, 1970; *Life in Mission,* Augsburg, 1977; *Spirituality: Aspects of Christian Life and Renewal,* 1980; *Small Congregations in Rural Settings: Aspects of Christian Presence and Ministry,* 1982; *New Pastor, New People,* 1983. Contributor to *Lutheran Standard, Event,* and *Mission '78 Youth Resource Manual.*

WORK IN PROGRESS: Research on the impact of science and technology upon faith-life, the concept of self, meaning of life and death, and the impact of science and technology on family-life; *Christian Faith and the Transformation of Ministry;* a research training program.

* * *

ADAMS, Richard N(ewbold) 1924-
(Stokes Newbold)

PERSONAL: Born August 4, 1924, in Ann Arbor, Mich.; son of Randolph Greenfield (a historian) and Helen Constance (Spiller) Adams; married Betty Virginia Hannstein (a teacher and writer), November 4, 1951; children: Walter Randolph, Tani Marilena, Gina Constance. *Education:* University of Michigan, A.B., 1947; Yale University, M.A., 1949, Ph.D., 1951. *Home:* 1506 Westlake Dr., Austin, Tex. 78746. *Office:* Department of Anthropology, University of Texas, Austin, Tex. 78712.

CAREER: Ethnological research and consultation in Guatemala and other Central American countries for Institute of Social Anthropology, Smithsonian Institution, U.S. Department of State, World Health Organization, and U.S. Operations Mission Educational Program; Michigan State University, East Lansing, professor of sociology and anthropology, 1956-62, researcher for Institute of Overseas Research in Peru, Bolivia, and Chile, 1958; University of California, Berkeley, visiting professor of anthropology, 1960-61; University of Texas at Austin, assistant director of Institute of Latin American Studies, 1962-67, professor of anthropology and chairman of department, 1962—. Consultant, Institute of Nutrition of Central America and Panama, Peace Corps, Ford Foundation, Agency for International Development. Board member and president of Texas Ballet Concerto, Inc., 1966-67; volunteer fireman, Westlake Hills, Tex. *Military service:* U.S. Naval Reserve, 1943-46; became lieutenant.

MEMBER: American Anthropological Association (fellow; member of executive board, 1970-72; president, 1976-77), American Association for the Advancement of Science (fellow; vice-president and chairman of Section "H," 1972 and 1973), American Sociological Society, American Ethnological Society, Society for Applied Anthropology (regional vice-president, 1958; executive committee member, 1959-61; vice-president, 1961-62; president, 1962-63), Latin American Studies Association (vice-president, 1967; president, 1968), Sigma Xi (fellow).

WRITINGS: The Home Made Poems, [London], 1934; *Un Analisis de las enfermedades y sus curaciones en una poblacion indigena de Guatemala,* translation from original English manuscript by Amalia G. de Ramirez, Instituto de Nutricion de Centro America y Panama, 1951, published as *Un Analisis de las creencias y practicas medicas en un pueblo indigena de Guatemala,* Ministerio de Educacion Publica (Guatemala), 1952; *Encuesta sobre la cultura de los ladinos en Guatemala,* translation by Joaquin Noval, Ministerio de Educacion Publica, 1956, 2nd edition, 1964; *Cultural Surveys of Panama-Nicaragua-Guatemala-El Salvador-Honduras,* Pan American Sanitary Bureau, 1957; *A Community in the Andes: Problems and Progress in Muquiyauyo,* University of Washington Press for American Ethnological Society, 1959.

(With Charles C. Cumberland) *United States University Co-operation in Latin America: A Study Based on Selected Programs in Bolivia, Chile, Peru, and Mexico,* Institute of Research on Overseas Programs, Michigan State University, 1960; (with others) *Social Change in Latin America Today: Its Implications for United States Policy,* introduction by Lyman Bryson, Harper for Council on Foreign Relations, 1960, published as *Social Change in Latin America Today,* Vintage Books, 1960; *Introduccion a la antropologia aplicada,* translation from original English manuscript and prologue by Jorge Skinner Klee, Ministerio de Educacion Publica, 1964; *Migraciones internas en Guatemala: Expansion agraria de los indigenas kekchies hacia El Peten,* translation from original English manuscript by Julio Vielman, Ministerio de Educacion Publica, 1965; *The Second Sowing: Power and Secondary Development in Latin America,* Chandler Publishing, 1967.

Crucifixion by Power: Essays on Guatemalan National Social Structure, 1944-1966, University of Texas Press, 1970; *Energy and Structure,* University of Texas Press, 1975; *Poder y control: la red de la expansion humana,* Mexico-CIS-INAN, 1977; *Paradoxical Harvest: Energy and Explanation in British History, 1870-1914,* Cambridge University Press, 1982.

University of Texas Offprint series, published by the Institute of Latin American Studies: *The Community in Latin America: A Changing Myth* (originally published in *Centennial Review,* summer, 1962), 1963; *Rural Labor in Latin America* (originally published in *Continuity and Change in Latin America,* edited by John J. Johnson, Stanford University Press, 1964), 1964; *Politics and Social Anthropology in Spanish America* (originally published in *Human Organization,* spring, 1964), 1964; *The Pattern of Development in Latin America* [and] *Desarrollo acelerado* (the former originally published in *Annals* of the American Academy of Political and Social Science, July, 1965; the latter originally published as "Sudden Development: Growth Patterns in Latin America" in *Americas,* August, 1965), 1965; *Ethics and the Social Anthropologist in Latin America* (originally published in *American Behavioral Scientist,* June, 1967), 1967; *Nationalization* (originally published in *Handbook of Middle American Indians,* Volume VI, edited by Robert

Wauchope, University of Texas Press, 1967), 1967; *Power and Power Domains* (originally published in *America Latina*, April-June, 1966), 1967; *Political Power and Social Structures* (originally published in *The Politics of Conformity in Latin America*, edited by Claudio Veliz, Oxford University Press, 1967), 1968.

Editor or compiler: *Political Changes in Guatemalan Indian Communities: A Symposium*, edited by Margaret W. Harrison and Robert Wauchope, Middle American Research Institute, Tulane University, 1957; (with Jack J. Preiss) *Human Organization Research: Field Relations and Techniques*, Dorsey for the Society for Applied Anthropology, 1960; (and author of introduction) *Responsibilities of the Foreign Scholar to the Local Scholarly Community*, Council on Educational Cooperation with Latin American Education and World Affairs, and Latin American Studies Association, 1961; (and author of introduction and notes, with Dwight B. Heath) *Contemporary Cultures and Societies of Latin America: A Reader in the Social Anthropology of Middle and South America and the Caribbean*, Random House, 1965; (with Raymond Fogelson and contributor) *The Anthropology of Power*, Academic Press, 1977.

Contributor: Benjamin D. Paul and W. B. Miller, editors, *Health, Culture and Community*, Russell Sage, 1955; Jorge Luis Arriola, editor, *Cultura indigena de Guatemala: Ensayos de antropologia social*, Ministerio de Educacion Publica, 1956; (and author of introduction) *Integracion social en Guatemala*, Seminario de Integracion Social Guatemalteca, Publicacion 3, [Guatemala], 1956; Frederick B. Pike, editor, *Freedom and Reform in Latin America*, University of Notre Dame Press, 1959.

Gertrude E. Dole and Robert L. Carneiro, editors, *Essays in the Science of Culture in Honor of Leslie A. White*, Crowell, 1960; *Social Change in Latin America Today*, Harper for Council on Foreign Relations, 1960; Lago Gladston, editor, *Human Nutrition, Historic and Scientific*, Institute of Social and Historical Medicine, 1960; David G. Mandelbaum, Gabriel W. Lasker, and Ethel Albert, editors, *The Teaching of Anthropology*, American Anthropological Association, 1963; Donald M. Valdes and Dwight G. Dean, editors, *Sociology in Use*, Macmillan, 1965; Wauchope, editor, *Handbook of Middle American Indians*, Volume VI, University of Texas Press, 1967; Claudio Veliz, editor, *Latin America and the Caribbean: A Handbook*, Anthony Blond, 1968; David L. Sills, editor, *International Encyclopedia of the Social Sciences*, Macmillan, 1968; *Survey of the Alliance for Progress* (hearings before Subcommittee on American Republics Affairs of the Committee on Foreign Relations), U.S. Senate, Ninetieth Congress, Second Session, 1969.

Social Anthropology of Latin America: Essays in Honor of Ralph Leon Beals, Latin American Studies Center, University of California, Los Angeles, 1970; Stanley Ross, editor, *Latin America in Transition: Problems in Training and Research*, State University of New York Press, 1970; *Contemporary Cultures and Societies of Latin America*, Random House, 1970; B. M. DuToit and Helen I. Safa, editors, *Migration and Urbanization: Models and Adaptive Strategies*, Mouton & Co., 1975; Joseph Spielberg and Scott Whiteford, editors, *Forging Nations*, Michigan State University Press, 1976; M. A. Selgson and John A. Booth, editors, *Political Participation in Latin America*, Holmes & Meier, 1979; Jack Gibbs, editor, *Social Control*, Sage Publications, 1982.

Contributor, under pseudonym Stokes Newbold, of an article to *Economic Development and Cultural Change*. Contributor of articles to numerous anthropology and sociology journals, including *American Anthropologist, Social Forces, Antropologia e Historia de Guatemala, Boletin de la Oficina Sanitaria Panamericana, Nutrition Reviews, Politica, Ethnohistory, Current Anthropology, Revista de Indias, Foro Internacional, Reviews in Anthropology,* and *Southwestern Journal of Anthropology.*

SIDELIGHTS: Richard N. Adams told *CA*: "I find, on reflection, that I generally write articles in a hope to inform others but that I write books for my own enjoyment."

The Second Sowing: Power and Secondary Development in Latin America and *Energy and Structure* have been published in Spanish.

* * *

ADAMS, Robert McCormick 1926-

PERSONAL: Born July 23, 1926, in Chicago, Ill.; son of Robert McCormick and Janet (Lawrence) Adams; married Ruth Salzman Skinner, July 24, 1953; children: Megan. *Education:* University of Chicago, Ph.B., 1947, M.A., 1952, Ph.D., 1956. *Office:* Oriental Institute, University of Chicago, 1155 East 58th St., Chicago, Ill. 60637.

CAREER: University of Chicago, Chicago, Ill., instructor, 1955-57, assistant professor, 1957-62, associate professor, 1962-63, professor of anthropology and Near East languages and civilizations, 1963-75, Harold H. Swift Distinguished Service Professor, 1975—, director of Oriental Institute, 1962-68, 1981—, dean of Division of Behavioral and Social Sciences, 1970-74, 1979-80. Visiting professor at Harvard University, 1962, and University of California, Berkeley, 1963; Lewis Henry Morgan Lecturer at University of Rochester, 1965; American School of Oriental Research, Baghdad School, annual professor, 1966-67, resident director, 1968-69, National Research Council, Division of Behavioral Science, member, 1967—, chairman of Assembly of Behavioral and Social Sciences, 1972-76. Trustee of National Humanities Center, 1976—, and Russell Sage Foundation, 1978. Has conducted field research in Iraq, Iran, Mexico, and Syria. *Military service:* U.S. Naval Reserve, active duty, 1944-46.

MEMBER: American Philosophical Society, National Academy of Sciences, American Association for the Advancement of Science (fellow), American Anthropological Association (fellow), American Academy of Arts and Sciences (fellow), Society for American Archaeology, Middle East Studies Association of North America (fellow), German Archaeological Institute, Sigma Xi.

WRITINGS: *Level and Trend in Early Sumerian Civilization*, University of Chicago Library, 1956; (editor with C. H. Kraeling) *City Invincible: A Symposium on Urbanization and Cultural Development in the Ancient Near East*, University of Chicago Press, 1960; *Land behind Baghdad: A History of Settlement on the Diyala Plains*, University of Chicago Press, 1965; *The Evolution of Urban Society: Early Mesopotamia and Prehispanic Mexico*, Aldine, 1966; (with Hans J. Nissen) *The Uruk Countryside: The Natural Setting of Urban Societies*, University of Chicago Press, 1972; (with others) *Irrigation's Impact on Society*, University of Arizona Press, 1974; (with Warren E. Johnston and Gordon A. King) *Some Effects of Alternative Energy Policies on California Annual Crop Production*, California Agricultural Experiment Station, 1978; (editor with Corinne S. Schelling) *Corners of a Foreign Field: Discussions about American Overseas Advanced Research*

Centers in the Humanities and Social Sciences, Rockefeller Foundation, 1979; *Heartland of Cities: Surveys of Ancient Settlement and Land Use on the Central Floodplain of the Euphrates*, University of Chicago Press, 1981. Contributor of more than eighty articles to professional journals. Advisory editor of archeology for *Encyclopaedia Britannica*.

SIDELIGHTS: Robert McCormick Adams's research is an ecologically oriented study of historic patterns of land use settlement and urbanization; he has a comparative interest in other centers of early civilization. *Avocational interests:* Skiing, mountaineering.

* * *

ADDAMS, Charles (Samuel) 1912-

PERSONAL: Born January 7, 1912, in Westfield, N.J.; son of Charles Huey (a manager for a piano company) and Grace M. (Spear) Addams; married Barbara Day, May 29, 1943 (divorced October, 1951); married Barbara Barb, December 1, 1954 (divorced, 1956); married Marilyn Matthews, May 31, 1980. *Education:* Attended Colgate University, 1929-30, University of Pennsylvania, 1930-31, and Grand Central School of Art, New York, N.Y., 1931-32. *Home:* 25 West 54th St., New York, N.Y. 10020; and Water Mill, N.Y.

CAREER: Worked briefly in New York, N.Y., for a Macfadden publication after submitting first cartoon to the *New Yorker* magazine in 1933; free-lance cartoonist, with work appearing regularly in the *New Yorker*, 1936—. Work exhibited at Fogg Art Museum, Rhode Island School of Design, Museum of the City of New York, University of Pennsylvania Museum, and Metropolitan Museum of Art. *Military service:* U.S. Army, Signal Corps, 1943-46. *Member:* Vintage Car Club of America, Armor and Arms Club, Coffee House. *Awards, honors:* Humor award, Yale University, 1954; special award of the Mystery Writers of America, 1961; honorary Doctor of Fine Arts, University of Pennsylvania, 1980.

WRITINGS—Cartoons: *Drawn and Quartered*, foreword by Boris Karloff, Random House, 1942, published as *D & Q: The Return of a Classic*, Simon & Schuster, 1962; *Addams and Evil*, introduction by Wolcott Gibbs, Random House, 1947; *Monster Rally*, foreword by John O'Hara, Simon & Schuster, 1950, reprinted, W. H. Allen, 1977; *Homebodies*, Simon & Schuster, 1954; *Nightcrawlers*, Simon & Schuster, 1957; (editor) *Dear Dead Days: A Family Album*, Putnam, 1959; *Black Maria*, Simon & Schuster, 1960; *The Penguin Charles Addams*, Penguin, 1962; *The Groaning Board*, Simon & Schuster, 1964; (with others) *Think Small*, Golden Press, 1967; *The Charles Addams Mother Goose*, Windmill Books, 1967; *My Crowd*, Simon & Schuster, 1970; *Charles Addams Favorite Haunts*, Simon & Schuster, 1976 (published in England as *Favorite Haunts*, W. H. Allen, 1977); *Creature Comforts: A New Collection of Classic Cartoons*, Simon & Schuster, 1981; (with others) *A Treasury of Windmill Books*, Windmill Books, 1981. Also contributor to biennial *New Yorker Album* and to *New Yorker War Album*, 1942.

Illustrator: John Kobler, *Afternoon in the Attic*, Dodd, 1950.

Contributor of cartoons to *Life*, *Collier's*, *Cosmopolitan*, and other publications.

SIDELIGHTS: The *New Yorker*'s resident master of macabre merriment since the mid-1930s, cartoonist Charles Addams specializes in making the fantastic and the absurd seem entirely commonplace. Explains a *Times Literary Supplement* critic:

"[Addams] can disturbingly convey the impression that, lunatic and monstrous as everything undoubtedly is, it is yet close to twentieth-century earth, and that Nightmare Lane leads directly into Fifth Avenue." As another *Times Literary Supplement* reviewer notes, however, "Addams mostly steers clear of the true horrors facing us in our day-to-day living," preferring instead to keep realistic touches and "serious" themes to a minimum.

An odd assortment of characters, some human and some not, people the typical Addams cartoon. "Monsters, young or old, four-legged or two-headed, prehistoric or contemporary, simpering or nonchalant, are very much Mr. Addams's affair," observes John Mason Brown in the *Saturday Review of Literature*. "His is a hobgoblin world of bats, spiders, broomsticks, snakes, cobwebs, and bloodletting morons in which every day is Hallowe'en." Despite the potentially offensive nature of his often gruesome subject matter, Brown continues, "nothing shocks [Addams] and no one is shocked by [Addams]. The more sinister his concepts are, the louder is our laughter and the greater our enjoyment. Clearly Mr. Addams invites us to enter a world which has nothing to do with the one in which we live except that, in the most glorious, undeviating, and giddy fashion, it turns all of its values topsy-turvy." In short, concludes the critic, Charles Addams has "the paradoxical distinction of having reduced the horrors of the present by having added to them. If only the other horrors were as laughable as the ones with which he delights us!"

MEDIA ADAPTATIONS: "The Addams Family" television series is based on characters created by Charles Addams and featured for many years in the *New Yorker*.

AVOCATIONAL INTERESTS: Vintage sports cars, Civil War history, archery, collecting medieval armor.

BIOGRAPHICAL/CRITICAL SOURCES: *New York Times*, October 5, 1947, October 15, 1950; *Times Literary Supplement*, November 15, 1947, July 22, 1977, December 25, 1981; *New York Herald Tribune Weekly Book Review*, December 7, 1947; *Saturday Review of Literature*, November 11, 1950; *New York Herald Tribune Book Review*, December 3, 1950; *Book World*, November 5, 1967; *Washington Post*, November 17, 1982.

* * *

AKENS, David S. 1921-

PERSONAL: Born April 16, 1921, in Lost Creek, Ky.; son of Claude Neuman (a newspaper publisher and teacher) and Nellie Geneva Akens; married Helen Morgan (a writer), August 21, 1953. *Education:* University of Miami, Coral Gables, Fla., B.A., 1950; University of Alabama, M.A., 1956; has studied writing at a number of other colleges and universities. *Home and office:* 6802 Jones Valley Dr. S.E., Huntsville, Ala. 35802.

CAREER: Free-lance writer and editor. International Harvester Co., Benham, Ky., editor of company magazine, 1948-49; high school English teacher, 1954-55.

WRITINGS—All published by Strode: *Rocket City U.S.A.*, 1959; *A Picture History of Rockets and Rocketry*, 1964; *John Glenn, First American in Orbit*, 1969; *Loss of Hearing and You*, 1970; *Little League Leader*, 1971; *Full-Time Football*, 1972; *Best Basketball Booster*, 1973; *World's Greatest Leaders: The Akens Book of Supernatural Records*, 1980; *University Jokes Told with Class*, 1982; *How to Get a Manuscript Published*, 1983. Contributor to newspapers and magazines.

WORK IN PROGRESS: A novel, *Beyond the 12-Mile Limit*.

AKINJOGBIN, I(saac) A(deagbo) 1930-

PERSONAL: Born January 12, 1930, in Ipetumodu (Ife), Nigeria; son of Joel Esudoyin (a farmer) and Bernice (Falowo) Akinjogbin; married Josephine Adebisi Odeloye, May 6, 1959; children: Adeolu, Olufemi, Yewande, Baderinwa, Olugbenga. *Education:* Attended Fourah Bay College, University of Sierra Leone; University of Durham, B.A. (with honors in history), 1957; School of Oriental and African Studies, Ph.D., 1963. *Religion:* Christian. *Home:* Isale-Apata, Ipetumodu (Ife), Nigeria. *Office:* Department of History, University of Ife, Ife, Nigeria.

CAREER: Yoruba Historical Research Scheme, Ibadan, Nigeria, junior research fellow, 1957-60; University of Ife, Ife, Nigeria, senior lecturer, beginning 1963, professor of history, 1968—, dean of faculty of arts, 1971-73, deputy vice-chancellor, 1974-76. Buel Gallagher Distinguished Professor, City College of the City University of New York, 1973-74. *Member:* International African Institute (London), Historical Association (Great Britain; honorary member), Historical Society of Nigeria (member of council; honorary general secretary, 1968-74). *Awards, honors:* Commonwealth scholar at University of London, 1960-63; Carnegie traveling fellow, 1970.

WRITINGS: (Contributor) I. Espie and J. F. Ade Ajayi, editors, *A Thousand Years of West African History,* Thomas Nelson, 1966; *Dahomey and Its Neighbours, 1708-1818,* Cambridge University Press, 1967; (editor) *The Story of Ketu,* 2nd edition, University of Ibadan Press, 1967; (editor) *Ewi Iwoyi* (modern Yoruba poetry), Collins, 1968; (contributor) Ajayi and M. Crowder, editors, *History of West Africa,* Volume I, Longman, 1971; *Topics on Nigerian Economic and Social History,* University of Ife Press, 1980; (contributor) O. Ikime, editor, *Groundwork of Nigerian History,* Heinemann Educational Books, 1980.

Also author of short stories and poems in Yoruba; translator of *Ede,* a short history, for Nigerian Ministry of Education, 1961. Contributor of articles on West African history to professional journals.

WORK IN PROGRESS: The Growth and Organisation of the Ife Kingdom.

SIDELIGHTS: I. A. Akinjogbin told *CA:* "There are two strands to my writing—the academic research oriented studies in history and the emotional (or rational) outcries in poems. Both are rooted in the same conviction (or illusion?) that life can be understood, improved, and enjoyed if critically watched and intelligently explained, and that human experiences of the Africans are part of the storehouse of human treasure and should be treated as such by all."

*   *   *

AKSENOV, Vassily
See AKSYONOV, Vassily (Pavlovich)

*   *   *

AKSYONOV, Vassily (Pavlovich) 1932-
(Vassily Aksenov)

PERSONAL: Given name transliterated as Vasily, Vasilii, Vasilli, and Vasilij, and surname transliterated as Aksehov in some sources; born August 20, 1932, in Kazan, U.S.S.R.; came to United States in 1980; son of Pavel Vassilievich and Evgenia Semenovna (Ginzburg) Aksyonov; married Kira Mendeleva, March 11, 1957; married second wife, Maya; children: (first marriage) Alexey. *Education:* First Leningrad Medical Institute, medical degree, 1956. *Politics:* Nonparty. *Religion:* Christian. *Home:* 1802 Wyoming Ave. N.W., Apt. 402, Washington, D.C. 20009.

CAREER: Physician, Leningrad Hospital, 1956-60; full-time writer, 1960—. Writer-in-residence, University of Southern California, 1981, George Washington University, 1982, and Goucher College, 1984. Fellow, Woodrow Wilson International Center, 1982. *Awards, honors:* Golden Prize in International Competition of Satirical Authors, Bulgaria, 1967.

WRITINGS—Novels, except as indicated: *Kollegi,* Soviet Writer Publishing House, 1961, translation by Margaret Wettlin published as *Colleagues,* Foreign Languages Publishing House (Moscow), 1961, translation by Alec Brown published under same title, Putnam, 1962; *Zvezdnyi bilet,* Youth Magazine, 1961, translation by Brown published as *A Starry Ticket,* Putnam, 1962, translation by Andrew R. MacAndrew published as *A Ticket to the Stars,* New American Library, 1963; *Apel'siny iz Marokko* (title means "Oranges from Morocco"), Youth Magazine, 1963; *Katapul'ta* (title means "Catapult"; short stories), Soviet Writer Publishing House, 1964.

Pora, moi drug, pora, Young Guard Publishing House, 1965, translation by Olive Stevens published as *It's Time, My Friend, It's Time,* Macmillan, 1969, published as *It's Time, My Love, It's Time,* Aurora Publishers, 1970; "Vsegda v prodazhe" (play; title means "Always on Sale"), first produced in Moscow at Sovremennik Theater, 1965; *Na polputi k lune* (title means "Halfway to the Moon"; short stories), Soviet Russia Publishing House, 1966; *Zatovarennaia bochkotara* (title means "The Empty Barrels"), Youth Magazine, 1968; *Zhal', chto vas ne bylo s nami* (title means "I Wish You Were with Us"; short stories), Soviet Writer Publishing House, 1969; *Moy dedushka pamjatnik* (title means "My Grandfather Is a Monument"), Children's Literature Publishing House, 1969.

Liubov' k elektrichestvu (title means "Love to the Electricity"), Youth Magazine, 1971; *The Steel Bird, and Other Stories* (short stories), translated by Rae Slonek and others, Ardis, 1979; (editor with Viktor Yerofeyev, Fazil Iskander, Andrei Bitov, and Yevgeny Popov) *Metropol* (anthology), Ardis, 1979, hardcover edition published as *Metropol: A Literary Almanac,* Norton, 1982; *Zolotaia nasha zhelezka,* Ardis, 1980; *Ozhog,* Ardis, 1980, translation by Michael Glenny published as *The Burn,* Houghton, 1984; *Aristofaniana Silyagushkami: Aristophaniana and the Frogs* (collection of plays), Hermitage, 1981; *Ostrov Krym,* Ardis, 1981, translation published as *The Island of Crimea,* Random House, 1983; *Bumazhnyi Peizazh* (title means "The Paperscape"), Ardis, 1983; "Tsaplya" (play; title means "The Heron"), produced in Paris at Theatre de Chaillot, February, 1984.

Also author of *Poiski zhanra* (title means "In Search of Genre") and play *Vash ubiytsa* (title means "Your Murderer"), published in *Performing Arts Journal,* spring, 1977. Former member of editorial board, *Yunost.*

SIDELIGHTS: In July, 1980, Russian novelist, playwright, and short story writer Vassily Aksyonov left his native land to join a growing number of his fellow countrymen in the West. A popular literary figure for nearly twenty years (especially among the so-called "Children of 1956," the first generation to come of age after Stalin's death), Aksyonov had long been subjected to the routine harassment and censorship many writers must face in the Soviet Union. During the 1970s, however, the crackdowns increased to the point where he was doing most of his work "for the drawer"—that is, for himself and not for publication. "I was becoming like a kind of iceberg," he explained to Michiko Kakutani in a *New York Times* interview. "Only a small part of my work was being published; the invisible part grew more and more. I was only one-third Aksyonov, and at last I became fed up. 'For what am I writing?' I thought. What is this pile of yellow paper—you retype it and retype it and send it all over the country to publishers, and everywhere it is rejected because they think it is dangerous."

In 1979, Aksyonov clashed with the government for what would prove to be the last time. In a move intended to challenge censorship laws, he and twenty-two other writers requested that an anthology of their banned works entitled *Metropol* be published. Soviet authorities refused the request and, as punishment, expelled the two youngest contributors to the collection from the Writers' Union. An angry Aksyonov then resigned from the same union in protest and was subsequently expelled from two other professional unions, leaving him without an official way of earning a living and therefore subject to prosecution under the law of *tuneyadstvo*—parasitism. At about the same time, incidents of physical harassment against the writer became more frequent and more threatening; his phone was tapped, the tires of his car were slashed, and mysterious vehicles veered suddenly in his direction. "I had no choice but to leave," Aksyonov told Kakutani. "I was under great psychological pressure, and I was exhausted from all the years of fighting—for every publication, every book. I was just looking for a peaceful place to write. It was a retreat after fighting."

Aksyonov has been a fighter for virtually his entire life. The son of parents who both spent eighteen years in exile in Siberia as Stalin's political prisoners, the author spent part of his youth in an orphanage for "Children of Enemies of the State." At the age of sixteen, he was allowed to join his mother in Siberia. Mindful of her own experience, she encouraged him to become a doctor because the doctors in the camps stood the best chance for survival. Aksyonov did indeed become a physician, but he soon abandoned the profession in order to pursue another, more compelling interest: writing fiction.

Aksyonov first experimented with fiction in the late 1950s while he was still a medical student in Leningrad. A member of a local literary club, he specialized in writing short stories, some of which were published in the Soviet journal *Yunost*. These early stories were largely autobiographical and, for the most part, adhered to the tenets of Socialist Realism "with its obligatory jargon and hortatory themes," as *Time*'s Patricia Blake observes. Aksyonov made a dramatic break with convention in 1961, however, with his novel *Zvezdnyi bilet,* published in English as *A Ticket to the Stars* and also as *A Starry Ticket*. Dealing with the forbidden subject of modern Soviet youth, *A Ticket to the Stars* shocked readers with its frank portrayal of what *Newsweek* writers Kenneth Woodward and Eloise Salholz describe as "the inner confusions, sexual ventures and spiritual yearnings" of the post-Stalin generation.

Soon dubbed "a Slavic J. D. Salinger," Aksyonov spent the next several years writing novels and short stories featuring, as Blake notes, "teenage runaways who craved *rokmuzyka*, wore Keds and *dzhinsy* and talked a nonstop street slang larded with Americanisms, just like real-life Russians." But the author was not entirely Western in his outlook, according to *Times Literary Supplement* reviewer Geoffrey Hosking. "For all their surface irreverence," explains the critic, "the young people whom Aksyonov and his associates portrayed were not deeply disaffected from Soviet society: their personal revolt was directed to the new and creative, and it usually ended with rededication to the building of socialism, conceived in the new post-Stalin spirit—a socialism replete with beat music, sputniks, transistor radios and very possibly (since 'convergence' was also in the air) even Coca-Cola." While some Soviet critics praised the novelist for his sensitivity to the problems and concerns of youth and for his attempts to rescue Russian literature from the drabness of Socialist Realism, others deplored his penchant for racy colloquial language and his preoccupation with the activities of rebellious and alienated members of the "Beatle generation."

Despite the controversial nature of his fiction, Aksyonov did not have a great deal of difficulty getting published during the early 1960s, a period of relative freedom in Soviet literature. From the mid-1960s onwards, however, he and other nonconformist writers began to encounter more and more resistance to their work. Explains Hosking: "One reason for this—though not the only one—was that 'youth prose' itself had developed notes of individual revolt, experimentation and subjectivity were becoming stronger, the ultimate rededication to socialism fainter. In Aksyonov's own work, the hoped for goal of a warm and brotherly society took on more stylized and metaphorical forms." By the end of the decade, Aksyonov had abandoned the youth theme entirely and was directing his efforts to avant garde satire and stylistic methods. "We had grown disappointed with the atheism and Marxism of our youth," the author said of himself and his contemporaries in a *Newsweek* article. "We wanted the spiritual freedom to think, to pray, to probe universal human questions."

In his book *Twentieth-Century Russian Drama: From Gorky to the Present,* Harold B. Segal notes that Aksyonov's newfound interest in the grotesque and the fantastic "found a felicitous creative outlet in dramatic writing before [it] became manifest . . . in his prose fiction." According to the critic, the Russian's plays from this era—"Always on Sale" and "Your Murderer"—are "satires rooted in a darkening vision of an increasingly conformist society." Daniel C. Gerould elaborates on this description in a *Performing Arts Journal* article. "In both plays," he writes, "we find extensive use of grotesque metamorphosis, the device of accelerating demagoguery producing craven conformity, an atmosphere of deepening nightmare followed by a brief and ironically triumphant epilogue, and a mirror-image opposition between a prissy, idealistic do-gooder and a raunchy, foul-mouthed con-man. . . . In the classic tradition of savage satire Aksyonov functions as a moralist and voices his outrage at human venality and folly." Both Segal and Gerould maintain that Aksyonov's work owes much to the avant-garde writers of the 1920s through the 1950s. In fact, remarks Gerould, "with these two plays, Aksyonov performed an invaluable service: he reestablished contact between modern Soviet drama and the great line of Russian and early Soviet satirists."

By the late 1960s Aksyonov had returned to writing prose fiction, though very little of his new work appeared in print in the Soviet Union. *Ozhog* (translated as *The Burn*), for example, published for the first time in 1980 by the American firm Ardis, was actually written between 1969 and 1975. As Hosking declares in his *Times Literary Supplement* review, this novel "is nothing less than the testimony of Aksyonov and his generation, a panorama of their hopes, their illusions and disillusions, and of the spiritual reappraisal which political and aesthetic reaction forced upon them." Part autobiography and part fiction, *Ozhog* is the story of Tolya von Shteinbok, a half-Jewish, half-Russian boy who witnesses his mother's arrest and the brutal beating of his best friend by security police. Cared for by his stepfather, Tolya grows up in the Siberian town where his mother lives as an exiled prisoner. He wants desperately to be like his classmates and to believe in what they all have been taught about the benevolence of the state, but he fears that his mother's status as a political outcast may make it impossible for him to do so. Complicating matters even further is Tolya's stepfather, a deeply religious man who impresses the boy with the depth of his faith and helps him discover "a whiff of freedom, of risk, of alienation from this world." Consequently, Tolya finds himself torn between two ways of life in a spiritual struggle that Aksyonov believes mirrors the one facing his generation.

The author unfolds his narrative in an unconventional manner. Dividing the novel into three parts, he begins the first part with a look at the 1970s as the youth culture has what Hosking calls "its final drunken fling, the hope and warmth degenerating into tawdry promiscuity and betrayal." The narrator for this section is a collective personality consisting of five young people (a writer, a sculptor, a jazz musician, a surgeon, and a scholar) whose lives constantly intermingle and who share the same childhood—that of Tolya von Shteinbok. On different occasions in the first part, all five catch a fleeting glimpse of a man they think is the security police agent who beat up their best friend many years before. The reappearance of this man sets the stage for a flashback to Tolya's postwar childhood, the focus of *Ozhog*'s second section. The third part then takes the reader back to the 1970s and Aksyonov's five young protagonists, all of whom, says Hosking, are left "to find their way forward in a world where [the] harbingers of both damnation and redemption now play a full part."

Commenting in *World Literature Today*, Vytas Dukas calls *Ozhog* an "unusual and rewarding work" that "borders on magic realism" with its blend of current events and imaginative fiction. He describes the author's prose as "vibrant" and has special praise for the poems and poetic devices he makes use of throughout the novel. In short, declares Dukas, "Aksyonov shows us [in *Ozhog*] that he is an excellent student of Gogol, Dostoevsky and Bulgakov in Russia and of Hemingway, Faulkner and Salinger in the USA. His language is rich and innovative. . . . [He] writes eloquently and expressively."

Though Hosking maintains that the first part of *Ozhog* is too long and that the hesitations and contradictions of the third part underscore the author's unfamiliarity with religious tradition, the critic nevertheless hails the novel as one of "the most significant works Aksyonov has yet published." Continues Hosking: "*Ozhog* is a rich and many-sided work, the product of self-examination as well as literary experimentation. It exhibits its author's weaknesses as well as his strengths, but as a whole it is the creation of a powerful imagination seeking a way forwards in the spiritual maelstrom of 1970s Moscow." With the publication of *Ozhog*, concludes the critic, Aksyonov has proven himself to be "a Western as well as a Russian writer," an artist who "will now reach, and be appreciated by, an international audience."

Since leaving the Soviet Union, Aksyonov has traveled and lectured throughout Western Europe and the United States; Washington, D.C., has become his home base. (Soviet authorities officially revoked Aksyonov's citizenship four months after his departure.) Unusually prolific, he is not at all like many of his fellow exiles who find that they are unable to write away from the sights and sounds of their native land. "I brought enough baggage with me in my head to last for the rest of my life," he assured *Time* reporter Blake. Furthermore, Aksyonov commented in the *New York Times* interview with Kakutani, he and other Soviet writers now living in the West have an obligation to continue their work. Explains the author: "Sometimes we think the new emigration is a brain drain. But sometimes I think it is not a tragedy, that it is our duty as writers now in the West to try to restore the links between Russian culture and Western culture, to prove we haven't become people without any spiritual life."

Aksyonov does not believe, however, that the future of Russian literature rests entirely in the hands of those writers who have fled to the West. He admits that "for a long time I thought that we had no new wave behind us, that after our so-called literature of the post-Stalin years, there would be no more. But with the support in literary circles for *Metropol*, we found there are many new writers who don't want to be utilized by the official literature. For that reason, *Metropol* was not a complete failure." In short, concludes Aksyonov, "there are many talented people inside Russia, and despite all the restrictions, this will never be emptied—from under the pavement, there is always green grass rising. Maybe some day I will be allowed to come back to see it."

BIOGRAPHICAL/CRITICAL SOURCES—Books: Max Hayward and Edward L. Crowley, editors, *Soviet Literature in the Sixties: An International Symposium*, Methuen, 1964; Harold B. Segel, *Twentieth-Century Russian Drama: From Gorky to the Present*, Columbia University Press, 1979; Katerina Clark, *The Soviet Novel: History as Ritual*, University of Chicago Press, 1981; *Contemporary Literary Criticism*, Volume XXII, Gale, 1982.

Periodicals: *Times Literary Supplement*, September 3, 1964, September 25, 1981; *Soviet Literature*, Number 3, 1967; *World Literature Today*, summer, 1979, spring, 1981, summer, 1981, winter, 1982; *New York Times*, October 24, 1979, December 20, 1979, September 20, 1980; *Time*, June 23, 1980, November 8, 1982; *Newsweek*, December 8, 1980, November 21, 1983; *Washington Post*, January 23, 1981, May 18, 1981; *Los Angeles Times Book Review*, January 23, 1983; *Washington Post Book World*, December 18, 1983; *Chicago Tribune Book World*, February 19, 1984.

—Sketch by Deborah A. Straub

* * *

ALAND, Kurt 1915-

PERSONAL: Born March 28, 1915, in Berlin, Germany; son of Paul and Frieda (Mueller) Aland. *Education:* University of Berlin, Lic. theol., 1939, Lic. theol. habil., 1941. *Home:* Einsteinstrasse 12, 44 Munster, Germany. *Office:* University of Munster, Munster, Germany.

CAREER: Lutheran clergyman. University of Berlin, Berlin, Germany, docent, 1946-47; Martin Luther University, Halle-Wittenberg, Germany, professor, 1947-58; University of Munster, Munster, Germany, professor of church history and New Testament, 1958—. Director of Institute for New Testament Textual Research; manager of Foundation for the Promotion of New Testament Research. *Member:* Saxonian Academy, Academy of the Netherlands, British Academy, Goettingen Academy, American Bible Society (honorary member), Society of Biblical Literature (United States; honorary member).

Awards, honors: D.theol., University of Goettingen; D.D., University of St. Andrews; D.Litt., Wartburg College, Waverly, Iowa.

WRITINGS: (Editor) Philipp J. Spener, *Pia desideria*, de Gruyter, 1940, 3rd edition, 1964; *Spener-Studien*, de Gruyter, 1943; *Apologie der Apologetik*, Christlicher Zeitschriftenverlag, 1948.

(Editor) F. Loofs, *Oeitfaden zum Studium der Dogmengeschichte*, 5th edition (Aland was not associated with earlier editions), Niemeyer Verlag, 1950, 7th edition, 1968; *Der Text des Kleinen Katechismus in der Gegenwart*, Guetersloher Verlagshaus, 1954; *Kirchengeschichte in Lebensbildern dargestellt*, Volume I, Wichern-Verlag, 1953, 3rd edition, 1962; *Der Arbeiten der Deutschen Akademie der Wissenschaften auf dem Gebiet der Religionsgeschichte*, Akademie-Verlag, 1955, 2nd edition, 1957.

(Editor with W. Matzkow) A. Julicher, *Itala*, de Gruyter, Volume III: *Lukasevangelium*, 1956, 2nd edition, 1976, Volume IV: *Johannesevangelium*, 1963, Volume II: *Markusevangelium*, 1970, Volume I: *Matthaeusevangelium*, 1972; (with E. Nestle) *Novum Testamentum Graece*, 22nd edition, United Bible Societies (London), 1956, 26th edition, 1979; *Novum Testamentum Graece et Latine*, 17th edition, Bibelanstalt, 1956, 22nd edition, 1963; (editor) H. Lietzmann, *Zeitrechnung der roemischen Kaiserzeit, des Mittelalters und der Neuzeit fuer die Jahre 1-2000 nach Christus*, 3rd edition (Aland was not associated with earlier editions), de Gruyter, 1956; *Die Handschriftenbestaende der polnischen Bibliotheken, insbesondere an griechischen und lateinischen Handschriften*, Akademie-Verlag, 1956; (editor) *Luther Deutsch und Lutherlexikon*, eleven volumes, Klotz Verlag, 1956, 4th edition, 1972; (with Ernst R. Reichert and Gerhard Jordan) *Hilfsbuch zum Lutherstudium*, Evangelische Verlaganstalt, 1957, 3rd edition, 1970; (editor with Frank Leslie Cross) *Studia Patristica*, Akademie-Verlag, 1957; (author of foreword and contributor) Adolf von Harnack, *Geschichte der altchristlichen Literatur bis Eusebius*, J. C. Hinrichs, 1958, 2nd edition, 1968.

Kirchengeschichtliche Entwuerfe: Alte Kirche, Reformation und Luthertum, Pietismus und Erweckungsbewegung, Guetersloher Verlagshaus, 1960; *Die Saeuglingstaufe im Neuen Testament und in der alten Kirche*, Kaiser-Verlag, 1961, 2nd edition, 1963, translation by G. R. Beasley-Murray published as *Did the Early Church Baptize Infants?*, Westminster, 1963; *Uber den Glaubenswechsel in der Geschichte des Christentums*, A. Toepelmann, 1961; *The Problem of the New Testament Canon* (lecture), Mowbray, 1962; *Kurzgefasste Liste der griechischen Handschriften des Neuen Testaments*, de Gruyter, 1963; (editor) *Synopsis Quattuor Evangeliorum*, United Bible Societies, 1964, 12th edition, 1982.

(With others) *The Authorship and Integrity of the New Testament: Some Recent Studies*, S.P.C.K., 1965; (editor) *Martin Luther's 95 Thesen*, Furche-Verlag, 1965, translation published as *Martin Luther's 95 Theses, with the Pertinent Documents from the History of the Reformation*, Concordia, 1968; *Der Weg zur Reformation, Zeitpunkt und Charakter des reformatorischen Erlebnisses Martin Luthers*, Kaiser-Verlag, 1965; (editor with M. Black, B. M. Metzger and A. Wikgren) *The Greek New Testament*, United Bible Societies, 1966, American Bible Society, 1967, 4th edition, 1983; *Studien zur Ueberlieferung des Neuen Testaments und seines Textes*, de Gruyter, 1967; *Repetitorium der Kirchengeschichte III: Reformation und Gegenreformation*, de Gruyter, 1967; *Quellen zur Geschichte des Papsttums und des Papsttums und des Katholizismus*, J.C.B. Mohr, 1967; *Von den Anfaengen bis zum Tridentinum*, J.C.B. Mohr, 1967; *Materialien zur neutestamentlichen Handschriftenkunde*, de Gruyter, 1968; (editor) *Works of I. H. von Wessenberg*, Herder-Verlag, Volume I, 1968, Volume IV, 1970, Volume III, 1983.

Saints and Sinners: Men and Ideas in the Early Church, Fortress, 1970; *Taufe und Kindertaufe, 40 Saetze zur Aussage des Neuen Testaments und dem historischen Befund*, Guetersloher Verlagshaus, 1971; *Synopsis of the Four Gospels* (Greek and English edition), United Bible Societies, 1972, 5th edition, 1982; *Martin Luther in der modernen Literatur: Ein kritischer Dokumentarbericht*, Luther Verlag, 1973; *Vollstaendige Konkordanz zum griechischen Neuen Testament*, de Gruyter, 1975-83; *Repertorium der griechischen christlichen Papyri, I Biblische Papyri*, de Gruyter, 1976, 2nd edition, 1980; *Die Reformatoren*, Guetersloher Verlagshaus, 1976; *Glanz und Niedergang der deutschen Universitaet. 50 Jahre deutscher Wissenschaftsgeschichte in Briefen an und von Hans Lietzmann (1892-1942)*, de Gruyter, 1979; *Neustamentliche Entwuerfe*, Kaiser-Verlag, 1979; *Four Reformers*, Augsburg, 1979.

Geschichte der Christenheit, Guetersloher Verlagshaus, Volume I: *Von den Anfaengen bis an die Schwelle der Reformation*, 1980, Volume II: *Von der Reformation bis in die Gegenwart*, 1982; *Von Jesus bis Justinian*, Guetersloher Verlagshaus, 1981; (with Barbara Aland) *Der Text des griechischen Neuen Testaments: Eine Einfuehrung in den Gebrauch der modernen Ausgaben sowie in Theorie und Praxis der neustamentlichen Textkritik*, Deutsche Bibelgesellschaft Stuttgart, 1982; *Die Reformation Martin Luthers*, Guetersloher Verlagshaus, 1982; *Die 95 Thesen Martin Luthers und die Anfaenge der Reformation*, Guetersloher Verlagshaus, 1983; (editor) *Martin Luthers 95 Thesen nebst dem Sermon von Ablass und Gnade*, 3rd revised edition, de Gruyter, 1983.

* * *

ALCOTT, Julia
See CUDLIPP, Edythe

* * *

ALDCROFT, Derek H. 1936-

PERSONAL: Born October 25, 1936, in Abergele, North Wales; son of Leslie Howard and Freda (Wallen) Aldcroft. *Education:* University of Manchester, B.A., 1958, Ph.D., 1962. *Politics:* Conservative. *Home:* 10 Linden Dr., Leicester, Leicestershire LE1 7RH, England. *Office:* Department of Economic History, University of Leicester, Leicester, Leicestershire LE1 7RH, England.

CAREER: University of Glasgow, Glasgow, Scotland, assistant lecturer in economic history, 1960-62; University of Leicester, Leicester, England, assistant lecturer, 1962-63; University of Glasgow, lecturer in economic history, 1964-67; University of Leicester, senior lecturer, 1967-70, reader, 1970-73; University of Sydney, Sydney, New South Wales, Australia, professor of economic history and head of department, 1973-76; University of Leicester, professor of economic history and head of department, 1976—. *Member:* Economic History Society (member of council).

WRITINGS: (Editor) *The Development of British Industry and Foreign Competition, 1875-1914*, Allen & Unwin, 1968; (with Harry Ward Richardson) *Building in the British Economy between the Wars*, Allen & Unwin, 1968; *British Railways in Transition: The Economic Problems of Britain's Railways since*

1914, Macmillan, 1968, St. Martin's, 1969; (with Harold James Dyos) *British Transport: An Economic Survey from the Seventeenth Century to the Twentieth*, Leicester University Press, 1969; (with Richardson) *The British Economy, 1870-1939*, Macmillan, 1969; (editor with Peter Fearon) *Economic Growth in Twentieth-Century Britain*, Macmillan, 1969, Humanities, 1970.

The Inter-War Economy: Britain, 1919-1939, Columbia University Press, 1970; (editor with Fearon) *British Economic Fluctuations, 1790-1970*, Macmillan, 1972; *Studies in British Transport History, 1870-1970*, David & Charles, 1974; *British Transport since 1914*, David & Charles, 1975; *From Versailles to Wall Street, 1919-1929*, University of California Press, 1977; *The European Economy, 1914-1970*, Croom Helm, 1977, St. Martin's, 1978, revised and enlarged edition published as *The European Economy, 1914-1980*, Croom Helm, 1980; (editor with Neil K. Burton) *British Industry between the Wars: Instability and Industrial Development, 1919-1939*, Scolar Press, 1979; *The East Midlands Economy*, Pointon York, 1979.

Rail Transport (bound with *Sea Transport* by Derrick Mort), Pergamon Press, 1981; (editor with P. L. Cottrell) *Shipping, Trade and Commerce*, Leicester University Press, 1981; (editor with Anthony Slaven) *Business, Banking and Urban History*, John Donald Publishers, 1982; *The British Economy between the Wars*, Philip Allan, 1983; (editor with Michael Freeman) *Transport in the Industrial Revolution*, Manchester University Press, 1983; *Full Employment: The Elusive Goal*, Harvester Press, 1984; (editor with Richard Rodger) *Bibliography of European Economic and Social History*, Manchester University Press, 1984. Member of advisory panel, *Economic Review*.

WORK IN PROGRESS: Research on "the constraints to full employment in the 1930's and 1980's and British economic growth in the twentieth century."

SIDELIGHTS: In a review of Derek H. Aldcroft's *British Industry between the Wars: Instability and Industrial Development, 1919-1939*, T. C. Barker writes in the *Times Literary Supplement:* "In [this] volume ten economic historians attempt [to look] at the performance of particular industries during the inter-war period.... This book is a courageous and commendable first shot at what is at present an impossible task, for the basic research has not yet been undertaken. [However,] this book provides new and significant insights into manufacturing problems between the wars. Above all, it brings about the need for much more research in this area."

AVOCATIONAL INTERESTS: Tennis, swimming, gardening, and the stock market.

BIOGRAPHICAL/CRITICAL SOURCES: Times Literary Supplement, April 18, 1980.

* * *

ALIBRANDI, Tom 1941-

PERSONAL: Born August 10, 1941, in Syracuse, N.Y.; son of John G. (in construction) and Elsya (Wilson) Alibrandi; children: John, Timothy, Sabin. *Education:* Attended University of Arizona, 1959-61; Syracuse University, B.A., 1963; University of California, Los Angeles, counseling certificate, 1974. *Home and office address:* P.O. Box 1118, Ben Lomond, Calif. 95005.

CAREER: Employed in construction management in Syracuse, N.Y., Los Angeles, Calif., and Montreal, Quebec, 1963-71; carpenter in Orange County, Calif., 1971-74; Family Development Program, Laguna Beach, Calif., counselor, 1975-79; writer. Director of youth programs for Orange County Alcoholism Program, 1975-79. *Awards, honors:* Grant from Orange County, Calif. 1976; Porgi Award from *West Coast Book Review,* 1979.

WRITINGS: Free Yourself, Major, 1975; *The Meditation Handbook,* Major, 1976; *Biorhythm: Get the Most Out of Your Life,* Major, 1976; *Young Alcoholics* (novel; also see below), Comp-Care, 1978; *Hallways: Poems of Transitions,* Chicken Walk, 1978; *Killshot* (novel; also see below), Pinnacle Books, 1979; *Uncle Joe Shannon,* Pinnacle Books, 1979; *Custody,* Pinnacle Books, 1979; *Burnout,* Pinnacle Books, 1981; *Blood Fortunes,* Dell, 1982.

Screenplays: "Young Alcoholics" (based on Alibrandi's novel of same title), TGB Productions, 1978; "Killshot" (based on Alibrandi's novel of same title), Samuel Goldwyn Jr. Productions, 1982.

Contributor to *Alcoholism Digest, Grapevine,* and *Modern People Newsweekly.*

WORK IN PROGRESS: Privileged Information, a non-fiction novel.

SIDELIGHTS: Tom Alibrandi told *CA:* "[I] started writing in 1974 after I hurt my back on a construction project. My hope is to write the truth as I see it, in such a fashion that a reader will feel as though it has happened to him/her. After ten published books, numerous magazine articles and two screenplays, I feel as though I've served my apprenticeship in writing."

BIOGRAPHICAL/CRITICAL SOURCES: Washington Post Book World, March 4, 1979.

* * *

ALIKI
See BRANDENBERG, Aliki Liacouras

* * *

ALLAMAND, Pascale 1942-

PERSONAL: Born September 22, 1942, in Montreux, Switzerland; daughter of Pierre (a travel agent) and Yvette (Milharoux) Allamand. *Education:* Ecole secondaire, Montreux, Switzerland, diploma, 1963. *Home and office:* Grand Rue 25, 1095 Lutry, Switzerland.

CAREER: Writer and illustrator of children's books. Apprentice photographer in Montreux, Switzerland, 1960-63; assistant to publicity and fashion photographer in Lausanne, Switzerland, 1963-70; free-lance photographic reporter in Lutry, Switzerland, 1970—.

WRITINGS—All juveniles; all self-illustrated: *The Boy and His Friend the Bear,* J. Cape, 1974; *The Pop Rooster,* translation by Michael Bullock, Scribner, 1975; *The Camel Who Left the Zoo,* Scribner, 1976; *The Little Goat in the Alps,* J. Cape, 1977; *A la Mode de Chez Nous* (cookbook; title means "Our Art of Cooking"), Payot, 1976; *Cocoa Beans and Daisies: How Swiss Chocolate Is Made,* Warne, 1978; *The Animals Who Changed Their Colors,* translation by Elizabeth Watson Taylor, Lothrup, 1979.

Illustrator of books by Nina Bawden: *William Tell,* Lothrup, 1981; *St. Francis of Assisi,* Lothrup, 1983.

WORK IN PROGRESS: A book about a celebrated man or woman, with Nina Bawden.

SIDELIGHTS: Pascale Allamand told *CA:* "If I make books for children, it is for three reasons: I love children, I love to paint, and I love to listen to stories and to tell them. Now at my age, as much as when I was small, I still love to listen to stories being told, whether they are for adults or children. So why shouldn't I tell them myself?"

* * *

ALLEN, Barbara
See STUART, (Violet) Vivian (Finlay)

* * *

ALLEN, Charlotte Vale 1941-
(Claire Vincent)

PERSONAL: Born January 19, 1941, in Toronto, Ontario, Canada; came to the United States in 1966; Canadian citizen; married Walter Bateman Allen, Jr., July 21, 1970 (divorced, 1976); married Barrie Baldaro (an actor and writer), January 23, 1980 (divorced, 1982); children: (first marriage) Kimberly Jordan Allen (daughter). *Education:* Attended drama school in Toronto, Ontario. *Politics:* No affiliation. *Religion:* No affiliation. *Home:* 25 Rowayton Woods Dr., Norwalk, Conn. 06854; and 29 Scarth Rd., Toronto, Ontario, Canada M4W 2S5. *Agent:* Paul R. Reynolds, Inc., 12 East 41st St., New York, N.Y. 10017.

CAREER: Actress and singer, 1959-63; revue performer and singer, 1963-71; insurance broker, 1971-74; writer, 1975—. Lecturer on the sexual abuse of children, 1980—.

WRITINGS—Novels, except as indicated: *Love Life*, Delacorte, 1976; *Hidden Meanings*, Warner Books, 1976; *Sweeter Music*, Warner Books, 1976; *Gentle Stranger*, Warner Books, 1977; *Another Kind of Magic*, Warner Books, 1977; *Mixed Emotions*, Warner Books, 1977; *Running Away*, New American Library, 1977; *Becoming*, Warner Books, 1977; *Julia's Sister*, Warner Books, 1978; (under pseudonym Claire Vincent) *Believing in Giants*, New American Library, 1978; *Acts of Kindness*, New American Library, 1979; *Moments of Meaning*, New American Library, 1979; *Promises*, Dutton, 1979.

Times of Triumph, New American Library, 1980; *Gifts of Love*, Dutton, 1980; *Daddy's Girl* (nonfiction), Wyndham Books, 1980; *The Marmalade Man*, Dutton, 1981; *Perfect Fools*, New English Library, 1981; *Intimate Friends*, Dutton, 1982; *Meet Me in Time*, Berkley Publishing, 1983. Also author, with Jo Kirkpatrick, of screenplay "Daddy's Girl," based on Allen's book of the same title.

WORK IN PROGRESS: A novel, for Berkley Publishing.

SIDELIGHTS: Charlotte Vale Allen told *CA* that although her books are about women, they are not just *for* women but "for everyone. I like to include issues of both social and emotional significance." Having written a number of successful novels in this vein, she published *Daddy's Girl*, an autobiographical work in which she comes to grips with a childhood made almost intolerable by her sexually abusive father. It is, writes Marilyn Murray Willison in the *Los Angeles Times Book Review,* "the harrowing tale of a childhood spent amidst a bitter, exploited mother and a manipulative and selfish father. Charlotte and her two older brothers were victims trapped by circumstance, but Charlotte bore the added indignity of being forced to suffer through her father's incestuous demands." *Library Journal* reviewer Janet Husband says that this is "altogether a powerful story, told with the considerable skill and restraint necessary to keep the facts from seeming sensational or maudlin." And Eleanor Wachtel, in a *Books in Canada* article, states that Allen "writes effectively. . . . She has written a genuinely troubling book, annoying, uncomfortable, and compelling."

Intertwined with the childhood recollections in *Daddy's Girl* are what Willison calls "verbal snapshots" of the author's struggle to free herself from her past. She had been conditioned to think of herself as ugly and unloveable, and thus "learning to love herself (much less a man) became a full-time assignment" during her adulthood. Writes Willison: "One finishes the book thinking that if it weren't for the kind and understanding attention of a high-school teacher (as well as the earlier ministrations of an aunt and uncle) the author would surely not be with us today." In addition to these early positive influences, Allen was aided by two friends, Norman and Lola, who helped her face her distasteful childhood and rebuild her life. As a result, she is able to write about her past with complete candor. As she says in *Daddy's Girl:* "It's impossible to forget what happened. I can't use Liquid Paper on 10 years of my life [from the age of seven to seventeen] and put a nice, thick white coat over it the way I do typing errors."

AVOCATIONAL INTERESTS: Needlepoint, tennis, photography; has studied drama, ballet, piano, art, and guitar.

BIOGRAPHICAL/CRITICAL SOURCES: Charlotte Vale Allen, *Daddy's Girl*, Wyndham Books, 1980; *Los Angeles Times Book Review*, September 18, 1980; *Library Journal*, December 1, 1980; *Books in Canada*, January, 1981.

* * *

ALTHER, Lisa 1944-

PERSONAL: Born July 23, 1944, in Tennessee; daughter of John Shelton (a surgeon) and Alice Margaret (Greene) Reed; married Richard Philip Alther (a painter), August 26, 1966; children: Sara Halsey. *Education:* Wellesley College, B.A., 1966. *Politics:* None. *Religion:* None. *Address:* c/o Alfred A. Knopf, Inc., 201 East 50th St., New York, N.Y. 10022.

CAREER: Atheneum Publishers, New York, N.Y., secretary and editorial assistant, 1967; free-lance writer, 1967—. Writer for Garden Way, Inc., Charlotte, Vt., 1970-71. Member of board of directors of Planned Parenthood of Champlain Valley, 1972. *Member:* P.E.N., National Writers' Union, Authors Guild, Authors League of America.

WRITINGS—Novels; published by Knopf: *Kinflicks*, 1976; *Original Sins*, 1981.

Other: (Author of introduction) Flannery O'Connor, *A Good Man Is Hard to Find*, Women's Press, 1980. Contributor of articles and stories to national magazines, including *Vogue, Cosmopolitan, Natural History, New Society, Yankee, Vermont Freeman, New Englander, New York Times Magazine,* and *New York Times Book Review*.

WORK IN PROGRESS: A novel.

SIDELIGHTS: In an age when most first fictions are ignored by readers and critics, Lisa Alther's *Kinflicks* made publishing news. Instead of a small press run, the 503-page novel boasted an initial printing of 30,000 hardback copies; it quickly ascended to the bestseller lists and was widely and favorably reviewed. In fact, Alther's satiric portrayal of a young woman's coming of age in the sixties so captivated the critics that it was immediately elevated to the company of J. D. Salinger's classic apprenticeship novel—*Catcher in the Rye*.

This comparison stems largely from the similarity between the novels' protagonists. In her search for a meaningful existence, Ginny Babcock emerges as a female Holden Caulfield. Like him, she is a survivor, and while the story of how adolescents survive is by now a familiar one, Alther's graphic depiction of Ginny's Tennessee teens, her flight north, and subsequent return south to her mother's deathbed rescues the novel from predictability. As a *New Yorker* critic puts it: "A number of other excellent writers have covered various parts of the turf covered here," but "no other writer has yet synthesized this material as well as Miss Alther has. In fact, it would not be an exaggeration to say that her cynical, clear-eyed, well-heeled, disaster-prone heroine, Ginny Babcock, can easily take her place alongside Holden Caulfield as a symbol of everything that is right and wrong about a generation." Furthermore, notes Valentine Cunningham in the *New Statesman,* "her account is often to be caught uproariously in the wry."

Cunningham's pun is an allusion to the comedic vein in which the story is written. Its broad social canvas, grim humor, and episodic structuring suggest a picaresque novel to some critics. Written in segments that alternate first person flashbacks with third person accounts of the present, *Kinflicks* affords two views of reality. The first is Ginny's, intimate, irreverent, at times burlesque; the second is more detached and serious, representing the author's point of view. "It doesn't always work—this tension between Ginny's wise-guy view of events and the way things actually work out," writes the *New York Times'* Christopher Lehmann-Haupt. "There are characters who shrivel into mere jokes—like the senile football coach who keeps shouting orders in the hospital room next door to Ginny's mother. And there are mere jokes that grow tiresome. . . . But when this tension works, it works marvelously—especially as a way of dramatizing Ginny's lack of identity (for how can she have an identity if she sees everything that happens to her as a joke?). Toward the end of the novel the strangest little things begin to move us a great deal."

Reviewers recognize that Alther's intent in splitting the narrative was to invest a comic novel with serious undertones, but they have differing opinions on the success of the technique. *New York Times Book Review* contributing critic Mary Cantwell believes "Miss Alther's alternation of the two points of view adds up to an almost flawless balance of light and dark, the skittery and the sad." But *Time's* Paul Gray finds the serious segments out of place in such a comedy. "Alther tries to make the illness and eventual death of Ginny's mother the rite of passage that will turn the daughter into a self-winding adult. But Mrs. Babcock, whose suffering and despair are movingly portrayed, seems to have been smuggled in from a different novel. *Kinflicks,* for better and worse, belongs to Ginny and her amusing, if hardly profound, moral: Sisterhood is Slapstick." But despite the imbalances Gray and other critics find in the novel, most agree that Alther's abilities shine through. "Lisa Alther has an honest talent for broad social comedy," observes Thomas R. Edwards in the *New York Review of Books,* "and it's the familiar, and forgivable, impulse to be 'serious' that makes *Kinflicks* too long, too much more than the rude portrait of failed contemporary desires and enthusiasms it was in its power to be."

In her second novel, *Original Sins,* Alther covers much the same territory she did in her first, only this time there are five protagonists. "*Kinflicks* followed a single heroine from her Tennessee upbringing through a series of wacky encounters up North with the countercultures of the '60s," Paul Gray explains in *Time.* "*Original Sins* quintuples its predecessor, offering five main characters, all Southerners, who try to grow up in a region and a country that are changing even faster than they are."

But whereas her first novel is a burlesque satire, bordering on farce, *Original Sins* "is a protest novel of a conventional sort, a compound of outrage and doctrine," according to Mark Schechner. "It is an all-out assault on the South for its rigidly maintained double standards on matters of race, sex, and class and for its failures to live up to its deficiencies," he continues in his *New Republic* review.

The novel opens with a prologue in which five children—"The Five" as they call themselves—are seated in a big beech known as The Castle Tree. Inseparable playmates, Sally and Emily Prince, Jed and Raymond Tatro, and their black cohort Donny are planning their futures together. As time passes and innocence fades, however, the realities of money, race, and class break them apart, and—as Schechner notes—"no measures ever after, not even the shotgun wedding of Jed and Sally, can join together what the facts of life have torn asunder."

As Alther chronicles their adventures, including the relocation of three of "The Five" to the North, she paints a broad social history of the sixties and seventies. Women's liberation, Vietnam, black power, civil rights, and the counterculture movement are among her subjects, but the portrait that emerges is unsatisfactory to some. Several critics charge that in her attempt to tell it all, to cover so much ground, Alther has sacrificed her characters' individuality. "The reader is haunted by the thought that the central characters, with the exception, perhaps, of the obstinately individualistic Emily, exist chiefly in order to illustrate differently developing states of political consciousness, as their progress from childhood to maturity is traced in often absorbing but sometimes oppressive detail," the *Times Literary Supplement* reviewer notes.

"The essential problem with those nearly 600 pages," Susan Wood writes in the *Washington Post Book World,* "is that they present every cliche you've ever heard about the South or about the political movements of the last two decades as though they are really, truly true: that is, with no sense of the complexities of individual lives, with no sympathy for the characters. These are not real people about whom we can care, merely stick figures."

Other reviewers object to Alther's use of dialect and her heavy-handed metaphors. Still others consider the book too preachy. But Cyra McFadden maintains that Lisa Alther's "excesses are those of overflowing talent and high spirits," and in her *Chicago Tribune Book World* review, McFadden proclaims *Original Sins* "a thoroughly endearing book." As Paul Gray puts it: "Alther takes risks that sometimes fail. She is willing to sacrifice plausibility for a comic effect, to put her characters through paces that occasionally seem dictated rather than inevitable. But such lapses are more than offset by the novel's page-turning verve and intelligence." Alther "gives generously, both to her readers and to the children of her imagination," he concludes.

BIOGRAPHICAL/CRITICAL SOURCES: Village Voice, March 8, 1976; *New York Times Book Review,* March 14, 1976, May 3, 1981; *New York Times,* March 16, 1976; *Saturday Review,* March 20, 1976, April, 1981; *Time,* March 22, 1976, April 27, 1981; *Washington Post Book World,* March 28, 1976, May 31, 1981; *New Yorker,* March 29, 1976, May 4, 1981; *New York Review of Books,* April 1, 1976; *New Statesman,* August 27, 1976, May 29, 1981; *Harper's,* May, 1976; *Contemporary*

Literary Criticism, Volume VII, Gale, 1977; *Nation,* April 25, 1981; *Ms.,* May, 1981; *Los Angeles Times,* June 4, 1981; *New Republic,* June 13, 1981; *Chicago Tribune Book World,* June 14, 1981; *Times Literary Supplement,* June 26, 1981.

—Sketch by Donna Olendorf

* * *

AMES, Norma 1920-

PERSONAL: Born August 17, 1920; daughter of Robert M. (a mail carrier) and Flora (Wiener) Knipple; married July 8, 1944 (divorced, 1956); children: Karyn. *Education:* Smith College, A.B. (magna cum laude), 1942; graduate study at Wellesley College, 1942, and at Institute of Arctic and Alpine Research, University of Colorado, 1964. *Home and office address:* Box 4233, Santa Fe, N.M. 87502.

CAREER: Curtiss-Wright Aircraft, Buffalo, N.Y., time study engineer, 1942-44; free-lance advertising copywriter and artist in Buffalo, 1944, and Santa Fe, N.M., 1944-46; worked as bookkeeper, chicken farmer, and at other jobs in Santa Fe, 1946-54; New Mexico Taxpayers Association, Santa Fe, research assistant, 1954-56; New Mexico Department of Game and Fish, Santa Fe, wildlife management officer, 1956-74, assistant chief of game management and supervisor of endangered species program, 1974-76, publications director, 1976-82; United States Fish and Wildlife Service, leader of Mexican Wolf Recovery Team, 1979—. Member, New Mexico Environmental Education Committee; New Mexico representative to Western Regional Environmental Education Council, 1971-74; researcher and breeder of Mexican wolves, 1971—.

MEMBER: Wildlife Society (chairman of conservation education committee, Mexico-Arizona section, 1969-72), National Audubon Society, American Association for the Advancement of Science, National Wildlife Federation, American Society of Mammalogists, North American Wolf Society, Wild Canid Survival and Research Center, North American Wildlife Park Foundation, Phi Beta Kappa, Sigma Xi. *Awards, honors:* Conservation Education Award of the Wildlife Society for *New Mexico Wildlife Management;* KOB wildlife and conservation award; Leopold Award from New Mexico chapter of Nature Conservancy.

WRITINGS: (Editor, contributor, and illustrator) *New Mexico Wildlife Management,* New Mexico Department of Game and Fish, 1967; *My Path Belated* (novel), Avon, 1970; *Whisper in the Forest* (novel), Avon, 1971; *Wildlife and People in New Mexico,* New Mexico Department of Game and Fish, 1979. Author of booklet series on mammals, birds, and fish, published by New Mexico Department of Game and Fish, 1960-64, and other department materials. Illustrator of *Woody Plants of New Mexico,* 1971, and *Woody Plants of the Southwest,* 1975. Contributor of articles to *New Mexico Wildlife, National Wildlife, Journal of North American Wolf Society,* and quarterly journal of American Association for the Advancement of Science; contributor of reviews to *Science Books and Films.*

WORK IN PROGRESS: A nonfiction book based on personal experiences and philosophies during work with wolves since 1971, and as leader of an international team of biologists responsible for recovering the Mexican wolf from the brink of extinction.

SIDELIGHTS: Norma Ames writes *CA:* "My acquisition of Mexican wolves in 1971 affected my whole life, including my literary output. Now, my work 'in progress' is, naturally, about wolves, but future books planned will include other kinds of wildlife.

"There is great need today for far more people to understand and cherish the natural world as it really is. The majority—who decide fates—still see the natural world as something expendable or exploitable or improvable or easily recreated by man. Direct exposure to nature is the best route to understanding and love, but most of urban America today can be exposed only through word and picture. Conveying understanding and love of nature will be a concern of my writing, whether nonfiction or fiction.

"In the near future, I also plan to return to fiction with human characters; my 'dime novels' of the early '70's were fun to do. More important, however, the novel permits an author to provide the reader with a sharpness of insight, a depth of philosophy, a flight of laughter, and a clutch of the heart, even in reporting events derived from the truth that is stranger than fiction (avoids libel suits, too!)."

* * *

ANCEL, Marc 1902-

PERSONAL: Born July 14, 1902, in Izeste, France; son of Leon (a director of a school for teachers) and Marie-Therese (Cambus) Ancel; married Yvonne Comte, August 12, 1935; children: Jacqueline (Mrs. Jean-Charles Sacotte), Jean-Pierre. *Education:* University of Paris, licence es lettres, licence en droit, and doctorat en droit. *Home:* 120 bis Boulevard du Montparnasse, 75014 Paris, France. *Office:* Institut de Droit Compare, Universite de Paris II, 28 rue Saint-Guillaume, 75007 Paris, France.

CAREER: Deputy district attorney, Valenciennes, France, 1929; temporary official in Ministry of Justice, 1930; University of Paris II, Institut de Droit Compare, Paris, France, secretary, 1932-34, secretary general, 1934-54, director of criminal science section, 1954—; Court of Appeal of Paris, Paris, beginning 1936, judge, beginning 1946, presiding judge of the chamber, beginning 1951; Supreme Court of Appeal of France, Paris, 1936—, judge, 1954-68, presiding judge in first division for civil cases, 1968-72, judge emeritus, 1982—; Centre Francais de Droit Compare, secretary general, 1956-68, president, 1968-82, honorary president, 1982—. Deputy public prosecutor, Rouen, France, 1934; judge, Tribunal de la Seine, 1940. Conseil de l'Europe, Comite Europeen pour les Problemes Criminels, president, 1957-62, member of scientific council, 1972-75; president, Association Internationale des Sciences Juridiques, UNESCO, 1966-68; member, United Nations International Committee against Racial Discrimination, 1970-75; president, Centre de Recherches de Politique Criminelle, 1973—.

MEMBER: Societe Internationale de Defense Sociale (president, 1966—), Institut de France (member of Academie des Sciences Morales et Politiques), Societe de Legislation Comparee (assistant secretary general, 1944-51; vice-president, 1951-66; president, 1966-69), Societe des Prisons et de Legislation Criminelle (president, 1981-84), Academy of Sciences (Hungary), Academy of Sciences (Union of Soviet Socialist Republics), Louisiana Law Institute (United States; honorary member), Instituto de Criminologia (Buenos Aires; honorary member). *Awards, honors:* Commandeur de la Legion d'Honneur; Officier de l'Ordre des Palmes Academiques; Officier de l'Ordre de la Sante Publique; Officier de l'Ordre de la Couronne (Belgium); Commandeur de l'Ordre du Merite (Italy); Commandeur de l'Ordre Equestre de Sainte-Agathe (San Marino);

Officier de l'Ordre National de la Cote-d'Ivoire; Commandeur d l'Ordre du Drapeau (Yugoslavia); medaille de l'Administration Penitentiaire et le l'Education Surveillee; LL.D., University of Geneva and University of Edinburgh.

WRITINGS—In English: *La Defense sociale nouvelle: Un Mouvement de politique criminelle humaniste*, Editions Cujas, 1954, translation and revision by J. Wilson and the author published as *Social Defence: A Modern Approach to Criminal Problems*, Routledge & Kegan Paul, 1965, Schocken, 1966, 3rd French edition, Editions Cujas, 1981; *The Death Penalty in European Countries*, Council of Europe, 1962.

In French: *La "Common Law" d'Angleterre* (title means "The Common Law of England"), Rousseau & Sons, 1927; (editor) *La Condition de la femme dans la societe contemporaine: Etat actuel des legislations concernant les droits politiques, l'activite professionnelle, la capacite civile, la situation de la femme dans la famille et la condition de la femme au regard du droit penal* (title means "The Condition of Women in Contemporary Society: The Present Status of Legislation Concerning Political Rights, Professional Activity, Civil Capacity, the Situation of Women in the Family, and the Condition of Women with Respect to Penal Law"), Recueil Sirey, 1938; *Traite de la capacite civile de la femme mariee d'apres la loi du 18 fevrier 1938*, [Paris], 1938, supplement, 1942; *L'Adoption dans les legislations modernes: Essai de synthese comparative suivi du releve systematique des legislations actuelles relatives a l'adoption* (title means "Adoption in Modern Legislation: An Essay in Comparative Synthesis Followed by a Systematic Statement of Existing Legislation Relating to Adoption"), Recueil Sirey, 1943, 2nd edition, 1958.

(Editor) *Les Grands Systemes penitentiaires actuels* (title means "The Great Penitential Systems of the Present Day"), [Paris], Volume I, 1950, Volume II, 1955; *Les Mesures de surete en matiere criminelle*, [Melun], 1950; *Les Methodes modernes de traitement penitentiaire*, Fondation Internationale Penale et Penitentiaire, 1951; *La Sentence indeterminee*, United Nations, 1953.

(Editor with Leon F. Julliot de la Morandiere) *L'Oeuvre juridique de Levy-Ullmann: Contribution a la doctrine moderne sur la science du droit et le droit compare* (title means "The Juridicial Work of Levy-Ullmann: Contribution to the Modern Doctrine on the Science of Law and Comparative Law"), Centre Francais de Droit Compare, 1955; *Introduction comparative aux codes penaux europeens*, [Paris], 1956; (editor with Antonin Besson) *La Prevention des infractions contre la vie humaine et l'integrite de la personne* (title means "The Prevention of Infractions against Human Life and the Integrity of the Person"), two volumes, Editions Cujas, 1956; (editor with Yvonne Marx and others) *Les Codes penaux europeens presentes dans leur texte actuel, avec un notice speciale sur chaque code et une introduction comparative generale* (title means "The European Penal Codes Presented in Their Existing Texts, with a Special Notice on Each Code and an Introduction"), six volumes, Centre Francais de Droit Compare, 1956-81; (editor with L. Radzinowicz) *Introduction au droit criminel de l'Angleterre* (title means "Introduction to British Criminal Law"), Editions de l'Epargne, 1959; (with Georges Levasseur) *Les Delinquants anormaux mentaux*, Editions Cujas, 1959.

(With Andre Besson) *Seuils d'age et legislation penale*, Editions Cujas, 1961; *Le Peine capitale*, United Nations, 1962; (editor and author of introduction) *La Reforme penale sovietique: Code penal, loi d'organisation judiciaire de la R.S.F.S.R. du 27 octobre 1960* (title means "Soviet Penal Reform: Penal Code, Code of Penal Procedure, Law of Judicial Organization for the R.S.F.S.R. of October 27, 1960"), Centre Francais de Droit Compare, 1962; (editor with Nikola Srzentic and others) *Le Droit penal nouveau de la Yougoslavie* (title means "The New Penal Law of Yugoslavia"), Editions de l'Epargne, 1962; (editor with Louis B. Schwartz) *Le Systeme penal des Etats-Unis d'Amerique* (title means "The Penal System of the United States of America"), Editions de l'Epargne, 1964; (editor with G. Bettiol) *Etudes en l'honneur de Jean Graven: La Protection des droits de l'homme selon les doctrines de la defense sociale moderne*, Librairie de l'Universite-Georg, 1969.

Utilite et methodes du droit compare: Elements d'introduction generale a l'etude comparative des droits (title means "Uses and Methods of Comparative Law: Elements of General Introduction to the Comparative Study of Law"), Editions Ides et Calendes, 1971; (with A. A. Piontkovsky) *Le Systeme penal sovietique*, Librairie Generale de Droit et de Jurisprudence, 1975; *Le Divorce a l'etranger: Etude de politique legislative comparee*, Documentation Francaise, 1975; *Le Juge du divorce: Politique judiciaire comparee*, Ministere de la Justice (Paris), 1978. Also author of *Le Probleme de l'enfance delinquante*, 1947.

Editor-in-chief, *Annuaire de Legislation Francaise et Etrangere*, Centre de Recherches de Politique Criminelle, 1949-68. Contributor to scholarly journals in France and abroad. Editor-in-chief, *Revue de Science Criminelle et de Droit Penal Compare*, 1936—, and *Archives de Politique Criminelle*, 1975—; *Revue Internationale de Droit Compare*, editor-in-chief, 1950-75, director, 1975—.

BIOGRAPHICAL/CRITICAL SOURCES: *Aspects nouveaux de la pensee juridique* (festschrift), two volumes, [Paris], 1975.

* * *

ANDERSEN, Ted
See BOYD, Waldo T.

* * *

ANDREASSEN, Karl
See BOYD, Waldo T.

* * *

ANICAR, Tom
See RACINA, Thom

* * *

ANTONOVSKY, Aaron 1923-

PERSONAL: Born December 19, 1923, in Brooklyn, N.Y.; son of Isaac (a laundryman) and Esther (Halperin) Antonovsky; married Helen Faigin (a psychologist), November 27, 1958; children: Avishai. *Education:* Brooklyn College (now Brooklyn College of the City University of New York), B.A., 1945; Yale University, M.A., 1952, Ph.D., 1955. *Politics:* Socialist. *Religion:* Jewish. *Home:* 10A Brosh St., Omer, Israel. *Office:* Israel Institute of Applied Social Research, P.O. Box 7150, Jerusalem, Israel; and Department of Health Sciences, Ben Gurion University of the Negev, Beersheva, Israel.

CAREER: Research associate, Yiddish Science Institute for Jewish Research, 1953-56; Brooklyn College (now Brooklyn College of the City University of New York), Brooklyn, N.Y., lecturer in sociology, 1955-59; research director of race relations, New York State Committee Against Discrimination, 1956-59; Israel Institute of Applied Social Research, Jerusalem, senior research associate, 1960—; Hebrew University of Jerusalem, Hadassah Medical School, Jerusalem, instructor in social medicine, 1962-73; Ben Gurion University of the Negev, Beersheva, Israel, Kunin-Lunenfeld Professor of Medical Sociology, 1973—. *Military service:* U.S. Army, 1943-45. *Member:* American Sociological Association, Israeli Sociological Association (national secretary, 1972-73). *Awards, honors:* Fulbright fellow, University of Tehran, 1959-60; U.S. Public Health Service fellow, Harvard University, 1965-66.

WRITINGS: (Editor with L. Lorwin) *Discrimination and Low Incomes,* New York State Committee Against Discrimination, 1960; (reviser and translator from the Yiddish) Elias Tcherikower, *The Early Jewish Labor Movement in the United States,* Yivo Institute for Jewish Research, 1961; (editor with John Kosa and I. K. Zola) *Poverty and Health: A Sociological Analysis,* Harvard University Press, 1969; (with A. M. Davies and Judith T. Shuval) *Social Functions of Medical Practice: A Study of Doctor-Patient Relationships in Israel,* Jossey-Bass, 1970; (with Alan Arian) *Hopes and Fears of Israelis,* Jerusalem Academic Press, 1972; (with A. D. Katz) *From the Golden to the Promised Land,* Academic Press and Norwood, 1979; *Health, Stress and Coping,* Jossey-Bass, 1979; (with N. Datan and B. Maoz) *A Time to Reap: The Middle Age of Women in Five Israeli Subcultures,* Johns Hopkins University Press, 1981. Contributor of articles to *Journal of Chronic Diseases, Social Science and Medicine,* and other periodicals.

WORK IN PROGRESS: Extensive research in medical sociology.

* * *

ARCHER, Ron
See WHITE, Theodore Edwin

* * *

ARD, Ben N(eal), Jr. 1922-

PERSONAL: Born December 6, 1922, in Dallas, Tex.; son of Ben Neal (a physician) and Maudie Lou (Yeattes) Ard. *Education:* University of California, Los Angeles, B.A., 1947; Oregon State University, M.S., 1954; University of Michigan, Ph.D., 1962. *Home:* 125 Cambon Dr., San Francisco, Calif. 94132. *Office:* Department of Counseling, San Francisco State University, San Francisco, Calif. 94132.

CAREER: Merrill-Palmer Institute, Detroit, Mich., fellow in marriage counseling and family life education, 1953-54; Volunteers of America, Los Angeles, Calif., counselor, 1954-55; California Tuberculosis and Health Association, San Francisco, counselor, 1955-56; Michigan State University, East Lansing, assistant professor of family life, 1956-59; University of Michigan, Ann Arbor, teaching fellow, 1959-60; Central Michigan University, Mount Pleasant, associate professor, 1960-61, professor of psychology, 1961-63; San Francisco State University, San Francisco, professor of counseling, 1963—. Psychologist in private practice, San Francisco, 1964—. *Member:* American Psychological Association, American Association for Marriage and Family Therapy, Society for the Scientific Study of Sex, California State Marriage Counseling Association (fellow; past president).

WRITINGS: (Editor) *Counseling and Psychotherapy,* Science & Behavior Books, 1966, revised edition, 1975; (co-editor) *Handbook of Marriage Counseling,* Science & Behavior Books, 1969, 2nd edition, 1976; (contributor) H. A. Otto, editor, *The New Sexuality,* Science & Behavior Books, 1971; (contributor) Albert Ellis, editor, *Growth through Reason,* Science & Behavior Books, 1971; *Treating Psychosexual Dysfunction,* Jason Aronson, 1974; *Rational Sex Ethics,* University Press of America, 1978; *Living without Guilt and/or Blame: Conscience, Superego and Psychotherapy,* Exposition Press, 1983. Contributor to journals of counseling and family life. Associate editor, *Family Coordinator: Journal of Education, Counseling, and Services.*

* * *

ARNOSKY, Jim 1946-

PERSONAL: Born September 1, 1946, in New York, N.Y.; son of Edward J. (a draftsman) and Marie (Telesco) Arnosky; married Deanna L. Eshleman, August 6, 1966; children: Michelle L., Amber L. *Education:* Attended high school in Pennsylvania. *Home:* South Ryegate, Vermont 05069.

CAREER: Draftsman in Philadelphia, Pa., 1964; Braceland Brothers (printers), Philadelphia, art trainee, 1965-66, creative artist, 1968-72; free-lance illustrator and writer, 1972—. *Military service:* U.S. Navy, 1966-68.

WRITINGS—Self-illustrated children's books: *I Was Born in a Tree and Raised by Bees,* Putnam, 1977; *Outdoors on Foot,* Coward, 1977; *Nathaniel,* Addison-Wesley, 1978; *Crinkleroot's Animal Tracks and Wildlife Signs,* Putnam, 1979; *A Kettle of Hawks,* Coward, 1979; *Mudtime and More Nathaniel Stories,* Addison-Wesley, 1979; *Drawing from Nature,* Lothrop, 1982; *Freshwater Fish and Fishing,* Four Winds, 1982; *Secrets of a Wildlife Watcher,* Lothrop, 1983; *Mouse Writing,* Harcourt, 1983.

Illustrator: Melvin Berger and Gilda Berger, *Fitting In: Animals in Their Habitats,* Coward, 1976; Miska Miles, *Swim, Little Duck,* Atlantic Monthly Press, 1976; Miles, *Chicken Forgets,* Atlantic Monthly Press, 1976; Miles, *Small Rabbit,* Atlantic Monthly Press, 1977; Marcel Sislowitz, *Look: How Your Eyes See,* Coward, 1977; Berniece Freschet, *Porcupine Baby,* Putnam, 1978; Freschet, *Possum Baby,* Putnam, 1978; Kaye Starbird, *Covered Bridge House,* Four Winds, 1979; Freschet, *Moose Baby,* Putnam, 1979; Eloise Jarvis McGraw, *Joel and the Magic Merlini,* Knopf, 1979; Betty Boegehold, *Bear Underground,* Doubleday, 1980; Margaret Bartlett and Preston Bassett, *Raindrop Stories,* Four Winds, 1980.

WORK IN PROGRESS: Drawing Life in Motion, for Lothrop.

SIDELIGHTS: Jim Arnosky told *CA:* "I had no formal art training but learned a great deal about drawing from my dad who is a skillful patent draftsman. With this training at home I began working in the art field as a trainee. . . . It wasn't until I had been on my own freelancing in illustration for nearly five year that I was introduced to the writing end of books. . . . Like solid, well-written poetry, writing for children emphasizes structure and the need for every word to count.

"I have always had a deep connection with the natural world and find its rhythm close to my own. I think of myself as an artist/naturalist. Most of my close friends are working naturalists, teachers, writers, photographers, farmers, and woodsmen. For four and a half years my wife, my two daughters, and I lived in a tiny cabin at the base of Hawk Mountain in Pennsylvania. There I matured as a writer and illustrator of natural subjects. . . . We have made our home in the hills of northern Vermont because its natural pace of life fits our needs best as a family and mine as a writer and illustrator.

"My books are autobiographical. I have difficulty contriving a story that doesn't come from a personal experience. (I admire writers who can.) The character Crinkleroot is a vehicle I use to express the teacher and father in me. He is an old grandfatherly woodsman who knows endless wonders about the natural world and teaches them to his readers through activities they can join in. The character Nathaniel is a caricature of the everyday part of me. He is a countryman. A gardener and outdoorsman. His individual approaches to living in the country sometimes lead into predicaments. Most of Nathaniel's wordless adventures are based on experiences of my own. Nathaniel's stories are wordless because, like myself, Nathaniel feels no need to talk when he's off on a walk or busy building or working around the farm. He is a perfect vehicle for me to share some of my own everyday adventures with youngsters."

AVOCATIONAL INTERESTS: Leisurely walking, growing food, fishing, fly-tying, training his team of Newfoundland dogs, watching wildlife, "thinking, listening, worrying, and smiling."

* * *

ARONSON, Elliot 1932-

PERSONAL: Born January 9, 1932, in Chelsea, Mass.; son of Harry and Dorothy Aronson; married Vera Rabinek, September 8, 1954; children: Hal, Neal, Julie, Joshua. *Education:* Brandeis University, B.A., 1954; Wesleyan University, Middletown, Conn., M.A., 1956; Stanford University, Ph.D., 1959. *Politics:* Radical. *Religion:* Jewish. *Home:* 1525 Laurent St., Santa Cruz, Calif. *Office:* Adlai Stevenson College, University of California, Santa Cruz, Calif. 95064.

CAREER: Harvard University, Cambridge, Mass., lecturer in social psychology, 1959-62; University of Minnesota, Minneapolis, associate professor and director of research, Laboratory for Research in Social Relations, 1962-64, professor of social psychology, 1964-65; University of Texas at Austin, professor of social psychology and director of social psychology program, 1965-74; University of California, Adlai Stevenson College, Santa Cruz, member of faculty, 1974—. Center for Advanced Study in the Behavioral Sciences, Stanford, Calif., visiting fellow, 1965-66, fellow, 1970-71, 1977-78; National Training Laboratories, intern in applied behavioral sciences, summer, 1970, professional member, 1970—. Licensed psychologist, state of Texas, 1970.

MEMBER: American Association for the Advancement of Science, American Psychological Association (fellow). *Awards, honors:* National Institute of Mental Health grants, 1966-71, 1968-75, 1970-71; Socio-Psychological Prize of American Association for the Advancement of Science, 1970; American Psychological Association Media Award 1973, for *The Social Animal;* distinguished teaching award and distinguished research in social psychology award, both 1980; Guggenheim fellowship, 1981-82; Gordon Allport Prize for Intergroup Relations, 1981.

WRITINGS: (Editor with Gardner Lindzey and contributor) *The Handbook of Social Psychology,* 2nd edition (Aronson was not associated with earlier edition), Addison-Wesley, Volume I: *Theories,* 1968, Volume II: *Research Methods,* 1969, Volume III: *The Individual in a Social Context,* 1969, Volume IV: *Group Psychology and Phenomena of Interaction,* 1969, Volume V: *Applied Social Psychology,* 1969, 3rd edition, 1984; (editor with R. P. Abelson, W. J. McGuire, T. M. Newcomb, and P. H. Tannenbaum, and contributor) *Theories of Cognitive Consistency: A Sourcebook,* Rand McNally, 1968; (editor) *Voices of Modern Psychology,* Addison-Wesley, 1969; *The Social Animal,* W. H. Freeman, 1972, 4th edition, 1984; *Readings about the Social Animal,* W. H. Freeman, 1973, 4th edition, 1984; (with Robert Helmreich) *Social Psychology,* Van Nostrand, 1973; (with J. M. Carlsmith and P. C. Ellsworth) *Methods of Research in Social Psychology,* Addison-Wesley, 1976; (with N. Blaney, J. Sikes, M. Snapp, and C. Stephan) *The Jigsaw Classroom,* Sage, 1978; (with A. Pines) *Burnout: From Tedium to Personal Growth,* Free Press, 1981.

Contributor: J. W. Atkinson, editor, *Motives in Fantasy, Action, and Society,* Van Nostrand, 1958; Shel Feldman, editor, *Cognitive Consistency,* Academic Press, 1966; Dorwin Cartwright and A. F. Zander, editors, *Group Dynamics,* 3rd edition, Harper, 1968; Leonard Berkowitz, editor, *Advances in Experimental Social Psychology,* Volume IV, Academic Press, 1969; W. J. Arnold and David Levine, editors, *Nebraska Symposium on Motivation: 1969,* University of Nebraska Press, 1969; C. G. McClintock, editor, *Experimental Social Psychology,* Holt, 1971.

Contributor of more than one hundred articles to psychology journals. Co-editor, "Bobbs-Merrill Reprint Series in Psychology," 1960—; consulting editor, *Journal of Personality and Social Psychology,* 1963—, *Journal of Experimental Social Psychology,* 1964—, and *Personality: An International Journal,* 1970—.

* * *

ARTOM, Guido 1906-1982

PERSONAL: Born June 15, 1906, in Turin, Italy; died March 6, 1982, in Milan, Italy; son of Alessandro (a physicist) and Elvira (Fubini) Artom: married Cristina Forges Davanzati (a translator), July 10, 1933; children: Elena (Mrs. Francesco Vicario), Sandra, Alessandro. *Education:* University of Rome, Doctor in Law, 1930. *Religion:* Roman Catholic. *Home:* 37 Via Manin, Milan 20121, Italy.

CAREER: Selezione dal *Reader's Digest,* Milan, Italy, books editor, 1948-71, general editorial consultant, 1971-82. Delegate of Italian publishers to European Common Market. *Military service:* Italian Army, Reserve officer. *Member:* Italian Publishers Association (member of board), Italian Professional Journalists Association. *Awards, honors:* Knight Commander of the Order of the Italian Republic; finalist in Strega Prize competition, 1981, for *I giorni del mondo.*

WRITINGS: (Editor) Henri Amedee Le Lorgne, Comte d'Ideville, *Il re, Il Conte e la Rosina,* Longanesi, 1959; *Napoleone e morto in Russia,* translation by Muriel Grindrod published as *Napoleon Is Dead in Russia,* Atheneum, 1970; *I Piemontesi a Roma,* Longanesi, 1974; *Cinque bombe per l'Imperatore,* Mondadori, 1974; *I Giudici scomparsi,* Mondadori, 1977; *Diario d'un diplomatico romano, 1862-1866,* Longanesi, 1979; *I giorni del mondo,* Longanesi, 1981; *La duchessa di Berry,* Rusconi, 1982. Regular contributor to *Storia Illustrata* (a monthly), and *Tuttolibri* (a weekly).

SIDELIGHTS: Guido Artom travelled frequently throughout Europe and in the United States. He spoke English, French, Spanish, and German.

BIOGRAPHICAL/CRITICAL SOURCES: Books, April, 1970; *New York Times Book Review,* April 19, 1970; *New Yorker,* May 23, 1970; *Best Sellers,* June 1, 1970.†

ASHE, Geoffrey (Thomas) 1923-

PERSONAL: Born March 29, 1923, in London, England; son of Arthur William (a travel agency general manager) and Thelma (Hoodless) Ashe; married Dorothy Irene Train (a teacher), May 3, 1946; children: Thomas, John, Michael, Sheila, Brendan. *Education:* University of British Columbia, B.A. (first class honours), 1943; Trinity College, Cambridge University, B.A. (first in English Tripos), 1948. *Religion:* Catholic. *Home:* Chalice Orchard, Well House Lane, Glastonbury, Somerset BA6 8BJ, England. *Agent:* (Literary) A. D. Peters, 10 Buckingham St., London WC2N 6BU, England.

CAREER: Writer. Polish University College, London, England, lecturer in English, 1948-50; Newman Neame (publishers), London, industrial research assistant, 1949-51; Ford Motor Co. of Canada, Windsor, Ontario, administrative assistant, 1952-54; Post Office Department, Toronto, Ontario, technical officer, 1954-55; Polytechnic, London, England, lecturer in management studies, 1956-67. Visiting professor of English, University of Southern Mississippi, 1982; Thomas Lamont Visiting Professor, Union College, Schenectady, N.Y., 1984; lecturer and contributor to television programs. *Member:* International Arthurian Society, Royal Society of Literature (fellow), Camelot Research Committee (co-founder; secretary).

WRITINGS: The Tale of the Tub: A Survey of the Art of Bathing through the Ages, Newman Neame, 1950; *King Arthur's Avalon: The Story of Glastonbury,* Collins, 1957; *From Caesar to Arthur,* Collins, 1960; *Land to the West: St. Brendan's Voyage to America,* Collins, 1962; *The Land and the Book,* Collins, 1965; *The Carmelite Order,* Carmelite Press, 1965; *Gandhi: A Study in Revolution,* Stein & Day, 1968; (editor and contributor) *The Quest for Arthur's Britain,* Pall Mall, 1968; *All about King Arthur* (juvenile), W. H. Allen, 1969, published in the United States as *King Arthur in Fact and Legend,* Ted Nelson, 1971.

Camelot and the Vision of Albion, Heinemann, 1971; (with others) *The Quest for America,* Pall Mall, 1971; *The Art of Writing Made Simple,* W. H. Allen, 1972; *The Finger and the Moon* (novel), Heinemann, 1973; *Do What You Will: A History of Anti-morality,* W. H. Allen, 1974; *The Virgin,* Routledge and Kegan Paul, 1976; *The Ancient Wisdom,* Macmillan, 1977; *Miracles,* Routledge and Kegan Paul, 1978; *A Guidebook to Arthurian Britain,* Longman, 1980; *Kings and Queens of Early Britain,* Methuen, 1982; *Avalonian Quest,* Methuen, 1982. Associate editor, *The Arthurian Encyclopedia,* Garland Press, in press. Author of play, "The Grass Island," 1964. Columnist in *Resurgence* magazine, 1973-78. Contributor to numerous periodicals, including *Speculum.*

SIDELIGHTS: The writings of Geoffrey Ashe represent an eclectic selection of religious, historical, and mythological topics. He has written extensively on the historical and literary aspects of Arthurian legend and has been involved with archaeological excavations in search of Camelot, but the scope of his works remains essentially diverse. "Geoffrey Ashe has written the best biography of Gandhi that I know," writes Henrietta Buckmaster in the *Christian Science Monitor,* and the critic's comments are a case in point, reflecting as they do Ashe's ability to range successfully over a wide variety of subject matter.

Gandhi: A Study in Revolution is "a model of fairness, proportion and restraint," according to Martin E. Marty in the *New York Times Book Review.* "In a time when Gandhi usually receives ideological or tractarian treatment, it is refreshing to have a simple narrative, a straight biography of a very human being." Marty makes reference to one of the central difficulties confronting the Gandhi biographer: overcoming the cult of personality and mythology surrounding the religious and political leader to reveal the "very human" man beneath. Describing the success with which Ashe copes with this problem, Francis Watson says in the *Spectator* that "Mr. Ashe has sunk his shafts in the immense material to convince us of what Einstein suggested we might one day scarcely believe, 'that such a one as this ever in flesh and blood walked upon this earth.' While the tribute is quoted, its suggestion of the superhuman is satisfactorily avoided."

Another formidable task for the biographer of Gandhi is the necessity of trying to tie together and balance the different periods in the Indian leader's life, while at the same time sifting through an enormous mass of detail. Philip Altbach, reviewing *Gandhi* in *Commonweal,* believes that the focus of the book is uneven: "Like most of Gandhi's other biographers, [Ashe] spends too much time on the South African experience and does not go into enough detail about India." Marty, however, disagrees: "The plot line of Gandhi's life in Britain, South Africa, and India is necessarily complex, [but] the reader will not be lost in detail. [Ashe's] quotations from Gandhi are pithy and pointed; the anecdotes are spare but illuminating." In a *Punch* article on the book, Honoria J. Scannard returns to Ashe's revelation of the man behind the myth as she summarizes the strengths of *Gandhi.* She asserts that Ashe's "greatest achievement is to present this eminently spiritual leader as a man who was also ruthlessly practical and passionately human."

While Ashe has written works on subjects as diverse as the cult of the Virgin Mary and the search for Camelot, the interrelated topics of religion, philosophy, and mythology have steadily run through a large proportion of his writings. Thus, while the relationship between Gandhi and Arthurian legend might not be immediately apparent, the two are part of a continuum of interests that find their expression in Ashe's *Camelot and the Vision of Albion.*

Writing in the *New Statesman,* Jonathan Raban calls the book "an enterprising foray into [the] rich seam of indigenous English mythology." The volume proposes the idea that Arthurian legend, in all of its many manifestations, reflects an innate desire in mankind for a golden age as embodied in a paradisal setting such as Camelot. According to Raban, Ashe's "real interest lies in the notion of a submerged 'British spirit,' personified by an Arthur/Albion figure. Ashe traces the theme of slumbering Albion through Shelley, 19th-century dissentient radicalism and the Mahatma Gandhi, [finishing] up in a state of hopeful suspense, with the Arthurian return just around the corner of the last chapter." The result is an attempt to synthesize a wide range of utopian thought and mythology around the central figure of Arthur, bringing together Greek and Celtic legend as well as the historical theories of writers such as Blake and Chesterton. It is a combination affirming what a *Booklist* reviewer terms the "timeless possibility for reinstatement and renewal . . . in the myths surrounding King Arthur."

BIOGRAPHICAL/CRITICAL SOURCES: Spectator, March 22, 1968; *Punch,* May 8, 1968; *Christian Science Monitor,* July 18, 1968; *New York Times Book Review,* July 21, 1968, August 29, 1977; *Times Literary Supplement,* October 16, 1969; *Commonweal,* March 13, 1970; *New Statesman,* January 15, 1971;

Booklist, May 15, 1972; *New York Review of Books*, November 11, 1976.

* * *

ASHLEY, Elizabeth
See SALMON, Annie Elizabeth

* * *

ASHLOCK, Robert B. 1930-

PERSONAL: Born September 17, 1930, in Indianapolis, Ind.; son of Hobert Dean (an engineer) and Juanita (Kinzer) Ashlock; married Julia Ann Bronnenberg, December 23, 1951; children: Joli Ann, Alan Dean. *Education:* Attended Ball State University, 1948-51, and Wheaton College, Wheaton, Ill., 1955; Butler University, B.S., 1957, M.S., 1959; Indiana University, Ed.D., 1965. *Religion:* Presbyterian. *Home:* 604 Hampton Cove, Clinton, Miss. 39056. *Office:* Graduate School of Education, Reformed Theological Seminary, 5422 Clinton Blvd., Jackson, Miss. 39209.

CAREER: Elementary school teacher and principal in Noblesville, Ind., 1957-64; University of Maryland, College Park, assistant professor, 1965-68, associate professor, 1968-73, professor of education, 1973-80, director of Arithmetic Center, 1972-80; currently member of staff of Graduate School of Education, Reformed Theological Seminary, Jackson, Miss. *Member:* National Education Association (life member), National Council of Teachers of Mathematics, Research Council for Diagnostic and Prescriptive Mathematics (president, 1979-81), Central Association of Science and Mathematics Teachers, Phi Delta Kappa.

WRITINGS: (Editor with Wayne Herman) *Current Research in Elementary School Mathematics*, Macmillan, 1970; *Error Patterns in Computation: A Semi-Programmed Approach*, C. E. Merrill, 1972, 3rd edition, 1982; (with James Humphrey) *Teaching Elementary School Mathematics through Motor Learning*, C. C Thomas, 1976; (with Martin L. Johnson, Wilmer L. Jones, and John W. Wilson) *Guiding Each Child's Learning of Mathematics*, C. E. Merrill, 1983. Contributor of about twenty-five articles and reviews to education journals.

SIDELIGHTS: Robert B. Ashlock told *CA:* "Most of my writings are concerned with helping children understand and enjoy success in arithmetic. I want them to perceive computation as a written record of observations in physical reality, something that makes sense. I also want the operations of arithmetic to make sense to children so they will know how to use them solving problems."

* * *

ATTICUS
See DAVIES, Hunter

* * *

AULETTA, Ken 1942-

PERSONAL: Born April 23, 1942, in New York, N.Y. *Education:* State University of New York College at Oswego, B.S., 1963; Syracuse University, M.A., 1965. *Politics:* "Registered Independent." *Home:* 544 East 86th St., New York, N.Y. 10028. *Office: New York Daily News*, 220 East 42nd St., New York, N.Y. 10017; and *New Yorker*, 43 West 43rd St., New York, N.Y. 10017.

CAREER: New York magazine, New York City, contributing editor, 1975-76; *Village Voice*, New York City, staff writer and weekly columnist, 1975-76; *New Yorker*, New York City, writer, 1977—; *New York Daily News*, New York City, political columnist, 1977—. Co-host of a weekly WNET-TV interview program, 1976—. *Awards, honors:* American Bar Association media award, 1976; Public Relations Society of America media award, 1976, for an article on New York's fiscal crisis, and 1977, for an article outlining an agenda to save the city; Amos Tuck Award for national economic reporting, Dartmouth College; finalist in the National Magazine Awards, Columbia University School of Journalism.

WRITINGS—All published by Random House: *The Streets Were Paved with Gold*, 1979; *Hard Feelings: Reporting on the Pols, the Press, the People and the City* (collection of essays), 1981; *The Underclass*, 1982; *The Art of Corporate Success*, 1984. Contributor of articles to *New York Times, New York Review of Books, More*, and *Esquire*.

SIDELIGHTS: Ken Auletta told *CA:* "Most of my work is concerned with political and economic and governmental matters, though I do stray off and write of the media frequently and, more recently, of multinational corporations. I very much enjoy having a regular magazine and newspaper outlet. Before resigning, that was the case at *New York* magazine and the *Voice*; it is again the case at the *New Yorker* and the *Daily News*. What I find is that the magazine work (or books) comes to represent those subjects that require more depth and thought and, because they afford more time, more careful writing. But magazines usually have a long leadtime, and the journalistic impulse is often satisfied by newspapers. There one can break a story, experience the communal sweat and nervousness of a city room, react quickly. A newspaperman, like a firefighter, responds to alarms; a magazine writer can set off his own alarms. There are advantages to each. By having a career that combines newspaper and magazine work, I like to think I have the best of both worlds."

Auletta's *The Streets Were Paved with Gold* is an analysis of the financial turmoil that plagued New York City during the 1970s. Writes Bob Kuttner in the *New York Times Book Review:* "For too many of our best political writers, politics itself becomes the central fascination. . . . But the point of politics, after all, is government. And unlike many of his colleagues who stay hooked on the easy adrenalin of day-to-day politics, Ken Auletta has gone on to explore government." Kuttner feels that *The Streets Were Paved with Gold* has "established Mr. Auletta as an astute critic of New York City government, with the patience and intellectual curiosity to plumb the fiscal muck and pull out an instructive, entertaining story."

Many observers blame the near-bankruptcy on a variety of factors outside of the control of the city. According to *Chicago Tribune Book World* reviewer Max J. Friedman, these include "the nation's economic ills, failure of state and federal governments to deal responsibly with welfare reform and hospital-cost containment, the energy crunch, and new voices of decentralized dissent and social activism." But Auletta finds that the government and citizens of New York compounded these problems unnecessarily. Kuttner explains that "rejecting all of the devil theories of New York's fiscal collapse, Mr. Auletta ascribed New York's woes to both the city's corrupt permanent government *and* the municipal unions; to New York's own overly generous version of the New Deal *and* to Washington's raw deal."

Julia Vitullo-Martin, in a *New York Review of Books* article, maintains that much of Auletta's book is a condemnation of the affluent lifestyle enjoyed by some highly visible New Yorkers rather than an analysis of the city's financial situation and that the author ignores New York's partially successful attempts to correct its own fiscal ills. She writes: "On the west side of Manhattan, once called Hell's Kitchen, a storefront church's neon sign flashes the message 'Sin will find you out.' *That* should have been the title of Ken Auletta's new book . . . because that is his theme. . . . He is distressed by what he sees as the city's blind revelry in the face of financial doom in 1975, a revelry that has started up once again with the influx of enormous private wealth to the city. He writes with the pain and the passion of one offended by sin." Among the excesses cited by Auletta: a $300-per-couple masquerade party at a disco; $4900 watches; $750,000 co-op apartments; $235 children's dresses; and $50-per-square-foot office rentals. The free-spending attitude of affluent citizens, he feels, helped to influence the city government toward fiscal irresponsibility. Furthermore, says Vitullo-Martin, "Auletta goes on at length about the fall of New York but gives short shrift to its salvation, temporary as that may be. The city *was* on the verge of catastrophe in June 1975. . . . Today the city has paid off all but a tiny amount of notes. . . . Default is remote. What happened? In 1975, the Municipal Assistance Corporation (MAC) was created by the state to save the city by forcing or cajoling—whichever worked—investors to trade in their short-term debt for long. They did. MAC solved the city's financing." And she feels that Auletta short-changes the effectiveness of this organization: "Anyone unfamiliar with MAC will not understand how it works from Auletta's description."

But many other observers agree with Auletta's assessment in *The Streets Were Paved with Gold* that the city was largely to blame for its financial difficulty. Alan K. Campbell (former dean of the Maxwell School of Citizenship and Public Affairs at Syracuse University), reviewing the book for the *New York Times Book Review*, states: "New York City used every financial and debt gimmick known to man and even invented some new ones to fill the budget gap, to the point that borrowing came to be considered a normal way to finance current services—in ordinary language, the city was living beyond its means." In addition to out-of-control borrowing, writes Friedman in the *Chicago Tribune Book World*, "Outrageous municipal union demands and settlements gave a new and disastrous meaning to collective bargaining in a governmental setting. How could political leaders bargain with unions who offered financial backing to those same politicians?"

Friedman calls *The Streets Were Paved with Gold* "an informed, impressive, multi-faceted examination of the people and events that led to the city's fiscal decline [and] near demise. . . . It is a classic study of opportunities lost, municipal profligacy, wasted labors, and technically balanced budgets, of well-meaning social goals and not-so-honest political realities." Campbell believes that the book is "a unique analysis of the causes of the New York City fiscal crisis" and states that "it substantially advances our understanding of the problem of New York City and clarifies the relevance of that problem to the rest of the nation." Concludes Friedman: "Auletta's book is a masterpiece—a shocking look backward and an equally frightening look ahead for this nation's ever-growing-older urban centers."

In another book dealing with problems facing big cities, Auletta looks at a group of people who exemplify hard-core poverty in the United States. As Charles Peters explains in the *New York Times Book Review*, Auletta's *The Underclass* "is not about poor people in general. It's about the underclass, those at the bottom—the long-term welfare recipients, street criminals, addicts and drifters who live outside the world of work and whose problems are not likely to be solved simply by the offer of a job." In researching the book, Auletta studied a number of job training programs, particularly those operated by the Manpower Demonstration Research Corporation (the M.D.R.C.), an institution funded by the federal government among other sources. According to Peters, the author "spent seven months with one group of 26 trainees in New York City attending classes designed, in his words, 'to instill the habit of work and to expunge bad habits.' He also visited M.D.R.C. programs in Mississippi and West Virginia and has read widely in the literature of poverty." The result, writes Max Benavidez in the *Los Angeles Times Book Review*, is "a responsible, in-depth study of people who have 'disappeared from the system.' The author has amassed and absorbed an extraordinary range of literature on the topic. He has talked with experts and has chronicled daily, direct experiences with the underclass. To his credit, he paints an unromanticized picture of the destitution that America so neatly ignores. . . . Auletta has written a first-rate sourcebook."

The subjects of Auletta's primary study, all participants in the M.D.R.C. program in New York, are "22 bona fide members of the 'underclass,'" writes Juan Williams in the *Washington Post Book World*, "who are being schooled in self-confidence and how to get and keep a job—such things as how to dress and speak at job interviews. Some soon depart, leaving Auletta with 15 to observe and talk to about the state of their lives, to ask how they see themselves in the rush of glamor and technology that is the state of the world but has nothing to do with them." Christopher Lehmann-Haupt of the *New York Times* notes that in this group "we meet the murderers, muggers, stickup men, drug addicts and welfare cheats of our darkest paranoia. We meet Pearl Dawson, killer and former alcoholic, who has been living alone on welfare in Jamaica, Queens. We meet Jerome Patterson, now going by the name Mohammed, a former 'warlord' for a Harlem gang who was convicted 10 times as a juvenile and has now lost count of the number of his arrests. We meet Leon Harris, who boasts he earned from $1,500 to $3,000 a day as a stickup man and used to write notes of apology to the loved ones of those he shot. We meet Jean Madison, who says she had eight children by the time she was 14 years old and 29 by the age of 38."

Williams is bothered by the fact that "there is some inconclusive end to the people Auletta observes. They graduate, don't graduate. They find jobs, lose jobs, can't get a job. Overall, the program that sponsored Auletta's sample finds that it has some success with long-term welfare recipients and former drug addicts but fails with former convicts and school dropouts." And Lehmann-Haupt maintains that this conclusion, stated by Auletta, is hardly surprising, considering that the M.D.R.C. program "puts welfare mothers in the same class as 'street criminals and hustlers' and 'traumatized ex-mental patients and alcoholics.'. . . Mothers on welfare are about the most direct and uncomplicated victims of poverty-through-unemployment that are possible to imagine."

Still, *The Underclass* has been widely praised for its thoroughness, for the seriousness of its subject matter, and for its author's dedication to his task. Writes Peter S. Prescott of *Newsweek*, "It offers a prodigious quantity of facts, statistics and argument, all of urgent concern to us all." In the *New York Times Book Review*, Peters credits Auletta for his fair-minded approach, noting that the author "is equally open to Oscar Lewis, a liberal anthropologist, and to Edward Banfield, a conservative political scientist, though he clearly does not accept the mythology of the extreme right that depicts the underclass as composed entirely of lazy, vicious, oversexed criminals. He sees these people as human beings, real and whole, and his empathy for even the most incorrigible of them is contagious." And even though he wishes Auletta's study had proven more conclusive, Juan Williams states that the author "brings a reporter's touch and an unbiased mind [to] *The Underclass*. That combination alone would be enough to set his book apart from the ones that preceded it, but Auletta goes a step further by bringing into the argument the people being argued about. By talking to poor people, by watching them—without voyeurism—push to the limits, he insists on testing the human ability to leave a bad way of life behind. . . . As an introduction and overview to the contemporary debate over American poverty—its roots and proposed solutions— Auletta's book is invaluable."

BIOGRAPHICAL/CRITICAL SOURCES: *New York Times Book Review*, March 25, 1979, August 10, 1980, June 27, 1982; *Chicago Tribune Book World*, April 8, 1979; *New York Review of Books*, May 17, 1979; *New York Times*, May 11, 1982; *Newsweek*, June 7, 1982; *Los Angeles Times Book Review*, June 13, 1982; *Washington Post Book World*, July 11, 1982.

—Sketch by Peter M. Gareffa

* * *

AUSTIN, Harry
See McINERNY, Ralph

* * *

AVERILL, Esther 1902-
(John Domino)

PERSONAL: Born July 24, 1902, in Bridgeport, Conn.; daughter of Charles Ketchum (a civil engineer) and Helen (Holden) Averill. *Education:* Graduate of Vassar College, 1923; attended Brooklyn Museum Art School. *Religion:* Episcopalian. *Home:* 30 Joralemon St., Apt. 11-A, Brooklyn, N.Y. 11201.

CAREER: Editor for *Women's Wear Daily*, New York City, beginning 1923; lived in Paris, France, 1925-35, working as free-lance journalist/photographer in field of fashion and decorative arts, later establishing The Domino Press and publishing books for children; returned to New York City, working in children's section of New York Public Library, and studying painting; full-time free-lance writer and illustrator. *Awards, honors: Cartier Sails the St. Lawrence* was selected as an American Library Association Notable Book.

WRITINGS: (With Lila Stanley) *Daniel Boone* (illustrated by Feodor Rojankovsky), Domino Press (Paris), 1931, revised edition, Harper, 1946; (with Stanley) *Powder: The Story of a Colt, a Duchess, and the Circus* (illustrated by Rojankovsky), Smith and Haas, 1933; *Flash: The Story of a Horse, a Coach-Dog and the Gypsies* (illustrated by Rojankovsky), Smith and Haas, 1934; (under pseudonym John Domino) *Fable of a Proud Poppy* (illustrated by Emile Lahner), Bookshop for Boys and Girls (Boston), 1934; *Political Propaganda in Children's Books of the French Revolution*, Colophon, 1935.

The Voyages of Jacques Cartier (illustrated by Rojankovsky), Domino Press (New York), 1937, revised edition published as *Cartier Sails the St. Lawrence*, Harper, 1956; (translator from the French) Jean Mariotti, *Tales of Poindi: A Legend of New Caledonia* (illustrated by Rojankovsky), Domino Press, 1938; *King Philip: The Indian Chief* (illustrated by Vera Belsky), Harper, 1950; *Eyes on the World*, Funk, 1969.

Self-illustrated juveniles; all published by Harper: *The Cat Club*, 1944; *The Adventures of Jack Ninepins*, 1944; *The School for Cats*, 1947; *Jenny's First Party*, 1948; *Jenny's Moonlight Adventure*, 1949; *When Jenny Lost Her Scarf*, 1951; *Jenny's Adopted Brothers*, 1952; *How the Brothers Joined the Cat Club*, 1953; *Jenny's Birthday Book*, 1954; *Jenny Goes to Sea*, 1957; *Jenny's Bedside Book*, 1959; *The Fire Cat*, 1960; *The Hotel Cat*, 1969; *Captains of the City Streets: A Story of the Cat Club*, 1972; *Jenny and the Cat Club: A Collection of Favorite Stories about Jenny Linsky*, 1973. Contributor of articles to *Colophon* and *Horn Book*.

WORK IN PROGRESS: A study of old French children's books and prints.

SIDELIGHTS: *The Cat Club*, which introduced Jenny Linsky, the shy little black cat with the bright red scarf, "launched me on my cat career," wrote Esther Averill, "for these little books of mine, as they appeared over the years, have brought me in touch with that wonderful world of true cat lovers. I mean the people who not only care for their own pets, but [who] also devote much time and effort to the humanitarian work of alleviating the suffering of the stray, abandoned cats of their communities. I wish that I might participate in such work more fully than I am able. It is sometimes heartbreaking work, and in no sense a 'hobby.'

"Jenny in real life was as shy as I have portrayed her. The number of books surprises me, for Jenny, when she was tiny, was so shy and plain that I felt that of all the cats I had had— many of them truly glamorous—she was the only one who would never have a 'story.' I did not suspect that Jenny's special brand of courage would carry her into so many adventures. The Cat Club, too, has expanded since she joined it in her first story—then there were only 12 members. Sometimes I feel that fate has made me a kind of Balzac of the Cat Club."

Esther Averill's Cat Club books have been published in German, Swedish, Danish, Afrikaans, and Japanese.

MEDIA ADAPTATIONS: *Jenny's Birthday Book* was filmed by Weston Woods, 1956; *Jenny and the Cat Club: A Collection of Favorite Stories about Jenny Linsky* was recorded as "Jenny and the Cat Club," selected stories read by Tammy Grimes, produced by Caedmon.

* * *

AVERY, June
See REES, Joan

* * *

AVI
See WORTIS, Avi

B

BAHR, Howard M. 1938-

PERSONAL: Born February 21, 1938, in Provo, Utah; son of Albert Frances (a soil scientist with U.S. Department of Agriculture) and Louie Jean (Miner) Bahr; married Rosemary Frances Smith, August 28, 1961; children: Bonnie Louise, Howard McKay, Rowena Ruth, Tanya Lavonne, Christopher Joseph, Laura Lee, Stephen Smith, Rachel Marie. *Education:* Brigham Young University, B.A. (with honors), 1962; University of Texas, M.A., 1964, Ph.D., 1965. *Religion:* Church of Jesus Christ of Latter-day Saints (Mormon). *Home:* 180 East 4320 N., Provo, Utah 84604. *Office:* Department of Sociology, Brigham Young University, Provo, Utah 84602.

CAREER: Columbia University, Bureau of Applied Social Research, New York, N.Y., project director of study on homelessness, 1965-68, research associate, 1966-68; Washington State University, Pullman, associate professor and associate rural sociologist, 1968-72, professor of sociology and rural sociologist, 1972-73, chairman of department, 1971-73; Brigham Young University, Provo, Utah, professor of sociology, 1973—, director of Family Research Institute, 1977-83. Lecturer in sociology, New York University, 1966-68 and Brooklyn College of the City University of New York, 1967; visiting lecturer, Columbia University, summer, 1968; visiting professor, University of Virginia, 1976-77. *Member:* American Sociological Association, National Council on Family Relations, Society for the Scientific Study of Religion, Rural Sociological Society, Tocqueville Society, Pacific Sociological Association, Southwestern Social Science Association. *Awards, honors:* Karl G. Maeser Research and Creative Arts Award, 1979.

WRITINGS: (Editor and contributor) *Disaffiliated Man: Essays and Bibliography on Skid Row, Vagrancy, and Outsiders,* University of Toronto Press, 1970; (editor with Bruce A. Chadwick and Robert C. Day, and contributor) *Native Americans Today: Sociological Perspectives,* Harper, 1971; (editor with Chadwick and Darwin L. Thomas, and contributor) *Population, Resources, and the Future: Non-Malthusian Perspectives,* Brigham Young University Press, 1972; (with Theodore Caplow) *Old Men Drunk and Sober,* New York University Press, 1973; *Skid Row: An Introduction to Disaffiliation,* Oxford University Press, 1973; (with Gerald R. Garrett) *Women Alone: The Disaffiliation of Urban Females,* Lexington Books, 1976; (with Chadwick and Joseph H. Stauss) *American Ethnicity,* Heath, 1979; (contributor) Louis Kreisberg, editor, *Research in Social Movements, Conflict, and Change,* Jai Press, 1980; (with Carol D. Harvey) *The Sunshine Widows: Adaptation to Sudden Bereavement,* Heath, 1980; (with Chadwick, Caplow, Reuben Hill, and Margaret Williamson) *Middletown Families: Fifty Years of Change and Continuity,* University of Minnesota Press, 1982; (with Spencer J. Condie and Kristen L. Goodman) *Life in Large Families: Views of Mormon Mothers,* University Press of America, 1982; (with Chadwick and Caplow) *All Faithful People: Change and Continuity in Middletown's Religion,* University of Minnesota Press, 1983; (with Goodman and Stan L. Albrecht) *Divorce and Remarriage,* Greenwood Press, 1983; (with Chadwick and Albrecht) *Social Science Research Methods,* Prentice-Hall, 1984.

Contributor to *International Encyclopedia of the Social Sciences,* 1968, and *Annual Review of Sociology,* 1983. Also contributor to social science journals. Associate editor of *Journal of Marriage and the Family,* 1978—, and *Rural Sociology,* 1978—; senior editor of *Acta Paedologica,* 1983—.

WORK IN PROGRESS: Additional books deriving from the Middletown II Project; an anthology on American Indians; a monograph on processes of disaffiliation or change in religious denomination.

SIDELIGHTS: Howard M. Bahr wrote *CA:* "I agree with Jacob Bronowski's notion that science and the arts are two main pathways leading to human knowledge, but that knowledge itself is a unitary whole. Bronowski said that 'human knowledge consists of the casting into rational form of the proof or disproof of what one may call intuitions—that is, hypotheses—in such a way that they can be shared with other people.' The usual mode of casting intuitions and evidence into rational or sharable form is writing. Early in my career an older colleague told me to 'write for yourself,' that is, to write according to standards that *I* thought were valid and on topics that were meaningful to me. Then, he said, I would have the satisfaction of having written according to the standards of good craftmanship as I understood them, and no editorial rejection or critic's denunciation could take away my personal satisfaction in work I thought well-done. Almost two decades of professional writing have affirmed part of that early advice.

"The scientific writer is rewarded or 'reinforced' at several stages in the process of producing an article or a book, among them the satisfaction when the piece is first completed, when it is accepted for publication, when galley or page proofs arrive, and when the finished product appears in journal or book form. For me, the strongest of these multiple or partial reinforcements happens when I finish a draft or revision of a piece and can honestly tell myself, 'this is well-done.' Even so, I now believe that I cannot afford the luxury of writing *only* for myself. The potential audience must be throughout the writing process, or the work may never be available to others. Unless it is published, the findings, insights, or observations I wish to add to the accumulation of human knowledge are unlikely to be recorded, archived, and retained for future use. I believe that quality scientific writing, or any writing, for that matter, involves successive revisions.

"In my revisions, I strive for three qualities: economy, elegance, and logical evolution or transition as one moves through the piece. Economy has to do with saying what one must say concisely, and it is achieved by pruning. Pruning involves taking each word, clause, and sentence and asking whether it says what it should, if it is necessary, and if it could be said in fewer or better words. Elegance in scientific writing has to do with both brevity and accuracy. It refers to precision, neatness, and simplicity. There is much attention to nuance and tone, to implication, connotation, and assumptions, as one edits for elegance. Finally, evolution as an ideal in writing has to do with flow, transition, and logical connection between passages. Proficiency in pruning, in writing as in horticulture, comes with practice. Great writers may be born, not made, but *good* writing is within the reach of most people who work at it."

* * *

BAILEY, Sydney D(awson) 1916-

PERSONAL: Born September 1, 1916, in Hull, England; son of Frank Burgess (a grain broker) and Elsie (a teacher; maiden name, May) Bailey; married Jennie Elena Brenda Friedrich (a social worker), April 26, 1945; children: Martin Dawson, Marion Elizabeth. *Education:* Attended secondary school in Worksop, Nottinghamshire, England. *Religion:* Society of Friends (Quakers). *Home and office:* 19 Deansway, East Finchley, London N2 0NG, England.

CAREER: National Newsletter, London, England, editor, 1946-48; Hansard Society for Parliamentary Government, London, secretary, 1948-54; Society of Friends (Quakers), New York City, representative to United Nations, 1954-58; Carnegie Endowment for International Peace, New York City, research fellow, 1958-60; writer, 1960—. Former chairman of Division of International Affairs, British Council of Churches; Council on Christian Approaches to Defence and Disarmament, founding member, former chairman, currently vice-president. Member of advisory committees of British Foreign Office. *Wartime service:* Society of Friends, attached to ambulance unit, 1940-46; served in China-Burma-India theater. *Member:* International Institute for Strategic Studies, Royal Institute of International Affairs, American Society for International Law.

WRITINGS: (Editor) *Aspects of American Government,* Hansard Society for Parliamentary Government, 1950; *Constitutions of British Colonies* (pamphlet), Hansard Society for Parliamentary Government, 1950; (editor) *Parliamentary Government in the Commonwealth,* Philosophical Library, 1951; *Lords and Commons* (pamphlet), H.M.S.O., 1951; (contributor) Norman J. Padelford, editor, *Contemporary International Relations Readings, 1950-1951,* Harvard University Press, 1951; *Parliamentary Government* (pamphlet), British Council, 1952, 2nd edition, 1958; *Ceylon,* Hutchinson, 1952; (editor) *The British Party System,* Praeger, 1952, 2nd edition, 1953; *Naissance du nouvelles democraties* (title means "The Birth of New Democracies"), Armand Colin, 1953; *Parliamentary Government in Southern Asia,* Institute of Pacific Relations, 1953; (editor) *Problems of Parliamentary Government in Colonies,* Hansard Society for Parliamentary Government, 1953; (editor) *The Future of the House of Lords,* Praeger, 1954; *British Parliamentary Democracy,* Houghton, 1958, 3rd edition, 1970.

The General Assembly of the United Nations, Praeger, 1960, 2nd edition, 1964, reprinted, Greenwood Press, 1978; *The Secretariat of the United Nations,* Praeger, 1962, 2nd edition, 1964, reprinted, Greenwood Press, 1978; *The Troika and the Future of the United Nations* (pamphlet), Carnegie Endowment for International Peace, 1962; (contributor) Saul H. Mendlovitz, editor, *Legal and Political Problems of World Order,* World Law Fund, 1962; *A Short Political Guide to the United Nations,* Praeger, 1963; (contributor) Evan Luard, editor, *The Evolution of International Organization,* Thames & Hudson, 1966; (contributor) *Peace Is Still the Prize,* S.C.M. Press, 1966; (contributor) Richard A. Falk and Mendlovitz, editors, *The Strategy of World Order,* World Law Fund, 1966; (contributor) Robert W. Gregg and Michael Barkun, editors, *The United Nations System and Its Functions,* Van Nostrand, 1968; *The Veto in the Security Council* (pamphlet), Carnegie Edowment for International Peace, 1968.

Voting in the Security Council, Indiana University Press, 1970; *Chinese Representation in the Security Council and General Assembly of the United Nations,* Institute for the Study of International Organization, 1970; (contributor) George Cunningham, editor, *Britain and the World in the Seventies,* Weidenfeld & Nicolson, 1970; *The Peaceful Settlement of International Disputes,* United Nations Institute for Training Research, 1970, 3rd edition, 1971; *Prohibitions and Restraints in War,* Oxford University Press 1972; *The Procedure of the United Nations Security Council,* Clarendon Press, 1975; (contributor) K. Venkata Raman, editor, *Dispute Settlement through the United Nations,* Oceana, 1977.

Christian Perspectives on Nuclear Weapons, British Council of Churches, 1981; (contributor) Davidson Nicol, editor, *Paths to Peace,* Pergamon, 1981; *How Wars End: The United Nations and the Termination of Armed Conflict, 1946-1964,* two volumes, Clarendon Press, 1982; (contributor) Paul Abrecht and Ninan Koshy, editors, *Before It's Too Late: The Challenge of Nuclear Disarmament,* World Council of Churches, 1983. Contributor of several hundred articles to periodicals, including *Economist, Spectator, Review of Politics, World Today, Survival, Theology, International Affairs,* and *American Journal of International Law.* Editor of *Parliamentary Affairs,* 1948-54.

WORK IN PROGRESS: A study of United Nations diplomacy after the war in the Middle East in June, 1967; a study of restrictions in the Christian tradition on the use of military force.

SIDELIGHTS: In a *New Society* review of Sydney D. Bailey's *How Wars End: The United Nations and the Termination of Armed Conflict, 1946-1964,* critic Adam Roberts notes that "there is a vast literature on how wars are fought; there is at least a respectable body of literature on how they begin; but much less is known about how they end." Bailey's book is an attempt to deal with this subject, which Roberts calls "both interesting and important, not least because, in this grossly over-armed world in which we live, stopping wars before they get out of hand is an obvious prerequisite for survival."

In his extensive research for *How Wars End,* Bailey read many hundreds of books and documents and found that since 1945 there have been about 150 "small wars" throughout the world. "Many of them," says Roberts, "ended without the direct involvement of the United Nations," but Bailey limits his study to seven well-documented cases in which the UN played a leading role. *Guardian* reviewer David Ennals notes that the UN "usually becomes involved [in conflicts] at the eleventh hour when the situation is already critical or when fighting has actually begun. And if it fails to achieve a ceasefire it is listed as another UN failure." Bailey concentrates on UN successes, analyzing the means by which peaceful settlements are achieved, and, more importantly, writes Ennals, suggesting "the enormously wide range of methods by which the services of the UN can be brought into play. . . . The simple message of this far from simple book is that the United Nations must be used to far greater effect than has so far been the case." In Bailey's words, the UN ought to "be engaged far more in prophylactic diplomacy."

Critics have found *How Wars End* to be noteworthy both for its scholarship and for its simplicity of style. E. C. Hodgkin, in a *Middle East* review, writes: "Most analysts of the UN write in prose as opaque as that used by its servants. Sydney Bailey is, happily, an exception. His style is terse and exact, his reasoning clear, and though he takes no sides he is not aloof from the conflicts he describes. It is refreshing to find a writer on such a subject who can quote Pepys and Saint-Simon to illustrate his arguments." Roberts states, "It is now so fashionable to decry the UN that this book's reminder that it has a crucial role to play in ending armed conflict is very welcome." And *Jewish Chronicle* reviewer Jon Kimche concludes, "Bailey's name will be blessed by every student, politician and diplomat for years to come for providing this invaluable information in such a compact, well-organised and accessible manner."

Sydney D. Bailey told *CA* that he began writing while recuperating in a Calcutta hospital during World War II: "I had been in China with a Quaker ambulance unit, and as we were constantly on the move and had no access to Western newspapers or radios, we knew almost nothing about what was happening in the outside world. After Japanese forces had occupied Burma, there were no land routes out of unoccupied China, so when I became seriously ill, the U.S. air force flew me over the Hump (the Himalayas) to India. I had a long spell in hospital, and after I'd read the few books in English in the hospital library, I began to occupy my time by writing a weekly newsletter on world affairs for my erstwhile colleagues in the Chinese interior.

"When I got back to London in 1944, I ran into George Orwell, who was then literary editor of the *Tribune.* Orwell asked me to review some books about China, and I soon graduated to writing short weekly pieces on Asian Politics. Orwell undoubtedly influenced my style: he once told me that economy and simplicity of language are essential if we are to resist tyranny.

"Although I remain unrepentently British, I have traveled widely and spent seven happy years in the United States. I seem to be drawn to trouble spots like Northern Ireland and the Middle East. I have been fortunate, because I have found friendship wherever I have traveled, and I have never felt threatened. Although my formal education ended when I was fifteen, I have tried to write as a scholar, but for practitioners rather than for other scholars. All my books deal with some aspect or other of building a more just and peaceful world, including seven volumes about the political functions of the United Nations. I know the UN has many defects, but it's the only UN we have. It is easy to criticise it, but the challenge is to improve it.

"I work at a cluttered desk overlooking a cheerful garden. I usually draft in my head first, often while driving, and then write in manuscript. When the material has been typed, I revise and abridge ruthlessly, as early in the day as possible, when my mind is still reasonably sharp. I find that editors and publishers are more cooperative with authors who submit intelligible typescripts. I have only one piece of advice to aspiring writers of nonfiction: Don't put everything you know into your first book."

AVOCATIONAL INTERESTS: Music, photography, people.

BIOGRAPHICAL/CRITICAL SOURCES: Guardian (Manchester), November 11, 1982; *New Society,* December 2, 1982; *Middle East,* January, 1983; *Jewish Chronicle,* May 27, 1983.

* * *

BAIRD, Joseph Armstrong (Jr.) 1922-

PERSONAL: Born November 22, 1922, in Pittsburgh, Pa.; son of Joseph A. (a physician) and L. C. Baird. *Education:* Oberlin College, B.A. (magna cum laude), 1944; Harvard University, M.A., 1947, Ph.D., 1951. *Home:* 1830 Mountain View Dr., Tiburon, Calif. 94920. *Office:* Department of Art History, University of California, Davis, Calif. 95616; and 872 North Point St., San Francisco, Calif. 94109.

CAREER: University of Toronto, Toronto, Ontario, 1949-53, began as lecturer, became instructor in art history; University of California, Davis, 1953—, began as instructor, currently professor of art history; proprietor of North Point Gallery, San Francisco, Calif. Curator and consultant, California Historical Society, 1961-62, 1967-70; cataloger of Robert B. Honeyman, Jr. Collection in Bancroft Library, University of California, Berkeley, 1964-65. Lecturer in United States and Mexico. *Member:* Society of Architectural Historians, American Society for Hispanic Art Historical Studies. *Awards, honors:* Award of Merit, California Historical Society.

WRITINGS: Time's Wondrous Changes: San Francisco Architecture, 1776-1915, California Historical Society, 1962; *The Churches of Mexico,* University of California Press, 1962; *California's Pictorial Letter Sheets, 1849-1896,* David Magee, 1967; *Historic Lithographs of San Francisco,* Burger & Evans, 1972; *The West Remembered,* California Historical Society, 1973; *Theodore Wares, the Japanese Years,* Oakland Museum, 1976; *Wine and the Artist,* Dover, 1979. Contributor of articles and reviews to professional journals.

* * *

BAJEMA, Carl Jay 1937-

PERSONAL: Born May 25, 1937, in Plainwell, Mich.; son of John A. (a grocer) and Jennie (Geukes) Bajema; married first wife, Ann Bos (a registered nurse), 1959; married second wife, Claudia Vanderwall, 1978; children: (first marriage) Mark Alan, Christopher Marshall; (second marriage) Rebecca Joy, Brandon Forrester. *Education:* Grand Rapids Junior College, A.A., 1957; Western Michigan University, B.S., 1959, M.A., 1961; Michigan State University, Ph.D., 1963. *Religion:* Agnostic.

Office: Department of Biology, Grand Valley State College, Allendale, Mich. 49428.

CAREER: Teacher of science in public schools of Grand Rapids, Mich., 1959-60; Mankato State College, Mankato, Minn., assistant professor of biology, 1963-64; Grand Valley State College, Allendale, Mich., assistant professor, 1964-68, associate professor, 1968-72, professor of biology, 1972—. Harvard University, research associate in population studies, School of Public Health, 1967-71, visiting professor of anthropology, 1974-75. Vice-president, Planned Parenthood Association of Kent County, 1965-66; member of board of directors, National Association for Repeal of Abortion Laws, 1969-72. *Member:* American Institute of Biological Sciences, American Association for the Advancement of Science, National Association of Biology Teachers, History of Science Society. *Awards, honors:* Population Council senior fellow at University of Chicago, 1966-67.

WRITINGS: (Editor) *Natural Selection in Human Populations*, Wiley, 1971; (editor) *Eugenics Then and Now*, Dowden, 1976; (with Garrett Hardin) *Biology: Its Principles and Implications*, W. H. Freeman, 1978; (editor) *Artificial Selection and the Development of Evolutionary Theory*, Hutchinson Ross, 1981; (editor) *Natural Selection Theory from the Speculations of the Greeks to the Quantitative Measurements of the Biometricians*, Hutchinson Ross, 1983; (editor) *Sexual Selection Theory before 1900*, Hutchinson Ross, 1984.

WORK IN PROGRESS: Research in the ongoing evolution of human behavior, and history of evolutionary thought.

* * *

BAKER, Donald W(hitelaw) 1923-

PERSONAL: Born January 30, 1923, in Boston, Mass.; son of Merrill Ellsworth (a cabdriver) and Ida Margaret (Dempsey) Baker; married Natalie Jane Krentz, May 2, 1945; children: Pamela Jane, Alison Jean. *Education:* Brown University, A.B., 1947, A.M., 1949, Ph.D., 1955; Harvard University, graduate study, summers, 1950-51. *Politics:* Left. *Religion:* Protestant. *Home:* 16 Harry Freedman Pl., Crawfordsville, Ind. 47933. *Office:* Department of English, Wabash College, Crawfordsville, Ind. 47933.

CAREER: Brown University, Providence, R.I., instructor in English, 1948-53; Wabash College, Crawfordsville, Ind., assistant professor, 1953-58, associate professor, 1958-69, professor of English, 1969-76, Milligan Professor of English, 1976—, director of drama, 1954-60, poet-in-residence, 1964—. Has given poetry readings and conducted workshops. *Military service:* U.S. Army Air Forces, aerial navigator, 1942-46; became first lieutenant.

MEMBER: American Association of University Professors, National Council of Teachers of English (member of national achievement awards advisory board, 1968-71), Modern Language Association of America, Great Lakes Colleges Association (director of New Writer's Awards, 1976—), Phi Beta Kappa. *Awards, honors:* McLain-McTurnan Award from Wabash College, 1967; National Endowment for the Arts fellowship, 1974-75.

WRITINGS: *Twelve Hawks and Other Poems*, privately printed, 1974; *Formal Application: Selected Poems, 1960-1980*, Barnwood Press, 1982; *Unposted Letters and Other Poems*, Barnwood Press, 1984.

Work represented in many anthologies, including *Sound and Sense*, edited by Perrine, 5th edition, and *Literature*, edited by Hogins. Contributor of poems to about sixty periodicals, including *Saturday Review*, *Nation*, *Atlantic*, *Poetry*, and *Carolina Quarterly*.

WORK IN PROGRESS: *Losing the Cities*, a book of short stories; *The Day Before*, poems; a novel.

SIDELIGHTS: Donald W. Baker told *CA:* "My writing is at present without much system. I'm not prolific and have a lot of trouble producing anything at all. Some of my poems persist: one of them, 'Formal Application,' is still being reprinted in anthologies. I'm happy about that. I hope to go on writing and teaching for a long time. I've done a lot of readings and workshops, and they're among my greatest pleasures, sharing what I've written and what I've learned with people who want to know."

Baker continues: "As I get older, I find my writing simplifying itself. I work towards simpler, clearer language. I also find it more and more difficult to write as well as I need to to satisfy myself. I like to get up early and write till I've produced something that pleases or moves me. That makes a happy day. I find myself looking backward more and more, getting poems out of my childhood and youth. The present serves as contrast and foil. But I write political poems, too, out of anger and frustration and fear for my children and grandchildren. Perhaps I should call them poems for peace. I'm most pleased now with making a short, clear, simple, dramatic poem that makes me smile or grieve when I read it again to myself. There's luck involved, but you also have to learn for a long time how to use your language and shape it. Most of us learn, too, that we'll never be 'great.'"

* * *

BAKER, Hugh D. R. 1937-

PERSONAL: Born December 15, 1937, in Essex, England; son of Baden Roberts and Evelyn (Fairman) Baker; married Susan Mary Elliott, September 30, 1961; children: Estella, Alexander Roberts, Stuart Roberts. *Education:* University of London, B.A., 1962, Ph.D., 1967. *Residence:* Hertfordshire, England. *Office:* School of Oriental and African Studies, University of London, London WC1E 7HP, England.

CAREER: University of London, School of Oriental and African Studies, London, England, lecturer in Chinese, 1967-80; reader in modern Chinese, 1980—, head of Contemporary China Institute, 1981—. Chinese language training advisor, Hong Kong government, 1974-75. *Military service:* Royal Air Force, 1956-58. *Member:* Royal Asiatic Society (Hong Kong branch), British Association for Chinese Studies.

WRITINGS: (Contributor of bibliography in Chinese and Japanese) Victor Purcell, *The Chinese in Southeast Asia*, Oxford University Press, 1965; *A Chinese Lineage Village, Sheung Shui*, Stanford University Press, 1968; (consultant editor) *Peoples of the Earth*, Volume XIII: *China, Japan and Korea*, Mondadori, 1973; *Ancestral Images: A Hong Kong Album*, South China Morning Post, 1979; *Chinese Family and Kinship*, Columbia University Press, 1979; *More Ancestral Images: A Second Hong Kong Album*, South China Morning Post, 1980; *Ancestral Images Again: A Third Hong Kong Album*, South China Morning Post, 1981; *New Peace Country: A Chinese Gazetteer of the Hong Kong Region*, Hong Kong University Press, 1983. Contributor to journals.

WORK IN PROGRESS: Documentary filmmaking and radio and television broadcasting on Chinese society and language; research on punning in Cantonese and on Chinese social organization; fiction based on his insights into oriental culture.

* * *

BALABAN, John B. 1943-

PERSONAL: Born December 2, 1943, in Philadelphia, Pa.; son of Phillip and Alice (Georgies) Balaban; married Lana Flanagan (a teacher), November 27, 1970. *Education:* Pennsylvania State University, B.A., 1966; Harvard University, M.A., 1967. *Home:* 356 Laurel Lane, State College, Pa. 16801. *Office:* Department of English, Pennsylvania State University, University Park, Pa. 16802.

CAREER: Pennsylvania State University, University Park, instructor, 1970-73, assistant professor, 1973-76, associate professor, 1976-82, professor of English, 1982—. Fulbright senior lecturer in Romania, 1976-77; Fulbright distinguished visiting professor in Romania, 1978. Has given readings of his poetry at colleges and universities all over the United States and in England, as well as on radio programs. Member of board of directors, Columbia University Translation Center, 1981—. Poetry judge for Academy of American Poets, 1978—, Pennsylvania Council of the Arts, 1979, and Poetry Society of America, 1980. *Wartime service:* Instructor in literature and descriptive linguistics at University of Can Tho, 1967-68, and Committee of Responsibility to Save War-Injured Children field representative in South Vietnam, 1968-69, as alternative to military service. *Member:* P.E.N. American Center, Association of Asian Scholars, Association of Literary Translators, Poetry Society of America.

AWARDS, HONORS: Woodrow Wilson fellow, 1966-67; Chris Award at Columbus Film Festival, 1969, for "Children of an Evil Hour"; Fulbright-Hays travel grant to Vietnam, 1971-72; National Endowment for the Humanities younger humanist fellow, 1972; Lamont Award from Academy of American Poets, 1974, for *After Our War;* Institute for Arts and Humanistic Study fellow, 1974 and 1977; National Book Award nomination, 1975, for *After Our War;* National Endowment for the Arts fellow, 1978; Steava Prize from Romanian Writers' Union, 1978; National Endowment for the Humanities grant, 1980; Vaptsarov Medal from Union of Bulgarian Writers, 1980.

WRITINGS: (Contributor) *Civilian Casualty, Social Welfare and Refugee Problems in South Vietnam,* U.S. Government Printing Office, 1969; *Vietnam Poems* (chapbook), Carcanet, 1970; (editor) *Vietnamese Folk Poetry,* Unicorn Press, 1974; *After Our War* (poems), University of Pittsburgh Press, 1974; *Letters from across the Sea/Scrisori de Peste Mare,* Dacia Press (Cluj, Romania), 1978; (editor) *Ca Dao Vietnam: An Anthology of Vietnamese Folk Poetry,* Unicorn Press, 1980; *Blue Mountain* (poems), Unicorn Press, 1982.

Films: "Children of an Evil Hour," Committee of Responsibility, Inc., 1969; "Harpers Ferry," Filmspace, 1977; "Graveyard at Bald Eagle Ridge," Filmspace, 1977. Also translator and consultant for film "Ca Dao Vietnam: Vietnamese Folk Poetry," 1982.

Contributor to anthologies, including *Demilitarized Zones,* edited by J. Barry and W. Ehrhart, East River Anthology, 1976; *Introduction to Poetry,* edited by E. Knapp, McCormick-Mathers, 1977; *The Gift Outright,* edited by Helen Plotz, Morrow, 1978; *Peace Is Our Profession,* edited by Barry, East River Anthology, 1981; *From A to Z: Two Hundred Contemporary American Poets,* edited by David Ray, Swallow Press, 1981. Contributor of poems, articles, translations, and reviews to periodicals, including *Sewanee Review, New England Review, Southern Review, Nation, Poetry Now, College English, Translation Review, Hudson Review, American Scholar, New York Times,* and *Directions in Literary Criticism.*

WORK IN PROGRESS: Translating modern Bulgarian poetry, with William Meredith; writing a chapbook of poems about Romania, and another book of poetry; translating the work of Ho Xuan Huong, a nineteenth-century poet; revising a novel; writing a film about Vietnamese poetry, for public television.

SIDELIGHTS: In his preface to *Blue Mountain,* John B. Balaban writes: "A few years ago I heard that out West you can spot poems ambling about off the highways like antelope, that, in fact, if you have a sharp eye and a quick hand, you could round up more poems in one afternoon than all the writers in Greenwich Village can conjure in a week. So, each summer for the past few years, I've set out in pursuit."

BIOGRAPHICAL/CRITICAL SOURCES: Poetry, April, 1978; John B. Balaban, *Blue Mountain,* Unicorn Press, 1982.

* * *

BALDUCCI, Ernesto 1922-

PERSONAL: Born August 6, 1922, in St. Fiora, Grosseto, Italy. *Education:* Attended University of Florence. *Home:* Badia Fiesolana, San Domenico di Fiesole, Florence, Italy.

CAREER: Roman Catholic priest.

WRITINGS: Papa Giovanni, Vallecchi, 1964, translation by Dorothy White published as *John, "The Transitional Pope,"* McGraw, 1965; *La Chiesa come Eucaristia,* Queriniana, 1970; *I servi inutili,* Cittadella, 1970; *Diario dell'esodo,* Vallecchi, 1971; *La fede dalla fede,* Cittadella, 1975; *Fede e scelta politica,* Mondadori, 1977; *Le ragioni della speranza,* Coines, 1977; *Il mandorlo e il fuoco,* Borla, Volume I, 1979, Volume II, 1980, Volume III, 1981; *Cittadini del mondo,* Principato, 1981; *Il terzo millennio,* Bompiani, 1981; *La pace, realismo di un'utopia,* Principato, 1983.

* * *

BALLOWE, James 1933-

PERSONAL: Surname is pronounced Ba-*loo;* born November 28, 1933, in Carbondale, Ill.; son of Frank Charles (a wholesaler) and Ruth (Maynard) Ballowe; married Jeanne Frances Sparks (a teacher), December 27, 1953; married second wife, Ruth Ganchiff (an arts administrator); children: (first marriage) Jeffrey Craig, Mary Elizabeth. *Education:* Millikin University, A.B., 1954; University of Illinois, M.A., 1956, Ph.D., 1963. *Home:* 124 Carriage Way, Apt. 109B, Burr Ridge, Ill. 60595. *Office:* Graduate School, Bradley University, Peoria, Ill. 61625.

CAREER: Decatur (Ill.) public schools, teacher of English and history, 1954-55; Millikin University, Decatur, Ill., assistant professor of English, 1961-63; Bradley University, Peoria, Ill., assistant professor, 1963-67, associate professor, 1967-71, professor of English, 1971—, chairman of department, 1971-74, interim associate dean of college of liberal arts and sciences, 1971, dean of Graduate School, 1974—, associate provost for academic affairs, 1978—. Illinois state Museum Board, member, 1976—, chairman of personnel committee. Member of board of trustees of Lakeview Museum for the Arts and Sciences, 1977-81 and Peoria Art Guild, 1978-81; trustee,

National Coal Museum, 1982. Campaign executive, United Way, 1979—; member of board, Illinois Writers, Inc., 1979-80. Chairman, Commission on the Arts and Humanities of City of Peoria, 1982—. *Military service:* National Guard, 1954-63; became sergeant. *Member:* Modern Language Association of America, American Studies Association, American Association of University Professors, American Civil Liberties Union, Council of Graduate Schools in the United States (member of task force on quality of master's programs, 1978—; member of task force on master's degrees, 1980—), Midwestern Association of Graduate Schools (member of executive committee), Illinois Association of Graduate Schools (chairman, 1979-80), Phi Kappa Phi. *Awards, honors:* Fulbright travel grant, 1967; awards from Illinois Arts Council, 1976 and 1979.

WRITINGS: (Editor) *George Santayana's America: Essays on Literature and Culture,* University of Illinois Press, 1967, 3rd edition, 1969; *The Coal Miners* (poetry), Spoon River Poetry Press, 1979. Work represented in anthologies, including: *A Sampler: New Poems and Some Poetry Talk,* Dunes House, 1976; Lucien Stryk, editor, *Prairie Voices,* Spoon River Poetry Press, 1980; David Pichaske, editor, *Beowulf to Beatles and Beyond,* Macmillan, 1981. Contributor of articles, poetry, and short stories to numerous periodicals, including *Encounter, American Quarterly, American Literature, Southern Review,* and *Salmagundi.*

WORK IN PROGRESS: Writing essays on literature and graduate studies.

SIDELIGHTS: James Ballowe told *CA:* "I do not find that poetry conflicts with research or administration. It is a way of keeping aware of myself and surroundings while engaged in more technical and mechanical activities. Reading and writing poetry improve everything else I do."

BIOGRAPHICAL/CRITICAL SOURCES: Kenyon Review, Volume XXX, number 4, 1968.

* * *

**BARAK, Michael
See BAR-ZOHAR, Michael**

* * *

BARBER, Benjamin R. 1939-

PERSONAL: Born August 2, 1939, in New York, N.Y.; children: Jeremy, Rebecca. *Education:* Albert Schweitzer College, Churwalden, Switzerland, Certificate, 1956; London School of Economics and Political Science, Certificate, 1959; Grinnell College, B.A. (with honors), 1960; Harvard University, A.M., 1963, Ph.D., 1966. *Home:* 924 West End Ave., New York, N.Y. 10025. *Agent:* Charlotte Sheedy Literary Agency, Inc., 145 West 86th St., New York, N.Y. 10024. *Office:* Department of Political Science, Rutgers University, New Brunswick, N.J. 08903.

CAREER: Albert Schweitzer College, Churwalden, Switzerland, lecturer in politics and ethics, 1963-65; University of Pennsylvania, Philadelphia, assistant professor of political science, 1966-69; Rutgers University, New Brunswick, N.J., assistant professor, 1969-70, associate professor, 1971-75, professor of political science, 1975—. Visiting assistant professor, Haverford College, 1968; visiting associate professor, Hunter College of the City University of New York, 1970; senior Fulbright-Hays research scholar, Essex University, 1976-77; visiting fellow, New York Institute for the Humanities, 1980-81; guest lecturer at Yale Drama School and at Hopkins Center, Dartmouth College.

MEMBER: American Political Science Association (co-chairperson of program committee, 1975-76), Conference for the Study of Political Thought (chairman, 1983-84), Authors Guild, Authors League of America, American Society of Composers, Authors, and Publishers, American Society for Political and Legal Philosophy, Academy of Political Science, International Political Science Association, Caucus for a New Political Science, Dramatists Guild. *Awards, honors:* Rutgers University Research Council grant, 1972-73; Guggenheim fellowship, and American Council of Learned Societies fellowship, 1980-81.

WRITINGS: (With C. J. Friedrich and M. Curtis) *Totalitarianism in Perspective: Three Views,* Praeger, 1969; *Superman and Common Men: Freedom, Anarchy and the Revolution,* Praeger, 1971; *The Death of Communal Liberty: A History of Freedom in a Swiss Mountain Canton,* Princeton University Press, 1974; *Liberating Feminism,* Continuum Books, 1975; *Marriage Voices* (novel), Simon & Schuster, 1981; *The Artist and Political Vision,* Transaction Books, 1982; *Strong Democracy: Participatory Politics for a New Age,* University of California Press, 1984. Also author of monograph, *Political Participation,* for Poynter Foundation.

Contributor: I. Wallerstein and P. Starr, editors, *The University Crisis Reader,* Volume II, Random House, 1971; F. Fleron and E. Hoffman, editors, *The Conduct of Soviet Foreign Policy,* Aldine-Atherton, 1971; J. A. Ogilvy, editor, *Self and World: Readings in Philosophy,* Harcourt, 1973; R. Edwards, editor, *Relevant Methods in Comparative Education,* UNESCO, 1973; J. B. Williamson, editor, *Social Problems: The Contemporary Debate,* Little, Brown, 1974; C. Bennett, editor, *Comparative Studies in Education: An Anthology,* Publications in Continuing Education, Syracuse University, 1975; Norman Daniels, editor, *Reading Rawls,* Basic Books, 1975.

R. Perruci, editor, *Introductory Sociology,* W. C. Brown, 1977; John Perry and Erna Perry, editors, *The Social Web,* 2nd edition, Canfield Press, 1977; George Roberts, editor, *Bertrand Russell: The Memorial Volumes,* Allen & Unwin, 1978; Robert H. Horwitz, editor, *Moral Foundations of the American Republic,* University Press of Virginia, 3rd edition, 1982; Michael Freeman and David Robertson, editors, *The Frontiers of Political Theory: Essays in a Revitalized Discipline,* St. Martin's, 1980.

Plays: "The People's Heart," first produced Off-Off Broadway at Theatre 3, November, 1969; "Delly's Oracle," first produced at Berkshire Theatre Festival, October, 1970; "Fightsong" (musical), produced in New York at Gene Frankel Theatre, 1975; (with Martin Best) "Journeys: A Musical Myth" (musical), produced in Hanover, N.H., at Hopkins Center, 1975. Also author of "The Bust," "Doors," and "Winning," all first produced in New York at Equity Showcase, and of "Home and the River" (opera/music theater).

Contributor of articles to *New York Times, Newsday, New Republic, London Review of Books, Harper's, Progressive,* and other periodicals. Editor, *Political Theory: An International Journal of Political Philosophy,* 1974—.

MEDIA ADAPTATIONS: "Journeys: A Musical Myth" was recorded by E.M.I. Records as "Knight on the Road."

BIOGRAPHICAL/CRITICAL SOURCES: U.S. News and World Report, February 9, 1975, July 7, 1975.

BARKS, Coleman (Bryan) 1937-

PERSONAL: Born April 23, 1937, in Chattanooga, Tenn.; son of Herbert Bernard (an educator) and Elizabeth (Bryan) Barks; married Kittsu Greenwood (an editorial assistant), 1962 (divorced); children: C. Benjamin, Cole Greenwood. *Education:* University of North Carolina, A.B., 1959, Ph.D., 1968; University of California, Berkeley, M.A., 1961. *Home:* 196 West View Dr., Athens, Ga. 30601. *Office:* English Department, University of Georgia, Athens, Ga. 30601.

CAREER: University of Southern California, Los Angeles, instructor in English, 1965-67; Univeristy of Georgia, Athens, assistant professor, 1967-72, associate professor of English, 1972—. Visiting professor, University of Michigan, 1974. *Member:* South Atlantic Modern Language Association. *Awards, honors:* Best poetry manuscript and best poem awards of Georgia Writers' Association, 1968; grants from National Endowment for the Arts, 1979, and Georgia Commission for the Arts, 1981; Guy Owen Poetry Prize from *Southern Poetry Review,* 1983.

WRITINGS: The Juice (poems), Harper, 1972; *New Words* (poems), Burnt Hickory, 1974; *We're Laughing at the Damage* (poems), Briarpatch, 1977; (translator from the Persian with Robert Bly) Laulana Jalal al-Din Rumi, *Night and Sleep,* Yellow Moon Press, 1981; (translator) Rumi, *Open Secret,* Threshold Books, 1983.

Contributor: William Cole, editor, *Pith and Vinegar: An Anthology of Short Humorous Poetry,* Simon & Schuster, 1969; Geof Hewitt, editor, *Quickly Aging Here: Some Poets of the 1970's,* Doubleday, 1969; *Twenty-three California Poets,* Ante-Echo, 1969; Cole, editor, *Poetry Brief: An Anthology of Short, Short Poems,* Macmillan, 1971; Fred Wolven and Duane Locke, editors, *New Generation: Poetry* (anthology), Ann Arbor Review, 1971; Frances McCullough, editor, *Earth, Air, Fire & Water,* Coward, 1971; Ann Colley and Judith Moore, editors, *Starting with Poetry* (anthology), Harcourt, 1973; *New Voices in American Poetry* (anthology), Winthrop Publishing, 1973; Cole, editor, *Half Serious* (anthology), Methuen, 1973; Guy Owen and Mary C. Williams, editors, *New Southern Poets: Selected Poems from Southern Poetry Review,* University of North Carolina Press, 1974.

Owen and Louis Rubin, editors, *Contemporary Southern Poetry,* University of North Carolina Press, 1975; *Poetry 2* (anthology), Scholastic Book Services, 1975; Robert Grey and Nancy Stone, editors, *White Trash* (anthology), New South, 1976; Owen, editor, *Southern Poetry,* Southern Poetry Review, 1976; Owen and Williams, editors, *Southern Poetry: The Seventies,* Southern Poetry Review, 1977; William Hedgepeth, editor, *The Hog Book,* Doubleday, 1978; Owen, editor, *Contemporary Southern Poetry: An Anthology,* Louisiana State University Press, 1979; *Southern Poetry since WW II* (anthology), Louisiana State University Press, 1980.

Contributor of about 250 poems to little magazines, including *Ann Arbor Review, Chelsea, Tennessee Poetry Journal, Poetry Review, New American* and *Canadian Poetry.*

WORK IN PROGRESS: A collection of poetry, *Ant Work;* another collection of translations of Rumi's works, with Robert Bly.

SIDELIGHTS: Writing in the *Dictionary of Literary Biography,* Barbara Lovell describes the poetry of Coleman Barks as "low key, but it turns out to be a reverberating poetry: phrases surface in the mind to insinuate themselves and turn out to be, after all, indelible—as do whole poems. His rhythms are subtle, his imagery—usually drawn from the ordinary, the everyday—astonishing in its exactitude and, more often than not, delivered with an almost throw-it-away gesture. But a Barks reader soon learns that there is nothing in this work to be thrown away, that while not confessional it rings of absolute, even relentless honesty while remaining what one critic, reaching for that ingrained wit and humor, calls 'sassy.'" Lovell also believes that it is precisely the low key quality of Barks's work that has kept him from being "more widely recognized in the courts of criticism" despite the fact that "his poetry is a singular achievement."

BIOGRAPHICAL/CRITICAL SOURCES: Dictionary of Literary Biography, Volume V: *American Poets since World War II,* Gale, 1980.

* * *

BARLAY, Stephen 1930-

PERSONAL: Born January 18, 1930, in Budapest, Hungary; immigrated to England, 1956; married Agi Semler (a photographer), September 9, 1956; children: Nicholas, Robin. *Education:* Read history and literature at Pazmany Peter University, Budapest, for four years. *Address:* c/o Hamish Hamilton Ltd., Garden House, 57-59, Long Acre, London WC2E 9J2, England.

CAREER: Free-lance writer, journalist, and broadcaster in Budapest, Hungary, 1948-56; employed in various positions, including barman, salesman, and waiter, in London, England, 1957-60; author and free-lance journalist, London, 1961—. *Military service:* Hungarian Army, 1952-53. *Member:* National Union of Journalists, Writers' Guild of Great Britain.

WRITINGS—Published by Hamish Hamilton, except as indicated; fiction: (With Peter Sasdy) *Four Black Cars,* translation by Paul Tabori, Putnam, 1958; *Blockbuster* (Book-of-the-Month Club selection), 1976, Morrow, 1977; *Remote Control,* Morrow, 1977; *Crash Course,* Harper, 1979; *In the Company of Spies,* Summit Books, 1981 (published in England as *Cuban Confetti,* Hamish Hamilton, 1981); *The Ruling Passion,* 1982; *The Price of Silence,* 1983.

Nonfiction: *Bondage: The Slave Traffic in Women Today,* Funk, 1968, revised edition, Ballantine, 1977 (published in England as *Sex Slavery: A Documentary Report on the International Scene Today,* Heinemann, 1968, revised edition, Hodder & Stoughton, 1975); *Aircrash Detective: The Quest for Air Safety,* 1969, revised edition, Hodder & Stoughton, 1975, published as *The Search for Air Safety: An International Documentary Report on the Investigation of Commercial Aviation Accidents* (U.S. Aviation and Space Book Club selection), Morrow, 1970, revised edition, Coronet, 1975; *Fire: An International Report,* 1972, Stephen Greene Press, 1973; *Double Cross: Encounters with Industrial Spies,* 1973, published as *The Secrets Business,* Crowell, 1974; *Fire, That Thin Red Line: The Case for Self-Defense,* Hutchinson, 1976.

Author of television and radio scripts: "This Is Your Chance" (quiz series), ATV (London), 1958; (with J. Elliott) "Double Dealers" (drama series), BBC-Radio, 1974, BBC-TV, 1976; "Point of No Return" (drama), BBC, 1976; "Blockbuster" (drama; based on his book of the same title), BBC, 1978; "The Price of Silence" (nine-part drama; based on his book of the same title), American Public Radio, 1983.

Contributor to anthologies, including *De Wereld Waarin Wij Wonen en Werken,* W. de Haan (Netherlands), 1961, and T.

Aczel, editor, *Ten Years After,* MacGibbon & Kee, 1966. Contributor to European periodicals.

SIDELIGHTS: In his youth, Stephen Barlay was involved in the Hungarian wartime resistance. By 1948, he had twice escaped from the Gestapo. He also participated in both the Hungarian Revolution and the new resistance. In 1956, he fled to London, where he continued his writing.

About *In the Company of Spies,* Newgate Callendar of the *New York Times Book Review* comments that this book "will keep any reader happily mystified for hours." He considers the novel "a bit too disorganized" yet admires it as a "skillful assemblage" of spy and mystery elements.

Miranda Seymour of the London *Times* labels *The Ruling Passion* an "impressive" novel, adding that it "successfully treads the dangerous path between the ludicrous and the sublime."

BIOGRAPHICAL/CRITICAL SOURCES: *New York Times Book Review,* September 20, 1981; *Times* (London), January 14, 1982.

* * *

BARNETT, Leonard (Palin) 1919-

PERSONAL: Born April 11, 1919, in Crewe, Cheshire, England; children: Andrew, Richard. *Education:* Attended University of Manchester; University of London, B.D. (with second class honors), 1945. *Home:* 12 Briarwood Rd., Stonleigh, Ewell, Epsom, Surrey KT17 2LY, England.

CAREER: Methodist minister, 1942—; currently minister of Cheam Methodist Church, Surrey, England; writer. Director, Methodist Holiday Hotels Ltd.; national secretary, Methodist Youth Department, 1949-58; regular BBC broadcaster on religious programs; also makes occasional television appearances. *Awards, honors:* L.H.D., Pfeiffer College, 1972.

WRITINGS: *Adventure with Youth,* Methodist Youth Department, 1952; *Starting out in Church Youth Club Work,* Methodist Youth Department; *Prayer-Time with Youth,* Methodist Youth Department, 1954; *A Prayer Diary for Youth,* Methodist Youth Department, 1955; *For Christian Beginners,* Methodist Youth Department, 1955; *Christian Responsibility for World Peace,* Epworth; *Talking to Youth,* National Sunday School Union, 1958.

Talking to Youth Again, National Sunday School Union, 1960; *A Boy's Prayer Diary,* Epworth, 1963; *A Girl's Prayer Diary,* Epworth, 1963; *Live for Kicks,* National Sunday School Union, 1964; (author of introduction) *Here Is Methodism: For Church Membership Groups and Other Interested People,* Epworth, 1966; *Star Quality,* National Christian Education Council, 1966; *Sex and Teenagers in Love,* Denholm House Press, 1967; *This I Can Believe,* Denholm House Press, 1969; *Sex and Sense,* International Bible Reading Association, 1969.

This Way to the Stars: Sermons for the Space Age, Epworth, 1971; *Good Times with God,* Hodder & Stoughton, 1975; *Homosexuality: Time to Tell the Truth,* Gollancz, 1975; *New Prayer Diary: For Young People and Others,* Hodder & Stoughton, 1975; *Sex and Young Lovers,* National Christian Education Council, 1979; *What Is Methodism?,* Epworth, 1980. Also author of *Getting It Over* and *The High Cost of Loving.*

Plays: *Pop! Goes the Patient,* Evans Bros., 1966. Also author of *Ten to Twelve,* Methodist Youth Department, *Boy on the Corner,* Evans Bros., *Windswept Week-end,* Evans, and *You've Got to Be Tough,* Methodist Youth Department. Feature writer, *Yours.*

* * *

BARNEY, Harry
See LOTTMAN, Eileen

* * *

BARNOUW, Erik 1908-

PERSONAL: Born June 23, 1908, in The Hague, Netherlands; son of Adriaan Jacob (a teacher) and Ann (Midgley) Barnouw; married Dorothy Beach, June 3, 1939; children: Jeffrey, Susanna, Karen. *Education:* Princeton University, A.B., 1929; University of Vienna, studied at Reinhardt Seminar, 1930. *Home:* 39 Claremont Ave., New York, N.Y. 10027. *Agent:* Harold Ober Associates, 40 East 49th St., New York, N.Y. 10017. *Office:* Columbia University, New York, N.Y. 10027.

CAREER: During early career, worked as broadcasting program director and writer for advertising agencies; Columbia Broadcasting System, New York City, writer and editor, 1939-40; National Broadcasting Co., New York City, editor of Script Division, 1942-44; U.S. War Department, Washington, D.C., supervisor of education unit, Armed Forces Radio Service, 1944-45; Columbia University, New York City, 1946—, began as assistant professor, became professor of dramatic arts, professor emeritus, 1973—, editor, Center for Mass Communication of Columbia University Press, 1949-71. Television and radio adapter for Theatre Guild, 1954-61. Chief of motion picture, broadcasting, and recorded sound division, Library of Congress, 1978-81. Producer of "Freedom to Read," Columbia University Bicentennial film, 1954, and "Hiroshima-Nagasaki, August 1945," Center for Mass Communication, 1970. President, International Film Seminars, Inc., 1960-67. Consultant on communication, U.S. Public Health Service, 1947-50.

MEMBER: Writers Guild (national chairman, 1957-59), Authors League of America (secretary, 1949-53), Society of American Historians, Society for Cinema Studies, National Academy of Television Arts and Sciences (member of board of governors, New York, 1958-61), American Civil Liberties Union (member of television-radio panel, 1946-73), Public Affairs Committee (member of board, 1961-65).

AWARDS, HONORS: George Foster Peabody Award for achievement in radio or television, 1944, for National Broadcasting Co. radio series, "Words at War"; Ohio State Institute for Education by Radio award, for best single program, 1948, for "The Conspiracy of Silence"; "Freedom to Read" was Edinburgh Film Festival selection, 1954; Gavel Award of American Bar Association and Sylvania Television Award for best noncommercial television series, 1959, for "Decision: The Constitution in Action"; Fulbright grant, 1961-62, for research in India on use of mass media; Guggenheim fellowship, 1969; Bancroft Prize, 1971, for *The Image Empire;* George Polk Award, 1971, for *A History of Broadcasting in the United States;* Silver Dragon award of Cracow Film Festival, 1972, for "Fable-Safe"; John D. Rockefeller III Fund fellowship, 1972; Woodrow Wilson fellowship, 1976; Indo-American fellowship, 1978-79; Eastman Kodak Gold Medal Award, 1982, for significant contributions as an innovative educator.

WRITINGS: *Handbook of Radio Writing,* Little, 1939; (editor) *Radio Drama in Action,* Rinehart, 1945; *Mass Communication:*

Television, Radio, Film, Press, Rinehart, 1956; *The Television Writer,* Hill & Wang, 1962; (with S. Krishnaswamy) *Indian Film,* Columbia University Press, 1963, 2nd edition, Oxford University Press, 1980; *A History of Broadcasting in the United States,* Oxford University Press, Volume I: *A Tower in Babel,* 1966, Volume II: *The Golden Web,* 1968, Volume III: *The Image Empire,* 1970; *Documentary: A History of the Non-Fiction Film,* Oxford University Press, 1974; *Tube of Plenty: The Evolution of American Television,* Oxford University Press, 1975; *The Sponsor: Notes on a Modern Potentate,* Oxford University Press, 1978; *The Magician and the Cinema,* Oxford University Press, 1981.

Films: (And producer, in consultation with Herbert Wechsler) "Decision: The Constitution in Action," (series of seven films), Center for Mass Communication and National Educational Television, 1957-59; "Memento," Center for Mass Communication, 1968; (and director) "Fable-Safe," Center for Mass Communication, 1971.

Television; adaptor; all for U.S. Steel Hour: Patterson Greene, "Papa Is All"; Roger Eddy, "The Women of Hadley"; Henrik Ibsen, "Hedda Gabler."

Author of radio documentary, "The Conspiracy of Silence," produced by ABC, 1948. Author, with Joshua Logan, of Princeton University Triangle Club musical, "Zuider Zee," 1928.

WORK IN PROGRESS: Editing the four-volume *International Encyclopedia of Communications,* for Oxford University Press and Annenberg School of Communications.

SIDELIGHTS: In his *New York Review of Books* article about Erik Barnouw's *A History of Broadcasting in the United States,* Leonard Ross recounts an anecdote involving Philo T. Farnsworth, the inventor of television. In 1927, Farnsworth and financial backer George Everson "gathered for a demonstration of Farnsworth's television apparatus. For the first time [the inventor] successfully transmitted several graphic designs, including a dollar sign. As Everson recalled later, 'It seemed to jump out at us on the screen.'" The overwhelming influence of money on the American broadcasting industry is an important theme of Barnouw's writings, including *A History of Broadcasting in the United States* and *The Sponsor: Notes on a Modern Potentate.*

A History of Broadcasting in the United States, which *New York Times Book Review* critic John Leonard calls the work that "everybody who writes about television steals from," covers, in three chronological categories, the high and low points of American radio and television history. Volume one, *A Tower in Babel,* recalls radio from its infancy until 1933; volume two, *The Golden Web,* examines the years 1933-1953, the peak period of radio programming; volume three, *The Image Empire,* takes up the story from 1953, when television was just beginning to hit its stride as the most formidable communication source in the world. The books illustrate events both dramatic (David Sarnoff's 72-hour marathon at the Wanamaker department store telegraph booth in 1912; as Sarnoff reports the sinking of the S.S. *Titanic,* President William Howard Taft orders all other wave lengths off the air) and whimsical (a profile of National Broadcasting Corp.'s "discovery," chimpanzee J. Fred Muggs, who almost singlehandedly rescues the fledgling "Today" show in 1953). Governmental controls of the air, technological achievements, and the study of broadcasting as a purely commercial enterprise are explored at length.

In a *New York Times Book Review* article, Eric F. Goldman describes Barnouw's "system" of the broadcasting industry as a "subtle one of men with inevitable instincts for money, status, power and a sense of fulfillment controlling powerful instruments which neither they nor most others have really tried to understand. The exploration of this theme permits the volumes to make their most salient contributions. Mr. Barnouw finds truth less on the flat surfaces than in the interstices; his emphasis is on complexity, conflicting interests, colliding drives, shadings, inherent difficulties. He spells out the full ambivalence of the figure who had so much to do with stating the original pattern of all broadcasting, Secretary of Commerce Herbert Hoover. [Barnouw] describes the rise of the corporate structures in a way which makes clear that men were fighting over a good many things apart from who makes money from the airwaves."

Nevertheless, the practice of making money from the airwaves pervades the entire broadcast industry. Thus it is the sponsor who perhaps exudes the greatest influence on the corporate structure; often the advertisers, as much as the government, control the content of the programs being broadcast. Barnouw's book *The Sponsor,* according to *Nation* critic John S. Rosenberg, is "the most incisive and well-written study to date of the economic structure and ideological impact of modern broadcasting." The author uses examples of advertiser influence throughout the book. One such story is of a 1950s dramatic presentation of the Nuremberg trials; the show's sponsor, a natural gas association, demanded that all references to "gas" (i.e. gas chambers) be deleted from the script.

"Barnouw is particularly effective in explaining what this [kind of] total sponsor control means," states *Washington Post Book World* reviewer Joel Swerdlow. Even today, "'newsmen' are selected via devices like the 'galvanic skin response tests' to make sure the audience will like them. 'Public service announcements' must be approved by the Advertising Council, the very people they're supposed to counterbalance." Another manifestation of sponsor control, according to Swerdlow's review, "is a revisionism that would make even Stalinist historians-blush. The stories are legend. One program portrayed the Civil War and never mentioned blacks or slavery. Lobbying by florists is notorious for keeping bereaved characters everywhere from saying, 'Send a charitable contribution instead of flowers.'"

Rosenberg sums up: "Although most viewers tend to view commercials as necessary interruptions in their favorite programs, Barnouw makes it abundantly clear [in *The Sponsor*] that the very purpose of the programs—a purpose that governs them from inception to airing—is to bring us to the commercials. Others have argued, as Barnouw does, that 'a network commercial is likely to promote not only a product but a way of life, a view of the world, a philosophy. . . .' What is unique about *The Sponsor* is the skill, subtlety and wisdom with which [the author's] observations on the structure of the media are woven together in such a slim and immensely readable volume."

BIOGRAPHICAL/CRITICAL SOURCES: *New York Review of Books,* April 8, 1971, March 9, 1972, April 6, 1978; *New York Times Book Review,* November 21, 1971, November 30, 1978; *Commonweal,* December 17, 1971; *Spectator,* February 14, 1976; Erik Barnouw, *The Sponsor: Notes on a Modern Potentate,* Oxford University Press, 1978; *Nation,* October 21, 1978; *Washington Post Book World,* June 18, 1978; *New York Times,* June 6, 1981.

—*Sketch by Susan Salter*

BARR, Pat(ricia Miriam) 1934-

PERSONAL: Born April 25, 1934, in Norwich, Norfolk, England; daughter of Spencer and Miriam Copping; married John Marshall Barr (a journalist), June 22, 1956 (deceased). *Education:* University of Birmingham, B.A. (honors), 1956; University College, London, M.A. (honors in English), 1964. *Politics:* Liberal. *Religion:* None. *Home:* 25 Montpelier Row, Blackheath, London S.E.3, England. *Agent:* Carol Smith Literary Agency, 2 John St., London WC1N 2HJ, England.

CAREER: Teacher of English at Yokohama International School, Yokohama, Japan, 1959-61, and with University of Maryland Overseas Program in Japan, 1961-62; assistant secretary of National Old People's Welfare Council, London, England, 1965-66; full-time writer, 1966—. *Awards, honors:* Winston Churchill fellowship, 1971, for nonfiction writing.

WRITINGS: The Coming of the Barbarians: The Opening of Japan to the West, 1853-1870, Dutton, 1967; *The Deer Cry Pavillion: A Story of Westerners in Japan, 1868-1905*, Macmillan, 1968; *A Curious Life for a Lady: The Story of Isabella Bird, a Remarkable Victorian Traveller*, Doubleday, 1970; *To China with Love: The Lives and Times of Protestant Missionaries in China, 1860-1900*, Doubleday, 1972; *The Memsahibs*, Secker & Warburg, 1976; *Taming the Jungle*, Secker & Warburg, 1977; *Framing the Female*, Kestrel, 1978; (with Ray Desmond) *Simla: A Hill Station in British India*, Scribner, 1978; *Japan*, David & Charles, 1980; *Chinese Alice*, Secker & Warburg, 1981; *Jade: A Novel of China*, St. Martin's, 1982. Contributor to *Homes & Gardens, Times Educational Supplement, Guardian,* and other periodicals.

WORK IN PROGRESS: A historical novel set in nineteenth century Japan, for St. Martin's.

SIDELIGHTS: Many of Pat Barr's books are historical studies of Japan and China. After living in the Orient for several years, Barr combined her fascination with the culture and history of this area with her talent for writing historical nonfiction. As a result, remarks a reviewer for the *Times Literary Supplement*, "[Pat] Barr has won a place for herself as a writer who can present, in a style both popular and elegant, the fruits of accurate research."

In a review of *The Deer Cry Pavilion: A Story of Westerners in Japan, 1868-1905,* Kenneth Lamott states in *Book World* that "Barr's lively and informative account . . . is really quite an extraordinary story involving some extraordinary characters. . . . Barr is an accomplished writer, and her story, witty and graceful as it is, cuts deeply below the brilliant surface description of life in emerging Japan. [This] is an admirable book.'' C. W. Stucki writes in *Library Journal* that Barr's book *The Coming of the Barbarians: The Opening of Japan to the West, 1853-1870* "is sometimes humorous, sometimes terrifying, and always interesting." And a writer for the *Times Literary Supplement* writes that in this book Barr "makes no pretense to Japanese scholarship or to a novel interpretation of the facts. . . . Barr earns high marks for the attractive and intelligent presentation of her tale."

According to a writer for *Choice*, Barr's book *To China with Love* is "a lively description of the life styles and personalities of British Protestant missionaries in China during the pioneering decades before the Boxer holocaust of 1900." As a critic for the *Times Literary Supplement* notes, "Barr's judgment of these people is warmed by a sympathy that is clear-headed in its charity."

In 1982 Barr published her first novel, *Jade: A Novel of China.* Set in nineteenth-century China, *Jade* tells the life of the daughter of English missionary parents. Orville Schell states in the *Los Angeles Times Book Review* that "Barr has put her Chinese historical backdrop to good purpose. . . . One must say that Barr has used history effectively to illustrate not only the . . . nature of [her heroine's experiences], but of China's anguished efforts to preserve cultural balance at a time when foreign encroachment compelled it to borrow science and technology from abroad." And Reid Beddow remarks in the *Washington Post Book World* that "at its best, *Jade* carries the reader along effortlessly. One certainly gets a sense of the sweep and variety of the old China. . . . Author Barr has woven what is evidently a lot of scholarly reading into her text."

In correspondence with *CA*, Barr explains how she happened to write her first novel. She states: "After publishing several works of nonfiction I decided to try my hand at historical fiction. . . . I was encouraged in this by my agent, Carol Smith, and my publishers, Secker & Warburg, and I had a considerable amount of unused or half-used background material to draw upon. I've now had sufficient success with my first novel . . . to give me confidence and I'm quite fascinated by the fictional challenge. The writing of a novel spills over into one's whole life and the limitations are one's own instead of being imposed by the available material as with nonfiction. Consequently there's always the hope of further development, of doing a little better next time. I am lucky in that I now thoroughly 'relish my habitual pursuit' and am earning sufficient money from it at long last to give me time to find out how far I can go."

BIOGRAPHICAL/CRITICAL SOURCES: Times Literary Supplement, September 28, 1967, February 6, 1969, January 5, 1974, October 30, 1981; *Library Journal,* October 1, 1967; *Book World,* June 1, 1969; *Choice,* December, 1973; *Washington Post Book World,* September 17, 1982, September 4, 1983; *Los Angeles Times Book Review,* September 19, 1982.

* * *

BARRANGER, M(illy) S(later) 1937-

PERSONAL: Born February 12, 1937, in Birmingham, Ala.; daughter of Clem C. (an engineer) and Mildred (Hilliard) Slater; married Garic Kenneth Barranger (an attorney), August 26, 1961; children: Heather D. *Education:* Alabama College (now University of Montevallo), B.A., 1958; Tulane University, M.A., 1959, Ph.D., 1964. *Home:* 1901 The Oaks, Chapel Hill, N.C. 27514. *Office:* Dramatic Art Department, University of North Carolina, 105 Graham 052A, Chapel Hill, N.C. 27514.

CAREER: Louisiana State University in New Orleans (now University of New Orleans), special lecturer in English, 1964-69; Tulane University, New Orleans, La., assistant professor, 1969-73, associate professor of theatre and speech, 1973-80, chairman of department, 1971-80; Visiting Young Professor in Humanities, University of Tennessee, 1981-82; University of North Carolina at Chapel Hill, professor of dramatic art and chairman of department, 1982—. Executive director of Tulane Center Stage theater, 1973-78; executive producer of Playmakers Repertory Company, 1982—. *Member:* American Theatre Association (vice-president of administration, 1975-77; president, 1978-79), National Theatre Conference, American Society for Theatre Research, Ibsen Society of America, Southeastern Theatre Conference.

WRITINGS: Barron's Simplified Approach to Ibsen, Barron's, Volume I: *Peer Gynt, A Doll's House, An Enemy of the People,*

1969, Volume II: *Ghosts, The Wild Duck, Hedda Gabler,* 1969; (editor with Daniel Dodson) *Generations: A Thematic Introduction to Drama,* Harcourt, 1971; (contributor) *Dictionary of Church History,* Westminster, 1971; *Theatre: A Way of Seeing,* Wadsworth, 1980; *Theatre: Past and Present,* Wadsworth, 1984. Contributor of articles to *College Language Association Journal, Modern Drama, Theatre Journal, Theatre News, Comparative Drama, Quarterly Journal of Speech,* and other journals.

WORK IN PROGRESS: Studies in Henrik Ibsen's late plays; *Radical Theatricality in Contemporary British Drama.*

AVOCATIONAL INTERESTS: Music, films, travel.

* * *

BARTLEY, Numan V(ache) 1934-

PERSONAL: Born October 29, 1934, in Ladonia, Tex.; son of Numan V. (a farmer) and Rosa (a nurse; maiden name, Rollin) Bartley; married Morraine Matthews, June, 1968. *Education:* East Texas State College, B.A., 1955; North Texas State University, M.A., 1961; Vanderbilt University, Ph.D., 1968. *Home:* 360 Segrest Cir., Athens, Ga. 30605. *Office:* Department of History, University of Georgia, Athens, Ga. 30601.

CAREER: Georgia Institute of Technology, Atlanta, instructor, 1964-66, assistant professor, 1966-70, associate professor of history, 1970-72; University of Georgia, Athens, associate professor, 1972-76, professor of history, 1976—. *Military service:* U.S. Navy, 1955-58, became lieutenant, junior grade. *Awards, honors:* Postdoctoral fellowships from Johns Hopkins University Institute of Southern History, 1969-70, University of Michigan Inter-University Consortium for Political Research, 1971, and Woodrow Wilson International Center for Scholars, 1972; Chastain Award for best book on the South, from Southern Political Science Association, 1976, for *Southern Politics and the Second Reconstruction;* Christ-Janer Award for creative research, 1980; E. Merton Coulter Award, Georgia Historical Society, 1982; National Endowment for the Humanities fellowship, 1984-85.

WRITINGS: The Rise of Massive Resistance: Race and Politics in the South during the 1950's, Louisiana State University Press, 1969; *From Thurmond to Wallace: Political Tendencies in Georgia, 1948-1968,* Johns Hopkins University Press, 1970; (with Hugh D. Graham) *Southern Politics and the Second Reconstruction,* Johns Hopkins University Press, 1976; (with Kenneth Coleman and others) *A History of Georgia,* University of Georgia Press, 1977; *The Creation of Modern Georgia,* University of Georgia Press, 1983. Contributor of articles to journals in his field.

WORK IN PROGRESS: A book on the modern South, 1945-1980.

SIDELIGHTS: In *The Rise of Massive Resistance: Race and Politics in the South during the 1950's,* Numan V. Bartley examines "resistance to reform during [that era], particularly in the area of education," according to Rice Estes, in *Library Journal.* The author "sees the 1957 clash of state and Federal forces [during the landmark integration of] Little Rock's Central High . . . as being more an accident of history than something planned by either side," says *New York Times Book Review* critic Larry L. King. "A lack of planning by Little Rock police and school officials, Governor Faubus and/or President Eisenhower—plus a mystifying breakdown in communications—encouraged chaos." And although King has criticism for what he calls Bartley's "dry-cleaned prose," the reviewer concludes that *The Rise of Massive Resistance* "is useful in making clear not only what happened when all of Dixie openly defied the nation, but what—with minimum planning and foresight—might have been largely avoided."

BIOGRAPHICAL/CRITICAL SOURCES: Library Journal, March 15, 1970; *New York Times Book Review,* June 21, 1970.

* * *

BAR-ZOHAR, Michael 1938-
(Michael Barak)

PERSONAL: Born January 30, 1938, in Sofia, Bulgaria; immigrated to Israel in 1948; son of Jacques M. (a dentist) and Ines (an opera singer; maiden name, Anavi) Bar-Zohar; married Galila Schlosberg (a teacher), October 8, 1958; children: Gilles. *Education:* Hebrew University of Jerusalem, B.A., 1959; Institut d'Etudes Politiques, University of Paris, M.A., 1959; Foundation Nationale de Sciences Politiques, Ph.D., 1963; Tel Aviv University, student of Middle East history and Arabic, 1973—. *Politics:* Labour Party (Israel). *Religion:* Jewish. *Home and office:* 14 Oppenheimer St., 69-395 Tel Aviv, Israel.

CAREER: Foreign correspondent in Paris, France, 1960-64, for several Israeli newspapers, including *Lamerhav,* and for Galei Zahal radio station; professional writer, 1964—. Press and public relations attache to General Moshe Dayan, Israeli Minister of Defense, 1967; member of central committee, Israel; Labour Party; elected to Knesset (Israeli Parliament), 1981—. Instructor in political science, Haifa University, beginning 1970; lecturer in Europe on Israel and the 1973 Yom Kippur War, 1974. *Military service:* Israeli Army and Air Force, beginning 1956; served in Air Force Intelligence, then in paratroops; took part in Six Day War, 1967, and in Yom Kippur War, 1973. *Awards, honors:* Sokolov Prize (Israeli equivalent of the Pulitzer Prize), and Foch Award of French Academy, both 1965, for *Suez: Ultra-Secret.*

WRITINGS—Nonfiction: *Suez: Ultra-Secret,* Fayard (Paris), 1964; *La Chasse aux savants allemands (1944-1960),* Fayard, 1964, translation by Len Ortzen published as *The Hunt for German Scientists,* Hawthorn, 1967; *Ben Gurion, le prophete arme,* Fayard, 1966, translation by Ortzen published as *The Armed Prophet: A Biography of Ben Gurion,* Arthur Barker, 1967, published as *Ben Gurion: The Armed Prophet,* Prentice-Hall, 1968; *Les Vengeurs,* Fayard, 1968, translation by Ortzen published as *The Avengers,* Arthur Barker, 1968, Hawthorn, 1969; *Historie secrete de la guerre d'Israel,* Fayard, 1968.

Embassies in Crisis: Diplomats and Demogogues behind the Six-Day War, Prentice-Hall, 1970; *Spies in the Promised Land: Iser Harel and the Israeli Secret Service,* translation by M. Stearns, Poynter, 1972; *The Third Truth,* translation by June P. Wilson, Houghton, 1973; *The Spy Who Died Twice,* translation from the French by Wilson and Walter B. Michaels, Houghton, 1975; *Ben-Gurion: A Biography* (originally published in three volumes in Israel, 1975-77), translation by Peretz Kidron, Weidenfeld & Nicolson, 1978, Delacorte, 1979; (with Eitan Haber) *The Quest for the Red Prince,* Morrow, 1983. Author of *The Book of the Paratroops,* 1969; also author of documentary film script "Ben-Gurion Remembers," based on his book *Ben-Gurion: A Biography.* Contributor of a series of syndicated articles to periodicals.

Novels; under name Michael Barak, except as indicated: *The Secret List of Heinrich Roehm,* Morrow, 1976; *The Enigma,*

Morrow, 1978 (published in England as *The Enigma Sacrifice,* Weidenfeld & Nicolson, 1978); (under name Michael Bar-Zohar) *The Deadly Document,* Delacorte, 1979; *The Phantom Conspiracy,* Morrow, 1980; *Double Cross,* New American Library, 1981.

SIDELIGHTS: Michael Bar-Zohar's *The Hunt for German Scientists* deals with the efforts of many countries to enlist the services of Germany's top scientists after World War II. These countries included the United States and the Soviet Union as well as France, South Africa, Argentina, and Egypt. "The atom and the rocket are Mr. Bar-Zohar's main themes," writes a *Times Literary Supplement* reviewer, "but he touches briefly on the small-scale French recruitment of German scientists and, more dramatically, on the Germans who went to work for Nasser, attracting the unwelcome attentions and parcel-bombs of the Israeli secret service." Bar-Zohar reminds us, Edwin Tetlow points out in the *Christian Science Monitor,* that "war is not only a matter of the firing of shot and shell but has secret facets which, even if less physically ghastly, are more dishonorable and sinister, and continue long after the guns have fallen silent." *New York Times Book Review* writer Willy Ley notes that the author "traveled extensively to interview the people who had been chased and transplanted" and feels that "he has produced a book that is interesting and often exciting reading."

In *The Avengers* Bar-Zohar chronicles the pursuit of Nazi war criminals that has been carried on by a group of dedicated individuals and governments since the end of World War II. The book is divided into three parts: The first covers the "early avengers," those who began their search immediately after the war; the second details the flight of some war criminals to other countries, particularly South American and Arab countries; and the third relates the long-term efforts of "avengers" to track down and prosecute such war criminals as Adolph Eichmann, as well as the continuing search for others, including Martin Bormann. *Library Journal* reviewer David Shavit finds that the book "may be seen as a companion" to *The Hunt for German Scientists,* dealing as it does with transplanted ex-Nazis. A *Choice* writer sees a similarity between *The Avengers* and famed Nazi-hunter Simon Wiesenthal's *The Murderers among Us* but believes that the value of Bar-Zohar's book lies in the fact that the author "has gathered much new material from interviews with 'avengers' who have not previously divulged their activities." Bar-Zohar's narrative skill draws praise from Leonard C. Schneider in a *Best Sellers* review, but, Schneider maintains, "the full value of the book is not just to be found in its descriptive passages. It is rightly called history and it joins the front line of those comparatively few works which look beyond atrocity to retribution. Although partisan, being written by a Jew about Jews, it is strongly objective. . . . The prose is sparse but powerful."

Bar-Zohar has written two well-received accounts of the life and times of David Ben-Gurion (one of the founders and first prime minister of Israel) *Ben-Gurion: The Armed Prophet* and *Ben-Gurion: A Biography.* A *Choice* reviewer notes that "Bar-Zohar had the unique opportunity to follow Ben-Gurion at work and at home for many months during the late 1950s and 1960s; Ben-Gurion granted him long and frequent interviews—a rare privilege." A critic for the *Economist,* calling *Ben-Gurion: The Armed Prophet* "a solid book," states that it is "useful to students on account of the unique nature of its source material, as well as of the author's candid judgments whenever he is writing from personal experience." Laurie May, in a *Library Journal* review, points out the book's "brisk style and timely subject" and finds that "Michael Bar-Zohar interprets [Ben-Gurion] as a man of the hour to bring the Israeli state into being." The *Choice* writer calls *Ben Gurion: A Biography* "no doubt the best English account of [Ben-Gurion's] life. . . . As a result [of Bar-Zohar's first-hand experience], the book contains much information that is not common knowledge even among scholars." Concludes David Pietrusza in the *National Review:* "[This book] provides a fascinating description of Ben-Gurion's takeover of the Zionist movement. . . . Bar-Zohar's prose is crisp and clean and his scholarship is detailed. The work should emerge as the standard biography."

MEDIA ADAPTATIONS: *The Enigma* was filmed as "Enigma" and starred Martin Sheen and Brigitte Fosse.

AVOCATIONAL INTERESTS: Scuba diving.

BIOGRAPHICAL/CRITICAL SOURCES: *Times Literary Supplement,* June 15, 1967, July 4, 1968; *New York Times Book Review,* September 17, 1967; *Christian Science Monitor,* September 18, 1967; *Economist,* November 25, 1967; *Jewish Quarterly,* winter, 1967-68; *Library Journal,* March 15, 1967; *Best Sellers,* March 1, 1969, June, 1979; *Choice,* September, 1969, May, 1979; *National Review,* September 28, 1979.

* * *

BASILE, Gloria Vitanza 1929-
(McKayla Morgan, Michaela Morgan)

PERSONAL: Born June 29, 1929, in Westfield, N.Y.; daughter of Alphonse and Guisepa (Guido) Vitanza; divorced; children: Louis, Robert, David. *Education:* Attended San Jose State University and University of California, Los Angeles. *Religion:* "Science of Mind." *Agent:* Andrew Ettinger Los Angeles Literary Agency, 6324 Tahoe Dr., Lake Hollywood, Calif. 90068.

CAREER: Gloria's (women's apparel shop), San Jose, Calif., owner and designer, 1950-56; actress for television and motion pictures, in Hollywood, Calif., 1956-62; music composer, 1956—; novelist, 1969—. Owner and designer of Down the Aisle (women's apparel shop), Beverly Hills, Calif., 1967-71. Director of actor's workshop in San Jose, Calif.; literary agent for motion pictures. *Member:* American Society of Composers, Authors, and Publishers, Authors Guild of Authors League of America, Screen Actors Guild, American Federation of Television and Radio Artists.

WRITINGS—All novels; all published by Pinnacle Books: *The Godson,* 1976, published as *The House of Lions,* 1978; (under pseudonym Michaela Morgan) *Madelaina,* 1977; *Appassionato,* 1978; *The Manipulators,* 1979; *Born to Power,* 1979; *Giants in the Shadows,* 1979; (under pseudonym Michaela Morgan) *Zanzara,* 1980; *Eye of the Eagle* (first novel in "Global 2000" trilogy), 1983; *Jackal Helix* (second novel in "Global 2000" trilogy), 1984; *Scorpion's Sting* (last novel in "Global 2000" trilogy), 1984. Also composer of music, under pseudonym McKayla Morgan.

WORK IN PROGRESS: Another trilogy.

SIDELIGHTS: Gloria Basile writes: "Having been raised in a highly prejudiced area in an era when Sicilian Italians were considered the lowest on the totem, the attitudes of my contemporaries were as puzzling as they were traumatic. Inclined to withdraw and survey the situation as if it were happening to another—not me, I found myself wondering at the differences in man. What makes one man better than the next or more acceptable? As a second generation Sicilian American,

I lacked true self identification until I was in my thirties. Poised between two world cultures, American and Sicilian, my childhood was one of ambivalence and moody introversion. However outgoing I was to offset these insecurities, by participating in school activities, and politics . . . I immersed myself in books, and became a voraciouos reader—anything I could lay my hands on.

"Over the years, after three children and two divorces, there still fermented inside me the need to know my roots—and to eliminate the childhood feelings of unworthiness cemented into my mentality by a bigoted people. I began to involve myself in extensive research to learn for myself what this stigma was concerning Italo-Sicilians. Out of this frustration and exhaustive research came *The Godson* and *Appassionato*, a story of post-war Sicily.

"In the late 1950's I pursued a career in Hollywood in the motion picture industry. Unsure [in] which facet of the industry I'd find my niche, I began as student of drama, actress, writer, composer, director, and worked up. I authored and composed lyrics and music for *Ballad of One Eyed Jacks* for the Brando movie. Hopefully, perhaps I may be able to produce a motion picture with the necessary integrity so terribly lacking in many of the films in recent years."

AVOCATIONAL INTERESTS: Travel (Mexico, Baja California, Italy, Sicily), free-form wall macrame, weaving, oil painting, botany, music.

* * *

BAUER, Yehuda 1926-

PERSONAL: Born April 6, 1926, in Prague, Czechoslovakia; son of Viktor (an engineer) and Uly (Fried) Bauer; married Shula White (a silk printer), December 20, 1955; children: Danit, Anat. *Education:* University of Wales, B.A., 1948, M.A., 1950; Hebrew University, Ph.D., 1960. *Home:* Kibbutz Shoval, Negev, Israel. *Office:* Institute of Contemporary Jewry, Hebrew University, Jerusalem, Israel.

CAREER: Lecturer at kibbutz seminars at Oranim and Giv'ath Haviva, Israel, 1954-61; Hebrew University, Jerusalem, Israel, professor, 1961—, head of department of Holocaust Studies, 1968—, head of Institute of Contemporary Jewry, 1973-77, and head of International Center for the Study of Antisemitism, 1982—. Member, scientific advisory committee, Yad Vashem, Jerusalem. *Military service:* Palmach (Jewish underground force), 1945-46; Israeli Army, 1948-49.

WRITINGS: Diplomatyah u-mahteret, [Merhavya], 1963, translation by Alton Winters published as *From Diplomacy to Resistance: A History of Jewish Palestine, 1939-1945*, Jewish Publication Society, 1970; (compiler) *ha-Tenu'ah hatsiyonit*, Institute of Contemporary Jewry, Hebrew University, 1963; *Flight and Rescue*, Random House, 1970; *They Chose Life: Jewish Resistance in the Holocaust*, American-Jewish Committee, 1973; *My Brother's Keeper*, Jewish Publication Society, 1974; *Ha'Brichah*, Sifriat Poalim, 1974; *The Holocaust in Historical Perspective*, University of Washington Press, 1978; *The Jewish Emergence from Powerlessness*, University of Toronto Press, 1979; *American Jewry and the Holocaust*, Wayne State University Press, 1981; *A History of the Holocaust*, F. Watts, 1982; *Ha'Shoah-Hebetim Historiim*, Sifriat Poalim, 1982. Also editor, with Nathan Rotenstreich, of *The Holocaust as Historical Experience*, Holmes & Meier.

Contributor to *Midstream, Jewish Heritage, Middle East Journal, Yad Vashem Studies, Zion, Yalkut Moreshet,* and other publications. Editor of historical section, *Hebrew Encyclopedia of Social Sciences,* 1965-71; member of editorial board, *Yalkut Moreshet* and *Yad Vashem Studies.*

WORK IN PROGRESS: A history of American Jewish aid to Jewish Holocaust survivors in Central Europe, 1945-53.

SIDELIGHTS: The Holocaust of World War II has been the primary subject of Yehuda Bauer's scholarly studies. Through his books Bauer seeks to discover the causes for the genocidal slaughter of millions of Jews in Nazi concentration camps. In *A History of the Holocaust*, Bauer traces the historical persecution of Jews and describes the antisemitic climate which gave rise to the Nazis. Max J. Friedman writes in the *Chicago Tribune Book World* that the book "is an important contribution to the Holocaust literature. It puts the Holocaust experience into the perspective of the ongoing antisemitism of history, thus giving readers pause to think about the consequences of their own prejudices and beliefs." Malcolm Boyd of the *Los Angeles Times Book Review* considers *A History of the Holocaust* to be "a scholarly work of prodigious scope."

BIOGRAPHICAL/CRITICAL SOURCES: Chicago Tribune Book World, November 26, 1978, September 26, 1982; *Los Angeles Times Book Review,* September 19, 1982.

* * *

BAUMBACH, Jonathan 1933-

PERSONAL: Born July 5, 1933; son of Harold M. (an artist) and Ida H. (Zackheim) Baumbach; married Elinor Berkman, September 10, 1956 (divorced, 1967); married Georgia Brown, June 10, 1969; children: (first marriage) David, Nina; (second marriage) Noah, Nicholas. *Education:* Brooklyn College (now of the City University of New York), A.B., 1955; Columbia University, M.F.A., 1956; Stanford University, Ph.D., 1961. *Home:* 42 Montgomery Pl., Brooklyn, N.Y. 11215. *Office:* Department of English, Brooklyn College of the City University of New York, Brooklyn, N.Y. 11210.

CAREER: Stanford University, Stanford, Calif., instructor in English, 1958-60; Ohio State University, Columbus, assistant professor of English, 1961-64; New York University, New York, N.Y., assistant professor of English and director of freshman English, 1964-66; Brooklyn College of the City University of New York, Brooklyn, N.Y., associate professor, 1966-70, professor of English, 1970—.

Member of board of directors, Teachers and Writers Collaborative, 1966—. Fiction Collective, co-founder, 1974, co-director, 1974-78, currently member of board of directors. Visiting professor, Tufts University, 1970-71, and University of Washington, 1978 and 1983. *Military service:* U.S. Army, 1956-58. *Member:* National Society of Film Critics (chairman, 1982-83). *Awards, honors:* Young Writers Award, *New Republic,* 1958; Yaddo fellowship, summers, 1963, 1964, and 1965; National Endowment for the Arts fellowship, 1969; Guggenheim fellow, 1978; Ingram-Merrill fellowship, 1983.

WRITINGS: "The One-Eyed Man Is King" (play), first produced at Theater East, New York City, 1956; *The Landscape of Nightmare: Studies in the Contemporary American Novel,* New York University Press, 1965; (contributor) W. R. Robinson, editor, *Man and the Movies,* Louisiana State University Press, 1967; (editor with Arthur Edelstein) *Moderns and Contemporaries: 12 Masters of the Short Story,* Random House, 1968, 2nd edition, 1977; (editor) *Writers as Teachers/Teachers as Writers,* Holt, 1970; (editor) *Statements: New Fiction from* the Fiction Collective, Braziller, 1975; (editor with Peter Spielberg) *Statements 2: New Fiction,* Fiction Collective, 1977; *The Return of Service* (story collection), University of Illinois Press, 1979.

Novels: *A Man to Conjure With,* Random House, 1965; *What Comes Next,* Harper, 1968; *Reruns,* Fiction Collective, 1974; *Babble,* Fiction Collective, 1976; *Chez Charlotte and Emily,* Fiction Collective, 1979; *My Father More or Less,* Fiction Collective, 1982.

Work appears in five anthologies. Contributor of short stories and articles to *Esquire, Kenyon Review, Partisan Review, Chicago Review, TriQuarterly, Nation* and other periodicals. Movie reviewer, *Partisan Review,* 1973—.

SIDELIGHTS: In his first book, *The Landscape of Nightmare: Studies in the Contemporary American Novel,* experimental writer Jonathan Baumbach examines the works of a number of postwar American novelists. "Baumbach explored each novel," Larry McCaffery of the *Dictionary of Literary Biography* writes, "in terms of how it portrays the nightmarish conditions of contemporary society and how each individual protagonist attempts to carve his own niche, or openly rebels against these conditions." In contrast to the novelists of an earlier generation who expressed the nightmarish quality of society "in terms of social defeats and victories," Bernard McCabe explains in *Commonweal,* the contemporary novelists Baumbach studies express it "in terms of the Self." It is this psychological approach that especially interests Baumbach. The novels he examines, Baumbach clarifies in his study, are concerned with "the confrontation of man with the objectification of his primordial self and his exemplary spiritual passage from innocence to guilt to redemption." Of particular importance to Baumbach, McCaffery reports, is "the way in which [these novels] make manifest the inner worlds and secret lives of their protagonists."

In his own novels, Baumbach also explores "inner worlds and secret lives," but does so through innovative narrative structures. Baumbach's narrative innovations have "placed him in the company of our most serious experimentalists," Jerome Klinkowitz explains in *The Life of Fiction.* The similarities and interrelationships between memories, dreams, our perceptions of the real world, and the images of popular culture are constant concerns in all of Baumbach's fiction. With his first novel, *A Man to Conjure With,* Baumbach "immediately established the shifting terrain of dream, memory, imagination, and public nightmare that his fiction would explore," writes McCaffery. Ironically, it is the most conventional of Baumbach's novels. As Klinkowitz explains, "there is experimentation [in *A Man to Conjure With*], but within traditional bounds; there is nothing unrealistic in the book except the character's dreams, which are clearly identified as such."

The novel concerns Peter Becker, who is trying to restore his marriage after being separated from his wife for many years. By piecing his life back together, Becker also hopes to reestablish a sense of personal identity. Speaking of Becker, Baumbach tells John Graham in *The Writer's Voice: Conversations with Contemporary Writers:* "It's as if all the details will add up to a picture of himself. And then, he can look at himself as he was. He has the idea, perhaps, that the man he was at twenty is still somewhere there, all the potentiality that was there at twenty and forgotten and lost. To look at himself at twenty is to come back there and start again, to recoup what he's lost."

"Much of the action," writes Klinkowitz, "takes place in Peter [Becker's] dreams, and his character is defined by them." Klinkowitz notes that Baumbach uses dreams in this novel to study the workings of the human imagination and to determine how dreams are expressed in language. Haskel Frankel of the *New York Times Book Review,* although admitting that "there is no question as to the author's talent, sensitivity, control and intelligence," believes *A Man to Conjure With* "adds up to nothing. We are introduced to a man by someone we respect, asked to study the man carefully—and then are never told the point of our studies." S. L. Bellman of *Saturday Review,* however, stresses the importance of the protagonist's dreams. This novel, he writes, "has the character of a weird Freudian nightmare that involves no stage effects or supernaturalism whatever." Also writing in *Saturday Review,* Henry S. Rasnik finds the novel "an ingenious portrait of a schlemiel-Everyman cracking up," while Emile Capouya of *Book Week* believes that "Baumbach writes with great elegance and wit. . . . He is inventive and amusing."

The dreams found in Baumbach's next novel, *What Comes Next,* "are indistinguishable from life," Klinkowitz states, since the protagonist, a college student named Christopher Steiner, is going mad. There is no specific catalyst for his madness. He is simply reacting to his society. "Too much violence in the street. Sex, bombing, suffocation, rape. Too much madness," as Baumbach describes it in the novel. The narrative is structured so as to reflect Steiner's deteriorating state of mind, interweaving his dreams and hallucinations with the real events around him. "Baumbach's short-jabbing prose, skirting the necessary edge of hysteria," writes McCabe, "thrusts the violent city at us. . . . Throughout the novel Baumbach works to dissolve ugly fact into fantasy, fantasy into fact, so that the nightmare and the reality are convincingly one."

C.D.B. Bryan of the *New York Times Book Review* compares Baumbach's handling of *What Comes Next* to the work of Nathaniel West. "Baumbach's writing," Bryan states, "like West's, is finely chiseled, keen and tough; his images are violent and garish; his hero, like [West's character] Miss Lonelyhearts, is obsessed by nightmares. . . . [But] Baumbach's value as a writer is that he makes the insanity of his hero seem appallingly sane."

In *Reruns,* Baumbach's narrator is again concerned with reassembling his life into a meaningful pattern. The narrator describes himself as "a hostage to the habit of rerunning the dead past in the cause of waking from the dream." Organized into a series of 33 short chapters, each a "dream-exorcism" as John Ager states in the *Carolina Quarterly,* the book presents the record of a man's life as a month's worth of short films at a cinema. Each chapter, or film, captures a life experience and retells it through dream logic and cinematic language. Some experiences are redone several times in different ways, as if the narrator were attempting to change the past through the power of his imagination. "These 'reruns,'" McCaffery explains, "are nightmarish, frantic, often violent episodes . . . whose characters and events are generated from a wide variety of cultural cliches, fairy tales, stories, and movies. . . . This is a world of terror, loneliness, and absurdity." Irving Malin of the *New Republic* agrees: "Usual routines are destroyed; only explosive energy remains. . . . The confusion, violence, humor, and madness are mixed so quickly that we . . . are overwhelmed."

By using cinematic techniques in *Reruns,* writes Michael Mewshaw in the *New York Times Book Review,* Baumbach attempts to capture in prose "the kind of simultaneous vision a movie or painting can express. He wants to show us objects and characters from mutually exclusive perspectives, to stretch our understanding of time and expand our comprehension of emotions so that contrary feelings will spring from the same experiences." Malin also sees the cinematic presentation as important to the novel's theme. "Baumbach," Malin writes, "asks important questions: does the individual gain self-knowledge by confronting his popular culture? What exactly is the value of dream (fantasy) in creating identity?" In *Reruns*, and the following novels, *Babble* and *Chez Charlotte and Emily*, McCaffrey believes, Baumbach explores "the role of the media (especially cinema) in creating societal norms and the individual's notion of self."

The characters and situations of popular culture form an important part of *Babble*, the adventures of a baby-hero. Because the novel is narrated by a 3-year-old, the conventions of fairy tales, comic books, and television are often used to tell the story, because these are the storytelling techniques most familiar to a small child. In this way, McCaffery writes, Baumbach investigates "the process whereby language is discovered and narrative patterns are imposed."

In contrast to Baumbach's previous novels, the distinctions between dream and reality are irrelevant in *Babble* because the baby narrator can make no such distinctions when relating his adventures. Fact, fantasy, and dream are intertwined into "a kind of surreal *Bildungsroman*," as McCaffery describes the book. Although the novel uses "the episodic form of *Reruns* and the beleaguered protagonists of both earlier novels," Thalia Selz writes in *fiction international*, "a transformation takes place in attitude. Baby, whom we seem prepared to label a clown, manages through patience and stratagem, to remain a hero in a dangerous world."

Like *Reruns* and *Babble*, *Chez Charlotte and Emily* is a fragmented narrative constructed much like a film montage. As Irving Malin writes in the *Hollins Critic*, it is a series of "stories within stories, boxes within boxes. The narrator writes about a couple; the couple write or fantasize about another couple; the third couple in turn have novelistic tendencies." All of the stories thus related are strongly reminiscent of the cinema, partly because the characters restage and reshoot scenes in varying ways, as might be done while making a movie. Other characters have the names of famous movie stars, while certain plot elements have their parallels in old movie scripts. The importance of these cinematic references, McCaffery points out, lies in the characters' ability to use their imaginations to restructure their world. "All these stories," McCaffery states, "are evidently metaphorical reflections of inner tensions, desires, and personality traits. . . . It is . . . through the agency of imagination and metaphor that [the characters] Joshua and Genevieve perpetuate themselves and their relationship, make love and communicate."

In his short story collection *The Return of Service*, Baumbach again uses the materials of popular culture. "Baumbach's stories," writes Terrence Winch of the *Washington Post Book World*, "show the influence of nonsense literature, literary satire and experimental fiction. There is a story about a story, a parody of a detective novel, an essay on a nonexistent, ridiculous novel, [and] a retelling of Hollywood's King Kong myth." Don Skiles of *American Book Review* believes that Baumbach's short stories "reflect the post-modern era, as they try for a form that synchs with a post-television age. . . . *The Return of Service* is a delight, a gratifying book to read, an adventurous, chance-taking work." Skiles defines Baumbach's concern as "the potential situation, the next curve in the road, the way another party might view the same events . . . ; the alternative ways in which a scene may be shot."

"Like many other postmodern writers," McCaffery states, "Baumbach's focus is not so much on the ambiguous, destructive, entropic 'outer world' as it is on the resources of the imagination in coping with this reality. The imagination for Baumbach . . . is instead a realm where man can freely manipulate the components of his experience (which is produced as much by symbols and media-produced substitutions as it is by the so-called real world) into structures of utility, order, and possibly even beauty."

CA INTERVIEW

CA interviewed Jonathan Baumbach by phone July 8, 1983, at work in Seattle, Washington.

CA: You've tried in your fiction to find, as you've said, "another way of getting at reality" besides the conventional novel. How do you feel about being called an "experimental" novelist?

BAUMBACH: I have no strong objection to it. But the word "experimental" is often used in a pejorative way, as if the work wasn't quite finished, but was just the trying out of something, and in that sense I resist the term. An alternate term that's been used is "innovative," though that's not in any way more exciting. I think probably all of these categories are just a way of not dealing with the work itself, of finding some rubric that includes it and thereby putting it safely away.

CA: When did you begin writing, or begin to know you wanted to be a writer?

BAUMBACH: I think I knew that I wanted to write when I was very young, a teenager or even pre-high school, though that doesn't necessarily mean that I knew I was going to *be* a writer. A lot of people want to do things when they're a certain age that have to do with childhood fantasies, and things change for them when they get older; so my becoming a writer may not have to do with that idea of myself as a child. But the wish was always there, and I think I was fairly clear about it when I was in college. I wrote plays first. I had a play done in New York in 1955, "The One-Eyed Man Is King."

CA: Is that the one you did as an M.F.A. thesis?

BAUMBACH: That's right.

CA: Were you, then, interested in the whole process of writing a play and getting it produced and perhaps directing it?

BAUMBACH: I had done it in college; I had written a play that I played in and also directed, so I don't think I had that in mind this time. In fact, I hadn't even thought of having it done. It just happened that I had my degree in playwriting at Columbia, and there were people around producing plays and someone wanted to see it; it was more circumstantial than something I had willed, though I did understudy the lead with the notion of playing it one night. I ended up not doing it, which I think was wise.

CA: You've written a lot about movies—as movie critic for Partisan Review *and in other places—and use cinematic kinds of devices in your fiction. Let's talk about how movies might have influenced your work. Did you get hooked on them early?*

BAUMBACH: Yeah. In fact, I've just written a piece on the relationship of movies to my work, which is coming out in a book that Bruce Kawin is editing, and so I've thought a lot about that recently. I think I was probably more interested in movies than books as a child, or interested in them in a different, more private way. One of the excitements of movies for me was that they were not sanctified by authority in those days. Almost no one talked about them as art. They were really an outlaw pleasure, so one could make them one's own. One knew that books and theater and music and painting were good for the life of the soul, and there was some aspect of duty involved in enjoying them, which is estranging for a child. So I spent a lot of time in movies as a kid. I certainly went every Saturday at some point, and I think there were probably times when I went twice a week, and there were double shows in those days. And I think my fantasies were largely tied up with movie images and iconographic figures in movies. What had interested me in fiction right from the start was a certain kind of dream ambience and the resonances it had. More and more it seemed to me that film images, particularly in the black-and-white film, are very much like dream images; the two began to merge for me and I used them interchangeably. So I would say that probably no other art form has had as much influence on my work.

CA: Do you think the movies had a lot to do with shaping your sense of humor?

BAUMBACH: I think that has more to do with growing up in Brooklyn. Everyone there was a stand-up comic. We all did routines on street corners, among ourselves. That's probably its origin, rather than movies. I don't even know that the movies I liked so much were comedies. I did like the Marx Brothers a great deal, though the best Marx Brothers films had come out before I was going to movies and I've only seen them in revival when I was older.

CA: I've read somewhere that you've made films. Is it true?

BAUMBACH: Not really. I have made films with a Super 8 camera, which is just play; I'm embarrassed to have them thought of as films. What I used to do every summer was get together a group of people who were around and improvise a scenario, and we would have some fun making these films. But they're not real films.

CA: Are you interested in doing any screenwriting, or have you done any?

BAUMBACH: I did a screen adaptation of my second novel, *What Comes Next,* but that was never made into a movie. From time to time, somebody has come to me and asked me to write a scenario or has been interested in a novel of mine, but it has turned out to be more thwarting than rewarding. I would like to write another screenplay if I didn't have to go through all that I've gone through the other times I've done it and if I was sure that it would end up becoming something, rather than just take six months out of my life. It's not the money that interests me, though money isn't bad to have; it's *doing* a movie. But commercial movies are so expensive that the percentages are against you, unless you do a lot of screenplays and get into it seriously.

CA: Do your own writing students come to you with any kind of literary background to provide them with reference points and examples in trying to find their own voices to write, or have they mostly grown up watching television instead of reading?

BAUMBACH: I have such a range of students, that's a hard question. I teach only graduate writing students now, and many of them are my age or just a little younger, so they've had backgrounds not so different from my own. I think kids are reading again now, and that there's been to some extent a movement away from visual media back to books, though this conclusion is from a very limited sampling and may just be a thoroughly subjective response. It's hard for me to compare my own undergraduate days with the undergraduate days of students that I have now, but I think overall my friends and I were better read than our counterparts now, though I'm not positive of that.

CA: You've studied and taught in other places, but you keep returning to New York. Is it the best emotional climate for your work?

BAUMBACH: I don't know that that's so. I originally moved back to New York with the idea that since I'd grown up there, the source of my work was there. I've been teaching at Brooklyn College for a long time now—since 1966. I've been away, but that's my permanent job and I own a house in Brooklyn. So it hasn't been a question of returning to Brooklyn so much as being a resident there and visiting other places, when I have some free time, just to open up new experiences. But I'm no longer committed to New York in that way. I think if some kind of opportunity showed up for me to be elsewhere, and it was workable for me, I would do it.

CA: How do you manage to juggle teaching and writing and editing? Do you try to maintain a regular writing schedule?

BAUMBACH: Yeah, I'm very compulsive and I think it's because I suspect I'm terribly lazy. I set myself four hours every morning. There was a period when I was doing it seven days a week, including major holidays. I've moderated that; I even allow myself weeks off, though I still try to work every morning at least three hours. And I've been fortunate that at Brooklyn College I've worked out my schedule so that I teach afternoons, sometimes into the evenings, and I tend to read student work at night, which leaves the mornings clear for myself.

CA: Are you working in the Fiction Collective now?

BAUMBACH: I'm marginally involved with it; I'm still on the board of directors and I still read manuscripts, but I'm not essentially involved with policy or doing much with it at the moment.

CA: It's changed a good bit since its founding, hasn't it?

BAUMBACH: Yeah. It has a lot of members now. Everyone who's done a book in it becomes a member, and there are over thirty—many people whom I never met, from around the country—and the people who are running it now are largely newer members. They see themselves as youth taking over.

CA: Do you think the future of publishing is going to rest more and more on small presses and groups like the Fiction Collective?

BAUMBACH: It seems as if it has to. The situation in commercial publishing gets more and more restrictive. I thought things would turn around at some point. But because of the expense of producing a book and the commitment of the publishing houses to making money with almost everything they do as opposed to taking chances on certain works or at certain points in an author's career—investing money in an author—it hasn't happened. I don't think most commercial publishers feel that they can take a chance with the young author who doesn't have an immediate audience. So, if literature is going to continue as we know it, I think small presses have inherited the burden. The university presses are beginning to recognize that and are publishing fiction—not only short fiction, but novels too. It's interesting. I think a lot of writers know this, yet it's not so much a public fact. The commercial presses, by and large, are not admitting what the restrictions are. It's still a well-kept secret and there's a sense that they're angry if one presents this to them as reality.

I still get calls from people who are interested in the Fiction Collective, and I put them on to members who can help them. Some of these people are writers with large reputations who have not gotten their last two books or so published. I have been surprised sometimes that a publisher won't take a chance on a writer who has had several books published and has a following. But publishers are not in control of their own business now. Just two or three firms are individually owned; almost every other publisher is part of a conglomerate. This limits very much what editors-in-chief are allowed to do, even with the best good will.

CA: *Do you think the so-called traditional novel is making a comeback—if indeed it ever went away?*

BAUMBACH: I think it's making a comeback in the sense that it's more in the public eye today, or even in the somewhat literary public eye, than it was a while back, though I think that had more to do with fashion than what's being written. And I think there's been a considerable amount of hostility toward the nonrealistic novel, or the experimental novel, and this is part of that backlash. But I don't know, really—I haven't read everything that's been published. The writers I like best are people still doing things that are relatively new or at least not following recognizable patterns.

CA: *Do you want to mention some of them?*

BAUMBACH: John Hawkes, Robert Coover, William Gass, Donald Barthelme.

CA: *Do you know any very new writers doing that sort of work?*

BAUMBACH: There are some in the Fiction Collective. There's a writer named Mark Legner who's quite interesting and very far-out. I think writers sense now that that's not the mode that has an audience, and no matter how much integrity a writer has, he can't be cut off completely from readers outside. I think there is a movement, even among what I think of as radical and innovative writers, toward working more with narrative than before.

CA: *Is there work in progress or something coming up in the near future that you'd like to talk about?*

BAUMBACH: I've just finished a draft of a new novel, which is much more direct than anything I've done before. I don't know that it's less difficult, but it deals much more directly with emotions than I think maybe anything since my first novel.

CA: *Is there anything that you haven't done that you'd like to try?*

BAUMBACH: I think there is, but I'm not sure what. I keep waiting for it to hit me. I feel what I do is not programmatic in any way; I follow intuition, and I've been fortunate enough to be able to write whatever I've wanted to write. It's an advantage not having to rely on writing to support myself. My instinct is that I want to attempt things that haven't been done before—not to force myself into strange grounds for their own sake, but to make certain discoveries which will open up my work.

This is related very much to the way I write. I've talked to students about it sometimes. (Students often want to find out what your method is, just as a way of checking to see if they're doing the right thing.) I try to work as nonintellectually as possible—to keep away from knowing what it is I'm doing, so that intuition is given full play, and to make discoveries in the process of writing. I can't write anything when I know its outcome. In fact, I don't even like to know what's going to happen on the next page, because I want to make it up as I go along. I find this works for me and keeps things interesting. It may be the only thing that works for me. If I know in advance what I'm going to do, I'm tired of it and I can't even put it down; I can't even work it up in some slightly different way. That may have something to do with why things come out the way they do in my work.

In this essay I've just finished, which is called "Seeing Myself in Movies," about how movies influence my work, I do analyses of both *Reruns* and *Chez Charlotte and Emily,* which seem to me the most cinematic of my books. Just thinking about them in these terms was completely new to me. It was like reading somebody else's work and writing an analysis of what someone else had done. And there were interesting discoveries for me but they scared me afterward; I thought, I didn't want to know this.

I think most serious writers work from unconscious sources, even those who think they know exactly what they're doing. We each try, I suspect, to find ways of getting to things we don't know we know. I always feel content with what I have when it's not something I knew I knew before, or something I hadn't expected to put down. After all, if our books aren't any smarter than we are, what good are they?

BIOGRAPHICAL/CRITICAL SOURCES—Books: Jonathan Baumbach, *The Landscape of Nightmare: Studies in the Contemporary American Novel,* New York University Press, 1965; Baumbach, *What Comes Next,* Harper, 1968; John Graham, *The Writer's Voice: Conversations with Contemporary Writers,* Morrow, 1973; Baumbach, *Reruns,* Fiction Collective, 1974; *Contemporary Literary Criticism,* Gale, Volume VI, 1976, Volume XXIII, 1983; Jerome Klinkowitz, *The Life of Fiction,* University of Illinois Press, 1977; *Dictionary of Literary Biography Yearbook: 1980,* Gale, 1981.

Periodicals: *Saturday Review,* April 17, 1965, October 26, 1968; *Commonweal,* September 24, 1965, December 13, 1968; *Book Week,* October 3, 1965; *New York Times Book Review,* November 21, 1965, October 13, 1968, October 13, 1974, January 13, 1980, July 27, 1980; *Kenyon Review,* January, 1966; *New Republic,* October 19, 1974; *Village Voice,* October 31, 1974; *Nation,* December 7, 1974; *Carolina Quarterly,* winter, 1975; *fiction international,* No. 6/7, 1976; *Hudson Review,* winter, 1976-77; *Chicago Review,* autumn, 1978; *Contemporary Literature,* winter, 1978; *Hollins Critic,* February, 1980; *Washington Post Book World,* March 30, 1980, May 3, 1982; *Sewanee Review,* July, 1980; *American Book Review,* March/April, 1981.

—Sketch by Thomas Wiloch

—Interview by Jean W. Ross

* * *

BAZIN, Germain (Rene Michel) 1907-

PERSONAL: Born 1907, in Paris, France; son of Charles and Jeanne Laurence (Mounier-Pouthot) Bazin; married Suzanne Comtesse Heller Bielotzerkowka, July, 1947. *Education:* Attended College Ste. Croix, Neuilly, College Ste. Croix, Orleans, and College de Pontlevoy; Sorbonne, University of Paris, Licencie en droit, diplome de l'Ecole du Louvre, Docteur es Lettres. *Religion:* Roman Catholic. *Home:* 23 quai Conti, Paris 75006, France. *Office:* Palais du Louvre, Paris, France.

CAREER: Began career in department of drawings of Ecole des Beaux Arts, Paris, France, 1928; Musee du Louvre, Paris, curator of department of paintings and drawings, 1937-51, director of department of paintings and drawings, 1951-65, director of restoration of paintings in French museums, beginning 1965, currently honorary curator-in-chief. Professor at Burssels Free University, 1934; professor of museum studies at Ecole du Louvre, 1941-70; research professor at York University, Toronto, Ontario. Director of numerous art exhibits in France and abroad; lecturer throughout Europe and in North and South America, 1945-63. Permanent delegate to International Commission for Care of Paintings; delegate to UNESCO conferences. *Military service:* French Army, Infantry, 1939-40; became captain.

MEMBER: Cercle de l'Union, Maison de l'Amerique Latine, Institut de France (Academie des Beaux-Arts), Accademia del diseguo (Florence, Italy), Accademia Clementina Bologna, Accademia Francesco Francia (Bologna, Italy), Academia nacional de Belas Artes (Lisbon, Portugal), Academie royale d'archeologie de Belgique, Academie royale des Sciences, Lettres et des Arts de Belgique, Instituto Coimbragense (Portugal).

AWARDS, HONORS: Legion of Honor (France), Officer, 1954, Commander of Arts and Letters; Officer of Order of Belgian Crown; Grand Officer of Ordre Leopold (Belgium); Officer Etoile Polaire (Sweden); Commander of Merit of the Italian Republic; Commander of the Cruzeiro do sul (Brazil), Officer of the Order of Santiago (Portugal); Prix Jeaubernet, for *Le Mont-Saint-Michel;* Grand Prix du rayonnement, Academie Francais.

WRITINGS: Le Mont-Saint-Michel, Auguste Picard, 1933, revised edition published as *Le Mont-Saint-Michel: Histoire et archeologie de l'origine a nos jours,* Hacker, 1979; (editor with Rene Huyghe) *Histoire de l'art contemporain: La peinture,* [France], 1935, reprinted, Arno, 1968; *La Peinture anglaise, 1730-1850,* A. Calavas, 1938; *La Peinture italienne aux XIV et XV siecles,* Hyperion, 1938, translation by Mary Chamot published as *Italian Painting in the Fourteenth and Fifteenth Centuries,* French and European Publications, 1938; *Renoir,* A. Skira, 1939, translation by L. Norton published as *Renoir,* Fama, 1947; *Memling,* Pierre Tisne, 1939, translation published as *Memling,* French and European Publications, 1939.

La Peinture francaise des origines au XVI siecle, Braun, 1940; *Rembrandt et la peinture hollandaise au Musee du Louvre,* Librairie des Arts Decoratifs, 1940; *La Pieta d'Avignon,* A. Skira, 1941; *Le Livre des saisons,* A. Skira, 1942; *Corot,* Pierre Tisne, 1942, 3rd revised edition, Hachette, 1973; *Fouquet,* A. Skira, 1942; *De David a Cezanne,* A. Skira, 1944; (contributor) *La Tapisserie francaise,* Pierre Tisne, 1946; *L'Epoque impressionniste,* Pierre Tisne, 1947, 2nd edition, 1953; *Primitifs francais: Enluminures et peintures des XIV et XV siecles,* A. Skira, 1948; (author of biographical notes) Rene Huyghe, *Les Contemporains,* Pierre Tisne, 1949; *Fra Angelico,* translation from the French manuscript by Marc Loge, edited by Andre Gloeckner, Heinemann, 1949.

Les grands Maitres hollandais, F. Nathan, 1950; (editor) *Histoire de la peinture moderne,* Hyperion (New York), 1950, translation by Rosamund Frost published as *History of Modern Painting,* Hyperion, 1951; (editor) *Histoire de la peinture classique,* Hyperion, 1950, translation by Frost published as *History of Classic Painting,* Hyperion, 1951; *Histoire de l'art de la prehistoire a nos jours,* Garamond, 1953, translation by Francis Scarfe published as *A Concise History of Art,* Thames & Hudson, 1958, 3rd edition, 1964, published as *A History of Art from Prehistoric Times to the Present,* Houghton, 1959; (author of text) *Louvre: Masterpieces of Italian Painting,* translation from the French manuscript by Ruth B. Davidson, New York Graphic Society, 1956; *L'Architecture religieuse baroque au Bresil,* two volumes, Museu de Arte (Sao Paulo), 1956-58; *Tresors de la peinture au Louvre,* A. Somogy, 1957, revised edition, 1966, translation by M. I. Martin published as *The Louvre,* Thames & Hudson, 1957, Abrams, 1958, 3rd revised edition, Thames & Hudson, 1971; *Tresors de l'Impressionnisme au Louvre,* A. Somogy, 1958, translation by S. Cunliffe-Owen published as *French Impressionists in the Louvre,* Abrams, 1958 (published in England as *Impressionist Paintings in the Louvre,* Thames & Hudson, 1958, 5th edition, 1964); *Musee de l'Ermitage,* Cercle d'Art, 1958; (author of preface) *Catalogue des peintures, pastels, sculptures impressionnistes,* Musee National du Louvre, 1959.

A Gallery of Flowers, translation by Jonathan Griffin from the French version of a work originally published in Germany under title *Das Blumenbouquet,* Thames & Hudson, 1960, Appleton, 1964; (author of introduction) *L'Italia vista dai pittori francesi del XVIII e XIX secolo,* [Rome], 1961; *The Loom of Art,* translation from the French manuscript by Griffin, Simon & Schuster, 1962; (contributor) *La Demeure et les Editions des Deux Mondes presentent les tapisseries de Mathieu Mategot,* La Demeure, 1962; *Gericault,* [Rouen], 1963; *Aleijadinho et la sculpture baroque au Bresil,* Le Temps, 1963; *Peinture classique du XVII siecle,* Impressions Darantiere, 1964; *Le message de l'absolu, de l'aube au crepuscule des images,* Hachette, 1964; *Baroque and Rococo,* translation by Griffin, Praeger, 1964, original French edition published as *Classique, baroque et rococo,* Larousse, 1965; *L'Aleijadinho: Un Michel Ange des Tropiques,* Le Temps, 1964; (author of text) Fundacao Calouste Gulbenkian, *Un Siecle de peinture francaise, 1850-1950,* [Lisbon], 1965; *Les Peintres d'avant garde,* Hachette, 1966; *Le Temps des Musees,* Desoer, 1966, translation by Jane van Nuis Cahill published as *The Museum Age,* Universe Books, 1967; *Histoire de la peinture classique et de la peinture moderne,* Gibert Jeune, 1967; *History of World Sculpture,* translation from the French manuscript by Madeline Jay, New York Graphic Society, 1968, reprinted, Alpine Fine Arts, 1982; *La Scultura Francese,* Fabbri, 1968; *Le monde de la sculpture des origines a nos jours,* J. P. Taillandier, 1968; *Destins du baroque,* Hachette, 1968; *The Baroque: Principles, Styles, Modes, Themes,* translation from the French manuscript by Pat Wardroper, New York Graphic Society, 1968; *Histoire de l'avant-garde en peinture du XIII au XX siecle,* Hachette, 1969, translation by Simon Watson Taylor published as *The Avant-Garde in Painting,* Simon & Schuster, 1969 (published in England as *The Avant-Garde in the History of Painting,* Thames & Hudson, 1969).

Edouard Manet, Fabbri, 1972; *Le langage des styles,* Somogy, 1976; *Les Palais de la Foi,* Office du Livre, Volume I, 1980, Volume II, 1981; *L'univers impressionniste,* Somogy, 1982.

Also author of *Presence de la sculpture du Paleolithique a nos jours,* UNB Books International. Co-editor of *Kindlers Malerei Lexikon,* Kindlers Verlag, 1964-71. Editor of and contributor to numerous art catalogues. Contributor to magazines and newspapers, including *L'Amour de l'Art.*

SIDELIGHTS: Germain Bazin, honorary curator-in-chief of the Louvre Museum in Paris, has authored numerous books on art and art history. His *History of World Sculpture* "is something of a tour de force, contriving to bring into single focus the whole history of sculpture from pre-history to modern times," writes a *Times Literary Supplement* critic, "[and the] book does precisely what it set out to do." A *Spectator* reviewer says *The Museum Age* "is a brilliant essay on the idea of a museum, traced from its inception in ancient Greece to its revival in the Renaissance . . . , and its transformation . . . into the publicly sponsored institutions familiar today."

In the *New York Times* S. L. Faison notes that like several other of Bazin's translated works, *French Impressionists in the Louvre* "has suffered considerably in translation." Yet, he maintains that this "cannot dim the luster of one of the finest works ever written on this major chapter of art history."

AVOCATIONAL INTERESTS: Rowing.

BIOGRAPHICAL/CRITICAL SOURCES: *Times Literary Supplement,* January 4, 1957, October 17, 1958, July 20, 1962, February 19, 1970, July 16, 1970; *Spectator,* December 12, 1958, July 12, 1968; *New York Times,* February 15, 1959; *New York Times Book Review,* October 25, 1959; *New York Review of Books,* March 12, 1970.

* * *

BECK, Hubert (F.) 1931-

PERSONAL: Born July 21, 1931, in Du Quoin, Ill.; son of Louis Carl (owner of a chicken hatchery) and Martina (Dierks) Beck; married Betty Lee Beaver, October 6, 1956 (divorced, July 8, 1982); children: Kathleen Ann, Cynthia Sue, Mary Lee, John Mark. *Education:* Concordia Seminary, St. Louis, Mo., B.A., 1953, M.Div., 1961; additional study at Concordia Seminary, St. Louis, and Lutheran School of Theology, Chicago, Ill. *Home:* 315 North College Main, College Station, Tex. 77840. *Office:* University Lutheran Chapel, Texas A&M University, College Station, Tex. 77843.

CAREER: Minister of Lutheran Church. Pastor of churches in Topeka, Kan., Charleston, and Des Plaines, Ill., 1956-67; Texas A&M University, College Station, pastor of University Lutheran Chapel, 1968—. *Member:* Lutheran Campus Ministers' Association, Kiwanis.

WRITINGS: *The Christian Encounters the Age of Technology,* Concordia, 1970; *The Way of God and the Ways of Men,* C.S.S. Publishing, 1972; *Thoughts for Today,* C.S.S. Publishing, 1972; *Why Can't the Church Be Like This?,* Concordia, 1973; (with Robert Otterstad) *Into the Wilderness,* Fortress, 1975; *Fantasies for Fantastic Christians,* Concordia, 1977; *How to Respond to the Cults,* Concordia, 1977; *Stay in the Son-Shine,* C.S.S. Publishing, 1980; *What Should I Believe?,* Concordia, 1980. Also author of tracts and theological papers. Contributor of articles to magazines. Editor of *Interconnections.*

WORK IN PROGRESS: A book of collected stories; devotion books based on Ecclesiastes and the Book of Revelation.

* * *

BECKER, Lucille F(rackman) 1929-

PERSONAL: Born February 4, 1929; daughter of Mark (a lawyer) and Sylvia (Schwartz) Frackman; married Robert F. Becker (a pension consultant), February 27, 1954; children: David, Daniel, Michael, Andrew. *Education:* Barnard College, B.A. (magna cum laude), 1949; University of Aix-Marseilles, diplome d'etudes francaises, 1950; Columbia University, M.A., 1954, Ph.D., 1958. *Office:* Department of French, Drew University, Madison, N.J. 07940.

CAREER: Columbia University, New York, N.Y., French instructor, 1954-58; Rutgers University, New Brunswick, N.J., French instructor, 1959-69; Drew University, Madison, N.J., professor of French, 1969—. *Member:* Modern Language Association, American Association of Teachers of French, American Association of University Professors, Phi Beta Kappa. *Awards, honors:* Fulbright scholar, 1949-50.

WRITINGS: (Contributor) *Montherlant vu par des jeunes,* La Table Ronde (Paris), 1959; (editor and author of introduction and notes with Alba della Fazia) Henry de Montherlant, *Le Maitre de Santiago,* Heath, 1965; *Henry de Montherlant: A Critical Biography,* Southern Illinois University Press, 1970; *Louis Aragon,* Twayne, 1971; (contributor) W. B. Fleischmann, editor, *Encyclopedia of World Literature in the Twentieth Century,* four volumes, Ungar, 1976; *Georges Simenon,* Twayne, 1977; *Francoise Mallet-Joris,* Twayne, 1984. Also contributor to reference books, including *Collier's Encyclopedia.* Contributor of articles to *Books Abroad, Yale French Studies, Romance Notes, French Review, Romanic Review,* and *Nation.*

* * *

BECKHAM, Stephen Dow 1941-

PERSONAL: Born August 31, 1941, in Coos Bay, Ore.; son of Ernest Dow (a teacher, logger, and salesman) and Anna M. (Adamson) Beckham; married Patricia Joan Cox (a music teacher), August, 1967; children: Andrew Dow, Ann-Marie C. *Education:* University of Oregon, B.A., 1964; University of California, Los Angeles, M.A., 1966, Ph.D., 1969. *Politics:* Democrat. *Religion:* Baptist. *Home:* 1389 Southwest Hood View Lane, Lake Oswego, Ore. 97034. *Office:* Department of History, Lewis and Clark College, Portland, Ore. 97219.

CAREER: Long Beach State College (now California State University, Long Beach), Long Beach, Calif., lecturer in history, 1968-69; Linfield College, McMinnville, Ore., assistant professor, 1969-72, associate professor of history, 1972-76; Lewis and Clark College, Portland, Ore., associate professor, 1977-81, professor of history, 1981—. Consultant to Coos, Lower Umpqua, and Sluslaw Indian Tribes, 1972—, Small Tribal Organization of Western Washington, 1973, Oregon Coastal Conservation and Development Commission, 1974-75, Oregon State Parks System, 1974-75, and Oregon State Historic Preservation Program, 1974—; member of technical advisory task force on estuaries and wetlands of Oregon State Land Conservation and Development Commission, 1975—; member of board of advisers, National Trust for Historic Preservation, 1977—. Expert witness for courts in Oregon and Washington in a number of cases concerning Indian tribes. *Member:* American Historical Association, Organization of American Historians, Western History Association. *Awards, honors:* Grant from National Endowment for the Humanities, 1972—.

WRITINGS: Requiem for a People: The Rogue Indians and the Frontiersmen, University of Oklahoma Press, 1971; *The Simpsons of Shore Acres,* Arago Books, 1971; *Lonely Outpost: The Army's Fort Umpqua,* Oregon Historical Society, 1971; *Coos Bay: The Pioneer Period, 1851-1890,* Arago Books, 1973; (editor and author of introduction) *Tall Tales from Rogue River: The Yarns of Hathaway Jones,* Indiana University Press, 1974; (contributor) William Loy and Allan Stuart, editors, *Historical Atlas of Oregon,* University of Oregon Press, 1976; *The Indians of Western Oregon: This Land Was Theirs,* Arago Books, 1977; *Identifying and Assessing Historical Cultural Resources,* Forest Service, U.S. Department of Agriculture, 1978.

(With Rick Minor and Kathryn Anne Toepel) *Cultural Resource Overview of the BLM Lake District, South-Central Oregon: Archaeology, Ethnography, History,* Department of Anthropology, University of Oregon, 1980; (with Minor and Toepel) *Cultural Resource Overview of BLM Lands in Northwestern Oregon: Archaeology, Ethnography, History,* Department of Anthropology, University of Oregon, 1980; (with Minor and Toepel) *Prehistory and History of BLM Lands in West-Central Oregon: A Cultural Resource Overview,* Department of Anthropology, University of Oregon, 1981; (with Minor and Toepel) *Native American Religious Practices in the Coastal Zone of Oregon,* Department of Anthropology, University of Oregon, 1984. Also author of *Land of the Umpqua: A History of Douglas County, Oregon,* 1984, and of television series "This Land Was Theirs: The Indians of the Oregon Coast," produced by Columbia Broadcasting System and Oregon Educational Broadcasting Co., 1971-72; contributor to *Handbook of the American Indian,* edited by William Sturtevant. Contributor to professional journals.

* * *

**BEDFORD, Ann
    See REES, Joan**

* * *

BELLMAN, Richard (Ernest) 1920-

PERSONAL: Born August 26, 1920, in New York, N.Y.; married, 1963; children: two. *Education:* Brooklyn College (now Brooklyn College of the City University of New York), B.A., 1941; University of Wisconsin—Madison, M.A., 1943; Princeton University, Ph.D., 1946. *Office:* Department of Mathematics, University of Southern California, Los Angeles, Calif. 90007.

CAREER: Truax Field, Madison, Wis., instructor in electronics, 1942-43; Princeton University, Princeton, N.J., instructor in mathematics, 1943-44; U.S. Navy, Radio and Sound Laboratory, San Diego, Calif., mathematician and physicist, 1944-45; U.S. Army, Los Alamos, N.M., mathematician and physicist, 1945-46; Princeton University, instructor, 1946-47, assistant professor of mathematics and research associate, 1947-48; Stanford University, Stanford, Calif., associate professor of mathematics, 1948-52; RAND Corp., Santa Monica, Calif., mathematician, 1952-65; University of Southern California, Los Angeles, professor of mathematics and electrical engineering, 1965—, professor of medicine in School of Medicine, 1974—, associate fellow of Institute of Higher Studies, 1975—. Associate of Center for the Study of Democratic Institutions, 1969-75. *Member:* American Mathematical Society, National Academy of Engineering, Society for Mathematical Biology (fellow), National Academy of Sciences.

AWARDS, HONORS: First Norbert Weiner Prize in Applied Mathematics from American Mathematical Society and Society for Industrial and Applied Mathematics, 1970; first Dickson Prize from Carnegie-Mellon University, 1970; D.Sc. from University of Aberdeen, 1973; D.Laws from University of Southern California, 1974; D.Math. from University of Waterloo, 1975; American Academy of Arts and Sciences fellowship, 1975; John von Neumann Theory Award from Institute of Management Sciences and Operations Research Society of America, 1976; Gold Medal from Institute of Electrical and Electronics Engineers, 1978; Heritage Medal from American Council for Control, 1983.

WRITINGS: Stability Theory of Differential Equations, McGraw, 1953; *Dynamic Programming,* Princeton University Press, 1957; (with others) *On Top Management Simulation,* American Management Association, 1957; *What Is Dynamic Programming?,* RAND Corp., 1959.

Introduction to Matrix Analysis, McGraw, 1960, 2nd edition, 1970; (with Edwin F. Beckenbach) *An Introduction to Inequalities,* Random House, 1961, 2nd edition, Springer-Verlag, 1965, 3rd edition, 1970; *A Brief Introduction to Theta Functions,* Holt, 1961; (editor) *A Collection of Modern Mathematical Classics: Analysis,* Dover, 1961; *Adapted Control Processes: A Guided Tour,* Princeton University Press, 1961; (with Stuart E. Dreyfus) *Applied Dynamic Programming,* Princeton University Press, 1962; (editor) *Symposium on Mathematical Optimization Techniques,* University of California Press, 1963; *A Mathematical Model of Drug Distribution in the Body,* RAND Corp., 1963; (with Robert E. Kalaba and Marcia C. Prestrud) *Invariant Imbedding and Radiative Transfer in Slabs of Finite Thickness,* American Elsevier, 1963; (with Kenneth L. Cooke) *Differential-Difference Equations,* Academic Press, 1963; (editor with Kalaba) *Selected Papers on Mathematical Trends in Control Theory,* Dover, 1964; (with Kalaba and H. H. Kagiwada) *Invariant Imbedding and Time-Dependent Transport Processes,* American Elsevier, 1964; *Perturbation Techniques in Mathematics, Physics, and Engineering,* Holt, 1964.

(With Kalaba) *Quasilinearization and Nonlinear Boundary-Value Problems,* American Elsevier, 1965; (with Kalaba) *Dynamic Programming and Modern Control Theory,* Academic Press, 1965; (with Kalaba and Jo Ann Lockett) *Numerical Inversion of the Laplace Transform: Applications to Biology, Economics, Engineering, and Physics,* American Elsevier, 1966; *Introduction to the Mathematical Theory of Control Processes,* Academic Press, Volume I, 1967, Volume II, 1971; *Modern Elementary Differential Equations,* Addison-Wesley, 1968, 2nd edition (with Cooke), 1971; *Some Vistas of Modern Mathematics: Dynamic Programming, Invariant Imbedding, and the Mathematical Biosciences,* University Press of Kentucky, 1968.

(With L. A. Zadeh) *Decision-Making in a Fuzzy Environment,* National Aeronautics and Space Administration, 1970; (with Cooke and Lockett) *Algorithms, Graphs, and Computers,* Academic Press, 1970; *Methods of Nonlinear Analysis,* Academic Press, Volume I, 1970, Volume II, 1973; (with John C. Hogan and Ernest M. Scheuer) *Programmed Statistics, with Chapters on Probability, Computer Theory, and Programmed Instruction,* Holt, 1970; (with E. Angel) *Dynamic Programming and Partial Differential Equations,* Academic Press, 1972; (with Charlene Paule Smith) *Simulation in Human Systems: Decision-Making in Psychotherapy,* Wiley, 1973; (with John Wilkinson) *The Dynamic Programming of Human Systems,* Mss Information, 1973; (with G. M. Wing) *An Introduction to Invariant Imbedding,* Wiley, 1975; *Introduction to Artificial Intelligence: Can Computers Think?,* Boyd & Fraser, 1978.

Analytic Number Theory: An Introduction, Addison-Wesley, 1980; (with A. Esogbue and I. Nabeshima) *Mathematical Aspects of Scheduling and Applications,* Pergamon, 1983; (with R. Roth) *Quasilinearization and the Identification Problem,* World Scientific Publishing (Singapore), 1983; *Mathematical Methods in Medicine,* World Scientific Publishing, 1983; *Elementary Matrix Theory,* World Scientific Publishing, in press; *Eye of the Hurricane: An Autobiography,* World Scientific Publishing, in press; *Selective Computation,* World Scientific Publishing, in press; (with R. Vasudevan) *Wave Propagation: An Imbedding Approach,* D. Reidel, in press; (with G. Adomian) *New Methods in Partial Differential Equations,* D. Reidel, in press; (with Roth) *The Laplace Transform,* World Scientific Publishing, in press; (with E. Stanley Lee) *Modern Applied Mathematics,* Pergamon, in press.

Also author of a number of technical pamphlets. Editor of "Mathematics in Science and Engineering" series, for Academic Press, and "Modern Analytic and Computational Methods in Science and Mathematics" series, for American Elsevier. Contributor of more than six hundred articles to professional journals. Editor of *Journal of Mathematical Analysis and Applications.*

WORK IN PROGRESS: An Introduction to the Mathematics of Coal Utilization Modeling, with E. Stanley Lee; *Differential-Difference Equations* and *Some New Methods in Approximation,* both with R. Roth.

* * *

BENCHLEY, Nathaniel (Goddard) 1915-1981

PERSONAL: Born November 13, 1915, in Newton, Mass.; died of a liver infection, December 14, 1981, in Boston, Mass.; son of Robert (a writer) and Gertrude (Darling) Benchley; married Marjorie Bradford, May 19, 1939; children: Peter Bradford, Nathaniel Robert. *Education:* Harvard University, B.S., 1938. *Address:* Box 244, Siasconset, Mass. 02564. *Agent:* Roberta Pryor, International Creative Management, 40 West 57th St., New York, N.Y. 10019.

CAREER: New York Herald Tribune, New York City, city reporter, 1939-41; *Newsweek,* New York City, assistant drama editor, 1946-47; free-lance writer and artist. *Military service:* U.S. Naval Reserve, 1941-45. *Member:* Coffee House and Century Association (both New York), Pacific Club (Nantucket, Mass.).

AWARDS, HONORS: Western Writers of America award for juvenile fiction, 1973, for *Only Earth and Sky Last Forever; Bright Candles* was named an American Library Association notable book, 1974.

WRITINGS—Adult books: *Side Street,* Harcourt, 1950; (editor) *The Benchley Roundup,* Harper, 1954; *Robert Benchley,* McGraw, 1955; *One to Grow On,* McGraw, 1958; *Sail a Crooked Ship,* McGraw, 1960; *The Off-Islanders,* McGraw, 1961; *Catch a Falling Spy,* McGraw, 1963; *A Winter's Tale,* McGraw, 1964; *A Firm Word or Two,* McGraw, 1965; *The Visitors,* McGraw, 1965; *The Monument,* McGraw, 1966; *Welcome to Xanadu,* Atheneum, 1968; *The Wake of the Icarus,* Atheneum, 1969; *Lassiter's Folly,* Atheneum, 1971; *The Hunter's Moon,* Little, Brown, 1972; *Humphrey Bogart,* Little, Brown, 1975; *Portrait of a Scoundrel,* Doubleday, 1979; *Sweet Anarchy,* Doubleday, 1979; *All Over Again,* Doubleday, 1981; *Speakeasy,* Doubleday, 1982.

Juvenile books; published by Harper, except as indicated: *Sinbad the Sailor,* Random House, 1960; *Red Fox and His Canoe,* 1964; *Oscar Otter,* 1966; *The Strange Disappearance of Arthur Cluck,* 1967; *A Ghost Named Fred,* 1968; *Sam the Minuteman,* 1969; *The Several Tricks of Edgar Dolphin,* 1970; *The Flying Lesson of Gerald Pelican,* 1970; *Feldman Fieldmouse,* 1971; *The Magic Sled,* 1972; *Small Wolf,* 1972; *The Deep Dives of Stanley Whale,* 1973; *Snorri and the Strangers,* 1976; *George the Drummer Boy,* 1977; *Kilroy and the Gull,* 1977; *Running Owl the Hunter,* 1979; *Walter, the Homing Pigeon,* 1981; *Snip,* Doubleday, 1981; *Demo and the Dolphin,* Harper, 1981.

Young adult books; all published by Harper: *Gone and Back,* 1971; *Only Earth and Sky Last Forever,* 1972; *Bright Candles: A Novel of the Danish Resistance,* 1974; *Beyond the Mists,* 1975; *A Necessary End: A Novel of World War Two,* 1976.

Other writings: *The Frogs of Spring* (three-act play; based on his novel *Side Street*), Samuel French, 1954; "The Great American Pastime" (screenplay), produced by Metro-Goldwyn-Mayer, 1956. Contributor of numerous articles and short stories to periodicals, including *New Yorker, Holiday, Esquire, McCall's, Ladies Home Journal,* and *Vogue.*

SIDELIGHTS: The most prolific member of an unusual literary family, Nathaniel Benchley wrote fifteen novels and nearly two dozen children's books during his forty-year career. Though he never attained the critical acclaim of his father Robert, the celebrated humorist, or the commercial success of his son Peter, the author of the best-seller *Jaws,* Nathaniel Benchley was a disciplined craftsman who produced a steady stream of literate and amusing books. His best-known novel, *The Off-Islanders,* combined many of the elements that typified his work. "The novel conveyed a mood of good-natured hilarity, in which decent and likable individuals undergo experiences that may be mildly harrowing but that never cause the reader to fear that things will not end happily, as in fact they do," explained Martin Weil in the *Washington Post.*

The novel, which was made into the movie "The Russians Are Coming, the Russians Are Coming," is a satiric depiction of the confusion that erupts in a Cape Cod village when a Russian submarine runs aground. Stranded on a sandbar, the Soviet captain sends some men ashore to steal a motorboat, but before they can accomplish their task, they are witnessed by some townspeople who think a full-scale invasion is underway.

"Mr. Benchley evidently is well acquainted with the New England islands," wrote a *Springfield Republican* reviewer, "and his character sketches of the independent, individualistic island people are basically sound even though considerably exaggerated in keeping with the burlesque nature of the story as a whole." Writing in the *New York Herald Tribune,* Al Morgan described the book as "a stylish, amusing piece of escape fiction, told with charm and wit at a breakneck pace." And in his *New York Times Book Review* critique, Edward Streeter observed: "Nat Benchley has said that being the son of Robert Benchley involved certain handicaps for a young writer. He need have no further concern. In *The Off-Islanders,* he has produced a book completely unlike anything his brilliant father ever wrote—and fully as good."

During the 1960s, Benchley turned his hand to children's writing "to get young people into the habit of reading instead of staring at the tube," he told *Publishers Weekly.* From a series of easy readers with fantastical plots, Benchley soon advanced to historical novels for young adults. Eschewed by some writers, the young adult books struck Benchley as a legitimate endeavor. "A lot of people believe that you should not have the so-called teen-age novel," he explained to Paul Janeczko in the *English Journal.* "They feel that you go straight from Tom Swift and the Hardy Boys to *Madame Bovary.* I don't think that's necessarily true, especially since there are so many kids now with, shall we say, limited reading ability. In the days when there was nothing to do *but* read, then people started on the 'classics' earlier. Nowadays, young people need a certain amount of help to show them what is possible."

Whether writing for youngsters or adolescents, Benchley advocated "telling a story as neatly and cleanly as possible," and it was his love of storytelling that led to *Only Earth and Sky Last Forever,* his first award-winning young adult book. While reading a series of articles in *American Heritage,* Benchley came upon an interview with an Indian survivor of the battle of the Little Big Horn—"an Indian," Benchley told Janeczko, "who only wanted to make a good impression on his girl. He had no idea it was Custer or anything like that." Benchley said he "found it enchanting that someone was involved in a monumental historical thing for his own interests." The author's enchantment soon assumed the shape of a historical novel in which a young Cheyenne named Dark Elk must prove his courage in order to win the lovely maiden Lahuka. "Reading Dark Elk's adventures, one feels that Benchley couldn't have written with more immediacy if he had ridden with Crazy Horse's band himself," observed Jean Mercier in *Publishers Weekly.* "The research is impressive and the characterizations effective. Although essentially a tragic story, it is lightened by the Benchley humor, notably in passages describing Dark Elk's early, fumbling efforts to prove his manhood."

Ten years before his death, Benchley moved from Manhattan to Nantucket—an island familiar to him since his boyhood and one which figured in many of his books. There, when he was not writing, "he painted the sea, fished the sea, and took his two sons onto the sea to teach them to respect it and, now and then, to hunt sharks," reported Russell Baker in the *New York Times.* "From these experiences his son Peter developed a fascination with sharks that eventually led him to write *Jaws.*"

MEDIA ADAPTATIONS: *Sail a Crooked Ship* was filmed by Columbia in 1961; *The Off-Islanders* was filmed as "The Russians Are Coming, the Russians Are Coming" by United Artists in 1966; *The Visitors* was filmed as "The Spirit Is Willing" by Paramount in 1966.

BIOGRAPHICAL/CRITICAL SOURCES: *San Francisco Chronicle,* July 12, 1961; *Springfield Republican,* July 16, 1961; *New York Herald Tribune,* July 23, 1961; *New York Times Book Review,* August 6, 1961, June 25, 1967, October 12, 1969, May 2, 1971, November 7, 1971, December 16, 1979; *Saturday Review,* August 12, 1961, March 13, 1971; *New York Times,* July 15, 1968; *New Republic,* October 18, 1969; *Publishers Weekly,* October 2, 1972; *Newsweek,* July 21, 1975; *English Journal,* September, 1976; *Washington Post,* March 24, 1979, November 5, 1979; *Los Angeles Times,* September 6, 1982; *Washington Post Book World,* November 9, 1982.

OBITUARIES: *Washington Post,* December 14, 1981; *New York Times,* December 15, 1981; *Newsweek,* December 28, 1981; *Publishers Weekly,* January 1, 1982; *Time,* January 4, 1982; *AB Bookman's Weekly,* February 22, 1982.†

* * *

BENCHLEY, Peter (Bradford) 1940-

PERSONAL: Born May 8, 1940, in New York, N.Y.; son of Nathaniel Goddard (an author) and Marjorie (Bradford) Benchley; married Wendy Wesson, September 19, 1964. *Education:* Harvard University, A.B. (cum laude), 1961. *Agent:* International Creative Management, 40 West 57th St., New York, N.Y. 10019.

CAREER: Novelist. *Washington Post,* Washington, D.C., reporter, 1963; *Newsweek,* New York, N.Y., associate editor, 1964-67; The White House, Washington, D.C., staff assistant to the President, 1967-69; free-lance writer and television news correspondent, beginning 1969. *Military service:* U.S. Marine Corps Reserve, 1962-63. *Member:* Coffee House, Spee Club, Hasty Pudding Institute of 1770.

WRITINGS—Novels, except as indicated; published by Doubleday, except as indicated: *Time and a Ticket* (nonfiction), Houghton, 1964; *Jonathan Visits the White House* (juvenile), McGraw, 1964; *Jaws* (also see below) 1974; *The Deep* (also see below), 1976; *The Island* (also see below), 1979; *The Girl of the Sea of Cortez,* 1982.

Screenplays: (Co-author) "Jaws" (based on his novel of the same title), Universal, 1975; (co-author) "The Deep" (based on his novel of the same title), Columbia, 1977; "The Island" (based on his novel of the same title), Universal, 1980.

Contributor to *Holiday, New Yorker, Diplomat, Moderator, Vogue, New York Herald-Tribune, New York Times Magazine, National Geographic,* and other periodicals.

SIDELIGHTS: Ever since he began exploring the Atlantic with his father, Peter Benchley has been fascinated by the sea. In 1974, the young writer turned that fascination to profit with a novel that was on the *New York Times* best-seller list for over forty weeks. *Jaws* "put sharks on the map and made him the most successful first novelist in literary history," according to Jennifer Dunning in the *New York Times Book Review.* Since then, all of Benchley's novels have concerned the ocean in one way or another. His first three—*Jaws, The Deep,* and *The Island*—are stories of high adventure in which an unexpected menace lurks in the water; his fourth—*The Girl of the Sea of Cortez*—is less dramatic and more lyrical, a sort of poetic fable with an environmental theme.

Peter Benchley inherited more than just a love of the sea from his father: his literary talents are a family legacy as well. His grandfather was the celebrated humorist Robert Benchley, and his father Nathaniel, also a writer, encouraged his son's interest by offering him, at fifteen, a small salary if he would write every day for a summer. By the time Peter was twenty-one, he had a literary agent from the same institution that represented his dad. Though Peter deemphasizes the role his heritage played in launching his career, Doubleday editor Thomas Congdon became increasingly aware of its importance when he and Benchley were discussing the proposal for *Jaws.* Most of the money in publishing is made by authors with proven track records, while first novels by unknown writers are generally ignored.

But the financial risk of publishing Benchley's first book of adult fiction was mitigated by his famous literary name. "I didn't realize it at the time," Congdon told the *Miami Herald,* "but Benchley did have a track record—his father and his grandfather."

Benchley's proposal also fit the formula of a best-seller. "First, its subject was something-about-which-the-general-public-knows-a-little-but-wants-to-know-more," explains a *Miami Herald* reporter. "Secondly, it conjured up a race memory: the external menace. Such situations as a fire in a skyscraper or a jumbo jet with a dead pilot at the controls. Such appeal to our survival instincts." Not only did *Jaws* catapult to the top of the best-seller lists, it also became an enormously successful motion picture. Benchley estimates that the combined revenue from the movie rights, paperback rights, magazine and book club syndications has provided him with enough income to write freely for ten years.

Despite its unqualified popularity, *Jaws* drew fire from some critics for what they perceived as weak characterization, contrived sub-plotting, and inappropriate allusions to Herman Melville's classic fish tale, *Moby Dick.* "Benchley claims he wanted to keep this a serious novel, as well as a best-seller, and that was probably his mistake," asserts Michael Rogers in the *Rolling Stone.* "None of the humans are particularly likable or interesting; the shark was easily my favorite character—and, one suspects, Benchley's also." Writing in the *New Statesman,* John Sparling concurs: "The characterisation of the humans is fairly rudimentary. . . . The shark, however, is done with exhilarating and alarming skill and every scene in which it appears is imagined at a special pitch of intensity." Other critics, including John Skow, are less appreciative. "Nothing works," writes Skow in *Time,* "not a hokey assignation between [the police chief's] wife and a predatory ichthyologist, and especially not an eat-'em up ending that lacks only Queequeg's coffin to resemble a bathtub version of *Moby Dick.*"

When asked how he felt about having his novel compared to Melville's, Benchley told *Palm Springs Life*: "I'm embarrassed. It isn't that kind of book, really. . . . It's a novel, and I think it's a good one, but it's a story not an allegory. I mean it's nice being a little bit rich and a little bit famous, but dammit, I didn't intend to rank with Melville."

One critic in tune with Benchley's intentions is Gene Lyons. "What one gets from Benchley, and this, I think, is the essence of his commercial genius, is *escape*," Lyons writes in the *New York Times Book Review.* "Instead of wallowing among the commonplaces of our culture's self-doubt, [his protagonists are] lucky enough to have An Adventure. But for the mundane accidents of fate, it might have been you or me."

Though the plots of Benchley's adventures occasionally strain the limits of credibility, their backgrounds are always carefully researched. In an author's note to *The Island,* his gruesome tale of seventeenth-century style pirates holed up on an island near the Bahamas, Benchley writes that he "consulted scores of books, and while I have endeavored to avoid any resemblance to real characters, I have tried equally hard to be faithful to historical reality." *Chicago Tribune Book World* contributing critic Lloyd Sachs thinks he succeeds: "Benchley has certainly done his homework on pirate lore—his portrait of the murderous but honorable buccaneer Jean-David Nau and his tenth-generation pirates, who are on the brink of extinction, is convincing and entertaining and more than a little affecting. Benchley succeeds in making their plight touching and funny with one small detail: that they have come to prize 6-12 insect repellent more than just about anything."

With the appearance of *The Island*—Benchley's third adventure novel—*Washington Post* reporter Joseph McLellan concluded that Benchley "writes according to a formula. The formula moreover is a simple one: take a lot of salt water and put into it something unexpected and menacing. Anybody can do it, and in the wake of *Jaws,* quite a few have tried. The problem (the writer's problem, not the reader's) is that nobody seems to do it quite as well as Benchley."

Despite a successful track record as an adventure novelist, Benchley abandoned his "formula" when he wrote *The Girl of the Sea of Cortez.* An idyllic tale of a young girl's fascination with the sea and its inhabitants, this book moves much more slowly than Benchley's thrillers—and that's too slowly, some critics say. "This could be a refreshing deviation [from the style of his previous novels], but Benchley doesn't tell a story," notes Lola D. Gillebaard in the *Los Angeles Times Book Review.* "His words describe rather than dramatize. Though his descriptions are often lyrical, this reader yearned for more conflict, more 'and then what happened?'" Writing in the *Washington Post Book World,* Thomas Gifford expresses a similar view: "When Benchley sticks to the manta ray, the girl, and the memories of her late father . . . , he is often effective, even poignant, moving. But out of water he is quickly beached and gasping his last. The problem is the plot."

Tony Bednarczyk, on the other hand, thinks that "the continual unveiling of thoughts, feelings, discoveries and wonderment about the underwater world," is what makes *The Girl of the Sea of Cortez* a success. Benchley's "book is dedicated to the infinite and mysterious wisdom of Nature," Bednarczyk concludes in *Best Sellers.* "It is not to be missed."

AVOCATIONAL INTERESTS: Guitar, tennis, sharks, the theater, films.

BIOGRAPHICAL/CRITICAL SOURCES—Books: *Contemporary Literary Criticism,* Gale, Volume IV, 1975, Volume VIII, 1978; *Authors in the News,* Volume II, Gale, 1976; Peter Benchley, *The Island,* Doubleday, 1979.

Periodicals: *New York Times,* January 17, 1974; *New York Times Book Review,* February 3, 1974, May 16, 1976, May 13, 1979, July 8, 1979, May 9, 1982; *Time,* February 4, 1974, July 5, 1982; *New Yorker,* February 18, 1974; *Rolling Stone,* April 11, 1974; *New Statesman,* May 17, 1974, June 22, 1979; *Palm Springs Life,* April, 1975; *Miami Herald,* June 8, 1975; *Newsweek,* May 10, 1976; *Washington Post,* September 1, 1978, April 30, 1979; *Detroit News,* May 6, 1979; *Chicago Tribune Book World,* May 13, 1979, August 8, 1982; *Washington Post Book World,* June 13, 1982; *Best Sellers,* August, 1982; *Los Angeles Times Book Review,* August 22, 1982.

—Sketch by Donna Olendorf

* * *

BENDER, Marylin 1925-

PERSONAL: Born April 25, 1925, in New York, N.Y.; daughter of Michael (a fashion merchant) and Janet (a fashion merchant; maiden name, Sloane) Bender; married Selig Altschul (an aviation consultant), 1959; children: James S. *Education:* Smith College, A.B., 1944; Columbia University, LL.B., 1947. *Address:* 1040 Park Ave., New York, N.Y. 10028.

CAREER: Journalist and writer of nonfiction books. *New York Journal American,* New York City, reporter, 1951-58; *Parade,*

New York City, writer, 1958-59; *New York Times,* New York City, reporter, 1959-76, editor of Sunday business section, 1976-77.

WRITINGS—Nonfiction: *The Beautiful People,* Coward, 1967; *At the Top,* Doubleday, 1975; (with husband, Selig Altschul) *The Chosen Instrument: Pan Am/Juan Trippe; The Rise and Fall of an American Entrepreneur,* Simon & Schuster, 1982; (with Monsieur Marc) *Nouveau Is Better Than No Riche at All,* Putnam, 1983. Contributor to magazines. Contributing editor, *Esquire,* 1978.

SIDELIGHTS: In her first book, *The Beautiful People,* Marylin Bender follows a number of developments in the world of *haute couture* that led to the clothing "revolution" of the 1960s. *Library Journal* reviewer D. L. Gustafson says that the book reads "like pages from a side venture into a fashion Who's Who," covering, as it does, a great many fashion-conscious celebrities as well as such famous designers as Givenchy, Courreges, Saint Laurent, and Cardin. It is, writes Gustafson, "an informed and informal report [that] succeeds as social and fashion history." Beverly Grunwald, in a *New York Times Book Review* article, states that Bender "followed the fads and fashions of the fun-tasting set with the serious detachment of a good journalist and the passion of a sociology major." The critic points out that "a good part of Miss Bender's book chronicles fashion history. She traces it from Dior's radical ankle length to [the] mini revolution. . . . The book is crammed with data about everyone from Paris's Courreges, who started it all with his daring white boot, to America's Kenneth, who excels at producing a well-scissored head." *Book World* reviewer George Frazier calls *The Beautiful People* an "enthralling study of the world of high fashion" and goes on to say that Bender "is a reporter who writes with rare objectivity. . . . Naturally [she] has done her homework, for the information she provides . . . is voluminous and detailed."

Bender's next book, *At the Top,* a collection of articles that originally appeared in the *New York Times* Sunday business section, offers a view of some of America's largest corporations, concentrating on the people who founded them and the people who run them. It is, writes J. D. Moorhead in the *Christian Science Monitor,* a "fascinating look" at American business, full of "success, money, glamour. Heady stuff." The companies profiled in *At the Top* include such giants as General Foods, Warner Communications, Braniff, Holiday Inns, Kohler, and Avon. According to W. H. Hoffman in a *Library Journal* article, Bender reveals that life at the top of these corporations "is characterized by 'views and vision—both clear and faulty—and . . . opportunities exploited or squandered.'" And much of the book, Hoffman finds, is devoted to "visions that have gone awry," such as the case of General Motors stubbornly attempting to market large, gas-guzzling cars during an energy crisis. Concludes Moorhead: "[Bender] knows how to spin journalistic prose. . . . She gives lucid instruction on how [the companies] grew up, and how they are getting along now."

In *The Chosen Instrument: Pan Am/Juan Trippe; The Rise and Fall of an American Entrepreneur,* co-authored with her husband, Selig Altschul, Bender again takes a look at corporate America, this time exploring the history of Pan American World Airways and its controversial founder, Juan Trippe. The book's title comes from Trippe's obsession with having Pan Am recognized as the "chosen instrument" of the United States government, with an officially sanctioned monopoly on international air routes. As *New York Times Book Review* writer Robert Lekachman explains, "Trippe's monomaniacal goal was Federal anointment of Pan Am as the sole carrier for freight and passengers, initially in Latin America and subsequently in trans-Pacific and trans-Atlantic markets." He appealed to several U.S. presidents and to Congress on patriotic grounds: Other countries, notably England and Germany, had established government-owned airlines that served as flagships for their national policies; in order to keep pace, the United States needed to designate one airline to carry our international standard. Although he was not without influence in Washington, Trippe was never to achieve this goal. Herbert Hoover was interested in the plan, but when Franklin D. Roosevelt succeeded him, any hope for a monopoly was extinguished. Still, Pan Am prospered. During World War II Trippe secured many lucrative military contracts, and after the war, the company's success continued with North Atlantic passenger service. Although Trippe never quite "gave up on his attempts to achieve monopoly," reports Lekachman, "his aspirations were repeatedly defeated by uncooperative politicians and militant trust-busters."

In a *New York Times* review of *The Chosen Instrument,* Susan Bolotin states, "More than a history of Pan Am specifically and aviation generally, more than a biography of 'Il Duce of the Airways,' . . . this book is a case study of 'networking' in action." Bender and Altschul point out that much of Pan Am's success was due to Trippe's connections with old Yale classmates. For a time, they maintain, "half of the Pan American board could sing 'The Whiffenpoof Song' with feeling." (Not coincidentally, the Pan Am Building was erected directly across from the Yale Club in New York City.) In fact, notes Lekachman, shortly after the First World War when Trippe, then a bored stockbroker, needed capital to support the founding of Pan Am, he "coaxed his rich college friends into financing a decidedly speculative venture," thus making them the company's first investors.

The story of Trippe and Pan Am "is told in considerable detail," writes a *Choice* reviewer, "lightened by a clear and simple style plus innumerable political, social, and personal anecdotes. . . . This is not merely a specific business case study; with it come many indications of how and why related institutions and persons behaved the way the did." More than just another business history, this is "good social history," states Boloton. And Lekachman concludes: "*The Chosen Instrument* is a refreshing change from those dull authorized chronicles whose authors trade discretion for access to corporate files. Although the authors hold Trippe, as the saying goes, in minimum high regard, they give him proper credit for the risks he took and the technical innovations in which Pan Am was a leader. . . . This is an exemplary tale, . . . a good story well told."

BIOGRAPHICAL/CRITICAL SOURCES: *Library Journal,* September 1, 1967, December 1, 1975; *Book World,* September 17, 1967; *Christian Science Monitor,* December 5, 1967, December 10, 1975; *New York Times Book Review,* October 15, 1967, July 25, 1982; *New Yorker,* October 21, 1967; *Reporter,* November 30, 1967; *Best Sellers,* February, 1976; *New York Times,* July 29, 1982; *Choice,* November, 1982; *Los Angeles Times Book Review,* October 26, 1983.

—Sketch by Peter M. Gareffa

* * *

BENDER, Thomas 1944-

PERSONAL: Born April 18, 1944, in San Mateo, Calif.; son

of Joseph C. (a politician) and Catherine (McGuire) Bender; married Sally Hill (a librarian), June 18, 1966 (divorced October 21, 1983); married Gwendolyn Wright (an architect, historian, and writer), January 14, 1984; children: (first marriage) David. *Education:* University of Santa Clara, B.A., 1966; University of California, Davis, M.A., 1967, Ph.D., 1971. *Residence:* New York, N.Y. *Office:* New York Institute for the Humanities, New York University, Washington Square, New York, N.Y. 10003.

CAREER: University of Wisconsin—Green Bay, assistant professor of history and urban studies, 1971-74; New York University, New York, N.Y., assistant professor, 1974-76, associate professor of history, 1976-77, Samuel Rudin Professor of the Humanities, 1977-82, university professor of the humanities, 1982—, fellow of New York Institute for the Humanities, 1977—, co-director, 1978-79. Visiting assistant professor, University of California, Davis, summer, 1972; chairman of Seminar on the City, Columbia University, 1976-78; visiting professor of urban affairs, Barnard College, 1983. Consulting editor, Oxford University Press, 1977—; consultant, Municipal Art Society of New York, 1978. *Member:* American Historical Association, Organization of American Historians, Intellectual History Group, American Studies Association. *Awards, honors:* Frederick Jackson Turner Prize from Organization of American Historians, 1975, for *Toward an Urban Vision: Ideas and Institutions in Nineteenth-Century America;* Guggenheim fellow, 1980-81.

WRITINGS: *Toward an Urban Vision: Ideas and Institutions in Nineteenth-Century America,* University Press of Kentucky, 1975; *Community: Social Change in America,* Rutgers University Press, 1978; (with Edwin Rozwenc) *The Making of American Society,* Knopf, 1978; (editor) Alexis de Tocqueville, *Democracy in America,* Random House, 1981.

Contributor: John Higham and Paul Conkin, editors, *New Directions in American Intellectual History,* Johns Hopkins University Press, 1979; Lisa Taylor, editor, *Cities,* Rizzoli International, 1982; Thomas L. Haskell, editor, *The Authority of Experts,* Indiana University Press, 1984; W. Sharpe and L. Walloch, editors, *Visions of the City,* Columbia University Press, 1984. Contributor to history, architecture, and education journals and to literary magazines, including *Nation, New York Times Book Review,* and *Partisan Review.*

WORK IN PROGRESS: Research on the cultural history of American cities and on the social foundations of intellectual life in cities (especially New York City), which will result in two books, *City-Culture: Architecture, Intellect, Politics and the Problem of Public Life* and *New York Intellectuals and the Quest for Metropolitan Culture.*

SIDELIGHTS: Thomas Bender explained to *CA* that when he "moved to New York University and, more important, New York City in 1974, I discovered metropolitan culture, both as an object of study and as an arena of my work. This discovery is at the base of my work in progress." He noted that his books and articles explore the theme of "the relation of knowledge and social experience . . . from different angles and using different historical phenomena and materials. For the most part, however, I have pursued this in the context of the historical development of urban life in the United States."

* * *

BENFORD, Gregory (Albert) 1941-

PERSONAL: Born January 30, 1941, in Mobile, Ala.; son of James Alton (a colonel in the U.S. Army) and Eloise (a teacher; maiden name, Nelson) Benford; married Joan Abbe (an artist), August 26, 1967; children: Alyson Rhandra, Mark Gregory. *Education:* University of Oklahoma, B.S., 1963; University of California, San Diego, M.S., 1965, Ph.D., 1967. *Residence:* Laguna Beach, Calif. *Agent:* Richard Curtis, 156 East 52nd St., New York N.Y. 10022. *Office:* Department of Physics, University of California, Irvine, Calif. 92717.

CAREER: Lawrence Radiation Laboratory, Livermore, Calif., fellow, 1967-69, research physicist, 1969-71; University of California, Irvine, assistant professor, 1971-73, associate professor, 1973-79, professor of physics, 1979—. Visiting fellow at Cambridge University, 1976 and 1979. Consultant to Physics International Co. *Member:* American Physical Society, Science Fiction Writers of America, Royal Astronomical Society. *Awards, honors:* Woodrow Wilson fellowship, 1963-64; Nebula Award from Science Fiction Writers of America, 1975, for novella *If the Stars Are Gods,* and 1981, for novel *Timescape;* British Science Fiction Association award, John W. Campbell Award from World Science Fiction Convention, and Dilmar Award for International Novel, all 1981, for *Timescape.*

WRITINGS—Science fiction novels: *Deeper Than the Darkness,* Ace Books, 1970, revised edition published as *The Stars in Shroud,* Putnam, 1979; *Jupiter Project,* Thomas Nelson, 1975; (with Gordon Eklund) *If the Stars Are Gods* (based on the authors' novella of the same title), Putnam, 1977; *In the Ocean of Night,* Dial, 1977; (with Eklund) *Find the Changeling,* Dell, 1980; *Shiva Descending,* Avon, 1980; *Timescape,* Simon & Schuster, 1980; *Against Infinity,* Simon & Schuster, 1983; *The Sea of Suns,* Simon & Schuster, 1984.

Contributor to anthologies, including: *Again, Dangerous Visions,* edited by Harlan Ellison, Doubleday, 1972; *Universe 4,* edited by Terry Carr, Random House, 1974; *New Dimensions, 5,* edited by Robert Silverberg, Harper, 1975.

Also author of a number of research papers. Contributor of articles and stories to magazines, including *Smithsonian, Natural History,* and *Omni.*

SIDELIGHTS: Gregory Benford's achievements in the field of physics, writes Mark J. Lidman in the *Dictionary of Literary Biography,* may overshadow his literary accomplishments. Benford holds a Ph.D. in theoretical physics and has done research on solid state physics, plasma physics, and high energy astrophysics, as well as astronomical research on the dynamics of pulsars, violent extragalactic events, and quasars. At the same time, his science fiction novels have earned him the respect of critics, fans, and his fellow writers. As a scientist, Lidman feels, Benford is "acutely aware of modern society's fascination with technology, but his novels also stress the negative aspects of living in a technological age. His works about alien contact have an appeal that is widespread in the 1980s, and his works which deal with science show us that we must learn to live intelligently in a technological world." The reviewer states that Benford's novels "are characterized by thoughtful composition and scientific expertise, and his work experience lends authenticity to his perspective on science."

Benford told *CA:* "I am a resolutely amateur writer, preferring to follow my own interests rather than try to produce fiction for a living. And anyway, I'm a scientist by first choice and shall remain so.

"I began writing from the simple desire to tell a story (a motivation sf writers seem to forget as they age, and thus turn into earnest moralizers). It's taken me a long time to learn how. I've been labeled a 'hard sf' writer from the first, but in fact I think the job of sf is to do it *all*—the scientific landscape, peopled with real persons, with 'style' and meaning ingrained, etc. I've slowly worked toward that goal, with many dead ends along the way. From this comes my habit of rewriting my older books and expanding early short stories into longer works (sometimes novels). Ideas come to me in a lapidary way, layering over the years. Yet, it's not the stirring moral message that moves me. I think writers are interesting when they juxtapose images or events, letting life come out of the stuff of the narrative. They get boring when they preach.

"To some extent, my novels reflect my learning various subcategories of sf. *Deeper than Darkness* (later revised into *The Stars in Shroud*) was the galactic empire motif; *Jupiter Project,* the juvenile; *If the Stars Are Gods* and *In the Ocean of Night,* both the cosmic space novel. *Timescape* is rather different; it reflects my using my own experiences as a scientist. Yet short stories, where I labored so long, seem to me just as interesting as novels. I learned to write there. Nowadays, my novels begin as relatively brisk plotlines and then gather philosophical moss as they roll. If all this sounds vague and intuitive, it is: That's the way I work. So I cannot say precisely why I undertake certain themes. I like Graham Greene's division of novels into 'serious' and 'entertainments,' though I suspect the author himself cannot say with certainty which of his own are which.

"It seems to me my major concerns are the vast landscape of science, and the philosophical implications of that landscape on mortal, sensual human beings. What genuinely interests me is the strange, the undiscovered. But in the end it is how people see this that matters most."

BIOGRAPHICAL/CRITICAL SOURCES: *Dictionary of Literary Biography, Yearbook: 1982,* Gale, 1983.

* * *

BENJAMINSON, Peter 1945-

PERSONAL: Born August 19, 1945, in Washington, D.C.; son of Albert (an electronics engineer) and Florence (a legal secretary; maiden name, Galinson) Benjaminson; married Susan Harrigan (a journalist), 1979; children: Anne White. *Education:* University of California, Berkeley, A.B., 1967; Columbia University, M.S., 1968. *Residence:* Vestal, N.Y.

CAREER: Journalist and writer. *Detroit Free Press,* Detroit, Mich., reporter and city-county bureau chief, 1970-76; *Atlanta Journal,* Atlanta, Ga., investigative, general assignment, and business reporter, 1980-81; State University of New York at Binghamton, assistant professor of English (journalism), 1981—. Interviewer for *Contemporary Authors,* Gale Research Co., 1979—. *Military service:* U.S. Army, 1968-70; became lieutenant. *Member:* Investigative Reporters and Editors. *Awards, honors:* Sloan fellow, Woodrow Wilson School of Public and International Affairs, Princeton University, 1976-77; first annual Jim Andrews Communicator Award for best book-length manuscript in the United States in the area of contemporary journalism, 1983, for *Death in the Afternoon: America's Big City Newspapers Struggle for Survival.*

WRITINGS: (With David Anderson) *Investigative Reporting,* Indiana University Press, 1976; *The Story of Motown,* Grove Press, 1978; *Death in the Afternoon: America's Big City Newspapers Struggle for Survival,* Andrews & McMeel, 1984.

SIDELIGHTS: CA asked Peter Benjaminson how he felt the investigative reporting demonstrated in the Watergate investigation affected reporters. He responded: "I, along with many other reporters, feel that the Watergate investigation a) showed what beneficial results could be achieved from an investigation partly based on not telling the truth (Woodward and Bernstein lying to the committee for the Re-election of the President employees they interviewed, as they themselves admit) and bending, if not breaking, the law and some ethical codes (interviewing or attempting to interview grand jurors, looking at other people's telephone bills, etc.) and b) made a lot of reporters and editors too arrogant and sure of themselves and too ready to see wrongdoing where there is none, or at least none that the public should be concerned about other than for reasons of gossip (as the post-Elizabeth Ray sex scandals, and perhaps even the Ray scandal itself, showed).

"I think the Watergate investigation also showed, once again, that nothing should be left to experts. I may be over-reflecting my own experiences, but I believe along with many others that war shouldn't be left to the generals, nor White House reporting to White House reporters, nor music industry reporting to music biz critics or executives."

Benjaminson's *The Story of Motown,* according to *Library Journal* reviewer Paul G. Feehan, is an account of the Detroit-based company that "rode to success on a stable of black composers," including Stevie Wonder, the Supremes, and the Temptations. Feehan notes that the book is based on "interviews with some upper echelon executives and with industry observers in general" and finds that, while Benjaminson's book may not be the definitive Motown history, it does relate all the "essential facts of a multi-million dollar venture." Benjaminson told *CA* that he views the Motown story "as a story of race in America and as a reflection of racial struggles—and of the eventually more-or-less successful integration of American society—in the music of that society."

BIOGRAPHICAL/CRITICAL SOURCES: *Journalism Quarterly,* winter, 1976; *Harper's,* September 6, 1976; *Columbia Journalism Review,* September/October, 1976; *Chronicle of Higher Education,* November 15, 1976; *Detroit News,* January 17, 1980; *Detroit Free Press,* January 20, 1980; *Library Journal,* March 1, 1980; *Investigative Reporters and Editors Journal,* spring, 1980.

* * *

ben-JOCHANNAN, Yosef 1918-

PERSONAL: Born December 31, 1918; married; wife's name, Gertrude. *Education:* "Not important to my writings." *Home:* 40 West 135th St., New York, N.Y. 10037. *Office:* Alkebu-lan Books and Education Materials Associates, 209 West 125th St., New York, N.Y. 10027.

CAREER: Egyptologist, historian, and writer. Adjunct professor of history and African studies, Cornell University, Ithaca, N.Y., 1970—; adjunct associate professor of history, Malcolm-King College, New York City; has taught or lectured at numerous colleges and universities in the United States, Europe, South America, and Africa; officer of educational trips to the Nile Valley (Ethiopia, Sudan, and Egypt) for Polo Travel. Chairman of board of directors, Alkebu-lan Foundation, Inc., New York City, and of Alkebu-lan Books and Education Materials Associates (a subsidiary of the Foundation). UNESCO and civilian adviser to the ambassador of Zanzibar, 1963-64. *Member:* Afro-American History Association, Society of African Historians and Anthropologists.

WRITINGS—All elementary and secondary school textbooks, published by Sadlier: (With others) *Africa: Land, People, Culture*, 1966; (with others) *Southern Neighbors*, 1966; (with others) *Southern Lands*, 1966.

All published by Alkebu-lan Books Associates: *Black Man of the Nile*, 1969; *African Origins of the Major "Western Religions,"* 1970; *Africa: Mother of "Western Civilization,"* 1971; (with George E. Simmonds) *The Black Man's North and East Africa*, 1972; *The Black Man of the Nile and His Family*, 1972, 3rd edition, 1981; *Cultural Genocide in the Black and African Studies Curriculum*, 1973; *A Chronology of the Bible: Challenge to the "Standard Version,"* 1973; *The Black Man's Religion*, three volumes, 1974.

All published by Alkebu-lan Books and Education Materials Associates: *Our Black Seminarians and Black Clergy without a Black Theology*, 1978; *The Saga of the "Black Marxists" versus the "Black Nationalists": A Debate Resurrected*, 1978; *Tutankhamon's African Roots Haley et al Overlooked*, 1978; *In Pursuit of George G.M. James' Study of African Origins in "Western Civilization,"* 1980; *They All Look Alike!; All of Them?*, four volumes, 1980-81; *The Alkebu-lanians of Ta-Merry's "Mysterious System," and the Ritualization of the Late Bro. Kwesie Adebisi*, 1982; *We the Black Jews: Witness to the "White Jewish Race" Myth*, 1983.

Author of pamphlets, *We the Black Jews*, written in Spanish, 1938, and *The Rape of Africa and the Crisis in Angola*, written in Portuguese and English, 1958; also author of recordings "Wake Up Black Man" (two records), 1973, "Egypt: The Golden Age" (one record), 1974, "The African in Ancient History before the Christian Era" (fifteen cassette tapes), 1976, "Africans of the Old Testament and Before" (fifteen cassette tapes), 1976, and "Christianity's African Roots" (one record), 1979.

WORK IN PROGRESS: Sixteen books.

SIDELIGHTS: Yosef Ben-Jochannan writes because of "the fact that the major presses did not want to publish anything other than the myths about African people. More so, because my teacher in eighth grade said that 'Negroes have no history.'"

BIOGRAPHICAL/CRITICAL SOURCES: Harold Cruse, *Crisis of the Negro Intellectual*, Morrow, 1967; Albert Cleage, Jr., *Black Christian Nationalism: New Directions for the Black Church*, Morrow, 1972; Henry Olela, *From Ancient Africa to Ancient Greece: An Introduction to the History of Philosophy*, Select Publishing (Atlanta), 1981; *Journal of African Civilizations*, November, 1982.

* * *

BENTON, John W. 1933-

PERSONAL: Born August 29, 1933, in Seattle, Wash.; son of Eric (a minister) and Virginia (Trowbridge) Benton; married Margaret Whaley (an administrative assistant), December 19, 1952; children: Marji Eileen, Connie Jean, Jim Edwin. *Education:* Attended Bethel Temple Bible School, Seattle, Wash., 1952-54. *Home and office address:* Walter Hoving Home, Box 194, Garrison, N.Y. 10524.

CAREER: Pastor of Assembly of God Church, 1958-63; Spokane Youth for Christ, Spokane, Wash., executive director, 1964; Teen Challenge, Inc., Brooklyn, N.Y., associate director, 1965—; Walter Hoving Home (rehabilitation home for girls), Garrison, N.Y., director, 1965—.

WRITINGS—For young people, except as indicated; all published by Revell: *Debs, Dolls, and Dope* (adult), 1968; *Carmen*, 1970; *Teenage Runaway* (adult), 1977; *Crazy Mary*, 1977; *Cindy*, 1978; *Patti*, 1979; *Suzie*, 1979; *Marji*, 1980; *Sherri*, 1980; *Lori*, 1980; *Marji and the Kidnap Plot*, 1980; *Debbie*, 1980; *Julie*, 1981; *Lefty*, 1981; *Vicky*, 1981; *Jackie*, 1981; *Marji and the Gangland Wars*, 1981; *Terri*, 1981; *Nikki*, 1982; *Connie*, 1982; *Valarie*, 1982; *Sheila*, 1982; *Denise*, 1982; *Do You Know Where Your Children Are?* (adult), 1982; *Stephanie*, 1983; *Candi*, 1983; *Sandi*, 1983; *Augie*, 1983. Also author of *I've Had It, Leah, How to Get Along with Everyone*, and *Traci*.

* * *

BENVENISTI, Meron (Shmuel) 1934-

PERSONAL: Born April 21, 1934, in Jerusalem, Palestine (now Israel); son of David and Lea (Friedman) Benvenisti; married Shoshana Lahav (a teacher), January 4, 1968; children: Eyal, Yuval, Sharon. *Education:* Hebrew University of Jerusalem, B.A. and B.Sc., 1961; Harvard University, Dr.PA., 1982. *Politics:* "Peace and civil rights movement." *Religion:* Jewish. *Home:* Ein Rogel 22, Jerusalem, Israel.

CAREER: Israeli Government, Jerusalem, director of economic and development department in Ministry of Tourism, 1960-65, administrator of Old City and East Jerusalem, 1967-71, city councillor of Jerusalem municipality, 1969-74, deputy mayor, 1974-78; free-lance writer, 1979—; director of West Bank Data Base Project, 1983—. *Military service:* Israel Defense Force, 1951-53.

WRITINGS: Mivtsarei Hatsalbanim B'Israel (title means "Crusader Castles in Israel"), Kiriyat Sepher (Jerusalem), 1965; *The Crusaders in the Holy Land*, translation by Pamela Fitton, Israel Universities Press, 1970, Macmillan, 1972; *Mul Hahoma Hasegura*, Weidenfeld & Nicolson, 1973, translation by Peretz Kidron published as *Jerusalem: The Torn City*, University of Minnesota Press, 1977; *Yerushalayim* (title means "The Peace of Jerusalem"), Hakibbutz Hamenchad, 1981. Contributor of map of crusader Palestine to atlas of Israel, 1960, 2nd edition, 1973.

WORK IN PROGRESS: The West Bank and Gaza; Zionism and Israel in the Eighties.

SIDELIGHTS: Meron Benvenisti's book *Jerusalem: The Torn City* "chronicles, with controlled passion and honest reporting, what has transpired in that extraordinary city during the decade since the Israeli army captured the Arab sector," writes Terence Smith of the *New York Times Book Review*. "It provides a case study of strained coexistence.... No one else, journalist, historian or bureaucrat, has attempted anything quite like this book."

AVOCATIONAL INTERESTS: Boating.

BIOGRAPHICAL/CRITICAL SOURCES: New York Times Book Review, June 12, 1977.

* * *

BERBRICH, Joan D. 1925-

PERSONAL: Born May 12, 1925, in Richmond Hill, N.Y.; daughter of John Adam and Dorothy (Scharen) Berbrich. *Education:* New York College for Teachers (now State University of New York at Albany), B.A., 1946; Columbia University, M.A., 1949; New York University, Ph.D., 1964. *Politics:*

Independent. *Religion:* Roman Catholic. *Home:* 5 Owen Ave., Glens Falls, N.Y. 12801.

CAREER: Mineola High School, Mineola, N.Y., English teacher, 1949-59, chairman of English department, 1959-75. Teacher of English, University of Connecticut, Storrs, summer, 1966; extension teacher of English, Nassau Community College, Garden City, N.Y., 1969-70.

WRITINGS: Three Voices from Paumanok: The Influence of Long Island on Cooper, Bryant, and Whitman, Friedman, 1969; (editor) *Sounds and Sweet Airs: The Poetry of Long Island,* Friedman, 1970; (editor) W. Oakley Cagney, *The Heritage of Long Island,* Friedman, 1970; (with M. Hecht and C. Cooper) *The Women, Yes,* Holt, 1973; (editor) *Stories of Crime and Detection,* McGraw, 1974; (editor) *Heaven and Hell,* McGraw, 1975.

Published by Amsco School Publications: *101 Ways to Learn Vocabulary,* 1971; *Wide World of Words,* 1975; *Writing Practically,* 1976; *Writing Creatively,* 1977; *Writing Logically,* 1978; *Writing about People,* 1979; *Writing about Fascinating Things,* 1980; *Writing about Curious Things,* 1981; *Writing about Amusing Things,* 1982; *Reading Today,* 1983. Contributor to literary and popular journals.

WORK IN PROGRESS: Reading around the World, for Amsco School Publications.

SIDELIGHTS: Joan Berbrich told *CA:* "Since I believe that writing is an art, not a happening, I have spent the last few years trying to understand and explain the 'how-to's' of writing. This seems important to me since good writing depends on clear thinking—and our contemporary world certainly needs that."

* * *

BERENDT, Joachim Ernst 1922-

PERSONAL: Born July 20, 1922, in Berlin, Germany; son of Ernst (a minister) and Maria (Hammerschmidt) Berendt; children: Christian. *Home:* Auf der Alm 11, D-7570 Baden-Baden, West Germany. *Office:* Sudwestfunk, Baden-Baden, West Germany.

CAREER: Sudwestfunk (Southwestern German Radio and Television Network), Baden-Baden, Germany, co-founder and broadcaster, 1945—; ARD (German TV), Baden-Baden, host and writer of "Jazz—Heard and Seen" series, 1954-72. Producer of over 250 jazz albums, including "Jazz Meets the World" series, 1969—; lecturer. Founder, American Folk Blues Festival, 1962, and Berlin Jazz Days, 1964; director, Olympic Games Jazz Festival, Munich, 1972. *Military service:* German Army; served in a panzer division in World War II. *Awards, honors:* Preis der Deutschen Fernsehkritik, 1957, for best musical television production of the year; Deutsche Bundesfilmpreis in Gold, 1962, for best film music of the year; Polish Cultural Award, 1978.

WRITINGS: Der Jazz, Deutsche Verlagsanstalt (Stuttgart), 1950; *Das Jazzbuch,* S. Fischer Verlag, 1953; *Jazz Optisch,* Nymphenburger Verlagshandlung, 1954; *Variationen uber Jazz,* Nymphenburger Verlagshandlung, 1956; *Blues,* Nymphenburger Verlagshandlung, 1957; *Prisma der Gegenwartigen Musik,* Furche, 1959; *Das Neue Jazzbuch: Entwicklung und Bedeutung der Jazzmusik,* S. Fischer Verlag, 1959, translation by Dan Morganstern published as *The New Jazz Book: A History and Guide,* Hill & Wang, 1962; (with Ed van der Elsken) *Foto-Jazz,* Nymphenburger Verlagshandlung, 1959; *Jazzlife,* Burda Druck und Verlag, 1961; *Blues, English-Deutsch,* Nymphenburger Verlagshandlung, 1962; *Das Jazzbuch: Von New Orleans bis Free Jazz,* S. Fischer Verlag, 1968, translation by Morganstern, Helmut Bredigkeit, and Barbara Bredigkeit published as *The Jazz Book: From New Orleans to Rock and Free Jazz,* Lawrence Hill, 1975.

Blues, Gerig, 1970; *Das Jazzbuch: von Rag bis Rock,* Fischer-Taschenbuch Verlag, 1975; *Ein Fenster aus Jazz,* S. Fischer Verlag, 1977; *Photo Story des Jazz,* Krueger Verlag, 1980, translation published as *Jazz: A Photo History,* Macmillan, 1981; *Mein Lesebuch,* S. Fischer Verlag, 1981; *Nada Brahma: Die Welt ist Klang,* Insel Verlag, 1983. Editor of "Calendar Jazz and Rock," 1954—.

SIDELIGHTS: CA asked Joachim Ernst Berendt what relationships he sees between European and American jazz. He reponded: "There is a strong influence of folk blues and archaic blues on today's scene. Contemporary jazz forms like soul and funk are unthinkable without the jazz tradition. Jazz as a whole is unthinkable without its tradition—not only in blues, but also in spirituals and gospel, and, of course, all the way back to West Africa (especially Yoruba and Dahomey cultures). The central figures of jazz are Louis Armstrong, Duke Ellington, Charlie Parker, John Coltrane, Miles Davis, Cecil Taylor, and Ornette Coleman.

"Jazz in Europe is considered much more as an art form than in America (where it is still part of the huge entertainment industry). European jazz from the twenties to the early sixties was not much more than an imitation of American jazz. But during the sixties, there was an emancipation process, and now, there are musicians in Europe who play their own kind of jazz, without looking much to America. For instance: German trombone player Albert Mangelsdorff, British saxophonist John Surman, Polish violinist Zbiggniew Seifert, etc. These musicians are using part of their own European tradition—in a way similar to American musicians using their tradition."

Berendt first became interested in jazz in 1935 when he was thirteen years old. "I was quite a radio fan," he told Hollie I. West in a *Washington Post* interview. "I got hooked listening to Benney Carter playing with the Ramblers." But jazz fell into disrepute with the Nazi government, and gradually the music was stifled. Berendt was drafted into the German Army and sent to the Russian front where he was injured and then returned to Germany. With the end of the war in sight, Berendt made his way into Allied territory. After the war, he resumed his musical interests, helping to found the Sudwestfunk radio and television network and broadcasting his popular "Jazz—Heard and Seen" TV series.

The author has visited the United States about thirty times, including 1976 when he joined in a Bicentennial conference, sponsored by the Smithsonian Institution, which featured international scholars discussing U.S. contributions to the world. Berendt explained to West: "Several of us said jazz was the most important American contribution.... Not film, comic strips, the atom bomb, politics. Many American scholars took issue with us. Americans have a very special relationship to jazz. In one sense, they know it. But they take it for granted. In Europe it's so much of an art form that it's special. It's a music of freedom and tolerance."

BIOGRAPHICAL/CRITICAL SOURCES: Washington Post, February 5, 1980.

BERESINER, Yasha 1940-

PERSONAL: Born June 12, 1940, in Turkey; son of Lazar David (a company chairman) and Rachel (Saltiel) Beresiner; married Zmira Goldman, January 7, 1964; children: Guy David, Dana. *Education:* Hebrew University of Jerusalem, LL.B., 1968. *Home address:* P.O. Box 97, London NW4 2LD, England. *Office:* Intercol London, 1A Camden Walk, Islington, London N3 3QR, England.

CAREER: Commodities & Equipment Ltd., London, England, director, 1969-74; Paramount International Coin Ltd., London, director, 1974-78; Stanley Gibbons Ltd., London, director, 1979-81; Intercol London, London, managing director, 1981—. *Military service:* Israeli Armed Forces, Paratroop Regiment, 1962-65. *Member:* International Bank Note Society (member of board of directors), Royal Numismatic Society (fellow), Numismatic Literary Guild (member of board of directors), American Numismatic Society, American Numismatic Association (life member), Latin American Paper Money Society (past president). *Awards, honors:* Writing award from Numismatic Literary Guild, 1974, for "Numismatic Scrapbook."

WRITINGS: *Catalogue of the Paper Money of Colombia*, Stanley Gibbons, 1973; *The Story of Paper Money*, David & Charles, 1974; *A Collector's Guide to Paper Money*, Stein & Day, 1977; *British County Maps Reference Guide*, ACC (Suffolk), 1983.

Author of columns in *International Banknote Journal*, 1971-74, in *Bank Note Reporter*, 1975, and in *Coins and Medals*, 1975—. Contributor of several hundred articles to numismatic journals in England and the United States, principally to *Numismatic*. Editor for Latin American Paper Money Society; former editor for International Bank Note Society.

WORK IN PROGRESS: *A Lexicon of Playing Card Terms*, publication expected in 1985.

SIDELIGHTS: Yasha Beresiner told *CA:* "My writing allows for a greater appreciation of my hobby; the inclination for research has always been present. Activities in society affairs led to editorships, beginning with editorial columns later developed into specialized articles which led to books. I consider a hobby to be essential to a more balanced way of life. Hard work on a hobby is always somehow less trying than normal work!"

He adds: "My cosmopolitan background (Russian father, Greek mother, Israel nationality and Israeli wife) led to fluent knowledge of English, Italian, Spanish, French, Hebrew, and Turkish, languages I use in travel; I know Latin America and Western Europe very well."

AVOCATIONAL INTERESTS: "Main interest outside collecting (I collect books, maps, coins, playing cards, prints, etc.) is sport. In judo I represented Israel at a students' Olympics in Tokyo in 1967; I am active still in golf. I enjoy bridge and backgammon."

BIOGRAPHICAL/CRITICAL SOURCES: *Bank Note Reporter*, September, 1976.

* * *

BERG, Lasse 1943-

PERSONAL: Born July 1, 1943, in Sweden; son of Edvard and Ebba (Kaeding) Berg; married Lisa Edfelt (a writer), 1965 (divorced, 1980); married Ingrid Lofstrom, 1982; children: Josefin, Mia, Linda. *Education:* University of Stockholm, Fil. Kand, 1970. *Agent:* Gidlunds Bokfoerlag, P.O. Box 12016, 11241 Stockholm, Sweden.

CAREER: Writer, 1970—. *Awards, honors:* United Nations Boerma Award, and *Arbetet* newspaper Lat leva-Award, both 1979, for *Mat och Makt*, co-authored by Lisa Berg.

WRITINGS: (With Lisa Berg) *Ansikte mot ansikte: Fascister och revolutionaerer i Indien*, Raben & Sjoegren, 1970, translation by Norman Kurtin published as *Face to Face: Fascism and Revolution in India*, Ramparts, 1971, revised edition, 1972; (with Lisa Berg and Stig T. Karlsson) *Varfoer jobbar Chand?* (juvenile; title means "Why Is Chand Working?"), Gidlund, 1971; (with Lisa Berg) *Uppvaknandet: Japan idag* (title means "Awakening: Japan Today"), Raben & Sjoegren, 1972; (with Lisa Berg) *Japan i Asien* (title means "Japan and Asia"), Utrikespolitiska Instituet, 1972; (with Lisa Berg) *Barn paa Bali* (juvenile; title means "Children in Bali"), Gidlund, 1974; (with Lisa Berg and Karlsson) *Japan: Framtiden har redan boerjat* (title means "Japan: The Future Has Started"), Gidlund, 1974; (with Lisa Berg and Karlsson) *Vi bor i vaerldens stoersta stad* (title means "Living in the Biggest City in the World"), Gidlund, 1974.

(With Lisa Berg) *Att leva i Bangladesh* (juvenile; title means "Living in Bangladesh"), Esselte Studium, 1975; (with Lisa Berg) *Tredje varlden* (title means "The Third World"), Gidlund, 1977; (with Lisa Berg) *Mat och Makt* (title means "Food and Power"), Gidlund, 1978; *Socialistisk experiment i Mocambique*, Swedish International Development Agency, 1980; *Asiatisk gryning* (title means "Asian Dawn"), Brevskolan, 1983. Also author of documentary radio and television scripts for Swedish Broadcasting Corp. Contributor to *Vi* and *Dagens Nyheter*.

WORK IN PROGRESS: *Along the Ganges*, an Indian travelogue.

SIDELIGHTS: Lasse Berg wrote *CA:* "By mixing grass-root level close-ups with analytical overviews I want to describe important political and economical trends in the Third World and its relation to the First and Second Worlds."

* * *

BERGER, Phil 1942-

PERSONAL: Born April 1, 1942, in Brooklyn, N.Y.; son of Jack (a grocer) and Fanny (Finkelstein) Berger; married; wife's name, Leslie. *Education:* Johns Hopkins University, B.A. (cum laude), 1964. *Residence:* New York, N.Y.

CAREER: *Greenwich Time* (newspaper), Greenwich, Conn., reporter, summers, 1963-64; Associated Press, Atlanta, Ga., newsman, 1964; *Sport* (magazine), associate editor, 1966-67; free-lance writer, 1966—. *Military service:* U.S. Army Reserve, 1967-71; active duty, 1965-66.

WRITINGS: *Championship Teams of the NFL*, Random House, 1968; *Heroes of Pro Basketball*, Random House, 1968; *Great Moments in Pro Football*, Messner, 1969; *Joe Namath: Maverick Quarterback*, Cowles, 1969; *Miracle on Thirty-Third Street: The New York Knickerbockers' Championship Season* (Literary Guild alternate selection), Simon & Schuster, 1970; *Great Running Backs in Pro Football*, Messner, 1970; *More Championship Teams of the NFL*, Random House, 1974; *The Last Laugh: The World of the Standup Comics* (Book-of-the-Month Club alternate selection), Morrow, 1975; (with Larry Borstein) *The Boys of Indy*, Corwin, 1977; *Where Are They Now?: Yesterday's Sports Heroes Today*, Popular Library, 1978. Contributor of more than three hundred stories and articles to popular magazines, including *New York, National Observer, Penthouse, Rogue, Cavalier, Look, Worlds of Tomorrow, Sport, Pageant, Parade,* and *Johns Hopkins,* and to newspapers, including *Village Voice* and *New York Post.*

AVOCATIONAL INTERESTS: Reading, basketball, tennis, distance running, New York City.

BIOGRAPHICAL/CRITICAL SOURCES: *New York Times,* October 22, 1970; *New York Post,* February 8, 1971; *San Francisco Chronicle,* April 9, 1975.†

* * *

BERLINER, Franz 1930-

PERSONAL: Born August 10, 1930, in Denmark; married Bibi Noergaard, 1952; children: Franz, Peter, Bolette. *Politics:* "As a human being, capable of thinking, I'm a pacifist." *Home:* Alleen 45, 8660 Skanderborg, Denmark.

CAREER: Author and journalist. *Soendags-BT,* Copenhagen, Denmark, weekly columnist, writing about children and their parents, 1965-71; *Politiken,* Copenhagen, daily critic on children's programs, 1969-83.

WRITINGS: *Tingelingelater,* Nyt Nordisk, 1956; *Godnat Skipper* (juvenile), Borgen, 1962; *Maane over fjeldet* (on Greenland), Borgen, 1964; *Stederne,* Borgen, 1966; *Boernene og vi* (child study), Berlingske, 1967; *Menneskenes Land* (juvenile), Bonniers, 1967, translation by Louise Orr published as *Summertime,* Collins, 1969; (with wife, Bibi Berliner) *Derude bag havet* (juvenile), Munksgard, 1968; *Groenland,* Carit Andersen, 1968.

Vestgroenland, Carit Andersen, 1970; *Haevneren,* Sesam, 1978; *Ulven,* Sesam, 1979; *Gaeslingen,* Sesam, 1980; *En dag den sommer,* Sesam, 1982; *Den Frygtloese,* Sesam, 1983.

Published by Gyldendal: *Evelyn* (short stories), 1954; *Hundene,* 1957; (contributor) *Boerne-og ungdomsboeger* (children's literature study), 1969; *Soefolket* (juvenile), 1970, translation by Lone Thygesen-Blecher published as *The Lake People,* Putnam, 1973; *En anden bog om Soefolket,* 1972; (with B. Berliner) *Alene hjemme* (juvenile), 1972; *Kahinoeen,* 1973; *Marinus,* 1978; (with B. Berliner) *Seksten dage i september,* 1980; *Hestestormen,* 1980; (with B. Berliner) *Koeb blomster,* 1981.

Author of television adaptation of *Menneskenes Land* for Danmarks Radio, 1969; also has written for Greenland and Danish radio. Editor, *Refleks* (encyclopedia for school children), 1973-77. Contributor of articles to magazines and newspapers, and book reviews to *Politiken.*

SIDELIGHTS: Franz Berliner spent five years in Greenland and has visited there several times since. He wrote the text of *Summertime* around drawings of Eskimo children done by Ingrid Vang Nyman, who was Danish but who did most of her work in Sweden. When she died in 1959 her son took her unpublished drawings to Berliner. *Media adaptations: Alene hjemme* played as Children's Theatre on *Filuren,* Aarhus, 1975.

BIOGRAPHICAL/CRITICAL SOURCES: *Books,* October, 1969. *Times Literary Supplement,* October 16, 1969.

* * *

BERTRAM, Jean De Sales

PERSONAL: Born in Burlington, Iowa; daughter of Val Randall (an orchestra conductor) and Ruth Cecilia (Gustafson) Bertram; divorced; children: Larkin Montgomery Bertram-Cox. *Education:* Women's College of the University of North Carolina (now University of North Carolina at Greensboro), B.A., 1942; University of Minnesota, M.A., 1951; Stanford University, Ph.D., 1963. *Office:* Department of Theatre Arts, School of Creative Arts, San Francisco State University, 19th at Holloway Ave., San Francisco, Calif. 94132.

CAREER: *Greensboro News-Record,* Greensboro, N.C., staff reporter, 1942-43; Burlington Industries, Greensboro, N.C., founder of public relations department, 1943-49; Minneapolis Vocational High School, Minneapolis, Minn., director of radio workshop, 1951-52; San Francisco State University, San Francisco, Calif., instructor, 1952-62, assistant professor, 1963-65, associate professor, 1966-71, professor of theater arts, 1972—.

MEMBER: Foundation for Biblical Research, National Story League, Western District National Story League, Storyland Story League of San Francisco, Phi Beta Kappa (president, Northern California chapter, 1963-65; delegate to triennial council, 1979, 1982), Omicron (California chapter; secretary, 1977-79; president, 1979-81; vice-president, 1981-83; permanent secretary, 1983—).

WRITINGS: *The Oral Experience of Literature,* Chandler, 1967; *The Actor Speaks: A Handbook for Actors and Students of the Voice,* 4th edition, Second Front, 1983.

Plays: "To Market, to Market," produced at University of Minnesota, 1950; "Symphonetic Easter Drama," produced at School of Creative Arts, San Francisco State University, San Francisco, Calif., 1955; "California Cameos," produced by California Historical Society, 1974; "American Cameos" (musical drama), produced by California Bicentennial Commission, 1976. Also author of "Black Beard, the Pirate," 1951.

Adaptations: Hans Christian Andersen, "The Emperor's New Clothes," produced by Children's Theatre of the West, 1954; Charles Dickens, "A Christmas Carol," produced in northern California, 1971-75. Also adapter of Biblical verses "The Cherry Tree" (based on Matthew 5: 22-24), produced in San Francisco, 1971-72, and "The Vision According to the Prophet Isiah," produced in San Francisco, 1972.

Also author of *Cosmorama-1972,* a twelve-minute poem on cosmic evolution. Contributor to *Educational Theatre Journal, Speech Teacher, Elementary English,* and *English Journal.*

WORK IN PROGRESS: *Jeremiah;* a collection of folk tales in China.

SIDELIGHTS: Jean De Sales Bertram told *CA:* "The difference between the way people talk and the way people write always has intrigued me. A native of Iowa, I was moved regularly back and forth between the Midwest and the South during my father's musical career. Every summer my southern idioms and drawl charmed friends and relatives in Iowa and Minnesota when my parents returned to their native states. Each autumn my midwestern accent and pacing invariably startled my southern playmates when my father resumed his activities in the south Atlantic states. Meanwhile, my mother taught me to read and established a routine for reading aloud half an hour by the clock every day. Even though the material presented very simple sentences such as 'Bay Ray had a cat,' I was admonished to speak with 'expression.' I remember vigorously protesting the animated rendition of these subject-verb-object statements, for even then I felt that too often the written word sounded stilted. Is it any wonder that these childhood experiences created in me an intense fascination with the voice as a means for conveying emotions and ideas?

"When I began writing in grammar school, I tried to let the characters in my stories talk as much as possible. Graduation from college found me working as a newspaper reporter, and while walking from one agency or contact to another on this job, my ears reveled in all the spoken rhythms I heard. Soon I became obsessed with the remembrances of these phrases and sentences, and every evening before dinner I began writing down what I had heard spoken during the day. . . . Some years later . . . during a playwrighting course at the University of Minnesota, several classmates asked, 'Where did you learn to write dialogue like that?' Then I realized that I had been listening to the sounds and rhythms of speech all of my life.

"Plays based on the Bible excite me for in these the word becomes all-powerful, and I am challenged by the compulsion to unite the formality of a written piece with the informality of the spoken form. Whenever I write I try to hear someone speaking the words on the page."

* * *

BESTER, Alfred 1913-

PERSONAL: Born December 18, 1913, in New York, N.Y.; son of James J. (a shoe merchant) and Belle (Silverman) Bester; married Rolly Goulko (an advertising executive), September 16, 1936. *Education:* University of Pennsylvania, B.A., 1935. *Politics:* "Emotional liberal." *Religion:* "Born Jewish but Animist by faith." *Address:* P.O. Box 202, Ottsville, Pa. 18942. *Agent:* Kirby McCauley, Ltd., 425 Park Ave. S., New York, N.Y. 10016.

CAREER: Free-lance writer in the 1940s and 1950s; editor of several popular magazines from the mid-1950s to the early 1970s, became senior editor of *Holiday* magazine; full-time writer beginning about 1972. *Member:* Science Fiction Writers of America. *Awards, honors:* Hugo Award for best novel, Science Fiction Writers of America, 1953, for *The Demolished Man.*

WRITINGS: Who He? (satirical novel), Dial, 1953 (published in England as *The Rat Race,* Panther, 1959); *The Life and Death of a Satellite* (nonfiction), Sidgwick & Jackson, 1967; (contributor) Brian W. Aldiss and Harry Harrison, editors, *Hell's Cartographers: Some Personal Histories of Science Fiction Writers* (nonfiction), Harper, 1975.

All science fiction: *The Demolished Man* (novel), Shasta Publications, 1953, new edition, edited by Lester Del Rey, Garland Publishing, 1975; *Tiger! Tiger!* (novel), Sidgwick & Jackson, 1955, reprinted, Penguin, 1974, published as *The Stars My Destination,* New American Library, 1957, illustrated edition, edited by H. V. Chaykin, published in two volumes, Baronet, 1979; *Starburst* (short stories), New American Library, 1958; *The Dark Side of the Earth* (short stories), New American Library, 1964; *An Alfred Bester Omnibus,* Sidgwick & Jackson, 1967; *The Computer Connection* (novel), Berkley Publishing, 1975 (published in England as *Extro,* Eyre Methuen, 1975); *The Great Short Fiction of Alfred Bester,* Berkley Publishing, Volume I: *The Light Fantastic,* 1976, Volume II: *Star Light, Star Bright,* 1976, published in one volume as *Starlight: The Great Short Fiction of Alfred Bester,* 1977; *Golem ^{100}* (novel), Simon & Schuster, 1980; *The Deceivers* (novel), Pinnacle Books, 1982.

Also author of comic scenarios in the 1940s, including "Superman" and "Batman"; author of radio scripts in the 1940s, including "Charlie Chan" and "The Shadow"; author of television scripts. Author of English libretti for Giuseppe Verdi's "La Traviata" and Modest Petrovich Moussorgsky's "The Fair at Sorochinsk." Contributor to *Holiday, Show, Venture,* and *Rogue.*

WORK IN PROGRESS: "My entire life is work in progress."

SIDELIGHTS: Although Alfred Bester hasn't published a large amount of science fiction, writes William L. Godshalk in the *Dictionary of Literary Biography,* "his impact on the genre has been enormous." He "is a science-fiction writer's writer," Peter Nicholls comments in *Washington Post Book World.* "He has been much admired by the old wave, the hard science men . . . but equally a hero to the young turks of the 1960s new wave, the writers of the left, the people who think that inner space has just as much to do with [science fiction] as outer space."

Bester established his reputation in his earliest science fiction novels *The Demolished Man* and *The Stars My Destination,* works described by Bud Foote in the *Detroit News* as recognized science fiction classics. *The Demolished Man* was Foote's introduction to "the not-yet-christened New Wave," and he points out that it was the first novel to win the newly-created Hugo Award. Bester's *The Stars My Destination* was "said by many people to be the best science fiction novel ever written," T. A. Shippey relates in the *Times Literary Supplement.* Bester turned away from science fiction while editing and contributing to *Holiday* magazine, but his reputation has remained intact. "As a science-fiction writer, Bester has never been prolific," writes Nicholls, "merely revolutionary."

Much of Bester's appeal is attributed to his eclecticism. In the opinion of *Village Voice* reviewer Robert Morales, for example, "*The Stars My Destination*—an incredible takeoff on *The Count of Monte Cristo,* and James Joyce pastiche—burlesqued the adventure novel into high art. Both story and novel excel in sheer lunatic excitement." Nicholls calls the book's main character "the archetypal Besterman, the 20th-century, pulp equivalent of the malcontent of Jacobean revenge dramas, brooding, sardonic, obsessed and murderous—at once ironic commentator and brutal actor in a dark, amoral world." Bester "is no unconscious myth-maker," Gerald Jonas notes in the *New York Times Book Review.* "He manipulates archetypal themes openly, zestfully, yet with an undertone of self-mockery, as if to let us know that he realizes the absurdity of his enterprise." Godshalk agrees that "his finest work is characterized by a serious playfulness."

The Computer Connection, for instance, is summarized by Godshalk as "a first-person narrative dictated to a diary-computer." In that novel, writes Jonas, Bester's "premises are so fantastic, his characters are so eccentric, his writing is so breathless that his work must either be swallowed whole, or rejected in its entirety." And, according to Godshalk, the novel *Golem ^{100}* is an attempt "to explode the parameters of print by combining words, musical scores, and graphics in order to create a new technique of synesthetic visio-narration. The experiment is successful because Bester links new techniques with traditional form."

Bester's writing is distinctive, however, in that it is not "technically oriented science fiction; [Bester's] scientific gadgetry is often not explained, and scientific developments—such as the terraforming of Venus and Mars—are left to the reader's imagination," Godshalk reports. "These are the givens of his fiction, and little is made of them. . . . A more important assumption of his fictive world is that man can develop unusual powers—telepathy, teleportation, and physical immortality—under unusual stress, and that once developed, these powers can be taught to others. . . . Bester emphasizes transformation through crisis, evolution through catastrophe."

The author, Godshalk concludes, "has remained constant in his concern with the basics of human passion and personal change. Technically he is an experimenter, and his influence can be charted in the works of such writers as John Brunner, Robert Silverberg, Clifford D. Simak, and Kurt Vonnegut, Jr."

The Demolished Man has been translated into Portuguese; *The Stars My Destination* has been translated into French.

BIOGRAPHICAL/CRITICAL SOURCES—Books: Thomas D. Clareson, editor, *SF: The Other Side of Realism*, Bowling Green University, 1971; Norman Spinrad, editor, *Modern Science Fiction*, Anchor Press, 1974; Darrell Schweitzer, interviewer, *Sf Voices*, T-K Graphics, 1976; Robert Scholes and Eric S. Rabkin, editors, *Science Fiction: History, Science, Vision*, Oxford University Press, 1977; Charles Platt, interviewer, *Dream Makers: The Uncommon People Who Write Science Fiction*, Berkley Publishing, 1980; David Cowart and Thomas L. Wymer, editors, *Dictionary of Literary Biography*, Volume VIII: *Twentieth-Century American Science-Fiction Writers*, Gale, 1981.

Periodicals: *Riverside Quarterly*, August, 1972; *Extrapolation*, May, 1975; *New York Times Book Review*, July 20, 1975, September 14, 1980; *Times Literary Supplement*, December 5, 1975; *Washington Post Book World*, May 25, 1980; *Village Voice*, May 26, 1980; *Detroit News*, July 27, 1980; *West Coast Review of Books*, September, 1982.

* * *

BIGIARETTI, Libero 1906-

PERSONAL: Born May 16, 1906, in Matelica, Italy; son of Lucano and Rosa (D'Andrea) Bigiaretti; married Matilde Crespi (a journalist). *Education:* Attended Liceo Artistico, Rome. *Home:* Via Francesco Denza 66, Rome, Italy.

CAREER: Journalist and writer, with principal vocational interest in contemporary arts. *Member:* Sindacato Nazionale Scrittori (Rome), Societe Europeenne de Culture, P.E.N., Societa Italiana degli Autori ed Editori (councillor). *Awards, honors:* Marzotto Prize, 1955, for *I Figli;* Viareggio Award, 1968, for *La Controfigura;* Chancian Award, 1968, for *Le Indulgenze;* Golden Pen Prize from Italian Council of Ministers for important contribution to Italian culture, 1982, for the entire body of his work.

WRITINGS: Una Amicizia difficile (novel), de Luigi, 1945, published as *Esterina: Un' Amicizia difficile*, Bompiani, 1962; *Incendi a Paleo*, Editrice Cultura Moderna, 1945; *Roma borghese*, Organizzazione Editoriale Tipografica, 1945; *Il villino* (novel), Garzanti, 1946, reprinted, Bompiani, 1974.

La Scuola dei ladri (three short novels), Garzanti, 1952; *I Figli*, Vallecchi, 1955, reprinted, Bompiani, 1974; *Disamore* (novel), Nistri-Lischi, 1956; *Carlone: Vita di un italiano*, Avanti, 1956; *Etruskische Wandmalerei*, W. Klein, 1956; *Schedario*, All'Insegna del Pesce d'Oro, 1956; *Disegni e dipinti di Bruno Caruso, 1952-1955* (text in Italian, English, and French), Priulla, 1957; *Carte romane*, Societa Editrice Internazionale, 1957; *Leopolda*, Sodalizio del Libro, 1957; *Uccidi o muori*, Vallecchi, 1958.

I Racconti (short stories), Vallecchi, 1961; *Il Congresso* (novel), Bompiani, 1963, translation by Joseph Green published as *A Business Convention*, Knopf, 1965 (translation published in England as *The Convention*, Macmillan, 1965); *Le Indulgenze*, Bompiani, 1963; *Cattiva memoria*, Nuova Accademia, 1965; *Il Dito puntato: Lettera all'editore con una riposta del medesimo* (correspondence with Valentino Bompiani), Bompiani, 1967; (with others) *Giovanni Pintori* (text in Italian and English), Bassoli, 1967; *La Controfigura* (novel), Bompiani, 1968; *Il Dissenso*, Bompiani, 1969.

Dalla donna alla luna (novel), Bompiani, 1972; *L'Uomo che manqia il leone* (short stories), Bompiani, 1974; *Le Stanze* (novel), Bompiani, 1976; *Due Senza* (novel), Bompiani, 1980; *Questa Roma*, Newton Compton, 1981; *A memoria d'nomo* (poems), Bagalona, 1983; *Il viaggiatore*, Rusconi, 1984.

SIDELIGHTS: Libero Bigiaretti told *CA* that, as a youth, he aspired to painting. Books, however, occupied much of his time and led him eventually from reading to writing. He found writing easy and developed no particular writing habits, composing as he went and where he could. As a reason for writing he says, "I wanted to write to learn and to elevate myself socially."

Bigiaretti believes that modern literature has "overrated the contributions of psychoanalysis and sociology. Flaubert and Dostoevski did not study sociology. Dante, Kafka, Melville did not know of psychoanalysis. Zola, Verga, Dickens did not study sociology."

His books are widely read and have been translated into all major languages. A filmscript based on his prize-winning novel, *La Controfigura*, has been written and produced.

* * *

BIRKS, Tony 1937-

PERSONAL: Born November 1, 1937, in Manchester, England; son of Edwyn Ainsworth (a publisher) and Nora Lilian (a writer) Birks; married Margaret Leslie Hay (an editor), July 14, 1972; children: Paul Raphael, Adam Nicholas. *Education:* Slade School of Fine Art, D.F.A., 1958; St. Edmund Hall, Oxford, M.A., 1961; University of Grenoble, ler Degre, 1964. *Home and office:* Marston House, Marston Magna, Yeovil, Somerset, England.

CAREER: Oxford School of Art, Oxford, England, lecturer in ceramics and sculpture, 1959-63; Thames & Hudson (publisher), London, England, art editor, 1964-68; George Rainbird Ltd., London, England, sponsor editor, 1968-71; Alphabet & Image Ltd., Sherborne, England, managing director, 1972—. *Awards, honors:* Slade sculpture prize, 1958; TV Westward award, 1973, for ceramics; National Book League award, 1980, for book design.

WRITINGS: The Art of the Modern Potter, Country Life Books, 1967, 2nd edition, Van Nostrand, 1977; *Building the New Universities*, David & Charles, 1972; *The Potter's Companion*, Dutton, 1974; *Meyer's Ornament*, Duckworth, 1974; (contributor) Emmanuel Cooper and Eileen Lewenstein, editors, *New Ceramics*, Van Nostrand, 1974; *Outline Guide to Pottery*, Blandford Press, 1975; *Pottery: A Complete Guide*, Pan Books, 1979, State Mutual Book, 1982; *Hans Coper*, Harper, 1984.

WORK IN PROGRESS: A biography of William Dampier.

SIDELIGHTS: Tony Birks writes briefly that he is "interested in all forms of design of all periods, especially architecture and carpets." *Avocational interests:* Tennis, sailing, theatre.

BIOGRAPHICAL/CRITICAL SOURCES: Times Literary Supplement, December 9, 1983.

* * *

**BLAKE, Jennifer
See MAXWELL, Patricia**

* * *

BLANK, Leonard 1927-

PERSONAL: Born May 10, 1927, in New York, N.Y.; son of Samuel and Mildred (Bernstein) Blank; married Bernice Bukaretsky, November 14, 1953; children: Jordan, Rona, Lyda. *Education:* Brooklyn College (now Brooklyn College of the City University of New York), B.A., 1949, M.A., 1952; New York University, Ph.D., 1955, additional study, 1961-67; Stanford University, postdoctoral study, 1955-57. *Home:* 4 Rumson Rd., Kendall Park, N.J. 08824. *Office:* Medical School, Rutgers University, New Brunswick, N.J. 08903.

CAREER: Diplomate in clinical psychology. Princeton Associates for Human Resources, Inc. (behavioral service firm), Princeton, N.J., president, 1968-78; Rutgers University, Graduate School, New Brunswick, N.J., adjunct associate professor of psychology, 1969-75, adjunct professor at Medical School, 1975—; director, New Jersey Institute for Psychotherapy, 1978—; Princeton Health Care Services, Inc., Princeton, president, 1982—. *Member:* American Psychological Association (fellow). *Awards, honors:* Distinguished Alumnus award, New York University, 1956.

WRITINGS: (Editor with Henry P. David) *Manpower and Psychology* (monograph), U.S. Government Printing Office, 1963; (editor with David) *Sourcebook for Training in Clinical Psychology,* Springer Publishing, 1964; *Psychological Evaluations in Psychotherapy,* Aldine, 1964; (editor with G. Gottsegen and M. Gottsegen) *Confrontation: Encounters in Self and Interpersonal Awareness,* Macmillan, 1971; *Age of Shrinks,* Darwin Press, 1979; *Psychology for Everyday Living,* Mayflower, 1980.

WORK IN PROGRESS: The Diogenes Group; Change and Behavior.

* * *

BOCOCK, Robert (James) 1940-

PERSONAL: Born September 29, 1940, in Lincoln, England; son of Frank William (a farmer) and Jessie (Drake) Bocock. *Education:* University of Leeds, B.A., 1962; University of London, diploma, 1963; Brunel University, Ph.D., 1973. *Home:* 10, Village Close, Belsize Ln., London N.W. 3, England. *Office:* Department of Sociology, Open University, Milton Keynes, Buckinghamshire, England.

CAREER: Brunel University, Uxbridge, England, lecturer in sociology, 1966-79; Open University, Buckinghamshire, England, currently lecturer in sociology. Annual lecturer at University of Birmingham; consultant to Richmond Fellowship. *Member:* International Conference of Sociology of Religion, British Sociological Association, Association of University Teachers, Association of Pastoral Care and Counseling.

WRITINGS: Ritual in Industrial Society, Allen & Unwin, 1974; *Freud and Modern Society,* Thomas Nelson, 1976; *An Introduction to Sociology,* Fontana, 1980; *Sigmund Freud,* Tavistock, 1983. Contributor to sociology journals.

WORK IN PROGRESS: Research on relations between psychoanalysis and sociology, on the sociology of morals, and on religion.

SIDELIGHTS: Robert Bocock writes: "I'm interested in the use of Freudian ideas to provide a basis for a view of man-in-society to act as a source of political legitimation in North American and West European societies, to provide an alternative to traditional Christianity (which has little appeal to bright young intellectuals in these societies), and as an alternative to Marxism (which is attractive to intellectuals, but lacks an awareness of human feelings). I aim to increase *tolerance of ambiguity* in individuals and organisations and between states."

* * *

BODE, Janet 1943-

PERSONAL: Surname is pronounced *Boe-*dy; born July 14, 1943, in New York; daughter of Carl J. (a writer and professor) and Margaret (Lutze) Bode. *Education:* University of Maryland, B.A., 1965; graduate study at Michigan State University and Bowie State College. *Residence:* New York, N.Y. *Agent:* Jean V. Naggar Literary Agency, 336 East 73rd St., Suite A, New York, N.Y. 10021.

CAREER: Writer. Has worked in Germany, Mexico, and the United States as personnel specialist, program director, community organizer, public relations director, and teacher. *Member:* National Writers Union, Authors Guild, Authors League of America. *Awards, honors:* Outstanding Social Studies Book Award, National Council for Social Studies, for *Rape: Preventing It; Coping with the Legal, Medical and Emotional Aftermath;* Best Books for Young Adults Citation, American Library Association, and selection as Notable Children's Trade Book in the Field of Social Studies, 1980, both for *Kids Having Kids: The Unwed Teenage Parent.*

WRITINGS: Kids School Lunch Bag (on the National School Lunch Program), Children's Foundation, 1972; *View from Another Closet: Exploring Bisexuality in Women,* Hawthorn, 1976; *Fighting Back: How to Cope with the Medical, Emotional and Legal Consequences of Rape,* Macmillan, 1978; *Rape: Preventing It; Coping with the Legal, Medical and Emotional Aftermath* (young adult), F. Watts, 1979; *Kids Having Kids: The Unwed Teenage Parent* (young adult), F. Watts, 1980.

Co-author of "Women against Rape" (television documentary film), 1975. Contributor of magazine articles to periodicals, including *Cosmopolitan, Redbook, New York, Medica,* and *Mademoiselle.*

WORK IN PROGRESS: Inconceivable, with Nora Coffey, for publication by Macmillan.

* * *

BODEY, Hugh (Arthur) 1939-

PERSONAL: Born January 15, 1939, in Bristol, England; son of A. E. (a chemist) and C. V. (Taylor) Bodey; married Mary Welch, July 28, 1962; children: Stephen, Andrew, Gillian. *Education:* University of Birmingham, B.A. (with honors), 1961; University of Exeter, education certificate, 1962. *Politics:* Liberal. *Religion:* Christian. *Home:* Belfield House, Poltimore, Devon EX4 0AE, England.

CAREER: Lydney Boys Secondary School, Lydney, Gloucestershire, England, teacher of history and religious studies, 1962-65; Rawthorpe County Secondary School, Huddersfield, Yorkshire, England, teacher, 1965-69; Colne Valley Museum, Golcar, Yorkshire, creator and first director, 1969-73; South Devon College of Arts and Technology, Torquay, Devon, England, lecturer in economic, industrial, and agrarian history, 1974—. Visiting lecturer, Huddersfield College of Education (Technical), 1970-74. *Member:* Society of Authors.

WRITINGS: Roads (history), Batsford, 1971; *A Bullet in My Trifle* (humor), privately printed, 1972; *Religion*, Batsford, 1973; *Industrial History in Huddersfield*, Huddersfield Public Library, 1973; *Twenty Centuries of British Industry*, David & Charles, 1975; *Discovering Industrial History and Archaeology*, Shire, 1975; *Teaching Kit: Factories*, Batsford, 1975; *Textiles*, Batsford, 1976; *Mining*, Batsford, 1976; (with Michael Hallas) *Elementary Surveying for Industrial Archaeologists*, Shire, 1977.

Roman People (young adult), David & Charles, 1981; *Immigrants and Emigrants*, David & Charles, 1982; *Nailmaking*, Shire, 1983. Contributor to *Industrial Archaeology*.

WORK IN PROGRESS: "Development of the textile industries in the Colne Valley, Yorkshire, England," for a Masters of Philosophy degree.

AVOCATIONAL INTERESTS: Gardening, photography, travel, wood turning, lecturing to adults on industrial history.

* * *

BOEGEHOLD, Betty (Doyle) 1913-
(Donovan Doyle)

PERSONAL: Surname is pronounced *Berg*-a-hold; born September 15, 1913, in New York, N.Y.; daughter of James and Myrtle Doyle; divorced; children: Karen Simon. *Education:* Wellesley College, B.A., 1935; Columbia University, M.A., 1943. *Politics:* Independent Democrat. *Religion:* Protestant. *Home:* 64 Sagamore Rd., Bronxville, N.Y. 10708. *Office:* Publications Division, Bank Street College, 610 West 112th St., New York, N.Y. 10025.

CAREER: Preschool teacher in New York City, 1936-40; elementary school teacher, librarian, assistant principal, and remedial reading specialist in Mount Vernon, N.Y., 1946-68; Bank Street College, New York City, senior editor of publications, staff writer, instructor in graduate programs, and director of writer's workshop, 1968—. Former owner of a nursery school. *Member:* Association for Childhood Education International, National Organization of Women, League of Women Voters, Common Cause, Citizens Council, Save the Children Foundation, Defenders of Wildlife, Animal Protection League, Wild Horse Organized Assistance, Fund for Animals, Friends of Animals, Phi Beta Kappa.

WRITINGS—Juveniles, except as indicated: *Three to Get Ready*, Harper, 1968; *Paw Paw's Run*, Dutton, 1969; *Pippa Mouse* (Junior Literary Guild selection), Knopf, 1973; *What the Wind Told*, Parents' Magazine Press, 1974; (with Cyndy Szekeres) *Here's Pippa Again* (Junior Literary Guild selection), Knopf, 1975; *Small Deer's Magic Tricks*, Coward, 1977; *Education before Five* (adult nonfiction), Teachers College Press, 1975; *Pippa Pops Out!*, Knopf, 1979; *Hurray for Pippa!*, Knopf, 1980; *Bear Underground*, Doubleday, 1980; *Chipper's Choices*, Coward, 1981; *In the Castle of Cats*, Dutton, 1981; (contributor and associate editor with William Hooks) *The Pleasure of Their Company: How to Have More Fun with Your Children* (adult nonfiction), Chilton, 1981.

Author of *The Carmen Book, The Jack Book, The Rosa Book,* and *The Victor Book*, all published by Macmillan. Also author, under pseudonym Donovan Doyle, of *Gray Gull, Bugs, The Old Woman Who Couldn't Keep a Secret, Almost There,* and *Perseus and Andromeda: A Retelling*, all published by Houghton.

Senior associate editor, "Bank Street Readers" series, Macmillan, 1967, and "Discovery" series, Houghton, 1976.

SIDELIGHTS: Betty Boegehold told *CA*: "I'm most interested in writing for young children—in using sensory images that will reach them—hopefully, in illuminating some small bit of their world, their concerns. I believe they deserve the best possible writing and the greatest respect—for books that touch them will not be forgotten by them. They are the most receptive of audiences—and should never be addressed as less wise than adults—only as less knowledgeable."

* * *

BOICE, James Montgomery 1938-

PERSONAL: Born July 7, 1938, in Pittsburgh, Pa.; son of G. Newton (an orthopedic surgeon) and Jean (Shick) Boice; married Linda Ann McNamara, June 9, 1962; children: Elizabeth Anne Horn, Heather Louise, Jennifer Sue. *Education:* Harvard University, A.B. (with high honors), 1960; Princeton Theological Seminary, B.D., 1963; University of Basel, D.Theol. (insigni cum laude), 1966. *Home:* 1827 Delancey Pl., Philadelphia, Pa. 19103. *Office:* Tenth Presbyterian Church, 1700 Spruce St., Philadelphia, Pa. 19103.

CAREER: Licensed in the Presbytery of Pittsburgh, Pa., 1963; *Christianity Today*, Washington, D.C., member of editorial staff, summers, 1962, 1963, assistant editor, 1966-68; Tenth Presbyterian Church, Philadelphia, Pa., pastor, 1968—; City Center Academy, Philadelphia, principal, 1983—. Speaker on "The Bible Study Hour" radio program originating in Philadelphia, 1969—.

WRITINGS: How God Can Use Nobodies, Victor Books, 1974, published as *Ordinary Men Called by God*, Victor Books, 1974; *Can You Run away from God?*, Victor Books, 1977; *Our Sovereign God*, Baker Book, 1977; *The Sovereign God*, Inter-Varsity Press, 1978; *God the Redeemer*, Inter-Varsity Press, 1978; *Awakening to God*, Inter-Varsity Press, 1979; (editor) *Making God's Word Plain*, Tenth Presbyterian Church, 1979; *Does Inerrancy Matter?*, Tyndale, 1980; *God and History*, Inter-Varsity Press, 1981; (editor) *Our Savior God*, Baker Book, 1981; *The Parables of Jesus*, Moody, 1983; *The Christ of Christmas*, Moody, 1983.

Published by Zondervan: *Witness and Revelation in the Gospel of John*, 1970; *Philippians: An Expositional Commentary*, 1971; *The Sermon on the Mount*, 1972; *How to Really Live It Up*, 1973, published as *How to Live the Christian Life*, Moody, 1982; *The Last and Future World*, 1974; *Commentary on the Gospel of John*, Volume I, 1975, Volume II, 1976, Volume III, 1977, Volume IV, 1978, Volume V, 1979; (contributor) Frank E. Gaebelin, editor, *The Expositor's Bible Commentary*, 1976; (editor) *The Foundation of Biblical Authority*, 1978; *The Epistles of John*, 1980; *Genesis*, Volume I, 1983; *The Minor Prophets*, Volume I, 1984. Contributor to religion periodicals.

WORK IN PROGRESS: Volumes II and III of *Genesis*; Volume II of *The Minor Prophets*.

BIOGRAPHICAL/CRITICAL SOURCES: *Time,* December 26, 1969.

* * *

BOMBECK, Erma 1927-

PERSONAL: Born February 21, 1927, in Dayton, Ohio; daughter of Cassius Edwin (a laborer) and Erma (Haines) Fiste; married William Bombeck (a school administrator), August 13, 1949; children: Betsy, Andrew, Matthew. *Education:* Attended Ohio University; University of Dayton, B.A., 1949. *Religion:* Roman Catholic. *Residence:* Paradise Valley, Ariz. 85253. *Mailing address:* Field Newspaper Syndicate, 1703 Kaiser Ave., Irvine, Calif. 92714.

CAREER: Author, columnist, humorist, and lecturer. *Dayton Journal-Herald,* Dayton, Ohio, writer, 1949-53; author of weekly column published in *Kettering-Oakwood Times,* 1963-65; author of thrice-weekly column, "At Wit's End," for *Dayton Journal-Herald,* 1965, syndicated to sixty-five newspapers by the Newsday Syndicate, 1965-67, and to over nine hundred newspapers by the Field Newspaper Syndicate, 1967—. Appears twice weekly on "Good Morning America," 1975—. Creator, writer, and executive producer of television series, "Maggie," produced by American Broadcasting Co., 1981. Appointed to the President's National Advisory Committee for Women, 1978. *Member:* Women in Communication, Sigma Delta Chi. *Awards, honors:* National Headliner Prize from Theta Sigma Phi, 1969; Mark Twain Award for Humor, 1973; received honorary doctorates from St. Scholastica College, Rosary College, Bowling Green University, College of Mount St. Joseph on the Ohio, Arizona State University, University of Dayton, Benedictine College, DePauw University, Southwestern at Memphis, and Loras College.

WRITINGS: At Wit's End (collection of columns; also see below), Doubleday, 1967; *Just Wait Till You Have Children of Your Own* (also see below), illustrations by Bil Keane, Doubleday, 1971; *I Lost Everything in the Post-Natal Depression* (also see below), Doubleday, 1973; *The Grass Is Always Greener over the Septic Tank,* McGraw, 1976; *If Life Is a Bowl of Cherries, What Am I Doing in the Pits?,* McGraw, 1978; *Aunt Erma's Cope Book: How to Get from Monday to Friday . . . in Twelve Days,* McGraw, 1979; *Motherhood: The Second Oldest Profession,* McGraw, 1983; *Erma Bombeck Giant Economy Size* (contains *At Wit's End, Just Wait Till You Have Children of Your Own,* and *I Lost Everything in the Post-Natal Depression*), Doubleday, 1983.

Also author of monthly column, "Up the Wall," published in *Good Housekeeping,* 1969-75. Contributor to *Reader's Digest, Family Circle, Redbook,* and *McCall's.*

SIDELIGHTS: Erma Bombeck has made a career of satirizing the various domestic crises confronting the average American household. Called everything from "America's Housewife-at-Large" by *People* to "the female Art Buchwald" by *Time,* Bombeck shares her views and opinions with millions of followers through her widely syndicated newspaper column "At Wit's End," television appearances, and her bestselling books. Diane Shah reports in *Newsweek* that "Bombeck assumes the role of straight woman in the mad world of suburbia. By rights that role should be a dud, but at a time when being a housewife is widely regarded as practically a social disease, Bombeck has become a pop phenomenon." And Seymour Rothman states in the *Toledo Blade,* "Erma's role in the column is that of a wife and mother who long ago has conceded defeat, but can't find anyone to surrender to."

Bombeck was drawn to the field of journalism at an early age. While attending high school, she worked part time as a copy girl for the *Dayton Journal-Herald* and during college she was employed as a reporter. After graduating from the University of Dayton with a degree in English, Bombeck became a staff writer for the newspaper, eventually writing feature articles for the women's section. In 1953, Bombeck resigned from her position with the *Dayton Journal-Herald* to start a family with her husband, Bill. Twelve years and three children later, Bombeck decided to return to journalism. As she explained in her book *If Life Is a Bowl of Cherries, What Am I Doing in the Pits?:* "I do not feel fulfilled cleaning chrome faucets with a toothbrush. It's my turn." Bombeck approached Ron Ginger, the editor of the *Kettering-Oakwood Times* (a local weekly newspaper), with her idea of writing a humorous column geared toward housewives. Ginger hired Bombeck and set her pay at three dollars per column. Bombeck's column soon became popular and attracted the attention of Glenn Thompson, the editor of the *Dayton Journal-Herald.* Thompson offered Bombeck a weekly salary of fifteen dollars to write three columns for his newspaper. Bombeck agreed to the offer. Sensing her potential, Thompson sent a sample of Bombeck's "At Wit's End" columns to the Newsday Syndicate suggesting they might be interested in syndicating the columns nationally. Newsday was impressed and signed Bombeck to a short-term contract. In 1967 with over sixty-five newspapers publishing her columns, Bombeck was offered a long-term contract with the Field Newspaper Syndicate, which she accepted.

Seymour Rothman of the *Toledo Blade* reports that the president of the Field Newspaper Syndicate, Robert G. Cowles, once remarked: "We've been selling Erma as a women's page feature, but we find more and more papers running her in other sections. One has her on the comic page, a number on the feature pages. . . . They found out before we did that she isn't strictly for women." Her seventeen-year partnership with the Field Newspaper Syndicate has proven profitable for Bombeck, with over 900 newspapers currently printing her column three times a week. According to a reviewer for *Time,* Bombeck's "enormous appeal contains no surprises. She has, as market researchers say, 'great demographics.' Her writing is aimed primarily at the millions of housewives whose world turns around car pools, P.T.A. meetings and Tupperware parties."

While she writes humorously about the average housewife's plight by using herself and her family as examples, Bombeck does not belittle the woman who chooses to stay at home. As she explains to an interviewer for *People:* "God knows I have laughed at her frustrations. I have dissected her and picked her apart. I have done everything to her you can imagine [over the] years. But she doesn't feel put down by it, she doesn't feel I am making fun of her, she is able to laugh at herself. If I get away with it, it's probably because I am basically one of them." Bombeck further explains to Peggy Rader of the *Akron Beacon Journal:* "My type of humor is almost pure identification. A housewife reads my column and says, 'But that's happened to ME! I know just what she's talking about!' You can't imagine what a great feeling that is for an American housewife. Basically women work alone when they're at home. They think no one is feeling what they are feeling, that no one understands their daily frustrations. But we do; we all do." Diane Shah writes in *Newsweek* that "Bombeck still prides herself on being 'just a housewife,' who really still does her own laundry." As Bombeck remarked to Shah, "I spend ninety per cent of my time living scripts and ten per cent writing them."

Lucille G. Crane feels that Bombeck helps her readers laugh at many of their problems. "Bombeck's humor is light, funny," Crane suggests in *Best Sellers*. "Household chores are always easier to do when done on her terms. Enjoyment is the key to her success, and most of her fans wish they could view life and its minor crises through her eyes. Common sense with humor is the Bombeck way." And *New York Times Book Review* critic Robert Lasson believes that women read Bombeck's books and columns because "women who inhabit the real world are told that they can achieve a fairy-tale existence simply by buying a certain vacuum cleaner or changing their brand of coffee.... They look around, these women, and something begins to dawn on them, 'Maybe I'm not the only one who isn't a [perfect] wife and mother.'" Bombeck's humor works, Lasson continues, "because it's not just wisecracks or one-liners or gags but marvelously comic insights that grow out of [her] life as organically as fungus forms between the bathroom tiles." Seymour Rothman writes in the *Toledo Blade* that "being funny is a skill, but being funny the way Erma is elevates it to an art. Erma takes a sobering situation and laces it with funny lines to an acceptable philosophic conclusion. The philosophy generally is 'Learn to enjoy frustration.'"

Bombeck's books are extensions of her columns. They are written to the same audience, about the same problems, with the same humor and insight that has endeared her to the readers of her columns. Richard R. Lingeman writes in a review of *If Life Is a Bowl of Cherries, What Am I Doing in the Pits?* published in the *New York Times Book Review*: "Her humor is precisely targeted on the large number of housewives in this country who share her experiences. Her style is a bit hectic and slapdash, sounding as though she scrawled the column on the back of a laundry list while stirring the evening's Hamburger Helper. It's the kind of style that is a half beat ahead of her readers, giving them a twitch of recognition and the feeling, 'I might have written that myself.'... Her humor is the coping kind—sarcastic shafts at fads and foibles." Although her first three books sold well, Bombeck's *The Grass Is Always Greener over the Septic Tank* sold over a half million copies in hardcover and stayed on the bestseller lists for over ten months. CBS-TV produced the book as a made-for-television movie with Carol Burnett and Charles Grodin in the lead roles. Bombeck's following three books, *If Life Is a Bowl of Cherries, What Am I Doing in the Pits?*, *Aunt Erma's Cope Book: How to Get from Monday to Friday . . . in Twelve Days*, and *Motherhood: The Second Oldest Profession* also made the bestseller lists.

Bombeck's success may be traced to the affinity between Bombeck and many of the women who read and identify with her writings. As Richard Lingeman observes: "One is left admiring Mrs. Bombeck for giving voice to a segment of the population that is not always heard from, but the trivia of whose lives may be, on the higher scale of things, as significant as anything that takes place in the male or sophisticated or urbane world. There is truth in the best of her humor, as well as sanity." But, as a *Newsweek* writer notes, Bombeck's humor appeals not only to suburban housewives: "Though her sensibility is strictly suburban, Bombeck manages to hit everybody's funny bone. [Once,] she was invited to speak to 3,500 farmers' wives in Kansas City. Fully 9,000 people turned up, and the crowd drew several hundred men as well. [And a] survey by the *Boston Globe* placed Bombeck high on the list of readers' favorites. Even a feminist like syndicated columnist Ellen Goodman admits to being a Bombeck fan." As Jane Holtz Kay states in *Ms.*: "Bombeck is not alone. She is out there where everybody's been headed this last quarter century: she is out there spinning her wheels to the suburbs in the greatest migration in American history.... And she is one of the few bards of this place and people."

MEDIA ADAPTATIONS: Two of Bombeck's lectures have been recorded and released as an album entitled "The Family That Plays Together Gets on Each Other's Nerves" by Warner Bros. Records in 1977; *The Grass Is Always Greener over the Septic Tank* was produced as a made-for-television movie by Columbia Broadcasting Systems in October, 1978.

CA INTERVIEW

CA interviewed Erma Bombeck by telephone on July 21, 1983, at her home in Paradise Valley, Arizona.

CA: Your "Justa Housewife" humor may have diverted millions of dollars from psychiatrists' pockets by helping women through the days of dirty diapers and screaming carpools. Did you have any idea when you started writing the column back in 1964 that it would make so many women laugh and feel better?

BOMBECK: Not a clue, no. It started off as an outlet for my own feelings, for my own survival, and that's truly all it was. When it was a weekly, I could hardly wait until the next week rolled around so I could get on with the next topic I wanted to get off my chest. It was a real bonus when people started to respond to it and say, "My god, lady, I feel the same way!" That had to be something of a plus for me. Here I was getting it all off my chest, and to find out that I was normal too (I never said *average*, but *normal*)—you can't imagine the relief! And I think that's probably what happened to most of us who were raised in an era of perfection where you do it all and you do it right; you don't complain about it, you just love it, because you're supposed to. To be so irreverent as to come right out and say, you know, this is not a religious experience . . . well, you wonder about yourself.

CA: Describing your own growing up in the Haymarket district of Dayton, Ohio, after your father died, you told Phyllis Batelle for Good Housekeeping *(April 1978): "We were poor. I'd just have been worried sick if I'd known. But I thought it was a really neat neighborhood." Where did the funniness come from? Were there lots of good times and laughter in your family?*

BOMBECK: Yes, and I don't know why. We had to be the strangest people in the world to laugh with so little to laugh about. My father died when I was nine. My mother had a fourth-grade education and got a job in a factory, and we lived with my grandmother. It was like one of those William Saroyan plays where you have a cast of fifty thousand and you're all related but you really don't know each other very well. We just moved around in this old house in this wonderfully integrated ethnic neighborhood. I went to synagogue on Saturday morning—I'm not Jewish. I went to a tent revival on Saturday night—I'm not a revivalist. I went to the Catholic church on Sunday, and at that time I was not a Catholic. It was one of those wonderful times when you made something to do and you had the friends to do it with, which is something my kids never had. They were in a very controlled neighborhood—you know how it is in the suburbs, where we all eat the same thing and think the same thoughts and wear the same pajamas and, my god, we are dull!

CA: Much of your humor centers on children and parenthood. Though the children in the column were semifictional, as you've said, and you were always careful not to violate your own children's privacy in your writing, were there ever times when the resemblance became too close and feelings were hurt?

BOMBECK: I'm not naive enough to think that I never got too close to the truth or too close to personal feelings. I don't *know* if I did, because my kids never told me. They've handled it so well and made it so easy for me. But I would suspect there have been times when they were maybe a little embarrassed by something I'd written. Maybe kids at school would say, "Did that really happen to you?" and they'd have to deal with that. Probably there were those moments. I didn't do it purposely to hurt anyone; it was just that I was caught up in a time of really writing some truths, and I'm afraid you get too close to it sometimes.

CA: How did you manage to write so steadily with the children at home?

BOMBECK: I don't know if this is a blessing or not, but I do seem to be able to block out everything around me. It could be from early reporting days, when there would be seventy-five people milling around the newsroom and you'd have to shut them out and think only of what was in your typewriter. It may have been that training, or it could have been the fact that I wanted to block it out. A psychiatrist could have a field day with me, I bet. But I always worked at home in the middle of some traffic pattern, whether it was outside of the only bathroom in the house or in the kitchen in front of the refrigerator. I always had people around me, and I could block it out and concentrate. I can do it now, just pull myself over to the side and think of anything else, and I won't even know there's anyone here. Maybe that's a blessing. I don't know.

CA: You've said you like the comedy of Bob Newhart, Steve Martin, Fred Allen, and Jonathan Winters. Are there any female performers you especially enjoy?

BOMBECK: Yes. All the comedians I like have one thing in common. They're all unique, fresh—they don't steal from anybody; they don't have to. They break new ground and they break rules that have not been broken before. I like that with comedy. I like the original models. Yes, there are women comedians I like. I've always credited Phyllis Diller with being the first who was irreverent about husbands, children, and housework. She really was the forerunner of us all. She was making jokes about rainbows over the diapers, and her dream in life was to have a stove that flushed. She was way out there before anyone else, and we all laughed and said, "Oh, isn't she crazy." Phyllis, you know, had five kids. She knew what she wrote and spoke about. Everyone said she was a stand-up comic, but she was more than that; she was reflecting a real social period out there that was just beginning to come into its own. Then, of course, there's Joan Rivers. I laugh at her, my god! Outrageous! How she has the guts to say the things she does, I don't know.

CA: Humor, however hyperbolic it may be, has to be rooted in some truth that its audience knows deep down. Has the shifting status of women over the past twenty years changed your audience?

BOMBECK: Yes, I suspect it has. I never had a great problem, though, and this has always surprised some people. A lot of men ask me, "Gosh, what does the women's movement think of you?" Well, the fact that they ask the question shows they know nothing about the women's movement. The women's movement was never against domesticity; it was very realistic about what we had. Consequently, I get along extremely well with the women's movement and consider myself a feminist, so I never had any problem with that. In order to function now, the humor has to be broader. It has to affect more women and it has to hit them where they live. In that respect, I think the audience has changed, which has changed the writing. The writing had to grow with the audience. You can't stagnate and be giving household hints when sixty percent of the women are holding down another job. What to do with nylon net is no longer important to them.

CA: In recent years you've been an active supporter of the Equal Rights Amendment. Before that, however, you were fairly apolitical, weren't you?

BOMBECK: I was. I wasn't in the closet—I mean, it's too crowded in there—but I was probably having some difficulty in justifying coming out for something like that and mixing it with the writing. I wasn't sure that I could or even that I wanted to, and I still have not dealt with the ERA in any column. All my speeches have been on my own, separate from my writing. But the feeling is not new; it's always been there.

CA: Was there something in particular that made you start speaking out?

BOMBECK: I had been sitting here thinking, this thing's going to happen; why wouldn't it? I couldn't see any problem with the words "equality under the law," because I'm a great believer in the law, and you change the law to fit your needs. That's what we've been doing for two hundred years. We have not lived one hundred percent by the Constitution; we've been interpreting. When the time came that I saw the ERA movement was faltering and there was a possibility that it might not succeed, I thought, I've got to get out there and do something about this. I think that was the prod I needed to become involved.

And I worked long and hard at it. I wasn't one of those celebrities who just went out and waved and smiled a lot. I did my homework, so I was on very firm ground. I knew why I believed as I did, and I was out to influence other people, no doubt about it. I didn't influence that many, obviously.

CA: Do you think the Equal Rights Amendment will be passed someday?

BOMBECK: It has to be. We fought for fifty years for the right to vote, you know. We've just begun with this.

CA: Let's talk about another one of your favorite topics. All of us over a certain age know about cod-liver oil and guilt. Do you think the current generation of young women is as affected by feelings of guilt and inadequacy as ours has been?

BOMBECK: Oh yes. Guilt will always be with us. I know. My mother invented guilt in 1927 and I remember her first remark to me was, "The fact that you were born during the Depression is probably a coincidence, but we will never be sure, will we?" And from then on it was one such remark after the other. Now I am also a carrier and have passed it on to my children, who will pass it on to their children. Yes, guilt sustains us, actually. It's the glue that keeps us all together.

CA: I think my favorite of your books is Aunt Erma's Cope Book: How to Get from Monday to Friday . . . in Twelve Days *(1979) because of its lovely satire on the self-help books that proliferated in the 1970s. Do you think we're over that phase?*

BOMBECK: Yes, absolutely. We are over it. I think we got bored to death thinking about ourselves. You know, I'm not that deep a person—maybe a sixteenth of an inch. Sometimes I go on book-promotion tours. You have to talk about yourself for five weeks. Well, I can sustain a thirty-minute phone conservation. Beyond that, your teeth begin to nod off. No one's really that interesting. But I do think the self-help books accomplished something. I'm not too sure what "get in touch with your feelings" means, but I think it got us on a positive note. We have been anti-everything for so long. That got us back to thinking about doing some good, starting with ourselves. Now I think it's time we stop thinking about ourselves and start thinking about the rest of the world. I hope so. Let's get on with it, because I'm really bored.

CA: It was a funny time, the '70s.

BOMBECK: In fact, my agent was here the other day and we were talking about how that book just made it. Timing is everything with books, and that period was beginning to wind down when the book came out. I think the paperback missed the market. It came out about a year later, and by then the fever had peaked and gone down. In the new book I've taken on motherhood. I should be safe with that; I think it's in for a while.

CA: Do you have trouble writing on schedule to meet your deadlines?

BOMBECK: I made a ridiculous statement about that just last week at the Academy of Achievement. That's a gathering of celebrities from every walk of life you could think of with selected exceptional high school students. You roam around for three days and these kids have access to you; they can sit at breakfast with you and ask questions about your career, and was success what you thought it would be, and all that. It's a real one-on-one thing. And one of the things I told them was that writer's block was like North Dakota: it did not exist. I'd never been to North Dakota; no one had ever seen it. Do you personally know anyone from North Dakota? Of course you don't! Well, I swear to you, everyone in the room was from North Dakota. I don't know where all those people came from, but there they were. It was terrible. That's probably the only thing they will remember. But, like North Dakota, writer's block does not exist. Write humor on demand? Of course you can. I hear these literary people all the time say you can't force anything. Of course you can. I do it three times a week, twenty years now.

CA: You were previously a member of the President's National Advisory Committee for Women. What has happened to the committee?

BOMBECK: It was abandoned. When one president goes out of office, the new president appoints this commission to serve as a sounding board for women everywhere: what they're thinking, what they want, what they need, what bills are relevant to them. This has been done since Eisenhower. When President Reagan came in, we wanted to resign and have him appoint a new group to take over. It never happened. We wrote many letters saying, we're still here; what are you going to do with us? Well, he did nothing with us. And so, as of this point, there is no commission. It's not a commission, you understand, that costs the taxpayers any money. Considering the brains of those forty women, the taxpayers could never have afforded them, not in their wildest imagination. We were volunteers. The only thing we had paid for us was our airplane ticket to Washington and back; we footed the bill for everything else. I felt that we did some good just by our being. But we have no commission now.

CA: Are you still giving lectures?

BOMBECK: No, I have not been on the lecture circuits for six years. When I started to do "Good Morning America," something had to give. I am a person; I only have so many hours in the day. And I thought to write three columns, and to write and perform two scripts a week and do the other things I do, something had to give. Lecturing was my least favorite thing. I don't like to travel. I don't like to leave home, I don't like to sit around watching cartoons in the morning in some strange hotel room, I don't like plastic on my glasses. So I stopped. I have given some benefit lectures since then for a few causes, like displaced homemakers, the Kidney Foundation, battered wives and children—groups that were cut to the bone financially and staged benefits to keep their doors open. But I'm not really lecturing.

CA: You give your husband a great deal of credit for his encouragement of your work, don't you?

BOMBECK: I sure do. It sounds very nonfeminist to say he allows me to *be*. But that's not an easy thing. I don't think people truly appreciate what men who are married to women like me in flashy professions have to put up with. People don't know what they're talking about when they say, "Well, why shouldn't they?" It's not just a matter of having a wife who is visible; there's more to it than that. These little part-time jobs we have really, and I mean *really*, take a lot away from our time with our husbands. It's not easy to be in their position. We ask for a great deal of understanding. We go places as a couple and the wife is swept up in some momentum while the husband is left by the door until somebody finally says, "What's your name? I'll make you a name tag." They suffer a lot of cruelties and lot of put-downs. It should never be that way, but unfortunately it is. For both my husband and me to work and try to have some kind of a personal and family life and to sustain a marriage that's thirty-four years old takes some effort on both our parts, and I must say he is amazing. He has a great deal of self-worth to put up with it.

CA: What writing are you doing for television now?

BOMBECK: Only what I perform myself. I've learned a lot with my ill-fated sitcom. I belong to a huge number of people who have bombed out—not that that makes you feel any better; everybody wants to be a success and be among the elite few. But it happens. Some member of the press called me right afterward and said, "Tell me what your feelings are at being a failure." I said, "You have the words wrong. I failed at something; I am not a failure." That's truly the way I felt, because I could see that so many people were in the same boat out there. There were something like fifteen new sitcoms at the time, and I think two of them survived. The mortality rate is amazing. I felt sorry for the cast and crew and all the people who worked so hard. But it was not devastating to me personally. I really learned a lot; I'd never written a script before in my life. (Maybe that showed!)

CA: Is there any kind of writing you haven't done that you'd like to try?

BOMBECK: I would like to try a play.

CA: You seem to be working harder than ever, at a time when you should, to borrow your words, "be eating chocolate sandwiches and getting up at the crack of noon." Does the future hold any plans for the rest that you've earned many times over?

BOMBECK: Well, you know, I quit every other day. I tell my friend Abigail Van Buren—"Dear Abby"—every five minutes, "I'm quitting. I'm quitting at the end of next week." She knows I'm lying. I get involved in all these things and I think, I don't need this, why am I doing this, and I have no answer for myself. Something else will come up that's challenging and I get excited about it. I'm just like a child; I think, oh, that would be so much fun to do. If I'm doing a special interview or some special segment for ABC, I get all excited about that as I watch it go together. It's just a real kick for me. I am still stimulated by all of it, and that's what keeps me going.

I think if you're bored, if you don't know it, your readers or your viewers are the first to know. I would feel myself sometimes during a lecture getting tired of hearing myself speak. That's deadly. If you don't have the enthusiasm, then how can you expect those people to keep awake out there in the audience? You have to bring some kind of your own vitality to what you're doing. That was not happening in the lectures toward the last, and I realized I was just exhausted from it. But whenever I get an idea that is brand new and fresh and I think, why didn't I think of that before, I get just like a kid.

BIOGRAPHICAL/CRITICAL SOURCES: Time, April 13, 1970, May 29, 1978; *Publishers Weekly,* July 19, 1971, June 11, 1973, March 13, 1978, September 10, 1978; *Best Sellers,* November 15, 1971, September 1, 1973, January, 1977, July, 1978, December, 1979; *New York Times Book Review,* October 7, 1973, July 3, 1977, April 30, 1978, November 18, 1979; *Toledo Blade,* February 16, 1975; *Akron Beacon Journal,* May 9, 1975; *Authors in the News,* Volume I, Gale, 1976; *Christian Science Monitor,* October 8, 1976; *Library Journal,* November 15, 1976, October 15, 1979; *Ms.,* June, 1977; Erma Bombeck, *If Life Is a Bowl of Cherries, What Am I Doing in the Pits?,* McGraw, 1978; *Newsweek,* January 2, 1978; *Good Housekeeping,* April, 1978; *Kirkus Reviews,* April 1, 1978, September 1, 1979; *People,* May 22, 1978, November 9, 1981.

—Sketch by Margaret Mazurkiewicz

—Interview by Jean W. Ross

* * *

BOONE, Daniel R. 1927-

PERSONAL: Born October 30, 1927, in Chicago, Ill.; son of Claude B. (a salesman) and Pearl L. (Richardson) Boone; married Mary M. Mosenthal, December 28, 1954; children: Penny, James, Robbie, Rebecca. *Education:* University of Redlands, B.A., 1951; Western Reserve University (now Case Western Reserve University), M.A., 1954, Ph.D., 1958. *Politics:* Democrat. *Religion:* Christian. *Office:* Department of Speech and Hearing Sciences, University of Arizona, Tucson, Ariz. 85721.

CAREER: Highland View Hospital, Cleveland, Ohio, chief of audiology and speech pathology, 1956-60; Western Reserve University (now Case Western Reserve University), Cleveland, assistant professor of speech pathology, 1960-63; University of Kansas, Kansas City, associate professor of speech pathology, 1963-66; University of Denver, Denver, Colo., professor of speech pathology, 1966-73; currently professor and director of speech pathology, University of Arizona, Tucson. Member of Board of Professional Services, American Cancer Society; member of board of directors, Cerebral Palsy Foundation. *Military service:* U.S. Army, 1945-47. *Member:* American Speech and Hearing Association (fellow; vice-president, 1969; president, 1976), Academy of Aphasia, Colorado Speech and Hearing Association (president, 1972), Arizona Speech-Language-Hearing Association, Sigma Xi.

WRITINGS: An Adult Has Aphasia, Interstate, 1965; *The Voice and Voice Therapy,* Prentice-Hall, 1971, 3rd edition, 1983; *Cerebral Palsy,* Bobbs-Merrill, 1972; (with Marcia Campbell) *The Microphonograph Program for Aphasia: Practice in Listening and Speaking Transcript,* Communication Skill Builders, 1983; (with Campbell) *The Microphonograph Program for Aphasia: Practice in Listening and Speaking Instructional Manual,* Communication Skill Builders, 1983. Also author of *Ripe Tomatoes, None, None, None,* and *Nostril Hair and Other Human Maladies,* all humor books. Contributor of over fifty articles to professional journals.

WORK IN PROGRESS: Human Communication and Its Disorders, for Prentice-Hall.

SIDELIGHTS: Daniel R. Boone told *CA:* "Writing for technical-professional books and articles is easier and more successful for me than writing fiction. That is, if one uses the external yardstick of commercial success, I have good luck with my professional writing as a professor of speech pathology. My gut level need, however, is to write fiction. After three attempts at writing humor books, each piece (*Ripe Tomatoes, None, None, None,* and *Nostril Hair and Other Human Maladies*) remains unpublished. Writing books about speech pathology topics requires an obvious discipline, responding to the need for professional peer review and the need to reference what one says. When I write fiction, I feel freer at the typewriter and am less likely to write, edit, rewrite. I suspect that it is this false feeling of freedom that contributes somewhat to the lack of quality that apparently characterizes my works of fiction. Publishers of texts and professional books seek me out as an author; the fiction editors hardly look at my unsolicited manuscripts."

* * *

BOUMAN, Pieter M(arinus) 1938-

PERSONAL: Born July 9, 1938, in Gent, Belgium; son of Jan-Arie (a bookkeeper) and Maria-Jozina (Moens) Bouman; married Irene Anderson Smith, May 24, 1978; children: (previous marriage) Anne-Marie, Irene, Peter. *Education:* Protestant Theological Faculty, Brussels, Licencie in Protestant Theology, 1961, Doctor in Protestant Theology, 1983; attended Protestant Theological Faculty, Paris, and University of Paris, Sorbonne, Institut des Hautes Etudes Religieuses, 1961-62. *Politics:* Socialist-Marxist. *Religion:* Reformed. *Office:* Parish Minister, United Protestant Church of Belgium, Louvain, Belgium.

CAREER: Ecumenical youth secretary for Belgium, Federation des Eglises Protestantes de Belgique, 1962-65; World Council of Churches, Geneva, Switzerland, and United Nations Food and Agriculture Organization, Rome, Italy, member of staff of Freedom from Hunger Campaign and Young World Program, 1965-68; general secretary, Ecumenical Youth Council for Europe, 1968-73; World Council of Churches, Geneva, Europe secretary, Programme Unit on Justice and Service, 1973-79; United Protestant Church of Belgium, Louvain, parish minister and personal adviser to president, 1979—. Staff officer for adult education, Stichting Lodewyk de Raet. *Member:* Sjaloom-Group (founding member).

WRITINGS: Can the World Share the Wealth?, Friendship, 1969; *Die Satten und die Habenichtse,* Burckhardthaus (West Germany), 1970; *Tears and Rejoicing: The History of European Inter-Church Aid, 1922-1956, a Critique,* I.D.S. (Brussels), 1983. Contributor to *Diepgang, Dux, Op Vrije Voeten, Risk,* and other ecumenical reviews.

WORK IN PROGRESS: Researching a short but comprehensive history of the Ecumenical movement and Protestantism in Belgium today.

SIDELIGHTS: Pieter M. Bouman has traveled in the Middle East, Africa, eastern and western Europe, United States, Canada, and Latin America.

* * *

BOURNE, L(arry) S(tuart) 1939-

PERSONAL: Born December 24, 1939, in London, Ontario, Canada; son of Stuart Howard (a mechanic) and Florence (Adams) Bourne; married Paula O'Neill (an educational researcher), August 14, 1967; children: David Stuart Alexander, Alexandra Lucy Elisabeth. *Education:* University of Western Ontario, B.A. (with honors), 1961; University of Alberta, M.A., 1963; University of Chicago, Ph.D., 1966. *Home:* 26 Anderson Ave., Toronto, Ontario, Canada M5P 1H4. *Office:* Centre for Urban and Community Studies, University of Toronto, 455 Spaldina Ave., Toronto, Ontario, Canada M5S 1A1.

CAREER: University of Toronto, Toronto, Ontario, assistant professor, 1966-69, associate professor, 1969-73, professor of geography, 1973—, Centre for Urban and Community Studies, associate director, 1969-72, director, 1972—. *Member:* Association of American Geographers, Canadian Association of Geographers, Canadian Association of University Teachers, Urban Studies Association, Regional Science Association, Land Economics Fraternity, Urban Affairs Association.

WRITINGS: Private Redevelopment of the Central City, University of Chicago, 1967; (editor) *Internal Structure of the City,* Oxford University Press, 1971, 2nd edition, 1982; (editor) *Urban Systems Development in Central Canada: Selected Papers,* University of Toronto Press, 1972; (editor) *The Form of Cities in Central Canada,* University of Toronto Press, 1973; (editor) *Urban Futures for Central Canada,* University of Toronto Press, 1974; *Urban Systems: Strategies for Regulation,* Oxford University Press, 1975; (editor) *Systems of Cities,* Oxford University Press, 1978; (editor) *Urban Housing Markets,* University of Toronto Press, 1979; *Geography of Housing,* Edward Arnold, 1981.

* * *

BOWKER, John (Westerdale) 1935-

PERSONAL: Born July 30, 1935, in London, England; son of Gordon Westerdale and Marguerite Bowker; married Margaret Roper (a university lecturer), June 22, 1963; children: David Charles. *Education:* Oxford University, B.A., 1958. *Home:* The Cottage, Bailrigg Lane, Lancaster, England. *Office:* Department of Religious Studies, University of Lancaster, Lancaster, England.

CAREER: Cambridge University, Cambridge, England, fellow of Corpus Christi College, 1962-74, university assistant lecturer, 1965, university lecturer, 1969; University of Lancaster, Lancaster, England, professor of religious studies, 1974—. Wilde Lecturer, Oxford University, 1972-75.

WRITINGS: The Targums and Rabbinic Literature: An Introduction to Jewish Interpretations of Scripture, Cambridge University Press, 1969; (contributor) *Making Moral Decisions,* S.P.C.K., 1969; *Problems of Suffering in Religions of the World,* Cambridge University Press, 1970; *The Sense of God: Sociological, Anthropological and Psychological Approaches to the Origin of the Sense of God,* Oxford University Press, 1973; *Uncle Bolpenny Tries Things Out,* Faber, 1973; *Jesus and the Pharisees,* Cambridge University Press, 1973; *The Religious Imagination and the Sense of God,* Oxford University Press, 1978; *Worlds of Faith: Religious Belief and Practice in Britain Today,* Ariel Books, 1983; (editor) *Senses and Culture: The Function and Management of Aggression and Cooperation in Biocultural Evolution,* Zygon, 1983.

WORK IN PROGRESS: A new approach to Christology based on the interpretation of the person of Christ in his original Jewish setting; a study of contemporary science and religion; editing *The Oxford Companion to Religions.*

* * *

BOYD, Waldo T. 1918-
(Ted Andersen, Karl Andreassen, Robert Parker)

PERSONAL: Born February 4, 1918, in Wiergor Township, Wis.; son of Walter S. (a farmer) and Mary S. (Reid) Boyd; married Anna B. Anker (an accountant and bookkeeper), July 19, 1941; children: Tahirih Ann (Mrs. Lowell Bell), Anna Ruhiyyih (Mrs. John Beaman). *Education:* Attended high school in West Des Moines, Iowa. *Politics:* "Uncommitted." *Religion:* Baha'i. *Mailing address:* P.O. Box 86, Geyserville, Calif. 95441.

CAREER: U.S. Navy, 1936-40, 1941-45, served as warrant radio electrician (radar) in South Pacific during World War II; teacher of electronics at technical high school in Des Moines, Iowa, 1945-47; field electronics engineer in Germany, Philco Corp., 1948-50; Dianetic Foundation, Wichita, Kan., director of public relations and publications, 1950-53; Aerojet-General Corp., Sacramento, Calif., manager of publications department, 1956-65; Baha'i School, Geyserville, Calif., manager, 1967-71. Electronics consultant to schools for the handicapped. Holds Federal Communications Commission general radiotelephone operator's license, California vocational teaching credential and is a licensed radio amateur, advanced class. *Member:* Authors League of America, Science Fiction Writers of America, California Writer's Club (president, 1966; president of central board, 1981-83).

WRITINGS: Your Career in the Aerospace Industry (Junior Literary Guild selection), Messner, 1966; *Your Career in Oceanology,* Messner, 1968; *The World of Cryogenics,* Putnam, 1968; *The World of Energy Storage,* Putnam, 1977; *Fiber Optics Communications: Experiments and Projects,* Sams, 1981. Contributor to *Popular Electronics, Popular Science, IF Science Fiction,* and other publications, some articles under pseudonyms.

WORK IN PROGRESS: *Baha'i: The Kingdom at Last; Cryptology for the Computer.*

SIDELIGHTS: Waldo T. Boyd wrote *CA:* "I began reading at an early age—four years. My mother had given me her favorite author's name, Ralph Waldo Emerson, and spent many hours reading to me as she cradled me in her arms. She recited poetry until I learned many of the epic poems by the time I could read, then introduced me to books of a kind not found among the adventures of Dick and Jane. I read the works of Shakespeare during my tenth year, and continued reading everything available from neighbor's bookshelves, particularly science fiction. Where reading blended into writing I don't quite recall, but there is a kinship.

"I joined the U.S. Navy at 18, and became a radioman and eventually a radar engineer, and continued to write. After discovering the Dvorak Simplified Keyboard my typing speed jumped to over 100 w.p.m., and I was 'hooked on writing' for life. I write with two feelings in my heart: I love learning, seeking always for Basic Truth, and to write is the best way to translate that learning to the world of the practical; secondly, I have a desire to share what I find with others.

"My advice to aspiring writers is to exercise an inquiring mind, and write, write, write. There can be not excuse for not writing at least one word a day, and as long as you are writing one, stretch a bit and put in a thousand for the day. You will develop your style by writing, and it will not hurt to read reams of poetry, the better to get some poetic nuance into your prose.

"It is seldom mentioned that there are a number of 'basic' professions. Among these are teaching, medicine, law, and communicating. If you are to be a writer, you will eventually find that you are once and forever, a communicator.

"I believe that much of the best material never sees the light of print. And far too much of what is printed becomes remaindered and lost to succeeding generations simply because the publisher cannot afford to keep books in the warehouse. Also, the art of reading is slowly withering as television becomes the prime source of news, science, drama, and education. And now the computer has entered the scene . . . who can predict its eventual impact on books?"

AVOCATIONAL INTERESTS: Building an electronic, computer peripheral Wurlitzer-style organ; experimenting with electrical effects on plant growth; conducting research into psi-functions of human beings, especially clairvoyance.

* * *

BOYLE, Robert H. 1928-

PERSONAL: Born August 21, 1928, in Brooklyn, N.Y.; son of Robert H. (a ship's engineer) and Elizabeth (Condouris) Boyle; married Jane C. Sanger, January 7, 1956 (died, 1975); married Kathryn Belous, July 31, 1977; children: (first marriage) Stephanie, Peter, R. Alexander. *Education:* Trinity College, Hartford, Conn., B.A., 1949; Yale University, M.A., 1950. *Politics:* Independent. *Religion:* Roman Catholic. *Home:* Lane Gate Rd., Cold Springs, N.Y. 10516. *Agent:* John Cushman Associates, 24 East 38th St., New York, N.Y. 10016. *Office: Sports Illustrated,* Time-Life Building, New York, N.Y.

CAREER: Employed by United Press, New York City, 1953-54; *Sports Illustrated,* New York City, staff writer, 1954-56; *Sports Illustrated* and *Time,* San Francisco, Calif., and Chicago, Ill., member of bureau and staff correspondent, 1956-60; *Sports Illustrated,* New York City, senior editor, 1960—.

Military service: U.S. Marine Corps, 1950-52; served as officer.

MEMBER: Hudson River Fishermen's Association (president). *Awards, honors:* Salmo Award, Theodore Gordon Flyfishers, 1965, for conservation articles in *Sports Illustrated;* Trinity College alumni medal, 1971; *Outdoor Life* Conservation Award, 1976, for work and writings on PCB contamination of the Hudson River; Conservation Communication Award, National Wildlife Federation, 1981, for articles on acid rain and the Florida environment.

WRITINGS: *Sport: Mirror of American Life,* Little, Brown, 1963; *The Hudson River,* Norton, 1969, expanded edition, 1979; (with others) *The Water Hustlers,* Sierra Club, 1971; (editor with Dave Whitlock) *The Fly Tyer's Almanac,* Crown, 1975; (editor with Whitlock) *The Second Fly Tyer's Almanac,* Lippincott, 1978; (with the Environmental Defense Fund) *Malignant Neglect,* Knopf, 1979; *Bass,* Norton, 1980; (with Eric Leiser) *Stoneflies for the Angler,* Knopf, 1982; (with son, R. Alexander Boyle) *Acid Rain,* Nick Lyons/Schocken, 1983; *At the Top of Their Game,* Nick Lyons/Schocken, 1983.

SIDELIGHTS: Robert Boyle's *Malignant Neglect* is "a detailed report on the cancer-causing agents that abound in our environment, how they cause cancer, and how many of them may be avoided or eliminated," writes Bayard Webster of the *New York Times.* Written with the Environmental Defense Fund, an ecology activist group, the book is, according to Philip Shabecoff of the *New York Times,* "a valuable work that makes clear that cancer is not a formless, irresistible scourge, but an enemy that can be thwarted. Not to read it would be to do oneself a disservice."

Boyle told *CA* he is "active in conservation work because I have no wish to see natural resources destroyed for what is mistakenly called progress." In 1980, Boyle signed an agreement with Hudson River utility companies on behalf of the Hudson River Fishermen's Association. The agreement put an end to a 17-year fight with Con Ed over the building of a pumped storage power plant. It also established the Hudson River Foundation for Science and Environmental Research, an independent foundation financed by the utilities. "My position," Boyle told *CA,* "was that the utilities had to pay for the damage they had done to the Hudson over the years. The Hudson is now the only river in the world with its own endowment."

BIOGRAPHICAL/CRITICAL SOURCES: *Washington Post,* June 7, 1979; *New York Times,* September 4, 1979, October 15, 1979, July 7, 1983; *Chicago Tribune Book World,* December 7, 1980; *New York Times Book Review,* July 24, 1983.

* * *

BRAINARD, Joe 1942-

PERSONAL: Born March 11, 1942, in Salem, Ark. *Home:* 8 Greene St., New York, N.Y. 10013. *Agent:* Fischbach Gallery, 29 West 57th St., New York, N.Y. 10019 (paintings).

CAREER: Painter, illustrator, and writer.

WRITINGS: *A Chair That Folds: A Collaborative Work by Joe Brainard and _____ (Sign Here),* Patsy Press, 1965; (with Ron Padgett) *100,000 Fleeing Hilda,* Boke Press, 1967; (with others) *Best & Company,* edited by Bill Berkson, [New York], 1969; *I Remember,* Angel Hair Books, 1970; *Bolinas Journal,* Big Sky, 1971; *Some Drawings of Some Notes to Myself,* Siamese Banana Press, 1971; (with Berkson) *Recent*

Visitors, Boke Press, 1971; *Selected Writings, 1962-1971,* Kulchur Foundation, 1971; (with Tom Clark) *Neil Young,* Boke Press, 1971; *The Banana Book,* Siamese Banana Press, 1972; *The Cigarette Book,* Siamese Banana Press, 1972; *The Friendly Way,* Siamese Banana Press, 1972; *I Remember More,* Angel Hair Books, 1972; (with Kenward Elmslie) *Shiny Ride,* Boke Press, 1972; (with Anne Waldman) *Self Portrait,* Siamese Banana Press, 1972; (illustrator) Waldman, *West Indies Poems,* Adventures in Poetry, 1972; *I Remember Christmas,* Museum of Modern Art, 1973; *New Work* (stories and poems), Black Sparrow Press, 1973; (illustrator) Robert Creeley, *The Class of '47,* Bouwerie Editions, 1973; (illustrator) Ted Berrigan, *The Drunken Boat,* [New York], 1974.

(With H. Freeman) *Brainard-Freeman Notebooks,* introduction by John Ashberry and Phil Demeyes, Gegenschein, 1975; (illustrator) Ashberry, *The Vermont Notebook,* Black Sparrow Press, 1975; (illustrator) Jonathan Williams, *gAy BCs: With Drawings by Joe Brainard (In the Action Comix Manner) / by Jonathan Williams (In the Absolutely Innocent, Dead-pan Manner of Kate Greenaway),* Final Press, 1976; (with Bill Berkson) *I Love You de Kooning,* The Authors and the Artists, 1977; *29 Mini-Essays,* Z Press, 1978; (illustrator) Elmslie, *The Champ,* Black Sparrow Press, 1978; *Nothing to Write Home About,* Little Caesar Press, 1981.

Also author of *Deep Freeze* and *Flesh Game,* both with Bill Berkson. Illustrator of *Living with Chris,* by Ted Berrigan, for Boke Press.

BIOGRAPHICAL/CRITICAL SOURCES: Nation, December 14, 1974; *Village Voice,* August 16, 1976, September 15, 1978; *Poetry,* December, 1976; *Village Voice Literary Supplement,* September, 1982.

* * *

BRALY, Malcolm 1925-1980

PERSONAL: Surname is pronounced *Braw*-lee; born July 16, 1925, in Portland, Ore.; died in an automobile accident, April 7, 1980, in Baltimore, Md.; son of James W. and Catherine (Cole) Braly; married second wife, Kristin; children: (first marriage) Steven, Ananda; (second marriage) Miriam. *Education:* Left high school before graduation. *Agent:* Knox Burger Associates, 39½ Washington Square South, New York, N.Y. 10012.

CAREER: Writer. Released from prison in 1965; University of Maryland, Baltimore County, writer-in-residence, 1980. *Awards, honors:* Mystery Writers of America scroll for *Felony Tank,* runner-up as best first mystery novel of 1961.

WRITINGS—Novels, except as indicated: *Felony Tank,* Fawcett, 1961; *Shake Him Till He Rattles,* Fawcett, 1963; *It's Cold Out There,* Fawcett, 1966; *On the Yard,* Little, Brown, 1967; *False Starts: A Memoir of San Quentin and Other Prisons,* Little, Brown, 1976; "On the Yard" (screenplay), Midwest Films, 1979; *The Protector,* Jove Publications, 1979. Contributor to *Esquire* and *Playboy.*

SIDELIGHTS: By the time he was forty years old, Malcolm Braly had spent some 17 years in prison for burglaries he had committed. Braly later drew upon his prison experiences when writing his books, recreating prison life in an honest and unadorned prose. His prison novel *On the Yard* and his nonfiction book *False Starts: A Memoir of San Quentin and Other Prisons* were thought by several critics to be among the finest books written in their genres.

On the Yard tells the story of Chilly Willy, a San Quentin inmate who runs the prison's black market and bookmaking operations. When Willy becomes too powerful, the prison authorities work to undermine his power and break him down. Braly presents a gallery of eccentric prison characters, including Stick, a young killer with Nazi sympathies who attempts a prison escape in a hot air balloon. But, Kenneth Lamott wrote in *Book World,* "Braly has given us a good deal more than an expertly presented gallery of grotesques. *On the Yard* is not only a taut and lean story, it is also a convincing testament to the final bankruptcy of a hundred years of our best thinking about prisons and prisoners." Richard Rhodes of the *New York Times Book Review* found an ambivalence in the story of Willy's destruction. "Braly," he wrote, "gives both sides of the story with the conviction of an intelligent inmate, trying to decide which side is right—and realizing, somewhere behind verbalization, that neither side can be right."

The simplicity and directness of Braly's writing and the painful honesty with which he approached his subject were praised by several critics. Braly, Lamott stated, "writes plainly and directly and has fashioned his story so that it drives ahead under its own power." Rhodes believed that "Braly wisely refuses to generalize San Quentin. He sticks to blunt specifics to make his case and makes it with an earnestness that is nevertheless complex and profound." "Braly," wrote H. Bruce Franklin in an article for *Contemporary Literature,* "magnificently describes the deadening sameness of prison, the fantasies that make possible life within it and that cause the extinction of many of these lives, the society of losers who play at being winners, the mindless power of the system and the impotent creativity of its victims, the ways in which the inmates reproduce the exploitative relationships of the capitalist society which has entrapped them, the diversity and potential of the thousands of lives concealed within prison uniforms." Lamott summed up his reaction to the book by calling it "virtually the only convincing novel of prison life I have read."

Braly again described prison life in *False Starts,* an autobiography about his years as a prisoner. "I went into prison a shy young man of 17," Braly told Henry Allen of the *Washington Post.* "I came out a bullshitter. But I never argued with society's right to imprison me as a burglar. A lot of prisoners are avid philosophers. When I was first in prison, everybody had a reason for being there, it was all psychoanalytic—their parents had split up, or whatever. I said no." Writing in *Newsweek* about Braly's memoir, Paul D. Zimmerman stated: "He recounts these experiences with none of the narcissism or self-pity found in so much confessional writing. Nor does he serve up the standard gothic horrors of prison literature." "[This book] rings true all the way through," Lamott wrote in the *New York Times Book Review,* ". . . and it's sharp, ironic, civilized and moving." William Cole of *Saturday Review* thought it "the best prison book I've ever read: taut, informative, even profound. The man is a *writer.*"

After looking at the crimes he had committed, and the almost deliberate ways he had given himself away, Braly concluded that most criminals wanted to be caught and punished "because basically," he told Allen, "they believe that what they're doing is wrong." When he came to terms with himself and accepted that he would have to change his ways if he wanted to live in outside society, Braly finally won parole. At the time of his death in 1980, he had been out of prison for fifteen years.

BIOGRAPHICAL/CRITICAL SOURCES: New York Times Book Review, October 22, 1967, February 29, 1976; *Book World,*

October 29, 1967; Malcolm Braly, *False Starts: A Memoir of San Quentin and Other Prisons,* Little, Brown, 1976; *Saturday Review,* January 24, 1976; *Newsweek,* March 15, 1976; *New Yorker,* April 5, 1976; *Washington Post Book World,* May 2, 1976; *The Author Speaks,* Bowker, 1977; *Contemporary Literature,* spring, 1977; *Washington Post,* April 11, 1979.

OBITUARIES: *New York Times,* April 9, 1980; *Washington Post,* April 10, 1980; *AB Bookman's Weekly,* April 21, 1980; *Newsweek,* April 21, 1980; *Publishers Weekly,* April 25, 1980.

* * *

BRANDENBERG, Aliki Liacouras 1929- (Aliki)

PERSONAL: Born September 3, 1929, in Wildwood Crest, N.J.; daughter of James Peter and Stella (Lagakos) Liacouras; married Franz Brandenberg (an author), March 15, 1957; children: Jason, Alexa Demetria. *Education:* Museum College of Art, Philadelphia, Pa., graduate, 1951. *Home:* 17, Regent's Park Terr., London NW1 7ED, England.

CAREER: Muralist and commercial artist in Philadelphia, Pa. and New York City, 1951-56, and Zurich, Switzerland, 1957-60; commercial artist, illustrator of children's books, and writer in New York City, 1960-77, and London, England, 1977—. *Awards, honors:* Children's Book Award of New York Academy of Sciences, 1977, for *Corn Is Maize: The Gift of the Indians.*

WRITINGS—All under name Aliki; self-illustrated: *The Story of William Tell,* A. S. Barnes, 1961; *My Five Senses,* Crowell, 1962; *My Hands,* Crowell, 1962; *The Wish Workers,* Dial, 1962; *The Story of Johnny Appleseed,* Prentice-Hall, 1963; *George and the Cherry Tree,* Dial, 1964; *The Story of William Penn,* Prentice-Hall, 1964; *A Weed Is a Flower: The Life of George Washington Carver,* Prentice-Hall, 1965; *Keep Your Mouth Closed, Dear,* Dial, 1966; *Three Gold Pieces,* Pantheon, 1967; *New Year's Day,* Crowell, 1967; *Hush Little Baby,* Prentice-Hall, 1968; *Diogenes,* Prentice-Hall, 1969; *The Eggs,* Pantheon, 1969; *My Visit to the Dinosaurs,* Crowell, 1969.

Fossils Tell of Long Ago, Crowell, 1972; *June 7,* Macmillan, 1972; *The Long Lost Coelacanth and Other Living Fossils,* Crowell, 1973; *Go Tell Aunt Rhody,* Macmillan, 1974; *Green Grass and White Milk,* Crowell, 1974; *At Mary Bloom's,* Greenwillow, 1976; *Corn Is Maize: The Gift of the Indians,* Crowell, 1976; *The Many Lives of Benjamin Franklin,* Prentice-Hall, 1977; *Wild and Woolly Mammoths,* Crowell, 1977; *The Twelve Months,* Greenwillow, 1978; *Mummies Made in Egypt,* Crowell, 1979; *The Two of Them,* Greenwillow, 1979.

Digging Up Dinosaurs, Crowell, 1981; *We Are Best Friends,* Greenwillow, 1982; *A Medieval Feast,* Harper, 1983; *Use Your Head, Dear,* Greenwillow, 1983.

Illustrator: Mickey Marks, *What Can I Buy?,* Dial, 1962; Dorothy Les Tina, *A Book to Begin On: Alaska,* Holt, 1962; Joan K. Heilbroner, *This Is the House Where Jack Lives,* Harper, 1962; Vivian L. Thompson, *The Horse That Liked Sandwiches,* Putnam, 1962; Bernice Kohn, *Everything Has a Size,* Prentice-Hall, 1964; Kohn, *Everything Has a Shape,* Prentice-Hall, 1964; Kohn, *One Day It Rained Cats and Dogs,* Coward, 1965; Betty Ren Wright, *I Want to Read!,* Whitman, 1965; Sean Morrison, *Is That a Happy Hippopotamus?,* Crowell, 1966; Helen Clare, *Five Dolls in the Snow,* Prentice-Hall, 1967; Wilma Yeo, *Mrs. Neverbody's Recipes,* Lippincott, 1968; Esther R. Hautzig, *A Home: A Visit in Four Languages,* Macmillan, 1968; Polly Greenberg, *Oh Lord, I Wish I Was a Buzzard,* Macmillan, 1968; Roma Gans, *Birds at Night,* Crowell, 1968; Jane Jonas Srivastava, *Weighing and Balancing,* Crowell, 1970.

Illlustrator; all by husband, Franz Brandenberg; published by Greenwillow, except as indicated: *I Once Knew a Man,* Macmillan, 1970; *Fresh Cider and Pie,* Macmillan, 1973; *No School Today!,* Macmillan, 1975; *A Secret for Grandmother's Birthday,* 1975; *A Robber! A Robber!,* 1976; *What Can You Make of It?,* 1977; *Nice New Neighbors,* 1977; *A Picnic Hurrah!,* 1978; *Six New Students,* 1978; *Everyone Ready?,* 1979.

It's Not My Fault!, 1980; *Leo and Emily,* 1981; *Leo and Emily's Big Ideas,* 1982; *Aunt Nina and Her Nephews and Nieces,* 1983; *Aunt Nina's Visit,* 1984; *Leo and Emily and the Dragon,* 1984.

SIDELIGHTS: Aliki Brandenberg told Dulcy Brainard of *Publishers Weekly* that before starting one of her nonfiction books for children she likes "to know nothing about a subject, then to absorb everything I can find about it, and *then* to select." Brainard believes that Brandenberg's "work as an illustrator is distinguished by both its range and a particular fitness of style to subject, picture to text."

BIOGRAPHICAL/CRITICAL SOURCES: *New York Times Book Review,* November 18, 1979, March 8, 1981, October 16, 1983; *Times Literary Supplement,* March 28, 1980; *Washington Post Book World,* May 9, 1982; *Publishers Weekly,* July 22, 1983.

* * *

BRANDENBERG, Franz 1932

PERSONAL: Born February 10, 1932, in Zug, Switzerland; son of Franz and Marie (Sigrist) Brandenberg; married Aliki Liacouras (an author and illustrator under name Aliki), March 15, 1957; children: Jason, Alexa Demetria. *Education:* Attended boarding school in Einsiedeln, Switzerland. *Home:* 17, Regent's Park Terr., London NW1 7ED, England.

CAREER: Began apprenticeship with publisher and bookseller in Lucerne, Switzerland, 1949; continued in book trade, 1952-60, working in bookshops or publishing houses in London, Paris, and Florence; literary agent in New York, N.Y., 1960-72; writer for children, 1970—.

WRITINGS—All juveniles; all illustrated by wife, Aliki; published by Greenwillow, except as indicated: *I Once Knew a Man,* Macmillan, 1970; *Fresh Cider and Pie,* Macmillan, 1973; *No School Today!,* Macmillan, 1975; *A Secret for Grandmother's Birthday,* 1975; *A Robber! A Robber!,* 1976; *I Wish I Was Sick, Too!,* 1976; *What Can You Make of It?,* 1977; *Nice New Neighbors,* 1977; *A Picnic Hurrah!,* 1978; *Six New Students,* 1978; *Everyone Ready?,* 1979.

It's Not My Fault!, 1980; *Leo and Emily,* 1981; *Leo and Emily's Big Ideas,* 1982; *Aunt Nina and Her Nephews and Nieces,* 1983; *Aunt Nina's Visit,* 1984; *Leo and Emily and the Dragon,* 1984.

WORK IN PROGRESS: "I am superstitious about talking about projects before they are finished."

SIDELIGHTS: Franz Brandenberg told *CA:* "Writing for children is my way of perpetuating my own childhood, which was very happy. Grandparents, aunts, and uncles played an important role in my family. We went to visit them; they came to visit us. One spinster aunt in particular, Aunt Nina, had a great influence on me. She took me on trips, introduced me to the circus and the theatre, and always brought me books. My latest series of picture books is about her.

"Neighbors, too, were important. We constantly climbed over each other's garden fences. The 'Leo and Emily' books are a result of these memories.

"Also our own children were a good source for stories. The 'Edward and Elizabeth' books were inspired by them. I am very lucky to have my wife illustrate my books, as she, naturally, understands me better than anyone else.

"I enjoy sharing my experiences with children, and I hope children enjoy reading about them."

Several of Brandenberg's books have been published in Japanese, Hebrew, French, German, Danish, and Swedish.

BIOGRAPHICAL/CRITICAL SOURCES: New York, December 17, 1973.

* * *

BRANDI, John 1943-

PERSONAL: Born November 5, 1943, in Los Angeles, Calif. *Education:* San Fernando Valley State College (now California State University, Northridge), B.F.A., 1965. *Home address:* Route 4, Box 51-A, Santa Fe, N.M. 87501.

CAREER: Writer and artist. Served as a Peace Corps volunteer in South America, 1965-68; poet-in-the-schools, Arts Division, State of New Mexico, during the 1970s; poet-in-the-parks, Carlsbad Caverns and Guadalupe Mountains, 1979. Has exhibited handmade books at Zora Gallery and Los Angeles Art Museum; has read poetry with jazz musicians in Santa Fe, N.M. Founder and editor, Tooth of Time Books. *Awards, honors: Portland State Review* prize for prose, 1971; P.E.N. American writers grant, 1973; grants from Arts Division, State of New Mexico, 1974-84; National Endowment for the Arts, fellowship in creative writing, 1979, grant to small presses, 1980-82, grant to edit children's poetry, 1981; Wittner Bynner Foundation grant, 1983.

WRITINGS: Tehachapi Fantasy, privately printed, 1964; *Poem Afternoon in a Square of Guadalajara* (prose poem), Maya Books, 1970; *Towards a Happy Solstice*, Christopher's Press, 1971; *Desde Alla*, Tree Books, 1971; *One Week of Mornings at Dry Creek*, Christopher's Press, 1971; *Y aun Hay Mas, Dreams and Explorations: New and Old Mexico*, Christopher's Press, 1972; *San Francisco Lastday Homebound Hangover Highway Blues*, Nail Press, 1973; *A Partial Exploration of Palo Flechado Canyon*, Nail Press, 1973; *Smudgepots: For Jack Kerouac* (prose poem), Nail Press, 1973; *The Phoenix Gas Slam* (prose poem), Nail Press, 1973; *Narrowguage to Riobamba*, Christopher's Press, 1975; (with Mal Warwick and Michael Scott) *Chimboraza: Life on the Haciendas of Highland Ecuador* (poems, narrations, and photographs), Akwesasne Notes Press, 1976; *Memorandum from a Caribbean Isle*, Blackberry Books, 1977; *Diary from Baja California*, Christopher's Press, 1978; *The Guadalupes: A Closer Look* (prose poem), Carlsbad Caverns Natural History Association, 1978; *Diary from a Journey to the Middle of the World*, Figures Press, 1980; *The Cowboy from Phantom Banks*, Floating Island Books, 1982; *Rite for the Beautification of All Beings* (prose poem), Toothpaste Press, 1983.

Poetry: *A Nothing Book*, privately printed, 1964; *Emptylots: Poems of Venice and L.A.*, Nail Press, 1971; *Field Notes from Alaska*, Nail Press, 1971; *Three Poems for Spring*, Nail Press, 1973; *August Poem*, Nail Press, 1973; *Firebook*, Smokey the Bear Press, 1974; *Turning Thirty Poems*, Duende Press, 1974; *In a December Storm*, Tribal Press, 1975; *Looking for Minerals*, Cherry Valley Editions, 1975; *In a September Rain*, Copper Canyon Press, 1976; *Poems from Four Corners*, Great Raven Press, 1978; *As It Is These Days*, Whistling Swan Press, 1979; *Andean Town Circa 1980*, Tooth of Time Books, 1980; *Poems for the People of Coyote*, Distant Longing Press, 1980; *Sky House/Pink Cottonwood*, Tooth of Time Books, 1980; *That Crow That Visited Was Flying Backwards*, Tooth of Time Books, 1982; *At the World's Edge*, Painted Stork Editions, 1983; *Zueikha's Book*, Doggerel Press, 1983; *Poems at the Edge of Day*, White Pine Press, 1983. Also author of *Hiding behind Open Doors*, 1981.

Author, with Jack Hirschman, of collage-poems *Interchange*, 1964, and *Kline Sky*, 1965; also author, with Szerlip, Wilson, and Karle, of *Four Dogs Mountain Songs*, 1980. Illustrator of *Tiny Talk*, a collection of poems by Laura Chester, 1972, of *Abra*, a children's story by David Meltzer, 1977, of *The Confounding*, a story by Steve Sanfield, 1981, and of *Only the Ashes*, a collection of translations by Sanfield, 1981.

SIDELIGHTS: John Brandi told *CA:* "I've had very little formal training in writing or painting. My parents, at an early age, encouraged me to write down memories and do drawings from my travels with them into deserts of the Southwest. I'm still adhered to this tradition, writing, illustrating, hand-illuminating my own books.

"New Mexico is a base where I work giving poetry/painting seminars for elderly, handicapped, blind, juvenile delinquents, prisoners, and public school children. Traveling out to places such as Burma, India, Nepal, Mexico, and Central America, I travel in again to sort out inner-thought geographies into prose, poetry, and expressionist paintings. Poetry for me is of course personal, an individual yet archetypal vision brought forward for others to view. At the same time it is my modest attempt toward world solidarity and peace."

* * *

BRECHER, Jeremy 1946-

PERSONAL: Born March 8, 1946, in Washington, D.C.; son of Edward M. (a writer) and Ruth (a writer; maiden name, Cook) Brecher. *Education:* Attended Reed College, 1963-65, and Institute for Policy Studies, 1965-68; Union Graduate School, Yellow Springs, Ohio, Ph.D., 1975. *Residence:* West Cornwall, Conn.

CAREER: Writer. Staff assistant to Representative Robert Kastenmeier in Washington, D.C., 1966; Friends Committee on National Legislation, Washington, D.C., member of staff, 1966-67; Council of Churches of Greater Washington, Washington, D.C., member of urban staff, 1968; Institute for Policy Studies, Washington, D.C., associate fellow, 1969-70; Yale University, New Haven, Conn., visiting lecturer in American studies and guest fellow, 1976-77; Institute for Labor Education and Research, New York, N.Y., member of staff, 1977; historical coordinator of Brass Workers History Project, 1981-83. Consultant to University of Connecticut, Mattatuck Historical Society, and Connecticut State Labor Council. *Member:* Work Relations Group. *Awards, honors:* Grant from National Endowment for the Humanities, 1982-84.

WRITINGS: Strike!, Straight Arrow Books, 1972, 3rd edition, South End Press, 1977; (editor with Rick Burns, Elizabeth

Long, Paul Mattick, Jr., and Peter Rachleff) *Root and Branch: The Rise of the Workers Movements*, Fawcett, 1975; (with Tim Costello) *Common Sense for Hard Times*, Two Continents Publishing, 1976, 2nd edition, 1977; (editor with others and author of introduction) *Le nouveau mouvement ouvrier Americain*, Spartakus (Paris), 1978; (contributor) Andrew Zimbalist, editor, *Case Studies on the Labor Process*, Monthly Review Press, 1979; (with Leon Zussman and Shirley Zussman) *Getting Together*, Morrow, 1979; (contributor) Ian Robertson, editor, *Social Problems*, 2nd edition (Brecher was not associated with earlier edition), Random House, 1980; (contributor) Patrick McGuire, editor, *Toward a Second Dimension: A Sociology Reader*, Kendall/Hunt, 1981; (editor with others) *Brass Valley: The Story of Working People's Lives and Struggles in an American Industrial Region*, Temple University Press, 1982; (contributor) Steve Shalom, editor, *Socialist Visions*, South End Press, 1983. Contributor to journals. Former editor of *Inter/Change*; associate editor of *Radical America*.

WORK IN PROGRESS: The Working People of Waterbury.

SIDELIGHTS: With the publication of *Strike!*, his American labor history, in 1972, Jeremy Brecher attracted critical attention for the book's blend of thorough historical research and socio-political analysis. "He has made an objective, minimally tendentious study of the American Experience," writes Richard Lingeman in the *New York Times*. "As a result this is a bracing draft of history." One of the distinguishing features of *Strike!* is its portrayal of a historical divergence between the interests of the American worker and those of organized trade unions. Focusing on this particular aspect of the work, Susan Lee and Peter Russell offer the following description of *Strike!* in the *New York Times Book Review:* "In his scholarly, genuinely stirring history of American workers, Brecher presents 'the true history of mass insurgence in America' as the struggle of 'authentic revolutionary movements against the establishment of state, capital, and trade unionism.' " However, Lee and Russell also point out what they believe to be an unjustified omission on Brecher's part: "[He] never assesses the argument that the fortunes of radical labor were tied to the political acumen of the American Socialist parties, that one need look no further than the bitter factionalism and tactical errors of the left to explain the failure of the radical labor movement."

Nonetheless, *Strike!* has been seen by a number of critics as a landmark in the study of American labor. Lingeman concludes: "The value of Mr. Brecher's book . . . is its tonic look at labor's past and its attempt to sketch a road map for the future. I commend it to the attention of management and labor, for both can learn something from it."

Strike! has been translated into Italian, Japanese, and German.

BIOGRAPHICAL/CRITICAL SOURCES: Jeremy Brecher, *Strike!*, Straight Arrow Books, 1972, 3rd edition, South End Press, 1977; *New York Times Book Review*, August 20, 1972; *New York Times*, August 23, 1972.

* * *

BRENNER, Barbara (Johnes) 1925-

PERSONAL: Born June 26, 1925, in Brooklyn, N.Y.; daughter of Robert Lawrence (a real estate broker) and Marguerite (Furboter) Johnes; married Fred Brenner (an illustrator), March 16, 1947; children: Mark, Carl. *Education:* Attended Seton Hall College (now University), 1942-43; also attended Rutgers University, 1944-46, New York University, and New School for Social Research. *Politics:* Independent.

CAREER: Prudential Insurance Co., copywriter, 1942-46; free-lance artist's agent, 1946-52; free-lance writer, mainly of juveniles, 1957—. Committee for a Sane Nuclear Policy, county chairman, 1960-61. *Member:* Authors Guild, Authors League of America. *Awards, honors:* N.Y. Herald Tribune Children's Spring Book Festival honor book award, 1961, for *Barto Takes the Subway; Book World* Spring Book Festival honor book award, 1970, and American Library Association notable book citation, both for *A Snake-Lover's Diary;* National Science Teachers Association and Children's Book Council award, 1974, for *Baltimore Orioles,* 1975, for *Lizard Tails and Cactus Spines,* 1977, for *On the Frontier with Mr. Audubon,* 1979, for *Beware! These Animals Are Poison,* and 1980, for *Have You Heard of a Kangeroo Bird?: Fascinating Facts about Unusual Birds;* American Library Association notable book citation, 1978, for *Wagon Wheels;* Best of the Best award, *School Library Journal,* 1982, for *On the Frontier with Mr. Audubon.*

WRITINGS—Juveniles, unless otherwise noted; several illustrated by her husband, Fred Brenner: *Somebody's Slippers, Somebody's Shoes,* W. R. Scott, 1957; *Barto Takes the Subway,* Knopf, 1961; *A Bird in the Family* (Junior Literary Guild selection), W. R. Scott, 1962; *Amy's Doll,* Knopf, 1963; *The Five Pennies,* Knopf, 1963; *Careers and Opportunities in Fashion* (young adult book), Dutton, 1964; *Beef Stew,* Knopf, 1965; *The Flying Patchwork Quilt,* Knopf, 1965.

Mr. Tall and Mr. Small, W. R. Scott, 1966; *Nicky's Sister,* Knopf, 1966; *Summer of the Houseboat,* Knopf, 1968; *Faces,* illustrated with photographs by George Ancona, Dutton, 1970; *A Snake-Lover's Diary,* W. R. Scott, 1970; *A Year in the Life of Rosie Bernard,* Harper, 1971; revised edition, Avon, 1983; *Is It Bigger Than a Sparrow?: A Box for Young Bird Watchers,* Knopf, 1972; *Walt Disney's "Three Little Pigs,"* Random House, 1972; *Bodies,* illustrated with photos by Ancona, Dutton, 1973; *If You Were an Ant,* Harper; 1973; *Walt Disney's "The Penguin That Hated the Cold,"* Random House, 1973; *Hemi: A Mule,* Harper, 1973; *Baltimore Orioles,* illustrated by J. Winslow Higginbottom, Harper, 1974; *Cunningham's Rooster,* illustrated by Anne Rockwell, Parents' Magazine Press, 1975; *Lizard Tails and Cactus Spines,* illustrated with photos by Merrit S. Keasey III, Harper, 1975.

Little One Inch, Coward, 1977; *On the Frontier with Mr. Audubon,* Coward, 1977; *We're Off to See the Lizard,* illustrated by Shelley Dietreichs, Raintree Editions, 1977; *Wagon Wheels,* illustrated by Don Bolognese, Harper, 1978; *Our Class Presents Ostrich Feathers: A Play in Two Acts* (first produced Off-Broadway, 1965), illustrated by Vera B. Williams, Parents' Magazine Press, 1978; *Beware! These Animals Are Poison,* illustrated by Jim Spanfeller, Coward, 1979; (with May Garelick) *The Tremendous Tree Book,* Four Winds Press, 1979; *Have You Ever Heard of a Kangeroo Bird?: Fascinating Facts about Unusual Birds,* illustrated by Irene Brady, Coward, 1980; *The Prince and the Pink Blanket,* illustrated by Nola Langner, Four Winds Press, 1980; *A Killing Season,* Four Winds Press, 1981; *Mystery of the Plumed Serpent,* Knopf, 1981; *Mystery of the Disappearing Dogs,* Knopf, 1982; *Love and Discipline* (adult book), Ballantine, 1983; *A Dog I Know,* Harper, 1983; *Bank Street's Family Guide to Home Computers* (adult book), Ballantine, 1984; *The Gorilla Signs Love,* Lothrop, 1984; *The Snow Parade,* Crown, 1984.

Contributor of articles to periodicals. Editor, Talkabout program, Adult Resource Books.

SIDELIGHTS: Barbara Brenner told *CA:* "All the circumstances of my life conspired to make me a writer—just lucky,

I guess. I grew up in Brooklyn, which supplied the color, and my mother had died when I was a year old, which supplied the sensitivity. We were poor, which gave me the social outlook and my father was ambitious for me, which developed the intellectual curiosity. Not to carry this any further, here I am, loving what I do and still surrounded by extraordinary stimuli. My husband is an artist, and we work together on books whenever we can. Our sons are both grown; one is a biologist, to whom I owe my interest in reptiles, and the other one is a musician, with whom I share an interest in music which has crept into at least one of my books. Our pet dogs and the wild animals here in rural Pennsylvania are rich sources of inspiration for my work."

AVOCATIONAL INTERESTS: Gardening, yoga, travel, birdwatching.

BIOGRAPHICAL/CRITICAL SOURCES: *Young Readers' Review*, April, 1966; *Library Journal*, July, 1968, May 15, 1970; *New York Times Book Review*, August 2, 1981.

* * *

BRESLAUER, George W. 1946-

PERSONAL: Born March 4, 1946, in New York, N.Y.; son of Henry Edward and Marianne (Schaeffer) Breslauer; married Yvette Assia, August 8, 1976. *Education:* University of Michigan, A.B., 1966, A.M. and Certificate in Russian Studies, 1968, Ph.D., 1973. *Office:* Department of Political Science, University of California, Berkeley, Calif. 94720.

CAREER: University of California, Berkeley, acting assistant professor, 1971-73, assistant professor, 1973-79, associate professor of political science, 1979—, acting chairman of Center for Slavic and East European Studies, 1982-84. *Member:* American Political Science Association, American Association for the Advancement of Slavic Studies, World Affairs Council, Phi Kappa Phi, Pi Sigma Alpha. *Awards, honors:* American Council of Learned Societies fellowship, 1968 and 1969-70; Social Science Research Council fellowship, 1969-70; National Academy of Sciences fellowship, 1970-71; Hoover Institution national fellow, 1975-76; American Association for the Advancement of Slavic Studies grant, 1979; Ford Foundation grant, 1982-83.

WRITINGS: (With Alexander Dallin) *Political Terror in Communist Systems*, Stanford University Press, 1970; (with Stanley Rothman) *Soviet Politics and Society*, West Publishing, 1977; *Five Images of the Soviet Future: A Critical Review and Synthesis*, Institute of International Studies, 1978; *Khrushchev and Brezhnev as Leaders: Building Authority in Soviet Politics*, Allen & Unwin, 1982.

Contributor: Chalmers Johnson, editor, *Change in Communist Systems*, Stanford University Press, 1970; Karl Ryavec, editor, *Soviet Society and the Communist Party*, University of Massachusetts Press, 1978; Stephen Cohen and others, editors, *The Soviet Union since Stalin*, Indiana University Press, 1980; Robert Wesson, editor, *The Soviet Union: Looking to the 1980's*, KTO Press, 1980; Seweryn Bialer and Thames Gustafson, editors, *Russia at the Crossroads*, Allen & Unwin, 1982; Alexander George, editor, *Managing Soviet-American Rivalry*, Westview, 1982.

Contributor of book reviews to journals, including *Russian Review* and *Dissent;* also contributor to numerous journals, including *Problems of Communism, American Political Science Review, Slavic Review,* and *Soviet Studies.* Member of advisory board, *Abstracts of Soviet and East European Emigre Periodical Literature*, 1982—. Member of editorial board, *Slavic Review*, 1983-85. Managing editor of international relations, *Soviet Union*, 1983—.

WORK IN PROGRESS: An essay for *World Politics;* a book chapter; a research project on the lessons drawn by the Soviets from their experience with U.S.-Soviet Third World competition during the 1970s.

* * *

BRETT, John Michael
See TRIPP, Miles (Barton)

* * *

BRETT, Michael
See TRIPP, Miles (Barton)

* * *

BRIGGS, Katharine Mary 1898-1980

PERSONAL: Born November 8, 1898, in London, England; died October 15, 1980, in Kent, England; daughter of Ernest Edward (an artist) and Mary (Cooper) Briggs. *Education:* Studied at Lansdowne House; Lady Margaret Hall, Oxford, M.A., 1926, Ph.D., 1952. *Religion:* Episcopalian. *Home:* Southolme, Sea View Rd., St. Margaret's Bay, Kent CT15 6EE, England. *Agent:* A. P. Watt & Son, 26 Bedford Row, London WC1R 2HL, England.

CAREER: Writer. Headed an amateur touring company for about fifteen years, produced plays in the Air Force, and wrote and produced plays locally in Perthshire and Oxfordshire, England. Visiting professor, University of Pennsylvania, 1970, and University of California at Berkeley, 1973. *Military service:* Women's Auxiliary Air Force, 1941-45. *Member:* International Institute of Arts and Letters (fellow), Folk-Lore Society (London; president, 1967-70), Bibliographical Society, Historical Association, American Folklore Society (life member), English Folk Dance and Song Society. *Awards, honors:* D.Litt., Oxford University, 1969.

WRITINGS: *The Legend of Maiden-Hair*, Stockwell, 1915; *The Garrulous Lady* (dramatic sketch), Golden Vista, 1931; *The Lisles of Ellingham*, Alden Press, 1935; *A History of 75 Years*, Henry Briggs & Son, 1935; *The Witches' Ride*, Capricornus, 1937; *Stories Arranged for Mime*, Capricornus, 1937; *The Fugitive* (one-act play), Capricornus, 1938; *The Peacemaker* (one-act play), Capricornus, 1938; *The Prince, the Fox and the Dragon*, Capricornus, 1938.

(With Winifred Briggs and Elspeth Briggs) *Whispers: An Experiment in Lino Cuts* (poems), Capricornus, 1940; *The Castilians*, Alden Press, 1949; *Lady in the Dark* (play), Capricornus, 1950; (with others) *The Twelve Days of Christmas*, Capricornus, 1952; *The Personnel of Fairyland: A Short Account of the Fairy People of Great Britain for Those Who Tell Stories to Children*, Alden Press, 1953, Bentley, 1954, reprinted, Singing Tree Press, 1971; *Hobberdy Dick*, Eyre & Spottiswoode, 1955, reprinted, Puffin Books, 1976; *Mime for Guides and Brownies*, Girl Guides Association, 1955; *Dunkeld and Birnam Guide*, Alden Press, 1956; *The Anatomy of Puck: An Examination of Fairy Beliefs among Shakespeare's Contemporaries and Successors*, Routledge & Kegan Paul, 1959, reprinted, Arno, 1977.

Pale Hecate's Team: An Examination of the Beliefs on Witchcraft and Magic among Shakespeare's Contemporaries and His Immediate Successors, Humanities, 1962, reprinted, Arno, 1977; (contributor) *Bruder Grimm Gedenken,* Elwert Verlag, 1963; *Kate Crackernuts,* Alden Press, 1963, revised edition, Kestrel, 1979, Greenwillow, 1980; (contributor) Allardyce Nicoll, editor, *Shakespeare Survey, 1964,* Cambridge University Press, 1964; (editor with Ruth Lyndall Tongue) *Folktales of England,* University of Chicago Press, 1965; (editor) Tongue, *Somerset Folklore,* Folk-Lore Society, 1965; *The Fairies in English Tradition and Literature,* University of Chicago Press, 1967 (published in England as *The Fairies in Tradition and Literature,* Routledge & Kegan Paul, 1967).

A Dictionary of British Folktales in the English Language, four volumes, Indiana University Press, Part A: *Folk-Tales,* two volumes, 1970 (published in England as *Folk Narratives,* Routledge & Kegan Paul, 1970), Part B: *Folk Legends,* two volumes, 1971, selections published as *British Folk Tales,* Pantheon, 1977 (published in England as *A Sampler of British Folk-Tales,* Routledge & Kegan Paul, 1977), new edition published as *British Folk Tales and Legends: A Sampler,* Paladin, 1977; *The Last of the Astrologers: Mr. William Lilly's History of His Life and Times from the Year 1608 to 1681,* 2nd edition, Folklore Society, 1974; *The Folklore of the Cotswolds,* Rowman, 1974; *An Encyclopedia of Fairies: Hobgoblins, Brownies, Bogies, and Other Supernatural Creatures,* Pantheon, 1976 (published in England as *A Dictionary of Fairies: Hobgoblins, Brownies, Bogies, and Other Supernatural Creatures,* Allen Lane, 1976), abridged edition published as *Abbey Lubbers, Banshees, and Boggarts: An Illustrated Encyclopedia of Fairies,* 1979; *The Vanishing People: Fairy Lore and Legends,* Pantheon, 1978 (published in England as *The Vanishing People: A Study of Traditional Fairy Beliefs,* Batsford, 1978); *Nine Lives: The Folklore of Cats,* Pantheon, 1980. Also author of numerous plays. Contributor to *Guider* and *Folklore.*

WORK IN PROGRESS: A book on legends of women through the centuries, for Pantheon.

SIDELIGHTS: British folklorist Katharine Mary Briggs, according to Israel Shenker in the *New York Times,* approached "omniscience in airy realms." When she spoke of fairies, says Shenker, "she [was] talking about creatures such as banshees, bogies, brownies, dwarfs, elves, giants, goblins, hags, mermaids and wizards, and [was] careful not to slight others such as Bugganes, Doonies, Feens, Guytrash, Mumpokers, Pechs, Piskies, Pwcas . . . and even Grigs, who are only pseudo-fairies."

However, Briggs often stressed that she was an "agnostic" about supernatural creatures. Shenker quoted her as saying: "I'm not a believer—my mind is evenly balanced. But many of the stories [about fairies] are very convincing, and I do believe that people really believe in them. If you're going to collect people's fairy beliefs, you have to keep an open mind, so the people don't think you're looking down on them."

"Her professional achievements were remarkable in a number of fields," states her *London Times* obituary. "As a meticulous scholar [Briggs] brought to folklore the rigorous canons of criticism that are essential to any discipline and as an accomplished historian she gained a penetrating and intuitive familiarity with the seventeenth century."

BIOGRAPHICAL/CRITICAL SOURCES: *Times Literary Supplement,* August 17, 1967, July 23, 1970; *Listener,* August 31, 1967; *Observer Review,* May 16, 1971; *The Witch Figure: Folklore Essays by a Group of Scholars in England Honouring the 75th Birthday of Katharine M. Briggs,* Routledge & Kegan Paul, 1973; *New York Times,* October 31, 1977; *Washington Post,* December 16, 1978, November 20, 1980.

OBITUARIES: *London Times,* October 25, 1980; *Publishers Weekly,* November 7, 1980.†

* * *

BRIGHAM, Besmilr 1923-

PERSONAL: Given name is pronounced Bess-miller; born September 28, 1923, in Pace, Miss.; daughter of Monroe and Bessye (Emmons) Moore; married Roy C. Brigham; children: Heloise (Mrs. Keith Wilson). *Education:* Mary Hardin-Baylor College, Belton, Tex., degree in journalism; New School for Social Research, graduate study. *Politics:* "No commitment." *Religion:* "No formal affiliation." *Home:* Route 1, Horatio, Ark. 71842.

CAREER: Free-lance author and poet. Poet-resident, Bryan Public Schools, Bryan, Tex., 1974. *Awards, honors:* National Endowment for the Arts fellowship grant for continuance of her work in poetry.

WRITINGS: *Agony Dance: Death of the Dancing Dolls,* Winepress Publishing, 1969; *Heaved from the Earth,* Knopf, 1971; *Death of the Wild* (poetry), Abbott House, 1984; *To Live As a Bird* (collected fiction), Abbott House, 1984. Also author of "The Thirteenth Mask: Games for an Easter Child" (script for dance/lyric drama), produced at Theatre of the Americas, East Lansing, Mich.

Contributor to anthologies: *31 New American Poets,* edited by Ron Schreiber, Hill & Wang, 1969; *New Directions #21,* New Directions, 1969; *New Directions #23,* New Directions, 1971; *Their Place in the Heat: Contemporary Poetry Statements,* Road Runner Press, 1971; *New Generation: Poetry,* edited by Fred Wolven, Ann Arbor Review Books, 1971; *I Love You All Day: It Is That Simple,* Abbey Press, 1971; *From the Belly of the Shark,* edited by Walter Lowenfels, Random House, 1973; *Rising Tides: Twentieth Century American Women Poets,* edited by Laura Chester and Sharon Barbra, Simon & Schuster, 1973; *Psyche: An Anthology of Modern American Women Poets,* edited by Barbara Segnitz and Carol Rainey, Dial Press, 1973; *I Hear My Sisters Saying,* edited by Dorothy Walters and Carol Konek, Crowell, 1976; *Arkansas Voices,* edited by Sarah M. Fountain, Rose Press, 1976.

Contributor of short stories to *Southern Review, Confrontation, Southwest Review, North American Review;* contributor of poetry to numerous journals and periodicals, including *Texas Quarterly, Atlantic, Harper's Bazaar, Confrontation, Prairie Schooner, Southwest Review, North American Review, New York Times, West Coast Review, Wisconsin Review, Beloit Poetry Journal, Granite,* and *Minnesota Review.*

WORK IN PROGRESS: "*The Rainbow House* (fiction) has grown from a singular collection to a study in three volumes: *Rainbow House, The Garden of Ix,* and *The Dark Field.* I have also been with *Fields of the Bell Lagoon* (poem), related (as is true of the fiction) to Central America. From what is happening there now, this is my only consolation. I am also with other structures from that emotional terrain, one that I hope to be on the last with soon: *Harry Smith: Passion at El Virgen,* set in Nicaragua back in the time of the old Somoza."

SIDELIGHTS: Besmilr Brigham told *CA:* "I wrote for a long time and put away. Early being trained in journalism, I had found that I had learned . . . all the wrong things, the tricks, a factual exposure that obliterated some way of passage into the interior. This, at times, has taken a strange adjustment. I had been trained in strictness, any deviation marked out with a black pen!

"After [*Heaved from the Earth*] was published, I felt again a horrifying exposure. I could put no collection together, not with assurance or interior certainty, as though another shadow had come in. I worked a year at Bryan, Texas . . . (the children were beautiful) and we went back from there again to Central America, the Caribbean coast, Honduras, Guatemala, settled on Lago Izabal. From this came 'Poems for the Lago,' now a part of the *Fields*. I have tried in these last years, and I'm still with it, to clear everything, all the work that I felt should be kept. And some people and places have stood by me.

"I have not left the medium of Poem, though I think a darkness is emerging; and the heavier canvas intrigues me. In some way, writing is projection; I like projecting into another mind, putting the pieces together, what I have seen, recognized, throwing an awareness . . . into the filling out of an event or occurrence, that I know very well that in some way happened, with all the 'embroidery' of that context.

"We have to find our own way; and if one is a writer, he or she also has to find a way to survive."

BIOGRAPHICAL/CRITICAL SOURCES: Their Place in the Heat: Contemporary Poetry Statements, Road Runner Press, 1971; *Crazy Horse,* Number 7, June, 1971; *Wisconsin Review,* summer, 1971; *Minnesota Review,* fall, 1971; *Poetry Society of America Bulletin,* February, 1972; *Texas Woman,* April-May, 1974.

* * *

BRINKS, Herbert J(ohn) 1935-

PERSONAL: Born May 25, 1935, in South Holland, Ill.; married Ruth Kortenhoven, 1957; children: Timothy, Steven, Marie, John. *Education:* Calvin College, A.B., 1957; University of Michigan, M.A., 1962, Ph.D., 1965. *Office:* Department of History, Calvin College, Grand Rapids, Mich. 49506.

CAREER: High school teacher of English, history, and Latin, in Allendale, Mich.; 1957-60; University of Michigan, Michigan Historical Collection, Ann Arbor, research assistant, 1961-62; Calvin College, Grand Rapids, Mich., assistant professor, 1962-68, professor of history, 1972—, Colonial Origins Collection, part-time curator, 1965-69, curator of manuscripts, 1972—; Michigan State University, East Lansing, assistant professor, 1969; Historical Society of Michigan, Ann Arbor, director, 1970-71. University of Michigan, teacher of extension courses in history at Grand Rapids, 1967, 1968, Flint and Detroit, 1970, and Dearborn Campus, 1971. Participant in numerous conferences.

MEMBER: American Historical Association, Organization of American Historians, Historical Society of Michigan, Michigan Archival Association. *Awards, honors:* Earhart Foundation fellowship, 1962, 1965; National Endowment for the Humanities summer grant, 1976-77; National Historical Publications and Records Commission grant, 1978-79; Fulbright-Hays Council for International Exchange of Scholars research grant, 1980-81.

WRITINGS: (Editor) *Guide to the Dutch-American Historical Collections of Western Michigan,* Dutch American Historical Commission, 1967; *Peter White,* Eerdmans, 1970; (editor with George S. May) *A Michigan Reader: 11,000 B.C. to A.D. 1865,* Eerdmans, 1973; *Schrijf Spoedig Terug! Brieven Van Immigranten in Amerika, 1847-1920,* Boekencentrum (Netherlands), 1978; (contributor) Francis X. Blovin, Jr., and Robert Warner, editors, *Sources for the Study of Migration and Ethnicity,* Bentley Historical Library (Ann Arbor, Mich.), 1979; (contributor) *Contemporary American Immigration,* Twayne, 1981; (contributor) *Dutch Immigration to North America,* Multicultural History Society of Ontario (Toronto), 1983.

Contributor of articles and fiction to numerous periodicals, including *Dialogue, Michigan History, Reformed Journal, Calvin Theological Journal,* and *Time Being.* Editor, Historical Society of Michigan *Chronicle,* 1969-71.

* * *

BRISTOL, Julius
See ABEL, Alan (Irwin)

* * *

BRISTOW, Gwen 1903-1980

PERSONAL: Born September 16, 1903, in Marion, S.C.; died August 16, 1980, in New Orleans, La.; daughter of Louis Judson (a minister) and Caroline Cornelia (Winkler) Bristow; married Bruce Manning, January 14, 1929 (deceased). *Education:* Judson College, A.B., 1924; attended Columbia University School of Journalism, 1924-25, and Anderson College. *Address:* Box 144, Encino, Calif. 91316. *Agent:* Brandt & Brandt, 101 Park Ave., New York, N.Y. 10017.

CAREER: Times-Picayune, New Orleans, La., reporter, 1925-34; full-time professional writer, beginning 1934. *Member:* Authors League of America, P.E.N. International (Los Angeles center president, 1969-71; international corresponding secretary, beginning 1971), Pen and Brush.

WRITINGS: (With husband, Bruce Manning) *The Invisible Host,* Mystery League, 1930, published as *The Ninth Guest,* Popular Library, 1975; (with Manning) *Gutenberg Murders,* Mystery League, 1931; (with Manning) *Two and Two Make Twenty-Two,* Mystery League, 1932; *Deep Summer,* Crowell, 1937, reprinted, Buccaneer Books, 1979; *The Handsome Road,* Crowell, 1938, reprinted, Buccaneer Books, 1979; *This Side of Glory,* Crowell, 1940, reprinted, Buccaneer Books, 1979; *Tomorrow Is Forever,* Crowell, 1943, reprinted, Buccaneer Books, 1976; *Jubilee Trail* (Literary Guild selection), Crowell, 1950; *Celia Garth* (Literary Guild selection), Crowell, 1959, reprinted, Popular Library, 1974; *Plantation Trilogy* (includes *Deep Summer, The Handsome Road, This Side of Glory,* and additional historical material to preface each book), Crowell, 1962; *Calico Palace,* Crowell, 1970; *Golden Dreams,* Crowell, 1980.

SIDELIGHTS: Gwen Bristow, who started her fiction-writing career by working with her husband, Bruce Manning, on mystery stories, became well known for her trilogy of novels depicting plantation life. *Deep Summer, The Handsome Road,* and *This Side of Glory* were occasionally criticized by some reviewers for their slow pacing and weak characterizations; nevertheless, the trilogy was ultimately praised by such critics as Margaret Wallace, who wrote in *The New York Times* of *This Side of Glory:* "There can be no question . . . of Gwen Bristow's solid and versatile talent as a novelist. Considered by itself, without reference to the two volumes which preceded it, *This Side of Glory* is a good story—a convincing study."

Bristow's novels were translated into numerous languages, including German, French, Spanish, Dutch, and Swedish.

MEDIA ADAPTATIONS: The Invisible Host was dramatized by Owen Davis under the title "The Ninth Guest," and filmed by Columbia with the latter title in 1931. *Tomorrow Is Forever* was filmed by RKO in 1946, and *Jubilee Trail* was filmed by Republic in 1953.

BIOGRAPHICAL/CRITICAL SOURCES: New York Times, March 31, 1940; *Times Literary Supplement*, July 13, 1940; *Atlantic Monthly*, January, 1944; *New York Times Book Review*, May 31, 1959.

OBITUARIES: Chicago Tribune, August 19, 1980.†

* * *

BROBY-JOHANSEN, R(udolf) 1900-

PERSONAL: Born November 25, 1900, in Aalborg, Denmark; son of Rasmus and Anna (Andersdatter) Johansen; married Karen Bjarnov, 1924 (died, 1927); married Aina Pogin (a magister artium), 1937; children: (first marriage) Hille Broby Madsen; (second marriage) Aud Broby Ilg, Bengta Broby Nielsen, Urs Broby-Johansen. *Education:* Studied at University of Copenhagen, and in Berlin, Dresden, and London "without taking any degrees on principle against all titles, degrees and examinations." *Home:* 74 Solsortvej, DK-2000 Kbh.F, Copenhagen, Denmark.

CAREER: Free-lance writer, principally on art subjects, and publicist. Lecturer on radio and television and at Scandinavian high schools. *Member:* Dansk forfatterforening, Danish Academy of Art. *Awards, honors:* "On principle: none. Exception: the reward of honor for authors from the Danish state"; Dr. phil.h.c., University of Goeteborg, 1981.

WRITINGS: Blod (poems; title means "Blood"), .DNSS Forlag, 1922, new edition, Gyldendal, 1968; *Kunst* (title means "Art"), .DNSS Forlag, 1922; *Bodsspil* (musical drama; title means "Play of Penitence"), Imorgen, 1925; *Kunst og klasse* (title means "Art and Class"), Fram Forlag (Oslo), 1932; *Kina klager* (poems; title means "China Complaint"), Hjorths Tryk, 1932; (with B. J. Aina) *Dainas* (Latvian folksongs), Hjorths Tryk, 1938.

Aesopske fabler, Hjorths Tryk, 1944, enlarged edition published as *Den lille Aesop*, Gyldendal, 1945, translation by B. Nordhjem published as *The Danish Aesop: 59 of the Old Animal Tales Retold*, Reitzel (Copenhagen), 1961; *Danmarks aeldste maleri* (title means "The Oldest Danish Painting"), Bording, 1945; *Omrids af Modens Historie set fra et koebenhavnsk modehus* (title means "Sketch of the History of Mode Seen from a Copenhagen Mode House"), Fonnesbech, 1947.

Farve faar Form: Papirets kunsthistorie (title means "Color and Form: The Art History of Paper"), Forenede papirfabrikker, 1960; (contributor) Gert Munch, editor, *En bog om Nyhavn*, Rosenkilde og Bagger, 1963; *Koebenhavn og dens beboere igar og idag* (title means "Copenhagen and Its Inhabitants Yesterday and Today"), Koebenhavns Magistrat, 1965; *Keysers Kunst, und Stilfibel*, Keysersche Verlags Buchhandlung (Munich), 1965; *Maleriets mestre* (title means "Masters of Painting"), Vinten, 1967; *Dagens dont gennem aartusinderne*, Fremad, 1969.

Dagens dont i Norden, Fremad, 1972; *Aret i Denmark* (title means "The Year in Denmark in Landscape Paintings"), F.D.B., 1973; *Svart pa vitt: Politiske teckningar* (title means "Black on White: Political Drawings"), Gidlunds (Stockholm), 1974; *Arbejdsbilledalbum* (title means "Album of Pictures with the Theme: Work"), Fremad, 1975; *Danske miljoeer* (title means "Danish Milieus"), F.D.B., 1975; *Med Broby i Vendsyssel og Hanherrederne: kunstvejviser*, Hamlet, 1978; *Med Broby pa Nord- og Midtfyn*, Hamlet, 1979; *Med Broby pa Sydfyn, Langeland, Tasinge, Aeroe og Samsoe*, Hamlet, 1979; *Med Broby i Nordvestjylland, Thy og Hardsyssel*, Hamlet, 1980; *Med Broby i Vest- og Syd-Sjaelland: fra Kalundborg til Vordingborg*, Hamlet, 1980.

Published by Gyldendal (Copenhagen), except as indicated: *Hverdagskunst, verdenskunst: En Oversigt over stilarternes ud vikling* (title means "Everyday Art, World Art"), 1943, published as *Hverdagskunst, verdenskunst: En Oversigt over Europas stiludvikling*, 1948, published as *Hvderdagskunst, verdenskunst: En Oversigt over Europas kunsthistorie*, 1958; *Den danske billedbibel de middelalderlige kalkmalerier* (title means "The Danish Picture Bible in Mediaeval Wall Paintings"), 1947; *Gennem det gamle Koebenhavn*, 1948, summary published as *Through Old Copenhagen*, Nationaltidende, 1948; *Gaga, Siksak og Holger*, 1949.

Verdensmestre: Ti malerbiografier med en indledning om farvens historie i Europa (title means "World Masters: Ten Biographies of Painters with the History of European Color"), 1950; *Krop og Klaer: Klaededragtens kunsthistorie*, 1953, 3rd edition, 1975, translation by Erik Friis and Karen Rush published as *Body and Clothes: An Illustrated History of the Art of Costume*, Reinhold, 1968; *Gennem det ny Koebenhavn* (title means "Through the New Copenhagen"), 1959, new edition, 1969.

Imprimatur (essays and a bibliography of his writings, 1922-60), 1960; *Hjemmets Pinakotek* (title means "Pinacotheca of the Home"), 1960; *Vi ser paa kunst fra oldtiden*, 1960; *Vor kunst* (title means "Our Art"), 1962, school edition published in three volumes as *Vi ser paa kunst* (title means "We Look at Art"); *H. C. Andersens Koebenhavn*, 1962, translation by Niels Haislund and Helen Fogh published as *Hans Andersen's Copenhagen*, 1963; *Historien om maleriet fra i Europa istid til nutid* (title means "History of Painting in Europe from the Ice Age to Our Time"), 1964; *Kunstordbog* (title means "Glossary of Art"), 1965; *Oldnordiske stenbilleder* (title means "Old Nordic Stone Pictures"), 1967, 2nd revised edition, 1973.

Skrift i sand (title means "Writings in the Sand"), 1970; *Hvad skal vi med toej?* (title means "Why Have We Clothing?"), 1971; *Kun kunst* (title means "Only Art"), 1971; *Den lystige historie om har og hat* (title means "The Funny History of Hair and Hat"), 1972; *Den triste historie om taerne* (title means "The Sad History of the Toes"), 1972; *Skolen i kunsten-kunsten i skolen* (title means "The School in Art—Art in the School"), 1974; *Sort pa hvidt: En politisk billedbog*, 1974; *Ismerne: Modernismens Kunsthistorie i 175 billeder*, 1977.

Also author of *Med Broby pa Lolland-Falster*, 1981, *Med Broby i Soenderjylland og pa Bornholm*, 1982, *Sort og roedt, Grafiske glimt*, 1982, *Med Broby i Sydjylland*, 1983, and *Med Broby i Nordsjaelland*, 1983. Also author of manuscripts for the films "Kalkmalerier" (title means "Mediaeval Wall Paintings"), 1954, and "Cement kriurafikset" (title means "The Crucifix of Beton"), 1968; also author of many television features about art.

SIDELIGHTS: R. Broby-Johansen, an antimilitarist, emphasizes that he has done no military service nor held any civil position, telling *CA*: "The last time any other person had command over me was when I was a child in school. . . . I have [written] what I wanted to [write], and sold it if anyone would print it; when not, I had the fun of [writing] it." About his work, Broby-Johansen told *CA:* "[I am] not a popularist in the usual sense of the word, but a scientist with an absolutely original and unorthodox approach to the problems of art history. [I] represent a sociological point of view in sharp opposition to the academic schools of art in the western as well as the eastern world."

Hverdagskunst, verdenskunst, Broby-Johansen's book on the history of art and decoration and ornament, is reprinted almost perennially in Denmark and has been translated into German, Norwegian, Swedish, Finnish, Hungarian, Latvian, and Czechoslovakian. Many of his other books have been translated into other languages.

BIOGRAPHICAL/CRITICAL SOURCES: R. Broby-Johansen, *Imprimatur* (essays and a bibliography of his writings, 1922-60), Gyldendal, 1960; Gert Munch, editor, *En bog om Nyhavn,* Rosenkilde og Bagger, 1963; *Drama,* spring, 1969; Dorthe Dester and Mette Kjeldsen, *Bibliography,* Gyldendal, 1975.

* * *

BROCK, Delia
   See EPHRON, Delia

* * *

BROOKS, Douglas
   See BROOKS-DAVIES, Douglas

* * *

BROOKS-DAVIES, Douglas 1942-
   (Douglas Brooks)

PERSONAL: Original name, Douglas Brooks; name legally changed in 1976; born March 10, 1942, in London, England; son of Douglas (an industrial chemist) and Margaret (Dean) Brooks; married Stevie Davies (a university lecturer and writer), February 12, 1976; children: Emily Jane, Grace Hannah, Robin Harry. *Education:* Brasenose College, Oxford, B.A., 1965; University of Liverpool, Ph.D., 1967. *Politics:* "Democratic socialist." *Religion:* "Superstitious atheist." *Home:* 3a Raynham Ave., Didsbury, Manchester M20 0BW, England. *Office:* Department of English, University of Manchester, Manchester, Lancashire, England.

CAREER: University of Leeds, Leeds, England, lecturer in English literature, 1967-70; University of Manchester, Manchester, England, lecturer, 1970-81, senior lecturer in English literature, 1981—.

WRITINGS: (Editor, under name Douglas Brooks) Henry Fielding, *Joseph Andrews and Shamela,* Oxford University Press, 1971; (editor with A. R. Humphreys; under name Douglas Brooks) Fielding, *Jonathan Wild and a Voyage to Lisbon,* Dent, 1973; (under name Douglas Brooks) *Number and Pattern in the Eighteenth-Century Novel,* Routledge & Kegan Paul, 1973.

(Editor) *Spenser: The Faerie Queene, a Selection,* Dent, 1976; *Spenser's Faerie Queene: A Critical Commentary on Books I and II,* Manchester University Press, 1977; *The Mercurian Monarch: Magical Politics from Spenser to Pope,* Manchester University Press, 1983; *Pope's "Dunciad" and the Queen of the Night: A Study in Emotional Jacobitism,* Manchester University Press, 1985. Founder and editor, "Literature in Context" series, Manchester University Press. Contributor to literature and language journals, including *Ariel* and *Essays in Criticism.* Member of editorial board, *Studies in Mystical Literature.*

SIDELIGHTS: Douglas Brooks-Davies comments: "I find many academic books (and academics) rather disturbingly impersonal. All my early writing was, similarly, impersonal. I hope I have now discovered the beauty and power of personal feeling and that this is now reflected in my writing and teaching." *Avocational interests:* Music (plays recorder, oboe, and viola), gardening.

* * *

BROUE, Pierre 1926-

PERSONAL: Born May 8, 1926, in France; son of Leon and Rene (Verrot) Broue; married Andree Jacquenet (a professor); children: Michel, Francoise, Catherine, Martine, Jean-Pierre. *Education:* University of Grenoble, diplome d'etudes superieures, 1952; University of Paris, Nanterre, doctorat es lettres (with high honors), 1972. *Politics:* "Militant Trotskyite." *Home:* 6 rue St. Ferjus, 38000 Grenoble, France. *Office:* Institut d'Etudes Politiques, BP 45, 38045 Saint Martin d'Heres, France.

CAREER: High school teacher of history in Nyons, Switzerland, and Beaune, Paris, and Moutereau-faut-Yonne, France, 1948-65; Institut d'Etudes Politiques, Saint Martin d'Heres, France, assistant historian, 1965-69, assistant master, 1969-72, lecturer, 1972-81, currently professor.

WRITINGS: (With Emile Temime) *La Revolution et la guerre d'Espagne,* two volumes, Editions de Minuit, 1961, translation by Tony White published as *The Revolution and the Civil War in Spain,* MIT Press, 1972; *Le Parti bolchevique: Histoire du P.C. de l'U.R.S.S.,* Editions de Minuit, 1963, 2nd edition, 1972; *Revolution en Allemagne, 1917-1923,* Editions de Minuit, 1971; *La Revolution espagnole, 1931-1939,* Flammarion, 1973; (with David King) *Trotsky: Iconographie,* Etudes et Documentation Internationales, 1979; *L'Assassinat de Trotsky,* Complexes, 1981.

Editor: Nikolai Ivanovich Bukharin, *ABC du communisme,* Maspero, 1963; *Les Proces de Moscou: Comptes rendus du commissariat du peuple a la justice, dossiers de la revision depuis le XXe congres du P.C. de l'U.R.S.S.,* Julliard, 1964; (and author of preface) *La Question chinoise dans l'Internationale communiste, 1926-1927,* Etudes et Documentation Internationales, 1965; *Pologne-Hongrie, 1956; ou, "Le Printemps en octobre,"* Etudes et Documentation Internationales, 1966; Leon Trotsky, *Le Mouvement communiste en France, 1919-1939,* Editions de Minuit, 1967; (and author of preface) *Ecrits a Prague sous la censure,* Etudes et Documentation Internationales, 1973; (and author of preface) *Le premier congres de l'Internationale communiste,* Etudes et Documentation Internationales, 1974; (and author of notes) Trotsky, *La Revolution espagnole, 1930-1940,* Editions de Minuit, 1975; Trotsky, *Oeuvres,* fifteen volumes, Institut Leon Trotsky and Etudes et Documentation Internationales, 1979-83. Contributor to history and political science journals.

WORK IN PROGRESS: Editing the next two volumes in the history of Communist international movement, covering the periods between the first and second congresses and the period of the second congress.

BROUN, Heywood Hale 1918-

PERSONAL: Surname rhymes with "croon"; born March 10, 1918; son of Heywood Campbell Broun (a newspaperman) and Ruth Hale (a journalist); married Jane Lloyd-Jones (an actress), 1949; children: Heywood Orren. *Education:* Swarthmore College, B.A., 1940. *Home:* 35 West 81st St., New York, N.Y. 10024.

CAREER: Sportswriter and columnist for *PM* and *New York Star*, New York, N.Y., before switching to acting; stage and television actor, beginning 1949, appearing on Broadway in "Bird Cage," "Pink Elephant," "Bells Are Ringing," and other productions. Sports broadcaster for Columbia Broadcasting System; became critic-at-large for "Sunday Morning," CBS. *Military service:* U.S. Army, Field Artillery; served with 9th Army in Europe; became technical sergeant. *Member:* Actors' Equity Association, Screen Actors Guild, American Federation of Television and Radio Artists, American Newspaper Guild, Phi Beta Kappa, Coffee House, Franklin Inn.

WRITINGS: (Editor) *The Collected Edition of Heywood Broun* (writings of his father), Harcourt, 1941; *A Studied Madness*, Doubleday, 1965; *Tumultuous Merriment*, Richard Marek, 1979; *Whose Little Boy Are You?: A Memoir of the Broun Family*, St. Martin's, 1983. Contributor to magazines.

SIDELIGHTS: Although he's worked successfully as an actor, a journalist, and an author, Heywood Hale Broun is perhaps best known as CBS's erudite sports commentator. Clad in his trademark multicolored madras jacket, Broun became a familiar figure to viewers during the more than ten years he covered professional and amateur sports. He distinguished himself in particular as a racetrack authority; as Charles Leroux notes in the *Chicago Tribune*, Broun has been known to carry only two pictures in his wallet—the first of his wife and son, the second of Triple Crown champion Secretariat. The writer is also the son of two famous, and controversial, journalists: socialist campaigner Heywood Campbell Broun and pioneering feminist Ruth Hale. Accordingly, two of Broun's critically-acclaimed books chronicle these aspects of his life. *Tumultuous Merriment* is a profile of athletes and their sports, culled from the author's sportscasting career; *Whose Little Boy Are You?: A Memoir of the Broun Family* recollects Broun's early years with his celebrated parents.

Tumultuous Merriment (the title derives from Samuel Johnson's definition of sport) "represents a sort of backward quest," says *Chicago Tribune Book World* writer Mitchell S. Ross. "It recovers all those events that rushed past with the weekly deadlines, separating those happenings whose charm was spontaneous rather than merely staged." Broun's book, continues Ross, "arrives at a serene and lively vision of the poetry and humor of sport. The beauty of the book lies less in its analysis of the current scene . . . than in its ability to express in its transcendent phrases those things that so many sports fans feel. It is the voice of an artist that says of the athlete in the age of free agentry, 'I want the players to have even more money if they will stop talking and acting like characters out of Sinclair Lewis' *Babbitt*.'"

Interspersed with the many anecdotes in *Tumultuous Merriment* is Broun's statement that the ever-increasing importance given to salaries and image consciousness have taken the true "merriment" from sports. While "this is not exactly a lightning-bolt of revelation," remarks Christopher Lehmann-Haupt in the *New York Times*, nevertheless "such arguments lend a semblance of gravity to [the author's] book. And they form a world on which his lighthearted reminiscences can alight."

"They probably shouldn't have gotten married," writes Broun of his parents in *Whose Little Boy Are You?*. "They probably should never have had a child; and they probably shouldn't, after seventeen years of marriage, have gotten divorced." The relationship Broun describes between himself and his progressive, fiercely independent parents underlines the autobiography. The writer also describes his childhood in the company of family friends Dorothy Parker, Alexander Woollcott, Paul Robeson, and Marc Connelly. Young "Woodie" was treated as an equal by the adults surrounding him and was expected to preside along with Heywood and Ruth (for the whole family was always on a first-name basis) at his parents' dinner parties. In a *Publishers Weekly* interview, Broun summarizes his childhood as a difficult one: "As children of the nineteenth century, my parents were smothered and kept in their place, so it was a big thing to raise a child in freedom. . . . But freedom to do what? Freedom to chat with Alex Woollcott?" As for his parents' political viewpoints, Broun says he sympathized with their liberal beliefs but experienced difficulty relating to Heywood and Ruth as he became older: "Usually a child becomes radical against conservative parents, but it would have been tough to get to the left of my father."

Whose Little Boy Are You? "makes absorbing reading not only as an account of life with two notable Americans but, more generally, as a record of a soul's struggle . . . to communicate with those who were nearest and dearest," comments *Washington Post*'s Joseph McLellan, who adds, "Broun might be surprised to discover how many of his fellow citizens with more ordinary parents have suffered from the same problem." The author is "no mere anecdote-monger; his memoir is a purgative examination of his failure in the eyes of his parents," concludes Barbara Shulgasser in the *New York Times Book Review*. The critic calls the work "a painfully honest book. . . . Broun has [now] by ordinary standards achieved success. Yet he recalls his childhood embarrassments with the urgency of one who still feels the hurt."

BIOGRAPHICAL/CRITICAL SOURCES: Heywood Hale Broun, *A Studied Madness*, Doubleday, 1965; Broun, *Tumultuous Merriment*, Richard Marek, 1979; *Los Angeles Times Book Review*, June 24, 1979; *New York Times*, July 4, 1979, May 13, 1983; *Chicago Tribune Book World*, July 8, 1979; *Chicago Tribune*, July 24, 1979; *Washington Post*, July 24, 1979, August 8, 1983; *New York Times Book Review*, July 29, 1979, June 5, 1983; Broun, *Whose Little Boy Are You?: A Memoir of the Broun Family*, St. Martin's, 1983; *Publishers Weekly*, June 3, 1983; *Time*, June 13, 1983.

* * *

BROWN, Frederick G(ramm) 1932-

PERSONAL: Born April 6, 1932, in Madison, Wis.; son of Fred E. (an accountant) and Meda (Gramm) Brown; married Barbara Ann Thaller (an art teacher), June 23, 1956; children: Jeffrey, Kirk, Daniel. *Education:* University of Wisconsin, B.A., 1954, M.A., 1955; University of Minnesota, Ph.D., 1958. *Religion:* Lutheran. *Home:* 2616 Kellogg, Ames, Iowa 50010. *Office:* Department of Psychology, Iowa State University, Ames, Iowa 50011.

CAREER: University of Missouri—Columbia, assistant professor of psychology and assistant director of testing and counseling, 1958-61; Iowa State University, Ames, assistant professor, 1961-64, associate professor, 1964-68, professor of psychology and education, 1968—. *Member:* American Psychological Association (fellow), American Educational Research Association, National Council on Measurement in Education, American Association for the Advancement of Science, Phi Beta Kappa. *Awards, honors:* National post-doctoral fellow, U.S. Office of Education, 1967-68; fellow, Center for Advanced Study in the Behavioral Sciences, 1967-68.

WRITINGS: Principles of Educational and Psychological Testing, Dryden Press, 1970, 3rd edition, Holt, 1983; *Measurement and Evaluation,* F. E. Peacock, 1971; *Guidelines for Test Use,* National Council on Measurement in Education, 1980; *Measuring Classroom Achievement,* Holt, 1981. Contributor to education and psychology journals.

* * *

BROWN, George Mackay 1921-

PERSONAL: Born October 17, 1921, in Stromness, Orkney Islands, Scotland; son of John and Mary Jane (Mackay) Brown. *Education:* Attended Newbattle Abbey College, 1951-53, 1956; University of Edinburgh, M.A., 1960, graduate study on the poetry of Gerard Manley Hopkins, 1962-64; Open University, M.A. *Religion:* Catholic. *Home:* 3 Mayburn Court, Stromness, Orkney Islands KW16 3DH, Scotland.

CAREER: Poet and author. *Member:* Royal Society of Literature (fellow). *Awards, honors:* Arts Council of Great Britain award for poetry, 1965; Society of Authors Travel Award, 1967; Scottish Arts Council award and Katherine Mansfield Menton short story prize, both 1969, for *A Time to Keep, and Other Stories;* officer, Order of the British Empire, 1974; honorary LL.D., Dundee University.

WRITINGS—Published by Hogarth, except as indicated: *The Storm, and Other Poems,* Orkney Press, 1954; *Loaves and Fishes* (poetry), 1959; *The Year of the Whale* (poetry), 1965.

The Five Voyages of Arnor (poetry), K. D. Duval, 1966; *A Calendar of Love* (stories), 1967, published as *A Calendar of Love and Other Stories,* Harcourt, 1968; *Twelve Poems,* Festival Publications, 1968; *A Time to Keep, and Other Stories,* 1969, Harcourt, 1970; *An Orkney Tapestry* (essays), Gollancz, 1969; "Witch" (play), first produced in Edinburgh, England, 1969.

A Spell for Green Corn (play; broadcast, 1967; adaptation produced at Perth Theatre, March, 1972), 1970; *Lifeboat and Other Poems,* 1971; *Poems New and Selected,* 1971, Harcourt, 1973; *Fishermen with Ploughs: A Poem Cycle,* 1971; *Greenvoe: A Novel,* Harcourt, 1972; (contributor of poem) Oliver Aston, *Water,* Evans Brothers, 1972; *Magnus: A Novel,* 1973; *The Two Fiddlers: Tales from Orkney,* 1974; *Hawkfall and Other Stoires,* 1974.

Letters from Hamnavoe (selected journalism), Gordon Wright Publishing, 1975; *Edwin Muir: A Brief Memoir,* Castlelaw Press, 1975; *From Stone to Thorn,* Abingdon, 1975; *Winterfold* (poetry), Chatto & Windus, 1976; *The Sun's Net* (short stories), 1976; *Witch, and Other Stories,* Longman, 1977; *Pictures in the Cave* (children's stories), Chatto & Windus, 1977; *Selected Poems,* 1977; *Under Brinkie's Brae* (selected journalism), Gordon Wright Publishing, 1979.

Six Lives of Fankle the Cat (children's stories), Chatto & Windus, 1980; *Portrait of Orkney,* 1981; *Andrina, and Other Stories,* Chatto & Windus, 1982; *Voyages* (poetry), 1984. Also author of television poem, "The Winter Islands," broadcast 1966; also author of several television and radio scripts, including "Orkney Trilogy," "Miss Barraclough," and "Andrina"; also author of stage works, "The Loom of Light," 1972, and "The Well," 1981. Also collaborator, with composer Peter Maxwell Davies, of musical works, including an opera, "Magnus," and a cantata, "Solstice of Light."

SIDELIGHTS: George Mackay Brown writes of life and nature in his native Orkney Islands. He has written novels, children's stories, essays, and media pieces, although he is best-known as a poet. His books often express religious, ritualistic themes, especially relating to Orkney living and his fictional Orkney town, Hamnavoe. Douglas Sealy states in the *Times Literary Supplement,* "Brown's books, with their insistence on the ritual of daily living, on the religious underpinning of our lives, and on the cyclic nature of our existence, are like a richly illuminated book of hours." Thomas J. Starr of the *Dictionary of Literary Biography* calls Brown "probably the greatest living Scottish writer."

Brown attempts to capture and re-create the reality of his homeland through both his prose and verse. A *Times Literary Supplement* reviewer comments that "Brown is a uniquely observant and skilful chronicler of life in his native Orkneys, past and present." In *Phoenix,* Harold Massingham concurs with the *Times Literary Supplement* observation, noting, "Brown knows where he is and writes with a local and natural authority." Massingham sees the same approach in Brown's poetry: "His local colour, in fact his total effect, is of a mature distillation and blend by an excellent and unmistakeable poet patiently subdued by, and to, the demands of his terrain." Reviewing *Voyages* for the *Times Literary Supplement,* Douglas Dunn maintains that "Brown's idealism is retrospective, fictionalizing a place and its meaning through an affectionate exploration of history which he holds up like a cupped treasure in the hands, and as an offering to the residual innocence of his native Orkney Islands."

Brown's work concentrates on traditional values and time-honored ethics. Dunn observes in *Poetry Nation* that "Brown, as a poet of remote island communities and unindustrial, non-urban landscapes, is at odds with the tradition of modern poetry." Dunn continues: "Brown's best poems are . . . full of names and characters, their typical vulnerabilities, and the virtues of the way of life their personalities prove. He celebrates an ideal of community." Sealy also recognizes traditional elements in Brown's poetry, asserting, "Brown, though he acknowledges the contemporary life of the islands intellectually, rejects it emotionally, so that his best poems are always instinct with nostalgia." In a *Times Literary Supplement* review, Dunn remarks upon Brown's traditional qualities in prose as well: "Since *A Calendar of Love* appeared in 1967, Brown has perfected a narrative style of great simplicity, its virtues drawn more from the ancient art of telling tales than from new-fangled methodologies of fiction."

About Brown's efforts in *Andrina and Other Stories,* Stuart Evans claims in the London *Times* that "this superb teller of tales who, whether he is writing in prose or verse, is always the poet, offers in this book a magical selection." Evans adds, "[The stories'] common strength, apart from George Mackay Brown's exquisite and unerring way with words, is in their humanity." Dunn also applauds Brown's work in the book, stating in the *Times Literary Supplement,* "In writing so controlled, . . . by a poet perfectly at ease with his imagination and a language natural to it, the effect of that apparent collision of old and new can only be fruitful and challenging, as well as, in this case, profoundly enjoyable."

This affinity between Brown's prose and poetry styles has also been noted by Starr, who calls Brown "a prose stylist with a poetic vision." Starr finds *Greenvoe,* Brown's novel of an imaginary island town, to be a superb example of Brown's artistry. "It is in *Greenvoe,*" he writes, "that Brown most successfully weaves all of [his recurring themes] into his own seamless garment.... *Greenvoe* is ... the culmination of all of George Mackay Brown's fictional concerns.... His novel ranks with *The Great Gatsby, Mrs. Dalloway,* and *The Spire* as among the great prose poems of this century."

Brown doesn't always garner critical praise, however. About *Six Lives of Fankle the Cat,* Charles Causley suggests in the *Times Literary Supplement* that "Brown's relaxed manner and somewhat loosely constructed narrative lack the cutting edge, the dramatic tension, . . . that we have grown to expect from his brilliant creation and re-creation of Orcadian myth and legend, for children and adults." Dunn complains in *Poetry Nation* that "unfortunately, Brown has now put forward a quaintly antithetical notion that there is a certain kind of real life for the good men of the Orkneys, and another kind of life in the cities of the mainland which is so vicious that it brings total punishment." Despite the occasional negative comment, most reviewers admire Brown's work. Evans observes in the *Times* that Brown's "characters greet the imagination with shy or confident assertion, leaving his readers richer for a chuckle or the hint of some sadness shared." Dunn remarks in *Poetry Nation* that in Brown's "best work, he solves all the problems of the poet who wants to be both bucolic, real, hard and northern."

In a brief commentary on his own writing, Brown told *CA:* "Since it seems to me that our civilization will possibly destroy itself before too long, I am interested in the labour and lives of the most primitive people of our civilization, the food-getters (crofters and fishermen) since it is those people living close to the sources of life who are most likely to survive and continue the human story; and since even their lives would be meaningless otherwise, I see religion as an illuminating and stabilising force in the life of a community. Out of these things I make my poems, stories, and plays."

Brown also told *CA* he considers the following "a kind of basic credo": "I believe in dedicated work rather than in 'inspiration'; of course on some days, one writes better than on others. I believe writing to be a craft like carpentry, plumbing, or baking; one does the best one can. Much mischief has been caused by a loose word like 'culture,' which separates the crafts into the higher arts like music, writing, sculpture, and the lowlier workaday arts (those, and the many others like them, that I have mentioned above). In 'culture circles,' there is a tendency to look upon artists as the new priesthood of some esoteric religion. Nonsense—and dangerous nonsense moreover—we are all hewers of wood and drawers of water; only let us do it as thoroughly and joyously as we can."

MEDIA ADAPTATIONS: The Two Fiddlers was adapted as "The Two Fiddlers: Opera in Two Acts" by Peter Maxwell Davies, with the libretto by Davies published by Boosey & Hawkes in 1978; the story "Andrina" of *Andrina, and Other Stories* was made into a television film by Bill Forsyth in 1982.

BIOGRAPHICAL/CRITICAL SOURCES: Times Literary Supplement, February 16, 1967, September 28, 1973, February 22, 1980, November 21, 1980, April 10, 1981, April 1, 1983, January 20, 1984; *Listener,* April 17, 1967; *Phoenix,* winter, 1971; Iain Crichton Smith, *Iain Crichton Smith, Norman MacCaig, George Mackay Brown,* Penguin Books, 1972; *Washington Post Book World,* November 26, 1972; *Hudson Review,* Volume XXVI, number 4, 1973-74; *Poetry Nation,* Number 2, 1974; *Contemporary Literary Criticism,* Volume V, Gale, 1976; Alan Bold, *George Mackay Brown,* Oliver & Boyd, 1978; *Dictionary of Literary Biography,* Volume XIV: *British Novelists since 1960,* Gale, 1983; *Times* (London), February 13, 1983.

* * *

BROWN, Irene Bennett 1932-

PERSONAL: Born January 31, 1932, in Topeka, Kan.; daughter of Paul Howard and Vesta (Helberg) Bennett; married Robert Ray Brown (a research chemist), November 2, 1951; children: Rourke Alan, Corey Wayne, Melia Elaine, Shana Leigh. *Education:* Attended high schools in Oregon. *Address:* Box 75, 149 West Union, Jefferson, Ore. 97352.

CAREER: Worked in Salem, Ore., as waitress, 1951, retail clerk, 1951-52, and long distance telephone operator, 1952-53; writer for children. *Member:* Society of Children's Book Writers (member of board of advisors), Western Writers of America, Authors Guild, Authors League of America, Kansas State Historical Society. *Awards, honors:* Pacific Northwest Writers Conference, editors award for juvenile stories, 1967, 1969, and for best children's book, 1975; Golden Spur award for best western juvenile book of 1982, Western Writers of America, for *Before the Lark.*

WRITINGS—Juvenile and young adult fiction: *To Rainbow Valley,* McKay, 1969; *Run from a Scarecrow,* Concordia, 1978; *Skitterbrain,* Nelson, 1978; *Wilson Whip* (Junior Literary Guild selection), Atheneum, 1979; *Morning Glory Afternoon* (Young Adult Literary Guild selection), Atheneum, 1981; *Before the Lark* (Junior Literary Guild selection), Atheneum, 1982; *Just Another Gorgeous Guy,* Atheneum, 1984.

Contributor of adult articles to *Westways, Northwest Living, Portland Oregonian, Oregon Journal,* and other publications; contributor of children's short stories and serials to *Five/Six, Friends, Fun for Middlers, Children's Friend,* and other magazines. Woman's editor, *Capitol Press* (Oregon farm weekly).

WORK IN PROGRESS: A novel, *Sometimes a Song,* about a girl's search of her past to learn her true identity; other novels for upper elementary and young adult readers.

SIDELIGHTS: "If I were to choose a theme for myself," Irene Bennett Brown writes, "it would be a framed quotation by author Robert Fontaine that hangs on my study wall: 'To be a writer is to reach, however awkwardly, for the stars, and move, however haltingly, in that direction.'

"I write what is in me to write, on subjects with which I have an emotional identity. I like to think that in turn I stir the emotions of my readers. A book for me begins, quite often, with wondering what would it be like if . . .? In *Before the Lark,* I wanted to know how it feels to have an affliction one cannot help and be shunned and ill-treated because of it. How does that person manage?

"Too many youngsters, I believe, are the object of injustice. They may be poor, or in a minority, or fat, plain, or any of the other endless stigmas. In *Before the Lark,* Jocey Royal is a social outcast because of a facial disfigurement, a harelip. I want kids to know, through reading my books about characters such as Jocey, that they are not alone. That injustice can be dealt with, and overcome, sometimes even gloriously.

"I find writing is work, but work I love. And days when the writing goes well, I'm ready to believe that a fairy godmother toe dances on the carriage of my typewriter."

BROWN, Ivor (John Carnegie) 1891-1974

PERSONAL: Born April 25, 1891, in Penang (now part of Federation of Malaya); died April 22, 1974, in London, England; son of William (a doctor) and Jean (Carnegie) Brown; married Irene Hentschel (a director of plays), January 4, 1916. *Education:* Attended Cheltenham College; Balliol College, Oxford, B.A. (with first class honors). *Politics:* "Capricious." *Religion:* Agnostic. *Home and office:* 20 Christchurch Hill, London N.W. 3, England. *Agent:* A. D. Peters & Co. Ltd., 10 Buckingham St., London WC2N 6BU, England.

CAREER: Writer and editor. *Manchester Guardian,* Manchester, England, drama critic, leader writer, and general journalist, 1921-35; drama critic for *Saturday Review,* 1923-30, *Observer,* 1929-54, *Week End Review,* 1930-34, *Sketch,* 1935-39, and *Punch,* 1940-42, all in London, England; *Observer,* editor, 1942-48, associate editor and honorary director, 1948-54; editor of *Theatre,* 1954-55; editor of *Drama,* 1956-74. Shute Lecturer in art of the theatre, Liverpool University, 1926; professor of drama, Royal Society of Literature, 1939. Director of drama, Council for Encouragement of Music and the Arts, 1940-42; chairman, British Drama League, 1954-65; governor of Old Vic and Shakespeare Memorial Theatres. Commentator for British Broadcasting Corp. radio. *Member:* Institute of Journalists (fellow), Critics' Circle (London, president, 1934-35), Authors' Society, Royal and Ancient Golf Club of St. Andrews, Garrick and Savile Clubs (both London). *Awards, honors:* Knight of Dannebrog (Denmark), 1949; LL.D., University of St. Andrews, 1950; D.Litt., University of Aberdeen, 1950; named Commander of the Order of the British Empire, 1957.

WRITINGS: Years of Plenty (novel), Secker, 1915, Doran, 1916; *Security,* Secker, 1916.

English Political Theory, Methuen, 1920, 2nd edition, 1929; *Lighting-Up Time,* Cobden-Sanderson, 1920; *The Meaning of Democracy,* Cobden-Sanderson, 1920, revised edition, Duckworth, 1950; *H. G. Wells,* Nisbet & Co., 1923, 2nd edition, 1929, reprinted, Folcroft, 1972; *Smithfield Preserv'd; or, The Divill, a Vegetarian* (interlude from quarto of 1925; produced by Critics' Circle at a private party in London, June 30, 1925), Samuel French (acting edition), 1925, privately printed for A. G. Leonard (Chicago), 1926; *Masques and Phases,* Cobden-Sanderson, 1926; *First Player: The Origin of Drama,* G. Howe, 1927, reprinted, Folcroft, 1974; *Parties of the Play,* Benn, 1928; *Essays of To-day and Yesterday,* Harrap, 1929; *Now on View* (essays), Methuen, 1929; *Art and Everyman,* Benn, 1929.

Brown Studies (essays), Eyre & Spottiswoode, 1930; *Puck, Our Peke,* Routledge, 1931; (with others) *A London Symphony,* London Committee of International Illumination Congress, 1931; *Marine Parade,* Gollancz, 1932; *I Commit to the Flames!* (essays), Hamish Hamilton, 1934; *Master Sanguine, Who Always Believed What He Was Told,* Hamish Hamilton, 1934, Harper, 1935; *The Heart of England,* foreword by J. B. Priestley, Scribner, 1935, 3rd edition, Batsford, 1951; *The Great and the Goods,* Hamish Hamilton, 1937; *I Made You Possible: A Play for the Girls of To-day in One Act,* Samuel French, 1937; (with George Fearon) *This Shakespeare Industry: Amazing Monument,* Harper, 1939 (published in England as *Amazing Monument: A Short History of the Shakespeare Industry,* Heinemann, 1939), reprinted, Greenwood Press, 1969, reprinted as *Amazing Monument: A Short History of the Shakespeare Industry,* Kennikat, 1970; (with Fearon) *The Shakespeares* [and] *The Birthplace* (the former by Brown, the latter by Fearon), Edward Fox, 1939; *Life within Reason,* Nicholson & Watson, 1939; *Down on the Farm* (one-act play), Samuel French, 1939.

(Contributor) James Lees-Milne, editor, *The National Trust: A Record of Fifty Years' Achievement,* Batsford, 1945; *The Old Vic "King Lear"* (critical review), Curtain Press, 1946; *William's Other Anne* (play), Samuel French, 1947; (with others) *Britain's Heritage: The Achievement of the National Trust, 1895-1945,* introduction by G. M. Trevelyan, Batsford, 1948; (editor and author of introduction) *"Observer" Profiles,* Wingate, 1948, reprinted, Arno, 1978; *Shakespeare* (biography), Doubleday, 1949, 2nd edition, revised and abridged, Collins, 1957, special edition, Time, Inc., 1962.

(Editor) *Shakespeare Memorial Theatre: A Photographic Record,* photographs by Angus McBean, Volume I: *1948-50,* foreword by Brown and Anthony Quayle, Reinhardt & Evans, 1951, Volume II: *1951-53* (includes a critical analysis by Brown), Max Reinhardt, 1953, Volume III: *1954-56* (includes a critical analysis by Brown), Max Reinhardt, 1956, Theatre Arts, 1957, Volume IV: *1957-59,* Max Reinhardt, 1959, Theatre Arts, 1960; *Winter in London,* Collins, 1951, Doubleday, 1952; (author of introduction) J. B. Priestley, *The Priestley Companion,* Heinemann, 1951; *Summer in Scotland,* Collins, 1952, Macmillan, 1953; (compiler) *The Bedside "Guardian"* (selections from the *Manchester Guardian,* 1951-52 to 1954-55) Collins, Volume I, 1952, Volume II, 1953, Volume III, 1954, Volume IV, 1955; (author of introduction) *The Complete Works of William Shakespeare,* four volumes, Nonesuch Press, 1953; (with Christopher Fry) *The Approach to Dramatic Criticism* [and] *An Experience of Critics* (the former by Brown and others, the latter by Fry), edited by Kaye Webb, prologue by Alec Guinness, Oxford University Press, 1953; *The Way of My World* (autobiography), Collins, 1954; (author of introduction) William Shakespeare, *Othello,* Folio Society (London), 1955; *Balmoral: The History of a Home,* Collins, 1955; *Pictures on the Wall* (one-act ghost play), Samuel French, 1955; *Emily's Night* (one-act play), Samuel French, 1957; *Dark Ladies,* Collins, 1957; *J. B. Priestley* (booklet; special issue of *British Book News*), Longmans, Green, 1957, revised edition, 1964; *William Shakespeare* (juvenile), Thomas Nelson, 1958; (editor) *A Book of England* (anthology), Collins, 1958; (author of introduction and notes on illustrations) *Royal Homes in Colour* (also see below), photographs by A. F. Kersting and others, Batsford, 1958.

London, Newnes, 1960, Macmillan, 1961; *Shakespeare in His Time,* Thomas Nelson, 1960, reprinted, Greenwood Press, 1976; (editor) *A Book of London* (anthology), Collins, 1961; (with Ralph Dutton) *Stately Homes in Colour* (single-volume edition of *Royal Homes in Colour,* by Brown, and *English Country Houses in Colour,* by Dutton), Batsford, 1961; *Mind Your Language!,* Bodley Head, 1962, Dufour, 1964; *Look at Theatres,* Hamish Hamilton, 1962; (compiler) *A Book of Marriage,* Hamish Hamilton, 1963; *How Shakespeare Spent the Day,* Bodley Head, 1963, Hill & Wang, 1964; *Dickens in His Time,* Thomas Nelson, 1963; *Shakespeare and His World,* Walck, 1964; *What Is a Play?,* Macdonald & Co., 1964; *London: An Illustrated History,* Studio Vista, 1965; *Shaw in His Time,* Thomas Nelson, 1965, reprinted, Greenwood Press, 1979; *Doctor Johnson and His World,* Lutterworth, 1965, Walck, 1966; *Jane Austen and Her World,* Lutterworth, 1966, Walck, 1967; *William Shakespeare,* Morgan-Grampian, Books, 1968, A. S. Barnes, 1969; *The Women in Shakespeare's Life,* Bodley Head, 1968, Coward, 1969.

Dickens and His World, Walck, 1970; (editor) *W. Somerset Maugham,* A. S. Barnes, 1970; (compiler and author of introduction) Robert Louis Stevenson, *Home from the Sea* (poems), Bodley Head, 1970; (compiler) *Charles Dickens, 1812-1870* (facsimile documents, broadsheets, and essays), Viking, 1970; *Shakespeare and the Actors,* Bodley Head, 1970, Coward, 1971; *Old and Young: A Personal Summing Up,* Bodley Head, 1971; *Conan Doyle: A Biography of the Creator of Sherlock Holmes,* Hamilton, 1972.

"Word-anthology" series; published by J. Cape, except as indicated: *A Word in Your Ear* (also see below), 1942; *Just Another Word* (also see below), 1943; *Book of Words* (contains *A Word in Your Ear* and *Just Another Word*), 1944, published as *A Word in Your Ear; and, Just Another Word,* foreword by J. Donald Adams, Dutton, 1945, reprinted, 1963, published as *Ivor Brown's Book of Words,* Greenwood Press, 1978; *I Give You My Word,* 1945, published with *Say the Word* (also see below) in a single volume as *I Give You My Word* [and] *Say the Word,* with an introduction by Adams, Dutton, 1948, reprinted, 1964; *Say the Word,* 1947; *No Idle Words,* 1948, published with *Having the Last Word* (also see below) in a single volume as *No Idle Words* [and] *Having the Last Word,* with an introduction by Adams, Dutton, 1951, reprinted, Greenwood Press, 1977; *Having the Last Word,* 1950; *I Break My Word,* 1951; *A Word in Edgeways,* 1953; *Chosen Words,* 1955, reprinted, Greenwood Press, 1978; *Words in Our Time,* 1958, reprinted, Greenwood Press, 1974; *Words in Season,* Hart-Davis, 1961, reprinted, Greenwood Press, 1974; *A Ring of Words,* Bodley Head, 1967, Transatlantic, 1972; *A Rhapsody of Words,* Bodley Head, 1969, Transatlantic, 1972; *Random Words,* Bodley Head, 1971; *A Charm of Names,* Bodley Head, 1972; *Words on the Level,* Bodley Head, 1973, Transatlantic, 1974.

Also author of *Journalism in Our Time* (oration delivered by Brown during the 37th Foundation Week of University College Union Society), [London], 1933, and of essays on dramatic criticism, Shakespeare, and poetic drama, published in *Transactions* of the Royal Society of Literature.

SIDELIGHTS: Ivor Brown once said that he began his literary career when he learned to spell, and that he never really specialized, preferring to practice journalism and authorship in several different forms. He was known as an essayist, novelist, journalist, playwright, and drama critic, as well as a "word-collector" whose research and speculations added much to the English language treasury of verbal meanings. A reviewer for the *Times Literary Supplement* wrote that "such guardians of English usage as Mr. Ivor Brown are much needed now and his onset against slipshod speech, pretentious writing and bureaucratic jargon should be taken to heart by everybody." In a review of *Mind Your Language!,* a *New York Times Book Review* writer found "the burden of Mr. Brown's message on simplicity and verbiage, on cliches and on the vitamin-rich qualities of slang in nourishing language . . . admirable in every way."

Brown's witty and imaginative approach to language carried over to his novels about English authors, which could be called social surveys of specific eras rather than histories, literary critiques, or biographies. Although offering little that was new in the way of interpretation, he documented the periods of his subjects (e.g., Jane Austen, Charles Dickens, Samuel Johnson) through detailed analyses of their lives and times, augmenting the text with carefully selected, annotated photographs. *Jane Austen and Her World* is a description of the actual world in which she lived, rather than the narrow one of which she wrote. Contemporary drawings, fashion, furniture, and architecture share pages with the social, political, economic, and cultural flavor of her environment. Similarly, Brown filled in the background of *Shaw in His Time* with Shaw's stated opinions on the politics, economics, religion, theatre, education, and status of women of his day. A *Times Literary Supplement* reviewer of the book noted that "Brown's judgments on every aspect of Shaw's prodigious achievement are valid in the light of his own keen participation in its circumstances. . . . It is the measure of Mr. Brown's advocacy that he proves beyond any doubt that G.B.S. played a leading seriocomic role in the blood and thunder melodrama of his time."

A meticulous and scholarly writer in any genre of his choice, Brown was perhaps best known for his ventures into Shakespeareana. *The Women in Shakespeare's Life* was his penultimate contribution to an ever-widening field of historical (and conjectural) literature about William Shakespeare and his family. A *New Yorker* reviewer wrote that this "is Mr. Brown's fourth book on Shakespeare, and there is not enough material for it . . . [His] two serious arguments are that the women in Shakespeare's family were more literate than has been held, and that his marriage was not that bad. His candidate for 'Mr. W.H.' is Pembroke, and for the Dark Lady is Mary Fitton, but he has no new evidence." James Sandoe, however, said in *Library Journal* that although "the index is inadequate, the bibliography a mild wave of the hand, . . . [the book's] judgment has a weight that does not need footnotes." Sandoe concluded that *The Women in Shakespeare's Life* "should lead readers contentedly to more of Mr. Brown's beguiling books."

BIOGRAPHICAL/CRITICAL SOURCES: Ivor Brown, *The Way of My World,* Collins, 1954; *Times Literary Supplement,* June 1, 1962, January 27, 1966; *New York Times Book Review,* April 26, 1964, January 24, 1965, May 7, 1967; *Young Readers' Review,* April, 1967; *Books and Bookmen,* December, 1967, August, 1970; *Observer Review,* June 30, 1968, April 25, 1971; *Plays and Players,* October, 1968; *Library Journal,* March 15, 1969; *New Yorker,* March 29, 1969; Brown, *Old and Young: A Personal Summing Up,* Bodley Head, 1971; *New York Times,* April 23, 1974.

OBITUARIES: *New York Times,* April 23, 1974.†

* * *

BROWNLOW, Kevin 1938-

PERSONAL: Born June 2, 1938, in Crowborough, Sussex, England; son of Robert Thomas and Nina (Fortnum) Brownlow. *Agent:* Harold Matson Co., Inc., 22 East 40th St., New York, N.Y. 10016.

CAREER: Film editor for World Wide Pictures, London, England, 1955-61, Samaritan Films, London, 1961-65, and Woodfall Films, London, 1965-68. Director, with Andrew Mollo, of "It Happened Here," 1966, and "Winstanley," 1975, of "Charm of Dynamite" (biographical film on Abel Gance, French movie innovator, for BBC-TV), and, with David Gill, "Hollywood" (thirteen-part television series), 1980, and "Unknown Chaplain" (three-part television series), 1983; also director of documentaries. *Member:* British Film Institute (former member of board of governors). *Awards, honors:* "It Happened Here" received Writers Guild award for best original screenplay, 1966; British Academy award nomination for editing, 1968, for "Charge of the Light Brigade"; British Film Institute special award for "Winstanley."

WRITINGS: How It Happened Here, Doubleday, 1968; *The Parade's Gone By . . .* (chronicle and analysis of silent films), Knopf, 1968; (editor) Karl Brown, *Adventures with D. W. Griffith,* Secker & Warburg, 1974; *The War, the West, and the Wilderness,* Knopf, 1979; *Hollywood: The Pioneers* (also see below; based on television series "Hollywood"), illustrated with photographs by John Kobol, Collins, 1980; "Hollywood" (television series), Thames Television, 1980; *Napoleon: Abel Gance's Classic Film,* Knopf, 1983. Also author of film scripts. Contributor of articles on film history to English film magazines.

SIDELIGHTS: Kevin Brownlow's research into the years of the silent film has resulted in a number of books dealing with such subjects as the early documentary, the innovators of the silent era, and French director Abel Gance's classic movie, "Napoleon."

In *The War, the West, and the Wilderness* Brownlow explores the intense, often dangerous methods used by Hollywood's early directors in filming features like "Nanook of the North" and "Terra Nova." According to the author, these films, shot entirely on location, often used actual participants in historical events recreating their actions for the camera. Thus, Mexican revolutionary Pancho Villa staged a raid for "The Life of General Francisco Villa" and British Prime Ministers Winston Churchill and David Lloyd George played themselves for a D. W. Griffith film. At the same time, some filmmakers exposed themselves to incredible risks in order to get a compelling shot. "If one can summarize the age that Brownlow celebrates, it is that of Herbert Ponting, recorder of Captain Robert Scott's expedition to the South Pole in 1910," says Richard Schickel of *Time.* "To record Scott's ship, the *Terra Nova,* slicing its way through polar ice, Ponting ordered a camera platform rigged to hang out ten feet from the starboard side of the ship. There, spread-eagled, unable to protect himself since his camera required both hands to operate, this mild-mannered banker's son conquered fear and seasickness to bring back an unforgettable image of heroic folly."

"A film book as beautiful and sane as this one is a very great rarity," writes *New Statesman* critic Russell Davies of *The War, the West, and the Wilderness.* "What distinguishes it from the spangled mass of reputation-mongering memoirs is that it is not really about the 'cinema industry' at all. It is about individuals at work, and the resourcefulness, courage and quickness of eye (or, in contrasting cases, trickery, hypocrisy and disregard for truth) they brought to the task of capturing, on silent film, what might be called the world's 'heroic grandeur.'"

The War, the West, and the Wilderness was followed by *Hollywood: The Pioneers,* a companion book to a thirteen-part Thames Television series Brownlow also wrote. Essentially compiling an homage to the stars both before and behind the camera, the author uses his interviews and John Kobol's often rare photographs to achieve a work that Lisa Mitchell calls "alive, entertaining, human, logical, concise and joyously easy to follow." Writing in the *Los Angeles Times Book Review,* Mitchell adds that *Hollywood* "is also a tribute to the pioneer still photographers, whose 'lighting techniques . . . created effects as rich and subtle as those of the great painters,' and whom Kobol, through indefatigable sleuthing and educated guessing, rescues from anonymity whenever possible."

Among the new information unearthed by Brownlow's interviews in *Hollywood* are facts such as that Harold Lloyd, famed for executing supposedly death-defying acts in his silent comedies, actually used a stuntman for the more perilous scenes, and that, according to Frank Rich's *Time* review, "Leading Man John Gilbert's career was not destroyed by his allegedly high-pitched voice but by the soupy dialogue of his first sound movies." The author, suggests Rich, "feels a true sense of loss about the era he describes. So many of the people and landmarks are gone now; so many early films have literally turned to dust. Brownlow holds that the advent of sound robbed movies of their power to stimulate the viewers' imaginations; once the audience no longer had to imagine voices, it ceased to be an active 'creative contributor to the process of making a film.'"

When French *auteur* Abel Gance made "Napoleon" in the 1920s, he found that his audience was not ready for the advanced filmmaking techniques he had utilized, such as subliminal cutting (adding visuals to a scene that would only last a fraction of a second), multiple-screen projection, and unrestricted mobility of the camera. The finished film was cut apart by its distributors and then was lost for decades. Brownlow, as early as his student days, took on the job of finding and reassembling the bits and pieces of the movie, enlisting the aid of the British Film Institute, the National Film Archive, Thames Television, and his partner, David Gill. Brownlow's efforts proved successful: in 1980, a restored, five-hour print of Gance's "Napoleon" enjoyed a triumphant tour of the United States and Great Britain, accompanied by a symphony orchestra to perform the film's score. The "Napoleon" screenings were sellouts at virtually every theater where they played.

Brownlow chronicles the challenging project in his book *Napoleon: Abel Gance's Classic Film.* Reviewing the work in the London *Times,* David Robinson notes that "the almost culpable modesty of [the author's] record cannot conceal the heroism of the effort; and the excitement that sustained him is communicated, so that the reader shares the thrill of every new sequence found, every obstacle overcome." The story of the film's second life, writes Robinson, "has sad and happy endings. The sad one is that with success (the resurrected 'Napoleon' has already earned [several] million dollars) came the inevitable unseemly wrangling over rights and profits. . . . The happy end is that Gance lived long enough to see his dream restored [the director died in 1981]." According to the critic, Brownlow writes as if *Napoleon* "were a letter to a friend, and the revelations of his feeling are touching: 'I'm in love with the whole film. It's part of me.'"

BIOGRAPHICAL/CRITICAL SOURCES: New York Times, December 11, 1968, July 5, 1979; *Newsweek,* February 26, 1979; *New York Times Book Review,* March 25, 1979, November 13, 1983; *Time,* April 2, 1979, May 5, 1980; *New Statesman,* June 8, 1979; *Film Comment,* July-August, 1979; *Village Voice,* July 9, 1979; Kevin Brownlow, *Hollywood: The Pioneers,* Collins, 1980; *Times Literary Supplement,* January 18, 1980, September 9, 1983; *Los Angeles Times Book Review,* March 9, 1980, November 20, 1983; *Washington Post Book World,* April 13, 1980; *Listener,* May 8, 1980; *Times* (London), June 9, 1983.

—Sketch by Susan Salter

* * *

BROXHOLME, John Franklin 1930- (Duncan Kyle)

PERSONAL: Born June 11, 1930, in Bradford, England; son of Norman F. (a valuer) and Margaret (Smith) Broxholme;

married Alison Millar Hair (a teacher), September 22, 1956; children: Helen, Christopher, Lindsay. *Education:* Educated in Bradford, England. *Home and office:* Oak Lodge, Valley Farm Rd., Newton, Sudbury, Suffolk, England. *Agent:* Rupert Crew Ltd., 1A King's Mews, Gray's Inn Rd., London WC1N 2JA, England.

CAREER: Telegraph & Argus (newspaper), Bradford, England, reporter, 1946-48, 1950-53; *Leicester-Mercury,* Leeds, England, sub-editor, 1953-56; *Yorkshire Post,* Leeds, member of staff in features department, 1956-57; Odhams Press Ltd., London, England, assistant editor of *Today—The New John Bull* (magazine), 1957-64, editor of *TV World* (magazine), 1964-68, editorial director of Odhams Magazines, 1968-69; full-time writer, 1969—. *Military service:* British Army Intelligence Corps, 1948-50. *Member:* Crime Writers' Association (chairman, 1976-77).

WRITINGS—Under pseudonym Duncan Kyle, except as indicated; published by St. Martin's, except as indicated: (Contributor under name John Franklin Broxholme) John Dodge, editor, *The Practice of Journalism,* Heineman, 1968; *A Cage of Ice,* 1970; *Flight into Fear,* 1972; *A Raft of Swords,* 1973; *The Suvarov Adventure,* 1974; *Terror's Cradle,* 1975; *Whiteout,* 1976; *In Deep,* 1976; *Black Camelot,* 1978; *Greenriver High,* 1979; *Stalking Point,* 1981; *The King's Commissar,* 1984.

WORK IN PROGRESS: Another book.

SIDELIGHTS: Under the pseudonym Duncan Kyle, John Franklin Broxholme "writes thinking man's thrillers," says a *Time* critic, "that invariably become best-sellers in Britain, and for good reason: they combine all too human characters, masterly plotting, and impeccable research." Reviewing *A Cage of Ice* in the *New York Times,* Thomas Lask finds the book thoroughly convincing: "Most of the action takes place in the middle of bare Arctic wastes with nothing but ice, snow, wind and water of polar cold to mark the landscape. Duncan Kyle . . . knows this white emptiness like his right hand; there is nothing bookish about his telling what it means to live in these subzero temperatures, what the merest exposure can do to human flesh, what safeguards have to be taken and how vehicles and other machines have to be coaxed to perform their functions." Lask calls the work "a good tight thriller that provides first-rate armchair excitement with a tension that doesn't let up until the last page."

BIOGRAPHICAL/CRITICAL SOURCES: New York Times, August 20, 1971; *Time,* October 30, 1978.

* * *

BRUGGER, Bill
  See BRUGGER, William

* * *

BRUGGER, William 1941-
  (Bill Brugger)

PERSONAL: Born January 9, 1941, in Brighton, England; son of William Brugger; married Suzanne Mary Pollard; children: Katherine Mary Elizabeth, Antony William Fabian, Max William Eugene. *Education:* School of Oriental and African Studies, London, B.A., 1964, M.Sc., 1968, Ph.D., 1972. *Home:* 7 Centre Way, Belair, South Australia, Australia 5052. *Office:* School of Social Sciences, Flinders University of South Australia, Bedford Park, South Australia, Australia 5042.

CAREER: Peking Second Foreign Languages Institute, Peking, China, teacher, 1964-66; University of London, London, England, member of staff of Contemporary China Institute, 1968-71; Flinders University of South Australia, Bedford Park, lecturer, 1972-75, senior lecturer, 1976-77, reader, 1978-80, professor of politics, 1980—.

WRITINGS—Under name Bill Brugger, except as indicated; published by Croom Helm, except as indicated: (Under name William Brugger) *Democracy and Organisation in the Chinese Industrial Enterprise, 1948-1953,* Cambridge University Press, 1976; *Contemporary China,* 1977; (editor) *China: The Impact of the Cultural Revolution,* 1978; (editor) *China since the "Gang of Four,"* 1980; *China: Liberation and Transformation, 1942-1962,* 1981; *China: Radicalism to Revisionism, 1962-1979,* 1981; (with K. Hannan) *Modernisation and Revolution,* 1983.

SIDELIGHTS: William Brugger's *Democracy and Organization in the Chinese Industrial Enterprise, 1948-1953* is, according to Andrew G. Walder in a *Journal of Asian Studies* review, "a meticulous, solidly researched account of China's experiences with various accounting, control, administrative, and incentive systems in the construction and iron and steel industries immediately following Liberation." Primary among these systems was the unsuccessful "Soviet model," an attempt to implement in China a number of principles that had evolved in the Soviet Union. These included "one-man management, national planning, material incentives and piecework systems of remuneration, and staff-line systems of command," writes Michael Gasster in the *Annals of the American Academy of Political and Social Science.* Walder notes that earlier books on the subject tended to blame the failure of the Soviet model on "the commitment of the [Chinese] Communist Party leadership—primarily Mao—to a set of 'egalitarian and participatory' revolutionary goals," while Brugger's analysis "deals more complexly with the concrete cultural and environmental barriers that served to render Soviet modes of organization inappropriate to China."

Basically, Brugger states that the Western concept of organization was firmly implanted in Czarist Russia and continued to dominate Soviet thinking after the Russian Revolution. This system, he feels, is characterized by "guilt," which is fostered by Western religions, and which leads to what Walder describes as an "individualistic, inner-directed, goal-seeking" population. The Far Eastern cultures, on the other hand, are characterized by "shame," which is promoted by the Eastern religions, and which places "a greater emphasis on the reactions and desires of other people for individual motivation and guidance." When these two philosophies came together in China, says Walder, "Soviet 'technological' conceptions conflicted with traditional Chinese 'human' conceptions of organization." In the end, the Chinese developed their own organizational model, one more in line with their tradition of human solidarity, and this is the system that ultimately replaced the Soviet model.

Joyce K. Kallgren, reviewing *Democracy and Organization in the Chinese Industrial Enterprise, 1948-1953* for the *American Political Science Review,* points out that Brugger originally intended to "describe how the Chinese government took over enterprises and brought worker participation into the factory," but at the request of some early manuscript readers he soon moved "into the broader questions of the logic of industrialization and the historical experience in which the Chinese efforts must be viewed. These broader concerns dictate much of the volume's organization." As a result, Kallgren finds that "the meticulous scholarship which buttresses the author's carefully stated observations and judgments on Chinese enterprises makes this volume important not only for the political economist or historian but also for the contemporary analyst." Gasster agrees that the book addresses the larger issues of "political development, industrialization, and organization theory" and believes that it will "come to be regarded as a major pioneering study." Concludes Walder: "This complex, well-documented analysis stands as a landmark study of the People's Republic's earliest attempts at industrial organization. . . . Future studies of China's participatory organizational experiments will certainly use Brugger's analysis as a point of reference."

BIOGRAPHICAL/CRITICAL SOURCES: *Annals of the American Academy of Political and Social Science*, November, 1976; *Times Literary Supplement*, April 1, 1977; *Journal of Asian Studies*, August, 1977; *American Political Science Review*, September, 1978.

* * *

BRULLER, Jean (Marcel) 1902-
(Vercors, J. Bruller Vercors)

PERSONAL: Born February 26, 1902, in Paris, France; son of Louis and Ernestine (Bourbon) Bruller; married Jeanne Barusseaud, 1931 (divorced); married Rita Barisse, 1957; children: Francois, Jean-Louis, Bertrand. *Education:* Attended University of Paris and a technical college, received diploma in electrical engineering; studied art in Paris after military service. *Home:* Moulin des Iles, 77120 St. Augustin, France.

CAREER: Novelist, essayist, and artist specializing in graphic art and engraving; founder with Pierre de Lescure of Editions de Minuit (publishing house for French Resistance movement), 1941; lecturer, 1945—. Designer of sets and costumes for Comedie Francaise, Paris, 1964. *Military service:* French Army, served in Alpine regiment in Tunis, 1940; became lieutenant. *Member:* P.E.N., French section (vice-president), Comite National des Ecrivains (honorary president). *Awards, honors:* Legion d'honneur; medaille de la Resistance; Council of Europe prize, 1982, for *One Hundred Years of French History*, Volume I: *Moi, Aristide Briand.*

WRITINGS—All under pseudonym Vercors: *Le Silence de la mer*, Editions de Minuit (Paris), 1941, published as *Les Silences de la mer*, Pantheon, 1943, translation by Cyril Connolly published as *The Silence of the Sea*, Macmillan, 1944 (published in England as *Put out the Light*), illustrated enlarged edition published as *Le Silence de la mer*, Club des Libraries de France (Paris), 1964; *La Marche a l'etoile*, Editions de Minuit, 1943, Pantheon, 1946, translation by Eric Sutton published as *Guiding Star*, Macmillan, 1946; *Le Songe*, Editions de Minuit, 1945; *Souffrance de mon pays*, Emile-Paul, 1945; *Le Sable du temps*, Emile-Paul, 1946; (author of introduction) Diego Brosset, *Un Homme sans l'Occident*, Editions de Minuit, 1946; *Les Armes de la nuit*, Editions de Minuit, 1946; *L'Imprimerie de Verdun*, Bibliotheque francaise, 1947; *Les Mots*, Editions de Minuit, 1947; *Les Yeux et la lumiere: Mystere a six voix*, A. Michel (Paris), 1948, 1950.

Plus ou moins homme (essays), A. Michel, 1950; *La Puissance du jour*, A. Michel, 1951; *Les Animaux denatures* (novel), A. Michel, 1952, translation by wife, Rita Barisse, published as *You Shall Know Them*, Little, Brown, 1953 (published in England as *Borderline*, Macmillan, 1954), published as *The Murder of the Missing Link*, Pocket Books, 1958; *Portrait d'une amitie et autres morts memorables*, A. Michel, 1954; *Les Pas dans la sable: L'Amerique, la Chine, et la France*, A. Michel, 1954; *Coleres* (novel), A. Michel, 1956, translation by Barisse published as *The Insurgents*, Harcourt, 1956, reprinted, Ayer Co., 1979; *Les Divagations d'un Francais en Chine* (self-illustrated), A. Michel, 1956; *P.P.C.; ou, Le Concours de Blois*, A. Michel, 1957, translation by Jonathan Griffin published as *For the Time Being*, Hutchinson, 1960; *Goetz*, Musee de Poche, 1958; *Sur ce Rivage*, A. Michel, Volume I: *Le Periple*, 1958, Volume II: *Monsieur Prousthe: Un Souvenir*, 1958, Volume III: *La Liberte de decembre* [and] *Clementine*, 1960, translation of volumes II and III by Barisse published as *Paths of Love*, Putnam, 1961, published in England as *Freedom in December*, Hutchinson, 1961; (editor) *Morale chretienne et morale marxiste*, La Palatine (Paris), 1960.

Sylva (novel), B. Grasset, 1961, translation by Barisse published under same title, Putnam, 1962; (with Paul Misraki) *Les Chemins de l'etre: Une Discussion*, A. Michel, 1965; (with Paul Silva-Coronel) *Quota; ou, Les Plethoriens* (novel), Stock, 1966, translation by Barisse published as *Quota*, Putnam, 1966; *La Bataille du silence: Souvenirs de minuit*, Presses de la Cite (Paris), 1967, translation by Barisse published as *The Battle of Silence*, Holt, 1968; *Le Radeau de la Meduse* (novel), Presses de la Cite, 1969, translation by Audrey C. Foote published as *The Raft of the Medusa*, McCall, 1971.

Liberte ou fatalite? Oedipe et Hamlet, Perrin (Paris), 1970; *Contes des Cataplasmes*, Editions G. P. (Paris), 1971; *Sillages* (novel), Presses de la Cite, 1972; *Sept Sentiers du desert*, Presses de la Cite, 1972; *Questions sur la vie a MM les biologistes*, Stock, 1973; *Comme un Frere*, Plon (Paris), 1973; *Tendre Naufrage* (novel), Presses de la Cite, 1974; *Ce que je crois* (essay), B. Grasset, 1975; *Je cuisine comme un chef* (cookbook), Seghers, 1976; *Les Chevaux du temps* (novel), Tchou, 1977; *Sens et non-sens de l'histoire* (essay), Galilee, 1978; *Camille; ou, l'enfant double* (children's book), G. P., 1978; *Le Piege a loup* (novella), Galilee, 1979; (with Olga Wormser-Migot) *Assez Mentir!* (essay), Ramsay, 1979; *One Hundred Years of French History*, Plon, Volume I: *Moi, Aristide Briand*, 1981, Volume II: *Les occasions perdues*, 1982.

Collections: *Three Short Novels* (includes "Guiding Star," "Night and Fog," and "The Verdun Press"), Little, Brown, 1947; *La songe precede de ce jour-la*, P. Seghers, 1950; *Le Silence de la mer et autres recits*, A. Michel, 1951; *Les Armes de la nuit et* [and] *La Puissance du jour*, A. Michel, 1951; *Les Animaux denatures* [and] *La Marche a l'etoile* (also see below), Livre de Poche, 1956.

Plays: *Zoo; ou, l'Assassin philanthrope* (based on *Les Animaux denatures;* first produced in Carcassonne, France, 1963), Theatre National Populaire, 1964, translation by James Clancy produced as "Zoo; or, The Philanthropic Assassin by Vercors: A Judicial, Zoological, and Moral Comedy in Three Acts," in Ithaca, N.Y., at Cornell University, March, 1968; (translator and illustrator) William Shakespeare, *Hamlet: Une Tragedie en cinq actes*, Editions Vialetay, 1965; (adaptor) "Oedipe-Roi" (based on work by Sophocles), first produced in La Rochelle, France, 1967, produced in Paris, France, 1970; "Le Fer et le velours," produced in Nimes, France, 1969; (adaptor) *Chat!* (based on Hungarian play by Istvan Orkeny), Gallimard, 1974; *Collected Theatre*, Volume I: *Zoo; ou, l'assassin philanthrope, Le Fer et le velours,* [and] *Le Silence de la mer,* Volume II: *For Shakespeare (Hamlet, Macbeth)*, Galilee, 1978.

Collections of art work under name Jean Bruller: "21 Recettes de Mort Violente," 1926, published as *21 Delightful Ways of Committing Suicide for the Use of Persons Who are Discouraged or Disgusted with Life for Reasons Which Do Not Concern Us, Covici, Friede, 1930; "Hypotheses sur les amateurs de peinture" (title means "Hypotheses on Art Lovers"), 1927; "Un Homme coupe en tranches" (title means "A Man Cut Up in Slices"), 1929; "Les Releves trimestriels," 1932-38; "Nouvelle cle des songes" (title means "A New Key to Dreams"), 1934; "L'Enfer" (title means "This Is Hell"), 1935; "Visions intimes et rassurantes de la guerre" (title means "Comforting Visions of the War"), 1936; "Silences," 1937; "La Danse des vivants" (title means "The Dance of the Living"), 1938. Art work has been exhibited world-wide, including Vienna, 1970, and Budapest and Cologne, 1971. Producer, under name J. Bruller Vercors, of *Callichromies*, reproductions of paintings based on his own process developed from silkscreen (includes works by Renoir, Van Gogh, Braque, and Picasso), 1952-58. Also illustrator of editions of Kipling, Racine, and others, and of children's books.

WORK IN PROGRESS: *Les Nouveaux Jours*, volume III of *One Hundred Years of French History*.

SIDELIGHTS: During the Nazi occupation of France in World War II, Jean Bruller, operating under the name Vercors, cofounded a clandestine publishing house in order to print and distribute literary works important to the Resistance. Editions de Minuit, or Midnight Press, produced more than twenty volumes of contemporary literature in direct defiance of both the German and Vichy governments. The first of these "midnight editions" was Bruller's own *The Silence of the Sea*. This short novel was widely read and translated into some thirty languages. Its publication in the United States is said to have aroused much fervent anti-Nazi sentiment. Each copy of the original edition included the following statement: "Propaganda is not our domain. We mean to safeguard our inner life and freely serve our art. The names matter little. It is no longer a question of petty personal fame."

The Battle of Silence is the story of the Midnight Press, containing Bruller's personal recollections of life in Nazi-ruled Paris. According to *New Yorker* reviewer Naomi Bliven, the book is "fascinating, for [the author] tells about the everyday problems of conducting a publishing business—selecting a manuscript, designing a book—while he and all his associates were in the disquieting situation of being liable at any moment to discovery, torture, and execution for having committed any part of the editorial process. His account is enthralling because it is matter-of-fact; it provides the circumstantial evidence—practical details and down-to-earth descriptions—that makes it easy for readers to envision the author's fantastic activities."

BIOGRAPHICAL/CRITICAL SOURCES: Vercors, *Le Silence de la mer*, Editions de Minuit (Paris), 1941, published as *Les Silences de la mer*, Pantheon, 1943, translation by Cyril Connolly published as *The Silence of the Sea*, Macmillan, 1944 (published in England as *Put out the Light*), illustrated enlarged edition published as *Le Silence de la mer*, Club des Libraries de France (Paris), 1964; *New Yorker*, March 9, 1946, November 8, 1969; *New York Herald Tribune Book Review*, June 28, 1953; *Atlantic*, February, 1969; R. D. Konstantinovic, *Vercors ecrivain et dessinateur* (monograph), C. Klincksieck, 1969; *New York Times Book Review*, October 24, 1971.

*   *   *

BUCHANAN, Patrick
See CORLEY, Edwin (Raymond)

BUDGE, Ian 1936-

PERSONAL: Born October 21, 1936, in Leeds, Yorkshire, England; son of John Elder (a pharmacist) and Elizabeth (Barnet) Budge; married Judith Beatrice Ruth Harrison (a teacher), July 17, 1964; children: Gavin Elder, Eileen Elizabeth. *Education:* University of Edinburgh, M.A. (with first class honors in history), 1959; Yale University, A.M. (with distinction), 1961, Ph.D., 1966. *Politics:* Scottish nationalist. *Religion:* Church of Scotland. *Home:* 4 Oxford Rd., Colchester, England. *Office:* Department of Government, University of Essex, Colchester, Essex, England.

CAREER: University of Edinburgh, Edinburgh, Scotland, assistant lecturer, 1962-64; University of Strathclyde, Glasgow, Scotland, assistant lecturer, 1963-64, lecturer, 1964-66; University of Essex, Colchester, England, lecturer, 1966-68, senior lecturer, 1968-71, reader, 1971-75, professor of government, 1975—, chairman of department, 1974-77. Executive director, European Consortium for Political Research, 1979-83; co-director, Social Science Research Council project for a computer survey analysis package for social scientists, 1969-71; director, summer school of European Consortium for Political Research, 1971, 1972, 1973, and summer school on West European Politics at European University Institute, 1984. Member of political science and international relations committee, Social Science Research Council, 1980-82.

WRITINGS: (With D. W. Urwin) *Scottish Political Behaviour: A Case Study in British Homogeneity*, Longmans, Green, 1966; *Agreement and the Stability of Democracy*, Makham, 1970; (with M. Margolis, J. S. Brand, and A.L.M. Smith) *Political Stratification and Democracy*, Macmillan, 1972; (with C. O'Leary) *Belfast: Approach to Crisis*, Macmillan, 1973; (editor with I. Crewe and D. J. Farlie) *Party Identification and Beyond*, Wiley, 1976; (with Farlie) *Voting and Party Competition*, Wiley, 1977; (with Farlie) *Explaining and Predicting Elections*, Allen & Unwin, 1983; (with D. McKay and others) *The New British Political System*, Longmans, 1983. Contributor to political science journals.

SIDELIGHTS: Ian Budge told *CA:* "My writing deals with research and theory on politics. Politics itself I regard as the most important of all collective activities. Depending on the political actions we undertake, we gain or lose cultural freedom, economic prosperity and all other desirable ends. I also believe that it is possible to build up a body of coherent, valid knowledge about politics which will help us make better decisions, so political science as a subject is vitally important and needs to be developed.

"Almost all my work has been on the way democracies work, particularly on how citizens choose between parties in elections, how the parties shape programmes which can be put up for popular endorsement, and how these then affect government action. This has thrown up various philosophical problems on the way (e.g. how do we know when a particular theory of these processes is correct or not?). So some of my research has been on such methodological and epistemological problems, always in the service of political theory, however.

"My conclusions are that although democracy is an imperfect system with many problems, it does allow for concerted rational action on the part of electors, parties and governments, probably to a greater extent than any other type of political arrangement that we have. This is a moral or normative conclusion that democracy is 'better,' stemming from factual research. I am interested in developing this type of argument, which brings in philosophical problems of the relationship between facts and morals—between the 'Is' and the 'Ought.' I don't think there can or should be a separation between 'factual' and 'moral' political theory. In the future I should like to get beyond the details of empirical research and write a general work which deals with the philosophical questions as a preliminary to systematising what we know about politics both from a factual and a moral point of view."

AVOCATIONAL INTERESTS: History, architecture, opera, walking, gardening, Italian politics and culture.

* * *

BUNNELL, Peter C(urtis) 1937-

PERSONAL: Born October 25, 1937, in Poughkeepsie, N.Y.; son of Harold C. (an engineer) and Ruth (Buckhout) Bunnell. *Education:* Rochester Institute of Technology, B.F.A., 1959; Ohio University, M.F.A., 1961; Yale University, M.A., 1965; *Home:* 40 McCosh Cir., Princeton, N.J. 08540. *Office:* Department of Art and Archaeology, Princeton University, Princeton, N.J. 08544.

CAREER: Museum of Modern Art, New York City, curator of photography, 1966-72; Princeton University, Princeton, N.J., visiting lecturer in department of art and archaeology, 1970-72, McAlpin Professor of the History of Photography and Modern Art, 1972—, faculty curator of photography, 1972—, director of art museum, 1973-78; writer. Visiting lecturer at Institute of Film and Television, New York University, 1968-70, department of art, Dartmouth College, 1968, and college seminar program, Yale University, 1973. Television host of special seventy-five-minute program, "Time, Light and Vision: The Art of Photography," for WNET-TV, New York City.

MEMBER: Society for Photographic Education (member of board of directors, 1968—; secretary, 1970-73; chairman, 1973-77), College Art Association (member of board of directors, 1975-79), Friends of Photography (member of board of trustees, 1974—; vice-president, 1977; president, 1978—), American Federation of Arts (member of exhibitions committee, 1978—), Photographic Historical Society of America. *Awards, honors:* Robert Chapman Bates fellow, Yale University, 1963-65; fellowship for studies in the history of photography, Polaroid Corp., 1965-66; Guggenheim fellowship, 1979.

WRITINGS: (Assistant to Egbert Haverkamp-Begeman, senior editor) *Color in Prints: European and American Color Prints, 1500 to the Present,* Art Gallery, Yale University, 1962; (with Russell Edson) *Jerry N. Uelsmann,* Aperture, 1970, revised and enlarged edition, 1973; *Eight Photographs/Edward Weston,* Doubleday, 1971; (editor with Alan Trachtenberg and Peter Neill) *The City: American Experience,* Oxford University Press, 1971; (author of introduction) Max Waldman, *Waldman on Theater,* Doubleday, 1971; *Barbara Morgan,* Morgan & Morgan, 1972; (author of introduction) Dianne Vanderlip, editor, *Photographic Portraits,* Moore College of Art, 1972; (editor with Robert Sobieszek) *The Literature of Photography,* sixty-two volumes, Arno, 1973; (author of introduction) *A Portfolio of Ten Photographs by Elliott Erwitt,* Witkin-Berley, 1974; *Jerry N. Uelsmann: Silver Meditations,* Morgan & Morgan, 1975; (author of introduction) *Helen Gee and the Limelight,* Carlton Gallery, 1977; (contributor) *Conversations with Wright Morris: Critical Views and Responses,* University of Nebraska Press, 1977; (editor with Robert Sobieszek) *The Sources of Modern Photography,* Arno, 1978; (author of introduction) *Aaron Siskind: 75th Anniversary Portfolio,* Light Gallery, 1979; *Lynton Wells: Paintings 1971-1978,* Art Museum, Princeton University, 1979; (editor) *A Photographic Vision: Pictorial Photography 1889-1923,* Peregrine Smith, 1980; *Altered Landscapes: The Photographs of John Pfahl,* Friends of Photography, 1981; (author of introduction) *Paul Caponigro: Photography 25 Years,* Photograph Gallery, 1981; (editor) *Edward Weston on Photography,* Gibbs M. Smith, 1983; *Emmet Gowin,* Corcoran Gallery of Art, 1983; *The Robert O. Dougan Collection of Historical Photographs and Photographic Literature,* Art Museum, Princeton University, 1983. Also author of *Nonsilver Printing Processes: Four Selections, 1886-1927,* Arno.

Publications include bibliographies and chronologies for *Paul Caponigro,* Grossman, 1967, 2nd edition, Aperture, 1972, *Mirrors Messages Manifestations,* Aperture, 1969, 2nd edition, 1982, *W. Eugene Smith,* Aperture, 1969, *Paul Strand: A Retrospective Monograph,* Aperture, 1971, and other bibliographies, exhibition brochures, and checklists. Editor with Nathan Lyons, *Photography 63* and *Photography 64,* George Eastman House. Contributor of articles and reviews to *Aperture, Arts in Virginia, Artscanada, Camera, Art in America, Afterimage, Creative Camera, Print Collector's Newsletter, Choice, New York Times Book Review,* and other periodicals.

WORK IN PROGRESS: A critical history of twentieth-century photography; monographs on photographers Alfred Stieglitz and Minor White; an anthology of writings on photography, 1917-1945; a collection of essays and reviews.

SIDELIGHTS: Peter C. Bunnell is the first McAlpin Professor of the History of Photography at Princeton University. He wrote *CA:* "The principal motivation in my writing is to expand the understanding of photography as a creative medium. In this endeavor I hope to speak both to the viewer of photographs and to the photographer. In each case the challenge is to broaden the conceptual and intellectual orientation through which photographs are usually made and interpreted. Photography has existed in something of an intellectual and critical vacuum for too long." He has traveled through England, France, Belgium, Holland, Germany, Austria, Japan, Switzerland, and Italy.

BIOGRAPHICAL/CRITICAL SOURCES: Time, April 13, 1970; *New York Times,* June 6, 1971, April 18, 1972; *Newsweek,* October 21, 1974; *Village Voice,* July 19, 1976.

* * *

BURKE, J(ackson) F(rederick Augustine) 1915-

PERSONAL: Born August 6, 1915, in Alameda, Calif.; son of Francis F.S. and Bessie Mae (Wood) Burke; married Rose de Sa Aleixo (a poet), December 25, 1958. *Education:* University of California, Berkeley, B.A., 1944. *Religion:* Roman Catholic. *Home and office:* 2130 Broadway, New York, N.Y. 10023.

CAREER: University of California, Berkeley, member of faculty; teacher of U.S. history and mathematics at Kamehameha Schools, Honolulu, Hawaii; New School for Social Research, Parsons Midtown Campus, New York, N.Y., instructor, 1982—; magazine editor.

WRITINGS—All novels: *Noah,* Bantam, 1969, reprinted, 1983; *Location Shots,* Harper, 1974; *Death Trick,* Harper, 1975; *The Kama Sutra Tango,* Harper, 1977; *Crazy Woman Blues,* Dutton, 1978; *Kelly among the Nightingales,* Dutton, 1979; *The Amazon Scam,* Carlyle, 1979. Contributor of more than one hundred stories and poems to magazines.

WORK IN PROGRESS: Juana, a novel based on the life of Sor Juana Ines de la Cruz, the seventeenth-century Mexican poet and first defender of women's rights in the New World; *The Man in the Glacier,* an adventure novel.

SIDELIGHTS: J. F. Burke's New York City-based mysteries are distinguished by the author's "way of catching the vibrations of every social level in the big town," according to Robert Friedman in the *New York Post. Location Shots* introduces raffish Sam Kelly, a black, balding, slightly portly hotel detective/private eye who "has a style of his own," as Jean M. White writes in the *Washington Post.* "He wears Sulka ties and a yellow straw boater, smokes Havana cigars and likes good women and good music." When a series of murders occurs at the seedy Hotel Castlereagh during the filming of a movie nearby, it is up to Kelly to solve the case, in what White describes as a "fresh, well-crafted private eye story."

In *Kelly among the Nightingales* the resourceful detective investigates the murders of an editor and a ghostwriter who were involved in writing the tell-all memoirs of Kelly's girlfriend, a successful madam. "Before he solves the case," says *Hudson Sun* critic Leo McConnell, "the murderer decides to do a number on Sam and his girl. Naturally, this makes Sam a little edgy but more determined to find out who the killer is and what motivates him or her. The result is a fast-paced mystery, filled with colorful characters, equally colorful dialogue and a bang-up finale."

Jazz pianist and amateur sleuth Joe Streeter is featured in two other Burke mysteries. *The Kama Sutra Tango* finds Streeter framed for the murder of his best friend—and he has only twenty-four hours to investigate Manhattan's downtown district to find the real killer. The novel is "dirty fun for the strong of stomach and grisly of heart," remarks a *Kirkus Reviews* critic. The disappearance of his girlfriend, a nightclub dancer, causes Streeter to sing the *Crazy Woman Blues,* in another Burke adventure. His search for Alice, the dancer, takes Streeter through Times Square and all over the city. Eventually the investigation widens to include assorted murders and the theft of some valuable jewels. In the end, though, justice prevails and the protagonists celebrate with a party at Streeter's nightclub.

Burke's novels have been translated into several languages; the author's manuscripts are collected at Mugar Memorial Library, Boston University.

MEDIA ADAPTATIONS: Location Shots, The Kama Sutra Tango, and *Crazy Woman Blues* have all been optioned for filming.

BIOGRAPHICAL/CRITICAL SOURCES: Washington Post, January 20, 1974; *Kirkus Reviews,* May 15, 1977; *New York Times Book Review,* August 14, 1977, June 10, 1979; *New York Post,* August 18, 1979; *Hudson Sun,* August 25, 1979.

* * *

BURROW, John W(yon) 1935-

PERSONAL: Born June 4, 1935, in Southsea, England; son of Charles Wyon (a salesman) and Alice (Vosper) Burrow; married Diane Dunnington, October 27, 1958; children: Laurence, Francesca. *Education:* Christ's College, Cambridge, B.A., 1957, M.A., 1960, Ph.D., 1961. *Office:* Arts Building, University of Sussex, Brighton, England.

CAREER: Cambridge University, Downing College, Cambridge, England, fellow, 1962-65; University of East Anglia, School of European Studies, Norwich, England, lecturer in history, 1965-69; University of Sussex, Brighton, England, reader, 1969-82, professor of history, 1982—. Visiting professor, University of California, Berkeley, 1981. *Awards, honors:* Wolfson Literary Prize for History, 1981.

WRITINGS—Published by Cambridge University Press, except as indicated: *Evolution and Society: A Study in Victorian Social Theory,* 1966; (editor and author of introduction) Charles R. Darwin, *The Origin of Species by Means of Natural Selection,* Penguin, 1968; (editor and author of introduction) Wihelm Humboldt, *The Limits of State Action: History and Theory of Political Science,* 1969; *A Liberal Descent: Victorian Historians and the English Past,* 1981.

WORK IN PROGRESS: A study of Edward Gibbon, for Oxford University Press.

SIDELIGHTS: In *A Liberal Descent: Victorian Historians and the English Past,* John W. Burrow examines the writings and opinions of five prominent nineteenth-century historians: Edward August Freeman, J. A. Froude, John Richard Green, William Stubbs, and Thomas B. Macaulay. "No summary can possibly do justice to the richness, subtlety, and originality of this book, to my mind one of the finest volumes on modern English intellectual history," John Clive remarks in the *New York Review of Books.* "[Burrow's] deep knowledge of the Victorian age has stood him in good stead in [this] book, which he intends not so much as a study of technical historiography as, in the words of Burckhardt, a record of what one age finds of interest in another."

Calling *A Liberal Descent* "a magnificent piece of historical archaeology," J. P. Kenyon writes in the *Times Literary Supplement* that "Burrow's [writing] style, subtly inquisitive and highly literary, has . . . reached full maturity. . . . It is a condensed style, sucking idea upon idea, meaning upon meaning, implication upon implication, down into an intellectual black hole; whence they are funnelled out the other end into a new world of lucidity."

BIOGRAPHICAL/CRITICAL SOURCES: Times (London), November 19, 1981; *Times Literary Supplement,* December 4, 1981; *New York Review of Books,* June 24, 1982.

* * *

BURROWAY, Janet (Gay) 1936-

PERSONAL: Born September 21, 1936, in Tucson, Ariz.; daughter of Paul M. (a tool and die worker) and Alma (a speech teacher; maiden name, Milner) Burroway; married Walter Eysselinck (a theatre director), March 18, 1961 (divorced, 1973); married William Dean Humphries, 1978; children: (first marriage) Timothy Alan, Tobyn Alexander. *Education:* Attended University of Arizona, 1954-55; Barnard College, B.A. (cum laude), 1958; Cambridge University, B.A. (with first class honors), 1960, M.A., 1965; additional study at Yale School of Drama, 1960-61. *Politics:* Liberal. *Home:* 240 DeSoto St., Tallahassee, Fla. 32303. *Office:* Department of English, Florida State University, Tallahassee, Fla. 32306.

CAREER: During her school years, worked for Young Men's Hebrew Association, *New Yorker,* and for UNICEF in Paris, France; supply teacher in Binghamton, N.Y., 1961-63; director of classical music program for schools in upstate New York, 1963; University of Sussex, Brighton, England, School of English and American Studies, 1965-70, began as assistant lecturer, became lecturer; University of Illinois at Urbana-Champaign, special assistant to the writing laboratory, 1971; Florida State University, Tallahassee, associate professor, 1971-77, professor of English and writing, 1977—. Regional director, New York State Expansion Program for Young Audiences, Inc., 1962-63; costume designer, Belgian National Theater at Ghent, 1965-70, and Gardner Centre for the Arts, University of Sussex, 1965-71.

AWARDS, HONORS: Pulitzer Prize nomination in literature, 1970, for *The Buzzards;* AMOCO award for excellence in teaching, Florida State University, 1974; National Endowment for the Arts creative writing scholarship, 1976.

WRITINGS: Descend Again (novel), Faber, 1960; *But to the Season* (poems), Keele University Press, 1961; *The Dancer from the Dance* (novel), Faber, 1965, Little, Brown, 1967; *Eyes* (novel), Little, Brown, 1966; *The Buzzards* (novel), Little, Brown, 1969; (contributor) Palmer Bovie, editor, *Five Roman Comedies,* Dutton, 1970; *The Truck on the Track* (juvenile; Junior Literary Guild selection), J. Cape, 1970, Bobbs-Merrill, 1971; *The Giant Jam Sandwich* (juvenile; National Scholastic Publications "Lucky Club" selection), J. Cape, 1972, Houghton, 1973; *Raw Silk* (novel), Little, Brown, 1977; *Material Goods* (poems), University Presses of Florida, 1980; *Writing Fiction: A Guide to Narrative Craft,* Little, Brown, 1982.

Plays: "Garden Party," produced at Barnard College, 1958; "The Fantasy Level," first produced at Yale School of Drama, 1961, produced at Playwrights' Theater, Tallahassee, Fla., 1979; "The Beauty Operators," first produced at Gardner Centre for the Arts, 1968, produced by Thames Television, London, England, 1970; "Hoddinott Veiling," produced by ATV Network Television, London, 1970; "Due Care and Attention," produced by ATV Network Television, 1973.

Contributor of poetry to anthologies, including *New Poems by American Poets No. 2,* Ballantine, 1957, *The Guinness Book of Poetry,* Putnam, 1961, and *Sound and Sense,* Harcourt, 1973. Contributor of articles to periodicals, including *Mademoiselle, Seventeen, Yale Review,* and *Story Quarterly.* Fiction reviewer, *New Statesman,* 1970-71 and 1975.

WORK IN PROGRESS: A novel, *Opening Nights,* and a play, "Division of Property."

SIDELIGHTS: "Janet Burroway is a writer of wide range and many voices," says Elizabeth Muhlenfeld in *Dictionary of Literary Biography.* "[Partly] because she has consciously avoided current trends, and [partly] because she lived abroad for eleven years, . . . her reputation has only recently begun to catch up with the consistently high quality of her work. Burroway's themes are universal—love, death, the implications of choice, human culpability—and in the broadest sense, her novels are profoundly moral. She creates a determinedly realistic world, a *comedie humaine* with tragic implications, where evil is most often the result of blindness."

Burroway is noted for the meticulous research she puts into her novels; her best-known work, *Raw Silk,* was a seven-year project. The story of the ill-fated marriage of an American woman to an English businessman, *Raw Silk* is narrated by the wife, Virginia Marbalestier. Virginia is "an engaging character; she speaks with wry intelligence and rare honesty, and she fastens onto the details of her life with a characteristic humor even when she is suffering most deeply," according to Muhlenfeld.

While Burroway "is not saying anything radically new in *Raw Silk,*" as Anatole Broyard points out in the *New York Times Book Review,* nevertheless "what makes [the novel] better than just another contemporary document are the good lines, like a form of personal attractiveness, which enliven its pages." Similarly, Mel Watkins, writing in the *New York Times,* finds that what sets *Raw Silk* apart "is Janet Burroway's superb stylistic gifts. . . . By focusing on the nuances of marital erosion, the silences, the minute fissures and crevices that go unnoticed until they become permanent breaches, [the author] has fashioned an affecting tale of ennui and dissolution."

"Hoddinnot Veiling" was Britain's independent television entry at the Monte Carlo festival in 1970. Janet Burroway's manuscripts and working papers are collected at the Strozier Library, Florida State University, in Tallahassee.

BIOGRAPHICAL/CRITICAL SOURCES: Newsweek, April 4, 1977; *New York Times Book Review,* April 10, 1977; *New York Times,* June 22, 1977; *Ms.,* August, 1977; *New Statesman,* August 12, 1977; *Times Literary Supplement,* October 14, 1977, May 22, 1982; *Dictionary of Literary Biography,* Volume VI: *American Novelists since World War II,* Gale, 1980.

* * *

BUSH, Barbara Holstein 1935-

PERSONAL: Born September 8, 1935, in California; daughter of Walter Edwin (an educator) and Beulah (an artist; maiden name, Williams) Holstein; married Richard Merrell Bush (a clergyman), June 16, 1956; children: Stephen, David, Gary, Patricia. *Education:* Los Angeles Harbor Junior College, A.A., 1954; California State University, Long Beach, B.A. (with great distinction), 1956. *Religion:* Protestant. *Home:* 27031 Pinjara Circle, Mission Viejo, Calif. 92691.

CAREER: Elementary school teacher in Los Angeles, Calif., 1956-57, Ewing Township, N.J., 1957-59, Princeton Township, N.J., 1959-60, Madera, Calif., 1965-66, and Mission Viejo, Calif., 1968-70. *Member:* P.E.O. Sisterhood, Pi Lambda Theta.

WRITINGS—Published by Zondervan, except as indicated: *I Can't Stand Cindy, Lord* (on her teaching experiences), 1976; *Ask Adam: A Shepherd and His Flock Face the Wolves Together,* Revell, 1978; *A Woman's Workshop on Mastering Motherhood,* 1981; *Walking in Wisdom: A Woman's Workshop on Ecclesiastes,* 1982; *Heart Trouble: A Woman's Workshop on Christian Character,* 1984. Author of column "Still Learning," in *Saddleback Valley News* (Mission Viejo), 1969-70.

SIDELIGHTS: Barbara Bush writes: "The area of prime importance to me in my writing is that of improved quality of life, especially in regard to human relationships. My approach will undoubtedly continue to be practical rather than theoretical, specifically trying to show how a personal relationship with Jesus Christ and an application of Biblical principles enriches daily life and mends torn interpersonal relationships.

"I sustain an enduring interest in the preservation of the family unit, public education, and church music, having served as church organist and choir director."

AVOCATIONAL INTERESTS: Travel (United States, Israel, Cyprus, Turkey, Greece), sewing and stitchery, reading.

* * *

BUSH, Martin H(arry) 1930-

PERSONAL: Born January 24, 1930, in Amsterdam, N.Y.;

son of Martin J. and Louise (Surento) Bush; married Elinor Seward, August 6, 1955 (divorced, December 23, 1969); children: Lisa Vail, Jennifer Seward, Pamela Lynn. *Education:* New York College for Teachers (now State University of New York at Albany), B.A., 1958, M.A., 1959; Syracuse University, Ph.D., 1966. *Home:* 8201 East Harry, Apt. 2204, Wichita, Kan. 67207. *Office:* Office of the Vice-President, Wichita State University, Wichita, Kan. 67208.

CAREER: New York State Department of Education, Albany, N.Y., acting senior historian, 1961-62, historical consultant, 1962-63; Syracuse University, Syracuse, N.Y., instructor in history, 1963-65, assistant dean, 1966-70; Wichita State University, Wichita, Kan., assistant vice-president, 1970-74, vice-president, 1974—, director of Edwin A. Ulrich Museum of Art, 1975—. *Military service:* U.S. Army, Intelligence, 1953-54.

WRITINGS: Francis Scott Key: Our National Anthem (brochure), New York State Education Department, 1964; (editor with H. L. Applegate and O. T. Barck) *Moses Dewitt Burnet, A Tour to the South: Travel Diary, 1815-1816,* Syracuse University, 1965; *American Political Cartoons: 1865-1965* (catalog), Syracuse University Library, 1966; *Boris Lovet-Lorski: The Language of Time* (catalog), introduction by Salvatore Quasimodo, Syracuse University Press, 1967; (author of introduction) *James Earle Fraser: American Sculptor* (catalog), Kennedy Galleries, 1969; *Ben Shahn: The Passion of Sacco and Vanzetti,* with an essay by Ben Shahn, Syracuse University Press, 1969; *Revolutionary Enigma: A Re-appraisal of General Philip Schuyler of New York,* Friedman, 1969.

Doris Caesar, introduction by Marya Zaturenska, preface by D. B. Wyndham Lewis, Syracuse University Press, 1970; *Goodnough,* commentary by Kenworth Moffett, Wichita State University, 1973; *Hanson,* Wichita State University, 1976; *Ernest Trova,* Ulrich Museum of Art, 1977; *Goodnough* (text and interview) Abbeville Press, 1982; (author of text) *The Photographs of Gordon Parks,* Ulrich Museum of Art, 1983. Contributor to *Notable American Women, School Letter, National Sculpture Review, Art News,* and *Art International.*

* * *

BUTLER, Octavia E(stelle) 1947-

PERSONAL: Born June 22, 1947, in Pasadena, Calif.; daughter of Laurice and Octavia M. (Guy) Butler. *Education:* Pasadena City College, A.A., 1968; attended California State University, Los Angeles, 1969. *Home address:* P.O. Box 6604, Los Angeles, Calif. 90055.

CAREER: Free-lance writer, 1970—. *Member:* Science Fiction Writers of America.

WRITINGS—Science fiction novels, except as indicated; published by Doubleday, except as indicated: *Patternmaster,* 1976; *Mind of My Mind,* 1977; *Survivor,* 1978; *Kindred* (mainstream novel), 1979; *Wild Seed,* 1980; *Clay's Ark,* St. Martin's, 1984.

Work represented in anthologies, including *Clarion,* edited by Robin Scott Wilson, New American Library, 1970, and *Chrysalis 4,* Zebra Books, 1979. Contributor to periodicals, including *Isaac Asimov's Science Fiction Magazine.*

WORK IN PROGRESS: A novel, tentatively entitled *Blindsight.*

SIDELIGHTS: Octavia Butler told *CA:* "I began writing when I was about ten years old for the same reason many people begin reading—to escape loneliness and boredom. I didn't realize then that writing was supposed to be work. It was too much fun. It still is. I began writing fantasy and science fiction because both inspire a high level of creativity and offer a great deal of freedom. However, I remember that when I began reading science fiction, I was disappointed at how little this creativity and freedom was used to portray the many racial, ethnic, and class variations. Also, I could not help noticing how few significant women characters there were in science fiction. Fortunately, all of this has been changing over the past few years. I intend my writing to contribute to the change."

In Butler's novels, writes Wayne Warga of the *Los Angeles Times,* "there is ample external action, . . . but her strength is with internal thought and emotion." The author explained to Warga that this may be "because I like being alone. I like working for myself. I need other people too, but not all the time." She also noted that her characters "are usually alienated and loners. They tend to be trapped into something that will help a lot of people. Or they volunteer. A lot of my work is about the courage of choice and circumstance. My friends tell me I write a lot about power, too, and I guess I do. I've felt powerless, so power appeals to me."

BIOGRAPHICAL/CRITICAL SOURCES: Los Angeles Times, January 30, 1981.

C

CALDWELL, John 1928-

PERSONAL: Born November 28, 1928, in Detroit, Mich.; son of John Homer and Dorothy (Briggs) Caldwell; married Hester Goodenough (a teacher), July 5, 1952; children: Timothy John, Sverre, Peter James, Jennifer. *Education:* Dartmouth College, B.A., 1950; Wesleyan University, M.A.L.S., 1965. *Residence:* Putney, Vt. 05346. *Office:* Putney School, Putney, Vt. 05346.

CAREER: Putney School, Putney, Vt., math teacher and athletic coach, 1953—. Three-time World Championships ski coach, twice U.S. Olympic ski team coach, U.S. ski team coach, 1966-72, and Australian Olympic cross-country ski team coach, 1980. U.S. Olympic ski team member, Oslo, 1952. *Military service:* U.S. Navy, 1950-52; became lieutenant junior grade.

WRITINGS—Published by Stephen Greene Press, except as indicated: *The Cross-Country Ski Book,* 1964, 6th edition, 1981; *The New Cross-Country Ski Book,* 1970; *Caldwell on Cross-Country,* 1975; *Cross-Country Skiing Today,* 1977; *Citizen Racing* (on cross-country marathon racing), Mountaineers, 1982. Contributing editor, *Skiing.*

WORK IN PROGRESS: Research on training, technique, and waxing for cross-country skiing.

SIDELIGHTS: John Caldwell has devoted much of his adult life to promoting the sport of cross-country skiing. A recognized expert on the subject, Caldwell has written *The Cross-Country Ski Book,* "the most successful book on cross-country skiing," according to Sally A. Lodge in *Publishers Weekly.* About his experience in the field, he told Lodge: "I suppose I'm the 'dean of cross-country coaches' or something like that. . . . I don't think I've ever actually been called that, but I've been around so long that I suppose I could be."

About the relationship between his teaching and coaching, Caldwell told *CA:* "I enjoy teaching. I think there is an important connection between the mental processes used in the teaching (and doing) of mathematics and the coaching of skiing. One must develop highly analytical thinking processes and then be able to express them."

AVOCATIONAL INTERESTS: Gardening, rowing, biking, hiking, maple syrup-making.

BIOGRAPHICAL/CRITICAL SOURCES Publishers Weekly, September 11, 1981.

CALDWELL, Lynton (Keith) 1913-

PERSONAL: Born November 21, 1913, in Montezuma, Iowa; married Helen Walcher, 1940; children: Edwin Lee, Elaine Lynnette. *Education:* University of Chicago, Ph.B. (with honors), 1935, Ph.D., 1943; Harvard University, M.A., 1938. *Home address:* Cedar Crest, 4898 Heritage Woods Rd., Bloomington, Ind. 47401. *Office:* Department of Political Science, Woodburn Hall, Indiana University, Bloomington, Ind. 47405.

CAREER: Indiana University at Bloomington, assistant professor of government and director of South Bend Center, 1938-44; Council of State Governments, Lexington, Ky., director of research and publications, 1944-47; Syracuse University, Maxwell Graduate School of Citizenship and Public Affairs, Syracuse, N.Y., professor of political science, 1947-55; University of California, Berkeley, visiting professor of political science, 1955-56; Indiana University at Bloomington, professor of political science, 1956—, Arthur E. Bentley Professor of Political Science, 1971—, professor of public and environmental affairs, 1971—.

Visiting member of faculty, University of Chicago, 1944-47; visiting professor of political science, University of Oklahoma, 1968. Co-director of Public Administration Institute in Turkey and the Middle East for the United Nations, 1954-55. Has been involved in special assignments and technical assistance in Colombia, Pakistan, India, the Philippines, Thailand, Indonesia, and with Central Treaty Organization. Member of environmental advisory board, U.S. Army Corps of Engineers; member of environmental science review committee, National Institutes of Health, 1966-67; member of environmental studies board, National Research Council, 1973-76; member of UNESCO Working Group on Environmental Education of Engineers. Consultant to National Aeronautics and Space Administration, Argonne National Laboratory, Oak Ridge National Laboratory, Office of Technology Assessment, and other government departments and agencies; served on National Commission on Materials Policy, 1971-73.

MEMBER: International Union for the Conservation of Nature and Natural Resources (life member), American Association for the Advancement of Science (fellow), American Society for Public Administration (member of council), National Academy of Public Administration, National Association for Environmental Education, Association for Politics and the Life Sciences, Society for International Development, Royal Society of Arts, Indiana Academy of Sciences, Cosmos Club.

AWARDS, HONORS: William E. Mosher Award from American Society for Public Administration, 1964, for article, "Environment: A New Focus for Public Policy"; National Science Foundation grants, 1965-76; guest scholar at Woodrow Wilson International Center for Scholars, Smithsonian Institution, 1970; Laverne Burchfield Award from American Society for Public Administration, 1972, for book review essay, "Environment: A Short Course in Semantics"; L.L.D. from Western Michigan University, 1977; Marshall E. Dimock Award from American Society for Public Administration, for article, "Biology and Bureaucracy: The Coming Confrontation."

WRITINGS: *The Administrative Theories of Hamilton and Jefferson,* University of Chicago Press, 1944, reprinted, Russell, 1964; *The Government and Administration of New York,* Crowell, 1954; *Government in Action: A Course of Training for Civic Leaders—Handbook for Universities* (booklet), American Foundation for Continuing Education, 1961; *Improving the Public Service through Training,* Agency for International Development, 1962; *Science, Technology, and Public Policy: A Syllabus for Advanced Study,* two volumes, Department of Government, Indiana University, 1968; *Science, Technology, and Public Policy: A Selective and Annotated Bibliography, 1945-1967,* two volumes, Department of Government, Indiana University, for National Science Foundation, 1968.

Environment: A Challenge to Modern Society, Natural History Press, 1970; *In Defense of Earth: International Protection of the Biosphere,* Indiana University Press, 1972; *Man and His Environment: Policy and Administration,* Harper, 1975; (with Lynton R. Hayes and Isabel M. MacWhirter) *Citizens and the Environment: Case Studies in Popular Action,* Indiana University Press, 1976; *Science and the National Environmental Policy Act: Redirecting Policy through Procedural Reform,* University of Alabama Press, 1983; *International Environmental Policy Emergence and Dimensions,* Duke University Press, 1984.

Editor: A. C. Conk and N. K. Savun, *Turkish Public Administration: A Report on the Rationalization of the State Organization,* Institute of Training for Public Service, Indiana University, 1961; *Environmental Studies: Papers on the Politics and Public Administration of Man-Environment Relationship,* Numbers I-IV, Institute of Public Administration, Indiana University, 1967; *Science and Public Policy in the American University,* Department of Government, Indiana University, 1969; (with Toufiq A. Siddigi) *Environmental Policy, Law, and Administration: A Guide to Advanced Study,* with supplementary bibliographies and author index, School of Public and Environmental Affairs, Indiana University, 1976; *A Study of Ways to Improve the Scientific Content and Methodology of Environmental Impact Analysis,* National Science Foundation, 1982.

Contributor: *Toward the Comparative Study of Administration,* Department of Government, Indiana University, 1957; *University Education and Public Service,* International Association of Universities, 1959.

Politics and Public Affairs, Institute of Training for Public Service, Indiana University, 1962; *Symposium on Management Training in Public Administrations,* Central Treaty Organization (Ankara, Turkey), 1964; Roscoe C. Martin, editor, *Public Administration and Democracy: Essays in Honor of Paul H. Appleby,* Syracuse University Press, 1965; Claude E. Hawley and Ruth G. Weintraub, editors, *Administrative Questions and Political Answers,* Van Nostrand, 1966; F. Fraser Darling and John P. Milton, editors, *Future Environments of North America,* Natural History Press, 1966; Bertram M. Gross, editor, *Action under Planning: The Guidance of Economic Development,* McGraw, 1967; Richard A. Humphrey, editor, *Universities and Development Assistance Abroad,* American Council on Education, 1967; Jerry R. Hopper and Richard I. Levin, editors, *Turkish Administrator: A Cultural Survey,* U.S. Agency for International Development, 1967; James C. Charlesworth, editor, *Theory and Practice of Public Administration: Scope, Objectives, and Methods,* American Academy of Political and Social Science, 1968; *Social Sciences and Environment,* University of Colorado Press, 1968; William R. Nelson, editor, *The Politics of Science,* Oxford University Press, 1968.

George W. Rogers, editor, *Change in Alaska: People, Petroleum, and Politics,* University of Alaska Press and University of Washington Press, 1970; Lorne H. Russurm and Edward Sommerville, editors, *Readings on Man's Natural Environment: A Systems Approach,* Wadsworth, 1970; Phillip O. Foss, editor, *Public Land Policy,* Associated University Press, 1970; Richard A. Cooley and Geoffrey Wandesforde-Smith, editors, *Congress and the Environment,* University of Washington Press, 1970; William W. Murdoch, editor, *Man and Environment,* Sinauer Associates, 1971; *A Time to Hear and to Answer,* University of Alabama Press, 1977; H. Flohr and W. Toennesmann, editors, *Politik und Biologie: Beiträge zur Life-Sciences Orientierung der Sozialwissenshaften,* Paul Parey Verlag, 1983; John B. Calhoun, editor, *Environment and Population,* Praeger, 1983; Michael Kraft and Norman Vig, editors, *Environmental Policy in the 1980s,* Congressional Quarterly, 1984.

Contributor to *American Behavioral Scientist, Human Ecology, Yale Review, BioScience, Religious Humanism, Technology and Culture,* and a number of public administration, law, history, and political science journals. Member of editorial board of *Public Administration Review,* 1948-51, *Natural Resources Journal, Environmental Conservation, Bulletin of Science, Technology, and Society,* and *Politics and the Life Sciences.*

WORK IN PROGRESS: Research on international aspects of environmental policy and the impact of bioscience and biotechnology on public policy.

* * *

CALLEN, Larry
See CALLEN, Lawrence Willard, Jr.

* * *

CALLEN, Lawrence Willard, Jr. 1927-
(Larry Callen)

PERSONAL: Born April 3, 1927, in New Orleans, La.; son of Lawrence Willard and Emily (Barrouquere) Callen; married Willa Carmouche (a learning disabilities diagnostician), December 6, 1958; children: Erin Andree, Alex David, Dashiel Noel, Holly Willa. *Education:* Attended Tulane University, 1944-45, 1953-54, and Loyola University, New Orleans, 1950-52; Florida State University, B.S., 1957; Louisiana State University, additional study, 1960-63. *Home:* 1117 Tiffany Rd., Silver Spring, Md. 20904. *Office:* U.S. Department of Labor, 601 D St. N.W., Washington, D.C. 20213.

CAREER: Jefferson Herald, New Orleans, La., associate editor, 1952-55; H. L. Peace Publications, New Orleans, associate editor of a fishing industry magazine, 1958-59; Louisiana Department of Employment Security, Baton Rouge, in unemployment insurance and employment services, 1959-63; U.S. Department of Labor, Washington, D.C., in employment services and unemployment insurance, 1963-78; free-lance writer, 1978—. *Military service:* U.S. Navy, 1945-46. U.S. Air Force, 1955-58.

WRITINGS—Under name Larry Callen; juvenile novels, except as indicated; *Pinch,* Atlantic-Little, Brown, 1976; *The Deadly Mandrake,* Atlantic-Little, Brown, 1978; *Sorrow's Song,* Atlantic-Little, Brown, 1979; *The Muskrat War,* Atlantic-Little, Brown, 1980; *Dashiel and the Night* (illustrated story for children), Dutton, 1981; *If the World Ends,* Atheneum, 1983; *The Fantastic Discovery* (illustrated story for children), Parker Brothers, 1984; *The Just-Right Family* (illustrated story for children), Parker Brothers, 1984.

WORK IN PROGRESS: "A collection of short stories about a kid who used to be me."

SIDELIGHTS: Lawrence Willard Callen, Jr. wrote *CA:* "There is a rather delicate middle ground between stories for children and stories for grownups. It's an elusive target. Story tellers who find it entertain both groups. I'm trying to find it.

"I am also totally sold on the value of the family in the intellectual, moral and emotional growth of the individual. I've indicated that in my books published so far.

"Maybe you would also like to know that most of *Pinch* was written on a commuter bus between my home in Silver Spring, Md., and my job in Washington, D.C. And a goodly portion of *The Deadly Mandrake* was written in a carpool over the same distance, and benefited from a great deal of kibitzing from fellow drivers.

"My hobbies are unrelated to writing. First is kid raising. We have four teenagers. I also have a few tropical fish and a cowrie collection. Cowries are salt water snails. I collect the shells. [Another hobby] is geneology. I occasionally dabble at this, trying to trace my family's journey prior to settling in Louisiana. We are Scotch-Irish. Progress is slow. I've only made it back to North Carolina."

* * *

CAMPBELL, Angus
See CHETWYND-HAYES, R(onald Henry Glynn)

* * *

CAMPBELL, Judith
See PARES, Marion (Stapylton)

* * *

CANTOR, Muriel G. 1923-

PERSONAL: Born March 2, 1923, in Minneapolis, Minn.; daughter of Leo and Bess (Willis) Goldsman; married Joel M. Cantor (a psychologist), August 6, 1944; children: Murray R., Jane O., James L. *Education:* University of California, Los Angeles, B.A., 1964, M.A., 1966, Ph.D., 1969. *Home:* 8408 Whitman Dr., Bethesda, Md. 20817. *Office:* Department of Sociology, American University, Washington, D.C. 20016.

CAREER: Immaculate Heart College, Los Angeles, Calif., instructor in sociology, 1966-68; American University, Washington, D.C., instructor, 1968-69, assistant professor, 1969-72, associate professor, 1972-76, professor of sociology, 1976—, chairperson of department, 1973-75, 1977-79. Visiting professor at University of California, Los Angeles, 1982. *Member:* American Sociological Association, Sociologists for Women in Society, Society for Study of Social Problems, Southern Sociological Society, Eastern Sociological Association, District of Columbia Sociological Society.

WRITINGS: Hollywood TV Producer, Basic Books, 1971; (with Phyllis L. Stewart) *Varieties of Work Experience,* Schenkman, 1974; (contributor) Jack Goldsmith and Sharon S. Goldsmith, editors, *The Police Community: Dimensions of an Occupational Subculture,* Palisades, 1974; *Prime-Time Television: Content and Control,* Sage Publications, 1980; (with Stewart) *Varieties of Work,* Sage Publications, 1982; (with Suzanne Pingree) *The Soap Opera,* Sage Publications, 1983. Contributor of articles and reviews to sociology journals. Editor, *SWS Newsletter* (national newsletter for Sociologists for Women in Society), 1977-79.

WORK IN PROGRESS: Television Entertainment: Political Realities and Public Policy.

* * *

CAPPS, Donald E(ric) 1939-

PERSONAL: Born January 30, 1939, in Omaha, Neb.; son of Holden F. (an accountant) and Mildred Linnea Theresa (Bildt) Capps; married Karen Docken, August 22, 1964; children: John Michael. *Education:* Lewis and Clark College, B.A., 1960; Yale University, Divinity School, B.D., 1963, S.T.M., 1965; University of Chicago, Divinity School, M.A., 1957, Ph.D., 1970. *Home:* 102 Ross Stevenson Circle, Princeton, N.J. 08540. *Office:* Princeton Theological Seminary, Princeton University, Princeton, N.J. 08540.

CAREER: University of Chicago, Divinity School, Chicago, Ill., assistant professor, 1969-74; University of North Carolina at Charlotte, associate professor of religious studies, 1974-76; Phillips University, Graduate Seminary, Enid, Okla., associate professor, 1976-79, professor, 1979-81; Princeton University, Princeton Theological Seminary, Princeton, N.J., professor, 1981—.

WRITINGS: (Editor with brother, Walter Holden Capps) *The Religious Personality,* Wadsworth, 1970; (editor with Frank E. Reynolds) *The Biographical Process,* Mouton & Co., 1976; (editor with Lewis Rambo and Paul Ransohoff) *Psychology of Religion: A Guide to Information Sources,* Gale, 1976; (editor with W. H. Capps and Gerald Bradford) *Encounter with Erikson,* Scholars Press, 1976; *Pastoral Care: A Thematic Approach,* Westminster, 1979; *Pastoral Counseling and Preaching,* Westminster, 1980; *Biblical Approaches in Pastoral Counseling,* Westminster, 1981; *Life Cycle Theory and Pastoral Care,* Fortress, 1983.

Contributor of articles to *Journal for the Scientific Study of Religion, Journal for the History of Behavioral Sciences, Journal of Religion, Pastoral Psychology, Theology Today,* and *Social Research.*

* * *

CAPPS, Walter H(olden) 1934-

PERSONAL: Born May 5, 1934; son of Holden F. (an accountant) and Mildred Linnea Theresa (Bildt) Capps; married

Lois Ragnihild Grimsrud, August 22, 1960; children: Lisa Margarit, Todd Holden. *Education:* Portland University, B.S., 1958; Augustana Theological Seminary, B.D. (summa cum laude), 1960; Yale University, S.T.M., 1961, M.A., 1963, Ph.D., 1965. *Home:* 1724 Santa Barbara St., Santa Barbara, Calif. 93101. *Office:* Department of Religious Studies, University of California, Santa Barbara, Calif. 93106.

CAREER: University of California, Santa Barbara, assistant professor, 1964-69, associate professor, 1969-73, professor of religious studies, 1973—, director, Institute of Religious Studies, 1970-76, and Robert Maynard Hutchins Center for the Study of Democratic Institutions, 1980-82. Visiting scholar, Warburg Institute, London, 1968-69, and Mansfield College, Oxford University, 1971. Member of board of theological education, Lutheran Church in America; member of board of directors, Pacific Lutheran Theological Seminary; member of Collegium, Pacific Lutheran University; president, Council on the Study of Religion and National Federation of State Humanities Councils; chairman of board, California Council for the Humanities and La Casa de Maria (Immaculate Heart College). *Member:* Society for Religion in Higher Education, American Academy of Religion, Society for the Scientific Study of Religion, American Association of University Professors. *Awards, honors:* Society for Religion in Higher Education fellow, 1968-69; University of California, Humanities Institute fellow, 1971-72, named professor of the year, 1982.

WRITINGS: (Editor and contributor) *The Future of Hope,* Fortress, 1970; (editor with brother, Donald E. Capps, and contributor) *The Religious Personality,* Wadsworth, 1970; (editor and contributor) *Ways of Understanding Religion,* Macmillan, 1972; *Time Invades the Cathedral,* Fortress, 1972; *Hope against Hope,* Fortress, 1976; (editor) *Seeing with a Native Eye,* Harper, 1976; (editor with D. E. Capps and Gerald Bradford) *Encounter with Erikson,* Scholars Press, 1976; (with Wendy Wright) *Silent Fire,* Harper, 1978; *The Unfinished War: Vietnam and the American Conscience,* Beacon Press, 1982; *The Monastic Impulse,* Crossroad, 1983. Contributor to *Revue Philosophique de Louvain, Heythrop Journal, Humanitas,* and other journals.

SIDELIGHTS: In his study *The Unfinished War: Vietnam and the American Conscience,* Walter H. Capps examines the theological and social implications of America's involvement in this country's most controversial war. According to Huston Horn's *Los Angeles Times Book Review* article, Capps feels that the American intervention in Vietnam left not only "a nationful of psychically scarred, uncomprehending veterans" but also a "conscience-stricken nation . . . still split down the middle. One camp calls for a more contemplative orientation toward human life, and a more benign American role in it. The other chafes to re-establish vibrant, vigorous and unrepentant American resolve through a reawakening of religious and political conservativism."

As Capps himself writes in *The Unfinished War:* "A world so easily divisible into such absolute contrasts is already severely fragmented. The real issue is whether healing can occur and wholeness be discovered before the trauma of the unfinished war is reenacted."

BIOGRAPHICAL/CRITICAL SOURCES: Walter H. Capps, *The Unfinished War: Vietnam and the American Conscience,* Beacon Press, 1982; *Los Angeles Times Book Review,* August 8, 1982, July 24, 1983.

CARENS, James Francis 1927-

PERSONAL: Born November 13, 1927, in Newbury, Mass.; son of James F. and Kathryn F. (Callahan) Carens; married Marilyn Mumford, June 7, 1961; children: Geoffrey Peter, Timothy Lawrence. *Education:* Harvard University, A.B., 1949; Yale University, M.A., 1951; Columbia University, Ph.D., 1959. *Home:* College Park, Lewisburg, Pa. 17837.

CAREER: Bucknell University, Lewisburg, Pa., instructor, 1955-59, assistant professor, 1959-65, associate professor, 1965-70, professor of English, 1970—; director of Bucknell University Press, 1969-72. *Member:* Modern Language Association of America, James Joyce Society, James Joyce Foundation.

WRITINGS: The Satiric Art of Evelyn Waugh, University of Washington Press, 1966; (editor and author of commentary) Oliver St. John Gogarty, *Many Lines to Thee: Letters to G.K.A. Bell from the Martello Tower at Sandycove, Rutland Square, and Trinity College, Dublin, 1904-1907,* Dolmen Press, 1971, Humanities, 1972; (editor and author of introduction) *The Plays of Oliver St. John Gogarty,* Proscenium Press, 1971; (contributor) *Modern Irish Literature,* Twayne, 1972; (contributor) *New Light on James Joyce,* Indiana University Press, 1972; (contributor) *Anglo-Irish Literature: A Review of Research,* Modern Language Association of America, 1976; *Surpassing Wit: Oliver St. John Gogarty, His Poetry and His Prose,* Columbia University Press, 1979; (editor) Eileen Sullivan, *Thomas Davis,* Bucknell University Press, 1979. Editor, "Irish Writers" series, Bucknell University Press, 1970—. Contributor of articles to professional journals.

BIOGRAPHICAL/CRITICAL SOURCES: Contemporary Literature, Volume 9, number 2, spring, 1968.†

* * *

CARLETON, Mark T. 1935-

PERSONAL: Born February 7, 1935, in Baton Rouge, La.; son of Roderick Lewis and Helen (Parker) Carleton; married Maureen O'Hearn, July 6, 1963 (divorced, 1982); children: Roderick Lewis, Michael Owen, Mark Albert. *Education:* Yale University, A.B., 1957; Stanford University, M.A., 1964, Ph.D., 1970. *Office:* Department of History, Louisiana State University, Baton Rouge, La., 70803.

CAREER: Foothill Junior College, Los Altos Hills, Calif., instructor in history, 1962-64; San Francisco State College (now University), San Francisco, Calif., instructor in history, 1964-65; Louisiana State University, Baton Rouge, lecturer, 1965-68, assistant professor, 1968-73, associate professor of history, 1973-76; Public Affairs Research Council of Louisiana, Inc., Baton Rouge, director of research, 1976-77; Louisiana State University, associate professor of history, 1977—. *Military service:* U.S. Marine Corps, 1957-60. U.S. Marine Corps Reserve, 1960-64. *Member:* Phi Beta Kappa. *Awards, honors:* Certificate of Commendation, American Association for State and Local History, 1973, for *Politics and Punishment;* Louisiana Literary Award from Louisiana Library Association, 1981, for *River Capital: An Illustrated History of Baton Rouge.*

WRITINGS: Study Guide to the Democratic Experience, Scott, Foresman, 1966, revised edition, 1968; *Politics and Punishment: The History of the Louisiana State Penal System,* Louisiana State University Press, 1971; (co-editor) *Readings in Louisiana Politics,* Claitors, 1975; *River Capital: An Illustrated History of Baton Rouge,* Windsor Publications, 1981; *Louisiana Politics: Festival in a Labyrinth,* Louisiana State

University Press, 1982; (co-author) *Louisiana: A History*, Forum Press, 1984. Contributor to *Dictionary of American History, Encyclopedia of Southern History, Biographical Dictionary of American Mayors: 1820 to the Present, Twentieth Century American Historians,* and *Dictionary of Literary Biography;* contributor of articles and reviews to *Labor History, Alabama Review, Louisiana History, Louisiana Studies, American Historical Review,* and *Journal of Southern History.* Managing editor, *Louisiana History,* 1968-69.

* * *

CARMICHAEL, Harry
See OGNALL, Leopold Horace

* * *

CARNER, Mosco 1904-

PERSONAL: Surname originally Cohen; born November 15, 1904, in Vienna, Austria; son of Rudolph and Selma (Liggi) Cohen; married Elisabeth Rode (a physician), February 17, 1962 (died, 1970); married Hazel Sebag-Montefione, April 25, 1976. *Education:* Vienna Music Academy, diploma, 1926; University of Vienna, Ph.D., 1928. *Home:* 14 Elsworthy Rd., London N.W. 3, England.

CAREER: State Theatre, Free City of Danzig (now in Poland), operatic conductor, 1930-33; conductor of major symphony orchestras in London, England, 1938-55; musical author and critic, London, 1949—. Member of British Broadcasting Corp. score reading panel, 1944-48, 1957-62, 1963-72. *Member:* Society for the Promotion of New Music (executive board, 1948-58), London Critics' Circle. *Awards, honors:* Silver medal of Italian government, 1963, for *Puccini: A Critical Biography.*

WRITINGS: (Author of preface) Rene Lenormand, *A Study of Twentieth-Century Harmony: A Treatise and Guide for the Student Composer of To-day,* Volume I: *Harmony in France to 1914,* B. F. Wood Music Co., 1940, published as *A Study of Twentieth-Century Harmony: Harmony in France to 1914 and Contemporary Harmony,* two volumes, Da Capo, 1975; *Dvorak,* Novello, 1940; *A Study of Twentieth-Century Music,* Joseph Williams, 1942; *Of Men and Music,* Joseph Williams, 1944; *A History of the Waltz,* Parrish, 1948; *Puccini: A Critical Biography,* Duckworth, 1958, Knopf, 1959, 2nd edition, Holmes & Meier, 1977.

(Author of introduction) Giuseppe Adami, editor, *Letters of Giacomo Puccini: Mainly Connected with the Composition and Production of His Operas,* new edition (Carner was not associated with previous edition), Harrap, 1974; *Alban Berg: The Man and the Work,* Duckworth, 1975, Holmes & Meier, 1977, revised edition, Duckworth, 1983; *"Madame Butterfly,"* Barrie & Jenkins, 1979; *Major and Minor,* Holmes & Meier, 1980; *Hugo Wolf Songs,* BBC Music Guides, 1982.

Contributor: G. Abraham, editor, *Schubert Symposium,* Lindsay Drummond, 1946; Abraham, editor, *Schumann Symposium,* Oxford University Press, 1952; R. Hill, editor, *The Concerto,* Penguin, 1952; A. Robertson, editor, *Chamber Music,* Penguin, 1957; A. Jacobs, editor, *Choral Music,* Penguin, 1963. Also contributor to *New Oxford History of Music,* 1975, and to *Grove's Dictionary of Music,* 5th and 6th editions.

Contributor to British newspapers and periodicals, including *Musical Times, London Times,* and *Daily Telegraph.* Music critic, *Time and Tide,* 1949-61, and *Evening News* (London), 1957-61.

WORK IN PROGRESS: Puccini's Tosca, for Cambridge University Press.

SIDELIGHTS: "The reputation that Mosco Carner has achieved by his full-length studies of Puccini and Berg has naturally thrown into the shade his achievements in other fields of musicology," states Martin Cooper in the *Times Literary Supplement.* Carner's *Major and Minor,* a collection of essays, then, says Cooper, "is an excellent reminder of the catholicity of [the author's] taste and the versatility of his mind."

"By far the longest and most significant of this collection is the essay on Beethoven's 'Fidelio'—its history, the comparison of the three versions and the sources on which the composer drew in planning the musical presentation of Bouilly's original drama," continues Cooper. "By detailed examination, Dr. Carner shows the specific qualities of each of Beethoven's librettists—Sonnleithner's dramatically diffuse original version corrected by Stephan von Breuning in the short-lived second version, and Treitschke's almost completely successful re-shaping of the work as we know it today."

Puccini: A Critical Biography and *Alban Berg: The Man and the Work* have been published in French and Italian editions.

AVOCATIONAL INTERESTS: Reading, travel, motoring, and swimming.

BIOGRAPHICAL/CRITICAL SOURCES: Listener, June 12, 1980; *Times Literary Supplement,* July 11, 1980.

* * *

CARR, Jess(e Crowe, Jr.) 1930-

PERSONAL: Born July 27, 1930, in Bland County, Va.; son of Jesse Crowe and Flossie (Mitchell) Carr; married Lois Domazet (a choir director), June 17, 1955; children: Marsha Ainslie, Susan Kay, Catherine Rae. *Education:* Coyne Technical School, Chicago, Ill., graduate. *Politics:* Independent. *Religion:* Baptist. *Home:* 1401 Madison St., Radford, Va. 24141.

CAREER: Self-employed businessman in southwestern Virginia, 1949-51, 1953-56; Commonwealth Press, Inc., Radford, Va., sales manager, 1956-62, vice-president and general manager, 1962-71, chairman of the board, 1977—; full-time writer, 1971—. Owner, Woodland Heights Sub-Division Co.; builder of homes and commercial buildings. *Military service:* U.S. Marine Corps, 1951-52. *Member:* Printing Industries of the Virginias (vice-president, 1967).

WRITINGS: A Creature Was Stirring and Other Stories, Commonwealth Press, 1970; *The Second Oldest Profession: An Informal History of Moonshining in America,* Prentice-Hall, 1972; *The Falls of Rabbor,* Moore Publishing, 1973; *The Saint of the Wilderness,* Commonwealth Press, 1974; *Birth of a Book,* Commonwealth Press, 1974; *The Frost of Summer,* Moore Publishing, 1975; *The Moonshiners,* Aurora, 1977; *Ship Ride down the Spring Branch and Other Stories,* Moore Publishing, 1978; *How a Book Is Born,* Moore Publishing, 1978; *Millie and Cleve,* Leisure Books, 1979; *A Star Rising,* Tower, 1980.

WORK IN PROGRESS: The Midas Touch; Death under the Trees; The Gift Horse and Other Stories; a sequel to *A Star Rising.*

AVOCATIONAL INTERESTS: Fishing, water skiing, boating, photography, playing folk guitar, collecting books.

CARSBERG, Bryan Victor 1939-

PERSONAL: Born January 3, 1939, in London, England; son of Alfred Victor (a chartered secretary) and Maryllia (Collins) Carsberg; married Margaret Graham, December 10, 1960; children: Debbie Anne, Sarah Jane. *Education:* London School of Economics and Political Science, M.Sc., 1967. *Religion:* None. *Home:* 14, The Great Quarry, Guildford, Surrey, England. *Office:* London School of Economics and Political Science, University of London, London, England.

CAREER: Bryan Carsberg & Co. (public accounting firm), Amersham, England, public accountant, 1962-64; University of London, London School of Economics and Political Science, London, England, lecturer in accounting, 1964-69; University of Manchester, Manchester, England, professor of accounting, 1969-78; assistant director, Financial Accounting Standards Board, 1978-81; University of London, London School of Economics and Political Science, Arthur Anderson Professor of Accounting and director of research, Institute of Chartered Accountants in England and Wales, 1981—. Visiting professor of business administration, University of California, Berkeley, 1974. Visiting lecturer in accounting, University of Chicago, Graduate School of Business, 1968-69. *Member:* Institute of Chartered Accountants in England and Wales. *Awards, honors:* W. B. Peat Medal and Prize, Institute of Chartered Accountants, 1960.

WRITINGS: An Introduction to Mathematical Programming for Accountants, Augustus M. Kelley, 1969; (editor with H. C. Edey) *Modern Financial Management,* Penguin, 1969; *Analysis for Investment Decisions,* Haymarket, 1974; (with E. V. Morgan and M. Parkin) *Indexation and Inflation,* Financial Times, 1975; *Economics of Business Decisions,* Penguin, 1975; (with A. Hope) *Investment Decisions under Inflation,* Institute of Chartered Accountants in England and Wales, 1976; (editor with Hope) *Current Issues in Accounting,* P. Allen, 1977; (editor with J. Arnold and R. Seapens) *Topics in Management Accounting,* P. Allen, 1980. Contributor to accounting and finance journals.

WORK IN PROGRESS: Books on modern financial reporting and current cost accounting.

* * *

CARTER, Angela 1940-

PERSONAL: Born May 7, 1940, in London, England; daughter of Hugh Alexander (a journalist) and Olive (Farthing) Stalker; married Paul Carter, September 10, 1960 (divorced, 1972). *Education:* University of Bristol, B.A., 1965. *Politics:* Labour Party. *Religion:* None. *Agent:* Deborah Rogers, 5-11 Mortimer St., London W1N 7RH, England.

CAREER: Journalist for newspapers in Croyden, Surrey, England, 1958-61; novelist, short-story writer, teacher, and critic. *Awards, honors:* John Llewllyn Rhys Memorial Prize, 1968, for *The Magic Toyshop;* Somerset Maugham Award, 1969, for *Several Perceptions;* Cheltenham Festival Literary Award, 1979, for *The Bloody Chamber and Other Stories.*

WRITINGS: Unicorn (poetry collection), Location Press (London), 1966; *The Sadeian Woman and the Ideology of Pornography,* Pantheon, 1979 (published in England as *The Sadeian Woman: An Exercise in Cultural History,* Virago, 1979); (contributor) *Sex and Sensibility: Stories by Contemporary Women Writers from Nine Countries,* Sidgwick & Jackson, 1981.

Novels: *Shadow Dance,* Heinemann, 1966, published as *Honeybuzzard,* Simon & Schuster, 1967; *The Magic Toyshop,* Heinemann, 1967, Simon & Schuster, 1968; *Several Perceptions,* Heinemann, 1968, Simon & Schuster, 1969; *Heroes and Villains,* Heinemann, 1969, Simon & Schuster, 1970; *Love,* Hart Davis, 1971; *The Infernal Desire Machines of Dr. Hoffman,* Hart Davis, 1972, published as *The War of Dreams,* Harcourt, 1974; *The Passion of New Eve,* Harcourt, 1977.

Story collections: *Fireworks: Nine Profane Pieces,* Quartet Books, 1974, published as *Fireworks: Nine Stories in Various Disguises,* Harper, 1981; *The Bloody Chamber and Other Stories,* Gollancz, 1979, Harper, 1980.

Juveniles: *Miss Z, the Dark Young Lady,* Simon & Schuster, 1970; *The Donkey Prince,* Simon & Schuster, 1970; *Comic and Curious Cats,* Crown, 1979; (translator) *The Fairy Tales of Charles Perrault,* Gollancz, 1977, Avon, 1979; (with Leslie Carter) *The Music People,* Hamish Hamilton, 1980; (editor) *Sleeping Beauty and Other Favourite Fairy Tales,* Gollancz, 1983.

Radio scripts: "Vampirella," 1976; "Come unto These Yellow Sands," 1979; "The Company of Wolves," 1980.

Contributor to *New Society, Vogue, Iowa Review, Tri-Quarterly,* and other publications.

WORK IN PROGRESS: A collection of journalism and reviews for Virago.

SIDELIGHTS: "Angela Carter," writes Caroline Moorehead of the *Times Literary Supplement,* "is a Gothic writer of allegory and metaphor, myth and symbolism." Carter combines elements from a number of literary genres into a unique style which makes her work "difficult to place," according to Lorna Sage of the *Dictionary of Literary Biography.* James Brockway echoes this appraisal in a review for *Books and Bookmen* in which he defines Carter as "our Lady Edgar Allan Poe. . . . But she is more still. Like all genuine art, hers breaks through the boundaries of one department of art and extends to others. So she is also a female [Waslaw] Nijinsky. . . . She is Aubrey Beardsley. . . . She has also the decadence, the hysteria, and the preciosity of [Joris Karl] Huysmans and [Maurice] Maeterlinck, the doll-like romance of [E.T.A.] Hoffmann. . . . She is also a female [Roman] Polanski. . . . And like all geniuses, she walks the tightrope on one side of which yawns the chasm of madness, on the other the chasm of bathos."

There are four elements in Carter's fiction that critics find recurring in all of her work: A lush, imagistic prose, Gothic themes, violence, and an undercurrent of eroticism. These elements can be found in her first novel, *Shadow Dance,* published in the United States as *Honeybuzzard.* The novel is set in an English junk shop which sells newly-fashionable Victorian antiques. The shop is owned by the weak Morris and his vicious partner Honeybuzzard. Honeybuzzard's girlfriend, Ghislaine, is a nymphomaniac whose face Honeybuzzard has mutilated. Sage finds these characters "an ambiguous threesome." Carter "sets a grotesque stage," writes P. L. Sandberg of *Saturday Review,* "and peoples it with characters who are often extravagantly Gothic. . . . She sets up outrageous tensions between her people and suggests many layers of meaning." Morris and Honeybuzzard prowl condemned houses at night, stripping them of items to sell in their shop. Sage believes that "the decay of ordinary possessions into 'antiques' forms a fitting metaphor for the decay of the characters' experience into theater." When Honeybuzzard goes mad and kills Ghislaine, Morris is finally moved to betray him to the police. Edwin Morgan of *New*

Statesman, although believing the novel "a little too fashionable" because of its portrayal of the late 1960s London youth culture, nonetheless believes that Carter "shows a decided talent for the grotesque scene, the nightmarish atmosphere, the alarming uncertainties of human relationships." Brockway enjoys the book because it has "an all but unbelievable quality: a *fresh* decadence."

"The fantasy motifs lurking in the background in *Shadow Dance*," writes Sage, "come into their own in *The Magic Toyshop*," Carter's second novel. It tells the story of Melanie, a teenaged girl, and her younger brother and sister who, suddenly orphaned, find themselves sent to live with an uncle they have never met. Uncle Philip owns a toyshop where he and his wife, struck dumb on their wedding night, and her two brothers live. The aunt and her brothers are, Sage writes, Uncle Philip's "creatures, as surely as the toys he carves." Gradually, Melanie and the children learn that though Uncle Philip rules the toyshop with dictatorial violence by day, his real passion is the building of a theater of life-sized puppets by night—a theater in which he desires Melanie to play the part of Leda in *Leda and the Swan*. "The plot [of *The Magic Toyshop*]," John Wakeman of the *New York Times Book Review* complains, "is grossly implausible, and seems constantly to be taking directions that surprise the author as much as the reader.... And yet the book succeeds, awkwardly but firmly welded together by the heat of its author's imagination. It leaves behind it a flavor, pungent and unsettling, which owes as much to its imperfections as to its virtues." "This story is weird and definitely not for children," admits William McCleary of *Library Journal*. Yet he finds the book "an extraordinary, even brilliant piece of writing."

Carter's third novel, *Several Perceptions*, also set in late 1960s England, tells the story of Joseph Harker, a young man who fails in his suicide attempt and so is forced to reconcile himself with the world. Plagued by hallucinations and macabre images, Harker gradually comes to terms with his life through his interaction with his eccentric neighbors, "a pageantlike array of 'fringe' figures who subsist on 1960s tolerance for impromptu, narcissistic performance," as Sage describes them. It is a nightmarish odyssey which ends with Harker's mock salvation at a Christmas party where "a series of ironic miracles" is staged, Sage writes. "The first three quarters of the book," writes Richard Boston of the *New York Times Book Review*, "gives a powerful account of the horror, the logic and the poetry of the schizophrenic's world.... But after [Carter's] early toughmindedness, one had hoped for a more telling denouement than the Spirit of Christmas." The reviewer for the *Times Literary Supplement* believes "it is hard to draw any logical conclusion from Miss Carter's series of images or perceptions. But anyone who has found her previous strange novels... sticking uncomfortably in the memory will appreciate that however macabre and sensational the scene is, Miss Carter is not simply an image-maker." Carter won the prestigious Somerset Maugham Award for *Several Perceptions*.

With *Heroes and Villains*, Carter abandoned the settings of her previous novels for the realm of science fiction. Set in a post-World War III world of barbarians and scattered remnants of civilization, the novel is largely a fable about the nature of civilized society. Carter's earlier nightmarish qualities are still present, particularly in the rituals of the barbarians, which allow "fantasies of aggression and possession to blossom into action," Sage writes. Marianne, a young girl in a civilized community, is drawn by fascination to join the barbarians. She "rejects the sterile rationality of [civilization]," writes Boston, "but she is also aware of the monsters that are brought forth [among the barbarians] by the sleep of reason." Brockway finds the novel "too obvious an invention, its hairy and bejewelled young savages too symbolic to be interesting." In contrast to this judgement, the *Times Literary Supplement* critic, thinks that the barbarians' "world is richly imagined.... The fantasy is made to work through the use of detail and the firmly established individuality of the characters," but the critic finds that "the occasional pretentiousness which creeps into the last part of the book... does spoil what is in many ways a remarkably effective novel." Boston judges it "a strange, compelling book" and asserts that Carter "tells her story with considerable skill. Her observation is sharp, and she writes extremely well."

The ironically titled *Love* is again set in Carter's familiar late 1960s England but, as Sage writes, it "is altogether blacker, more erotic, and more lucidly nasty" than her previous novels. The novel details the relationship between Lee, a young teacher, his wife Annabel, a disturbed woman who rarely talks or moves, and Lee's brother Buzz, a voyeur who only experiences the world through photographs. "Mixing the grim, the exotic, the farcical," writes Anita Van Vactor of *Listener*, "Miss Carter traces the growth of a three-way symbiosis, a hermetic mythology decorated by Annabel's suicide attempts." Lee's efforts to escape the relationship by taking a mistress or throwing out his brother are ineffective because of his ultimate devotion to Annabel. "Again [Carter] is concerned," writes the *Times Literary Supplement* reviewer, "with the darker side of sibling affection and the type of love that consumes. [She] is extremely good at twining the macabre and unlikely with the possible.... Carter should add to her reputation by this taut study of strangeness."

Carter returned to an imaginary landscape in *The War of Dreams*, published in England as *The Infernal Desire Machines of Dr. Hoffman*. Using the surrealist goal of manifesting unconscious desires as the basis for her story, she creates Dr. Hoffman, a scientist who discovers "how to set the unconscious free," Sage writes, "and he begins to infiltrate reality with guerilla images that slide out of mirrors to mingle with the citizenry." When the government bureaucrat Desiderio is beseiged with these hallucinations, he sets off on a quest to find Dr. Hoffman and destroy him. "Along the way," writes William Hjortsberg of the *New York Times Book Review*, "he meets a macabre traveling carnival, an Indian tribe living on river-barges and speaking a kind of birdsong, a troupe of Moroccan acrobats who juggle the dismembered parts of their own bodies, a 'connoisseur of catastrophe,' black African cannibals, Mongolian pirates, a herd of centaurs, and Albertina, Dr. Hoffman's beautiful, Oriental-looking daughter." He also visits a "surreal brothel where android prostitutes enact the transformation of flesh into vegetable, animal, machine," Sage writes. In the end, Desiderio destroys the dream machines of Dr. Hoffman and saves reality. He "chooses the real, chooses contentment rather than ecstasy, reason rather than passion," writes J. D. O'Hara of the *Washington Post Book World*. "So does Carter." Ironically, despite the protagonist's restoration of the real world, *The War of Dreams* marked Carter "more decisively than any of her work up to that point," Sage believes, "as an aggressive anti-realist."

This anti-realist approach is also found in Carter's next novel, *The Passion of New Eve*, a violent sexual odyssey that takes Evelyn, an Englishman who abandons his pregnant girlfriend, from New York to California. Along the way he is captured in the desert by Amazons and surgically transformed into a woman, resides for a time with a Charles Manson-like cult, and finally meets his favorite movie actress, who turns out to be a transvestite. As Peter Ackroyd of *Spectator* writes, it "is a simple story of rape, castration, and apocalypse." Ackroyd particularly believes that Carter's "uneasy tone, perched somewhere between high seriousness and farce, unsettles the narrative as it leaps from one improbability to the next." Unfortunately, he also believes that the "language is so grandiose and verbose it can only transmit fantasies and visions—and no novel can survive for long on such a meagre diet."

Sage sees *The Passion of New Eve* as being closely related to the themes presented in Carter's nonfiction book *The Sadeian Woman and the Ideology of Pornography*. This feminist study of pornography argues that the Marquis de Sade created in his pornographic novels truthful portraits of women as they exist in modern society. "In the looking-glass of Sade's misanthropy," Carter writes in the book, "women may see themselves as they have been and it is an uncomfortable sight." In his novels *Justine* and *Juliette*, Sade portrays two kinds of women: the first a passive sex object, the second a dominant tyrant. These, Carter believes, are the only two possibilities for women in an unfree society. What makes Sade unusual as a pornographer, and of special interest to feminists, Carter writes, was his "claiming rights of free sexuality for women, and in installing women as beings of power in his imaginary worlds. This sets him apart from all other pornographers at all times and most other writers of his period."

There are echoes of *The Sadeian Woman* in Carter's collection *Fireworks: Nine Stories in Various Disguises*. Michele Slung of the *Washington Post Book World* writes that "reading *Fireworks*, I thought of Carter's 'ideology of pornography,' for these tales are nearly all exquisite while at the same time aggressively obscene. Like sinister fruits, they cause us to become addicted to their bizarre flavor." Victoria Glendinning of *New Statesman* finds that the stories "are the result of [Carter's] preoccupation with the imagery of the unconscious. . . . The real world [blossoms] strangely. The tales are full of puppets, mirrors, forests, sequined eyes, shells, flowers and diffuse lust." Although decrying what she sees as the familiarity of Carter's subjects, a familiarity she attributes to Carter's use of archetypal elements, Glendinning concludes: "Angela Carter is a genius of a word-spinner."

Sexual themes are also prevalent in Carter's second story collection, *The Bloody Chamber and Other Stories*, a collection Linda Rolens of the *Los Angeles Times Book Review* describes as "stories with disturbing eroticism" that are composed of "sexuality and violence." "An obsession . . . with sadistic power and masochistic sacrifice pervades *The Bloody Chamber*," writes Alan Friedman of the *New York Times Book Review*. Retelling old fairy tales in contemporary language, Carter's stories differ from the originals in one important way. "The difference is sex," as Carolyn G. Heilbrum of the *Washington Post Book World* writes. "[Carter] gives women an active part in the stories. In Carter's versions we are delighted to find women who are lusty and clever, animals who are tender and loving, and stories with a narrative pull like Scheherazade's." Susan Kennedy of the *Times Literary Supplement* believes that Carter's stories have "the power, not only to cause us to think again, and deeply, about the mythic sources of our common cultural touchstones, but to plunge us into hackle-raising speculation about aspects of our human/animal nature." "Carter . . . has tried her hand," Rolens states, "at the near impossible and succeeded: She has transformed classic fairy tales into potent adult tales."

Sage finds that although Carter has won several major literary awards, "her preoccupations as a writer—deepened and defined over the years—remain radically at odds with the puritanism and the conventional realism that characterize much British fiction." Moorehead also sees Carter as a unique writer, one whose "imaginary worlds are so original, so bizarre, and so full of talent that they have the clarity of dreams."

BIOGRAPHICAL/CRITICAL SOURCES—Periodicals: *New Statesman*, July 8, 1966, November 14, 1969, August 16, 1974; *Saturday Review*, February 18, 1967; *Library Journal*, February 1, 1968; *New York Times Book Review*, February 25, 1968, March 2, 1969, September 13, 1970, September 8, 1974, February 17, 1980, June 14, 1981; *Times Literary Supplement*, August 1, 1968, November 20, 1969, June 18, 1971, February 8, 1980, July 4, 1981; *Listener*, May 20, 1971, September 26, 1974; *Washington Post Book World*, August 18, 1974, February 24, 1980, June 28, 1981; *Books and Bookmen*, February, 1975; *Spectator*, March 26, 1977; *New Review*, June/July, 1977; *Los Angeles Times Book Review*, March 16, 1980.

Books: *Contemporary Literary Criticism*, Volume V, Gale, 1976; Angela Carter, *The Sadeian Woman and the Ideology of Pornography*, Pantheon, 1979; *Contemporary Issues Criticism*, Volume I, Gale, 1982; *Dictionary of Literary Biography*, Volume XIV: *British Novelists since 1960*, Gale, 1983.

—Sketch by Thomas Wiloch

* * *

CASTAGNOLA, Lawrence A. 1933-

PERSONAL: Surname is pronounced Cas-ta-no-la; born June 3, 1933, in Sacramento, Calif.; son of Ferdinand (a certified public accountant) and Louise Castagnola. *Education:* Attended University of Santa Clara, 1951-54; Gonzaga University, B.A., M.A., 1957; Alma College, M.A., 1964. *Home:* 1345 Stewart Rd., Sacramento, Calif. 95825.

CAREER: Entered Society of Jesus (Jesuits) in 1951; ordained a priest in 1964. High school teacher in San Francisco, Calif., 1957-60; chaplain at Fort Worden Treatment Center for Juveniles, Port Townsend, Wash., 1965; teacher at Jesuit High School, Sacramento, Calif., 1965-71; founder and director of a home for emotionally disturbed boys, Sacramento, 1970-83; currently teacher at St. Francis High School, Sacramento.

WRITINGS: Let Your Lamps Be Burning, St. Paul Publications, 1966; *Pastoral Reflections*, St. Paul Publications, 1967; *I Love Youth: It's Teenagers I Hate*, B. Herder, 1970; *Confessions of a Catechist*, Alba, 1970; *I Love Troublemakers: It's Trouble I Hate*, privately printed, 1978; *A View from Andrew's Pocket*, privately printed, 1980, 1981; *The Bookeating Monster*, Acca (Thailand), 1983.

* * *

CATUDAL, Honore M(arc, Jr.) 1944-

PERSONAL: Born October 17, 1944, in Washington, D.C.; son of Honore M. (a government official) and Gertrude (Hemm) Catudal; married Renate Goerz, April 1, 1967; children: Raymond, Sandra. *Education:* Free University of Berlin, Zertifikat, 1968; Syracuse University, B.A. (cum laude), 1969; American University, M.I.S., 1971, Ph.D., 1973. *Religion:* Catholic. *Office:* Department of Politics, St. John's University, Collegeville, Minn. 56321.

CAREER: St. John's University, Collegeville, Minn., assistant professor of international relations, 1973—. *Military service:*

U.S. Army, 1962-65. *Member:* International Studies Association, Oral History Association, American Society of International Law, American Political Science Association, Conference Group on German Politics, Phi Alpha Theta, Pi Sigma Alpha. *Awards, honors:* Phi Alpha Theta prize, 1969, for essay on Steinstuecken.

WRITINGS: Steinstuecken: A Study in Cold War Politics, privately printed, 1971; *The Enclave Problem of Western Europe,* University of Alabama Press, 1977; *The Diplomacy of the Quadripartite Agreement on Berlin: A New Era in East-West Relations,* Berlin Verlag (Berlin), 1978; *A Balance Sheet of the Quadripartite Agreement on Berlin,* Berlin Verlag, 1978; *Kennedy and the Berlin Wall Crisis: A Case Study in U.S. Decision-Making,* International Publications Service, 1980. Contributor to national and international journals in the fields of geography, history, political science, and international relations.

WORK IN PROGRESS: Two books, *Playing the China Card: U.S.-Chinese Relations 1969-1983,* and *Does Deterrence Deter: Myth of Reality?*

SIDELIGHTS: Honore M. Catudal's writing on Berlin and enclaves (pieces of one state situated in another) stems from his experience as an army private stationed in the divided city during the early 1960s. There he served as a security guard for Rudolph Hess.

While in college, he traveled to Washington, D.C., New York City, and Cambridge, to interview more than a dozen military and diplomatic officials, who at one time or another have been deeply involved in a Berlin crisis. Among those he talked with were Dwight Eisenhower, Lucius Clay, Maxwell Taylor, James Gavin, Dean Rusk, Robert Murphy, Foy Kohler, Eleanor Dulles, and Allen Dulles.

Catudal spent his "junior year abroad" as a student in Berlin, and took out a second residence in the small enclave community of Steinstuecken, legally part of the American sector but lying as a separate "island" inside East Germany. Encouraged by its 180 inhabitants, who made their personal archives available to him, he proceeded to write its political history. Before Catudal was suddenly barred by East German border guards in 1968, he was one of the few outsiders ever to visit the cut-off village.

When the four-power talks on Berlin got underway in 1970, Catudal proposed that the Steinstuecken enclave be joined to the mainland through an exchange of territory. This idea was soon injected into the conversations with the Russians by American diplomats. The Russians, after some preliminary discussion, accepted the idea of a territorial swap; when the quadripartite accord was finally signed in 1971, the inhabitants of Steinstuecken were provided with a Western controlled corridor linking their village with the rest of West Berlin.

AVOCATIONAL INTERESTS: Chess, tennis, long-distance running.

BIOGRAPHICAL/CRITICAL SOURCES: Washington Post, January 2, 1972; *Bunte,* September 21, 1972.

* * *

**CAVALLO, Evelyn
See SPARK, Muriel (Sarah)**

**CEBULASH, Mel 1937-
(Ben Farrell, Glen Harlan, Jared Jansen, Jeanette Mara)**

PERSONAL: Surname is pronounced *Seb*-yu-lash; born August 24, 1937, in Jersey City, N.J.; son of Jack (a mailman) and Jeanette (Duthie) Cebulash; married Deanna Penn, August 19, 1962 (divorced); married Dolly Hasinbiller, June 19, 1977; children: (first marriage) Glen Harlan, Benjamin Farrell, Jeannette Mara. *Education:* Jersey City State College, B.A., 1962, M.A., 1964; University of South Carolina, graduate study, 1964-65. *Religion:* Jewish. *Address:* c/o Pitman Learning, 19 Davis Dr., Belmont, Calif. 94002.

CAREER: Junior high school teacher of reading in Teaneck, N.J., 1962-64; Fairleigh Dickinson University, Rutherford, N.J., instructor in reading clinic, 1965-67; Scholastic Magazines, Inc., New York, N.Y., editor for language arts, 1966-76; Bowmar/Noble Publishing Co., Los Angeles, Calif., editor-in-chief, 1976-80; currently publisher, book division, Pitman Learning, Belmont, Calif. *Military service:* U.S. Army, 1955-58. U.S. Army Reserve, 1958-61. *Member:* Authors Guild, Authors League of America, Mystery Writers of America (regional vice-president, 1982-83). *Awards, honors:* Author Award of New Jersey Association of Teachers of English, 1969, for *Through Basic Training with Walter Young.*

WRITINGS: The Grossest Book of World Records, Pocket Books, 1978; *The Champion's Jacket,* Creative Education, 1979; *I'm an Expert,* Scott, Foresman, 1982; *Ruth Marini of the Dodgers,* Lerner Book Co., 1983; *Ruth Marini—Dodger Ace,* Lerner Book Co., 1983; *Ruth Marini—World Series Star,* Lerner Book Co., in press.

Published by Scholastic Book Services: (Adaptor) *Monkeys, Go Home* (based on Walt Disney film), 1967; *Through Basic Training with Walter Young,* 1968; (adaptor) *The Love Bug* (based on Walt Disney film), 1969; *Man in a Green Beret and Other Medal of Honor Winners,* 1969; (adaptor) *The Boatniks* (based on Walt Disney film), 1970; *The Ball That Wouldn't Bounce,* 1972; (under pseudonym Glen Harlan) *Petey the Pup,* 1972; (under pseudonym Jared Jansen) *Penny the Poodle,* 1972; (adaptor) *Herby Rides Again* (based on Walt Disney film), 1974; *Dic-tion-ar-y Skilz,* 1974; (adaptor) *The Strongest Man in the World* (based on Walt Disney film), 1975; *Blackouts,* 1979; *The Spring Street Boys Team Up,* 1982; *The Spring Street Boys Settle a Score,* 1982; *The Spring Street Boys Hit the Road,* 1982; *The Spring Street Boys Go for Broke,* 1982.

Published by Random House: *Baseball Players Do Amazing Things,* 1973; *Football Players Do Amazing Things,* 1975; *Basketball Players Do Amazing Things,* 1976; *The 1,000 Point Pro Sports Quiz Book: Football,* 1979; *The 1,000 Point Pro Sports Quiz Book: Basketball,* 1979; *The 1,000 Point Pro Sports Quiz Book: Baseball,* 1980.

Published by Bowmar/Noble: *Math Zingo,* 1978; *Reading Zingo,* 1978; *Big League Baseball Reading Kit,* 1979; *Spanish Math Zingo,* 1979; *Crosswinds Reading Program,* 1979; *A Horse to Remember,* 1980.

Contributor of short stories to university literary journals. Contributing editor, *Scholastic Scope* (magazine). Editor, "ACTION Reading Kit" series, Scholastic Book Services, 1970.

WORK IN PROGRESS: A mystery novel.

SIDELIGHTS: Mel Cebulash writes: "The idea of writing entered my mind when I was a senior in college. The first short story I tried was published, and although the stories that followed didn't meet with the same approval, my small measure of success was enough to sustain a continuing effort.

"Just before my first child was born, I left teaching and moved into writing and editing as a full-time activity. My parents and friends looked upon the move as the foolish pursuit of a far-fetched dream. Fortunately, years of reading had led me to believe in the possibility of dreams. My writing has ranged from picture book stories for children to books for adults. I have been especially interested in stories and books for young people who have difficulty in reading, and I suppose these efforts have been most rewarding to me.

"Most of my fiction stems either directly or indirectly from experience. I use experience for ideas, but I allow the writing to shape the experience into something new—something that hasn't happened to me or anyone else.

"I've been pleased by the sales of my books, but my real joy in writing has come from the letters I've received from young people. When I think I'm all alone with a typewriter, I remind myself of the many friends I've made through writing."

AVOCATIONAL INTERESTS: The literature and popular music of the 1930s, the works of James T. Farrell ("a friend and inspiration").

* * *

CHAFE, William H(enry) 1942-

PERSONAL: Born January 28, 1942, in Boston, Mass.; son of William Robinson and Elsie (Crabtree) Chafe; married Lorna Waterhouse, July 12, 1964; children: Christopher Robert, Jennifer Elizabeth. *Education:* Harvard University, A.B. (magna cum laude), 1962; Union Theological Seminary, New York, N.Y., graduate study, 1962-63; Columbia University, M.A., 1966, Ph.D., 1971; Cornell University, summer graduate study, 1967. *Home:* 820 Tinkerbell Rd., Chapel Hill, N.C. 27514. *Office:* Department of History, Duke University, Durham, N.C. 27706.

CAREER: Columbia Grammar School, New York, N.Y., instructor in history and comparative religion, 1963-65; Vassar College, Poughkeepsie, N.Y., instructor in history, 1970-71; Duke University, Durham, N.C., assistant professor of history, 1971—, associate director of Oral History Program, 1971—. *Awards, honors:* National Endowment for the Humanities summer fellow, 1972, fellow, 1974; Rockefeller Humanities fellow, 1978; Robert F. Kennedy Book Award, 1981, for *Civilities and Civil Rights: Greensboro, North Carolina, and the Black Struggle for Freedom;* award from Mayflower Corp., 1981; National Humanities Center fellow, 1981-82.

WRITINGS: (Contributor) Robert C. Twombly, editor, *Blacks in White America since 1865,* McKay, 1971; *The American Woman: Her Changing Social, Political, and Economic Roles, 1920-1970,* Oxford University Press, 1972; (contributor) James T. Patterson, editor, *The United States since 1930,* Burgess, 1974; *Women and Equality: Changing Patterns in American Culture,* Oxford University Press, 1977; *Civilities and Civil Rights: Greensboro, North Carolina, and the Black Struggle for Freedom,* Oxford University Press, 1980; (editor with Howard Sitkoff) *A History of Our Time,* Oxford University Press, 1983. Contributor to *Journal of Southern History, Michigan History,* and *New England Social Studies Bulletin.*

SIDELIGHTS: According to Sandra Salmans' *Times Literary Supplement* review of *Civilities and Civil Rights: Greensboro, North Carolina, and the Black Struggle for Freedom,* William H. Chafe's book "focuses on the period from 1945 to 1975 during which Greensboro and the rest of the country witnessed the evolution, through peaceable rallies to bloody riots, of the modern civil-rights movement. . . . By putting Greensboro under the microscope, [Chafe provides] an interesting insight into the forces within a community that resisted the black struggle for freedom."

Randall Kennedy writes in the *New Republic* that Chafe's "history of race relations in Greensboro . . . is infused with the spirit of the dissent it chronicles. Thoughtful, well written, and thoroughly researched, it is a work of disciplined, committed scholarship that is likely to inspire imitation. . . . *Civilities and Civil Rights . . .* is as suggestive about future actions as it is instructive about the past. It represents the sort of scholarly advocacy that honors the historian's calling."

Similarly, James Reston, Jr. points out in a *New York Times Book Review* article that Chafe's book "is social history at its best. . . . It fulfills history's highest value by speaking to the present and to the future."

BIOGRAPHICAL/CRITICAL SOURCES: New York Review of Books, September 15, 1977, October 7, 1982; *New Republic,* February 16, 1980; *New York Times Book Review,* April 6, 1980; *Times Literary Supplement,* April 24, 1981.

* * *

CHAMBERS, Aidan 1934-

PERSONAL: Born December 27, 1934, in Chester-le-Street, County Durham, England; son of George Kenneth Blacklin (a funeral director) and Margaret (Hancock) Chambers; married Nancy Lockwood (former editor of *Children's Book News*), March 30, 1968. *Education:* Attended Borough Road College, London, England, 1955-57. *Home and office:* "Lockwood", Station Rd., Woodchester, Stroud, Gloucestershire GL5 5EQ, England.

CAREER: Teacher of English and drama at various schools in England, 1957-68; full-time writer, 1968—. Publisher, as Thimble Press, of *Signal: Approaches to Children's Books,* and *Young Drama: The Magazine about Child and Youth Drama.* Has produced children's plays for stage and written and presented several radio and television programs. *Military service:* Royal Navy, 1953-55. *Member:* Society of Authors.

WRITINGS—For young people, except as noted: *Johnny Salter* (play), Heinemann Educational Books, 1966; *The Car* (play), Heinemann Educational Books, 1967; *Cycle Smash* (novel), Heinemann, 1967; *The Chicken Run* (play), Heinemann Educational Books, 1968; *Marle* (novel), Heinemann, 1968; *The Reluctant Reader* (adult), Pergamon, 1969; (with wife, Nancy Chambers) *Ghosts,* Macmillan, 1969.

(With N. Chambers) *World Zero Minus,* Macmillan, 1971; *More Haunted Houses,* Pan Books, 1973; (editor) *Book of Ghosts and Hauntings,* Kestrel Books, 1973; *Introducing Books to Children* (adult), Heinemann Educational Books, 1973, revised edition, Horn Book, 1983; *Great British Ghosts,* Pan Books, 1974; *Great Ghosts of the World,* Pan Books, 1974; *Flyers and Flying,* Kestrel Books, 1976; *Funny Folk,* Heinemann, 1976; (editor) *Cops and Robbers,* Kestrel Books, 1977; *Ghost Carnival,* Heinemann, 1977; *Breaktime* (novel), Bodley Head, 1978; *Animal Fair,* Heinemann, 1979.

Fox Tricks, Heinemann, 1980; (editor) *Ghosts That Haunt You,* Kestrel Books, 1980; (editor) *Loving You Loving Me,* Macmillan, 1980; *Seal Secret* (novel), Bodley Head, 1980; (editor)

Ghost after Ghost, Kestrel Books, 1982; *Dance on My Grave* (novel), Bodley Head, 1982; *The Dream Cage* (play), Heinemann, 1982; *The Present Takers* (novel), Bodley Head, 1983.

Contributor to *Winter Tales for Children 4,* Macmillan. General editor, Macmillan "Topliners" series, books designed for adolescents reluctant to read the usual fiction found in publishers' lists. Author of column "Letter from England," in *Horn Book* (magazine). Contributor to *Books and Bookmen, Times Educational Supplement, Teachers' World,* and *Books for Your Children.* Reviewer for *Children's Book News.*

WORK IN PROGRESS: Criticism of current children's fiction; novels and stories.

SIDELIGHTS: According to *Times Literary Supplement* reviewer Edward Blishen, Aidan Chambers remarks in the foreword to *Ghosts That Haunt You* that "as a writer of ghost stories, [Chambers] had received many letters from young readers, telling him about their own encounters with the supernatural. This led him to wonder why more writers did not put young ghosts, or young victims of ghosts, into their stories. And that in its turn led to this collection of ten tales."

BIOGRAPHICAL/CRITICAL SOURCES: Drama, winter, 1968; *Times Literary Supplement,* October 16, 1969, July 18, 1980, November 26, 1982, September 30, 1983; *New York Times Book Review,* April 29, 1979.

* * *

CHAMBERS, Dewey W. 1929-

PERSONAL: Born March 23, 1929, in King City, Calif.; son of Ned and Mabel (Woods) Chambers; married Judith A. McMillin (vice-president of student life, University of the Pacific), June 12, 1970. *Education:* San Jose State College (now University), A.B., 1952, M.A., 1960; Wayne State University, Ed.D., 1965. *Religion:* Christian. *Home:* 3636 Merrimac Circle N., Lincoln Village W., Stockton, Calif. 95207. *Office:* University of the Pacific, Stockton, Calif. 95204.

CAREER: Elementary school teacher, San Carlos Elementary School District, San Carlos, Calif., 1952-59; San Francisco State College (now University), San Francisco, Calif., demonstration-laboratory teacher, 1959-62; Wayne State University, Detroit, Mich., instructor in education, 1962-65; University of the Pacific, Stockton, Calif., assistant professor, 1965-68, associate professor, 1968-70, professor of education, 1970—.

Professor of education, University of California, Davis, Extension, 1966-67, 1971-72, and University of California, Santa Cruz, Extension, 1972. Visiting professor at Wisconsin State University—Platteville, 1966, and State University of New York College at Fredonia, 1970; guest professor, State University of Wisconsin, 1966, New York State University, 1969, Oakland University, 1974, and University of California, Irvine, 1975. Guest lecturer, San Marcos University, Lima, Peru, 1961. Producer, "The Frederick Burk Story" (television special) for KGO-TV, 1963. Lecturer, "University Classroom on the Air," for K.U.O.P. Radio, 1968-69. Member of board of trustees, Pacific Collegiate School, 1974-75. Has served on numerous committees. Consultant to television series, "The Wonderful World of Children's Literature," ABC-TV, 1967. Consultant to several organizations, including Xerox Microreading Libraries of Xerox Corp., 1971, Far West Regional Laboratory of Education Research, 1974, and Coronet Film Corp., 1974-75, 1976-77.

MEMBER: International Reading Association, National Education Association, National Council of Teachers of English (member of board of directors, 1969-72), California College and University Faculty Association, California Teachers Association, Commonwealth Club of California (member of literary jury, 1969-83), Phi Delta Kappa, Phi Delta Phi.

AWARDS, HONORS: Golden Apple Award, *San Francisco News,* 1958; named notable American of the bicentennial era, American Biographical Institute, 1976; Mortar Board Faculty Recognition award, 1979, School of Education distinguished professor award, 1982, all university distinguished professor award, 1982, all from University of the Pacific.

WRITINGS: Children's Literature: Storytelling and Creative Drama, W. C. Brown, 1970; *Children's Literature in the Curriculum,* Rand McNally, 1971; (contributor) Paul C. Burns and Leo Schell, editors, *Elementary School Language Arts: Selected Readings,* Rand McNally, 1969; (editor) *Adventuring with Books,* Citation Press, 1973; (editor) *Folk and Other Tales from the Mother Lode,* University of the Pacific Press, 1974; (with Heath Lowry) *The Language Arts: A Pragmatic Approach,* W. C. Brown, 1975; *The Oral Tradition: Storytelling and Creative Drama,* W. C. Brown, 1977; *The Keys to Success,* Smith Corona Corp., 1979; (editor) *Tales of the Delta Fox,* University of the Pacific Press, 1982. Also author, with Sandra Anselmo and B. Jan Timmons, of "In My Neighborhood I Wonder about the Supermarket" (children's filmstrip), 1980.

Monographs: (With Shirley Jennings) *The Achievement Patterns of Eight Linguistic Sets of Children in a Pluralistic Community,* Bureau of Research and Field Services, School of Education, University of the Pacific, 1975; (with P. Roberts) *Have a Star Spangled Bicentennial with Children's Literature,* Sacramento (Calif.) Public Library, 1976; (editor) *Ukipau* (folk and other tales of the New Hawaiians), University of the Pacific, 1977. Contributor of articles to education journals. Book reviewer for *Elementary English,* 1964-65, and *Pacific Historian,* 1966.

BIOGRAPHICAL/CRITICAL SOURCES: I. Leif, *Children's Literature: A Historical and Contemporary Bibliography,* Whitson Publishing, 1977; *Pacific Review,* December, 1979.

* * *

CHAPMAN, Christine 1933-

PERSONAL: Born June 10, 1933, in Detroit, Mich.; daughter of Duncan Stewart (a businessman) and Esther (a teacher; maiden name, Goodrich) Patton; married William Thomas Chapman (a foreign correspondent), September, 1956; children: Peter T., Daniel S. *Education:* Wells College, B.A., 1954; George Washington University, M.A., 1965. *Politics:* Democrat. *Residence:* Tokyo, Japan. *Agent:* Helen Brann Agency, Inc., 14 Sutton Pl. S., New York, N.Y. 10022.

CAREER: Scholastic, New York, N.Y., staff writer, 1954-56; *Charleston News & Courier,* Charleston, S.C., part-time staff writer, 1956-58; teacher of English at private schools in Charleston, S.C., 1958-60, and Washington, D.C., 1962-66; Sidwell Friends School, Washington, D.C., English teacher, 1966-77; lecturer in English literature and Composition at Tsuda College and Chiba University, Tokyo, Japan, 1977—.

WRITINGS: America's Runaways, Morrow, 1976; *The New Youth,* Asahi Press, 1981; *Today's Youth,* Asahi Press, 1984. Contributor to magazines and newspapers, including *International Herald Tribune.*

WORK IN PROGRESS: "A murder mystery set in present-day Japan in which the characters, Americans and Japanese, bring to a boil passions engendered during the Occupation."

SIDELIGHTS: Christine Chapman writes: "Federal and state governments, the police, psychiatry, and the schools contribute, erroneously, to the idea of runaways as delinquents or as mentally ill children. In *America's Runaways* I tried to show what was happening to more than a million children who leave home suddenly each year for many reasons, most centering on the family."

* * *

CHARLES, Henry
See HARRIS, Marion Rose (Young)

* * *

CHERRY, (Edward) Colin 1914-1979

PERSONAL: Born June 23, 1914, in St. Albans, England; died November 23, 1979, in England; son of Arthur Leonard and Margaret Ellen Cherry; married Heather Blanche White, 1956; children: Lucy Helen, Anna Frances. *Education:* University of London, B.Sc., 1936, M.Sc., 1940, D.Sc., 1958. *Politics:* Labour. *Religion:* "Not a member of any church." *Home:* Combe House, Chichester Rd., Dorking, Surrey, England. *Office:* Department of Electrical Engineering, Imperial College of Science and Technology, University of London, London SW7 2BT, England.

CAREER: General Electric Co., Research Laboratories, London, England, member of scientific staff, 1936-45; College of Technology, Manchester, lecturer, 1945-47; University of London, Imperial College of Science and Technology, London, lecturer, 1947-52, reader, 1952-58, Henry Mark Pease Professor of Telecommunication, 1958-79. Member of assessment board of Open University and of St. Dunstan's Scientific Committee. Member of United Kingdom National Commission for UNESCO. *Member:* British International Studies Association, Institution of Electrical Engineers, British Experimental Psychology Society, Royal Horticultural Society, Royal Society of Arts. *Awards, honors:* Fourth Marconi International Fellowship, 1978, granted in recognition of scientific achievement for the benefit of humanity in the field of communications science or technology; honorary associate of the City and Guilds of London Institute.

WRITINGS: *Pulses and Transients in Communication Circuits*, Chapman & Hall, 1949; *On Human Communication: A Review, a Survey, and a Criticism*, M.I.T. Press, 1957, 3rd edition, 1978; *World Communication: Threat or Promise?: A Sociotechnical Approach*, Wiley, 1971, 2nd edition, 1978; (editor) *Pragmatic Aspects of Human Communication*, Reidel, 1974. Contributor of about one hundred and twenty articles to technical journals.

WORK IN PROGRESS: Before his death, Colin Cherry was writing a book about the social significance of information technology, *The Second Industrial Revolution?*, which is now being prepared for publication.

SIDELIGHTS: Colin Cherry commented to *CA*: "I have always been highly critical of the traditional teaching of technology, especially that of communication, arguing that is meaningful if considered only as a political matter. My students are largely drawn from developing countries and this has forced me to study the nature of the human communication process socially, psychologically, and philosophically in order to understand and advise better on specification of telecommunication systems to be of real value to development. I have travelled widely and lectured in some thirty countries of Europe, North and South America, and Asia."

AVOCATIONAL INTERESTS: Gardening, foreign travel, watercolor.

OBITUARIES: *AB Bookman's Weekly*, December 24-31, 1979.†

* * *

CHETIN, Helen 1922-

PERSONAL: Born July 6, 1922; daughter of Guy Edward (a physician) and Helen (Collins) Campbell; married Adnan Chetin (a geologist); children: Timur, Sara. *Education:* Attended University of Texas, 1943-45. *Home and office:* 1665 Euclid Ave., Berkeley, Calif. 94709.

CAREER: Stanford University, Institute for Mathematical Studies in the Social Sciences, Stanford, Calif., writer, 1966-71; New Seed Press (publisher of children's books), Berkeley, Calif., editor, 1973—. *Awards, honors: Tales from an African Drum* was selected for the Child Study Association book list.

WRITINGS: *Tales from an African Drum*, Harcourt, 1971; *Perihan's Promise, Turkish Relatives and the Dirty Old Iman*, Houghton, 1973; *How Far Is Berkeley?*, Harcourt, 1977; *Frances Ann Speaks Out: My Father Raped Me*, New Seed Press, 1978; *The Lady of the Strawberries*, PMA (Canada), 1978; *Angel Island Prisoner 1922*, New Seed Press, 1982. Editor, *The Wild Iris*, 1973-78.

WORK IN PROGRESS: Poetry; a historical novel about an Ottoman harem.

SIDELIGHTS: *The Lady of the Strawberries* has been published in French and German editions.

* * *

CHETWYND-HAYES, R(onald Henry Glynn) 1919-
(Angus Campbell)

PERSONAL: Born May 30, 1919, in Middlesex, England; son of Henry (a movie theatre manager) and Rose May (Cooper) Chetwynd-Hayes. *Education:* Educated in England. *Politics:* Liberal. *Religion:* Church of England. *Home and office:* 42A Church Rd., Richmond, Surrey TW10 6LN, England. *Agent:* London Management, 235/241 Regent St., London W1A 2JT, England.

CAREER: Writer and editor, 1973—. Salesman in London, England, for Harrods Ltd., Army and Navy Stores, and Bourne & Hollingsworth Ltd.; showroom and exhibition manager for Peerless Build-In Furniture Ltd. *Military service:* British Army, 1939-46. *Member:* Society of Authors.

WRITINGS—All fiction: *The Man from the Bomb*, John Spencer, 1959; *The Dark Man*, Sidgwick & Jackson, 1964, published as *And Love Survived*, Zebra Books, 1979; *The Unbidden*, Tandem Books, 1971, Pyramid Press, 1975; *Cold Terror*, Tandem Books, 1973, Pyramid Press, 1975; *The Elemental*, Fontana Books, 1974; *The Night Ghouls*, Fontana Books, 1975; *The Monster Club*, New English Library, 1975; *Terror by Night*, Pyramid Press, 1976; *Tales of Fear and Fantasy*, Fontana Books, 1977; *The Cradle Demon and Other Stories of Fantasy and Terror*, Kimber, 1978; (author of novelization) *Dominique*, Star Books, 1978; *The Brats*, Kimber, 1979; *The*

Partaker, Kimber, 1980; *Kamtellar*, Kimber, 1980; (author of novelization) *The Awakening*, Magnum Books, 1980; *Tales of Darkness*, Kimber, 1981; *Tales from Beyond*, Kimber, 1982.

Editor and contributor; published by Fontana Books: *Cornish Tales of Terror*, 1971; (under pseudonym Angus Campbell) *Scottish Tales of Terror*, 1972; *Welsh Tales of Terror*, 1973; *Ninth Fontana Book of Great Ghost Stories*, 1973; *Tenth Fontana Book of Great Ghost Stories*, 1974; *Eleventh Fontana Book of Great Ghost Stories*, 1975; *Terror Tales from Outer Space*, 1975; *Gaslight Tales of Terror*, 1976; *Twelfth Fontana Book of Great Ghost Stories*, 1976; *Thirteenth Fontana Book of Great Ghost Stories*, 1977; *Fourteenth Fontana Book of Great Ghost Stories*, 1978; *Fifteenth Fontana Book of Great Ghost Stories*, 1979; *Sixteenth Fontana Book of Great Ghost Stories*, 1980; *Seventeenth Fontana Book of Great Ghost Stories*, 1982.

Published by Armada Books: *First Armada Monster Book* (juvenile), 1975; *Second Armada Monster Book*, 1976; *Third Armada Monster Book*, 1977; *Fourth Armada Monster Book*, 1978; *Fifth Armada Monster Book*, 1979; *Sixth Armada Monster Book*, 1981.

Also editor and contributor to *Doomed to the Night*, published by Kimber. Contributor to periodicals, including *Reveille*.

WORK IN PROGRESS: Eighteenth Fontana Book of Great Ghost Stories; "Yesterday's Phantoms," a thirteen-part television series.

SIDELIGHTS: Many of R. Chetwynd-Hayes' books have been translated into German.

MEDIA ADAPTATIONS: "From beyond the Grave," a film based on four stories by R. Chetwynd-Hayes, was made by Amicus Films for Warner Brothers in 1974; "Something in the Woodwork," a television adaptation of his story "Household," was shown on the program "Night Gallery"; *The Monster Club* was made into a film in 1980.

* * *

CHILDS, Marquis W(illiam) 1903-

PERSONAL: Born March 17, 1903, in Clinton, Iowa; son of William Henry (a lawyer) and Lilian Malissa (Marquis) Childs; married Lu Prentiss, August 26, 1926 (died June, 1968); married Jane Neylan McBain, August 6, 1969; children: (first marriage) Prentiss, Malissa. *Education:* University of Wisconsin, A.B., 1923; University of Iowa, A.M., 1925. *Home:* 2703 Dumbarton Ave. N.W., Washington, D.C. 20007. *Office:* 1701 Pennsylvania Ave. N.W., Washington, D.C. 20036.

CAREER: United Press International, reporter in Chicago and Midwest, 1923, in New York, 1925-26; *St. Louis Post Dispatch*, St. Louis, Mo., feature writer, 1926-30; free-lance writer, 1930-34; *St. Louis Post Dispatch*, special correspondent and member of Washington, D.C., staff, 1934-68. Columnist for United Feature Syndicate, 1944-54. Eric W. Allen Memorial Lecturer at University of Oregon, 1950; lecturer at Columbia University School of Journalism.

MEMBER: Sigma Delta Chi, Kappa Sigma, Overseas Writers Club (president, 1943-45), Century Club (New York), Gridiron Club (president, 1957); Washington Press Club, Metropolitan Club, and Cosmos Club (all Washington). *Awards, honors:* LL.D., Upsala College, 1943; Order of the North Star (Sweden), Sigma Delta Chi award, 1945, for best Washington correspondent; University of Missouri award for journalism, 1951; Litt.D., University of Wisconsin, 1966, and University of Iowa, 1969; Pulitzer Prize for commentary (first time awarded), 1969.

WRITINGS—Nonfiction: *Sweden: Where Capitalism Is Controlled*, John Day, 1934; *Sweden: The Middle Way*, Yale University Press, 1936, second revised and enlarged edition, 1947; *They Hate Roosevelt!*, Harper, 1936; *Washington Calling!*, Morrow, 1937; *This Is Democracy: Collective Bargaining in Scandinavia*, Yale University Press, 1938; (with William T. Stone) *Toward a Dynamic America: The Challenge of a Changing World*, Foreign Policy Association, 1941; *This Is Your War*, Little, Brown, 1942; *I Write from Washington*, Harper, 1942; (author of new evaluation) Brooks Adams, *America's Economic Supremacy*, Harper, 1947, reprinted, Books for Libraries, 1971; *The Farmer Takes a Hand: The Electric Power Revolution in Rural America*, Doubleday, 1952, reprinted, DaCapo Press, 1974; (with Douglass Cater) *Ethics in a Business Society*, Harper, 1954, reprinted, Greenwood Press, 1973; *The Ragged Edge: The Diary of a Crisis*, Doubleday, 1955; *Eisenhower, Captive Hero: A Critical Study of the General and the President*, Harcourt, 1958; (editor with James Reston) *Walter Lippmann and His Times*, Harcourt, 1959, reprinted, Books for Libraries, 1968; *Sweden: The Middle Way on Trial*, Yale University Press, 1980; *Mighty Mississippi: Biography of a River*, Ticknor & Fields, 1982.

Novels: *The Cabin*, Harper, 1944; *The Peacemakers*, Harper, 1961; *Taint of Innocence*, Harper, 1967.

Contributor to periodicals, including *Saturday Evening Post, Life, New Republic, Yale Review,* and *Reader's Digest.*

SIDELIGHTS: A distinguished columnist, on the Washington staff of the *St. Louis Post Dispatch* for over thirty years, Marquis W. Childs won a Pulitzer Prize in 1969 for his incisive political analysis and commentary. Childs established his reputation as an astute political observer in 1936 with the publication of his highly regarded *Sweden: The Middle Way*. This book, wrote Walter Thompson in a 1936 *American Political Science Review* article, was "an able and up-to-date discussion of cooperation, cooperative housing, the state power system, state railways, state ownership of industries, government monopolies, liquor control, the social-democratic regime, [and the] future prospects" of the Swedish economic and social system. *Books* reviewer H. G. Leach called it "striking observation, faithful reporting, vigorous journalism of a high order." And Agnes Rothery, in the *Saturday Review of Literature*, stated that "Childs presents his well assembled material with such authenticity that his book may be unqualifiedly recommended to all students of these subjects."

The impact of *Sweden: The Middle Way* is evident from the commentary of more recent writers, such as Michael Harrington of the *New Republic*. In 1980 Harrington wrote that the book "had the great merit of rescuing an extremely important social and economic experiment from behind a linguistic curtain which was impenetrable for all but a tiny fraction of the world." Adds Steven Kelman of the *Washington Post Book World*: "*The Middle Way* . . . was a widely read and influential book on Sweden that launched the country as a model for many who longed for a humane alternative to the Depression era extremes of fascism and Stalinism. That Sweden has received an attention from scholars and from those interested in social policy far disproportionate to its population of 8 million and its peripheral status in world affairs, has in a significant measure been due to the image of the country established in books such as *The Middle Way*."

As a young man, a native of the Mississippi River town of Clinton, Iowa, Childs had been fascinated with the history and lore of the river. At the age of twenty-nine he had even begun writing a book on the subject but abandoned the project in order to concentrate on his primary vocation, reporting. Following his retirement from journalism, Childs "turned back to his labor of youthful love," says *Washington Post Book World* reviewer Jonathan Yardley, and published *Mighty Mississippi: Biography of a River*. A *New Yorker* writer notes: "The center of Mr. Childs' portrait is the steamboat era . . . and the end of that much romanticized [time] with the emergence of the railroads. . . . Mr. Childs is a thoughtful writer, and his reflections on the Mississippi and its importance in our history are always interesting, and often even arresting." Yardley finds that "Childs provides quick, perceptive and often witty glimpses of a history that, in less selective hands could go on for volume upon volume." Yardley concludes that even though the subject is a much romanticized one, "there is no sentimentalizing in 'Mighty Mississippi.' It is a forthright, clear-eyed story that . . . manages to do what its author wishes: 'It reflects the vigor, the passion, the love of life, of that mighty stream.'"

BIOGRAPHICAL/CRITICAL SOURCES: *Saturday Review of Literature*, February 15, 1936; *Books*, February 16, 1936; *American Political Science Review*, June, 1936; *Economist*, September 19, 1936; *Washington Post Book World*, April 13, 1980, June 30, 1982; *New Republic*, May 3, 1980; *New Yorker*, August 30, 1982; *Choice*, November, 1982.

* * *

CHISHOLM, Matt
See WATTS, Peter Christopher

* * *

CLAIBORNE, Robert (Watson, Jr.) 1919-

PERSONAL: Born May 15, 1919, in High Wycombe, Buckinghamshire, England; son of Robert W. (an attorney) and Virginia (McKenney) Claiborne; married Adrienne Aaron, August 26, 1945 (divorced, 1965); married Sybil Resnik Nukanen (a writer), April 24, 1965; children: (first marriage) Amanda Susan, Samuel McKenney; (second marriage) Jan Stacy (stepson). *Education:* Attended Massachusetts Institute of Technology, 1936-37, Antioch College, 1937-39; New York University, A.B. (magna cum laude), 1942. *Agent:* Sanford Greenburger Associates, 825 Third Ave., New York, N.Y. 10022.

CAREER: Lathe operator, factory worker, and union official in New Jersey and New York, 1942-46; folksinger and music teacher in New York City, 1946-57; *Scientific American*, New York City, associate editor, 1957-60; *Medical World News*, New York City, associate, news, and managing editor, 1960-64; *Life Science Library*, New York City, editor, 1964-65. Lecturer on ecology for New School for Social Research, 1971-72. *Member:* National Association of Science Writers, National Writers Union, Authors Guild, Authors League of America.

WRITINGS: (With Samuel Goudsmit) *Time*, Time, Inc., 1966; (with Walter Modell and Al Lansing) *Drugs*, Time, Inc., 1968; *Climate, Man and History*, Norton, 1970; *On Every Side the Sea*, American Heritage Press, 1971; *The First Americans*, Time-Life, 1973; (editor with Victor McKusick) *Medical Genetics*, HP Publishing, 1973; *God or Beast: Evolution and Human Nature*, Norton, 1974; *The Birth of Writing*, Time-Life, 1974; *The Summer Stargazer: Astronomy for Absolute Beginners*, Coward, 1975, revised edition, Penguin, 1981; (editor with Gerald Weissman) *Cell Membranes: Biochemistry, Cell Biology & Pathology*, HP Publishing, 1975; (with Lionel Casson and Bryan M. Fagen) *Mysteries of the Past*, American Heritage Press, 1977; *Our Marvelous Native Tongue: The Life and Times of the English Language*, Times Books, 1983.

Contributor of articles and reviews to *Harper's*, *Nation*, *New York Times*, *Village Voice*, *Science Digest*, *Smithsonian*, and other periodicals. Part-time senior editor for *Hospital Practice*, 1966—.

WORK IN PROGRESS: *The Wild Cell—Seed of Cancer*, for Harcourt; *Saying What You Mean: A Commonsense Guide to American Usage*, for Norton; with Norman Javitt, *Living with Gallstones*; *Dossiers: Secret Agents from ASHENDEN to SMILEY*.

SIDELIGHTS: Robert Claiborne's study *Our Marvelous Native Tongue: The Life and Times of the English Language* traces English back to its roots in several other languages, such as the Indo-European dialects and the Italic vocabulary. The inspiration for the work, as the author writes in the preface of the book, began "when I was ten and studying French with my mother. To help me remember the meaning of French *siege* (seat) she pointed out that it was obviously related to English 'siege,' in which an army *sits* down around a town and waits for it to surrender. This incident, and doubtless many similar ones now forgotten, began my lifelong fascination with words: where they came from, why they mean what they do and how different words are related."

"Basically, I tend to think of myself as a teacher whose medium happens to be print rather than the classroom," Claiborne told *CA*. "But since (unlike most teachers) I don't have a captive audience, I also try to be a storyteller, though my stories are of course fact, not fiction. Because I believe in playing fair with the reader, I try to present not just conclusions but the facts and reasoning that underlie the conclusions. I have an abiding hatred of writers (names on request) who justify nonsensical propositions by distorting facts or simply inventing them—and try to show them up when I get the chance."

AVOCATIONAL INTERESTS: Aikido, body-surfing, bird-watching, gardening, photography, poker, travel, and writing letters to the editor.

BIOGRAPHICAL/CRITICAL SOURCES: *Best Sellers*, June 1, 1970; *Washington Post*, December 3, 1974; Robert Claiborne, *Our Marvelous Native Tongue: The Life and Times of the English Language*, Times Books, 1983; *New Yorker*, June 6, 1983; *New York Times Book Review*, September 18, 1983.

* * *

CLARK, David
See HARDCASTLE, Michael

* * *

CLAYTON, (Francis) Howard 1918-

PERSONAL: Born May 20, 1918, in St. John's, Newfoundland, Canada; son of Arthur (an Anglican minister) and Ella (Warren) Clayton; married Helen Margaret Doig, July 29, 1942; children: Elizabeth, Margaret, John. *Education:* University of Birmingham (England), Bachelor of Commerce, 1949; University of London, teaching certificate, 1957. *Politics:* Conservative. *Religion:* Anglican. *Home:* 2A Brownsfield Rd., Lichfield, Staffordshire, England.

CAREER: Birmingham Regional Hospital Board, Birmingham, England, hospital administrator, 1949-56; Wednesbury College of Commerce, Staffordshire, England, lecturer, 1957-63; Tamworth College of Further Education, Staffordshire, lecturer, 1963-67; writer and free-lance lecturer, 1967—. Elected councillor on Lichfield District Council, 1976, served as chairman of council, 1982-83. *Military service:* British Army, 1939-45; served in Royal Artillery; became lieutenant; lost left leg in action during World War II. *Member:* Newcomen Society (London), Victorian Society (London).

WRITINGS: The Atmospheric Railways, privately printed, 1966; *The Duffield Bank and Eaton Railways,* Oakwood Press, 1968; *Atlantic Bridgehead: The Story of Transatlantic Communications,* Garnstone Press, 1968; (with M. Jacot and R. Buttrell) *Miniature Railways,* Volume I, Oakwood Press, 1971; *Coaching City: A Glimpse of Georgian Lichfield,* Dragon Press (Bala, Wales), 1971; *Cathedral City: A Look at Victorian Lichfield,* privately printed, 1978, revised edition, 1981; *The Great Swinfen Case,* Regency Press, 1980. Contributor to *Country Life* and *Railway Magazine.*

WORK IN PROGRESS: A book about Lichfield in the Civil War of 1642.

SIDELIGHTS: Howard Clayton told *CA:* "I began by lecturing and giving talks on subjects which interested me—mainly local history, industrial history and railway history. This naturally involved a good deal of research. It seemed sensible to use this material for writing—first for magazine articles and then for books. I found I enjoyed writing, and so I have continued."

* * *

CLAYTON, James L. 1931-

PERSONAL: Born July 28, 1931, in Salt Lake City, Utah; son of Ernest (an educator) and Olita (Melville) Clayton; married Geraldine Horsley, June 13, 1957; children: Creed, Catherine, Andrea. *Education:* University of Utah, B.A., 1958; Cornell University, Ph.D., 1964. *Home:* 1445 Arlington Dr., Salt Lake City, Utah 84103. *Office:* 310 Park Bldg., University of Utah, Salt Lake City, Utah 84112.

CAREER: Hamilton College, Clinton, N.Y., instructor in history, 1962-63; University of Utah, Salt Lake City, instructor, 1963-64, assistant professor, 1964-66, associate professor, 1967-71, professor of history, 1971—, University Distinguished Honors Professor, 1977—, director of honors programs, 1967-70, dean of Graduate School, 1978—. Visiting assistant professor at Dartmouth College, 1966-67; visiting professor at U.S. Air Force bases in Germany and Greece, 1975; Reynolds Lecturer, 1976. Member of Utah State Medical School Admissions Board, 1968-69, and Graduate Record Examination Board, 1982—. *Military service:* U.S. Army, Counterintelligence Corps, 1953-55. *Member:* Council of Graduate Schools in the United States, Western Association of Graduate Schools (president, 1981-82), Phi Kappa Phi.

AWARDS, HONORS: Voelker Foundation grant, New York University, 1960; Social Science Research Council travel grant, 1962; Distinguished Teaching Award, University of Utah, 1966; Solon J. Buck Prize, 1967, for best article published in *Minnesota History* in 1967; American Philosophical Society grant, 1970; Thiokol Corp. grant, 1980.

WRITINGS: (Editor with Alfred Cave) *American Civilization: A Documentary History,* W. C. Brown, 1966, revised edition, 1969; (editor) *The Economic Impact of the Cold War,* Harcourt, 1970; *A Farewell to the Welfare State,* University of Utah, 1976; *Does Defense Beggar Welfare?,* National Strategy Information Center, 1979; *On the Brink: Defense, Deficits, and Welfare Spending,* Ramapo, 1983.

Contributor: Davis Bobrow, editor, *Components of Defense Policy,* Rand McNally, 1965; David Ellis, editor, *The Frontier in American Development,* Cornell University Press, 1969; Seymour Melman, editor, *The War Economy,* St. Martin's, 1971. Contributor of articles to *Western Political Quarterly, Dialogue: A Journal of Mormon Thought, Minnesota History, Pacific Historical Review, Financial Post, Nation, Playboy,* and other periodicals.

WORK IN PROGRESS: A monograph, *The Economic Consequences of American Wars; The Limits of Greatness,* a monograph on the rise and limitations of the American welfare state.

SIDELIGHTS: James L. Clayton told *CA:* "My primary purpose in writing is to use the lessons of history to help solve current problems. Fiscal issues have been my primary concern, especially those which relate to defense and our growing indebtedness."

AVOCATIONAL INTERESTS: Skiing, especially high alpine three-pin excursions into the Wasatch Mountains.

* * *

CLOUSE, Robert Gordon 1931-

PERSONAL: Born August 26, 1931, in Mansfield, Ohio; son of Garry R. (a teacher) and Marian (Culp) Clouse; married Bonnidell A. Barrows (a professor of psychology), June 18, 1955; children: Gary R., Kenneth D. *Education:* William Jennings Bryan College (now Bryan College), B.A., 1954; Grace College, B.D. and M.Div., 1957; University of Iowa, M.A., 1960, Ph.D., 1963. *Politics:* Democrat. *Home:* 2122 South 21st St., Terre Haute, Ind. 47802. *Office:* Department of History, Indiana State University, Terre Haute, Ind. 47809.

CAREER: Minister of the Brethren Church. Pastor in Cedar Rapids, Iowa, 1957-60; Indiana State University, Terre Haute, associate professor, 1963-70, professor of history, 1970—. Visiting professor, Indiana University, 1964-65, and 1968-69. *Member:* National Fellowship of Brethren Ministers, American Historical Association, American Society of Church History, Society for Reformation Research, Central Renaissance Conference (president, 1968-69). *Awards, honors:* Grants from Folger Shakespeare Library, 1964, American Philosophical Society, 1968, Institute for Advanced Christian Studies, 1970, Newberry Library, 1972, Lilly Library, 1976, and National Endowment for the Humanities, 1977, 1980, and 1983.

WRITINGS: (With Robert D. Linder and Richard V. Pierard) *Protest and Politics: Christianity and Contemporary Affairs,* Attic Press, 1968; (with Peter Toon) *Puritans, the Millennium, and the Future of Israel,* James Clarke, 1970; (with Linder and Pierard) *The Cross and the Flag,* Creation House, 1972; (editor) *The Meaning of the Millennium: Four Views,* Inter-Varsity Press, 1977; (with Pierard) *Streams of Civilization: The Modern World to the Nuclear Age,* Volume II, Mott Media, and CLP Publishers, 1979; *The Church in the Age of Orthodoxy and the Enlightenment: Consolidation and Challenge from 1600 to 1800,* Concordia, 1980; (editor) *War: 4 Christian Views,* Inter-Varsity Press, 1981; (editor) *Wealth and Poverty: 4 Christian Views,* Inter-Varsity Press, 1983. Contributor to theology journals.

WORK IN PROGRESS: A history of the Christian church.

CLOUTIER, Cecile
See CLOUTIER-WOJCIECHOWSKA, Cecile

* * *

CLOUTIER-WOJCIECHOWSKA, Cecile 1930-
(Cecile Cloutier; Cecile de Lantagne, a pseudonym)

PERSONAL: Born June 13, 1930, in Quebec City, Quebec, Canada; daughter of Adrien (a civil servant) and Maria (de Lantagne) Cloutier; married Jerzy Wojciechowski (a university professor), December 27, 1966; children: Marie-Berenice, Eve-Moira. *Education:* Laval University, B.A., 1951, M.A., 1953, L.esL., 1953, D.E.S., 1954; Sorbonne, University of Paris, D.deL.U., 1961. *Home:* 44 Farm Greenway, Don Mills, Toronto, Ontario, Canada M3A 3M2. *Office:* Department of French, University of Toronto, Toronto, Ontario, Canada.

CAREER: University of Ottawa, Ottawa, Ontario, assistant professor of French literature and aesthetics, 1958-64; University of Toronto, Toronto, Ontario, 1964—, began as associate professor, currently professor of French and Quebec literatures and aesthetics. Lecturer, Royal Ontario Museum, 1966, New York University, 1966, and at learned societies in Ottawa, 1967. Consultant to Canadian Council of the Arts and Canadian Humanities Council.

MEMBER: Modern Language Association of America, Association of Teachers of French, Association Canadienne des professeurs de francais, Societe des ecrivains, Societe des poetes, P.E.N., Societe d'Esthetique, American Society of Aesthetics, Le Societe des gens de Lettres de France, Societe des ecrivains de France et d'outre-mer. *Awards, honors:* Silver medal from Societe des ecrivains de France, 1960, for *Mains de sable;* Canada Council scholar, 1964-65 and 1967-68; Cocteau prize from Center for Continuing Education, 1964; prizes for poetry from the Canadian Centennial Commission, 1968.

WRITINGS—Under name Cecile Cloutier; poetry: *Mains de sable,* Editions de L'Arc (Quebec), 1960; *Cuivre et soies, suivi de Mains de sable,* Editions du Jour (Montreal), 1964; *Cannelles et craies,* J. Grassin (Paris), 1969; *Paupieres,* Librairie Deom (Montreal), 1970; (contributor) John Robert Columbo, editor, *How Do I Love Thee: Sixty Poets of Canada (and Quebec) Select and Introduce Their Favourite Poems from Their Own Work,* M. G. Hurtig, 1970; *Cablogrammes,* G. Chambelland (Paris), 1972; *Springtime of Spoken Words,* Hounslow (Toronto), 1978; *Chaleuils,* L'Hexagone (Montreal), 1978; *Pres,* Editions Saint-Germain des Pres (Paris), 1983. Contributor of articles, sometimes under pseudonym Cecile de Lantagne, and of poetry to French and French-Canadian journals.

WORK IN PROGRESS: Four books of poetry, *L'Echangeur, Pain, Vin d'ombre et de lumiere,* and *Bagues;* two volumes of essays, *De Poesia quebecence* and *Au pied de courant.*

AVOCATIONAL INTERESTS: Crafts, travel, languages (Cecile Cloutier has studied Polish, German, Russian, Spanish, Chinese, Sanskrit, Eskimo, Latin, and Greek).

* * *

COAN, Richard Welton 1928-

PERSONAL: Born January 24, 1928, in Martinez, Calif.; son of Otis Welton (an instructor in English) and Dorothy (a secretary; maiden name, Wilson) Coan; children: Lisa Coan Cooper, Cynthia, Angela. *Education:* Los Angeles City College, A.A., 1946; University of California, Berkeley, A.B., 1948, M.A., 1950; University of Southern California, Ph.D., 1955. *Home:* 2136 North Marion Blvd., Tucson, Ariz. 85712. *Office:* Department of Psychology, University of Arizona, Tucson, Ariz. 85721.

CAREER: University of Illinois at Urbana-Champaign, research associate in psychology, 1955-57; University of Arizona, Tucson, assistant professor, 1957-60, associate professor, 1960-64, professor of psychology, 1964—. *Member:* American Psychological Association, Association for Humanistic Psychology, Society for Multivariate Experimental Psychology.

WRITINGS: The Optimal Personality: An Empirical and Theoretical Analysis, Columbia University Press, 1974; *Hero, Artist, Sage, or Saint?: A Survey of Views on What Is Variously Called Mental Health, Normality, Maturity, Self-Actualization, and Human Fulfillment,* Columbia University Press, 1977; *Psychologists: Personal and Theoretical Pathways,* Irvington, 1979; *Psychology of Adjustment: Personal Experience and Development,* Wiley, 1983.

Contributor: S. V. Zagona, editor, *Studies and Issues in Smoking Behavior,* University of Arizona Press, 1967; V. S. Sexton and H. Misiak, editors, *Historical Perspectives in Psychology,* Brooks/Cole, 1971; O. K. Buros, editor, *The Sixth Mental Measurements Yearbook,* Gryphon, 1972; Buros, editor, *The Seventh Mental Measurements Yearbook,* Gryphon, 1972; R. M. Dreger, editor, *Multivariate Personality Research,* Claitors, 1972. Contributor to psychology journals.

WORK IN PROGRESS: Books on the evolution of consciousness and the masculine and feminine.

SIDELIGHTS: Richard Coan writes: "My primary areas of research have been personality theory and patterns of theoretical orientation in psychology, but I have a general interest in the symbolic systems of mankind. I want to understand the psychological roots common to science, art, mythology, religion, and philosophy." *Avocational interests:* Musical composition, writing poetry.

* * *

COE, Richard N(elson) 1923-

PERSONAL: Born October 27, 1923, in Rustington, Sussex, England; son of Frederick Augustus (a barrister) and Stella Mary Coe; married Valentina Zhukova, September 3, 1949 (divorced, 1969); married Ada Biagi, February 2, 1972; children: (first marriage) Antonia Marion Thais, Andrew Ivan Daniel; (second marriage) Terence Mark-Antony, Dominic Eugene Graburn, Laura-Julia Gabrielle. *Education:* Oriel College, Oxford, M.A., 1949; University of Leeds, Ph.D., 1954. *Office:* Department of French and Italian, University of California, Davis, Calif. 95616.

CAREER: University of Leeds, Leeds, England, 1950-62, began as assistant lecturer, became lecturer in French; University of Queensland, Brisbane, Australia, senior lecturer in French, 1962-63; University of Melbourne, Parkville, Victoria, Australia, reader in French, 1963-65; University of Warwick, Coventry, England, reader in French, 1966-69; University of Melbourne, Melbourne, Victoria, professor of French, 1969-72; University of Warwick, professor of French, 1972-79, dean of faculty of humanities, 1973-75; University of California, Davis, professor of French and comparative literature, 1979—. *Military service:* British Army, 1943-46; served in the Middle East. *Member:* Australian Academy of the Humanities (fellow).

WRITINGS: (Translator and editor) Stendhal, *Life of Rossini*, Calder, 1956; *Rome, Naples and Florence*, Calder, 1959; *Morelly: Ein Rationalist auf dem Wege zum Sozialismus*, Ruetten & Loening, 1961; *Eugene Ionesco*, Grove, 1961 (published in England as *Ionesco*, Oliver & Boyd, 1961); *Samuel Beckett*, Grove, 1964 (published in England as *Beckett*, Oliver & Boyd, 1964); *Crocodile*, Faber, 1964; *The Vision of Jean Genet*, Grove, 1968; (editor) *The Theatre of Jean Genet: A Casebook*, Grove, 1970; *Lives of Haydn, Mozart and Metastasio*, Calder, 1971; *When the Grass Was Taller*, Yale University Press, 1984. Member of editorial boards, *Australian Journal of French Studies* and *Journal of the American-Romanian Academy of Arts and Sciences*.

WORK IN PROGRESS: Books on Stendhal and nineteenth-century opera.

SIDELIGHTS: Richard N. Coe is competent in Bulgarian, Russian, and German. *Avocational interests:* Theater, travel, and ornithology.

BIOGRAPHICAL/CRITICAL SOURCES: Encounter, May, 1968; *Books and Bookmen,* May, 1968; *New Republic,* August 31, 1968; *New Leader,* October 21, 1968; *Books Abroad,* summer, 1969.

* * *

COHEN, Peter Zachary 1931-

PERSONAL: Born October 27, 1931; married; wife's name, Suzanne; children: Jay, Todd. *Education:* University of Wyoming, B.S., 1953, M.A., 1961. *Home:* Route 1, Alta Vista, Kan. 66834. *Office:* Department of English, Kansas State University, Manhattan, Kan. 66502.

CAREER: Kansas State University, Manhattan, 1961—, began as instructor, currently associate professor of English. Member of Wabaunsee County (Kan.) Planning Commission, 1969—. *Military service:* U.S. Army, 1954-56. *Member:* American Association of University Professors, Authors League of America, Authors Guild, and several wildlife organizations. *Awards, honors:* Friends of American Writers Award, 1973, for *Foal Creek*.

WRITINGS—All juveniles; published by Atheneum, except as indicated: *The Muskie Hook,* 1969; *The Bull in the Forest* (Junior Literary Guild selection), 1969; *Morena* (Junior Literary Guild selection), 1970; *the Authorized Autumn Charts of the Upper Red Canoe River Country,* 1972; *Foal Creek,* 1972; *Bee,* 1975; *The Cannon in the Park* (children's play; first produced in Hoxie, Kan. at Continental Theatre, September, 1975), Modern Theatre for Youth, 1975; *Deadly Game at Stony Creek,* Dial, 1978; *Calm Horse, Wild Night* (Junior Literary Guild selection), 1982; *The Great Red River Raft,* Albert Whitman, 1984. Author of two movie scripts for Xerox Educational Films.

SIDELIGHTS: Peter Zachary Cohen lives on a small farm "raising sheep, horses and chickens under fence, [and] coyotes, rabbits, owls, and the evening stars, too, I guess, by letting them run loose." He says that he returns from contacts with the field-and-stream-out-of-doors "with a renewed sense of wonder at the world," and he writes "to try to discover more about the 'whys' and 'what ifs' of the attitudes and situations I feel and observe."

BIOGRAPHICAL/CRITICAL SOURCES: PTA Magazine, September, 1969; *Book World,* November 9, 1969, May 7, 1972; *Publishers Weekly,* March 20, 1972; *New York Times Book Review,* January 21, 1979.

* * *

COHEN, Robert 1938-

PERSONAL: Born July 14, 1938; son of Lester Ellis (an attorney) and Lydia (Goldblatt) Cohen; married Lorna Buck, November 13, 1972; children: (previous marriage) Michael Geoffrey; (present marriage) Whitney Lane. *Education:* University of California, Berkeley, B.A., 1961; Yale University, D.F.A., 1965. *Home:* 1360 Bluebird Canyon Dr., Laguna Beach, Calif. 92651. *Office:* School of Fine Arts, University of California, Irvine, Calif. 92717.

CAREER: Connecticut College, New London, drama director, 1964-65; University of California, Irvine, 1965—, began as assistant professor, currently professor of drama and chairman of department. Actor and director.

WRITINGS: Giraudoux: Three Faces of Destiny, University of Chicago Press, 1969; *Acting Professionally,* Mayfield, 1972, 3rd edition, Barnes & Noble, 1983; (with John Harrop) *Creative Play Direction,* Prentice-Hall, 1974, 2nd edition, 1983; *Acting Power,* Mayfield, 1977; *Theatre,* Mayfield, 1982; *Acting One,* Mayfield, 1984. Contributor to *On Stage Studies, Theatre Survey, Contemporary Literature, Theatre Journal, Drama Review,* and *Los Angeles Times.*

* * *

COLES, John M(orton) 1930-

PERSONAL: Born March 25, 1930, in Woodstock, Ontario, Canada; son of John L. (an investment broker) and Alice (Brown) Coles; married Mona Shiach, December 20, 1958; children: Joanne, Steven, Alison, Ian. Education: University of Toronto, B.A., 1952; Cambridge University, diploma, 1957, Sc.D., 1980; University of Edinburgh, Ph.D., 1959. *Home:* Fitzwilliam College, Cambridge, England. *Office:* Department of Archaeology, Fitzwilliam College, Cambridge University, Cambridge, England.

CAREER: Cambridge University, Fitzwilliam College, Cambridge, England, lecturer in archaeology and anthropology, 1960-75, reader, 1976-79, professor of European prehistory, 1980—. *Member:* Royal Society of Arts (fellow), Society of Antiquaries (fellow), British Academy (fellow).

WRITINGS: (Editor with D. A. Simpson) *Studies in Ancient Europe: Essays Presented to Stuart Piggott,* Leicester University Press, 1968, Humanities, 1969; (with E. S. Higgs) *The Archaeology of Early Man,* Praeger, 1969; *Field Archaeology in Britain,* Methuen, 1972; *Archaeology by Experiment,* Scribner, 1973; *Experimental Archaeology,* Academic Press, 1979; (with A. F. Harding) *The Bronze Age in Europe,* Methuen, 1979; (with B. J. Orme) *Prehistory of the Somerset Levels,* Somerset Levels Project, 1980. Also contributor to *Proceedings* of Prehistoric Society and *Proceedings* of Society of Antiquaries of Scotland. Contributor to journals, including *Antiquity.*

WORK IN PROGRESS: The Archaeology of Wetlands, for publication by Edinburgh University Press; *Images in a Landscape.*

COLLINS, Will
See CORLEY, Edwin (Raymond)

* * *

COLWELL, Eileen (Hilda) 1904-

PERSONAL: Born June 16, 1904, in Robin Hoods Bay, Yorkshire, England; daughter of Richard Harold (a Methodist minister) and Gertrude (Mason) Colwell. *Education:* University College School of Librarianship, London, Diploma of Librarianship, 1924. *Religion:* Christian. *Home:* 60 Priory Rd., Loughborough, Leicester, England.

CAREER: Children's librarian in Bolton, Lancaster, England, 1924-26; Borough of Hendon, London, England, children's librarian, 1926-67; Loughborough School of Librarianship, Loughborough, Leicester, England, lecturer on children's literature, 1967-69. Storyteller on "Playschool" and "Jackanory" television programs for children. *Member:* International Federation of Library Associations, Youth Libraries Group of Library Association (founding member; chairman at various times). *Awards, honors:* Member of Order of British Empire, 1965, for service to children in libraries and in the book world; honorary Doctor of Literature, 1975.

WRITINGS: How I Became a Librarian, Nelson, 1956; *Eleanor Farjeon: A Monograph,* Bodley Head, 1961; *Storytelling,* Bodley Head, 1980.

Editor: *Tell Me a Story,* Penguin, 1962; (and contributor) *Storyteller's Choice,* Bodley Head, 1963; (and contributor) *Tell Me Another Story,* Penguin, 1964; (and contributor) *A Second Storyteller's Choice,* Bodley Head, 1965; (and contributor) *Hallowe'en Acorn,* Bodley Head, 1966; (and contributor) *Time for a Story,* Penguin, 1967; (and contributor) *The Youngest Storybook,* Bodley Head, 1967; *The Princess Splendour,* Longmans, Green, 1969; (and contributor) *Bad Boys,* Penguin, 1972; *Round about and Long Ago,* Longman Young Books, 1972; *Tales from the Islands,* Kestrel Books, 1975; (and contributor) *The Magic Umbrella and Other Stories for Telling,* Bodley Head, 1976; *Humblepuppy and Other Stories for Telling,* Bodley Head, 1978; *The Devil's Bridge and Other Stories,* Macmillan Education, 1979; *Lost Land and Other Stories,* Macmillan Education, 1979; *More Stories to Tell,* Penguin, 1979; *Bedtime Stories,* Ladybird Books, 1982. Contributor to professional library and reviewing journals.

WORK IN PROGRESS: A collection of stories for children; an autobiography.

SIDELIGHTS: Eileen Colwell told *CA:* "My main interests throughout my life have been children and their natural complement, storytelling. I became a children's librarian at a time when children's libraries were rare in this country, with the resolve that as many children as possible should have an opportunity to know books, not just *any* books but the best I could find. . . . Nearly everything interesting in my life has been bound up with my chosen career. I read manuscripts for publishers, review books and travel about the country lecturing on children's literature and storytelling. These activities have taken me to most European countries and across the Atlantic and to Japan and, most important of all, brought me valued friendships with people of like interests."

BIOGRAPHICAL/CRITICAL SOURCES: Nancy Larrick, *A Parent's Guide to Children's Reading,* 3rd edition, Doubleday, 1969.

COOK, Terry 1942-

PERSONAL: Born May 22, 1942, in Chicago, Ill.; son of Lewis Ray and Marie (Roberts) Cook; married Virginia Destro, August 12, 1968; children: Anastasia, Christopher. *Education:* Attended Lehigh University, 1960-64. *Home address:* P.O. Box 123, Chester, N.J. 07930. *Office:* Cook Publishing Co., 14 Schooley's Mountain Rd., Drawer G, Long Valley, N.J. 07853-0446.

CAREER: Writer of column, "New Jersey News" for *Drag News,* 1963; *Drag World,* Los Angeles, Calif., associate editor, 1965-66; *Car Craft,* Los Angeles, feature editor, 1966-68, editor, 1968-71; *Hot Rod,* Los Angeles, editor, 1972-74; *Vans and Trucks,* East Northport, N.Y., editor, 1975-76; *Car and Driver,* New York, N.Y., editorial staff writer, 1976-77; *T-Shirt Retailer and Screen Printer* (trade publication), Long Valley, N.J., owner and publisher, 1979—. Also producer of annual car show, Lead East, for custom cars, street hot rods, and pre-1963 vintage autos. Member of Chester Planning Board. *Military service:* U.S. Army Reserve, 1968-74.

WRITINGS: Vans and the Truckin' Life, Abrams, 1977; *Getting Started in the Retail Shirt Business,* Cook Publishing Co., 1980.

WORK IN PROGRESS: Research on three-dimensional films and printed matter (including posters, books, and comics).

SIDELIGHTS: Terry Cook remarks: "I am extremely self-motivated. During my tenure as magazine editor, newsstand sales rose substantially. When I left each magazine, its newsstand sales dropped. I believe in 'telling it like it is,' assuming you do thorough research."

BIOGRAPHICAL/CRITICAL SOURCES: Hot Rod, February, 1972; *Car Craft,* April, 1972.

* * *

COPLIN, William D(avid) 1939-

PERSONAL: Surname rhymes with "*rope*-in"; born September 22, 1939, in Baltimore, Md.; son of Isidor (a salesman) and Dubbie (Lebowitz) Coplin; married Merry Roseman, September 2, 1963 (divorced, May, 1976); married Vickie J. Bradley, July, 1977; children: Britt, Deborah, Laura, Richard. *Education:* Johns Hopkins University, B.A., 1960; American University, M.A., 1962, Ph.D., 1964; post-doctoral study at University of Michigan, 1968-69. *Office:* Public Affairs and Citizenship Program, 105 Maxwell Hall, Maxwell School of Citizenship and Public Affairs, Syracuse University, Syracuse, N.Y. 13210.

CAREER: Instructor in political science at Howard University and American University, both Washington, D.C., 1962-64; Wayne State University, Detroit, Mich., assistant professor, 1964-67, associate professor of political science, 1967-69; Syracuse University, Syracuse, N.Y., associate professor, 1969-72, professor of political science, 1972—, director of International Relations Program, 1970-75, director of Public Affairs and Citizenship Program of Maxwell School of Citizenship and Public Affairs, 1975—. Lecturer, Foreign Service Institute, 1973-75. Member of executive committee of Consortium for International Studies Education, 1972-77. Director of political risk services, Frost and Sullivan, Inc., 1979—. Consultant to Industrial College of the Armed Forces, 1967-69, National War College and Consolidated Analysis Centers, Inc., both 1971, Department of State, External Research Bureau, 1972, *New York Times* Educational Division for College Utilization, 1975-

78, and Presidential Commission to Study the Organization of the Government for the Conduct of Foreign Policy, 1975-76.

MEMBER: International Studies Association (chairman of Education Commission, 1971-75), Association of Political Risk Analysts (member of board of directors, 1980—), American Political Science Association (chairman of International Relations Panels, 1974), American Society of International Law (member of executive council, 1975-77), Social Science Education Consortium. *Awards, honors:* National Science Foundation faculty fellowship, 1968-69; New York State Assembly Intern Program faculty fellowship, 1977-78; Distinguished Alumni Award, American University, 1982.

WRITINGS: The Functions of International Law, Rand McNally, 1966; (editor) *Simulation in the Study of Politics,* Markham, 1968.

(Editor with Charles W. Kegley, Jr.) *A Multi-Method Introduction to International Politics: Readings in Observation, Explanation, and Prescription,* Markham, 1971, 2nd edition published as *Analyzing International Relations: A Multi-Method Introduction,* Praeger, 1975; (with Michael K. O'Leary and Stephen L. Mills) *Participant's Guide to PRINCE: Concepts, Environments, Procedures,* International Relations Program, Syracuse University, 1971; *Introduction to International Politics: A Theoretical Overview,* Markham, 1971, 3rd edition, Prentice-Hall, 1980; (with O'Leary) *Everyman's PRINCE: A Guide to Understanding Political Problems,* Duxbury, 1972, 2nd edition, 1976; *PS-6: Introduction to the Analysis of Public Policy from a Problem Solving Perspective,* Policy Study Associates, 1973; (with Mills and O'Leary) *PRINCE-DOWN Student Manual: A Gaming Approach to the Study of Policy Issues,* International Relations Program, Syracuse University, 1973; (with others) *A Description of the PRINCE Model,* Learning Resources in International Relations, 1974; (with others) *American Foreign Policy,* Duxbury, 1974.

(With O'Leary) *Quantitative Techniques in Foreign Policy Forecasting and Analysis,* Praeger, 1975; (with O'Leary and Robert F. Rich) *Toward the Improvement of Foreign Service Reporting,* U.S. Government Printing Office, 1975; *An Introduction to the Analysis of Public Policy Issues from a Problem-Solving Perspective,* Learning Resources in International Studies, 1975; (with O'Leary) *PS-17: Introduction to the Analysis of Public Policy,* Policy Studies Associates, 1978; (editor) *Teaching Policy Studies: What and How,* Lexington Books, 1978.

(With O'Leary) *Basic Policy Studies Skills,* Policy Studies Associates, 1981; (with O'Leary) *Political Risks in Thirty Countries: A Euromoney Report,* Euromoney Publications, 1981; (with O'Leary) *Turkey: The Problems of Transition,* Euromoney Publications, 1982; (with O'Leary) *Political Risks in Thirty-Five Countries: A Euromoney Report,* Euromoney Publications, 1983; (with O'Leary) *Political Risk from Territorial Disputes: A Global Survey,* Frost & Sullivan, 1983.

Contributor: Richard A. Falk and Wolfram F. Hanrieder, editors, *International Law and Organization,* Lippincott, 1968; Michael Barkun and Robert W. Gregg, editors, *The United Nations System,* Van Nostrand, 1968; Abdul A. Said, editor, *Theory of International Relations: The Crisis of Relevance,* Prentice-Hall, 1968; James N. Rosenau, editor, *International Politics and Foreign Policy: A Reader in Research and Theory,* revised edition, Free Press, 1969; Gregg and Kegley, editors, *After Vietnam: The Future of American Foreign Policy,* Doubleday, 1971; *Instruction in Diplomacy: Scope, Objectives, and Methods,* American Academy of Political and Social Science, 1972; (with O'Leary and J. McMaster) *Technological Forecasting and Social Change,* Elsevier, 1979.

Also author, with Leonard Stitleman, of exercises for the "American Government Simulation" series, Science Research Associates, 1969, and of teaching materials for *Learning Packages in International Relations.* Author of student manual and editor of test item catalogue for "Mentorex for American Politics," a testing-tutorial system, for Cognitive Systems, Inc., 1970. Co-author of pamphlet, "A Description of the PRINCE Model," International Relations Program, Syracuse University, 1972, and of "Three Two-Person Games: A Slide Tape Introduction to Game Theory Concepts in the Study of International Interactions," Center for Instructional Development and International Relations Program of Syracuse University, 1973. Co-author and co-editor, with O'Leary, of *World Political Risk Forecasts,* 1979—. Contributor to *Political Science Annual,* Volume II, Bobbs-Merrill, and *Proceedings of the National Gaming Council,* both 1969, *Sage International Yearbook of Foreign Policy Studies,* 1974, and numerous other conference proceedings. Also contributor to political science journals. Member of editorial board of *Simulation and Games,* 1971-75; editor of *Policy Studies Journal,* 1978—, and, with O'Leary, *Political Risk Letter,* 1979—, for Frost & Sullivan.

WORK IN PROGRESS: Political Risk Forecasting for Twenty-Five Countries.

SIDELIGHTS: William D. Coplin told *CA:* "All of my writing, except for a few esoteric ones required to gain promotion and tenure, has been to achieve one purpose: assist the individual to understand and deal with the political, social, and economic conditions he or she faces. If the social sciences have any value at all, it is in providing tools for analysis; and if these tools are any good, it is in helping people make better decisions. I take as a matter of faith that people can improve their understanding and control the social world by thinking more systematically and clearly. With this goal, there has been no need to pretend, as many of my colleagues in the social sciences have, that my writing transmits scientific knowledge or, as is usually the case, discusses how I have searched for the elusive knowledge through massive computer based data sets or the ideas of the great thinkers. My writing works if it helps the student, the businessman, the civil servant, and the citizen cope."

* * *

**CORLEY, Edwin (Raymond) 1931-1981
(Patrick Buchanan, Will Collins, David Harper, William Judson)**

PERSONAL: Born October 22, 1931, in Bayonne, N.J.; died of a heart attack, November 7, 1981, in Gulfport, Miss.; son of Gordon and Lillian (Neal) Corley; married Elizabeth Zekauskas, July 5, 1963; children: Richard, Elizabeth, Eugene. *Education:* Self-educated. *Agent:* John Cushman Associates, Inc., 25 West 43rd St., New York, N.Y. 10036.

CAREER: Theatrical stage manager, New York City, 1952-54; publisher of *Off-Broadway* (magazine), New York City, 1954-58; advertising copywriter, New York City, 1958-69; vice-president, Compton Agency, 1966-68; vice-president, Dancer-Fitzgerald-Sample, 1969; full-time writer and filmmaker. Films include "Next Stop 28th," 1960, "Up the Avenue," 1961, and "Saturday Night on Channel 2," 1962. *Military service:* U.S. Air Force, 1947-52. *Member:* Authors

Guild, Authors League of America. *Awards, honors:* Robert Flaherty award for "Up the Avenue" and "Saturday Night on Channel 2"; the latter also received the silver medal, Cannes Film Festival.

WRITINGS—All novels: *Siege*, Stein & Day, 1969; *The Jesus Factor*, Stein & Day, 1970; *Farewell, My Slightly Tarnished Hero*, Dodd, 1972; *Acapulco Gold*, Dodd, 1973; *Shadows*, Stein & Day, 1975; *Sargasso*, Doubleday, 1977; *Air Force One*, Doubleday, 1978; *The Genesis Rock*, Doubleday, 1980; *Long Shots*, Doubleday, 1981.

Under pseudonym Patrick Buchanan; suspense novels: *A Murder of Crows*, Stein & Day, 1971; *A Parliament of Owls*, Stein & Day, 1972; *A Requiem of Sharks*, Dodd, 1973; *A Sounder of Swine*, Dodd, 1974.

Under pseudonym Will Collins: *Grizzly*, Pyramid, 1976.

Under pseudonym David Harper: *Hijacked*, Dodd, 1970; *Big Saturday*, Dodd, 1971; *The Green Air*, Mason & Lipscomb, 1973; *The Patchwork Man*, Dodd, 1975; *The Hanged Man*, Dodd, 1976; *The Last Superbowl*, Curtis, 1976.

Under pseudonym William Judson: *Alice and Me*, Arthur Fields, 1973; *Winter Kill*, Talmy Franklin, 1974; *Cold River*, Mason & Lipscomb, 1975; *Kilman's Landing*, Mason-Charter, 1975.

Also author of plays "Five Plays for Two Men," produced in Tokyo, 1951, "Goodnight Sweet Prince," produced in Tokyo, 1951, "Hedda," produced in New York, 1958, and "Letta Rip," produced in St. Louis, 1961. Author of column "Good Books," syndicated to nearly one hundred newspapers.

WORK IN PROGRESS: A novel about Hurricane Camille; *Out-Takes*, a novel of real-life Hollywood; a frontier novel, *Where the Trail Divides*, under pseudonym Will Collins; *Wolf Bay*, an adventure story of hand logging in Alaska at the turn of the century, under pseudonym William Judson.

SIDELIGHTS: *The Jesus Factor* has been translated into German.

MEDIA ADAPTATIONS: *Hijacked* was adapted into the film "Skyjacked," produced by Metro-Goldwyn-Mayer in 1972.

BIOGRAPHICAL/CRITICAL SOURCES: New York Times Book Review, April 12, 1981; *Los Angeles Times Book Review*, May 24, 1981.

OBITUARIES: New York Times, November 10, 1981; *Publishers Weekly*, November 20, 1981.†

* * *

CORNFELD, Gaalyah 1902-

PERSONAL: Born May 26, 1902, in Rosh Pina, Palestine (now Israel); son of Leon Arieh (a philologist) and Sarah (Korsonsky) Cornfeld; married Lilian Kert (a nutritionist and writer of cookbooks), 1924; children: Gibeon. *Education:* Attended Lycee Francais, Cairo, Egypt. *Religion:* Jewish. *Home:* 185 Hayarkon St., Tel Aviv 63453, Israel.

CAREER: Editor, historian, and journalist, 1942-47; Twersky Publishing House, Tel Aviv, Israel, acting director, 1945-48; in private business, 1950-52; Hebrew Book Publishers Association, Tel Aviv, general secretary, 1952-59; Hamikra Baolam Publishing Ltd., Tel Aviv, director and chief editor, 1957—. Director and chief editor, G. and L. Cornfeld, Publishers.

WRITINGS: (Editor) *Adam to Daniel: An Illustrated Guide to the Old Testament and Its Background*, Macmillan, 1960; (editor) *Daniel to Paul: Jews in Conflict with Graeco-Roman Civilization*, Macmillan, 1962; *Epic of the Maccabees*, Macmillan, 1962; (editor) *Pictorial Biblical Encyclopedia: A Visual Guide to the Old and New Testaments*, Macmillan, 1964; (with Bernard Rosenblatt) *Two Generations of Zionism*, Shengold Publishers, 1967; (compiler) *War for Redemption and Peace* (trilingual edition, Hebrew, English, and French), [Israel], 1967; (with Pirsume Yerushalayim) *Jerusalem at Large*, Jerusalem Publications, 1968.

(Editor) Benjamin Mazar, *The Mountain of the Lord*, Doubleday, 1975; (general editor) *Josephus: The Jewish War*, Zondervan, 1982; (editor with D. N. Freedman) *Archaeology of the Bible: Book by Book*, Harper, 1982; *The Historical Jesus*, Macmillan, 1983. Also author of *This Is Mesada*, *I Love Jerusalem*, and *Albums of Israel*, 1970 and 1972; editor of *Excavations on the Temple Mount and the City of David*, by B. Mazar. Contributor of articles and essays to American publications since 1936.

WORK IN PROGRESS: An illustrated Bible; a Bible archaeology.

SIDELIGHTS: Gaalyah Cornfeld speaks French, English, Hebrew, and Arabic; he has a large photographic archive on Biblical background and Near Eastern archaeology and is considered an authority on the Middle East. His books have been translated into a number of languages, including German, Swedish, Danish, and Japanese. *Avocational interests:* Archaeology, photography, country hiking, studying nature.

* * *

CORRIVEAU, Monique (Chouinard) 1927-

PERSONAL: Born September 6, 1927, in Quebec, Quebec, Canada; daughter of Francois Xavier (a lawyer) and Bernadette (Rouillard) Chouinard; married Bernard Corriveau (a law notary), September 29, 1951; children: Matthieu, Francois, Bernadette, Marie-Noel, Thomas, Pascal, Vincent, Sophie, Isabelle, Jeanne. *Education:* Attended University of Toronto, 1946-48; Laval University, B.A., 1950, B.Ph., 1950. *Religion:* Catholic.

CAREER: Writer. *Member:* Societe des Ecrivains Canadiens. *Awards, honors:* Prix de l'Association Canadien des Educateurs de Langue Francaise, 1958, for *Le Secret de Vanille*, and 1959, for *Les Jardiniers du hibou;* Prix du Concours Litteraire de la Province de Quebec, 1964, and Medaille de l'Association des Bibliothecaires du Canada, 1966, both for *Le Wapiti;* Prix du Concours Litteraire de la Province de Quebec, 1966, for *Le Maitre de Messire;* Prix de la Commission du Centenaire de Canada, 1967, for *Cecile;* Prix Michelle Le Normand from Societe des Ecrivains Canadiens, 1971, for cumulated work.

WRITINGS—Juveniles, except as indicated: *Le Secret de Vanille*, Editions du Pelican (Quebec), 1958, revised edition, Editions Jeunesse (Montreal), 1972; *Les Jardiniers du hibou*, Editions Jeunesse, 1963; *Le Wapiti*, Editions Jeunesse, 1964, translation by J. M. L'Heureux published as *The Wapiti*, Macmillan, 1968; *La Maitre de Messire*, Editions Jeunesse, 1965; *Max*, Editions Jeunesse, 1965, school text edition edited by G. A. Klinck, Copp, 1966; *La Petite Fille du printemps*, Editions Jeunesse, 1966; *Max au rallye*, Editions Jeunesse, 1968, school text edition edited by Klinck, Bellhaven House, 1970; *Cecile*, illustrated by daughter, Marie-Noel Corriveau, Editions Jeunesse, 1968; *Le Temoin* (adult novel), Cercle de Livre de France (Montreal), 1969.

Le Garcon au cerf-volant, Fides, 1974; *Les Saisons de la mer*, Fides, 1975; *Patrick et Sophie en fusee*, Editions Heritage, 1975; *Compagnon du soleil*, Volume I: *L'oiseau de feu*, Volume II: *La lune noir*, Volume III: *Le temps des chats*, Fides, 1976; *La mort des autres, 1916-1918*, Fides, 1980. Also author of four puppet plays.

WORK IN PROGRESS: Two juveniles, *Max contre Macbeth* and *Max en planeur; Les Montcorbier*, historical fiction for adults written in a series of eight or ten "parallel novels" with her sister.†

* * *

CORTAZAR, Julio 1914-1984
(Julio Denis)

PERSONAL: Born August 26, 1914, in Brussels, Belgium; held dual citizenship in Argentina and (beginning 1981) France; died February 12, 1984, of a heart attack in Paris, France; son of Julio Jose and Maria Herminia (Descotte) Cortazar; married former spouse Aurora Bernardez, August 23, 1953. *Education:* Received degrees in teaching and public translating; attended Buenos Aires University.

CAREER: Writer. High school teacher in Bolivar and Chivilcoy, both in Argentina, 1937-44; teacher of French literature, University of Cuyo, Mendoza, Argentina, 1944-45; manager, Argentine Publishing Association (Camara Argentina del Libro), Buenos Aires, Argentina, 1946-48; public translator in Argentina, 1948-51; free-lance translator for UNESCO, Paris, France, 1952-84. Member of jury, Casa de las Americas Award. *Awards, honors:* Prix Medicis, 1974, for *Libro de Manuel;* Ruben Dario Order of Cultural Independence awarded by Government of Nicaragua, 1983.

WRITINGS: (Under pseudonym Julio Denis) *Presencia* (poems; title means "Presence"), El Bibliofilo (Buenos Aires), 1938; *Los reyes* (play; title means "The Monarchs"), Gulab y Aldabahor (Buenos Aires), 1949; *Bestiario* (stories; title means "Bestiary"; also see below), Editorial Sudamericana (Buenos Aires), 1951; *Final del juego* (stories; also see below), Los Presentes (Mexico), 1956, expanded edition, Editorial Sudamericana, 1964, translation by Paul Blackburn published as *End of the Game, and Other Stories* (includes stories from *Final del juego, Bestiario,* and *Las armas secretas* [also see below]), Pantheon, 1967, published as *Blow-Up, and Other Stories,* Collier, 1968; *Las armas secretas* (stories; title means "The Secret Weapons"; also see below), Editorial Sudamericana, 1959, reprinted with introduction by Susana Jakfalvi, Ediciones Catedra (Madrid), 1979.

Los premios (novel), Editorial Sudamericana, 1960, translation by Elaine Kerrigan published as *The Winners,* Pantheon, 1973; *Historias de cronopios y de famas* (also see below), Ediciones Minotauro (Buenos Aires), 1962, translation by Paul Blackburn published as *Cronopios and Famas,* Pantheon, 1969; *Rayuela* (novel), Editorial Sudamericana, 1963, translation by Gregory Rabassa published as *Hopscotch,* Pantheon, 1966; *Cuentos* (includes stories from *Bestiario, Final del juego, Las armas secretas,* and *Historias de cronopios y de famas*), Casa de las Americas (Havana), 1964; *Todos los fuegos el fuego* (stories; also see below), Editorial Sudamericana, 1966, translation by Suzanne Jill Levine published as *All Fires the Fire, and Other Stories,* Pantheon, 1973; *La vuelta al dia en ochenta mundos* (essays, poetry, and stories; title means "Around the Day in Eighty Worlds"), Siglo Veintiuno Editores (Mexico), 1967; (contributor) *Buenos Aires de la fundacion a la angustia,* Ediciones de la flor (Buenos Aires), 1967; *El perseguidor y otros cuentos* (stories), Centro Editor para America Latina (Buenos Aires), 1967.

62: Modelo para armar (novel), Editorial Sudamericana, 1968, translation by Rabassa published as *62: A Model Kit,* Pantheon, 1972; (with others) *Cuba por argentinos,* Editorial Merlin (Buenos Aires), 1968; *Buenos Aires, Buenos Aires* (includes French and English translations), Editorial Sudamericana, 1968; *Ultimo round* (essays, poetry, and stories; title means "Last Round"), Siglo Veintiuno Editores, 1969; *Viaje alrededor de una mesa* (title means "Trip around a Table"), Cuadernos de Rayuela (Buenos Aires), 1970; (with Oscar Collazos and Mario Vargas Llosa) *Literatura en la revolucion y revolucion en la literatura,* Siglo Veintiuno Editores, 1970; *Relatos* (contains *Bestiario, Final del juego, Las armas secretas,* and *Todos los fuegos el fuego*), Editorial Sudamericana, 1970.

La isla a mediodia y otros relatos (contains twelve previously published stories), Salvat Editores, 1971; (contributor) *Literatura y arte nuevo en Cuba,* Editorial Estela (Barcelona), 1971; *Pameos y meopas* (poetry), Editorial Llibres de Sivera (Barcelona), 1971; *Prosa del observatorio,* Editorial Lumen (Barcelona), 1972; *Libro de Manuel* (novel), Editorial Sudamericana, 1973, translation by Rabassa published as *A Manual for Manuel,* Pantheon, 1978; *La casilla de los Morelli,* edited by Jose Julio Ortega, Tusquets, 1973; *Octaedro* (stories; title means "Octahedron"; also see below), Editorial Sudamericana, 1974; *Antologia,* La Libreria, 1975; *Fantomas contra los vampiros multinacionales* (title means "Fantomas Takes on the Multinational Vampires"), Excelsior (Mexico), 1975; (contributor) *Humanario,* La Azotea (Buenos Aires), 1976; *Ceremonias* (contains *Final del juego* and *Las armas secretas*), Seix Barral, 1977; *Alguien que anda por ahi y otros relatos* (stories), Alfaguara (Madrid), 1977, translation by Rabassa published as *A Change of Light and Other Stories* (also contains *Octaedro*), Knopf, 1980; *Territorios,* Siglo Veintiuno Editores, 1978; *Un tal Lucas,* Ediciones Alfaguara, 1979, translation by Rabassa published as *A Certain Lucas,* Knopf, 1984.

Queremos tanto a Glenda, Ediciones Alfaguara, 1980, translation by Rabassa published as *We Love Glenda So Much,* Knopf, 1983; *Paris: The Essence of an Image,* Roto-Vision, 1981; (with Carol Dunlop) *Los autonautas de la cosmopista,* [Barcelona], 1983.

Translator: Alfred Stern, *Filosofia de la risa y del llanto,* Iman (Buenos Aires), 1950; Lord Houghton, *Vida y cartas de John Keats,* Iman, 1955; Marguerite Yourcenar, *Memorias de Adriano,* Editorial Sudamericana, 1955; Edgar Allan Poe, *Obras en prosa,* two volumes, Revista de Occidente, 1956; Poe, *Cuentos,* Editorial Nacional de Cuba, 1963; Poe, *Aventuras de Arthur Gordon Pym,* Instituto del Libro (Havana), 1968; Poe, *Eureka,* Alianza (Madrid), 1972.

Also translator of works by G. K. Chesterton, Andre Gide, Jean Giono, and Daniel Defoe, published in Argentina between 1948 and 1951. Contributor to numerous periodicals, including *Revista Iberoamericana, Cuadernos Hispanoamericanos, Books Abroad,* and *Casa de las Americas.*

SIDELIGHTS: Argentine author Julio Cortazar was "one of the world's greatest writers," according to novelist Stephen Dobyn. "His range of styles," Dobyn wrote in the *Washington Post Book World,* "his ability to paint a scene, his humor, his endlessly peculiar mind makes many of his stories wonderful. His novel *Hopscotch* is considered one of the best novels written by a South American."

A popular as well as a critical success, *Hopscotch* not only established Cortazar's reputation as a novelist of international merit but also, according to David W. Foster in *Currents in the Contemporary Argentine Novel,* prompted wider acceptance in the United States of novels written by other Latin Americans. For this reason many critics, such as Jaime Alazraki in *The Final Island,* viewed the book as "a turning point for Latin American literature." A *Times Literary Supplement* reviewer, for example, called *Hopscotch* "the first great novel of Spanish America."

Still other critics, including novelists Jose Donoso and C.D.B. Bryan, saw the novel in the context of world literature. Donoso, in his *The Boom in Spanish American Literature: A Personal History,* claimed that *Hopscotch* "humanized the novel." Cortazar was a writer, Donoso continued, "who [dared] to be discursive and whose pages [were] sprinkled with names of musicians, painters, art galleries, . . . movie directors [, and] all this had an undisguised place within his novel, something which I would never have dared to presume to be right for the Latin American novel, since it was fine for Thomas Mann [a German novelist] but not for us." In the *New York Times Book Review,* Bryan stated: "I think *Hopscotch* is the most magnificent book I have ever read. . . . No novel has so satisfactorily and completely and beautifully explored man's compulsion to explore life, to search for its meaning, to challenge its mysteries. Nor has any novel in recent memory lavished such love and attention upon the full spectrum of the writer's craft."

Cortazar attempted to perfect his craft by constant experimentation. In his longer fiction he pursued, as Leo Bersani observed in the *New York Times Book Review,* both "subversion and renewal of novelistic form." This subversion and renewal was of such importance to Cortazar that often the form of his novels overshadowed the action that they described. Through the form of his fiction Cortazar invited the reader to participate in the writer's craft and to share in the creation of the novel.

Hopscotch is one such novel. In *Into the Mainstream: Conversations with Latin-America Writers,* Luis Harss and Barbara Dohmann wrote that *Hopscotch* "is the first Latin American novel which takes itself as its own central topic or, in other words, is essentially about the writing of itself. It lives in constant metamorphoses, as an unfinished process that invents itself as it goes, involving the reader in such a way to make him part of the creative impulse." Thus, *Hopscotch* begins with a "Table of Instructions" that tells the reader that there are at least two ways to read the novel. The first is reading chapters one to fifty-six in numerical order. When the reader finishes chapter fifty-six he can, according to the instructions, stop reading and "ignore what follows [nearly one hundred more short chapters] with a clean conscience." The other way of reading suggested by the instructions is to start with chapter seventy-two and then skip from chapter to chapter (hence, the title of the book), following the sequence indicated at the end of each chapter by a number which tells the reader which chapter is next. Read the second way, the reader finds that chapter 131 refers him to chapter fifty-eight and chapter fifty-eight, to chapter 131, so that he is confronted with a novel that has no end. With his "Table of Instructions" Cortazar forces the reader to write the novel while he is reading it.

Cortazar's other experimental works include *62: A Model Kit* (considered a sequel to *Hopscotch*), *A Manual for Manuel,* *Ultimo round* ("Last Round"), and *Fantomas contra los vampiros multinacionales* ("Fantomas Takes on the Multinational Vampires"). *62: A Model Kit* is based on chapter sixty-two of *Hopscotch* in which a character, Morelli, expresses his desire to write a new type of novel. "If I were to write this book," Morelli states, "standard behavior . . . would be inexplicable by means of current instrumental psychology. . . . Everything would be a kind of disquiet, a continuous uprooting, a territory where psychological causality would yield disconcertedly."

In *62: A Model Kit* Cortazar attempted to put these ideas into action. Time and space have no meaning in the novel: although it takes place in Paris, London, and Vienna, the characters move and interact as if they are in one single space. The characters themselves are sketchily presented in fragments that must be assembled by the readers. Chapters are replaced by short scenes separated by blank spaces on the pages of the novel. Cortazar noted in the book's introduction that once again the reader must help create the novel: "The reader's option, his personal montage of the elements in the tale, will in each case be the book he has chosen to read."

A Manual for Manuel continues in the experimental vein. Megan Marshall described the book in *New Republic* as "a novel that merges story and history, a supposed scrapbook of news clippings, journal entries, diagrams, transcripts of conversations, and much more." The book, about the kidnapping of a Latin American diplomat by a group of guerillas in Paris, is told from the double perspective of an unnamed member of the group who takes notes on the plans for the kidnapping and a nonmember of the group, Andres, who reads the notes. Periodically, these two narrations are interrupted by the inclusion of English-, French-, and Spanish-language texts reproduced in the pages of the novel. These texts, actual articles collected by Cortazar from various sources, form part of a scrapbook being assembled for Manuel, the child of two of the members of the group. On one page, for example, Cortazar reprinted a statistical table originally published in 1969 by the U.S. Department of Defense that shows how many Latin Americans have received military training in the United States. The reader reads about the compilation of the scrapbook for Manuel, while at the same time reading the scrapbook and reacting to the historical truth it contains.

Other such experimentation is found in *Ultimo round,* a collection of essays, stories, and poetry. William L. Siemens noted in the *International Fiction Review* that this book, like *Hopscotch* and *62: A Model Kit,* "is a good example of audience-participation art." In *Ultimo round,* he declared, "it is impossible for the reader to proceed in a conventional manner. Upon opening the book the reader notes that there are two sets of pages within the binding, and he must immediately decide which of them to read first, and even whether he will go through by reading the top and then the bottom of page one, and so on."

Cortazar's brief narrative *Fantomas contra los vampiros multinacionales* is yet another experiment with new forms of fiction. It presents, in comic book form, the story of a "superhero," Fantomas, who gathers together "the greatest contemporary writers" to fight the destructive powers of the multinational corporations. Chilean Octavio Paz, Italian Alberto Moravia, and American Susan Sontag, along with Cortazar himself, appear as characters in the comic book. Although short, the work embodies several constants in Cortazar's fiction: the comic (the comic book form itself), the interplay of fantasy and reality (the appearance of historical figures in a fictional work), and a commitment to social activism (the portrayal of the writer as a politically involved individual). These three elements, together with Cortazar's experiments with the novelistic form, are the basic components of Cortazar's fiction.

Cortazar explained how these elements function together in his essay, "Algunos aspectos del cuento" ("Some Aspects of the Story"), which Jaime Alazraki quoted in *The Final Island*. His work, Cortazar claimed, was "an alternative to that false realism which assumed that everything can be neatly described as was upheld by the philosophic and scientific optimism of the eighteenth century, that is, within a world ruled more or less harmoniously by a system of laws, of principles, of causal relations, of well defined psychologies, of well mapped geographies. . . . In my case, the suspicion of another order, more secret and less communicable [was one of the principles guiding] my personal search for a literature beyond overly naive forms of realism."

Whatever the method, whether new narrative forms, unexpected humor, incursions into fantasy, or pleas for a more humane society, Cortazar strove to shake the reader out of traditional ways of thinking and seeing the world and to replace them with new and more viable models. Dobyn explained in the *Washington Post Book World*, "Cortazar wants to jolt people out of their self-complacency, to make them doubt their own definition of the world."

The humor in Cortazar's work often derived from what a *Time* reviewer referred to as the author's "ability to present common objects from strange perspectives as if he had just invented them." Cortazar, declared Tom Bishop in *Saturday Review*, was "an intellectual humorist. . . . [He had] a rare gift for isolating the absurd in everyday life [and] for depicting the foibles in human behavior with an unerring thrust that [was] satiric yet compassionate."

Hopscotch is filled with humorous elements, some of which Saul Yurkievich listed in *The Final Island*. He included "references to the ridiculous, . . . recourse to the outlandish, . . . absurd associations, . . . juxtaposition of the majestic with the popular or vulgar, . . . puns, . . . [and] polyglot insults." John Leonard called absurdity "obligatory" in a work by Cortazar and gave examples of the absurd found in *A Manual for Manuel*, "a turquoise penguin [is] flown by jet to Argentina; the stealing of 9,000 wigs . . . and obsessive puns." In an interview with Evelyn Picon Garfield, quoted in *Books Abroad*, Cortazar called *Cronopios and Famas* his "most playful book." It is, he continued, "really a game, a very fascinating game, lots of fun, almost like a tennis match."

This book of short, story-like narratives deals with two groups of creatures described by Arthur Curley in *Library Journal* as the "warm life-loving *cronopios* and practical, conventional *famas* . . . imaginary but typical personages between whom communication is usually impossible and always ridiculous." One portion of the book, called "The Instruction Manual," contains detailed explanations of various everyday activities, including how to climb stairs, how to wind a clock, and how to cry. In order to cry correctly, the author suggested thinking of a duck covered with ants. With these satiric instructions Cortazar, according to Paul West in *Book World*, "cleanses the doors of perception and mounts a subtle, bland assault on the mental rigidities we hold most dear." By forcing us to think about everyday occurrences in a new way, Cortazar, Malva E. Filer noted in *Books Abroad*, "expresses his rebellion against objects and persons that make up our everyday life and the mechanical ways by which we relate to them." Filer continued: "In Cortazar's fictional world [a] routine life is the great scandal against which every individual must rebel with all his strength. And if he is not willing to do so, extraordinary elements are usually summoned to force him out of this despicable and abject comfort."

These "extraordinary elements" enter into the lives of Cortazar's characters in the form of fantastic episodes which interrupt their otherwise normal existences. Alexander Coleman observed in *Cinco maestros: Cuentos modernos de Hispanoamerica* ("Five Masters: Modern Spanish-American Stories"): "Cortazar's stories start in a disarmingly conversational way, with plenty of local touches. . . . But something always seems to go awry just when we least expect it." "Axolotl," a short story described by novelist Joyce Carol Oates in the *New York Times Book Review* as her favorite Cortazar tale, begins innocently: a man describes his trips to the Parisian botanical gardens to watch a certain type of salamander called an axolotl. But the serenity ends when the narrator admits, "Now I am an axolotl." In another story, a woman has a dream about a beggar who lives in Budapest (a city the woman has never visited). The woman ends up actually going to Budapest where she finds herself walking across a bridge as the beggar woman from her dream approaches from the opposite side. The two women embrace in the middle of the bridge and the first woman is transformed into the beggar woman—she can feel the snow seeping through the holes in her shoes—while she sees her former self walk away. In yet another story, a motorcyclist is involved in a minor traffic accident and suddenly finds himself thrown back in time where he becomes the victim of Aztec ritual sacrifice. Daniel Stern noted in *Nation* that with these stories and others like them "it is as if Cortazar is showing us . . . that it is essential for us to reimagine the reality in which we live and which we can no longer take for granted."

Although during the last years of his life Cortazar was so involved with political activism that Jason Weiss described him in the *Los Angeles Times* as a writer with hardly any time to write, the Argentine had early in his career been criticized "for his apparent indifference to the brutish situation" of his fellow Latin Americans, according to John Leonard in the *New York Times*. Evidence of his growing political preoccupation is found in his later stories and novels. Leonard observed, for instance, that *A Manual for Manuel* "is a primer on the necessity of revolutionary action," and William Kennedy in the *Washington Post Book World* noted that the newspaper clippings included in the novel "touch[ed] the open nerve of political oppression in Latin America." Many of the narratives in *A Change of Light, and Other Stories* are also politically oriented. Oates described the impact of one story in the *New York Times Book Review*. In "Apocalypse at Solentiname," a photographer develops his vacation photographs of happy, smiling people only to discover pictures of people being tortured. Oates commented, "The narrator . . . contemplates in despair the impotence of art to deal with in any significant way, the 'life of permanent uncertainty . . . in . . . almost all of Latin America, a life surrounded by fear and death.'"

Cortazar's fictional world, according to Alazraki in *The Final Island*, "represents a challenge to culture." This challenge is embedded in the author's belief in a reality that reaches beyond our everyday existence. Alazraki noted that Cortazar once declared, "Our daily reality masks a second reality which is neither mysterious nor theological, but profoundly human. Yet, due to a long series of mistakes, it has remained concealed under a reality prefabricated by many centuries of culture, a culture in which there are great achievements but also profound aberrations, profound distortions." Bryan further explained these ideas in the *New York Times Book Review*: Cortazar's "surrealistic treatment of the most pedestrian acts suggest[ed] that one way to combat alienation is to return to the original receptiveness of childhood, to recapture this original innocence, by returning to the concept of life as a game."

Cortazar confronted his reader with unexpected forms, with humor, fantasy, and unseemly reality in order to challenge him to live a more meaningful life. He summarized his theory of fiction (and of life) in an essay, "The Present State of Fiction in Latin America," which appeared in *Books Abroad*. The Argentine concluded: "The fantastic is something that one must never say good-bye to lightly. The man of the future . . . will have to find the bases of a reality which is truly his and, at the same time, maintain the capacity of dreaming and playing which I have tried to show you . . . , since it is through those doors that the Other, the fantastic dimension, and the unexpected will always slip, as will all that will save us from that obedient robot into which so many technocrats would like to convert us and which we will not accept—ever."

MEDIA ADAPTATIONS: The story, "Las babas del diablo," from the collection *Las armas secretas* was the basis for Michaelangelo Antonioni's 1966 film "Blow Up."

AVOCATIONAL INTERESTS: Jazz, movies.

BIOGRAPHICAL/CRITICAL SOURCES: Casa de las Americas, numbers 15-16, 1962; *New York Times Book Review*, March 21, 1965, April 10, 1966, June 15, 1969, November 26, 1972, September 9, 1973, November 19, 1978, November 9, 1980, March 4, 1984; *New York Review of Books*, March 25, 1965, April 28, 1966, April 19, 1973, October 12, 1978; *Saturday Review*, March 27, 1965, April 9, 1966, July 22, 1967, September 27, 1969; *America*, April 17, 1965, July 9, 1966, December 22, 1973; *New Yorker*, May 18, 1965, February 25, 1974; *Books Abroad*, fall, 1965, winter, 1968, summer, 1969, winter, 1970, summer, 1976; *New Republic*, April 23, 1966, July 15, 1967, October 21, 1978, October 25, 1980; *Time*, April 29, 1966, June 13, 1969, October 1, 1973; *Commentary*, October, 1966; Luis Harss and Barbara Dohmann, *Into the Mainstream: Conversations with Latin-American Writers*, Harper, 1967; *Library Journal*, July, 1967, September, 1969, September 15, 1980; *National Review*, July 25, 1967; *Christian Science Monitor*, August 15, 1967, July 3, 1969, December 4, 1978; *Nation*, September 18, 1967; *Novel: A Forum on Fiction*, fall, 1967; Alexander Coleman, editor, *Cinco maestros: Cuentos modernos de Hispanoamerica*, Harcourt, Brace, & World, 1969; *Atlantic*, June, 1969, October, 1973; *Book World*, August 17, 1969.

Jose Vasquez Amaral, *The Contemporary Latin American Narrative*, Las Americas, 1970; Jose Donoso, *Historia personal del "boom,"* Editorial Anagrama (Barcelona), 1972, translation by Gregory Kolovakos published as *The Boom in Spanish American Literature: A Personal History*, Columbia University Press, 1977; Helmy F. Giacoman, editor, *Homenaje a Julio Cortazar*, Anaya, 1972; *Virginia Quarterly Review*, spring, 1973; *Revista Iberoamericana*, July-December, 1973; *Times Literary Supplement*, October 12, 1973, December 7, 1979; *Washington Post Book World*, November 18, 1973, November 5, 1978, November 23, 1980, May 1, 1983; *Hispania*, December, 1973; *Contemporary Literary Criticism*, Gale, Volume II, 1974, Volume III, 1975, Volume V, 1976, Volume X, 1979, Volume XIII, 1980, Volume XV, 1980; *International Fiction Review*, January, 1974, January, 1975; *Hudson Review*, spring, 1974; David W. Foster, *Currents in the Contemporary Argentine Novel*, University of Missouri Press, 1975; Evelyn Picon Garfield, *Julio Cortazar*, Frederick Ungar, 1975; *World Literature Today*, winter, 1977, winter, 1980; Jaime Alazraki and Ivar Ivask, editors, *The Final Island*, University of Oklahoma Press, 1978; *Chicago Tribune*, September 24, 1978; *New York Times*, November 13, 1978, March 24, 1983; *Listener*, December 20, 1979.

Chicago Tribune Book World, November 16, 1980, May 8, 1983; *Los Angeles Times Book Review*, December 28, 1980, June 12, 1983; *El Pais*, April 19, 1981; *Los Angeles Times*, August 28, 1983.

OBITUARIES: New York Times, February 13, 1984; *Washington Post*, February 13, 1984; *Los Angeles Times*, February 14, 1984; *Times* (London), February 14, 1984; *Chicago Tribune*, February 14, 1984; *Toronto Globe and Mail*, February 18, 1984; *Village Voice Literary Supplement*, March, 1984.†

—Sketch by Marian Walters

* * *

CORY, Ray
See MARSHALL, Mel(vin D.)

* * *

COVEY, Stephen R. 1932-

PERSONAL: Born October 24, 1932, in Salt Lake City, Utah; son of Stephen Glenn and Louise (Richards) Covey; married Sandra Merrill, August 14, 1956; children: Cynthia, Maria, Stephen, Michael Sean, David, Catherine, Colleen, Jenny, Joshua. *Education:* University of Utah, B.S., 1952; Harvard University, M.B.A., 1957; Brigham Young University, D.R.E., 1976. *Religion:* Church of Jesus Christ of Latter-day Saints. *Home:* 2160 North Oakcrest Lane, Provo, Utah 84604. *Office:* 381 West 2230 N., Suite 360, Provo, Utah 84604.

CAREER: Church of Jesus Christ of Latter-day Saints, president of mission in Ireland, 1962-65; Brigham Young University, Provo, Utah, administrative posts, 1965-69, associate professor, 1970-83, adjunct professor of organizational behavior, 1983—; consultant in organizational behavior. Guest lecturer, Brookings Institution, Washington, D.C., 1961—.

WRITINGS: Spiritual Roots of Human Relations, Deseret, 1970; *How to Succeed with People*, Deseret, 1971; *The Divine Center*, Bookcraft, 1982; (with Truman Madsen) *Marriage and Family*, Bookcraft, 1983.

WORK IN PROGRESS: A business book on organizational behavior.

* * *

COWEN, Roy C(hadwell) 1930-

PERSONAL: Born August 2, 1930, in Kansas City, Mo.; son of Roy Chadwell (a businessman) and Mildred F. (Schuetz) Cowen; married Hildegard Bredemeier, October 6, 1956. *Education:* Yale University, B.A., 1952; University of Goettingen, Dr. Phil., 1961. *Religion:* Methodist. *Home:* 2874 Baylis Dr. N., Ann Arbor, Mich. 48104. *Office:* Department of German, University of Michigan, Ann Arbor, Mich. 48109.

CAREER: University of Michigan, Ann Arbor, instructor, 1960-64, assistant professor, 1964-67, associate professor, 1967-71, professor of German, 1971—, chairman of department, 1979—. *Military service:* U.S. Navy, 1952-56. *Member:* Modern Language Association of America, Internationale Vereinigung fuer Germanische Sprach-und Literaturwissenschaft. *Awards, honors:* Senior fellowship, National Endowment for the Humanities, 1972-73.

WRITINGS: (Editor) Christian Dietrich Grabbe, *Scherz, Satire, Ironie und tiefere Bedeutung,* Blaisdell, 1969; (editor) Franz Grillparzer, *Des Meeres und der Liebe Wellen,* Blaisdell, 1969; (editor) Georg Buechner, *Dantons Tod,* Blaisdell, 1969; *Neunzehntes Jahrhundert (1830-1880),* Francke-Verlag, 1970; *Christian Dietrich Grabbe,* Twayne 1972; *Naturalismus: Kommentar zu einer Epoche,* Winkler-Verlag, 1973, 2nd edition, 1977; (editor and contributor) Grabbe, *Werke in zwei Baenden mit cinem Vommentarbande,* Hanser Verlag, 1975-77, 3rd edition, 1981; *Hauptmann-Kommentar zum dramatischen Werk,* Winkler-Verlag, 1980; *Hauptmann-Kommentar zum nichtdramtischen Werk,* Winkler-Verlag, 1981; (editor) *Dramen des deutschen Naturalismus: Gerhart Hauptmann bis Karl Schoenherr,* two volumes, Winkler-Verlag, 1981. Contributor to journals in United States and Germany.

* * *

COWLES, Virginia (Spencer) 1912-1983

PERSONAL: Born August 24, 1912, in Brattleboro, Vt.; died September 17, 1983 (some sources cite September 16, 1983), in an automobile accident in southwest France; daughter of Edward Spencer (a physician and psychiatrist) and Florence Wolcott (Jaquith) Cowles; married Aidan M. Crawley (a British politician), 1945; children: Harriette, Andrew, Randall. *Education:* Educated privately. *Home:* 19 Chester Sq., London S.W. 1, England.

CAREER: Columnist for the Boston (Mass.) *Breeze* in the early 1930s; then fashion magazine and free-lance writer in New York, N.Y.; free-lance newspaper correspondent covering the Spanish Civil War, 1936-37; roving war correspondent for the *London Sunday Times* and the *London Daily Telegraph,* covering the Russian invasion of Finland, the German invasion of France, the North African campaign, the Italian campaign, and the Allied invasion of France and Germany 1938-45. Special assistant to the American ambassador, American Embassy, London, England, 1942-43. *Awards, honors:* Order of the British Empire, 1947.

WRITINGS—All nonfiction: *Looking for Trouble* (journalistic experiences), Harper, 1941; *How America Is Governed,* Lutterworth, 1944; *No Cause for Alarm,* Harper, 1949 (published in England as *No Cause for Alarm: A Study of Trends in England Today,* Hamish Hamilton, 1949); *Winston Churchill: The Era and the Man,* Harper, 1953; *Gay Monarch: The Life and Pleasures of Edward VII,* Harper, 1956 (published in England as *Edward VII and His Circle,* Hamish Hamilton, 1956); *The Phantom Major: The Story of David Stirling and His Desert Command,* Harper, 1958 (published in England as *The Phantom Major: The Story of David Stirling and the S.A.S. Regiment,* Collins, 1958, junior edition, 1962).

The Great Swindle: The Story of the South Sea Bubble, Harper, 1960; *The Kaiser,* Harper, 1963; *1913: The Defiant Swan Song,* Weidenfeld & Nicolson, 1967, published as *1913: An End and a Beginning,* Harper, 1968; *The Russian Dagger: Cold War in the Days of the Czars,* Harper, 1969; *The Romanovs,* Harper, 1971; *The Rothschilds: A Family of Fortune,* Knopf, 1973; *The Last Tsar and Tsarina,* Weidenfeld & Nicolson, 1977; *The Astors,* Weidenfeld & Nicolson, 1979.

The Great Marlborough and His Duchess, Weidenfeld & Nicolson, 1983. Contributor of articles to various periodicals, including *Vogue* and *Harper's.*

SIDELIGHTS: Virginia Cowles was the author of many nonfiction works, including biographies of such famous leaders as Winston Churchill, Edward VII, and Kaiser Wilhelm II and such well-known families as the Romanovs, the Rothschilds, and the Astors.

Cowles's first biography, *Winston Churchill: The Era and the Man,* won the praise of many reviewers for being what a critic for the *Springfield Republican* termed "a first-class piece of biographical writing." Geoffrey Bruun wrote in the *New York Herald Tribune Book Review* that "in preparing this lively, competent . . . study, Virginia Cowles made full use of her exceptional advantages. . . . Her descriptions of the man, his character, motivations, mannerisms, moods, working habits are shrewd and objective and her insights into the British temperament, prejudices, parliamentary techniques and personalities enrich her pages."

"What Miss Cowles has done is to produce a lively, shrewd and in some ways, original study of the most versatile, vivacious and oldest of the great figures of the contemporary world," declared Denis Brogan in the *New York Times.* "Cowles succeeds admirably in what she really set out to do: to make us see in him not merely the heroic figure of 1940-45, but the man who, just before his finest hour, had apparently had two political careers killed under him and was unlikely to have another chance." And Alastair Buchan remarked in *New Republic* that "Cowles, who by her wartime writing and her earlier books has shown that she is a first-class journalist and observer of the English scene, has been remarkably successful. She has written a biography in the true sense, not merely a personal history written backwards, as is so often the case, judging the boy in terms of the man."

Gay Monarch: The Life and Pleasures of Edward VII was Cowles's second biographical study. Bruun commented in another *New York Herald Tribune* review: "In her biography of Winston Churchill, . . . Virginia Cowles revealed her talent for analyzing a statesman in personal terms and relating him to his era. Now she has done the same for Edward VII in a similar anecdotal style and has produced an equally entertaining book. It is, in some respects, an even better book, for it is based on wider research, has a larger cast of characters, and assesses them more shrewdly."

"Cowles writes a clear, masculine and economical English," a reviewer for the *Times Literary Supplement* stated. "Her quotations from letters and contemporary memoirs are apposite and well chosen, and her comments, with a few exceptions, judicious. . . . Cowles has written a sensible, readable book, avoiding both irony and mockery, and doing justice to a likable, even rather endearing man."

Cowles was also noted for her studies of wealthy and influential families in such works as *The Romanovs, The Rothschilds: A Family of Fortune,* and *The Astors.* As in her biographies of individuals, Cowles presented her families in a sensitive and lively manner without ignoring their place in history. For example, a *Times Literary Supplement* critic stated that *The Romanovs* "is popular history; and from Miss Cowles's first sentence . . . she sets a brisk and at times breathtaking pace. It is the kind of colourful, personal history that reads with the compelling excitement of a novel." And in a *Library Journal* review of *The Rothschilds,* S. R. Herstein remarked: "In this splendid biography, Cowles brings the Rothschild legend to life. Perhaps the word biography is too narrow, for Cowles has written a lively social history, placing the family within the European context and using narrative, anecdote, and copious illustration." As for *The Astors,* said Kristiana Gregory in the *Los Angeles Times,* it is "as much a history lesson as a breathless peak into three-storied yachts and rambling manors with parlors paved in silver dollars. . . . Cowles surveys this legendary family with tales, photos and drawings as colorful as a royal garden.''

Many reviewers believed it was Cowles's skill at making her interesting and powerful characters come alive that really made her writing popular with readers. For instance, J. H. Plumb commented in the *New York Times Book Review* that the Romanovs "were a splendidly exotic bunch from first to last and Virginia Cowles, an amateur historian of practiced skill, makes the most of them.'' And a reviewer wrote in the *New Yorker* that *The Astors* is "a lively illustrated account of a family once celebrated for its wealth and extravagance both in the United States and in Great Britain. . . . This is not so much a saga of rags to riches as it is the epic of an entire tribe's struggle to attain normality."

Cowles achieved recognition for more than just her biographical studies. *Looking for Trouble*, hailed by *Library Journal* as "one of the most interesting books to come from the war zones," is a collection of Cowles's memoirs of her years as a newspaper correspondent covering events such as the Spanish Civil War and the outbreak of World War II in Europe and England. "As the compact yet comprehensive record of a woman correspondent's unique experience, her story makes one of the most engrossing and most illuminatingly effective books that the war has produced," declared Katherine Woods in the *New York Times*. Linton Wells noted in the *Saturday Review of Literature*: "*Looking for Trouble* certainly integrated events and personalities into a compact picture which is as absorbing as it is worthwhile—absorbing because it vividly depicts a courageous American newspaper woman struggling for her stories in the flaming vortex of war; worthwhile because it reveals clearly the history-making things she saw and heard as one nation after another died." And a reviewer for *Spectator* stated: "Cowles is a good journalist, with a nose for news, a very personal talent for putting news over freshly, and an ability rare among members of her profession to indicate the relation of the small episode to the larger issue. This book is a triumphant monument to her prescience in being consistently in the right place at the right time over a number of years."

BIOGRAPHICAL/CRITICAL SOURCES: *Spectator,* August 1, 1941; *Saturday Review of Literature,* August 9, 1941; *New York Times,* August 10, 1941, May 24, 1953; *Library Journal,* August, 1941, February 15, 1964, November 1, 1973; *Springfield Republican,* June 21, 1953; *New York Herald Tribune Book Review,* July 5, 1953, October 21, 1956; *New Republic,* July 6, 1953; *Times Literary Supplement,* July 27, 1956, November 19, 1971; *New York Times Book Review,* March 15, 1964, December 5, 1971; *New Yorker,* January 14, 1980; *Los Angeles Times,* February 3, 1980.

OBITUARIES: *Chicago Tribune,* September 18, 1983; *Times* (London), September 19, 1983; *New York Times,* September 20, 1983.

—Sketch by Margaret Mazurkiewicz

* * *

COX, Keith (Kohn) 1931-

PERSONAL: Born April 21, 1931, in Austin, Tex.; son of Lambuth and Pearl Cox; married Sue Johnson (a teacher), July 1, 1961; children: Suzanne, Gregory. *Education:* University of Texas, B.B.A., 1953, M.B.A., 1959, Ph.D., 1963. *Politics:* Democrat. *Religion:* Presbyterian. *Home:* 7315 Carew, Houston, Tex. 77074. *Office:* Department of Marketing, University of Houston, Cullen Blvd., Houston, Tex. 77004.

CAREER: Kent State University, Kent, Ohio, assistant professor of marketing, 1963-67; University of Houston, Houston, Tex., 1967—, began as associate professor, became professor of marketing. *Member:* American Marketing Association (vice-president in education, 1975; vice-president in finance, 1976; president, 1979).

WRITINGS: (Editor) *Analytical Viewpoints in Marketing,* Prentice-Hall, 1968; *Experimentation for Marketing Decisions,* Intext Publishing, 1969; (editor with Ben Enis) *Marketing Classics,* Allyn & Bacon, 1969, 4th edition, 1981; (with Enis) *The Marketing Research Process,* Goodyear Publishing, 1972; (with Philip Kotler) *Marketing Management and Strategy,* Prentice-Hall, 1972, 3rd edition, 1984; (editor with Vern J. McGinnis) *Strategic Market Decisions: A Reader,* Prentice-Hall, 1982.

* * *

COYNE, John (P.) 1940-

PERSONAL: Born 1940 in Chicago, Ill.; son of Thomas and Mary (Kilcourse) Coyne; married Judith Wederholt (an editor). *Education:* St. Louis University, B.A.; Western Michigan University, M.A.; attended Georgetown University and George Washington University. *Home:* LaBranche Rd., Austerlitz, N.Y. 12017. *Agent:* Peter Lampack, 60 West 68th St., New York, N.Y. 10023.

CAREER: Writer. Worked for Peace Corps in Ethiopia, 1962-67; has worked as a high school and college teacher; State University of New York at Old Westbury, became dean of students.

WRITINGS: (With Tom Hebert) *This Way Out: A Guide to Alternative College Education in the United States, Europe, and the Third World,* Dutton, 1972; (editor) *Better Golf,* Follett, 1972; (editor) *The New Golf for Women,* Doubleday, 1973; (with Hebert) *By Hand: A Guide to Schools and Careers in Crafts,* Dutton, 1974; (editor) *The Penland School of Crafts Book of Jewelry Making,* Bobbs-Merrill, 1975; (editor) *The Penland School of Crafts Book of Pottery,* Bobbs-Merrill, 1975; (with Hebert) *Getting Skilled: A Guide to Private Trade and Technical Schools,* Dutton, 1976, 2nd edition, National Association of Trade and Technical Schools, 1982; (with Jerry Miller) *How to Make Upside-Down Dolls,* Bobbs-Merrill, 1977.

Novels; published by Putnam, except as indicated: *The Piercing,* 1979; *The Legacy* (based on the film of the same title), Berkley, 1979; *The Searing,* 1980; *Hobgoblin,* 1981; *The Shroud,* 1982.

WORK IN PROGRESS: A novel, *Brothers and Sisters.*

SIDELIGHTS: The variety of books that John Coyne has produced throughout his career reflects his many interests. The author's two "Penland School of Crafts" books contain conversations with craftsmen from the famous Penland School in North Carolina, as well as instructions in each craft. The Penland faculty members are among the best craftsmen in the country and have earned the school a fine reputation in its field. *New York Times Book Review* critic Beth Gutcheon has praise for Coyne's books on the Penland method of pottery and jewelry making, saying, "If you have some experience in one of these crafts, and if the work and the talk in these handsome books fails to move you, feel your pulse to see if you're alive."

In addition to the craft books, Coyne has written about golf instruction and college alternatives. More recently he has turned to horror novels, with some success. *The Piercing,* his first novel, tells the story of the rape of twelve-year-old Betty Sue Wadkins, molested in the Appalachian woods by the devil, who is disguised as a hillbilly. Soon after, Betty Sue becomes a stigmatic, bleeding from wounds in her hands and feet each week. Five years later this fact becomes public and, as a *Critic* writer describes it, "Betty Sue is turned into a full-flowing stigmatic who does her thing on National TV." Mixed reviews greeted *The Piercing;* the *Critic* writer, for example, calls the novel a "putrid puddle of gagging, sensational, tasteless, ultimately pointless fiction," while Michele Slung in the *Washington Post Book World* contends that Coyne "has concocted a swift-moving plot, one that's intelligently done, if not terribly subtle" and says the book provides readers with "an interlude of ghastly pleasure."

Hobgoblin, a tale of terror centering on a role-playing game, was criticized by Joseph McLellan in the *Washington Post* for its "loose ends and failures of character motivation." Ultimately, though, McLellan finds the novel "a decent story about life in a small town high school, and the problems for a new boy in town who is rather shy and withdrawn and handicapped by a preppy background. [Coyne] is very good at characterizing the young thugs who tend to dominate the scene in many high schools these days, and he is intriguing in his invention of 'Hobgoblin,' an elaborate, complex game of the 'swords and sorcery' genre, based on old Irish legends and played with cards, dice and a dazzling variety of exotic characters."

CA INTERVIEW

CA interviewed John Coyne on August 30, 1983, at his home in Austerlitz, New York.

CA: You've co-authored guides to educational institutions, written and edited how-to books that are really more than how-to books, and most recently written novels that deal with the occult. That variety suggests an assortment of interests in your background. How did you come to be a writer?

COYNE: I always wanted to be a writer. I wanted to be a novelist, and I was using these other forms to get to a position where I could write novels full-time. A lot of these books I did, particularly the craft books and the books that I edited, were used as a way of making money so that I could buy some time in which to write a novel. From 1971 up until 1979, when I published *The Piercing,* I wrote seven novels that are all unpublished. When *The Piercing* came along, it finally was an idea that clicked. But I gained a lot of experience not only by writing books about craft and education, but also by writing for educational magazines, general-content magazines, travel magazines; I still do travel pieces for a variety of magazines when I'm not writing novels.

CA: Did the guidebooks on schools come about through your professional involvement in education?

COYNE: Yes. I graduated from St. Louis University and obtained a master's degree at Western Michigan University. Then I joined the Peace Corps in 1962 and was in the first group of volunteers to go into Ethiopia. After that I was asked by Harris Wofford, a friend of mine who was starting an experimental college in the State University of New York at Old Westbury, to go with him to help organize this college; I became a dean and stayed for a couple of years.

It was during this period that I met Tom Hebert, and we decided that a book could be written for students looking for experimental schools. That became *This Way Out* (1972). It was about alternatives to college, ways a student could put together an academic degree by studying in the United States, studying overseas, learning on his own. It came in the wave of experimentation in education in the early '70s.

That led to our doing two more books for Dutton on education. *By Hand* (1974) was about ways that some of the people we were meeting were obtaining degrees and making a living by working in crafts—pottery, ceramics, glassblowing, weaving, woodworking, and so on. *Getting Skilled* (1976) is a look at proprietary schools, for-profit schools where you can learn to be an electrician or a deep-sea diver—marketable skills.

CA: And the beautiful "Penland School of Crafts" books, on jewelry making and pottery, came along in 1975; they must have grown out of your research for By Hand.

COYNE: That's right. When I was doing *By Hand* I went to Penland, which I knew about from friends of mine who had been there, and stayed for a couple of weeks interviewing and obtaining information on crafts. Then I decided that they really should do a series of books. I talked to the director of the Penland School, Bill Brown, and he agreed. So I went back to Penland a year or so later and stayed there to do the books.

What Penland does is bring teachers in for the summer or other short periods of time. I would interview them and they would do a project while I was there; then I edited and designed the material into the books. We were going to do many more, but unfortunately they did not sell enough to justify the expense that we put into them, so we couldn't get the publishers to continue the series. It was a wonderful project and I'm still interested in it. I've written about Penland for a number of publications including the *Smithsonian* magazine.

CA: During those years you also edited some books on golf, Better Golf *(1972) and* The New Golf for Women *(1973). Had golf been an earlier interest of yours?*

COYNE: Yes. I had been raised near a golf course and had caddied and worked at a golf course during my whole adolescence. I was just doing what all writers do—use what they know to develop ideas that would sell to publishers. I would then write the books in a relatively short time, maybe one or two months, and get enough money to allow me to work on a novel for six or eight months.

That's how I spent the '70s until 1976, when *The Piercing* was sold as an idea to G. P. Putnam and caught on the wave of the cult/horror novels, and that developed into where I am now. At the moment I'm trying to move from writing this type of novel into what I would call general fiction.

CA: When did your fascination with the occult begin?

COYNE: It began while I was at the McDowell Colony working on another book, which I wrote a hundred pages of and couldn't sell. So I was trying to make a decision whether I should continue to write fiction or just give up the attempt, because nothing that I had been doing was working, and I was looking at the bestseller list. *Carrie* had just come out. And I thought, what is there that I have some familiarity with that might fit into a particular genre—Western or romance or detective story? The current fascination with horror books began, I believe, with *Rosemary's Baby* and *The Exorcist.* And then *Carrie* was made into a very successful movie, and that started Stephen

King. I remembered that I had been fascinated as a young boy by stigmata and various stories about stigmata, so I began then to do some research and I developed a plot that is the hook of *The Piercing*, which is about a stigmatic girl found by a priest in the mountains of western North Carolina (though the book doesn't say it's western North Carolina). The publishers liked it so much that they asked me to do the novelization of the movie "The Legacy," and that in turn led to my doing *The Searing*; then came *Hobgoblin* and then *The Shroud*, which came out in paperback in July 1983.

CA: The genre is obviously very popular. Do you have any ideas about why horror has such an appeal to people now?

COYNE: I think it has had a phenomenal development, and I attribute that to a couple of things. One is the success of the movie "The Exorcist" and the movie "Carrie," which were visually very gripping and spawned the development of more movies of that kind. Usually in hard times people want some sort of escape literature. We went through a particularly bad time, and I think that was a factor. And these kinds of books run in cycles. I actually think the cycle is over with; we've seen the sudden growth of so many of these books in paperback racks, and I think it's faded now, to be replaced by the more typical mystery story, though there'll continue to be people like Stephen King and Peter Straub who will publish every year or so and do fairly well.

CA: Your novels are carefully and sometimes intricately plotted. How much of the plot do you outline before you begin to write?

COYNE: On all of the novels that I've done so far of this kind, I've done very little plotting. I have an idea of what I'm going to do, and I have sort of a general idea of how the book will end, but I do not know the specifics at all. I write by painting myself into a corner! When I get into the corner, then I have to figure out how to get out of there, and if I do it imaginatively enough, it not only surprises me, it surprises the reader as well.

CA: So you have some fun in the process too?

COYNE: Yes. If I knew what the book was going to be about, I wouldn't want to write it. It's a discovery for me too. And often I'm really surprised at how it turns out.

CA: I suspect you do a lot of research for the novels.

COYNE: I do. For *The Shroud*, I had to do research in Africa, the American West, Nazism, the Reformation, the Counter-Reformation. The most gruesome research that I did was for the part in which a body is embalmed. In fact, I found it very difficult to write those scenes.

CA: Do you generally enjoy the research?

COYNE: I do. I found that when I was doing research on topics for magazine articles, I would do enough research to write a book. You do get fascinated. One of the nice things about being a writer is that you're continually doing something new, continually learning something new, and in my case it's always in a different area. *Hobgoblin* is a book about fantasy games, role-playing games; and not only did I play these games to learn what the fascination was, but I also had to do some study in Irish mythology to develop a credible game for the book. I had a lot of letters from young people especially, asking me where they could buy the game Hobgoblin. But it exists, of course, only in the book.

CA: Do you write with the possibility of a movie in mind?

COYNE: No. I *am* aware, as a writer, that with the number of tantalizing and powerful visual images out there today in movies and television, one has to grab the reader very quickly and keep the reader's attention because there's so much that can take his mind into something else. So I write with the sense that people today are learning by visual images rather than by reading alone. And I think that that has affected my writing. I am also that kind of a writer. But although people say that my work sometimes reads like a screenplay, this has not been my intent. And the truth of that, of course, is evident in the fact that none of my books have been made into movies.

CA: Is there any talk of movies?

COYNE: No.

CA: Would you be interested in doing screenplays?

COYNE: Oh, sure. I like to write articles; I like to write short stories; I would love to do a play. Any writer that writes wants to do everything. I would like to do a screenplay just to go through the process and see what it was like. But I much prefer writing novels because in the novel you're alone; you're allowed to develop it until you reach the point of sending it to the editor. Screenwriting is a much more communal kind of process. There are so many people involved in the movie once the script is done, through the rewrite of the script, to the producer, the director, and the actors. I think it's much easier to write a novel and get it published than it is to write a screenplay or a teleplay and get it produced.

CA: What kind of reading do you enjoy?

COYNE: I find that I don't read as much now as I did when I was in high school and college. Then I was really reading almost a book a day; now I probably read a book a week. I don't read much when I'm writing, and if I do read something, I'll read nonfiction or an entirely different kind of thing from what I'm working on. Very seldom will I read another current book unless it's by a friend of mine. But I do tend to go back and reread the books that meant a lot to me when I was growing up. Every year I will read, almost religiously, Hemingway's *The Sun Also Rises*, Salinger's *Catcher in the Rye*, and Faulkner's *Light in August*. I read strictly for pleasure. And I tend also to spend more time reading nonfiction now than I did when I was younger.

CA: What kind of writing schedule do you keep?

COYNE: I keep fairly regular hours. I try to get working at least by eight o'clock in the morning. I got a word processor about a year ago, and that has affected my production. I used to write, for example, five pages a day. I tried to do a thousand words a day. I'm finding that with this word processor I'm writing a lot more pages and I'm editing a lot more when I go through it. I try to write at least one to two thousand words a day in rough-draft form, and that means I usually work until about three o'clock. I might have something to eat for lunch, but it is very quick. Then around three or three-thirty I take a break and jog three or four miles and read the newspaper and do things like that.

In the evening I tend to do household chores—answering letters, paying bills, that kind of stuff. My wife is an editor, and if she comes home with manuscripts to read, then I might do some more work. Actually, I work every day when I'm writing something specific. I thought that once I was successful I'd quit doing that, but I've found out that I'm working on something every day. I work rather intensely in the process of finishing a novel, which can take anywhere from five to eight months, and then I don't do anything big for several months. I might do a travel piece. I might go someplace where my wife and I will take a vacation. Then I will think up a new idea and go back into the process again.

CA: How do you divide your time between New York City and Austerlitz?

COYNE: The way we're dividing it now is that on Wednesday I go down to the city and on Friday night Judy and I drive up here to Austerlitz, which is about two and a half hours north of the city in the New York Berkshires. Then she goes back either Sunday night or Monday. This will change with the weather; in the winter I'll spend more time in the city.

CA: You said earlier that you'd like to get into a more general kind of fiction. Are there specific works in progress or future plans you'd like to talk about?

COYNE: Yes, I'm currently working on a project that I hope will be a book called *Brothers and Sisters*, which is a contemporary story of a Midwest Irish-Catholic family.

CA: Is there any advice you'd give aspiring writers?

COYNE: I think there is a real misconception about the writer's life. This is probably considered one of the most romantic occupations of the Western World, as being a rock star is. The major problem with being a professional writer, full-time, is that it is extremely difficult to make a living at it. There are very few writers, as surveys will indicate, who are able to write full-time. They have to combine writing with something else. Anybody who wants to write has to be realistic and understand that the chances of making it into a full-time career are one or two percent.

What I had to do until I was quite old, before I could devote full time to writing, was a variety of things—work for the government, teach high school and college, be a dean, and that sort of thing. But that was all useful, because no experience is wasted on a writer. And I think the worst thing that can happen to a writer is to become an academic writer whose whole experience is teaching at college. That sort of life has nothing to do with the way the world is run. I think that you need the experience of dealing with a different world if you want to be any kind of writer, regardless of what you write about. It absolutely doesn't make any difference what topic; you just need that experience in your data bank of knowledge.

The other thing I'd say is about learning this craft of writing: The only way to learn how to write a novel is to write a novel. I was in a creative writing program at St. Louis University called the Writers' Institute; I went to St. Louis University because of it. It was created by James Cronin in 1948 and dissolved shortly after I left, in 1959 or 1960. In that program we had to write every day and turn in a thousand words a week in assignments. That discipline of sitting down every day and writing is incredibly valuable. Every time I write a novel I'm a better writer at the end of it than I was at the beginning. But there are no magic tricks.

BIOGRAPHICAL/CRITICAL SOURCES: Saturday Review World, February 9, 1974; *Smithsonian*, November, 1975; *New York Times Book Review*, December 7, 1975; *Critic*, February 1, 1979; *Washington Post Book World*, March 25, 1979; *Washington Post*, December 19, 1981; *Los Angeles Times*, October 2, 1983.

—Interview by Jean W. Ross

* * *

CROSBIE, John S(haver) 1920-

PERSONAL: Born May 1, 1920, in Montreal, Quebec, Canada; son of Thomas Champion and Margaret Ruth (Shaver) Crosbie; married Catherine Patricia James, November 19, 1971; children: Peter, Stephen, Andrew, Kathryn, Charles. *Education:* Attended University of New Brunswick and University of Toronto. *Home:* 107 Ridge Dr., Toronto, Ontario, Canada M4T 1B6. *Office:* Magazine Association of Canada, 44 Eglinton West, Suite 501, Toronto, Ontario, Canada MAR 1A1.

CAREER: Canadian Broadcasting Corp., Halifax, Nova Scotia and Toronto, Ontario, Canada, announcer and producer, 1942-44; Purdy Productions, Toronto, managing director, 1944-46; Dancer-Fitzgerald-Sample Ltd., Toronto, assistant general manager, 1946-49; Canadian Advertising Agency Ltd., Montreal, Quebec, Canada, general manager, 1949-50; J. Walter Thompson Co. (advertising agency), New York, N.Y., employed in Toronto office, 1950-58, became vice-president in Chicago, Ill., 1958-64, and San Francisco, Calif., 1965-66; Magazine Association of Canada, Toronto, president, 1967—. Director and former chairman of Canadian Advertising Advisory Board; former vice-chairman of United Appeal, Toronto. *Military service:* Officer in the Canadian Army, 1940-42.

MEMBER: Metropolitan Club and Canadian Club (both New York City) Granite Club (Toronto).

WRITINGS: Canada and Its Leaders, Baxter, 1968; *Crosbie's Dictionary of Puns*, Simon & Schuster (Canada), 1972, 2nd edition, Harmony, 1977; *The Mayor of Upper Upsalquitch*, McGraw, 1973; *The Incredible Mrs. Chadwick*, McGraw, 1975; *Crosbie's Book of Punned Haiku*, Workman, 1979; *The World's Worst Puns*, Harmony, 1982. Also author of radio and television scripts. Contributor to magazines.

WORK IN PROGRESS: Chairman of the Bored, The International Save the Pun Foundation.

BIOGRAPHICAL/CRITICAL SOURCES: Los Angeles Times Book Review, June 27, 1982; *Chicago Tribune Book World*, July 4, 1982.

* * *

CROSS, Richard K(eith) 1940-

PERSONAL: Born May 19, 1940, in Hackensack, N.J.; son of Gordon Keith and Marguerite (Grossmann) Cross; married Christa Maria Wolf, December 18, 1970; children: Catherine, Anna. *Education:* Princeton University, A.B. (magna cum laude), 1962; Stanford University, M.A., 1966, Ph.D., 1967. *Office:* Department of English, University of Maryland, College Park, Md. 20742.

CAREER: Dartmouth College, Hanover, N.H., instructor in English, 1966-68; University of California, Los Angeles, assistant professor, 1968-74, associate professor, 1974-80, professor of English, 1980-83, vice-chairman of department, 1976-77; University of Maryland, College Park, professor of English and chairman of department, 1983—. Fulbright lecturer, University of Wuerzburg, 1971-72. *Awards, honors:* Humanities Institute fellow, 1970, 1974; American Council of Learned Societies grant-in-aid, 1973.

WRITINGS: Flaubert and Joyce: The Rite of Fiction, Princeton University Press, 1971; *Malcolm Lowry: A Preface to His Fiction,* University of Chicago Press, 1980; (contributor) Suzanne Ferguson, editor, *Critical Essays on Randall Jarrell,* G. K. Hall, 1983. Contributor to *Twentieth Century Literature, Contemporary Literature, Modern Fiction Studies, Modern Philology, Nineteenth-Century Fiction,* and *Parnassus.*

* * *

CRUMBLEY, D. Larry 1941-

PERSONAL: Born January 18, 1941, in Kannapolis, N.C.; son of Carl Donald and Velvia Crumbley; married Donna D. Loflin (divorced, January, 1983); children: Stacey, Dana, Heather. *Education:* Pfeiffer College, B.S. (cum laude), 1963; Louisiana State University, Baton Rouge, M.S., 1965, Ph.D., 1967. *Home address:* P.O. Box 9027, College Station, Tex. 77840. *Office:* Department of Accounting, School of Business, Texas A & M University, College Station, Tex. 77843.

CAREER: Seidman & Seidman, Baton Rouge, La., staff accountant, 1967; Pennsylvania State University, University Park, assistant professor of accounting, 1967-69; Arthur Andersen & Co., New York, N.Y., faculty resident, 1969-70; certified public accountant in the state of North Carolina, 1970; University of Florida, Gainesville, associate professor of accounting, 1970-73, 1975; University of Southern California, University Park, director of master of taxation program, 1975; Texas A & M University, School of Business, College Station, graduate faculty research fellow in department of accounting, 1975—. Adjunct assistant professor, Graduate School of Business, New York University, 1970. *Member:* American Institute of Certified Public Accountants, National Tax Association, American Taxation Association (former president), American Accounting Association, Texas Society of Certified Public Accountants, Phi Kappa Phi, Beta Gamma Sigma, Beta Alpha Psi. *Awards, honors:* Ford Foundation grant, 1966-67; Humble Oil Company fellowship, 1966-67; College of Business Administration research awards, 1976-77.

WRITINGS: (With Michael Davis) *Organizing, Operating and Terminating Subchapter S Corporations,* Estate Tax Publishing Co. (Aberdeen), 1970, revised edition, Lawyers & Judges Publishing, 1975; (with Ronald Copeland and Joseph Wojdak) *Advanced Accounting,* Holt, 1971; *A Practical Guide to the Preparation of Gift Tax Returns,* Estate Tax Publishing Co., 1971, revised edition, Lawyers & Judges Publishing, 1977; *A Practical Guide to Preparing an Estate Tax Return,* Lawyers & Judges Publishing, 1977; *West's Federal Taxation,* two volumes, West Publishing, 1977.

The Federal Income Tax: Sources and Applications, Prentice-Hall, 1980; *Readings in Oil Industry Accounting,* Pennwell Publishing, 1980; *Donate Less to the IRS,* Vestal, 1981; *Estate Planning in the '80s,* American Management Association, 1982; *Readings in Crude Oil Windfall Profit Tax,* Pennwell Publishing, 1982; *Readings in Selected Tax Problems of the Oil Industry,* Pennwell Publishing, 1982. Co-author of a column, "Tax Notes for the Young Practitioner," in *Taxation for Accountants.* Contributor of about two hundred articles on accounting and taxation to professional journals. Editor of *Oil and Gas Tax Quarterly;* co-editor of *Texas Tax Service;* also editor of various hobby-related columns for *Coin World, Philatelic Reporter and Digest,* and *Linn's World Stamp Almanac.*

* * *

CUBAN, Larry 1934-

PERSONAL: Born October 31, 1934, in Passaic, N.J.; son of Morris (a jobber) and Fanny (Janoff) Cuban; married Barbara Joan Smith (a secretary), June 15, 1958; children: Sondra, Janice. *Education:* University of Pittsburgh, B.A., 1955; Western Reserve University (now Case Western Reserve University), M.A., 1958; Stanford University, Ph.D., 1974. *Religion:* Jewish. *Home:* 2846 Kipling St., Palo Alto, Calif. 94306. *Office:* School of Education, Stanford University, Stanford, Calif. 94305.

CAREER: Teacher in public schools in Pennsylvania and Ohio, 1955-63; Cardozo Project in Urban Teaching, Washington, D.C., master teacher of history, 1963-65, director, 1965-67; Roosevelt High School, Washington, D.C., teacher of history, 1967-68; District of Columbia Public Schools, Washington, D.C., director of staff development, 1969-70; Roosevelt High School, teacher of history, 1970-71; Virginia Public Schools, Arlington, superintendent, 1974-81; Stanford University, Stanford, Calif., associate professor in School of Education, 1981—. Member, President's Advisory Committee for Teacher Corps, 1967-69; director, U.S. Commission on Civil Rights, 1968. Consultant to National Institute for Education, National Teacher Corps, and various public school systems, colleges, and universities, 1964—.

WRITINGS: The Negro in America, Scott, Foresman, 1964, revised edition published as *The Black Man in America,* 1971; *To Make a Difference: Teaching in the Inner City,* Free Press, 1970; (with Philip Roden) *The Promise of America,* Scott, Foresman, 1971; (editor) *Youth as a Minority,* National Council for the Social Studies, 1972; *Urban School Chiefs under Fire,* University of Chicago Press, 1976; *How Teachers Taught: Constancy and Change in American Classrooms, 1890-1980,* Longman, 1984.

Editor of "Contemporary Civilization" series, published by Scott, Foresman: *Japan,* 1970; *India,* 1971; *Russia,* 1972; *Kenya,* 1972; *Mexico,* 1972. Contributor to numerous periodicals, including *Teachers College Record, Harvard Educational Review, Saturday Review, Educational Leadership, Journal of Negro Education, Washington Post,* and *Kappan.*

* * *

CUDLIPP, Edythe 1929-
(Julia Alcott, Jane Horatio, Carrie Jordan, Nicole Norman, Maureen Norris, Rinalda Roberts, E. F. Van Zandt)

PERSONAL: Born September 4, 1929, in Jamestown, N.Y.; daughter of Edwin F. and Edna (Van Zandt) Cudlipp; married Bruce Stewart Lachlan, Jr., October 1, 1970 (divorced, 1974). *Education:* Mount Holyoke College, B.A., 1951; University of Heidelberg, further study, 1955. *Home:* 82 Horatio St., New York, N.Y. 10014. *Agent:* Lucianne Goldberg Agency, 255 West 8th St., New York, N.Y. 10024.

CAREER: U.S. Army, civilian editor in Heidelberg, Germany, 1957-62; *American Businessman,* Washington, D.C., writer,

1963-65; *This Week*, New York City, associate editor, 1965-67; *Coronet*, New York City, senior editor, 1967-70; freelance writer, 1970—. *Member:* Authors Guild, Authors League of America.

WRITINGS: Understanding Women's Liberation, Paperback Library, 1971; (under pseudonym Jane Horatio) *A Matter of Life and Death*, Award Books, 1971; (with Jane Sorensen) *The New Way to Become the Person You'd Like to Be*, McKay, 1973; (under pseudonym Rinalda Roberts) *The Four Marys*, Popular Library, 1976; *Furs: An Appreciation of Luxury, A Guide to Value*, Hawthorne, 1978; *Vitamins: What They Are and Why You Need Them*, Grosset, 1978; *Jewelry: An Appreciation of Luxury, A Guide to Value*, Dutton, 1980; (under pseudonym Carrie Jordan) *Rivals for Love*, Playboy Paperbacks, 1981.

Under pseudonym Julia Alcott; published by Signet: *A Long Lost Love*, 1976; *The Key to Her Heart*, 1976; *Island of Love*, 1977.

Under pseudonym Nicole Norman; published by Pocket Books: *Heather Song*, 1980; *The Firebird*, 1981.

Under pseudonym Maureen Norris; published by Jove: *Starry Eyed*, 1983; *Seaswept*, 1984.

WORK IN PROGRESS: Research for an historical romance and a nonfiction book.

SIDELIGHTS: Edythe Cudlipp told *CA*: "Flexibility as to subject in fiction and non-fiction is the key to survival in freelancing—which is good, since to me part of the fun of writing is the challenge of the new and different."

* * *

CURRY, Peggy Simson 1911-

PERSONAL: Born December 30, 1911, in Dunure, Ayrshire, Scotland; daughter of William Andrew (a rancher) and Margaret (Anderson) Simson married William Seeright Curry (an educator), July 21, 1937; children: Michael Munro. *Education:* University of Wyoming, B.A., 1936. *Politics:* Republican. *Religion:* Presbyterian. *Home and office:* 3125 Garden Creek Rd., Casper, Wyo. 82601. *Agent:* August Lenninger Literary Agency, Inc., 437 Fifth Ave., New York, N.Y. 10016.

CAREER: Casper College, Casper, Wyo., instructor in creative writing, 1952—. Lecturer at various colleges and writers' conferences 1952—. Poet-in-residence, State of Wyoming poetry-in-schools program, 1971—. *Member:* Western Writers of America, Kappa Kappa Gamma, P.E.O. Sisterhood. *Awards, honors:* Spur Award, Western Writers of America, 1957, 1970; Kappa Kappa Gamma Distinguished Alumni award, 1964; University of Wyoming Distinguished Alumni award, 1968; poet laureate of Wyoming, 1981.

WRITINGS: Fire in the Water (novel), McGraw, 1951; *Red Wind of Wyoming* (poetry), Allan Swallow, 1955, revised edition, Spirit Mound Press, 1977; *So Far from Spring* (novel), Viking, 1956; *The Oil Patch* (novel), McGraw, 1959; *Creating Fiction from Experience*, Writer, Inc., 1964, revised edition, 1975; *A Shield of Clover* (juvenile novel), McKay, 1970; (contributor) *Women Poets of the West*, Boise State University, 1979; (contributor) *The West*, Doubleday, 1980; *Summer Range* (poetry), Dooryard Press, 1981; (contributor) *Westward the Women*, Doubleday, 1984. Contributor to *New York Times, Saturday Evening Post, Christian Science Monitor, Reader's Digest, Good Housekeeping,* and *Boys' Life*. Poet's column in *Chicago Sunday Tribune* and in other publications.

WORK IN PROGRESS: Shindig, a novel; a book of poems.

* * *

CURTIS, (Hubert) Arnold 1917-

PERSONAL: Born May 20, 1917, in London, England; son of Frank Hubert and Elizabeth Ethel (Ward) Curtis; married Almaria Daphne Wingfield Digby, March 9, 1948; children: Stephanie, Jill. *Education:* New College, Oxford, B.A., 1939, M.A., 1959. *Address:* P.O. Box 10, Limuru, Kenya.

CAREER: Chief of East Africa Mission, International Refugee Organization, 1947-50; staff member, British Council for Aid to Refugees, 1951; Kenya Ministry of Education, Nairobi, 1952-73, secretary, Institute of Education, 1964-66, inspector of teacher education, 1966-73. *Wartime service:* Friends Ambulance Unit, 1940-44; United Nations Relief and Rehabilitation Administration, Middle East and Greece, 1944-47.

WRITINGS: Africa (youth book), Oxford University Press, 1969; *Conversation Practice*, East Africa Publishing House, 1970; *Write Well* (junior composition textbook), Oxford University Press, 1975; (co-author) "New Peak" juvenile series, Oxford University Press, 1962-65; (co-author) "Pivot English Course" series, Longmans (Kenya), 1965-69; (editor) "Kenya Primary Geography" series, ten volumes, Evans Brothers Ltd. (London), 1977-81; (editor with Mrs. Elspeth Huxley) *Pioneers' Scrapbook*, Evans Brothers, Ltd. (London), 1980; "Know Your English" series, three volumes, East Africa Publishing House (Nairobi), 1983—.

BIOGRAPHICAL/CRITICAL SOURCES: Times Literary Supplement, June 26, 1969.

D

DAM, Kenneth W. 1932-

PERSONAL: Born August 10, 1932, in Marysville, Kan.; son of Oliver W. (a farmer) and Ida (Heupplesheuser) Dam; married Marcia Wachs (a college professor), June 7, 1962; children: Eliot, Charlotte. *Education:* University of Kansas, B.S., 1954; University of Chicago, J.D., 1957. *Home:* 5609 South Kenwood Ave., Chicago, Ill. 60637. *Office:* Office of the Deputy Secretary, Department of State, Washington D.C. 20520.

CAREER: U.S. Supreme Court, Washington, D.C., law clerk, 1957-58; Cravath, Swaine & Moore (law firm), New York, N.Y., associate, 1958-60; University of Chicago, Chicago, Ill., visiting assistant professor, 1960-61, associate professor, 1961-64, professor of law, 1964-71; U.S. Office of Management and the Budget, Washington, D.C., assistant director, 1971-73; U.S. Council on Economic Policy, Washington, D.C., executive director, 1973; University of Chicago, professor of law, 1974-76, Harold J. and Marion F. Green Professor of Law, 1976—, provost, 1980-82; U.S. Department of State, Washington, D.C., deputy secretary of state, 1982—. Member, Council on Foreign Relations; member of board of directors, Chicago Council on Foreign Relations. *Member:* American Bar Association, American Law Institute. *Awards, honors:* LL.D., New School for Social Research, 1983.

WRITINGS: (With Lawrence Krause) *The Treatment of Foreign Income,* Brookings Institution, 1964; *The GATT: Law and International Economic Organization,* University of Chicago Press, 1970; *Oil Resources: Who Gets What How?,* University of Chicago Press, 1976; (with George P. Shultz) *Economic Policy beyond the Headlines,* Stanford Alumni Association, 1977; *The Rules of the Game: Reform and Evolution in the International Monetary System,* University of Chicago Press, 1982. Contributor to law journals.

SIDELIGHTS: Kenneth W. Dam writes *CA* that he is "interested in the borderline between the legal system and the economic system." His area of expertise is international economy and diplomacy.

* * *

DANGERFIELD, Harlan
See PADGETT, Ron

DANIELS, Arlene Kaplan 1930-

PERSONAL: Born December 10, 1930, in New York, N.Y.; daughter of Jacob (a storekeeper) and Elizabeth (Rathstone) Kaplan; married Richard Rene Daniels (a hospital administrator), June 9, 1956. *Education:* University of California, Berkeley, B.A. (with honors), 1952, M.A., 1954, Ph.D., 1960. *Politics:* Democrat. *Religion:* Agnostic. *Office:* Department of Sociology, Northwestern University, Evanston, Ill. 60201.

CAREER: University of California, Berkeley, principal investigator for School of Public Health, 1957-58, instructor in speech, 1959-61; Mental Research Institute, Palo Alto, Calif., research associate, 1961-66; San Francisco State College (now University), San Francisco, Calif., associate professor of sociology, 1966-69; Scientific Analysis Corp., San Francisco, research associate, 1968-75; Northwestern University, Evanston, Ill., professor of sociology and director of program on women, 1974—. *Member:* American Sociological Association, Society for the Study of Social Problems.

AWARDS, HONORS: U.S. Army Research and Development Command grant, 1963-66; National Institute of Mental Health fellowship in law and psychiatry at School of Criminology, University of California, Berkeley, 1965-66; child health and human development grant, 1967-70; Social Science Research Council, faculty research award, 1970-71; Ford Foundation fellowship, 1975-76.

WRITINGS: (Contributor) Gideon Sjoberg, editor, *Politics, Ethics and Social Research,* Schenkman, 1967; (editor with Rachel Kahn-Hut) *Academics on the Line,* Jossey-Bass, 1970; (contributor) Tamotsu Shibutani, editor, *Human Nature and Collective Behavior,* Prentice-Hall, 1970; (contributor) Hans P. Dreitzle, editor, *Recent Trends in Sociology,* Macmillan, 1970; (contributor) Eliot Freidson and Judith Lorber, editors, *Medical Men and Their Work,* Atherton, 1971; *A Survey of Research Concerns on Women's Issues,* Association of American Colleges, 1975; (contributor) Marcia Millman and Rosabeth Kanter, editors, *Another Voice,* Doubleday, 1975; (editor with Gaye Tuchman and James Benet) *Hearth and Home,* Oxford University Press, 1978.

(Editor with Benet) *Education: Straitjacket or Opportunity?,* Transaction Books, 1980; (editor with Kahn-Hut) *Women and Work,* Oxford University Press, 1980; (editor with Alice Cook and Val Lorwin) *Women and Trade Unions in Eleven Indus-*

trialized Countries, Temple, 1984. Contributor to psychiatry and sociology journals.

WORK IN PROGRESS: Invisible Careers: Women Leaders in the Volunteer World, for University of Chicago Press.

* * *

DANKY, James Philip 1947-

PERSONAL: Born October 3, 1947, in Los Angeles, Calif.; son of Philip Harper (a probation officer) and Elizabeth (an elementary school principal; maiden name, James) Danky; married second wife, Christine Schelshorn, August 13, 1981; children: Matthew Philip. *Education:* Ripon College, A.B., 1970; University of Wisconsin—Madison, M.A.L.S., 1973. *Religion:* None. *Residence:* Stoughton, Wis. *Office:* State Historical Society of Wisconsin, 816 State St., Madison, Wis. 53706.

CAREER: Department of Public Social Services of Los Angeles County, Los Angeles, Calif., welfare clerk, 1970-71; Department of Social Services of Jefferson County, Jefferson, Wis., social worker, 1971-72; State Historical Society of Wisconsin, Madison, order librarian, 1973-76, newspapers and periodicals librarian, 1976—. *Member:* American Library Association, American Historical Association, State Historical Society of Wisconsin.

WRITINGS: Undergrounds: A Union List of Alternative Periodicals in Libraries of the United States and Canada, State Historical Society of Wisconsin, 1974; (editor with Eleanor McKay) *Women's History: Resources of the State Historical Society of Wisconsin,* State Historical Society of Wisconsin, 1975, 4th edition, 1982; (compiler with Neil Strache) *Hispanic Americans in the United States: A Union List of Periodicals and Newspapers Held by the Library of the State Historical Society of Wisconsin and the Libraries of the University of Wisconsin—Madison,* State Historical Society of Wisconsin, 1979; (compiler with Strache, Maureen E. Hady, Susan Bryl, and Erwin Welsh) *Black Periodicals and Newspapers: A Union List of Holdings in Libraries of the University of Wisconsin and the Library of the State Historical Society of Wisconsin,* second revised edition, State Historical Society of Wisconsin, 1979; (compiler with Hady) *Asian American Periodicals and Newspapers: A Union List of Holdings in the Library of the State Historical Society of Wisconsin and the Libraries of the University of Wisconsin—Madison,* State Historical Society of Wisconsin, 1979; (editor with Elliott Shore) *Alternative Materials in Libraries: A Handbook,* Temple University Libraries, 1979, revised and enlarged edition, Scarecrow, 1982; *Genealogical Research: An Introduction to the Resources of the State Historical Society of Wisconsin,* State Historical Society of Wisconsin, 1979.

(Compiler) *Women's Periodicals and Newspapers from the Eighteenth Century to 1981: A Union List of the Holdings of Madison, Wisconsin Libraries,* G. K. Hall, 1982; (editor) *Index to Wisconsin Native American Periodicals, 1897-1981,* Greenwood Press, 1983; (editor) *Native American Periodicals and Newspapers, 1828-1982: Bibliography, Publishing Record, and Holdings,* Greenwood Press, 1983; (editor with Sanford Berman) *Alternative Library Literature: A Biennial Anthology,* Oryx, 1984.

Editor of proceedings of Conference on Book Publishing in Wisconsin, 1977, Conference on Periodical Publishing in Wisconsin, 1978, and Conference on the Native American Press in Wisconsin and the Nation, 1982. Co-editor of column "Wisconsin History Checklist" in *Wisconsin Magazine of History,* 1973-74 and 1976-77; author of column "Alternative Periodicals" in *Wilson Library Bulletin,* 1975-77. Editor of *Collectors' Network News,* 1977-78.

WORK IN PROGRESS: A union list of labor union periodicals in the United States and Canada; research on librarians as advocates; an analytical history of publishing in Wisconsin; research on periodical publishing as an indication of social tension.

SIDELIGHTS: James Philip Danky writes: "In writing and editing, my emphasis has been to create works that are useful in promoting an alternative or progressive viewpoint of the events in the world. In suggesting that a wide range of materials and ideas promotes social diversity, I am attempting to blend politics, culture, and library science."

AVOCATIONAL INTERESTS: Raising pigs.

* * *

DAVEY, Gilbert (Walter) 1913-

PERSONAL: Born June 7, 1913, in London, England; son of Walter (a director of an advertising company) and Ethel (Franklin) Davey; married Angela Gross, October 7, 1939; children: Claire. *Education:* Attended Stationers' Company's School. *Religion:* Church of England. *Home:* 54 Cumberland House, St. Mary's Court, Peterborough, Cambridgeshire PE1 1UN, England.

CAREER: Worked in insurance field prior to World War II, including a period with Lloyd's of London; Pearl Assurance Co., Ltd., West End Branch, London, England, assistant branch manager, 1947-67, assistant manager of North London region, 1967-77, also assistant manager of general branch accounts, Peterborough division of head office. Auxiliary Fire Service, Watford, Hertfordshire, England, commandant, 1939-41; Chief Regional Fire Officer, Cambridge, England, staff officer, 1941-44. *Military service:* British Army, 1943-47; served on staff of military governor, Berlin, Germany; became major.

WRITINGS—Edited by Jack Cox: *Fun with Radio,* Edmund Ward, 1957, revised edition, 1978; *Fun with Short Waves,* Edmund Ward, 1960, revised edition published as *Fun with Short Wave Radio,* 1979; *Fun with Electronics,* Edmund Ward, 1962, revised edition, Kaye & Ward, 1972; *Fun with Transistors,* Edmund Ward, 1964, revised edition, Kaye & Ward, 1971; *Fun with Hi-Fi,* Kaye & Ward, 1973; *Fun with Silicon Chips in Modern Radio,* Kaye & Ward, 1981. Radio correspondent, *Boy's Own Paper,* 1946-67; contributor to *Boy's Own Annual, Practical Wireless,* and other periodicals.

WORK IN PROGRESS: An autobiographical history of radio receiver designs for home construction in the United Kingdom.

* * *

DAVID, Anne 1924-

PERSONAL: Born July 4, 1924, in New York, N.Y.; daughter of William (a printer) and Florence (Korn) Rauchman; married Harold (Hal) David (a songwriter and lyricist), December 24, 1946; children: James Andrew, Craig Warren. *Education:* New York University, B.E., 1945. *Home:* 24 West 55th St., New York, N.Y. 10019. *Office:* Budget and Credit Counseling Service, New York, N.Y.

CAREER: Elementary teacher in public schools in Baldwin, N.Y., 1945-48, and Valley Stream, N.Y., 1949; Roslyn Public

Schools, Roslyn, N.Y., volunteer worker as chairman of various parent groups, teacher, tutor of disadvantaged children, beginning 1956, chairman of legislation for Coordinated Council, 1970-71; budget counselor for Nassau County Family Service Association, 1976-79, and Budget and Credit Counseling Service, 1979—. Member of board of directors, League of Women Voters, Roslyn, 1961-69; Commissioner to Commemorate U.N. Day, Roslyn Village Government, 1968-70. Organizer of community service programs for high school seniors, Roslyn.

WRITINGS—Published by Cornerstone Library: *A Guide to Volunteer Services: Help Yourself by Helping Others,* 1970; *Get out and Stay out of Debt,* 1981. Editor of local news column for Roslyn Public Schools Coordinated Council, 1965-69.

WORK IN PROGRESS: Marriage in America, an examination of long-term relationships.

SIDELIGHTS: Anne David told *CA:* "In 1971, based on research done for *A Guide to Volunteer Services,* I opened a clearinghouse for volunteers and agencies utilizing the services of volunteers. We operated this successful community service (never a fee) as volunteers, by volunteers, for volunteers until 1976, having placed more than 1,500 people in more than 300 agencies throughout Nassau County, N.Y."

* * *

DAVIES, Hunter 1936-
(Atticus)

PERSONAL: Born January 7, 1936, in Renfrew, Scotland; son of John Hunter and Marion (Brechin) Davies; married Margaret Forster (a writer), June 11, 1960; children: Caitlin, Jake, Flora. *Education:* University of Durham, B.A., 1957. *Home:* 11 Boscastle Rd., London NW5, England. *Office: Punch,* 27 Tudor St., London EC4, England.

CAREER: Writer. *Evening Chronicle,* Manchester, England, reporter, 1958-60; *Sunday Times,* London, England, reporter, 1960, columnist under pseudonym Atticus, 1961-67; editor of *Colour* magazine, 1975-77; *Punch,* London, columnist, 1979—.

WRITINGS: Here We Go, Round the Mulberry Bush (novel), Heinemann, 1965, Little, Brown, 1966; (editor) *The New "London Spy": A Discreet Guide to the City's Pleasures* (nonfiction), Blond, 1966, David White, 1967; *The Other Half* (nonfiction), Heinemann, 1966, published as *The Other Halves,* Stein & Day, 1968; *The Beatles: The Authorized Biography,* McGraw-Hill, 1968.

(Editor and contributor with seventeen others) *I Knew Daisy Smuten* (communal novel), Coward, 1970; *The Rise and Fall of Jake Sullivan* (novel), Little, Brown, 1970; *A Very Loving Couple* (novel), Weidenfeld & Nicolson, 1971; *The Glory Game,* Weidenfeld & Nicolson, 1972, St. Martin's, 1973; *Body Charge,* Sphere, 1974; *A Walk along the Wall,* Weidenfeld & Nicolson, 1974; *George Stephenson* (biography), Weidenfeld & Nicolson, 1975; *The Creighton Report,* Hamish Hamilton, 1976; *A Walk Around the Lakes,* Weidenfeld & Nicolson, 1979.

William Wordsworth: A Biography, Atheneum, 1981; *Father's Day,* Weidenfeld & Nicolson, 1981; *The Grades: The First Family of British Entertainment,* Weidenfeld & Nicolson, 1981; *A Walk along the Tracks,* Weidenfeld & Nicolson, 1982; *England!,* Futura, 1982; *Great Britain: A Celebration,* Hamish Hamilton, 1982; *Flossie Teacake's Fur Coat,* Bodley Head, 1982; *British Book of Lists,* Hamlyn, 1982.

MEDIA ADAPTATIONS: Here We Go, Round the Mulberry Bush and *The Rise and Fall of Jake Sullivan* have been filmed.

BIOGRAPHICAL/CRITICAL SOURCES: Commentary, April, 1969; *Times Literary Supplement,* July 23, 1970; *New York Times Book Review,* February 24, 1974, December 14, 1980; *New York Times,* October 29, 1980; *Washington Post,* November 13, 1980.

* * *

DAVIS, Robert Murray 1934-

PERSONAL: Born September 4, 1934, in Lyons, Kan.; son of Matthew Cary (a dealer) and Elizabeth (Murray) Davis; married Barbara Hillyer, December 28, 1958 (divorced, April 3, 1981); children: Megan, Jennifer, John. *Education:* Rockhurst College, B.S., 1955; University of Kansas, M.A., 1958; University of Wisconsin, Ph.D., 1964. *Office:* Department of English, University of Oklahoma, 760 Van Vleet, Norman, Okla. 73019.

CAREER: Loyola University, Chicago, Ill., assistant professor of English, 1962-65; University of California, Santa Barbara, assistant professor of English, 1965-67; University of Oklahoma, Norman, 1967—, currently professor of English. Visiting professor, University of New Brunswick, St. John, summer, 1981; Fulbright lecturer, Eotvos University, Budapest, 1981; visiting lecturer, University of Paris, spring, 1983; United States Information Service lecturer in France, Yugoslavia, Hungary, and Germany, spring, 1983. *Member:* Modern Language Association of America, South Central Modern Language Association. *Awards, honors:* National Endowment for the Humanities summer stipend, 1969.

WRITINGS: (Editor) *The Novel: Modern Essays in Criticism,* Prentice-Hall, 1969; (editor) *Evelyn Waugh,* B. Herder, 1969; (editor) *Steinbeck,* Prentice-Hall, 1972; (editor) *Modern British Short Novels,* Scott, Foresman, 1972; (with others) *Evelyn Waugh: A Checklist of Primary and Secondary Material,* Whitston Publishing, 1972; (with others) *Donald Barthelme: A Bibliography,* Archon, 1977; *A Catalogue of the Evelyn Waugh Collection,* Whitson, 1981; *Evelyn Waugh, Writer,* Pilgrim, 1981; *A Bibliography of Evelyn Waugh,* Whitson, in press. Contributor to scholarly journals. Associate editor, *Genre.*

WORK IN PROGRESS: A book on the use of Western motifs in avant-garde fiction; an edition of Evelyn Waugh's juvenilia; a selection of Owen Wister's nonfiction; a collection of bibliographical essays.

BIOGRAPHICAL/CRITICAL SOURCES: Times Literary Supplement, August 21, 1981, July 9, 1982.

* * *

DAWSON, Mildred A(gnes) 1897-

PERSONAL: Born June 4, 1897; daughter of Henry and Emma Margaret (Fuller) Dawson. *Education:* Iowa State Teachers College (now University of Northern Iowa), B.A. and Critic Teacher Diploma, 1922; University of Chicago, M.A., 1928; New York University, Ed.D., 1936.

CAREER: Teacher in Sumner, Iowa, 1916-19, 1924-25; Indiana Normal School (now Indiana University of Pennsylvania), Indiana, Pa., critic teacher, 1922-24; Iowa State Teachers College (now University of Northern Iowa), Cedar Falls, teacher of education, 1925-27; University of Chicago, Chicago, Ill., research assistant in educational psychology, 1928-29; University of Wyoming, Laramie, assistant professor of education and chairman of department, 1929-35; University of Georgia, Athens, associate professor and chairman of department, 1936-37; University of Tennessee, Knoxville, professor of education and chairman of department, 1937-45; F. A. Owen Publishing Co., Dansville, N.Y., books editor, 1945-47; director of elementary education, Kingston, N.Y., 1947-49; professor of education at State Teachers College (now State University of New York College at Fredonia), 1949-52, and Appalachian State Teachers College (now Appalachian State University), Boone, N.C., 1952-54; Sacramento State College (now California State University, Sacramento), Sacramento, Calif., professor of education and children's literature, 1954-65, professor emeritus, 1965—; writer on educational subjects, 1965—.

MEMBER: International Reading Association (president), National Council of Teachers of English (past chairman of elementary section), National Conference on Research in English (past president), National Society for the Study of Education, American Association of University Women, League of Women Voters, Delta Kappa Gamma (past state president), Pi Lambda Theta, Kappa Delta Pi.

WRITINGS: (With F. H. Dingee) *Directing Learning in the Language Arts*, Burgess, 1942, revised edition, 1948; (with J. M. Miller and others) *Language for Daily Use*, Grades 3-6, World Book, 1948, reprinted, Harcourt, 1973; *Language Teaching in Grades 1 and 2*, World Book, 1949, revised edition, 1957; (with Miller and others) *Language for Daily Use*, Grades 7-8, World Book, 1949-50; *Teaching Language in the Grades*, World Book, 1951; (with Bonnie Scales) *Language for Daily Use*, Grade 2, World Book, 1952; (with Marian Zollinger) *Guiding Language Learning*, World Book, 1957, 2nd edition (with Zollinger and Ardell Elwell), Harcourt, 1963; (with Henry A. Bamman) *Fundamentals of Basic Reading Instruction*, Longmans, Green, 1959, 3rd edition, McKay, 1973; (with F. H. Dingee) *Children Learn the Language Arts*, Burgess, 1959.

(Editor with M. A. Choate) *How to Help a Child Appreciate Poetry: One Hundred Poems to Express with Voice and Action*, Fearon, 1960; (with Bamman and R. J. Whitehead) *Oral Interpretation of Children's Literature*, W. C. Brown, 1964; (editor) *Children, Books, and Reading*, International Reading Association, 1964; *Let's Talk and Write*, Harcourt, 1965; (with G. Newman) *Language Teaching in Kindergarten and the Early Primary Grades*, Harcourt, 1966; (with others) *Adventures in Reading*, Benefic, 1967; (compiler) *Developing High School Reading Programs*, International Reading Association, 1967; (with Newman) *Oral Reading and Linguistics*, Benefic, 1969; (compiler) *Teaching Word Recognition Skills*, International Reading Association, 1970; (with Herman F. Benthul) *Fun Sounds*, Benefic, 1973; (with Benthul) *Gay Sounds*, Benefic, 1973; (contributor) Bamman, editor, *Five Words Long*, 3rd edition (Dawson was not associated with previous editions), Addison-Wesley, 1978; (with Alberta Collins) *Alphabet Soup*, revised edition (Dawson was not associated with previous edition), Addison-Wesley, 1978; (contributor) Bamman, editor, *Six Impossible Things*, revised edition (Dawson was not associated with previous edition), Addison-Wesley, 1978.

Also author, with Bamman, of "Target" reading cassette series, Addison-Wesley, 1972. Author of pamphlet on reading skills, and editor of a series of instructor pamphlets published by F. A. Owen, 1946-47. Contributor to "Kaleidoscope Readers" series and "Cornerstone Readers" series, both published by Addison-Wesley. Contributor to education publications.

AVOCATIONAL INTERESTS: Gardening, bird lore, palmistry, reading, bridge, spectator sports, fishing.†

* * *

DEARDEN, James S(hackley) 1931-

PERSONAL: Born August 9, 1931, in Barrow-in-Furness, England; son of John Clifford (a company director) and Polly (Shackley) Dearden; married Jillian Roma Cheverton, September 20, 1958; children: Sarah Jane. *Education:* Attended Bembridge School, 1945-49. *Politics:* Conservative. *Religion:* Church of England. *Home:* Hillway House, Bembridge, Isle of Wight, England. *Office:* Ruskin Galleries, Bembridge School, Isle of Wight, England.

CAREER: Tantivy Press (publishers), London, England, advertising manager, 1952-57; Bembridge School, Isle of Wight, England, curator of Ruskin Galleries, 1957—. Curator of Ruskin Collection at Brantwood, Coniston, England. *Military service:* British Army, 1949-51; became second lieutenant. British Army Emergency Reserve, 1951-60; became captain. *Member:* Bibliographical Society, Printing Historical Society, Ruskin Society (secretary), Turner Society, Old Bembridgians Association (president), Isle of Wight Foot Beagles. *Awards, honors:* Named Companion of the Guild of St. George.

WRITINGS: Catalogue of the Pictures by John Ruskin and Other Artists at Brantwood, Coniston, Education Trust, 1960; *Ruskin Association Books* (catalog of books from Ruskin's library now in Ruskin Galleries), Yellowsands Press, 1962; (editor) *The Professor: Arthur Severn's Memoir of John Ruskin*, Allen & Unwin, 1967; *Books from Ruskin's Library* (now in collection at Brantwood, Coniston), Yellowsands Press, 1967; *A Short History of Brantwood*, Association for Liberal Education, 1967, 2nd edition, 1974.

(Editor) John Ruskin, *Iteriad*, Graham, 1969; *Facets of Ruskin*, Skilton, 1970; (with K. G. Thorne) *Ruskin and Coniston*, Covent Garden Press, 1971; *John Ruskin*, Shire Publications, 1973, 2nd edition, Brantwood Trust, 1981; *Turner's Isle of Wight Sketchbook*, Hunnyhill Publications, 1979; (editor) *Sale and Exhibition Catalogues Relating to John Ruskin, His Work and His Collection*, Oxford Microfilm Publications, 1981; (contributor) R. E. Rhodes and D. I. Janik, editors, *Studies in Ruskin*, Ohio University Press, 1982.

General editor of "Ruskin Research" series. Contributor of articles representing original research on Ruskin to *The Library, Apollo, Book Collector, Connoisseur*, and other journals. Editor of *Ruskin Newsletter*, 1969—.

WORK IN PROGRESS: Portraits of John Ruskin; a catalog of Ruskin's library; an international check-list of locations of all Ruskin material; a biography of Thomas Sunderland, 1744-1823.

SIDELIGHTS: James S. Dearden told *CA:* "As curator of the world's largest Ruskin collection, at Bembridge and Brantwood, Coniston, I am interested in all aspects of Ruskin studies, with a particular emphasis on biographical and bibliographical research. The care of the Ruskin collection and the collaboration with other scholars studying Ruskin are my profession and hobby. Bembridge School has its own private printing press, of which I am in charge. This involves a certain amount of teaching. My hobbies include the collecting of books relating to the English Lake District, bibliography, printing history, and illuminated manuscripts, and collecting eighteenth-century English watercolors. My vocation and hobbies all sprang from an original interest in the local history of my own village in north Lancashire."

* * *

d'EASUM, Cedric (Godfrey) 1907-
(Dick d'Easum)

PERSONAL: Born April 29, 1907, in Canada; came to the United States in 1910, naturalized citizen; son of Basil C. (a priest) and Ethel A. (Stacey) d'Easum; married Mary E. Williamson, June 18, 1935. *Education:* University of Idaho, B.A., 1930; also attended Colorado State University and University of Wyoming. *Politics:* Republican. *Religion:* Episcopalian. *Home and office:* 1086 Krall St., Boise, Idaho 83702.

CAREER: Idaho Statesman, Boise, reporter and author of column, "Two Cents Worth," 1932-43; State Fish and Game Department, Boise, news director, 1943-49; University of Idaho, Extension Service, Boise, editor, 1949-72; writer, 1972—. Member of Boise Green Belt Committee, 1974—. *Military service:* U.S. National Guard, 1926-29. U.S. Army Reserve, Infantry, 1930-40. *Member:* Kiwanis (president, 1972), Masons (state grand historian, 1969), Elks.

WRITINGS—All under name Dick d'Easum: *Fragments of Villainy* (essays), Caxton, 1959; *Sawtooth Tales,* Caxton, 1977; *Dowager of Discipline: The Life of Dean of Women, Permeal French,* University Press of Idaho, 1981; (with George L. Yost) *Idaho: The Fruitful Land,* Symms-York, 1981; *The Idanha: Guests and Ghosts of an Historic Idaho Inn,* Caxton, 1984. Author of weekly column in *Idaho Statesman,* 1943-76.

WORK IN PROGRESS: A novel of cattle rustling in early Idaho; a biography, with Walter Sparks, of Jack Simplot, potato king.

* * *

d'EASUM, Dick
See d'EASUM, Cedric (Godfrey)

* * *

de BETANCOURT, Cressy
See DOBKIN De RIOS, Marlene

* * *

DEBRECZENY, Paul 1932-

PERSONAL: Surname is pronounced *Deb*-bret-sen-ee; born February 16, 1932, in Budapest, Hungary; came to United States in 1960, naturalized in 1966; son of Zsigmond (a statistician) and Margit (Csanady) Debreczeny; married Gillian M. Butterworth, October 30, 1959; children: Louise, Martin. *Education:* Eotvos University of Budapest, B.A. in Russian language and literature, 1953, B.A. in Hungarian language and literature, 1955; University of London, Ph.D., 1960. *Politics:* Democrat. *Home:* 304 Hoot Owl Lane, Chapel Hill, N.C. 27514. *Office:* Department of Slavic Languages, University of North Carolina, Chapel Hill, N.C. 27514.

CAREER: Institute of Literature, Hungarian Academy of Sciences, Budapest, Hungary, research fellow, 1955-56; Pergamon Press, Oxford, England, translation editor, 1959-60; Tulane University, New Orleans, La., assistant professor, 1960-66, associate professor of Russian, 1966-67; University of North Carolina at Chapel Hill, associate professor, 1967-74, professor, 1974-83, alumni distinguished professor of Russian literature, 1983—, chairman of department, 1974-79, chairman of Humanities Division, 1983—. *Member:* Modern Language Association of America, American Association of Teachers of Slavic and East European Languages, American Association for the Advancement of Slavic Studies. *Awards, honors:* Summer research grants from American Philosophical Society, Tulane University, and University of North Carolina; awarded key to city of New Orleans, 1967; International Research and Exchanges Board research grants, 1973, 1982; National Endowment for the Humanities research grant, 1979-80.

WRITINGS: Nikolay Gogol and His Contemporary Critics, American Philosophical Society, 1966; (editor and translator with Jesse Zeldin) *Literature and National Identity: Nineteenth-Century Russian Critical Essays,* University of Nebraska Press, 1970; (editor with Thomas Eekman) *Chekhov's Art of Writing: A Collection of Critical Essays,* Slavica, 1977; *Temptations of the Past* (novel), Hermitage, 1982; (editor and translator) *Alexander Pushkin: Complete Prose Fiction,* Stanford University Press, 1983; *The Other Pushkin: A Study of Alexander Pushkin's Prose Fiction,* Stanford University Press, 1983; (editor) *American Contributions to the Ninth International Congress of Slavists,* Volume II, Slavica, 1983. Guest editor for two special issues on Pushkin, *Canadian-American Slavic Studies,* summer, 1976, spring, 1977, and for a special issue on Turgenev, summer, 1983.

WORK IN PROGRESS: The Image of Alexander Pushkin in Russian Cultural Consciousness.

* * *

De GREGORI, Thomas R(oger) 1935-

PERSONAL: Born May 5, 1935, in Cleveland, Ohio; son of James V. (an engineer) and Mary Anne (Tambascio) De Gregori; married Gayle Sutherland, October 22, 1960; children: Alice, James, Roger. *Education:* University of New Mexico, B.A., 1959, M.A., 1960; University of Texas, Ph.D., 1965. *Politics:* Democrat. *Religion:* None. *Home:* 2327 Goldsmith, Houston, Tex. 77030. *Office:* Department of Economics, University of Houston, Houston, Tex. 77004.

CAREER: University of Khartoum, Khartoum, Sudan, visiting lecturer, 1962-63; Case Institute of Technology (now Case Western Reserve University), Cleveland, Ohio, assistant professor of economics, 1963-67; University of Houston, Houston, Tex., associate professor, 1967-75, professor of economics, 1975—, chairman of department, 1969-71, research associate of Institute for International Business Analysis, 1982—. Adjunct professor, Center for International Studies, St. Thomas University, 1981—. Executive associate of Denver Research Institute, 1978—. Lecturer and consultant on technology and economic development to numerous countries, including India, Pakistan, Nepal, Thailand, and Tanzania. Also consultant to several U.S. government agencies. *Military service:* U.S. Marine Corps Reserve. *Member:* American Economic Association, Association for Evolutionary Economics (member of board of directors, 1981—), Society for the History of Technology, African Studies Association, Economic History Association.

WRITINGS: (With Oriol Pi-Sunyer) *Economic Development: The Cultural Context,* Wiley, 1969; *Technology and the Economic Development of the Tropical African Frontier,* Press of Case Western Reserve University, 1969; *Technology and Economic Change: Essays and Inquiries,* McLouglin Associates, 1977.

Contributor: Z. A. Konczacki and J. M. Konczacki, editors, *The Economic History of Tropical Africa,* Frank Cass, 1978; Richard Weekes, editor, *Ethnographic Survey of the Muslim World,* Greenwood Press, 1978, 2nd edition, in press; Louis J. Rodriguez, editor, *The Dynamics of Growth: An Economic Profile of Texas,* Madrona Press, 1978; Warren J. Samuels, editor, *The Economy as a System of Power,* Transaction Books, 1979; John Q. Adams, editor, *Institutional Economics: Contributions to the Development of Holistic Economics,* Martinus Nijhoff, 1980.

Also author of monograph, *U.S. Dependence on Southern African Minerals.* Author with June Ferrill of four-act play, "Only Connect." Scriptwriter of video tape programs, "Transportation," "The Family," "The Role of Government in the Lives of Citizens," and "Ethical Complications of Genetic Counseling." Contributor of numerous articles and book reviews to *Journal of Economic Issues, Technology and Culture, Journal of Developing Areas, Administration and Society, Topic: A Journal of the Liberal Arts, American Journal of Economics and Sociology, Forum, Journal of Economic History, Growth and Change: A Journal of Regional Development,* and other journals. Member of editorial board of *Journal of the American Studies Association of Texas, 1975-76,* and *Journal of Economic Issues,* 1976-80.

WORK IN PROGRESS: Science, Technology and the Process of Development.

SIDELIGHTS: Thomas R. De Gregori's book, *Technology and the Economic Development of the Tropical African Frontier,* has been widely and favorably reviewed in scholarly journals. Ian Parker calls the book "a powerful work of synthesis, which integrates a vast amount of primary and secondary source material and brings it imaginatively to bear on some of the more challenging problems of African economic development. The wide-ranging bibliography in De Gregori's study is 87 pages in length, and the text itself displays in abundance the rare and valuable scholarly gift of a disciplined eclecticism."

Michael T. Pledge finds the book "an important addition to the growing literature on Africa and on economic development. It is important for economic development, not because of its departure from traditional analysis, but because of its scholarly investigation of African development and its insights into the process of development in general. Its value is enhanced by its interdisciplinary presentation of the topic and can be profitably read by individuals in many different disciplines."

BIOGRAPHICAL/CRITICAL SOURCES: Journal of Developing Areas, Volume V, number 2, January, 1971; *World Affairs Bulletin,* Volume V, number 6, March, 1971; *Professional Geographer,* Volume XXIII, number 2, April, 1971; *Technology and Culture,* Volume XII, number 2, April, 1971; *American Anthropologists,* Volume LXXIII, number 4, August, 1971; *Journal of Modern African Studies,* Volume IX, number 3, October, 1971; *Political Science Quarterly,* Volume LXXXVII, number 1, March, 1972; *American Political Science Review,* Volume LXVI, number 2, June, 1972; *Agricultural History,* Volume XLVI, number 4, October, 1972; *Economic Development and Cultural Change,* Volume XXI, number 2, January, 1973; *Africa Today,* Volume XX, number 4, fall, 1973.

* * *

**de LANTAGNE, Cecile
See CLOUTIER-WOJCIECHOWSKA, Cecile**

DELIUS, Anthony (Ronald St. Martin) 1916-

PERSONAL: Born June 11, 1916, in Simonstown, South Africa; son of Edwin St. Martin (an officer in the Royal Navy) and Mignonne (Elliott) Delius; married Christina Truter, August, 1941; children: Christonie (daughter), Peter Nicholas. *Education:* Rhodes University, B.A., 1938. *Address:* 30 Graemesdyke Ave., London SW14 7BJ, England.

CAREER: Saturday Post (now *Evening Post*), Port Elizabeth, Cape Province, South Africa, co-founder, 1947, editor and political correspondent, 1947-50; *Cape Times,* Cape Town, South Africa, parliamentary correspondent, 1951-54, 1958-67; British Broadcasting Corp., Africa Service, London, England, writer, 1968-77; free-lance writer, 1977—. *Military service:* South African Directorate of Military Intelligence, 1940-45; became captain. *Awards, honors:* South African Poetry Prize, 1960; Central News Agency Ltd. award (South Africa), for *Border.*

WRITINGS: Young Traveller in South Africa, Phoenix House, 1947, 2nd revised edition, 1959; *The Unknown Border* (poems), Balkema, 1954; *The Long Way Round* (travel), Timmins, 1956; *The Last Division* (satirical verse), Human & Rousseau, 1959; *The Fall: A Play about Rhodes,* Human & Rousseau, 1960; *A Corner of the World: Thirty-Four Poems,* Human & Rousseau, 1962; *The Day Natal Took Off* (prose satire), Human & Rousseau, 1963; *Black South-Easter* (verse), New Coin, 1966; *Border* (novel), David Philip, 1976. Also author of "Upsurge in Africa" included in the Canadian Institute of International Affairs "Behind the Headlines" series, 1960. Contributor to *New Yorker, Reporter, Washington Post, Encounter, Guardian,* and other magazines and newspapers. Former co-editor, *Standpunte* (Cape Town); member of editorial board, *Contrast* magazine (Cape Town), beginning 1962.

SIDELIGHTS: A collection of Anthony Delius's manuscripts is housed in Rhodes University, Grahamstown, South Africa.†

* * *

DEMARET, Pierre 1943-

PERSONAL: Born October 24, 1943, in Algeria; son of Pierre and Suzette (Gornes) Demaret. *Politics:* Liberal. *Religion:* None. *Home:* 61 Avenue Philippe Auguste, Paris 11, France 75011.

CAREER: Journalist in Paris, 1966-74; free-lance writer, 1974—.

WRITINGS: Guide Solar des Pieds-Noirs, Solar, 1972; (with Jean Mabire) *La Brigade Frankreich,* Fayard, 1973; (with Christian Plume) *Objectif de Gaulle,* Laffont, 1973, translation by Richard Barry published as *Target de Gaulle: The Thirty-One Attempts to Assassinate the General,* Secker & Warburg, 1974, published as *Target de Gaulle: The True Story of the Thirty-One Attempts on the Life of the French President,* Dial, 1975; (compiler) Pierre Rostaing, *Le Prix d'un Serment, 1941-1945: Des Plaines de Russie a l'enfer de Berlin,* Table Ronde, 1975; (editor with Christian Plume) Jacques Bonny, *Mon pere, l'inspecteur Bonny,* Laffont, 1975; (with Jean Michel Charlier) *Hoover: La main de fer qui a tenu six presidents Americains,* Laffont, 1976; *Borghese, le prince noir des hommes-tor-pilles,* Laffont, 1977; (editor) *Patents, Territorial Restrictions and European Economic Community Law,* Verlag Chemie, 1978. Also author of television scripts, "Les Dossiers noirs" and "Le Prince Borghese et les hommes Terpilles."

WORK IN PROGRESS: *Usiage: Vichy et la Resistance,* for Table Ronde.†

* * *

DEMURA, Fumio 1940-

PERSONAL: Born September 15, 1940, in Yokohama, Japan; son of Shitoshi and Masu (Kawashima) Demura. *Education:* Attended Nihon University. *Home:* 901 East 19th St., Santa Ana, Calif. 91706. *Office:* 1429 North Bristol St., Santa Ana, Calif. 91706.

CAREER: Karate instructor. Writer. *Awards, honors:* Named All Japan Karate Champion, 1961 and 1962; elected to Black Belt Hall of Fame, 1969; Golden Fist award, 1974.

WRITINGS—All published by O'Hara Publications: *Shito-ryn Karate,* 1971; *Nunchaku: Karate Weapon of Self-Defense,* 1971; *Sai: Karate Weapon of Self-Defense,* 1974; (with John G. Allee) *Bo: Karate Weapon of Self-Defense,* 1976; (with Dan Ivan) *Advanced Nunchaku,* 1976; (with Ivan) *Street Survival: A Practical Guide to Self-Defense,* 1979; *Tonfa: Karate Weapon of Self-Defense,* 1982.†

* * *

DENIS, Julio
See CORTAZAR, Julio

* * *

DENVER, Rod
See EDSON, J(ohn) T(homas)

* * *

DENZIN, Norman K(ent) 1941-

PERSONAL: Born March 24, 1941, in Iowa City, Iowa; son of Kenneth F. (a foreman) and Betty (Townsley) Denzin; married Evelyn K. Hurlbut, February 1, 1963 (divorced); children: Johanna, Rachel. *Education:* University of Iowa, A.B., 1963, Ph.D., 1966. *Home:* 607 South New St., Champaign, Ill. 61820. *Office:* Department of Sociology, University of Illinois, Urbana, Ill. 61801.

CAREER: University of Illinois at Urbana-Champaign, assistant professor of sociology, 1966-69; University of California, Berkeley, assistant professor of sociology, 1969-71; University of Illinois at Urbana-Champaign, associate professor, 1971-73, professor of sociology, 1973-80, professor of criticism, interpretive theory, and sociology, 1981—. Consulting sociologist, Federal Offenders Rehabilitation Project, Seattle, Wash., 1967-68. Referee on grant applications, National Foundation on the Arts and Humanities, 1970. *Member:* International Sociological Association (secretary of biography and society research group, 1982—), American Sociological Association (secretary-treasurer of social psychology section, 1978-80), American Anthropological Association, American Psychological Association, American Association for Public Opinion Research, Society for the Study of Symbolic Interaction (vice-president, 1976-78), Society for the Sociological Study of Social Problems, Society for the Psychological Study of Social Issues, Society for the Study of Applied Anthropology, Pacific Sociological Society, Midwest Sociological Society.

WRITINGS: (Editor and contributor with Stephen P. Spitzer) *The Mental Patient: Studies in the Sociology of Deviance,* McGraw, 1968.

The Research Act: A Theoretical Introduction to Sociological Methods, Aldine, 1970, 2nd edition, McGraw, 1978; (contributor) Eliot Freidson and Janet Lobeser, editors, *Medical Men and Their Work,* Atherton, 1970; (Contributor) Anthony L. Guenther, editor, *Criminal Behavior and Social Systems: Contributions of American Society,* Rand McNally, 1970; (editor and contributor) *Sociological Methods: A Sourcebook,* Aldine, 1970, 2nd edition, McGraw, 1977; (editor and contributor) *The Values of Social Science,* Aldine, 1970, 2nd edition, Dutton, 1973; (with others) *Social Relationships,* Aldine, 1970; (contributor) Gregory P. Stone and Harvey A. Farberman, editors, *Social Psychology through Symbolic Interaction,* Ginn-Blaisdell, 1970; (contributor) Jack D. Douglas, editor, *Understanding Everyday Life,* Aldine, 1970; (contributor) Douglas, editor, *Deviance and Respectability: The Social Construction of Moral Meanings,* Basic Books, 1970; (contributor) Douglas, editor, *Situations and Structures: Introduction to Sociology,* Free Press, 1970; (editor) *Children and Their Caretakers,* Dutton, 1973.

(With Alfred R. Lindesmith and A. R. Strauss) *Social Psychology,* 4th edition (Denzin was not associated with previous editions), Dryden, 1975, 5th edition, 1982; (with Lindesmith and Strauss) *Readings in Social Psychology,* 2nd edition (Denzin was not associated with previous edition), Holt, 1975; *Childhood Socialization,* Jossey-Bass, 1977; (editor) *Studies in Symbolic Interaction: A Research Annual,* six volumes, Jai Press, 1978-84; *On Understanding Emotion,* Jossey-Bass, 1984.

Contributor to numerous journals, including *Social Forces, Journal of Health and Social Behavior, Mental Hygiene, Sociological Quarterly, Social Problems, American Sociological Review, American Sociologist, American Journal of Sociology, Newsociety, Pacific Sociological Review, Word, Quest,* and *Slavic Review.* Special issue editor, *Trans-action,* June-July, 1971; associate editor of *Sociological Quarterly,* 1972-82, *Urban Life,* 1972—, and *Contemporary Sociology* 1978-81; editorial referee, *American Journal of Sociology.*

WORK IN PROGRESS: *Studies in Interpretation; Interpreting the Lives of Ordinary People;* developing the conceptual and empirical foundations of a critical, interpretive point of view in the human disciplines.

SIDELIGHTS: Norman K. Denzin told *CA:* "[My] basic position is that human conduct can only be understood by grasping the historical perspectives, languages and points of view of those we study. Instrumental works have been by G. H. Mead, C. H. Cooley, H. Blumer, C. Peirce, W. James, J. Dewey, A. Smith, E. Husserl, M. Scheler, S. Freud, Karl Marx, Martin Heidegger, Jean-Paul Sartre, and Merlea-Ponty. [The] basic question guiding my work is 'How is meaning constructed and lived in the lives of ordinary people and how may we, as interpretive scholars, ground our understandings in the spoken prose of the people we study?' "

* * *

DESMOND, Robert W(illiam) 1900-

PERSONAL: Born July 31, 1900, in Milwaukee, Wis.; son of William John (in real estate) and Lillian Amy (Wilce) Desmond; married Dorothy Christian, 1927 (deceased); married Emily Virginia Wall, March 17, 1949; children: (first marriage) Richard S. (deceased); (second marriage) Christopher R., Carolyn V. *Education:* University of Wisconsin, Madison, A.B., 1922; School of International Studies, Geneva, Switzerland, certificate, 1929; University of Minnesota, M.A., 1930; London School of Economics and Political Science, London, Ph.D., 1936. *Home:* 314 Ricardo Pl., La Jolla, Calif. 92037.

CAREER: Free-lance writer. *Milwaukee Journal,* Milwaukee, Wis., reporter, rewriter, and on copydesk, 1922-25; *Miami Herald,* Miami, Fla., on copydesk and city desk, 1925-26; *New York Herald,* Paris edition, Paris, France, on copydesk, 1926-27; University of Michigan, Ann Arbor, instructor in journalism, 1927-28; University of Minnesota, Minneapolis, instructor, 1928-29, assistant professor of journalism, 1929-32; *Christian Science Monitor,* Boston, Mass., editorial writer, editor, associate editor, and news editor in London bureau, 1931, 1933-38; Northwestern University, Evanston, Ill., professor of journalism, 1938-39; University of California, Berkeley, professor of journalism, 1939-68, professor emeritus, 1968—, chairman of department, 1939-54, 1962-63, 1967; *San Diego Union,* San Diego, Calif., on copydesk and other departments, 1969-74.

Visiting professor at Stanford University, 1938; Fulbright lecturer at University of Amsterdam, 1955-56, University of Baghdad, 1965-66, and University of Teheran, 1968-69; lecturer at University of Strasbourg, 1956, 1958, 1960. Member of press staff at Williamstown Institute of Politics, 1932; on foreign desk at *New York Times,* 1941; worked for *San Francisco Examiner,* 1942, *Louisville Courier-Journal,* summer, 1955, North American Newspaper Alliance (NANA), 1955-56, *Hartford Times,* summer, 1964, and *San Francisco Chronicle,* 1968; academic director of foreign assignment tour in Europe, 1952; author of "Conceived in Liberty," a column syndicated by Copley News Service, 1971-75. News commentator on KSFO-Radio, 1941-42; member of UNESCO Commission on Technical Needs of the Mass Media, 1947, 1949; consultant to *Encyclopedia Americana* and International Press Institute. *Military service:* U.S. Army, Infantry, 1918, 1943-44; served in European theater; became major.

MEMBER: American Association of Schools and Departments of Journalism (president, 1947-48), Association for Education in Journalism, Torch Club (local president, 1976-77), Sigma Delta Chi (and its Key Club). *Awards, honors:* Citation from California State Senate, 1968; distinguished service award from University of Wisconsin, 1980; distinguished service awards from Sigma Delta Chi, 1981, and in 1982 for *Crisis and Conflict: World News Reporting between Two Wars, 1920-1940.*

WRITINGS: Newspaper Reference Methods, University of Minnesota Press, 1933; *Press and World Affairs,* Appleton, 1937; (with Francis James Brown, Charles Hodges, Joseph Slabey Roucek) *Contemporary World Politics,* Wiley, 1940, revised edition, 1941; *The Professional Training of Journalists* (brochure), UNESCO, 1949; *Les tendances de l'enseigement du journalisme aux Etats-Unis* (title means "Trends in the Teaching of Journalism in the United States"), Etudes de Press, 1959; *Professional Secrecy and the Journalist,* International Press Institute, 1962; *The Information Process: World News Reporting to the Twentieth Century,* University of Iowa Press, 1978; *Windows on the World: World News Reporting, 1900 to 1920,* University of Iowa Press, 1981; *Crisis and Conflict: World News Reporting between Two Wars, 1920-1940,* University of Iowa Press, 1982; *Tides of War,* University of Iowa Press, 1984. Contributor to magazines. Member of editorial staff of *Journalism Quarterly,* 1955-65.

WORK IN PROGRESS: Two books completing the history of international news coverage.

SIDELIGHTS: Robert W. Desmond writes: "My professional activities, as noted, have been divided between active journalism and teaching journalism, with the two often combined, or with return to active journalism in summer months (while teaching). All graduate work was in the area of political science and international relations, with a special research and professional interest in the area of world news reporting. Travel beyond the United States and Canada has been concentrated in Europe and the Middle East, but has also included the Far East, parts of Africa, Cuba, Mexico, and the West Indies."

* * *

DETRO, Gene 1935-

PERSONAL: Born November 26, 1935, in Oakland, Calif. *Education:* San Francisco State College (now University), B.A., 1958. *Politics:* None. *Religion:* "Has stopped looking for outward forms from other sources. Takes what comes."

CAREER: United Press International, San Francisco, Calif., 1954-56, began as copyboy, became staff writer; *News-Sentinel,* Seaside, Calif., editor, 1957-59; Kofman Newspapers, Alameda County, Calif., section editor and writer, 1960-67; Synanon Foundation, Mitchell, Calif., member of research staff and editor of monthly magazine, 1968-70; Desiderata School, Sacramento, Calif., teacher of writing and magazine production, 1971; *Oregon Journal,* Portland, poetry critic, beginning 1971; Portland State University, Portland, teacher of poetry workshops, 1975—. Founding director of Portland Poetry Festival, 1973-74; member of board of directors of Portland Poetry Center; consultant to Oregon Arts Commission.

WRITINGS: Extensions (poems), Moon Graphics, 1972; *The Honey Dwarf* (novel), Dustbooks, 1974; *Mary Militant,* Holmgangers, 1979; *Moon Horns, Razor Door,* Holmgangers, 1981; *The Mary Caper,* Sunburst Press, 1982; *When All the Wild Summer,* Holmgangers, 1983. Critic for *Small Press Review.*

WORK IN PROGRESS: A Red Hood's for Riding, a novel based on the fairy tale "Red Riding Hood."

BIOGRAPHICAL/CRITICAL SOURCES: Northwest Review, autumn, 1975.†

* * *

DHRYMES, Phoebus J(ames) 1932-

PERSONAL: Born October 1, 1932, in Cyprus; came to United States in 1951, naturalized in 1954; son of Demetrios and Kyriaki (Neophytou) Dhrymes; married Beatrice Bell Fitch, 1972; children: Phoebus, Jr., Philip Andrew, Alexander Robert. *Education:* University of Texas, B.A., 1957; Massachusetts Institute of Technology, Ph.D., 1961. *Religion:* Greek Orthodox. *Home:* 107 White Plains Rd., Bronxville, N.Y. 10708. *Office:* Department of Economics, Columbia University, New York, N.Y. 10027.

CAREER: Harvard University, Cambridge, Mass., assistant professor of economics, 1962-64; University of Pennsylvania, Philadelphia, associate professor, 1964-67, professor of economics, 1967-73; Columbia University, New York, N.Y., professor of economics, 1973—, Wesley Clair Mitchell Research Professor, 1977. *Military service:* U.S. Army, 1952-54. *Member:* American Economic Association, American Statistical Association (fellow), Economic Studies Society, Econometric Society (fellow). *Awards, honors:* Natural Science Foundation fellowship, 1961-62; Guggenheim fellowship, 1965-66; Ford Foundation faculty research fellowship, 1968-69.

WRITINGS: Distributed Lags: Problems of Formulation and Estimation, Holden-Day, 1970, new edition, North-Holland

Publishing, 1983; *Econometrics: Statistical Foundations and Applications,* Harper, 1970, new edition, Springer-Verlag, 1974; *Domestic Consequences of an Overvalued Currency,* Economic Planning Center (Athens), 1978; *Introductory Econometrics,* Springer-Verlag, 1978; *Mathematics for Econometrics,* Springer-Verlag, 1978. Editor, *International Economic Review,* 1964-71; co-editor, *Journal of Econometrics,* 1972-77; member of board of editors, *Greek Economic Review,* 1978—.

* * *

DICK, Ignace 1926-

PERSONAL: Born 1926, in Aleppo, Syria; son of Joseph and Angelique Dick. *Education:* Attended Seminary of St. Ann, Jerusalem; University of Louvain, Ph.D. *Home address:* Greek Catholic Archbishopric, P.O. Box 146, Aleppo, Syria.

CAREER: Priest of Roman Melkite Catholic Church.

WRITINGS: *Qu'est-ce que l'Orient chretien?,* Casterman (Tournai), 1966, translation by C. Gerard Guertin published as *What Is the Christian Orient?,* Newman, 1967; (with Edelby) *Vatican II: Decret sur les eglises orientales catholiques,* Editions du Cerf, 1970; *Theodore Abuqurra: Traite de l'existence du Createur et de la vraie religion* (in French and Arabic), [Beirut], 1982; *Sens et vicissitudes de l'uniatisme: L'Ecartelement de la double fidelite,* [Beirut], 1982.

* * *

DILLON, Millicent (Gerson) 1925-

PERSONAL: Born May 24, 1925, in New York, N.Y.; daughter of Ephraim (a salesman) and Clara (a nurse; maiden name, Millman) Gerson; married Murray L. Lesser, June 1, 1948 (divorced, 1959); married David F. Dillon, January 18, 1964 (divorced, 1966); children: (first marriage) Wendy, Janna. *Education:* Hunter College (now of the City University of New York), A.B., 1944; San Francisco State University, M.A., 1966. *Religion:* Jewish. *Home:* 4062 Ben Lomond Dr., Palo Alto, Calif. 94306. *Agent:* Maxine Groffsky, 2 Fifth Ave., New York, N.Y. 10011. *Office:* News and Publications, Stanford University, Stanford, Calif. 94305.

CAREER: Assistant physicist on government projects at Princeton University, 1944-45, and Oak Ridge, Tenn., 1947; Standard Oil Co., Kettleman Hills Oil Field, technical assistant, 1946; Los Angeles County, Hawthorne, Calif., case worker in social services department, 1949-52; Foothill College, Los Altos Hills, Calif., instructor in English, 1968-71, part-time instructor, 1971-74; Stanford University, Stanford, Calif., writer for news and publications office, 1974—. *Member:* Authors Guild, Authors League of America, P.E.N. *Awards, honors:* National Endowment for the Humanities fellowship, 1977.

WRITINGS: *Baby Perpetua and Other Stories,* Viking, 1971; *The One in the Back Is Medea* (novel), Viking, 1973; (contributor) William Abrahams, editor, *Prize Stories: The O. Henry Awards,* Doubleday, 1980; *A Little Original Sin: The Life and Work of Jane Bowles,* Holt, 1981. Contributor to *Nation, Threepenny Review,* and *Ascent.*

WORK IN PROGRESS: *We Are All Artists,* a novel.

SIDELIGHTS: Although she produced only a handful of writings during her career, Jane Bowles was admired for her talent by such literary figures as Tennessee Williams, Alan Sillitoe, and Carson McCullers. The author was also a notorious free spirit of her times: a limping, Jewish lesbian ("Crippie, the Kike Dyke," as she sometimes referred to herself), Bowles had many affairs while married to the noted composer/novelist Paul Bowles. The two of them lived and worked in South America and North Africa until Jane's death in 1973 following a series of strokes. Millicent Dillon examines the many facets of the writer in her book *A Little Original Sin: The Life and Work of Jane Bowles.*

"Janes Bowles' life, as her biographer . . . tells us," writes Ben Pleasants in the *Los Angeles Times Book Review,* "was lived without much regard for anyone but Jane Bowles. From her early days in Woodmere, Long Island (where she went around painting all the cars in her neighborhood with red paint), to her final battles and betrayals with an Arab lover, it became apparent the Bowles was not destined for a quiet post in the Harvard Library; what she wanted from life were the heights and the depths, both explored at length. Dillon captures all the drama, the despair, the neurosis and the comedy with a carefully researched and skillfully written book." *Chicago Tribune Book World* critic Edmund White praises Dillon for the fact that the biographer "never cheaply psychoanalyzes [her] subject but rather presents the woman and her work with sensitivity and admiration." Bowles, according to Laurie Stone, reviewing *A Little Original Sin* in the *Village Voice,* "lives in the book. Dillon accomplished the difficult feat of making an alledgedly fascinating figure actually appear fascinating. She is a better chronicler than analyst, and the text flags during her faint hearted probes into Jane's sexuality and writer's block. But her appreciation of Jane's power is infectious, and the biography is an inviting introduction to Bowles's work."

BIOGRAPHICAL/CRITICAL SOURCES: *Washington Post Book World,* August 2, 1981; *Chicago Tribune Book World,* August 9, 1981; *Village Voice,* August 19, 1981; *Los Angeles Times Book Review,* August 30, 1981; *New York Times Book Review,* September 13, 1981; *Time,* September 14, 1981.

* * *

DOBKIN De RIOS, Marlene 1939-
(Cressy de Betancourt)

PERSONAL: Born April 12, 1939, in New York, N.Y.; daughter of Bernard (a salesman) and Anne (a bookkeeper; maiden name, Schwartz) Dobkin; married Yando Rios (an artist), November 7, 1969; children: Gabriela, Ivy-nam. *Education:* Queens College (now Queens College of the City University of New York), B.A., 1959; New York University, M.A., 1963; University of California, Riverside, Ph.D., 1972. *Home:* 2517 East Santa Fe, Fullerton, Calif. 92631. *Office:* Department of Anthropology, California State University, Fullerton, Calif. 92634.

CAREER: City University of New York, New York, N.Y., part-time lecturer in anthropology at City College and Brooklyn College, 1964-66; University of Massachusetts, Boston, instructor in anthropology, 1966-67; California State University, Los Angeles, assistant professor of anthropology, 1967-68; California State University, Fullerton, assistant professor, 1969-72, associate professor, 1972-78, professor of anthropology, 1978—.

Field secretary for Admiralty Islands-New Guinea Expedition of American Museum of Natural History, spring, 1965; research associate at Institute of Social Psychiatry of National University of San Marcos, Lima, Peru, 1968-69; visiting scientist at Smithsonian Institution, summer, 1970; research anthropologist at Metropolitan State Hospital, Norwalk, Calif., 1970—, psychotherapist at Day Treatment Center and Spanish

Language Ward, 1973; associate researcher in anthropology at California College of Medicine at University of California, Irvine, 1974—; post-doctoral researcher and lecturer in Medical Anthropology Program, University of California, San Francisco, 1975-76; resident director of Intercollegiate Study Center, Lima, 1978-79; consultant to National Commission on Marihuana and Drug Abuse, 1973, National Academy of Sciences, Riverside, California Department of Mental Health, University of Washington Social Welfare Institute, Veterans Administration Hospital, Long Beach and Westwood, Calif., Institute of Higher Studies, Santa Barbara, Calif.

MEMBER: American Anthropological Association (fellow), Royal Anthropological Institute (fellow), American Association for the Advancement of Science, Ethnopharmacology Society (president, 1979-81), Southwestern Anthropological Association (president, 1979-80). *Awards, honors:* American Council of Learned Societies travel grant, Lima, Peru, 1970; Second National Commission on Marihuana and Drug Abuse contract, 1971; National Institute on Drug Abuse travel grant, University of Chicago, 1974; U.S. Public Health Service grant, University of California, San Francisco, 1975-76; National Institute on Alcohol Abuse and Alcoholism grant, 1975-76; National Institute of Mental Health post-doctoral fellowships, Medical Anthropology Program, University of California, San Francisco, 1975-76, and Summer Institute on Neurobiology and the Addictions, University of California, Irvine, 1977.

WRITINGS: (Contributor) Michael J. Harner, editor, *Hallucinogens and Shamanism,* Oxford University Press, 1972; *Visionary Vine: Psychedelic Healing in the Peruvian Amazon,* Chandler Publishing, 1972; (contributor) Ramon de la Fuente and Maxwell Weisman, editors, *Psychiatry: Proceedings of the Fifth World Congress of Psychiatry,* Volume II, Excerpta Medica, 1973; (contributor) *Drug Use in America: Problems in Perspective,* Volume I, U.S. Government Printing Office, 1973; (contributor) Thomas Fitzgerald, editor, *Social and Cultural Identity: Problems of Persistence and Change,* University of Georgia Press, 1974.

(Contributor) Vera Rubin, editor, *Cannabis and Culture,* Mouton (The Hague), 1975; *The Wilderness of Mind: Sacred Plants in Cross-cultural Perspective,* Sage Publications, 1976; (contributor) Brian du Toit, editor, *Drugs, Rituals and Altered States of Consciousness,* Balkema Press (Amsterdam), 1976; (contributor) J. Westermeyer, editor, *Anthropology and Mental Health,* Mouton, 1976; (contributor with William Emboden) G. Meyer and K. Blum, editors, *New World Folk Medicine,* University of Texas Press, 1979; (contributor) Stanley Krippner and S. Cohen, editors, *LSD into the Eighties,* Orenda-Unity, 1981. Also contributor to *Anthropology and Experience,* edited by Joan Koss, and *La relacion entre las creencias en la brujeria y la enfermedad psicosomatica,* edited by A. Chirif.

Contributor to professional journals. Associate editor in ethnopharmacology of *Medical Anthropology Newsletter;* member of editorial review board of *Journal of Psychedelic Drugs* and *Journal of Ethnopharmacology.*

WORK IN PROGRESS: *Don Hilde: An Amazon Urban Healer.*†

* * *

DOERINGER, Peter B(rantley) 1941-

PERSONAL: Born February 26, 1941, in Boston, Mass.; son of Frank Atchley and Elizabeth (Musser) Doeringer; married Suzannah J. Fabing, June 19, 1965. *Education:* Harvard University, A.B., 1962, A.M., 1965, Ph.D., 1966. *Home:* 16 Maple Ave., Cambridge, Mass. 02139. *Office:* Department of Economics, Boston University, 270 Bay St. Rd., Boston, Mass. 02215.

CAREER: Harvard University, Cambridge, Mass., instructor, 1966-67, assistant professor of economics, 1967-72, associate professor of political economy, 1972-74; Boston University, Boston, Mass., professor of economics, 1974—. Lecturer at London School of Economics and Political Science, University of London, 1971-72. Consultant to Equal Employment Opportunity Commission, 1966-67, to U.S. Department of Labor, 1967—, and to Organization for Economic Cooperation and Development, 1972-73; Boston Area Manpower Planning Council, member, 1970-72, acting chairman, 1971. *Member:* American Arbitration Association, American Economic Association, Industrial Relations Research Association.

WRITINGS: (Editor) *Programs to Employ the Disadvantaged,* Prentice-Hall, 1969; (with Michael J. Piore) *Internal Labor Markets and Manpower Analysis,* Heath, 1971; (with Bruce Vermeulen) *Jobs and Training in the Eighties: Vocational Policy and the Labor Market,* Nijhoff, 1981; (editor) *Industrial Relations in International Perspective,* Holmes & Meier, 1981; *Workplace Perspectives on Education and Training,* Nijhoff, 1981. Author of several research reports on problems in economics for the U.S. and Boston city governments. Contributor of articles to professional journals.†

* * *

DOGAN, Mattei 1920-

PERSONAL: Born October 16, 1920, in Rumania; son of Ian and Giselle Dogan. *Education:* Sorbonne, University of Paris, 1946-50, Docteur es Lettres, Diplome de l'Institut d'Etudes Politiques, Diplome d'Etudes Superieures de Philosophie, Diplome d'Etudes Superieures d'Histoire. *Home:* 72 Blvd. Arago, Paris 13, France. *Office:* Centre National de la Recherche Scientifique, 82 rue Cardinet, Paris 17, France.

CAREER: French sociologist and political scientist. Centre National de la Recherche Scientifique, Paris, France, research associate, 1952-55, master of research, 1955-63, deputy director of research, 1963-64, director of research, 1969—. Director, Bureau d'Analyses Sociologiques Europeenes, Paris, 1970-78; visiting professor of political science, University of California, Los Angeles, 1973—. Member of committee for social and economic development, Delegation Generale a la Recherche Scientifique et Technique, 1966-69. Visiting professor at University of Trento, Italy, 1967, Indiana University, 1971, Yale University, 1972, and Institute of Statistical Mathematics, Tokyo, 1975; organizer of several international scientific conferences.

MEMBER: International Sociological Association (president of social ecology committee, 1970—), International Political Science Association (chairman of committee on political elites, 1971—), International Social Science Council (member of standing committee on social science data archives, 1966—), French Sociological Association, French Political Science Association (member of executive council, 1970-78), French National Committee of Scientific Research, Centre d'Etudes Sociologiques (member of executive board, 1964-68). *Awards, honors:* Silver Medal of National Center of Scientific Research, 1966; award of Academie des Sciences Morales et Politiques.

WRITINGS: (With Jacques Narbonne) *Les Francaises face a la Politique,* Colin, 1956; (editor) *Le Comportement Politique,* Centre National de la Recherche Scientifique, 1966; (editor with O. Petracca) *Partiti Politici Strutture Sociali in Italia,* Editore Communita (Milan), 1968; (editor with S. Rokkan) *Quantitive Ecological Analysis in the Social Sciences,* M.I.T. Press, 1969, new edition published as *Social Ecology,* 1974.

(Editor with R. Rose) *European Politics: A Reader,* Little, Brown, 1971; (editor) *The Mandarins of Western Europe,* Halsted, 1975; (co-author) *Report on German Universities,* International Council on the Future of the University, 1977; *La Comparaison internationale en sociologie politique,* Litec (Paris), 1980; *Sociologie politique comparative,* Economica, 1981; (with D. Pelassy) *How to Compare Nations,* Chatham House, 1983; (co-author) *Il Systema politico italiano tra crisi e innovazione,* University of Turin, 1983; *Religion, classe et politique en France,* Economica, 1984.

Contributor: M. Duverger, editor, *Partis politiques et classes sociales,* A. Colin, 1955; Institut de Sociologie Solvay, editors, *La Condition sociale de la femme,* Bruxelles, 1956; M. Duverger, F. Goguel, and J. Touchard, editors, *Les Elections de 1956,* A. Colin, 1957; J. Fauvet and H. Mendras, editors, *Les Paysans et la politique,* A. Colin, 1958; Association Francaise de Science Politique, editors, *Le Referendum et les elections de 1958,* A. Colin, 1960; D. Marvick, editor, *Political Decision Makers,* Free Press, 1961; L. Hamon, editor, *Les Nouveaux comportements politiques de la classe ouvriere,* Presses Universitaires de France, 1962; A. Spreafico and J. LaPalombara, editors, *Elezioni e comportamento politico in Italia,* Communita (Milan), 1963; R. Boudon and P. Lazarsfeld, editors, *Le Vocabulaire des sciences sociales,* Mouton, 1965; S. M. Lipset and S. Rokkan, editors, *Party Systems and Voter Alignments,* Free Press, 1967; O. Stammer, editor, *Party Systems, Party Organizations and the Politics of New Masses,* Institut fuer politische Wissenschaft (Berlin), 1968.

S. Kertesz, editor, *The Task of Universities in a Changing World,* University of Notre Dame Press, 1971; *Science et theorie de l'opinion publique,* Retz (Paris), 1981; *Liber amicorum leo moulin,* Lemaire (Brussels), 1982; Myron Weiner and Ergun Ozbudun, editors, *Competitive Elections in Developing Countries,* American Enterprise Institute, 1983; Ali Kazancigl and Ozbudun, editors, *Ataturk: Fondateur d'un etat moderne,* UNESCO, 1983.

More than forty essays and articles have been published in French, English, Italian, Spanish, and German journals. Member of editorial review board of *Revue Francaise de Sociologie,* 1965-71, *Affari Sociali Internazionali,* 1973-78, and *Comparative Political Studies,* 1971—.

WORK IN PROGRESS: Pluralist Democracies in Western Europe.

SIDELIGHTS: Sociologie politique comparative was translated into Japanese.

* * *

DOGGETT, Frank 1906-

PERSONAL: Born May 4, 1906, in Jacksonville, Fla.; son of John L. (an attorney) and Carrie (Van Deman) Doggett; married Dorothy Emerson, March 16, 1934; children: Dorothy Jean (Mrs. Herschel E. Shepard), John L. *Education:* Rollins College, A.B., 1931; Emory University, M.A., 1933. *Religion:* Episcopalian. *Home:* 310 Sixth St., Atlantic Beach, Fla. 32003.

CAREER: D. U. Fletcher Senior High School, Neptune Beach, Fla., principal, 1937-69; writer. *Military service:* U.S. Naval Reserve, 1943-65; retired as lieutenant commander. *Member:* Modern Language Association of America. *Awards, honors:* D.Let., University of Florida; National Endowment for the Humanities senior fellowship, 1981.

WRITINGS: Stevens' Poetry of Thought, Johns Hopkins Press, 1966; (editor with Robert Buttel) *Wallace Stevens: A Celebration,* Princeton University Press, 1980; *Wallace Stevens: The Making of the Poem,* Johns Hopkins Press, 1980. Contributor to *PMLA, English Literary History, Studies in English Literature,* and other journals.

WORK IN PROGRESS: With Dorothy Emerson, a study of Wallace Stevens's symbolic universe.

SIDELIGHTS: Wallace Stevens scholar Frank Doggett first caught critics' attention in 1966 with his book *Stevens' Poetry of Thought.* The study was then called "the best book on Stevens that has yet appeared" by Marie Borroff in the *Yale Review.* Borroff continues, "Whether or not one feels that all [the author's] interpretations are equally convincing, there is no doubt that Doggett is equal to the demands of Stevens's art at its most difficult, and he shows himself fully aware that the meanings of Stevens's symbolic language are neither predictable nor fully consistent."

More recently, Doggett's exploration of the poet has resulted in *Wallace Stevens: A Celebration,* edited by Doggett and Robert Buttel, and the critical study *Wallace Stevens: The Making of the Poem.* The former work contains contributions by such writers as Irwin Ehrenpreis, Helen Vendler, and Joseph Riddel. *Times Literary Supplement* reviewer Stephen Fender labels *Wallace Stevens: A Celebration* "an apt tribute to one of the major poets of the century, a collection of essays exemplifying the widest range of scholarly and critical approaches: everything from bio-snippets to post-structuralist analysis, and even two posthumous contributions from the poet himself."

Of *Wallace Stevens: The Making of the Poem,* Lucy Beckett says: "[The] book, a less ambitious enterprise than [*Stevens' Poetry of Thought,*] uses some of the many passages of specific explanation in Stevens's letters to support fresh readings of a selection of the poems. It also traces the course of some ideas, images and methods upon which Stevens meditated and worked variations throughout his career." Although Beckett, in her *Times Literary Supplement* article, warns that "the better a poem is, . . . the less adequate any single reading of it will be," the critic finds that Doggett's "careful and tactful exposition of Stevens's habits of composition and his hedging of his argument with constant reminders of the dangers of overdefinite limitation of meaning, make it clear that he is perfectly aware of this." Concludes Beckett, "It is no adverse criticism of this mild and civilized book to say that it constantly reminds one of the truism that the only satisfactory words in which to describe what a poem is about are the words of the poem."

BIOGRAPHICAL/CRITICAL SOURCES: American Literature, March, 1967; *Yale Review,* March, 1967; *New York Times,* May 3, 1980; *Times Literary Supplement,* May 30, 1980, October 24, 1980; *New York Times Book Review,* June 1, 1980.

* * *

DOHERTY, Catherine de Hueck 1900-

PERSONAL: Born August 15, 1900, in Nijni-Novgorod, Russia (now U.S.S.R.); immigrated to Canada, 1921; became Canadian citizen; daughter of Theodore (a diplomat) and Emma (a concert pianist; maiden name, Thompson) de Kolyschkine; married Boris de Hueck, January 25, 1915 (deceased); married

Edward Doherty, June 25, 1943 (deceased); children: (first marriage) George Theodore. *Education:* Attended Princess Oblensky College; University of Petrograd (now Leningrad), M.A. *Politics:* Liberal. *Religion:* Roman Catholic. *Home and office:* Madonna House Apostolate, Combermere, Ontario, Canada K0J 1L0.

CAREER: Nurse in Russia, Scotland, and Canada; after arriving in America, worked as waitress, salesclerk, laundress, and maid; Leigh Emmerich Lecture Bureau, New York, N.Y., 1925-30, began as lecturer, became lecture manager and lecture buyer; member and director general of Lay Apostolate of Catholic Action (organization which establishes religious study centers called Madonna Houses), in Toronto, 1930-38, in New York City, 1938-48, in Combermere, Ontario, 1948—. *Military service:* Served as nurse in Russian Army, 1916-17; received St. George Medal for "exceeding bravery under fire" and the Medal of the Order of St. Anne.

AWARDS, HONORS: Poverello Medal, College of Stuebenville, 1957; St. John of Jerusalem Medal (Great Britain), 1959; certificate of appreciation, Royal Canadian Air Force, 1960; Pro Ecclesia et Pontiface Medal, Roman Catholic Church, 1960; Pius X Award, 1965; Aquinas Award, 1966; Franciscan International Award, 1970; Medal of the Order of the Ladies of Galilee, 1970; Teresa of Avila Award, College of St. Teresa (Winona, Minn.), 1975; Order of Canada Medal, Government of Canada, 1977; President's Medal, College of St. Benedict (St. Joseph, Minn.), 1977; Academie Francaise Award, 1977, for *Poustinia;* Queen's Medal (Great Britian), 1978; D.H.L., St. Ursala College (Cleveland), 1978; Athol Murray Humanities Award, Athol Murray College, 1979; D.H.L., St. Mary-of-the-Woods College, 1979; D.H.L.,Wadhams College (Ogdensburg, N.Y.), 1979.

WRITINGS: Friendship House, Sheed, 1947; *Dear Bishop,* Sheed, 1947; *Dear Seminarian,* Bruce Publishing (Milwaukee), 1950; *My Russian Yesterdays,* Bruce Publishing, 1951; *Dear Sister,* Bruce Publishing, 1953; *Where Love Is God Is,* Bruce Publishing, 1953; *Stations of the Cross,* privately printed, 1954; *Out of the Crucible,* St. Paul Publications, 1961.

Poustinia, Ave Maria Press, 1975; *The Gospel without Compromise,* Ave Maria Press, 1976; *Not without Parables,* Ave Maria Press, 1976; *Sobernost,* Ave Maria Press, 1977; *Strannik,* Ave Maria Press, 1978; *The People of the Towel and the Water,* Dimension Books, 1978; *Apostolic Farming,* privately printed, 1978; *Fragments of My Life* (autobiography), Ave Maria Press, 1979; *I Live on an Island,* Ave Maria Press, 1979; *Dear Father,* Alba House, 1979; *Unknown Mysteries of Our Lady,* Dimensions Books, 1979; *Doubts, Loneliness, Rejection,* Alba House, 1981; *Molchanie,* Crossroad Publishing Co., 1982; *Urodivoi, Fools for God,* Crossroad Publishing, 1983.

Contributor of numerous articles to religion journals. Editor of monthly religious newspapers, *Social Forum,* 1934-38, *Friendship House News,* 1938-48, and *Restoration,* 1948.

WORK IN PROGRESS: Journey Inward: Poetic Meditations.

* * *

DOMINO, John
See AVERILL, Esther

* * *

DONABEDIAN, Avedis 1919-

PERSONAL: Born January 7, 1919, in Beirut, Lebanon; came to the United States in 1955, naturalized citizen, 1960; son of Samuel (a physician) and Maritza (Der-Hagopian) Donabedian; married Dorothy Salibian (a professor of nursing), September 15, 1945; children: Haig, Bairj, Armen. *Education:* American University of Beirut, B.A., 1940, M.D., 1944; Harvard University, M.P.H., 1955. *Politics:* "Equal opportunity elitist!" *Religion:* Protestant. *Home:* 1739 Ivywood, Ann Arbor, Mich. 48103. *Office:* School of Public Health, University of Michigan, 109 Observatory St., Ann Arbor, Mich. 48109.

CAREER: English Mission Hospital, Jerusalem, Israel, physician and acting superintendent, 1945-47; American University of Beirut, Beirut, Lebanon, instructor in physiology, 1948-50, clinical assistant in dermatology, 1948-54, university physician, 1949-54, director of University Health Service, 1951-54; United Community Services of Metropolitan Boston, Boston, Mass., medical associate, 1955-57; New York Medical College, New York, N.Y., assistant professor, 1957-60, associate professor of preventive medicine, 1960-61; University of Michigan, Ann Arbor, associate professor, 1961-64, professor of medical care organization, 1964—. Senior member of National Academy of Sciences Institute of Medicine; honorary fellow of American College of Hospital Administrators.

MEMBER: American Public Health Association (fellow), Association of Teachers of Preventive Medicine. *Awards, honors:* Dean Conley Award from American College of Hospital Administrators, 1969; Norman A. Welch Award from National Association of Blue Shield Plans, 1976, and Elizur Wright Award from American Risk and Insurance Association, 1978, both for *Benefits in Medical Care Programs.*

WRITINGS: A Guide to Medical Care Administration, Volume II: *Medical Care Appraisal: Quality and Utilization,* American Public Health Association, 1969; *Aspects of Medical Care Administration: Specifying Requirements for Health Care,* Harvard University Press, 1973; *Benefits in Medical Care Programs,* Harvard University Press, 1976; *Explorations in Quality Assessment and Monitoring,* Health Administration Press, Volume I: *The Definition of Quality and Approaches to Its Assessment,* 1980, Volume II: *The Criteria and Standards of Quality,* 1982, Volume III: *The Methods and Findings of Quality Assessment and Monitoring: An Illustrative Analysis,* 1984. Contributor to medical and public health journals.

WORK IN PROGRESS: Research on the assessment and monitoring of the quality and appropriateness of medical care.

SIDELIGHTS: Avedis Donabedian writes briefly: "For some years now my major interest has been in collecting and systematizing available information in the field of health services administration. This work will continue probably until my retirement and will represent my contribution to my field."

* * *

DONALDSON, Frances (Annesley) 1907-

PERSONAL: Born January 13, 1907, in Harrow, England; daughter of Frederick (a playwright) and Leslie (Hoggan) Lonsdale; married John Donaldson (in Parliament), February 20, 1935; children: Thomas Hay, Rose Albinia (Mrs. Nicholas Deakin), Catherine Frances (Mrs. Mark Jennings). *Education:* Educated in Bromley, England. *Politics:* Labour. *Religion:* None. *Home:* 1 Chalcot Crescent, London NW1L, England.

CAREER: Farmer and writer.

WRITINGS: Freddy Lonsdale, Lippincott, 1958; *The Marconi Scandal,* Harcourt, 1963; *Evelyn Waugh: Portrait of a Country*

Neighbour, Chilton, 1968; *The Actor-Managers,* Regnery, 1970; *Edward VIII,* Lippincott, 1975; *King George VI and Queen Elizabeth,* Weidenfeld & Nicolson, 1977; *P. G. Wodehouse: A Biography,* Knopf, 1982 (published in England as *P. G. Wodehouse: The Authorized Biography,* Weidenfeld & Nicolson, 1982).

SIDELIGHTS: Frances Donaldson's *P. G. Wodehouse* is "a wonderfully researched biography," writes Christopher Warman in the *London Times,* "which tells you all you need to know" about the popular British-American humorist who created such memorable characters as Bertie Wooster, Lord Emsworth, Psmith, and the redoubtable valet Jeeves. Donaldson first met Wodehouse in 1921 when, at the age of fourteen, she became friends with his stepdaughter Leonora, and through the years she maintained contact with the Wodehouse family. Thus, notes Warman, when she undertook the biography she "had the advantage of access to all Wodehouse's important private papers."

"Donaldson seems an eminently qualified Wodehouse biographer," states *Chicago Tribune Book World* reviewer Alzina Stone Dale. "Her portrait of Pelham Grenville Wodehouse, familiarly known as 'Plum' or 'Plummy,' suggests that Wodehouse was a sweet, pathologically shy artist, who sketches his period by enlarging upon the stock figures of musical comedy: the silly ingenue, the dragon aunt, the masterly butler. . . . In Donaldson's capable hands, this story of P. G. Wodehouse comes across, like its subject, as sweet, silly and a little sad." And Heywood Hale Broun, in the *Washington Post Book World,* says that "no one who loves the Wodehouse oeuvre should miss reading [Donaldson's] biography. . . . His essential likeableness and, to use an old-fashioned word, decency, come breathing out of Donaldson's pages like a whiff of good pipe smoke mixed with country air."

Several reviewers, including Leslie Raddatz of the *Los Angeles Times,* feel that Wodehouse's life was too dull for a full-length biographical study. Raddatz writes: "Although Donaldson tries valiantly to link the persons and events in Wodehouse's career to the delightful characters he created . . . or to deny such connections as perceived by others, he remains, sad to say, 'a fairly uninteresting man.'" Raddatz feels that "one does not read *about* P. G. Wodehouse. One reads P. G. Wodehouse."

Still, many critics, although agreeing that Wodehouse did not live a terribly exciting life, believe Donaldson's book to be a definitive and worthwhile study of the writer. Indeed, maintains Charles Champlin in the *Los Angeles Times Book Review,* "the wonder of the biography is that she sustains a great interest in a man who seemed resolute in his wish to be uninteresting, except on paper." Champlin notes that this "beautifully composed, affectionate but absolutely judicious biography arrives a bit later than the several books marking the Wodehouse centenary in 1981. It is worth waiting for because it is—whether the reader is or isn't a Wodehouse enthusiast—a superior piece of biographical research and a careful job of literary placement."

BIOGRAPHICAL/CRITICAL SOURCES: *Washington Post Book World,* June 6, 1982; *Los Angeles Times Book Review,* July 4, 1982; *Chicago Tribune Book World,* July 25, 1982; *Los Angeles Times,* September 9, 1982; *London Times,* September 16, 1982; *Times Literary Supplement,* November 12, 1982.

* * *

DONALDSON, (Charles) Ian (Edward) 1935-

PERSONAL: Born May 6, 1935, in Melbourne, Australia; son of William Edward (a physician) and Elizabeth (Weigall) Donaldson; married Tamsin Jane Procter (a linguist), March 6, 1962; children: Benjamin, Sadie. *Education:* University of Melbourne, B.A. (with honors), 1957; Magdalen College, Oxford, B.A. (with honors), 1960, M.A., 1964; attended Merton College, Oxford, 1962. *Politics:* Labour. *Religion:* None. *Home:* 22 Dugan St., Deakin, Canberra, Australian Capital Territory 2600, Australia. *Office:* Humanities Research Centre, Australian National University, Canberra, Australian Capital Territory 2601, Australia.

CAREER: University of Melbourne, Parkville, Victoria, Australia, senior tutor in English, 1958; Oxford University, Oxford, England, lecturer in English and fellow of Wadham College, 1962-69; Australian National University, Canberra, Australian Capital Territory, professor of English, 1969—, director of Humanities Research Centre, 1974—. Visiting assistant professor at University of California, Santa Barbara, 1967-68. *Member:* International Association of University Professors of English, Australasian and Pacific Society for Eighteenth-Century Studies, Australian Universities Language and Literature Association, Australia Academy of the Humanities (fellow), American Society for Eighteenth-Century Studies.

WRITINGS: *The World Upside-Down: Comedy from Jonson to Fielding,* Clarendon Press, 1970; (editor) *Ben Jonson: Poems,* Oxford University Press, 1975; *The Rapes of Lucretia: A Myth and Its Transformations,* Clarendon Press, 1982; (editor) *Jonson and Shakespeare,* Macmillan, 1983; (editor) *Transformations in Modern European Drama,* Macmillan, 1983. General editor of "HRC" series, Macmillan, 1979—. Theater reviewer for *Guardian,* 1961-69; co-editor of *Essays in Criticism,* 1965-69; member of editorial board of *Oxford Review,* 1966-69, *A.U.M.L.A.,* 1973-77, and *Southern Review,* 1975-77.

WORK IN PROGRESS: Editing, with wife, Tamsin Donaldson, *Seeing the First Australians;* two books on comedy; editing a volume of works by Ben Jonson.

* * *

DORFMAN, John 1947-

PERSONAL: Born April 19, 1947, in Chicago, Ill.; son of Isaiah Sol (a lawyer) and Lillian (a secretary; maiden name, Schley) Dorfman; married Deborah Levinson, June 20, 1971; children: Laura, Jessica. *Education:* Princeton University, A.B., 1969; Columbia University, M.F.A., 1972. *Home:* 3547 Flanders Dr., Yorktown Heights, N.Y. 10011. *Office:* Forbes, 60 Fifth Ave., New York, N.Y. 10011. *Agent:* Dominick Abel Literary Agency, Inc., 498 West End Ave., New York, N.Y. 10024.

CAREER: *Home News,* New Brunswick, N.J., reporter, 1970-72; Associated Press, New York City, reporter, 1972-73; *Consumer Reports,* Mount Vernon, N.Y., assistant editor, 1973-74; free-lance writer, 1974-81; *Forbes,* New York City, associate editor, 1981—. Consultant to *Consumer Reports. Member:* American Society of Journalists and Authors, U.S. Chess Federation. *Awards, honors:* Certificate of merit from American Bar Association, 1974, for *Consumer Reports* series on landlord-tenant relations.

WRITINGS: *Consumer Survival Kit,* Praeger, 1975; *A Consumer's Arsenal,* Praeger, 1976; *Well-Being: An Introduction to Health,* Scott, Foresman, 1980; *Consumer Tactics Manual,* Atheneum, 1980; *Family Investment Guide,* Atheneum, 1981;

Stock Market Directory, Doubleday, 1982. Contributor to *Chicago, Money, Playboy, Parade,* and *Consumer Reports.*

WORK IN PROGRESS: *Center Counter Game,* a novel.

SIDELIGHTS: John Dorfman writes that he is interested in "fiction writing, business and the arts. My first novel, *The Brontosaurus Affair,* remains unpublished to date."

* * *

DOSS, Margot Patterson

PERSONAL: Born in St. Paul, Minn.; daughter of Eugene Northrop (a certified public accountant) and Irene (Watson) Patterson; married John Whinham Doss (a pediatrician), June 7, 1947; children: Richard, Alexander, Jock, Gordon. *Education:* Illinois Wesleyan University, B.A.; graduate study at New School for Social Research and University of Chicago. *Politics:* Democrat. *Religion:* Episcopalian. *Home:* 1331 Greenwich St., San Francisco, Calif. 94109; and Box 447, Bolinas, Calif. 94924. *Office:* San Francisco Chronicle, San Francisco, Calif. 94119; and Box E, Pago Pago, American Samoa 96799.

CAREER: Feature writer for *Baltimore Sun, Milwaukee Sentinel, Peoria Journal Transcript,* and *Bloomington* (Ill.) *Pantagraph,* 1943-60; *San Francisco Chronicle,* San Francisco, Calif., weekly columnist, 1960—. Instructor in nature, University of California Outdoor Environmental classes, 1969-82, and Pacific Heights Community College, 1972-79; lecturer at Foothill College, 1972, and San Francisco State University, 1973. Personality on weekly television show, "Evening Magazine," on KPIX-TV, 1976-82. *Member:* San Francisco Press Club, Sierra Club (life member), Oceanic Society (life member).

WRITINGS: *San Francisco at Your Feet,* Grove, 1962, revised edition, 1974; *Bay Area at Your Feet,* Chronicle Publishing, 1970; *Golden Gate Park at Your Feet,* Chronicle Publishing, 1970; *Walks for Children in San Francisco* (juvenile), Grove, 1970; *Paths of Gold,* Chronicle Books, 1974; (contributor) *Richtig Reisen,* Dumont, 1976; *There There,* Presidio Press, 1978; *A Walkers Yearbook,* Presidio Press, 1983. Contributor to magazines.

AVOCATIONAL INTERESTS: Conservation and ecology, history of California, letterpress printing, wild herbs and gardening, trail finding and trail building.

* * *

DOTTS, Maryann J. 1933-

PERSONAL: Born November 11, 1933, in Pittsburgh, Pa.; daughter of Charles A. and Mary J. (Dryer) Dreese; married M. Franklin Dotts (an editor), August 9, 1958 (divorced, 1982); children: Ruthann C. *Education:* National College, Kansas City, Mo., A.B., 1956; Scarritt College for Christian Workers, M.A., 1974; George Peabody College for Teachers, M.L.S., 1975. *Religion:* United Methodist. *Address:* Mulberry Street United Methodist Church, P.O. Box 149, Macon, Ga. 31202.

CAREER: Director of Christian education at United Methodist churches in Erie, Pa., 1956-58, and Arlington Heights, Ill., 1958-61; Riverside Church, New York, N.Y., teacher and supervisor, 1965-67; Upper Room Library and Museum, Board of Discipleship, Nashville, Tenn., librarian and cataloguer, 1975; Belle Meade United Methodist Church, Nashville, director of Christian education, 1976-79; Andrew Price Memorial United Methodist Church, Nashville, director of Christian education, 1980-84; Mulberry Street United Methodist Church, Macon, Ga., director of Christian education, 1984—. *Member:* Church and Synagogue Library Association (member of board of directors, 1976-77, president, 1978-79), Christian Educators Fellowship, Tennessee Conference Christian Educators Fellowship, Tennessee Association of Young Children, Nashville Association of Young Children.

WRITINGS: *I Am Happy* (juvenile), Abingdon, 1971; (with husband, M. Franklin Dotts) *Clues to Creativity: Providing Learning Experiences for Children,* three volumes, Friendship Press, 1974-76; *The Church Resource Library,* Abingdon, 1975; *When Jesus Was Born* (juvenile), Abingdon, 1979. Author of curriculum material for United Methodist Church, 1963—.

WORK IN PROGRESS: *Librarian's Guide to Displays;* a book of chorale readings of the Bible for children; *Cooking with Young Children;* a handbook for volunteer librarians; a book on the relationships of colors, sizes, and shapes.

AVOCATIONAL INTERESTS: Camping, Chinese cooking, needlepoint, travel.

* * *

DOVEGLION
See VILLA, Jose Garcia

* * *

DOVER, K(enneth) J(ames) 1920-

PERSONAL: Born March 11, 1920, in Croydon, England; son of Percy Henry James (a civil servant) and Dorothy (Healey) Dover; married Audrey Latimer, March 17, 1947; children: Alan Hugh, Catherine Ruth. *Education:* Balliol College, Oxford, M.A., 1947; Merton College, Oxford, additional study, 1948. *Politics:* "Left of center." *Religion:* Agnostic. *Office:* Corpus Christi College, Oxford University, Oxford, England.

CAREER: Oxford University, Balliol College, Oxford, England, fellow and tutor in classics, 1948-55; University of St. Andrews, St. Andrews, Scotland, professor of Greek, 1955-76; dean of Faculty of Arts, 1960-63, 1973-75; Oxford University, Corpus Christi College, president, 1976—. Visiting lecturer, Harvard University, 1960; Sather Visiting Professor of Classics, University of California, Berkeley, 1967. *Military service:* British Army, 1940-45; served in Africa and Italy; became lieutenant; mentioned in dispatches. *Member:* British Academy (fellow; president, 1978-81), Royal Society of Edinburgh (fellow), Society for the Promotion of Hellenic Studies (president, 1971-74), Society for the Promotion of Roman Studies, Classical Association (president, 1976), Linguistics Association of Great Britain. *Awards, honors:* Knighted, 1977.

WRITINGS: *Greek Word Order,* Cambridge University Press, 1960; (author of commentary) Thucydides, *History of the Peloponnesian War,* Books 6 and 7, Clarendon Press, 1965; (editor and author of introduction and commentary) Aristophanes, *Clouds,* Clarendon Press, 1968; *Lysias and the Corpus Lysiacum,* University of California Press, 1968; (editor and author of introduction and commentary) Theocritus, *Selected Poems,* Macmillan, 1971; *Aristophanic Comedy,* University of California Press, 1972; *Greek Popular Morality,* Basil Blackwell, 1975; *Greek Homosexuality,* Duckworth, 1978; *The Greeks,* BBC Publications, 1980; (editor and author of commentary with A. W. Gomme and A. Andrews) *Historical Commentary* on *Thucydides,* Clarendon Press, 1981. Contributor to classical journals. Co-editor, *Classical Quarterly,* 1962-68.

WORK IN PROGRESS: Writing on the language of Greek comedy and prose literature; an edition of Aristophanes' *Frogs,* with commentary.

SIDELIGHTS: K. J. Dover is "a Hellenist of unimpeachable credentials," says Erich Segal in the *New York Times Book Review.* Segal's remarks occur in a review of Dover's groundbreaking text on Hellenic society, *Greek Homosexuality.* Long recognized as a historically important aspect of Greek society during the classical period, the topic of homosexuality has in Segal's words "been all but ignored" by historians. "Clearly," he says, "this has been a difficult subject for scholars to deal with." *Greek Homosexuality* is thus an attempt to shed light on an important issue.

The book outlines the role of male sexual relations in Greek education, sport, and philosophy, drawing on classical art and literature for examples. *Greek Homosexuality* is a "sound, scholarly . . . work," according to a reviewer for the *Christian Century.* While Segal singles out a possible weakness in the study, remarking that "there may be some who will regret that Mr. Dover does not really explain *why* the Greeks so enthusiastically adopted their idiosyncratic mode of life," he goes on to add: "One cannot underestimate the importance of Mr. Dover's book. With philological brilliance and scholarly objectivity, he presents facts that can no longer be ignored. It is a step toward understanding the complex nature of the Greeks, whom we claim as cultural fathers."

In addition to Greek, Dover is competent in Italian, Spanish, German, Dutch, and French.

AVOCATIONAL INTERESTS: "Unspoilt natural scenery, fauna and flora, comparative and historical linguistics, the processes of change in ethics, religion and society, psychopathology."

BIOGRAPHICAL/CRITICAL SOURCES: *New York Times Book Review,* April 8, 1979; *Christian Century,* July 16, 1980; *Times Literary Supplement,* April 3, 1981.

* * *

DOYLE, Donovan
See BOEGEHOLD, Betty (Doyle)

* * *

DRAGONWAGON, Crescent 1952-
(Ellen Parsons)

PERSONAL: Name at birth, Ellen Zolotow; name legally changed; born November 25, 1952, in New York, N.Y.; daughter of Maurice (a biographer) and Charlotte (a children's book writer; maiden name, Shapiro) Zolotow; married second husband, Crispin Dragonwagon (an archaeologist), March 20, 1970 (divorced August 10, 1975); married third husband, Ned Shank (an architectural marketer), October 20, 1978. *Education:* Educated in Hastings-on-Hudson, N.Y., and Stockbridge, Mass. *Home address:* 312 Arizona St., Atlanta, Ga. 30307; and Dairy Hollow, Eureka Springs, Ark. 72632.

CAREER: Full-time writer. Participant in artist-in-the-schools programs in Eureka Springs, Arkansas, and Atlanta, Georgia. Fellow at Ossabow Island, 1982. Lecturer on writing at National Council of Teachers of English Conference, 1980, American Association of School Librarians, 1982, Oklahoma Writers Conference, 1982, Ohio River Valley Writers Conference, 1983, and Omega Institute, 1983. Co-owner of Dairy Hollow House (a bed-and-breakfast inn), Eureka Springs, Arkansas. *Member:* Authors Guild, Authors League of America, American Society of Journalists and Authors, American Civil Liberties Union. *Awards, honors: To Take a Dare* was named an American Library Association notable book of the year, 1982.

WRITINGS—Children's books, except as indicated; published by Harper, except as indicated: (Under pseudonym Ellen Parsons) *Rainy Day Together,* 1970; *The Commune Cookbook* (cookbook), Simon & Schuster, 1971; *The Bean Book* (cookbook), Workman Publishing, 1972; *Putting Up Stuff for the Cold Time* (cookbook), Workman Publishing, 1973; *Strawberry Dress Escape,* Scribner, 1975; *When Light Turns into Night,* 1975; *Wind Rose,* 1976; *Stevie Wonder* (biography), Flash Books, 1976; *Will It Be Okay?,* 1977; *Your Owl Friend,* 1979; *If You Call My Name,* 1982; (with Paul Zindel) *To Take a Dare* (young adult novel), 1982; *Message from Avocadoes* (poems), August House, 1982; *I Hate My Brother Harry,* 1983; *Katie in the Morning,* 1983; *Always, Always,* Macmillan, 1984; *Alligator Arrived with Apples: A Thanksgiving Potluck Alphabet,* Macmillan, 1984; *Coconut,* 1984; *Jemima Remembers,* Macmillan, 1985; *Just Like in the Movies* (young adult novel), 1985.

Contributor to popular magazines, including *Cosmopolitan, Seventeen, Organic Gardening, New Ingenue, McCalls, Aphra, Los Angeles, Atlanta, New Age, Arkansan, Arkansas Times,* and *Arkansas Gazette.*

SIDELIGHTS: *To Take a Dare* by Crescent Dragonwagon and Paul Zindel "stakes a claim to be this season's most talked about 'Young Adult' novel—sure to scandalize many parents at the same time that it hooks a large audience of worldly wise teens," says Joyce Milton in the *New York Times Book Review.* The book is narrated by sixteen-year-old runaway Chrysta Perretti, a former juvenile delinquent and aspiring Punk Queen, and takes a frank look at adolescent drinking, drug abuse, and sex. "On my thirteenth birthday my father called me a slut once too often, my dog was hit by a car, and I lost my virginity—what was left of it," she declares in the opening sentence. "It's almost a certainty that [*To Take a Dare*] will be a target of censors because of the uncompromising, flat-out raw language the narrator and others use and because of Chrissie's experiences," predicts a *Publishers Weekly* reviewer.

However, despite Chrysta's questionable character at the beginning of the book and "for all its punk bravado," says Milton, *To Take a Dare* "is as moralistic as any Hollywood romance of the Production Code era." After running away from home Chrysta develops a painful venereal disease that leaves her permanently sterile and is threatened with rape by her boss and with death by a twelve-year-old runaway she has taken in. Eventually, though, she lands in a small resort town and at age sixteen begins a career as a cook, makes friends who help her through the bad times, and wins the love of a caring boy. Her experiences—both good and bad—"somehow teach her she has a lot of strength, love and other good qualities in spite of her unhappy childhood," writes a *School Library Journal* critic, "and the messages about not running away from oneself, caring about others and being willing to ask for help when necessary are made quite obvious toward the end." Says the *Publishers Weekly* writer: "The novel is strong stuff but it is a voice that should be heard. Millions like the narrator fall into the freedom trap each year and need help. Chrissie is luckier than most."

Commenting on her work, Crescent Dragonwagon told *CA*: "I have always seen myself as a writer first. Not a children's book writer as such, or a novelist, or a poet, or a magazine writer, or a cookbook author—though I have done each of these types of writing. Writing is the lens through which I focus on the world and the things in it which trouble me, or interest me, or give me pleasure. The particular subject or feeling I am looking at through the lens determine what form the finished piece of writing will take. The exception to this rule is when I'm working on a novel, however; for there the characters soon take over and do it *their* way, from *their* perspective—which may be very different from mine.

"I feel lucky to have a profession which allows me to explore so many interests, while allowing me to stay true to the main and abiding interest in my life: writing. I have always known that this is what I wanted to do—and that, too, is lucky. It makes possible the persistent striving which underlies craft, talent, experience, gift and good fortune.

"I also feel writing is a highly utilitarian profession. To quote from a poem of mine called 'Looking for Bones in Her House,' 'She can write about anything that happens to her!'"

AVOCATIONAL INTERESTS: Gardening, reading, cooking, movies of the 1920s, '30s, and '40s, antiques, historic preservation, white water canoeing, environmentalism, anti-nuclear movement, theater.

BIOGRAPHICAL/CRITICAL SOURCES: Publishers Weekly, March 19, 1982; *New York Times Book Review,* April 25, 1982; *School Library Journal,* May, 1982.

* * *

DRUMMOND, Harold D. 1916-

PERSONAL: Born June 8, 1916, in Bettsville, Ohio; son of Ray Waldo and Velma (Foor) Drummond; married Catherine Street, August 30, 1939; children: H. Evan. *Education:* Attended Westminster College, Salt Lake City, Utah, 1933-35; Colorado State College (now University of Northern Colorado), A.B., 1937, M.A., 1940; Stanford University, Ed.D., 1948. *Office:* University of New Mexico, Albuquerque, N.M. 87131.

CAREER: Teacher and elementary school principal in Texas, 1938-42; George Peabody College for Teachers, Nashville, Tenn., professor of elementary education, 1947-60; University of New Mexico, Albuquerque, professor of elementary education, 1960-79, professor emeritus, 1979—, associate dean for Curriculum and Instruction. Acting professor of education assigned to University of the Philippines, Stanford University, 1954-55. *Military service:* U.S. Naval Reserve, 1942-45; became lieutenant. *Member:* National Education Association, Association for Supervision and Curriculum Development (president, 1965), Professors of Curriculum, National Council for the Social Studies, National Council for Geographic Education, Phi Delta Kappa, Phi Kappa Phi, Kappa Delta Pi.

WRITINGS: (With Charles R. Spain and John I. Goodlad) *Educational Leadership and the Elementary School Principal,* Rinehart, 1956.

Senior author and rewriter of teachers' manuals; texts originally written by De Forest Stull and Roy W. Hatch: *A Journey through Many Lands,* Allyn & Bacon, 1960, 4th edition, 1981; *Journeys through the Americas,* Allyn & Bacon, 1960, 4th edition, 1981; *The Eastern Hemisphere,* Allyn & Bacon, 1961, 5th edition, 1983; *The Western Hemisphere,* Allyn & Bacon, 1961, 5th edition, 1983; *Journeys through the United States and Canada,* Allyn & Bacon, 1966. Contributor to education journals. Member of editorial advisory board, *Childcraft,* 1957-60, 1967-80.

SIDELIGHTS: Harold D. Drummond has visited sixty-five countries gathering material for his writings.

AVOCATIONAL INTERESTS: Photography.

* * *

DRUON, Maurice (Samuel Roger Charles) 1918-

PERSONAL: Born April 23, 1918, in Paris, France; son of Rene Druon de Reyniac and Leonilla Samuel-Cros; married Madeleine Marignac, September 25, 1968. *Education:* Educated in Paris, France, at Faculte des Lettres and Ecole des Sciences Politiques. *Home:* 73 rue de Varenne, Paris 7e, France; and Abbaye de Faize, les Artigues-de-Lussac, 33570 Lussac, France. *Office:* c/o Institut de France, 23 quai de Conti, Paris 6e, France. *Agent:* Andre Berheim, 55 avenue George V, Paris 8e, France.

CAREER: Writer. War correspondent, 1944-45. Minister of cultural affairs of France, 1973-74; deputy for Paris, Comite Central du Rassemblement pour la Republique, 1978; member, Conseil Franco-Britannique. Honorary president, Association des Laureats du Concours General. *Military service:* French Cavalry, officer, 1940. Escaped from France through Spain, 1942, and served with Free French Forces in England, 1942-44. *Member:* French Academy, Societe des Gens de Lettres, Societe des Auteurs et Compositeurs Dramatiques, Societe des Auteurs Compositeurs et Editeurs de Musique, Conseil Litteraire de Monaco, Academie de Bordeaux, Savile Club (London). *Awards, honors:* Prix Goncourt, 1948, for *Les Grandes Familles;* Monaco Literary Council Prize for the whole of his work, 1966; officer of the Legion of Honor; commander of Arts and Letters; commander of cultural merit of Monaco; commander, Royal Order of Phoenix (Greece) and Order of Tunisia; grand cross, Order of Merit (Italy) and Order of Aztec Eagle (Mexico); grand officer, Order of Merit (Malta), Order of the Lion (Senegal), and Order of Honor (Greece).

WRITINGS—Novels: *La Derniere Brigade,* Grasset, 1946, reprinted, Edito-Service, 1973, translation by Humphrey Hare published as *The Last Detachment: The Cadets of Saumur, 1940,* Hart-Davis, 1957, revised French edition, Societe des Editions, 1965; *Les Grandes Familles* (first novel in trilogy "La Fin des hommes"; also see below), Julliard, 1948, reprinted, Edito-Service, 1972, translation by Edward Fitzgerald published as *The Rise of Simon Lachaume,* Dutton, 1952; *La Chute des corps* (second novel in trilogy "La Fin des hommes"; also see below), Julliard, 1950, reprinted, Edito-Service, 1973; *Rendez-vous aux enfers* (third novel in trilogy "La Fin des hommes"; also see below), Julliard, 1951, reprinted, Edito-Service, 1973; *La Volupte d'etre,* Julliard, 1954, reprinted, Edito-Service, 1973, translation by Moura Budberg published as *The Film of Memory,* Scribner, 1955, published as *A Matter of Time,* New American Library, 1976, revised French edition, Club des Editeurs, 1958.

Les Rois maudits (title means "The Accursed Kings"), Volume I: *Le Roi de fer,* Del Duca, 1955, reprinted, Edito-Service, 1972, translation by Hare published as *The Iron King,* Scribner, 1956, published as *The Ardent Infidels,* Ace Books, 1977, new French edition, Del Duca/Plon, 1965, Volume II: *La Reine etranglee,* Del Duca, 1955, reprinted, Edito-Service, 1972, translation by Hare published as *The Strangled Queen,* Hart-

Davis, 1956, Scribner, 1957, new French edition, Del Duca/Plon, 1966, Volume III: *Les Poisons de la couronne,* Del Duca, 1956, reprinted, Edito-Service, 1972, translation by Hare published as *The Poisoned Crown,* Scribner, 1957, new French edition, Del Duca/Plon, 1966, Volume IV: *La Loi des males,* Del Duca, 1956, reprinted, Edito-Service, 1972, translation by Hare published as *The Royal Succession,* Scribner, 1958, new French edition, Del Duca/Plon, 1966, Volume V: *La Louve de France,* Del Duca, 1959, translation by Hare published as *The She-Wolf of France,* Hart-Davis, 1960, Scribner, 1961, new French edition, Del Duca/Plon, 1966, Volume VI: *Le Lis et le lion,* Del Duca, 1960, translation by Hare published as *The Lily and the Lion,* Hart-Davis, 1961, Scribner, 1962, new French edition, Del Duca/Plon, 1966, Volume VII: *Quand un roi perd la France,* Plon, 1977; *L'Hotel de Mondez* (also see below), Julliard, 1956; *Alexandre le grand; ou, Le Roman d'un dieu,* Del Duca, 1958, repirnted, Livre de Poche, 1974, new edition published as *Alexandre le dieu,* 1961, translation by Hare published as *Alexander the God,* Scribner, 1961; *The Curtain Falls: A Modern Trilogy* (one-volume translation of trilogy "La Fin des hommes"; contains *The Magnates* [translation of *Les Grandes Familles*], *Feet of Clay* [translation of *La Chute des corps*], and *Rendezvous in Hell* [translation of *Rendez-vous aux enfers*]), translation by Hare, Hart-Davis, 1959, Scribner, 1960; *Les Memoires de Zeus,* Hachette, Volume I: *L'Aube des dieux,* 1963, translation by Hare published as *The Memoirs of Zeus,* Scribner, 1964, Volume II: *Les Jours des hommes,* 1965.

Other works: *Lettres d'un Europeen* (essays), Julliard, 1944, expanded edition published as *Lettres d'un Europeen, 1943-1970,* Plon, 1970; (translator) Edward Sackville-West, *Ithaque delivree* (dramatic poem; translation of *The Rescue*), A. Michel, 1947; *Megaree* (play; produced, 1942; also see below), Julliard, 1949; *Remarques* (essays), Julliard, 1952; (with uncle, Joseph Kessel) *Le Coup de grace* (play; produced, 1952), Gallimard, 1953; *Tistou les pouces verts* (juvenile; also see below), Del Duca, 1957, translation by Hare published as *Tistou of the Green Thumbs,* Scribner, 1958 (published in England as *Tistou of the Green Fingers,* Hart-Davis, 1958), revised French edition, Plon, 1968; *Theatre* (plays; includes "Megaree," "Un Voyageur," and "La Contessa"), Julliard, 1962; *Des Seigneurs de la plaine a l'Hotel de Mondez* (collection), Julliard, 1962, translation by Hare published as *The Black Prince and Other Stories,* Hart-Davis, 1962, published as *The Glass Coffin and Other Stories,* Scribner, 1963; *Bernard Buffet* (essays), Hachette, 1964, translation by A. M. Sheridan Smith published under same title, Methuen, 1965, October House, 1966; *Paris, de Cesar a Saint Louis* (essay; also see below), Hachette, 1964, translation by Hare published as *The History of Paris from Caesar to St. Louis,* Hart-Davis, 1969, Scribner, 1970; *Le Pouvoir* (maxims), Hachette, 1964.

Les Tambours de la memoire: mai 1945-mai 1965, Plon, 1965; *Le Bonhour des uns . . .* (collection; includes *Tistou les pouces verts*), Plon, 1967; *Ces Messieurs de Rothschild,* Editions P. Tisne, 1967; (contributor) *Belles Histoires de chevaux,* Gautier-Languereau, 1968; *L'Avenir en dessarroi,* Plon, 1968; (with Jacques Suffel) *Vezelay, colline eternelle* (also see below), Union Generale d'Editions, 1968; *Une Eglise qui se trompe de siecle: Reponses et commentaires de Luc Baresta,* Plon, 1972; *Au Pas de la vie,* Edito-Service, Volume I: *Les Epreuves et les esperances, 1939-1946,* 1973, Volume II: *Les Rivages et les sources,* 1974, Volume III: *Les Lectures et les amities,* 1975, Volume IV: *Les Idees et les moeurs,* 1975; *Nouvelles et recits* (includes *Les Seigneurs de la plaine, L'Hotel de Mondez, Le Bonheur des uns . . .* , and *Tistou les pouces verts*), Edito-Service, 1973; *Regards sur l'histoire: Paris, de Cesar a Saint Louis, Vezelay, colline eternelle, Melanges historiques pour Charles de Gaulle,* Edito-Service, 1973; *La Parole et le pouvoir,* Plon, 1974; *Politique et civilisation: Discours,* Edito-Service, 1975; *Bernard Buffet* (exhibition catalog), Musee Postal (Paris), 1978; (with others) *Hommage a Jean Sainteny,* Plon, 1978.

Also author of film scripts "Les Grandes Familles," 1958, and "Film of Memory," 1972, both adaptations of his novels, and of "Le Baron de l'Ecluse," 1958, an adaptation of a novel by Georges Simenon; author, with Kessel, of "Le Chant des partisans," the song of the French Resistance, with music by Anna Marly.

Contributor to *La Nef, Revue de Paris, Paris Match, Figaro Litteraire, Lettres Francaises, Nouvelles Litteraires, Marie Claire,* and *Elle.*†

* * *

DUBIE, Norman (Evans) 1945-

PERSONAL: Born April 10, 1945, in Barre, Vt.; son of Norman E., Sr. (a clergyman) and Doris (a registered nurse) Dubie; married Francesca Stafford, December 28, 1968 (divorced); married Pamela Stewart (a poet and teacher), November 28, 1975 (divorced January 3, 1980); married Jeannine Savard (a poet), June 18, 1981; children: (first marriage) Hannah. *Education:* Goddard College, B.A., 1969; University of Iowa, M.F.A., 1971. *Politics:* None. *Religion:* "Some." *Home:* 700 West Brown, No. 6, Tempe, Ariz. 85281. *Office:* Department of English, Arizona State University, Tempe, Ariz. 85281.

CAREER: University of Iowa, Iowa City, lecturer at Writers Workshop, 1971-74; Ohio University, Athens, assistant professor of English, 1974-75; Arizona State University, Tempe, writer-in-residence, 1975-76, lecturer, 1976-83, professor of English, 1983—, director of graduate writing program, 1976—. Poetry director for Prison Writers and Artists Workshop, 1973-74; has given poetry readings all over the United States. *Awards, honors:* Bess Hokin Prize from *Poetry* and Modern Poetry Association, 1976, for "The Negress, Her Monologue of Dark Crepe"; Guggenheim fellowship, Mexico, 1977-78; The Norman Dubie collection is housed at the University of Iowa.

WRITINGS—Poetry: *Alehouse Sonnets,* University of Pittsburgh Press, 1971; *The Prayers of the North American Martyrs,* Penumbra Press, 1975; *Popham of the New Song,* Graywolf, 1975; *In the Dead of the Night,* University of Pittsburgh Press, 1975; *The Illustrations,* Braziller, 1977; *A Thousand Little Things,* Cummington Press, 1977; *The City of the Olesha Fruit,* Doubleday, 1979; *Odalisque in White,* Porch Publications, 1979; *The Everlastings,* Doubleday, 1980; *The Window in the Field,* Razorback Press (Denmark), 1981; *Selected and New Poems,* Norton, 1983.

Contributor: *The American Poetry Anthology: Poets under Forty,* Avon, 1975; *Poetry as Process: Fifty Contemporary American Poets,* edited by Alberta Turner, McKay, 1977; *The Face of Poetry: One Hundred Poets,* Gallimaufry, 1977; *The Longman Anthology of Contemporary American Poetry,* edited by Friebert and Young, Longman, 1983; *The Morrow Anthology of Young American Poets,* edited by Smith and Bottoms, Morrow, 1984. Contributor of articles and poems to literary journals, including *American Poetry Review, Iowa Review, Poetry, Field, Antioch Review,* and *New Yorker.* Poetry editor of *Iowa Review,* 1971-72, and *Now,* 1973-74.

WORK IN PROGRESS: The Book of Lamentations.

SIDELIGHTS: Poet "Norman Dubie's work manifests a powerful disposition to relocate his imagination out of its own time and place," according to Vernon Shetley in the *New York Review of Books*. This relocation may involve the use of a historically significant locale for the setting of a poem (ancient Egypt) or perhaps the life of an artist from the past (Renoir). In a review of *The Everlastings*, Shetley draws a close parallel between Dubie's techniques and those of the creator of the dramatic monologue, Robert Browning: "One might say that Browning takes a tape recorder to the past, Dubie a camera. [The latter] seeks to evoke emotion through a highly particularized rendering of a world of objects." In Shetley's view, Dubie's methods are not always successful, however, and the poet has been both praised and criticized for his use of elaborate detail and imagery. Susan Wood focuses on this issue in the *Washington Post Book World*, saying that despite the "beautiful, elegant surface," of many of Dubie's works, "one was simply not given enough information for understanding. Why *this* detail and not *that* one, and what is to be our attitude toward the poem?"

Wood feels, however, that Dubie overcomes these problems in *The City of the Olesha Fruit*, where "the exquisitely rendered details seem to be there for a reason." Katha Pollitt, writing in the *Nation*, expresses a similar point of view: "[His] lush images . . . fold into one another in a way that is often pleasing to the inner eye." She states that Dubie's "poetic strategies" are "widely admired and much imitated" and goes on to add: "Dubie is obviously a determined and gifted poet, with energy to burn."

BIOGRAPHICAL/CRITICAL SOURCES: Washington Post Book World, August 19, 1979; *Nation*, July 5, 1980; *New York Review of Books*, April 29, 1982.

*   *   *

DUGGER, Ronnie 1930-

PERSONAL: Born April 16, 1930, in Chicago, Ill.; son of William Leroy and Mary (King) Dugger; married Jean Williams (a teacher), June 13, 1950 (divorced, 1978); married Patricia Blake (a writer), June 29, 1982; children: (first marriage) Gary McGregor, Celia Williams. *Education:* University of Texas, B.A., 1950; graduate study at University of Texas and Oxford University. *Address:* P.O. Box 1466, Austin, Tex. 78767. *Agent:* Edward J. Acton, Inc., 825 Third Ave., New York, N.Y. 10022. *Office: The Texas Observer*, 600 W. Seventh St., Austin, Tex. 78701.

CAREER: Worked as newscaster, sports announcer, and sports writer for *San Antonio Express*, San Antonio, Tex., political reporter for International News Service, British correspondent for Texas newspapers, assistant to the executive director for writing and research of National Security Training Commission, Washington, D.C.; *Texas Observer*, Austin, editor, 1954-61, 1963-66, editor and publisher, 1966—. Special correspondent to newspapers and magazines. Member of national advisory council of American Civil Liberties Union. *Member:* Authors Guild, Authors League of America, P.E.N., Texas Institute of Letters, Texas Philosophical Society.

WRITINGS: Dark Star: Hiroshima Reconsidered in the Life of Claude Eatherly of Lincoln Park, Texas, World, 1967; (editor) *Three Men in Texas; Bedichek, Webb, and Dobie: Essays by Their Friends in the "Texas Observer*," University of Texas, 1967; *Our Invaded Universities: Form, Reform, and New Starts*, Norton, 1974; *The Politician: The Life and Times of Lyndon Johnson; the Drive for Power, from the Frontier to Master of the Senate*, Norton, 1982; *On Reagan: The Man and His Presidency*, Macmillan, 1983. Columnist; contributor of articles to periodicals.

SIDELIGHTS: Describing Ronnie Dugger's *The Politician: The Life and Times of Lyndon Johnson; the Drive for Power, from the Frontier to Master of the Senate* in the *New York Times Book Review*, Aaron Latham writes: "Reading it is like being locked in a room alone with Lyndon Johnson: the book preaches at you, it is sometimes outrageous, but it twists your arm and makes you keep on reading." Dugger conducted a series of interviews with Johnson in 1967 and 1968 and his work is both a biography of Johnson and an interpretation of American and world politics in the light and aftermath of his policies. "This is Dugger's view of today's world as revealed through a partial retelling of the life of Lyndon Johnson," asserts Dan Balz in the *Washington Post Book World*. Crucial to Dugger's understanding of Johnson is the author's belief that the president's upbringing and exposure to the mythology of the old Texas west had a profound impact on his ideals. And in the view of Peter Wyden in the *Los Angeles Times Book Review*, Dugger "is at his best tracing Johnson's greed, grandiosity and crudeness to the cowboy past of his frontier forefathers."

Several critics have commented on what they perceive to be Dugger's hostile approach to his subject. John Bartlow Martin says in the *Chicago Tribune Book World* that "[*The Politician*] is decidedly not a friendly book." Writing in the *National Review*, William Murchison offers a similar opinion: "Dugger . . . doesn't like Johnson. Let him count the ways, which are various—and which make a well-researched book . . . less persuasive than it ought to be." Murchison adds, however, that "Dugger has, through personal interviews and years of laborious research, turned up much that's interesting and informative. Johnson's early life is recounted better here than in any other book I know of." Donald Morrison also focuses on Dugger's aggressive approach in *Time*: "Every other Johnsonian swagger, pronunciamento and claim is held up to the light for flaws and cracks. His book is very light on endearing anecdotes . . . but Dugger is a digger—wide-ranging, thorough, judicious." Latham says of Johnson, "No one book seems large enough to hold him. A whole shelf is required to tell his story. Ronnie Dugger has made a welcome contribution to that bookshelf."

BIOGRAPHICAL/CRITICAL SOURCES: Washington Post Book World, April 25, 1982, November 13, 1983; *Chicago Tribune Book World*, May 2, 1982; *New York Times Book Review*, May 9, 1982, January 8, 1984; *Time*, May 10, 1982; *Los Angeles Times Book Review*, May 30, 1982; *National Review*, October 1, 1982; *Times Literary Supplement*, January 7, 1983.

*   *   *

DUKORE, Bernard F. 1931-

PERSONAL: Born July 11, 1931, in New York, N.Y.; married Margaret Mitchell, 1974 (divorced, 1983). *Education:* Brooklyn College (now Brooklyn College of the City University of New York), A.B., 1952; Ohio State University, M.A., 1953; University of Illinois, Ph.D., 1957. *Home:* 46-043 Puulau Pl., Kaneohe, Hawaii 96744. *Office:* Department of Drama and Theatre, University of Hawaii, Honolulu, Hawaii 96822.

CAREER: Hunter College in the Bronx (now Herbert H. Lehman College of the City University of New York), Bronx,

N.Y., instructor in drama, 1957-60; University of Southern California, Los Angeles, assistant professor of drama, 1960-62; California State College at Los Angeles (now California State University, Los Angeles), 1962-66, began as assistant professor, became associate professor of drama; City University of New York, New York, N.Y., 1966-72, began as associate professor, became professor of drama; University of Hawaii, Honolulu, professor of drama, 1972—. Visiting fellow at Humanities Research Centre, Australian National University, 1979. *Military service:* U.S. Army, 1954-56; became sergeant. *Member:* American Educational Theatre Association, American Society for Theatre Research. *Awards, honors:* Guggenheim fellow, 1969-70; American Theatre Association fellow, 1975; National Endowment for the Humanities fellow, 1976-77.

WRITINGS: (Editor and author of introduction) George Etherege, *The Man of Mode*, Chandler Publishing, 1962; (editor with Ruby Cohn) *Twentieth Century Drama: England, Ireland, United States*, Random House, 1966; *Saint Joan: A Screenplay by Bernard Shaw*, University of Washington Press, 1968; (editor with Daniel C. Gerould) *Avant-Garde Drama: Major Plays and Documents, Post World War I*, Bantam, 1969; (editor with Robert O'Brien) *Tragedy: Ten Major Plays*, Bantam, 1969; *Bernard Shaw, Director*, University of Washington Press, 1970; (editor) John Gassner, *A Treasury of the Theatre*, Volume II, revised edition (Dukore was not associated with first edition), Simon & Schuster, 1970; (compiler) *Drama and Revolution*, Holt, 1970; (compiler) *Documents for Drama and Revolution*, Holt, 1970; *Bernard Shaw, Playwright: Aspects of Shavian Drama*, University of Missouri Press, 1973; *Dramatic Theory and Criticism*, Holt, 1974.

Seventeen Plays: Sophocles to Baraka, Crowell, 1976; *Where Laughter Stops: Pinter's Tragicomedy*, University of Missouri Press, 1976; *Money and Politics in Ibsen, Shaw, and Brecht*, University of Missouri Press, 1980; (editor and author of introduction) *The Collected Screenplays of Bernard Shaw*, University of Georgia Press, 1980; *The Theatre of Peter Barnes*, Heinemann Educational, 1981; (compiler) *Bernard Shaw's "Arms and the Man": A Composite Production Book*, Southern Illinois University Press, 1982; *Harold Pinter*, Grove, 1982; *American Dramatists, 1918-1945*, Grove, 1984. Contributor to *Tulane Drama Review, Educational Theatre Journal, Modern Drama, Theatre Survey*, and other drama journals.

BIOGRAPHICAL/CRITICAL SOURCES: *Times Literary Supplement*, March 20, 1981.

* * *

DUMONT, Jean-Paul 1940-

PERSONAL: Born May 23, 1940, in Vendome, France; son of Paul-Ursin (a physician) and Genevieve Dumont. *Education:* Sorbonne, University of Paris, A.B., 1964; University of Pittsburgh, Ph.D., 1972. *Office:* Department of Anthropology, University of Washington, Seattle, Wash. 98195.

CAREER: Anthropological fieldwork among Panare Indians of Venezuelan Guiana, 1967-69; Fordham University, Bronx, N.Y., instructor, 1970-71, assistant professor of anthropology, 1972; University of Washington, Seattle, Wash., assistant professor, 1975-79, associate professor of anthropology, 1979—. Visiting assistant professor at universities of Paris, Nantes, and Tours, 1972, and at Queens College of City University of New York, 1973-74; visiting lecturer, Princeton University, 1974-75.

MEMBER: American Anthropological Association (fellow), American Ethnological Association, Society for Psychological Anthropology, Association for Asian Studies, University of Washington Center for Studies in Demography and Ecology, School of International Studies Religion Studies Group. *Awards, honors:* Research training fellowship from Social Science Research Council, 1976-77; Fulbright-Hayes research fellowship, 1980-81; grant from Social Science Research Council and American Council of Learned Societies, 1982-83; fellowship from Council for International Exchange of Scholars, 1982-83.

WRITINGS: (With J. Monod) *Le Foetus Astral*, Bourgois, 1970; *Hasard Coagule* (poetry), Bourgois, 1970; *Flocs* (poetry), Bourgois, 1972; (contributor) R. Jaulin, editor, *Le Livre Blanc de l'Ethnocide en Amerique*, Fayard, 1972; (contributor) *De l'Ethnocide*, Union Generale d'Editions, 1972; (contributor) *Essais de Semiotique Poetique*, Larouse, 1972.

Under the Rainbow: Nature and Supernature Among the Panare Indians, University of Texas Press, 1976; (contributor) E. B. Basso, editor, *Essays on the Carib Culture, Society and Language*, University of Arizona Press, 1977; (contributor) W. C. McCormack and S. A. Wurm, editors, *Language and Thought: Anthropological Issues*, Mouton, 1977; (contributor) S. A. Freed, editor, *Anthropology and the Climate of Opinion*, New York Academy of Sciences, 1977; *The Headman and I: Ambivalence and Ambiguity in Anthropological Fieldwork*, University of Texas Press, 1978; (with P. U. Dumont) *Adele, Adele, Adele*, Bourgois, 1979; (with Dumont) *Le Cercle Amoureux d'Henry Legrand*, Gallimard, 1979.

WORK IN PROGRESS: Another book on the Panare.

* * *

DUNN, Judy
See SPANGENBERG, Judith Dunn

* * *

DUNN, Mary Lois 1930-

PERSONAL: Born August 18, 1930, in Uvalde, Tex.; daughter of F. S. (a railroad signal maintainer) and Ruth Alice (Hawkes) Dunn. *Education:* Stephen F. Austin State College (now Stephen F. Austin University), B.A., 1951; Louisiana State University, M.S. in L.S., 1957. *Politics:* "Presently Republican—vote for the man, not the party." *Religion:* Southern Baptist.

CAREER: Houston Independent School District, Houston, Tex., librarian, 1951—. Consultant to Texas Educational Agency on Title II ESEA, 1965. *Member:* American Library Association, Texas Library Association, Houston Association of School Librarians, Phi Beta Mu. *Awards, honors:* Sequoyah Children's Book Award of Oklahoma (determined by vote of children in grades four through nine), 1972, for *The Man in the Box: A Story from Vietnam*.

WRITINGS: *The Man in the Box: A Story from Vietnam*, McGraw, 1968; (with John G. Maguire) *Patty Hearst*, 2nd edition, Merit Publications, 1975; (with Ardath Mayhar) *The Absolutely Perfect Horse*, Harper, 1983.

WORK IN PROGRESS: A book on motorcycles, for young people.

SIDELIGHTS: Mary Lois Dunn and Ardath Mayhar's *The Absolutely Perfect Horse* is the tale of Annie Braeden, a young girl who dreams of acquiring the ideal horse. When the time comes for her to buy one, however, she brings home a sickly old pony, much to the consternation of family and friends. Her impulse to adopt the beast is repaid, though, when he saves the lives of her two brothers. Carol Van Sturm, writing in the *Washington Post Book World,* calls the book "a tight compelling story, with rich diversity of unique, memorable characters." Reviewing the work in *Booklist,* Denise M. Wilms concludes, "There is an undeniable sentimental streak here, but strong characterizations and a good plot compensate to make this very satisfying reading."

BIOGRAPHICAL/CRITICAL SOURCES: *Booklist,* April 15, 1983; *Washington Post Book World,* May 8, 1983.†

* * *

DUNN, Stephen 1939-

PERSONAL: Born June 24, 1939, in New York, N.Y.; son of Charles F. (a salesman) and Ellen (Fleishman) Dunn; married Lois Kelly (a yoga teacher), September 26, 1964; children: Andrea Ellen, Susanne. *Education:* Hofstra University, B.A., 1962; New School for Social Research, graduate study, 1964-66; Syracuse University, M.A., 1970. *Home:* 445 Chestnut Neck Rd., Port Republic, N.J. 08241. *Agent:* Philip G. Spitzer Literary Agency, 111-25 76th Ave., Forest Hills, N.Y. 11375. *Office:* Stockton State College, Pomona, N.J., 08240.

CAREER: Williamsport Billies, Williamsport, Pa., professional basketball player, 1962-63; National Biscuit Co., New York City, copywriter, 1963-66; Zipp-Davis Publishing Co., New York City, assistant editor, 1967-68; Southwest Minnesota State University, Marshall, assistant professor of creative writing, 1970-73; Stockton State College, Pomona, N.J., poet-in-residence, 1974—. Visiting professor, University of Washington, 1980, and Columbia University. *Military service:* U.S. Army, 1962. *Member:* American Association of University Professors. *Awards, honors:* Academy of American Poets, New York Poetry Center "Discovery '71" Award; National Endowment for the Arts fellowship, 1974, 1981; Theodore Roethke Prize, 1977, and Helen Bullis Prize, 1982, both from *Poetry Northwest.*

WRITINGS—All poetry; published by Carnegie-Mellon University Press, except as indicated: *Five Impersonations,* Ox Head Press, 1971; *Looking for Holes in the Ceiling,* University of Massachusetts Press, 1974; *Full of Lust and Good Usage,* 1976; *A Circus of Needs,* 1978; *Work and Love,* 1981; *Not Dancing,* 1984.

WORK IN PROGRESS: A collection of long poems.

SIDELIGHTS: Stephen Dunn lived in Spain for a year and has spent other periods in Europe. He writes: "My poetry must speak for itself; I have no comments about it."

* * *

DUNNING, (Arthur) Stephen (Jr.) 1924-

PERSONAL: Born October 31, 1924, in Duluth, Minn.; son of Arthur Stephenson and Julia (Hunter) Dunning; married Florence Jane Danielson, September 2, 1950; children: Steven, Elizabeth, Julia, Sarah. *Education:* Carleton College, B.A., 1949; University of Minnesota, B.A. and M.A., 1951; Florida State University, Ph.D., 1959. *Religion:* Unitarian Universalist. *Home:* 517 Oswego, Ann Arbor, Mich. 48104. *Office:* Department of English, University of Michigan, Ann Arbor, Mich. 48109.

CAREER: Teacher of English at junior and senior high schools, 1951-59; Duke University, Durham, N.C., assistant professor, 1959-61, associate professor of education, 1961-62; Northwestern University, Evanston, Ill., associate professor of education and co-director, Curriculum Center in English, 1962-64; University of Michigan, Ann Arbor, professor of education and professor of English, 1964—. Poet-in-the-schools for Michigan Council for the Humanities, 1982. Director of National Council of Teachers of English institutes in Minneapolis, Phoenix, and Durham, 1968, and Commission on Literature, 1972-74. Senior consultant in English, Scholastic Book Services, 1968-82. *Military service:* U.S. Army Air Forces, 1943-45. *Member:* National Council of Teachers of English (committee chairman, 1962-66; president-elect, 1974; president, 1974-75), American Association of University Professors, Michigan Council of Teachers of English (chairman of publications committee, 1965-67; president, 1968-69), Conference on English and Education (member of executive committee, 1966-72; chairman of executive committee, 1970-72).

AWARDS, HONORS: Panhandler Award, 1977, for poems; Alumni Achievement Award, Carleton College, 1978; Fries Award, Michigan Council of Teachers of English, 1976; Michigan Council for the Arts creative artist grant, 1983.

WRITINGS: *Teaching Literature to Adolescents: Poetry,* Scott, Foresman, 1966; *Teaching Literature to Adolescents: Short Stories,* Scott, Foresman, 1968; (with Ruth Clay and Andrew Carrigan) *Poetry,* Scholastic Book Services, 1970; (with Henry Maloney) *Superboy/Supergirl,* Scholastic Book Services, 1971; (with Lahna Diskin and Maloney) *Short Story,* Scholastic Book Services, 1973; (with M. Joe Eaton and Malcolm Glass) *Poetry II,* Scholastic Book Services, 1974; (with Alan B. Howes) *Literature for Adolescents: Teaching Poems, Stories, Novels, and Plays,* Scott, Foresman, 1975; *Who Am I?,* Scholastic Book Services, 1978; *Dreams,* Scholastic Book Services, 1978; *Handfuls of Us* (poems), Croissant and Co., 1980; *Walking Home Dead* (poems), Stone County Press, 1981; *Do You Fear No One* (poems), Pancake Press, 1982.

Editor: (With Dwight L. Burton) *Courage,* Scholastic Book Services, 1960; (with Carol Lee) *Frontiers,* Scholastic Book Services, 1961; (with Robert Smith and Jane Sprague) *Small World,* Scholastic Book Services, 1964; (with Edward Lueders and Hugh L. Smith) *Reflections on a Gift of Watermelon Pickle, and Other Modern Verse,* text edition, Scott, Foresman, 1966, trade edition, Lothrop, 1967; (with Lueders and Smith) *Some Haystacks Don't Even Have Any Needle, and Other Complete Modern Poems,* Lothrop, 1969; *English for the Junior High Years,* National Council of Teachers of English, 1969; *Mad, Sad and Glad,* Scholastic Book Services, 1970.

Supervising editor of twelve literature units published by Scholastic Book Services, 1961-64, and revisions, 1972—; editor of series of long-playing records, "Today's Poets: Their Poems/Their Voices," Volumes I-V, Scholastic Records, 1967.

WORK IN PROGRESS: A book of poems, *Say It with Me,* for Word Works; a collection of prose poems, *Menominee; Poetry Workshop,* with William Stafford.

SIDELIGHTS: Stephen Dunning told *CA:* "I'd been teaching and writing for years before I began writing poems. In the fall of 1975 I promised myself I'd 'practice poetry' every day. Of course, I haven't. But poetry writing is now the center of my writing life.

"Until 1975, I'd written mainly to publish. It seemed natural to send these early poems out to magazines. After I published forty or fifty, without noticeably changing the world, I realized that the energy going into the effort to publish was mis-directed. It was the poems, not their publication! So publishing became more a casual thing. Then I liked the doing of it—the actual writing time—even more.

"I think of myself as a developing (eight-year-old) poet captured in an older body. That gives me 'advantages.' For example, I know specific ways to practice. (Students and others I work with sometimes don't.) I've learned not to edit and polish too soon—not until I've expanded a poem many whichways. I almost always get good stuff from expanding, stuff to pare down and groom. I've learned from copying good poems, too: copying taught me to slow myself as a reader, to pay close attention. And I've learned that writing poems is a way to find out (often about myself), not a way to tell.

"Does all this lean toward [the] question: 'What advice would you give aspiring writers?' I think so, but there are more obvious things. First, of course, *read*. Think and talk about what you read. Next, *practice*. Practice! Regular routines work for many writers—rising early to write; or putting in so much time [a] day. Some days I start off by copying (or copy-changing) a poem that has in it some quality I want to practice. I also trick myself—put my attention on something like form or rhyme in order to free my un-self-conscious self. I believe in practicing, and in re-writing; I believe in 'the luck' that sometimes comes with practice and re-write.

"Isn't wanting to be a poet different from wanting to be another kind of author? Poetry seems close to journal-keeping, or personal writing. Stories and essays seem written more for others, but poetry [is] more for oneself. I write mainly for myself, anyway. I advise young poets to set sights high (for example, try to write poems as good as those of your poet heroes or heroines); to practice regularly and rigorously; and to join with others who write, who care about themselves *as writers*. Of course you can help such people; and they can help you. Friends who matter most to me now are writing friends."

* * *

DYE, Thomas R(oy) 1935-

PERSONAL: Born December 16, 1935, in Pittsburgh, Pa.; son of James C. and Marguerite A. (Dewan) Dye; married Joan G. Wohleber, June, 1957; children: Roy Thomas, Cheryl Price. *Education:* Pennsylvania State University, B.A., 1957, M.A., 1959; University of Pennsylvania, Ph.D., 1961. *Home:* 2321 Killarney Way, Tallahassee, Fla. 32308. *Office:* Policy Sciences Program, Florida State University, Tallahassee, Fla. 32306.

CAREER: University of Wisconsin—Madison, assistant professor of political science, 1962-63; University of Georgia, Athens, assistant professor, 1963-65, associate professor of political science and chairman of department, 1965-68; Florida State University, Tallahassee, professor of government, 1968—, chairman of department, 1969-72, director of Policy Sciences Program, 1978—. Visiting professor at Bar Ilan University, 1972, and University of Arizona, 1976. *Military service:* U.S. Air Force Reserve, 1957-62; became first lieutenant. *Member:* American Political Science Association (secretary, 1969-72), Southern Political Science Association (member of executive council; president, 1976-77), Phi Beta Kappa, Omicron Delta Kappa. *Awards, honors:* U.S. Office of Education research grants, 1966-67, 1969-70; National Science Foundation grants, 1967, 1970-71; National Institutes of Health research grant, 1973-76.

WRITINGS: (With Oliver P. Williams, S. Charles Liebman, and Harold Herman) *Suburban Differences and Metropolitan Policies*, University of Pennsylvania Press, 1965; *Politics, Economics, and the Public*, Rand McNally, 1966; (editor with Brett W. Hawkins) *Politics in the Metropolis: A Reader in Conflict and Cooperation*, C. E. Merrill, 1967; *Politics in States and Communities*, Prentice-Hall, 1969, 5th edition, in press; (with Lee Greene and George S. Parthemos) *American Government: Theory, Structure, and Process*, Wadsworth, 1969; (compiler) *American Public Policy*, C. E. Merrill, 1969.

(With Harmon Zeigler) *The Irony of Democracy*, Wadsworth, 1970, 6th edition, 1984; *The Politics of Equality*, Bobbs-Merrill, 1971; *Understanding Public Policy*, Prentice-Hall, 1972, 4th edition, 1984; *Power and Society*, Brooks/Cole, 1975, 3rd edition, 1983; *Who's Running America?: Institutional Leadership in the United States*, Prentice-Hall, 1976, 2nd edition published as *Who's Running America?: The Carter Years*, 1979, 3rd edition published as *Who's Running America?: The Reagan Years*, 1983; *Policy Analysis: What Governments Do, Why They Do It, and What Difference It Makes*, University of Alabama Press, 1976; (with Zeigler) *American Politics in the Media Age*, Brooks/Cole, 1983.

Contributor: *The Legislative Process in Congress and the States*, Institute of Public Administration, Pennsylvania State University, 1961; Robert E. Crew, editor, *State Politics*, Wadsworth, 1966; Michael N. Danielson, editor, *Metropolitan Politics*, Little, Brown, 1966; Samuel C. Patterson, editor, *American Legislative Process: A Reader*, Van Nostrand, 1967; Peter Woll, editor, *American Government: Readings and Cases*, Little, Brown, 1968; Aaron Wildavsky and Nelson Polsby, editors, *American Governmental Institutions*, Rand McNally, 1968.

Donald P. Sprengel, editor, *Comparative State Politics: A Reader*, Wadsworth, 1970; Ira Sharkansky and Richard I. Hofferbert, editors, *Politics and Policies in States and Communities*, Little, Brown, 1970; Walter G. Hack, editor, *Educational Administration: Selected Readings*, Allyn & Bacon, 1970; David A. Morgan and Samuel Kirkpatrick, editors, *Urban Political Analysis: A Systems Approach*, Free Press, 1970; Oliver Walter, editor, *Political Scientists at Work*, Duxbury, 1971; Robert N. Spadaro, editor, *The Policy Vacuum*, Lexington Books, 1975; Frank P. Scioli and Thomas J. Cook, editors, *Methodologies for Analyzing Public Policies*, Lexington Books, 1975; Stuart Nagel, editor, *Policy Studies and the Social Sciences*, Lexington Books, 1975.

Editor of "Policy Analysis" series, Bobbs-Merrill. Contributor of numerous articles, essays, and reviews to social science journals.

WORK IN PROGRESS: Writing on state politics, on inequality, political leadership, and political systems, and on public policy.

* * *

DYKE, John 1935-

PERSONAL: Born November 24, 1935, in Alcester, England; son of Arthur (a cobbler) and Cissie (a lady's maid; maiden name, Hale) Dyke; married Jennifer Carter, April 17, 1965; children: William, James, Anna. *Education:* Birmingham College of Art, N.D.D., 1962. *Politics:* Socialist. *Home:* 58 Southfield Rd., High Wycombe, Buckinghamshire HP13 5LA, England.

CAREER: Served with Fleet Air Arm, Royal Navy 1952-59; art teacher in London, England, 1963-65; Methuen & Co. Ltd.

(publishers), London, graphic designer, 1965-66; free-lance author and illustrator, 1962—. Lecturer in graphic design at art schools.

WRITINGS—Self-illustrated: *Peter and the Pier,* Dobson, 1968; *Columbus Mouse,* Macmillan, 1973; *Magic Colour,* Macmillan, 1974; (with Nic Tucker) *In the Picture,* Longman, 1976; *Pigwig,* Methuen, 1978; *Pigwig and the Pirates,* Methuen, 1979; *Pigwig and the Crusty Diamonds,* Methuen, 1982; *Barrington the Circus Mouse,* Methuen, 1984.

Illustrator: Ann-Cath Vestly, "The Eight Children" series, Methuen, 1973-79; Joan Redmayne and Edward Ramsbottom, *Secret Island,* Macmillan, 1975; Ann Thwaite, *Rose in the River,* Hodder & Stroughton, 1975; Dorothy Edwards, *Dad's New Car,* Methuen, 1976; Ves Magee, *Oliver the Famous Birdman,* Longman, 1976; Fran Hunia, *The Three Bears,* Ladybird Books, 1976; Redmayne and Ramsbottom, *In the Air,* Macmillan, 1977; Marion Green, *The Magician Who Lived on the Mountain,* Hodder & Stoughton, 1977; Hunia, *The Three Billy Goats Gruff,* Ladybird Books, 1977; Hunia, *The Elves and the Shoemaker,* Ladybird Books, 1978; Hunia, *The Sly Fox and the Little Red Hen,* Ladybird Books, 1979; Vernon Mills, *Tom Thumb,* Ladybird Books, 1979. Contributor to numerous periodicals.

WORK IN PROGRESS: Sammy at the Fair.

E

ECO, Umberto 1932-

PERSONAL: Born January 5, 1932, in Alessandria, Italy; son of Giulio and Giovanna (Bisio) Eco; married Renate Ramge (a teacher), September 24, 1962; children: Stefano, Carlotta. *Education:* University of Turin, Ph.D., 1954. *Home:* Via Melzi d'Eril 23, 20154 Milano, Italy. *Office:* Universita di Bologna, Via Guerrazzi 20, Bologna, Italy.

CAREER: RAI (Italian Radio-Television), Milan, Italy, editor for cultural programs, 1954-59; University of Turin, Turin, Italy, assistant lecturer, 1956-63, lecturer in aesthetics, 1963-64; University of Milan, Milan, lecturer on faculty of architecture, 1964-65; University of Florence, Florence, Italy, professor of visual communications, 1966-69; Milan Polytechnic, Milan, professor of semiotics, 1969-71; University of Bologna, Bologna, Italy, associate professor, 1971-75, professor of semiotics, 1975—. Visiting professor, New York University, 1969, 1976, Northwestern University, 1972, University of California, San Diego, 1975, Yale University, 1977, 1980, 1981, and Columbia University, 1978. Lecturer on semiotics (the study of signs) at various institutions throughout the world, including University of Antwerp, Ecole Pratique des Hautes Etudes, University of London, Nobel Foundation, University of Warsaw, University of Budapest, University of Toronto, Murdoch University—Perth, and Amherst College. Member of the Council for the United States and Italy. *Military service:* Italian Army, 1958-59.

MEMBER: International Association for Semiotic Studies (secretary-general, 1972-79, vice-president, 1979—), James Joyce Foundation (honorary trustee). *Awards, honors:* Premio Strega and Premio Anghiari, both 1981, both for *Il nome della rosa;* named honorary citizen of Monte Cerignone, Italy, 1982; Prix Medicis for best foreign novel, 1982, for French version of *Il nome della rosa; Los Angeles Times* fiction prize nomination, 1983, for *The Name of the Rose.*

WRITINGS—In Italian: *Il problema estetico in San Tommaso* (title means "The Aesthetic Problem in Saint Thomas"), Edizioni di Filosofia, 1956, 2nd edition published as *Il problema estetico in Tommaso d'Aquino,* Bompiani, 1970; *Filosofi in liberta,* Taylor (Turin), 1958, 2nd edition, 1959; (contributor) *Momenti e problema di storia dell'estetica,* Marzorati, 1959.

Opera aperta: forma e indeterminazione nelle poetiche contemporanee (includes *Le poetiche di Joyce;* also see below), Bompiani, 1962, revised edition, 1972; *Diario minimo,* Mondadori, 1963, 2nd revised edition, 1976; *Apocalittici e integrati: Comunicazioni di massa e teoria della cultura di massa,* Bompiani, 1964, revised edition, 1977; *Le poetiche di Joyce,* Bompiani, 1965, 2nd edition published as *Le poetiche di Joyce dalla "Summa" al "Finnegans Wake,"* 1966; *Appunti per una semiologia delle comunicazioni visive* (also see below), Bompiani, 1967; (author of introduction) Mimmo Castellano, *Noi vivi,* Dedalo Libri, 1967; *La struttura assente* (includes *Appunti per una semiologia delle comunicazioni visive*), Bompiani, 1968, revised edition, 1983; *La definizione dell'arte* (title means "The Definition of Art"), U. Mursia, 1968; (editor) *L'uomo e l'arte,* Volume I: *L'arte come mestiere,* Bompiani, 1969; (editor with Remo Faccani) *I sistemi di segni e lo strutturalismo sovietico,* Bompiani, 1969, 2nd edition published as *Semiotica della letteratura in URSS,* 1974.

(Editor) *Socialismo y consolacion: Reflexiones en torno a "Los misterios de Paris" de Eugene Sue,* Tusquets, 1970, 2nd edition, 1974; *Le forme del contenuto,* Bompiani, 1971; (editor with Cesare Sughi) *Cent'anni dopo: Il ritorno dell'intreccio,* Bompiani, 1971; *Il segno,* Isedi, 1971, 2nd edition, Mondadori; (editor with M. Bonazzi) *I pampini bugiardi,* Guaraldi, 1972; (editor) *Estetica e teoria dell'informazione,* Bompiani, 1972; (contributor) *Documenti su il nuovo medioevo,* Bompiani, 1973; (editor) *Eugenio Carmi: una pittura de paesaggio?,* G. Prearo, 1973; *Il costume di casa: Evidenze e misteri dell'ideologia italiano,* Bompiani, 1973; *Beato di Liebana: Miniature del Beato de Fernando I y Sancha,* F. M. Ricci, 1973; *Il superuomo di massa: Studi sul romanzo popolare,* Cooperativa Scrittori, 1976, revised edition, Bompiani, 1978; (co-editor) *Storia di una rivoluzione mai esistita l'esperimento Vaduz,* Servizio Opinioni, RAI, 1976; *Dalla periferia dell'Impero,* Bompiani, 1976; *Come si fa una tesi di laurea,* Bompiani, 1977; *La definizione dell'arte,* Garzanti, 1978; *Lector in fabula: La cooperazione interpretative nei testi narrativa* (also see below), Bompiani, 1979; (contributor) *Carolina Invernizio, Matilde Serao, Liala,* La Nuova Italia, 1979; (contributor) *Convegno su realta e ideologie dell'informazione, Milan, 1978,* Il Saggiatore, 1979; (with others) *Perche continuiamo a fare e a insegnare arte?,* Cappelli, 1979.

Sette anni di desiderio, Bompiani, 1983.

In English translation: (Editor with G. Zorzoli) *Storia figurata delle invenzioni: Dalla selce scheggiata al volo spaziali,* Bompiani, 1961, translation by Anthony Lawrence published as *The Picture History of Inventions from Plough to Polaris*, Macmillan, 1963, 2nd Italian edition, Bompiani, 1968; (editor with Oreste del Buono) *Il caso Bond*, Bompiani, 1965, translation by R. Downie published as *The Bond Affair*, Macdonald, 1966.

(Editor with Jean Chesneaux and Gino Nebiolo) *I fumetti di Mao*, Laterza, 1971, translation by Frances Frenaye published as *The People's Comic Book: Red Women's Detachment, Hot on the Trail, and Other Chinese Comics,* Anchor Press, 1973; *Il nome della rosa*, Bompiani, 1980, translation by William Weaver published as *The Name of the Rose*, Harcourt, 1983.

In English: *A Theory of Semiotics*, Indiana University Press, 1976, translation from original English manuscript published as *Trattato di semiotica generale*, Bompiani, 1975; *The Role of the Reader: Explorations in the Semiotics of Texts*, Indiana University Press, 1979, revised Italian edition published as *Lector in fabula: La cooperazione interpretative nei testi narrativa*, Bompiani, 1979.

Semiotics and the Philosophy of Language, Indiana University Press, 1984; (editor with T. Sebeok) *Sign of the Three: Dupin, Holmes, Pierce*, Indiana University Press, 1984.

Many of Umberto Eco's books have been translated into foreign languages, including German, French, and Spanish. Contributor to numerous encyclopedias, including *Enciclopedia Filosofica* and *Encyclopedic Dictionary of Semiotics*. Also contributor to proceedings of the First Congress of the International Association for Semiotic Studies. Columnist for *Il giorno, La stampa, Corriere della Sera*, and other newspapers and magazines. Contributor of essays and reviews to numerous periodicals, including *Espresso, Corriere della Sera, Times Literary Supplement, Revue Internationale de Sciences Sociales*, and *Nouvelle Revue Francaise*.

Member of editorial board, *Semiotica, Poetics Today, Degres, Structuralist Review, Text, Communication, Problemi dell'informazione,* and *Alfabeta;* nonfiction senior editor, Casa Editrice Bompiani, Milan, 1959-75; editor, *VS—Semiotic Studies*.

WORK IN PROGRESS: Semiotics and the Philosophy of Language.

SIDELIGHTS: No one expected *The Name of the Rose* to become an internationally acclaimed best-seller, least of all Umberto Eco, the man who wrote the book. A respected Italian scholar, Eco had built his literary reputation on specialized academic writing about semiotics—the study of how cultures communicate through signs. Not only was *The Name of the Rose* his first novel, it was also a complex creation, long on philosophy and short on sex—definitely not blockbuster material, especially not in Italy where the market for books is small. Eco himself considered the initial press run of 15,000 copies excessive, according to the *Times*. That was in 1980. By 1983, *The Name of the Rose* had been translated into more than twenty languages, won several of Europe's most prestigious literary prizes, and sold nearly a million and a half hardback copies worldwide. Today the novel is considered a publishing phenomenon, and people in the book business are still asking themselves why.

Some experts attribute its success to the current interest in fantasy literature. "For all its historical accuracy, *The Name of the Rose* has the charm of an invented world," Drenka Willen, Eco's editor at Harcourt Brace Jovanovich, told *Newsweek*. Others chalk it up to snob appeal. "Every year there is one great *unread* best-seller. A lot of people who will buy the book will never read it," Howard Kaminsky, president of Warner Books, suggests in that same *Newsweek* article.

But perhaps the most plausible explanation is the one offered by Franco Ferrucci in the *New York Times Book Review:* "The answer may lie in the fact that Mr. Eco is the unacknowledged leader of contemporary Italian culture, a man whose academic and ideological prestige has grown steadily through years of dazzling and solid work." In addition to semiotics—a field that he almost singlehandedly legitimatized—Eco is an expert on logic, literature, aesthetics, and history. In fact, in Eco's opinion, the science of semiotics embraces not only these, but all aspects of culture. Academics have been reading Eco's hypotheses for years in specialized texts such as *A Theory of Semiotics* and *The Role of the Reader: Explorations in the Semiotics of Texts*. While these works are unintelligible to the public at large, some of Eco's concepts have begun to filter down. "Only a specialist or a panicky grad student would read a book called *A Theory of Semiotics*," Walter Kendrick observes, "but a general reader might well pick up a semiotic novel if it promised to give the gist of the matter without bogging down in jargon. For most readers," Kendrick continues in the *Village Voice Literary Supplement*, "*The Name of the Rose* is worth reading as a sugarcoated version of that otherwise unpalatable subject."

On one level *The Name of the Rose* is a murder mystery in which a number of Catholic monks are inexplicably killed. The setting is an ancient monastery in northern Italy, the year is 1327, and the air is rife with evil. Dissention among rival factions of the Franciscan order threatens to tear the church apart, and each side is preparing for a showdown. On one side stand the Spiritualists and the emperor Louis IV who endorse evangelical poverty; on the other, the corrupt Pope John XXII and the monks who believe that the vow of poverty will rob the church of earthly wealth and power. In an effort to avoid a confrontation, both sides agree to meet at the monastery—a Benedictine abbey that is considered neutral ground. To this meeting come William of Baskerville, an English Franciscan empowered to represent the emperor, and Adso, William's disciple and scribe. Before the council can convene, however, the body of a young monk is discovered at the bottom of a cliff, and William, a master logician in the tradition of Sherlock Holmes, is recruited to solve the crime, assisted by Adso, in Watson's role. As the murders proliferate in seeming fulfillment of an apocalyptic prophecy, the sleuths engage in passionate debates about the meaning of scriptures. These theological digressions, which are grounded in fact and frequently studded with Latin quotations, lend a historical dimension to the book. What's more, the evidence that William and Adso pursue involves secret symbols and coded manuscripts—in other words, semiotics.

Nowhere is the importance of decoding symbols more apparent than in the library—an intricate labyrinth that houses all types of books, including volumes on pagan rituals and black magic. The secret of the maze is known to only a few, among them the master librarian whose job it is to safeguard the collection and supervise the circulation of appropriate volumes. William suspects that the murders relate to a forbidden book—a rare work with "the power of a thousand scorpions"—that some of the more curious monks have been trying to obtain. "What the temptation of adultery is for laymen and the yearning for riches is for secular ecclesiastics, the seduction of knowledge is for monks," William explains to Adso. "Why should they not have risked death to satisfy a curiosity of their minds, or have killed to prevent someone from appropriating a jealously guarded secret of their own?"

After being put off the track by a number of red herrings, William finally locates the prohibited book and the "Antichrist" who has committed the murders. To reveal the culprit would spoil the story, but it can be reported that the volume in question turns out to be the "lost" second volume of Aristotle's *Poetics*, which extols comedy as a force for good. This the murderer could not stand. As Gerard Reedy explains in his *America* review, the killer "fears that this authoritative explication of comic genres will undermine the seriousness of truth." Believing that Christ never laughed, the murderer cannot abide the laughter of others. He "did a diabolical thing because he loved his truth so lewdly that he dared anything in order to destroy falsehood," William explains to Adso, adding: "Perhaps the mission of those who love mankind is to make people laugh at the truth, *to make truth laugh,* because the only truth lies in learning to free ourselves from insane passion for the truth."

This statement appears to reflect Eco's attitude as well as William's. "It is almost too obvious that William is Mr. Eco himself," Franco Ferrucci points out in the *New York Times Book Review*. Writing in the *Village Voice Literary Supplement*, Walter Kendrick explains the connection between William's philosophy and modern semiotics: "Throughout the book, the naive realism of Adso, the narrator, bumps heads with the nominalism of William, his mentor. Realism and nominalism were schools of medieval philosophy. . . . But the two positions correspond rather well to the common sense of a modern reader and the apparent nihilism of a semiotician. . . . Baldly stated, realism maintains that the names of things are directly attached to the essence of what they denote, that universals are 'realer' than particulars. Nominalism attributes no reality to names; they are merely human ways of organizing a world that would otherwise be unmanageable."

Some medievalists have suggested that this is a distinctly modern point of view, out of place in William's world. His comment upon finally solving the case is revealing. "I behaved stubbornly," he tells Adso, "pursuing a semblance of order, when I should have known well there is no order in the universe." Kendrick points out that "such an idea goes far beyond all the heresies for which fourteenth-century people were burned at the stake; not only shouldn't William have known it, he wouldn't have thought it for another 600 years." While acknowledging the inaccuracy, Walter Goodman excuses it in the name of poetic license. "In this novel," he writes in the *New York Times,* "imagination carries the day. William of Baskerville may be an anachronism, but Mr. Eco wants us to know that his rationality, tolerance and compassion would have added light to what used to be known as the Dark Ages." In a letter to *CA,* Eco contests these criticisms. "Many medievalists say that I am correctly mirroring the most advanced ideas of the fourteenth century," he writes, adding that the novel has prompted several articles in academic journals as well as a symposium at the University of Louvain.

If William speaks for reason, Adso—the young novice who, in his old age, will relate the story—represents the voice of faith. Ferrucci believes that Adso reflects the author's second side: "The Eco who writes *The Name of the Rose* is Adso: a voice young and old at the same time, speaking from nostalgia for love and passion. William shapes the story with his insight; Adso gives it his own pathos. He will never think, as William does, that 'books are not made to be believed but to be subjected to inquiry'; Adso writes to be believed."

Another way Eco's novel can be interpreted is as a parable of modern life. The vehement struggle between church and state mirrors much of recent Italian history with its "debates over the role of the left and the accompanying explosion of terrorist violence," writes Sari Gilbert in the *Washington Post.* Eco acknowledges the influence that former Italian premier Aldo Moro's 1978 kidnapping and death had on his story, telling Gilbert that it "gave us all a sense of impotence," but he also warned that the book was not simply a *roman a clef.* "Instead," he told Herbert Mitgang in a *New York Times Book Review* article, "I hope readers see the roots, that everything that existed then—from banks and the inflationary spiral to the burning of libraries—exists today. We are always approaching the time of the anti-Christ. In the nuclear age, we are never far from the Dark Ages."

BIOGRAPHICAL/CRITICAL SOURCES—Periodicals: *Journal of Communication,* autumn, 1976; *Art Journal,* winter, 1976-77; *Language in Society,* April, 1977; *Times Literary Supplement,* July 8, 1977; *Language,* Volume LIII, number 3, 1977; *American Anthropologist,* September, 1978; *International Philosophical Quarterly,* June, 1980; *Corriere della Sera,* June 1, 1981; *Quaderni Medievali,* June 11, 1981; *New York Times,* June 4, 1983; *New York Times Book Review,* June 5, 1983; July 17, 1983; *Time,* June 13, 1983; *Wall Street Journal,* June 20, 1983; *Newsweek,* July 4, 1983; September 26, 1983; *Maclean's,* July 18, 1983; *New York Review of Books,* July 21, 1983; *Harper's,* August, 1983; *America,* August 13, 1983; *People,* August 29, 1983; *New Republic,* September 5, 1983; *Times* (London), September 29, 1983, November 3, 1983; *Village Voice Literary Supplement,* October, 1983; *Washington Post,* October 9, 1983; *Merkur,* Volume XXXVII, number 1, 1983.

Books: Eco, *The Name of the Rose,* translation by William Weaver, Harcourt, 1983; *Contemporary Literary Criticism,* Volume XXVIII, Gale, 1984.

—Sketch by Donna Olendorf

* * *

EDGAR, David 1948-

PERSONAL: Born February 26, 1948, in Birmingham, England; son of Barrie (a TV producer) and Joan (Burman) Edgar. *Education:* Manchester University, B.A. (with honors), 1969. *Politics:* Socialist. *Religion:* None. *Agent:* Michael Imison, 81 Shaftesbury Ave., London W.1, England.

CAREER: Playwright. Leeds Polytechnic, Leeds, England, fellow in creative writing, 1972-74; Birmingham Repertory Theatre, Birmingham, England, resident playwright, 1974-75. *Member:* Association of Cinematograph, Television and Allied Technicians, Writers' Guild, Theatre Writers' Union. *Awards, honors:* United Kingdom/United States Bicentennial Arts fellow, 1978-79; John Whiting Award, Arts Council of Great Britain for "Destiny"; Society of West End Theatres award for best play, Antoinette Perry Award ("Tony"), and New York Drama Critics Circle award for best play, all 1982, for "The Life and Adventures of Nicholas Nickleby"; Emmy Award nomination, Academy of Television Arts and Sciences, 1983, for the television production of "The Life and Adventures of Nicholas Nickleby"; *Maydays* was named best new play by a number of periodicals, including *Plays and Players, Punch, The Stage,* and *Daily Express.*

WRITINGS—Plays: "Two Kinds of Angel" (one-act), first produced in Bradford, England, at Bradford University Theatre, July, 1970, produced in London at Basement Theatre, February, 1971; "A Truer Shade of Blue," first produced in Bradford at Bradford University Theatre, August, 1970; "Bloody Rosa," first produced in Bradford at Bradford University Theatre, September, 1970, produced in Edinburgh, Scotland, at Edinburgh Festival, August, 1971; "Still Life: Man in Bed," first produced in Edinburgh at Pool Theatre, May, 1971, produced in London, England, at Little Theatre, July, 1972; "Acid," first produced in Bradford at Bradford University Theatre, July, 1971, produced in Edinburgh at Edinburgh Festival, August, 1971; "The National Interest" (one-act), produced by General Will (theatre company), August, 1971; "Conversation in Paradise," first produced in Edinburgh at Edinburgh University Theatre, October, 1971; "Tedderella," first produced in Edinburgh at Pool Theatre, December, 1971, produced in London at Bush Theatre, January 10, 1973.

"The Rupert Show" (one-act), first produced in Bradford at Bradford University Theatre, produced by General Will, January, 1972; "The End," first produced in Bradford at Bradford University Theatre, March, 1972; "Excuses Excuses" (two-act), first produced in Coventry, England, at Belgrade Theatre, May, 1972, produced in London at Open Space Theatre, July, 1973, produced as "Fired" by Second City Theatre Co., January, 1975; "Rent: Or, Caught in the Act," produced by General Will, May, 1972, produced in London at Unity Theatre, June, 1972; "State of Emergency" (one-act), first produced by General Will, August, 1972, produced in London at Royal Court Theatre Upstairs, November 7, 1972; (with Tony Bicat, Howard Brenton, Brian Clark, Francis Fichs, David Hare, and Snoo Wilson) "England's Ireland," first produced in Amsterdam, Netherlands, at Mickery Theatre, September, 1972, produced in London at Round House Theatre, October 2, 1972; "Road to Hanoi," first produced by Paradise Foundry (theatre company), October, 1972; "Not with a Bang But a Whimper," first produced in Leeds, England, at Leeds Polytechnic Theatre, November, 1972; "Death Story," first produced in Birmingham, England, at Birmingham Repertory Studio Theatre, November, 1972, produced in New York by Manhattan Theatre Club, March, 1975.

(With Brenton) "A Fart for Europe" (one-act), produced in London at Royal Court Theatre Upstairs, January 18, 1973; (with others) "Up Spaghetti Junction," first produced in Birmingham at Birmingham Repertory Studio Theatre, February, 1973; "Gangsters" (also see below), produced in London at Soho Polytechnic Lunchtime Theatre, February 13, 1973; "Baby Love" (one-act; also see below), first produced in Leeds at Leeds Playhouse, March 16, 1973, produced in London at Soho Polytechnic Lunchtime Theatre, May 28, 1973; "Liberated Zone," produced in Bingley, England, at Bingley College of Education, June, 1973; "The Case of the Workers' Plane" (two-act), produced in Bristol, England, at Bristol New Vic, June, 1973, revised play produced as "Concorde Cabaret" (also see below), by Avon Touring Co., January, 1975; "Operation Iskra" (three-act), produced by Paradise Foundry, September 4, 1973; "The Eagle Has Landed" (also see below), produced in Liverpool, England, at Liverpool University, November, 1973.

"The Dunkirk Spirit," produced by General Will, January, 1974; *Dick Deterred* (two-act; produced in London at Bush Theatre, February 25, 1974, produced in New York at Redfield Theatre, January, 1983), Monthly Review Press, 1974; "The All-Singing All-Talking Golden Oldie Rock Revival Ho Chi Minh Peace Love and Revolution Show," produced in Bingley at Bingley College of Education, March, 1974; "Man Only Dines," produced in Leeds at Leeds Polytechnic Theatre, June, 1974; "O Fair Jerusalem," produced in Birmingham at Birmingham Repertory Studio Theatre, May, 1975; "Summer Sports," first produced in Birmingham by Birmingham Arts Lab, July, 1975, produced in London at Bankside Globe Theatre, August 7, 1975, produced as "Blood Sports" at Bush Theatre, June 28, 1976; "The National Theatre," produced in London at Open Space Theatre, October 14, 1975; "Events Following the Closure of a Motorcycle Factory," produced in Birmingham at Birmingham Repertory Studio Theatre, February, 1976; "Saigon Rose" (also see below), produced in Edinburgh at Traverse Theatre, July, 1976, produced in New York at Westside Mainstage, November, 1982; *Destiny* (also see below; first produced in Stratford, England, at Other Place, September 22, 1976, produced on the West End at Aldwych Theatre, May 12, 1977), Eyre Methuen, 1976; "The Perils of Bardfrod," produced in Bradford at Theatre in the Mill, Bradford University, November, 1976.

Wreckers (first produced in Exeter, England, by 7:84 Theatre Co., February 10, 1977, produced in London at Half Moon Theatre, April 19, 1977), Eyre Methuen, 1977; "Our Own People," first produced by Pirate Jenny (theatre company), November, 1977, produced in London at Royal Court Theatre, January 9, 1978; *Ball Boys*, Pluto Press, 1978; (adaptor) *The Jail Diary of Albie Sachs* (also see below; produced in London at Warehouse Theatre, June 16, 1978, produced in New York by Manhattan Theatre Club, November, 1979), Collings, 1978; (adaptor) *Mary Barnes* (first produced in Birmingham at Birmingham Repertory Studio Theatre, August 31, 1978, produced in London at Royal Court Theatre, January 10, 1979, produced in New York at New York Theatre Studio, July, 1983), Eyre Methuen, 1979; *Teendreams* (produced in Bristol at Vandyck Theatre, January 26, 1979), Eyre Methuen, 1979.

(Adaptor) *The Life and Adventures of Nicholas Nickleby* (also see below; based on the Charles Dickens novel; first produced on the West End by Royal Shakespeare Co. at Aldwych Theatre, June 21, 1980, produced on Broadway at Plymouth Theatre, October 5, 1981), Dramatists Play Service, 1982; *Maydays* (produced in London at Barbican Theatre, 1983), Eyre Methuen, 1983.

Scripts; produced for television, except as indicated: "The Eagle Has Landed" (based on play of the same title), Granada Television, 1973; "Sanctuary" (based on the author's play "Gangsters"), Scottish Television, 1973; "I Know What I Meant," Granada Television, 1974; "Baby Love" (based on play of the same title), British Broadcasting Corp. (BBC), 1974; "Concorde Cabaret" (based on play of the same title), Harlech Television, 1975; (with Robert Muller and Hugh Whitemore) "Censors," BBC, 1975; "The Midas Touch," BBC, 1975; "Ecclesiastes" (radio play), BBC Radio 4, 1977; "Destiny" (based on play of the same title), BBC, 1978; "Saigon Rose" (radio play; based on play of the same title), BBC Radio 3, 1979; "The Jail Diary of Albie Sachs" (based on play of the same title), BBC, 1980; "The Life and Adventures of Nicholas Nickleby" (based on play of the same title), Channel Four, 1982, syndicated in America by Mobil Showcase Theatre, 1983. Also author of "Lady Jane," for Paramount.

Contributor: V. E. Mitchell, editor, *The London Fringe Theatre*, Burnham House, 1975; Wilfrid van der Will, editor, *Workers and Writers*, Department of German, Birmingham University, 1975; James Vinson, editor, *Contemporary Dramatists*, St. James Press, 1977; Ramon Delgado, editor, *Best*

Short Plays of 1982, Chilton, 1982; Robert Giddings, editor, *The Changing World of Charles Dickens*, Barnes & Noble, 1983. Also contributor to periodicals, including *Plays and Players, New Edinburgh Review,* and *Socialist Review.*

SIDELIGHTS: Although best known as the adaptor of Charles Dickens's *The Life and Adventures of Nicholas Nickleby* into the highly-publicized theatre event of the 1980-81 season, David Edgar is more notable as one of the most outspoken—and prolific—playwrights of Britain's New Left. Since 1970, when "Two Kinds of Angel" premiered, Edgar has seen more than forty subsequent plays and musicals successfully staged.

Most of Edgar's work reflects his interest in the "agitprop" (extremely liberal) politics of Britain's counterculture; his dramatic style often draws from the encompassing, audience-involving mode popularized by Bertolt Brecht. One scene from "The Jail Diary of Albie Sachs," for instance, calls for the audience to join the political-prisoner title character in remaining absolutely quiet for two minutes. This gesture "actually conveys the nature of prison solitude," says Michael Billington in the *New York Times.* "The relief with which the audience shuffles and coughs at the end of that period says a lot about the torture of confinement."

The theme of imprisonment is also explored in Edgar's adaptation "Mary Barnes," the true story of a woman's harrowing treatment for schizophrenia at an East London "therapy community." The play, according to Stanley Weintraub in his *Dictionary of Literary Biography* article, examines "not only what constitutes madness by societal standards but also whether or not society is guilty of complicity in the maladjustment of a talented human being, whether or not the mind's potential is wasted in order to seize easy solutions for controlling a 'mad' person, and whether or not one can even talk of sanity in a less-than-sane society."

In a lighter vein, the playwright created a musical farce, "Dick Deterred," which compares the Nixon administration to the court of the corrupt King Richard III. This work features such characters as H. R. (Bob) Buckingham, the king's chief of staff, and Eugene McClarence, "duke and Senator from Minnesota, [who] is done in by Richard, Mayor of Chicago," as Richard F. Shepard writes in a *New York Times* review. With another comedy, "Rent: Or, Caught in the Act," Edgar prefigured his success with adapting "Nicholas Nickleby" by giving his characters Dickensian names like Mr. Devious (of the legal firm of Devious, Devious, and Downright Dishonest) and Honest Tom Hard-Done-By, the corruptable hero of the piece. "State of Emergency" and "Operation Iskra" constitute two more titles of what Weintraub calls the author's "agitprop cartoons."

Running eight and one half hours, Edgar's "Nicholas Nickleby" set transatlantic records as the longest play ever produced and, in New York, for the most expensive theatre ticket price ever legally set. While many objected to the one-hundred dollar price for the two evenings of entertainment (hardier playgoers could opt to see the entire show in one day), *Time* magazine critic Richard Corliss points out that at twenty cents per minute, "Nicholas Nickleby" was one of Broadway's biggest bargains. In adapting Dickens's book, Edgar observes to Corliss, the author faced "a twofold challenge: to convert a rambling, complexly plotted novel into a play in a few months, and to respond to ideas from the two directors [Trevor Nunn and John Caird], from Designer John Napier, from Composer Stephen Oliver and all those actors." The challenge was met with overwhelming success: "Nicholas Nickleby" went on to win several theatre awards in both artistic and technical categories. The production also captured praise such as the kind Bernard Levin writes in the *Times.* Levin describes the event as "a celebration of love and justice that is true to the spirit of Dickens's belief that those are the fulcrums on which the universe is moved, and the consequence is that we come out not merely delighted but strengthened, not just entertained but uplifted, not only affected but changed."

Edgar told *CA:* "The aim of my work is to create a theatre of public life, as a counter to the domestic drama which dominates theatre and television on both sides of the Atlantic. I have recently become interested in adaptation of historical and contemporary works in pursuit of this aim."

AVOCATIONAL INTERESTS: Cooking.

BIOGRAPHICAL/CRITICAL SOURCES: Ronald Hayman, *British Theatre since 1955,* Oxford University Press, 1979; *New York Times,* March 18, 1979, March 6, 1980, October 5, 1981, January 10, 1982, November 30, 1982, January 24, 1983; Catherine Itzin, *Stages in the Revolution,* Eyre Methuen, 1980; *Times* (London), July 8, 1980, October 22, 1983; Simon Trussler, editor, *New Theatre: Voices of the Seventies,* Eyre Methuen, 1981; *Time,* October 5, 1981; *Newsweek,* October 12, 1981; *Dictionary of Literary Biography,* Volume XIII: *British Dramatists since World War II,* Gale, 1982.

* * *

EDSON, J(ohn) T(homas) 1928- (Rod Denver, Chuck Nolan)

PERSONAL: Born February 17, 1928, in Worksop, Nottinghamshire, England; son of Thomas John (a coal miner) and Eliza Charlotte (Gill) Edson; married Dorothy Mary Thompson, December 14, 1957 (divorced, 1974); children: Leslie Brian, Raymond, Steven, Peter John, Samantha Diane, Mark William James. *Education:* Attended schools in Nottinghamshire. *Politics:* None ("against all organised political groups"). *Religion:* Church of England ("nominally"). *Home:* 1 Cottesmore Ave., Melton Mowbray, Leicestershire LE13 0HY, England. *Agent:* Rosica Colin, 4 Hereford Sq., London SW7 4TU, England.

CAREER: Haulage hand at a stone quarry in Steetley, England, 1943-46; British Army, Royal Army Veterinary Corps, dog trainer, 1946-58, serving as sergeant in Germany, Malaya, Hong Kong, North Africa, Kenya, and Cyprus (combat duty in Kenya and Cyprus); owner of a fish and chip shop in Melton Mowbray, England, 1958-62; also worked in Mowbray, as a production hand in Petfoods Industries, 1962-65, and as a postman, 1965-68; writer of western novels. *Member:* Western Writers of America, Royal Army Veterinary Corps Old Comrades Association, Northampton Lower Forty Club (honorary member). *Awards, honors:* Second prize in western section of Brown, Watson's Literary Contest, for *Trail Boss.*

WRITINGS—Published by Brown, Watson, except as indicated: *Trail Boss,* 1961; *The Hard Riders,* 1962; *The Texan,* 1962; *Rio Guns,* 1962; *The Ysabel Kid,* 1962; *Sagebrush Sleuth,* 1962; (under pseudonym Rod Denver) *Arizona Ranger,* 1962, later reprinted under his own name; (under pseudonym Chuck Nolan) *Quiet Town,* 1962, later reprinted under his own name; *Waco's Debt,* 1962; *The Rio Hondo Kid,* 1963; *Apache Rampage,* 1963; *The Fastest Gun in Texas,* 1963; *The Drifter,* 1963; *The Half Breed,* 1963; *Gun Wizard,* 1963; *Gunsmoke Thunder,* 1963; *Wagons to Backsight,* 1964; *Waco Rides In,* 1964; *The Rushers,* 1964; *The Rio Hondo War,* 1964; *Trigger Fast,* 1964;

The Wildcats, 1965; *The Peacemakers*, 1965; *Troubled Range*, 1965; *The Fortune Hunters*, 1965; *Slaughter's Way*, 1965, Bantam, 1969; *The Man from Texas*, 1965; *The Trouble Busters*, 1965; *Trouble Trail*, 1965; *The Cowthieves*, 1965; *The Bull Whip Breed*, 1965, Bantam, 1969; *Guns in the Night*, 1966; *A Town Called Yellowdog*, 1966; *The Devil Gun*, 1966, Bantam, 1969; *The Colt and the Sabre*, 1966; *The Law of the Gun*, 1966; *Return to Backsight*, 1966; *The Fast Gun*, 1967; *The Big Hunt*, 1967; *Terror Valley*, 1967; *Comanche*, 1967; *Hound Dog Man*, 1967; *Sidewinder*, 1967.

Published by Corgi Books, except as indicated: *The Floating Outfit*, 1967; *The Rebel Spy*, 1968; *The Bad Bunch*, 1968; *The Hooded Riders*, 1968; *Calamity Spells Trouble*, 1968; *Rangeland Hercules*, 1968; *McGraw's Inheritance*, 1968; *The Making of a Lawman*, 1968, Bantam, 1971; *The Professional Killers*, 1968; *The Town Tamers*, 1969, Bantam, 1973; *Cold Deck, Hot Lead*, 1969; *The Bloody Border*, 1969; *The Small Texan*, 1969; *The Second Draw*, 1969; *Cuchilo*, 1969; *The Deputies*, 1969; *Goodnight's Dream*, 1969; *From Hide and Horn*, 1969, Bantam, 1974.

Under the Stars and Bars, 1970; *Kill Dusty Fog*, 1970; *Back to the Bloody Border*, 1970; *White Stallion: Red Mare*, 1970; *Point of Contact*, 1970; *The Owlhoot*, 1970; *A Horse Called Mogallon*, 1971; *Hell in the Palo Duro*, 1971; *Slip Gun*, 1971; *Run for the Border*, 1971; *Bad Hombre*, 1971; *Go Back to Hell*, 1972; *The South Will Rise Again*, 1972; *Two Miles to the Border*, 1972; *You're in Command Now Mr. Fog*, 1973; *The Big Gun*, 1973; *Set Texas Back on Her Feet*, 1973; *.44 Calibre Man*, 1973; *Blonde Genius*, 1973; *The Hide and Tallow Men*, 1974; *The Quest for Bowie's Blade*, 1974; *Sixteen Dollar Shooter*, 1974; *Young Ole Devil*, 1975; *Bunduki and Dawn*, 1975; *Sacrifice for the Quagga God*, 1975; *Get Urrea*, 1975; *Ole Devil and the Caplocks*, 1976; *Ole Devil and the Mule Train*, 1976; *Doc Leroy, M.D.*, 1977; *Ole Devil at San Jacinto*, 1977; *Mr. J. G. Reeder, Meet Cap. Fog!*, 1977; *Texas Ranger*, 1977; *Set A-Foot*, 1977; *Beguinage*, 1978; *Fearless Master of the Jungle*, 1978; *Beguinage Is Dead*, 1978; *The Remittance Kid*, Corgi-Severn House, 1978; *The Whip and the War Lance*, Corgi-Severn House, 1979; *You're a Texas Ranger, Alvin Fog*, 1979; *J. T.'s Hundredth*, 1979; *The Gentle Giant*, 1979.

J. T.'s Ladies, 1980; *Rapido Clint*, 1980; *Calamity, Mark and Belle*, 1980; *The Justice of Company 'Z'*, 1980; *Master of Triggernometry*, 1981; *Old Moccasions on the Trail*, Corgi-Severn House, 1981; *Waco's Badge*, 1982; *A Matter of Honour*, 1982; *White Indians*, 1982; *Cut One, They All Bleed*, 1983; *The Hide and Horn Saloon*, Corgi-Severn House, 1983; *Wanted! Belle Starr*, 1983; *Ole Devil's Hands and Feet*, 1983; *Buffalo Are Coming!*, 1984; *The Return of Rapido Clint and Mr. J. G. Reeder*, 1984; *Is-a-Man*, 1984.

Writer of serials, series, short stories, and nonfiction for *Rover*, *Hotspur*, and *Victor*.

WORK IN PROGRESS: *The Amazons of Zillikian; More Justice from Company 'Z'; Waco and Doc Leroy; J. T.'s Ladies Ride Again*, an anthology of Edson's leading female protagonists.

SIDELIGHTS: A wire service photograph of J. T. Edson brandishing two plastic guns appeared in American newspapers in the spring of 1970 under the caption "Paper Cowboy," with the explanation that "England's answer to Zane Grey" was forced to work out action scenes for his books with fake revolvers because British police claim he doesn't need real ones. Edson says that his writing "is of action, adventure, escapist variety, written purely for the enjoyment of people who like that kind of a story . . . while also earning a comfortable living for myself. . . . I have become hooked on the fictionist genealogy style of writing perfected by Philip Jose Farmer. This allows me to tie in various of my Western characters with the protagonists of the 'Bunduki' series of books. . . . All my work is action-escapism-adventure motivated and I try to steer clear of the 'message' style of writing.'' Edson goes on to say: "I refuse to accept the frequently made statement that the traditional type of Western novel is not wanted by the reading public and my sales figures seem to prove me correct. One thing I will not do is produce books featuring the 'liberal' anti-hero. My pet hate is journalists who label me a 'postman-turned-author,' or pretend to think I need to dress in 'cowboy' clothes to write. To me this is merely an extension of their middle class 'liberal' snobbery. I was a moderately, if not financially successful writer before I became a postman. If they have to use a label, I would prefer to be called an ex-regular soldier turned author which is correct."

J. T. Edson was made an honorary admiral in the Texas Navy, an honorary commodore in the Powder River Navy, Wyoming, and an honorary deputy sheriff of Travis County, Texas, and of Thurston County, Washington. Edson's books have been translated into Danish, Dutch, Swedish, Norwegian, German, Afrikaans, and Serbo-Croatian.

AVOCATIONAL INTERESTS: Fishing, golf, collecting police concealment holsters, "adding to my collection of Japanese replica-nonfiring firearms," and building up his reference library.

BIOGRAPHICAL/CRITICAL SOURCES: *Times*, February 24, 1968; *Sunday Mirror*, April 28, 1968.

* * *

EDWARDS, David L(awrence) 1929-

PERSONAL: Born January 20, 1929, in Cairo, Egypt; son of Lawrence Wright (a civil servant) and Phyllis Edwards; married Hilary Phillips; children: Helen, Katharine. *Education:* Magdalen College, Oxford University, B.A., 1952, M.A., 1959. *Office:* 51 Barthside, London SE1 9JE, England.

CAREER: Ordained a priest of the Church of England. S.C.M. Press, London, England, managing director and editor, 1959-66; Cambridge University, Cambridge, England, fellow and dean of King's College, 1966-70; canon of Westminster and rector of St. Margaret's, London, 1970-78; Norwich Cathedral, Norwich, England, dean, 1978-83; Southwark Cathedral, London, provost, 1983—. Curate, St. Martin-in-the-Fields, London, 1958-66.

WRITINGS: *Not Angels but Anglicans*, S.C.M. Press, 1958; *This Church of England*, Church Information Office, 1962; *God's Cross in Our World*, Westminster, 1963; *F. J. Shirley: An Extraordinary Headmaster*, S.P.C.K., 1969; *The Last Things Now*, S.C.M. Press, 1969; *Religion and Change*, Harper, 1969, revised edition, Hodder & Stoughton, 1974.

Leaders of the Church of England, 1828-1944, Oxford University Press, 1971, revised edition published as *Leaders of the Church of England, 1828-1978*, Hodder & Stoughton, 1978; *St. Margaret's, Westminster*, Pitkin, 1972; *What Is Real in Christianity?*, Westminster, 1972; *The British Churches Turn to the Future: One Man's View of the Church Leaders' Conference, Birmingham, 1972*, S.C.M. Press, 1973; *Ian Ramsey, Bishop of Durham: A Memoir*, Oxford University Press, 1973; *What Anglicans Believe*, Mowbray, 1974, published as *What*

Anglicans (Episcopalians) Believe, Forward Movement Publications, 1975; *Jesus for Modern Man: An Introduction to the Gospels in Today's English Version,* Fontana for the Bible Reading Fellowship, 1975; *A Key to the Old Testament,* Collins, 1976; *Your Faith,* Mowbray, 1978; *A Reason to Hope,* Collins & World, 1978.

Christian England, Volume I: *Its Story to the Reformation,* Oxford University Press, 1981, Volume II: *From the Reformation to the Eighteenth Century,* Eerdmans, 1983.

Compiler; all abridged from *Good News Bible in Today's English* version: *Good News in Acts,* Collins, 1974, published as *Good News in Acts: The Acts of the Apostles in Today's English Version,* Fontana for the Bible Reading Fellowship, 1975; *Today's Story of Jesus,* Collins & World, 1976; *The Catholic Children's Bible,* Collins, 1979; *The Children's Bible,* Collins, 1979.

Editor: *The Honest to God Debate: Some Reactions to the Book "Honest to God,"* Westminster, 1963; *Preparing for the Ministry of the 1970s: Essays on the British Churches by H.G.G. Herklots, James Whyte and Robin Sharp,* S.C.M. Press, 1964; *Christians in a New World,* S.C.M. Press, 1966; *Unity: The Next Step?,* S.P.C.K., 1972.

Also author of *A History of the King's School, Canterbury,* Faber, and *Movements into Tomorrow,* S.C.M. Press.

SIDELIGHTS: In his book, *Religion and Change* (1969), David L. Edwards considers the challenges to religion which have arisen during the twentieth century. As John H. Wright observes in his review for *Commonweal,* Edwards "has attempted to survey and evaluate the social and intellectual forces operating in twentieth-century Christianity and to project both a new shape for the Christian church and a new statement of Christian belief." While Edwards himself described his purpose in writing this book as "absurdly audacious," many reviewers deem the study a success. "Here," remarks the *Times Literary Supplement* reviewer, "is a quite superb account of the present scene combining a scholarly depth with a breadth of vision. While it is a masterly survey, brilliant in its detail, there are excellent summaries and many constructive insights. It should be prescribed reading for all concerned with the Christian faith and its institutions as well as with the well-being of humanity."

BIOGRAPHICAL/CRITICAL SOURCES: *Times Literary Supplement,* July 31, 1969, August 21, 1969, January 28, 1972, October 13, 1972, January 18, 1974, February 5, 1982; *Commonweal,* December 26, 1969; *Commentary,* January, 1970.

* * *

EDWARDS, Dorothy   1914-1982

PERSONAL: Born November 6, 1914, in Teddington, Middlesex, England; died August 9, 1982 in Reigate, Surrey, England; daughter of Charles and Alice (Saunders) Brown; married Francis P. Edwards (a lecturer on communications, medieval research, and drama), 1942; children: Jane Brunt, Francis C. F. *Education:* Educated in England. *Politics:* Liberal. *Religion:* Christian.

CAREER: Author of children's books and television and radio plays, lecturer, and storyteller. Editor, producer, and scriptwriter, "Listen with Mother" series for British Broadcasting Corp. Radio. *Member:* Society of Authors, Radiowriters Association, Writer's Action Group, Society of Women Writers and Journalists. *Awards, honors:* Children's Rights Workshop "The Other Award," 1975, for *Joe and Timothy Together.*

WRITINGS—Juvenile; all published by Methuen, except as indicated: *Tales of Joe and Timothy,* 1969; *Listen! Listen!,* B.B.C. Publications, 1970; *Peter Nicknock and the Cuckoo Clock,* Transworld Publishers, 1971; *Roger's Trains,* Transworld Publishers, 1971; *Joe and Timothy Together,* 1971; *Listen and Play Rhymes,* two books, 1972; (editor) *"Listen with Mother" Stories,* B.B.C. Publications, 1972; *Look, Look a Cookery Book,* 1972; *Look, Look My Garden Book,* 1972; *Sam's Wooly Hat,* Transworld Publishers, 1973; *Janie's Cooking Day,* Transworld Publishers, 1973; (editor) *The Read to Me Story Book,* 1974; *The Magician Who Kept a Pub,* Kestrel Books, 1975; *A Wet Monday,* 1975; *A Look, See and Touch Book,* 1976; *A Walk Your Fingers Story,* 1976; *Dad's New Car,* 1976; *Going Fishing,* 1976; (editor) *Once, Twice, Thrice Upon a Time,* Lutterworth, 1976; (editor) *Once, Twice, Thrice and Then Again,* Lutterworth, 1976; (editor) *Read Me Another Story Book,* Methuen, 1976; *Here's Sam,* Methuen, 1979; *Ghosts and Shadows,* Lutterworth, 1980; *Crash,* Hippo Books, 1980; (editor) *Storytime,* Methuen, 1980; *A Strong and Willing Girl,* Methuen, 1980; *The Witches and the Grinnygog,* Faber, 1981.

"My Naughty Little Sister" series; published by Methuen, except as indicated: *My Naughty Little Sister,* 1952; *More Naughty Little Sister Stories,* 1957; *When My Naughty Little Sister Was Good,* 1968; *All About My Naughty Little Sister,* 1969; *My Naughty Little Sister's Friends,* 1969; *My Naughty Little Sister and Bad Harry,* 1974; *My Naughty Little Sister Goes Fishing,* Methuen, 1976; *My Naughty Little Sister and Bad Harry's Rabbit,* 1977, Prentice-Hall, 1981; *My Naughty Little Sister at the Fair,* 1979.

Contributor of short stories to books and anthologies; also contributor of short stories, articles, and verse to numerous periodicals.

SIDELIGHTS: Dorothy Edwards once wrote *CA:* "My interests are wide. In my time I ran an antique shop and also wrote for and ran a drama school for the Surrey Community Players. I am very absorbed by my husband's researches in mediaeval drama, art, and culture and interested too in music and films.

"When I was small I lived in Teddington on the River Thames, and the places in my stories are all there, including the place where my little sister fell in the river. I write my stories for under-fives mainly for reading aloud or telling and they were first heard on 'Listen with Mother' where they proved very successful and have been ever since.

"I am a grandmother, very happy in the company of small children, and very enthusiastic for the work done by the Federation of Childrens' Books Group, who are doing so much to see that the child gets to the book."

OBITUARIES: London *Times,* August 12, 1982.†

* * *

EDWARDS, Norman
See WHITE, Theodore Edwin

* * *

EDWARDS, Philip   1923-

PERSONAL: Born February 7, 1923, in Barrow-in-Furness, England; son of Robert Henry (in politics) and Bessie (Pritchard) Edwards; married Hazel Valentine, July 8, 1947 (deceased); married Sheila Wilkes, May 8, 1952; children: (second marriage) Matthew, Charles, Richard, Catherine. *Education:* University of Birmingham, B.A., 1942, M.A., 1946, Ph.D., 1960. *Home:* 12 South Bank, Oxton, Birkenhead L43 5UP, England. *Office address:* University of Liverpool, P.O. Box 147, Liverpool L69 3BX, England.

CAREER: University of Birmingham, Birmingham, England, lecturer in English, 1946-60; Trinity College, University of Dublin, Dublin, Ireland, professor of English literature, 1960-66; University of Essex, Colchester, England, professor of literature, 1966-74; University of Liverpool, Liverpool, England, professor of English literature, 1974—. Visiting professor, University of Michigan, 1964-65, Williams College, 1969, and Otago University, New Zealand, 1980. *Military service:* British Navy, 1942-45; became sub-lieutenant. *Awards, honors:* Fellow, Harvard University, 1954-55.

WRITINGS: Sir Walter Raleigh, Longmans, Green, 1953; (editor) Thomas Kyd, *The Spanish Tragedy,* Methuen, 1958; *Thomas Kyd and Early Elizabethan Tragedy,* Longmans, Green, 1965; (with Roger Joseph McHugh) *Jonathan Swift, 1667-1967: A Dublin Tercentenary Tribute,* Dolmen Press, 1967; *Shakespeare and the Confines of Art,* Barnes & Noble, 1968.

(Editor) William Shakespeare, *King Lear,* Macmillan, 1975; (editor) Shakespeare, *Pericles, Prince of Tyre,* Penguin, 1976; (editor with Colin Gibson) *The Plays and Poems of Philip Massinger,* Oxford University Press, 1976; *Threshold of a Nation: A Study in English and Irish Drama,* Cambridge University Press, 1979; (editor with Inga-Stina Ewbank and G. K. Hunter) *Shakespeare's Styles: Essays in Honour of Kenneth Muir,* Cambridge University Press, 1980. Contributor to *Shakespeare Survey* and other journals.

WORK IN PROGRESS: An edition of Shakespeare's *Hamlet* for Cambridge University Press; a book on Shakespeare for Oxford University Press.

SIDELIGHTS: In *Threshold of a Nation: A Study in English and Irish Drama,* "Philip Edwards has had the original and interesting idea," writes Katharine Worth of the *Times Literary Supplement,* "of examining the English drama of Shakespeare's time and the Irish drama of Yeats's time under the same light. His approach is so fruitful that one can only wonder why it was never tried before." Worth finds the book a "spirited, scholarly, and absorbing study." Edwards' book *Shakespeare's Styles: Essays in Honour of Kenneth Muir* has also drawn praise. Katherine Duncan-Jones of the *Times Literary Supplement* describes the collection of essays as offering "a high level of originality and interest" and believes that "the book deserves to become a critical classic."

BIOGRAPHICAL/CRITICAL SOURCES: Times Literary Supplement, February 29, 1980, October 3, 1980.

* * *

EGAN, Gerard 1930-

PERSONAL: Born June 17, 1930, in Chicago, Ill. *Education:* Loyola University, Chicago, A.B., 1953; M.A. (philosophy), 1959, M.A. (clinical psychology), 1963, Ph.D., 1969. *Office:* Community and Organization Development, Loyola University, Chicago, Ill. 60611.

CAREER: Loyola University of Chicago, Chicago, Ill., 1969—, began as assistant professor, currently professor of psychology. Consultant to various organizations and institutions. *Member:* American Psychological Association, American Association for Humanistic Psychology, American Association for Counseling and Development.

WRITINGS—All published by Brooks/Cole: *Encounter: Group Processes for Interpersonal Growth,* 1970; (editor) *Encounter Groups: Basic Readings,* 1971; *Face to Face: The Small Group Experience and Interpersonal Growth,* 1973; *The Skilled Helper: A Model for Helping and Human Relations Training,* 1975, 2nd edition published as *The Skilled Helper: Model, Skills, and Methods for Effective Helping,* 1982; *Exercises in Helping Skills,* 1975, 2nd edition, 1981; *Interpersonal Living: A Skills/Contract Approach to Human Relations Training in Groups,* 1976, instructor's manual (with M. Bacchi), 1978; *You and Me: The Skills of Human Communication in Everyday Life,* 1977, instructor's manual (with J. W. Bryer, Jr.) published as *Training the Skilled Helper,* 1979; (with M. Cowan) *People in Systems: A Model Development for the Human Services Professions and Education,* 1979; (with Cowan) *Moving into Adulthood: Themes and Variations in Self-Directed Development,* 1980; *Change Agent Skill for Helping and Human-Service Professionals,* in press.

Contributor: W. Hunt, editor, *Human Behavior and Its Encounter Groups,* Schenkman, 1971; E. E. Whitehead, editor, *The Parish: Community and Ministry,* Paulist Press, 1978; W. Burke, editor, *The Cutting Edge: Current Theory and Practice in Organization Development,* University Associates, 1978; E. K. Marshall and P. D. Kurtz, editors, *Interpersonal Helping Skills: A Guide to Training Methods, Programs, and Resources,* Jossey-Bass, 1982; D. Larson, editor, *Teaching Psychological Skills: Models for Giving Psychology Away,* Brooks/Cole, 1983.

Also author of series of eight videotapes on the eight steps of a problem-management model of counseling, Loyola University Media Services, 1982. Contributor of articles to various professional journals, including *Journal of Applied Behavioral Science, Journal of Community Psychology,* and *Cognitive Therapy and Research.*

WORK IN PROGRESS: Being In a Group: Models, Working Knowledge, and Skills for Effective Group Participation, for Brooks/Cole.

SIDELIGHTS: Gerard Egan told *CA:* "I have entered the world of organizations, institutions, and communities as a consultant and this is reflected in my current writing. Writing, together now with the consulting I do, has been and is the principal instrument of my professional development."

* * *

EKWALL, Eldon E(dward) 1933-

PERSONAL: Born August 28, 1933, in Martland, Neb.; son of Arthur Clarence (a farmer) and Bessie G. (Ingels) Ekwall; married Maxine Rains, January 26, 1956 (deceased); married Carol Ann Morrow, May 12, 1982; children: (first marriage) Dwight, Cindy (deceased). *Education:* University of Nebraska, B.Sc., 1959, M.Ed., 1961; University of Arizona, Ed.D., 1966. *Religion:* Methodist. *Home:* 3605 O'Keefe, El Paso, Tex. 79902. *Office:* Reading Center, Department of Curriculum and Instruction, University of Texas, El Paso, Tex. 79968.

CAREER: Public school teacher and administrator in Benedict, Neb. and San Manuel, Ariz., 1959-67; New Mexico Highlands University, Las Vegas, assistant professor of education, 1967-68; University of Kansas, Lawrence, assistant professor of education, 1968-69; University of Texas at El Paso, 1969—, began as associate professor, currently professor of education. *Military service:* U.S. Army, 1953-55. *Member:* International Reading Association (former president of Lawrence Area and El Paso County councils; former member of board of directors of Arizona State chapter), National Education Association (life member), Organization of Teacher Educators in Reading, Professors of Reading Education, Phi Delta Kappa.

WRITINGS: Locating and Correcting Reading Difficulties, C. E. Merrill, 1970, 4th edition, 1985; *Psychological Factors in the Teaching of Reading,* C. E. Merrill, 1973; *Diagnosis and Remediation of the Disabled Reader,* Allyn & Bacon, 1976, 2nd edition, 1983; *Corrective Reading System,* Pyrotechnics, 1976; *Teachers Handbook on Diagnosis and Remediation in Reading,* Allyn & Bacon, 1977; *Elkwall Reading Inventory,* Allyn & Bacon, 1979; (with James L. Shanker) *Diagnostic-Prescriptive Phonics Lessons,* Allyn & Bacon, 1981; (with Shanker) *Teaching Developmental Reading in the Elementary School,* C. E. Merrill, 1985. Senior author and co-inventor of *Rx Reading Program;* also author of several monographs on the effectiveness of reading skills. Contributor of articles to periodicals, including *Arizona Teacher, Science Teacher, Reading Teacher, Journal of Learning Disabilities, Elementary English, School Science and Math,* and *Texas Outlook.*

WORK IN PROGRESS: Conducting study of oral and silent reading speeds of children in grades one through nine.

SIDELIGHTS: Eldon E. Ekwall told *CA* that he is "especially interested in the differences in results in students' scores when tested individually and using group diagnostic tests . . . and in methods of teaching comprehension."

* * *

ELBOW, Peter (Henry) 1935-

PERSONAL: Born April 14, 1935, in New York, N.Y.; son of William C. and Helen (Platt) Elbow; married Linda Smickle, September 1, 1964 (divorced March, 1968); married Caroline Cambell Pelz (a social worker), July 8, 1972; children: two. *Education:* Williams College, B.A. (magna cum laude), 1957; Exeter College, Oxford, B.A., 1959, M.A., 1963; graduate study at Harvard University, 1959-60; Brandeis University, Ph.D., 1969. *Home:* 11 New York Ave., Stony Brook, N.Y. 11790. *Office:* Department of English, State University of New York at Stony Brook, Stony Brook, N.Y. 11794.

CAREER: Massachusetts Institute of Technology, Cambridge, instructor in humanities, 1960-63; Franconia College, Franconia, N.H., member of English faculty and chairman of core curriculum, 1963-65, associate dean of faculty, 1964-65; Massachusetts Institute of Technology, lecturer, 1968-69, assistant professor of literature, 1969-72; Evergreen State College, Olympia, Wash., member of faculty, 1972-81; State University of New York at Stony Brook, director of writing programs, 1982—. Teacher of evening writing classes in Roxbury, Mass., 1968-72. Consultant to writing programs at various colleges and universities. *Member:* National Council of Teachers of English, Society for Values in Higher Education, Phi Beta Kappa. *Awards, honors:* Honorary Woodrow Wilson fellowship, 1957; Danforth fellowship, 1957; essay prize from English Institute, 1966; Kent postdoctoral fellowship, Wesleyan University Center for Writing, 1981-82.

WRITINGS: Thoughts on Writing Essays (student handbook), Franconia College, 1965; *Writing without Teachers,* Oxford University Press, 1973; *Oppositions in Chaucer,* Wesleyan University Press, 1975; *Writing with Power: Techniques for Mastering the Writing Process,* Oxford University Press, 1981.

Contributor: Philip Damon, editor, *Literary Criticism and Historical Understanding,* Columbia University Press, 1967; Don Flourney, editor, *The New Teachers,* Jossey-Bass, 1971; *Writing; Voice and Thought,* National Council of Teachers of English, 1971; Henry B. Maloney, editor, *Goal-Making for English Teaching,* National Council of Teachers of English, 1973; Gerald Grant, editor, *On Competence: An Analysis of a Reform Movement in Higher Education,* two volumes, Syracuse Research Corporation, 1978; Jack Noonan and Kenneth Eble, editors, *New Directions for Teaching and Learning,* Jossey-Bass, 1981; Richard Martin and Eble, editors, *Sourcebook for College Teachers,* Jossey-Bass, 1981.

Contributor to education and literature journals, and to *Christian Century.*

SIDELIGHTS: Peter Elbow writes: "I had to get interested in writing twice. First in school when a couple of teachers encouraged me and it seemed to come naturally. Then again in my late twenties after I had grown completely frightened and blocked about writing in college and graduate school."

* * *

ELCOCK, Howard J(ames) 1942-

PERSONAL: Born June 6, 1942, in Shrewsbury, England; son of George (a coal merchant) and Marion S. (Edge) Elcock. *Education:* Queen's College, Oxford, B.A., 1964, B.Phil., 1966, M.A., 1968. *Politics:* Labour Party. *Religion:* Anglican. *Home:* 23, Wolsingham Rd., Gosforth, Newcastle-upon-Tyne NE3 4RP, England. *Office:* School of Government, Faculty of Professional Studies, Newcastle-upon-Tyne Polytechnic, Newcastle-upon-Tyne NE1 8ST, England.

CAREER: University of Hull, Hull, Yorkshire, England, lecturer, 1966-77, senior lecturer in politics, 1977-81; Newcastle-upon-Tyne Polytechnic, Newcastle-upon-Tyne, England, head of School of Government, 1981—. Member, Humberside County Council, 1973-81. *Member:* Political Studies Association, Royal Institute of Public Administration, Fabian Society, Royal Yachting Association, Elgar Society, Yorkshire Ouse Sailing Club, Tynemouth Sailing Club.

WRITINGS: Administrative Justice, Longmans, Green, 1969; *Portrait of a Decision: The Council of Four and the Treaty of Versailles,* Methuen, 1972; *Political Behavior,* Methuen, 1976; (with Stuart Haywood) *The Buck Stops Where? Accountability and Control in the NHS,* University of Hull, 1980; (with Michael Wheaton) *Local Government: Politicians, Professionals and the Public in Local Authorities,* Methuen, 1982; (with others) *What Sort of Society? Economic and Social Policy in Modern Britain,* Martin Robertson & Co., 1982. Contributor to *Historical Journal, Public Administration, Public Administration Bulletin,* and *Political Studies.*

WORK IN PROGRESS: A book on decentralization in government in England; a study of members of district health authorities; a volume of case-studies on improving public policy.

AVOCATIONAL INTERESTS: Dingy sailing, music.

BIOGRAPHICAL/CRITICAL SOURCES: Times Literary Supplement, October 15, 1982.

ELKINS, Dov Peretz 1937-

PERSONAL: Born December 7, 1937, in Philadelphia, Pa.; married Elaine Rash, June 12, 1960; children: Hillel Michael, Jonathan Saul, Shira Batya. *Education:* Gratz College, Teacher's Diploma, 1958; Temple University, B.A., 1959; Jewish Theological Seminary of America, M.H.L., 1962, Rabbi, 1964; Hebrew University of Jerusalem, additional study, 1962-63; Colgate Rochester Divinity School, D.Min., 1976; University Associates, M.H.R.D., 1983. *Office address:* Growth Associates, Box 18429, Rochester, N.Y. 14618-0429.

CAREER: Rabbi at Har Zion Temple, Philadelphia and Radnor, Pa., 1966-70, at Jacksonville Jewish Center, Jacksonville, Fla., 1970-72, and at Temple Beth El, Rochester, N.Y., 1972-76; Growth Associates (human relations consulting firm), Rochester, president, 1976—. Jewish chaplain, Haverford State Hospital, 1967-70; faculty member of department of theology, Villanova University, 1969-70. Member of commission of Jewish chaplaincy, National Jewish Welfare Board, 1967-70; member of board, Philadelphia Zionist Organization, 1968-70. Consultant in couple and family therapy, individual and group counseling, and consulting for educational and industrial organizations. *Military service:* U.S. Army, chaplain, 1964-66. *Awards, honors:* Issac Siegel Memorial Award, National Jewish Welfare Board, Jewish Book Council of America, 1964, for *Worlds Lost and Found: Discoveries in Biblical Archaeology;* honorary doctorate from Colgate Rochester Divinity School, 1976.

WRITINGS: (With Azriel Eisenberg) *Worlds Lost and Found: Discoveries in Biblical Archaeology* (juvenile), Abelard, 1964; *So Young to Be a Rabbi* (essay collection), Yoseloff, 1969; (with Eisenberg) *Treasures from the Dust,* Abelard, 1972; *Rejoice with Jerusalem,* Media Judaica, 1972; *A Tradition Reborn: Sermons and Essays on Liberal Judaism,* A. S. Barnes, 1973; *God's Warriors: Heroic Stories of Jewish Military Chaplains,* Jonathan David, 1974.

Proud to Be Me: Raising Self-Esteem in Individuals, Families, Schools and Minority Groups, Growth Associates, 1975, revised edition published as *Glad to Be Me: Raising Self-Esteem in Yourself and Others,* Prentice-Hall, 1976; *Shepherd of Jerusalem: A Biography of Chief Rabbi Abraham Isaac Kook,* Shengold, 1976; *Humanizing Jewish Life: Judaism and the Human Potential Movement,* A. S. Barnes, 1976; *Teaching People to Love Themselves: A Leader's Handbook of Theory and Technique for Self-Esteem and Affirmation Training,* Growth Associates, 1977; *Clarifying Jewish Values,* Growth Associates, 1977; *Jewish Consciousness Raising,* Growth Associates, 1977; *Experiential Programs,* Growth Associates, 1978; *Self-Concept Sourcebook,* Growth Associates, 1979; *Twelve Pathways to Feeling Better about Yourself,* Growth Associates, 1980.

Sermons included in *Best Jewish Sermons,* Jonathan David, 1966 and 1968, in *Sermons on Jewish Holidays and Festivals,* National Jewish Welfare Board, 1966, and in *Sermons for Special Occasions,* Jonathan David, 1967. Columnist for Seven Arts Feature Syndicate. Contributor of articles to numerous periodicals. Editor, *Benineinu;* contributing editor, *Judaica Book Guide.* Book review editor, *Torch;* regular reviewer, *The Jewish Exponent* and *The Jewish Advocate.*

WORK IN PROGRESS: Meeting Your Jewish Self: Personal Growth for Jews; Exercises in Creativity.

SIDELIGHTS: Dov Peretz Elkins is a certified instructor for Parent Effectiveness Training (P.E.T.) and Teacher Effectiveness Training (T.E.T.). Elkins told *CA* his "specialty is integrating religion, education, and behavioral sciences." His latest focus is promoting holistic health and wellness lifestyle.

* * *

ELLIOTT, Osborn 1924-

PERSONAL: Born October 25, 1924, in New York, N.Y.; son of John and Audrey (Osborn) Elliott; married Deirdre Spencer, May 8, 1948 (divorced December 28, 1972); married Inger Abrahamsen McCabe (a designer and photographer), October 20, 1973; children: Diana, Dorinda, Cynthia. *Education:* Harvard University, A.B., 1946. *Home:* 10 Gracie Sq., New York, N.Y. 10028. *Office:* Graduate School of Journalism, Columbia University, 116th St. and Broadway, New York, N.Y. 10027.

CAREER: New York Journal of Commerce, New York City, reporter, 1946-49; *Time,* New York City, contributing editor, 1949-52, associate editor, 1952-55; *Newsweek,* New York City, senior business editor, 1955-59, managing editor, 1959-61, editor, 1961-69, editor-in-chief, 1969-72, president and chief executive officer, 1971-72, editor, 1972-75, chairman of board, 1972-76, editor-in-chief, 1975-76; Columbia University, Graduate School of Journalism, New York City, dean, 1979—. Lecturer. Director, *Washington Post* Co., 1961. Member of board of overseers of Harvard College, 1965-71. Trustee of American Museum of Natural History, Asia Society, New York Public Library, 1968-72, St. Paul's School, 1969-73, and Winston Churchill Foundation, 1970-73. Chairman of Citizens Committee for New York City, 1975—. *Military service:* U.S. Naval Reserve, 1944-46; became lieutenant junior grade.

MEMBER: Council on Foreign Relations, American Academy of Arts and Sciences (fellow), Harvard Club, Coffee House Club, Racquet Club and Tennis Club (all New York). *Awards, honors:* D.H.L. from Michigan State University, 1972.

WRITINGS: Men at the Top, Harper, 1959; *The World of Oz,* Viking, 1979. Also editor of *The Negro Revolution in America,* 1964.

SIDELIGHTS: Osborn Elliott's *The World of Oz* is the story of the author's tenure as editor of *Newsweek* magazine during the 1960s and early 1970s. "This is one of those rare books that is exactly what it purports to be," says David Shaw in the *Los Angeles Times Book Review:* "one man's chatty account of his work, his friends and his feelings during a particularly contentious and controversial time in contemporary American history. He writes knowledgeably and amusingly about . . . Newsweek's rivalry with Time, the war in Vietnam, the civil rights movement, feminism, [and] student activism." Jean Strouse, reviewing the book in *Newsweek,* describes it as "an engaging memoir."

BIOGRAPHICAL/CRITICAL SOURCES: Newsweek, May 12, 1980; *Los Angeles Times Book Review,* June 1, 1980; *Time,* June 9, 1980; *New York Times Book Review,* June 15, 1980; *Washington Post Book World,* June 15, 1980.

* * *

ELWARD, James (Joseph) 1928-
(Rebecca James)

PERSONAL: Surname is pronounced *el-*word; born November 22, 1928, in Chicago, Ill.; son of Joseph F. and Dasianne (Lenert) Elward. *Education:* Attended Loyola University, 1946-48; Catholic University, A.B., 1950. *Politics:* Democrat. *Re-

ligion: Roman Catholic. *Home:* 140 Riverside Dr., New York, N.Y. 10024. *Agent:* Joan Stewart, William Morris Agency, 1350 Avenue of the Americas, New York, N.Y. 10019.

CAREER: Head writer and assistant writer for various television programs on all three major networks, 1956—. Actor and director at various summer stock theatres, 1955-70. *Military service:* U.S. Army, 1950-52. *Member:* Actor's Equity, Players Club. *Awards, honors:* Award from Writers' Guild, 1956, for best comedy script of the year.

WRITINGS—Plays: (Contributor) *Writers Guild Anthology of Prize Television Plays,* Random House, 1956; *Upbeat* (three-act), Dramatic Publishing Co., 1960; (author of libretto) *The Man on the Bearskin Rug* (one-act opera), Boosey & Hawkes, 1963; *Friday Night* (contains three one-acts, "The River," "Passport," and "Mary Agnes Is 35"; first produced Off-Broadway at Pocket Theatre, February, 1965), Dramatists Play Service, 1970; *Best of Friends* (three-act; first produced in London at Strand Theatre, February, 1970), Dramatists Play Service, 1970. Also author of two-act play, *Hallelujah!,* first produced in New York at Lambs Club, and three unproduced plays, "A Perfect Stranger," "Subject to Change," and "Finale."

Television scripts: "The Remittance Man," produced on "Matinee Theatre," 1956; "Upbeat," produced on "U.S. Steel Hour," 1957; "Victim," produced on "U.S. Steel Hour," 1957; "Hide Me in the Mountains," CBC (Canada), 1960; "Music Power," ABC, September, 1968.

Television serial scripts: "Look Up and Live," and "Lamp Unto My Feet," CBS, 1961-63; "The Secret Storm," CBS, 1963-67; "The Young Marrieds," ABC, 1964; "Love Is a Many Splendored Thing," CBS, 1968; "The Guiding Light," CBS, 1969; "The Doctors," NBC, 1970; "Where the Heart Is," CBS, 1970.

Novels; under pseudonym Rebecca James, except as indicated: *Storms End,* Doubleday, 1975; *The House Is Dark,* Doubleday, 1976; *Tomorrow Is Mine,* Doubleday, 1979; (with Helen Van Slyke; under name James Elward) *Public Smiles, Private Tears: The Last Novel,* Harper, 1982. Also author of *Ask for Nothing More,* Harper.

* * *

EMANUEL, James A. 1921-

PERSONAL: Born June 15, 1921, in Alliance, Neb.; son of Alfred A. (a farmer and railroad worker) and Cora Ann (Mance) Emanuel; married Mattie Etha Johnson, 1950 (divorced, 1974); children: James A., Jr. (deceased). *Education:* Howard University, A.B. (summa cum laude), 1950; Northwestern University, M.A., 1953; Columbia University, Ph.D., 1962. *Politics:* Democrat. *Office:* Department of English, City College of the City University of New York, Convent Ave. at 138th St., New York, N.Y. 10031.

CAREER: Canteen steward in Civilian Conservation Corps, Wellington, Kan., 1939-40; weighmaster with an iron company, Rock Island, Ill., 1941-42; U.S. War Department, Office of the Inspector General, Washington, D.C., confidential secretary to assistant inspector general of the Army, 1942-44; Army and Air Force Induction Station, Chicago, Ill., chief of pre-induction section (as civilian), 1950-53; YWCA Business and Secretarial School, New York City, teacher of English and commercial subjects, 1954-56; City College of the City University of New York, New York City, instructor, 1957-62, assistant professor, 1962-70, associate professor, 1970-73, professor of English, 1973—. Fulbright professor, University of Grenoble, France, 1968-69, and University of Warsaw, Poland, 1975-76. Visiting professor, University of Toulouse, France, 1971-73 and 1979-81. Has given readings of his poetry in universities, schools, and before civic groups in America and Europe. Consultant on Black literature with New York State Education Department and boards of education, 1970. *Military service:* U.S. Army, Infantry, 1944-46; served in Netherlands, East Indies, and the Philippines; became staff sergeant; received Army Commendation Ribbon.

MEMBER: Fulbright Alumni Association. *Awards, honors:* John Hay Whitney Foundation Opportunity fellowship, 1952-54; Eugene F. Saxton Memorial Trust fellowship, 1964-65.

WRITINGS: Langston Hughes, Twayne, 1967; *The Treehouse and Other Poems,* Broadside Press, 1968; (editor with Theodore Gross) *Dark Symphony: Negro Literature in America,* Free Press, 1968; *At Bay,* Broadside Press, 1968; *Panther Man,* Broadside Press, 1970; (with McKinley Kantor and Lawrence Osgood) *How I Write/2,* Harcourt, 1972, new edition, 1975; *Black Man Abroad: The Toulouse Poems,* Lotus Press, 1978; *A Chisel in the Dark (Poems: Selected and New),* Lotus Press, 1980; *A Poet's Mind,* Regents Publishing, 1983; *The Broken Bowl: New and Uncollected Poems,* Lotus Press, 1983. Also author of *Snowflakes and Steel: My Life as a Poet, 1971-1980,* a manuscript autobiography written at the request of the Jay B. Hubbell Center for American Literary Historiography at Duke University and deposited there in 1981.

Contributor of essays: Addison Gayle, editor, *Black Expression,* Weybright & Talley, 1969; Richard Abcarian, editor, *Native Son: A Critical Handbook,* Wadsworth, 1970; Gayle, editor, *The Black Aesthetic,* Doubleday, 1971; Therman B. O'Daniel, editor, *Langston Hughes, Black Genius,* Morrow, 1971; James Vinson, editor, *Contemporary Novelists,* St. James Press, 1972; Lloyd W. Brown, editor, *The Black Writer in Africa and the Americas,* Hennessey & Ingalls, 1973; Donald B. Gibson, editor, *Modern Black Poets,* Prentice-Hall, 1973; Jay Martin, editor, *A Singer in the Dawn: Reinterpretations of Paul Laurence Dunbar,* Dodd, 1975; Sy M. Kahn and Martha Raetz, editors, *Interculture: A Collection of Essays and Creative Writing . . . ,* Wilhelm Braumueller, 1975; Rayford Logan and Michael Winston, editors, *Dictionary of American Negro Biography,* Norton, 1982.

Poems anthologized in *Sixes and Sevens* (London), 1962, *American Negro Poetry,* 1963, *New Negro Poets: U.S.A.,* 1964, *Anthologie de la Poesie Negro-Americaine: 1770-1965* (Paris), 1966, *Kaleidoscope: Poems by American Negro Poets,* 1967, and about one hundred other volumes. General editor, "Broadside Critics" series on Black poetry. About ninety poems have been published in periodicals, including *Phylon, Negro Digest, Renaissance,* and *Imprints Quarterly;* also contributor of book reviews to *Books Abroad* and *New York Times Book Review,* and of articles to scholarly journals.

WORK IN PROGRESS: A seventh volume of poems, tentatively entitled *Black Tender.*

SIDELIGHTS: James A. Emanuel told *CA:* "I compose poems at the typewriter whenever possible. . . . I like to break new ground in Black American literature: *Snowflakes and Steel, A Poet's Mind,* and *The Broken Bowl* are innovative in format; I hope that they will encourage readers to study Black literature more closely than ever." He adds that *Dark Symphony: Negro Literature in America* "was meant to overcome almost thirty years of neglect of Black literature by American publishers of anthologies and literary histories."

According to *Black American Poetry: A Critical Commentary*, Emanuel seems "destined to become one of the major Black poets." His poems have been read on a British Broadcasting Corp. program in England and on the Voice of America program "The Whole World Is Listening." They have also been used in the Broadway show "A Hand Is on the Gate" and included in dramatic presentations on the college circuit. His greatest satisfaction, though, came from writing *Langston Hughes*, "a book evolving from my racial pride."

Emanuel's own readings have taken him to Africa, England, France, Austria, Poland, Hungary, Romania, and elsewhere in Europe, where much of his poetry and prose since 1970 has been written. "My European experiences," he says, "have confirmed my faith in literary art and in Blackness as one of its deepest sources."

Langston Hughes has been translated into French.

BIOGRAPHICAL/CRITICAL SOURCES: *Negro Digest*, April, 1965, June, 1966, January, 1968, January, 1969; *Times Literary Supplement*, July 8, 1965; *Negro American Literature Forum*, Volume I, number 1, fall, 1967; *Nation*, December 4, 1967; *New York Times Book Review*, November 26, 1968; *Ramparts*, October, 1969; *Road Apple Review*, winter, 1971-72; *The Crowell Handbook of Contemporary Poetry*, Crowell, 1973; *The Paperback*, University of Warsaw, June, 1976; *Black American Poetry: A Critical Commentary*, Monarch, 1977; *Black American Literature Forum*, Volume XIII, number 3, 1979; *Pregled 219*, [Belgrade, Yugoslavia], 1982.

* * *

EMORY, Alan (Steuer) 1922-

PERSONAL: Name legally changed in 1951; born May 7, 1922, in New York, N.Y.; son of Henry (a state Supreme Court justice) and Ethel (a labor arbitrator; maiden name, Steuer) Epstein; married Nancy Goodman (a musician and teacher), October 15, 1950; children: Marc D., John A., Katharine B. *Education:* Harvard University, A.B., 1943; Columbia University, M.S., 1947. *Religion:* Unitarian. *Home:* 6302 Crosswoods Cir., Falls Church, Va. 22044. *Office:* 1001 National Press Bldg., Washington, D.C. 20045.

CAREER/WRITINGS: *Watertown Daily Times*, Watertown, N.Y., city reporter, 1947-48, state editor, 1948-49, legislative correspondent, 1949-51, Washington correspondent, 1951—, writer of editorial page column, "From Washington," 1951—. United Features-North American Newspaper Alliance, Washington, D.C., writer of syndicated column appearing in 200 newspapers, 1954-80. Washington correspondent for *Oswego Palladium Times*, 1951-80, *Schenectady Gazette*, 1954—, *Middletown Record*, 1956-62, and *Binghamton Sun Bulletin*, 1962-64; special correspondent, Radio Press International, New York, N.Y., 1959-60; Washington columnist, *Empire State Report*, 1980—.

Notable assignments include coverage of all national conventions since 1952, a series on Alaska, 1958, Richard Nixon's trips to the Soviet Union, 1959 and 1972, President Eisenhower's South African trip, 1960, a series on Venezuela, 1966, a series on Russia, 1972, a series on tax policy, a series on acid rain in Canada, 1981, a series on China, 1981, and a series on Western Europe based on interviews with heads of state and opposition leaders in Germany, Italy, Great Britain, and members of the North Atlantic Treaty Organization (NATO), 1983.

Lecturer; occasional panelist on NBC's "Meet the Press." Director and vice-president of Lake Barcroft (Va.) Community Association, and Watertown (N.Y.) and Massena (N.Y.) Little Theatres.

Contributor of articles to magazines and newspapers, including *Business Week, Reporter, Nation, Electrical World, Washington Post, Washington Star, Editor and Publisher, Quill,* and to a book on the 1981 national convention, published by the Society of Professional Journalists. Also author of booklets on Alaska, 1958, Venezuela, 1966, the Soviet Union, 1972, and Washington, D.C. *Military service:* U.S. Army, European theater of operations, 1943-46; became staff sergeant.

MEMBER: National Press Club (member of speakers' committee), White House Correspondents' Association, Washington Press Club, Sigma Delta Chi (Washington professional chapter; treasurer, 1972-73; vice-president, 1973-74; president, 1974-75; director, 1975-80; foundation treasurer, 1978—), Gridiron Club of Washington, D.C. (member of producers' committee; music chairman of executive committee, 1982). *Awards, honors:* Thomas L. Stokes award from the Washington Journalism Center, 1968, for a series of articles concerning the future of atomic power in New York state; elected to Washington Hall of Fame, Society of Professional Journalists, Sigma Delta Chi, 1979.

SIDELIGHTS: A series of articles written by Alan Emory, was helpful in affecting a reversal of the Nixon administration's policy concerning the use of individual income tax records by federal agencies.

* * *

ENGEL, Marian 1933-

PERSONAL: Born May 24, 1933, in Toronto, Ontario, Canada; daughter of Frederick Searle (a teacher) and Mary (Fletcher) Passmore; married Howard Engel (a broadcaster), January 27, 1962 (divorced, 1977); children: William Lucas and Charlotte Helen Arabella (twins). *Education:* McMaster University, B.A., 1955; McGill University, M.A., 1957. *Politics:* New Democratic Party. *Home:* 70 Marchmount Rd., Toronto, Ontario, Canada MGG 2A9. *Agent:* Virginia Barber, 353 West 21st St., New York, N.Y. 10011.

CAREER: Writer. Montana State University, lecturer at extension in Missoula, 1957-58; Study School, Montreal, Quebec, teacher, 1958-60; St. John's School (Royal Air Force school), Nicosia, Cyprus, teacher, 1963; writer-in-residence, University of Alberta, Edmonton, 1977-78, and University of Toronto, 1980-81. Chairman, Writers' Union of Canada, 1973-74; member, Toronto Book Prize committee, 1974-77; trustee, Toronto Public Library Board, 1974-77. *Member:* Writers Union of Canada, Association of Canadian TV and Radio Artists. *Awards, honors:* Canada Council senior arts fellowship, 1968, 1973, 1976; Governor General's award for best novel in English in Canada, 1976, for *Bear; Lunatic Villas* was co-winner of the City of Toronto Book Awards, 1982; Engel was made an officer of the Order of Canada, 1982.

WRITINGS—Novels, except as noted: *No Clouds of Glory*, Harcourt, 1968, published as *Sarah Bastard's Notebook*, Paperjacks, 1971; *The Honeyman Festival*, St. Martin's, 1970; *Monodromos*, Anansi, 1973, published as *One Way Street*, Hamish Hamilton, 1975; *Joanne: The Last Days of a Modern*

Marriage, Paperjacks, 1975; *Inside the Easter Egg* (short stories), Anansi, 1975; *Bear,* Atheneum, 1976; *The Glassy Sea,* McClelland & Stewart, 1978, St. Martin's, 1979; *The Year of the Child,* St. Martin's, 1981 (published in Canada as *Lunatic Villas,* McClelland & Stewart, 1981); *The Islands of Canada,* Hurtig, 1982.

Juveniles: *Adventurer at Moon Bay Towers,* Irwin Clarke, 1974; *My Name Is Not Odessa Yarker,* Kids Can Press, 1977.

Author of scripts for Canadian Broadcasting Corp. radio on Lawrence Durrell, Henry Miller, Leonard Woolf, and other literary figures. Contributor of short stories and articles to numerous magazines and newspapers, including *MacLean's, Saturday Night, Redbook, Toronto Globe and Mail,* and the *New York Times Book Review.*

WORK IN PROGRESS: A novel; literary essays; book reviews.

SIDELIGHTS: Marian Engel is a respected Canadian writer whose work remains better known in her native country than in the United States. While her publications range from children's books to adult nonfiction, she is regarded primarily as a novelist; her fictions appeal to scholars as well as the reading public, for they are deft creations, painstakingly crafted and underpinned with serious themes. She writes frequently of women—"more-than-ordinarily sensitive women" according to Joyce Carol Oates—and though her heroines seem unexceptional, they are actually complex women, wrestling with crucial issues and assuming new roles. Often their crises propel them beyond mundane interests, evoking spiritual concerns. Engel "has always been a recorder of those brief, wondrous moments when the human seems to touch upon something larger than or different from itself," Oates explains in a *Canadian Forum* review.

Nowhere is this preoccupation more evident than in *Bear*—a fictive *tour de force* that won Engel a 1976 Governor General's award and that many consider her finest book. Described by *Choice* as "a bizarre, and perhaps ultimate, chapter in the familiar Canadian identity quest," *Bear* chronicles the rebirth of Lou, a "slug-pale," prematurely aged archivist employed by Ontario's Historical Institute. "In the winter," the story begins, "she lived like a mole, buried deep in her office, digging among maps and manuscripts." Though she loves her profession, the prolonged isolation has left Lou vaguely dissatisfied. "It was," she explains, "as if life in general had a grudge against her. Things persisted in turning grey. . . . After five years she now felt that in some way [the seclusion of her job] had aged her disproportionately, that she was as old as the yellowed papers she spent her day unfolding." When an island estate in remote northern Ontario is bequeathed to the Institute, Lou welcomes the task of inspecting its library and cataloging the books. "For her," explains *Newsweek*'s Margo Jefferson, "the assignment becomes a voyage away from cities, orderly history and human beings into nature, animal life, legend and self-fulfillment."

The only objectionable feature of the arrangement is that Lou must tend to the bear that lives in a log hut behind the main house. A legacy from the former owner, this is one of a long line of bears that have inhabited the island since it was first settled by the Cary family in the nineteenth century. "It seems that from the start Colonel Cary, a dandy fascinated by Byron and Shelley, romantically as one with Swinburne and the pre-Raphaelites, saw something heroic and virile in bears," writes Webster Schott in the *Washington Post Book World*. "He and his heirs kept a bear in a hutch near the house for as long as anyone could remember." Though Lou is not an animal lover, she accepts responsibility for feeding the beast, which is "indubitably male." In the process of cataloging, Lou soon discovers the old Colonel's handwritten notes about bear lore and legend interspersed among his books and finds herself more and more fascinated by the beast outside. They eat together, swim together, defecate together. Before long, Lou has unchained him and invited him into the house where, one night, he explores her nude body with his tongue.

While the *Saturday Review* critic charges that, from the moment Lou says "'I love you, bear,' . . . her behavior becomes too extreme and too implausible to be read without snickering," most critics praise Engel's treatment of this difficult subject. Among them is Doris Grumbach, who writes in the *New York Times Book Review* that Lou's "need of the bear is like any human need; for warm contact, for sexual pleasure, for uncritical acceptance. Only at the beginning does she wonder: 'What a strange thing to do. To have done. To have done to me.'" Nor does *Saturday Night* contributing critic Anne Montagnes consider the sex scenes inappropriate: "Except to the quaintly fastidious, there is nothing offensive, only profound tenderness. In fact, at the point where concupiscence tempts the story toward wet-lipped perversion (Bear gets an erection and Lou . . . presents herself animal-style to him), Bear, with one slash of his non-retractable claws, restores sanity."

In his scholarly study, Donald S. Hair explains why the "breaking and re-establishing" of the bestiality taboo is essential to Lou's rebirth. "When a barrier as strong as that is broken," he writes in *Canadian Literature,* "all barriers begin to fall, and a new unity can begin forming itself. But the re-establishing of the taboo is equally crucial. The barrier begins to reappear when Lou becomes aware of the fact that she has broken it. Instinctively, she turns to human contact, and tries, unsuccessfully, to find release with Homer [the local shopkeeper]. The climactic moment is Lou's attempt to have intercourse with the bear: 'He reached out one great paw and ripped the skin on her back.' In terms of the realism of the novel, the bear is simply proving to be the wild creature that Homer has regularly warned Lou about. But in symbolic terms, the bear releases Lou into her full human identity by marking the limits of kinship, and finally separating animal from human. The pain and the blood suggest a rebirth and certainly Lou feels that she has been reborn."

But there is more to Engel's story than Lou's rebirth. Read as a parable, Bear reenacts what *Harper's* calls "the Romanticism of those who, like the Carys, have sought to live in the wilderness on their own, imported terms." Like the nineteenth-century British settlers, Lou comes to the island prepared to solve its mysteries through erudition, and, throughout her stay, she carefully records each book and scrap of paper she finds. But the scholarly techniques that have served her so well in the city prove ineffectual in the Canadian north. Writing in the *Times Literary Supplement*, Jane Miller explains why: "The island has mysteries no archivist can penetrate and it produces in Lou a clarity of vision which is not a historian's. The bear has a history as the island has, and both are to be understood through love rather than scholarship." Or, as Webster Schott puts it: "The presence of the bear, chain gone, free in the house, is greater than history." On still a broader level, *Bear* laments the separation of all men from their animal past. Civilization has disconnected man from his physical history.

Despite the levels of meaning and symbolic patterns interwoven throughout the book, *Bear* remains a well-integrated novel.

"We have no sense that actions are forced or details thrust upon us," notes Donald S. Hair. "Everything is carefully observed and fully realized. If, as Margaret Avison has said, the devil is etc., there is no devil in the book. We live 'sweetly and intensely' with Lou and her bear, exploring, like her, the infinite richness of simplicity."

The heroine of Engel's subsequent novel is another alienated loner—this time a divorcee named Marguerite Heber Bowen. Rita, as she is called, is middle-aged when *The Glassy Sea* opens and living alone on an isolated island, an existence dictated by the terms of her divorce from an ambitious Ontario politician who wants her out of the way. Written as two slices of the present sandwiched around a long letter explaining Rita's past, the novel traces her journey from girlhood to university student to Anglican nun, and then, following the dissolution of her order, sketches in rapid succession her marriage, motherhood, divorce and exile, ending with her return to the convent to establish a women's hostel.

Though some critics find fault with the novel's structure, most consider her subject important. Engel "is writing about the religious life of a woman, a modern woman with a strong hunger for purity, which she well knows is an odd and difficult taste in this age," explains Mary Gordon in the *New York Times Book Review*. Writing in the *Canadian Forum*, Katherine Govier calls *The Glassy Sea* "a thinker's book, perhaps, a *gut* thinker's book. . . . Engel is asking about faith for the faithless (it was good taste rather than belief that took Rita into the order, she admits), and love and sex for the loveless."

At the end of the novel, when Rita returns to the convent to open a shelter for battered women, she knows what she wants: "a core of women helping other women to put their lives . . . in order. The casualties are coming in greater and greater numbers, and though I would like to take the men, too, and cry, 'Off with the old, on with the new,' and 'You must love one another or die!' it is women I am committed to working with and I shall do that." According to *Washington Post* reviewer Joseph McLellan, "it is a thing worth saying, and its worth is compounded in this book by the quirky elegance with which it is said."

Engel's next novel, a satiric comment on Toronto life, marks a departure from her earlier style. "I wanted to get out of the lush, descriptive writing I'd done before," she told *Quill and Quire*'s Michael Ryval. "It was beginning to say nothing, and I wanted to say the way things really are in Toronto, not the usual pieties." The inspiration for *Lunatic Villas* was a remark one of her children made while Engel was teaching at the University of Alberta. "Things were fairly grim in Edmonton for my kids," she explained to Ryval. "I was having a great time. But they didn't fit in at all. Edmonton is terribly straight. In Toronto, they feel quite normal and part of a community of kids whose parents are writers, filmmakers and CBC producers. Anyway, one day they told me *my* life was absolutely disgusting. That's when I discovered they were watching all these junky TV programmes, and they believed we should all live like the people in Eight is Enough. . . . In those terms, my life is a failure. And I was unnerved. Until I thought it was funny."

Engel's answer to her children was a comedy about an unconventional, but loving, mother who resides in an unfashionable Toronto neighborhood (Rathbone Place, a.k.a. Ratsbane, later nicknamed Lunatic Villas). Here, amid unmade beds and grimy floors, divorcee and free-lance writer Harriet Ross is raising her brood of unruly children. Though natural mother to only one child, Harriet has acquired an additional six through marriages and circumstance. Soon they are joined by Mrs. Saxe, a little old English lady who arrives on her bicycle one snowy night, bringing, according to the *Maclean's* reviewer, "unexpected insights and warmth, knitting street and family together." There is also an assortment of odd neighbors and friends, so many characters and incidents, in fact, that Doris Cowan writes in *Books in Canada* that it sometimes seems Engel "is quite deliberately packing the novel with everything she has observed or discovered since the last one was written, whether it fits or not."

Some reviewers find the digressions distracting; others, including Cowan, argue that the technique works successfully: "You pick up the threads as you read, and if you miss a few, if names are introduced abruptly and mysterious references are made, it doesn't matter: the important themes will be back." In this story, Michelle Gadpaille has identified the nature of love, "specifically that seven-eighths of love that is loyalty, commitment, and responsibility, that brings its rewards slowly, and is not in the least romantic or sentimental," as one important theme. "What originality there is in *Lunatic Villas*, she continues in *Canadian Literature*, "comes . . . from its unspectacular rejection of idealized pictures of parenthood and childhood. In *Lunatic Villas* children are presented as children: they may be strong, but they cannot replace fathers; sweet, but they can be seduced by money; vulnerable, but they can survive away from home." Praising its artful "fusion of laughter and reality," Leo Simpson concludes in *Quill and Quire* that *Lunatic Villas* "sparkles wittily throughout, and contains an earnest volume's worth of truth about the way lives are lived by women and children."

CA INTERVIEW

CA interviewed Marian Engel by telephone May 17, 1983, at her home in Toronto.

CA: When did you begin to write, or to think seriously about being a writer?

ENGEL: I started to write when I was a child. I used to sell little things to the Sunday-school papers; they had a contest every month. From that, of course, I thought I'd be a great instant writer when I grew up. But, like everyone else, I had to go through my apprenticeship.

CA: So you had early encouragement, at least from the Sunday-school paper. What about parents and teachers? Did they encourage you?

ENGEL: I think they did. My mother was smart. She simply used to say, "Oh, it's very hard." I think if she had taken any more interest in it than that, I would have perversely dropped it. But she knew that I liked the challenge. She had a typewriter, and somehow there were always paper and stamps around.

CA: Much of your prose is quite poetic. Did you write poetry earlier, or were you influenced in a conscious way by poetry?

ENGEL: Oh, very much. I wrote poetry earlier. I hoped to be a poet. That went away when I was twenty-one, and I realized that if it does go away, you're not a poet. But also we had done a lot of poetry at home. We used to memorize poetry when we did the dishes—we would do Longfellow and Tennyson. And I think that sticks with you.

CA: Who were your literary heroes or influences?

ENGEL: I suppose practically everyone. I went to university at a time when my English department was all enthralled with T. S. Eliot. And then I did my graduate work with Hugh MacLennan, the Canadian novelist, at McGill. He was a great mentor for me.

CA: Like some of the women in your fiction, you've gone away from home for extended periods of time—to the United States (Montana), France, England, and Cyprus. How do you think living away from Canada has affected your work either directly or indirectly?

ENGEL: When I grew up in Canada, it was such a small world. It was a place you had to get away from, and of course I swore I was never coming back, that I was never going to be a provincial and live in this terrible country. That has changed now. I don't think anybody needs to leave. People still do, of course. We all rush around trying to find better weather. But living in Europe (I was there for three years) gave me a wonderful perspective on this country. I came back and it seemed very silent, very empty, and I couldn't get over the landscape. It's all so beautiful. We came back, I remember, in the fall, I think in November, and sailed down the St. Lawrence River. It was blazing with color, and so magnificent! There's nothing in Europe like that. But people seemed very quiet and subdued. And I think if I were away for a couple of years again, I would again be maddened when I came back by the fact that they're quiet and subdued and conservative.

CA: In her discussion of your work in Book Forum, *Ann Hutchinson noted that "success is almost a bad word in Canada," and that this compounds the problems women in particular have in becoming successful and dealing with success, a theme you have dealt with in your fiction. Would you comment on this?*

ENGEL: I've often had conversations with people who were successful and feeling very unpopular. It does seem to be true; I guess that is a puritanical thing, and you must have some of that left in the United States, too. To be successful in a career is to leave modesty behind. It's also to be conspicuous, and therefore you become a target. I am not so successful that I have had much trouble with it. Margaret Atwood is a person who has really suffered. People are getting over it now, but she went through a period of not being able to do anything right for the great public. Again, I think Canada is growing up. We're getting used now to having our own culture heroes, and that makes it a bit better. Unfortunately, we have no movie stars, so they use the writers for public appearances.

CA: Was it on winning the 1977 Governor General's Award for Bear *that you became something of a public figure?*

ENGEL: I think it was when I was chairman of the Writers' Union of Canada. I did a lot of press work and a lot of television work, so I leapt into prominence. I found that very difficult because, unless you look like a movie star, you feel like a fool. I have since learned always to demand a make-up person and then it's much better, but still it is making yourself into a target, and I never quite know what to do with public appearances. But I'm better at them than I used to be, and there are advantages. We have a scheme whereby the Canada Council pays you for public appearances, for readings. Sometimes that's very handy income, and it is a wonderful way of traveling around the country; but you have to be in the mood for it. I have never really liked meeting new people, and I am sometimes kind of unreliable—I growl at them if I am in the wrong mood—so I find it all terrifying.

CA: You've done reviews for the New York Times Book Review. *Would you comment on the importance of reviews and the quality of reviews in this country as compared with Canada?*

ENGEL: I haven't reviewed for the *Times* for many, many years. I don't know why they dropped me—I think because I was getting out of touch with American books. You can't keep up with everything, you know. The more I got absorbed into the Canadian scene, read my contemporaries, the fewer Americans I read. The Canadian book world tends to be ingrown, I think, to a larger extent than the American. I think the *New York Times* is good, though it seems to have a tendency to promote books more than Canadian reviews do. Of course, we're like that. We jump on each other. In Canada the scene is still small enough that people tend to attack each other in a way that doesn't happen in the *Times*. So, what I like getting in Toronto is the new Iris Murdochs and Doris Lessings, because then I don't have any ax to grind.

The difference between the American and Canadian literary scenes is quite interesting to me. You have a much larger one and one likes to think it's less quarrelsome, though I don't know. But we have been building a very interesting literary outlook in this country and it looks as if it's lasting. When I started out I thought I was going to be the only person who was going to be a novelist in my generation. To my delight, there are twenty, maybe twenty-five of us who are really good. There were a whole bunch of kids growing up during the war who came out wanting to write novels, and we've all succeeded. That's somehow very exciting, because you've got lots of talented people to sharpen your claws on.

CA: Do you think Canada appreciates its writers more than we do in the United States, or in a different way?

ENGEL: Canadians are very conservative and I think very shocked by some of us, and they don't know what to do with others of us, but when you go out and meet the public you do find people who are very, very grateful for what you've done. There are always people coming up and saying, "I really like your book. I was having a bad time during my life and I sat down and read that, and I laughed and shared those feelings." That's very gratifying. The other nice thing is that there's a lot of literary material on radio and it reaches people in the smaller places, the isolated places. I'm sure that happens in the United States too, but I don't think you have our kind of national radio. It has become much more gratifying to be a Canadian writer than it was thirty years ago.

CA: You've done a lot of teaching. Have teaching and writing been mutually beneficial, or has the teaching been more of a struggle?

ENGEL: I found teaching an awful struggle. My father was a teacher, so they always wanted me to teach, and it's an honorable thing to do. On the other hand, to write and teach and keep house is just too much for me, so I avoid teaching when I can. I'm not teaching now. I think I have a certain amount to teach my students, and they certainly have something to teach me, but I get very impatient with having to go out and do those kinds of things when a day could be a writing day.

CA: Do you maintain a regular daily writing schedule?

ENGEL: I do when I'm in the middle of something. I'm not at the moment, so I'm hanging loose. But when I'm really writing, and I'm going to have to discipline myself and yell at myself, I find the best thing to do is get up in the morning and not read the paper, but just go straight to the typewriter and get at it again. I don't know about anybody else, but I only last two or three hours at most. Then I do the rest of the things. But I find if I start anything else in the morning, that writing energy is shot.

CA: Through your work as chairman of the Writers' Union of Canada (1973-1974), a member of the Toronto Book Prize Committee (1974-1977), and writer-in-residence at the University of Alberta (1977-1978), you've probably had a great deal of contact with other writers.

ENGEL: Yes, and I was also on the Library Board as a trustee. That was done on purpose. Some of us felt that they weren't spending enough of their money on books, and certainly not on Canadian books. So five of us moved in and became a majority of the trustees. These were appointments, and it took us a long time to figure out how to get them; we were very much helped by the fact that our generation had moved into City Hall at that time. That job was sometimes agony. I hadn't realized how heavy political work is. Everybody always caucuses at 5 o'clock. Well, who's going to make the supper?

But we did a tremendous amount of political work those two years. The library system was going to be changed in a way that we felt would be very unsatisfactory for the citizens—certainly for book-loving citizens—and we simply voted things down. We said books, more books. No athletic programs, more books! We were finding that a disproportionate amount of money was being spent in the rich neighborhoods, of course, and there were all kinds of political things going on. But we had a lot of librarians on our side, and that helped. I wasn't a leader in the movement; I was very much a follower. I voted with people who could handle statistics, and we did manage to get some reforms. We kept a good library system in this city and tried to update it. It was a great political insight for me, though I'd never want to do it again.

CA: Has all your contact with other writers enriched your own work in any way?

ENGEL: Oh, I think immensely, yes. It was very interesting when we founded the union. (Now the union has changed, of course. More writers have moved in, so it isn't that little intense group of novelists who founded it anymore. But most of us original people are still there, even though we don't control it.) I think that just to sit down in a room with a bunch of people who do the same crazy thing was very good for us. And we exchange a lot of information—the union has to a degree become an information center. It has done a lot of work on contracts, and relationships with agents and editors.

CA: You write a lot about women and women's problems. Do you consider yourself a feminist?

ENGEL: I'm not a radical feminist, but I'm a feminist and I've been one since I was about sixteen. I couldn't see why I was inferior because I was female. I'm not interested, however, in programmatic feminist writing for myself, and people inside the movement often want feminists to do that. They say, "Why don't you show women as successful in our terms?" I write about what I see and feel. Many of my friends are successful, and I ought to say more about their lives; but most women are still floundering; pressure is still against us: I write about that world, not the utopian world.

CA: In addition to novels, juvenile fiction, short stories, and articles, you've written scripts on literary figures for Canadian Broadcasting Corporation radio. Have you done any writing for television?

ENGEL: I've done two plays, neither of which was produced. It's hard for me to write without visual descriptions, which I am good at.

CA: Were you involved in the production of the radio scripts that you wrote?

ENGEL: No, I wasn't. I was then married to a radio producer and I used to stay out of the building when those things were going on.

CA: Would you like to be involved in radio or television production at all?

ENGEL: No, not particularly. It's very technical work. Someone has just produced a radio play based on my novel *The Year of the Child*. It was aired last Saturday night, and I didn't hear it because I thought that the fee was under negotiation through my agent so I didn't think it would be on yet. It was written and dramatized quite nicely, I'm told. But when these things are scheduled, you don't always hear about them. That is how remote they are. I don't do as much with radio because I divorced radio. I just let them pay me for things now.

CA: Is there any kind of writing you'd like to do that you haven't tried yet?

ENGEL: I want to do some real literary essays, although I don't know whether I'm up to it. Last year when I supported myself by doing a column in the family page of the *Toronto Star*, I discovered that I did not *want* a half million readers and that there was a lot people wanted to know about me that I didn't want to tell; but I discovered also that I could invent a popular style and hold an audience. After a while we all got tired of it and it was canceled and I was glad. Now I would like to slide up to the other end of the scale and try to do some thinking writing. But I think that's going to be very difficult for me. I'm working on a novel now, and when I finish that I'll try the other kind of writing, because that's one thing I haven't done in Canada. I didn't get involved with the little magazines and wasn't able to do serious criticism. I'm getting very interested in the mental processes that create different forms.

CA: How do you feel about your own career at this point? Are you happy with what you've done?

ENGEL: Yes, in a way. I was appointed to the Order of Canada this year. That is gratifying. People are beginning to phone up about reprinting the old books, which is nice. I think I've done well. I certainly haven't done everything I want to do, and, you know, you do run out of energy eventually. I'm fifty now, and I can't work as hard as I did when I was forty. On the other hand, I know more and there's more that I want to do, and perhaps just writing about writing is one of the logical conclusions too.

BIOGRAPHICAL/CRITICAL SOURCES—Books: *Eleven Canadian Novelists*, Anansi, 1972; David Helwig, *The Human Element, Second Series*, Oberon, 1981.

Periodicals: *New York Times Book Review*, February 25, 1968, August 15, 1976, September 9, 1979; *Saturday Night*, October, 1970, May, 1976, May, 1981; *Canadian Forum*, May, 1976, March, 1979; *New York Times*, July 26, 1976, August 14, 1979; *Newsweek*, August 16, 1976; *Washington Post Book World*, August 29, 1976; *Saturday Review*, September 18, 1976, May, 1981; *Harper's*, October, 1976; *Choice*, January, 1977; *New Statesman*, April 1, 1977; *Times Literary Supplement*, April 1, 1977; *Books in Canada*, August-September, 1979, April, 1981, March, 1982; *Washington Post*, September 4, 1979; *Quill and Quire*, March, 1981, April, 1981; *Maclean's*, March 9, 1981, *Canadian Literature*, spring, 1982, autumn, 1982.

—Sketch by Donna Olendorf
—Interview by Jean W. Ross

* * *

ENGLISH, Maurice 1909-1983

PERSONAL: Born October 21, 1909, in Chicago, Ill.; died November 18, 1983, in Philadelphia, Pa.; son of Michael and Agnes (Sexton) English; married Fanita Blumberg (a psychotherapist), April 25, 1945; children: Jonathan Brian, Deirdre Elena. *Education:* Harvard University, A.B. (magna cum laude), 1933. *Home:* 724 Pine St., Philadelphia, Pa. 19106.

CAREER: Free-lance journalist in U.S. and Europe, 1933-53; foreign correspondent in France and Spain, 1938-41; editor in chief of international division of National Broadcasting Co., 1941-43; editor and publisher of *Chicago Magazine*, 1953-56; free-lance writer, 1957-61; University of Chicago Press, Chicago, Ill., managing editor, 1961-63, senior editor, 1963-69; Temple University Press, Philadelphia, Pa., founder and director, 1969-76; University of Pennsylvania Press, Philadelphia, director, beginning 1979. Founder of Pulvinar Press, 1975. Read poetry at Library of Congress, 1978. *Member:* American Association of University Presses, Phi Beta Kappa, Harvard Club (New York), Franklin Inn Club (Philadelphia). *Awards, honors:* Ferguson Award, Friends of Literature, 1964, for *Midnight in the Century;* Fulbright fellowship in creative writing, 1966-67.

WRITINGS: (Contributor) *The New Yorker Book of Verse*, Harcourt, 1935; (contributor) Selden Rodman, editor, *100 Modern Poets*, Pellegrini & Cudahy, 1949; (editor) *The Testament of Stone: Themes of Idealism and Indignation from the Writings of Louis Sullivan*, Northwestern University Press, 1963; *Midnight in the Century* (poems), Prairie School Press, 1964; (translator with others) *The Selected Poems of Eugenio Montale*, New Directions, 1965; (contributor) Robert Cromie, editor, *Where Steel Winds Blow*, McKay, 1969; *A Savaging of Roots* (poems), Pas de Loup Press, 1974. Also author of *Choosing the God*, 1976, and play "The Saints in Illinois."

WORK IN PROGRESS: "The Seven Ages," a play; *A Bone Hieroglyph and Other Poems.*

SIDELIGHTS: Maurice English once wrote *CA*, "It's better to just write and publish, and not offer all sorts of explanations, which rarely go beyond the first four lines in *Midnight in the Century:* ''Since no one is someone without a disguise / And the truths of the parlor in the bedroom are lies / And my everyday self is a shoddy disgrace, / I have put on these masks to show you my face.''"

MEDIA ADAPTATIONS: Maxims and Minims, a choral composition by Sydney Hodkinson based on English's *Midnight in the Century*, was premiered at the Eastman School of Music in 1978.

AVOCATIONAL INTERESTS: Translating from French, Italian, and Spanish, poetry readings, lecturing and teaching on "what is American about American poetry."

OBITUARIES: Publishers Weekly, December 16, 1983.†

* * *

EPHRON, Delia 1944-
(Delia Brock)

PERSONAL: Born July 12, 1944, in Los Angeles, Calif.; daughter of Henry (a writer) and Phoebe (a writer; maiden name, Wolkind) Ephron; married Dan Brock (divorced). *Education:* Barnard College, B.A., 1966. *Residence:* Los Angeles, Calif.

CAREER: Writer.

WRITINGS: (With Lorraine Bodger; under name Delia Brock) *The Adventurous Crocheter*, Simon & Schuster, 1972; (with Bodger) *Glad Rags*, Simon & Schuster, 1975; *How to Eat Like a Child, and Other Lessons in Not Being a Grown-Up*, Viking, 1978; (with Bodger) *Crafts for All Seasons*, Universe, 1980; *Teenage Romance: Or How to Die of Embarrassment*, Viking, 1981; *Santa and Alex*, Little, Brown, 1983. Contributor to magazines, including *Vogue*, *Esquire*, *New York Times Magazine*, and *New York*.

WORK IN PROGRESS: A screenplay for Walt Disney Productions.

SIDELIGHTS: Delia Ephron's book, *How to Eat Like a Child, and Other Lessons in Not Being a Grown-Up*, is a humorous collection of essays about childhood covering such topics as birthdays, Christmas, sibling torture, car rides, school, and pets. The title piece, originally published in the *New York Times Magazine*, was a child's view of the proper way to consume peas, mashed potatoes, ice cream, fried eggs, spinach, and other assorted foods.

For her next collection of essays, *Teenage Romance: Or How to Die of Embarrassment*, Ephron interviewed about seventy-five teenagers in New York and California. She tells *People*: "They say teens today are more sophisticated, but I believe they're just as nervous and embarrassed as ever. The girls still worry about getting pregnant [from] kissing; the boys are as preoccupied as ever with 'getting it.'"

MEDIA ADAPTATIONS: How to Eat Like a Child was adapted into a musical special for the National Broadcasting Corp.

BIOGRAPHICAL/CRITICAL SOURCES: New York Times, November 17, 1978; *Reader's Digest*, March, 1979, August, 1979; *Saturday Evening Post*, May, 1979; *People*, October 12, 1981; *Nation*, November 21, 1981; *Washington Post Book World*, August 22, 1982; *New York Times Book Review*, September 5, 1982.†

* * *

EPHRON, Nora 1941-

PERSONAL: Born May 19, 1941, in New York, N.Y.; daughter of Henry (a writer) and Phoebe (a writer; maiden name, Wolkind) Ephron; married Dan Greenburg (a writer), April 9,

1967 (divorced); married Carl Bernstein (a journalist), April 14, 1976 (divorced); children: (second marriage) Jacob, Max. *Education:* Wellesley College, B.A., 1962. *Agent:* Lynn Nesbit, International Creative Management, 40 West 57th St., New York, N.Y. 10019.

CAREER: New York Post, New York City, reporter, 1963-68; free-lance journalist, 1968-72; *Esquire* magazine, New York City, columnist and contributing editor, 1972-73; *New York* magazine, New York City, contributing editor, 1973-74; *Esquire,* senior editor and columnist, 1974-76. *Awards, honors:* Penney-Missouri award from University of Missouri Journalism School and J. C. Penney & Co., 1973; D.H.L. from Briarcliff College, 1974; with Alice Arden, nomination for outstanding original screenplay, American Academy of Motion Picture Arts and Sciences, 1984, for "Silkwood."

WRITINGS—Published by Knopf, except as indicated: *Wallflower at the Orgy,* Viking, 1970; *Crazy Salad: Some Things about Women,* 1975; *Scribble, Scribble: Notes on the Media,* 1979; *Heartburn,* 1983; (with Alice Arden) "Silkwood" (screenplay), Twentieth Century-Fox, 1983. Author of "Women" column, in *Esquire,* 1972-73, in *New York,* 1973-74, and of "Media" column in *Esquire,* beginning 1974. Contributor of articles to *Esquire, New York, Oui, McCall's,* and *Cosmopolitan.*

SIDELIGHTS: Nora Ephron is no stranger to public scrutiny. In the early 1960s her parents, writers Henry and Phoebe Ephron, based their successful play "Take Her, She's Mine" on their eldest daughter's letters home from Wellesley College. Later Nora Ephron would gain a reputation as an acerbic, often autobiographical reporter and columnist, regularly writing for such publications as *New York* magazine and *Esquire.* Finally, Ephron would chronicle her much-publicized breakup with second husband Carl Bernstein in her novel *Heartburn.*

"I've always written about my life," Ephron explained to Stephanie Mansfield in a *Washington Post* interview coinciding with the release of *Heartburn.* "That's how I grew up. 'Take notes. Everything is copy.' All that stuff my mother said to us. I think that it would have been impossible for me to go through the end of my marriage and not written about it, because although it was the most awful thing I've ever been through . . . it was by *far* the most interesting." As a result of her novel and columns, Ephron has become a media figure; she once told Lois Gould in a *New York Times Book Review* interview that she thinks "the day of the purely objective, invisible reporter is over [and] the reporter has become not only visible, but touchable. There seems to be such a hunger on the part of the reading public to know about the writer, and [the writer's life] somehow becomes more interesting than the event." Ephron is, however, a reluctant celebrity. In *Scribble, Scribble,* one of her books of collected columns, she writes: "I am tired of the first person singular noun. I am tired of reading how this journalist serves her guests dinner on the bed and about how that journalist has a Shetland pony with a nervous tic."

Nevertheless, the confessional nature of *Heartburn* surprised many critics and made its author a prime topic on the New York-Washington, D.C., media cocktail-party circuit. Indeed, the events in Ephron's life that inspired the book seem the perfect ingredients for a popular novel: A well-known writer (Ephron), on her second marriage to an acclaimed journalist (Carl Bernstein, of the *Washington Post* and Watergate fame), finds out while she is seven months pregnant with their second child that her husband is having an affair with the daughter of a former prime minister (Margaret Jay, the wife of British Ambassador Peter Jay). In *Heartburn,* the heroine, Rachel Samstat, a famous author of cookbooks, learns while she is pregnant that her second husband, political columnist Mark Feldman, has been seeing a socialite, one Thelma Rice, described by the narrator as "a fairly tall person with a neck as long as an arm and a nose as long as a thumb, and you should see her legs, never mind her feet, which are sort of splayed." The novel recounts the last six weeks of Rachel and Mark's marriage.

"How awfully lucky for those who treat them badly . . . that when journalists get mad they reach for a typewriter instead of a gun," says Grace Glueck in the *New York Times Book Review,* citing the often vengeful nature of *Heartburn.* Art Seidenbaum also takes note of this when he remarks in the *Los Angeles Times Book Review:* "How could [Ephron] publish a *roman* so shamelessly *a clef,* exposing the warts, peccadilloes and worse of family, ex-husbands and friends? How awful (yet how juicy) to describe ['Mark Feldman'] as 'capable of having sex with a Venetian blind,' or to mention that first husband 'Charlie' (presumably [Ephron's first husband] humorist Dan Greenburg) 'was so neurotic he . . . put hospital corners on the newspapers he lined the hamster cage with.'"

What some critics, such as Rhoda Koenig and Garrett Epps, found to their disliking, however, was not so much the novel's nature, but its tone and style. Koenig, reviewing the book in *New York,* for instance, finds that in *Heartburn,* "as in other novels whose heroines have been battered by feminism and the sexual revolution, there's a half-formed anger about the state of the relations between men and women. The old, cute games won't work, but the women, not knowing what else to do, just go on playing them without any conviction. These women might make amusing minor characters, but as heroines they flounder around too much, alternately wistful and sour, dragging the books down with them." Ephron's book in particular, states Koenig, "solicits our sympathy . . . in a very dictatorial way: Actions are stated rather than dramatized, characters are labeled rather than portrayed. Every image has been pre-digested for us—it's a monologue by a Venus's-flytrap." *New Republic* reviewer Epps finds the author's heroine "shallow, snobbish, self-important [and] provincial" and he feels that "a writer who is demanding our attention should either sell her book by invitation only or else give us something to admire. I found precious little admirable about *Heartburn*—not the cliche-ridden, *Cosmo*-coy writing, not the lifestyle it describes, not the values it embodies."

On the other hand, Grace Glueck sees *Heartburn* as "[bristling] ferociously with wit, [but] not entirely lacking in soul." Ephron, according to the critic, "has a great way with short, brisk dialogue and a knack for reporting on what upscale people say and do to one another. And she delivers her entire . . . tale of woe in a well-sustained voice: the strained tones of affronted Jewish-princesshood." According to *Time* magazine's Stefan Kanfer, the author "refuses to allow a note of self-pity; even her title is derisive. Humiliations are always relieved by pratfalls: Mark has been spending time on the psychiatrist's couch—unfortunately, Thelma is on it with him. Rachel's mother breathes her last, and when a nurse covers her with a sheet the old lady sits up, sings 'Ta da!', checks out of the hospital and files for divorce." "Simultaneously funny and touching, . . . Ephron's novel careers along, leaning into the curves, in the kind of hip, urban-Jewish voice that distances pain with one-liners," says Cyra McFadden. Writing about *Heartburn* in the *Chicago Tribune Book World,* McFadden continues: "On the surface, it's the print version of a standup comedy routine. Behind the fast patter, though, and in concert with it, is another voice. It's also Rachel's and while muted, it interrupts now and then to insist, 'This hurts.' Up to her ankles in the rubble of what she thought was the perfect marriage, she can salvage what's left of herself only by taking a broad, comic overview of How Life Is.''

''The question *Heartburn* raises is this: Can Ephron's novel be read by anyone familiar with the author or her writing as a bittersweet novel of how love doesn't work—as Ephron's 'Annie Hall'?,'' asks Jesse Kornbluth in a *New York* article. ''Or is Rachel Samstat so close to Nora Ephron that a reader who knows more than a little about her can't help taking it as a form of nonfiction fiction?'' Kornbluth further notes: ''*Heartburn* is not just a scrambled transcript of incidents from Nora Ephron's life—the end of the book, for example, is liberally sprinkled with the kind of wisdom that must have cost a lot of tears and therapy—but this psychologizing may be too little too late to neutralize the chitchat that has preceded it. And given [the author's] past writing, gossip-minded readers may not be wrong to gobble the book for its dish. Ephron, as everyone who's read her knows, is one of our greatest prosecutorial talents.'' ''Long after the chatter has abated,'' concludes Kanfer, ''*Heartburn* will be providing insights and laughter. . . . [As] Nora Ephron is about to learn, leaving well is the best revenge.''

MEDIA ADAPTATIONS: *Heartburn* has been optioned for a film.

BIOGRAPHICAL/CRITICAL SOURCES: *New York Times Book Review,* June 27, 1975, July 13, 1975, April 16, 1978, April 24, 1983; *Ms.,* November, 1975; *Houston Post,* November 4, 1975; *Authors in the News,* Volume II, Gale, 1976; *Commonweal,* June 18, 1976; *Newsweek,* April 24, 1978, April 11, 1983; *Time,* May 29, 1978, April 11, 1983; *Critic,* August 15, 1978; Nora Ephron, *Scribble, Scribble,* Knopf, 1979; *Chicago Tribune,* November 4, 1979, December 14, 1983; *People,* January 14, 1980; *Contemporary Literary Criticism,* Volume XVII, Gale, 1981; Ephron, *Heartburn,* Knopf, 1983; *New York,* March 14, 1983, May 9, 1983; *Washington Post,* March 30, 1983, April 25, 1983, December 14, 1983; *Chicago Tribune Book World,* April 17, 1983; *Los Angeles Times Book Review,* April 17, 1983; *New Republic,* May 23, 1983; *Times* (London), September 15, 1983.

—Sketch by Susan Salter

* * *

ERNST, Kathryn (Fitzgerald) 1942-

PERSONAL: Born November 12, 1942, in New York, N.Y.; daughter of Joseph Michael (a physician) and Helen Ann (a social worker; maiden name, Dougherty) Fitzgerald; married John Lyman Ernst, December 11, 1971 (divorced April, 1977). *Education:* Wells College, B.A., 1963; New York University, graduate study, 1963-64. *Residence:* New York, N.Y. *Office:* Kathryn F. Ernst Associates, Inc., 80 East End Ave., New York, N.Y. 10028.

CAREER: Prentice-Hall, Inc., Englewood Cliffs, N.J., assistant editor of executive letters, 1963-64, associate editor, 1964-65; Small Business Administration, Washington, D.C., confidential assistant for public affairs, 1965-66; Donaldson, Lufkin & Jenrette, New York City, portfolio analyst, 1966-67; Prentice-Hall, Inc., assistant editor in Trade Division, 1968, director of children's books, 1969-74, assistant vice-president in Trade Division, 1974-75; Franklin Watts, Inc., New York City, editor-in-chief, 1975-76, vice-president and editorial director, 1976-77; International Telephone and Telegraph Corp., New York City, staff operations executive, 1977-78, manager of marketing projects and operations planning for Educational, Transportation, and Building Services Group, 1978-80; A. G. Becker, New York City, managing director of institutional equity, 1980-82; Kathryn F. Ernst Associates, Inc., New York City, president, 1982—.

AWARDS, HONORS: Outstanding achievement award from Small Business Administration, 1966; Christopher Award for Editorial Achievement from Christopher Brothers, 1972, for acquiring and publishing anonymously written *Go Ask Alice,* Prentice-Hall, 1971; outstanding science book award from National Science Teachers Association, 1977, for *Mr. Tamarin's Trees;* named to YWCA Academy of Achievers, 1979.

WRITINGS—Juveniles, except as indicated: *Danny and His Thumb,* illustrations by Tomie de Paola, Prentice-Hall, 1973; *Mr. Tamarin's Trees,* illustrations by Diane de Groat, Crown, 1976; *Owl's New Cards,* Crown, 1977; *Charlie's Pets,* illustrations by Arthur Cumings, Crown, 1978; *Indians: The First Americans,* illustrations by Richard Smolinski, F. Watts, 1979; *The Complete Calorie Counter for Dining Out* (adult), Jove Publications, 1981; *The Complete Carbohydrate Counter for Dining Out* (adult), Jove Publications, 1981; *ESP McGee and the Mysterious Magician,* Avon, 1983.

WORK IN PROGRESS: A six book series of computer mystery novels for young people, for Random House.

* * *

EURICH, Nell 1919-

PERSONAL: Born July 28, 1919, in Norwood, Ohio; daughter of Clayton W. and Edah (Palmer) Plopper; married Alvin C. Eurich (an educator), March 15, 1953; children: Juliet Ann, Donald Alan. *Education:* Stephens College, A.A., 1939; Stanford University, B.A., 1941, M.A., 1943; Columbia University, Ph.D., 1959. *Home:* 24 West 55th St., New York, N.Y. 10019; and Hubbell Mountain Rd., Sherman, Conn. 06784.

CAREER: University of Texas, Main University (now University of Texas at Austin), Austin, Tex., director of student union, 1942-43; Barnard College, New York City, resident counselor, 1944-46; Woman's Foundation, New York City, assistant to president, 1947-49; New York College For Teachers (now State University of New York at Albany), Albany, N.Y., officer in charge of public relations, 1949-52; Stephens College, Columbia, Mo., acting president, 1952, director of development, 1953-54; New York University, New York City, assistant professor of English, 1959-64; New College, Sarasota, Fla., academic dean and acting president, 1965; City of Aspen, Aspen, Colo., director of project to reorganize the public high school curriculum, 1966; Vassar College, Poughkeepsie, N.Y., professor of English and dean of faculty, 1967-70; Manhattanville College, Purchase, N.Y., professor of English, 1971-75, provost and dean of faculty, 1971-75; senior consultant to International Council for Educational Development, 1975—.

National Endowment for the Humanities, member of national selection committee and chairman of Rocky Mountain regional committee, 1966-67, consultant, 1970-71; Marshall Scholarships, member of Middle States commission, 1967-68, chairman of Northeastern region, 1969-71; member, U.S. Commission on Instructional Technology, U.S. Department of Health,

Education, and Welfare, 1968-69; member of judges panel for Federal Woman's award, 1969—; Academy for Educational Development, consultant, 1970-71, senior consultant, 1980—; member of career minister review board, U.S. Department of State, 1972; member of regional panel, White House Commission on Fellows, 1973; member of mid-Atlantic committee, Rhodes Scholarships, 1976; member of Carnegie Council on Policy Studies in Higher Education, 1977-80. Trustee of New College Foundation, 1975—, Bennington College, 1976-83, Carnegie Foundation for the Advancement of Teaching, 1977—, and 17-24 Corp., 1978—; former trustee of New College, Salisbury School, Bank Street College of Education, Hudson Guild Neighborhood House, and Rocky Mountain School.

MEMBER: Modern Language Association of America, American Association of Colleges, World Society for Ekistics, National Council of Women of the United States (honorary member), Aspen Institute for Humanistic Studies, Institute for Advanced Studies in Medicine and the Humanities, Society for the Right to Die (member of executive committee, 1976—). *Awards, honors:* D.H.L., Manhattanville College, 1975.

WRITINGS: *Science in Utopia: A Mighty Design*, Harvard University Press, 1967; (contributor) Alvin Toffler, editor, *Learning for Tomorrow*, Random House, 1974; (contributor) . . . *From Parnassus: A Volume of Essays for Jacques Barzun*, Harper, 1976; (editor) *Systems of Higher Education*, International Council for Educational Development, 1978; *Systems of Higher Education in Twelve Countries: A Comparative View*, Praeger, 1981. Also author, with B. Schwenkmeyer, of *Great Britain's Open University*, 1971. Contributor of articles to educational journals.

* * *

EVANS, Jessica
    See LOTTMAN, Eileen

* * *

EWEN, Stuart 1945-

PERSONAL: Born June 13, 1945, in New York, N.Y.; son of Sol Joshua (a dentist) and Sylvia (a librarian; maiden name, Scott) Ewen; married Elizabeth Wunderlich (a college teacher), October 5, 1966; children: Paul Scott, Sam Travis. *Education:* University of Wisconsin, Madison, B.A., 1968; University of Rochester, M.A., 1969; State University of New York at Albany, Ph.D., 1974. *Politics:* "Share Jose Yglesias' wish to overthrow capitalism." *Residence:* New York, N.Y. *Office:* Hunter College of the City University of New York, 695 Park Ave., New York, N.Y. 10021.

CAREER: Student Non-Violent Coordinating Committee (SNCC), Atlanta, Ga., field secretary in Mississippi, 1964- 65; *Connections* (underground newspaper), Madison, Wis., editor, 1967-68; writer, 1968-71; State University of New York Empire State College, Albany, assistant professor of history, 1971-77; Hunter College of City University of New York, New York, N.Y., professor of media studies, 1977—. Seminar associate at Columbia University, 1976-77. *Member:* Ad-Hoc Committee for Thinking. *Awards, honors:* Woodrow Wilson fellowship, 1969; award from American Library Association, 1976, for *Captains of Consciousness*.

WRITINGS: (Editor with wife Elizabeth Ewen, John Kaufman, and Michael Cherniavsky) *Social Textures of Western Civilization*, Wiley, 1972; *Captains of Consciousness: Advertising and the Social Roots of the Consumer Culture*, McGraw, 1976; (with E. Ewen) *Channels of Desire: Mass Images and the Shaping of American Consciousness*, McGraw, 1982. Contributor to journals, including *Liberation, Radical America, Cultural Studies, Journal of Communication, Harvard Educational Review,* and *Processed World*.

WORK IN PROGRESS: *Style: The Politics of Appearance in American Culture*, an analysis of the impact and uses of mass forms of style in American society.

SIDELIGHTS: Stuart Ewen writes: "My work focuses on the development of mass culture as a significant aspect of industrial capitalist society. Rather than writing internal and anecdotal history of the mass media industries, I have attempted to locate these industries within the broad social history of monopoly capitalism. While much of my writing has been scholarly, I see my work as essentially political. The power of mass produced images in our lives requires a historical understanding, a political analysis, and a radical response."

In his book, *Channels of Desire: Mass Images and the Shaping of American Consciousness,* Ewens analyzes the relationship between capitalism and the growth of mass culture. His "central thesis is that the rise of consumer culture lies in a crisis of industrialism at the turn of the century," according to Lary May in the *Los Angeles Times Book Review.* "Responding to major conflicts between capital and labor, big business began to generate consumer goods and images promising a realm of escape. Naturally . . . escape appealed most to those suffering in the new order: immigrants, laborers and women." Though he believes that Ewens overemphasizes the role played by big business in the manipulation of the masses, May finds *Channels of Desire* "a valuable book."

Channels of Desire has been translated into French.

BIOGRAPHICAL/CRITICAL SOURCES: *Los Angeles Times Book Review,* August 22, 1982.

F

FABER, Charles F(ranklin)   1926-

PERSONAL: Born December 6, 1926, in Monroe County, Iowa; son of Richard A. (a farmer) and Inez (McAlister) Faber; married Patricia Jane Utt, June 8, 1947; children: Deborah, Daniel, Melinda. *Education:* Coe College, B.A., 1948; Columbia University, M.A., 1952; Northern Illinois University, graduate study, 1957-58; University of Chicago, Ph.D., 1961. *Home:* 3569 Cornwall Dr., Lexington, Ky. *Office:* Department of Educational Administration and Supervision, University of Kentucky, Lexington, Ky. 40506.

CAREER: Principal and teacher in public schools in Bethany, Ill. and Geneva, Ill., 1949-59; University of Chicago, Chicago, Ill., instructor in education, 1959-61; Iowa State University, Ames, assistant professor of education, 1961-64; George Peabody College for Teachers (now George Peabody College for Teachers of Vanderbilt University), Nashville, Tenn., professor of education and chairman of department of educational administration, 1964-71; University of Kentucky, Lexington, professor of education and chairman of department of educational administration and supervision, 1971—.

Member of various school survey teams from University of Chicago, Iowa State University, and George Peabody College for Teachers; member of various committees on educational improvement and finance; coordinator, Study of Administrative Organization, Chattanooga Public Schools, 1969. Lecturer to and participant in panel discussions for educational and civic organizations. *Member:* National Association of Elementary School Principals, Phi Delta Kappa.

WRITINGS: (With Walter Hartrick) *School Program Characteristics Opinionnaire*, Midwest Administration Center, University of Chicago, 1960; (editor) *Tenth Annual Report of the Midwest Administration Center*, Midwest Administration Center, University of Chicago, 1961; *Toward Improved School Administration*, W. K. Kellogg Foundation, 1962; (with Holmes and Daryl Hobbs) *An Analysis of Factors Related to School District Quality in TENCO*, Iowa State University Extension Service, 1962; (with Hobbs and Holmes) *Comparison of Measures of School District Quality in TENCO—1961-62 and 1962-63*, Iowa State University Extension Service, 1963; *Education Holds Our Future*, State of Iowa, Department of Public Instruction, 1964; *Project MID-TENN*, Metropolitan Nashville-Davidson County School System, 1966.

(With Gilbert Shearron) *Elementary School Administration: Theory and Practice*, Holt, 1970; *A Manual for School Board Members*, Center for Professional Development, University of Kentucky, 1976; (with Lois J. Barnes and Donald Martin, Jr.) *Legal Rights and Responsibilities of Kentucky Teachers and Pupils*, Center for Professional Development, University of Kentucky, 1980; *A Guide for School Board Members*, Center for Professional Development, University of Kentucky, 1981.

All privately printed: (With Virgil S. Lagomarcina and Glenn E. Holmes) *A Proposed Plan for School District Reorganization in Poweshiek, Iowa, Mahaska, Keokuk, Washington, and Jefferson Counties*, 1962; (with James C. LaPlant and Robert A. Pittillo, Jr.) *School Organization in Chattanooga, Tennessee*, 1969; *Greatest Country Music Hits of All Time*, 1974; *The Country Music Almanac*, Volume I: *1922-1943*, 1978, Volume II: *1944-1978*, 1979.

Contributor: *School District Organization in St. Louis County, Missouri*, Department of Education, University of Chicago, 1960; *An Educational Survey of the Palos Community Consolidated School District #118*, Department of Education, University of Chicago, 1961; David B. Guralnik and Richard H. Hinze, editors, *Webster's New World Dictionary and Student Handbook*, elementary edition, Southwestern Co., 1966; Ernest Q. Campbell, editor, *Problems in Urban Educational Planning*, Central Midwestern Regional Educational Laboratory, 1967; *School Law Update, 1977*, National Organization on Legal Problems in Education, 1978; *School Law Update, 1982*, National Organization on Legal Problems in Education, 1983.

Contributor; all published by Division of Surveys and Fields Services, George Peabody College for Teachers: *Organization of School Systems in Georgia*, 1965; *Vermilion Parish Public Schools*, 1969; *Stanly County Public Schools*, 1971; *Monroe Public Schools*, 1971; *Charlottesville Pattern for School Improvement*, 1973; *Alleghany County Public Schools*, 1973; *Little Rock Public Schools*, 1974; *Fort Wayne Public Schools*, 1975.

Contributor to *Peabody Journal of Education, Phi Delta Kappan, Journal of Teacher Education, Journal of Educational Research, American School Board Journal*, and other periodicals.

FALCO, Maria J(osephine) 1932-

PERSONAL: Born July 7, 1932, in Wildwood, N.J.; daughter of John and Mafalda (Barbieri) Falco. *Education:* Immaculata College, A.B., 1954; Fordham University, M.A., 1958; Bryn Mawr College, Ph.D., 1963; postgraduate study at Carnegie-Mellon University, 1983. *Home:* 4008 Harvard Ave., Metairie, La. 70002. *Office:* College of Arts and Sciences, Loyola University, New Orleans, La. 70118.

CAREER: Immaculata College, Immaculata, Pa., instructor, 1957-60, assistant professor of history and political science, 1960-63; Washington College, Chestertown, Md., assistant professor of political science, 1963-64; research assistant for U.S. Senatorial candidate from Pennsylvania, with National Center for Education in Politics faculty fellowship, 1964-65; Le Moyne College, Syracuse, N.Y., assistant professor, 1966-68, associate professor of political science, 1968-73, chairman of department, 1967-73; Stockton State College, Pomona, N.J., professor of political science, 1973-76; University of Tulsa, Tulsa, Okla., chairman of social and behavioral sciences faculty, 1976-79; Loyola University, New Orleans, La., dean of College of Arts and Sciences, 1979—. President of Syracuse chapter of New Democratic Coalition, 1970-71. Member, American Council on Education, 1979—; member, board of directors, American Conferences of Academic Deans, 1984—.

MEMBER: American Political Science Association, American Academy of Political and Social Science, American Association of University Professors (vice-president of Le Moyne College chapter, 1971-72), Association of American Colleges, Association of Jesuit Colleges and Universities, Women's Caucus for Political Science (president, 1976-77), Foundations of Political Theory Group, Women's Equity Action League, Common Cause, Public Citizen, Southwest Political Science Association. *Awards, honors:* Fulbright fellow at University of Florence, 1954-55; postdoctoral research fellowship at Yale University, 1965-66; National Science Foundation summer grant for Interuniversity Consortium for Political Research at University of Michigan, 1968; named outstanding educator in the United States, 1975.

WRITINGS: (Contributor) Rocco Tresolini and John Frost, editors, *Readings in American National Government and Politics,* Prentice-Hall, 1966; *Truth and Meaning in Political Science: An Introduction to Political Inquiry,* C. E. Merrill, 1973, 2nd edition, University Press of America, 1983; (editor) *Through the Looking Glass: Epistemology and the Conduct of Inquiry, an Anthology,* University Press of America, 1979; *"Bigotry!": Ethnic, Machine, and Sexual Politics in a Senatorial Election,* Greenwood Press, 1980. Contributor to professional journals. Consulting editor, *Political Parties and the Civic Action Groups.*

* * *

FALK, Richard A(nderson) 1930-

PERSONAL: Born November 13, 1930, in New York, N.Y.; son of Edwin Albert (an attorney and naval historian) and Helene (Pollak) Falk; married second wife, Maria Gabler (an electronic engineer), March 29, 1963; married third wife, Florence Gross, December 15, 1967; children: (first marriage) Christopher; (following marriages) Dimitri, Noah. *Education:* University of Pennsylvania, B.S., 1952; Yale University, L.L.B., 1955; Harvard University, S.J.D., 1962. *Office:* Woodrow Wilson School, Princeton University, Princeton, N.J.

CAREER: Admitted to the Bar of New York, 1956. Ohio State University, Columbus, 1955-62, began as assistant professor, became associate professor of law; Princeton University, Woodrow Wilson School, Princeton, N.J., associate professor of law, 1961-65, Albert G. Milbank Professor of International Law and Practice, 1965—, acting director, Center of International Studies, 1975. Director, North American section, World Order Models Project; member of Council on Foreign Relations; trustee, Procedural Institute of International Law and Fund for Peace, Institute for World Order, National Parks and Conservation Association. Member, editorial policy board, Public Broadcasting Laboratory, 1967-68; member of advisory board, Amnesty International. Consultant to U.S. Senate Foreign Relations Committee, 1967, and to U.S. Arms Control and Disarmament Agency, World Law Fund, and Naval War College. Counsel before International Court of Justice, 1965, 1972-73; counsel to Ethiopa and Liberia in the Southwest Africa Cases. *Military service:* U.S. Coast Guard Reserve, 1951-57.

MEMBER: International Law Association, International Studies Association, American Society of International Law (member of executive committee, 1964-67, 1975—, and of board of review and development, 1965-69, 1976—; vice-president, 1970-72, 1974-75), Foreign Policy Association (member of board of directors), American Political Science Association, Lindisfarne Association (fellow). *Awards, honors:* Ford Foundation fellow, 1958-59; McCosh Faculty fellow, 1965; Center for Advanced Study in Behavioral Sciences fellow, 1968-69; Institute for World Order senior fellow, 1974—.

WRITINGS: (With Sigmund Timberg, Thomas Aron, and Roland Stanger) *Essays on International Jurisdiction,* Ohio State University Press, 1961; (with Quincy Wright, Julius Stone, and Stanger) *Essays on the International Law of Espionage,* Ohio State University Press, 1962; *Law, Morality, and War in the Contemporary World,* Praeger, 1963; *Indirect Aggression and Disarmament,* Princeton University, Center of International Studies, 1963; *The Role of Domestic Courts in the International Legal Order,* Syracuse University Press, 1964; *The Authority of the United Nations over Non-Members,* Princeton University, Center of International Studies, 1965; *The Aftermath of Sabbatino,* edited by Lyman M. Tondel, Jr., Oceana, 1965; (co-author) *On Minimizing the Use of Nuclear Weapons: Three Essays by Richard A. Falk, Robert C. Tucker, and Oran R. Young,* Princeton University, Center of International Studies, 1966; *Legal Order in a Violent World,* Princeton University Press, 1968; *The Six Legal Dimensions of the Vietnam War,* Princeton University, Center of International Studies, 1968; *Erosion of the Rule of Law in South Africa,* International Commission of Jurists (Geneva), 1968.

The Status of Law in International Society, Princeton University Press, 1970; *This Endangered Planet: Prospects and Proposals for Human Survival,* Random House, 1971; *A Global Approach to National Policy,* Harvard University Press, 1975; *Statecraft in an Era of World Order, Decay, and Renewal,* Australian National University Research School of Pacific Studies, 1975; *A Study of Future Worlds,* Free Press, 1975; *Future Worlds,* Foreign Policy Association, 1976.

(With Burns H. Weston and Anthony A. D'Amato) *International Law and World Order: An Introductory Problem-Oriented Coursebook,* West Publishing, 1980; *A World Order Perspective on Authoritarian Tendencies,* World Order Models Project (New York), 1980; *Human Rights and State Sovereignty,* Holmes & Meier, 1981; *Toward a Just World Order,* Westview, Volume I, 1982; (with Robert Lifton) *Indefensible Weapons: The Case against Nuclearism,* Basic Books, 1982.

Editor: (With R. J. Barnet) *Security in Disarmament*, Princeton University Press, 1965; (with Saul Mendlovitz) *The Strategy of World Order*, four volumes, World Law Fund, 1966; (with Mendlovitz) *Disarmament and Economic Development*, World Law Fund, 1966; (with Mendlovitz) *International Law*, World Law Fund, 1966; (with Mendlovitz) *Toward a Theory of War Prevention*, World Law Fund, 1966; (with Mendlovitz) *The United Nations*, World Law Fund, 1966; (with Wolfram F. Hanrieder) *International Law and Organization: An Introductory Reader*, Lippincott, 1968; (and compiler) *The Vietnam War and International Law*, Princeton University Press, Volume I, 1968, Volume II, 1969, Volume III, 1971, Volume IV, 1976.

(With C. E. Black) *The Future of the International Legal Order*, Princeton University Press, Volume I, 1970, Volume II, 1971, Volume III-IV, 1972; (with Gabriel Kolko and Lifton) *Crimes of War: A Legal, Political-Documentary, and Psychological Inquiry into the Responsibility of Leaders, Citizens, and Soldiers for Criminal Acts in Wars*, Random House, 1971; Wright and others, *The International Law of Civil War*, Johns Hopkins Press, 1971; (with Mendlovitz) *Regional Politics and World Order*, W. H. Freeman, 1973.

(With Samuel I. Kim) *The War System: An Interdisciplinary Approach*, Westview, 1980.

Contributor to law journals. Member of editorial board, *World Politics*, 1962-68, *American Journal of International Law*, 1964—, *Foreign Policy*, 1970—, and *Alternatives*, 1975—.

SIDELIGHTS: As Albert G. Milbank Professor of International Law and Practice at Princeton University, Richard A. Falk appears to be a member of the establishment, but his writings reveal him to be a freethinker, proposing radical solutions to man's problems on earth. In his book *This Endangered Planet: Prospects and Proposals for Human Survival*, Falk outlines four main threats to man's future—the threat of nuclear war (arising from the political division of the world into nation-states), overpopulation, depletion of natural resources, and the increasing deterioration of the earth's environment. While urgent, Falk's message "is delivered unstridently and bolstered by scholarly evidence from . . . a wide range of fields," according to Charles G. Bolte in the *New Republic*. "It is the essence of Falk's book that a drastic systems change is possible without violence," Bolte continues. "He builds a political model of a cooperative system of world order and describes a set of transition strategies that might bring it into being. He does not avoid the difficulties."

In a subsequent book, Falk outlines several means for achieving the expanded world organization he envisions. *A Study of Future Worlds* starts "from the premise that the present order of big-power world management is a war system in which military, economic, and political forces are manipulated to maintain the present structure of power," according to Harold Taylor in the *Saturday Review*. "It is a structure that necessarily divides the world into winners and losers and gives the powerful among the world's elites, inside and outside governments, nearly all the world's benefits, while leaving nothing for the masses except a protracted struggle for survival."

Falk's solution involves enlisting the support of transnational organizations and agencies, many of which already operate outside the present system of national governments, in establishing a "central guidance system" for world management. Included in his proposals are recommendations for revamping the United Nations, so that the organization would be expanded in both size and power, while reflecting more accurately the interests of all the world's peoples and not just the superpowers.

According to Harold K. Jacobson in the *Annals of the American Academy of Political and Social Science*, "Falk argues that the first step toward the creation of his preferred world order must be the mobilization of segments of opinion, especially in the industrial countries and particularly in the United States. His book is important because it will surely stimulate debate and consequently catalyze this mobilization. He viewed his book as a contribution to education, and he has surely achieved his purpose handsomely."

BIOGRAPHICAL/CRITICAL SOURCES: *New Republic*, April 24, 1971, May 15, 1971; *Science Books*, December, 1972; *American Political Science Review*, March, 1975; *Saturday Review*, June 28, 1975; *Annals of the American Academy of Political and Social Science*, November, 1975; *Contemporary Issues Criticism*, Volume I, Gale, 1982.†

* * *

FANCUTT, Walter 1911-

PERSONAL: Born February 22, 1911, in Blackburn, Lancashire, England; son of James (a baker) and Bertha (Fletcher) Fancutt; married Amy F. M. Hawkins, December 29, 1933. *Education:* Attended All Nations Bible College, 1928-31, and Central School of Arts, London, England, 1957-60. *Politics:* Liberal. *Home:* 4 B St. Boniface Gardens, Ventnor, Isle of Wight PO38 1NN, England.

CAREER: Baptist minister in London, England, 1933-45; officiating chaplain to Armed Forces, 1942-50; minister of churches in Andover, Hampshire, England, 1945-52, Isle of Wight, England, 1952-57; Mission to Lepers, London, editorial secretary, 1957-69, editorial consultant, 1969—. Member of council, Baptist Union of Great Britain, 1948; president, Southern Baptist Association, 1950, 1984. *Member:* Society of Authors, Rotary Club of Mill Hill, Rotary Club of Ventnor. *Awards, honors:* National prize, Centre of Religious Journalism, 1942, for patriotic poem.

WRITINGS: *The Royal Review: A Poem*, Newman Watts, 1942; *The Kingsgate Pocket Poets*, eight volumes, Kingsgate Press, 1943-46; (editor) *Then Came Jesus*, Kingsgate Press, 1944; *From Vision to Advance*, Holmes (Andover), 1950; *The Story of Whitchurch Baptist Church*, Holmes (Andover), 1952; *In This Will I Be Confident: A Little Book of Confident Living for Every Day*, Kingsgate Press, 1957; *Beyond the Bitter Sea*, Mission to Lepers, 1958; (editor) *Escaped as a Bird*, Mission to Lepers, 1962, revised edition, 1970; *Present to Heal*, Mission to Lepers, 1964; *The Mission to Lepers: 90 Years of Leprosy Service, 1874 Despair, 1964 Hope*, Mission to Lepers, 1966; *Daily Remembrance: A Prayer Cycle for the Leprosy Mission*, Mission to Lepers, 1966; *The Imprisoned Splendour*, Mission to Lepers, 1970; *With Strange Surprise*, Leprosy Mission, 1974; *The Southern Baptist Association and Its Churches*, Holmes, Andover, 1974; *The Luminous Cloud*, A. James, 1980; *East Dene*, Ventnor Local History Society, 1982. Also author of *His Excellent Greatness*, Clarendon Press. Contributor to *Poetry Review* and to religious journals. Editor, *Without the Camp, Lamplighter*, 1957-70.

AVOCATIONAL INTERESTS: Collection of portrait engravings from sixteenth-century onwards.

FARB, Peter 1929-1980

PERSONAL: Born July 25, 1929, in New York, N.Y.; died of leukemia, April 8, 1980, in Boston, Mass.; son of Solomon and Cecelia (Peters) Farb; married Oriole Horch (a museum director), February 27, 1953; children: Mark Daniel, Thomas Forest. *Education:* Vanderbilt University, B.A. (magna cum laude), 1950; graduate study at Columbia University, 1950-51. *Politics:* Independent. *Home:* 39 Pokeberry Ridge, Amherst, Mass. 01002.

CAREER: Argosy, New York City, feature editor, 1950-52. Free-lance writer and researcher in the science and natural history of North America, 1953-1980. Editor-in-chief of Panorama (publishing project), Columbia Broadcasting System, 1960-61; curator of American Indian cultures, Riverside Museum, New York City, 1964-71; visiting lecturer, Yale University, 1971-72, fellow, Calhoun College, 1971-78; trustee, University of Massachusetts Libraries, beginning 1976. Consultant, Smithsonian Institution, 1966-71; judge, National Book Awards Committee, 1971. Member of board of directors, Allergy and Asthma Foundation of America, 1970-73.

MEMBER: American Association for the Advancement of Science (fellow), American Anthropological Association, Ecological Society of America, Society for American Archaeology, Society of American Historians (fellow), Society of Magazine Writers, New York Entomological Society (former secretary), P.E.N., Phi Beta Kappa, Omicron Delta Kappa. *Awards, honors: Face of North America: The Natural History of a Continent* was chosen as an American Library Association notable book.

WRITINGS: Living Earth, Harper, 1959; *The Story of Butterflies and Other Insects,* Harvey, 1959; *The Insect World,* Constable, 1960; *The Story of Dams: Hydrology for the Young Scientist,* Harvey, 1961; *The Forest,* Time, Inc., 1961, 2nd edition, 1978; (co-editor) *Prose by Professionals,* Doubleday, 1961; *The Insects,* Time, Inc., 1962, 2nd edition, 1977; *The Story of Life: Plants and Animals through the Ages,* Harvey, 1962; *Ecology,* Time, Inc., 1963, revised edition, 1979; *Face of North America: The Natural History of a Continent* (Book-of-the-Month Club selection and Outdoor Life Book Club selection), Harper, 1963, young reader's edition, 1964; *The Land and Wildlife of North America,* Time, Inc., 1964, 2nd edition, 1978.

(With John Hay) *The Atlantic Shore,* Harper, 1966; *The Land, Wildlife, and Peoples of the Bible,* Harper, 1967; *Man's Rise to Civilization as Shown by the Indians of North America from Primeval Times to the Coming of the Industrial State* (Book-of-the-Month Club selection, Book Find Club selection, and History Book Club of London selection), Dutton, 1968, 2nd edition published as *Man's Rise to Civilization: The Cultural Ascent of the Indians of North America,* 1978; *Yankee Doodle,* Simon & Schuster, 1970; *Word Play: What Happens When People Talk* (Book Find Club selection and Modern Psychology Book Club selection), Knopf, 1974; *Humankind* (Book-of-the-Month Club selection and History Book Club selection), Houghton, 1978.

(With George Armelagos) *Consuming Passions: The Anthropology of Eating,* Houghton, 1980.

Also author of *The Forest Reader,* 1964. Editor, "North American Nature Series," Harper, beginning 1964. Columnist, *Better Homes and Gardens,* 1959-63, and contributor of science and nature articles to *Reader's Digest* and other national magazines. Member of editorial board, journal of New York Entomological Society.

WORK IN PROGRESS: The Human Experience: A Textbook of Anthropology, with Irven DeVore.

SIDELIGHTS: Peter Farb was a naturalist, linguist, anthropologist, and author who popularized the natural human sciences in his many books. At home in a number of disciplines and willing to travel anywhere to complete research, Farb produced works ranging in subject from the geological formation of North American mountains and rivers (*Face of North America: The Natural History of a Continent*) to the latest scientific findings about homo sapiens (*Humankind*).

At his death, Farb had just completed a study of the eating habits of different societies, entitled *Consuming Passions: The Anthropology of Eating*—a book he co-authored with George Armelagos. This study postulated that "to know what, where, how, when, and with whom people eat is to know the character of their society." In her *Washington Post* review of *Consuming Passions,* Carole Sugarman notes that the book "should be enough to satisfy anyone's craving to know how eating affects rites of passage, sex, vocabulary, religion, gift-giving, taboos and other aspects of human existence."

Many of Farb's books have been translated into foreign languages, and his lively writing style and grasp of scientific subjects helped his books set sales records for works on natural history.

BIOGRAPHICAL/CRITICAL SOURCES: Peter Farb and George Armelagos, *Consuming Passions: The Anthropology of Eating,* Houghton, 1980; *Washington Post,* August 28, 1980; *New York Times,* August 30, 1980; *Los Angeles Times Book Review,* September 28, 1980.

OBITUARIES: New York Times, April 9, 1980; *Chicago Tribune,* April 10, 1980; *Los Angeles Times,* April 14, 1980; *AB Bookman's Weekly,* April 21, 1980; *Publishers Weekly,* May 6, 1980.†

* * *

FARLEY, Eugene J. 1916-

PERSONAL: Born September 18, 1916, in Newark, N.J.; son of Matthew E. and Mary (O'Toole) Farley; married Alice Reichl, June 27, 1942; children: David, Dennis. *Education:* Montclair State College, B.A., 1938, M.A., 1946; Rutgers University, Ed.D., 1964. *Home address:* P.O. Box 964, Columbia, Md. 21044.

CAREER: South Orange-Maplewood School District, Maplewood, N.J., teacher, 1947-56, counselor, 1956-76. Director of basic education and high school equivalency in adult school, South Orange, N.J., 1966-69. Consultant, adult education, 1966—, TV High School, 1967, Your Future Is Now, 1972; consultant in pre-retirement counseling, 1977—. *Military service:* U.S. Army, Medical Administration Corps, 1941-45; became captain. *Member:* American Psychological Association, National Council of Senior Citizens, Maryland Psychological Association, Maryland Gerontological Association.

WRITINGS—Published by Barron's, except as indicated: (With Clyde Weinhold and Arthur Crabtree) *High School Certification through G.E.D. Tests,* Holt, 1967; *How to Prepare for the High School Equivalency Examination: Reading Interpretation Tests,* 1970; (with wife, Alice R. Farley) *Developing Reading Skills for the High School Equivalency Examinations* in Social Studies, Science, and Literature, 1972; (with A. R. Farley) *Getting Ready for the High School Equivalency Exam: Beginning Preparation in Reading and English*, 1973; *Barron's Preview Examination to Prepare for High School Equivalency Tests*, 1973.

(With A. R. Farley) *How to Prepare for the High School Equivalency Examination: The Reading Skills Test*, 1980; (with A. R. Farley) *How to Prepare for the High School Equivalency Examination: The Social Studies Test*, 1981; (with A. R. Farley) *How to Prepare for the High School Equivalency Examination: The Science Test*, 1983.

Also editor of five books for Barron's.

WORK IN PROGRESS: Revisions to two books and the equivalency exam, for Barron's.

* * *

FARNIE, D(ouglas) A(ntony) 1926-

PERSONAL: Born March 31, 1926, in Salford, Lancashire, England; son of Arthur and Ethel (Farrington) Farnie; married Edna Verina Eato. *Education:* University of Manchester, B.A., 1951, M.A., 1953; University of Natal, Ph.D., 1969. *Home:* 31 Parksway, Swinton, Manchester M27 1JN, England. *Office:* Department of History, University of Manchester, Manchester M13 9PL, England.

CAREER: University of Natal, Durban, lecturer in history, 1954-60; University of Manchester, Manchester, England, lecturer, 1961-71, senior lecturer, 1972-80, reader in economic history, 1980—. Participant in the Eighth International Conference on Business History, Fuji, Japan, 1981. Visiting lecturer, University of Bonn, 1982. *Military service:* British Army, 1944-48; became sergeant. *Member:* Historical Association, Economic History Society.

WRITINGS: *East and West of Suez: The Suez Canal in History, 1854-1956*, Clarendon Press, 1969; *The English Cotton Industry and the World Market, 1815-1896*, Clarendon Press, 1979; *The Manchester Ship Canal and the Rise of the Port of Manchester, 1894-1975*, Manchester University Press, 1980. Contributor to economic, historical, and literary journals, including *The Bulletin of the John Rylands Library*.

WORK IN PROGRESS: A history of the trade in textile machinery, linking the spread of the cotton industry in the world to its decline in Lancashire and relating both to the export industry which grew to maturity in Lancashire side by side with the cotton industry.

SIDELIGHTS: D. A. Farnie told *CA:* "The theme of the Suez book, the changing pattern of relationships between Europe and Asia, was partly a delayed product of my military service in India and Egypt. During my service in the Suez Canal zone, at Ismailia and Kentara, I developed no particular interest in the history of Egypt but I read Gibbon's *Decline and Fall* as an introduction to the study of history, which to me then meant the history of Europe. When I undertook research into the history of the cotton industry in 1951-53, I became aware of the importance of the Indian market for Lancashire during the era of its greatest expansion and I also explored the influence of the opening of the Canal on the export trade to the East."

* * *

FARR, Judith 1937-

PERSONAL: Born March 13, 1937, in New York, N.Y.; daughter of Russell John (a musician) and Frances (Wissell) Banzer; married George F. Farr, Jr. (a deputy director, National Endowment for the Humanities), June 30, 1962; children: Alec Winfield. *Education:* Marymount Manhattan College, B.A., 1957; Yale University, M.A., 1959, Ph.D., 1965. *Politics:* Democrat. *Religion:* Episcopalian. *Home:* 2542 North Vermont St., Arlington, Va. 22207. *Office:* Department of English, Georgetown University, Washington, D.C. 20057.

CAREER: Vassar College, Poughkeepsie, N.Y., instructor in English, 1961-63; St. Mary's College, St. Mary's, Calif., assistant professor of English, 1964-68; State University of New York College at New Paltz, assistant professor, 1968-71, associate professor of English, beginning 1971; Georgetown University, visiting professor, 1977-78, associate professor of English, 1978—.

WRITINGS: (Editor) *Twentieth-Century Interpretations of "Sons and Lovers,"* Prentice-Hall, 1970; (contributor) Maynard Mack and George deForest Lord, editors, *Poetic Traditions of the English Renaissance* (anthology), Yale University Press, 1982; *The Life and Art of Elinor Wylie*, Louisiana State University Press, 1983. Also contributor to anthologies, *Riverside Anthology III*, 1958, and *New Campus Writing #4*, 1963. Contributor of poetry, fiction, and criticism to *Manhattan Poetry Review*, *American Literature*, and *Minnesota Review*.

WORK IN PROGRESS: A novel, *The Right Place*; a book of criticism, *The "Indestructible Estate" of Emily Dickinson*.

SIDELIGHTS: Judith Farr told *CA:* "There is little to say about my writing except that, apart from my husband and child, it absorbs me most." *Avocational interests:* Eighteenth-century French art, history, and decoration, French literature, collecting eighteenth-century English china and furniture.

* * *

FARRELL, Ben
See CEBULASH, Mel

* * *

FEINBERG, Gerald 1933-

PERSONAL: Born May 27, 1933, in New York, N.Y.; son of Leon (a journalist and poet) and Florence (Weingarten) Feinberg; married Barbara Silberdick (a free-lance editor and writer), August 9, 1968; children: two sons. *Education:* Columbia University, B.A., 1953, M.A., 1954, Ph.D., 1957. *Office:* Physics Department, Columbia University, New York, N.Y. 10027.

CAREER: Institute for Advanced Study, Princeton, N.J., member of School of Mathematics, 1956-57; Brookhaven National Laboratory, Upton, N.Y., research associate, 1957-59; Columbia University, New York, N.Y., assistant professor, 1959-61, associate professor, 1961-65, professor of physics, 1965—, head of department, 1980-82. Adjunct assistant professor and consultant to physics department, New York University, 1959; fellow, Churchill College, Cambridge University, 1963-64. *Member:* American Physical Society (fellow), New York Academy of Sciences. *Awards, honors:* Alfred P. Sloan Foundation fellow, 1960-64; Guggenheim Foundation fellow, 1973-74.

WRITINGS: *The Prometheus Project: Mankind's Search for Long-Range Goals*, Doubleday, 1969; *What Is the World Made Of*, Doubleday-Anchor, 1977; *Consequences of Growth*, Seabury, 1977; (with Robert Shapiro) *Life Beyond Earth*, Morrow,

1980. Contributor to *Proceedings of the Royal Society* and to science journals.

WORK IN PROGRESS: A book on the future of science, for Simon & Schuster; research in elementary particle physics.

SIDELIGHTS: In their book *Life Beyond Earth*, physicist Gerald Feinberg and chemist Robert Shapiro draw on some of the most advanced ideas in their fields to postulate the possibility of extraterrestrial life. While some scientists maintain that unfavorable galactic conditions make life outside earth's atmosphere unlikely, Feinberg and Shapiro argue that extraterrestrial life probably does exist in some form. The trap that many of us fall into is expecting life on other planets to resemble life on earth. By looking only for parallel civilizations, we may miss what life there is in space.

Ours is a carbon-based system of life, but Feinberg and Shapiro see no reason why other chemical life forms—including some based on silicon—are not possible. "In a series of carefully constructed and clearly demarcated speculations," writes Timothy Ferris in the *New York Times Book Review*, "they envision how living organisms could thrive not only on planets unlike earth but even within such seemingly hostile settings as gas clouds wafting through space or upon the fiery surfaces of stars." According to Malcolm W. Browne's *Books of the Times* review, their most startling idea "suggests life forms consisting of energy rather than matter, living in the thin interstellar gas of galaxies and having dimensions spanning light-years."

Though these ideas are bound to provoke controversy, the *New Yorker* concludes: "For people who like to read about solid scientific speculation, this is an exhilarating, informative, and ultimately liberating book."

BIOGRAPHICAL/CRITICAL SOURCES: New York Times, February 25, 1969; *New Yorker*, June 30, 1980; *Books of the Times*, September, 1980; *New York Times Book Review*, November 29, 1981.

* * *

FERGUSON, Robert W(illiam) 1940-

PERSONAL: Born January 23, 1940, in Anaconda, Mont.; son of William Irving and Grace (Kerr) Ferguson; married Dolores Lillian, November 4, 1964; children: Michelle Ann, William Robert. *Education:* Fullerton Junior College, A.A., 1961; California State University, Los Angeles, B.S., 1967; graduate study at Orange Coast College, 1968, and University of California, Los Angeles, 1970; California State University, Long Beach, M.S., 1972; U.S. International University, Ph.D., 1977. *Home:* 925 Vista Del Gaviota, Orange, Calif. 92665. *Office:* 28000 Marguerite Pkwy., Mission Viejo, Calif. 92675.

CAREER: City of Orange, Calif., police patrolman, 1962-64, investigator, 1964-65, alcohol, narcotics, and vice investigator, 1965-68, sergeant, 1968-69; Saddleback College, Mission Viejo, Calif., instructor in administration of justice, 1969-71, director of administration program, 1971—. Instructor at Saddleback College, 1968-69; lecturer at California State University, Los Angeles, Pepperdine University, and Chapman College. Member of California Community College Task Force for Criminal Justice Curriculum Development. *Member:* California Association of Administration of Justice Educators (vice-chairman, 1973), Saddleback College Faculty Association (president, 1972), California Teachers Association.

WRITINGS: Ferguson: Memoirs and Reminiscences of Montana (family biography), Harlow Press, 1973; *The Nature of Vice Control in the Administration of Justice*, West Publishing, 1974; *Readings in Concepts of Criminal Law*, West Publishing, 1975; *Drug Abuse Control*, Holbrook, 1975; *Concepts of Criminal Law*, Holbrook, 1976; *Artistry in Cabochons*, Gembooks, 1976; (with Allan H. Stokke) *Legal Aspects of Evidence*, Harcourt Legal & Professional Publications, 1978.

Also author of *The Criminal Justice Process: Principles and Procedures*, 1977.

AVOCATIONAL INTERESTS: Sporting activities, youth groups.†

* * *

FERICANO, Paul F(rancis) 1951-

PERSONAL: Born January 16, 1951, in San Francisco, Calif.; son of Frank Paul and Josephine (Anello) Fericano; married Katherine Judeen Daly, October 14, 1972; children: Kate. *Education:* Attended various universities in California, 1969-75. *Politics:* "Stoogism." *Religion:* "Catholic Stoogism." *Address:* P.O. Box 236, Millbrae, Calif. 94030. *Agent:* Elizabeth Trupin, JET Literary Associates, Inc., 124 East 84th St., Suite 4A, New York, N.Y. 10028.

CAREER: Writer and poet. Has worked as dishwasher, waiter, washing machine repairman, gardener, carpenter, clown, playground supervisor, truck driver, warehouseman, disc-jockey, house painter, Santa Claus, and in various other occupations; editor, *The West Conscious Review* and *Crow's Nest Magazine*, 1974-77; worked for California Poetry-in-the-Schools program, 1978-79; conducted poetry workshops at Western Federal Penitentiary, Pittsburgh, Pa., 1980, 1984. *Member:* National Writers Union. *Awards, honors:* American Association of University Women fiction award, 1969; Creative Artists Award for poetry, 1976; International Poet award, 1982.

WRITINGS—Poetry, except as indicated: *Beneath the Smoke Rings*, Dithyramb Poetry Series, 1976; *The Cancer Quiz*, Scarecrow Books, 1977; *Loading the Revolver with Real Bullets*, Second Coming Press, 1977; *The Ventriloquist*, Poetry Exchange, 1978; *The Answer*, Hearthstone Press, 1979; *The Condition of Poetry in the Modern World: A Stoogist Manifesto* (prose), Pour Souls Press, 1980; *Sinatra, Sinatra*, Pour Souls Press, 1982; *Commercial Break*, Pour Souls Press, 1982. Contributor to *Wormwood Review, Mother Jones, Poetry Now, Total Abandon, Northern Pleasure*, and other magazines.

WORK IN PROGRESS: A collection of poems, tentatively entitled *The Secret Dreams of Nelson Rockefeller;* a novel dealing with social diseases.

SIDELIGHTS: Paul F. Fericano told *CA:* "Everything I write is derived from the contemporary scene, which gives me an unlimited supply of both the banal and incredible; from a Nancy Reagan snub, to a poorman's diet, and back to a Nancy Reagan snub. For any writer, living in the America of the eighties offers tremendous challenges to explore, with words, true deeds of heroism. I make no bones about being linked with the progressive movement, but I also have no pretensions about who I am and what I can and cannot do as an individual and as a writer and poet. Today stupidity, in its silliest and most dangerous form, continues to manifest itself in our lives—from what we watch on TV, to who we believe when we step into a voting booth. We are witnessing new witch hunts, book burnings, religious abuse, deteriorating civil liberties, winnable nuclear war solutions, and a smiling complacency for the man who sits in the highest office unprecedented since voters welcomed Warren G. Harding into their lives and futures.

"Still, there is a growing discontent with, and mounting distrust for, a democratic system that appears to be eating itself into permanent lockjaw—all in the name of a 'better way.' So, I ask myself, what is your job as a writer in America? What can you, a mere poet, hope to accomplish against a backdrop that, at first glance, could be the invention of some drugged-up, paranoid, Hollywood screen producer? My answer is clear: nothing. With dreams of immortality cast out from my life, though, real progress begins. And in that, as a writer on the American scene, I feel I can accomplish a great deal more. For any writer, that should be it. I am an informal historian poking my nose into places others keep telling me it doesn't belong. I long ago stopped wondering and caring if my work will be read by future generations. I write for people, today, now. My tools are true laughs, and laughable truths. And if I can reach and react with those tools, I'll be in pretty good shape to continue nose-poking (as well as eye-poking) for some time."

BIOGRAPHICAL/CRITICAL SOURCES: CODA: Poets and Writers, July, 1976.

* * *

FERN, Alan M(axwell) 1930-

PERSONAL: Born October 19, 1930, in Detroit, Mich.; son of Martin (a teacher) and Rose (Coral) Fern; married Lois Ann Karbel (a librarian), March 17, 1957. *Education:* University of Chicago, A.B., 1950, M.A., 1954, Ph.D., 1960. *Home:* 3605 Raymond St., Chevy Chase, Md. 20815. *Office:* National Portrait Gallery, Smithsonian Institution, Washington, D.C. 20560.

CAREER: University of Chicago, Chicago, Ill., instructor, 1953-60, assistant professor of humanities, 1960-61; Library of Congress, Prints and Photographs Division, Washington, D.C., assistant curator of prints, 1961-62, curator of prints, 1962-64, head of processing and curatorial section, 1964-73, assistant chief of division, 1964-73, chief of division, 1973-76, director of research department, 1976-78, director for special collections, 1978-82; Smithsonian Institution, National Portrait Gallery, Washington, D.C., director, 1982—. Also taught at Art Institute of Chicago, Institute of Design, Pratt Institute, and University of Maryland. *Member:* College Art Association (director), Print Council of America (former president), American Antiquarian Society, Cosmos Club, Grolier Club, Baltimore Bibliophiles, Double Crown Club (honorary member).

WRITINGS: (Editor) Lucien Pissarro, *Notes on the Eragny Press, and a Letter to J. B. Manson*, Cambridge University Press, 1957; (with others) *Art Nouveau*, New York Museum of Modern Art, 1960; *Word and Image: Posters from the Collection of the Museum of Modern Art*, edited by Mildred Constantine, New York Museum of Modern Art, 1968.

Leonard Baskin (catalog of an exhibition), National Collection of Fine Arts, Smithsonian Institution, 1970; (author of introduction) *American Prints in the Library of Congress*, Johns Hopkins Press, 1970; (contributor) J. Sutter, editor, *The Neo-Impressionists*, Ides et Calandes (Neuchatel), 1970, New York Graphic Society, 1971; (co-author) *Revolutionary Soviet Film Posters*, Johns Hopkins Press, 1974; (contributor) *Lasansky: Printmaker*, University of Iowa Press, 1975; (contributor) *Fritz Eichenberg*, C. N. Potter, 1977; *Lance Hidy's Posters*, Alphabet Press, 1983.

Contributor to *New York Times Book Review, Apollo, Architectural Review, Book-Collector's Quarterly, Chicago Review, College Art Journal,* and other publications. Former book review editor, *Art Journal*.

* * *

FERNEA, Elizabeth Warnock 1927-

PERSONAL: Surname is pronounced *Fur*-nee-ah; born October 21, 1927, in Milwaukee, Wis.; daughter of David Wallace (a chemist) and Elizabeth (Meshynsky) Warnock; married Robert Alan Fernea (a social anthropologist), June 8, 1956; children: Laura Ann, David Karim, Laila Catherine. *Education:* Reed College, B.A., 1949; graduate study, Mount Holyoke College, 1949-50, and University of Chicago. *Politics:* Democrat. *Religion:* Roman Catholic. *Home:* 3003 Bowman Rd., Austin, Tex. 78703. *Agent:* A. Watkins, Inc., 77 Park Ave., New York, N.Y. 10016. *Office:* Center for Middle Eastern Studies, University of Texas, Austin, Tex. 78712.

CAREER: Reed College, Portland, Ore., director of public relations, 1950-54; University of Chicago, Chicago, Ill., admissions counselor and promotion assistant, 1954-56; U.S. Information Agency, contract reporter and writer in Baghdad, Iraq, 1956-58; University of Chicago, member of public relations staff, 1958-59; University of Texas at Austin, Center for Middle Eastern Studies, research associate, 1973—, instructor, 1975—. Lecturer on women in the Middle East at numerous conferences and symposia in the United States and abroad. Member, board of directors, American New East Refugee Aid, America-Mideast Educational and Training Services, and Austin Ballet Theater. Chairman, film and media committee, Center for Middle Eastern Studies; coordinator, Resource Sharing Program, 1979—. Member of Travis County Democratic Women's Committee and Lay Citizen Advisory Committee on Textbooks, Austin Independent School District. Faculty advisor; consultant, Mellon Foundation Project on Women and Social Change, Smith College, 1978.

MEMBER: Middle Eastern Studies Association of North America, Texas Institute of Letters. *Awards, honors:* Named outstanding woman in Literature, Texas America Association of University Women, 1978; National Endowment for the Humanities film grant, 1978, 1980, 1981.

WRITINGS: Guests of the Sheik, Doubleday, 1965, published as *Guests of the Sheik: An Ethnography of an Iraqi Village*, 1969; *A View of the Nile*, Doubleday, 1970; *A Street in Marrakech*, Doubleday, 1975; (editor with Marilyn Duncan) *Texas Women in Politics*, Foundation for Women's Resources (Austin, Tex.), 1977; (editor and translator with Basima Qattan Bezirgan) *Middle Eastern Muslim Women Speak*, University of Texas Press, 1977. Also author of films "Some Women of Marrakech," broadcast in 1977, and "Saints and Spirits," produced in 1979.

Contributor: (With husband, Robert A. Fernea) Alice Taylor, editor, *Focus on the Middle East*, Praeger, 1971; (with R. A. Fernea) Nikki Keddie, editor, *Scholars, Saints and Sufis*, University of California Press, 1972; (contributor of translation with Bezirgan) Jacques Berque, *Cultural Expressions in Arab Society*, University of Texas Press, 1978; (with James Malarkey and Sabra Webber) *History of the Family and Kinship: A Select International Bibliography*, Kraus, 1979. Contributor of reviews to periodicals. Contributing editor, *Texas Books in Review*.

WORK IN PROGRESS: A film, "Reformers and Revolutionaries: Middle Eastern Women."

SIDELIGHTS: Elizabeth Warnock Fernea told *CA:* "*Guests of the Sheik* grew out of the two years spent with my husband in a small village in Iraq (while he did anthropological field research)." Fernea's films "Some Women of Marrakech" and "Saints and Spirits" were shown at the Margaret Mead Film Festival of the American Museum of Natural History.

* * *

FETSCHER, Iring 1922-

PERSONAL: Born March 4, 1922, in Marbach, Germany; son of Rainer (a university professor) and Clara (Mueller) Fetscher; married Elisabeth Goette (a translator), June 7, 1957; children: Caroline, Sebastian, Justus, Christiane. *Education:* University of Tuebingen, Ph.D., 1950, habilitation, 1959. *Politics:* Social Democratic Party. *Home:* Ganghoferstrasse 20, Frankfurt am Main, West Germany. *Agent:* Joan Daves, 59 East 54th St., New York, N.Y. 10022. *Office:* University of Frankfurt, Mertonstrasse 17, Frankfurt am Main 6, West Germany.

CAREER: University of Tuebingen, Tuebingen, West Germany, assistant, 1950-55, lecturer in philosophy, 1959-63; University of Frankfurt, Frankfurt am Main, West Germany, professor of political philosophy, 1963—; New School for Social Research, New York, N.Y., Theodor Heuss professor of political philosophy, 1968-69. Researcher, German Research Association, 1955-59. Member of programme commission, Social Democratic Party, Germany. *Military service:* German Army, 1940-45; received Iron Cross, first class. *Member:* P.E.N., International Institute for Political Philosophy (member of board, 1969—), International Commission of Law.

WRITINGS: Von Marx zur Sowjetideologie, Hessische Landeszentrale fuer Heimatdienst, 1956, 21st edition, Diesterweg, 1981; *Die Freiheit im Lichte des Marxismus-Leninsmus,* Bundeszentrale fuer Heimatdienst, 1959; *Rousseaus politische Philosophie: Zur Geschichte des demokratischen Freiheitsbegriffs,* Luchterhand, 1960, 3rd edition, Surkamp, 1975; *Rechtsradikalismus,* Europaeische Verlags-Anstalt, 1967; *Modelle internationale Ordnung,* Internationaler Arbeitskreis Sonnenberg, 1967; *Karl Marx und der Marxismus,* Piper, 1967, published as *Marx and Marxism,* Herder & Herder, 1971; *Politkwissenschaft,* Fischer, 1968, published as *Grossbritannien: Gesellschaft, Staat, Ideologie,* Athenaeum Fischer Taschenbuch, 1972; *Vor- und Fruehformen des Sozialismus,* Arbeitstexte Verlag, c. 1969.

Die Demokratie, Kohlhammer, 1970; *Hegels Lehre vom Menschen,* Frommann, 1970; *Hegel, Groesse und Grenzen,* Kohlhammer, 1971; *Wer hat Dornroeschen wachgekuesst?: Das Maerchen Verwirrbuch,* Claassen, 1972; *Modelle der Friedenssicherung,* Piper, 1972; *Demokratie zwischen Sozialdemokratie und Sozialismus,* Kohlhammer, 1973; *Marxistische Portraets,* Frommann-Holzboog, 1975; *Herrschaft und Emanzipation: Zure Philosophie des Buergertums,* Piper, 1976; *Terrorismus und Reaktion,* Bund-Verlag, 1977, expanded edition published as *Terrorismus und Reaktion in der Bundesrepublik Deutschland und in Italien,* Rowohlt, 1981; (with Werner Hofmann and Wolfgang Abendroth) *Ideengeschichte der sozialen Bewegung des 19. und 20. Jahrhunderts,* de Gruyter, 1979; *Ueberlebens: Bedingungen der Menschheit,* Piper, 1980; (with Alfred Blatter and others) *Wie geht es weiter?,* Lenos, 1980; *Vom Wohl: Fahrtstext zure neuen Lebensqualitaet,* Bund-Verlag, 1982.

Editor: Iosif Stalin, *Uber dialektischen und historischen Materialismus,* Diesterweg, 1956; Paul Yorck von Wartenburg, *Bewusstseinsstellung und Geschichte: Ein Fragment aus dem philosophischen Nachlass,* M. Niemeyer, 1956; Auguste Comte, *Rede ueber den Geist des Positivismus,* Meiner, 1956; *Der Marxismus,* three volumes, Piper, 1962-65; Karl Marx and Friedrich Engels, *Studienausgabe,* four volumes, Fischer, 1966; Thomas Hobbes, *Leviathan,* Luchterhand, 1966; Paul Lafargue, *Das Recht auf Faulheit und Persoenliche Erinnerungen an Karl Karx,* Europaeische Verlagsanstalt, 1966; *Der Sozialismus: Vom Klassenkampf zum Wohlfahrtsstaat,* Desch, 1968; *Der Kommunismus,* Desch, 1969; Marx, *Manifest der Kommunistischen Partie,* Reclam, 1969; Marx, *Pressefreiheit und Zensur,* Europaeische Verlags-Anstalt, 1969; (and compiler) Marx, *Deutsche Geschichte im 19. Jahrhundert,* Fischer, 1969.

Vladimir Il'ich Lenin, *Studienausgabe,* Fischer, 1970—; (and compiler) *Hegel in der Sicht der neueren Forschung,* Wissenschaftliche Buchgesellschaft, 1973; *Marxisten gegen Antisemitismus,* Hoffmann und Campe, 1974; (with Milan Machovec) *Marxisten und die Sache Jesu,* Kaiser, 1974; *Grundbegriffe des Marxismus,* Hoffmann und Campe, 1976; (with Horst E. Richter) *Worte machen keine Politik,* Rowohlt, 1976; Willy Brandt, *Geschichte als Auftrag: Willy Brandts Reden zur Geschichte der arbeiterbewegung, Berlin und Bonn,* Desch, 1981.

General editor, *Marxismusstudien,* four volumes, Mohr, 1957-68. Editor, *Politische Texte,* 1964-72.

Contributor: Ferdinand Alguie, *Descartes,* translated from the French by Christoph Schwarze, Frommann, 1962; Werner Post, *Verdirbt Relition den Menschen?,* Patmos, 1969; Detlef Horster, *Ist die Epoche des Faschismus beendet?,* J. Metzler, 1971; Fritz Buesser, *Karl Marx im Kreuzverhoer der Wissenschaften,* Artemis-Verlag, 1974; *Jugend und Terrorismus,* Juventa-Verlag, 1979. Also contributor to proceedings of the 27th international Geneva conference.

SIDELIGHTS: Iring Fetscher told *CA:* "Fascism and War were the first important experiences of my life. I turned to philosophy and history in order to find out about it and to help build up a better free society. Next came the disillusion with socialism as practiced in East Germany and the Soviet Union, and finally the insight developed by the 'Club of Rome' study on the 'Limits of Growth.'"

CA asked Fetscher what he felt was the future of political philosophy in Germany. He responded: "Conservative theories will very probably center around the concept of the late professor Arnold Gehlen (institutions as relief conferring) and less around nationalism as in the past. Technocratic conservatism argues that the 'man in the street' is generally incapable of judging adequately the more and more complex problems of contemporary government, so that the democratic consent has to be manipulated for the sake of effective and competent management by elites.

"Progressive thought will turn away from any form of dogmatic Marxism which seems to be discredited not only by the Soviet Union but as well by the very conservative and bureaucratic East German regime which is a combination of Prussianism and Soviet imports. A combination of decentralisation (wherever it can be afforded), of changes in styles of life (of individual and social 'aims') and of more equality will be justified as the only possible alternative for a centralized anonymous dictatorship in the service of technological growth and/ or of the necessary adaptation of the individuals to the requirements of a less quickly growing economy (and therefore less and less acceptable inequality). The theoretical basis of such an image will be a combination of critical evaluations of the economic system, of a genetical approach to civilization (Norbert Elias, etc.) and of anthropology (genetic psychology). The elaboration of a kind of political ethic will be necessary, which would allow a critique of—for instance—happiness as pleasure, needs as demands for consumer goods, and freedom as free enterprise for the few."

CA asked Fetscher if he could foresee a political joining of East and West Germany in the future, and if it is possible, what first steps are needed. He said: "I do not think that in a foreseeable future there is any chance of reuniting East and West Germany. The actual governing elite of East Germany has no interest whatsoever in such a move, neither would they accept an abdication of their rulership, which would be the inevitable outcome of a common parliament (where the majority would be anti-Communist), nor have they any realistic hope of winning Communist majorities in West Germany. The only chance for such an evolution would be (1) a change in the Soviet Union towards democracy and a real lessening of tensions, (2) a change within East Germany (or West Germany) which would bring the two different societies nearer to each other. Maybe in the long run Eurocommunism, if it should be successful in Italy, Spain, France, and also if a complete split with the Eastern Communist countries could be avoided, could have such an influence . . . but I think such an evolution very unlikely.

"The only realistic basis for a reunification is the fact that until now still a rather great part (certainly a majority) of the East German population would prefer to become members of the West German State. The constant contact via radio, television, letters and smuggled-in books and/or newspapers has until now prevented a complete separation. Nevertheless the fact that the East German population has now 44 years of dictatorship behind it and the West German population at least 28 years of experience in parliamentary liberal democracy accounts for deepgoing differences, which become bigger every day."

Several of Fetscher's books have been translated into Spanish and Italian.

* * *

FINDLEY, Timothy 1930-

PERSONAL: Born October 30, 1930, in Toronto, Ontario, Canada; son of Allan Gilmore and Margaret (Bull) Findley. *Education:* Findley was self-educated beyond the ninth grade after illness had interrupted his formal education. *Agent:* Nancy Colbert & Associates, 303 Davenport Rd., Toronto, Ontario, Canada M5R IK5.

CAREER: Actor for fifteen years; was a charter member of Stratford (Ontario) Shakespeare Festival, 1953; went from Canada to England as protege of Alec Guinness; contracted with H. M. Tennant Productions, London, England, 1954-55, to appear in *The Prisoner* (with Alec Guinness), 1954, *The Matchmaker* (with Ruth Gordon), 1955, and *Hamlet* (with Paul Scofield), 1955; toured with *The Matchmaker* in the United States, 1956-57; wrote advertising copy at a small radio station in Canada; presently full-time professional writer. Playwright-in-residence, National Arts Centre, Ottawa, Canada, 1974-75; writer-in-residence, University of Toronto, 1978-79. *Member:* Authors Guild, Authors League of America, Writers' Union of Canada (chairman, 1977-78), Association of Canadian Television and Radio Artists.

AWARDS, HONORS: Canada Council Junior Arts Award, 1968; Major Armstrong Award, 1970, for radio drama, "The Journey"; Association of Canadian Television and Radio Artists award, 1975, for "The National Dream"; Governor General's Award for fiction in English, and City of Toronto Book Award, both 1977, both for *The Wars;* Canada Council Senior Arts Award, 1978; ANIK Award, 1980, for television documentary, "Dieppe: 1942"; D.Litt., Trent University, 1982.

WRITINGS—Novels: *The Last of the Crazy People,* Meredith, 1967; *The Butterfly Plague,* Viking, 1969; *The Wars* (also see below), Clarke, Irwin, 1977; *Famous Last Words,* Clarke, Irwin, 1981.

Plays: *Can You See Me Yet?* (first produced in Ottawa at the National Arts Centre, March 1, 1976), Talonbooks, 1977; "John A.—Himself," first produced by Theatre London in London, Ontario, 1979.

Screenplays; produced by the Canadian Broadcasting Corp. (CBC-TV), except as indicated: "The Paper People," 1967; "Don't Let the Angels Fall," National Film Board of Canada-Columbia, 1969; "The Whiteoaks of Jalna" (based on the novels by Mazo de la Roche), 1971-72; (with William Whitehead) "The National Dream," 1974; (with Whitehead) "Dieppe: 1942," 1979; "The Wars" (based on his novel of the same title), Nielsen-Ferns, National Film Board of Canada, 1983.

Also author of a number of other television, radio, and film documentaries, including "The Journey" (radio drama), 1970. Author of novellas, including *Hello Cheeverland, Goodbye,* 1978, and *Lemonade,* 1981. Contributor of short stories to *Tamarack Review, New Orleans Review, Esquire, Cavalier,* and other periodicals; also contributor of critical reviews and essays to magazines and newspapers, including *Toronto Globe and Mail, Toronto Life,* and *Saturday Night.*

WORK IN PROGRESS: Two novels, *Bingo the Cat* (working title) and *Songs.*

SIDELIGHTS: Timothy Findley is a Canadian actor-turned-novelist who started writing when he was in his teens. "At that time I had glandular fever," he told *Books.* "I was in bed for the whole of one winter and did little more than sleep, wake up, eat, and go back to sleep." When he wasn't sleeping, Findley wrote what he calls "a kind of modern day romance." His serious writing began almost a decade later when he wrote a story entitled "About Effie" to prove a point to actress Ruth Gordon with whom he was performing at the time.

"We had been to an exhibition of paintings in Manchester, all done by people under thirty years of age," he explained in an interview with Alison Summers in *Canadian Literature.* "I was in my twenties then. When we came out, Ruth asked me 'Why are you people so damned negative about everything? All those pictures were black, depressing, ugly. Can't you say *yes* to anything?' Aloud I said to her, 'I don't think we're negative, Ruth.' I had an argument, or rather a pleasant conversation, with her. Secretly I decided, 'I'll prove that we're not.' I went back to my digs and I wrote a story." As Findley told *Books,* it was "a very sad and negative story. But she loved it." Gordon lent him an old typewriter, showed his story to Thornton Wilder, and suggested that perhaps literature, not theatre, was his natural milieu.

Since that time, Findley has written four novels and three novellas, as well as numerous short stories, plays, and films. An actor no longer, he still infuses his writing with the pageantry of the stage. "The importance of sound, spectacle, and style to a full appreciation of Findley's fictions, whether they be scripts intended to be *listened to* on the radio, scripts intended to be *seen* on television, the movie screen, or the theatre-stage, or whether they be the texts of short-stories and novels, cannot be overemphasized," John F. Hulcoop writes in *Canadian Literature*. "His work compels the critic to recover his senses (*see* more, *hear* more) by making direct appeals to the viewer-listener-reader through sight, sound and style: these are what force us to pay attention—to look and listen and mark his words."

In addition to stylistic similarities, Findley's fictions share some common themes. Fraught with violence, laced with images of fire, his books abound in symbolic details that reveal man's basic fears. "Everyone is so afraid of life itself that they would prefer to be locked up in an insane asylum," Findley commented in a 1981 CBC interview. In several of his novels, including *The Last of the Crazy People* and *The Butterfly Plague*, Findley examines individuals who do insane things in order to clarify what, in his words, is "bright and good."

Peter Klovan believes that this idea receives its most powerful treatment in Findley's 1977 novel, *The Wars*. "Here," Klovan writes in *Canadian Literature*, the device of a story-within-a-story is used to illustrate how a personality transcends elemental forces even while being destroyed by them. . . . As Findley's narrator realizes, 'People can only be found in what they do.' His problem in *The Wars* is to understand the actions of Robert Ross, a young Canadian officer, who when caught up in a German offensive during the Great War, tries and fails to save one hundred and thirty horses from being killed. Robert's failure leaves him horribly burned, and in many ways is simply the inevitable outcome of the pattern of futility which characterized his brief life. . . . But, in the process, Robert's struggle is raised to mythological proportions as a metaphor of fate and man's place in the universe, so that an apparent defeat is turned into a triumph. Indeed, 'tragic' is not too strong a term to describe *The Wars*."

In his subsequent novel, a curious mixture of fact and fiction entitled *Famous Last Words*, Findley resurrects a literary character from an Ezra Pound poem, Hugh Selwyn Mauberley, and "makes him into an expatriate Poundian protege, a noted novelist who has followed Ezra into the byways of the fascist disaster," writes Stephen Koch in the *Washington Post Book World*. According to Hulcoop, the allure of fascism is another recurring Findley theme. "All his works . . . are concerned with the different facets of what, at some level or other, 'allows fascism to be': a 'what' going beyond politics, a spiritual sickness the symptoms of which are fear, hatred, a lack of love which makes cruelty possible, and a failure of imagination which betrays us into confusing the truly beautiful with the allure of the high and the mighty."

BIOGRAPHICAL/CRITICAL SOURCES: *Saturday Night*, May, 1967; *Books*, June, 1967; *New York Times Book Review*, June 16, 1967, July 9, 1978, August 15, 1982; *Canadian Forum*, June, 1968; *Fiddlehead*, summer, 1968; *Times Literary Supplement*, March 5, 1970; *New Yorker*, August 21, 1978, August 9, 1982; *Canadian Literature*, winter, 1981, autumn, 1982; *Profiles in Canadian Literature*, number 51, 1982; Margaret Atwood, *Second Words*, Anansi Press, 1982; *New York Times*, June 22, 1982; *Washington Post Book World*, July 18, 1982; *Newsweek*, July 19, 1982; *Chicago Tribune Book World*, August 1, 1982; *Time*, August 2, 1982; *Los Angeles Times Book Review*, August 29, 1982.

FINE, Reuben 1914-

PERSONAL: Born October 11, 1914, in New York, N.Y.; son of Jacob (a businessman) and Bertha (Nedner) Fine; married Charlotte Margoshes (a psychologist), September 1, 1937; children: Benjamin, Ellyn June. *Education:* City College of New York (now City College of the City University of New York), B.S., 1933, M.S., 1939; University of Southern California, Ph.D., 1948.

CAREER: Private practice as psychologist and psychoanalyst, Los Angeles, Calif., 1945-48, and New York City, 1948—; University of Southern California, Los Angeles, member of faculty, 1945-48; City College (now City College of the City University of New York), New York City, instructor in psychology, 1948-53; Veterans Administration, New York City, clinical psychologist, 1948—; Elmhurst General Hospital, Queens, N.Y., attending psychologist and supervisor of psychotherapy, Psychiatric Division, 1961—. Director of Center for Creative Living, 1963—, Center for Psychoanalytical Training, 1972—, and Foundation for Formation of Psychoanalytic Universities, 1972—. Visiting professor at City College of the City University of New York, 1953-61, University of Amsterdam, 1961, Lowell Institute of Technology, 1967-69, University of Florence, 1968, and Adelphi University, 1969—. President of Institute for Psychoanalytic Training and Research. Consultant to U.S. Navy. Chess master, 1933-50, co-world champion, 1946-48. *Military service:* U.S. Navy, 1944-45, civilian scientist; received distinguished service award. *Member:* American Psychological Association (fellow, council representative), Society for Projective Techniques (fellow), National Psychological Association for Psychoanalysis (vice-president), U.S. Chess Foundation, New York Psychological Association (director, 1958-68).

WRITINGS—Chess books: (Editor with Fred Reinfeld) *A. Alekhine vs. E. D. Bogoljubow: World's Chess Championship*, McKay, 1934; (editor with Reinfeld) *Dr. Lasker's Chess Career*, Black Knight Press, 1935; (reviser) Larry Evans, *Modern Chess Openings*, 6th edition, McKay, 1939; *Basic Chess Endings*, McKay, 1941; (editor) Emanuel Lasker, *Manual of Chess*, revised edition, Dutton, 1942; *Chess the Easy Way*, McKay, 1942, reprinted, Cornerstone, 1963; *The Ideas Behind the Chess Openings*, McKay, 1943, revised edition, 1949; *Chess Marches On!*, Chess Review, 1945, published as *Fifty Chess Lessons from Modern Master Play*, Capricorn, 1963, published as *Fifty Chess Masterpieces, 1941-1944*, Dover, 1977; *Practical Chess Openings*, McKay, 1948, reprinted, 1973; *The World's a Chessboard*, McKay, 1948, published as *Great Moments in Modern Chess*, Dover, 1965.

(Editor) *World's Great Chess Games*, Crown, 1951, reprinted, Dover, 1983; *The Middle Game in Chess*, McKay, 1952; *Lessons from My Games: A Passion for Chess*, McKay, 1958, reprinted, Dover, 1983; (editor with Reinfeld) *Lasker's Greatest Chess Games, 1889-1914*, Dover, 1963; (with son, Benjamin Fine) *The Teenage Chess Book*, McKay, 1965; *Psychology of the Chess Player*, Dover, 1965, with new appendix, 1967.

(Author of comments and annotations) *The Final Candidates Match, Buenos Aires, 1971: Fischer versus Petrosian*, Hostel Chess Association, 1971; *Bobby Fischer's Conquest of the World's Chess Championship: The Psychology and Tactics of the Title Match*, McKay, 1973.

Psychology books: *Freud: A Critical Re-Evaluation of His Theories*, McKay, 1962, revised edition published as *The Development of Freud's Thought: From the Beginnings (1886-1900) Through Id Psychology (1900-1914) To Ego Psychology (1914-1939), Jason Aronson, 1973; The Healing of the Mind: The Technique of Psycoanalytic Psychotherapy, McKay, 1971; Psychoanalytic Psychology, Jason Aronson, 1975; A History of Psychoanalysis, Columbia University Press, 1979; The Intimate Hour, Avery, 1979; The Psychoanalytic Vision: A Controversial Reappraisal of the Freudian Revolution, Free Press, 1981; The Logic of Psychology: A Dynamic Approach, University Press of America, 1983.

SIDELIGHTS: As an expert in the fields of psychology and chess, Reuben Fine is noted for the many books he has produced on these subjects. An advocate of Freudian psychology, Fine wrote A History of Psychoanalysis to refute the argument that the Freudian theory is not yet well enough accepted to be a basis for fact. As the author states in the work: "Freud laid a solid foundation upon which the building is still being constructed. The foundation, like Einstein's relativity and Darwin's evolution, is so solid that it probably will never change, but the building can be altered in many ways."

BIOGRAPHICAL/CRITICAL SOURCES: Reuben Fine, A History of Psychoanalysis, Columbia University Press, 1979; New York Times Book Review, August 5, 1979.†

* * *

**FINLAY, Fiona
See STUART, (Violet) Vivian (Finlay)**

* * *

FINNEGAN, Ruth H(ilary) 1933-

PERSONAL: Born December 31, 1933, in Londonderry, Northern Ireland; daughter of Thomas (a university administrator) and Lucy Agnes (a professional lecturer; maiden name, Campbell) Finnegan; married David John Murray (a university professor), September 7, 1963; children: Rachel Clare, Kathleen Anne, Brigid Aileen. Education: Oxford University, Diploma in Anthropology (with distinction), 1959, B.Litt., 1960, D.Phil., 1963. Home: 125 Church Green Rd., Bletchley, Milton Keynes MK3 6DE, England. Office: Faculty of Social Sciences, Open University, Milton Keynes MK7 6AA, England.

CAREER: University College of Rhodesia and Nyasaland (now University of Zimbabwe), Salisbury, Southern Rhodesia (now Harare, Zimbabwe), lecturer in social anthropology, 1963-64; University of Ibadan, Ibadan, Nigeria, lecturer, 1965-67, senior lecturer in sociology, 1967-69; Open University, Milton Keynes, England, lecturer in sociology, 1969-72, senior lecturer in comparative social institutions, 1972-75, 1978-82, reader in comparative social institutions, 1982—. Reader in sociology, University of South Pacific, Suva, Fiji, 1975-78. Member of social anthropology committee, 1978-82, social affairs committee, 1982—, and Social Science Research Council (United Kingdom).

WRITINGS: Survey of the Limba People of Northern Sierra Leone, H.M.S.O., 1965; Limba Stories and Story-Telling, Clarendon Press, 1967; Oral Literature in Africa, Clarendon Press, 1970; (editor with Robin Horton) Modes of Thought: Essays on Thinking in Western and Non-Western Societies, Faber, 1973; Oral Poetry: Its Nature, Significance and Social Context, Cambridge University Press, 1977; (editor) The Penguin Book of Oral Poetry, Allen Lane, 1978, published as A World Treasury of Oral Poetry, Indiana University Press, 1978; (editor with Raymond Pillai) Essays on Pacific Literature, Fiji Museum, 1978; (editor with Stuart Brown and John Fauvel) Conceptions of Inquiry, Methuen, 1981.

General editor with Peter Burke of "Cambridge Studies in Oral and Literate Culture" series, Cambridge University Press, 1979—.

WORK IN PROGRESS: Research on local musical groups and musical activities in Milton Keynes, tentatively entitled Music in Milton Keynes.

* * *

FINNERAN, Richard J(ohn) 1943-

PERSONAL: Born December 19, 1943, in New York, N.Y.; son of Edward G. and Maude Florence (Rudden) Finneran; married Mary M. FitzGerald, 1976. Education: New York University, B.A., 1964; University of North Carolina, Ph.D., 1968. Home: 906 Beau Chene Dr., Mandeville, La. 70448. Office: Department of English, Newcomb College, Tulane University, New Orleans, La. 70118.

CAREER: University of Florida, Gainesville, instructor in English, 1967-68; New York University, New York, N.Y., instructor in English, 1968-70; Tulane University, Newcomb College, New Orleans, La., assistant professor, 1970-74, associate professor, 1974-77, professor of English, 1977—. Member: International Association for the Study of Anglo-Irish Literature (member of executive committee, 1973-82), American Association of University Professors, Modern Language Association of America (chairman of Celtic group, 1972, and Anglo-Irish Group, 1979), South Atlantic Modern Language Association (chairman of Irish studies section, 1977), South Central Modern Language Association (chairman of Anglo-Irish group, 1972). Awards, honors: Centenary fellowship to Yeats International Summer School at Sligo, Ireland, 1965; National Endowment for the Humanities summer stipend, 1975.

WRITINGS: (Editor) William Butler Yeats, John Sherman and Dhoya, Wayne State University Press, 1969; (editor) William Butler Yeats: The Byzantium Poems, C. E. Merrill, 1970; The Prose Fiction of W. B. Yeats, Dolmen Press, 1973; (editor) Letters of James Stephens, Macmillan, 1974; (editor and contributor) Anglo-Irish Literature: A Review of Research, Modern Language Association of America, 1976; (co-editor) Letters to W. B. Yeats, Macmillan, 1977; (editor) The Correspondence of Robert Bridges and W. B. Yeats, Macmillan, 1977; The Olympian and the Leprechaun: W. B. Yeats and James Stephens, Dolmen Press, 1978.

Editing Yeats's Poems, Macmillan, 1983; (editor and contributor) Recent Research on Anglo-Writers, Modern Language Association of America, 1983; (editor) The Poems of W. B. Yeats: A New Edition, Macmillan, 1983; (editor) Yeats: An Annual of Critical and Textual Studies, Cornell University Press, 1983. Co-general editor, "Collected Edition of the Works of W. B. Yeats"; series editor, "Poems in the Cornell Yeats." Contributor to language journals.

AVOCATIONAL INTERESTS: Tennis, basketball, football, music.

* * *

FISHER, Seymour 1922-

PERSONAL: Born May 13, 1922, in Baltimore, Md.; son of

Sam (a cleaning store owner) and Jean (Miller) Fisher; married Rhoda Lee Feinberg (a psychologist), March 22, 1947; children: Jerid Martin, Eve Phyllis. *Education:* University of Chicago, M.A., 1943, Ph.D., 1948. *Home:* 4855 Armstrong Rd., Manlius, N.Y. 13104. *Office:* Department of Psychiatry, Upstate Medical Center, State University of New York, Syracuse, N.Y. 13210.

CAREER: Illinois Neuropsychiatric Institute, Chicago, public health fellow in clinical psychology, 1945-48; Elgin State Hospital, Elgin, Ill., chief psychologist, 1949-51; Veterans Administration Hospital, Houston, Tex., research psychologist, 1952-56; Baylor University College of Medicine (now Baylor College of Medicine), Houston, U.S. Public Health Service career research investigator and associate professor of psychology, 1957-61; State University of New York Upstate Medical Center, Syracuse, professor of psychology, 1961—. *Member:* American Psychological Association.

WRITINGS: (With Sidney Cleveland) *Body Image and Personality,* Van Nostrand, 1958, revised edition, Dover, 1968; *Body Experience in Fantasy and Behavior,* Appleton, 1970; *The Female Orgasm,* Basic Books, 1973; *Body Consciousness,* Prentice-Hall, 1973; (with wife, Rhoda Fisher) *What We Really Know about Child Rearing,* Basic Books, 1976; (with Roger Greenberg) *The Scientific Credibility of Freud's Theories and Therapy,* Basic Books, 1977; (with Greenberg) *The Scientific Evaluation of Freud's Theories and Therapy: A Book of Readings,* Basic Books, 1978; (with Fisher) *Pretend the World Is Funny and Forever: A Psychological Analysis of Comedians, Clowns, and Actors,* Erlbaum, 1982.

* * *

FITZGERALD, Ernest A. 1925-

PERSONAL: Born July 24, 1925, in Crouse, N.C.; son of James Boyd (a minister) and Hattie (Chaffin) Fitzgerald; married Frances Perry, August 25, 1945; children: James Boyd, Patricia Anne. *Education:* Attended Pfeiffer College; Western Carolina College (now University), A.B. (cum laude), 1947; Duke University, B.D., 1951; summer graduate study, Emory University. *Office address:* West Market Street United Methodist Church, P. O. Box 870, Greensboro, N.C. 27402.

CAREER: Has served pastorates in Methodist churches in the Webster Circuit, 1944-47, the Liberty Circuit, 1947-50, Asheboro, 1950-55, Asheville, 1955-59, Charlotte, 1959-64, and Greensboro, 1964-66, all in North Carolina; senior minister of Centenary United Methodist Church, Winston-Salem, N.C., beginning 1966; currently affiliated with West Market Street United Methodist Church, Greensboro, N.C. Joined Western North Carolina Conference in 1946, served as Chairman of Television, Radio and Film Commission for four years, member of Commission on Christian Social Concerns, Board of Pensions, committee on Methodist information, structure committee of Southeastern Jurisdictional Consultation on Larger Churches, and vice-chairman of committee on conference structure; also member of board of global ministries and of board of the ordained ministry. Official visitor to World Methodist Conference in London, England, 1966; Staley Christian Scholar Lecturer; member of Evangelistic Mission, Dominican Republic. Delegate, Jurisdictional Conference, 1968, 1972, 1976, World Methodist Conference, Denver, Colo., 1971; participant in Southeastern Jurisdictional Laity Conference, 1977. Member of board of trustees of Institute of Homeletical Studies, National United Methodist Foundation for Higher Education, Western North Carolina Conference Methodist Foundation, Triad United Methodist Home, United Way of Forsyth County, Pfeiffer College, Misenheimer, N.C., and board of visitors, Duke University Divinity School, Durham, N.C. *Member:* Masons, Rotary Club, Torch Club. *Awards, honors:* Distinguished Alumni Award from Pfeiffer College, 1965, and Duke University, 1973; D.D., High Point College, 1968.

WRITINGS: There's No Other Way, Abingdon, 1970; *The Structures of Inner Peace,* Fisher-Harrison Corp., 1973; *You Can Believe!,* Abingdon, 1975; *Living under Pressure,* Fisher-Harrison Corp., 1976; *A Time to Cross the River,* Fisher-Harrison Corp., 1977; *How to Be a Successful Failure,* Atheneum, 1978; *God Writes Straight with Crooked Lines,* Atheneum, 1980; *Diamonds Everywhere: Appreciating God's Gifts,* Abingdon, 1983.

Contributor of articles to religious magazines, including *Upper Room Disciplines* and *Church School.*

AVOCATIONAL INTERESTS: Operating ham radio, woodworking, boating, waterskiing, reading, flying, mechanics.

* * *

FitzRALPH, Matthew
See McINERNY, Ralph

* * *

FLUTE, Molly
See LOTTMAN, Eileen

* * *

FLYNN, Don
See FLYNN, Donald R(obert)

* * *

FLYNN, Donald R(obert) 1928-
(Don Flynn; house pseudonym: Kate Williams)

PERSONAL: Born November 18, 1928, in St. Louis, Mo.; son of George Joseph and Mary (Foley) Flynn; married Charlotte J. Bayton (a free-lance writer), October 26, 1957; children: Kevin, Christopher, Colin. *Education:* University of Missouri, B.A., 1952. *Agent:* Nina Resnick, Fifi Oscard Associates, 19 West 44th St., New York, N.Y. 10036. *Office: New York Daily News,* 220 East 42nd St., New York, N.Y. 10017.

CAREER: Newspaper reporter, *St. Joseph Gazette,* St. Joseph, Mo., 1953-54, *Topeka State-Journal,* Topeka, Kan., 1955-56, *Kansas City Star,* Kansas City, Mo., 1956, *Chicago Daily News,* Chicago, Ill., 1957-58, and *New York Journal-American,* 1959-65, and *New York Herald Tribune,* 1966, both New York City; *New York Daily News,* New York City, reporter and writer, 1967—. *Member:* Authors League of America, Dramatists Guild, Writers Guild of America, East.

WRITINGS—Under name Don Flynn; plays: "Now It Makes Sense" (three-act comedy), first produced in Bellport, L.I., at Gateway Playhouse, August 26, 1969; "Pull the Covers Over My Head" (three-act drama), first produced Off-Off Broadway at The Actor's Place, fall, 1969; "A Money-Back Guarantee" (one-act comedy), first produced Off-Off-Broadway at American Theatre, fall, 1969.

"The Petition" (one-act comedy), first produced in Waterford, Conn., at Eugene O'Neill Memorial Theatre Center, summer,

1970; "The Man Who Raped Kansas" (two-act comedy), first produced at Gilford Playhouse, August 3, 1970, produced as "Keep Krap Out of Kansas," in Long Island at Arena Players Repertory Theater, 1982; "Something That Matters" (two-act comedy), first produced Off-Off-Broadway at American Theatre, 1973; "A Meaningful Relationship," first produced in New York at the Shandol Theatre, 1974.

"The Pilgrims Landed Just Down the Road" (three-act comedy), first produced in Long Island at Arena Players Repertory Theater, 1982; "Around the Corner from the White House" (two-act comedy), first produced in New York at No Smoking Playhouse, 1983. Also author of "The Black Sheep," produced Off-Off-Broadway at The Actor's Place.

Novels: *Murder Isn't Enough*, Walker & Co., 1982.

Young adult novels; written with wife, Charlotte J. Bayton Flynn, under house pseudonym Kate Williams; "Sweet Valley High" series; published by Bantam: *Power Play*, 1983; *Dear Sister*, 1984; *Too Easy*, 1984.

Also author under name Don Flynn of two episodes of "One of the Boys," starring Mickey Rooney, for NBC-TV, 1981; author of dramatic series "Street Cop," optioned by CBS-TV, and comedy series "Room Nine," optioned by Columbia Pictures.

BIOGRAPHICAL/CRITICAL SOURCES: *New York Times Book Review*, November 13, 1983.

* * *

FOLEY, (Anna) Bernice Williams 1902-

PERSONAL: Born November 20, 1902, in Wigginsville, Ohio; daughter of Karl Howland (president of a wholesale grocers' concern) and Bertye (a poet; maiden name Young) Williams; married Warren Massey Foley (an executive with Standard Oil Co.; deceased); children: Williams Massey, Karlanne (Mrs. William Scully Hauer). *Education:* Attended University of Cincinnati, 1920-24, Nanking Language College, Nanking, China, 1925-26, and Columbia University, 1931; Jesus College, Oxford, graduate school certificate, 1969. *Politics:* Conservative. *Religion:* Mormon. *Home:* 10224 Linden Ln., Overland Park, Kan. 66207.

CAREER: WKRC, Cincinnati, Ohio, fashion commentator, 1934; WSAI, Cincinnati, fashion commentator, 1938; WCPO-TV, Cincinnati, fashion commentator, 1947-50; Mabley & Carew Department Store, Cincinnati, special events coordinator, 1951-66; Martha Kinney Cooper Ohioana Library, Columbus, Ohio, director, 1966-76. Lecturer at Evening College, University of Cincinnati, 1948-49; lecturer on creative writing for American Association of University Women and other groups. Member of board of directors of Ohio Poetry Day, 1968-76.

MEMBER: American Women in Radio and Television (Educational Foundation Hi-O chapter chairman, 1970), English Speaking Union (Columbus branch president, 1966-69), National League of American Pen Women, Overseas Press Club, Freedoms Foundation of Valley Forge, Women in Communications, Daughters of the American Revolution, Society of Ohio Archivists, Ohio Historical Society, Ohio Academy of History, Ohio Arts Council (member of literary advisory panel, 1966-70), Ohio Press Women, Ohio Press Club, Faculty Club of Ohio State University, Theta Sigma Phi, Kappa Kappa Gamma, Sigma Delta Chi. *Awards, honors:* Woman of the Year award, Kappa Kappa Gamma, 1974; First Award, Ohio Press Women, 1975, for *Ohioana Quarterly;* Freedoms Foundation of Valley Forge award and First Award, Ohio Press Women, both 1976, for *Ohioana Year Book;* plaque and portrait placed in Women's Hall of Fame, Columbus, Ohio, 1982.

WRITINGS: *Star Stories* (juvenile), McCall Publishing, 1970; *Spaceships of the Ancients*, Veritie, 1978; *Why the Cock Crows Three Times*, Child's World, 1980; *The Gazelle and the Hunter*, Child's World, 1980; *A Walk among Clouds*, Child's World, 1980.

Also author of children's stories. Former columnist, Cincinnati *Times-Star*, columnist for *Forest Hills Journal* and *Community Journal*, 1970-76. Editor of *Ohioana Quarterly*, 1966-76, and *Ohioana Year Book*, 1966-76, book reviewer for Sunday edition of *Columbus Dispatch;* former book reviewer for Cincinnati *Enquirer*.

WORK IN PROGRESS: A book of stories of Korean legends in English for children.

AVOCATIONAL INTERESTS: Swimming, hiking, travel ("I've made twenty or more trips to Europe, the Orient, the Caribbean, Russia, and North Africa").

* * *

FONER, Eric 1943-

PERSONAL: Born February 7, 1943, in New York, N.Y.; son of Jack Donald (a professor) and Liza (Kraitz) Foner; married Naomi Achs (an associate producer of a children's television workshop), June 20, 1965 (divorced, 1977); married Lynn Garafola (a writer on dance), May 1, 1980. *Education:* Columbia University, B.A., 1963, Ph.D., 1969; Oxford University, B.A., 1965. *Home:* 606 West 116th St., New York, N.Y. 10027. *Office:* Department of History, Columbia University, New York, N.Y. 10027.

CAREER: Columbia University, New York City, assistant professor of history, 1969-73; City College of the City University of New York, New York City, associate professor of history, 1973-82; Columbia University, professor of history, 1982—. *Member:* American Historical Association, Southern History Association, Phi Beta Kappa. *Awards, honors:* American Council of Learned Societies fellowship, 1972-73; Guggenheim fellowship, 1975-76.

WRITINGS: *Free Soil, Free Labor, Free Men: The Ideology of the Republican Party before the Civil War*, Oxford University Press, 1970; *Nat Turner*, Prentice-Hall, 1971; *Tom Paine and the American Revolution*, Oxford University Press, 1976, published as *Tom Paine and Revolutionary America*, 1977; *Politics and Ideology in the Age of the Civil War*, Oxford University Press, 1980; *Nothing but Freedom: Emancipation and Its Legacy*, Louisiana State University Press, 1983.

Editor; published by Hill & Wang, except as indicated: *America's Black Past: A Reader in Afro-American History*, Harper, 1971; Richard D. Brown, *Modernization: The Transformation of American Life, 1600-1865*, 1976; James R. Green, *The World of the Worker and Labor in Twentieth Century America*, 1978; Julie R. Jeffrey, *Frontier Women: The Trans-Mississippi West, 1840-1880*, 1979; Harvard Sitkoff, *The Struggle for Black Equality, 1954-1980*, 1981; Carl Kaestle, *Pillars of the Republican: Common Schools and American Society, 1790-1860*, 1983.

Contributor of reviews to *New York Times* and *New York Review of Books;* contributor of articles to *Journal of American History, Journal of Negro History*, and *New York History*.

WORK IN PROGRESS: A volume on Reconstruction for "New American Nation" series.

SIDELIGHTS: Eric Foner's *Free Soil, Free Labor, Free Men: The Ideology of the Republican Party before the Civil War* interprets the philosophy of the Republican party before the Civil War. William W. Freehling writes in the *New York Review of Books* that Foner "supplies the best guide yet written to the Republican position in the years before the Civil War." Freehling goes on to explain that Foner "suggests that antebellum Southerners may indeed have been something other than paranoid in fearing that Republicans were abolitionists."

According to David Donald writing in the *New York Times Book Review, Free Soil, Free Labor, Free Men* "is a useful and fair-minded summary of what Republicanism meant in the 1850's, and it is especially valuable as a corrective to older historical stereotypes.... This carefully researched, fair-minded book ought to kill some of the hoary myths about the early Republicans. [Foner] finds little evidence to suggest that Republicans used antislavery as a cloak for economic policies."

Writing about another Foner book, *Politics and Ideology in the Age of the Civil War,* J. H. Silbey states in *American Historical Review:* "[Foner] is excellent at delineating the dominant ideologies and linking them to political events.... Foner also recognizes the early importance of intersectional political parties in resisting and containing sectional confrontation, but he emphasizes their demise in the face of popular sectional ideologies.... This is an important and invigorating book." And C. V. Woodward remarks in *New Republic* that Foner's "basic contention is that 'the coming of the Civil War is the story of the intrusion of sectional ideology into the political system.'... Like many books that stress the importance of the Civil War, this one skips over the way and jumps from causes to consequences. But it has important things to say about both—and especially about the latter. The author is dead right in fixing on control of black labor as the basic issue of Reconstruction."

BIOGRAPHICAL/CRITICAL SOURCES: Library Journal, July, 1970; *Virginia Quarterly Review,* autumn, 1970; *New York Times Book Review,* October 18, 1970; *New York Review of Books,* September 23, 1971; *New Republic,* November 22, 1980; *American Historical Review,* October, 1981; *Village Voice Literary Supplement,* November, 1983.

* * *

FONTAINE, Andre (Lucien Georges) 1921-

PERSONAL: Born March 30, 1921, in Paris, France; son of Georges (a trader) and Blanche (Rochon-Duvigneaud) Fontaine; married Isabelle Cavaille, June 15, 1943; children: Jean-Marc, Agnes, Laurent. *Education:* University of Paris, Licence en droit, 1940, Licence es lettres, 1941, Diplomes d'etudes superieures de droit public et d'economie politique, 1942. *Religion:* Catholic. *Office:* Le Monde, 5 rue des Italiens, 75627 Paris, CEDEX 9, France.

CAREER: Reporter, *Temps Present,* 1946-47; *Le Monde,* Paris, France, 1947—, began as assistant news editor, foreign editor, 1951-69, editor in chief, 1969—. Member of board, Banque Indosuez, Institut Francais des Relations Internationales, and Centre des Hautes Etudes de l'Afrique et de l'Asie Modernes. *Member:* Presse Diplomatique Francaise. *Awards, honors:* Prix de la Communaute Atlantique, 1960; officer, Lion of Finland (Belgium) and Order of Vasa (Sweden); knight of Dannebrog (Denmark) and Crown of Belgium; commander, Order of Merit of the Italian Republic and Order of Tudor Vladimirescu; named Atlas International Editor of the Year, 1976; Prix des Ambassadeurs, 1983.

WRITINGS—Published by Fayard, except as indicated: *L'Alliance atlantique a l'heure du degel,* Calmann-Levy, 1960; *Histoire de la guerre froide,* Volume I, 1966, Volume II, 1967, translation published as *History of the Cold War,* Volume I: *From the October Revolution to the Korean War, 1917-1950,* translation by D. D. Paige, Pantheon, 1968, Volume II: *From the Korean War to the Present,* translation by Renaud Bruce, Pantheon, 1969; *La Guerre civile froide,* 1969; *Le Dernier Quart du siecle,* 1976; *La France au bois dormant,* 1978; *Un Seul Lit pour deux reves: Histoire de la "detente," 1962-1981,* 1981.

SIDELIGHTS: In his two-volume study *History of the Cold War,* French journalist Andre Fontaine maintains that the conflict between the United States and the Soviet Union dates not from 1945 but from 1917. Rejecting both the orthodox view that Russia is entirely to blame for East-West tensions and the revisionist view that America must take full responsibility for the Cold War, Fontaine offers readers a synthesis that avoids extremes of opinion. In fact, declares Michael Harrington in the *New Republic,* "the value of this *History of the Cold War* is that it is not a factional, polemical work. It is a sober narrative of well-known facts with unobtrusive and interesting interpretations."

Fontaine's focus, notes Stephen Rosenfeld in the *Washington Post,* "is on events, on the choices as they appeared to contemporary actors, on the possibilities they took or missed." F. Y. Blumenfeld makes a similar observation, stating in a *Newsweek* review of *History of the Cold War* that the author "concentrates almost exclusively on the political aspects of the struggle. He obviously believes that the manipulations of the world leaders are what determined the era." According to the *New Yorker* critic, the resulting account of international events and personalities "is an urbane, thoughtful piece of work."

"Fontaine has undertaken a formidable task," asserts Anthony Eden in *Book World.* "It is a tribute to his objectivity and sense of purpose that he has given us a book which is both informative and stimulating.... [He] points out what he judges to be the errors of the past, and they could help to guide us in the present." Even though he occasionally disagrees with some of the author's interpretations, Eden's fellow *Book World* reviewer Anthony Hartley also finds Fontaine to be "an agile and instructive guide through the ugly mazes" of postwar foreign relations.

Several critics, including Gaddis Smith and Seyom Brown, are considerably less impressed by Fontaine and his book. "[*History of the Cold War*] is flawed by factual errors, distortion and some mistranslation," writes Smith in the *New York Times Book Review.* "[Fontaine's] study revises little and confuses much.... Few of [his] interpretations would disturb the hardest of American cold warriors, although his historical inaccuracies left this historian spluttering." Brown, commenting in the *Saturday Review,* is also critical of *History of the Cold War.* "[Fontaine's] apparent lack of central hypothesis—either explicit or implicit—makes this an exasperating study to read, almost totally lacking in narrative drive though it deals with events of the highest dramatic content," declares the reviewer. "As literature it is a failure; as history it is incomplete, and as social science it is riddled with contradictory explanations."

Rosenfeld, who admits that "it is simple enough to challenge Fontaine" on one point or another, nevertheless believes that "it is more valuable, and more fun, to read him, to engage one's mind with his, to see how the jumble of events of the last two decades smooths out into rational patterns and insights of an interesting modern man." Concludes the critic: "*History of the Cold War* is not the last word, but it is a fascinating word in the West's continuing story."

BIOGRAPHICAL/CRITICAL SOURCES: *Book World,* March 10, 1968, July 6, 1969; *Newsweek,* March 18, 1968; *New York Times Book Review,* March 24, 1968; *New Republic,* March 30, 1968; *New York Times,* May 2, 1968, May 3, 1968, August 2, 1969; *Christian Science Monitor,* July 11, 1968; *Washington Post,* August 2, 1969; *New Yorker,* September 13, 1969; *Saturday Review,* October 18, 1969.

* * *

FORBES, Daniel
See KENYON, Michael

* * *

FORNARI, Franco 1921-

PERSONAL: Born April 18, 1921, in Piacenza, Italy; son of Attilio and Maria (Vermi) Fornari; married Bianca Bertonazzi (a psychoanalyst), December 27, 1947; children: Gigliola, Maurizio, Silvia, Massimo, Ilaria. *Education:* University of Milan, graduate in medicine and surgery, libero Docente of psychology. *Home and office:* Via Plinio 63, Milano, Italy 20129.

CAREER: University of Milan, Milan, Italy, director of Institute of Psychology of Facolta di Lettere e Filologia, 1972—, founder of l'Instituto di Polemologia. *Member:* International Psychoanalytical Society, Societa Psicanalitica Italiana (past president), Societa Italiana de Psicologia, Societa Italiana di Psichiatria. *Awards, honors:* Premio Letterairo S. Dona di Piave, 1969, for *Angelo a capofitto.*

WRITINGS—Published by Feltrinelli (Milan), except as indicated: *La Vita affettiva originaria del bambino,* 1963; *Psicanalisi della guerra atomica,* Comunita (Milan), 1964; *Nuovi orientamenti della psicanalisi,* 1966, revised edition, 1970; *Psicanalisi della guerra,* 1966, translation by Alenka Pfeifer published as *The Psychoanalysis of War,* Anchor Press, 1974; (compiler) *Dissacrazione della guerra,* 1969; *Angelo a capofitto,* Rizzoli, 1969.

Mussolini's Gadfly, Vanderbilt University Press, 1971; *Genitalita e cultura,* 1975; *I fondamenti di una teoria psicoanalitica del linguaggio,* Boringhieri, 1979; *Il codice vivente,* Boringhieri, 1981; *La malattia dell'Europa,* 1981; *La lezione freudiana,* 1982. Also author of numerous scientific papers on psychoanalysis and related subjects.

* * *

FORSYTH (OUTRAM), Anne 1933-

PERSONAL: Born March 17, 1933, in Dunfermline, Scotland; daughter of James Whyte and Catherine (Marshall) Forsyth; married D. H. Outram. *Education:* University of St. Andrews, M.A., 1953. *Home:* 4 East Ridgeway, Cuffley, Hertfordshire, England.

CAREER: *Fife Herald,* Cupar, Fife, Scotland, reporter, 1953-55; *Manchester Evening News,* Manchester, England, reporter, 1955-57; Halle Concerts Society, Manchester, secretary to Sir John Barbirolli, 1957-59; *Woman's Own,* London, England, 1959-64, began as sub-editor, became assistant home editor; Macmillan & Co., London, editor in overseas department, 1964-69; Routledge & Kegan Paul Ltd., London, editorial manager, 1969-70; Evans Brothers Ltd., London, managing editor of Overseas and English Language Teaching Books, 1970-78; editorial manager, Bell & Hyman, 1979-81.

WRITINGS: *English for Everyone,* Macmillan, 1969; *Cheap and Cheerful, Homemaking on a Budget,* Mills & Boon, 1973; *Table Settings for All Occasions,* Mills & Boon, 1975; *Your Own Place,* Oliver & Boyd, 1976; (with others) *Practical Homemaking,* Bell & Hyman, 1980; *Baxter the Travelling Cat,* Hodder & Stoughton, 1981; (co-author) *Beginning Cookery,* Bell & Hyman, 1981; *Sam's Wonderful Shell,* Hamish Hamilton, 1982; *Monster Monday,* Hamish Hamilton, 1983.

BIOGRAPHICAL/CRITICAL SOURCES: *Books and Bookmen,* September, 1969.

* * *

FOULKES, Fred K. 1941-

PERSONAL: Born July 27, 1941; son of Clarence R. and Constance (Klee) Foulkes. *Education:* Princeton University, A.B., 1963; Harvard University, M.B.A., 1965, D.B.A., 1968. *Home:* 50 Follen St., Cambridge, Mass. 02138. *Office:* School of Management, Boston University, Boston, Mass. 02215.

CAREER: Chemical Bank New York Trust, New York, N.Y., trainee, 1963; Harvard University, Graduate School of Business Administration, Boston, Mass., research associate in business, 1966; Chrysler Corp., Detroit, Mich., labor relations staff, 1967; formerly associate professor of business administration at Harvard University, Graduate School of Business Administration; Boston University, School of Management, Boston, professor of management policy and director of Human Resources Policy Institute, 1980—. *Member:* Industrial Relations Research Association, Phi Beta Kappa, Omicron Delta Epsilon.

WRITINGS: *Creating More Meaningful Work,* American Management Association, 1969; (contributor) Harold L. Sheppard and Neal Q. Herrick, editors, *Where Have All the Robots Gone?: Worker Dissatisfaction in the Seventies,* Free Press, 1972; *Personnel Policies in Large Nonunion Companies,* Prentice-Hall, 1980; (with E. Robert Livernash) *Human Resources Management: Text and Cases,* Prentice-Hall, 1982; (editor) *Employee Benefits Handbook,* Warren, Gorham & Lamont, 1982. Contributor to *Compton Yearbook,* 1974. Contributor of article to *Harvard Business Review* and *Harvard Business School Bulletin.*

WORK IN PROGRESS: Research on job enrichment, personnel's changing role, career planning and development, personnel practices of large, nonunion employers in the United States, robotics, and executive compensation.

* * *

FOX, Mary Virginia 1919-

PERSONAL: Born November 17, 1919, in Richmond, Va.; daughter of George Henry (a realtor) and Leila Virginia (Merrell) Foster; married Richard Earl Fox (a manufacturer); children: Phillip Richard, Thomas George, William Earl. *Education:* Northwestern University, B.S. (with honors), 1940.

Politics: "Very flexible." *Religion:* United Church of Christ. *Home:* 2841 Century Harbor, Middleton, Wis. 53562.

CAREER: Writer. *Member:* National League of American Pen Women, American Society of Journalists and Authors, Council for Wisconsin Writers.

WRITINGS—All juveniles: *Apprentice to Liberty*, Abingdon, 1960; *Treasure of the Revolution*, Abingdon, 1961; *Ambush at Fort Dearborn*, St. Martin's, 1962; *Ethel Barrymore: A Portrait*, Reilly & Lee, 1970; *Pacifists: Adventures in Courage*, Reilly & Lee, 1971; *Lady for the Defense: A Biography of Belva Lockwood*, Harcourt, 1975.

Barbara Walters: The News Her Way, Dillon, 1980; *Jane Fonda: Something to Fight For*, Dillon, 1980; *Jane Goodall: Living Chimp Style*, Dillon, 1981; *Janet Guthrie: Foot to the Floor*, Dillon, 1981; *The Skating Heidens*, Enslow, 1981; *Mister President: Ronald Reagan*, Enslow, 1982; *Justice Sandra Day O'Connor*, Enslow, 1983.

Writer of material for other publishers, including Harper, Science Research Associates, Lyons & Carnahan, and David Cook. Contributor to *Encyclopaedia Britannica*; author of radio scripts and travel articles.

WORK IN PROGRESS: Aboard the Space Shuttle, for Messner.

SIDELIGHTS: Mary Virginia Fox traveled with her husband, Richard Earl Fox, who was advising industry in undeveloped countries, 1966-69, living in the Philippines, Iran, Colombia, and Tunisia.

* * *

FOX, Stephen R. 1945-

PERSONAL: Born February 28, 1945, in Boston, Mass.; son of Kenneth R. (a textile engineer) and Eleanor (a librarian; maiden name, Pihl) Fox. *Education:* Williams College, A.B., 1966; Brown University, Ph.D., 1971. *Politics:* Independent. *Religion:* "Non-institutional."

CAREER: Free-lance writer. *Member:* American Historical Association, Organization of American Historians, Alliance of Independent Scholars (Cambridge, Mass.), P.E.N. (New England).

WRITINGS: The Guardian of Boston, William Monroe Trotter, Atheneum, 1970; *John Muir and His Legacy: The American Conservation Movement*, Little, Brown, 1981; *The Mirror Makers: A History of Twentieth-Century American Advertising and Its Creators*, Morrow, 1984.

Contributor of occasional articles and reviews to *Orion Nature Quarterly, Boston Globe*, and to the journal of the Theodore Roosevelt Association.

SIDELIGHTS: Stephen R. Fox told *CA*: "I got my doctorate with the idea of becoming a history professor, but I found that I disliked teaching. So I have worked as a free-lance since 1973, making my living at editing and research jobs at first, then as a full-time writer in recent years. I remain enough of an academic to want to write books that are intellectually respectable—that the *Journal of American History* will not give the back of its hand to—but I also must try to please a trade publisher and a general reading audience. Hard to find topics that satisfy both constituencies.

"Ideologically, I am anti-modernist. This viewpoint lurks behind everything I write, especially my book on John Muir and the conservation movement. The greatest single influence on my anti-modernist perspective has been Rowland Berthoff's book *An Unsettled People* (Harper, 1971). Anti-modernism has also been well explicated in *No Place of Grace* by Jackson Lears (Pantheon, 1981). To me, this perspective represents an alternate radical tradition, congruent in some ways with Marxism, but without the typical Marxist prejudices against religion, folk cultures, and non-urban life. Actually it is more radical than Marxism, which shares the materialist and rationalistic superstitions of the urban-industrial culture that afflicts us.

"When people ask how I decided to be a writer, I always say I didn't choose it; I can't imagine myself doing anything else."

BIOGRAPHICAL/CRITICAL SOURCES: New York Times Book Review, June 21, 1981.

* * *

FRANCIS, Philip
See LOCKYER, Roger

* * *

FRANKLIN, Harry 1906-

PERSONAL: Born January 20, 1906, in London, England; son of Frederick L. (an engineer) and Isabella (Middlemast) Franklin; married Hilda Hadfield, August 30, 1928; children: Henry Clive, Tonia Franklin, Hilda Tilley. *Education:* Exeter College, Oxford, B.A., 1927, Dip.Ed., 1928; Lincoln's Inn, Barrister-at-Law, 1938. *Religion:* Church of England. *Home:* Warren House, Warren Lane, Froxfield, Petersfield, Hampshire, England.

CAREER: Colonial Service, Northern Rhodesia (now Zambia), 1929-51, serving variously as inspector of education, district commissioner, and resident magistrate, 1929-41, director of Information and Broadcast Services, 1941-45; Northern Rhodesia government, Minister of Education and Social Services, 1954-59, member of Legislative Council, 1959-60, Minister of Transport and Works, 1961-62; farmer, near Lusaka, Zambia. War correspondent, 1942-45. *Member:* Commonwealth Parliamentary Association. *Awards, honors:* Order of the British Empire.

WRITINGS: Ignorance Is No Defence, Longmans, Green, 1941; *Unholy Wedlock: The Failure of the Central African Federation*, Allen & Unwin, 1963; *Crash*, Robert Hale, 1968; *Don't Go to Centa*, Robert Hale, 1970; *The Flag Wagger*, Shepheard-Walwyn, 1976. Author of radio scripts for Canadian Broadcasting Corp., British Broadcasting Corp., and National Broadcasting Co. Contributor of short stories to magazines, articles to *Spectator, Guardian, Observer, Times*, and other newspapers.

SIDELIGHTS: Harry Franklin commented, "Writing is hard work. I don't know why I do it." His travels have covered all of Africa, most of Europe, the Middle East, Southeast Asia, Canada, and America.

* * *

FREEMAN, Roger L(ouis) 1928-

PERSONAL: Born July 27, 1928, in New York, N.Y.; son of Andrew A. (a writer) and Mary Alice (a chemist; maiden name, Newton) Freeman; married Francisca Paquita (a registered nurse), June 25, 1966; children: Robert Carlos, Cristina, Rosalind. *Education:* Attended Middlebury College, 1948-51; New York University, B.A., 1966, M.A., 1973. *Religion:* Congregationalist. *Home address:* P.O. Box 259, Sudbury, Mass. 01776-0259.

CAREER: Military Sea Transportation Service, Brooklyn, N.Y., radio officer, 1952-59; Bendix Radio, Towson, Md., senior engineer in Spain, 1959-62; International Telephone and Telegraph Communications Systems, Paramus, N.J., member of technical staff, 1962-66; Page Communication Engineers, Washington, D.C., staff engineer, 1966-70; International Telephone and Telegraph Laboratories, Madrid, Spain, assistant technical director, 1970-78; Raytheon Co., Equipment Division, Sudbury, Mass., senior principal engineer and program manager, 1978—. Founder and president, Eaton Grange Co., Inc., 1981; member of faculty, Northeastern University. *Military service:* U.S. Naval Reserve, 1946-70, active duty, 1946-48; became lieutenant senior grade.

MEMBER: Institute of Electrical and Electronics Engineers (senior member; former secretary of Spain section), Armed Forces Communications and Electronics Association. *Awards, honors:* Civil service award from U.S. Navy, 1958, for outstanding service in high latitude operations; commendation from Bogota, Colombia, Ministry of Telecommunication, 1968.

WRITINGS: *A Visitor's Guide to Madrid,* Editorial Everest, 1971; *English-Spanish/Spanish-English Dictionary of Telecommunications Terms,* Cambridge University Press, 1972; *Telecommunication Transmission Handbook,* Wiley, 1975, 2nd edition, 1981; *Telecommunication System Engineering,* Wiley, 1980; *Reference Manual for Telecommunication Engineers,* Wiley, 1984. Contributor to telecommunications journals.

WORK IN PROGRESS: Radio System Design for Telecommunications and *Glossary of Telecommunication Terminology,* both for Wiley; *The Joys of Spanish: A Compendium of Castilian Colloquialisms;* a novel, tentatively entitled *Memories of a Merchant Mariner.*

SIDELIGHTS: Roger L. Freeman explained to *CA* that he is equally interested in technical and cultural writing, alternating between the fields of telecommunications and Hispanic studies.

* * *

FREUND, Philip (Herbert) 1909-

PERSONAL: Surname rhymes with "joined"; born February 5, 1909, in Vancouver, British Columbia, Canada; son of Henry (a businessman) and Gussie (Robinson) Freund. *Education:* Cornell University, B.A. (cum laude), 1929, M.A., 1931. *Home:* 1025 Fifth Ave., New York, N.Y. 10028. *Agent:* Bertha Klausner International Literary Agency, Inc., 71 Park Ave., New York, N.Y. 10016.

CAREER: City University of New York, New York City, lecturer at Film Institute at City College, 1945-66, lecturer in English at Hunter College, 1945-79; Fordham University, New York City, 1957—, began as adjunct assistant professor, professor of communication arts, 1966-76, professor emeritus, 1976—. Taught at Cornell University, 1946, University of British Columbia, 1948-50, and Baruch College, 1948-53; guest lecturer at Boston College, 1966, and New York University, 1967. President of Herbert Robinson Fund, Inc., 1960-70. Former consultant to Secretary of the Army, Anti-Defamation League of B'nai B'rith, Young America Films, and Film Research Associates. *Military service:* U.S. Army, Signal Corps, 1941-45; served as head of Scenario Board of Review in film section of Signal Corps Photographic Centre. *Member:* Sigma Delta Chi, New Dramatists Committee. *Awards, honors:* Bureau of New Plays fellowship, 1937; awarded Bene merenti by Fordham University.

WRITINGS: (Contributor) *Cornell Plays,* Samuel French, 1932; *The Merry Communist* (fantasy), Pilgrim House, 1934; (author of critical preface) Kimi Gengo, *To One Who Mourns at the Death of the Emperor,* Pilgrim House, 1934; *The Snow and Other Stories,* Pilgrim House, 1935; *Book of Kings* (first novel in trilogy; also see below), Pilgrim House, 1937; *The Evening Heron* (novel), Pilgrim House, 1937; *Dreams of Youth* (novel), Pilgrim House, 1938; (with Marie-Jeanne) *Yankee Ballerina* (juvenile), Dodd, 1939.

The Dark Shore (novel), Washburn, 1941; *The Young Greek and the Creole* (stories), Pilgrim House, 1944; *Three Exotic Tales,* Pilgrim House, 1945; *Edward Zoltan* (second novel in trilogy; also see below), Beechhurst Press, 1946; *How to Become a Literary Critic,* Beechhurst Press, 1947, revised edition published as *The Art of Reading the Novel,* Collier, 1965; (with Marie-Jeanne) *Opera Ballerina* (juvenile), Dodd, 1947; *Stephanie's Son* (third novel in trilogy; also see below), Beechhurst Press, 1947; *Easter Island* (novel), Beechhurst Press, 1947; *The Zoltans* (trilogy; includes *Book of Kings, Edward Zoltan,* and *Stephanie's Son*), Beechhurst Press, 1948; *A Man of Taste and Other Stories,* Beechhurst Press, 1949.

Private Speech (poetry), W. H. Allen, 1951, Pilgrim House, 1952; *Saturnalia and the Nomads* (first novel in trilogy; also see below), Secker & Warburg, 1956; *The Rooftop and Eurasia* (second novel in trilogy; also see below), Secker & Warburg, 1957; *How the World Began* (third novel in trilogy; also see below), Secker & Warburg, 1958; *The Volcano God* (trilogy; includes *Saturnalia and the Nomads, The Rooftop and Eurasia,* and *How the World Began*), British Book Center, 1959; (editor and author of critical preface) Otto Rank, *The Myth of the Birth of the Hero and Other Essays,* Vintage Press, 1959.

The Beholder: Seven Tales of Sebastian Romm, W. H. Allen, 1961, British Book Center, 1962; *The Devious Ways* (stories), W. H. Allen, 1962, London House, 1963; *Myths of Creation* (belles lettres), W. H. Allen, 1964, Washington Square Press, 1966, reprinted, Transatlantic, 1975; (author of critical preface) Joseph Conrad, *Lord Jim,* Collier, 1965; *The Spymaster* (stories), W. H. Allen, 1965, Washburn, 1966; *The Young Artists* (stories), W. H. Allen, 1966.

Searching, W. H. Allen, 1972, Paul Eriksson, 1975. Short stories have been anthologized. Editor of several biographies.

Plays: *Mario's Well* (one-act), Samuel French, 1940; *Prince Hamlet* (one-act, fourteen scenes; first produced Off-Broadway at Sunset Theatre, 1972), Bookman Associates, 1953; *Three Off-Broadway Plays* (includes "The Fire Bringers," "The Peons" [produced Off-Broadway at the Brander Matthews Theatre], and "The Brooding Angel" [produced Off-Broadway at the Key Theatre]), Pitman, 1968; *Three Poetic Plays* (includes "Flame and Cedar," "Jocasta," and "The Bacchae"), W. H. Allen, 1970; *More Off-Broadway Plays* (includes "Charles IV," "Edge of the Jungle" [produced at New York Shakespeare Public Theatre Annex], and "Miss Lucy in Town"), Transatlantic, 1974. Also author of "Simon, Simon," published in *One-Act Play Magazine,* 1935.

Writer of television scripts for "Kraft Theater, "Chrysler Theater," "General Electric Theater," "Jane Wyman Theater," "Matinee Theater," and others. Writer of over twenty-five documentary films. Also contributor of stories and articles to magazines and journals, including *New York Times Magazine* and *Saturday Evening Post.*

WORK IN PROGRESS: Two scholarly projects: a book-length study of the plays of Eugene O'Neill and a multi-volume history of world theatre.

SIDELIGHTS: Philip Freund has travelled widely, including trips to Russia, Poland, Jordan, Egypt, Morocco, India, Cambodia, Nepal, Sri Lanka, Ecuador, and Venezuela. Freund's writings have been translated into German, Italian, Spanish, Japanese, Urdu, and Thai.

AVOCATIONAL INTERESTS: Collecting art.

* * *

FRIED, Charles 1935-

PERSONAL: Born April 15, 1935, in Prague, Czechoslovakia; brought to United States in 1941, naturalized in 1948; son of Anthony (an executive) and Marta (Winterstein) Fried; married Anne Summerscale (a high school teacher), June 13, 1959; children: Charles Gregory, Antonia Catherine. *Education:* Princeton University, A.B., 1956; Oxford University, B.A.Juris., 1958, M.A., 1961; Columbia University, LL.B., 1960. *Office:* Law School, Harvard University, Cambridge, Mass. 02138.

CAREER: Admitted to District of Columbia and Massachusetts Bars; U.S. Supreme Court, Washington, D.C., law clerk to Associate Justice John M. Harlan, 1960-61; Harvard University, Law School, Cambridge, Mass., assistant professor, 1961-65, professor of law, beginning 1965, currently Carter Professor of General Jurisprudence. Associate reporter, model code pre-arraignment procedure, American Law Institute, 1964. Consultant to U.S. Treasury Department, Transportation and Justice Department, and to the White House. *Member:* American Society for Political and Legal Philosophy (vice-president), National Academy of Science, Institute of Medicine, Phi Beta Kappa. *Awards, honors:* Guggenheim fellow, 1971-72.

WRITINGS: An Anatomy of Values; Problems of Personal and Social Choice, Harvard University Press, 1970; *Medical Experimentation: Personal Integrity and Social Policy,* American Elsevier, 1974; *Right and Wrong,* Harvard University Press, 1978; *Contract as Promise: A Theory of Contractual Obligation,* Harvard University Press, 1981. Contributor to law journals.

SIDELIGHTS: Recent violation of human rights by government agencies and corporate officials has led to a renewed interest in ethical theory. One theorist addressing himself to basic questions of right and wrong is Harvard law professor Charles Fried. In his book, *Right and Wrong,* Fried argues *against* philosophers who define conduct as moral or immoral on the basis of its outcome. These utilitarians, as they are called, follow a formula first outlined in the late 1700s which posits that an action can be justified if it produces the greatest good for the greatest number. Fried disagrees. In his opinion, some actions are always wrong—lying or intentionally murdering innocents, for example—no matter how much good they may produce.

Fried's rigid moral standards stem from the idea that human life is deserving of respect, and they reflect what he calls "the value of personhood." When we murder or lie to a person, we are showing disrespect for his being. As Alasdair MacIntyre explains in the *New Republic:* "I violate the respect for another's rationality when I lie to him or her, just as I violate the integrity of another's person if I assault or murder him." Thus it is wrong to torture a prisoner of war, for instance, even though doing so might reveal information that would save many lives.

Stephen Rowntree writes in *America* that Fried's "argument is worth making because there are so many occasions when it is plausible to claim that violating the rights of a few is necessary for the greater good. But from such a position comes the justification for much of the brutality that increasingly characterizes police, military and government actions today."

And Steven Kelman expresses a similar view: "An approach such as Fried's is indeed an important corrective to utilitarian calculations that are often all too ready to sacrifice individuals—be they 'unproductive' ghetto dwellers or the handicapped on the one side, or 'overprivileged' capitalists on the other—on the altar of the greatest good." Later on in that same *New Leader* article, Kelman commends Fried for "having produced a well-written and provocative volume, containing discussions of many important issues."

BIOGRAPHICAL/CRITICAL SOURCES: Charles Fried, *Right and Wrong,* Harvard University Press, 1978; *New Republic,* May 6, 1978; *New York Times Book Review,* June 25, 1978; *New Leader,* July 3, 1978; *America,* November 18, 1978.

* * *

FRIED, Eleanor L.
See FURMAN, Eleanor L.

* * *

FRIED, John J(ames) 1940-

PERSONAL: Surname is pronounced freed; born November 3, 1940; in Quito, Ecuador; came to United States in 1950, naturalized in 1956; son of Philip and Jeanette (Rosenheck) Fried; married Christiane Hommey, September 8, 1968. *Education:* University of Michigan, M.A., 1961; Columbia University, M.S., 1963. *Home:* 1206 Alvira, Los Angeles, Calif. 90035.

CAREER: Formerly free-lance writer and reporter for *Detroit News,* United Press International, and *Life; Press-Telegram,* Long Beach, Calif., medical science writer, 1979-81, editorial pages editor, 1981—. *Member:* National Association of Science Writers, National Conference of Editorial Writers, Sigma Delta Chi. *Awards, honors:* Clarion Award, Women in Communication, 1980, 1981; Pulitzer Prize finalist, Meritorious Public Service, 1981; Sigma Delta Chi Distinguished Service Award, 1981; Los Angeles Press Club journalism awards for excellence, 1981, 1982.

WRITINGS: The Mystery of Heredity, John Day, 1971; *Vasectomy: Truth and Consequences,* Saturday Review Press, 1972; *Life along the San Andreas Fault,* Saturday Review Press, 1973; (with E. B. Dietrich) *Code Arrest: A Heart Stops,* Saturday Review Press, 1974; (editor) Howard Wilcox, *Hothouse Earth,* Praeger, 1975; *The Vitamin Conspiracy,* Saturday Review Press, 1975; (with Lucas Yanker) *Animal Doctor,* Saturday Review Press, 1976; *Vitamin Politics,* Prometheus Books, 1984.

Contributor to *New Leader, New Republic, Sports Illustrated, Reader's Digest, New York Times Sunday Magazine, Playgirl,* and *Free Enterprise.*

* * *

FRIEDHEIM, Robert L(yle) 1934-

PERSONAL: Born August 1, 1934, in New York, N.Y.; son

of Joseph N. and Blanche (Vogel) Friedheim; married Robin Rudolph (an editor), June 17, 1956; children: Amy, Jessica. *Education:* Columbia University, B.A., 1955, M.A., 1957; University of Washington, Seattle, Ph.D., 1962. *Office:* Institute for Marine and Coastal Studies, University of Southern California, University Park, Los Angeles, Calif. 90089-0341.

CAREER: Purdue University, Lafayette, Ind., assistant professor, 1961-66, associate professor of political science, 1966; Center for Naval Analyses, Arlington, Va., 1966-76, began as researcher, director of Law of the Sea Project, 1972-76; University of Southern California, Los Angeles, professor of international relations, 1976—, associate director, Institute for Marine and Coastal Studies, 1976—, director, Sea Grant Program, 1980—, director, master of marine affairs program, 1982—. *Military service:* U.S. Army, Intelligence, 1957-58. *Member:* International Studies Association, American Political Science Association, American Society of International Laws, Marine Technology Society. *Awards, honors:* American Council of Learned Societies grant, 1962; Purdue University research grants, 1963, 1964; Center for Naval Analyses fellowship, 1971-72; National Science Foundation grant, 1974-75; Office of Naval Research grant, 1978-80.

WRITINGS: The Seattle General Strike, University of Washington Press, 1964; *Offshore Boundaries and Zones,* Ohio State University Press, 1967; (co-author) *The Navy and the Common Sea,* U.S. Government Printing Office, 1972; (co-author) *Forecasting Outcome of Multilateral Negotiations,* Center for Naval Affairs, Volume I, 1977; (co-author and editor) *Managing Ocean Resources,* Westview, 1979; (co-author and editor) *Making Marine Policy,* Westview, 1981; (co-author) *Japan and the New Ocean Regime,* Westview, 1984. Also author of numerous studies for Center for Naval Analyses.

Contributor: L. Alexander, editor, *The Law of the Sea,* Ohio State University Press, 1967; *Pacem in Maribus,* Royal University Press of Malta, 1971; George H. Quester, editor, *Readings on International Politics,* Little, Brown, 1971; Robert Jordan, editor, *Multinational Cooperation: Economic, Social and Scientific Development,* Oxford University Press, 1972; John Lawrence Hargrove, editor, *Who Protects the Ocean?,* West Publishing, 1975; Michael MacGuire, Ken Booth, and John McDonnell, editors, *Soviet Naval Policy, Objectives, and Constraints,* Praeger, 1975; Don Walsh, editor, *Law of the Sea: Issues in Ocean Resource Management,* Praeger, 1977; J. Schmidhauser and J. Totten, editors, *The Whaling Issue in U.S.-Japanese Relations,* Westview, 1978.

Also contributor to *Monograph Series in World Affairs,* University of Denver Press, 1968-69, and to proceedings of the twelfth conference of the Law of the Sea Institute, in Honolulu, Hawaii, 1979. Contributor of reviews and articles on labor and international diplomacy to numerous periodicals, including *Pacific Northwest Quarterly, World Politics, Environmental Management, Ocean Development and International Law,* and *Journal of Maritime Law and Commerce.*

* * *

FRIEDRICH, Paul 1927-

PERSONAL: Born October 22, 1927, in Cambridge, Mass.; son of Carl Joachim and Lenore (Pelham) Friedrich; married Lore Enig, January 9, 1950; married Margaret Hardin (a college professor), February 26, 1966; married Deborah Gordon, August 9, 1975; children: (first marriage) Maria Elizabeth, Susan Guadalupe, Peter Roland; (second marriage) Kanya. *Educa-*

tion: Harvard University, B.A., 1950, M.A., 1951; Yale University, Ph.D., 1957. *Home:* 5550 South Dorchester, Chicago, Ill. 60637. *Office:* Department of Anthropology, University of Chicago, 1126 East 59th, Chicago, Ill. 60637.

CAREER: University of Connecticut, Storrs, instructor in anthropology and sociology, 1956-57; Harvard University, Cambridge, Mass., instructor in anthropology, 1957-58; Deccan College, Poona, India, junior linguistic scholar, 1958-59; University of Pennsylvania, Philadelphia, assistant professor of anthropology and linguistics, 1959-62; University of Chicago, Chicago, Ill., associate professor, 1962-67, professor of anthropology and linguistics, 1967—. Associate professor of linguistics, University of Michigan, summers, 1960, 1961, and University of Indiana, summer, 1964. *Military service:* U.S. Army, 1946-47. *Member:* Linguistic Society of America, American Anthropological Association. *Awards, honors:* Social Science Research Council fellow in Mexico, 1966-67; Guggenheim fellow, 1982-83.

WRITINGS: On the Meaning of the Tarascan Suffixes of Space, published with *On the Classification in the Athapascan, Eyak, and the Tlingit Verb* by Michael E. Krauss, Waverly, 1969; *Agrarian Revolt in a Mexican Village,* Prentice-Hall, 1970, revised edition, University of Chicago Press, 1977; *Proto-Indo-European Trees: The Arboreal System of a Prehistoric People,* University of Chicago Press, 1970; *The Tarascan Suffixes of Locative Space: Meaning and Morphotactics,* Indiana University Press, 1971; *On Aspect Theory and Homeric Aspect,* published with *Dialectal Developments in Chinookian Tense-Aspect Systems: An Aural-Historical Analysis* by Michael Silverstein, University of Chicago Press, 1974; *A Phonology of Tarascan,* Department of Anthropology, University of Chicago, 1975; *Proto-Indo-European Syntax,* Journal of Indo-European Studies, 1975.

Neighboring Leaves Ride This Wind (poems), Friedrich, 1976; *The Meaning of Aphrodite,* University of Chicago Press, 1978; *Bastard Moons* (poems), Friedrich, 1978, revised edition, Benjamin and Martha Waite Press, 1979; *Language, Context, and the Imagination,* introduction by Anwar S. Dil, Stanford University Press, 1979; (with Dell Hymes and Joseph Greenberg) *On Linguistic Anthropology: Essays in Honor of Harry Hoijer, 1979,* edited by Jacques Maquet, Udena, 1980. Also author of *Tarascan: From Meaning to Sound.*

WORK IN PROGRESS: Researching poetics and various aspects of linguistics; work on another volume of poetry.

SIDELIGHTS: Paul Friedrich has competence in Spanish, Greek, German, Russian, and Tarascan, and reads French and several other languages.

* * *

FUCHS, Lucy 1935-

PERSONAL: Born April 13, 1935, in Ohio; daughter of Frank X. (a machinist) and Mary (Honigford) Weber; married Frank J. Fuchs (a teacher), August 14, 1971. *Education:* University of Dayton, B.S., 1961; Ohio State University, M.A., 1967; Florida State University, M.S., 1973; University of South Florida, Ph.D., 1984. *Politics:* Democrat. *Religion:* Roman Catholic. *Home and office:* 505 South Oakwood Ave., Brandon, Fla. 33511.

CAREER: High school French teacher in Cincinnati, Ohio, 1966-69; Florida State University, Tallahassee, counselor, 1969-71; social worker in Tampa, Fla., 1971-73; Hillsborough County

Elementary School, Hillsborough, Fla., teacher, beginning 1974; St. Leo College, St. Leo, Fla., professor, 1980—. Instructor in sociology and French at Hillsborough Community College, 1972—. *Member:* International Reading Association.

WRITINGS—All published by Bouregy: *Wild Winds of Mayaland* (novel), 1978; *Dangerous Splendor,* 1978; *Shadow of the Walls,* 1980; *Pictures of Fear,* 1981. Also author of three school workbooks. Contributor of numerous articles and children's stories to education and religion periodicals and children's magazines, including *Highlights for Children, Primary Treasure,* and *Our Little Friend.*

WORK IN PROGRESS: A novel; a nonfiction book.

SIDELIGHTS: Lucy Fuchs comments: "I write because I am not happy when I am not writing. I have learned very much from other writers, both through personal conversations and from publications of writers, such as the magazines for writers. I am interested in just about everything, especially people as they relate to each other."

AVOCATIONAL INTERESTS: Travel, religion, reading, crafts, gardening, cooking.

* * *

FULLER, R(ichard) Buckminster (Jr.) 1895-1983

PERSONAL: Born July 12, 1895, in Milton, Mass.; died of a heart attack, July 1, 1983, in Los Angeles, Calif.; son of Richard Buckminster (a merchant) and Caroline Wolcott (Andrews) Fuller; married Anne Hewlett, July 12, 1917 (died July, 1983); children: Alexandra Willets (deceased), Allegra (Mrs. Robert Snyder). *Education:* Attended Harvard University, 1913-15, and U.S. Naval Academy, 1917. *Home:* 200 Locust, Philadelphia, Pa. 19106. *Office address:* P.O. Box 696, Edwardsville, Ill. 62025.

CAREER: Writer and lecturer. Richards, Atkinson & Kaserick, Boston, Mass., apprentice machine fitter, 1914; Armour & Co., New York, N.Y., apprentice, 1915-17, assistant export manager, 1919-21; national account sales manager, Kelly Springfield Truck Co., 1922; president, Stockade Building System, 1922-27; 4-D Co., Chicago, Ill., founder, 1927, president, 1927-32; assistant director of research, Pierce Foundation-American Radiator-Standard Sanitary Manufacturing Co., 1930; Dymaxion Corp., Bridgeport, Conn., founder, 1932, director and chief engineer, 1932-36, vice-president and chief engineer, 1941-42; assistant to director of research and development, Phelps Dodge Corp., 1936-38; technical consultant, *Fortune* magazine, 1938-40.

Chief of mechanical engineering section, Board of Economic Warfare, 1942-44; special assistant to director, Foreign Economic Administration, 1944; chairman of board and administrative engineer, Dymaxion Dwelling Machines, 1944-46; Fuller Research Foundation, Wichita, Kan., chairman of board of trustees, 1946-54; president, Geodesics, Inc., 1954-56; Synergetics, Inc., Raleigh, N.C., president, 1954-59; Southern Illinois University, Carbondale, 1956-83, began as research professor, became professor emeritus; Plydomes, Inc., Des Moines, Iowa, president, beginning 1957; Tetrahelix Corp., Hamilton, Ohio, chairman of board, beginning 1959. Chairman of board, Buckminster Fuller Institute, beginning 1959; trustee, Research and Design Institute, 1966; director, Temcor Corporation, 1967; University of Detroit, Detroit, Mich., R. Buckminster Fuller Professor of Architecture, beginning 1970.

Trowbridge Lecturer, Yale University, 1955; Hill Foundation Lecturer, St. Olaf's College, 1957; Lorado Taft Lecturer, University of Illinois, 1960; Charles Eliot Norton Professor of Poetry, Harvard University, 1961-62; Ullman Lecturer, Brandeis University, 1962; San Jose State College, visiting professor of engineering, 1966, world fellow in residence, University City Science Center, beginning 1972; visiting professor, Iowa State University, 1966; visiting professor or lecturer at many universities around the world. U.S. representative to American-Russian Protocol Exchange, U.S.S.R., 1959.

Consultant to Time, Inc., 1938-40, Ford Foundation and Calcutta (India) Planning Organization, beginning 1961, governor of North Carolina, beginning 1962, Space Science Laboratory of General Electric, 1963, U.S. Steel Space Team, 1964, John Deere and Co., 1964, American Association of University Women, 1965, NASA and ASTRA, beginning 1965, and U.S. Institute of Behavioral Research, beginning 1965. Director of Oceanographic Study, New York, N.Y.; member of board of trustees, New York Cancer Research Institute, beginning 1964, and International Corporation, beginning 1964; member of board of trustees of overseers in art, Brandeis University, beginning 1965; architect/trustee for "Denationalized World Man Territory," Cyprus, beginning 1966; president of board of directors, Harmony Hill Music Foundation, beginning 1966; member of council, Internal Advisory Council of the National Pollution Control Foundation, 1966. *Military service:* U.S. Navy, 1917-19; became lieutenant.

MEMBER: World Academy of Art and Science (fellow), World Society for Ekistics (vice-president; international president, 1975-77), International Society for Stereology, Royal Society of Arts (Benjamin Franklin life fellow), Royal Institute of British Architects, Society of Venezuelan Architects, Mexican College and Institute of Architects, Institute for Advanced Philosophic Research, Mensa (international president, 1975-83), Institute of General Semantics (fellow and honorary trustee), Institute of Human Ecology, American Association for the Advancement of Science (life fellow), American Institute of Architects (honorary life member), National Academy of Sciences (member of Building Research Institute), National Institute of Arts and Letters (life member), American Society of Professional Geographers, American Association of University Professors, American Academy of Arts and Letters (academician, 1980), American Society for Metals, Society of Architectural Historians, Harvard Engineering Society, Lincoln Academy of Illinois, Architectural League of New York, Phi Beta Kappa, Sigma Xi, Alpha Rho Chi, Tau Sigma Delta, Century Club (New York), New York Yacht Club, Northeast Harbor Fleet, Camden Yacht Club, Somerset Club (Boston), Authors Club (London).

AWARDS, HONORS: Award of merit from New York chapter of American Institute of Architects, 1952; Award of merit from U.S. Marine Corps, 1954; Gran Premio, Trienniale de Milano, 1954, 1957; Centennial Award, Michigan State University, 1955; gold medal scarab, National Architectural Society, 1958; gold medal, Philadelphia chapter of American Institute of Architects, 1960; Frank P. Brown Medal, Franklin Institute, 1960; Allied Professions gold medal, American Institute of Architects, 1963; Plomade de Oro Award, Society of Mexican Architects, 1963; Brandeis University Special Notable Creative Achievement Award of the Year, 1964; Delta Phi Delta Gold Key Laureate, 1964; Industrial Designers Society of America Award of Excellence, 1966; Graham Foundation fellow, 1966-67; Lincoln Academy of Illinois, fellow and Order of Lincoln Medal, 1967; gold medal, National Institute of Arts and Letters, 1968; named Humanist of the Year, American Association of Humanists, 1969; Dean's Award, State University of New York, 1980; named to Housing Hall of Fame, 1981; Presidential Medal of Freedom, 1983.

Recipient of about forty honorary doctorate degrees, including: Dr. Design, University of North Carolina, 1954; Dr. Arts, University of Michigan, 1955; D.Sc., Washington University, 1957, University of Colorado, 1964; Doctor of Fine Arts, Southern Illinois University, 1959, University of New Mexico, 1964; H.H.D., Rollins College, 1960; Doctor of Letters, Clemson University, 1964; Doctor of Humane Letters, Monmouth College, 1965, Long Island University, 1966; Doctor of Engineering, Clarkson College, 1967. "Buckminster Fuller Recognition Day" declared by University of Colorado, 1963, state of Massachusetts, 1977, cities of Boston and Cambridge, 1977, state of Minnesota, 1978, state of Illinois, 1980, city of Buffalo, 1980, city of Austin, 1981.

WRITINGS: *4D Time-Lock*, privately printed, 1927, reprinted, N.M. Lama Foundation, 1972; *Nine Chains to the Moon*, Lippincott, 1938, reprinted, Doubleday, 1971; (with others) *New Worlds in Engineering*, Chrysler Co., 1940; *Industrialization of Brazil*, Board of Economic Warfare, 1943; *Survey of the Industrialization of Housing*, U.S. Foreign Economics Administration, 1944.

Geoscope—1960, edited by James Robert Hillier, Princeton University, 1960; *New Approaches to Structure*, [Washington, D.C.], 1961; *Untitled Epic Poem of the History of Industrialization*, Jonathon Williams, 1962; *No More Second Hand God, and Other Writings*, Southern Illinois University Press, 1963; *Ideas and Integrities: A Spontaneous Autobiographical Disclosure*, edited by Robert W. Marks, Prentice-Hall, 1963; *Education Automation: Freeing the Scholar to Return to His Studies*, Southern Illinois University Press, 1963; *Charles Eliot Norton 1961-62 Lectures at Harvard University*, Harvard University Press, 1963; *Governor's Conference with Buckminster Fuller*, Governor's Office (Raleigh), 1963; (with John McHale) *World Design Science Decade, 1965-1975: Inventory of World Resources, Human Trends and Needs—Phase 1 of 5 Two-year Increments of World Retooling Design Decade Proposed to the International Union of Architects*, Southern Illinois University, 1963; (with McHale) *World Resources Inventory, Human Trends and Needs*, Southern Illinois University, 1963; *World Design Science Decade, 1965-1975: The Design Initiative* (includes phase 1, [1964], document 2, also brief outlines of phases 2, 3, 4, and 5), Southern Illinois University, 1964.

Comprehensive Thinking, edited by McHale, Southern Illinois University, 1965; *What I Am Trying to Do*, Cape Goliard, 1968; (author of foreword) Isamu Noguchi, *A Sculptor's World*, Harper, 1968; (contributor) Richard Kostelanetz, editor, *Beyond Left and Right: Radical Thought for Our Times*, Morrow, 1968; *Operating Manual for Spaceship Earth*, Southern Illinois University Press, 1969; (with others) *The Arts and Man*, Prentice-Hall, 1969; *Utopia or Oblivion: The Prospects for Humanity*, Bantam, 1969; *Reprints and Selected Articles*, Bern Porter, 1969; *Planetary Planning*, Jawaharlal Nehru Memorial Fund, 1969; *Fifty Years of the Design Science Revolution and the World Game: A Collection of Articles and Papers on Design*, Southern Illinois University, 1969.

(With others) *Approaching the Benign Environment: The Franklin Lectures in the Sciences and Humanities*, University of Alabama Press, 1970; *I Seem to Be a Verb*, Bantam, 1970; (author of introduction) Samuel Rosenberg, *The Come As You Are Masquerade Party*, Prentice-Hall, 1970; *The Buckminster Fuller Reader*, edited by James Miller, J. Cape, 1970; *The World Game: Integrative Resource Utilization Planning Tool*, Southern Illinois University, 1971; *Old Man River: An Environmental Domed City*, Parsimonious Press, 1972; (editor with Henry Dreyfuss) *Symbol Sourcebook: An Authoritative Guide to International Graphic Symbols*, McGraw, 1972; *Intuition*, Doubleday, 1972, second revised edition, Impact, 1983; *Buckminster Fuller to Children of Earth*, Doubleday, 1972; *Earth, Inc.*, Doubleday-Anchor, 1973; (with Robert W. Marks) *The Dymaxion World of Buckminster Fuller*, Doubleday, 1973; *Synergetics: Explorations in the Geometry of Thinking*, Macmillan, 1975; *And It Came to Pass—Not to Stay*, Macmillan, 1976; (with Edgar J. Applewhite) *Synergetics Two: Explorations in the Geometry of Thinking*, Macmillan, 1979; *R. Buckminster Fuller on Education*, edited by Robert D. Kahn and Peter H. Wagschal, University of Massachusetts Press, 1979.

(With Kiyoshi Kuromiya) *Critical Path*, St. Martin's, 1981; *Tetrascroll*, St. Martin's, 1982; *Grunch of Giants*, St. Martin's, 1983. Also produced recordings "Designing Environments," Big Sur Recordings, 1976, "Anticipating Tomorrow's Schools," [Philadelphia], 1975, and "R. Buckminster Fuller Thinks Aloud," Credo 2. Contributor to journals. Editor, *Convoy* (magazine), 1918-19; publisher, *Shelter* (magazine), 1931-32; editor and author, "Notes on the Future" column, *Saturday Review*, beginning 1964.

SIDELIGHTS: In 1927, when he was thirty-two years old, Richard Buckminster ("Bucky") Fuller, Jr., stood at the shores of Lake Michigan and contemplated whether to take his life. Despondent over the death of his four-year-old daughter, in disgrace with his family because he was the first Fuller in five generations to have been expelled (twice) from Harvard University, the young man had also just lost his job and was a debt-ridden alcohol abuser. As he would later recall, Fuller paused for a while at the lake's edge on "a jump-or-think basis." The answer came to him, as a *New York Times* article reported, when Fuller realized that "you do not have the right to eliminate yourself. You do not belong to you. You belong to the universe." With that, Fuller turned from the shore and embarked on what would become an illustrious career as one of America's most innovative engineers and inventors, as well as a noted philosopher, poet, educator, and environmentalist.

Best known for his invention of the geodesic dome, the self-described "citizen of the twenty-first century" was a major exponent of using science to improve life on what he coined Spaceship Earth. Acclaim, even acceptance, did not come easily at first; early in his career Fuller was regarded by some as a crackpot because of such utopian inventions as the Dymaxion House, a fully self-sufficient dwelling capable of being built on a pre-fab basis, and the Dymaxion Bathroom, the whole of which could be produced *en masse*, like an auto body. Perhaps the most controversial of these early innovations was the Dymaxion Car. Built in the 1930s, the car was an egg-shaped three-wheeler which could get 40 miles per gallon and reach speeds of up to 120 miles per hour. The promising prototype succumbed to poor publicity after a 1935 accident in which, as the *New York Times* stated, "one of the cars collided with a sedan in Chicago and both vehicles overturned. By the time reporters arrived, the other car . . . had been towed away. The driver of the Dymaxion car was killed, and under such headlines as 'Three Wheeled Car Kills Driver,' newspaper accounts did not mention that another car had been involved."

Despite such setbacks, Fuller's enthusiasm for Dymaxion products (the word is an amalgam of "dynamic," "maximum" [efficiency], and "ion" [of power]) and other futuristic concepts continued unabated. And while the tide of public approval began to turn his way with the production of the Dymaxion Ariocean World Map, the first flat chart that displayed the entire surface of the earth without distortion, Fuller's reputation as an engineer of vision was cemented with the 1947 unveiling of the geodesic dome.

Defining geodesic as "the most economical momentary relationship among a plurality of points and events," the self-taught architect had designed that rare thing—a "structure [that] occurs in nature and can be built by man," according to the *New York Times*. The dome is "as self-sufficient as a butterfly's wing and as strong as an egg shell," the *Times* continued. "It depends on no heavy vaults or flying buttresses to support it. Its strength is derived instead from a complex of alternating squares and triangles which produce a phenomenal strength-to-weight ratio when pressure is applied to any point on the structure. It crops up all over in nature—in viruses, in the cornea of the eye. Fuller patented it in 1953—almost like getting a patent on gravity." Within a short time of its introduction, the geodesic dome was being used as everything from a cover for an automobile plant to a hangar for a Marine Corps helicopter station. "Radomes" housed radar equipment along miles of the Distant Early Warning Lines in the Arctic. Russian premier Nikita Khruschev was impressed by the structure and invited its inventor—"Mr. J. Buckingham Fuller"—to lecture to Soviet engineers.

Indeed, lecturing and generally promoting the wonders of the new technological age were as important to Fuller as were any of his other projects. America's countercultural youth of the 1960s were especially attracted to the scientist-philosopher, who championed the environment with his energy-efficient designs. In a 1970 *Saturday Review* article, Harold Taylor explained further Fuller's popularity with the young: "[They] are . . . prepared to accept the fact that the very conception of wealth as accumulation of capital is in the present circumstances obsolete, and that wealth is to be measured not by the amounts of money in banks but [, as Fuller insisted,] by the amounts of energy, physical and mental, that are available to solve the problem of making the world work for its inhabitants." The philosopher himself stated this idea more flatly in a 1976 *New York Times Magazine* profile: "There is no energy shortage. There is no energy crisis. There is a crisis of ignorance."

As an author, Fuller often described a technological utopia waiting for those willing to shed the old ideas about science and society. A passage from his study *Synergetics: Explanations in the Geometry of Thinking*, for instance, predicts a future "moving intuitively toward an utterly classless, raceless, omnicooperative, omniworld humanity." Naturally, some critics took exception to this kind of speculation; Robert Wood and O. B. Hardison, Jr. found *Synergetics* an engrossing if somewhat difficult read. Wood, writing in *Saturday Review*, was "exasperated" by the book's "approach to evidence and validation. . . . [The author] interweaves strangely disparate elements: fact and value, commentary on life and the universe, quantity and quality, evidence and inference. And he does this majestically, carelessly, in a manner calculated to infuriate the conscientious scholar in whatever field he happens to be writing about." However, the critic suggested that the sheer weight of Fuller's arguments (the book runs almost 900 pages) and the enthusiasm with which he expressed them made the work valuable. The author, concluded Wood, infused his book with "a genuinely American idiom, of liberalism and expansion and progress. So *Synergetics* is best *read*, not studied. But this reading should be done in 'takes,' with time in between for contemplation. Fuller's work is best understood as a special celebration of the American experience and as such, it deserves our heartfelt appreciation."

New York Times Book Review critic Hardison called *Synergetics* "a kind of *summa theologica* of Fuller's mathematics, philosophy and design theories." Citing the numerous graphs, charts, and equations the author included in the work, Hardison remarked that as a reader "you grope for analogies. The Notebooks of Leonardo. The Opera of Paracelsus. Pascal's *Pensees*. Or Alexander Pope's remark about Creation: 'A mighty maze, but not without a plan.' [The book] is alternately brilliant and obscure, opaque and shot through with moments of poetry. What becomes clear with patience is that the virtues and the liabilities are one. *Synergetics* could not have been written in any other way because its language and mathematics are vehicles for a vision. They embody the vision and if they were different the vision itself would be different—perhaps impossible to express, but certainly impossible to express convincingly."

One of the last major books published before his death, Fuller's *Critical Path* was called by its author "by far the most important thing" he had ever done, according to Guy Murchie in the *Chicago Tribune Book World*. Essentially a long-range plan for the revitalization of Spaceship Earth, *Critical Path* employs some of the author's most startling scientific views, as well as an admonishment for its readers to stop being wary of technology and to start appreciating the potential gifts that science offers. For instance, Fuller wrote that the "most effective educational system for human beings . . . is to be derived from the home video cassette system and supporting books, the pages of which are also to be called forth on world-satellite-interlinked video 'library' screens as published in any language." "Some will consider . . . *Critical Path* too far up in the clouds for practical use because they are biased against technology," stated Murchie, "but if they could only let themselves consider his message with a fully open mind, I think they just might discover something profoundly spiritual there."

Shortly after Fuller's death, Norman Cousins had this to say about the futurist in *Saturday Review*: "The great poets have attempted to describe the human mind and spirit, but I doubt that any of them have done so more provocatively than Bucky. The reason perhaps is that Bucky was not only inspired and nourished by the weightless and all-embracing entity called the human mind, but he had a way of opening our minds to the phenomena within them. In this way, he introduced us to ourselves."

BIOGRAPHICAL/CRITICAL SOURCES—Books: Buckminster Fuller and Robert W. Marks, *The Dymaxion World of Buckminster Fuller*, Reinhold, 1960; John McHale, *R. Buckminster Fuller*, Braziller, 1962; Sidney Rosen, *Wizard of the Dome: R. Buckminster Fuller, Designer for the Future*, Little, Brown, 1969; Hugh Kenner, *Bucky: A Guided Tour of Buckminster Fuller*, Morrow, 1973; Alden Hatch, *Buckminster Fuller: At Home in the Universe*, Crown, 1974; G. W. Close, *R. Buckminster Fuller*, Council of Planning Libraries, 1977; Athena V. Lord, *Pilot for Spaceship Earth: R. Buckminster Fuller, Architect, Inventor and Poet* (for juveniles), Macmillan, 1978; R. Snyder, editor, *R. Buckminster Fuller*, St. Martin's, 1980.

Periodicals: *Business Week*, May 10, 1958; *Time*, October 20, 1958, January 10, 1964, March 10, 1967, March 1, 1968, May 11, 1970; *Newsweek*, July 13, 1959, August 5, 1963; *New*

York Times Magazine, August 23, 1959, April 23, 1967, July 6, 1975; New Yorker, October 10, 1959; New York Times Book Review, July 28, 1963, May 5, 1968, April 20, 1969, June 29, 1975, April 19, 1981, July 17, 1983; Architectural Forum, October, 1963; Times Literary Supplement, September 6, 1963, August 6, 1964, September 11, 1969, October 28, 1983; Science Digest, October, 1964; Horizon, summer, 1968; Saturday Review, May 2, 1970, May 31, 1975, September-October, 1983; Washington Post, June 10, 1970; Nation, June 15, 1970; Life, February 26, 1971; New York Times, August 28, 1978; People, July 21, 1980; Chicago Tribune Book World, March 22, 1981; Los Angeles Times Book Review, April 26, 1981, September 19, 1982; Times (London), April 14, 1983; National Review, July 22, 1983.

OBITUARIES: New York Times, July 3, 1983; Washington Post, July 3, 1983; Times (London), July 4, 1983; Newsweek, July 11, 1983; Time, July 11, 1983.†

—Sketch by Susan Salter

* * *

FURMAN, Eleanor L. 1913-
   (Eleanor L. Fried)

PERSONAL: Born February 20, 1913, in New York, N.Y.; married second husband, Sylvan S. Furman (assistant commissioner of New York State Department of Mental Hygiene), 1961; children: (first marriage) Ellen J. Sklar; stepchildren: Emily, Laura, Hester. Education: Barnard College, B.A., 1933. Home: 680 West End Ave., New York, N.Y. 10025; and R.D. 2, West Stockbridge, Mass. 01266.

CAREER: Fashion Institute of Technology, New York, N.Y., director of placement, 1947-73, professor emeritus, 1973—.

Secretary-treasurer and member of board, Bill of Rights Foundation. Member: National Vocational Guidance Association, American College Personnel Association, Personnel Association of New York.

WRITINGS: (Under name Eleanor L. Fried) Is the Fashion Business Your Business?, Fairchild, 1958, 3rd edition, 1970; (under name Eleanor L. Fried; with Catherine Avent) Starting Work, Parrish, 1965; Retirement: You're in Charge, Praeger, 1984. Editor, MVAC Newsletter.

* * *

FURST, Alan 1941-

PERSONAL: Born February 20, 1941, in New York, N.Y. Education: Oberlin College, A.B., 1962; Pennsylvania State University, M.A., 1967. Agent: Melanie Jackson, Suite 2805, 1500 Broadway, New York, N.Y. 10036.

CAREER: Writer. Awards, honors: Fulbright fellowship, 1969-70.

WRITINGS—Novels: Your Day in the Barrel, Atheneum, 1976; The Paris Drop, Doubleday, 1980; The Caribbean Account, Delacorte, 1981; Shadow Trade, Delacorte, 1983.

Contributor to Esquire.

WORK IN PROGRESS: A novel.

BIOGRAPHICAL/CRITICAL SOURCES: New York Times Book Review, February 3, 1980, November 1, 1981; Los Angeles Times Book Review, April 27, 1980; Best Sellers, October, 1981.

G

GALLOWAY, Joseph L(ee) 1941-

PERSONAL: Born November 13, 1941, in Bryan, Tex.; son of Joseph L. and Marian (Dewvall) Galloway; married Theresa Null, September 9, 1966; children: Lee Tyler, Joshua Joseph. *Education:* Attended Victoria College, 1959. *Residence:* Bayside, Tex. *Office:* U.S. News and World Report, 2400 N St. N.W., Washington, D.C. 20037.

CAREER/WRITINGS: Victoria Advocate, Victoria, Tex., reporter, 1959-61; United Press International, New York, N.Y., reporter in Kansas City, Mo., 1961, capital correspondent in Topeka, Kan., 1962-64, war correspondent in Saigon, 1965-66, editor in Tokyo, Japan, 1967, manager in Jakarta, Indonesia, 1968-73, manager for South Asia, New Delhi, 1973-74, manager for Southeast Asia, Singapore, 1974-75, bureau manager in Moscow, 1976-79, manager in Los Angeles, Calif., 1980-83; *U.S. News and World Report,* Washington, D.C., West Coast manager in Los Angeles, 1983-84, special assignment writer in Washington, D.C., 1984—. Member, advisory board, Los Angeles City College journalism department. Notable assignments include coverage of war in Indochina, India-Pakistan War of 1971, student uprisings in Sri Lanka, 1971, Moscow dissident trials, 1979, and Carter-Brezhnev summit in Vienna, 1979.

MEMBER: Foreign Correspondents Association (president in Indonesia, 1973), Foreign Correspondents of Southeast Asia, Press Club of India, Marine Corps Combat Correspondents Association, Foreign Correspondents Club of Tokyo, Greater Los Angeles Press Club, Sigma Delta Chi.

SIDELIGHTS: Joseph L. Galloway told *CA:* "Never have quite understood why *CA* invited a plowhorse to share these pages with such a collection of skittish thoroughbreds. Still don't. As to why I do what I do, I was born curious and no other profession licenses curiosity so readily as does journalism. Being a reporter, as one of my colleagues commented, certainly beats growing up. Well said and as good a reason for doing it as any I have heard.

"Another colleague and beloved friend, who disappeared into a North Vietnamese prison camp in Cambodia in 1971 and is listed as missing/presumed dead, added another short explanation of it all: Vietnam was what we had instead of happy childhoods.

"One is not invited to become maudlin in such short space, but in Indochina we learned to mourn almost before we had learned to love, burying the best and brightest of a generation of young reporters, photographers and, yes, those we covered, the soldiers who shared foxholes and food and bad water and fears.

"Two old men I had the honor to know, interview, and cover as a kid reporter—Harry Truman of Independence, Mo. and Alf M. Landon of Topeka, Kan.—sent me out into the world from the Midwest with strict orders to look, listen, and learn. Fifteen years passed before I considered that I had done enough to satisfy their injunctions and come home.

"My ears ring with the cries of the dying, the shouts of triumph, the murmurs of small joys, the thundering defiance of Anatoly Shcharansky judging those who dared try to judge him, the shuffle of boots going into battle and bare feet fleeing it. My job is to remember it and share it, that none of it, even the most senseless parts of it, be lost or have been done in vain.

"Finally, now having sons four and six years old, I have given hostages to the world of 2050 and even beyond, and I hope to pass on to them a world certainly no worse for what I have done and learned and perhaps one that even is better."

* * *

GAMBLE, Andrew (Michael) 1947-

PERSONAL: Born August 15, 1947, in London, England; son of Marcus Elkington (a company director) and Joan (Westall) Gamble; married Christine Jennifer Rodway (a social worker), June 15, 1974; children: Tom, Corinna, Sarah. *Education:* Cambridge University, B.A., 1968, Ph.D., 1975; University of Durham, M.A., 1969. *Home:* 193 Rustlings Rd., Sheffield S11 7AD, England. *Office:* Department of Political Theory and Institutions, University of Sheffield, Sheffield S10 2TN, England.

CAREER: University of Sheffield, Sheffield, England, lecturer, 1973-82, reader in political economy and political theory, 1982—. *Member:* Political Studies Association. *Awards, honors:* Isaac Deutscher Memorial Prize, 1972, for *From Alienation to Surplus Value;* Mitchell Prize, 1977.

WRITINGS: (With Paul Walton) *From Alienation to Surplus Value,* Sheed, 1972; *The Conservative Nation,* Routledge &

Kegan Paul, 1974; (with Walton) *Capitalism in Crisis: Inflation and the State,* Macmillan, 1976; *Britain in Decline,* Beacon Press, 1981; *Introduction to Modern Social and Political Thought,* Macmillan, 1981; (with Stuart Walkland) *The Party System and Economic Policy,* Oxford University Press, 1984.

Contributor: H. M. Drucker, editor, *Multi-Party Politics,* Macmillan, 1979; A. Layton-Henry, editor, *Conservative Party Politics,* Macmillan, 1980; J. Barry Jones, editor, *Perspectives on Political Economy,* Frances Pinter, 1983; V. Bogdanor, editor, *Liberal Party Politics,* Oxford University Press, 1983; Stuart Hall and Martin Jacques, editors, *The Politics of Thatcherism,* Lawrence & Wishart, 1983; David Coates and Gordon Johnston, editors, *Socialist Arguments,* Martin Robertson, 1983; Drucker, editor, *Developments in British Politics,* Macmillan, 1983.

WORK IN PROGRESS: Thatcherism and the British State, for Macmillan.

SIDELIGHTS: Andrew Gamble told *CA:* "My recent work has focused on the rise of the New Right in Britain, the nature of 'Thatcherism' and problems of political economy. Making things comprehensible to as many people as possible is what matters most to me in my writing. My outlook on most things was permanently transformed by being at university during the extraordinary years of the late 1960s."

AVOCATIONAL INTERESTS: "The fortunes of Sheffield United Football Club," the music of Bob Dylan.

* * *

GANDLEY, Kenneth Royce 1920-
(Oliver Jacks, Kenneth Royce)

PERSONAL: Born December 11, 1920, in Croyden, England; son of John Mathew and Ethel (Saunders) Gandley; married Stella Amy Parker (an editor), March 16, 1946. *Education:* Self-educated. *Religion:* Church of England. *Home and office:* 3, Abbotts Close, Abbotts Ann, Andover, Hampshire, England. *Agent:* David Higham Associates, 5-8 Lower John St., Golden Sq., London W1R 4HA, England.

CAREER: Business and Holiday Travel, London, England, managing director, 1948-72, member of board of directors, 1948—; full-time writer, 1972—. *Military service:* British Army, Infantry, 1939-46; served in Africa; became captain. *Member:* Crime Writers Association, Writers Action Group, Landsdown Club (London). *Awards, honors: The Third Arm* was named a best book of 1981 by the *New York Times; 10,000 Days* was named a best book of 1982 by the *London Daily Mail.*

WRITINGS—Mystery novels; under name Kenneth Royce: *My Turn to Die,* Barker, 1958; *The Soft Footed Moor,* Barker, 1959; *The Long Corridor,* Cassell, 1960; *No Paradise,* Cassell, 1961; *The Night Seekers,* Cassell, 1962; *The Angry Island,* Cassell, 1963; *The Day the Wind Dropped,* Cassell, 1964; *Bones in the Sand,* Cassell, 1967; *A Peck of Salt,* Cassell, 1968; *A Single to Hong Kong,* Hodder & Stoughton, 1969.

The XYY Man (book club selection), McKay, 1970; *The Concrete Boot* (book club selection), McKay, 1971; *The Miniatures Frame* (book club selection), Simon & Schuster, 1972; *The Masterpiece Affair* (book club selection), Simon & Schuster, 1973; *Spider Underground,* Hodder & Stoughton, 1973; *Trap Spider,* Hodder & Stoughton, 1974; *The Woodcutter Operation,* Simon & Schuster, 1975; *Bustillo,* Coward, 1976; *The Satan Touch* (book club selection), Hodder & Stoughton, 1979; *The Third Arm,* McGraw, 1980; *10,000 Days* (book club selection), McGraw, 1981; *Channel Assault,* McGraw, 1983.

Mystery novels; under pseudonym Oliver Jacks: *Man on a Short Leash,* Stein & Day, 1974; *Assassination Day,* Stein & Day, 1976; *Autumn Heroes,* Hodder & Stoughton, 1977, St. Martin's, 1978; *Implant,* Collins, 1981.

WORK IN PROGRESS: The Stalin Account, under Royce; *Breakout,* under Jacks.

SIDELIGHTS: Kenneth Royce Gandley is a prolific British mystery writer whose novels are marked by fast action and a taut, lively style. Writing in the *New York Times Book Review,* Newgate Callendar describes his book *The Third Arm* as "thoroughly believable; there is none of the amateur-besting-professional nonsense. And it is written in clean, flowing prose with some sharp dialogue."

Gandley told *CA* that he began writing "in halfpenny exercise books at the age twelve. I illustrated the stories myself and sold them for one penny—which only goes to show that I may have been an early starter at writing, but already I was a lousy businessman. But I still enjoy my writing. Seventy-five percent of my income from writing comes from outside my own country."

MEDIA ADAPTATIONS: The XYY Man, The Concrete Boot, The Masterpiece Affair, The Miniatures Frame, Trap Spider, and *The Woodcutter Operation* have all been adapted for television.

AVOCATIONAL INTERESTS: Travel, sports, jazz, antiques.

BIOGRAPHICAL/CRITICAL SOURCES: New York Times Book Review, October 17, 1971, May 4, 1975, September 5, 1976, December 26, 1976, April 30, 1978, June 8, 1980; *Washington Post Book World,* April 20, 1980.

* * *

GARD, Joyce
See REEVES, Joyce

* * *

GARFIELD, Sol L(ouis) 1918-

PERSONAL: Born January 8, 1918, in Chicago, Ill.; son of Julius (a grocer) and Rebecca (Friedman) Garfield; married Amy L. Nusbaum, December 25, 1945; children: Ann, Joan, Stanley, David. *Education:* Northwestern University, B.S., 1938, M.A., 1939, Ph.D., 1942. *Home:* 7030 Waterman Ave., University City, Mo. 63130. *Office:* Department of Psychology, Washington University, St. Louis, Mo. 63130.

CAREER: Veterans Administration, Mendota, Wis., chief psychologist, 1946-47, Mental Hygiene Clinic, Milwaukee, Wis., chief psychologist, 1949-51, Downey, Ill., chief of psychology service, 1951-57; University of Connecticut, Storrs, associate professor of psychology, 1947-49; University of Nebraska, College of Medicine, Omaha, associate professor, 1957-59, professor of medical psychology, 1959-63; Missouri Institute of Psychiatry, St. Louis, principal research scientist, 1963-64; Columbia University, Teachers College, New York, N.Y., professor of psychology, 1964-70; Washington University, St. Louis, Mo., professor of psychology, 1970—. Lecturer, Northwestern University, 1952-57. Consultant, Veterans Administration, 1958-76, National Institute of Mental Health, 1961-64 and 1982-86, Peace Corps, 1964-70. *Military service:* U.S. Army, 1942-46; became second lieutenant. *Member:* American Association for the Advancement of Science (fellow), American Psychological Association (fellow; president of Division of Clinical Psychology, 1965-66).

WRITINGS: *Introductory Clinical Psychology: An Overview of the Functions, Methods and Problems of Contemporary Clinical Psychology,* Macmillan, 1957; (editor with A. E. Bergin) *Handbook of Psychotherapy and Behavior Change: An Empirical Analysis,* Wiley, 1971, 2nd edition, 1978; *Clinical Psychology: The Study of Personality and Behavior,* Aldine, 1974, 2nd edition, 1983; *Psychology: An Eclectic Approach,* Wiley, 1980.

Contributor: A. Burton and R. E. Harris, editors, *Clinical Studies of Personality,* Harper, 1955; J. M. Wepman and R. W. Heine, editors, *Concepts of Personality,* Aldine, 1963; N. Ellis, editor, *Theory and Research in Mental Deficiency,* McGraw, 1963; B. B. Wolman, editor, *Handbook of Clinical Psychology,* McGraw, 1965; E. F. Hammer, editor, *Use of Interpretation in Treatment,* Grune, 1968.

Psychology of the Education Process, McGraw, 1970; A. Mahrer and L. Pearson, editors, *Creative Developments in Psychotherapy,* Press of Case Western Reserve University (Cleveland), 1971; A. S. Gurman and A. M. Razin, editors, *Effective Psychotherapy: A Handbook of Research,* Pergamon, 1977; A. E. Kazdin, A. S. Bellack, and M. Hersen, editors, *New Perspectives in Abnormal Psychology,* Oxford University Press, 1980; C. E. Walker, editor, *Clinical Practice of Psychology: A Practical Guide for Mental Health Professionals,* Pergamon, 1981; Wolman, editor, *The Therapist's Handbook,* 2nd edition, Van Nostrand, 1982.

Also contributor to *Quantitative Techniques for the Evaluation of the Behavior of Psychiatric Patients,* 1982, and *Clinical Psychology in Great Britain,* 1983.

Consulting editor, *Journal of Abnormal Psychology,* 1964-70; *Journal of Consulting and Clinical Psychology,* consulting editor, 1964-78, editor, 1979-84.

WORK IN PROGRESS: Preparing 3rd edition of *Handbook of Psychotherapy and Behavior Change,* for Wiley; preparing articles on psychology, psychotherapy, and related issues to contribute to texts.

* * *

GARNER, William 1920-

PERSONAL: Born in 1920, in Grimsby, Lincolnshire, England; married Gwen Owen, 1944. *Education:* University of Birmingham, B.Sc. (with honors), 1941. *Agent:* Roberta Pryor, International Creative Management, 40 West 57th St., New York, N.Y. 10019; and Elaine Greene Ltd., 31 Newington Green, London N16 9PU, England.

CAREER: Free-lance writer, London, England, 1947-49; public relations director, Monsanto Co., London, 1949-64, and Massey-Ferguson Ltd., Toronto, Ontario (corporate staff based in London), 1964-66; full-time novelist, 1967—. *Military service:* Royal Air Force, 1941-46; became flight lieutenant. *Member:* Writer's Guild of Great Britain.

WRITINGS: *Overkill,* New American Library, 1966; *The Deep, Deep Freeze,* Putnam, 1968; *The Us or Them War,* Putnam, 1969; *The Manipulators,* Bobbs-Merrill, 1970 (published in England as *The Puppet-Masters,* Collins, 1970); *Strip Jack Naked,* Bobbs-Merrill, 1971 (published in England as *The Andra Fiasco,* Collins, 1971); *Ditto, Brother Rat,* Collins, 1973; *A Big Enough Wreath,* Putnam, 1975; *The Moebius Trip,* Putnam, 1980; *Think Big, Think Dirty,* St. Martin's, 1983; *Rats' Alley,* Heinemann, 1984.

WORK IN PROGRESS: The third part of a trilogy of which *Think Big, Think Dirty* and *Rats' Alley* were the first and second parts.

SIDELIGHTS: William Garner's espionage novels have been translated into Japanese and Russian. He writes: "Strongly motivated. Views on almost everything that matters. Views on what matters might differ from those of many."

Film options have been sold on five of Garner's books.

BIOGRAPHICAL/CRITICAL SOURCES: *New York Times Book Review,* June 9, 1968, January 18, 1976; *Times Literary Supplement,* April 14, 1983.

* * *

GAROS, Stephanie
See KATZ, Steve

* * *

GARRETT, Gerald R. 1940-

PERSONAL: Born September 21, 1940, in Mount Vernon, Wash.; son of Kenneth J. and Odessa P. (Wells) Garrett; married Marcia Pope (a professor of sociology and a lawyer), June 10, 1967 (divorced June 10, 1976). *Education:* Whitman College, A.B., 1962; Washington State University, M.A., 1966, Ph.D., 1970. *Office:* Graduate Program in Applied Sociology, University of Massachusetts—Boston, Harbor Campus, Boston, Mass. 02125.

CAREER: University of Wisconsin, Whitewater, instructor in sociology, 1966-67; Carroll College, Waukesha, Wis., assistant professor of sociology, 1967-68; Washington State University, Pullman, research fellow in sociology, 1968-70; University of Massachusetts—Boston, Harbor Campus, Boston, professor of sociology, 1970—, director, Graduate Program in Applied Sociology, 1982—. Research associate at Columbia University, 1969, 1970; lecturer at University of Maryland, European Division, Heidelberg, Germany, 1976-77, and Boston University Overseas Programs, Seckenheim, West Germany, 1978—; visiting associate professor at Washington State University, 1977-78, and University of Alaska, Fairbanks, 1978; visiting professor, Troy State University/Europe, Wiesbaden, West Germany, 1978-79. Member of National Task Force on Higher Education and Criminal Justice, 1975-76.

MEMBER: Academy of Criminal Justice Sciences, Society for the Study of Social Problems (program chairman, 1980-81), American Sociological Association, American Society of Criminology, Eastern Sociological Society (program chairman, 1981-82), Northeastern Association of Criminal Justice Educators, Massachusetts Sociological Association.

WRITINGS: (With H. M. Bahr) *Disaffiliation among Urban Women,* Columbia, 1971; (with Bahr) *Women Alone,* Heath, 1976; (with Richard Rettig and Manuel J. Torres) *Manny: A Criminal-Addict's Story,* Houghton, 1977.

Contributor: Bahr, editor, *Skid Row: An Introduction to Disaffiliation,* Oxford University Press, 1973; Jack Kinton, editor, *Professionalization in America: Police Roles in the 1970's,* Social Science & Sociological Resources, 1975; Jack and Joann Delora, editors, *Intimate Life Styles,* Goodyear Publishing, 1976; Joseph Scott and Simon Dinitz, editors, *Criminal Justice Planning,* Praeger, 1978; E. J. Hunter and Steven Nice, editors, *Military Families: Adaptation to Stress,* Praeger, 1979; C. Ford and J. Eddy, editors, *Women and Alcohol,* W. C. Brown, 1980;

C. Larson, *Crime, Correction and Society,* General Hall, 1984. Contributor to numerous professional journals.

WORK IN PROGRESS: Research on alcoholism in women, alcohol problems in the military, alcohol prevention and education, and correctional education; evaluations research; two book manuscripts, *Alcohol and Social Life* and *The Natural History of a Policeman's Career.*

* * *

GAVRON, Daniel 1935-

PERSONAL: Born December 7, 1935, in London, England; son of Nathan (a patent attorney) and Lily (Ettman) Gavron; married Angela Jacobs (a teacher of blind children), September 20, 1957; children: Etan, Ilana, Assaf. *Education:* Attended School of Oriental and African Studies, London, 1955-59. *Politics:* Social Democrat. *Religion:* "Jewish-Agnostic." *Home:* Motza Elite, Jerusalem, Israel.

CAREER: Regional Tourist Office, Arad, Israel, tourist officer, 1961-63; Kaiser Engineers, Sdom, Israel, secretary, 1963-67; University of the Negev, Beersheba, Israel, public relations officer, 1967-71; Israel National Radio, Jerusalem, news editor and senior reporter, 1971-80, head of English News, 1980-82; *Jerusalem Post,* Jerusalem, Israel, night editor and feature writer, 1982—. Founder-settler of Arad, new town in the Negev, chairman of Arad Settlers Committee, 1963; former leader in Habonim youth movement and former kibbutz member. *Military service:* Israel Defense Forces (Reserves), 1961—.

WRITINGS: The End of Days (historical novel), Jewish Publication Society (Philadelphia), 1970; *Walking through Israel* (nonfiction), Houghton, 1980; *Israel after Begin* (nonfiction), Houghton, 1984. Contributor to a number of journals, including *Commentary.*

WORK IN PROGRESS: The Other Foot, a modern novel of Israel; *An Israel Social History.*

SIDELIGHTS: Daniel Gavron wrote *CA:* "My project for a series of novels on Israel today has been postponed with only one written, one sketched out, and none published. It's difficult to sell fiction, and I've found that a sort of personalized journalism has a ready market. These are the forms of *Walking through Israel* and *Israel after Begin* and (in slightly weightier form) will be the form of *An Israel Social History.*

"I still like the fictional form, but my editors seem to think the journalistic form more suited to my style. As my object is to bring the reality of modern Israel before the interested American reader, I am also happy to achieve this journalistically. But I hope to return to the novel series, "Towers in the Desert," one day. Meanwhile I am filling in the time between nonfiction projects with *The Other Foot,* a contemporary Israeli thriller."

BIOGRAPHICAL/CRITICAL SOURCES: Los Angeles Times Book Review, November 9, 1980.

* * *

GELFOND, Rhoda 1946-

PERSONAL: Born May 15, 1946, in Philadelphia, Pa.; daughter of Jacob Allen and Frances (Takiff) Gelfond; married Victor Berman. *Education:* University of Pennsylvania, B.A., 1968; Johns Hopkins University, M.A., 1970; Brown University, M.A., 1972; Simmons College, M.L.S., 1976. *Religion:* Jewish. *Home:* 6403 Ruffin Rd., Chevy Chase, Md. 20015.

CAREER: Poet and songwriter. Poet-in-the-schools, Rhode Island State Arts Council, 1970-71, Pennsylvania Arts Council, 1973—, and New Hampshire Arts Council, 1976-77; instructor in poetry, Boston Center for Adult Education, 1976. *Member:* Academy of American Poets, New England Poetry Club, Pennsylvania Poetry Society. *Awards, honors:* Academy of American Poets Prize, 1971; Winfield Townley Scott Memorial Award, 1972.

WRITINGS: The First Trail (poems), Hellcoal Press of Brown University, 1972; *Laughing Past History,* Copper Beech Press, 1976. Contributor to anthologies, including *New Poets, 1970* and *Instant Anthology.* Contributor to periodicals, including *Coldspring Journal* and *Baltimore Sun.*

WORK IN PROGRESS: A collection of poems, *Daily Bread.*

SIDELIGHTS: "The concern with words in my poetry," Rhoda Gelfond told *CA,* "is somehow connected with an attempt to work them out of tightened etymology and into present action and new meanings . . . a kind of 'raying out' of language."

* * *

GEORGE, Mary Carolyn Hollers Jutson 1930-
(Mary Carolyn Hollers Jutson)

PERSONAL: Born June 5, 1930, in San Antonio, Tex.; daughter of James P. (a dentist) and Helen Marley Hollers; married second husband, W. Eugene George, May, 1980; children: (first marriage) Robert M. T., Jr., Scott Hollers. *Education:* Mary Baldwin College, B.A., 1951; University of Texas, M.A., 1970. *Religion:* Episcopal. *Address:* P.O. Box 4426, Austin, Tex. 78765. *Office:* Department of Art, San Antonio College, 1300 San Pedro, San Antonio, Tex. 78284.

CAREER: San Antonio College, San Antonio, Tex., 1970—, began as assistant professor, currently associate professor of art history. Member of board of trustees of San Antonio Art Institute, and Texas board of review for National Register of Historic Places, 1976-81. *Member:* Society of Architectural Historians (Texas chapter president, 1978), San Antonio Conservation Society. *Awards, honors:* Community excellence award from San Antonio chapter of American Institute of Architects, 1973; Emily Smith Medallion for Distinguished Service from Mary Baldwin College, 1975; grants from Texas Society of Architects, 1982-83, and San Antonio Conservation Society, 1984.

WRITINGS: (Under name Mary Carolyn Hollers Jutson) *Alfred Giles: An English Architect in Texas and Mexico,* Trinity University Press, 1972; *Mary Bonner: Impressions of a Printmaker,* Trinity University Press, 1982; (contributor) Adolf K. Placzek, editor, *Macmillan Encyclopedia of Architects,* Macmillan, 1982.

WORK IN PROGRESS: O'Neil Ford, Architect: His Life and Work.

* * *

GETZ, Gene A(rnold) 1932-

PERSONAL: Born March 15, 1932, in Francesville, Ind.; son of John A. (a farmer) and Matilda (Honegger) Getz; married Elaine Holmquist, June 11, 1956; children: Renee Elaine, Robyn Lynn, Kenton Gene. *Education:* Moody Bible Institute, diploma, 1952; attended Eastern Montana College of Education (now Eastern Montana College), 1952-53; Rocky Mountain College, B.A., 1954; Wheaton College, Wheaton, Ill., M.A.,

1958; New York University, Ph.D., 1969. *Home:* 10929 Fernald, Dallas, Tex. 75218. *Office address:* Center for Church Renewal, P.O. Box 863173, Plano, Tex. 75086.

CAREER: Engaged in radio ministry with Montana Gospel Crusade and youth director of Church of the Air, Billings, Mont., 1952-54; assistant pastor of community church in Hinsdale, Ill., 1954; director of Christian education at Bible church in Lisle, Ill., 1956-58; Moody Bible Institute, Chicago, Ill., instructor in Christian education, 1956-68, director of evening school, 1963-68; Dallas Theological Seminary, Dallas, Tex., associate professor of Christian education, beginning 1968; affiliated with Center for Church Renewal, Plano, Tex., 1978—. Fellowship Bible Church, Dallas, pastor, 1972-81; Fellowship Bible Church North, Plano, pastor, 1981—. Visiting professor, Word of Life Summer Institute of Camping, Schroon Lake, N.Y., 1964-68. President, Space Age Communications, Dallas. *Member:* National Association of Professors of Christian Education, National Sunday School Association (former president of Research Commission).

WRITINGS—published by Moody: *Audio-Visuals in the Church,* 1959, revised edition published as *Audiovisual Media in Christian Education,* 1972; *The Vacation Bible School in the Local Church,* 1962; *The Christian Home,* 1967; (with Roy B. Zuck) *Christian Youth: An In-Depth Study,* 1968; *The History of the Moody Bible Institute,* 1969; *The Story of the Moody Bible Institute,* 1969; (editor with Zuck) *Adult Education in the Church,* 1970; (with Zuck) *Ventures in Family Living,* 1971; *Sharpening the Focus of the Church,* 1974.

Published by Regal Books: *The Measure of a Man,* 1974; *The Measure of a Church,* 1975; *Measure of a Christian: Studies in Philippians,* 1976; *Abraham: Trials and Triumphs,* 1976; *Moses: Moments of Glory, Feet of Clay,* 1976; *The Measure of a Family,* 1976; *The Measure of a Woman,* 1977; *Measure of a Christian: Studies in Titus,* 1978; *When You Feel Like a Failure—Take a Lesson from David,* 1978; *The Measure of a Marriage,* 1980; *Nehemiah: A Man of Prayer and Persistence,* 1981; *Joshua: Defeat to Victory,* 1983; *Joseph: From Prison to Palace,* 1983; *Measure of a Christian: Study in James I,* 1983.

Published by Victor Books: *Building Up One Another,* 1976; *Loving One Another,* 1979; *Encouraging One Another,* 1981; *Praying for One Another,* 1982. Contributor to religious journals.

WORK IN PROGRESS: Measure of a Christian: Studies in James II-V; Serving One Another; When the Pressure's On—Take a Lesson from Elijah.

* * *

GIBBONS, Gail 1944-

PERSONAL: Born August 1, 1944, in Oak Park, Ill.; daughter of Harry George (a tool and die designer) and Grace (Johnson) Ortmann; married Glenn Gibbons, June 25, 1966 (died May 20, 1972); married Kent Ancliffe (a builder), March 23, 1976; children: (stepchildren) Rebecca, Eric. *Education:* University of Illinois, B.F.A., 1967. *Home address:* Corinth, Vt. 05039. *Agent:* Florence Alexander, 80 Park Ave., New York, N.Y. 10016.

CAREER: WCIA-Television, Champaign, Ill., artist, 1967-69; Bob Howe Agency, Chicago, Ill., staff artist, 1969-70; WNBC-Television, House of Animation, New York, N.Y., staff artist, 1970-76; free-lance writer, 1976—. Makes graphic slides, distributed by United Press International, for use on television news programs.

AWARDS, HONORS: New York City Art Director Club award, 1979, for *The Missing Maple Syrup Sap Mystery;* American Institute of Graphic Arts award, 1979, for *Clocks and How They Go;* National Science Teachers Association/Children's Book Council award, 1980, for *Locks and Keys,* and 1982, for *Tool Book;* certificate of appreciation from U.S. Postmaster General, 1982, for *The Post Office Book: Mail and How It Moves.*

WRITINGS—All self-illustrated juveniles: *Willy and His Wheel Wagon* (Junior Literary Guild selection), Prentice-Hall, 1975; *Salvador and Mister Sam: A Guide to Parakeet Care,* Prentice-Hall, 1976; *Things to Make and Do for Halloween,* F. Watts, 1976; *Things to Make and Do for Columbus Day,* F. Watts, 1977; *Things to Make and Do for Your Birthday,* F. Watts, 1978; *The Missing Maple Syrup Sap Mystery,* Warne, 1979; *Clocks and How They Go,* Crowell, 1979.

Locks and Keys, Crowell, 1980; *The Too Great Bread Bake Book,* Warne, 1980; *Trucks,* Crowell, 1981; *The Magnificent Morris Mouse Clubhouse,* F. Watts, 1981; *Tool Book,* Holiday House, 1982; *The Post Office Book: Mail and How It Moves,* Crowell, 1982; *Christmas Time,* Holiday House, 1982; *Boat Book,* Holiday House, 1983; *Paper, Paper, Everywhere,* Harcourt, 1983; *Thanksgiving Day,* Holiday House, 1983; *New Row!,* Crowell, 1983; *Sun Up, Sun Down,* Harcourt, 1983.

Illustrator: Jane Yolen, *Rounds about Rounds,* F. Watts, 1977; Judith Enderle, *Good Junk,* Dandelion Press, 1979; Catharine Chase, *Hot & Cold,* Dandelion Press, 1979; Chase, *The Mouse in My House,* Dandelion Press, 1979; Chase, *My Balloon,* Dandelion Press, 1979; Chase, *Pete, the Wet Pet,* Dandelion Press, 1979; Chase, *The Mouse at the Show,* Dandelion Press, 1980; Joanna Cole, *Cars and How They Go,* Crowell, 1983.

SIDELIGHTS: Gail Gibbons told *CA:* "I became interested in writing children's books when in college—one of my instructors was involved in illustrating children's books. I did a children's show, 'Take a Giant Step,' for National Broadcasting Corp. for two years, doing all the artwork; this made me more interested in writing and drawing for children."

BIOGRAPHICAL/CRITICAL SOURCES: New York Times Book Review, November 18, 1979, September 26, 1982; *Chicago Tribune Book World,* December 12, 1982.

* * *

GIL, David G(eorg) 1924-

PERSONAL: Surname legally changed, 1952; born March 16, 1924, in Vienna, Austria; came to United States in 1957, naturalized in 1963; son of Oskar and Helene (Weisz) Engel; married Eva A. Bresslauer, August 2, 1947; children: Daniel, Gideon. *Education:* Hebrew University, Jerusalem, Israel, B.A., 1957; University of Pennsylvania, M.S.W., 1958, D.S.W., 1963. *Politics:* Socialist. *Home:* 29 Blossomcrest Rd., Lexington, Mass. 02173. *Office:* Florence Heller Graduate School for Advanced Studies in Social Work, Brandeis University, Waltham, Mass. 02254.

CAREER: Counselor and teacher at Boys' Village for Dependent, Neglected, and Delinquent Boys, Department of Social Welfare, Jewish Community Council for Palestine, 1943-45; probation officer, Department of Social Welfare, Government of Palestine, 1945-48; Ministry of Social Welfare, Tel Aviv, Israel, senior probation officer, 1950-51, assistant director,

1951-53, chief supervisor, 1955-57; Jewish Family Service, Philadelphia, Pa., family counselor and family life educator, 1957-59; Association for Jewish Children, Philadelphia, supervisor and research associate, 1959-63; Massachusetts Society for the Prevention of Cruelty to Children, Boston, director of research, 1963-64; Brandeis University, Florence Heller Graduate School for Advanced Studies in Social Work, Waltham, Mass., assistant professor of child welfare, 1964-66, associate professor of social welfare, 1966-69, professor of social policy, 1969—.

Lecturer, Hebrew University, 1955-57, and Smith College, 1979-81; member of faculty, Harvard University, 1973; adjunct professor of sociology, Tufts University, 1973-77; visiting professor, George Warren Brown School of Social Work, Washington University, 1975—, McGill University, 1977, and University of Nebraska, 1978-79. Boston University, School of Social Work, member of faculty, Division of Continuing Education, 1972, member of research curriculum review committee, 1972. Member of professional advisory committee, Martha Eliot Center, 1967-68; member of steering committee, Program for Advanced Social Work Training in Teaching and Consultation in Child Treatment, Judge Baker Guidance Center, 1967-71; co-chairman of Committee to Develop an Adequate Standard of Living for Massachusetts, 1971; member of national advisory board, National Committee to Abolish Corporal Punishment in Schools, 1973; member of Massachusetts Committee for National Health Insurance, 1973—; member of board of directors, American Parents Committee, 1974—; member of professional advisory board, National Committee for Prevention of Child Abuse, 1974-82; member of external review committee, University of Minnesota School of Social Development, 1975; member of program committee, Consortium on Peace Research, Education, and Development, 1975-76; member of Langdon Associates, 1975—. Consultant to National Commission on the Causes and Prevention of Violence, 1968, National Science Foundation, 1973-74, Minnesota Systems Research, Inc., 1974-75, National Incidence of Child Abuse Study, 1975, Metropolitan College, Boston University, 1975, Westat, Inc., 1976-77, Ontario Council on Graduate Studies, 1979, and Center for Social Development and Humanitarian Affairs, United Nations, 1980-81. *Military service:* Israeli Army, 1948-49; conscientious objector, served as welfare officer.

MEMBER: International Peace Research Association, National Association of Social Workers, Academy of Certified Social Workers, American Sociological Association, Child Welfare League of America (member of publication advisory committee, 1964-71; member of research committee, 1968-71), American Ortho-Psychiatric Association, American Association of University Professors (member of executive committee of Brandeis University chapter, 1968), American Association for the Advancement of Science, American Bar Association (member of advisory committee on child abuse legislation, 1974-75), American Civil Liberties Union, Democratic Socialists of America, Union of Radical Political Economists, Association for Humanist Sociology (vice-president, 1978-79; president, 1980-81); Radical Alliance of Social Service Workers, New American Movement, American Humanist Association, War Resisters League, Child Welfare League of America (member of publications advisory committee, 1964-71; member of research committee, 1968-71), Asia Society (member of panel on Vietnam, Laos, and Cambodia, 1974—).

WRITINGS: Implications for Doctoral Education in Social Welfare of an Examination of the Concept of Motivation, Brandeis University, Papers in Social Welfare, 1965; (editor and compiler) *Doctoral Dissertations in Social Work Related to the Field of Child Welfare,* Children's Bureau, U.S. Department of Health, Education, and Welfare, 1966; (with John H. Noble) *Public Knowledge, Attitudes and Opinions about Physical Child Abuse in the United States,* Brandeis University, Papers in Social Welfare, 1967; *Nationwide Survey of Legally Reported Physical Abuse of Children,* Brandeis University, Papers in Social Welfare, 1968; *Physical Abuse of Children: One Manifestation of Violence in American Society,* National Commission on the Causes and Prevention of Violence, 1968.

Abusing Parents: Cultural and Class Factors, Virginia Commonwealth University, 1970; (editor) *Violence against Children: Physical Child Abuse in the United States,* Harvard University Press, 1970, revised edition, 1973, paperback edition published with new preface and appendix, 1978; *Unravelling Social Policy: Theory, Analysis, and Political Action towards Social Equality,* Schenkman, 1973, 3rd edition, 1981; *The Challenge of Social Equality: Essays on Policy, Social Development, and Political Practice,* Schenkman, 1976; (editor) *Child Abuse and Violence,* American Orthopsychiatric Association, 1979; *Beyond the Jungle: Essays on Human Possibilities, Social Alternatives, and Radical Practice,* Schenkman, 1979.

(Author of foreword) Richard Volpe, Margot Breton, and Judith Milton, editors, *The Maltreatment of the School-aged Child,* Heath, 1980; (author of foreword) Ellie Winberg and Tom Wilson, editors, *Single Rooms: Stories of an Urban Subculture,* Schenkman, 1981.

Contributor: H. Aptekar, editor, *Social Work Practice, 1966,* National Conference on Social Welfare, Columbia University Press, 1966; Ray E. Helfer and C. H. Kempe, editors, *The Battered Child,* University of Chicago Press, 1968; *Social Security: The First 35 Years,* University of Michigan Press, 1966.

Alan Gorr, editor, *The School in the Social Setting: Source Readings,* Mss Educational Publishing, 1971; Mason P. Thomas, Jr., editor, *Proceedings of the Second Governor's Conference on Child Abuse and Neglect,* University of North Carolina, Institute of Government, 1972; Urie Bronfenbrenner, editor, *Influences on Human Development,* Dryden, 1972; Alvin L. Schorr, editor, *Children and Decent People,* Basic Books, 1974; Jerome Leavitt, editor, *The Battered Child: Selected Readings,* General Learning Press, 1974; Robert Brenner, editor, *Children and Youth in America,* Harvard University Press, 1974; Suzanne K. Steinmetz and Murray A. Straus, editors, *Violence in the Family,* Dodd, 1974.

Louis Lowy, editor, *Social Welfare Policy,* Xerox Individualized Publishing, 1975; Susan B. Harris, editor, *Child Abuse: Present and Future,* National Committee for Prevention of Child Abuse, 1975; Tropman, Dluhy, Lind, Vasey, and Croxton, editors, *Strategic Perspectives on Social Policy,* Pergamon, 1976; Ann H. Beuf and Dorothy Kurz, editors, *Childhood: A Social Construct,* Xerox Individualized Publishing, 1977; Daniel Porter Kimble, editor, *Contrast and Controversy in Modern Psychology,* Goodyear Publishing, 1977; Pamela Cantor, editor, *Understanding a Child's World: Readings in Infancy through Adolescence,* McGraw, 1977; Constance M. Lee, editor, *Child Abuse: A Reader and Source Book,* Open University Press, 1978; Sheila Maybanks and Marvin Bryce, editors, *Home-Based Services for Children and Families: Policy, Practice, and Research,* C. C Thomas, 1978; J. M. Ekelaar and S. Katz, editors, *Family Violence,* Butterworth & Co., 1978; Judith Areen, editor, *Cases and Materials on Family*

Law, Foundation Press, 1978; Jesse A. Goldner, editor, *Child Abuse and Neglect and the Law,* Institute on Child Behavior and Development, University of Iowa, 1979; Volpe, Breton, and Milton, editors, *Schools and the Problem of Child Abuse,* University of Toronto Press, 1979; Wolfgang Merten and Eberhard Windaus, editors, *Forum Kindesmisshandlung-Praevention, Intervention, Nachsorge,* Kinderschutz-Zentrum, 1979; Richard Bourne and Eli H. Newberger, editors, *Critical Perspectives on Child Abuse,* Heath, 1979.

Social Policy and Social Services, Ginn, 1980; William Feigelman, editor, *Prescription for Better Days: Readings on Policy Alternatives for America's Social Problems,* W. C. Brown, 1980; Joanne V. Cook and Roy T. Bowles, editors, *Child Abuse: Commission and Omission,* Butterworths, 1980; Leroy H. Pelton, editor, *The Social Context of Child Abuse,* Human Sciences, 1981; Anne Crichton, editor, *Health Policy Making,* Health Administration Press, 1981; John F. Jones and Rama S. Pandey, editors, *Social Development: Conceptual, Methodological and Policy Issues,* St. Martin's, 1981; Bill Roberts, editor, *Abuse in Families,* Open University Press, 1982.

Contributor to professional journals, including *Journal of Health and Social Behavior, Social Service Review, Journal of Marriage and the Family, Journal of Education for Social Work, Child Welfare, Children, Humanity and Society,* and *Social Work.* Member of editorial board, *American Journal of Orthopsychiatry,* 1973-77, *Humanity and Society,* 1976-66, and *Social Development Issues,* 1976—. Consulting reader, *American Sociological Review,* 1973—; associate editor, *Journal of Sociology and Social Welfare,* 1974—, and *Children and Youth Services Review,* 1978; consulting editor, *Evaluation and Health Professions,* 1977—, and *Journal of International and Comparative Social Welfare,* 1981—.

* * *

GILBERT, Herman Cromwell 1923-

PERSONAL: Born February 23, 1923, in Mariana, Ark.; son of Van Luther (a minister) and Cora (Allen) Gilbert; married Ivy McAlpine, July 19, 1949; children: Dorthea, Vincent Newton. *Education:* Completed two years of a three-year correspondence course in law, LaSalle Extension University, 1941; attended IBM Educational Center. *Politics:* Independent Democrat. *Religion:* Protestant. *Home:* 11539 South Justice St., Chicago, Ill. 60643. *Office:* Path Press, Inc., 53 West Jackson Blvd., Chicago, Ill. 60604.

CAREER: AFL-CIO, United Packinghouse Workers of America, Chicago, Ill., program coordinator, 1955-57; Illinois Department of Labor, Bureau of Employment Security, Chicago, manager of automated systems section, 1957-70, assistant employment security administrator, 1970-81; administrative assistant and chief of staff to Congressman Gus Savage (2nd District, Illinois, Democrat), 1981-82. Executive vice-president, Path Press, Chicago, 1968—; publicity director, Chicago League of Negro Voters and Protest at the Polls. Member of joint Federal-State Committee on Automated Systems, Interstate Conference of Employment Security Agencies. *Military service:* U.S. Army Air Forces, 1943-46; attended Armed Forces Institute, 1944-45; became staff sergeant. *Member:* Society of Midland Authors.

WRITINGS: The Uncertain Sound (novel), Path Press, 1969; *The Negotiations* (novel), Path Press, 1983. Author of column, "This Needs Saying," in Chicago's *Westside Booster,* 1959-60. Managing editor of Citizen Newspapers, 1965-67.

WORK IN PROGRESS: The Campaign, a novel which deals with attempts of black independent politicians to gain political power in Chicago; *This Needs Saying,* a book of essays updating and extending ideas first introduced in his newspaper column of the same title; *The American Way,* a satirical novel of conflicts, sellouts, and accommodations in a state agency in the mid-1970s; *Cotton Patch to Computer,* an autobiography.

SIDELIGHTS: Herman Cromwell Gilbert told *CA:* "As is clear from the broad range of activities in which I have been engaged over the years, writing itself has been somewhat of a sidelight. However, this does not mean that I have taken my writing lightly, only that I have placed a higher value on making a decent living for my family and sending my children through college. Now that these things have been achieved, I am free to spend the remainder of my life writing.

"I have always been clear about the types of books I wanted to write: books that helped push Black Americans along the road to full equality by spotlighting radical situations and making these situations plausible through clearly delineated characters. These things I think I have accomplished in both of my published novels, *The Uncertain Sound,* which deals with school integration, interracial love, and unionism in a southern Illinois town in 1950, and *The Negotiations,* which dramatizes the efforts of blacks to negotiate a separate state in the late 1980s. The nonfiction and autobiographical writings in which I am currently engaged are following this same intent."

* * *

GILDNER, Gary 1938-

PERSONAL: Born August 22, 1938, in West Branch, Mich.; son of Theodore Edward (a carpenter) and Jean (Szostak) Gildner; married Judith McKibben, January 5, 1963; children: Gretchen. *Education:* Michigan State University, B.A., 1960, M.A., 1961. *Home:* 2915 School St., Des Moines, Iowa 50311. *Office:* Department of English, Drake University, Des Moines, Iowa 50311.

CAREER: Wayne State University, Detroit, Mich.; writer for department of university relations, 1961-62; Northern Michigan University, Marquette, instructor in English, 1963-66; Drake University, Des Moines, Iowa, associate professor of English, 1966—; Reed College, Portland, Ore., writer-in-residence (on leave from Drake University), 1983-85. *Awards, honors:* Robert Frost fellow at Bread Loaf Writers' Conference, 1970; National Endowment for the Arts fellow, 1971, 1976; Yaddo fellow, 1972, 1973, 1975, 1976, 1978; MacDowell Colony fellow, 1974; Theodore Roethke prize, 1976; William Carlos Williams prize, 1977; Helen Bullis prize, 1979.

WRITINGS—Poetry, except as indicated: *First Practice,* University of Pittsburgh Press, 1969; *Digging for Indians,* University of Pittsburgh Press, 1971; *Nails,* University of Pittsburgh Press, 1975; (editor with Judith Gildner, and contributor) *Out of This World: Poems from the Hawkeye State* (anthology), Iowa State University Press, 1975; *Letters from Vicksburg,* Unicorn Press, 1976; *The Runner and Other Poems,* University of Pittsburgh Press, 1978; *Jabon,* Breitenbush, 1981; *The Crush* (stories), Ecco Press, 1983; *Blue Like the Heavens: New and Selected Poems,* University of Pittsburgh Press, 1984.

Contributor to anthologies, including: *Best Little Magazine Fiction, 1970,* edited by Curt Johnson, New York University Press, 1970; *I Love You All Day,* edited by Philip Dacey and Gerald Knoll, Abbey Press, 1970; *Poetry Brief,* edited by William

Cole, Macmillan, 1971; *An Introduction to Poetry,* edited by X. J. Kennedy, Little Brown, 1971, revised edition, 1976; *Poems One Line and Longer,* edited by Cole, Grossman, 1973; *Poetry: Points of Departure,* Winthrop, 1974; *The American Poetry Anthology,* edited by Daniel Halpern, Avon, 1975; *Heartland II: Poets of the Midwest,* edited by Lucien Stryk, Northern Illinois University Press, 1975; *The Sporting Spirit,* edited by Robert Higgs and Neil Isaacs, Harcourt, 1977; *Fifty Contemporary Poets,* edited by Alberta Turner, McKay, 1977; *The Treasury of American Poetry,* edited by Nancy Sullivan, Doubleday, 1978; *A Geography of Poets,* edited by Edward Field, Bantam, 1979.

WORK IN PROGRESS: Two novels, *The Second Bridge* and *Thrasher;* a collection of short stories, *The Rainbow Farm;* more poems.

SIDELIGHTS: Gary Gildner writes: "I wrote *Letters from Vicksburg* during a cold, wet week in March of 1975. All winter I hadn't written much that made me happy. *Nails* was finished—had been for a while and was about to come out—and maybe I was pushing too hard to come up with poems that were not like the poems in that book. Or maybe I was doing something else 'wrong.' I don't know. Anyway, I was in a dry spell. And sloppy weather never helps. One day I picked up the civil war letters that Judy had left in my room . . . and right away I was taken with this fellow—this cocky, frightened, proud, lonely, semi-literate young soldier from Iowa who was on his way to Vicksburg and writing home to his wife about it. I began to fool with the idea of using the letters in some kind of exercise that might help open me up. The story was good, that is the bones were there, but his presentation, as the English teacher might say, was ignorant: he spelled mainly by ear, . . . he used no punctuation, and he rambled. I thought, what are these letters *not* like? Well, I decided, they are about as far from the sonnet as Yogi Berra's batting style, so why don't I 'translate' them into that sober shape—just as an exercise, just as a way of getting away from myself, and just to be contrary? I may have been feeling a bit cocky too, at this point, though God knows why. I wrote drafts of the first two or three and liked them; I liked them even better after removing some screws here and there and letting them breathe as fully as they wanted to. Somewhere in the middle of number four, I think, I started to get that feeling which you can't describe but which feels *good,* and the exercise became something else then. . . . I departed from the letters, as I say elsewhere, whenever it seemed necessary or fruitful; but I tried to remain faithful to their grammar, their 'stance'. . . . I stayed with the sonnet plan throughout, but I felt absolutely no guilt taking out hardware whenever the voice got tight on me."

BIOGRAPHICAL/CRITICAL SOURCES: *Los Angeles Times,* November 30, 1983.

* * *

GILL, (Ronald) Crispin 1916-

PERSONAL: Born March 10, 1916, in Plymouth, England; son of Joseph Henry (a builder) and Margaret Jane (Crispin) Gill; married Mary Beatrice Grills Foot, August 4, 1939 (died February 19, 1971); married Betty Theed, August 26, 1972; children: (first marriage) Jane Elford (Mrs. Tony Parker), Crispin Owen, Sarah Margaret Foot (Mrs. Michael Mitchell). *Education:* Attended secondary school in Plymouth, England, 1926-34. *Religion:* Church of England. *Home:* The Grey House, Kingsand, Torpoint, Cornwall PL10 1NP, England.

CAREER: *Western Morning News,* Plymouth, England, reporter, 1934-38, sub-editor, 1939, chief sub-editor, 1946-47, news editor, 1948-49, assistant editor, 1950-71; *Countryman* (magazine), Burford, Oxfordshire, England, editor, 1971-81. Member of Friends of Buckland Abbey Committee, 1951-71, and Dartmoor National Park Committee, 1954-66; chairman of Plymouth Lifeboat Committee, 1967-71. West Devon scout commissioner, 1951-64. *Military service:* British Army, Royal Army Service Corps, 1940-46; became captain. *Member:* Society for Nautical Research, Hakluyt Society, Royal Institution of Cornwall, Devon and Cornwall Record Society, Devonshire Association, Royal Western Yacht Club of England.

WRITINGS—Published by David & Charles, except as indicated: *The West Country,* Oliver & Boyd, 1962; *Plymouth: A New History,* Volume I: *Ice Age to the Elizabethans,* 1966, Volume II: *1603 to the Present Day,* 1979; (with Frank Booker and Tony Soper) *The Wreck of the Torrey Canyon,* Taplinger, 1967; *Plymouth in Pictures,* 1968; *Sutton Harbour,* Sutton Harbour Improvement Co., 1970; (editor) *Dartmoor: A New Study,* 1970; *Mayflower Remembered: A History of the Plymouth Pilgrims,* Taplinger, 1970; *The Isles of Scilly,* 1975; *Dartmoor,* 1976; (editor) *The Countryman's Britain,* 1976; *The Countryman's Britain in Pictures,* 1977.

AVOCATIONAL INTERESTS: The sea, travel, and maritime history.

* * *

GILL, David (Lawrence William) 1934-

PERSONAL: Born July 3, 1934, in Chislehurst, Kent, England; son of Donald James Walton and Marjorie Maud (Paramor) Gill; married Irene Zuntz (a lecturer), July 5, 1958; children: Thomas, Nicholas, Jaquetta. *Education:* University College, London, B.A. (honors in German), 1955; University of Birmingham, Certificate in Education, 1960; University of London (external), B.A. (honors in English), 1970. *Home:* 32 Boyn Hill Rd., Maidenhead, Berkshire, England. *Office:* Buckinghamshire College of Higher Education, Queen Alexander Rd., High Wycombe, Buckinghamshire, England.

CAREER: Bedales School, Hampshire, England, teacher of German and English, 1960-62; Nyakasura School, Fort Portal, Uganda, teacher of English, 1962-64; Magdalen College School, Oxford, England, teacher of German and English, 1965-71; Newland Park College of Education, Buckinghamshire, England, lecturer, 1971-79; Buckinghamshire College of Higher Education, Buckinghamshire, lecturer, 1979—. *Military service:* British Army, Royal Signals, 1955-57. *Awards, honors: Birmingham Post* poetry prize, 1960.

WRITINGS: *Men with Evenings* (poems), Chatto & Windus, 1966, Wesleyan University Press, 1967; *The Pagoda and Other Poems,* Chatto & Windus, 1969, Wesleyan University Press, 1970; *Peaches and Apercus,* Poet & Peasant Books, 1974; *In the Eye of the Storm: Fifty Years of Ondva Iysohorsky,* Hub Publications, 1976; *The Upkeep of the Castle,* Hub Publications, 1978. Contributor of poetry to periodicals, including *Listener, Observer, Critical Quarterly,* and *Country Life.*

WORK IN PROGRESS: A fifth collection of his poems; *One Potato, Two Potato,* action verse for children, for Macmillan Education.

SIDELIGHTS: David Gill writes *CA:* "As time runs out in the northern hemisphere, the subject matter for poetry shrinks. Without the threat of nuclear war hanging over Europe, there would be love, nature, time, death on a human scale, and a thousand and one personal experiences to turn into poetry: As it is, poets have to turn resistance-fighters, narrow their eyes, and sharpen their weapons. As humanity gets swallowed up in the terrible triumph of bigotry and technology, poets need to assert ordinary human values. It is tempting to write a throwaway poetry (Who can look forward to generations of reprints of Palgrave's Golden Treasury?)—but even the holocaust is no excuse for bad verse. South African poets *have* to write about Apartheid because it is part of their human condition. They do so with resentment. We have to write about the Bomb. We do so, with resentment of those who have made the nuclear arms race their bread and butter."

* * *

GILL, Jerry H. 1933-

PERSONAL: Name legally changed, 1965; born February 7, 1933, in Lynden, Wash.; son of Walter and Virginia (McGinnis) Gauthier. *Education:* Westmont College, B.A., 1956; University of Washington, Seattle, M.A., 1957; New York Theological Seminary, B.D., 1960; Duke University, Ph.D., 1966. *Office:* Department of Philosophy, Barrington College, Barrington, R.I. 02806.

CAREER: Clergyman; ordained, 1956; Seattle Pacific College, Seattle, Wash., assistant professor of philosophy and religion, 1960-64; Southwestern at Memphis, Memphis, Tenn., assistant professor of philosophy, 1966-69; Eckerd College, St. Petersburg, Fla., 1969-77, began as associate professor, became professor of philosophy; Eastern College, St. Davids, Pa., professor of Christianity and culture, 1977-83; Barrington College, Barrington, R.I., professor of philosophy, 1983—. *Member:* American Philosophical Association, American Academy of Religion.

WRITINGS: Ingmar Bergman and the Search for Meaning, Eerdmans, 1967; (editor) *Philosophy Today,* Macmillan, Number I, 1968, Number II, 1969, Number III, 1970; (editor) *Philosophy and Religion,* Burgess, 1968; (editor) *Essays on Kierkegaard,* Burgess, 1969; *The Possibility of Religious Knowledge,* Eerdmans, 1971; *Ian Ramsey,* Allen & Unwin, 1976; *Wittgenstein and Metaphor,* University Press of America, 1981; *On Knowing God,* Westminster, 1981; *Toward Theology,* University Press of America, 1982; *Metaphilosophy,* University Press of America, 1982. Contributor to theology and philosophy journals.

WORK IN PROGRESS: Books on art and incarnation, Flannery O'Connor, and a dialogical apologetica.

* * *

GILLIE, Oliver (John) 1937-

PERSONAL: Born October 31, 1937, in North Shields, England; son of John Calder (an optician) and Ann (an artist; maiden name, Philipson) Gillie; married Louise Panton (a television producer), November 15, 1969; children: Lucinda, Juliet. *Education:* University of Edinburgh, B.Sc. (summa cum laude), 1960, Ph.D., 1966; Stanford University, graduate study, 1960-61. *Residence:* London, England. *Agent:* Harold Matson Co., Inc., 276 Fifth Ave., New York, N.Y. 10001. *Office: Sunday Times,* 200 Gray's Inn Rd., London W.C.1, England.

CAREER: University of Edinburgh, Edinburgh, Scotland, assistant lecturer in genetics, 1961-65; Medical Research Council, London, England, researcher, 1965-68; *Science Journal,* London, biological sciences editor, 1968-69; *General Practitioner,* London, editor, 1970-71; *Sunday Times,* London, medical correspondent, 1971—. *Member:* Royal Society of Medicine (fellow), Genetical Society, National Union of Journalists, Association of Science Writers, Medical Journalists Association.

AWARDS, HONORS: Co-winner with wife, Louise Panton, of Glaxo science writers' prize, 1975, for articles on childbirth; Order of the Bifurcated Needle from World Health Organization, 1976, for services in eradication of smallpox; Specialist Writer of the Year award from British National Press, 1977; Royal Jubilee Medal from Her Majesty Queen Elizabeth II, 1977; British Science Writer of the Year award, 1979; Medical Journalist of the Year award, shared with Ian Yeomans, 1980, for articles on heart transplantation.

WRITINGS: The Living Cell, Thames & Hudson, 1970; *Who Do You Think You Are?* Saturday Review Press, 1976; *How to Stop Smoking,* Granada, 1977; (with Derrick Mercer) *The "Sunday Times" Book of Body Maintenance,* M. Joseph, 1978, published as *The Complete Book of Body Maintenance,* Norton, 1979; (with Caroline Conran and Michael Bateman) *The World's Best Food for Health and Long Life,* Houghton, 1981 (published in England as *The "Sunday Times" Guide to the World's Best Food,* Hutchinson, 1981); (with Angela Price and Sharon Robinson) *The "Sunday Times" Self-Help Directory,* Granada, 1982.

* * *

GILLIES, John 1925-

PERSONAL: Born December 15, 1925, in Chicago, Ill.; son of Anton J. (a clergyman) and Anna (a social worker; maiden name, Batutis) Gillies; married Carolyn Young (a librarian), March 18, 1950; children: Laurie Gillies Yarbrough, Stephen, Andrew. *Education:* Attended Wheaton College, Wheaton, Ill., 1945, 1947, Northwestern University, 1947-49, and University of Texas, 1956-57. *Politics:* Independent. *Religion:* Presbyterian. *Home:* 9303 Hunters Trace E., Austin, Tex. 78758.

CAREER: Presbyterian Church of the United States, Atlanta, Ga., audiovisual director, 1961-65; Christian Rural Overseas Program/Church World Service, Elkhart, Ind., communication director, 1965-72; communications consultant, 1972-74; State Department of Public Welfare, Austin, Tex., director of educational media production, 1974-77; Christian Rural Overseas Program, Austin, Tex., regional director for Texas, 1977-79; free-lance writer, 1979—. Interim director, Texas Conference of Churches, 1982. Has also worked as mass communications missionary in Brazil, advertising executive, announcer, television director, and newscaster. *Military service:* U.S. Army, 1945-46.

MEMBER: Authors Guild, Authors League of America, American Federation of Television and Radio Artists, Screen Actors Guild, Religious Public Relations Council (past member of board of governors). *Awards, honors:* Blue ribbon from Educational Film Library Association, 1964, for filmstrip script "Gold D. Lox and the Five Bears"; bronze medal from Religious Arts Festival, 1973, for "The Retreat."

WRITINGS: A Primer for Christian Broadcasters, Moody, 1955; *The Martyrs of Guanabara,* Moody, 1976; *A Guide to Caring for and Coping with Aging Parents,* Thomas Nelson, 1981; (with Walter Price), *Antiochus,* Moody, 1982.

Plays: "The Firemakers" (musical play), first produced in Bristol, Ind., at Frontier Theatre, July 1, 1974; *The Retreat* (one-act; first produced in Sacramento, Calif., at Religious Arts

Festival, 1973), Contemporary Drama Service, 1980; *Give Us a Sign* (one-act; first produced as "The Sign Painter"), Contemporary Drama Service, 1980.

Also author of several dozen radio, film, filmstrip, and television scripts.

WORK IN PROGRESS: Research on Hannah More and other nineteenth-century evangelical Anglican social reformers in England, for a novel.

SIDELIGHTS: John Gillies writes: "I am vitally interested in history, believing that there are authentic heroes and heroines yet to be described and popularized. I have found many of these in church history, particularly in script assignments; I am infatuated with the sometimes not-so-saintly saints who have made life and our world more livable. I am a first-generation American and I still have hope and excitement about this country."

AVOCATIONAL INTERESTS: Travel (Europe and the Middle East; has lived in Argentina), amateur photography, semi-professional singing and acting.

* * *

GILLQUIST, Peter E. 1938-

PERSONAL: Born July 13, 1938, in Minneapolis, Minn.; son of William Parker Gillquist (with Minnesota State Highway Department); married Marilyn Grinder, May 14, 1960; children: Wendy Jo, Gregory Ray, Ginger Ann, Terri Beth, Heidi Lou, Peter Jon. *Education:* University of Minnesota, B.A., 1960; additional study at Dallas Theological Seminary, 1960-61, and Wheaton College, Wheaton, Ill., 1961-62. *Politics:* Conservative. *Religion:* Orthodox Christian. *Home:* 6684 Pasado Rd., Isla Vista, Calif. 93117. *Office:* c/o Thomas Nelson, Inc., Elm Hill Pike and Nelson Place, Nashville, Tenn. 37214-1000.

CAREER: Campus Crusade for Christ, district director, later regional director in Illinois, 1960-68; Memphis State University, Memphis, Tenn., director of development, 1969-72; Thomas Nelson, Inc. (publishers), Nashville, Tenn., editor, 1976—. Presiding Bishop, Evangelical Orthodox Church, 1979—. *Member:* Alpha Delta Sigma, Sigma Alpha Epsilon.

WRITINGS—Published by Zondervan, except as indicated: *Love Is Now*, 1970; *Farewell to the Fake I.D.: An Extraordinary Handbook for Spiritual Survival in Our Pressurized Society*, 1971; *Let's Quit Fighting About the Holy Spirit*, 1975; *The Physical Side of Being Spiritual*, 1979; *Why We Haven't Changed the World*, Revell, 1981. Managing editor of *Collegiate Challenge*, 1962-68.

WORK IN PROGRESS: *Going Back Home: A Pilgrimage to the Historic Faith.*

* * *

GINSBURG, Herbert (Paul) 1939-

PERSONAL: Born September 26, 1939, in New York, N.Y.; son of Isaiah (an occupational therapist) and Lillian (Ringler) Ginsburg; married Jane Knitzer (a psychologist), November 24, 1974; children: Deborah, Rebecca, Jonathan, Lizbeth, Susan. *Education:* Harvard University, B.A., 1961; University of North Carolina, Ph.D., 1965. *Office:* Graduate School of Education, University of Rochester, Rochester, N.Y. 14627.

CAREER: Cornell University, Ithaca, N.Y., assistant professor, 1965-69, associate professor of psychology, 1969-76; University of Maryland, Baltimore, professor of psychology, 1976-79; University of Rochester, Graduate School of Education, Rochester, N.Y., professor, 1979—.

WRITINGS: (With Sylvia Opper) *Piaget's Theory of Intellectual Development*, Prentice-Hall, 1969; *The Myth of the Deprived Child*, Prentice-Hall, 1972; *Children's Arithmetic: The Learning Process*, Van Nostrand, 1977; *The Development of Mathematical Thinking*, Academic Press, 1983.

WORK IN PROGRESS: Research on cognition and personality.

* * *

GLEN, Duncan (Munro) 1933-

PERSONAL: Born January 11, 1933, in Cambuslang, Lanarkshire, Scotland; son of John Kennedy and Margaret (Tennent) Glen; married Margaret Eadie, January 4, 1957; children: Ian Kenneth, Alison Rosemary. *Education:* Educated at Rutherglen Academy, and then Edinburgh College of Art, 1953-56. *Home:* 25 Johns Rd., Radcliffe-on-Trent, Nottingham, England. *Office:* Trent Polytechnic, Burton St., Nottingham, England.

CAREER: H. M. Stationery Office, London, England, typographer, 1958-60; Watford College of Technology, Watford, Hertfordshire, England, lecturer in typographic design, 1960-63; Robert Gibson & Sons Ltd. (publishers), Glasgow, Scotland, editor, 1963-65; Preston Polytechnic, Preston, Lancashire, England, lecturer, 1965-69, senior lecturer in graphic design, 1969-74, head of graphic design division, 1974-78; Trent Polytechnic, Nottingham, head of department of visual communication, 1978—. Founder and owner of Akros Publications, 1965—. *Military service:* Royal Air Force, national service, 1956-58.

WRITINGS—Published by Akros Publications, except as indicated: *Hugh MacDiarmid: Rebel Poet and Prophet*, Drumalban Press, 1962; *Hugh MacDiarmid and the Scottish Renaissance*, Chambers, 1964; *The Literary Masks of Hugh MacDiarmid*, Drumalban Press, 1964; *Scottish Poetry Now*, 1966; *Idols: When Alexander Our King Was Dead: Poem*, 1967; (editor) *Poems Addressed to Hugh MacDiarmid*, 1967; *Kythings and Other Poems*, Caithness Books, 1969; *Sunny Summer Sunday Afternoon in the Park?*, 1969; (editor) *Selected Essays of Hugh MacDiarmid*, Cape, 1969, University of California Press, 1970.

Unnerneath the Bed: Poem, 1970; (editor) *The Akros Anthology of Scottish Poetry, 1965-70*, 1970; *A Small Press and Hugh MacDiarmid*, 1970; (with Hugh MacDiarmid) *The MacDiarmids: A Conversation*, 1970; *In Appearances: A Sequence of Poems*, 1971; *Clydesdale: A Sequence of Poems*, 1971; (editor) *Whither Scotland?*, Gollancz, 1971; *The Individual and the Twentieth-Century Scottish Literary Tradition*, 1971; *Feres: Poems*, 1971; (editor) *Hugh MacDiarmid: A Critical Survey*, Scottish Academic Press, 1972, University of California Press, 1973; *A Journey Past: A Poem*, privately printed, 1972; *A Cled Score: Poems*, 1974; (compiler) *A Bibliography of Scottish Poets from Stevenson to 1974*, 1974.

Mr. & Mrs. J. L. Stoddart at Home: A Poem, 1975; (with John Brook) *The New Buildings of Preston*, Harris Press, 1975; (editor with Nat Scammacca) *La Nuova Poesia Scozzese*, Celebes, 1976; *Five Literati*, Ham's Press, 1976; *Weddercock*, privately printed, 1976; *Gaitherings: Poems in Scots*, 1977; *Forward from Hugh MacDiarmid*, 1977; *Hugh MacDiarmid: An Essay*, 1977; *Realities Poems*, 1980; *On Midsummer Evenin Merriest of Nichts?*, 1981; (editor) *Akros Verse, 1965-1982*, 1982; *The State of Scotland: A Poem*, 1983; *Have Pen Will*

Travel (autobiography), Ramsay Head Press, 1984; *The Turn of the Earth: A Sequence of Poems*, 1984. Editor, *Akros*, 1965-83, *Graphic Lines*, 1975-78.

SIDELIGHTS: Duncan Glen told *CA*, "Scottish literary renaissance has given me the sense of belonging to a Scottish culture . . . rather than a subsidiary of English literature with only parochial interests."

* * *

GLIEWE, Unada (Grace) 1927-
(Unada)

PERSONAL: Given name is pronounced You-*nay*-dah; born July 10, 1927, in Rochester, N.Y.; daughter of Edwin Herman (a carpenter) and Unada (Hinckley) Gliewe. *Education:* Syracuse University, B.F.A. (magna cum laude), 1949. *Politics:* Democrat (usually). *Religion:* Lutheran. *Home:* 2300 Pine St., Philadelphia, Pa. 19103.

CAREER: O'Brien Advertising Agency, Rochester, N.Y., staff artist, 1950-54; Lutheran Board of Parish Education, Philadelphia, Pa., staff artist, 1954-67; free-lance illustrator and writer. *Member:* Plays and Players (associate arts member), Philadelphia Children's Reading Round Table.

WRITINGS—Self-illustrated children's books: *Ricky's Boots*, Putnam, 1970; *Andrew's Amazing Boxes*, Putnam, 1971; *The Marvelous Monster of Mulligan Heights*, Houghton, 1981.

Illustrator under name Unada: Patricia Miles Martin, *Dolly Madison*, Putnam, 1967; Ruby L. Radford, *Sequoya*, Putnam, 1967; Martha M. Welch, *Saucy*, Coward, 1968; Bayard Dominick, *Joe, a Porpoise*, Astor-Honor, 1968; Ned Hoopes, *Ali Baba and the Forty Thieves*, Dell, 1968; Lynn Gessner, *Trading Post Girl*, Fell, 1968; Oren Arnold, *The Great Sleepy Gun Animal Hunt*, Fell, 1968; Gertrude Weaver, *The Emperor's Gift*, Thomas Nelson, 1969; Martin, *That Cat: One, Two, Three*, Putnam, 1969.

Anne Malcolmson, *Captain Ichabod Paddock: Whaler of Nantucket*, Walker & Co., 1970; Peggy Mann, *Twenty-Five Cent Friend*, Coward, 1970; Marion E. Gridley, *Pontiac*, Putnam, 1970; *Our Gifts* (children's prayers), C. R. Gibson, 1971; N.J.W. Sellers, *Charley's Clan*, Albert Whitman, 1973; *My Book Book*, Lippincott, 1973; Jo Anne Wold, *Well, Why Didn't You Say So?*, Albert Whitman, 1975; Dorothy Hamilton, *Rosalie*, Herald Press, 1977; Jo Anne S. Hoffman, *Martin's Invisible Invention*, Judson, 1977; Ida DeLage, *The Old Witch and the Dragon*, Garrard, 1979; Cara Lynn Phillips, *Doing Right Makes Me Happy*, Standard, 1982. Also illustrator of textbooks and readers for Lippincott, Fortress, Judson, and Westminster.

* * *

GLUCK, Jay 1927-

PERSONAL: Born January 11, 1927, in Detroit, Mich.; son of Harry J. (a musician) and Lillian Mary Veronica Friar (Campbell-Phillips) Gluck; married Sumiye Hiramoto (a writer), May 9, 1955; children: Cellin Phillip, Garet Arthur. *Education:* Attended City College (now City College of the City University of New York), 1943-44, and George Washington University, 1946-47; University of California, Berkeley, B.A. in anthropology, 1949; Asia Institute School for Asian Studies, New York, N.Y., graduate study, 1950-51. *Politics:* Democrat by Oriental resignation. *Religion:* "Jew by temper; Buddhist inclination." *Agent:* Ruth Aley, Maxwell Aley Associates, 145 East 35th St., New York, N.Y. 10016. *Office:* SOPA, 6-6, Nishiyama-cho, Ashiya 659, Japan.

CAREER: Asian Publications, Tokyo, Japan, editor of *Asian Weekly, View,* and *Preview,* 1952-53; Orient Asia Grafix, Tokyo, owner, publisher, and editor of *Anone* fortnightly and *Orient Digests,* 1953-57; Wakayama National University, Wakayama, Japan, professor of English, 1957-64; SOPA, Shiraz, Iran, and Ashiya, Japan, owner and publisher, 1963—. Publisher and editor of art books in English, Persian, and German for National Iranian Radio and Television and by appointment to Her Majesty the Empress, 1976-78. Restorer, with wife, Sumiye Gluck, of Narenjestan Palace for use as Asia Institute of Pahlavi University, Shiraz; assistant director of Asian Institute of Pahlavi University, 1966-70. Art collector and museum consultant on Near Eastern art; designer and restorer of American House, a museum of Americana in Kobe, Japan; restorer of 100-year-old home as Museum for Gluck Collection of Persian Art, Kobe, 1983; director of Persia House Museum. *Military service:* U.S. Navy, 1943-45.

WRITINGS: Ah So (cartoon misadventures of a foreigner in Japan), Orient Asia Grafix (Tokyo), 1953, revised edition, 1982; *Zen Combat* (martial arts of Japan), Ballantine, 1964, revised edition, 1984; (translator with Grace Suzuki and others, and editor) *Ukiyo: Stories of the "Floating" World of Postwar Japan,* Universal Library, 1964; (with wife, Sumiye Gluck) *Japan Inside Out* (guidebook), five volumes, Asia Institute Books, 1964-65, new edition, (with son, Garet Arthur Gluck), 1983-84; (editor) *Survey of Persian Art,* Asia Institute Books, Volume XV: *A Bibliography of Pre-Islamic Persian Art,* 1975, Volume XVI: *A Bibliography of Islamic Persian Art,* 1978; (with photographer, Sachiko Saeki) *Pocket Dictionary of the Silk Road* (in Japanese), Shinshindo Publications (Kyoto), 1978; *330 Pieces from the Gluck Collection* (catalogue; in Japanese), Asahi Newspapers and Seibu Culture Center, 1981.

Also author of two documentary films for Iranian National Television; author of *100 Pieces from the Gluck Collection at Tekisui Museum* (catalogue), 1978. Also contributor to *A Survey of Persian Handicraft,* 1977. Translator with wife, S. Gluck, and editor-publisher of series on agriculture and anthropology of Southeast Asia, Asia Institute Books for Kyoto National University Center for Southeast Asian Studies, 1966-67. Also editor and contributor of photographs and addenda to several volumes in "Library of Introductions to Persian Art" series, which was suspended by the Iranian revolution in 1978. Also contributor to *Encyclopedia of Sexual Behavior.* Former columnist, *Japan Times,* Tokyo. Contributor of more than four hundred articles to various Asian publications. Roving editor, *France-Asie/Asia,* 1960-66.

WORK IN PROGRESS: Editing and contributing to Volume XVII, XVIII, and XIX of *Survey of Persian Art; Kamikaze,* a novel on the Mongol empire; completing a biography of the late Arthur Upham Pope, begun by Robert Payne and Rexford Stead, who both died in 1983; assembling a collection of Pope's offbeat stories on Asia.

SIDELIGHTS: Jay Gluck describes himself to *CA* as a "dilettante of the type one laughingly refers to today as an Asian expert." He commuted quarterly between Iran and Japan from 1963-78, and he indicates that he regrets he did not record his impressions of the Iranian milieu just prior to the revolution in 1978: "It is a writer's rent for the space and air he takes up to see life more critically and record this, regardless of the immediate cost it threatens to—but usually does not—demand. Failure to do so costs more later and these payments never cease. The Zen adage that he who knows is silent and he who speaks out knows not is now seen to be but a sad commentary, and not the instructions for evidencing wisdom the young accolyte smugly took them for."

A Survey of Persian Handicraft has been published in Farsi (Persian) and will be translated into Japanese.

* * *

GODWIN, Joscelyn 1945-

PERSONAL: Born January 16, 1945, in Kelmscott, Oxford, England; came to the United States in 1966, naturalized in 1980; son of Edward (an artist and writer) and Stephanie (an artist and writer; maiden name, Allfree) Godwin; married Sharyn Louise Cook (a musician), July 31, 1971 (divorced, 1979); married Janet Matthews, November 21, 1979; children: (second marriage) Ariel. *Education:* Magdalene College, Cambridge, B.A., 1965, Mus.B., 1966, M.A., 1970; Cornell University, Ph.D., 1969. *Home address:* R.D. 1, Earlville, N.Y. 13332. *Office:* Department of Music, Colgate University, Hamilton, N.Y. 13346.

CAREER: Cleveland State University, Cleveland, Ohio, instructor in music, 1969-71; Colgate University, Hamilton, N.Y., assistant professor, 1971-76, associate professor, 1976-82, professor of music, 1982—. Church organist, 1969-75. *Member:* Royal College of Organists (fellow), American Musicological Society. *Awards, honors:* Abingdon Prize from Cambridge University, 1966, for "String Trio"; Harding Prize from Royal College of Organists, 1966.

WRITINGS: (Composer) *Epistle to Harmodius,* Novello, 1966; (composer) *A Few Thoughts for Treble Recorder,* Modern Music for Recorders, 1966; (author of preface and notes) Henry Cowell, *New Musical Resources,* Something Else Press, 1969; (translator) Werner Walcker-Meyer, *The Roman Organ of Acquinum,* Musikwissenschaftliche Verlagsgesellschaft, 1973; (editor) *Schirmer Scores: A Repertory of Western Music,* Schirmer Books, 1975; (editor) *Marco Attilio Regolo,* Harvard University Press, 1975; *Robert Fludd: Hermetic Philosopher and Surveyor of Two Worlds,* Thames & Hudson, 1979; *Athanasius Kircher: A Renaissance Man and the Quest for Lost Knowledge,* Thames & Hudson, 1980; *Mystery Religions in the Ancient World,* Thames & Hudson, 1981. Contributor to *Dictionary of Twentieth Century Music* and to music and religion journals.

WORK IN PROGRESS: An anthology of musical esotericism in the West, tentatively entitled *Music, Mysticism, and Magic,* for Faber; a work, tentatively entitled *The Harmonious Universe,* for Thames & Hudson.

SIDELIGHTS: Author, composer, and organist Joscelyn Godwin told *CA* that his recent work "describes the circuitous route I am having to take in order to reach a better understanding of music in the light of my philosophical interests." Those interests encompass a broad range of time and thought and include such subjects as hermeticism (the study of the astrological and occult writings attributed to Hermes Trismegistus), the role of music in the universe, and the "Perennial Philosophy," a concept central to Godwin's work that attempts to unify and find a common purpose in man's religious experience.

One of Godwin's most widely reviewed works, *Mystery Religions in the Ancient World,* is described by Mary Beard in the *Times Literary Supplement* as "a book not of history, but of theosophy. Ancient religion has been rescued from the hands of 'unbelieving academics' and 'Christian chauvinists,' and the Mysteries are seen to play their part in the 'Perennial Philosophy,' as 'attempts, each valid for its time and place, to point the way to the true goal of human existence!'"

Godwin defined for *CA* the relationship between *Mystery Religions in the Ancient World* and two of his previous works, *Robert Fludd: Hermetic Philosopher and Surveyor of Two Worlds* and *Athanasius Kircher: A Renaissance Man and the Quest for Lost Knowledge:* "Fludd and Kircher were two universal men of the Renaissance for whom music was a fundamental element of their attempt to grasp the cosmos as a whole. Both were deeply concerned with hermeticism, and Kircher especially with the mystery religions of antiquity. Hence [*Mystery Religions in the Ancient World*], which approaches these religions with the question, 'how are we to empathize with these believers?'"

While Beard faults Godwin's approach, she nevertheless points out the value of his purpose, declaring of *Mystery Religions in the Ancient World:* "There is something of interest here. [As a work of mysticism] this book is, I suspect, quite par for the course. Moreover, the recurring and shifting notion of the 'Perennial Philosophy,' from its inception in sixteenth-century Italy, through Leitniz, Huxley, and beyond, is certainly worth attention; as is also . . . the intellectual make-up of Godwin himself."

Having explored the religious implications of his earlier work through the writing of *Mystery Religions in the Ancient World,* Godwin has returned to music. He explains the present and future course of his work: "I have assembled in my anthology a continuous stream of 'musical hermeticism' as it appears in the West and Islam. This is the source material on which *The Harmonious Universe* presents my own ideas. Although I have written exclusively about Western esotericism, I hope later to move in spirit to the East, where I feel more at home philosophically. But the *Sophia Perennis* to which I and my friends are devoted knows no boundaries of time or place."

BIOGRAPHICAL/CRITICAL SOURCES: Times Literary Supplement, January 15, 1982.

* * *

GOODRUM, Charles A(lvin) 1923-

PERSONAL: Born July 21, 1923, in Pittsburg, Kan.; son of Bernie Loy (a city park director) and Mae (Beaver) Goodrum; married Donna Belle Mueller, September 2, 1950; children: Christopher Kent, Julia Belle, Geoffrey Paul. *Education:* University of Wichita (now Wichita State University), student, 1941-43, 1945-46, B.A., 1964; attended Princeton University, 1943-44; Columbia University, M.A., 1949. *Home:* 2808 Pierpont St., Alexandria, Va.

CAREER: University of Wichita (now Wichita State University), Wichita, Kan., librarian in charge of circulation, 1947-48; Library of Congress, Washington, D.C., Legislative Reference Service, reference librarian, 1949-50, political science bibliographer, 1950-53, librarian, 1953-62, coordinator of research, 1963-70, Congressional Research Service, assistant director, 1970-76, Office of the Librarian of Congress, director of Office of Planning and Development, 1976-78. Writer and consultant, 1978—. *Military service:* U.S. Army, 1943-46.

WRITINGS: I'll Trade You an Elk, Funk, 1967; *The Library of Congress,* Praeger, 1974, 2nd revised edition, with Helen W. Darymple, Westview, 1982; *Dewey Decimated* (mystery novel), Crown, 1977; *Carnage of the Realm* (mystery novel),

Crown, 1979 (published in England as *Dead for a Penny*, Gollancz, 1979); *Treasures of the Library of Congress*, Abrams, 1980; (with Darymple) *Guide to the Library of Congress*, Library of Congress, 1983. Contributor to *Atlantic, New Yorker*, and library journals.

WORK IN PROGRESS: A historical novel; two murder mysteries, a detective story set in a famous library of rare books, and a French farce.

SIDELIGHTS: Charles A. Goodrum writes *CA* that he tries "to keep the word processor working between fairly dignified nonfiction, and light casual entertainments." His mystery novels have both been detective stories set in a famous library of rare books, as is one of his works in progress. One of Goodrum's nonfiction books, *Treasures of the Library of Congress*, is described by *New York Times Book Review* critic Frances Taliaferro as "a large handsome volume whose text suggests the remarkable range of the Library's 76 million items; abundant photographs document the richness of books and objects that are the best of their kind." *Washington Post Book World* reviewer Herman W. Liebert reports that, here, Goodrum "writes with humor, a sure feel for the little-known and the unexpected, and a sense of the ticking of history's clock. No one who cares about our present as the child of its past and the parent of its future can read his book without being freshly instructed and deeply moved."

MEDIA ADAPTATIONS: I'll Trade You an Elk was produced by Walt Disney Studios as a made-for-television movie.

BIOGRAPHICAL/CRITICAL SOURCES: Washington Post Book World, November 16, 1980; *New York Times Book Review*, February 8, 1981.

* * *

GOODWIN, R(ichard) M(urphey) 1913-

PERSONAL: Born February 24, 1913, in New Castle, Ind.; son of William Murphey (a farmer) and Mary (Florea) Goodwin; married Jacqueline Wynmalen, June 24, 1937. *Education:* Harvard University, B.A. (summa cum laude), 1934, Ph.D., 1941; Oxford University, B.A., 1936, B.Litt., 1937. *Politics:* "Formerly Communist, now Socialist (member British Labour Party)." *Religion:* None. *Home:* Dorvis's Ashdon, Essex, England. *Office:* Istituto di Economia, Piazza S. Francesco, 53100 Siena, Italy.

CAREER: Harvard University, Cambridge, Mass., instructor, 1942-45, assistant professor of economics, 1945-50; Cambridge University, Cambridge, England, lecturer and fellow, 1952-67, reader in economics, 1967-79; University of Siena, Siena, Italy, professor of economics, 1979—. Painter. *Member:* Econometric Society (fellow), Royal Economic Society. *Awards, honors:* Rhodes scholar.

WRITINGS: Elementary Economics from the Higher Standpoint, Cambridge University Press, 1970; *Essays in Economic Dynamics*, Macmillan, 1982; *Essays in Linear Economic Structures*, Macmillan, 1983.

SIDELIGHTS: R. M. Goodwin spends approximately half his time painting, pointing out that "this is not an avocation but of equal importance in my life to the writing and teaching of economics."

* * *

GOTTMAN, John M(ordechai) 1942-

PERSONAL: Born April 26, 1942, in the Dominican Republic; divorced, 1981. *Education:* Fairleigh Dickinson University, B.S. (magna cum laude), 1962; Massachusetts Institute of Technology, M.S., 1964; University of Wisconsin—Madison, M.A., 1967, Ph.D., 1971; University of Colorado, postdoctoral study, 1971-72. *Home:* 1830 Valley Rd., Champaign, Ill. 61820. *Office:* Department of Psychology, University of Illinois, Champaign, Ill. 61820.

CAREER: Fairleigh Dickinson University, Rutherford, N.J., instructor in mathematics, 1959-60; University of California, Berkeley, instructor in mathematics, 1964; Lawrence Radiation Laboratory, Berkeley, computer programmer, 1964-65; University of Wisconsin—Madison, school psychologist at Center of Community Leadership Development, 1967-68; Central University High School, investigator, 1968-69, director of high school equivalency program and counselor in vocational placement, 1969; researcher for public schools of Madison, Wis., and associate director of Instructional Research Laboratory, 1969-71; Indiana University at Bloomington, assistant professor, 1972-74, associate professor of psychology, 1974-76; University of Illinois at Urbana-Champaign, professor of psychology, 1976—. *Awards, honors:* Woodrow Wilson fellowship, 1962-63; U.S. Public Health Service grant, 1973-76; National Institute of Mental Health Research Scientist Development Award, 1979-83.

WRITINGS: (With R. Clasen) *Evaluation in Education: A Practitioner's Guide*, F. E. Peacock, 1972; (with S. R. Leiblum) *How to Do Psychotherapy and How to Evaluate It: A Manual for Beginners*, Holt, 1974; (with G. V. Glass and V. Willson) *Design and Analysis of Time Series Experiments*, Colorado University Associated Press, 1975; (with J. Gonso, C. Notarius, and H. Markman) *A Couple's Guide to Communication*, Research Press, 1976; (contributor) A. E. Bergin and S. L. Garfield, editors, *Handbook of Psychotherapy and Behavior Change*, Wiley, 2nd edition (Gottman was not associated with first edition), 1978; (contributor) T. Kratochwill, editor, *Strategies to Evaluate Change in Single Subject Research*, Academic Press, 1978; (with others) *Marital Interaction: Experimental Investigations*, Academic Press, 1979.

Time-Series Analysis: A Comprehensive Introduction for Social Scientists, Cambridge University Press, 1981; (editor with Steven Asher) *Development of Children's Friendships*, Cambridge University Press, 1981; (with Esther A. Williams) *A User's Guide to the Gottman-Williams Time Series and Analysis Computer Programs for Social Scientists*, Cambridge University Press, 1982; *How Children Become Friends* (monograph), Society for Research in Child Development, 1983. Co-editor of films, including "Otto: A Case Study in Abnormal Behavior," 1974, "Otto: From a Psychoanalytic Perspective," 1975, and "Otto: From a Phenomenological Perspective," 1975; co-author of films, including "Marital Conflict," 1975, "Will You Be My Friend?," and "Behavioral Interviewing with Couples," 1976. Contributor of articles and reviews to professional journals.

* * *

GRAHAM, Robert G. 1925-

PERSONAL: Born June 11, 1925, in St. Louis, Mo.; children: Lisa Gail, Nicole Marie, Scott Robert. *Education:* University of Illinois, B.S., 1949; University of Texas, M.B.A., 1963, Ph.D., 1965. *Politics:* Republican. *Religion:* Protestant. *Home:* 119 Sunset, Berea, Ohio 44017. *Office:* Baldwin-Wallace College, Berea, Ohio 44017.

CAREER: Frontier Homes Corp., Meadville, Pa., sales manager, 1958-60; Oregon State University, Corvallis, assistant professor, 1965-67, associate professor, beginning 1967, chairman of department of business environment and organizational behavior, beginning 1969; Sangamon State University, Springfield, Ill., professor, 1972-75; University of Wisconsin—Parkside, Kewasha, professor, 1975-78; Baldwin-Wallace College, Division of Business Administration, Berea, Ohio, director of undergraduate studies, 1978—. President, P.D.M., Inc. Consultant, Pacific Northwest Bell Telephone Co., 1966. *Military service:* U.S. Army, Infantry, 1943-46; became first lieutenant. *Member:* Academy of Management, Society of Personnel Administration, Western Academy of Management, Pacific Northwest Personnel Managers Association.

WRITINGS: (With C. F. Gray) *Business Games Handbook*, American Management Association, 1969; *Dictionary of Systems Management*, Mohican Publishing, 1983; *Dictionary of Acronyms*, Mohican Publishing, 1983. Contributor to business and personnel journals. Editor, *Northwest Business Management*, 1968-71.

WORK IN PROGRESS: A text on systems management; a text on project management.

* * *

GRANT, Anthony
See PARES, Marion (Stapylton)

* * *

GREEN, Andrew (Malcolm) 1927-

PERSONAL: Born July 28, 1927, in London, England; son of Arthur Alfred (a secretary) and May Edith (Simpson) Green; married Hazel Hunter, September 8, 1951 (divorced, 1971); married Norah Bridget Cawthorne, 1979. *Education:* Educated in England. *Politics:* "Democratic." *Home:* Scribes Church Cottages, Mountfield, Robertsbridge, East Sussex, England.

CAREER: G. B. Kalee, London, England, assistant general manager, 1952-54; S. N. Bridges, London, advertising and publicity manager, 1954-64; Trade and Technical Press, Morden, England, group editor, 1964-67; Thomson Organization, London, editorial director, 1967-71; Malcolm Publications, London, managing director, 1972-75; writer, 1972—. Tutor of adult courses in parapsychology throughout Surrey, East Sussex, West Sussex, and Kent counties; has appeared on radio and television broadcasts. *Military service:* British national service, 1945-52; served in the Life Guards, Household Cavalry, 1945-48, and Territorial Army, Parachute Regiment, 1948-52; became captain.

MEMBER: Institute of Service Management (founder, 1961), British Institute of Management, Institute of Scientific and Technical Communicators (fellow), Royal Society of Arts (fellow), Society for Psychical Research, Borderline Science Investigation Group (president, 1977). *Awards, honors:* M.Phil., 1975; certificate of award, American Parapsychology Research Fellowship of California, 1982.

WRITINGS: *Mysteries of Surrey*, Napier, 1972; *Mysteries of Sussex*, Napier, 1973; *Mysteries of London*, Napier, 1973; *Ghost Hunting: A Practical Guide*, Garnstone, 1973, Fontana, 1977; (editor) *Our Haunted Kingdom*, Wolfe, 1973, Mayflower, 1975; *Ghosts of the South East*, David & Charles, 1976; *Haunted Houses*, Shire, 1976; *Phantom Ladies*, Bailey Bros. & Swinfen, 1977; *Ghosts of Tunbridge Wells*, Hilton, 1978; *The Ghostly Army*, Macdonald Educational, 1980; *Ghosts of Today*, Kaye & Ward, 1980. Contributor to *Times Educational Supplement, Prediction, Nursing Times, Wireless World, Social Work Today, Doctor, Police Journal*, and other periodicals. Editor, *Freight Forwarder*, 1971-75, *Mobil News for Industry*, 1972-75.

WORK IN PROGRESS: "A definitive work on apparitions"; an examination of "recent 'possession' cases."

SIDELIGHTS: Andrew Green told *CA*: "My constant aim is to promote parapsychology and the serious study of this neo-science." His purpose in writing "is to provide constant evidence of genuine phenomena, to strengthen the need for a rational approach, and to offset distortions and sensationalism by the popular media."

AVOCATIONAL INTERESTS: Archaeology and gardening.

* * *

GREEN, Lawrence W(inter) 1940-

PERSONAL: Born September 16, 1940, in Bell, Calif.; son of Clifton Lawrence and Ora Elizabeth (Winter) Green; married Judith M. Ottoson (in educational policy), May 1, 1982; children: Beth, Jennifer. *Education:* University of California, Berkeley, B.S., 1962, M.P.H., 1966, D.P.H., 1968. *Home:* 3020 Lafayette St., Houston, Tex. 77005. *Office address:* Center for Health Promotion Research and Development, University of Texas Health Science Center at Houston, P.O. Box 20708, Houston, Tex. 77025.

CAREER: Ford Foundation, Dacca, Bangladesh, training associate, 1963-65; University of California, Berkeley, lecturer in health education, 1968-70; Johns Hopkins University, Baltimore, Md., assistant professor, 1970-72, associate professor, 1972-77, professor of health education, 1977-81, head of Health Education Division, 1972-81, assistant dean of School of Hygiene and Public Health, 1975-76; University of Texas Health Science Center at Houston, professor of community medicine and director of Center for Health Promotion Research and Development, 1981—.

Visiting lecturer at Harvard University, 1981-82. Founding member of Pregnancy Testing and Counseling Center and Family Planning Training Institute, Planned Parenthood Association of Maryland, 1972-74; member of expert panel on consumer health education, National Institute of Health, 1975-76; member of advisory committee on planning, National Center for Health Education, 1975. Consultant to World Health Organization, National Center for Health Services Research, National Heart, Lung, and Blood Institute, Arthur D. Little Co., Abt Associates, Medical Research Council of New Zealand, and the state health departments of California, District of Columbia, Hawaii, Kentucky, Louisiana, Ohio, Pennsylvania, Rhode Island, and Texas. *Military service:* U.S. Public Health Service, 1962.

MEMBER: International Union for Health Education, American Public Health Association (member of governing council, 1974-76), Society for Public Health Education (chairman of research and studies committee and monograph committee; president, 1983-84), Association for the Advancement of Health Education, American School Health Association, Society for Prospective Medicine, Society for Preventive Oncology, American Academy of Physical Education, American Academy of Behavioral Medicine Research, Society for Behavioral Medicine. *Awards, honors:* Beryl J. Roberts Award for research in health education, Society for Public Health Education, 1972, for monograph *The Dacca Family Planning Experiment;* Distinguished Career Award, American Public Health Association, 1978; Presidential Citation, Association for the Advancement of Health Education, 1981; National Health Science Honorary Award, Eta Sigma Gamma, 1982.

WRITINGS: Status Identity and Preventive Health Behavior, School of Public Health, University of California, Berkeley, 1970; (with Harold C. Gustafson, William Griffiths, and David Yaukey) *The Dacca Family Planning Experiment: A Comparative Evaluation of Programs Directed at Males and at Females* (monograph), School of Public Health, University of California, Berkeley, 1972; (with Carl Anderson) *Community Health,* Mosby, 1972, 4th edition, 1982; (with Virginia Wang) *Not Forgotten but Still Poor,* University of Maryland Cooperative Extension, 1974; (with Marshall Kreuter, Sigrid G. Deeds, and Kay B. Partridge) *Health Education Planning: A Diagnostic Approach,* Mayfield, 1980; (with Connie C. Kansler) *The Professional and Scientific Literature in Patient Education,* Gale, 1980; (with Rebecca Parkinson) *Managing Health Promotion in the Workplace: Guidelines for Implementation and Evaluation,* Mayfield, 1982.

With Karol Josef Krotki; all published by Pakistan Institute of Development Economics: *Seven Years of Clinic Experience under the "Traditional Planned Parenthood Approach" in Karachi: A Baseline for Evaluating the Next Phase of Family Planning in Pakistan,* 1965; *Demographic Implications of the First Six Years of Family Planning in Karachi, 1958-1964,* 1966.

Contributor to public health and other professional journals. Editor of *Health Education Monographs.* Member of editorial boards of *Health Education Quarterly, Journal of Public Health Policy, Journal of Community Health,* and *Journal of Family and Community Health.*

WORK IN PROGRESS: Measurement and Evaluation in Health Education, with Frances M. Lewis, for Mayfield Publishing.

SIDELIGHTS: Lawrence W. Green writes *CA:* "The field of health education has been given considerable attention and priority in recent health policy decisions and legislative actions of the federal government. The need for scientific literature on the effectiveness of health education in relation to life-style changes such as diet, exercise, accident prevention, and smoking has made work on evaluation of health education of interest to government planners, legislative analysts, hospital and health administrators, and others."

* * *

GREENE, Jonathan Edward 1943-

PERSONAL: Born April 19, 1943, in New York, N.Y.; married Alice-Anne Kingston, June 5, 1963 (divorced); married Dobree Adams, May 23, 1974; children: Michal Tara (deceased), Kora Radella; stepchildren: Hunter Purdy, John Purdy. *Education:* Bard College, B.A., 1965; additional study at University of California, Wagner College, and University of Kentucky. *Address:* P.O. Box 106, Frankfort, Ky. 40602-0106.

CAREER: Gnomon Press, Frankfort, Ky., publisher, 1965—; University Press of Kentucky, Lexington, production manager and designer, 1967-75.

WRITINGS—Poetry: *The Reckoning,* Matter Books, 1966; *Instance,* Buttonwood Press, 1968; *The Lapidary,* Black Sparrow Press, 1969; *A 17th Century Garner,* Buttonwood Press, 1969; *An Unspoken Complaint,* Unicorn Press, 1970; *Glossary of the Everyday,* Coach House Press (Toronto), 1974; *Scaling the Walls,* Gnomon Press, 1974; *Peripatetics,* Truck Press, 1978; *Once a Kingdom Again,* Sand Dollar, 1979; *Quiet Goods,* Larkspur Press, 1980; *Idylls,* Iron Mountain Press, 1983; *Small Change for the Long Haul,* Station Hill Press, 1984; *Trickster Tales,* Toothpaste Press, 1984. Poems included in several anthologies and periodicals.

WORK IN PROGRESS: A book of poems, *Anniversaries.*

* * *

**GREENFIELD, Darby
See WARD, Philip**

* * *

**GREENWOOD, Edward Alister 1930-
(Ted Greenwood)**

PERSONAL: Born December 4, 1930, in Melbourne, Victoria, Australia; son of George Frederick (an architect) and Ilma (McDonald) Greenwood; married Florence Lorraine Peart (a kindergarten director), January 15, 1954; children: Catherine, Meredith, Alister, Emma. *Education:* Melbourne Teachers' College, Primary Teaching Qualification, 1949; Royal Melbourne Institute of Technology, Diploma of Art, 1959. *Politics:* Uncommitted. *Religion:* "Personal." *Home and office:* Hilton Rd., Ferny Creek, Victoria 3786, Australia.

CAREER: Education Department of Victoria, Melbourne, Australia, primary teacher, 1948-56; lecturer in art education at Melbourne Teachers' College, Melbourne, 1956-60, and Toorak Teachers' College, Toorak, Melbourne, 1961-68; currently writer, illustrator, and craft reviewer for the *Age* newspaper. Deputy-chairman of Community Arts Board, Australia Arts Council, 1978-83.

AWARDS, HONORS: Picture Book of the Year Award, 1968, for illustrations in *Sly Old Wardrobe,* and commendation, 1969, for *Obstreperous,* both from the Children's Book Council of Australia; high commendation from Children's Book Council of Australia, 1974, for *Joseph and Lulu and the Prindiville House Pigeons,* which was also named to the Hans Christian Anderson Honours List, 1974; Visual Arts award for illustration from Australian Council for the Arts, and commendation from the Children's Book Council of Australia, 1976, both for *Terry's Brrrmmm GT;* commendation from the Children's Book Council of Australia for *The Pochetto Coat.*

WRITINGS—All under name Ted Greenwood; all children's books; published by Hutchinson: *The Pochetto Coat,* 1978; *The Boy Who Saw God,* 1980; *Flora's Treasures,* 1982.

All self-illustrated children's books; published by Angus & Robertson, except as indicated: *Obstreperous,* 1970; *Aelfred,* 1970; *V.I.P.,* 1971; *Joseph and Lulu and the Prindiville House Pigeons,* 1972; *Terry's Brrrmmm GT,* 1975; *Curious Eddie,* 1977; *Ginnie,* Kestrel, 1979; *Everlasting Circle,* Hutchinson, 1981; *Marley and Friends,* 1983.

Illustrator of children's books: Ivan Southall, *Sly Old Wardrobe,* Cheshire, 1968, St. Martin's, 1970; *Children Everywhere* (Australian section; text by Southall), Field Enterprises Educational Corp., 1970.

WORK IN PROGRESS: Warts and All, a collaboration with a medical practitioner about children's conceptions and misconceptions about their bodies and health; *Ship Rock,* a picture book about change and decay; *The House of Mr. Materlink,* a "sound book" taped for the blind.

SIDELIGHTS: Edward Alister Greenwood is particularly interested in cultivating the senses of children "in an age where so many experiences come to them in a vicarious form." "Although the illustrated book is such a form," he comments, "I hope my books will act as catalysts for activity by those who read and look at them."

* * *

GREENWOOD, Ted
See GREENWOOD, Edward Alister

* * *

GRENIER, Mildred 1917-

PERSONAL: Born February 1, 1917, in Maysville, Mo.; daughter of Clarence W. (a farmer) and Mary Ann (Bottorff) Bromley; married Joseph G. Grenier (a public school teacher), December 24, 1942; children: Joseph Kent (killed in Vietnam), Candace Jeanette. Education: Attended Maryville State Teachers College and Furman University; Missouri Western State College, B.S., 1975. Politics: Republican. Religion: Methodist. Home address: 1811 Lovers Lane Hts., St. Joseph, Mo. 64505.

CAREER: Public school teacher in Fairport, Mo., 1936-39, and in Osborn, Mo., 1939-43; nursery school teacher in Columbia, S.C., 1944-46; Missouri Western State College, St. Joseph, teacher of creative writing, 1974-79. Member: National League of American Pen Women (president, 1960-62; president of Missouri chapter, 1962-64; historian, 1964-66; treasurer, 1966-68; secretary, 1970-72), Missouri Writers Guild (first vice-president, 1983-84). Awards, honors: First prize in International Instructor Stories for Children Awards, 1965; has won four awards in Writer's Digest contests, two from Freedoms Foundation, and local, state, regional, and national awards from National League of American Pen Women.

WRITINGS: Christmas Every Day, A. D. Freese, 1961; How High Is the Sky? (juvenile), Herald House, 1968; How Kids Can Earn Cash, Fell, 1970; The Wagon and the Star, Standard Publishing, 1971; God Made Our World, C. R. Gibson, 1972; The Quick and Easy Guide to Making Money at Home, Fell, 1974; How to Win Recipe and Cooking Contests, R and D Services, 1978; Pictorial History of St. Joseph, Donning, 1981; Special Day Prayers for the Very Young Child, Concordia, 1983; Capsule Course for the Freelance Writer, Pilot Books, 1983. Contributor of more than two thousand items to more than one hundred publications, including Ladies' Home Journal, Saturday Evening Post, Jack and Jill, New York Herald Tribune, Kansas City Star and Times, and Christian Herald.

* * *

GRIEB, Kenneth J. 1939-

PERSONAL: Born April 3, 1939, in Buffalo, N.Y.; son of Joseph J. and Ida Grieb. Education: University of Buffalo (now State University of New York at Buffalo), B.A., 1960, M.A., 1962; Indiana University, Ph.D., 1966. Home: 1505 Porter Ave., Oshkosh, Wis. 54901. Office: Department of History, University of Wisconsin, Oshkosh, Wis. 54901.

CAREER: Indiana University at South Bend, resident lecturer in history, 1965-66; University of Wisconsin—Oshkosh, assistant professor, 1966-70, associate professor, 1970-74, professor of history, 1974—, John McNary Rosebush University Professor, 1983—, coordinator of Latin American studies, 1968-77, coordinator of international studies, 1977—, director of Interdisciplinary Center, 1978—. Member: American Historical Association, Organization of American Historians, Latin American Studies Association, Conference on Latin American History (chairman of Caribe-Centro America committee, 1979-80), Society for Historians of American Foreign Relations, Midwest Association for Latin American Studies (president, 1972-73), Wisconsin Council of Latin Americanists (president, 1970-71), Phi Alpha Theta. Awards, honors: Doherty Foundation fellow in Mexico, 1964-65.

WRITINGS: The United States and Huerta, University of Nebraska Press, 1969; (co-editor) Latin American Government Leaders, Arizona State University Press, 1970, 2nd edition, 1975; (co-author) Essays on Miguel Angel Asturias, Latin American Center, University of Wisconsin—Milwaukee, 1973; (contributor) Richard E. Greenleaf and Michael C. Meyer, editors, Research in Mexican History: Topics, Methodology, Sources, and a Practical Guide to Field Research, University of Nebraska Press, 1973.

The Latin American Policy of Warren G. Harding (monograph), Texas Christian University Press, 1976; (contributor) Jules David, editor, Perspectives in American Diplomacy, Arno Press, 1976; Guatemalan Caudillo: The Regime of Jorge Ubico, Guatemala, 1931-1944, Ohio University Press, 1979; (editor) Research Guide to Central America and the Caribbean, University of Wisconsin Press, 1984.

Consulting editor of "The World of Latin America" series, Forum Press, 1982—. Contributor of articles and reviews to historical journals. Member of board of editors of Americas, 1976—, and Historian, 1981—.

WORK IN PROGRESS: United States Relations with Central America, 1930-1945; Mexico and the Second World War; The Regime of General Manuel Avilla, Comacho: Mexico 1940-1946; A Bibliography of Central America.

* * *

GROSS, Feliks 1906-

PERSONAL: Born June 17, 1906, in Cracow, Poland; came to United States in 1941, naturalized in 1955; son of Adolf (a lawyer) and Augusta (Alexander) Gross; married Priva Baidaff (a professor of art history), 1937; children: Eva Helena Gross Friedman. Education: University of Cracow, Magister Juris, 1929, Dr.Juris, 1930; further study of political science in Paris, France, 1931. Home: 310 West 85th St., New York, N.Y. 10024. Office: Graduate Center, City University of New York, 33 West 42nd St., New York, N.Y. 10036; and Polish Institute of Arts and Sciences in America, 59 East 66th St., New York, N.Y. 10021.

CAREER: Active in Workers University Association (adult education movement in Poland), 1925-39, and director of its Labor Social Science School, Cracow, 1934-38; University of London, London School of Economics and Political Science, London, England, occasional lecturer in social anthropology, 1939-40; New Europe and World Reconstruction (monthly journal), New York City, editor, 1942-45; City University of New York, professor of sociology and anthropology at Brooklyn College, Brooklyn, N.Y., and Graduate Center, New York City, 1946-77, professor emeritus, 1977—, president of university Academy for Humanities and Sciences, 1980—.

Visiting professor and director of Institute of International Affairs, University of Wyoming, summers, 1945-52; visiting professor, New York University, 1945-68, Woodrow Wilson School of Foreign Affairs, University of Virginia, 1951 and 1954-56,

University of Vermont, 1956, and Columbia University, 1973; senior Fulbright lecturer, University of Rome, 1957-58, 1964-65, and 1974, University of Pavia, 1958, and Diplomatic Institute of the Italian Foreign Office, University of Florence, 1977; lecturer at other universities in the United States and Europe. Member of research council, Foreign Policy Research Institute, Philadelphia, 1966-76. Secretary-general, Central-East European Planning Board (Czechoslovakia, Greece, Yugoslavia, and Poland), 1942-45; president, Taraknath Das Foundation, 1965; member of board of directors, International League of Human Rights. Consultant, National Committee for Prevention and Causes of Violence, 1969.

MEMBER: International Institute of Sociology, American Sociological Association, American Association for the Advancement of Slavic Studies, Academy of Political Science, Polish Institute of Arts and Sciences in America (vice-president, 1964; director, 1975), Authors League of America, New York Academy of Sciences, Sigma Xi.

AWARDS, HONORS: Carnegie scholar in Paris, 1931; recipient of grants from Public Affairs Foundation, New York University, 1962-63, Sloane Foundation, 1963, Research Foundation of the City University of New York, 1966-67, 1971, and 1974, American Council of Learned Societies, 1969, National Science Foundation, 1972, Rockefeller Foundation, 1974, Italian National Research Council, 1974, and Brooklyn College Foundation, 1975; Order of Phoenix (Greece) for scholarly work, 1963.

WRITINGS: (With Zygmunt Gross) *Socjologia Partii Politycznej* (title means "Sociology of Political Parties"), [Cracow], 1928, 2nd edition, Czytelnik, 1946; *Koczownictwo: Studja nad Nomadyznem i nad Wyply wem Tegoz na spoleczenstwo* (title means "Nomadism: Studies on Nomadism and Its Influence on Society"; includes summaries in English), introduction by Bronislaw Malinowski, Instytut Popierania Nauki, 1936; (editor with Zygmunt Myslakowski) *Robotnicy Pisza* (title means "Biographies of Workers"), Ksiegarnia Powszechna, 1937; *Proletariat i Kultura* (title means "Proletariat and Culture"), Proletariatum Ksiegarnia Powszechna, 1938.

Crossroads of Two Continents: A Democratic Federation of East-Central Europe, Columbia University Press, 1945; *The Polish Worker: A Study of a Social Stratum* (large part written in Polish), translation by Norbert Guterman, Roy, 1945; *Socjalism Humanistyczny* (title means "Humanistic Socialism"), Polish Socialist Alliance (New York), 1946; (editor) *European Ideologies: A Survey of Twentieth-Century Political Ideas,* introduction by Robert M. MacIver, Philosophical Library, 1948; (editor with Rex Hopper and Samuel Koenig) *Sociology* (readings), Prentice-Hall, 1954; (editor with Basil J. Vlavianos) *The Struggle for Tomorrow: Modern Political Ideologies of the Jewish People,* Arts (New York), 1954; *Foreign Policy Analysis,* preface by Adolf A. Berle, Jr., Philosophical Library, 1954; *The Seizure of Political Power in a Century of Revolutions,* Philosophical Library, 1958; *Druga Rewolucja Przemyslowa* (title means "Second Industrial Revolution"), Swiatlo (Paris), 1958.

O Wartosciach Spolecznych (title means "On Social Values"), Polish Institute of Arts and Sciences in America, 1961; *Uwagi o Zmianie Spolecznej,* introduction by Norman Thomas, Democratic Press and Liberty Publications (London), 1964; *World Politics and Tension Areas,* New York University Press, 1966; *Valori Sociali e Struttura* (title means "Social Values and Structure"), Institute of Empirical Research, University of Rome, 1967; *Violence in Politics,* Mouton, 1973; *Il Paese: Values and Social Change in an Italian Village,* New York University Press, 1974; *Contadini, Rocche, Contrade,* University of Rome, 1974; *The Revolutionary Party: Essays in the Sociology of Politics,* Greenwood Press, 1974; *Ethics in the Borderland: An Inquiry into the Nature of Ethnicity and Reduction of Tensions,* Greenwood Press, 1978; *Ideologies, Goals, and Values,* Greenwood Press, 1983.

Contributor: Joseph E. Roucek, editor, *Central-Eastern Europe,* Prentice-Hall, 1946; Roucek, *Contemporary Sociology,* Philosophical Library, 1958; *La Fonction publique internationale et l'action internationale d'assistance technique,* [Paris], 1958; Kirkham, Levy, and Croty, editors, *Assassination and Political Violence,* U.S. Government Printing Office, 1970; *Boundaries and Regions,* Lint, 1973; Sidney Hook and others, editors, *The Philosophy of the Curriculum,* Prometheus Press, 1975; L. Pellicani, editor, *Sociologia dei mutamenti rivoluzionari,* Vallecchi, 1976.

Associate editor and contributor, *Slavonic Encyclopedia,* Philosophical Library, 1949. Author of syndicated column for Asian and Latin American newspapers, Foreign News Service, 1962-63. Contributor to journals in the United States, Belgium, Sweden, India, Mexico, Germany, Poland, Costa Rica, Italy, and France.

WORK IN PROGRESS: A new edition of *Proletariat i Kultura.*

SIDELIGHTS: Feliks Gross told *CA:* "I did not write for money. At its best, scholarly books bring a welcome, but a limited, income. I signed flat fee contracts on books that sold well just to finish a project. Nor did I write for academic promotion. I had sufficient publications. With a very heavy teaching load for several decades, writing called for self-discipline, early rising—just about 4:30 or 5:00 A.M.—and long hours of work.

"Why do we write books? I asked myself many times. Sometimes—most of the time—it is like mountain climbing. I could not explain why I did it and even enjoyed it. Most of the time we cannot explain why. But, in all honesty, there is often a sentiment of compelling duty to share views and findings in areas the writer considers relevant; at times it is a feeling of discovery. In spite of it all—so it seems to me—in honest writing there is less of a profit motive, less of a search for material gain, even publicity and vainglory, than most people assume.

"Research and writing are for me difficult and demanding tasks. However, once the material is gathered, and the effort reduced to writing and editing, the search for essentials still persists with a compelling sentiment of need for further reduction of text and ideas to the most relevant.

"At times, pleasant was the final work of editing, which I have often done in a garden, in the fresh air under an old apple tree on an island off the coast of Maine."

*　*　*

GRUBER, Ruth

PERSONAL: Born in New York, N.Y.; daughter of David and Gussie (Rockower) Gruber; married Philip Hope Michaels (a lawyer), February 4, 1951 (died, February 14, 1968); married Henry Rosner, September, 1974 (died, March 16, 1982); children: (first marriage) Celia Joyce, David Morris. *Education:* New York University, B.A.; University of Wisconsin, M.A.; University of Cologne, Ph.D. *Religion:* Jewish. *Residence:* New York, N.Y.

CAREER: U.S. Department of the Interior, Washington, D.C., special assistant to Secretary of Interior and field representative for Alaska, 1941-46; *New York Post,* New York City, foreign correspondent, 1946; *New York Herald Tribune,* New York City, special foreign correspondent, 1947-65. Lecturer, Hunter College of the City University of New York, 1961-66. Co-chairman, Women's Division of United Jewish Appeal of Greater New York, 1950—. *Member:* Arctic Institute of North America, American Society of Journalists and Authors, P.E.N., Overseas Press Club of America, Writers Guild of America, National Council of Women of the United States, Society of the Silurians. *Awards, honors:* Ford Foundation travel and study grant to Israel, 1964; National Jewish Book Award, 1979, for *Raquela: A Woman of Israel.*

WRITINGS: *I Went to the Soviet Arctic,* Simon & Schuster, 1939, revised and enlarged edition, Viking, 1944; *Destination Palestine: The Story of the Haganah Ship Exodus 1947,* Current Books, 1948; *Israel without Tears,* A. A. Wyn, 1950; *Israel Today: Land of Many Nations,* Hill & Wang, 1958, revised edition, 1963; *Puerto Rico: Island of Promise,* Hill & Wang, 1960; (editor) *Science and the New Nations,* Basic Books, 1961; *Israel on the Seventh Day,* Hill & Wang, 1968; *Felisa Rincon de Gautier: The Mayor of San Juan,* Crowell, 1972; (with Marjorie Margolies) *They Came to Stay,* Coward, 1975; *Raquela: A Woman of Israel,* Coward, 1978; *Haven: The Unknown Story of 1,000 World War II Refugees,* Coward, 1983. Also author of scripts for NBC-TV program, "Eternal Light." Columnist, *Haddassah* magazine, 1961—. Contributor to magazines, including *Look, Saturday Review, Commentary, Nation, New Republic,* and *Ms.*

SIDELIGHTS: Ruth Gruber was a special assistant to Secretary of the Interior Harold Ickes in June of 1944 when President Franklin D. Roosevelt announced that temporary haven would be provided to 1,000 mostly Jewish refugees who had made their way to Italy during World War II. Gruber was selected to escort them by ship to a former U.S. army camp in Oswego, N.Y. and to help them settle in once they arrived. She describes the experience in *Haven: The Unknown Story of 1,000 World War II Refugees.* In a *New York Times* review, Richard F. Shepard indicates that, here, Gruber "combines the thorough knowledge of the insider with the writing skill of the professional to tell the story of this unusual footnote to history." Once they were established in the compound, the camp residents had to contend with the fact that they lived in a kind of limbo, without even the status of immigrants. As a condition of asylum, the refugees had been required to sign a contract stipulating that, at war's end, they would return to Europe, but many of them hadn't expected that they would be forced to live up to it. And, as legal "guests" of the United States, they were unable to apply for immigrant status although some already had relatives in the country. Ironically, due to a labor shortage at a nearby frozen food plant, several residents of the camp found themselves working in town next to large numbers of POWs, who could look forward to returning to a more secure life in Europe than the refugees.

Roosevelt had promised Congress that the refugees would eventually go back to Europe, but after his death and Truman's succession a change in policy was implemented. In January of 1946, the refugees were transported to Canada where they were able to obtain visas that allowed them to enter the United States as immigrants. Gruber provides readers with an update on the lives of several of these immigrants and their families in the final chapter of *Haven.* Shepard concludes that "it is a touching story . . . in which the writer has put us in the full picture and humanized it with anecdote and specific people." *Washington Post Book World* critic Frances A. Koestler adds that "in the mounting mass of documentation on the 10 million lives lost in the Holocaust, the events described in this book constitute little more than a footnote, yet, as sometimes happens, a footnote can provide a sharper shaft of illumination than the text it annotates."

BIOGRAPHICAL/CRITICAL SOURCES: *Washington Post Book World,* August 28, 1983; *New York Times,* August 30, 1983.

* * *

GRUNDY, Kenneth W(illiam) 1936-

PERSONAL: Born August 6, 1936, in Philadelphia, Pa.; son of William and Alma (Hahn) Grundy; married Martha J. Paxson, June 25, 1960; children: William MacIntyre, Thomas Paxson, Anne Edmunds. *Education:* Ursinus College, B.A. (with honors), 1958; Pennsylvania State University, M.A., 1961, Ph.D., 1963. *Home:* 2602 Exeter Rd., Cleveland Heights, Ohio 44118. *Office:* Department of Political Science, Case Western Reserve University, Cleveland, Ohio 44106.

CAREER: San Fernando Valley State College (now California State University, Northridge), Northridge, Calif., assistant professor of political science, 1963-66; Case Western Reserve University, Cleveland, Ohio, associate professor, 1966-74, professor of political science, 1974—. Visiting assistant professor at Pennsylvania State University, summer, 1965; visiting senior lecturer at Makerere University, 1967-68; Fulbright professor at University of Zambia, 1977; Fulbright professor at National University of Ireland, University College, Galway, 1979-80; Armington professorship, 1983-84. Visiting scholar at Institute of Social Studies (the Hague), 1972-73.

MEMBER: International Studies Association, African Studies Association (fellow), Inter-University Seminar on the Armed Forces and Society (member of executive council, 1976—). *Awards, honors:* Rockefeller Foundation grant for Uganda, 1967-68; Center on International Race Relations grant for southern Africa, 1969-71; Social Science Research Council grant, 1972-73 (for England and the Netherlands), 1979-80; Earhart Foundation grant, 1979-80; Bradlow fellow, South African Institute of International Affairs, 1982.

WRITINGS: (Contributor) William H. Friedland and Carl G. Rosberg, Jr., editors, *African Socialism,* Stanford University Press, 1964; *Conflicting Images of the Military in Africa,* East African Publishing House, 1968; *Guerrilla Struggle in Africa: Analysis and Preview,* Grossman, 1971; *Confrontation and Accommodation in Southern Africa: The Limits of Independence,* University of California Press, 1973; (with Michael Weinstein) *The Ideologies of Violence,* C. E. Merrill, 1974; *We're Against Apartheid, But . . .* (monograph), University of Denver, 1974.

Defense Legislation and Communal Politics (monograph), Ohio University, 1978; (co-editor and contributor) *Evaluating Transnational Programs in Government and Business,* Pergamon, 1979; *Soldiers without Politics: Blacks in the South African Armed Forces,* University of California Press, 1983; *The Rise of the South African Security Establishment* (monograph), South African Institute of International Affairs, 1983.

Also contributor of chapters to books. Contributor of more than one hundred articles and reviews to academic and literary journals and popular magazines, including *Saturday Review, Yale Review,* and *Virginia Quarterly Review.* Book review editor, *International Journal of Comparative Sociology,* 1973-82; special editor, *Armed Forces and Society,* January, 1976; contributing editor, *Current History,* 1982—.

WORK IN PROGRESS: An extended study of South African defense and foreign policy, especially relating to the role of the security establishment in policy-making.

SIDELIGHTS: Kenneth W. Grundy told *CA:* "There has been a regrettable dichotomy drawn between scholarly writing and popular writing, as if the two cannot coexist, least of all be present in the same piece. Technical writing must be arcane, obscure, comprehensible to none but the professional scientist. Popular writing must be simple, without depth or subtlety. Nonsense. I regard it my task to bring the two together and to make international issues understandable to interested citizens. Social scientists are responsible for communicating their findings to the public as well as to other specialists. Both have important roles in the public policy process, and both must be well-informed to perform their roles properly."

Grundy adds: "Writing for me is a joy, not a chore. I regret how difficult it is to find the time to do as much as I would like to do. This is so, not because all other tasks are unpleasant, but because so many other tasks are also fun. Teaching is pleasant. So is doing things with my family. Choices have to be made from among a variety of enjoyments, and herein lies the dilemma—how to squeeze forty hours out of a day without becoming thoroughly frustrated."

* * *

GUILES, Fred Lawrence 1920-

PERSONAL: Born November 17, 1920, in Des Moines, Iowa; son of Fred Lawrence (a sales manager) and Lelia (Hanson) Guiles. *Education:* Columbia University, B.S., 1950. *Politics:* Independent liberal. *Religion:* Protestant. *Address:* c/o Franklin R. Weissberg, 505 Park Ave., New York, N.Y. 10022.

CAREER: St. John Associates, Inc., New York, N.Y., public relations work, 1950-69; free-lance writer, 1969—. *Military service:* U.S. Army, 1942-46; served in Italy and Philippines.

WRITINGS: Norma Jean: The Life of Marilyn Monroe, McGraw, 1969; *Marion Davies,* McGraw, 1972; *Hanging on in Paradise,* McGraw, 1975; *Tyrone Power: The Last Idol,* Doubleday, 1979; *Stan: The Life of Stan Laurel,* Stein & Day, 1981; *Jane Fonda: The Actress in Her Time,* Doubleday, 1982. Also author of two plays, "Song for a Certain Midnight" and "The Dead Survivors."

WORK IN PROGRESS: A revised biography of Marilyn Monroe; *The Sunset Blues,* a novel.

SIDELIGHTS: Chicago Tribune Book World critic Bruce Cook describes Fred Lawrence Guiles's *Norma Jean: The Life of Marilyn Monroe* as the "first now-it-can-be-told biography of Marilyn Monroe." Norman Mailer used the work as a reference when he wrote about the actress in his book *Marilyn,* according to Stephen Farber in the *New York Times Book Review.* Guiles is currently at work on a revision of *Norma Jean,* which may supply readers with a more clearly-defined portrait of the actress than the original provided. Many critics found the biography reliable, but it left them wanting to know more. *Commentary* critic Michael Wood indicates that *Norma Jean* "is pleasant enough, decent, well-intentioned, well-researched." However, comments *New York Times Book Review* critic Andrew Sarris, Guiles "never conveys the magical magnification of a little blonde girl with a large head, an often dumpy body, a stammering breathlessness, and a warm, muddled mind into the stuff that so many dreams were made of."

"Bravely, protectively, and sometimes a little disingenuously, Mr. Guiles goes back over it all," comments *New York Times* reviewer John Leonard, "the foster homes, the first marriage when she was 16, the early modeling, the various Svengalis, the studio contracts, lovers, stardom, despair, breakdowns and death." Still, writes Leonard, "the woman remains elusive, undefined." In the words of Wood, "*Norma Jean* is a readable, gentle, intelligent book. It simply falls down on the crucial question: how innocent was Marilyn? How ruthless was she in digging for protectors and then ditching them? How much did she sleep around to get ahead? How much did it hurt to be close to her? Guiles goes discreet here." "Unfortunately," indicates Sarris, "the facts (at least, those unearthed here by Fred Lawrence Guiles) are considerably less interesting than the fantasies evoked by any one picture of Marilyn Monroe in her familiar pose of sensual supplication."

Also about the film industry, Guiles's *Hanging on in Paradise,* "is the first book-length nonfiction account of the writers who came to Hollywood at the height of the studio system," writes Harold Meyerson in *Harper's.* Here, Farber indicates, Guiles focusses upon the period between 1930 and 1950, when such writers as Lillian Hellman, F. Scott Fitzgerald, and Dorothy Parker made their contributions to film. During that time, writes Farber, "many European artists uprooted by Fascism ended up in Los Angeles along with the New York exiles; for a decade or so the town must have been almost as lively and stimulating as Paris in the twenties." Describing the era as "Hollywood's Golden Age," Farber calls the book "a kind of composite biography of the Hollywood writer, at a time when the movie capital was also the cultural and intellectual center of the world."

Guiles writes about an equally glamorous age—concentrating primarily on the late 1910's to the early 1930's—in *Marion Davies,* a biography of the 19-year-old Ziegfield Follies showgirl who became the lifetime mistress of publishing tycoon William Randolph Hearst and, thereby, one of the richest women in the world. *New York Times Book Review* critic Nunnally Johnson describes it as "not a story that the righteous will be able to get much comfort out of." "Whatever the official wages of sin," he remarks, "Miss Davies wound up with holdings estimated to be worth in excess of $20,000,000, a reward for love unlikely to be topped under the present tax structure." Budd Schulberg points out in *New Republic* that Davies was "able to offer William Randolph Hearst himself a cool million when his regal compulsion for what Veblen calls conspicuous consumption (began) to drain even his fabulous resources."

Davies also enjoyed a long and mostly successful career as a film comedienne, despite a stutter which might have hindered her when the industry switched from silent films to talkies. According to a *Times Literary Supplement* reviewer, "Mr. Guiles's admirably detailed filmography lists no fewer than forty-six film titles (including one serial of some thirty episodes) spread over twenty years, 1917-37." But the legend is that any success she enjoyed was predicated upon Hearst's use of his papers to publicize and praise her to the public. Later in her career, Davies's life was fictionalized in "Citizen Kane," a film that portrayed her thinly disguised counterpart, Susan Alexander, as an incompetent provided with a brief singing career by her benefactor, who forced her upon an ungracious public. In Guiles's opinion, however, Davies was a talented comedienne. His thesis is that Hearst's attempts to promote her through his papers, in addition to his misguided efforts to push her towards a stardom as a serious actress, hurt rather than helped her career, and the film "Citizen Kane" compounded the damage, since the public tended to accept the movie as truth.

As Schulberg relates, *Marion Davies* is "a researcher's avalanche of Marionalia. If you are interested in what Marion had for brunch in her 15-room 'bungalow' on the MGM lot on September 12, 1925 (probably straight gin), chances are the meticulous Mr. Guiles will be able to supply the information." The *Times Literary Supplement* critic reports that "the balance [Guiles] achieves between the professional career of Marion Davies and her, after all, equally fascinating private life with Hearst is exemplary, and the book is in general a model of what such books should be." On the whole, concludes Johnson, *Marion Davies* "is an impressive chronicling of as gaudy a legend as this century has to offer."

AVOCATIONAL INTERESTS: Conservation and animal rescue programs.

BIOGRAPHICAL/CRITICAL SOURCES: New York Times, June 17, 1969; *New York Times Book Review,* August 3, 1969, September 24, 1972, May 18, 1975; *Commentary,* September, 1969; *New Republic,* January 6 & 13, 1973; *Times Literary Supplement,* May 18, 1973; *Harper's,* July, 1975; *New Yorker,* April 20, 1981; *West Coast Review of Books,* May, 1982; *Chicago Tribune Book World,* June 13, 1982, April 3, 1983.

—Sketch by Candace Cloutier

* * *

GUNN, Bill
See GUNN, William Harrison

* * *

GUNN, William Harrison 1934-
(Bill Gunn)

PERSONAL: Born July 15, 1934, in Philadelphia, Pa.; son of William Harrison and Louise (Alexander) Gunn. *Education:* Attended public schools in Philadelphia, Pa. *Politics:* Democrat. *Residence:* New York, N.Y. *Agent:* Bertha Case, 42 West 53rd St., New York, N.Y.

CAREER: Actor on stage, television, and films, 1955—; writer. *Military service:* U.S. Navy.

WRITINGS—All under name Bill Gunn; novels: *All the Rest Have Died,* Delacorte, 1964; *Rhinestone Sharecropping* (also see below), Reed, Cannon, 1981.

Stage plays: "Marcus in the High Grass," produced in New York by Theatre Guild, 1959; "Johnnas," produced in New York at Chelsea Theatre, 1968; *Black Picture Show* (produced in New York at Vivian Beaumont Theatre), Reed, Cannon, 1975; "Rhinestone" (musical; based on novel *Rhinestone Sharecropping),* produced in New York at Richard Allen Center, 1982. Also author of "Celebration," produced in Los Angeles at Mark Taper Forum.

Screenplays: (With Ronald Ribman) "The Angel Levine" (adaptation of novel by Bernard Malamud), United Artists, 1970; "The Landlord" (adaptation of a novel by Kristin Hunter), United Artists, 1970; "Ganja and Hess" (released under title "Blood Couple"), Kelly-Jordon Enterprises, 1973. Also author of "Don't the Moon Look Lonesome" (adaptation of a novel by Don Asher); associated with "The Greatest," Columbia, 1976.

WORK IN PROGRESS: A novel, *The Death Game;* plays.

SIDELIGHTS: Bill Gunn, an actor and director, is the author of two plays based on his experiences as a screenwriter in Hollywood. The first, "Black Picture Show," is described by Jack Kroll of *Newsweek* as being "about a black artist who has to sell out to the devilish white culture in order to survive." But, Kroll adds, "there's more to the play than that. . . . The leading character is Alexander, a poet and writer whose sanity appears to have snapped in his lifelong attempt to make it as a black artist in a white, anti-art society. Beginning in a mental institution [where Alexander has been confined,] the play breaks back into time to show how the pressure built up."

Critics Ted E. Kalem and Brendan Gill argue with Gunn's depiction of a writer's compromise with the Hollywood system. "What is Gunn driving at?," asks Kalem in *Time.* "He is saying that Alexander, an artist of seemingly impeccable integrity, has sold out and has been destroyed by his yen for lucre. This is twaddle. No artist has ever been corrupted or humiliated by the quest for cash unless he was a willing accomplice." And Gill, while calling the author an "obviously gifted" playright, wonders in *New Yorker:* "Why is it worse for a black to sell out to a white than for a white to sell out to a white, or, for that matter, for a black to sell out to a black? Except on grounds of racial snobbery, with its implication that all blacks ought to be able to be counted on to behave more honorably than all whites, why should the question of color arise?"

"Rhinestone," a stage musical Gunn adapted from his novel *Rhinestone Sharecropping,* is "apparently inspired by [the author's] involvement with the 1976 Hollywood film biography of Muhammad Ali, 'The Greatest,'" according to Frank Rich's *New York Times* review. The critic finds fault with Gunn's characterization in this play: "The hero and the other black characters are vaguely written martyrs or naifs; the moguls are absurdly caricatured racist villains. By Act III, there's little left for the two sides to do but scream at one another in a simplistically polarized debate that strains credibility to the breaking point." Even so, states Rich, "one finds patches of good writing [in 'Rhinestone,'] starting with a haunting opening monologue in which [the protagonist's] father . . . recounts how the producer David Belasco once exploited a Harlem vaudeville troupe during an earlier show-business era," "The main problem is that Gunn is consumed with hate for not only Hollywood . . . but also, it seems, the whole white race," writes John Simon in *New York.* "What then, is left? The odd line flashing with honest anger, the occasional bit of searing sarcasm redolent of pain." Simon concludes, "There is a genuine ache in Gunn's play, but even ache needs to be sculptured, orchestrated, dramatized."

BIOGRAPHICAL/CRITICAL SOURCES: Philadelphia Bulletin, December 1, 1974; *Newsweek,* January 20, 1975; *New Yorker,* January 20, 1975; *Time,* January 20, 1975; *New York,* January 27, 1975, December 6, 1982; *Contemporary Literary Criticism,* Volume V, Gale, 1976; *Authors in the News,* Volume I, Gale, 1976; *Los Angeles Times Book Review,* May 9, 1982; *New York Times,* December 23, 1982.†

H

HALL, C(onstance) Margaret 1937-

PERSONAL: Born August 11, 1937, in Lancashire, England; came to the United States in 1962; daughter of John (a quarry owner) and Madeline (a teacher; maiden name, Brooks) Hall; married Robert T. Cole (a lawyer, in international law), October 25, 1959; children: Elizabeth Anne, Tanya Helen, Judith Amy. *Education:* London School of Economics and Political Science, London, B.Sc. (with honors), 1960; American University, M.A., 1969, Ph.D., 1970. *Home:* 4846 Langdrum Lane, Chevy Chase, Md. 20015. *Office:* Department of Sociology, Georgetown University, Washington, D.C. 20015.

CAREER: Instructor at English state schools, 1957-59, and private schools in Belgium, 1960-62; American University, Washington, D.C., professorial lecturer in sociology, 1970; Georgetown University, Washington, D.C., assistant professor, 1970-75, associate professor of sociology, 1975—, chairman of department, 1976-80, 1983—. Research associate of Family Center, Department of Psychiatry, Georgetown University Medical Center, 1976—; research associate of Kennedy Institute Center for Population Research, 1975—. Private practice in clinical sociology, 1971—. Clinical consultant to Community Mental Health Services, Frederick, Md., 1971-76.

MEMBER: American Sociological Association, Clinical Sociology Association, Sociologists for Women in Society, Society for the Scientific Study of Religion, District of Columbia Sociological Society, Phi Kappa Phi.

WRITINGS: The Sociology of Pierre Joseph Proudhon, 1809-1865, Philosophical Library, 1971; *Vital Life: Questions in Social Thought,* Christopher, 1973; *Field Notes: And Butterflies Beget Butterflies,* Libra, 1977; *Pilgrim: Explorations in Life-Space,* Libra, 1978; *Bric-a-Brac,* Antietam, 1978; *Woman Unliberated: Difficulties and Limitations in Changing Self,* Hemisphere Publishing, 1979; *Pearls,* Antietam, 1979; *Giving Birth,* Antietam, 1979; *The Bowen Family Theory and Its Uses,* Jason Aronson, 1981; *Individual and Society: Basic Concepts,* Antietam, 1979, 2nd edition, 1981; *Journal,* Antietam, 1983.

Contributor: Frances D. Andres and Joseph P. Lorio, editors, *Georgetown Family Symposia: A Collection of Selected Papers,* Volume I, Family Section, Department of Psychiatry, Georgetown University Medical Center, Volume I, 1974, Volume II, 1977; Ronald W. Manderscheid and Frances E. Manderscheid, editors, *Systems Science and the Future of Health,* Groome Center, Sibley Hospital, 1976. Also contributor to *Sociological Research Symposium,* edited by J. Sherwood Williams and others, 1975. Contributor to *Journal for the Scientific Study of Religion, Journal of Family Counseling, The Family,* and *Sociological Review Monograph.*

WORK IN PROGRESS: Books on aging and development of family theory; research includes cross-cultural substantiation of family theory and aging studies.

SIDELIGHTS: C. Margaret Hall told *CA:* "I am interested in writing books as a means of communication with others. A current research interest is aging and how this experience is affected by family relationships and personal and social 'beliefs.'"

* * *

HALL, N(orman) John 1933-

PERSONAL: Born January 1, 1933, in Orange, N.J.; son of Norman C. and Lucille (Hertlein) Hall; married Marianne E. Gsell, October 13, 1968; children: Jonathan. *Education:* Seton Hall University, A.B., 1955, M.A., 1967; Catholic University of America, S.T.B., 1959; New York University, Ph.D., 1970. *Home:* 44 West 10th St., New York, N.Y. 10011. *Office:* Department of English, Bronx Community College of the City University of New York, Bronx, N.Y. 10453.

CAREER: New York University, New York City, part-time lecturer in English, 1967-70; Bronx Community College of the City University of New York, Bronx, N.Y., assistant professor, 1970-75, associate professor, 1975-78, professor of English, 1978—; Graduate School and University Center of the City University of New York, New York City, professor, 1980—. Part-time lecturer in English, New School for Social Research, 1970-74. *Member:* Modern Language Association of America. *Awards, honors:* Research awards from American Council of Learned Societies, 1973, and from City University of New York; fellowships from National Endowment for the Humanities, 1974, Guggenheim Foundation, 1977, and American Council of Learned Societies, 1980.

WRITINGS: (Editor) Anthony Trollope, *The New Zealander,* Clarendon Press, 1972; *Salmagundi: Byron, Allegra, and the Trollope Family,* Beta Phi Mu, 1975; *Trollope and His Illustrators,* Macmillan (London), 1980; (editor) *The Trollope Crit-*

ics, Macmillan (London), 1981; (editor) *The Letters of Anthony Trollope,* Stanford University Press, 1983. Contributor to literature journals.

WORK IN PROGRESS: Trollope: A Biography, for Clarendon Press.

* * *

HANSON, Earl D(orchester) 1927-

PERSONAL: Born February 15, 1927, in Shahjahanpur, India; son of Harry Albert (a missionary) and Jean (Dorchester) Hanson; married Carlota Ferne Kinzie, June 10, 1948 (divorced August 30, 1973); married Evelyn Fairheller (a university administrator), January 4, 1975; children: (first marriage) Mardi Jean Hanson d'Alessandro, Stanley Royce, Kenric Mark. *Education:* Bowdoin College, A.B. (cum laude), 1945; Indiana University, Ph.D., 1954. *Office:* College of Science in Society, Wesleyan University, Middletown, Conn. 06457.

CAREER: Yale University, New Haven, Conn., instructor, 1954-57, assistant professor of zoology, 1957-60; Wesleyan University, Middletown, Conn., associate professor, 1960-63, professor of biology, 1963-81, Fisk Professor of Natural Science, 1972—, professor of biology and science in society, 1981—, chairman of department of biology, 1968-71, chairman of College of Science in Society, 1975-78, 1979—.

Research associate at Osaka University, 1960-61; guest professor at University of Tuebingen, 1967-68; visiting professor at Madurai-Kamaraj University and Gujarat University, 1978-79; visiting university fellow at Sri Venkateswara University and Gujarat University, 1981; fellow at East-West Center, Honolulu, 1983. Commission on Undergraduate Education in the Biological Sciences, member, 1963-67, member of executive committee, 1963-65, chairman, 1965-67; member of regional selection board for Woodrow Wilson fellowships, 1964-65; member of Haddam Conservation Commission, 1969-73; life sciences panel member, Council for International Exchange of Scholars, 1981-84. Member of corporation of Bermuda Biological Station, 1959—, and Middlesex Memorial Hospital, 1967-75. *Military service:* U.S. Marine Corps Reserve, active duty, 1945-46.

MEMBER: American Association for the Advancement of Science, American Association of University Professors, American Institute of Biological Sciences (member of governing board, 1971-74), Science, Technology and Society Association, National Science Teachers Association, Society of Protozoologists, Federation of American Scientists, New York Academy of Sciences, Connecticut Academy of Arts and Sciences, Connecticut Academy of Science and Engineering, Phi Beta Kappa, Sigma Xi. *Awards, honors:* Lalor faculty summer research award, 1956, 1957; Fulbright fellowship, 1960-61, 1978-79; Guggenheim fellowship, 1960-61; Harbison Distinguished Teaching Award, Danforth Foundation, 1970; National Science Foundation grants.

WRITINGS: Animal Diversity, Prentice-Hall, 1961, 3rd edition, 1972; (editor with E. C. Dougherty, Z. N. Brown, and W. D. Hartman, and contributor) *The Lower Metazoa: Comparative Biology and Phylogeny,* University of California Press, 1963; (contributor) G. W. Kidder, editor, *Chemical Zoology,* Volume I, Academic Press, 1967; (contributor) Robert G. Page, editor, *Preparation for the Study of Medicine,* University of Chicago Press, 1969.

(Contributor) W. J. van Wagtendonk, editor, *Paramecium: A Current Survey,* Elsevier, 1973; (contributor) D. H. Prescott, editor, *Methods in Cell Physiology,* Volume III, Academic Press, 1974; *The Origin and Early Evolution of Animals,* Wesleyan University Press, 1977; (with David Lockard and Peter Jensch) *Biology: The Science of Life* (high school textbook), Houghton, 1980; *Understanding Evolution,* Oxford University Press, 1981; (editor and contributor) *Recombinant DNA Research and the Human Prospect,* American Chemical Society, 1983. Also contributor to *Encyclopaedia Britannica.* Contributor of about fifty articles to science journals.

WORK IN PROGRESS: Myths and Paradigms: An Inquiry into Our Creative and Cognitive Resources.

SIDELIGHTS: Earl D. Hanson told *CA:* "My present interests are aimed at bringing together the enormous resources of what we know with what we need to know. Never before in the history of this earth have we known so much about food production, but yet more people are malnourished today than ever before. Never before have we known so much about what determines the quality of our environment, yet we are abusing and polluting it on a scale never seen before. And so on in one area of major human concern after another—population, resources, energy utilization, etc. Somehow we must use our creative and intellectual resources more effectively than they are presently being used."

* * *

HANSON, Peggy 1934-

PERSONAL: Born December 3, 1934, in Shreveport, La.; daughter of Paul David and Edna (Alexander) Pugh; married H. P. Hanson, August 15, 1955; married second husband, Nicolas P. Stein (a major, U.S. Army Aviation), June 17, 1970; children: (first marriage) Michael Lee, Patricia Suzanne. *Education:* Attended Trinity University, San Antonio, one year. *Religion:* Agnostic. *Home:* 2007 Sierra, Kemah, Tex. 77565.

CAREER: Spent fifteen years in data processing as operator, supervisor, and teacher; lived two years in Saigon, Vietnam as a civilian technical representative for U.S. Army, and three years in Germany; University of Texas Medical Branch at Galveston, assistant to director of Data Processing Center, 1973-76; proprietor of a design studio in Houston, Tex., 1976-77; founder and owner of Writer's Ink (a professional writing service specializing in technical and non-technical manuscripts for corporate customers); currently free-lance writer.

WRITINGS: Keypunching, Prentice-Hall, 1966, 4th edition, in press; *Operating Data Entry Systems,* Prentice-Hall, 1977; *Moving to America: A Guide for Foreign Nationals,* [India], 1984; *The Texas Instruments Professional Computer,* Prentice-Hall, 1984.

WORK IN PROGRESS: Two novels, one a romantic adventure entitled *Seek Not the Dead,* the other a horror story entitled *The Labyrinth at Maxcanu.*

SIDELIGHTS: Peggy Hanson told *CA:* "I want to move from technical writing to fiction writing exclusively within the next few years. Technical writing pays handsomely, but fiction writing is lots more fun. I never expect to be considered a major writer, but my fondest wish is that when the reader puts down one of my books, he will always say, 'That was a damn good story; I really enjoyed it.'"

* * *

HANZLICEK, C(harles) G(eorge) 1942-

PERSONAL: Born August 23, 1942, in Owatonna, Minn.; son

of George John (a machinist) and Freda (Schuenke) Hanzlicek; married Dianne Staley, May 11, 1968; children: Leah Rose. *Education:* University of Minnesota, B.A., 1964; University of Iowa, M.F.A., 1966. *Politics:* "Irrational." *Religion:* "Without." *Home:* 738 East Lansing Way, Fresno, Calif. 93704. *Office:* Department of English, California State University, Fresno, Calif. 93740.

CAREER: California State University, Fresno, 1966—, began as assistant professor, professor of English, 1975—. *Awards, honors:* National Endowment for the Arts fellowship, 1976; Devins Award, Devins Foundation, 1977-78, for *Stars.*

WRITINGS—Poems, except as indicated: *The Voices* (translations of Rainer Maria Rilke), Is It As Press, 1970; *Living in It,* Stone Wall Press, 1971; *A Bird's Companion* (versions of American Indian songs), Licklog Press, 1974; *Stars,* University of Missouri Press, 1977; *Calling the Dead,* Carnegie-Mellon University, 1982; *A Dozen for Leah,* Brandenburg Press, 1982; *When There Are No Secrets,* Carnegie-Mellon University, in press.

WORK IN PROGRESS: Translations, with Dana Habova, of selected poems by Czech poet Vladimir Holan.

SIDELIGHTS: C. G. Hanzlicek told *CA:* "My main teaching interests are in the fields of creative writing and literature of the American Indian. My chief aim as a poet is to write with clarity, total clarity. If I am misunderstood, I have written badly. In terms of subject matter, I am more interested in emotions than in ideas, more drawn to the life of the body than the life of the mind. The great Irish poet, W. B. Yeats, said somewhere that the only two things worth writing about are sex and death. He meant that in the broadest sense, of course, and I tend to agree. I take poetry seriously, and therefore try to write serious poems."

AVOCATIONAL INTERESTS: Photography.

* * *

HARDCASTLE, Michael 1933-
(David Clark)

PERSONAL: Born February 6, 1933, in Huddersfield, England. *Education:* Attended schools in Huddersfield, England, until eighteen. *Home:* 17 Molescroft Park, Beverly, East Yorkshire HU17 7EB, England.

CAREER: Writer. Newspaper reporter and feature writer, 1956-67. *Military service:* British Army, 1951-56; served with Royal Educational Corps in Africa.

WRITINGS—Juveniles: *Aim for the Flag,* Heinemann, 1967, Follett, 1969; *The Big One,* Thomas Nelson, 1974; *The Chase,* Thomas Nelson, 1974; *On the Run,* Thomas Nelson, 1974; *Heading for Goal,* Thomas Nelson, 1974; *Flare Up,* Thomas Nelson, 1975; *Get Lost,* Thomas Nelson, 1975; *Money for Sale,* Heinemann Educational, 1975; *The Chasing Game,* Michael Hardcastle Publications, 1976; *The Hidden Enemy,* Michael Hardcastle Publications, 1976; *Fire on the Sea,* Longman, 1978; *Crash Car,* Longman, 1978; *Holiday House,* Longman, 1978; *Strong Arm,* Longman, 1978; *Behind the Goal,* Pelham Books, 1980; *Top Soccer,* Harrap, 1980; *Top Fishing,* Harrap, 1980; *Top Speed,* Harrap, 1981; *The Gigantic Hit,* Pelham Books, 1982; *Hooked!,* Longman, 1983.

Published by Heinemann: *Soccer Is Also a Game,* 1966; *Shoot on Sight,* 1967; *Goal,* 1969; *Don't Tell Me What to Do,* 1970; *Playing Ball,* 1972; *Goals in the Air,* 1972; *Island Magic,* 1973; *The Demon Bowler,* 1974; *Life Underground,* 1975; *Where the Action Is,* 1976; *Top of the League,* 1979.

Published by Benn: *Dive to Danger,* 1969; *Walk for Us,* 1969; *Stop That Car,* 1970; *Reds and Blues,* 1970; *Strike,* 1970; *Smashing,* 1970; *Come and Get Me,* 1971; *Live in the Sky,* 1971; *Shelter,* 1971; *A Load of Trouble,* 1971; *Blood Money,* 1971; *It Wasn't Me,* 1971; *In the Net,* 1971; (under pseudonym David Clark) *Goalie,* 1972; (under pseudonym David Clark) *Splash,* 1972; (under pseudonym David Clark) *Run,* 1973; (under pseudonym David Clark) *Top Spin,* 1973; (under pseudonym David Clark) *Grab,* 1974; (under pseudonym David Clark) *Winner,* 1974; (under pseudonym David Clark) *Volley,* 1975; (under pseudonym David Clark) *Roll Up,* 1975; *Go for Goal,* 1980; *Hot Wheels,* 1980; *Racing Bike,* 1980; *Snakerun,* 1980.

Published by Methuen: *United,* 1973; *Away from Home,* 1974; *Free Kick,* 1974; *The Saturday Horse,* 1977; *Soccer Special,* 1978; *The Switch Horse,* 1980; *Half a Team,* 1980; *Roar to Victory,* 1982; *Fast from the Gate,* 1982; *Caught Out,* 1983; *The Team That Wouldn't Give In,* 1984.

Published by Collins Educational, all in 1974: *Last Across; The Match; Dead of Night; Road Race; A Hard Man; Catch; Day in the Country; The Long Drop.*

Published by Armada Books: *The First Goal,* 1976; *Breakaway,* 1976; (contributor) Diana Pullein Thompson, editor, *True Horse and Pony Stories,* 1976; *On the Ball,* 1977; *Shooting Star,* 1977; *Goal in Europe,* 1978; *Kick Off,* 1981; *Attack!,* 1982.

* * *

HARLAN, Glen
See CEBULASH, Mel

* * *

HARPER, David
See CORLEY, Edwin (Raymond)

* * *

HARRIFORD, Daphne
See HARRIS, Marion Rose (Young)

* * *

HARRIS, Marion Rose (Young) 1925-
(Rose Young; pseudonyms: Henry Charles, Daphne Harriford, Keith Rogers)

PERSONAL: Born July 12, 1925, in Cardiff, South Wales; daughter of Robert Henry and Marion (Phillips) Young; married Kenneth Mackenzie Harris (director of a furnishing company), August 18, 1943; children: Roger Mackenzie, Pamela Daphne, Keith Mackenzie. *Education:* Attended Gillingham School and Cardiff Technical College. *Home and office:* Walpole College, Long Dr., Burnham, Buckinghamshire SL1 8AS, England.

CAREER: Writer. Private secretary to managing director of builder's merchant, 1942-46; free-lance journalist, 1946—; editor of Regional Feature Service, 1964-71; W. Foulsham & Co. Ltd., Slough, Buckinghamshire, England, editorial controller, 1974-83. Child care consultant for *Here's Health;* London correspondent for *Irish Leather and Footwear Journal* and *Futura* (fashion trade magazine). Furnishing consultant to builders, architects, and magazines, designing interiors for show houses at Ideal Homes Exhibition, Olympia, London, England, 1963-64, and for building estates in England. *Member:* Romantic Novelists Association, Society of Authors, Thames Valley Writers.

WRITINGS: *Fresh Fruit Dishes,* Jenkins, 1963, reprinted, 1977; *Making a House a Home,* Pan Books, 1963; *The Awful Slimmer's Book,* Wolfe, 1967; *Teach Your Mum Flower Arranging,* Wolfe, 1968; (contributor) *Dairy Book of Home Management,* Milk Marketing Board, 1969; (under pseudonym Henry Charles) *Twenty-Five Easy to Grow Vegetables: In Any Size Plot,* Foulsham, 1975; (under pseudonym Daphne Harriford) *Fix It Yourself: Indoor Repairs,* Foulsham, 1975; (under pseudonym Keith Rogers) *Fix It Yourself Plumbing: Basic Repairs and Maintenance,* Foulsham, 1975; (under name Rose Young) *When the Clouds Clear,* International Publishing Co., 1975; *Captain of Her Heart,* R. Hale, 1976; (under name Rose Young) *Love Can Conquer,* International Publishing Co., 1976; (under name Rose Young) *Secret of Abbey Place,* International Publishing Co., 1977; *Just a Handsome Stranger,* Hamlyn, 1983.

Scriptwriter for British Broadcasting Corp. schools broadcast, "Do Manners Matter," and for "Home This Afternoon" series. Contributor of short stories to magazines; contributor of articles on a variety of subjects, including home, fashion, child care, furnishings, and beauty, to provincial newspapers and magazines, trade publications, and women's magazines, including *Top Secretary, Homefinder, Cupid Chronicle, Home Overseas, Moneymaker,* and *Writer's Review.*

WORK IN PROGRESS: Six romance novels, *A Year and a Day, A Kiss in Time, Girl with Six Fingers, Love Is Where Your Heart Is, 13 Albert Terrace,* and *Master of Her Fate; Dreadful Dragons,* for children; *How a Computer Can Help You.*

SIDELIGHTS: Marion Rose Harris told *CA:* "Romance, so often scorned by the 'serious' fiction writer, can be as therapeutic for women as sports are for men. Transporting them from their mundane daily round into romantic fantasy can prove more beneficial than valium or any other sedative. Romantic fiction often helps the reader to sort out her own marital problems, or avoid some of the pitfalls, so it could even be claimed that it has some educational value."

* * *

HARRISON, Barbara 1941-

PERSONAL: Born January 22, 1941, in New York, N.Y.; daughter of Alexander (in hotel management) and Ann (Sukulak) Harrison. *Education:* Attended schools in New York and Vermont. *Politics:* Democrat. *Religion:* Roman Catholic. *Home and office:* 400 East 57th St., New York, N.Y. 10022.

CAREER: Playboy Organization, New York, N.Y., publicity director, 1963-68; former public relations consultant for a film production firm, Cinegraphique, and volunteer worker in political campaigns.

WRITINGS—All novels: *The Pagans,* Avon, 1970; *City Hospital,* Avon, 1975; *The Gorlin Clinic,* Avon, 1975; *Rhinelander Pavillion,* Zebra Books, 1980; *Rhinelander Center,* Zebra Books, 1981; *This Cherished Dream,* Zebra Books, 1984. Also author of *The Wildings,* published by Dell.

WORK IN PROGRESS: A family saga.

HATTON, Ragnhild Marie 1913-

PERSONAL: Born February 10, 1913, in Bergen, Norway; daughter of Gustav Ingolf and Marie (Rikheim) Hanssen; married Harry Hatton, June 24, 1936; children: Peter Harry Sverre, Paul Gustav. *Education:* University of Oslo, Cand.Mag., 1936; University College, London, Ph.D., 1947. *Politics:* Liberal. *Religion:* Church of England. *Home:* 49 Campden St., Kensington, London W.8, England. *Office:* London School of Economics and Political Science, University of London, Houghton St., Aldwych, London W.C.2, England.

CAREER: University of London, London, England, student and part-time teacher, 1937-49, assistant lecturer, 1949-50, lecturer, 1950-58, reader in history, 1958-68, professor of history at London School of Economics and Political Science, 1968-81, dean, Faculty of Economics, 1974-78, professor emeritus, 1981—, Creighton Lecturer, 1982. Member, London Honours Board of Examiners in History, 1964-68; external examiner in history for University of Nottingham, 1965-69, University of Edinburgh, 1965-70, Queens University, Belfast, 1972-73, and University of Warwick, 1975-77. *Member:* Association of University Teachers, Royal Historical Society (fellow; member of council, 1979-83), Historical Association, Anglo-Netherlands Society, Anglo-Norse Society, Anglo-Swedish Society, Swedish Academy (foreign corresponding member), La Academia Panamanena de la Historia (corresponding member), American Historical Association (honorary foreign member, 1981). *Awards, honors:* Appointed Knight First Class of Norwegian Order of Saint Olav, 1983.

WRITINGS: *Diplomatic Relations between Great Britain and the Dutch Republic, 1714-1720,* East & West, 1950; (editor with J. S. Bromley) *William III and Louis XIV: Essays 1680-1720 by and for Mark A. Thomson,* University of Toronto Press, 1967; (contributor) K. Bourne and D. C. Watt, editors, *Studies in International History,* Longmans, Green, 1967; *Charles XII of Sweden,* Weidenfeld & Nicolson, 1968, Weybright & Talley, 1969; *Europe in the Age of Louis XIV,* Thames & Hudson, 1969, Harcourt, 1970, new edition, Norton, 1979; *War and Peace, 1680-1720* (inaugural lecture), Weidenfeld & Nicolson, 1969.

(Contributor) J. C. Rule, editor, *Louis XIV and the Craft of Kingship,* Ohio State University Press, 1970; (editor with M. S. Anderson) *Studies in Diplomatic History: Essays in Memory of David Bayne Horn,* Longmans, Green, 1970; (editor) E. Lund, M. Pihl, and J. Sloek, *A History of European Ideas,* Hurst & Co., 1971; *Louis XIV and His World,* Putnam, 1972; (contributor) Paul Fritz and David Williams, editors, *The Triumph of Culture: Eighteenth-Century Perspectives,* A. M. Hakkert, 1972; (contributor) T. Hunczak, editor, *Russian Imperialism from Ivan the Great to the Revolution,* Rutgers University Press, 1974.

(Author of introduction) Francoise-Marie Arouet de Voltaire, *The History of Charles XII King of Spain,* translated by Antonia White, Folio, 1976; (editor and contributor) *Louis XIV and Absolutism,* Macmillan, 1976; (editor and contributor) *Louis XIV and Europe,* Macmillan, 1976; (contributor) A. G. Dickens, editor, *The Courts of Europe: Politics, Patronage and Royalty, 1400-1800,* Thames & Hudson, 1977; *George I: Elector and King,* Harvard University Press, 1978; (contributor) *Les Relations Franco Autrichiennes sous Louis XIV,* Saint-Cyr-Coetquidan, 1983.

Also author of a pamphlet, *Charles XII,* 1974. General editor, "Men in Office" series, Thames & Hudson, 1975—. Contributor to *The New Cambridge Modern History*, Volumes VI and VII, and to history journals, including *European Studies Review, Journal of Modern History*, and *XVII Siecle*.

WORK IN PROGRESS: A history of Europe from 1688 to 1740, for Fontana; *The Northern Crowns;* a study of the Spanish succession issue, for Oxford University Press; a book on Louis XIV for Allen & Unwin and University of California Press.

SIDELIGHTS: Ragnhild Marie Hatton told *CA:* "I love my undergraduate and postgraduate teaching in England, Europe, [North America], and . . . as far south as Panama. . . . I delight in my archival, museum, and library research trips in England and abroad, but I also feel that historians ought, where they have the inclination, to transmit the results of their research to the general educated public and to students of history, young and old. [I] have therefore—quite apart from the works aimed at professional historians—found much joy in writing scholarly history in a form easily digestible . . . [and] with plenty of illustrations. One of my books has more than two hundred illustrations; another has more than a hundred. . . . My [biographies] are carefully (and sumptuously) illustrated. Unfortunately, the present high cost of including illustrations has postponed the publication of a [book] I have much enjoyed researching: *The Northern Crowns*, intended to both elucidate the national treasures of [the Scandinavian] countries and to convince the Scandinavians of what they owe to royal and court initiative and patronage in the past. More than six hundred illustrations have been collected and commented on for the seven chapters."

* * *

HAVILAND, Virginia 1911-

PERSONAL: Born May 21, 1911, in Rochester, N.Y.; daughter of William J. and Bertha (Esten) Haviland. *Education:* Cornell University, B.A., 1933. *Politics:* Democrat. *Home:* Harbour Square, 520 N St. S.W., Washington, D.C. 20024. *Office:* Children's Book Section, Library of Congress, Washington, D.C. 20540.

CAREER: Boston (Mass.) Public Library, beginning 1934, children's librarian, 1941-48, branch librarian, 1948-52, reader's adviser for children, 1952-63; Library of Congress, Washington, D.C., head of Children's Book Section, 1963—. Lecturer, Simmons College, School of Library Science, 1957-62, and Trinity College, 1969—; Hewins Lecturer, New England Library Association. Chairman, Newbery-Caldecott Award Committee (American Library Association), 1953-54; judge, *New York Herald Tribune* Children's Spring Book Festival Awards, 1955-57; International Hans Christian Andersen Award, member of jury, 1959—, president of jury, 1971-74; judge, *Book World* Children's Spring Book Festival Awards, 1969; judge, National Book Awards, 1969. Representative of American Library Association at European conferences of International Board on Books for Children and International Federation of Library Associations.

MEMBER: International Board on Books for Children (member of executive board), International Federation of Library Associations (member of executive committee), P.E.N., Authors Guild, Authors League of America, American Library Association (chairman of Children's Library Association, 1954-55, chairman of book evaluation committee, 1962-63), National Council of Administrative Women in Education, National Society of Women Geographers, District of Columbia Library Association, Washington Children's Book Guild, Pi Lambda Theta. *Awards, honors:* Recipient of Regina Medal and Grolier Award, both 1976.

WRITINGS: *Travelogue Storybook of the Nineteenth Century*, Horn Book, 1950; *William Penn, Founder and Friend*, Abingdon, 1952; *Ruth Sawyer*, Walck, 1965; (editor) Louise S. Bechtel, *Books in Search of Children: Essays and Speeches*, Macmillan, 1969; (editor with William Jay Smith) *Children and Poetry*, Library of Congress, 1970, 2nd revised edition, 1979; (editor) *The Wide World of Children's Books*, Library of Congress, 1972; (editor) *The Fairy Tale Treasury*, Coward, 1972; *Childrens' Books of International Interest*, American Library Association, 1972; *Children and Literature: Views and Reviews*, Scott, Foresman, 1973; (author of introduction) *Yankee Doodle's Literary Sampler of Prose, Poetry, and Pictures*, Crowell, 1974; (compiler with Margaret N. Coughlin) *Samuel Langhorne Clemens: A Centennial for Tom Sawyer*, Library of Congress, 1976; *Legends of North America*, Collins & World, 1979; (with others) *The Best of Children's Books, 1964-1978*, illustrated by Debbie Dieneman, Library of Congress, 1980.

"Favorite Fairy Tales" series; published by Little, Brown: *Favorite Fairy Tales Told in England*, 1959; . . . *in France*, 1959; . . . *in Germany*, 1959; . . . *in Ireland*, 1961; . . . *in Norway*, 1961; . . . *in Russia*, 1961; . . . *in Scotland*, 1963; . . . *in Spain*, 1963; . . . *in Poland*, 1963; . . . *in Italy*, 1965; . . . *in Sweden*, 1966; . . . *in Czechoslovakia*, 1966; . . . *in Japan*, 1967; . . . *in Greece*, 1970; . . . *in Denmark*, 1971; . . . *in India*, 1973.

Also editor of *One Hundred Best Books for Children*, 1956, and *Children's Literature: A Guide to Reference Sources*, 1966. Narrator of "Folklore in the Culture of the Child," an educational cassette, 1977. Contributor to *Horn Book, Wilson Library Bulletin*, and other journals. Associate editor of *Horn Book*, beginning 1952.

WORK IN PROGRESS: Publishing program of Children's Book Section, Library of Congress.†

* * *

HAVLICE, Patricia Pate 1943-

PERSONAL: Born February 2, 1943, in Cleveland, Ohio; daughter of Edward A. (a machinist) and Theresa (Makuc) Pate; married Richard F. Havlice (a chemical engineer), September 9, 1967. *Education:* Ursuline College for Women, B.A., 1965; University of Michigan, M.A.L.S., 1966. *Home:* 1803 Neptune Ln., Houston, Tex. 77062.

CAREER: Cuyahoga County Public Library, Cleveland, Ohio, adult services librarian, 1966-67; Ohio State University Library, Columbus, junior reference librarian, 1967-68; Indiana University, Northwest Regional Campus Library, Gary, senior reference librarian, 1969-70.

WRITINGS—Published by Scarecrow, except as indicated: *Art in Time* (index to all the pictures in the art section of *Time* magazine), 1970; *Index to American Author Bibliographies*, 1971; *Index to Artistic Biography*, 1973, 1st supplement, 1981; *Index to Literary Biography*, 1975, 1st supplement, 1983; *Popular Song Index*, 1975, 2nd supplement, 1984; *World Painting Index*, 1977, 1st supplement, 1982; *And So to Bed: An Annotated Bibliography of Diaries Published in English*, 1984; *Earth Scale Art: A Bibliography and Index to Reproductions*, McFarland & Co., 1984; *Oral History: An Annotated Bibliography*, McFarland & Co., 1984.

SIDELIGHTS: Patricia Pate Havlice told *CA:* "My pet peeve is people who are so inconsiderate as to die out of alphabetical order while I am correcting proofs for the various indexes I've compiled." *Avocational interests:* Needlework, quilting, reading.

* * *

HAYDEN, Naura 1942-

PERSONAL: Born September 29, 1942, in Los Angeles, Calif.; daughter of John E. (a newspaperman) and N. Elizabeth (Bussins) Hayden; married Theodore Geiser (an attorney), June 4, 1975 (divorced). *Education:* Attended University of California at Los Angeles and Berkeley. *Religion:* "Believer in Love." *Agent:* Julian Bach Literary Agency, Inc., 747 Third Ave., New York, N.Y. 10017.

CAREER: Actress, singer, and writer on health, love, and marriage. *Member:* International Academy of Preventive Medicine (honorary fellow).

WRITINGS: The Hip, High-Prote, Low-Cal, Easy-Does-It Cookbook, Dodd, 1973; *Everything You've Always Wanted to Know About Energy But Were Too Weak to Ask,* Hawthorn, 1976; *Isle of View (Say It Out Loud),* Arbor House, 1980; *Astro-Logical Love,* Bibli O'Phile Publishing Co., 1983; *How to Satisfy a Woman Every Time and Have Her Beg for More,* Dutton, 1983.

SIDELIGHTS: "My profession is acting and singing, both of which I love to do," Naura Hayden told *CA,* "but I also love to write books, write music, make television appearances as a personality, come up with business ideas, and turn people on to health! I have enormous energy and love to use it constructively. I have a new record album out titled 'And Then She Wrote,' and I starred in an Off-Broadway musical, 'Be Kind to People Week.' I have also completed a movie in which I star, 'The Perils of P. K.,' a zany comedy."

BIOGRAPHICAL/CRITICAL SOURCES: People, May 30, 1977.

* * *

HEINZ, William Frederick 1899-1976

PERSONAL: Born August 10, 1899, in Greymouth, New Zealand; died March 29, 1976; son of Emil Philip and Emma Louise Heinz; married. *Education:* Educated in secondary school in Greymouth, New Zealand. *Home:* 335 Cambridge Ter., City 1, Christchurch, New Zealand.

CAREER: Plumber in the family firm, 1918-32; sound engineer in Westrex Theatre, 1932-41; New Zealand Radio Corp., Wellington, radio engineer, 1941-43; Ministry of Supply, South Westland, New Zealand, manager of mica mine, 1944-45; theatre engineer in Christchurch, New Zealand, 1946-48; in the electronics business in Christchurch, 1948-52; Christchurch Drainage Board, Christchurch, head of trade waste department, 1952-68; writer, 1968-76. Gave broadcast talks. Member of regional committee of Westland Historic Places Trust.

WRITINGS: Prospecting for Gold, Pegasus, 1952, 5th edition, 1975; *The Story of Shantytown,* Pegasus, 1972; (compiler) *Bright Fine Gold: Stories of the New Zealand Gold Fields,* A. H. & A. W. Reed, 1974; *New Zealand's Last Goldrush: Kumara,* A. H. & A. W. Reed, 1976. Editor of "Men of the West" series for Christchurch Press, beginning 1973.

WORK IN PROGRESS: A Gold Digger's Scrap Book, an autobiography.

SIDELIGHTS: William Frederick Heinz once wrote *CA:* "The importance of the Gold Rush in New Zealand from 1861 had a remarkable impact on the settlement of the colony. It is only now that we are beginning to realise the implications of the mixing of the peoples of many European and Asian countries, not forgetting the Australian and Californian gold miners, who as prospector explorers added many Place Names to New Zealand." Heinz explored most of the geologically interesting parts of New Zealand and, as a mountaineer, had to his credit several first ascents of alpine peaks. He carried out field research on the West Coast gold drifts, prospecting and advisory work on the antimony lode at Endeavour Inlet, research into the rarer metals, and prospecting for radioactive rocks and gem stones.

BIOGRAPHICAL/CRITICAL SOURCES: Christchurch Press, October 11, 1975.†

* * *

HEMMING, John (Henry) 1935-

PERSONAL: Born January 5, 1935, in Vancouver, British Columbia, Canada; son of Henry Harold and Alice (Weaver) Hemming. *Education:* Attended Eton College, Windsor, England, 1948-53, and McGill University, 1953-54; Oxford University, B.A., 1957, M.A., 1960, D.Litt., 1981. *Politics:* None. *Religion:* None. *Office:* Municipal Journal Ltd., 178-202 Grand Portland St., London W1 NGNH, England; and Royal Geographical Society, 1 Kensington Gore, London SW7 2AR, England.

CAREER: Maclean-Hunter Publishing Co., Toronto, Ontario, assistant editor, 1957-59; deputy leader in Brazil, Iriri River Exploration Party, 1961; Brintex Exhibitions Ltd., London, England, managing director, 1963-70; Municipal Journal Ltd., London, deputy chairman, 1965-76, chairman, 1976—. Trustee of *Geographical Magazine* and *Survival International,* both London. *Military service:* Canadian Army, Militia Artillery, 1958-59; became first lieutenant. *Member:* Royal Geographical Society (director, 1975—), Anglo-Brazilian Society (council member), Travellers Club, Beefsteak Club. *Awards, honors:* Robert Pitman Literary Prize, 1970, and Christopher Book Award, 1971, both for *The Conquest of the Incas.*

WRITINGS: The Conquest of the Incas, Harcourt, 1970; (coauthor) *Tribes of the Amazon Basin in Brazil,* Charles Knight, 1973; *Red Gold: The Conquest of the Brazilian Indians,* Macmillan, 1978; *The Search for El Dorado,* Michael Joseph/Dutton, 1978; *Machu Picchu,* Newsweek, 1981; *Monuments of the Incas,* New York Graphic Society/Little, Brown, 1982; *The New Incas,* Pyramid, 1983; (editor) *Change in the Incas,* two volumes, Manchester University Press, 1984. Contributor to *Sunday Times, Observer, Sunday Telegraph,* and other publications in England. Assistant editor, *Civic Administration* (Toronto).

SIDELIGHTS: John Hemming "is well known for his elegant, graceful writing about South American Indian civilizations," asserts a *New York Times Book Review* critic. Calling *Monuments of the Incas* "a magnificent survey of the Inca remains," the reviewer adds, "In this book [Hemming] gives a fairly complete account of the Inca buildings and culture in an impressively concise text."

Hemming told *CA* that he has "a deep concern with the fate of original or primitive tribes clashing with modern society. The Spanish conquest of Inca Peru was one of the first colonial invasions of the Americas; but lesser invasions are still taking place, as native peoples find their homelands occupied in the name of progress."

He has traveled quite widely in all continents, including a crossing of an unusual part of the Sahara and of the Syrian desert, a major exploration of an unknown part of Brazil, and visits to remote tribes in Brazil, Peru, and central Africa.

BIOGRAPHICAL/CRITICAL SOURCES: *New Statesman*, July 10, 1970; *Economist*, July 11, 1970; *Observer Review*, August 9, 1970; *Book World*, October 11, 1970; *New York Times Book Review*, December 12, 1982.

* * *

HEMPHILL, Paul 1936-

PERSONAL: Born February 18, 1936, in Birmingham, Ala.; son of Paul (a truck driver) and Velma Rebecca (an employee of the U.S. Government; maiden name, Nelson) Hemphill; married Susan Milliage Olive, September 23, 1961 (divorced, 1975); married Susan Farran Percy (a magazine editor), November 6, 1976; children: (first marriage) Lisa, David, Molly; (second marriage) Martha. *Education:* Auburn University, B.A., 1959. *Home:* 1090 Alta Ave. N.E., Atlanta, Ga. 30307. *Agent:* Sterling Lord Agency, 660 Madison Ave., New York, N.Y. 10021.

CAREER: Sportswriter for newspapers in Birmingham, Ala., Augusta, Ga., and Tampa, Fla., 1958-64; *Atlanta Journal*, Atlanta, Ga., columnist, 1964-69; free-lance writer, 1969—. Visiting lecturer at University of Georgia, fall, 1973; instructor in journalism at Florida A&M University, beginning 1975. Commentator on "All Things Considered" radio show; guest on "Today" and "McNeill-Lehrer Report" television shows. *Military service:* Alabama Air National Guard, active duty, 1961-62; served in France. *Awards, honors:* Nieman fellow at Harvard University, 1968-69; literary achievement award from Georgia Writers Association, 1970, for *The Nashville Sound*.

WRITINGS: *The Nashville Sound: Bright Lights and Country Music*, Simon & Schuster, 1970; (with Ivan Allen, Jr.) *Mayor: Notes on the Sixties*, Simon & Schuster, 1971; *The Good Old Boys*, Simon & Schuster, 1974; *Long Gone: A Novel*, Viking, 1979; *Too Old to Cry*, Viking, 1981. Author of columns appearing in *San Francisco Examiner*, 1976, *Baltimore Sun*, *USA Today*, *Atlanta Constitution*, *Sport*, and *Country Music*. Contributor to periodicals, including *Life*, *Playboy*, *Cosmopolitan*, *Mademoiselle*, *Atlantic*, *New York Times Magazine*, *True*, *Sports Illustrated*, and *TV Guide*. Senior editor, *Atlanta* (magazine), 1980.

WORK IN PROGRESS: *A Walk with the Wolves*; *The Holy Ghost*, "a sweeping generational novel covering forty years in the lives of a western North Carolina family," for Macmillan.

SIDELIGHTS: Paul Hemphill says he is "a committed 'Southern writer.' The South is all I know—my blood, my instincts, my viewpoint. I also believe a writer is giving a more honest view of the world if he lives and works Out There, going to the typewriter every day, more or less writing memos to Shakespeare and Cervantes and Dickens and the rest, telling them what went on around here yesterday. I have turned down chances to work in other places, for more money, because the South is where I belong."

Hemphill's writings have all emerged from the Southern experience. His first book, *The Nashville Sound: Bright Lights and Country Music*, is a journalistic overview of the rise to popularity of country and western music. Christopher Lehmann-Haupt of the *New York Times* writes that Hemphill has described this phenomenon "delightfully, by mixing together history and spot interviews and on-the-scene reportage in a book that reads as smoothly and sparklingly as a bluegrass breakdown."

Craig McGregor similarly comments on the book in a *New York Times Book Review* article: "Hemphill describes the scene in a racy, impressionistic style, mixing profiles of singers . . . with on-the-spot accounts of Friday night at Tootsie's Orchid Lounge, Saturday night at the Grand Ole Opry and several nights on the road with Bill Anderson and the Po' Boys. . . . His book," continues McGregor, "is like a huge pop collage, as immensely detailed and trivial as a Rauschenberg and, by its end, one has a real feeling for the scene: its tawdriness, its triumphs, its money-greed, its racism, its smash-ups and pillheads and ego-trips, and the painful spectacle of genuinely creative, semi-'folk' artists ripping themselves apart in pursuit of a Cadillac-and-ranch-house success. That's what commercialism means, and we should be grateful to Hemphill for describing it so horrifyingly well."

In his 1979 book, *Long Gone: A Novel*, Hemphill tells the story of a baseball team called the Graceville Oilers and their chase for the 1956 pennant in the Class D Alabama-Florida League. Hemphill himself played on the real-life team of the same name in his youth, and this experience apparently lent much to the background of the novel, for, as Stephen Goodwin points out in a *Washington Post* review, "there's plenty going on in this short novel, and Hemphill keeps the narrative hurtling forward. The dim and shabby ballparks, the burger joints and honky-tonks, the hot and buggy Southern towns—these are the only stops, and Hemphill knows his territory. He knows the histories of the hopefuls and the has-beens, the waitresses, the widow, the washed-up sportswriter, the louts of the country club."

Lloyd Sachs, writing in the *Chicago Tribune Book World*, finds that *Long Gone* is "an irresistibly affectionate, gritty, caustically funny portrait of a time and place—the Florida Panhandle of the mid-'50s—that never strives for effect or deep meaning, serving up instead an intoxicating blend of fresh, offbeat characters and a relaxed, smooth narrative."

Reviewer Pete Axthelm comments in *Newsweek* that, "as a writer, Hemphill has a good high hard one [with *Long Gone*]. His evocative opening scene, among others, bears comparison to Faulkner in his lighter moods. And once he has backed the reader away from the plate with the fast ball, Hemphill can also deliver some tantalizing slow curves. . . . Hemphill has set us up in the style of the craftiest of moundsmen—and slipped a first-rate novel past us."

"Hemphill is a Southerner," writes Al Burt in the *Miami Herald*, "now and forever, illuminating the absurdities tenderly, the cruelties and false prophets with a venom that tells you he has suffered a special pain because of them."

BIOGRAPHICAL/CRITICAL SOURCES: *New York Times*, April 27, 1970, January 26, 1981; *New Republic*, June 27, 1970; *New York Times Book Review*, July 19, 1970, September 22, 1974, January 18, 1981; *New York Review of Books*, November 4, 1971; *Miami Herald*, November 30, 1975; *Authors in the News*, Volume II, Gale, 1976; *Newsweek*, August 20, 1979; *Washington Post*, August 27, 1979, February 14, 1981; *Chicago Tribune Book World*, October 7, 1979.

HENDRICKSON, Robert A(ugustus) 1923-

PERSONAL: Born August 9, 1923, in Indianapolis, Ind.; son of Robert A. (a lawyer) and Eleanor Riggs (Atherton) Hendrickson; married Virginia Reiland Cobb (an actress), February 3, 1951; children: Alexandra Kirk, Robert Augustus III. *Education:* Attended Yale University, 1941-43, and University of Bescancon, 1945; Sorbonne, University of Paris, Certificat, 1946; Harvard University, LL.B., 1948. *Office:* Condert Brothers, 200 Park Ave., New York, N.Y. 10166.

CAREER: Admitted to Indiana Bar, 1948, and New York Bar, 1949; Lord, Day & Lord (law firm), New York City, attorney, 1948-52; Surrogates of New York County, New York City, law assistant, 1952-54; Breed, Abbott, Morgan (law firm), New York City, attorney, 1954-67; Lovejoy, Wasson, Lundgren & Ashton (law firm), New York City, partner, beginning 1967; currently affiliated with Condert Brothers, New York City. Visiting professor of law, University of Miami, 1976. Lecturer on estate planning and other subjects at law institutes in a number of states. Member of board of directors, St. Martin's Press, Inc., and Mason/Charter Publishers, Inc.; trustee of International Center for the Disabled and St. Hilda's and St. Hugh's School. President, The Church Club of New York, Inc., 1976—. Chairman of board of governors, New York Young Republican Club, 1954. *Military service:* U.S. Army, 1943-46; became first lieutenant; received Bronze Star, Purple Heart with oak-leaf cluster, Presidential Unit Citation, and battle stars for the Ardennes, Rhineland, and Central Europe campaigns.

MEMBER: American Bar Association, Maritime Law Association, American Foreign Law Association (president, 1983—), Consular Law Society (president, 1982-83, chairman, 1983—), Carl Duisberg Society (chairman and director), New York State Bar Association, Indiana Bar Association, Bar Association of the City of New York.

WRITINGS: Interstate and International Estate Planning, Practising Law Institute, 1968; (contributor) *Successful Estate Planning Ideas and Methods,* Prentice-Hall, 1968; *The Future of Money,* Prentice-Hall, 1970; (contributor) Jacob K. Lasser, *J. K. Lasser's Estate Tax Techniques,* [New York], 1970; *Estate Planning for the Migrant Executive,* Practising Law Institute, 1971; *The Cashless Society,* Dodd, 1972; *Hamilton,* Mason/Charter, Volume I: *1757-1789,* Volume II: *1789-1804,* 1976; *The Rise and Fall of Alexander Hamilton,* Van Nostrand, 1981; (with William K. Steven) *Current Legal Aspects of International Estate Planning,* American Bar Association, 1981; (with Neal R. Silverman) *Changing the Situs of a Trust,* Seminar Press, 1982. Contributor to law journals.

SIDELIGHTS: The Future of Money has been published in British, German, and Japanese editions.

* * *

HENKE, Emerson O(verbeck) 1916-

PERSONAL: Born February 20, 1916, in Stendal, Ind.; son of George Arthur and Sarah (Overbeck) Henke; married Beatrice Arney, June 6, 1939; children: Michael, Pamela (Mrs. Mark Bailes). *Education:* Evansville College (now University of Evansville), B.S., 1937; Indiana University, M.S., 1939, D.B.A., 1953. *Politics:* "Conservative." *Religion:* Presbyterian. *Home:* 3317 Lake Shore Dr., Waco, Tex. 76708. *Office:* Department of Accounting, Baylor University, Waco, Tex. 76706.

CAREER: Accountant in Evansville, Ind., with Iglehart Milling Co., 1937-38, and Hoosier Lamp & Stamping Co., 1939-40; Evansville College (now University of Evansville), Evansville, instructor, 1940-41, assistant professor, 1941-43, associate professor, 1943-45, professor of accounting, 1945-48; Baylor University, Waco, Tex., professor of accounting, 1948-78, distinguished professor of accounting, 1978-81, J. E. Bush Professor of Accounting, 1981—, chairman of department, 1948-67, dean of Hankamer School of Business, 1967-77. Visiting professor at University of Miami, summer, 1946, and University of Texas at Austin, spring, 1966; American Institute of Certified Public Accountants distinguished visiting professor at University of Denver, 1971-72. Certified public accountant in Texas and Indiana. Has served as deacon, elder, and Sunday school teacher in Presbyterian Church, Waco.

MEMBER: American Institute of Certified Public Accountants (research consultant, 1959-63), American Accounting Association (past chairman of national research committee; vice-chairman of public sector section, 1977-78; chairman of public sector section, 1978-79), Municipal Finance Officers Association, Association of Governmental Accountants, Texas Society of Certified Public Accountants (president of Central Texas chapter, 1960-61), Beta Alpha Psi (past president), Beta Gamma Sigma, Rotary Club, Waco Philosopher's Club.

AWARDS, HONORS: Named "Most Popular Business Professor," 1964-65, and "Outstanding Professor," 1980, both at Baylor University; named "Outstanding Educator" by Outstanding Educators of America, 1971, 1972, and 1973; Alumni Certificate of Excellence, University of Evansville, 1978; inducted into University of Evansville Athletic Hall of Fame, 1983.

WRITINGS: (Contributor) *Accounting Teacher's Guide,* Southwestern, 1953; *Accounting for Nonprofit Organizations: An Exploratory Study,* Bureau of Business Research, Indiana University, 1965; *Accounting for Nonprofit Organizations,* Wadsworth, 1966, 3rd edition, 1983; (with Walstein Smith) *CPA Review Outline,* Prentice-Hall, 1969; (contributor) Sidney Davidson, editor, *Handbook of Modern Accounting,* McGraw, 1970; *Introduction to Accounting: A Conceptual Approach,* Petrocelli Books, 1974; (with Roderick L. Holmes and Lucian G. Conway, Jr.) *Managerial Use of Accounting Data: A How-to Guide for Understanding Accounting Data and Making It Work for You,* Gulf Publishing, 1978; *Introduction to Nonprofit Organization Accounting,* Wadsworth, 1980; (contributor) John C. Burton, editor, *Handbook of Accounting and Auditing,* Warren Publishing, 1981; (with C. William Thomas) *Auditing: Theory and Practice,* Kent Publishing, 1983. Contributor of articles on business and accounting to professional journals, including *Accounting Review* and *Journal of Accountancy.*

AVOCATIONAL INTERESTS: Fishing, water skiing, snow skiing, ballroom dancing, square dancing, tennis, and other sports.

* * *

HEPPLE, Bob (Alexander) 1934-

PERSONAL: Born August 11, 1934, in South Africa; son of Alexander (a journalist) and Josephine (Zwarenstein) Hepple; married Shirley Goldsmith (a secretary), July 7, 1960; children: Brenda, Paul Alexander. *Education:* University of the Witwatersrand, B.A., 1954, LL.B., 1957; Cambridge University, LL.B., 1966. *Religion:* None. *Office:* Faculty of Law, University College, 4 Endsleigh Gardens, London WC1H 0EG England.

CAREER: University of the Witwatersrand, Johannesburg, South Africa, lecturer in law, 1959-62; attorney in private practice and advocate of Supreme Court of South Africa, 1958-63; detained and imprisoned for ninety days without trial in 1963 on grounds of political activities against apartheid policies of the South African Government; upon his release he took refuge in England; Gray's Inn, London, England, barrister-at-law, 1966—; University of Nottingham, Nottingham, England, lecturer in law, 1966-68; Cambridge University, Cambridge, England, lecturer in law and fellow of Clare College, 1968-76; chairman of Industrial Tribunals, England and Wales, 1975—; University of Kent at Canterbury, professor of law, 1976-77; University of London, University College, London, England, professor of English law, 1982—.

WRITINGS: Race, Jobs, and the Law in Britain, Allen Lane, 1968, 2nd edition, Penguin, 1970; (with Paul O'Higgins) Public Employee Unionism in the United Kingdom: The Legal Framework, Institute of Labor and Industrial Relations, University of Michigan and Wayne State University, 1971; (with O'Higgins) Individual Employment Law: An Introduction, Sweet & Maxwell, 1971, 2nd edition published as Employment Law, 1976, 4th edition, 1981; (editor) Encyclopedia of Labour Relations Law, Sweet & Maxwell, 1972; (with M. H. Matthews) Tort: Cases and Materials, Butterworth & Co., 1974, 2nd edition, 1980; (editor with others) Bibliography of the Literature on British and Irish Labour Law, Mansell, 1975; (with Glanville Williams) Foundations of the Law of Tort, Butterworth & Co., 1976, 2nd edition, 1984; (with J. Loewenberg and others) Compulsory Arbitration, Lexington Books, 1976; (editor with others) Labour Relations Statutes and Materials, Sweet & Maxwell, 1979; (with others) Labour Law in Great Britain and Ireland to 1978, Sweet & Maxwell, 1981; (contributor) Comparative Labour Law, Kluwer-Harrap Handbooks, 1982.

Contributor to *International Encyclopedia of Labor Law and Relations.* Contributor to law and industrial relations journals. Founding editor, *Industrial Law Journal,* 1972-77.

WORK IN PROGRESS: Books on labor relations law and tort.

BIOGRAPHICAL/CRITICAL SOURCES: Statesman, June 21, 1968; Listener, July 18, 1968; Cambridge Law Journal, November, 1970; British Journal of Industrial Relations, March, 1971.

* * *

HEREN, Louis (P.) 1919-

PERSONAL: Born February 6, 1919, in London, England; son of William F. (a printer) and Beatrice H. (Keller) Heren; married Patricia C. O'Regan, June 16, 1948; children: Patrick, Katherine, Sarah, Elizabeth. *Education:* Educated in London, England. *Politics:* Liberal. *Religion:* Roman Catholic. *Home:* Fleet House, Vale of Health, London N.W.3, England.

CAREER: Times, London, England, war correspondent in Kashmir, 1947, Israel, 1948, Korea, 1950, and Indo-China, 1951, foreign correspondent in India, 1947, Israel and Middle East, 1948-50, Far East, 1951-53, and India and Pakistan, 1953-55, chief correspondent in Germany, 1955-60, and in Washington, D.C., 1960-70, London deputy editor and foreign editor, 1970-81. *Military service:* British Army, 1939-46; served in Europe, Burma and the Far East. *Member:* National Press Club (Washington, D.C.). *Awards, honors:* Hannan Swaffer Award (now British Press Award) as International Reporter of the Year, 1967; John F. Kennedy Memorial Award and American Academy of Achievement Award, both for *New American Commonwealth,* 1968.

WRITINGS: New American Commonwealth, Harper, 1968; No Hail, No Farewell, Harper, 1970; Growing Up Poor in London, Hamish Hamilton, 1974; Story of America, Times Newspapers, 1976; Growing Up on the Times, Hamish Hamilton, 1978; Alas, Alas for England: What Went Wrong with Britain, Hamish Hamilton, 1981; The Powerless Press, Orbis Publishing, 1984. Contributor to magazines.

SIDELIGHTS: Louis Heren's *Alas, Alas, for England: What Went Wrong with Britain* traces the growth of England's bureacratic system and its political and economic difficulties, all within the context of the country's decline as a world power. Charles Champlin, writing in the *Los Angeles Times Book Review,* calls it an "indictment of a complacent and moribund capitalism, unimaginative unionism, an unbalanced political system giving Parliament too much power and the prime minister too little, and critically errant philosophical attitudes." Acknowledging that the causes of Britain's economic and political stagnation are various and complex, Heren's focus is largely on what Alfred Friendly describes in the *Times* as personal failures, "personal mistakes in deciding on *Weltpolitik,* personal failures of will and nerve to block minority tyranny in the trade union movement, personal irresponsibility in the face of the tyranny of Parliament." These failures, according to Friendly, are detailed in a "score of deft portraits, each of only a few paragraphs, of the principal figures determining the nation's political and economic course." He concludes: "They add their share of sparkle to a book admirably organized and argued in singularly precise language."

BIOGRAPHICAL/CRITICAL SOURCES: Atlantic, February, 1968; Time, February 9, 1968; Book World, February 25, 1968; New Republic, March 16, 1968; Reporter, April 18, 1968; New York Times Book Review, August 9, 1970; New York Times, August 19, 1970; New York Review of Books, November 19, 1970; Times Literary Dupplement, October 19, 1973; Times (London) March 19, 1981; Punch, May 13, 1981; Los Angeles Times Book Review, June 7, 1981.

* * *

HERRON, Orley R., Jr. 1933-

PERSONAL: Born November 16, 1933, in Olive Hill, Ky.; son of Orley R. (a vice-president of sales for a rubber band company) and Hyllie Ann (Weaver) Herron; married Donna Jean Morgan, August 24, 1956; children: Jill, Morgan, Mark. *Education:* Wheaton College, Wheaton, Ill., B.A., 1955; Michigan State University, M.A., 1959, Ph.D., 1965. *Office:* Office of the President, National College of Education, 2840 Sheridan Rd., Evanston, Ill. 60201.

CAREER: Presbyterian Church, River Forest, Ill., director of youth, 1956-58; Michigan State University, East Lansing, head resident adviser, 1958-61; Westmont College, Santa Barbara, Calif., dean of students, 1961-67; University of Mississippi, University, associate professor of education, 1967-68; Indiana State University, Terre Haute, assistant to the president, 1968-70; Greenville College, Greenville, Ill., president, 1970-77; National College of Education—Main Campus, Evanston, Ill., president, 1977—. *Member:* American Personnel and Guidance Association, National Association of Student Personnel Administrators, Phi Delta Kappa.

WRITINGS: The Role of the Trustee, International Textbook, 1969; (co-author) Input/Output, Moody, 1970; (editor) New

Dimensions in Student Personnel Administration, International Textbook, 1970; *Christian Executive in a Secular World,* Thomas Nelson, 1979; *Who Controls Your Child?,* Thomas Nelson, 1980; *Honor Thy Children,* Thomas Nelson, 1980. Contributor of about twenty articles to journals, including *College and University Business.*

AVOCATIONAL INTERESTS: Sports, music.

* * *

HESS, Lilo 1916-

PERSONAL: Born in 1916 in Erfurt, Germany. *Education:* Educated in European schools. *Home:* R.D. 1, Stroudsburg, Pa. 18360.

CAREER: Animal photographer for magazines; writer and illustrator of children's books. *Awards, honors: Animals That Hide, Imitate and Bluff* was selected one of the Child Study Associations' Books of the Year.

WRITINGS—Author and photographic illustrator; published by Scribner, except as indicated: *Christine, the Baby Chimp,* G. Bell, 1954; *Rabbits in the Meadow,* Crowell, 1963; *Easter in November,* Crowell, 1964; *Shetland Ponies,* Crowell, 1964; *The Timid Sheep,* Crowell, 1965; *Sea Horses,* 1966; *Foxes in the Woodshed,* 1966; *Pigeons Everywhere,* 1967; *The Curious Raccoons,* 1968; *The Remarkable Chameleon,* 1968; *The Misunderstood Skunk,* 1969.

Animals That Hide, Imitate and Bluff, 1970; *The Praying Mantis, Insect Cannibal,* 1971; *Mouse and Company,* 1972; *Problem Pets,* 1972; *Monkeys and Apes without Trees,* 1973; *A Snail's Pace,* 1974; *A Pony to Love,* 1975; *Small Habitats,* 1976; *A Puppy for You,* 1976; *A Dog by Your Side,* 1977; *Life Begins for Puppies,* 1978; *The Amazing Earthworm,* 1979.

Listen to Your Kitten Purr, 1980; *Bird Companions,* 1981; *Diary of a Rabbit,* 1982; *Making Friends with Guinea Pigs,* 1983; *A Cat's Nine Lives,* 1984; *The Good Luck Dog,* 1985.

Illustrator: Dorothy C. Hogner, *Odd Pets,* Crowell, 1951; Irmengarde Eberle, *Fawn in the Woods,* Crowell, 1962. Photographs published in *Natural History Magazine, Life, Look, Parents' Magazine, New York Times Magazine, This Week,* and in European periodicals.

WORK IN PROGRESS: *Secrets of a Meadow,* for Scribner.

* * *

HESSE, Mary (Brenda) 1924-

PERSONAL: Surname rhymes with "dressy"; born October 15, 1924, in Reigate, England; daughter of Ethelbert Thomas (an accountant) and Brenda Nellie (Pelling) Hesse. *Education:* Imperial College of Science and Technology, London, B.Sc., 1947, Ph.D., 1948; University College, London, M.Sc., 1949. *Religion:* Church of England. *Home:* 39 Highsett, Hills Rd., Cambridge, England. *Office:* Department of History and Philosophy of Science, Cambridge University, Free School Lane, Cambridge CB2 3RH, England.

CAREER: University of Leeds, Leeds, England, lecturer in mathematics, 1951-55; University of London, University College, London, England, lecturer in history and philosophy of science, 1955-59; Cambridge University, Cambridge, England, lecturer, 1960-68, university reader, 1968-75, professor of philosophy of science, 1975—, member of council of senate, 1962-66. Visiting professor at Yale University, 1962-63, University of Minnesota, 1966, University of Chicago, 1968, and University of Notre Dame, 1972. Stanton Lecturer, Cambridge University, 1978-80; Gifford Lecturer, University of Edinburgh, 1983. *Member:* British Society for the Philosophy of Science, British Society for the History of Science (member of university grants committee, 1980—), British Academy (fellow).

WRITINGS: *Science and the Human Imagination,* S.C.M. Press, 1953; *Forces and Fields,* Littlefield, 1961; *Models and Analogies in Science,* Sheed, 1963, enlarged edition, University of Notre Dame Press, 1966; *In Defence of Objectivity* (lecture), British Academy, 1973; *The Structure of Scientific Inference,* University of California Press, 1974; (editor) *Applications of Inductive Logic,* Clarendon Press, 1979; *Revolutions and Reconstructions in the Philosophy of Science,* Indiana University Press, 1980. Contributor to professional journals. Editor, *British Journal for the Philosophy of Science,* 1965-69.

WORK IN PROGRESS: Research in the philosophy of social sciences and the philosophy of religion.

* * *

HIGMAN, Francis M(ontgomery) 1935-

PERSONAL: Born September 17, 1935, in Georgetown, Guyana; son of Ernest (a clergyman) and Anne (Corp) Higman; married Ruth Benson (a teacher), July 19, 1960; children: Clarie, Julian, Sophia. *Education:* St. John's College, Oxford, B.A., 1959, M.A., 1964, B. Litt., 1964. *Religion:* Anglican. *Home:* 70 Dunster Rd., West Bridgford, Nottingham NG2 6JE, England. *Office:* Department of French, University of Nottingham, Nottingham NG7 2RD, England.

CAREER: University of Bristol, Bristol, England, lecturer in French, 1961-70; University of Dublin, Trinity College, Dublin, Ireland, professor of French, 1970-78; University of Nottingham, Nottingham, England, professor of French, 1979—. *Military service:* Royal Air Force, 1954-56. *Member:* Society for French Studies, Association of University Teachers. *Awards, honors:* Ordre National du Merite, 1978.

WRITINGS: *The Style of John Calvin in His French Polemical Treatises,* Oxford University Press, 1967; (editor with K. Cameron and K. M. Hall) Theodore de Beze, *Abraham Sacrifiant,* Droz, 1967; (editor) John Calvin, *Three French Treatises,* Athlone Press, 1970; (contributor) T. C. Cave, editor, *Ronsard the Poet,* Methuen, 1973; *Censorship and the Sorbonne,* Droz, 1979; (editor) Guillaume Farel, *Le Pater noster,* Droz, 1982; (contributor) J. F. Gilmont, editor, *Palaestra Typographica,* Verviers, Gason, 1984.

WORK IN PROGRESS: Other studies on Calvin and Reformation literature in French.

SIDELIGHTS: Francis M. Higman writes: "Teaching foreign languages has made me peculiarly aware that the way we think is partly conditioned by the language we happen to use. My work, technical as it may seem, is all centered on the period at which the modern French language—and thus the modern French mentality—was just taking shape." Higman spent ten years of his youth in South America.

* * *

HILL, Draper
See HILL, L(eroy) Draper, Jr.

HILL, L(eroy) Draper, Jr. 1935-
(Draper Hill)

PERSONAL: Born July 1, 1935, in Boston, Mass.; son of Leroy Draper (an investment banker) and Jean (Thompson) Hill; married Sarah Adams, April 22, 1967; children: Jennifer, Jonathan. *Education:* Harvard University, B.A. (magna cum laude), 1957; University College, London, additional study, 1960-63. *Home:* 368 Washington Rd., Grosse Pointe, Mich. 48230. *Office:* Detroit News, 615 West Lafayette Blvd., Detroit, Mich. 48231.

CAREER: Quincy Patriot Ledger, Quincy, Mass., reporter and cartoonist, 1957-60, 1963-64; *Worcester Telegram* and *Evening Gazette,* Worcester, Mass., editorial cartoonist, 1964-71; *Commercial Appeal,* Memphis, Tenn., editorial cartoonist, 1971-76; *Detroit News,* Detroit, Mich., editorial cartoonist, 1976—. One-man shows at Originals Only, 1973, and Brooks Memorial Art Gallery, 1975. Member of advisory board, Swann Foundation for Caricature and Cartoon, 1980—. *Member:* Association of American Editorial Cartoonists (second vice-president, 1972-74; first vice-president, 1974-75; president, 1975-76), Club of Odd Volumes (Boston), Signet Society (Harvard). *Awards, honors:* Fulbright scholar in England, 1960-62; Guggenheim fellow, 1983-84.

WRITINGS—Under name Draper Hill: *The Crane Library,* trustees of Thomas Crane Public Library (Quincy, Mass.), 1962; *Cartoon and Caricature from Hogarth to Hoffnung,* Arts Council of Great Britain, 1962; *Mr. Gillray: The Caricaturist,* Phaidon, 1965; (editor) *Fashionable Contrasts: 100 Caricatures by James Gillray,* Phaidon, 1966; *James Gillray, 1756-1815: Drawings* (catalogue), Arts Council of Great Britain, 1967; *Illingworth: On Target,* Boston Public Library, 1970; *The Lively Art of J. P. Alley, 1885-1934* (catalogue), Brooks Memorial Art Gallery, 1973; (with James Roper) *The Decline and Fall of the Gibbon,* Inadvertent Press, 1974; (author of introduction) *I Feel I Should Warn You,* Preservation Press, 1975; (editor) *The Satirical Etchings of James Gillray,* Dover, 1976. Contributor to *Encyclopedia of Collectibles,* 1978.

WORK IN PROGRESS: A biography of the cartoonist, Thomas Nast.

* * *

HILLING, David 1935-

PERSONAL: Born February 21, 1935, in Eastbourne, Sussex, England; son of William Roderick (a travel agent) and Jessie Katheleen (Hobbs) Hilling; married Wendy Elizabeth Hubbard, September 8, 1962; children: Hugh Richard, Christopher James. *Education:* University College of Wales, Aberystwyth, B.Sc. (with upper second class honors), 1957; University of London, Postgraduate Certificate in Education, 1958, Ph.D., 1974; University of Wales, M.Sc., 1961. *Home:* 4 Torrington Rd., Berkhamsted, Hertfordshire HP4 3DD, England. *Office:* Bedford College, University of London, Regent's Park, London NW1 4NS, England.

CAREER: University of Ghana, Accra, lecturer in geography, 1961-66; University of London, Bedford College, London, England, lecturer, 1966-78, senior lecturer in geography, 1978—. Transport consultant for United Nations Economic Commission for Africa, 1970-72; consultant for shipping lines. *Member:* Royal Geographical Society (fellow), Geographical Association, Institute of British Geographers, Maritime Economists Group, Chartered Institute of Transport, African Studies Association of the United Kingdom. *Awards, honors:* Vivian Bulkeley-Johnson Trophy, Inland Waterways Association of Britain, 1978, for contributions to commerical use of waterways.

WRITINGS: (Contributor) C. A. Fisher, editor, *Essays in Political Geography,* Methuen, 1968; (editor with Brian Stewart Hoyle, and contributor) *Seaports and Development in Tropical Africa,* Macmillan, 1970; (with J. I. Clarke, and others) *An Advanced Geography of Africa,* Hulton Educational Publications, 1975; *Barge Carrier Systems: Inventory and Prospects,* Benn, 1977; (editor) *Barge Systems Conference Proceedings, New Orleans, 1980,* Polytech International, 1981; (editor and contributor with Hoyle) *Seaport Systems and Spatial Change,* Wiley, 1984. Also author of scripts for British Broadcasting Corp. school broadcasts. Also contributor to encyclopedias and directories. Contributor of about thirty articles to geography journals, including *Geographical Magazine* and *Geography.*

WORK IN PROGRESS: A textbook on the geography of Africa; a textbook on transport and developing countries.

* * *

HILTON, Suzanne 1922-

PERSONAL: Born September 3, 1922, in Pittsburgh, Pa.; daughter of Edwin P. (an insurance broker) and Helen (McFeely) McLean; married Warren Mitchell Hilton (an insurance engineer), June 15, 1946; children: Edwin Bruce, Diana Lester. *Education:* Attended Pennsylvania College for Women (now Chatham College), 1940-43; Beaver College, B.A., 1945. *Religion:* Methodist. *Home:* 301 Runnymede Ave., Jenkintown, Pa. 19046.

CAREER: Former researcher and copywriter for advertising department of Westminster Press, Philadelphia, Pa.; public relations director for Jenkintown School District, Jenkintown, Pa. Researcher and writer of local history. *Member:* Author's Guild, Philadelphia Children's Reading Round Table. *Awards, honors: The Way It Was—1876* was selected as one of the best books of the year, 1975, by *New York Times;* Legion of Honor, Chapel of Four Chaplains, 1978; award for nonfiction, Drexel University School of Library and Information Science, 1979; Golden Spur Award, Western Writers of America, 1981, for *Getting There: Frontier Travel without Power.*

WRITINGS—Young adult books; all published by Westminster: *How Do They Get Rid of It?* (Junior Literary Guild selection), 1970; *How Do They Cope with It?,* 1970; *It's Smart to Use a Dummy* (Junior Literary Guild selection), 1971; *It's a Model World* (Junior Literary Guild selection), 1972; *Beat It, Burn It, and Drown It,* 1974; *The Way It Was—1876,* 1975.

Who Do You Think You Are?: Digging for Your Family Roots, 1976; *Here Today and Gone Tomorrow* (Junior Literary Guild selection), 1978; *Getting There: Frontier Travel without Power* (Junior Literary Guild selection), 1980; *We, the People: The Way We Were, 1783-1793* (Junior Literary Guild selection), 1981; *Faster Than a Horse* (Junior Literary Guild selection), 1983.

Also associate editor and contributor, *Montgomery County: The Second Hundred Years.* Contributor of short stories and articles to periodicals. Editor, Old York Road Historical Society *Bulletin.*

WORK IN PROGRESS: A book on history using resources from original manuscripts.

SIDELIGHTS: Suzanne Hilton told *CA:* "As a schoolchild, I never really liked history. Today I'm fascinated by it, trying to bring a new lively dimension to writing about the past. The people I write about really lived and still sound alive through their letters and diaries. I hope that my books can help spark young peoples' interest in what otherwise might be a dull task of memorizing dates. I have read several hundred diaries to pluck the most interesting tales written while the memory of an adventure was still ripe in the mind of the diary-writer.''

She also mentions that she and her husband "often use a tired old VW camper to carry us from one interesting historical location to another for still more research and diary-snooping. We have been doing some genealogical research along the way as well."

AVOCATIONAL INTERESTS: Sailing and gunkholing up the little streams that run into Chesapeake Bay.

* * *

HINTZ, (Loren) Martin 1945-

PERSONAL: Born June 1, 1945, in New Hampton, Iowa; son of Loren (a flier) and Gertrude (an office manager; maiden name, Russell) Hintz; married Sandra Lee Wright (a writer and literary agent), May 1, 1971; children: Daniel, Stephen, Kate. *Education:* College of St. Thomas, St. Paul, Minn., B.A., 1967; Northwestern University, M.A., 1968. *Politics:* Liberal. *Religion:* Roman Catholic. *Home and office:* 2879 North Grant Blvd., Milwaukee, Wis. 53210. *Agent:* Ray Pvechner, 3210 South 7th St., Milwaukee, Wis. 53215.

CAREER: Free-lance writer and photographer. *Milwaukee Sentinel*, Milwaukee, Wis., reporter and editor, 1968-75. Worked as a case worker for American Red Cross, 1968-71; associate member of School of the Sisters of St. Francis.

MEMBER: Society of American Travel Writers (vice chairman, Central States, 1978-79; chairman, Central States, 1979-83; member of national board, 1981-83), American Society of Journalists and Authors, Society of Children's Book Writers, Society of Professional Journalists (president, Milwaukee chapter, 1976), Caledonian Society, Circus Model Builders of America, Northwest Territorial Alliance (public relations officer), Midwest Travel Writers' Association, Wisconsin News Photographers Association, Wisconsin Soccer Press and Radio Association, Milwaukee Kickers (soccer club; member of board of directors, 1972-74), Milwaukee Press Club, Clan Donald (Midwest district), Sigma Delta Chi (member of board of directors of Milwaukee chapter, 1972-74; president-elect, 1975-76; president, 1976).

AWARDS, HONORS: Kicker of the year award from Milwaukee Kickers, 1970; school bell award from Wisconsin Education Association, 1971, for educational news coverage; community service award from Inland Daily Press Association, 1974; second place in short nonfiction contest, 1979, and runner-up in juvenile nonfiction contest, 1983, both from Council of Wisconsin Writers; photography, newspaper, and magazine writing awards from Central States chapter of Society of American Travel Writers, 1982 and 1983.

WRITINGS: (With wife, Sandra Hintz) *We Can't Afford It*, Raintree, 1976; *The If I Can't Be Ordained, I'll Cook Book*, Thomas More Press, 1978; *Computers in Our Society, Today and Tomorrow*, F. Watts, 1983.

Contributor: *Four-Wheel Drive North American Trail Guide*, Rand McNally, 1978; *Circus Workin's*, Messner, 1980; *Tons of Fun*, Messner, 1982; *The Universal Story*, Universal Foods, 1982.

Contributor to "Land of Enchantment" series, published by Children's Press: *Land of Enchantment: Norway*, 1982; . . . *Finland*, 1983; . . . *West Germany*, 1983; . . . *Italy*, 1983; . . . *Chile*, 1984; . . . *Morocco*, 1984; . . . *Switzerland*, 1984; . . . *Argentina*, 1984; . . . *Sweden*, 1984. Contributor to magazines and newspapers, including *Billboard, Amusement Business, Scouting, Exclusively Yours, Compass*, and *Wisconsin Trails*.

WORK IN PROGRESS: "The Reunion," a play; a collection of short stories; articles for periodicals.

SIDELIGHTS: Martin Hintz has played and coached soccer for the Milwaukee Kickers and has covered the World Cup Soccer Championships in Mexico and West Germany. He has written numerous articles as followups to his travels in Chile and Poland, as well as to other countries "in turmoil." During his college years, he worked for Royal American Shows, the largest carnival in the United States, and has used that experience as the basis for many short stories.

"All these experiences," Hintz told *CA*, "help keep the problems of society in perspective, as well as provide a basis for understanding our common humanity with all its joys and sorrows."

* * *

HIPP, George
See ABRAMS, George J(oseph)

* * *

HODGE, Francis (Richard) 1915-

PERSONAL: Born December 17, 1915, in Geneva, N.Y.; son of Richard Duane (a barber) and Mabel Ella (Clark) Hodge; married Beulah Bernice Wiley (a television producer), June 1, 1942; children: Elizabeth Jean (Mrs. James Flack II). *Education:* Hobart College, B.A., 1939; Cornell University, M.A., 1940, Ph.D., 1948. *Home:* 1109 Bluebonnet Lane, Austin, Tex. 78704. *Office:* Department of Drama, University of Texas, Austin, Tex. 78712.

CAREER: Carroll College, Waukesha, Wis., instructor in drama, 1940-42; Cornell University, Ithaca, N.Y., instructor in drama, 1948; University of Texas at Austin, assistant professor, 1949-55, associate professor, 1955-62, professor of drama, 1962-79, professor emeritus, 1979—. Director of one hundred plays in the United States and Canada; supervisor of the production of over three hundred plays, including one hundred new one-act plays. Visiting assistant professor, University of Iowa, 1948-49; professor of drama, summers, University of Colorado, 1960, Banff School of Fine Arts, 1961-68, and University of British Columbia, 1962. *Military service:* U.S. Army Air Forces, 1942-45; became staff sergeant. *Member:* International Society for Theatre Research, American Theatre Association (fellow), Speech Communication Association, American Society for Theatre Research, Theatre Library Association, Phi Kappa Phi. *Awards, honors:* Golden Anniversary award, Speech Association of America, 1965, for *Yankee Theatre*.

WRITINGS: (Contributor) *A History of Speech Education in America*, Appleton-Century-Crofts, 1954; (contributor) Leroy Robert Shaw, editor, *German Theatre Today*, University of Texas Press, 1964; *Yankee Theatre: The Image of America on the Stage, 1825-1850*, University of Texas Press, 1964; (author of introduction) Noah Ludlow, *Dramatic Life As I Found It*, Benjamin Blom, 1966; *Play Directing: Analysis, Communi-*

cation, and Style, Prentice-Hall, 1971, 2nd edition, 1982; (contributor) *The American Theatre: A Sum of Its Parts,* Samuel French, 1971; (editor) *Innovations in Stage and Theatre Design* (essays), American Society for Theatre Research and Theatre Library Association, 1972. Contributor to journals, including *American Historical Review, Theatre Arts, Theatre Annual, Quarterly Journal of Speech, Educational Theatre Journal, Texas Quarterly, Southern Speech,* and *Theatre Survey.* Editor, *Educational Theatre Journal,* 1966-68.

WORK IN PROGRESS: Theatre and Audience in America.

SIDELIGHTS: Francis Hodge has traveled extensively in Europe and Asia, studying folk festivals, antique theatres, contemporary stagings, and audiences. He told *CA:* "I write about the theatre as one way I can help keep this hand-crafted form alive against the onslaught of the electronic media and the disassociations of the urban explosion in our time. I am looking for converts by helping young people understand its differences, its societal functions, its meanings and meanderings throughout its history."

BIOGRAPHICAL/CRITICAL SOURCES: Writer, November, 1971; *Quarterly Journal of Speech,* April, 1972.

* * *

**HODGSON, David
See LEWIS, David**

* * *

HOFFMAN, Phyllis M(iriam) 1944-

PERSONAL: Born September 7, 1944, in Brooklyn, N.Y.; daughter of Morris and Bertha (Levine) Hoffman. *Education:* State University of New York at Binghamton, B.A. (magna cum laude), 1965; Bank Street Colledge of Education, M.A., 1974. *Home:* 49 Eighth Ave., New York, N.Y. 10014. *Office: Peanut Butter,* Scholastic Book Services, 50th West 44th St., New York, N.Y. 10036.

CAREER: Harper & Row Publishers, Inc., New York City, children's book editor, 1966-70; Abelard-Schuman Ltd., New York City, children's book editor, 1970-72; Little Star of Broome Day Care Center, New York City, group teacher, 1975-77; Harcourt Brace Jovanovich, Inc., New York City, editor in reading department, 1978-82; Scholastic Book Services, New York City, editor of *Peanut Butter* magazine, 1983—.

WRITINGS—All children's books: *Steffie and Me,* Harper, 1970; (editor of German translation) Hans Christian Andersen, *The Ugly Duckling,* Abelard, 1972; *Happy Halloween,* Atheneum, 1982; *Play Ball with the Yankees,* Atheneum, 1983.

* * *

HOGG, Ian V(ernon) 1926-

PERSONAL: Born October 29, 1926, in Durham, England; son of William Vernon (an attorney) and Mary Eleanor (Whalley) Hogg; married Anna Teresa Trebinska, March 10, 1962; children: George, Leslie, Alexandra. *Education:* Attended schools in Durham and St. Albans, Hertfordshire, England, 1932-40. *Politics:* Conservative. *Religion:* Protestant. *Home and office:* 15 Packers Hill, Upton-upon-Severn, Worcestershire, England. *Agent:* Watson, Little Ltd., Suite 8, 26 Charing Cross Rd., London SW 1, England.

CAREER: British Army, 1945-72, served in Europe, Hong Kong, and in the Korean War, 1950-52; Royal Military College of Science, Shrivenham, Swindon, Wiltshire, England, member of instructional staff of Royal Artillery, 1953-72, retired as master gunner. *Member:* Royal Artillery Historical Society, Institute of Journalists, Royal United Services Institute for Defence Studies, American Defense Preparedness Association.

WRITINGS: Military Pistols and Revolvers: The Handguns of the Two World Wars, Arco, 1970; *The Guns, 1939-1945,* Ballantine, 1970; *German Secret Weapons of World War II,* Arms & Armour Press, 1970; *Barrage: The Guns in Action,* Ballantine, 1971; *The Guns, 1914-1918,* Ballantine, 1971; *German Pistols and Revolvers,* Arms & Armour Press, 1971; (with John S. Weeks) *Military Small Arms of the Twentieth Century,* Arms & Armour Press, 1973; (with L. F. Thurston) *British Artillery of the First World War,* Ian Allen, 1973; *Artillery,* MacDonald & Janes, 1973; *Rail Gun,* John Batchelor, 1973; *Weapons of the Arab-Israeli War,* Phoebus Publishing, 1973; *Coast Defences of England and Wales,* David & Charles, 1974; *Grenades and Mortars,* Ballantine, 1974; *A History of Artillery,* Hamlyn, 1974; *Infantry Weapons,* Phoebus Publishing, 1974; *German Secret Weapons,* Phoebus Publishing, 1974.

German Artillery of World War Two, Arms & Armour Press, 1975; *Gas: The Story of Chemical Warfare,* Ballantine, 1975; *Fortress: The History of Military Defence,* MacDonald, 1975; (with J. H. Batchelor) *Armies of the American Revolution,* Leo Cooper, 1975; *Allied Secret Weapons,* Phoebus Publishing, 1975; *Modern Soviet Weapons,* Phoebus Publishing, 1975; *The Machine Gun,* Phoebus Publishing, 1975; *The Guns of World War Two,* MacDonald, 1976; *Encyclopedia of Infantry Weapons,* Bison Books, 1977; *World Pistols,* Arms & Armour Press, 1977; (contributor) *The Japanese War Machine,* Bison Books, 1977; (contributor) *The Russian War Machine,* Bison Books, 1977; (contributor) *Hitler's Decisive Battles,* Quarto Publications, 1977.

British and American Artillery of World War Two, Arms & Armour Press, 1978; *The Tank Story,* Phoebus Publishing, 1978; *Guns and How They Work,* Marshall Cavendish, 1978; *Encyclopedia of Firearms,* Quarto Press, 1978; *Naval Gun,* Blandford Press, 1978; *Anti-Aircraft,* MacDonald & Janes, 1978; *Armor in Conflict,* MacDonald & Janes, 1980; (with Weeks) *Encyclopedia of Military Vehicles,* Quarto Press, 1980; *A History of Fortification,* Orbis Publishing, 1981; *The Cartridge Guide,* Arms & Armour Press, 1982; *Patton: A Biography,* Bison Books, 1982; *The Israeli War Machine,* Quarto Press, 1983; (with C. Chant) *The Nuclear War File,* Ebury Press, 1983; *Modern Small Arms,* Bison Books, 1983.

Contributor to periodicals, including *War Monthly, Weapons & Warfare, Guns Review, Defense Afrique,* and *National Defense.* Editor, *Jane's Military Review,* 1982—, and *Jane's Infantry Weapons,* 1983—; military editor, *Defence* and *Miltronics,* both 1978-82; contributing editor, *Jane's Defence Review,* 1982—.

WORK IN PROGRESS: A Collector's Guide to Revolvers, for publication by Arms & Armour Press; *The British Army: A Design History,* a history of the repercussions of weapon design on tactics, for publication by Ian Allen.

SIDELIGHTS: Ian V. Hogg told *CA:* "Since 1978 my work has become more involved with defence journalism, culminating in my appointment as editor of *Jane's Infantry Weapons* and, through this, as a contributing editor for *Jane's Defence Review.* In 1984 this magazine is to become a weekly publication, which will mean a great deal more journalism, though I expect to be able to produce an occasional book under the Jane's imprint."

HOLYER, Erna Maria 1925-
(Ernie Holyer)

PERSONAL: Born March 15, 1925, in Weilheim, Germany; came to United States in 1956, naturalized citizen; daughter of Mathias (a hotel, theater, and farm owner) and Anna (Goldhofer) Schretter; married Friedrich Rupp, May 27, 1943; married second husband, Gene Wallace Holyer (president of Holyer Construction Co.), August 24, 1957. *Education:* San Jose City College, A.A., 1964; attended College of San Mateo, San Jose State University, and University of California, Santa Cruz, 1965-74. *Home:* 1314 Rimrock Dr., San Jose, Calif. 95120.

CAREER: Free-lance writer, mainly for children; painter, with several one-woman shows. Teacher of creative writing in San Jose adult education program. *Member:* California Writers Club.

WRITINGS—Juveniles; under pseudonym Ernie Holyer: *Rescue at Sunrise, and Other Stories*, Review & Herald, 1965; *Steve's Night of Silence, and Other Stories*, Review & Herald, 1966; *A Cow for Hansel*, Review & Herald, 1967; *At the Forest's Edge*, Southern Publishing, 1969; *Song of Courage*, Southern Publishing, 1970; *Lone Brown Gull, and Other Stories*, Review & Herald, 1971; *Shoes for Daniel*, Southern Publishing, 1974; *Sigi's Fire Helmet*, Pacific Press Publishing Association, 1974; *The Southern Sea Otter*, Steck, 1975; *Reservoir Road Adventure*, Baker Book, 1982.

Contributor: G. Tabler, editor, *Und Wieder Scheint die Sonne* (anthology), Advent Verlag, 1974; D. F. Kellerman, editor, *Language Experiences in Reading*, Encyclopaedia Britannica Educational Corp., 1975; Richard T. Scott, editor, *Point 32 Program*, Reader's Digest Press, 1978. Also contributor of several book-length serials and more than 200 short stories and articles to magazines and newspapers.

WORK IN PROGRESS: Elisha Brooks, "the story of a Michigan backwoods boy who crossed the Plains in 1852 and, starving and half-orphaned, struggled to get himself an education in California"; *The Brown Dawn*, "a novel set in a small town in Germany during 1923-33, the time of Hitler's rise to power."

SIDELIGHTS: Erna Maria Holyer wrote *CA*: "My decision to write germinated one hot August day in 1943. My only sister lay in her casket, blond, beautiful, and oh, so still. At twenty-three, she hadn't had time to make her mark in life. A world was lost to me, the essence of a person I loved gone forever. Stunned, I poured my shock into a poem. Who cares about people after they die? Who recalls their uniqueness? Who remembers their tragedies and joys?

"I agonized about survival. Theodor Storm charmed me through his novellas and poems, holding me in a web of enchantment. Richard Wagner moved me deeply through his librettos and musical dramas. Superb writers both, they had committed their inner spirit to paper and, in doing so, remained alive.

"My head burst with fantasies, philosophies and observations. Like Parsifal, the guileless fool, I bumbled into a wondrous, if startling, world. A book of fairytales took shape and was accepted by a Munich publisher. The illustrator completed the beautiful color plates just before a currency devaluation bankrupted the publisher in 1948. I continued to write, eventually switching to English, a language learned as an adult. My children's stories appeared in a variety of magazines starting in 1960. Readers loved them, I was told. Educators felt these 'Ernie Holyer stories' had a positive influence on the young.

"My aim is to create beauty, inspire readers, and leave something of lasting value. Often, I ask myself, 'What comes next?' Time, the writer's ally and enemy, is passing. Partially completed manuscripts slumber uneasily in drawers and filing cabinets. False starts, right starts, who knows? Should I finish these, or start a new tale that begs to be told? I wish for the wisdom of Solomon, the faith of Job, the courage of David. Once the decision to write is made, one charges ahead like the immature Parsifal, suffering setbacks, succumbing to lures and detours, reveling in joys and despair. All this in search of the Holy Grail, the work that will endure. It's a growing process, a labor of love, a quest without guarantees attached. The creative spirit is a powerful drive, seeking expression, needing to communicate, wanting to share. Vincent Van Gogh once wrote, 'If one has fire within oneself and a soul, they cannot be hidden under a bushel . . . because what one has within oneself will out!'"

* * *

HOLYER, Ernie
See HOLYER, Erna Maria

* * *

HORATIO, Jane
See CUDLIPP, Edythe

* * *

HORWITZ, Julius 1920-

PERSONAL: Born August 18, 1920, in Cleveland, Ohio; son of Samuel (a merchant) and Jennie (Chazin) Horwitz; married Lois J. Sandler (a school secretary), June 1, 1947; children: Jonathan Seth, David Aaron. *Education:* Attended Ohio State University, 1940-42, 1946, and Columbia University, 1947-50; New School for Social Research, B.A., 1953. *Religion:* Hebrew. *Home:* 10 Stuyvesant Ave., Larchmont, N.Y. 10538. *Agent:* Ned Leavitt, William Morris Agency, 1350 Avenue of the Americas, New York, N.Y. 10019.

CAREER: New York City (N.Y.) Department of Welfare, social investigator, 1956-62; New York State Senate, Albany, consultant on public welfare to majority leader, 1963-65; New York State Joint Legislative Committee on Public Health, Albany, consultant, 1965-67; City of New York, director of Medicaid Information Office, 1967-70; Health Insurance Plan of New York, New York City, director of public relations, 1970—. Faculty member, The New School, Center for New York City Affairs. *Military service:* U.S. Army Air Forces, 1942-45; received Europe-Africa-Middle Eastern theater ribbon with six Bronze Stars, and Distinguished Unit Citation.

MEMBER: Authors League of America, P.E.N., New School Alumni Association (president; ex-officio member, board of trustees, 1970-74), Central Bureau for the Jewish Aged (member, board of directors, 1972—). *Awards, honors:* Guggenheim fellowship for writing, 1954, 1963; Silver Gavel award, American Bar Association, 1967; Silver Bunny Award, *Playboy*, for best short story of 1975.

WRITINGS—Novels; except as indicated: *The City* (short stories), World Publishing, 1953; *The Inhabitants*, World Publishing, 1960; *Can I Get There by Candlelight*, Atheneum, 1964; *The W.A.S.P.*, Atheneum, 1967; *The Diary of A.N.: The Story of the House on West 104th Street*, Coward, 1970; *The Married Lovers*, Dial, 1973; *Natural Enemies*, Holt, 1975; *Landfall*, Holt, 1977; *The Best Days*, Holt, 1980.

Contributor: *New Light on Juvenile Delinquency,* Wilson, 1967; *Psychology in Action,* Macmillan, 1967; *Children's Behavior,* Exposition Press, 1968; *Readings in American Government,* Crowell, 1968; *Patterns of Power: Social Foundations of Education,* Pitman Publishing, 1968; *Cities in Trouble,* Quadrangle, 1970; *Politics and Progress,* Silver Burdett, 1971; *Economic Analysis and Policy,* Prentice-Hall, 1971; *Social Problems in America,* Wiley, 1972; *Social Crisis,* Crowell, 1974. Contributor of short stories and articles to periodicals, including *Commentary, Midstream, Contact, New York Times Sunday Magazine,* and *Reader's Digest.*

WORK IN PROGRESS: A novel, for Cornelia and Michael Bessie Books.

SIDELIGHTS: Written from the perspective of an author who spent years working for New York City's public welfare system, Julius Horwitz's early novels chronicle the deprived, often dangerous world of that city's downtrodden. Three of these books, *The Inhabitants, The W.A.S.P.,* and *The Diary of A.N.,* depict characters whose poverty and helplessness drive them to desperate acts.

Critics tend to view these novels as gripping, sometimes shocking portrayals of urban life. Daniel Talbot, of the *New York Herald Tribune Book Review,* however, finds fault with the author's handling of character dialogue, noting that in *The Inhabitants* "the uneducated unfortunates speak like philosophers." In a similar vein, *New York Times Book Review* writer Claude Brown complains that Horwitz makes all of the residents of Harlem "sound like dull welfare case-histories" in *The W.A.S.P.* Nevertheless, most critics recommend Horwitz's books. "[The author] is no simple humanitarian or sociology-directed student of life," asserts Martin Tucker in *Saturday Review.* "His eye is on people and not their type; he is more interested in behavior than status. The result is a novel [*The Inhabitants*] that is filled with magnificently incisive portraits." And *Saturday Review* writer Zena Sutherland finds *The Diary of A.N.* "a biting indictment and a brutally real and moving fictionalization of the plight of the ghetto child."

Horwitz's later novels, *The Married Lovers, Natural Enemies,* and *Landfall* among them, examine the conflicts and traumas faced by New York's upper classes. In *The Married Lovers,* described by James R. Frakes in the *New York Times Book Review* as a "journal of high-fashion *angst,*" David, a surgeon, attempts suicide when he learns of his wife's infidelity. During his recovery in the hospital, David attempts to analyze what went wrong in his marriage. *New York Times* critic Anatole Broyard calls *The Married Lovers* "a bright but uneasy offspring of the maxims of La Rochefoucald and *Human Sexual Inadequacy* by Masters and Johnson." D.A.N. Jones, in the *Times Literary Supplement,* remarks that in *The Married Lovers* the three main characters "all . . . speak in the best sort of American English, a spare, graceful, aphoristic style, which is pleasing to read but makes the novel implausible—as if Socrates, Xanthippe and Diotima were all on one wavelength." Ultimately, though, Jones feels the author uses his "exceptional verbal fluency merely to illustrate confusion, irrationality and failure in communication. His elegant book is well worth reading, particularly by the married and the marriageable."

"Considering that [*Natural Enemies*] is about the awfulness of a marriage, of middle age and of pretty much everything that is going on these days, it manages to be disconcertingly original," says Jane Miller in the *Times Literary Supplement.* The story of a publisher who, out of depression and confusion, decides to kill his wife, his children, and himself, *Natural Enemies* examines one man's reaction to the pressures of modern American society. Although Anatole Broyard, in a *New York Times* article, takes exception to the way Horwitz handles his subject—"It is my feeling that the author is an exhibitionist of indignation, a phenomenon not at all uncommon in the contemporary novel"—Jane Miller contends that the book "works so well because the vision of the world provided by the hero's disintegration is always understandable as the product of his state of mind and the circumstances of his life." Anne Tyler greeted *Landfall,* a novel about incest, with similar comment. She states in the *New York Times Book Review:* "The tone in [the novel] is thoughtful and unstrained, and the characters are believable. [They] may be bound together partly by inertia and despair, but [they] have the complexity that we stub our toes on every day in real life."

Julius Horwitz's books have been translated into several languages, including French, Italian, German, Dutch, Hungarian, Spanish, and Danish.

MEDIA ADAPTATIONS: *Natural Enemies* was adapted into a film and released by Cinema 5 in 1979.

BIOGRAPHICAL/CRITICAL SOURCES: *New Yorker,* August 27, 1960, June 6, 1975; *New York Herald Tribune Book Review,* August 28, 1960; *Saturday Review,* September 10, 1960, February 21, 1970; *Time,* September 8, 1967; *New York Times Book Review,* September 10, 1967, March 22, 1970, September 16, 1973, September 14, 1975, July 31, 1977; *Newsweek,* March 9, 1970; *Village Voice,* March 12, 1970; *New York Times,* May 17, 1970, June 3, 1973, June 3, 1975; *Times Literary Supplement,* December 13, 1974, October 24, 1975; *Contemporary Literary Criticism,* Volume XIV, Gale, 1980.

* * *

**HOWARD, Hartley
See OGNALL, Leopold Horace**

* * *

HOWLETT, John (Reginald) 1940-

PERSONAL: Born April 4, 1940, in Leeds, England; son of Reginald (a civil servant) and Leila (Cagna) Howlett; married Ada Angela Finocchiaro, June 10, 1967; children: Isabel, Suzanne Louise. *Education:* Jesus College, Oxford, B.A. (with honors), 1962. *Home:* Orchard House, Stone-in-Oxney, Tenterden, Kent, England. *Agent:* Michael Imison, Van Loewen, Ltd., 28 Kingly St., London W1R 5LB, England.

CAREER: Full-time writer, 1966—.

WRITINGS: *James Dean* (biography), Simon & Schuster, 1975; *The Christmas Spy,* Hutchinson, 1975, Harcourt, 1976; *Tango November,* Hutchinson, 1976; *Frank Sinatra,* Plexus, 1979.

Also author of script, "Shaheen," produced on Italian television network RAI, and of musical play, "Dean," produced in London, 1977.

WORK IN PROGRESS: *Orange,* a novel; "Occupation Democrat, Destination Hell," a television thriller series; "Venetian Shadows," a television series.

MEDIA ADAPTATIONS: A story Howlett wrote with David Sherwin was adapted into a screenplay entitled "If," produced by Paramount, 1969.

HUDSON, Liam 1933-

PERSONAL: Given name is pronounced *Lee*-um; born July 20, 1933, in London, England; son of Cyril and Kathleen Hudson; married Elizabeth Ward, 1955; married second wife, Bernadine Jacot de Boinod, 1965; children: three sons, one daughter. *Education:* Attended Exeter College, Oxford, 1954-57. *Home:* 34 North Park, Garrards Cross, Bucks, England. *Office:* Psychology Department, Brunel University, Uxbridge, Middlesex, England.

CAREER: Cambridge University, Cambridge, England, researcher at Psychological Laboratory, 1957-65, fellow of King's College, 1966-68; University of Edinburgh, Edinburgh, Scotland, professor of educational sciences and director of Research Unit on Intellectual Development, beginning 1968; professor of psychology, Brunel University, Uxbridge, Middlesex, England. Member, Institute for Advanced Study, Princeton, N.J., 1974-75.

WRITINGS: Contrary Imaginations, Methuen, 1966, published as *Contrary Imaginations: Psychological Study of the English Schoolboy,* Penguin, 1968; *Frames of Mind: Ability, Perception and Self-Perception in the Arts and Sciences,* Methuen, 1968, Norton, 1970; (editor) *The Ecology of Human Intelligence,* Penguin, 1970; *The Cult of the Fact,* J. Cape, 1972, published as *The Cult of the Fact: A Psychologist's Autobiographical Critique of His Discipline,* Doubleday, 1973; *Originality,* Oxford University Press, 1973.

Human Beings: The Psychology of Human Experience, Doubleday, 1975 (published in England as *Human Beings: An Introduction to the Psychology of Human Experience,* J. Cape, 1975); *The Nympholepts,* J. Cape, 1978; *Bodies of Knowledge: Psychological Significance of the Nude in Art,* Weidenfeld & Nicolson, 1982.

AVOCATIONAL INTERESTS: Painting, photography.

BIOGRAPHICAL/CRITICAL SOURCES: New Statesman, January 17, 1969.

* * *

HUFFMAN, Franklin E(ugene) 1934-

PERSONAL: Born January 28, 1934, in Harrisonburg, Va.; son of Rudolph Bernard and Stella (Zigler) Huffman; married Marcia Russell, June 9, 1962 (divorced); married Sandra Iliescu, January 14, 1974; children: (first marriage) Russell Franklin, David Kenneth; (second marriage) Christopher Gregory, Samantha Alexandra. *Education:* Bridgewater College, B.A., 1955; graduate study at American University, 1960, Cornell University, 1960-64, and School of Oriental and African Studies, London, 1964-65; Cornell University, Ph.D., 1967. *Home:* 410 Winston Court, Ithaca, N.Y. 14850. *Office:* Department of Modern Languages and Linguistics, 414 Morrill Hall, Cornell University, Ithaca, N.Y. 14853.

CAREER: High school teacher of French, history, and geography in Weyers Cave, Va., 1958-60; Yale University, New Haven, Conn., assistant professor of Southeast Asian languages, 1967-72; Cornell University, Ithaca, N.Y., associate professor of linguistics, 1972-79, professor of linguistics and Asian studies, 1979—. *Military service:* Conscientious objector; served as French interpreter with International Voluntary Services in Laos, Indochina, 1956-58.

MEMBER: Linguistic Society of America, Association for Asian Studies, American Oriental Society, American Siam Society.

Awards, honors: London-Cornell Project fellow at University of London, 1964-65; Fulbright research fellow in Thailand and Cambodia, 1964-66; Guggenheim fellowship for research in Southeast Asia, 1970-71; Ford Foundation fellow, Thailand, 1976; National Science Foundation grant for research in Thailand, 1979-81; Fulbright-Hays Faculty Research Grant, Thailand, 1983-84.

WRITINGS—Published by Yale University Press, except as indicated: *Cambodian System of Writing and Beginning Reader, with Drills and Glossary,* 1970; *Modern Spoken Cambodian,* 1970; *Intermediate Cambodian Reader,* 1972; *Cambodian Literary Reader and Glossary,* 1977; *English-Khmer Dictionary,* 1978; *Intermediate Spoken Vietnamese,* Cornell University Southeast Asia Program, 1980; *English for Speakers of Khmer,* 1983.

WORK IN PROGRESS: Studies in Mon-Khmer Linguistics; Bibliography of Mainland Southeast Asian Linguistics.

SIDELIGHTS: Franklin E. Huffman is fluent in Thai, Cambodian, and French, and speaks some German, Spanish, Burmese, and Lao.

* * *

HUME, Robert D. 1944-

PERSONAL: Born July 25, 1944, in Oak Ridge, Tenn.; son of David Newton (a college professor) and Aloyse (Bottenwiser) Hume; married Kathryn Irvine (a college teacher), June 18, 1966. *Education:* Haverford College, B.A. (with honors), 1966; University of Pennsylvania, Ph.D., 1969. *Politics:* Independent. *Religion:* None. *Office:* Department of English, Pennsylvania State University, University Park, Penn. 16802.

CAREER: Cornell University, Ithaca, N.Y., assistant professor, 1969-74, associate professor of English, 1974-77; Pennsylvania State University, University Park, professor of English, 1977—, associate head of department, 1979-83. *Member:* Modern Language Association of America, American Society for Eighteenth-Century Studies, Society for Theatre Research, Phi Beta Kappa. *Awards, honors:* Woodrow Wilson fellow, 1966; Guggenheim fellow, 1983-84.

WRITINGS: Dryden's Criticism, Cornell University Press, 1970; *The Development of English Drama in the Late Seventeenth Century,* Clarendon Press, 1976; (co-editor) *"The Country Gentleman": A "Lost" Play and Its Background,* University of Pennsylvania Press, 1976; (co-editor) Elizabeth Polwhele, *The Frolicks; or, the Lawyer Cheated,* Cornell University Press, 1977; (editor) *The London Theatre World, 1660-1800,* Southern Illinois University Press, 1980; (co-editor) *Vice Chamberlain Coke's Theatrical Papers, 1706-1715,* Southern Illinois University Press, 1982; *The Rakish Stage,* Southern Illinois University Press, 1983; (co-author) *Producible Interpretation: Eight English Plays, 1675-1707,* Southern Illinois University Press, 1984. Editor for English and American literature annual eighteenth-century bibliography in *Philological Quarterly,* 1971-74.

WORK IN PROGRESS: Revision of Parts I and II of *The London Stage, 1660-1800;* an Oxford English text, *Buckingham;* an edition of Downes' *Roscius Anglicanus; A Register of English Theatrical Documents, 1660-1737.*

* * *

HUNNINGS, Neville March 1929-

PERSONAL: Born August 12, 1929, in Enfield, Middlesex,

England; son of Thomas March and Elsie Maud (Batter) Hunnings; married Maerta Cecilia Edsman (a pediatrician), October 13, 1962; children: Thomas Ingemar March, Nicholas Olof March, Ann Christina Cecilia. *Education:* King's College, London, LL.B., 1953, LL.M., 1956, Ph.D., 1964. *Home:* 11 Russell Hill, Purley, Surrey, England. *Office:* European Law Centre Ltd., 4 Bloomsbury Sq., London WC1A 2RL, England.

CAREER: Practiced law, London, England, 1954-58; Central Office of Information, London, information officer, 1958-62; British Institute of International and Comparative Law, London, senior research officer, 1964-72; Common Law Reports Ltd., London, general editor, 1972-78; European Law Centre Ltd., London, director, 1978—. Visiting lecturer in European law at Civil Service College, London, 1973-79, King's College, University of London, 1973-74, and Queen Mary College, University of London, 1975-81. *Military service:* Royal Air Force, 1948-49; became sergeant. *Member:* Society for Theatre Research.

WRITINGS: Film Censors and the Law, Allen & Unwin, 1967, Hillary, 1968; (contributor) *Censura e cinema,* Publicacoes dom Quixote (Lisbon), 1969; (co-editor) *Legal Problems of an Enlarged European Community,* Stevens, 1972; (contributor) Stanley Henig, *Power and Decision In Europe,* Europotentials Press, 1980; *Gazetteer of European Law,* two volumes, European Law Centre, 1983. Contributor to *Britannica Book of the Year, Annual Register of World Events,* and other legal and film publications. Editor, *Common Market Law Reports, European Commercial Cases;* European law editor, *Journal of Business Law;* assistant editor, *Index to Foreign Legal Periodicals.*

WORK IN PROGRESS: Censorship in a Free Society; Films of Menace; Manual of Legal Citations: Western Europe; research on the comparative law on obscenity and on film copyright.

* * *

HUNTLEY, James Robert 1923-

PERSONAL: Born July 27, 1923, in Tacoma, Wash.; son of Wells James (a business executive) and Laura (Berquist) Huntley; married second wife, Colleen Grounds, May 27, 1967; children: (first marriage) Mark Edward, David Farrington, Virginia Christine, Jean Elizabeth. *Education:* University of Washington, Seattle, B.A. (magna cum laude), 1948, graduate study, 1951; Harvard University, M.A., 1956. *Home:* Waterwood, 401 South Bay Lane, Port Ludlow, Wash. 98365.

CAREER: Variously employed as community recreation director, YMCA secretary, and technician for Pan American World Airways, Seattle, Wash., 1942-49; consultant, State of Washington Parks and Recreation Commission, 1949-52; U.S. Foreign Service, exchange-of-persons officer in Frankfurt and Nuremberg, Germany, 1952-54, director of U.S. Information Agency information center, Hof/Saale, Germany, 1954-55, assistant to U.S. President's Coordinator for Hungarian Relief, 1956, European regional affairs officer for U.S. Information Agency, Washington, D.C., 1956-58, and deputy public affairs officer for U.S. Mission to the European Communities, Brussels, Belgium, 1958-60; Atlantic Institute, Paris, France, founder and executive secretary, 1960-63, director of North American office, Washington, D.C., 1963-65; Ford Foundation, New York, N.Y., program associate in International Affairs Division, 1965-67; Council of the Atlantic Colleges, London, England, secretary general, 1967-68; free-lance writer and consultant on international affairs, 1968-74; Battelle Memorial Institute, Seattle, Wash., fellow and head of research in advanced international systems, 1974-83; president of Atlantic Council of the United States, 1983—. Member of board of trustees, World Affairs Council of Seattle, Federal Union, and Atlantic Council of the United States. *Military service:* U.S. Navy, 1943-46.

MEMBER: English-Speaking Union, American Friends of Wilton Park, Phi Beta Kappa, DACOR Club (Washington, D.C.), Rainier Club (Seattle).

WRITINGS: (Co-editor) *The Atlantic Community: A Force for Peace,* National Association of Secondary School Principals, 1963; *The NATO Story,* Manhattan Publishing, 1965, 2nd edition, 1969; (with W. R. Burgess) *Europe and America: The Next Ten Years,* Walker & Co., 1970; *Uniting the Democracies,* New York University Press, 1980. Contributor to *Orbis, Futures, European Community, Atlantic Community Quarterly, Dialogue, Washington Quarterly,* and other journals.

SIDELIGHTS: James Robert Huntley told *CA:* "The American people understand the international environment most inadequately. In the popular mind it is extremely difficult to reconcile our national ideals of democracy, liberty, and justice under law with the dog-eat-dog character of a world in which, by and large, national sovereignties are still king. In my writing, I strive to interpret the need for and show development of international institutions with force of law as a necessary replacement for power politics. The growing ties between the practicing democracies constitute the core of this hopeful change."

* * *

HURD, Michael John 1928-

PERSONAL: Born December 19, 1928, in Gloucester, England; son of John Edwin George and Amy Florence (Hatton) Hurd. *Education:* Pembroke College, Oxford, M.A., 1953. *Home:* 4 Church St., West Liss, Hampshire, England.

CAREER: Professor of music theory, Royal Marines School of Music, 1953-59; free-lance composer, writer, and lecturer, 1959—. Conductor of Alton Choral Society and Petersfield Operatic Society. *Military service:* British Intelligence Corps, 1947-49.

WRITINGS: Immortal Hour: The Life and Period of Rutland Boughton, Routledge & Kegan Paul, 1962; *Young Person's Guide to Concerts,* Routledge & Kegan Paul, 1962, Roy, 1965; *Young Person's Guide to Opera,* Routledge & Kegan Paul, 1963, Roy, 1965; *Sailors' Songs and Shanties,* Walck, 1965; *Young Persons' Guide to English Music,* Roy, 1965; *Soldiers' Songs and Marches,* Walck, 1966; *Benjamin Britten,* Novello, 1966; *The Composer,* Oxford University Press, 1968; *An Outline History of European Music,* Novello, 1968; *Elgar,* Crowell, 1969.

Mendelssohn, Faber, 1970, Crowell, 1971; *Vaughan Williams,* Crowell, 1970; *The Ordeal of Ivor Gurney,* Oxford University Press, 1978; *The Oxford Junior Companion to Music,* Oxford University Press, 1978; *The Orchestra,* Phaidon, 1981. Composer of choral, orchestral, and chamber music, songs, and operas, all published by Novello.

WORK IN PROGRESS: A Concise History of British Music, for Oxford University Press; musical compositions.

SIDELIGHTS: In spite of his considerable output as an author, Michael John Hurd told *CA* he would mainly like to be considered a composer.

* * *

HUSON, Paul (Anthony) 1942-

PERSONAL: Surname is pronounced "Hew-sun"; born September 19, 1942, in London, England; immigrated to United States in 1968; son of Edward Richard (an author) and Olga (a motion picture costume designer; maiden name, Lehmann) Huson. *Education:* University College, London, Slade Diploma of Fine Art, 1964, graduate study in cinema arts, 1964-65. *Residence:* Los Angeles, Calif. *Agent:* (Literary) The Helen Brann Agency, Inc., 14 Sutton Pl. S., New York, N.Y. 10022; (film and television) Creative Artists Agency, Inc., 1888 Century Pk. E., Suite 1400, Los Angeles, Calif. 90067.

CAREER: Toured United States and opened an exhibition of his paintings in Houston, Tex., 1965; assistant designer for a London play and a Vienna State Opera production, 1965-66; British Broadcasting Corp. Television, London, England, designer, 1966-67; assistant art director for Columbia Pictures-BCC Films Ltd. production of "Otley," and visual coordinator of Columbia Pictures' "The Virgin Soldiers," London, 1967-68. Played the part of Edward V in the film version of Shakespeare's "Richard III" starring Laurence Olivier, 1956. *Member:* Authors Guild of America, Academy of Television Arts and Sciences, American Society for Psychical Research, Writers Guild of America West, Association of Cinematograph, Television and Allied Technicians (London).

WRITINGS—Nonfiction, except as indicated; self-illustrated: *Mastering Witchcraft: A Practical Guide for Witches, Warlocks and Covens,* Putnam, 1970; *The Devil's Picturebook: The Complete Guide to Tarot Cards, Their Origins and Their Usage,* Putnam, 1971; *The Coffee Table Book of Witchcraft and Demonology,* Putnam, 1973; *Mastering Herbalism: A Practical Guide,* Stein & Day, 1974; *How to Test and Develop Your ESP,* Stein & Day, 1975; *The Keepsake* (fiction), Warner Books, 1981. Also creator of and author of scripts for two television series, "Tucker's Witch," 1982, and "The Hamptons," 1983; also author of two teleplays, "The Bermuda Triangle," Playboy Productions, and "Ghost Riders," Talent Associates. Contributor to *Witches Almanac* and *Fate Magazine.*

SIDELIGHTS: Paul Huson told *CA:* "I didn't begin writing professionally until I emigrated to the United States in 1968. Having difficulty finding work in the area of film art direction here was a marvellous excuse to try my hand at writing. I suppose writing and illustrating my own books has given me the greatest creative satisfaction I have known. The goal, literary that is, in all my writing so far is enchantment—I attempt to evoke in my readers my own sense of wonder and involvement in the occult or paranormal, to guide them into those mysterious realms." He has this advice for aspiring writers: "Write about your obsessions and try and share them with your reader. Write clearly and unpretentiously." Many of Paul Huson's books have been translated into French, Italian, Danish, and Spanish.

BIOGRAPHICAL/CRITICAL SOURCES: Modern Screen, August, 1970; *True,* October, 1970; *Boston Morning Globe,* July 16, 1974; *Journal of Parapsychology,* Volume XXXIX, number 4, December, 1975.

HUTCHINGS, Raymond 1924-

PERSONAL: Born November 18, 1924, in Westcliff-on-Sea, England; son of Dudley Albert and Winifred Alice (Bennett) Hutchings; married Karen Langemark, April 2, 1949; children: Stella, Theresa (Mrs. Nigel Philip Repper), Julian, Nicholas. *Education:* St. John's College, Cambridge, B.A., 1947, M.A., 1953; University of London, Ph.D., 1958. *Home and office:* 168 Turnpike Link, Croydon CRO 5NZ, England.

CAREER: Member of British Foreign Office and Foreign Service, 1952-68, 1973-75; British Embassy, Moscow, Soviet Union, junior attache, 1954, second secretary, 1957-59; Royal Institute of International Affairs, London, England, research specialist in Soviet studies, 1968-72; Harvard University, Russian Research Center, Cambridge, Mass., research fellow, 1972-73. University of Maryland, lecturer, 1962, visiting professor, 1972; lecturer, University of Southern California, 1962; senior research fellow in economic history, Australian National University, 1964-68; visiting professor, Pennsylvania State University, 1973, University of Texas, 1976. Has given annual lecture tours in North America, 1973—. *Military service:* British Army, 1943-46; became sergeant. *Member:* National Association for Soviet and East European Studies (treasurer, 1968-72), American Association for the Advancement of Slavic Studies, Royal United Services Institute for Defence Studies.

WRITINGS: Soviet Economic Development, Basil Blackwell, 1971, 2nd edition, 1982; *Seasonal Influences in Soviet Industry,* Oxford University Press, for Royal Institute of International Affairs, 1971; *Soviet Science Technology Design: Interaction and Convergence,* Oxford University Press, for Royal Institute of International Affairs, 1976; *Chronological Patterns in the Presentation of Soviet Economic Statistics,* Bundesinstitut fuer ostwissenschaftliche und internationale Studien, 1982; *The Soviet Budget,* Macmillan, 1983; *The Structural Origins of Soviet Industrial Expansion,* Macmillan, 1984.

Contributor: G. Schoepflin, editor, *The Soviet Union and Eastern Europe,* Anthony Blond, 1970; W. Gumpel and Dietmar Keese, editors, *Probleme des Industrialismus im Ost und West,* Gunter Olzog, 1973; M. McGwire, editor, *Soviet Naval Developments,* Praeger, 1973; J. Hardt, editor, *Soviet Economic Prospects for the Seventies,* Joint Economic Committee, 1973; A. Brown and others, editors, *The Cambridge Encyclopedia of Russia and the Soviet Union,* Trewin Coppleston Publishing, 1982. Senior editor of *Abstracts: Soviet and East European Series,* 1980—; project editor of a multilingual economics dictionary, 1981—. Contributor of more than sixty articles and reviews to professional journals; regular contributor to the Economist Intelligence Unit.

WORK IN PROGRESS: Research in Soviet arms export trends; study of Soviet policy on disclosing information; research in Albanian economics, with emphasis on migration policy.

SIDELIGHTS: Raymond Hutchings told *CA:* "Almost thirty years of reading, writing, or reflecting about Russia, or looking at Russia, had to take a different turn after 1971 when I found myself included on the list of Britons banned from re-entering the U.S.S.R. Fortunately, in the areas of study in which I was then engaged, this offered little or no handicap, but for travel and exploration on the spot some other country or countries had to be substituted. During the last five years, I have learned to read Bulgarian and Albanian. In April 1983 I visited Albania. There is much to do in analysis and explanation of the Albanian economy and I have begun work in this sphere.

"Although fully switched into the network of academic literature about the Soviet Union and Eastern Europe, I have no continuous academic post. But, on the other hand, I have experience speaking in different institutions . . . which is possibly unrivalled—a total of seventy-eight [institutions] at the last count. Apparently I am better known in North America than in Britain, but I prefer that to the other way round, just as I prefer being locked out of the Soviet Union to being locked in.

"By the way, I am not writing or researching all the time—I don't think anybody could. I also have a tiny but unique business of making small things out of shell, and this brings me as much satisfaction, though in a different way, as my main occupation. It has been gratifying to see how evidence has built up in support of my theory about cyclical patterns which originate in the mechanism of the long-time plans: Soviet arms exports and various aspects of Soviet budgetary behaviour are amongst the phenomena that are found to exhibit such a pattern, which is also illustrated in Soviet economic statistics. In general, I think that future research on the Soviet Union has to pay more attention to Soviet policies in disclosing or not disclosing information. It is amazing how many people do not take account of this."

I

INGRAMS, Doreen 1906-

PERSONAL: Born January 24, 1906, in London, England; daughter of Edward (a member of Parliament and privy councillor) and Isabella (Scott) Shortt; married Harold Ingrams (a political officer with service in Arabia), June 3, 1930; children: two daughters. *Education:* Privately educated in London, England, and in Switzerland. *Home:* 3 Westfield House, Tenterden, Kent, England.

CAREER: British Broadcasting Corp., London, England, senior assistant in Arabic Service, 1956-68. Lecturer for Central Office of Information. Member of executive committee, Council for the Advancement of Arab-British Understanding. *Member:* United Nations Association (vice-chairman of Tenterden branch). *Awards, honors:* Co-winner with her husband of Founders Medal of Royal Geographical Society and of Lawrence of Arabia Medal of Royal Central Asian Society.

WRITINGS: *A Survey of Social and Economic Conditions in the Aden Protectorate*, H.M.S.O., 1949; *A Time in Arabia*, J. Murray, 1970; *Palestine Papers, 1917-1922: Seeds of Conflict*, J. Murray, 1972; *The Arab World* (booklets and film strip), EMC Corp., 1974; *Mosques and Minarets*, EMC Corp., 1974; *New Ways to Ancient Lands*, EMC Corp., 1974; *Tents to City Sidewalks*, EMC Corp., 1974; *The Awakened: Women of Iraq*, Third World Publications, 1984. Contributor to *Middle East Handbook*, 1971, and to *Gulf Handbook*, 1976-77.

BIOGRAPHICAL/CRITICAL SOURCES: *Listener*, December 31, 1970.

* * *

INMAN, Billie (Jo) Andrew 1929-

PERSONAL: Born May 16, 1929, in Thurber, Tex.; daughter of Robert A. (an oilfield worker) and Gussie (Oyler) Andrew; married George D. Inman (an elementary school principal), May 23, 1950; children: Paul David, Laura Lou. *Education:* Midwestern University, B.A., 1950; Tulane University, M.A., 1951; Texas Technological College (now Texas Tech University), graduate study, summer, 1954; University of Texas at Austin, Ph.D., 1961. *Religion:* Unitarian-Universalist. *Home:* 5531 East North Wilshire Dr., Tucson, Ariz. 85711. *Office:* Department of English, University of Arizona, Tucson, Ariz. 85721.

CAREER: Teacher of English in public schools in Lubbock, Tex., and Borger, Tex., 1951-54; West Texas State College (now University), Canyon, instructor in English, 1955-57; University of Texas at Austin, special instructor, 1961-62; University of Arizona, Tucson, instructor, 1962-63, assistant professor, 1963-68, associate professor, 1968-72, professor of English, 1972—, director of freshman English, 1967-71, director of graduate studies, 1973-74. Director of National Defense Education Act Institute in English, University of Arizona, 1965. *Member:* Modern Language Association of America. *Awards, honors:* National Endowment for the Humanities fellowship, 1982-83.

WRITINGS: (With Ruth Gardner) *Aspects of Composition*, Harcourt, 1970, 2nd edition, 1979; *Walter Pater's Reading, 1858-1873*, Garland Publishing, 1981; (contributor) Philip Dodd, editor, *Walter Pater: An Imaginative Sense of Fact*, Frank Cass & Co., 1981; (contributor) Alain Sullivan, editor, *British Literary Magazines*, Volume III, Greenwood Press, 1984. Contributor to *Philological Quarterly*, *Texas Studies in Literature and Language*, *19th-Century Fiction*, *Victorian Newsletter*, *Papers on Language and Literature*, *Prose Studies*, and *English Literature in Transition*. Co-editor, *Pater Newsletter*.

WORK IN PROGRESS: *Walter Pater's Reading, 1874-1894*.

BIOGRAPHICAL/CRITICAL SOURCES: *Pater Newsletter*, spring, 1982; *Papers of the Bibliographical Society of America*, Volume LXXVI, number 4, 1982.

* * *

INMAN, Will 1923-

PERSONAL: Original name, William Archibald McGirt, Jr.; name legally changed in 1973; born May 4, 1923, in Wilmington, N.C.; son of William Archibald (in the real estate and insurance business) and Delia Ellen (a registered nurse; maiden name, Inman) McGirt; married Barbara Ann Sherman, June 12, 1969 (divorced March 1, 1973); children: William Stanley. *Education:* Duke University, A.B., 1943. *Politics:* "Democrat—believe in group work but not when group diminishes value of individual." *Religion:* "Kaurian." *Home:* 2551 West Mossman Rd., Tucson, Ariz. 85746.

CAREER: Poet. Publisher and editor of *Kauri* (poetry newsletter), 1964-71, editor, 1980—; Montgomery College, Rockville, Md., member of English faculty, 1969-73; member of staff of Arizona Department of Developmental Disabilities, 1978—. Vice-president of Free University of New York, mid-

1960's; artist-in-residence, American University, Washington, D.C., spring, 1967; coordinator, Free University at American University, spring, 1968. Has read poetry on radio and at colleges and universities.

WRITINGS: Lament and Psalm, New Athenaeum Press (Crescent City, Fla.), 1960; *I Am the Snakehandler*, New Athenaeum Press, 1960; *A River of Laughter*, New Athenaeum Press, 1961; *Honey in Hot Blood*, Bitterroot Press, 1962; *108 Verges Unto Now*, Carlton Press, 1964; *Selected Poems from 108 Prayers for J. Edgar*, published as a special edition of *Epos*, New Athenaeum Press, 1965; *108 Tales of a Po' Buckra from the Lower Cape Fear*, Kauri, 1965; *A Congress of the Winds*, reproduced from typewritten copy, 1966; *Black Power: A Search for Umbra Within*, reproduced from typewritten copy, 1966; *A Generation of Heights*, Goliards Press, 1969; (editor) *Fired Up With You!*, Border Press, 1977; *The Walkers in the Tongue*, edited by Benet Tvedten, Blue Cloud, 1977; *Voice of the Beech Oracle*, edited by Paul Mariah, ManRoot Press, 1977; *Speak Changes*, edited by Natalie Hough de Combray, Lake Avenue Press, 1983; *A Way Through for the Damned*, edited by Jerry Craven, Pierides Press, 1983. Also contributor to *Whose Heaven, Whose Earth?*, Knopf.

Poetry has been published in numerous anthologies, including: *Poets of North Carolina*, edited by R. Walser, University of North Carolina Press, 1963; *New Orlando Poetry Anthology*, Volume II, edited by Anca Vrbovska, New Orlando Publications, 1963; *Of Poetry and Power* (John F. Kennedy memorial), Basic Books, 1964; *Where Is Vietnam?: American Poets Respond*, edited by Walter Lowenfels, Anchor Books, 1967; *Only Humans with Songs to Sing*, edited by Dan Georgakas, Smyrna Press, 1967; *In a Time of Revolution*, edited by Lowenfels, Random House, 1969; *Mad Windows*, edited by Phil Perry, Literary Press, 1969; *Southern Poetry Review: A Decade of Poems*, edited by Guy Owen and Mary C. Williams, [Raleigh, N.C.], 1969.

North Carolina Poetry, edited by Owen, Southern Poetry Review Press, 1970; *Campfires of the Resistance: Poetry from the Movement*, edited by Todd Gitlin, Bobbs-Merrill, 1971; *The East Side Scene: American Poetry, 1960-65*, edited by Allen De Loach, Anchor Books, 1972; *Poems from the Capital*, edited by Ron Arck, Bethesda Press, 1972; *For Neruda, For Chile*, edited by Lowenfels, Beacon Press, 1975; *Southwest*, edited by Karl Kopp, Red Earth Press, 1977; *Orgasms of Light*, edited by Winston Leyland, Gay Sunshine Press, 1977; *A Long Line of Joy*, edited by William J. Robson, privately printed, 1978; *The Face of Poetry*, edited by LaVerne Harrell Clark, Heidelberg Graphics, 1979; *Focus 101* (poet biographies), edited by Clark, Heidelberg Graphics, 1979; *Images from the High Plains*, edited by Craven, Staked Plains Press, 1979. Also author of several unpublished novels and books of poetry. Has recorded "New Jazz Poets" for Broadside Records. Author of weekly column, "Conchsound in the Hills," in *News-Herald* (Franklin, Pa.). Contributor of short stories, poetry and articles to journals and newspapers. Editor of American issue, *Poet*, 1964.

SIDELIGHTS: Will Inman is "concerned with the interpenetration of opposites in fullest most exquisite balance, spiritual awareness with social concern, intellect with intuition, individual with group, man with nature." He continued: "I would root my social concern into my deepest spiritual connection. Modern man can learn much of elemental human possibilities by meditating on tribal attitudes, not to go back to tribal exclusiveness, but toward embracing all mankind as the new tribe, with true reverence for self and for nature as indivisible."

ISAACS, Jacob
See KRANZLER, George G(ershon)

* * *

ISRAEL, Fred L. 1934-

PERSONAL: Born February 8, 1934, in New York, N.Y.; son of Jack C. (a teacher) and Evelyn (Wallach) Israel. *Education:* City College (now City College of the City University of New York), B.S., 1955; Columbia University, M.A., 1956, Ph.D., 1959. *Office:* Department of History, City College of the City University of New York, New York, N.Y. 10031.

CAREER: City College of the City University of New York, instructor, 1956-63, assistant professor, 1963-67, associate professor, 1967-74, professor of American history, 1974—. *Member:* American Historical Association, Organization of American Historians. *Awards, honors:* Louis Knott Koontz Award from Pacific Coast branch of American Historical Association, 1962; Scribes Award from the American Bar Association, 1971, for *The Justices of the United States Supreme Court*.

WRITINGS—Published by Chelsea House, except as indicated: (Contributing editor) *Guide to Historical Literature*, Macmillan, 1961; *Nevada's Key Pittman*, University of Nebraska Press, 1963; (editor and author of commentary) *The Chief Executive: Inaugural Addresses of the Presidents from Washington to Johnson*, Crown, 1965; *The War Diary of Breckinridge Long*, University of Nebraska Press, 1966; (editor) *The State of the Union Messages of the Presidents: 1789-1966*, three volumes, 1966; (editor) *Major Peace Treaties of Modern History, 1648-1967*, five volumes, 1967-80; (editor with Leon Friedman) *The Justices of the United States Supreme Court*, five volumes, 1969-78; (editor with Arthur M. Schlesinger, Jr.) *History of American Presidential Elections, 1789-1968*, nine volumes, 1971—; *Major Presidential Decisions*, 1980; (editor) *1897 Sears Roebuck Catalogue*, 1981; (editor with Schlesinger) *The Coming to Power: Critical Presidential Elections in American History*, 1981.

SIDELIGHTS: In his review of Fred L. Israel's biography, *Nevada's Key Pittman*, J. P. Nichols comments in *American Historical Review*: "[This book] aims at, and achieves, a rather devastating portrayal of Pittman by himself. With the barest minimum of author's comment, Israel lets Pittman's letters and other papers demonstrate how he maintained himself as Nevada's lawyer at Washington from 1913 to 1940." And G. C. Fite remarks in *Journal of American History* that "it is refreshing to read a biography of a second-rate political figure by an author who has not tried to make a silk purse out of a sow's ear. *Nevada's Key Pittman* is a thoughtful and provocative biography."

Writing about Israel's *The State of the Union Messages of the Presidents: 1789-1966*, W. C. Kiessel explains in *Library Journal*: "[The] messages through the perspective of our Presidents, give the major events and trends of our dramatic heritage. [This set] is indispensable in the study of American political history."

BIOGRAPHICAL/CRITICAL SOURCES: American Historical Review, January, 1964, January, 1967; *Journal of American History*, June, 1964; *America*, August 20, 1966; *Library Journal*, September 1, 1966.

J

JACKS, Oliver
   See GANDLEY, Kenneth Royce

* * *

JACKSON, Wilma   1929-

PERSONAL: Born December 17, 1929, in Chicago, Ill.; daughter of R. L. (a minister) and Sophia (a beautician and teacher; maiden name, Shaw) Littlejohn; married Gordon Chester Jackson (an auto company employee); children: Carole Lynn Harris, Linda Kathryn Luten, Shelley Susanne Bethay, Jill. *Education:* Attended Wilson Junior College and Flint Community College; Michigan State University, certificate in Counseling-Substance Abuse, 1976; University of Michigan, B.G.S., 1977. *Politics:* Democrat. *Religion:* Protestant. *Home:* 2018 Whittlesey St., Flint, Mich. 48503. *Agent:* Scott Meredith, 845 Third Ave., New York, N.Y. 10022. *Office:* Medi-Rary Literary Agency, 615 Lippincott Blvd., Flint, Mich. 48503.

CAREER/WRITINGS: Chicago Defender, Chicago, Ill., feature writer, 1955-57; *Flint Herald,* Flint, Mich., social news columnist, 1956-58; Associated Negro Press, women's editor, 1957-62; *Chicago Defender,* columnist, 1959-60; Negro Press International, theatrical editor, 1962-63; *Sepia* magazine, writer of column "Just Ask Me," 1963-78; Medi-Rary Literary Agency, Flint, director, 1972—; *Flint Journal,* Flint, writer of column "Dear Wilma," 1982-84. Columns contributed to teen magazines include "Confidentially Speaking," "Guess Who?" "Data 'N Chatter," "Dear Soul Sister," "Star Treks," and "Where the Soul Is." Contributor of articles to *Negro Digest, Tan,* and *Ebony.* Member of board of directors, *Flint Gazette.* Market research interviewer for Barlow Survey Service, 1958-60; lecturer in creative writing, University of Michigan, 1977; instructor in psychology of counseling, Jordan College, 1982-83; instructor in creative writing, Continuing Education Division, Mott Community College. *Member:* National Association of Media Women (founder of Flint, Mich., chapter; president, 1977, 1984; member of board of directors), Links, Inc. (charter member of Flint chapter), National Negro Business and Professional Women's Clubs, Inc., Urban League Guild, Flint Writer's Club. *Awards, honors:* Journalism awards from Flint Writer's Club, 1969-73, 1975, 1977.

WORK IN PROGRESS: Dear Wilma, a collection of advice columns; *Just Ask Me Again,* a collection of answers to questions about celebrities in show business.

SIDELIGHTS: Wilma Jackson told *CA:* "I like people. I have always found meeting and sharing and exchanging ideas an enriching experience. One is naturally limited to one-to-one sort of conversations because of lack of time, proximity and other variables. So I wander, explore, ponder and put it all down on paper so I can 'talk' to the masses. Places visited can be seen again and the adventure comes alive for me (and I hope others) when recollections are put down in print. I write also, I must confess, for the sheer joy of writing, letting thoughts leap to life on paper.

"Having reached the grand stage of grandmotherhood (Alshaya, Alexis, Nikole and Angelique), and having become 'mom' to teenagers and adults while counseling at the John F. Kennedy Center (a pre-vocational alternative high school) and Jordan College, I discovered [that] having some answers to a lot of questions gave me an ice-breaking way to communicate quickly. Hence, two years ago the *Flint Journal* invented 'Dear Wilma,' an advice column slanted at teenagers, but word seems to have gotten around and I suspect some of my readers are past sweet sixteen. God has been good to me to grant me this entry, to expand my creativity in such a way that keeps my enthusiasm whirling and I pray brings a chuckle to teens who are troubled. Life is a venture. Writing is THE adventure."

* * *

JAMES, Cy
   See WATTS, Peter Christopher

* * *

JAMES, Rebecca
   See ELWARD, James (Joseph)

* * *

JANGER, Allen R(obert)   1932-

PERSONAL: Born September 5, 1932, in Chicago, Ill.; son of Max and Myrtle (Levy) Janger; married Inez Kurn, September 11, 1960; children: Edward, Matthew, Michael. *Education:* Attended University of Chicago, 1949-55, and London School of Economics and Political Science, 1955-56. *Office:* The Conference Board, 845 Third Ave., New York, N.Y. 10022.

CAREER: The Conference Board (formerly National Industrial Conference Board), New York, N.Y., 1960—, began as senior specialist in organization and developmental research, became executive director, management systems group, 1982—. *Military service:* U.S. Army, 1957-59.

WRITINGS—Published by National Industrial Conference Board: (With Harold Steiglitz) *Top Management Organization in Divisionalized Companies*, 1965; *Personnel Administration: Changing Scope and Organization*, 1966; *Managing Programs to Employ the Disadvantaged*, 1970.

Published by The Conference Board: (With Ruth G. Shaeffer) *Employing the Disadvantaged: A Management Perspective*, 1972; *Corporate Organization Structures*, Volume I: *Manufacturing*, 1973, Volume II: *Financial Enterprises*, 1974, Volume III: *Service Companies*, 1977; *The Personnel Function: Changing Objectives and Organization*, 1977; *Matrix Organization of Complex Businesses*, 1978; *Organization of Joint Ventures*, 1980; (with Ronald E. Berenbeim) *External Forces on Corporate Decision Making: A Growing International Problem*, 1981.

* * *

**JANSEN, Jared
See CEBULASH, Mel**

* * *

JARES, Joe 1937-

PERSONAL: Surname is pronounced Jars; born September 2, 1937, in Huntington Park, Calif.; son of Frank August (a wrestler) and Dorothy (Pepper) Jares; married Sue Ellen Wolins (a photo editor, writer, and researcher), May 14, 1967; children: Hayley Joanne, Julie Michele. *Education:* University of Southern California, B.A., 1959. *Religion:* Agnostic. *Home:* 9701 Cresta Dr., Los Angeles, Calif. 90035. *Agent:* Julian Bach, Jr., 747 Third Ave., New York, N.Y. 10017. *Office:* Sports Department, *Daily News*, Box 400, Los Angeles, Calif. 90051.

CAREER: United Press International (UPI), Los Angeles, Calif., staff writer, 1959; *Los Angeles Herald-Express*, Los Angeles, sports writer, 1959-60; United Press International, staff writer, 1960-61; *Los Angeles Times*, Los Angeles, staff writer, 1961-65; *Sports Illustrated* (magazine), associate editor in New York, N.Y., then Beverly Hills, Calif., 1965-81; *Daily News*, Los Angeles, sports editor, 1982—. *Military service:* Air National Guard, 1959-62; Air Reserve, 1962-65. *Member:* U.S. Basketball Writers Association, Phi Beta Kappa, Sigma Delta Chi, Phi Kappa Phi. *Awards, honors:* Award for best sports story of the year from California Associated Press, 1964; award for best sports story of the year from Los Angeles Press Club, 1964.

WRITINGS: (With Ed Lindop) *White House Sportsmen*, Houghton, 1964; (with Walt Frazier) *Clyde*, Holt, 1970; *Basketball: The American Game*, Follett, 1971; *Whatever Happened to Gorgeous George?*, Prentice-Hall, 1974; (with John Robinson) *Conquest: A Cavalcade of U.S.C. Football*, Neff, 1981; (with Ken Sprague) *The Athlete's Body*, J. P. Tarcher, 1981.

* * *

JAY, Douglas (Patrick Thomas) 1907-

PERSONAL: Born March 23, 1907, in Woolwich, England; son of Edward Aubrey Hastings (a barrister) and Isobel (Craigie) Jay; married M. C. Garnett, September 30, 1933 (divorced, 1972); married Mary Lavinia Thomas (an administrator), May 27, 1972; children: Peter, Martin, Catherine (Mrs. Stewart Boyd), Helen (Mrs. David Kennard). *Education:* Attended Winchester College, 1920-26; New College, Oxford, B.A., 1929, M.A., 1930. *Politics:* Labour. *Religion:* None. *Agent:* David Higham, 5-8 Lower John St., Golden Square, London W1R 4HA, England. *Office:* Causeway Cottage, Minster Lovell, Oxfordshire, England.

CAREER: Oxford University, Oxford, England, fellow of All Souls College, 1930-37, 1968—; British Parliament, London, England, Labour member, 1945-83. Economic secretary to the British Treasury, 1947-50, financial secretary to the Treasury, 1950-51; president of the Board of Trade, British Cabinet, 1964-67.

WRITINGS: *The Socialist Case*, Faber & Faber, 1937; *Who Is to Pay for the War and the Peace*, Routledge & Kegan Paul, 1940; (with others) *The Road to Recovery*, Fabian Society, 1948; *Socialism in the New Society*, Longmans, Green, 1962, St. Martin's, 1963; *After the Common Market*, Penguin, 1968; *Change and Fortune*, Hutchinson, 1980.

SIDELIGHTS: Throughout Douglas Jay's memoirs, *Change and Fortune*, runs "an assertion of Englishness that is characteristic," writes London *Times* reviewer David Wood. According to Wood, Jay's "opposition to the United Kingdom's entry to the European Economic Community, which undoubtedly led to his dismissal from the Wilson Cabinet, was always strongly founded on his judgment of English, or perhaps I should say British, interests." *Times Literary Supplement* critic Janet Morgan indicates that *Change and Fortune* "shows with what persistence and devotion he applied himself to realizing the aims of the Labour Party and improving the condition of the country he so deeply loved."

Morgan points out that, in the book, Jay "gives the impression of having endured his career, rather like his preparatory school, rather than enjoying it." However, in conclusion, she comments that "describing people, with humour and sensitivity, appears to be Mr. Jay's strength as a writer. His political history may be dry and laboured but he understands character, illuminating with a telling anecdote, remembering a quotation or trick of behavior that has struck him. Intellectually rigorous and personally austere, he is by no means dessicated. Parts of his book are extremely moving, when he speaks, for instance, of his children, the countryside, the death of his greatly loved sister, the difficulties of his constituents' lives, the unparalleled happiness of release from a frightening school. He is a most interesting mixture, and so are his memoirs."

BIOGRAPHICAL/CRITICAL SOURCES: *Times* (London), August 11, 1980; *Times Literary Supplement*, September 5, 1980.

* * *

JEEVES, Malcolm A(lexander) 1926-

PERSONAL: Born November 16, 1926, in Stamford, England; son of Alexander F. T. and Helena M. (Hammond) Jeeves; married Ruth E. Hartridge, April 7, 1955; children: Sarah M. E., Joanna M. H. *Education:* St. John's College, Cambridge, B.A. (with honors), 1951, M.A., 1954, Ph.D., 1956; additional study at Harvard University, 1953-54. *Religion:* Protestant. *Home:* 7 Hepburn Gardens, St. Andrews, Scotland. *Office:* Department of Psychology, University of St. Andrews, St. Andrews, Scotland.

CAREER: University of Leeds, Leeds, Yorkshire, England, lecturer in psychology, 1956-59; University of Adelaide, Adelaide, Australia, professor of psychology and head of department, 1959-69, dean of Faculty of Arts, 1963-64; University of St. Andrews, St. Andrews, Scotland, professor of psychology and head of department, 1969—, vice-principal, 1981—. Inter-Varsity Fellowship, president of Australia branch, 1969, president of Great Britain branch, 1974. *Military service:* British Army of the Rhine, 1945-48; became lieutenant. *Member:* Experimental Psychology Society, British Psychological Society (fellow), Australian Psychological Society (fellow). *Awards, honors:* Rotary Foundation fellow at Harvard University, 1953-54.

WRITINGS: (Co-author) *Where Science and Faith Meet*, Inter-Varsity, 1952; *Contemporary Psychology and Christian Belief and Experience* (pamphlet), Tyndale, 1960; (with Zoltan Paul Dienes) *Thinking in Structures*, Hutchinson, 1965; *Scientific Psychology and Christian Belief*, Inter-Varsity, 1966; (editor) *The Scientific Enterprise and Christian Faith*, Tyndale, 1969; (with Dienes) *The Effects of Structural Relations upon Transfer*, Hutchinson, 1970; *Experimental Psychology: An Introduction for Biologists*, Arnold, 1974; *Psychology and Christianity: The View Both Ways*, Inter-Varsity, 1976; (with G. B. Greer) *Analysis of Structural Learning*, Academic Press, 1983; (editor and contributor) *Behavioral Science and Christianity*, Inter-Varsity, 1984; (co-author) *Free to Be Different*, Marshall, Morgan & Scott, 1984. Contributor to science journals.

WORK IN PROGRESS: Neuropsychological studies of interhemispheric relations.

AVOCATIONAL INTERESTS: Music, walking, and fly-fishing.

* * *

JENNER, W(illiam) J(ohn) F(rancis) 1940-

PERSONAL: Born October 5, 1940, in Birmingham, England; married Delia Davin (an academic; divorced); married Eileen Candler (a teacher; divorced); children: (first marriage) Lucy; (second marriage) Rachel, Matthew. *Education:* Oxford University, B.A., 1962, D.Phil., 1976. *Office:* Department of Chinese Studies, University of Leeds, Leeds LS2 9JT, England.

CAREER: Foreign Languages Press, Peking, China, translator, 1963-65; University of Leeds, Leeds, England, lecturer in Chinese studies, 1965—.

WRITINGS: (Translator) Aisin Gioro Pu Yi, *From Emperor to Citizen* (autobiography of last emperor of China), Foreign Languages Press (Peking), Volume I, 1964, Volume II, 1965; (editor and translator, with additional translations by Gladys Yang) *Modern Chinese Stories*, Oxford University Press, 1970; (contributor) *Mouvements populaires et societes secretes en Chine aux xme et xxe siecles*, Maspero, 1970; *Memories of Loyang: Yang Hsuan-Chih and the Lost Capital*, Clarendon Press, 1981; (translator) Wu Cheng'en, *Journey to the West*, Foreign Languages Press, Volume I, 1982, Volume II, 1983, Volume III, in press; (translator) Lu Xun, *Selected Poems*, Foreign Languages Press, 1982. Contributor of reviews and articles on China to periodicals.

WORK IN PROGRESS: Long-term research on Chinese history and literature, ancient, mediaeval, and modern; translations of modern and classical Chinese literature.

SIDELIGHTS: In his work *Memories of Loyang: Yang Hsuan-Chih and the Lost Capital*, W.J.F. Jenner traces the transient history of China's capital city, Loyang, during the fourth through sixth centuries A.D. "From legendary antiquity it was part of the political game in China that capital cities could be moved about the board; and the Wei Dynasty—one of the many 'barbarian' regimes which jostled for power in northern China . . .—followed this hallowed Chinese tradition,'' says Raymond Dawson in a *Times Literary Supplement* review of the book. "On and off, Dr. Jenner has spent almost half his lifetime [studying Chinese history], so his book will not always be easy reading for the stranger making his first visit to this world; but [ancient historian Yang Hsuan-Chih's record of Loyang] is the earliest surviving substantial description of a Chinese city, and such long-term devotion to it has produced an extremely valuable contribution to our understanding of a little-known period."

BIOGRAPHICAL/CRITICAL SOURCES: Times Literary Supplement, April 9, 1982, June 24, 1983.

* * *

JENSEN, Julie
See McDONALD, Julie

* * *

JOHNSON, Haynes Bonner 1931-

PERSONAL: Born July 9, 1931, in New York, N.Y.; son of Malcolm Malone (an editor and writer) and Ludie (Adams) Johnson; married Julia Erwin, September 21, 1954 (divorced); children: Katherine Adams, David Malone, Stephen Holmes, Sarah Brooks, Elizabeth Haynes. *Education:* University of Missouri, B.J., 1952; University of Wisconsin—Madison, M.S., 1956. *Politics:* Independent. *Religion:* Episcopalian. *Home:* 3201 Broad Branch Terrace N.W., Washington, D.C. 20008. *Office: Washington Post*, 1150 15th St. N.W., Washington, D.C. 20071.

CAREER: Wilmington News-Journal, Wilmington, Del., reporter, 1956-57; *Washington Star*, Washington, D.C., 1957-69, began as reporter, successively became national rewriteman, assistant city editor, and national assignments reporter; *Washington Post*, Washington, D.C., national correspondent, 1969-73, assistant managing editor, 1973-77, columnist, 1977—. Lecturer at colleges and universities; Ferris Professor of Journalism at Princeton University, 1975 and 1978. Commentator on television programs "Today" and "Washington Week in Review." *Military service:* U.S. Army, 1952-55; became first lieutenant. *Member:* National Press Club, Phi Gamma Delta, Gridiron Club (Washington, D.C.), Nassau Club (Princeton, N.J.).

AWARDS, HONORS: Grand Award for reporting and Public Service Award, Washington Newspaper Guild, both 1962 and 1968; Front Page Award for political reporting, American Newspaper Guild, 1964; Pulitzer Prize in national reporting, 1966, for coverage of the civil rights demonstrations in Selma, Ala.; Headliners Award for national reporting, 1968; Sigma Delta Chi Award for general reporting, 1969; Duke University fellow in communications, 1973-74.

WRITINGS: Dusk at the Mountain—The Negro, the Nation, and the Capital: A Report on Problems and Progress, Doubleday, 1963; (with Manuel Artime, Jose Perez San Roman, Erneido Oliva, and Enrique Ruiz-Williams) *The Bay of Pigs: The Leaders' Story of Brigade 2506*, Norton, 1964 (published in England as *The Bay of Pigs: The Invasion of Cuba by Brigade 2506*, Hutchinson, 1965); (author of introduction and epilogue)

David Lowe, *Ku Klux Klan: The Invisible Empire,* Norton, 1967; (with Bernard M. Gwertzman) *Fulbright: The Dissenter,* Doubleday, 1968.

(With George C. Wilson, Peter A. Jay, and Peter Osnos) *Army in Anguish* (articles originally published in *Washington Post,* September-October, 1971), Pocket Books, 1972; (with Nick Kotz) *The Unions,* Pocket Books, 1972; (with Richard Harwood) *Lyndon,* Praeger, 1973; (editor) *The Fall of a President,* introduction by Benjamin C. Bradlee and Howard Simons, Delacorte, 1974; *The Working White House,* illustrated with photographs by Frank Johnston, Praeger, 1975; *In the Absence of Power: Governing America,* Viking, 1980.

WORK IN PROGRESS: A novel about Washington in World War II.

SIDELIGHTS: The son of the late Pulitzer Prize-winning reporter and editor Malcolm Johnson, Haynes Bonner Johnson has distinguished himself as a newspaperman and political commentator in his own right. Whereas his father was awarded the 1948 Pulitzer Prize in local reporting for his "Crime on the Water Front" series in the *New York Sun,* Johnson himself won the 1966 Pulitzer in national reporting (thereby becoming part of the only father and son to receive Pulitzers in the history of American journalism) for his coverage of the civil rights demonstrations in Selma, Alabama. A veteran of more than twenty-five years of working in the nation's capital—first for the *Washington Star,* then the *Washington Post*—Johnson is considered "one of the most perceptive, the best-informed, and the most level-headed reporters in Washington," says former London *Times* editor Godfrey Hodgson in the *Washington Post Book World.* Presidents and congressional leaders have sought his advice and help, and thousands of television viewers know him for his reports on the Public Broadcasting Service (PBS) program "Washington Week in Review." Johnson's books on affairs of national interest, particularly *The Bay of Pigs: The Leaders' Story of Brigade 2506* and *In the Absence of Power: Governing America,* have accordingly attracted much attention.

The Bay of Pigs is the story of "Brigade 2506," the task force of Cuban exiles organized, trained, and directed by the U.S. Central Intelligence Agency (CIA) to overthrow Premier Fidel Castro in April, 1961. The book "is not, and does not purport to be, a complete history of the [disastrous] invasion and of the events that led up to it," notes Ernest Halperin in the *New York Review of Books.* "The reader is mercifully spared an account of the various political groups in Miami, their complicated maneuvers and intrigues, their combinations and internal disputes."

Basing his report largely on interviews with the four principal brigade leaders and other survivors of the invasion force, Johnson "offers what unquestionably is the most coherent, detailed and complete account of the brigade's adventures," writes Tad Szulc in the *New York Times Book Review.* "In putting it all together as a narrative told in terms of individual and recognizable human beings, instead of the previous treatments of the expeditionary force as a faceless and anonymous entity, Mr. Johnson has done a superb and exciting job of writing. He describes the despair of the brigade's commanders, physically exhausted and morally shattered by their defeat, but still hoping for the impossible miracle of a last-minute rescue by their American allies—or, at least, for a few hours of American air-cover over the beachhead. It is to Mr. Johnson's credit that he has not sought to embellish his story with adjectives and superfluous comments, but lets it tell itself in crisp dialogue of the shouted commands and of the commonplace remarks that men in battle make to each other."

Halperin believes the book greatly increases one's respect for the men of the brigade, "whose performance at first glance seemed to have been unimpressive. [Johnson's] vivid and completely convincing description of the battle, with all its horror and confusion, shows that they fought well and bravely under competent leadership and only gave in when their supply of ammunition was exhausted." But Halperin disagrees with Johnson's claim that the final responsibility for the Bay of Pigs fiasco rests with the CIA: "Johnson cites some instances in which, according to him, the President was misinformed on various details by the CIA. He also reports that according to statements by the military and political leaders of the brigade, a CIA man told them to proceed with the invasion [regardless of White House orders]. This has been denied by the agent in question, and even if it were true, it could hardly have been anything other than irresponsible talk by an individual. The basic fact is that all the important decisions concerning the invasion were made by the top policymakers of two administrations, and not by the CIA. The CIA was entrusted with the execution of these decisions."

Harold Lavine, however, maintains in *Saturday Review* that "there is ample evidence in Johnson's book to support the belief that, after a while, the [CIA agents] became so obsessed with the idea of invading Cuba they were ready to lie to anyone, the President, the Cuban exile leaders, the brigade leaders, anyone, to carry out their plans." The CIA agents, Lavine explains, "occasionally acted as though Dwight D. Eisenhower and later John F. Kennedy were impertinent outsiders. Twice, they made preparations to defy Kennedy's orders if these orders should displease them. At the very last moment, while men were dying on the beaches, they ignored a White House decision with cheery good will."

Szulc, too, points out that Johnson "documents his charges abundantly, describing how the CIA inexplicably changed an earlier plan for multiple guerrilla landings, which might have succeeded, into the blueprint for the one-thrust invasion, which never had a reasonable chance of victory." Lavine concludes that though there are minor gaps in the story, "Johnson has written a powerful and convincing book that will long remain a definitive one."

In the Absence of Power, an examination of President Jimmy Carter's experiences with Congress, the bureaucracy, and the press during his first thirty months in office, suggests that Carter's inability to get key legislation through Congress reflects a nationwide breakdown of party loyalty, discipline, and power. Johnson believes the breakdown is "so severe and so ominous," says Walter Karp in the *New Republic,* "that America today stands in imminent danger of becoming ungovernable."

Though many reviewers share Johnson's concern, several dismiss his explanation of Carter's legislative failures. Lowell Ponte, for example, writes in the *Los Angeles Times Book Review* that despite the diminishing authority of political machines, labor unions, and Capitol Hill bosses, "power seems not so much absent as up for grabs." Ponte believes that Johnson, "in his criticisms of Carter, . . . unwittingly reflects the mind-set of those Washington Old Insiders the voters elected Carter to replace."

According to Walter Karp, Johnson's explanation "not only contradicts the facts, it contradicts itself. . . . Carter's failure, in Johnson's view, stems in large measure from his unwillingness to cooperate with Democratic leaders. The implication of this is obvious. Democratic leaders are powerful men and Carter's defiant conduct turned them into powerful adversaries. This is a perfectly reasonable proposition but it saws off the other leg of Johnson's explanation, namely that the party leaders are not powerful men at all, but rather, loyal and impotent ones; the real opposition to Carter's bills coming from the 'new breed' of post-Watergate Democrats whom the 'loyal' leaders no longer can control."

Godfrey Hodgson resolves the apparent conflict in the book this way: "What has happened, I think, is that Haynes Johnson has to some extent confused two books, either of which he is exceptionally well-qualified to write. One is a narrative history of the Carter presidency. He has done this with great skill. . . . The other was a book about the profound malfunctions of American government. I happen to believe Haynes Johnson is right in his judgment that the American people show some signs of being unwilling to govern themselves. As he points out, they certainly show every sign of being unwilling to be taxed adequately to provide the services they expect. But I also believe that these problems go further back in time, and deeper into the structure of the society, than Jimmy Carter's experience in his first thirty months in office."

BIOGRAPHICAL/CRITICAL SOURCES: *Saturday Review*, May 25, 1963, May 16, 1964; *Newsweek*, May 18, 1964; *New York Times Book Review*, May 24, 1964, September 22, 1968, April 27, 1980; *Reporter*, June 18, 1964; *New Republic*, June 27, 1964, April 5, 1980; *New York Review of Books*, July 9, 1964; *Times Literary Supplement*, February 18, 1965, August 7, 1969; *Book World*, August 18, 1968; *Washington Post Book World*, April 6, 1980; *Los Angeles Times Book Review*, April 27, 1980.

—Sketch by James G. Lesniak

* * *

JOHNSON, Oliver A(dolph) 1923-

PERSONAL: Born February 16, 1923, in Everett, Wash.; son of Gustaf A. and Olga (Toll) Johnson; married Carol Jeanne Pence, March 21, 1946; children: Julie Mae, Stuart Earle, Elizabeth Ann, Melinda Jean. *Education:* Linfield College, B.A., 1944; Yale University, M.A., 1950, Ph.D., 1951; Oxford University, graduate study, 1950-51. *Home:* 4381 Picacho Dr., Riverside, Calif. 92507. *Office:* Department of Philosophy, University of California, Riverside, Calif. 92521.

CAREER: Yale University, New Haven, Conn., instructor in philosophy, 1951-52; Institute for Philosophical Research, San Francisco, Calif., fellow, 1952-53; University of California, Riverside, assistant professor, 1953-59, associate professor, 1959-65, professor of philosophy, 1965—, chairman of department, 1963-71. Distinguished visiting professor, University of Delaware, 1983. *Military service:* U.S. Naval Reserve, active duty, 1943-46; became lieutenant junior grade. *Member:* American Philosophical Association (secretary-treasurer, Pacific division), Royal Institute of Philosophy.

WRITINGS: *Ethics: A Source Book*, Holt, 1958, published as *Ethics: Selections from Classical and Contemporary Writers*, 1965, 4th edition, 1978; (editor with John Louis Beatty) *Heritage of Western Civilization*, Prentice-Hall, 1958, 5th edition, 1981; *Rightness and Goodness*, Nijhoff, 1959; (editor) *Man and His World*, McKay, 1964; *Moral Knowledge*, Nijhoff, 1966; *The Moral Life*, Allen & Unwin, 1969, Humanities, 1970; *The Problem of Knowledge*, Nijhoff, 1974; *Skepticism and Cognitivism*, University of California Press, 1978; (editor) *The Individual and the Universe*, Holt, 1981.

JOHNSON, S(amuel) Lawrence 1909-1978

PERSONAL: Born August 16, 1909, in Tyne Dock, England; brought to United States in 1910, naturalized in 1930; died September 11, 1978; son of Samuel and Florence (Woody) Johnson; married Alice Duncan, November 9, 1935; children: S. Thomas, Mrs. Robert Foulks, Lawrice Kay. *Education:* Carleton College, B.A., 1930; Andover Newton Theological School, M.Div., 1933; attended New England Conservatory of Music, Harvard University, and Hebrew University of Jerusalem. *Home:* 1430 John Wesley Cir., Birmingham, Ala. 35210.

CAREER: Ordained minister of Congregational Church, 1933; Pilgrim Congregational Church, Birmingham, Ala., pastor, beginning 1961, became pastor emeritus. *Member:* Philosophical Society of England (fellow), Society of Biblical Literature, National Association of Professors of Hebrew, Southern Association of Marriage Counselors, Masons, Rotary, Hi 12. *Awards, honors:* D.D., Piedmont College, 1954.

WRITINGS—Published by Abingdon, except as indicated: *"Come unto Me," Said the Master*, Department of the Ministry of Congregational Churches, 1949; *The Pig's Brother, and Other Children's Sermons*, 1970; *The Squirrel's Bank Account*, 1972; *Cats and Dogs Together*, 1975; *Captain Ducky*, 1976; *The Mouse's Tale*, 1978; *The Cross-Eyed Bear*, 1980. Contributor of articles to *Christian Sun*, *Upper Room Disciplines*, and other periodicals.

WORK IN PROGRESS: Children's sermons.†

* * *

JONES, Douglas C(lyde) 1924-

PERSONAL: Born December 6, 1924, in Winslow, Ark.; son of Marvin Clyde (an auto mechanic) and Bethel (Stockburger) Jones; married Mary Arnold (a sales clerk), January 1, 1949; children: Mary Glenn, Martha Claire, Kathryn Greer, Douglas Eben. *Education:* University of Arkansas, B.A., 1949; graduate study at U.S. Army Command and General Staff College, 1961; University of Wisconsin—Madison, M.S., 1963. *Home:* 1987 Greenview Dr., Fayetteville, Ark. 72701. *Agent:* George Wieser, Wieser & Wieser, Inc., Box 608, Millwood, N.Y. 10546.

CAREER: Writer and artist. U.S. Army, career officer, 1943-68, retiring as lieutenant colonel; served in Pacific Theater during World War II, later as commander of infantry rifle companies in Europe and Korea, and as information officer with Philadelphia Army Air Defense Command; chief of Armed Forces Press Branch, Office of Assistant Secretary of Defense for Public Affairs, The Pentagon, Washington, D.C., 1966-68. University of Wisconsin—Madison, member of faculty in School of Journalism and Mass Communication, 1968-74, visiting lecturer, 1974—. Has exhibited paintings of Plains Indians in one-man show at Washington Gallery of Art, 1967, and in Fayetteville, Ark., and Tulsa, Okla. *Awards, honors*—Military: Army Commendation Medal (three times); Legion of Merit, 1968. Civilian: Golden Spur Award, Western Writers of America, 1976, for *The Court-Martial of George Armstrong Custer*; *Elkhorn Tavern* was named best novel of 1980 by Friends of American Writers.

WRITINGS—Novels, except as indicated: *The Treaty of Medicine Lodge* (nonfiction), University of Oklahoma Press, 1966;

The Court-Martial of George Armstrong Custer, Scribner, 1976; *Arrest Sitting Bull,* Scribner, 1977; *A Creek Called Wounded Knee,* Scribner, 1978; *Winding Stair,* Holt, 1979 (published in England as *The Winding Stair Massacre,* Allen & Unwin, 1980); *Elkhorn Tavern,* Holt, 1980; *Weedy Rough,* Holt, 1981; *The Barefoot Brigade,* Holt, 1982; *Season of Yellow Leaf,* Holt, 1983. Contributor of articles and reviews to periodicals, including *Kansas Historical Quarterly* and *Journalism Quarterly.*

WORK IN PROGRESS: Two nineteenth-century based novels.

SIDELIGHTS: Douglas C. Jones "has to be one of the most knowledgeable and imaginative writers of the American West," says Jay Daly in the *School Library Journal.* A retired army officer, Jones became a best-selling author in 1976 with the publication of *The Court-Martial of George Armstrong Custer,* an "obviously well-researched and unquestionably readable first novel," according to James R. Frakes in the *New York Times Book Review.* Since then, Jones has produced a string of successful novels that Jeff Nathan claims in the *Los Angeles Times Book Review* demonstrate his skill as "a superb storyteller and authentic chronicler of the American West."

The Court-Martial of George Armstrong Custer and the two novels that followed it, *Arrest Sitting Bull* and *A Creek Called Wounded Knee,* form a "de facto trilogy," notes Alan Cheuse in the *New York Times Book Review,* since they chronologically deal with U.S.-Indian relations. *The Court-Martial of George Armstrong Custer* is an exercise in the historical imagination—the premise being that Custer somehow survived the Little Big Horn massacre, only to be court-martialed for his actions. Though Walter Clemons maintains in *Newsweek* that the "initial gimmick remains merely a gimmick" and says "Custer is hauled back from the grave and never brought to convincing life in any of the book's invented scenes," Robert McGeehin states in *Best Sellers* that the "setting, personalities, and testimony are convincing and suspenseful."

James R. Frakes also considers *The Court-Martial of George Armstrong Custer* exceptional. Calling it a "harbinger of a new fictional genre—the imaginative staging of a whole series of trials that *might* have occured," he praises Jones's handling of the subject: "Douglas C. Jones is not untalented; he apparently knows military law and American Indians, and his present-tense style is taut and disciplined. His subject here is unusually provocative. Besides its political implications and its elements of Greek tragedy, 'there are more intrigues in this case . . . than in the Arabian Navy.'"

Arrest Sitting Bull further develops the matter of the Little Big Horn and its aftermath: the quelling of the Indian uprising and the death of Sitting Bull. Noting that the book "avoids both cowboy movie cliches and racist formulations about the Rapacious White Usurper," Jane Larkin Crain says in the *New York Times Book Review* that it "is written with supple and effective simplicity; the narrator's stoic awareness of the enormity of history itself gives this narrative a compelling dignity that distinguishes it from more run-of-the-mill popularizing treatments of the American West."

A Creek Called Wounded Knee re-enacts what Sylvia Martin describes in the *Chicago Tribune Book World* as "the definitive last scene in the tragedy of the American Indian." Though Martin believes Jones's use of the present tense occasionally forces him to "sink into a mire of 'had had's,'" she nevertheless points out the merit of Jones's rendering: "Excellence rears up now and again like a struggling stallion. Jones depicts each side, placing us now with the Indians, now with the whites, so that we approach the fatal rendezvous with the fears, confusions, and misunderstandings of both. He does not disguise the fact that his sympathies are with the Indians . . . but avoids the pit of sentimentality, taking his cue from that great indian history by Dee Brown, *Bury My Heart at Wounded Knee.* That was a broad canvas. Here we see as through an enlarging glass the clash of two incompatible cultures." Alan Cheuse has similar praise for the book: "The pages describing the battle. . . , if not some of the laconic scenes leading up to it, will burn into your mind. Mr. Jones's prose here is less fine than in his earlier novels, but *A Creek Called Wounded Knee* is 'honest civilized work with a hammer and forge.'"

Although Jones is best known for his U.S. Cavalry-Sioux Indian trilogy, his other novels exhibit the same level of skill and authenticity, according to critics. *Winding Stair,* for example, is "a significant and highly entertaining contribution to the popular literature of the West," writes Brian Garfield in the *New York Times Book Review.* "The historical research is seamless—the story never slows down to admit dull exposition. *Winding Stair* convinces the reader, utterly, that this is how life must have been in that place at that time."

"The realism evoked by [*Weedy Rough*] is as strong as that in [Jones's] historical novels," says John Thomas Stovall in the *Chicago Tribune Book World.* Set in a small Southern town in the years following World War I, *Weedy Rough* is a departure from the time and place that Jones's readers have come to expect. But Stovall believes the book "isn't that radical a departure" for Jones, because "his narrative technique and thorough depiction of people and place make the novel seem realistic, almost factual. Even though 'Weedy Rough' is a change, Jones's skill is still there."

Elkhorn Tavern, moreover, "has the makings of a classic Western," insists Michael Malone in the *New York Times Book Review.* "It has the beauty of 'Shane' and the elegiac dignity of 'Red River' without the false glamour or sentimentality of those classic Western films. . . . Mr. Jones is at home among the ridges and hardwoods of a frontier valley; he knows what moves in its forests, how the land changes under the seasons. He holds us still and compels us to notice what we live in."

MEDIA ADAPTATIONS: *The Court-Martial of George Armstrong Custer* was adapted for television and broadcast on "Hallmark Hall of Fame," NBC-TV, 1978.

BIOGRAPHICAL/CRITICAL SOURCES: *New York Times Book Review,* November 21, 1976, December 11, 1977, November 19, 1978, October 28, 1979, November 16, 1980, October 3, 1982, December 11, 1983; *Newsweek,* December 20, 1976; *Best Sellers,* April, 1977, December, 1977; *Chicago Tribune Book World,* November 5, 1978, December 28, 1980, October 25, 1981; *Los Angeles Times Book Review,* November 11, 1979; *Washington Post,* December 20, 1979; *Los Angeles Times,* October 1, 1980; *Washington Post Book World,* October 5, 1980; *School Library Journal,* January, 1981.

—Sketch by James G. Lesniak

* * *

JONES, Jeanne 1937-

PERSONAL: Born May 17, 1937, in Los Angeles, Calif.; daughter of Jesse Ross (a manufacturer) and Kathryn (Jones) Castendyck; married Joseph Bush (a physician), November 4, 1965 (died July 2, 1968); married Robert Letts Jones, April 15, 1972; children: Thomas Barton Beek, David Benjamin Beek. *Education:* Attended Northwestern University and University of Southern California. *Religion:* Episcopal. *Home address:* P.O. Box 1212, La Jolla, Calif. 92038. *Agent:* Margaret McBride Liberary Agency, Box 8730, La Jolla, Calif. 92038.

CAREER: Writer. President and founder of Angelitos del Campo (auxiliary to American Diabetes Association). *Member:* National Federation of Press Women, Authors Guild, Authors League of America, San Diego Opera Association (member of board of directors). *Awards, honors:* First place in adult books from National Federation of Press Women, 1972, for *The Calculating Cook: A Gourmet Cookbook for Diabetics and Dieters.*

WRITINGS—Published by 101 Productions, except as indicated: *The Calculating Cook: A Gourmet Cookbook for Diabetics and Dieters,* 1972; *Diet for a Happy Heart,* 1975, revised edition published as *Diet for a Happy Heart: A Low-Cholesterol, Low-Saturated Fat, Low-Calorie Cookbook,* 1981; *Fabulous Fiber Cookbook,* 1977, revised edition, 1979; *Jeanne Jones' Party Planner and Entertaining Diary,* 1979; *Secrets of Salt-Free Cooking: A Complete Low Sodium Cookbook,* 1979; (with James Thomas Cooper) *The Fabulous Fructose Recipe Book,* M. Evans, 1979.

(With Karma Kientzler) *Fitness First: A Fourteen-Day Diet and Exercise Program,* 1980; *Ambition's Woman* (novel), M. Evans, 1981; *More Calculated Cooking: Practical Recipes for Diabetics and Dieters,* 1981; *Jeanne Jones' Food Lovers' Diet,* Scribner, 1982; *Stuffed Spuds: One Hundred Meals in a Potato,* M. Evans, 1982; (with Dick Duffy) *Best Restaurants in San Diego County,* 1983; (with Donna Swajeski) *The Love in the Afternoon Cookbook: Recipes from Your Favorite ABC-TV Soap Operas, Ryans Hope, One Life to Live, All My Children,* M. Evans, 1983; *Jet Fuel: New Food Strategy for the High Performance Person,* Villard, 1984.

* * *

JONES, R(ichard) Ben(jamin) 1933-

PERSONAL: Born January 29, 1933, in Bakewell, England; son of W. F. (a local government officer) and E. M. (Stubbs) Jones; married Anne Veronica Price (an educator), July 28, 1958; children: Lucy, Flora, Amy. *Education:* Exeter College, Oxford, B.A. (with first class honors), 1956, B.Litt. and M.A., 1960. *Politics:* "Left of centre." *Religion:* Church of England. *Home:* Yew Court, 93 Stockton Lane, York, England.

CAREER: London Education Authority, London, England, administrator, 1958-60; King Edward's School, Bath, England, schoolmaster and head of history department, 1960-64; Oakham School, Oakham, England, housemaster, careers master, and head of arts faculty, 1964-74; Goole Grammar School, Goole, Humberside, England, head of department of humanities, 1974—. Adult education lecturer, 1959-65; moderator and chief examiner in history, politics, and European studies, University of London and Cambridge Local Examination Board; chief examiner, AEB. *Military service:* Royal Air Force, national service, 1951-53. *Member:* Goole Historical Association (chairman).

WRITINGS: The French Revolution, Funk, 1967; *Economic and Social History of England: 1770-1790,* Longman, 1971, 2nd edition, 1979; *The Hanoverians: A Century of Growth, 1714-1815,* Blond Educational, 1972; (editor) *Practical Approaches to the New History: Suggestions for the Improvement of Classroom Method,* Hutchinson Educational, 1973; *Napoleon: Man and Myth,* Hodder & Stoughton, 1974; *The Victorians: A Century of Achievement,* Hart-Davis, 1975; *The Making of Contemporary Europe,* Hodder & Stoughton, 1980; (editor and contributor) *History of Britain* (secondary school textbook), Hodder & Stoughton, Volume II: *Britain: 1450-1760,* 1983, Volume IV: *Britain: 1760-1914,* 1983, Volume V: *Britain: 1914-1980's,* in press; *Nineteenth-Century Britain,* Hodder & Stoughton, 1984. General editor, "London History" series. Contributor to history journals. Editor, *Bulletin of Historical Research,* 1958-60, *History,* 1970, and *Teaching History.*

WORK IN PROGRESS: A humanities course; Volume I of *History of Britain.*

SIDELIGHTS: R. Ben Jones writes: "One of the things I have come to believe is that students are fed on too thin a diet. They need to be asked to think things out, not simply to remember lists of facts or basic patterns of information. This belief inspires each of my volumes, which draw upon contemporary sources as well as a wide range of secondary works. The *History of Britain* is a series that deliberately sets out and fosters in adolescents the idea of the 'New History' calling for work at greater depth than is common in many textbooks for these age groups."

* * *

JORDAN, Carrie
See CUDLIPP, Edythe

* * *

JORSTAD, Erling (Theodore) 1930-

PERSONAL: Born October 13, 1930, in Kenyon, Minn.; son of Oscar Edwin and Laura (Voxland) Jorstad; married Helen Haban (a college teacher), August 25, 1956 (divorced, 1979); children: Eric, Laura. *Education:* St. Olaf College, B.A., 1952; Harvard University, M.A., 1953; University of Wisconsin, Ph.D., 1957. *Religion:* Lutheran. *Home:* 1130 Highland Ave., Northfield, Minn. 55057. *Office:* Department of History, St. Olaf College, Northfield, Minn. 55057.

CAREER: St. Olaf College, Northfield, Minn., instructor, 1956-58, assistant professor, 1958-61, associate professor, 1961-69, professor of history, 1969—. Visiting professor of history at Chiang Mai University, Thailand, 1977. *Military service:* Minnesota National Guard, 1955-57; became second lieutenant. *Member:* American Historical Association, Organization of American Historians, American Association of University Professors, American Society of Church History, Society for Religion in Higher Education, Upper Midwest Historical Society (secretary, 1958-60), Phi Beta Kappa. *Awards, honors:* Minnesota Historical Society research fellowship, 1959; American Association of State and Local History grant-in-aid, 1960; Danforth Foundation research fellowship, 1963-64; American Philosophical Society research grant, 1970-71; recipient of several St. Olaf College faculty development grants.

WRITINGS: The Politics of Doomsday: The Fundamentalists of the Far Right, Abingdon, 1970; *The Instant Giant: American Radicalism in the 1960s,* College Notes, 1970; *Love It or Leave It?: A Dialog on Loyalty,* Augsburg, 1972; *That New-Time Religion: The Jesus Revival in America,* Augsburg, 1973; *The Holy Spirit in Today's Church,* Abingdon, 1973; *Bold in the Spirit: Lutheran Charismatic Renewal in America,* Augsburg, 1974; *The Politics of Moralism: The New Christian Right in America,* Augsburg, 1981; *Evangelicals in the White House: The Cultural Maturation of Born Again Christianity,* Edwin Mellen, 1981. Contributor to *Dialog, Christian Scholar, Lutheran Quarterly, Concern, Ecumenist, Theology Today,* and

Minnesota History; also contributor of reviews to *Journal of Presbyterian History, Lutheran Quarterly, Christianity Today,* and *Fides et Historia.*

WORK IN PROGRESS: *Counting Down to Doomsday: The New Apocalyptic Vision in America.*

SIDELIGHTS: "My two major interests are religion and politics," Erling Jorstad told *CA.* "Since I am neither a politician nor a minister, I follow my interests by studying the relationships between these two fields. I write because I hope to reach a wide audience and because I find both my teaching and writing are enhanced by sustained scholarly research. Writing is a form of teaching; and in the classroom I have the opportunity to try out new ideas before starting the writing process on a new project. One major fringe benefit has been the large number of invitations to speak to various groups about my research. This is good not only for my ego and wallet, but it gives me the opportunity to realize that there really are people out there who have read my material. In turn, I learn from them what interests them, and often this helps shape the direction of my latest research project.

"My field of investigation is contemporary American religious life. This means I am writing instant history, something close to journalism. This creates some hazards, such as finding someone else is bringing out a book before you are on the same subject. But it has rewards also, because it gives me a sense of engagement and participation in the current scene in America. I attempt to be as objective as possible, and at the same time to put my scholarship to work for causes in which I believe."

AVOCATIONAL INTERESTS: Classical music, aquatic sports, and bicycle touring.

* * *

JUCKER, Sita 1921-

PERSONAL: Born April 21, 1921, in Switzerland; daughter of Hans (a manager of a factory) and Delly (Kaehr) Bruder; married Werner Jucker (an architect), October 11, 1947; children: Andreas, Thomas. *Education:* Studied at Ecole des Beaux Arts, Geneva, Ecole Paul Colin, Paris, and Kunstgewerbeschule, Basel. *Home:* Greifenseestrasse 56, 8603 Schwerzenbach, Switzerland.

CAREER: Artist and illustrator; does book illustrating and bookcovers. Has worked as a shop window decorator, clothing designer, publicity employee, and newspaper and magazine illustrator. *Member:* Gesellschaft Schweizerischer Malerinnen, Verband Schweizerischer Grafiker.

WRITINGS—Published by Artemis Verlag (Zurich), except as indicated: (Illustrator) Ursina Ziegler, *Squaps, der Mondling* (picture book), 1969, translation by Barbara Kowal Gallob published as *Squaps, the Moonling,* Atheneum, 1969; (with Ziegler) *Peppino,* 1971, translation published by Atheneum, 1971; (illustrator) H. C. Artmann, *Omepul* (picture book), 1973, translation published as *Angus,* Methuen, 1973.

(Illustrator) Regine Schindler, *Hen Laugfuss* (picture book), 1975, published as *Mr. Longfoot,* Methuen, 1975; *Der grosse Uk* (picture book), translation published as *The Friendly Monster,* Methuen; *Die Maus bambino* (picture book), Bohem Press (Zurich), 1982; (illustrator) U. von Wiese, *Die Prinzessin, die nicht schlafen konnte* (picture book), Bohem Press, 1982; *Kiwitan ein Suchbuch,* Bohem Press, 1984.

Also illustrator: Dino Larese, *Regula,* Verlag Sauerlaender; Margrit Studer, *Mein Buch,* Flamberg Verlag; Hans Schranz, *Was kuemmert mich Maeni,* Flamberg Verlag; Annemarie Meyer-Dalbert, *Hexlein hilftsuchen,* Rascher-Verlag; Alois Dickerhoff, *Wendelau und Gueldenhaar,* Fussli-Verlag; Ursula Geiger, *Komm bald Christine,* Blaukreuz-Verlag; Gobi Walter, *D'Wiehnachtsgschicht,* Zwingli-Verlag; Gunvor Fossum, *In Kukeberg geschieht etwas,* Verlag H. R. Sauerlaender & Co.; Roman Brodmann, *Tagebuch mit Aphrodite,* Turicum-Verlag; Johanna Stratenwerth, *Arma und der Reiter,* Verlag Ernst Kaufman; Olga Meyer, *Tapfer und treu,* Verlag Sauerlaender; Heinrich Ryssel, *Sterne und Sternchen,* Werner Classen-Verlag; Schindler, *Auf der Shassenach Weihnachteh,* Kaufmann Verlag; Colette Buechergilde Gutenberg, *Die Fessel.*

Also illustrator of seven books by Jenifer Wayne for Albert Mueller-Verlag, and Heinemann, including *Merry by Name, The Day the Ceiling Fell Down, The Ghost Next Door, Kitchen People, The Night the Rain Came In,* and *Ollie;* also illustrator of elementary texts and other books.

* * *

JUDSON, John 1930-

PERSONAL: Born September 9, 1930, in Stratford, Conn.; son of Irving John (a motel proprietor) and Edna (Hewitt) Judson; married Joanne Carol Aker, October 30, 1959; children: William Nicholas (died, 1972), Lisa Ann, Gary James, Sara Lea. *Education:* Colby College, A.B., 1958; attended University of Maine, 1962-63; State University of Iowa, M.F.A., 1965. *Office:* Department of English, University of Wisconsin—LaCrosse, LaCrosse, Wis. 54601.

CAREER: Semi-professional baseball player in Maine and Iowa; worked in research and development for electronics firms in Connecticut and Massachusetts; high school and college preparatory school teacher in Iowa and Maine; University of Wisconsin—LaCrosse, 1965—, began as assistant professor, currently professor of English. *Military service:* U.S. Air Force, 1951-55; received Korean medal.

WRITINGS: (With John Stevens Wade) *Two from Where It Snows,* Northeast, 1964; *Surreal Songs,* Juniper, 1968, revised edition, 1969; *Within Seasons,* Colby College, 1968; (editor with others) *Voyages to the Inland Sea: Essays and Poems,* Center for Contemporary Poetry, Volume I, 1971, Volume II, 1972, Volume III, 1973, Volume IV, 1974, Volume V, 1975, Volume VI, 1976, Volume VII, 1977; (editor) *The Long Poem,* Juniper Press, 1972; *Finding Words in Winter,* Elizabeth Press, 1973; *Ash Is the Candle's Wick,* Juniper Press, 1975; *Routes from the Onion's Dark,* Pentagram Press, 1976; (editor) *Northeast,* Juniper Press, 1977; *A Purple Tale,* New Rivers Press, 1978; *North of Athens,* Spoon River Poetry Press, 1980; *Reasons Why I Am Not Perfect,* Sparrow, 1982. Contributor of poems to periodicals. Poetry editor, *Northeast,* 1962—.

WORK IN PROGRESS: A book of poems; a novel.

SIDELIGHTS: John Judson has traveled in Mexico, Canada, Japan, Korea, and the United States.

* * *

JUDSON, William
See CORLEY, Edwin (Raymond)

* * *

JUTSON, Mary Carolyn Hollers
See GEORGE, Mary Carolyn Hollers Jutson

K

KAHN, David 1930-

PERSONAL: Born February 7, 1930, in New York, N.Y.; son of Jesse (a lawyer) and Florence (a glass manufacturer; maiden name, Abraham) Kahn; married Susanne Fiedler, October 22, 1969; children: Oliver, Michael. *Education:* Bucknell University, A.B., 1951; Oxford University, Ph.D., 1974. *Politics:* Democrat. *Religion:* Jewish. *Home:* 120 Wooleys Lane, Great Neck, N.Y. 11023. *Office: Newsday,* Melville, N.Y. 11747.

CAREER: Free-lance writer. *Newsday* (Long Island daily), Garden City, N.Y., reporter, 1955-63; *Herald Tribune,* Paris, France, deskman, 1965-67; New York University, New York, N.Y., associate professor of journalism, 1975-79; *Newsday,* Melville, N.Y., assistant op-ed editor, 1979—. *Member:* American Cryptogram Association (president, 1965-67), American Historical Association, American Committee for the History of the Second World War, New York Cipher Society (president, 1955-62).

WRITINGS: Two Soviet Spy Ciphers, privately printed, 1960, later published by Central Intelligence Agency; *Plain-text in the New Unabridged,* Crypto Press, 1963; *The Codebreakers: The Story of Secret Writing,* Macmillan, 1967; *Hitler's Spies: German Military Intelligence in World War II,* Macmillan, 1978; *Kahn on Codes,* Macmillan, 1983; (adaptor) Pierre Lorain, *Clandestine Operations: The Arms and Techniques of the Resistance, 1941-44,* Macmillan, 1983. Contributor to *Encyclopedia Americana,* and to *Atlantic, Scientific American, Foreign Affairs, Military Affairs, New York Times Magazine,* and *Cryptogram.* Editor and founder of *Cryptologia.*

SIDELIGHTS: David Kahn's works are the stuff of which spy thrillers are made: international intrigue, codes, and military intelligence. Kahn, however, has chosen to chronicle actual events and real personalities, writing history rather than fiction. Among his works concerned with things covert and enigmatic is *The Codebreakers: The Story of Secret Writing,* called "a classic history of cryptography," by Joseph E. Persico in the *Washington Post Book World.* The book traces the course of code making and breaking from ancient times to the present, and while such a topic might not seem a likely subject for popular success, the book in fact sold well. Myra McPherson, writing in the *Washington Post,* offers this explanation: "[Kahn] laced the heavy material in 'The Codebreakers' with fascinating asides—from Plutarch to pig latin. . . . [His] spoon-feeding of fact after fact produced the nearly impossible—a thousand-page tome on a subject hardly destined to titillate, became a best seller (75,000 in hardback)." David Hunt calls *The Codebreakers* a "brilliant book" in the *Times Literary Supplement,* and to Jack Beatty in *Newsweek* it is a "much-admired study." The book grew out of Kahn's long-standing interest in cryptography. McPherson points out that "when [the author] was 12, he was walking past the public library in Great Neck, L.I., and 'stopped in my tracks when I saw this book about codes with this terrific title, *Secret and Urgent.* It hooked me—and I never grew up.'"

In the view of a number of critics, the appeal of Kahn's works is partly the product of his ability to combine erudition and enthusiasm. McPherson describes him as "both a serious historian and purveyor, at times, of glib but interesting generalizations. . . . His books [are] a mix of the anecdotal, massive research and impressive analysis." In his review of Kahn's *Hitler's Spies: German Military Intelligence in World War II,* Hunt expresses a similar opinion regarding the author's effective blend of scholarship and storytelling: "He pays proper attention to the really essential weapons of military intelligence: prisoners and captured documents . . . and intercepted enemy communications. Nevertheless, he knows what the public wants . . . and makes sure that he prints plenty of spy stories."

As the reader makes his or her way through the stories and scholarly details contained in *Hitler's Spies,* a pattern gradually emerges. In Persico's words, Kahn "has provided fare for the spy-thriller buff and a clear verdict on Germany's secret warfare: 'At every one of the strategic turning points of World War II, her intelligence failed.'" Those failures range from the comical pair of German agents who were landed on the Maine coast and spent their money on themselves rather than on gathering intelligence, to the disastrous situation that Persico describes in his review: "German agents reporting from Britain were actually a serious liability. They had all come under British control and were feeding their presumed masters deliciously misleading information." As Kahn asserts however, even successful and accurate intelligence was of little use to the German war effort. Beatty describes why: "There was one overwhelming flaw in the German totalitarian order: all of the information from the various services came together in one place only—the turbid mind of Adolf Hitler—and 'no facts,' writes Kahn, 'could ever have convinced Hitler that he was wrong.'"

Describing Kahn's characteristic approach to his subjects, a *New Yorker* critic states that "[he] teaches the layman everything he can possibly grasp about an arcane speciality." That Kahn is both a respected historian and best-selling author at the same time is acknowledged by a number of writers. Leonard Bushkoff, in his *New York Times Book Review* article on *Hitler's Spies*, summarizes those qualities that contribute to the appeal and value of Kahn's works: "His judgments are balanced, authoritative, without either the banality or the sensationalism that often marks popularizing writers. The bibliography is ample, carefully subdivided, meant for use and not merely display. A serious book, clearly: handcrafted, meant to last."

BIOGRAPHICAL/CRITICAL SOURCES: *Christian Science Monitor*, October 5, 1967; *Book World*, November 26, 1967; *New York Times Book Review*, January 7, 1968, June 18, 1978; *New Republic*, February 10, 1968; *Time*, February 16, 1968, July 10, 1978; *American Historical Review*, July, 1968; *Newsweek*, June 26, 1978; *Washington Post*, July 9, 1978; *New Yorker*, July 10, 1978; *Washington Post Book World*, August 13, 1978; *Times Literary Supplement*, October 10, 1978.

* * *

KARL, Jean E(dna) 1927-

PERSONAL: Born July 29, 1927, in Chicago, Ill.; daughter of William (a salesman) and Ruth (Anderson) Karl. *Education:* Mount Union College, B.A., 1949. *Home:* 136 East 36th St., New York, N.Y. 10016. *Office:* 597 Fifth Ave., New York, N.Y. 10017.

CAREER: Scott, Foresman and Co., Chicago, Ill., junior editorial assistant and assistant editor, 1949-56; Abingdon Press, New York City, children's book editor, 1956-61; Atheneum Publishers, New York City, director of children's book department, 1961—, vice-president, 1964—. Chairman, American Library Association/Children's Book Council joint committee, 1963-65; president, Children's Book Council, 1965; co-director of seminar on children's publications, School of Library Science, Case Western Reserve University, 1969; trustee, Mount Union College, 1974-77. *Member:* American Association of Publishers (member of Freedom to Read Committee, 1974-80; member of executive board, General Trade Division, 1975-77). *Awards, honors:* D.Litt., Mount Union College, 1969.

WRITINGS: *From Childhood to Childhood: Children's Books and Their Creators*, John Day, 1970; *The Turning Place: Stories of a Future Past*, Dutton, 1976; *Beloved Benjamin Is Waiting*, Dutton, 1978; *But We Are Not of Earth*, Dutton, 1981. Contributor of articles to *Publishers' Weekly, Wilson Library Bulletin, Writer,* and other professional and educational periodicals.

* * *

KATZ, Samuel 1914-
(Shmuel Katz)

PERSONAL: Born December 9, 1914, in Johannesburg, South Africa; son of Alexander Zyskind (a builder) and Luba (Breslov) Katz; divorced. *Education:* Attended University of the Witwatersrand, 1930. *Politics:* Zionist. *Religion:* Jewish. *Home:* 155 Dizengoff St., Tel Aviv, Israel.

CAREER: Commissioner of the Union of South Africa, Jerusalem, Palestine, secretary, 1936-39; *Jewish Standard,* London, England, editor, 1940-42, 1945-46; *Daily Express,* London, staff member, 1943-45; settled in Palestine, 1946; member of high command, Irgun Zvai Leumi, 1947-48; Herut Movement, co-founder, 1948, member of executive committee, 1948-51; member of Knesset (Herut Party), 1949-51; Karni Publishers Ltd., Tel Aviv, Israel, manager, 1951-76; Megiddo Publishing Co. Ltd., Tel Aviv, manager, 1962-76; adviser to prime minister, 1977-78. New Zionist Organization, member of administrative committee, London, 1940-42, member of world executive committee, London and Jerusalem, 1945-46; member of executive committee, Land of Israel Movement, 1967-77.

WRITINGS: (Translator) Vladimir Jabotinsky, *Story of the Jewish Legion*, Ackerman, 1945; (translator) Menachem Begin, *The Revolt*, Schuman, 1951; *Days of Fire*, Doubleday, 1968; *Battleground*, Bantam, 1973, new edition, 1977; *The Hollow Peace*, Dvir (Tel Aviv), 1981; *Battletruth*, Dvir, 1983. Political columnist, *Ma'ariv* and *Jerusalem Post*, 1978—. Contributor to journals in Israel, South Africa, Great Britain, and the United States.

* * *

KATZ, Shmuel
See KATZ, Samuel

* * *

KATZ, Steve 1935-
(Stephanie Garos)

PERSONAL: Born May 14, 1935, in Bronx, N.Y.; son of Alexander (a salesman) and Sally (Goldstein) Katz; married Patricia Bell, June 10, 1956 (separated); children: Avrum, Nikolai, Rafael. *Education:* Cornell University, B.A. (with honors), 1956; University of Oregon, M.A., 1959. *Residence:* Boulder, Colo. *Agent:* Georges Borchardt, Inc., 136 East 57th St., New York, N.Y. 10022. *Office:* Department of English, University of Colorado, Boulder, Colo. 80309.

CAREER: English Language Institute, Lecca, Italy, staff member, 1960; faculty member overseas, University of Maryland, 1961-62; Cornell University, Ithaca, N.Y., assistant professor, 1963-68; University of Iowa, Iowa City, lecturer at Writer's Workshop, 1969-1970; Brooklyn College of the City University of New York, Brooklyn, N.Y., writer-in-residence, 1970-71, co-director of Projects in Innovative Fiction, 1971-73; Queens College of the City University of New York, Flushing, N.Y., adjunct assistant professor, 1973-75; University of Notre Dame, Notre Dame, Ind., associate professor of English, 1976-78; University of Colorado, Boulder, associate professor of English, 1978—. Has done radio work. *Member:* P.E.N., Writers Guild, Authors League of America. *Awards, honors:* P.E.N. grant, 1972; Creative Artists Public Service grant, 1976; National Education Association grant, 1976, 1982.

WRITINGS: *The Lestriad* (novella), limited edition, Edizioni Milella (Italy), 1962; *The Weight of Antony* (poems), Eibe Press, 1964; *The Exagggerations of Peter Prince* (novel), Holt, 1968; *Creamy and Delicious* (stories), Random House, 1970; (under pseudonym Stephanie Garos) *Posh* (novel), Grove, 1971; *Saw* (novel), Knopf, 1972; *Cheyenne River Wild Track* (poems), Ithaca House, 1973; *Moving Parts* (novel), Fiction Collective, 1977; *Wier and Pouce* (novel), Sun & Moon, 1984; *Stolen Stories* (short fiction), Fiction Collective, 1984.

Also author of screenplays, including "Hex," Twentieth-Century Fox, "Mendozz the Jew," "Toussaint," and "Chicago Needs Show." Work represented in anthologies, including *Stories from Epoch, Modern Occasions, Experiments in Prose, Innovative Fiction,* and *Statements.* Contributor of stories and poems to periodicals, including *Chicago Review, Paris Review, Northwest Review, Choice, Outsider, Le Nouveau Commerce,* and *In Transit.* Past editor, *Northwest Review* and *Epoch.*

WORK IN PROGRESS: A novel, *Florry of Washington Heights.*

SIDELIGHTS: Steve Katz told *CA:* "Lived in Southern and Northern Italy. Speak Italian. Studied Tai Chi Chuan for eight years. Have done extensive readings of both fiction and poetry. Have read for WBAI and participated in an award-winning radio broadcast of original radio works for WXXI in Rochester. My fiction reflects my feeling that it is necessary for our survival to reorder our perception of the world."

BIOGRAPHICAL/CRITICAL SOURCES: New York Times Book Review, September 8, 1968, October 1, 1972; *Newsweek,* September 9, 1968; *Nation,* September 23, 1968; *National Observer,* October 7, 1968; *Kenyon Review,* Issue 5, 1968; Jerome Klinkowitz, *Life of Fiction,* University of Illinois Press, 1978; *Critique,* summer, 1983.

* * *

KEELING, Jill Annette (Shaw) 1923-

PERSONAL: Born January 29, 1923, in Chesterfield, Derbyshire, England; daughter of Thomas Kenyon (an engineer) and Ileene Vera (Foster) Shaw; married Clinton Harry Keeling (a self-employed zoologist), August 24, 1953 (divorced, 1974); children: Anthony, Jeremy, Diana, Phoebe. *Education:* Bedford College for Women, London, B.A. (with honors), 1944. *Politics:* None. *Religion:* Agnostic. *Home:* Tyddn Seion, Nebo, Penygroes, Caernarfon, Gwynedd, North Wales, United Kingdom. *Office:* Centre for Educational Zoology, 31 North St., Whitwick, Leicestershire, England.

CAREER: St. George's School, Ascot, Berkshire, England, English teacher, 1944-45; Ashover Zoological Gardens, Ashover, Derbyshire, England, superintendent, 1954-74; Centre for Educational Zoology, Whitwick, Leicestershire, England, director, 1975—. Consultant to National Trust. *Member:* Kinnean Society (fellow), Military and Hospitaller Order of St. Lazarus of Jerusalem.

WRITINGS: Variations on a Theme, Stockwell, 1957; *Ask of the Beasts,* Anthony Blond, 1960; *The Old English Sheepdog,* W. & G. Foyle, 1961, 2nd edition, 1975; (with Clinton Harry Keeling) *Keeling's Ark,* Harrap, 1970; (with Terry K. Mills) *Animals for Schools,* Harrap, 1973. Contributor to *Countryman, Chambers's Journal, International Zoo Year Book, Teacher's World,* and other journals.

WORK IN PROGRESS: Animal Inventions and *And They Shall Teach Thee,* both for Blond & Briggs.

SIDELIGHTS: "I have always wanted to write," Jill Annette Keeling told *CA,* "and produced two short 'novels' and a few poems before I was ten—unpublished, I may add! Nowadays my writing is almost incidental to my main work, which takes the form of lecturing. I believe very strongly that ninety percent of Man's problems come about because he has forgotten that he, too, is an animal, so I currently live for most of the year in a motorized caravan, travelling the length and breadth of England accompanied by some twenty or thirty animal 'friends' who range from invertebrates and amphibians to reptiles, birds, and mammals, introducing them to school children in the hope of instilling a proper respect not only for their fellow creatures on this planet, but for their whole environment. Man *is* an animal, and governed by the same ecological laws as the rest of them—he isn't God almighty; if he doesn't realize this soon, he is in a fair way to end for ever that greatest miracle of planet earth—life in all its diversity."

* * *

KELLER, Karl 1933-

PERSONAL: Born May 29, 1933, in Manti, Utah; son of Calvin T. and Lillie B. Keller; married Ruth Anderson, July 27, 1956; children: Kristen, Michael, Chad, James, Mather. *Education:* University of Utah, B.A., 1958, M.A., 1959; University of Minnesota, Ph.D., 1964. *Politics:* Left. *Religion:* "Gone." *Home:* 2595 Ocean Front Walk, San Diego, Calif. 92109. *Office:* Department of English, San Diego State University, San Diego, Calif. 92182.

CAREER: University of Minnesota, Minneapolis, instructor in English, 1959-64; State University of New York College at Cortland, assistant professor of English, 1964-66; San Diego State University, San Diego, Calif., assistant professor, 1966-69, associate professor, 1969-72, professor of English, 1972—. *Member:* Modern Language Association of America. *Awards, honors:* Fulbright scholar in France, 1973; Huntington Library fellowship, 1975; American Council of Learned Societies grant, 1980-81.

WRITINGS: (With Clifton Fadiman) *American Literature, Post 1945: Future Resources and Development,* Famous Writers, 1970; *The Example of Edward Taylor,* University of Massachusetts Press, 1975; *The Only Kangaroo among the Beauty: Emily Dickinson and America,* Johns Hopkins University Press, 1979. Member of board of editors of *Dialogue,* 1964-74, and *American Quarterly;* member of bibliography staff of *American Literature,* 1967-72.

WORK IN PROGRESS: Solomon Stoddard on the Beginnings of an American Literature; The Mormons Are Coming, the Mormons Are Coming; San Diego, Writing.

SIDELIGHTS: Karl Keller's *The Only Kangaroo among the Beauty: Emily Dickinson and America* is a "rare combination in literary criticism," according to Suzanne Juhasz in *Library Journal,* being both "scholarly and creative, sophisticated and pragmatic." Keller's study attempts to focus on Dickinson and her works within the context of the writings and personalities of many of the major literary figures of her day, including Whitman, Emerson, Thoreau, and Hawthorne. Keller's purpose, says Willis J. Buckingham in *American Literature,* "in exploring Dickinson's affiliations with American writers, is to describe a range of possibilities. . . . Each pairing will tell us something about Dickinson as well as the figure she is placed alongside." This process, Buckingham believes, is more or less successful depending upon the particular pairing, but in the view of Helen McNeil, the results "[place] Dickinson surprisingly close to the center of a well-populated mid- and later nineteenth-century American cultural scene."

Writing in the *Times Literary Supplement,* McNeil identifies *The Only Kangaroo among the Beauty* as part of a reforming trend in Dickinson scholarship, part of the transition from "Dickinson as myth" to a more accurate picture of her as poet. In McNeil's words, "The 'new' Emily Dickinson is still in the making," and Keller's work serves to "locate [the poet] culturally and artistically." How effective is Keller's approach?

Despite misgivings about the book's handling of the language of Dickinson's poems, Buckingham concludes that "nowhere has the subject of Dickinson's literary relations been approached with such sustained verve and savvy, and nowhere has it yielded so many bracing discriminations."

BIOGRAPHICAL/CRITICAL SOURCES: *Library Journal*, February 1, 1980; *Times Literary Supplement*, December 12, 1980; *American Literature*, Volume LII, January, 1981.

* * *

KELLEY, Donald R(eed) 1931-

PERSONAL: Born February 17, 1931, in Elgin, Ill.; son of Walter Louis and Helen (Davis) Kelley; married former wife, Nancy Lief (a teacher), June 4, 1962; married second wife, Bonnie Smith (an historian), June 30, 1979; children: (first marriage) John Reed; (second marriage) Patrick, Patience. *Education:* Harvard University, B.A., 1953; Columbia University, M.A., 1956, Ph.D., 1962; graduate study at University of Paris, 1958-59. *Home:* 312 Wilmot Rd., Rochester, N.Y. 14618. *Office:* Department of History, University of Rochester, Rochester, N.Y. 14627.

CAREER: Queens College of the City University of New York, Flushing, N.Y., lecturer in history, 1960-63; Southern Illinois University, Carbondale, assistant professor of history, 1963-65; State University of New York at Binghamton, assistant professor, 1965-68, associate professor, 1968-71, professor of modern European history, 1971-72; Harvard University, Cambridge, Mass., visiting professor, 1972-73; University of Rocheser, Rochester, N.Y., professor of history, 1973—. *Military service:* U.S. Army, 1953-55. *Member:* American Academy of Arts and Sciences, American Historical Association, Renaissance Society of America, Mediaeval Academy of America. *Awards, honors:* Fulbright fellowship, 1958-59; American Philosophical Society grant, 1964, 1971; Newberry Library grant, 1965; American Council of Learned Societies fellowship, 1967-68; Institute for Advanced Study, fellow, 1969-70, 1977-78; Folger Shakespeare Library Grant, 1970; Guggenheim fellowship, 1974-75, 1980-81; National Endowment for the Humanities fellowship, 1977-78.

WRITINGS: *Foundations of Modern Historical Scholarship*, Columbia University Press, 1970; *Francois Hotman: A Revolutionary's Ordeal*, Princeton University Press, 1973; *The Beginning of Ideology*, Cambridge University Press, 1981; *Historians and the Law in France, 1804-1848*, Princeton University Press, 1984.

Contributor to a number of professional journals. Member of editorial board of *Journal of the History of Ideas* and *French Historical Studies*.

WORK IN PROGRESS: *The Human Measure: Social Thought and the Western Legal Tradition*.

SIDELIGHTS: Donald R. Kelley told *CA:* "I have made a hobby (though it is also the focus of my work) of trying to build intellectual bridges from my field, history, over to other disciplines, including philosophy, literature, religion, law, political science and sociology. Judging by the hospitality of various scholarly journals, the efforts seem to me to be successful for every case except the last, and even sociology I haven't yet given up on."

BIOGRAPHICAL/CRITICAL SOURCES: *Times Literary Supplement*, January 14, 1983.

KELLY, Dave
See KELLY, David M(ichael)

* * *

KELLY, David M(ichael) 1938-
(Dave Kelly)

PERSONAL: Born June 23, 1938, in Grand Rapids, Mich.; son of Peter Earl (a laborer) and Margaret (Weisel) Kelly; married Sylvia Hayden Neahr (an English teacher), September 12, 1960; children: Jordu, Colette, Willow (all daughters). *Education:* Michigan State University, B.A. (journalism), 1961, M.A., 1962; University of Iowa, M.F.A., 1966. *Politics:* "Yes." *Religion:* "No." *Home address:* P.O. Box 53, Geneseo, N.Y. 14454. *Office:* Department of English, State University of New York College, Geneseo, N.Y. 14454.

CAREER: State University of New York College at Geneseo, poet-in-residence, associate professor of English, and director of creative writing, 1967—. *Awards, honors:* National Endowment for the Arts, discovery grant, 1970, 1976, poetry fellowship, 1976-77; Lamont Award finalist, 1972, for *Instruction for Viewing a Solar Eclipse;* New York State Council on the Arts Creative Artists Public Service fellowship, 1974-75, 1978-79; special distinction award from Elliston Foundation, 1980, for *Filming Assassinations;* received three fellowships for summer work in poetry from the State University of New York Faculty Research Foundation.

WRITINGS—All under name Dave Kelly; all poetry: *The Night of the Terrible Ladders*, Hors Commerce Press (Torrance, Calif.), 1966; *All Here Together*, Lillabulero Press, 1969; *Summer Study*, Runcible Spoon Press, 1969; *Dear Nate*, Runcible Spoon Press, 1969; *Instruction for Viewing a Solar Eclipse*, Wesleyan University Press, 1972; *In These Rooms*, Red Hill Press, 1976; *Poems in Season*, Texas Portfolio Editions, 1977; *Filming Assassinations*, Ithaca House, 1979; *Great Lakes Cycle*, Steps Inside Press, 1980; *Northern Letter* (chapbook), Nebraska Review, 1980.

Others: *At a Time: A Dance for Voices*, Basilisk, 1972; *Did You Hear They're Beheading Bill Johnson Today?*, Stone Press, 1974; *The Flesh-Eating Horse and Other Sagas*, Bartholomew's Cobble Press, 1976. Contributor of poetry to over one hundred and fifty periodicals, including *Nation*, *Paris Review*, *Modern Letters*, *Poetry Now*, *Prairie Schooner*, and *American Poetry Review*.

WORK IN PROGRESS: Several 50- and 60-poem "slim volumes"; a 200-page collected volume.

SIDELIGHTS: David M. Kelly told *CA:* "I am occasionally seized by the unhappy conviction that I belong to a species on the verge of its extinction and deserving of it. This of course colors my recent enjoyment of hobbies and pastimes including raising and running sled dogs, swimming, enjoying the sun, cooking and eating after somewhat of a gourmet fashion and faulty guitar playing. Important writers include, among many, Neruda, Lorca, Merwin, Chambers, Logan."

BIOGRAPHICAL/CRITICAL SOURCES: *December*, 1969; *Nickel Review*, November 25, 1969; *Democrat and Chronicle*, March 22, 1970; *Westigan Review*, Number 3, 1970 (special issue dedicated to Kelly's work); *Mid American Review*, spring, 1983.

KELMAN, Steven 1948-

PERSONAL: Born May 1, 1948, in New York, N.Y.; son of Kurt (a patent agent) and Sylvia (an attorney; maiden name, Etman) Kelman. *Education:* Harvard University, B.A. (summa cum laude), 1970, Ph.D., 1978; University of Stockholm, additional study, 1970-71. *Politics:* "Democratic socialist." *Religion:* Jewish. *Home:* 21 Stoner Ave., Great Neck, N.Y. 11021. *Office:* John F. Kennedy School of Government, Harvard University, Cambridge, Mass. 02138.

CAREER: Associate professor of public policy, John F. Kennedy School of Government, Harvard University. *Awards, honors:* Fulbright scholar in Sweden, 1970-71.

WRITINGS: Push Comes to Shove: The Escalation of Student Protest, Houghton, 1970; *Behind the Berlin Wall: An Encounter in East Germany,* Houghton, 1972; *Regulating America, Regulating Sweden: A Comparative Study of Occupational Safety and Health Policy,* MIT Press, 1980; *What Price Incentives?,* Auburn House, 1981. Contributor to *New Republic, Public Interest, New Yorker, Commentary, Harper's, New Leader* and *Life.*

WORK IN PROGRESS: A book on the policymaking process in America.

SIDELIGHTS: During his senior year at Harvard University, Steven Kelman wrote *Push Comes to Shove: The Escalation of Student Protest,* a book about student radicalism. George Keller states in *Book World* that Kelman's study "is bold, searing and squarely in the new camp of radical middle criticism. It is probably the most revealing book on student swingers and revolutionaries to apper this far. With sympathy, wit and remarkable political sense, Kelman demonstrates that the hip radicals are just as earnest, hypocritical, well-intentioned and silly as others have shown martini-drinking suburbanite golfers to be." And C. M. Curtis comments in the *Christian Science Monitor* that "Kellman's critique of the SDS [Students for a Democratic Society] movement . . . is pungent and closely argued. . . . Kelman is intelligent and resourceful, and his stylish, supremely confident book deserves close reading by anyone who can still be animated by the amibitions or excesses of the student left."

In 1971 the *New Yorker* sent Kelman on assignment to East Germany to observe the everyday lives of the citizens of that country. Kelman wrote a number of articles for the *New Yorker* reporting his experiences, and in *Behind the Berlin Wall: An Encounter in East Germany,* Kelman expands on these articles. M. R. Yerburgh remarks in *Library Journal* that Kelman's "coverage is objective and interesting, yet at the same time seems to confirm our stereotyped suspicions of what life is surely like in the Soviet sphere. It's conventional wisdom vindicated." And in *Newsweek* S. K. Oberbeck believes that "though Kelman injects a bit too much nailbiting . . . drama into his litany of police-state anxieties . . . , he does survey a good spectrum of the population in this incredibly bleak-sounding dictatorship."

AVOCATIONAL INTERESTS: Learning foreign languages (has mastered French, German, and Swedish).

BIOGRAPHICAL/CRITICAL SOURCES: Book World, May 10, 1970; *Christian Science Monitor,* August 14, 1970; *New York Review of Books,* September 24, 1970; *Library Journal,* September 1, 1972; *Newsweek,* October 30, 1972; *Best Sellers,* January 15, 1973.

KELTON, Elmer 1926-
(Lee McElroy)

PERSONAL: Born April 29, 1926, in Andrews, Tex.; son of R. W. (a cowman) and Beatrice (Parker) Kelton; married Anna Lipp, July 3, 1947; children: Gary, Stephen, Kathryn. *Education:* University of Texas, B.A. in Journalism, 1948. *Politics:* "Very independent." *Religion:* Methodist. *Home:* 2460 Oxford, San Angelo, Tex. 76804. *Office address: Livestock Weekly,* Box 3306, San Angelo, Tex. 76901. *Agent:* John Payne, Lenniger Literary Agency, 104 East 40th St., New York, N.Y. 10016.

CAREER: San Angelo Standard-Times, San Angelo, Tex., farm and ranch editor, 1948-63; *Ranch* (magazine), San Angelo, editor, 1963-68; *Livestock Weekly,* San Angelo, associate editor, 1968—. Free-lance writer. *Military service:* U.S. Army, Infantry, 1944-46; served in Europe. *Member:* Western Writers of America (director, 1960-62 and 1963-64; president, 1962-63), Sigma Delta Chi. *Awards, honors:* Spur Awards for best western novel from Western Writers of America, 1957, for *Buffalo Wagons,* 1972, for *The Day the Cowboys Quit,* 1974, for *The Time It Never Rained,* and 1982, for *Eyes of the Hawk;* Award of Merit from Texas Civil War Centennial Commission, 1962, for *Bitter Trail;* Best Southwest Novel of the Year Award from Border Regional Library Association, 1972, for *The Day the Cowboys Quit;* Western Heritage Award from National Cowboy Hall of Fame, 1974, for *The Time It Never Rained,* and 1979, for *The Good Old Boys;* state awards from Associated Press for news stories and pictures.

WRITINGS—Published by Ballantine, except as indicated: *Hot Iron,* 1956; *Buffalo Wagons,* 1957; *Barbed Wire,* 1957; *Shadow of a Star,* 1959; *The Texas Rifles,* 1960; *Donovan,* 1961; *Bitter Trail,* 1962; *Horsehead Crossing,* 1963; *Massacre at Goliad,* 1965; *Llano River,* 1966; *After the Bugles,* 1967; *Captain's Rangers,* 1969; *Hanging Judge,* 1969; *The Day the Cowboys Quit,* Doubleday, 1971; *The Time It Never Rained,* Doubleday, 1973; *The Good Old Boys,* Ace Books, 1979; *The Wolf and the Buffalo,* Doubleday, 1980; (author of text) *Frank McCarthy: The Old West,* Greenwich Press, 1981.

Under pseudonym Lee McElroy; all published by Doubleday: *Joe Pepper,* 1975; *Long Way to Texas,* 1976; *Eyes of the Hawk,* 1981.

Contributor of about fifty short stories to magazines and several hundred articles to farm periodicals.

SIDELIGHTS: Elmer Kelton explains his early interest in western life to Carlton Stowers of the *Dallas News:* "I was fortunate . . . to grow up around cowboys who talked constantly about the old days, the range wars and cattle drives and the struggles of early cowmen who settled West Texas. Ranch cowboys are great storytellers. They have their own tales to tell, and they also have those handed down by their fathers and grandfathers. I expect in the retelling they are embellished a little, but a germ of truth is still there."

Kelton shares with *CA* his thoughts on writing western novels: "There are three kinds of truth in the telling of our past: fact, folklore and fiction. Each has its place. Formal history tells what happened, when, where, and to whom. But the formal historian is bound by the necessity to document his statements. He is not free to speculate upon the 'whys' of it all.

"Folklore often tells us more about people than formal history does. It is not bound by the restrictions which fetter the historian. Fiction gives the writer freedom to combine the best elements of fact and folklore, plus his own creativity, to illuminate areas the light of the other two may not reach. With fiction we are able to stir the senses and emotions and, by personalizing history, give it a reality the reader might otherwise never experience.

"This does not give us a moral right to distort or falsify. The historical fiction writer has a moral obligation to remain true to the spirit of his subject matter, to create rather than to destroy."

BIOGRAPHICAL/CRITICAL SOURCES: *Dallas News,* May 12, 1974; *Authors in the News,* Volume I, Gale, 1976.

* * *

KEMP, Gene 1926-

PERSONAL: Born December 27, 1926, in Wigginton, England; daughter of Albert (an electrician) and Alice (Sutton) Rushton; married Norman Charles Pattison, August 20, 1949 (divorced, May, 1958); married Allan William George Kemp (a National Union of Railwaymen divisional officer), August 23, 1958; children: (first marriage) Judith Eve; (second marriage) Chantal Alice, Richard William. *Education:* University of Exeter, degree in English (with honors), 1945. *Politics:* Labour. *Religion:* Church of England. *Home and office:* 16 Waverley Ave., Exeter, Devonshire EX4 4NL, England. *Agent:* Gerald Pollinger, Lawrence Pollinger Ltd., 18 Maddox St., Mayfair, London W1R 0EU, England.

CAREER: Writer. Saint Sidwell's School, Exeter, England, teacher, 1963-77. Governor of Central Schools in Exeter; lecturer at Rolle College, 1974-75. Member of Council for the Advancement of State Education and of general management committee of Exeter Labour Party. *Member:* National Union of Teachers, National Association for the Teaching of English.

WRITINGS—For children; published by Faber, except as indicated: *The Prime of Tamworth Pig,* 1972, Merrimack Book Service, 1979; *Tamworth Pig Saves the Trees,* 1973, Merrimack Book Service, 1978; *Tamworth Pig and the Litter,* 1975, Merrimack Book Service, 1978; *The Turbulent Term of Tyke Tyler,* 1977; *Christmas with Tamworth Pig,* 1977, Merrimack Book Service, 1979; *Gowie Corby Plays Chicken,* 1979; (editor) *Ducks and Dragons: Poems for Children* (anthology), illustrations by Carolyn Dinan, 1980; *Dog Days and Cat Naps,* 1980; *Clock Tower Ghost,* 1981; *No Place Like,* 1983; *Charlie Lewis Plays for Time,* 1984; *The Well,* 1984.

AVOCATIONAL INTERESTS: Politics, reading folklore, myths, and adult literature ("I like Saul Bellow a lot"), amateur archaeology (visiting iron-age forts), gardening.

BIOGRAPHICAL/CRITICAL SOURCES: *Times Literary Supplement,* March 25, 1977.

* * *

KENYON, Michael 1931-
(Daniel Forbes)

PERSONAL: Born June 26, 1931, in Huddersfield, Yorkshire, England; son of George (an engineer) and Madeleine (Roberts) Kenyon; married Catherine Bury (a schoolteacher), June 3, 1961; children: Lucy Jane, Kate Madeline, Polly. *Education:* Oxford University, B.A. and M.A., 1954; Duke University, graduate student, 1954-55. *Home:* 156 Rue Nationale, 46000 Cahors, France. *Agent:* Richard Scott Simon, Ltd., 32 College Cross, London NW1, England.

CAREER: Reporter on *Bristol Evening Post,* Bristol, England, 1955-58, *News Chronicle,* London, England, 1958-60, and *Guardian,* London, 1960-64; University of Illinois at Urbana-Champaign, visiting lecturer in journalism, 1964-66; full-time professional writer, living in Jersey, the Channel Islands, Great Britain, 1966-72, London, England, 1972-76, and Cahors, France; Southampton College, Long Island, N.Y., visiting lecturer in journalism and crime fiction, 1977-78. *Military service:* Royal Air Force, pilot officer, 1949-51.

WRITINGS: *Green Grass* (novel), Macmillan (London), 1970; *Brainbox and Bull* (juvenile adventure), Argus & Robertson, 1976.

Mystery novels: *May You Die in Ireland,* Morrow, 1965; *The Trouble with Series Three,* Morrow, 1967 (published in England as *The Whole Hog,* Collins, 1967); *Out of Season,* Collins, 1969; *The 100,000 Welcomes,* Coward, 1971; *The Shooting of Dan McGrew,* Collins, 1972; *A Sorry State,* McKay, 1974; (under pseudonym Daniel Forbes) *Mr. Big,* Coward, 1975, published under name Michael Kenyon, Collins, 1975; *The Rapist,* Collins, 1977, published under pseudonym Daniel Forbes, Coward, 1978; *The Molehill File,* Coward, 1978 (published in England as *Deep Pocket,* Collins, 1978); *The Elgar Variation,* Coward, 1981; *Zigzag,* Collins, 1981; *Man at the Wheel,* Doubleday, 1982; *The God Squad Bod,* Collins, 1982; *A Free Range Wife,* Doubleday, 1983. Contributor to *Gourmet.*

SIDELIGHTS: Michael Kenyon is a prolific author of crime and mystery novels, several of which feature the poetic sleuth Detective-Inspector "'enry" Peckover, who is introduced in *The Molehill File.* In this novel, according to a *Time* critic, Peckover links "the murder of a Mayfair tart to a web of political, financial, and sexual hanky-panky" that involves some prominent government figures.

The Elgar Variation finds Peckover investigating the murder of a housekeeper by an English lord. Alan Chesne, in a *New York Times* review of the book, describes Kenyon as a writer who displays "a puckish energy that permits him to take some risks in depicting his characters and the complex social situations that they inhabit."

AVOCATIONAL INTERESTS: Peace and quiet.

BIOGRAPHICAL/CRITICAL SOURCES: *Observer,* July 11, 1965, January 2, 1983; *Spectator,* July 23, 1965; *New York Times Book Review,* August 1, 1965, February 6, 1983, November 20, 1983; *Times Literary Supplement,* September 12, 1965, January 1, 1982; *Time,* July 17, 1978; *New York Times,* February 8, 1981.

* * *

KERENSKY, Oleg 1930-

PERSONAL: Born January 9, 1930, in London, England; son of Oleg Alexander (a chartered civil engineer) and Nathalie (Bely) Kerensky. *Education:* Christ Church, Oxford, B.A. (with honors), 1951, M.A., 1953. *Home:* 110 Bank St., New York, N.Y. 10014.

CAREER: British Broadcasting Corp. (BBC), London, England, sub-editor for BBC News, 1953-55, diplomatic correspondent, 1955-63, deputy editor of *Listener,* 1963-68; *Daily Mail,* London, ballet critic, 1957-71; *New Statesman,* London, ballet critic, 1968-79; *International Herald Tribune,* Paris,

France, London ballet critic, 1971-79; New York correspondent for *Stage*, 1979—.

WRITINGS: *World of Ballet*, Coward, 1970 (published in England as *Ballet Scene*, Hamish Hamilton, 1970); *Anna Pavlova*, Dutton, 1973; *The New British Drama*, Hamish Hamilton, 1977; *The Guiness Guide to Ballet*, Guiness Superlatives, 1981. Contributor to *Times* (London), *Guardian, Dancing Times*, and other publications.

SIDELIGHTS: Oleg Kerensky, grandson of Alexander Fedorovitch Kerensky, prime minister of Russia in 1917, is "very interested in Soviet affairs and politics generally." His interests extend to all aspects of the theater, including opera.

About *The Guiness Guide to Ballet*, Julie Kavanaugh of the *Times Literary Supplement* comments that the book "provides good, basic information" on the international ballet world. While the reviewer criticizes both the photographs and the chapter on critics, she states that "the value of Kerensky's book lies in its compression and accessibility."

BIOGRAPHICAL/CRITICAL SOURCES: *New Statesman*, September 18, 1970; *Times Literary Supplement*, June 25, 1982.

* * *

KETCHUM, William C(larence), Jr. 1931-

PERSONAL: Born March 29, 1931, in Columbia, Mo.; son of William Clarence and Mildred Ann (Roberts) Ketchum; married Erica Stoller, August 9, 1982; children: Rachael Forbes, Aaron Roberts. *Education:* Union College and University, Schenectady, N.Y., B.A., 1953; Columbia University, J.D., 1956. *Home:* 241 Grace Church St., Rye, N.Y. 10580. *Office:* New School for Social Research, New York, N.Y. 10011.

CAREER: Member of Bar of State of New York; attorney with law firms in New York City, prior to 1969; Civil Court, New York City, attorney, 1969-76; New School for Social Research, New York City, instructor in fine arts, 1971—. *Military service:* U.S. Naval Reserve, active duty, 1956-60; became lieutenant. *Member:* New York Historical Society, New York State Bar Association, Association of the Bar (New York City). *Awards, honors:* Ambassador of Honor book award, English Speaking Union, 1983, for *American Folk Art of the 20th Century*.

WRITINGS: *Early Potters and Potteries of New York State*, Funk, 1970; *The Pottery and Porcelain Collector's Handbook*, Funk, 1971; *American Basketry and Woodenware*, Macmillan, 1974; *A Treasury of American Bottles*, Bobbs-Merrill, 1975; *Hooked Rugs*, Harcourt, 1976; *The Catalog of American Antiques*, Rutledge Books, 1977; *The Catalog of American Collectibles*, Mayflower Books, 1979; *Collecting American Craft Antiques*, Dutton, 1980; *Auction*, Sterling, 1980; *Western Memorabilia*, Hammond, 1980; *Toys and Games*, Smithsonian Institution, 1981; *Furniture*, Volume II: *Post Federal*, Smithsonian Institution, 1981; *The Catalog of World Antiques*, Rutledge Books, 1981; *Boxes*, Smithsonian Institution, 1982; *American Furniture, Cupboards, Chests and Related Pieces*, Knopf, 1982; *Pottery and Porcelain*, Knopf, 1983; *American Folk Art of the 20th Century*, Rizzoli, 1983.

Contributor to *Western Collector, Spinning Wheel, Antiques Journal, Early American Life*, and *Americana;* also contributor to newsletters *Pontil* and *Pottery Collectors*.

WORK IN PROGRESS: A book on Victorian crafts; a book on international furniture styles.

SIDELIGHTS: William C. Ketchum has had "extensive foreign travel and residence abroad," including Spain, France, the British Isles, Portugal, Italy, Morocco, Switzerland, Canada, Mexico, Chile, Japan, Taiwan, the Philippines, Korea, and Hong Kong. *Avocational interests:* Antique collecting and dealing, fishing, historical research.

BIOGRAPHICAL/CRITICAL SOURCES: *Los Angeles Times Book Review*, December 14, 1980.

* * *

KIESLING, Christopher (Gerald) 1925-

PERSONAL: Surname is pronounced Keys-ling; born August 15, 1925, in Chicago, Ill.; son of Edward Joseph (in advertising) and Florence (Fiset) Kiesling. *Education:* Pontifical Philosophical Faculty of St. Thomas, River Forest, Ill., Ph.L., 1950; University of St. Thomas Aquinas, Rome, Italy, S.T.L., 1956; Pontifical Theological Faculty of Immaculate Conception, Washington, D.C., S.T.D., 1965. *Home:* Dominican Community, 97 Waterman Place, St. Louis, Mo. 63112. *Office:* Aquinas Institute, 3642 Lindell Blvd., St. Louis, Mo. 63108.

CAREER: Entered Order of Preachers (Dominicans), 1947, ordained Roman Catholic priest, 1954; Aquinas Institute of Theology, Dubuque, Iowa, professor of theology, 1956-76; Aquinas Institute, St. Louis, Mo., professor of theology, 1981—. Research fellow, Divinity School, Yale University, 1970-71. Director of formation, Province of St. Albert, 1975-81. Lecturer and retreat master. *Member:* North American Academy of Liturgy, Catholic Theological Society of America, American Society for Eighteenth-Century Studies.

WRITINGS: (Contributor) Reginald Masterson, editor, *Seeking the Kingdom*, B. Herder, 1961; (contributor) Masterson, editor, *Theology in the Catholic College*, Priory Press, 1961; (contributor) T. A. O'Meara and C. D. Weisser, editors, *Paul Tillich in Catholic Thought*, Priory Press, 1964; *Before His Majesty*, Aquinas Library, 1965; *The Spirit and Practice of the Liturgy*, Priory Press, 1965.

The Future of the Christian Sunday, Sheed, 1970; (contributor) James Michael Lee and Patrick C. Rooney, editors, *Toward a Future for Religious Education*, Pflaum Standard, 1970; *Any News of God?*, Pflaum Standard, 1971; *Confirmation and Full Life in the Spirit*, St. Anthony Messenger Press, 1973; (contributor) Karen Hurley, editor, *Why Sunday Mass?*, St. Anthony Messenger Press, 1973; (contributor) Leonard Swidler and Arlene Swidler, editors, *Women Priests*, Paulist Press, 1977; *Celibacy, Prayer, and Friendship*, Alba House, 1978.

Contributor to *McGraw's New Catholic Encyclopedia for Home and School;* also contributor to numerous religious periodicals, including *Modern Liturgy, New Catholic World, Studies in Formative Spirituality, Worship, Review for Religious, Cross and Crown, Theological Studies, Living Light, Chicago Studies, Journal of Ecumenical Studies*, and *Our Family*. Editor, *Spirituality Today*, 1977—.

WORK IN PROGRESS: A book on liturgy and social justice; a book on theology of religious life.

SIDELIGHTS: Christopher Kiesling told *CA:* "Writing helps me clarify my own stance before the questions which life poses. Through writing I can help others find their way through life. It is very satisfying to learn that someone across the country or on the other side of the world was helped by something I had written."

KINDLEBERGER, Charles P(oor), II 1910-

PERSONAL: Born October 12, 1910, in New York, N.Y.; son of E. Crosby and Elizabeth Randall (McIlvaine) Kindleberger; married Sarah Bache Miles, May 1, 1937; children: Charles P., Richard S., Sarah, E. Randall. *Education:* University of Pennsylvania, A.B., 1932; Columbia University, M.A., 1934, Ph.D., 1937. *Home address:* Bedford Rd., Lincoln, Mass. 01773.

CAREER: Federal Reserve Bank of New York, New York City, researcher in international trade and finance, 1936-39; Federal Reserve System, Washington, D.C., member of board of governors, 1940-42; Joint Economic Committee of the United States and Canada, Washington, D.C., American secretary, 1941-42; Office of Strategic Services, Washington, D.C., American secretary, 1941-42; Office of Strategic Services, Washington, D.C., member of staff, 1942-44, 1945; U.S. Department of State, Washington, D.C., chief of German and Austrian Economic Affairs division, 1945-48; Massachusetts Institute of Technology, Cambridge, Mass., associate professor, 1948-51, professor of economics, 1951-76, professor emeritus, 1976—, chairman of faculty, 1965-67. Member of staff, Bank for International Settlements, 1939-40. *Military service:* U.S. Army, 1944-45; became major; received Bronze Star and Legion of Merit. *Member:* American Academy of Arts and Sciences, American Economic Association (president-elect, 1984), St. Anthony Club, Phi Beta Kappa, Delta Psi.

WRITINGS: *International Short-term Capital Movements,* Columbia University Press, 1937; *The Dollar Shortage,* M.I.T. Press, 1950; *International Economics,* Irwin, 1953, revised edition, 1973; *The Terms of Trade,* M.I.T. Press, 1956; *Economic Development,* McGraw, 1958, revised edition, 1965; *Foreign Trade and the National Economy,* Yale University Press, 1962; *Economic Growth in France and Britain, 1851-1950,* Harvard University Press, 1964; *Europe and the Dollar,* M.I.T. Press, 1966; *Europe's Postwar Growth,* Harvard University Press, 1967; *American Business Abroad,* Yale University Press, 1969; *Power and Money,* Basic Books, 1970; (editor) *The International Corporation,* M.I.T. Press, 1970; (editor) *North American and Western European Economic Policies,* St. Martin's, 1971; *The Great Depression,* University of California Press, 1973; *Economic Response: Comparative Studies in Trade, Finance and Growth,* Harvard University Press, 1978; *Manias, Panics and Crashes: A History of Financial Crises,* Basic Books, 1978; *International Money: A Collection of Essays,* Allen & Unwin, 1981; *A Financial History of Western Europe,* Allen & Unwin, 1984.

BIOGRAPHICAL/CRITICAL SOURCES: *New Statesman,* November 3, 1967.

* * *

KING, Martin
See MARKS, Stan(ley)

* * *

KINGSTON, (Frederick) Temple 1925-

PERSONAL: Born December 30, 1925, in Toronto, Ontario, Canada; son of George Frederick (an Anglican primate) and Florence B. (Brown) Kingston; married Pauline Boyd Smith, June 15, 1951; children: Frederick, Elizabeth, Paul, Rebecca. *Education:* University of Toronto, B.A., 1947, M.A., 1950, L.Th., 1950, B.D., 1952; Oxford University, D.Phil., 1954; University of Basel, postdoctoral study, 1957. *Home:* 833 Kildare Rd., Windsor, Ontario, Canada. *Office:* Canterbury College, University of Windsor, 172 Patricia Rd., Windsor, Ontario, Canada.

CAREER: Anglican clergyman; Anglican College of British Columbia, Vancouver, professor of theology, 1953-59; University of Windsor, Canterbury College, Windsor, Ontario, professor of philosophy, 1959—, principal, 1965—. Visiting professor, Laval University, Quebec, Quebec, 1983. *Military service:* Royal Canadian Naval Reserve, chaplain, 1945—. *Member:* Canadian Philosophical Association, Aristotelian Society, Mind Association, Royal Institute of Philosophy, Humanities Association of Canada. *Awards, honors:* Canada Council fellowship to Oxford University, 1968-69; Cultural Exchange scholarship to France, 1974; Canada Council research grant, France, 1975.

WRITINGS—Published by Canterbury College, University of Windsor, except as indicated: *French Existentialism: A Christian Critique,* University of Toronto Press, 1961; (editor) *Anglicanism and Principles of Christian Unity,* 1972; (editor) *Anglicanism and Contemporary Social Issues,* 1973; (editor) *The Church and Industry,* 1974; (contributor) Gilbert Ryle, editor, *Contemporary Aspects of Philosophy,* Ariel Press, 1976; (editor) *The Church and the Arts,* 1977; (editor) *Anglicanism and the Essentials of the Faith,* 1978; (editor) *Anglicanism and the Lambeth Conference,* 1978; (editor) *Living Christian Spirituality,* 1978; (editor) *The Reality of God in the Contemporary World,* 1982. Also editor of *The Church and Ethics in Public Life,* 1975; author of *On the Importance of Residence Life to Higher Education.*

WORK IN PROGRESS: *George Berkeley: Doctrine of Spirit; Contemporary French Philosophy; Philosophy of Dialog: Cultures of Ontario and Quebec.*

* * *

KIRCHNER, Audrey Burie 1937-

PERSONAL: Born August 23, 1937, in Lancaster, Pa.; daughter of John Sawyer (a contractor) and Florence (Snyder) Burie; married Leo J. Kirchner (in industrial sales), April 23, 1977. *Education:* Millersville State College (now University), B.S.Ed., 1959, M.Ed., 1961; University of Maryland, doctoral study, 1977—. *Politics:* Republican. *Religion:* Roman Catholic. *Home:* 668 West Vine St., Lancaster, Pa. 17603. *Office:* Jenkins School, Millersville State University, Millersville, Pa. 17551.

CAREER: Millersville State University, Millersville, Pa., 1962—, began as associate professor, currently professor of education, teacher at Jenkins School for Children, 1962—. *Member:* Association for Childhood Education International, International Reading Association, Council for Exceptional Children, National Association for the Education of Young Children, Millersville State University Faculty Association.

WRITINGS: (With Mary Ann Heltshe) *Reading with a Smile,* Acropolis Books, 1975; *Basic Beginnings,* Acropolis Books, 1979; *Encounters with Joy,* Acropolis Books, 1984; *Giggles, Smiles and Crocodiles,* Acropolis Books, 1984. Contributor to education journals.

SIDELIGHTS: Audrey Burie Kirchner writes: "I have loved working with young children. Each day in the classroom has been exciting and I am deeply satisfied as I watch these children grow to adulthood. My writings are an attempt to share workable, successful learning activities with other teachers and the college students I teach."

* * *

KISH, Kathleen Vera 1942-

PERSONAL: Born June 21, 1942, in Trenton, N.J.; daughter of Stephen E. (an engineer) and Veronica J. (Lupsa) Kish. *Education:* University of California, Berkeley, B.A., 1964; University of Wisconsin—Madison, M.A., 1965, Ph.D., 1971. *Home:* 5723-B Bramblegate Rd., Greensboro, N.C. 27409. *Office:* Department of Romance Languages, University of North Carolina, Greensboro, N.C. 27412.

CAREER: University of North Carolina at Greensboro, lecturer, 1969-71, assistant professor, 1971-76, associate professor, 1976-83, professor of Spanish, 1983—. *Member:* International Courtly Literature Society, Asociacion Internacional de Hispanistas, Modern Language Association of America, Hispanic Society of America (corresponding member), American Society for Eighteenth-Century Studies, American Association of Teachers of Spanish and Portuguese, Renaissance Society of America, Society for Spanish and Portugese Historical Studies, South Atlantic Modern Language Association (chairman of Spanish section, 1976), University of North Carolina at Greensboro Musical Arts Guild, University of California Alumni Association, Phi Beta Kappa, Alpha Mu Gamma, Sigma Delta Pi. *Awards, honors:* Fulbright fellowship to Madrid, 1966-67; National Endowment for the Humanities grant, 1979.

WRITINGS: An Edition of the First Italian Translation of the "Celestina," University of North Carolina Press, 1973; (contributor) Alan M. Gordon and Evelyn Rugg, editors, *Actor del Sexto Congreso Internacional de Hispanistas,* University of Toronto, 1980; (contributor) Gilbert Paolini, editor, *La Chispa '81,* Tulane University, 1981; (contributor) Beth Miller, editor, *Women in Hispanic Literature: Icons and Fallen Idols,* University of California Press, 1983; (editor and author of introduction with Ursula Ritzenhoff) Christof Wirsung, *Ain Hipsche Tragedia (1520) and Ainn Recht Liepliches Buchlin (1534),* Georg Olms Verlag, 1983. Contributor to language, literature, and Spanish studies journals. Editorial assistant for *Romance Philology,* 1964; member of editorial board of *Celestinesca,* 1977—; editor of *La Coronica,* 1979-81.

WORK IN PROGRESS: Studying translations and stage adaptations of *La Celestina;* research on the Spanish ballad tradition, parallelism in medieval verse, and eighteenth-century Spanish poetry.

SIDELIGHTS: Kathleen Vera Kish writes: "Currently, my motivation springs from within, although my students provide important positive reinforcement. Fellowships and research grants are equally significant; without them day-to-day duties can stifle research and writing." She has studied Spanish, French, Italian, German, Latin, Russian, Arabic, and Portuguese, and has traveled in Spain, the rest of Europe, Tunisia, Venezuela, and South Africa.

* * *

KLAAS, Joe 1920-

PERSONAL: Surname is pronounced "class"; born March 24, 1920, in San Francisco, Calif.; son of Otto Henry (a transportation executive) and Isabel Emma (Schwesinger) Klaas; married Betty Jane Stanley, June 8, 1947; children: Marc, Anthony, Marianna, Juliet, Jonathon, Elizabeth. *Education:* University of Washington, B.A., 1946, M.A., 1952. *Politics:* Democrat. *Religion:* "God." *Office address:* P.O. Box 222614, Carmel, Calif. 93922.

CAREER: Alaska Broadcasting System, Anchorage, news director, 1947-49; KUJ, Walla Walla, Wash., program director, 1949-50; Fisher Broadcasting Co., Seattle, Wash., account executive, 1954-56; KITO, San Bernardino, Calif., general manager, 1957-59; Crowell-Collier Broadcasting Co., Oakland, Calif., sales manager, 1959-61; Churchill Broadcasting Co., San Francisco, Calif., account executive, 1961-67; American Broadcasting Co., San Francisco, account executive, 1967-79. Talent scout and screenwriter for Mardi Gras Productions, 1957-59. Member, Twelve Step House, San Francisco. *Military service:* Royal Air Force, pilot, 1941-42; became sergeant; received Distinguished Service Medallion. U.S. Army Air Forces, 1942-45; became lieutenant colonel; received Air Medal with five oak leaf clusters, Purple Heart. U.S. Air Force Reserve, 1945-70. *Member:* Authors Guild, Alcoholic Rehabilitation Association (member of board of directors), Sigma Delta Chi.

WRITINGS: Maybe I'm Dead, Macmillan, 1955; (contributor) *American Men at Arms,* Little, Brown, 1967; *Amelia Earhart Lives: A Trip through Intrigue to Find America's First Lady of Mystery,* McGraw, 1970; *Vlucht door de hell,* Elsevier, 1980; *Twelve Steps to Happiness: A Handbook for All Twelve-Steppers,* Hazelden Foundation, 1982; *De Manzaner affaire,* Elsevier, 1983. Author of record album, "Twelve Steps: The Road to Recovery, Serenity and Happiness," Hazelden Foundation, 1980.

WORK IN PROGRESS: A novel, *Aufwiedersehen, Mein Fuherer.*

SIDELIGHTS: Joe Klaas has traveled widely in England, France, Belgium, Germany, Czechoslovakia, Hungary, Austria, Switzerland, Italy, Spain, Tunisia, Algeria, Morocco, Poland, China, the Netherlands, Mexico, Canada, Alaska, Central America, and islands in the South Pacific. He told *CA:* "[I] firmly believe that each of us can turn his will and his life over to the care of God and thereby achieve the freedom to do everything he wants to do. When you do what you want to do, you are a success. I believe everyone should do what he wants to do in total freedom. Any compromise of one's own wants is failure. Most people, starting with childhood, form a pattern of turning themselves down, which is a habit of failure. I do what I want to do and am free and successful. I fought for freedom, gave up to God, and won it."

AVOCATIONAL INTERESTS: Skin diving, riding horses.

* * *

KLEEBERG, Irene (Flitner) Cumming 1932-

PERSONAL: Born April 21, 1932, in Chicago, Ill.; daughter of James Coale (an advertising executive) and Elsie (a professional volunteer; maiden name, Battin) Cumming; married Fred Martin Kleeberg (a printing consultant), October 20, 1957; children: John Martin, Margaret Anne. *Education:* Wellesley College, B.A., 1954. *Politics:* "Registered Democrat, Socialist at heart." *Religion:* Humanist.

CAREER: Thames Advertising Service Ltd., London, England, copywriter, 1954-55; L. Bamberger & Co., Newark, N.J., buyer, 1955-56; *Women's Wear Daily,* New York City, editor,

1956-58; American correspondent for several British trade publications, beginning 1958; *Homesewing Trade News,* New York City, fashion and education editor, beginning 1971. Volunteer, New York City Commission for the United Nations and Consular Corps, 1966—; chairman, Seventeenth Precinct Community Council (police department), 1966-68; member of board of directors, International Community Center, 1973—; member of acquaintanceship committee, New York Wellesley Club, 1973—. *Member:* Authors Guild, Authors League of America, Women's Fashion Fabrics Association (vice-president), Embroiderer's Guild of Great Britain, Danish Handicraft Guild. *Awards, honors:* Certificate of Merit from the police department, City of New York; Certificate of Appreciation from the City of New York.

WRITINGS: Make Your Own Pants and Skirts, Bantam, 1971, revised edition, 1972; *Making School Clothes for Boys and Girls,* Bantam, 1971; *The Blue Jeans Book,* Bantam, 1972; (translator) Rob Herwig, *128 House Plants You Can Grow,* Macmillan, 1972; *Fashion Tops,* Drake, 1973; *Bicycle Repair,* F. Watts, 1973; *Sewing for Bazaars,* Bantam, 1974.

(Editor) *The Butterick Fabric Handbook: A Consumer's Guide to Fabrics for Clothing and Home Furnishings,* Butterick Publishing, 1975; *Bicycle Touring,* F. Watts, 1975; *The Butterick Home Decorating Handbook: A Consumer's Guide to Selecting, Purchasing, and Caring for Home Furnishings,* Butterick Publishing, 1976; *Christianity,* F. Watts, 1976; (editor with R. Patrick Cash) *The Management of Fashion Merchandising: A Symposium,* National Retail Merchants Association, 1977; *The Home Energy Saver: All the Facts You Need to Save Energy Dollars,* Butterick Publishing, 1977; (editor) Rite van der Klip, *Crochet,* Two Continents Publishing, 1977; *Going to Camp,* F. Watts, 1978; *The Moving Book: How Not to Panic at the Thought,* Butterick Publishing, 1978. Contributor of articles to *Women's Wear Daily, Baby Talk, Stores Magazine,* and numerous other trade publications.

WORK IN PROGRESS: Translation from the Dutch of a book on dominoes; research on college admissions procedures.

SIDELIGHTS: As a volunteer for the New York City Commission for the United Nations and Consular Corps, Irene Cumming Kleeberg helps newly arrived foreign diplomats and their families with their adjustment to the city of New York. She is competent in French and Dutch, and knows some Italian and Spanish.†

* * *

KNAPPER, Christopher (Kay) 1940-

PERSONAL: "K" in surname is silent; born March 4, 1940, in Crewe, England; son of Harold Alfred Kay (a tool-fitter) and Hilda (Nevitt) Knapper. *Education:* University of Sheffield, B.A. (honors), 1961; University of Saskatchewan, Ph.D., 1969. *Politics:* Socialist. *Religion:* Atheist. *Home:* 630 Rockway Dr., Kitchener, Ontario, Canada N2G 3BA. *Office:* Teaching Resource Office, University of Waterloo, Waterloo, Ontario, Canada N2L 3GI.

CAREER: Cutlery Research Council, Sheffield, England, editorial, information, and liaison officer, 1961-62; University of Sheffield, Sheffield, independent research worker in department of psychology, 1962-66; University of Regina, Regina, Saskatchewan, instructor and special lecturer, 1966-69, assistant professor, 1969-71, associate professor, 1971-76, professor of psychology, 1976, chairman of department, 1969-76; University of Waterloo, Waterloo, Ontario, professor of psychology and environmental studies and teaching resource person, 1977—. University of Regina, co-chairman of M.A. program in communications, 1971-72, chairman of advisory committee to School of Social Work, 1971-73, adjunct professor of psychology, 1978-80. Canada Council, referee of research grant applications, 1972-75, member of doctoral fellowship selection committee, 1975, chairman of committee, 1976. Visiting scientist, University of Lethbridge, 1973, and University of Osaka, 1982. Research fellow, University of Waikato (New Zealand), 1974; visiting fellow, Western Australian Institute of Technology, 1982. Member of committee on teaching and learning, Council of Ontario Universities, 1978-80.

MEMBER: International Association of Applied Psychology, British Psychological Society (fellow), Canadian Psychological Association, Canadian Association of University Teachers (chairman of professional orientation committee, 1971-73; member of curriculum, research, and education committee, 1971-73; treasurer and chairman of finance and management committee, 1972-73; member of executive committee, 1972-73; member of board of directors, 1972-73, 1974-76; member of teaching effectiveness subcommittee, 1973—; member of academic freedom and tenure committee, 1974-76), Canadian Society for the Study of Higher Education, American Psychological Association (foreign affiliate; visiting scientist, 1973), American Educational Research Association, American Association for Higher Education, Society for the Psychological Study of Social Issues, Psychological Society of Saskatchewan (secretary, 1967-69), Regina Film Society (executive president, 1969-70). *Awards, honors:* Canada Council fellowship for work on psychology of clothes, 1968; Federal Department of Transportation grant, 1973, for investigation of psychological factors in automobile safety; Canada Council research grant, 1973-74, to study teaching effectiveness and training strategies in Commonwealth universities.

WRITINGS: (With Peter B. Warr) *The Perception of People and Events,* Wiley, 1968; (with A. J. Cropley and R. J. Moore) *A Quasi-Clinical Strategy for Safety Research: A Case Study of Attitudes to Seat Belts,* Federal Department of Transportation (Ottawa), 1973; (with Cropley) *Property and Insurance: A Study of Public Opinion,* University of Regina, 1975; (editor) *Scaling the Ivory Tower: Appraising College and University Teaching,* Clarke, Irwin, 1976; (with Cropley) *Social and Interpersonal Factors in Driving,* University of Regina, 1976; (editor with G. L. Geis, C. E. Pascal, and B. M. Shore) *If Teaching Is Important . . . : The Evaluation of Instruction in Higher Education,* Clarke, Irwin, 1977; *The Evaluation of Instructional Technology,* Croom Helm, 1980; (with Shore, S. F. Foster, G. G. Nadeau, N. Neill, and V. Sim) *Guide to the Teaching Dossier: Its Preparation and Use,* Canadian Association of University Teachers, 1980; (editor) *New Directions for Teaching and Learning: Expanding Learning through New Communications Technologies,* Jossey-Bass, 1982; (with L. Gerter and G. Wall) *Energy, Recreation, and the Urban Field,* University of Waterloo, in press.

Contributor: P. Heilmann, editor, *Materialen zur Einfuehrung in die Publizistik-Wissenschaft,* Volume I, Institute of Publicity, Free University of Berlin, 1966; *Proceedings of the First International Conference on Driver Behaviour,* International Drivers' Behaviour Research Association (Paris), 1974; P. Stringer and H. Wenzel, editors, *Transportation Planning for a Better Environment,* Plenum, 1976; D. M. R. Taplin, editor, *Advances in Research on the Strength and Fracture of Material,* Pergamon, 1977; W. H. Ittelson and D. Burkhardt, editors, *Environmental Assessment of Socio-economic Systems,* Plenum, 1978; G. M. Stephenson and J. M. Davis, editors, *Progress in Applied Social Psychology,* Wiley, 1981; M. Argyle, editor, *Social Skills and Work,* Methuen, 1981; B. Sheehan, editor, *New Directions for Institutional Research—Information Technology: Innovation and Applications,* Jossey-Bass, 1982; E. Avedon, editor, *Data-Based Teaching in the Social Sciences,* UNESCO, in press; F. B. Lovis and E. D. Taggs, editors, *Informatics Education for All Students at University Level,* North-Holland Publishing, in press.

Contributor to numerous journals, including *Journal of Social Psychology, British Journal of Social and Clinical Psychology,* and *Canadian Psychologist;* also contributor to magazines and newspapers. Referee, *Canadian Journal of Behavioural Science,* 1974, 1975; abstracter, *Psychological Abstracts.* Editor, *Design in Sheffield,* 1964; member of editorial board, *Canadian Psychology,* 1979-81; guest editor, *International Review of Applied Psychology,* 1980.

WORK IN PROGRESS: A book on lifelong learning and higher education.

SIDELIGHTS: Christopher Knapper wrote *CA:* "Although I am a fairly prolific writer of academic books and papers, I do not really consider this to be 'creative' writing in the sense of writing a poem or novel. I have lately become increasingly interested in writing for a general audience—as opposed to academics, in the hope of communicating ideas and issues to a wider public. It gives me great pleasure to be praised for the clarity and fluency of writing style—even in an academic monograph. A British colleague and I have recently completed a study of academics' approaches to the writing task. I find my own methods quite unusual. I dictate rough notes on a pocket dictaphone (often when walking the five miles to work), and then have a secretary transcribe the tapes on a word processor. I do my own editing on the word processor."

* * *

KNOEPFLE, John 1923-

PERSONAL: Surname pronounced "Know-full"; born February 4, 1923, in Cincinnati, Ohio; son of Rudolph (a salesman) and Catherine (Brickley) Knoepfle; married Margaret Godfrey Sower, December 26, 1956; children: John Michael, Mary Catherine, David Edmund, James Girard (deceased), Christopher Brickley. *Education:* Xavier University, Cincinnati, Ohio, Ph.B., 1947, M.A., 1949; St. Louis University, Ph.D., 1967. *Politics:* Democrat. *Religion:* Catholic. *Office:* Brookens 390, Sangamon State University, Springfield, Ill. 62708.

CAREER: WCET (educational television), Cincinnati, Ohio, producer-director, 1953-55; Ohio State University, Columbus, assistant instructor, 1956-57; Southern Illinois University, East St. Louis, lecturer, 1957-61; St. Louis University High School, St. Louis, Mo., lecturer in English, 1961-62; Maryville College of the Sacred Heart, St. Louis, Mo., assistant professor of English, 1962-66; St. Louis University, St. Louis, Mo., associate professor and director for creative writing, 1967-71; Sangamon State University, Springfield, Ill., professor of literature, 1972—. Also affiliated with Mark Twain Summer Institute, 1962-64, and Washington University College, 1963-66. Consultant to Project Upward Bound, 1965-70. *Military service:* U.S. Navy, 1942-46; became lieutenant junior grade; received Purple Heart. *Member:* Modern Language Association, American Studies Association.

WRITINGS: (Translator with James Wright and Robert Bly) *Twenty Poems of Cesar Vallejo,* Sixties Press, 1961, published as *Neruda and Vallejo: Selected Poems,* Beacon Press, 1971; *Rivers into Islands,* University of Chicago Press, 1965; *Affair of Culture and Other Poems,* Juniper, 1969; *After Gray Days and Other Poems,* Crabgrass Press, 1969; *Songs for Gail Guidry's Guitar,* New Rivers Press, 1969.

The Intricate Land, New Rivers Press, 1970; *Dogs and Cats and Things like That: Poems for Children,* McGraw, 1971; *The Ten-Fifteen Community Poems,* Back Door, 1971; *Our Street Feels Good: Poems for Children,* McGraw, 1972; *Whetstone,* BkMk, 1972; *Deep Winter Poems,* Three Sheets, 1972; *Thinking of Offerings,* Juniper, 1975; *A Box of Sandalwood,* Juniper, 1978; *A Gathering of Voices,* Rook, 1978; (editor with Dan Jaffe) *Frontier Literature: Images of the American West,* McGraw, 1979; *Poems for the Hours,* Uzzano, 1979.

Contributor to anthologies: *From the Hungarian Revolution,* edited by David Ray, Cornell University Press, 1967; *Heartland: Poets of the Midwest,* edited by Lucien Stryk, Northern Illinois University Press, 1967; *Voyages to the Inland Sea,* edited by John Judson, Juniper, 1971; *Regional Perspectives: America's Literary Heritage,* edited by John Gordon Burke, American Library, 1973; *Late Harvest: Plains and Prairie Poets,* BkMk, 1977; *Five Missouri Poets,* edited by Jim Barnes, Chariton Press, 1979; *Prairie Voices: A Collection of Illinois Poets,* edited by Stryk, Illinois Arts Council Foundation, 1980. Also contributor to *Poems at the Gate,* 1964.

SIDELIGHTS: John Knoepfle's poetry speaks of his life in the Midwest. Because Midwestern poets are rarely recognized by modern critics, says Dan Jaffe in *Great Lakes Review,* Knoepfle, who "has been producing poems of enormous resonance," remains generally unknown.

The poet, writes Jaffe, "does not write one or two kinds of poems. One of the indications of his strength is the variety of textures, attitudes, subjects, and tactics found in his poems. He can be cryptically epigrammatic, journalistically surreal, and religiously sardonic. Do those sound like paradoxes? He is a landscape poet and a political poet. At times he searches our history and our folklore, at others creates nightmares. He is a poet of gentleness who probes the inhumane. He lays it out without comment in one poem; the next poem is a riddle. To be sure there is a Knoepfle personality, a quality of language and concern that marks all of the poems, but I hesitate to label it."

BIOGRAPHICAL/CRITICAL SOURCES: Minnesota Review, No. 3, 1968; *Great Lakes Review,* No. 3, 1976; *Focus Midwest,* 14, 1980.

* * *

KOCSIS, Robert
See KOSSEZ, Robes

* * *

KOLB, Harold H(utchinson), Jr. 1933-

PERSONAL: Born January 16, 1933, in Boston, Mass.; son of Harold Hutchinson (a commercial artist) and Ottille (Moss) Kolb; married Jean Burgin, March 9, 1957; children: Kathryn, Lee. *Education:* Amherst College, A.B., 1955; University of Michigan, M.A., 1960; Indiana University, Ph.D., 1968. *Home address:* Route 1, Box 319, Covesville, Va. 22931. *Office:*

Department of English, Wilson Hall, University of Virginia, Charlottesville, Va. 22903.

CAREER: Valparaiso University, Valparaiso, Ind., instructor in English, 1960-62; Indiana University at Bloomington, teaching associate, 1962-65, fellow, 1965-67; University of Virginia, Charlottesville, assistant professor, 1967-70, associate professor, 1970-81, professor of English, 1981—, director of American studies program, 1973—, director and co-director of programs in teaching, 1975—. Guest professor of American studies, University of Bonn, 1982. Instructor and faculty coordinator, American Academy of Judicial Education, 1976-80; director, Canadian judicial writing program, 1981—. Consultant and grant administrator, National Endowment for the Humanities, 1972-81. *Military service:* U.S. Navy, aviator, 1955-59. U.S. Naval Reserve, 1959-76; became commander. *Member:* Modern Language Association of America (regional associate, 1972-74; member of delegate assembly, 1983-86). *Awards, honors:* Summer research faculty fellowships, University of Virginia, 1969 and 1970; Guggenheim fellowship, 1970-71; sesquicentennial associateship, Center for Advanced Studies, University of Virginia, 1976.

WRITINGS: The Illusion of Life: American Realism as a Literary Form, University Press of Virginia, 1969; *A Field Guide to the Study of American Literature,* University Press of Virginia, 1976; *A Writer's Guide: The Essential Points,* Harcourt, 1980; (contributor) Philip Beidler and Sarah Davis, editors, *The Mythologizing of Mark Twain,* University of Alabama Press, 1984; (contributor) Jerry W. Ward, editor, *The New American Literary History,* Modern Language Association of America, 1984.

Contributor of articles on American literature and history, composition, and pedagogy to professional publications, including *Journal of Popular Culture, American Literary Realism, Virginia Quarterly Review, College English,* and *Cresset.*

WORK IN PROGRESS: Mark Twain as Humorist.

* * *

KOPP, Anatole 1915-

PERSONAL: Born November 1, 1915, in St. Petersburg, Russia (now Leningrad, U.S.S.R.); son of Alexandre and Helene (Margulis) Kopp; married Claudine Retail (a lawyer), July 3, 1953; children: Pierre. *Education:* Graduate of Ecole Speciale d'Architecture, Paris, 1936, and Ecole des Beaux Arts, Paris, 1939; Massachusetts Institute of Technology, M.Arch., 1943. *Politics:* "Left." *Religion:* "Jewish origin; no religion." *Home:* 119 rue Notre Dame des Champs, Paris VI, France.

CAREER: Architect and planner, Paris, France, 1953—. Associate member, B.E.R.U. (planning agency), Paris, 1960—; professor in department of planning, University of Paris VIII. *Military service:* French Army, 1939-40; became sergeant. U.S. Army, 1943-45. *Member:* Cercle d'Etudes d'Architecture.

WRITINGS: Ville et revolution, Anthropos, 1967, translation by Thomas E. Burton published as *Town and Revolution: Soviet Architecture and City Planning, 1917-1935,* Braziller, 1970; *Changer la vie—changer la ville,* Union Generale d'Editions (Paris), 1975; *L'Architecture de la periode stalinienne,* Presses Universitaires de Grenoble, 1978; *Architecture et mode de vie: Textes commentes des annees vingt en U.R.S.S.,* Presses Universitaires de Grenoble, 1979; *France, 1945-1955: L'Architecture de la reconstruction—Solutions obligees ou occasions perdues?,* Editions de Moniteur, 1982. Director, *Espaces et Societes* (quarterly).

WORK IN PROGRESS: Research on the architecture and planning of the New Deal period in the United States.

AVOCATIONAL INTERESTS: Photography, Russian contemporary literature and life, the 1930s in American politics and culture.

* * *

KOSSEZ, Robes 1935-
(Robert Kocsis)

PERSONAL: Original name, Robert Kocsis; born September 1, 1935, in South Ozone Park, N.Y.; son of Frank J. and Mary (Ondyke) Kocsis. *Education:* Hofstra College (now University), B.A., 1957. *Home:* 118 West 69th St., New York, N.Y. 10023. *Agent:* Scott Hudson Ltd., 215 East 76th St., New York, N.Y. 10021.

CAREER: Playwright; actor in regional theatres, summer stock, Off-Broadway productions, and tours, 1957—. *Member:* Actors' Equity Guild, Dramatists Guild.

WRITINGS—All unpublished plays; under name Robert Kocsis; "A Dash of Spirits," first produced on the West End at Wyndham's Theatre by Repertory Players, March 22, 1964; "Some Winter Games," first produced at Red Barn Theatre, August 17, 1965; "The Seven Deadly Arts," first produced at Westport (Conn.) County Playhouse, August 14, 1967; "The Wolves" (three-act), first produced at the Washington (D.C.) Theatre Club, January 21, 1970; "A Place without Mornings," first produced in Stratford, Conn., at American Shakespeare Festival, August 18, 1971, produced Off-Broadway at Theatre De Lys, 1972.

Under name Robes Kossez: "Me Jack You Jill," first produced Off-Broadway at Cherry Lane Theatre, 1975, produced on Broadway at John Golden Theatre, 1976; "Red, White and Very Blue," first produced Off-Broadway at Provincetown Playhouse, 1975; "Dracula," first produced on Martha's Vineyard by the Vineyard Players, 1975; "Circus of Dreams," first produced Off-Off Broadway at American Folk Theatre, 1980.

WORK IN PROGRESS: "Along Came a Spider" and "A Family Matter."

SIDELIGHTS: "The Wolves" has also been produced throughout Germany and Austria from 1971-81.

BIOGRAPHICAL/CRITICAL SOURCES: Washington Post, January 23, 1970; *Variety,* February 18, 1970.

* * *

KOVRIG, Bennett 1940-

PERSONAL: Born September 8, 1940, in Budapest, Hungary; married Marina Kuchar (a teacher), June 10, 1967. *Education:* University of Toronto, B.A., 1962, M.A., 1963; University of London, Ph.D., 1967. *Home:* 48 Wilgar Rd., Toronto, Ontario, Canada. *Office:* Department of Political Science, University of Toronto, Toronto, Ontario, Canada.

CAREER: University of Toronto, Toronto, Ontario, assistant professor, 1968-70, associate professor, 1970-74, professor of political science, 1974—, chairman of department of political science, 1979—. *Member:* Canadian Institute of International Affairs, Canadian Political Science Association.

WRITINGS: *The Hungarian People's Republic*, Johns Hopkins Press, 1970; (contributor) Peter A. Toma, editor, *The Changing Face of Communism in Eastern Europe*, University of Arizona Press, 1970; *The Myth of Liberation: East-Central Europe in U.S. Diplomacy and Politics since 1941*, Johns Hopkins University Press, 1973.

(Contributor) Charles Gati, editor, *The International Politics of Eastern Europe*, Praeger, 1976; *Communism in Hungary from Kun to Kadar*, Hoover Institution, 1979; (contributor) Teresa Rakowska-Harmstone and Andrew Gyorgy, editors, *Communism in Eastern Europe*, Indiana University Press, 1979; (contributor) Milorad M. Drachkovitch, editor, *East Central Europe: Yesterday, Today, Tomorrow*, Hoover Institution, 1982; (contributor) N. F. Dreisziger and others, editors, *Struggle and Hope: The Hungarian-Canadian Experience*, McClelland & Stewart, 1982.

Author of annual chapter in Richard F. Starr, editor, *Yearbook on International Communist Affairs*, Hoover Institution, 1972-82. Contributor to *International Journal*, *Historical Journal*, and *Survey*.

WORK IN PROGRESS: Several studies on Eastern Europe and East-West relations.

* * *

KRAMER, Aaron 1921-

PERSONAL: Born December 13, 1921, in Brooklyn, N.Y.; son of Hyman and Mary (Click) Kramer; married; two children. *Education:* Brooklyn College (now Brooklyn College of the City University of New York), B.A., 1941, M.A., 1951; New York University, Ph.D., 1966. *Politics:* Independent. *Home:* 96 Van Bomel Blvd., Oakdale, N.Y. 11769. *Agent:* John Payne, Lenniger Literary Agency, 437 Fifth Ave., New York, N.Y. 10016. *Office:* Department of English, Dowling College, Oakdale, N.Y. 11769.

CAREER: New York Guild for the Jewish Blind, New York, N.Y., lecturer, 1955-58, dramatics director, 1958-59; high school teacher of English in Bogota, N.J., 1959-61; Dowling College, Oakdale, N.Y., 1961—, began as instructor, associate professor, 1966-70, professor, 1970—, graduate professor of English, 1975-78. Lecturer in English, Queens College of the City University of New York, 1966-68; lecturer in Shakespearean studies, University of Guanajuanto, 1974; guest poetry teacher at many schools and colleges. Originator and director of poetry therapy program, Hillside Hospital, Glen Oaks, N.Y., 1956-60; co-director of poetry therapy program, Cleary School for the Deaf, Ronkonkama, N.Y. and Central Islip State Hospital, 1969-78. Producer of poetry programs on radio; judge of various Poetry Society of America contests, 1948-58; chairman of judges for Reynolds Lyric Award, 1956, and Arthur Davison Ficke Memorial Award, 1957; judge for *Lyric* (magazine) Awards, 1974.

MEMBER: International Academy of Poets, P.E.N. American Center, Edna St. Vincent Millay Society, Dramatists Guild, Authors League of America, American Society of Composers, Authors, and Publishers, Association for Poetry Therapy, Northeast Modern Language Association, Walt Whitman Birthplace Association (trustee, 1980—).

AWARDS, HONORS: Award for New York State Poetry Day prize poem, "Nocturne," 1953; Reynolds Lyric Award of *Lyric* (magazine), 1961, for "Forest Vapors"; *Lyric* (magazine) Award, 1967, for "Cadenza"; Virginia Prize of *Lyric* (magazine) and Hart Crane Memorial Award, 1969, for "A Hundred Planets"; annual American Society of Composers, Authors, and Publishers awards, 1971-81, 1983; Outstanding Educators of America awards, 1971, 1972, 1974; All Nations Poetry Contest Awards, Triton College, 1975, for "For Three Days," "Wedding in Los Angeles," and "Grandparents in London," 1976, for "Three Young Men," 1977, for "At Four Minutes to One," and 1978, for "The Hidden Beach"; University of Michigan Musical Theatre Award, 1978; Memorial Foundation for Jewish Culture fellowship, 1978-79. Musical works and a film incorporating his poetry have won several other prizes.

WRITINGS—Poetry: *Another Fountain*, privately printed, 1940; *Till the Grass Is Ripe for Dancing*, Harbinger House, 1943; *Thru Our Guns*, privately printed, 1945; *The Glass Mountain*, B. Ackerman, 1946; *The Thunder of the Grass*, International Publishers, 1948; *The Golden Trumpet*, International Publishers, 1949; *Thru Every Window*, William-Frederick, 1950; *Denmark Vesey*, privately printed, 1952; *Roll the Forbidden Drums!*, Cameron & Kahn, 1954, reprinted, Rogers Book Service, 1978; (with Saul Lishinsky) *The Tune of the Calliope*, Yoseloff, 1958; *Moses*, O'Hare Books, 1962; *Rumshinsky's Hat*, Yoseloff, 1964; *Henry at the Grating*, Folklore Center, 1968; *On the Way to Palermo*, A. S. Barnes, 1973; *O Golden Lane!*, Dowling College Press, 1976; *Carousel Parkway*, A. S. Barnes, 1980; *The Burning Bush: Poems and Other Writings, 1940-1980*, Cornwall Books, 1983; *In Wicked Times*, Black Buzzard, 1983.

Other books: (With others) *Seven Poets in Search of an Answer*, B. Ackerman, 1944; (translator with F. Ewen) *The Poetry and Prose of Heinrich Heine*, Citadel, 1948; (translator and editor) Morris Rosenfeld, *The Teardrop Millionaire*, Emma Lazarus Federation, 1955; (translator) *Songs and Ballads: Goethe, Schiller, Heine*, O'Hare Books, 1963; (translator) Rainer Maria Rilke, *Visions of Christ: A Posthumous Cycle of Poems*, edited by S. Mandel, University of Colorado Press, 1967; *The Prophetic Tradition in American Poetry: 1835-1900*, Fairleigh Dickinson University Press, 1968; (with others) *Poetry Therapy*, Lippincott, 1969; (translator) *Poems by Abraham Reisen*, Dowling College Press, 1971; (editor) *Melville's Poetry: Toward the Enlarged Heart*, Fairleigh Dickinson University Press, 1972; (compiler) *On Freedom's Side*, Macmillan, 1972; (with others) *Poetry the Healer*, Lippincott, 1973; (with others) *Paumanok Rising*, Street Press, 1980; (with others) *The Mainstreamed Library*, American Library Association, 1982; *Mob Psychology*, F. Watts, in press.

Scripts: "Tell This Blood," music by Lukas Foss, Cleveland Music Festival, 1946; "United Nations Cantata," music by Richard Neumann, American Music Festival, 1947; "When Every Tear Is Turned to Stone," commissioned by United Nations Film Division, 1949; "Ballad of August Bondi," music by Serge Hovey, Brooklyn Academy of Music, 1955; "In Us Lives the Music," Carnegie Hall, 1956; "A Garland of Music," New York Town Hall, 1957; "The Tinderbox," music by Tristram Cary, British Broadcasting Corp., 1957.

(With others) "An Autumn Sequence," music by Donald Swann, British Broadcasting Corp., 1970; "Chelm," music by Eugene Glickman, Garden City Cathedral, 1970; "Neglected Poems of Herman Melville," British Broadcasting Corp., 1973; "The Ghost of Amsterdam," music by Pauline Konstantin, Nassau Community College, 1976; (translator) "The Emperor of Atlantis," music by Viktor Ullmann, San Francisco Opera, 1977; "Rain Song," music by Michael Cherry, Columbia University concert, Siena, Italy, 1977; "Heavenly Express," music by

Arnold Black, WQXR, 1977; "Five Songs of Death and Life," music by Eugene Glickman, Carnegie Hall, 1977; "Death Takes a Holiday," British Broadcasting Corp., 1979; "Moses the Emancipator," Wilshire-Ebell Theatre, Los Angeles, Calif., 1979; (author of lyrics) "The Beautiful Dream of Ilya Ilyich Oblomov," book by John Barnes, music by Black, abridged version produced in Waterford, Conn., at Eugene O'Neill Theatre Center, 1983.

Reader of his own and other works for "Serenade," a Folkways album and "On Freedom's Side: The Songs and Poems of Aaron Kramer," a Freneau album; recorded some of his poetry for Library of Congress, 1982. Poems have been used as texts by many composers and choreographers. Work anthologized in *From Goethe to Ibsen, Poems of the United Nations, The Jews in the United States, Lift Every Voice, Treasury of Jewish Poetry,* and other collections.

Contributor to journals and newspapers, including *Carleton Miscellany, Massachusetts Review, Prairie Schooner, San Francisco Review, Midstream, Mediterranean Review, Modern Poetry Studies, Journal of Humanistic Psychology, Denver Quarterly, Kenyon Review, Poet Lore, New England Review, Psychiatry, New York Times,* and *Poetry Northwest;* former staff contributor to *Harlem Quarterly, Sing Out,* and *Village Voice;* co-editor of *West Hills Review: A Whitman Journal,* 1979—. Member of editorial board, Cross-Cultural Communications, 1979—.

WORK IN PROGRESS: To Nineveh!, an anthology of Yiddish social poetry; with L. Buck, *To Break the Silence,* essays on poetry for the disabled; *Yiddish Lullabies,* an anthology of translations, for Shalom Verlag; translating and editing *The Poems of Ingeborg Bachmann,* with S. Mandel.

SIDELIGHTS: Aaron Kramer told *CA:* "My advice [to aspiring writers] is as it has been for every workshop I've conducted. First off, the aspiring writer should consider what it is to which he aspires. If the goal is publication, then he should research the field thoroughly and bend all his efforts toward creating the sort of work that is currently accepted. If a second goal is to win critical approval, literary prizes, and representation in anthologies, then he should carefully study the influential reviewers and adopt the kind of writing which most consistently wins awards and is anthologized.

"If, on the other hand, he aspires to achieve his own voice, even though it has a currently unpopular 'ring' (for example, if his mode is the rhymed stanza)—if his goal is visionary or prophetic, if his preference is for clarity, melody and expansiveness rather than allusive density, harshness and extreme condensation—then he must be prepared, in the exclusive club of twentieth-century American poetry, to go unpublished or, if published by some miracle, to remain largely unnoticed. A vicious two-inch comment in *Choice* may, in fact, represent the peak of his public career!

Kramer adds that he has "been influenced by such poets as Walt Whitman, Emily Dickinson, Herman Melville, and Gerard Manley Hopkins, in terms not of their technique but their spirit. Although they would have enjoyed an appreciative audience, they were willing either to publish their own work or to go unpublished through life. These are among my heroes, and I consider it no accident that a later time has awarded each of them the prizes and praises to which they did not aspire."

KRANZLER, George G(ershon) 1916-
(Gershon Kranzler; Jacob Isaacs, a pseudonym)

PERSONAL: Born January 27, 1916, in Stuttgart, Germany (now West Germany); son of Meyer L. and Hanna (Adler) Kranzler; married Trude Neuman, December 4, 1944; children: Harvey, Chani, Elliot M., Shari. *Education:* Columbia University, M.A., 1943, Ph.D., 1954; University of Wuerzburg, Ph.D., 1948. *Religion:* Jewish. *Home:* 6701 Park Heights Ave., Baltimore, Md. 21215. *Office:* Department of Sociology, Towson State University, Baltimore, Md. 21204.

CAREER: High school principal in New York, N.Y., and Baltimore, Md., 1945-65; Towson State University, Baltimore, professor of sociology, 1966—. Part-time instructor at Johns Hopkins University, Evening College, 1967—. *Member:* American Sociological Association, National Education Association, National Association of Secondary School Principals, Society of Education, American Association of University Professors. *Awards, honors:* Seltzer-Brodsky Prize, 1967, for *The Face of Faith: An American Hassidic Community.*

WRITINGS: Williamsburg, U.S.A., Volume I: *Williamsburg, a Jewish Community in Transition: A Study of the Factors and Patterns of Change in the Organization and Structure of a Community in Transition,* Feldheim, 1961, Volume II: *The Face of Faith: An American Hassidic Community,* Baltimore Hebrew College Press, 1972; *The Broken Bracelet: A Historical Novel for Young Jews,* Merkos L'Inyonei Chinuch, 1967; *Yoshko the Dumbbell, and Other Stories,* Feldheim, 1969; *The Secret Code, and Other Stories for Boys,* Merkos L'Inyonei Chinuch, 1971; *Seder in Herlin, and Other Stories for Girls,* Merkos L'Inyonei Chinuch, 1971.

Contributor: *Hebrew School Education,* Mesorah Publications, 1970; *The Torah Personality,* Mesorah Publications, 1980; *Dimensions of the Orthodox Jewish Community,* Ktav, 1981; *Holocaust,* Mesorah Publications, 1981; *The Best of "Our World,"* Mesorah Publications, 1981.

Under name Gershon Kranzler: *Jewish Youth Companion: Stories, Games, and Adages for the Jewish Year,* Merkos L'Inyonei Chinuch, 1957, revised and enlarged edition, 1984; *Galuth Melodies: Stories for Young and Old,* three volumes, 3rd edition, Merkos L'Inyonei Chinuch, 1957, 4th edition, 1971; (with Nissan Mindel) *Who, What, When, Where: Interesting Facts from Jewish History, Law, and Lore,* Merkos L'Inyonei Chinuch, 1959; *The Golden Shoes, and Other Stories,* Feldheim, 1960; *At B.A.T.T.,* Merkos L'Inyonei Chinuch, 1978; *The Silver Matzoth,* Feldheim, 1981.

Also author, under pseudonym Jacob Isaacs, of *Our People,* five volumes, published by Merkos L'Inyonei Chinuch. Contributor of chapters to books and numerous articles to periodicals.

WORK IN PROGRESS: People of Faith and *A Generation Later,* Volumes III-IV of *Williamsburg, U.S.A.;* a textbook, *The Sociology of the Contemporary Jewish Community.*

* * *

KRANZLER, Gershon
See KRANZLER, George G(ershon)

* * *

KRIEGEL, Leonard 1933-

PERSONAL: Born May 25, 1933, in Bronx, N.Y.; son of Fred

and Sylvia (Breittholz) Kriegel; married Harriet May Bernzweig, August 24, 1957; children: Mark Benjamin, Eric Bruce. *Education:* Hunter College (now Hunter College of the City University of New York), B.A., 1955; Columbia University, M.A., 1956; New York University, Ph.D., 1960. *Residence:* New York, N.Y. *Agent:* Elaine Markson Literary Agency, 44 Greenwich Ave., New York, N.Y. 10011. *Office:* Department of English, City College of the City University of New York, New York, N.Y. 10033.

CAREER: Long Island University, Brooklyn, N.Y., assistant professor of English, 1960-61; City College of the City University of New York, New York, N.Y., 1961—, began as assistant professor, currently professor of English, Fulbright lecturer, University of Leiden, 1964-65, University of Groningen, 1968-69, University of Paris, 1981. *Awards, honors:* Guggenheim fellow, 1971-72; Rockefeller fellow, 1976.

WRITINGS: (Editor) *The Essential Works of the Founding Fathers,* Bantam, 1964; *The Long Walk Home,* Appleton, 1964; *Edmund Wilson,* Southern Illinois University Press, 1971; *Working Through: An Autobiographical Journey in the Urban University,* Saturday Review Press, 1973; (with Abraham Lass) *Stories of the American Experience,* New American Library, 1973; *Notes for the Two Dollar Window,* Dutton, 1976; *Of Man and Manhood,* Hawthorn, 1979; *Quitting Time* (novel), Pantheon, 1982.

WORK IN PROGRESS: A novel.

SIDELIGHTS: Leonard Kriegel had produced several notable nonfictions, including the sociological study *Of Men and Manhood,* before publishing his first novel, *Quitting Time,* in 1982. The former is an exploration of masculine images and responsibility in modern society. "Our ideas of what a man is . . . no longer sustain us, and they no longer generate belief in our capacity to hand our own sense of manhood on to the next generation," writes Kriegel in the work. The question of mind-body dualism enters the author's argument. "The athlete may be a contemporary hero," Kriegel states, "but he is not necessarily a model of manhood." A man "is not just the sum of his physical effort, after all."

In a *New York Times Book Review* article about *Of Men and Manhood,* Vance Broujaily finds the author "a Socratic teacher, inviting debate, raising questions, offering clarification. He has written a book to be read slowly, in agreement or disagreement, one that provokes a restless urge to amplify."

Quitting Time tells the story of Barney Kadish, labor leader and Communist, who in the 1920s attempts to organize the workers of New York's garment district. Caught up in the emotionally and politically unstable milieu of pre-World War II Manhattan, Barney Kadish, according to Fred Setterberg in a *Nation* review, "cannot answer this question: How is a radical to live in America?" The author, Setterberg continues, "writes beautifully of ordinary people who see history as their personal crucible. He writes with grace about uncommon courage. Most of all, his characters merit our concern; we feel that their risks were worth taking. The story of individual sacrifice and collective achievement is not made to begin or end with the life of Barney Kadish; *Quitting Time* is suffused with the idea of possibility, with hope for another time when the world is 'fresh and open and promising. And we are young enough to change it.'"

BIOGRAPHICAL/CRITICAL SOURCES: Leonard Kriegel, *Of Men and Manhood,* Hawthorn, 1979; *New York Times Book Review,* December 9, 1979; *Nation,* December 22, 1979, May 29, 1982; Kriegel, *Quitting Time,* Pantheon, 1982; *Washington Post Book World,* April 3, 1982.

* * *

KRIESBERG, Louis 1926-

PERSONAL: Born July 30, 1926, in Chicago, Ill.; son of Max (a furrier) and Bessie (Turner) Kriesberg; married Lois Ablin (an anthropologist), 1959; children: Daniel, Joseph. *Education:* University of Chicago, Ph.B. (with honors), 1947, M.A., 1950, Ph.D., 1953; attended summer sessions at Columbia University, 1946, University of California, Berkeley, 1947, and Johns Hopkins University, 1953. *Religion:* Jewish. *Home:* 247 Kensington Pl., Syracuse, N.Y. 13210. *Office:* Department of Sociology, Syracuse University, Syracuse, N.Y.

CAREER: Columbia University, New York, N.Y., instructor in sociology, 1953-56; University of Cologne, Cologne, Germany, Fulbright research scholar, 1956-57; University of Chicago, Chicago, Ill., senior fellow in law and behavioral sciences, 1957-58, research associate and senior study director of National Opinion Research Center, 1958-62; Syracuse University, Syracuse, N.Y., associate professor, 1962-66, professor of sociology, 1966—, chairperson of department, 1974-77, research associate at Youth Development Center, 1962-68. Research associate in International Relations Program, Northwestern University, 1968.

MEMBER: International Sociological Association (member of executive committee, 1982—), International Studies Association, International Peace Research Association, American Sociological Association (chairperson of world conflicts section, 1976), Society for the Study of Social Problems (member of C. Wright Mills Award Committee, 1965-66; chairperson of Committee on Standards and Freedom of Research Publication and Teaching, 1966-67; chairperson of International Tensions Committee, 1969-71; member of board of directors, 1973-76; president, 1983-84), American Association of University Professors, Eastern Sociological Society (member of nominations committee, 1969; member of contributed papers committee, 1973; member of executive committee, 1977-81). *Awards, honors:* Marshall Field fellowship, 1950-51; Ford Research Training fellowship, 1952-53; I. P. Gellman Award from Eastern Sociological Society, 1981.

WRITINGS: (With Seymour S. Bellin) *Fatherless Families and Housing: A Study in Dependency,* Syracuse University Youth Development Center, 1965; (editor and author of introduction) *Social Processes in International Relations: A Reader,* Wiley, 1968; *Mothers in Poverty: A Study of Fatherless Families,* Aldine, 1970; *The Sociology of Social Conflicts,* Prentice-Hall, 1973, 2nd edition published as *Social Conflicts,* 1982; (editor) *Research in Social Movements, Conflicts and Change,* Jai Press, Volume I, 1978, Volume II, 1979, Volume III, 1980, Volume IV, 1981, Volume V, 1983; *Social Inequality,* Prentice-Hall, 1979.

Contributor: Hans L. Zetterberg, editor, *Sociology in the United States of America,* UNESCO, 1956; Ida Harper Simpson and Richard L. Simpson, editors, *Social Organization and Behavior: A Reader in General Sociology,* Wiley, 1964; Perry Bliss, editor, *Readings in Behavioral Sciences and Marketing,* 2nd edition (Kriesberg was not associated with previous edition), Allyn & Bacon, 1967; Howard S. Becker, David Riesman, Blanche Geer, and Robert Weiss, editors, *Institutions and the Person: Essays Presented to Everett C. Hughes,* Aldine, 1968; P. Meadows and E. Mizruchi, editors, *Readings in Urban Sociology,* Addison-Wesley, 1969.

Kenneth E. Boulding, editor, *Peace and the War Industry*, Aldine, 1970, 2nd edition, 1973; Charles V. Willie, editor, *The Family of Black People*, C. E. Merrill, 1970; G. W. Thielbar and S. D. Feldman, editor, *Issues in Social Inequality*, Little, Brown, 1972; L. R. Stuart and L. E. Abt, editor, *Children in Separation and Divorce*, Viking, 1972; W. Heydebrand, editor, *Comparative Organizations*, Prentice-Hall, 1973; Michael Haas, editor, *Behavioral International Relations*, Chandler Publishing, 1974; M. Abrahamson, E. H. Mizruchi, and C. Hornung, editors, *Stratification and Mobility*, Macmillan, 1976; Raj P. Mohan, editor, *Management and Complex Organizations in Comparative Perspectives*, Greenwood Press, 1979; M. Olsen and M. Micklin, editors, *Handbook of Applied Sociology: Frontiers of Contemporary Research*, Praeger, 1981; William M. Evan, editor, *Knowledge and Power in a Global Society*, Sage Publications, 1981; Carolyn M. Stephensen, editor, *Alternative Methods for International Security*, University Press of America, 1982; Burns H. Weston, editor, *Toward Nuclear Disarmament and Global Security*, Westview, 1983.

Also contributor of articles to numerous periodicals, including *American Journal of Sociology, International Social Science Journal, Christian Century, Journal of the American Medical Association, Public Opinion Quarterly, Social Forces*, and *Journal of the American College of Dentists*. Book review editor, *American Journal of Sociology*, 1962; associate editor, *Social Problems*, 1967-69. Member of board of associate editors, *Journal of Voluntary Action Research*, 1976—; member of editorial board of *Journal of Political and Military Sociology*, 1981—, and *Peace and Change: A Journal of Peace Research*, 1981.

WORK IN PROGRESS: An examination of efforts at de-escalating international conflicts using cases from U.S.-Soviet and Israeli-Arab relations.

* * *

KUHLMAN, Kathryn 1910(?)-1976

PERSONAL: Born in Concordia, Mo.; died February 20, 1976, in Tulsa, Okla.; daughter of Joe (the mayor of Concordia) and Emma (Walkenhorst) Kuhlman. *Residence:* Pittsburgh, Pa. *Address:* c/o Bethany Fellowship, Inc., 6820 Auto Club Rd., Minneapolis, Minn. 55438.

CAREER: Kathryn Kuhlman Foundation (religious organization), Pittsburgh, Pa., and Los Angeles, Calif., president, beginning 1954. Originator of daily radio broadcasts throughout the United States and overseas, and of weekly television shows broadcast in United States and Canada, beginning 1966; twenty-two missions have been established by Kathryn Kuhlman Foundation overseas, including missions in Nicaragua, India, Hong Kong, Republic of South Africa, and Viet Nam. Had held public services in United States, and in Sweden and Israel. *Awards, honors:* Medal of Honor from Vietnamese military, 1970; D.H.L. from Oral Roberts University, 1972; recipient of U.S. Capitol Building flag, commemorating twenty-five years of preaching in Pittsburgh, 1972; named a colonel of Kentucky; presented with keys to cities of Pittsburgh and Los Angeles.

WRITINGS—Published by Bethany Fellowship, except as indicated: *I Believe in Miracles*, Prentice-Hall, 1962; (compiler) *God Can Do It Again*, Prentice-Hall, 1969; *Captain Le Vrier Believes in Miracles*, 1973; *Nothing Is Impossible with God*, Prentice-Hall, 1974; *10,000 Miles for a Miracle*, 1974; *How Big Is God?* (juvenile), 1974; *Standing Tall*, 1975; *Never Too Late*, 1975; *From Medicine to Miracles*, 1978; *A Glimpse into Glory*, 1979.

SIDELIGHTS: Kathryn Kuhlman was regarded as one of the foremost "faith healers" of her time. At the height of her success during the 1960s, thousands reportedly flocked to the "miracle services" at which she presided. Although surrounded by controversy—the sick and lame among her followers were said to be suffering only from delusions of their ailments—Kuhlman nonetheless made her career as public as possible, travelling throughout the United States and broadcasting her sermons over radio and television.

Born into a Baptist home in Concordia, Missouri, Kuhlman once said she first felt the calling towards religion at about age thirteen. Calling faith "that quality or power by which the things desired become the things possessed," the evangelist wrote in *I Believe in Miracles:* "You cannot have faith without results any more than you can have motion without movement. . . . Although we trust in the Lord, it is *faith* which has action and power."

BIOGRAPHICAL/CRITICAL SOURCES: Kathryn Kuhlman, *I Believe in Miracles*, Prentice-Hall, 1962; H. K. Hosier, *Kathryn Kuhlman*, Marshall, Morgan & Scott, 1977; J. Buckingham, *Daughter of Destiny*, Pocket Books, 1978.

OBITUARIES: New York Times, February 22, 1976; *Newsweek*, March 1, 1976.†

* * *

KURZ, Mordecai 1934-

PERSONAL: Born November 29, 1934, in Nathanya, Israel; son of Moses and Sarah (Krauss) Kurz; married; children: one. *Education:* Hebrew University of Jerusalem, B.A., 1957; Yale University, M.A., 1958, Ph.D., 1961; Stanford University, M.S., 1960. *Home:* 931 Casanueva Pl., Stanford, Calif. 94305. *Office:* Department of Economics, Stanford University, Stanford, Calif. 94305.

CAREER: Stanford University, Stanford, Calif., research associate of Institute for Mathematical Studies in the Social Sciences, 1961-62, assistant professor of economics, 1962-63; Hebrew University of Jerusalem, Jerusalem, Israel, lecturer, 1963-64, senior lecturer in economics, 1964-66; Stanford University, visiting associate professor, 1966-67, associate professor, 1967-68, professor of economics, 1969—, economic consultant to Stanford Research Institute. Director of economics, Institute for Mathematical Studies in the Social Sciences. Research associate, National Bureau of Economic Research, 1979-82. Consultant to several organizations; special economic consultant to government of Canada. Special economic advisor, President's Commission on Pension Policy, 1978-79. *Military service:* Israeli Armed Forces, 1952-54.

MEMBER: Econometric Society (fellow; member of program committee, 1980; chairman of program committee, 1984), American Economic Association. *Awards, honors:* Ford Management fellow, 1958; Yale University fellow, 1959; Ford Faculty fellow, 1973; Guggenheim fellow, 1977-78.

WRITINGS: Components of Economic Growth of National Output, Stanford Research Institute, 1967; (with K. J. Arrow) *Public Investment, the Rate of Return, and Optimal Fiscal Policy*, Johns Hopkins Press, 1970.

Contributor: (With P. Dhrymes) *Determinants of Investment Behavior*, Universities-National Bureau Conference Series, 1967;

H. W. Kuhn and G. B. Szegoe, editors, *Mathematical Systems Theory and Economics,* Springer-Verlag, 1968; M. Balch, D. McFadden, and S. Wu, editors, *Essays on Behavior under Uncertainty,* North Holland Publishing, 1974; B. Ballasa and R. Nelson, editors, *Economic Progress, Private Values and Public Policy* (essays in honor of William Fellner), North Holland Publishing, 1977; Michael J. Boskin, editor, *Federal Tax Reform,* Institute for Contemporary Studies, 1978; Boskin, editor, *Economics and Human Welfare: Essays in Honor of Tibor Scitovsky,* Academic Press, 1979.

C. Campbell, editor, *Controlling the Cost of Social Security,* American Enterprise Institute, 1982; J. Ronen, editor, *Entrepreneurship,* Lexington Books, 1983; George R. Feiwel, editor, *Trends in Contemporary Microeconomics,* Macmillan, 1983. Also contributor, with A. Hart, to *Forming Coalitions,* 1983. Contributor of numerous articles to economic journals. Associate editor, *Journal of Economic Theory*.

* * *

KYLE, Duncan
   See BROXHOLME, John Franklin

L

LAFFERTY, R(aphael) A(loysius) 1914-

PERSONAL: Born November 7, 1914, in Neola, Iowa; son of Hugh David (an oil-lease broker) and Julia Mary (a teacher; maiden name, Burke) Lafferty. *Education:* Attended University of Tulsa, 1932-33; further study with International Correspondence Schools, 1939-42. *Politics:* Independent. *Religion:* Roman Catholic. *Home:* 1715 South Trenton Ave., Tulsa, Okla. 74120. *Agent:* Virginia Kidd, Box 278, Milford, Pa. 18337.

CAREER: Clark Electrical Supply Co., Tulsa, Okla., buyer, 1935-42, 1946-50, and 1952-71; free-lance writer, 1971—. *Military service:* U.S. Army, 1942-46; became staff sergeant; received New Guinea Campaign Star. *Member:* Authors Guild, Science Fiction Writers of America. *Awards, honors:* Nebula Award nomination, Science Fiction Writers of America, 1968, for *Past Master,* 1970, for *Fourth Mansions,* and 1971, for *The Devil Is Dead;* Hugo Award nomination, World Science Fiction Convention, 1968, for *Past Master;* Phoenix Award, 1971; Hugo Award, World Science Fiction Convention, 1973, for short story "Eurema's Dam"; E. E. Smith Memorial Award, 1973.

WRITINGS—Science fiction novels, except as indicated: *Past Master,* Ace Books, 1968; *The Reefs of Earth,* Berkley Publishing, 1968; *Space Chantey,* Ace Books, 1968; *Fourth Mansions,* Ace Books, 1969.

Nine Hundred Grandmothers (story collection), Ace Books, 1970; *Arrive at Easterwine: The Autobiography of a Ktistec Machine,* Scribner, 1971; (contributor) *Four Futures: Four Original Novellas of Science Fiction,* Hawthorn, 1971; *The Fall of Rome* (historical novel), Doubleday, 1971; *The Flame Is Green* (historical novel), Walker & Co., 1971; (contributor) Robert Silverberg, editor, *New Dimensions II,* Doubleday, 1972; *Okla Hannali* (historical novel), Doubleday, 1972; *Strange Desires* (story collection), Scribner, 1972; *Does Anyone Else Have Something Further to Add?: Stories about Secret Places and Mean Men,* Scribner, 1974; (with Gene Wolfe and Walter Mondy) *In the Wake of Man: A Science Fiction Triad* (novellas), Bobbs-Merrill, 1975.

Funnyfingers and Cabrito (story collection), Pendragon Press, 1976; *Horns on Their Heads* (story collection), Pendragon Press, 1976; *Not to Mention Camels,* Bobbs-Merrill, 1976; *Apocalypses* (contains novellas "Where Have You Been, Sandaliatis?" and "The Three Armegeddons of Enniscorthy Sweeney"), Pinnacle Books, 1977; (contributor) Terry Carr, editor, *Universe 7,* Doubleday, 1977.

(Contributor) Carr, editor, *Universe 10,* Doubleday, 1980; *Aurelia,* Donning, 1982; *Golden Gate and Other Stories,* Corroboree Press, 1982; *Annals of Klepsis,* Ace Books, 1983; *Through Elegant Eyes: Stories of Austro and the Men Who Know Everything,* Corroboree Press, 1983; (contributor) Arthur W. Shea, editor, *The Year's Best Fantasy Stories 9,* DAW Books, 1983; *Ringing Changes* (story collection), Ace Books, 1984.

"The Devil Is Dead" trilogy: *The Devil Is Dead,* Avon, 1971; *Archipelago: The First Book of "The Devil Is Dead" Trilogy,* Manuscript Press, 1979; *More Than Melchisedech,* Donning, 1983.

Contributor of over 150 short stories to *Magazine of Fantasy and Science Fiction, New Mexico Quarterly Review,* and other periodicals.

SIDELIGHTS: R. A. Lafferty is one of those writers, Gerald Jonas of the *New York Times Book Review* believes, "who usually [publishes] under a science fiction label but whose stories stretch the definitions of 'reasonableness' to the breaking point. [Lafferty is really] a teller of tall tales." Often based on absurd or satirical premises, Lafferty's short stories are developed in a logical manner, following their unlikely and humorous premises to their natural conclusion. He has written stories about a speeded-up world in which fads last only a few hours, about a child's shoebox camera that makes things disappear, and about a group of archeologists who unearth an old chimney which not only tells them of the past, but of the present and future as well. Jonas finds that Lafferty writes "a rollicking, never-look-back prose that almost [demands] to be read aloud." "Lafferty's stories," Mary Weinkauf states in *Science Fiction and Fantasy Book Review,* "represent the best in science fiction—whimsical examinations of the notions and obsessions of the most exotic animal [man]."

Lafferty's novels display the same freewheeling inventiveness as do his stories. Speaking of the novel *Aurelia,* Thom Gunn of *Science Fiction and Fantasy Book Review* describes what makes this book different from more conventional works of science fiction. It is, he writes, "decidedly not in the 'hard' SF tradition of gadgetry and physics; this book is rather a whimsical Magical Mystery Tour. [It features] a shifting kaleidoscope of cartoon characters . . . all bopping about a daffy Dali-esque canvas of comic surrealism, a big glittering junkyard of linguistic effects, literalized puns, and overstated symbolism. . . . At its best it is a firework celebration of imagination."

More often, Lafferty combines this comic exuberance with a concern for the eternal struggle between good and evil, approaching this subject from a surprisingly traditional Roman Catholic perspective. But, as Patricia Ower of the *Dictionary of Literary Biography* points out, Lafferty's "vision, despite his Roman Catholicism, does not incline to the positive. It is at best ironic and comic in a black vein." In an article for *Extrapolation,* Dena C. Bain sees Lafferty as "a shaper of myth who . . . bases his mythological pictures on the mystical tradition of the West, and on the attempt of man to transcend the rational and expand his perception of the cosmos." Bain further sees Lafferty as primarily concerned with a theological struggle. "To Lafferty," Bain writes, "the mystical Christian archetypes of good and evil represent the eternal struggle between forces of darkness and light in a dualistic universe, and he creates out of his own beliefs an ethic as well as a cosmology."

In *The Devil Is Dead,* for example, Lafferty chronicles the struggle between two "archetypal groups of dark forces" for control of humanity, Bain writes. These two groups—the "Demons," the descendents of aliens, and the "Elder Race," an ancient group of prehumans—have been battling for centuries and, even though the climactic battle at novel's end is certain to destroy them both, they are destined to rise once again and renew their struggle. Told in a rambunctious style heavily influenced by Irish folktales, the struggle features a menagerie of characters, including a mermaid, a king, and various devils and aliens. The "convoluted plot," Ower writes, "[makes] it difficult for the narrator, Finnegan, and therefore for the reader, to tell exactly who the devil is, who is on which side of the fight, and who is really dead." Ower sees the "strange logic and metamorphoses of the novel" as "most strongly rooted in the world of dreams."

Another Lafferty novel concerned with this theological struggle is *Fourth Mansions,* a novel about "'returnees,' people who reincarnate themselves in order to prevent mankind's breakthrough to a higher plane of existence," as Ower explains. The struggle between the returnees and the "Harvesters," a rival group seeking to push mankind to a higher evolutionary level, is chronicled by Freddy Foley, a reporter investigating the failures of human history. As James Blish writes in the *Magazine of Fantasy and Science Fiction,* the novel's "genre is rare but well known: Heraldic fantasy with a religious intent." Despite its serious intentions, the novel manages to be "a light, entertaining book," Ower states. Blish finds that Lafferty's style is "cadenced without being pseudo-bardic, he relies heavily on extravagant metaphors, and he often bursts into verse, much of it original and all of it good."

In *Past Master,* Lafferty treats the question of religion in another manner, creating the society of Astrobe, a utopian world which has denied the religious side of man's nature and in so doing has destroyed man's essence. Designed in accordance with the ideas of Sir Thomas More, Astrobe finds itself being abandoned by its citizens. They leave the cities, where all of man's traditional fears and wants no longer exist, to live in Cathead, "Astrobe's largest city," explains Harold L. Berger in *Science Fiction and the New Dark Age,* "a monstrous, festering cancer of a city, a sprawl of twenty million ground down by hunger, plague, poisonous stench, and breaking labor, an infernal place of short life and bodies rotting in the streets." The leaders of Astrobe bring Thomas More forward in time to examine their society and suggest a solution to this perplexing situation.

What More finds is that Astrobe has cut man off from his unconscious mind and made all nonmaterial ideas illegal. Religion, superstition, and psychic phenomena, for example, are suppressed. Because of mechanical thought-police who can literally read minds and instantly kill those who think incorrectly, the cities of Astrobe have become inhuman and sterile places to live. As the leaders of Astrobe seek to deny the human unconscious, "the archetypes of the collective unconscious are able to assume physical reality," Bain writes. More finally "allies himself with the rebels of the slums and the group of archetypal figures," Bain states, ". . . and his death at the end of the novel triggers the revolution that will destroy the world and bring about the birth of a new order."

"Though prolific," writes Ower, "[Lafferty] has been neglected, and his lot has been relative obscurity perhaps traceable to the limited appeal of his religious themes." Ower sees this situation changing. Because Lafferty has been praised by other science fiction writers for his "virtues of vitality, absurd vision, and underground humor," Ower believes "these qualities may yet lead to a broad readership for R. A. Lafferty."

Lafferty's "The Devil Is Dead" trilogy was published out of sequence, the first book not finding a publisher until several years after the second was published. A collection of Lafferty's manuscripts is housed at the McFarlin Library at the University of Tulsa.

BIOGRAPHICAL/CRITICAL SOURCES—Books: Harold L. Berger, *Science Fiction and the New Dark Age,* Bowling Green University, 1976; Paul Walker, *Speaking of Science Fiction: The Paul Walker Interviews,* Luna Press, 1978; *Dictionary of Literary Biography,* Volume VIII: *Twentieth-Century American Science Fiction Writers,* Gale, 1981.

Periodicals: *Magazine of Fantasy and Science Fiction,* May, 1968, May, 1971, January, 1972, January, 1976; *Galaxy,* September, 1968, January, 1972, October, 1975; *Punch,* January 1, 1969; *Washington Post Book World,* July 18, 1971, August 13, 1972; *New York Times Book Review,* August 8, 1971, October 3, 1976; *Wall Street Journal,* August 24, 1972; *Booklist,* September 1, 1976; *New York Times,* October 3, 1976; *Spectator,* January 14, 1978; *Times Literary Supplement,* January 17, 1978; *Village Voice Literary Supplement,* May, 1982; *Extrapolation,* summer, 1982; *Science Fiction and Fantasy Book Review,* December, 1982, June, 1983.

—Sketch by Thomas Wiloch

* * *

LAIRD, Dugan 1920-

PERSONAL: Born July 6, 1920, in Rockwell City, Iowa; son of Joseph D. (a farmer) and Viola Dugan (Day) Laird. *Education:* University of Northern Iowa, B.A., 1941; Northwestern University, M.A., 1948, Ph.D., 1952; also attended University of Wyoming and University of Minnesota. *Home:* 9 Willowick Dr., Decatur, Ga. 30038.

CAREER: Emporia State Teachers College (now Emporia State University), Emporia, Kan., instructor in speech and theatre, 1946-47; University of Minnesota, Minneapolis, instructor in public speaking, 1947-48; Northwestern University, Evanston, Ill., instructor in speech, 1948-51; United Air Lines, Chicago, Ill., instructor and training manager, 1952-70; writer, speaker, and consultant, 1970—. Has led conferences and workshops for training and development in Canada, England, Morocco, India, Greece, Germany, and Ireland. *Member:* American Society for Training and Development, National Society for Performance and Instruction. *Awards, honors:* Awards from American Society of Training and Development, 1971, 1976, for contributions to the training profession.

WRITINGS: (With J. R. Hayes) *Level-Headed Letters,* Hayden, 1964; *Business Writing Skills: A Workbook,* Addison-Wesley, 1970; *Training Methods for Skills Acquisition,* American Society for Training and Development and Agency for International Development, 1972; *A User's Look at the Audio-Visual World,* National Audio-Visual Association, 1973, revised edition, 1977.

Approaches to Training and Development, Addison-Wesley, 1978; *Writing for Results: Principles and Practice,* Addison-Wesley, 1978; (with Ruth House) *Training Today's Employees,* CBI Publishing, 1983; (with Lloyd S. Baird and Craig Eric Schneier) *The Training and Development Sourcebook,* Human Resource Development Press, 1983; (with House) *Interactive Classroom Instruction,* Scott, Foresman, 1984.

SIDELIGHTS: Dugan Laird writes that he is "now concerned primarily with adult learning and the science of instruction."

* * *

LAMONT, Marianne
See RUNDLE, Anne

* * *

LANE, Carolyn 1926-

PERSONAL: Born June 4, 1926, in Providence, R.I.; daughter of Harry T. (president of Blocker Air Conditioning Corp.) and Margaret (Breitenfeld) Blocker; married M. Donald Lane, Jr. (an architect), April 28, 1951; children: Jay Donald. *Education:* Connecticut College, B.A., 1948. *Home:* Ward Rd., Salt Point, N.Y. 12578.

CAREER: Author, playwright, illustrator, and artist. Has designed and executed sets for local theatrical organizations. *Member:* Authors Guild, Dramatists Guild, Society of Children's Book Writers, Authors League of America. *Awards, honors:* Community Children's Theatre, Kansas City, Mo., twelfth annual merit award, 1963, and Pioneer Drama Service Award, 1967, both for play "Turnabout Night at the Zoo"; Pioneer's Best Children's Play, 1969, for "The Wayward Clocks"; Theatre Guild of Webster Groves, Mo., One-Act Play Contest, first prize, 1969, for "The Last Grad," second prize, 1980, for "The Scheme of the Driftless Shifter"; Weisbrod One-Act Playwriting Contest, first prize, 1982, for "Cousin Ernestine."

WRITINGS—Children's books: *Uncle Max and the Sea Lion,* Bobbs-Merrill, 1970; *Turnabout Night at the Zoo* (based on play of same title; also see below), Abingdon, 1971; *The Voices of Greenwillow Pond,* Houghton, 1972; *The Winnemah Spirit,* Houghton, 1975; *Princess,* Scholastic Book Services, 1979; *Echoes in an Empty Room,* Holt, 1981; *Princess and Minerva,* Scholastic Book Services, 1981.

Plays: *Turnabout Night at the Zoo* (children's play), Pioneer Drama Service, 1967; *The Wayward Clocks* (children's play), Pioneer Drama Service, 1969; *The Last Grad* (one-act adult drama), Baker's Plays, 1970; *Child of Air* (one-act adult drama), Pioneer Drama Service, 1972; *Tales of Hans Christian Andersen* (children's play), Pioneer Drama Service, 1978; *The Runaway Merry-Go-Round* (children's play), Pioneer Drama Service, 1978; *The World of the Brothers Grimm* (children's play), Pioneer Drama Service, 1979; *The Ransom of Emily Jane* (one-act adult drama), Pioneer Drama Service, 1980; *The Scheme of the Driftless Shifter* (one-act adult), Baker's Plays, 1981. Also author of one-act play, "Cousin Ernestine."

WORK IN PROGRESS: Several children's books; a musical play for children.

SIDELIGHTS: Carolyn Lane wrote *CA:* "I consider writing for children to be both a pleasure and a responsibility. The pleasure is in giving free rein to imaginings and fancies that authors for adults may never enjoy, and in experiencing anew the delights, the sorrows, the excitements of a child's world. It is in writing for children that I keep the child in me forever alive, maintaining the sense of wonder that is often lost to adults. The responsibility is in giving young readers the very best work of which I am capable, in the hope of inspiring an enjoyment of reading that will last a lifetime."

* * *

LANGSTAFF, Nancy 1925-

PERSONAL: Born May 3, 1925, in Brooklyn, N.Y.; daughter of John (a businessman) and Elinor (a pianist; maiden name, Smith) Woodbridge; married John Meredith Langstaff (a writer and teacher), April 3, 1948; children: John Elliot, Peter Gary, Deborah Graydon. *Education:* Vassar College, B.A., 1945; attended Art Students League of New York and Cranbrook Academy of Art, 1946-47; Lesley College, M.A., 1974. *Home:* 9 Burlington St., Lexington, Mass. 02173. *Office:* Lesley College Graduate School, 29 Everett St., Cambridge, Mass. 02238.

CAREER: Teacher at an elementary independent school in McLean, Va., 1955-66; studied and traveled abroad, 1966-69; Cambridge Friends School, Cambridge, Mass., elementary school teacher, 1969-78; Lesley College Graduate School, Cambridge, Mass., core faculty member of Creative Arts in Learning, 1979—. Music teacher to President John F. Kennedy's children at the White House, 1963, and at Wheelock College and Lesley College, 1974-78.

WRITINGS: A Tiny Baby for You (juvenile), Harcourt, 1956; (with husband, John Langstaff) *Jim along Josie* (adult), Harcourt, 1970; *Teaching in an Open Classroom,* National Association of Independent Schools, 1975; *Exploring with Clay,* Early Childhood Education International, 1981. Contributor to *Independent Schools Bulletin.*

WORK IN PROGRESS: Study of ways that active involvement in music can enhance aspects of early reading and language development.

SIDELIGHTS: Nancy Langstaff told *CA:* "An absorption that is evidenced in all my work concerns the exciting potentials for learning that children evidence when encouraged to use their own initiative, responsibility, and creativity."

* * *

LANIER, Alison Raymond 1917-
(G. Alison Raymond)

PERSONAL: Born April 1, 1917, in New York, N.Y.; daughter

of Edward H. (a physician) and Isabel (Ashwell) Raymond; married Albert G. Lanier (a lawyer), September 9, 1967. *Education:* Bryn Mawr College, A.B. (cum laude), 1938. *Home:* 66 Little Brook Rd., Wilton, Conn. 06897.

CAREER: Proxy Parents, New York City, owner and director, 1938-40; Bryn Mawr College, Bryn Mawr, Pa., assistant director of public relations and director of residence hall, 1940-42; International Child Welfare Union, Geneva, Switzerland, co-director in New York office of overseas schools, 1946-50; Pennsylvania Civil Defense Organization, Harrisburg, deputy for eastern area, 1950-54; Committee of Correspondence, New York City, executive director, 1954-61; Carnegie Endowment for International Peace, New York City, director of Hospitality Information Services, 1961-64; employed with Foreign Policy Association, 1965-66; Overseas Briefing Associates, New York City, founder and president, 1967-80. Instructor at New School for Social Research and U.S. Department of State Foreign Service Institute, Washington, D.C.; director of orientation and seminars (at intervals) for Council on Student Travel. Consultant to numerous corporations. Chairman of overseas selection, Girl Scouts of America. *Military service:* U.S. Navy, Women's Reserve, 1942-63; active duty, 1942-46; retired as commander.

MEMBER: International Consultants Foundation, Society for International Education, Training and Research, Society for International Development, American Society for Training and Development, American Association of University Women (member of board).

WRITINGS: (Under name G. Alison Raymond) *Half the World's People,* Appleton-Century-Crofts, 1965; *Living in Europe,* Scribner, 1973; *Living in the U.S.A.,* Scribner, 1973, 6th edition, Intercultural Press, 1981; *China Today: The Family,* Harper, 1974; *China Today: Molding the Mind of a Nation,* Harper, 1974; *Your Manager Abroad: How Welcome? How Prepared?,* American Management Association, 1975; (contributor) *Fodor's Guide to the U.S.A.,* Fodor's, 1976; *Petromarkets '78,* Middle East American Business Conference, 1977; *Overseas Assignment Directory Service,* Knowledge Industry Publications, 1977; *Basic Handbook for International Transfer,* Overseas Briefing Associates, 1978.

"Update" series; published by Overseas Briefing Associates, except as indicated: *Update: Columbia,* 1973; . . . *Netherlands,* 1973; . . . *Egypt,* 1975, 3rd edition, Intercultural Press, 1982; . . . *Indonesia,* 1975, 4th edition, Intercultural Press, 1982; . . . *Iran,* 1975, 2nd edition, 1978; . . . *Japan,* 1975, 5th edition, Intercultural Press, 1981; . . . *Saudi Arabia,* 1975, 4th edition, Intercultural Press, 1981; . . . *Spain,* 1975; . . . *Germany,* 1976, 3rd edition, Intercultural Press, 1980; . . . *Hong Kong,* 1976, 4th edition, Intercultural Press, 1980; . . . *South Korea,* 1976, 5th edition, Intercultural Press, 1981; . . . *Kuwait,* 1976, 3rd edition, Intercultural Press, 1982; . . . *Lebanon,* 1976; . . . *Mexico,* 1976, 4th edition, 1981; . . . *Singapore,* 1976, 4th edition, Intercultural Press, 1982; . . . *Venezuela,* 1976, 5th edition, Intercultural Press, 1981; . . . *Brazil,* 1977, 4th edition, Intercultural Press, 1982; . . . *France,* 1977, 3rd edition, Intercultural Press, 1980; . . . *Nigeria,* 1977, 4th edition, Intercultural Press, 1982; . . . *United Arab Emirates,* 1977, 3rd edition, Intercultural Press, 1982; . . . *Bahrain and Qatar,* 1978, 3rd edition, Intercultural Press, 1982; . . . *Belgium,* 1978, 2nd edition, Intercultural Press, 1980; . . . *Britain,* 1978, 3rd edition, Intercultural Press, 1980; . . . *Iraq,* 1978; . . . *Taiwan,* 1978, 3rd edition published as *Update: Republic of China,* Intercultural Press, 1980, 4th edition, Intercultural Press, 1982.

Also author of feature stories for U.S. Information Agency. Contributor to *Annals of the American Academy of Political and Social Science;* contributor of articles to trade journals.

SIDELIGHTS: Alison Raymond Lanier told *CA:* "My writings—and practically everything else I have done in my life—have been centered primarily on intercultural differences throughout the world as they have developed from differing national and ethnic pasts. I am keenly interested in how such differences affect living and working together in this shrinking (and increasingly interrelated) world.

"I have tried to catch some of the essential factors in books, articles, and corporate briefings in order to help Americans relate more easily to people of other countries, and vice versa.

"Over the years I have organized seminars in thirty-seven countries in Europe, Latin America, the Middle East, Africa, and Asia, and have worked with many thousands of students on international student ships. . . . All of this has been grist to my writing mill."

Half the World's People has been translated into French; *Living in the U.S.A.* has been translated into Japanese, Chinese, French, Portugese, Spanish, and Arabic.

* * *

LASLETT, John H(enry) M(artin) 1933-

PERSONAL: Born May 7, 1933, in Watford, England; son of George H. R. (a minister) and Evelyn (Alden) Laslett; married Barbara R. Tauber (a sociologist), September 26, 1959 (divorced September, 1983); children: Michael, Sarah. *Education:* Oxford University, B.A., 1957, M.A., and D.Phil., 1962; Northwestern University, graduate study, 1958-59. *Office:* Department of History, University of California, Los Angeles, Calif. 90024.

CAREER: University of Liverpool, Liverpool, England, assistant lecturer in political theory and institutions, 1961-62; University of Chicago, Chicago, Ill., assistant professor of social sciences, 1962-64, assistant professor of history, 1964-68; University of California, Los Angeles, associate professor, 1968-75, professor of history, 1975—, joint appointee to Institute of Industrial Relations, 1982-83. *Military service:* British Army, Intelligence, 1952-54. *Member:* American Historical Association, Society for the Study of Labour History. *Awards, honors:* Willett Faculty Research Award, University of Chicago, 1964; Social Science Research Council fellow, 1970-71.

WRITINGS: The Workingman in American Life, Houghton, 1968; *Labor and the Left: A Study of Radical and Socialist Influences in the American Labor Movement, 1881-1924,* Basic Books, 1970; (with Seymour M. Lipset) *Failure of a Dream? Essays in the History of American Socialism,* Doubleday-Anchor, 1974, new edition, University of California Press, 1984; *Reluctant Proletarians: A Comparative History of American Socialism,* Greenwood Press, 1984; *Nature's Noblemen: The Fortunes of the Independent Collier in Scotland and the American Midwest, 1855-1889,* University of California, Los Angeles, Institute of Industrial Relations, 1984. Contributor to history journals.

WORK IN PROGRESS: Research into comparative coal mining communities in Britain and America; research into U.S. working class history and culture; research into immigration.

LASLETT, Peter 1915-
(Thomas Ruffell)

PERSONAL: Born in 1915, in Bedford, England; son of Russell and Eveline (Alden) Laslett; married Janet Clark; children: George Robert. *Education:* Cambridge University, M.A., 1940. *Politics:* Labour. *Office:* Trinity College, Cambridge University, Cambridge, England.

CAREER: British Broadcasting Corp., London, England, producer, 1947-55; Cambridge University, Trinity College, Cambridge, England, reader in politics and history of social structures, 1960—. Founder of the University of the third Asc, 1981—. *Military service:* Royal Navy, 1940-46.

WRITINGS: (Editor) *The Physical Basis of Mind: A Series of Broadcast Talks,* Blackwell, 1950; (editor) *Philosophy, Politics, and Society: A Collection,* Macmillan, 1956, revised and enlarged edition, Barnes & Noble, Volume I, 1963, Volume II (with W. G. Runciman), 1962, Volume III (with Runciman), 1967, Volume IV (with Runciman and Quentin Skinner), 1972, Volume V (with James Fishkin), 1978.

(Editor and author of introduction) John Locke, *Two Treatises on Government: A Critical Edition with an Introduction and Apparatus Criticus,* Cambridge University Press, 1960, 2nd edition, New American Library, 1965; *The World We Have Lost,* Methuen, 1965, 2nd edition, 1971, Scribner, 1966, 2nd edition, 1973, 3rd edition, 1983; (editor) Locke, *The Library of John Locke,* Oxford University Press, 1965, 2nd edition, Clarendon Press, 1971; (editor) *Anglo-American Conference on the Mechanization of Library Services, Brasenose College, Oxford University, 1966,* Mansell, 1967.

(Editor with Richard Wall, and author of introduction) *Household and Family in Past Time: Comparative Studies in the Size and Structure of Domestic Group over the Last Three Centuries in England, France, Serbia, Japan, and Colonial North America, with Further Materials from Western Europe,* Cambridge University Press, 1972; *Family Life and Illicit Love in Earlier Generations,* Cambridge University Press, 1977.

Bastardy and Its Comparative History, Arnold, 1980.

Has also produced "Historical Demography, 1450-1800," B.F.A. Educational Media, 1972.

WORK IN PROGRESS: A book tentatively entitled *Britain! Be Your Own Asc!*

BIOGRAPHICAL/CRITICAL SOURCES: L'Express, October 6, 1969.

* * *

LEAHY, Syrell Rogovin 1935-

PERSONAL: Given and middle names are accented on second syllable; surname is pronounced *Lay*-he; born January 4, 1935, in Brooklyn, N.Y.; daughter of Samuel (an optometrist) and Dora (a teacher; maiden name, Cedar) Rogovin; married Daniel J. Leahy (a professor of mathematics), August 25, 1963; children: Joshua, Melinda. *Education:* Cornell University, B.A., 1956; Phillipps Universitat, graduate study, 1956-57; Columbia University, M.A., 1959, additional graduate study, 1959-61. *Politics:* "Frequently Democrat." *Religion:* Jewish. *Home and office:* 19 Country Squire Rd., Old Tappan, N.J. 07675. *Agent:* Claire Smith, Harold Ober Associates, Inc., 40 East 49th St., New York, N.Y. 10017.

CAREER: Textbook writer in New York City, 1961-62; International Business Machines Corp., Yorktown Heights, N.Y., linguistic researcher, 1962-65; teacher of remedial courses for adults in New York City, 1966-69; American Telephone & Telegraph Co., New York City, writer of training materials, 1970—. *Member:* Linguistic Society of America, Authors Guild, Authors League of America.

WRITINGS: Modern English Sentence Structure, Random House, 1964; *Baby Care,* McGraw, 1966; (with Harry Huffman) *Programmed College English,* McGraw, 1968; *A Book of Ruth* (novel), Simon & Schuster, 1975; *Circle of Love* (novel), Putnam, 1980; *Family Ties* (novel), Putnam, 1982.

WORK IN PROGRESS: A sequel to *Family Ties.*

SIDELIGHTS: Syrell Rogovin Leahy told *CA:* "As writing has become an increasingly important and time-consuming part of my life, I have relinquished more and more of the outside work I used to do. Now I accept only the occasional, short-term job, partly to get out of the house for a brief period to see what the world is doing. What I have learned is that the work that I do—alone and quietly, with only my typewriter and the people I have invented—is the most fun I have ever had."

* * *

LEARY, Edward A(ndrew) 1913-

PERSONAL: Born May 3, 1913, in Bridgeport, Conn.; son of Edward J. (a printer) and Edna (Hill) Leary; married Rosemary Waters, July 4, 1942; married Linda Wohlfeld (an executive with Blue Cross/Blue Shield), March 9, 1961; children: Tim, Karen, Regina, Andrew. *Education:* "Left college the summer of enrollment with a touring stock company," 1943. *Politics:* Independent. *Religion:* "Nonsectarian." *Home:* 7314 Manchester Dr., Apt. A, Indianapolis, Ind. 46260.

CAREER: Ed Leary & Associates (public relations counselors), Indianapolis, Ind., president, 1962-82; Ball State University, Muncie, Ind., instructor in writing for radio and television, 1982—. Creative director and account supervisor of major accounts for advertising agencies in New York, Cleveland, and Chicago. *Military service:* U.S. Army, 1942-45. *Member:* Indianapolis Press Club, Indianapolis Literary Club. *Awards, honors:* Indiana University award, 1967, for *The Nineteenth State, Indiana;* Indiana Press Club award for journalistic excellence, 1976.

WRITINGS: The Nineteenth State, Indiana, E. Leary, 1966, revised edition, Sycamore Press, 1977; *Indianapolis: The Story of a City,* Bobbs-Merrill, 1970; (editor) *Indiana Almanac and Fact Book,* Sycamore Press, 1977; *Pictorial History of Indianapolis,* Downing, 1980; *Enterprise,* Hook Drug Co., 1984; *Do All the Good You Can,* Methodist Hospital of Indiana, 1984.

Also author of filmscript "At Home in Indiana," of scripts for radio series "House of Mystery," and of slide presentations. Former columnist, *Indianapolis Star.*

AVOCATIONAL INTERESTS: Motion pictures, U.S. history (especially the Civil War, 1920's, and New Deal era), radio and TV, Lincoln, U.S. government, ecology, and theater.

SIDELIGHTS: Edward A. Leary told *CA:* "I wish I were not driven to write. It's damned hard work; in fact, the hardest work I do. I agree with Olin Miller who once said: 'Writing is the hardest way of earning a living, with the possible exception of wrestling alligators.'"

LEBEAUX, Richard 1946-

PERSONAL: Born March 2, 1946, in New York, N.Y.; son of Lincoln (a physician) and Thelma (a psychologist; maiden name, Westerman) Lebeaux; married Ellen Abraham (a social worker), October 7, 1973; children: Rachel. *Education:* Middlebury College, A.B. (summa cum laude), 1968; Harvard University, M.A.T., 1970; additional graduate study at Brandeis University, 1970-71; Boston University, Ph.D., 1975. *Religion:* Jewish. *Home:* 955 Marigold Ave., East Lansing, Mich. 48823. *Office:* Department of American Thought and Language, Michigan State University, East Lansing, Mich. 48824.

CAREER: High school English teacher in Needham, Mass., 1969-70; St. Louis Community College at Forest Park, St. Louis, Mo., instructor in American civilization and English, 1975-76; Michigan State University, East Lansing, instructor in American civilization and English, 1975-76, assistant professor, 1976-81, associate professor of American thought and language, 1981—. *Member:* American Studies Association, Modern Language Association of America, College English Association, Thoreau Lyceum, Thoreau Society, Phi Beta Kappa.

WRITINGS: Young Man Thoreau, University of Massachusetts Press, 1977; (contributor) Joel Meyerson, editor, *Studies in the American Renaissance, 1981,* Twayne, 1981; (contributor) Raymond D. Gozzi, editor, *Thoreau's Psychology: Eight Essays,* University Press of America, 1983; *Thoreau's Seasons,* University of Massachusetts Press, 1984; (contributor) Samuel Baron and Carl Pletsch, editors, *Psychology and the Biographer,* International Universities Press, in press. Contributor to *American Examiner.*

WORK IN PROGRESS: Research on the "moratorium" in the lives of American writers and in American culture, life cycle studies of American writers, failure in American culture, men and masculinity in America, biography, journal writing, American folk music from the 1930's to the present, and the singer-songwriter in America.

SIDELIGHTS: Richard Lebeaux writes: "I am committed to teaching and writing which explores what it means to be human and which considers—directly and indirectly—how a life is to be lived. I am concerned with fostering human liberation and a respect for diversity, coupled with a recognition of how much we have in common, how interdependent we are, and how much we need each other."

AVOCATIONAL INTERESTS: Song writing, singing, playing the guitar, camping, hiking, sports, New England.

* * *

LEECH, Geoffrey N(eil) 1936-

PERSONAL: Born January 16, 1936, in Gloucester, England; son of Charles Richard (a bank employee) and Dorothy (Foster) Leech; married Frances Berman, July 29, 1961; children: Thomas, Camilla. *Education:* University College, London, B.A., 1959, M.A., 1962, Ph.D., 1969; Massachusetts Institute of Technology, graduate study, 1964-65. *Religion:* Church of England. *Home:* 12 Clougha Ave., Lancaster, England. *Office:* Department of Linguistics and Modern English Language, University of Lancaster, Bailrigg, Lancaster, England.

CAREER: Clarendon School, South Oxhey, Hertfordshire, England, assistant schoolmaster, 1960-61; University of London, University College, London, England, assistant lecturer, 1962-65, lecturer in English, 1965-69; University of Lancaster, Bailrigg, Lancaster, England, reader in English, 1969-74, professor of linguistics and modern English languages, 1974—. *Military service:* Royal Air Force, 1954-56; became senior aircraftsman. *Member:* Philological Society, Linguistic Association of Great Britain. *Awards, honors:* Harkness fellow at Massachusetts Institute of Technology, 1964-65.

WRITINGS: English in Advertising: A Linguistic Study of Advertising in Great Britain, Longmans, Green, 1966; *A Linguistic Guide to English Poetry,* Longmans, Green, 1969; *Towards a Semantic Description of English,* Longmans, Green, 1969, Indiana University Press, 1970; *Meaning and the English Verb,* Longman, 1971; (with Randolph Quirk, Sidney Greenbaum, and Jan Svartvik) *A Grammar of Contemporary English,* Longman, 1972; *Semantics,* Penguin Books, 1974, revised edition, 1981.

(With Svartvik) *A Communicative Grammar of English,* Longman, 1975; *Explorations in Semantics and Pragmatics,* Benjamins, 1980; (editor with Greenbaum and Svartvik) *Studies in English Linguistics: For Randolph Quirk,* Longman, 1980; (with Michael H. Short) *Style in Fiction,* Longman, 1981; (with Margaret Deuchar and Robert Hoogenraad) *English Grammar for Today,* Macmillan, 1982; *Principles of Pragmatics,* Longman, 1983. Contributor of articles and essays to journals.

WORK IN PROGRESS: With Randolph Quirk, Sidney Greenbaum, and Jan Svartvik, *A Grammar of English* (working title), for publication by Longman; a research project, with Roger Garside, Geoffrey Sampson, and others, entailing a large-scale analysis of a computer corpus of English and development of automatic probabilistic parsing methods.

AVOCATIONAL INTERESTS: Music (playing piano and organ), conservation.

* * *

LEHMAN, Yvonne 1936-

PERSONAL: Born April 3, 1936, in Piedmont, S.C.; married Howard N. Lehman (a retired employee of Federal Bureau of Prisons), September 28, 1958; children: Lori Susan, Lisa Kay, David Andrew, Cindy Carol. *Education:* Attended School of Christian Writing, Minneapolis, Minn., John A. Logan College, and University of North Carolina at Asheville. *Religion:* Southern Baptist. *Home address:* P.O. Box 188, Black Mountain, N.C. 28711.

CAREER: Free-lance writer. *Member:* National League of American Pen Women (former national librarian; president of Asheville, N.C. branch), Romance Writers of America, Inspirational Romance Writers Conference (founder and director), Appalachian Writers Conference, Western North Carolina Christian Writers Conference (founder and director of Blue Ridge Assembly). *Awards, honors:* Dwight L. Moody Award for excellence in Christian literature, 1968; first place in National League of American Pen Women biennial contest, 1974, for *Dead Men Don't Cry,* and third place, 1982, for *Fashions of the Heart;* prize for best article in *Writer's Digest* contest, 1977, for "Joni," and 1983, for "Inspirational Romance Writing."

WRITINGS: Red Like Mine, Zondervan, 1970; *Dead Men Don't Cry,* Zondervan, 1973; *Fashions of the Heart,* David Cook, 1981; *In Shady Groves,* Chosen Books, 1983; *Mountain Man,* Zondervan, 1984. Also author of *Verliebt in einen Farbigen,* 1978. Author of weekly column for *Illinois Baptist,* 1970. Contributor to periodicals, including *Young Family, Vista, Home*

Life, Live, Lutheran Digest, Moody Monthly, Asheville Citizen-Times, Mature Living, Christian Writer, and *Marriage and Family Living.* Nonfiction editor, *Pen Woman.*

WORK IN PROGRESS: A historical novel; "contemporary inspirational romances."

* * *

LEHN, Cornelia 1920-

PERSONAL: Born December 15, 1920, in Leonidavka, U.S.S.R.; became a Canadian citizen; daughter of Gerhard G. (a farmer) and Sara (Ens) Lehn. *Education:* Bethel College, North Newton, Kan., B.A., 1957; attended Mennonite Biblical Seminary, 1958-59; University of Iowa, M.A., 1969. *Religion:* Mennonite. *Home:* 9103 Hazel St. S., Chilliwack, British Columbia, Canada V2P 5N5.

CAREER: Did relief work under the Mennonite Central Committee for four years, working in Germany, 1950, 1951; General Conference Mennonite Church Central Office, Commission on Education, Newton, Kan., editor, 1959-70, director of children's work, 1970-82; free-lance writer, 1982—.

WRITINGS—Published by Faith & Life: *God Keeps His Promise: A Bible Story Book for Kindergarten Children,* 1970; *Peace Be with You,* 1980; *Involving Children and Youth in Congregational Worship,* 1982; *The Sun and the Wind,* 1983; *I Heard Good News Today,* 1983. Editor of kindergarten curriculum materials published by Faith & Life and Herald Press. General editor of "Foundation" series, published by Evangel, Faith & Life, Mennonite Publishing House, and Mennonite Brethren Publishing. Editor of *Der Kinderbote* and *Junior Messenger.*

* * *

LEISER, Burton M. 1930-

PERSONAL: Surname is pronounced *lee*-sur; born December 12, 1930, in Denver, Colo.; son of Nathan (in retail furniture business) and Eva Mae (Newman) Leiser; married Miriam Waid (a teacher), August 10, 1954 (divorced); married C. Barbara Hurowitz Tabor, June 9, 1967 (divorced); children: Shoshana Yafah, Illana Devorah, Phillip B.; stepchildren: Ellen Beth Tabor, David Lawrence Tabor, Susan Ruth Tabor. *Education:* University of Chicago, B.A., 1951; graduate study at University of Colorado, 1951-52, and New York University, 1955-57; Yeshiva University, M.Heb.Lit., 1956; Brown University, Ph.D., 1968; Drake University, J.D., 1981. *Politics:* Democrat. *Religion:* Jewish. *Home:* 11 Meadow Pl., Briarcliff Manor, N.Y. 10510. *Office:* Department of Philosophy, Pace University, 78 North Broadway, White Plains, N.Y. 10603.

CAREER: Teacher and principal at Hebrew schools in Rhode Island and Massachusetts, 1957-64; University of Denver, Denver, Colo., instructor in philosophy, 1962-63; Fort Lewis College, Durango, Colo., instructor in philosophy, 1963-65; State University of New York at Buffalo, assistant professor, 1965-68, associate professor of philosophy, 1968-70; Sir George Williams University, Montreal, Quebec, visiting associate professor, 1969-70, associate professor of Judaic studies, 1970-72; Drake University, Des Moines, Iowa, professor of philosophy and chairman of department, 1972-83; Pace University, White Plains, N.Y., Edward J. Mortola Professor of Philosophy, 1983—.

MEMBER: International Society of Legal and Social Philosophy, American Philosophical Association, American Society for Value Inquiry (president), Society for Political and Legal Philosophy, Society for Philosophy and Public Policy, University Centers for Rational Alternatives, American Association of University Professors, Authors Guild, American Professors for Peace in the Middle East (member of national executive committee), Authors League of America.

AWARDS, HONORS: Research grants from State University of New York Research Foundation and Memorial Foundation for Jewish Culture, 1966-68, 1970-71, Exxon Education Foundation, 1975-77, Drake University, 1975, 1981, and National Endowment for the Humanities, 1979.

WRITINGS: Custom, Law, and Morality: Conflict and Continuity in Social Behavior, Doubleday, 1969; *Liberty, Justice, and Morals: Contemporary Value Conflicts,* Macmillan, 1973, 3rd edition, in press; *Values in Conflict: Life, Liberty, and the Rule of Law,* Macmillan, 1981. Contributor to philosophy, religion, and law journals.

WORK IN PROGRESS: Genocide and *The Essence of Judaism.*

SIDELIGHTS: Burton M. Leiser told *CA:* "Philosophers in the English-speaking world have lately written at length about ordinary language in the most obscure jargon. In attempting to impress their colleagues with their humility, they adopt such absurd mannerisms as qualifying substantive assertions with 'It seems to me that it is the case that. . . .' And to demonstrate their technical competence, they riddle their articles with special symbols and letters in upper and lower case, in roman and italic type, and in Greek. They have impressed, bored, and bewildered one another. They have also cut themselves off from intelligent users of ordinary language who might have been interested in what they had to say, if only they could have made sense of it.

"When philosophers, from Plato to Sartre and Russell, have written lucidly about real issues, they have found an eager audience. The dogmatic assertion that a philosopher can achieve popularity only by sacrificing philosophical integrity is simply false. Every author who is eager to have his work published should remember that publishers are just as eager to find works from which readers will derive pleasure and enlightenment. Once one finds those delightful combinations of words that are aesthetically pleasing and intellectually edifying, the rest is easy."

* * *

LENT, John A(nthony) 1936-

PERSONAL: Born September 8, 1936, in East Millsboro, Pa.; son of John (a railroad worker) and Rose Marie (Marano) Lent; married Martha Meadows, June 17, 1961; children: Laura, Andrea, John Vincent, Lisa, Shahnon. *Education:* Ohio University, B.S.J. (with honors), 1958, M.S. (with highest honors), 1960; graduate study at University of Guadalajara, summer, 1961, and Syracuse University, 1962-64; University of Oslo, certificate, 1962; Sophia University, Tokyo, certificate, 1965; University of Iowa, Ph.D. (with highest honors), 1972. *Home:* 669 Ferne Blvd., Drexel Hill, Pa. 19026. *Office:* Department of Journalism, Temple University, Philadelphia, Pa. 19122.

CAREER: West Virginia Institute of Technology, Montgomery, instructor in English and journalism and director of public relations, 1960-62, 1965-66; Wisconsin State University—Eau Claire (now University of Wisconsin—Eau Claire), assistant professor of journalism, 1966-67; Marshall University, Huntington, W. Va., assistant professor of journalism, 1967-69; Universiti Sains Malaysia, Penang, Malaysia, coordinator and lecturer in mass communications, 1972-74; Temple University, Philadelphia, Pa., associate professor, 1974-76, professor of communications, 1976—. Visiting lecturer, De La Salle College, Manila, Philippines, 1964-65; visiting associate professor, University of Wyoming, 1969-70.

MEMBER: International Association of Mass Communication Research, Inter-American Press Association, Association for Asian Studies, Asia Mass Communication Research and Information Centre, Latin American Studies Association, Caribbean Studies Association, Malaysia/Singapore/Brunei Studies Group (founding chairman), Philippine Studies Group, Sigma Delta Chi, Sigma Tau Delta, Phi Alpha Theta, Kappa Tau Alpha. *Awards, honors:* Fulbright scholar to Philipines, 1964-65; Benedum Research Award; vice-chancellor research awards, Universiti Sains Malaysia; library collections at Ohio University and Alvina T. Burrows Institute named for Lent; two Broadcast Preceptor awards, 1979.

WRITINGS: *Journalism Study of New York Colleges and High Schools,* Newhouse Communications Research Center, Syracuse University, 1963; (editor) *Readings on the Foreign Press,* West Virginia Institute of Technology, 1965; *Philippine Mass Communications Bibliography: First Cumulation of Sources on Areas of Advertising, Journalism, Newspaper, Magazine, Public Relations, Radio, Television, Movies,* [Fort Worth], 1966; *Newhouse, Newspapers, Nuisances: Highlights in the Growth of a Communications Empire,* Exposition Press, 1966; *Three Research Studies,* West Virginia Institute of Technology, 1966; *Philippine Mass Communications: Before 1811, after 1966,* Philippine Press, 1967.

(Editor) *The Asian Newspapers' Reluctant Revolution,* Iowa State University Press, 1971; *Asian Mass Communications: A Comprehensive Bibliography,* School of Communications and Theater, Temple University, 1974; (contributor) Alan Wells, *Mass Communications: A World View,* National Press, 1974; *Commonwealth Caribbean Mass Communications,* State University of New York Press, 1975; *Third World Mass Media and Their Search for Modernity: The Case of Commonwealth Caribbean, 1717-1976,* Bucknell University Press, 1977; (editor) *Cultural Pluralism in Malaysia: Polity, Military, Mass Media, Education, Religion, and Social Class,* Center for Southeast Asian Studies, Northern Illinois University, 1977; (editor) *Broadcasting in Asia and the Pacific: A Continental Survey of Radio and Television,* Temple University Press, 1978; (editor) *Malaysian Studies: Present Knowledge and Research Trends,* Center for Southeast Asian Studies, Northern Illinois University, 1979; *Topics in Third World Mass Communications,* Asian Research Service, 1979; *Development News,* AMIC, 1979.

Caribbean Mass Communications: A Comprehensive Bibliography, African Studies Association, 1981; (author of introduction) *Newspapers in Asia: Contemporary Trends and Problems,* Heinemann Educational, 1982; *New World and International Information Order: A Bibliography and Resource Guide,* AMIC, 1982.

Also contributor of chapters to books and co-author of filmstrip "Pied Type, A Load of Coal and the Laser"; compiler of slide presentations on Asia and the Caribbean for Vis-Com, Inc., 1972 and 1975. Contributor of over two hundred articles to about eighty periodicals, including *Journalism Quarterly, Television Quarterly, Quill, Gazette* (Amsterdam), *Asian Studies, Philippine Studies, European Broadcast Review, Silliman Journal* (Philippines), and *Estudios Orientales* (Mexico). Bibliographer for *Journalism Quarterly;* founding editor of *Berita: Newsletter of Malaysia/Singapore/Brunei Studies Group* and *Asian Studies at Temple Newsletter;* associate editor of *International Communications Bulletin,* 1970-72; assistant editor of *Media History Digest* and *Communication Booknotes;* member of editorial board of *Crossroads, World Media Report, Philippine Research Bulletin, India Review, Human Rights Quarterly,* and *Asian Profile.*

WORK IN PROGRESS: Books on Asian films; *World Media Bibliography;* research on transnationalizing telecommunications in Southeast Asia; Caribbean and Asian bibliographies on mass media; *International Communications Textbook.*

SIDELIGHTS: John A. Lent has traveled in Europe, Asia, Latin America, and the Caribbean. He developed and taught the first international communications courses at University of Wisconsin—Eau Claire, Marshall University, University of Wyoming, and Universiti Sains Malaysia. He has also supervised archeological excavations in Canada, edited an underground newspaper, and helped organize FREE, a group for racial equality in West Virginia. Lent has chaired and organized panels, lectured, presented papers, and spoken at national and international conferences and symposia in Venezuela, Korea, Dominican Republic, Curacao, the Virgin Islands of the United States, Martinique, Colombia, Cuba, the United States, England, Mexico, St. Lucia, Jamaica, Philippines, Malaysia, Laos, India, Thailand, Singapore, East Germany, Trinidad, Tobago, and Canada. He feels writing comes from rigid discipline, and he writes at long stretches—usually going on an all-night schedule for months.

* * *

LEONARD, Elmore 1925-
(Emmett Long)

PERSONAL: Born Oct. 11, 1925, in New Orleans, La.; son of Elmore John (a salesman) and Flora (Rive) Leonard; married Beverly Cline, July 30, 1949 (divorced May 24, 1977); married Joan Shepard, September 15, 1979; children: (first marriage) Jane Freels, Peter, Christopher, William, Katherine. *Education:* University of Detroit, Ph.B., 1950. *Religion:* Catholic. *Residence:* Birmingham, Mich. 48011. *Agent:* H. N. Swanson, 8523 Sunset Blvd., Los Angeles, Cal. 90069.

CAREER: Writer. Campbell-Ewald Advertising Agency, Detroit, Mich., copywriter, 1950-61; free-lance writer of industrial and educational motion pictures, many for Encyclopaedia Britannica Films, 1961-63; head of Elmore Leonard Advertising Company, 1963-66. *Military service:* U.S. Naval Reserve, 1943-46. *Member:* Writers Guild of America, West, Mystery Writers of America, Western Writers of America, Authors League of America, Authors Guild. *Awards, honors: Hombre* was selected as one of twenty-five best Western novels of all time by Western Writers of America, 1977.

WRITINGS—Novels: *The Bounty Hunters,* Houghton, 1953; *The Law at Randado,* Houghton, 1955; *Escape from 5 Shadows,* Houghton, 1956; *Last Stand at Saber River,* Dell, 1957; *Hombre,* Ballantine, 1961; *The Big Bounce,* Gold Medal, 1969; *The Moonshine War,* Doubleday, 1969; *Valdez Is Coming,* Gold Medal, 1970; *Forty Lashes Less One,* Bantam, 1972; *Mr. Majestyk,* Dell, 1974; *Fifty-Two Pickup,* Delacorte, 1974; *Swag,* Delacorte, 1976; *Unknown Man No. 89,* Delacorte, 1977; *The Hunted,* Dell, 1977; *The Switch,* Bantam, 1978; *Ryan's Rule,* Dell, 1978; *Gunsight,* Bantam, 1979; *City Primeval: High*

Noon in Detroit, Arbor House, 1980; *Gold Coast*, Bantam, 1980; *Split Images*, Arbor House, 1981; *Cat Chaser*, Arbor House, 1982; *Stick*, Arbor House, 1983; *LaBrava*, Arbor House, 1983.

Screenplays: "The Moonshine Wars" (based on his novel of the same title), Metro-Goldwyn-Mayer, 1970; "Joe Kidd," Universal, 1973; "Mr. Majestyk" (based on his novel of the same title), United Artists, 1974. Also author of "Split Images" (based on his novel of the same title), "Stick" (based on his novel of the same title), Universal, "LaBrava" (based on his novel of the same title), Universal, and "The Rosary Murders" (based on the novel of the same title by William X. Kienzle).

SIDELIGHTS: "After writing 23 novels, Elmore Leonard has been discovered," writes Herbert Mitgang in the *New York Times*, capturing the rapid growth that Leonard's critical stock has experienced in recent years. Following three decades of moderate success with his novels and short stories, Leonard is receiving the kind of attention in both reviews and interviews befitting an author whom Richard Herzfelder in the *Chicago Tribune* calls "a writer of thrillers whose vision goes deeper than thrill." While the plots of Leonard's books remain inherently action-packed and suspenseful, he is, says *Washington Post Book World* critic Jonathan Yardley, "[being] praised for accomplishments rather more substantial than that of keeping the reader on tenterhooks." These accomplishments, which Yardley describes as "[raising] the hard-boiled suspense novel beyond the limits of genre and into social commentary," have led critics previously inclined to pigeonhole Leonard as a crime or mystery novelist to dispense with such labels in their assessments of his work. In the process, several critics have chosen to mention Leonard's name alongside those of other writers whose literary achievements transcend their genres, among them Ross Macdonald and Dashiell Hammett. Such comparisons are "flattering, but hardly accurate," according to Grover Sales in the *Los Angeles Times Book Review*. "Leonard is an original. His uncanny sense of plot, pace and his inexhaustible flair for the nervous rhythms of contemporary urban speech have caught the spirit of the '80s."

Leonard began his writing career in the early 1950's, submitting cowboy stories to western magazines, and eventually turned his hand to western novels while pursuing a parallel career as an advertising copywriter for a firm in Detroit. The latter was not an occupation much to Leonard's liking, however. "He says matter-of-factly that he hated the work," notes Bill Dunn in a *Publishers Weekly* interview, "but it allowed him precious time and a steady paycheck to experiment with fiction, which he did in the early morning before going off to work." Leonard told Dunn: "Sometimes I would write a little fiction at work, too. I would write in my desk drawer and close the drawer if somebody came in."

Leonard's first novel, *The Bounty Hunter*, was published in 1953, and its choice of subject matter reflects the fact that the author was determined from the beginning of his career that his writing should be a practical as well as a creative pursuit, that he would be a seller of books as well as a writer of them. Leonard explained to Beaufort Cranford in *Michigan Magazine* that "It seemed best to pick a genre and I chose westerns, probably because I like western movies. I subscribed to *Arizona Highways* and started reading about cowboys and Apaches and the cavalry—all that was very big in the '50s—and just did research. I decided I wasn't going to be a literary writer, that I wouldn't end up in the quarterlies. So if I was going to be a commercial writer, I had to learn how to do it." His decidedly professional approach to writing paid off, and Leonard continued to publish western novels at a prolific rate through the end of the decade, turning out two pages a day between five and seven A:M. before going to work.

After the publication of *Hombre* in 1961, Leonard left the advertising agency in order to be able to devote more time to fiction, but as he told Cranford: "From '61 to '65 I didn't write *any*, though I had already done five books and about 30 short stories and sold a couple of movies." During those four years Leonard continued to produce advertising materials for his own company, while at the same time writing promotional and educational films for various concerns, including Encyclopaedia Britannica. With the success of the 1967 film version of *Hombre*, starring Paul Newman, the author was finally able to turn his energies to full-time writing. The demand for western novels had diminished, however, and Leonard gradually turned to new subjects and settings for his books. He explained to Gay Rubin in the *Detroiter:* "I began writing westerns because there was a market for them. Now of course there is an interest in police stories . . . suspense, mystery, crime." These elements became a part of Leonard's fiction, and according to Dunn, "In the last 10 years [Leonard has] trained his sights on modern thrillers, which many reviewers feel is his proper genre."

The question of genre is one that chafes Leonard, for whom labels of any kind have little appeal. "I don't try to write a particular kind of book," he explained to Cranford. "Reviewers have tried to categorize me, but I think I'm finally being recognized for what I write. I certainly write crime stories, there's always crime in there. I hope there's suspense too." In his *Chicago Tribune* review of Leonard's *City Primeval: High Noon in Detroit*, Larry Kart states that the author's books are "not 'detective stories' or 'mysteries,' although there is considerable suspense in his work, but novels that depict real criminals in the real world." "I think that I'm really writing novels, not mysteries," Leonard told Mitgang, "but I don't want to sound pretentious. I do like to read that I write clean prose and that my stuff is considered economical."

Both the economy of Leonard's prose and what critic Newgate Callendar in the *New York Times Book Review* describes as the author's "infallible ear" for dialog have brought comparisons—not with other writers of suspense fiction—but with Ernest Hemingway. Leonard acknowledged Hemingway's influence to Herzfelder: "*For Whom the Bell Tolls* taught me how to write westerns. I could understand what Hemingway was doing—the way he uses all the senses, the feel and smell of a gun." Leonard is not fond of working with either description or narration, however, preferring instead, he told Bruce Cook in the *Washington Post Book World*, "to move my story with dialogue. I try to keep physical description to a minimum. I'm not interested so much in situations as I am in characters." The result of Leonard's attention to conversation and character, writes David Lehman in *Newsweek,* is that when his characters speak, whether the setting is a corporate boardroom or the street, the dialog "never rings false." In his review of the novelist's *Cat Chaser*, Callendar asserts that "Leonard exactly reproduces the speech of all classes, and . . . he is especially interested in underworld or fringe-of-the-underworld types." Reviewing the same book in the *New York Times*, John Leonard believes that the novelist is "better at dialog than anybody else on the block I can think of except Philip Roth."

One of the author's techniques for keeping his dialog polished and real is simply to listen: to stockbrokers, policemen, or whomever a fictional situation requires. Leonard told Marilyn Stasio in the *Chicago Tribune* that while doing the research for his novel *City Primeval* he "sat around the [Detroit] homicide squad room for a couple of months. I got a lot of good dialog, good sounds—not just from the cops, but from witnesses, suspects, lawyers." He insists, however, that the process of learning to write dialog by listening is more complex than simply borrowing overheard conversations. "The dialog in my novels is mostly made up," he explained to Mitgang. "It isn't the words that are authentic but, rather, the rhythm of the way people talk. Only once in a while do I hear whole sentences spoken when I'm listening for material."

His gift for dialog notwithstanding, Leonard's rise as a serious writer has as much to do with the content of his works as it does with the craft they display. Kart believes that Leonard's "special virtue as a novelist is the way in which he slams one kind of violence (and the assumptions that underlie it) against another—to the point where his books are, simultaneously, social comedies as precisely tuned as anything this side of Oscar Wilde and realistic portraits of people who would just as soon kill you as not." A number of other writers have also focused on Leonard's ability to capture the dark humor that underlies the violent situations his characters frequently find themselves in. Yardley speaks of "an acute, funny and sometimes very bitter picture of a world that is all too real and recognizable, yet a world that rarely makes an appearance in the kind of fiction that is routinely given serious consideration."

Leonard's protagonists are usually men living at the edge of society, characters who may have taken a wrong turn somewhere but whose basic morality and outlook places them head and shoulders above their surroundings. As Leonard explained to Cranford, "Even when the main character is . . . an armed robber, he's still a decent human being with feelings, and you realize that early on." While these men might not always triumph in the difficult circumstances they are placed in, their struggles are universal—"Their lives add up to social commentary," believes Mitgang.

Writing in the *Washington Post Book World*, Michele Slung moves away from the individual strengths of Leonard's novels as she summarizes their effect as a whole: "The satisfactions of . . . Leonard are more than the charm of his heroes and the richness of his supporting cast, more even than his twisty plots. It's become a cliche, to acclaim creative works as 'American,' but that, I think, is what the sum of the Leonard parts is—sunshine and violence, optimism and disarray, filtered through Leonard's own forthright individualism and consistently lightened by his quizzical humor."

Reviewing Leonard's novel *LaBrava* in the *New York Times*, Christopher Lehman-Haupt says, "As usual, [the author's] dialog is so authentic that it dances off the page." And John F. Vesely describes the novel in the *Detroit News* as Leonard "writing at his peak," an assessment in line with the author's own professed ambitions. For while the income from his writings has always been a major motivating factor in his approach to his work, he told Cook that "about 1976 or 1977, it occurred to me that I could make a name for myself and not just money. Now, as I see it, there's been a gradual shift in my work, so that there's a little more emphasis on—I don't know how else to put it—the literary side." Leonard summed up his future aspirations for Herzfelder: "After 32 years, I'm still trying to get better and I still think I can get better. It took me a long time to realize that a lot of readers like what I like, and if I write what they like, they'll read it."

MEDIA ADAPTATIONS: Film adaptations of Leonard's work include "3:10 to Yuma," Columbia Pictures, 1957, "Hombre," Twentieth Century-Fox, 1967, "The Big Bounce," Warner Bros., 1969, and "Valdez is Coming," United Artists, 1971.

AVOCATIONAL INTERESTS: Travel.

BIOGRAPHICAL/CRITICAL SOURCES: Detroiter, June, 1974; *Authors in the News,* Volume II, Gale, 1976; *New York Times Book Review,* May 22, 1977, September 5, 1982, March 6, 1983, December 27, 1983; *Washington Post,* October 6, 1980; *Chicago Tribune,* February 4, 1981, April 8, 1983, December 8, 1983; *Washington Post Book World,* February 7, 1982, July 4, 1982, February 20, 1983; *Detroit News,* February 23, 1982, October 23, 1983; *Newsweek,* March 22, 1982, July 11, 1983; *New York Times,* June 11, 1982, April 28, 1983, October 7, 1983, October 29, 1983; *Publishers Weekly,* February 25, 1983; *Los Angeles Times Book Review,* February 27, 1983; *Chicago Tribune Book World,* April 10, 1983, October 30, 1983; *Michigan Magazine* (Sunday magazine of the *Detroit News*), October 9, 1983.

—Sketch by Robert T. Wilson

* * *

LEONARD, John 1939-

PERSONAL: Born February 25, 1939, in Washington, D.C.; son of Daniel D. and Ruth (Woods) Leonard; married Christiana Morison, June 13, 1959 (divorced, 1976); remarried; children: Andrew Warren. *Education:* Attended Harvard University, 1956-58; University of California, Berkeley, B.A., 1962.

CAREER: Writer. *National Review,* Boston, Mass., editorial apprentice, 1959-60; Station KPFA-Radio, Berkeley, Calif., book reviewer and drama and literature program producer, 1963-64; publicity writer in Boston, Mass., 1964-67; *New York Times,* New York City, member of staff, 1967-69, book reviewer, 1969-70, book review editor, 1971-76, chief cultural critic, 1977-83; *Variety,* New York City, member of editorial staff, beginning 1983. *Awards, honors: Black Conceit* was nominated for a National Book Award.

WRITINGS: The Naked Martini, Delacorte, 1964; *Wyke Regis,* Delacorte, 1966; *Crybaby of the Western World,* Doubleday, 1969; *Black Conceit,* Doubleday, 1973; *This Pen for Hire,* Doubleday, 1973; *Private Lives in the Imperial City,* Knopf, 1979. Contributor to little literary magazines.

WORK IN PROGRESS: A satiric spy story set in southern California.

SIDELIGHTS: Private Lives in the Imperial City is a collection of sixty-nine columns John Leonard wrote between 1977 and 1979 for the *New York Times.* Leonard, says Anstiss Drake in a *Chicago Tribune Book World* review of the book, "can write like a wizard; he wraps his self-analysis in leaves of witty wisdom so that the excellent among his pieces become delectable and memorable morsels. Although he can be cosily identified with, he is a cut above the ordinary columnist of the domestic scene."

An *Atlantic* reviewer finds that Leonard's columns "sing variations on a single theme: the honor of parenthood, the courage of domesticity, the glory of ordinariness. Which is fine, and more than fine, except that the repeated celebration of one's own humility in the daily *New York Times* is a chancy proposition. It is not easy to be the Erma Bombeck of the Upper East Side."

Leonard himself talks about the origin of the "Private Lives" column with Nora Ephron in a *New York Times Book Review* article. "In 1976," says Leonard, "I'd gone through a divorce, I'd quit my job as a sort of commissar of literary culture, I was sleeping in hotel rooms and on the couches of friends, and the [*New York*] *Times* really didn't know what to do with me. I must have been wandering through the newsroom with a typewriter on my back, looking like the definition of middle-class anxiety, when Arthur Gelb [*New York Times* deputy managing editor] suggested I try out a column for the new Wednesday section. His notion was that it would be about daily life, domestic problems, children, friends. . . . Not bitter, although bittersweet was all right. Leave out the sex and politics. To my surprise, and probably to Gelb's, it turned out to be enormous fun, like writing a short story on deadline once a week. . . . It asks what I hope are moral questions: How do you want your children to grow up? What do you think is decent and fair? Who are your friends, and why? How do you behave when nobody's looking? The big problem with it, I think, is that its obsessions and compulsions are so upper-middle-class. If I'm writing about my personal life, my psychic yard goods, I'm writing a lot of the time about a townhouse in Manhattan and a vacation in Greece and private schools and tulips. These aren't typical American situations. They're privileges. I'm Jill Clayburgh instead of Erma Bombeck."

Leonard reviews his own book in the *Nation:* "And so the Erma Bombeck of the Great Pickle Section of the *New York Times* sees fit to inflict on a hapless public sixty-nine of his Wednesday morning thumb-suckers. It was hard enough for some of us to work up much interest in his cats and his stoop and his coffee grinder and his fondue pot and his qualms on the first go-round; a book-length rerun is an exacerbation. One is tempted to suggest that he be sensitive on his own time, not ours."

BIOGRAPHICAL/CRITICAL SOURCES: *New York Times Book Review*, October 28, 1973, April 22, 1979; *Newsweek*, November 12, 1973; *Time*, December 31, 1973; *National Review*, January 18, 1974; *Washington Post Book World*, April 18, 1979; *Chicago Tribune Book World*, April 22, 1979; *Atlantic*, May, 1979; *Nation*, May 5, 1979.†

* * *

LEONARD, Phyllis G(rubbs) 1924-

PERSONAL: Born October 4, 1924, in Westerville, Ohio; daughter of Maynard Lee (a paper hanger) and Lura McEwen (Steele) Grubbs; married Walter Magruder Leonard (a writer and photographer), January 31, 1948. *Education:* Attended Cleveland College (now Case Western Reserve University), 1942-44; Universidad de San Carlos, certificate, 1948; American Graduate School of International Management, certificate, 1949. *Politics:* "Conservative and proud to be an American." *Religion:* Protestant, "not much of a church-goer but try to practice everyday Christianity." *Home and office:* P.O. Box 400, Tombstone, Ariz. 85638. *Agent:* Phyllis Westberg, Harold Ober Associates, 40 East 49th St., New York, N.Y. 10017.

CAREER: Leonard Insurance Agency, Phoenix, Ariz., partner with husband, 1952-63, president, 1963-71; Leonard Corp. (family firm), Phoenix, president, 1971—. President of Insurance Women of Phoenix, Inc., 1956, and of Tombstone City Library Board; free-lance writer, 1971—. *Member:* Authors Guild, Authors League of America, Society of Southwestern Authors, Friends of the Cochise County Library (member of board of directors). *Awards, honors:* First prize for fiction in Arizona Press Women's annual communications contest and second prize for adult fiction in National Federation of Press Women's annual communications contest, both 1974, both for *Prey of the Eagle;* first prize for fiction, Society of Southwestern Authors, 1976, for *Phantom of the Sacred Well.*

WRITINGS: *Prey of the Eagle*, McKay, 1974; *Phantom of the Sacred Well*, McKay, 1976; *Warrior's Woman*, Coward, 1977; *The Street of the Madwoman*, Coward, 1977; *Tarnished Angel*, Coward, 1980; *Mariposa*, Dell, 1983; *Beloved Stranger*, Dell, 1984. Contributor of articles to magazines, including *Christian Science Monitor, Mankind, American Horseman, National Parks and Conservation, American Girl, Child Life, Iron Worker, True Frontier,* and *Pacific Discovery.*

WORK IN PROGRESS: A novel set in New Mexico, 1916.

SIDELIGHTS: Phyllis G. Leonard wrote *CA:* "I dreamed of being a novelist since I was small. I like archaeological and historical material best, including little-known trivia. (E.g., I used the fact that the Mayas worshipped Cortes' horse as a god in *Phantom of the Sacred Well.*) I feel my 'mission' is to be a top-notch tale-spinner, combining entertainment with education through my careful research. If I can inspire readers to broaden intellectual horizons through curiosity about authentic data I've used, as well as enjoy the books as escape literature, I will feel I have given them a 'baker's dozen.' I hope to continue specializing in Latin American cultures and Amerindian civilizations, but as a lifelong history buff will write novels with other backgrounds, too. Philosophically, although I realize good guys may not always win, . . . I remain optimistic about life and tend to be a romantic pragmatist. My books have had happy endings and generally will."

When asked where she finds her authentic data and little-known trivia, Leonard replied: "How do I research a book? Taking *Warrior's Woman* as an example—by choosing several excellent references by authorities such as Prescott, Soustelle, Peterson, Von Hagen, Parry, and others, I immerse myself in them, then get relevant books mentioned in their bibliographies and study those. (E.g., heroine's adventures in *Warrior's Woman* were involved with Cortes' conquest of Mexico; I studied him so narrative would be accurate in every detail from the scar on his lip to the banner's motto.) I also read good fiction: Marshall, Shedd, Shellabarger, Madariaga for different viewpoints. Translations from Spanish and Nahuatl records are invaluable for on-the-spot flavor. The subjects for *Warrior's Woman* ranged from armor and Aztecs to wolfhounds and witchcraft. Research is a joy to me and I feel a great obligation to readers to be as accurate as humanly possible. If sources don't agree or if they admit some lack of information, I use common sense, qualifying the statement in some way so the reader can make up his own mind.

"As to where I find little-known trivia such as Cortes' horse's name or how Toledo blades were made, sometimes it's sheer luck; other times it's the result of hours of assiduous digging, reading, and detective work. The latter is great fun and usually uncovers other research gems. This so-called trivia brings the past to vivid life and makes readers feel they are right there. Libraries, after all, are the treasurehouses of the world.

"I have specialized in Latin American and Amerindian backgrounds in . . . four novels because of a deep fascination for these areas which began at American Graduate School of International Management. There, my husband and I (as newlyweds) studied Spanish and Central and South American countries' commerce, customs, etc. in preparation for a foreign trade career (that we did not follow). These studies, plus the summer in Guatemala in 1948, plus southern European travel later, came to fruition first in articles and then novels. *However, and I emphasize this, if publishers ask for novels placed in other areas, I'll be able to do those, too, applying my research techniques. [After all,]* Tarnished Angel *is set in San Francisco, 1850,* Mariposa *here in Cochise County, 1875-94, and* Beloved Stranger *in Santa Fe, 1880."*

CA asked Leonard what her working habits were like. "Nothing unusual, I'm afraid. I now have a lovely office where I have a writing desk and a desk for clerical and general work. Hours are 10 AM to 6 PM, generally, with snack and chat breaks with my husband. I do the first draft of the novel in longhand—*just* the right word is a passion—then type the second draft which is polished numerous times before a typed manuscript is ready for the publisher. I keep the drapes closed so I won't daydream over desert skies, quail and rabbits in front of the window, or wind in the trees! The house also has to be neat while I'm working or I'm up straightening things! Although difficult at times creatively and financially, writing is a joy, and I hope I'll be fortunate enough to emulate Nora Lofts, Anya Seton, J. Briskin, Susan Howatch, and others of like talent in versatility and output."

The Street of the Madwoman has been translated into German and Spanish, *Phantom of the Sacred Well* into French, and *Prey of the Eagle* into German.

AVOCATIONAL INTERESTS: Bird-watching, camping, trailering to beauty spots of the Southwest; work with local humane society, art association, clinic auxiliary, and Vigilettes ("we wear gowns from 1880s for tourists from all over the world").

BIOGRAPHICAL/CRITICAL SOURCES: *Arizona Republic,* February 14, 1974; *Phoenix,* September, 1974; *Books of the Southwest,* August-September, 1983.

* * *

LESTER, David 1942-

PERSONAL: Born June 1, 1942, in London, England; U.S. citizen; son of Harry (a bookie) and Kathleen (Moore) Lester; married Jean Mercer (a psychologist and author under names Gene Lester and Jean Mercer), April 15, 1967 (divorced, 1977); married Mary E. Murrell (a professor of criminal justice), July 20, 1979; children: (first marriage) Simon. *Education:* Cambridge University, B.A., 1964, M.A., 1968; Brandeis University, M.A., 1966, Ph.D., 1968. *Politics:* None. *Religion:* None. *Home:* R.D. 3, 166 Jackson Rd., Berlin, N.J. 08009. *Office:* Psychology Program, Richard Stockton State College, Pomona, N.J. 08240.

CAREER: Wellesley College, Wellesley, Mass., instructor, 1967-68, assistant professor of psychology, 1968-69; Suicide Prevention and Crisis Service, Buffalo, N.Y., research director, 1969-71; Richard Stockton State College, Pomona, N.J., associate professor, 1971-74, professor of psychology, 1975—, chairman of the department, 1971-74. Instructor and clinical associate, State University of New York at Buffalo, 1969-71; research associate, Philadelphia General Hospital, 1971-75. *Awards, honors:* National Institute of Mental Health research grant, 1967-68.

WRITINGS—Published by C. C Thomas, except as indicated: (Editor) *Explorations in Exploration,* Van Nostrand, 1969; (with first wife, Gene Lester) *Suicide: The Gamble with Death,* Prentice-Hall, 1971; *Why Men Kill Themselves,* 1972, 2nd edition published as *Why People Kill Themselves,* 1983; (editor with G. Brockopp) *Crisis Intervention and Counseling by Telephone,* 1973; *Comparative Psychology: Phyletic Differences in Behavior,* Alfred Publishing, 1973; *A Physiological Basis for Personality Traits,* 1974; (with G. Lester) *Crime of Passion: Murder and the Murderer,* Nelson-Hall, 1975; *Unusual Sexual Behavior: The Standard Deviations,* 1975; *The Use of Alternative Modes for Communication in Psychotherapy: The Computer, the Book, the Telephone, the Television, the Tape Recorder,* 1977; (editor) *Gambling Today,* 1979.

(With B. Sell and K. Sell) *Suicide: A Guide to Information Sources,* Gale, 1980; *Psychotherapy for Offenders,* Pilgrimage Press, 1981; (editor) *The Elderly Victim of Crime,* 1981; (with wife, Mary E. Murrell) *Introduction to Juvenile Delinquency,* Macmillan, 1981; *The Psychological Basis for Handwriting Analysis,* Nelson-Hall, 1981; *The Structure of the Mind,* University Press of America, 1982; *Gun Control: Issues and Answers,* 1984; (with A. Levitt) *Insanity and Incompetence: Case Studies in Forensic Psychology,* Pilgrimage Press, 1984.

Contributor of over five hundred articles to *Journal of Clinical Psychology, American Anthropologist, Journal of General Psychology, Nature, Clinical Psychologist, Omega,* and other professional journals. Founder and co-editor, *Crisis Intervention,* 1969-71; member of editorial advisory board, Institute for Scientific Information, 1969-70, and *Current Contents (Social and Behavioral Sciences);* member of editorial board, *Omega,* 1971—.

SIDELIGHTS: David Lester told *CA:* "At this time in my life, I am growing tired of writing yet more books on psychological topics and social science issues. I am much more excited by my fledgling attempts to write [opinion-editorials] for newspapers, articles for magazines, and fiction. Even minor successes in these areas please me much more than my scholarly works. At present, I am in the midst of writing two detective stories, but I am still uncertain whether I will complete them and eventually see them in print."

* * *

LEUCHTENBURG, William E(dward) 1922-

PERSONAL: Born September 28, 1922, in Ridgewood, N.Y.; son of William Henry (a postal clerk) and Lauretta (McNamara) Leuchtenburg; married Jean Matilda McIntire, December 21, 1948 (divorced, July 22, 1982); children: Thomas, Christopher, Joshua. *Education:* Cornell University, B.A., 1943; Columbia University, M.A., 1944, Ph.D., 1951. *Home:* 505 Hawthorne Lane, Chapel Hill, N.C. 27514. *Office:* Department of History, University of North Carolina at Chapel Hill, Chapel Hill, N.C. 27514.

CAREER: New York University, New York City, instructor in economics, 1947; Smith College, Northampton, Mass., 1949-51, began as instructor, became assistant professor of government; Harvard University, Cambridge, Mass., assistant professor of American history, 1951-52; Columbia University, New York City, associate, 1952-54, associate professor, 1954-59, professor of American history, 1959-71, De Witt Clinton Professor of History, 1971-83, associate chairman of department of history, 1958-61, 1967-70, and 1973-75; University of North Carolina at Chapel Hill, Chapel Hill, N.C., William Rand Kenan, Jr. Professor of History, 1982—.

Harmsworth Professor of American History, Oxford University, 1971-72; visiting professor, Duke University Law School, 1982; Betty Lou Fletcher Goodman Scholar, Peace College,

1982. Lecturer, Salzburg Seminar in American Studies, summer, 1956; fellow, Center for Advanced Study in the Behavioral Sciences (Stanford, Calif.), 1961-62, University of Michigan Seminar on Methods in Historical Analysis, summer, 1965, National Humanities Center, 1978-79 and Mellon senior fellow, 1979-81, Woodrow Wilson Center for International Affairs, 1982, and Queen's College, Oxford University.

Member of visiting committees of colleges, including Oberlin College, 1970, and Swarthmore College, 1974. Trustee, Smith College, 1980-83, and National Humanities Center, 1981—. Liberal Party, director for Queens County, and New York state youth director, 1944-45; New England field director for National Council for a Permanent Fair Employment Practices Commission, 1945-46; Americans for Democratic Action, national field representative, 1948, and Massachusetts state director, 1948-49. Member, National Study Commission on Records and Documents of Federal Officials, 1975-77, Program Committee for Fifteenth International Congress of Historical Sciences (Bucharest), 1980, Study Group on the Commemoration of U.S. Senate Bicentenary, and Franklin Delano Roosevelt Centennial Committee.

Western field representative and delegate analyst for W. Averell Harriman, Democratic National Convention, 1952; elections analyst, National Broadcasting Co. (NBC), 1962, 1964, 1968, 1972. Assistant editor, American Labor Conference on International Affairs, 1945; editorial advisory board, Franklin Delano Roosevelt Library, 1971-76. Member of advisory committee, John F. Kennedy Memorial Library, 1965-68, New York Center for Visual History, U.S. Senate Historical Office, Center for the Study of the Consumer Movement, and Studies Center of the University of Oklahoma. Consultant, Ford Foundation, 1965-66, National Broadcasting Co. (NBC), 1981-82, American Broadcasting Co. (ABC), 1982-83, Project '87, 1983—, and Oxford University Press; advisor, Social Security Administration. *Military service:* U.S. Army, 1943.

MEMBER: American Academy of Arts and Sciences (fellow), Society of American Historians (president, 1978-81), Organization of American Historians (member of executive board, 1968-71), American Historical Association (national program chairman, 1966), Century Association, Committee on Sociological History, Massachusetts Historical Society (corresponding member), Phi Beta Kappa. *Awards, honors:* Bancroft Prize from Columbia University and Francis Parkman Prize from Society of American Historians, both 1964, both for *Franklin D. Roosevelt and the New Deal, 1932-1940;* National Endowment for the Humanities fellow, 1968-69; M.A. (honorary), Oxford University, 1971; Guggenheim fellow, 1975-76.

WRITINGS: Flood Control Politics, Harvard University Press, 1953, reprinted, 1972; *The Perils of Prosperity, 1914-1932,* University of Chicago Press, 1958; *Franklin D. Roosevelt and the New Deal, 1932-1940,* Harper, 1963; *New Deal and Global War,* Time-Life, 1964; *The Great Age of Change,* Time-Life, 1964; (author of introduction) Edwin R. Lewinson, *John Purroy Mitchel,* Astra Books, 1965; (with Samuel Eliot Morison and Henry Steele Commager) *The Growth of the America Republic,* two volumes, Oxford University Press, 1969, revised edition, 1980.

A Troubled Feast: American Society since 1945, Little, Brown, 1973, revised edition, 1983; (author of introduction) Peter Joseph, *Good Times: An Oral History of America in the 1960s,* Charterhouse, 1973; *War and Social Change in Twentieth Century America,* Mary Baldwin College, 1977; (author of introduction and advisory editor) *Political Parties,* Arno, 1977; (with Morison and Commager) *A Concise History of the American Republic,* Oxford University Press, 1977, revised edition, 1983; (with Anthony Quinton, George W. Ball, and David Owen) *Britain and the United States: Four Views to Mark the Silver Jubilee,* Heinemann, 1979; *In the Shadow of FDR: From Harry Truman to Ronald Reagan,* Cornell University Press, 1983.

Editor: Theodore Roosevelt, *The New Nationalism,* Prentice-Hall, 1961; Woodrow Wilson, *The New Freedom,* Prentice-Hall, 1961; Walter Lippmann, *Drift and Mastery,* Prentice-Hall, 1961; *Franklin D. Roosevelt: A Profile,* Hill & Wang, 1967; *The New Deal: A Documentary History,* Harper, 1968; *The Unfinished Century: America since 1900,* Little, Brown, 1973.

Contributor: Allan Nevins, editor, *Times of Trial,* Knopf, 1958; John Braeman, Robert H. Bremner, and Everett Walters, editors, *Change and Continuity in Twentieth-Century America,* Ohio State University Press, 1964; editors of *Life* magazine, *The First World War,* Time, Inc., 1965; Aida DiPace Donald, *John F. Kennedy and the New Frontier,* Hill & Wang, 1966; Daniel J. Boorstin, editor, *An American Primer,* University of Chicago Press, 1966; Richard W. Leopold, Arthur S. Link, and Stanley Coben, editors, *Problems in American History,* Volume II, Prentice-Hall, 1966, revised edition, 1972; Philip B. Kurland, editor, *The Supreme Court Review: 1966,* University of Chicago Press, 1966; Stephen E. Ambrose, editor, *Institutions in Modern America: Innovation in Structure and Process,* Johns Hopkins Press, 1967; Harold Hyman and Leonard W. Levy, editors, *Freedom and Reform,* Harper, 1967; C. Vann Woodward, editor, *The Comparative Approach to American History,* Basic Books, 1968; Harold M. Hollingsworth and William F. Holmes, editors, *Essays on the New Deal,* University of Texas Press, 1969; Victor Hoar, editor, *The Great Depression: Essays and Memoirs from Canada and the United States,* Copp Clark, 1969.

John A. Garraty, *Interpreting American History: Conversations with Historians,* Volume II, Macmillan, 1970; Arthur M. Schlesinger, Jr. and Fred L. Israel, editors, *History of American Presidential Elections, 1789-1968,* Volume III, McGraw, 1971; Garraty and Peter Gay, editors, *The Columbia History of the World,* Harper, 1972; George N. Atiyeh, editor, *Arab and American Cultures,* American Enterprise Institute for Public Policy Research, 1977; Michael V. Namorato, editor, *Have We Overcome?,* University Press of Mississippi, 1979. Also contributor to *The Humanist as Citizen.*

Editor, "Contemporary American History" series, Columbia University Press; co-editor, Prentice-Hall's "Classics in History" series and Harper's "American Perspectives" series. Contributor to *Dictionary of American Biography;* also to journals, including *New York Times Book Review, American Heritage, American Historical Review, Atlantic Monthly, New Republic,* and *Washington Post Book World.* Editorial board, fifty-eight volume "Politics and People" series, Arno, 1974. Editorial board, *Columbia University Forum,* 1960-64; board of directors, *American Journal, 1900-2000;* advisory board, *America: History and Life;* editorial advisory board, *Political Science Quarterly* and *American Heritage.* Editorial consultant, *Columbia Encyclopedia.*

WORK IN PROGRESS: Final volume of "Oxford History of the United States" and a book on the Supreme Court crisis of 1937, both for Oxford University Press; an essay on the class aspect of electoral behavior in the Great Depression.

BIOGRAPHICAL/CRITICAL SOURCES: *New York Times Book Review,* December 25, 1983.

* * *

LEVENDOSKY, Charles (Leonard) 1936-

PERSONAL: Born July 4, 1936, in Bronx, N.Y.; son of Charles Leonard (an army officer) and Laura (Gregorio) Levendosky; married Charlotte Anne Jaeger (an elementary teacher), July 15, 1961; children: Alytia Akiko, Ixchel Nicole. *Education:* University of Oklahoma, B.S., 1958, B.A., 1960, graduate study, 1960-61; New York University, M.A. in Ed., 1963. *Address:* (Permanent) c/o Mrs. Charles Levendosky, 4841 Crisp Way, San Diego, Calif. 92117. *Office address:* P.O. Box 3033, Casper, Wyo. 82602.

CAREER: High school teacher of mathematics and science in Christiansted, St. Croix, U.S. Virgin Islands, 1963-65, and in New York City, 1966-68; New York University, New York City, part-time instructor for Project Apex, 1967-68, instructor, 1968-70, assistant professor of English, 1970-71; Georgia Southern College, Statesboro, poet-in-residence and associate director of Project Radius of Georgia Commission on the Arts, summers, 1971, 1972; Wyoming Council on the Arts, Casper, poet-in-residence and director of Poetry Programs of Wyoming, 1972-82; *Casper Star-Tribune,* Casper, arts editor, columnist, and opinion and editorial page editor, 1982—. *Military service:* U.S. Army, 1961-62 ("given a discharge after proving my reluctance to be made into a killing machine"). *Member:* P.E.N., International Platform Association. *Awards, honors:* Teacher of the Year Award, 1965; National Endowment for the Arts fellow, 1974-75; Governor's Award for the Arts, 1983, for contributions to the arts of Wyoming.

WRITINGS: perimeters (an extended poem), Wesleyan University Press, 1970; (contributor) R. Kostelanetz, editor, *Breakthrough Fictioneers* (anthology), Something Else Press, 1972; *small town america* (poem), engravings by Bernard Solomon, Boxwood Press, 1974; *words & fonts* (poster poems), graphics by Solomon, Council on the Arts, 1975; *aspects of the vertical* (poetry), Point Riders Press, 1978; *Distances* (poetry), Dooryard Press, 1980; *Wyoming Fragments* (poetry), Buffalo Point Press, 1981; *Nocturnes* (poetry), Dooryard Press, 1982. Also author of libretto "From Hell to Breakfast." Contributor of poetry and reviews to *Parnassus, Poetry in Review, Paintbrush,* and other magazines. Member of advisory board, *New York Quarterly.*

WORK IN PROGRESS: The third volume of a projected quartet tentatively entitled *boomtown wyoming,* to be a continuation of *perimeters* and *aspects of the vertical.*

SIDELIGHTS: Charles Levendosky wrote to *CA:* "In the past twenty years I have collaborated with filmmakers, composers, graphic artists, choreographers, and musicians [in the] belief that the range and concept of poetry must be expanded. Each of these collaborations, conversely, has taught me something about the possibilities of poetry on the page. I have learned as much about 'language' from these experiments as I have writing poetry for twenty-five years."

In 1978 Levendosky was invited to perform at the Eleventh International Festival of Sound Poetry held in Toronto.

* * *

LEVI, Primo 1919-

PERSONAL: Born July 31, 1919, in Turin, Italy; son of Cesare (a civil engineer) and Ester (Luzzati) Levi; married Lucia Morpurgo (a teacher), September 8, 1947; children: Lisa, Renzo. *Education:* University of Turin, degree in chemistry, 1941. *Religion:* Jewish. *Home:* Corso Re Umberto 75, Turin, Italy.

CAREER: Partisan in Italian Resistance, 1943; deported to Auschwitz Concentration Camp in Oswiecim, Poland, and imprisoned there, 1943-45; SIVA (paints, enamels, synthetic resins), Settimo, Turin, Italy, technical executive, 1948-74. *Awards, honors:* Premio Campiello (Venice literary prize), 1963, for *La Tregua,* and 1982, for *Se non ora, quando?;* Premio Bagutta (Milan literary prize), 1967, for *Storie Naturali;* Premio Strega (Rome literary prize), 1979, for *La chiave a stella;* Premio Viareggio (Viareggio literary prize), 1982, for *Se non ora, quando?*

WRITINGS: Se Questo e un Uomo, F. de Silva (Turin), 1947, 11th edition, Einaudi, 1967, translation by Stuart Woolf published as *If This Is a Man,* Orion Press (New York), 1959, published as *Survival in Auschwitz: The Nazi Assault on Humanity,* Collier, 1961, new edition, 1966 (published in England as *If This Is a Man,* Bodley Head, 1966), dramatic version in original Italian (with Pieralberto Marche), Einaudi, 1966; *La Tregua,* Einaudi, 1958, 8th edition, 1965, translation by Woolf published as *The Reawakening,* Little, Brown, 1965 (published in England as *The Truce: A Survivor's Journey Home from Auschwitz,* Bodley Head, 1965); *Storie Naturali,* Einaudi, 1967; (with Carlo Quartucci) *Intervista Aziendale* (radio script), Radiotelevisione Italiana, 1968.

Vizio di Forma, Einaudi, 1971; *Il sistema periodico,* Einaudi, 1975; *Shema: Collected Poems,* Menard, 1976; *La chiave a stella,* Einaudi, 1978; *Se non ora, quando?,* Einaudi, 1982, translation published as *If Not Now, When?,* Summit Books, in press.

SIDELIGHTS: Primo Levi told *CA:* "My uncommon experience as a concentration camp inmate and as a survivor has deeply influenced my later life and has turned me into a writer. The two books [*Se Questo e un Uomo* and *Le Tregua*] . . . are a chronicle of my exile and an attempt to understand its meaning."

If This Is a Man and *The Reawakening,* the English translations of *Se Questo e un Uomo* and *Le Tregua,* have been widely praised for their portrayal of Levi's imprisonment and subsequent return home. W. J. Cahnman, for example, reviewing *If This Is a Man* in *American Journal of Sociology,* writes: "Here is literally a report from hell: the detached, scientific, unearthly story of a man who descended to the nether world at Auschwitz and returned to the land of the living." Levi's "lack of personal bitterness is almost unnatural, especially when it is realised that he wrote so soon after the German retreat brought him his freedom," notes G. F. Seddon in the *Manchester Guardian.* "Levi's more outstanding virtue is his compassionate understanding of how in these conditions men cease to be men, either give up the struggle or in devious ways win it, usually at the expense of their fellow men."

Sergio Pacifici points out in *Saturday Review* that like *If This Is a Man, The Reawakening* is more than an intimate and accurate diary. "It is a plea for self-restraint and generosity in human relations that may well be heeded in our own critical times," he says. "Levi's lucid and wise reflections on the nature of man deserve more than a mere hearing. *The Reawakening* must take its honored place next to Carlo Levi's *Christ Stopped at Eboli,* Andre Schwartz-Bart's *The Last of the Just,* and *The Diary of Anne Frank.*"

BIOGRAPHICAL/CRITICAL SOURCES: *Saturday Review,* January 2, 1960, May 15, 1965; *Times Literary Supplement,* April 15, 1960, December 3, 1982; *Manchester Guardian,* April 22, 1960, February 12, 1965; *American Journal of Sociology,* May, 1960; *Observer,* January 26, 1965; *New York Times Book Review,* November 7, 1965.

* * *

LEWIS, David 1942-
(David Hodgson)

PERSONAL: Born April 6, 1942, in London, England. *Education:* Educated in France, Germany, and the United Kingdom. *Agent:* Joan Daves, 54 East 54th St., New York, N.Y. *Address:* The Darbies, East Dean, Eastbourne, Sussex, England.

CAREER: Began journalism career as photographer; worked for two years at the Central London Polytechnic School of Photography; became free-lance magazine photographer, contributing to *Paris Match, Stern,* and *Life;* was appointed editorial director of Features International, a British news syndicate, and worked for them as a journalist and photographer for several years; currently full-time writer. Director of Action on Phobias. Lecturer and broadcaster.

WRITINGS: (With Peter Hughman) *Most Unnatural: An Inquiry into the Stafford Case,* Penguin, 1971; (with Hughman) *Just How Just?,* Secker & Warburg, 1975; *Sexpionage: The Exploitation of Sex by Soviet Intelligence,* Harcourt, 1976; (with Robert Sharpe) *The Success Factor: How to Be Who You Want to Be,* Crown, 1976; *Hitler: The Secret Life of Adolf Hitler,* Hanau, 1977; (with Sharpe) *Thrive on Stress: How to Make It Work for You,* Souvenir Press, 1977, published as *Thrive on Stress: How to Make It Work to Your Advantage,* Warner Books, 1978; *The Secret Language of Your Child: How Children Talk Before They Can Speak,* Souvenir Press, 1978; (with Sharpe) *The Anxiety Antidote: How to Beat the Fear Response,* Souvenir Press, 1979; (with James Greene) *The Hidden Language of Your Handwriting: The Remarkable New Science of Graphonomy and What It Reveals about Personality, Health and Emotions,* Souvenir Press, 1980; *How to Be a Gifted Parent: Realise Your Child's Potential,* Souvenir Press, 1980; (with Greene) *Thinking Better,* Rawson Associates, 1982. Also author of *You Can Teach Your Child Intelligence,* Souvenir Press, *Know Your Own Mind,* Penguin, *Your Child's Drawings: Their Hidden Meaning,* Hutchinson, and *Fight Your Phobia and Win,* Sheldon Press.

Under pseudonym David Hodgson; all published by Transatlantic: *All about Photographing Animals and Birds,* 1975; *All about Action Photography,* 1976; *Dive, Dive, Dive: A Guide to Sport Diving,* 1976.

WORK IN PROGRESS: Research at the University of Sussex.

SIDELIGHTS: David Lewis writes *CA:* "After working as a journalist for a number of years, I resigned as director of Britain's major independent syndication service to return to academic studies. In great part this decision was motivated by covering stories in Northern Ireland and other world trouble spots. I decided I could make better use of my time than in reporting tragedies. Subsequently, [I] obtained a first class honours degree in psychology and a Ph.D. at the University of Sussex.

"I have a special research interest in the effects of the emotions on intellectual attainment. I am currently a director of Action on Phobias, a charity which I set up in order to provide help for phobic sufferers. I am also involved in helping children think more effectively through a special home-based training programme which I have created. Currently more than a thousand families are working with my methods."

Lewis indicates that his books on the psychology of stress and on child development have been published in more than thirty countries.

* * *

LEWIS, James, Jr. 1930-

PERSONAL: Born March 7, 1930, in Newark, N.J.; son of James and Marie (Wilkerson) Lewis; married Valdmir M. Cummins, August 17, 1954; children: Michael, Patricia, Terence. *Education:* Hampton Institute, B.S., 1953; Columbia University, M.S., 1957; East Coast University, Ed.D., 1970; Harvard University, postdoctoral study, 1970-71; Antioch College, Ph.D., 1971. *Office:* EIC/NE, 2 Babcock Pl., West Orange, N.Y. 07052.

CAREER: Industrial arts teacher in Jersey City, N.J., 1956-57; Wyandanch (N.Y.) public schools, special education teacher, 1957-59, director of special education, 1959-66, elementary principal, 1966-67, district principal, 1967-72; Villanova University, Villanova, Pa., associate professor of education, 1972-73; Medgar Evers College of the City University of New York, Brooklyn, N.Y., professor of education, and chairman of division of technical education, 1973-74; Central Berkshire Regional School District, Dalton, Mass., superintendent of schools, 1974; executive director, Educational Improvement Center Northeast, 1974— . Consultant to National Center for Education Research and Development, New York State Department of Education, 1970-71. *Military service:* U.S. Army Reserve, 1955-67; became major.

MEMBER: American Association of School Administrators, National Education Association, American Association of University Professors, National Alliance of Black School Educators, Association for Supervision and Curriculum Development, American Society of Training and Development, American Management Association, National Society of Corporate Planners, Massachusetts Association of School Superintendents, New Jersey Association of School Administrators. *Awards, honors:* Alfred North Whitehead fellow, Harvard University, 1970-71.

WRITINGS—Published by Parker Publishing, except as indicated: *A Contemporary Approach to Nongraded Education,* 1969; *The Tragedies in American Education,* Exposition, 1971; *Differentiating the Teaching Staff,* 1971; *Administering the Individualized Instruction Program,* 1971; (with Robert M. Bookbinder and Raymond R. Bauer) *Critical Issues in Education: A Problem-Solving Guide for School Administrators,* Prentice-Hall, 1972; *Appraising Teacher Performance,* 1973; *School Management by Objectives,* 1974; *Administrator's Complete Guide to Individualized Instruction: A Professional Handbook,* 1977.

BIOGRAPHICAL/CRITICAL SOURCES: School Management, March, 1969; *Think,* October, 1969.

* * *

LIEBER, Robert J(ames) 1941-

PERSONAL: Born September 29, 1941, in Chicago, Ill.; son

of Nathan R. and Beatrice (Bespalow) Lieber; married Nancy Lee Isaksen, June 20, 1964; children: Benjamin Yves, Keir Alexander. *Education:* University of Wisconsin, B.A. (with honors), 1963; University of Chicago, NDEA Title IV fellow in political science, 1963-64; Harvard University, Ph.D., 1968, Knox traveling fellow in London, 1966-67; St. Antony's College, Oxford, visiting fellow, 1969-70. *Office:* Department of Government, Georgetown University, Washington, D.C. 20057.

CAREER: United Nations Student Intern, New York, N.Y., 1962; University of California, Davis, assistant professor, 1968-72, associate professor, 1972-77, professor of political science, 1977-81, chairman of department, 1975-76 and 1977-80; Georgetown University, Washington, D.C., professor of government, 1982—. Visiting scholar, Inter-University Consortium for Political Research, Ann Arbor, Mich., summer, 1968; research associate, Harvard University Center for International Affairs, 1974-75. Fellow of Woodrow Wilson International Center for Scholars, 1980-81.

MEMBER: American Political Science Association, American Civil Liberties Union, International Studies Association, Phi Beta Kappa. *Awards, honors:* Social Science Research Council postdoctoral research training fellowship, 1969-70; Council on Foreign Relations International Affairs fellowship, 1972; Guggenheim fellowship, 1973; Rockefeller International Relations fellowship, 1978-79.

WRITINGS: British Politics and European Unity: Parties, Elites, and Pressure Groups, University of California Press, 1970; *Theory and World Politics,* Winthrop Publishing, 1972; (co-author) *Contemporary Politics: Europe,* Winthrop Publishing, 1976; *Oil and the Middle East War,* Harvard University Center for International Affairs, 1976; (co-editor and contributor) *Eagle Entangled: U.S. Foreign Policy in a Complex World,* Longman, 1979; (editor and contributor) *Will Europe Fight for Oil?,* Praeger, 1983; (co-editor and contributor) *Eagle Defiant: U.S. Foreign Policy in the 1980s,* Little, Brown, 1983; *The Oil Decade: Conflict and Cooperation in the West,* Praeger, 1983.

Contributor of articles to periodicals, including *International Affairs* (London), *American Political Science Review, International Security, Politique Etrangere, Harpers, New York Times,* and *Washington Post.*

WORK IN PROGRESS: Writing on European-American relations and on U.S. foreign policy.

* * *

LIFTON, Betty Jean

PERSONAL: Born in New York, N.Y.; daughter of Oscar and Hilda Kirschner; married Robert Jay Lifton (a professor of psychiatry), March 1, 1952; children: Kenneth Jay, Karen. *Education:* Barnard College, B.A., 1948. *Agent:* Berenice Hoffman, Berenice Hoffman Literary Agency, 215 West 75th St., New York, N.Y. 10023.

CAREER: Children's author, playwright, and journalist. *Awards, honors: New York Herald Tribune* award, 1960, for *Kap the Kappa,* and 1970, for *Return to Hiroshima;* National Book Award nomination, 1975, for *Children of Vietnam.*

WRITINGS: Joji and the Dragon, Morrow, 1957; *Mogo the Mynah,* Morrow, 1958; *Joji and the Fog,* Morrow, 1959; *Kap the Kappa,* Morrow, 1960; *The Dwarf Pine Tree,* Atheneum, 1963; *Joji and the Amanojaku,* Norton, 1965; *The Cock and the Ghost Cat,* Atheneum, 1965; *The Rice-Cake Rabbit,* Norton, 1966; *Many Lives of Chio and Garo,* Norton, 1966; *Taka-Chan and I: A Dog's Journey to Japan,* Norton, 1967; *The One-Legged Ghost* (Junior Literary Guild selection), Atheneum, 1968; *Kap and the Wicked Monkey,* Norton, 1968; *The Secret Seller,* Norton, 1968; *A Dog's Guide to Tokyo,* Norton, 1969.

Return to Hiroshima (Junior Literary Guild selection), Atheneum, 1970; "Moon Walk" (children's play), first produced on Broadway at City Center, November 26, 1970; *The Mud Snail Son,* Atheneum, 1971; *The Silver Crane,* Seabury, 1971; (with Thomas C. Fox) *Children of Vietnam,* Atheneum, 1972; *Good Night, Orange Monster,* Atheneum, 1972; (editor) *Contemporary Children's Theater,* Avon, 1974; *Twice Born: Memoir of an Adopted Daughter,* McGraw, 1975; *Jaguar, My Twin,* Atheneum, 1976; *Lost and Found: The Adoption Experience,* Dial, 1979; *I'm Still Me,* Knopf, 1981. Contributor to newspapers and periodicals.

SIDELIGHTS: Betty Jean Lifton sees the institution of legal adoption as a procedure built on pretense and deception, calling it in *Lost and Found: The Adoption Experience* "The Game of As If." Her own experience as an adopted child, chronicled in *Twice Born: Memoir of an Adopted Daughter,* convinced her that the typical "identity crisis" of adolescence is aggravated and prolonged by being adopted. "What [Lifton] didn't know, all wisdom to the contrary, *did* hurt her," writes Julia Whedon in the *New York Times Book Review.* "She worried about herself. She felt ashamed, counterfeit. She hid her doubts and feelings until they festered. To save herself she had to find herself; she began her own rescue at thirty." Whedon believes that Lifton "makes a very strong case for open access to adoption records and common cause with those relatively new private agencies organized to help others as Mrs. Lifton, independently and courageously, helped herself."

BIOGRAPHICAL/CRITICAL SOURCES: New York Times Book Review, December 1, 1972, November 2, 1975, July 15, 1979, April 26, 1981; Betty Jean Lifton, *Twice Born: Memoir of an Adopted Daughter,* McGraw, 1975; Lifton, *Lost and Found: The Adoption Experience,* Dial, 1979; *Washington Post Book World,* April 22, 1979.

* * *

LIN, Florence (Shen)

PERSONAL: Married K. Y. Lin (in investments); children: Flora, Kay. *Education:* Attended University of Nanking. *Home:* 4525 Henry Hudson Parkway, Bronx, N.Y. 10471.

CAREER: Cooking teacher and writer, specializing in Chinese food and nutrition. Teacher at China Institute in America, 1960—. Has conducted more than a hundred cooking demonstrations. Consultant to metropolitan restaurants and major food processors.

WRITINGS—Published by Hawthorn: *Florence Lin's Chinese Regional Cookbook: A Guide to the Origins, Ingredients, and Cooking Methods of Over Two Hundred Regional Specialties and National Favorites, with Special Sections on Chinese Eating and Cooking Utensils, Planning and Preparation of Menus, Chinese Teas, Wines, and Spirits,* 1975; *Florence Lin's Chinese Vegetarian Cookbook,* 1976; *Florence Lin's Chinese One-Dish Meals,* 1978; *Florence Lin's Cooking with Fire Pots,* 1979.

SIDELIGHTS: As a young woman, Florence Lin traveled extensively with her father, visiting all the important cities of China. The dinners that accompanied each visit gave her opportunities to sample the more unusual delicacies, as well as the finer preparations of the more common. In 1965 and 1969, she returned to the Far East to survey and study the markets, food businesses, and the cooking. Now, she teaches her students to prepare Chinese foods, properly order a meal in a Chinese restaurant, and comfortably find their way among the myriad grocery shops in lower Manhattan's Chinatown. She offers beginners' courses and conducts an advanced course in banquet dishes, Chinese hors d'oeuvres, and a variety of Dim Sum.

* * *

LIND, Alan R(obert) 1940-

PERSONAL: Born January 21, 1940, in Chicago, Ill.; son of Albin Matthias (an auditor) and Minnette (Swanson) Lind. *Education:* University of Chicago, B.A. (liberal arts) and B.A. (business administration), 1962; graduate study at Northwestern University, 1964-67. *Politics:* Democratic. *Religion:* Evangelical Covenant. *Home:* 141 Hemlock, Park Forest, Ill. 60466.

CAREER: Illinois Central Magazine, Chicago, Ill., editorial assistant, 1964-66, assistant editor, 1966-71; *Illinois Central Gulf News,* Chicago, editor, 1971-75; Burson-Marsteller (public relations firm), Chicago, technical writer, 1975-77; account executive, Gardner, Jones & Co. (public relations firm), 1977-78; account executive, Hill & Knowlton, Inc. (public relations firm), 1979—. Co-founder, publisher and general editor of Prototype Publications, Park Forest, Ill., 1972—; publications director of Central Electric Railfans' Association, 1974. Founder of Transport History Press; lecturer at American Management Association seminars, 1973. *Military service:* U.S. Army Reserve, 1963-69.

MEMBER: International Association of Business Communicators, International Platform Association, American Judicature Society, Association of Railroad Editors, Professional Photographers of America, National Museum of Transport, Chicago Press Club, Chicago Historical Society, Industrial Editors Association of Chicago, Chicago Association of Business Communicators, Chicago Gallery of Photography (exhibiting member, 1970-71), Park Forest Racquet Club. *Awards, honors:* Golden Trumpet Award from Publicity Club of Chicago, 1981 and 1982.

WRITINGS: (Editor with W. D. Randall) *From Zephyr to Amtrak,* Prototype Publications, 1972; (editor with Randall) *Monarchs of Mid-America,* Prototype Publications, 1973; *Chicago Surface Lines: An Illustrated History,* Transport History Press, 1974, 3rd revised edition, 1979; *Horsecars to Streamliners: An Illustrated History of the St. Louis Car Company,* Transport Historical Press, 1978. Mass transit and commuter railroad columnist, *Passenger Train Journal,* 1982—.

WORK IN PROGRESS: A book on the Illinois Central Railroad's motive power.

SIDELIGHTS: Alan R. Lind once wrote *CA:* "Passenger transportation is my field, particularly travel by main line railroad train, and urban transportation by streetcar, motor bus, trolley bus, subway, and elevated. Concern about pollution, the gas shortage, and a re-ordering of national priorities have made both main line train travel and urban public transportation increasingly important.... In searching for material on transportation, I have visited every continental state and seen much of Canada. My camera is always with me on these trips."

LIPPITT, Gordon L(eslie) 1920-

PERSONAL: Born August 20, 1920, in Fergus Falls, Minn.; son of Walter Otis and Lois (Garvey) Lippitt; married Phyllis E. Parker, June 6, 1942; children: Anne (Mrs. Thomas Rarich), Mary (Mrs. Bruce Burner), Constance J. (Mrs. Robert Ridgway). *Education:* Springfield College, Springfield, Mass., B.S., 1942; Yale University, B.D., 1946; University of Nebraska, M.A., 1947; American University, Ph.D., 1959. *Politics:* Democrat. *Home:* 5605 Lamar Rd., Washington, D.C. 20016. *Office:* School of Government and Business Administration, George Washington University, Washington, D.C. 20006.

CAREER: Industrial Recreation Federation, New Haven, Conn., director, 1942-45; executive secretary of University of Nebraska YMCA, 1945-49; Union College, Schenectady, N.Y., assistant professor of psychology, 1949-50; National Education Association, Washington, D.C., program director of National Training Laboratories and assistant director of Division of Adult Education Service, 1950-59; George Washington University, Washington, D.C., professor of behavioral science, 1959—, founder and director of Center for the Behavioral Sciences, 1960-65. Mutual Security Agency, Productivity Division, Paris, France, education and training specialist, 1952-53, chief of industrial training and education branch, 1953-54.

Program director, White House Conference on Children and Youth, 1950; Rufus Jones Lecturer, American Friends Service Committee, 1966; visiting scholar, University of California, Los Angeles, 1967. Leadership Resources, Inc., president, 1960-67, chairman of board, 1967-68; member of board of directors, Washington YMCA, 1965-73, Petroleum Exploration and Drilling Fund, 1968-70, and Data Financial Corp., 1969; chairman of the board, International Consultants Foundation, 1973—, and Organization Renewal, Inc., 1974—. President of Glenwood Manor Estates, Deland, Fla., 1968—, Franklin Parker Corp., 1970-73, and Project Associates, Inc., Washington, D.C., 1973—.

MEMBER: World Futurist Society, American Psychological Association, National Education Association (life member), Academy of Management, American Society for Public Administration, Society for the Psychological Study of Social Issues, American Management Association, American Society for Training and Development (member of board of directors, 1965-69; president, 1969), Society for Personnel Administration, American Association of University Professors.

AWARDS, HONORS: National Award of Young Men's Christian Associations, 1942; Distinguished Civilian Service Award, U.S. Army, 1962; Dow Leadership Award, Hillsdale College, 1970; LL.D., Springfield College, 1971; Annual Authors Award, Training Officers Conference, 1974; Torch Award, 1975, and Gordon Bliss Award, 1982, both from American Society for Training and Development; McHenry Award, Industrial Management Council, 1983, for contributions to management.

WRITINGS: (Editor) *Leadership in Action,* National Institute of Applied Behavioral Science, 1957; (with Edith W. Seashore) *The Leader and Group Effectiveness,* Association Press, 1962; *Quest for Dialogue,* Friends General Conference, 1966; *Organization Renewal,* Prentice-Hall, 1969, 2nd edition, 1982; (with others) *Optimizing Human Resources: Readings in Individual and Organization Development,* Addison-Wesley, 1971; *Visualizing Chance,* University Associates, 1973; (with F. Taylor) *Management Development and Training Handbook,* McGraw, 1975; (co-author) *Consulting Process in Action,* University Associates, 1978; (co-author) *Systems Thinking,* International Consultants Foundation, 1981.

Also author of more than three hundred articles and pamphlets. Guest columnist for *Nation's Cities*, 1967-68, and *Training and Development Journal*, 1982-83. Editor, *Journal of Social Issues*, 1960.

SIDELIGHTS: Gordon L. Lippitt told *CA* that early in his writing career, he felt a need to fulfill his ego by impressing his colleagues and leaving a memory for his grandchildren. Later, he realized "whether one communicates in a manner that the reader can understand, use, and value [is far more important and] a continuing challenge."

* * *

LISTON, Robert A. 1927-

PERSONAL: Born August 23, 1927, in Youngstown, Ohio; son of Benjamin Furman and Lola (Carder) Liston; married Jean Altman, September 8, 1950; children: Cynthia Kay, Stephen Ward, Felicia Kay. *Education:* Hiram College, A.B., 1949. *Home:* 30 Marvin Ave., Shelby, Ohio 44875. *Agent:* Curtis Brown Ltd., 575 Madison Ave., New York, N.Y. 10022.

CAREER: Former newspaperman in Marion, Ohio, 1954, Mansfield, Ohio, 1954-56, and on *Baltimore News American*, Baltimore, Md., 1956-64; now full-time free-lance writer. *Military service:* U.S. Army, Infantry, 1952-53; served in Korea. *Awards, honors:* Christopher Book Award, 1974, for *The Right to Know: Censorship in America*.

WRITINGS: *Sargent Shriver: A Candid Portrait*, Farrar, Straus, 1964; *Your Career in Law Enforcement*, Messner, 1965, revised edition, 1973; *Your Career in Civil Service*, Messner, 1966; *Your Career in Transportation*, Messner, 1966; *Great Detectives*, Platt, 1966; *Tides of Justice*, Delacorte, 1966.

On the Job Training and Where to Get It, Messner, 1967, revised edition, 1973; *Your Career in Selling*, Messner, 1967; *The Dangerous World of Spies and Spying*, Platt, 1967; (with Robert M. N. Crosby) *The Waysiders: Reading and the Dyslexic Child*, Delacorte, 1968 (published in England as *Reading and the Dyslexic Child*, Souvenir Press, 1969); *Downtown: Our Challenging Urban Problems*, Delacorte, 1968; *Politics from Precinct to President*, Delacorte, 1968; *What You Should Know about Pills*, Pocket Books, 1968; *The Pros*, Platt & Monk, 1968; (with Surrey Marshe) *The Girl in the Centerfold*, Dell, 1969.

Slavery in America: The History of Slavery (Child Study Association book list), McGraw, 1970; *The American Poor* (Child Study Association book list), Delacorte, 1970; *Greetings, You Are Hereby Ordered for Induction: The Story of the Draft*, McGraw, 1970; *The Limits of Defiance: Strikes, Rights and Government*, F. Watts, 1971; *Young Americans Abroad*, Messner, 1971; *Dissent in America*, McGraw, 1971; *Edge of Madness: Prisons and Prison Reform in America*, F. Watts, 1972; *Slavery in America: The Heritage of Slavery*, McGraw, 1972; *Who Shall Pay?: Taxes and Tax Reform in America*, Messner, 1972, revised edition, 1976; *When Reason Fails: Psychotherapy in America*, Macrae, 1972; *Presidential Power: How Much Is Too Much?*, McGraw, 1972; *The American Political System*, Parents Magazine Press, 1972.

The Right to Know: Censorship in America, F. Watts, 1973; *The United States and the Soviet Union: A Background Book on the Struggle for Power*, Parents Magazine Press, 1973; *The Ugly Palaces: Housing in America*, F. Watts, 1974; *Violence in America: A Search for Perspective*, Messner, 1974; *Healing the Mind: Eight Views of Human Nature*, Praeger, 1974; *Who Really Runs America?*, Doubleday, 1974; *Who Stole the Sunset?: Dilemmas in Morality*, Thomas Nelson, 1974; *Defense against Tyranny: A Balance of Power in Government*, Messner, 1975; *We, the People?: Congressional Power*, McGraw, 1975; *Getting in Touch with Your Government*, Messner, 1975.

Promise or Peril?: The Role of Technology in Society, Thomas Nelson, 1976; *Patients or Prisoners?: The Mentally Ill in America*, F. Watts, 1976; *By These Faiths: Religions for Today*, Messner, 1977; *The Charity Racket*, Thomas Nelson, 1977; *Why We Think as We Do*, F. Watts, 1977; *Terrorism*, Thomas Nelson, 1977; *Women Who Ruled: Cleopatra to Elizabeth II*, Messner, 1978; *The Great Teams: Why They Win All the Time*, Doubleday, 1979. Also author, under pseudonyms, of ten novels. Contributor to national magazines.

SIDELIGHTS: Robert A. Liston writes: "I am heavily committed to writing books for teenagers, a field I never considered when I began to write. . . . The secret is to write *up* to teenagers, for they know more than adults."

Liston's books have been published in Britain and translated into Dutch, German, Swedish, Italian, and Japanese.

* * *

Lo BELLO, Nino 1921-

PERSONAL: Born September 8, 1921, in Brooklyn, N.Y.; son of Joseph and Rosalie (Moscarelli) Lo Bello; married Irene Helen Rooney, February 22, 1948; children: Susan, Thomas. *Education:* Queens College (now Queens College of the City University of New York), B.A., 1947; New York University, M.A., 1948, graduate study, 1948-50. *Politics:* Liberal. *Religion:* Roman Catholic. *Home:* 24 Lenaugasse, 3400 Weidling bei Vienna, Austria. *Agent:* Paul Gitlin, 7 West 51st St., New York, N.Y. 10019.

CAREER: Newspaper reporter in Brooklyn, N.Y., 1946-50; University of Kansas, Lawrence, instructor in sociology, 1950-56; Rome correspondent for *Business Week* and McGraw-Hill's *World News*, 1957-62, and *New York Journal of Commerce*, 1962-64; *New York Herald Tribune*, New York, N.Y., economic correspondent in Vienna, Austria, 1964-66; free-lance writer. Visiting professor at Denison University, 1956, and University of Alaska, 1974. *Military service:* U.S. Army, 1942-46. *Member:* Overseas Press Club of America, Foreign Press Club of Rome, Press Club of Vienna.

WRITINGS: *The Vatican Empire*, Trident, 1969; *Vatican, U.S.A.*, Simon & Schuster, 1972; *European Detours*, Hammond, Inc., 1981; *The Vatican Papers*, New English Library, 1982; *Vatikan im Zwielicht*, Econ Verlag, 1983. Contributor of more than 1,500 articles to periodicals.

WORK IN PROGRESS: Two books.

SIDELIGHTS: Nino Lo Bello told *CA*: "It has not been my purpose, in writing frequently about the Vatican, to demean the Roman Catholic religion (the one I grew up with and practice), either in the eyes of Catholics or non-Catholics. I make no judgment on the validity of the faith, for I recognize that the religion gives many people solace and joy. Furthermore, though I have not sought to rebut any Catholic tenets, I have concerned myself with certain imperfections and failings among the men who run the Church. As a journalist I have attempted in my books always to be as professionally objective as is humanly possible and let the facts speak for themselves.

"Whoever takes it upon himself to write about the Vatican could easily give the impression that he is an expert. There are, in my opinion, no experts on the Vatican. There are, indeed, Vatican-watchers, Vatican theorists, and Vaticanologists—but there are no Vatican experts. This reminds me of a story: During an audience one day when a dozen cardinals, bishops, and assorted clerics were present, and Pope Pius XII was in one of his rare good moods, he asked two young priests the same question: 'How long have you been in the Vatican?' The first man replied, 'Three weeks.' 'Then,' said the pope, 'you are an expert on the Vatican!' The second man gave as his reply, 'Three years.' 'Then,' said the pope, 'you know nothing about the Vatican!'"

AVOCATIONAL INTERESTS: Opera ("opera buff supreme").

BIOGRAPHICAL/CRITICAL SOURCES: New York Times, February 3, 1969; *Saturday Review,* February 8, 1969; *Commonweal,* February 28, 1969; *New York Times Book Review,* June 29, 1969; *Christian Science Monitor,* July 31, 1969.

* * *

LOCHMAN, Jan Milic 1922-

PERSONAL: Born April 3, 1922, in Nove Mesto, Czechoslovakia; son of Josef and Marie (Jelinek) Lochman; married Eliska Jerabek, September 19, 1952; children: Vera, Tomas, Marek. *Education:* Studied at Hus Faculty of Theology, Prague, 1945-46, University of St. Andrews, 1946-47, and University of Basel, 1947-48; Hus Faculty of Theology, Th.D., 1948. *Home:* Heuberg 33, 4051, Basel, Switzerland. *Office:* University of Basel, Basel, Switzerland.

CAREER: Clergyman of Czech Brethren Church; Comenius Faculty of Theology, Prague, Czechoslovakia, professor of theology, 1950-68; Union Theological Seminary, New York, N.Y., professor of theology, 1968-69; University of Basel, Basel, Switzerland, professor of theology, beginning 1969, Rector Magnificus, 1981-83. Noble Lecturer, Harvard University, 1970-71; visiting lecturer at other universities in the United States and in many European countries. Member of central committee, World Council of Churches; chairman of theological department, World Alliance of Reformed Churches, 1970-82. *Awards, honors:* D.D., University of Aberdeen, 1973.

WRITINGS: Nabozenske mysleni ceskeho obrozeni (title means "Religious Thought of the Czech Enlightenment"), Kalich, 1952; *Theologie und kalter Krieg* (booklet), Hefte aus Burgscheidungen, 1960; *Die Bedeutung geschichtlicher Ereignisse fuer ethische Entscheidungen,* EVZ Verlag, 1963; *Die Not der Versoehung,* Herbert Reich Evangelischer Verlag, 1963; (with Gerhard Bassarak) *Gemeinde in der veraenderten Welt,* Evangelische Verlagsanstalt, 1963; *Duchovni odkaz obrozeni: Dobrovsky, Bolzano, Kollar, Palacky* (title means "Legacy of the Enlightenment"), Kalich, 1964.

Herrschaft Christi in der saekularisierten Welt (booklet), EVZ Verlag, 1967; (with M. R. Shaull and Charles C. West) *Zur Theologie der Revolution,* Kaiser Verlag, 1967; *Church in a Marxist Society: A Czechoslovak Church,* Harper, 1970; *Perspektiven politischer Theologie,* TVZ Verlag, 1971; *Das radikale Erbe,* TVZ Verlag, 1972; *Christus oder Prometheus?,* Furche Verlag, 1972; (with Fritz Buri and Heinrich Ott) *Dogmatik im Dialog,* three volumes, Guetersloher Verlagshaus, 1973-76; *Traegt oder truegt die christliche Hoffnung?,* TVZ Verlag, 1974.

Marx begegnen, Guetersloher Verlagshaus, 1975, translation by Edwin H. Robertson published as *Encountering Marx,* Fortress, 1977; *Living Roots of Reformation,* Augsburg, 1979; *Reconciliation and Liberation,* Fortress, 1980; *Signposts to Freedom,* Augsburg, 1982; *Theology of Praise,* Knox, 1982; *Das Glaubensbekenntnis,* Guetersloher Verlagshaus, 1982; *Vom Sinn der Feste,* Reinhardt, 1982; *Comenius,* Imba, 1983.

WORK IN PROGRESS: An English translation of *Das Glaubensbekenntnis,* for publication by Fortress.

* * *

LOCKYER, Roger 1927-
(Philip Francis)

PERSONAL: Born November 26, 1927, in London, England; son of Walter (a businessman) and May-Florence (Cook) Lockyer. *Education:* Pembroke College, Cambridge, B.A. (with first class honors in history), 1950, M.A., 1955. *Politics:* Liberal. *Home:* 64 Fielding Rd., London W4 1HL, England.

CAREER: Lycee Louis-le-Grand, Paris, France, assistant in English, 1951-52; Haileybury and Imperial Service College, Hertford, England, head of history department, 1952-53; Ernest Benn Ltd. (publishers), London, England, assistant editor, "Blue Guides," 1953-54; Lancing College, Sussex, England, head of history department, 1954-61; University of London, London, temporary lecturer in history at Royal Holloway College, Englefield Green, Surrey, 1961-63, lecturer in history at Goldsmiths' College, 1963-64, and at Royal Holloway College, 1964—. *Military service:* Royal Navy, instructor, 1946-48; became lieutenant. *Member:* Economic History Society, Historical Association, Past and Present Society, Victorian Society, National Trust, London Library.

WRITINGS: (Editor) *The Trial of Charles I,* Folio Society, 1959; (with John Thorn and David Smith) *History of England,* Benn, 1961; (editor and author of introduction) *Cavendish's Life of Wolsey,* Folio Society, 1962; (under pseudonym Philip Francis; editor and author of introduction) *John Evelyn's Diary,* Folio Society, 1963; *Tudor and Stuart Britain, 1471-1741,* Longmans, Green, 1964; *The Monarchy,* Blond Educational, 1965; (editor) Richard Hyde Clarendon, *The History of the Great Rebellion,* Oxford University Press, 1967; (translator and adapter with John Thorn and D. Smith) Therese Henrot, *Histoire de l'Angleterre,* Gerard, 1968; *Henry VII,* Longmans, Green, 1968, Harper, 1971; (editor and author of introduction) Francis Bacon, *The History of the Reign of King Henry the Seventh,* Folio Society, 1971; *Habsburg and Bourbon Europe, 1470-1720,* Longman, 1974; *Buckingham: The Life and Political Career of George Villiers, First Duke of Buckingham, 1592-1628,* Longman, 1981.

SIDELIGHTS: "Almost everything about George Villiers, first Duke of Buckingham . . . is exceptional," writes Michael Ratcliffe in his London *Times* review of Roger Lockyer's historical study *Buckingham.* A court favorite of King James I, Villiers quickly rose to positions of political power, in which he was frequently accused of corruption; at the same time he was a military leader of disasterously poor ability. Villiers was assassinated at age thirty-six by lieutenant John Felton (Villiers had rejected a captain's commission for Felton) and at the funeral, according to Ratcliffe's review, "the drummers kept up a rattling tattoo to drown possible growls of rejoicing from the crowds, and the soldiers carried their arms on their shoulders, just in case, instead of trailing them in tribute on the ground."

"The career of Buckingham has never before been explored with the thoroughness of Roger Lockyer's scholarly and often arresting biography," states *Times Literary Supplement* critic

Patrick Collinson, "and consequently it is now better understood, and in a sense condoned. For unless the biographer begins with an overtly antagonistic purpose, his identification with his subject is almost bound to lead in a sympathetic direction and, in the case of a vilified figure like Buckingham, into an exercise in rehabilitation. Consequently, [the author's] impressive study reads as a contribution to the current work of revision which is ridding early Stuart history of its heroes and villians, playing down the sense of inexorable advancing constitutional crisis, and explaining the political conflicts of the age in terms of honest misunderstandings occuring within a malfunctioning political system."

AVOCATIONAL INTERESTS: Looking at buildings, reading novels and poetry, theater-going, cooking and eating.

BIOGRAPHICAL/CRITICAL SOURCES: Times (London), December 10, 1981; *Times Literary Supplement,* October 29, 1982.†

* * *

LOEB, Robert H., Jr. 1917-

PERSONAL: Born November 1, 1917, in New York, N.Y.; son of Robert H. (a stockbroker) and Irma (Fried) Loeb; married, 1937 (divorced); married Bette Harmon, September 6, 1943 (deceased); married Jeanne Starr (a dance teacher), July 2, 1964; children: (second marriage) Karen, Robert H. III. *Education:* Attended schools in Switzerland for four years as a boy; attended Brown University for three and one-half years (quit in senior year), and Columbia University. *Politics:* "Cultural Materialist." *Religion:* Episcopalian. *Home address:* R.R. 2, Box 88, Pomfret Center, Conn. 06259. *Agent:* Raines & Raines, 475 Fifth Ave., New York, N.Y. 10017.

CAREER: Writer. Worked on Wall Street for several years; *Esquire,* Chicago, Ill., 1944-47, began as promotion man, became aviation, games, cook, and drink editor; Pegasus Books, Inc. (mail order publishing business), Chicago, president, 1947-50; Norman, Craig & Kummel Agency, New York City, copywriter, 1952-54; Ted Bates & Co., New York City, copywriter, 1954-66. *Military service:* Served in Royal Canadian Air Force and U.S. Army Air Forces during World War II (long since a pacifist). *Member:* Episcopal Peace fellowship.

WRITINGS: Wolf in Chef's Clothing: The Picture Cook and Drink Book for Men, Wilcox & Follet, 1950, published as *The New Wolf in Chef's Clothing,* Follett, 1958; *Date Bait: The Younger Set's Picture Cookbook,* Wilcox & Follett, 1952; *She Cooks to Conquer,* Funk, 1952; *Nip Ahoy: The Picture Bar Guide,* Wilcox & Follett, 1954; *How to Wine Friends and Affluent People,* Follett, 1965; *Manners at Work: How They Help You toward Career Success,* Association Press, 1966; *Manners to Love by for Young Couples,* Association Press, 1971; (with Jean C. Vermes) *Male Power: The Young Man's Guide to Good Grooming,* Association Press, 1971. Also author of *What You Should No before Your Operation, Macho Medicine: From Eve to Ms., What Our Pets Want Us to Know about Vets, but Can't Tell Us,* and two novels.

All for young people: *He-Manners,* Association Press, 1954, revised edition, 1970; *Mary Alden's Cook Book for Children,* Wonder Books, 1955; *She-Manners,* Association Press, 1959, revised edition, 1970; *Manners for Minors,* Association Press, 1964; *The Sins of Bias,* M. Evans, 1970; *His and Hers Dating Manners,* Association Press, 1970; (with John P. Maloney) *Your Legal Rights as a Minor,* F. Watts, 1974; *New England Village: Everyday Life in 1810,* Doubleday, 1976; *Your Guide to Voting,* F. Watts, 1977; (with Vidal S. Clay) *Breaking the Sex-Role Barrier,* F. Watts, 1977; *Crime and Capital Punishment,* F. Watts, 1978; *Meet the Real Pilgrims: Everyday Life on Plimoth Plantation in 1627,* Doubleday, 1979; *Marriage: For Better or Worse,* F. Watts, 1980.

WORK IN PROGRESS: An adult nonfiction work that describes the social conditions of mill workers in the early nineteenth century.

SIDELIGHTS: Robert H. Loeb, Jr. writes: "Although I spent the past 15-20 years writing books for young adults (with a few juveniles thrown in), I am going back to the adult market for two very pragmatic reasons: young adults scarcely read, and the sales of such books are comparatively limited. It's too bad because they do need to be enlightened. But then, too, so do adults.

"In addition to a novel I completed with a very modest amount of aid from the Connecticut Commission on the Arts, I have finished a second one. However, neither of my agents will send it out and I'm having a problem getting editors to even read it. The solution would obviously be to write trash. But I can no more do that than a comparatively happily married woman could turn a few tricks for extra cash. Or could she?"

* * *

LOEPER, John J(oseph) 1929-
(Jay Lowe, Jr.)

PERSONAL: Born July 9, 1929, in Ashland, Pa.; son of Peter H. (a jeweler) and Mary (Monaghan) Loeper; married Jane B. Knawa, June 13, 1959. *Education:* Pennsylvania State University, A.B.S.; Trenton State College, B.S., M.A.; Protestant Episcopal University, London, Ph.D. *Religion:* Roman Catholic. *Residence:* New Hope, Pa. *Agent:* James Brown Associates, Inc., 25 West 43rd St., New York, N.Y. 10036.

CAREER: Teacher in Lambertville, N.J., 1952-56, and Princeton, N.J., 1956-59; Hatboro (Pa.) public schools, guidance counselor, 1959-61, administrator, 1961—. Guest lecturer, Bergische Universitat, 1975. President, New Hope-Solebury Board of Education; member of board of directors, New Hope Public Library. *Member:* National Education Association, Pennsylvania State Education Association. *Awards, honors:* American Educators Medal, Freedoms Foundation, 1965.

WRITINGS—Juvenile books, except as indicated; published by Atheneum, except as indicated: *Men of Ideas,* 1970; *Understanding Your Child through Astrology* (adult nonfiction), McKay, 1970; *Going to School in 1776,* 1975; *The Flying Machine,* 1976; *The Shop on High Street,* 1977; *The Golden Dragon: By Clipper Ship around the Horn,* 1978; *Mr. Marley's Main Street Confectionery,* 1979; *Galloping Gertrude,* 1981; *By Hook and Ladder,* 1982; *Away We Go!,* 1982; (self-illustrated) *The House on Spruce Street,* 1983; *Going to School in 1876,* 1984. Contributor of articles to education journals and to *Gourmet, Coronet,* and *Cats Magazine;* also contributor of drama reviews to newspapers.

WORK IN PROGRESS: A historical novel.

SIDELIGHTS: John J. Loeper writes: "My greatest pleasure comes from the letters I receive from my readers, especially the young readers. These let you know that your writing is being appreciated and enjoyed. And there is always pleasure in seeing your work in print. It makes the work and the waiting worthwhile."

AVOCATIONAL INTERESTS: Paintings in oils and watercolors.

BIOGRAPHICAL/CRITICAL SOURCES: Philadelphia Inquirer, October 17, 1982.

* * *

LOFLAND, John (Franklin) 1936-

PERSONAL: Born March 4, 1936, in Milford, Del.; married Lyn Hebert (a university professor), January 2, 1965. *Education:* Swarthmore College, B.A., 1958; Columbia University, M.A., 1960; University of California, Berkeley, Ph.D., 1964. *Home:* 523 E St., Davis, Calif. 95616. *Office:* Department of Sociology, University of California, Davis, Calif. 95616.

CAREER: University of Michigan, Ann Arbor, assistant professor of sociology, 1964-68; Sonoma State College (now Sonoma State University), Rohnert Park, Calif., associate professor of sociology, 1968-70; University of California, Davis, associate professor, 1970-74, professor of sociology, 1974—. *Member:* American Sociological Association, Pacific Sociological Association (president, 1980-81).

WRITINGS: Doomsday Cult: A Study of Conversion, Proselytization and Maintenance of Faith, Prentice-Hall, 1966, enlarged edition, Irvington, 1977; (with wife, Lyn H. Lofland) *Deviance and Identity,* Prentice-Hall, 1969; *Analyzing Social Settings: A Guide to Qualitative Observation and Analysis,* Wadsworth, 1971, second edition (with Lofland), 1984; *Doing Social Life,* Wiley, 1976; (with H. Bleackley) *State Executions,* Patterson Smith, 1977; (editor) *Social Strategies,* Sage Publications, 1977; *Crowd Lobbying,* University of California Institute of Governmental Studies, 1982; (with M. Fink) *Symbolic Sit-Ins,* University Press of America, 1982; *Protest: Essays on Collective Behavior and Social Movements,* Transaction Books, in press. Editor, *Urban Life: A Journal of Ethnographic Research,* 1972-75.

WORK IN PROGRESS: Human Gatherings: The Sociology of People in Assembly; Organizing for Social Change: Dynamics of Social Movement Organizations.

* * *

LONDON, Artur 1915-

PERSONAL: Born February 1, 1915, in Ostrava, Czechoslovakia; moved to France, 1963; naturalized French citizen, 1971; son of Emil and Berta (Lippe) London; married Elizabeth Ricol, 1946; children: Francoise, Gerard, Michel. *Education:* Attended public schools. *Politics:* Socialist. *Religion:* None. *Home:* 22-26 rue du Sergent Bauchat, Paris 12, France.

CAREER: Joined Communist Party at the age of 13; fought in the Spanish Civil War; joined French Army, 1939; active in the French Resistance during World War II and deported to concentration camp by the Nazis; Government of Czechoslovakia, Prague, Under Secretary of Foreign Affairs, 1949-51; arrested for treason and sentenced to prison term; released in 1958; moved to France, 1963. *Awards, honors*—Military: Legion d'honneur, Croix de guerre avec palmes, and Medaille de la Resistance. Made Officier de la Legion d'honneur, 1983. Other: Prix d'Aujourd'hui, 1969, for *L'Aveu.*

WRITINGS: Spanelko, Spanelko, Editions Politique (Prague), 1963; *L'Aveu,* Gallimard (Paris), 1968, translation by Alastair Hamilton published as *The Confession,* Morrow, 1970 (published in England as *On Trial,* Macdonald, 1970); *Se Levantaron antes del Alba,* Ediciones Peninsula (Barcelona), 1978; "Le Merle Siffleur" (play), first produced in Geneva, Switzerland, at Theatre de Carrouge, in November, 1980.

SIDELIGHTS: As a loyal member of the Communist Party for many years, Artur London fought against the Fascists during the Spanish Civil War, worked in the French Resistance during the Nazi occupation and, with the Soviet takeover of Eastern Europe in the late 1940s, served as the Under Secretary of Foreign Affairs for the communist government of Czechoslovakia.

London was serving in this position in 1951 when he and 13 other top Czech government officials were arrested and charged with treason. The defendants were accused of attempting to overthrow the government, and "of Trotskyism, Titoism, Zionism, and conspiracy with the West," as Mary-Kay Wilmers writes in *Listener.* The arrests were part of a general suppression of political independence in Eastern Europe by the Stalinist regime of the Soviet Union. During this same period, government officials in other satellite countries were also arrested and tried on serious charges. These trials, writes Edward Crankshaw in the *Observer,* were how Soviet leader Joseph Stalin "sought to demonstrate his absolute dominion over Central Europe. . . . The trials were ordered, devised, organized, and rehearsed in detail by the Soviet Secret Police . . . and modelled precisely on the notorious Moscow trials of the late 1930s."

The arrests of London and other Czech officials was also a move by the Soviets to remove Jewish leaders from political office. Eleven of the fourteen Czechs arrested were Jews. The same proportion held true for those arrested in Hungary and Bulgaria. "They were nearly all Jews," writes Crankshaw. "Stalin was killing off the Jews." Bernard Hrico of *Best Sellers* sees Stalin as having relied on native antisemitism to blunt criticism of the arrests. "Trumped-up charges against London," he writes, "would be easy because he was a Jew. He was victimized by neo-Nazi antisemitism which respected neither person nor principle."

London and the other defendants were found guilty after a show trial during which each defendant "confessed" to outlandish charges and denounced each other for crimes against the state. London's crime was leading a "Trotskyist conspiracy" against the regime. Eleven of the fourteen defendants were executed. London and two others received prison sentences.

In *The Confession,* London describes the ordeal of his arrest, trial, and prison term. The book, Hrico writes, "deals at great length with London's surveillance, arrest, trial, torture, and conditionings. The anguish and misery of London becomes that of the reader who suffers with him, spends nights and days in absolute horror." "London," Crankshaw explains, "was held in isolation, starved, beaten, brutalized, threatened, cajoled, under almost incessant interrogation for 20 months on end, his 'confessions' endlessly, brutally, lovingly tailored to tally with new confessions of others, to incriminate still more."

Because of his arrest and conviction, London came to renounce communism. He writes in *The Confession:* "It was the bureaucratic deformation of socialism, the suppression of criticism, the deification of the Party by the formulae 'the Party is always right' and 'the Party needs you' which put us on the wrong track." Although London regrets "his own acquiescence in these formulae," as Wilmers writes, he still has faith in a non-Soviet style socialism. "He still believes," Wilmers points out, "that 'the truth will triumph' and be 'wedded for ever with the "Internationale'"''

MEDIA ADAPTATIONS: *The Confession* was filmed in France in 1970.

BIOGRAPHICAL/CRITICAL SOURCES: *L'Express,* September 1-7, 1969, May 4-10, 1970; *Observer,* October 25, 1970; *Listener,* November 5, 1970; *Best Sellers,* December 15, 1970.

* * *

LONDON, Herbert I(ra) 1939-

PERSONAL: Born March 6, 1939, in New York, N.Y.; son of Jack (a salesman) and Esta (Epstein) London; married Vicki London, November 27, 1977; children: Stacy, Nancy. *Education:* Columbia University, B.A., 1960, M.A., 1961; New York University, Ph.D., 1966. *Religion:* Jewish. *Home:* 2 Washington Sq. Village, New York, N.Y. 10012. *Office:* New York University, 715 Broadway, New York, N.Y. 10003.

CAREER: New School for Social Research, New York City, instructor in American studies, 1966; Australian National University, Canberra, Australia, research associate, 1966-67; New York University, New York City, assistant professor, 1967-69, associate professor, 1969-76, professor of social studies, 1976—, director of "University without Walls," 1971-76, dean of Gallatin Division, 1976-77. Consultant, Hudson Institute, Institute for Advancement of Urban Education. *Member:* American Association of University Professors, American Historical Association, American Political Science Association, Pop Culture Association. *Awards, honors:* Anderson fellowship; Fulbright award; honorary degree from University of Aix Marseille.

WRITINGS: (Editor with Arnold Spinner) *Education in the Twenty-first Century* (papers from symposium sponsored by Center for Field Research and Social Services, New York University), Interstate, 1969; *Non-White Immigration and the White Australian Policy,* New York University Press, 1970; *Fitting In,* Grosset, 1974; *Social Science Theory, Structure and Application,* New York University Press, 1975; *The Overheated Decade,* New York University Press, 1976.

The Seventies: Counterfeit Decade, University Press of America, 1980; *Myths That Rule America,* University Press of America, 1981; *Closing the Circle: A Cultural History of the Rock Revolution,* Nelson-Hall, 1984; *Why Are They Lying to Our Children?,* Stein & Day, 1984. Contributor of articles to numerous periodicals, including *National Review, Saturday Review, New York Times, Washington Post, American Scholar,* and *Chronicles of Culture.*

WORK IN PROGRESS: A play based on the life of composer Harry Von Tilser.

SIDELIGHTS: Herbert I. London was the director of New York University's "University without Walls," a program established by nineteen American colleges and universities in 1971 to make college-level education more flexible and available to persons of all ages. Funded by grants from the U.S. Office of Education and the Ford Foundation, and administered by the Union for Experimenting Colleges and Universities at Antioch College, "University without Walls" offered degree credit for such off-campus activities as government and business internships, service in VISTA and the Peace Corps, travel abroad, and independent study.

London told *CA* that "playing college and professional basketball as well as making rock records in the late '50s" account for his current interest in pop culture.

* * *

LONG, Emmett
See LEONARD, Elmore

* * *

LONG, William Stuart
See STUART, (Violet) Vivian (Finlay)

* * *

LONGACRE, William A(tlas) II 1937-

PERSONAL: Born December 16, 1937, in Hancock, Mich.; son of William A. (a professor) and Doris (Green) Longacre. *Education:* Attended Michigan College of Mining and Technology (now Michigan Technological University), 1955-56; University of Illinois, B.A., 1959; University of Chicago, M.A., 1962, Ph.D., 1963. *Home:* 2133 West Window Rock Dr., Tucson, Ariz. 85745. *Office:* Department of Anthropology, University of Arizona, Tucson, Ariz. 85721.

CAREER: Field Museum of Natural History, Chicago, Ill., field assistant in anthropology, 1959-61, research assistant, 1961-64; University of Arizona, Tucson, assistant professor, 1964-68, associate professor, 1968-74, professor of anthropology, 1974—, director of Archaeological Field School, 1966—. Adjunct professor of anthropology, University of Hawaii, 1981—. University of Illinois at Urbana-Champaign, visiting assistant professor of anthropology, 1964, visiting lecturer at Chicago Undergraduate Division, summer, 1964. Visiting associate professor, Yale University, 1971-72; visiting professor, University of the Philippines, 1975-76 and 1979-80. Fellow, Center for Advanced Study in the Behavioral Sciences, 1972-73. *Member:* American Anthropological Association (fellow), American Association for the Advancement of Science (fellow), Society for American Archaeology, Arizona Academy of Science, Sigma Xi. *Awards, honors:* Woodrow Wilson fellowships, 1959-60, 1960-61, 1963.

WRITINGS—Editor: (And contributor) *Reconstructing Prehistoric Pueblo Societies,* University of New Mexico Press, 1970; Francois Bordes, *A Tale of Two Caves,* Harper, 1972; E. N. Wilmsen, *Lindenmeier: A Pleistocene Hunting Society,* Harper, 1974; T. P. Culbert, *The Lost Civilization: The Story of the Classic Maya,* Harper, 1974; (with J. N. Hill, Fred Plog, G. J. Gumerman, and D. Green) *World Archaeology,* Routledge & Kegan Paul, 1974.

Contributor: Sally R. Binford and Lewis R. Binford, editors, *New Perspectives in Archeology,* Aldine, 1968; Jennings and Hoebel, editors, *Readings in Anthropology,* McGraw, 1972; Ernestine Green, editor, *In Search of Man,* Little, Brown, 1973; *Research and Theory in Current Archaeology,* Wiley, 1973; *Man in Adaptation: The Biosocial Background,* 2nd edition (Longacre was not associated with previous edition), Aldine, 1974; Murray J. Leaf, editor, *Frontiers of Anthropology,* D. Van Nostrand, 1974; C. Moore, editor, *Reconstructing Complex Societies,* American Schools of Oriental Research, 1974; Ezra B.W. Zubrow, editor, *Demographic Anthropology: Quantitative Approaches,* University of New Mexico Press, 1976; Ian Hodder and others, editors, *Pattern of the Past: Studies in Honour of David Clarke,* Cambridge University Press, 1981.

Also author of foreword for *Prehistoric Southwestern Craft Arts,* by Clara Lee Tanner, University of Arizona Press, 1976. Contributor to *International Encyclopedia of the Social Sciences;* also contributor of numerous articles to various journals.

* * *

LOOMES, Brian 1938-

PERSONAL: Born in 1938, in Leeds, England. *Education:* University of Leeds, B.A., 1962. *Home and office:* Calf Haugh Farmhouse, Pateley Bridge, North Yorkshire, England.

CAREER: Antiques dealer, specializing in country clocks, 1966—. *Member:* Society of Genealogists (fellow).

WRITINGS—Published by David & Charles, except as indicated: *Yorkshire Clockmakers,* Dalesman Publishing, 1972; *The White Dial Clock,* 1974; *Westmorland Clocks and Clockmakers,* 1975; *Lancashire Clocks and Clockmakers,* 1976; *Country Clocks and Their London Origins,* 1976; *Watch and Clock Makers of the World,* NAG Press, 1976; *Complete British Clocks,* 1978; *The Early Clockmakers of Great Britain,* NAG Press, 1980. Also author of television script "Sanctuary," 1980.

WORK IN PROGRESS: Grandfather Clocks and Casework.

AVOCATIONAL INTERESTS: "Self-sufficiency, cultivation, gardening, and returning to the land."

* * *

LOTTMAN, Eileen 1927-
(Harry Barney, Jessica Evans, Molly Flute, Samantha Mellors, Maud Willis)

PERSONAL: Born August 15, 1927, in Minneapolis, Minn.; daughter of Myer (a certified public accountant) and Goldye (Cohn) Shubb; married Evan Lottman (a motion picture film editor), August 25, 1956; children: Jessica. *Education:* Attended University of Iowa, 1945-50. *Home:* 15 West 72nd St., New York, N.Y. 10023.

CAREER: Held numerous odd jobs, 1950-53; Arthur P. Jacobs Co., New York City, film press agent, 1953-64; G. P. Putnam's Sons, New York City, publicity director, 1964-68; Dell Publishing Co., New York City, publicity director, 1968-69; Bantam Books, New York City, editor, 1969-71; free-lance writer, 1971—. Instructor in screenwriting, Brooklyn College of the City University of New York, 1980-83.

WRITINGS—Novels: *The Hemlock Tree,* Popular Library, 1975; *Summersea,* Coward, 1975; *After the Wind,* Dell, 1979; (under pseudonym Harry Barney) *The Package,* Dell, 1980; *The Brahmins,* Delacorte, 1982; (co-translator from the French) Charlotte Wagner, *Sweet Cakes,* Pinnacle Books, 1983.

Novelizations of film and television scripts: (Under pseudonym Maud Willis) *The Devils's Rain,* Dell, 1975; (under pseudonym Maud Willis) *Doctors' Hospital,* Pocket Books, 1975; *The Bionic Woman: Welcome Home, Jaime,* Berkeley Books, 1976; *The Bionic Woman: Extracurricular Activities,* Berkeley Books, 1977; (under pseudonym Molly Flute) *Through the Looking Glass,* Dell, 1977; *The Greek Tycoon,* Warner Books, 1978; (under pseudonym Jessica Evans) *Blind Sunday,* Scholastic Book Services, 1978; (under pseudonym Samantha Mellors) *The Orphan,* Jove, 1979; *All Night Long,* Jove, 1980; *Rich and Famous,* Bantam, 1981; *Dynasty,* Bantam, 1983.

Also author of four study guides on the making of films for Universal Pictures. Author of column "Under Covers," published in *Village Voice,* 1974-75, and of columns appearing in *Publishers Weekly* and other periodicals. Contributor of numerous book reviews and articles to various newspapers and magazines.

WORK IN PROGRESS: A play; a series of educational computer games; a musical based on her novel *Summersea.*

SIDELIGHTS: Eileen Lottman once wrote *CA:* "I write for fun and money. I wrote my first book in order to pay for a flute, which I took up when I began free-lancing and found I had time to practice. My husband's work allows us to travel the best way—three to six months in each new place. I feel extraordinarily lucky, may never try to write for art's sake."

* * *

LOUIS, Paul P(anickavede) 1918-

PERSONAL: Born September 26, 1918, in Pallithode, India; son of Louis Paulose (a farmer) and Achamma (Therath) Panickavede. *Education:* St. Joseph Pontifical Seminary, Ph.L., 1944, S.T.L., 1947; University of San Francisco, B.S., 1955; University of Detroit, M.B.A., 1956; Michigan State University, D.Ed., 1960. *Politics:* None. *Home:* 9715 Sheehan Rd., Centerville, Ohio 45459. *Office:* Department of Economics, University of Dayton, Dayton, Ohio 45409.

CAREER: Ordained diocesan Roman Catholic priest, 1947. St. John Bosco Manufacturing Co., Kerala, India, president, 1949-53; Aquinas College, Grand Rapids, Mich., instructor, 1957-58; Nazareth College, Kalamazoo, Mich., instructor, 1958-59; University of San Diego, San Diego, Calif., assistant professor of business and economics, 1959-63; University of Dayton, Dayton, Ohio, associate professor, 1964-72, professor of economics, 1972—. Associate pastor of Roman Catholic church in Miamisburg, Ohio, 1970. Founder of St. Rita's Poor Home; director of Catholic Charities, 1949-53. Chairman, Beekman Motors, Inc., 1975. Founder and director of India Cultural Center; president of Farmer's Cooperative, 1948-52; founder of Milk for Babies Club, 1966-72.

MEMBER: American Economic Association, American Education Association, Society for Advancement of Management, Alpha Kappa Psi. *Awards, honors:* Papal Chamberlain Award from Pope Paul VI, 1965.

WRITINGS: Exotic Recipes of India: A Cookbook, Colonial Printers, 1960; *Readings in the History of Economic Thought,* McCutchan, 1971; *Success Unlimited,* Orient House, 1974; *Dictionary of Economics,* Orient House, 1980. Author of *Economic Geography: Economic Growth and Development,* University of Dayton Press. Also author of fourteen books in Malayalam language, 1947-52. Editor of *Labour,* 1949-53.

WORK IN PROGRESS: Makers of American Business.

* * *

LOWBURY, Edward (Joseph Lister) 1913-

PERSONAL: Born December 6, 1913, in London, England; son of Benjamin William (a physician) and Alice (Halle) Lowbury; married Alison Young (a musician), June 12, 1954; children: Ruth, Pauline, Miriam. *Education:* University College, Oxford, B.A., 1936, B.M. and B.Ch., 1939; London Hospital Medical College, London, M.A., 1940; Oxford University, D.M., 1957. *Home:* 79 Vernon Rd., Birmingham 16, England.

CAREER: Member of scientific staff, Medical Research Council of Great Britain, 1947—; Birmingham Accident Hospital,

Birmingham, England, bacteriologist in Medical Research Council Burns Research Unit, 1949-79; University of Aston, Birmingham, honorary professor of medical microbiology, 1979—. Honorary research fellow, University of Birmingham, 1950—. Adviser in bacteriology, Birmingham Regional Hospital Board, 1960—; honorary director, Hospital Infection Research Laboratory, Birmingham, 1966-79. Consultant to United States on hospital-acquired infection, World Health Organization, 1965. *Military service:* Royal Army Medical Corps, 1943-47; became major.

MEMBER: Royal College of Pathologists (fellow), Royal College of Physicians (fellow), Royal College of Surgeons (fellow), Royal Society of Literature (fellow), Society for General Microbiology, Society for Applied Bacteriology, Pathological Society of Great Britain and Ireland, British Medical Association. *Awards, honors:* John Keats Memorial Lecturer award, 1973; Everett Evans Memorial Lecturer award, 1977; D.Sc., University of Aston, 1977; A. B. Wallace Memorial Lecturer and Medal, 1978; LL.D., University of Birmingham, 1980; Officer of the Order of the British Empire (O.B.E.).

WRITINGS—Poetry, except as indicated: *Fire,* [Oxford], 1934; *Crossing the Line,* Hutchinson, 1947; *Metamorphoses,* Keepsake Press, 1958; (with Terence Heywood) *Facing North,* Mitre Press, 1960; *Time for Sale,* Chatto & Windus, 1961; (contributor of poetry) Palgrave, editor, *Golden Treasury* (anthology), Oxford University Press, 1964; *New Poems,* Keepsake Press, 1965; *Daylight Astronomy,* Wesleyan University Press, 1968; *Figures of Eight,* Keepsake Press, 1969; (with wife, Alison Young, and Timothy Salter) *Thomas Campion: Poet, Composer, Physician* (biography), Barnes & Noble, 1970; *Green Magic* (poems for young people), Chatto & Windus, 1972; *The Night Watchman,* Chatto & Windus, 1974; (with G. A. Ayliffe) *Drug Resistance in Antimicrobial Therapy* (technical), C. C Thomas, 1974.

(Editor with others) *Control of Hospital Infection: A Practical Handbook* (technical), Chapman & Hall, 1975, 2nd edition, 1981; *Poetry and Paradox: Poems and an Essay,* Keepsake Press, 1976; (with others) *Troika: A Selection of Poems,* Daedalus Press, 1977; *Selected Poems,* Celtion Press, 1978; *A Letter from Masada,* Keepsake Press, 1982; *Goldnesh,* Celandine Press, 1983; (editor) *The Poetical Works of Andrew Young,* Secker & Warburg, in press.

Also contributor of chapters and articles to numerous books, among them *The Scientific Basis of Medicine, Textbook of British Surgery, Recent Advances in Surgery, Recent Advances in Clinical Pathology, Chamber's Encyclopedia,* and *Encyclopedia of Poets.*

Also contributor to *A Map of Modern Verse,* "The Poet Speaks" (recordings), and other collections. Contributor of poetry and medical and scientific articles to periodicals, including *Encounter, London Magazine, Times Literary Supplement, New York Times,* and *Southern Review.* Editor, *Equator* (Nairobi), 1945-46.

WORK IN PROGRESS: To Shirk No Idleness: A Critical Biography of Andrew Young.

SIDELIGHTS: The two sides of the double life Edward Lowbury leads as a medical man and as a poet are "excitingly contrasted," he notes, adding: "I write at weekends and on holiday, but store up memories and experiences for use at these times. The collaborative study on Thomas Campion reflects an interest of many years in Elizabethan music and poetry, and incidentally gave me an insight into the divided life of a seventeenth-century doctor-poet who was also a fine composer."

BIOGRAPHICAL/CRITICAL SOURCES: Southern Review, Volume VI, 1970.

* * *

LOWE, Jay, Jr.
  See LOEPER, John J(oseph)

* * *

LUCE, Don 1934-

PERSONAL: Born September 20, 1934, in East Calais, Vt.; son of Collins Andrew (a farmer) and Margaret (Sanders) Luce. *Education:* University of Vermont, B.S., 1957; Cornell University, M.S., 1958. *Religion:* Congregationalist. *Residence:* East Calais, Vt. 05650.

CAREER: International Voluntary Services, Saigon, Vietnam, director, 1958-67; Cornell University, Ithaca, N.Y., research associate, 1968; World Council of Churches, Geneva, Switzerland, executive secretary, 1969; Clergy and Laity Concerned, Inc., New York City, director, 1974-78; Southeast Asia Resource Center, New York City, co-director, 1979—.

WRITINGS: (With John Sommer) *Viet Nam: The Unheard Voices,* foreword by Edward M. Kennedy, Cornell University Press, 1969; (with Holmes Brown) *Hostages of War,* Clergy & Laity Concerned, Inc., 1973; (editor with Cora Weiss and author of afterword) Van Tien Dung, *Our Great Spring Victory,* Monthly Review Press, 1977; *Oh Freedom,* Clergy & Laity Concerned, Inc., 1977; *Shadows from a Cabin Night,* Southeast Asia Resource Center, 1979; (editor with Lee Sun Al) *The Wish: Poems of Korea,* Friendship, 1983. Also author, with Becky Cantwell, of *Made in Taiwan: A Human Rights Investigation,* Southeast Asia Resource Center; also editor, with Jacqui Chagnon, of *Of Quiet Courage: Poems from the Viet War,* 1974.

BIOGRAPHICAL/CRITICAL SOURCES: Saturday Review, June 28, 1969; *New York Times Book Review,* July 20, 1969.

* * *

LUEBKE, Frederick Carl 1927-

PERSONAL: Born January 26, 1927, in Reedsburg, Wis.; son of Frederick J. (a teacher) and Martha (Kretzmann) Luebke; married Norma Wukasch (an editor), August 12, 1951; children: Christina, John, David, Thomas. *Education:* Concordia Teachers College, River Forest, Ill., B.S., 1950; Claremont Graduate School, M.A., 1958; University of Nebraska, Ph.D., 1966. *Home:* 3117 Woodsdale Blvd., Lincoln, Neb. 68502. *Office:* Department of History, University of Nebraska, Lincoln, Neb. 68588.

CAREER: Teacher in elementary and secondary schools in Pomona and Los Angeles, Calif., 1951-61; Concordia Teachers College, Seward, Neb., 1961-68, began as assistant professor, became associate professor of history; University of Nebraska, Lincoln, associate professor, 1968-72, professor of history, 1972—, director, Center for Great Plains Studies, 1983—. Scholar-in-residence, Rockefeller Foundation Study and Conference Center, Bellagio, Italy, 1982. *Member:* Organization of American Historians, Immigration History Society, Western History Association. *Awards, honors:* Danforth Foundation teacher grants, 1964, 1965; National Endowment for the Humanities fellowship, 1967; senior Fulbright research fellowship, University of Stuttgart, 1974-75; Newberry Library fellowship, 1977, 1978.

WRITINGS—Published by University of Nebraska Press, except as indicated: *Immigrants and Politics: The Germans of Nebraska, 1880-1900*, 1969; (editor and contributor) *Ethnic Voters and the Election of Lincoln*, 1971; *Bonds of Loyalty: German-Americans and World War I*, Northern Illinois University Press, 1974; (contributor) John Higham, editor, *Ethnic Leadership in America*, Johns Hopkins University Press, 1978; (co-editor and contributor) *The Great Plains: Environment and Culture*, 1979; (editor and contributor) *Ethnicity on the Great Plains*, 1980; (contributor) Stephan Thernstrom, editor, *Harvard Encyclopedia of American Ethnic Groups*, Harvard University Press, 1980; (contributor) Paul Schach, editor, *Languages in Conflict*, 1980; (co-editor) *Vision and Refuge: Essays on the Literature of the Great Plains*, 1982; (contributor) Michael P. Malone, editor, *Historians and the American West*, 1983. Contributor of articles to scholarly journals.

WORK IN PROGRESS: Research on the history of the German ethnic group in Brazilian society, 1890-1920, with particular reference to World War I.

* * *

LUNDBERG, Donald E(mil) 1916-

PERSONAL: Born June 10, 1916, in Waterloo, Iowa; son of Emil T. (a moulder) and Jennie (Hampton) Lundberg; married Carolyn Brown, 1942; children: Alan, Derek, Lance. *Education:* Iowa State Teachers College (now University of Northern Iowa), B.A., 1941; Duke University, M.A., 1942; Cornell University, Ph.D., 1946. *Religion:* Protestant. *Office:* Department of Hotel and Restaurant Management, California State Polytechnic University, Pomona, Calif. 91768; and Schiller International University, Chateau Pourtales, rue Melanie, 67 Strasbourg, France.

CAREER: Cornell University, Ithaca, N.Y., assistant professor of hotel administration, 1946-49; Idaho State College (now University), Pocatello, professor of psychology and dean of students, 1949-50; Florida State University, Tallahassee, professor of hotel and restaurant management and head of department, 1950-59; University of New Hampshire, Durham, chairman of department of hotel administration, 1959-62; University of Massachusetts—Amherst, head of department of hotel, restaurant, and travel administration, 1963-73; California State Polytechnic University, Pomona, chairman of department of hotel and restaurant management, 1973-83, professor emeritus, 1983—; Schiller International University, Strasbourg, France, director of masters program in hotel/travel management, 1984—.

Visiting lecturer, Ithaca College, 1946-50; lecturer, Ealing Technical College and University of Surrey, 1968, and University of Kentucky, 1968-70. Research associate, University of Hawaii, 1970. Lecturer for Club Managers Association of America, and to personnel management workshops in United States and Canada. Manager of resorts. Consultant, U.S. Department of Commerce, Catering Education Research Institute, Industrial Training Board for Hotel and Catering Industry, and to universities and businesses. *Military service:* U.S. Navy, 1942-45; became lieutenant. U.S. Naval Reserve, 1945-68; became commander. *Member:* International Society of Food Service Consultants (former president), International Epicurean Circle, Sigma Xi.

WRITINGS: Personnel Practices in Hotels, Cornell University, 1947; *Personnel Management in Hotels and Restaurants*, Burgess, 1949.

(With Vernon C. Kane) *Business Management: Hotels, Motels, and Restaurants*, Peninsular Press, 1952; (editor) *Motel Management Correspondence Course*, American Motels, Inc., 1953; *Operating Manual for Navy Messes and Clubs Ashore*, Bureau of Naval Personnel and U.S. Air Force, 1954; (editor) *Readings in Club Management*, privately printed, 1956; *Inside Innkeeping*, W. C. Brown, 1956.

Adventure in Costa Rica, Dixie Publishers, 1960, revised edition published as *Costa Rica*, 1968; (with Peter Dukas) *How to Operate a Restaurant*, Ahrens, 1960; (with James A. Armatas) *The Management of People in Hotels, Restaurants and Clubs*, W. C. Brown, 1964, revised edition, 1980; *The Logic of Cookery*, privately printed, 1964, revised edition published as *The Logic of Cooking*, 1977; (with Lendal H. Kotschevar) *Understanding Cooking*, University of Massachusetts, 1965, revised edition, 1984.

The Hotel and Restaurant Business, Cahners, 1970, 2nd revised edition, 1984; (with Joseph Amendola) *Understanding Baking*, Cahners, 1971; *The Tourist Business*, Cahners, 1971, 2nd revised edition, 1984; *Front Office Human Relations*, privately printed, 1979; *International Travel and Tourism*, Grid Publishing, 1984; *The Restaurant: From Concept to Operation*, Grid Publishing, 1984. Contributor to *American Motel Magazine*, *Club Management*, *Hotel Management*, *Institutions*, and other publications. Consulting editor, *Drive-In Management*. Editorial director, Ahrens Publishing Co.; book editor, "Hotel and Restaurant Book" series, W. C. Brown, 1956-70.

* * *

LYMAN, Stanford M(orris) 1933-

PERSONAL: Born June 10, 1933, in San Francisco, Calif.; son of Arthur H. (a grocer) and Gertrude (Kramer) Lyman. *Education:* University of California, Berkeley, A.B., 1955, M.A., 1957, Ph.D., 1961. *Politics:* Independent. *Religion:* Jewish. *Home:* 122 Spring St., Apt. 2-S, New York, N.Y. 10012. *Office:* Department of Sociology, New School for Social Research, 66 West 12th St., New York, N.Y. 10011.

CAREER: University of British Columbia, Vancouver, instructor, 1960-62, assistant professor of sociology, 1962-63; University of California Extension, Berkeley, associate professor and head of liberal arts department, 1963-64; Sonoma State College (now University), Rohnert Park, Calif., associate professor of sociology and chairman of department, 1964-68; University of Nevada at Reno, 1968-70, began as associate professor, became professor of sociology; University of California, San Diego, associate professor of sociology, 1970-72; New School for Social Research, Graduate Faculty of Political and Social Science, New York, N.Y., professor of sociology, 1972-81, professor of sociology and Asian studies, 1981—, chairman of department of sociology, 1972-75.

Lecturer in Southeast Asia for United States Information Service, 1975; senior member, Linacre College, Oxford University, 1975; Fulbright lecturer, Doshisha University and Ryukoku University, Kyoto, Japan, 1981-82. *Member:* American Sociological Association, Chinese American Historical Society, Center for Japanese American Studies, Society for the Study of Symbolic Interaction, Eastern Sociological Society, Phi Beta Kappa.

WRITINGS: *The Oriental in North America,* University of British Columbia Extension Service, 1962; (with Marvin B. Scott) *Sociology of the Absurd,* Appleton, 1970; (with Scott) *The Revolt of the Students,* C. E. Merrill, 1970; *The Asian in the West,* Desert Research Institute, University of Nevada, 1970; *The Black American in Sociological Thought: A Failure of Perspective,* edited by Herbert Hill, Putnam, 1972; *Chinese Americans,* Random House, 1974; (with Scott) *The Drama of Social Reality,* Oxford University Press, 1975.

The Asian in North America, American Bibliographic Center-Clio Press, 1977; (editor with Richard Harvey Brown) *Structure, Consciousness and History,* Cambridge University Press, 1977; *The Seven Deadly Sins: Society and Evil,* St. Martin's, 1978; (with Arthur J. Vidich) *American Sociology: Worldly Rejections of Religion and Their Directions,* Yale University Press, 1984. Advisory editor, *Pacific Sociological Review, Symbolic Interactionism, Amerasia Journal, Journal of Ethnic Studies,* and *Phylon Quarterly.*

WORK IN PROGRESS: With Arthur J. Vidich, *Sociology,* for publication by F. Watts; *The Chinese and the Amerinds: A Study in Social Anthropology.*

LYONS, Arthur (Jr.) 1946-

PERSONAL: Born January 5, 1946, in Los Angeles, Calif.; son of Arthur and Shirley (Hamilton) Lyons. *Education:* University of California, Santa Barbara, B.A., 1967. *Residence:* Palm Springs, Calif.

CAREER: Writer; proprietor of a restaurant in Palm Springs, Calif., 1980—.

WRITINGS: *The Second Coming: Satanism in America,* Dodd, 1970; *The Dead Are Discreet,* Mason/Charter, 1974; *All God's Children,* Mason/Charter, 1975; *The Killing Floor,* Mason/Charter, 1976; *Dead Ringer,* Mason/Charter, 1977; *Castles Burning,* Holt, 1979; *Hard Trade,* Holt, 1981; *At the Hands of Another,* Holt, 1983; *Bad Sign,* Holt, 1984.

BIOGRAPHICAL/CRITICAL SOURCES: *New York Times Book Review,* January 16, 1977, May 10, 1981.

M

MACAROV, David 1918-

PERSONAL: Born November 20, 1918, in Savannah, Ga.; son of Isaac (a manufacturer) and Fannie (Schoenberg) Macarov; married Frieda Rabinowitz (a registered nurse), December 5, 1946; children: Varda, Frances, Raanan, Annette. *Education:* University of Pittsburgh, B.Sc., 1951; Western Reserve University (now Case Western Reserve University), M.Sc., 1954; Brandeis University, Ph.D., 1968. *Religion:* Jewish. *Home:* Nayot 8, Jerusalem, Israel. *Office:* School of Social Work, Hebrew University, Jerusalem, Israel.

CAREER: Hebrew University of Jerusalem, Paul Baerwald School of Social Work, Jerusalem, Israel, associate professor of social welfare and planning, 1959—, director, Joseph J. Schwartz Graduate Program for Training Directors and Senior Personnel for Community Centers, 1970-75. Visiting professor at Adelphi University, 1975-77, and University of Melbourne, 1977. *Military service:* U.S. Army Air Forces, 1942-45; served in China, Burma, and India; received Distinguished Unit Citation and battle cluster. Israel Defence Forces, 1947-49; became squadron leader.

MEMBER: International Association of Social Workers, International Society for Social Economics (board member), World Future Society (Israel coordinator), Society for the Reduction of Human Labor (chairman), National Association of Social Workers, American Council on Social Work, National Conference of Jewish Communal Service, Council on Social Work Education, Society for Human Development, Industrial Relations Research Association.

WRITINGS: Incentives to Work: The Effects of Unearned Income, Jossey-Bass, 1970; *The Short Course in Development Training,* Massada, 1973; (contributor) D. Thursz and J. L. Vigilante, editors, *Meeting Human Needs: An Overview of Nine Countries,* Sage Publications, Volume I, 1975, Volume II, 1977; *Administration in the Social Work Curriculum,* Council on Social Work Education, 1976; *The Design of Social Welfare,* Holt, 1978; *Work and Welfare: The Unholy Alliance,* Sage Publications, 1980; *Worker Productivity: Myths and Reality,* Sage Publications, 1982; (contributor) H. Didsbury, editor, *Working Now and in the Future,* World Future Society, 1983.

MacDOUALL, Robertson
See MAIR, George Brown

* * *

MacDOUGALL, Mary Katherine

PERSONAL: Born in Mount Auburn, Ill.; daughter of F. D. (a newspaper editor and publisher) and Kitty May (Alexander) Slate; married Wayne Fox McMeans (deceased); married Harold Alexander MacDougall (deceased); children: (first marriage) David, Nancy McMeans Richey; (second marriage) Alexander, Kent, Alan Ross MacDougall. *Education:* Attended Alma College, one year; University of Michigan, B.A. and graduate study; University of Texas, graduate study. *Home:* 2511 Hartford Rd., Austin, Tex. 78703.

CAREER: Former teacher in secondary schools and at University of Texas, editor of trade journal, and member of editorial staff of newspapers in Port Huron, Mich., Abilene, Tex., and Austin, Tex.; Unity Center of Positive Prayer, Austin, Tex., currently founding minister. Has radio program.

WRITINGS: Black Jupiter, Broadman, 1960; *What Treasure Mapping Can Do for You,* Unity Books, 1968; *Prosperity Now,* Unity Books, 1969; *Healing Now,* Unity Books, 1970; *Making Love Happen,* Doubleday, 1970; *Happiness Now,* Unity Books, 1971; *Dear Friend,* CSA Press, 1980; *Dear Me,* CSA Press, 1984. Contributor of short stories and several hundred articles to magazines.

WORK IN PROGRESS: Three books.

SIDELIGHTS: Mary Katherine MacDougall writes: "For as long as I have any memory, I have had the consistent desire: to be a channel of help to others, to learn more about God and me, and to write. People are my vocation and avocation. They have seemed to be delayers but delays that come to us and that we do not instigate are always for good, for the better or for our protection in some way. . . . As teachers always learn more from teaching than the students, writers get more benefit from their writing than readers can. This is one reason why a writer should never write anything that is not helpful to his own growth and progress." *What Treasure Mapping Can Do for You, Healing Now,* and *Prosperity Now* have been translated into Spanish.

MACKEY, Ernan
See McINERNY, Ralph

* * *

MACKINLOCK, Duncan
See WATTS, Peter Christopher

* * *

MacKINNON, Edward M(ichael) 1928-

PERSONAL: Born June 30, 1928, in Boston, Mass.; son of Michael Andrew (a realtor) and Anna (MacIsaac) MacKinnon; married Barbara A. Bacon (a philosophy professor), March 4, 1972; children: Jennifer Ann, Kathleen Elizabeth. *Education:* Boston College, B.A., 1949, M.A. (philosophy), 1954; Harvard University, M.A. (physics), 1955; St. Louis University, Ph.D., 1958; Weston College, S.T.L., 1962. *Politics:* Democrat. *Home:* 2045 Manzanita Dr., Oakland, Calif. 94611. *Office:* Department of Philosophy, California State University, Hayward, Calif. 94542.

CAREER: Boston College, Chestnut Hill, Mass., assistant professor, 1965-67, associate professor, 1967-69, professor of philosophy, 1969-71; California State University, Hayward, professor of philosophy, 1971—, chairman of department, 1979—. *Member:* American Philosophical Association, American Physical Society, Philosophy of Science Association, American Association for the Advancement of Science, American Association of University Professors, Sigma Xi.

WRITINGS: Truth and Expression (Hecker Lectures), Paulist/Newman, 1971; *The Problem of Scientific Realism,* Appleton, 1971; *Scientific Explanation and Atomic Physics,* University of Chicago Press, 1982; *Basic Reasoning,* Prentice-Hall, in press. Contributor to journals in his field. Associate editor, *Continuum,* 1967-70, *Philosophy Forum,* 1968—.

* * *

MacNUTT, Francis S. 1925-

PERSONAL: Born April 22, 1925, in St. Louis, Mo.; son of Joseph Scott (a portrait painter) and Agnes (a ballet dancer; maiden name, Cady) MacNutt; married Judith C. Sewell, 1980; children: Rachel Ellen, David Scott. *Education:* Harvard University, B.A., 1948; Catholic University of America, M.F.A., 1950; Aquinas Institute of Theology, Ph.D., 1958. *Politics:* Independent. *Religion:* Roman Catholic. *Home:* 342 Rowena, Dunedin, Fla. 33528.

CAREER: Entered Ordo Praedicatorum (Order of Preachers—Dominicans), 1950, ordained Roman Catholic priest, 1956; Aquinas Institute of Theology, Dubuque, Iowa, professor of homiletics, 1958-66; Catholic Homiletic Society, St. Louis, Mo., executive director, 1966-69; Thomas Merton Foundation, St. Louis, Mo., director, 1970-80; Christian Healing Ministries, Inc., Clearwater, Fla., president, 1981—. Member of National Service Committee of Catholic Charismatic Renewal, 1976-80. *Military service:* U.S. Army, Medical Corps, 1944-46.

MEMBER: National Audubon Society, Common Cause. *Awards, honors:* Franciscan International Award, 1977, for contribution to the knowledge of healing through prayer; honorary warden of International Order of St. Luke.

WRITINGS: Gauging Sermon Effectiveness, Priory Press, 1960; *Teach Us to Love: Sisters' Conference Needs,* B. Herder, 1964; *How to Prepare a Sermon,* Novalis, 1970; *Healing,* Ave Maria Press, 1974; *The Power to Heal,* Ave Maria Press, 1977; *The Prayer That Heals,* Ave Maria Press, 1981. Founding editor of *Preaching: A Journal of Homiletics,* 1965-70.

SIDELIGHTS: Francis S. MacNutt told *CA:* "*Healing* has had an effect upon the thinking and practice of many Christians (especially Catholics) in encouraging a renewal of the practice of praying for healing. In conjunction with the writings of Ruth Stapleton, Agnes Sanford, Barbara Shlemon, and many others, this book seems to have effected a real change in many churches in the past few years."

He adds: "Agnes Sanford called *Healing* 'the most scholarly and comprehensive book on Christian healing that I have ever read.' It has been translated into ten languages, and 600,000 copies have been printed in the American edition."

* * *

MacTHOMAIS, Ruaraidh
See THOMSON, Derick S(mith)

* * *

MAGARY, Kerstin Fraser 1947-

PERSONAL: Born March 20, 1947, in Oakland, Calif.; daughter of Peter E. (a printing salesman) and Frances Euphrosyne (a teacher; maiden name, Olsson) Fraser; married Alan Magary (a writer, editor, and publisher), April 8, 1972. *Education:* Attended University of California, Berkeley, 1965; Mills College, Oakland, Calif., B.A., 1969; Stanford University, M.B.A., 1978. *Home:* 1440 16th Ave., San Francisco, Calif. 94122. *Agent:* Max Gartenberg, 15 West 44th St., New York, N.Y. 10036.

CAREER: World Airways, Oakland, Calif., flight attendant, 1969; Bank of America International, San Francisco, Calif., researcher and writer, 1969-71; free-lance writer and photographer in eastern Africa, New York, and California, 1971-82; Wilton, Coombs & Colnett Advertising, San Francisco, advertising account executive, 1974-75; Gensler & Associates (architects), San Francisco, editor, beginning 1975; Southern Pacific Transportation Co., San Francisco, manager, 1978—. Member of Women's Transportation Seminar. *Member:* Heritage, SPUR, San Francisco Zoological Society, San Francisco Junior Chamber of Commerce, Sierra Club.

WRITINGS: (Editor with husband, Alan Magary, and John Hirsch) *Fodor's Europe on a Budget,* Fodor/McKay, 1972, 4th revised edition, 1975; (with A. Magary) *East Africa: A Travel Guide,* Harper, 1975; (with A. Magary) *Across the Golden Gate: California's North Coast, Wine Country, and Redwoods,* Harper, 1980.

WORK IN PROGRESS: South of San Francisco: A Guide, for Harper.

* * *

MAIR, George Brown 1914-
(Robertson MacDouall)

PERSONAL: Born May 27, 1914, in Troon, Scotland; son of Alexander (a businessman) and Catherine (Robertson) Mair; married Geertruide van der Poest Clement, February 21, 1940; children: Alexander Craig van der Poest Clement, George Leonard Robertson. *Education:* University of Glasgow, M.B.

and Ch.B., 1936, M.D. and F.R.C.S. (Edinburgh), 1939, F.R.F.P.S. (Glasgow), 1943. *Religion:* Theist. *Home:* Upper Kinneil House, Old Polmont, Stirlingshire, Scotland. *Agent:* Scottish Lecture Agency, Brisbane Street, Greenock, Scotland; Laurence Pollinger Ltd., 18 Maddox St., Mayfair, London W1R 0EU, England.

CAREER: University of Durham, Durham, England, assistant professor of surgery, 1945-53; Law Hospital, Lanarkshire, Scotland, surgeon, 1953-68; director of medical clinic in central Scotland, 1954-68. Cosmetic surgeon in Rotterdam, 1977-80. Celebrity lecturer on Pacific and Orient Lines summer cruises, 1953-62. Founder of Scottish Exit, a voluntary euthanasia group. Leader of Royal Scottish Geographical Society expeditions to Greece, Turkey, and Anatolia. Former examiner, General Nursing Council, Scotland; former demonstrator-lecturer in anatomy, University of Glasgow. *Member:* British Medical Association, Crime Writers Association, Mystery Writers of America, Guild of Travel Writers, P.E.N. (Scotland), Society of Authors, National Book League.

WRITINGS: Surgery for Abdominal Hernia, E. J. Arnold, 1948; (under pseudonym Robertson MacDouall) *Surgeon's Saga,* Heinemann, 1950; *Doctor Goes East,* P. Owen, 1952; *Doctor Goes North,* P. Owen, 1958; *Doctor Goes West,* P. Owen, 1958.

Destination Moscow, Jenkins, 1960; *Doctor in Turkey,* T. Allen, 1961; *The Day Khrushchev Panicked,* Random House, 1962; *Death's Foot Forward,* Jarrolds, 1963, Random House, 1964; *Miss Turquoise: The Second David Grant Story,* Jarrolds, 1964, published as *Miss Turquoise: A David Grant Story,* Random House, 1965; *Live, Love and Cry,* Jarrolds, 1965; *Kisses from Satan: A David Grant Story,* Nelson, Foster & Scott, 1966; *The Girl from Peking,* Jarrolds, 1967; *Black Champagne,* Jarrolds, 1968; *Goddesses Never Die,* Jarrolds, 1969.

A Wreath of Camellias, Jarrolds, 1970; *Crimson Jade,* Jarrolds, 1971; *Paradise Spells Danger,* Jarrolds, 1973; *Confessions of a Surgeon,* Luscombe, 1974; *A Guide to Package Holidays,* New English Library, 1974; *Escape from Surgery,* Luscombe, 1975; *How to Die with Dignity,* Scottish Exit, 1980, supplement, 1980.

SIDELIGHTS: George Brown Mair told *CA:* "I have frequently wondered why books are written at all—especially since 'best-sellers' are not too common. But especially do I view with suspicion authors who talk about 'inspiration.' Inspiration is a prime essential for poets, and of these there are few. Rhymesters—yes! Poets—few!

"My own motives for writing books have been simple. A first book concerning one aspect of surgery was intended to impress my seniors and hasten promotion. The second, a fantasy autobiography written under a pseudonym was a good example of wishful thinking. It outlined, I suppose, the sort of future which my subconscious must have hoped for at that time. A number of travel books were then presented to the book world because I wished to share treasured experiences with other people. And even in the early 1950s I had quite a number of treasured experiences which most people tended to disbelieve. I had a whimsical idea that if they were dealt with in book form rather than as small talk that sceptics might be converted. Which they were!

"The series of ten David Grant books [was] merely an outlet for my own aggressions during a difficult phase of life. I caused my hero, David Grant, to deal with sundry villains as I, personally, would have liked to deal with certain people with nuisance value in my own life. This probably saved me from some sort of 'nervous breakdown' since, when the frustrating decade had been weathered, I no longer felt any desire to involve my strong-arm man in mayhem.

"The Confessions and Escape books are but the first two volumes of what may become an autobiographical trilogy. Sadly, however, a brief reference to 'euthanasia' caused a global furor and involved me in the sensitive field of flirting with dangerous laws in [an] effort to have some of them amended. And that, in turn, plunged me up to the neck in suggesting how terminally ill people might control their own destinies and 'die with dignity.' One side effect of this was to cause me to found a voluntary euthanasia organization called Scottish Exit, which now has members in about seventy countries.

"My advice to aspiring writers is to expect nothing, but to remember that no one can say what will become a best-seller until they hear the rhythmic sound of feet marching towards the libraries.

"I have no strong views about the contemporary literary scene but tend to disapprove of wrapping convincing fiction around dangerous historical facts."

Mair's books have been published in Japanese, Dutch, Italian, German, and Norwegian editions.

AVOCATIONAL INTERESTS: Collecting Georgian and earlier antiques, Sevres porcelain, and symbols of religious worship in pre-history, with emphasis on Minoan, Hittite, Buddhist, and Athenian civilizations.

BIOGRAPHICAL/CRITICAL SOURCES: Glasgow Evening Citizen, February 13, 1963.

* * *

MALABRE, Alfred L(eopold, Jr.) 1931-

PERSONAL: Surname is pronounced Ma-*larb;* born April 23, 1931, in New York, N.Y.; son of Alfred L. and Marie (Cassidy) Malabre; married Mary Patricia Wardropper; children: Richard, Ann, John. *Education:* Yale University, B.A., 1952; Columbia University, M.S., 1953. *Politics:* Independent. *Home:* 320 East 72nd St., New York, N.Y. 10021. *Office: Wall Street Journal,* 22 Cortlandt St., New York, N.Y. 10007.

CAREER: U.S. Navy, career officer, 1953-56, retiring as lieutenant; worked as rewrite man on *Hartford Courant,* 1957-58; *Wall Street Journal,* New York City, worked on Midwest edition in Chicago, Ill., 1958-60, worked with London bureau, 1960-61, Bonn bureau chief, 1961-62, economics reporter with New York City bureau, 1962-68, news editor for economics, 1968-72, news editor, 1972—. *Member:* Pilgrims Society of the United States. *Awards, honors:* Poynter fellow at Yale University, 1976.

WRITINGS: Understanding the Economy: For People Who Can't Stand Economics, Dodd, 1976; *America's Dilemma: Jobs vs. Prices,* Dodd, 1978; *Investing for Profit in the Eighties,* Doubleday, 1982.

Work represented in anthologies, including *Here Comes Tomorrow* and *The World of the Wall Street Journal.* Author of column "Outlook" in *Wall Street Journal.* Contributor to *Encyclopaedia Britannica* and *Dow Jones Investors Handbook,* and to popular magazines, including *Harper's, Money, Saturday Review, Reporter,* and *Science Digest.*

SIDELIGHTS: Reviewing Alfred L. Malabre's book *Investing for Profit in the Eighties,* Karen Arenson of the *New York*

Times Book Review finds it "a readable book that explains how the economy shrinks and expands in periodic business cycles and how you can plan investments around those cycles." Of particular value, Michael M. Thomas of the *Washington Post Book World* believes, is Malabre's recounting of his less successful investment experiences. "Here's a man," writes Thomas, "who's been burned by investmentdom's best and brightest; he displays his scars, tells us wherefrom they came, and thereby teaches a lesson to be ignored at our peril." Malabre told *CA* that an "understanding of our economic system and the forces that move our economy is vital to the country's well-being."

BIOGRAPHICAL/CRITICAL SOURCES: *New York Times Book Review*, October 17, 1982; *Washington Post Book World*, March 6, 1983.

* * *

MALO, John W. 1911-

PERSONAL: Born April 11, 1911, in Ringo, Kan.; son of John (a farmer) and Helen (Kocol) Malo; married Renee B. Mier (a free-lance artist), November 24, 1935; children: Kenneth, Marcia. *Education:* Northwestern University, B.S. in Ed., 1934; studied at University of Warsaw, 1935, and University of Chicago; DePaul University, M.A. in Ed., 1947. *Home:* 9633 Surrey Rd., Castle Rock, Colo. 80104.

CAREER: Foreman High School, Chicago, Ill., teacher and coach, 1941-56, counsellor, 1956-60, assistant principal, 1960-71. Canoeing guide in hinterland of Canada. *Member:* Outdoor Writers Association of America, Association of Great Lakes Outdoor Writers, Rocky Mountain Outdoor Writers (member of board).

AWARDS, HONORS: Coach of the Year Award of Chicagoland Prep Writers, 1953; Ford Foundation fellowship for study and travel, 1953-54; citation in annual competition sponsored by Evinrude Motors and Outdoor Writers Association of America, 1970, for *Canoeing;* Thermos Award, 1972, for "excellence in writing and personal endeavor on outdoor recreation."

WRITINGS: *Canoeing* (youth book), Follett, 1969; *Malo's Complete Guide to Canoeing and Canoe-Camping,* Quadrangle, 1969, 4th edition, New York Times Books, 1983; *Wilderness Canoeing,* Macmillan, 1971; *Snowmobiling: The Guide,* Macmillan, 1971; *All-Terrain Adventure Vehicles,* Macmillan, 1972; *Complete Guide to Houseboating,* Macmillan, 1974; *Motor-Camping around Europe,* Stackpole, 1974; *Tranquil Trails,* Greatlakes Living Press, 1977; *Midwest Canoe Trails,* Contemporary, 1978; *Fly Fishing for Panfish,* Dillon, 1981; *Family Guide to Warm Water Fishing,* Jande-Hagan, 1983. Writer of magazine and newspaper articles on canoeing.

SIDELIGHTS: John W. Malo first became interested in canoeing as a teenager and has been exploring stateside and Canadian wilderness streams and introducing young people to outdoor life ever since. Praising Malo's work in this field, the Outdoor Writers Association of America, cited Malo for ". . . creating an awareness of the recreational potential of the nation's waterways, and the need for preservation of the natural beauty of these waters." He has traveled by canoe in unmapped areas of Canada, kayaked in the Dnieper River in the Carpathians, and paddled a dugout canoe in British Honduras and Guatemala. He also has tried gold panning and uranium prospecting in the American West and fished in both fresh and salt water.

MALONE, Michael P. 1940-

PERSONAL: Born April 18, 1940, in Pomeroy, Wash.; son of John A. (a merchant) and Delores (Cheyne) Malone; married Gail E. Wilcox, August 4, 1962 (divorced, 1982); married Kathleen Campbell, 1982; children: (first marriage) John Thomas, Molly Christine. *Education:* Gonzaga University, B.A., 1962; Washington State University, Ph.D., 1966. *Religion:* Catholic. *Home:* 49 Hitching Post, Bozeman, Mont. 59715. *Office:* Department of History, Montana State University, Bozeman, Mont. 59715.

CAREER: Texas A & M University, College Station, assistant professor of history, 1966-67; Montana State University, Bozeman, 1967—, began as assistant professor, became professor of history, 1974—, head of department of history and philosophy, 1976-79, dean of graduate studies, 1979—. *Member:* Organization of American Historians, Pacific Northwestern History Association, Western History Association, Montana Historical Society (vice-president). *Awards, honors:* National Science Foundation summer grant, 1971, 1972.

WRITINGS: (Editor with Richard B. Roeder) *The Montana Past: An Anthology,* University of Montana Press, 1969, 2nd edition, 1973; *C. Ben Ross and the New Deal in Idaho,* University of Washington Press, 1970; (with Roeder) *Montana: A History of Two Centuries,* University of Washington Press, 1976; *The Battle for Brute: Mining and Politics on the Northern Frontier, 1864-1906,* University of Washington Press, 1981; (editor) *Historians and the American West,* University of Nebraska Press, 1983.

Contributor to *Pacific Historical Review, Idaho Yesterdays, Montana,* and *Pacific Northwest Quarterly.* Member of editorial board, *Western Historical Quarterly* and *Pacific Northwest Quarterly;* book review editor, *Montana: The Magazine of Western History.*

WORK IN PROGRESS: A history of the western United States, with R. W. Etulain and K. H. Owens.

* * *

MALTIN, Leonard 1950-

PERSONAL: Born December 18, 1950, in New York, N.Y.; son of Aaron I. and Jacqueline (Gould) Maltin; married Alice Tlusty, 1975. *Education:* Attended New York University, 1968-72. *Religion:* Jewish. *Office:* c/o "Entertainment Tonight," 1549 North Vine St., Los Angeles, Calif. 90028.

CAREER: *Film Fan Monthly* (magazine), Teaneck, N.J., editor and publisher, 1966-75; general editor, Popular Library film series, 1973-77; member of faculty, New School for Social Research, New York City, 1973-82; currently film critic for, and contributor of feature stories to, syndicated television series "Entertainment Tonight." Curator, American Academy of Humor, 1975-76; guest programmer, film department, Museum of Modern Art, New York City, 1976. Consultant and writer, Showtime division of Viacom International, 1976-80. *Member:* Society for Cinephiles, Sons of the Desert.

WRITINGS: *TV Movies,* New American Library, 1969, revised edition, 1984; *Movie Comedy Teams,* New American Library, 1970, revised edition, 1974; *Behind the Camera: The Cinematographer's Art,* New American Library, 1971, published as *The Art of the Cinematographer,* Dover, 1978; *The Great Movie Shorts,* Crown, 1972, published as *Selected Short Subjects,* DaCapo, 1983; *The Disney Films,* Crown, 1973; *Carole Lombard,* Pyramid Publications, 1976; (with Richard W. Bann)

Our Gang: The Life and Times of the Little Rascals, Crown, 1977; *The Great Movie Comedians*, Crown, 1978; *Of Mice and Magic: A History of American Animated Cartoons*, McGraw, 1980.

Editor: *The Real Stars*, Curtis Books, 1973; *The Laurel and Hardy Book*, Curtis Books, 1973; *The Real Stars #2*, Curtis Books, 1973; *Hollywood: The Movie Factory*, Popular Library, 1976; *Hollywood Kids*, Popular Library, 1977; *The Whole Film Sourcebook*, New American Library, 1983.

Contributor: *A Concise History of the Cinema*, A. S. Barnes, 1971; *The Compleat Guide to Film Study*, National Council of Teachers of English, 1972; *The American Film Heritage*, Acropolis Books, 1972; *Directors in Action*, Bobbs-Merrill, 1973; *The Movie Buff's Book*, Volume II, Pyramid Publications, 1977. Contributor to *Esquire, New York Times, Saturday Review, TV Guide, Film Comment, Variety, American Film, Millimeter, Print*, and other periodicals.

WORK IN PROGRESS: Revised editions of *TV Movies* and *Movie Comedy Teams*, both for New American Library, and *The Disney Films*, for Crown.

SIDELIGHTS: Few movie buffs have turned their enthusiasm for films into a lucrative career as effectively as Leonard Maltin has. At age sixteen Maltin assumed editorship of *Film Fan Monthly* and within a short time increased the magazine's circulation dramatically. By the time he was contracted to produce the popular series *TV Movies*, his editor, Patrick O'Connor, had to conceal Maltin's age "lest the Bantam brass suspect that O'Connor had taken leave of his senses" in hiring a seventeen-year-old, according to *Los Angeles Times* writer Charles Champlin.

"No, I haven't seen 15,000 movies," states Maltin, noting in *Film Comment* the first question he is often asked when people learn about his association with *TV Movies*. The author explains that the extensive compilation of facts and ratings on virtually every film ever likely to appear on television is a result of contributions by several editors, including Mike Clark, Alvin Marill, Rob Edelman, and Maltin's wife, Alice Tlusty. "I don't agree with them all the time," says Maltin of the four-star rating system used by the contributors, "nor they with me." But the greatest challenge in producing the guide, acknowledges the author, is not in critique but in accuracy. For instance, "the very name of a film can be the subject of dispute. A film may be known officially as *Neil Simon's I Ought to Be in Pictures* or *Irving Berlin's Blue Skies*, but no one actually refers to it that way except lawyers for the lucky parties involved. . . . Some titles that involve punctuation (*Blowup*, no hyphen, *E. T. The Extra-Terrestrial*, no comma) . . . may be rendered differently in the on-screen credits and in official advertising."

Establishing a particular movie's running time constitutes "the biggest single headache in compiling [the] book," says Maltin. He tells Champlin, "Ask four people at a studio what the running time of a film was and you'll get four different answers." By the time a movie is released, re-released, and finally sold to television, Maltin explains, its length may be altered several times. He offers an example in *Film Comment* of what he calls a hopeless case: The Marx Brothers classic "A Night at the Opera." "MGM Television states that the film is 96 minutes long. . . . But one film buff, who times movies with a stopwatch, told me that it ran no more than 90 minutes. Then I heard from a film editor at a TV station who had just clocked a brand-new print from MGM at 91 minutes on the nose. I decided to check with Films Incorporated. . . . [Their] result: 93 minutes. Next, I turned to MGM's home-video division, only to find that their version ran 87 minutes—because it had been 'time-compressed' for videocassette release. Finally, I prevailed upon Dennis Murphy at MGM/UA to commission someone at his studio library to run a complete 35mm fine-grain negative through a timer, which yielded a response of 92 minutes—the first and only time that particular number came up!"

Maltin finds temporary relief from these "headaches" by writing a number of books dealing with many aspects of film history, including a study of cinematography, a synopsis of movie comedians, and a critically-acclaimed work delving into the history of American animated cartoons, *Of Mice and Magic*. The author also appears regularly as a film critic on the syndicated television series "Entertainment Tonight." He told *CA* that he finds no small irony in the fact that more people see one of his critiques on any given evening than have purchased all his books put together.

BIOGRAPHICAL/CRITICAL SOURCES: *Saturday Review*, September 17, 1967; *New York Times*, May 6, 1976; *Los Angeles Times Book Review*, October 12, 1980; *Chicago Tribune*, November 12, 1980; *New York Times Book Review*, December 21, 1980; *Film Comment*, September-October, 1982; *Los Angeles Times*, December 2, 1982.

* * *

MANN, Peter H. 1926-

PERSONAL: Born September 5, 1926, in Huddersfield, Yorkshire, England; son of Frank Drury and Annie (Hinchliffe) Mann; married Margaret Hartshorne, December 28, 1950; children: Hilary, Richard, Lucy. *Education:* University of Leeds, B.A., 1950; University of Liverpool, M.A. (by research), 1952; University of Nottingham, Ph.D., 1955. *Politics:* "Secret ballot." *Residence:* England. *Office:* 158 Station Rd., Cropston, Centre for Library and Information Management, Loughborough University, Leicester, England.

CAREER: University of Liverpool, Liverpool, England, research assistant, department of social science, 1950-52; University of Nottingham, Nottingham, England, research fellow, 1952-54; University of Sheffield, Sheffield, England, lecturer, 1954-64, senior lecturer, 1964-72, reader in sociology, 1972-83; Loughborough University, Centre for Library and Information Management, Leicester, England, director, 1983—. *Military service:* British Merchant Navy, radio officer, 1943-47. *Member:* Association of University Teachers, National Trust.

WRITINGS: *An Approach to Urban Sociology*, Humanities, 1965; *Methods of Sociological Enquiry*, Schocken, 1968; (with J. L. Burgoyne) *Books and Reading*, Deutsch, 1969; *Books: Buyers and Borrowers*, Deutsch, 1971; *Students and Books*, Routledge & Kegan Paul, 1974; *The Facts about Romantic Fiction*, Mills & Boon, 1974; *From Author to Reader: A Social Study of Books*, Routledge & Kegan Paul, 1982. Editor, *British Universities Annual*, 1967-69.

WORK IN PROGRESS: Research in problems of the management of libraries of all types.

SIDELIGHTS: The result of fifteen years of research into the British book industry, Peter H. Mann's *From Author to Reader: A Social Study of Books* is "packed with statistical data on, among other things, publishing, distribution of bookshops and sales levels; book buying by the general public, public libraries, universities and local authorities; and the social demography of book buying and borrowing," according to Jim McGuigan in *New Statesman.*

Both McGuigan and *Times Literary Supplement* reviewer Nigel Cross criticize the author for too often "stating the obvious while neglecting all the interesting questions about the social construction of literary categories and the actual interchange and tensions between them," as McGuigan states. However, Cross also notes that Mann "makes some sensible suggestions for increasing readership both through libraries and bookshops. He points out that although librarians have read the [book reviews] . . . , most borrowers and purchasers depend on the publisher's blurb as a guide to the merit and content of a novel. Mann suggests that the card index might carry some critical commentary, or at least cross-reference: 'if you like C. S. Forester why not try Joseph Conrad?'; that reviews should be prominently displayed, and that prize-winning novels should be identified. He believes that booksellers could be more daring and display books by themes as well as by category and publishers' imprint. So a novel about India, for example, might be shelved in the travel section."

BIOGRAPHICAL/CRITICAL SOURCES: *New Statesman,* October 15, 1982; *Observer,* November 7, 1982; *Times Literary Supplement,* December 31, 1982; *London Review of Books,* February 17, 1983.

* * *

**MANNERS, Alexandra
   See RUNDLE, Anne**

* * *

MANZALAOUI, Mahmoud (Ali)   1924-

PERSONAL: Surname is pronounced *Man-za-la-*wee; born May 13, 1924, in London, England; son of Hussein Sadek (a landowner) and Fatma (Deif) Manzalaoui; married M. H. Kirkley. *Education:* University of Cairo, B.A., 1944; Oxford University, B.Litt., M.A., D.Phil. *Home:* 4258 West 14th Ave., Vancouver, British Columbia, Canada. *Office:* Department of English, University of British Columbia, Vancouver, British Columbia, Canada V6T 1W5.

CAREER: University of Alexandria, Alexandria, Egypt, assistant lecturer, 1949-54, lecturer, 1954-61, associate professor, 1961-68, professor of English, 1968-69; University of British Columbia, Vancouver, professor of English, 1969—. Visiting fellow, Clare Hall, Cambridge University, 1968-69; visiting senior member, St. Anthony's College, Oxford University, 1974-75. Member of Committee for Encouragement of Tourism, Alexandria, Egypt, 1966-67. *Member:* Amici Thomae Mori, Oxford and Cambridge Club (London).

WRITINGS: (Editor) *Arabic Writing Today,* Volume I: *The Short Story,* Volume II: *The Drama,* University of California Press, 1969-77; (contributor) D. Brewer, editor, *Writers and Their Background: Geoffrey Chaucer,* G. Bell, 1974, Ohio University Press, 1975; *"Secretum Secretorum": Nine English Versions,* Volume I, Early English Text Society, 1976; (with P. Heyworth) *Medieval Studies for J. A. W. Bennett,* Oxford University Press, 1981. Contributor to *Times Educational Supplement, Etudes anglaises, Journal of Courtauld and Warburg Institutes,* and other publications.

WORK IN PROGRESS: Volume II of *"Secretum Secretorum": Nine English Versions* and cognate articles.

**MARA, Jeanette
   See CEBULASH, Mel**

* * *

MARCHAND, Leslie A(lexis)   1900-

PERSONAL: Born February 13, 1900, in Bridgeport, Wash.; son of Alexis (an inventor) and Clara (Buckingham) Marchand; married Marion Knill Hendrix (an artist and writer), July 8, 1950. *Education:* University of Washington, Seattle, B.A. 1922, M.A., 1923; Columbia University, Ph.D., 1940; attended Sorbonne, University of Paris, 1927-28, and University of Munich, summer, 1932. *Home address:* P.O. Box 189, Avon, N.C. 27915.

CAREER: Alaska Agricultural College and School of Mines (now University of Alaska), Fairbanks, professor of English and French, 1923-27, 1934-35; Columbia University, New York, N.Y., lecturer in English, 1936-37; Rutgers University, New Brunswick, N.J., instructor, 1937-42, assistant professor, 1942-46, associate professor, 1946-53, professor of English, 1953-66, professor emeritus, 1966—. Instructor at University of Washington, Seattle, summer, 1924, visiting professor, summers, 1925, 1958; instructor at Columbia University, summers, 1929-31, visiting professor, summers, 1945-46, 1965; visiting professor at University of California, Los Angeles, summer, 1949, University of Illinois, summer, 1954, Arizona State University, 1966-67, and Harvard University, summer, 1969; Fulbright professor at University of Athens, 1958-59; professorial lecturer at Hunter College of the City University of New York, 1960-62; Berg Visiting Professor at New York University, 1962-63; John Cranford Adams Professor of English at Hofstra University, 1967-68.

MEMBER: International P.E.N., Modern Language Association of America, Keats-Shelley Association of America (member of board of directors), Byron Society (vice-president), Phi Beta Kappa.

AWARDS, HONORS: Book of the year award from New Jersey Association of Teachers of English, 1958, for *Byron: A Biography;* grants from American Council of Learned Societies, 1964, 1971, Carl and Lily Pdorzheimer Foundation, 1970, American Philosophical Society, 1970, and National Endowment for the Humanities, 1972-73, 1974-75, 1976-79; Guggenheim fellowship, 1968-69; James Russell Lowell Prize from Modern Language Association of America, 1974, for *Byron's Letters and Journals;* D.H.L. from University of Alaska, 1976; D.Litt. from Rutgers University, 1981; Royal Society of Literature fellow, 1981.

WRITINGS: *The Athenaeum: A Mirror of Victorian Culture,* University of North Carolina Press, 1941; (editor and author of introduction) *Letters of Thomas Hood from the Dilke Papers in the British Museum,* Rutgers University Press, 1945; (editor and author of introduction) *Selected Poetry of Lord Byron,* Random House, 1951, revised edition, 1967; (contributor) Klaus W. Jones, editor, *The Maugham Enigma,* Citadel, 1954; *Byron: A Biography,* three volumes, Knopf, 1957; (editor and author of introduction) *Lord Byron: "Don Juan,"* Houghton, 1958; (contributor) Rudolf Kirk and C. F. Main, editors, *Essays in Literary History,* Rutgers University Press, 1960; *Byron's Poetry: A Critical Introduction,* Houghton, 1965.

Byron: A Portrait, Knopf, 1970; (editor) *Byron's Letters and Journals,* Harvard University Press, Volume I: *In My Hot Youth,*

1973, Volume II: *Famous in My Time,* 1973, Volume III: *Alas! the Love of Women,* 1974, Volume IV: *Wedlock's the Devil,* 1975, Volume V: *So Late into the Night,* 1976, Volume VI: *The Flesh Is Frail,* 1976, Volume VII: *Between Two Worlds,* 1977, Volume VIII: *Born for Opposition,* 1978, Volume IX: *In the Wind's Eye,* 1979, Volume X: *A Heart for Every Fate,* 1980, Volume XI: *For Freedom's Battle,* 1981, Volume XII: *The Trouble of an Index,* 1982; *Lord Byron: Selected Letters and Journals,* Harvard University Press, 1982.

Reporter and city editor of *Fairbanks Daily News-Miner,* summer, 1926; night wire filing editor for Associated Press (Newark Bureau), 1943-44. Author of "The Once Over," a column in *MS: A Magazine for Writers,* 1930. Contributor to *Encyclopedia Americana, Collier's Encyclopedia,* and *Encyclopaedia Britannica.* Contributor of about eighty articles and reviews to scholarly journals and to magazines and newspapers, including *Spectator, Christian Science Monitor, New York Times,* and *Saturday Review.*

SIDELIGHTS: George Gordon, Lord Byron, apart from being one of the most popular poets of nineteenth-century England, was also one of the most enthusiastic and prolific letter-writers of his day. His known correspondence amounts to nearly 3,000 letters, encompassing in subject matter every facet of the poet's public and private affairs. Collecting and editing this vast body of material has been the ten-year project of Byron scholar Leslie A. Marchand, who has produced twelve volumes of the poet's letters and journals.

Citing Marchand's four-decade involvement in researching Byroniana, James Atlas says in the *New York Times Book Review* that Marchand's work is "more than a matter of diligent library research. [The author] belongs among those intrepid literary historians portrayed in Richard Altick's *The Scholar Adventurers,* where an entertaining account of his search . . . can be found. Like Col. Ralph Isham and Chauncey Brewster Tinker, who recovered Boswell's journals from Malahide Castle in Scotland through persistence and scholarly detective work, Professor Marchand was convinced from the start that a great many of Byron's papers remained at large and set off for Europe in the summer of 1947 determined to recover them."

The result of Marchand's comprehensive research has proven successful; the twelve volumes of *Byron's Letters and Journals* have been met with praise from scholars and critics on both sides of the Atlantic. A comment typical of most critics comes from Michael Ratcliffe, reviewing Volume XI of the series, *For Freedom's Battle,* in the London *Times:* "Byron's unique greatness of spirit has perhaps never been acknowledged so readily as today. That we possess such a brilliant and exhilerating portrait of the man (as distinct from the poet) is due . . . supremely to Leslie Marchand, for his three-volume Life (1957) and for this reading edition of the journals and letters— . . . almost three times as many as in any other collection."

BIOGRAPHICAL/CRITICAL SOURCES: Richard D. Altick, *The Scholar Adventurers,* Macmillan, 1950; *Times Literary Supplement,* April 4, 1980, April 24, 1981; *Times* (London), April 23, 1980; *New York Times Book Review,* August 3, 1980, November 7, 1982; *New York Times,* November 4, 1982.

* * *

MARIANI, Paul L(ouis) 1940-

PERSONAL: Born February 29, 1940, in New York, N.Y.; son of Paul Patrick (a day-camp foreman) and Harriet (Green) Mariani; married Eileen Spinosa (a kindergarten teacher), August 24, 1963; children: Paul, Mark, John. *Education:* Manhattan College, Bronx, N.Y., B.A., 1962; Colgate University, M.A., 1964; City University of New York, Ph.D., 1968. *Politics:* Democrat. *Religion:* Roman Catholic. *Office:* Department of English, Bartlett Hall, University of Massachusetts, Amherst, Mass. 01003.

CAREER: Colgate University, Hamilton, N.Y., instructor in English, 1963-64; John Jay College of Criminal Justice of the City University of New York, New York, N.Y., assistant professor of English, 1967-68; University of Massachusetts—Amherst, assistant professor, 1968-71, associate professor, 1971-75, professor of English, 1975—. Robert Frost fellow in poetry, Bread Loaf Writers' Conference, 1980; Robert Frost Professor of English, Bread Loaf School of English, 1982. *Member:* Modern Language Association of America, Hopkins Society. *Awards, honors:* National Endowment for the Humanities fellowship, 1973, 1981-82; *William Carlos Williams: A New World Naked* won the New Jersey Writers Award and was nominated for an American Book Award, both 1982.

WRITINGS: *A Commentary on the Complete Poems of Gerard Manley Hopkins,* Cornell University Press, 1970; *William Carlos Williams: The Poet and His Critics,* American Library Association, 1975; *Timing Devices: Poems,* Pennyroyal Press, 1977; *William Carlos Williams: A New World Naked,* McGraw, 1981; *Crossing Cocytus: Poems,* Grove Press, 1982; *A Useable Past: Essays, 1973-1983,* University of Massachusetts Press, 1984; *Prime Mover: Poems,* Grove Press, 1985.

Contributor to *Massachusetts Review, Hudson Review, Tendril, Nation, Iowa Review, Prairie Schooner,* and other journals. Associate editor, *William Carlos Williams Review.*

WORK IN PROGRESS: A biography of John Berryman, for Morrow.

SIDELIGHTS: William Carlos Williams, one of the most distinguished American poets of the twentieth century, was a champion of the American ideal in poetry; he shunned the examples of such contemporaries as Ezra Pound and T. S. Eliot, who had left the United States to live and write in England and Europe. As a result, Williams was often ignored by the critics and reading public of his age. In *William Carlos Williams: A New World Naked,* biographer Paul L. Mariani says of his subject's existence: "It had indeed been quite a life: the uphill struggle of an American revolutionary to establish—against the incredible odds of neglect, misinterpretation, dismissal—an American poetic based on a new measure and a primary regard for the living, protean shape of the language as it was actually used. It had been a fight, a magnificent fight, against the academy, against the numbing sclerosis of the universities, against the very scholars of the language (there were none, Williams insisted), against special interests of all kinds, and [he'd] had to create a strategy and sometimes even desperate homemade measures where none had existed before."

"Williams' life, in its devotion to poetry and refusal to compromise, is a model for poets," remarks Louis Simpson in the *Washington Post Book World.* "It deserves to be researched thoroughly and have all the parts put in order so that we may understand them. Paul Mariani has done the job—I doubt that there will be a more thorough and reliable biography of Williams in our time. . . . There are so many facts, so many incidents and conversations! Mariani has followed the usual method of American biographers: he has put everything in so as not to risk leaving anything out."

Indeed, finds Gilbert Sorrentino, the author "is relentless in detailing the shabby treatment accorded Williams throughout the whole of his career, a record of intellectual misprision that invented a Williams who was, and still is—with endemic regularity—thought of as a kind of amiable primitive, an unsophisticated scribbler, a simple small-town doctor who wrote on the side, but wrote, mind you, without quite knowing what he was doing: the literary equivalent of Grandma Moses or the New Jersey version of *vers libre*'s gift to the world, Carl Sandburg." Commenting on Mariani's biography in the *New York Times Book Review*, Sorrentino continues: "[The author] shatters these idiocies by a careful examination of Williams's work in poetry, fiction and criticism, setting it against the general somnambulism of the time. In a sense, this book may be read as a kind of graph of the reactionary shoddiness of the American critical mind in the face of a modern master, and I half suspect that . . . Mariani intends us to read it this way because of the attention he has paid to this facet of Williams's career."

In detailing every facet of his subject's life, Mariani, according to Anatole Broyard of the *New York Times*, "does not know when he is showing Dr. Williams in an unflattering light. He seems to find some of the doctor's crude or simplistic remarks examples of his 'honesty' or lack of affectation. This devoted family man, this hard-working small-town physician, this poet, sometimes sounds like an ordinary redneck with . . . his reference to Hart Crane as a 'crude homo' or his fondness for sexual and scatological imagery." Broyard notes that "there is something grotesque in the assumption that reading a man's poetry entitles us to learn all the worst things about him, as if to prove that poetry is not a sissified affair, or that a poet can be as vulgar or as foolish as anyone else. The effect here is to elevate the vulgar rather than the poetry."

Karl Shapiro, on the other hand, argues that "one reads biographies for gossip, really. It is charming in retrospect to hear that Williams had a whirlwind love affair with one of the female editors of *Poetry Chicago*, and that he had to call the police to chase a mad, oversexed, syphilitic German baroness out of his garage." Shapiro, in the *Chicago Tribune Book World*, states: "This is not to say that Mariani diminishes his subject. Reduction to the human is not only endearing but allows true greatness to come into focus."

"This is a definitive biography in certain respects," concludes *New Republic* critic Robert Coles. "Time haunted the busy doctor, the versatile writer, and time dominates this book, which is narrated with a strong chronological (rather than interpretive) emphasis, though Mariani does allow himself an occasional critical digression. His writing is energetic, fast-paced, a bit tough—not unlike the manner of the busy New Jersey writer and physician himself. This is a long book, and some will judge that parts of it ought to have been cut. But William Carlos Williams was *sui generis*, a citizen well worth inclusion in his own magnificent social history (good God, he did *that* brilliantly, too!) *In the American Grain;* and it is a pleasure to have so much of his exceptional life run by one's eyes, reach one's mind and heart again."

"Increasingly, I have turned to the poem as my forum, a pit in which I wrestle with the shadows for the elusive prize of light," Paul L. Mariani told *CA*. "In prose it is biography, the life of the poet, so that I may better see how others did it before me. The poems deal with the self, especially earlier versions of that self, with the issues of our time as these press themselves upon us and—finally—with the extraordinary powers of the imagination. At the heart of it all—poetry, criticism, biography—it is the fascination with the language itself."

BIOGRAPHICAL/CRITICAL SOURCES: Paul L. Mariani, *William Carlos Williams: A New World Naked*, McGraw, 1981; *Chicago Tribune Book World*, November 15, 1981; *New York Times Book Review*, November 22, 1981; *New Republic*, November 25, 1981; *New York Times*, November 28, 1981; *Los Angeles Times Book Review*, December 13, 1981; *Los Angeles Times*, December 30, 1981; *Washington Post Book World*, January 3, 1982; *Commonweal*, October 8, 1982; *William Carlos Williams Review*, fall, 1983.

—Sketch by Susan Salter

* * *

MARILL, Alvin H(erbert) 1934-

PERSONAL: Born January 10, 1934, in Brockton, Mass.; son of Morris (a jeweler) and Rose (a ballet teacher; maiden name, Sampson) Marill; married Sandra R. Lelyveld, August 30, 1959; children: James, Steven. *Education:* Boston University, B.S., 1955. *Residence:* Glen Rock, N.J. 07452.

CAREER: WBOS Radio, Boston, Mass., music director, 1958-62; WNAC Radio and Television, Boston, producer, writer, and music director, 1962-67; WRFM-WNYW Radio, New York City, director of music programming, 1967-69; RCA Records, New York City, publicist and public information writer, 1969-72; Tatham, Laird & Kudner Direct Marketing, New York City, senior writer/editor, partner, 1973-81; RCA Direct Marketing, New York City, senior writer/editor, manager, 1981—. Free-lance publicist, 1972-73. *Military service:* U.S. Army, 1956-58. *Member:* Alpha Epsilon Rho.

WRITINGS: (With Alan G. Barbour and James R. Parish) *Boris Karloff: An Illustrated Career Study*, Cinefax, 1968; (with Barbour and Parish) *Errol Flynn: An Illustrated Career Study*, Cinefax, 1968; (with Parish) *The Cinema of Edward G. Robinson*, A. S. Barnes, 1972; *Katharine Hepburn: An Illustrated Study*, Pyramid Publications, 1973; *The Films of Anthony Quinn*, Citadel, 1975; (editor) *Moe Howard and the Three Stooges*, Citadel, 1977; *Samuel Goldwyn Presents*, A. S. Barnes, 1977; *The Films of Sidney Poitier*, Citadel, 1978; (with Dennis Belafonte) *The Films of Tyrone Power*, Citadel, 1978; *Robert Mitchum on the Screen*, A. S. Barnes, 1978; *Movies Made for Television, 1964-79*, Arlington House, 1980; *Movies Made for Television, 1979-84*, New York Zoetrope, 1984. Author of "The Television Scene," a monthly column in *Films in Review*. Contributor to journals, including *Screen Facts, Record World,* and *Image*. Associate editor, *TV Movies*.

* * *

MARKHAM, Meeler 1914-

PERSONAL: Born March 8, 1914, in Fort Worth, Tex.; son of Henry Nathan (a builder and carpenter) and Mattie (Sanders) Markham; married Myrtie Manlove (a secretary), June 18, 1937; children: Edwin. *Education:* Attended Howard Payne College, 1934-35, University of Texas, 1936, Texas Christian University, 1943, and Southwestern Baptist Theological Seminary, 1943-45, 1947. *Office:* 214 Harralton Circle, Devine, Tex. 78016.

CAREER: Worked with U.S. Soil Conservation Service in Texas, 1937-40; ordained deacon in Baptist Church, 1938, and minister, 1941; U.S. Army, Quartermaster Corps, Fort Sam Houston and Fort Worth, Tex., began as inspector, became supervisor, then chief inspector, 1941-43; pastor of churches in Somerset, Tex., 1941-42, Carrizo Springs, Tex., 1945-51, and Mercedes, Tex., 1951-55; Lower Rio Grande Baptist Association, Harlingen, Tex., superintendent of missions, 1955-60; Kansas Convention of Southern Baptists, Wichita, secretary of department of missions, 1960-65; Southern Baptist Home Mission Board, Division of Associational Missions, Atlanta, Ga., secretary of mission property services, 1966-70, director of associational publications, 1971-76; director of missions, Frio River Baptist Association, 1976-81; Trinity Baptist Church, Lytle, Tex., pastor, 1981. Former member of executive board, Baptist General Convention of Texas. *Member:* Masons, Rotary International.

WRITINGS: This Confident Faith, Broadman, 1968; (contributor) *Every Day, Five Minutes with God,* Broadman, 1969; *History of Frio River Baptist Association,* Frio River Baptist Association, 1981. Writer of pamphlets and booklets. Contributor to magazines.

WORK IN PROGRESS: The Bible Story; Basic Mission Concepts.

* * *

MARKS, Stan(ley) 1929-
(Martin King)

PERSONAL: Born April 25, 1929, in London, England; taken to Australia at the age of two; son of Sidney (in clothing business) and Sally (Bernstein) Marks; married Eve Mass (a designer of toys), July 15, 1951; children: Lee (daughter; deceased), Peter. *Education:* Attended University of Melbourne. *Home:* 348 Bambra Rd., Caulfield, Melbourne, Victoria, Australia 3162. *Office:* Australian Tourist Commission, St. Kilda Rd., Melbourne, Victoria, Australia 3004.

CAREER: Began working for an Australian country newspaper at the age of seventeen; later a reporter and theater critic for *Melbourne Herald,* Melbourne, Australia; reporter for newspapers in England, 1951, and in Montreal, Quebec, and Toronto, Ontario, 1952-53; correspondent for Australian newspapers in New York, N.Y., 1954-55; returned to Australia to become public relations supervisor of Australian Broadcasting Commission, Melbourne, 1958-64; public relations officer of Trans Australia Airlines, 1965-67; Australian Tourist Commission, Melbourne, public relations manager, 1968—. *Member:* Australian Journalists Association, Australian Society of Authors, Society of Australian Travel Writers.

WRITINGS—Published by Methuen, except as indicated: *God Gave You One Face* (novel), R. Hale, 1964; (contributor) *Walkabout's Book of Best Australian Stories,* Landsdowne Press, 1968; *Graham Is an Aboriginal Boy,* photographs by Brian McArdle, 1968, Hastings House, 1969; *Fifty Years of Achievement,* 1972; *Animal Olympics* (stories), 1972-76; *Rarua Lives in Papua New Guinea,* 1974; *Ketut Lives in Bali,* 1976; *Boy of Indonesia,* 1976; (author of text) William Andrew David Brodie, *St. Kilda Sketchbook,* Rigby, 1980.

Author of plays "When a Wife Strikes," 1970, and "Everybody Out," and of a collection of scripts, "Is She Fair Dinkum?"; also author *Malvern Sketchbook, Australia Welcomes You,* and of stories for two records for children, *Animal Olympics* and *Montague the Mouse Who Sailed with Captain Cook.* Co-originator of a comic strip, "Ms.," for Australian newspapers, including *Melbourne Herald, Auckland Star,* and *Christchurch Star,* 1975—. Contributor of feature stories and articles to Australian and overseas journals; some of the articles were published under the pseudonym Martin King.

WORK IN PROGRESS: A novel and a film script.

SIDELIGHTS: Stan Marks has a strong interest in the arts, youth, and promoting better understanding between nations. As early as 1951 he suggested that an All-British Commonwealth Arts Festival should be held regularly; later he began urging that a Youth Council be established at the United Nations to get the world's young closer to policy making. A Commonwealth Arts Festival eventually was held, and the Youth Council idea brought him an invitation to the 1960 White House Conference on Youth. He also has advocated an "Ideas Bank" for international peace, where people might send suggestions to be sifted for possible discussion ("just one good idea might save that button being pushed"). His books reflect those concerns and his interest in aborigines.

While researching his book *Graham Is an Aboriginal Boy,* Marks lived for ten days with the Arunta tribe near Alice Springs in Australia's Northern Territory, learning to hunt with a boomerang and to enjoy a diet of bush bananas and figs. He has also lived in other villages in New Guinea and Bali while researching his books. Marks told *CA* that these experiences have shown him that "all people really require same things, especially ability to survive with some dignity—a sense which over the centuries (I guess, since dawn of time) certain peoples, of all races, creeds and self-righteousness, have felt they knew the answers and could dictate (or impose their) wills on others.

"I feel, if we still have time, the hope is in today's youngsters, but with all the factions, isms, those who have all the answers, fanatics (of all ilks) and so many sects, creeds and groups, I wonder whether the young have a chance.

"I also worry about the international communications explosion. With all the power of good in our world-wide TV, radio, computer and other links, we seem to be misusing it, not using it at all or letting it all take its chance. Why this incredible leaning towards violence in our entertainments and leisure activities? Why? Is it really something in our inborn natures? Why are so many ready to die for something—is it easier than to TRY and live for it? No, I'm not a cynic, maybe a little sceptical; but is that bad? I do not feel an invasion from the outside would unite us—I feel some earth power would join with the invaders for some gain or whatever. Will we learn? Are we meant to? Isn't it time we came together to give today's people a chance—not future generations? When do we start to think of all peoplekind? I hope, in some small way, my writings, especially Children Everywhere books, have sown some seeds of better understanding of each other, of the importance of each person, that no one has the only answer. With so much to live for, people seem bent on destruction."

* * *

MARMOR, J(udd) 1910-

PERSONAL: Born May 1, 1910, in London, England; brought to United States in 1911, naturalized in 1916; son of Clement Kalman (a writer) and Sarah (Levene) Marmor; married Katherine Stern, May 1, 1938; children: Michael Franklin. *Education:* Columbia University, A.B., 1930, M.D., 1933; New York Psychoanalyst Institute, psychoanalytic training, 1937-41. *Home:* 655 Sarbonne Rd., Los Angeles, Calif. 90077. *Office:* Suite 909, 10889 Wilshire Blvd., Los Angeles, Calif. 90024.

CAREER: St. Elizabeth's Hospital, Washington, D.C., intern, 1933-35; Montefiore Hospital, New York City, resident neurologist and later fellow, 1935-37; private practice of psychiatry, psychoanalysis and neurology, New York City, 1937-46, Los Angeles, Calif., 1946—; Cedar-Sinai Medical Center, Los Angeles, director of Divisions of Psychiatry, 1965-72; University of Southern California, School of Medicine, Los Angeles, Franz Alexander Professor of Psychiatry, 1972-80, adjunct professor of psychiatry, 1980—. Psychiatrist, Brooklyn State Hospital, 1937; senior attending psychiatrist, Los Angeles County General Hospital, 1954. Instructor and associate in neurology, Columbia College of Physicians and Surgeons, 1938-40; adjunct neurologist in charge of neurology clinic, Mt. Sinai Hospital, New York City, 1939-46.

Lecturer, New School of Social Research, New York City, 1942-43; instructor, American Institute of Psychoanalysis, 1943; lecturer in psychiatry, New York Medical College, 1944-46; University of California, Los Angeles, lecturer, 1948-49, visiting professor of social welfare, 1949-64, clinical professor of psychiatry in School of Medicine, 1953-80. Visiting professor of psychology, University of Southern California, 1946-49. Southern California Psychoanalytic Institute, training analyst, 1953—, president, 1956-57. Senior attending psychiatrist, Los Angeles County General Hospital, 1954-80. Senior consultant, Veteran's Administration, Los Angeles, 1946-50; psychiatric consultant, Brentwood Veteran's Administration Hospital, 1955-65. Diplomate, National Board of Medical Examiners, 1935, and American Board of Psychiatry and Neurology, 1939.

Vice-president, Psychosomatic Research Foundation; member of board of directors of Behavioral Science Research Foundation, Neumeyer Foundation, Human Interaction Research Institute, and Theater Group of Los Angeles Center for Performing Arts; member of Council on Mental Health of Western Interstate Community for Higher Education. Chairman of Contemporary Art Council, Los Angeles County Museum of Art. *Military service:* U.S. Public Health Service (duty with U.S. Navy), 1944-45.

MEMBER: American Academy for the Advancement of Science, American Academy of Psychoanalysis (fellow; president, 1965-66), American Medical Association (fellow), American Psychiatric Association (life fellow; president, 1975-76), American Orthopsychiatric Association (fellow; member of board of directors, 1968-71), American College of Psychiatrists (fellow), New York Academy of Medicine (life fellow), American Psychoanalytic Association, American Fund for Psychiatry (member of board of directors, 1955-57), Group for the Advancement of Psychiatry (member of board of directors, 1968-70; president, 1973-75), Southern California Psychiatric Society, Southern California Psychoanalytic Society (president, 1960-61), Los Angeles County Medical Society, Phi Beta Kappa, Alpha Omega Alpha.

AWARDS, HONORS: Silver Medal for distinguished service in field of psychiatry, from College of Physicians and Surgeons, Columbia University, 1966; D.H.L., Hebrew Union College, 1972; Bowis Award for outstanding achievements and leadership in the field of psychiatry, American College of Psychiatrists, 1978; Humanitarian award, Camelback Hospital Foundation, 1979; Outstanding Achievement award, Bay Area Physicians for Human Rights, 1980; Founders award, American Psychiatric Association, 1982; Performance award, Mental Health Association, 1982.

WRITINGS: *Psychiatrists and Their Patients: A National Study of Private Office Practice,* Joint Information Service of American Psychiatric Association and National Association for Mental Health, 1975. Also author of "You've Got to Be Taught to Hate," a twenty-eight minute tape for Center for the Study of Democratic Institutions.

Editor: *Psychiatric Aspects of the Prevention of Nuclear War,* Group for the Advancement of Psychiatry, 1964; *Sexual Inversion: The Multiple Roots of Homosexuality,* Basic Books, 1965; *Modern Psychoanalysis: New Perspectives and Directions,* Basic Books, 1968; *Psychiatry in Transition: Selected Papers,* Brunner-Mazel, 1974; *Homosexual Behavior: A Modern Reappraisal,* Basic Books, 1980; (with S. Woods) *The Interface between Dynamic Psychotherapy and Behavioral Therapy,* Plenum, 1980.

Contributor: R. W. Sellars, editor, *Philosophy for the Future,* Macmillan, 1949; *Psychoanalysis and the Social Sciences,* International Universities Press, 1958; S. Liebman, editor, *Emotional Forces in the Family,* Lippincott, 1959; J. Masserman, editor, *Current Psychiatric Therapies,* Grune, 1961; L. Salzman and Masserman, editors, *Modern Concepts of Psychoanalysis,* Philosophical Library, 1962; Masserman, editor, *Science and Psychoanalysis,* Grune, 1962; *The Encyclopedia of Mental Health,* F. Watts, 1963; *The Psychological Basis of Medical Practice,* Harper, 1963; A. Larson, editor, *A World without War,* McGraw, 1963.

M. Schwebel, editor, *Human Survival and the Behavioral Sciences,* Science & Behavior Books, 1965; (with V. Bernard and P. Ottenberg) Kats and Felton, editors, *Health and the Community,* Free Press, 1965; G. Usdin, editor, *Psychoneurosis and Schizophrenia,* Lippincott, 1966; *Birth Control: A Continuing Controversy,* C. C Thomas, 1967; S. Rosenbaum and I. Alger, editors, *The Marriage Relationship,* Basic Books, 1968; W. Gray and others, editors, *General Systems Theory and Psychiatry,* Little, Brown, 1968; *Current Trends in Psychiatry,* Forest Hospital Foundation (Des Plaines, Ill.), 1968; I. Galdston, editor, *Psychoanalysis in Present-Day Psychiatry,* Brunner, 1969; T. Rose, editor, *Violence in America,* Random House, 1969.

Contributor of more than three hundred articles to scientific journals. Member of editorial boards, *Psychiatry Digest, Contemporary Psychoanalysis, Archives of Sexual Behavior, Comprehensive Psychiatry, American Journal of Psychoanalysis, International Journal of Family Psychiatry,* and *American Journal of Psychoanalysis.*

SIDELIGHTS: J. Marmor told *CA:* "It has been my firm conviction in all of my writing that both theory and practice should rest on a sound foundation of scientific thought. Where theory fails to do so, one must be prepared to alter the theory. Where practice fails to do so, and yet is pragmically effective, one must continue to search for an explanation of the effectiveness that falls within scientifically verifiable boundaries. Psychiatry is a field in which there has always been a profusion of diverse approaches and claims; this has never been more true than it is now. If we are ever to find our way out of this confusing maze of claims and counterclaims, it will only be by clinging steadfastly to the compass of scientific thought and method.

"An important factor in my own efforts has been my resistance from the beginning to the siren call of simplistic, unitary, or 'linear' explanations of complex problems. Rather, I have always tended to think of causation in psychiatry, in field-theoretical terms, as a resultant of the interaction of many variables.

"Another continuing theme in my writing has been the search for common denominators underlying the numerous divergent views that characterize our field. I have tried to maintain a historic perspective about it as a discipline in the process of development and change, rather than as a fixed and immutable one. If I can take any credit as a psychiatrist who has lived and worked in the midst of the profound changes that have taken place in our field over the past half century, it is that I have tried to keep an open mind to new currents of thought, and have not been afraid to modify either my theories or my practices in the light of new developments.

"Finally, in most of my writings, there has been a consistent concern with betterment of the human predicament. This preoccupation may, of course, be part of the complex motivational pattern that so often shapes an interest in psychiatry in the first place, but in my case, it also stems from a background deeply steeped in a concern for social justice."

* * *

MARRUS, Michael R(obert) 1941-

PERSONAL: Born February 3, 1941, in Toronto, Ontario, Canada; son of Elliott Lloyd and Lillian (Brenzel) Marrus; married Carol Randi Greenstein (a teacher), May 13, 1971; children: two. *Education:* University of Toronto, B.A., 1963; University of California, Berkeley, M.A., 1964, Ph.D., 1968. *Office:* Department of History, University of Toronto, Toronto, Ontario, Canada M5S 1A1.

CAREER: University of Toronto, Toronto, Ontario, assistant professor, 1968-73, associate professor, 1973-77, professor of history, 1978—. Visiting fellow, St. Antony's College, Oxford, 1978-80; visiting professor, University of California, Los Angeles, 1982. *Awards, honors:* With Robert O. Paxton, History Prize and Book Prize nominations, both from *Los Angeles Times,* and National Jewish Book Award, all 1982, for *Vichy France and the Jews;* Guggenheim fellowship, 1984-85.

WRITINGS: The Politics of Assimilation: A Study of the French Jewish Community at the Time of the Dreyfus Affair, Clarendon Press, 1971; (editor) *The Emergence of Leisure,* Harper, 1974; (with Robert O. Paxton) *Vichy France and the Jews,* Basic Books, 1981; *Refugees and the International Order in Europe,* Oxford University Press, in press. Contributor of articles on French and Jewish history to journals.

SIDELIGHTS: Following the German occupation of June, 1940, France was divided into two zones. Occupied France, an area including Paris and the northern and western coasts, operated under German control. Unoccupied France—also known as Vichy France—was administered by Marshal Henri Petain. The fate of the Jews in Occupied France has been well known for years. However, the historical view of Vichy France was one of a benevolent state where the Jews and other immigrants were relatively safe. This thesis has been challenged by Michael R. Marrus and Robert O. Paxton in their study *Vichy France and the Jews.*

According to David Lindsey's *Los Angeles Times Book Review* article, "a widely held impression is that Vichy generally protected Jews in its area and only under German pressure initiated discrimination and persecution. Not so, say [the authors]. They begin this work by examining the roots of anti-Semitism in France. As many Jewish refugees reached France in the 1930s from other parts of Europe and Algeria, French antagonism toward the newcomers grew. The soil, then, was already prepared when Vichy and the Unoccupied Zone were born. In a short time and without German prompting, the Vichy regime imposed restrictions on the naturalization of refugees . . . and restricted entry into law and medical professions. . . . Although designed primarily to protect French citizens, these measures were vigorously applied against Jews."

"Paxton and Marrus offer a conclusive account of the reasons for [Vichy collaboration with the Germans]," says *New Republic* critic David Pryce-Jones. "Petin and [Vice-Premier Pierre] Laval may have been cynically indifferent to what happened to Jews, but many of their associates were anti-Semites in the classical Dreyfus-affair mold. Anti-Semitism with a French rather than a German accent was defended with nationalistic pride as a proper assertion of French authority in a properly French sphere. Thus expropriated Jewish property might be more advantageously 'Aryanized' into French, instead of German, hands." The book's indictment, continues Pryce-Jones, "falls on the average Frenchman who, like his counterpart in Germany, handed his conscience over to the state. The Rene Bousquets [Bousequet was a Vichy police official who complied with German demands] and the gendarmes and the anti-Jewish police and the thousands of 'Aryanizing' bureaucrats and the numberless profiteers each contributed in his way to putting French Jews at the mercy of mass-murderers. Accomplices like these, some active and some passive, were indispensable to the Germans, who otherwise never could have mobilized the manpower to impose the Final Solution upon France."

In writing *Vichy France and the Jews,* the authors "provide a graphic and often heartrending account of official cruelty, administrative callousness, public prejudices and popular indifference; the section on Vichy's concentration camps is particularly eloquent," observes Stanley Hoffmann in the *New York Times Book Review.* "Their exhaustive research and the sobriety of their prose make this indictment far more powerful than previous works on the subject."

BIOGRAPHICAL/CRITICAL SOURCES: New York Times Book Review, November 1, 1981; *New Republic,* November 18, 1981; *Los Angeles Times Book Review,* November 29, 1981; *New York Review of Books,* December 3, 1981; *Commentary,* January, 1982; *Times Literary Supplement,* July 23, 1982.

* * *

MARSDEN, George (Mish) 1939-

PERSONAL: Born February 25, 1939, in Harrisburg, Pa.; son of Robert Samuel (a clergyman) and Bertha (a teacher; maiden name, Mish) Marsden; married Lucie Commeret, June 30, 1969; children: Gregory, Brynn. *Education:* Haverford College, B.A. (with honors), 1959; Yale University, M.A., 1961, Ph.D., 1965; Westminster Theological Seminary, B.D., 1963. *Politics:* Independent. *Religion:* Christian Reformed. *Home:* 844 Dallas S.E., Grand Rapids, Mich. 49507. *Office:* Department of History, Calvin College, Grand Rapids, Mich. 49506.

CAREER: Yale University, New Haven, Conn., assistant instructor, 1964-65; Calvin College, Grand Rapids, Mich., instructor, 1965-66, assistant professor, 1966-70, associate professor, 1970-73, professor of history, 1974—; writer. Visiting professor, Trinity Evangelical Divinity School, 1976-77. *Member:* American Historical Association, American Society of Church History, Presbyterian Historical Society, Conference on Faith and History. *Awards, honors:* Younger humanist fellowship from National Endowment for the Humanities, 1971-

72; Calvin Center for Christian Scholarship fellowship, 1979-80, research fellowship, 1982-83; *Fundamentalism and American Culture* named book of the year, *Eternity* (magazine), 1981.

WRITINGS: *The Evangelical Mind and the New School Presbyterian Experience,* Yale University Press, 1970; *The American Revolution* (pamphlet), National Union of Christian Schools, 1973; (editor with Frank Roberts) *A Christian View of History?,* Eerdmans, 1975; *Fundamentalism and American Culture: The Shaping of Twentieth-Century Evangelicalism,* Oxford University Press, 1980; (editor with Mark A. Noll and others) *Eerdmans Handbook to Christianity in America,* Eerdmans, 1983; (with Noll and Nathan O. Hatch) *The Search for Christian America,* Crossway Books, 1983; (editor) *Evangelicalism and Modern America,* Eerdmans, 1984.

Contributor: David Wells and John Woodbridge, editors, *The Evangelicals,* Abingdon, 1975; W. Stanford Reid, editor, *John Calvin: His Influence in the Western World,* Zondervan, 1982; Noll and Hatch, editors, *The Bible in America,* Oxford University Press, 1982; Ronald A. Wells, editor, *The Wars of America: Christian Views,* Eerdmans, 1982; Mary Douglas and Steven M. Tipton, editors, *Religion and America: Spirituality in a Secular Age,* Beacon Press, 1983; Ronald Stone, editor, *Reformed Faith and Politics,* University Press of America, 1983; Ashley Montagu, editor, *Science and Creationism,* Oxford University Press, 1983; Alvin Plantinga and Nicholas Wolterstorff, editors, *Faith and Rationality,* University of Notre Dame Press, 1984; C. T. McIntire and R. A. Wells, editors, *History and Historical Understanding,* Eerdmans, 1984. Also contributor to several church periodicals. Associate editor, *Christian Scholar's Review,* 1970-77; editor, *Reformed Journal,* 1980—.

SIDELIGHTS: In his work *Fundamentalism and American Culture: The Shaping of Twentieth-Century Evangelicalism,* George Marsden, according to *Commentary* critic Peter Skerry, "traces the roots of fundamentalism in the evangelical fervor that swept ante-bellum America, what has come to be known as the Second Great Awakening. From towns along the Erie Canal in New York to the farthest reaches of the Western frontier, revivals and camp meetings were everywhere in evidence. This religious fervor gradually spilled over into social reform movements such as abolitionism, temperance, and Sabbatarianism. What these varied efforts had in common was an intense optimism about America and its future."

Noting that "belief in science and the progress it fosters was an important part of what [the author] calls the 'evangelical consensus,'" Skerry points out that the striking blow of Darwinism caused upheaval in the church "not merely [because] Darwin challenged the biblical version of creation. A much more profound challenge, according to Marsden, was Darwin's method of forming and testing hypotheses. His reliance on the speculative constructs that had been rejected by Baconian science challenged the evangelical consensus at its epistemological core. From within that consensus Darwinism appeared to open up not only science, but American democracy and religion itself, to a radical subjectivism."

Marsden's study ends with the victory of "agnostic cosmopolitan liberals," as *Times Literary Supplement* writer David Martin puts it, in the landmark Scopes "monkey trial" of 1925. Stating that fundamentalism "is just as complex a scene today as [the author] describes in the late nineteenth century," Martin concludes: "One cannot equate fundamentalism, evangelicalism and the moral majority. One cannot assure that a right-wing stance is inevitable, since in other parts of the world the same phenomenon is politically volatile. One cannot guess how far practices like faith healing and exorcism will continue to penetrate even the liberal mainstream. It is certain only that here we have a cautionary tale, important both for the defective social theory of liberals, and their continued survival. They should read, mark, learn and inwardly digest Dr. Marsden's book."

BIOGRAPHICAL/CRITICAL SOURCES: George Marsden, *Fundamentalism and American Culture: The Shaping of Twentieth-Century Evangelicalism,* Oxford University Press, 1981; *Commonweal,* February 27, 1981; *Times Literary Supplement,* December 18, 1981; *Commentary,* May, 1982.

* * *

**MARSHALL, Joanne
  See RUNDLE, Anne**

* * *

**MARSHALL, Mel(vin D.) 1911-
  (Ray Cory, Carlton Mitchell, Zeke Tyler)**

PERSONAL: Born October 8, 1911, in San Antonio, Tex.; son of Carl S. and Della (Duncan) Marshall; married Aldine Thompson, May 22, 1937. *Home:* 330 First St., Phillips, Tex. 79071. *Agent:* August Lenniger, Lenniger Literary Agency, Inc., 437 Fifth Ave., New York, N.Y. 10016.

CAREER: Active in newspapers and broadcasting in South and Southwest, 1929-46; *Pittsburg News* (weekly), Pittsburg, Calif., owner and publisher, 1946-47; Pittsburg Broadcasting Co., Inc. (KECC), Pittsburg, secretary-treasurer and general manager, 1946-57; Pittsburg Daily News Publishing Co., Pittsburg, director and publisher, 1947-49; president and general manager of Humboldt Broadcasters, Inc., Arcata, Calif., 1957-64, and Del Norte Broadcasters, Inc., Crescent City, Calif., 1958-64; free-lance writer and photographer, 1965—; president, Context, Inc. (consultants in writer/publisher computer use), 1979—. Consultant on news and editorial presentation for radio and television stations. *Member:* Western Writers of America (president, 1976-77).

WRITINGS—Nonfiction: *Steelhead* (Field & Stream Book Club selection), Winchester Press, 1971; *The Care and Repair of Fishing Tackle,* Winchester Press, 1976; *How to Make Your Own Lures and Flies,* Funk, 1976; *How to Make Your Own Fishing Rods,* Outdoor Life Book Club, 1978; *How to Fish,* Winchester Press, 1978; *How to Choose and Use Lumber, Plywood, Panelboards and Laminates,* Harper, 1979; *How to Repair, Reupholster and Refinish Furniture,* Harper, 1979; *Sierra Summer,* University of Nevada Press, 1979; *Yard Buildings,* Doubleday, 1981.

Cookbooks: *The Delectable Egg,* Simon & Schuster, 1968; *Cooking over Coals,* Winchester Press, 1971; *Fish Cookery,* Harper, 1971; *The Family One-Pot Cookbook,* Ace Books, 1973; *The Family Poultry and Fowl Cookbook,* Ace Books, 1973; *The Family Cookout Cookbook,* Ace Books, 1973; *Real Living with Real Foods,* Fawcett, 1974; *The Perfect Host,* Winchester Press, 1975; *The Complete Book of Outdoor Cookery,* Van Nostrand, 1983.

Western fiction; published by Ballantine, except as indicated: *Longhorns North,* 1969; *Buffalo!,* 1969; *McQuade,* 1971; *Long Rider,* 1971; *Drift Fence,* 1971; *Two Funerals for Tombstone,*

1973; *Buffalo Hunt,* 1975; *Sheepherder's Gold,* Fawcett, 1980; *Gato,* Dell, 1980; *Lannigan's Revenge,* Dell, 1980.

Western fiction; all under pseudonym Ray Cory; published by Avalon, except as indicated: *Valley of Death,* 1966; *Trail of Vengeance,* 1966; *Guns on the Pedernales,* 1967; *Riders of Tierra Roja,* 1969; *Hell Canyon,* Award, 1973.

Western fiction; under pseudonym Zeke Tyler; published by Dell: *Foxx!,* 1981; *Foxx's Gold,* 1981; *Foxx Hunting,* 1982; *Foxx's Herd,* 1982; *Foxx's Vixen,* 1982; *Foxx's Foe,* 1983.

Other writings: (Under pseudonym Carlton Mitchell) *Hot Oil* (mystery/suspense novel), Belmont Tower, 1980. Also author of twenty-five adult western novels under undisclosed pseudonyms. Contributor to *Argosy, Gourmet, Outdoor Life, Sports Afield, Ladies Home Journal,* and numerous trade and regional periodicals.

SIDELIGHTS: Mel Marshall told *CA*: "The suggestion of some of my contemporaries that I'm either a syndicate or a book packager, with a lot of work by others published under my name or my pseudonyms is not true. While still in my teens, cutting my teeth on newspaper stories and radio drama, I learned to write fast and use the correct words the first time; the habit still persists. Even before switching from typewriter to computer, I was turning out Western fiction at the rate of a chapter a day. The computer makes it only a bit faster by eliminating the on-paper revision and by enabling me to consolidate chapters into one file for an uninterrupted full-manuscript printout."

Editions of the author's novels have appeared in numerous European countries.

* * *

MARTIN, Jose L(uis) 1921-
(Ramar Yunkel)

PERSONAL: Born July 11, 1921, in Vega Baja, Puerto Rico; son of Isidoro (an accountant) and Carmen (Montes) Martin; married Blanca Rodriguez (a teacher); children: five. *Education:* University of Puerto Rico, B.A., 1942, M.A., 1953; Columbia University, Ph.D., 1965. *Residence:* New York, N.Y. *Office:* Department of Spanish, Inter-American University of Puerto Rico, San German, Puerto Rico 00753.

CAREER: University of Puerto Rico, Rio Piedras, 1952-58, began as instructor, became assistant professor of Spanish and humanities; Columbia University, New York City, 1958-60, began as lecturer, became instructor of Spanish and Spanish-American literature; Queens College of the City University of New York, Flushing, N.Y., instructor in Spanish, 1960-65; Inter-American University of Puerto Rico, San Juan, associate professor of Spanish, 1966-68; Illinois State University, Normal, associate professor of Spanish-American literature, 1968-71; City College of the City University of New York, New York City, associate professor of Puerto Rican literature and stylistics, 1971-76; Inter-American University of Puerto Rico, San German, assistant professor of Spanish, 1976—. Visiting professor, New York University, summer, 1960; associate professor, Hofstra University, summer, 1964; member of board of directors, Institute of Puerto Rico, 1972—. *Military service:* U.S. Army, 1943-46; became staff sergeant.

MEMBER: Modern Language Association of America, Asociation of Teachers of Spanish and Portuguese, Instituto Internacional de Literatura Iberoamericana, Instituto de Literatura Puertorriquena, Asociacion de Escritores de Puerto Rico, Sigma Delta Pi (honorary member). *Awards, honors:* Diploma from Nueva Narrativa Hispanoamericana, 1971; Order of Don Quixote, from Sigma Delta Pi, 1973; Institute of Puerto Rico in New York literature award, 1975.

WRITINGS: *La Poetica de Oppenheimer* (title means "The Poetry of Oppenheimer"), Editorial Asomante, 1952; *Agonia del Silencio* (poetry; title means "Agony of Silence"), Editorial Orfeo, 1953; *Analisis Estilistico de Tapia* (title means "Stylistic Analysis of Tapia"), Institute of Puerto Rican Culture, 1958; *Meditaciones Puertorriquenas* (title means "Puerto Rican Meditations"), Departamento de Instruccion Publica, 1959.

Arco y Flecha (title means "Bow and Arrow"), Editorial Club de la Prensa, 1961; *La Poesia de Jose Eusebio Caro* (title means "The Poetry of Jose Eusebio Caro"), Instituto Caro y Cuervo (Bogota), 1966.

Romancero del Cibuco (title means "Ballads from the Cibuco"), Editorial Orion, 1970; (under pseudonym Ramar Yunkel) *El Retorno: Sueno* (title means "The Return"), Editorial Latino-Americana, 1971; *Hostos Escritor,* Institute of Puerto Rican Culture, 1971; *La critica metodica de Anderson Imbert,* Cuadernos Hispanoamericana, 1972; *La yuxtaposicion tiempoespecial en el francotirador de P. L. Soto,* Nueva Narrativa Hispanoamericana, 1972; *El sabor de la carne,* G. del Toro (Madrid), 1973; *Critica estilistica* (title means "Stylistic Criticism"), Editorial Gredos, 1973; *Literatura hispanoamericana contemporanea,* Editorial Edil, 1973; *La narrativa de Vargas Llosa,* Editorial Gredos, 1974; *La peninsula en la Edad Media,* Editorial Teide, 1976. Also author of *El teatro de Rene Marques,* Institute of Puerto Rican Culture.

Contributor to periodicals, including *La Torre, Revista del Instituto de Cultura Puertorriquena, Prensa Literaria, Cuadernos Hispanoamericanos,* and *Sin Nombre.* Founder and former editor, *Ateneo, Olimpo,* and *Aulas;* former co-editor, *Pegaso* and *Orfeo.*

WORK IN PROGRESS: A novel, *Bridge to Eternity,* under pseudonym Ramar Yunkel.

SIDELIGHTS: Jose L. Martin has traveled extensively in the United States, Latin America, and Europe. He paints in oils and has shown his work at exhibitions in San Juan and New York.†

* * *

MARTIN, Judith (Sylvia) 1938-
(Miss Manners)

PERSONAL: Born September 13, 1938, in Washington, D.C.; daughter of Jacob (an economist) and Helen (a teacher; maiden name, Aronson) Perlman; married Robert Martin (a scientist), January 30, 1960; children: Nicholas Ivor, Jacobina Helen. *Education:* Wellesley College, B.A., 1959. *Home:* 1651 Harvard St. N.W., Washington, D.C. 20009. *Office:* Vanity Fair, 350 Madison Ave., New York, N.Y. 10017.

CAREER: *Washington Post,* Washington, D.C., reporter, beginning 1960; currently critic-at-large, *Vanity Fair,* New York, N.Y. Author of "Miss Manners," a weekly newspaper column, distributed by United Features Syndicate, 1978—. Member of faculty at George Washington University, 1978. President of board of trustees of Georgetown Day School. *Member:* White House Correspondents Association, State Department Correspondents Association, Washington Press Club.

WRITINGS—Published by Atheneum, except as indicated: *The Name on the White House Floor* (collection of columns), Coward, 1973; *Miss Manners' Guide to Excruciatingly Correct Behavior* (collection of columns), 1981; *Gilbert: A Comedy of Manners*, 1982; *Miss Manners' Guide to Rearing Perfect Children*, 1984.

WORK IN PROGRESS: Style and Substance, a novel.

SIDELIGHTS: "Dear Miss Manners," pleads a follower of Judith Martin's column, "What is your opinion of people who purposely leave the price tag on gifts in order for the giftee to be aware of the generosity of the giftor?" "Gentle Reader," she replies, "that the least they can do is to scream as the person is opening the present, lean over and pull the price tag off, and drop it into a nearby ashtray, where it can be left to be examined at leisure by everyone."

As America's leading arbiter of the social graces, Judith Martin, a.k.a. Miss Manners, has guided the readers of her syndicated newspaper column down the path of proper behavior with both characteristic humor and common sense. Not content to merely recapitulate the ideas of such classic etiquette experts as Emily Post and Amy Vanderbilt, Martin told *CA* that she "extends" traditional modes of behavior to fit today's social practices. In her writings Martin stresses manners over morals, noting the difference: "In manners, as distinct from morals, . . . the only recognized act is one that has been witnessed." Thus, Miss Manners doles out advice on potentially sticky modern situations, from the overnight arrangements of unmarried couples (board them in separate bedrooms and try to ignore the nocturnal traffic in the hallways) to the proper response upon learning one has given one's partner a venereal disease (send flowers and a note of apology, as one would do with any other social *faux pas*). Of course, she is always open to such perennial posers as which fork to use with which course at a large table setting (when in doubt, work from the outside fork inwards) and how to gracefully devour an ear of corn (left-to-right, typewriter style).

The surge of interest in good manners has kept Martin busy with interviews, lectures, and promotional tours for her popular compilation *Miss Manners' Guide to Excruciatingly Correct Behavior*. The writer attributes this renewed attraction to etiquette to the fact that, starting in the middle part of this century, "manners degenerated for many reasons, all of which have marvelous names—honesty, self-expression and creativity," as she relates to a *U.S. News and World Report* columnist, adding, "people have found out what it is like to live in a rude world, and they can't stand it."

For Martin, Jerry Adler explains in *Newsweek,* life is "a constant exchange of social obligations, beginning as a newborn—who is enjoined to receive guests, if he wishes to do so while sleeping, with his face turned toward the center of the room. After death, our friends are warned against the self-indulgent fantasy that we wouldn't have wanted them to give up the company barbeque to attend our funeral. For all those occasions in between, Miss Manners gives explicit, pertinent, and absolutely self-assured advice."

Only two things seem to faze the usually unflappable Miss Manners. The first involves those readers who ask her to provide a witty or vengeful comeback to those who have been rude to them. "Well," Martin insists in her *CA* interview, "I'm not in the rudeness business; I'm in the politeness business." The second problem concerns certain critics who imply that, as Elaine Kendall writes in the *Los Angeles Times,* "since the questions and answers are all couched in the same deft prose, it's clear [Martin] writes the entire column herself."

Not so, maintains Miss Manners. Her Gentle Readers send in all their own questions (although Martin will admit to some cutting), and the columnist is "quite proud of [them]. They *do* try to adopt my tone," she tells *Publishers Weekly*'s Jennifer Crichton.

Martin herself was the object of a controversy regarding manners in the 1960s when, as a reporter for the *Washington Post,* she apparently violated press protocol at Julie Nixon's wedding reception and was subsequently barred from Tricia Nixon's nuptials. Martin defends her behavior to this day; she remarks to Crichton: "I didn't barge in on this little family wedding in a tiny chapel. This was a huge public event. And I didn't do anything rude, burp at the table or something. It was a lot less sexy and more technical than that. I had written things about the Nixons they didn't much care for, the Nixons called up the *Washington Post* and said they'd rather I not attend, and the *Post* said, 'You're tangling with the wrong folks.' We boycotted the whole thing."

Fortunately, Martin was able to use such experiences as inspirational fodder for her novel *Gilbert* (appropriately subtitled *A Comedy of Manners*). The story of a young man's determination to make his way in the political and social whirl of Washington, D.C., *Gilbert,* which Martin had begun researching during her college days at Wellesley, satirizes the rigid etiquette and finely drawn lines of protocol pervading Washington's high ranks. For instance, title character Gilbert Fairchild learns early in life that "it is more effective to be tall and barely civil than short and eagerly sociable. This did not affect his height, but it taught him when to shut up."

Although some critics find fault with the novel—Susan Issacs, in the *Washington Post Book World,* cites slow character development, for example—others praise *Gilbert* as a highly attuned look at modern social-climbing techniques. *Chicago Tribune Book World* reviewer Michael Killan states: "One finishes the first half clutching one's sides—and also for analogies: *Catcher in the Rye* as done by *Catch-22*. A Jewish *Tom Jones*. *Felix Krull,* with genuine yuks. Harry Flashman let loose in Cambridge and Washington." The author, says Killan, "pins each [character] specimen to the board wriggling and squirming. After reading her treatment of a typical Washington embassy party, no one would dare feel impressed by one again."

But while Martin's portrayals may be "wicked," as Tracy Young puts it in the *New York Times Book Review,* and her novel "deft and sly, . . . there is no more savagery in her humor than in a circus. Even the manipulative Gilbert is an essentially sunny character. Surrounded by the self-deluded, [he] is honest with himself, if no one else." The critic concludes: "In *Gilbert* Judith Martin has chosen to ignore the anguished psyche and create a confection so cleverly written it begs to be quoted promiscuously. A wise choice, and a tasteful one as well."

CA INTERVIEW

CA interviewed Judith Martin on August 26, 1983, at work in Washington, D.C.

CA: Since you're best known as Miss Manners, let's begin by talking about the importance of her topic. How would she explain it, for example, to a child of my acquaintance who said, "I hate manners most of all!" or to an adult whose behavior would seem to express that same sentiment?

MARTIN: The answer to both is, "Do you like people being mean and insulting to you?" No, of course not. Well, it doesn't take too much sophistication to understand that unless we have a social consensus that we will be polite to one another, we are all going to be victims. And the unpleasantness of being a victim is going to outweigh the advantage to one's laziness or moodiness of not having to be polite oneself.

CA: Did you see the recent Newsweek *report (August 29, 1983) called "Minding Manners Again"?*

MARTIN: I did see it. They called me—tracked me down in Bayreuth, Germany, to talk about the whole thing. I disagreed with the premise. In fact, I'm just writing about this myself. I thought the idea of an etiquette camp as remedial etiquette for children who weren't taught manners at home—which, of course, is the proper way to do it—was a good idea. But I was a bit horrified when I saw the things in the story. To me they represent what everybody mistakenly thinks etiquette is and therefore hates it. There is a widespread feeling that etiquette is a kind of a secret ritual of the rich, knowing all kinds of little inside tips in order to make everybody else feel dreadful. When you start teaching a child to kiss the hand of a lady (which couldn't be more incorrect, among other things) or you start telling children how to behave in a limousine—children who don't know how to behave on the bus!—you are simply encouraging this insane idea that it's an initiation to manners of rich people who want to be mean to poor people. Well, that is not what manners are all about. It's very nice to know how to behave in a limousine; I'm not arguing with that. An elderly European may kiss the hand of a woman, although only a married woman—you never kiss the hand of an unmarried woman. It's a ritual, not an appropriate ritual to Americans and certainly not appropriate to children. I have nothing against the refinements of etiquette, but if you emphasize the ones that seem to have a certain unpleasant snob value and ignore the basics, it's as if you sent children to nutrition camp and then fed them nothing but very complicated pastries.

CA: There does seem to be more interest, though, in general good behavior than there has been for the last fifteen years or so. Why do you think this is happening?

MARTIN: Because people cannot stand the abrasiveness level of this society anymore. There is a definite interest, and I keep looking for signs that it's going to translate itself into people understanding that they cannot correct the situation by going around delivering smart put-downs to people who are rude to them. I still get a lot of letters asking me to suggest ways for people to be rude in return to people who have been rude to them. Well, I'm not in the rudeness business; I'm in the politeness business. And when people finally understand that the only solution is to be polite themselves and to teach their children to be polite, we will have the answer. Now, one reason people are reluctant to do this is because they also mistakenly see politeness as allowing other people to walk all over them. That isn't true. Etiquette covers a wide range of behavior, some of which is designed to make other people feel *terrible,* but still in a polite manner. I mean, we don't have the duel anymore, we don't have the slap across the face with gloves, but that was very much a part of the etiquette of its day. A refusal to allow people to mistreat you can be done politely; that is certainly within the range of etiquette. What is *not* within the range is being rude in return. That simply increases the level of rudeness and I, at least, am trying to decrease it. I think that the people who are taking a new interest in etiquette are doing so because they just can't bear the rudeness and they want to decrease it, too.

CA: You see a definite link between manners and history. Would you comment on that?

MARTIN: There is no such thing as being entirely without manners. It's not a question of whether we want manners or not. Manners are a part of human society, always—good manners, bad manners, different kinds of manners—just as language is. And just as language varies from place to place and from society to society, and sometimes among different groups within the society, so do manners. My interest in manners grew out of my interest in history. How did people behave in a given time and place? I began reading etiquette books because I thought the surest way to find out what everybody was doing in a society was to read one of their etiquette books; whatever they were being told not to do, they must have been doing, or no one would have to tell them not to do it!

There's also a concept that manners are written in stone. I must say, I occasionally try to encourage this concept, but basically it isn't true. It's whatever the society agrees upon. It's a form of communication that covers all behavior among human beings. It doesn't cover what goes on churning inside your soul or between you and your god, but it covers everything else. It's extremely interesting to see what different groups or different societies choose to consider unacceptable behavior. And, of course, that develops and changes.

CA: In one article you mentioned the Victorian era and how the manners of that time related to the changes growing out of the Industrial Revolution.

MARTIN: Yes, the interesting periods in history for manners are times of change or times when things have gotten so terribly complicated that it becomes an aesthetic ritual in itself. And that's what we have the best documentation on, because that's when etiquette books are written. When children only have to imitate their parents, they don't have to read etiquette books any more than they have to read language books to learn their own language. They just do what their parents do. In places of social mobility, such as the United States, people who are changing the social subdivision they are in have to find out what the different manners are.

This is best exemplified in the Industrial Revolution in Victorian England because of the changeover in the economy. The land-based economy was no longer the greatest source of money. Wheat coming in from Canada to England lowered the price of domestic wheat, and there were a great many other reasons that the agricultural economy was changing, the major one, of course, being the growth of industry. So new fortunes were being made. Obviously the people who have the means are always going to want to be in the control group, and the people who are losing out are going to resist it. The reason Victorian manners got so complicated was that the fading aristocrats kept throwing up barriers to keep the rising industrialists from moving up to the upper classes. Well now, they didn't really keep them from doing this.

There are societies in which the aristocracy is completely closed, where the aristocracy has all but died out, such as in most European countries. It's viable in England because while the landed aristocracy was saying, "Oh, those people are so vulgar," they were nevertheless marrying their sons to the daughters of these industrialists, a lot of them American industrialists.

They would typically say—and this is what makes British nineteenth-century novels so much fun—"Isn't it terrible, you know, young Lord So-and-So has fallen madly in love with this American girl and her parents are impossible, but after all, she's a sweet young thing." And they take her in and they do her over so that she has the manners of the upper class, and what do they get? They get her father's fortune! The British aristocracy has survived very nicely on this principle. But more and more manners are invented because of this little game they are playing.

There was a tremendous interest in manners in the Renaissance. It was a time of wonderful buildings and incredible paintings; the aesthetic pleasures of living were rising. One can only surmise, but I imagine that people said, "Well then, but why are we behaving like such pigs?" So standards of how to make deportment aesthetically pleasing began developing, and a great many etiquette books were written. There are a number of etiquette books from ancient Greek and Roman times because of the interest in philosophy, the interest in ideal behavior. What is the epitome to which human beings can rise in terms of their behavior?

All religious tracts involved great emphasis on what you could really call etiquette. The Bible is full of how to behave. In addition to the rules on morality, there are ones that are strictly manners. When you have an interest in improving the level of human behavior, it has to include a large percentage of manners. So, for different reasons, many periods in history have been periods of tremendous interest in etiquette, whether they actually call it that or not. Modern Japanese manners are so complicated that Japan is full of etiquette books. Theirs is a society in a great state of change, but there is an effort to preserve forms and manners rather than just completely tossing them aside as we did here. There is a comparable period in medieval Europe when manners had developed into such a complicated system that typically a nobleman would send his son to be a servant to another knight so that he could learn the system by experience, because he couldn't learn it from just hanging around the house—or the castle, as the case may be.

CA: What area of behavior now do you think causes the greatest etiquette or manners problems?

MARTIN: Right now it's the very basic elements of everyday living for the masses. This idea that how to order in a French restaurant is a major problem is ridiculous, or the situation that I am typically presented by television hosts: "I sit down at the table," they will say, "and there are five forks and I panic because I don't know which to use." My answer is, "No, you don't." I mean how many times do you sit down at a table with five forks? Practically never. And if you do, it's a very simple system; you take the one on the outside. If you make a mistake, this is probably the least detectable etiquette felony you will ever commit, because there would be nothing ruder than for the hostess or anyone else to look at your place setting to see which fork you're using. Nobody is going to notice. And if you use the wrong fork you're still going to come out even because they gave you the right number. If you used the fish fork for the salad, you can use the salad fork for the fish. Also, if it is a five-fork dinner, the footman is assigned to see to it that you have the proper equipment. If you drop something on the floor, he's got to go and replace it; that's his job. It's nonsense to say that this is a problem. It's not.

The problem is: How do I go through an ordinary day, take a bus or a drive, buy something in a store, get a sandwich in a coffee shop, or do *anything* without being insulted? How do I even come home without someone sitting down—a friend or, for many people, a relative—saying, "I want to be completely honest with you," and then insulting you. That's the problem. The problem is that some people have brought up their children mainly with the idea that they should be uninhibited, which is a sort of Jean-Jacques Rousseau concept that the child is born a noble savage and civilization is bad for him. People who brought up their children like that can't stand their children, because the children bad-mouth them and are rude to them. Those are the problems. I yield to no one in my admiration for a pleasantly designed and properly used fork, but the forks are not the problem.

CA: Right after graduation from Wellesley, you went to work for the Post, *where you've written (in addition to "Miss Manners") pieces on social life in Washington, and film and drama criticism. After manners, what have you most enjoyed writing about?*

MARTIN: I love criticism. I am now doing it as critic-at-large for *Vanity Fair*. Fiction, of course, is my great love—or another one of my great loves; I'm rather promiscuous about my literary love affairs. If you think of it as a mother who loves all her children it's not quite as offensive as if you think of it as a romantic simile.

CA: You started the novel Gilbert *right out of Wellesley also, didn't you?*

MARTIN: I had sketches for it, yes. The idea really came from dormitory talk at Wellesley. I thought, why is everybody so miserable? Here we are in this magnificent setting with nothing to do but read and write and enjoy ourselves.

CA: Was writing a very early ambition?

MARTIN: Yes, and specifically, from the time I was in my early teens, I wanted to be a drama critic and I wanted to be a novelist. I've been fortunate enough to live to see these dreams come true.

CA: You said that you particularly admire the work of Jane Austen, Anthony Trollope, Henry James, and Edith Wharton. Are there current writers whose work you like?

MARTIN: Yes, but I tend more to dabble with current writers. I don't have a current writer at the moment who is an absolute passion that I would read over and over and over again, and perhaps that's a fault of mine in that I feel there is a patina that comes with age. I was once assigned to write a story about a previously unknown sex scandal involving well-known writers, and I was about to be very indignant with the editor for assigning it to me, on the grounds that "I don't do this kind of thing," when I found out it was about an affair that George Eliot had before she went to live with Henry Lewes. Then I was interested. But what is the difference? Am I putting in a glamour from age that I would not consider a part of current things? I don't know whether I am guilty of that, but indeed, I'm afraid I must say that my favorite writers are all dead, which makes life difficult for me because they rarely publish new books.

Stendhal is another of my great favorites, and Thackeray. I keep a shelf of books, aside from the library in the house, of my all-time favorite writers, who are the people we've just named. It's a shelf that takes between five and eight years to read through, presuming I'm going about my normal, everyday life. Fortunately, I have a rather bad memory, and so by the time I get down to the bottom, I have forgotten the details of the early books and I can go back and start all over. I read Jane Austen again last year. I hadn't read her for perhaps ten years, and I had forgotten enough so that it was not just revisiting, but a lot of it was fresh to me, which is a wonderful feeling. My mother once said to me, "Old age is a marvelous thing, dear. All you need is two good books!"

CA: Where do you do most of your writing, and what kind of writing schedule do you keep?

MARTIN: The schedule is all theoretical because my life has changed so much in the last year. Up until that time I went in to work every day at the *Post* except that I spent one day a week, which I usually took out of vacation time or comp time for overtime, working on my novel. I'm no longer at the *Post*. My regular job is with *Vanity Fair*. Also, in the last year, I've been doing an enormous amount of promotion in connection with my books—television, radio, and things like that—and I've still got more to go. But when I finish that, my idea is that I will spend five days a week writing: one day a week for my column, whatever time it takes for my *Vanity Fair* piece, and the rest on the new novel. I have a little office in a town house I have just bought and share with another writer.

CA: Do you find it easier working away from home?

MARTIN: I can't work in my own house, simply because I would spend the time rearranging drawers that don't need rearranging. I always had office space at the *Post; Vanity Fair*, of course, is in New York so I need an office in Washington, and that was why I acquired a marvelous, pleasant little house where I have all my files and research books and do my work.

CA: Do you ever consult other etiquette authorities in deciding on answers to the questions you get?

MARTIN: Not living ones, because my philosophy somewhat disagrees with that of other etiquette writers, which is really why I went into the business. In this century, or at least after World War I, etiquette writing came to be the "Oh, use your common sense and do whatever makes you feel comfortable" kind of thing. My feeling was always that if you went by that rule, which is all very well for many areas of your life, you wouldn't need to consult an etiquette book, would you? I am perhaps more tradition-oriented on the one hand, and on the other hand, I love what I call making up tradition. That is a contradiction in terms, of course, but I mean evolving traditional patterns to fit new situations. That comes out of my own head. I do have a modest collection—everything I can get my hands on—of historic etiquette books.

CA: Do you get a lot of letters from people who disagree with your answers?

MARTIN: Only on certain topics. If I venture to put down the prejudice—though this is traditional, not something I've made up—that the title *Doctor* is used for a medical doctor but a Ph.D. does not use the term socially, then I get millions of letters from people saying, "I worked hard for this degree and I'm going to use it!" Well, you work hard for your salary too, but you don't tell everybody what it is. If I quote the correct system of using *Senior, Junior, II, III*, and so on, with names, which is that they move along as the eldest person dies, I get furious letters from people who say that *Junior* is part of their name. If I say that spaghetti is not correctly eaten with a tablespoon either here or in Italy, I get furious letters from people who believe it is. It's the picky points that people get upset over. I can make huge, sweeping statements about matters that deeply touch on everybody's lives, how they should bring up their children or how they should treat their spouses, and I never get a letter of disagreement.

CA: Do you enjoy the television appearances and book promotion tours as much as you seem to?

MARTIN: Yes and no. I do have a lot of fun with it. I've loved theater all my life and here I am, setting out in middle age to be a vaudeville actress. This is what it amounts to, you know; I go from city to city and I do eight shows a day and I come on between the animal act and the stripper and do my bit. But, in fact, it has taken so much of my time in the last year or so that the new schedule I just quoted to you does not allow for such things. But if I have a book coming out, I do it intensely for a short period. For example, week after next, I'm going to do a week of promotion in England because the British editions of *Miss Manners' Guide* and *Gilbert* are coming out. Then I'm home for a week and then I'm going to do four intensive weeks of traveling around the United States for television and radio appearances for the paperback edition of *Miss Manners' Guide*. But after that, I'm not going to do anything until the following year, when my next book will be out. You're right, I enjoy it. I have a splendid time with it. You know, so many writers complain, and rightly so, that television appearances are really completely unrelated to the skills or motivation or anything to do with writing. But it just happens, as I say, that I discovered I *love* being an old vaudeville actress. But I can't be that and a writer as well; I have too many writing projects going to spare any regular time for the other.

CA: What's in progress?

MARTIN: The next Miss Manners book will be out probably in the fall of 1984. I don't have a deadline on the second novel.

CA: Would you like to try something completely unlike what you've done before?

MARTIN: I don't want to take on something new. I think it would really be unbearably greedy if I told you I had a list of unfulfilled professional desires and secret ambitions, because I have such an embarrassment of riches in writing novels, writing criticism regularly, and writing a regular syndicated column. I feel very lucky that so many things I wanted to do have worked out, and that I'm able to do them all.

BIOGRAPHICAL/CRITICAL SOURCES: Judith Martin, *Miss Manners' Guide to Excruciatingly Correct Behavior*, Atheneum, 1981; Martin, *Gilbert: A Comedy of Manners*, Atheneum, 1982; *Harper's*, June, 1982; *New York Times Book Review*, June 6, 1982, January 2, 1983; *Washington Post Book World*, June 13, 1982, December 26, 1982; *Newsweek*, July 5, 1982; *New York Times*, July 10, 1982; *Chicago Tribune Book World*, July 30, 1982, February 13, 1983; *People*, August 9, 1982; *Publishers Weekly*, October 29, 1982; *New Republic*, December 6, 1982; *U.S. News and World Report*, December 6, 1982; *Times Literary Supplement*, October 21, 1983.

—*Sketch by Susan Salter*
—*Interview by Jean W. Ross*

MARTIN, Les
See SCHULMAN, L(ester) M(artin)

* * *

MARTIN, Nancy
See SALMON, Annie Elizabeth

* * *

MARTIN, Roderick 1940-

PERSONAL: Born October 18, 1940, in Lancaster, England; son of Reginald (a mechanic) and Edna (Josephson) Martin; married Jan Sergeant, August 17, 1963; children: Catherine Susannah, Sarah Frances, James Nicholas Alexander. *Education:* Balliol College, Oxford, B.A. (with first class honors), 1961; University of Pennsylvania, graduate study, 1961-62; Nuffield College, Oxford, D.Phil., 1965. *Home:* 62 Lonsdale Rd., Oxford, England. *Office:* Trinity College, Oxford University, Oxford, England.

CAREER: University of York, Heslingdon, England, lecturer in modern history, 1964-66; Oxford University, Oxford, England, lecturer at Jesus College, 1966-69, university lecturer in politics and sociology, and fellow of Trinity College, 1969—. Visiting senior lecturer, Monash University, 1975. *Member:* British Sociological Association. *Awards, honors:* Arthur Andersen travelling fellow.

WRITINGS: Communism and the British Trade Unions, 1924-1933: A Study of the National Minority Movement, Oxford University Press, 1969; (editor with D.E.H. Whiteley) *Sociology, Theology and Conflict,* Barnes & Noble, 1969; (with R. H. Fryer) *Redundancy and Paternalist Capitalism,* Allen & Unwin, 1973; *The Sociology of Power,* Routledge & Kegan Paul, 1977; *New Technology and Industrial Relations in Fleet Street,* Oxford University Press, 1981; (with R. Undy) *Ballots and Trade Union Democracy,* Blackwell, 1984; (with Judith Wallace) *Working Women in Recession,* Oxford University Press, in press.

WORK IN PROGRESS: Various research projects in industrial relations.

* * *

MARTINES, Julia
See O'FAOLAIN, Julia

* * *

MARTINES, Lauro 1927-

PERSONAL: Born November 22, 1927, in Chicago, Ill.; married Julia O'Faolain (a novelist); children: Lucien Christopher. *Education:* Drake University, A.B., 1950; Harvard University, Ph.D., 1960. *Politics:* Liberal independent. *Religion:* None. *Home:* 15 Glenloch Rd., London N.W.3, England. *Agent:* A. D. Peters, 10 Buckingham St., Adelphi, London WC2N 6BU, England. *Office:* History Department, University of California, Los Angeles, Calif. 90024.

CAREER: Reed College, Portland, Ore., assistant professor of history, 1958-62; University of California, Los Angeles, professor of history, 1966—. *Military service:* U.S. Army, 1945-47. *Member:* American Historical Association, Renaissance Society of America, Mediaeval Academy of America, Dante Alighieri Society of Florence (Italy). *Awards, honors:* Awards from Guggenheim Memorial Foundation, American Council of Learned Societies, American Philosophical Society, Harvard University, Ford Foundation, and National Endowment for the Humanities; citation for distinguished achievement from Society for Italian Historical Studies, for *The Social World of the Florentine Humanists.*

WRITINGS: The Social World of the Florentine Humanists, Princeton University Press, 1963; *Lawyers and Statecraft in Renaissance Florence,* Princeton University Press, 1968; *Violence and Civil Disorder in Italian Cities, 1200-1500,* University of California Press, 1972; (with wife, Julia O'Faolain) *Not in God's Image: Women in History from the Greeks to the Victorians,* Harper, 1973; *Power and Imagination: City-States in Renaissance Italy,* Knopf, 1979.

Contributor of articles and reviews to professional journals in America and Italy. Member of board of editors, *Viator: Medieval and Renaissance Studies.*

WORK IN PROGRESS: A study of society and history in English Renaissance poetry.

SIDELIGHTS: The author of *Power and Imagination: City-States in Renaissance Italy,* Lauro Martines is generally regarded as an expert in that renowned era of Italian history. In the preface to *Power and Imagination,* the author notes that the book's title "is my way of referring to, and altering, the more conventional distinction between 'society' and 'culture.' In telling a story which courses across five centuries, I was driven to pursue a central theme, a thread more easily visible than 'society.' I chose to center attention on the fortunes of 'power' because, in tracing the movement of political authority, I was also compelled, all the way along, to track the direction of social and economic change. And I chose 'imagination' over 'culture' because my supreme concern is with relations between dominant social groups (power) and the articulated, formal, refined, or idealizing consciousness of those who speak for the powerful. In this interplay, the workings of imagination tend to be foremost."

Martines's theory, according to Christopher Lehmann-Haupt in the *New York Times,* is "that nothing about Renaissance art and culture is anything more than the reflection of the needs and concerns of the period's ruling elite. Even the weakness of the culture is reflected in that art and scholarship. And at the very high-water mark of the High Renaissance, . . . this weakness of the culture had already begun to undermine it." Peter Burke likewise finds that the author "looks at the arts with the eye of a politician." In his *New York Review of Books* article about *Power and Imagination,* Burke quotes Martines as stating, "Before we daze ourselves with notions about the period's universal love of art, let it be remembered that popes Julius II and Leo X used artists such as Raphael and Michelangelo to glorify themselves personally, their families and their office." "Martines discusses the arts primarily as propaganda, ideology, self-assertion," continues Burke. "He sees portraits as designed to reflect flattering self-images. He looks at palaces as embodiments of the desire of the political elite to dominate the space within the walls of their city. Like the towers built by the warring nobles of the twelfth and thirteenth centuries, Renaissance palaces are 'affirmations of power.'"

Burke, however, thinks Martines's argument is one-sided. "[The author] sees that art was used by the rich, the well-born, and the powerful as a mode of self-assertion, and illustrates this point with some vivid examples. The trouble is that he sees little else," comments the critic, who also notes, "It is easy enough for [Martines] to quote examples of humanists who made successful careers in government and of rulers who were interested in ideas, but the less successful intellectuals and the less cultivated members of the ruling class escape his attention." In the *Times Literary Supplement,* John Larner has measured praise for *Power and Imagination,* saying: "There is much of interest here both for scholars and a more general audience. Yet how far the reader will be convinced by the detailed interpretations of the relations between art and the social order will probably depend on how far he accepts the credibility of any detailed sociology of culture." Ultimately, though, Larner suggests that "even those who may be sceptical of the author's general theses will still find here a great deal to instruct and entertain them."

Lehmann-Haupt also recommends the book, finding that "much of what is stimulating about the theory lies in how Professor Martines employs it as a tool to analyze the art and culture of the period." The critic, furthermore, is "especially impressed with [the author's] organization of history. For example, when confronted by a series of differing items—be they constitutions or dukes or voting systems—instead of describing each one of them by turn, he first extracts what is typical in them and then summarizes their variations." "To the writing of history," concludes Lehmann-Haupt, "we welcome Professor Martines's sense of order."

BIOGRAPHICAL/CRITICAL SOURCES: Lauro Martines, *Power and Imagination: City-States in Renaissance Italy,* Knopf, 1979; *New York Times,* April 11, 1979; *New Yorker,* April 16, 1979; *New York Review of Books,* October 11, 1979; *Times Literary Supplement,* July 25, 1980.

* * *

MARX, Anne

PERSONAL: Born in Bleicherode, Germany; came to United States in 1936, naturalized in 1938; daughter of Jakob (a physician) and Susanne (Weinberg) Loewenstein; married Frederick E. Marx (a real estate consultant), February 12, 1937; children: Thomas J., Stephen L. *Education:* Graduated from University of Heidelberg Medical School; University of Berlin Medical School, M.S., 1933; attended Orthopedic Clinic of University of Frankfurt am Main, 1934-35. *Home:* 315 The Colony, Tallwood Lane, Hartsdale, N.Y. 10530. *Office:* Frederick E. Marx Corp., Inc., 200 Park Ave., New York, N.Y. 10016; and Harwood Bldg., Scarsdale, N.Y. 10583.

CAREER: Vice-president of Frederick E. Marx Corp., New York City. Fairleigh Dickinson University, Madison, N.J., staff member of poetry workshop, 1962-64; Iona College, Writers' Conference, New Rochelle, N.Y., director of poetry workshop, 1964-70; Wagner College, New York City Writers' Conference, fellow, 1965; Arkansas Writers' Conference and South & West Conventions, principal speaker, 1966-71; Poetry Society of America Poetry Workshop, New York City, guest critic, 1970-71; Council for the Arts in Westchester, Inc., Westchester, N.Y., chairman of poetry division, 1970; New York Public Library, Donnell Library Center, New York City, director of poetry reading series, 1970-74; workshop leader at conventions, National League of American Pen Women, 1974, 1976, 1977; speaker, Arts Center of Jakarta, Indonesia, 1979; poetry workshop leader, Scarsdale Cultural Center, 1980.

MEMBER: Poetry Society of America (fellow, 1964; member of executive board, 1965-70; vice-president, 1970-72), Poetry Society of Great Britain, National League of American Pen Women (president of Westchester County branch, 1962-64; North Atlantic regional chairman, 1964-66; New York state president, 1982-84), Academy of American Poets, National Federation of State Poetry Societies, Composers, Artists and Authors of America, Inc. (poetry editor, 1974-78), Poetry Society of Pennsylvania, New York Poetry Forum.

AWARDS, HONORS: Poetry awards from National Federation of Women's Clubs, 1957, 1958, 1959, and National Federation of State Poetry Societies, 1962, 1965, 1966; National Sonnet prizes, 1959 and 1968; American Weave Chapbook award, 1960, for *Into the Wind of Waking;* annual Braithwaite Contest, 1960; Countess d'Esternaux gold medal, 1965; Greenwood Prize (Great Britain), 1966; South & West Publications award, 1966, for *By Grace of Pain;* award, Ivan Franko Memorial Competition, 1966; Atlantic Award, 1967; Mason Sonnet Prizes, World Order of Narrative Poets, 1970, 1971, 1972, 1974, 1975, and 1980; Cecil Hemely Memorial Prize, Poetry Society of America, 1974; named Poet of the Year, New York Poetry Forum, 1981; Della Miller Memorial Prize, 1982; numerous other awards in American and English poetry contests.

WRITINGS—Poetry: *Ein Buechlein: German Lyrics,* Kaufman Verlag, 1935; *Into the Wind of Waking,* foreword by John Holmes, American Weave Press, 1960; *The Second Voice,* Fine Editions Press, 1963; *By Grace of Pain,* South & West Publications, 1966; *By Way of People,* Golden Quill Press, 1970; *A Time to Mend: Selected Poems, 1960-1970,* Living Poets Library, 1973; *Hear of Israel and Other Poems,* Golden Quill Press, 1975; *40 Love Poems for 40 Years,* Highmarks House, 1977; *Face Lifts for All Seasons,* Golden Quill Press, 1980; *45 Love Poems for 45 Years,* Highmarks House, 1982. Also co-editor of an anthology, *Pegasus in the Seventies,* 1975.

Work appears in anthologies, including: *The World's Love Poetry,* Bantam, 1960; *Discourses on Poetry,* South & West Publications, 1967; *The Illustrated Treasury of Poetry for Children,* edited by David Ross, Grosset, 1970; *Spring World, Awake,* edited by M. C. Luckhardt, Abingdon, 1970; *From Deborah and Sappho to the Present,* New Orlando Publications, 1976; *Americana Anthology,* Cross-Cultural Communications, 1976; *American Women Poets,* Olivant Press, 1976; *Port-Folio,* Howard Publishing, 1978; *A Grandmother Is for Loving,* C. R. Gibson, 1981; *The Study and Writing of Poetry: American Women Poets Study Their Craft,* Whitston Publishing, 1982; *Great Poems,* Collins & World, 1983.

Contributor of poetry to magazines, including *Poet Lore, Midwest Review, Poet/India, Ukranian Review,* and *New York Quarterly.* Poetry editor, *Pen Woman,* 1974-78.

WORK IN PROGRESS: Articles on contemporary poetry and poets; collections of new poems; "A Practical Workshop for Impractical Poets."

SIDELIGHTS: Anne Marx told *CA:* "As a bilingual poet, I am especially intrigued with the mystery of language communicating in the unique way we call poetry. Born and educated in Germany, I always knew poetry to be a spontaneous natural activity for me. Being expelled from my homeland meant giving up not only a beloved language but also the writing of poetry, my most meaningful means of communication. It took twenty years until English became my most natural voice, the preferred tool for writing. The differences in my two languages, as well as in my two backgrounds, intrigue me now. Aided by a thorough early foundation in Latin, a fair command of French, and by my present extensive annual travel abroad, I am searching for new ways to overcome language barriers, especially in poetry. Translations are never enough."

BIOGRAPHICAL/CRITICAL SOURCES: Beaux Arts, spring, 1957; Poetry Society Bulletin, October, 1959, October, 1963, November, 1964, November, 1966, November, 1968, November, 1970; Villager, October, 1960, February, 1971; Il Giornale Dei Poetei, April, 1961; Essence, winter, 1967-68; Poet Lore, spring, 1968, winter, 1971, summer, 1974; Pen Woman, May, 1969, June, 1983; Book Exchange (London), November, 1970; Encore, November, 1975, January, 1976; New York Times, March 1, 1981; Wormser Zeitung (Germany), March, 1983.

* * *

MARX, Wesley 1934-

PERSONAL: Born November 2, 1934, in Los Angeles, Calif.; son of Edward Howard (a business executive) and Kathleen (Woods) Marx; married Judith Mell, August 25, 1962; children: Christopher, Heather, Tyler. Education: Stanford University, B.A., 1956. Home and office: 18051 Butler, Irvine, Calif. 92715.

CAREER: Independent-Star News, Pasadena, Calif., reporter, 1960-61; free-lance writer, 1961—; University of California, Irvine, lecturer in social ecology, 1975—. Contributing editor, Los Angeles Magazine, 1961-64. Editorial consultant, General Dynamics, 1964; correspondent, National Observer, Los Angeles, 1965-66. Lecturer in marine affairs at universities, including Louisiana State University, Notre Dame University, Oregon State University, Iowa State University, and California State University, Fullerton. Member of California's Attorney General's Environmental Task Force, 1970-76. Trustee, Center for Law in Public Interest, 1979—; Governor's appointee, California Tahoe Regional Planning Agency, 1981—. Consultant on marine elements to California Coastal Zone Conservation Commission (south coast), 1974. Military service: U.S. Marine Corps, 1956-59; became first lieutenant.

MEMBER: American Planning Association, Water-Pollution Control Federation, Friends of the University of California at Irvine Library. Awards, honors: Orange County Authors Award from University of California at Irvine Friends of the Library, 1967, and James D. Phelan Award, 1968, both for The Frail Ocean; Orange County Authors Award, 1978, for Acts of God, Acts of Man.

WRITINGS: The Frail Ocean, Coward, 1967; Man and His Environment: Waste, Harper, 1971; Oilspill, Sierra Club, 1971; The Protected Ocean, Coward, 1972; The Pacific Shore, Dutton, 1974; Acts of God, Acts of Man, Coward, 1977; The Oceans: Our Last Resource, Sierra Club, 1981.

Contributor: Frederick Tietze and James McKeown, editors, The Changing Metropolis, Houghton, 1964; Carey McWilliams, editor, The California Revolution, Grossman, 1968; Garrett De Bell, editor, The Environmental Handbook, Ballantine, 1970; Maurice Strobbe, editor, Understanding Environmental Pollution, Mosby, 1971; Les Line, editor, What We Save Now, Houghton, 1973; Walt Anderson, editor, Politics and Environment, Goodyear Publishing, 1975; H. J. Walker, editor, Geoscience and Man, Louisiana State University, 1975; Grady Clay, editor, Water and the Landscape, McGraw, 1979; Kathleen Courrier, editor, Life after '80: Environmental Choices We Can Live With, Brick House Publishing, 1980.

Contributor to periodicals, including Atlantic, American Heritage, Nation, Reader's Digest, Audubon, and Smithsonian.

WORK IN PROGRESS: Writing on coastal management and ocean politics at the national and international level, including pollution, military exploitation, fishery management, seabed mining, and hazards planning; research on origin and development of varied human perspectives toward natural waterforms.

SIDELIGHTS: "From Ocean City to Orange County," Wesley Marx writes in Acts of God, Acts of Man, "we have been attempting to control the wrong agent of disaster. Nature creates hazards; man, particularly urban man, creates disasters. Urbanization, rather than hurricanes and fault zones, needs to be controlled." In this study the author describes floods, hurricanes, and earthquakes "as natural as raindrops or sunsets. . . . What distinguishes them is their high energy." These natural phenomena become calamitous, according to Marx, when buildings are constructed in their paths. Joan Hanauer, in a Washington Post article, finds that Marx "sets forth our civilization's stupidity in building in places where it should not, where it is obviously on 'a collision course with disaster.'"

"I don't expect [Acts of God, Acts of Man] to be a popular book; it is too straightforward and raises too many painful issues," says Los Angeles Times critic Robert Kirsch. However, "Marx accepts the obligation of suggesting alternate policies to the traditional cycle of relief and deterrence." John S. Rosenberg, in a Smithsonian review, calls the book "particularly useful in pointing out what we gain from designing with nature: 'When we urbanize floodplains, we sacrifice other critical land uses such as outdoor recreation and agriculture. By keeping floodplains as open space, we not only reduce hazard risk but gain these critical uses.' We exchange potential misery and suffering for valuable amenities generally lacking in urban America. Best of all, the book indicates how relatively moderate the costs are for achieving these gains."

AVOCATIONAL INTERESTS: Photography, ocean body-surfing, and scuba diving in kelp sea forests off California.

BIOGRAPHICAL/CRITICAL SOURCES: Nation, June 26, 1972; Wesley Marx, Acts of God, Acts of Man, Coward, 1977; Los Angeles Times, May 30, 1977, March 25, 1982; Smithsonian, June, 1977; Washington Post, June 11, 1977.

* * *

MASON, George E(van) 1932-

PERSONAL: Born March 9, 1932, in Cortland, N.Y.; son of Evan E. and Norma (Barnes) Mason; married Gloria M. Gulino, July 3, 1953; children: Victoria, Joseph, Elizabeth, William, Christopher. Education: Cortland State Teachers College (now State University of New York College at Cortland), B.S., 1953; Syracuse University, M.S., 1958, Ph.D., 1963. Politics: Democrat. Home: 405 Riverhill, Athens, Ga. 30606. Office: College of Education, University of Georgia, Athens, Ga. 30602.

CAREER: Elementary teacher in North Syracuse, N.Y., 1955-57; Board of Cooperative Educational Services, Theresa, N.Y., reading specialist, 1957-60; Florida State University, Tallahassee, associate professor and head of department of elementary education, 1963-66; University of Georgia, Athens, associate professor, 1966-71, professor of reading, 1971—. Military service: U.S. Army, 1953-55. Member: International Reading Association, National Reading Conference, National Society for the Study of Education, College Reading Association, Phi Delta Kappa.

WRITINGS: (With Edwin H. Smith) *Teaching Reading in Adult Basic Education*, Florida State Department of Education, 1965; (with William D. Sheldon) *Winner's Circle*, Allyn & Bacon, 1970; *On the Level*, Allyn & Bacon, 1975; *Full Count*, Allyn & Bacon, 1975; *A Primer on Teaching Reading*, E. E. Peacock, 1981; (with Jay S. Blanchard and Danny B. Daniel) *Computer Applications in Reading*, International Reading Association, 1979, revised edition, 1983.

WORK IN PROGRESS: Research on television and reading.

* * *

MASSEY, James Earl 1930-

PERSONAL: Born January 4, 1930, in Ferndale, Mich.; son of George Wilson (a minister) and Elizabeth (Shelton) Massey; married Gwendolyn Inez Kilpatrick (a registered nurse), August 4, 1951. *Education:* Attended Detroit Conservatory of Music, 1946, University of Detroit, 1949-50, 1953-54, and Salzburg Mozarteum, Austria, 1952; Detroit Bible College, B.R.E., B.Th., 1961; Oberlin College, M.A., 1964; University of Michigan, graduate study, 1967-68. *Politics:* Democrat. *Home:* 700 Chestnut, Anderson, Ind. 46012. *Office:* Mass Communications Board of the Church of God, 1303 East Fifth St., Anderson, Ind. 46011.

CAREER: Ordained to the ministry of the Church of God, 1951; Church of God of Detroit, Detroit, Mich., associate pastor, 1953-54; Metropolitan Church of God, Detroit, founder and senior pastor, 1954-76, honorary pastor-at-large, 1976—; Jamaica School of Theology, Kingston, president, 1963-66; Anderson College and School of Theology, Anderson, Ind., professor of religion, campus pastor, 1969-77; Church of God, Mass Communications Board, Anderson, speaker, "Christian Brotherhood Hour" (international radio broadcast of the Church of God), 1977-82. Member of board of directors, Detroit Council of Churches, 1967-69. Member of board of directors, National Religious Broadcasters, 1978—, and Warner Press, Inc. *Military service:* U.S. Army, 1951-63.

MEMBER: National Association of the Church of God (historian, 1957—; chairman, commission on higher education, 1968—; vice-chairman, publication board, 1968—; chairman, committee on Christian unity, 1969-81), National Negro Association of Evangelicals (member of board of directors, 1969—), Inter-Varsity Christian Fellowship (corporation member, 1970—), National Committee of Black Churchmen, National Association of College and University Chaplains. *Awards, honors:* D.D., Asbury Theological Seminary, 1972; Danforth Foundation Underwood fellow, 1972; Staley Distinguished Christian Scholar, 1977.

WRITINGS: The Growth of the Soul, privately printed, 1955; *An Introduction to the Negro Churches in the Church of God Reformation Movement*, Shining Light Survey Press, 1957; *"When Thou Prayest": An Interpretation of Christian Prayer according to the Teachings of Jesus*, Warner Press, 1960; *The Worshiping Church: A Guide to the Experience of Worship*, Warner Press, 1961; *Raymond S. Jackson: A Portrait*, Warner Press, 1967.

The Soul Under Siege (A Fresh Look at Christian Experience), Warner Press, 1970; *The Hidden Disciplines*, Warner Press, 1972; *The Responsible Pulpit*, Warner Press, 1974; *The Sermon in Perspective*, Baker Book, 1976; (editor) *Christian Brotherhood Hour Study Bible*, Thomas Nelson, 1980; *Designing the Sermon*, Abingdon, 1980; (editor with Wayne McCown) *Hermeneutics: Interpreting God's Word for Today*, Warner Press, 1982; (editor) *Educating for Service*, Warner Press, 1983.

Contributor to periodicals and journals, including *Christianity Today*, *Methodist Herald*, *Christian Century*, *Pulpit*, and *Covenant Quarterly*. Member of editorial board, *Christian Scholar's Review* and *Leadership;* contributing editor, *Vital Christianity*.

WORK IN PROGRESS: Howard Thurman: A Theological Biography; a revision of *An Introduction to the Negro Churches in the Church of God Reformation Movement*, with the new title *The Church of God and the Negro; Christian Theology and Social Experience*.

AVOCATIONAL INTERESTS: Beethoven's music, stamp collecting, oil painting, travel.

* * *

MAST, Gerald 1940-

PERSONAL: Born May 13, 1940, in Los Angeles, Calif.; son of George A. (a pharmacist) and Bess (Gorelnik) Mast. *Education:* University of Chicago, B.A., 1961, M.A., 1962, Ph.D., 1967. *Residence:* Chicago, Ill. *Agent:* Richard A. Balkin, Balkin Agency, 880 West 181st St., New York, N.Y. 10033. *Office:* Department of English and Humanities, University of Chicago, 5811 South Ellis Ave., Chicago, Ill. 60637.

CAREER: Oberlin College, Oberlin, Ohio, instructor in English, 1965-67; College of Staten Island of the City University of New York, Staten Island, N.Y., associate professor of performing and creative arts, 1967-78; University of Chicago, Chicago, Ill., professor of English and humanities, 1978—. Director of professional and university plays in Chicago, New York City, and Provincetown, Mass., 1961—; actor and extra in Hollywood movies, 1948-63. *Member:* Modern Language Association of America, Writer's Guild, Actor's Equity Association, Society for Cinema Studies.

WRITINGS: A Short History of the Movies, Bobbs-Merrill, 1971, 3rd edition, 1981; *The Comic Mind: Comedy and the Movies*, Bobbs-Merrill, 1973; *Filmguide to Rules of the Game*, Indiana University Press, 1973, 2nd edition, University of Chicago Press, 1979; (with Marshall Cohen) *Film Theory and Criticism: Introductory Readings*, Oxford University Press, 1974, 3rd edition, 1985; *Film/Cinema/Movie: A Theory of Experience*, Harper, 1977; *Howard Hawks, Storyteller*, Oxford University Press, 1982; *The Movies in Our Midst: Readings in the Cultural History of Film in America*, University of Chicago Press, 1982.

Contributor of articles to periodicals and film journals, including *New Republic*, *Cinema Journal*, *Critical Inquiry*, and *Quarterly Review of Film Studies*.

WORK IN PROGRESS: Singing, Dancing, Feeling, Thinking: The American Musical on Stage and Film, for Overlook Press.

SIDELIGHTS: Gerald Mast's study of director Howard Hawks, entitled *Howard Hawks, Storyteller*, traces the career of the man responsible for such films as *The Big Sleep*, *Bringing Up Baby*, and *Red River*, attempting to show that in addition to being popular, Hawks's films are the product of a serious and artistically ambitious artist. Mast portrays the director's own words regarding his work as far too modest, and in the words of *New York Times Book Review* critic Seymour Peck, "attempts to discover whether there wasn't more to the Hawks career than the casual, seemingly artless goal that Hawks proclaimed of 'telling a good story' and having 'fun.'" Peck describes *Howard Hawks, Storyteller* as "particularly impressive," and elaborates on the author's methods: "Throughout, Mr. Mast demonstrates the development in each film of the Hawks themes of work, friendship, honor and love—the unity of personal, moral and vocational commitments. It is an illuminating and fascinating demonstration. His case for Hawks is eloquent, exciting, often persuasive, entertaining and—yes, fun."

BIOGRAPHICAL/CRITICAL SOURCES: *Los Angeles Times Book Review*, May 10, 1981, November 7, 1982; *New York Times Book Review*, December 19, 1982; *Times Literary Supplement*, August 12, 1983.

* * *

MATHIAS, Frank Furlong 1925-

PERSONAL: Born May 23, 1925, in Maysville, Ky.; son of Charles Lindsay (a salesman) and Nancy (Furlong) Mathias; married Florence Duffy, August 23, 1958; children: Nancy Browning, Frank Furlong, Susan Elizabeth. *Education:* University of Kentucky, B.A., 1950, M.A., 1961, Ph.D., 1966; graduate study at Mexico City College, 1950-51. *Politics:* Democrat. *Religion:* Roman Catholic. *Home:* 2728 Corlington Dr., Dayton, Ohio 45440. *Office:* Department of History, Box 155, University of Dayton, Dayton, Ohio 45409.

CAREER: Dance band musician in Ohio Valley area, 1940-55; National Airlines, Miami, Fla., ticket agent, 1951; U.S. Steel, Beaumont, Tex., messenger, 1951; high school teacher of Spanish and English in the public schools of Cincinnati, Ohio, 1951-52; in sales promotion for Lorillard Tobacco Co. in eastern Kentucky, 1953-57; West Virginia Institute of Technology, Montgomery, member of staff of history department, 1962-63; University of Dayton, Dayton, Ohio, 1963—, became professor of history. *Military service:* U.S. Army, Infantry, 1943-46; served in South Pacific theater; became sergeant; received Luzon Invasion Bronze Arrow. *Member:* Organization of American Historians, American Catholic Historical Association, Southern Historical Association, Kentucky Historical Association, Ohio Academy of History.

WRITINGS: (Editor) *Incidents and Experiences in the Life of Thomas W. Parsons*, University Press of Kentucky, 1975; *Albert D. Kirwan: A Man for All Seasons*, University Press of Kentucky, 1975; *GI Jive: An Army Bandsman in World War II*, University Press of Kentucky, 1982.

Contributor: *A History of Nicholas County, Kentucky*, [Danville, Ky.], 1976; *Kentucky: Its History and Heritage*, Forum Press, 1978; *Teaching Mountain Children*, Appalachian Consortium Press, 1978. Contributor of articles and book reviews to religion and history journals.

WORK IN PROGRESS: A political history of Kentucky, 1820-1850.

* * *

MATTHEWS, William 1942-

PERSONAL: Born November 11, 1942, in Cincinnati, Ohio; son of William P., Jr. and Mary E. (Sather) Matthews; married Marie Harris (a teacher), May 4, 1963 (divorced, 1974); children: William, Sebastian. *Education:* Yale University, B.A., 1965; University of North Carolina at Chapel Hill, M.A., 1966. *Home:* 245 Avenue C, Apt. 10-D, New York, N.Y. 10019. *Office:* Atlantic Monthly Press, 8 Arlington St., Boston, Mass. 02116.

CAREER: Wells College, Aurora, N.Y., instructor in English, 1968-69; Cornell University, Ithaca, N.Y., assistant professor of English, 1969-74; University of Colorado, Boulder, associate professor of English, beginning 1974; University of Washington, Seattle, professor of English, 1978-83; currently affiliated with Atlantic Monthly Press. Visiting lecturer, University of Iowa, 1976-77; visiting professor, University of Houston, 1981, 1983. Co-director of Lillabulero Press and co-editor of *Lillabulero* (poetry journal), 1966-74; member of editorial board for poetry, Wesleyan University Press, 1969-74; advisory editor, L'Epervier Press, 1976—. Member of literature panel, National Endowment for the Arts, 1976—; member of board of directors, Associated Writing Programs, 1977—. *Awards, honors:* National Endowment for the Arts fellowship, 1974; Guggenheim fellowship, 1980-81.

WRITINGS—Poetry books, except as indicated: *Broken Syllables*, Lillabulero Press, 1969; *Ruining the New Road*, Random House, 1970; *The Cloud*, Barn Dream Press, 1971; *Sleek for the Long Flight*, Random House, 1972; *An Oar in the Old Water* (pamphlet), Stone Press, 1974; *Sticks and Stones*, Pentagram Press, 1975; (with Mary Feeney, translator from the French) Jean Follain, *Removed from Time* (pamphlet), Tideline Press, 1977; (with Feeney, translator from the French) Follain, *A World Rich in Anniversaries*, Grilled Flowers Press, 1979; *Rising and Falling*, Atlantic-Little, Brown, 1979; *Flood*, Atlantic-Little, Brown, 1982; *A Happy Childhood*, Atlantic-Little, Brown, 1984.

Contributor to numerous anthologies; also contributor of articles and reviews to periodicals. Advisory editor, *Tennessee Poetry Journal*, 1970-72; poetry editor, *Iowa Review*, 1976-77; contributing editor, *Gumbo*, 1977—.

WORK IN PROGRESS: A book of poetry; a book of essays.

SIDELIGHTS: The themes underlying the poetry of William Matthews, according to Ken McCullough in a *Dictionary of Literary Biography* article, range from the acceptance of death and karmic responsibility to suspicion and childhood reminiscences, and even to basketball and jazz. The poet's work is "eclectic," says McCullough, "but from the beginning he has had a strong individual voice. . . . One senses in Matthews a no-nonsense discrimination that has allowed him to station himself between the Brahmins and the Faustians—to take psychic risks yet survive them." And although McCullough characterizes some of Matthews's early work with metaphors and similes as "facile [and] gratuitous" and calls the poet's posture "almost cavalier," the critic stresses that by the publication of *Sleek for the Long Flight*, "[Matthews] had eliminated this tendency. [He] does, however, employ the metaphysical conceit in an effective manner in [his first] book and throughout his work."

BIOGRAPHICAL/CRITICAL SOURCES: *Ohio Review*, spring, 1972; *Ironwood*, Volume III, 1973; *Words*, winter, 1974; *Black Warrior Review*, spring, 1975; *Aegis*, fall, 1975; *Washington Post Book World*, August 19, 1979; *New York Times Book Review*, October 21, 1979; *Dictionary of Literary Biography*, Volume V: *American Poets since World War II*, Gale, 1980.

* * *

MATURA, Mustapha 1939-

PERSONAL: Born December 17, 1939, in Trinidad, West Indies; son of Chandra (a salesman) and Violet (Rivers) Mathura; married Marian Walsh, October 5, 1961; children: Ann Simone, Dominic, Cayal. *Education:* Educated in Roman Catholic intermediate school. *Agent:* Judy Daish, 122 Wigmore St., London W1, England.

CAREER: Worked as office boy, stock clerk, insurance salesman, and tally clerk in Trinidad, West Indies, 1954-61; worked as hospital porter, cosmetic display assistant, and stockroom assistant in England, 1961-68; full-time writer, 1968—. Founder and chairman, Black Theatre Co-operative; advisor, International Theatre Institute. *Awards, honors:* John Withing Award from Arts Council of Great Britain, 1970; George Devine Award from English Stage Co., 1972, for "As Time Goes By"; named most promising writer by *Evening Standard,* 1975, for "Play Mas"; named Director of the Year, *Caribbean Times,* 1982.

WRITINGS—Plays: *As Times Goes By and Black Pieces* ("Black Pieces" first produced in London, 1970; "As Time Goes By" first produced in London, 1971), Calder & Boyars, 1972; *Play Mas* (first produced in London at Royal Court Theatre, 1974; first produced in New York City, 1976), Marion Boyars, 1976; *Nice, Rum an Coca Cola, and Welcome Home Jacko* ("Nice" first produced in London, 1973; "Rum an Coca Cola" first produced in London, 1976, first produced in New York City at the Brooklyn Academy of Music, October, 1977; "Welcome Home Jacko" first produced in London, 1979, first produced in New York City at the Black Theater Cooperative, May, 1983), Eyre Methuen, 1980; *Independence and Meetings* ("Independence" first produced in 1979; "Meetings" first produced in London, 1981, first produced in New York City at the Phoenix Theater, March 30, 1981), Eyre Methuen, 1982.

Unpublished plays: "Bakerloo Line" (one-act play), first produced in London at the Almost Free Theatre, 1972; "Black Slaves, White Chains" (one-act play), first produced in London at Theatre Upstairs, 1975; "Bread," first produced in London at the Young Vic Theatre, 1976; "More, More," first produced in London, 1978; "Another Tuesday," first produced in London, 1978; "A Dying Business," first produced in London, 1980; "One Rule," first produced in London, 1981.

Screenplays: "Murders of Boysie Singh," 1972. Also co-author of television series "No Problems," 1983.

SIDELIGHTS: Mustapha Matura's plays depict Caribbean blacks confronting modern white society. "His sharp depiction," writes Richard Eder in the *New York Times,* "of the illusions, strains and breakages of a third world people trying to cope with contemporary life, matches pain with humor and knows the beauty as well as the futility of what is vanishing." Speaking of "Meetings," Mel Gussow writes in the *New York Times* that "the play begins as a sardonic social satire and gradually grows darker and darker until it becomes a nightmare vision, something close to an apocalypse." Gussow concludes that Matura is "a gifted playwright."

Matura told *CA:* "I respond differently to each new play I write, as I imagine the actor does to a character and so it should be—be it the exploration of a character, the possibilities of a situation, or the surprising number of meanings to a line. So it would be less than accurate, and misleading, to find one common perception throughout my work. It is constantly changing and that's why I do it. I create a world on paper and find I have also done so in my consciousness."

BIOGRAPHICAL/CRITICAL SOURCES: Race Today, [London], 1974; *New York Times,* October 28, 1977, March 31, 1981, May 25, 1983.

MAUTNER, Franz H(einrich) 1902-

PERSONAL: Born June 8, 1902, in Vienna, Austria; came to United States in 1938; son of Adolf Albert and Gabriele Mautner; married Hedwig Herrmann (a teacher), December 24, 1928 (deceased); children: Johanna Elisabeth (Mrs. Thomas Plaut), Mary Helen. *Education:* Attended University of Heidelberg, 1921; University of Vienna, Dr.Phil., 1926. *Home:* 408 Walnut Lane, Swarthmore, Pa. 19081.

CAREER: Classical grammar school teacher of German and French, Vienna, Austria, 1927-29; University of Besanon, Besanon, France, lecturer in German, 1929-30; teacher at classical grammar school in Vienna, 1930-32, professor of German and French, 1933-38; Indiana University at Bloomington, assistant professor of German, 1939-40; Hobart College, Geneva, N.Y., assistant professor of German, 1941-44; Ohio Wesleyan University, Delaware, assistant professor of language and literature, 1944; U.S. Department of State, Washington, D.C., professional writer in German, 1945; Ohio Wesleyan University, assistant professor of language and literature, 1946-48; Kenyon College, Gambier, Ohio, associate professor of German and comparative literature, 1948-52; Sarah Lawrence College, Bronxville, N.Y., lecturer in German, 1953-55; Swarthmore College, Swarthmore, Pa., associate professor, 1955-58; professor of German, 1958-72, professor emeritus, 1972—.

Dozent at People's University (Vienna), 1936-38; lecturer at Johns Hopkins University, 1939, and Queens College (now Queens College of the City University of New York), 1953-55; visiting professor at Princeton University, 1962, University of Pennsylvania, 1964, Bryn Mawr College, 1971, and Cornell University, 1975.

MEMBER: International Arthur Schnitzler Research Association, Internationale Vereinigung fuer germanische Sprach- und Literaturwissenschaft, International Nestroy Society, International Comparative Literature Association, International Association for Studies in German Langauage and Literature, Modern Language Association of America, Modern Humanities Research Association, American Association of Teachers of German, American Council for the Study of Austrian Literature (vice-president, 1969-72), Lichtenberg Gesellschaft, Deutsche Akademie fuer Sprache und Dichtung, Phi Beta Kappa. *Awards, honors:* American Council of Learned Societies scholarship, 1954; Guggenheim fellowship, 1964-65, and 1968-69; Austrian Cross of Honor (first class) for Arts and Letters, 1969.

WRITINGS: Johann Nestroy und seine Kunst (title means "Johann Nestroy and His Art"), O. Lorenz, 1937; *Moerikes "Mozart auf der Reise nach Prag"* (title means "Moerike's 'Mozart on His Journey to Prague'"), Scherpe-Verlag, 1957; *Lichtenberg: Geschichte seines Geistes* (title means "Lichtenberg: A History of His Mind"), de Gruyter, 1968; *Nestroy,* Stiehm, 1974; *Wort und Wesen* (title means "Words and Essence"), Insel-Verlag, 1974.

Editor: Nestroy, *Der Talisman* (title means "The Talisman"), Scho, 1935, revised edition, 1958; Nestroy, *Ausgewaehlte Werke* (title means "Selected Writings"), O. Lorenz, 1938; (translator and editor with Henry Hatfield) *The Lichtenberg Reader: Selected Writings of Georg Christoph Lichtenberg,* Beacon Press, 1959; Lichtenberg, *Gedankenbuecher* (title means "Books of Thoughts"), Fischer Buecherei, 1963, revised edition, Stiehm, 1967; Nestroy, *Das Maedl aus der Vorstadt* (title means "The Girl from the Suburb"), Reclam, 1968; (with Hatfield) Lichtenberg, *Lichtenberg: Aphorisms and Letters,* Cape Editions, 1969; Nestroy, *Komoedien* (title means "Comedies"), three volumes, Insel-Verlag, 1970; *Nestroy-Brevier* (title means "Nestroy Breviary"), Insel-Verlag, 1981.

Contributor: *Das Deutsche Drama* (title means "The German Drama"), August Bagel, 1958; *Georg Buechner,* Wissenschaftliche Buchgesellschaft, 1965; *Adalbert Stifter: Studien und Interpretationen* (title means "Adalbert Stifter: Studies and Interpretation"), Stiehm, 1968; *Wie, warum, und zu welchem Ende wurde ich Literaturhistoriker?* (title means "How, Why, and to What End Did I Become a Literary Historian?"), Suhrkamp, 1972; *Handbuch des deutschen Dramas,* August Bagel, 1980.

Contributor to *Columbia Dictionary of Modern European Literature, Fischer-Lexikon: Literatur,* and *Handbook of Austrian Literature.* Contributor to academic journals and festschriften.

WORK IN PROGRESS: Research on comedy and language and on methods of literary history and criticism; editing a five-volume collection of Lichtenberg's writings and letters.

AVOCATIONAL INTERESTS: Mountain climbing, swimming.

BIOGRAPHICAL/CRITICAL SOURCES: *Listener,* February 19, 1970.

* * *

MAXWELL, Patricia 1942-
(Patricia Ponder; Jennifer Blake, Maxine Patrick, pseudonyms; Elizabeth Treahearne, a joint pseudonym)

PERSONAL: Born March 9, 1942, in Winn Parish, La.; daughter of John H. (an electrician) and Daisy (Durbin) Ponder; married J. R. Maxwell (a retail automobile dealer), August 1, 1957; children: Ronnie, Ricky, Delinda, Kathy. *Home address:* Rural Route 1, Box 133, Quitman, La. 71268.

CAREER: Writer. *Member:* National League of American Pen Women, Romance Writers of America.

WRITINGS: *The Secret of Mirror House,* Fawcett, 1970; *Stranger at Plantation Inn,* Fawcett, 1971; (with Carol Albritton, under joint pseudonym Elizabeth Treahearne) *Storm at Midnight,* Ace Books, 1973; *Dark Masquerade,* Fawcett, 1974; *The Bewitching Grace,* Popular Library, 1974; *The Court of the Thorn Tree,* Popular Library, 1974; *Bride of a Stranger,* Fawcett, 1974.

(Under pseudonym Jennifer Blake) *Love's Wild Desire,* Popular Library, 1977; *The Notorious Angel,* Fawcett, 1977, published under pseudonym Jennifer Blake, 1983; (under name Patricia Ponder) *Haven of Fear,* Manor Books, 1977; (under name Patricia Ponder) *Murder for Charity,* Manor Books, 1977; *Sweet Piracy,* Fawcett, 1978; *Night of the Candles,* Fawcett, 1978; (under pseudonym Maxine Patrick) *The Abducted Heart,* Signet, 1978; (under pseudonym Jennifer Blake) *Tender Betrayal,* Popular Library, 1979; (under pseudonym Maxine Patrick) *Bayou Bride,* Signet, 1979; (under pseudonym Maxine Patrick) *Snowbound Heart,* Signet, 1979; (under pseudonym Jennifer Blake) *The Storm and the Splendor,* Fawcett, 1979.

(Under pseudonym Maxine Patrick) *Love at Sea,* Signet, 1980; (under pseudonym Maxine Patrick) *Captive Kisses,* Signet, 1980; (under pseudonym Jennifer Blake) *Golden Fancy,* Fawcett, 1980; (under pseudonym Jennifer Blake) *Embrace and Conquer,* Fawcett Columbine, 1981; (under pseudonym Maxine Patrick) *April of Enchantment,* Signet, 1981; (under pseudonym Jennifer Blake) *Royal Seduction,* Ballantine, 1983; *Midnight Waltz,* Ballantine, 1984; (under pseudonym Jennifer Blake) *Surrender in Moonlight,* Ballantine, 1984.

Contributor of poetry, short stories, and articles to newspapers; contributor to *Vignettes of Louisiana History* and *Louisiana Leaders.*

WORK IN PROGRESS: A novel, *Fierce Eden,* for Ballantine.

SIDELIGHTS: Patricia Maxwell told *CA:* "I write for the classic reason, to entertain, but also for the joy of the mental exercise and for that rare moment of euphoria that comes when the writer's subconscious takes over and pours out the story with little interference from the conscious mind. The [Jennifer] Blake historical romances give me particular pleasure because of a love affair with history that is of long standing. I like to recreate the past as closely as possible. If I can take readers with me back in time, if I can make them see what I see, feel what I feel, even if only for a brief moment, then I am satisfied."

* * *

MAYS, Buddy (Gene) 1943-

PERSONAL: Born September 11, 1943, in Albuquerque, N.M.; son of Carl (an electrician) and Ethel (Boggus) Mays; married Mary Helen Now, October 20, 1973 (divorced June 1, 1977). *Education:* Attended New Mexico State University, 1967-70. *Politics:* None. *Home and office address:* P.O. Box 44, Truth or Consequences, N.M. 87901.

CAREER: Free-lance writer and photographer. *Albuquerque Tribune,* Albuquerque, N.M., photographer, 1970-72; Philmont Scout Ranch, Cimarron, N.M., instructor in mountaineering, 1972; KOAT-TV, Santa Fe, N.M., reporter, 1974-75. *Military service:* U.S. Coast Guard, 1961-65; received Gold Lifesaving Medal and expert rifleman medal. *Member:* Society of American Travel Writers. *Awards, honors:* Pulitzer Prize nomination, 1977, for feature photography on the American cowboy in the the Southwest.

WRITINGS: *Wildwaters,* Chronicle Books, 1977; *A Pilgrim's Notebook Guide to Western Wildlife,* Chronicle Books, 1977; *People of the Sun,* University of New Mexico Press, 1979; *Ancient Cities of the Southwest,* Chronicle Books, 1982; *Children of the Ancients,* Chronicle Books, 1984; *Bed and Breakfast, Colorado,* Chronicle Books, 1985. Contributor of articles and photographs to various magazines, including *Time, Newsweek, Forbes, Outdoor Life, Sports Afield,* and *Sunset.*

SIDELIGHTS: Buddy Mays writes: "My entire world revolves around nature, and most of my books, articles, and photographs are aimed toward doing my part to save what is left for future generations. Hopefully my books and articles make readers aware that our wild land is in trouble and only they can help."

* * *

MAZER, Norma Fox 1931-

PERSONAL: Born May 15, 1931, in New York, N.Y.; daughter of Michael and Jean (Garlen) Fox; married Harry Mazer (a novelist), February 12, 1950; children: Anne, Joseph, Susan, Gina. *Education:* Attended Antioch College and Syracuse University. *Politics:* "I believe in people—despise institutions while accepting their necessity." *Religion:* "Jewish by birth, pantheistic by nature." *Home and office:* Brown Gulf Rd., Jamesville, N.Y. 13078.

CAREER: Writer, 1964—. *Awards, honors:* A Figure of Speech was nominated for National Book Award, 1973; Lewis Carroll Shelf Award from University of Wisconsin, 1975, for *Saturday the Twelfth of October;* awards for *Dear Bill, Remember Me?* include Christopher Award, outstanding book of the year award from *New York Times,* best book of the year award from *School Library Journal,* and best book for young adults from American Library Association, all 1976; *The Solid Gold Kid* named an American Library Association best book for young adults, 1977, and International Reading Association-Children's Book Council children's choice, 1978; *Up in Seth's Room* named American Library Association best book for young adults, 1979; awards for *Mrs. Fish, Ape, and Me, the Dump Queen* include Austrian Children's Books list of honor, and German Children's Literature prize, both 1982; Edgar Award, Mystery Writers of America, 1982, for *Taking Terri Mueller.*

WRITINGS—Juvenile and young adult fiction; published by Delacorte, except as indicated: *I, Trissy,* 1971; *A Figure of Speech,* 1973; *Saturday the Twelfth of October,* 1975; *Dear Bill, Remember Me?,* 1976; (with husband, Harry Mazer) *The Solid Gold Kid,* 1977; *Up in Seth's Room,* 1979; *Mrs. Fish, Ape, and Me, the Dump Queen,* Dutton, 1980; *Taking Terri Mueller,* Avon, 1981; *When We First Meet,* Four Winds, 1982; *Summer Girls, Love Boys and Other Short Stories,* 1982; *Someone to Love,* 1983; *Downtown,* Avon, 1983.

Contributor of stories and articles to magazines, including *Jack and Jill, Ingenue, Calling All Girls, Child Life, Boys and Girls,* and *Redbook.*

WORK IN PROGRESS: Several novels, a short story.

SIDELIGHTS: "It's not hard to see why Norma Fox Mazer has found a place among the most popular writers for young adults these days," says Suzanne Freeman in the *Washington Post Book World.* "At her best, Mazer can cut right to the bone of teenage troubles and then show us how the wounds will heal. She can set down the everyday scenes of her characters' lives in images that are scalpel-sharp. . . . Mazer has taken great care to get to know the world she writes about. She delves into the very heart of it with a sure and practiced hand."

Mazer's stories reflect the conflicts and decisions facing young people in a contemporary society. In *Taking Terri Mueller,* for instance, the thirteen-year-old protagonist seeks to reunite with her mother, whom she has not seen since her parents were divorced when the girl was five. "Mazer makes it clear from start to finish that this is a book which bears a message," points out Freeman. "It is dedicated to 'parents who are still waiting for their children to return.' And a note at the end of the text gives readers a number to call 'If you think Terri's story is your story and there is a parent looking for you.' But Mazer does not take the easy way out in this book. There are no good guys or bad guys. There are no easy answers."

The author told *CA:* "I seem to deal in the ordinary, the everyday, the real. I should like in my writing to give meaning and emotion to ordinary moments. In my books and stories I want people to eat chocolate pudding, break a dish, yawn, look in a store window, wear socks with holes in them. . . ."

AVOCATIONAL INTERESTS: Reading, racketball in winter, "living in summer on our land in Canada with sun, rain, wind, and water, and without electricity, telephone, newspaper, radio, indoor plumbing, stove, refrigerator, lights, etc., etc., etc."

BIOGRAPHICAL/CRITICAL SOURCES: New York Times Book Review, October 19, 1975, November 14, 1976, January 20, 1980, March 13, 1983; *New York Times,* December 21, 1976; *Contemporary Literary Criticism,* Volume XXVI, Gale, 1983; *Washington Post Book World,* April 10, 1983.

* * *

McCLUSKEY, Neil Gerard 1921-

PERSONAL: Born December 15, 1921, in Seattle, Wash.; son of Patrick John and Mary Genevieve (Casey) McCluskey. *Education:* Gonzaga University, A.B., 1944, M.A., 1945; Alma College, Los Gatos, Calif. (now Jesuit School of Theology at Berkeley), S.T.L., 1952; graduate study at University of Geneva, 1952-54, and in France; Columbia University, Ph.D., 1958. *Home:* 4455 Douglas Ave., Riverdale, N.Y. 10471. *Office:* BHRAGS, Inc., 1212 East New York Ave., Brooklyn, N.Y. 11212.

CAREER: Seattle University, Seattle, Wash., assistant professor of philosophy, 1954-55; *America,* New York City, education editor, 1955-60; Gonzaga University, Spokane, Wash., associate professor of education, 1960-63, dean of faculties and academic vice-president, 1963-66; University of Notre Dame, Notre Dame, Ind., professor of education, 1966-69, dean and director of Institute for Studies in Education, 1969-71; City University of New York, Herbert H. Lehman College, New York City, professor and dean of education, 1971-75, Graduate School and University Center, New York City, director of gerontological studies, 1975-80; currently affiliated with BHRAGS (Brooklyn's Haitian Ralph and Good Shepherd Centers), Inc., Brooklyn, N.Y. Columbia University, faculty of permanent seminar on higher education, 1958—, visiting professor, 1965, 1966; lecturer, Oppenheimer College of Social Studies, Rhodesia, 1962.

MEMBER: American Association for Higher Education, American Historical Association, American Association of University Professors, American Educational Research Association, Religious Education Association (member of executive committee and board of directors), National Council on Religion and Public Education (chairman of board of directors), Catholic Commission on Intellectual and Cultural Affairs, Phi Delta Kappa.

WRITINGS: Public Schools and Moral Education, Columbia University Press, 1958, reprinted, Greenwood Press, 1975; *Catholic Viewpoint on Education,* Doubleday, 1959; (editor) *Catholic Education in America,* Teachers College, Columbia University, 1964; *Catholic Education Faces Its Future,* foreword by Theodore M. Hesburgh, Doubleday, 1968; (editor) *The Catholic University: A Modern Appraisal,* University of Notre Dame, 1970; (editor with Edgar F. Borgatta) *Aging and Society: Current Research and Policy Perspectives,* Sage, 1980; (editor with Borgatto) *Aging and Retirement: Prospects, Planning, and Policy,* Sage, 1981.

* * *

McCOMB, David G(lendinning) 1934-

PERSONAL: Born October 26, 1934, in Kokomo, Ind.; son of John F. (in civil service) and Jennie (Glendinning) McComb; married Mary Alice Collier, September 6, 1957; children: Katherine, Susan, Joe. *Education:* Southern Methodist University, B.A., 1956; Stanford University, M.B.A., 1958; Rice University, M.A., 1962; University of Texas, Ph.D., 1968. *Religion:* Unitarian Universalist. *Home:* 2024 Manchester Dr., Fort Collins, Colo. 80526. *Office:* Department of History, Colorado State University, Fort Collins, Colo. 80523.

CAREER: South Texas Junior College (now University of Houston Downtown College), Houston, instructor in history, 1962; San Antonio College, San Antonio, Tex., assistant professor of history, 1962-66; University of Houston, Houston, instructor in history, 1966-68; University of Texas at Austin, research associate in oral history, 1968-69; Colorado State University, Fort Collins, assistant professor, 1969-72, associate professor, 1972-77, professor of history, 1977—, chairman of department, 1975-80.

MEMBER: North American Association for Sports History, American Association for State and Local History, Organization of American Historians, Oral History Association, Society for the History of Technology, Western History Association, State Historical Society of Colorado, Texas State Historical Association. *Awards, honors:* Tullis Prize, Texas State Historical Association, 1969, for *Houston: The Bayou City;* award of merit, American Association for State and Local History, for oral history work in Colorado.

WRITINGS: *Houston: The Bayou City,* University of Texas Press, 1969, revised edition published as *Houston, a History,* 1981; *Big Thompson: Profile of a Natural Disaster,* Pruett, 1980; *Agricultural Technology and Society in Colorado,* Colorado State University, 1981; (co-author) *Colorado: A History of the Centennial State,* Colorado Associated University Press, 1982.

WORK IN PROGRESS: History of Galveston, Texas; oral history of the Olympic Training Center in Colorado Springs.

* * *

McCOMBS, Maxwell E(lbert) 1938-

PERSONAL: Born December 3, 1938, in Birmingham, Ala.; son of Max E. and Gertrude (Smith) McCombs; married Zoe Helen Collins; children: Mary Elizabeth, Leslie Ann. *Education:* Tulane University, B.A., 1960; Stanford University, M.A., 1961, Ph.D., 1966. *Office:* Communications Research Center, Syracuse University, Syracuse, N.Y. 13210.

CAREER: *New Orleans Times-Picayune,* New Orleans, La., general assignment reporter, 1961-62, state supreme court reporter, 1962-63; University of California, Los Angeles, lecturer, 1965-66, assistant professor of journalism, 1966-67; University of North Carolina, Chapel Hill, assistant professor, 1967-69, associate professor of journalism, 1969-73; Syracuse University, Syracuse, N.Y., John Ben Snow Professor of Newspaper Research, 1973—, director of Communications Research Center, 1973—. Visiting lecturer at University of Wisconsin, Madison, summer, 1970, Northwestern University, summers, 1974-75, and University of Missouri, summer, 1980. *Military service:* U.S. Army Reserve, information officer, 1963-67. *Member:* Association for Education in Journalism, American Newspaper Publishers Association (director of News Research Center, 1975—), A. G. Bell Association, American Association for Public Opinion Research.

WRITINGS: *Mass Communication on the Campus,* Communication Board, University of California, Los Angeles, 1967; *Mass Media in the Marketplace,* Journalism Monographs, 1972; (editor with Donald Shaw and David Gray, and contributor) *Handbook of Reporting Methods,* Houghton, 1976; (editor with Shaw, and contributor) *The Emergence of American Political Issues: The Agenda-Setting Function of the Press,* West, 1977; (with George Comstock, Steven Chaffee, Natan Katzman, and Donald Roberts) *Television and Human Behavior,* Columbia University Press, 1978; (with Lee Becker) *Using Mass Communication Theory,* Prentice-Hall, 1979; (with David Weaver, Doris Graber, and Chaim Eyal) *Media Agenda-Setting in a Presidential Election: Issues, Images, Interests,* Praeger, 1981.

Contributor: *New Educational Media in Action: Case Studies for Planners,* Volume III, UNESCO, 1967; Phillip Tichenor and F. G. Kline, editors, *Current Perspectives in Mass Communication Research,* Volume I, Sage Publications, 1972; D. M. Kovenock, J. W. Prothro and others, editors, *Explaining the Vote: Presidential Choices in the Nation and the States, 1968,* Institute for Research in Social Science, University of North Carolina, Chapel Hill, 1973; Roy Moore and other editors, *Gathering and Writing News: Selected Readings,* College and University Press, 1975; Steven Chaffee, editor, *Political Communication,* Sage Publications, 1975; Ronald Ostman and Hamid Mowlana, editors, *International Yearbook of Drug Addiction and Society,* Volume III: *Communication Research and Drug Education,* Sage Publications, 1976; James Grunig, editor, *Decline of the Global Village,* General Hall, 1976; Jim Richstad, editor, *New Perspectives in International Communication,* East-West Center Communications Institute, 1977; Laurily K. Epstein, editor, *Women and the News,* Hastings House, 1978; Sidney Kraus, editor, *The Great Debates: Carter vs. Ford, 1976,* Indiana University Press, 1979.

Michael Emery and Ted Smythe, editors, *Readings in Mass Communication: Concepts and Issues in the Mass Media,* W. C. Brown, 1980; Guido Stempel and Bruce Westley, editors, *Research Methods in Mass Communication,* Prentice-Hall, 1981; Earl Newsom, editor, *The Newspaper,* Prentice-Hall, 1981; G. C. Wilhoit, editor, *Mass Communication Review Yearbook,* Sage Publications, Volume II, 1981, Volume III (edited by Charles Whitney and Ellen Wartella), 1982; Dan Nimmo and Keith Sanders, editors, *Handbook of Political Communication,* Sage Publications, 1981. Contributor of about forty articles and reviews to professional journals and to newspapers.

WORK IN PROGRESS: *The Art and Science of Advanced Reporting,* with Donald Shaw and Gerry Keir, for Longman.

* * *

McDONALD, Jill (Masefield) 1927-1982

PERSONAL: Born October 30, 1927, in Wellington, New Zealand; died January 2, 1982, in London, England; daughter of Reginald Bedford (an architect) and Cecily Sutherland (Chambers) Hammond; married Alec McDonald, March 27, 1948 (divorced September 21, 1960); children: Glen Rohan (Mrs. Philip Spicer), Murray James. *Education:* Attended University of Auckland, 1946-48. *Home and office:* 43 Blackheath Rd., London S.E.10, England.

CAREER: Free-lance illustrator, 1953-57; Department of Education, Wellington, New Zealand, art editor for School Publications Branch, 1957-65; free-lance illustrator and writer, 1965-82. Affiliated with Puffin Books and creator of the "Puffin Club" feature in *Puffin Post.*

WRITINGS—For children; all self-illustrated: *Counting on an Elephant,* Puffin, 1975; *Maggy Scraggle Loves the Beautiful Ice-Cream Man,* Kestrel, 1977; *The Happyhelper Engine,* Methuen, 1980.

Illustrator: Norman Hunter, *Puffin Book of Magic*, Puffin, 1968; Margaret Greaves, *Gallery*, Methuen, 1968; John Cunliffe, *Farmer Barnes at the Country Fair*, Lion Press, 1969; Janet Aitcheson, *The Pirates Tale*, Puffin, 1970, Harper, 1971; John F. Waters, *The Royal Potwasher*, Methuen, 1972; Greaves, *Little Jacko*, Methuen, 1973; Greaves, *The Dagger and the Bird*, Methuen, 1973; Carolyn Sloan, *The Penguin and the Vacuum Cleaner*, Puffin, 1974, McGraw, 1975; Hunter, *Professor Branestawm's Learning Do-It-Yourself Handbook*, Bodley Head, 1976; Cunliffe, *Farmer Barnes and the Goats*, Deutsch, 1976; Albert Burton, Jr., *Codes for Kids*, Puffin, 1981.

WORK IN PROGRESS: More books for children.

SIDELIGHTS: Jill McDonald once wrote *CA:* "My mother taught me to see the world around me and, also, what was going on inside my head. My father taught me I could get where I wanted to be if I worked at it hard enough. No complaints about my childhood, though I had an appetite for much more horror and melodrama than came my way. That was partly why I needed to gobble up books as fast as the public library would lend them to me. Five books a week was the limit which generally meant that Thursday and Friday I had nothing to read.

"I always liked drawing and writing, but so do many little kids. I think why I keep on doing it is because it nourishes a basic belief in the essential rightness and order of life in the face of frequent and chaotic evidence to the contrary. Writing a story or painting a picture pulls together all the tatty little bits and pieces skittering around my head and gives them a pattern and shape.

"Motivation for getting anything actually finished is usually that I need the money. I don't really know what makes me start in the first place. Probably best not to think too much about this—I feel chaotic and dispersed if I don't and at my very best if I do. I very much like the freshness and wonder with which little kids view the world and so like to write and draw for them. On the other hand I have a steadily growing list of unborn pictures and stories which no way fit within a child's-eye view and which are becoming more and more strident in their demand to see themselves on paper."

OBITUARIES: *Times* (London), January 8, 1982.†

*   *   *

McDONALD, Julie 1929-
(Julie Jensen)

PERSONAL: Born June 22, 1929, in Audubon County, Iowa; daughter of Alfred J. (a farmer) and Myrtle (Faurschou) Jensen; married Elliott R. McDonald, Jr. (an attorney), May 6, 1952; children: Beth Pearson, Elliott R. III. *Education:* University of Iowa, B.A. and Certificate in Journalism, 1951. *Politics:* Republican (moderate). *Religion:* Presbyterian. *Home:* 2802 East Locust St., Davenport, Iowa 52803.

CAREER: Rockford Register-Republic and Morning Star, Rockford, Ill., women's editor, 1951-52; *Quad-City Times*, Davenport, Iowa, feature writer and fine arts critic, 1962-82; *Rock Island Argus*, Rock Island, Ill., arts writer, 1983—. Iowa Arts Council, chairman, 1969-73, writer-in-the-schools, beginning 1974. Lecturer in English, Black Hawk College, Moline, Ill., 1965; lecturer in journalism, St. Ambrose College, Davenport, 1974—. Clarinetist, formerly playing with Rockford Symphony Orchestra, currently with Bettendorf Community Band. Liaison director, Scott County Association for Mental Health, 1956-58; secretary, Scott County Republican Central Committee, 1957-74. *Member:* P.E.O. Sisterhood, Authors Guild, Authors League of America, Davenport Writers' Club, Questers Study Club, Phi Beta Kappa.

AWARDS, HONORS: Quad-City Writer of the Year, 1969; honorary doctorate of letters, St. Ambrose College, 1972; Governor's Media in the Arts Award, 1975; Friends of American Writers Award, 1979, for *Petra;* first place in state and national competitions for fiction, National Federation of Press Women, and Johnson Brigham Award, Iowa Library Association, both 1983, for *The Sailing Out.*

WRITINGS: Baby Black, Angus Journal, 1960; *Amalie's Story* (novel), Simon & Schuster, 1970; *Pathways to the Present* (originally published as a fifty-part historical series in the *Quad-City Times*), Boyar Books, 1977; (contributor) Clarence Andrews, editor, *Growing Up in Iowa*, Iowa State University Press, 1978; *Petra* (novel), Iowa State University Press, 1978; (contributor) Clarence Andrews, editor, *Christmas in Iowa*, Midwest Heritage Press, 1979; *Ruth Buxton Sayre: First Lady of the Farms* (biography), Iowa State University Press, 1980; *The Sailing Out* (novel), Iowa State University Press, 1982; *Delectably Danish: Recipes and Reflections*, Penfield Press, 1982.

Also author of novel *Earth Tones*, as yet not published; author of two three-act plays for Davenport Junior Theatre and a three-act play, "High Rise," produced by Playcrafters, Moline; also author of a historical play, "Time and the River," produced by Quad-City Center for Performing Arts. Contributor of two short novels to *Redbook.* Contributor of articles to newspapers under name Julie Jensen.

WORK IN PROGRESS: The Ballad of Bishop Hill, for Askild and Karnekull (Stockholm), and *Margaret in Love*, both novels.

SIDELIGHTS: Julie McDonald writes *CA:* "Working with children in the State Arts Council's Writers-in-the-Schools program has helped me sort out why and how I function as a writer. Trying to transmit a vision always makes it much more one's own."

McDonald indicates that "as a lifelong midwesterner, I have spent my writing life sifting midwestern experience for fictional truth. That truth in its quiet solidity is not destined for best-sellerdom, but I am satisfied to attempt its expression with all the honesty and craft I can muster. I believe that attention must be paid to this life in this place because there is value in it for people everywhere. . . . I am astonished by letters from readers who think my novels are true stories, but I shouldn't be, as I do a great deal of research to make them seem real. As a fledgling biographer, I still feel the strictures of being an intruder in another person's life, but this is one of the problems of dealing with a living subject."

AVOCATIONAL INTERESTS: Paintings, drawings, and prints ("collect modestly"), Scottish Deerhounds, and Friends of the Public Library projects.

*   *   *

McDONALD, Walter (Robert) 1934-

PERSONAL: Born July 18, 1934, in Lubbock, Tex.; son of Charles Arthur (a painter) and Vera Belle (Graves) McDonald; married Carol Ham, August 28, 1959; children: Cynthia, David, Charles. *Education:* Texas Technological College (now Texas

Tech University), B.A., 1956, M.A., 1957; University of Iowa, Ph.D., 1965. *Religion:* Christian. *Office:* Department of English, Texas Tech University, Lubbock, Tex. 79409.

CAREER: U.S. Air Force, career officer, 1957-71, instructor at U.S. Air Force Academy, 1960-62, 1965-66, assistant professor, 1966, associate professor of English, 1967-71, retired as major; Texas Tech University, Lubbock, associate professor, 1971-75, professor of English, 1975—, director of creative writing, 1972—.

MEMBER: P.E.N., Modern Language Association of America, National Council of Teachers of English, Conference of College Teachers of English (member of council, 1977-80), South Central Modern Language Association, Texas Institute of Letters, Texas Association of Creative Writing Teachers (president, 1974-76). *Awards, honors:* Voertman's Poetry Award, Texas Institute of Letters, 1976, for *Caliban in Blue and Other Poems;* best story award, Texas Institute of Letters, 1976, for "The Track"; National Education Association creative writing fellowship, 1984.

WRITINGS: (Editor with Frederick Kiley) *A "Catch-22" Casebook,* Crowell, 1973; *Caliban in Blue and Other Poems,* Texas Tech Press, 1976; (editor with James White) *Texas Prize Stories and Poems,* Texas Center for Writers Press, 1978; *One Third Leads to Another,* Cedar Rock Press, 1978; *Anything, Anything,* L'Epervier, 1980; *Burning the Fence,* Texas Tech Press, 1981; *Working against Time,* Calliope Press, 1981. Contributor of stories, poems, and articles to literary journals, including *TriQuarterly, Poetry,* and *American Poetry Review.*

WORK IN PROGRESS: Poetry; fiction.

* * *

McELROY, Lee
See KELTON, Elmer

* * *

McFARLAND, Philip (James) 1930-

PERSONAL: Born June 20, 1930, in Birmingham, Ala.; son of Thomas Alfred (a lawyer) and Lucile (a teacher; maiden name, Sylvester) McFarland; married Patricia Connors (a teacher), July 23, 1960; children: Philip James, Jr., Joseph Thomas. *Education:* Oberlin College, B.A., 1951; St. Catharine's College, Cambridge, M.A., 1964. *Home:* 18 Independence Ave., Lexington, Mass. 02173. *Agent:* John Cushman Associates, Inc., 242 West 27th St., New York, N.Y. 10001. *Office:* Concord Academy, Concord, Mass. 01742.

CAREER: Houghton Mifflin Co., Boston, Mass., textbook editor, 1958-64; traveled and lived in Europe, 1964-66; Concord Academy, Concord, Mass., English teacher, 1966—; writer. *Military service:* U.S. Naval Reserve, active duty, 1951-54; became lieutenant junior grade.

WRITINGS: A House Full of Women (novel), Simon & Schuster, 1960; (with Allan A. Glatthorn, Harold Fleming, and others) *Composition: Models and Exercises,* Harcourt, 1971; (with others) "Focus on Literature" series, Houghton, 1972, revised edition, 1978; *Sojourners: A Narrative of the Human Adventure as Lived by Some Historic Dreamers and Sufferers, Including John Brown, Aaron Burr, Sir Walter Scott, Mary Shelley, John Jacob Astor and Washington Irving,* Atheneum, 1979; *Seasons of Fear* (fiction), Schocken, 1984.

WORK IN PROGRESS: Sea Dangers (nonfiction).

SIDELIGHTS: Philip McFarland's *Sojourners,* according to *Chicago Tribune Book World* critic James R. Mellow, "is not a plodding textbook account of the birth of the American nation.... Nor is the book strictly a 'biography,' as it is billed, of Washington Irving, America's first great man of letters. It is both more and less than either of these; a stirring narrative of life and times in 19th-century America from the duel between Aaron Burr and Alexander Hamilton in 1804 to the death of Irving and the hanging of the abolitionist leader John Brown in 1859—a period that marked the coming of age and the end of innocence in American society."

More specifically, *Sojourners* traces the development of American society through the eyes of Irving who, as both writer and ambassador, crossed paths with some of the most illustrious names of the nineteenth century. McFarland describes, for instance, Irving's relationship with the young widow Mary Shelley (author of the gothic classic *Frankenstein*) and speculates on how the life and death of her husband, poet Percy Bysshe Shelley, affected them. "In epochal biography," notes R.W.B. Lewis in his *New York Times Book Review* article about *Sojourners,* "the relationship can be a casual one. Irving once rode with Aaron Burr in a stagecoach from Fredericksburg to Richmond.... That is warrant enough for [the author] to launch into the histrionic narrative of Burr from his soldiering days through the fateful duel with Hamilton, the bizarre adventuring in the Southwest and the trials that followed, the later years of wandering in disgrace."

Critic James Atlas finds both the format of McFarland's work and the author's writing style distracting. The reviewer particularly objects to what he sees as McFarland's dwelling on one theme—"that we are mortal," as Atlas writes in his *New York Times* review. "Time and again, . . . McFarland marvels over this immutable and unpleasant fact.... Yes, one longs to cry, it is miraculous, unnerving, tragic that people die; but can't this author allow his subjects to live on the page without reminding us that they are really dead?"

On the other hand, Mellow and Lewis find *Sojourners* a satisfying study of American history. Lewis cites McFarland's dramatic imagery, remarking that the author displays "an almost Faulknerian intensity" about the subjects of his work and that "by quickening such images . . . into being [he] makes *Sojourners* a constantly beguiling and informative experience." And Mellow finds that McFarland has "an unfailing eye for the color and excitement of the age, and he has written one of the most absorbing cultural histories I have read."

BIOGRAPHICAL/CRITICAL SOURCES: Chicago Tribune Book World, November 11, 1979; *New York Times Book Review,* December 30, 1979; *New York Times,* January 5, 1980; *Village Voice Literary Supplement,* October, 1982.

* * *

McGRADY, Patrick M(ichael), Jr. 1932-

PERSONAL: Born July 17, 1932, in Shelton, Wash.; son of Patrick Michael (a journalist) and Grace Helen (Robinson) McGrady; married Elizabeth Rosenbaum, March 4, 1964; married second wife, Colleen Yvonne Bennett (a painter), January 7, 1967 (divorced, 1976); children: (first marriage) Ilya Andreas; (second marriage) Vanessa Veveya Totote, Ian Bennett Franklin. *Education:* Institut d'Etudes Politiques de Paris, Certificat d'etudes politiques, 1953; Yale University, B.A., 1954. *Home and office:* 221 West 82nd St., New York, N.Y. 10024; and 3111 Paradise Bay Rd., Port Ludlow, Wash. 98365. *Agent:*

Julian Bach Literary Agency, 747 Third Ave., New York, N.Y. 10017.

CAREER: Associated Press, Minneapolis, Minn., newsman, 1954-55; United Press, newsman in Boston, Mass., and Albany, N.Y., both 1954; *Chicago Sun-Times,* Chicago, Ill., newsman, 1955-56; Congress for Cultural Freedom, Paris, France, news editor, 1956-57; National Broadcasting Company, Inc., New York City, television editor for "Briefing Session," 1957-58; Fund for the Republic, New York City, consultant, 1958-59; Immedia, Inc. (broadcasting productions), New York City, president, 1959-62; *New Leader,* New York City, promotion manager, 1962; *Newsweek,* Moscow, U.S.S.R., bureau chief, 1963; Young & Rubicam, New York City, consultant on international programming, 1965; free-lance writer and journalist, 1966—. Frequent guest on radio and television talk programs; lecturer and consultant.

MEMBER: American Society of Journalists and Authors (president, 1975-76), American Association for the Advancement of Science, Gerontological Society, American Aging Association (member of board of directors), American Geriatrics Society, National Association of Science Writers, Yale Club of New York. *Awards, honors:* The Youth Doctors was included on *Book World*'s list of the one hundred best books of 1968.

WRITINGS: Television Critics in a Free Society, Fund for the Republic, 1960; *The Youth Doctors,* Coward, 1968; *The Love Doctors,* Macmillan, 1972; (editor) *Emily Wilkens' Secrets from the Super Spas,* Grosset, 1976; (with Nathan Pritikin) *The Pritikin Program for Diet and Exercise,* Grosset, 1979; (with Richard J. Corriere) *The Friendship Connection,* Morrow, 1984. Contributor to numerous publications, including *Esquire, Ladies' Home Journal, Look, London Sun, Status, Book World,* and *Woman's Day.*

SIDELIGHTS: The Pritikin Program for Diet and Exercise spent fifty-two weeks on the *New York Times* bestseller list.

* * *

McINERNY, Ralph 1929-
(Harry Austin, Matthew FitzRalph, Ernan Mackey, Monica Quill)

PERSONAL: Born February 24, 1929, in Minneapolis, Minn.; son of Austin Clifford (a mechanical engineer) and Vivian (Rush) McInerny; married Constance Terrill Kunert, January 3, 1953; children: Cathleen, Mary Hosford, Anne Policinski, David, Elizabeth, Daniel. *Education:* St. Paul Seminary, St. Paul, Minn., B.A., 1951; University of Minnesota, M.A., 1952; Laval University, Ph.D. (summa cum laude), 1954. *Politics:* Independent. *Religion:* Roman Catholic. *Home:* 2158 Portage Ave., South Bend, Ind. *Agent:* Ellen Levine, 370 Lexington Ave., New York, N.Y. 10017. *Office address:* Box 495, University of Notre Dame, Notre Dame, Ind. 46556.

CAREER: Creighton University, Omaha, Neb., instructor in philosophy, 1954-55; University of Notre Dame, Notre Dame, Ind., assistant professor, 1955-59, associate professor of philosophy, beginning 1959, Michael P. Grace Professor of Medieval Studies and director of Medieval Institute, 1978—. Member of Catholic Commission on Intellectual and Cultural Affairs. *Military service:* U.S. Marine Corps, 1946-47.

MEMBER: American Catholic Philosophical Association (council, 1966—), American Philosophical Association, Metaphysical Society of America, Soren Kierkegaard Society, Fellowship of Catholic Scholars, Society for Christian Philosophy, Authors Guild, Authors League of America, Mystery Writers of America, Writers Guild. *Awards, honors:* Fulbright research grant, Belgium, 1959-60; National Endowment for the Humanities fellowship; honorary doctorate, Benedictine College.

WRITINGS: The Logic of Analogy: An Interpretation of St. Thomas, Nijhoff, 1961; *History of Western Philosophy,* Volume I, Regnery, 1963; *Thomism in an Age of Renewal,* Doubleday, 1966; *Jolly Rogerson* (novel), Doubleday, 1967; *Studies in Analogy,* Nijhoff, 1968; *From the Beginnings of Philosophy to Plotinus,* University of Notre Dame Press, 1969; *A Narrow Time,* Doubleday, 1969; *Philosophy from Augustine to Ockham,* University of Notre Dame Press, 1970; *The Priest,* Harper, 1973; *Gate of Heaven,* Harper, 1975; *Rogerson at Bay,* Harper, 1976; *Romanesque,* Harper, 1977; *Spinnaker,* Gateway-Regnery, 1977; *Abecedary,* Juniper, 1979.

Published by Vanguard: *Quick as a Dodo,* 1978; *Bishop as Pawn,* 1978; *Lying Three,* 1979; *Second Vespers,* 1980; *Thicker Than Water,* 1981; (under pseudonym Monica Quill) *Not a Blessed Thing!,* 1981; (under pseudonym Monica Quill) *Let Us Prey,* 1982; *The Grass Widow,* 1983.

Contributor of scholarly articles to professional journals and symposia; also contributor, sometimes under pseudonyms, of short fiction to magazines. Author of columns for *Quodlibets, South Bend Tribune,* and *National Catholic Register;* editor, *New Scholasticism,* 1966—.

BIOGRAPHICAL/CRITICAL SOURCES: New York Times Book Review, July 26, 1981, January 31, 1982, November 6, 1983; *Washington Post Book World,* August 17, 1980, January 17, 1982.

* * *

McKINNELL, James 1933-

PERSONAL: Born March 22, 1933, in Linn Township, Walworth County, Wis.; son of James Charles (a farmer) and Margaret (Wiedenhoft) McKinnell; married Letha Miriam Miller (a teacher), March 22, 1959; children: James, Andrew. *Education:* Grinnell College, B.A., 1957; Eden Theological Seminary, graduate study, 1957-58; Bethany Theological Seminary, B.D., 1961, D.Min., 1978. *Home:* 6909 Auburn Rd., Rockford, Ill. 61103. *Office:* First Church of the Brethren, 6909 Auburn Rd., Rockford, Ill. 61103.

CAREER: Farmer in Walworth, Wis., 1950-53; pastor of Chester Center Church near Grinnell, Iowa, 1955-57, and of Churches of the Brethren in Hagerstown, Md., 1959-60, Worthington, Minn., 1961-67, and New Paris, Ind., 1967-74; First Church of the Brethren, Rockford, Ill., pastor, 1974—. Chairman of Migrant Service Committee of Elkhart and Kosciusko counties, Indiana, 1968-69. *Member:* Rockford Clergy Association, Phi Beta Kappa.

WRITINGS: Now about Peace, Brethren Press, 1971; *Church Growth and the Brethren,* Brethren Press, 1979; (reviser) *Congregational Goals Discovery Plan,* Brethren Press, 1979. Contributor to church publications.

WORK IN PROGRESS: The Promises of God; What It Means to Be a Member of the Family of God; an article, "Relational Webs in the Ministry of Jesus."

SIDELIGHTS: James McKinnell writes: "I was raised on a dairy farm in southern Wisconsin, the eldest son of a Scotch-Irish father and German mother. I attended country-school and a small high school in Walworth, Wisconsin. I intended to make farming my career, when an encounter with Jesus Christ led me to begin training for the ministry at Grinnell College. After completing college, I began to search for a theological school that was affiliated with a Christian denomination that had an active pacifist program. I chose the Church of the Brethren. Since completing doctoral studies, I have become a consultant and writer in the areas of church growth and goal setting."

AVOCATIONAL INTERESTS: Camping, mechanics and inventing, research on his family tree.

* * *

McLUHAN, (Herbert) Marshall 1911-1980

PERSONAL: Born July 21, 1911, in Edmonton, Alberta, Canada; died after a long illness, December 31, 1980, in Toronto, Ontario, Canada; son of Herbert Ernest (a real estate and insurance salesman) and Elsie Naomi (an actress and monologuist; maiden name, Hall) McLuhan; married Corinne Keller Lewis, August 4, 1939; children: Eric, Mary (Mrs. Thomas James Colton), Teresa, Stephanie, Elizabeth, Michael. *Education:* University of Manitoba, B.A., 1932, M.A., 1934; Cambridge University, B.A., 1936, M.A., 1939, Ph.D., 1942. *Religion:* Roman Catholic. *Home:* 3 Wychwood Park, Toronto, Ontario, Canada M6G 2V5.

CAREER: University of Wisconsin—Madison, instructor, 1936-37; St. Louis University, St. Louis, Mo., instructor in English, 1937-44; Assumption University, Windsor, Ontario, associate professor of English, 1944-46; University of Toronto, St. Michael's College, Toronto, Ontario, associate professor, 1946-52, professor of English, 1952-80, creator (by appointment) and director of Center for Culture and Technology, 1963-80. Lecturer at numerous universities, congresses, and symposia in the United States and Canada; Albert Schweitzer Professor of Humanities at Fordham University, 1967-68. Chairman of Ford Foundation seminar on culture and communications, 1953-55; director of media project for U.S. Office of Education and National Association of Educational Broadcasters, 1959-60. Appointed by Vatican as consultor of Pontifical Commission for Social Communications, 1973. Consultant to Johnson, McCormick & Johnson Ltd. (public relations agency), Toronto, 1966-80, and to Responsive Environments Corp., New York City, 1968-80. *Member:* Royal Society of Canada (fellow), Modern Language Association of America, American Association of University Professors.

AWARDS, HONORS: Governor General's Literary Award for critical prose, 1963, for *The Gutenberg Galaxy: The Making of Typographic Man;* Fordham University Communications Award, 1964; D.Litt. from University of Windsor, 1965, Assumption University, 1966, Grinnell College, 1967, Simon Fraser University, 1967, St. John Fisher College, 1969, University of Edmonton, 1972, and University of Western Ontario, 1972; Litt.D. from University of Manitoba, 1967; Molson Prize of Canada Council for outstanding achievement in the social sciences, 1967; Carl-Einstein-Preis, German Critics Association, 1967; Companion of the Order of Canada, 1970; Institute of Public Relations President's Award (Great Britain), 1970; LL.D. from University of Alberta, 1971; Christian Culture Award, Assumption University, 1971; Gold Medal Award, President of the Italian Republic, 1971, for original work as philosopher of the mass media; President's Cabinet Award, University of Detroit, 1972.

WRITINGS: "Henry IV": A Mirror for Magistrates (originally published in *University of Toronto Quarterly*), [Toronto], 1948; *The Mechanical Bride: Folklore of Industrial Man,* Vanguard, 1951, reprinted, Beacon Press, 1967; *Counterblast,* privately printed, 1954, revised and enlarged edition, designed by Harley Parker, Harcourt, 1969; (editor and author of introduction) Alfred Lord Tennyson, *Selected Poetry,* Rinehart, 1956.

(Editor with Edmund Carpenter) *Explorations in Communication* (anthology), Beacon Press, 1960; *The Gutenberg Galaxy: The Making of Typographic Man,* University of Toronto Press, 1962, New American Library, 1969; *Understanding Media: The Extensions of Man* (originally written as a report to U.S. Office of Education, 1960), McGraw, 1964; (compiler and author of notes and commentary with Richard J. Schoeck) *Voices of Literature* (anthology), two volumes, Holt (Toronto), 1964-65, Volume I published as *Voices of Literature: Sounds, Masks, Roles,* 1969.

(With Quentin Fiore) *The Medium Is the Massage: An Inventory of Effects* (advance excerpt published in *Publishers Weekly,* April 3, 1967), designed by Jerome P. Agel, Random House, 1967; (with V. J. Papanek and others) *Verbi-Voco-Visual Explorations* (originally published as Number 8 of *Explorations*), Something Else Press, 1967; (with Fiore) *War and Peace in the Global Village: An Inventory of Some of the Current Spastic Situations That Could Be Eliminated by More Feedforward* (excerpt entitled "Fashion: A Bore War?" published in *Saturday Evening Post,* July 27, 1968), McGraw, 1968; (with Parker) *Through the Vanishing Point: Space in Poetry and Painting,* Harper, 1968; *The Interior Landscape: The Literary Criticism of Marshall McLuhan, 1943-1962,* edited and compiled by Eugene McNamara, McGraw, 1969.

Culture Is Our Business, McGraw, 1970; (with Wilfred Watson) *From Cliche to Archetype,* Viking, 1970; (with Barrington Nevitt) *Executives—Die-Hards and Dropouts: Management Lore in the Global Village,* Harcourt, 1971; (with Nevitt) *Take Today: The Executive as Dropout,* Harcourt, 1972; (author of introduction) Harold Adams Innis and Mary Quale, editors, *Empire and Communications,* University of Toronto Press, 1972; (author of foreword) Willy Blok Hanson, *The Pelvic Tilt: Master Your Body in Seven Days,* McClelland & Stewart, 1973.

(With Sorel Etrog) *Spiral,* Fitzhenry & Whiteside, 1976; (with Robert Logan) *Libraries without Shelves,* Bowker, 1977; (with son, Eric McLuhan, and Kathy Hutchon) *City as Classroom: Understanding Language and Media,* Book Society of Canada, 1977; (with Pierre Babin) *Autre homme, autre chretien a l'age electronique,* Chalet, 1978; (with E. McLuhan and Hutchon) *Media, Messages, and Language: The World as Your Classroom,* preface and introduction by David A. Sohn, National Textbook Co., 1980.

Contributor: Bernard Rosenberg and David Manning White, editors, *Mass Culture,* Free Press of Glencoe, 1957; G. Legman, editor, *The Compleat "Neurotica," 1948-1951,* Hacker Art Books, 1963; *The Electronic Revolution* (published as a special issue of *American Scholar,* spring, 1966), United Chapters of Phi Beta Kappa, 1966; Gerald Emanuel Stearn, editor, *McLuhan—Hot and Cool: A Primer for the Understanding of and a Critical Symposium with a Rebuttal by McLuhan,* Dial, 1967; Stanley T. Donner, editor, *The Meaning of Commercial Television* (University of Texas-Stanford University seminar held in Asilomar, Calif., 1966), University of Texas Press, 1967; Richard Kostelanetz, editor, *Beyond Left and Right: Radical Thoughts for Our Times,* Morrow, 1968; Bernard Bergonzi, editor, *Innovations,* Macmillan, 1968; *Exploration of the Ways, Means, and Values of Museum Communication with the Viewing Public* (seminar held at the Museum of the City of New York, October 9-10, 1967), Museum of the City of New York, 1969; Lauro de Oliveira Lima, *Mutacoes em educacao Segundo McLuhan,* Editora Vozes, 1971.

Author of a multimedia bulletin, *The Marshall McLuhan DewLine Newsletter,* published monthly by Human Development Corp., beginning 1968. General editor, with Ernest Sirluck and Schoeck, of "Patterns of Literary Criticism" series, seven volumes, University of Chicago Press and University of Toronto Press, 1965-69. Contributor of articles and essays to numerous periodicals, including *Times Literary Supplement, Vogue, American Scholar, Kenyon Review, Sewanee Review, Family Circle, Encounter,* and *Daedalus. Explorations,* coeditor with Carpenter, 1954-59, editor, beginning 1964; member of editorial board, *Media and Methods,* beginning 1967.

SIDELIGHTS: "The medium is the message," quipped Marshall McLuhan, and the world took notice. Summarized in this aphorism, McLuhan's novel insights into the functions of mass media and their implications for the future of our technological culture earned him both international acclaim and vitriolic criticism. He was variously called a prophet, a promoter, a poet, a prankster, an intellectual mad-hatter, a guru of the boob tube, a communicator who could not communicate, and a genius on a level with Newton, Darwin, Freud, Einstein, and Pavlov. Considered the oracle of the electronic age by advertising, television, and business executives who often admitted not understanding much of what he said, McLuhan made pronouncements on a vast range of contemporary issues, including education, religion, science, the environment, politics, minority groups, war, violence, love, sex, clothing, jobs, music, computers, drugs, television, and automobiles; all these pronouncements, however, were based on his belief that human societies have always been shaped more by the nature of the media used to communicate than by the content of the communication. Though he expressed his ideas in an abstruse style that reflected a predilection for puns, in books that declared the book obsolete, his influence was, and is, unmistakable. "One must admit regardless of whether he agrees with McLuhanism," observes Richard Kostelanetz in *Master Minds,* that McLuhan was "among the great creative minds—'artists'—of our time."

Contrary to his public image, McLuhan was by training a man of letters. At the University of Manitoba, he first studied engineering because of an avowed "interest in structure and design," notes Kostelanetz, but later changed his major to English literature and philosophy. After earning his first M.A. in 1934 with a thesis on "George Meredith as a Poet and Dramatic Parodist," McLuhan pursued medieval and Renaissance literature abroad at Cambridge University, ultimately producing a doctoral thesis on the rhetoric of Elizabethan writer Thomas Nashe. His writing career began with a critical study of Shakespeare's "Henry IV," and his contributions to professional journals included essays on T. S. Eliot, Gerard Manley Hopkins, John Dos Passos, and Alfred Lord Tennyson. Kostelanetz points out that even after McLuhan became known as a communications theorist, "academic circles regard[ed] him as 'one of the finest Tennyson critics.'"

A combination of circumstances, however, gradually led McLuhan to transcend his literary upbringing. The lectures of I. A. Richards and F. R. Leavis at Cambridge initiated an interest in popular culture that blossomed when McLuhan, a Canadian whose first two teaching jobs were in the United States, found himself "confronted with young Americans I was incapable of understanding," he said in *Newsweek.* "I felt an urgent need to study their popular culture in order to get through."

McLuhan's first published exploration of the effects of mass culture on those engulfed in it was *The Mechanical Bride: Folklore of Industrial Man.* The book deals with "the pop creations of advertising and other word-and-picture promotions as ingredients of a magic potion, 'composed of sex and technology,' that [is] populating America with creatures half woman, half machine," writes Harold Rosenberg in the *New Yorker.* Exposing the effects of advertising on the unconscious, the book describes the "mechanical bride" herself as that peculiar mixture of sex and technology exemplified in attitudes toward the automobile.

Kostelanetz believes that although the book was "sparsely reviewed [in 1951] and quickly remaindered, *The Mechanical Bride* has come to seem in retrospect, a radical venture in the study of American mass culture. Previous to McLuhan, most American critics of integrity were disdainfully horrified at the growing proliferation of mass culture—the slick magazines, the comic books, the Hollywood movies, radio, television. . . . McLuhan, in contrast, was probably the first North American critic to inspect carefully the forms the stuff in the mass media took and then wonder precisely how these forms influenced people; and while he was still more scornful than not, one of his more spectacular insights identified formal similarities, rather than differences, between mass culture and elite art."

Specifically, McLuhan noticed the abrupt apposition of images, sounds, rhythms, and facts in modern poems, symphony, dance, and newspapers. Discontinuity, he concluded in *The Mechanical Bride,* is a central characteristic of the modern sensibility: "[It] is in different ways a basic concept of both quantum and relativity physics. It is the way in which a Toynbee looks at civilization, or a Margaret Mead at human cultures. Notoriously, it is the visual technique of a Picasso, the literary technique of James Joyce."

Following *The Mechanical Bride* and his promotion to full professor at St. Michael's College of the University of Toronto, McLuhan expanded his study of the relationship between culture and communication. From 1953 to 1955 he directed a Ford Foundation seminar on the subject and, with anthropologist Edmund Carpenter, founded a periodical called *Explorations* to give seminar members an additional forum for their ideas. By the late 1950s, his reputation as a communications specialist extended into the United States, earning him an appointment as director of a media project for the U.S. Office of Education and the National Association of Educational Broadcasters. The University of Toronto acknowledged his growing importance by naming him the first director of its Center for Culture and Technology, founded in 1963 to study the psychic and social consequences of technology and the media.

McLuhan's work during this period culminated in what many regard as his two major books, *The Gutenberg Galaxy: The Making of Typographic Man*—which in 1963 won Canada's highest literary honor, the Governor General's Award—and *Understanding Media: The Extensions of Man,* which eventually brought him worldwide renown. Drawing on his own impressive erudition, the analytical techniques of modern art criticism, and the theories of, among others, political economist Harold Adams Innis, McLuhan presented in these books his view of the history of mass media as central to the history of civilization in general. Borrowing Buckminster Fuller's metaphor that a tool of man's is essentially an extension of man, McLuhan claimed that the media not only represent extensions of the human senses but that they, by their very nature as determinants of knowledge, dictate "the character of perception and through perception the structure of mind," summarizes James P. Carey in *McLuhan: Pro and Con*. "The medium"—more than the content—"is the message" because it shapes human perception, human knowledge, human society.

Thus, according to McLuhan in *The Gutenberg Galaxy*, the rise of the printing press revolutionized Western civilization. By placing an overemphasis on the eye, rather than the ear of oral cultures, print reshaped the sensibility of Western man. Human beings came to see life as they saw print—as linear, often with causal relationships. Print accounted for such phenomena as linear development in music, serial thinking in mathematics, the liberal tradition, nationalism, individualism, and Protestantism (the printed book encouraged thinking in isolation; hence, individual revelation). By giving man the power to separate thought from feeling, it enabled Western man to specialize and to mechanize, but it also led to alienation from the other senses and, thus, from other men and from nature itself.

The theme of alienation was "central to the argument of Innis," notes Carey, "[but McLuhan went] beyond this critique and argue[d] that the reunification of man, the end of his alienation, the restoration of the 'whole' man will result from autonomous developments in communications technology." The electronic media of the modern era—telegraph, radio, television, movies, telephones, computers—according to McLuhan in *Understanding Media*, are reshaping civilization by "moving us out of the age of the visual into the age of the aural and tactile." Because electronic media create a mosaic of information reaching us simultaneously through several senses, our sensibility is being radically transformed—as evidenced, for example, by the revolution in modern art. This redistribution and heightening of sensory awareness signifies a return to our tribal roots, where communication was multisensory and immediate. United by electronic media, the world is rapidly becoming a "global village," where all ends of the earth are in immediate touch with one another.

From this view of history branded "informational technological determinism" by Kostelanetz, McLuhan extrapolated numerous ideas in *The Gutenberg Galaxy, Understanding Media*, and subsequent books about the effects of education (the book is passe; one needs to be "literate" in many media), the concept of childhood, the landscape of social organization, the problem of personal privacy, war and propaganda, moral relativism, "hot" and "cool" media (a "cool" medium requires more sensory and mental participation than a "hot" one), the generation gap, television (those who worry about the programs on TV—a "cool" medium—are missing its true significance), modern art, and other topics. "McLuhan's performance was breathtaking," writes John Leonard in the *New York Times*. "He ranged from physics to Cezanne, from Africa to advertising, from the Moebius strip to Milman Parry's treatise on the oral character of Yugoslav epic poetry. Euclidean space, chronological narrative, artistic perspective, Newtonian mechanics, and capitalist economics were all called into question. They were lies of the dislocating eye."

McLuhan's ideas, however, were not as neatly nor as modestly presented as this brief summary might suggest, for he considered his books "probes"—invitations to explore—rather than carefully articulated arguments. McLuhan, notes Kostelanetz, believed "more in probing and exaggerating—'making discoveries'—than in offering final definitions, as well as raising . . . critical discourse to a higher level of insight and subtlety. For this reason, he [would] in public conversation rarely defend any of his statements as absolute truths, although he [would] explain how he developed them. 'I don't agree or disagree with anything I say myself' [was] his characteristic rationale."

To further dramatize his "probes," McLuhan eschewed the traditional, print-age, linear, expository structure of introduction, development, elaboration, and conclusion, attempting instead "to imitate in his writing the form of the TV image, which he describe[d] as 'mosaic,'" says Rosenberg. A typical McLuhan book or paragraph, according to Kostelanetz, "tends to make a series of analytic statements, none of which become an explicitly encompassing thesis, though all of them approach the same body of phenomena from different angles or examples. These become a succession of exegetical glosses on a mysterious scriptural text, which is how McLuhan analogously regard[ed] the new electronic world. . . . This means that one should not necessarily read his books from start to finish—the archaic habit of print-man. True, the preface and first chapter of *The Mechanical Bride* . . . really do *introduce* the themes and methods of the book; but beyond that, the chapters can be read in any order. The real introduction to *The Gutenberg Galaxy* is the final chapter, called 'The Galaxy Reconfigured'; even McLuhan advise[d] readers to start there; and the book itself is all but a galaxy of extensive printed quotations."

In addition to these stylistic features, McLuhan had a "predilection for positively blood-curdling puns," says a *New Republic* contributor, as well as a penchant for aphorisms. Deliberately punning on his famous dictum "The medium is the message," for example, McLuhan titled his 1967 photo-montage *The Medium Is the Massage: An Inventory of Effects* to convey his belief that instead of neutrally presenting content, "all media work us over completely. They are so pervasive in their personal, political, esthetic, psychological, moral, ethical, and social consequences that they leave no part of us untouched, unaffected, unaltered. The medium is the massage." He said the 1967 book was designed to clarify the ideas in *Understanding Media* by depicting "a collide-oscope of interfaced situations."

McLuhan's habitual, mosaic mixture of fact and theory, pun and picture, came to be characterized as "McLuhanese," which George P. Elliott describes in *McLuhan—Hot and Cool* as "deliberately antilogical: circular, repetitious, unqualified, gnomic, outrageous." The late Dwight Macdonald refers to "McLuhanese" in *Book Week* as "impure nonsense, nonsense adulterated by sense," and in another *Book Week* article Arthur M. Schlesinger, Jr., calls it "a chaotic combination of bland assertion, astute guesswork, fake analogy, dazzling insight, hopeless nonsense, shockmanship, showmanship, wisecracks, and oracular mystification, all mingling cockily and indiscriminately in an endless and random monologue . . . , [which] contains a deeply serious argument."

The novelty of McLuhan's ideas coupled with their unconventional presentation gave rise by the late 1960s "to an ideology . . . and a mass movement producing seminars, clubs, art exhibits, and conferences in his name," reports James P. Carey. One of the most frequently quoted intellectuals of his time, McLuhan became, in Carey's words, "a prophet, a phenomenon, a happening, a social movement." Advertising and television executives hailed him as the oracle of the electronic age, although as Alden Whitman states in the *New York Times*, "he did not think highly of the advertising business. 'The hullabaloo Madison Avenue creates couldn't condition a mouse,' he said." In 1965, avant-garde composer John Cage visited him in Toronto to discuss his insights. Publisher William Jovanovich later invited him to collaborate on a study of the future of the book. McLuhanisms soon appeared everywhere, including the popular American television show "Rowan and Martin's Laugh-In." And in 1977, Woody Allen persuaded him to make a cameo appearance in the Oscar-winning film "Annie Hall" to defend his theories.

Despite winning a great deal of admiration, McLuhan was also feared and rejected, "especially . . . by journalists and television personalities who saw themselves threatened by his analyses because they did not understand either him or his equally important sources," says E. C. Wheeldon in the London *Times*. He was often denounced as a fakir, a charlatan, and—because he considered TV the most influential medium of the electronic age—a guru of the boob tube. Critics charged him with over-simplification, faulty reasoning, inconsistency, confusion of myth and reality, as well as undermining the entire humanist tradition, and these charges continue to be leveled.

John Simon, writing in *McLuhan: Pro and Con,* considers McLuhan's "worst failing" to be "the wholesale reinterpretation of texts to prove his preconceived argument," and others scoff at McLuhan's attempt to explain virtually every social and cultural phenomenon in terms of the media. "For McLuhan," writes Harold Rosenberg, "beliefs, moral qualities, social action, even material progress play a secondary role (if that) in determining the human condition. The drama of history is a crude pageant whose inner meaning is man's metamorphosis through the media. As a philosophy of cultural development, *Understanding Media* is on a par with theories that trace the invention of the submarine to conflicts in the libido."

In the *New York Review of Books,* D. W. Harding praises McLuhan's "probes" as maneuvers that try "to break free from self-inhibition and sterile dispute," yet he believes they are ultimately self-defeating: "How in the face of independent common sense could McLuhan get away with, for example, his claim that primitive cultures are oral and auditory and ours is visual? Questionable even in the limited context of the psychiatrist's article he bases it on, the notion as a generalization is wildly implausible. The American Indians' skill in tracking, the bedouins' astonishing capacity for reading camel spoor, these are ordinary instances of the familiar fact that in many habitats the survival of a primitive people depended on constant visual alertness, acute discrimination, and highly trained inference from visual data. . . . One is left with the truism that we read a lot and preliterates don't. The implications of that fact are well worth exploring, but we get no help from stories of alteration in some physiologically and psychologically undefined 'sensory ratio.'"

"McLuhan is a monomaniac who happens to be hooked on something extremely important," concludes Tom Nairn in the *New Statesman,* "but the colossal evasiveness, the slipshod reasoning, and weak-kneed glibness accompanying the mania make him dangerous going. . . . Capable of the most brilliant and stimulating insight into relationships other historians and social theorists have ignored, he systematically fails to develop this insight critically. Consequently, his view of the connection between media and society is an unbelievable shambles: his dream-logic turns necessary conditions into sufficient conditions, half-truths into sure things, the possible into a *fait accompli.*"

The overriding source of irritation for many readers is McLuhan's intricate style. John Fowles, for example, finds *From Cliche to Archetype* "as elegant and as lucid as a barrel of tar." The book, according to Fowles in *Saturday Review,* "makes one wonder whether Marshall McLuhan's celebrated doubts over the print medium don't largely stem from a personal incapacity to handle it. Perhaps the graceless style, the barbarously obscuring jargon, the incoherent hopping from one unfinished argument into the middle of the next are all meant to be subtly humorous. But the general effect is about as subtle and humorous as a Nazi storm trooper hectoring the latest trainload of Jews. It is all barked fiat: off with your head if you dare to disagree."

David Myers suggests in *Book World* that, ultimately, it is "as a poet and only as a poet that McLuhan can be read without exasperation," and others seem to agree. Kenneth Burke maintains in the *New Republic* that McLuhan "transcends the distinction . . . between 'prove' and 'probe,' both from the Latin *probare.* 'Proof' requires a considerable sense of continuity; 'probing' can be done at random, with hit-and-run slogans or titles taking the place of sustained exposition. And in the medium of books, McLuhan with his 'probing' has 'perfected' a manner in which the non sequitur never had it so good." "Even at his worst," insists Tom Wolfe in *Book World,* "McLuhan inspires you to try to see and understand in a new way, and in the long run this may prove to be his great contribution."

The aim of McLuhan's "poetry," however, remains a matter of dispute. James P. Carey, who considers McLuhan "a poet of technology," claims his work "represents a secular prayer to technology, a magical incantation of the gods, designed to quell one's fears that, after all, the machines may be taking over. . . . McLuhan himself is a medium and that is his message." But McLuhan maintained that rather than predicting the future of our technological age, he was merely extrapolating current processes to their logical conclusions. "I don't *approve* of the global village," he once told a *Playboy* interviewer, "I say we live in it." Writing in *McLuhan: Pro and Con,* John Culkin supports the detachment of McLuhan's viewpoint: "Too many people are eager to write off Marshall McLuhan or to reduce him to the nearest and handiest platitude which explains him to them. He deserves better. . . . He didn't invent electricity or put kids in front of TV sets; he . . . merely [tried] to describe what's happening out there so that it can be dealt with intelligently. When someone warns you of an oncoming truck, it's frightfully impolite to accuse him of driving the thing."

Richard Kostelanetz, moreover, believes that McLuhan was "trenchantly a humanist." He quotes McLuhan as saying, "By knowing how technology shapes our environment, we can transcend its absolutely determining power. . . . My entire concern is to overcome the determination that results from people trying to ignore what is going on. Far from regarding technological change as inevitable, I insist that if we understand its components we can turn it off any time we choose. Short of turning it off, there are lots of moderate controls conceivable."

Whether McLuhan was a poet of technology, a detached observer, or a trenchant humanist, "what remain paramount are his global standpoint and his zest for the new," concludes Harold Rosenberg. "As an artist working in a mixed medium of direct experience and historical analogy, he [gave] a needed twist to the great debate on what is happening to man in this age of technological speedup. [Whereas] other observers . . . [repeated] criticisms of industrial society that were formulated a century ago, . . . McLuhan, for all his abstractness, . . . found positive, humanistic meaning and the color of life in supermarkets, stratospheric flight, the lights blinking on broadcasting towers. In respect to the maladies of de-individuation, he . . . dared to seek the cure in the disease, and his vision of going forward into primitive wholeness is a good enough reply to those who would go back to it.''

MEDIA ADAPTATIONS: A happening entitled "McLuhan Megillah," based on *Understanding Media* and *The Gutenberg Galaxy* and combining dance, film, painting, poetry, sculpture, and other art forms, was produced at Al Hansen's Third Rail Time/Space Theatre in Greenwich Village in January of 1966. A McLuhan television special based on *The Medium Is the Massage* was produced on NBC-TV, March 19, 1967. In September of 1967, Columbia Records released a four-track LP (Columbia CL 2701, stereo 9501), based on *The Medium Is the Massage* and produced by Jerome P. Agel.

CA INTERVIEW

On February 27, 1982, *CA* talked by phone with Donald F. Theall, President of Trent University in Peterborough, Ontario, about the late Marshall McLuhan. Dr. Theall is a former student of McLuhan's and author of *The Medium Is the Rear View Mirror: Understanding McLuhan.*

CA: You were a graduate student of Marshall McLuhan's at St. Michael's College at the University of Toronto and secretary of his first culture and communications seminar. What kind of relationship did he have generally with his students? Was he very accessible to them?

THEALL: Oh yes. Marshall was always very open to any student who really wanted to work on the kinds of problems he was interested in. And this made the seminar an extremely exciting one for the students who were involved in it. He was really just at the beginning of his career; *The Mechanical Bride* had just been published. It was an especially interesting period for the students who worked with him, particularly since he was very, very accessible during that period of time.

CA: Not an ivory-tower figure at all?

THEALL: Marshall was never an ivory-tower figure anyway. As his writing suggests, he's far from one who confined himself in the university. He had a very good sense of what was going on in the world around him, a wide and catholic set of interests.

CA: Did his students in any way significantly affect his writing or the development of his theories at that point?

THEALL: I think that all through Marshall's career there was a very necessary kind of symbiotic relationship with students. He was a converser. He liked to talk. He liked sounding boards. And therefore he liked the interplay of ideas. My own feeling, having been a student of his at that period of time, was that his students were really of great importance to him. They helped shape and form the processes of his mind. A great deal of what he has to say in his writings about dialogue and communication, conversation and communication, would relate to the type of student-teacher rapport that Marshall needed and wanted.

CA: Later, when he began to work as a consultant to businesses, he never left teaching even for a short while, did he?

THEALL: No, he never left teaching. Of course I did not have direct contact with him at that time. I was then at McGill, so I don't know what his relationship with students was like at firsthand. But having spoken to many of his students of that period, I would say he continued to have this close relationship with students to formulate most of what he did in terms of dialogue and interchange and conversation.

CA: He was the sort of man who might be disliked by more orthodox thinkers. Did he suffer much ill will from his colleagues?

THEALL: I think one would have to say that he did not have the easiest time in the University of Toronto in the 1950s, or, in fact, possibly subsequently. Anyone who has very new, groundbreaking, forward-looking ideas, as McLuhan did, is bound to disturb people with more traditional roots. I think also his way of working was somewhat chaotic and creative and anarchistic in a world that's used to a good deal more order and restraint.

CA: Much of his writing is not easy to understand. Was this also true of his public speaking and his classroom lectures?

THEALL: It could vary considerably. He could be very direct, very open, very simple at times. At other times his public speeches could be as enigmatic and aphoristic as his books were. I think it depended really on his mood and the particular stage of development of the topic he was pursuing. I have heard him give very straightforward and articulate public lectures, and he was certainly well liked as a lecturer by the students in the period I was at St. Michael's.

CA: How did he react to his own becoming a myth?

THEALL: I wasn't as close to him then. I'm not quite sure when he became a myth. It's a little hard to date, too. It's not a sort of instantaneous process; it's a gradual one. One thing which Marshall had was an immensely good sense of humor, and I think he always saw a certain irony in coming to be a myth. I think he generally kept a remove from being swept up by a sense of self-importance, which often disturbs people in that kind of situation. I'm not sure that the process with the demands it made on him didn't at times exhaust him a good deal. He needed a great deal of sustenance from books and ideas and discussions with students and people close to him.

CA: Being misunderstood didn't seem to bother him?

THEALL: No, I don't think it bothered him. I think in some ways he felt there was a kind of magic in it, the kind of magic that went back to the French symbolists, that in mystery there is an ambivalence which leads to a greater depth of meaning and perhaps greater truth. He probably was deliberately cryptic at times to intensify the possibilities of meaning.

CA: He said that he didn't believe everything he wrote, but rather used certain statements as "probes" to get the reader thinking. Has this presented a great obstacle to a really objective analysis of his thinking?

THEALL: I think it may have. I don't think it *should*. In fact he himself offers many of the clues to his own methodology. It may have been a misreading of Bacon's essay style that led him to suggest that in the Baconian kind of essay you threw together a lot of ideas as the mind followed them through a problem. He felt he followed the same sort of pattern, moving through the mind in the process of thinking through a question. And I believe he thought that was how he should be read. However, most people today won't easily read that way, and that leads to some of the tension between his method and his readers.

CA: What are the main gaps in the critical assessment of his work?

THEALL: I don't think there are many good books on McLuhan that go beyond introductions to his work. There have been very few people willing to deal with him at great length. Probably the essays are more important, more helpful, than most of the books. I would think that the kind of book Dennis Duffy wrote is probably a quite helpful introduction to Marshall's work. I've always felt my book was a very good analysis of his method and his intellectual interests, and I think the two collections of essays *McLuhan: Pro and Con* and *McLuhan—Hot and Cool* contain some of the better essays that have been done on him. Probably the most important criticism of his work—from a left-wing point of view, but a very thoughtful and provocative criticism—is in a book called *The Critical Twilight* by a man named John Fekete. But I think, as I say in a paper I've just finished for an anthology George Gerbner of the University of Pennsylvania is bringing out, that he's left a series of very important questions which as yet haven't even been entertained.

CA: What does McLuhan's work offer for the ordinary person, the person who's not a philosopher?

THEALL: Stimulation. For example, the kinds of books that he did in mid-career like *The Medium Is the Massage* and *War and Peace in the Global Village* can be picked up by a reader because they are multimedia essays, and they can lead to some very stimulating kinds of ideas. A classroom text he wrote, *City as Classroom,* is a fairly lucid text for school students. I think lots of people enjoy ideas but don't want to get into the complexities of something like *The Gutenberg Galaxy.* Certainly businessmen read him rather avidly during a considerable period of time and seem to have found a good deal in his work that stimulated them.

CA: It was reported in the papers after McLuhan's stroke in 1980 that his retirement from the University of Toronto, which had been previously postponed, would be put into effect and his Center for Culture and Technology there would be closed down. His son Eric was packing up papers and getting things ready to move. Had it been completely dismantled by the time he died?

THEALL: I can't answer that precisely. I think probably the University of Toronto is now creating a kind of multidisciplinary communications program in honor of McLuhan. The seminar still goes on at St. Michael's College; a group of people participating in that tries to continue some of McLuhan's work. But in many ways the *Center* was Marshall. I mean, it wasn't a question of dismantling the Center; it was a question that the Center and Marshall were almost coterminous. I think personally that a center of that type ought to be continued. But the particular one that existed would have changed in any case, because there was only one Marshall McLuhan.

CA: It was physically a very small place, wasn't it?

THEALL: Yes, it was in what had been a coach house behind some older buildings that were used for university purposes dating back to the nineteenth century.

CA: What do you consider his most significant contribution to the academic community?

THEALL: I think in the long run it will turn out to be his having indicated the very important role that the humanities and humanistic and artistic perspectives have to play in very crucially new areas of interdisciplinary studies—in communications, in the whole field of the evolving information society. And I think he discovered that there were important perceptions in the arts, in the tradition of the humanities, which people were disregarding in a movement towards positivisitic science and technology that could be in the long run crucial not only to enriching our academic knowledge but to our *survival.* I suppose there are hundreds of things one could say about Marshall; one could go on for a very long period of time.

But I think the greatest tragedy would be if, now that he has died and the Center has ceased to be, the work he started was not followed out because of the paradoxes, the difficulties that seem to be implicit in it. Because I still think, and I think even some of his better critics like Fekete think, that there is much in that work which we haven't even begun to explore in terms of questions about the human value of the arts and the artistic process in understanding the process of communications, which is becoming so vital to us. These challenges are still there. I think, to a degree, the fact that groups like the International Communication Association and the Canadian Communication Association recently have been devoting symposia to McLuhan is recognition of this.

BIOGRAPHICAL/CRITICAL SOURCES—Books: Marshall McLuhan, *The Mechanical Bride: Folklore of Industrial Man,* Vanguard, 1951; McLuhan, *The Gutenberg Galaxy: The Making of Typographic Man,* University of Toronto Press, 1962; McLuhan, *Understanding Media: The Extensions of Man,* McGraw, 1964; Quentin Fiore and McLuhan, *The Medium Is the Massage: An Inventory of Effects,* Bantam, 1967; Gerald Emanuel Stearn, editor, *McLuhan—Hot and Cool: A Primer for the Understanding of and a Critical Symposium with a Rebuttal by McLuhan,* Dial, 1967; Harry H. Crosby and George R. Bond, compilers, *The McLuhan Explosion* (casebook on McLuhan and *Understanding Media*), American Book Co., 1968; Sidney Walter Finkelstein, *Sense and Nonsense of McLuhan,* International Publishers, 1968; Raymond Rosenthal, editor, *McLuhan: Pro and Con,* Funk, 1968; Dennis Duffy, *Marshall McLuhan,* McClelland & Stewart, 1969; Richard Kostelanetz, *Master Minds: Portraits of Contemporary American Artists and Intellectuals,* Macmillan, 1969; Theodore L. Gross, *Representative Men,* Free Press, 1970; Jonathan Miller, *Marshall McLuhan,* Viking, 1971; Donald F. Theall, *The Medium Is the Rear View Mirror: Understanding McLuhan,* McGill-Queens University Press, 1971; John Fekete, *The Critical Twilight: Explorations in the Ideology of Anglo-American Literary Theory from Eliot to McLuhan,* Routledge & Kegan Paul, 1978.

Periodicals: *New York Times,* October 21, 1951, February 27, 1967, September 7, 1967, January 1, 1981.

Book Week, June 7, 1964, March 19, 1967; *Time,* July 3, 1964, March 3, 1967, January 12, 1981; *Times Literary Supplement,* August 6, 1964, September 28, 1967; *New York Review of Books,* August 20, 1964, November 23, 1967, January 2, 1969; *Nation,* October 5, 1964, May 15, 1967, December

4, 1967, December 8, 1969; *New Statesman,* December 11, 1964, September 22, 1967.

Commentary, January, 1965; *New Yorker,* February 27, 1965; *Books,* September, 1965, January, 1967; *Harper's,* November, 1965, June, 1967; *Life,* February 25, 1966; *Newsweek,* February 28, 1966, March 6, 1967, September 23, 1968, January 12, 1981; *New York Times Book Review,* May 1, 1966, March 26, 1967, September 8, 1968, December 21, 1969, July 12, 1970, December 13, 1970; *Village Voice,* May 12, 1966, December 26, 1970; *Vogue,* July, 1966; *Esquire,* August, 1966; *Saturday Review,* November 26, 1966, March 11, 1967, May 9, 1970, November 21, 1970; *Commonweal,* January 20, 1967, June 23, 1967; *New York Times Magazine,* January 29, 1967; *Saturday Night,* February, 1967; *Kenyon Review,* March, 1967; *Antioch Review,* spring, 1967; *Critic,* August, 1967; *Listener,* September 28, 1967, October 19, 1967; *American Dialog,* autumn, 1967; *Western Humanities Review,* autumn, 1967; *Book World,* October 29, 1967, September 15, 1968, July 27, 1969, November 30, 1969, December 6, 1970; *Partisan Review,* summer, 1968; *National Review,* November 19, 1968; *Canadian Forum,* February, 1969; *Playboy,* March, 1969; *Sewanee Review,* spring, 1969.

New Republic, February 7, 1970, June 10, 1972; *Twentieth-Century Literature,* July, 1970; *Books and Bookmen,* March, 1971; *L'Express,* February 14-20, 1972; *Christian Science Monitor,* May 17, 1972.

Maclean's Magazine, January 7, 1980, March 17, 1980; *Chicago Tribune,* January 1, 1981; *Times* (London), January 2, 1981; *Publishers Weekly,* January 23, 1981.

OBITUARIES: *Chicago Tribune,* January 1, 1981; *New York Times,* January 1, 1981; *Times* (London), January 2, 1981; *Newsweek,* January 12, 1981; *Time,* January 12, 1981; *AB Bookman's Weekly,* January 19, 1981; *Publishers Weekly,* January 23, 1981.

[Sketch verified by Donald F. Theall]

—Sketch by James G. Lesniak
—Interview by Jean W. Ross

* * *

McNEISH, James 1931-

PERSONAL: Born October 23, 1931, in Auckland, New Zealand; son of Arthur William (an army officer) and Geraldine (a violinist; maiden name, Bosworth) McNeish; married Felicity Wily, July 16, 1960 (divorced, August 31, 1964); married Helen Schnitzer (a photographer and author), December 27, 1968; children: (first marriage) Kathryn Ann. *Education:* University of Auckland, B.A., 1952. *Residence:* New Zealand. *Agent:* George Greenfield, John Farquharson Ltd., 162 Regent St., London W1R 5TB, England.

CAREER: Writer. *New Zealand Herald,* Auckland, New Zealand, journalist and arts editor, 1950-58; teacher in London, England, 1960-62; free-lance radio broadcaster and radio documentary producer, 1962—. Founder and director, with wife Helen, of Bridge in New Zealand (private educational travel trust), 1974—. *Military service:* Territorial Service Army of New Zealand. *Member:* P.E.N. International. *Awards, honors:* Katherine Mansfield fellowship, 1973; New Zealand Government scholarship, 1979; Berlin Kuenstler program fellowship, 1983.

WRITINGS: *Fire under the Ashes* (biography of Danilo Dolci), Hodder & Stoughton, 1965, Beacon Press, 1966; *Mackenzie* (novel), Hodder & Stoughton, 1970; *The Mackenzie Affair* (novel), Hodder & Stoughton, 1972; (with Marti Friedlander) *Larks in a Paradise,* Collins, 1974; *The Glass Zoo* (novel), St. Martin's, 1976; *As for the Codwits* (autobiographical diary), Hodder & Stoughton, 1977; (with Brian Brake) *Art of the Pacific,* Oxford University Press, 1979; *Belonging: Conversations in Israel,* Holt, 1980; *Joy* (novel), Hodder & Stoughton, 1982; (with wife, Helen McNeish) *Walking on My Feet* (biography), Collins & World, 1983.

Author of plays "1895," "The Rocking Cave," and "The Mouse Man," produced in Auckland, New Zealand, at Mercury Theatre, 1973-76. Also author of penal report to New Zealand Minister of Justice, 1974.

WORK IN PROGRESS: A novel based on the life of an Olympic runner who, at the age of twenty-six, achieved world fame and shortly after died falling beneath a train.

SIDELIGHTS: James McNeish told *CA:* "New Zealanders live on the edge of the world looking out. If they go away and stay too long, they usually suffer an identity crisis. If they become celebrities, the crisis is that much worse. Few come through unscathed, and some not at all."

BIOGRAPHICAL/CRITICAL SOURCES: *Times Literary Supplement,* August 12, 1983.

* * *

McPHERSON, Sandra 1943-

PERSONAL: Born August 2, 1943, in San Jose, Calif.; daughter of Walter James (a physical education professor) and Frances (Gibson) McPherson; married Henry D. Carlile (an English professor and poet), July 22, 1966; children: Phoebe. *Education:* Attended Westmont College, 1961-63; San Jose State College (now University), B.A., 1965; University of Washington, Seattle, graduate study, 1965-66. *Home:* 7349 Southeast 30th Ave., Portland, Ore. 97202.

CAREER: Honeywell, Inc., Seattle, Wash., technical writer, 1966; University of Iowa, Writers' Workshop, Iowa City, member of faculty, 1974-76, 1978-80; University of California, Berkeley, visiting faculty member, 1981; member of faculty, Oregon Writers' Workshop, Pacific Northwest College of Art, 1981—. Member, Forum on Individuality, White House Conference on Children, 1970. Has given poetry readings at universities and schools around the United States.

AWARDS, HONORS: Helen Bullis Prize, *Poetry Northwest,* 1968; Ingram Merrill Foundation grant, 1972, and 1984; Bess Hokin prize for poetry, 1972; Emily Dickinson Prize, Poetry Society of America, 1973; National Endowment for the Arts grant, 1974-75, and 1980; Blumenthal-Leviton-Blonder prize for poetry, 1975; Guggenheim Foundation fellowship, 1976-77; National Book Award nomination, 1979, for *The Year of Our Birth;* recipient of Northwest Booksellers Prize for *Radiation; Elegies for the Hot Season* was one of the first three books of verse chosen for National Council on the Arts program to aid university presses.

WRITINGS—All poetry collections: *Elegies for the Hot Season,* Indiana University Press, 1970, reprinted, Ecco Press, 1982; *Radiation,* Ecco Press, 1973; *The Year of Our Birth,* Ecco Press, 1978; *Sensing,* Meadow Press, 1980; *Patron Happiness,* Ecco Press, 1983.

Work appears in anthologies, including: *Best Poems of 1968,* Borestone Mountain Poetry Awards, 1969; *American Literary*

Anthology III, Viking, 1970; *Rising Tides: Twentieth Century American Women Poets,* Washington Square Press, 1973; *No More Masks!, No More Mythologies!,* Doubleday, 1973; *Modern Poetry of Western America,* Brigham Young University Press, 1975; *The American Poetry Anthology: Poets under Forty,* Avon, 1975.

Contributor of poetry to various periodicals, including *Nation, New Yorker, Poetry, New Republic, Field, Iowa Review, Harper's, Ironwood, Poetry Northwest,* and *Antaeus.*

SIDELIGHTS: Speaking of *Elegies for the Hot Season,* Sandra McPherson's first collection of poetry, Jonathan Galassi of *Poetry* notes a similarity to "Sylvia Plath in the stark, basic pictures that give shape to this poet's deepest insights." Valerie Trueblood of *American Poetry Review* believes "this is the world at its plainest and most sign-giving. . . . McPherson has a gift . . . for bringing the physical world close without blinking at it."

This unadorned presentation is continued in *Radiations,* a collection which "seemed to clear a space for itself among the books of the year," writes Trueblood, "and to sit in its own ring of light." There are two distinct kinds of poems in this collection, David Cavitch of the *New York Times Book Review* believes. The first are poems which "express a sensitive young woman's decorous thoughts around the house," while in the others "McPherson connects her personal existence to large, contemporary metaphors, and her simple, homebody language acquires the overtones of fierce truth, coolly delivered."

"The poles of McPherson's imagination in [*The Year of Our Birth*] are absence and presence," Margaret Gibson states in *Library Journal,* "as she traces the process of consciousness in fragments of childhood and in moments which touch adult lives." J. C. Oates of *New Republic* finds that despite "too many poems that read like facile exercises," the book contains "beautifully-rendered poems with the lucidity of parables."

BIOGRAPHICAL/CRITICAL SOURCES: *Poetry,* August, 1971, May, 1975; *New York Times Book Review,* November 17, 1974; *Library Journal,* February 15, 1978; *American Poetry Review,* July, 1978; *New Republic,* December 9, 1978.

* * *

McWHINNEY, Edward 1926-

PERSONAL: Born May 19, 1926, in Sydney, New South Wales, Australia; son of Matthew Andrew and Evelyn Annie (Watson) McWhinney; married Emily Ingalore (an economist and stockbroker), June 27, 1951. *Education:* University of Sydney, LL.B., 1949; Yale University, LL.M., 1951, Sc.Jur.D., 1953; Academy of International Law, The Hague, Diploma in International Law, 1951. *Home:* 1949 Beach Ave., Vancouver, British Columbia, Canada V6G 1Z2. *Office:* Department of Politics, Simon Fraser University, Burnaby, Vancouver, British Columbia, Canada V5A 156.

CAREER: Yale University, New Haven, Conn., lecturer in law, 1951-53, assistant professor of political science and fellow of Silliman College, 1953-55; University of Toronto, Toronto, Ontario, professor of international and comparative law and member of Centre for Russian Studies, 1955-66; McGill University, Montreal, Quebec, professor of law and director of Institute of Air and Space Law, 1966-71; Indiana University, Bloomington, professor of law and director of international and comparative legal studies, 1971-74; Simon Fraser University, Vancouver, British Columbia, professor of international law and relations and chairman of department of politics, 1974—. Visiting professor at Ecole Libre des Hautes Etudes, 1952, Luxembourg, 1959, 1960, University of Heidelberg and Max-Planck Institut, 1960-61, National University of Mexico, 1965, University of Paris and University of Madrid, 1968, University d'Aix-Marseille, 1969, Institut Universitaire, Luxembourg, 1972, 1974, 1976, The Hague Academy of International Law, 1973, Aristotelian University of Thessaloniki, 1975, University of Nice, 1976-77, Jagellonian University of Cracow, 1976, University of Paris, 1982, and College of France, Paris, 1983. Queen's counsel, Canada, 1967—; royal commissioner, Quebec, 1968-72; royal commissioner, British Columbia, 1974-75. Legal consultant to United Nations, 1953-54, U.S. Naval War College, 1961-68, Government of Ontario, 1965-71, Government of Quebec, 1969-70, 1974-75, and Government of Canada, 1979. Special advisor, Canadian delegation to the United Nations, 1981-83. *Military service:* Australian Air Force, 1943-45; became flying officer (first lieutenant).

MEMBER: American Society of International Law (member of executive council, 1965-68), Canadian Society of International Law (chairman of executive committee, 1972-75), Institut de Droit International (Paris; membre titulaire), American Foreign Law Association. *Awards, honors:* Rockefeller Foundation fellowship, 1960-61, 1966-68; Canada Council fellowship, 1960-61.

WRITINGS: *Judicial Review in the English-Speaking World,* University of Toronto Press, 1956, 4th edition, 1969; (editor and contributor) *Canadian Jurisprudence: The Civil Law and Common Law in Canada,* University of Toronto Press, 1958.

Foederalismus und Bundesverfassungsrecht, Quelle & Meyer, 1961; *Constitutionalism in Germany,* Sijthoff, 1962; *Comparative Federalism,* University of Toronto Press, 1962, 2nd edition, 1965; *Peaceful Coexistence and Soviet-Western International Law,* Sijthoff, 1964; (editor and contributor) *Law, Foreign Policy, and the East-West Detente,* University of Toronto Press, 1964; *Federal Constitution-Making for a Multi-National World,* Sijthoff, 1966; *International Law and World Revolution,* Sijthoff, 1967; (editor with Martin A. Bradley) *The Freedom of the Air,* Oceana, 1968; *Conflict ideologique et Ordre public mondial,* A. Pedone (Paris), 1969; (editor with Bradley) *New Frontiers in Space Law,* Oceana, 1969.

(Editor and contributor) *The International Law of Communications,* Oceana, 1971; (editor and contributor) *Aerial Piracy and International Law,* Oceana, 1971; (editor and contributor with P. Pescatore) *Federalism and Supreme Courts and the Integration of Legal Systems,* Editions UGA (Brussels), 1973; *The Illegal Diversion of Aircraft and International Law,* Sijthoff, 1975; *The International Law of Detente,* Sijthoff, 1978; *The World Court and the Contemporary International Law-Making Process,* Sijthoff, 1979; *Quebec and the Constitution, 1960-1978,* University of Toronto Press, 1979.

Constitution-Making: Principles, Process, Practices, University of Toronto Press, 1981; *Conflict and Compromise: International Law and World Order in a Revolutionary Age,* Holmes & Meier, 1981. Also author of *Canada and the Constitution,* 1982, and *United Nations Law-Making,* 1983.

Contributor to *International Encyclopaedia of the Social Sciences* and *Encyclopaedia Britannica.* Contributor of articles and essays to *Harvard Law Review, Revue Generale de Droit/International Public,* and other journals in the United Kingdom, United States, France, Germany, Spain, and India.

WORK IN PROGRESS: *Federalism and Nationalism;* studies on relations between the West, the Communist countries, and the Third World; science and technology and international law; communications and broadcasting and international law; *Supreme Courts and Judicial Law-Making.*

SIDELIGHTS: Edward McWhinney is fluent in French and German and competent in Russian, Italian, and Spanish. *Avocational interests:* Golf, tennis, swimming, walking.

* * *

MEETER, Glenn 1934-

PERSONAL: Born May 5, 1934, in Hammond, Ind.; son of John Arthur and Joan (Hoekman) Meeter; married Marlene Meyerink, August 10, 1955; children: Barbara Ann, Nancy Lynn, Joel Arthur, Alison Joan. *Education:* Calvin College, A.B., 1955; Vanderbilt University and George Peabody College for Teachers (now George Peabody College for Teachers of Vanderbilt University), M.A.T. (joint degree), 1956; University of Iowa, Ph.D., 1966. *Politics:* Democrat. *Religion:* Congregationalist. *Home:* 140 Tilton Park Dr., DeKalb, Ill. 60115. *Office:* Department of English, Northern Illinois University, DeKalb, Ill. 60115.

CAREER: High school English teacher in Lansing, Ill., 1956-60; University of Southern California, Los Angeles, assistant professor, 1964-69, associate professor of English, 1969; Northern Illinois University, DeKalb, associate professor, 1969-80, professor of English, 1980—, director of undergraduate English studies. Visiting associate professor of English at Baylor University, summer, 1978. *Member:* Modern Language Association of America, Conference on Christianity and Literature. *Awards, honors:* Graves Award from Pomona College and American Council of Learned Societies, 1968-69, for study; Breadloaf scholarship, 1970, for short story "Waiting for Daddy."

WRITINGS: *Bernard Malamud and Philip Roth*, Eerdmans, 1968; (contributor) Frank N. Magill, editor, *Magill's Literary Annual*, Salem Press, 1972; (contributor) Jerome K. Klinkowitz and J. L. Somer, editors, *The Vonnegut Statement*, Delacorte, 1973; (editor with Robert Detweiler) *The Faith and Fiction: The Modern Short Story*, Eerdmans, 1979; *Letters to Barbara* (novel), Eerdmans, 1981. Short stories anthologized in *Innovative Fiction*, edited by Klinkowitz and Somer, Dell, 1972, *Redbook's Famous Fiction*, edited by Anne Mollegen Smith, Redbook Books, 1977, and *Experimentelle amerikanische Prosa*, edited by Brigitte Scheer-Schaezler, Reclam, 1977. Contributor of stories to magazines and literary journals, including *Atlantic, Redbook, Chicago Review, South Dakota Review, Ohio Review,* and *Epoch.*

WORK IN PROGRESS: A novel, *Wedding Journey.*

BIOGRAPHICAL/CRITICAL SOURCES: *Christian Century,* May 26, 1982.

* * *

MELLORS, Samantha
See LOTTMAN, Eileen

* * *

MERRITT, E. B.
See WADDINGTON, Miriam

MEYERSON, Edward L(eon) 1904-1980

PERSONAL: Born September 14, 1904, in New York, N.Y.; died July 7, 1980; son of Meyer and Celia (Reisman) Meyerson; married Alice Tannenbaum (a dramatic reader), June 29, 1930; children: Philip. *Education:* Attended Crane Junior College, 1921-23; Northwestern University, Diploma in Commerce, 1925; graduate study at Loyola University of Chicago, 1926-27, and New School for Social Research, 1953-57; also received J.D. *Home and office:* 1414 San Carlos Ave., Apt. 106, San Carlos, Calif. 94070.

CAREER: Writer. Licensed public accountant in New York City, 1928-66; Credit Exchange, New York City, credit consultant, 1966-71; Wadsworth Publishing Co., Belmont, Calif., editor and accounting and credit manager, 1971-74. Lecturer at City College (now City College of the City University of New York) and at Henry George School of Social Science, both during 1950's. Director of poetry workshops in San Carlos and Redwood City, Calif.; gave poetry readings in California and on radio programs. *Member:* World Poetry Society, Poetry Society of America, Academy of American Poets, New York Poetry Forum. *Awards, honors:* First prize from *Voices International,* 1968, for poem "Hurry, Feet, Hurry"; poetry prize from *South and West* literary festival, 1969, for "Haight-Ashbury"; second prize in poetry from *South and West,* 1972, for "Liturgy for the Living," first prize, 1974, for short story "Blood of Christ."

WRITINGS—Poetry: *Parcae,* Poets Press, 1934; *Flying Dust,* Poetry Publications, 1937; *The Seed Is Man: A Collection of Poetry and an Essay on Ezra Pound,* William-Frederick, 1967, published as *Seed Is Man: Poems of Maturity,* 1973; *Chameleon,* Branden Press, 1971; (editor) *San Carlos Poetry Workshop Anthology,* four volumes, San Carlos Fine Arts Commission, 1974-78; *Liturgy for the Living: Selected Poems, 1960-1975,* Golden Quill, 1976. Contributor of articles and reviews to magazines and newspapers. Assistant book editor for *South and West.*†

* * *

MICKS, Marianne H(offman) 1923-

PERSONAL: Born April 30, 1923, in Seneca Falls, N.Y.; daughter of Ransom Rathbone and Emma Louise (Hoffman) Micks. *Education:* Smith College, A.B., 1945; Columbia University, M.A., 1948; Church Divinity School of the Pacific, B.D., 1957; Yale University, Ph.D., 1960. *Religion:* Christian. *Office:* Department of Biblical Theology, Virginia Theological Seminary, Alexandria, Va. 22304.

CAREER: Prior to 1960, worked in university ministry with National Council of Episcopal Church at Smith College, Northampton, Mass., and University of California, Berkeley; Western College, Oxford, Ohio, chairman of department of religion, 1960-66, dean and professor of religion, 1966-74; Virginia Theological Seminary, Alexandria, professor of biblical and historical theology, 1974—. Member of Episcopal Church Joint Commission on Ecumenical Relations, 1967-73, general board of examining chaplains, 1971—, and theological committee, 1974—. *Member:* Society of Biblical Literature, American Academy of Religion, Society for Values in Higher Education (fellow), Phi Beta Kappa. *Awards, honors:* D.D., Church Divinity School of the Pacific, 1968.

WRITINGS: *Introduction to Theology,* Seabury, 1964, revised edition, 1983; *The Future Present: The Phenomenon of Christian Worship, Seabury, 1970; (editor with Charles P. Price) Reginald H. Fuller and others, *Toward a New Theology of Ordination: Essays on the Ordination of Women*, Virginia Theological Seminary, 1976; (with Thomas E. Ridenhour) *Lent*, Fortress, 1979; *The Joy of Worship*, Westminster, 1982; *Our Search for Identity: Humanity in the Image of God*, Fortress, 1982.†

* * *

MIDDLEMAS, Keith
See MIDDLEMAS, Robert Keith

* * *

MIDDLEMAS, Robert Keith 1935-
(Keith Middlemas)

PERSONAL: Born May 26, 1935, in Alnwick, England; son of Robert James (a solicitor) and Eleanor Mary Middlemas; married Susan Tremlett, August 30, 1958; children: Sophie, Lucy, Annabel, Hugo. *Education:* Pembroke College, Cambridge, first class honors in history, 1958; has also received D.Phil. and D.Litt. *Religion:* Church of England. *Home:* Ashurst, Sussex, England. *Office:* Department of History, University of Sussex, Falmer, Brighton, England.

CAREER: House of Commons, London, England, clerk, 1958-66; University of Sussex, Falmer, Brighton, England, reader in history, 1966—. Chairman, Findon Conservation Association, 1969-72. *Military service:* British Army, Northumberland Fusiliers, lieutenant, 1953-55. Territorial Army, 1955-65. *Member:* Association of Contemporary Historians, National Rifle Association (Great Britain), Marylebone Cricket Club, Fly Fishers Club.

WRITINGS: Command the Far Seas: A Naval Campaign of the First World War, Hutchinson, 1961; *The Master Builders: Thomas Brassey, Sir John Aird, Lord Cowdray, Sir John Norton-Griffiths*, Hutchinson, 1963; *The Clydesiders: A Left-Wing Struggle for Parliamentary Power*, Hutchinson, 1965; (author of introduction) Maureen Stafford, *British Furniture through the Ages*, Coward, 1966; (under name Keith Middlemas; with Derek Cecil Davis) *Colored Glass*, C. N. Potter, 1968 (published in England as *Coloured Glass*, Jenkins, 1968); (under name Keith Middlemas; with John Barnes) *Baldwin* (biography of Stanley Baldwin), Weidenfeld & Nicolson, 1969, published in America as *Life of Baldwin*, Macmillan, 1970; (editor under name Keith Middlemas) Thomas Jones, *Whitehall Diary*, three volumes, Oxford University Press, 1969.

Continental Coloured Glass, Barrie & Rockliff, 1970; *Antique Glass in Color*, Doubleday, 1971; (under name Keith Middlemas) *The Strategy of Appeasement*, Quadrangle, 1972 (published in England as *Diplomacy of Illusion*, Weidenfeld & Nicolson, 1972); (under name Keith Middlemas) *Edward VII*, Weidenfeld & Nicolson, 1972, new edition, 1975; (under name Keith Middlemas) *Life and Times of George VI*, Weidenfeld & Nicolson, 1974; (under name Keith Middlemas) *Double Market: Art Theft and Art Thieves*, Tiptree Book Services, 1974; (under name Keith Middlemas) *Cabora Bassa: Engineering and Politics in Southern Africa*, Weidenfeld & Nicolson, 1975; (under name Keith Middlemas) *Politics in Industrial Society: The British Experience since 1911*, Andre Deutsch, 1979; *Power and the Party: Changing Faces of Communism in Western Europe since 1968*, Andre Deutsch, 1980; *Industry Unions and Government: Twenty-one Years of NEDC*, Macmillan, 1984.

WORK IN PROGRESS: The Changing Nature of the Modern State: Britain 1940-1980, for Andre Deutsch.

SIDELIGHTS: Times Literary Supplement critic Paul Addison calls Robert Keith Middlemas's *Politics in Industrial Society* "the most challenging book so far attempted on the political history of twentieth-century Britain, and in critical respects the challenge succeeds. A corporate state in embryo has been located and defined for the first time. The concepts of 'corporate bias' and 'continuous contract' have been matched against the archives and shown to work. The simpler faiths which cling to parliamentary processes have been subjected to a chilling blast of scepticism. The Middlemas thesis, it is safe to forecast, will colour all further discussion. And while the constitutional problem is likely to remain one of the great open questions, [the author] will deserve most of the credit for posing it in the first place."

AVOCATIONAL INTERESTS: Collecting antiques and works of art; rifle shooting (member of British team competing in Canada, 1955), tennis, squash, hunting game.

BIOGRAPHICAL/CRITICAL SOURCES: Spectator, June 21, 1969, October 11, 1969; *Times Literary Supplement*, July 17, 1969, May 2, 1980.

* * *

MIDDLEMISS, Robert (William) 1938-

PERSONAL: Born April 24, 1938, in Hartlepool, England; came to the United States in 1965, naturalized citizen, 1976; son of Robert William (a foreman) and Mary (Kelly) Middlemiss; married Deborah Louise Cass, September 8, 1962 (marriage ended, 1974); married Elizabeth Marie Dixon (a counselor), May 17, 1975; children: (second marriage) Whitney Faulkner (daughter). *Education:* Sir George Williams University, B.A., 1963; McGill University, B.L.S., 1964; Adelphi University, graduate study, 1965-66. *Home:* 3 Heritage Dr., Newnan, Ga. 30263. *Agent:* Alison Clemente, Charles R. Byrne Agency, 128 East 56th St., New York, N.Y. 10022.

CAREER: Armstrong Cork Co., Montreal, Quebec, laboratory technician, 1953-54; United Aircraft Corp., Longueuil, Quebec, production clerk, 1954-56; Federal Department of Transport, Ottawa, Ontario, marine engineer, 1956-59; York University, Toronto, Ontario, assistant acquisitions librarian, 1964-65; Adelphi University, Garden City, N.Y., acquisitions librarian, 1965-67; Indiana State University, Terre Haute, librarian and head of acquisitions department, 1967-71, lecturer in library science, 1970-71; B. H. Blackwell Ltd., Oxford, England, library services adviser, 1971-72; Media Fair, Inc., Vienna, Va., vice-president, 1973-79; Educational Activities, Inc., Baldwin, N.Y., Georgia sales consultant, 1979-84; Neumann Associates, New Berlin, Wis., vice-president of marketing and communications, 1984—. *Member:* Dixie Council of Authors and Journalists (member of board of trustees).

WRITINGS: The Parrot Man (novel), Fawcett, 1977; *The Lofoten Run*, Fawcett, 1979; *The Pelican's Clock*, Fawcett, 1981.

WORK IN PROGRESS: A satire on suburbia, entitled *Ms. Pilgrim's Progress*.

SIDELIGHTS: Robert Middlemiss told *CA:* "My published works have been spy thrillers, using violence to make statements about human nature. In my current work I am trying to accomplish the same goals by using humor."

MILLER, Cecilia Parsons 1909-

PERSONAL: Born July 15, 1909, in Mansfield, Ohio; daughter of Walbridge and Katherine Hooker (Whiteman) Parsons; married H. Lionel Miller (a writer), May 13, 1934; children: Thomas Kenyon, Daniel Benjamin, Damaris Ray (Mrs. Roger E. Milo), Elisabeth Walbridge (Mrs. Wayne R. Thompson) (all adopted). *Education:* Hillsdale College, B.A., 1932. *Religion:* Protestant. *Home:* 264 Walton St., Lemoyne, Pa. 17043.

CAREER: Writer. Arts Festival of Greater Harrisburg, member of executive committee, 1966—, vice-president, 1972-73, president, 1973-74. President, Presbyterian Interracial Fellowship of Great Harrisburg, 1968-70. *Member:* National Federation of State Poetry Societies (president, 1959-60; past vice-president and secretary; member of advisory board), Pennsylvania Poetry Society (president, 1957-61, 1977-81; historian), Harrisburg Arts Council (charter member; secretary, 1970-71, 1972; president, 1973-74), Harrisburg Manuscript Club (secretary), Chi Omega Alumnae. *Awards, honors:* Recipient of over twenty awards for poetry, including second place award from National Federation of State Poetry Societies, 1966, for *To March to Terrible Music,* Carl Sandburg Award from North Carolina Poetry Society, 1971, first place award from National Federation of State Poetry Societies, 1974, Ogden Nash Award, 1974, and awards from Pennsylvania Poetry Society, Poetry Society of Michigan, South Dakota Poetry Society, Kentucky State Poetry Society, and Delaware Poetry Society.

WRITINGS—Poetry, except as indicated: *Not Less Content,* Keystone Press, 1960; *Peculiar Honors,* Keystone Press, 1962; (contributor) *La Poesie Contemporaine aux Etats-Unis* (anthology), La Revue moderne, 1962; (contributor) *Commemorative Anthology: John F. Kennedy,* Swordsman Publishing, 1964; *To March to Terrible Music,* South & West, 1967; (contributor) *Kentucky Harvest* (anthology), D. Brandenburg, 1968; *Stand at the Edge,* South & West, 1970; *Glow in the Sky,* Obadiah Holmes Press, 1976; (editor) *Belfry and Hearth: Carlisle Poets,* Obadiah Holmes Press, 1976; (editor) *Not Just Any July: Keysner Poets,* Obadiah Holmes Press, 1976; *Keeping an Eye on June* (haiku and senryu), Obadiah Holmes Press, 1977; *Shorts in the Circuit: Light Verse,* Obadiah Holmes Press, 1978.

Also author of *Space Where Once a Husband Stood* (poetry), 1972, for Coretta Scott King; also author of novels, short stories, and articles. Contributor to numerous anthologies. Editor of two annuals, Pennsylvania Poetry Society *Prize Poems,* 1958-69, 1975-76, 1979—, and National Federation of State Poetry Societies annual, 1968-69; editor of *Winds of Liberty,* Bicentennial anthology for Harrisburg Manuscript Club; also editor of six collections of poetry for local poets. Editor of Pennsylvania Poetry Society *Newsletter,* 1957-69, 1979—; National Federation of State Poetry Societies, founder and editor of newsletter, *Strophes,* 1963-66, member of editorial committee, 1965-67.

WORK IN PROGRESS: Six poetry manuscripts; ten novels.

SIDELIGHTS: Cecilia Parsons Miller told *CA:* "Nurtured to be a writer, I met with encouragement at home and at school. Our family of children is an acquired one (four adopted children), and the process of acquiring them demanded both time and energy. Keeping them on the right track took even more, as adopted children usually have built-in difficulties. None of ours was less than twenty-one months when they arrived, and habits had been formed.

"In 1956 I began to concentrate on my writing; I've ended up with thirteen novels to date, all of them dear to my heart, all needing polish and final typing. [I've also written] perhaps thirty short stories and numerous articles; seemingly there are not enough hours in the day to get them marketed. A few have been published.

"With poetry I have been luckier. I still find myself distracted by community projects; participating in the anti-nuclear program since 1970, we are at present desperately trying to prevent the re-opening of Unit I at Three Mile Island, that large piece of insanity built in the middle of a river subject to flooding, adjacent to an international airport, too close to the state capital/capitol. The health and future of this area has been at risk since 1974 when Unit I went on line; since the accident, the already blighted residents are rightfully fearful of the future. The NRC commissioners, who were here in November, 1982, act as though they can't read; all this talk about emotional stress when they should be worried about getting our medical bills dumped on them.

"The outlet with poetry has given me a release valve and a sense of satisfaction. A winning poem in the annual contest of the National Federation of State Poetry Societies is titled 'The Fearsome Periphery of Three Mile Island.'"

AVOCATIONAL INTERESTS: Environmental concerns, horticulture, collecting ("amateur status only"), eleven grandchildren, two great-grandchildren.

* * *

MILLER, Hugh 1937-

PERSONAL: Born April 27, 1937, in Wishaw, Lanarkshire, Scotland; son of James Weir (an engineer) and Alice (Waddell) Miller; married Anne McNeil, 1958 (divorced, 1966); married Margaret Elizabeth Jenson, January 25, 1967; children: (first marriage) Lesley (daughter); (second marriage) James, Rachel. *Education:* Attended University of Glasgow, Stow College, and London Polytechnic.

CAREER: Scottish Independent Television, Glasgow, Scotland, editorial assistant, 1958-60; technical and photographic assistant to a forensic pathologist at University of Glasgow, 1960-62; Unique Studios, London, England, manager, 1963-64, co-owner, 1965-70; writer, beginning 1972. Former trustee of Jude Trust.

WRITINGS—Novels; published by New English Library, except as indicated: *The Open City,* 1973; *Drop Out,* 1973; *Short Circuit,* 1973; *Kingpin,* 1974; *Double Deal,* 1974; *Feedback,* 1974; *Ambulance,* St. Martin's 1975; *The Dissector,* St. Martin's, 1976; *A Soft Breeze from Hell,* 1976; *Kingpin,* 1976; *The Saviour,* 1977; *Terminal 3,* Futura Publications, 1978; *The Mourning Brooch,* 1978; *The Rejuvenators,* 1979. Also author of *Olympic Bronze,* 1979, and *Head of State,* 1979.

Books for sleight-of-hand and paranormalist entertainers: *A Pocketful of Miracles,* Unique Books, 1969; *Secrets of Gambling,* Unique Books, 1970; *Professional Presentations,* Tannen, 1971; *Koran's Legacy,* Repro 72, 1973; *Hypnotism,* Supreme Magic Co., 1977.

Scripts for instructional films: "Basic Post Mortem Technique," Advent Productions (London), 1962; "Close-Up with Cards," Davis Films (Chicago), 1971. Also author of documentary filmscript, "Levels," 1973.

Editor, *Bulletin,* 1967-69, and *Gen,* 1968-71.

SIDELIGHTS: Hugh Miller writes: "The drive central to all my fiction is an impulse towards presenting the reader with a balanced amalgam of entertainment, enlightenment, and concern. The colorations and distortions of professional and emotional commitments, produced in ordinary people, provide a foundation for viable fiction; the same stresses, working on extraordinary people, can make a fascinating additive to the structure. I make it my personal concern to ensure—as best I can—that the quality of escape in my work is such that readers are not merely anaesthetised for a time, but emerge with some change of outlook applicable to everyday existence."

AVOCATIONAL INTERESTS: Photography, hi-fi.

BIOGRAPHICAL/CRITICAL SOURCES: Coventry Telegraph, August 28, 1974.

* * *

MILLER, Wilma H(ildruth) 1936-

PERSONAL: Born March 8, 1936, in Dixon, Ill.; daughter of William A. (an electrician) and Ruth (Hanson) Miller. Education: Northern Illinois University, B.S., 1958, M.S., 1961; University of Arizona, Ed.D., 1967. Religion: Protestant. Home: 302 North Coolidge, Normal, Ill. 61761. Office: Department of Education, Illinois State University, Normal, Ill. 61761.

CAREER: Elementary school teacher in Dixon, Ill., 1958-63, and Tucson, Ariz., 1963-64; Wisconsin State University (now University of Wisconsin—Whitewater), Whitewater, assistant professor of reading, 1965-68; Illinois State University, Normal, associate professor, 1968-72, professor of education, 1972—. Visiting professor at Western Washington State College (now Western Washington University), 1970. Member: International Reading Association, American Educational Research Association, Illinois Association for Higher Education, Kappa Delta Pi, Pi Lambda Theta. Awards, honors: Citation of merit, International Reading Association, 1968, for doctoral dissertation; Illinois State University summer fellowship, 1970.

WRITINGS—Published by Center for Applied Research in Education, except as indicated: Identifying and Correcting Reading Difficulties in Children, 1971; (editor) Elementary Reading Today: Selected Articles, Holt, 1972; The First R: Elementary Reading Today, Holt, 1972, 2nd edition, 1977; Diagnosis and Correction of Reading Difficulties in Secondary School Students, 1973; Reading Diagnosis Kit, 1974, 2nd edition, 1978; Reading Correction Kit, 1975, 2nd edition, 1982; Corrective Reading Skills Activity File, 1977; Reading Activities Handbook, Holt, 1980; Teaching Elementary Reading Today, Holt, 1983. Contributor to Reading Teacher, Elementary English, Elementary School Journal, Clearinghouse, Illinois School Research, and other publications. Editor of Reading Clinic, 1975-77.

* * *

MILLER, Zane L. 1934-

PERSONAL: Born May 19, 1934, in Lima, Ohio; son of Paul Jennings (a railroadman) and Beryl (Dutton) Miller; married Janet Smith, December 27, 1955. Education: Miami University, Oxford, Ohio, B.S., 1956, M.A., 1959; University of Chicago, Ph.D., 1966. Politics: Democrat. Home: 812 Dunore Rd., Cincinnati, Ohio. Office: Department of History, University of Cincinnati, Cincinnati, Ohio 45221.

CAREER: Northwestern University, Evanston, Ill., instructor in American history, 1964-65; University of Cincinnati, Cincinnati, Ohio, assistant professor, 1965-70, associate professor, 1970-74, professor of history, 1974—, co-director of Center for Neighborhood and Community Studies, 1981—. Member: American Historical Association, Organization of American Historians, American Association of University Professors, Southern Historical Association, Ohio Academy of History. Awards, honors: National Science Foundation grant; National Endowment for the Humanities fellow; Social Science Research Council research fellow; Newberry Library fellow; Ohio Academy of History book award, for Suburb: Neighborhood and Community in Forest Park, Ohio, 1935-1976.

WRITINGS: Boss Cox's Cincinnati, Oxford University Press, 1968; (editor with Henry D. Shapiro) Science and Society in the West: Selected Writings of Dr. Daniel Drake, University Press of Kentucky, 1970; (contributor) Kenneth Jackson and Stanley K. Schultz, editors, Cities in American History, Knopf, 1972; (contributor) James F. Richardson, editor, The American City: Historical Studies, Xerox College Publishing, 1972; The Urbanization of Modern America: A Brief History, Harcourt, 1973; (contributor) Raymond Mohl and Richardson, editors, The Urban Experience, Wadsworth, 1973; (contributor) Leo Schnore, editor, The New Urban History, Princeton University Press, 1975; (contributor) Alexander Callow, editor, The Urban Bosses, Oxford University Press, 1976; (with Shapiro) Clifton: Neighborhood and Community in an Urban Setting, Laboratory in American Civilization, University of Cincinnati, 1976; (with George Roth) Cincinnati's Music Hall, Jordan & Co., 1978.

(Editor with Paula Dubeck) Urban Professionals and the Future of the Metropolis, Kennikat, 1980; (contributor) Greer, editor, Ethnics, Machines, and the American Urban Future, Schenkman, 1981; Suburb: Neighborhood and Community in Forest Park, Ohio, 1935-1976, University of Tennessee Press, 1981; (editor with Thomas M. Jenkins) The Planning Partnership, Sage Publications, 1982. Contributor to history journals.

WORK IN PROGRESS: A work on W.E.B. Du Bois.

* * *

MILLS, Barriss 1912-

PERSONAL: Born January 26, 1912, in Cleveland, Ohio; son of Charles Wendell (a businessman) and Emma (Barriss) Mills; married Iola Jones (an artist), August 7, 1937; children: John, Russell, William Barriss, Robert. Education: Dartmouth College, A.B., 1934; University of Chicago, M.A., 1936; University of Wisconsin, Ph.D., 1942. Politics: Independent. Home: 915 North Chauncey Ave., West Lafayette, Ind. 47906.

CAREER: Iowa State University of Science and Technology, Ames, instructor in English, 1937-40; Michigan State University, East Lansing, instructor in English, 1942-44; Iowa State University of Science and Technology, assistant professor, 1944-46, associate professor of English, 1946-47; University of Denver, Denver, Colo., associate professor, 1947-48, professor of English, 1948-50, chairman of department, 1947-50; Purdue University, Lafayette, Ind., professor of English, 1950-73, chairman of department, 1950-62. Teacher of poetry and poetry writing at Writers' Workshop, Chautauqua, N.Y., summer, 1965. Awards, honors: Best poetry award at Indiana University's Indiana Author's Day, 1964, for The Idylls of Theokritos: A Verse Translation.

WRITINGS—Poetry, except as indicated: The Black and White Geometry, Sparrow Press, 1955; Parvenus & Ancestors, Sparrow Press, 1959; (translator) The Idylls of Theokritos: A Verse

Translation, Purdue University Press, 1963; *Occasions and Silences,* Scrip Press (England), 1964; *Aftermath,* Goosetree Press, 1965; (translator) *The Carmina of Catullus: A Verse Translation,* Purdue University Press, 1965; *Letter to Felix,* Scrip Press, 1968; (translator) *Epigrams from Martial: A Verse Translation,* Purdue University Press, 1969; (with George Mills) *Broken Present,* Barking Dog Press, 1972; (with others) *A Suit of Four,* Purdue University Press, 1973; (with others) *Indiana Indiana,* Vagrom Chapbooks, 1975.

Published by Elizabeth Press: *Domestic Fables: Selected Poems,* 1971; (translator) *The Soldier and the Lady: Poems of Archilochos and Sappho,* 1975; *Roughened Roundnesses,* 1976; *The Unheroic Muse: Essays on Five Classical Poets* (nonfiction), 1978; (translator) *The Eclogues of Vergil: A Verse Translation,* 1980; *Poems from the Greek Anthology,* 1981.

Contributor of articles and poems to literary journals. Associate editor, *Poet & Critic,* 1961-62.

SIDELIGHTS: In *Indiana Indiana,* Barriss Mills writes: "I think of poetry as counterstatement—an antidote to verbal buffeting from the media. We're bullied by politicians, pundits, PR men, ad men, telling us what to think and feel. . . . Poetry restores us to ourselves and to things that really count: nature and the seasons, our work, love, youth and age, family and friends. And honest words." Explaining his motivation for translating Greek and Latin poets, Mills told CA that he attempts "to reestablish, for myself at least, some contact with our longer past at a time when winds of change are blowing through the daily headlines and our press, our politicians, and our preoccupations are as fickle as the weathercock."

AVOCATIONAL INTERESTS: Making stoneware pots, bowling, growing house plants from seed.

BIOGRAPHICAL/CRITICAL SOURCES: Barriss Mills and others, *Indiana Indiana,* Vagrom Chapbooks, 1975.

* * *

MINCHINTON, W(alter) E(dward) 1921-

PERSONAL: Born April 29, 1921, in Dulwich, London, England; son of Walter Edward (a clerk) and Anne (Clark) Minchinton; married Marjorie Sargood (a medical social worker), August 18, 1945; children: Paul Richard, Anne Border, Susan Clare, David Walter. *Education:* London School of Economics and Political Science, B.Sc., 1947. *Home:* 53 Homefield Rd., Exeter EX1 2QX, England. *Office:* Department of Economic History, University of Exeter, Exeter EX44RJ, England.

CAREER: University of Wales, University College of Swansea, assistant lecturer, 1948-50, lecturer, 1950-59, senior lecturer in history, 1959-64; University of Exeter, Exeter, England, professor of economic history, 1964—, head of department, 1964-83. Visiting professor, Fourah Bay College, University of Sierra Leone, 1965, and LaTrobe University, 1981-82. *Military service:* British Army, Royal Signals, 1942-45; became lieutenant. *Member:* Economic History Society, Royal Economic Society, British Agricultural History Society, Royal Historical Society (fellow). *Awards, honors:* Alexander Prize of Royal Historical Society, 1953, for article, "Bristol: The Metropolis of the South West in the Eighteenth Century"; Rockefeller Foundation research fellow, 1959-60.

WRITINGS: *The British Tinplate Industry: A History,* Oxford University Press, 1957; *The Port of Bristol in the Eighteenth Century,* Bristol Branch of the Historical Association, 1962; *Industrial Archaeology in Devon,* Devon County Council, 1968, 4th edition, 1984; *Devon at Work,* David & Charles, 1974; *Windmills of Devon,* Exeter Industrial Archaeology Group, 1977; *A Guide to Industrial Archaeology Sites in Britain,* Paladin Books, 1984.

Editor: *The Trade of Bristol in the Eighteenth Century,* Bristol Record Society, 1957; *Politics and the Port of Bristol in the Eighteenth Century,* Bristol Record Society, 1963; *Essays in Agrarian History,* two volume reprints edition, Augustus M. Kelley, 1968; *Industrial South Wales, 1750-1914: Essays in Welsh Economic History,* Augustus M. Kelley, 1968; *Mercantilism: System or Expediency?,* Heath, 1969; (and author of introduction) *The Growth of English Overseas Trade in the Seventeenth and Eighteenth Centuries,* Methuen, 1969, Barnes & Noble. 1970.

Wage Regulation in Pre-industrial England, David & Charles, 1971; (with Peter Harper) *American Manuscripts in the House of Lords Record Office,* Microform Review, 1983; *The Statistics of the Virginia Slave Trade, 1698-1775,* Virginia State Library, 1984.

Editor; all published by University of Exeter: *Farming and Transport in the South West,* 1972; (with H. E. S. Fisher) *Transport and Shipowning in the West Country,* 1973; *Population and Marketing: Two Studies in the History of the South-West,* 1976; *Capital Formation in South-West England,* 1978; *Reactions to Social and Economic Changes, 1750-1939,* 1979; *Agricultural Improvement: Medieval and Modern,* 1981.

* * *

MINTER, David L. 1935-

PERSONAL: Born March 20, 1935, in Midland, Tex.; son of Kenneth Cruse (a minister) and Frances (Hennessy) Minter; married Caroline Sewell, December 22, 1957; children: Christopher Sewell, Frances Elizabeth. *Education:* North Texas State University, B.A., 1957, M.A., 1959; Yale University, B.D., 1961, Ph.D., 1965. *Home:* 2121 McClendon, Houston, Tex. 77025. *Office:* Emory College, Emory University, Atlanta, Ga. 30322.

CAREER: Yale University, New Haven, Conn., Danforth instructor in English, 1964-65; University of Hamburg, Hamburg, Germany, university lecturer, 1965-66; Yale University, lecturer in English, 1966-67; Rice University, Houston, Tex., assistant professor, 1967-69, associate professor, 1969-73, professor of English, 1973-80; Emory University, Atlanta, Ga., professor of English and dean of Emory College, 1981—. Visiting associate professor, Columbia University, 1971, and Washington University, 1972. *Member:* Modern Language Association of America.

WRITINGS: *The Interpreted Design as a Structural Principle in American Prose,* Yale University Press, 1969; (editor) *Twentieth-Century Interpretations of "Light in August,"* Prentice-Hall, 1970; *William Faulkner: His Life and Work,* Johns Hopkins University Press, 1980.

SIDELIGHTS: David Minter's *William Faulkner: His Life and Work* "is not only a first-rate biography, it could easily be used as a pattern for one of those family generation novels. . . . His biography is equipped with all the furniture of a scholarly treatise—notes and sources, extensive analyses—yet he manages to keep these unobtrusive most of the time, and the book is as readable as a serious novel of character," asserts Dee Brown in the *Chicago Tribune Book World.* Brown further describes the work as "well-organized, fairly complete, and clearly well-written," yet also observes, "If any fault is to be found with this literary biography it is in the sometimes over-long discussions and analyses of each of Faulkner's novels, during which Minter occasionally lapses into a classroom manner." Brown concludes, however, that the biography "should take its place near the front of any collection of Faulkneriana."

Malcolm Cowley, in a *New York Times Book Review* article, shares Brown's aversion to the scholarly passages, noting, "Mr. Minter writes what we have come to recognize as academic prose, abstract, humorless, long-winded and full of quotations from other scholars, each identified in a footnote." Cowley nevertheless comments that "much of what he [Minter] says is sensitive and informative." About the overall work, Lachlan Mackinnon of the *Times Literary Supplement* states, "The great virtue of David Minter's book is that he knows that the question of who a man was is less interesting than that of whom he wished to become."

BIOGRAPHICAL/CRITICAL SOURCES: Chicago Tribune Book World, October 26, 1980; *Washington Post Book World,* November 9, 1980; *New York Times Book Review,* February 23, 1981; *Times Literary Supplement,* May 29, 1981.

* * *

MISS MANNERS
See Martin, Judith (Sylvia)

* * *

MITCHELL, Austin (Vernon) 1934-

PERSONAL: Born September 19, 1934, in Baildon, Yorkshire, England; son of Richard and Mary (Butterworth) Mitchell. *Education:* University of Manchester, B.A., 1956, M.A., 1957; Oxford University, D.Phil., 1963. *Politics:* "Perverse, but always left of center." *Religion:* Agnostic Anglican. *Home:* Longfield, Triangle, Halifax, West Yorkshire, England. *Office:* 1 Abbey Park Rd., House of Commons, Westminster, London, England.

CAREER: University of Otago, Dunedin, New Zealand, lecturer in politics, 1957-63; University of Canterbury, Christchurch, New Zealand, senior lecturer in politics, 1963-67; Oxford University, Nuffield College, Oxford, England, official fellow, 1967—; House of Commons, Westminster, London, England, elected Member of Parliament for Grimsby, 1977—. Appeared on regular weekly television program in New Zealand for two years; has appeared on Yorkshire television with British Broadcasting Corp. *Member:* Political Studies Association, Association of University Teachers, National Union of Journalists, APEX.

WRITINGS: (With R. M. Chapman and W. K. Jackson) *New Zealand Politics in Action,* Oxford University Press, 1962; *Waitaki Votes,* Otago University Press, 1962; *Government by Party,* Whitcombe & Tombs, 1966; *The Whigs in Opposition,* Clarendon Press, 1967; *Politics and People in New Zealand,* Whitcombe & Tombs, 1969; (with Sid Waddell) *Teach Thyssen Tyke,* Frank Graham, 1971; *Yorkshire Jokes,* Frank Graham, 1971; *The Half-Gallon Quarter-Acre Pavlova Paradise,* Whitcombe & Tombs, 1974; *Can Labour Win Again?,* Fabian Society, 1979; *Westminster Men,* Metheun, 1982; *The Case for Labour,* Longman, 1983; *Four Years in the Death of the Labour Party,* Metheun, 1983.

WORK IN PROGRESS: People's Democracy—Government and Politics in New Zealand; British Public Opinion with the Labour Government, 1974-79.

SIDELIGHTS: Austin Mitchell told *CA*: "My career has continued its remorseless downhill slide first from academe to television then into politics. If this goes on I may eventually have to work for a living."

* * *

MITCHELL, Carlton
See MARSHALL, Mel(vin D.)

* * *

MITCHELL, David (John) 1924-

PERSONAL: Born January 24, 1924, in London, England; son of James Watt (a grain broker) and Clare (Hayden) Mitchell; married Valerie Eva Bennett (divorced); married Cecelia Hopkinson (divorced); children: (second marriage) Timothy Jason. *Education:* Trinity College, Oxford, M.A. (with honors), 1947. *Politics:* "Armchair anarchist." *Religion:* "Christian agnostic." *Home:* 20 Mountacre Close, Syndenham Hill, London SE26, England.

CAREER: Staff writer for *Picture Post,* 1947-52; Pictorial Press (photo-journalistic agency), London, England, owner and editor, 1953-56; Central Office of Information, London, picture editor, 1957-65; free-lance writer, 1965—. *Military service:* Royal Air Force, pilot trainee, 1942-44.

WRITINGS: Monstrous Regiment: The Story of the Women of the First World War, Macmillan, 1966 (published in England as *Women on the Warpath: The Story of the Women of the First World War,* J. Cape, 1966); *The Fighting Pankhursts,* Macmillan, 1967; *The Pankhursts,* Heron Books, 1970; *1919 Red Mirage,* Macmillan, 1970; (contributor) Stephen W. Sears, editor, *The Horizon History of the British Empire,* American Heritage Press, 1973; *Bernardo O'Higgins,* Verlag Plata, 1976; *Pirates,* Dial, 1976; *Queen Christabel: A Biography of Christabel Pankhurst,* Macdonald & Jane's, 1977; (contributor) Robert James Maddox, editor, *Readings in American History,* Dushkin, 1978; *The Jesuits: A History,* F. Watts, 1981; *The Spanish Civil War,* F. Watts, 1983. Contributor of articles and book reviews to a number of periodicals, including *Times* (London), *New Statesman, History Today, Times Literary Supplement, New Society* and *Sunday Times Magazine.*

WORK IN PROGRESS: A study of "the mythology-scatology/reality of monks, nuns, and perhaps of the Confessional," tentatively entitled *Dirty Habits.* Also, "if enough 'villains' would contact me, I'd like to attempt an off-beat World War II coverage on 'misfits' (like myself) in the armed forces. In 1914-18, we might have been shot; in 1939-45, we were often treated more leniently, perhaps referred to psychiatrists and discharged as more trouble than worth."

SIDELIGHTS: David Mitchell told *CA* that he decided to try to earn a living as a writer in 1965 after a lifetime of prevarication or muddled preparation. He lived in Spain from 1965 "until devaluation of the pound, marital disaster, and rising local prices in 1973 forced a return to the United Kingdom." Though he has written books and articles on suffrage-feminist themes, he is not a convinced "women's libber." His main interest is in "utopian, often fanatical characters, beautiful (or at least sympathetic) losers," and he has a keen interest in the Spanish anarchist movement and the early stages of Italian fascism. He finds it hard to believe in the brotherhood of Man but longs to get involved in a brotherhood of men. On the other hand, however, he finds full commitment to any system of belief impossible and considers the doctrine of original sin the best available working clue to human behavior and human history.

AVOCATIONAL INTERESTS: "Single parenting, reading (especially re-reading), desultory traditional jazz listening, revisiting Spain, travel journalism in general."

* * *

MITCHELL, James 1926-
(James Munro)

PERSONAL: Born March 12, 1926, in South Shields, England; son of James William (a fitter) and Mina Mitchell; married Norma Halliday (a teacher), August 1, 1953; children: Simon John, Peter James. *Education:* Saint Edmund Hall, Oxford, B.A., 1948, M.A., 1949. *Home:* 62 Marsden Rd., South Shields, England. *Agent:* Hughes Massie Ltd., 31 Southampton Row, London WC1B 5HL, England. *Office:* College of Art, Backhouse Park, Sunderland, England.

CAREER: Actor and travel agent in United Kingdom and Paris, France, 1948-50; Technical College, South Shields, England, lecturer in English, 1950-59; television writer in London, England, 1959-63; College of Art, Sunderland, England, lecturer in liberal studies, 1963—. *Member:* Screen Writers' Guild, Society of Film and Television Arts. *Awards, honors:* British Crime Writers' Association Award for *A Way Back.*

WRITINGS: Here's a Villain, Morrow, 1958; *A Way Back,* Morrow, 1959; *Soldier in the Snow,* Faber & Faber, 1961; *Steady Boys Steady* (also see below), P. Davies, 1961; *Among African Sands,* P. Davies, 1963; *A Magnum for Schneider,* Jenkins, 1969, published as *A Red File for Callan,* Simon & Schuster, 1971; *Ilion Like a Mist,* Cassell, 1969; *The Winners,* Cassell, 1970; *Russian Roulette,* Morrow, 1973; "Innocent Bystanders" (filmscript; based on novel of the same title; also see below), Paramount, 1973; *Smear Job,* Hamish Hamilton, 1975, Putnam, 1977; *Death and Bright Water,* Morrow, 1975; *When the Boat Comes In,* Hamish Hamilton, Book One, 1976, Book Two: *The Hungry Years,* 1976, Book Three: *Upwards and Onwards,* 1977; *Goodbye Darling,* Hamish Hamilton, 1979.

Under pseudonym James Munro: *The Man Who Sold Death,* Barrie & Jenkins, 1964, Knopf, 1965, reprinted, Charter Books, 1980; *Die Rich, Die Happy,* Barrie & Jenkins, 1965, Knopf, 1966; *Money That Money Can't Buy,* Barrie & Jenkins, 1967, Knopf, 1968; *Innocent Bystanders,* Barrie & Jenkins, 1969, Knopf, 1970.

Contributor of reviews to *New Statesman, Books and Art,* and *John O'London's.* Author of twelve television plays, and of film script, "Steady Boys Steady." Creator of "Callan" television series, 1967.

WORK IN PROGRESS: Research on mass media, eighteenth-century life in England, and the writing skills of painters and sculptors.

SIDELIGHTS: James Mitchell speaks French and Spanish. He commented to *CA*: "I am interested in the novel, which I rate far higher than all television and most films. I like writing thrillers, and reading thrillers which read like latter-day Gothic novels, i.e., I like reading Chandler. Teaching and writing are the two things I like doing best. I'm lucky to be able to do both."†

MOHR, Gordon 1916-
(Jack Mohr)

PERSONAL: Born January 1, 1916, in Chicago, Ill.; son of Herman (an engineer) and Millicent (Mohr) Mansfield; married Ruth Satterthwaite, December 28, 1958 (divorced); married Doris S. Grone, July 7, 1972; children: Dwight Gordon. *Education:* Attended Moody Bible Institute, 1934-35, and Minot State College, 1947-48. *Politics:* Conservative ("critical of foreign policy and bitterly anti-communist without being a radical rightist"). *Religion:* Baptist. *Home:* 113 Ballentine St., Bay St. Louis, Miss. 39520.

CAREER: U.S. Army, 1942-64, retiring as lieutenant colonel; served eight years in Korea and Japan and five years in Ethiopia; taken prisoner by communists in 1948, tortured, and stood before People's Court and firing squad. Public lecturer on communism, 1951—, appearing for American Opinion Speaker's Bureau, Belmont, Mass., 1965—; publisher of *Christian Patriot Crusader* newsletter; national military coordinator for Citizens Emergency Defense System. *Awards, honors*—Military: Silver Star; Bronze Star with two clusters; Purple Heart with three clusters; Commendation Medal with cluster; Korean Distinguished Service Cross; and three Presidential Unit citations. Other: Doctor of Letters, Freelandia Institute (Cassville, Mo.), 1976.

WRITINGS—Under name Jack Mohr: *Hyenas in My Bedroom,* A. S. Barnes, 1969; *Destination Somewhere,* Southwest Radio Church Publications (Oklahoma City, Okla.), 1971; *Formula for Survival,* Southwest Radio Church Publications, 1972; *Point of No Return,* Southwest Radio Church Publications, 1973; *Invasion from Hell,* Southwest Radio Church Publications, 1975; *Psychopolitics: The Communist Art of Brainwashing,* Tabernacle Publishing, 1976; *The Satanic Counterfeit,* Hoffman Publishing, 1980; *Know Your Enemies,* Hoffman Publishing, 1981; *Satan's Kids,* Hoffman Publishing, 1982.

AVOCATIONAL INTERESTS: Game conservation.

* * *

MOHR, Jack
See MOHR, Gordon

* * *

MOLLENKOTT, Virginia R(amey) 1932-

PERSONAL: Born January 28, 1932, in Philadelphia, Pa.; daughter of Robert Franklin (a chiropractor) and May (Lotz) Ramey; married Friedrich H. Mollenkott (a teacher), June 17, 1954 (divorced); children: Paul F. *Education:* Bob Jones University, B.A., 1953; Temple University, M.A., 1955; New York University, Ph.D., 1964. *Politics:* Independent. *Religion:* Episcopal. *Home:* 11 Yearling Trail, Mt. Laurel Lakes, Hewitt, N.J. 07421. *Office:* Department of English, William Paterson College, 300 Pompton Rd., Wayne, N.J. 07470.

CAREER: Temple University, Philadelphia, Pa., instructor in English, 1954-55; Shelton College, Ringwood, N.J., instructor, 1955-56, associate professor of English and chairperson of department, 1956-63; Nyack Missionary College, Nyack, N.Y., chairperson of English department, 1963-67; William Paterson College, Wayne, N.J., associate professor, 1967-74, professor of English, 1974—, chairperson of department, 1972-76. Member of Task Force of Women of Faith in the '80s, 1980—. Stylistic consultant to New International Version Bible Translation Committee, 1970-75. *Member:* Modern Language

Association of America (assembly delegate, 1975-78; member of executive committee, Division on Religion and Literature, 1977-81), Milton Society of America (member of executive committee, 1975-78), National Council of Teachers of English, Conference on Christianity and Literature (member of board of directors, 1974-77), National Council of Churches (member of Inclusive Language Lectionary Committee, 1981—), New York University English Graduate Association (member of steering committee, 1963—; president, 1967-68).

WRITINGS: *Adamant and Stone Chips: A Christian Humanist Approach to Knowledge,* Word, Inc., 1967; *In Search of Balance,* Word, Inc., 1969; (editor) *Adam among the Television Trees: An Anthology of Verse by Contemporary Christian Poets,* Word, Inc., 1971; *Women, Men and the Bible,* Abingdon, 1977; (with Letha Scanzoni) *Is the Homosexual My Neighbor?: Another Christian View,* Harper, 1978; *Speech, Silence, Action!: The Cycle of Faith,* Abingdon, 1980; *The Divine Feminine: Biblical Imagery of God as Female,* Crossroad, 1983; (co-editor) *An Inclusive Language Lectionary,* Westminster, 1983; (with Catherine Barry) *Views from the Intersection,* Crossroad, 1984.

Contributor: Ted Hipple, editor, *Readings for Teaching in Secondary Schools,* Macmillan, 1973; J. Max Patrick and Roger B. Rollins, editors, *Trust to Good Verses: Essays in Honor of Robert Herrick,* University of Pittsburgh Press, 1974; James D. Simmonds, editor, *Milton Studies VI,* University of Pittsburgh Press, 1975; Paul Jewett, editor, *Man as Male and Female,* Eerdmans, 1975; *The Milton Encyclopedia,* Bucknell University Press, 1978; J. M. Patrick and Roger H. Sundell, editors, *Milton and the Art of Sacred Song,* University of Wisconsin Press, 1979; Virginia Hearn, editor, *Our Struggle to Serve: The Stories of 15 Evangelical Women,* Word, Inc., 1979; Gerald H. Anderson and Thomas F. Stransky, *Liberation Theologies in North America and Europe,* Paulist/Newman, 1979; Lina Mainiero, editor, *American Women Writers: A Critical Reference Guide from Colonial Times to the Present,* Ungar, 1982.

Also contributor to *The Christian Ministry in a World of Crisis,* 1970, *Spinning a Sacred Yarn: Women Speak from the Pulpit,* 1982, and *Peacemakers: Christian Voices from the New Abolitionist Movement,* edited by Jim Wallis, 1983. Contributor to journals, including *Christianity Today, Studies in Philology, Today's Education, Christian Century, Christianity and Crisis,* and *Journal of English and Germanic Philology.* Assistant editor, *Seventeenth-Century News;* chief bibliographer, Conference on Christianity and Literature *Newsletter,* 1967-78; member of editorial board, *Studies in Mystical Literature,* 1982—.

WORK IN PROGRESS: A book on biblical hermeneutics; a book on New Age Evangelism; an article for *Studies in Formative Spirituality;* many articles for various journals on the importance of inclusive God-language and male-female mutuality.

SIDELIGHTS: Virginia R. Mollenkott writes *CA* that "the possibility of nuclear holocaust leaves little time for human transformation. Nevertheless I have faith that global synergy may yet be achieved through God's grace and human effort. All of my work attempts to contribute to a transformation from machismo to mutuality."

* * *

MOORE, Thomas Gale 1930-

PERSONAL: Born November 6, 1930, in Washington, D.C.; son of Charles Godwin (a naval officer) and Beatrice (McLean) Moore; married Cassandra Chrones (a college teacher), December 28, 1958; children: Charles, Antonia. *Education:* Attended Massachusetts Institute of Technology, 1949-51; George Washington University, B.A., 1957; University of Chicago, M.A., 1959, Ph.D., 1961. *Religion:* None. *Home:* 3766 La Donna, Palo Alto, Calif. 94306. *Office:* Hoover Institution, Stanford, Calif. 94305.

CAREER: Chase Manhattan Bank, New York, N.Y., foreign research economist, 1960-61; Carnegie Institute of Technology (now Carnegie-Mellon University), Pittsburgh, Pa., assistant professor of economics, 1961-65; Michigan State University, East Lansing, associate professor of economics, 1965-68; U.S. Council of Economic Advisers, Washington, D.C., senior staff economist, 1968-70; Michigan State University, professor of economics, 1970-74; Hoover Institution, Stanford, Calif., senior fellow and director of domestic studies program, 1974—. Adjunct scholar, American Enterprise Institute, 1972—, and CATO Institute, 1982—. Member of U.S. Department of Commerce's Economic Advisory Board, 1971-73; member of advisory committee of RAND and the National Science Foundation, 1975-76; member of advisory board of the Reason Foundation, 1982—, and of the Urban Institute, 1982-84; member of Governor Reagan's Energy Policy Advisory Group, 1980, Governor Reagan's Regulatory Policy Advisory Group, 1980, and President-elect Reagan's transition team of the Interstate Commerce Commission, 1980. Stanford Savings and Loan, member of board of directors, 1979-82, chairman of board of directors, 1982. *Military service:* U.S. Navy, 1951-55. *Member:* American Association for the Advancement of Science, American Economic Association, Western Economic Association, Southern Economic Association.

WRITINGS: (Contributor) *Studies in Banking Competition and the Banking Structure,* U.S. Treasury, 1966; *The Economics of the American Theater,* Duke University Press, 1968; (contributor) Walter Adams, editor, *The Structure of American Industry,* 4th edition (Moore was not associated with earlier editions), Macmillan, 1971; *Freight Transportation Regulation,* American Enterprise Institute, 1972; (contributor) *Public Claims on U.S. Output,* American Enterprise Institute, 1973; *Trucking Regulation: Lessons from Europe,* American Enterprise Institute, 1976; *Uranium Enrichment and Public Policy,* American Enterprise Institute, 1978; (contributor) E. J. McAllister, editor, *Agenda for Progress,* Heritage Foundation, 1981; (contributor) A. Rabushka and P. Duignan, editors, *The United States in the 1980's,* Hoover Press, 1980.

Contributor to *Arts Management* and to banking and economic journals. Member of advisory board of *Journal of Post-Misesian Economics,* 1983—.

* * *

MOORE, Trevor Wyatt 1924-

PERSONAL: Born July 21, 1924; son of Glendon Hazelitt (a retail executive) and Ruth Edna (Wyatt) Moore; married Marcena M. Idle, June 10, 1944; children: Marci (Mrs. J. Louis Dettling), Trevor Wyatt Dunstan II, Gregory Benedict, John Joseph, Veronica Ruth, David Michael, Martha Elizabeth, Francesca Maria, Peter Mark. *Education:* Northwestern University, student, 1947-48; Loyola University, Chicago, Ill., Ph.B., 1950; Nagoya University, Ph.D., 1960; Orthodox Seminary, New York, Th.L., 1971. *Address:* Holy Resurrection Cathedral Rectory, 1611 Wallace St., Philadelphia, Pa. 19130.

CAREER: Ordained priest of Orthodox Catholic Church, 1970; elected and consecrated Bishop of Philadelphia, Pa., 1971; elevated to Archbishop, Orthodox Catholic Archdiocese of Philadelphia, 1971; elevated to Metropolitan, 1973; became Metropolitan-Primate, Holy Eastern Orthodox Church of the United States, 1975. *Christian Art,* Chicago, Ill., editorial director, 1962-63; *Anno Domini,* Jenkintown, Pa., editor, 1963-64; *St. Joseph Magazine,* Saint Benedict, Ore., art editor, 1966-69; *WAY/Catholic Viewpoints,* San Francisco, Calif., contributing editor, 1968—; *Christian Century,* Chicago, editor-at-large, 1971-76. Chairman, American Conference of Orthodox Bishops, 1976-77; president, Holy Synod, Holy Eastern Orthodox Church of the United States, 1977—; chairman of advisory board, Hahnemann Medical College and Hospital Mental Health/Mental Retardation Center, Philadelphia, 1976-79. Lecturer, World Center for Liturgical Studies. *Wartime service:* U.S. Merchant Marine, 1942-46; became senior staff officer.

MEMBER: Royal Society of Arts (England; fellow), American Society for Church Architecture (corporate member), Guild for Religious Architecture (associate member). *Awards, honors:* American College and Seminary of the Orthodox Catholic Church (New York), D.D., 1971, D.Ed., 1971, D.Th., 1972; "Old Master" honors, Purdue University, 1972; D.D. from Universidad de los Pueblos de las Americas (San Juan, P.R.), 1973; Ecumenical Legion of Honor award, Chapel of the Four Chaplins, Temple University, 1976; Renaissance Award, City of Philadelphia, 1978; Masterman Community Service Award, 1980.

WRITINGS: Where the Action Is, World Center for Liturgical Studies, 1969; (with wife, Marcena Moore) *Sex, Sex, Sex,* Ave Maria Press and Pilgrim Press, 1969; *The Service of the Twelve Passion Gospels* (Holy Friday Matins), Resurrection Press, 1979; (editor) *Eastern Orthodox Prayers,* Resurrection Press, 1982; *Matins for Holy Saturday,* Resurrection Press, 1983; *Journey to the Kingdom,* Resurrection Press, 1983. Also author of audio-visual production, *Miracles of Jesus Christ,* 1983. Contributor to *Christian Century* and other periodicals.

WORK IN PROGRESS: Contributions of the Russian-American Orthodox Church to American Ecclesiastical History, for Resurrection Press; *The Divine Liturgy of St. John Chrysostom,* with rubrical notes and commentary.

SIDELIGHTS: Trevor Moore and his wife described the troubled life of an activist family in suburbia in "Why They Ran Us Out of Jenkintown," which appeared in *Look.* They said that harassment (their sidewalk had been painted black, the house pelted with eggs, and their children, who printed an underground newspaper, beaten at school) reached one peak after the publication of *Sex, Sex, Sex.* Eventually, total family involvement in the peace movement led to termination of the lease on their rented house and an eviction notice. Moore adds that his political activism and role of clergyman have led to work on "a theology of survival of the person and human spirit, *not* to be confused with the fanatical goals of the contemporary 'survivialist cult.' " Moore also notes that "the duties and pressures of administering a national Orthodox-Greek Catholic Church, a cathedral parish and social services center and many civic duties, as well as travel to all parishes, missions and schools leaves little time at present for anything but theological writing, a circumstance which is often frustrating but dictated by ecclesiastical vocation."

BIOGRAPHICAL/CRITICAL SOURCES: Look, October 20, 1970; *Christian Century,* March 3, 1971.

MORAN, James Sterling 1909-
(Jim Moran)

PERSONAL: Born November 24, 1909, in Woodstock, Va.; son of J. Sterling and Nellie (Bryant) Moran; married Linda Howes, January 6, 1976. *Education:* Educated in public schools. *Politics:* "Apolitical." *Religion:* "Anhhhh." *Office:* Jim Moran Associates, 200 Fifth Ave., New York, N.Y. 10010.

CAREER: Varied career as lecturer on sightseeing bus, door-to-door salesman, aviator, teacher of classical guitar, sound engineer, airport engineer, and newspaperman before entering publicity business in 1938; currently head of Jim Moran Associates, New York, N.Y. Guest on hundreds of television programs in role of world traveler interested in archaeology, primitive people, unusual inventions, practical jokes, and publicity stunts; has appeared on "The Tonight Show Starring Johnny Carson," "Today," "David Frost Show," "Steve Allen Show," "Ernie Kovacs Show," and "Jack Paar Show."

WRITINGS: Sophocles, the Hyena: A Fable (juvenile), McGraw, 1954; *Miserable: A Story about a Dinosaur* (juvenile), Bobbs-Merrill, 1960; *Why Men Shouldn't Marry,* Lyle Stuart, 1969; *The Frustrations of the Irish,* Cornerstone Library, 1971; *The Classical Women* (photographs), Playboy Press, 1972; *How I Became an Authority on Sex,* Stein & Day, 1973; *The Wonders of Magic Squares,* Vintage Books, 1981.

WORK IN PROGRESS: Linda and the Magic Bubbles, for children; *The God Biz,* a history of religion; untitled memoirs.

SIDELIGHTS: The Classical Woman has been translated into Italian; *Why Men Shouldn't Marry* has been translated into French and Finnish. Moran has been the subject of three television documentaries.

BIOGRAPHICAL/CRITICAL SOURCES: Saturday Review, April 5, 1969.

* * *

MORAN, Jim
See MORAN, James Sterling

* * *

MORGAN, (Walter) Jefferson 1940-

PERSONAL: Born March 30, 1940, in Salt Lake City, Utah; son of Thomas Ralph (an executive) and Althea (a pharmacist and nurse; maiden name, Ball) Morgan; married Patricia Williams, 1960 (divorced, 1965); married Jinx Adams (a writer), March 26, 1971; children: Stacy, Derick, Coulter, *Education:* University of California, teaching credential, 1967; also attended Diablo Valley College, Oakland City College, University of Chicago, University of California, Berkeley, Stanford University, and Harvard University. *Home and office address:* P.O. Box 9827, St. Thomas, Virgin Islands 00801. *Agent:* Carl Brandt, Brandt & Brandt, 1501 Broadway, New York, N.Y. 10036.

CAREER: Oakland Tribune, Oakland, Calif., copyboy, 1957-58, police reporter, 1958-59, assistant state editor, 1959-60, courthouse bureau chief, 1960-63, city desk rewrite man, 1963-69, special writer, 1969-76, author of column "Dining with Wine," 1976; free-lance writer, 1976—. Western U.S. correspondent for Manchester *Guardian,* 1967—. Instructor at

Peralta Colleges, 1967-69. Member of Society of Nieman Fellows. *Member:* Royal Commonwealth Society, Confrerie de la Marmite, San Francisco Press Club, Harvard Club. *Awards, honors:* Newswriting prizes from Associated Press, 1966, 1969, 1971, 1973; William F. Knowland Award, 1966, 1969, 1970; first prize from San Francisco Press Club, 1970, 1973; Nieman fellow at Harvard University, 1971-72; McQuade Award from Association of Catholic Newsmen, 1974; award from California Taxpayers Association, 1974.

WRITINGS: Guide to California Wines, Dutton, 1968, 3rd edition, 1975; *Adventures in the Wine Country,* Chronicle Books, 1971, revised edition, 1976; *Why Have They Taken Our Children?,* Delacorte, 1978; (with Donald T. Lunde) *The Die Song: A Journey into the Mind of a Mass Murderer,* Norton, 1980. Contributor to popular magazines, including *Reader's Digest, National Wildlife, Bon Appetit, Parade,* and *Travel and Leisure.*

WORK IN PROGRESS: Magazine writing.

SIDELIGHTS: The Die Song: A Journey into the Mind of a Mass Murderer is a study of Herbert Mullin, a paranoid schizophrenic, and is based on psychiatrist Donald T. Lunde's examination of this convicted killer. Calling the writing "excellent," *Los Angeles Times Book Review* critic Robert Kirsch adds that what is made clear in *The Die Song* "is the skewed nature of the person in the grip of his disorder, the swing between normal behavior and the grip of a delusional system that seems to the killer logical and determined."

BIOGRAPHICAL/CRITICAL SOURCES: New York Times Book Review, March 30, 1980; *Los Angeles Times Book Review,* April 13, 1980.

* * *

**MORGAN, McKayla
See BASILE, Gloria Vitanza**

* * *

**MORGAN, Michaela
See BASILE, Gloria Vitanza**

* * *

MORGAN, Roger P(earce) 1932-

PERSONAL: Born March 3, 1932, in Burton, England; son of Donald Emlyn (a school principal) and Esther (Pearce) Morgan; married Annie-Francoise Combes (a university teacher); children: Caroline, Mark, Patrick, Benedict. *Education:* Cambridge University, B.A., 1953, M.A., 1957, Ph.D., 1959; graduate study at University of Paris, 1953-54, and University of Hamburg, 1955. *Politics:* Labour.

CAREER: University of London, London, England, tutor in social studies, 1957-59; University College of Wales, Aberystwyth, lecturer in international politics, 1959-63; University of Sussex, Brighton, England, lecturer in history and international relations, beginning 1963. Visiting professor of public law and government at Columbia University; research associate at Center for International Affairs, Harvard University, 1965-66. Lecturer to adult education groups, American student groups visiting Europe, and university extension courses. *Member:* Political Studies Association, Royal Institute for International Affairs, Institute for Strategic Studies, Association of University Teachers.

WRITINGS: The German Social Democrats and the First International: 1864-1872, Cambridge University Press, 1965; *Modern Germany,* Hamish Hamilton, 1966; (with James L. Henderson and others) *Since 1945: Aspects of Contemporary World History,* Methuen, 1966.

(Editor) *Germany, 1870-1970: A Hundred Years of Turmoil,* Macdonald & Co., 1970; (editor with Karl Kaiser) *Britain and West Germany: Changing Societies and the Future of Foreign Policy,* Oxford University Press for the Royal Institute of International Affairs, 1971; *The New Communications Technology and Its Social Implications,* International Broadcast Institute, 1971; *Western European Politics since 1945: The Shaping of the European Community,* Batsford, 1972; (editor) *The Study of International Affairs: Essays in Honour of Kenneth Younger,* Oxford University Press, 1972; *High Politics, Low Politics: Toward a Foreign Policy for Western Europe,* Sage, 1973; *The United States and West Germany, 1945-1973: A Study in Alliance Politics,* Oxford University Press, 1974; *The Unsettled Peace: A Study of the Cold War in Europe,* BBC Publications, 1974; (editor) *Mid-Century World,* Newsweek, 1975; (editor) *Sunrise and Stormclouds,* Newsweek, 1975; (editor) *Decade of Crisis,* Newsweek, 1975; *West Germany's Foreign Policy Agenda,* Sage, 1978.

Moderates and Conservatives in Western Europe, Heinemann Educational Books, 1982. Contributor of articles and book reviews to periodicals.

AVOCATIONAL INTERESTS: Music.†

* * *

MORRIS, A(ndrew) J(ames) A(nthony) 1936-

PERSONAL: Born November 7, 1936, in Caerphilly, Wales; son of George (a coalworker) and Minnie (Smart) Morris; married Cicely Alison Rosser (a social worker), December 22, 1958; children: Anthony John Lloyd, Fiona Eleanor. *Education:* London School of Economics and Political Science, LL.B., 1958, M.A., 1963; Institute of Education, London, B.A., 1959, D.Litt., 1967. *Home:* 50 Marlborough Park S., Belfast BT9 6HS, Northern Ireland. *Office:* History Department, University of Ulster, Jordanstown Campus, Newton Abbey, Northern Ireland.

CAREER: Schoolmaster, 1959-62, and 1964-66; University of London, London School of Economics and Political Science, London, England, senior research officer, 1967-73; Ulster College, Jordanstown, Northern Ireland, professor of philosophy, politics, and history, 1974-84, head of department; University of Ulster, Jordanstown Campus, Newton Abbey, Northern Ireland, professor of history and head of department, 1984—. Visiting professor at University of North Carolina at Charlotte, 1973, University of Witwatersrand, Johannesburg, 1981, 1982; research fellow, Nuffield Foundation, 1982-83.

WRITINGS: Parliamentary Democracy in the Nineteenth Century, Pergamon, 1967; *Radicalism against War, 1906-14,* Longman, 1972, Rowman & Littlefield, 1974; (editor and contributor) *Edwardian Radicalism, 1900-1914,* Routledge & Kegan Paul, 1974; *C. P. Trevelyan, 1870-1958: Portrait of a Radical,* Blackstaff, 1977, St. Martin's, 1978; *The Scaremongers: The Advocates of War and Rearmament,* Routledge & Kegan Paul, 1984. Contributor of articles and reviews to political science and history journals. Editor of *Moirae,* 1976-84.

WORK IN PROGRESS: Several books and essays on various aspects of the political history of Edwardian England.

MORRIS, Tina 1941-

PERSONAL: Born April 8, 1941; children: two daughters. *Education:* "Irrelevant." *Home:* Forge Farm, Garstang Rd., Bilsborrow, Preston, Lancashire, England.

CAREER: "Irrelevant."

WRITINGS: Flowers of Snow: City Poems, Screeches Publications, 1964; (editor) *Victims of Our Fear,* Screeches Publications, 1964; *Whether You or I Love or Hate: Poems of Love,* Screeches Publications, 1965; *A Song of the Great Peace,* edited by Dave Cunliffe, B.B. Books, 1967; (editor with Cunliffe) *Thunderbolts of Peace and Liberation,* B.B. Books, 1969; (contributor) *New Writers VII,* Calder & Boyars, 1969; (with T. K. Metcalf) *Uncreated Stars,* B.B. Books, 1970; *Tree* (poems), Court Poetry Press, 1978; *A Child's Picture of the World,* Speed Limit Press, 1979. Contributor to journals and little magazines.

WORK IN PROGRESS: "A long-lasting love affair with trees currently drives me to express the spirit of trees (as I feel it) in many ways—prose, poetry, novels, children's books (if I keep trying, I'll get it right eventually!)."

SIDELIGHTS: Tina Morris told *CA:* "With two young daughters, a large food-producing garden, and a vast family of assorted hairies to care for, I'm spared the effort of feeling I *ought* to be writing in any spare moments. Now, to achieve anything, I find I have to forget all the pencil-sharpening routines and really get 'stuck-in.' It's wonderful discipline!"

She added that she is "thoroughly frustrated by the publishing world. I *don't* have a stack of rejection slips but I *do* have a pile of letters from publishers praising my work then always, alas, saying that they can't/won't publish it because it isn't COMMERCIAL enough and/or short stories just don't sell. . . . My one consolation is that the writing comes first—as both joy and agony—and the attempt to get published is just a side-effect!"

A *Times Literary Supplement* reviewer states that Tina Morris's early work "qualifies . . . for the dream label. Bizarre violence, rape, incest, sensations of gestation and death alternate in a planned but confusing way in a series of connecting paragraphs written in the new international avant-garde prose. . . . But despite the mannerisms Miss Morris rarely loses one's attention. This kind of dream material is becoming routine in current 'underground' literature, but she manages to evoke many of her personal nightmare images with chilling effect."

BIOGRAPHICAL/CRITICAL SOURCES: Times Literary Supplement, August 29, 1969.

* * *

MORRIS, William 1913-

PERSONAL: Born April 13, 1913, in Boston, Mass.; son of Charles Hyndman (an attorney) and Elizabeth Margaret (Hanna) Morris; married Jane Frazer, August 7, 1939; married Mary Elizabeth Davis (a writer), February 8, 1947; children: Ann Elizabeth (Mrs. Paul Downie), Susan McLeod, John Boyd, William Frazer, Mary Elizabeth, Evan Nathanael. *Education:* Harvard University, A.B., 1935. *Politics:* Independent Democrat. *Religion:* Episcopalian. *Home:* 355 Sound Beach Ave., Old Greenwich, Conn. 06870. *Office:* 27 West 44th St., New York, N.Y. 10036.

CAREER: Newman School, Lakewood, N.J., instructor in English and Latin, 1935-37; G. & C. Merriam Co. (publisher), Springfield, Mass., member of college department staff, 1937-43; Grosset & Dunlap, Inc., New York City, managing editor, 1945-47, executive editor, 1947-53, editor-in-chief, 1953-60; Grolier, Inc., New York City, executive editor, *International Encyclopedia,* 1960-62, editor-in-chief, *Grolier Universal Encyclopedia,* 1962-64; American Heritage Publishing Co., New York City, editor-in-chief, *American Heritage Dictionary,* 1964-71; Xerox Family Education Services, New York City, editor-in-chief, *Xerox Intermediate Dictionary* and *Weekly Reader Beginning Dictionary,* 1971-75. *Military service:* U.S. Maritime Service, 1943-45; served in various combat areas as communications officer; became lieutenant junior grade.

MEMBER: National Council of Teachers of English, Modern Language Association of America, American Library Association, Society for General Semantics; Dutch Treat Club (president emeritus), Society of Salurians, Overseas Press Club, Coffee House, and Harvard Club (all New York); Old Greenwich Boat Club.

WRITINGS: (Editor) *Words: The New Dictionary,* Grosset, 1947, revised edition (with Charles P. Chadsey and Harold Wentworth) published as *The Grosset Webster Dictionary,* 1953, new edition, 1966; (editor) *Concise Biographical Dictionary,* Grosset, 1949; (editor with wife, Mary Morris) *The Concise Dictionary of Famous Men and Women,* revised edition, Grosset, 1951; *It's Easy to Increase Your Vocabulary* (juvenile), Harper, 1957, revised edition, Penguin, 1975; (with M. Morris) *The Word Game Book,* Harper, 1959, revised edition, Penguin, 1975; (with M. Morris) *Dictionary of Word and Phrase Origins,* Harper, Volume I, 1962, Volume II, 1967, Volume III, 1971; *The William Morris Self-Enrichment Vocabulary Program,* Grolier, 1965; (editor-in-chief) *The American Heritage Dictionary of the English Language,* American Heritage Publishing Co., 1969, new college edition, 1975.

Your Heritage of Words (juvenile), Dell, 1970; (editor and author of introduction) Harriet Wittels and Joan Greisman, *The Young People's Thesaurus* (juvenile), Grosset, 1973; (editor-in-chief) *The Xerox Intermediate Dictionary* (juvenile), Xerox Family Education Services, 1973, published as *The Ginn Intermediate Dictionary,* Ginn, 1977; (editor-in-chief) *The Weekly Reader Beginning Dictionary* (juvenile), Xerox Family Education Services, 1973; (with M. Morris) *Harper Dictionary of Contemporary Usage,* Harper, 1975, 2nd edition, 1983; (with M. Morris) *Morris Dictionary of Word and Phrase Origins,* Harper, 1977.

Editor, "Berlitz Self-Teacher Language Books" series, 1949-53. Consulting editor, *Funk & Wagnalls New Standard Dictionary,* international edition, 1954-58, and *New College Standard Dictionary,* 1958-60. Author of column "William Morris on Words," Bell-McClure Syndicate, 1954-68; author, with M. Morris, of column "Words, Wit, and Wisdom," *Los Angeles Times* Syndicate, 1968-75, and United Feature Syndicate, 1975—. Contributor to *Esquire, Saturday Review, Changing Times, Today's Living,* and other magazines.

SIDELIGHTS: William Morris told *CA:* "I began my writing career by submitting samples of a column about language to a couple of newspaper syndicates. After a year or so, one of them started to run it. That was nearly thirty years ago, and it's still running here and in Mexico and Japan. It has never made much money for me, but it has been the source of much material for books that my wife Mary and I have done and that, on the whole, have been very profitable. I edited the first

American Heritage Dictionary and am enormously proud of my creation. I worked on salary for American Heritage Publishing Co. (plus a few unfulfilled promises) and have often regretted not insisting on a royalty—as I have on all my later works. However, the fame of having created the most exciting American dictionary of this century has led to lectures, TV work, and other things that might not otherwise have come my way."

Several of Morris's books have been translated into Japanese.

* * *

MORTON, Alexander C(lark) 1936-

PERSONAL: Born December 10, 1936; son of Jay Morton (a publisher of newspapers) and Gladys (Arth) Molasky; married; wife's name, Marlena. *Education:* Attended Pennsylvania Military College. *Office:* International Publishing Co., 665 Lavilla Dr., Miami Springs, Fla. 33166.

CAREER: Member of sales and editorial staff of *Hollywood Herald,* Hollywood, Fla., 1958, and WITU-TV, Hallandale, Fla., 1959; Clear Pools, Inc., Hollywood, owner, 1959-65; Home News Publishing, Hialeah, Fla., member of sales and editorial staff, 1964-66; International Publishing Co., Miami Springs, Fla., publisher of *Airline and Travel Food, Duty Free International, Jockey Club Winner's Circle, Grove Isle Club,* and *Passenger and Inflight Services* magazines, 1966—. *Military service:* U.S. Army, 1953-56; became captain. *Member:* U.S. Junior Chamber of Commerce (past international director and international senator).

WRITINGS: (Compiler) *Annual Guide to Careers as an Airline Stewardess,* International Publishing Co., 1968; *What You Need to Know for a Career as an Airline Stewardess,* Cowles, 1968; *The Official 1981-82 Guide to Airline Careers,* Arco, 1981; *The Official 1982-83 Guide to Airline Careers,* Arco, 1982; *The Official 1982-83 Guide to Travel Agent and Travel Careers,* Arco, 1982; *The Official Guide to Food Service and Hospitality Management,* Arco, 1983.

* * *

MOSS, Cynthia J(ane) 1940-

PERSONAL: Born July 24, 1940, in Ossining, N.Y.; daughter of Julian B. (a newspaper publisher) and Lillian (Drion) Moss. *Education:* Smith College, B.A., 1962. *Home and office address:* P.O. Box 48177, Nairobi, Kenya. *Agent:* Wendy Weil, Julian Bach Literary Agency, Inc., 747 Third Ave., New York, N.Y. 10017.

CAREER: Newsweek, New York, N.Y., reporter and researcher, 1964-68; full-time research assistant studying elephant behavior and ecology in Lake Manyara, Tanzania, 1968; assistant to veterinary researchers in Nairobi, Kenya, 1969; research assistant to environmental physiologist on the Athi Plains, Kenya, 1970, and in Tsavo National Park, Kenya, 1970; part-time free-lance journalist, 1970-71; *Wildlife News,* Washington, D.C., editor, 1971—; co-director, Amboseli Elephant Research Project, Amboseli, Kenya, 1979—. Research fellow, Animal Research and Conservation Centre, New York Zoological Society. Part-time research assistant in Amboseli, 1972-75. Research associate, Sub-Department of Animal Behaviour, Cambridge University. Lecturer on elephant social organization and behavior. *Member:* East African Natural History Society. *Awards, honors:* African Wildlife Leadership Foundation grant, 1975; American Book Award nomination for best science paperback book, 1982, for *Portraits in the Wild: Behaviour Studies of East African Mammals;* received grants from the Merlin Foundation and the New York Zoological Society.

WRITINGS: Portraits in the Wild: Behaviour Studies of East African Mammals, Houghton, 1975, 2nd edition, University of Chicago Press, 1982; (contributor) R. Hinde, editor, *Relationships and Social Structure of Some Non-human Primates,* Blackwell Scientific Publications, in press; (editor with David Western) *The Amboseli Elephants,* University of Chicago Press, in press. Author of research report used in making the film "The African Elephant," for Cinema Center Films, 1969. Contributor to various periodicals, including *Smithsonian, Swara, International Wildlife, Nature,* and *Ms.* Member of editorial board, *Elephant.*

WORK IN PROGRESS: A popular book on author's work studying the Amboseli elephants.

SIDELIGHTS: Cynthia J. Moss is a wildlife biologist who has lived in East Africa since 1968 studying elephant behavior and other aspects of African wildlife. P. D. Zimmerman explains in *Newsweek:* "In the 1960's, a new generation of young scientists began trickling into East Africa to study the peculiarities of wild animals. . . . In many cases, the work of these wildlife pioneers provided the first systematic study of creatures previously known largely through myth and random observation. Cynthia Moss [popularizes] fresh information without in any way vulgarizing it."

In 1975, Moss published *Portraits in the Wild: Behaviour Studies of East African Mammals.* According to a reviewer for *Choice,* Moss selected "typical species of several mammal groups and [reported] on the scientific studies that have been or are being made on their behavior and ecology." Jane E. Brody writes in the *New York Times* that "the leisurely descriptions of the various animals and how they have been studied are replete with intriguing and often surprising details."

AVOCATIONAL INTERESTS: Camping in wild parts of East Africa; horseback riding on the Athi plains.

BIOGRAPHICAL/CRITICAL SOURCES: Publishers Weekly, September 22, 1975; *Newsweek,* December 1, 1975; *Choice,* March, 1976; *New York Times,* September 7, 1982, February 15, 1983, November 15, 1983.

* * *

MOSSE, George L(achmann) 1918-

PERSONAL: Born September 20, 1918, in Berlin, Germany; naturalized U.S. citizen; son of Hans (a publisher) and Felicia Lachmann-Mosse. *Education:* Attended Cambridge University, 1936-39; Haverford College, B.S., 1941; Harvard University, Ph.D., 1946. *Home:* 36 Glenway, Madison, Wis. *Office:* Department of History, University of Wisconsin—Madison, Madison, Wis. 53706.

CAREER: University of Iowa, Iowa City, 1945-55, began as instructor, became associate professor; University of Wisconsin—Madison, 1955—, began as associate professor, became professor of history, John C. Bascom Professor of History, 1965—. Visiting professor at Stanford University, 1963-64, Jewish Theological Seminary of America, 1977, Capetown University, 1980, and University of Munich, 1982-83; Hebrew University, Jerusalem, visiting professor, 1969-70, 1972, 1974, 1976, 1978, Koebner Professor of History, 1979—; visiting fellow at Australian National University, 1972, 1979. Member of board of directors of Wiener Library, 1973—, and Leo

Baeck Institute, 1978—; member of board of overseers of Tauber Center for Jewish Studies, Brandeis University, 1980—. Educational consultant, Coronet Instructional Films, 1954—. Consultant, U.S. High Commission in Germany (U.S. Information Service), 1951, 1955.

MEMBER: American Society for Reformation Research (president, 1961-62), American Historical Association, American Society for Church History, American Association of University Professors (president, Iowa Conference, 1953-54). *Awards, honors:* Huntington Library grant, 1953; Social Science Research Council grant, 1961; E. Harris Harbison Prize, Danforth Foundation, 1970; D.Litt., Carthage College, 1973; "Aqui Storia" prize, 1975.

WRITINGS: The Struggle for Sovereignty in England: From the Reign of Queen Elizabeth to the Petition of Right, Michigan State College Press, 1950, reprinted, Octagon, 1968; *The Reformation,* Holt, 1953, 3rd revised edition, 1963; *The Holy Pretence: A Study of Christianity and Reason of State from William Perkins to John Winthrop,* Basil Blackwell, 1957, reprinted, Fertig, 1968.

The Culture of Western Europe: The Nineteenth and Twentieth Centuries, Rand McNally, 1961, 2nd edition, 1974; *The Crisis of German Ideology: The Intellectual Origins of the Third Reich,* Grosset, 1964, reprinted, Schocken, 1981; (compiler with Walter Ze'ev Laqueur) *1914: The Coming of the First World War,* Harper, 1966; (with Laqueur) *The Left-Wing Intellectuals between the Wars, 1919-1939,* Gannon, 1966; (with Helmut Georg Koenigsberger) *Europe in the Sixteenth Century,* Holt, 1968; (author of introduction) Max Nordau, *Degeneration,* Fertig, 1968.

Germans and Jews: The Right, the Left, and the Search for a "Third Force" in Pre-Nazi Germany, Fertig, 1970; *The Nationalization of the Masses: Political Symbolism and Mass Movements in Germany from the Napoleonic Wars through the Third Reich,* Fertig, 1977; *Toward the Final Solution: A History of European Racism,* Fertig, 1977; *Interviste Sul Nazismo,* Laterza, 1977, translation published as *Nazism: A Historical and Comparative Analysis of National Socialism,* Transaction Books, 1978; *Masses and Man: Nationalist and Fascist Perceptions of Reality,* Fertig, 1980.

Editor: (With Hill, Cameron, and Petrovich) *Europe in Review: Readings and Sources since 1500,* Rand McNally, 1957, revised edition, 1964; *Nazi Culture: Intellectual, Cultural, and Social Life in the Third Reich,* Grosset, 1966; (and contributor) *International Fascism, 1920-1945,* Harper, 1966; *Socialism and War,* Weidenfeld & Nicolson, 1966; *History Today in USA, Britain, France, Italy, Germany, Poland, India, Czechoslovakia, Spain, Holland, Sweden,* Weidenfeld & Nicolson, 1967; (with Laqueur) *Literature and Politics in the Twentieth Century,* Harper, 1967; *Literature and Society,* Weidenfeld & Nicolson, 1967; (with Laqueur) *The New History: Trends in Historical Research and Writing since World War Two,* Harper, 1967; *Education and Social Structure in the Twentieth Century,* Harper, 1967; *The Middle East,* Weidenfeld & Nicolson, 1968; *Reappraisals: A New Look at History,* Weidenfeld & Nicolson, 1968; *Urbanism: The City in History,* Weidenfeld & Nicolson, 1969; *The Great Depression,* Weidenfeld & Nicolson, 1969.

Generations in Conflict, Weidenfeld & Nicolson, 1970; (with B. Vago) *Jews and Non-Jews in Eastern Europe, 1918-1945,* Wiley, 1974; (with Laqueur) *Historians in Politics,* Sage Publications, 1974; *Police Forces in History,* Sage Publications, 1974; *International Fascism: New Thoughts and New Approaches,* Sage Publications, 1979.

Contributor: Schuyler, editor, *The Making of English History,* Dryden, 1952; Stuart Woolf, editor, *The Nature of Fascism,* Weidenfeld & Nicolson, 1958.

Entscheidungsjahr 1933, J.C.B. Mohr, 1964; S. Burell, editor, *Religious Ideas and Institutions of Western Civilization,* Macmillan, 1964; *Studies of the Leo Baeck Institute,* Ungar, 1967; Brison Gooch, editor, *Interpreting European History,* Dorsey Press, 1967; *Foundations of the Nineteenth Century,* Fertig, 1968; Peter N. Stearns, editor, *A Century for Debate,* Dodd, 1969.

New Cambridge Modern History, Volume IV: *The Decline of Spain and the Thirty Years War,* Cambridge University Press, 1970; *Zur Geschichte Der Jeden in Deutschland Im 19. Und 20. Jahrhundert,* Leo Baeck Institute, 1971; Robert J. Scall, editor, *Forces of Order and Movement in Europe,* Houghton, 1971; David Daiches and David Thorlby, editors, *Literature and Western Civilization,* Aldus Books, 1972; Boyers, editor, *The Legacy of Refugee Intellectuals,* Schocken, 1972; Eugene Kamenka, editor, *Nationalism: Yesterday and Today,* Australian National University Press, 1973; Reinhold Grimm and Johst Hermand, editors, *Popularitat und Trivialitat,* Athenaum Verlag (Frankfurt), 1974; Grimm and Hermand, editors, *Geschichte im Gegenwartsdrama,* Kohlhammer, 1977; Klaus Vondung, editor, *Das Kriegserlebnis,* Gottingen, 1979; (with Stephen Lampert) Joel E. Dimsdale, editor, *Survivors, Victims and Perpetrators: Essays on the Nazi Holocaust,* Westbury Press, 1979; *Aldo Moro: L'intelligenza e gli avvenimenti, Testi 1959-1978,* Garzanti, 1979.

Kamenka, editor, *Community,* Edward Arnold, 1980; Grimm and Hermand, editors, *Faschismus und Avant Garde,* Atheneum, 1980; Volker R. Berghahn and Martin Kitchem, editors, *Germany in the Age of Total War,* Croom Helm, 1981. Also contributor to *Fascism: An Anthology,* edited by Nathaniel Greene, 1968, *Manners, Morals, Movements,* edited by Werner Braatz and others, 1970, and *Deutsches Utopisches Denken im 20. Jahrhundert,* edited by Grimm and Hermand, 1974. Contributor to encyclopedias and yearbooks; contributor to numerous academic journals. Co-editor, *Journal of Contemporary History,* 1965—.

SIDELIGHTS: George L. Mosse's work has been translated into Polish, Italian, Spanish, and French.

BIOGRAPHICAL/CRITICAL SOURCES: New York Times Book Review, July 12, 1970, February 8, 1981; *Commentary,* October, 1970; *Times Literary Supplement,* July 23, 1971, September 26, 1975, December 23, 1977.

* * *

MOTHER MARY ANTHONY
    See WEINIG, Jean Maria

* * *

MOURSUND, David G. 1936-

PERSONAL: Born November 3, 1936, in Eugene, Ore.; son of Andrew F. (a professor) and Lulu (Vorleck) Moursund; married Janet Peck (a professor), August 12, 1961; children: Elizabeth Ann, David Andrew, Russell Alan, Jennifer Lee. *Education:* University of Oregon, B.A., 1958; University of Wisconsin—Madison, M.A., 1960, Ph.D., 1963. *Home:* 2420

Olive, Eugene, Ore. 97405. *Office:* Department of Computer and Information Science, University of Oregon, Eugene, Ore. 97403.

CAREER: Michigan State University, East Lansing, assistant professor, 1963-66, associate professor of mathematics, 1966-67; University of Oregon, Eugene, associate professor of mathematics, 1967-69, head of department of computer science, 1969-75, associate professor, 1975-76, professor of computer science, 1976—. International Council for Computers in Education, Inc., founder and president, 1979—. Co-founder of Oregon Council for Computer Education, 1971; member of advisory board, Apple Education Foundation. Consultant. *Military service:* U.S. Army, 1958-59; became second lieutenant. *Member:* Association for Computing Machinery, American Mathematical Association, Phi Beta Kappa.

WRITINGS: (With Charles Duris) *Elementary Theory and Application of Numerical Analysis,* McGraw, 1967; *How Computers Do It,* Wadsworth, 1969; *Problem Analysis and Solution Using FORTRAN IV,* Wadsworth, 1970; (editor with Dunlap) *Computers in Education Resource Handbook,* University of Oregon Press, 1973, 5th revised edition, 1977; *BASIC Programming for Computer Literacy,* McGraw, 1978; (with Karen Billings) *Are You Computer Literate?,* dilithium, 1979; (with Billings) *Problem Solving with Calculators,* dilithium, 1979.

School Administrator's Introduction to Instructional Use of Computers (monograph), International Council for Computers in Education, 1980, 3rd revised edition, 1983; *Calculators in the Classroom: With Applications for Elementary and Middle School Teachers,* Wiley, 1981; *Introduction to Computers in Education for Elementary and Middle School Teachers,* International Council for Computers in Education, 1981; *Parent's Guide to Computers in Education* (monograph), International Council for Computers in Education, 1983. Also author of booklets on educational computing published by International Council for Computers in Education. Editor-in-chief, *Computing Teacher,* 1979—.

* * *

MUELLER, Gerhard G(ottlob) 1930-

PERSONAL: Born December 4, 1930, in Eineborn, Germany; naturalized U.S. citizen, 1957; son of Gottlob Karl (a farmer) and Elisabeth Charlotte (Hossack) Mueller; married Coralie George, June 7, 1958; children: Kent, Elisabeth, Jeffrey. *Education:* College of Sequoias, A.A., 1954; University of California, Berkeley, B.S. (with honors), 1956, M.B.A., 1957, Ph.D., 1962. *Home:* 9660 Northeast 34th St., Bellevue, Wash. 98004. *Office:* 262 Mackenzie Hall, University of Washington, Seattle, Wash. 98195.

CAREER: Certified Public Accountant. FMC Corp., San Jose, Calif., accountant, 1957-58; University of Washington, Seattle, assistant professor, 1960-63, associate professor, 1963-67, professor of accounting, 1967—, coordinator of faculty research in Graduate School of Business Administration, 1968-69, chairman of department of accounting, 1969-78, director of graduate professional accounting program, 1979—. Research fellow at Price Waterhouse Co., 1962-64; visiting professor at Cranfield School of Management, England, 1973, 1974, and University of Zurich, 1973-74. Consultant to U.S. Treasury Department, 1963-68, and American Institute of Certified Public Accountants, 1967-74; consultant to several business and professional service firms; expert legal witness, international lecturer, and leader of management seminars.

Member: American Institute of Certified Public Accountants, American Accounting Association (chairman of committee on international accounting, 1964-67; academic vice-president, 1970-71), Society for International Development, Academy of International Business (fellow), Northwest Accounting Research Group, Washington Society of Certified Public Accountants, Alpha Gamma Sigma, Beta Alpha Psi, Beta Gamma Sigma. *Awards, honors:* National Outstanding Accounting Educator Award, American Accounting Association, 1982.

WRITINGS: International Accounting, Macmillan, 1967, 2nd edition published as *International Accounting II,* Prentice-Hall, 1984; (editor with Kenneth Berg and Lauren Walker) *Readings in International Accounting,* Houghton, 1968; (editor with Charles H. Smith and contributor) *Accounting: A Book of Readings,* Holt, 1970, 2nd edition, Dryden, 1976; *A New Introduction to Accounting,* Price Waterhouse Foundation, 1971; (editor with Konrad W. Kubin) *A Bibliography of International Accounting,* 3rd edition (Mueller not associated with earlier editions), International Accounting Studies Institute, University of Washington, 1973; (author of foreword) George M. Scott and others, *An Introduction to Financial Control and Reporting in Multinational Enterprises,* Bureau of Business Research, University of Texas, 1973.

(Author of foreword) Michael Lafferty, *Accounting in Europe,* Woodhead-Faulkner, 1975; (with Robert G. May and Thomas H. Williams) *A New Introduction to Financial Accounting,* Prentice-Hall, 1975, 2nd edition, 1980; (with May and Williams) *A Brief Introduction to Managerial and Social Uses of Accounting,* Prentice-Hall, 1975; (with Frederick D. S. Choi) *An Introduction to Multinational Accounting,* Prentice-Hall, 1978; (editor with Choi and contributor) *Essentials of Multinational Accounting: An Anthology,* University Microfilms, 1979; (editor with Seiichi Sato and others) *A Compendium of Research on Information and Accounting for Managerial Decision and Control in Japan,* American Accounting Association, 1982.

"Accounting Practices" monograph series; published by University of Washington: *Accounting Practices in the Netherlands,* 1962; *. . . in Sweden,* 1962; *. . . in Argentina,* 1963; *. . . in West Germany,* 1964; (with Hiroshi Yoshida) *. . . in Japan,* 1968.

Contributor: John J. Coyle and Edward J. Mock, editors, *Readings in International Business,* International Textbook Co., 1965; Paul Garner and Kenneth B. Berg, editors, *Readings in Accounting Theory,* Houghton, 1966; Richard N. Farmer, editor, *International Management,* Dickenson, 1968; (with V. K. Zimmerman) Schuyler F. Otteson, editor, *Internationalizing the Traditional Business Curriculum,* Bureau of Business Research, Indiana University, 1968.

Abram Mey Tachtig Jaar—Liber Amicorum, Uitgeuersmaatschappij W. De Haan, 1970; R. Wixon, W. G. Kell, and N. M. Bedford, editors, *Accountant's Handbook,* Ronald, 1970; Etienne Cracco, editor, *International Business: 1970,* Institute for International Business and Economic Development Studies, Michigan State University, 1970; A. Kapoor and Phillip D. Grub, editors, *The Multinational Enterprise in Transition,* Darwin Press, 1972; (with L. M. Walker and Fawzi Dimian) C. J. Gibson, G. G. Meredith, and R. Peterson, editors, *Accounting Concepts: Readings,* Cassell Australia Ltd., 1972; *Management Accounting for Multinational Corporations,* Volume II, National Association for Accountants, 1974.

(With W. R. Gregory and R. N. Tabor) P. P. LeBreton, editor, *The Assessment and Development of Professionals: Theory and*

Practice, University of Washington, 1976; T. J. Burns and H. S. Hendrickson, editors, *The Accounting Sampler,* 3rd edition, McGraw, 1976; Ian Tilley and Peter Jubb, editors, *Capital, Income and Decision Making: Introductory Readings in Accounting,* Holt-Saunders, 1977; *International Accounting, Auditing and Tax Issues,* Business International, 1979; W. John Brennan, editor, *The Internationalization of the Accounting Profession,* Canadian Institute of Chartered Accountants, 1979; (with L. Walker) *Notable Contributions to the Periodical International Accounting Literature: 1975-78,* American Accounting Association, 1979.

Contributor to proceedings and annals; contributor of articles and reviews to numerous business and accounting journals.

WORK IN PROGRESS: A comprehensive assessment of state of the art international accounting.

AVOCATIONAL INTERESTS: Skiing and other outdoor activities.

* * *

MUELLER, Robert Kirk 1913-

PERSONAL: Surname is pronounced "Miller"; born July 25, 1913, in St. Louis, Mo.; son of E. R. Otto and Lucille (Flaugher) Mueller; married Jane Elizabeth Konesko (an artist), December 27, 1939; children: Lucy Alison (Mrs. Paul White), Patricia Kirk (Mrs. Elmer Hilpert), James Arno. *Education:* Washington University, B.S., 1934; University of Michigan, M.S., 1935; Harvard University, graduate study, 1950. *Religion:* Protestant. *Home:* Huckleberry Hill, Lincoln, Mass. 01773. *Office:* Arthur D. Little, Inc., Acorn Park, Cambridge, Mass. 02140.

CAREER: Monsanto Co., St. Louis, Mo., 1935-68, general manager, 1952-61, vice-president, director, and member of executive committee, 1963-68; Arthur D. Little, Inc., Cambridge, Mass., beginning 1968, vice president, 1973-77, chairman of board of directors, 1977—. Shawinigan Resins Corp., president, 1952-61, chairman of board of directors, 1961-63; director, Hospital Efficiency Corp. Member of board of directors of Massachusetts Mutual Life Insurance Co., Massachusetts Mutual Income Investors, Inc. (also member of executive committee), Bay Banks, Inc., and Salzburg Seminars in American Studies (also member of executive committee). Trustee, Colby-Sawyer College and International Academy of Management. *Wartime service:* Manager of Longhorn Ordnance Works, Karnack, Tex., 1944-46.

MEMBER: American Management Association (life member; member of international council and president's council), American Institute of Chemical Engineers, American Chemical Society, Society of Chemical Industry, American Association for the Advancement of Science (fellow), Institute of Directors (London), New York Academy of Science, Metropolitan Club (New York), Algonquin Club (Boston), Eccentric Club (London), Colony Club (Springfield, Mass.), Harvard Faculty Club.

WRITINGS: *Probability Controls,* Funk, 1950; *Risk Survival and Power,* American Management Association, 1970; *The Innovation Ethic,* AMACOM, 1971; *Board Life,* AMACOM, 1974; *Buzzwords,* Van Nostrand, 1974; *Behind the Boardroom Door,* Crown, 1984.

Published by Lexington Books: *Metadevelopment: Beyond the Bottom Line,* 1977; *New Directions for Directors: Behind the Bylaws,* 1978; *Career Conflict: Management's Inelegant Dysfunction,* 1978; *Board Compass: What It Means to Be a Director in a Changing World,* 1979; *The Incomplete Board: The Unfolding of Corporate Governance,* 1981; *Board Score: How to Judge Boardworthiness,* 1982.

SIDELIGHTS: Robert Mueller's books have been published in French, German, and Japanese.

* * *

MUNRO, James
See MITCHELL, James

* * *

MURPHY, James J(erome) 1923-

PERSONAL: Born September 9, 1923, in San Jose, Calif.; son of James Joseph (a clerk) and Marie Therese (Utzerath) Murphy; married Kathleen Woods, February 7, 1948; children: Sheila Maureen, Brian Robert. *Education:* Saint Mary's College of California, B.A., 1947; Stanford University, M.A., 1950, Ph.D., 1957. *Religion:* Roman Catholic. *Home:* 915 Villanova Dr., Davis, Calif. 95616. *Office:* Department of Rhetoric, University of California, Davis, Calif. 95616.

CAREER: United Press International (UPI), San Francisco, Calif., newsman, 1947-48; Stanford University, Stanford, Calif., assistant professor of speech, 1954-59; Princeton University, Princeton, N.J., assistant professor of speech, 1959-65; University of California, Davis, associate professor, 1965-68, professor of rhetoric, 1968—, vice-chancellor, 1968-69, associate dean, College of Letters and Science, 1972-75, chairman, department of rhetoric, 1975—. *Military service:* U.S. Army Air Forces, 1943-45. U.S. Air Force Reserve, 1945-69; retired as major. *Member:* Modern Language Association of America, Speech Communication Association, International Society for the History of Rhetoric, Mediaeval Academy of America, Medieval Association of the Pacific (president, 1966-70), Pacific Philological Association. *Awards, honors:* Anniversary Award for Distinguished Scholars, Speech Association of America, 1965; American Council of Learned Societies fellow, 1971-72; annual book award, Speech Communication Association, 1975, for *Rhetoric in the Middle Ages.*

WRITINGS: (With Jon M. Ericson) *The Debater's Guide,* Bobbs-Merrill, 1961; (editor and author of introduction and notes) Quintilian, *On the Early Education of the Citizen-Orator* (Book I and chapters 1-10 of Book II of *Institutio oratoria*), translation by John Selby Watson, Library of Liberal Arts, 1966; (editor with Peter Kontos) *Teaching Urban Youth,* Wiley, 1967; (editor) *Demosthenes' "On the Crown": A Critical Study of a Masterpiece of Ancient Oratory,* translation by John J. Keaney, Random House, 1967; (editor and translator) *Three Medieval Rhetorical Arts,* University of California Press, 1971; (editor) *Medieval Rhetoric: A Select Bibliography,* University of Toronto Press, 1971; (editor) *A Synoptic History of Classical Rhetoric,* Random House, 1972; *Rhetoric in the Middle Ages: A History of Rhetorical Theory from Saint Augustine to the Renaissance,* University of California Press, 1974; (editor and contributor) *Medieval Eloquence: Studies in the Theory and Practice of Medieval Rhetoric,* University of California Press, 1977; (compiler) *Renaissance Rhetoric: A Short-Title Catalogue,* Garland, 1981; (editor and contributor) *The Rhetorical Tradition and Modern Writing,* Modern Language Association, 1982; (editor and contributor) *Renaissance Eloquence: Studies in the Theory and Practice of Renaissance Rhetoric,* University of California Press, 1983.

Contributor of over twenty articles to periodicals, including *Medieval Studies, Speech Monographs, Philological Quarterly,* and *Journal of the American Forensic Association.* Editor, *Rhetorica: A Journal of Rhetoric;* member of editorial boards, *Philosophy and Rhetoric* and *Language and Communication.*

WORK IN PROGRESS: With Carole Newlands, *The Attack of Peter Ramus on Quintilian: A Translation of "Rhetoricae distinctiones in Quintilianum" (1549),* for Northern Illinois University Press.

SIDELIGHTS: James J. Murphy told *CA:* "There is an ancient Greek saying that 'he who does not know rhetoric will be a victim of it.' Since human communication has always been a dominant force in our civilization, I've long been interested in tracing its history to see how its future can be shaped. I always tell students they must study the history of rhetoric so they won't spent their time re-inventing the wheel—that is, redoing what someone else has already done. When you look at it that way, the history of rhetoric is a fascinating subject that tells us a good deal about every stage of our civilization."

Rhetoric in the Middle Ages: A History of Rhetorical Theory from Saint Augustine to the Renaissance has been published in Italian.

* * *

MUSSER, Joe
    See MUSSER, Joseph L.

* * *

MUSSER, Joseph L.   1936-
    (Joe Musser)

PERSONAL: Born August 15, 1936, in Morton Grove, Ill.; son of Joseph R. and Nellie (Weathers) Musser; married Nancy Green, July 29, 1956; children: Kerry, Kevin, Bruce, David, Laurinda. *Home:* 2712 Capri Ct., Rockford, Ill. 61111. *Office:* 610 East State St., Rockford, Ill. 61104.

CAREER: Worked for newspaper in Rockford, Ill., 1952-61; WMBI Radio, Chicago, Ill., employee, 1961-66; free-lance writer and producer, 1966-72, 1974-75; Bibles for the World, Wheaton, Ill., vice-president, 1972; Four Most Productions, Inc., Wheaton, president, 1973; Quadrus Media Ministry, Inc., Rockford, president, 1975—. Assistant director, Bedford Center for Creative Study, Glen Ellyn, Ill., 1968—. *Military service:* Illinois National Guard, 1954-62; became staff sergeant. *Member:* Fellowship of Christians in the Arts, Media and Entertainment. *Awards, honors:* First Prize in Radio Competition, Festival of Arts in Birmingham, Ala., 1966, for radio drama "Dawn at Checkpoint Alpha"; Best Book of the Year Award, Campus Life and EPA, for *Joni;* Best Book of the Year runner-up in biography category, 1983, for *Josh.*

WRITINGS—Published by Zondervan: (With Tom Skinner) *Black and Free,* 1968; (editor) *Voice of the Morning* (novel), 1968; *Behold a Pale Horse* (novel), 1970, revised edition published as *The Coming World Earthquake,* Tyndale, 1982; (editor) *Words of Revolution,* 1972; (with Joni Eareckson) *Joni,* 1976.

Other publishers: (Co-author) *Dare to Believe,* Creation House, 1974; (with Tommy and Sally John) *The Tommy John Story,* Revell, 1978; (with Paul Moore) *The Shepherd of Times Square,* Nelson, 1979; *Josh: The Excitement of the Unexpected* (biography of Josh McDowell), Here's Life Publishers, 1981; *Beyond the Next Mountain* (novelization of motion picture), Tyndale, 1982. Also author of three unpublished books; also author of screenplays for film and television, including "The Rapture," 1972; also author of radio plays, including "Dawn at Checkpoint Alpha."

WORK IN PROGRESS: A novel; two screenplays; a biography.

SIDELIGHTS: Joni, a 3.5 million-copy best-seller, has been translated and published overseas in over two dozen countries.

* * *

MYERS, J(ohn) William   1919-

PERSONAL: Born December 1, 1919, in Huntington, W.Va.; son of Condon William (an engraver) and Mary Olive (Fox) Myers; married Nancy Hortense Paxton, July 6, 1942 (died 1954); married Helen File Fleming, November 28, 1981; children: Martha Ann (Mrs. Philip L. Parks), Lenora Ellen (Mrs. James Johns), Nancy Louise (Mrs. Gerald D. Smith), John Charles. *Education:* Ohio Wesleyan University, B.A., 1951; Bowling Green State University, M.A., 1952. *Politics:* Liberal Democrat. *Address:* 105 Fulton St., Lyons, Ohio 43533.

CAREER: Ordained a Methodist minister in 1948; minister, Ohio Annual Conference of the Methodist Church, 1944-54; transferred to the Unitarian Church, 1956; Horton Unitarian Universalist Church, Horton, Mich., currently minister. Journeyman letterpress and lithographic printer, editor, publisher, book designer, and free-lance writer, 1954—. Lecturer on poetry and religion. *Member:* American Academy of Poets, Poetry Society of America, Catholic Poetry Society of America, American Translators Association, Ohio Poetry Society, Poetry Society of Virginia. *Awards, honors:* Nomination for Pulitzer Prize in Poetry, 1964, for *Green Are My Words;* London Literary Circle award, 1967, for poem, "Prayer for a House I Never Had."

WRITINGS—Poetry; published by New Merrymount Press, except as indicated: *Evening Exercises,* Humanist Education Press, 1956; *These Mown Dandelions,* Ohio Poetry Review Press, 1959; *My Mind's Poor Birds,* Elgeuera Press, 1963; *Alley to an Island,* 1963; *Green Are My Words,* 1964; *Sun Bands and Other Poems,* Georgetown Press, 1964; *Anatomy of a Feeling,* 1966; *Variations on a Nightingale,* 1968; *A Greene County Ballad,* 1972; *The Sky Is Forever,* 1974; *Something Will Be Mine,* 1976; *Annotations 1951,* 1977; *Stones of Promise,* 1977; (translator of Friedrich Nietzsche's text to the Frederick Delius choral work) *A Mass of Life,* 1980; *Homage to Dionysius: Selected Poems of Friedrich W. Nietzsche in Translation,* 1982; *Juliet and God* (poetic play), 1983.

Also translator from the German of poetry of Johann W. Von Goethe, Friedrich Hoelderlin, Joseph von Eichendorff, Friedrich Rueckert, Edward Moerike, Reiner Kunze, Gottfried Keller, Richard Dehmel, Stefan Anton George, Hermann Hesse, Franz Werfel, and Karl Krolow. Contributor of poems to over sixty journals and newspapers, including *American Weave, Bitterroot, Cardinal Poetry Quarterly, Descant, Free Lance, Hartford Courant, Laurel Review, Meanjin Quarterly, New York Herald Tribune, South and West,* and *Spirit;* contributor of bibliographies to *Twentieth Century Literature* and *Dasein: The Quarterly Review.* Reviewer for *Chicago Sun-Times.* Editor, *Mid-Lakes Humanist* (American Humanist Association publication), 1956-59, *Ohio Poetry Review,* 1957-59, *Anthropos, the Quarterly of Humanist Poetry,* 1958-59, *Ohio Poetry Society Bulletin,* 1958-59, and *Poetry Dial,* 1959-61; poetry editor, *Humanist,* 1961-62; advisory and contributing editor, *Dasein: The Quarterly Review,* 1962—.

WORK IN PROGRESS: Opus Guyandotte, a collection of poems; *A Long Time Learning,* an autobiography; *White Rocks: A Poetic Legend.*

SIDELIGHTS: J. William Myers told *CA:* "As I approach what are doubtless the last decades of my life there is a perspective—to chase a metaphor is the enduring thing. So I desire, down deep, to fly above this time of cheap ethics, unbelievable illiteracy and a fear of man's demise, to live in the hope something of mine will sing beyond the ruin. This means I have purposed to make use of the symbol knowing it to be a symbol and never to be mistaken for reality."

AVOCATIONAL INTERESTS: Cooking, baking, making wines.

BIOGRAPHICAL/CRITICAL SOURCES: Columbus Dispatch, May 22, 1969; *Observer-Reporter* (Washington, Pa.), June 23, 1969; *Record-Outlook* (McDonald, Pa.), November 18, 1971; *Newark Advocate,* May 1, 1978; *Adrian Telegram,* February 9, 1980.

N

NANDY, Pritish 1947-

PERSONAL: Born January 15, 1947, in Bhagalpur, Bihar, India; son of Satish Chandra (a schoolteacher) and Prafulla Nandy; married Rina Mumtaz, January 17, 1966 (divorced); married Rina Biswas, February 10, 1977; children: (first marriage) Teesta, Kushan; (second marriage) Rangita, Ishita. *Education:* Educated in Calcutta. *Politics:* None. *Religion:* None. *Home:* 93 Gitanjali, Walkeshwar Rd., Bombay 400006, India.

CAREER: Guest Keen Williams Ltd., Calcutta, India, publicity and public relations manager, 1969-82; Times of India Group (publishing house for newspapers and magazines), Bombay, India, publishing director, 1982—. Free-lance writer, photographer, and graphic designer. Has participated in poetry readings and seminars throughout the world. Member of advisory board of Sahitya Akademi. *Awards, honors:* Numerous awards for poetry, editing, photography, and graphic design, including being named a Padmashri by the President of India, 1977.

WRITINGS—Poetry: *Of Gods and Olives: Twenty-one Poems,* Writers Workshop (Calcutta), 1967; *On Either Side of Arrogance,* Writers Workshop, 1968; *I Hand You in Turn My Nebbuk Wreath: Early Poems,* Dialogue Publications, 1968; *From the Outer Bank of the Brahmaputra,* New Rivers Press, 1969; *Masks to Be Interpreted in Terms of Messages,* Writers Workshop, 1970; *Madness Is the Second Stroke,* Dialogue Publications, 1971; *The Poetry of Pritish Nandy,* Oxford (Calcutta), 1973; *Dhritarashtra Downtown, Zero: A Poem,* Dialogue Publications, 1974.

Riding the Midnight River: Selected Poems of Pritish Nandy, Arnold Heinemann, 1975; *Lonesong Street,* Poets Press, 1975; *In Secret Anarchy,* Arnold Heinemann, 1976; *A Stranger Called I,* Arnold Heinemann, 1976; *Tonight, This Savage Rite,* Arnold Heinemann, 1977; *The Nowhere Man,* Arnold Heinemann, 1977; *Pritish Nandy, Thirty,* Arnold Heinemann, 1978; *Anywhere Is Another Place,* Arnold Heinemann, 1979; *The Rainbow Last Night,* Arnold Heinemann, 1981.

Editor of anthologies: *Poetry from India,* Dialogue Publications, 1970; *Indian Poetry in English, 1947-1972: An Anthology,* Oxford (Calcutta), 1972; *Indian Poetry in English Today,* Sterling, 1973; *Modern Indian Poetry,* Heinemann, 1974; *Bengali Poetry Today,* Michigan State University, 1974; *Strangertime,* [New Dehli], 1977; *Love,* Vikas Publishing, 1978; *Modern Indian Literature,* Arnold Heinemann, 1978.

Translator: *The Complete Poems of Samar Sen,* Writers Workshop, 1970; *Subhas Mukhopadhyay: Poet of the People,* Dialogue Publications, 1970; *Poems from Bangladesh,* Perspective Publications, 1971; *The Prose Poems of Lokenath Bhattacharya,* Dialogue Publications, 1971; *Bangladesh: Voice of a New Nation,* Lyrebird, 1972; *Shesh Lekha: The Last Poems of Rabindranath Tagore,* Dialogue Publications, 1973; *The Songs of Mirabai,* Arnold Heinemann, 1975; *The Poetry of Kaifi Azmi,* Poets Press, 1975; *The Giraffe Flames: Poems by Sunil Gangopadhyay,* Poets Press, 1976.

Also author of *Rites for a Plebeian Statue: An Experiment in Verse Drama,* Writers Workshop (Calcutta), 1969, first produced on All India Radio, 1970. Editor of *Dialogue India;* poetry editor of *Illustrated Weekly of India.*

MEDIA ADAPTATIONS: Pritish Nandy has made a recording of his poetry entitled "Lonesong Street," 1977. Two films have been made based on his poetry, "Pritish Nandy's Lonesong Street" and "Pritish Nandy's Hideout."

BIOGRAPHICAL/CRITICAL SOURCES: Subhoranjan Dasgupta, *Pritish Nandy,* Arnold Heinemann, 1976; Subhas Saha, *The Wings of Night: A Study of Pritish Nandy's Work,* Prayerbooks (Calcutta), 1978.

* * *

NATANSON, Maurice (Alexander) 1924-

PERSONAL: Born November 26, 1924, in New York, N.Y.; son of Charles (an actor) and Kate (Scheer) Natanson; married Lois Lichenstein, January 21, 1949; children: Charles, Nicholas, Kathy. *Education:* Lincoln Memorial University, A.B., 1945; New York University, M.A., 1948; University of Nebraska, Ph.D., 1950; New School for Social Research, D.S.Sc. (summa cum laude), 1953. *Politics:* Democrat. *Religion:* Jewish. *Office:* Department of Philosophy, Yale University, New Haven, Conn. 06520.

CAREER: University of Nebraska, Lincoln, instructor, 1950-51; New School for Social Research, New York, N.Y., lecturer in philosophy, Graduate Faculty, 1952-53; University of Houston, Houston, Tex., assistant professor, 1953-56, associate professor of philosophy, 1956-57; University of North Carolina, Chapel Hill, associate professor, 1957-62, professor of philosophy, 1962-65; University of California, Santa Cruz, professor of philosophy and fellow of Cowell College, 1965-

76; Yale University, New Haven, Conn., professor of philosophy, 1976—. Distinguished visiting professor, Pennsylvania State University, 1963; visiting professor, University of California, Berkeley, 1964-65; guest professor, University of Konstanz, 1974. *Member:* American Philosophical Association, International Phenomenological Society, Society for Phenomenology and Existential Philosophy. *Awards, honors:* American Council of Learned Societies scholar, 1951-53, fellow in Europe, 1961-62; University of California, senior faculty fellowship, 1967-68; National Endowment for the Humanities, senior fellow, 1971-72; National Book Award in philosophy and religion, 1974, for *Edmund Husserl: Philosopher of Infinite Tasks*.

WRITINGS: *A Critique of Jean-Paul Sartre's Ontology*, University of Nebraska Press, 1951, reprinted, Haskell House, 1972; *The Social Dynamics of George H. Mead*, Public Affairs, 1956, reprinted, Nijhoff, 1973; (contributor) *For Roman Ingarden*, Nijhoff, 1959; (contributor) *The Critical Matrix*, Georgetown University Press, 1961; (contributor) *The World of Thomas Wolfe*, Scribner, 1962; *Literature, Philosophy, and the Social Sciences*, Nijhoff, 1962; (contributor) *Psychiatrie der Gegenwart*, two volumes, Springer, 1963; *The Journeying Self: A Study of Philosophy and Social Role*, Addison-Wesley, 1970; *Edmund Husserl: Philosopher of Infinite Tasks*, Northwestern University Press, 1973; *Phenomenology, Role, and Reason: Essays on the Coherence and Deformation of Social Reality*, C. C Thomas, 1974.

Editor: Alfred Schutz, *The Problem of Social Reality*, Nijhoff, 1962; *Philosophy of the Social Sciences: A Reader*, Random House, 1963; (with Henry W. Johnstone, Jr.) *Philosophy, Rhetoric, and Argumentation*, Pennsylvania State University Press, 1965; *Essays in Phenomenology*, Nijhoff, 1966; *Psychiatry and Philosophy*, Springer, 1969; *Phenomenology and Social Reality*, Nijhoff, 1970; *Phenomenology and the Social Sciences*, two volumes, Northwestern University Press, 1973; Gaston Berger, *Recherches sur les Conditions de la connaissance essai d'une theoretique Pure*, Garland Publishing, 1979; Kurt Stavenhagen, *Absolute Stellungnahmen: Eine ontologische untersuchung uber das wesen der Religion*, Garland Publishing, 1979; Adolf Sternberger, *Der Verstandene tod: Eine Untersuchung zu Martin Heideggers Existenzialontologie*, Garland Publishing, 1979; Hermann Lotze, *Logic*, two volumes, Garland Publishing, 1980; James F. Ferrier, *Philosophical Works: Phenomenology—Background, Foreground and Influences*, three volumes, Garland Publishing, 1980.

Contributor to philosophy and social science journals. Member of board of editors, *Philosophy and Phenomenological Research;* consulting editor, "Northwestern University Studies in Phenomenology and Existential Philosophy" series; book review editor, *Man and World*.

WORK IN PROGRESS: Studies in the philosophy of death; two books for children, illustrated by Rosekrans-Hoffman.†

* * *

NATHAN, David 1926-

PERSONAL: Born December 9, 1926, in Manchester, England; son of Joseph and Doris (Ingleby) Nathan; married Norma Ellis, March 31, 1957; children: Paul, John. *Education:* "Rudimentary." *Politics:* Ex-Socialist. *Religion:* None. *Home:* 16 Augustus Close, Brentford Dock, Brentford, Middlesex, England. *Agent:* Harvey Unna and Stephen Durbridge Ltd., 14 Beaumont Mews, Marylebone High St., London W1N 4HE, England.

CAREER: Copyboy on newspaper in Manchester, England, 1942-44; reporter on newspapers in Lancashire, England, 1947-49, and Nottingham, England, 1949-52; *Daily Mail*, London, England, syndication news editor, 1952-54; *Daily Herald & Sun*, London, reporter, 1955-60, theater critic, 1960—. Assistant editor and theatre critic, *Jewish Chronicle*, London. *Military service:* Royal Navy, 1944-47. *Member:* National Union of Journalists, Writers Guild. *Awards, honors:* Royal Television Society Writer's Award, for "A Good Human Story."

WRITINGS: (With Freddie Hancock) *Hancock: A Biography*, Kimber & Co., 1969; *The Freeloader* (novel), W. H. Allen, 1970; *The Laughtermakers*, P. Owen, 1971; "A Good Human Story" (television play), produced by Granada, 1977; "The Belman of London" (radio play), produced by BBC Radio 3, 1982; "The Bohemians" (radio play), produced by BBC Radio 4, 1983; *Portrait of a Star: Glenda Jackson*, Sunflower Books, 1984.

Also author of comedy television scripts for "That Was the Week That Was," "Not So Much a Programme," "BBC3," and "At the 11th Hour"; also author of screenplay of his novel, *The Freeloader*, for production by Associated British.

WORK IN PROGRESS: A television play; a radio play.

* * *

NEEDLEMAN, Jacob 1934-

PERSONAL: Born October 6, 1934, in Philadelphia, Pa.; son of Benjamin and Ida (Seltzer) Needleman; married Carla Satzman (a writer), August 30, 1959; children: Raphael, Eve. *Education:* Harvard University, B.A., 1956; University of Freiburg, graduate study, 1957-58; Yale University, Ph.D., 1961. *Residence:* San Francisco, Calif. *Agent:* Marlene Gabriel, 333 West 56th St., New York, N.Y. 10019. *Office:* Department of Philosophy, San Francisco State University, San Francisco, Calif. 94132.

CAREER: West Haven Veterans Administration Hospital, West Haven, Conn., clinical psychology trainee, 1960-61; Rockefeller Institute, New York, N.Y., research associate, 1961-62; San Francisco State University, San Francisco, Calif., 1962—, began as assistant professor, 1962-66, became associate professor, 1966, currently professor of philosophy, chairman of department, 1968-69. Visiting scholar, Union Theological Seminary, 1967-68; director, Center for the Study of New Religions, 1977-83; lecturer in psychiatry and consultant in medical ethics, University of California, San Francisco, 1981-84. *Member:* American Philosophical Association, American Academy of Religion.

AWARDS, HONORS: Fulbright scholarship in Germany, 1957-58; Fels Foundation fellowship in Munich, 1959; Society for Religion in Higher Education grant, 1967-68; grants from Marsden Foundation and Ella Lyman Cabot Trust for research for *The New Religions*, 1969; grants from Marsden Foundation and Far West Institute, 1975; Rockefeller Foundation humanities fellowship, 1977-78.

WRITINGS: *Being-in-the-World*, Basic Books, 1963, published with new introduction, Torchbooks, 1968; (translator) Erwin Straus, *The Primary World of Senses*, Free Press of Glencoe, 1963; (contributor of translation) *Essays on Ego Psychology*, International Universities Press, 1964; (co-editor) *Care of Patients with Fatal Illness*, New York Academy of Sciences, 1969; (contributor) Austin H. Kutscher, editor, *Death and Bereavement*, C. C Thomas, 1969.

The New Religions, Doubleday, 1970; (author of foreword) Lizelle Reymond, *To Live Within,* Doubleday, 1971; (author of foreword) Reymond, *My Life with a Brahmin Family,* Penguin, 1972; (author of foreword) Maurice Nicoll, *The New Man,* Penguin, 1972; (author of foreword) Leo Schaya, *The Universal Meaning of the Kabbalah,* Penguin, 1973; *Religion for a New Generation,* Macmillan, 1973, 2nd edition, 1976; (editor) *The Sword of Gnosis,* Penguin, 1973; (contributor) E. Wyschogrod, *The Phenomenon of Death,* Harper, 1974; (editor) *Sacred Tradition and Present Need,* Viking, 1974; *A Sense of the Cosmos,* Doubleday, 1975; *On the Way to Self Knowledge: Sacred Tradition and Psychotherapy,* Knopf, 1976; (editor) *Understanding the New Religions,* Seabury, 1978; (editor) *Speaking of My Life: The Art of Living in the Cultural Revolution,* Harper, 1979; (contributor) J. Sulzberger, editor, *Search,* Harper, 1979.

Lost Christianity, Doubleday, 1980; *Consciousness and Tradition,* Cross Roads, 1982; *The Heart of Philosophy,* Knopf, 1982. General editor of "Penguin Metaphysical Library," sixteen volumes. Contributor of articles and reviews to journals in his field.

WORK IN PROGRESS: A study of the spiritual role of the physician in contemporary society.

SIDELIGHTS: Jacob Needleman told *CA:* "I write to people who, like myself, are searching for a way to maintain or return to the questions of the heart that a child puts to the universe: who am I? why am I on earth? how can I find out the meaning of my life? Some time ago I discovered how easy it was to forget these questions when surrounded by sophisticated books and other people's opinions and the promises of clever theorists. I seem to feel my humanity only when I come closer to this search, and if anything of that is expressed in my writing, I am very glad."

* * *

NELSON, Peter 1940-

PERSONAL: Born July 30, 1940, in St. Louis, Mo.; son of Ralph Arnold and Catherine (English) Nelson. *Education:* Occidental College, B.A., 1964; California State University, Los Angeles, graduate study, 1965; University of California, Irvine, M.F.A., 1969. *Home:* 256 East Mendocino, Altadena, Calif. 91001. *Office:* Stella Polaris Gallery, 303 Boyd St., Los Angeles, Calif. 90013.

CAREER: M.S.E.I. (public relations firm), Palm Springs, Calif., publicist, 1965-66; Fawcett-McDermott Associates (advertising firm), Honolulu, Hawaii, staff associate, 1966; Pasadena Art Museum, Pasadena, Calif., editorial consultant, 1967-70, media director, 1969-70; University of Hawaii, Honolulu, instructor, 1968-69, 1970-73, assistant professor of English, 1973-79; Stella Polaris Gallery (visual and performing arts), Los Angeles, Calif., owner and director, 1981—. Visiting professor, Maharishi International University, Fairfield, Iowa, 1975-76, 1980, 1981.

WRITINGS: Between Lives (poems), Ironwood Press, 1974; *Spring into Light* (poems), Green Tree Press, 1978.

WORK IN PROGRESS: Several collections of poems.

SIDELIGHTS: Peter Nelson has traveled and lived in the Pacific, Asia, and Europe.

NELSON, Richard K(ing) 1941-

PERSONAL: Born December 1, 1941, in Madison, Wis.; son of Robert King (a state employee) and Florence (Olson) Nelson. *Education:* University of Wisconsin, B.S., 1964, M.S., 1968; University of California, Santa Barbara, Ph.D., 1971. *Home address:* P.O. Box 2808, Sitka, Alaska 99835.

CAREER: University of California, Santa Barbara, research fellow in anthropology, 1968-71; University of Hawaii, Honolulu, assistant professor of anthropology, 1971-72; Memorial University of Newfoundland, St. Johns, assistant professor of anthropology, 1972-73; University of Alaska, Fairbanks, research associate, 1973-77; University of California, Santa Barbara, visiting lecturer, 1978; University of California, Santa Cruz, visiting lecturer, 1979; University of Alaska, visiting professor, 1980, affiliate associate professor, 1982—. Member of field expeditions to Kodiak Island, Alaska, 1961, Anangula Island in the Aleutians, 1963, and four extended ethnographic field studies among Alaskan Eskimos and Athapaskan Indians.

WRITINGS: Alaskan Eskimo Exploitation of the Sea Ice Environment, Arctic Aeromedical Laboratory, U.S. Air Force, 1966; *Hunters of the Northern Ice,* University of Chicago Press, 1969; *Hunters of the Northern Forest,* University of Chicago Press, 1973; (co-author) *Kuuvangmiit: Contemporary Subsistence Living in the Latter Twentieth Century,* National Park Service, 1977; (co-author) *Tracks in the Wildland: A Portrayal of Koyukon and Nunamiut Subsistence,* National Park Service, 1978.

Shadow of the Hunter: Stories of Eskimo Life, University of Chicago Press, 1980; *Harvest of the Sea: Coastal Subsistence in Modern Wainwright,* North Slope Borough (Barrow, Alaska), 1982; *Make Prayers to the Raven: A Koyukon View of the Northern Forest,* University of Chicago Press, 1983; *The Athapaskans: People of the Boreal Forest,* University of Alaska Museum (Fairbanks), 1983.

WORK IN PROGRESS: Co-author, *The Space Between: Nature and Man in Interior Alaska.*

* * *

NEWBOLD, Stokes
See ADAMS, Richard N(ewbold)

* * *

NISHIHARA, Masashi 1937-

PERSONAL: Surname is accented on second syllable; born August 4, 1937, in Osaka, Japan; son of Chikao and Yoneko Nishihara; married Susuko Osawa (a linguist), December, 1968; children: Aya, Mitsu (daughters). *Education:* University of North Carolina, student, 1959-60; Kyoto University, B.A., 1962; University of Michigan, M.A., 1968, Ph.D., 1972. *Home:* 21-3, 2-chome, Hashirimizu, Yokosuka-shi, Kanagawa-ken 239, Japan. *Office:* Defense Academy, 1-chome, Hashirimizu, Yokosuka-shi, Kanagawa-ken 239, Japan.

CAREER: Center for Japanese Social and Political Studies, Tokyo, Japan, research assistant, 1962-64; Kyoto University, Center for Southeast Asian Studies, Kyoto, Japan, head of Jakarta Liaison Office, 1970-72; Kyoto Sangyo University, Kyoto, Japan, associate professor, 1973-75, professor of Southeast Asian politics, 1975-77; Defense Academy, Yokosuka, Japan, professor of international relations, 1977—. Visiting research fellow, Rockefeller Foundation, New York, N.Y., 1981-82. *Member:* Japan Society of International Relations,

Association of Asian Political and Economic Studies, International Studies Association, International Institute for Strategic Studies Trilateral Commission, Research Institute for Peace and Security.

WRITINGS: Golkar and the Indonesian Elections of 1971, Modern Indonesia Project, Cornell University, 1972; (with Robert E. Ward, Frank J. Shulman and Mary Espey) *The Allied Occupation of Japan, 1945-1952: An Annotated Bibliography of Western Languages Materials,* American Library Association, 1975; *The Japanese and Sukarno's Indonesia,* University Press of Hawaii, 1976; *Tonan Ajia no seijiteki fuhai* (title means "Political Corruption in Southeast Asia"), Sobunsha, 1976; (contributor) Tadashi Yamamoto and Bae-ho Han, editors, *Korea and Japan,* Korea University, 1978; (contributor) *Southeast Asian Affairs, 1980,* Institute of Southeast Asian Affairs, 1980; (contributor) Ryukichi Imai and John Barton, editors, *Arms Control II,* Oelgeschager, Gunn & Hain, 1981; (contributor) *Motto shiritai Indoneshia* (title means "Indonesia yet to Be Learned About"), Kobundo, 1982; (editor) *Nihon gaiko no hiseishiki chaneru* (title means "Informal Channels in Japanese Diplomacy"), Japanese Association of International Relations, 1983. Contributor to international security and Asian studies journals.

WORK IN PROGRESS: Research on Japan's role in Asia and in Western security.

SIDELIGHTS: Masashi Nishihara writes: "I have been concerned about the lack of academic interest in the role of human personal contacts between the Japanese and other Asian countries. Pre-war and wartime contacts between the Japanese and Indonesians had lots to do with postwar binational relations. I wanted to uncover this in my book from Hawaii Press. I wish to do similar things, in the future, about other countries. It is important to me to know what Japan has done to our neighbors, for I am concerned about the future of Asia as a whole."

BIOGRAPHICAL/CRITICAL SOURCES: Wakai Chikara (title means "Young Power"), February, 1977.

* * *

NOEL HUME, Ivor 1927-

PERSONAL: Born 1927 in London, England; son of Cecil and Gladys Mary (Bagshaw Mann) Noel Hume; married Audrey Baines. *Education:* Attended Framingham College, Suffolk, England, 1936-39, and St. Lawrence College, Kent, England, 1942-44. *Home address:* P.O. Box 1711, Williamsburg, Va. 23185. *Office:* Department of Archaeology, Colonial Williamsburg, Va. 23185.

CAREER: Guildhall Museum, London, England, archaeologist responsible for recovery of antiquities in postwar London, 1949-57; Colonial Williamsburg, Va., chief archaeologist, 1957-64, director of department of archaeology, 1964-72, resident archaeologist, 1972—. Honorary research associate, Smithsonian Institution, 1959—. Vice-chairman, Governor's advisory committee, Virginia Research Center for Historical Archaeology, 1969-70, member, 1971-76; member of review panel, National Endowment for the Humanities, 1973-77, and of Institute for Early American History and Culture, 1974-77. Consultant to government of Jamaica, 1967-69. *Military service:* Indian Army, 1944-45; invalided out.

MEMBER: American Association of Museums, Zoological Society of London (fellow), Society of Antiquaries of London (fellow), Society for Historical Archaeology, Society for Post-Medieval Archaeology (vice-president, 1967-76), Kent Archaeological Society, Virginia Archeological Society. *Awards, honors:* Society of Colonial Wars in the State of New York best book award and American Association for State and Local History award of merit, both 1964, for *Here Lies Virginia;* special award for historical archaeology, University of South Carolina, 1975; L.H.D., University of Pennsylvania, 1976.

WRITINGS: Archaeology in Britain, Foyle, 1953; (with A. Noel Hume) *Handbook of Tortoises, Terrapins and Turtles,* Foyle, 1954; *Treasure in the Thames,* Muller, 1956; *Great Moments in Archaeology,* Phoenix House, 1957; *Here Lies Virginia* (American Heritage selection), Knopf, 1963; *1775, Another Part of the Field,* Knopf, 1966; *Historical Archaeology,* Knopf, 1968; *A Guide to Artifacts of Colonial America,* Knopf, 1969; *All the Best Rubbish,* Harper, 1974; *Early English Delftware from London and Virginia,* University Press of Virginia, 1977; *Martin's Hundred,* Knopf, 1982, published as *Martin's Hundred: The Discovery of a Lost Colonial Virginia Settlement,* Dell, 1983.

Author of two pseudonymous novels in England, 1971 and 1972; author and director of film "Doorway to the Past," 1968; author and narrator of television films "The Williamsburg File," 1976, and "Search for a Century," 1980. Also author of pamphlets and more than forty archaeological reports, studies and articles on glass and ceramics published in British and American journals, including *Archaeologia Cantiana, Illustrated London News, Antiques, Journal of Glass Studies, Connoisseur, Apollo,* and *Country Life.*

SIDELIGHTS: In 1976 archaeologist Ivor Noel Hume, while examining the site of Carter's Grove, an eighteenth-century Virginia mansion, made a startling discovery—the remains of an early seventeenth-century settlement called Martin's Hundred. The 220 English settlers who built the small community had arrived in the New World some time before the *Mayflower* sailed. They faced a treacherous existence; those pioneers who managed to survive disease and starvation were massacred during an Indian uprising in 1622. And yet, as Noel Hume declares in his book *Martin's Hundred,* the excavation and identification of the site yielded many valuable facts about the living conditions and sociology of America's earliest known immigrants.

For instance, the author "tells us how pottery used by the landholding class can be distinguished from that used by servants and gives us the mathematical formula for dating a site by the size of the stem end of a clay tobacco pipe," says Frederika Randall in her *Nation* review of *Martin's Hundred.* "He traces a few rusty chain links to a coat of mail and a fragment of blue and white tile to an example of delftware depicted in a seventeenth-century Dutch painting. He ponders the gash in the skull of one of the soggy skeletons and decides, finally, that a blow from a garden spade was the probable cause of death."

But "if the importance of the Martin's Hundred site is historical, the emphasis of Noel Hume's book is on the archeological," writes *Newsweek* critic Peter S. Prescott. The reviewer notes that the author "is especially candid regarding the difficulties and disappointments attending his profession. . . . The archeologist works under strain—'Everything he does is destructive'—but the rewards are greater: 'It is the thrill of a chase that excites an archaeological historian, pursuing the proof with all the intensity of a hunter, the adrenalin flowing until the moment of the kill; then an instant of elation—and it's done. The excitement drains away.'"

BIOGRAPHICAL/CRITICAL SOURCES: Ivor Noel Hume, *Martin's Hundred,* Knopf, 1982; *Washington Post Book World,*

July 4, 1982; *Newsweek,* July 5, 1982; *Nation,* August 7-14, 1982; *Times Literary Supplement,* January 7, 1983.†

* * *

NOLAN, Chuck
See EDSON, J(ohn) T(homas)

* * *

NORMAN, Nicole
See CUDLIPP, Edythe

* * *

NORRIS, Maureen
See CUDLIPP, Edythe

* * *

NORTHUMBRIAN GENTLEMAN, The
See TEGNER, Henry (Stuart)

* * *

NOVAK, Maximillian E(rwin) 1930-

PERSONAL: Born March 26, 1930, in New York, N.Y.; son of George and Elsie (Loewy) Novak; married Demetra Palamari, June 13, 1954 (divorced, 1963); married Estelle Gershgoren (an assistant professor of English), August 21, 1966; children: (second marriage) Ralph, Daniel, Rachel. *Education:* University of California, Los Angeles, B.A., 1952, M.A., 1954, Ph.D., 1958; St. John's College, Oxford, D.Phil., 1961. *Religion:* Jewish. *Home:* 451 South El Camino Dr., Beverly Hills, Calif. 90212. *Office:* Department of English, University of California, 405 Hilgard Ave., Los Angeles, Calif. 90024.

CAREER: University of California, Los Angeles, professor of English, 1962—, Clark Library Professor, 1973-74. *Member:* International Association of University Professors of English, Modern Language Association of America, American Society for Eighteenth-Century Studies, Oxford Society. *Awards, honors:* Fulbright-Hays fellowship, 1955-57; Guggenheim fellowship, 1965-66; American Philosophical Society fellowship, 1979; National Endowment for the Humanities fellowship, 1980-81.

WRITINGS: Economics and the Fiction of Daniel Defoe, University of California Press, 1962; *Defoe and the Nature of Man,* Clarendon Press, 1963; (with Herbert Davis) *The Uses of Irony* (pamphlet), Clark Library, 1966; (editor with George R. Guffey) John Dryden, *Works,* Volume X, University of California Press, 1970; *Congreve,* Twayne, 1971; (with Aubrey Williams) *Congreve Consider'd* (pamphlet), Clark Library, 1971; (with Edward Dudley) *The Wildman Within,* Pittsburgh University Press, 1972; (editor with David Rodes) Thomas Southerne, *Oroonoko,* Regents Drama Series, 1976; (editor) *English Literature in the Age of Disguise,* University of California Press, 1977; *Realism, Myth and History in Defoe's Fiction,* University of Nebraska Press, 1983; *Eighteenth-Century English Literature,* Macmillan, 1983; (editor with Guffey and Alan Roper) Dryden, *Works,* Volume XIII, University of California Press, 1984. Editor, Augustan Reprint Society.

WORK IN PROGRESS: A biography of Daniel Defoe, with Paula Backscheider; a critical study of I. J. Singer, with wife, Estelle Novak.

SIDELIGHTS: Maximillian E. Novak's special areas of interest are the novel in general, eighteenth-century literature, Jewish-American fiction, and Restoration and eighteenth-century drama.

NOVAK, Robert D(avid) 1931-

PERSONAL: Born February 26, 1931, in Joliet, Ill.; son of Maurice Pall (a chemical engineer) and Jane Anne (Sanders) Novak; married Geraldine Williams, November 10, 1962; children: Zelda, Alexander Augustus Williams. *Education:* Attended University of Illinois, 1948-52. *Home:* 6417 Tilden Lane, Rockville, Md. 20852. *Office:* Room 1312, 1750 Pennsylvania Ave. N.W., Washington, D.C. 20006.

CAREER: Reporter for *Joliet Herald-News,* Joliet, Ill., 1948-50, and *Champaign-Urbana Courier,* Urbana, Ill., 1950-51; correspondent in Lincoln and Omaha, Neb., Indianapolis, Ind., and Washington, D.C., for Associated Press, 1954-58; *Wall Street Journal,* New York City, Washington correspondent, 1958-63; New York Herald Tribune Syndicate, New York City, author of column "Inside Report," 1963-66; author of column, Publisher's Hall Syndicate, 1966—. *Member:* National Press Club, Sigma Delta Chi.

WRITINGS: The Agony of the GOP, 1964, Macmillan, 1965; (with Rowland Evans, Jr.) *Lyndon B. Johnson: The Exercise of Power,* New American Library, 1966; (with Evans) *Nixon in the White House: The Frustration of Power,* Random House, 1971; (with others) *The Mass Media and Modern Democracy,* edited by Harry M. Clor, Rand McNally, 1974; (with Evans) *The Reagan Revolution: An Inside Look at the Transformation of the U.S. Government,* Dutton, 1981.

Contributor to *Saturday Evening Post, Reporter, New Republic, Esquire, National Observer, Economist,* and other publications.

SIDELIGHTS: The Reagan Revolution: An Inside Look at the Transformation of the U.S. Government, written by newspaper columnists Robert D. Novak and Rowland Evans, Jr., is a study of the administration of President Ronald Reagan. It argues that Reagan's economic policies will change the United States as dramatically as did the policies of President Franklin D. Roosevelt.

In flattering terms, Novak and Evans outline Reagan's career and discuss the development of his conservative economic and political ideas. Charles Kaiser of *New Republic* takes exception to the authors' assertion that Reagan's "string of roles in B-movies is actually the best possible preparation for the most dangerous job in the world." Because of such assertions throughout the book, Kaiser believes that *The Reagan Revolution* "provides powerful evidence of the authors' determination to transform themselves from journalists into official publicists for their newest hero."

James Fallows of the *New York Times Book Review* agrees. The authors "suggest in every possible way that the changes instituted by the new administration were long overdue," he writes. "What is best about Mr. Evans and Mr. Novak, in contrast to many other newspaper columnists," he continues, "is that they still believe in legwork. Their column attempts to be reportorial rather than oracular. . . . When they stick to reporting in this new book, they produce a competent if unexciting summary of how the administration developed and sold its policies."

BIOGRAPHICAL/CRITICAL SOURCES: Time, December 2, 1966; *Christian Science Monitor,* September 14, 1981; *New Republic,* September 30, 1981; *New York Times Book Review,* October 4, 1981; *National Review,* November 13, 1981.

NUELLE, Helen S(hearman) 1923-

PERSONAL: Born August 1, 1923, in St. Louis, Mo.; daughter of George S. and Winafred (Burns) Shearman; married Raymond Nuelle (a cost accountant), June 4, 1949; children: Adrienne (Mrs. Lawrence W. Laughlin). *Education:* Attended high school in St. Louis, Mo. *Politics:* Independent. *Religion:* Roman Catholic. *Home:* 2525 Yorkshire Dr., Florissant, Mo. 63033. *Agent:* Donald MacCampbell, Inc., 12 East 41st St., New York, N.Y. 10017.

CAREER: Office worker; writer. *Member:* Missouri Historical Society.

WRITINGS—All gothic novels; except as indicated: *Evil Lives Here,* Avalon, 1973; *The Haunting of Bally Moran,* Woodhill, 1976; *Sins of the Past,* Woodhill, 1977; *Land Where Our Fathers Died* (murder mystery), Woodhill, 1978; *Surrender to Love,* Dell, 1978; *The Danger in Loving,* Dell, 1980; *The Long Enchantment,* Dell, 1980; *The Treacherous Heart,* Dell, 1981.

WORK IN PROGRESS: A gothic mystery, *The Pictures at Peacock Hill.*†

* * *

NYE, Joseph S(amuel), Jr. 1937-

PERSONAL: Born January 19, 1937, in South Orange, N.J.; son of Joseph Samuel (a stockbroker) and Else (Ashwell) Nye; married Mary Harding, 1961; children: John, Benjamin, Daniel. *Education:* Princeton University, A.B. (summa cum laude), 1958; Oxford University, B.A., 1960; Harvard University, Ph.D., 1964. *Religion:* Unitarian Universalist. *Home:* 1932 Massachusetts Ave., Lexington, Mass. 02173. *Office:* John F. Kennedy School of Government, Harvard University, 79 John F. Kennedy St., Cambridge, Mass. 02138; and Center for International Affairs, Harvard University, 1737 Cambridge St., Cambridge, Mass. 02138.

CAREER: Harvard University, Cambridge, Mass., instructor, 1964-66, assistant professor, 1966-69, associate professor, 1969-71, professor of government, 1971—, program director for Center for International Affairs, 1969-72. Visiting professor, Institut Universitaire des Hautes Etudes Internationales, 1968, and School of International Affairs, Carleton University, 1973; visiting fellow, Royal Institute of International Affairs, 1974. Carnegie Endowment for International Peace, member of committee on travel and maintenance awards, 1970-75; chairman of panel on U.S. security and the future of arms control, 1981—; member of nuclear energy policy study, Ford Foundation, 1975-76; member of Trilaterial Commission, 1979—. Member of Rhodes scholarship selection committee for New Hampshire, 1967, and Massachusetts, 1970-72; member of visiting committee, Georgetown University School of Foreign Service, 1972-77; trustee, Wells College, 1974-77. Consultant to U.S. government agencies and departments and to Ford Foundation, 1973, 1975, and 1976, United Nations department of economic and social affairs, 1973-74, and Paine, Webber, Mitchell, Hutchins, Inc., 1979—; special advisor, Aspen Institute for Humanistic Studies, 1982—; member of advisory panel, Office of Technology Assessment, 1982—.

MEMBER: International Institute for Strategic Studies, Institute for International Economics (member of advisory committee, 1981—), World Peace Foundation (member of board of directors, 1972-77 and 1981—), World Association for International Relations (founding member), United Nations Association (member of board of directors, 1973—), Atlantic Institute for International Affairs (member of board of governors, 1974-77), Council on Foreign Relations (member of committee on studies, 1972-77), Committee for Economic Development (member of research advisory committee, 1973; chairman, 1974-76), Overseas Development Council (member of board of directors, 1983), American Society of International Law (member of board of review and development, 1973), American Academy of Arts and Sciences (member of committee on international security studies, 1982—), National Academy of Arts and Sciences (member of ocean policy committee, 1969-75; member of commission on international relations, 1977-82; member of committee on international security and arms control, 1980-82), American Political Science Association (member of program committee, 1971; chairman of Helen Dwight Reid award committee, 1973). *Awards, honors:* Rhodes scholar, 1958-60.

WRITINGS: Pan Africanism and East African Integration, Harvard University Press, 1965; (editor) *International Regionalism,* Little, Brown, 1968; *Peace in Parts: Integration and Conflict in Regional Organization,* Little, Brown, 1971; (editor with Robert O. Keohane) *Transnational Relations and World Politics,* Harvard University Press, 1972; (with Ernst B. Haas and Robert L. Butterworth) *Conflict Management by International Organizations,* General Learning Press, 1972; (with Keohane) *Power and Interdependence: World Politics and Transition,* Little, Brown, 1977; (editor with David A. Deese) *Energy and Security,* Ballinger, 1980; (with others) *Living with Nuclear Weapons,* Harvard University Press, 1983. Also author of *Managing U.S.-Soviet Relations,* Council on Foreign Relations.

Contributor: J. Butler and A. Castagno, editors, *Papers on Africa,* Praeger, 1967; Leon N. Lindberg and Stuart A. Scheingold, editors, *Regional Integration: Theory and Research,* Harvard University Press, 1970; Cyril Black and Richard Falk, editors, *The Future of International Legal Order,* Volume IV, Princeton University Press, 1972; Lawrence B. Krause and Walter S. Salant, editors, *European Monetary Unification and Its Meaning for the United States,* Brookings Institution, 1973; Robert Cox and Harold Jacobson, editors, *The Anatomy of Influence: Decision Making in International Organization,* Yale University Press, 1973; C. Fred Bergsten, editor, *The Future of the International Economic Order,* Heath, 1973; Fred Greenstein and Nelson Polsby, editors, *The Handbook of Political Science,* Addison-Wesley, 1975; *Annual Editions: World Politics,* Dushkin, 1982; Harry Blechman, editor, *Rethinking the U.S. Strategic Posture: A Report from the Aspen Consortium on Arms Control and Security Issues,* Ballinger, 1982; Samuel P. Huntington, editor, *The Strategic Imperative: New Policies for American Security,* Ballinger, 1982.

Contributor to professional journals. Member of editorial board, *Ocean Development and International Law,* 1967, *Foreign Policy,* 1970-76 and 1979—, and *International Security,* 1979; *International Organization,* member of board of editors, 1968—, chairman, 1972-74.

AVOCATIONAL INTERESTS: Skiing, squash, fishing.

BIOGRAPHICAL/CRITICAL SOURCES: New York Times Book Review, August 16, 1981, June 26, 1983; *Washington Post Book World,* July 3, 1983.

O

O'CONNELL, Timothy E(dward) 1943-

PERSONAL: Born August 21, 1943, in Plainfield, N.J.; son of Desmond H. (a businessman) and Rosemary (McGough) O'Connell. *Education:* St. Mary of the Lake Seminary, B.A., 1965, S.T.B., 1967, S.T.L., 1969; Fordham University, Ph.D., 1974. *Office:* Institute of Pastoral Studies, Loyola University of Chicago, 6525 North Sheridan Rd., Chicago, Ill. 60626.

CAREER: Archdiocese of Chicago, Chicago, Ill., ordained Roman Catholic priest, 1969; Loyola University of Chicago, Chicago, director of liturgy, 1967-68; associate pastor of Roman Catholic church in Oak Lawn, Ill., 1969-70; St. Mary of the Lake Seminary, Mundelein, Ill., assistant professor, 1973-76, associate professor, 1976-81, professor of moral theology, 1981-82, chairman of department, 1975-82; Loyola University of Chicago, Institute of Pastoral Studies, director, 1982—. *Member:* American Academy of Religion, Catholic Theological Society of America, American Society of Christian Ethics.

WRITINGS: What a Modern Catholic Believes about Suffering and Evil, Thomas More Association, 1972; *Changing Roman Catholic Moral Theology: A Study in Josef Fuchs,* University Microfilms, 1974; *Contemporary Meditations on Personal Holiness,* Thomas More Association, 1975; *Principles for a Catholic Morality,* Seabury, 1978. Contributor to theology journals and other magazines, including *Chicago Studies, Thought, Critic,* and *America.*

* * *

ODELL, Robin 1935-

PERSONAL: Born December 19, 1935, in Totton, England; son of Samuel Arthur and Dorothy (Lickfold) Odell; married Joan Bartholomew, September 19, 1959. *Education:* Educated in England. *Politics:* Liberal. *Religion:* Agnostic. *Home:* 15 Churchill Crescent, Sonning Common, Reading RG4 9RU, England. *Office:* Water Research Centre, Medmenham, Marlow SL7 2HD, England.

CAREER: University of Southampton, Southampton, England, laboratory technician in department of zoology, 1951-54, assistant museum curator, 1956-62; University Institute of Education in Southampton, technical demonstrator, 1962-68; Water Research Centre, Marlow, England, publications manager, 1968—. Member, Institute of Public Relations and Institute of Scientific and Technical Communicators. *Military service:* British Army Medical Service, 1954-56. *Member:* Society of Authors, Crime Writers' Association (Great Britain), Rationalist Press Association, Paternosters, Our Society (crimes club), Southampton Humanist Society (secretary, 1962-68). *Awards, honors:* F.C.C. Watts Memorial Prize, 1957; International Humanist and Ethical Union Prize, 1960; special Edgar award from Mystery Writers of America, 1980, for *The Murderers' Who's Who.*

WRITINGS: Jack the Ripper in Fact and Fiction, Harrap, 1965; (with Tom Barfield) *Humanist Glossary,* Pemberton, 1967; *Exhumation of a Murder,* Harrap, 1975; (with J.H.H. Gaute) *The Murderers' Who's Who,* Harrap, 1978; (with Gaute) *Lady Killers,* Granada, 1980; (with Gaute) *Lady Killers 2,* Granada, 1981; (with Gaute) *Murder "Whatdunit",* Harrap, 1982; (with Gaute) *Murder Whereabouts,* Harrap, 1985. Contributor to *Crimes and Punishment Encyclopedia, Psychology, Ethical Outlook, Humanist, New Zealand Rationalist,* and *Pulse.*

SIDELIGHTS: Robin Odell told *CA:* "The question most frequently asked is, 'Why write about such a gruesome subject as murder?' Murder is about finality which is why it fascinates and mystifies. Most murders have qualities which form the basis of popular interest. Ordinary people can identify with the circumstances which lead to the possibility of murder—that much is within their experience—but the forces which breach the threshold of violence are part of the consuming mystery. That is why the subject is worth writing about and there is no finer account of murder in the English language than that of Thomas de Quincey in his 'Murder Considered as One of the Fine Arts,' published in 1827."

* * *

O'DELL, Scott 1903-

PERSONAL: Born May 23, 1903, in Los Angeles, Calif.; son of Bennett Mason and May Elizabeth (Gabriel) O'Dell; married Jane Rattenbury, 1948. *Education:* Attended Occidental College, 1919, University of Wisconsin, 1920, Stanford University, 1920-21, and University of Rome, 1925.

CAREER: Formerly a cameraman and a book editor for a Los Angeles newspaper; full-time writer, 1934—. *Military service:* U.S. Air Force.

AWARDS, HONORS: Rupert Hughes Award, 1960, John Newbery Medal, 1961, Southern California Council on Literature for Children and Young People notable book award, 1961, Hans Christian Andersen award of merit, 1962, William Allen White Award, 1963, German Juvenile International Award, 1963, and Nene Award, 1964, all for *Island of the Blue Dolphins;* Newbery honor award, 1967, and German Juvenile International Award, 1968, both for *The King's Fifth;* Newbery honor awards, 1968, for *The Black Pearl,* and 1971, for *Sing Down the Moon;* Hans Christian Andersen Medal, 1972; University of Southern Mississippi medallion, 1976; Regina Medal, 1978; *Focal* Award, Los Angeles Public Library, 1981.

WRITINGS: Representative Photoplays Analyzed: Modern Authorship, Palmer Institute of Authorship, 1924; *Woman of Spain: A Story of Old California* (novel), Houghton, 1934; *Hill of the Hawk* (novel), Bobbs-Merrill, 1953; (with William Doyle) *Man Alone,* Bobbs-Merrill, 1953; *Country of the Sun: Southern California, an Informal History and Guide,* Crowell, 1957; *The Sea Is Red: A Novel,* Holt, 1958; (with Rhoda Kellogg) *The Psychology of Children's Art,* Communications Research Machines, 1967.

Juveniles; all published by Houghton: *Island of the Blue Dolphins,* 1960; *The King's Fifth,* 1966; *The Black Pearl,* 1967; *The Dark Canoe,* 1968; *Journey to Jericho,* 1969; *Sing Down the Moon,* 1970; *The Treasure of Topo-el-Bampo,* 1972; *The Cruise of the Arctic Star,* 1973; *Child of Fire,* 1974; *The Hawk That Dare Not Hunt by Day,* 1975; *Zia,* 1976; *The 290,* 1976; *Carlota,* 1977; *Kathleen, Please Come Home,* 1978; *The Captive,* 1979; *Sarah Bishop,* 1980; *The Feathered Serpent,* 1981; *The Spanish Smile,* 1982.

WORK IN PROGRESS: The Amethyst Ring.

SIDELIGHTS: Scott O'Dell's novel *Island of the Blue Dolphins* tells the story of Karana, an Indian girl who lives alone on an island. Although she is alone, she "not only manages to exist but to wring a measure of comfort, beauty, even joy in her solitude," writes E. L. Buell of the *New York Times Book Review.* The novel is based on the true story of a nineteenth-century woman who lived on a remote island off the coast of California. "Years of research must have gone into this book," writes the *Horn Book* reviewer, "to turn historical fact into so moving and lasting an experience." The *Chicago Sunday Tribune* critic has a similar appraisal. *Island of the Blue Dolphins,* he writes, "has the timeless, enduring quality of a classic. Reading it should be a deeply moving experience for anyone over 10." M. S. Libby of the *New York Herald Tribune Book Review* calls it "a book not written to fulfill any need or with any audience in mind, but simply because the subject has seized the author's imagination, and he had to write it." "This is a remarkable book," Charlotte Jackson of the *San Francisco Chronicle* concludes, "written with such restraint that it becomes all the more powerful."

MEDIA ADAPTATIONS: Island of the Blue Dolphins was filmed by Universal in 1964. *The Black Pearl* was filmed in 1976.

BIOGRAPHICAL/CRITICAL SOURCES—Periodicals: *New York Times Book Review,* March 27, 1960, February 24, 1980, May 4, 1980, January 10, 1982; *Horn Book,* April, 1960; *Chicago Sunday Tribune,* May 8, 1960; *New York Herald Tribune Book Review,* May 8, 1960; *San Francisco Chronicle,* May 8, 1960; *Washington Post Book World,* March 9, 1980, January 9, 1983.

Books: John Rowe Townsend, *Written for Children: An Outline of English Language Children's Literature,* Lippincott, 1965; Cornelia Meigs, editor, *A Critical History of Children's Literature,* Macmillan, 1969; Constantine Georgiou, *Children and Their Literature,* Prentice-Hall, 1969; Townsend, *A Sense of Story: Essays on Contemporary Writing for Children,* Lippincott, 1971; *Children's Literature Review,* Volume I, Gale, 1976.

* * *

O'DELL, William F(rancis) 1909-

PERSONAL: Born January 24, 1909, in Detroit, Mich.; son of Frank Trevor and Garnett (Aikman) O'Dell; married Bess Baer, June 10, 1933; children: Peggy (Mrs. J. Thomas Pinckard), David T. *Education:* University of Illinois, B.S., 1930. *Home:* 5707 Shell Point Village, Ft. Myers, Fla. 33908.

CAREER: Penton Publishing Co., Cleveland, Ohio, staff member, 1933-37; Ross Federal Research Corp., New York, N.Y., vice-president, 1937-44; Statistical Research Co., Chicago, Ill., managing director, 1944-45; Market Facts, Inc. (marketing research consultants), Chicago, president, 1945-64, chairman, 1964-73; University of Virginia, McIntire School of Commerce, Charlottesville, professor of marketing, 1964-75. *Member:* American Marketing Association (president, 1960-61), American Association of University Professors.

WRITINGS: The Marketing Decision, American Management Association, 1968; (co-author) *Marketing Decision Making,* South-Western, 1976, 3rd edition, 1984; *How to Make Lifetime Friends—With Peers and Parents,* Exposition Press, 1978; *Twelve Families: An American Experience,* Gateway, 1981. Contributor to business, geneology, and marketing journals. Member of editorial staff, *Journal of Marketing.*

* * *

OEHSER, Paul H(enry) 1904-

PERSONAL: Surname is pronounced *O*-zher; born March 27, 1904, in Cherry Creek, N.Y.; son of Henry Christian (a farmer) and Agnes (Abbey) Oehser; married Grace M. Edgbert (an artist), October 4, 1927; children: Gordon Vincent, Richard Edgbert. *Education:* Greenville College, A.B., 1925; also studied at University of Iowa, summer, 1924, and took graduate courses at intervals at American University, 1925-30. *Politics:* Democrat. *Home:* 9012 Old Dominion Dr., McLean, Va. 22102.

CAREER: U.S. Department of Agriculture, Bureau of Biological Survey, Washington, D.C., assistant editor, 1925-31; Smithsonian Institution, Washington, D.C., editor, U.S. National Museum, 1931-50, assistant chief of Editorial Division, 1946-50, chief of Editorial and Publication Division and public relations officer, 1950-66; National Geographic Society, Washington, D.C., editor of scientific publications, 1966-78. Member of boards of directors, Greater Washington Educational Television Association, 1958-64, and Westminster School, Annandale, Va., 1967—.

MEMBER: Wilderness Society (member of governing council, 1966-77, and honorary council, 1977—), Thoreau Society (president, 1961), American Ornithologists' Union, Washington Academy of Sciences (fellow), Columbia Historical Society, Philosophical Society of Washington, Literary Society of Washington (corresponding secretary and treasurer, 1972—), Biological Society of Washington, Washington Biologists' Field Club (president, 1964-67), History of Science Club, Cosmos Club (president, 1974), Palaver Club. *Awards, honors:* Cosmos Club Distinguished Service Award, 1968.

WRITINGS: Sons of Science: The Story of the Smithsonian Institution and Its Leaders, Henry Schuman, 1949, reprinted, Greenwood Press, 1968; *Fifty Poems,* Sherwood House (Washington, D.C.), 1954; *The Smithsonian Institution,* Praeger, 1970; *The Witch of Scrapfaggot Green,* Pin Willow Press, 1981; *The Smithsonian Institution,* Westview, 1983. Editor, *Proceedings of the Eighth American Scientific Congress,* 1940, twelve volumes; general editor, *The United States Encyclopedia of History,* 1967-68. Contributor of articles, reviews, and verse to journals, encyclopedias, and newspapers. Managing editor, *Journal of the Washington Academy of Sciences,* 1939-59; editor, *Arlington Historical Magazine,* 1939-62, and *Bulletin* of the Cosmos Club, 1951-69.

SIDELIGHTS: Paul H. Oehser told *CA:* "I remember a quatrain recited to me long ago by a physicist of the National Bureau of Standards—a critique of sorts of a certain kind of writing: 'He wrote in neither verse nor prose / But simply laid his words in rows— / Not up and down as Webster penned / But row on row and end on end.'"

* * *

O'FAOLAIN, Julia 1932-
(Julia Martines)

PERSONAL: Surname is pronounced O'Fay-lawn; born June 6, 1932, in London, England; daughter of Sean (a writer) and Eileen (Gould) O'Faolain; married Lauro Martines (a professor and historian); children: Lucien Christopher. *Education:* University College, Dublin, received B.A. and M.A.; graduate study at Universita di Roma and Sorbonne, University of Paris. *Home:* 15 Glenloch Rd., London N.W.3, England. *Agent:* Deborah Rogers, Ltd., 49 Blenheim Cres., London W.11, England; and International Creative Management, 40 West 52nd St., New York, N.Y. 10019.

CAREER: Writer, translator, and language teacher. *Awards, honors: No Country for Young Men* was named to the Booker Prize short list.

WRITINGS: (Translator, under name Julia Martines) Gene Brucker, editor, *Two Memoirs of Renaissance Florence: The Diaries of Buonaccorso Pitti and Gregorio Dati,* Harper, 1967; (translator, under name Julia Martines) Piero Chiara, *A Man of Parts,* Little, Brown, 1968; *We Might See Sights! and Other Stories,* Faber, 1968; *Godded and Codded,* Faber, 1970, published as *Three Lovers,* Coward, 1971; (editor with husband, Lauro Martines) *Not in God's Image: Women in History from the Greeks to the Victorians* (nonfiction), Harper, 1973; *Man in the Cellar* (short stories), Faber, 1974; *Women in the Wall* (novel; New Fiction Society selection in England), Viking, 1975; *Melancholy Baby, and Other Stories,* Poolberg Press, 1978; *No Country for Young Men* (novel), Allen Lane, 1980; *Daughters of Passion* (short stories), Allen Lane, 1982; *The Irish Signorina* (novel), Allen Lane, 1984.

Contributor to anthologies: *London Magazine Stories,* edited by Alan Ross, London Magazine Editions, 1967, 1969, 1971; *Winter's Tales,* edited by A. D. Maclean, Macmillan, 1973; *Bitches and Sad Ladies,* edited by Pat Rotter, Harper Magazine Press, 1975; *Winter's Tales,* edited by Maclean, Macmillan, 1973, 1980, 1982; *The Bodley Head Book of Irish Short Stories,* edited by David Marcus, Bodley Head, 1980; *The Penguin Book of Irish Short Stories,* edited by Benedict Kiely, Penguin, 1981; *Fathers: Reflections by Daughters,* edited by Ursula Owen, Virago, 1983; *Firebird 3: Writing Today,* edited by Robin Robertson, Penguin, 1984.

Contributor of short stories and reviews to *New Yorker, Kenyon Review, Saturday Evening Post, Vogue, Critic, Cornhill Magazine, Nova, Cosmopolitan, Times* (London), *Irish Press, New York Times, Washington Post, Hibernia, Triquarterly, The Fiction Magazine, Observer,* and other periodicals. Also contributor to "Kaleidoscope," a British Broadcasting Corporation radio program.

WORK IN PROGRESS: A novel set in the last years of papal Rome, before the city was annexed by Italy.

SIDELIGHTS: When Julia O'Faolain's book *Three Lovers* appeared, the inevitable comparisons between her novel and the work of her father, novelist and short-story writer Sean O'Faolain, were made. *Book World* critic J. R. Franks dismisses the issue by saying: "Yes, Julia O'Faolain is Sean's daughter. No, she does not write like her father. And maybe, if [*Three Lovers*] is a fair harbinger, she'll become the family-member whose name is used for identification." Franks's opinion is echoed by Sally Beauman, who notes in the *New York Times Book Review* that the author "writes firmly, with a voice all her own." Praising O'Faolain's "well planned, intelligent, concise" style, Beauman finds the author's writing "more pointed than that of [her father] with a cold female eye for the egocentricities of masculine behavior."

Two of O'Faolain's notable works focus on women in history. *Not in God's Image: Women in History from the Greeks to the Victorians,* edited by O'Faolain and her husband, Lauro Martines, is described by a *Christian Century* writer as a collection of readings from primary sources that "documents the subjection of women in Western civilization." An *Economist* critic states that "as a source-book on the history of women, [*Not in God's Image*] stands in a class quite of its own. . . . The authors deal skilfully with the constant larding of hypocrisy, ranging from recipes for damaged maidenhoods to advice on concealing intellect." Mary Ellmann also admires the work, writing in the *New York Review of Books* that O'Faolain's effort is "distinguished by genuine scholarship. Its feminist sympathy is apparent . . . but it pursues the point by hard work, not by swishy emotion. And what a picture unfolds!"

Women in the Wall, a novel based on the life of Queen Radegund, who in the sixth century founded the monastery of the Holy Cross, is another example of O'Faolain's interest in women's place in history. According to *Times Literary Supplement* critic Lalage Pulvertaft, by adapting such characters as Queen Radegund and St. Agnes, the author tampered with history to "try and answer fundamental questions about women's role in society." Pulvertaft expresses criticism for O'Faolain's motives in writing *Women in the Wall:* "In her fashionable wish to explain visions as sexuality, vocations as perverted power mania, [the author] misses the nub of the matter; that God, through Christ, had challenged women as well as men to be individuals, even if this meant attacking the institutions of society."

Doris Grumbach, on the other hand, reviewing the book for *New Republic,* calls O'Faolain "a novelist of great talent whose interest has . . . come close to a Poe-ian obsession with immurement. . . . The force of language, the subtle and entirely successful recreation by means of it of the spirit as well as the events of Gallic life 13 centuries ago, at the end of the Roman era and the beginning of the Christian, make *Women in the Wall* a remarkably modern historical novel, poignant and powerful. It absorbs the reader into a time when women were chattels, when 'inherited land followed the spear not the spindle,'—into a time when the greatest conquerer was not of the flesh but of the spirit, when the full force of early Christianity made fanatics and saints of its believers."

With *No Country for Young Men*, O'Faolain "tackles the legacy of Republicanism in Southern Ireland through the story of one family," according to Hermoine Lee in the *Observer*. This story follows the efforts of an American sympathizer in Ireland who, while conducting research for a pro-Republican film, is drawn into the lives of a family whose members have involved themselves in the Irish cause for years. Writing a novel that spans three generations is "an ambitious undertaking," says Patricia Craig in the *Times Literary Supplement;* however, the critic finds the book somewhat "unsure of its own purpose. *No Country for Young Men* is not a political thriller, not a stark tragedy, not a documentary of social behaviour, not a story of personal relations, not a family saga, not a piece of historical fiction; but it contains . . . elements of all these.''

Other critics, though, found more to praise in the novel. Lee, while acknowledging that "at times the novel edges toward lecture-topics," concludes nonetheless that the book's "strong grasp of the relation between a family and a national history transcends its occasional imaginative sagginess." The work "reflects a concern for the nation that emerged from the Troubles, and a worry about the new Troubles," states William Trevor in *Hibernea*. Trevor continues: "As a novel, it is old-fashioned in the very best sense, tidily knitting together its disparate strands, athletically leaping about in time and place, telling several stories at once." And *Guardian* reviewer Robert Nye, while noting that there "have been many novels about twentieth century Ireland and its problems," says that *No Country for Young Men* is "one of the very best books of its kind that it has ever been my pain and my pleasure to read."

Irish issues also surface in *The Obedient Wife*, but in a different setting. The tale of a Catholic housewife's infatuation with an Irish Catholic priest in Los Angeles, *The Obedient Wife* is "a novel about failures of instinct, as well as . . . social and conjugal failures," according to Patricia Craig in another *Times Literary Supplement* review. Craig adds: "There is plenty of scope for comedy in Julia O'Faolain's novel, but she has chosen not to present her material in a comic mode. . . . Instead she coolly assesses the circumstances and traits that have got her characters into their present predicament, and still more coolly allows their defects and misapprehensions to become apparent in the course of the narrative." *The Obedient Wife*, comments Craig, "is an exceptionally polished work; if its ending disappoints feminists, who require gestures of social rebelliousness from their fiction, just as Catholic readers used to require wholesomeness in theirs, it is none the less appropriate, in that it represents an assertion of the values its heroine has lived by.''

O'Faolain is one of "the very few Irish writers who [is] truly international in range," declares Roger Garfitt in his contribution to the book *Two Decades of Irish Writing: A Critical Survey*. "Where she differs most sharply . . . from other Irish writers is in choosing to work from within the contemporary flux of modes and passions. Her characters generally have comparative economic freedom. . . . They do not escape, though, essentially the same challenges: only in their case the pressure comes from within, generally as a conflict between the direction of their own vitality and the assumptions of the way they have been brought up." Concludes Garfitt: "There is a power of mind behind her work, as well as an irreverently perceptive eye, that catches the intensity of human drives, the essential seriousness of the effort to live, without swallowing any of the trends in self-deception. She is an acute observer, who is involved at a level of concern deeper than the substance of her observations."

BIOGRAPHICAL/CRITICAL SOURCES: *Listener,* June 20, 1968, September 26, 1974, June 3, 1982; *London Magazine,* September, 1968, November, 1970, October/November, 1974; *Best Sellers,* May 1, 1971; *New York Times Book Review,* May 9, 1971; *Book World,* June 13, 1971; *Saturday Review,* July 3, 1971; *Economist,* February 17, 1973; *Choice,* December, 1973, October, 1975; *New York Review of Books,* November 1, 1973; Julia O'Faolain, *Women in the Wall,* Viking, 1975; Douglas Dunn, editor, *Two Decades of Irish Writing: A Critical Survey,* Dufor, 1975; *Times Literary Supplement,* April 4, 1975, June 13, 1980, July 23, 1982; *New Republic,* May 10, 1975; Patrick Rafroidi and Maurice Harmon, editors, *The Irish Novel in Our Times,* Volume III, Publications de l'Universite de Lille, 1975-1976; *Contemporary Literary Criticism,* Gale, Volume VI, 1976, Volume XIX, 1981; *Observer,* June 1, 1980; *Guardian,* June 5, 1980; *Hibernea,* June 5, 1980; *New Statesman,* June 6, 1980, November 12, 1982; *Dictionary of Literary Biography,* Volume XIV, Gale, 1983.

—Sketch by Susan Salter

* * *

O'FAOLAIN, Sean 1900-

PERSONAL: Name originally John Francis Whelan, changed to Gaelic variant, 1918; born February 22, 1900, in Cork, Ireland; son of Denis and Bridget (Murphy) Whelan; married Elleen Gould, June, 1928; children: Julia, Stephen. *Education:* University College at Cork of National University of Ireland, B.A., 1921, M.A., 1925; Harvard University, M.A., 1929. *Home:* 17 Rosmeen Park, Dunlaoire, County Dublin, Ireland. *Agent:* A. P. Watt, 26/28 Bedford Row, London W.C.1, England.

CAREER: Fought in Irish Revolution, 1918-21; Irish Republican Army, director of publicity, 1923; Princeton University, Princeton, N.J., and Boston College, Boston, Mass., lecturer in English, both 1929; St. Mary's College, Strawberry Hill, England, lecturer in English, 1929-33; full-time author, 1932—. *Member:* Arts Council of Ireland (director, 1957-59), Irish Academy of Letters. *Awards, honors:* John Harvard fellowship, 1928-29; Femina Prize nomination, 1932, for *Midsummer Night Madness and Other Stories;* D.Litt., Trinity College, Dublin, 1957.

WRITINGS—Short stories: *Midsummer Night Madness and Other Stories,* Viking, 1932; *There's a Birdie in the Cage,* Grayson, 1935; *The Born Genius: A Short Story,* Schuman's, 1936; *A Purse of Coppers: Short Stories,* J. Cape, 1937, Viking, 1938; *Teresa and Other Stories,* J. Cape, 1947, published as *The Man Who Invented Sin and Other Stories,* Devin-Adair, 1948; *The Finest Stories of Sean O'Faolain,* Little, Brown, 1957 (published in England as *The Stories of Sean O'Faolain,* Hart-Davis, 1958); *I Remember! I Remember! Stories,* Little, Brown, 1962; *The Heat of the Sun: Stories and Tales,* Little, Brown, 1966; *The Talking Trees and Other Stories,* Little, Brown, 1970; *Foreign Affairs and Other Stories,* Little, Brown, 1976; (with others) *One True Friend and Other Irish Stories,* Structural Readers, 1977; *Selected Stories of Sean O'Faolain,* Little, Brown, 1978; *Collected Stories,* Constable, 1980.

Novels: *A Nest of Simple Folk,* J. Cape, 1933, Viking, 1934; *Bird Alone,* Viking, 1936; *Come Back to Erin,* Viking, 1940, reprinted, Greenwood Press, 1972; *And Again?*, Constable, 1979.

Biographies: *The Life Story of Eamon De Valera*, Penguin, 1934; *Constance Markievicz; or, The Average Revolutionary*, J. Cape, 1934, revised edition published as *Constance Markievicz*, Sphere Books, 1968; *King of the Beggars: A Life of Daniel O'Connell, the Irish Liberator, in a Study of the Rise of the Modern Irish Democracy, 1775-1847*, Viking, 1938, abridged edition, Parkside Press (Dublin), 1945, reprinted, Greenwood Press, 1975; *De Valera*, Penguin, 1939; *The Great O'Neill: A Biography of Hugh O'Neill, Earl of Tyrone, 1550-1616*, Duell, Sloan & Pearce, 1942, reprinted, Mercier Press, 1970; *Newman's Way: The Odyssey of John Henry Newman*, Devin-Adair, 1952 (published in England as *Newman's Way*, Longmans, Green, 1952); *Vive Moi!* (autobiography), Little, Brown, 1964 (published in England as *Vive Moi! An Autobiography*, Hart-Davis, 1965).

Travel: *An Irish Journey*, Longmans, Green, 1940; *A Summer in Italy*, Eyre & Spottiswoode, 1949, Devin-Adair, 1950; *An Autumn in Italy*, Devin-Adair, 1953 (published in England as *South to Sicily*, Collins, 1953).

Other: (Editor) *Lyrics and Satires from Tom Moore*, Cuala Press (Dublin), 1929, reprinted, Biblio Distribution Centre, 1971; (editor) *The Autobiography of Theobald Wolfe Tone*, Thomas Nelson, 1937; *She Had to Do Something: A Comedy in Three Acts* (first produced in Dublin, 1937), J. Cape, 1938; (compiler) *The Silver Branch: A Collection of the Best Old Irish Lyrics, Variously Translated*, Viking, 1938, reprinted, Books for Libraries, 1968; *The Story of Ireland* (history), Collins, 1943; (editor and author of foreword) Samuel Lover, *Adventures of Handy Andy*, Parkside Press, 1945; (author of preface) D 83222, *I Did Penal Servitude*, Metropolitan Publishing (Dublin), 1945; *The Irish*, Penguin, 1947, published as *The Irish: A Character Study*, Devin-Adair, 1949, revised and updated edition, Penguin, 1969, published as *The Story of the Irish People*, Avenel, 1982; *The Short Story* (criticism and stories), Collins, 1948, Devin-Adair, 1951; *The Vanishing Hero: Studies in Novelists of the Twenties*, Eyre & Spottiswoode, 1956, Little, Brown, 1957, published as *The Vanishing Hero: Studies of the Hero in the Modern Novel*, Grosset, 1957; (editor) *Short Stories: A Study in Pleasure*, Little, Brown, 1961.

Contributor of short stories and articles to numerous magazines, journals, and other periodicals. Editor, *Bell* (Irish periodical), 1940-45.

SIDELIGHTS: "Of all the significant O's in twentieth century Irish literature," notes Paul A. Doyle in *Best Sellers*, "Sean O'Casey is the most humorous and flamboyant, Liam O'Flaherty the most emotional and unpolished, Frank O'Connor the most satiric and whimsical, and Sean O'Faolain the most versatile and profound." One of modern Ireland's greatest chroniclers, O'Faolain has produced many memorable novels, short stories, and nonfiction works during his career, which spans more than fifty years.

Born John Francis Whelan in County Cork, Ireland, O'Faolain from an early age was inhibited, according to Gordon Henderson's *Dictionary of Literary Biography* article about the author, by "his father's unquestioning respect for authority, his mother's excessive piety, and the preoccupation both had with rising above their peasant-farmer origins." He was also influenced by the plays at the nearby Cork Opera House, and spent much of his time during his youth watching the dramatic presentations of such classics as *The Scarlet Pimpernel* and *The Prisoner of Zenda*. One play in particular had a dramatic effect on O'Faolain. Lennox Robinson's "The Patriot," a story set in an Irish shopkeeper's parlor, elicited a strong reaction from the boy. As O'Faolain relates in Henderson's article: "For years I had seen only plays straight from the West End of London. . . . Here was a most moving play about Irish peasants, shop-keeping and farming folk, men and women who could have been any one of my uncles and aunts down the country. It brought me strange and wonderful news—that writers could also write books and plays about the common everyday reality of Irish life."

Perhaps the most important event of O'Faolain's early years, however, was the Easter Rebellion of 1916. Although at first he opposed the uprising, motivated by his father's unwavering loyalty to the crown, O'Faolain soon became outraged at the brutal way the British forces "crushed the rebellion and then systematically executed its leaders," as Henderson puts it. "Fired with a new sense of nationalism," he continues, "[O'Faolain] was soon taking lessons in the Irish language and, at eighteen, joined other young men and women at a summer school for Gaelic speakers in the mountains of West Cork." At the same age, the young man unofficially changed his name from the anglicized John Whelan to the Gaelic Sean O'Faolain. He then joined the Irish Volunteers, an organization that later produced some members of the militant Irish Republican Army (IRA). And while O'Faolain eventually became involved with IRA activities—he was the group's publicity director at age twenty-three—the writer avoided the extreme, often violent tactics for which that organization would become infamous. "To have cast me for the role of a gunman would have been like casting me as a bull-fighter," explains O'Faolain in Henderson's piece. It was during this tumultuous period in Irish history that O'Faolain began his writing career.

The author's early works, including the novels *A Nest of Simple Folk* and *Bird Alone*, explore the lives of people caught up in various stages of "The Troubles." Leo O'Donnell, the lead character of *A Nest of Simple Folk*, for example, is seen over a period of sixty-two years, starting in 1854 and ending with the Easter Rebellion. O'Donnell, imprisoned for several years because of his Fenian involvement (the Fenians, an Irish nationalistic group, were established in the nineteenth century), "grows old futilely pursuing patriotic dreams," as Henderson writes, and passes his strong sense of Gaelic pride on to his nephew, Denis Hussey, a character modeled after O'Faolain himself. As both a political story and a poignant character study, *A Nest of Simple Folk* is "a memorable work, memorable as an instance of the power and passion of memory," according to Donat O'Donnell, reviewing the novel in *Renascence*.

Bird Alone, banned as obscene by Ireland's Censorship Board, opens with the elderly Corney Crone looking back over his life as a builder in Cork. The book focuses on his relationship with his grandfather, a staunch Fenian who helps shape young Crone's political viewpoint. Later, ostracized because of both his Irish activism and a scandal involving a woman who dies while giving birth to his child, Crone becomes a recluse, a "bird alone," living in an attic room.

"This is one of the very few modern novels . . . in which the treatment of character bears the stamp of a complete and subtle mastery," comments V. S. Pritchett about *Bird Alone*. In his *Christian Science Monitor* article, Pritchett continues: "The sympathy is profound to the point of tears—and they are often tears of that convinced laughter which comes when one says,

These people are round, whole, real and lovable and yet have that quality of mysteriousness which leaves us . . . in questioning wonder before even those whom we know very well." The reviewer deems *Bird Alone* "the genre piece of a master." William Troy, on the other hand, has praise not for the characters in the novel, but for its setting. County Cork is presented, Troy declares in *Nation*, as "more real and interesting than any of its inhabitants. This is managed partly through the fluid poetic style and partly through a formal framework which makes possible the rapid transitions and vivid condensations of the memory." Troy does have criticism for *Bird Alone*—he says he received an impression "of conflicts unresolved, of ambiguities remaining suspended"—but he ultimately cites the book's "flowing current of exquisitely modulated language." This view is shared by *Boston Transcript* critic A. B. Tourtellot, who finds that the novel's "major flaw . . . is the inadequate treatment of the story as a story." However, Tourtellot concludes, *Bird Alone* is "a fine and rich book, but fine and rich chiefly because of the craftsmanship of its author and not because of the strength of the story."

Although his novels and books of criticism have been well received, O'Faolain is also generally regarded as an accomplished short-story writer. In his collections the author examines the many aspects of modern Irish life. "His stories are typically dense, lush, complex, and rich—his is not an art of understatement," finds Gary Davenport in a *Hudson Review* article. "[O'Faolain] has two major themes: what it means to be Irish, and what it means to be an Irish Catholic. [The author] is a loyal but critical Irishman; he is capable of denouncing Irish provincialism of both the nationalist and religious genres, but unlike [Bernard] Shaw he denounces it from within: he lives in Ireland and he remains a Catholic. . . . And these stories are full to bursting of life. Landscape provides much of this richness—especially the fecund landscape of his native Cork: low thick clouds, endless rain, sodden earth. And the characters who live in this environment partake of its sense of being outside time."

"In regard to style," says Paul A. Doyle in his book *Sean O'Faolain*, "[the author] favors the technique of uniting suggestion and compression. He uses the words 'engrossed' and 'active' in reference to good style. The beginning of the narrative must at once establish the mood of the story and then the writer works carefully word by word, sentence by sentence, toward the total effect—the innermost illumination which is really the story . . . behind the story." Doyle notes: "The superior stories in [O'Faolain's collections] are characterized by subtlety, compassion, understanding, irony, and a perceptive awareness of the complexity of human nature. Themes and insights are suggested and implied rather than flatly stated, and the themes are significant. In these superior stories O'Faolain demonstrates authorial objectivity and detachment; he avoids description for its own sake; and he successfully infuses a poetic mood—subdued and delicate—over the narratives. Overall, then, it may be affirmed that stories such as 'A Broken World,' 'The Man Who Invented Sin,' 'The Silence of the Valley,' 'Up the Bare Stairs'—to mention a few—exemplify considerable artistry and expert control of modern short story techniques."

"Although the tone in his stories is sometimes satiric," offers Henderson, "[the author] more often withholds judgement of his characters' actions or adopts the stance of an understanding observer. In this respect O'Faolain says he took Chekhov as his model and acknowledges that he also learned from Chekhov to de-emphasize plot, advance the action indirectly by implication, strive for compression, and suffuse his stories with a poetic mood." O'Faolain's reputation as an important modern author, Henderson concludes, "rests most firmly on his short stories. . . . His later stories have won a wide popular audience in such mass-market circulation magazines as *Colliers, McCall's*, . . . and *Playboy*. Their popular appeal, however, does not reduce his stature as a writer of serious fiction. Like [James] Joyce and [Frank] O'Connor, he took the short story as he received it from Maupassant and Chekhov and transformed it into something uniquely his own and uniquely Irish."

O'Faolain's letters and manuscripts are collected at the Bancroft Library, University of California, Berkeley.

MEDIA ADAPTATIONS: Two of O'Faolain's short stories, "Mother Matilda's Book" and "The Man Who Invented Sin," were adapted into plays and broadcast by Granada Television Ltd. in England, August 19, 1970.

AVOCATIONAL INTERESTS: Travel and gardening.

BIOGRAPHICAL/CRITICAL SOURCES—Books: Benedict Keily, *Modern Irish Fiction: A Critique,* Golden Eagle Books (Dublin), 1950; Donat O'Donnell, *Maria Cross: Imaginative Patterns in a Group of Modern Irish Writers,* Oxford University Press, 1952; Sean O'Faolain, *Vive Moi!* (autobiography), Little, Brown, 1964; Maurice Harmon, *Sean O'Faolain: A Critical Introduction,* University of Notre Dame Press, 1966; Paul A. Doyle, *Sean O'Faolain,* Twayne, 1969; *Contemporary Literary Criticism,* Gale, Volume I, 1973, Volume VII, 1977, Volume XIV, 1980; Joseph Storey Rippier, *The Short Stories of Sean O'Faolain: A Study in Descriptive Techniques,* Barnes & Noble, 1976; *Dictionary of Literary Biography,* Volume XV: *British Novelists, 1930-1959,* Gale, 1983.

Periodicals: *Nation,* January 24, 1934; *Christian Science Monitor,* August 12, 1936; *Boston Transcript,* October 10, 1936; *New Republic,* February 15, 1939; *Renascence,* autumn, 1950; *Dublin Magazine,* April-June, 1955; *New York Times Book Review,* May 12, 1957, January 25, 1976, November 26, 1978, October 30, 1983; *Newsweek,* January 8, 1962; *Irish University Review,* spring, 1976; *New Statesman,* April 23, 1976, September 28, 1979; *Time,* June 26, 1976; *South Atlantic Quarterly,* summer, 1976; *Hudson Review,* spring, 1979; *London Magazine,* June, 1980; *Times Literary Supplement,* November 7, 1980, November 20, 1981, December 3, 1982; *Los Angeles Times,* December 28, 1983; *Chicago Tribune Book World,* February 12, 1984.

—Sketch by Susan Salter

* * *

OGNALL, Leopold Horace 1908-1979
(Harry Carmichael, Hartley Howard)

PERSONAL: Born June 20, 1908, in Montreal, Quebec; died April 12, 1979; son of Harry Henry and Elizabeth (Jacobson) Ognall; married Cecilia Sumroy, July 5, 1932; children: Harry Henry, Michael John, Margaret Rose (Mrs. Wilfred Ellenbogen). *Education:* Attended Rutherglen Academy, Glasgow, Scotland. *Religion:* Jewish. *Home:* 18 Avondale Court, Shadwell Lane, Leeds 17, Yorkshire, England. *Agent:* A. D. Peters, 10 Buckingham St., Adelphi, London WC2N 6BU, England.

CAREER: Mystery and crime novelist. Before becoming full-time writer, worked in father's business, then as newspaper reporter and editor of local weekly, correspondence manager in mail order firm, ten years, efficiency engineer for British government, four years. *Member:* Society of Authors (North of England committee), P.E.N. (fellow), Authors' Club, Crime Writers Association, Yorkshire Medico-Legal Society.

WRITINGS—Under pseudonym Harry Carmichael; published by Collins, except as indicated: *The Vanishing Trick*, 1952; *Death Leaves a Diary*, 1952; *Deadly Nightcap*, 1953, reprinted, 1973; *School for Murder*, 1953; *Why Kill Johnny?*, 1954; *Death Counts Three*, 1954; *Noose for a Lady*, 1955; *Money for Murder*, 1955; *The Screaming Rabbit*, Simon & Schuster, 1955; *The Dead of the Night*, 1956; *Justice Enough*, 1956; *Emergency Exit*, 1957; *Put Out That Star*, 1957; *Into Thin Air*, 1957, Doubleday, 1958; *James Knowland: Deceased*, 1958; *A Question of Time*, 1958; *Or Be He Dead*, Doubleday, 1958; *Stranglehold*, 1959, reprinted, Severn House, 1976; *Marked Man*, Doubleday, 1959; *The Seeds of Hate*, 1959.

Requiem for Charles, 1960; *Alibi*, 1961, Macmillan, 1962; *Confession*, 1961; *The Late Unlamented*, Doubleday, 1961; *The Link*, 1962; *Of Unsound Mind*, Doubleday, 1962; *Vendetta*, Macmillan, 1963; *Flashback*, 1964; *Safe Secret*, 1964, Macmillan, 1965; *Post Mortem*, 1965, Doubleday, 1966; *Suicide Clause*, 1966; *The Condemned*, 1967; *Murder by Proxy*, 1967; *A Slightly Bitter Taste*, 1968.

Death Trap, 1970, McCall Publishing, 1971; *Remote Control*, 1970, McCall Publishing, 1971; *The Quiet Woman*, 1971, Saturday Review Press, 1972; *Most Deadly Hate*, 1971, Saturday Review Press, 1974; *Naked to the Grave*, 1972, Saturday Review Press, 1973; *Too Late for Tears*, 1973, Saturday Review Press, 1975; *Candles for the Dead*, 1973, Saturday Review Press, 1976; *The Motive*, 1974, Dutton, 1976; *False Evidence*, 1976; *A Grave for Two*, 1977; *Life Cycle*, 1978.

Under pseudonym Hartley Howard; all published by Collins: *The Last Appointment*, 1951; *The Last Vanity*, 1951; *The Last Deception*, 1951; *Death of Cecilia*, 1952; *Bowman Strikes Again*, 1953; *The Other Side of the Door*, 1953; *Bowman at a Venture*, 1954; *Bowman on Broadway*, 1954; *No Target for Bowman*, 1955; *Sleep for the Wicked*, 1955; *A Hearse for Cinderella*, 1956; *The Bowman Touch*, 1956; *The Long Night*, 1957; *Key to the Morgue*, 1957; *Sleep My Pretty One*, 1958; *The Big Snatch*, 1958; *Deadline*, 1959; *The Armitage Secret*, 1959; *Extortion*, 1960; *Fall Guy*, 1960; *I'm No Hero*, 1961; *Time Bomb*, 1961; *Double Finesse*, 1962; *Count-down*, 1962; *The Stretton Case*, 1963; *Department K*, 1964; *Out of the Fire*, 1965; *Portrait of a Beautiful Harlot*, 1966; *Counterfeit*, 1966; *Routine Investigation*, 1967; *The Eye of the Hurricane*, 1968; *The Secret of Simon Cornell*, 1969; *Cry on My Shoulder*, 1970; *Room 37*, 1970; *Million Dollar Snapshot*, 1971; *Murder One*, 1971; *Epitaph for Joanna*, 1972; *Nice Day for a Funeral*, 1972; *Highway to Murder*, 1973; *Dead Drunk*, 1974; *Treble Cross*, 1975; *Payoff*, 1976; *One-Way Ticket*, 1978; *The Sealed Envelope*, 1979.

WORK IN PROGRESS: Additional books.

SIDELIGHTS: Leopold Horace Ognall once told *CA*: "My motivation since the age of ten has been the desire to write. When I eventually became a full-time professional, I was additionally motivated by the urge to provide for a wife and family. I am vocationally interested in a wide range of subjects and could be described as a man who knows a little about everything and not very much about anything.

"If I have any remaining ambition," Ognall concluded, "it is to go on writing as long as I go on living. That way I shall hope to keep my mind alive."

A total of sixty Ognall books have been published in nine foreign languages in Europe and South America; many books have been serialized in newspapers and magazines in Britain, North Africa, and Scandinavia.

MEDIA ADAPTATIONS: *Department K* was filmed by Columbia in 1968 as "Assignment K"; *A Slightly Bitter Taste* was produced as a television play.

AVOCATIONAL INTERESTS: Beer, books, and Beethoven.

BIOGRAPHICAL/CRITICAL SOURCES: *Best Sellers*, January 15, 1971; *Saturday Review*, February 27, 1971.

OBITUARIES: *Times* (London), April 16, 1979.†

*   *   *

O'HAIR, Madalyn (Mays) Murray 1919-

PERSONAL: Born April 13, 1919, in Pittsburgh, Pa.; daughter of John Irvin (a civil engineer) and Lena (Scholle) Mays; married second husband, Richard Franklin O'Hair (an intelligence agent), October 18, 1965 (died, 1976); children: William J. Murray III, Jon G. Murray, Robin Murray-O'Hair. *Education*: Attended University of Toledo, 1936-37, and University of Pittsburgh, 1938-39; Ashland College, B.A., 1948; graduate study at Western Reserve University (now Case Western Reserve University), 1948-49, and Ohio Northern University, 1949-51; South West Texas College of Law, LL.B., 1953, converted to J.D., 1975; Howard University, M.P.S.W., 1954; Minnesota Institute of Philosophy, Ph.D., 1971. *Politics*: "Individual Anarchist." *Religion*: American Atheist. *Office*: American Atheists, Inc., 2210 Hancock Dr., Austin, Tex. 78756.

CAREER: Supervisor of psychiatric social workers with state welfare, probation, and family and children's agencies in Houston, Tex., 1952-56, and Baltimore, Md., 1959-63; U.S. Department of Health, Education and Welfare, Washington, D.C., staff attorney, 1956-59; American Atheist Center, Austin, Tex., founder, 1959; American Atheists, Inc., Austin, founder, 1965; director, American Atheist Radio series (broadcast on 4,160 stations), 1968-76, and American Atheist Television Forum (broadcast on 32 stations), 1980—. Founder, Charles E. Stevens American Atheist Library and Archives, Inc., 1970. *Military service*: Women's Army Corps, 1943-46; became second lieutenant. *Member*: Society of Separationists (founder; secretary, 1965-75, president, 1975—).

WRITINGS—Published by American Atheist Press, except as indicated: *Why I Am an Atheist*, 1965; *What on Earth Is an Atheist!*, 1966; *The American Atheist*, 1967; *An Atheist Epic: Bill Murray, the Bible, and the Baltimore Board of Education*, 1968; *The Atheist World*, 1969.

An Atheist Speaks, 1970; *Let Us Prey: An Atheist Looks at Church Wealth*, 1970; *All about Atheists*, 1971; *Understanding Atheism*, 1971; *An Atheist Believes*, 1971; *Atheism: Its Viewpoint*, 1972; (author of introduction) *Atheist Magazines: A Sampling, 1927-1970*, Arno, 1972; (editor) *The Atheist Viewpoint*, 25 volumes, Arno, 1972; *Letters from Atheists*, 1972; *Letters from Christians*, 1973; *Freedom Under Siege: The Impact of Organized Religion on Your Liberty and Your Pocketbook*, J. P. Tarcher, 1974; *Religious Factors in the War in Vietnam*, 1975; *Everyday Atheism*, 1975.

The American Atheist Radio Series of Ingersoll the Magnificent, 1977; *Women and Atheism: The Ultimate Liberation*, 1979; *An Atheist Primer*, 1980; *Nobody Has a Prayer*, 1982; *James Lick: American Atheist*, 1983; (with son, Jon G. Murray)

All the Questions You Ever Wanted to Ask American Atheists, with All the Answers, 1983; *Jesus Christ: Super Fraud,* 1984; *An Original Theory in Respect to the Origin of Religion,* 1984. Contributor to *American Atheist Magazine.* Advisory editor on atheism, *New York Times* and Arno Press.

WORK IN PROGRESS: Research on religion, "its origins, its evolution, its political interventions in diverse nations, its wealth, its insanity."

SIDELIGHTS: Atheist Madalyn Murray O'Hair made legal history in 1959 when she and her eldest son sued the Baltimore Public Schools in protest against mandatory school prayers and Bible reading in the classroom. The Supreme Court ruled in her favor in 1963, declaring forced prayers in public schools to be unconstitutional. The issue, O'Hair has said, was not freedom of religion, but freedom *from* religion.

O'Hair claims to have been an atheist since the age of 12, when she "read the Bible one weekend and realized it was a perfectly bizarre book," she tells Jim Gallagher of the *Detroit Free Press.* "Nobody who reads the Bible can believe it.... The Old Testament is about a vicious, ugly, hate-ridden God, and the New Testament is about an incompetent one."

Because of her views, O'Hair and her family have often been the targets of assault and harassment. "Our house was attacked scores of times," she tells *CA.* "Our car was destroyed; my eldest son was attacked physically hundreds of times; I was severely beaten; my mother was knocked unconscious by policemen; and my father suffered a fatal heart attack during an assault on our house."

O'Hair's atheist activism has continued unabated, however. She has filed a number of lawsuits against such things as the tax exemption for church property, the words "In God We Trust" on American currency, and the reciting of prayers before NASA space flights. In 1977 she and fundamentalist preacher "Big Bob" Harrington staged a series of debates on Christianity and atheism, playing to packed houses across the country. "People are seeing someone who's not afraid to stand up to one of these . . . evangelists," O'Hair explained to *Newsweek* at the time. "If nobody else will tell them they're nuts, I will."

Stressing the irrational nature of religion and the negative effects she sees it having on believers, O'Hair argues that atheism is a liberation from superstition. "We must learn to use the scientific method and reason to solve problems," she tells Gallagher, "not irrationality, and the churches personify the essence of irrational thinking." O'Hair told *CA:* "It becomes increasingly important to evaluate, honestly, the impact of religion in our culture and the residual impact of religion on our institutions. It is also necessary to sort out fact from religious propaganda and to [promote] a thoroughly rational approach to living and a culture predicated thereon."

Although her beliefs have earned her the title "the most hated woman in America," according to *Newsweek,* O'Hair's atheist organization, the Society of Separationists, has grown steadily over the years, now claiming some 60,000 members. The American Atheist Press, American Atheist Book of the Month Club, and television and radio shows all help spread O'Hair's message of atheism. "We're here to stay," O'Hair told *Newsweek,* "and the religious community had . . . better find that out."

BIOGRAPHICAL/CRITICAL SOURCES: *Life,* June 19, 1964; *Saturday Evening Post,* July 11, 1964; *Esquire,* October, 1964; *Playboy,* October, 1965; Madalyn Murray O'Hair, *An Atheist Epic: Bill Murray, the Bible, and the Baltimore Board of Education,* American Atheist Press, 1968; *Newsweek,* February 9, 1970, December 1, 1975, September 19, 1977; *Time,* February 9, 1970; *Christian Century,* February 11, 1970; *Washington Post,* February 18, 1970; *New York Times Magazine,* May 16, 1976; *Christianity Today,* August 26, 1977, October 7, 1977; *People,* June 2, 1980.

* * *

OLIVER, Roland Anthony 1923-

PERSONAL: Born March 30, 1923, in Srinagar, Kashmir; son of D. G. and Lorimer Janet (Donaldson) Oliver; married Caroline Florence Linehan, 1947; children: one daughter. *Education:* King's College, Cambridge, M.A. and Ph.D. *Home:* 7 Cranfield House, Southampton Row, London WC1, England; Frilsham Woodhouse, Hermitage, Berkshire, England.

CAREER: Attached to British Foreign Office, 1942-45; School of Oriental and African Studies, London, England, lecturer, 1948-58; University of London, London, England, reader in African history, 1958-63, professor of the history of Africa, 1963—. Organizer of international conferences on African history and archaeology, 1953-61. Franqui Professor, University of Brussels, 1961; visiting professor, Northwestern University, 1962, Harvard University, 1967; president, British Institute in Eastern Africa. *Member:* Royal African Society (council member), Academie Royale des Sciences d'Outremer (Brussels; corresponding member), Minority Rights Group (chairman), Athenaeum Club. *Awards, honors:* Haile Selassie I Prize Trust Award, 1966.

WRITINGS: *The Missionary Factor in East Africa,* Longmans, Green, 1952, 2nd edition, 1965; *How Christian Is Africa?,* Highway Press, 1956; *Sir Harry Johnston and the Scramble for Africa* (illustrated), Chatto & Windus, 1957, St. Martin's, 1958.

(Editor) *The Dawn of African History,* Oxford University Press, 1961, 2nd edition, 1968; (with John D. Fage) *A Short History of Africa,* Penguin, 1962, New York University Press, 1963, 5th edition, Penguin, 1975; (with Matthew Gervase) *History of East Africa* (also see below), Volume I, Clarendon Press, 1963; *African History for the Outside World,* School of Oriental and African Studies, 1964; (editor with Caroline Oliver) *Africa in the Days of Exploration,* Prentice-Hall, 1965; (with Anthony Atmore) *Africa Since 1800,* Cambridge University Press, 1967, 3rd edition, 1981; (editor) *The Middle Age of African History,* Oxford University Press, 1967; (with Gervase) *History of Africa: The Early Period* (consists of first six chapters of *History of East Africa*), Oxford University Press, 1967; (compiler and editor with Fage) *Papers in African Prehistory,* Cambridge University Press, 1970; (with Brian M. Fagan) *Africa in the Iron Age: c 500 B.C. to A.D. 1400,* Cambridge University Press, 1975.

(With Atmore) *The African Middle Ages, 1400-1800,* Cambridge University Press, 1981. General editor, with Fage, of *Cambridge History of Africa,* eight volumes, Cambridge University Press, 1976-85.

* * *

OLSON, Helen Kronberg

PERSONAL: Born in Mt. Angel, Ore.; daughter of Paul and Christine Kronberg; married Anthony Perillo (deceased); married John Harold Olson (a representative for an electronics company); children: (first marriage) Paul Anthony Perillo. *Education:* Mt. Angel College, B.S., 1952, also graduate study. *Politics:* Democrat. *Home:* 20739 Hazelnut Ridge Rd. N.E., Scotts Mills, Ore. 97375.

CAREER: Marion County Welfare, Salem, Ore., child welfare caseworker, 1960-63; Oregon State Hospital, Salem, social worker, 1964-65; art and elementary school teacher in Marion County, Ore.; full-time writer and tree farmer.

WRITINGS—Children's books: *Stupid Peter and Other Tales: New Stories to Read Together* (original children's folk tales), Random House, 1970; (contributor) *The Real Book of First Stories* (anthology), edited by Dorothy Haas, Rand McNally, 1974; (contributor) *The Princess Book* (anthology), edited by Haas, Rand McNally, 1975; (contributor) *The Witch Book* (anthology), edited by Haas, Rand McNally, 1976; *The Secret of Spirit Mountain* (wilderness suspense novel), Dodd, 1980; *The Strange Thing That Happened to Oliver Wendell Iscovitch* (humorous novel), Dodd, 1983.

Also author of an unpublished children's book. Contributor of short stories to numerous publications, including *Humpty Dumpty, Children's Playmate, Encyclopaedia Britannica, Scholastic Magazine,* and *Adventure.*

WORK IN PROGRESS: A children's mystery novel; a humorous picture book.

SIDELIGHTS: Helen Kronberg Olson told *CA:* "As soon as I learned to read I became an insatiable reader—and a literary critic. There were many good children's books, and the satisfaction I received from them I still treasure today. But, then there were the books that didn't make it. I skipped whole passages and raged at disappointing endings. Now, as a children's author, I only write what both the child and adult in me fully enjoy reading."

AVOCATIONAL INTERESTS: Reading, travelling.

BIOGRAPHICAL/CRITICAL SOURCES: Silverton Appeal Tribune, November 26, 1970; *Statesman* (Salem), December 13, 1970; *The Oregonian,* December 19, 1970.

* * *

O'MALLEY, William J(ohn) 1931-

PERSONAL: Born August 18, 1931, in Buffalo, N.Y.; son of William John (a food distributor) and Beatrice (an office manager; maiden name, Foley) O'Malley. *Education:* Attended College of the Holy Cross, 1949-51; attended seminaries in New York, 1951-55; Fordham University, B.A., 1956, M.A., 1957; Woodstock College, B.Th., 1963, M.Div., 1964; graduate study at St. Bueno's College, 1964-65, Royal Academy of Dramatic Art, 1967, Northwestern University, 1969, and Jesuit School of Theology (Berkeley), 1974. *Home:* 1800 Clinton Ave. S., Rochester, N.Y. 14618.

CAREER: Entered Society of Jesus (Jesuits), 1951, ordained Roman Catholic priest, 1963; high school teacher in New York, N.Y., 1957-60; McQuaid Jesuit High School, Rochester, N.Y., English and theology teacher, 1965—. Played Father Joe Dyer in "The Exorcist," released by Warner Brothers, 1973; has acted in and directed numerous plays. Consultant to American Education Publications, 1964-68, Education Testing Service, and National Assessment of Writing, 1971-72.

WRITINGS: An Approach to English (syllabus and teaching manuals), Buffalo Province Educational Association, 1965; (contributor) Robert Beauchamp, editor, *The Structure of Literature,* American Education Publications, 1969; *Meeting the Living God,* Paulist/Newman, 1973; *The Fifth Week,* Loyola University Press, 1976; *The Roots of Unbelief,* Paulist/Newman, 1976; *A Book about Praying,* Paulist/Newman, 1976; *The Living Word,* Paulist Press, Volume I: *Scripture and Myth,* 1980, Volume II: *How the Gospels Work,* 1980; *The Voice of Blood,* Orbis, 1980; *Phoenix: Twenty-Five Years of McQuaid Jesuit High School,* Northeastern Publications, 1980.

Also author of "Capers," an unproduced filmscript on vocations, "Phoenix," a modernization of the Gospel narratives, and several musical adaptations of books and plays. Contributor of articles to *Jesuit Educational Quarterly, A.E.P. Challenges,* and other education and Catholic periodicals.

WORK IN PROGRESS: "This year I began a humungoid and doubtless hubristic project: a novel about the 2,500 priests who were prisoners in Dachau. It will begin 30 January 1933, the day Hitler took power, and trace three lives through 30 April 1945. Since, as of January, 1984, I've written 300 pages covering only the first year, any fool could tell this will end up—if I live long enough—two or three thousand-page books. I don't mind a bit. In fact, working on it is so mesmerizing I really don't care if it's even published. Well. . . ."

SIDELIGHTS: William J. O'Malley told *CA:* "I'm a priest-teacher-director, any one of which is enough to exhaust your twenty-four hour day or your fifty-two year old cleric. As a Puritan of Kamikaze dedication, I spend my days making certain that I will not die bored." O'Malley has acted in more than twelve plays and has directed more than fifty. Because of his role in "The Exorcist," he has been invited to make several television appearances.

* * *

O'NEILL, William L. 1935-

PERSONAL: Born April 18, 1935, in Big Rapids, Mich.; son of John Patrick (an oil and gas contractor) and Helen (Marsh) O'Neill; married E. Carol Knollmueller, August 20, 1960; children: Cassandra Leigh, Catherine Lorraine. *Education:* University of Michigan, A.B., 1957; University of California, Berkeley, M.A., 1958, Ph.D., 1963. *Home:* 232 Harrison Ave., Highland Park, N.J. 08904. *Office:* Department of History, Rutgers University, New Brunswick, N.J. 08903.

CAREER: University of Pittsburgh, Pittsburgh, Pa., visiting assistant professor of history, 1963-64; University of Colorado, Boulder, assistant professor of history, 1964-66; University of Wisconsin—Madison, assistant professor, 1966-69, associate professor of history, 1969-71; Rutgers University, New Brunswick, N.J., professor of history, 1971—. Visiting associate professor, University of Pennsylvania, 1969-71. *Military service:* U.S. Army Reserve, 1960-66 (six months active duty). *Member:* American Historical Association, Organization of American Historians, Authors Guild, Phi Beta Kappa. *Awards, honors:* National Endowment for the Humanities fellowship, 1979-80.

WRITINGS: Divorce in the Progressive Era, Yale University Press, 1967; *Everyone Was Brave: The Rise and Fall of Feminism in America,* Quadrangle, 1969; *The Woman Movement: Feminism in the United States and England,* Barnes & Noble, 1969; *Coming Apart: An Informal History of America in the 1960's,* Quadrangle, 1971; (co-author) *Looking Backward: A Re-introduction to American History,* McGraw, 1974; *The Progressive Years: America Comes of Age,* Dodd, 1975; *The Last Romantic: A Life of Max Eastman,* Oxford University Press,

1978; *A Better World: The Great Schism—Stalinism and the American Intellectuals,* Simon & Schuster, 1982.

Editor: *Echoes of Revolt: "The Masses," 1911 to 1917,* Quadrangle, 1966; *American Society since Nineteen Forty-Five,* Quadrangle, 1969; *Women at Work,* Quadrangle, 1972; *The American Sexual Dilemma,* Holt, 1972; *Insights and Parallels: Problems and Issues in American Social History,* Burgess, 1973. Contributor to professional journals.

SIDELIGHTS: William L. O'Neill sheds new light on the history of radical politics in the United States in his books *The Last Romantic: A Life of Max Eastman* and *A Better World: The Great Schism—Stalinism and the American Intellectuals.* O'Neill's biography of Max Eastman provides a new look at a man who began his career as the editor of the radical journal *The Masses* and ended up as a supporter of Senator Joseph McCarthy and a contributing editor to *Reader's Digest. A Better World* is a study of the American intellectual community's support of, and eventual disenchantment with, the Stalinist regime of Soviet Russia.

The long political career of Max Eastman took him from the far left wing to the far right wing, and involved him in many of the major political events and movements of the twentieth century. Eastman began his career in 1912 as the editor of *The Masses,* a socialist political journal. In the years before World War I, he turned *The Masses* into an influential and freewheeling journal of art and politics, publishing some of the most important writers and artists of the time. "For a brief time," Clancy Sigal of the *Nation* writes, "the paper was the rallying point for almost everything that was then alive and irreverent in American culture." *"The Masses,"* Sigal quotes O'Neill as writing, "was not so much a publishing venture as a movement, even for some a way of life." During World War I, Eastman wrote a series of outspoken editorials against U.S. involvement in the war. These editorials earned him two separate trials for subversion. Due partly to his passionate courtroom oratory Eastman was acquitted both times, although he lost many of his socialist readers over his stand on the war issue.

The Russian Revolution of 1917 seemed to embody Eastman's dream of a socialist society. He hoped, writes Jerome Charyn in the *New York Times Book Review,* that the revolution "would install a society of prophets, artists, and social engineers. He was willing to abandon himself to that experiment." In 1922 Eastman visited the Soviet Union and took a Russian wife. A strong supporter of communist leaders Nikolai Lenin and Leon Trotsky, Eastman was at first enthusiastic about the revolution. But once Joseph Stalin assumed power on the death of Lenin, and Eastman's in-laws and many of his revolutionary friends were executed, he became disillusioned. "He was one of those," writes David Caute in the *New Statesman,* "who had cheerfully excused the suppression of the non-Party opposition in Russia yet expressed shock-horror-outrage when the same implacable laws of human engineering were brought to bear on his own friends inside the fold."

In 1929, Trotsky himself was exiled from the Soviet Union. Eastman became the first American Trotskyist, and during the 1920s and 1930s, he translated Trotsky's monumental *History of the Russian Revolution* and wrote a number of books critical of the Stalinist regime. Perhaps the most important of these was *Artists in Uniform,* a study of Stalin's persecution of Russian writers and artists. The book caused Stalin to label Eastman a "gangster of the pen."

Eastman's relationship with the exiled Trotsky was always shaky. The Russian Revolution had convinced Eastman that Marxism was "unscientific" and therefore fatally flawed. His continuing questioning of orthodox Marxist doctrine during the 1930s finally led to a break with Trotsky. By 1941, Eastman's analysis of the faults in Marxist theory had moved him far to the political right. He rejected socialism entirely in a 1941 article for *Reader's Digest,* arguing instead in favor of democracy, which Eastman claimed could only flourish in a capitalist society. Ironically, many on the left wing were growing disenchanted with Stalin at this time and began to take seriously Eastman's earlier anti-Stalinist writings—writings that were far to the left of Eastman's current political position. During the 1940s he worked as a contributing editor of *Reader's Digest,* writing articles on socialism and free enterprise. Later he moved to the more conservative *National Review.* In the 1950s Eastman emerged as a supporter of Senator Joseph McCarthy's sometimes-hysterical anti-communist investigations.

"On one level," writes John K. Roth of the *Los Angeles Times Book Review,* "O'Neill's study of Max Eastman is a record of innocence lost and realism gained. . . . O'Neill likes Max Eastman. He esteems the man's honesty, enjoyment of life, his struggles with the politics of right and wrong." Terry Eagleton of *Books and Bookmen* judges *The Last Romantic* to be "an admirably detailed portrait of the American Trotskyite-turned-McCarthyite, Max Eastman. Apart from some dubious Oedipal speculations at the outset, Professor O'Neill steers cautiously clear of 'depthful' political or psychoanalytical probings of Eastman and is content for the most part to give us the biographical facts." Although deploring O'Neill's discomfort when relating the details of Eastman's many love affairs and criticizing the sometimes "moralistic" tone O'Neill uses, Charyn nonetheless believes that "we do owe something to Professor O'Neill. He has 'rescued' Max Eastman [from obscurity]."

O'Neill again deals with radical politics in *A Better World,* a book Eric M. Breindel of *Commentary* describes as "a careful, systematic study of the struggle between those American intellectuals who supported or apologized for Stalinism and their adversaries, from the period of the New Deal on." Dennis Wrong of *New Republic* calls it "as accurate a one-volume account as we are likely to have for a very long time of the opinions over two crucial decades of the leading American intellectuals on all major domestic and international events pertaining to Communism and the Soviet Union."

O'Neill's detailed presentation and examination of the pro-Soviet positions of certain literary and political journals proves a bit uncomfortable for some reviewers. The *New Republic* and the *Nation* are particularly singled out for their alleged pro-Soviet pronouncements during the 1930s and 1940s. Maurice Isserman, reviewing the book for the *Nation,* finds that O'Neill is "right" about the *Nation.* "Many American radicals," Isserman writes, "have yet to face up to the uncomfortable fact that they, or their predecessers on the left, apologized for the second most vicious system of political tyranny to appear in the twentieth century." However, Isserman thinks that O'Neill has been unfair in his condemnation. He quotes selected *Nation* editorials from the 1940s which criticized Soviet policy, and argues that O'Neill's quotations proving the opposite are equally selective and misleading. "Progressive intellectuals of the 1930s . . . should be held responsible for the illusions they shared and promoted," Isserman believes, "but they deserve fairer treatment than the selective retribution O'Neill visits upon them." The *New Republic* reviewer, Dennis Wrong, feels differently about how his magazine is portrayed. "One feels immense gratitude to O'Neill," he writes, "for having faithfully reported a record that has been the subject of so much mythmaking." Wrong agrees that, at times, the *New Republic* had "sacrific[ed] honesty . . . upon the altar of hope" when reporting on the Soviet Union in the 1940s.

"One of the singular merits of *A Better World*," Abraham Brumberg writes in the *Washington Post Book World*, "is to remind us that the tendency to romanticize the Soviet Union was not confined . . . to 'knee-jerk liberals.' It characterized a good part of the conservative establishment as well. This was true of the *Saturday Evening Post*, *Time*, and even that bastion of philistine anti-communism, *Reader's Digest*. . . . O'Neill is scrupulously fair and objective."

In the second half of *A Better World*, O'Neill turns his attention to the 1950s and the anti-communist hysteria of the time. It is here where O'Neill "begins to break new ground," writes Alan Brinkley of the *New York Times Book Review*. "[O'Neill argues] that the left wing itself was to blame for its plight; that the callousness of intellectuals who apologized for Stalinism and the dishonesty of those who, when pressed, tried to deny their communist sympathies altogether made McCarthyism not only possible but in some respects even necessary." "O'Neill treats the McCarthy era," writes Breindel, "in a particularly thoughtful manner. He examines the harsh public record—the hearings, the loyalty oaths, the show-business blacklist, and all the rest—but does not scant the prior political activities of most of the victims."

A Better World, Brinkley writes, "is a serious book by a respected scholar. . . . It is well-researched, carefully argued and highly provocative. But like most studies of the age of McCarthy, this is not so much a work of history as a polemic." "By clarifying this often muddied history and setting it into measured analytical perspective," Breidnel writes, "William O'Neill's book makes an important contribution both to scholarship and to the cause of political honesty."

BIOGRAPHICAL/CRITICAL SOURCES: *New York Times*, November 17, 1978; *Los Angeles Times Book Review*, November 19, 1978, May 22, 1983; *New York Review of Books*, December 7, 1978; *New York Times Book Review*, December 10, 1978, January 9, 1983; *Village Voice*, December 18, 1978; *Progressive*, January, 1979; *New Republic*, January 20, 1979, March 14, 1983; *Nation*, February 10, 1979, March 19, 1983; *New Statesman*, March 2, 1979; *Economist*, March 17, 1979; *Books and Bookmen*, July, 1979; *National Review*, December 24, 1982; *Commentary*, March, 1983; *Washington Post Book World*, March 27, 1983.

—Sketch by Thomas Wiloch

* * *

ONO, Chiyo 1941-

PERSONAL: Born February 26, 1941, in Tokyo, Japan; daughter of Rei (a Noh player) and Ryuko Kondoh; married Yoh Ono (a master of a training ship), August 7, 1960; children: Sayuri. *Education:* Attended Fuji Women's College, 1962. *Home:* 8-406, Jingumae 6-25, Shibuya Ku, Tokyo, Japan.

CAREER: Author and illustrator of picture books, poetry, and Japanese elementary school textbooks.

WRITINGS—All self-illustrated: *Okaerinasai Otohsan*, PHP-Kenkyusho, 1980; *Yuki ni natta Kumasan*, Dainippon Kaiga, 1980; *Hoh Hoh*, Dainippon Kaiga, 1981; *Kuzunoha Gitsune*, Soiku-Sha, 1983; *Ichiban Utsukushii Hana*, Soiku-Sha, 1983. Published by Shiko-Sha Co. (Tokyo): *Hitoripotti no Neko*, 1967; *Watashi no Geta* (juvenile), 1969, translation published as *Which Way, Geta?*, Thomas Nelson, 1970; *Maigo ni natta Ohmu*, 1970, translation published as *The Boy and the Bird*, John Day, 1970; *Itodenwa*, Shiko-Sha Co., 1971; *Mina Kamisama no Okurimono*, 1978; *Kawa*, 1979; *Huttekuru*, 1983. Also author and illustrator, *Otasuke Nekosan*, Shiko-Sha Co.

SIDELIGHTS: Chiyo Ono told *CA*: "Since I grew up as the daughter of a famous Noh player, I love Japanese traditional culture very much; I want to make the picture books of Noh so that people in the world might understand and enjoy it." *Watashi no Geta* has also been published in French.

* * *

OSKAMP, Stuart 1930-

PERSONAL: Born May 31, 1930, in Oak Park, Ill.; son of Alfred Stuart (a professor) and Catharine (Willard) Oskamp; married Barbara Harvey, December 26, 1955 (divorced, 1972); married Catherine Cameron, December 18, 1973; children: David, Karen. *Education:* Grinnell College, B.A. (with honors), 1951; Stanford University, Ph.D., 1960. *Office:* Department of Psychology, Claremont Graduate School, Claremont, Calif. 91711.

CAREER: Center for Advanced Study in the Behavioral Sciences, Stanford, Calif., assistant psychologist, 1956; Stanford University, Stanford, assistant psychologist, 1957-59; Veterans Administration Hospital, Palo Alto, Calif., trainee in clinical psychology, 1957-59; Veterans Administration Mental Hygiene Clinic, San Francisco, Calif., trainee in clinical psychology, 1959-60; Claremont Graduate School, Claremont, Calif., assistant professor, 1960-64, associate professor, 1964-70, professor of psychology, 1970—. Research psychologist, Palo Alto Medical Research Foundation, 1960; U.S. Peace Corps, field assessment officer in Hilo, Hawaii, 1963; psychologist with Tri-City Mental Health Authority, Pomona, Calif., 1964-66; research associate at Institute of Social Research, University of Michigan, 1966-67, and University of Bristol, 1971. American Psychological Association visiting scientist, 1967-68; academic visitor, London School of Economics and Political Science, University of London, 1981. *Military service:* U.S. Naval Reserve, 1951-55; became lieutenant. *Member:* American Psychological Association, Society for the Psychological Study of Social Issues, American Association of University Professors, Western Psychological Association, Phi Beta Kappa, Sigma Xi.

WRITINGS: (With R. M. Suinn) *The Predictive Validity of Projective Measures: A Fifteen-Year Evaluative Review of Research*, C. C Thomas, 1969; (contributor) L. S. Wrightsman, *Social Psychology in the Seventies*, Brooks/Cole, 1972, 2nd edition, 1977; *Attitudes and Opinions*, Prentice-Hall, 1977; (contributor) A. S. Kahn, editor, *Social Psychology*, W. C. Brown, 1984; *Applied Social Psychology*, Prentice-Hall, 1984; (editor) *Applied Social Psychology Annual*, Sage, 1984. Contributor to psychology journals. Advisory editor, *Journal of Consulting and Clinical Psychology*, 1969-73, and *Population and Environment*, 1978—.

WORK IN PROGRESS: Research on attitudes, social issues, and applied social psychology.

SIDELIGHTS: Stuart Oskamp told *CA*: "One of my most satisfying activities is working with individual graduate students to plan and design research projects which are both rigorous and relevant to important questions. Through all of my work runs the theme of applying social psychological methods and findings to the solution of social problems and public policy issues.... Other satisfying moments have come in reaching for high standards in my avocational activities such as choral and solo singing, photography, and coaching my son's and daughter's soccer teams."

* * *

OSWALT, Wendell H(illman) 1927-

PERSONAL: Born June 26, 1927, in Youngstown, Ohio; son of Elmer J. and Sarah (Hillman) Oswalt; married Helen Louise Taylor, February 27, 1946; children: William M., Pamela K., Ivar. *Education:* University of Alaska, B.A., 1952; University of Arizona, Ph.D., 1959. *Office:* Department of Anthropology, University of California, Los Angeles, Calif. 90024.

CAREER: University of Alaska, College, research associate in anthropology, 1955-57; University of California, Los Angeles, assistant professor, 1959-65, associate professor, 1965-69, professor of anthropology, 1969—, chairman of department, 1973-76. Field researcher in Alaska, 1947—; visiting professor at University of Alaska, summers, 1960, 1962, 1964. *Military service:* U.S. Coast Guard, 1945-46. *Member:* American Anthropological Association (fellow), American Association for Advancement of Science.

WRITINGS: Napaskiak: An Alaskan Eskimo Community, University of Arizona Press, 1963; *Mission of Change in Alaska,* Huntington Library, 1963; *This Land Was Theirs: A Study of the North American Indian,* Wiley, 1966, 3rd edition published as *This Land Was Theirs: A Study of North American Indians,* 1978; *Alaskan Eskimos,* Chandler, 1967; *Understanding Our Culture: An Anthropological View,* Holt, 1970; (editor) *Modern Alaskan Native Material Culture,* University of Alaska Museum, 1972; *Other Peoples, Other Customs: World Ethnography and Its History,* Holt, 1972; *Habitat and Technology: The Evolution of Hunting,* Holt, 1973; (with others) *An Anthropological Analysis of Food-Getting Technology,* Wiley, 1976; *Eskimos and Explorers,* Chandler & Sharp, 1979; *Historic Settlements along the Kuskokwim River, Alaska,* Alaska Division of State Libraries and Museums, Department of Education, 1980; *Kolmakovskiy Redoubt: The Ethnoarchaeology of a Russian Fort in Alaska,* Institute of Archaeology, University of California, Los Angeles, 1980. Contributor of articles to professional journals.

* * *

OWEN, Tom
See WATTS, Peter Christopher

P

PADGETT, Ron 1942-
(Harlan Dangerfield)

PERSONAL: Born June 17, 1942, in Tulsa, Okla.; married; children: one son. *Education:* Columbia University, A.B., 1964. *Home:* 342 East 13th St., New York, N.Y. 10003.

CAREER: Worked as an auto mechanic and drove transcontinental cargo transport before 1962; St. Mark's-in-the-Bowery, New York City, poetry workshop instructor, 1968-69; poet in various New York City Poets in the Schools Programs, 1969-76; writer in the community, South Carolina Arts Commission, 1976-78; St. Mark's Poetry Project, New York City, director, 1978-81; Teachers and Writers Collaborative, New York City, director of publications, 1982—. Co-founder of Full Court Press (publishing house), New York City, 1973. *Awards, honors:* Boar's Head Poetry Prize and George E. Woodberry Award, both from Columbia University, both 1964; Gotham Book Mart Avant-Garde Poetry Prize, 1964; Fulbright fellowship in Paris, 1965-66; Poets Foundation grants, 1965, 1968; New York City Academy of Arts and Letters grant, 1966, 1971; National Endowment for the Arts fellowship, 1983.

WRITINGS—Poetry collections, except as indicated: *In Advance of the Broken Arm,* "C" Press, 1964; (with Ted Berrigan and Joe Brainard) *Some Things,* "C" Press, 1964; *2/2 Stories for Andy Warhol,* "C" Press, 1965; *Sky,* Goliard Press, 1966; (with Berrigan) *Bean Spasms,* Kulcher Press, 1967; *Tone Arm,* Once Press (Essex, England), 1967; (with Brainard) *100,000 Fleeing Hilda,* Boke, 1967; (with Tom Clark) *Bun,* Angel Hair Books, 1968; *Great Balls of Fire,* Holt, 1969; (with Jim Dine) *The Adventures of Mr. and Mrs. Jim and Ron,* Cape Goliard Press, 1970; *Sweet Pea,* Aloes, 1971; *Poetry Collection,* Strange Faeces Press, 1971; (with Brainard) *Sufferin' Succotash* [bound with *Kiss My Ass* by Michael Brownstein], Adventures in Poetry, 1971; (with Berrigan and Clark) *Back in Boston Again,* Telegraph, 1972; *Antlers in the Treetops* (novel), Coach House Press, 1973; (with Dine) *Oo La La,* Petersburg Press, 1973; *Crazy Compositions,* Big Sky, 1974; (with others) *The World of Leon,* Big Sky, 1974; *Toujours l'amour,* SUN, 1976; *Arrive by Pullman,* Generations (Paris), 1978; *Tulsa Kid,* Z Press, 1979; *Triangles in the Afternoon,* SUN, 1980.

Editor: (With Berrigan) Tom Veitch, *Literary Days,* "C" Press, 1964; (with David Shapiro) *An Anthology of New York Poets,* Random House, 1970; (with Bill Zavatsky) *The Whole Word Catalogue 2,* Teachers and Writers Collaborative/McGraw, 1976; (with Nancy Larson Shapiro) *The Point: Where Teaching and Writing Intersect,* Teachers and Writers Collaborative, 1983.

Plays: (With Berrigan) *Seventeen: Collected Plays,* "C" Press, 1965; (adaptor with Johnny Stanton) Henry Carey, *Chrononhotonothologos,* Boke, 1971.

Translator: Guillaume Apollinaire, *The Poet Assassinated,* Holt, 1968; Pierre Cabanne, *Dialogues with Marcel Duchamp,* Viking, 1970; (with Zavatsky) Valery Larbaud, *The Poems of A. O. Barnabooth,* Mushinsha (Tokyo), 1974; Blaise Cendras, *Kodak,* Adventures in Poetry, 1976.

SIDELIGHTS: Ron Padgett belongs to the New York school of poetry, a school that "relies on highly sophisticated, urban statement, seemingly artless when it is most artificial, and ingenuous when it is most shrewd," writes Gilbert Sorrentino in the *New York Times Book Review.* "The poems defy criticism by proffering the reader a brilliantly polished but false naivete. This is consciously done." Sorrentino judges Padgett to be one of "the most accomplished" poets of the New York school.

In much of his poetry, Padgett focuses on the ordinary and everyday and "brilliantly transforms mundane experience into the subject of poetry, through subtle humor, wordplay, and a childlike fascination with the world," writes Caroline G. Bokinsky in the *Dictionary of Literary Biography.* Reviewing *Great Balls of Fire* for *Library Journal,* Bill Katz also notes Padgett's concern for the commonplace. He finds that "the title indicates [Padgett's] basic involvement with the modern cliche scene of American life yet fails to point up his tremendous skill with delicate thought and basic intelligence." In a review of *Triangles in the Afternoon* and *Tulsa Kid* for the *American Book Review,* Donna Brook writes that Padgett's poems deal with such commonplace things as Cheez-Its, chocolate milk, and kitchen matches. She believes that "for both what he discusses and how he goes about discussing it . . . , Ron Padgett can be called a champion of American language and experience."

"I feel good about Padgett's work," Brook concludes, "the way it wakes, shakes, and charms, and I carry it around even when I don't coherently defend it to myself." "Ron Padgett," Bokinsky writes, "never ceases from exploring the mystery of the commonplace while giving pleasure as he illuminates the trivial."

BIOGRAPHICAL/CRITICAL SOURCES: Richard Kostelanetz, editor, *The New American Arts*, Horizon, 1966; *Village Voice*, December 7, 1967, January 24, 1977; *New York Times Book Review*, March 31, 1968, September 19, 1976; *Poetry*, December, 1968, January, 1972; *Times Literary Supplement*, January 23, 1969; *Newsweek*, March 3, 1969; *Library Journal*, October 1, 1969; *New Republic*, December 13, 1969; *Yale Review*, June, 1970; *Dictionary of Literary Biography*, Volume V: *American Poets since World War II*, two volumes, Gale, 1980; *American Book Review*, March/April, 1981.

* * *

PAGE, Martin 1938-

PERSONAL: Born June 30, 1938, in London, England; son of Basil Lloyd and Mary (Hacker) Page; married Jillian Vera Robertson. *Education:* Pembroke College, Cambridge, B.A. (with honors). *Agent:* John Farquharson Ltd., Bell House, 8 Bell Yard, London WC2A 2JU, England; Harold Matson Co., Inc., 276 Fifth Ave., New York, N.Y. 10001.

CAREER: *Manchester Guardian*, Manchester, England, reporter, 1960-62; *Daily Express*, London, England, foreign correspondent, then diplomatic correspondent, 1962-65, with two years in Moscow and war coverage in Algeria, Congo (now Zaire), Vietnam, Borneo, and India; free-lance writer in London, 1965—. *Member:* P.E.N., Society of Authors, National Union of Teachers, Cambridge University Union.

WRITINGS: *The Day Khruschev Fell*, Hawthorn, 1965; (with David Burg) *Unpersoned: The Fall of Nikita Sergeyevitch Khruschev*, Chapman & Hall, 1966; *The Yam Factor, and Other Insights into the Lives and Customs of the Executive Tribes of America*, Doubleday, 1972 (published in England as *The Company Savage: Life in the Corporate Jungle*, Cassell, 1972); (compiler) *Kiss Me Goodnight, Sergeant-Major: The Songs and Ballads of World War II*, Hart-Davis, 1973; *The Lost Pleasures of the Great Trains*, Morrow, 1975; (editor) *For Gawdsake Don't Take Me!: The Songs, Ballads, Verses, Monologues, etc. of the Call-Up Years, 1939-1963*, Hart-Davis, 1976; *The Pilate Plot*, Coward, 1978. Author of television scripts. Contributor to periodicals, including *Atlantic*, *Vogue*, *Newsday*, and *Sunday Times* and *Times* (both London).

WORK IN PROGRESS: Research into British politics and monarchy during the crisis of 1936.

SIDELIGHTS: Martin Page has traveled extensively in Europe, Africa, the Middle East, Far East, and Australia.†

* * *

PALMER, Bernard 1914-
(John Runyan)

PERSONAL: Born November, 1914, in Central City, Neb.; son of Ben H. (in monument business) and Stella (Jarvis) Palmer; married June Berger, June 20, 1934 (died September 28, 1939); married Marjorie Matthews (a writer), December 12, 1940; children: (first marriage) James Barrett (deceased); (second marriage) Morris Jay, Bonnie Lou (Mrs. Douglas Young), Janice Kay (Mrs. Edward Fowler). *Education:* Attended Kearney State College, 1933, and Hastings College, 1940. *Politics:* Republican. *Religion:* Protestant (Evangelical Free Church of America). *Home:* 1013 14th Ave., Holdrege, Neb. 68949. *Office:* 421 East Ave., Holdrege, Neb. 68949.

CAREER: Palmer Bros. Monument Co., Holdrege, Neb., stonecutter and shop foreman, 1957-67, vice-president, 1962-74, president, 1974—, chairman of board of directors, 1974—; writer, 1967—. Member of board of directors, Tyndale Foundation, 1963—. *Member:* Gideons International (past president of Nebraska chapter), Kiwanis.

WRITINGS—Published by Moody, except as indicated: *Parson John*, Eerdmans, 1942; *Storm Winds*, Eerdmans, 1942; *Visibility Zero*, Zondervan, 1944; *Dark Are the Shadows*, Zondervan, 1945; *Dangerous Mission*, Zondervan, 1945; *Mission of Mercy*, Hitchcock, 1946; *Goon Walford Fights Back*, Van Kampen, 1946; *Withering Grass*, Van Kampen, 1949.

Radio Stories, Back to the Bible, 1950; *Radio Stories #3*, Back to the Bible, 1952; *Sky Pilot Gang Busters*, Sky Pilot Press, 1955; *Jungle Jim*, 1956; *Storm on the Muskeg*, 1957; *New Skipper of the Flying Swede*, 1957; (with wife, Marjorie Palmer) *Miracle of the Prairies*, 1958, new edition published as *Beacon on the Prairies*, Briercrest Bible Institute, 1970.

Andy Logan and the Oregon Trail Mystery, 1961; *Mystery of Dungu Re*, 1961; *Tattered Loin Cloth*, 1962; *Adventure in Tanganyika*, 1963; *Yukuma the Brave*, 1963; *The Wind Blows Wild*, 1968; *Sue Riley and the Mysterious Cargo*, 1968; *Across the Deep Valleys*, Nebraska Christian Press, 1969.

My Son, My Son, 1970; *So Restless, So Lonely*, Bethany Fellowship, 1970; *Seek No Tomorrow*, 1971; *Whisper the Robin*, Zondervan, 1972; *God Understands*, 1973; (with M. Palmer) *The Winds of God Are Blowing*, Tyndale, 1973; (with Irene Hanson) *The Wheelbarrow and the Comrade*, 1973; *Amsterdam Rebel*, 1973; (with Fred Eggerichs) *A Bag without Holes*, Bethany Fellowship, 1975; *Frosty Roberts and the Golden Jade Mystery*, 1975; *Silent Thunder*, Bethany Fellowship, 1975; *The Davis Triplets and the Film Action*, 1975; *White Water on the Yukon*, 1975; *Pattern for a Total Church*, Victor Books, 1975; *I'm a Louie, Atsa Phil*, 1975.

Yoneko, Back to the Bible, 1976; *People's Church on the Go*, Victor Books, 1976; (with M. Palmer) *How Churches Grow*, Bethany Fellowship, 1976; *McTaggart's Promise*, David Cook, 1978; *Who Made? Who Tells? Who Cares? Who Loves?*, Bethany Fellowship, 1979; *Run for the West*, David Cook, 1979; *Nothing Is Impossible*, 1979; *What'll You Have to Drink*, Horizon House, 1979.

Ted and the Secret Club, Victor Books, 1980; *Hitched to a Star*, 1981; *Breck's Choice*, Horizon House, 1981; (with M. Palmer) *The Flood*, Bethel Publishing, 1982; (with M. Palmer) *Who Helps*, Bethel Publishing, 1982; (with M. Palmer) *Who Shows*, Bethel Publishing, 1982; (with M. Palmer) *Light a Small Candle*, Free Church Publications, 1983.

"Bradley" series; published by Back to the Bible: *The Mysterious Letter*, 1975; *Mystery of the New Sky*, 1975; *Jon and the Break-in Mystery*, 1976; *Trena and the Old Diary*, 1976; *Homesteading in Standing Bear's Territory*, 1976; *Princess Pat Saves the Day*, 1977; *Trena's Rodeo Vial*, 1977; *Mystery of the Missing Fossil*, 1977.

"Brigade Boys" series; published by Moody: *Brigade Boys and the Flight to Danger*, 1960; *. . . and the Phantom Radio*, 1960; *. . . in the Arctic Wilderness*, 1961; *. . . and the Disappearing Stranger*, 1961; *. . . and the Basketball Mystery*, 1963.

"Career" series; published by Moody: (With M. Palmer) *Student Nurse*, 1960; (with M. Palmer) *Barbara Nichols, Fifth Grade Teacher*, 1960; *Big Season*, 1960; *Mystery of the Musty Ledger*, 1960; *Peggy Archer, Missionary Candidate*, 1961; *Brad Foster, Engineer*, 1962; (with M. Palmer) *Karen Simms*,

Private Secretary, 1963; *Randy Warren, First Term Missionary,* 1963; *Cal Henderson, M.D.,* 1963; *Jim Shelton, Radio Engineer,* 1964; (with M. Palmer) *Sandra Emerson, R.N.,* 1966; *Lee Sloan, Missionary Pilot,* 1966; *Dennis Harper, Missionary Journalist,* 1966.

"Danny Orlis" series; published by Moody, except as indicated: *Danny Orlis Stories,* Back to the Bible, 1953; *Danny Orlis and the Point Barrow Mystery,* Good News Publishing, 1954; *. . . and the Angle Inlet Mystery,* 1954; *. . . and the Strange Forest Fires,* 1955; *. . . and the Hunters,* 1955; *. . . Goes to School,* 1955; *. . . and the Rocks that Talk,* 1955; *. . . on Superstition Mountain,* 1956; *. . . Makes the Team,* 1956; *. . . Changes Schools,* 1956; *. . . and the Wrecked Plane,* 1956; *. . . and the Big Indian,* 1956; *. . . and the Sacred Cave,* 1957; *. . . Star Back,* 1957; *. . . and the Boy Who Would Not Listen,* 1957; *. . . Plays Hockey,* 1957; *. . . and His Big Chance,* 1958; *. . . and the Contrary Mrs. Forester,* 1958; *. . . and the Man from the Past,* 1959; *. . . , Big Brother,* 1959; *. . . on the Valiant,* 1959; *. . . and Marilyn's Great Trial,* 1959.

Danny Orlis and the Mystery of the Sunken Ship, 1960; *. . . and Ron Orlis in the Canadian Wilderness,* 1960; *. . . in the Mysterious Zandeland,* 1960; *. . . and the Time of Testing,* 1961; *. . . , Bush Pilot,* 1961; *. . . and Hal's Great Victory,* 1962; *. . . and the Drug Store Mystery,* 1962; *. . . and Ron's Call to Service,* 1963; *. . . and the Headstrong Linda Penner,* 1963; *. . . and the Ordeal at Camp,* 1963; *. . . and Linda's Struggle,* 1964; *. . . and the Ice Fishing Escapade,* 1964; *. . . and Linda's New Mother,* 1965; *. . . and Ron in the Mexican Jungle Mystery,* 1965; *. . . and the Defiant Kent Gilbert,* 1965; *. . . and Robin's Big Battle,* 1965; *. . . and the Old Mine Mystery,* 1966; *. . . and Kent's Encounter with the Law,* 1966; *. . . and Robin's Rebellion,* 1966; *. . . and Robin's Big Mistake,* 1966; *. . . and Jim's Northern Adventure,* 1967; *. . . and Kent Gilbert's Tragedy,* 1967; *. . . and the Teen-Age Marriage,* 1967; *. . . and the Guatemala Adventure,* 1967; *. . . and Fritz McCloud, High School Star,* 1968; *. . . and Excitement at the Circle R,* 1968; *. . . and Jim Morgan's Scholarship,* 1968; *. . . and Trouble on the Circle R Ranch,* 1968; *. . . and the Accident that Shook Fairview,* 1968; *. . . : Bid for Victory,* 1969; *. . . and the Dry Gulch Mystery,* 1969; *. . . and Johnny's New Life,* 1969.

Danny Orlis and DeeDee's Defiance, 1970; *. . . and DeeDee's Best Friend,* 1970; *. . . and the Football Feud,* 1971; *. . . and the Crisis at Cedarton,* 1971; *. . . and the Bewildered Runaway,* 1971; *. . . and the Mexican Kidnapping,* 1971; *. . . and the Canadian Caper,* 1972; *. . . and the Alaskan Highway Adventure,* 1972; *. . . : Forced Down,* 1972; *. . . and the Live-in Tragedy,* 1972; *. . . and the Colorado Challenge,* 1972; *. . . and Doug's Big Disappointment,* 1973; *. . . and the Ski Slope Emergency,* 1973; *. . . and the Mystery at Northwest High,* 1973; *. . . and the Girl Who Dared,* 1974; *. . . and the Mysterious Intruder,* 1974; *. . . and the Mysterious Intruder,* 1974; *. . . and the Rock Point Rebel,* 1974; *. . . and the Model Plane Mystery,* 1975.

"Dell Norton" series; published by Moody: *The Wild Float Trip,* 1958; *The Vanishing Mountain Lion,* 1958; *The Echo Mountain Hermit,* 1958; *Dell Norton in the Ozarks,* 1958; *Dell Norton and the Hidden Cave,* 1959.

"Felicia Cartwright" series; published by Moody: *Felicia Cartwright and the Frantic Search,* 1958; *. . . and the Missing Sideboard,* 1958; *. . . and the Green Medallion,* 1958; *. . . and the Uncut Diamond,* 1958; *. . . and the Case of the Twisted Key,* 1959; *. . . and the Case of the Frightened Student,* 1959; *. . . and the Case of the Lonely Teacher,* 1960; *. . . and the Case of the Dancing Fire,* 1960; *. . . and the Case of the Troubled Rancher,* 1961; *. . . and the Case of the Storm-Scarred Mountain,* 1961; *. . . and the Case of the Hungry Fiddler,* 1962; *. . . and the Case of the Antique Bookmark,* 1963; *. . . and the Case of the Lost Puppy,* 1965; *. . . and the Case of the Knotted Wire,* 1966; *. . . and the Case of the Honorable Traitor,* 1967; *. . . and the Case of the Black Phantom,* 1968; *. . . and the Case of the Lone Ski Boot,* 1969; *. . . and the Case of the Bad-Eyed Girl,* 1970; *. . . and the Case of the Pink Poodle,* 1970.

"Golden Boy" series: *Golden Boy,* Van Kampen, 1954; *. . . : Outlaw,* Van Kampen, 1954; *. . . and the Counterfeiters,* Scripture Press, 1958.

"Halliway Boys" series; published by Moody: *The Halliway Boys on Crusade Island,* 1957; *. . . and the Disappearing Staircase,* 1958; *. . . on the Secret Expedition,* 1958; *. . . on a Dangerous Voyage,* 1958; *. . . and the Mysterious Treasure Map,* 1960; *. . . and the Missing Film Mystery,* 1960; *. . . on Forbidden Mountain,* 1962; *. . . on a Secret African Safari,* 1962.

"Little Feather" series; published by Zondervan: *Little Feather Goes Hunting,* 1946; *. . . at Big Bear Lake,* 1947; *. . . Rides Herd,* 1947; *. . . and the Mystery Mine,* 1948; *. . . at Tonak Bay,* 1950; *. . . and the Secret Package,* 1951; *. . . and the River of Grass,* 1953.

"Lori Adams" series; published by Moody: *Lori Adams and the Old Carter House Mystery,* 1969; *. . . and the Adopted Rebel,* 1971; *. . . and the River Boat Mystery,* 1971; *. . . and the Jungle Search,* 1974.

"Mel Webb" series; published by Moody: *Mel Webb and the Border Collie,* 1964; *. . . on the Danger Trail,* 1964; *. . . and the Stolen Dog Mystery,* 1964.

"Mickey Turner" series; published by Moody: *The Fire Detectives,* 1955; *Trapped on Sugar Loaf Mountain,* 1955; *Mickey Turner and the Phantom Dog,* 1955; *Mickey Turner, Ranger's Son,* 1955.

"Orlis Twins" series; published by Moody: *The Orlis Twins and the Secret of the Mountain,* 1959; *. . . and the High School Gang,* 1959; *. . . Live for Christ,* 1959; *. . . and the New Coach,* 1960; *. . . and Mike's Last Chance,* 1960; *. . . and Ron's Big Problem,* 1961; *. . . and Jim Morgan's Ordeal,* 1962; *. . . and Roxie's Triumph,* 1963.

"Pat Collins" series; revised editions published as "Jim Dunlap" series; published by Moody: *Pat Collins and the Peculiar Dr. Brockton,* 1957, revised edition published as *Jim Dunlap and the Strange Doctor Brockton,* 1967; *Pat Collins and the Hidden Treasure,* 1957; *Pat Collins and the Wingless Plane,* 1957, published as *Jim Dunlap and the Wingless Plane,* 1968; *Pat Collins and the Captive Scientist,* 1958; *Pat Collins and the Mysterious Orbiting Rocket,* 1958, published as *Jim and the Mysterious Orbiting Rocket,* 1968; *Pat Collins and the Secret Engine,* 1967.

"Pioneer Girls" series; all with M. Palmer; published by Moody: *Pioneer Girls and the Mystery of Oak Ridge Manor,* 1959; *. . . and the Mystery of the Missing Cocker,* 1959; *. . . and the Strange Adventures on Tomahawk Hill,* 1959; *. . . at Caribou Flats,* 1959; *. . . and the Secret of the Jungle,* 1962; *. . . and the Mysterious Bedouin Cave,* 1963; *. . . and the Dutch Mill Mystery,* 1968.

"Powell Family" series; published by Accent Books: *Rebel of the Lazy H Ranch*, 1980; *The Case of the Missing Dinosaur*, 1981; *Clue of the Old Sea Chest*, 1981; *The Mystery at Poor Boy's Folly*, 1981.

"Ted and Terri" series; published by Moody: *Ted and Terri and the Broken Arrow*, 1971; *. . . and the Crooked Trapper*, 1971; *. . . and the Troubled Trumpeter*, 1971; *. . . and the Stubborn Bully*, 1971; *. . . and the Secret Captive*, 1971.

Under pseudonym John Runyan; "Biff Norris" series; published by Moody: *Biff Norris and the Clue of the Lonely Landing Strip*, 1962; *. . . and the Clue of the Worn Saddle*, 1962; *. . . and the Clue of the Nervous Stranger*, 1962; *. . . and the Clue of the Golden Ram*, 1962; *. . . and the Clue of the Midnight Stage*, 1963; *. . . and the Clue of the Lavender Mink*, 1964; *. . . and the Clue of the Gold Ring*, 1965; *. . . and the Clue of the Angry Fisherman*, 1966; *. . . and the Clue of the Disappearing Wolf*, 1967; *. . . and the Clue of the Mysterious Letter*, 1968; *. . . and the Clue of the Half-Burned Book*, 1969.

Under pseudonym John Runyan; "Tom Barnes" series; published by Moody: *Tom Barnes and the Substitute Second Baseman*, 1964; *. . ., Blocking Back*, 1966; *. . ., Forward*, 1968.

Ghostwriter of *God Is for the Alcoholic*, by Jerry Dunn, Moody, 1965. Author of weekly radio series, "Saturday Youth Program," broadcast in United States and abroad by Back to the Bible Broadcast, 1950-76. Contributor to screenplay, "My Son, My Son" (based on book of the same title), and to "Silent Thunder," and an additional film for Ken Anderson Films (Winona Lake, Inc.). Contributor to *Christian Life*. Member of board of publications, Evangelical Free Church of America, 1965-71, 1971-74, 1980—.

SIDELIGHTS: Bernard Palmer told *CA*: "I was born and raised on the prairies of Nebraska, along the fringe of the cattle country. I didn't realize it when I was growing up but I could not have had a better background for writing children's stories. My father promoted a number of rodeos over a period of several years and we went from one of his shows to another, getting acquainted with the kids of the contestants and developing a love for horses. An uncle was teaching on a western South Dakota Indian Reserve and on frequent visits there I rode horseback with both white and Indian companions over the Badlands.

"My grandfather lived in northern Minnesota and our yearly visit to his farm taught me much about the north woods, fishing, and boating. When I was given an assignment to do the 'Danny Orlis' stories for radio and books it seemed natural for me to think first of the north country. I have always had a deep love for northern United States and Canada and learned enough as a kid to write intelligently about them.

"I wrote my first story, a murder mystery with eleven killings and I don't remember how many broken bones, shootings and stabbings when I was in junior high school. I had a sort of travelling library in my homeroom. I would write a page and pass it to the boy behind me, who read it and gave it to someone else. There must have been a dozen or more who read it before it got back to me.

"Still, I didn't consider writing as a profession until my first and only year in college. I had failed the English test and was put in the 'dumbbell' class. The teacher, with more courage than wisdom, had us write a short story as an assignment. By the time I had finished setting it on paper I knew writing was for me. I had never done anything half so intriguing.

"I set to it at once, thinking I would use it to help put myself through college. The harsh reality of rejection slips soon blew a hole in that dream, but did nothing to lessen my determination. I gave myself ten years to get a major piece of work published. It took me eight and a half years before I signed my first book contract. However, I know now that if I hadn't made progress in the first ten years I would have given myself another ten. I was hooked for life.

"Writing, at least for my wife [Marjorie Palmer] and I who work together as a team, has not been as rewarding financially as some have the impression professional writing is, but there have been other benefits. We have been privileged to go places denied to most, except the very wealthy. We have met some of the most interesting men and women in the country and have tucked away in memory the intriguing stories of people and organizations, some of which cannot be published.

"Our most difficult piece of writing was the tragic-victorious story of the life and death of our oldest son, Barry *(My Son, My Son)*. It was also made into a movie to be shown in churches and schools and has helped many young men and women and their parents.

"Looking back over a lifetime of writing I have made many mistakes and failures but there is not one thing I would change."

AVOCATIONAL INTERESTS: Travel, fishing, boating.

BIOGRAPHICAL/CRITICAL SOURCES: *Christian Life*, February, 1970.

* * *

PALMER, (Nathaniel) Humphrey 1930-

PERSONAL: Born November 6, 1930, in Keighley, England; son of William Nathaniel (a teacher) and Dorothy (Procter) Palmer; married Elizabeth Packiam Theophilus (a lecturer), December 20, 1956; children: Jeremy Mohan. *Education:* Christ Church, Oxford, B.A. (in classics and philosophy; with first class honors), 1953, M.A., 1956, B.A. (in theology), 1958; University of Wales, Ph.D., 1966. *Office address:* Philosophy Department, University College, University of Wales, P.O. Box 78, Cardiff CF1 1XL, Wales.

CAREER: Christ Church College, Kanpur, India, lecturer in philosophy and English, 1956-58; University of Wales, University College, Cardiff, assistant lecturer, 1958-60, lecturer, 1960-68, senior lecturer, 1968-74, reader in philosophy, 1974—, assistant dean of Faculty of Theology, 1968-70, chairman of Religious Studies Board, 1983-84. Lecturer, Madras Christian College, 1962-64. External examiner in theology, University of Bristol. *Military service:* National service as conscientious objector, 1953-55.

WRITINGS: (With wife, Elizabeth Palmer) *Common Tamil Words*, Christian Literature Society, 1964; *The Logic of Gospel Criticism*, St. Martin's, 1968; (translator from the German) L. Nelson, *Progress and Regress in Philosophy*, Basil Blackwell, Volume I, 1970, Volume II, 1971; *Analogy*, St. Martin's, 1973; (editor with A. F. Thyagaraju) J. R. Macphail, *The Parables of Jesus King and Teacher*, Christian Literature Society, 1976; (editor) Macphail, *The Sermons of Jesus King and Teacher*, Christian Literature Society, 1977; (editor) Macphail, *The Kingdom and the King*, Christian Literature Society, 1977; *Arguing for Beginners*, University College, Cardiff, 1979.

(Translator from the German) Immanuel Kant, *Kant's Critique of Pure Reason: An Introductory Version*, University College, Cardiff, 1983; (translator from the German with D. Evans) *Understanding Arguments*, University College, Cardiff, 1983.

Contributor to *Listener, Spectator,* and to philosophy and theology journals.

WORK IN PROGRESS: A book, *Presupposition and Transcendental Inference.*

SIDELIGHTS: Humphrey Palmer told *CA:* "With two colleagues, I have tried to promote the specific study of reasoning in schools. Many young people enjoy arguing just as they enjoy boxing or net ball, and it has rather more application to their other studies. They should be given the chance to learn the rules.

"I have also been keen that the study of religions—and not just Christianity—should continue to form part of a humane education."

AVOCATIONAL INTERESTS: Simple gadgetry.

* * *

PALMER, Marjorie 1919-

PERSONAL: Born October 2, 1919, in Randolph, Neb.; daughter of Locie Floyd (a farmer) and Maud (Jay) Matthews; married Bernard Palmer (a writer and company president), December 12, 1940; children: Morris Jay, Bonnie Lou (Mrs. Douglas Young), Janice Kay (Mrs. Edward Fowler); stepchildren: James Barrett (deceased). *Education:* Attended high school in Wilcox, Neb. *Politics:* Republican. *Religion:* Protestant (Evangelical Free Church of America). *Home:* 1013 14th Ave., Holdrege, Neb. 68949. *Mailing address:* Box 502, Holdrege, Neb. 68949.

CAREER: Author. *Member:* Gideons International (past president of Nebraska chapter auxiliary).

WRITINGS: (With Ethel Bowman) *The Bride's Book of Ideas,* Tyndale, 1970; (with Bowman) *The Young Mother's Book of Ideas,* Tyndale, 1973; *God Helps David,* Moody, 1983; *God Saves Noah,* Moody, 1983.

With husband, Bernard Palmer: *Miracle of the Prairies,* Moody, 1958, new edition published as *Beacon on the Prairies,* Briercrest Bible Institute, 1970; *The Winds of God Are Blowing,* Tyndale, 1973; *How Churches Grow,* Bethany Fellowship, 1976; *The Flood,* Bethel Publishing, 1982; *Who Helps,* Bethel Publishing, 1982; *Who Shows,* Bethel Publishing, 1982; *Light a Small Candle,* Free Church Publications, 1983.

"Career" series; all with B. Palmer; published by Moody: *Student Nurse,* 1960; *Barbara Nichols, Fifth Grade Teacher,* 1960; *Karen Simms, Private Secretary,* 1963; *Sandra Emerson, R.N.,* 1966.

"Pioneer Girls" series; all with B. Palmer; published by Moody: *Pioneer Girls and the Mystery of Oak Ridge Manor,* 1959; *. . . and the Mystery of the Missing Cocker,* 1959; *. . . and the Strange Adventures on Tomahawk Hill,* 1959; *. . . at Caribou Flats,* 1959; *. . . and the Secret of the Jungle,* 1962; *. . . and the Mysterious Bedouin Cave,* 1963; *. . . and the Dutch Hill Mystery,* 1968.

WORK IN PROGRESS: More children's books.

SIDELIGHTS: Marjorie Palmer told *CA:* "I grew up in a little Nebraska town. My favorite pastime was reading. I would take my book on a nice summer day and go out to one of our old apple trees. There, high on a limb with the tree trunk as my backrest I would while away the hours reading. Sometimes I would get so absorbed in a book that my mother's calls were ignored for as long as possible. And being a bookworm has continued until this day.

"My husband, Bernard Palmer, was an aspiring young author even before I met him, and a year or so after our marriage his first novel was published. We began to attend writer's conferences together and there I became acquainted with the basics of writing. I became a critic, reading and rereading each page as it came from my husband's typewriter. On the trips to conferences, and later to visit editors, I sometimes hesitated to leave our four children and go traipsing off to Chicago. Our neighbor, Granny Magill told me: 'Margie, you get ready and go with Bernie. He wants you to go with him now, and if you keep saying no, he will go alone. And soon he won't ask you to go at all.'

"So we began to research together and did much of plotting stories together. When our oldest son was big enough to do a little babysitting, we would go out and drive around town talking out a plot, for it was about the only place we could find for complete quiet from four normal kids.

"The year of our twenty-fifth wedding anniversary, one son, one daughter, and one foster daughter were married. Soon the new brides were coming to me saying: 'Mom, how do you do this, or that? How do you keep the food all warm enough to serve, and what do you do when you get unexpected company, etc.' And one of them said, 'Why don't you write a book with all of this in it?'

"With that incentive, a dear friend and I got our heads together and came up with *The Bride's Book of Ideas* and later *The Young Mother's Book of Ideas.*"

* * *

PAPAS, William

PERSONAL: Born in South Africa of a Greek father and a German mother; married second wife, Theresa Pares, 1970. *Education:* Attended art school in South Africa, and continued his studies in Beckenham, England, 1947. *Address:* Villa Theo, Ermioni, Argolis, Greece.

CAREER: Abandoned formal studies to hitchhike around Europe, sketching and working as a dishwasher in Sweden, a walking billboard advertising schnappes in Germany, and a riveter's helper in England; returned to South Africa in 1951 and joined the staff of the *Cape Times,* Capetown, as an artist and illustrator; in 1954 decided to travel overland to England but his jeep broke down thirty miles out, so he abandoned the trip and tried his hand at farming, 1954-56, and then trucking; finally reached England in 1959 with a large portfolio of drawings and his family of four; did a cartoon strip, "Bella and Lujah," and editorial cartoons for *Sunday Times,* London, 1959-66, and did feature drawings and political cartoons for the *Guardian,* London, 1959-69, and for *Punch,* 1966-70; writer and illustrator of children's books, 1964—. Has exhibited art work in Jerusalem, Israel, 1981, Geneva, Switzerland, 1983, and in Athens, Greece. *Military service:* South African Air Force.

WRITINGS—Self-illustrated juveniles: *The Press,* Oxford University Press, 1964; *Tasso,* Coward, 1967; *No Mules,* Oxford University Press, 1967, Coward, 1968; *Taresh the Tea Planter,* Oxford University Press, 1968, World Publishing, 1969; *A Letter from India,* Oxford University Press, 1968, F. Watts, 1969; *A Letter from Israel,* Oxford University Press, 1968, F. Watts, 1969; *Theodore; or, The Mouse Who Wanted to Fly,*

Oxford University Press, 1969; *Elias the Fisherman*, Oxford University Press, 1970; *The Monk and the Goat*, Oxford University Press, 1971; *The Long Haired Donkey*, Oxford University Press, 1972; *Instant Greek*, privately printed, 1972; *The Most Beautiful Child*, Oxford University Press, 1973; *The Zoo*, Oxford University Press, 1974; *Yes, Yes, Yes*, privately printed, 1974.

Adult books: *People of Old Jerusalem*, Holt, 1980.

Illustrator: Charles Downing, *Tales of the Hodja*, Walck, 1965; Theodore Papas, *The Story of Mr. Nero*, Coward, 1966; Jonathan Stone, *The Law*, Oxford University Press, 1966; Dumas, *Captain Pamphiles Adventures*, Oxford University Press, 1971; Flynn, *Mister God, This is Anna*, Collins, 1974; W. H. Nelson, *The Londoners*, Random House, 1974; Skurzynski, *Two Fools and a Faker*, Lothrop, 1977; Malcolm Muggeridge, *In the Valley of This Restless Mind*, Collins, 1977; Pope John Paul I, *Illustrimi*, Collins, 1978; C. S. Lewis, *The Screwtape Letters*, new edition, Collins & World, 1979.

WORK IN PROGRESS: A pictorial record of Greek villagers and village life tentatively entitled *The Vanishing Greeks*.

SIDELIGHTS: William Papas considers his book illustrating a form of "elongated cartooning," especially when the children's books are on social and political themes. He has fulfilled his ambition to devote most of his time to painting and illustrating on a little island in Greece.

BIOGRAPHICAL/CRITICAL SOURCES: Young Readers' Review, March, 1967; *New Statesman*, November, 1968; *Chicago Tribune Book World*, December 7, 1980.

* * *

PARES, Marion (Stapylton) 1914-
(Judith Campbell, Anthony Grant)

PERSONAL: Surname is pronounced "pairs"; born November 7, 1914, in West Farleigh, Kent, England; daughter of Walter John (a lieutenant commander, Royal Navy) and Dorothy (Chetwynd-Stapylton) Fletcher; married Humphrey Pares (a farmer and company director), June 5, 1937; children: Penelope Iris (Mrs. Peter Furler), Susan Caroline (Mrs. John Gray), Theresa Judith (Mrs. William Papas), Frances Campbell (Mrs. Nigel Harland). *Education:* Educated at boarding school in England. *Politics:* "Traditionally Conservative—but interest lukewarm. Nor overfond of *any* politicians!" *Religion:* "Basically Church of England, but not great upholder of any man-made forms of religion." *Agent:* A. M. Heath & Co. Ltd., 40-42 William IV St., London WC2N 4DD, England.

CAREER: "Spent the years prior to marriage in the normal occupations and amusements for one of my day and age. Always said I 'would write,' but bar normal spate of adolescent poetry, did nothing about it. Wrote a lot during war years while husband abroad, but nothing published . . . until around 1958, when some very modest publishing began to push writing to the fore." Member of Associated Speakers lecture agency.

WRITINGS—Under pseudonym Judith Campbell, except as indicated: *Four Ponies* (juvenile fiction), Muller, 1958; *Merrow Ponies* (juvenile fiction), Muller, 1960; *Family Pony* (nonfiction; illustrated with family photographs and drawings by daughter, Susan Caroline Pares), Lutterworth, 1961; *The Queen Rides* (nonfiction), Lutterworth, 1964, Viking, 1965; *Horses in the Sun* (nonfiction), M. Joseph, 1966, Sportshelf, 1969; *Police Horses*, David & Charles, 1967, A. S. Barnes, 1968; *Anne: Portrait of a Princess*, Cassell, 1969; *Pony Events*, Batsford, 1969; *The World of Horses*, Hamlyn, 1969.

The World of Ponies, Hamlyn, 1970; *Horses and Ponies*, Grosset, 1971, enlarged edition, Hamlyn, 1972; *Elizabeth and Philip*, Regnery, 1972; *Princess Anne and Her Horses*, Brockhampton Press, 1972; *Family on Horseback*, Lutterworth, 1972; *The Champions*, Arthur Barker, 1973; *Royalty on Horseback*, Sidgwick & Jackson, 1974; *The Horseman's World*, Ridge Press, 1975; *Eventing*, Weidenfeld & Nicolson, 1976.

Queen Elizabeth II, Crown, 1980; (under pseudonym Anthony Grant) *The Mutant*, R. Hale, 1980; *Your Own Pony Club*, Lutterworth, 1981; *Charles: A Prince of Our Time*, Octopus Books, 1981; *The Royal Partners: The Queen's 35 Years of Marriage*, Hale, 1982; *Royal Horses*, New English Library, 1983.

Also author of *Anne and Mark*, published by Sidgwick & Jackson. Author of a series of articles for the children's page of the *Sunday Times*, 1960-63; author of monthly columns on the countryside and country living for the *Daily Telegraph*, 1962-63, and the children's magazine *Look and Learn*, 1966.

WORK IN PROGRESS: A television documentary based on *Royal Horses*; *Ponies and Palaces*, a lighthearted account of the people Pares has met and the places she's visited because of her interest in horses.

SIDELIGHTS: Brought up on a fruit farm, remote in the Kentish downs, Marion Pares has always lived in the country, with interests centered on farming, horses and ponies of the family variety, and wild flowers. The wanderings of four travel-minded daughters (one worked her way around the world; another spent a year in Crete) propelled her out of the countryside in 1965 to Jordan, where she studied King Hussein's stud of Arabian horses, those of the police force and Royal Guard, and camels of the Desert Patrol. *Horses in the Sun* resulted.

In researching *Horses in the Sun* and *The Queen Rides*, she was allowed to ride many of the horses. It was "a sometimes hilarious experience for someone who has spent her life riding rotund ponies belonging to our daughters." Research for *The Queen Rides* was done at the Royal Mews where Queen Elizabeth was "incredibly helpful and patient" in helping the author get what she wanted.

In the spring of 1966 Mrs. Pares and her husband went to Crete and the Pelopenese to do a film on village life and the flowers. In the fall they went to Iran for another film and material for *The World of Horses* and *The World of Ponies*. She has also researched material in Greece and France, often accompanied by her husband, and visited the United States in 1974 to gather information for *Horseman's World*. "If the films and books are successful," Mrs. Pares said, "we would like to make the ends of the earth the limits of our activity."

Mrs. Pares reported that she ran "a 'shoe-string' riding club . . . for local children with no other chance of riding. . . . They, under supervision, did all the work and provided me with a lot of reference!"

Her books have appeared in multiple translations, including Swedish, German, French, Italian, Danish, Dutch, and Norwegian.

* * *

PARKER, Robert
See BOYD, Waldo T.

PARSONS, Denys 1914-

PERSONAL: Born March 12, 1914, in London, England; son of Alan (a drama critic) and Viola (daughter of British actor-manager Sir Herbert Beerbohm Tree) Parsons; married Frances Burke (a bio-statistician), May 28, 1962; children: two sons. *Education:* University College, London, B.Sc., 1936; Imperial College of Science and Technology, London, M.Sc., 1938. *Home:* 21 Kingsley Pl., London N6 5EA, England. *Agent:* A. M. Heath & Co. Ltd., 40-42 William IV St., London WC2N 4DD, England.

CAREER: Revertex Sales Co. Ltd., London, England, rubber and plastics research, 1939-45; Realist Film Unit Ltd., London, director of educational and industrial films, 1945-51; National Research Development Corp. (development and exploitation of new inventions), London, manager of information and public relations services, 1952-73; British Library, London, head of press and public relations section, 1973-80; self-employed piano tuner, 1980—. *Member:* Society for Psychical Research.

WRITINGS: (Compiler) *Musical Appreciation*, British Films Institute, 1948; *It Must Be True*, Macdonald & Co., 1952; *Can It Be True?*, Macdonald & Co., 1953; *All Too True*, Macdonald & Co., 1954; *True to Type*, Macdonald & Co., 1955; *Nothing Brightens a Garden Like Primrose Pants*, Hanover House, 1955; *Many a True World*, Macdonald & Co., 1958; *Never More True*, Macdonald & Co., 1960; (editor) *What's Where in London: The BP Guide to Shops and Services*, K. Mason, 1961, 7th edition published as *What's Where in London with BP: Denys Parsons' Offbeat Guide to London Shops and Services*, 1972; *Say It Isn't So*, A. S. Barnes, 1962; (editor) *The Directory of Tunes and Musical Themes*, S. Brown, 1975; *The Denys Parsons Puzzle Book*, Sphere, 1979.

Published by Pan Books: *Funny Ha Ha and Funny Peculiar*, 1965; *Funny Ho Ho and Funny Fantastic*, 1967; *Funny Amusing and Funny Amazing*, 1969; *Funny Convulsing and Funny Confusing*, 1971; *Fun-tastic!*, 1971; *Even More Fun-tastic!*, 1972; (with Betty James) *London for You: A Beginner's Guide*, 1973; *Funny Funny Funny*, 1976; (editor) *Funny Ribtickebus and Funny Ridiculous*, 1979; *The Best of Shrdlu*, 1981.

Contributor to periodicals, including *Journal of Society for Psychical Research*, *New Scientist*, and *Games*.

WORK IN PROGRESS: A book of humorous reminiscences.

* * *

PARSONS, Ellen
See DRAGONWAGON, Crescent

* * *

PATRICK, Maxine
See MAXWELL, Patricia

* * *

PAULDEN, Sydney (Maurice) 1932-

PERSONAL: Born September 6, 1932, in Eccles, England; son of Abe (a grocer) and Polly (Wallis) Paulden; married Mirkka-Liisa Levonius (a secretary for her husband), December 1, 1956 (died October, 1977); married Malinran Somrongpun, June, 1982; children: (first marriage) Raymond Levonius, Kai Andrew, Jan Eric. *Education:* Downing College, Cambridge, B.A., 1954, M.A., 1959. *Politics:* None. *Religion:* None. *Home:* "Windsmoor," the Ridges, Finchampstead, Wokingham, Berkshire, England.

CAREER: Hulton Press Ltd., London, England, industrial editor, 1956-59; Envoy Journals Ltd., London, editorial director, 1959-68; writer. *Military service:* British Army, 1954-56; became sergeant. *Awards, honors:* Winston Churchill Memorial Trust fellowship, 1969; Queen Elizabeth Silver Jubilee Medal, 1977.

WRITINGS: Plan Your Export Drive, Arlington Books, 1965; (with Colin McMillan) *Export Agents: A Complete Guide to Their Selection and Control*, Cahners, 1968, 2nd edition published as *Sales Manager's Guide to Selection and Control of Export Agents*, 1969; (with Bill Hawkins) *Whatever Happened at Fairfields?*, Gower Press, 1969.

Market Europe—The Trendsetters, British National Export Council, 1971; *Hardy Heating International*, British Broadcasting Corp. (BBC) Publications, 1971; *Yan and the Gold Mountain Robbers* (juvenile), Abelard, 1975; *Yan and the Firemonsters* (juvenile), Abelard, 1976; *Yan and the Battle for Bergania* (juvenile), Abelard, 1977; *How to Deliver on Time* (on management), Gower Press, 1977; *The Deadly Gang* (juvenile), Methuen, 1980.

Also author of *Joint Export Marketing Groups*, 1973. Regular contributor to *Times* (London), *Guardian*, *Financial Times* and *Euromoney Trade Finance Report*. Editor, *D and B Creditnews*.

SIDELIGHTS: Sydney Paulden told *CA*: "Whatever is written should be enjoyable to read and easily digestible. This applies to fiction and non-fiction. . . . Children's book writing is not so far removed from business book writing. I want my children's books to be exciting adventures that, at the same time, convey a sense of more profound implications." He is fluent in French and German and has varying degrees of competency in Spanish, Italian, Swedish, and Finnish.

MEDIA ADAPTATIONS: Hardy Heating International was produced as a series of ten television programs by BBC, 1971; *Yan and the Gold Mountain Robbers* was also produced as a television program by BBC, 1976.

* * *

PAYNE, Michael 1941-

PERSONAL: Born January 17, 1941, in Dallas, Tex.; son of Fred G. and Jocie M. (Lundberg) Payne; married second wife, Laura Asherman, December 26, 1973; children: (first marriage) Jeffrey Michael; (second marriage) Albert George, Edward Allen. *Education:* Attended University of California, Berkeley, 1958-59, 1961; Southern Oregon College, B.A., 1962; University of Oregon, Ph.D., 1969. *Home:* 1704 Jefferson Ave., Lewisburg, Pa. 17837. *Office:* Department of English, Bucknell University, Lewisburg, Pa. 17837.

CAREER: Medford Senior High School, Medford, Ore., English teacher, 1962-63; University of Oregon, Eugene, English instructor and assistant director of English composition, 1966-69; Bucknell University, Lewisburg, Pa., assistant to full professor, 1969-80, Presidential Professor, 1982—, head of department of history, 1980-82, head of department of English, 1982—. Writer for Oregon Curriculum Study Center, 1966, 1969; fellow, Folger Shakespeare Library, 1973. *Member:* Modern Language Association of America, Shakespeare Association of America, National Council of Teachers of English, College English Association, American Schools of Oriental Research. *Awards, honors:* National Endowment for the Humanities fellow, 1974; Lindback Award for Distinguished Teaching, 1976.

WRITINGS: (Editor with Glen Love) *Contemporary Essays on Style,* Scott, Foresman, 1969; *Irony in Shakespeare's Roman Plays,* Humanities, 1976; (contributor) *Perspectives on Hamlet,* Bucknell University Press, 1976; *Shakespeare: Contemporary Critical Approaches,* Bucknell University Press, 1980; *Joseph Priestly: Three Views,* Bucknell University Press, 1981. Contributor of articles to numerous publications, including *English Journal, Modern Fiction Studies, Essays in Criticism, Shakespeare Quarterly, College Literature, Pennsylvania English,* and *Biblical Archaeologist.* Associate editor, *Bucknell Review.*

WORK IN PROGRESS: A study of myth in the works of William Blake.

* * *

PEISSEL, Michel (Francois) 1937-

PERSONAL: Surname is pronounced Pay-sell; born February 11, 1937, in Paris, France; son of Georges (a diplomat) and Simone (Ladeuille) Peissel; married former wife Marie Claire deMontaignac, June, 1963; married Mildred Lynard Allen, 1981; children: (first marriage) Olivier, Jocelyn. *Education:* Attended University of Ottawa and Harvard University, 1958-59; Sorbonne, University of Paris, Doctorate in Anthropology, 1969. *Home:* Calle del Puig, Cadaques, Gerona, Spain.

CAREER: Explorer and writer. Participated in an expedition down the Quintana-Roo coast of the Yucatan Peninsula, Mexico, 1958, led an anthropological expedition to the Mount Everest area of the Himalayas, 1959, and a second Quintana-Roo expedition, 1961; one of the few westerners to enter Mustang, a feudal kingdom between Tibet and Nepal, where he spent the spring of 1964; made an expedition across Bhutan, another Himalayan country, 1968; led an expedition through Nepal, 1972; participated in an expedition in quest of Mayan waterways, 1975; did field work in Ladakh and Zanskar, regions in the Himalayas, 1975-78; participated in filming expedition to Zanskar to make four-part BBC documentary "The Last Place on Earth," 1978; led International Ganges Hovercraft Expedition, 1980; conducted research on Minaro in Ladakh and Pakistan, 1980-83. *Member:* Explorers Club (New York), Himalayan Society, Rallye L'Aumance (hunt club; Vitray, France). *Awards, honors:* National Association of Independent Schools Book Award, 1963, for *The Lost World of Quintana-Roo.*

WRITINGS: The Lost World of Quintana-Roo, Dutton, 1963; *Tiger for Breakfast,* Dutton, 1966; *Mustang: The Forbidden Kingdom,* Dutton, 1967 (published in England as *Mustang: A Lost Tibetan Kingdom,* Collins, 1968); *Lords and Lamas: A Solitary Expedition Across the Secret Himalayan Kingdom of Bhutan,* Heinemann, 1970; *Bhoutan: Royaume d'Asie inconnu,* Editions B Arthaud Sarl, 1971; *Cavaliers of Kham: The Secret War in Tibet,* Heinemann, 1972, published as *The Secret War in Tibet,* Little, Brown, 1973; *The Great Himalayan Passage: Across the Himalayas by Hovercraft,* Collins, 1974, published as *The Great Himalayan Passage: The Story of an Extraordinary Adventure on the Roof of the World,* Little, Brown, 1975; *Himalaya Continent Secret,* Flammarion, 1977; *The Mayan Gates of Gold,* Laffont, 1978; *Zanskar: The Hidden Kingdom,* Dutton, 1979. Contributor of about 150 feature stories to periodicals, including *Geo, L'Express, National Geographic, McCalls, Europea,* and *Gazetta Illustrada.*

WORK IN PROGRESS: The Himalayans, a photobook for Perlinger Verlag; *Operation Ibex: The Discovery of the Greek El Dorado in Little Tibet;* a study of the Mayan independence movements.

SIDELIGHTS: Michel Peissel's *Zanskar: The Hidden Kingdom* concerns a medieval Buddhist community of 12,000 that still thrives in a valley in the western Himalayas. According to Jan Morris in *Spectator,* part of the region's history includes "a prophecy that Zanskar would one day be a meeting place for fairies. If M. Peissel were not an explorer of high reputation, one might be tempted to suppose that he had made the whole place up."

Peissel's work on his explorations in the Yucatan Peninsula, *The Lost World of Quintana-Roo,* has been published in France, Sweden, Spain, Czechoslovakia, U.S.S.R., and England. *Mustang: The Forbidden Kingdom* has been translated into French, German, Russian, and Spanish.

BIOGRAPHICAL/CRITICAL SOURCES: New York Times Book Review, June 25, 1967; *New Yorker,* August 5, 1967; *New Statesman,* September 15, 1967; *Books and Bookmen,* April, 1968; *Observer Review,* August 11, 1968; *Listener,* December 26, 1968; *London Times,* February 9, 1972, June 7, 1972, December 14, 1972; *L'Express,* November 20-26, 1972; *Wall Street Journal,* January 2, 1980; *Spectator,* February 16, 1980.

* * *

PEJOVICH, Svetozar 1931-

PERSONAL: Born March 22, 1931, in Belgrade, Yugoslavia; U.S. citizen; son of Mitar (an accountant) and Zorka (Civrich) Paige (originally Pejovich); married Lilliana Davinich, May 25, 1958; children: Alexandra, Brenda, Philip. *Education:* University of Belgrade, LL.B., 1955; Georgetown University, Ph.D. (with honors), 1963. *Religion:* Eastern Orthodox. *Office:* Department of Economics, Texas A&M University, College Station, Tex. 77843; and School of Management, University of Dallas, Irving, Tex. 75061.

CAREER: St. Mary's College, Winona, Minn., associate professor of economics, 1962-66; University of Dallas, Irving, Tex., associate professor of economics, 1966-67; Texas A&M University, College Station, member of faculty, 1967-70; Ohio University, Athens, professor of economics, beginning 1970; currently professor of economics at Texas A&M University and dean of School of Management at University of Dallas. *Member:* American Economic Association, National Tax Association, Catholic Economic Association, Alpha Kappa Psi. *Awards, honors:* Ford Foundation fellowship; grants from U.S. Department of Labor, National Science Foundation, 1966-67, Relm Foundation, 1967-68, and American Association of Learned Societies, 1968-69.

WRITINGS: The Market-Planned Economy of Yugoslavia: A Schumpeterian Interpretation, University of Minnesota Press, 1966; (with Eirik Grundtvig Furubotn) *TheEconomics of Property Rights,* Ballinger, 1974; (editor) *Governmental Controls and the Free Market: The U.S. Economy in the 1970s,* Texas A&M University Press, 1976; (editor) *Individual Freedom: Selected Works of William H. Hutt,* Greenwood Press, 1977; (editor) *The Codetermination Movement in the West: Labor Participation in the Management of Business Firms,* Lexington Books, 1978; *Life in the Soviet Union: A Report Card on*

Socialism, Fisher Institute, 1979; *Fundamentals of Economics: A Property Rights Approach,* Fisher Institute, 1979; (editor) *Philosophical and Economic Foundations of Capitalism,* Lexington Books, 1982. Contributor to *National Tax Journal, Western Economic Journal, Social Order,* and other periodicals. Associate editor, *Review of Social Economics,* beginning 1967.

WORK IN PROGRESS: A textbook, *Towards a Theory of Comparative Economics;* research on the role of technical schools in improving the skill and earning power of labor in rural America.

SIDELIGHTS: Svetozar Pejovich is competent in Slavic languages and German. *Avocational interests:* Chess.†

* * *

PENNIMAN, Howard R(ae) 1916-

PERSONAL: Born January 30, 1916, in Steger, Ill.; son of Rae Ernest (a merchant) and Alethea (Bates) Penniman; married Morgia Anderson, December 30, 1940; children: Barbara Jean, Ruth Mary, William Howard, Catherine Clara, Matthew Francis. *Education:* Louisiana State University, B.A., 1936, M.A., 1938; University of Minnesota, Ph.D., 1941. *Religion:* Episcopal. *Home:* 1409 Red Oak Dr., Silver Spring, Md. *Office:* Department of Government, Georgetown University, Washington, D.C.

CAREER: University of Alabama, University, instructor in political science, 1941-42; Yale University, New Haven, Conn., instructor in department of government, 1942-45, assistant professor, 1945-48; U.S. Central Intelligence Agency, Washington, D.C., staff member, 1948-49; U.S. Department of State, Washington, D.C., assistant chief of External Research Staff, 1949-52, staff member of Psychological Strategy Board, 1952-53, chief of External Research Staff, 1953-55; U.S. Information Agency, chief of Overseas Book Division, 1955-57; Georgetown University, Washington, D.C., professor of government, 1957—, head of department, 1959-63. Adjunct scholar, American Enterprise Institute, 1971. Visiting lecturer in political science at Connecticut College for Women (now Connecticut College), 1944-45, University of Minnesota, 1947, New School for Social Research, 1947-48, and University of Puerto Rico, 1950. Delegate to Maryland Constitutional Convention, 1967-68; co-chairman of Montgomery County Committee on Drug Abuse, 1969-70; trustee, Montgomery College, 1971—. Elections consultant to American Broadcasting Companies, 1968—. *Military service:* U.S. Army, 1945-46.

MEMBER: International Political Science Association, American Political Science Association (president of Washington, D.C. chapter, 1958-59), Pi Gamma Mu, Pi Sigma Alpha, Sigma Delta Chi. *Awards, honors:* Social Science Research Council field fellow, 1940-41; Fulbright research fellow in France, 1964-65.

WRITINGS: (Editor and author of introduction) John Locke, *On Politics and Education,* W. J. Black, 1947; (editor) *Sait's American Parties and Elections,* Appleton, 1948, revised edition, 1952; (with H. Zink and G. Hathorn) *American Government and Politics: National, State and Local,* Van Nostrand, 1958; (with Zink and Hathorn) *Government and Politics in the United States,* Van Nostrand, 1961, revised edition (with Ferber and Hathorn), 1965; *The American Political Process,* Van Nostrand, 1962; *Decision in South Vietnam,* Free Society Association, 1967; (with Ralph W. Winter, Jr.) *Campaign Finances: Two Views of the Political and Constitutional Implications,* American Enterprise Institute for Public Policy Research, 1971; *Elections in South Vietnam,* American Enterprise Institute for Public Policy Research, 1972.

Editor; all published by American Enterprise Institute for Public Policy Research: *Canada at the Polls: The General Elections of 1974,* 1975; *Britain at the Polls: The Parliamentary Elections of 1974,* 1975; *France at the Polls: The Presidential Election of 1974,* 1975; *Australia at the Polls: The National Elections of 1975,* 1977; *Italy at the Polls: The Parliamentary Elections of 1976,* 1977; *Ireland at the Polls: The Dail Elections of 1977,* 1978; *Israel at the Polls: The Knesset Elections of 1977,* 1979; *The Australian National Elections of 1977,* 1979.

New Zealand at the Polls: The General Election of 1978, 1980; *Venezuela at the Polls: The National Elections of 1978,* 1980; *The French National Assembly Elections of 1978,* 1980; *Britain at the Polls, 1979: A Study of the General Election,* 1981; *Canada at the Polls, 1979 and 1980: A Study of the General Elections,* 1981; *Greece at the Polls: The National Elections of 1974 and 1977,* 1981; *Italy at the Polls, 1979: A Study of the Parliamentary Elections,* 1981.

Contributor to professional journals. Columnist for *America,* 1958-64.†

* * *

PERKINSON, Henry J(oseph) 1930-

PERSONAL: Born November 27, 1930, in Philadelphia, Pa.; son of Thomas F. and Helen (Kerner) Perkinson; married Audrey Wesley, March 28, 1953; children: Anthea, Aleta, Amelie, Ariel, Sam. *Education:* University of Pennsylvania, B.S., 1952; graduate study at University of London, 1954-55; Harvard University, M.Ed., 1956, Ed.D., 1959. *Residence:* Shohola, Pa. *Office:* School of Education, New York University, Washington Sq., New York, N.Y. 10003.

CAREER: Kent State University, Kent, Ohio, assistant professor of education, 1959-62; New York University, New York, N.Y., 1962—, currently professor of educational history. *Military service:* U.S. Army, 1952-54; became first lieutenant. *Member:* History of Education Society (president, 1970-71). *Awards, honors:* Italian government fellow at University of Naples, 1958-59.

WRITINGS: (Editor with Paul Nash) *The Educated Man: Studies in the History of Educational Thought,* Wiley, 1965, reprinted, Robert E. Krieger, 1980; *The Imperfect Panacea: American Faith in Education, 1865-1965,* Random House, 1968, 2nd edition published as *The Imperfect Panacea: American Faith in Education, 1865-1976,* 1977; *The Possibilities of Error: An Approach to Education,* McKay, 1971; *Two Hundred Years of American Educational Thought,* McKay, 1976; (with Ronald M. Swartz and Stephanie G. Edgerton) *Knowledge and Fallibilism: Essays on Improving Education,* New York University Press, 1980; *Since Socrates: Studies in the History of Western Educational Thought,* Longman, 1980; *Learning from Our Mistakes,* Greenwood, in press. Editor, *History of Education Quarterly,* 1965-71.

* * *

PERLMAN, John N(iels) 1946-

PERSONAL: Born May 13, 1946, in Alexandria, Va.; son of Ellis S. (in congressional liaison work for Washington Metropolitan Area Transit Authority) and Bertha (Jessen) Perlman; married Janis Hadobas, May 26, 1967; children: Nicole Jeanne Kachina. *Education:* Ohio State University, B.A., 1969; Iona College, M.S., 1981. *Home:* 1632 Mamaroneck Ave., Mamaroneck, N.Y. 10543.

CAREER: Teacher for Poetry-in-the-Schools programs in St. Paul, Minn., Georgia, California, and at Hommocks School, Larchmont, N.Y., 1971-73; Ohio State University, Columbus, visiting instructor in poetry, 1973; Hommocks School, teacher of language arts and creative writing, 1973—. National Endowment for the Arts, Washington, D.C., poetry consultant, 1971—; Casper, Wyo., poet-in-residence for Wyoming Community Colleges, 1971-72. *Awards, honors:* Academy of American Poets awards, 1968, 1969; Vanderwater Prize, 1969.

WRITINGS—Poetry; published by Elizabeth Press, except as indicated: *Kachina*, Ohio State University Press, 1971; *Three Years Rings*, 1972; *Dinner 650 Warburton Ave.*, 1973; *Notes toward a Family*, 1975; *The Hudson: A Weave*, Jordan Davies Press, 1976; *Nicole*, 1976; *Self Portrait*, 1976; *Swath*, 1978; *Homing*, 1981; *Powers*, Kachina Press, 1982; *A Wake of*, Tamarisk Press, 1983; *Longtrail*, Longhouse, 1985. Contributor of poems to *Origin, Elizabeth, First Issue, Grosseteste Review, Longhouse,* and *Tamarisk.*

WORK IN PROGRESS: The Gravity; Eyes Alight.

SIDELIGHTS: John N. Perlman comments: "There is the deep faith that poetry is communicable because [it is] prior to word and coeval with humanity. Reading is acquired over time and with familiarity, but the poetic experience is before time and encounter, as touched and touch without severence or degree. Thus are the terms *writer* and *reader* foregone. What seemed to rise from heart through mind likewise seems from mind to plumb past heart. Each and all so moved, absolved at last of *poetry*, inspirited, confirmed."

* * *

PETERS, F(rancis) E(dward) 1927-

PERSONAL: Born June 23, 1927, in New York, N.Y.; son of Frank L. and Marguerite (Quinlan) Peters; married Mary Battistessa (an executive secretary), 1966; children: Peter Paul. *Education:* St. Louis University, A.B., 1950, M.A., 1952; Princeton University, Ph.D., 1961. *Office:* Near East Center, New York University, New York, N.Y. 10012.

CAREER: New York University, New York, N.Y., assistant professor, 1961-64, associate professor of classics, 1964-69, professor of history and Near Eastern language and literature, 1969—. *Member:* American Oriental Society, Middle East Studies Association, Phi Beta Kappa.

WRITINGS: Greek Philosophical Terms: A Historical Lexicon, New York University Press, 1968; *Aristotle's Arabus*, E. J. Brill, 1968; *Aristotle and the Arabs: The Aristotelian Tradition in Islam*, New York University Press, 1969; *The Harvest of Hellenism*, Simon & Schuster, 1971; *Allah's Commonwealth*, Simon & Schuster, 1974; *Ours: The Making and Unmaking of a Jesuit*, Richard Marek, 1981; *The Children of Abraham: Judaism, Christianity and Islam*, Princeton University Press, 1983.

WORK IN PROGRESS: The History of the Arabs Before Islam; A Social and Economic History of Medieval Islam.

SIDELIGHTS: F. E. Peters writes: "I am a historian of the Near East from 300 B.C. to 1200 A.D., and so also of Hellenistic Judaism, early Christianity, and medieval Islam. I am trained in Greek, Latin, Syriac, and Arabic, with extensive travels in the Islamic world from Morocco to India, but chiefly in Syria.

"My [earlier work was] concentrated upon the transition from the world of Greco-Roman antiquity to the new world of Islam. I have spent much of my career studying the passage of ideas from the Greeks to Islam, but more recently I have turned to institutions, and more particularly to the transition of the city and its life from a Greco-Roman milieu to an Islamic one: how the physical shape, functions and classes of the city of late antiquity changed into the present profile of an Islamic city. Much of my travelling [has been] devoted to an observation of urban geography (quarters, arrangement of street patterns, marketplaces, walls, etc.) as they reflect upon the preindustrial city. Near Eastern cities are rapidly changing and so the historical evidence is equally rapidly being effaced. Dead cities like Petra and Palmyra may remain frozen forever, but the nonindustrialized part of living cities like Damascus [and] Aleppo are being altered faster than the historian can record and study them.

"For some years I worked on the urban development of the cities in the lava lands of southern Syria, but more recently I have attempted to bring the skills of the urban historian to bear on the city of Jerusalem, a far more complex subject than Damascus or Aleppo, for example, since it is above all else a holy city. The holy city in the Near East seems to have its own morphology which sometimes reinforces and sometimes contradicts the normal patterns of urban development in the Near East. This is the focus of my present work.

"There are now three books complete in manuscript on this subject: *Mecca and Jerusalem: The Typology of the Holy City in the Near East; The Distant Shrine: Jerusalem under the Muslims;* and *A Reader on Jerusalem: The Holy City through the Eyes of Chroniclers, Visitors, Pilgrims and Prophets from David to the Beginning of Modern Times.*"

BIOGRAPHICAL/CRITICAL SOURCES: Washington Post Book World, August 23, 1981.

* * *

PETERS, Margot 1933-

PERSONAL: Born May 13, 1933, in Wausau, Wis.; daughter of Edgar J. and Elsie (a journalist; maiden name, Merkel) McCullough; married Peter Ridgway Jordan; children: Marc, Claire. *Education:* University of Wisconsin, Madison, B.A., 1961, M.A., 1965, Ph.D., 1969. *Home:* 511 College St., Lake Mills, Wis. 53551. *Office:* Department of English, University of Wisconsin, Whitewater, Wis. 53190.

CAREER: Northland College, Ashland, Wis., assistant professor of English, 1963-66; University of Wisconsin—Whitewater, assistant professor, 1969-74, associate professor, 1974-77, professor of English, 1977—. Kathe Tappe Vernon Chair of Biography, Dartmouth College, 1978; participant, International Symposium of Biography, 1980. *Member:* Modern Language Association of America, Authors Guild, Authors League of America, Bronte Society, Bernard Shaw Society, Women's Caucus for the Modern Languages. *Awards, honors:* Award from Friends of American Writers, 1975, for *Unquiet Soul;* American Council of Learned Societies fellowship, 1976-77; George M. Freedly award, Banta award, and Council of Wisconsin Writers award, all for *Bernard Shaw and the Actresses.*

WRITINGS: Charlotte Bronte: Style in the Novel, University of Wisconsin Press, 1973; *Unquiet Soul: A Biography of Charlotte Bronte*, Doubleday, 1975; (contributor) Michael Holroyd, editor, *The Genius of Bernard Shaw*, Holt, 1979; *Bernard Shaw and the Actresses*, Doubleday, 1980; (author of introduction) Dan H. Laurence, editor, *Mrs. Warren's Profession in Bernard Shaw: Early Texts*, Garland, 1981; *Mrs. Pat: The Life of Mrs. Patrick Campbell*, Knopf, 1984. Contributor to scholarly and literary magazines and journals.

SIDELIGHTS: Of Margot Peters's study *Bernard Shaw and the Actresses*, London *Times* critic Philippa Toomey says: "This is a fascinating book, and it is a pity about the title, which has the air of a music-hall joke. . . . [The work is] a serious and excellent biography illustrating the influence that women had on Shaw and his work. He claimed that women never played an important part in his life, and [the author] deftly and amusingly demonstrates that this was not so."

As Peters relates, the renowned playwright carried on various relationships with numerous women throughout his career, notably with actresses Ellen Terry and Mrs. Patrick Campbell. "It was the mother-figure that particularly appealed to him," notes Michael Holroyd in a *Times Literary Supplement* review. "His ideal woman was a mother-and-wife in whose love he could be born again and with whom he could enjoy a second happy childhood eclipsing the first. But as his experiences with Ellen Terry show, he feared to break the illusion with physical contact." Citing the strict chronological sequencing of the work, Holroyd finds that Peters has applied "so many strands to this story that she is forced to break off, recapitulate, pull up some other strand, then start forward again. As we get particularly interested in one aspect of the story we are abruptly switched to another." However, while the critic feels that "the [stylistic] experiment may not be wholly successful, the book is full of good sense, careful research and a fine percipience. Margot Peters has not only thought but felt; not only read but experienced. Her attitude to Shaw seems to be one of admiration and exasperation mixed—which creates an authentic atmosphere for the ambivalent feelings of these actresses towards Shaw."

BIOGRAPHICAL/CRITICAL SOURCES: Times Literary Supplement, May 1, 1981; *Times* (London), June 4, 1981.

* * *

PETERSON, Carolyn Sue 1938-

PERSONAL: Born June 23, 1938, in Carthage, Mo.; daughter of Harry A. and Clara (a nutrition aide; maiden name, Johnson) Peterson; children: Angie (adopted). *Education:* Joplin Junior College, A.A., 1957; University of Missouri, A.B., 1959, graduate study, 1964-66; University of Denver, M.A.L.S., 1960; further graduate study at Northwest Missouri State College, 1966-68. *Home:* 3002 Illingworth Ave., Orlando, Fla. 32806. *Office:* Orlando Public Library, 10 North Rosalind, Orlando, Fla. 32801.

CAREER: Town and Country Regional Library, Joplin, Mo., children's librarian, 1960-62; Northwest Missouri State University, Maryville, instructor in library science, and librarian at university elementary, junior high, and high schools, 1962-68; University of Colorado, Boulder, instructor in library science, 1968-70; Orlando Public Library, Orlando, Fla., head of children's department, 1970—; co-owner and co-editor of Moonlight Press, 1981—.

MEMBER: American Library Association, Association for Library Service (member of publications support committee, 1978-83; member of Caldecott committee, 1980-81), Southeastern Library Association (member of Children's Division executive committee, 1982-83), Florida Library Association (president of Children's Caucus, 1976-77). *Awards, honors:* Outstanding Library Development Award, Florida Library Association, Outstanding Library Service Award, Southeastern Library Association, John Cotton Dana Award, American Library Association, and CINE Golden Eagle Award, all for Peterson's innovative programs at Orlando Public Library; American Book Award nominee in Reference Division, 1980, Outstanding Reference Book, American Library Association, 1980, and recommended reference source for school media centers by School Library Journal, all for *Index to Children's Songs*.

WRITINGS: Reference Books for Elementary and Junior High School Libraries, Scarecrow, 1970, revised edition, 1975; (contributor) *Start Early for an Early Start* (anthology), American Library Association, 1976; (with Ann D. Fenton) *Index to Children's Songs*, H. W. Wilson, 1979; (with Brenny Hall) *Story Programs: A Source Book of Materials*, Scarecrow, 1980; (with Fenton) *Reference Books for Children*, Scarecrow, 1981; (with Fenton) *Christmas Story Programs*, Moonlight Press, 1981.

Also author of filmstrip, "Sharing Literature with Children," Orlando Public Library, 1974. Contributor of poems and articles to education and library journals and to children's magazines, including *Jack and Jill* and *Child Life*.

WORK IN PROGRESS: Story Programs for Older Children; Story Programs for Two-Year-Olds.

SIDELIGHTS: Carolyn Sue Peterson told *CA*: "Since my professional concerns revolve primarily around children, books, and reading, I have attempted through writing as well as action to promote interest in all three. I believe that children who are reared with a love for books will become reading adults and that adults who read will become enlightened and concerned citizens. With whatever facilities at my disposal, I want to contribute to the welfare and growth of children, for they are our most valuable resources."

AVOCATIONAL INTERESTS: Guitar, archery, music, computers, hiking, the women's movement.

* * *

PETTES, Dorothy E.

PERSONAL: Born in Brooklyn, N.Y.; daughter of Robert M. and Florence E. (Robb) Pettes. *Education:* University of California, Los Angeles, A.B., 1936; University of California (now University of California, Berkeley), graduate study, 1937-38; University of Chicago, A.M., 1948. *Politics:* Democratic. *Religion:* Episcopalian. *Home:* 341 Tideway Dr., Apt. 116, Alameda, Calif. 94501.

CAREER: University of California, Berkeley, School of Social Welfare, faculty member, 1951-69; University of Newcastle-upon-Tyne, Newcastle-upon-Tyne, England, faculty member, 1969-79. *Military service:* U.S. Navy, Women's Reserve (WAVES), 1942-45. *Member:* American Association of Social Workers, Association of Social Work Teachers. *Awards, honors:* Fulbright senior fellowship in England, 1964-66.

WRITINGS: Supervision in Social Work: A Method for Student Training and Staff Development, Verry, 1967; (with Priscilla Young and Joyce Warham) *Administration and Staff Super-*

vision in the Child Care Service (monograph), Association of Child Care Officers (London), 1968; *Staff and Student Supervision: A Task-Centred Approach,* Allen & Unwin, 1979.

AVOCATIONAL INTERESTS: Photography.

* * *

PHELAN, John Leddy 1924-1976

PERSONAL: Born July 19, 1924, in Fall River, Mass.; died July 25, 1976; son of Joseph P. (a manufacturer) and Rose (Dunn) Phelan. *Education:* Harvard University, A.B., 1947; University of California, Berkeley, M.A., 1948, Ph.D., 1951. *Politics:* Democrat. *Home:* 5457 Lake Mendota Dr., Madison, Wis. *Office:* History Department, University of Wisconsin, Madison, Wis. 53706.

CAREER: University of Wisconsin—Milwaukee, lecturer, 1956, assistant professor, 1956-58, associate professor of history, 1958-60; University of Wisconsin—Madison, associate professor, 1960-64, professor of history, 1964-76. Member of executive council, Milwaukee County Council of Democratic Party, 1958-60. Chairman, Conference of Latin American History, 1973. *Member:* American Historical Association, Academy of American Franciscan History. *Awards, honors:* Fulbright scholar in France, 1951-52; Newberry Library fellow, 1953-55; Guggenheim fellow, 1960-61.

WRITINGS: *The Millennial Kingdom of the Franciscans in the New World: A Study of the Writings of Geronimo de Mendieta, 1525-1604,* University of California Press, 1956, 2nd revised edition, 1970; *The Hispanization of the Philippines: Spanish Aims and Filipino Responses, 1565-1700,* University of Wisconsin Press, 1959; *The Kingdom of Quito in the Seventeenth Century: Bureaucratic Politics in the Spanish Empire,* University of Wisconsin Press, 1968; *The People and the King: The Comunero Revolution in Colombia, 1781,* University of Wisconsin Press, 1978. Editor of *The Ordinances Issued by the Audiencia of Manila for the Alcaldes Mayores (1642, 1696, and 1739),* 1960. Contributor of articles on the Spanish Empire and modern Latin America to journals. Member of board of editors, *Hispanic-American Historical Review,* 1962-70.

WORK IN PROGRESS: *Reform, Revolt, and Revolution in the Spanish Empire, 1590-1800.*

SIDELIGHTS: *The Millennial Kingdom of the Franciscans in the New World: A Study of the Writings of Geronimo de Mendieta, 1525-1604* has been published in Spanish.

BIOGRAPHICAL/CRITICAL SOURCES: *South Atlantic Quarterly,* winter, 1969.†

* * *

PHILLIPS, Bernard S. 1931-

PERSONAL: Born June 4, 1931, in New York, N.Y.; son of Morris (an owner of a retail butcher shop) and Suzan (Greenstone) Pustilnik; married Marjorie Ruth Birnbach (an instructor in early childhood education), January 30, 1955; children: David, Michael. *Education:* Columbia University, B.A., 1952; Washington State University, M.A., 1954; Cornell University, Ph.D., 1956. *Politics:* Independent. *Home:* 12 Trotting Horse Dr., Lexington, Mass. 02173. *Office:* Department of Sociology, Boston University, 100 Cummington St., Boston, Mass. 02215.

CAREER: University of North Carolina at Chapel Hill, School of Public Health, assistant professor of social psychology, 1956-58; University of Illinois at Urbana-Champaign, assistant professor of sociology, 1959-61; Boston University, Boston, Mass., assistant professor, 1961-63, associate professor, 1963-72, professor of sociology, 1972—. Consultant to Puerto Rico Department of Education, 1968. Visiting professor at Florida State University, 1969, and University of Hawaii at Manoa, 1974. *Member:* American Sociological Association (fellow), Eastern Sociological Society. *Awards, honors:* Japan Area Development Center visiting scholar award, 1968.

WRITINGS: *Social Research: Strategy and Tactics,* Macmillan, 1966, 3rd edition, 1976; *Sociology: Social Structure and Change,* Macmillan, 1969; *Worlds of the Future: Exercises in Sociological Imagination,* C. E. Merrill, 1972; *Sociology: From Concepts to Practice,* McGraw, 1979; *Sociological Research Methods,* Dorsey, 1985. Co-founder and co-editor, *Sociological Practice,* 1976-78.

SIDELIGHTS: Bernard S. Phillips told *CA,* "My . . . work centers on how to wed the abstract concepts of sociology to concrete situations, whether described by social scientists or poets or portrayed by dramatists."

* * *

PHILLIPS, David Atlee 1922-
(George Spelvin)

PERSONAL: Born October 31, 1922, in Fort Worth, Tex.; son of Edwin (a lawyer) and Mary (an executive; maiden name, Young) Phillips; married Helen Haasch, June 5, 1948 (divorced, 1967); married Virginia Simmons (an educator), March 28, 1968; children: David Jr., Maria, Christopher, Deborah, Bryan, Wynne, Todd. *Education:* Attended College of William and Mary, 1940-41, Texas Christian University, 1941-42, and University of Chile, 1948-49. *Politics:* Democrat. *Religion:* Protestant. *Home:* 8224 Stone Trail Dr., Bethesda, Md. 20817.

CAREER: Worked as writer and actor in New York, N.Y., 1940-48; *South Pacific Mail,* Santiago, Chile, editor and publisher, 1948-54; Central Intelligence Agency, Washington, D.C., intelligence officer, 1950-75, chief of Western Hemisphere division, 1973-75; professional lecturer, 1975—; has appeared on numerous television shows, including "60 Minutes" and "Today," on behalf of Association of Former Intelligence Officers. *Military service:* U.S. Army Air Forces, 1944-45; became staff sergeant; received Air Medal with cluster and Purple Heart. *Member:* Association of Former Intelligence Officers (founder and president, 1975—). *Awards, honors:* Intelligence Medal of Merit, 1955; Distinguished Intelligence Medal, 1975.

WRITINGS: *The Night Watch: 25 Years of Peculiar Service,* Atheneum, 1977; *The Carlos Contract* (novel), Macmillan, 1978; *The Great Texas Murder Trials* (novel), Macmillan, 1979. Editor, under pseudonym George Spelvin, *Periscope* (a quarterly for intelligence professionals), 1975-78; contributing editor, *Defense Electronics.*

SIDELIGHTS: For David Atlee Phillips, "a 25-year veteran of C.I.A.'s clandestine services, spying proved a rewarding and often pleasant career," writes David Wise in the *New York Times Book Review.* "Then, abruptly, everything changed. In December 1974, Seymour Hersh revealed in the *New York Times* that the C.I.A. had been spying on Americans. Suddenly there was the Rockefeller Commission, the Congressional Investigations, a riptide of daily news stories, books criticizing the Agency, the Justice Department poking around. . . . Clearly, it wasn't fun any more." Phillips told *CA* that he retired from his position as chief of the Western Hemisphere Division in 1975 "to participate in the current controversy concerning intelligence in America." Upon leaving the agency, he founded the Association of Former Intelligence Officers, an organization of C.I.A. retirees that takes an active role in the debate and now boasts a membership of 3,500. Discussing the association's position on intelligence issues, Phillips indicated to *CA* that "we believe in Congressional oversight and legislation for intelligence operations—but that an adequate intelligence capability is essential. We have *some* success in explaining the role of intelligence and improving the tarnished image of intelligence men and women."

A nonfictional account of Phillips's experiences within the Central Intelligence Agency, *The Night Watch: 25 Years of Peculiar Service* also attempts to refute criticisms of the agency. *New York Times* reviewer John Leonard writes that, in *The Night Watch*, Phillips "introduces his agency as a bunch of fun-loving white hats who, on the whole, would have preferred retiring somewhere to raise rabbits if it weren't for this problem of Communist terrorists about whom they have to fill out so many tedious 3 x 5 cards. He deplores excess and assassination. . . . The method of *The Night Watch* is to admit mistakes and light up a filter-tipped extenuation. Thus: the C.I.A. shouldn't mess around at home, and oughtn't to have tried to abolish Salvador Allende—or anybody else—abroad, but we mean well."

BIOGRAPHICAL/CRITICAL SOURCES: New York Times Book Review, March 6, 1977, January 21, 1979, August 26, 1979; *New York Times*, March 10, 1977; *Nation*, April 29, 1978; *New York Review of Books*, February 8, 1979.

* * *

PHIPPS, William E(ugene) 1930-

PERSONAL: Born January 28, 1930, in Waynesboro, Va.; son of Charles Henry (a clergyman) and Ruth (Patterson) Phipps; married Martha Ann Swezey, December 21, 1954; children: Charles, Anna, Ruth. *Education:* Davidson College, B.S., 1949; Union Theological Seminary in Virginia, B.D., 1952; University of St. Andrews, Ph.D., 1954; University of Hawaii, M.A., 1963. *Home:* Lincoln Ave., Elkins, W.Va. 26241. *Office:* Davis and Elkins College, Elkins, W.Va. 26241.

CAREER: Presbyterian clergyman. Peace College, Raleigh, N.C., professor of Bible, 1954-56; Davis and Elkins College, Elkins, W.Va., professor of religion and philosophy and chairman of department, 1956—. *Military service:* U.S. Army Reserve, 1955-63; became first lieutenant. *Member:* American Academy of Religion, American Association of University Professors, West Virginia Philosophical Society (president, 1968-69), Phi Alpha Theta, Rotary.

WRITINGS: Was Jesus Married?: The Distortion of Sexuality in the Christian Tradition, Harper, 1970; *The Sexuality of Jesus: Theological and Literary Perspectives*, Harper, 1973; *Recovering Biblical Sensuousness*, Westminster, 1975; *Influential Theologians on Woman*, University Press of America, 1980; *Encounter through Questioning Paul*, University Press of America, 1983. Contributor to *New York Times* and to religious journals.

WORK IN PROGRESS: A publication "that focuses on the growth of supernaturalism in the course of Christianity."

SIDELIGHTS: William E. Phipps writes: "I think that significant personal qualities are best revealed when someone expresses opinions about the opposite sex. Thus, I have used this index of character in searching scriptures and theological writings. In theory, most religious figures hold that inequity is iniquity, but few are fully conscious of the gender injustices that are embedded in the cultural patterns that they accept."

BIOGRAPHICAL/CRITICAL SOURCES: Christian Century, November 25, 1970, March 3, 1971, April 28, 1971.

* * *

PIASECKI, Bruce 1955-

PERSONAL: Born February 1, 1955, in West Islip, N.Y.; son of Walter John Piasecki and Lillian Kureczko. *Education:* Cornell University, B.A. (summa cum laude), 1976, Ph.D., 1981. *Politics:* "More critical than political." *Religion:* "Presently searching." *Home:* 358 Oakwood Ave., West Islip, N.Y. 11795. *Office:* Center for Liberal Studies, Clarkson College of Technology, Potsdam, N.Y. 13676.

CAREER: Cornell University, Ithaca, N.Y., assistant teacher of writing, 1976-77; currently assistant professor at Center for Liberal Studies, Clarkson College of Technology, Potsdam, N.Y. *Awards, honors:* Long Island award from C. W. Post Center, 1974; New York Poetry Forum's Narrative Award, 1976; awards from Cornell Council on the Arts, 1976, Carnegie Fund for Authors, 1977, P.E.N. American Center, 1977, and Fund for Investigative Journalism, 1983.

WRITINGS: (Editor) *The First Anthology*, Society of Humanities, 1974; *Stray Prayers* (poems), Ithaca House, 1976; *Beyond Dumping: New Strategies for Controlling Toxic Wastes*, Greenwood Press, 1984. Contributor to *Washington Monthly*, *Amicus Journal*, *Business and Society Review*, and other periodicals. Editor, *Praxis*, 1977-78.

WORK IN PROGRESS: A cultural history of American environmentalism, *In Nature We Trust: Origins and Demise of American Confidence in Nature*.

* * *

PINCHER, H(enry) Chapman 1914-

PERSONAL: Born March 29, 1914, in Ambala, Punjab State, India; son of Richard Chapman (an army officer) and Helen (an actress; maiden name, Foster) Pincher; married Constance Sylvia Wolstenholme, 1965; children: Patricia Chapman, Michael Chapman. *Education:* Attended University of London, 1932-36. *Home and office:* Church House, 16 Church St., Kintbury, Newbury, Berkshire, England.

CAREER: Staff member at Liverpool Institute, 1936-40; *Daily Express*, London, England, 1946-79, began as defense editor, became science editor and medical editor, assistant editor and chief defense correspondent, 1972-79; free-lance journalist, novelist, and business consultant, 1979—. *Military service:* British Army, specialist on rocket weapons, 1940-46; became staff captain. *Awards, honors:* Fellow, King's College, University of London, 1979; D.Litt., University of Newcastle upon Tyne, 1979.

WRITINGS: Into the Atomic Age, Hutchinson, 1946; *Breeding of Farm Animals*, Penguin, 1946; *A Study of Fishes*, Doubleday, 1948; *Evolution*, Jenkins, 1950; *Spotlight on Animals*, Hutchinson, 1950; (with Bernard Blake Wicksteed) *It's Fun Finding Out*, 2nd series, Daily Express, 1950; *Sleep: How to Get More of It*, Daily Express, 1954; *Not with a Bang* (novel), New American Library, 1965; *The Giantkiller*, Weidenfeld &

Nicolson, 1967; *The Penthouse Conspirators,* M. Joseph, 1970; *Sex in Our Time,* Weidenfeld & Nicolson, 1973; *The Skeleton at the Villa Wolkonsky,* M. Joseph, 1974; *The Eye of the Tornado,* M. Joseph, 1976; *The Four Horses,* M. Joseph, 1978; *Inside Story: A Documentary of the Pursuit of Power,* Sidgwick & Jackson, 1978, Stein & Day, 1979; *Dirty Tricks: A Novel,* Stein & Day, 1980; *Their Trade is Treachery,* Sidgwick & Jackson, 1981; *The Private World of St. John Terrapin,* Sidgwick & Jackson, 1982; *The Spy of the Century,* Sidgwick & Jackson, 1984.

SIDELIGHTS: *Not with a Bang* has been translated into Italian.

* * *

PINCUS, Edward R. 1938-

PERSONAL: Born July 6, 1938, in New York, N.Y.; son of Jules and Anne (Schehr) Pincus; married Jane Kates (a craftswoman and author), June 22, 1960; children: Sami, Benjamin. *Education:* Brown University, A.B., 1960; additional study at La Scola Normale Superiore di Pisa, 1960-61; Harvard University, M.A., 1966. *Address:* P.O. Box 72, Roxbury, Vt. 05669.

CAREER: Cambridgeport Film Corp., Cambridge, Mass., president, 1965—; Massachusetts Institute of Technology, Cambridge, lecturer, 1969-70, assistant professor, 1970-72, associate professor, 1972-76, adjunct professor of filmmaking, 1977-80; Harvard University, Cambridge, visiting lecturer, 1980-83. *Member:* Society of Motion Picture and Television Engineers. *Awards, honors:* Fulbright fellow, 1960-61; Woodrow Wilson fellow, 1961-62; National Endowment for the Arts fellow, 1970, 1974, and 1980; Guggenheim fellow, 1972-73.

WRITINGS: Guide to Filmmaking, New American Library, 1969, hardcover edition, Regnery, 1972; *Filmaker's Handbook,* Plume, 1984.

WORK IN PROGRESS: Various filmmaking projects.

BIOGRAPHICAL/CRITICAL SOURCES: Roy Levin, *Documentary Explorations,* Doubleday, 1971.

* * *

PINION, F(rancis) B(ertram) 1908-

PERSONAL: Born December 4, 1908; married Marjorie Fidler, August, 1935; children: Andrew, Catherine. *Education:* Cambridge University, B.A., 1930, M.A., 1936; Oxford University, diploma in education, 1944. *Residence:* Sheffield, Yorkshire, England.

CAREER: Headmaster of a grammar school in England, 1950-61; University of Sheffield, Sheffield, England, lecturer, 1961-68, senior lecturer, 1968-73, reader in English studies, 1973-74, sub-dean of Faculty of Arts, 1965-74. Visiting lecturer in English, University of Michigan, 1964-65. Lecturer at universities in the United States and Norway. Active in promoting work of the American Field Service in Yorkshire and East Midlands region, and former chairman of the committee for the selection of British students placed in America. *Member:* Thomas Hardy Society (honorary vice-president), D. H. Lawrence Society. *Awards, honors:* Litt.D. from Cambridge University, 1981.

WRITINGS—All published by Macmillan, except as indicated: *Educational Values in the Age of Technology,* Pergamon, 1964; (author of critical commentary) Thomas Hardy, *The Mayor of Casterbridge,* 1966; *A Hardy Companion,* 1968; *A Jane Austen Companion,* 1973; *A Bronte Companion,* 1975; *A Commentary on the Poems of Thomas Hardy,* 1976; *Thomas Hardy: Art and Thought,* 1977; *A D. H. Lawrence Companion,* 1978; *A George Eliot Companion,* 1981; *A Wordsworth Companion,* 1983; *A Tennyson Companion,* 1984.

Editor: Robert Browning, *The Ring and the Book* (abridged edition), 1957; *A Selection of Shelley's Poetry,* 1958; Thomas Hardy, *Tess of the d'Urbervilles,* 1959; *A Wordsworth Selection,* 1963; Browning, *Men and Women,* 1963; *A Lamb Selection,* 1965; Browning, *Dramatis Personae,* Collins, 1969; (with Evelyn Hardy) *One Rare Fair Woman,* 1972; *Thomas Hardy and the Modern World,* Thomas Hardy Society, 1974; Hardy, *The Mayor of Casterbridge,* 1975; Hardy, *The Woodlanders,* 1975; Hardy, *Two on a Tower,* 1975; (and contributor) *Budmouth Essays on Thomas Hardy,* Thomas Hardy Society, 1976; (and contributor) *A George Eliot Miscellany,* Thomas Hardy Society, 1982.

Editor of other selections of poetry for school use, published 1941-64. Contributor to professional journals. Editor, *Thomas Hardy Society Review,* 1975.

WORK IN PROGRESS: A T. S. Eliot Companion.

* * *

PINKWATER, Daniel Manus 1941- (Manus Pinkwater)

PERSONAL: Born November 15, 1941, in Memphis, Tenn.; son of Philip (a ragman) and Fay (Hoffman) Pinkwater; married Jill Schutz (a writer and illustrator), October 12, 1969. *Education:* Bard College, B.A., 1964; also studied at Art Institute of Chicago, Harvard University, University of Liverpool, and University College, Nairobi, Kenya. *Politics:* Republican. *Religion:* Taoist. *Home:* 22 Hudson Pl., Hoboken, N.J. 07030.

CAREER: Writer and illustrator of children's books. Art instructor at Children's Aid Society, New York City, 1967-69, Lower West Side Visual Arts Center, New York City, 1969, Henry Street Settlement, New York City, 1969, and Bonnie Brae Farm for Boys, Millington, N.J., 1969; Inner City Summer Arts Program, Hoboken, N.J., assistant project director, 1970. Has exhibited his prints at Brooklyn Museum, St. John's University, State University of New York College at Potsdam, Carleton College, First Zen Institute, and the First Hawaii National Print Exhibition.

WRITINGS—All juveniles; self-illustrated, except as indicated: *Wizard Crystal,* Dodd, 1973; *Magic Camera,* Dodd, 1974; *Lizard Music,* Dodd, 1976; *The Big Orange Splot,* Hastings House, 1977; (with wife, Jill Pinkwater) *Superpuppy: How to Choose, Raise, and Train the Best Possible Dog for You,* illustrated by J. Pinkwater, Seabury, 1977; *The Blue Seed Thing,* Prentice-Hall, 1977; *The Hoboken Chicken Emergency,* Prentice-Hall, 1977; *Fat Men from Space,* Dodd, 1977; *The Last Guru,* Dodd, 1978; *Return of the Moose,* Dodd, 1979; *Alan Mendelsohn: The Boy from Mars,* Dutton, 1979; *Yobgorgle: Mystery Monster of Lake Ontario,* Clarion Books, 1979; *Pickle Creature,* Four Winds, 1979.

(With Luqman Keele) *Java Jack,* Crowell, 1980; *The Wuggie Norple Story,* illustrated by Tomie de Paola, Four Winds, 1980; *The Magic Moscow,* Four Winds, 1980; *Tooth-Gnasher Superflash,* Four Winds, 1981; *The Worms of Kukumlima,* Dutton, 1981; *Attila the Pun,* Four Winds, 1981; *The Snarkout Boys and the Avocado of Death,* Lothrop, 1982; *Young Adult*

Novel, Crowell, 1982; *Slaves of Spiegel,* Four Winds, 1982; *I Was a Second Grade Werewolf,* Dutton, 1983; *The Snarkout Boys and the Baconburg Horror,* Lothrop, 1983; *Ducks!,* Little, Brown, 1983; *Devil in the Drain,* Dutton, 1983.

Under name Manus Pinkwater: *The Terrible Roar,* Knopf, 1970; *Bear's Picture,* Holt, 1972; *Fat Elliot and the Gorilla,* Four Winds, 1974; *Blue Moose,* Dodd, 1975; *Three Big Hogs,* Seabury, 1975; *Wingman,* Dodd, 1975; *Around Fred's Bed,* illustrated by Robert Mertens, Prentice-Hall, 1976.

WORK IN PROGRESS: "Much."

SIDELIGHTS: Peter Andrews writes in the *New York Times Book Review:* "One of the things I most admire about [Daniel Manus] Pinkwater when he is at his best is the reckless way he refuses to try for the fey bemusement that is the hallmark of so many children's humor books. He is shameless in trying to make the reader laugh out loud—the most difficult feat in English letters. . . . Mr. Pinkwater has been rightly praised as a children's author who does not treat his audience as if they are all little darlings."

AVOCATIONAL INTERESTS: Everything.

BIOGRAPHICAL/CRITICAL SOURCES: New York Times Book Review, April 25, 1982.

* * *

PINKWATER, Manus
See PINKWATER, Daniel Manus

* * *

PINSKER, Sanford 1941-

PERSONAL: Born September 28, 1941, in Washington, Pa.; son of Morris David (a salesman) and Sonia (Molliver) Pinsker; married Ann Getson (a teacher), January 28, 1968; children: Matthew, Beth. *Education:* Washington and Jefferson College, B.A., 1963; University of Washington, Seattle, M.A., 1965, Ph.D., 1967. *Religion:* Jewish. *Home:* 700 North Pine St., Lancaster, Pa. 17603. *Office:* Department of English, Franklin and Marshall College, Lancaster, Pa. 17604.

CAREER: Franklin and Marshall College, Lancaster, Pa., assistant professor, 1967-73, associate professor of English, 1973—. *Member:* Modern Language Association of America, Multi-Ethnic Literature of the United States, James Joyce Society, Northeast Modern Language Association.

WRITINGS: The Schlemiel as Metaphor, Southern Illinois University Press, 1971; *Still Life and Other Poems,* Greenfield Review Press, 1975; *The Comedy That "Hoits": An Essay on the Fiction of Philip Roth,* University of Missouri Press, 1975; *Between Two Worlds: The American Novel in the 1960's,* Whitston Publishing, 1978; *Philip Roth: Critical Essays,* G. K. Hall, 1982; *Memory Breaks Off and Other Poems,* Northwoods Press, in press; (co-author) *America and the Holocaust,* Penkevill Publishing, in press.

WORK IN PROGRESS: Studies of Pacific Northwest poets; a book on American humor.

SIDELIGHTS: Sanford Pinsker told *CA:* "Auden once said that the important things to learn were how to laugh and how to pray. For me, poetry seems an ideal place to do both. Criticism, on the other hand, happens when ideas are clear enough to fit into prose."

PIPER, William Bowman 1927-

PERSONAL: Born December 7, 1927, in Lexington, Ky.; son of Lewis A. (a teacher) and Anna (a teacher; maiden name Zink) Piper; married Katharine Welles, August 22, 1955; children: Henry, Walter, Anthony, Anne. *Education:* Harvard University, B.A. (magna cum laude), 1951; Columbia University, M.A., 1952; University of Wisconsin, Ph.D., 1958. *Home:* 2132 Dryden Rd., Houston, Tex. 77030. *Office:* Department of English, Rice University, Houston, Tex. 77001.

CAREER: Cornell University, Ithaca, N.Y., instructor in English, 1958-61; University of Louisville, Louisville, Ky., assistant professor of English, 1961-64; Western Reserve University (now Case Western Reserve University), Cleveland, Ohio, associate professor of English, 1964-69; Rice University, Houston, Tex., professor of English, 1969—. *Military service:* U.S. Army, 1946-48; became staff sergeant. *Member:* Modern Language Association of America, American Society for Eighteenth-Century Studies, South Central Modern Language Association. *Awards, honors:* Fulbright scholar, 1957-58.

WRITINGS: Laurence Sterne, Twayne, 1965; *The Heroic Couplet,* Press of Case Western Reserve University, 1969; (editor with Robert A. Greenberg) *The Critical Swift,* Norton, 1972; *An Anthology of Heroic Couplet Poetry,* University Microfilms, 1977; *Evaluating Shakespeare's Sonnets,* Rice University Studies, 1979. Contributor of essays, reviews, and poems to literary journals.

WORK IN PROGRESS: The Literature of Common Sense; Immaterialist Aesthetics.

SIDELIGHTS: William Bowman Piper told *CA:* "All my work is devoted to preserving literary experience as a reliable body of knowledge and, consequently, as a reliable foundation of culture."

* * *

PLANK, Robert 1907-1983

PERSONAL: Born January 17, 1907, in Vienna, Austria; died July 15, 1983, in Cleveland, Ohio. *Education:* University of Vienna, LL.D., 1931; University of California, M.S.W., 1948. *Home:* 2387 Overlook Rd., Cleveland, Ohio 44106. *Office:* Department of Psychology, Case Western Reserve University, Cleveland, Ohio 44106.

CAREER: Psychiatric social worker, 1940-60, supervising clinical social worker, U.S. Veterans Administration, 1960-71; Case Western Reserve University, Cleveland, Ohio, adjunct associate professor of psychology and English, beginning 1969. *Military service:* U.S. Army, 1943-45; received Bronze Star Medal and four battle stars. *Member:* American Orthopsychiatric Association (fellow), Science Fiction Research Association, Conference of Utopian Scholars.

WRITINGS: The Emotional Significance of Imaginary Beings, C. C Thomas, 1968; *George Orwell's Guide through Hell: A Psychological Study of the Novel Nineteen Eighty-Four,* North River Press, 1984.

Contributor: M. R. Hillegas, editor, *Shadows of Imagination,* Southern Illinois University Press, 1962; E. Barmeyer, editor, *Science Fiction,* W. Fink, 1972; F. Rottensteiner, editor, *Po-*

laris I., Insel-Verlag, 1973; J. Lobdell, editor, *A Tolkien Compass,* Open Court, 1975.

Joseph Olander and Martin Greenberg, editors, *Arthur C. Clarke,* Taplinger, 1977; Olander and Greenberg, editors, *Robert A. Heinlein,* Taplinger, 1978; Jack Williamson, editor, *Teaching Science Fiction: Education for Tomorrow,* Owlswick, 1980; Eric S. Rabkin and others, editors, *The End of the World: The Imagination of Catastrophe,* Southern Illinois University Press, 1983. Contributor to professional journals.

SIDELIGHTS: Robert Plank once told *CA:* "Some difficult concepts can be explained more easily by reference to a cartoon in the *New Yorker.* There is a cartoon by Charles Addams where the gentleman who often appears in his work shows a photograph album to a boy, presumably his grandson. The caption (I am not trying to quote verbatim): 'This is your Uncle Jack, of whom it can be truly said that the world is a worse place for his having lived in it.' Without this help, the meaning of life might be a difficult concept.

"The tradition I grew up in, the Austrian Socialist labor and youth movement, did not deem it sufficient to live so that the world would thereby become a better place; it called for efforts to organize it to that end. Hence my interest in Utopism. When I became a psychiatric social worker in the United States, I found that science fiction often was a pseudonym for utopia and that the fantasies of SF [science fiction] authors closely resembled those of our patients. Hence my interest in SF.

"Eventually I retired from my social work job, and my interest in fantasies of patients dried up. At the same time utopias began again to sail under their own flag. So my interest in SF waned, my interest in utopias remained. The more I studied them, the more I got hung up (this, I think, is the proper word) on the work of George Orwell. Genius is the magnet that attracts and holds the steel filings. This metaphor may be limping, but within it I am one of those specks of metal dust."

* * *

PLANTE, David 1940-

PERSONAL: Born March 4, 1940, in Providence, R.I.; son of Anaclet Joseph Adolph and Albina (Bison) Plante. *Education:* Attended University of Louvain, Belgium, 1959-60; Boston College, B.A., 1961. *Home:* 38 Montagu Square, London W1, England. *Agent:* Deborah Rogers Ltd., 49 Blenheim Crescent, London W11, England; and Georges Borchardt, 136 East 57th St., New York, N.Y. 10022.

CAREER: Writer, living in England since 1966. English School, Rome, Italy, teacher, 1961-62; *Hart's Guide to New York,* New York, N.Y., researcher, 1962-64; Boston School of Modern Languages, Boston, Mass., teacher, 1964-65; teacher, St. John's Preparatory School, Mass., 1965-66; University of Tulsa, Tulsa, Okla., writer-in-residence, 1979-82. *Awards, honors:* Henfield Fellow, University of East Anglia, 1975; British Arts Council grant; *The Family* was nominated for a National Book Award, 1979; Guggenheim grant, 1983; Prize for Artistic Merit, American Academy-Institute of Arts and Letters, 1983.

WRITINGS—Novels, except as indicated: *The Ghost of Henry James,* Gambit, 1970; *Slides,* Gambit, 1971; *Relatives,* J. Cape, 1972; *The Darkness of the Body,* J. Cape, 1974; (contributor) Giles Gordon, editor, *Beyond Words: Eleven Writers in Search of a New Fiction* (collection), Hutchinson, 1975; *Figures in Bright Air,* Gollancz, 1976; *The Family* (first novel in trilogy), Farrar, Straus, 1978; *The Country* (third novel in trilogy), Atheneum, 1981; *The Woods* (second novel in trilogy), Atheneum, 1982; *Difficult Women: A Memoir of Three* (nonfiction), Atheneum, 1983. Regular contributor to *New Yorker;* has contributed to *Paris Review, Transatlantic Review,* and *Tri Quarterly.*

WORK IN PROGRESS: The Foreigner, a novel for Atheneum.

SIDELIGHTS: David Plante's writing has been abundant and variegated. *Publishers Weekly* critic John F. Baker indicates that Plante "began his writing life as a very deliberate experimentalist, has worked through in his most admired works to date, the trilogy *The Family, The Country,* and *The Woods,* to a form of intensely heightened naturalism, and has now branched out in *Difficult Women* into a kind of deadpan literary memoir."

Although Plante is primarily a novelist, *Difficult Women: A Memoir of Three* is a nonfictional portrait of three literary figures, novelist Jean Rhys, feminist writer Germaine Greer, and literary hostess Sonia Orwell, George Orwell's widow. In the book, Plante examines his friendships with the three, friendships motivated in part by his interest in the women's "difficult" dispositions, but also by their standing in the literary world. Orwell was able to introduce Plante to many in her large circle of friends, including Rhys, and, to Plante, Rhys in particular represented the intellectual cafe society that flourished in Paris during the 1920's. Vivian Gornick writes in the *New York Times Book Review* that Plante describes "the spectacular exaggerations of will and character the three women embody." And according to *Saturday Review* critic Andrea Barnet, "Plante raises these psychological portraits to the narrative pitch of fiction. He brings each to life with a dramatic precision that is formidable." "It's as if Mr. Plante were staring out over a wild and rugged typography of femaleness and wondering how one lives in such a land," maintains Anatole Broyard in the *New York Times.*

Patricia Blake writes in *Time,* however, that "though he purports to have given them a sympathetic hearing, Plante seems curiously ambivalent, not only about this trio, but about the entire sex." *Harper's* critic James Wolcott also finds the book's tone offensive. Describing it as a "racy, chatty, celebrity-cruising memoir," he theorizes that Plante, "a writer's writer" held in high critical regard for his quiet literary accomplishments, "wanted to break out of his modest niche in the literary world and cut a larger swath." "The mistake," he writes, "was in taking such a tacky approach. In dishing Jean Rhys, Sonia Orwell, and Germaine Greer in *Difficult Women,* David Plante has not only nudged his lance into the sickly creature that was once chivalry, but he's done violence to his own respectable name."

Plante firmly established his literary reputation with his trilogy, three earlier novels that relate the story of the Francoeurs, a large, working-class, Roman Catholic family with a mostly French-Canadian, partially American Indian heritage. Told from the viewpoint of the young writer son, Daniel, the novels describe his passage from adolescence to adulthood and his family's disintegration: His mother suffers a breakdown and becomes senile, while his father grows into a bitter, senile old age and finally dies. The first novel of that trilogy, *The Family,* writes John Calvin Batchelor in the *Village Voice,* "represents a departure so radical and unprecedented from the experimental directions Plante has unsuccessfully worked" in his first five shorter novels "that one is obliged once again to assert that all things are possible for those who make-believe." With *The Family,* asserts Batchelor, Plante has returned to "a fictionist's primary responsibility—storytelling."

In such early experimental novels as *The Darkness of the Body*, Plante often left the details of character and setting deliberately vague, in order for the reader to focus upon the inner emotional life of the protagonists. And he frequently disregarded conventional narrative. His first novel, for instance, *The Ghost of Henry James*, is described by Baker as "a fragmented narrative that was a deliberate tribute to the master." "Plante has applied the Jamesian mood to a contemporary situation," writes Jonathan Yardley in the *New York Times Book Review*, and the result is something more or less than a novel, since, according to a *Times Literary Supplement* critic, it is also "'a functional analysis' of the work of Henry James." The point of the exercise, writes Denis Donoghue in the *New York Review of Books*, "is to write the kind of story that James might write if he had the luck to live in 1970, free of social restraint."

Such experimentation can be found throughout Plante's earliest writing. *New York Times Book Review* critic Jonathan Strong indicates that the title of Plante's work *Slides* refers to "the 67 vignettes in which the story is told. They *are* slides (rather than home movies) because they each focus on one moment of tension that breaks off unresolved, leaving it for us to imagine what happens next." And in his fifth novel, *Figures in Bright Air*, Plante told Baker in an interview, "I'd got away from narrative altogether, trying to create something that reverberates, as music does."

Not all reviewers agree with Batchelor that Plante's experimental efforts were completely "unsuccessful," though. A *Times Literary Supplement* reviewer comments in qualification that, in his earlier works, Plante "gives the impression of a talented writer somehow trapped by the elaborateness of his own ingenuities." Mary Sullivan in the *Listener* maintains that "*Slides* induces a series of satisfactions all the deeper for being not quite graspable." And although Richard Freedman in *Book World* describes *The Ghost of Henry James* as "overrich and too highly technicolored, festering in elegant decadence, and ideal for inhaling with a Campari-and-soda," *New York Times Book Review* critic Jonathan Yardley calls it "in many respects a remarkable piece of work." Plante's trilogy may represent a return to traditional narrative, but as Plante sees it, the books are not a repudiation of the experimental work, but instead, a logical progression from it. He indicated to Baker: "I always wanted to write [the trilogy], and in a way all my earlier work was an attempt to prepare myself for it, trying to learn a craft."

Batchelor believes *The Family* is a significant improvement over Plante's previous efforts. In *The Family*, he writes, Plante "has finally permitted his serious ideas to live in recognizable, admirable human beings who dream, build, brag, stumble, collapse and get up again." The book describes the emotional breakdown of Reena Francoeur, Daniel's mother, but in Batchelor's opinion, the story is about the father, Jim Francoeur, "a hard, taciturn, disciplined man who has worked unflinchingly for 40 years at the same tool shop. His temperament dominates the family; and it is his rise to near success as a foreman, a local Republican candidate, and a home-owner, and his fall to near hopelessness as an unemployed, heavily indebted, and cruelly, intractably frightened old man that defines the plot."

Plante uses "only the simple vocabulary of his working-class characters [to plunge] us into a hermetic, devout, French-Catholic world," writes Elizabeth Peer in *Newsweek*. This family situation is particularly "claustrophobic," maintains Anne Stevenson in the *Times Literary Supplement*, "contained as it is within a Catholic French-speaking parish in a Protestant New England city at a time (the late 1950s) when the old-fashioned life of the parish is under threat from the mass-making (or in this case, possibly, Mass-breaking) forces of American society."

"Plante is very good at creating this world," confirms Susan Wood in *Washington Post Book World*, "the weight of its oppression, as he describes the ugliness of the factories, the churches, the schools, the houses. One flinches at the conversations of Matante Oenone, Jim's sister, which tend toward lurid descriptions of poverty and death, or at the nuns' equally lurid descriptions of the sufferings of the saints and martyrs, and the passion of Christ. Also depressing are the long and detailed conversations within the family, those double binds in which conflicting messages of love and hate are so often sent." "Through the eyes of adolescent Daniel, the sixth son," states Peer, "we experience the unpredictable shifts of family chemistry."

Although the viewpoint in *The Family* is Daniel's, the story is told in the third person. In *The Country*, the Francoeur children are grown, and the events—the elderly Francoeurs' retreat into senility and the father's death—are related in the first person by Daniel who lives in London, returning only to visit. The book's subject, according to A. Alvarez in the *New York Review of Books*, "is the numbing grief grown children feel as they watch their parents descend into helplessness and death." *Washington Post Book World* critic Jonathan Yardley states that "the novel, like its subject, is neither glamorous nor sexy. Plante's prose is spare, measured, quietly insistent; though the novel is brief, it conveys the labored pace of a long dying. It also conveys both the ordinariness and the extraordinariness of dying, its universality and its uniqueness." The work is described in the *New York Times Book Review* by Mary Gordon as "a haunting lament, a controlled cry of loss and knowledge won through language, sorrow, memory, impossible and comprehending love."

Despite its subject matter, "self-control dominates *The Country*," writes *Time* reviewer Paul Gray. "Plante is a minimalist with language; his prose reduces events to small, discrete moments. He uses words less to evoke a scene than to catalogue it." "This flat style may look easy," he writes, "but what Plante accomplishes with it is not." *Nation* reviewer Brina Caplan points out that Plante's "narrator follows action and speech with the watchful precision of an Indian ancestor tracking game through the woods. No word is wasted, and every word reports something seen, heard or touched. As a result, *The Country* is written in spare prose that isolates the external facts of ordinary life, reminding us of their inherent order and gravity."

Calling Plante a "highly visual writer," *Newsweek* reviewer Jean Strouse indicates that he "gives the physical feeling of this world . . . along with the bleak, claustrophobic atmosphere of the senior Francoeurs' lives." *New Republic* critic Jack Beatty adds that "it is Plante's grip on the objective method of narration, his commitment to what Henry James called scenic rendering, that allows him, in the long flashback at the country house, to turn from brother to brother and from mother to father in quick defining strokes of description and dialogue." "The novel," writes Strouse, "moves through small emblematic, almost ceremonial moments—as if you were watching a film in freeze frame with the sound off." Alvarez comments that "it is like watching a whole movie in slow motion: discreet movements, each frozen and complete in itself, and a slightly distorted soundtrack, full of Chekhovian gaps and silences, through which the characters mutely hint at feelings they do not otherwise care to articulate."

Yet Yardley maintains that "*The Country* has one unfortunate weakness. Its intensity occasionally lapses into humorlessness; when seriousness becomes solemnity, as Plante is inclined to let it do, what we get is huffing and puffing." And A. N. Wilson in the *Times Literary Supplement* prefers some of Plante's experimental fiction to *The Country*, which he finds overly realistic and subjective. He writes: "I do not know whether *The Country* is an insufficiently transformed piece of autobiography, or whether the failure is owing to the possibly delicate nature of his material." The novel, in his opinion, "lacks the crisp detachment and originality of mind displayed in David Plante's earlier novels *Relatives* and *The Ghost of Henry James*."

Most reviewers, however, consider *The Country* a remarkable achievement. Beatty, for instance, concludes that "throughout the novel there are even hints that the world is lit by a mystery beyond death. This is suggested in an insistent imagery of light breaking into darkened rooms and illuminating the tops of trees at dusk; and it is made explicit early in the novel when Daniel sees his father standing alone in the woods [surrounded by his ancestors]. This preserving place seems to be a fusion of the Catholic notion of the communion of saints with Daniel's projection of his primordial Indian descent, and it surrounds the action of the novel like a ring of light from a far country to which all the characters are going. It adds a note of the numinous to this lovely painful book."

The completive novel of the trilogy, *The Woods,* was originally published last, but since it concerns Daniel's first two years of college and the intervening summers he spends at the lake where his family vacations, it should fall second chronologically, as it was written. A slim book, it is divided into three parts, "The Reflection," "The Woods," and "The War," which present three scenes from the young writer's life during a period when he fears being drafted into the army. In the novel, Daniel also comes to accept his preference for homosexuality, but overall, according to Jack Beatty in *New Republic,* the work "is about the adolescent dread of selfhood and its loneliness." R. Z. Sheppard in *Time* writes that "few periods are as difficult to pin down as that brief limbo between the end of youth and the beginning of adulthood. The mysteries of the physical and the spiritual, the image and the imagination are fresh and beckoning."

Although *The Woods* is part of the trilogy, its concerns are dissimilar to those of *The Family* and *The Country*. Here, writes *New York Times Book Review* critic Edith Milton, "Mr. Plante is not interested in the sociology of Daniel's world or in the psychology of the people he shares it with; he explores instead the boundary between Daniel's ruthlessly insignificant everyday existence and the vast landscape of his inner apathy, examining through Daniel's eyes the proposition that matter and spirit are irreversibly divided from each other and that both are irrevocably alien to him."

Chicago Tribune Book World reviewer L. M. Rosenberg maintains that the book is built around "one peculiar but interesting question, namely: What does it mean to live inside a body?" "Central to the novel is the philosophical notion of body as idea," agrees Rosalind Belben in the *Times Literary Supplement,* "the body not confined to flesh and blood but a configuration projected by the mind into 'a space' outside." "The focus," writes Beatty, "is on Daniel's consciousness, specifically on his preoccupation with 'the space, large and empty' which he sees behind people as a kind of enveloping presence. (It is a version of the existentialist notion of 'the encompassing,' and while Daniel is drawn toward it as to a great mystery, readers who think existentialism vaporous will not pass page two.)"

"Young Daniel Francoeur, Plante's protagonist, feels what seems a uniquely Roman Catholic variety of metaphysical lust," maintains *Newsweek* critic Gene Lyons. "He craves not so much to make love as to uncover spiritual mysteries." *New York Review of Books* critic Robert Towers points out that "Plante manages to surround almost every object and every inconsequential event with a kind of luminescent space, like a halo. By following Daniel's attention as it moves very slowly from one thing to the next, he produces an effect of hallucinatory realism, in which each detail seems to exist in its own right, to have a quasimystical 'thingness' about it, quite apart from whatever significance it may or may not have in the larger picture.

The result is a paucity of active narrative. According to Milton, "leitmotifs create the real fictional texture of the novel, which has a surface almost without incident, indeed almost without narrative." And *Washington Post Book World* critic Jonathan Yardley considers that "texture" overly cerebral. In *The Woods,* he writes, "Plante has made the mistake of intellectualizing what is not, in point of fact, an intellectual or rational process: an adolescent's struggle to come to terms with a world considerably more ambiguous than he is capable, at this point, of understanding. Not merely does Daniel Francoeur spend too much time feeling sorry for himself, but he does so in thoughts and language that are quite implausible for one of his inexperience and immaturity."

Milton agrees that *The Woods* is not without fault, but argues that "it is also a brilliantly original work, intense, illuminating and compelling. Eccentric enough to be beyond the pale of most critical judgement, its virtues certainly are worth considerably more than its faults." As Le Anne Schreiber explains in the *New York Times,* Plante attempts to describe "states of mind so elusive that they can only be intimated; his is a world of vague apprehensions and diffuse longings, and to enter it is to feel perpetually suspended on the verge of something. Revelation seems imminent until one realizes that for David Plante the sense of imminent revelation is a permanent condition."

CA INTERVIEW

CA interviewed David Plante by telephone June 23, 1983, at his London home.

CA: You were first published in London, after you'd been living in London for several years, but you'd done a lot of writing before that in New York, hadn't you?

PLANTE: Yes, I was writing a novel while I was in New York working for *Hart's Guide to New York City.* I wrote five or six novels before I went to New York from Boston. There was never a question in my mind about writing; I always had. But when I graduated from college, I thought, now the next step is to get published. And I went to New York with that in mind. It was a total disaster on my part. Nothing seemed to work. I came to London in 1966, where I met people who were interested in what I was writing.

CA: Had you begun The Ghost of Henry James *(1970), your first novel, in New York?*

PLANTE: No. I wrote that in London. Actually, *Slides,* my second published novel, was written first—also in London.

The publisher said they would accept *Slides* if they liked the next novel. So I went ahead and wrote *The Ghost of Henry James*, and they published it first.

CA: The Ghost of Henry James was a tribute to James, whom you've called "an obsession." Cynthia Ozick has recently written about her obsession with James, which she says delayed her finding her own voice. Have you had a similar problem?

PLANTE: Yes, and not only with James. Other major writers become obsessions. This has been said much more eloquently by other people. These writers get in the way somehow. It's a dangerous thing even to suggest that one feels one must try to "defeat" them. Who is one to defeat these great writers? Nevertheless, there is the feeling of having somehow to deal with them in whatever minor, fumbling, and insignificant way one can.

With pretty much every novel I write there's a writer in the background. In all my novels up to the family novels there's been a writer, usually an American and usually a New England writer, whom I have in mind. It's one of the many tricks one uses to try to give one's book some kind of unity, direction, integrity. If I keep one writer in mind, and sort of ask him questions, even though I may disagree with what I imagine he would answer, it gives me a certain focus. But I should keep this idea to myself, because it sounds literary, even presumptuous.

CA: Having a home in London, a place in Italy, and a job as writer-in-residence at the University of Oklahoma in Tulsa, do you feel that you belong, either physically or in a literary sense, more to one place than another?

PLANTE: Oh, I'm totally American. There's never been any question of that. And I'll tell you, I think this whole question of expatriatism is open to reassessment. I've certainly had a lot of experience living abroad; I've lived abroad now pretty much half my life. Before I moved to London, I lived in Belgium and Rome, then went to New York for a few years and then came to London. Being an expatriate implies being cut off, cutting oneself off, from one's country. It implies that one is saying, I'm no longer an American; I've adopted a foreign culture, manners, and speech. I don't feel I've done that at all. As a matter of fact, living abroad has heightened my awareness of America. It's given me an edge to my self-consciousness, made me think about being an American in a way I wouldn't have thought had I stayed in America.

I don't feel out of touch at all. I get back to America in seven hours. Here we are, talking over the Atlantic Ocean as if you were around the corner. And I don't feel British. I'm not a British writer, and I'm certainly not an Italian writer! So simply by the process of elimination I would be American. But I'm American in much more positive ways; I think all my obsessions and preoccupations are American.

CA: Does moving from place to place affect your writing in any way that you can tell?

PLANTE: That's impossible to say. The American writer Robert Coover lived in England for about nine years, and I used to see him from time to time. He said that he decided to move back to America because he felt he was losing his American idiom, and when he went back to America and turned on the television set he wouldn't understand the advertisements or sometimes even the jokes because he wouldn't know what they were about. Well, I'm not an idiomatic writer. And in a curious way, even though English is my first language, I always think of it as my second language, as language that I'm always having to think about, wonder about, and invent, that I can't take for granted. I think moving around helps me not to take it for granted.

CA: Do you write as well while you're teaching, or does the schedule make it difficult?

PLANTE: My course load is kept to a minimum; they're very kind in Tulsa. I'm not going back this year, by the way. I got a Guggenheim grant, so I decided to take off the whole year to write.

CA: On the subject of teaching, you've said that you feel creative writing can't really be taught. What can the teacher do for aspiring writers?

PLANTE: Make the students aware in a way that they hadn't been aware before. I think that if a "teacher" can do anything, he can instill in writers a degree of awareness, so that when they are on a street or in a restaurant or on a bus, they'll look and listen and taste and smell and touch with a higher degree of awareness than they would have before. If a teacher can do that, he's done a great deal. And I think there is something helpful in talking about writing. Writing is a very mysterious thing. I try to give the students a sense of the real, great mystery of writing. It helps them, because if they begin to think of writing as a mystery, they're going to treat it with much more . . . I don't want to use the word *reverence*, but they're going to take more care in writing their sentences and their paragraphs. Again, it's a question of not taking it for granted.

CA: Is that related to what you've said in the past about being in touch with something under the surface of consciousness, something not intended or willed, that must be allowed to come out?

PLANTE: Oh yes, very, very much. I'm sure that my own best bits of writing occur when I have no idea what I'm writing—when I'm not intending anything, but I do sense that there's some kind of intention which is not my intention.

CA: Does that become easier? Are there tricks to encouraging that state of mind?

PLANTE: Yes, technical tricks. One that I can think of (and I really shouldn't be saying this, because of course all tricks are embarrassing) is repetition, repeating words in slightly different ways. At the end of a paragraph in which a word is repeated, you find that the repetition produces a certain effect which you can't really calculate. It goes beyond your contriving, though you have contrived it to the degree that you've repeated a word, hoping that with the repetition slightly different meanings of the word will be revealed. And in the context of the paragraph or the page, this creates an overall impression.

CA: Does letting his subconscious thought play such a part in writing have to preclude the writer's thinking about his readership, and how readers will receive the work?

PLANTE: First, I should say that what I am trying to allow to make its own impression is not, I believe, some dark, unknowable presence from my unconscious. I don't have much interest in my unconscious. The sense I want to be the soul of my writing is the sense of being able to understand if *only* one had the eyes to see and the ears to hear. This has to do with the conscious mind, everybody's conscious mind. Now, I think a great deal about readers. One thing I never want to do (though I'm certain I must do it) is bore my readers. I want at every moment to make them aware, *conscious,* as they hadn't been before. I cut out anything that I think may not suggest something to the reader, anything that would be slack information.

CA: You recently told John F. Baker for Publishers Weekly *(December 24, 1982): "People in England take prose for granted. American prose is superior because it's often so unexpected." Would you elaborate on that?*

PLANTE: I do believe that, with a few exceptions, English prose style is now taken entirely for granted. You pick up a contemporary English novel in a book shop and read a page and it seems rather flat, some of it even rather flaccid, and taken for granted. It doesn't have the edge to it, the inventiveness, that American writing often has. I'm talking about my contemporaries now, or people even younger than I. You feel that Americans know that there is a difference between the written and the spoken language, and that writing requires a degree of self-conscious craft, whereas the English tend to think that if you can speak, you can write—that the written word comes out of the spoken word. Well, I'm not saying that's not true, but at the moment it seems to produce rather flat English prose, for the most part.

CA: Do America and England treat their writers very differently?

PLANTE: Yes, they do. There's much more reverence for writers in America than in England. That is lovely, but also very dangerous, because America seems more and more to treat its writers as celebrities, which doesn't happen in England. James Baldwin is a name that just popped into my mind as an example of what happens in America, where the writer becomes a kind of guru, and then is dropped, and is destroyed. There's great success, and then destruction of some kind.

I'd like to read a study of this, what happens to, not just writers, but celebrities in America. You can think of absurd examples—singers, movie stars. In England, writers are not treated in a particularly special way. In fact, sometimes you think they're not treated in any special way at all. There's a certain flatness about being a writer here, not excitement. But that's sort of safe, and one gets on with one's work.

CA: The earlier fiction, before The Family *and* The Country *and* The Woods, *was very experimental. Were you trying to get away from narrative altogether, as you said about* Figures in Bright Air? *Were you working toward a specific goal with the experimentation?*

PLANTE: I was working toward an abstraction of some kind. I was self-consciously involved in literature in all those books, which I don't think is a bad thing for a writer to be. I've often heard writers whom I respect very much say, "Oh, for God's sake, don't be that terrible thing, a writer! Don't write *literature!*" Well, yes, I can appreciate that and I think it is a good warning, but, on the other hand, I think it can also be greatly to one's advantage to be very interested in "literature" and, when you write, to use your self-consciousness as a "writer." And I did that. I certainly don't regret it; I've learned a great deal. I suppose if I was aiming toward anything, it was some kind of pure literature, something that didn't refer outside itself, to history or sociology or psychology or religion or any of the other disciplines, but toward something totally self-contained as a work of literature. For imaginative writing to survive, it must go beyond history, sociology, psychology, religion. It must. And I don't feel that I've turned from one way of writing to another abruptly. Although I haven't been able to explain it to myself properly, I feel the family novels were in some way a continuation of what I had been doing before.

CA: Was it hard to come back to the stuff of your own boyhood and growing up as a subject for those family novels?

PLANTE: No, because I had always had it in mind to do it. It was always something that I felt I was preparing myself for, so it was a great pleasure finally to get down to do it.

CA: Did you set out to write a trilogy?

PLANTE: No, I didn't. But I found that each aspect that I wanted to cover demanded a separate book, and it ended up being a trilogy. Also, you see, they were published out of the order in which they were written. *The Family* was written first. Then *The Woods* was written and then *The Country.* And because of problems with the publisher of *The Family* in America, another publisher published *The Country* before *The Woods.* They all three are going to come out in paperback in September in the right order. *The Woods* really needs to have *The Family* on either side of it; it's a kind of interlude and it needs two stronger novels on either side. So, when it's read in paperback, it'll have its proper position.

CA: Difficult Women, *your first nonfiction book, is a subjective treatment of novelist Jean Rhys, Sonia Orwell (the widow of George Orwell), and feminist writer Germaine Greer. How did that book come about?*

PLANTE: It's a bit complicated. I had helped Jean Rhys with her autobiography, which was published unfinished, and I thought I'd really like to explain to myself, to get down on paper, what my involvement was in the unfinished biography. A certain amount of it, I must confess, comes from the diary I had kept while I was helping Jean. I showed the memoir of Jean to Francis Wyndham, Jean's literary executor. He seemed very enthusiastic about it and was responsible for having it published in the *Paris Review.*

Then my English publisher asked if I'd be interested in writing a biography of Jean Rhys. I said, "No—well, maybe." But I wasn't terribly enthusiastic about it. I don't fancy myself a biographer. But in any case I had lunch with Francis Wyndham and spoke to him about it. He said that he was going to abide by Jean's stipulation in her will that there be no official biography, so he couldn't help me. However, he wouldn't be against my writing a book about Jean in a very personal way, as I had written the memoir. Then he said, very frankly, "Are you interested in writing more?" I said I didn't think so. And he said, "Why don't you do a collection of people similar to Jean, and call it *Difficult Women*?" So the idea came from Francis Wyndham and I went away thinking about Jean, questioning myself about my particular attraction to Jean, and thinking, who are the other women in my life whom I'm close to who also present the same curious attraction that Jean did, for whatever reason? And I thought of Sonia Orwell and Germaine Greer. I thought it would be interesting for me to take an entirely personal point of view—not a biographical point of view but an *autobiographical* one—and examine what it was that attracted me to these frankly difficult women who are also extraordinary. That's how I wrote the book.

CA: Are there kinds of writing you haven't done that you'd like to do?

PLANTE: Yes, I think I would quite like to write a play, though it's such a different thing from writing a novel that one would have to learn the craft from the beginning, not from the point of view of a novelist, but from that of a playwright. That, of course, would take a very long time. But I'd like to write a play. And from time to time, I write, not poems, but prayers. I'm not a believer at all, but I find that at idle moments I write a prayer and that satisfies me for now. There's a prayer at the end of *The Family*. It was written completely apart from the novel and then at a certain point I thought, that would make a very good ending. That's the only one I've ever published, and I don't know if I'd ever publish another. But I do write them from time to time.

CA: Is there work in progress you'd like to talk about?

PLANTE: I just finished a novel; I'm putting the last touches to it now. It's set in Barcelona and revolves around a black woman whom I knew when I lived in Barcelona many years ago and her lover, who is a white American. It's all rather peculiar; there's no way I can describe it.

CA: How do you feel about your own writing and your career at this point?

PLANTE: I feel I've only begun. I have buried in my mind the plots for about twenty more novels. That's a lot, and that might occupy me for the rest of my life, but I really do feel I've only begun. Maybe, maybe I've taken one step, but there are many more steps to take. I do believe that. Also I think it's very important that one should always consider that one's an amateur. The moment you start thinking, well, here I am, I'm a professional writer, you're in danger because you start taking things for granted. And that's a terrible thing to do.

I feel I've been very lucky. I was in New York just recently, because I got an award in literature from the American Academy and Institute of Arts and Letters. It was wonderful being in New York. In book shops, I saw a hundred different publications, all doing short stories and poems. That just doesn't exist here; there are only three or four literary magazines, and they're not terribly interesting. And I'm very, very lucky in that the *New Yorker* is taking my work. Sitting there on the stage at the awards ceremony among writers I had heard of, read, seen photographs of, I must admit that I thought to myself, this is where I belong.

I don't want to put England down in any way. I got my start in England; all my initial support was given to me by England. There was a time when I had no money at all and was struggling to work. The Arts Council here gave me £3000 as a grant, even though I wasn't really eligible. They said they thought I had integrated myself enough into the English world of writers. I was first published here. I had some novels published here which were never published in America. All those so-called experimental novels were well received in England.

With the publication of *The Family* things have changed, and I get much less attention in England now than I do in America. It's as though England has been disappointed in me because I've gone ahead and become totally American. I never denied I was. I'm very grateful to England for what has happened here, but it's in America that I feel what is happening now is important.

BIOGRAPHICAL/CRITICAL SOURCES: Times Literary Supplement, March 19, 1970, April 16, 1971, July 7, 1972, February 1, 1974, July 2, 1976, April 28, 1978, March 13, 1981, January 29, 1982, February 25, 1983; *New Statesman,* March 13, 1970, March 12, 1971, June 16, 1972, February 1, 1974, April 2, 1976, March 13, 1981, February 4, 1983; *Spectator,* March 14, 1970, March 27, 1971, February 2, 1974, April 10, 1976, February 6, 1982; *Observer,* March 15, 1970, March 14, 1971, June 18, 1972, January 27, 1974, April 4, 1976; *Listener,* March 19, 1970, March 18, 1971, June 15, 1972, February 7, 1974, April 1, 1976; *Publishers Weekly,* June 29, 1970, June 7, 1971, August 26, 1974, December 24, 1982; *Book World,* November 1, 1970; *New York Review of Books,* November 5, 1970, August 17, 1978, November 19, 1981, December 16, 1982; *New York Times Book Review,* November 29, 1970, December 6, 1970, August 22, 1971, October 20, 1974, July 2, 1978, October 4, 1981, August 15, 1982, January 16, 1983; *Bookseller,* March, 1971; *Choice,* March, 1971; *Books and Bookmen,* May, 1971, July, 1972; *Guardian Weekly,* June 24, 1972, February 2, 1974; *Contemporary Review,* April, 1974.

Contemporary Literary Criticism, Gale, Volume VII, 1977, Volume XXIII, 1983; *Newsweek,* July 24, 1978, September 14, 1981, September 6, 1982; *Washington Post Book World,* August 27, 1978, September 27, 1981, August 8, 1982; *Saturday Review,* September 2, 1978, March-April, 1983; *Village Voice,* April 23, 1979; *Chicago Tribune Book World,* October 4, 1981, September 19, 1982, March 6, 1983; *New Republic,* October 7, 1981, October 11, 1982; *Time,* October 12, 1981, August 2, 1982, February 7, 1983; *Nation,* February 6, 1982; *New York Times,* July 19, 1982, January 15, 1983; *New Yorker,* September 20, 1982; *Harper's,* January, 1983; *Times* (London), January 27, 1983; *Village Voice Literary Supplement,* February, 1983.

—Sketch by Candace Cloutier
—Interview by Jean W. Ross

* * *

PLOG, Fred (Thomas III) 1944-

PERSONAL: Born July 19, 1944, in Fort Monmouth, N.J.; son of Fred Thomas, Jr. and Phyllis (Gessert) Plog; married Gayle Gillham, April 11, 1966; children: Stephen Joseph, Thomas Edward, Amy Elizabeth, Katherine Marie. *Education:* Northwestern University, B.A., 1966; University of Chicago, M.A., 1968, Ph.D., 1969. *Home:* 4041 Sotol Dr., Las Cruces, N.M. 88001. *Office:* Department of Sociology/Anthropology, New Mexico State University, Las Cruces, N.M. 88003.

CAREER: Field Museum of Natural History, Chicago, Ill., research assistant, 1967-69; University of California, Los Angeles, assistant professor of anthropology, 1969-72; State University of New York at Binghampton, associate professor of anthropology, 1972-75; Arizona State University, Tempe, associate professor of anthropology, 1976-81; New Mexico State University, Las Cruces, professor of sociology/anthropology, 1981—. *Member:* Phi Beta Kappa, Phi Eta Sigma, Delta Sigma Rho, Sigma Xi.

WRITINGS: (Editor with Paul Bohannon) *Beyond the Frontier,* Natural History Press, 1967; (with Paul S. Martin) *Arizona*

Archaeology, Natural History Press, 1973; *The Study of Prehistoric Change,* Seminar Press, 1974; (with C. Jolly) *Physical Anthropology and Archaeology,* Knopf, 1975; (with D. Bates) *Cultural Anthropology,* Knopf, 1976; (with Bates and Jolly) *Anthropology: Decisions, Adaptation, and Evolution,* Knopf, 1976; (with A. E. Dittert) *Generations in Clay,* Northland, 1980.

WORK IN PROGRESS: Studies of the southwestern United States's cultural ecology.

* * *

POLKING, Kirk 1925-

PERSONAL: Born December 21, 1925, in Covington, Ky.; daughter of Henry (a salesman) and Mary (Hull) Polking. *Education:* Studied in evening courses at American University, 1944, and at University of Cincinnati and Xavier University at intervals, 1944—. *Politics:* Independent. *Religion:* Roman Catholic. *Home:* 529 Constitution Sq., Cincinnati, Ohio 45230. *Office:* F & W Publishing Co., 9933 Alliance Rd., Cincinnati, Ohio 45242.

CAREER: U.S. War Department, Washington, D.C., administrative assistant, 1943-45; F & W Publishing Co., Cincinnati, Ohio, editorial assistant on *Modern Photography* and *Writer's Digest,* 1948-52, circulation manager of *Farm Quarterly,* 1952-57; free-lance writer, 1957-63; F & W Publishing Co., editor of *Writer's Digest,* 1963-73, editor of *Artists Market,* 1973-75, director of Writer's Digest School, 1976—. *Member:* Author's Guild, National Federation of Press Women, National League of American Pen Women, Women in Communications. *Awards, honors:* Women in Communications Headliner Award, 1970.

WRITINGS: Let's Go with Lewis and Clark, Putnam, 1963; *Let's Go with Henry Hudson,* Putnam, 1964; *Let's Go See Congress at Work,* Putnam, 1966; *Let's Go to an Atomic Energy Town,* Putnam, 1968; (editor with others) *The Beginning Writer's Handbook,* Writer's Digest, 1968, revised edition published as *The Beginning Writer's Answer Book,* 3rd revised edition, 1984; (editor) *How to Make Money in Your Spare Time by Writing,* Cornerstone Library, 1971; *The Private Pilot's Dictionary and Handbook,* Arco, 1974; (editor with Leonard Mergnus) *Law and the Writer,* Writer's Digest, 1978; (editor) *Jobs for Writers,* Writer's Digest, 1980; *Oceans of the World: Our Essential Resource,* Putnam, 1983. Editor or co-editor, *The Writer's Market,* 1964-71.

WORK IN PROGRESS: New home study courses in writing and art.

AVOCATIONAL INTERESTS: Flying (obtained private pilot's license in 1968).

* * *

PONDER, Patricia
See MAXWELL, Patricia

* * *

POPENOE, David 1932-

PERSONAL: Surname is pronounced *Pop*-en-oe; born October 1, 1932, in Los Angeles, Calif; son of Paul (a family life specialist) and Betty (Stankovitch) Popenoe; married Katharine Sasse, July 18, 1959; children: Rebecca, Julia. *Education:* Antioch College, A.B., 1954; University of Pennsylvania, M.C.P., 1958, Ph.D., 1963. *Politics:* Democrat. *Religion:* Religious Society of Friends (Quaker). *Home:* 92 Moore St., Princeton, N.J. 08540. *Office:* Lucy Stone Hall, Rutgers University, New Brunswick, N.J. 08903.

CAREER: Philadelphia Redevelopment Authority, Philadelphia, Pa., program planner, 1956-58; Newark Central Planning Board, Newark, N.J., senior planner, 1958-59; Rutgers University, New Brunswick, N.J., assistant director of research and education in Urban Studies Center, 1961-64, director of academic affairs in Urban Studies Center, 1965-69, associate professor of urban planning at Livingston College, 1967-69, associate professor of sociology at Douglass College, 1969-77, professor of sociology, 1977, chairman of department of sociology, 1979—. Adjunct professor of public administration, New York University, 1964-65, 1967-68; lecturer in department of sociology, University of Pennsylvania, 1965-69; visiting professor, University of Stockholm, 1972-73, 1974, 1977. *Military service:* U.S. Army, 1954-56.

MEMBER: International Sociological Association, American Sociological Association, American Institute of Certified Planners, American Association of University Professors, American Planning Association, Eastern Sociology Society, Society for the Advancement of Scandinavian Studies.

WRITINGS: (Editor) *The Urban-Industrial Frontier: Essays on Social Trends and Institutional Goals in Modern Communities,* Rutgers University Press, 1969; (editor with Robert Gutman) *Neighborhood, City and Metropolis: An Integrated Reader in Urban Sociology,* Random House, 1970; *Sociology* (introductory text), Prentice-Hall, 1971, 5th edition, 1983; *The Suburban Environment: Sweden and the United States,* University of Chicago Press, 1977; *Private Pleasure, Public Plight: American Metropolitan Community Life in Comparative Perspective,* Transaction Books, 1984.

Contributor: P. P. Indik and F. K. Berrien, editors, *People, Groups and Organizations,* Teachers College Press, 1968; Paul Meadows and Ephraim H. Mizruchi, editors, *Urbanism, Urbanization, and Change: Comparative Perspectives,* Addison-Wesley, 1969; Marcia P. Effrat, editor, *The Community: Approaches and Applications,* Free Press, 1974; V. Karn and C. Ungerson, editors, *The Consumer Experience in Housing,* Gower Press, 1980; G. R. Wekerle and others, editors, *New Space for Women,* Westview, 1980; J. John Palen, editor, *City Scenes,* Little, Brown, 1981.

Contributor of articles and reviews in the area of sociology, urban studies, and social planning to professional journals. Editor with Robert Gutman of a special issue of *American Behavioral Scientist* devoted to urban studies, February, 1963; editor of *Urban Education,* April, 1971.

* * *

POPPER, Frank J. 1944-

PERSONAL: Born March 26, 1944, in Chicago, Ill.; son of Hans (a physician) and Lina (Billig) Popper; married Deborah Epstein, August 9, 1968; children: two. *Education:* Haverford College, A.B. (with high honors), 1965; graduate study at Massachusetts Institute of Technology, 1965-66; Harvard University, M.P.A., 1968, Ph.D., 1972. *Home:* 10 North Eighth Ave., Highland Park, N.J. 08904. *Office:* Urban Studies Department, Rutgers University, New Brunswick, N.J. 08903.

CAREER: Twentieth Century Fund, New York, N.Y., research associate, 1968-69; Public Administration Service, Chicago,

Ill., research associate, 1971-73; American Society of Planning Officials, Chicago, senior research associate, 1973-74; Twentieth Century Fund Project on the Politics of State Land-Use Planning, Chicago, director, 1975-81; Resources for the Future, Washington, D.C., Gilbert White Fellow, 1982-83; Rutgers University, New Brunswick, N.J., associate professor in urban studies department, 1983—. Senior associate, Environmental Law Institute, Washington, D.C., 1979-80.

WRITINGS: *The President's Commissions,* Twentieth Century Fund, 1970; (co-author) *Urban Nongrowth: City Planning for People,* Praeger, 1976; *The Politics of Land-Use Reform,* University of Wisconsin Press, 1981; (co-editor) *Land Reform, American Style,* Rowman & Allanheld, 1984. Also contributor to major government reports. Contributor to political science, city planning, environmental, and medical journals.

WORK IN PROGRESS: *The LULU: Coping with Locally Unwanted Land Uses,* for publication by Resources for the Future; *The Survival of the American Frontier.*

* * *

PORTER, Joe Ashby 1942-

PERSONAL: Born July 21, 1942, in Kentucky; son of Lawrence (a machinist and coal miner) and Margaret (Wise) Porter. *Education:* Harvard University, B.A., 1964; Pembroke College, Oxford, graduate study, 1964-65; University of California, Berkeley, M.A., 1966, Ph.D., 1973. *Home:* 1007 Buchanan Blvd. N., Durham, N.C. 27701. *Office:* Department of English, Duke University, Durham, N.C. 27706.

CAREER: University of Virginia, Charlottesville, assistant professor of English, 1970-73; University of Baltimore, Baltimore, Md., assistant professor of English, 1976-77; Shoreline Community College, Seattle, Wash., assistant professor of English, 1977-78; Murray State University, Murray, Ky., assistant professor of English, 1978-80; Duke University, Durham, N.C., assistant professor of English, 1980—. Assistant professor at Towson State College, 1976-77. *Member:* Modern Language Association of America, Associated Writing Programs, South Atlantic Modern Language Association. *Awards, honors:* Fulbright fellowship, 1964-65; National Endowment for the Arts fellowship, 1979-80; National Endowment for the Arts/P.E.N. syndicated fiction award, 1983.

WRITINGS: *Eelgrass* (novel), New Directions, 1977; *The Drama of Speech Acts: Shakespeare's Lancastrian Tetralogy,* University of California Press, 1979; *The Kentucky Stories,* Johns Hopkins University Press, 1983.

Work anthologized in *The Best American Short Stories, The Pushcart Prize, New Directions: An International Anthology,* and *Contemporary American Fiction.* Contributor of articles and stories to periodicals, including *South Atlantic Review, Occident, Minnesota Review, Antaeus, Sun and Moon,* and *Triquarterly.*

WORK IN PROGRESS: A scholarly study of the figure of Mercutio in *Romeo and Juliet;* two novels; assorted short fiction.

SIDELIGHTS: Joe Ashby Porter, who has lived in France and speaks the language, writes that French literature is one of the major influences on his work. He has also lived in England and North Africa.

POST, Gaines, Jr. 1937-

PERSONAL: Born September 22, 1937, in Madison, Wis.; son of Gaines (a professor) and Katherine (Rike) Post; married Jean Bowers, July 19, 1969; children: Katherine, Daniel. *Education:* Cornell University, B.A., 1959; Oxford University, B.A., 1963; Stanford University, M.A., 1965, Ph.D., 1969. *Residence:* Claremont, Calif. *Office:* Dean of Faculty, Claremont McKenna College, Claremont, Calif. 91711.

CAREER: University of Texas at Austin, assistant professor, 1969-74, associate professor of history, 1974-83; Claremont McKenna College, Claremont, Calif., dean of faculty, 1983—. *Military service:* U.S. Army, 1959-61; became first lieutenant. *Member:* American Historical Association. *Awards, honors:* Rhodes scholarship, 1961-63.

WRITINGS: *The Civil-Military Fabric of Weimar Foreign Policy,* Princeton University Press, 1973; (with others) *The Humanities in American Life: Report of the Commission on the Humanities,* University of California Press, 1980.

WORK IN PROGRESS: A book on British foreign policy and defense in the 1930s.

SIDELIGHTS: Gaines Post told *CA:* "I inherited my interest in history from my father, a mediaeval historian. I became especially interested in German history and civil-military relations while stationed in Germany." *Avocational interests:* Backpacking, wine tasting, tree pruning.

* * *

POULIN, A(lfred A.), Jr. 1938-

PERSONAL: Born March 14, 1938, in Lisbon, Me.; son of Alfred A. (a laborer) and Alice (Michaud) Poulin; married Basilike H. Parkas; children: Daphne. *Education:* St. Francis College, Biddeford, Me., B.A. (cum laude), 1960; Loyola University, Chicago, Ill., M.A., 1962; University of Iowa, M.F.A., 1968. *Home:* 92 Park Ave., Brockport, N.Y. 14420. *Office:* Department of English, State University of New York College at Brockport, Brockport, N.Y. 14420.

CAREER: St. Francis College, Biddeford, Me., instructor in humanities, 1962-64; University of Maryland, European Division, Heidelberg, Germany, instructor in English, 1965; University of New Hampshire, Durham, instructor in English, 1965-66; St. Francis College, assistant professor of English, 1968-71, chairman of humanities department, 1969-71, assistant to president, 1971; State University of New York College at Brockport, 1971—, began as assistant professor, currently professor of English. Resident at Corporation of Yaddo, 1977, 1980; visiting professor at University of Athens, December, 1980, May, 1981, May, 1982. Founding editor and publisher of BOA Editions, 1976—; founding executive director and chairman of board of New York State Literary Center, Inc., 1978-81. Director of Brockport Writers Forum, 1971-78; New York State Council on the Arts, panelist on literature program, 1977-80, member of task force on the individual writer, 1980-81. Consultant to publishing companies and literary organizations. *Awards, honors:* Danforth Foundation associate, 1970-74; Research Foundation of the State University of New York fellowships and grants, 1972, 1973, 1974, 1977, 1979; National Endowment for the Arts creative writing fellowship, 1974, grant, 1982; translation award, Translation Center, Columbia University, 1976, for *The Sonnets to Orpheus.*

WRITINGS: (Editor, with David DeTurk, and contributor) *The American Folk Scene: Dimensions of the Folksong Revival,*

Dell, 1967; (editor) *Contemporary American Poetry*, Houghton, 1971, 4th edition, in press; (editor) *Making in All Its Forms: Contemporary American Poetics and Criticism*, Dutton, 1972; *In Advent: Poems*, Dutton, 1972; *Catawba: Omens, Prayers and Songs*, Graywolf Press, 1977; *The Widow's Taboo: Poems after the Catawba*, Mushinsha, 1977; *The Nameless Garden: Poems*, Croissant, 1978; *The Slaughter of Pigs: A Sequence of Poems* (chapbook), Ohio Review, 1981; (editor) *A Ballet for the Ear: Interviews, Reviews and Essays by John Logan*, University of Michigan Press, 1982.

Translator; from the French, except as indicated: (From the German) Rainer Maria Rilke, *Duino Elegies* [and] *The Sonnets to Orpheus*, Houghton, 1977; Rilke, *Saltimbanques*, Graywolf Press, 1979; Rilke, *The Roses and the Windows*, Graywolf Press, 1979; Anne Hebert, *Poems*, Quarterly Review of Literature, 1980; Rilke, *The Astonishment of Origins*, Graywolf Press, 1982; Rilke, *Orchards*, Graywolf Press, 1982; Rilke, *The Migration of Powers*, Graywolf Press, 1983.

Contributor of poems and translations to numerous anthologies; contributor of poems, translations, essays, and reviews to magazines and journals, including *Atlantic*, *Esquire*, *Ms.*, *Journal of Modern Literature*, *Modern Poetry Studies*, and *New England Review*. Contributing editor, *American Poetry Review*, 1972—.

WORK IN PROGRESS: Writing *Begin Again: Poems, Cave Dwellers: Poems*, and *The Dangerous Widows and Other Eskimo Tales*; translating *Ode to the Saint Lawrence: The Poems of Gatien Lapointe*; editing *I Sing the Body Electric: Sexuality in American Poetry, Contemporary American Poetry*, Volume II, *Modern American Poetry*, and *The Figure of Experience: An Introduction to Poetry*; translating and editing *Like a Singing Tree: Contemporary French Poetry of Canada* and an expanded edition of *Poems* by Anne Hebert.

SIDELIGHTS: A. Poulin, Jr. told *CA*: "For good or ill, I have chosen not to be exclusively a poet. I have not isolated my work as a poet from my interest in the popular arts, especially songwriting, from my critical interest in the poetry and criticism of others, from the challenge of editing, or from my activities as a teacher. I am convinced that each of these feeds on the other, is strengthened by such interchange. Besides, a man—at least this man—survives on a number of levels, each with its own stress of energy and identity."

Selections from *The Widow's Taboo: Poems after the Catawba* have been translated into Greek.

BIOGRAPHICAL/CRITICAL SOURCES: Washington Post Book World, December 5, 1982.

* * *

POWELL, (Caryll) Nicolas (Peter) 1920-

PERSONAL: Born May 20, 1920, in Johannesburg, South Africa; son of Owen Price (a mining engineer) and Nora (Webb) Powell. *Education:* Attended University of Strasbourg, 1937-38; Peterhouse, Cambridge, B.A., 1941, M.A., 1945. *Religion:* Church of England. *Home:* 11 Somerset St., Kingsdown, Bristol BS2 8NB, England. *Agent:* David Higham Associates, 5-8 Lower John St., London W1R 4HA, England.

CAREER: Affiliated with British Council, London, England, 1949-51, second secretary of embassy in Bonn, West Germany, 1954-59, in Cologne, West Germany, 1959-62, in London, 1962-68, in Vienna, Austria, 1968-75, and in Amsterdam, Netherlands, 1975-80. *Military service:* Royal Marines, Commandos, 1940-49; prisoner of war in Italy, 1942-43; received Distinguished Service Order. *Member:* Society of Authors, Royal Society of Literature (fellow), Vienna Secession (honorary corresponding member), Reform Club, Victorian Society. *Awards, honors:* Order of the British Empire, 1975; Josef Hoffmann Ehrung Award from Vienna Secession, 1975; Goldenes Verdienstzeichen des Landes Wien, 1981.

WRITINGS: The Hills Remain (novel), Bodley Head, 1947; *The Drawings of Henry Fuseli*, Faber, 1951; *From Baroque to Rococo*, Praeger, 1959; *Great Palaces*, Weidenfeld & Nicolson, 1964; *Fuseli: The Night Mare*, Viking, 1973; *The Sacred Spring: The Arts in Vienna, 1898-1918*, New York Graphic Society, 1974; *Travellers to Trieste*, Faber, 1977. Contributor to *Encyclopaedia Britannica* and to *New Yorker*, *Burlington Magazine*, and *Geographical Magazine*.

SIDELIGHTS: Nicolas Powell told *CA* that his main interests are baroque architecture in Austria and Germany, Viennese *Jugendstil*, Henry Fuseli, and eighteenth- and nineteenth-century English drawings. He has traveled in Italy, Morocco, southern Germany, and Austria, and spent his childhood in France and Belgium.

BIOGRAPHICAL/CRITICAL SOURCES: Hilary St. George Saunders, *The Green Beret*, M. Joseph, 1949.

* * *

PRAGER, Arthur

PERSONAL: Born in New York, N.Y. *Residence:* Sag Harbor, N.Y. *Agent:* Daniel M. O'Shea, Jr., 888 8th Ave., New York, N.Y. 10019. *Office:* 7 Washington Square N., New York, N.Y. 10003.

CAREER: Attache at U.S. Embassy, Taipei, Taiwan and U.S. Consulate, Hong Kong, 1955-59; New York University, New York City, assistant professor of air science, 1959-62; Office of the Mayor, New York City, member of staff, 1962—. Executive director, Royal Oak Foundation. Consultant to Twentieth Century-Fox Film Corp. and Book-of-the-Month Club. *Military service:* U.S. Army Air Forces, 1943-46; became captain; received Distinguished Flying Cross.

WRITINGS: Rascals at Large: Or, the Clue in the Old Nostalgia, Doubleday, 1971; *The Mahogany Tree: An Informal History of "Punch,"* Hawthorn, 1978.

Scripts: "Mouseterpiece Theatre," Walt Disney Cable Television, 1983.

Contributor of articles and reviews to *Saturday Review* and *American Heritage*.

SIDELIGHTS: In *The Mahogany Tree: An Informal History of "Punch,"* Arthur Prager traces the history of England's most popular humor magazine. Named after the long table around which the magazine's staff holds its meetings, the book "is rich in history and in characters of all sorts," writes Joe Mysak of *National Review*. "Be certain, if it happened at *Punch*, at any time in the 138 years of the British humor magazine's existence, it is in this book."

Begun in 1841, *Punch* quickly established itself as the leading humor magazine of its day and attracted some of the most famous of English writers as contributors. The magazine "was quite radical in the early days," Robert M. Strozier of the *New York Times Book Review* states, "[and] a vigilant foe of privilege and pomposity." Strozier relates, however, that "*Punch*, [Prager] says, enjoyed its greatest success and power early on, but by 1880 it had become stuffy, establishment and bland. The magazine has had its ups and downs since then."

Prager relates this history in "a likeable tone; his affection for his subject is tangible," the *New Yorker* critic believes, "and he is quick to point out when the old jokes are still alive." Prager's use of "roll-call" history—the listing of names and biographical sketches of all those associated with the magazine—strikes the *New Yorker* critic as hard to follow. Mysak, too, deplores the "names, names, names," especially in the second half of the book. Nonetheless, Strozier considers the book "a good, brisk, affectionate (though not notably ambitious) introduction to a magazine that has come to be considered a national institution."

BIOGRAPHICAL/CRITICAL SOURCES: *New Yorker*, May 7, 1979; *New York Times Book Review*, July 1, 1979; *Economist*, August 11, 1979; *National Review*, December 21, 1979.

* * *

PRESTON, Ivy (Alice) Kinross 1914-

PERSONAL: Born November 11, 1914, in Timaru, Canterbury, New Zealand; daughter of Andrew (a farmer) and Lily (Ward) Kinross; married Percival Edward James Preston (a farmer), October 14, 1937 (died, 1956); children: David Robin, Peter Ronald, Diane Jeane, Lynnette Ruth. *Education:* Attended schools in Canterbury, New Zealand. *Politics:* Labour. *Religion:* Presbyterian. *Home:* 95 Church St., Timaru, New Zealand.

CAREER: Novelist. *Member:* P.E.N., New Zealand Women Writers Society, Romantic Novelists' Association (London), Romance Writers of America, South Island Writers Association, Timaru Writers Guild.

WRITINGS—Published by R. Hale, except as indicated: *The Silver Stream* (autobiography), Pegasus Press, 1959; *Where Ratas Twine*, Wright & Brown, 1960; *None So Blind*, Wright & Brown, 1961; *Magic in Maoriland*, Wright & Brown, 1962; *Rosemary for Remembrance*, 1962; *Island of Enchantment*, 1963; *Tamarisk in Bloom*, 1963; *Hearts Do Not Break*, 1964; *The Blue Remembered Hills*, 1965; *The Secret Love of Nurse Wilson*, 1966; *Enchanted Evening*, 1966; *Hospital on the Hill*, 1967; *Nicolette*, 1967; *Red Roses for a Nurse*, 1968; *Ticket of Destiny*, 1969; *April in Westland*, 1969.

A Fleeting Breath, 1970, Beagle Books, 1971; *Interrupted Journey*, 1970, Beagle Books, 1971; *Portrait of Pierre*, 1970, Beagle Books, 1971; *Petals in the Wind*, 1971; *Release the Past*, 1972; *Romance in Glenmore Street*, 1973, Ace Books, 1978; *Voyage of Destiny*, 1973; *Moonlight on the Lake*, 1974; *The House above the Bay*, 1975; *Sunlit Seas*, 1975; *Where Starts May Lead*, 1976; *One Broken Dream*, 1977; *Mountain Magic*, 1978; *Summer at Willowbank*, 1979.

Interlude in Greece, 1980; *Nurse in Confusion*, 1981; *Enchantment at Hillcrest*, 1982.

Also co-author of *Springbrook*, 1971; author of radio scripts. Contributor of short stories and articles to *New Zealand Playdate, New Zealand Farmer, Arena, New Zealand Home Journal*, and other magazines.

WORK IN PROGRESS: A novel, *Fair Accuser;* an updated autobiography; a biography of Preston's great-grandmother, an early New Zealand pioneer.

SIDELIGHTS: Ivy Kinross Preston told *CA:* "I began my writing career with a love story—my own. *The Silver Stream* tells of my meeting, marriage, and nineteen happy years with my husband and ends with his death from cancer at the age of forty-four. Since then I have continued to write love stories simply because I believe in the force of love in the world."

Preston's books have been translated into French, Italian, Dutch, Norwegian, Greek, Danish, and German.

BIOGRAPHICAL/CRITICAL SOURCES: Ivy Kinross Preston, *The Silver Stream*, Pegasus Press, 1959; *New Zealand Weekly News*, July 15, 1959; *Christchurch Star*, December 1, 1960; *New Zealand Women's Weekly*, January 23, 1963; *Timaru Herald*, July 7, 1963, December 12, 1963.

* * *

PREWITT, Kenneth 1936-

PERSONAL: Born March 16, 1936, in Alton, Ill.; son of Carl K. and Louise (Carpenter) Prewitt; married Anne Biggar, September 6, 1963; children: Jennifer Ann, Geoffrey Douglas. *Education:* Southern Methodist University, B.A., 1958; Washington University, M.A., 1959; Stanford University, Ph.D., 1963. *Home:* 30 Scenic Dr., Hastings-on-Hudson, N.Y. 10706. *Office:* Social Science Research Council, 605 Third Ave., New York, N.Y. 10158.

CAREER: Washington University, St. Louis, Mo., assistant professor of political science, 1963-64; Makerere University College, Kampala, Uganda, visiting professor of political science, 1964-65; University of Chicago, Chicago, Ill., beginning 1964, assistant professor to professor of political science, 1976-79, director of National Opinion Research Center, 1979—; president, Social Science Research Council, New York, N.Y. Research associate in political science, Stanford University, 1968-69; also taught at Institute of Development Studies, University of Nairobi, Nairobi, Kenya, 1970-72; fellow, Center for Advanced Study in the Behavioral Sciences, 1983-84. *Member:* American Political Science Association, Association for the Advancement of Science. *Awards, honors:* Guggenheim fellowship, 1983-84.

WRITINGS: (Editor with Louis Knowles) *Institutional Racism in America*, Prentice-Hall, 1969; (with Richard E. Dawson) *Political Socialization: An Analytic Study*, Little, Brown, 1969, 2nd edition, 1977; *Recruitment of Political Leaders: A Study of Citizen-Politicians*, Bobbs-Merrill, 1970; *Education and Political Values*, East African Publishing House, 1971; *Labyrinths of Democracy*, Bobbs-Merrill, 1973; *Introduction to American Government*, 4th edition, Harper, 1983.

BIOGRAPHICAL/CRITICAL SOURCES: *Washington Post*, February 24, 1970.

* * *

PRISCO, Salvatore III 1943-

PERSONAL: Born October 1, 1943, in Jersey City, N.J.; son of Salvatore (a businessman) and Libra (Deputato) Prisco; married Dorothy DeSteno (a fashion instructor), July 15, 1967; children: Lisa Natalie. *Education:* St. Peter's College, B.S., 1964; Rutgers University, M.A., 1965, Ph.D., 1969. *Home:* 510 Hamilton Dr., Hackettstown, N.J. 07840. *Office:* Department of Humanities, Stevens Institute, Hoboken, N.J. 07030.

CAREER: University of Alabama, University, assistant professor, 1969-72, associate professor of history, 1972-74; Union College, Cranford, N.J., lecturer in history, 1975-76; Stevens Institute, Hoboken, N.J., associate professor in humanities,

1977—. Member of governing board of Civil Liberties Union, Tuscaloosa, Ala., 1970-71. *Member:* Organization of American Historians, Academy of Political Science, American Historical Association, Society for Historians of American Foreign Relations. *Awards, honors:* Windham Foundation research grant, 1972-73; National Endowment for the Humanities summer grant, 1979.

WRITINGS: *John Barrett: Progressive Era Diplomat,* University of Alabama Press, 1973; *An Introduction to Psychohistory,* University Press of America, 1980. Contributor to history journals. Abstract editor of *Historical Abstracts,* 1972-75, and *America: History and Life,* 1972-75.

WORK IN PROGRESS: A collective biography of Progressive Era American diplomats, 1890-1920.

AVOCATIONAL INTERESTS: Travel, tennis.

Q

QUEBEDEAUX, Richard (Anthony) 1944-

PERSONAL: Born October 16, 1944, in Los Angeles, Calif.; son of Thomas Crawford (an electrical engineer) and Annette (Scheyer) Quebedeaux. *Education:* University of California, Los Angeles, B.A. (with honors), 1966, M.A., 1970; Harvard University, S.T.B. (cum laude), 1968; Oxford University, D.Phil., 1975. *Politics:* Democrat. *Religion:* United Church of Christ. *Address:* 2236 Channing Way, Berkeley, Calif. 94704.

CAREER: United Church Board for Homeland Ministries, New York, N.Y., consultant on church renewal, 1975-77; Unification Theological Seminary, Barrytown, N.Y., consultant, 1978-80; New Ecumenical Research Association, Barrytown, senior consultant, 1980—. *Member:* American Society of Authors and Journalists, Harvard Club (New York). *Awards, honors:* Ecumenical scholarship from World Council of Churches, 1969-70, for Mansfield College, Oxford.

WRITINGS: The Young Evangelicals, Harper, 1974; *The New Charismatics: The Origins, Development, and Significance of Neo-Pentecostalism,* Doubleday, 1976; *The Worldly Evangelicals,* Harper, 1978; *I Found It!: The Story of Bill Bright and Campus Crusade for Christ,* Harper, 1979; (author of introduction) Arthur C. Piepkorn, *Profiles in Belief,* Volume IV: *Evangelical, Fundamentalist, and Other Christian Bodies,* Harper, 1979; (editor with Rodney Sawatsky) *Evangelical-Unification Dialogue,* Rose of Sharon Press, 1979; *By What Authority: The Rise of Personality Cults in American Christianity,* Harper, 1982; (editor) *Lifestyle: Conversations with Members of the Unification Church,* Rose of Sharon Press, 1982; *The New Charismatics II,* Harper, 1983; (contributor) Glen Evans, editor, *The Complete Guide to Writing Nonfiction,* Writer's Digest Books, 1983. Contributor to religious magazines.

WORK IN PROGRESS: Contribution to *Encyclopedia of Religion in America,* for Scribner.

SIDELIGHTS: Richard Quebedeaux's book *The Worldly Evangelicals* is, according to Kenneth A. Briggs in a *New York Times* review, "the best analysis of a huge segment of America's religious life that has come along since the revivalistic boom began a few years ago. Besides providing insightful and useful information, it is written with flair and coy humor."

BIOGRAPHICAL/CRITICAL SOURCES: New York Times, November 17, 1978.

QUILL, Monica
See McINERNY, Ralph

* * *

QUIRK, Lawrence J. 1923-

PERSONAL: Born September 9, 1923, in Lynn, Mass.; son of Andrew L. and Margaret Quirk. *Education:* Suffolk University, B.A. (cum laude), 1949; Boston University, graduate study, 1949-50. *Home:* 74 Charles St., New York, N.Y. 10014.

CAREER: Writer for film magazines, and former editor of *Screen Life, Screen Parade, Screen Stars, Movie World,* and *Hollywood Stars;* editor and publisher of *Quirk's Reviews* (film publication), 1972—; also worked in earlier years for *Lynn Item,* Lynn, Mass., *Boston Record-American,* Boston, Mass., *New York World-Telegram and Sun,* and as film critic for *Motion Picture Herald, Motion Picture Daily,* and other periodicals. *Military service:* U.S. Army, 1950-53; public relations assignments, 1951-53; became sergeant. *Awards, honors:* Walt Whitman Award, 1979, for *Some Lovely Image.*

WRITINGS—Published by Citadel, except as indicated: *Robert Francis Kennedy,* Holloway, 1968; *The Films of Joan Crawford,* 1968; *The Films and Career of Ingrid Bergman,* 1970; *The Films of Paul Newman,* 1971, revised edition, 1981; *The Films of Fredric March,* 1971; (author of introduction) *Anthology of Photoplay Magazine, 1928-1940,* Dover, 1971; *The Films of William Holden,* 1973; *The Great Romantic Films,* 1974; *The Films of Robert Taylor,* 1975; *Some Lovely Image* (novel), Quirk Publishing, 1976; *The Films of Ronald Colman,* 1976; *The Films of Warren Beatty,* 1979; *The Films of Myrna Loy,* 1980; *The Films of Gloria Swanson,* 1984. Contributor to *Variety, Photoplay, Modern Screen, New York Times, Films in Review,* and *Theatre.*

WORK IN PROGRESS: A biography of James R. Quirk of *Photoplay; Lauren Becall, Her Life and Films.*

SIDELIGHTS: Lawrence J. Quirk is a nephew of James R. Quirk, founder of *Photoplay* and editor and publisher of the magazine during its greatest days (the twenties). Lawrence J. Quirk originated the James R. Quirk Awards in 1973, for meritorious achievements in film-related fields. The award has been given to over twenty-two people, including Lillian Gish, Joan Crawford, and Blanche Sweet.

R

RABEN, Joseph 1924-

PERSONAL: Born September 3, 1924, in New York, N.Y.; son of Abraham (a pharmacist) and Frances (a teacher; maiden name, Goldner) Raben; married Marguerite Bloch (an editor), June 8, 1952; children: Jeremy, Elizabeth. *Education:* University of Wisconsin, B.A., 1944; Indiana University, M.A., 1949, Ph.D., 1954. *Office address:* Paradigm Press, P.O. Box 1057, Osprey, Fla. 33559.

CAREER: Princeton University, Princeton, N.J., instructor in English, 1952-54; Queens College of the City University of New York, Flushing, N.Y., instructor, 1954-61, assistant professor, 1962-67, associate professor, 1967-70, professor of English, 1970-84; Paradigm Press, Osprey, Fla., director, 1984—. Philips Lecturer, Haverford College, 1968; visiting lecturer, University of Pisa, 1970, 1972. Chairman of working group on humanities, International Federation of Information Processing, 1971—; member of advisory committee to Associated Universities on National Institute for Information Systems, 1968; organizer, Conference on Data Bases in the Humanities and Social Sciences, 1979—. Consultant to International Business Machines Corp., 1964, 1981, and to RAND Corp., 1969. *Military service:* U.S. Army, 1945-46; editor of translations in Tokyo, 1946. *Member:* Modern Language Association of America, Association for Literary and Linguistic Computing (member of advisory board), Association for Computers and the Humanities (founder; president, 1980-83). *Awards, honors:* American Council of Learned Societies fellow for computer-oriented research in humanities, 1964.

WRITINGS: (Contributor) George Gerbner and others, editors, *The Analysis of Communication Content*, Wiley, 1969; (contributor) Carlos A. Cuadra, editor, *Annual Review of Information Science and Technology*, Encyclopaedia Britannica for American Society for Information Science, 1971, (editor) *Computer-Assisted Research in the Humanities: A Directory of Scholars Active*, Pergamon, 1977; (editor with Gregory A. Marks) *Data Bases in the Humanities and Social Sciences* (proceedings of a 1979 International Federation for Information Processing Conference), North-Holland Publishing, 1980; (contributor) Martha E. Williams, editor, *Annual Review of Information Science and Technology* Encyclopaedia Britannica for American Society for Information Science, 1981. Founder and editor of *Computers and the Humanities Journal*, 1966—; founder and director of *SCOPE: Scholarly Communication—Online Publishing and Education* newsletter, 1983—.

SIDELIGHTS: Joseph Raben writes: "The motivation to establish a journal to further the interaction of computers and humanistic research was a recognition that each field would ultimately appreciate its need for the other. Complex machinery requires imaginative, inquiring minds to exploit its potential; the humanities require all the aid that technology can supply for the routine functions that support the high-level activity: indexes, concordances, bibliographies, text collations, photocomposition. In my editorial and authorial activities, I have sought to explain the benefits of this interaction to appropriate audiences around the world."

* * *

RACINA, Thom 1946-
   (Tom Anicar, Lisa Wells)

PERSONAL: Born June 4, 1946, in Kenosha, Wis.; son of Frank (a dry cleaner) and Esther (Benko) Racina. *Education:* Attended University of New Mexico, 1964-66; Art Institute of Chicago, B.F.A., 1969, M.F.A., 1971. *Politics:* Democrat. *Home:* 3449 Waverly Dr., Los Angeles, Calif. 90027. *Agent:* Rhoda A. Weyr, William Morris Agency, 1350 Avenue of the Americas, New York, N.Y. 10019.

CAREER: Goodman Theatre, Chicago, Ill., assistant director, 1966-69, playwright-in-residence, 1969-71; writer, 1971—; children's television writer for Hanna-Barbera, 1972-73; associate head writer for "General Hospital," American Broadcasting Companies, Inc., 1980—. Has worked as a church organist, a price-check boy on roller skates in a discount store, a night club pianist, and a piano teacher.

WRITINGS—Novels: *Lifeguard*, Warner Paperback, 1976; (under pseudonym Tom Anicar) *Secret Sex*, New American Library, 1976; *The Great Los Angeles Blizzard*, Putnam, 1977; *Quincy, M.E.*, Berkley, 1977; *Kojak in San Francisco*, Berkley, 1977; *Palm Springs*, Seaview, 1978; *FM*, Jove, 1978; *Sweet Revenge*, Berkley Publishing, 1978; *Tomcat*, Ace Books, 1981; (under pseudonym Lisa Wells) *Magda*, Ace Books, 1982.

Musical plays for children: (adaptor) William Shakespeare, "A Midsummer Night's Dream," first produced in Chicago, Ill., at Goodman Theatre, 1968; *Allison Wonderland*, Samuel French,

1970; *The Marvelous Misadventure of Sherlock Holmes*, Samuel French, 1971.

Plays; both first produced in Chicago, Ill., at Goodman Theatre: "Allison," January 30, 1970; "Sherlock," July 6, 1971.

WORK IN PROGRESS: Three, a novel.

SIDELIGHTS: Racina writes: "I have no desire to write literature, only the kind of books I like to read, novels which are real escapist entertainment. The motivation to do much and do it well and be happy at the same time comes from a long history of battling the disease pancreatitis. Having been faced with death several times, it is always a joy to have one more pain-free day to be able to write a few more pages."

AVOCATIONAL INTERESTS: Travel (including the Soviet Union), gourmet cooking, swimming, driving his BMW, playing the piano, and "sharing an eleven room house with two cats, Saxon and Sherman, and a dog named Herschel."

BIOGRAPHICAL/CRITICAL SOURCES: New York Times Book Review, November 13, 1977.

* * *

RADICE, Betty 1912-

PERSONAL: Born January 3, 1912, in Hessle, Yorkshire, England; daughter of William Clarke (a solicitor) and Mabel (Brown) Dawson; married Italo de Lisle Radice (a senior civil servant in H. M. Treasury), September 16, 1935; children: Thomas Evasio, Catherine Lucy (deceased), Teresa Mary (deceased), Charles William, John de Lisle. *Education:* St. Hilda's College, Oxford, B.A., 1935, M.A. *Home:* 65 Cholmeley Crescent, London N6 5EX, England; and Old Post Office, Berrick Salome, Oxfordshire, England. *Office:* Penguin Books Ltd., Harmondsworth, Middlesex, England.

CAREER: Westminster Tutors, London, England, tutor, 1935-40; Channing School, London, senior classics mistress, 1956-62; Penguin Books Ltd., Harmondsworth, England, joint editor of "Penguin Classics," 1964—. Private tutor in classics and English. *Member:* Classical Association, Royal Society of Literature, Royal Society of Arts (fellow), Roman Society, London Classical Society, Virgil Society. *Awards, honors:* Honorary fellow of St. Hilda's College, Oxford University, 1981.

WRITINGS—Editor and translator, except as indicated; published by Penguin, except as indicated: *The Letters of the Younger Pliny*, 1964; Terence, *The Comedies*, Volume I, 1965, Volume II, 1967, revised edition published in one volume, 1976; Pliny the Younger, *Letters and Panegyricus*, two volumes, Loeb Classical Library, 1969; (compiler and author of introduction) *Who's Who in the Ancient World*, Stein & Day, 1971, revised edition, Penguin, 1973; (translator) Erasmus, *Praise of Folly*, 1971, revised edition, Folio Society, 1974; *The Letters of Abelard and Heloise*, 1974, Folio Society, 1977; (translator) Livy, *Rome and Italy*, 1982; (author of introduction) Horace, *The Odes and Epodes*, 1983; (editor) Edward Gibbon, *Memoirs of My Life*, 1984.

Also translator of other works from Greek, Latin, and Italian for Officina Bodoni (Verona).

WORK IN PROGRESS: Letters of Abelaerd and Heloise, a translation for Oxford Mediaeval Texts; *Terence*, two volumes, for Loeb Classical Library; translations of *The Collected Works of Erasmus*, Volumes XXVII and XXVIII, for University of Toronto Press; an eight-volume edition of Edward Gibbon's *Decline and Fall of the Roman Empire*, for Folio Society.

AVOCATIONAL INTERESTS: Foreign travel, music, literature, and grandchildren.

* * *

RADL, Shirley L(ouise) 1935-

PERSONAL: Born August 24, 1935, in Calif.; daughter of Robert C. (a contractor) and Henrietta Joyce (Kenna) Rogers; married Calvin A. Radl (an engineer), October 20, 1956; children: Lisa, Adam. *Politics:* Democrat. *Home:* 220 Miramonte Ave., Palo Alto, Calif. 94306. *Agent:* Rhoda Weyr, William Morris Agency, 1350 Avenue of the Americas, New York, N.Y. 10019.

CAREER: Executive secretary, Sylvania Electronics, 1959-65; Zero Population Growth, Inc., Los Altos, Calif., national executive director, 1969-71; National Organization for NONparents, Palo Alto, Calif., national executive director, 1972-73; president, Quality of Life, Inc., 1973—. Lecturer. *Member:* Authors Guild, Authors League of America.

WRITINGS: Mother's Day Is Over, Charterhouse, 1973; (with Carol A. Chetkovich) . . . *And the Pursuit of Happiness*, Metamorphosis Press, 1976; *The New Mother's Survival Guide*, Rawson Associates, 1979; (with Philip G. Zimbardo) *The Shyness Workbook*, A & W Publishers, 1979; (with Zimbardo) *The Shy Child*, McGraw, 1981; *The Invisible Woman: Target of the Religious New Right*, Delacorte, 1983. Contributor of articles to periodicals, including *Glamour* and *Cosmopolitan*.

SIDELIGHTS: Shirley L. Radl told *CA*: "I do not consider myself a writer but instead one who is moved to write by specific circumstances or because of an avid interest in a subject. I am passionately interested in the prevention of child abuse and to that end have done several articles for major publications and organized a crisis intervention hotline in my own community. If another major work is forthcoming, it will probably deal with something within the culture that affects us all, such as social pressure to conform, coercion, etc."

BIOGRAPHICAL/CRITICAL SOURCES: Los Angeles Times Book Review, September 11, 1983.

* * *

RAGAWAY, Martin A(rnold) 1928-

PERSONAL: Born January 29, 1928, in Brooklyn, N.Y.; son of Philip (a pharmacist) and Evelyn (Mandelbaum) Ragaway; married Donna Jo Whitman, 1952 (divorced, 1959); married Connie Hunter Webber, 1969 (divorced, 1972); children: (first marriage) Jill; (second marriage) Philip. *Education:* New York University, B.S., 1945. *Home:* 1172 Casa Verde Way, Palm Springs, Calif. 92262. *Office: Funny Funny World*, 8625 Holloway Dr., Los Angeles, Calif. 90069.

CAREER: New York Mirror, New York, N.Y., assistant Brooklyn editor; became writer for television films and radio; currently editor and publisher of *Funny Funny World*, Los Angeles, Calif. *Member:* Alpha Phi Sigma. *Awards, honors:* Emmy Awards from Academy of Television Arts and Sciences for material written for Dick Van Dyke, and for material written for Red Skelton; awards from Writer's Guild, for material written for Dick Van Dyke, and for writing Alan King's "Wonderful World of Aggravation"; received National Scholastic Award for material written for Bill Cosby.

WRITINGS—Published by Price, Stern, except as indicated: (With Milton Berle) *Out of My Trunk*, Blue Ribbon Books,

1945; *Good News/Bad News Book,* 1972; *The World's Worst Golf Jokes,* 1972; *The World's Worst Doctor Jokes,* 1972, revised edition, 1979; *The World's Worst Lawyer Jokes,* 1972; *The World's Worst Psychiatrist Jokes,* 1974; (editor with L. L. Sloan) *World's Worst Show Me Jokes,* 1978; *The Good News Is There's More Bad News,* 1978; *The Prince: How to Tell a Spoiled American Male,* 1979; *How to Get a Teenager to Run away from Home,* 1980; *Did You Hear about the Amerikanski . . .?,* 1981; *How to Tell if Your Paranoia Is Real!,* 1981; *Sex before Golf,* 1982; *Don't Think about Retiring Until . . . ,* 1982; *I Don't Tawuk Funny,* 1983.

Films: "The Milkman," Universal, 1950; "Abbot and Costello in the Foreign Legion," Universal, 1950; "Ma and Pa Kettle Go to Town," Universal, 1950; "Lost in Alaska," Universal, 1952; "Ma and Pa Kettle Go to the Fair," Universal, 1952.

Author of television and radio material for performers, including Milton Berle, Dinah Shore, Bob Hope, Alan King, Dick Van Dyke, Red Skelton, Jackie Gleason, and Lucille Ball. Contributor to magazines and newspapers.

SIDELIGHTS: Martin A. Ragaway writes: "*Funny Funny World* has twenty correspondents around the world and possibly the most elite circulation list including heads of state, congressmen, senators, college presidents, etc. I take humor very seriously. Life is a strait jacket if you insist on adhering to it humorlessly. I probably know more about the funny, odd, strange wacky things happening around the world than any other human being alive. My daily goal: To contribute to the sum total of human laughter."

* * *

RAGOSTA, Millie J(ane) 1931-
(Melanie Randolph)

PERSONAL: Born March 1, 1931, in Huntingdon, Pa.; daughter of Chester Earl (a printer) and Maximilla (Heck) Baker; married Vincent Anthony Ragosta (an insurance agent), February 4, 1950; children: Vincent, Kathleen, Arthur, Kevin, Ruth, Joseph, John, Anthony, Margaret, William, Rosemary. *Education:* Attended high school in Huntingdon, Pa. *Politics:* Liberal Republican. *Religion:* Roman Catholic. *Home:* 319 East Linn St., Bellefonte, Pa. 16823. *Agent:* Julie Fallowfield, McIntosh & Otis, Inc., 475 Fifth Ave., New York, N.Y. 10017.

CAREER: Writer, 1966—. *Member:* Bellefonte Women's Club.

WRITINGS—Published by Doubleday, except as indicated: *The Lighthouse* (gothic novel), Avalon, 1971; *House of the Evil Winds* (gothic novel), Bouregy, 1973; *Lorena Veiled* (gothic novel), Ballantine, 1974; *Taverna in Terrazzo* (gothic novel), Ballantine, 1975; *King John's Treasure* (gothic novel), 1976; *Witness to Treason* (historical novel), 1977; *The House on Curtin Street* (historical romance), 1979.

Gerait's Daughter (historical romance), 1981; *The Winter Rose* (historical romance), 1982; *The Dream Weaver* (contemporary romance), 1983; (under pseudonym Melanie Randolph) *Heart Full of Rainbows,* Berkley/Jove, 1983; *Sing Me a Love Song* (contemporary romance), 1984.

Author of weekly column of family humor for *Twin Circle Catholic Newspaper* (Los Angeles). Contributor of articles and stories to magazines, including *Family Digest.*

WORK IN PROGRESS: Made in Heaven, a contemporary romance; *The Druid's Lass,* a historical romance.

SIDELIGHTS: Millie J. Ragosta comments: "I began writing at the age of thirty-five because I was the mother of ten children and was overwhelmed with the need to do something just for myself. But, being convinced a mother is needed at home, it had to be something I could do there. I produced my last baby and the first of eight books. I started with gothics because I had so much to learn, but now I am doing historical fiction, my favorite."

She adds: "Our family of husband Vince and I and eleven children has increased by four grandchildren. We've moved one block from the three-story Victorian house [that was the] setting of *The House on Curtin Street* into a one-story, 1939 rambling cottage built from salvage material when the Bellefonte 1911-vintage high school was widely damaged by fire in 1938. I'm now making even more books, not babies! Though both are delightful, at this point in my life, the books are more practical."

* * *

RAKOSI, Carl
See RAWLEY, Callman

* * *

RAMSAY, William M(cDowell) 1922-

PERSONAL: Born August 3, 1922, in Huntsville, Tex.; son of Charles Summer (a minister) and Catherine (McKay) Ramsay; married DeVere Maxwell, April 27, 1954; children: William McDowell, Jr., John Alston. *Education:* Southwestern at Memphis, A.B., 1946; Union Theological Seminary in Virginia, B.D., 1949; University of Edinburgh, Ph.D., 1954; additional study at Columbia University, 1966-67. *Politics:* Democrat. *Address:* Box 235, McKenzie, Tenn. 38201. *Office:* Bethel College, McKenzie, Tenn. 38201.

CAREER: Ordained Presbyterian minister, 1950; pastor of churches in Knoxville, Tenn., 1950-54, and Paducah, Ky., 1954-59; Presbyterian Board of Christian Education, Richmond, Va., associate director of adult education, 1959-69; King College, Bristol, Tenn., professor of philosophy, 1969-79; Bethel College, McKenzie, Tenn., Hannibal Seagle Professor of Religion and Philosophy, 1979—. *Military service:* U.S. Army, Infantry, 1943-46.

WRITINGS: The Christ of the Earliest Christians, John Knox, 1959; *The Meaning of Jesus Christ,* John Knox, 1964; (with John Leith) *The Church: A Believing Fellowship,* John Knox, 1965; *Cycles and Renewal: Trends in Protestant Lay Education,* Abingdon, 1969; *The Layman's Guide to the New Testament,* John Knox, 1981. Also author of articles, church school materials, and other educational materials for Presbyterian Board of Christian Education. Contributor of weekly page to *Outlook.*

* * *

RANDOLPH, Melanie
See RAGOSTA, Millie J(ane)

* * *

RANK, Hugh (Duke) 1932-

PERSONAL: Born November 3, 1932, in Chicago, Ill.; son of Hugh A. (a salesman) and Margaret (McGreevy) Rank; married Lee Novak (a teacher), August 31, 1958; children: Elizabeth, Christopher, James-Jonathan, David. *Education:* University of

Notre Dame, B.A., 1954, M.A., 1955, Ph.D., 1969. *Home:* 834 Pin Oak Lane, Park Forest South, Ill. 60466. *Office:* College of Arts and Sciences, Governors State University, Park Forest South, Ill. 60466.

CAREER: Arizona State University, Tempe, instructor in English, 1959-60, 1961-62; St. Joseph's College, Rensselaer, Ind., assistant professor of English, 1962-67; Sacred Heart University, Fairfield, Conn., associate professor of English, 1968-72; Governors State University, Park Forest South, Ill., professor of English, 1972—. Founder and publisher, Counter-Propaganda Press. *Military service:* U.S. Army, public information officer, 1955-58; served in Germany; became first lieutenant.

MEMBER: National Council of Teachers of English, Conference on College Composition and Communication, Illinois Consumer Educators. *Awards, honors:* Fulbright award, 1967-68; George Orwell Award from National Council of Teachers of English, 1976, for distinguished contribution toward honesty and clarity in public language.

WRITINGS: The American Scene, Gyldendal, 1969, 2nd edition, 1971; *The U.S.A.: A Commentary,* Litton International, 1972; *Edwin O'Connor,* Twayne, 1974; (editor) *Language and Public Policy,* National Council of Teachers of English, 1974; *The Counter-Propaganda File,* Counter-Propaganda Press, 1976; *The Pitch: How to Analyze Advertising,* Counter-Propaganda Press, 1982; *The Pep Talk: How to Analyze Political Language,* Counter-Propaganda Press, 1984. Also author of numerous one-page teaching aids. Contributor of articles to language and literary journals, including *New England Quarterly,* and poems to "little" magazines.

SIDELIGHTS: Hugh Rank told *CA:* "Since 1972, my research has centered on propaganda analysis; interest in eighteenth-century rhetoric led me, via Jonathan Edwards and Perry Miller, back to Aristotle's *Rhetoric.* Re-examining my own priorities, I felt that I should apply my own effort to analyze the language and persuasion of our contemporary 'professional persuaders'—especially advertising and political propaganda. When the National Council of Teachers of English created a Committee on Public Doublespeak in 1972 (mandated to help 'prepare children to cope with commercial propaganda'), I became the original chairman, attempting to create a useful technique to teach the young how to analyze sophisticated persuasion. For nearly four years, my main project was the creation of a new schema as a structure to organize propaganda analysis; by re-sorting twenty-five existing taxonomies, eliminating the jargon, I produced a simple pattern, 'Intensify/Downplay,' which can be applied to verbal, nonverbal, and other symbolic human communication. Copyright was released to the public domain so that texts could freely incorporate it. In 1976, the Committee on Public Doublespeak endorsed the schema. This was followed by a series of one-page teaching aids, designed to be photocopied, [for use] in teaching individuals the patterns of persuasion used by *any* persuader, commercial or political, left or right."

AVOCATIONAL INTERESTS: "Lieben und arbeiten."

BIOGRAPHICAL/CRITICAL SOURCES: Daniel Dieterich, *Teaching about Doublespeak,* National Council of Teachers of English, 1976.

* * *

RAPER, Arthur F(ranklin)   1899-1979

PERSONAL: Born November 8, 1899, near Lexington, N.C.; died August 10, 1979, in Virginia; son of William Franklin (a farmer) and Julia (Crouse) Raper; married Martha Elizabeth Jarrell, June 12, 1930; children: Charles, Harrison, Arthur Jarrell, Margaret Raper Hammun. *Education:* University of North Carolina, A.B., 1924, Ph.D., 1931; Vanderbilt University, M.A., 1925. *Politics:* "Usually a Democrat." *Religion:* "At first Moravian, then Methodist by marriage." *Home:* 10801 Miller Rd., Oakton, Va. 22124.

CAREER: Commission on Interracial Cooperation, Atlanta, Ga., research secretary, 1926-39; Agnes Scott College, Decatur, Ga., acting professor of sociology, 1932-39; Carnegie-Myrdal Study of the American Negro, New York, N.Y., research associate, 1939-40; U.S. Department of Agriculture, Bureau of Agricultural Economics, Greene County, Ga., social science analyst, 1940-42, social science analyst and principal social scientist in Washington, D.C., 1942-52; U.S. Mutual Security Agency, Economic Cooperation Administration, Far East Division, Washington, D.C., consultant, working with Philippines Council on field study of local rural life, 1952; U.S. Agency for International Development, Washington, D.C., Foreign Operations Administration, Mutual Security Mission to China, project evaluation adviser in Taiwan, 1952-54, International Cooperation Administration, consultant to Community Development Division on Middle East and South Asia, 1954-55, regional community development adviser in the Middle East and North Africa, 1955-58, member of training development staff and Career Development Division, 1958, assistant chief of orientation and counseling branch in Office of Personnel, 1958-61, acting chief, 1961-62. Conducted weekly graduate seminars at Catholic University, Washington, D.C., late 1950's to early 1960's; Michigan State University, East Lansing, senior advisor for Overseas Program to Pakistan Academy for Rural Development in Comilla, East Pakistan, 1962-64, member of Pakistan Project, 1964-65, visiting professor of sociology and Asian studies, 1964-67. Consultant on agrarian reform to Allied Occupation Command, Japan, 1947, 1948, 1949. Trustee of Delta Cooperative Farms, Inc., 1946-52; member of board of National Sharecroppers' Fund. Executive Secretary of Council on a Christian Social Order, 1938-40. *Member:* American Sociological Association, Rural Sociological Society, Society for International Development, Southern Sociological Association, Southern Regional Council, Phi Beta Kappa.

WRITINGS: The Tragedy of Lynching, University of North Carolina Press, 1933, revised edition, Patterson Smith, 1969; *Preface to Peasantry: A Tale of Two Black Belt Counties,* University of North Carolina Press, 1936, revised edition, Atheneum, 1968; (with Ira De A. Reid) *Sharecroppers All,* University of North Carolina Press, 1941, reprinted, Russell, 1971; *Tenants of the Almighty,* Macmillan, 1943, reprinted, Arno, 1971.

(With Carl C. Taylor, Douglas Ensminger, and others) *Rural Life in the United States,* Knopf, 1950; (with Herbert Passin and others) *The Japanese Village in Transition,* General Headquarters, Supreme Commander for Allied Powers (Tokyo), 1950; (contributor) Louis W. Jones, editor, *The Changing Status of the Negro in Southern Agriculture,* Tuskegee Institute, 1950; (with wife, Martha J. Raper) *Guide to Agriculture, U.S.A.,* U.S. Government Printing Office, 1951, revised by Catherine Senf, 1955; (contributor) L. A. Potts, editor, *Land Tenure in the Southern Region,* Tuskegee Institute, 1951; *Rural Taiwan: Problem and Promise,* Joint Commission on Rural Reconstruction in China, 1953; *Urban and Industrial Taiwan: Crowded and Resourceful,* U.S. Mutual Security Mission to China, 1954.

(With Harry L. Case and others) *Rural Development in Action: The Comprehensive Experiment at Comilla, East Pakistan,* Cornell University Press, 1970; (contributor) Carle C. Zimmerman and Richard E. Dewors, editors, *Sociology of Underdevelopment,* Copp, 1970. Also author of several pamphlets and an orientation manual for foreign visitors on rural life in the United States. Contributor of about thirty-five articles to professional journals.

WORK IN PROGRESS: Research on current social and economic conditions; preparing personal papers for submission to the Southern Historical Collection at University of North Carolina Library.

SIDELIGHTS: In 1951, Arthur F. Raper organized a study for the International Motion Picture Division of the U.S. Department of State on appropriate rural audio-visual materials for eleven Asian countries. *Avocational interests:* Growing organic beef, fruits, and vegetables; participating in civic and church activities.

OBITUARIES: Washington Post, August 12, 1979.†

* * *

RATNER, Rochelle 1948-

PERSONAL: Born December 2, 1948; daughter of Herman (a business executive) and Esther (Tischler) Ratner. *Education:* Studied at Bread Loaf Writers' Conference, 1968, and New School for Social Research, 1969. *Home:* 314 East 78th St., New York, N.Y. 10021. *Office address:* American Book Review, Box 188, Cooper Station, New York, N.Y. 10003.

CAREER: East Village Other (newspaper), New York City, book review editor, 1970-71; *Soho Weekly News,* New York City, columnist, 1975-82; *American Book Review,* New York City, executive editor, 1978—. Worked for Poetry-in-the-Schools programs in New York, New Hampshire, and South Carolina.

WRITINGS—Poems, except as indicated: *A Birthday of Waters,* New Rivers Press, 1971; *False Trees,* New Rivers Press, 1973; (translator) Paul Colinet, *Selected Prose Poems,* Clown War Press, 1975; *Mysteries,* Ragnarok Press, 1976; *Pirates's Song,* Jordan Davies Press, 1976; *The Tightrope Walker,* Pennyworth Press, 1977; *Graven Images,* illustrated by Bernard Solomon, Boxwood Press, 1977; *Quarry,* New Rivers Press, 1978; *Combing the Waves,* Hanging Loose Press, 1979; *Sea Air in a Grave Ground Hog Turns Toward,* Segull Publications, 1980; *Hide and Seek,* Ommation Press, 1980; *Practicing to Be a Woman: New and Selected Poems,* Scarecrow, 1982; *Women Writing in America: Trying to Understand What It Means to Be a Feminist* (criticism), Contact II, 1984. Contributor of poetry, articles, and fiction to numerous literary journals and reviews, including *Nation, Sumac, Shenandoah, National Jewish Monthly, Pequod, Poetry Review,* and *New Women's Times.* Book reviewer, *Library Journal,* 1975—; co-editor, *Hand Book,* 1978—.

WORK IN PROGRESS: A critical book exploring the use of persona in American poetry (tracing it to its British roots in Browning, Tennyson, and Hardy); an autobiographical fiction fantasy, *Peer Group;* more poems.

SIDELIGHTS: "I write from my experiences with myself," Rochelle Ratner says, "not from the landscape around me as much as I like to think I do. If I went to other places, my poems would most likely remain with the imagery I've been using all along—that of the sea, and my childhood." Her poetry writing continues, the author adds, "spurred by a visit to Israel, and the problems and pleasures of living part-time in a rural environment after years in the city."

* * *

RAWLEY, Callman 1903-
(Carl Rakosi)

PERSONAL: Original name, Carl Rakosi; name legally changed; born November 6, 1903, in Berlin, Germany; came to United States in 1910; son of Hungarian nationals, Leopold and Flora (Steiner) Rakosi; married Leah Jaffe, May 6, 1939; children: Barbara, George. *Education:* University of Wisconsin, B.A., 1924, M.A., 1926; University of Pennsylvania, Master of Social Work, 1940. *Religion:* Jewish. *Home:* 128 Irving Street, San Francisco, Calif. 94122.

CAREER: University of Texas at Austin, instructor, 1928-29; Cook County Bureau of Public Welfare, Chicago, Ill., social worker, 1932-33; Federal Transient Bureau, New Orleans, La., supervisor, 1933-34; Tulane University of Louisiana (now Tulane University), Graduate School of Social Work, New Orleans, field work supervisor, 1934-35; Jewish Family Welfare Society, Brooklyn, N.Y., caseworker, 1935-40; Jewish Social Service Bureau, St. Louis, Mo., case supervisor, 1940-43; assistant director of Jewish Children's Bureau and Bellefaire (residential treatment center for disturbed children), both Cleveland, Ohio, 1943-45; Jewish Family and Children's Service, Minneapolis, Minn., executive director, 1945-68; private practice in psychotherapy and marriage counseling, 1958-68; Yaddo, Saratoga Springs, N.Y., resident writer, 1968-75. Writer-in-residence, University of Wisconsin, 1969-70; member of faculty, National Poetry Festival, 1973; visiting poet, Michigan State University, 1974.

MEMBER: National Association of Social Workers (president of South Minnesota chapter, 1959-61), National Conference of Jewish Communal Service (vice-president, 1957-58), Family Service Association of America (chairman of Midwest regional committee, 1961-64; chairman of committee on long-range planning, 1964-66). *Awards, honors:* National Endowment for the Arts award, 1969, fellowship, 1972 and 1979.

WRITINGS—All under name Carl Rakosi: *Selected Poems,* New Directions, 1941; *Amulet,* New Directions, 1967; *Two Poems,* Modern Editions Press, 1971; *Ere-Voice,* New Directions, 1971; *Ex Cranium, Night,* Black Sparrow Press, 1975; *My Experiences in Parnassus,* Black Sparrow Press, 1977; *History,* Oasis Books (London), 1981; *Droles de Journal,* Toothpaste Press, 1981; *Collected Prose,* National Poetry Foundation, 1983; *Spiritus, I,* Pig Press (England), 1983.

Contributor to anthologies, including *Objectivists Anthology,* edited by Louis Zukofsky, *America, a Prophesy,* edited by Rothenberg and Quasha, *The American Literary Anthology,* No. 3, edited by Louis Simpson, *Poems One Line and Longer,* edited by William Cole, *Heartland II,* edited by Lucien Stryk, and *Modern Things,* edited by Parker Tyler. Contributor of poetry to journals, including *Paris Review, Quarterly Review of Literature, Poetry, Massachusetts Review, Transition,* and *Exile.*

SIDELIGHTS: Callman Rawley told *CA:* "Between the years 1939 and 1965 I wrote no poetry. Was stimulated to write again by the interest of Andrew Crozier, a young British poet. *Amulet* represents my work to 1967 and revisions of earlier poems." Rawley is a member of the older Objectivist group of poets, "reflecting the influence" of Ezra Pound and William Carlos Williams, according to a *Choice* reviewer. "Like Williams's [poetry]," writes *New York Times Book Review* critic R. W. Flint, "his writing has obviously been nourished every step of the way by the rigors and rewards of exacting work well outside the literary orbit."

BIOGRAPHICAL/CRITICAL SOURCES: *New York Times Book Review*, January 28, 1968, November 16, 1975; *Prairie Schooner*, fall, 1968; *Contemporary Literature*, spring, 1969; *Iowa Review*, winter, 1971; *Choice*, July-August, 1972; *Margins*, February, 1975; *Preview*, June, 1975; *Chicago Review*, winter, 1979; *The American Book Review*, May-June, 1982.

* * *

RAY, Dorothy Jean 1919-

PERSONAL: Born October 10, 1919, in Cedar Falls, Iowa; daughter of Oscar Theodore and Vina (Younker) Tostlebe; married Stanley Freeland Thompson, May 17, 1942; married second husband, Verne Frederick Ray (an anthropologist), February 2, 1955; children: (first marriage) Eric Stanley Thompson. *Education:* Iowa State Teachers College (now University of Northern Iowa), B.A., 1941; graduate study at Radcliffe College, 1948-50, and University of Washington, Seattle, 1954-55. *Address:* Box 586, Port Townsend, Wash. 98368.

CAREER: University of Alaska, Geophysical Institute, College, administrative assistant, 1952-53; independent anthropologist and writer. Research anthropologist for several Indian land cases heard before Indian Claims Commission. *Awards, honors:* Grants from Arctic Institute of North America, 1950, and American Philosophical Society, 1968.

WRITINGS—Published by University of Washington Press, except as indicated: *Artists of the Tundra and the Sea*, 1961; *Eskimo Masks: Art and Ceremony*, photographs by Alfred A. Blaker, 1967; *Graphic Arts of the Alaskan Eskimo*, Indian Arts and Crafts Board, 1969; *The Eskimos of Bering Strait, 1650-1898*, 1975; *Eskimo Art: Tradition and Innovation in North Alaska*, 1977; (collaborator) Louis L. Renner, *Pioneer Missionary to the Bering Strait Eskimos: Bellarmine Lafortune, S.J.*, Binford & Mort, 1979; *Aleut and Eskimo Art: Tradition and Innovation in South Alaska*, 1981. Contributor to *Anthropological Papers of the University of Alaska*, *Polar Notes*, *Journal of the West*, *Beaver* (Winnipeg), *Alaska*, *The Alaska Journal*, and other journals.

WORK IN PROGRESS: *Ethnohistory in the Arctic: The Bering Strait Area*, for Limestone Press.

AVOCATIONAL INTERESTS: Playing piano and flute, taking off for the wilderness with a packsack on her back.

* * *

RAY, Mary (Eva Pedder) 1932-

PERSONAL: Born March 14, 1932, in Rugby, England; daughter of William John (a teacher) and Dora (Moule) Ray. *Education:* Attended Birmingham College of Art and Crafts, 1950-52; College of the Ascension, Birmingham, England, London Diploma of Social Studies, 1954. *Religion:* Church of England. *Home:* Pandora, 24 Richmond Dr., Herne Bay, Kent, England.

CAREER: Church social worker in Sheffield, England, 1957-61; old people's welfare worker for Warwickshire County Council, 1961-62; civil servant in Birmingham and London, England, 1962-78.

WRITINGS—Published by Faber, except as indicated: *The Voice of Apollo*, J. Cape, 1964, Farrar, Strauss, 1966; *The Eastern Beacon*, J. Cape, 1965, Farrar, Strauss, 1967; *Standing Lions*, 1968, Meredith, 1969; *Spring Tide*, 1969; *Living in Earliest Greece*, 1969; *Shout against the Wind*, 1970; *A Tent for the Sun*, 1971; *The Ides of April*, 1974; *Sword Sleep*, 1975; *Beyond the Desert Gate*, 1977; *Song of Thunder*, 1978; *Rain from the West*, 1980; *The Windows of Elissa*, 1982; *The Golden Bees*, 1984.

SIDELIGHTS: Mary Ray's historical novels have received critical praise. Ann Evans of the *Times Literary Supplement*, for example, finds that *The Windows of Elissa*, a novel set in ancient Carthage, possesses "vision and immediacy." "There are few writers," Evans believes, "who can reconstruct history with such authority as this, or imbue it with such a depth of human insight. It requires not only a genuine and scholarly knowledge of a historical period . . . but a quality of imagination which can inhabit time past as though it were the only reality."

Mary Ray told *CA*: "Since I was a child of about six I have never felt any strangeness or distance about what I have learned about the people of Greece and Rome and of earlier civilizations. I was at home in the periods in the way that some people are at home in a place or a country. I started writing about Roman Britain, because I knew what the places looked like, and for me it is important that the three strands of actual geographical firsthand knowledge, historical research and imagination should all be as strong as I can make them. After I was able to go to Greece regularly I particularly enjoyed writing about the people who had lived there. I became fascinated by what was the same for me—smells and weather and mountains and ants, and what was quite different—slavery, pain and the worship of different Gods.

"Looking back I can see that certain themes are usually important in my books. Creative people have a habit of turning up as characters, as making things—from jam to fine art—is very important to me, and my creative people often have to fight to be able to practice their skills as in my experience one does in real life. I also enjoy writing about the very old and the very young, which is a hangover from working in residential homes for mothers and babies and the old when I was a social science student. I am also obsessed by a theme very common in children's books—. . . how and when, when one is young, you become able to come to terms with what life brings. I suppose this is because for children's writers their own childhood is still very alive. We remember the things that it was painful to learn, what we had to fight for and what we had to accept; the characters in our books follow where we went or the way we wish we had gone."

BIOGRAPHICAL/CRITICAL SOURCES: *Times Literary Supplement*, March 28, 1980, March 26, 1982.

* * *

RAYMOND, G. Alison
See LANIER, Alison Raymond

* * *

RAYNER, Mary 1933-

PERSONAL: Born December 30, 1933, in Mandalay, Burma; daughter of A. H. and Yoma Grigson; married E. H. Rayner, 1960 (divorced, 1982); children: Sarah, William, Benjamin. *Education:* University of St. Andrews, M.A. (second class honors), 1954. *Residence:* Twickenham, Middlesex, England.

Address: c/o Macmillan London Ltd., 4 Little Essex St., London W.C.2, England.

CAREER: Former production assistant at Hammond, Hammond Ltd. (publisher), London, England; Longmans, Green & Co. Ltd. (publisher), London, England, copywriter, 1959-62; free-lance book illustrator, 1974—. *Member:* Society of Authors.

WRITINGS—All self-illustrated juveniles; published by Atheneum, except as indicated: *The Witchfinder,* Morrow, 1976; *Mr. and Mrs. Pig's Evening Out,* 1976; *Garth Pig and the Ice Cream Lady,* 1978; *The Rain Cloud,* 1980; *Mrs. Pig's Bulk Buy,* 1981.

Illustrator: Daphne Ghose, *Harry,* Lutterworth, 1973; Stella Nowell, *The White Rabbit,* Lutterworth, 1975; Griselda Gifford, *Because of Blunder,* Gollancz, 1977; Gifford, *Cass the Brave,* Gollancz, 1978; Partap Sharma, *Dog Detective Ranjha,* Macmillan, 1978.

Work appears in anthologies, *Allsorts Six,* edited by Ann Thwaite, Methuen, 1974; *Allsorts Seven,* edited by Thwaite, Methuen, 1975; *Young Winters' Tales Seven,* edited by M. R. Hodgkin, Macmillan, 1976; *All Sorts of Poems,* edited by Thwaite, Angus & Robertson, 1978. Contributor of stories to *Cricket.*

SIDELIGHTS: Mary Rayner's *Mr. and Mrs. Pig's Evening Out* is considered by Elaine Moss of the *Times Literary Supplement* to have "style, wit, excitement, high drama, and pathos." "If humour and terror (resolved) are the ingredients of treasured nursery stories," Moss believes, "[*Mr. and Mrs. Pig's Evening Out*] will be loved till its sturdy binding falls off."

BIOGRAPHICAL/CRITICAL SOURCES: Times Literary Supplement, July 16, 1976, July 24, 1981; *New York Times Book Review,* October 23, 1977, October 12, 1980, June 7, 1981, November 1, 1981.

* * *

RE, Edward D(omenic) 1920-

PERSONAL: Born October 14, 1920, in Santa Marina, Italy; U.S. citizen, brought to United States in 1928; son of Anthony and Marina (Maetta) Re; married Margaret Ann Corcoran (an attorney), June 3, 1950; children: Mary Ann, Anthony John, Marina, Edward, Victor, Margaret, Matthew, Joseph, Mary Elizabeth, Mary Joan, Mary Ellen, Nancy Madeline. *Education:* St. John's University, B.S. (cum laude), 1941, LL.B. (summa cum laude), 1943; New York University, J.S.D., 1950. *Office:* U.S. Court of International Trade, Federal Plaza, New York, N.Y. 10007.

CAREER: Pratt Institute, Brooklyn, N.Y., instructor in legal aspects of engineering, 1947-48; St. John's University, School of Law, Brooklyn, N.Y., instructor, 1947-49, assistant professor, 1949-50, associate professor, 1950-51, professor, 1951-61, adjunct professor, 1969-80, distinguished professor of law, 1980—; Foreign Claims Settlement Commission of the United States, Washington, D.C., chairman, 1961-68; assistant secretary of state for Educational and Cultural Affairs, Washington, D.C., 1968-69; U.S. Customs Court (now U.S. Court of International Trade), New York, N.Y., judge, 1969-77, chief judge, 1977—. Visiting professor, Georgetown University, School of Law, 1962-67; New York Law School, adjunct professor, 1972-82, Martin Distinguished Visiting Professor, 1982—. Board of Higher Education of the City of New York, member, 1958-69, member emeritus, 1969—. *Military service:* U.S. Army Air Forces, 1943-47. U.S. Air Force Reserve, Judge Advocate General's Department, retired as colonel; received Air Force Commendation Medal, 1961.

MEMBER: American Bar Association (chairman, international and comparative law section, 1965-67, member, house of delegates, 1976-78), American Society of International Law, Consular Law Society, Judge Advocate's Association, Foreign Law Association (president, 1971-73), Federal Bar Council (president, 1973-74), American Law Institute, American Arbitration Association, National Panel of Arbitrators, National Catholic Educational Association, Reserve Officers Association, New York State Bar Association.

AWARDS, HONORS: Honorary doctorate from University of Aquila, Italy, 1960; Interfaith Award from Morgenstern Foundation, 1961; LL.D. from St. Mary's College (Notre Dame, Ind.), 1968, St. John's University, 1968, Maryville College (St. Louis, Mo.), 1969, New York Law School, 1976, Brooklyn College of the City University of New York, 1978, Nova University, 1980, and Roger Williams College, 1982; L.H.D. from College of Staten Island of the City University of New York, 1982, and DePaul University, 1982; other awards from educational, cultural, religious, and civic organizations.

WRITINGS: Foreign Confiscations in Anglo-American Law, Oceana, 1951; *Brief Writing and Oral Argument,* Oceana, 1951, 5th edition, 1983; (with Lester B. Orfield) *Cases and Materials on International Law,* Bobbs-Merrill, 1955, revised edition, 1965; *Selected Essays on Equity,* Oceana, 1955; (contributor) Grindel, editor, *Concept of Freedom,* Regnery, 1955; (contributor) *Le Regime matrimonial dans les legislations contemporaines,* Institut de Droit Compare de l'Universite de Paris, 1957; (with Zechariah Chafee, Jr.) *Cases and Materials on Equity,* Foundation Press, 1958, 5th edition, 1967.

(Contributor) *International Arbitration: Liber Amicorum for Martin Domke,* Nijhoff, 1967; *Cases and Materials on Equity and Equitable Remedies,* Foundation Press, 1975; *Freedom's Prophet: Selected Writings of Zechariah Chafee, Jr.,* Oceana, 1981; *Cases and Materials on Remedies,* Foundation Press, 1982. Contributor of numerous articles and reviews to legal journals.

* * *

RECHCIGL, Miloslav, Jr. 1930-

PERSONAL: Surname is pronounced "wrecks-eagle"; born July 30, 1930, in Mlada Boleslav, Czechoslovakia; came to U.S. in 1950, naturalized in 1955; son of Miloslav (a member of the parliament of the First Czechoslovakian Republic) and Marie (Rajtrova) Rechcigl; married Eva Marie Edwards, August 23, 1953; children: John Edward, Karen Marie. *Education:* Cornell University, B.S., 1954, M.N.S., 1955, Ph.D., 1958. *Home:* 1703 Mark Lane, Rockville, Md. 20852. *Office:* Agency for International Development, U.S. Department of State, Washington, D.C. 20523.

CAREER: Cornell University, Ithaca, N.Y., research associate in department of biochemistry, 1958; U.S. Public Health Service, National Cancer Institute, Bethesda, Md., research fellow, 1958-60, senior investigator, laboratory of biochemistry, 1960-68, grants associate, 1968-69; U.S. Department of Health, Education, and Welfare, Health Services and Mental Health Administration, Washington, D.C., special assistant for nutrition and health to the director of Regional Medical Programs Service, 1969-70; U.S. Department of State, Agency for International Development, Washington, D.C., nutrition advisor,

1970—, Office of Research and Institutional Grants, assistant director, 1973-74, acting director, 1974-75, director of interregional research staff, 1975-78, chief of Research and Methodology Division, 1979—, currently research advisor to Office of the Science Advisor.

Executive secretary, nutritional advisory committee of Health Service and Mental Health Administration, U.S. Department of Health, Education and Welfare, 1969-70, and Research and Institutional Grants Council, 1970-74, and research advisory committee, 1971—, both Agency for International Development; Agency for International Development representative, U.S. Department of State USC/FAR Committee, 1972—; delegate to White House Conference on Food, Nutrition and Health, 1969, and Agricultural Research Policy Advisory Committee, U.S. Department of Agriculture, Working Conference on Research to Meet United States and World Food Needs, 1975. Consultant, U.S. Department of Agriculture, 1969-70, U.S. Department of Treasury, 1973, U.S. Office of Technology Assessment, 1977—, and U.S. Food and Drug Administration, 1979—.

MEMBER: International Society for Cell Biology, International Society for Research on Civilization Diseases and Vital Substances, International College of Applied Nutrition (fellow), Society for International Development, Intercontinental Biographical Association (fellow), International Platform Association, Czechoslovak Society of Arts and Sciences (director-at-large, 1968-72; vice-president, 1968-74; president, 1974-78; member of presidential collegium, 1978—; program chairman of 1st Congress, 1962, and 2nd Congress, 1964; chairman of nominating committee, 1979), Society for Geochemistry and Health, Society for Developmental Biology, Society for Biological Rhythm, Society of Research Administrators, Institute of Food Technologists, Society for Experimental Biology and Medicine, History of Science Society, Association for the Advancement of Slavic Studies, American Society of Biological Chemists, American Society for Cell Biology, American Institute of Biological Sciences, American Institute of Animal Science, Federation of American Societies for Experimental Biology, American Public Health Association, American Association for Cancer Research, American Association for the Advancement of Science (fellow), American Chemical Society (member of joint board-council committee on international activities, 1975-76), American Institute of Chemists (fellow and member of council, 1972-74), American Institute of Nutrition, Council of the National Cancer Institute of Scientists, New York Academy of Sciences, Washington Academy of Science (fellow and delegate, 1972—), District of Columbia Institute of Chemists (president-elect, 1971-72; president, 1972-74; councilor, 1974-79), Chemical Society of Washington, Delta Tau Kappa (honorary member), Sigma Xi, Phi Kappa Phi, Cornell Club (Washington, D.C.), Cosmos Club (Washington, D.C.).

WRITINGS: Czechoslovakia and Its Arts and Sciences: A Selective Bibliography in the Western European Languages, Mouton, 1964; (with Zdenek Hruban) *Microbodies and Related Particles: Morphology, Biochemistry, and Physiology,* Academic Press, 1969; *World Food Problem: A Selective Bibliography of Reviews,* CRC Press, 1975.

Editor: *The Czechoslovak Contribution to World Culture,* Mouton, 1964; *Czechoslovakia Past and Present,* Mouton, Volume I: *Political, International, Social and Economic Aspects,* Volume II: *Essays on the Arts and Sciences,* 1968; (and contributor) *Enzyme Synthesis and Degradation in Mammalian Systems,* Karger, 1971; (and compiler with wife, Eva Rechcigl) *Biographical Directory of the Members of the Czechoslovak Society of Arts and Sciences in America, Inc.,* Czechoslovak Society of Arts and Sciences in America, 1972, new edition, 1978; (and contributor) *Food, Nutrition, and Health,* with introduction by Jean Mayer, Karger, 1973; *Man, Food, and Nutrition: Strategies and Technological Measures for Alleviating the World Food Problem,* CRC Press, 1973; *Comparative Animal Nutrition,* Karger, Volume I: *Carbohydrates, Lipids, and Accessory Growth Factors,* 1976, Volume II: *Nutrient Elements and Toxicants,* 1977, Volume III: *Nitrogen, Electrolytes, Water, and Energy Metabolism,* 1979; *Nutrition and the World Food Problem,* Karger, 1979; *Handbook of Nutritional Requirements in a Functional Context,* two volumes, CRC Press, 1981; *Handbook of Agricultural Productivity,* two volumes, CRC Press, 1981.

Contributor: A. A. Albanese, editor, *Newer Methods of Nutritional Biochemistry,* Academic Press, 1963; Catherine E. Forest Weber and George Weber, editors, *Advances in Enzyme Regulation,* Volume II, Pergamon, 1964; F. Homburger, editor, *Progress in Experimental Tumor Research,* Volume X, Karger, 1968; *Handbook of Biochemistry,* CRC Press, 1968, 2nd edition, 1970; Anthony San Pietro, editor, *Regulatory Mechanisms for Protein Synthesis in Mammalian Cells,* Academic Press, 1968; P. L. Horecky, editor, *East Central Europe: A Guide to Basic Publications,* University of Chicago Press, 1969.

Editor-in-chief of CRC Handbook Series in Food and Nutrition, 1977—, and of "Comparative Animal Nutrition" Series, 1977—, both for CRC Press.

Compiler of "Critical Bibliography of the History of Science and Its Cultural Influences" for *Isis* (quarterly of History of Science Society). Contributor to journals. Editor of conference proceedings. Abstractor and translator, *Chemical Abstracts,* 1958—. Chairman of publications committee, Czechoslovak Society of Arts and Sciences in America, and editor of congress proceedings. Co-editor of *International Journal of Cycle Research,* 1969-74; member of editorial board, *The Journal of Applied Nutrition,* 1970—, and *Nutrition Reports International,* 1977-80.

BIOGRAPHICAL/CRITICAL SOURCES: Miloslav Rechcigl, Jr., editor, *The Czechoslovak Contribution to World Culture,* Mouton, 1964.

* * *

REDMOND, Eugene B. 1937-

PERSONAL: Born December 1, 1937, in East St. Louis, Ill.; son of John Henry and Emma (Hutchinson) Redmond. *Education:* Southern Illinois University, B.A., 1964; Washington University, M.A., 1966. *Home:* 1925 Seventh Ave., No. 7L, New York, N.Y. 10026. *Office:* Department of English, California State University, Sacramento, Calif. 95819.

CAREER: East St. Louis Beacon, East St. Louis, Ill., associate editor, 1961-62; *Monitor,* East St. Louis, contributing editor, 1963-65, executive editor, 1965-67, editorial page and contributing editor, 1967—; Southern Illinois University at Edwardsville, East St. Louis branch, teacher-counselor in Experiment in Higher Education, 1967-68, poet-in-residence and director of language workshops, 1968-69; Oberlin College, Oberlin, Ohio, writer-in-residence and lecturer in Afro-American studies, 1969-70; California State University, Sacramento, professor of English and poet-in-residence in ethnic studies,

1970—. Visiting writer-in-residence, Southern University and Agricultural and Mechanical College, 1971-72; instructor of Afro-American literature, Oak Park School of Afro-American Thought, Sacramento City College, 1971; visiting lecturer, University of Leiden, summer, 1978; visiting professor and writer, University of Wisconsin, 1978-79; visiting professor, University of Nigeria, 1980; lecturer and reader at other colleges and universities in the United States and Canada. Coordinator of Annual Third World Writers and Thinkers Symposium, 1972—; director of Henry Dumas Creative Writing Workshop, 1974—, and of Interracial-Intercultural Communications through the Arts, East St. Louis School District, 1977. Founder-publisher, Black River Writers Press. Member of board of directors, Olatunji Counseling Educational Center, East St. Louis, and IMPACT. Member of board and chairman of publicity, Young Disciples Foundation. Senior consultant, Performing Arts Training Center, East St. Louis, 1967—; consultant, Ghetto Communications Workshop Planners. *Military service:* U.S. Marines, 1958-61.

MEMBER: Congress of Racial Equality, American Newspaper Guild, National Newspaper Publishers Association, National Association of African American Educators, California Association of Teachers of English, African Association of Black Studies, California Writers Club, Northern California Black English Teachers Association.

AWARDS, HONORS: First prize, Washington University Annual Festival of the Arts, 1965, for poem "Eye in the Ceiling"; first prize of *Free Lance* (magazine), 1966, for poem "Grandmother"; Literary Achievement Award, Sacramento Regional Arts Council, 1974; Best of the Small Press Award, Pushcart Press, 1976; Poet-Laureate, East St. Louis, Ill., 1976; faculty research award, California State University, Sacramento, 1976; California Arts Council grant, 1977; Illinois Arts Council grant, 1977; New York Council on the Arts grant, 1977-78; National Endowment for the Arts creative writing fellowship, 1978.

WRITINGS—Poetry, except as indicated: *A Tale of Two Toms,* Monitor, 1968; *A Tale of Time and Toilet Tissue,* Monitor, 1969; *Sentry of the Four Golden Pillars,* Black River Writers, 1970; *River of Bones and Flesh and Blood,* Black River Writers, 1971; *Songs from an Afro/Phone,* Black River Writers, 1972; *In a Time of Rain and Desire: New Love Poems,* Black River Writers, 1973; *Consider Loneliness as These Things,* Centro Studi E Scambi Internazionali, 1973; *Drumvoices—The Mission of Afro-American Poetry: A Critical History* (nonfiction), Doubleday-Anchor, 1976.

Editor: (And contributor) *Sides of the River,* Bethany Press, 1969; Henry Dumas, *Ark of Bones, and Other Stories* (fiction), Random House, 1974; Dumas, *Play Ebony, Play Ivory,* Random House, 1974; Dumas, *Jonoah and the Green Stone,* Random House, 1976; *Griefs of Joy: Selected Afro-American Poetry for Students,* Black River Writers, 1977; Dumas, *Rope of Wind, and Other Stories* (fiction), Random House, 1978.

Work represented in anthologies, including: *Tambourine,* Washington University Press, 1966; *The New Black Poetry,* International Publishers, 1969; *Today's Negro Voices,* Simon & Schuster, 1969; *A Galaxy of Black Writing,* Moore Publishing, 1969; *Giant Talk: Anthology of Third World Writings,* Random House, 1974; *open poetry,* Random House, 1975; *A Documentary History of the Little Magazine since 1950,* Pushcart, 1978; *Calafia: The California Poetry,* Y'bird, 1979.

Also author of plays, "Shadows before the Mirror," "Cry Cry Winds through the Throats of Horns and Drums," "Drum Voices," "The Night John Henry Was Born," "If You Need Me Why Don't You Know It?: A Blues Ballet," and "9 Poets with the Blues," performed live and on television in Sacramento, Calif. Contributor to and performer (second lead) in multi-media ballet "Ode to Taylor Jones," produced and directed by Katherine Dunham. Contributor of poetry and articles to numerous journals and newspapers. Contributing editor, *Confrontation: A Journal of Third World Literature.*

WORK IN PROGRESS: Adapting his own work and that of other writers for television.

SIDELIGHTS: Eugene B. Redmond told *CA:* "Motherless and fatherless at age eight, I was raised in part by a grandmother and a group of neighborhood fathers—friends of my older brother and members of the Seventh Day Adventist Church I attended.... I try to make maximum use of formal training and general experience. At the very center of this writer's life and work is the desire and struggle for Black self-determination and respect for basic humanity." Redmond notes that he has been influenced by "Langston Hughes, Melvin Tolson, Theodore Roethke, Smokey Bill Robinson, Yevgeny Yevtushenko, blues, jazz lyrics, and the movement currently underway." He is "concerned with dynamics of Black Block Voting, Black Language, Third World politics and writings, [and feels] indebted to Fannon.... I perform regularly, acting and reading poetry with the Performing Arts Training Center (directed by Katherine Dunham, friend and critic) ..., [and am] involved with music and basic rhythms—the key to 'style' of Black writing. I also play the percussive instruments.... [I] acquired speaking knowledge of Japanese while in Far East with Marines. [I have also] spent some time in Laos."

MEDIA ADAPTATIONS: Redmond has recorded *Bloodlinks and Sacred Places,* readings of his poetry with musical accompaniment.

* * *

REES, Albert (Everett) 1921-

PERSONAL: Born August 21, 1921, in New York, N.Y.; son of Hugo R. and Rosalie (Landman) Rees; married Candida Kranold, July 15, 1945; married second wife, Marianne Russ, June 22, 1963; children: (first marriage) David; (second marriage) Daniel, Jonathan. *Education:* Oberlin College, B.A., 1943; University of Chicago, M.A., 1947, Ph.D., 1950. *Home:* 32 Turner Ct., Princeton, N.J. 08540. *Office:* 630 Fifth Ave., New York, N.Y. 10111.

CAREER: Roosevelt College (now University), Chicago, Ill., instructor in economics, 1947-48; University of Chicago, Chicago, assistant professor, 1948-54, associate professor, 1954-61, professor of economics and chairman of department, 1961-66; Princeton University, Princeton, N.J., professor of economics, 1966-79, provost, 1975-77; Alfred P. Sloan Foundation, New York, N.Y., president, 1979—. Research associate, National Bureau of Economic Research, 1953-54; staff member, Council of Economic Advisers, 1954-55; fellow, Center for Advanced Study in the Behavioral Sciences, 1959-60. Member of board of directors, Social Science Research Council, 1966-72; member, New Jersey Public Employment Relations Commission, 1968-69. *Member:* American Economic Association.

WRITINGS: Real Wages in Manufacturing, 1890-1914, Princeton University Press, 1961; (editor with Earl J. Hamilton and Harry G. Johnson) *Landmarks in Political Economy,* University of Chicago Press, 1962; *The Economics of Trade Unions,*

University of Chicago Press, 1962; (with George P. Shultz) *Workers and Wages in an Urban Labor Market,* University of Chicago Press, 1970; *Economics of Work and Pay,* Harper, 1973; *Striking a Balance: Making National Economic Policy,* University of Chicago Press, 1984. Also editor of *International Encyclopedia of the Social Sciences.*

Contributor: *Interpreting the Labor Movement,* Industrial Relations Research Association, 1952; *The Measurement and Behavior of Unemployment,* Princeton University Press, 1957; Philip D. Bradley, editor, *The Public Stake in Union Power,* University Press of Virginia, 1959; *Wages, Prices, Profits, and Productivity,* American Assembly, Graduate School of Business, Columbia University, 1959; *The Price Statistics of the Federal Government,* National Bureau of Economic Research, 1961. Contributor of about twenty articles to economic, labor relations, and business journals. Editor, *Journal of Political Economy,* 1954-59.

* * *

REES, Joan 1927-
(Joan Alice Gladys Rees; pseudonyms: June Avery, Ann Bedford, Susan Strong)

PERSONAL: Born May 8, 1927, in London, England; daughter of George William Robert (a company director) and Alice (Bedford) Rees; married Frank Louis Cyprien (a visual aids adviser), April 20, 1965. *Education:* University of London, Diploma in Literature. *Politics:* "Internationally-minded liberal." *Religion:* Unaffiliated. *Home:* Flat 20, Harraby Green, Broadstone, Dorsetshire BH18 8NG, England. *Agent:* J. F. Gibson's Literary Agency, Box 173, London SW3, England.

CAREER: Journal of British Kinematograph Society, London, England, editorial assistant, 1953-55; United Nations Food and Agriculture Organization, Rome, Italy, editorial assistant, 1957-64; writer. *Member:* Society of Authors, Romantic Novelists Association, Jane Austen Society, Keats-Shelley Memorial Association.

WRITINGS: First Adventure, John Gresham, 1962; *Lesson of Love,* John Gresham, 1962; *Voyage to Happiness,* John Gresham, 1963; *Ticket to Romance,* John Gresham, 1963; *Crossroads of Love,* John Gresham, 1964; *Bright Star: The Story of John Keats and Fanny Brawne,* Harrap, 1968; *The Queen of Hearts,* R. Hale, 1974; *Jane Austen: Woman and Writer,* St. Martin's, 1976; *The Bride in Blue,* R. Hale, 1978; *The Lass from the Sea,* R. Hale, 1979; *The Winter Queen,* R. Hale, 1983. Also author of *The Summer of 1560,* 1977. Author of short stories.

Under name Joan Alice Gladys Rees, published by John Gresham: *First Love,* 1965; *Between Strangers,* 1967; *The Decoy,* 1967.

Under pseudonym June Avery: *Voyage of Dreams,* John Gresham, 1967.

Under pseudonym Ann Bedford: *Adventure in Rome,* John Gresham, 1965.

Under pseudonym Susan Strong; published by R. Hale: *This Thing Called Love,* 1969; *My Own True Love,* 1971; *Error of Judgement,* 1977; *Love Remembered,* 1979; *Will to Love,* 1982; *Drama of Love,* 1982; *By Love Cast Out,* 1982.

WORK IN PROGRESS: A biography of Shelley's Jane Williams; a Bronte study.

SIDELIGHTS: Joan Rees has spent a number of months in India and visited many other countries, including Thailand, North Africa, and Australia. *Avocational interests:* Music and the theater.

BIOGRAPHICAL/CRITICAL SOURCES: Good Housekeeping (British edition), January, 1964; *Times* (London), August 5, 1968.

* * *

REES, Joan Alice Gladys
See REES, Joan

* * *

REEVES, Joyce 1911-
(Joyce Gard)

PERSONAL: Born in 1911, in London, England. *Education:* Lady Margaret Hall, Oxford, B.A. *Home:* 1 Eliza Cottages, Charing, Ashford, Kent TN27 0JG, England.

CAREER: Author. Served as an administrative officer with the Ministry of Economic Warfare, London, England, and with the Supreme Headquarters of the Allied Expeditionary Force, Frankfurt, Germany, 1940-45; studio potter, 1947-56; has also taught school and worked for a literary agent. *Member:* Society of Authors.

WRITINGS—All under pseudonym, Joyce Gard: (Adaptor) Jules Verne, *Journey to the Centre of the Earth,* Hutchinson Educational, 1961; *Woorroo* (illustrated by Ronald Benham), Gollancz, 1961; *The Dragon of the Hill,* Gollancz, 1963; *Talargain the Seal's Whelp,* Gollancz, 1964, published as *Talargain,* Holt, 1965; *Smudge of the Fells,* Gollancz, 1965, Holt, 1966; *The Snow Firing,* Gollancz, 1967, Holt, 1968; *The Mermaid's Daughter,* Holt, 1969; *Handysides Shall Not Fall,* Kaye & Ward, 1975; *The Hagwaste Donkeys,* Pelham Books, 1976.

Under name Joyce Reeves, translator from the French on the subject of contemporary art. Contributor of book reviews to the *Times Literary Supplement, Growing Point,* and *Junior Bookshelf.*

SIDELIGHTS: Joyce Reeves uses a combination of fact and fiction in her novels, which have been highly praised by numerous book reviewers. "Vivid, excellent writing, the skillful blending of fantasy and history and a plot filled with suspense make this an outstanding work," commented a *New York Times* critic about the author's novel, *Talargain.*

Of the *The Mermaid's Daughter,* a review in the *Times Literary Supplement* said: "The rich and rapturous telling will undoubtedly thrill . . . impressionable adolescent girls of sensibility and spirituality."

"Writing was the only thing I ever wanted to do, but owing to circumstances beyond my control, I was not able to get down to it seriously till rather late in life," Reeves told *CA.* "I staked my hopes on a novel for adults which caused me much mental torment, but it failed to find a publisher. In the aftermath there sprang up a happy crop of children's novels which came, not easily—writing is never easy for me—but at least without anguish. Just as suddenly that harvest ended.

"I have never been able to make books at will, even when it was essential to pay the bills, and my last attempt at a children's novel simply didn't work. It was set in the Shetland Islands—I was there before they discovered North Sea oil—a remote and beautiful landscape of barren moorland rich in archaeological sites, which drew my spirit with magnetic force away from fiction and into the prehistoric past. Since then I have been digging deeper and deeper into archaeology and am now working on a book on Britain in the Dark Ages.

"One of the nicest things that happened to me as a children's writer was when two rather special American children's librarians, Cornelia Jones and Olivia Way, came to see me in London and subsequently included me in their book, *British Children's Writers*. . . . I was so pleased to be numbered among their selection."

AVOCATIONAL INTERESTS: Contemporary art, archaeology, gardening, and listening to classical music.

BIOGRAPHICAL/CRITICAL SOURCES: New York Times Book Review, May 23, 1964; *Times Literary Supplement*, June 26, 1969; Cornelia Jones and Olivia Way, *British Children's Writers*, American Library Association, 1976.

* * *

REID, Barbara 1922-

PERSONAL: Born April 18, 1922, in New York, N.Y.; daughter of Louis Raymond (a newspaperman) and Helen (Dickey) Reid. *Education:* Wheaton College, Norton, Mass., B.A. (magna cum laude), 1942. *Politics:* Registered Democrat. *Religion:* Episcopalian. *Home:* 138 West 11th St., New York, N.Y. 10011.

CAREER: Writer. Previously worked as secretary and editorial assistant, Frederick R. Rinehart Co., New York, N.Y. *Member:* Author's Guild of America, Poets and Writers, Phi Beta Kappa. *Awards, honors:* Grants from Mary Roberts Rinehart Foundation, 1967, and P.E.N., 1983.

WRITINGS: (Ghost writer) *Horace Havemeyer, 1886-1956*, privately printed by Havemeyer family, 1957; *Carlo's Cricket* (juvenile), McGraw, 1967; *Miguel and His Racehorse* (juvenile), Morrow, 1974; *The Tears of San Lorenzo* (novella), Apple-Wood, 1977; (with sister-in-law, Ewa Malewicz Reid) *The Cobbler's Reward* (juvenile), Macmillan, 1978; (contributor) William Abrahams, editor, *Prize Stories, 1981: The O. Henry Awards*, Prentice-Hall, 1981.

Also author of novel *Moon in the Yellow River*, as yet unpublished. Contributor of articles and stories to magazines and journals, including *Harper's Bazaar*, *Ladies' Home Journal*, *Sewanee Review*, *Hudson Review*, *Descant*, and *Quartet*.

WORK IN PROGRESS: A short story.

SIDELIGHTS: Barbara Reid has traveled and lived abroad a good deal, particularly in France, Italy, and England.

* * *

REID, Clyde H. 1928-

PERSONAL: Born December 13, 1928, in Peoria, Ill.; son of Clyde Henderson (a businessman) and Marguerite (Barham) Reid; married second wife, Jennifer Hewitt Kraut, February 12, 1972 (divorced, 1980); children: (first marriage) Laurie Beth, Eric James, Robin Joye; (second marriage) Kelton Jud. *Education:* Bradley University, B.S., 1949; Pacific School of Religion, M.A., 1952, B.D., 1953; Boston University, Th.D., 1960; postdoctoral study, Menninger Foundation, 1964-65, and C. G. Jung Institute, Zurich, 1972-73. *Home:* 1035 Tantra Park Circle, Boulder, Colo. 80303.

CAREER: Clergyman of United Church of Christ. Bradley University, Peoria, Ill., assistant dean of students, 1949-50; University Congregational Church, Seattle, Wash., minister to students, 1953-54; minister of Congregational churches in Seattle, 1954-57, and Dunstable, Mass., 1957-59; Union Theological Seminary, New York City, assistant professor of practical theology, 1960-64; United Church of Christ, Board for Homeland Ministries, New York City, secretary for evangelism, 1965-67; Institute for Advanced Pastoral Studies, Bloomfield Hills, Mich., associate director, 1967-70; Iliff School of Theology, Denver, Colo., associate professor, 1971-74; Center for New Beginnings, Denver, executive director, 1974-80; psychotherapist in private practice, 1980—. Member of faculty, Colorado Institute for Transpersonal Psychology. Lecturer and leader of retreats, conferences and workshops throughout North America. *Member:* International Communication Association, Society for the Advancement of Continuing Education for Ministry, Association for Humanistic Psychology, Society for the Scientific Study of Religion, American Association of Pastoral Counselors (diplomate), Association for Past Life Research and Therapy (member of board of directors).

WRITINGS: I Belong, United Church Press, 1964; *Why I Belong*, United Church Press, 1964; *The God-Evaders*, Harper, 1966; *The Empty Pulpit*, Harper, 1967; (contributor) *The Creative Role of Interpersonal Groups in the Church Today*, Association Press, 1968; *Groups Alive—Church Alive*, Harper, 1969; *21st-Century Man Emerging*, Pilgrim, 1971; *Help! I've Been Fired*, Pilgrim, 1971; *Celebrate the Temporary*, Harper, 1972; *Let It Happen*, Harper, 1973; *The Return to Faith*, Harper, 1974; (contributor) *You and Communication in the Church*, Word Books, 1974; *You Can Choose Christmas*, Word Books, 1975; *Dreams: Discovering Your Inner Teacher*, Winston Press, 1983. Contributor to *Christian Century* and religious education journals. Guest editor, special issue of *Pastoral Psychology*, March, 1967.

WORK IN PROGRESS: Journey Inward: Journey Out Past Life, Present Life.

SIDELIGHTS: Clyde H. Reid told *CA*: "I continue to explore the frontiers between spirituality and psychology. One of the most fertile areas for my research in this convergence is the exploration of Jungian psychology with its emphasis on the deeper Self and the unfolding patterns in the human psyche. Past life therapy is one of the exciting frontiers this work has led me into." *The Empty Pulpit* has been translated into German.

BIOGRAPHICAL/CRITICAL SOURCES: Pastoral Psychology, March, 1967.

* * *

REISMAN, Arnold 1934-

PERSONAL: Born August 2, 1934, in Lodz, Poland; naturalized U.S. citizen; son of Isidor and Rose (Yoskowitz) Reisman; married second wife, Ellen G. Kronheim, August 3, 1980; children: (first marriage) Miriam, Ada, Deborah, Nina. *Education:* University of California, Los Angeles, B.S., 1955, M.S., 1957, Ph.D., 1963. *Religion:* Jewish. *Home:* 18428 Parkland Dr., Shaker Heights, Ohio 44122. *Office:* Department of Operations Research, Case Western Reserve University, Cleveland, Ohio 44106.

CAREER: City of Los Angeles, Calif., assistant mechanical engineer in department of water and power, 1955-57; California State College at Los Angeles (now California State University,

Los Angeles), assistant professor, 1957-61, associate professor of engineering, 1961-66; University of Wisconsin—Milwaukee, visiting associate professor of engineering and business administration, 1966-67, visiting associate professor of engineering, 1967-68; Case Western Reserve University, Cleveland, Ohio, associate professor, 1968—, professor of operations research, 1971—. Visiting professor, University of Hawaii, 1971, Hebrew University of Jerusalem and Japan-America Institute of Management Science, both 1975, Ben Gurion University, 1984. Associate research engineer, Western Management Science Institute, 1964-65; vice-president, University Associates, Inc., Cleveland, 1968—. Member of board of directors of several corporations and nonprofit institutions. Consultant to federal departments, health service institutions, and to industry.

MEMBER: Operations Research Society of America, Institute of Management Sciences, American Society of Mechanical Engineers, American Association for the Advancement of Science (fellow; former member of council), American Society for Engineering Education, American Institute of Industrial Engineers (senior member), American Association of University Professors, Society for Advanced Medical Systems (fellow), New York Academy of Sciences, Phi Delta Kappa, Sigma Xi. *Awards, honors:* Named among outstanding educators in America, 1971; named engineer of the year for the city of Cleveland, 1973.

WRITINGS: (Editor and contributor) *Engineering: A Look Inward, a Reach Outward*, University of Wisconsin Press, 1967; *Engineering Economics: A Unified Approach*, Reinhold, 1970; *Managerial and Engineering Economics: A Unified Approach*, Allyn & Bacon, 1971; (with Burton V. Dean, Michael Salvador, and Muhittin Oral) *Industrial Inventory Control*, Gordon & Breach, 1972; (editor with Michael D. Mesarovic) *Systems Approach and the City*, North Holland Publishing, 1972; (with A. K. Rao) *Discounted Cash Flow Analysis: Stochastic Extensions*, American Institute of Industrial Engineers, 1973; (editor with M. L. Kiley and contributor) *Health Care Delivery Planning*, Gordon & Breach, 1973; *Systems Analysis in Health-Care*, Lexington Books, 1979; *Materials Management for Health Services*, Lexington Books, 1981; (with Jon D. Clark) *Computer System Selection: An Integrated Approach*, Praeger, 1981; (with wife, Ellen Reisman) *Welcome Tomorrow*, North Coast Publishing, 1982; *Enfoque de sistemas en la administracion de materiales en hospitales*, Pan American Health Organization, 1983.

Contributor: E. S. Buffa, editor, *Models for Production and Operations Management*, Wiley, 1963; Buffa, editor, *Readings in Production and Operations Management*, Wiley, 1966; Leslie Holliday, editor, *Integration of Technologies*, Hutchinson, 1966; Richard H. P. Kraft, editor, *Strategies of Educational Planning*, Florida State University Press, 1968; E. F. Schlifer, editor, *Library System Distribution Network Design*, Jerusalem Academic Press, 1973; J. W. Clark, editor, *Clinical Dentistry*, Harper, 1977.

Also contributor to J. R. Longstreet and W. G. Modrow, editors, *Readings in Finance*, D. M. Mark, H. Aly and D. M. Albanito, editors, *Models in Financial Management*, Holden-Day, R. L. Schultz and D. P. Slevin, editors, *Implementing Operations Research/Management Science*, American Elsevier, and *International Handbook on Data Processing*, 1977. Editor, "Operations Management" series, Wiley, 1972—. Author of a number of research reports. Contributor of more than one hundred articles to scholarly and professional journals.

REMINGTON, Robin Alison 1938-

PERSONAL: Born January 15, 1938, in Boston, Mass.; daughter of Bradford Austin and Mabelle (Therrien) Remington; married Paul Wallace. *Education:* Southwest Texas State College (now University), A.B., 1958; Indiana University, M.A., 1961, Ph.D., 1966. *Home:* 1707 University Ave., Columbia, Mo. 65201. *Office:* Department of Political Science, University of Missouri, Columbia, Mo. 65211.

CAREER: Massachusetts Institute of Technology, Cambridge, research associate in communist studies, Center for International Studies, 1966-73, lecturer in humanities department, 1970; University of Missouri—Columbia, associate professor, 1974-80, professor of political science, 1980—. Visiting lecturer, Boston University, 1972-73, and Yale University, 1973-74. Exchange scholar to Belgrade, Yugoslavia, Institute of International Politics and Economics, 1970-71.

MEMBER: American Political Science Association, American Association for Southeast European Studies (member of executive council, 1976-77). *Awards, honors:* Fulbright fellow, 1981; American Council of Learned Societies grant, 1982; University of Missouri—Columbia Alumnae Anniversary Award, 1983.

WRITINGS: (Editor) *Winter in Prague: Documents on Czechoslovak Communism in Crisis*, MIT Press, 1969; *The Warsaw Pact: Case Studies in Communist Conflict Resolution*, MIT Press, 1971; *The International Relations of Eastern Europe: A Guide to Information Sources*, Gale, 1978.

Contributor: John Wells and Maria Wilhelm, editors, *The People vs. Presidential War*, Dunellen Publishing, 1970; Catherine McArdle Kelleher, editor, *Political-Military Systems: Comparative Perspectives*, Sage Publications, Inc., 1974; Frank B. Horton III and others, editors, *Comparative Defense Policy*, Johns Hopkins University Press, 1974.

William E. Griffiths, editor, *The Soviet Empire: Expansion and Detente*, Lexington Books, 1976; Charles Gati, editor, *The International Politics of Eastern Europe*, Praeger, 1976; Gary K. Bertsch and Thomas W. Ganschow, editors, *Comparative Communism: The Soviet, Chinese, and Yugoslav Models*, W. H. Freeman, 1976; Judy Bertelsen, editor, *Nonstate Nations in International Politics: Comparative System Analyses*, Praeger, 1977; Jerzy J. Wiatr and Richard Rose, editors, *Comparing Public Policies*, PAN (Warsaw), 1977; Dale Herspring and Ivan Volyges, editors, *Comparative Communist Civil-Military Relations*, Westview, 1978; Phillip Petersen, editor, *Soviet Policy in the Post-Tito Balkans: Studies in Communist Affairs*, Volume IV, U.S. Government Printing Office, 1979; Teresa Rakowska-Harmstone and Andrew Gyorgy, editors, *Communism in Eastern Europe*, Indiana University Press, 1979.

V. V. Aspaturian and others, editors, *Eurocommunism between East and West*, Indiana University Press, 1981; Stephen Fischer-Galati, editor, *Eastern Europe in the 1980s*, Westview, 1981; Roger E. Kanet, editor, *Soviet Foreign Policy in the 1980s*, Praeger, 1982; Bojana Tadic and Ranko Petkovic, editors, *Nonalignment in the Eighties*, [Belgrade], 1982; Daniel E. Nelson, editor, *Soviet Allies: The Warsaw Pact and the Issue of Reliability*, Westview, 1983.

Contributor to *East European Quarterly, Survey, Orbis, Current History*, and other journals.

WORK IN PROGRESS: An essay, "Functions of Nonalignment: A Cross-Systems Comparison of Domestic-Foreign Policy Linkages in India and Yugoslavia"; research into "the usefulness of the 'penetration' model of Communist civil-military relations using Yugoslav and Polish case-studies."

SIDELIGHTS: "My research is devoted to the study of Communist political systems," Robin Alison Remington told *CA*, "because I am concerned that an overwhelming amount of American policy-making time, energy, and resources is dissipated due to our stereotypic fears of these societies. I genuinely believe that understanding the world we live in is as important to defense as the 1984 $305 billion budget proposed by this administration. Ignorance is more expensive than the MX missile. Moreover, the political/economic imperatives of the North-South dialogue can not be buried in East-West rhetoric. Both superpowers in the 1980s have an increasing problem of translating their undeniable power into influence."

* * *

RENKEN, Aleda 1907-

PERSONAL: Born June 21, 1907, in Jefferson City, Mo.; daughter of John L. and Lilly (Kaeppel) Beck; married C. J. Renken (a Civil Service employee), June 14, 1931; children: John, Elizabeth (Mrs. Terrance Boone), Tim, Anne (Mrs. Anthony Marshall), Steve. *Education:* Attended Warrensburg Teachers College, University of Missouri, and Lincoln University, Jefferson City, Mo. *Religion:* Lutheran. *Home:* Route 2, Holts Summit, Mo.

CAREER: Department of Conservation, Jefferson City, Mo., circulation manager of *Conservationist*, beginning 1953; currently free-lance writer. *Member:* Jefferson City Writers Guild. *Awards, honors:* Writer of the Year award from Missouri State Writers Guild.

WRITINGS—Juvenile; published by Concordia, except as indicated: *Kathy*, F. Watts, 1967; *Never the Same Again*, Westminster, 1971; *Jeff and the Bad Guy*, 1973; *Picked-on Pat*, 1973; *Rough Rapids Ahead*, 1974; *The Two Christmases*, 1974; *Adventure on Padre Island*, 1975; *Mystery of Cottage Cove*, 1975; *Trouble at Briden High*, 1978; *Grandma Haley*, 1981; *Donnie's Dangers*, 1981; *Pat's Problem*, 1981. Contributor of articles and short stories to *Conservationist*, *Wee Wisdom*, and *Cresset*.

AVOCATIONAL INTERESTS: Fishing, hiking, oil painting, and bowling.†

* * *

RESCHER, Nicholas 1928-

PERSONAL: Born July 15, 1928, in Germany; naturalized U.S. citizen in 1944; son of Erwin Hans (an attorney) and Meta (Landau) Rescher; first married in 1951; married second wife, Dorothy Henle, February 10, 1968; children: Elizabeth, Mark, Owen, Catherine. *Education:* Queens College (now Queens College of the City University of New York), B.S., 1949; Princeton University, M.A., 1950, Ph.D., 1951. *Home:* 5818 Aylesboro Ave., Pittsburgh, Pa. 15217. *Office:* Department of Philosophy, University of Pittsburgh, Pittsburgh, Pa. 15260.

CAREER: Princeton University, Princeton, N.J., instructor in philosophy, 1951-52; RAND Corp., Santa Monica, Calif., research mathematician, 1954-57; Lehigh University, Bethlehem, Pa., associate professor of philosophy, 1957-61; University of Pittsburgh, Pittsburgh, Pa., professor of philosophy, 1961-70, university professor, 1970—, director of Center for Philosophy of Science, 1981—. *Military service:* U.S. Marine Corps, 1952-54. *Member:* International Union of History and Philosophy of Science (secretary general, 1970-75), Royal Asiatic Society of Great Britain and Ireland (fellow), Sigma Xi. *Awards, honors:* Ford Foundation fellow, 1959-60; L.H.D., Loyola University (Chicago), 1970; Guggenheim fellow, 1971-72; honorary member, Corpus Christi College, Oxford University, 1975.

WRITINGS: On the Probability of Nonrecurring Events, Holt, 1959; (with Olaf Helmer-Hirschberg) *On the Epistemology of the Inexact Sciences*, RAND Corporation, 1960; *An Introduction to Logic*, St. Martin's, 1964; *Hypothetical Reasoning*, North-Holland Publishing, 1964; *The Logic of Commands*, Routledge & Kegan Paul, 1966; *Temporal Modalities in Arabic Logic*, Reidel, 1967; *The Philosophy of Leibniz*, Prentice-Hall, 1967; *Distributive Justice: A Constructive Critique of the Utilitarian Theory of Distribution*, Bobbs-Merrill, 1967; *Topics in Philosophical Logic*, Reidel, 1968; *Many-Valued Logic*, McGraw, 1969; *Introduction to Value Theory*, Prentice-Hall, 1969; (editor with Kurt Baier) *Values and the Future*, Free Press, 1969.

Scientific Explanation, Free Press, 1970; (editor and contributor) *Essays in Honor of Carl G. Hempel*, Reidel, 1970; (with Michael E. Marmura) *The Refutation by Alexander of Aphrodisias of Galen's Treatise on the First Mover*, Karachi Publications of the Central Institute of Islamic Research, 1970; (with Alastair Urquhart) *Temporal Logic*, Springer-Verlag, 1971; *Conceptual Idealism*, Basil Blackwell, 1973; *The Coherence Theory of Truth*, Clarendon Press, 1973; *The Primacy of Practice*, Basil Blackwell, 1973; *Studies in Modality*, Basil Blackwell, 1974; *A Theory of Possibility: A Constructivistic Conceptualistic Account of Possible Individuals and Possible Worlds*, Basil Blackwell, 1975; *Plausible Reasoning: An Introduction to the Theory and Practice of Plausibilistic Inference*, Van Gorcum, 1976; *Methodological Pragmatism: A Systems-Theoretic Approach to the Theory of Knowledge*, New York University Press, 1977; *Dialectics: A Controversy-Oriented Approach to the Theory of Knowledge*, State University of New York Press, 1977; *Peirce's Philosophy of Science*, University of Notre Dame Press, 1978; *Cognitive Systematization*, Rowman & Littlefield, 1979; (with Robert Brandom) *The Logic of Inconsistency: A Study in Nonstandard Possible-World Semantics and Ontology*, Rowman & Littlefield, 1979; *Leibniz: An Introduction to His Philosophy*, Rowman & Littlefield, 1979.

Scepticism, Rowman & Littlefield, 1980; *Empirical Inquiry*, Rowman & Littlefield, 1981; *Leibniz's Philosophy of Nature: A Group of Essays*, Reidel, 1981; *Mid-Journey: An Unfinished Autobiography*, University Press of America, 1982; *Risk: A Philosophical Introduction to the Theory of Risk Evaluation and Management*, University Press of America, 1982.

All published by University of Pittsburgh Press: *Al-Farabi: An Annotated Bibliography*, 1962; (translator and author of introduction and notes) Al-Farabi, *Short Commentary on Aristotle's "Prior Analytics"*, 1963; *Studies in the History of Arabic Logic*, 1963; *The Development of Arabic Logic*, 1964; *Al-Kindi: An Annotated Bibliography*, 1964; (editor) *Galen and the Syllogism: An Examination of the Thesis That Galen Originated the Fourth Figure of the Syllogism in the Light of New Data from Arabic Sources*, 1966; (editor) *The Logic of Decision and Action* (essays), 1967; *Studies in Arabic Philosophy*, 1968; *Essays* in *Philosophical Analysis: Historical and Systematic,* 1969; *Welfare: The Social Issues in Philosophical Perspective,* 1972; *A Theory of Possibility,* 1975; *Unselfishness: The Role of the Vicarious Affects In Moral Philosophy and Social Theory,* 1975; *Scientific Progress: A Philosophical Essay on the Economics of Research in Natural Science,* 1978; *Unpopular Essays on Technological Progress,* 1980; *Induction,* 1980. Editor of *American Philosophical Quarterly,* 1964—.

WORK IN PROGRESS: A book entitled *The Limits of Science.*

SIDELIGHTS: Nicholas Rescher writes *CA* that he believes that "writing is a tool of inquiry in philosophy. We are never fully clear about our ideas until we set them down on paper with the I's dotted and the T's crossed. Accordingly, *nulla dies sine linea* is a sound motto for a philosopher."

The Primacy of Practice and *Cognitive Systematization* have been translated into Spanish; *Dialectics: A Controversy-Oriented Approach to the Theory of Knowledge* has been translated into Japanese; *Scientific Progress: A Philosophical Essay on the Economics of Research in Natural Science* has been translated into German.

AVOCATIONAL INTERESTS: Historical and biographical reading.

BIOGRAPHICAL/CRITICAL SOURCES: Times Literary Supplement, October 19, 1973, April 19, 1974, August 22, 1980; Ernest Sosa, editor, *The Philosophy of Nicholas Rescher,* Reidel, 1979; Robert Almeder, editor, *Praxis and Reason: Studies in the Philosophy of Nicholas Rescher,* University Press of America, 1982.

* * *

REUTHER, Ruth E. 1917-

PERSONAL: Born February 27, 1917, in Gainesville, Tex.; daughter of Edwin Jerry (a railroad clerk) and Grace (Patrick) Huffaker; married James Richard Reuther (an optometrist), January 26, 1941; children: Alma Grace (Mrs. B. E. Richardson). *Education:* Cooke County Junior College, A.A., 1936; North Texas State Teachers College (now North Texas State University), B.S., 1938; additional study at Midwestern University (now Midwestern State University) and Oklahoma University. *Politics:* Democrat. *Religion:* Baptist. *Home:* 4450 Phillips, Wichita Falls, Tex. 76308.

CAREER: Free-lance writer. Teacher in Wichita Falls, Tex., 1958-73. Former member of Gainesville Community Circus. *Member:* International Reading Association, National Federation of Poets, National Education Association, Texas State Teacher's Association, Texas Parents and Teachers (life member), Poetry Society of Texas (past vice-president), Wichita County Historical Commission, Wichita Falls Poetry Society (past president), Order of the Eastern Star, Kappa Delta Pi, Delta Kappa Gamma. *Awards, honors:* Cokesbury Award runner-up, 1971; awards from Poetry Society of Texas, 1976, and National Federation of Poets, 1983.

WRITINGS: Wife of Four Hobbies, Pageant, 1957; *Gray C: Circus Horse* (juvenile), Houghton, 1970; *Texas Is My Home,* Foundation Publishers, 1982; *A Century of Faithful Witness,* Evans, 1983. Contributor of short stories and articles on meditation to numerous magazines.

WORK IN PROGRESS: A religious novel; a children's book.

SIDELIGHTS: Ruth E. Reuther told *CA:* "I prefer to write children's books because it is my belief that if you write a good one, you are 'writing a memory.' I have also found that writing a memory of God's children can be a rewarding experience. Each of us has one book we remember best from childhood. I hope that *Gray C: Circus Horse* will be that book for some child." *Avocational interests:* Gardening, photography.

* * *

REYNOLDS, Clark G(ilbert) 1939-

PERSONAL: Born December 11, 1939, in Pasadena, Calif.; son of William Gilbert (a golf professional) and Alma (Clark) Reynolds; married Constance Caine, August 3, 1963; children: Dwight Dale, Ward William, Colleen Elizabeth. *Education:* University of California, Santa Barbara, B.A., 1961; Duke University, M.A., 1963, Ph.D., 1964. *Office address:* P.O. Box 986, Mt. Pleasant, S.C. 29464.

CAREER: U.S. Naval Academy, Annapolis, Md., assistant professor of history, 1964-68; University of Maine, Orono, associate professor, 1968-74, professor of history, 1974-76; chairman and professor of humanities, U.S. Merchant Marine Academy, 1976-78; curator, Patriots Point Naval and Maritime Museum, 1978—. *Member:* North American Society for Oceanic History, American Historical Association, American Military Institute, U.S. Naval Institute.

WRITINGS: (With J. J. Clark) *Carrier Admiral,* McKay, 1967; *The Fast Carriers: The Forging of an Air Navy,* McGraw, 1968; *Command of the Sea: The History and Strategy of Maritime Empires,* Morrow, 1974, revised edition published in two volumes, 1983; *Famous American Admirals,* Van Nostrand, 1978; *The Carrier War,* Time-Life, 1982. Contributor to journals, including *American Neptune, Royal United Services Institution Journal* (England), and *Military Affairs.*

WORK IN PROGRESS: The Fighting Lady; Admiral John H. Towers and the Rise of Naval Aviation.

BIOGRAPHICAL/CRITICAL SOURCES: New York Times Book Review, January 12, 1969; *U.S. Naval Institute Proceedings,* October, 1973.

* * *

REYNOLDS, Paul Davidson 1938-

PERSONAL: Born March 5, 1938, in Mattoon, Ill.; son of John Tom (a petroleum engineer) and Barbara (Barteldes) Reynolds; married Anne-Marie Therese Lair (a college professor), 1965; children: Christopher Mosdale, Nicole. *Education:* University of Kansas, B.S., 1960; Stanford University, M.B.A., 1964, M.A., 1966, Ph.D., 1969. *Home:* 4222 Grimes Ave.S., Minneapolis, Minn. 55416. *Office:* Department of Sociology, University of Minnesota, Minneapolis, Minn. 55455.

CAREER: San Francisco State College (now University), San Francisco, Calif., lecturer in sociology, 1967-68; University of California, Riverside, assistant professor of sociology, 1968-70; University of Minnesota, Minneapolis, assistant professor, 1970-72, associate professor, 1972-80, professor of sociology, 1980—. Consultant to American Psychological Association, 1971, and UNESCO, 1975-76. *Military service:* U.S. Army, Ordnance Corps, 1960-61, 1962; became first lieutenant. U.S. Army Reserve, 1962-68. *Member:* American Sociological Association, American Association for the Advancement of Science.

WRITINGS: A Primer in Theory Construction, Bobbs-Merrill, 1971; (contributor) I. Drapkin and E. Viano, editors, *Victim-*

ology: A New Focus, Heath, 1975; (compiler) *Value Dilemmas Associated with the Development and Application of Social Science,* UNESCO, 1975; *Ethical Dilemmas and Social Science Research,* Jossey-Bass, 1979; *Ethics and Social Science Research,* Prentice-Hall, 1982. Contributor to *International Social Science Journal, Behavioral Science, Journal of Educational Psychology, American Sociological Review,* and other publications.

WORK IN PROGRESS: Organizations: The Major Issues.

SIDELIGHTS: Paul Davidson Reynolds wrote *CA:* "Words are difficult material for expressing ideas, but the best we have."

* * *

RICE, Anne 1941-

PERSONAL: Born October 4, 1941, in New Orleans, La.; daughter of Howard (a sculptor) and Katherine (Allen) O'Brien; married Stan Rice (a poet), October 14, 1961; children: Michele (deceased), Christopher. *Education:* Texas Woman's University, student, 1959-60; San Francisco State College (now University), B.A., 1964, M.A., 1971; graduate study at University of California, Berkeley, 1969-70. *Home:* 3887 17th St., San Francisco, Calif. 94114.

CAREER: Writer. Held a variety of jobs, sometimes two at a time, including waitress, cook, theater usherette, and insurance claims examiner. *Member:* Authors Guild. *Awards, honors:* Joseph Henry Jackson Award, honorable mention, 1970.

WRITINGS: Interview with the Vampire, Knopf, 1976; *The Feast of All Saints,* Simon & Schuster, 1980; *Cry to Heaven,* Knopf, 1982. Contributor of numerous book reviews to *San Francisco Chronicle* and *San Francisco Bay Guardian.*

WORK IN PROGRESS: A sequel to *Interview with the Vampire;* a novel, *A Dark and Secret Place,* "about an orphan boy involved with the prostitution underground in late Victorian England, much of it set against the background of the Oscar Wilde trial"; a collection of horror stories.

SIDELIGHTS: Best-selling author Anne Rice "deserves a place among those responsible writers who strive to combine the accuracy of history with the vitality of fiction," claims Penelope Mesic in the *Chicago Tribune Book World.* Rice has gained a reputation for what Valerie Miner, writing in the *Los Angeles Times Book Review,* calls her "intricate, stunning imagination." Explaining that her dramatic flair is rooted in childhood, Rice told *CA:* "I was brought up a Catholic in New Orleans, and the religion, atmosphere, and history of the city profoundly influenced my writing. In many ways, mine was a nineteenth-century childhood, and I have always felt like something of an outsider in America. Perhaps this is the reason I tend to write about outcasts: vampires in my first novel (monstrous outcasts doomed to appear human, to hunger literally for the human, but never to be human); the *gens de couleur libre* in *The Feast of All Saints* (mulatto and quadroon outcasts who in spite of wealth and breeding are never accepted into New Orleans white society); and the castrati in my third novel (the mutilated male opera sopranos of the eighteenth century who were worshipped for their voices, sought after as lovers, but always regarded as freaks)."

Written in six weeks, *Interview with the Vampire* launched Rice's career by selling more than one-and-a-half million copies and gaining much critical attention. Called "a revisionist vampire book that's deservedly become a kind of classic" by Gregory Sandow in the *Village Voice Literary Supplement,* the novel illustrates the author's penchant for vivid, provocative prose. As Sandow points out: "Anne Rice is not afraid of blood: her vampires are killers. They swoon in blood, and find their senses sharpened but their sensibilities dulled." Yet, as Rice explains in a *Los Angeles Times* interview with Kathy MacKay, she tried to look beyond the fantastic world of the book's subject to examine very human concerns. "Both [*Interview with the Vampire* and *The Feast of All Saints*] in a strange way are concerned with the question of brotherhood.... I am obsessed by the question of how we live in our day and age when the faith in authority symbols is lost. How do we find guidance from others? In both novels the main characters find out they must fall back on themselves."

Rice's protagonist in *The Feast of All Saints,* Marcel Ste. Marie, is one of the 18,000 *gens de couleur libre,* or free people of color, who occupied an almost forgotten place in New Orleans during the 1840s. The children of white slave owners and their black or mulatto mistresses, free people of color developed an isolated community of intellectuals, artists, and craftsmen who although free—even owning slaves themselves—had neither the right to vote nor the right of free speech. According to Anne Edwards in *Washington Post Book World,* the free people of color set themselves above blacks who could claim no white blood, creating "a society riddled with snobbery, without any sense of their own place in history or for that matter the foresight to see that their insular, multi-class-structured life was a certain path to extinction." Notes Edwards, "A parallel exists with the white aristocracy of the south at the same time."

Rice spent ten years researching the history of these people for *The Feast of All Saints,* traveling with her husband, poet Stan Rice, to Haiti and Louisiana. While the book does examine the social, cultural, and historical plight of the *gens de couleur libre,* it does not constantly address their lack of rights. Instead, the author focuses on individual characters' choices, desires, and disappointments. The resulting book is not only about race, Rice tells MacKay, but makes a moral statement "about life and ... characters who are examples of how to behave." Marcel Ste. Marie is raised as a gentleman, dependent largely on his absentee father's patronage for present material comforts and future educational opportunities. When left penniless as a young man, Miner explains, Marcel must reevaluate his situation. "Once [he] acknowledges there is no order to obey—not the church, nor the system of patronage, nor the American democracy—he begins to take charge of his own life."

Reviewers consistently note the novelist's talent for interesting the reader in the fates of her characters. Miner comments that Rice "recovers [a] hidden history" by "writing with a fascination for her individual characters and an intimate affection for New Orleans." "Rice is extremely clever at texturing her characters and their personal stories," adds Edwards. Rhoda Koenig, however, calls *The Feast of All Saints* "a sluggish, humid novel," and states in the *New York Times Book Review* that the book "falls somewhere between serious historical fiction and enjoyable trash." Miner disagrees, believing the book "is rare, combining a 'real story,' a profound theme and exquisite literary grace." Other reviewers express more reserved opinions. While admitting that she finds the narrative "desperately in need of an editor's unmerciful blue pencil," Edwards feels it "has a strange and compelling drive to it.... There is drama and melodrama rising and falling in a wild pulse beat on every page." Concludes Mesic: "Ann Rice has a talent for the panoramic, for the large structures of plot.... *The Feast of All Saints* is an honest book, a gifted book, the substantial execution of a known design. . . . [It] has the popular novel's uncanny ability of mirroring our attitudes, our wishes, our vision of ourselves."

"*Cry to Heaven,* like Anne Rice's [earlier novels], is bold and erotic, laced with luxury, sexual tension, music," states Alice Hoffman in the *New York Times Book Review.* "Here passion is all, desires are overwhelming, gender is blurred." Set in Italy in the eighteenth century, the book traces the lives of two castrati, male sopranos in the prestigious Italian opera. Michiko Kakutani in the *New York Times* calls the work "a dark, humid melodrama filled with assassinations, attempted suicides and incestuous couplings . . . animated by such operatic passions as ambition and revenge." It provides "not only a Baroque portrait of 18th-century Italy, but also a fitting showcase for its author's gothic imagination," Kakutani adds.

Reviewers again commend Rice's characterization. "Indeed," writes Kakutani, "it is a testament to Mrs. Rice's ability to portray Tonio's state of mind that the initial curiosity his anomalous condition elicits in a reader is quickly replaced by genuine concern about his choices and his fate." While admitting that "there are times when the novelist seems not to trust herself—the tension is sometimes heightened in ways that seem false," Hoffman summarizes: "*Cry to Heaven* is so daring and imaginative that it may frighten off some readers, even offend them by its baroque quality. This is a novel dazzling in its darkness, and there are times when Mrs. Rice seems like nothing less than a magician: It is a pure and uncanny talent that can give a voice to monsters and angels both."

"For me, writing is the grand passion, the activity which makes my life worthwhile," Rice told *CA.* "For twenty years I have been married to Stan Rice, who is a poet, and his works . . . have influenced me enormously. . . . We live in a restored Victorian [house] in the heart of San Francisco's Castro District, enjoying a very urban existence, attending the symphony and ballet, seeing good films, enjoying frequent local poetry readings, haunting the local bookstores, writing for hours in the local cafes. At home we are perpetually in the atmosphere of clicking typewriters, booklined walls, passionate conversation about this person, that idea, this theme. It is a rich and marvelous life." Attributing her success to a willingness to take risks, Rice comments to MacKay: "I think somewhere along the line I realized that fear of failure prevents us from doing a lot of things. . . . You've got to dare to be great. You may fail magnificently, but if you do, it's OK—you've given it your full try."

AVOCATIONAL INTERESTS: Traveling, ancient Greek history, archaeology, social history since the beginning of recorded time, old movies on television, and, she adds, "I enjoy going to boxing matches—am fascinated by performers of all kinds, and by sports which involve one man against another or against a force."

BIOGRAPHICAL/CRITICAL SOURCES: Chicago Tribune Book World, January 27, 1980; *Washington Post Book World,* January 27, 1980; *Los Angeles Times Book Review,* February 3, 1980, December 19, 1982; *Chicago Tribune,* February 10, 1980; *New York Times Book Review,* February 17, 1980, October 10, 1980; *Village Voice Literary Supplement,* June, 1982; *New York Times,* September 8, 1982.

—Sketch by Nancy Hebb

* * *

RICHARDSON, John Martin, Jr. 1938-

PERSONAL: Born March 12, 1938, in New York, N.Y.; son of John Martin and Marguerite (Pentz) Richardson; married Janice Bartlett (a fashion designer), December 30, 1960; children: Heather Bradford. *Education:* Dartmouth College, B.A., 1960; University of Minnesota, Ph.D., 1968. *Politics:* Democrat. *Religion:* Society of Friends. *Office:* School of International Service, American University, Washington, D.C. 20016.

CAREER: Case Western Reserve University, Cleveland, Ohio, assistant professor of political science, 1969-75; American University, Washington, D.C., associate professor and director of Center for Technology and Administration, 1975-78, professor of applied systems analysis, 1978-79, professor of international affairs and applied systems analysis, 1980—. *Military service:* U.S. Navy, 1960-65; became lieutenant. *Member:* World Future Society, American Political Science Association, U.S. Association for the Club of Rome, Society for Computer Simulation, The Hunger Project, Royal African Society, Wright Ingraham Institute, Carrying Capacity. *Awards, honors:* Social Science Research Council postdoctoral research training fellowship, 1969; named "One of the Twenty Most Effective Decision-Makers in the World," international selection committee of the Simulation Councils of America.

WRITINGS: Partners in Development, Michigan State University Press, 1968; (with Donella Meadows and Gerhart Bruckmann) *Groping in the Dark: The First Decade of Global Modeling,* Wiley, 1982; (editor) *Making It Happen: A Positive Guide to the Future,* U.S. Association for the Club of Rome, 1982.

Contributor: R. T. Holt and J. E. Turner, editors, *The Methodology of Comparative Research,* Free Press, 1970; (with Thomas Pelsoci) Kan Chen, editor, *Urban Dynamics: Extensions and Reflections,* San Francisco Press, 1971; (with Pelsoci) M. D. Mesarovic and A. Reisman, editors, *Systems Approach and the City,* North-Holland Publishing, 1972; *Water, 1973,* American Institute of Chemical Engineers, 1973; R. L. Chartrand, editor, *Information Technology Serving Society,* Pergamon, 1979; Jacques Richardson, *Models of Reality,* Lomond, 1984. Contributor of numerous scholarly papers to conferences and seminars. Also contributor to journals.

WORK IN PROGRESS: A comprehensive sourcebook on the end of hunger.

SIDELIGHTS: John Martin Richardson, Jr., told *CA:* "I believe that writing is an essential step in analyzing an issue, putting our thoughts in systematic order, offering opportunity for our ideas to be challenged and therefore improved and sharpened, and providing means to stimulate interest or at least awareness from other people in the issues we think important to the community. However, we have to always bear in mind that words have their own limits in conveying ideas and feelings of the writer, words being concrete and static means used to express abstract and rapidly changeable agents such as ideas and feelings."

* * *

RICHARDSON, Robert (Dale, Jr.) 1934-

PERSONAL: Born June 14, 1934, in Milwaukee, Wis.; son of Robert Dale (a clergyman) and Lucy (Marsh) Richardson; married Elizabeth Hall, November 7, 1959; children: Elizabeth, Anne. *Education:* Harvard University, B.A., 1956, Ph.D., 1961. *Home:* 2400 South Jackson St., Denver, Colo. 80210. *Office:* Department of English, University of Denver, Denver, Colo. 80210.

CAREER: Harvard University, Cambridge, Mass., instructor in English, 1961-63; University of Denver, Denver, Colo., assistant professor, 1963-68, associate professor, 1968-72, professor of English, beginning 1972, Phipps Professor of Humanities, 1979-82, head of department of English, 1968-73. Visiting professor, Harvard University summer school, 1976, Queens College and Graduate Center, City University of New York, 1978, Sichuan University, 1983. Member of board of directors, David R. Godine Publishers; trustee, Meadville-Lombard Theological School, University of Chicago. *Member:* Modern Language Association of America, American Studies Association, American Association of University Professors, American Civil Liberties Union, Phi Beta Kappa. *Awards, honors:* Huntington Libraries fellow, 1973-74.

WRITINGS—All published by Indiana University Press: *Literature and Film,* 1969; (with Burton Feldman) *The Rise of Modern Mythology,* 1972; *Myth and Literature in the American Renaissance,* 1978. Also author of *Myth and Romanticism,* a reprint series of fifty-two volumes of major myth sources used by the English Romantics. Contributor of articles and reviews to professional journals. *Denver Quarterly,* associate editor, 1967-76, book review editor, 1976—; member of editorial board, *Western Review.*

WORK IN PROGRESS: A study of Henry David Thoreau; a study of Ralph Waldo Emerson's Italian journey.

SIDELIGHTS: The subjects of Robert Richardson's critical study of *Myth and Literature in the American Renaissance,* including Nathaniel Hawthorne and Herman Melville, "are also originators and renewers of myth," notes *Sewanee Review* critic Harold Beaver. "They compel us to believe in the 'grand creations of the mythic imagination.'" Beaver cites Richardson's belief that, for instance, "underlying and informing *Moby Dick* is nothing less than a conception of myth as a necessary category of the imagination." "The diagnosis is right," Beaver continues. "[Classical scholars] Bayle . . . , Diderot and Holbach may have been intent on a natural supernaturalism. . . . But Hawthorne as much as Melville, with his Ahab and White Whale, was concerned with a supernatural naturalism."

BIOGRAPHICAL/CRITICAL SOURCES: New Republic, October 25, 1969; *Books Abroad,* spring, 1971; *Critique,* November, 1977; Robert Richardson, *Myth and Literature in the American Renaissance,* Indiana University Press, 1979; *Sewanee Review,* spring, 1980.

* * *

RIMMER, C(harles) Brandon 1918-

PERSONAL: Born February 21, 1918, in Los Angeles, Calif.; son of Harry (a clergyman and writer) and Mignon (Brandon) Rimmer; married Florence Caldwall (a teacher), July 2, 1942; children: David, Paul Douglas, Daniel Harry, Donna. *Education:* University of Southern California, B.A., 1950; Fuller Theological Seminary, M.Div., 1956. *Religion:* Non-denominational. *Address:* 14698 Nordhoff St., Panorama City, Calif. 91402.

CAREER: First Presbyterian Church of Hollywood, Hollywood, Calif., in Christian education department; served as pastor of nondenominational church, 1957-64; Baird Aviation, Burbank, Calif., commercial pilot; Electronic Calculating Service, Los Angeles, Calif., began as corporation pilot, became sales manager for scientific computer applications; manager of bookstore in Glendale, Calif., 1971-78; writer, 1971—. *Military service:* U.S. Army Air Forces, pilot in "The Devil's Brigade," 1941-47; became captain; received Distinguished Flying Cross.

WRITINGS: Mayhem and Mercy, Creation House, 1972; *Religion in Shreds,* Creation House, 1973; *Harry,* Creation House, 1973; (with Bill Brown) *The Unpredictable Wind,* Thomas Nelson, 1974; *Tell the Rock I'm Alive,* Successful Living, 1975; *The Dirks Escape,* Jeremy Books, 1979 (published in England as *The Escapes of Gerhard Dirks,* Kingsway Publications, 1979); *Torn for the Healing,* Jeremy Books, 1981.

* * *

RINZLER, Alan 1938-

PERSONAL: Born October 26, 1938, in New York, N.Y.; son of Harvey (a doctor) and Evelyn (Rothman) Rinzler; married second wife, Cheryl Rudenko; children: (first marriage) Ben, Jonathan, Peter; (second marriage) Lara. *Education:* Harvard University, B.A., 1960. *Religion:* Jewish. *Office:* GPI Publications, Cupertino, Calif.

CAREER: Editor at Simon & Schuster, Inc., Macmillan Publishing Co., Inc., and Holt, Rinehart & Winston, Inc., all New York City; president, Straight Arrow Books, San Francisco, Calif.; editorial director, Bantam Books, Inc., New York City; currently director of book division, GPI Publications, Cupertino, Calif.

WRITINGS: (Editor) *The New York Spy,* David White, 1967; (with Max Wolff) *The Educational Park: A Guide to Its Implementation,* Center for Urban Education, New York, 1970; (editor) *Youth Manifesto,* Macmillan, 1970; *Bob Dylan: The Illustrated Record,* Crown, 1978.

* * *

RISTE, Olav 1933-

PERSONAL: Born April 11, 1933, in Volda, Norway; son of Olav (a headmaster) and Bergliot (Meidell) Riste; married Ruth Pittman (a cyto-technician), June 15, 1964. *Education:* University of Oslo, Cand.philol., 1959; St. Antony's College, Oxford, D.Phil., 1963. *Home:* Husarveien 18, Billingstad 1362, Norway.

CAREER: United Nations, New York, N.Y., special interne, 1956-57; Norwegian Armed Forces, War Historical Department, Oslo, Norway, civil historian, 1964-80; National Defence College, Research Centre for Defence History, Oslo, director, 1980—. Occasional lecturer, University of Oslo, 1964-80; research fellow, Harvard University, 1967-68; visiting professor, Free University of Berlin, 1972-73; adjunct professor of history, University of Bergen, 1980—; guest scholar, Woodrow Wilson International Center for Scholars, 1982. *Military service:* Norwegian Army, Signal Corps, one year.

WRITINGS: The Neutral Ally: Norway's Relations with Belligerent Powers in the First World War, Humanities, 1965, 3rd edition, 1983; (editor, and author with Johannes Andenaes and Magne Skodvin) *Norway and the Second World War,* J. G. Tanum, 1966; (with Berit Noekleby) *Norway 1940-1945: The Resistance Movement,* International Publications Service, 1970, 3rd edition, 1978; *'London-regjeringa': Norge i krigsalliansen 1940-1945,* Det Norske Samlaget, Volume I: *1940-1942, Proevetid,* 1973, Volume II: *1942-1945, Vegen heim,* 1979. Contributor to historical journals.

WORK IN PROGRESS: A research project on Norway's postwar national security policy.

ROACH, Marilynne K(athleen) 1946-

PERSONAL: Born July 15, 1946, in Cambridge, Mass.; daughter of William Lawrence (a house painter) and Priscilla (Dunbar) Roach. *Education:* Massachusetts College of Art, B.F.A., 1968. *Religion:* Christian. *Residence:* Watertown, Mass. 02172.

CAREER: Mosaic Tile Co., Boston, Mass., designer, 1968-70; free-lance writer and illustrator in Watertown, Mass., 1970—. *Awards, honors: The Mouse and the Song* named Children's Book Showcase title, 1975; Breadloaf Writers' Conference fellowship, 1977.

WRITINGS: The Mouse and the Song, Parents' Magazine Press, 1974; (adaptor from the Latin work of Quintus Horatius Flaccus) *Two Roman Mice,* Crowell, 1975; *Dune Fox,* Atlantic-Little, Brown, 1977; *Encounters with the Invisible World* (short stories), Crowell, 1977; *Presto: Or, the Adventures of a Turnspit Dog,* Houghton, 1979; (illustrator) Peter C. Horton, *So You Want to Fix up an Old House,* Little, Brown, 1979; (illustrator) Horton, *Coal Comfort,* Little, Brown, 1980; *Down to Earth at Walden,* Houghton, 1980. Contributor to *Boston Globe.*

WORK IN PROGRESS: An epic fantasy adventure set in seventeenth-century New England, tentatively titled *An Expedition to Norumbega.*

SIDELIGHTS: Presto: Or, the Adventures of a Turnspit Dog, follows the travels of a plucky terrier in eighteenth-century London. Presto had spent most of his life in a turnspit, "a devilish device by which a roast was kept turning on a spit by means of a small dog's running constantly within a wheel," as Selma G. Lanes describes it in a *New York Times Book Review* article. Escaping from this terrible life, Presto explores London, meeting in his wanderings a company of pickpockets, forgers, innkeepers, actors, puppeteers, and of course several other dogs. And although the terrier's adventures often result in danger, the author, says Lanes, "does not dwell on injustice and cruelty, but rather on fortitude and imagination, loyalty and affection—those qualities which enable heroes to prevail over blind chance." The book, Lanes concludes, is "a tour de force of unobtrusive scholarship woven into a rich and suspenseful tale. . . . Not since Natalie Babbitt's [*Tuck Everlasting*] has there been so original a novel for children." *Washington Post Book World* critic Leon Garfield recommends *Presto* not only to children but to their parents, saying that adults would be "surprised by the high spirits, the stylishness and the honest delight in storytelling."

MEDIA ADAPTATIONS: Two stories appearing in *Encounters with the Invisible World* have been adapted for film: "The Ghost in the Shed" was presented as an animated cartoon for Columbia Broadcasting System in 1970; "The Orchard Murder" was adapted into a live-action film by John Hoover.

BIOGRAPHICAL/CRITICAL SOURCES: Washington Post Book World, November 11, 1979; *New York Times Book Review,* December 16, 1979, January 18, 1981.

* * *

ROBBINS, Martin 1931-

PERSONAL: Born July 10, 1931, in Denver, Colo.; son of Sam M. (a businessman) and Evelyn (Bricker) Robbins. *Education:* University of Colorado, B.A. (cum laude), 1952; State University of Iowa, M.A., 1959; Brandeis University, Ph.D., 1968. *Religion:* Jewish. *Office:* Radcliffe Institute, Cambridge, Mass. 02138.

CAREER: State University of Iowa, Iowa City, public relations feature writer, 1959-61; Northeastern University, Boston, Mass., assistant professor of English, 1963-73; Harvard College, Cambridge, Mass., teacher of writing, 1973-76; member of faculty, giving seminars, at Radcliffe Institute, Cambridge. Senior Fulbright-Hays lecturer, National University of Buenos Aires, 1973; visiting associate professor of drama, Boston University, 1974; teacher of short story writing, Boston College, 1974. Public relations feature writer, Yeshiva University, 1960. Gives poetry readings, lecture-recitals, and song recitals; has appeared on WHDH-TV, WGBH-TV, and WBZ, as lecturer, discussant, singer, and interviewer. *Member:* P.E.N., New England Poetry Club.

WRITINGS—Poetry: *A Refrain of Roses,* Alan Swallow, 1965; *A Reply to the Headlines: Poems 1965-70,* Swallow Press, 1970; *A Week Like Summer,* X Press, 1979; *A Year with Two Winters,* X Press, 1984.

Unpublished plays: "The Seasons of His Mercies: John Donne at St. Paul's, Christmas, 1624," first produced in Boston at Church of the Advent, December 21, 1969; "The Revolution Starts Inside" (one-act), first produced in Boston at Northeastern University, April 23, 1970; "Mussorgsky on Seeing the Pictures at an Exhibition" (dramatic monologue with music and choreography), first performed at Northeastern University, April 3, 1971.

"To Form a More Perfect Union" (a dramatic oratorio), first performed at College of William and Mary, December 4, 1976; "In Praise of Light" (short drama with medieval music), first performed in Boston at "First Night" celebration, December 31, 1981; "Images of Boston" (narration to musical impressions), first performed in concert and on WGBH-FM radio, 1981-82.

Also translator from the Armenian, *Land, Love, Century: New and Selected Poems,* by Gevorg Emin. Contributor to numerous periodicals, including *Art International, Sewanee Review, Webster Review, Radcliffe Quarterly, Saturday Review, English Language Notes,* and *New Republic.*

WORK IN PROGRESS: A full-length play, "An Overcoat for Joe Zero": a novella, *Requiem for a River.*

AVOCATIONAL INTERESTS: Fishing, hiking.

* * *

ROBERTS, Brian 1930-

PERSONAL: Born March 19, 1930, in London, England; son of Henry Albert (an engineer) and Edith (Watts) Roberts. *Education:* St. Mary's College, Twickenham, England, Teacher's Certificate, 1955; University of London, Diploma in Sociology, 1958. *Religion:* Roman Catholic. *Home:* North Knoll Cottage, 15 Bridge St., Frome BA11 1BB, Somerset, England. *Agent:* Harold Ober Associates, Inc., 40 East 49th St., New York, N.Y. 10017.

CAREER: Free-lance writer. Teacher in England and South Africa, 1958-67. *Military service:* Royal Navy, 1949-53.

WRITINGS: Ladies in the Veld, J. Murray, 1965; *Cecil Rhodes and the Princess,* Lippincott, 1969; *Churchills in Africa,* Taplinger, 1971; *The Diamond Magnates,* Scribner, 1972; *The Zulu Kings,* Scribner, 1974; *Kimberley: Turbulent City,* David

Philip (Capetown), 1976; *The Mad Bad Line: The Family of Lord Alfred Douglas,* Hamish Hamilton, 1981; *Randolph: A Study of Churchill's Son,* Hamish Hamilton, 1984. Contributor to newspapers and magazines in England and South Africa.

SIDELIGHTS: Brian Roberts has written several books on South African history and the people involved in making that history. *Cecil Rhodes and the Princess,* his 1969 book, is a dual biography of Cecil Rhodes and Catherine Radziwill. Radziwill was a Polish-born princess whose unsuccessful attempts to win Rhodes's affection resulted in political and social scandal. A *Times Literary Supplement* reviewer comments that "this is the first detailed study of Princess Radziwill to have been written, and the record of her early political and journalistic intrigues provides an illuminating background to her later activities in South Africa. For this, and for his exploration behind the public image of Rhodes to discover the person of flesh, blood and even emotion, Mr. Roberts has delved deeply. The result is an absorbing, controversial dual biography."

"After writing in diverting style on Cecil Rhodes and Princess Radziwill," says another *Times Literary Supplement* critic, Roberts "has chosen a more . . . important South African theme" for his next book, *Churchills in Africa.* As history of the period of the 1890s and the early 1900s, "when South Africa cast its strongest spell, . . . it makes a good story, and Mr. Roberts has told it well, in a fluent style and with an impartiality that is rare."

In his next volume on South African history, *The Diamond Magnates,* Roberts writes about the four fortune hunters of the 1870s who ultimately founded the world's largest diamond mining company, DeBeer's of South Africa. Roberts, "who is deeply versed in South African history," says a *Times Literary Supplement* reviewer, "has produced a most readable and well-researched study of what were indeed the Klondyke days." Roberts presents "an entertaining and well-documented account of this group of men as they fought each other for supremacy."

In his 1974 book, Roberts writes a history of the Zulu nation in southeast Africa during the nineteenth century. *The Zulu Kings,* says Alden Whitman in a *New York Times Book Review* article, "is the first tempered account we have . . . of the rise of the Zulu nation. It is an impressive feat, not only for its scholarship and its attention to oral tradition, but also for its grasp of the Zulu experience and its evocation of the Zulu ethos."

BIOGRAPHICAL/CRITICAL SOURCES: *Observer Review,* July 6, 1969, November 20, 1970; *Times Literary Supplement,* July 31, 1969, August 1, 1971, October 6, 1972; *New York Times,* August 5, 1969; *Washington Post Book World,* July 22, 1973; *New York Times Book Review,* July 20, 1975.

* * *

ROBERTS, John R. 1934-

PERSONAL: Born March 7, 1934, in Indiana; son of Paul D. and Irene (McMurray) Roberts; married Lorraine Bielski (a teacher), August 5, 1955; children: Stephanie, Mary, Claire, Milissa, Lisa, John. *Education:* Indiana State University, B.A. (magna cum laude), 1955; University of Illinois, M.A., 1957, Ph.D., 1962. *Politics:* Independent. *Religion:* Roman Catholic. *Home:* 407 Longfellow, Columbia, Mo. 65201. *Office:* Department of English, University of Missouri, Columbia, Mo. 65201.

CAREER: University of Wisconsin—Madison, assistant professor of English, 1962-66; University of Detroit, Detroit, Mich., associate professor of English, 1966-68; University of Missouri—Columbia, associate professor, 1968-72, professor of English, 1972—, chairman of department, 1974-80. Visiting scholar, Cambridge University, 1981. *Member:* Modern Language Association of America, Milton Society of America, Central Renaissance Conference, Friends of Bemerton, Friends of Milton's Cottage.

WRITINGS: *A Critical Anthology of English Recusant Devotional Prose: 1558-1603,* Duquesne University Press, 1966; *An Annotated Bibliography of the Criticism of John Donne: 1912-1967,* University of Missouri Press, 1973; *Essential Articles for the Study of John Donne's Poetry,* Archon Books, 1975; *George Herbert: An Annotated Bibliography of Modern Criticism, 1905-1974,* University of Missouri Press, 1978; *Essential Articles for the Study of George Herbert's Poetry,* Archon Books, 1979; *John Donne: An Annotated Bibliography of Modern Criticism, 1967-1978,* University of Missouri Press, 1982. Contributor to literature journals.

* * *

ROBERTS, John Storm 1936-

PERSONAL: Born February 24, 1936, in London, England; son of Alexander Storm (an accountant) and Ernestine (Bickford) Roberts; married Jane Mary Lloyd, 1959 (divorced, 1980); married Anne Needham; children: Stephen Storm, Alice Amanda. *Education:* Christ Church, Oxford, B.A. (with honors in modern languages), 1959. *Politics:* Liberal. *Religion:* None. *Home:* 123 Congress St., Brooklyn, N.Y. 11201.

CAREER: *Geographical Magazine,* London, England, editorial assistant, 1959-62; sub-editor on local newspapers in England, 1962-63, and on *East African Standard,* Nairobi, Kenya, 1963-66; *Interbuild,* London, assistant editor, 1967; writer on African urban music and producer of radio programs on the same topic, 1967-70; *Africa Report,* New York, N.Y., managing editor, 1970-71, editor, 1971-73; free-lance writer, 1974-80; senior editor, *Nuestro* magazine, 1980; editor, *World Broadcast News,* 1981-83. Founder of Original Music, a distributor of contemporary African recordings and books on Black, African, and other ethnic music.

WRITINGS: *A Land Full of People: Life in Kenya Today,* Praeger, 1967; *Black Music of Two Worlds,* Praeger, 1972; *The Latin Tinge,* Oxford University Press, 1979. Also author of radio plays and dramatized documentaries; also contributor to books. Contributor of hundreds of articles on Black, African, Caribbean, and Latin music to journals in half a dozen countries; contributor of poetry to several journals and magazines; contributor of short detective fiction to *Ellery Queen* magazine.

WORK IN PROGRESS: A book on the music of the whole Caribbean; other works on his musical specialties.

SIDELIGHTS: John Storm Roberts writes *CA* that he used to see himself as "a fiction writer who wrote about music on the side. As my published fiction is restricted to a few short stories, and I have a modest international reputation for my musical work, I have had to revise that assessment. But as they used to say about the Brooklyn Dodgers, 'Wait'll next year!'"

Roberts indicates that he is best known for his work on Black, African, Caribbean and Latin music, which, in addition to his written contributions, has included recording field trips to the Caribbean, and the compilation and production of record albums. Writing about Roberts's book *Black Music of Two Worlds,* a *Times Literary Supplement* reviewer comments that "Mr. Roberts's own acquaintance both in field conditions and on disc or tape with this immense range of [Afro-American] music, dance and folk poetry seems indisputable, and the information he proffers both fascinates and stimulates."

Roberts speaks French, German, Spanish, Swahili, and some Italian and Arabic.

BIOGRAPHICAL/CRITICAL SOURCES: Times Literary Supplement, July 27, 1967, October 26, 1973; *New York Times Book Review,* November 11, 1979.

* * *

ROBERTS, Rinalda
See CUDLIPP, Edythe

* * *

ROBINSON, Donald W(ittmer) 1911-1980

PERSONAL: Born July 4, 1911, in Williamsport, Pa.; died September 12, 1980; son of Francis Martin (an officer, U.S. Navy) and Anna (Laedlein) Robinson; married Esther Louise Stanbro, December 14, 1950. *Education:* Harvard University, A.B., 1932; University of Pennsylvania, Ph.D., 1944. *Politics:* Independent. *Religion:* Unitarian Universalist. *Address:* 3775 Modoc Rd., Apt. 40, Santa Barbara, Calif. 93105. *Office:* Special Publications, Phi Delta Kappa, Eighth and Union, Bloomington, Ind. 47401.

CAREER: Taught American history at high schools in Upper Darby, Pa., Brookline, Mass., and Berkeley, Calif., 1936-46; University of Tampa, Tampa, Fla., professor of education, 1946-48; Colorado Women's College (now Temple Buell College), Denver, Colo., assistant to president, 1948-49; University of Mississippi, University, associate professor of education, 1949-51; California College of Arts and Crafts, Oakland, executive dean, 1951-55; teacher of social studies and head of department, Sequoia Union School District, Calif., 1956-62; Phi Delta Kappa (international education fraternity), Bloomington, Ind., associate editor and director of special publications, beginning 1962; National Association of Secondary School Principals, Washington, D.C., staff member, beginning 1968. Project director, National Council of Social Studies, 1965-66; member of National Curriculum Committee, Unitarian Universalist Association, beginning 1972. Consultant, U.S. Office of Education. *Member:* Phi Delta Kappa.

WRITINGS: (With Harold Oyer, Daniel Roselle, and Elmer Pflieger) *Promising Practices in Civic Education,* National Council for the Social Studies, 1967; (editor) *As Others See Us: An International View of American History,* Houghton, 1969; *A World to Gain,* U.S. National Committee, UNESCO, 1969; (editor) *Verdict on America: Readings from Textbooks of Other Countries,* Houghton, 1974. Also author of published lecture, *Professional Responsibility and Contemporary Problems,* Bureau of Educational Materials and Research, College of Education, Louisiana State University, 1974. Columnist, writing "Scraps from a Teacher's Notebook" for *Phi Delta Kappan.* Contributor to *Saturday Review* and education journals.

WORK IN PROGRESS: Editing *Fifty Years of the "Kappan,"* an anthology.†

ROGERS, Keith
See HARRIS, Marion Rose (Young)

* * *

ROOSEVELT, James 1907-

PERSONAL: Born December 23, 1907, in Hyde Park, N.Y.; son of Franklin Delano (a president of the United States) and Anna Eleanor (a writer and lecturer; maiden name Roosevelt) Roosevelt; married Betsey Cushing (divorced, 1940); married Romelle Schneider (divorced, 1956); married Irene Kitchenmaster (divorced, 1969); married Mary Winskill (a teacher), October 3, 1969. *Education:* Harvard University, graduate, 1930; Boston University, graduate study, 1931. *Religion:* Episcopal. *Office:* James Roosevelt & Co., 120 Newport Center Dr., Suite 206, Newport Beach, Calif. 92660.

CAREER: Roosevelt & Sargent, Inc. (insurance), Boston, Mass., organizer and president, 1931-37; in motion picture industry, 1938-40; Roosevelt & Sargent, Inc., executive vice-president of west coast office, 1946; U.S. House of Representatives, Washington, D.C., congressman from 26th California district, 1955-66, serving on committee on education and labor and select small business committee; United Nations, New York City, U.S. ambassador to Economic and Social Council, 1966-68; I.O.S. Development Co. (mutual funds), Geneva, Switzerland, vice-president, 1968-71; James Roosevelt & Co. (business consultants), Newport Beach, Calif., president, 1971—; Whittier College, Whittier, Calif., Richard M. Nixon Professor of Political Science. Member of President's Commission on Executive Exchange. Armand Hammer Human Rights and Peace Conference, participant, 1979, 1980, and 1981.

Lecturer in social ecology at University of California at Irvine, 1973, Woodbury University, and Chapman College. Trustee, National Foundation-March of Dimes, estate of Franklin D. Roosevelt, Chapman College, and the Georgia Warm Springs Foundation. Vice-president, Eleanor Roosevelt Cancer Foundation. Member of board, Eleanor Roosevelt Institute and South Coast Repertory. *Military service:* U.S. Marine Corps Reserve, 1940-45; became brigadier general; received Navy Cross and Silver Star Medal. *Member:* Metropolitan Club, Harvard Club. *Awards, honors:* National Conference of Christians and Jews Humanitarian Award, 1981.

WRITINGS: (With Sidney Shalett) *Affectionately, F.D.R.: A Son's Story of a Lonely Man,* Harcourt, 1959; (editor) *The Liberal Papers,* Anchor Books, 1962; (with Bill Libby) *My Parents: A Differing View,* Playboy Press, 1976; (with Sam Toperoff) *A Family Matter* (novel), Simon & Schuster, 1980.

SIDELIGHTS: James Roosevelt, the eldest son of the late U.S. president Franklin Delano Roosevelt, reveals the personal side of his father in the biography *Affectionately, F.D.R.: A Son's Story of a Lonely Man.*

The biography, writes J. M. Burns of the *New York Times Book Review,* tells of "not one father, but of three—the vigorous, overpowering father of the days before polio, the gallant cripple fighting his way back to active life . . . and the public figure in Albany and Washington. The first two fathers come through brilliantly in these pages; the picture of the 'public' father adds little to what we already know." Because of its anecdotal nature, the book reveals much about Roosevelt's family life. Walter Trohan of the *Chicago Sunday Tribune* finds the book "warm and affectionate [and] sprinkled with intimate stories." E. M. Mills of the *Christian Science Monitor* believes that the book "includes many hitherto undisclosed intimate details." "This book," Burns writes, "adds a whole new dimension to our knowledge of Roosevelt—his role as father—and also a whole new dimension of unresolved complexity."

Several critics believe that, whatever the reader's political persuasion, the book's portrait of Roosevelt will be entertaining and appealing. Mills, for example, believes that *Affectionately, F.D.R.* "should prove engrossing for both friend and nonadmirer." The *Springfield Republican* reviewer finds that the reason for this appeal is that "even [Roosevelt's] most confirmed political foes never questioned the great personal charm of the late President, and this warm human quality shines brightly through the pages of this book."

BIOGRAPHICAL/CRITICAL SOURCES: *Christian Science Monitor,* October 8, 1959; *Chicago Sunday Tribune,* October 11, 1959; *New York Times Book Review,* October 18, 1959, January 2, 1977, July 20, 1980; *Saturday Review,* October 24, 1959; *Springfield Republican,* November 29, 1959; *Psychology Today,* March, 1977; *Economist,* September 24, 1977.

* * *

ROOT, William Pitt 1941-

PERSONAL: Born December 28, 1941, in Austin, Minn.; son of William Pitt (a farmer and show business director) and Bonita (Hilbert) Root; married Judith Bechtold, 1965 (divorced, 1970); children: Jennifer Lorca. *Education:* University of Washington, B.A., 1964; University of North Carolina at Greensboro, M.F.A., 1967; Stanford University, additional study, 1968-69. *Home:* Rancho Linda Vista, Oracle, Ariz. 85623.

CAREER: Todd Shipyards, Seattle, Wash., general helper, 1959; stock clerk, warehouseman, teamster, in Seattle, Wash., and Long Beach, Calif., 1960-64; Sweet Chariot Bar, Seattle, Wash., bouncer, 1964-65; Slippery Rock State College, Slippery Rock, Pa., instructor in English, 1967; Michigan State University, East Lansing, assistant professor of writing, 1967-68; lecturer in writing, Mid-Peninsula Free University, 1969-70; Amherst College, Amherst, Mass., writer-in-residence, 1971; poet in Poet-in-the-Schools Programs in Vermont, Idaho, Texas, Montana, Arizona, and Oregon, 1971-77; writer-in-residence at University of Southwestern Louisiana, Lafayette, and Wichita State University, Wichita, Kans., 1976; University of Montana, Missoula, visiting writer-in-residence, 1977-78, 1980-81, and 1983-84; Interlochen Arts Academy, Interlochen, Mich., visiting writer-in-residence, 1979.

AWARDS, HONORS: First prize in Academy of American Poets University Poetry Contest, 1966; Atlantic Young Poet award, 1967; Wallace Stegner creative writing fellowship, Stanford University, 1968-69; Rockefeller creative writing grant, 1969; John Simon Guggenheim Memorial Fellowship, 1970; National Endowment for the Arts creative writing grant, 1973; International Poetry Film Festival Orpheus Award, 1975, for screenplay co-authored by Ray Rice, "Song of the Woman and the Butterflyman"; Pushcart Prize, 1978, 1982; United States/United Kingdom Exchange Artist Fellowship, 1978-79; Stanley Kunitz Award, 1982.

WRITINGS—Poetry: *The Storm and Other Poems,* Atheneum, 1969; *Striking the Dark Air for Music,* Atheneum, 1973; *The Port of Galveston,* Galveston Arts Center, 1974; (editor) *What a World, What a World! Poetry by Young People in Galveston Schools,* Pipedream Press, 1974; *Coot and Other Characters: Poems New and Familiar,* Confluence, 1977; *A Journey South,* Graywolf, 1977; *7 Mendocino Songs,* Mississippi Mud Press, 1977; *Reasons for Going It on Foot,* Atheneum, 1981; *In the World's Common Grasses,* Moving Parts Press, 1981; *Fireclock,* Four Zoas Press, 1981; *The Unbroken Diamond: Nightletter to the Mujahideen,* Pipedream Press, 1983; *Invisible Guests,* Confluence, 1984; (translator) *Selected Odes of Pablo Neruda,* Four Zoas Press, 1984.

Also author, with Ray Rice, of screenplays, "Song of the Woman and the Butterflyman," 1975, "Seven for a Magician," 1976, and "Faces from the Poems of William Pitt Root," 1978.

WORK IN PROGRESS: A children's story, *The Man Who Used to Be the World's Greatest Hunter;* three poetry collections, *Faultdancing, Under the Umbrella of Blood,* and *Sea-Grape Tree & the Miraculous;* two short-story collections, *Tree of Water and Other Stories,* and *Who's to Say This Isn't Love? and Other Stories.*

SIDELIGHTS: William Pitt Root told *CA:* "In *The Storm and Other Poems* I was occupied mostly with the effort of locating my own earliest heart; most of the poems are retrospective and yearn. With *Striking the Dark Air for Music,* I determined to locate and explore some of the forms of despair isolating me from my own vitality; after those somewhat ritual 'Reckonings' comes a sequence of 'Songs,' energies which are expansive rather than constrictive, celebrations rather than analyses. (Poetry of confession is of most value when as in the work of Roethke it records transformations and the growth spurred by painful admissions; when it merely documents an essential failure of spirit, it profanes the tradition it assumes.)

"*Coot and Other Characters* is a gathering of old and new poems all of which describe or dramatize particular people ranging from a Vietnam veteran to a Black rioter, from an old lady lapsing into senility to a gang of dirty bikers. Coot himself is an old prospector flushed out of the Colorado Rockies by a ski resort development; his reflections on the various worlds he has lived through constitute some of my most successful poetry to date. Most recent are the poems of *Faultdancing,* which include sequences about the Sonora Desert and the Mendocino coast and a long work, *Fireclock,* which incorporates and 'heals' a nightmare of a particularly gruesome sort. While *Coot and Other Characters* tends to portray individuals caught up in their circumstances, *Faultdancing* rests on visions extending beyond circumstance.

"*Reasons for Going It on Foot* is a culmination of one aspect in my work (gleaning fruits after having laid some personal demons to rest for awhile) and a start in that other direction out of myself and into the world of larger concerns and other interests, including various levels of political awareness. Henry Miller once said that for a man to be absorbed in the lives of others, his own life must be f——ed-up. Despite the lives one might adduce in his support, he's clearly wrong in being so narrow. Youth is commonly self-absorbed, disentangling what is essential from what is circumstantial, but as that struggle progresses it is natural for awareness to expand—compassionate concern is perhaps the richest complication of such growth, provided, of course, that the mind keeps pace with the heart. Stupidity can only charm its equals while avarice, if it is cunning, has the whole world for an audience."

BIOGRAPHICAL/CRITICAL SOURCES: *Virginia Quarterly Review,* autumn, 1969; *New York Times,* August 15, 1970; *Clarion-Ledger* (Jackson, Miss.), September 5, 1976; *Chowder Review,* October 11, 1978; *Hudson Review,* autumn, 1981;

New York Times Book Review, September 6, 1981; William Heyen, editor, *Generation of 2,000: Thirty Contemporary Poets*, Ontario Review Press, 1984.

* * *

ROSENBERG, Shirley Sirota 1925-

PERSONAL: Born June 30, 1925, in New York, N.Y.; daughter of Charles and Donia (Rudoy) Sirota; married Jerome David Rosenberg (a physicist), August 27, 1947; children: Jonathan, Hindy. *Education:* Brooklyn College (now Brooklyn College of the City University of New York), B.A., 1946. *Home:* 116 East 4th St. S.E., Washington, D.C. 20003.

CAREER: Brooklyn Examiner, Brooklyn, N.Y., managing editor, 1946-49; *Washington Ledger*, Washington, D.C., manager editor, 1953-55; free-lance writer, 1957—; Washington correspondent, *Parents' Magazine*, 1967-77; Smithsonian Institution, Washington, D.C., editor-in-chief of ICP program, 1972-77; SSR, Inc., Washington, D.C., currently president and editor-in-chief. Consultant to Children's Bureau, U.S. Department of Health, 1967, Office of Deputy Assistant Secretary for Population and Family Planning, 1967-68, and National Institute on Alcohol Abuse and Alcoholism, 1971-72. *Awards, honors:* Blue Pencil Award, National Association of Government Communicators, 1981, for *National Energy Transportation Study*.

WRITINGS—Published by U.S. Government Printing Office, except as indicated: (With Frances G. Conn) *The First Oil Rush*, Duell, Sloan & Pearce, 1967; (editor) *First Special Report to the U.S. Congress on Alcohol and Health, from the Secretary of Health, Education, and Welfare*, 1971, revised edition, National Institute on Alcohol Abuse and Alcoholism, 1971; *Northern Tier Pipeline*, 1979; *National Energy Transportation Study*, 1981. Regular contributor to magazines and newspapers, including *Friends, Look, Parents', Family Weekly, Washington Star*, and *Washington Post*.

* * *

ROSIER, Bernard 1931-

PERSONAL: Born October 23, 1931, in Melun, France; married Anne Scheid (a psychologist), February 15, 1958; children: Benedicte, Claire, Bruno, Marc. *Education:* Institut National Agronomique, Paris, Ingenieur Agronome, 1955; Centre d'Etude des Programmes Economiques, Paris, Dipl.C.E.P.E., 1964; University of Grenoble, Sc.D., 1967; Faculte des Sciences economiques de France, Agrege de Sciences economiques, 1970. *Home:* Le Petit Roquefavour, Aix-en-Provence, France. *Office:* CEDEC, University of Aix-Marseille, Chateau-Lafarge, Route des Milles, 12390 Aix-les-Milles, France.

CAREER: Societe Grenobloise d'Etudes et d'Applications Hydrauliques, Grenoble, France, director of studies, 1958-61; Institut National Agronomique, Paris, France, assistant master in agricultural development and planning, 1961-67; University of Grenoble, Faculty of Economic Sciences, Grenoble, faculty member, 1967-74, professor, 1970-74; University of Aix-Marseille, Faculty of Economic Sciences, Aix-en-Provence, France, professor, 1974—. Director, Centre de Recherche en Developpement Compare, Dynamique et Prospective economiques (CEDEC). Professor, Institut des Sciences Politiques, Paris. Consultant to UNESCO.

WRITINGS: (With Rene Dumont) *Nous allons a la famine*, Editions du Seuil, 1966, translation published as *The Hungry Future*, Praeger, 1969; *Agriculture moderne et socialisme: Une experience yougoslave*, Presses Universitaires de France, 1968; *Structures agricoles et developpement economique*, Mouton, 1969; (editor and co-author) *Modeles de Planification decentralisee*, Presses Universitaires de Grenoble, 1973.

Croissance et crise capitalistes, Presses Universitaires de France, 1975, 2nd edition, 1984; (co-author) *L'Occident en desarroi: Ruptures d'un systeme economique*, Editions Dunod (Paris), 1978; (with Pierre Dockes) *Rythmes economiques; crises et changement social: Une perspective historique*, Editions La Decouverte/Maspero, 1983; (co-author) *Approches du developpement endogene*, Presses UNESCO, 1984.

Also author of numerous research reports for UNESCO. Contributor to economics journals in France and Europe.

WORK IN PROGRESS: Changement technique, division du travail et rapports sociaux, with Pierre Dockes; *Elements d'economie politique; Systemes economiques compares*.

* * *

ROSSINI, Frederick A(nthony) 1939-

PERSONAL: Born September 20, 1939, in Washington, D.C.; son of Frederick D. (a scientist) and Anne (Landgraff) Rossini; married Maria Miranda (an architect), June 5, 1964; children: Anthony J., Laura M., Jon D. *Education:* Spring Hill College, B.S., 1962; University of California, Berkeley, Ph.D., 1968. *Residence:* Atlanta, Ga. *Office:* School of Social Sciences, Georgia Institute of Technology, Atlanta, Ga. 30332.

CAREER: University of California, Berkeley, acting assistant professor of physics, 1968, fellow in philosophy, 1969-71; National Aeronautics and Space Administration, Ames Research Center, Moffat Field, Calif., research associate, 1971-72; Georgia Institute of Technology, Atlanta, assistant professor, 1972-76, associate professor, 1976-80, professor of social sciences, 1980—, director of Technology and Science Policy Program, 1980-82, director of Technology Policy and Assessment Center, 1981—, associate director of Office of Interdisciplinary Programs, 1983—.

MEMBER: International Association for Impact Assessment (co-founder and treasurer, 1981—), International Association for the Study of Interdisciplinary Research, Society for Philosophy and Technology, Policy Studies Organization, American Association for the Advancement of Science, Sigma Xi. *Awards, honors:* National Institute of Mental Health fellowship, 1969-71; National Academy of Sciences grant, 1971-72.

WRITINGS: (With Patrick Kelly, Melvin Kranzberg, and others) *Technological Innovation: A Critical Review of Current Knowledge*, San Francisco Press, 1977; (with A. L. Porter, S. R. Carpenter, and A. T. Roper) *A Guidebook for Technology and Impact Analysis*, North-Holland Publishing Co., 1980; (with Porter) *Integrated Impact Assessment*, Westview, 1983. Contributor to journals in physics and social and policy sciences. Co-editor-in-chief, *Impact Assessment Bulletin*, 1981-84; associate editor, *Technological Forecasting and Social Change*, 1980—.

WORK IN PROGRESS: Interdisciplinary Research, with A. L. Porter and D. E. Chublin.

SIDELIGHTS: Frederick A. Rossini told *CA:* "My driving intellectual research interest is the question of simultaneously relating to many representations of the world. Philosophy has traditionally concerned itself with developing a single set of premises or working toward a single conclusion. It is time to learn to understand and live comfortably with the manifold or alternative representations of the world."

He adds: "The new information technologies are playing a major role in structuring our representations of the world. It remains to be seen how these will affect our self-perceptions and lifeworld."

* * *

ROTHSCHILD, Lincoln 1902-1983

PERSONAL: Born August 9, 1902, in New York, N.Y.; died March 29, 1983, in Dobbs Ferry, N.Y.; son of Joseph J. (a businessman) and Mary Ellen (Smith) Rothschild; married second wife, Elisabeth Hitchings (a teacher), November 14, 1953; children: Peggy, Jack; stepchildren: Anne, Christina. *Education:* Columbia University, A.B., 1923, A.M., 1933; attended Art Students League, 1923-25. *Home:* 63 Livingston Ave., Dobbs Ferry, N.Y. 10522.

CAREER: Columbia University, Columbia College, New York City, instructor in art history, 1925-34; Works Progress Administration, Federal Art Project, New York City, director of New York Unit, "Index of American Design," 1937-41; worked as a wood patternmaker in various plants for the war industry, 1942-46; Adelphi College, Garden City, Long Island, N.Y., assistant professor of art and head of department, 1946-50; Artists Equity Association, New York City, national executive director, 1951-57; Riverdale Country School, New York City, instructor in humanities and industrial arts, 1957-64; City College of the City University of New York, New York City, lecturer in art history, 1964-68. *Member:* College Art Association, American Society for Aesthetics, American Artists Congress (treasurer, 1936-41), Art Students League of New York (member of board of directors, 1931).

WRITINGS: Sculpture through the Ages, McGraw, 1942; *Style in Art,* Thomas Yoseloff, 1960; *Hugo Robus* (monograph), American Federation of Arts, 1960; (contributor) F. V. O'Connor, editor, *The New Deal Art Projects,* Smithsonian Institution Press, 1971; *To Keep Art Alive: The Effort of Kenneth Hayes Miller, American Painter, 1876-1952,* Art Alliance, 1974; *Forms and Their Meaning in Western Art,* A. S. Barnes, 1976; *Susan Kahn,* Art Alliance, 1980. Contributor to art journals. Founder and editor of *Pragmatist in Art,* 1964-78.

SIDELIGHTS: "Art has a direct relation to its socio-economic background," Lincoln Rothschild told *CA.* "I try to expound the connection so as to make the history of art a significant, basic interest of the social sciences."

OBITUARIES: New York Times, April 5, 1983.†

* * *

ROVIT, Earl (Herbert) 1927-

PERSONAL: Born May 26, 1927, in Boston, Mass.; son of Samuel and Francis (Ehrenberg) Rovit; married Honey V. Weissenfeld, 1953; children: Sam Brian, Rebecca Laughlin. *Education:* University of Michigan, A.B., 1950; Boston University, M.A., 1951, Ph.D., 1957. *Home:* 15 East 21st St., New York, N.Y. *Office:* City College of the City University of New York, New York, N.Y. 10031.

CAREER: Bates College, Lewiston, Me., instructor, 1953-55; University of Louisville, Louisville, Ky., instructor, 1955-57, assistant professor, 1957-61, associate professor of English, 1961-64; Wesleyan University, Middletown, Conn., associate professor of English, 1964-65; City College of the City University of New York, New York, N.Y., assistant professor of English, 1965—. University of Freiburg, Fulbright professor of American literature, 1960-61. *Military service:* U.S. Army, 1945-47. *Member:* Modern Language Association of America, American Studies Association. *Awards, honors:* Guggenheim fellow, 1965-66, National Endowment for the Humanities senior fellow, 1978-79.

WRITINGS: Herald to Chaos: The Novels of Elizabeth Madox Roberts, University of Kentucky Press, 1960; *Ernest Hemingway,* Twayne, 1963; *The Player King,* Harcourt, 1965; *A Far Cry,* Harcourt, 1967; *Crossings,* Harcourt, 1973; *Saul Bellow: A Collection of Critical Essays,* Prentice-Hall, 1975. Contributor to *Books Abroad, Nation, Yale Review, American Scholar,* regional literary journals.

SIDELIGHTS: Earl Rovit's novels are noted for their intricate structures and themes. Often demanding works, his novels have been compared to those of Pirandello, James Joyce, and Bernard Malamud. *The Player King,* for instance, is a surprisingly complex work for a first novel. Rich with literary and mythological allusions, *The Player King* is a multi-layered fable, with each section overlapping and intertwining with the others: an opening and closing dialogue between the author and his Yiddish alter ego frames the journal of Leo, a young writer who has written a novel also entitled *The Player King* (which forms the main narrative); also included are parodies of reviews of Rovit's *The Player King* and a fictitious *Paris Review* interview with Rovit.

"This account may suggest an excess of artifice," writes *Saturday Review*'s Granville Hicks after describing the structure of the novel, "and it is true that Rovit is highly self-conscious, but at least he squarely faces one of the dilemmas of the contemporary novelist. As he makes clear by a multiplicity of literary allusions, he is a man of these times, familiar with the literature of these times, and he refuses to make the world he writes about simpler than that in which he lives." One *Choice* reviewer comments that "beneath this framework [in the novel] there is incorporated a phantasmagoria of motifs and references to Orpheus, the Fisher King, the philosophy of Jonathan Edwards, being and nothingness, and the course of American intellectual development from Puritan Boston to Jewish New York."

An important theme in *The Player King,* as the *Choice* critic mentions, is the role of the Jew in American letters. Robert Alter in *Commentary* argues that *The Player King* "could serve as a textbook introduction to [the] whole literary image of the Jew. . . . According to Rovit, or rather one of his several personae, the two great myths of Christian literature, Christ and Faust, the Victim and Victimizer, are dead and their place is now taken by the myth of the Jew, at once a grotesque figure of fun and an uncanny shaman-hero. . . . There is unresolved irony here: it is hard to know just what is meant seriously and what satirically. This very irresolution is Rovit's way of hanging onto both the grotesque mask and the sentimental image behind the mask. But the mythicized Jew, sheltering in that 'mysterious greasy black of the ghetto,' is clearly present . . . , for all the ingenious disguises Rovit provides him."

Although the novel has generally been praised, *The Player King* is not immune from criticism. Some critics find it overly self-conscious: the allusions and references simply become too much, its clever form is distracting. "*The Player King* is to fiction what op art is to painting," says Martin Levin in a *New*

York Times Book Review article in which he satirizes Rovit's style by analysing the hidden meanings in the novel—including such trivialities as the fact that the name Earl means "man." "There is cerebral sport in all this," Levin continues, "and the evidence of a vigorous intellect at work. But Mr. Rovit wears his learning heavily. Leo is ponderous; David facetious rather than witty, and Earl Rovit is a shade precious." Hicks also finds that the author's literary tricks sometimes get out of hand: "The novel that depicts chaos is likely, of course, to become chaotic, as Rovit's sometimes does; but he is bold and resourceful, and in so far as the novel is a failure it is a brave and admirable one."

A Far Cry also exhibits many of the characteristics of *The Player King:* it has an unusual structure—in this case two parallel stories told in alternate chapters—and a theme that also revolves around the Jew. The first story takes place in Renaissance Venice where the Jewish usurer Lazarro dello Strologo bears the burden of guilt for a murder committed by his daughter's gentile lover in order to save the Jewish community. The second tale is that of Sheldon Pfiest, slowly dying of cancer of the prostate in a Catholic hospital in New York. Pfeist was the leader of a religion whose main ritual was a symbolic re-enactment of an atomic explosion which revolves around his phallus and in which the female disciples (or "angels") were renamed after movie stars.

"A capacity for lived and imagined pain unites the two characters [in *A Far Cry*]," writes Peter Collier in the *New York Times Book Review.* "The central themes of the book come from the predominantly Jewish mainstream in American letters, but Rovit's implementation is wholly unique. He approaches the particularly modern problem of guilt and redemption by constructing two parallel but completely independent narratives; he then attempts to fuse them, by an act of imagination, within the cosmic frame of Christ's passion." Hicks, again writing in *Saturday Review,* maintains that "the point of the book, of course, lies in the contrast between the two deaths. Because of his faith and his sense of the community of true believers, Lazzaro is able to come to terms with himself and his fate, to endure great suffering, and to die peacefully. Sheldon, with nothing more to sustain him than a makeshift and egocentric religion, dreads death, and, though the miracles of medicine reduce his physical suffering, his mental anguish is acute.... [Rovit suggests] that death could be better endured when men were able to believe in God. What makes the novel impressive is his success in breathing life into two such different characters."

A number of reviewers concur that Rovit is more successful in *A Far Cry* than in *The Player King*. "This long, rich, mature novel displays once again the fascination with telling a story on two levels that Earl Rovit demonstrated in his well-reviewed first novel 'The Player King,'" says a *Publishers Weekly* critic. "This time Mr. Rovit seems to have his material much more tightly in grasp." Hicks notes that "Rovit's narrative [in *A Far Cry*] drives ahead with great power, and the writing is the best he has done." Collier considers *A Far Cry* to be "both deft and audacious. Rovit, demonstrating a respect for traditional craftsmanship, endows each of the narratives with its own suspense and catharsis. And even though his fusion of the respective fates of Lazzaro and Pfeist into a single cohesive statement about the human condition fails to evolve from the symbolic nexus, remaining largely implied (as opposed to achieved), he has written a powerful book."

"The surface of Earl Rovit's third novel, *Crossings,* is intricate and resplendently original," declares Mark Taylor in *Commonweal,* and indeed once again Rovit uses an experimental form to relay his story. The narrative of *Crossings* is divided into two parts, chronicling the events of a single day from either of two directions. The events of the novel are told by four major characters as they perceive them, "so the act of reading *Crossings* becomes a process of making judgements and then balancing, modifying, and correcting them as new reports come in from elsewhere, reports that are equally true but equally prejudiced and thus never quite a confirmation, though rarely an explicit contradiction, of what one has been led to believe," says Taylor. "But since the book starts at both ends, two narratives unfold simultaneously in opposite directions, meaning, in a way, that there are really two books here, and emphasizing, in each reader's irreversible choice of which one to read, the relentless consequences of choice, and even of belief in choice, within the novel itself."

Crossings takes place in Connecticut in 1886. Clovis Enfield is in labor with her first child. "By different psychological routes [Rovit] brings four persons ... to the same point in time, the day of the child's birth in 1886," notes *Library Journal* reviewer Karen Horny. "Not all the background is filled in but the essence is there: the impact of the birth, the expectation and effect of death, the cruelty which covers vulnerability when people are unable to cope with their own needs or those of the others close to them." A *Publishers Weekly* critic calls *Crossings* "an interesting experiment and one that works well" and notes that Rovit's approach to his story "by no means detracts from the book's strong and sensitive portrayal of people caught in life, moved by birth to reflect on other imponderables."

Taylor also believes that *Crossings*'s strengths go beyond its unique structure. "These particulars of design ally *Crossings* with much of the most ambitious contemporary fiction, which seeks to blur its identity as fiction by actively involving the reader in the novelistic process, making him a character in the work, and a force in its eventual outcome," says Taylor. "It would be a mistake, however, to insist too strongly on the experimental, postmodernist nature of *Crossings,* for not only does it develop a complex historical theme, but beneath its glittering surface are the enduring rhythms of literature, and of myth, that resist ultimate isolation and reductive categorization."

BIOGRAPHICAL/CRITICAL SOURCES: *New York Times Book Review,* April 18, 1965, July 2, 1967; *Saturday Review,* June 12, 1965, June 24, 1967; *Choice,* July/August, 1965; *Commentary,* September, 1965; *Publishers Weekly,* April 24, 1967, September 17, 1973; *Library Journal,* August, 1973; *Commonweal,* July 26, 1974; *Contemporary Literary Criticism,* Gale, Volume VII, 1977.

—Sketch by Heidi A. Tietjen

* * *

ROYCE, Kenneth
See GANDLEY, Kenneth Royce

* * *

RUEFF, Jacques (Leon) 1896-1978

PERSONAL: Born August 23, 1896, in Paris, France; died April 23, 1978, in Paris, France; son of Adolphe (a doctor) and Caroline (Levy) Rueff; married Christiane Vignat, April 13, 1937; children: Marie-Caroline, Passerose (daughter). *Education:* Ecole Polytechnique, diploma, 1921; additional study at Ecole Libre des Sciences Politiques, 1922-23. *Home:* 51 rue de Varenne, Paris 75007, France. *Office:* Institut de France, 23 quai de Conti, Paris 75006, France.

CAREER: French government economic official. Served as inspector of finances, 1923-26; junior assistant to French premier and finance minister Raymond Poincare, 1926-27; League of Nations Secretariat, member of economics and financial section, 1927-30, served on financial stabilization missions to Greece and Bulgaria, 1927, and Portugal, 1928; French Embassy, London, England, financial attache, 1930-31; Ecole Libre des Sciences Politiques, Paris, France, professor of economics, 1931-40; French Department of Treasury, Paris, Mouvement General des Fonds, assistant director, 1934-36, director, 1936; special counselor of state, 1937-39; assistant governor of Bank of France, 1939-41; chairman of Military Mission for German and Austrian Affairs, 1944; chairman of Paris Conference for German Reparations, 1945; French delegate to Reparations Commission in Moscow, Soviet Union, 1945; president of Interallied Agency for Reparation, Brussels, Belgium, 1946-52; Court of Justice of European Communities, Luxembourg, Luxembourg, judge, 1952-57; chief justice, 1957-62, member of social and economic council, beginning 1962; Institut de France, Paris, chancellor, beginning 1963.

Faculty member at University of Paris, Institut de Statistique, 1923-30, and Institut d'Etudes Politiques, 1945-48. Economic advisor to Allied commander-in-chief of occupied Germany, 1945; alternate French delegate to first and second general assembly of United Nations; president of Committee for Reorganization of French Finances, 1958; vice-president of Committee for Suppression of Obstacles to Economic Expansion, 1959-60; member of French Economic and Social Council, 1962; chairman of European subsidiary of Lincoln National Life Insurance Co. *Military service:* French Army, 1915-18; served in artillery and with American Expeditionary Force; became lieutenant.

MEMBER: International Statistical Institute (vice-president), Conseil International de la Philosophie et des Sciences Humaines (UNESCO; president, 1949-53; honorary president), Academie Francaise, Academie des Sciences Morales et Politiques, College des Sciences Sociales et Economiques (president, beginning 1960), Compagnie de Reassurances Nord-Atlantique (president, beginning 1963), Societe Elysees-Valeurs (president, beginning 1967), Academie Royale des Sciences, Lettres et Arts (Belgium; associate member), Academia Nazionale dei Lincei (Italy; associate member), Societe de Statistique de Paris (honorary president), Societe d'Economie Politique de Paris (honorary president), Institut Atlantique a Paris (vice-president, beginning 1962).

AWARDS, HONORS: Croix de guerre, three citations; Commander, Palmes academiques; Grand Cross of Order of Chene (Luxembourg); Grand Officer of Order of Leopold (Belgium), Order of Orange Nassau (Holland), Order of Saint Charles (Monaco), and Polonia Restituta (Poland); Grand Prix Andre-Arnoux, 1967; Grand-Croix de la Legion d'honneur, 1968; grande medaille de vermeil from the city of Paris, 1970.

WRITINGS: Des Sciences physiques aux sciences morales, Alcan, 1922, revised edition with additional commentary published as *Des Sciences physiques aux sciences morales: Un Essai de 1922, reconsidere en 1969,* Payot, 1969, translation by Herman Green published as *From the Physical to the Social Sciences: Introduction to a Study of Economic and Ethical Theory,* Johns Hopkins Press, 1929; *Sur une Theorie de l'inflation,* Berger-Levrault, 1925; *Theorie des phenomenes monetaires,* Payot, 1927; *Les Problemes actuels du credit,* Alcan, 1930.

L'Ordre social, two volumes, Recueil Sirey, 1945, 3rd edition, revised with new preface, in one volume, M. T. Genin, 1967; *Il faut choisir: Monnaie saine ou Etat totalitaire,* Editions SEDIF, 1947; *La Nouvelle Conception des relations economiques internationales,* Editions SPID du Comite d'Action Economique et Douaniere, 1947; *Epitres aux dirigistes,* Gallimard, 1949.

Discours aux independants, M. T. Genin, 1951; *La Regulation monetaire et le probleme institutionnel de la monnaie,* Recueil Sirey, 1953; *Un Instrument d'analyse economique: La Theorie des vrais et des faux droits,* College Libre des Sciences Sociales et Economiques, 1955; *L'Ordre dans la nature et dans la societe,* Diogene, 1955; *Mission et responsabilite des elites dans une civilisation de masses,* Centre Economique et Social de Perfectionement des Cadres, 1956.

L'Age de l'inflation, Payot, 1963, translation by A. H. Meeus and F. G. Clarke published as *The Age of Inflation,* Regnery, 1964; (with Fred Hirsch) *The Rose and the Rule of Gold: An Argument,* Department of Economics, Princeton University, 1965; *Discours de reception de Jacques Rueff a l'Academie francaise et response de M. Andre Maurois,* Gallimard, 1965; *Le Lancinant Probleme des balances de paiements,* Payot, 1965, translation by Jean Clement published as *Balance of Payments: Proposals for the Resolution of the Most Pressing World Economic Problem of Our Time,* Macmillan, 1967; *Les Dieux et les rois: Regards sur le pouvoir createur,* Hachette, 1967, translation by George Robinson and Roger Glemet published as *The Gods and the Kings: A Glance at Creative Power,* Macmillan, 1973; *Les Fondements philosophiques des systemes economiques,* Payot, 1967.

Le Peche monetaire de l'Occident, Plon, 1971, translation by Glemet published as *The Monetary Sin of the West,* Macmillan, 1972; *Combat pour l'ordre financier: Memoires et documents pour sevir a l'histoire du dernier demi-siecle,* Plon, 1972; *La Reforme du systeme monetaire international,* Plon, 1973; (author of introduction) Jean Cocteau, *Mon premier voyage,* Vialetey, 1973; *La Creation du monde: Comedie-Ballet en 5 journees,* Plon, 1974; *De l'Aube au crepuscule: Autobiographie de l'auteur,* Plon, 1977; *Theorie monetaire,* Plon, 1979; *Politique economique,* Plon, 1979.

Contributor: (And editor) *Les Doctrines monetaires a l'epreuve des faits,* Alcan, 1932; *Monnaie d'hier et de demain,* Editions SPID du Comite d'Action Economique et Douaniere, 1952; *Enquete sur la liberte,* Hermann, 1953; M. H. Sennholz, editor, *On Freedom and Free Enterprise,* Van Nostrand, 1955; L. Sommer, editor, *Essays in European Thought,* [Princeton, N.J.], 1960.

Author of opera-ballet, "La Creation du monde"; also author of or contributor to economic pamphlets, reports, and research papers, including *Rapport sur la situation financiere de la France: Plan de stabilisation,* Imprimerie Nationale, 1958, and, with Louis Armand, *Rapport sur la suppression des obstacles a l'expansion economique,* two volumes, Imprimerie Nationale, 1960. Contributor to numerous conference proceedings and to English and French language journals in his field.

SIDELIGHTS: Jacques Rueff, the first economist elected to the French Academy (l'Academie Francaise), was an adviser to the French government and a leading advocate of the full gold standard as a foundation for economic stability. As early as 1931, he warned that the Great Depression had been provoked by the inflationary effect of the gold-exchange standard, a temporary device approved in 1922 by the war-ruined countries of Europe that allowed them to use foreign currencies such as the British sterling pound and the American dollar as reserves in place of gold. "The system could only lead to inflation and bust, which arrived in 1929," wrote John L. Hess in the *New York Times Book Review.* "When the same system was resurrected at Bretton Woods as World War II ended, Rueff predicted it would lead to the same result."

Rueff wrote and lectured widely on the dangers of inflation and possible economic collapse. Noting that the internal purchasing power of nearly every world currency had vastly declined since World War I, he believed that even a minor international incident or a small economic disturbance could trigger another global collapse. He criticized the monetary policies of the United States and their principal spokesman, John Maynard Keynes, for not only tolerating but also encouraging inflation. As late as 1972, he repeated his prediction that the United States would never eliminate its balance of payments deficit until there was a radical change in the international monetary system that generated it.

Rueff exerted his greatest influence as an adviser to President Charles de Gaulle at the beginning of the Fifth Republic. In 1958 he "helped Antoine Pinay put across a stabilization of the franc that was a model of its kind," reported Hess. "In a few months, the nation turned from bankruptcy to a surplus of payments and growing reserves. (This was in the midst of the Algerian war, as Rueff would point out in arguing that peace in Asia would not of itself solve the United States deficit.)" His austerity reform program included a drastic reduction in borrowing, the removal of nearly all quota restrictions for international trade, and the creation of a new franc (worth 100 old francs). Though the pressure of the inflationary dollars from without gradually weakened the effort at equilibrium within, the recovery in France was so successful that a decade later John Ardagh, in *The New French Revolution,* called the Rueff Plan "the [de Gaulle] regime's greatest economic achievement."

BIOGRAPHICAL/CRITICAL SOURCES: John Ardagh, *The New French Revolution,* Harper, 1968; *National Review,* February 27, 1968; *Times Literary Supplement,* July 30, 1971; *New York Times Book Review,* March 26, 1972; Jacques Rueff, *De l'Aube au crepuscule: Autobiographie de l'auteur,* Plon, 1977; *New York Times,* April 25, 1978; *Washington Post,* April 25, 1978.

OBITUARIES: New York Times, April 25, 1978; *Washington Post,* April 25, 1978; *Time,* May 8, 1978.†

* * *

**RUFFELL, Thomas
See LASLETT, Peter**

* * *

**RUFFLE, The
See TEGNER, Henry (Stuart)**

* * *

RUFFRIDGE, Frank(lin James) 1931-

PERSONAL: Born February 23, 1931, in Jamesville, Mich.; son of Franklin (a critic) and Constance (Trouncer) Ruffridge; married Helena Ima Freech (a psychiatrist), February 23, 1955; children: Franklin III, Constance. *Education:* Westport College, A.B., 1958; graduate study at various universities. *Politics:* "Responsible freedom." *Home:* 221 Lewiston Rd., Grosse Pointe Farms, Mich. 48236.

CAREER: Writer. Ran away from home at fourteen and tried in vain to join the Marines by lying about his age; worked at many odd jobs, 1945-54, including water boy at a zoo, errand boy for a team of oil-well drillers, assistant to a government chicken inspector, and "travelling bartender" for a large caterer; while in college, worked as a bartender and as a distributor of leaflets. Director, annual community Arts and Oddities Carnival, 1971-76. *Member:* American Club, Time and Truth Society, Zoo Society. *Awards, honors:* Zoo Society grant, 1959, for work on a manuscript concerning alligator preservation (never completed); Time and Truth Society best book award, 1971, for *Everything You Never Needed to Know.*

WRITINGS: Zoos I Have Known, Zoo Society, 1959; *My Most Unforgettable Zoo,* Zoo Society, 1960; *What's in a Dictionary Besides Words?,* privately printed, 1962; *My Life as an Inspector of Chickens, Including an Entirely New Method of Chicken-Sexing,* privately printed, 1963; *Time Doesn't Really Fly!,* Reps Publishing, 1965; *Dictionary Reading for Fun and Profit,* Reps Publishing, 1967; (translator from the English with Everett S. Tuffnell) Bernard Owill, *Je lis seulement au nuit,* privately printed, 1969.

Everything You Never Needed to Know, Demo Publishing, 1971; *Many's the Time . . . ,* Bore Press, 1972; *Who Invited You?,* Demo Publishing, 1974; *I've Been Meaning to Tell You: All the Things Not to Say to a Crazy Person,* Bore Press, 1976; (editor) *Nonsense, My Dear* (anthology of light verse), Bore Press, 1978; *Natural Nemeses: Tales of Gales, Gophers, and Grubs,* Reps Publishing, 1978; *The Wear of Where: Appropriate Apparel,* How-To Handbooks, 1980; *Mens sana in corpore sano,* Ursidae Books, 1982; *Cabin Fever!,* Canadian Knights Press, 1984. Contributor of light verse, reviews, and articles to periodicals, including *Bore Quarterly* and several animal behavior journals.

SIDELIGHTS: Frank Ruffridge told *CA:* "I've *done* a lot of weird things in my life, and now I'm trying to *write* about them. People are too complacent. They should be *jolted.* (My wife thinks I'm crazy, but she may be right—she's a psychiatrist!) What we need to think about is Time and Nature and Animals, instead of war and money and status. I believe thinking should be a *passionate* process. My thoughts tend to run to the wild—bears, wilderness, and the parallels between human and nonhuman animal behavior in uncivilized surroundings, for example."

AVOCATIONAL INTERESTS: Making drinks, telling jokes in the mirror, walking, philosophizing.

* * *

RULE, Jane (Vance) 1931-

PERSONAL: Born March 28, 1931, in Plainfield, N.J.; daughter of Arthur Richards (a businessman) and Jane (Packer) Rule. *Education:* Mills College, B.A., 1952. *Home address:* The Fork, R.R. 1, Galiano, British Columbia, Canada V0N 1P0. *Agent:* Georges Borchardt, Inc., 136 East 57th St., New York, N.Y. 10022.

CAREER: Concord Academy, Concord, Mass., teacher of English, 1954-56; University of British Columbia, Vancouver, assistant director of International House, 1958-59, lecturer in

English, 1959-70, visiting lecturer in creative writing, 1973-74. Has worked variously as typist, teacher of handicapped children, change girl in a gambling house, and store clerk, mostly for background material.

MEMBER: Phi Beta Kappa. *Awards, honors:* Canadian Authors' Association, best novel of 1978 award, for *The Young in One Another's Arms,* best short story of 1978 award, for "Joy"; Literature Award, Gay Academic Union, 1978; award of merit, Fund for Human Dignity, 1983.

WRITINGS: The Desert of the Heart (novel), Macmillan Co. of Canada, 1964, World Publishing, 1965, reprinted, Naiad Press, 1983; *This Is Not for You* (novel), McCall Publishing Co., 1970; *Against the Season* (novel), McCall Publishing Co., 1971; *Theme for Diverse Instruments* (short stories), Talonbooks, 1975; *Lesbian Images* (criticism), Doubleday, 1975; *The Young in One Another's Arms* (novel), Doubleday, 1977; *Contract with the World* (novel), Harcourt, 1980; *Outlander* (short stories and essays), Naiad Press, 1981.

Work represented in anthologies: *Best Short Stories of 1972,* Oberon, 1972; *Contemporary Voices,* Prentice-Hall, 1972; *New Canadian Short Stories,* Oberon, 1975; *Stories from Pacific and Arctic Canada,* Macmillan, 1975; *After You're Out,* Links Books, 1975; Bob Weaver, editor, *Small Wonders,* CBC, 1982; Ed Jackson and Stan Persky, editors, *Flaunting It,* Pink Triangle Press, 1982. Author of column "So's Your Grandmother," in *Body Politic.* Contributor of reviews and articles to literature journals and other periodicals, including *Redbook, Chatelaine, San Francisco Review, Housewife, Canadian Literature, Queen's Quarterly,* and *Globe and Mail.*

WORK IN PROGRESS: Articles and short stories.

SIDELIGHTS: Jane Rule lived in England at one period. She has a number of foster children under the Foster Parents' Plan and has visited them in Greece and Italy. *Media adaptations: The Desert of the Heart* is to be made into a feature film by Desert Heart Productions, for release in 1984.

AVOCATIONAL INTERESTS: Civil liberties and international aid programs, gardening, collecting paintings.

BIOGRAPHICAL/CRITICAL SOURCES: Los Angeles Times Book Review, October 5, 1980; *Contemporary Literary Criticism,* Volume XXVII, Gale, 1984.

* * *

RUNDLE, Anne
(Marianne Lamont, Alexandra Manners, Joanne Marshall, Jeanne Sanders)

PERSONAL: Born in Berwick-on-Tweed, England; daughter of George Manners (a soldier) and Annie (Sanderson) Lamb; married Edwin Charles Rundle (a civil servant), October 1, 1949; children: Anne M. H. (Mrs. Bruce D. Kelly), James, Iain. *Education:* Attended public schools in Berwick-on-Tweed, England. *Politics:* Conservative. *Religion:* Church of England. *Home and office:* Cloy Cottage, Knowe Rd., Brodick, Arran KA27 8BY, Scotland. *Agent:* John McLaughlin, 31 Newington Green, London N16 9PU, England.

CAREER: Writer. British Civil Service, Berwick-on-Tweed and Newcastle-on-Tyne, England, civil servant, 1942-50. *Awards, honors:* Netta Muskett Award of Romantic Novelists Association, 1967, for *The Moon Marriage;* Romantic Novelists Association major awards, 1970, for *Cat on a Broomstick,* and 1971, for *Flower of Silence;* named Daughter of Mark Twain, 1974, in recognition of *Follow a Shadow.*

WRITINGS—Published by Hutchinson, except as indicated: *The Moon Marriage,* 1967; *Swordlight,* 1968; *Forest of Fear,* 1969; *Rakehell,* 1970; *Dragonscale* (juvenile), 1969; *Tamlane* (juvenile), 1970; *Lost Lotus,* R. Hale, 1972; *Amberwood,* R. Hale, 1973, Bantam, 1974; *Heronbrook,* Bantam, 1974; *Judith Lammeter,* Bantam, 1976; *Grey Ghyll,* St. Martin's, 1978.

Under pseudonym Marianne Lamont: *Dark Changeling,* 1970, Avon, 1973; *Green Glass Moon,* 1970; *Bitter Bride Bed,* 1971; *Nine Moons Wasted,* Putnam, 1976; *Horns of the Moon,* Constable, 1979; *A Serpent's Tooth,* Constable, 1983.

Under pseudonym Alexandra Manners: *The Stone Maiden,* Putnam, 1973; *Candles in the Wood,* Putnam, 1974; *The Singing Swans,* Putnam, 1975; *Cardigan Square,* Putnam, 1977; *Sable Hunter,* Collins, 1977; *Wilford's Daughter,* Putnam, 1978; *White Moths,* Collins, 1979; *Echoing Yesterday,* Corgi, 1983; *Karran Kinrade,* Corgi, 1983; *The Red Bird,* Corgi, 1984; *The Gaming House,* Corgi, 1984.

Under pseudonym Joanne Marshall: *Cuckoo at Candlemas,* Jenkins, 1968; *Cat on a Broomstick,* Jenkins, 1969; *The Dreaming Tower,* Jenkins, 1969; *Flower of Silence,* Mills & Boon, 1970, Avon, 1974; *Babylon Was Dust,* Mills & Boon, 1971; *Wild Boar Wood,* Mills & Boon, 1972, Avon, 1973; *The Trellised Walk,* Mills & Boon, 1973; *Sea-Song,* Mills & Boon, 1973; *Follow a Shadow,* Putnam, 1974; *Valley of Tall Chimneys,* Collins, 1975; *Last Act,* Putnam, 1976; *The Peacock Bed,* St. Martin's, 1978.

Under pseudonym Jeanne Sanders: *Spindrift,* R. Hale, 1974.

AVOCATIONAL INTERESTS: Painting, reading, walking.

* * *

RUNYAN, John
See PALMER, Bernard

* * *

RUSE, Gary Alan 1946-

PERSONAL: Born August 24, 1946, in Miami, Fla.; son of Layton Newman (an electronics technician) and Virginia Mae (Singer) Ruse. *Education:* University of Miami, Coral Gables, Fla., B.A., 1968. *Politics:* "Registered Democrat; hopeful skeptic." *Religion:* "Currently unaffiliated." *Residence:* Miami, Fla.

CAREER: William Morrow & Co., New York, N.Y., book illustrator, 1968; free-lance writer and artist, 1971—. *Military service:* U.S. Army, Engineer Corps, 1969-70; served in Vietnam; received Commendation Medal with oak leaf cluster. *Member:* Science Fiction Writers of America; Mystery Writers of America, Authors Guild, Authors League of America.

WRITINGS—All novels: *Houndstooth,* Prentice-Hall, 1975; *A Game of Titans,* Prentice-Hall, 1976; *The Gods of Cerus Major,* Doubleday, 1982. Contributor to *Analog.*

WORK IN PROGRESS: A Victorian adventure novel, *Darkwinter;* a fantasy adventure novel, *Morlac;* several science fiction novels.

SIDELIGHTS: Gary Alan Ruse told *CA:* "I became interested in writing out of a love for reading and daydreaming. . . . I write the kind of stories I like to read and have always been most impressed by writers who are primarily good story-tellers. . . . my basic outlook does, and I hope will, remain the same: writing is often hard work, but it is simply too much fun to avoid." Urging his readers to let him know their ideas, Ruse says: "If you like something I've written, or even if you dislike something, don't be afraid to let me know, care of the publisher. I'd love to hear readers' opinions."

* * *

RUSSELL, Clifford S(pringer) 1938-

PERSONAL: Born February 11, 1938, in Holyoke, Mass.; son of Kenneth Clifford (a plant manager) and Helen (a teacher; maiden name, Springer) Russell; married Louise Bennett (an economist), February 3, 1965. *Education:* Dartmouth College, B.A. (summa cum laude), 1960; Harvard University, Ph.D., 1968. *Home:* 4344 Verplanck Pl. N.W., Washington, D.C. 20016.

CAREER: Makerere University, Kampala, Uganda, assistant lecturer in economics, summer, 1964; Social Security Administration, Office of Research and Statistics, Baltimore, Md., economic statistician, summer, 1965; Wayne State University, Detroit, Mich., instructor in economics, summer, 1966; Resources for the Future, Washington, D.C., staff member, 1968—, director of regional and urban studies program, 1974-75, director of Division of Institutions and Public Decisions, 1975-77, director of Quality of the Environment Division, 1981—. Guest researcher at University of Bergen, 1976. Member of executive committee and board of trustees of Environmental Defense Fund. Member of environmental studies board, National Academy of Science, 1983-85; consultant to Organization for Economic Co-operation and Development. *Military service:* U.S. Navy, 1960-63; executive officer of "U.S.S. Nipmuc," 1962-63. *Member:* American Economic Association, Association of Environmental and Resource Economists (member of board, 1981-83). *Awards, honors:* Woodrow Wilson fellowship, 1964-68.

WRITINGS: (With David Arey and Robert Kates) *Drought and Water Supply: Implications of the Massachusetts Experience for Municipal Planning,* Johns Hopkins Press, 1970; *Residuals Management in Industry: A Case Study of Petroleum Refining,* Johns Hopkins Press, 1973; (editor) *Ecological Modeling in a Resource Management Framework,* Resources for the Future, 1975; (with William J. Vaughan) *Steel Production: Processes, Products, and Residuals,* Johns Hopkins Press, 1976; (with Walter O. Spofford, Jr., and Robert A. Kelly) *Environmental Quality Management: An Application to the Lower Delaware Valley,* Resources for the Future, 1976; (editor) *Safe Drinking Water: Current and Future Policy Problems,* Resources for the Future, 1978; (editor) *Collective Decision Making: Applications from Public Choice Theory,* Resources for the Future, 1979; (with William J. Vaughan) *Freshwater Recreational Fishing: The National Benefits of Water Pollution Control,* Resources for the Future, 1982; (and editor with Janusz Kindler) *Modeling Water Demands,* Academic Press, 1984.

Contributor: Allen V. Kneese and Blair T. Power, editors, *Environmental Quality Analysis: Theory and Method in the Social Sciences,* Johns Hopkins Press, 1972; Robert Dorfman, Henry Jacoby, and H. A. Thomas, editors, *Models for Managing Regional Water Quality,* Harvard University Press, 1973; *The Management of Water Resources in England and Wales,* Saxon House, 1974; Jerome Rothenberg and I. G. Heggie, editors, *The Management of Water Quality and the Environment,* Macmillan, 1974; Edwin T. Haefele, editor, *The Governance of Common Property Resources,* Johns Hopkins Press, 1974; Edwin Mills, editor, *Economic Analysis of Environmental Problems,* National Bureau of Economic Research, 1975; Gardner M. Brown and James A. Crutchfield, editors, *Economics of Ocean Resources,* University of Washington Press, 1983; Erhard F. Joeres and Martin H. David, editors, *Buying a Better Environment,* University of Wisconsin Press, 1983; Allen Kneese, editor, *Handbook of Resource and Environmental Economics,* North-Holland Publishing, 1984.

Contributor of about twenty-five articles and reviews to economic and scientific journals. Member of executive committee and editorial board of *Land Economics;* member of editorial board of *Economic Perspectives.*

* * *

RYAN, Kevin 1932-

PERSONAL: Born October 7, 1932, in Mt. Vernon, N.Y.; married, 1964, wife's name Marilyn; children: two daughters, one son. *Education:* University of Toronto, B.A., 1955; Columbia University, M.A., 1960, summer graduate study, 1962; Stanford University, Ph.D., 1966; Harvard University, postdoctoral study, 1970-71. *Home:* 127 Commonwealth Ave., Chestnut Hill, Mass. 02167. *Office:* School of Education, Boston University, 605 Commonwealth Ave., Boston, Mass. 02215.

CAREER: High school English teacher in Suffern, N.Y., 1959-63; Stanford University, Stanford, Calif., instructor in education, 1965-66; University of Chicago, Graduate School of Education, Chicago, Ill., assistant professor and director of master of arts in teaching program, 1966-69, director of teacher trainers program, 1969-72, associate dean of training program, 1972-73, associate professor of education, 1973-75; Ohio State University, Columbus, professor of education, 1975-82, associate dean for program development, 1975-78; Boston University, Boston, Mass., professor of education, 1982—.

Visiting professor, Harvard University, 1973, and 1974. Senior study director, National Opinion Research Center, 1974-75. Instructor, Naval Officer's Candidate School, summer, 1963. Member of administrative policy commission, ERIC-Clearinghouse Teacher Education, U.S. Office of Education, 1973. Consultant, Commission for Public School Personnel Policies in Ohio, 1971-73. *Military service:* U.S. Naval Reserve, 1955-59; active duty, 1959-65; became lieutenant. *Member:* American Educational Research Association, American Association of Colleges for Teacher Education, Association for Supervision and Curriculum Development, Phi Delta Kappa. *Awards, honors:* Alfred North Whitehead fellow at Harvard University, 1970-71; American Association of Colleges for Teacher Education certificate of recognition, 1975; Fulbright-Hays Scholar, 1980.

WRITINGS: (With Dwight William Allen) *Microteaching,* Addison-Wesley, 1969; (editor) *Don't Smile until Christmas: Accounts of the First Year of Teaching,* University of Chicago Press, 1970; (contributor) J. L. Olivero and E. G. Buffe, editors, *Educational Manpower,* Indiana University Press, 1970; (contributor) Robert Maidment, editor, *Criticism, Conflict, and Change: Readings in American Education,* Dodd, 1970; (author of foreword) James Lewis, Jr., *Differentiating the Teaching Staff,* Parker Publishing, 1971; (with James M. Cooper) *Those Who Can, Teach,* Houghton, 1972, 3rd edition, 1980; (compiler with Cooper) *Kaleidoscope: Selected Readings in Education,* Houghton, 1972, 3rd edition, 1980; (contributor) Cooper, editor, *Differentiated Staffing,* Saunders, 1972.

(Editor) *Teacher Education,* University of Chicago Press, 1975; (editor with David E. Purpel) *Moral Education,* McCutchan, 1976; (with others) *Biting the Apple: Accounts of First Year Teachers,* Longman, 1980; (with wife, Marilyn Ryan) *Making a Marriage,* St. Martin's, 1982.

Multi-media instructional materials: (With others) "Teaching Skills for Elementary and Secondary School Teachers," General Learning Corporation, 1969; "Values for Youth: New Approaches to Moral Education," Thomas More Association, 1975. Contributor to education journals.

* * *

RYKEN, Leland 1942-

PERSONAL: Born May 17, 1942, in New Sharon, Iowa; son of Frank (engaged in farming) and Eva (Bos) Ryken; married Mary Graham, August 22, 1964; children: Philip Graham, Margaret Lynn, Nancy Elizabeth. *Education:* Central College (now Central University of Iowa), B.A., 1964; University of Oregon, Ph.D., 1968. *Politics:* Independent. *Religion:* Presbyterian. *Home:* 1118 North Howard, Wheaton, Ill. 60187. *Office:* Department of English, Wheaton College, Wheaton, Ill. 60187.

CAREER: Wheaton College, Wheaton, Ill., professor of English, 1968—.

WRITINGS: The Apocalyptic Vision in "Paradise Lost," Cornell University Press, 1970; *The Literature of the Bible,* Zondervan, 1974; (contributor) Kenneth Gros Louis, editor, *Literary Interpretations of Biblical Narratives,* Abingdon, 1974; *Triumphs of the Imagination: Literature in Christian Perspective,* Inter-Varsity Press, 1979; *The Christian Imagination: Essays on Literature and the Arts,* Baker Book, 1981; (co-editor and contributor) *Milton and Scriptural Tradition: The Bible into Poetry,* University of Missouri Press, 1984; (editor) *A Library of Literary Criticism: The Testament,* Ungar, 1984. Editor of *Heroes of Genesis, Heroines of the Bible, Parables and Portraits of the Bible,* for Literature of the Bible, Inc., 1976, 1977. Contributor to scholarly journals.

WORK IN PROGRESS: Books on literature in Christian perspective, the Bible as literature, and on Puritanism.

BIOGRAPHICAL/CRITICAL SOURCES: Virginia Quarterly Review, summer, 1970.

S

SABLE, Martin Howard 1924-

PERSONAL: Born September 24, 1924, in Haverhill, Mass.; son of Benjamin (a distributor) and Ida (Saberlinsky) Sable; married Minna Gibbs, February 5, 1950; children: James S., Charles D. *Education:* Boston University, A.B., 1946, M.A., 1951; Universidad Nacional Autonoma de Mexico, Doctorate, 1952; Simmons College, M.S., 1959. *Home:* 4518 North Larkin St., Milwaukee, Wis. 53211. *Office:* School of Library and Information Science, University of Wisconsin—Milwaukee, Milwaukee, Wis. 53201.

CAREER: Northeastern University, Boston, Mass., staff librarian and bibliographer, 1959-63; California State College at Los Angeles (now California State University, Los Angeles), language librarian, 1963-64; Los Angeles County Library, Hawthorne, Calif., reference librarian, 1964-65; University of California, Los Angeles, assistant research professor at Latin American Center, 1965-68; University of Wisconsin—Milwaukee, School of Library and Information Science, associate professor 1968-72, professor, 1972—. Visiting professor at Hebrew University of Jerusalem, 1972-73. Bibliographer, Office of Latin American Studies, Harvard University, 1962-63. *Member:* Institute of International Education, International Federation for Documentation, Library Association of Colombia (honorary member), American Library Association, Conference on Latin American History, Association of American Library Schools, Latin American Studies Association, American Association of University Professors, Midwest Association for Latin American Studies, North Central Council of Latin Americanists.

WRITINGS: A Selective Bibliography in Science and Engineering, G. K. Hall, 1964; *Master Directory for Latin America,* Latin American Center, University of California (Los Angeles), 1965; *Periodicals for Latin American Economic Development, Trade and Finance: An Annotated Bibliography,* Latin American Center, University of California, 1965; *A Guide to Latin American Studies,* two volumes, Latin American Center, University of California, 1967; *UFO Guide: 1947-1967,* Rainbow Press, 1967; *Communism in Latin America, an International Bibliography: 1900-1945,* Latin American Center, University of California, 1968; *A Bio-Bibliography of the Kennedy Family,* Scarecrow, 1969; *Urbanization Research, with Special Reference to Latin America: An Inventory,* Center for Latin American Studies, University of Wisconsin—Milwaukee, 1969.

Latin American Agriculture: A Bibliography, Center for Latin American Studies, University of Wisconsin—Milwaukee, 1970; *Latin American Studies in the Non-Western World and Eastern Europe,* Scarecrow, 1970; *Latin American Urbanization: A Guide to the Literature, Organizations and Personnel,* Scarecrow, 1971; *International and Area Studies Librarianship: Case Studies,* Scarecrow, 1973; *The Guerrilla Movement in Latin America,* University of Wisconsin—Milwaukee, 1977; *Exobiology: A Research Guide,* Green Oak, 1978; *A Guide to Nonprint Materials for Latin American Studies,* Blaine Ethridge, 1979.

The Latin American Studies Directory, Blaine Ethridge, 1981; *A Bibliography of the Future for Arts-Recreation-Culture, Communication, Economy-Employment, Education, Health and Wellbeing, Housing, Land Use, Public Safety, and Transportation,* Goals for Greater Milwaukee 2000, 1981; *Materials on Latin America for Elementary and Secondary Schools,* 3rd edition (Sable was not associated with previous editions), Center for Latin American Studies, University of Wisconsin—Milwaukee, 1982; *The Protection of the Library: An International Bibliography,* Haworth Press, 1984. Also author of *Latin American Jewry: A Research Guide,* 1977.

Contributor: Jose Rubia Barcia and M. A. Zeitlin, editors, *Unamuno: Creator and Creation,* University of California Press, 1967. Contributor to *Encyclopedia of Library and Information Science,* to "Scripta Hierosolymitana" series, and to periodicals, including *New England Modern Language Association Bulletin, Current History, American Documentation, International Library Review, Herald of Library Science, Inter-American Review of Bibliography, European Studies Newsletter,* and *Behavioral and Social Science Librarian.*

WORK IN PROGRESS: A Checklist of the Writings of Pioneer Latinamericanists in the United States of America, Latin American Research Resources, and *A Bibliography of Holocaust Bibliographies and Directory.*

SIDELIGHTS: "Learning is the greatest adventure of all," Martin Howard Sable told *CA.* "Contributions to knowledge and progress distinguish mankind from the rest of the animal kingdom. I am grateful for the great teachers I've been privileged to learn from, many of whom I attempt to emulate in my teaching methods. I hope to have been instrumental in my students' success in their respective careers."

* * *

SACHS, Mendel 1927-

PERSONAL: Born April 13, 1927, in Portland Ore.; son of Samuel (a rabbi) and Florence (Farber) Sachs; married Yetty Herman, June 22, 1952; children: Robert, Daniel, Carolyn, Michael. *Education:* University of California, Los Angeles, A.B., 1949, M.A., 1950, Ph.D., 1954. *Home:* 95 Carriage Cir., Williamsville, N.Y. 14221. *Office:* Department of Physics, State University of New York, Buffalo, N.Y. 14260.

CAREER: University of California, Livermore, physicist in radiation laboratory, 1954-56; Lockheed Missiles and Space Co., Palo Alto, Calif., research scientist, 1956-61; San Jose State College (now University), San Jose, Calif., assistant professor of physics, 1957-61; McGill University, Montreal, Quebec, research professor of physics, 1961-62; Boston University, Boston, Mass., associate professor of physics, 1962-66; State University of New York at Buffalo, professor of physics, 1966—. *Military service:* U.S. Navy, 1945-46. *Member:* British Society for the Philosophy of Science.

WRITINGS: Solid State Theory, McGraw, 1963; (contributor) R. Cohen and M. Wartofsky, editors, *Boston Studies in the Philosophy of Science,* Volume III, Humanities, 1968; *The Search for a Theory of Matter,* McGraw, 1971; *The Field Concept in Contemporary Science,* C. C Thomas, 1973; (contributor) C. A. Hooker, editor, *Contemporary Research in the Foundations and Philosophy of Quantum Theory,* D. Reidel, 1973; *Ideas of the Theory of Relativity,* Israel Universities, 1974; *Ideas of Matter,* University Press of America, 1981; *General Relativity and Matter,* D. Reidel, 1982.

Contributor of articles to numerous periodicals, including *International Journal of Theoretical Physics, Nuovo Cimento, British Journal for Philosophy of Science, La Recherche, Nature, American Journal of Physics,* and *Foundations of Physics.* Member of editorial board, *Annales Fond. L. de Broglie.*

WORK IN PROGRESS: Research in general relativity applied to astronomical and elementary particle problems, foundations of quantum theory, and philosophy and history of science.

SIDELIGHTS: Mendel Sachs told *CA:* "The major part of my writing experience in theoretical physics and the philosophy of physics has been concerned with a single question: Is the basis of Einstein's theory of general relativity broad enough to explain the fundamental nature of matter in all domains of present-day experimental knowledge in physics, from elementary particle physics to cosmology? My research results so far imply that the answer is affirmative, provided that a) in particle physics, the current concepts of quantum theory are abandoned (as Einstein anticipated), though its mathematical form is maintained in special applications of low energy physics, as a linear approximation, and b) in astrophysics, some of the contemporary ideas must be *abandoned,* such as the cosmological 'single big bang' model, the 'cosmological principle,' asserting that the matter of the universe is homogeneously and isotropically distributed, and the notion about the existence of black hole stars as actual mathematical singularities of a space-time metric.

"Instead of these ideas, a general field theory of matter, based entirely on Einstein's principle of relativity, entails numerous (and continuously differentiable) variables only to represent matter, where instead of a model in terms of separable 'things' (galaxies, stars, people, or protons), the matter of the universe is characterized by a genuine continuum, where field concentrations play the role of the 'apparent' things, analogous to the role of the ripples of a pond, as continuous (though distinguishable) manifestations of the entire pond, rather than things in it.

"An important result of this research program is its resounding negative conclusion to Einstein's question in his debate with Bohr, 'Did God play with dice when He created the universe?' For general relativity theory, as a fundamental theory of matter, is a fully deterministic field theory of the universe, in the spirit of the Spinozist philosophical outlook, where the (linear) probability calculus, called 'quantum mechanics,' turns out to be a mathematical approximation for a fully covariant, nonlinear field theory of inertia, which has no probability interpretation in its general form. The fundamental continuous field variables, according to this view of matter, then entail a genuine unification of the force manifestations of matter, of all types, with its inertial manifestations, in the form of a unified field theory, that in principle entails any domain of matter, from elementary particle physics to cosmology."

* * *

SACKMAN, Harold 1927-

PERSONAL: Born May 11, 1927, in New York, N.Y.; son of Louis and Lena Sackman; married Kathleen Kiviat, 1951; children: Jeffrey, Sharon, Amy. *Education:* City College (now City College of the City University of New York), B.S., 1948; Columbia University, M.A., 1949; Fordham University, Ph.D., 1953. *Home:* 13609 Bayliss Rd., Los Angeles, Calif. 90049. *Office:* School of Business and Economics, California State University, Los Angeles, Calif. 90032.

CAREER: Fordham University, Bronx, N.Y., research associate working on Air Force projects, 1951-53; Psychological Research Associates, Washington, D.C., research associate, 1952-53; RAND Corp., Santa Monica, Calif., social scientist in Systems Research Laboratory, 1953-54; Systems Development Corp. (independent nonprofit organization supported by U.S. Government and foundations), Santa Monica, supervisor of problem design group in air defense program, 1954-58, scientist working on SAGE computer program, 1959-63, senior human factors scientist, 1964-66, senior research scientist, 1968-70; University of Southern California, Social Science Research Institute, Los Angeles, Calif., senior psychologist, 1970-71; Kansas State University, Manhattan, professor of computer science and chairman of department, 1971-72; RAND Corp., senior psychologist, 1972-76; California State Polytechnic University, School of Business, Pomona, professor of information systems, 1976-77; University of California, Irvine, lecturer, 1977-78; University of Manchester, Grade School of Business, Manchester, England, professor and senior research fellow, 1978-79; California State University, Los Angeles, professor of business information systems, 1979—. Lecturer, University of California, Los Angeles, 1968-71. Vice-president of planning and member of board of directors and of the executive committee, San Fernando Valley Child Guidance Clinic, 1975-81. Research consultant to numerous businesses, organizations, and institutions. *Military service:* U.S. Naval Reserve, active duty as electronics technician, 1945-46.

MEMBER: American Psychological Association (associate member), American Federation of Information Processing Societies, American Association for the Advancement of Science, Association for Computing Machinery, Phi Beta Kappa.

WRITINGS: Computers, System Science, and Evolving Society, Wiley, 1967; (contributor) Perry E. Rosove, editor, *Developing Computer-Based Information Systems,* Wiley, 1967; (contributor) William C. McGee, editor, *Effective Program Development: The Choices,* Data Processing Digest, 1969; (contributor) K. deGreene, editor, *Systems Psychology,* McGraw, 1970; (contributor) Geroge F. Weinwurm, editor, *On the Management of Computer Programming,* Auerbach, 1970; (editor with Norman Nie and contributor) *The Information Utility and Social Choice,* AFIPS Press, 1970; *Man-Computer Problem Solving,* Mason & Lipscomb, 1970; *Mass Information Utilities and Social Excellence,* Mason & Lipscomb, 1971; (contributor) Alan F. Westin, editor, *Information Technology in a Democracy,* Harvard University Press, 1971; (editor with R. L. Citrenbaum and contributor) *Online Planning,* Prentice-Hall, 1972; (editor with H. Borko and contributor) *Computers and the Problems of Society,* AFIPS Press, 1972; (editor with B. Boehm and contributor) *Planning Community Information Utilities,* AFIPS Press, 1972.

(Editor with E. Mumford and contributor) *Human Choice and Computers,* North Holland Publishing, 1975; *Delphi Critique: Expert Opinion, Forecasting, and Group Process,* Heath, 1975; (contributor) Anthony Debons and William J. Cameron, editors, *Perspectives in Information Science,* NATO Advanced Study Institutes, 1975; (editor and contributor) *State of the Art Report on Man-Computer Communications,* Infotech International, 1979; *Social Management of Future Computer Network Information Services,* Trident Publishers, 1981; *Collected Papers on Computers and Society,* Trident Publishers, 1984, Volume I: *Social Impacts and Social Theory,* Volume II: *Systems Methodology and Experimental Studies.* Also author of reports for U.S. Air Force, Social Science Research Institute and other organizations, and papers on man-computer communications and system test and evaluation. Contributor of articles to journals, including *Journal of the Association for Computing Machinery, Machine Design, Journal of the Human Factors Society,* and *Policy Analysis.*

SIDELIGHTS: Harold Sackman wrote *CA:* "Fresh out of graduate school as a fledgling psychologist in 1955, I was introduced to the Buck Rogers world of the first large-scale, realtime, command and control system—the Cape Cod prototype of our computer-based continental air defense system. Watching 100 military operators fighting simulated air battles over American airspace in the vast, dimly lit Air Defense Direction Center, hunched over eerie phosphorescent TV screens, aiming light guns at rapidly changing alphanumeric and geographic displays, I knew that the 21st century had arrived. It subsequently became clear that except for the vagaries of the marketplace, there was no social plan to harness the awesome potential of computers in the public interest. I have since dedicated my professional efforts as a psychologist and information scientist toward explicating the vital public stakes and the polarizing gap between the information rich and the information poor with the exponential growth of computer-aided services. I continue to hope that cooperative, long-range social planning may eventually give us the best rather than the worst of possible computer worlds for posterity."

* * *

SACKSON, Sid 1920-

PERSONAL: Born February 4, 1920, in Chicago, Ill.; son of Aaron J. (an engineer) and Esther (Rosen) Sackson; married Bernice P. Berdick, September 7, 1941; children: Dana R., Dale E. Friedman. *Education:* City College (now City College of the City University of New York), B.S., 1943. *Religion:* "No organized religion." *Home and office:* 1287 Arnow Ave., Bronx, N.Y. 10469.

CAREER: Writer and inventor of games. Licensed civil engineer; U.S. Department of the Navy, Brooklyn, N.Y., civilian chief engineering draftsman, 1940-46; Corbett-Tinghir Co., New York City, engineering designer, 1946-48; City of New York, Traffic Department, traffic engineer, 1948-51; Dorr Co., Stanford, Conn., engineering designer, 1951-55; Shapiro Associates, New York City, engineer and programmer, 1955-70.

WRITINGS—Juveniles, except as indicated: *A Gamut of Games* (adult), Random House, 1969, revised edition, Pantheon, 1982; *Beyond Tic Tac Toe: Challenging and Exciting New Games to Be Played with Colored Pens or Pencils,* Pantheon, 1975; (contributor) *The Family Creative Workshop,* Plenary, 1976; *Beyond Solitaire: Challenging New Games for One to Play with Colored Pens or Pencils,* Pantheon, 1976; *Beyond Words: Exciting New Word Games,* Pantheon, 1977; *Beyond Competition: Six Dynamic Games for Two or More Players to Win Together,* Pantheon, 1977; *Calculate!: Use Your Calculator and Your Wits in 6 Challenging Games for 2 or More Players,* Pantheon, 1979; *Playing Cards around the World,* Pantheon, 1981. Author of game review column, "Briefings," in *Strategy and Tactics,* 1969-81. Contributing editor, *Games,* 1978—.

WORK IN PROGRESS: Game reviews and original games for several magazines; research on old and new games.

SIDELIGHTS: Game creator, collector, and historian Sid Sackson is the author of *A Gamut of Games,* described by Robert F. Sayre in the *Nation* as a "suitably light-spirited and yet precisely written and illustrated description of thirty-eight new and different games." Not merely a collection of Sackson's own inventions, the book also contains his research into the history of games and their place in society. One of Sackson's historical anecdotes follows the development of the popular board game Monopoly, whose origins can be traced to "The Landlord's Game," patented by a woman in 1904. In Sayre's words, "Sackson has a fascinating store of information about games," having sought them out "in the Patent Office and in foreign museums and libraries."

"A game is for fun, but Sid Sackson takes it one step further: the game as an art form," says Barbara Karlin in the *New York Times Book Review.* Karlin's remarks appear in a review of Sackson's *Tic Tac Toe: Challenging and Exciting New Games to Be Played with Colored Pens or Pencils.* The book consists of a series of games in which the players alternately color patterns of lines and geometric figures. The completion of the games then yields an abstract work of art, each one in the style of a different contemporary artist, each one an example of what Sayre calls Sackson's "splendid variety of the hard and the easy, the quick and the cerebral."

Sackson described for *CA* how his passion for games developed: "When I was in first grade, the high point of the day would occur when the teacher distributed pages from a magazine and instructed us to circle the words we knew. The positioning of the circles and their relationship to each other interested me much more than the words themselves. I evolved rules for joining the circles, set objectives for the growing chains, and thereby created my first game.

"Now, many years after my initial discovery of games in the first grade, I am just as intrigued by what makes a game tick as I was then. I have created several hundred games of my own, but I am just as fascinated by one created by a friend, one I buy in a store, or one I rediscover in a library or museum. With this as a spur—and helped by travels throughout North America and Europe—my collection of games and books on games (in eight languages) has continued to grow. It is now recognized as the largest private collection, and very probably the largest anywhere. Although final arrangements have not been completed, the collection will ultimately be donated to a museum or a university."

The games that Sackson has invented and published include "Acquire," "Sleuth," "Bazaar," "Executive Decision," "Venture," "Monad," "Focus," "Major Battles and Campaigns of General George S. Patton," "Major Campaigns of General Douglas MacArthur," "Totally," "The Harry Lorayne Memory Game," "Sly," "Can't Stop," "Temptation Poker," and "Domination."

BIOGRAPHICAL/CRITICAL SOURCES: *Nation*, March 9, 1970; *New York Times Book Review*, November 16, 1975.

* * *

SAGER, Clifford J. 1916-

PERSONAL: Born September 28, 1916, in New York, N.Y.; son of Max and Lena (Lipman) Sager; children: Barbara (Mrs. Dickson Parsons), Philip, Anthony, Rebecca. *Education:* Pennsylvania State University, B.S., 1937; New York University, M.D., 1941; New York Medical College, certificate in psychoanalysis, 1949. *Office:* 65 East 76th St., New York, N.Y. 10021.

CAREER: Licensed to practice medicine in New York, New Jersey, and California; Montefiore Hospital, New York City, intern, 1941-42; Bellevue Hospital, New York City, fellow in psychiatry, 1942, 1946-48; New York Medical College, New York City, director of therapeutic service and associate dean of Postgraduate Center for Mental Health, 1948-60, professor of psychiatry and director of partial hospitalization programs, family treatment and study unit, 1960-70; Metropolitan Hospital, New York City, attending psychiatrist, 1960-70; Mount Sinai Medical School, New York City, clinical professor of psychiatry, 1970-80; New York Hospital-Cornell Medical Center, New York City, clinical professor of psychiatry, 1980; attending psychiatrist at Payne Whitney Clinic, 1980—. Associate director, department of psychiatry (family and group therapy), and attending physician, Beth Israel Medical Center, New York City; chief of applied behavioral sciences and attending physician, Gouverneur Hospital, New York City, 1971-74; psychiatric director, Jewish Board of Family and Children Services, New York City, 1974—. *Military service:* U.S. Army, medical corps, 1942-46; became captain.

MEMBER: American Psychiatric Association, American Medical Association, Academy of Psychoanalysis, American Orthopsychiatric Association, American Group Psychotherapy Association (member of board of directors, 1962—; president, 1968-70), Society of Medical Psychoanalysts (president, 1960-61), American Board of Psychology and Neurology, Eastern Society for Sex Therapy (president, 1976-77), New York Society for Clinical Psychiatry.

WRITINGS: (Contributor) Alfred H. Rifkin, editor, *Schizophrenia in Psychoanalytic Office Practice*, Grune, 1957; (author of introduction) John G. Howells, *The Theory and Practice of Family Psychiatry*, C. C Thomas, 1963; (contributor) Jules Masserman, editor, *Current Psychiatric Therapies*, Grune, 1965; (contributor) Silvano Arieti, editor, *American Handbook of Psychiatry*, Volume III, Basic Books, 1966; (contributor) Alfred M. Freedmand and H. I. Kaplan, editors, *Comprehensive Textbook of Psychiatry*, Williams & Wilkins, 1967; (contributor) S. E. Waxenberg, Thomas L. Brayboy, S. Slipp, and Barbara R. Waxenberg, editors, *Progress in Community Mental Health*, Grune, 1969.

(With Brayboy and B. Waxenberg) *The Black Ghetto Family in Therapy: A Laboratory Experiment*, Grove, 1970; (with Helen Singer Kaplan) *Progress in Group and Family Therapy*, Brunner, 1972; *Marriage Contracts and Couple Therapy: Hidden Sources of Intimate Relationships*, Brunner, 1976; (with Bernice Hunt) *Intimate Partners: Hidden Patterns in Love Relationships*, McGraw, 1979; *Treating the Remarried Family*, Brunner, 1983. Also contributor of chapters to numerous textbooks.

Contributor to *Mental Hygiene, American Journal of Psychotherapy, Journal of Neurological and Mental Diseases, Psychoanalytic Review, International Journal of Group Psychotherapy, Journal of Psychology,* and other professional journals. Member of editorial board, *Family Process, American Journal of Orthopsychiatry, International Journal of Group Psychotherapy,* and *Divorce;* editor, *Journal of Sex and Marital Therapy.*

WORK IN PROGRESS: Various articles on marriage, family, and sex for professional journals.

* * *

SALMON, Annie Elizabeth 1899-
(Elizabeth Ashley, Nancy Martin)

PERSONAL: Born September 26, 1899, in Croydon, England; daughter of Arthur and Annie (Griggs) Martin; married Leslie Bernard Salmon (a telecommunications engineer), September 10, 1932 (died, 1966); children: Joan Frances (Mrs. Leslie George Oppitz), Brenda Elizabeth (Mrs. Graham Whitworth Salmon). *Education:* Attended elementary schools in Croydon and Norwood, England. *Politics:* Conservative.

CAREER: Canadian Customs Department, London, England, secretary to investigator of values, 1922-32; Canadian customs consultant in England, 1932-33; writer, 1938—. *Member:* Society of Authors, Society of Women Writers and Journalists, Women's Press Club of London (chairman, 1961), Croydon Writers' Circle (honorary life member; president). *Awards, honors:* Berwick Sayers Memorial Prize from Croydon Writers' Circle, 1966-67.

WRITINGS—Juveniles, except as indicated; under pseudonym Nancy Martin: *Bumps,* University of London Press, 1942; *Stories for Judy and Elizabeth and Jane* (Bible stories), Victory Press, 1943; *The Holy Land,* Edinburgh House Press, 1944; *The Shepherds' Message* (nativity play), Religious Education Press, 1944; *Abwa and Her Picture,* Edinburgh House Press, 1946, 2nd edition, 1950; *Jolly Jinks,* Victory Press, 1946; *No Music for Diana,* GB Publications Ltd., 1948; *Belindamay and Her Sixpence,* Victory Press, 1949; *Belindamay and Her White Mice,* Victory Press, 1949.

Africa, Edinburgh House Press, 1950; *Young Farmers at Gaythorne,* Macmillan, 1953; *Call the Vet,* Macmillan, 1953; *Young Farmers in Denmark,* Macmillan, 1954; *Purley Congregational Church* (adult), privately printed, 1954; *Adventure on the Alm* (geography), Macmillan, 1955; *Young Farmers in Scotland,* Macmillan, 1956; *Fifty Years of Progress* (adult), privately printed, 1957; *Vet in the Making,* Macmillan, 1957; *Occupation for Kay,* Macmillan, 1958; *Ann and Peter in Denmark,* Muller, 1959.

Jean Behind the Counter, Macmillan, 1960; *Finn the Fisherboy* (geography), Macmillan, 1961; *Probation Officer,* Macmillan, 1962; *Jean, Teenage Fashion Buyer,* Macmillan, 1964; *Three Horses,* Macmillan, 1964; *Three Dogs,* Macmillan, 1965; *Call the Nurse,* Macmillan, 1966; *Chi-Chi the Giant Panda* (nonfiction), Arlington Books, 1966; *Call the Courier,* Macmillan, 1967; *Three at the Zoo,* Macmillan, 1968; *Teresa Joins the Red Cross,* Macmillan, 1968; *The Post Office: From Carrier Pigeon to Confravision* (nonfiction), Dent, 1969.

Red Cross Challenge, Macmillan, 1970; *Four Girls in a Store,* Macmillan, 1971; *The Fire Service Today* (nonfiction), Dent, 1972; *William Carey: The Man Who Never Gave Up* (biography), Hodder & Stoughton, 1974; *Search and Rescue: The Story of the Coastguard,* David & Charles, 1974; *Prayers for Children and Young People,* Hodder & Stoughton, 1975, Westminster, 1976; *Pilots of Sea and River Craft,* Terence Dalton Ltd., 1977; *The Great Doctor: The Story of Albert Schweitzer,* Wheaton, 1978; *Enjoying Retirement,* Lion Publishing, 1979.

River Ferries, Dalton, 1980; *In a Changing World,* John Grooms Association for the Disabled, 1982; *Man with a Vision,* Wheaton, 1983. Also author of *Children's Bible Stories from the New Testament,* 1982, and *Children's Bible Stories from the Old Testament,* 1983.

Children's books; under pseudonym Elizabeth Ashley: *The Wonderful Holiday,* Ward Lock, 1957; *Happy Venture,* Evangelical Publishers, 1959; *The Caravan Family,* Evangelical Publishers, 1961; *A Garden for Trudy,* Evangelical Publishers, 1962; *Seven Tiny Stories About Jesus,* Dean & Son, 1963; *Day by Day Stories About Jesus,* Dean & Son, 1964; *Ten Stories About Jesus,* Dean & Son, 1965; *Alison's Choice,* Evangelical Publishers, 1965; *Wonderful Stories Jesus Told,* Dean & Son, 1967; *The Story of Jesus,* Dean & Son, 1967; *The Christmas Story,* Dean & Son, 1969; *Della's Discovery,* Evangelical Publishers, 1970; *Another Book About Jesus,* Dean & Son, 1972; *A Child's Story of Jesus,* Dean & Son, 1982.

Author of scripts for British Broadcasting Corp.

WORK IN PROGRESS: A biography, for Wheaton & Co.

SIDELIGHTS: Annie Elizabeth Salmon writes that she began by writing stories and books for very young children, and as her own children grew older, began writing for older children. She has conducted research for her writing in coal mines, hospitals, coastguard stations, naval air stations, and helicopter ports. Her books have been published in German, Norwegian, Swedish, Dutch, and Finnish.

* * *

SALZANO, F(rancisco) M(auro) 1928-

PERSONAL: Born July 27, 1928, in Cachoeira do Sul, Brazil; son of Francisco (a medical doctor) and Onelia (Pertille) Salzano; married Thereza Torres, March 20, 1952; children: Felipe, Renato. *Education:* Federal University of Rio Grande do Sul, Sc. Bach., 1950, licentiate, 1952, Priv.Doc., 1960; University of Sao Paulo, fellow, 1951, Ph.D., 1955. *Home:* Venancio Aires, 1092, Apt. 11, Porto Alegre, Rio Grande do Sul, Brazil. *Office:* Departamento de Genetica, Federal University of Rio Grande do Sul, Caixa Postal 1953, Porto Alegre, Rio Grande do Sul, Brazil.

CAREER: Federal University of Rio Grande do Sul, Porto Alegre, Rio Grande do Sul, Brazil, instructor, 1951-60, assistant professor, 1960-67, associate professor, 1967-81, professor of genetics, 1981—. Institute of Natural Sciences, researcher, 1952-62, head of genetics section, 1963-68, director, 1968-71. *Member:* International Union of Anthropological and Ethnological Sciences (vice-president, 1978—), International Association of Human Biologists (secretary-general, 1974-80), Latin American Genetics Society (member of board, 1972-76, 1983-85), Brazilian Society of Genetics (president, 1966-68), Brazilian Society for the Advancement of Science (member of council, 1961-77, 1979-83), Brazilian Academy of Sciences. *Awards, honors:* Rockefeller Foundation fellow, 1956-57. Silver medal of Sociedade Brasileira para o Progresso do Ciencia, 1973, for distinguished service to the sciences in Brazil.

WRITINGS: O Problema das especies cripticas: Estudos no sub-grupo bocainensis (Drosophila), Instituto de Ciencias Naturais, Universidade Federal do Rio Grande do Sul, 1956; *Estudos geneticos e demograficos entre os indios do Rio Grande do Sul,* Instituto de Ciencias Naturais, Universidade Federal do Rio Grande do Sul, 1961; (with Newton Freire-Maia) *Populacoes brasileiras: Aspectos demograficos, geneticos e antropologicos,* Companhia Editora Nacional and Universidade de Sao Paulo, 1967, translation published as *Problems in Human Biology: A Study of Brazilian Populations,* text edition, Wayne State University Press, 1970.

(Editor) *The Ongoing Evolution of Latin American Populations,* C. C Thomas, 1970; (editor) *The Role of Natural Selection in Human Evolution,* North-Holland, 1975; *Pindorama, a inocencia perdida,* Vozes, 1975; *Voci e soa heranca,* Civilizacao Brasileira, 1979; *Genetica odontologica,* T. A. Queiroz/Universidade de Sao Paulo, 1982; *A genetica e a lei,* T. A. Queiroz, 1983.

Contributor of 440 scientific papers to journals and books in Brazil, Mexico, the United States, Europe, and India.

WORK IN PROGRESS: Research in human genetics, including population structure and polymorphisms, chromosome aberrations, problems of medical interest, and studies of twins.

SIDELIGHTS: F. M. Salzano told *CA* that he was at first involved with research in animal genetics. After a one-year stay at the human genetics department of the University of Michigan, however, he became interested in human genetics. He has traveled extensively in Brazil's interior, conducting Indian group studies.

* * *

SANCTUARY, Gerald 1930-

PERSONAL: Born November 22, 1930, in Bridport, England; son of John C. T. (a physician) and Maisie (Brooks) Sanctuary; married Rosemary L'Estrange, July 28, 1956; children: Celia, Nigel, Thomas, Charles, Sophie. *Education:* Attended Bryanston School, Blandford, England, and Law Society's School of Law, London. *Home:* 100 Fishpool St., St. Albans, Hertfordshire, England. *Office:* 123 Golden Ln., London, England.

CAREER: Hasties (attorneys), London, England, partner, 1957-63; National Marriage Guidance Council, London, field secretary, 1963-65, national secretary, 1965-69; Sex Information and Educational Council of the U.S. (SIECUS), New York, N.Y., director for international services, 1969, executive director, 1969-71; The Law Society, London, secretary of professional and public relations, 1971-79; Royal Society for Mentally Handicapped Children and Adults, London, legal adviser, 1979—. Speaker at conferences on the family and marriage in Europe, Africa, and United States; assisted in formation of Family Service Council of Kenya, 1967. Liveryman and honorary legal adviser, Guild of Air Pilots and Air Navigators of London; freeman of City of London. *Military service:* Royal Air Force, 1953-55. *Member:* American Association of Marriage Counselors (clinical member).

WRITINGS: *Marriage under Stress,* Verry, 1968; (with Constance Whitehead) *Divorce—and After: A Handbook for the Divorced and Separated,* Gollancz, 1970; *Before You See a Solicitor,* Oyez, 1973, 2nd edition, 1983; *After I'm Gone: What Will Happen to My Handicapped Child?,* Souvenir Press, 1984. Contributor to journals.

AVOCATIONAL INTERESTS: Amateur drama (has played seven Shakespearean roles and many other parts).

* * *

SANDE, Theodore Anton 1933-

PERSONAL: Born November 21, 1933, in New London, Conn.; son of Lars Anton and Viola (Edgecombe) Sande; married Solveig Inga-Maj Imselius, August 6, 1960; children: Susanne Ingrid, Lars Michael. *Education:* Rhode Island School of Design, B.Sc., 1956; Yale University, M.Arch., 1961; University of Pennsylvania, Ph.D., 1972. *Religion:* Episcopalian. *Home:* 2735 Landon Rd., Shaker Heights, Ohio 44122. *Office:* 10825 East Blvd., Cleveland, Ohio 44106.

CAREER: Hakon Ahlberg, Stockholm, Sweden, designer and architect, 1960; Washburn, Luther & Rowley, Attleboro, Mass., designer, 1961-62; Barker & Turoff Associates, Providence, R.I., designer, 1962-63; Turoff Associates, Providence, junior partner, 1964-67; Turoff & Sande, Providence, partner, 1968-70; self-employed architect and consultant in Cranston, R.I., 1970, Drexel Hill, Pa., 1970-72, and Williamstown, Mass., 1972-75; National Trust for Historic Preservation, Washington, D.C., director of professional services, 1975-76, director of planning and development, 1977-78, vice-president for historic properties, 1979-80; Western Reserve Historical Society, Cleveland, Ohio, executive director, 1981—. Certified by National Council of Architectural Registration Boards; registered architect in Rhode Island and Massachusetts.

Lecturer in art at Williams College, 1972-75; faculty member of Clark Art Institute, 1973-75; visiting professor of architecture at Rensselaer Polytechnic Institute, 1973-74, and University of Pennsylvania, spring, 1976, 1977; adjunct professor of history and American studies at Case Western Reserve University; lecturer at University of Michigan, Brown University, Worcester Polytechnic Institute, University of Vermont, Rhode Island School of Design, and Smithsonian Institution. Has exhibited drawings in Providence, R.I. Co-chairman of Conference on Industrial Archaeology, Smithsonian Institution, 1971; member of North Adams Historic District Study Commission, 1974, and of scientific committee of Ecomusee (Le Creusot, France), 1976. Trustee of William H. Hall Free Library, 1970, American Precision Museum, 1973-76, and Ohio Museums Association, 1982—. Consultant to Connecticut Historic Preservation Society, 1782 Quaker Meeting House Restoration, and other organizations. *Military service:* U.S. Navy Reserve, 1956-66, active duty as air intelligence officer, 1956-60; became lieutenant.

MEMBER: American Association of Museums, Society of Architectural Historians, Society for Industrial Archeology (founder; first president, 1971-72; member of board of directors, 1973-76), Royal Oak Foundation, Rowfant Club. *Awards, honors:* George Frazer Award, Rhode Island chapter of American Institute of Architects, 1956, for excellence in architectural design; Frank Miles Day Prize, University of Pennsylvania, 1972.

WRITINGS: *Industrial Archeology: A New Look at the American Heritage,* Stephen Greene Press, 1976; (co-editor) *Historic Preservation of Engineering Works,* American Society of Civil Engineers, 1981. Also editor of *New England Textile Mill Survey,* 1971, and contributor to *Guidebook to Philadelphia Architecture,* 1974. Contributor of articles and reviews to history, technology, architecture, and archaeology journals.

* * *

SANDERS, Jeanne
See RUNDLE, Anne

* * *

SANDERS, Pieter 1912-

PERSONAL: Born September 21, 1912, in Schiedam, Netherlands; son of Pieter (an architect) and Ina (Habraken) Sanders; married June 24, 1937; wife's name, Ida; children: Pieter, Frederieke (Mrs. Willard B. Taylor), Martijn. *Education:* Attended University of Leiden, 1930-34, Ph.D., 1945. *Religion:* Protestant. *Home:* 134 Burg. Kanppertlaan, 3117 BD Schiedam, Netherlands.

CAREER: Admitted to bar, 1936; private law practice, 1936-59; Netherlands School of Economics, Rotterdam, professor of corporation law, beginning 1959; Erasmus University of Rotterdam, Rotterdam, began as professor of commercial law and comparative law, became emeritus professor, 1980—. Member of board of directors, K.L.M. (Royal Dutch Airlines), Ryn Schelde Verolme Shipyards, OGEM, and other corporations. Trustee of Museum Boymans van Beuningen, Rotterdam, and Stedelyh Museum, Amsterdam.

WRITINGS: *Aantasting van arbitrale vonnissen* (attack on arbitral awards), Tjeenk Willink, 1940; (general editor) *Arbitrage International Commercial: International Commercial Arbitration,* Nijhoff, Volume I, 1956, Volume II, 1960, Volume III, 1965; *Societas Europea* (inaugural lecture), Kluwer, 1959.

Het Nationaal Steunfonds (history of financing the underground movement in the Netherlands during World War II; includes summary in English), Nijhoff, 1960; *Vorentwurf eines Statuts fuer Europaeische Aktiengesellschaften* (draft for a European stock corporation), European Commission, 1967, English edition published as *European Stock Corporation,* Commerce Clearing House, 1969; *N.V. and B.V.,* Kluwer, 1976, 3rd edition, 1981; *Trends in the Field of International Commercial Arbitration* (Hague Academy Lecture, 1975), Nijhoff, 1976; *Dutch Company Law,* Oyez Publishing, 1977.

General editor, *Yearbook on Arbitration,* Kluwer, Volumes I-X, 1976-85.

WORK IN PROGRESS: N.V. and B.V., 4th edition; *The New Dutch Arbitration Law,* for publication by Tjeenk Willink; a chapter on arbitration for *Encyclopedia of Comparative Law,* for publication by Hamburg Zweigert/Drobnig.

AVOCATIONAL INTERESTS: Comparative art ("modern, compared with African and pre-Columbian"), architecture.

SANFORD, Leda 1933-

PERSONAL: Born October 11, 1933, in Tuscany, Italy; came to the United States in 1939, naturalized in 1939; daughter of Fausto Giovannetti (an artist) and Josephine (Lunardi) Giovannetti Cole; married Howard Sanford (divorced); married Mort Gordon, 1982; children: (first marriage) Robert Wayne, Scott Howard. *Education:* Fashion Institute of Technology, New York City, A.A.S., 1953; additional study at University of Pennsylvania, 1977. *Home:* 160 East 65th St., New York, N.Y. 10021.

CAREER/WRITINGS: Teens and Boys (magazine), New York City, 1966-72, began as editorial assistant, editor-in-chief, 1971-72; *Men's Wear* (magazine), New York City, editor-in-chief, 1972-75; *American Home* (magazine), New York City, president, publisher, and editor-in-chief, 1975-77; *Chief Executive* (magazine), New York City, editor-in-chief and publisher, 1978-79; *Attenzione* (magazine), New York City, editor-in-chief and publisher, 1979-82; *Bon Appetit* (magazine), New York City, publisher and vice-president, 1982-83. Chairman of men's wear committee for COTY fashion awards, 1975. Author of column "For Your Information from the Desk of Leda Sanford," *American Home*, 1975-77. Contributor to *Folio* and other magazines. *Member:* Italy-America Chamber of Commerce (member of executive board), Fashion Group, Fashion Institute of Technology Alumni Association, Advertising Women of New York, Columbus Citizens Committee. *Awards, honors:* Forum of Italian-American Educators Award, 1980; Mortimer C. Ritter Award, Fashion Institute of Technology Alumni Association, 1981; Amita Award, Chamber of Commerce of Lucca, Italy, 1981.

WORK IN PROGRESS: A book about her years in magazine publishing.

SIDELIGHTS: Leda Sanford admits in *Folio* that after graduating from high school at age sixteen, she wanted more than anything "to be the editor of a magazine, live in a Manhattan penthouse, [and] be a glamorous and strong woman." Her career ambitions were stifled for years by her mother, who believed that journalism was no place for a lady. Not until age thirty-three, following fashion designing, marriage, the birth of two sons, a suburban lifestyle and a divorce, did her journalism dream begin to come true. But the delay had little effect on Sanford's success. Within six years, she worked her way up from editorial assistant to editor-in-chief of the trade magazine *Teens and Boys* and then became the first woman editor of *Men's Wear*. Since then, she has published and edited such magazines as *American Home, Attenzione,* and *Bon Appetit* with an intensity that makes it "impossible to react unemotionally to her," notes Ira Ellenthal in *Folio*.

When she became president, publisher, and editor-in-chief of *American Home* in 1975, Sanford faced the difficult task of rescuing a debt-ridden giant from collapse. The Charter Company, which acquired the struggling magazine from John Mack Carter, was losing about $100,000 an issue, according to Philip H. Dougherty in the *New York Times,* and its chairman, Raymond K. Mason, looked to Sanford to reverse the trend. Believing that *American Home* needed a more enthusiastic, more aggressive staff to execute the magazine's repositioning, Sanford fired several salesmen and replaced them with saleswomen—a move that led certain trade media to brand her as a woman who fires men. Ellenthal quotes a publishing analyst as saying, "Believe it or not, some people have neither forgotten nor forgiven [Sanford's move]."

But Sanford's main effort was devoted to changing the editorial content of *American Home*. Convinced that women's service magazines had become voyeuristic, "glorified *Photoplays*" in their efforts to compete with television, Sanford wanted *American Home* to support and inform the woman of today, but in a less radical fashion than the feminist publications like *Ms*. "Interesting as it was," she remarks in *Folio*, "I never want to repeat the experience of trying to turn around a magazine. . . . As you revitalize or change the editorial, you attempt to attract a new audience, a costly undertaking. At the same time, you can't afford to dump all the old readers overboard because you need them to renew your rate bases. Trying to pick up new readers fast enough to replace old ones is a tough proposition. Circulation pressures tend to cause an ambivalence that holds you back from following through completely on your editorial goals."

After two and a half years of repositioning, Charter merged *American Home* with *Redbook,* and Sanford became head of *Chief Executive*. A year later (1979), she met fast-food magnate Jeno Paulucci, developed a plan to start a magazine for people with roots or interest in Italy, and introduced *Attenzione*. Italian-born and fluent in the language, Sanford acknowledges in *Folio* that she "was as emotionally involved with *Attenzione* as Gloria Steinem is with *Ms*." She describes the magazine as "the first non-ethnic/ethnic publication," differing from general interest magazines only in the "emphasis and degree to which we [used] the Italian connection."

Ellenthal reports that even though *Attenzione* was "nurtured lovingly by Sanford and a small dedicated staff, it . . . ran aground in treacherous circulation waters. Locating its exact market proved costly and tedious." Sanford admits there were problems but believes the magazine was canceled prematurely: "The last issue produced by the original staff had forty pages of advertising and the editorial product was a gem. It's not fair to call a magazine a failure when it's not given enough time to mature."

From her experience in the business, Sanford offers in another *Folio* article this advice to aspiring publishers: "First of all, be absolutely sure in your own mind what you believe about the product, the audience, your goals, and where the magazine fits into the total scheme of publishing. Second, *don't compromise*. Compromise kills in publishing; while fine tuning and adjustments are necessary, compromise is usually the beginning of the end. Third, tight budgetary controls and monthly reviews of the financial state of affairs are essential because early detection of problems can often save the 'patient.' Circulation expenses and income are the quicksand of publishing. . . . In regard to personnel, . . . give people you trust a lot of rope. If you don't trust them, hang over their shoulders. Don't expect, inspect. Misplaced confidence, misplaced authority, misplaced freedom can drag you down. Direct strongly. A new magazine doesn't have time to be polite."

BIOGRAPHICAL/CRITICAL SOURCES: Chicago Daily News, January 14, 1976; *Philadelphia Inquirer,* February 23, 1976; *Detroit Free Press,* April 16, 1976; *Fort Lauderdale News,* May 18, 1976; *Miami Herald,* May 20, 1976; *New York Times,* June 15, 1976; *Folio,* February, 1982, November, 1982.

* * *

SARNO, Ronald A(nthony) 1941-

PERSONAL: Born September 26, 1941, in Jersey City, N.J.;

son of Anthony Vincent (an accountant) and Philomena (Pilla) Sarno; married Una McGinley, July 26, 1975. *Education:* Attended Bellarmine College, Plattsburgh, N.Y., 1959-63, and Weston College, 1963-66; Boston College, A.B., 1965, M.A., 1966; Woodstock College, M.Div., 1972; New York University, candidate for Ph.D. *Politics:* Democrat. *Home:* 52 Charles St., Little Ferry, N.J. 07643. *Office:* 225 Park Avenue S., Suite 734, New York, N.Y. 10003.

CAREER: Parochial high school teacher of English and religion, New York City, 1966-69; facilitator, high school human relations workshops, National Conference of Christians and Jews, 1968-71; U.S. Christian Life Communities, national college moderator, 1970-75, east region representative, 1975-79; St. Joseph's Hospital and Medical Center, Paterson, N.J., administrative assistant in department of pediatrics, 1976-79; Mountainview Medical Associates, P.C., Nyack, N.Y., administrator, 1980-82; Caldwell College, Caldwell, N.J., chief development officer, 1982-83; Family Dynamics, Inc., New York City, director of development and public relations, 1983—. Associate director, St. Ignatius Retreat House, Manhasset, N.Y., 1972-75. Lecturer on mass media, St. Peter's College, Jersey City, N.J., 1970; lecturer on New Testament, St. John's University, Jamaica, N.Y., 1975. *Member:* International Platform Association, National Federation of Fund Raising Executives, Federation of Christian Ministries, Loyola Christian Life Community, Lions Club of Little Ferry (secretary, 1983—).

WRITINGS: Achieving Sexual Maturity, Paulist/Newman, 1969; *Let Us Proclaim the Mystery of Faith,* Dimension, 1970; *The People of Hope,* Liguorian, 1971; *The Cruel Caesars: Their Impact on the Early Church,* Alba House, 1976; (with Len Badia) *Morality: How to Live It Today,* Alba House, 1979. Also author of *Prayers for Modern, Urban, Uptight Man;* also editor of *Liturgical Handbook for Christian Life Communities,* 1974. Contributor to *Jesuit Yearbook.* Contributor of about twenty-five articles to periodicals, including *America* and *Chicago Studies.* Assistant editor, *Sacred Heart Messenger,* 1967; contributing editor, *National Jesuit News,* 1971-72.

WORK IN PROGRESS: Modern Communication Theory and Catholic Religious Education, 1950-1980, a doctoral dissertation.

SIDELIGHTS: Ronald A. Sarno told *CA:* "I always feel slightly outdated when writing because I really believe that media have far more influence on people today than print. However, I have also found that my writing has always received an appreciative, if limited audience. I am in the unusual position of telling print-oriented readers how much influence the non-print media have on their lives, especially on religious and philosophical opinions."

* * *

SAUNDERS, Thomas 1909-

PERSONAL: Born February 21, 1909, in Crossgates, Scotland; married Janet Agnes Clark, 1940; children: Thomas Glen, James Clark, Allan John. *Education:* University of Manitoba, B.A., 1935; Manitoba College, L.Th., 1938; United College, D.D., 1959. *Home:* 527 Oxford St., Winnipeg, Manitoba, Canada.

CAREER: Served as United Church of Canada minister in rural Manitoba, Winnipeg, and West Vancouver; *Winnipeg Free Press,* Winnipeg, Manitoba, literary editor, 1960-76. *Military service:* Canadian Army, World War II; served as chaplain.

WRITINGS—Poetry, except as indicated; published by Ryerson, except as indicated: *Scrub Oak,* 1949; *Horizontal World,* 1951; (contributor) Bliss Carman, Lorne Pierce, and V. B. Rhodenizer, editors, *Canadian Poetry in English* (anthology), 1954; *Something of a Young World's Dying,* 1958; *The Devil and Cal McCabe; or, The Tale of the Cowman's Corns: A Story in Verse,* 1960; (contributor) E. W. Mandel and J. G. Pilon, editors, *Poetry 62* (anthology), 1961; *Red River of the North and Other Poems of Manitoba,* Peguis, 1969; *Beyond the Lakes* (prose), Peguis, 1978; *A Proud Heritage,* Peguis, 1982.

* * *

SAWEY, Orlan (Lester) 1920-

PERSONAL: Surname rhymes with "joy"; born May 8, 1920, in Grit, Tex.; son of Francis Bennett (a farmer) and Catherine Lavinia (Gary) Sawey; married Nina Geneva Ewing, April 2, 1942; children: Sara Catherine, Bennett Charles, Timothy Ewing. *Education:* Texas College of Arts and Industries (now Texas A & I University), B.A., 1942; University of Texas, M.A., 1947, Ph.D., 1953. *Politics:* Skeptic. *Religion:* Church of Christ. *Home and office:* 305 Merritt St., South Boston, Va. 24592.

CAREER: Preacher of Church of Christ, 1942—. Texas College of Arts and Industries (now Texas A & I University), Kingsville, instructor, 1947-50, assistant professor of English, 1952-55; Harding College, Searcy, Ark., associate professor, 1955-56, professor of English, 1956-58; Lincoln Memorial University, Harrogate, Tenn., professor of English and head of department, 1958-60; University of Virginia, Clinch Valley College, Wise, professor of English and chairman of department, 1960-62; Appalachian State University, Boone, N.C., professor of English, 1962-65; Pan American College, Edinburg, Tex., professor of English and head of department, 1965-69, director of Division of Arts and Sciences, 1966-68; Texas A & I University, professor of English, 1969-77, chairman of department, 1971-75. Guitarist and folk singer for more than forty years. *Military service:* U.S. Army, Medical Department, 1942-46; became technical sergeant. *Member:* Western American Literature Association, Southwestern American Literature Association, Texas Folklore Society.

WRITINGS: Bernard DeVoto, Twayne, 1969; (editor with wife, Nina Sawey) *She Hath Done What She Could: The Reminiscences of Hettie Lee Ewing,* [Dallas], 1974; *Charles A. Siringo,* Twayne, 1981. Also author of religion papers. Contributor to newspapers and literary and folklore journals.

WORK IN PROGRESS: Fiction.

SIDELIGHTS: Orlan Sawey told *CA:* "I probably should not appear in a list of contemporary writers, because I never have thought of myself as a professional writer. Since I have preached longer than I have taught in colleges and universities, much of my writing has been in obscure religious papers of limited interest. I have done many newspaper book reviews. I have always written about things which interested me, with little concern about whether my readers were interested.

"The two biographies published by Twayne are not typical Twayne productions. The DeVoto book is an extended essay on DeVoto's interest in the American West, forced into the TUSAS format. The Siringo book is about old Charlie Siringo, cowboy during the open-range period of the cattle industry and Pinkerton detective for more than twenty years. I admired his spunk in his life and in his writing, and I let this admiration show. One of the house readers suggested that the book was not a typical Twayne book, but the scholar-reader said, 'It's interesting. Print it!' It slipped by, too.

"The best I can say is that I have had fun writing; my teaching supported my writing (and my preaching). I wasn't hungry."

* * *

SCAER, David P(aul) 1936-

PERSONAL: Born March 13, 1936, in Brooklyn, N.Y.; son of Paul Henry (a Lutheran pastor) and Victoria (Zimmermann) Scaer; married Dorothy Hronetz (a registered nurse and instructor), June 18, 1960; children: David Paul, Jr., Stephen Charles, Peter James. *Education:* Concordia College, Bronxville, N.Y., A.A., 1955; Concordia Theological Seminary, St. Louis, Mo., B.A., 1957, M.Div., 1960, Th.D., 1963; graduate study at Kansas State University, 1958-59, and University of Muenster, 1960-62; postdoctoral study at University of Heidelberg, 1969. *Politics:* Republican. *Religion:* Lutheran. *Home:* 1912 Brandywine Trail, Fort Wayne, Ind. 46825; and Pocono Pines, Pa. 18350. *Office:* Concordia Theological Seminary, Fort Wayne, Ind. 46825.

CAREER: Ordained Lutheran clergyman, 1962; University of Illinois at Urbana-Champaign, part-time instructor in Bible and ethics, 1966-76; Concordia Theological Seminary, Fort Wayne, Ind. (formerly in Springfield, Ill.), assistant professor, 1966-69, associate professor, 1969-77, professor of systematic theology, 1977—. Member of Illinois Right to Life, 1973-76. *Member:* Society of Biblical Literature, Evangelical Theological Society, Concordia Historical Society. *Awards, honors:* John W. Behnken postdoctoral fellowship for study in Europe, 1969.

WRITINGS: The Lutheran World Federation Today, Concordia, 1971; *The Apostolic Scriptures,* Concordia, 1971; *What Do You Think of Jesus?,* Concordia, 1973; *Getting into the Story of Concord: A History of the Book of Concord,* Concordia, 1977; (editor and contributor) *Luther's Catechisms—450 Years,* Concordia Seminary Press, 1979; *James: The Apostle of Faith,* Concordia, 1983; Also author of *A Latin Ecclesiastical Dictionary,* 1978.

Contributor: *Tensions in Contemporary Theology,* Moody, 1976, 3rd revised edition, 1979; *The History of Christian Doctrine,* Baker, 1979; *Perspectives on Evangelical Lutheran Theology,* Baker, 1979; *Die eine heilige christliche Kirche,* Martin Luther Verlag, (Erlangen), 1981. Contributor to *Christianity Today, Cresset, Lutheran Witness,* and *Concordia Journal.* Editor, *Concordia Theological Quarterly.*

* * *

SCARGILL, (David) Ian 1935-

PERSONAL: Born March 22, 1935, in Batley, England; son of Arthur Firth (an electrical engineer) and Evelyn (Goodall) Scargill; married Mary Leslie Branch (a novelist), August 8, 1964; children: Katherine Eugenie. *Education:* St. Edmund Hall, Oxford, B.A. (with first class honors), 1957, M.A. and D.Phil., both 1961. *Religion:* United Reformed Church. *Home:* 25 Portland Rd., Oxford, England. *Office:* School of Geography, Oxford University, Mansfield Rd., Oxford, England.

CAREER: Oxford University, Oxford, England, departmental demonstrator, 1959-64, fellow of St. Edmund Hall, 1962—, lecturer in geography, 1964—. Magistrate in Oxford; trustee of Oxford Preservation Trust. *Member:* Royal Geographical Society (fellow), Geographical Association, Institute of British Geographers.

WRITINGS: Economic Geography of France, Macmillan, 1968; *The Dordogne Region of France,* David & Charles, 1974; *The Form of Cities,* Bell & Hyman, 1979; (with A. G. Crosby) *Oxford and Its Countryside,* Oxford Books, 1982. Editor of "Problem Regions of Europe" series, seventeen books, Oxford University Press, 1972—. Contributor to geography and town planning journals.

WORK IN PROGRESS: Urban France.

SIDELIGHTS: Ian Scargill told *CA:* "My principal interests lie in the study of France, where I have a cottage, and in the contemporary problems of cities. I am a magistrate, sitting on the Oxford City Bench, and my spare time is mainly devoted to the conservation work of the Oxford Preservation Trust."

* * *

SCHAFF, Adam 1913-

PERSONAL: Born March 10, 1913, in Lwow, Poland (in a section now part of the Soviet Union); son of Maks (a barrister) and Ernestyna (Felix) Schaff; married Anna Kibrik, July 15, 1935 (died March, 1975); married Teresa Tonczak, 1976; children: Ewa. *Education:* University of Lwow, M.A., 1935; graduate study, Ecole des Sciences Politiques et Economiques, Paris; Soviet Academy of Sciences' Institute of Philosophy, doctor's degree, 1945. *Office:* Institute of Philosophy and Sociology, Polish Academy of Sciences, Nowy Swiat 72, Warsaw, Poland. *Agent:* Agencja Autorska, Hipoteczna 2, Warsaw, Poland.

CAREER: University of Warsaw, Warsaw, Poland, professor of philosophy, 1948-70, professor emeritus, 1970—; University of Vienna, visiting professor, 1969-72, honorary professor of philosophy, 1972-82. Director, Institute of Philosophy and Sociology, Warsaw, Poland, 1956-68. Participant in the underground communist movement since his youth; member and chief ideologist of central committee of Polish United Worker's Party, 1954-68. Past president of board of directors, European Center for Social Sciences, Vienna; member, International Institute of Philosophy, Paris. *Member:* Polish Academy of Sciences (chairman of philosophy committee, 1951-68), Bulgarian Academy of Sciences (foreign member). *Awards, honors:* Honorary doctorates from University of Michigan, 1967, Sorbonne, University of Paris, 1975, and University of Nancy, 1982.

WRITINGS: Pojecie i slowo (title means "Concept and Word"), Ksiazka, 1946; *Wstep do teorii marksizmu* (title means "Introduction to the Theory of Marxism"), Ksiazka, 1947; *Pogadanki ekonomiczne* (title means "Economical Essays"), Ksiazka, 1947; *Pogadanki o materializmie historycznym* (title means "Essays on Historical Materialism"), Ksiazka & Wiedza, 1948.

Narodziny i rozwoj filozofii marksistowskiej (title means "The Rise and Growth of Marxist Philosophy"), Ksiazka & Wiedza, 1950; *Z zagadnien marksistowskiej teorii prawdy* (title means "The Problems of the Marxist Theory of Truth"), Ksiazka & Wiedza, 1951; *Obiektywny charakter praw historii* (title means "The Objective Nature of the Laws of History"), Panstwowe Wydawnictwo Naukowe, 1955; *Aktualne zagadnienia polityki kulturalnej* (title means "Actual Problems of Cultural Policy"), Panstwowe Wydawnictwo Naukowe, 1956; *Spor o zagadnienie moralnosci* (title means "Dispute on the Problems of Morality"), Ksiazka & Wiedza, 1958; *Glowne zagadnienia i kierunki filozofii: Teoria pozanania* (title means "Main Problems and Trends of Philosophy: Theory of Knowledge"), Panstwowe Wydawnictwo Naukowe, 1958.

Wstep do semantyki, Panstwowe Wydawnictwo Naukowe, 1960, translation by Olgierd Wojtasiewicz published as *Introduction to Semantics,* Pergamon, 1962; *Marksizm a egzystencjalism* (essays), Ksiazka & Wiedza, 1961 (subsequent expanded Polish editions published as *Filozofia Czlowieka),* translation published as *A Philosophy of Man,* Monthly Review Press, 1963; *Jezyk a poznanie* (title means "Language and Cognition"), Panstwowe Wydawnictwo Naukowe, 1964, translation by Wojtasiewicz published as *Language and Cognition,* edited by Robert S. Cohen, McGraw, 1973.

Marksizm a jednostka ludzka (title means "Marxism and the Individual"), Panstwowe Wydawnictwo Naukowe, 1965, translation by Wojtasiewicz published as *Marxism and the Human Individual,* edited by Cohen, introduction by Erich Fromm, McGraw, 1970; *Szkice z filizofii jezyka* (title means "Essays in the Philosophy of Language"), Ksiazka & Wiedza, 1968; *Historia i prawda* (title means "History and Truth"), Ksiazka & Wiedza, 1970; *Structuralizm i Marksizm* (title means "Structuralism and Marxism"), Ksiazka & Wiedza, 1976.

Alienation as a Social Phenomenon, Pergamon, 1980; *Stereotypen und das menschliche Handeln* (title means "Stereotypes and Human Activity"), Wien Europaverlag, 1981; *Kommunistische Bewegung auf dem Scheidewej* (title means "Communist Movement at Crossroad"), Wien Europaverlag, 1982. Contributor of about 250 essays and articles to periodicals. Editor of *Mysl Wspolczesna,* 1946-51, and *Mysl Filozoficzna,* 1951-56.

SIDELIGHTS: Adam Schaff's books have been translated into many languages, including German, Spanish, Italian, and English.

BIOGRAPHICAL/CRITICAL SOURCES: *New York Review,* April 25, 1968.

* * *

SCHELL, Jonathan 1943-

PERSONAL: Born August 21, 1943, in New York, N.Y. *Education:* Graduate study in Far Eastern history at Harvard University; also studied in Tokyo, Japan, for one year. *Office: New Yorker,* 25 West 43rd St., New York, N.Y. 10036.

CAREER: Writer. *New Yorker,* New York, N.Y., contributing editor, 1968—. *Awards, honors:* National Institute and American Academy of Arts and Sciences award in literature, 1973; *Los Angeles Times* Book Prize and National Book Critics Circle Prize nomination, both 1982, for *The Fate of the Earth.*

WRITINGS—All published by Knopf; all originally serialized in the *New Yorker: The Village of Ben Suc,* 1967; *The Military Half: An Account of Destruction in Quang Ngai and Quang Tin,* 1968; *The Time of Illusion,* 1976; *The Fate of the Earth,* 1982.

SIDELIGHTS: Jonathan Schell's first two books are graphic descriptions of the systematic destruction of South Vietnamese villages by American forces in the winter and summer of 1967. In *The Village of Ben Suc,* Schell relates the story of a small farming community thirty miles northeast of Saigon. The town, located on a corner of the "Iron Triangle"—forty square miles of jungle well known as a Viet Cong stronghold—had supposedly become a major conduit for Viet Cong arms and ammunition. The entire area had been under the civil and military control of the National Liberation Front for so many years, writes Schell, that "to villagers of Ben Suc the [NLF] was not a band of roving guerrillas but the full government of their village." Attempts, since 1964, by South Vietnamese troops to dislodge the Communists had proven futile. For this reason, in January of 1967, U.S. forces stepped in, evacuated the 3500 inhabitants of Ben Suc, and leveled the town.

Schell, on his way home from a year of graduate study in Tokyo, "accompanied the operation from the beginning," states John Dillon in the *Christian Science Monitor.* "He swooped into Ben Suc with the first 60 helicopters.... He watched the village taken, the people forcibly removed, the houses burned, bulldozed, and bombed. The author's style is simple reporting. He lets the events speak." In a *New York Times Book Review* article, John Mecklin writes that in *The Village of Ben Suc,* a "relentlessly exacerbating book, a brilliant 24-year-old Harvard post-graduate student has registered a stinging indictment on the performance of his own generation in Vietnam.... It should be required reading in the Pentagon." Mecklin finds that the book "performs a public service in suggesting how poorly American military commanders ... understand the nature of Asian guerrilla warfare" and that it "is written with a skill that many a veteran war reporter will envy, eloquently sensitive, subtly clothed in an aura of detachment, understated, extraordinarily persuasive."

In his next book, *The Military Half: An Account of Destruction in Quang Ngai and Quang Tin,* Schell continues to elaborate on the same theme. This time, writes Eliot Fremont-Smith in the *New York Times,* he reports "in remarkably sensitive and lucid detail, the destruction, mostly from the air, of the homes and villages and inhabitants of two rural, mountainous provinces which lie athwart the main north-south [Vietnamese] artery, Highway No. 1, along the coast south of Hue." During this operation, Schell flew as an observer in the small two-seat planes of the Forward Air Control (FAC), whose task it was to locate targets for jet fighter-bombers. According to Fremont-Smith, the pilots of these planes were supposed to "tell which villages, houses ..., forest trails, and even individual people—seen from 1,500 to 5,000 feet above—are 'friendly' and which are not." Much of Schell's criticism of this system centers on the arbitrariness with which air strikes were guided. For instance, an individual who looked up at a passing FAC plane was presumed to be a Viet Cong intending to report the aircraft's direction; a person sighted in an area ordered by dropped leaflets to be cleared was also presumed to be unfriendly, even though a large percentage of rural Vietnamese were illiterate and thus unable to read the pamphlets. The result of such dubious sightings was massive air strikes—bombings, napalm drops, and strafing. Schell reports that as of fall, 1967, seventy percent of the villages in Quang Ngai had been obliterated, and forty percent of the population was living in refugee camps.

While acknowledging *The Military Half* as "an excellent descriptive narrative which provides the reader with a vivid portrait of the war's techniques and characters," Steven C. Schueller of the *National Review* maintains that Schell "witnessed action in a limited area," a criticism that was also leveled by a few reviewers of *The Village of Ben Suc.* But Jonathan Mirsky, in a *Nation* article, disagrees, stating that when the first book was published "some reviewers twisted madly, attempting to explain away the destruction of [the village] as an unfortunate but probably *isolated* incident." Mirsky himself "had visited not only Ben Suc but all the surrounding area," and found that "such wide-scale wiping out was common." Of *The Military*

Half, Mirsky concludes: "I know no book which has made me angrier and more ashamed. If upon finishing it one still says only 'war is hell' one's soul may be in mortal danger. Putting Dr. Spock, Father Berrigan, and hundreds of anonymous draft refusers in prison for protesting the crimes described by Jonathan Schell is an act of social perversion."

Schell's *The Time of Illusion,* published in 1976, is an account of the Nixon presidency from January, 1969, when Richard Nixon took office, to August, 1974, when, in the midst of the Watergate scandal, he became the first U.S. president to resign. Schell asserts that, beginning with the Kennedy administration, there has been a growing tendency on the part of the leaders of the United States to place more importance on image than on substance and to place above all else the illusion of American "credibility" in the eyes of the rest of the world. Thus, writes Robert Sherrill in the *New York Times Book Review,* "when Nixon set about hiring spies, burglars, sabateurs, con men, extortionists,... and using I.R.S. officials and F.B.I. officials and C.I.A. officials and local police to destroy the anti-war opposition, he was, says Schell, doing it in the sincere belief that he was saving not only his own country, but the world." Sherrill expresses the opinion that Schell may be "a bit too relentless in his pursuit of Nixon" but feels that overall the author's "careful reconstruction of the convoluted chaos and frenzied contradiction of the Nixon years, his portrayal of this strange isolated creature who played with the world like Captain Queeg played with steelies, is not merely fascinating; it is inspired." Roderick Nordell of the *Christian Science Monitor* believes that at the time of the book's writing it was "probably too soon to nail things down with Mr. Schell's degree of certitude." Still, Nordell says that Schell "offers a provocative, early entry in solving the mystery of how-did-it-all-happen-in-America." And *Library Journal* reviewer R. J. Masters states, "This is likely to become one of the classic accounts of the Vietnam-Watergate era."

The best selling and most widely discussed of Schell's books is *The Fate of the Earth,* which is, according to *Chicago Tribune Book World* writer Richard Rhodes, "the first accurate, honest, full-scale examination of the certain and probable consequences of nuclear war." The work is divided into three parts: first, an explanation of how atomic bombs are made and why the human race cannot possibly survive a major nuclear confrontation; second, a discourse on our responsibility to future generations—as Schell says, "We have always been able to send people to their death, but only now has it become possible to prevent all birth and so doom all future human beings to uncreation"; and third, a condemnation of the deterrence theory—Schell believes that as long as nuclear weapons are at the disposal of fiercely nationalistic world leaders, the extinction of life on earth will remain an imminent possibility.

Noting that there have been thousands of commentaries on the possible effects of a nuclear war, Max Lerner, writing in the *New Republic,* asserts that *The Fate of the Earth* "will become the classic statement of the emerging consciousness. It is a mix of technical information on nuclear destruction and ecological fallout; philosophical reflections on the extinction of the human species; and a (too brief) discussion of the political choices that lie before us." *Los Angeles Times* book editor Art Seidenbaum says that among all the available anti-nuclear literature, "Schell's work is the most hideous and the most persuasive for two reasons: First, his repeated theme is larger than life-or-death, the examination of extinction, extinction for human beings present and yet unborn, extinction of the once-life-sustaining planet we inhabit; second, his reporting and his speculating and his evidence are presented absolutely unhysterically."

Reviewing *The Fate of the Earth* for the *Washington Post Book World,* Jerome B. Wiesner (president emeritus of Massachusetts Institute of Technology and science adviser to Presidents Kennedy and Johnson) reports that "Schell spent five years interviewing groups of scientists in various fields of study where the effects of nuclear war are being explored. Those lines of inquiry included the possible effects on human beings physically and psychologically, on the biosphere and the life support system in which they live, on the economy by which their needs are met, and on the organized society which brought civilization to its present high level. He found that these separate effects of a nuclear war reinforced each other to a degree not appreciated even by the experts; that the many different aspects of a nuclear war would interact on each other to such an extent that the total damage would be far worse than most of us had thought."

How much worse? Schell states that "now there are some fifty thousand [nuclear] warheads in the world, possessing the explosive yield of roughly twenty billion tons of TNT, or one million six hundred thousand times the yield of the bomb that was dropped by the United States on the city of Hiroshima." In addition, Rhodes says that Schell's research has concluded: "A 10,000-megaton nuclear attack—well within Soviet capabilities—would subject every city and town [in the United States] down to 1,500 population to a full megaton of flesh-charring heat, crushing blast, and lethal radiation. The primary zone of destruction—the zone, as it were, directly under the bombs—would encompass one-sixth of the total land mass of the nation."

Such revelations have led several reviewers, including Seidenbaum of the *Los Angeles Times,* to label *The Fate of the Earth* "the most important, dismaying book of the year." In the *New Republic,* Max Lerner writes: "Only rarely has a book made political history on a scale as grand as this one seems destined to. It was true of Harriet Beecher Stowe's *Uncle Tom's Cabin* before the Civil War, of Zola's *J'accuse* at the time of the Dreyfusards, of John Maynard Keynes's *Economic Consequences of the Peace* after World War I. There is a similar vatic quality about Schell's book; it speaks from and to the spirit that seems to have seized our time—the deep undeniable stirrings among millions of every political persuasion. However formidable the book's grisly calculus of death and its involved rumination, there is also a note of passion that meets the passion of the reader." Concludes Kai Erikson in the *New York Times Book Review:* "This is a work of enormous force. There are moments when it seems to hurtle, almost out of control, across an extraordinary range of fact and thought. But in the end, it accomplishes what no other work has managed to do in the 37 years of the nuclear age. It compels us—and compel *is* the right word—to confront head on the nuclear peril in which we all find ourselves.... Albert Einstein once said that 'the unleashed power of the atom has changed everything save our modes of thinking,' but the kinds of conversation to which Schell now invites us will go a long way toward improving that situation."

BIOGRAPHICAL/CRITICAL SOURCES: *New York Times Book Review,* October 29, 1967, January 18, 1976, April 11, 1982; *Best Sellers,* November 1, 1967; *Time,* November 17, 1967; *Christian Science Monitor,* December 2, 1967, March 9, 1976; *Nation,* January 8, 1968, August 5, 1968; *New York Times,*

June 10, 1968, April 8, 1982; *National Review*, March 25, 1969; *Newsweek*, January 12, 1976, April 19, 1982; *New York Review of Books*, June 24, 1976; *Washington Post Book World*, April 18, 1982; *Chicago Tribune Book World*, April 18, 1982; *Los Angeles Times*, April 21, 1982; *New Republic*, April 28, 1982; *Times Literary Supplement*, July 16, 1982; Jonathan Schell, *The Fate of the Earth*, Knopf, 1982.†

—Sketch by Peter M. Gareffa

* * *

SCHERER, F(rederic) M(ichael) 1932-

PERSONAL: Born August 1, 1932, in Ottawa, Ill.; son of Walter King (a merchant) and Margaret (Lucey) Scherer; married Barbara Silbermann, August 17, 1957; children: Thomas M., Karen A. Main, Christina A. *Education:* University of Michigan, A.B., 1954; Harvard University, M.B.A., 1958, Ph.D., 1963. *Home:* 35 Wellesley Rd., Swarthmore, Pa. 19081. *Office:* Department of Economics, Swarthmore College, Swarthmore, Pa. 19081.

CAREER: Harvard University, Graduate School of Business Administration, Boston, Mass., member of faculty, 1958-63; Princeton University, Princeton, N.J., assistant professor of economics, 1963-66; University of Michigan, Ann Arbor, associate professor, 1966-69, professor of economics, 1969-72; International Institute of Management, Berlin, Germany, social research fellow, 1972-74; U.S. Federal Trade Commission, Bureau of Economics, Washington, D.C., director, 1974-76; Northwestern University, Evanston, Ill., professor of economics, 1976-82; Swarthmore College, Swarthmore, Pa., professor of economics, 1982—. Consultant on national security policy, technological change, the patent system, and antitrust matters. *Military service:* U.S. Army, 1954-56.

MEMBER: American Economic Association, Federation of American Scientists, European Association for Research in Industrial Economics, Southern Economic Association. *Awards, honors:* Lanchester Prize of Operations Research Society of America, 1964, for *The Weapons Acquisition Process: Economic Incentives;* National Science Foundation grant.

WRITINGS: (With others) *Patents and the Corporation*, privately printed, 1958, revised edition, 1959; (with M. J. Peck) *The Weapons Acquisition Process: An Economic Analysis*, Division of Research, Harvard Business School, 1962; *The Weapons Acquisition Process: Economic Incentives*, Division of Research, Harvard Business School, 1964; *Industrial Market Structure and Economic Performance*, Houghton, 1970, revised edition, 1980; (with others) *The Economics of Multi-Plant Operation: An International Comparisons Study*, Harvard University Press, 1975; *Technology and Growth: Schumpeterian Perspectives*, MIT Press, 1984. Contributor to economics and technology journals.

WORK IN PROGRESS: The behavioral consequences of mergers and divestitures.

* * *

SCHNACKENBURG, Rudolf 1914-

PERSONAL: Born January 5, 1914, in Kattowitz, Germany; son of Leopold (an engineer) and Anna (Christ) Schnackenburg. *Education:* University of Breslau, Dr. theol., 1937; University of Munich, Habilitation for New Testament Exegesis, 1947. *Home:* Erthalstrasse 22d, 87 Wuerzburg, Federal Republic of Germany. *Office:* Universitaet Wuerzburg, 87 Wuerzburg, Neue Universitaet, Sanderring 2, Federal Republic of Germany.

CAREER: Roman Catholic priest; University of Dillingen, Dillingen, Germany, assistant professor, 1952-55; University of Bamberg, Bamberg, Germany, ordinary professor, 1955-57; University of Wuerzburg, Wuerzburg, Germany, professor of New Testament exegesis and biblical theology, 1957—. Former consultant to Pontifical Bible Commission and to Secretariat for Promoting Christian Unity (Rome); member of Pontifical Theological Commission and of a number of ecumenical groups. Lecturer at University of Notre Dame, fall, 1965, and participant in various congresses in the United States. *Member:* Studiorum Novi Testamenti Societas (president, 1966-67), Society of Biblical Literature (honorary member). *Awards, honors:* Dr. theol. h.c., Innsbruck University, 1970.

WRITINGS: Die Johannesbriefe, Herder (Freiburg), 1953, 5th edition, 1975; *Die sittliche Botschaft des Neuen Testamentes*, Max Hueber, 1954, revised and enlarged German edition, 1962, translation of revised edition by J. Holland-Smith and W. J. O'Hara published as *The Moral Teaching of the New Testament*, Herder, 1965; *Gottes Herrschaft und Reich*, Herder, 1959, translation by John Murray published as *God's Rule and Kingdom*, Herder & Herder (New York), 1963, 2nd enlarged edition, 1968.

La Theologie du Nouveau Testament, Desclee de Brouwer (Brussels), 1961, translation by David Askew published as *New Testament Theology Today*, Herder & Herder, 1963; *Baptism in the Thought of St. Paul: A Study in Pauline Theology*, Herder & Herder, 1964; *Von der Wahrheit die freimacht*, A. Pustet (Munich), 1964, translation by Rodelinde Albrecht published as *The Truth Will Make You Free*, Herder & Herder, 1966; *Das Johannesvangelium*, Herder, Volume I, 1965, Volume II, 1971, Volume III, 1975, translation of Volume I by Kevin Smith published as *The Gospel According to St. John*, Herder & Herder, 1968, Volume II, Burns & Oates, 1979, Volume III, Burns & Oates, 1982; *Present and Future: Modern Aspects of New Testament Theology* (lecture series), University of Notre Dame Press, 1966; *Die Kirche im Neuen Testament: Ihre Wirklichkeit und theologische Deutung, ihr Wesen und Geheimnis*, Herder, 1966, translation by W. J. O'Hara published as *The Church in the New Testament*, Herder & Herder, 1965; *Das Evangelium nach Markus*, Patmos-Verlag, Volume I, 1966, Volume II, 1971, translation published as *The Gospel According to St. Mark*, Herder & Herder, 1970; *Christliche Existenz nach dem Neuen Testament*, Koesel-Verlag, Volume I, 1967, Volume II, 1968, translation by F. Wieck published in two volumes as *Christian Existence in the New Testament*, University of Notre Dame Press, 1968.

Schriften zum Neuen Testament, Koesel-Verlag, 1971; *Glaubensimpulse aus dem Neuen Testament*, Patmos-Verlag, 1973, translation by Jeremy Moiser published as *Belief in the New Testament*, Paulist Press, 1974 (published in England as *The Will to Believe: Meditation on New Testament Themes*, Darton, Longman & Todd, 1974); *Christ: Present and Coming*, Fortress, 1978; *Der Brief an die Epheser*, Neukirchen, 1982.

Editor of several book series. Editor, *Biblische Zeitschrift*, 1957—.

BIOGRAPHICAL/CRITICAL SOURCES: Christian Century, February 26, 1969.

SCHNEIDER, Stephen H(enry) 1945-

PERSONAL: Born February 11, 1945, in New York, N.Y.; son of Samuel (an educator) and Doris (an educator; maiden name, Swarte) Schneider. *Education:* Columbia University, B.S., 1966, M.S., 1967, Ph.D., 1971. *Politics:* "Support for candidates with long-term perspective." *Office:* National Center for Atmospheric Research, P.O. Box 3000, Boulder, Colo. 80307.

CAREER: Goddard Institute for Space Studies, New York, N.Y., postdoctoral research associate, 1971-72; National Center for Atmospheric Research, Boulder, Colo., fellow, 1972-73, deputy head of climate project, 1973-78, acting leader of climate sensitivity group, 1978-80, head of visitor programs and deputy director of advanced study program, 1980—. Lecturer and writer. *Member:* American Meteorological Society, American Geophysical Union, American Association for the Advancement of Science, Federation of American Scientists, Sigma Xi.

WRITINGS: (With Lynne Mesirow) *The Genesis Strategy: Climate and Global Survival*, Plenum, 1976; (with Lynne Martin) *The Primordial Bond: Exploring Connections between Man and Nature through the Humanities and Science*, Plenum, 1981; (with Randi S. Londer) *The Coevolution of Climate and Life*, Sierra Club, 1984. Editor, *Climatic Change*, 1975—. Contributor to *Science, New Engineer, Journal of Atmospherical Science, Nature,* and other periodicals.

SIDELIGHTS: The Primordial Bond: Exploring Connections between Man and Nature through the Humanities and Science studies present-day environmental problems from both scientific and humanistic perspectives. Authors Stephen H. Schneider and Lynne Martin argue that neither perspective alone provides a clear understanding of the situation nor the means by which to improve it. "They feel," writes Richard Severo in the *New York Times,* "that both scientists and humanists have a responsibility for cooperatively producing answers to the problems created since the Industrial Revolution." David Burns of the *Washington Post* calls *The Primordial Bond* "a provocative and highly readable discussion of the limitations of both science and humanism in confronting [environmental] issues." Burns considers the book's treatment of the environment to be "the clearest description currently available of the global, biological, and chemical cycles on which life depends, and human disruptions of those cycles."

Schneider told *CA* how he began his writing career: "I am a research scientist concerned with both the effects of climate on society and the converse. From considerable experience in Washington I became convinced that many of the warnings from scientists and others about potential climate-related crises were being ignored by governmental officials who were preoccupied with events whose relative time span is, at most, as far away as the next election. The need to 'go public' was apparent and led to my writing *The Genesis Strategy: Climate and Global Survival* for a popular audience. The book and attendant media, government, and lecture appearances have helped to put certain issues before the public. Despite some academic resistance to public airing of uncertain scientific issues, I intend to continue to study, write and speak on the urgent need for society to anticipate potential long-term consequences of its short term policies with emphasis on issues with a technological component."

BIOGRAPHICAL/CRITICAL SOURCES: Washington Post, July 18, 1981; *New York Times,* September 1, 1981.

SCHNELL, George A(dam) 1931-

PERSONAL: Born July 13, 1931, in Philadelphia, Pa.; son of Earl Blackwood and Emily (Bernheimer) Schnell; married Mary Lou Williams (in real estate sales), June 21, 1958; children: David Adam, Douglas Powell, Thomas Earl. *Education:* West Chester State College, B.S., 1958; Pennsylvania State University, M.S., 1960, Ph.D., 1965. *Politics:* Democrat. *Religion:* Reformed Church. *Home:* 4 Joalyn Rd., New Paltz, N.Y. 12561. *Office:* Department of Geography, Hamner House 1, State University of New York College at New Paltz, New Paltz, N.Y. 12561.

CAREER: State University of New York College at New Paltz, assistant professor, 1962-65, associate professor, 1965-68, professor of geography, 1968—, chairman of department, 1969—. Visiting professor, University of Hawaii, summer, 1966; adjunct professor, Empire State College, 1974—. *Military service:* U.S. Army, 1952-54. *Member:* Association of American Geographers, National Council on Geographic Education, Pennsylvania Academy of Science, Pennsylvania Geographic Society. *Awards, honors:* National Science Foundation summer fellow, 1965.

WRITINGS: (Contributor) John M. Sherwig, *Guineas and Gunpowder,* Harvard University Press, 1969; (editor with George J. Demko and Harold M. Rose) *Population Geography: A Reader,* McGraw, 1970; (with Kenneth Corey and others) *The Local Community: A Handbook for Teachers,* Macmillan, 1971; (contributor) Lewis Brownstein, *Education and Rural Development in Kenya: A Case Study of Primary School Graduates,* Praeger, 1972; (contributor) Q. H. Stanford, editor, *The World's Population: Problems of Growth,* Oxford University Press (Canada), 1972; (contributor) *Readings on West Virginia and Appalachia,* Kendall-Hunt, 1976; (with Mark Stephen Monmonier) *The Study of Population: Elements, Patterns, Processes,* C. E. Merrill, 1983; (contributor with Monmonier) S. K. Majumdar and E. W. Miller, editors, *Pennsylvania Coal: Resources, Technology, and Utilization,* Pennsylvania Academy of Science, 1983. Also author of audio units, "Weather, Climate, and Man," Learning Systems, Inc., 1971. Contributor to proceedings; contributor to geography and other professional journals. Member of editorial board, *Pennsylvania Academy of Science,* 1968—; member of editorial and advisory board, Pennsylvania Coal Project; guest editor, *Pennsylvania Geographer,* 1973.

WORK IN PROGRESS: Research project, "U.S. Population Trends by Race."

SIDELIGHTS: George A. Schnell told *CA:* "I enjoy teaching very much, especially undergraduates, and am especially gratified to see them go on to succeed in graduate and professional schools and gain positions of responsibility. This success is very much based upon their ability to communicate—to write—and helping them to learn to write has become an important part of my role in their academic lives."

*   *   *

SCHOENFELD, David 1923-

PERSONAL: Born October 26, 1923, in New York, N.Y.; son of Harry (a restaurateur) and Anna (Blatt) Schoenfeld; married Madalynne Geller (a librarian), December 23, 1944. *Education:* Brooklyn College (now Brooklyn College of the City

University of New York), B.A., 1945; University of Southern California, M.B.A., 1947. *Religion:* Jewish. *Home:* 21 Albemarle Rd., White Plains, N.Y. 10605. *Office:* J.C. Penney, 1301 Avenue of the Americas, New York, N.Y. 10019.

CAREER: Fleetwood Cleaners, Mount Vernon, N.Y., proprietor, 1947-62; Lincoln High School, Yonkers, N.Y., teacher of economics, beginning 1962; President's Committee on Consumer Interests, Washington, D.C., director for consumer education, 1967-69; Consumers Union of United States, Inc., director for educational services, 1969-74; J.C. Penney, New York, N.Y., manager of consumer relations, 1974—. Writer-consultant, New York State Education Department. *Military service:* U.S. Army, 1943-46; became technical sergeant.

MEMBER: National Council for Social Studies, Council on Consumer Information, Society of Consumer Affairs Professionals, Association for Consumer Research, National Business Education Association, American Home Economics Association, American Council on Consumer Interests, Middle States Council for Social Studies, New York State Council on Economic Education, Hudson Valley Council on Economic Education, Jewish War Veterans. *Awards, honors:* Fellowship grant, New York State, 1963.

WRITINGS: (Editor with James E. Mendenhall) *Consumer Education in Lincoln High School,* Consumers Union, 1965; (with Arthur Natella) *The Consumer and His Dollars,* Oceana, 1966, 3rd edition, 1975; *Course Outline for Consumer Economics,* Oceana, 1966.

Director of "Consumer Education Materials Project"; published by Educational Services Division, Consumers Union of United States: *Elementary Level: Consumer Education,* 1972; *Consumer Education in Junior and Community Colleges, Postsecondary, Vocational, and Technical Institutes,* 1972; *Adult Consumer Education in the Community,* 1973; *Early Childhood: Consumer Education,* 1973; *Preparing the Consumer Educator,* 1973; *Secondary Level: Consumer Education,* 1973.†

* * *

SCHULMAN, L(ester) M(artin) 1934-
(Les Martin)

PERSONAL: Born September 3, 1934, in Brooklyn, N.Y.; son of David and Rose (Tirnauer) Schulman; married Janet Schuetz (a writer of juvenile books), May 19, 1957; children: Nicole. *Education:* Antioch College, B.A., 1955. *Politics:* "Alienated." *Religion:* None. *Home and office:* 290 Riverside Dr., Apt. 7B, New York, N.Y. 10025. *Agent:* Marilyn Marlow, Curtis Brown, Ltd., 575 Madison Ave., New York, N.Y. 10022.

CAREER: Popular Library, Inc., New York City, editor, 1963-65; Bantam Books, Inc., New York City, editor, 1966-67; Dell Publishing Co., New York City, editor, 1967-69; free-lance writer and editor, 1969—. *Military service:* U.S. Army, 1957-59.

WRITINGS—Editor; all juvenile anthologies except as indicated: *Come Out of the Wilderness* (Black anthology), Popular Library, 1965; *Winners and Losers,* Macmillan, 1968; *The Loners: Short Stories about the Young and Alienated,* Macmillan, 1970; *The Cracked Looking Glass: Stories of Other Realities,* Macmillan, 1971; *Travelers,* Macmillan, 1972; *A Woman's Place,* Macmillan, 1974; *Autumn Light: Illuminations of Age,* Crowell, 1978.

Under pseudonym Les Martin; adaptations of films; all published by Random House: *Raiders of the Lost Ark,* 1981; *Bladerunner,* 1982; *Indiana Jones and the Temple of Doom,* 1984.

WORK IN PROGRESS: A novel for young adults; a suspense novel.

* * *

SCHULTE, Elaine L(ouise) 1934-
(Elaine L. Young)

PERSONAL: Born November 18, 1934, in Indiana; daughter of Dietrich and Louise (Matthew) Young; married Frank L. Schulte (a business executive and photographer), October 1, 1955; children: Gregory L., Richard M. *Education:* Purdue University, B.S., 1956. *Home address:* P.O. Box 746, Rancho Sante Fe, Calif. 92067.

CAREER: J. Walter Thompson (advertising agency), Los Angeles, Calif., member of staff, 1956-57; writer, 1957—. Lecturer at conferences, colleges, schools and libraries throughout the country. Lecturer at California community colleges. *Member:* Presbyterian Church of the U.S.A., National League of Pen Women, Alpha Chi Omega.

WRITINGS: Zack and the Magic Factory (juvenile novel), Thomas Nelson, 1976; *Whither the Wind Bloweth* (young adult novel), Avon, 1982; *On Wings of Love* (adult novel), Zondervan, 1983. Also author of unpublished novel, "Flame of Love." Contributor of articles, stories, and poems to national and foreign magazines, sometimes under name Elaine L. Young.

WORK IN PROGRESS: Two adult novels, a young adult novel, and a juvenile novel.

SIDELIGHTS: Elaine Schulte remarks: "My direction in writing has changed to inspirational novels, short stories, and articles since 1979. It seems my interest in archaeology has finally been useful, and I hope that 'Flame of Love,' my latest novel, in which archeology is of interest during the heroine's pilgrimage in the footsteps of the Apostle Paul, will soon be published."

Elaine Schulte lived in Belgium for three years and traveled extensively throughout Europe and Africa. Many of her travel articles have been syndicated to major U.S. newspapers.

AVOCATIONAL INTERESTS: Archaeology (has explored archaeological sites in Turkey and Greece), history.

* * *

SCHULTZ, Mort(on) J(oel) 1930-

PERSONAL: Born October 13, 1930, in New York, N.Y.; son of William J. and Dorothy (Meyers) Schultz; married Janice Peck, June 15, 1952; children: Howard, Steven. *Education:* Rutgers University, B.Letters, 1952, M.A., 1962. *Home and office:* 6755 West Broward Blvd., Apt. 403A, Plantation, Fla. 33317.

CAREER: U.S. Department of the Army, Edison, N.J., civilian magazine editor, 1954-58; Lockheed Electronics Co., Plainfield, N.J., public relations representative, 1958-63; free-lance writer, 1963—. *Military service:* U.S. Army, Infantry, 1952-54; became first lieutenant. *Member:* American Society of Journalists and Authors, National Association of Home and Workshop Writers, Society of Automotive Engineers.

WRITINGS: Photographic Reproduction, McGraw, 1963; *The Teacher and Overhead Projection,* Prentice-Hall, 1965; *Teach-*

ing Ideas That Make Teaching Fun, Parker & Son, 1969; *Practical Handbook of Painting and Wallpapering,* Fawcett, 1969; *How to Fix It,* McGraw, 1971; *A Thousand One Questions and Answers About Your Car,* McGraw, 1973.

Popular Mechanics Complete Car Repair Manual, Hearst Books, 1975; *Popular Mechanics Complete Appliance Repair Manual,* Hearst Books, 1975; *McGraw-Hill Illustrated Auto Repair Course,* McGraw, 1978; *Wiring,* Creative Homeowner Press, 1980; *Crown's Diesel Engine Repair Manual,* Crown, 1984.

Contributor of articles to periodicals, including *Better Homes and Gardens, Motor, Homeowner, Popular Mechanics, Family Circle, Reader's Digest,* and *Popular Science.*

SIDELIGHTS: Mort Schultz told *CA:* "I came to specialize in the field of car repair by having been associated with automobiles practically since day one. My family operated auto sales agencies until Pearl Harbor Day and after V-J Day, and as I was growing up I became experienced in auto mechanics and auto sales. However, cars are by no means my only interest. For example, I write books and magazine articles on home repair and boating, because I am interested in both subjects, and I realize that they are important to many people. My background in auto mechanics has made the mastery of home and boat mechanics relatively easy.

"Other subjects that interest me enough to research them thoroughly so I can write about them include aviation, energy, science, technology, and the military."

* * *

SCHULTZ, Samuel J(acob) 1914-

PERSONAL: Born June 9, 1914, in Mountain Lake, Minn.; son of David D. (a farmer) and Anna (Eitzen) Schultz; married Eyla June Tolliver (a real estate seller), June 17, 1943; children: Linda Sue (Mrs. Norwood Anderson), David Carl. *Education:* John Fletcher College, B.A., 1940; Faith Theological Seminary, B.D., 1944; Harvard University, S.T.M., 1945, Th.D., 1949. *Home:* 18 Lois Lane, Lexington, Mass. 02173. *Office:* Department of Bible and Theology, Wheaton College, Wheaton, Ill. 60188.

CAREER: Ordained to ministry of Christian and Missionary Alliance, 1944; pastor of churches in Pine River, Minn., 1940-41, Brockton, Mass., 1944-45, and Belmont, Mass., 1945-47; Gordon College, Wenham, Mass., instructor in Bible, 1946-47; assistant professor of Bible and history at Bethel College and Seminary, St. Paul, Minn., 1947-49, and St. Paul Bible College, St. Paul, 1948-49; Wheaton College, Wheaton, Ill., assistant professor, 1949-54, associate professor, 1954-59, Samuel Robinson Professor of Bible and Theology, 1959-80, professor emeritus, 1980—, chairman of department of Bible and philosophy, 1957-63, chairman of Division of Biblical Education and Philosophy, 1963-67, chairman of Division of Biblical Studies, 1972-80. Supply pastor in Winnetka, Ill., 1950-52, 1960, and Hingham, Mass., 1958-59. Public speaker on archaeology and biblical subjects. Member of board of education, Bethel College and Seminary, 1960-65; former member of board, Institute of Basic Youth Conflicts, and The Watchman Association, Inc.

MEMBER: Society of Biblical Literature, Evangelical Theological Society, American Society of Oriental Research, Phi Sigma Tau. *Awards, honors:* Wheaton College Alumni Association research-study grant, 1958; New York University grant for research in Israel, 1966.

WRITINGS: The Old Testament Speaks, Harper, 1960, 2nd edition, 1970; *Law and History: Old Testament Survey,* Evangelical Teacher Training Association, 1964, 3rd edition, 1980; *The Prophets Speak,* Harper, 1968; *Deuteronomy: Gospel of Love,* Moody, 1971; *The Gospel of Moses,* Harper, 1974; (contributor) *The Living and Active Word of God: Studies in Honor of Samuel J. Schultz,* Eisenbrauns, 1983; *Leviticus: An Everyman's Commentary,* Moody, 1983. Contributor to *Christianity Today.* Editor, *Journal of the Evangelical Theological Society,* 1961-75.

WORK IN PROGRESS: Commentaries for *Word Bible Commentary,* for Word Books; *The Message of the Prophets,* for Pillar Book series in Amharic for Ethiopia; *Genesis* for Reader's Scriptural Guide, to be published by Zondervan.

* * *

SCHUYLER, Keith C. 1919-

PERSONAL: Surname is pronounced Skyler; born June 10, 1919, in Berwick, Pa.; son of Glenn W. and G. Ethel (Kirchner) Schuyler; married Eloise Jean Helt, January 17, 1942; children: Keith C., Jr., Brian J., Bradley K. *Education:* Attended school in Berwick, Pa. *Politics:* Republican. *Religion:* Episcopalian. *Home address:* R.D. 2, Berwick, Pa. 18603. *Office address:* R.D. 3, Box 3120D, Berwick, Pa. 18603.

CAREER: Berwick Enterprise, Berwick, Pa., 1937-51, began as reporter and photographer, became city editor; flight instructor and charter pilot in Berwick, 1946-49; Chamber of Commerce, Berwick, executive secretary, 1951-55; Connecticut Mutual Life Insurance Co., agent in Berwick, 1955—; free-lance writer, mainly on sports. Member of board, International Bowhunter Education Foundation. *Military service:* U.S. Army Air Forces, 1942-45; commander of B-24 on bombing missions over Germany; became first lieutenant. *Member:* Authors Guild, Outdoor Writers of America (former member of board), National Rifle Association (member of board), Trout Unlimited (first vice-president of Pennsylvania branch), Pennsylvania Outdoor Writers Association (past president), Veterans of Foreign Wars, American Legion, Masons.

WRITINGS: Lures: The Guide to Sport Fishing, Stackpole, 1955; *Elusive Horizons,* A. S. Barnes, 1969; *Archery: From Golds to Big Game,* A. S. Barnes, 1970; *Bow Hunting for Big Game,* Stackpole, 1974; *A Last Time to Listen,* Cedar Press, 1977; *Getting Your Start in Flyrod Fishing,* McKay, 1979. Author of columns, "Fins, Furs & Feathers," published in *Berwick Enterprise,* 1938—, "About Hunting & Fishing," published in *V.F.W. Magazine,* 1952-80, "Straight from the Bowstring," published in *Pennsylvania Game News,* 1963—.

SIDELIGHTS: Keith C. Schuyler wrote *CA:* "With six books and well over 3,000 local, state and national columns and a fistful of magazines articles and fiction, I have still managed to make a comfortable living—selling life insurance. But for the typewriter, my material existence could have been much more profitable. My life could have been as routine as a time clock. My memories could be confined to ledger statements and dirty diapers.

"Like the wild gander, I mated for life and missed none of the view in season. My pen, still searching, has written my own epitaph. It can't be read, but I have lived it. And I ask no more."

SCHWARZ, Richard W(illiam) 1925-

PERSONAL: Born September 12, 1925, in Wataga, Ill.; son of George William (a farmer) and Mildred (Imschweiler) Schwarz; married Joyce Anderson, June 11, 1950; children: Constance Kay, Richard Paul, Dwight Luther. *Education:* Emmanuel Missionary College, B.A., 1949; University of Illinois, M.S., 1953; University of Michigan, M.A., 1959, Ph.D., 1964. *Politics:* Republican. *Religion:* Seventh-Day Adventist. *Home:* 229 North Maplewood Dr., Berrien Springs, Mich. 49103. *Office:* Administration Bldg., Andrews University, Berrien Springs, Mich. 49104.

CAREER: Broadview Academy, La Grange, Ill., librarian, 1949-53; Adelphian Academy, Holly, Mich., librarian, 1953-55; Andrews University, Berrien Springs, Mich., instructor, 1955-58, assistant professor, 1958-63, associate professor, 1963-68, professor of history and chairman of department, 1968-77, vice president for academic administration, 1977—. Guest lecturer, Michigan State University Extension Service, 1967. *Military service:* U.S. Naval Reserve, 1944-46. *Member:* Association of Seventh-Day Adventist Historians, Phi Beta Kappa, Phi Alpha Theta.

WRITINGS: John Harvey Kellogg, M.D., Southern Publishing, 1970; (contributor) W. Johns and R. Utt, editors, *The Vision Bold,* Review & Herald, 1977; *Lightbearers to the Remnant,* Pacific Press, 1979; (contributor) George Knight, editor, *Early Adventist Educators,* Andrews University Press, 1983. Contributor to *Dictionary of American Biography.*

Contributor of book reviews to *Seminary Studies* and *Library Journal* and articles to *American Historical Review, Illinois State Historical Journal, Adventist Heritage,* and *Spectrum.* Editor, *Seventh-Day Adventist Historians Newsletter,* 1968-72.

SIDELIGHTS: Richard W. Schwarz, whose life-long interest has been teaching, has co-directed two student study tours of Europe. He spent over ten years in research for his biography and several articles on John Harvey Kellogg, and is a frequent speaker on Kellogg at historical societies.

Schwarz told *CA:* "*Lightbearers to the Remnant* was prepared under the auspices of the Department of Education of the General Conference of Seventh-Day Adventists as a college-level textbook on church history. It has been adopted in all Seventh-Day Adventist colleges in North America and many overseas."

* * *

SEIDLER, Grzegorz Leopold 1913-

PERSONAL: Born September 18, 1913, in Stanislawow, Poland; son of Teodor (a lawyer) and Eugenia (Dawidowicz) Seidler; married Alina Bogusz (an editor), March 1, 1969. *Education:* Jagiellonian University, Doctorate, 1938; additional study at University of Vienna and Oxford University. *Home:* Raabego 7m, 17 Lublin, Poland. *Office:* Faculty of Law, Marii Curie-Sklodowskiej University, Plac Marii Curie-Sklodowskiej 5, 20-031 Lublin, Poland.

CAREER: Jagiellonian University, Krakow, Poland, lecturer in history of philosophy, 1945-50; Marii Curie-Sklodowskiej University, Lublin, Poland, chair of philosophy of law, 1950—, rector, 1959-69. Visiting professor at Christian-Albrechts-University, Kiel, West Germany, 1980-81; visiting fellow at Cambridge University, 1981-82. Director of Polish Cultural Institute, London, England, 1969-71. *Awards, honors:* Banner of Labour first class, and Commander's Cross with star of Order of Polonia Restituta (both state decorations); honorary doctorate, Marii Curie-Sklodowskiej University and Academy of Economics, Krakow.

WRITINGS: Technika prac parlamentarnych, privately printed, 1938; *O istocie wladzy panstwowej,* Ksiegarnia Powszechna (Krakow), 1946; *Ewolucja problemow budzetowych w polskim prawie konstytucyjnym,* Ksiaznica (Krakow), 1946; *Rozwazania nad norma ustrojowa,* Ksiaznica, 1947; *Wladza ustawodawcza i wykonawcza,* Swiat i Wiedza (Krakow), 1948; *Teoria panstwa i prawa,* Panstwowe Wydawnictwo Naukowe (Krakow), 1951; *Wspolczesne kierunki w nauce prawa,* Panstwowe Wydawnictwo Naukowe, 1951; *Mysl polityczna Starozytnosci,* Wydawnictwo Literackie (Krakow), 1955, 3rd edition, 1961; *Doktryny prawne imperializmu,* Panstwowe Wydawnictwo Naukowe, 1957, 3rd edition, Wydawnictwo Lubelskie, 1979.

Soziale Ideen in Byzanz, Akademie-Verlag (Berlin), 1960; *Mysl polityczna Sredniowiecza,* Wydawnictwo Literackie, 1961; *The Emergence of the Eastern World,* Oxford University Press, 1968; *Mysl polityczna czasow nowozytnych,* Wydawnictwo Literackie, 1972; *Przedmarksowska mysl polityczna,* Wydawnictwo Literackie, 1974; (contributor) Roman Schnur, editor, *Staatsraeson: Studien zur Geschichte politischen Begriffs,* Duncker & Humblot (Berlin), 1975; *Z zagadnien filozofii prawa,* Wydawnictwo Lubelskie, 1978; *Two Essays in Political Theory,* University of Pittsburgh, 1979; *W nurcie Oswiecenia,* Wydawnictwo Lubelskie, 1984.

Contributor to *Slavic Review, Studies on Voltaire and the Eighteenth Century,* and journals in Poland and Germany. Editor-in-chief of *Annales Universitatis Mariae Curie-Sklodowska,* 1955—.

WORK IN PROGRESS: Research on main ideas in European culture, including allegories and symbols as factors shaping consciousness.

SIDELIGHTS: Grzegorz Seidler told *CA:* "My studies aim at achieving a broad synthesis, so that the history of political thought would become fairly coherent and focused on principal evolutionary tendencies. In my opinion studies in the history of political thought of necessity lead to a comparison of our own value system and our ideas with those of the past. Only a past that is united with the present is significant in the shaping of human consciousness, which is always being formed in the present."

Seidler's *Doktryny prawne imperializmu* was published in Czech, Ukrainian, Russian, Hungarian, and Bulgarian translations; several of his other books have also appeared in translation.

* * *

SENDY, Jean 1910-1978

PERSONAL: Born November 16, 1910, in St. Petersburg, Russia (now Leningrad, U.S.S.R.); died April, 1978. *Education:* Attended Sorbonne, University of Paris. *Politics:* "Strictly non-believer." *Religion:* Gnostic. *Home:* 68 rue J. J. Rousseau, Paris 75001, France.

CAREER: Formerly a journalist and translator; writer. *Military service:* Served with French regular army and with French Underground.

WRITINGS: Les Cahiers de cours de Moise, Julliard, 1963; *Les Dieux nous sont nes,* Grasset, 1966; *La Lune: Cle de la Bible,* Julliard, 1968, translation by Lowell Blair published as *The Moon: Outpost of the Gods,* Berkley, 1975; *Nous autres gens du Moyen Age,* Julliard, 1969; *Ces Dieux qui firent le ciel et la terre: Le Roman de la Bible,* R. Laffont, 1969, translation by Blair published as *Those Gods Who Made Heaven and Earth: The Novel of the Bible,* Berkley, 1972; *L'Ere du verseau: Fin de l'illusion humaniste,* R. Laffont, 1970, translation published as *The Coming of the Gods,* Berkley, 1973; *Plaidoyer pour un genocide,* Julliard, 1972; (translator) Donald Kenrick and Grattan Puxon, *Destins gitans: Des Origines a la "solution finale,"* Calmann-Levy, 1974; *Les Temps messianiques,* R. Laffont, 1975.†

* * *

SHAHANE, Vasant Anant 1923-

PERSONAL: Born December 18, 1923, in Parbhani, India; son of Anant Vasant (a lawyer) and Laxmi (Desai) Shahane; married Ratnaprabha Pradhan (a lecturer in English), June 7, 1946; children: Neelima (daughter), Deepak (son). *Education:* Attended Osmania University, 1940; Bombay University, B.A. (with honors in English literature), 1944, LL.B., 1946, M.A., 1947; University of Leeds, Ph.D., 1957. *Home:* 3-4-1013/22 Barkatpura, Hyderabad 27, Andhra Pradesh, India 500027. *Office:* Department of English, Osmania University, Hyderabad 7, Andhra Pradesh, India 500007.

CAREER: Osmania University, Hyderabad, Andhra Pradesh, India, lecturer, 1947-56, reader, 1957-64, professor, 1965-72, senior professor of English, 1972—, principal of University College of Arts and Commerce, 1973-74, dean of Faculty of Arts, 1974, 1975, 1976-79. Visiting professor of English, Wisconsin State University—LaCrosse (now University of Wisconsin—La Crosse), 1967-68, and Wayne State University, 1970-71. Chief warden, Osmania University hostels. *Member:* All India English Teachers' Conference (general secretary), Indian Association for English Studies (general secretary), Modern Language Association of America, PEN (India). *Awards, honors:* Fulbright travel fellowship to United States, 1966; award for distinguished achievement in English literature, 1974; Best University Teacher Award, Andhra Pradesh State Government, 1980.

WRITINGS: Shalaka (collection of short stories in Marathi language), Nagpur Prakashan, 1950; *Pashchimekadacha Wara* (collection of critical essays in Marathi), Sushama Prakashan, 1953; *E. M. Forster: A Reassessment,* Kitab Mahal, 1962; *Ideas and Ideals,* S. Chand, 1963; (editor) *Modern One-Act Plays,* Macmillan (Madras), 1963; (editor) *Prose for Our Time,* Longmans, Green (Madras), 1966; (editor) *Perspectives on E. M. Forster's "A Passage to India": A Collection of Critical Essays,* Barnes & Noble, 1968.

Khushwant Singh, Twayne, 1972; *Rudyard Kipling: Activist and Artist,* Southern Illinois University Press, 1973, 2nd edition, 1975; (editor) *E. M. Forster: A Study in Double Vision,* Arnold-Heinemann (New Delhi), 1975, Verry, 1976; *Focus on "A Passage to India,"* Orient Longman (Madras), 1975, South Asia Books, 1976; *Ruth Prawer Jhabvala,* Inter-Culture Associates, 1976, second edition, Arnold-Heinemann, 1983.

(Editor with M. Sivarama-Krishna) *Indian Poetry in English: A Critical Assessment,* Macmillan, 1980; (editor with M. N. Sarma) *The Flute and the Drum: Studies in Sarojini Naidu's Poetry and Politics,* Avon Press, 1980; (editor with Saros Cowasjee) *Modern Indian Fiction,* Vikas Publishing House, 1981; (editor) *Approaches to E. M. Forster,* Arnold-Heinemann, 1981; *"A Passage to India": E. M. Forster,* Longman, 1982; *T. S. Eliot's "The Waste Land": A Study,* Macmillan, 1982.

Contributor: M. K. Naik, editor, *Critical Essays on Indian Writing in English,* Dharwar, 1971; Naik, editor, *The Image of India in Western Creative Writing,* Macmillan, 1971; Naik, editor, *Indian Studies in American Fiction,* Macmillan, 1974; *Essays and Studies: Festschrift in Honour of Professor K. Viswanatham,* Machilipatnam, 1977; *CERVT: E. M. Forster Special Volume,* University of Montpellier, 1977; Manuel and Panikar, editors, *English in India,* Macmillan, 1978; Ramesh Mohan, editor, *Indian Writing in English,* Orient Longman, 1978; Krishna Nandan Sinha, editor, *Indian Writing in English,* Heritage Publishers, 1979; Naik, editor, *Aspects of Indian Writing in English,* Macmillan, 1979; G. K. Das and John Beer, editors, *E. M. Forster: A Human Exploration,* Macmillan, 1979; A. K. Srivastava, editor, *Alien Voice: Perspectives on Commonwealth Literature,* Print House, 1981; C. T. Thomas and others, editors, *Focus on Literature Essays in Memory of C. A. Sheppard,* Macmillan, 1982; Judith S. Herz and Robert K. Martin, editors, *E. M. Forster: Centenary Revaluations,* Macmillan, 1982.

Author of study notes for Walt Whitman's *Leaves of Grass,* Cliff Notes, 1969. Contributor to *Ungar's Encyclopedia of World Literature in the Twentieth Century,* 1982, and *Encyclopedia of Indian Literature,* 1983; contributor of articles and reviews to academic journals, including *Studies in Romanticism, English Studies,* and *Journal of Indian Writing in English.* Editor of *Osmania Journal of English Studies.*

WORK IN PROGRESS: Prajapati, a novel.

SIDELIGHTS: Vasant Anant Shahane told *CA:* "I have written a novel based on my experiences of post-Independence India covering the period from 1947 to 1983. The novel is entitled *Prajapati* (the Lord of the universe), who is the father and guide of angels, devils, and men. The novel has a mythical structure, and its narrative is woven round several myths of Prajapati in Indian mythology—from the great god, Brahma, to a diminutive god.

"The story is also deeply concerned with political Prajapatis of modern India who rule the country. The theme also encompasses the Hindu caste system (in four divisions), and each section attempts to project the development of an individual as well as the caste to which he belongs. Thus, *Prajapati* projects an image of contemporary India."

* * *

SHANOR, Donald Read 1927-

PERSONAL: Born July 11, 1927, in Ann Arbor, Mich.; son of William Wilson (an engineer) and Katherine (Read) Shanor; married Constance Collier (a medical editor), November 24, 1951; children: Rebecca Read, Elizabeth Lynne. *Education:* Northwestern University, B.S., 1951; Columbia University, M.A., 1964. *Politics:* Liberal Democrat. *Home:* 285 Riverside Dr., New York, N.Y. 10025. *Agent:* A. L. Hart, Fox-Chase Agency, 419 East 57th St., New York, N.Y. 10022. *Office:* Graduate School of Journalism, Columbia University, New York, N.Y. 10027.

CAREER: During his early career was factory and railroad worker; American Forces Network, Frankfurt, Germany, editor/reporter, 1952-54; United Press International, editor/reporter in Frankfurt, Germany, London, England, New York City, and at the United Nations, 1954-65; Columbia University, New York City, lecturer in journalism, 1965-67; *Chicago Daily News,* Chicago, Ill., correspondent in Eastern and Western Europe and the Mideast, 1967-71; Columbia University,

1971—, began as associate professor, currently professor of journalism and international affairs. Ford Foundation consultant on Third World media, 1981—. *Military service:* U.S. Navy, 1945-46. *Member:* Society of Professional Journalists, Association for Education in Journalism, American Council on Germany.

WRITINGS: The New Voice of Radio Free Europe (monograph), Columbia University Press, 1967; *Soviet Europe*, Harper, 1975; *The Soviet Triangle: Russia's Relations with China and the West in the Eighties*, St. Martin's, 1980; (co-author) *News from Abroad and the Foreign Policy Public*, Foreign Policy Association, 1980.

Contributor of articles on Poland, Austria, and Switzerland to *Collier's Encyclopedia Yearbook*, 1970—. Also contributor to periodicals, including *Atlantic Monthly* and *New Leader*. Contributing editor, *World Press Review*, 1973—; advisory editor, *Columbia Journalism Review*, 1971—.

WORK IN PROGRESS: A Nation of Dissidents (tentative title); *Voices from the Third World*.

SIDELIGHTS: Donald Read Shanor told *CA* that the kind of writing he is doing now isn't a great deal different from what he was producing as a daily journalist, except in one all-important aspect: he can now measure his time to research and report in months and even years instead of hours or days. "Where the daily journalist may have at best a five minute scan of the clips or their electronic equivalent for background, [I] can take the time to do a complete 'ghost draft' of [my] chapters, writing a draft of the book on the basis of information already available. The next step, however, is crucial: going out and doing the reporting and further original research, using the ghost draft only as a way of beginning to learn the subject, as a key to knowing what questions to ask. In the final version, almost all of the ghost draft disappears (hence its name), since it is superseded by better, newer, more focused information and writing."

AVOCATIONAL INTERESTS: Carpentry, hiking.

* * *

SHARMAT, Marjorie Weinman 1928-

PERSONAL: Born November 12, 1928, in Portland, Me.; daughter of Nathan (a wholesaler and manufacturer of dry goods and men's furnishings) and Anna (Richardson) Weinman; married Mitchell Brenner Sharmat (a realtor), February 24, 1957; children: Craig Lynden, Andrew Richard. *Education:* Attended Lasell Junior College, 1946-47; graduate of Westbrook Junior College, 1948. *Residence:* Tucson, Ariz. *Agent:* Harold Ober Associates, 40 East 49th St., New York, N.Y. 10017.

CAREER: Writer. Yale University, New Haven, Conn., circulation staff member of university library, 1951-54, circulation staff member of law library, 1954-55. Writer of greeting card verse and advertising copy.

AWARDS, HONORS: Recipient of "book of the year" citations from Library of Congress, 1967, for *Rex*, 1976, for *Mooch the Messy*, and 1979, for *Griselda's New Year*, from the Child Study Association, 1971, 1973-76, 1978, and 1979, and from *Saturday Review, Newsweek, Ladies Home Journal,* and *Ms.*; recipient of "best book of the season" citations from the "Today Show," 1972, for *Nate the Great*, and 1975, for *Maggie Marmelstein for President*, and from *House and Garden*; "Classroom Choices" citations from International Reading Association and Childrens' Book Council, 1976-82; Tower Award, Westbrook College, 1975; first runner-up of Arizona Young Readers' Award, 1978-79; Irma Simonton Black Honor Book Award, 1980, for *Gila Monsters Meet You at the Airport*; *Edgemont* was named "notable trade book in the field of social studies" by the National Council for the Social Studies; also recipient of numerous other awards and award nominations.

WRITINGS—Juveniles, except as indicated: *Rex*, Harper, 1967; *Goodnight, Andrew, Goodnight, Craig*, Harper, 1969.

Gladys Told Me to Meet Her Here, Harper, 1970; *A Hot Thirsty Day*, Macmillan, 1971; *51 Sycamore Lane*, Macmillan, 1971; *Getting Something on Maggie Marmelstein*, Harper, 1971; *A Visit with Rosalind*, Macmillan, 1972; *Nate the Great*, Coward, 1972; *Sophie and Gussie*, Macmillan, 1973; *Morris Brookside, a Dog*, Holiday House, 1973; *Nate the Great Goes Undercover*, Coward, 1974; *Morris Brookside Is Missing*, Holiday House, 1974; *I Want Mama*, Harper, 1974.

I'm Not Oscar's Friend Anymore, Dutton, 1975; *Walter the Wolf*, Holiday House, 1975; *Burton and Dudley*, Holiday House, 1975; *Nate the Great and the Lost List*, Coward, 1975; *Maggie Marmelstein for President*, Harper, 1975; *The Lancelot Closes at Five*, Macmillan, 1976; *The Trip, and Other Sophie and Gussie Stories*, Macmillan, 1976; *Mooch the Messy*, Harper, 1976; *Edgemont*, Coward, 1977; *I'm Terrific*, Holiday House, 1977; *I Don't Care*, Macmillan, 1977; *Nate the Great and the Phony Clue*, Coward, 1977; (contributor) Ann Durell, editor, *Just for Fun*, Dutton, 1977; *A Big Fat Enormous Lie*, Dutton, 1978; *Nate the Great and the Sticky Case*, Coward, 1978; *Thornton the Worrier*, Holiday House, 1978; *Mitchell Is Moving*, Macmillan, 1978; *Mooch the Messy Meets Prudence the Neat*, Coward, 1979; *Scarlet Monster Lives Here*, Harper, 1979; *Mr. Jameson and Mr. Phillips*, Harper, 1979; *The 329th Friend*, Four Winds, 1979; (with husband, Mitchell Sharmat) *I Am Not a Pest*, Dutton, 1979; *Uncle Boris and Maude*, Doubleday, 1979; *Octavia Told Me a Secret*, Four Winds, 1979; *Say Hello, Vanessa*, Holiday House, 1979; *Griselda's New Year*, Macmillan, 1979; *The Trolls of 12th Street*, Coward, 1979.

Little Devil Gets Sick, Doubleday, 1980; *What Are We Going to Do about Andrew?*, Macmillan, 1980; *Taking Care of Melvin*, Holiday House, 1980; *Sometimes Mama and Papa Fight*, Harper, 1980; (with Mitchell Sharmat) *The Day I Was Born*, Dutton, 1980; *Grumley the Grouch*, Holiday House, 1980; *Gila Monsters Meet You at the Airport*, Macmillan, 1980; *Nate the Great and the Missing Key*, Coward, 1981; *Twitchell the Wishful*, Holiday House, 1981; *Chasing after Annie*, Harper, 1981; *Rollo and Juliet, Forever!*, Doubleday, 1981; *The Sign*, Houghton, 1981; *Lucretia the Unbearable*, Holiday House, 1981; *The Best Valentine in the World*, Holiday House, 1982; *Two Ghosts on a Bench*, Harper, 1982; *Nate the Great and the Snowy Trail*, Coward, 1982; *Mysteriously Yours, Maggie Marmelstein*, Harper, 1982; *Square Pegs* (young adult; novelization of television program), Dell, 1982; *Frizzy the Fearful*, Holiday House, 1983; *I Saw Him First* (young adult), Dell, 1983; *How to Meet a Gorgeous Guy* (young adult), Dell, 1983; *Rich Mitch*, Morrow, 1983; *Who's Afraid of Ernestine?*, Putnam, 1984; *The Story of Bentley Beaver*, Putnam, 1984; *Bartholomew the Bossy*, Macmillan, 1984; *How to Meet a Gorgeous Girl* (young adult), Dell, 1984; *Sasha the Silly*, Holiday House, 1984; (contributor) Donald Gallo, editor, *Fourteen, Fifteen, Sixteen* (young adult), Dell, 1984.

Contributor to magazines and newspapers.

WORK IN PROGRESS: Two children's books for Oxford University Press; a young adult novel for Dell.

SIDELIGHTS: Marjorie Weinman Sharmat's books have been published in England, Japan, Israel, Canada, the Netherlands, Australia, New Zealand, Denmark, France, Germany, and Sweden.

MEDIA ADAPTATIONS: I'm Not Oscar's Friend Any More was made into a television film and presented as part of the CBS-TV Library Special, "The Wrong Way Kid"; *Gila Monsters Meet You at the Airport* was made into a pilot film for the PBS-TV "Reading Rainbow" series; *Nate the Great Goes Undercover* was made into a film.

AVOCATIONAL INTERESTS: Playing piano, drawing.

BIOGRAPHICAL/CRITICAL SOURCES: Frederic Raphael and Kenneth McLeish, *The List of Books,* Harmony House, 1981; Nancy Larrick, *A Parents' Guide to Children's Reading,* 4th edition, Doubleday, 1982.

* * *

SHEEHAN, Susan 1937-

PERSONAL: Born August 24, 1937 in Vienna, Austria; came to United States in 1941; naturalized, 1946; daughter of Charles and Kitty C. (Herrmann) Sachsel; married Neil Sheehan (a reporter for *New York Times*), March 30, 1965; children: Maria Gregory, Catherine Fair. *Education:* Wellesley College, B.A., 1958. *Home:* 4505 Klingle St. N.W., Washington, D.C. 20016. *Agent:* Robert Lescher, 155 East 71st St., New York, N.Y. 10021. *Office: New Yorker* Magazine, 25 West 43rd St., New York, N.Y. 10036.

CAREER: Esquire-Coronet (magazines), New York City, editorial researcher, 1959-60; free-lance writer in New York City, 1960-62; *New Yorker* (magazine), New York City, staff writer, 1962—. Member of literature panel of the District of Columbia Commission on Arts and Humanities, 1979—. Member of advisory committee on employment and crime, Vera Institute of Justice, 1978—; consultant on 42nd St. redevelopment project for New York City Department of City Planning. Judge, Robert F. Kennedy Journalism Awards, 1980, 1984. *Member:* National Mental Health Association. *Awards, honors:* Guggenheim fellowship, 1975-76; Sidney Hillman Foundation Award, 1976, for "A Welfare Mother"; Gavel Award from American Bar Association, 1978, for *A Prison and a Prisoner;* Woodrow Wilson Center for International Scholars fellowship, 1981; Mental Health Media Award for individual reporting from National Mental Health Association, 1981, for article "The Patient"; Pulitzer Prize for best nonfiction work, 1982, and American Book Award nomination for general nonfiction, 1983, both for *Is There No Place on Earth for Me?;* Distinguished Alumni Award, Wellesly College, 1984; Ford Foundation fellowships; Phi Beta Kappa.

WRITINGS—All nonfiction: *Ten Vietnamese* (collection of sketches), Knopf, 1967; *A Welfare Mother* (first printed in *New Yorker*), introduction by Michael Harrington, Houghton, 1976; *A Prison and a Prisoner* (first printed in *New Yorker*), Houghton, 1978; *Is There No Place on Earth for Me?* (first printed as "The Patient" in *New Yorker*), Houghton, 1982; *Kate Quinton's Days* (first printed in *New Yorker*), Houghton, 1984.

Contributor to magazines, including *New York Times Sunday Magazine, Atlantic, New Republic, Harper's, Holiday,* and *McCall's.*

WORK IN PROGRESS: A biography of Alfred Knopf, for Houghton.

SIDELIGHTS: Journalist Susan Sheehan specializes in long, difficult stories that lay open the lives of people to whom her affluent *New Yorker* readers are not ordinarily exposed. Four of these accounts—of a welfare recipient, a convicted thief, a mental patient, and an elderly woman on Medicaid—have been published in book form. Sheehan's account of a schizophrenic woman, first published in the *New Yorker* as "The Patient" and then as a book entitled *Is There No Place on Earth for Me?*, won a Pulitzer Prize for general nonfiction in 1982 and received an American Book Award nomination.

In her work Sheehan attempts to examine systems and institutions through the presentation of an individual case. In *A Welfare Mother* Sheehan takes on the governmental public assistance programs, in *A Prison and a Prisoner* she looks at Green Haven maximum security prison and the New York penal system, in *Is There No Place on Earth for Me?* she scrutinizes Creedmoor Psychiatric Center as well as many of the methods for treating the mentally ill, and in *Kate Quinton's Days* she tackles the Medicaid program and the treatment of the elderly in the United States. In a *Village Voice* review of *Is There No Place on Earth for Me?*, Vince Aletti points out that in psychiatric patient Sylvia Frumkin, Sheehan "has found . . . a 'representative' figure whose history illuminates a system or an institution, not in a flash of revelation but through painstaking accumulation of data and insight. Sheehan's scrupulous, vivid case histories are constructed bit by bit, fine webs of evidence and observation, dense with fact but charged with feeling. . . . Sheehan's focus on Sylvia is hardly a narrow one; Sylvia is the entry point, the key that begins to unlock the institution. Starting with her, Sheehan takes every tangent, follows every lead, and attempts to follow up every loose end—all with obvious delight in the serendipitous fact." Writing about *A Prison and a Prisoner,* Kenneth Lamont states in the *Washington Post Book World:* "Susan Sheehan's cool and altogether admirable book does not describe an unusual prisoner in an unusual prison. Quite the contrary, I was reminded on almost every page of my own experiences teaching school in San Quentin 25 years ago. I knew [subject George] Malinow in a half-dozen incarnations." *Newsweek's* Peter S. Prescott states that in *A Prison and A Prisoner* Sheehan "wisely has chosen as narrow a focus as possible; an intense look at a single prisoner is more likely to provide reliable insights into the whole system than is a broad and superficial survey."

Sheehan spends months researching her articles and, in order to catch and record the smallest details, she often stays with her subjects for stretches at a time, observing and interviewing them and everyone with whom they are involved. Before she began writing *Is There No Place on Earth for Me?*—a book Meg Rosenfeld of the *Washington Post* calls a "reportorial tour de force"—Sheehan had compiled 1000 pages of her own notes and observations as well as an additional 1000 pages of material on the treatment Sylvia Frumkin had received for the past seventeen years. Sheehan's technique, says Rosenfeld, "is a kind of total immersion, observation and interviews combined with extensive library research. At Creedmoor, she insinuated herself so completely that she became the proverbial fly on the wall. She calls it 'third person invisible.'" In an interview with *Chicago Tribune* reporter Peter Gorner, Sheehan recalls, "I literally live with my subjects when I'm on a story. When I profiled Carmen Santana, the welfare mother, I slept in the same bed with her. I found myself in a room where heroin was being dealt, wondering all the time how I was going to explain my presence when the police came."

Sheehan writes her profiles in a straightforward, documentary style that Prescott refers to as her "plain gray worsted prose." For instance, in *A Welfare Mother* Sheehan spends seven pages recording Carmen Santana's purchases after she received her biweekly assistance check. In *A Prison and a Prisoner* she details the events of inmate George Malinow's day, often recording it in minute-by-minute fashion. *Is There No Place on Earth for Me?* begins with a vivid account of one of Sylvia Frumkin's psychotic breakdowns. "Susan Sheehan is a master of the *New Yorker* style," comments Willard Gaylin in the *New Republic*. "[*Is There No Place on Earth for Me?*] is a written version of what in movies would be called cinema verite." The sparse unemotional prose Sheehan uses in her books is carried through in her approach to her material. "Massive research and clear, dry, unsentimental prose style characterize Sheehan's work," notes Gorner in his *Chicago Tribune* article on *Is There No Place on Earth for Me?*. "[Sheehan] is a camera who reports on what she learns and observes, neither excoriating or lauding—'I try not to affix blame,' she says. 'Blame is not very useful.'"

All of Sheehan's profiles have been well-received, both by critics and the public. For example, Sara Sanborn, writing in *Saturday Review*, considers *A Welfare Mother* to be "a perfect little book. The excellence of *A Welfare Mother* lies in the sureness of vision, discipline, and patience that kept it small; a more self-indulgent writer could have made it twice as long and half as good. Its purity is its impact. . . . This is a book of life on its own terms; it makes the pious generalizations of both right and left look even more futile than usual. *A Welfare Mother* is a fine achievement, a book that should be read."

However, a number of critics find that Sheehan's approach to her subject in *A Welfare Mother* detracts from the story she presents; Sheehan's style is too controlled and factual, thus lacking in emotion. "Unfortunately, Mrs. Santana seldom emerges as anyone other than a welfare recipient," says Susan Jacoby in the *New York Times Book Review*. "One of Mrs. Santana's sons is a drug addict, and her attitude toward that is disposed of in two quick sentences. Does a mother on welfare bleed less than other mothers when she learns her son is mainlining heroin? In this instance, as in many others, a major weakness of the piece is its lack of direct quotation." Richard Lingeman of the *New York Times* sees this as a possible problem of reprinting a magazine article as a book; "Mrs. Sheehan's style . . . is cool, objective, self-effacing, pitched in an even, controlled tone; the facts of Mrs. Santana's life, the comings-and-goings of her typical days, the highs and lows are all extruded through this mold in a smooth controlled flow," writes Lingeman. "While this style may have worked well in a magazine piece, in a book, out of the context of the magazine, it suddenly seems to shrink and flatten out. . . . Mrs. Sheehan's journalistic commitment is praiseworthy, and her book does offer some insight into the welfare system through the eyes of one of its victims—or beneficiaries, if you will. But laughter, tears and emotions are missing. The author has distanced the reader too much, providing neither emotional involvement nor material for thought." However, despite raising similar objections in the *Washington Post Book World*, Kristen Hunter maintains: "Susan Sheehan has chosen to concentrate on only one life. Considering that life's scope, having distilled its essence into slightly more than 100 pages is a remarkable feat."

In a *New York Times Book Review* article in which he praises Sheehan for her insights into the penal system in *A Prison and a Prisoner*, Fred J. Cook states, "The bulging prisons of America incarcerate a full-sized criminal army, composed overwhelmingly of incorrigibles and growing at a rate that outstrips facilities to contain them." *A Prison and a Prisoner*, Cook continues, "is a marvelous work of detailed reporting, . . . [and] Sheehan presents this picture [of the prisons] in all its hopelessness. She not only delves into the mechanics of the prison system and the daily life of the prisoner, but she gets inside their skulls as well." *A Prison and a Prisoner* also examines the changes in philosophy of the correctional system from reformist (which aims at rehabilitation of the prisoners) to hard-line (which entails incarcerating prisoners simply to keep them off the streets and spurns rehabilitation programs such as job training). "George Malinow, 57, a payroll-robbing recidivist from Brooklyn, is a complex figure and living repository of correction history," observes James Lieber in the *Nation*. "Incarcerated all but three years since 1938, he participated in the state's early reform experiments in Walkill, hardened big-house years at Sing Sing, and survived Attica by nesting on a roof. . . . These institutions and others . . . have distinct, often bizarre rules and flavors that Sheehan understands. The prisons come to seem like strange city-states within a not always harmonious league."

Although Sheehan paints a vivid picture of prison life, the absence of emotion in her style once again works against her in some critics' minds. Her book lacks focus in that she does not present the reader with any conclusions, contends the *New York Times*'s Anatole Broyard. "I don't know quite what to make of '*A Prison and a Prisoner*,'" declares Broyard. "Susan Sheehan is a good observer as well as a determined researcher, yet when I had finished her book, I felt at a loss to say what she thought—or wanted me to think—about the prisons and the particular prisoner she describes. . . . [She] gives us an accurate but curiously passive picture of the current issues in prison management. When she tells us the prevalent view in penology now is that rehabilitation does not work, I was not sure whether she was reporting a trend or expressing an evaluation of her material."

"Susan Sheehan never says . . . [that prisons do not work]," says *Newsweek*'s Prescott in agreement with Broyard's view that Sheehan offers the reader few conclusions of her own. "A cool reporter determined to be as objective as she can, she leaves it to her reader to infer her conclusions." Kenneth Lamont finds this absence of opinion one of the book's strengths rather than one of its weaknesses: "*A Prison and a Prisoner* . . . is not a reformer's book, complete with recommendations for an increased food budget, more vocational training, enlarged visiting hours, and all the dreary rest," he says in *Washington Post Book World*. "It is a much better and more important book than that, for it comes to grips with reality and portrays it superbly. The world it describes is often absurd and shot through with black humor, precisely the sort of reality that reduces official society to muscle-bound helplessness." Concludes Prescott: "Thoughtless reviewers will doubtless complain that [Sheehan] offers no solutions to the dilemma of our prisons. Never mind; reporters are not social engineers. It is achievement enough that they describe a situation as it is—and this Sheehan has done remarkably well."

Also writing on the same issue of neutrality in *A Prison and a Prisoner*, *Nation* reviewer James Lieber differs from the other critics in that he does believe that Sheehan comes to a conclusion and that "she manages without opining to make a point that is arguably reactionary, possibly dangerous." Lieber finds that in her presentation Sheehan presents a more than sympathetic view of prison officials' beliefs that few of the men in prisons like Green Haven are suffering and that her choice of Malinow as her subject serves to confirm this view. And Malinow, says Lieber, is not necessarily representative of the prison population. "The message is clear that Malinow does best when given maximal structure, when put in a box," the critic notes. "Because [Sheehan] has chosen Malinow as opposed to equally valid counterimages available (rebellious, retarded, junkie, nonwhite, etc.), she is able to slip into easy generalizations about a population of 1,800 [at Green Haven].... Something doesn't fit. In my job [as an assistant public defender] we try to keep defendants out of state pens even when the alternative is the county jail. The reason is that state time is hard time, and for reasons that range from noise to separation, those who draw it hit bottom and grow old before their years. Taking her cue from the administration, Sheehan regards the regular suicide attempts as ploys to get attention, drugs and transfers rather than as reflections of despair." Cook in the *New York Times Book Review* also finds that Sheehan makes some conclusions about the penal system but suggests that "the most chilling aspect of Susan Sheehan's account is the conclusion that nothing has worked—and nothing in the foreseeable future is likely to work."

Of all of Sheehan's books, however, it is *Is There No Place on Earth for Me?* that has gained the greatest attention. Its notoriety derives from its sometimes harrowing presentation of life in a psychiatric hospital but especially from the bizarre and often darkly humorous personality of its main subject, Sylvia Frumkin. "I have schizophrenia—cancer of the nerves. My body is overcrowded with nerves. This is going to win me the Nobel Prize for medicine," declares Frumkin in one of her numerous highspeed monologues in *Is There No Place on Earth for Me?*

"Cancer of the nerves. Sylvia Frumkin is the lunatic poet of the nut house," writes Megan Rosenfeld in the *Washington Post*, "summoning from the dark mess of her mind amazing screeds that ring like a bell in the fog. 'The body is run by electricity. My wiring is all faulty . . . ,' she said once. On another day her vision was this: 'My skin is just like the lawn. I'm going to tear it off and pluck out the bed of dandelions. This isn't schizophrenia, it's terminal acne. . . .'" And it is Frumkin's vision of the world and of herself that keeps the reader so intensely interested, despite the fact that she is, as Maggie Scarf says in the *New York Times Book Review,* "an unlikely heroine, voraciously greedy (for food and attention), overweight, hostile and assaultive . . . [, prone to] excesses of . . . speechifying, and . . . preposterous appearance and behavior." To Vince Aletti in the *Village Voice,* she "emerges as an unlikely and unforgettable heroine, at once the most appealing and appalling character you're likely to encounter in a book this year." According to Willard Gaylin in the *New Republic,* Sylvia Frumkin "is not a 'lovable eccentric.' She is not even very likable. But she will break your heart."

Sylvia Frumkin was first diagnosed as a schizophrenic at the age of fourteen and entered Creedmoor Psychiatric Center in Queens, New York for the first time a year and a half later. By the time Sheehan met her seventeen years later Frumkin had been in and out of mental institutions ten times; one hospitalization lasted two years. It is through Frumkin that Sheehan is able to enter the nightmarish world of the insane and to explore the labyrinth of hospitals, drugs, megavitamins, electroconvulsive treatments, and insulin shock therapy that comprise part of the darker side of America's approach to the mentally ill. "Susan Sheehan, with extraordinary explicitness, takes us through each hospitalization," explains Gaylin. "The central institution is Creedmoor, not one of the ornaments of the New York State mental health system. What happens at Creedmoor is often infuriating: wrong medications wrongly administered, insensitivity, bureaucratic mess and meanness." The *New York Times*'s Christopher Lehmann-Haupt comments: "If Sylvia's plight is foremost in our awareness while reading 'Is There No Place on Earth for Me?,' Mrs. Sheehan's narrative handling of it is not far behind. What is especially impressive is how effortlessly she moves back and forth between this case in particular and the status of mental disease in general. At one moment, she is giving us a limpid explanation of the difference between anti-anxiety and anti-psychotic, or neuroleptic, drugs, and how the latter are thought to go about mitigating the psychotic phase of schizophrenia. The next moment we are in the hospital with Sylvia, watching her move like a perpetual-motion machine gone mad—witnessing that special combination of intelligence and grandiosity that makes her, in at least one doctor's opinion, 'a genius at being insane.'"

Is There No Place on Earth for Me? points out many of the changes in the approach to treating the mentally ill, as well as many of the shortfalls in the methods of those treatments and in the philosophies behind them. Creedmoor, says Gaylin, "is the kind of institution that has contributed to the recent crusade for 'deinstitutionalization' with its simplistic assumption that if only there were no institutions there would be no mental disease. Sylvia herself knows better. On reading in a Creedmoor form that their 'philosophy of treatment' is that 'the individual with a problem is best served in his own environment,' she responds, 'I'm against polluting the environment, always have been.'" At the same time, however, Sheehan is determined "not to affix blame" to any one person or institution. Meg Greenfield reports in *Washington Post Book World* that "it is true that the book reveals some terrible lapses in institutional conduct, for instance, and some dangerous shortages of money, expertise and common sense among those charged with the care of Miss Frumkin when she is at her most violent or deranged. But I was struck by the reverse of this as a general matter: the enormous number of individuals and groups and institutions that have taken extra initiatives and invested money and energy to try to help Miss Frumkin—relatives, church folk, doctors, case workers, hospital attendants and administrators. She has been the beneficiary, if that is the word for it, of all those many reforms and bright ideas we editorial writers like to pronounce the good and self-evident solution: halfway houses and rehabilitation programs and vocational training and God knows what all for nearly two decades. What we learn is humility, that there are some human conditions and complexities that we can't 'fix' with a bright idea."

Sheehan's book has been praised as perhaps a clearer portrait of mental illness than many of the books that have preceded it. "If only Ken Kesey had met Sylvia Frumkin before he took his fanciful flight over the cuckoo's nest," speculates Gaylin. "Or Peter Shaffer [author of 'Equus'] had talked to her before he littered the Broadway stage with his horse manure (or R. D. Laing would talk to her—as soon as possible), a confused and unsuspecting public would have been spared a lot of mischievous information. . . . To romanticize an illness as severe as schizophrenia is a sin against the sufferer. To minimize it by assuming that kindness and proper care are enough is to trivialize the problem. Susan Sheehan does neither. She honestly and directly indicates, with infinite detail and patience, the anguish and the agony that mental illness always wreaks on its victim, and on those in contact with her, particularly those who love her."

BIOGRAPHICAL/CRITICAL SOURCES: *Saturday Review,* July 10, 1976; *Washington Post Book World,* July 18, 1976, May 21, 1978, April 11, 1982; *New York Times Book Review,* August 8, 1976, July 9, 1978, May 2, 1982; *New York Times,* August 27, 1976, May 13, 1978, April 7, 1982; *National Review,* September 17, 1976; *Newsweek,* May 15, 1978, April 5, 1982; *Nation,* September 2, 1978; *Chicago Tribune Book World,* April 18, 1982; *Village Voice,* April 20, 1982; *New Republic,* May 12, 1982; *Chicago Tribune,* May 17, 1982; *Ms.,* June, 1982; *America,* July 31, 1982; *Washington Post,* August 1, 1982.

—Sketch by Heidi A. Tietjen

* * *

SHERMAN, Jane 1908-

PERSONAL: Born June 14, 1908, in Beloit, Wis.; daughter of Horace Humphrey (an advertising writer) and Florentine (an opera singer; maiden name, St. Clair) Sherman; married Ned Lehac (a science teacher and musical composer), February 8, 1940. *Education:* Attended high school in Elmhurst, N.Y. *Home:* 8 Huguenot St., New Paltz, N.Y. 12561.

CAREER: Professional dancer; toured the Far East with Ruth St. Denis, Ted Shawn and Denishawn Dancers, 1925-26, and the United States, 1926-27; toured the United States with the Ziegfeld Follies, 1927-28; member of Humphrey-Weidman concert dancers, 1928; performed in Broadway productions "The Third Garrick Gaities," "9:15 Revue," and "Hello, Daddy," 1928-30; danced with Rockettes at Radio City Music Hall in New York, N.Y., 1934-35; traveled and studied in Europe, 1935-44; *Seventeen,* New York City, fiction editor, 1944-45; United Nations Information Center, New York City, secretary to head of Radio Division, 1946; writer, 1946—. Reconstructor of Denishawn dances for performances in concert by the Vanaver Caravan of New York, the New Jersey Center for the Performing Arts, and the Dancemakers of St. Petersburg, Fla., 1980—. Lecturer on Denishawn Dance at colleges and conferences throughout the United States.

AWARDS, HONORS: De la Torre Bueno Prize from Dance Perspectives Foundation and Wesleyan University Press, 1974-75, for *Soaring: The Diary and Letters of a Denishawn Dancer in the Far East, 1925-1926;* National Endowment for the Humanities grant, 1977-78.

WRITINGS: *Soaring: The Diary and Letters of a Denishawn Dancer in the Far East, 1925-1926,* Wesleyan University Press, 1976; *The Drama of Denishawn Dance,* Wesleyan University Press, 1979; *Denishawn: The Enduring Influence,* G. K. Hall, 1983; (with Barton Mumaio) *One Step at a Time: The Story of Barton Mumaw from Denishawn to Jacob's Pillow to Broadway and Beyond,* Dance Horizons, 1985.

For children: *The Real Book about Dogs,* F. Watts, 1951; *The Real Book about Horses,* F. Watts, 1952; *The Real Book about Bugs,* F. Watts, 1952; *The Real Book of Amazing Scientific Facts,* F. Watts, 1953; *The Real Book about Snakes,* F. Watts, 1955; *The Little House that Moved,* Grosset, 1972.

Work anthologized in *The Best in Children's Books,* Doubleday, 1959 and *Catch Your Breath,* Gerrard, 1973.

Also author, with husband, Ned Lehac, of an educational newspaper column and other material for the Hudson Valley Citizens Watch on nuclear safety. Contributor of stories, poems, articles, and reviews to magazines, including *Dance Magazine, Dance Chronicle, Dance Scope, Cue,* and *Hudson Valley,* and to newspapers.

SIDELIGHTS: Jane Sherman writes *CA:* "Long after I stopped writing children's books to pursue other interests, I was impelled to return to the typewriter by the recognition that the great period in American dance represented by [the work of] Ruth St. Denis and Ted Shawn was being distorted by current dance writers and historians. Younger generations of dancers were ignorant of the philosophies and techniques of those very pioneers from whose ideas, works, and pupils developed the modern dance we know today.

"My first dance book, *Soaring,* therefore sought to contribute a picture of these artists, St. Denis and Shawn, as I had known them, both as teachers and as performers. It described their fifteen month tour of the Far East in 1925-26, when I was the youngest member of their company. This was the first time the countries of the Orient had been visited by a modern Western dance group. I was convinced by the reaction to this book that it was essential for future historians to have additional accurate records of those dances of the past, so my next book, *The Drama of Denishawn Dance,* describes in detail fifty-six works in the Denishawn repertory I had known. In my third book, *Denishawn: The Enduring Influence,* I continued to present a history of that seminal institution which made a uniquely valuable contribution to American modern dance and American theatrical culture in general, particularly through the innovative techniques of those remarkable products of Denishawn: Martha Graham, Doris Humphrey, Louis Horst, and Charles Weidman.

"Recently I have been able to help companies realize on the concert stage many of the original Denishawn dances in which I had either appeared countless times or had seen frequently performed. These reconstructed works of mine have been performed in various parts of the country, especially at the famous Jacob's Pillow Dance Festival which was originally founded by Ted Shawn in 1932. It has been most rewarding to enable young modern dancers to experience with their own bodies, or see with their own eyes, what some of the creations of their 'ancestors' were really like."

Several of Sherman's books have been translated into Urdu, Portuguese, Danish, and Chinese.

* * *

SHIBLES, Warren 1933-

PERSONAL: Born July 10, 1933, in Hartford, Conn.; son of Stanley Neil and Jean (Russell) Shibles; married Patricia Pell, August, 1957; married second wife, Carolyn Foster, 1976; children: (first marriage) Garth, Kirsten, Eric. *Education:* University of Connecticut, B.A., 1958; University of Colorado, M.A., 1963; Indiana University, graduate study, 1963-66. *Religion:* "Philosopher-Atheist." *Address:* Box 342, Whitewater, Wis. 53190. *Office:* Department of Philosophy, University of Wisconsin, Whitewater, Wis. 53190.

CAREER: Parsons College, Fairfield, Iowa, lecturer in philosophy, 1966-67; University of Wisconsin—Whitewater, assistant professor of philosophy and chairman of department, 1967—; Language Press, Whitewater, director, 1970—. *Military service:* U.S. Army, 1953-55. *Member:* American Philosophical Association, American Association of University Professors, Writers Association. *Awards, honors:* University of Wisconsin research grant, 1974-75.

WRITINGS—Published by Language Press, except as indicated: *Philosophical Pictures*, 1969; *Wittgenstein, Language and Philosophy*, 1969, revised edition, 1974; *Models of Ancient Greek Philosophy*, Vision Press, 1971; *An Analysis of Metaphor*, Mouton, 1971; *Metaphor: An Annotated Bibliography and History*, 1971; (editor) *Essays on Metaphor*, 1972; *Tudor Figures of Rhetoric*, 1972; *Death: An Interdisciplinary Analysis*, 1974; *Emotion: The Method of Philosophical Therapy*, 1974; *Humor: A Comprehensive Classification and Analysis*, 1978; *Rational Love*, 1978.

"Teaching Young People to Be Critical" series, published by Language Press in 1978: *Good and Bad Are Funny Things: A Rhyming Book; Ethics for Children; Emotion: A Critical Analysis for Children; Humor: A Critical Analysis for Children; Time: A Critical Analysis for Children*.

Contributor of poetry to various journals and anthologies. Also contributor of over fifty articles to journals, including *Philosophy Today, International Studies in Philosophy, Philosophy and Phenomenological Research, Journal of Value Inquiry*, and *Journal of Aesthetic Education*.

WORK IN PROGRESS: A book on lying and another book on humor for adults.

SIDELIGHTS: Warren Shibles told CA: "My goal is to promote honest, open inquiry and to inquire into and clarify the most relevant aspects of knowledge for understanding humanism and for living an aesthetic life. Most people, however, seem to refuse to inquire and even to oppose it."

* * *

SHIKES, Ralph E. 1912-

PERSONAL: Born September 20, 1912, in Boston, Mass.; son of David (a realtor) and Rebecca Charlotte (Herson) Shikes; married Elizabeth Todd, February 10, 1940; married second wife, Ruth Collins, September 19, 1958; children: (first marriage) Katherine Todd; (second marriage) Jennifer Collins. *Education:* Harvard University, A.B. (magna cum laude), 1933. *Politics:* Independent. *Home:* 16 West 77th St., New York, N.Y. 10024.

CAREER: American Book Co., New York City, staff member, 1934-38; Viking Press, New York City, staff member, 1938-41; Limited Editions Club, New York City, staff member, 1941-42; Office of War Information, Washington, D.C., staff member, 1942-43; Editorial Projects, Inc., New York City, president, 1952-58; Science & Medicine Publishing Co., New York City, president, 1958-73. President, Public Concern Foundation; member of board of directors, Bill of Rights Foundation; treasurer, Creative Arts Rehabilitation Foundation. *Military service:* U.S. Army, 1943-45; editor of *Daily Pacifican*. *Member:* National Association of Science Writers, Authors League of America, College Art Association.

WRITINGS: *Slightly Out of Order*, Viking, 1958; *The Indignant Eye: The Artist as Social Critic in Prints and Drawings from the 15th Century to Picasso*, Beacon Press, 1969; (contributor) *The Artist in the Service of Politics*, MIT Press, 1977; (with Paula Hays Harper) *Pissarro: His Life and Work*, Horizon Press, 1980; *Wit, Bite and Irony: Painters as Caricaturists since Delacroix*, Horizon Press, 1984. Editor of numerous anthologies. Managing editor, *The Washington Spectator*.

SIDELIGHTS: About *Pissarro: His Life and Work*, John Russell comments in the *New York Times Book Review:* "Ralph E. Shikes and Paula Harper are animated in their biography by due respect and regard for Pissarro. . . . They are neither cranky nor pretentious. They have assembled a good corpus of illustrations. They never stray far from the direct first-person quotations on which modern biography has come to rely for authenticity." However, Russell, upon closer examination, complains about the book's overall effect: "But this book seems to this reader to lack bite, sweep and command. There is no sign, to begin with, that the paintings have been looked at with either a fresh or a deeply informed eye." Russell concludes that the book "does not change the way in which we look at Pissarro's work. . . . But there is nothing cheap or presumptuous about 'Pissarro: His Life and Work,' and it has been carried through to an honest if limited conclusion."

Yet Lucy Lippard admires the work, observing in the *Nation* that "Ralph Shikes and Paula Harper have provided an honest portrait of an honest man—as solid and likable as their subject—while adding depth to his popular nice-guy image." She adds that "one of the most interesting aspects of this book is its lively image of the Impressionists arguing and discussing both art and politics as they moved toward group action in the first artist-organized exhibitions."

BIOGRAPHICAL/CRITICAL SOURCES: *New York Times*, July 11, 1980; *New York Times Book Review*, July 20, 1980; *Atlantic*, August, 1980; *New Yorker*, August 25, 1980; *Nation*, September 20, 1980.

* * *

SHINGLETON, Royce (Gordon, Sr.) 1935-

PERSONAL: Born October 25, 1935, in Stantonsburg, N.C.; son of Wiley Thomas (a merchant and farmer) and Lossie (Vick) Shingleton; married Ruth Bennett (a medical records administrator), June 10, 1962; children: Royce Gordon, Jr., Justin Thomas. *Education:* East Carolina University, B.S., 1958; Appalachian State University, M.A., 1964; Florida State University, Ph.D., 1971. *Home:* 2323 Pheasant Dr., Albany, Ga. 31707. *Office:* Social Science Division, Albany Junior College, Albany, Ga. 31707.

CAREER: Dinwiddie High School, Dinwiddie, Va., history and English teacher, 1960-61; Greene Central High School, Snow Hill, N.C., social studies teacher, 1961-63; Lees-McRae College, Banner Elk, N.C., dean of men, 1964-65; Georgia State University, Atlanta, history instructor, 1968-73; Oglethorpe University, Atlanta, faculty member, 1973-77; Albany Junior College, Albany, Ga., member of faculty in Social Science Division, 1977—. *Military service:* U.S. Army, 1958-60; served as administrative assistant in West Germany. *Member:* Thronateeska Heritage Foundation, Southeastern Writers Association, Georgia Association of Historians, Phi Alpha Theta. *Awards, honors:* Nonfiction award, Southeastern Writers Association, 1981, for *Richard Peters: Champion of the New South* manuscript.

WRITINGS: (Editor) *America in the Making*, McCutchan, 1969; *John Taylor Wood: Sea Ghost of the Confederacy* (National Historical Society Book Club selection), University of Georgia Press, 1979. Also author of *Richard Peters: Champion of the New South*. Contributor of articles to various history journals.

AVOCATIONAL INTERESTS: Tennis.

* * *

SHIPMAN, David 1932-

PERSONAL: Born November 4, 1932, in Norwich, England;

son of Alfred Herbert and Edith (Deeks) Shipman. *Education:* Attended Merton College, Oxford, 1954-55. *Agent:* Frances Kelly Agency, 9 King Edward Mansions, 629 Fulham Rd., London SW6, England.

CAREER: Victor Gollancz Ltd., and Methuen & Co. Ltd., London, England, assistant sales manager, 1955-61; representative in Europe for U.S. publisher, Curtis Circulation, 1961-63; free-lance European representative for several British publishers, 1964-66; writer and film historian, 1968—. Guest lecturer on cinema, University of East Anglia, 1972.

WRITINGS: The Great Movie Stars: The Golden Years, Crown, 1970, revised edition, Hill & Wang, 1981; *The Great Movie Stars: The International Years,* Angus & Robertson, 1972, St. Martin's, 1973, revised edition, Hill & Wang, 1981; *Brando,* Doubleday, 1975; *The Story of Cinema,* Volume I: *From the Beginnings to "Gone with the Wind,"* Hodder & Stoughton, 1982, St. Martin's, 1984; Volume II: *From "Citizen Kane" to the Present Day,* St. Martin's, 1984; *The Good Film and Video Guide,* Hodder and Stoughton/Consumers' Association, 1984. Associate editor, *Films and Filming,* 1983—.

WORK IN PROGRESS: A history of science fiction and fantasy movies, for publication by Hamlyn Publishing Group; *A Screen for Venus: Sex in the Cinema,* for publication by Hamish Hamilton.

* * *

SHIVANANDAN, Mary 1932-

PERSONAL: Born January 6, 1932, in Rangoon, Burma; came to the United States in 1960, naturalized in 1971; daughter of Sir John Francis (in Indian Civil Service) and Jean Newton (Simpson) Sheehy; married Kandiah Shivanandan (an astrophysicist), September 17, 1960; children: John Uthya-Surian, Marianne Gauri. *Education:* Newnham College, Cambridge, B.A. (honors), 1954, M.A., 1967. *Politics:* Democrat. *Religion:* Roman Catholic. *Home and office:* 4711 Overbrook Rd., Bethesda, Md. 20816.

CAREER: Canadian Broadcasting Corp., assistant radio producer in Toronto, Ontario, 1956-58, and Montreal, Quebec, 1958-60; *Mid East,* Washington, D.C., associate editor, 1968-69; American University, Washington, D.C., associate research scientist in foreign area studies, 1969-70; *New American Encyclopedia,* Washington, D.C., associate editor-in-chief, 1971-72; free-lance writer, 1972—; director, KM Assos., 1980—. Lecturer to women's groups and schools; has broadcast over Canadian Broadcasting Corp., British Broadcasting Corp., and Australian Broadcasting Corp.

WRITINGS: Bobtail and Bubtail (juvenile), Thacker & Co., 1945; *Gamal Abdul Nasser,* SamHar Press, 1973; (with Richard F. Nyrop, Beryl L. Benderly, and others, and contributor) *Area Handbook for Pakistan,* U.S. Government Printing Office, 1971, 4th edition, 1975; (with Nyrop, Benderly, and others, and contributor) *Area Handbook for Ceylon,* U.S. Government Printing Office, 1971; (with Nyrop, Benderly, and others, and contributor) *Area Handbook for India,* U.S. Government Printing Office, 3rd edition, 1975; *Natural Sex,* Rawson Wade, 1979; (co-editor) *Natural Family Planning: Development of Natural Programs,* International Federation for Family Life Promotion, 1984. Author of column "Perspectives, News Briefs," in *Marriage & Family Living,* 1977-81. Contributor to magazines and newspapers, including *Washingtonian, Rolling Stone,* and *U.S. Catholic.* Contributing editor, *Marriage & Family Living,* 1977-81. Editor of family planning columns for Family Enrichment Features, 1983—, and NFP Newsletter Distribution Service, 1984—.

SIDELIGHTS: Mary Shivanandan writes: "Having traveled since childhood (born in Burma, educated in England and Australia, worked in Canada and the United States . . .), I have a cosmopolitan outlook. Experience, supplemented by research, has given me insight into the ways of life and modes of thought of varied cultural and religious groups. This adds more perspective to my present writing on the family.

"After contributing for several years to books, magazines, newspapers and radio on general interest, political, scientific and international topics, I am now writing almost exclusively in the field of marriage, family, and natural family planning. I am not only writing on these topics myself but enabling others, through my editing and other communication skills, to express their experience in these areas."

BIOGRAPHICAL/CRITICAL SOURCES: CBC Times, Volume XVII, number 10, 1964.

* * *

SHIVERS, Jay S(anford) 1930-

PERSONAL: Born July 7, 1930, in New York, N.Y.; son of Ted M. and Mabel (Sinkoff) Shivers; married Rhoda Goldstein (a teacher), February 14, 1951; children: Jed Mark. *Education:* Indiana University, B.S., 1952; New York University, M.A., 1953, additional study, 1953-55; University of Wisconsin, Ph.D., 1958. *Politics:* Independent. *Home:* South Eagleville Rd., Storrs, Conn. 06268. *Office:* U-34, University of Connecticut, Storrs, Conn. 06268.

CAREER: Hillside Psychiatric Hospital, Glen Oaks, N.Y., recreational leader, 1952-53; Goldwater Memorial Hospital, Welfare Island, N.Y., director of recreational rehabilitation, 1953; University of Wisconsin—Madison, instructor in education, 1955-57; U.S. Veterans Administration Hospital, Madison, Wis., recreational supervisor, 1957-58; Mississippi Southern College (now University of Southern Mississippi), Hattiesburg, professor of recreational service education and chairman of department, 1958-62; University of Connecticut, Storrs, assistant professor, 1962-66, associate professor, 1967-69, professor of recreational service education, 1970—. Visiting summer professor at Eastern Washington State College (now Eastern Washington University), 1963, and California State College at Hayward (now California State University, Hayward), 1967. Chairman of Mansfield (Conn.) Park Planning Committee, 1962—, Mansfield Recreational Services, 1965—, and Connecticut Older Worker Employee Network, 1982—. Member of scientific committee, Van Cle Foundation, 1976. *Military service:* U.S. Army, Counter-Intelligence Corps, special agent, 1953-55.

MEMBER: International Recreation Association, World Leisure and Recreation Association, International Playground Association, International Rehabilitation Association, National Recreation and Park Association, Society of Professional Recreation Educators, National Therapeutic Recreational Society, American Association for Health, Physical Education and Recreation, American Academy of Leisure Science (founding fellow, 1980), American Association of University Professors, United World Federalists, Connecticut Recreation and Park Association, Sierra Club, Phi Delta Kappa.

AWARDS, HONORS: Certificate of Achievement from Hospital Section, American Recreation Society, 1965; Honor Award of Connecticut Recreation Society, 1968; National Literary Award of National Recreation and Park Association, 1979; Distinguished Service Award of National Therapeutic Recreational Society, 1983.

WRITINGS: *Horizons Unlimited: The Organization of Recreational Services in the State of Mississippi,* Mississippi Recreation Association, 1959; (with George Hjelte) *Public Administration of Park and Recreational Services,* Macmillan, 1962; *Leadership in Recreational Service,* Macmillan, 1963; *Principles and Practices of Recreational Service,* Macmillan, 1967.

Camping: Management, Counselling, Program, Appleton, 1971; *Planning Recreational Places,* A. S. Barnes, 1971; (with Hjelte) *Public Administration of Recreational Services,* Lea & Febiger, 1972; (with C. R. Calder) *Recreational Crafts for School and Community,* McGraw, 1974; (with Hollis F. Fait) *Therapeutic Recreational Service,* Lea & Febiger, 1975; *Essentials of Recreational Service,* Lea & Febiger, 1978; *Perceptions of Recreation and Leisure,* Holbrook, 1978; (with H. Ibrahim) *Leisure: Emergence and Expansion,* Hwong Publishing, 1979.

Recreational Leadership: Group Dynamics and Interpersonal Relations, Princeton Publishing, 1980, 2nd edition, 1985; (with Fait) *Recreational Service for the Aging,* Lea & Febiger, 1980; (with Joseph W. Halper) *The Crisis in Urban Recreational Service,* Fairleigh Dickenson University Press, 1981; *Special Recreational Service: Therapeutic and Adapted,* Lea & Febiger, 1984; (with Charles Bucher) *Recreation for Today's Society,* 2nd edition (Shivers was not associated with 1st edition), Prentice-Hall, 1984; *Recreational Safety: The Standard of Care,* Associated University Presses, 1985.

Also author of master plans for recreational service in various towns. Contributor of more than fifty articles to recreation and rehabilitation journals. Member of editorial board, 1962-69, and editor, 1964-66, of annual *Recreation in Treatment Centers.*

WORK IN PROGRESS: *Camping: Organization and Operation,* for Wiley.

* * *

SHULMAN, Frank Joseph 1943-

PERSONAL: Born September 20, 1943, in Boston, Mass.; son of Murray (a civil engineer) and Edna (Altman) Shulman. *Education:* Harvard University, A.B. (magna cum laude), 1964; additional study at Hebrew University of Jerusalem, 1964-65, and Inter-University Center for Japanese Language Studies, 1967-68; University of Michigan, M.A. (East Asian studies), 1968, M.A. (library science), 1969, doctoral candidate, 1974—. *Office:* East Asia Collection, McKeldin Library, University of Maryland, College Park, Md. 20742.

CAREER: University of Michigan, Center for Japanese Studies, Ann Arbor, bibliographer and librarian, 1970-75; University of Maryland, McKeldin Library, College Park, curator of East Asia Collection, 1976—. Library consultant to the Groupe d'Etudes et de Documentation sur le Japon Contemporain, Ecole Pratique des Hautes Etudes, 1974. *Member:* International Association of Orientalist Librarians, Association for Asian Studies (vice-president of mid-Atlantic region, 1980-81; member of executive group of committee on East Asian libraries, 1982-83; member of board of directors, 1983-86), American Historical Association, Association for the Bibliography of History, Independent Scholars of Asia, European Association for Japanese Studies, Middle East Librarians' Association, Asiatic Society of Japan, Japan-American Society of Washington, D.C., District of Columbia Library Association. *Awards, honors:* Carnegie Library Science Endowment fellowship, 1969; awarded grants for bibliographical work by the American Council of Learned Societies, 1969, Memorial Foundation for Jewish Culture, 1973, Japan-United States Friendship Commission, 1978, Henry Luce Foundation, 1980, and Japan Foundation, 1982.

WRITINGS: (with Robert Ward) *Allied Occupation of Japan, 1945-1970: An Annotated Bibliography of Western-Language Materials,* American Library Association, 1974; (with Teresa S. Yang and Thomas C. Kuo) *East Asian Resources in American Libraries,* Paragon, 1977.

Editor and compiler: *Japan and Korea: An Annotated Bibliography of Doctoral Dissertations in Western Languages, 1877-1969,* American Library Association, 1970; *Doctoral Dissertations on South Asia, 1966-1970: An Annotated Bibliography Covering North America, Europe and Australia,* Center for South and Southeast Asian Studies, University of Michigan, 1971; *Doctoral Dissertations on China: A Bibliography of Studies in Western Languages, 1945-1970,* University of Washington Press, 1972; *American and British Doctoral Dissertations on Israel and Palestine in Modern Times,* Xerox University Microfilms, 1973; *Doctoral Dissertations on China, 1971-1975: A Bibliography of Studies in Western Languages,* University of Washington Press, 1978; (with Archie R. Crouch) *Mid-Atlantic Directory to Resources for Asian Studies,* Mid-Atlantic Region, Association for Asian Studies, 1980; *Doctoral Dissertations on Japan and on Korea, 1969-1979: An Annotated Bibliography of Studies in Western Languages,* University of Washington Press, 1982.

Contributor of numerous articles, book reviews, reports, and papers to professional journals, including *Journal of Asian Studies, Monumenta Nipponica, Library Quarterly, Journal of Korean Affairs, Asian Studies Professional Review, Committee on East Asian Libraries Bulletin,* and many others. Editor for doctoral dissertations, *Newsletter of the Association for Asian Studies,* 1969-71, and *Asian Studies Professional Review,* 1971-74. Assistant editor, *Bibliography of Asian Studies* of the Association for Asian Studies, 1970-71; editor, *Doctoral Dissertations on Asia: An Annotated Bibliographical Journal of Current International Research,* 1975—.

WORK IN PROGRESS: *Doctoral Dissertations on China and Inner Asia, 1976-1980,* for the University of Washington Press; *Doctoral Dissertations in Jewish Studies and Related Subjects, 1945-1980; A Bibliography on Jewish History and Civilization, the Old Testament, the Ancient Near East, the State of Israel, and Contemporary Jewish Affairs,* for Greenwood Press; *Doctoral Dissertations on Southeast Asia, 1968-1975: An Annotated Bibliography of International Research,* for University of Michigan; *A Century of U.S.-Korean Relations, 1882-1982: A Bibliography of Western-Language Books, Articles, and Theses,* for the Woodrow Wilson International Center for Scholars, Smithsonian Institution; *The Allied Occupation of Japan: A Bibliography of Western-Language Publications from the Years 1970-1983,* for the Center for Japanese Studies, University of Michigan.

SIDELIGHTS: Frank Shulman has long been interested in the subject of Japan's postwar economic and political relations with the Middle East. He has a very extensive personal library collection on Asia.

SIEGEL, Adrienne 1936-

PERSONAL: Born June 10, 1936, in New York, N.Y.; daughter of Nathan (a physician) and Jean (an attorney; maiden name, Mark) Spitzer; married Martin Siegel (a professor of history), May 7, 1972. *Education:* University of Pennsylvania, B.S., 1957; Columbia University, M.A., 1959; New York University, Ph.D., 1973. *Home:* 330 West Jersey St., Elizabeth, N.J. 07202. *Office:* Department of History, Long Island University, Brooklyn Center, Brooklyn, N.Y. 11201.

CAREER: William Howard Taft High School, New York, N.Y., teacher of history, 1959-62; James Madison High School, New York, N.Y., teacher of history, 1962-77; Long Island University, Brooklyn Center, Brooklyn, N.Y., assistant professor of history, 1977—. Member of Brooklyn College Honor Academy Collaborative, 1982. Associate of Columbia University City Seminar; member of Columbia University Post Doctoral Seminars in Urban History. *Member:* Organization of American Historians, Institute for Research in History (fellow). *Awards, honors:* Danforth Associate, 1972; Alumnae Club Key and Pin Award, New York University, 1973; fellowship and Founder's Day Award, New York University; Fulbright Fellowship to India, 1978.

WRITINGS: Philadelphia, Oceana, 1975; *The Image of the American City in Popular Literature, 1820-1870,* Kennikat, 1981; *John Marshall,* Associated Faculty Press, 1984. Contributor to *Journal of American History, North Dakota Quarterly,* and *Journal of Popular Culture.*

SIDELIGHTS: Adrienne Siegel told *CA:* "What people have thought of their cities is as much a reality as what has happened in them. The impact of the media in fashioning the perceptions of Americans to their urban communities has been the focus of my research for the last several years." *Avocational interests:* Travel, theater, ballet, music, gourmet cooking, sailing, motorcycling.

BIOGRAPHICAL/CRITICAL SOURCES: Publishers' Weekly, June 2, 1975; *Interact,* December, 1975.

* * *

SILVAROLI, Nicholas J. 1930-

PERSONAL: Born December 4, 1930, in Buffalo, N.Y.; son of Nicholas Amrigo and Caroline (De Paula) Silvaroli; married Margaret M. Masterson (a teacher), August 22, 1952 (divorced May 12, 1975); children: Diane, Christine, Pamela. *Education:* State Teacher's College (now State University of New York at Fredonia), B.A., 1953; State University College of Education at Buffalo (now State University of New York at Buffalo), M.A., 1960; Syracuse University, Ed.D., 1963. *Politics:* Independent. *Religion:* Unitarian Universalist. *Home:* 706 East Colgate, Tempe, Ariz. 85283. *Office:* College of Education, Arizona State University, Tempe, Ariz. 85281.

CAREER: Teacher in public schools of Williamsville, N.Y., 1956-60; Arizona State University, Tempe, director of Reading Center, 1964, associate professor, 1965-70, professor of education, 1970—. Director of annual migrant teacher institutes in Arizona. Former member of a musician's local union. *Military service:* U.S. Army, 1953-55; became sergeant. *Member:* International Reading Association (chairman of committee on automation in reading), National Society for the Study of Education, National Committee for Research in Education, Phi Delta Kappa.

WRITINGS: Classroom Reading Inventory, W. C. Brown, 1966, 4th edition, 1980; (with John C. Edwards) *Reading Improvement Program,* W. C. Brown, 1968; (with William D. Sheldon) *This Cool World* (young adult book), Allyn & Bacon, 1970; (with Jann Skinner and J. O. "Rocky" Mayner) *Oral Language Evaluation,* EMC Corp., 1977; (with Warren Wheelock) *Teaching Reading: A Decision Making Process,* W. C. Brown, 1980; (with Dennis J. Kear and Michael E. McKenna) *A Classroom Guide to Reading Assessment and Instruction,* Kendall/Hunt, 1982.

AVOCATIONAL INTERESTS: Flying (private pilot with visual flight rules rating), playing the piano.

* * *

SIMIC, Charles 1938-

PERSONAL: Born May 9, 1938 in Yugoslavia; came to United States in 1949; son of George (an engineer) and Helen (Matijevic) Simic; married Helene Dubin (a dress designer), October 25, 1965; children: Anna. *Education:* New York University, B.A., 1966. *Politics:* None. *Religion:* Eastern Orthodox. *Address:* Old Mountain Rd., Northwood, N.H. 03261. *Office:* Department of English, University of New Hampshire, Durham, N.H. 03824.

CAREER: Aperture (photography magazine), New York, N.Y., editorial assistant, 1966-74; University of New Hampshire, Durham, associate professor of English, 1974—. *Military service:* U.S. Army, 1961-63. *Awards, honors:* P.E.N. International Award for Translation, 1970; Guggenheim fellowship, 1972-73; National Endowment for the Arts fellowship, 1974-75, and 1979-80; Edgar Allan Poe Award, American Academy of Poets, 1975; National Institute of Arts and Letters and American Academy of Arts and Letters Award, 1976; National Book Award nomination, 1978, for *Charon's Cosmology;* Harriet Monroe Poetry Award, University of Chicago, 1980; Di Castignola Award, Poetry Society of America, 1980; P.E.N. Translation Award, 1980; Ingram Merrill fellowship, 1983-84.

WRITINGS—Poetry: *What the Grass Says,* Kayak, 1967; *Somewhere among Us a Stone Is Taking Notes,* Kayak, 1969; *Dismantling the Silence,* Braziller, 1971; *White,* New Rivers Press, 1972, revised edition, Logbridge-Rhodes, 1980; *Return to a Place Lit by a Glass of Milk,* Braziller, 1974; *Biography and a Lament,* Bartholemew's Cobble (Hartford, Conn.), 1976; *Charon's Cosmology,* Braziller, 1977; *Brooms: Selected Poems,* Edge Press, 1978; *School for Dark Thoughts,* Banyan Press, 1978; *Classic Ballroom Dances,* Braziller, 1980; *Austerities,* Braziller, 1982; *Weather Forecast for Utopia and Vicinity,* Station Hill Press, 1983.

Translator: Ivan V. Lalic, *Fire Gardens,* New Rivers Press, 1970; Vasko Popa, *The Little Box,* Charioteer Press, 1970; *Four Modern Yugoslav Poets,* Lillabulero (Ithaca, N.Y.), 1970; (and editor with Mark Strand) *Another Republic,* Viking, 1976; *Key to Dream, According to Djordje,* Elpenor, 1978; Popa, *Homage to the Lame Wolf,* Field (Oberlin, Ohio), 1979; (with Peter Kastmiler) Slavko Mihalic, *Atlantis,* Greenfield Review Press, 1983; (with others) Henri Michaux, *Translations: Experiments in Reading,* O ARS, 1983.

Poetry appears in anthologies, including: *The Young American Poets,* edited by Paul Carroll, Follett, 1968; *The Contemporary American Poets,* edited by Mark Strand, World Publishing, 1969; *Major Young American Poets,* edited by Al Lee, World Publishing, 1971; *America a Prophesy,* edited by George Quasha and Jerome Rothenberg, Random House, 1973; *Shake the Ka-*

leidoscope: A New Anthology of Modern Poetry, edited by Milton Klonsky, Pocket Books, 1973; *The New Naked Poetry,* edited by Stephen Berg and Robert Mezey, Bobbs-Merrill, 1976; *The American Poetry Anthology,* edited by Daniel Halpern, Avon, 1976; *A Geography of Poets,* edited by Edward Field, Bantam, 1979; *Contemporary American Poetry, 1950-1980,* Longman, 1983; *The Norton Anthology of Poetry,* Norton, 1983.

Contributor of poems to over 100 magazines, including *New Yorker, Poetry, Nation, Kayak, Atlantic, Esquire, Chicago Review,* and *New Republic.*

SIDELIGHTS: Although the poetry of Charles Simic has garnered much critical admiration—and a score of imitators—its unique enigmatic quality makes it difficult for critics to describe. Robert B. Shaw of *New Republic* defines Simic's poems as "at once weighty and evasive, and describing them is about as easy as picking up blobs of mercury with mittens on."

Simic's poetry draws heavily on European folklore. "The real figures in his poems," writes Stanley Plumley in the *New York Times Book Review,* "are from primitive folklore, tales, a medieval shadow-world of the literature of memory." Simic also uses the literary forms of folklore. "The poetic structures are oral," Zora Devrnja of *Poet and Critic* says of Simic's poems. "Simic works with skeletal narratives formed by incremental repetition, traditional dialogues, proverbs, riddles, nursery rhymes." Simic's folk world, "a network of omens and images," as Paul Zweig describes it in the *Village Voice,* "produces a delightful simplicity."

Several critics point to Simic's concern with what a critic for *Virginia Quarterly Review* calls a "pre-verbal, pre-conceptual consciousness." Simic examines this consciousness, the critic continues, by using "childhood, folklore, eroticism, foods, animals, and plants" in his poems. Similarly, Alan Williamson of *Poetry* finds that Simic's poetry "has often urged on us the importance of the pre-civilized, even the pre-human, portion of ourselves."

The Yugoslavian poet Vasco Popa, whose books Simic has translated into English, has been a substantial influence on Simic's work. The folklore of their native Yugoslavia figures prominently in both men's poetry, but Simic adds to this a simplicity of style and an intense concentration upon common objects. It is this concentration that gives his poems their surreal intensity. Simic, writes Shaw, looks "so long and fixedly at common objects that they acquire haloes of strangeness, and become disquietingly animated." Victor Contoski sees a religious element in Simic's fascination with inanimate objects. He writes in *Chicago Review:* "Time and again [Simic] speaks of things in religious terms. Knives in a butcher shop glitter 'like altars / In a dark church.' He is baptized in the sight of a dying pig. He addresses his shoes as sacred objects. . . . Things are, simply put, sacramental." Contoski also finds that "Simic's efforts to interpret the relationship between the animate and inanimate have led to some of the most strikingly original poetry of our time, a poetry shockingly stark in its concepts, imagery, and language."

Simic's "determined concentration on the most common things," Shaw believes, "makes reality strange and, even when terrifying, strangely inviting." J. D. McClatchy of *Poetry* also sees an eerie quality in Simic's work. He writes in a review of *Classic Ballroom Dances* that Simic's poems are "haunted, wryly imaginative, darkly self-possessed [and are] distinguished by their unnerving attention to objects, dream images, cognitive traps." "It is strangely hellish," is how Geoffrey Thurley describes Simic's work in *The American Moment: American Poetry in the Mid-Century.* Thurley goes on to write that Simic's poetry seems "almost as if it is expecting at any moment to break into the black-and-white horror film to which it is the technicolor contrast. . . . Simic creates a world in which only emptiness finally exists: it is a world of silence, waiting for the unspeakable to happen, or subsisting in the limbo left afterwards." This grim approach is also found in *Classic Ballroom Dances,* a collection of poems about European history. In this book, Simic "is hounded by the past," writes Vernon Young in *Hudson Review,* "the past of Europe, which he retells as a succession of mini-Grimm fairy tales at their most monstrous, peopled with goblins, witches, men marching, blood and bones, phantom horses in the snow, Mongols and foxes; in short, all the paraphernalia of what [Simic] himself calls the Great Dark Night of History."

Dismantling the Silence, a poetry collection that incorporates many of the poems found in Simic's two earlier collections, has drawn particular critical praise. Shaw writes in *Poetry* that he has "met with very few volumes as imaginatively fertile, in which so many of the poems are instantly memorable." Young believes that "Simic can scarcely improve on the bizarre juxtapositions and the hobgoblin midnights of the soul which he envisioned in [*Dismantling the Silence*]."

Later Simic collections have sometimes been judged to be less successful than his earlier work. Speaking of *Austerities,* for example, Williamson writes in the *New York Times Book Review* that it is "a slightly disappointing book, unlikely to dispel the impression that the poet has not quite fulfilled the promise of his brilliant early *Dismantling the Silence.*" L. M. Rosenberg of the *Chicago Tribune Book World,* however, finds the same book appealing: "I love [Simic's] humor, his observations of the sad, the forlorn, and the homely." Rosenberg points out that "a surreal feeling of disquiet is one of Simic's celebrated trademarks; I am just as fond of his more emotional, and concurrently more mystical, work [as found in *Austerities*]." Bruce Bennett of *Nation* admits that *Austerities* deals with "a climate almost unremittingly harsh" but "despite the bleakness, the experience of reading *Austerities* is not austere. For one thing, there is abundant humor, albeit of the gallows variety. . . . There is the pleasure afforded by the poems themselves: precise and pungent, clean and spare, they make Simic's grim vision more than palatable."

Because of the distinctive nature of his writing, Diane Wakoski finds it difficult to define Simic. She writes in *Poetry:* "I have not yet decided whether Charles Simic is America's great living surrealist poet, a children's writer, a religious writer, or simple-minded. My decision in this matter is irrelevant actually because, whatever he is, his poetry is cryptic and fascinating."

BIOGRAPHICAL/CRITICAL SOURCES: *Poetry,* December, 1968, September, 1971, March, 1972, February, 1975, November, 1978, July, 1981; *Village Voice,* April 4, 1974; *Virginia Quarterly Review,* spring, 1975; *Choice,* March, 1975; *Poet and Critic,* Volume IX, number 1, 1975; *Contemporary Literary Criticism,* Volume VI, 1976, Volume IX, 1978, Volume XXII, 1982; *Georgia Review,* winter, 1976; *New Republic,* January 24, 1976; *Antioch Review,* spring, 1977; *Chicago Review,* Volume XLVIII, number 4, 1977; Geoffrey Thurley, *The American Moment: American Poetry in the Mid-Century,* St. Martin's, 1978; *New York Times Book Review,* March 5, 1978, October 12, 1980, May 1, 1983; *Washington Post Book World,* November 2, 1980; *Hudson Review,* spring, 1981; *Boston Review, March/April, 1981; *Ploughshares,* Volume VII, number 1, 1981; *Chicago Tribune Book World,* June 12, 1983; *Gargoyle,* Number 22/23, 1983.

—Sketch by Thomas Wiloch

* * *

SIMMONS, James W(illiam) 1936-

PERSONAL: Born April 20, 1936, in London, Ontario, Canada; son of James William and Sara (Clark) Simmons; married Harriet Xanthakos, August 30, 1964; children: two. *Education:* University of Western Ontario, B.Sc., 1959; University of Chicago, M.A., 1962, Ph.D., 1964. *Politics:* New Democratic Party. *Religion:* Agnostic. *Office:* Department of Geography, University of Toronto, Toronto, Ontario, Canada.

CAREER: University of Western Ontario, London, assistant professor, 1963-66, associate professor of geography, 1966-67; University of Toronto, Toronto, Ontario, associate professor, 1967-75, professor of geography, 1975—. Consultant to Metropolitan Toronto Urban Renewal Study, 1964-65. *Member:* Canadian Association of Geographers, Association of American Geographers, Canadian Political Science Association, Regional Science Association, Canadian Regional Science Association.

WRITINGS: The Changing Pattern of Retail Location, Department of Geography, University of Chicago, 1964; *Toronto's Changing Retail Complex,* Department of Geography, University of Chicago, 1966; (with Robert Simmons) *Urban Canada,* Copp Clark, 1969, 2nd edition, 1974; (editor with Larry S. Bourne) *The Form of Cities in Central Canada,* University of Toronto Press, 1973; (with Alan M. Baker and Marie Truelove) *Patterns of Residential Movement in Metropolitan Toronto,* University of Toronto Press, 1974; (editor with Bourne and others) *Urban Futures for Central Canada,* University of Toronto Press, 1974; (editor with Bourne) *Systems of Cities: Readings on Structure, Growth, and Policy,* Oxford University Press (New York), 1978.

All published by Centre for Urban and Community Studies, University of Toronto: *Patterns of Interaction within Ontario and Quebec,* 1970; *Net Migration within Metropolitan Toronto,* 1971; (with Baker) *Household Movement Patterns,* 1972; *Canada as an Urban System: A Conceptual Framework,* 1974; *Canada: Choices in a National Urban Strategy,* 1975.

Contributor to professional journals.

* * *

SIMON, John Y. 1933-

PERSONAL: Born June 25, 1933, in Highland Park, Ill.; son of Jay (a banker) and Jane (Younker) Simon; married Harriet Furst, July 22, 1956; children: Philip, Ellen. *Education:* Swarthmore College, B.A., 1955; Harvard University, M.A., 1956, Ph.D., 1961. *Home:* 805 Glenview Dr., Carbondale, Ill. 62901. *Office:* Ulysses S. Grant Association, Morris Library, Southern Illinois University, Carbondale, Ill. 62901.

CAREER: Ohio State University, Columbus, instructor in history, 1960-62, on leave, 1962-64; Southern Illinois University at Carbondale, executive director and managing editor, Ulysses S. Grant Association, 1962—, associate professor, 1964-71, professor of history, 1971—. *Member:* American Historical Association, Organization of American Historians, Association for Documentary Editing (chairman of steering committee, 1978; past president, 1978-79; president-elect, 1979-80; president, 1980-81; past president, 1981-82), Illinois Association for the Advancement of History (president, 1983-84), Illinois State Historical Society (vice-president, 1966-67; director, 1967-70), Illinois Sesquicentennial Commission (member of historians' advisory committee, 1965-68). *Awards, honors:* Illinois State Historical Society award of merit, 1970; Harry S Truman Award from Kansas City Civil War Round Table, 1972; Fletcher Pratt Award from Civil War Round Table of New York, 1973; Moncado Prize Award from American Military Institute, 1982; Founds Award from Confederate Memorial Literary Society, 1983; distinguished service award from Association for Documentary Editing, 1983; D. H. L. from Lincoln College, 1983.

WRITINGS: Ulysses S. Grant Chronology, Ohio Historical Society, 1963; (editor) *General Grant by Matthew Arnold with a Rejoinder by Mark Twain,* Southern Illinois University Press, 1966; (contributor) *Illinois Civil War Sketches,* Civil War Centennial Commission of Illinois, 1966; (editor) *The Papers of Ulysses S. Grant,* Southern Illinois University Press, Volume I: *1837-61,* 1967, Volume II: *April-September, 1861,* 1969, Volume III: *October 1, 1861-January 7, 1862,* 1970, Volume IV: *January 8-March 31, 1862,* 1972, Volume V: *April 1, 1862-August 31, 1862,* 1973, Volume VI: *September 1-December 8, 1862,* 1977, Volume VII: *December 9, 1862-March 31, 1863,* 1979, Volume VIII: *April 1-July 6, 1863,* 1979, Volume IX: *July 7-December 31, 1863,* 1982, Volume X: *January 1-May 31, 1864,* 1982, Volume XI: *June 1-August 15, 1864,* 1984, Volume XII: *August 16-November 15, 1864,* 1984; (author of foreword) Thomas M. Pitkin, *The Captain Departs: Ulysses S. Grant's Last Campaign,* Southern Illinois University Press, 1973; (editor) *The Personal Memoirs of Julia Dent Grant,* Putnam, 1975; (author of foreword) William M. Anderson, *They Died to Make Men Free: A History of the 19th Michigan Infantry in the Civil War,* Hardscrabble, 1980; (with David L. Wilson) *Ulysses S. Grant: Essays and Documents,* Southern Illinois University Press, 1981.

Member of advisory committee, *Papers of Daniel Chester French,* 1975—; member of editorial board, *The Papers of Jefferson Davis,* Louisiana State University Press, 1980—, and *Documentary History of the First Federal Elections,* University of Wisconsin Press, 1980—. Contributor of articles on Ulysses S. Grant to *Encyclopaedia Britannica* and *World Book Encyclopedia.* Contributor to numerous journals, including *Journal of the Illinois State Historical Society, Civil War History, Journal of American History, Military Affairs,* and *Ohio History.* Civil War editor, *Manuscripts,* 1967-72. Editor of Ulysses S. Grant Association's *Newsletter,* 1963-73.

SIDELIGHTS: John Y. Simon is considered to be one of America's leading experts on Ulysses S. Grant. As editor of the multi-volume *The Papers of Ulysses S. Grant,* Simon explores the life of the great military leader and eighteenth president of the United States by examining an estimated thirty thousand documents. These documents include such items as Grant's personal, official, and military correspondence with his family, friends, members of his staff, and commanders.

R. J. Haylik suggests in *Library Journal* that "this collection . . . will help to assure General Grant his proper place in history as an extraordinary man who had his share of human failing, but had an inner strength." And R. N. Current states in the *Annals of the American Academy of Political and Social Science* that Simon's editing is "excellent" and that in the second volume in this series the writings "reproduced are, naturally, most valuable for the biography of Grant himself, though they also shed light on the mobilization of Illinois forces, the response of confused and divided Missourians, and the beginnings of military activity in the Mississippi Valley.''

A reviewer writes in the *New Yorker* that *The Papers of Ulysesses S. Grant* "is an enterprise of archival importance. . . . Grant [was] a good writer: he dispensed with rhetoric, ordered his thoughts in a clear array, and expresses them to the point. [Many] letters are to Julia Dent Grant, his fiancee for four long years, and through them we perceive a rather different person from the taciturn and colorless figure of many histories, for here, speaking for himself, is a man of quick feelings and perceptions, very much alive to what went on about him, and a man, dogged by what would seem heartbreaking bad luck, who never let a phrase of self-pity escape him.'' Finally, a writer for *Choice* comments that "the personal letters to wife, father, and father-in-law are the most interesting because they reveal the intimate Grant.''

BIOGRAPHICAL/CRITICAL SOURCES: New Yorker, August 26, 1967; *Library Journal*, September 15, 1967; *Times Literary Supplement*, September 28, 1967; *Choice*, February, 1970; *Annals of American Academy of Political Social Science*, March, 1970; *New York Times*, December 1, 1982.

* * *

SIMS, George (Frederick Robert) 1923-

PERSONAL: Born August 3, 1923, in London, England; son of George (a company director) and Ada (Harrison) Sims; married Beryl Simcock, August 7, 1943; children: Christopher George, Linda Daphne, Timothy Edward. *Education:* Educated in Harrow, England. *Home:* Peacocks, Hurst, Reading, Berkshire, England. *Agent:* Anthony Sheil Associates Ltd., 2-3 Morwell St., London WC1B 3AR, England.

CAREER: Worked in Fleet Street, London, England, as a trainee for the Press Association, 1940-42; G. F. Sims (rare books), Hurst, Reading, Berkshire, England, proprietor, 1947—. *Military service:* British Army, 1942-47; became sergeant.

WRITINGS: The Swallow Lovers, privately printed, 1942; *Poems*, Fortune Press, 1944; *The Immanent Goddess* (verse), Fortune Press, 1944; *A Catalogue of Letters, Manuscript Papers and Books of Frederick Rolfe, Baron Corvo*, G. F. Sims, 1949; (contributor of short story) John Pudney, editor, *Pick of Today's Short Stories 7*, Putnam & Co., 1956; *Some Cadences: Poems Written in 1945*, privately printed, 1960.

Suspense novels: *The Terrible Door*, Horizon, 1964; *Sleep No More*, Harcourt, 1966; *The Last Best Friend*, Stein & Day, 1967; *The Sand Dollar*, Gollancz, 1969; *Deadhand*, Gollancz, 1971; *Hunters Point*, Gollancz, 1973; *The End of the Web*, Walker & Co., 1976; *Rex Mundi*, Gollancz, 1978; *Who Is Cato?*, Macmillan, 1981; *The Keys of Death*, Macmillan, 1982; *Coat of Arms*, Macmillan, 1984.

Also author, *A Catalogue of Llewelyn Powys Manuscripts*, G. F. Sims. Contributor to anthologies. Contributor of stories and articles to periodicals.

SIDELIGHTS: George Sims told *CA:* "In a generous critique of my books which appeared in *Twentieth-Century Crime and Mystery Writers* (Macmillan, 1980), Harry Keating animadverted on the fact that I have always been an amateur writer in the sense that I have not had to rely on my books to provide a basic income. But I do not see that being an amateur writer, in that sense, is a bad thing. Having another career has meant that I have never been under economic pressure to produce a book and have waited until some subject or theme was compelling.

"I once read a newspaper paragraph about a famous art collection which had disappeared since the Nazi occupation of Paris. I had the urge to go there, conduct enquiries, and see if I could make a factual book out of the quest. But I realised that this project would take up too much time for a non-professional writer, and I dropped the plan; instead I wrote a novel of suspense, *The Last Best Friend*, using the same theme.''

AVOCATIONAL INTERESTS: Travel (particularly in the Mediterranean and West Indies), underwater swimming, movies and "everything to do with them.''

BIOGRAPHICAL/CRITICAL SOURCES: Twentieth-Century Crime and Mystery Writers, Macmillan, 1980; *Observer*, May 10, 1981, May 9, 1982; *Times Literary Supplement*, June 19, 1981.

* * *

SIMSOVA, Sylva 1931-

PERSONAL: Born February 24, 1931, in Prague, Czechoslovakia; children: Cyril, Debora. *Education:* University College, London, F.L.A., 1957, M.Phil., 1975, P.G.Dip.Comp., 1983. *Office:* School of Librarianship, Polytechnic of North London, Ladbroke House, 62-66 Highbury Grove, London N5 2AD, England.

CAREER: Islington Public Library, London, England, junior assistant, 1951-55; Hackney Public Library, London, senior assistant, 1955-58; Stoke Newington Public Library, London, branch librarian, 1958-60; Finchley Public Library, London, district librarian, 1960-64; Polytechnic of North London, School of Librarianship, London, assistant lecturer, 1964-66, lecturer, 1966-70, senior lecturer in librarianship, 1971—. *Member:* Library Association.

WRITINGS: (Editor) *Lenin, Krupskaia and Libraries*, translation by G. Peacock and Lucy Prescott, Shoe String Press, 1968; (editor) *Nicholas Rubakin and Bibliopsychology*, translation by Monique MacKee and Peacock, Shoe String Press, 1968; (with MacKee) *A Handbook of Comparative Librarianship*, 1970, 2nd revised and enlarged edition, Bingley, 1975; (with A. D. Burnett and R. K. Gupta) *Studies in Comparative Librarianship*, Library Association, 1973.

(With W. T. Chin) *Information Sheets on Chinese Readers*, Polytechnic of North London, School of Librarianship, 1981; *Library Needs of the Vietnamese in Britain*, Polytechnic of North London, School of Librarianship, 1982; *A Primer of Comparative Librarianship*, Bingley, 1982; (with Chin) *Library Needs of Chinese in London*, Polytechnic of North London, School of Librarianship, 1982.

Contributor: J. S. Kujoth, editor, *Libraries, Readers and Book Selection*, Scarecrow, 1969; Kujoth, editor, *Reading Interests of Children and Young Adults*, Scarecrow, 1970; B. Katz and R. Burgess, editors, *Library Lit. 4: The Best of 1974*, Scarecrow, 1975; I. McIlwaine, editor, *Bibliography and Reading: A Festschrift in Honour of Ronald Stavely*, Scarecrow, 1983. Contributor to numerous periodicals, including *International Library Review, Library Association Record, Library World, Books and Bookmen, Bookseller, Libri*, and *Journal of Librarianship*.

WORK IN PROGRESS: Research on the subjective dimensions of readability.

SIDELIGHTS: Sylva Simsova told *CA:* "The guiding theme of my work is the relationship between the library and its users both in the social and individual aspect." She lists her professional interests as comparative librarianship, library services to ethnic groups, and the psychology of reading. *Avocational interests:* Hiking, camping, open-air life, reading, music and other cultural pursuits, philosophy, psychology.

* * *

SINGER, C(harles) Gregg 1910-

PERSONAL: Born June 3, 1910, in Philadelphia, Pa.; son of Arthur Gregg (a bridge architect) and Edith (a teacher; maiden name, Lord) Singer; married Marjorie Pouder, September 6, 1939; children: Marjorie Jean Singer Satterwaite, Richard Gregg, Terrie Elizabeth Singer Speicher, Robert Adams. *Education:* Haverford College, A.B., 1933; University of Pennsylvania, A.M., 1935, Ph.D., 1940. *Politics:* Conservative. *Religion:* Presbyterian. *Home:* 319 Wake Dr., Salisbury, N.C. 28144. *Office Address:* Atlanta School of Biblical Studies, P.O. Box 150, Avondale Estates, Atlanta, Ga. 30002.

CAREER: Wheaton College, Wheaton, Ill., 1944-48, began as associate professor, became professor of history, chairman of department; Salem College, Winston-Salem, N.C., professor of history, 1948-54, chairman of department; Belhaven College, Jackson, Miss., professor of history, 1954-58, chairman of department; Catawba College, Salisbury, N.C., professor of history, 1958-77, chairman of department, 1958-75; Atlanta School of Biblical Studies, Atlanta, Ga., professor of church history, 1977—. Area director of War Manpower Commission, 1942-44.

WRITINGS: South Carolina in the Confederation, privately printed, 1941, reissued, Porcupine Press, 1976; *A Theological Interpretation of American History,* Craig Press, 1964, revised edition, Presbyterian & Reformed, 1981; (contributor) Barb Henry, editor, *Christian Faith and Modern Philosophy,* Channel Press, 1964; *Toynbee,* Baker Book, 1965; *John Calvin: His Roots and Fruits,* Presbyterian & Reformed, 1967; (contributor) Ronald Nash, editor, *The Philosophy of Gordon Clark,* Presbyterian & Reformed, 1968; (contributor) E. H. Geehan, editor, *Jerusalem and Athens,* Presbyterian & Reformed, 1971; *The Unholy Alliance,* Arlington House, 1975; (contributor) Gary North, editor, *Foundations of Christian Scholarship,* Ross House Books, 1976; *Christian Approaches: To Philosophy, to History,* Presbyterian & Reformed, 1978; *From Rationalism to Irrationality,* Presbyterian & Reformed, 1979. Also author, with G. Russell Evans, of *The Church and the Sword.* Contributor to *Encyclopedia of Christianity* and *Dictionary of Christianity.* Contributor to professional journals and *Christianity Today.*

WORK IN PROGRESS: The Decline of Western Thought.

SIDELIGHTS: C. Gregg Singer remarks: "I never dreamed I would become a writer. I started to write articles about thirty years ago and in 1964 I produced my first book as a result of my sketches of Augustine, Calvin, the Puritans, and the American Revolution. Its success led to requests to do more writing—and I have done it."

* * *

SIRACUSA, Joseph M(arcus) 1944-

PERSONAL: Born July 6, 1944, in Chicago, Ill.; son of John P. (a business executive) and Josephine M. Siracusa; married Sally Johnson (an artist), December 21, 1968; children: Joseph Anthony, Joy Christine. *Education:* University of Denver, B.A., 1966, M.A., 1968; University of Colorado, Ph.D., 1971; also attended University of Vienna, 1964-65. *Politics:* Independent. *Religion:* Roman Catholic. *Residence:* St. Lucia, Queensland, Australia. *Office:* Department of History, University of Queensland, St. Lucia, 4067 Queensland, Australia.

CAREER: University of Colorado, Boulder, instructor in history, 1969-71; Merrill Lynch, Pierce, Fenner & Smith, Inc., member of executive training program in Boston, Mass., and New York, N.Y., 1972-73; University of Queensland, St. Lucia, Australia, lecturer, 1973-75, senior lecturer, 1976-80, reader in American diplomatic history, 1981—. Visiting professor of history, Fletcher School of Law and Diplomacy, 1980-81. Licensed by New York and American Stock Exchanges and Chicago Board of Trade.

MEMBER: American Historical Association, Organization of American Historians, Society for Historians of American Foreign Relations, Australian Institute of International Affairs, Australian-New Zealand American Studies Association, Australian Historical Association, Association of Contemporary Historians (London), Society for the Study of Internationalism, Australian Defense and Foreign Policy Association. *Awards, honors:* Grants from University of Colorado, 1971, University of Queensland, 1973-83, Australian Government, 1975-76, 1980-81, and Harry S Truman Library Institute for National and International Affairs, 1975, 1977.

WRITINGS: (Editor) *New Left Diplomatic Histories and Historians: The American Revisionists,* Kennikat, 1973; *The American Diplomatic Revolution: A Documentary History of the Cold War, 1941-1947,* Holt, 1976; (editor with Glen St. John Barclay) *Australian-American Relations since 1945: A Documentary History,* Holt, 1976; (editor with Barclay, and contributor) *The Impact of the Cold War: Reconsiderations,* Kennikat, 1977; (contributor) John A. Moses, editor, *The Historical Discipline and Culture in Australasia,* University of Queensland Press, 1977; (with Julius W. Pratt and Vincent P. DeSantis) *A History of United States Foreign Policy,* Prentice-Hall, 4th edition (Siracusa was not associated with earlier editions), 1977; (with Daniel M. Smith) *The Testing of America, 1914-1945,* Forum Press, 1979.

(Contributor) C. L. Egan, editor, *Essays in Twentieth Century American History Dedicated to Professor Daniel M. Smith,* University Press of America, 1982; (contributor) Richard Dean Burns, editor, *Guide to American Foreign Relations since 1700,* Clio Press, 1982; *The Changing of America, 1945-1982,* Forum Press, 1984. Contributor of articles and reviews to history, politics, and international studies journals. *Australian Journal of Politics and History,* acting editor, 1976-77, associate editor, 1977—; *World Review,* editor, 1984—.

SIDELIGHTS: Joseph M. Siracusa told *CA:* "I have been deeply motivated by the erosion of standards in the writing of American history during the past fifteen years. What has passed for scholarship, not to mention profundity, seemed to me at best rubbish. In fact, the time traveler who unearths our culture in several thousand years will have great difficulty in distinguishing between our fiction and our nonfiction."

AVOCATIONAL INTERESTS: Tennis, walking, "breathing in fresh air."

SISSON, Rosemary Anne 1923-

PERSONAL: Surname rhymes with "listen"; born October 13, 1923, in London, England; daughter of Charles Jasper (a professor) and Vera (Ginn) Sisson. *Education:* University College, London, B.A. (with honors), 1946; Cambridge University, M.Lit., 1948. *Politics:* Conservative. *Religion:* Church of England. *Agent:* Andrew Mann Ltd., 1 Old Compton St., London W.1, England.

CAREER: Writer. University of Wisconsin—Madison, instructor in English, 1949-50; University of London, University College, London, England, assistant lecturer in American literature, 1950-54; University of Birmingham, Birmingham, England, assistant lecturer in English, 1954-55; *Stratford-upon-Avon Herald*, Stratford-upon-Avon, England, drama critic, 1955-57. Member of Coventry Cathedral Drama Council. *Military service:* Royal Observer Corps, 1943-45. *Member:* Writers Guild of Great Britain, Writers Guild of America. *Awards, honors:* Repertory Players Award, 1964, for "The Royal Captivity."

WRITINGS: The Adventures of Ambrose, Harrap, 1951, Dutton, 1952; *The Impractical Chimney-Sweep*, Macmillan, 1956, F. Watts, 1957; *The Isle of Dogs*, Macmillan, 1959; *The Young Shakespeare*, Parrish, 1959; *The Young Jane Austen*, Parrish, 1962; *The Young Shaftesbury*, Parrish, 1964; *The Exciseman*, R. Hale, 1973; *The Killer of Horseman's Flats*, Doubleday, 1973; *The Stratford Story*, W. H. Allen, 1975, published as *Will in Love*, Morrow, 1976; *Escape from the Dark*, W. H. Allen, 1976, published as *The Littlest Horse Thieves*, Pocket Books, 1976; *The Queen and the Welshman* (also see below), W. H. Allen, 1979; *The Manions of America* (based on a story by Agnes Nixon; also see below), Dell, 1981.

Plays: *The Queen and the Welshman* (acting edition), Samuel French, 1958, reprinted, Arrow Books, 1980; *Fear Came to Supper* (acting edition), Samuel French, 1959; *The Dark Horse*, Samuel French, 1979. Also author of produced plays "The Splendid Outcasts," "Home and the Heart," "The Royal Captivity," "Bitter Sanctuary," and, with Robert Morley, "A Ghost on Tiptoe."

Screenplays: "Anstice"; "Ride a Wild Pony" (adaptation of James Aldridge's *A Sporting Proposition*), Walt Disney Productions; "Pit Ponies," Walt Disney Productions; (with David Swift) "Candleshoe," Walt Disney Productions, 1978; (with Brian Cleens and Harry Soalding) "The Watcher in the Woods," Walt Disney Productions, 1981; "The Wind in the Willows" (animated version), Cosgrove Hall Productions.

Television plays: "The Vagrant Heart"; "The Man from Brooklyn"; "The Ordeal of Richard Feverel" (adaptation of the novel by George Meredith); "The Mill on the Floss" (adaptation of the novel by George Eliot); "Catherine of Aragon" ("Six Wives of Henry VIII" series); "Beyond Our Means"; "Let's Marry Liz"; "The Irish R.M."; "Mistral's Daughter" (adaptation of the novel by Judith Krantz).

Plays anthologized in *Plays of the Year*, Flek Books, 1958, 1959, and in "Heritage of Literature" series, Longmans, Green, 1962. Script writer of episodes in British Broadcasting Corp. television series, "Compact," "Upstairs, Downstairs," "Within These Walls," and "The Duchess of Duke Street." Author of script for mini-series "The Manions of America," E.M.I. and American Broadcasting Companies (ABC-TV). Contributor of poetry and short stories to magazines, and articles to *Sunday Times*.

SIDELIGHTS: Rosemary Anne Sisson told *CA:* "From my earliest childhood, my sole ambition was to be an actress, and my dearest love was the theatre. This ambition was frustrated by the outbreak of the Second World War while I was still at school, and when I began writing novels, it was as a sort of desperate second-best. It was not until I wrote my first play that I realized that my ambition could be fulfilled by writing plays for others to act, instead of acting them myself.

"I wrote seven more plays before that first one was produced, and rewrote the first one seven times before its production in 1957 turned me into a professional writer. Its adaptation for television led me into writing my first original play for television, and, many years later, television led to my writing my first film. But it has only been since I returned to writing novels as well that I have realized that all my writing is essentially theatrical—to act a story out in the minds and hearts of an audience. The different media demand different crafts, but in them all, my ambition is essentially that first ambition of all, and I feel profoundly grateful to have been allowed to fulfill it."

AVOCATIONAL INTERESTS: Riding, gardening, cooking, housework.

* * *

SIZER, John 1938-

PERSONAL: Born September 14, 1938, in Grimsby, England; son of John Robert (a docks foreman) and Mary (Hawley) Sizer; married Valerie Davies, October 10, 1965; children: Richard John, Stuart James, Jonathan Matthew. *Education:* Attended Grimsby College of Technology, 1954-61; University of Nottingham, B.A., 1964. *Home:* 317 Beacon Rd., Loughborough, England. *Office:* Department of Management Studies, Loughborough University of Technology, Loughborough LE11 3TU, England.

CAREER: Clover Dairies Ltd., Grimsby, England, assistant accountant, 1958-61; G.K.N. Ltd., Smethwick, England, financial analyst, 1964-65; University of Edinburgh, Edinburgh, Scotland, lecturer in accounting, 1965-68; London Graduate School of Business Studies, London, England, senior lecturer in accounting, 1968-70; Loughborough University of Technology, Loughborough, England, professor of financial management, 1970—, dean of School of Human and Environmental Studies, 1973-76, senior pro vice-chancellor, 1980-82. *Member:* Institute of Cost and Management Accountants, American Accounting Association, British Institute of Management, Society for Research into Higher Education. *Awards, honors:* Leverhulme Prize, Institute of Cost and Management Accountants.

WRITINGS: An Insight into Management Accounting, Penguin, 1969, 2nd edition, 1979; *Kosteninformatie in het bedrijfsbeleid*, Het Spectrum, 1970; *Case Studies in Management Accounting*, Longman, 1974, Penguin, 1976; *Nocoes Basicas de Contabilidade Gerencial*, Edicao Saravia, 1980; (editor and contributor) *Readings in Management Accounting*, Penguin, 1980; *Perspectives in Management Accounting*, Heinemann/I.C.M.A., 1981; (editor with Alfred Morris) *Resources and Higher Education*, Monograph 51, Society for Research into Higher Education, 1983. Contributor to management and accounting journals.

WORK IN PROGRESS: Management accounting case histories; management of financial reductions in institutions of higher education.

SIDELIGHTS: John Sizer told *CA:* "Academics have to stretch themselves if they are to stretch their students. Writing is a demanding, stretching, but also satisfying, experience. A book is a snapshot of one's views at a point in time, of views that are constantly changing, developing, and maturing. Thus, a collection of one's past writings is like a family photograph album."

* * *

SKIDMORE, Max J(oseph, Sr.) 1933-

PERSONAL: Born December 25, 1933, in Springfield, Mo.; son of Joseph Franklin and Gladys (Watt) Skidmore; married Patricia Bassett, April 15, 1954 (divorced); married Charlene Campbell, June 20, 1976; children: (first marriage) Max Joseph, Jr. *Education:* Southwest Missouri State College (now University), B.S. and B.S. in Education, 1956; University of Missouri, M.Ed., 1956; Brookings Institution, graduate study, 1959-60; University of Minnesota, Ph.D., 1964. *Politics:* Democrat. *Religion:* Unitarian. *Residence:* Portales, N.M. *Office:* College of Liberal Arts and Sciences, Eastern New Mexico University, Portales, N.M. 88130.

CAREER: Teacher in Missouri public schools, 1954-55; superintendent of schools, Climax Springs, Mo., 1956-57; Department of Health, Education and Welfare, Washington, D.C., Social Security Administration, management analyst, 1959-62, Office of Commissioner of Social Security, administrative assistant, 1962-64, U.S. Office of Education, program review officer, 1964-65; University of Alabama, Tuscaloosa, associate professor of political science and director of American studies program, 1965-68; Southwest Missouri State University, Springfield, Mo., professor of political science and head of department, 1968-82; Eastern New Mexico University, Portales, N.M., dean of college of arts and sciences, 1982—. Senior Fulbright lecturer and director, American Studies Research Centre, Hyderabad, India, 1978-79. Visiting professor at University of Colorado, Colorado Springs, summer, 1968, and University of Nebraska at Omaha, summer, 1972. Consultant to various municipalities and educational institutions.

MEMBER: American Political Science Association, American Studies Association, American Academy of Political and Social Science, American Association of University Professors, Mid-Continent American Studies Association (president, 1976-1977), Southeastern American Studies Association (executive board member, 1966-68), Southern Political Science Association, Western Political Science Association, Missouri Political Science Association (president, 1971-72), Council on Human Relations (Tuscaloosa; member of board of directors, 1966-68).

WRITINGS: Medicare and the American Rhetoric of Reconciliation, University of Alabama Press, 1970; *Word Politics: Essays on Language and Politics,* James Freel, 1972; (with Marshall Carter Wanke) *American Government,* St. Martin's, 1974, 3rd edition, 1981; *American Political Thought,* St. Martin's, 1978; (with James Barnes and Marshall Carter) *The World of Politics,* St. Martin's, 1980, 2nd edition, 1984; (contributor) B. K. Shrivastava and Thomas W. Casstevens, editors, *American Government and Politics,* Humanities, 1980.

Contributor of articles and reviews to *Mississippi Quarterly, School and Community, American Quarterly, Phi Delta Kappan, Progressive, Greek Review of Social Research, American Studies, Political Science Quarterly,* and other periodicals. Member of editorial board, *American Studies,* 1972-80, 1981-85; editor, *Indian Journal of American Studies,* 1978-79.

WORK IN PROGRESS: Additional work on language and politics, political thought, and American politics; "I am even guilty, occasionally, of poetry."

SIDELIGHTS: Max J. Skidmore told *CA* that his "central motivation in writing [is] human and non-human survival and the development of human potential [which implies] two fundamental considerations: political and ecological (i.e., to provide survival at a humane level). Basic to these considerations are the paradoxical needs to prevent community or governmental actions that stifle individual potential, and the prevention of the excesses of possessive individualism that stifle community potential (and even community and individual awareness of the difficulties)."

* * *

SKIPPER, James K(inley), Jr. 1934-

PERSONAL: Born September 14, 1934, in Columbus, Ohio; son of James Kinley (a college professor) and Dorothy (Lewis) Skipper; married Joan Lois McCown, June 12, 1958; children: James Kinley III, John Frederic. *Education:* Northern Illinois University, B.S., 1956; Northwestern University, M.A., 1960, Ph.D., 1964. *Home:* 2214 Thornridge Drive, Toledo, Ohio 43614. *Office:* Department of Sociology, Virginia Polytechnic Institute and State University, Blacksburg, Va. 14061.

CAREER: Research associate at Presbyterian-St. Luke's Hospital, Chicago, Ill., 1960-62, and Yale University, New Haven, Conn., 1963-65; Case Western Reserve University, Cleveland, Ohio, assistant professor, 1965-67, associate professor of sociology, 1967-71; University of Western Ontario, London, professor of sociology, 1970-72; Medical College of Ohio, Toledo, professor of community and family medicine, 1972-78; Bowling Green State University, Bowling Green, Ohio, member of staff of department of health services, 1979-82; Virginia Polytechnic Institute and State University, Blacksburg, member of faculty of department of sociology, 1983—. Visiting professor at University of Hawaii, summer, 1968. Consultant to Cleveland Vocational Guidance and Rehabilitation Service, 1965-70, Case Western Reserve University Dental School, 1966-67, Howard Advertising Agency, Inc., 1966-67, and Department of Health, Education, and Welfare, 1968-70. *Military service:* U.S. Army, active duty, 1957-58. U.S. Army Reserve, 1957-63; became sergeant first class. *Member:* American North Central Sociological Association.

WRITINGS: (Editor with Robert Leonard and contributor) *Social Interaction and Patient Care,* Lippincott, 1965; (with Phyllis N. Hallenbeck and Stephen L. Fink) *How the Severely Disabled Client Perceives Problems of Daily Living,* Vocational Guidance and Rehabilitation Services, 1966; (with Emily Mumford) *Sociology in Hospital Care,* Harper, 1967; (editor with Mark Lefton and Charles McCaghy and contributor) *Approaches to Deviance: Theories, Concepts and Research Findings,* Appleton, 1968; (editor with Lefton and McCaghy) *In Their Own Behalf: Voices from the Margin,* Appleton, 1968, 2nd edition, 1974; (editor with Powhatan Wooldridge and Leonard) *Behavioral Science, Social Practice, and the Nursing Profession,* Press of Case Western Reserve University, 1968; *Boys and Girls in White: An Analysis of the First Six Classes at MCO,* Medical College of Ohio, 1976; (with Wooldridge and Leonard) *Methods of Clinical Experimentation to Improve Patient Care,* Mosby, 1978; (with others) *Deviance: Voices from the Margin,* Wadsworth, 1981. Contributor to health, education, and sociology periodicals in the United States and Canada.

445

SKLARE, Marshall 1921-

PERSONAL: Born October 21, 1921, in Chicago, Ill.; son of Irving (a businessman) and Bee (Lippman) Sklare; married Rose Bernards (an editor), June 8, 1947; children: Daniel, Judith, Joshua. *Education:* Attended Northwestern University, 1938-39, 1940-43; University of Chicago, M.A., 1945; Columbia University, Ph.D., 1953. *Religion:* Jewish. *Home:* 12 Nathan Rd., Newton Centre, Mass. 02159. *Office:* Lown Building, Brandeis University, Waltham, Mass. 02254.

CAREER: American Jewish Committee, New York City, director, Division of Scientific Research, 1953-66; Yeshiva University, New York City, professor of sociology, 1966-70; Brandeis University, Waltham, Mass., professor of American Jewish studies and sociology, 1970—, director of Center for Modern Jewish Studies, 1980—. Fulbright lecturer, Hebrew University of Jerusalem, 1965-66.

WRITINGS: Conservative Judaism: An American Religious Movement, Free Press of Glencoe, 1955, revised edition, Schocken, 1972; (with M. Vosk) *The Riverton Study: How Jews Look at Themselves and Their Neighbors,* American Jewish Committee, 1957; (editor) *The Jews: Social Patterns of an American Group,* Free Press of Glencoe, 1958; (with J. Greenblum) *Jewish Identity on the Suburban Frontier: A Study of Group Survival in the Open Society,* Basic Books, 1967, second edition, University of Chicago Press, 1979; *America's Jews,* Random House, 1971; (editor) *The Jew in American Society,* Behrman, 1974; *The Jewish Community in America,* Behrman, 1974; (editor) *Understanding American Jewry,* Transaction Books, 1982; (editor) *American Jews: A Reader,* Behrman, 1983.

WORK IN PROGRESS: A Sociological Analysis of American Jewry.

* * *

SLIDE, Anthony 1944-

PERSONAL: Born November 7, 1944, in Birmingham, England; son of Clifford Frederick and May (Eaton) Slide. *Education:* Attended grammar school in Birmingham, England. *Politics:* "Liberally conservative." *Religion:* None. *Office:* 4118 Rhodes Ave., Studio City, Calif. 91604.

CAREER: Silent Picture (quarterly devoted to the art and history of silent film), London, England, founder and editor, 1968-74; American Film Institute, Washington, D.C., associate archivist, 1972-75; Academy of Motion Picture Arts and Sciences, National Film Information Service, Beverly Hills, Calif., resident film historian, 1975-80; free-lance writer and researcher, 1980—. Organizer of first silent film festival ever held in England, 1970; research associate, American Film Institute, 1971-72; consultant on silent film programming, National Film Theatre, London. Lecturer at Museum of Modern Art, Pacific Film Archive, Columbia University, and Library of Congress.

WRITINGS: Sir Michael Balcon (monograph), British Film Institute, 1969; *Lillian Gish* (monograph), British Film Institute, 1969; (with Paul O'Dell) *Griffith and the Rise of Hollywood,* A. S. Barnes, 1970; (with O'Dell) *Early American Cinema,* A. S. Barnes, 1971; *The Griffith Actresses,* A. S. Barnes, 1973; (with Edward Wagenknecht) *The Films of D. W. Griffith,* Crown, 1975; *The Idols of Silence,* A. S. Barnes, 1976; *The Big V: A History of the Vitagraph Company,* Scarecrow, 1976; *Early Women Directors,* A. S. Barnes, 1977, revised edition, Da Capo Press, 1984; *Aspects of American Film History Prior to 1920,* Scarecrow, 1978; *Films on Film History,* Scarecrow, 1979; *The Films of Will Rogers* (monograph), Academy of Motion Picture Arts and Sciences, 1979.

The Kindergarten of the Movies: A History of the Fine Arts Studio, Scarecrow, 1980; (with Wagenknecht) *Fifty Great American Silent Films: 1912-1920,* Dover, 1980; *The Vaudevillians,* Arlington House, 1981; *Great Radio Personalities in Historic Photographs,* Dover, 1982; *A Collector's Guide to Movie Memorabilia,* Wallace-Homestead, 1983; (editor) *International Film, Radio and Television Journals,* Greenwood Press, 1984; *Great Silent Stars in Historic Photographs,* Dover, 1985.

Editor, "Selected Film Criticism" series; published by Scarecrow: *Selected Film Criticism: 1896-1911,* 1982; . . . *1912-1920,* 1982; . . . *1921-1930,* 1982; . . . *1931-1940,* 1982; . . . *1941-1950,* 1983; . . . *1951-1960,* 1984; . . . *Foreign Films, 1930-1950,* 1984; . . . *1900-1919,* 1985; . . . *1920-1930,* 1985; . . . *1931-1950,* 1985.

Also editor of "Filmmakers" series for Scarecrow. Contributor of articles on the history of film to numerous periodicals. Member of editorial board, *Quarterly Review of Film Studies.*

WORK IN PROGRESS: Fifty Great British Films: 1932-1982, for Dover.

SIDELIGHTS: Anthony Slide told *CA,* "I consider myself a working film scholar, one who makes his living by writing, researching and lecturing on film history, without the aid of grants or academic affiliations."

* * *

SMALL, Melvin 1939-

PERSONAL: Born March 14, 1939, in New York, N.Y.; son of Herman Z. and Ann (Ashkenazy) Small; married Sara Jane Miller, October 23, 1958; children: Michael, Mark. *Education:* Dartmouth College, B.A., 1960; University of Michigan, M.A., 1961, Ph.D., 1965. *Home:* 1815 Northwood, Royal Oak, Mich. 48073. *Office:* History Department, Wayne State University, Detroit, Mich. 48227.

CAREER: Wayne State University, Detroit, Mich., assistant professor, 1965-70, associate professor, 1970-75, professor of history, 1976—, chairman of department, 1979—. Visiting assistant professor, University of Michigan, summer, 1968; visiting professor, Aarhus University, Aarhus, Denmark, 1972-74, 1983. *Member:* American Historical Association, Organization of American Historians, Society for Historians of American Foreign Relations, Peace Science Society (member of executive council, 1976-79). *Awards, honors:* Fellow, Center for Advanced Study in the Behavioral Sciences, 1969-70; American Council of Learned Societies, study fellow, 1969-70, grant, 1983; grant, Lyndon B. Johnson Library, 1982.

WRITINGS: (Editor) *Public Opinion and Historians,* Wayne State University Press, 1970; (with J. David Singer) *The Wages of War,* Wiley, 1972; *Was War Necessary?,* Sage Books, 1980; (with Singer) *Resort to Arms,* Sage Books, 1982.

Contributor: James N. Rosenau, editor, *International Politics and Foreign Policy,* Free Press, 1969; Francis A. Beer, editor, *Alliances,* Holt, 1970; Julian R. Friedman and others, editors, *Alliances in International Politics,* Allyn & Bacon, 1970; James Short and Marvin Wolfgang, editors, *Collective Violence,* Aldine, 1972; William Coplin and Charles Kegley, editors, *Ana-*

lyzing International Relations, Praeger, 1975; Alexander De Conde, editor, *Dictionary of the History of American Foreign Policy*, Scribner, 1978; Paul Loren, editor, *Diplomacy: New Approaches in History, Theory, and Policy*, Free Press, 1979; Charles Kegley and Pat McGowan, editors, *Challenges to America*, Sage Books, 1979. Contributor to journals in his field.

WORK IN PROGRESS: Protest and Policy: The Impact of the Anti-War Movement on Decision Makers, 1965-1971.

* * *

SMART, (Roderick) Ninian 1927-

PERSONAL: Born May 6, 1927, in Cambridge, England; son of William Marshall (a professor) and Isabel (Carswell) Smart; married Libushka Clementina Baruffaldi, July 17, 1954; children: Roderick, Luisabel, Caroline, Peregrine. *Education:* Oxford University, B.A., 1951, B.Phil. and M.A., 1954. *Politics:* Social Democrat. *Religion:* Church of England. *Office:* Department of Religious Studies, University of California, Santa Barbara, Calif. 93106.

CAREER: University College of Wales, Aberystwyth, assistant lecturer, 1952-55; University of London, King's College, London, England, lecturer in the history and philosophy of religion, 1956-61; University of Birmingham, Birmingham, England, H. G. Wood Professor of Theology, 1961-67; University of Lancaster, Lancaster, England, professor of religious studies, 1967-82; University of California, Santa Barbara, professor of religious studies, 1976—. Visiting professor at University of Wisconsin, 1965, Princeton University, 1972, Otago University, 1972, University of Queensland, 1980, University of Cape Town, 1982, and Harvard University, 1983. Visiting lecturer in philosophy, Yale University, 1955-56; visiting lecturer, Banaras Hindu University, summer, 1960; Teape Lecturer, University of Delhi, 1964; Gifford Lecturer, University of Edinburgh, 1979-80. *Military service:* British Army, Intelligence Corps, 1945-48; served overseas in Ceylon; became captain. *Member:* Aristotelian Society, Athenaeum Club (London).

WRITINGS: Reasons and Faiths, Routledge & Kegan Paul, 1958; *A Dialogue of Religions*, S.C.M. Press, 1960; (editor) *Historical Selections in the Philosophy of Religion*, Harper, 1962; *Philosophers and Religious Truth*, S.C.M. Press, 1964, 2nd edition, 1969; *Doctrine and Argument in Indian Philosophy*, Allen & Unwin, 1964; *The Teacher and Christian Belief*, James Clarke, 1966; *Secular Education and the Logic of Religion*, Faber, 1968; *The Yogi and the Devotee*, Allen & Unwin, 1968; *The Religious Experience of Mankind*, Scribner, 1969.

Buddhism and the Death of God, University of Southampton, 1970; *The Philosophy of Religion*, Random House, 1970, 2nd revised edition, 1976; *The Concept of Worship*, Macmillan, 1972; *The Phenomenon of Religion*, Macmillan, 1973; *The Science of Religion and the Sociology of Knowledge: Some Methodological Questions*, Princeton University Press, 1974; *Mao*, Collins, 1974; *The Long Search*, BBC Publications, 1977; (with Donald Harder) *New Movements in the Study and Teaching of Religious Education*, M. Temple Smith, 1978; *In Search of Christianity*, Harper, 1979.

Epistles of John, Christadelphian, 1980; *Beyond Ideology: Religion and the Future of Western Civilization*, Harper, 1981; (editor with Richard Hecht) *Sacred Texts of the World: A Universal Anthology*, Crossroad (New York), 1982; *Worldviews: Crosscultural Explorations in Human Beliefs*, Scribner, 1983.

Also author of *The Phenomenon of Christiantiy*, 1979. Contributor to philosophy and theology journals. Editorial consultant, BBC-TV series, "The Long Search."

WORK IN PROGRESS: A book on religions and ideologies.

SIDELIGHTS: In his book, *In Search of Christianity*, Ninian Smart "is intrigued by his quarry's quick-change artistry as found around the world," writes Huston Horn in the *Los Angeles Times Book Review*. "[Smart] observes the heterogeneous array of Christian dogmas and customs and certitudes and hunches with the affectionate and wondering trust one feels at Pasadena's New Year's Rose Parade: Like high priests, the white-suited tournament officials insist there really is a conceptual theme beneath all the floral trappings; it's up to the beholder to believe. . . . Smart says: 'It is not possible to define an essence of Christianity, beyond saying that the faith relates to Christ.' But . . . the face of Christ . . . has seldom for long retained shape and focus. Thus, Smart suspects, it is possible finally to speak only of Christianities, and only of sociologies of the various Christianities. . . . 'The beginning of understanding it,' he concludes, 'is noticing its strangeness.'"

Smart told *CA*: "I have tried in my writings to illuminate problems of philosophy and the history and nature of religion and religions. When I have the ideas I usually write fast. *The Concept of Worship* was written in eight days in Princeton in 1971. But sometimes I do a lot of revision. Though some of the stuff is technical I believe in clarity. I write best in my wife's home in North Italy: the sun seems to warm the brain."

AVOCATIONAL INTERESTS: Cricket, painting.

BIOGRAPHICAL/CRITICAL SOURCES: New York Times Book Review, February 9, 1969, July 16, 1969; *Commonweal*, April 4, 1969; *Christian Century*, May 7, 1969; *Los Angeles Times Book Review*, September 16, 1979; *Los Angeles Times*, February 30, 1983.

* * *

SMILEY, Virginia Kester 1923-

PERSONAL: Born February 21, 1923, in Rochester, N.Y.; daughter of Harold P. and Isabell (Fleming) Kester; married Robert P. Smiley (a gravure engraver), September 8, 1945; children: Suzanne, Kimberly. *Education:* Attended public schools in Rochester, N.Y. *Politics:* Republican. *Religion:* Protestant. *Home:* 669 Webster Rd., Webster, N.Y. 14580.

CAREER: Writer. Worked in Rochester, N.Y., as a telephone operator, 1941-42, secretary at a hospital, 1942-43, and in the offices of Hickok Manufacturing Co., 1943-44, and Birdseye-Snyder Co., 1944-45. *Member:* Mystery Writers of America, Genessee Valley Writers (former secretary).

WRITINGS—Published by Bouregy, except as noted: *Little Boy Navaho* (juvenile), Abelard, 1954; *The Buzzing Bees* (juvenile), Abelard, 1956; *Swirling Sands*, Dodd, 1958; *Nurse Kate's Mercy Flight*, Ace Books, 1968; *A Haven for Jenny*, 1970; *High Country Nurse*, 1970; *A Horse for Matthew Allen*, Ginn, 1972; *Under Purple Skies*, 1972; *Guest at Gladehaven*, Dell, 1972; *Mansion of Mystery*, Dell, 1973; *Nurse for Morgan Acres*, 1973; *Nurse of the Grand Canyon*, 1973; *Cove of Fear*, 1974; *Nurse for the Civic Center*, 1974; *Libby Williams, Nurse Practitioner*, 1975; *Liza Hunt, Pediatric Nurse*, 1976; *Nurse Delia's Choice*, 1977; *Nurse Karen's Summer of Fear*, 1979; *Love Rides the Rapids*, 1980; *Sugarbush Nurse*, 1981; *Starburst*, Berkley Publishing, 1982. Contributor of short stories to juvenile and teen magazines.

WORK IN PROGRESS: The Long Road Home, for Dell, and *Sugarbush Spring,* for Simon & Schuster, both novels for young adults; a suspense/romance novel, *Pacer's Ransom,* for Avon.

SIDELIGHTS: Virginia Kester Smiley told *CA:* "I write 'light' nurse romances and 'light' mystery and suspense romances because I believe there is a need for this type of book . . . something to pick up and read easily in an evening, in a bus, on a plane, etc. I think with so many serious adult type novels being published there is a need for romances. I do an occasional juvenile because I enjoy writing for the young. Whenever I find a fan letter from a child in my mailbox, the hours I spend glued to the typewriter are worthwhile. The trend in books has changed in [recent] years, with the sensual books very much 'in.' They are 'escape' reading with a huge following. *Starburst* was my first attempt at this type."

* * *

SMITH, D(avid) W(arner) 1932-

PERSONAL: Born November 14, 1932, in Loughborough, England; son of John Sidney (a farmer) and Ellen (Wootton) Smith; married Olaug Synnevag (a librarian), June 27, 1963; children: Ingrid Marie, Anne Catherine. *Education:* University of Leeds, B.A., 1954, Ph.D., 1961. *Politics:* "Left of centre." *Home:* 208 Glengrove Ave. W., Toronto, Ontario, Canada M4R 1P3. *Office:* Department of French, Victoria University, University of Toronto, 73 Queen's Park Crescent, Toronto, Ontario, Canada M5S 1K7.

CAREER: Memorial University of Newfoundland, St. John's, assistant professor of French, 1960-63; University of Toronto, Victoria University, Toronto, Ontario, assistant professor, 1963-67, associate professor, 1967-71, professor of French, 1971—, chairman of department at Victoria University, 1972-75, and at University of Toronto, 1975-80.

WRITINGS: Helvetius: A Study in Persecution, Clarendon Press, 1965, reprinted, Greenwood Press, 1982; *Helvetius's Library,* Institute et musee Voltaire (Geneva), 1971; (editor with others) *Correspondance generale d'Helvetius,* University of Toronto Press, Volume I: *1737-56,* 1981, Volume II: *1758-1760,* 1984.

* * *

SMITH, David M(arshall) 1936-

PERSONAL: Born July 16, 1936, in Birmingham, England; son of James Marshall and Elizabeth (McIlquam) Smith; married Margaret Ruth Harrup (a sociologist), August, 1961; children: Michael, Tracey. *Education:* University of Nottingham, B.A., 1958, Ph.D., 1961. *Politics:* Socialist. *Religion:* None. *Home:* 41 Traps Hill, Laughton, Essex, England. *Office:* Department of Geography and Earth Science, Queen Mary College, University of London, Mile End Rd., London E1 4NS, England.

CAREER: Research assistant in Staffordshire County Planning and Development Office, England, 1961-63; University of Manchester, Manchester, England, lecturer in geography and planning, tutor in extramural studies, 1963-66; Southern Illinois University, Carbondale, visiting assistant professor, 1966-67, associate professor of geography, 1967-70; University of Florida, Gainesville, associate professor of geography and urban studies, 1970-72; University of London, Queen Mary College, London, England, professor of geography, 1973—, head of department, 1981—.

Visiting lecturer, University of Natal, Durban, South Africa, and University of the Witwatersrand, Johannesburg, South Africa, 1972-73; visiting associate professor, University of New England, 1973. Affiliated with Anglo-Soviet Cultural Exchange, 1977, 1982. Consultant to Ministry of Public Building and Works and National Buildings Record, 1961-66, Regional Development Service of Greek Government, 1965-66, South East Lancashire and North East Cheshire Transportation Study, 1966, city of Tampa, Fla., 1971-72, and government of Peru, 1976. *Member:* Association of American Geographers, Institute of British Geographers. *Awards, honors:* American Philosophical Society research award, 1967, 1968, 1970.

WRITINGS: The Industrial Archaeology of the East Midlands, David & Charles, 1965; *Industrial Britain: The North West,* David & Charles, 1969; *Industrial Location: An Economic Geographical Analysis,* Wiley, 1971, 2nd edition, 1981; *The Geography of Social Well-Being in the United States,* McGraw, 1973; (with wife, Margaret R. Smith) *The United States: How They Live and Work,* David & Charles, 1973; *Patterns in Human Geography,* David & Charles, 1975; *Human Geography: A Welfare Approach,* St. Martin's, 1977; *Where the Grass Is Greener: Living in an Unequal World,* Penguin Books, 1979, Johns Hopkins University Press, 1982; *Living under Apartheid: Aspects of Urbanization and Social Change in South Africa,* Allen & Unwin, 1982.

Editor of "Industrial Britain" series, David & Charles, 1965—.

Contributor to geography, regional planning, and social studies journals, including *East Midland Geographer, Journal of Industrial Archaeology, Regional Studies, Environment and Planning,* and *Tijdschrift voor Economische en Sociale Geografie.*

* * *

SMITH, Jack (Clifford) 1916-

PERSONAL: Born August 27, 1916, in Long Beach, Calif.; son of Charles Franklin (a salesman) and Anna Mary (Hughes) Smith; married Denise Bresson (an executive administrator), June 17, 1939; children: Curtis Bresson, Douglas Franklin. *Education:* Attended Bakersfield College. *Religion:* "No affiliation." *Home:* 4251 Camino Real, Los Angeles, Calif. 90065. *Office: Los Angeles Times,* Times-Mirror Sq., Los Angeles, Calif. 90053.

CAREER: Honolulu Advertiser, Honolulu, Hawaii, copy editor, 1940-42; *Los Angeles Daily News,* Los Angeles, Calif., reporter, 1946-49; *Los Angeles Herald-Express,* Los Angeles, reporter, 1950-53; *Los Angeles Times,* Los Angeles, reporter and rewrite man, 1953-58, author of column "Jack Smith," 1958—. *Military service:* U.S. Marine Corps, combat correspondent, 1944-46. *Awards, honors:* National Headliners Award for best column of regional interest, 1975.

WRITINGS: Three Coins in the Birdbath (collection of newspaper columns), Doubleday, 1965; *Smith on Wry* (collection of columns), Doubleday, 1970; *God and Mrs. Gomez* (autobiographical account), Reader's Digest Press, 1974; *The Big Orange* (collection of articles from *Westways*), Ritchie, 1976; *Spend All Your Kisses, Mr. Smith* (collection of columns), McGraw, 1978; *Jack Smith's L.A.* (collection of columns), McGraw, 1980; *How to Win a Pullet Surprise* (collection of columns), F. Watts, 1982. Contributor to *Westways.*

BIOGRAPHICAL/CRITICAL SOURCES: New York Times, January 22, 1979.

SMITHGALL, Elizabeth
See WATTS, Elizabeth (Bailey) Smithgall

* * *

SMYKAY, Edward W(alter) 1924-

PERSONAL: Born February 24, 1924, in South River, N.J.; son of Walter and Agnes (Bogucki) Smykay; married Ann Haenssler, 1947; children: Robert, Richard, Ronald, Anne Marie. *Education:* Rutgers University, B.S., 1948; University of Maine, M.S., 1952; University of Wisconsin, Ph.D., 1956. *Office:* Department of Marketing, University of Baltimore, Charles at Mount Royal, Baltimore, Md. 21201.

CAREER: Marquette University, Milwaukee, Wis., 1953-56, began as instructor, became assistant professor of economics; Michigan State University, East Lansing, assistant professor of marketing and transportation, 1956-76; University of Baltimore, Baltimore, Md., professor of marketing and chairman of department, 1979—. Lecturer to marketing and economic associations in Japan, Canada, and United States. *Military service:* U.S. Army Air Forces, 1943-46; became second lieutenant. *Member:* American Economic Association, American Marketing Association, American Society of Traffic and Transportation, National Council of Physical Distribution Management (president, 1966-67), Associated Traffic Clubs of America (vice-president), Midwest Economics Association.

WRITINGS: (With Donald J. Bowersox and Frank H. Mossman) *Physical Distribution Management: Logistics Problems of the Firm*, Macmillan, 1961, revised edition (with Bowersox and Bernard J. LaLonde), 1968, 3rd edition (sole author), 1973; (editor) *Essays on Physical Distribution Management*, Traffic Service Corp., 1961; (with LaLonde) *Bibliography on Physical Distribution Management*, Marketing Publications, 1967; (with LaLonde) *Physical Distribution: The New and Profitable Science of Business Logistics*, Dartnell, 1967; *Physical Distribution Management: Total Systems Route to New Profits*, [New York], 1967; (compiler with Bowersox and LaLonde) *Readings in Physical Distribution Management: The Logistics of Marketing*, Macmillan, 1969.

(With Joan Breibart) *Introductory Marketing: A Programmed Approach*, Macmillan, 1971; (with Mary A. Higby and Brian F. Harris) *Marketing Processes: A Decision Making Approach*, Mindelhall, 1977, *Marketing Channels*, Mindelhall, 1980. Contributor to *Encyclopaedia Britannica*.†

* * *

SMYTH, David 1929-

PERSONAL: Born February 7, 1929, in Buenos Aires, Argentina; son of Currell Hutchinson (a manager) and Jessie (Dodds) Smyth; married Elli Helene Dusterhoft (a nurse), November 9, 1968; children: Clifford Dieter. *Education:* Cambridge University, M.A., 1951. *Politics:* Independent. *Religion:* "Protestant agnostic." *Home:* 8 Beechwood Ave., Metuchen, N.J. *Agent:* Arthur Pine, 1780 Broadway, New York, N.Y. 10019. *Office:* Associated Press, 50 Rockefeller Center, New York, N.Y. 10020.

CAREER: Associated Press, New York, N.Y., Latin American news editor, 1963-72, financial editor, 1973—. *Military service:* Argentine Army, 1952. *Member:* New York Financial Writers Association.

WRITINGS: The Speculator's Handbook, Regnery, 1974; *You Can Survive Any Financial Disaster*, Contemporary Books, 1976; *Unusual Investments That Could Make You Rich*, Contemporary Books, 1978. Contributor of articles to *Nation* and *Freeman*.

* * *

SNYDER, Gerald S(eymour) 1933-

PERSONAL: Born June 4, 1933, in New York, N.Y.; son of David and Minnie (Beenstock) Snyder; married Arlette Amsellem, August 2, 1961; children: Michele, Daniel. *Education:* Missouri School of Journalism, B.J., 1958; Middlebury College, Graduate School of Spanish at University of Madrid, graduate study, 1961-62.

CAREER: Religious News Service, New York City, writer, 1958-60, and free-lance writer in Europe and North Africa, 1958-62; United Press International, New York City, reporter and writer, 1962-66; National Geographic Society, Washington, D.C., writer, 1966-71; free-lance writer, 1961—. *Military service:* U.S. Army, 1954-56. *Member:* Lewis & Clark Trail Heritage Foundation. *Awards, honors:* Feature writing award from Sigma Delta Chi, 1958.

WRITINGS: In the Footsteps of Lewis and Clark, National Geographic Society, 1970; *The Computer: How It's Changing Our Lives*, U.S. News & World Report, 1972; *The Religious Reawakening in America*, U.S. News & World Report, 1972; *Let's Talk about Computers*, Jonathan David, 1973; *Your Car: How to Buy It, Take Care of It, and Save Money*, U.S. News & World Report, 1973; *1994: The World of Tomorrow*, U.S. News & World Report, 1973; *The Right to Be Let Alone*, Messner, 1975, new edition, 1976; (editor) Wallace Stettinius, *Management Planning and Control: The Printers Path to Profitability*, Printing Industries of America, 1975; *The Right to Be Informed: Censorship in the United States*, Messner, 1976, revised edition, 1978; *The Royal Oak Disaster*, Kimber & Co., 1976, Presidio Press, 1978; *Is There a Loch Ness Monster?: The Search for a Legend*, Messner, 1977.

Are There Alien Beings?: The Story of UFOs, Messner, 1980; *Human Rights*, F. Watts, 1980; *Test Tube Life: Scientific Advance and Moral Dilemma*, Messner, 1982. Contributor to national magazines, including *National Observer*.

WORK IN PROGRESS: A book on the Philippine resistance movement in World War II; a book on German submarine missions in World War II; research for a book on Palestine during World War II.

AVOCATIONAL INTERESTS: Raising children, collecting stamps, watching sports, reading.†

* * *

SOLBERG, Carl 1915-

PERSONAL: Born March 20, 1915, in Minneapolis, Minn.; son of Carl K. (a Lutheran clergyman) and Sina (a social worker; maiden name, Varland) Solberg; married Barbara Selmer (a piano teacher), March 5, 1945; children: Carl, Richard, Sara, Andrew. *Education:* St. Olaf College, B.A., 1935; Oxford University, M.A. and B.Litt., both 1939. *Home:* 4 Francis Lane, Port Chester, N.Y. 10573. *Agent:* International Creative Management, 40 West 57th St., New York, N.Y. 10019. *Office:* Roothbert Fund, Inc., 815 Second Ave., New York, N.Y. 10017.

CAREER: Time, Inc., New York, N.Y., member of editorial staff, 1939-70; Roothbert Fund, Inc., New York City, director, 1958—, president, 1970—. Lecturer at Columbia University, 1963-66. *Military service:* U.S. Navy, 1942-45.

WRITINGS: Riding High: America in the Cold War, Mason & Lipscomb, 1973; *Oil Power,* Mason/Charter, 1976; *Conquest of the Skies,* Little, Brown, 1979; *Hubert Humphrey: A Biography,* Norton, 1984.

SIDELIGHTS: Carl Solberg's *Riding High: America in the Cold War* is "an opinionated, jazzy survey of the years between Hiroshima and the test-ban treaty," writes Barton J. Bernstein in *Nation.* Calling the work "the first concise history of the U.S. roughly from 1947 to 1967," Timothy Foote explains in *Time:* "[Solberg] deals to some extent with the textures of everyday living—the rush to the suburbs and the rise of the barbecue pit, James Dean fan clubs and bomb shelters. But his main aim is to describe the enormous effect of the cold war on American life." Bernstein considers the resulting book "an ambitious but uneven volume that reflects hard work, wide reading and a willingness to reconsider cherished notions."

BIOGRAPHICAL/CRITICAL SOURCES: Time, September 9, 1974; *Nation,* September 21, 1974, January 25, 1975; *Christian Science Monitor,* February 19, 1976.

* * *

SOLIDAY, Gerald Lyman 1939-

PERSONAL: Born November 25, 1939, in Wooster, Ohio; son of Vaughn Gerald and Mary A. (Snell) Soliday; married Donna Warren, May 26, 1961; children: Elizabeth Anne, Karin Tamara. *Education:* Ohio State University, B.A., 1961, M.A., 1963; Harvard University, Ph.D., 1969. *Home:* 7737 El Padre, Dallas, Tex. 75248. *Office:* Department of History, University of Texas at Dallas, Box 688, Richardson, Tex. 75080.

CAREER: Brandeis University, Waltham, Mass., assistant professor of history, 1968-76; University of Texas at Dallas, associate professor of history and history of ideas, 1976—. *Member:* Bruno Walter Society, Western Association of German Studies. *Awards, honors:* American Council of Learned Societies grant, summer, 1969; Alexander von Humboldt Foundation fellowship to Germany, 1972-74, summers, 1978, 1980.

WRITINGS: Community in Conflict: Frankfurt Society in the Seventeenth and Early Eighteenth Centuries, University Press of New England, 1974; (editor) *History of the Family and Kinship: A Select International Bibliography,* H. P. Kraus, 1980.

WORK IN PROGRESS: A Social History of Marburg, Germany: The Sixteenth through the Eighteenth Centuries; A Study of Marriage Patterns and Social Mobility in Frankfurt, Germany: The Seventeenth to the Early Eighteenth Century.

* * *

SOMERVILLE, Mollie

PERSONAL: Born in New York, N.Y.; divorced; children: Richard C.J., Margaret Ann S. Wiegert. *Education:* Attended Cornell University and Columbia University. *Home:* 1414 17th St. N.W., Washington, D.C. 20036.

CAREER: Daughters of the American Revolution, Washington, D.C., writer-in-residence, 1962—. Lecturer to student groups, patriotic and hereditary societies, and organizations related to American history. *Member:* Authors Guild, Authors League of America, National League of American Pen Women (Capital branch), Association for the Preservation of Virginia Antiquities, Manuscript Society (Washington, D.C. branch).

WRITINGS: In Washington, Daughters of the American Revolution, 1965; *Alexandria, Virginia: George Washington's Home Town* (guidebook), Newell-Cole, 1966; *Washington Walked Here: Alexandria on the Potomac,* Acropolis Books, 1970, 2nd edition, 1982; *Women of the American Revolution,* Daughters of the American Revolution, 1974; (contributor) *Alexandria: A Composite History,* Volume I, Alexandria Bicentennial Commission, 1975; *Washington Landmark,* Daughters of the American Revolution, 1976; *Historic and Memorial Buildings of the Daughters of the American Revolution,* Daughters of the American Revolution, 1979. Contributor to periodicals, including *DAR Magazine.*

WORK IN PROGRESS: The FDR White House: Memoirs, a tribute on the centennial anniversary of Anna E. Roosevelt's birth.

* * *

SPANGENBERG, Judith Dunn 1942-
(Judy Dunn)

PERSONAL: Born October 6, 1942, in New Jersey; daughter of T. C. Tristram and Phoebe (a photographer; maiden name, Pierson) Dunn; married Thomas Craig Spangenberg (an advertising executive), December 18, 1965; children: Tyler Craig. *Education:* Sweet Briar College, B.S., 1964. *Religion:* Protestant. *Home:* 36 Smith Ridge Rd., South Salem, N.Y. 10590.

CAREER: J. C. Penney Co., New York City, copywriter, 1964-65; Ogilvy & Mather Advertising Agency, New York City, editor of house organ, 1966-67; free-lance writer, 1968—.

WRITINGS—Under name Judy Dunn, except as indicated: (With father, Tris Dunn, and mother, Phoebe Dunn) *Things,* Doubleday, 1968; (with T. Dunn and P. Dunn) *Animal Friends,* Creative Educational Society, 1971; (with T. Dunn and P. Dunn) *Feelings,* Creative Educational Society, 1971; (with T. Dunn and P. Dunn) *Friends,* Creative Educational Society, 1971; (with T. Dunn and P. Dunn) *Having Fun,* Creative Educational Society, 1971; (under name Judith Dunn Spangenberg) *Our Time Is Now* (poetry), illustrated with photographs by P. Dunn, Hallmark, 1973.

Published by Random House; illustrated with photographs by P. Dunn: *The Little Duck,* 1976; *The Little Lamb,* 1977; *The Little Goat,* 1978; *The Little Rabbit,* 1980; *The Animals of Buttercup Farm,* 1981; *The Little Kitten,* 1983; *The Little Puppy,* 1984.

Contributor of poems to numerous journals, 1961-66.

* * *

SPARK, Muriel (Sarah) 1918-
(Evelyn Cavallo)

PERSONAL: Born February 1, 1918, in Edinburgh, Scotland; daughter of Bernard (an engineer) and Sarah Elizabeth (Uezzell) Camberg; married S. O. Spark, 1937 (divorced); children: Robin (son). *Education:* Attended schools in Edinburgh, Scotland. *Religion:* Roman Catholic. *Residence:* Italy. *Agent:* Harold Ober Associates, Inc., 40 East 49th St., New York, N.Y. 10017.

CAREER: Writer. Wrote news items for political intelligence department of British government, 1944-45; affiliated with *Argentor* (jewelry trade magazine); press agent for businessmen; founder, *Forum* (literary magazine), 1949; part-time editor, Peter Owen Ltd. (publishing company). *Member:* Royal Society of Literature (fellow), Poetry Society (general secretary, 1947-49), P.E.N., American Academy and Institute of Arts and Letters (honorary member). *Awards, honors: Observer* short story prize, 1951, for "The Seraph and the Zambesi"; Prix Italia, 1962, for radio play adaptation of *The Ballad of Peckham Rye;* Yorkshire Post Book of the Year Award, 1965, and James Tait Black Memorial Prize, 1966, both for *The Mandelbaum Gate;* commander, Order of the British Empire, 1967; LL.D., University of Strathclyde, 1971; Booker McConnell Prize nomination, 1981, for *Loitering with Intent.*

WRITINGS—Fiction; novels, except as indicated: *The Comforters* (also see below), Lippincott, 1957, reprinted, Perigee Books, 1984; *Robinson,* Lippincott, 1958; *Memento Mori* (also see below), Macmillan (London), 1958, Lippincott, 1959, reprinted, Perigee Books, 1982; *The Go-Away Bird and Other Stories* (short stories), Macmillan (London), 1958, Lippincott, 1960; *The Ballad of Peckham Rye* (also see below), Lippincott, 1960, reprinted, Perigee Books, 1982; *The Bachelors,* Macmillan (London), 1960, Lippincott, 1961, reprinted Perigee Books, 1984; *Voices at Play* (short stories and radio plays), Macmillan (London), 1961, Lippincott, 1962; *The Prime of Miss Jean Brodie,* Macmillan (London), 1961, Lippincott, 1962; *A Muriel Spark Trio* (contains *The Comforters, Memento Mori,* and *The Ballad of Peckham Rye*), Lippincott, 1962; *The Girls of Slender Means,* Knopf, 1963, reprinted, Perigee Books, 1982; *Doctors of Philosophy* (play; first produced in London, 1962), Macmillan (London), 1963, Knopf, 1966; *The Mandelbaum Gate,* Knopf, 1965; *Collected Stories I* (short stories), Macmillan (London), 1967, Knopf, 1968; *The Public Image,* Knopf, 1968; *The Very Fine Clock* (juvenile), Knopf, 1968; *The Driver's Seat,* Knopf, 1970; *Not to Disturb,* Macmillan (London), 1971, Knopf, 1972; *The Hothouse by the East River,* Viking, 1973; *The Abbess of Crewe,* Viking, 1974; *The Takeover* (also see below), Viking, 1976; *Territorial Rights,* Coward, 1979; *Loitering with Intent,* Coward, 1981; *Bang-Bang You're Dead and Other Stories,* Panther Books, 1983; *The Only Problem,* Coward, 1984.

Poetry: *The Fanfarlo and Other Verse,* Hand and Flower Press, 1952; *Collected Poems I,* Macmillan (London), 1967, Knopf, 1968, published as *Going Up to Sotheby's and Other Poems,* Panther Books, 1982.

Nonfiction: *Child of Light: A Reassessment of Mary Wollstonecraft Shelley,* Tower Bridge Publications, 1951, reprinted, Richard West, 1978; (with Derek Stanford) *Emily Bronte: Her Life and Work,* P. Owen, 1953, London House and Maxwell, 1960, reprinted, Merrimack Book Service, 1982; *John Masefield,* Nevill, 1953, Norwood, 1978.

Editor: (And author of introductions with Stanford) *Tribute to Wordsworth,* T. Brun, 1950, reprinted, Kennikat, 1970; (and author of introduction) *A Selection of Poems by Emily Bronte,* Grey Walls Press, 1952; (with Stanford) *My Best Mary: The Letters of Mary Shelley,* Wingate, 1953; *The Letters of the Brontes: A Selection,* University of Oklahoma Press, 1954 (published in England as *The Bronte Letters,* Nevill, 1954); (with Stanford) *Letters of John Henry Newman,* P. Owen, 1957.

Also author of a film adaptation of *The Takeover.* Contributor of short stories to the *New Yorker* and of poems, articles, and reviews to magazines and newspapers, occasionally under the pseudonym Evelyn Cavallo. Editor, *Poetry Review,* 1947-49; review editor, *European Affairs,* 1949-50.

SIDELIGHTS: Often described as one of the best, yet one of the most unappreciated, of today's novelists, Muriel Spark puzzles those readers and critics with an affinity for labels and categories. Explains Richard Sullivan in *Book World:* "For those who take comfort in instant classification Muriel Spark keeps posing a mischievous problem. She's elusive. There is no question about her quality: her work to date has demonstrated it.... Yet she doesn't fit neatly into any pigeonhole.... She is—and probably without bothering in the least about it, prefers to be—an original."

Spark had already achieved some recognition as a critic and poet when she entered what was virtually her first attempt at fiction, the short story "The Seraph and the Zambesi," in a 1951 Christmas writing contest sponsored by the *Observer.* The fanciful tale of a troublesome angel who bursts in on an acting troupe staging a holiday pageant on the banks of Africa's Zambesi River, "The Seraph and the Zambesi" won top honors in the competition and attracted a great deal of attention for its unconventional treatment of the Christmas theme. Several other stories set in Africa and England followed; soon Spark's successes in fiction began to overshadow those in criticism and poetry.

In 1954 Spark's publisher, Macmillan, urged her to try writing a novel. Spark reluctantly agreed. "I thought it was an inferior way of writing," she told Frank Kermode in a *Partisan Review* interview. "So I wrote a novel to work out the technique first, to sort of make it all right with myself to write a novel at all."

At the same time she was working out the technique for writing a novel, Spark was "working out" something else far more important in her life—her conversion to Roman Catholicism. The daughter of a Jewish father and a Presbyterian mother, Spark had for many years practiced the Anglican faith. During the early 1950s, however, the inadequacy of her old beliefs became more and more unsettling; soon she found herself searching for new and better answers in the works of English theologian John Cardinal Newman, an early nineteenth-century Anglican convert to Catholicism. Reading Newman, explains Spark in *Twentieth Century,* "helped me find a definite location," and her eventual conversion, though marked by tremendous spiritual and physical turmoil, "provided my norm ... something to measure from."

With financial and moral support from both Macmillan and author Graham Greene, Spark struggled for nearly three years to sort out the aesthetic, psychological, and religious questions raised by her conversion and her attempt at writing longer fiction. Drawing on the tenets of her new faith, which she believes is especially "conducive to individuality, to finding one's own individual point of view," the young writer formulated her own theory of the novel. According to Kermode in his book *Continuities,* this theory suggests that "a genuine relation exists between the forms of fiction and the forms of the world, between the novelist's creation and God's." In essence, Spark sees the novelist as very God-like—omniscient and omnipotent, able to manipulate plot, character, and dialogue at will. Viewed in this light, Kermode and others contend, Spark's first novel, *The Comforters,* is obviously "an experiment designed to discover whether ... the novelist, pushing people and things around and giving 'disjointed happenings a shape,' is in any way like Providence."

Because Spark's Catholicism figures so prominently in *The Comforters* and subsequent works, it is "much more than an item of biographical interest," in the opinion of Victor Kelleher. Comments Kelleher in *Critical Review:* "Spark does not stop short at simply bringing the question of Catholicism into her work; she has chosen to place the traditionally Christian outlook at the very heart of everything she writes. . . . [Her tales proclaim] the most basic of Christian truths: that all man's blessings emanate from God; that, in the absence of God, man is nothing more than a savage." Catharine Hughes makes a similar assessment of Spark's religious sentiment in an article in *Catholic World*. Observes the critic: "[Spark satirizes] humanity's foibles and incongruities from a decidedly Catholic orientation. One is conscious that she is a writer working within the framework of some of Christianity's greatest truths; that her perspective, which takes full cognizance of eternal values, is never burdened by a painful attempt to inflict them upon others."

Despite their acknowledgment of Spark's unmistakably Catholic outlook, most critics hasten to point out that she is not at all what is usually thought of as a "Catholic writer." "[There] is a difference between a Catholic who writes novels and a Catholic Novelist," declares D. J. Enright in his book *Man Is an Onion*. "This latter term evokes, even if it shouldn't, an unholy mixture of the Claudelic, the Mauriacesque and the Greenean, a browbeating either direct or indirect, a stifling odour of incense or of fallen sweat or of both. Mrs. Spark's writing seems to me altogether dissimilar: even a lapsed Wesleyan can approach her without too painful a sense of intimidation or exclusion. . . . Granville Hicks has faintly deplored her as 'a gloomy Catholic, like Graham Greene and Flannery O'Connor, more concerned with the evil of man than with the goodness of God.' Far from gloomy, I would even have thought [Spark] positively funny, and . . . concerned with the evil of man no more than is to be expected in a fair-minded though shrewd observer of humanity. . . . Spark neither despises nor hates her fellow humans nor dotes simple-mindedly on her Catholicism. . . . What emerges [in her work] is a chastened Christianity not so far removed in matters of this world from the chastened humanism which is the only sort of humanism our age can allow."

Ann Dobie also takes issue with those who label Spark a "Catholic novelist." In *Critique: Studies in Modern Fiction*, Dobie insists that "it is doubtful that a reader who is not aware of [the author's] religious affiliation would know that she is a Roman Catholic. Muriel Spark is never didactic about her religion. Her purpose is to intrigue, not teach. She awakens the reader's imagination and curiosity instead of making firm the ideas which she brings to the novel. . . . Spark's novels are therefore written to express a moral or spiritual truth. Though they entertain by their wit and originality, their basic purpose lies in their endeavor to make a statement about the nature of the universe and man's place in it."

At first glance, however, Spark's novels do not seem to reflect her strong religious and moral preoccupations. In terms of setting, for example, the author usually chooses to locate her modern morality tales in upper-class urban areas of England or Italy. Her "fun-house plots, full of trapdoors, abrupt apparitions, and smartly clicking secret panels," as John Updike describes them in a *New Yorker* article, focus on the often bizarre behavior of people belonging to a small, select group: elderly men and women linked by long-standing personal relationships in *Memento Mori;* unmarried male and female residents of the same London district in *The Bachelors;* students and teachers at a Scottish girls' school in *The Prime of Miss Jean Brodie;* servants on a Swiss estate in *Not to Disturb;* guests at a pair of neighboring Venetian hotels in *Territorial Rights*. The "action" in these stories springs from the elaborate ties Spark concocts between the members of each group—ties of blood, marriage, friendship, and other kinds of relationships. Commenting in her study of the author, critic Patricia Stubbs observes that the use of such a technique reflects Spark's fascination with "the way in which the individual varies in different settings, or different company." "By taking this restricted group of protagonists," explains Stubbs, "[Spark] is able to create multiple ironies, arising from their connecting and conflicting destinies: by her selection of such a restricted canvas, she can display the many facets of her creatures' personalities, and the different roles which they, or society, decree they should play."

Like her settings and plots, Spark's characters belie her strong Catholic convictions. In fact, as many reviewers have noticed, she has few qualms about depicting her coreligionists (who figure prominently in her fiction) in a manner that creates a decidedly objectionable image for their faith. For instance, Robert Maurer, writing in the *Saturday Review*, describes Spark's cast of characters as a "strange collection of eccentrics, self-deceivers, misfits, and purveyors of reprehensible madness." Because of their interrelatedness, all are equally important to the story line, though one or two usually stand out somewhat from the rest. These protagonists, most often female Catholic converts, "are frequently intelligent and talented women who, because they demand much of life, insist on a broad view of its possibilities," reports Dobie. "At the same time they desire the security of certain ultimate laws which limit man's actions." Spark generally portrays them in the midst of a struggle to understand themselves and their chaotic environments within the context of their religion. Though their struggle may be a noble one, they are not necessarily heroic or even very likable people. According to Gail Kessler Kmetz in *Ms.*, the typical Spark heroine "believes herself to be above ordinary standards of right and wrong. . . . She is an autocrat, an elitist, a tyrant convinced that God's standards are identical to her own." In short, remarks Derek Stanford in his study of the author, Spark's protagonists, "encased in the self-love of their own rightness or superiority, . . . do not attract us to identify ourselves with them or their self-willed fates."

Secondary characters fare little better in most of Spark's novels; as Dobie notes, they are among those "despicable people" who "misuse religious faith to achieve their own gain: money, social position, personal pride." Mean-spirited liars, meddlers, and bores, they are Catholic only in that they have "the articles of an ancient creed built into their grid of reflexes, predispositions, and quirks," writes Updike. Yet as Samuel Hynes points out in *Commonweal*, they are not truly evil: "[Spark] is not, like that other distinguished convert, Graham Greene, devil-ridden; the diabolic creatures who turn up in her books are more grotesque than terrifying, and their deeds are rather annoying than destroying. They are . . . the kind of people who bring out the pettiness and uncharitableness in us, not the kind who lead us to damnation."

Spark often emphasizes the diabolicism of a particular person or event by introducing supernatural forces into a setting that is otherwise quite ordinary. The appearance of these inscrutable forces is always unpredictable, and they may take a variety of forms: an enigmatic stranger with unusual powers, disembodied voices, untraceable telephone calls. Whatever their form, they exert considerable influence over human activities; according to Dobie, however, their purpose is neither to harm nor to help, but to disrupt routine, provoke thought, and inspire spiritual growth. As such, the supernatural is as important an element in Spark's world as the natural.

Both Hynes and Dobie view this intrusion of the supernatural as "a more pervasive, less specific" manifestation of Spark's religious feeling, to use Hynes's words. Explains Dobie: "Those characters [in Spark's fiction] who recognize [supernatural forces] for what they are acquire 'vision.' . . . That is, such characters are given the opportunity to comprehend more fully the nature of themselves and the world. If the characters accept the opportunity, their new concept of reality is a liberating one, for the limitations which they had previously accepted are destroyed by a new grasp of the enormity of the real world which reaches far beyond what the human being can observe by his senses and prove by his reason." In short, as Dobie and many others have concluded, Spark makes us take a second look at the world and the people we think we know; she transfigures the commonplace, blending the ordinary and the supernatural ("complementary parts of a whole and rich reality") in such a way that "a new concept of reality emerges, one which is closer to truth."

In contrast to the complexities of plot, characterization, and theme in her fiction, Spark is noted for what Stubbs refers to as a "frugality of method." Precise, economical, and matter-of-fact, her prose leaves most readers "wondering why other writers must babble on and on to twice that length," declares a reviewer for *Time*. States Edmund White in the *New York Times Book Review:* "Details, no matter how prosaic, are presented with the utmost clarity, even severity, and this classic exactitude holds our interest, for it is the tone of the professor during the opening lectures of a course that we know is quickly going to get bewilderingly out of hand. . . . Dozens of scenes are compressed into a single slim volume, but each is displayed in the dry, unemphatic, seemingly leisurely style for which the author is renowned." Malcolm Bradbury makes a similar observation in *Critical Quarterly*, remarking that Spark's books "possess a high tactical authority and a singular clarity so that every compositional decision, every rhetorical device, every perspective in every sentence has the high economy of, for example, one of Hemingway's better stories, the same air of exchanging language at the very best possible rate." As White asserts, "this efficiency and orderliness . . . are [Spark's] real artistic achievements."

In the tradition of the intellectual novelist, Spark avoids florid descriptions of the physical world, preferring instead to concentrate on dialogue, on "the play of ideas and experiences upon the mind, and the interplay of minds upon each other," in Hynes's words. Her characterizations are quick, sharp, and concise; in a *New Statesman* article, for instance, Walter Allen writes that the author "pins [her types] to the page quivering in their essential absurdity." As a result, says *Newsweek* reviewer Raymond A. Sokolov, "a [typical Spark] character is born, with a deft flick of the author's wrist, in an effortless few pages."

Spark teams her technical virtuosity with an elegant, acerbic wit and condescending attitude that most readers find highly entertaining. As Melvin Maddocks declares in *Life:* "Reading a Muriel Spark novel remains one of the minor pleasures of life. Like a perfect hostess, she caters to our small needs. In the manner available to only the best British novelists, she ordains a civilized atmosphere—two parts what Evelyn Waugh called creamy English charm, one part acid wit. She peoples her scene discriminatingly, showing a taste for interesting but not overpowering guests. . . . As the evening moves along, she has the good sense to lower the drawing-room lights and introduce a pleasantly chilling bit of tension—even violence—just to save us all, bless her, from the overexquisite sensibilities of the lady novelist."

Charles Alva Hoyt traces the source of Spark's humor to her conception of the novelist as a God-like figure. Noting in the book *Contemporary British Novelists* that Spark is "a thoroughly mischievous writer," Hoyt goes on to explain: "By that I do not mean only that she plays tricks upon her characters—although she does—or upon the reader—she treats him even worse—but that she also views the universe itself as mischievous. The cosmos is neither void of all sense, nor is it sentient but preoccupied: it is both aware of individuals and fond of meddling with them for its own amusement. . . . [Spark's universe] reveals its playfulness in an almost continuous flow of irony, but it is quite as fond of comedy as it is of tragedy. There is furthermore in her work an almost irresponsible impertinence towards everyday reality. . . . What we have here is . . . not the scientist's or the theologian's attempt to reason the demons out of the thunderstorm, but the magician's effort to make the demons do his bidding."

Yet, as Barbara Grizzuti Harrison reminds readers in a *New York Times Book Review* article, Spark is at heart "a profoundly serious comic writer whose wit advances, never undermines or diminishes, her ideas." This sentiment is shared by Harrison's fellow *New York Times Book Review* critic Leonard Graver, who writes: "Sinister metaphysical farce has always been one of Muriel Spark's specialities. . . . [But] lurid entertainment is only part of [her] intention. She has always been a novelist who wishes to tease readers into serious thought. . . . [Her work] has the cleverness to entertain and the intelligence to provoke thought."

The effects of Spark's malevolent wit are intensified by the air of authorial omniscience and condescension that permeates her fiction. Reflecting what David Pryce-Jones describes in the *London Magazine* as a desire "to observe man disposing what God has proposed," Spark deliberately sets up a distance between herself and her characters (and, to a somewhat lesser extent, between herself and her readers) that clearly gives the impression she knows much more than she cares to reveal. One is always well aware, says Hoyt, of "the cool, clever female mind in control. This level scrutiny from the distance plays continuously though mildly upon every frenzied human action like the soft, semi-contemptuous gaze of the household cat. Muriel Spark is ever the reasonable recorder of unreason: she is the Jane Austen of the surrealists." As such, maintains a *Times Literary Supplement* critic, Spark "makes it refreshingly clear that modern satire can be more than anger or tittle-tattle."

Not all reviewers, however, are quite as charmed by Spark's biting humor and cool detachment. To some, these trademarks of her writing are a source of uneasiness. States Thomas R. Brooks in the *New Leader:* "On the surface, [a typical Spark novel] might pass for a decaying comedy of manners. . . . Yet underneath the deftly paced plot and the gleaming prose there lurks a disconcerting darkness that goes beyond black humor. The trouble, I think, is that the characters are dislikable to a degree that is fatal." *Los Angeles Times* critic Jascha Kessler asserts that this is because "the narrator [Spark] usually employs is too often the stereotypical convert, joyless and sexless; sometimes it's a disembodied voice, literally a spook; or it's intellectualist, bored by the drab English, or English (African) colonial, life; or it's neuter, hysterical, grim, as though suffering from menopause from the onset of puberty, and wishing only to find refuge or surcease from the life of the whole person. And that refuge is too easily found in an attitude that is self-consciously catty and complacent, spiritualistic rather than spiritual, smug about rosaries, icons, rituals, embarrassed by faith and not exalted or empowered by it, as though faith demands a show of warmth that is in poor taste."

Gillian Tindall, on the other hand, believes that it is the author's omniscient tone that makes her characters so unattractive. Says Tindall in the *New Statesman:* "[Spark's] insistence that for all her characters the future *is already there,* and that she can reveal it if she has a mind to, tends to belittle them and, by depriving them of self-determination, turns them into demented automata." Christopher Ricks views Spark's tendency to create unsympathetic characters in more negative terms. In a *New York Review of Books* article, Ricks declares: "[Spark's works] exemplify more than any other writing known to me, a body of work guilty of all that which it finds most hateful and which it most eagerly exposes. . . . 'Merciless,' the reviewers have always said. Leave aside the question of why something which is a vice in life becomes a virtue in literature; but why fabricate characters at whose expense you can then exercise your mercilessness?"

According to a few critics, Spark's omniscient tone also gives her work an overall air of inconsequentiality. Margaret Drabble, for instance, notes in the *New York Times Book Review* that Spark is "an enigmatic novelist, and her forte is to imply that she knows much more than . . . she chooses to say. . . . She writes of the rich, the clever, the sophisticated, the experienced; the innocent and the unknowing receive hardly more than a derisory nod or an astonished salute in her collected works. . . . [Her characters] are the jet set of fiction. . . . But, as ever, Muriel Spark raises the question: what lies beneath this dazzling game? Anything? Nothing? And, as ever, she leaves us on our own . . . to try to answer it. At times one suspects she may not know the answer herself. It is easy to appear knowing if one says little, or if one works . . . on the level of tediously protracted fantasy." Commenting in *The Modern English Novel,* Bernard Harrison also characterizes Spark's novels as "too spun-out. They seem all surface, and a rather dry, sparsely furnished, though elegant and mannered surface at that. . . . [They] seem, while one is reading them, to be profoundly, if obscurely, preoccupied with morality, not to say moral theology. Indeed they seem to be about nothing else. But there is no denying the obscurity. . . . Nothing is ever fully explained or given depth."

Even Maurer, who believes that requesting Spark to "alter these characteristics in her work would be [asking] her to surrender her uniqueness—and, one hastens to add, much of her delight and pleasure," has reservations about her "self-controlled poise, the intellectuality of her pessimism, her crisp sort of kindness, her impatience with moral obliquity." In short, observes the critic, "one wonders how vast a reserve of sympathy lies beneath the iceberg of her consciousness, and how far beyond trickery her work would go if she let it show through."

John Updike suspects that differences between American and English sensibilities account for much of the negative criticism reviewers have expressed regarding Spark's coolly distant attitude. Though he himself finds that "her hard, unflecked prose seems laid on from a calculated distance that this admirer, sometimes, would be relieved to see reduced," he nevertheless maintains that "detachment is the genius of her fiction. We are lifted above her characters, and though they are reduced in size and cryptically foreshortened, they are all seen at once, and their busy interactions are as plain and pleasing as a solved puzzle. The use by a serious author of [such techniques] may strike American readers as incongruous. We are accustomed to honest autobiographical shapelessness. . . . Our novels tend to be about education rather than products of it; they are soul-searching rather than worldly-wise. English fiction, for all the social and philosophical earthquakes since Chaucer, continues to aspire, with the serenity of a treatise, to a certain dispassionate elevation above the human scene. Hence its greater gaiety and ease of contrivance, its (on the whole) superior finish, and its flattering air of speaking to the reader who, himself presumably educated, may be spared the obvious."

Others also find Spark's attitude appropriate and not at all callous. "There is certainly a remoteness, a lack of ordinary compassion, in [Spark's] dealing with characters," admits Kermode in the *New Statesman.* "But this is part of the premise of her fiction; if we feel sorry in the wrong way, it's because our emotions are as messy and imprecise as life, part of the muddle she is sorting out." Hynes makes a similar observation, stating: "Compassion is there, but Mrs. Spark's religion protects her from that too-easy compassion which we call sentimentality. She is neither cold nor soft-hearted; on the whole she is amiably disposed toward her characters, finds material for comedy in them, and records their nastier qualities without rancor. . . . If she is detached in her attitude toward her characters, this is understandable in a novelist who sees people in terms of the designs into which they fit."

Despite all that has been written about her and her fiction, Muriel Spark remains an enigma to most critics, concerning herself as she does "with matters beyond reality, with forces that do not lend themselves to facile explanations," according to Florence Rome in the *Chicago Tribune Book World.* Described by Sybille Bedford in the *Saturday Review* as "an artist, a serious—and most accomplished—writer, a moralist engaged with the human predicament, wildly entertaining, and a joy to read," Spark has nevertheless, in Stubbs's opinion, "succeeded triumphantly in evading classification." Updike, too, contends that Spark possesses a truly exceptional talent—a talent that without a doubt makes her an unclassifiable "original." In fact, he declares in the *New Yorker,* Spark "is one of the few writers of the language on either side of the Atlantic with enough resources, daring, and stamina to be altering, as well as feeding, the fiction machine."

Shirley Hazzard also counts herself among those who believe Muriel Spark is indeed "a remarkable writer." Elaborating on the subject in a lengthy *New York Times Book Review* article, Hazzard states: "At this moment when, in all the arts, novelty is frequently confused with quality, Mrs. Spark's writings demonstrate how secondary—in fact, how incidental—are innovations of style and form to the work of the truly gifted. . . . When the word 'humorous' has little currency in literature or in life, her wit is employed to produce effects and insights only matched in contemporary fiction, in this reviewer's opinion, by the glittering jests of Vladimir Nabokov. At a time when our 'tolerance' tends to take the form of general agreement that we are all capable of the worst crimes had we but the conditions for committing them, Mrs. Spark interests herself instead in our capacities for choice and in the use we make of them; and in those forces of good and evil that she picks out unerringly, often gleefully, beneath their worldly camouflage." Noting that the author "does not posture instructively, nor does she shade her work to appease reviewers and gladden the hearts of publishing companies," Hazzard concludes that Muriel Spark writes for the best possible reason: "She writes to entertain, in the highest sense of that word—to allow us the exercise of our intellect and imagination, to extend our self-curiosity and enrich our view."

MEDIA ADAPTATIONS: Several of Muriel Spark's novels have been adapted for the stage, film, and television. A dramatization of *Memento Mori* was produced on stage in 1964. Jay Presson Allen's dramatization of *The Prime of Miss Jean Brodie*, published by Samuel French in 1969, was first produced in Torquay, England, at the Princess Theatre beginning April 5, 1966, then in Boston at the Colonial Theatre from December 26, 1967, to January 6, 1968, and finally on Broadway at the Helen Hayes Theatre beginning January 9, 1968. Allen also wrote the screenplay for the 1969 film version of the same novel, a Twentieth Century-Fox production starring Maggie Smith. John Wood's dramatization of *The Prime of Miss Jean Brodie* was produced in London at Wyndham's Theatre in 1967. A six-part adaptation appeared on public television in England in 1978 and in the United States in 1979. *The Driver's Seat* was filmed in 1972, and in 1974 *The Girls of Slender Means* was adapted for television. *The Abbess of Crewe* was filmed and released in 1976 under the title "Nasty Habits."

CA INTERVIEW

CA interviewed Muriel Spark by telephone June 30, 1983, at her apartment in Rome, Italy.

CA: In a review of your Collected Stories I, *Shirley Hazzard said that you write "to entertain, in the highest sense of that word—to allow us the exercise of our intellect and imagination, to extend our self-curiosity and enrich our view." Is that a good and accurate comment?*

SPARK: I think it's a very appreciative one. I do write to entertain; I write to give pleasure, but that doesn't always mean to amuse. One can give pleasure by making people sad or happy. I think that is very good praise coming from Shirley Hazzard, whom I admire myself very much.

CA: You said you thought the novel was an "inferior way of writing" and did the first one, The Comforters, *as a kind of trial to "work out the technique."*

SPARK: Yes, that used to be my view, that it was a lazy form of writing poetry. Now your critic the late Allen Tate said a novel is a poem or it is nothing. It has to be seen from the poetic point of view. That doesn't mean that there has to be poetic speech and that it has to be rather lush, like Lawrence Durrell's writing, but that there has to be a poetic conception. To me, poetry is the first thing and a novel is, to me, a poem.

CA: Were you convinced at once that the novel was a good form for you, or did it take several novels to convince you?

SPARK: I was convinced right away.

CA: Do you think beginning to write novels later in your career—after writing poetry, criticism, and short stories—made it easier somehow than it would have been if you'd done it at first?

SPARK: I think that there was less fumbling about. I could go straight at it because I had accumulated a lot of experience in life. I had something to write about. I'd also had an apprenticeship in the use of words because I was always very interested in formal poetry. I used to try every different type of meter and rhyme.

CA: Did you find that writing novels gave you some kind of satisfaction that was missing in writing poetry?

SPARK: Yes, I did. I found that it was releasing, that it was not nearly so constricted. One's imagination could really run free in a good stream and one could plan on a much more complicated basis than one would plan a poem. I love to have complex plots.

CA: Yes, I know. How much of the structure of a novel do you have worked out, even if only in your mind, before you begin to write it?

SPARK: Hardly any, but a great deal of that is unconscious, I think. It's almost a musical sense; I do find that as I'm writing, I construct, and the construction is very much bound up with the rest of the form and the theme. What I'm writing about gives shape to what I'm writing.

CA: The beginning of your career as a novelist came around the time of your conversion to Roman Catholicism. You've said that you find Catholicism "conducive to individuality, to finding one's own individual personal point of view." Can you explain how that works?

SPARK: I don't know how it would work for other people, but it works for me. I can only speak for myself. I think it's a matter of finding one's self. It certainly was my religion. I can't conceive of not believing anything and I can't conceive of believing any other religion. I stuck there. And joining the church did have a simultaneously releasing effect on my creativity. The two coincided. I had been an Anglican for a long time and had thought it good, but it wasn't right for me.

CA: Much of the literary criticism written about your work centers on the concept of you as a Catholic writer. How do you feel about that label?

SPARK: I think that's fair enough. That ties in with your previous question. You see, freedom to write is also freedom to think. It also means that the things that impede one from expressing oneself, from expressing one's imaginative life, are quite small and unimportant when one comes up against a big thing like the Catholic religion. I don't go along with all the small points of Catholicism, the nonessentials. I don't always agree with what the pope does and says, and all that, but I think that in the broad historical sense the church does teach you to see things in proportion. This has a very, very releasing effect. Nothing matters very much of things that previously seemed to matter a great deal, and yet *everything* matters a great deal. It's a paradox.

CA: Do you keep up with the reviews of your books and the critical writing on your work?

SPARK: No, I don't. I do read many works of criticism. I get quite fascinated. My main reading is the *New York Review of Books*. The criticisms of my own work I can't keep up with because, unless the publisher sends them to me, I don't get them. I get the reviews when they come out in England and America, but I can't read the German ones, and I can't read Finnish and at least seventy different languages the reviews come out in. So I really have no idea what people are saying or thinking. Occasionally I get a nice letter in English from a foreign country, so I know my work is being read in that part of the world.

CA: There's quite a large body of literary criticism on your work.

SPARK: I know there have been an awful lot of books and articles written about my work. Some are valid and some are not. Some are very, very good, especially the ones by people who don't know me personally. People who know me personally tend to rush in and elaborate on all sorts of things that have absolutely nothing to do with my work.

CA: You've said that you don't rewrite. Do you, as critic Patricia Stubbs suggested in writing about The Comforters, *"hear" the novel while it is being written?*

SPARK: In some way I do. I've got a sense of voices. I don't actually hear physical voices, but I have a sense of the sound. I don't rewrite a good deal. Sometimes I do if I have a book with one or two difficult chapters, and I'm not sure whether I should use the first person to begin with. Just lately sometimes I do rewrite a bit, but on the whole, not much. It's pretty clean manuscript by the time it's finished.

CA: Some of your critics have accused you of a lack of compassion for your characters. Do you ever get emotionally involved with the characters in the process of writing, in a way that doesn't show up in the finished product?

SPARK: I always do, but I don't show it. I think that way the stark reality comes across more. And I don't think many of the younger critics would say that. At first, when I started to write, it was rather more shocking. I think people have become used to what I'm about. I don't believe in sentimentalizing, but there is emotional content, naturally.

CA: You've spoken in the past of having an unstructured writing schedule. Has that changed for you?

SPARK: No, it hasn't. I don't sit down to write every day, but if I'm not writing, I'm thinking about it every day. And then I do a long stretch. I make time, and I enjoy that. I really love doing that.

CA: Do you get away from it ever, say between books, and forget about it altogether, or is that impossible now?

SPARK: No, it's not impossible. It's very difficult to get away from . . . well, not quite the business side, because agents and other people do that, but to get away from reminders that one is an author. But I do manage. I go off to France with a friend, I travel a great deal, and I do manage to get away—but not away from ideas, ever. I live very much in a world of ideas.

CA: You talked briefly with Victoria Glendinning for the New York Times Book Review *about depression as "the enemy," but an enemy you can defeat by knowing you can wait it out. Do the periods of depression have any relationship to the progress of your writing or to what you're writing about?*

SPARK: Sometimes. But sometimes it's got more to do with weather—thunder, atmospheric conditions, things like that. Or some news I've had. We all have ups and downs, you know. My periods of depression last for such a short time that it's not really worth considering doing anything about them.

CA: In a 1970 address to the American Academy of Arts and Letters, you called for the abolition of sentiment and emotion in the arts, saying that satire and ridicule were the only "living art form for the future." Do you still feel that way?

SPARK: I don't want to abolish emotion and sentiment, but I do think that if you want to effectively speak out for an idea, the way to do it is more to ridicule. Satire is far more important, it has a more lasting effect, than a straight portrayal of what is wrong. I think that a lot of the world's problems should be ridiculed, but ridiculed properly rather than, well, wailed over. People go to the theater, for instance, and see a play about some outrage or other, and then they come away feeling that they've done something about it, which they haven't. But if these things are ridiculed, it sticks and the perpetrators will stop doing it.

I do believe in satire as a very, very potent art form. The only difficulty I see about what I said to the Academy of Arts and Letters is that in the countries where satire is needed most, the people go to jail if they write it. I once wrote a satire about Watergate, called *The Abbess of Crewe*. Do you know that was a bestseller in the Soviet Union? But if any of their writers had written an anti-Kremlin satire, he would've been put in jail or in a lunatic asylum. That is the trouble. Where it's needed most, in the totalitarian states, the authorities will not allow ridicule.

CA: Several of your books have been adapted for the stage, the movies, radio, and television, the best known probably being The Prime of Miss Jean Brodie. *Do you mind seeing them changed, as they inevitably are, from the original?*

SPARK: No, I don't. I'll tell you, in a way I've been very lucky because I've always had good adaptors, and *Jean Brodie* seems to have been a good vehicle for the actresses who have played the part, because they have been very good. I'm rather interested to see what can be done in another form, actually.

CA: Are there any movies or television plays in the offing now?

SPARK: Yes, I think that in Germany they're doing *Not to Disturb*. In America there's a project now coming up to do *Memento Mori* as a stage play. I'm negotiating that right at the moment. There are always things in different parts of the world, you know.

CA: Did you do a screen adaptation yourself?

SPARK: I did a screen adaptation of a novel of mine called *The Takeover*. I was very happy and so were the producers. It was going to be done by Joe Losey and I hope will be done one day, but the producer, a young German, took a fall; he had a big financial loss and he couldn't go ahead with it although he'd paid everyone up to date and had the casting. It was very, very sad, but I still have hopes of it. I did enjoy doing that movie script. It really was an unusual thing for me, to turn my own book into a play, and of course I added to it. I changed it a bit.

CA: Are you pretty much settled in Rome now? Do you plan to stay?

SPARK: I really live in the country, in Tuscany, with a friend who has a house there. I have a place in Rome, but I only come here to have a little social life, answer letters, things like that. I usually write in the country. But I do go to France and Germany quite a lot, and to England, of course, and to the United States quite often.

CA: How long did you live in New York?

SPARK: Four years.

CA: Did you find it hard to work there?

SPARK: It was very hard to work there towards the end; it was much too distracting. But I thought it thrilling all the same. It's an exciting life.

CA: Are there current works in progress or future plans that you'd like to talk about?

SPARK: When I finish what I'm working on now, I want to get together a book of short stories. I did a couple this year. I always write short stories and I still write poems. There was a book of poems published in England recently. The novel I'm writing now is very unusual, not like anything I've done before. But I don't want to talk about it, because it spoils the magic.

BIOGRAPHICAL/CRITICAL SOURCES—Books: Derek Stanford, *Muriel Spark: A Biographical and Critical Study,* Centaur Press, 1963; Charles Shapiro, editor, *Contemporary British Novelists,* Southern Illinois University Press, 1965; Donald E. Stanford, editor, *Nine Essays in Modern Literature,* Louisiana State University Press, 1965; Karl Malkoff, *Muriel Spark,* Columbia University Press, 1968; Frank Kermode, *Continuities,* Random House, 1968; D. J. Enright, *Man Is an Onion: Reviews and Essays,* Chatto & Windus, 1972; Patricia Stubbs, *Muriel Spark,* Longman, 1973; Peter Kemp, *Muriel Spark,* Elek, 1974, Barnes & Noble, 1975; *Contemporary Literary Criticism,* Gale, Volume II, 1974, Volume III, 1975, Volume V, 1976, Volume VIII, 1978, Volume XIII, 1980, Volume XVIII, 1981; Gabriel Josipovici, editor, *The Modern English Novel: The Reader, the Writer and the Work,* Open Books, 1976; Ruth Whittaker, *The Faith and Fiction of Muriel Spark,* Macmillan (London), 1978; *Dictionary of Literary Biography,* Volume XV: *British Novelists, 1930-1959,* Gale, 1983.

Periodicals: *Manchester Guardian,* February 12, 1957; *Spectator,* February 22, 1957, November 3, 1961, December 22, 1967, June 7, 1968; *New Statesman and Nation,* February 23, 1957; *Commonweal,* August 23, 1957, September 18, 1959, February 23, 1962, December 3, 1965, January 14, 1966; *New York Times,* September 1, 1957, October 19, 1958, March 29, 1972, November 26, 1974, October 7, 1976, May 19, 1979, May 28, 1981; *Yale Review,* autumn, 1957, December, 1958, January, 1959, June, 1959, June, 1961; *Times Literary Supplement,* June 27, 1958, March 4, 1960, October 11, 1960, November 3, 1961, October 25, 1963, October 14, 1965, September 25, 1970, May 22, 1981; *New Statesman,* July 5, 1958, March 28, 1959, March 5, 1960, October 15, 1960, November 3, 1961, September 27, 1963, September 25, 1970, March 2, 1973, April 27, 1979; *New York Times Book Review,* May 17, 1959, August 28, 1960, September 29, 1968, March 26, 1972, October 3, 1976, May 20, 1979, May 31, 1981; *New Yorker,* June 13, 1959, August 27, 1960, September 30, 1961, September 14, 1963, January 27, 1968, June 8, 1981; *Atlantic,* August, 1959, October, 1968.

Time, August 15, 1960, January 19, 1962, January 13, 1967, November 1, 1968, October 26, 1970, June 11, 1979, July 6, 1981; *Saturday Review,* November 19, 1960, April 8, 1961, January 20, 1962, September 14, 1963, October 16, 1965, October 5, 1968, September 18, 1976; *Chicago Sunday Tribune,* January 1, 1961; *Catholic World,* August, 1961; *Twentieth Century,* autumn, 1961; *New Republic,* January 29, 1962; *Critique: Studies in Modern Fiction,* Volume V, no. 2, 1962, Volume XII, no. 1, 1970, Volume XV, no. 1, 1973; *Partisan Review,* spring, 1963; *Book Week,* September 15, 1963; *Harper,* November, 1963; *New York Review of Books,* October 28, 1965, December 19, 1968, November 28, 1974, November 11, 1976; *Listener,* December 7, 1967, September 24, 1970; *London Magazine,* July, 1968; *Books and Bookmen,* July, 1968, April, 1973; *Los Angeles Times,* July 14, 1968; *Book World,* September 29, 1968, November 23, 1969; *Saturday Review,* October 5, 1968; *Life,* October 11, 1968; *Newsweek,* October 21, 1968, November 30, 1970, May 18, 1981; *Best Sellers,* November 1, 1968, November 1, 1970; *Christian Science Monitor,* November 14, 1968; *Kenyon Review,* Volume XXXI, no. 2, 1969.

Nation, October 5, 1970; *New Leader,* November 30, 1970, July 30, 1979; *Critical Quarterly,* autumn, 1972; *Hudson Review,* autumn, 1972; *Chicago Tribune Book World,* April 29, 1973, May 24, 1981; *Ms.,* May, 1976; *Washington Post Book World,* October 3, 1976, June 24, 1979, May 24, 1981; *Critical Review,* Number 18, 1976; *Washington Post,* May 4, 1979; *Detroit News,* June 21, 1981.

—Sketch by Deborah A. Straub
—Interview by Jean W. Ross

[Sketch verified by Craig Tenney of Harold Ober Associates literary agency]

* * *

SPEAIGHT, George Victor 1914-

PERSONAL: Surname is pronounced Spate; born September 6, 1914, in Bishop's Hatfield, England; son of Frederick William and Emily (Elliot) Speaight; married Mary Mudd (schools officer of London Museum), 1946; children: Anthony Hugh, Margaret Isabella Mary. *Education:* Attended Haileybury College. *Politics:* "Radical conservative liberal." *Religion:* "Progressive Roman Catholic." *Home:* 6 Maze Rd., Kew Gardens, Richmond, Surrey, England.

CAREER: George Rainbird Ltd. (publishers), London, England, editorial director. *Member:* International Federation for Theatre Research, Union Internationale de la Marionette (member of honor), Royal Society of Arts (fellow), British Puppet and Model Theatre Guild (vice-president), Society for Theatre Research (chairman).

WRITINGS: Juvenile Drama: The History of the English Toy Theatre, Macdonald & Co., 1946, revised and enlarged edition published as *The History of the English Toy Theatre,* Plays, Inc., 1969; *The History of the English Puppet Theatre,* De Graff, 1955, revised edition published as *Punch and Judy: A History,* Plays, Inc., 1970; (editor) *The Memoirs of Charles Dibdin the Younger,* Society for Theatre Research, 1956; (editor) *Bawdy Songs of the Early Music Hall,* David & Charles, 1975; *The Book of Clowns,* Macmillan, 1980; *A History of the Circus,* A. S. Barnes, 1980; (editor) Henry Whiteley, *Memories of Circus etc.,* Society for Theatre Research, 1981; (editor) *The Life and Travels of Richard Barnard,* Society for Theatre Research, 1981.

BIOGRAPHICAL/CRITICAL SOURCES: *Spectator*, April 18, 1969; *Punch*, July 1, 1970.

* * *

SPEAIGHT, Robert (William) 1904-1976

PERSONAL: Born January 14, 1904, at St. Margaret's Bay, Kent, England; died November 4, 1976; son of Frederick William (a company director) and Emily Isabella (Elliot) Speaight; married Esther Evelyn Bowen, 1935; married Bridget Laura Bramwell Bosworth-Smith, May 28, 1951; children: Patrick William Ellis, Teresa Clare Davison, Crispin John. *Education:* Attended Haileybury and Imperial Service College, 1918-22; Lincoln College, Oxford, M.A. (honors), 1925. *Politics:* Conservative. *Religion:* Roman Catholic. *Home and office:* Campion House, Benenden, Kent, England. *Agent:* David Higham Associates Ltd., 76 Dean St., London W.1, England.

CAREER: British actor, author, and lecturer. Started theatrical career with Liverpool Repertory Theatre, 1926; toured Egypt with Shakespearina company, 1927; played leading Shakespearian roles at Old Vic, 1931-32; created role of Becket in T. S. Eliot's "Murder in the Cathedral," 1935; played St. Thomas More in Robert Bolt's "A Man for All Seasons" in Australia, 1962-63; has appeared in dozens of other roles in England, United States, Canada, France, Scotland, and Wales. Lecturer for British Council on tours abroad; lecturer in United States, 1961, 1962, 1965. Broadcaster and recording artist for English poetry on Argo and Spoken Arts records. *Member:* Royal Society of Literature (fellow), Beefsteak and Garrick Clubs. *Awards, honors:* Commander of Order of the British Empire, 1958; Legion of Honour, officer, 1969.

WRITINGS: Mutinous Wind, Davies, 1932; *The Lost Hero,* Davies, 1934; *Legend of Helena Vaughan,* Putnam, 1936 (published in England as *The Angel in the Mist,* Cassell, 1936); *St. Thomas of Canterbury,* Putnam, 1938 (published in England as *Thomas Becket,* Longmans, Green, 1938, 2nd edition, 1949); *The Unbroken Heart,* Cassell, 1939; *Acting: Its Idea and Tradition,* Cassell, 1939; *Drama Since 1939,* Longmans, Green, 1948; (with others) *Drama, the Novel, Poetry, Prose Literature,* Dent, 1949.

George Eliot, Roy, 1954, 2nd edition, Barker, 1968; *William Poel and the Elizabethan Revival,* Harvard University Press, 1954; *Nature in Shakespearian Tragedy,* Macmillan, 1956; *The Life of Hilaire Belloc,* Farrar, Straus, 1957, reprinted, Darby Books, 1981; (editor) *Hilaire Belloc, Letters,* Macmillan, 1958; *The Christian Theatre,* Hawthorn, 1960; *William Rothenstein,* Eyre & Spottiswoode, 1962; *Ronald Knox in His Writings,* Sheed, 1965; *The Life of Eric Gill,* Kenedy, 1965; *Teilhard de Chardin: A Biography,* Collins, 1967, published as *The Life of Teilhard de Chardin,* Harper, 1968.

Vanier: Soldier, Diplomat and Governor General: A Biography, Collins, 1970; *The Property Basket: Recollections of a Divided Life* (autobiography), Collins, 1970; (with others) *Teilhard de Chardin: Remythologization,* Argus Communications, 1970; (editor) William Bridges-Adams, *Letter Book,* Society for Theatre Research, 1971; *Essays by Divers Hands: Being the Transactions of the Royal Society of Literature,* Volume XXXVII, Oxford University Press, 1972; *Shakespeare on the Stage: An Illustrated History of Shakespearian Performance,* Little, Brown, 1973; *George Bernanos: A Study of the Man and the Writer,* Harvill Press, 1973; *A Companion Guide to Burgandy,* Collins, 1975; *Francois Mauriac: A Study of the Writer and the Man,* Chatto & Windus, 1976; *Furia: A Novel Based on the Murder of the Poet Garcia Lorca,* Weidenfeld & Nicholson, 1976; *Shakespeare: The Man and His Achievement,* Stein & Day, 1977. Contributor to periodicals.

SIDELIGHTS: Robert Speaight was notable both as an actor and a theatre scholar. Among the books he produced during his four-decade career is a critical study, *Shakespeare: The Man and His Achievement.* Addressing the general audience in this work, the author contended that the themes of Shakespeare's plays were related to the bard's personal life. S. Schoenbaum, in his *New Republic* review of the book, noted that some readers will "inevitably disagree with some of what Speaight says. But the theatrical approach to [Shakespeare's life] is an extremely important one, and the author is so wise, and agreeably avuncular . . . that his audience will return to the theater . . . with a renewed sense of the ever-fresh vitality of a prodigal body of dramatic writing."

Speaight was fluent in French; some of his works were translated into that language.

AVOCATIONAL INTERESTS: Walking, riding.

BIOGRAPHICAL/CRITICAL SOURCES: New Republic, November 17, 1973, June 29, 1974, May 21, 1977; William B. Wahl, *Poetic Drama Interviews,* Institut fuer Englische Sprache und Literatur, Universitat Salzburg, 1976; *Spectator,* January 22, 1977; *New York Times,* June 23, 1977.†

* * *

SPELVIN, George
See PHILLIPS, David Atlee

* * *

SPENCER, Colin 1933-

PERSONAL: Born July 17, 1933, in London, England; son of Harry (a master builder) and Gypsy (Heath) Spencer; married Gillian Ghapman (an archaeologist), October 2, 1959 (divorced, 1969). *Education:* Studied at Brighton Art College. *Politics:* Socialist. *Religion:* Humanist. *Home:* 44, Lonsdale Sq., London N.1, England. *Agent:* JCA Literary Agency, Inc., 242 West 27th St., New York, N.Y. 10001.

CAREER: Full-time writer and painter. Paintings exhibited in Cambridge and London. *Military service:* British Army, Royal Army Medical Corps, 1950-52. *Member:* Writer's Guild of Great Britain (chairman, 1982-83).

WRITINGS—Novels, except as indicated: *An Absurd Affair,* Longmans, Green, 1961; *Anarchists in Love* (Book I of quartet), Eyre & Spottiswoode, 1963, published as *The Anarchy of Love,* Weybright, 1967; *Poppy, Mandragora and the New Sex,* Anthony Blond, 1966; *Asylum,* Anthony Blond, 1966; *The Tyranny of Love* (Book II of quartet), Weybright, 1967; *Lovers in War* (Book III of quartet), Anthony Blond, 1970; *Panic,* Secker & Warburg, 1971; *How the Greeks Kidnapped Mrs. Nixon,* Quartet Books, 1974; *The Victims of Love* (Book IV of quartet), Quartet Books, 1978; *Gourmet Cooking for Vegetarians* (nonfiction), Deutsch, 1978; *Good & Healthy* (nonfiction), Robson Books, 1983.

Plays: "The Ballad of the False Barman" (musical; music by Clifton Parker), first produced in London at Hampstead Theatre Club, 1966; "Spitting Image" (first produced in London at Hampstead Theatre Club, 1968; produced on West End at Duke of York's Theatre, 1968; adapted for American stage by Donald Driver and produced Off-Broadway at Theatre de Lys, February 19, 1969), published in *Plays and Players*, September, 1968; "The Trail of St. George," first produced at Soho Theatre, March 8, 1972; "The Sphinx Mother," first produced in Salzburg, Austria, 1972; "Why Mrs. Newstadter Always Loses," first produced in London, 1972; "Summer at Camber—39," first produced in London, 1973; "Keep It in the Family," first produced at Soho Theatre, 1978.

Also author of television documentary, "Vandal Rule OK," produced by Independent Television, 1979. Food columnist for the *Guardian*; contributor to *London*, *Transatlantic Review*, and other periodicals.

SIDELIGHTS: Commenting on Colin Spencer's *The Anarchy of Love* and *The Tyranny of Love*, Guy Davenport notes in *National Review* that the two novels are "vividly drawn, wonderfully heard, and quite powerfully written. . . . England has many writers more polished than Mr. Spencer, but none quite so wildly energetic in his passion for reality." As a *Times Literary Supplement* critic explains, the two books join with *Lovers in War* and *The Victims of Love* to create a quartet that tells "the continuing story of the Simpson family whose personal—principally sexual—problems have led to fragmentation of both family and individual life."

Spencer's 1971 work *Panic* is "a study of dual obsessions: of pederasty and child murder on the one hand, and on the other the overwhelming, morbid desire of the father of a murdered girl to come face to face with her killer," according to another *Times Literary Supplement* reviewer. "The book is set in Brighton, and how good Mr. Spencer is at extracting the last drop of atmosphere from that over-described town," adds Susan Hill in *New Statesman*. Hill concludes, "[Spencer] makes [the seaside resort's] beautiful extravagances seem peculiarly sinister."

BIOGRAPHICAL/CRITICAL SOURCES: National Review, November 5, 1968; *Washington Post*, December 24, 1968; *Transatlantic Review*, spring, 1970; *New Statesman*, February 20, 1970, October 29, 1971; *Spectator*, January 15, 1972, February 18, 1978.

* * *

SPERBER, Murray A(rnold) 1940-

PERSONAL: Born November 30, 1940, in Montreal, Quebec, Canada; son of Lawrence L. (a retailer) and Gladys (Epstein) Sperber; married Aneta Wharry (a photographer), March 26, 1966. *Education:* Purdue University, B.A., 1961; University of California, Berkeley, M.A., 1963, Ph.D., 1974. *Politics:* "Left." *Religion:* Jewish. *Home address:* 333 South Lincoln St., Bloomington, Ind. 47401. *Office:* Department of English, BH-442, Indiana University, Bloomington, Ind. 47405.

CAREER: College of the Holy Names, Oakland, Calif., instructor in English, 1964-65; University of California, Extension Divisions in San Francisco and Berkeley, instructor in English, 1966-68; Indiana University at Bloomington, lecturer, 1971-74, assistant professor, 1974-78, associate professor of modern literature, film, and creative writing, 1978—. *Member:* American Federation of Teachers. *Awards, honors:* Canada Council fellow in England and France, 1969-71.

WRITINGS: (Editor) *And I Remember Spain: A Spanish Civil War Anthology*, Macmillan, 1974; (editor) *Arthur Koestler: A Collection of Critical Essays*, Prentice-Hall, 1977; *Politics and Literature: A Textbook*, Hayden, 1978; *George Orwell*, Unger, 1984. Contributor to literature and film journals.

SIDELIGHTS: Murray A. Sperber once told *CA*: "In my writing and teaching, I attempt to persuade people that politics informs all of life, including literature and film, and that the serious question for the artist is not how to escape from politics (those who try to flee merely serve the regime in power) but how best to become aware of politics and how best to integrate this awareness into one's life and work. Colleagues tell me that politics and literature is no longer fashionable; I reply that I'm in it for the duration."

* * *

SPERRY, Len 1943-

PERSONAL: Born December 1, 1943, in Milwaukee, Wis.; son of Leonard V. (an engineer) and Wanda R. (a nurse; maiden name, Sadowski) Sperry; married, 1967; children: one. *Education:* St. Mary's College, Winona, Minn., A.B. (cum laude), 1966; Northwestern University, Ph.D., 1970; Alfred Adler Institute, postdoctoral certificate in psychotherapy, 1972; U.S. International University, Ph.D. (clinical psychology), 1976. *Politics:* Independent. *Religion:* Roman Catholic.

CAREER: Chicago Archdiocesan Schools, Chicago, Ill., member of psychological service, 1968-69; DePaul University, Chicago, instructor of education, 1969-70; St. Mary's College and Notre Dame University, South Bend, Ind., assistant professor of educational psychology, 1970-71; Marquette University, Milwaukee, Wis., associate professor of educational psychology, 1971-74; University of Wisconsin—Milwaukee, visiting associate professor of educational psychology, 1974-75; U.S. International University, San Diego, Calif., clinical supervisor in psychology, beginning 1975. Consultant, Illinois State Commission on Urban Education, 1970, and American Appraisal Associates, 1972. *Member:* American Educational Research Association, American Psychological Association, American Personnel and Guidance Association, Wisconsin Society of Adlerian Psychology (president, 1974-75), Phi Delta Kappa.

WRITINGS: (Editor) *Learning Performance and Individual Differences*, Scott, Foresman, 1972; (co-author) *Modular Education Programming*, American Appraisal Co., 1973; (with L. R. Hess) *Contact Counseling: Developing People in Organizations*, Addison-Wesley, 1974; *Developing Skills in Contact Counseling*, Addison-Wesley, 1975; (with D. J. Mickelson and P. H. Hunsaker) *You Can Make It Happen: A Guide to Self-Actualization and Organizational Change*, Addison-Wesley, 1977; *The Together Experience: Getting, Growing, and Staying Together in Marriage*, Beta Book, 1978; *The Decision Book*, Beta Book, 1980. Contributor to psychology journals. Member of editorial board, *Reading Improvement Journal*, 1973.†

* * *

STANSKY, Peter (David Lyman) 1932-

PERSONAL: Born January 18, 1932, in New York, N.Y.; son of Lyman (a lawyer) and Ruth (Macow) Stansky. *Education:* Yale University, B.A., 1953; King's College, Cambridge, B.A., 1955, M.A., 1959; Harvard University, Ph.D., 1961. *Office:* Department of History, Stanford University, Stanford, Calif. 94305. *Agent:* Wallace & Sheil Agency, Inc., 177 East 70th St., New York, N.Y. 10021.

CAREER: Harvard University, Cambridge, Mass., instructor, 1961-64, assistant professor of history, 1964-68; Stanford University, Stanford, Calif., associate professor, 1968-74, professor, 1974-75, Frances and Charles Field Professor of History, 1975—. *Member:* American Historical Association, Conference of British Studies. *Awards, honors:* Guggenheim fellowship, 1966-67 and 1974-75; American Book Award nomination, with William Abrahams, 1981, for *Orwell: The Transformation.*

WRITINGS: Ambitions and Strategies, Oxford University Press, 1964; (with William Abrahams) *Journey to the Frontier: Two Roads to the Spanish Civil War,* Little, Brown, 1966; (editor) *The Left and War,* Oxford University Press, 1969; (editor) *John Morley Nineteenth-Century Essays,* University of Chicago Press, 1970; (with Abrahams) *The Unknown Orwell,* Knopf, 1972; *England since 1867,* Harcourt, 1973; (editor) *Churchill: A Profile,* Hill & Wang, 1973; (editor) *The Victorian Revolution,* F. Watts, 1973; (with Abrahams) *Orwell: The Transformation,* Knopf, 1979; *Gladstone: A Progress in Politics,* Little, Brown, 1979. Articles and reviews have appeared in *Victorian Studies, Partisan Review, History Today,* and other history journals.

SIDELIGHTS: Peter Stansky, in an interview with Alice Adams for the *New York Times Book Review,* explains how he and joint author William Abrahams came to write their in-depth literary biographies of George Orwell: "Actually it goes back . . . to the early 50's, when I was an undergraduate at Yale. My senior thesis was about young English writers who took part in the Spanish Civil War, on the side of the Republic, and I paid particular attention to John Cornford and Julian Bell, whose stories [Abrahams] and I would write about in *Journey to the Frontier*—and to George Orwell. You couldn't write about Englishmen in Spain and leave out Orwell. There was never a thought of *not* writing about him. What we hadn't thought, taking up the topic, was that it would evolve in so complex a way and over so many years. Perhaps if we had known what was ahead, we might have been too intimidated to begin."

The authors' years of research resulted in two lengthy volumes, *The Unknown Orwell* (1972) and *Orwell: The Transformation* (1979). While the former work examines Orwell's early years, *The Transformation* is "a close portrait of the making of a political writer and revolutionary" between 1933 and 1937, according to Eric Homberger in the *Times Literary Supplement.* A *New York Times* reviewer explains: "To get at the truth behind the [Orwell] image is only the incidental purpose of Mr. Abraham's and Mr. Stansky's project. What they were primarily concerned with when they undertook their study was to discover how Eric Blair, the sensitive, introverted son of an officer in the Bengal civil service, transformed himself into the George Orwell who has come down to posterity." The task "required a special sensitivity, for Orwell's work appears so clear and above board as to require little exegesis, and his stature as 'one of the few contemporary writers who really matter,' as Irving Howe put it, demands a scrupulous respect," comments Ivan R. Dee in *Chicago Tribune Book World.* "The authors *have* dealt sensitively—even delicately—with the details of Orwell's life," Dee adds.

In contending with the lack of primary material on Orwell (his papers are protected in conformance with his wish that no biography be written about him), Stansky and Abrahams should be forgiven, believes Dee, for creating a work that is "less than full-bodied." While calling the book "generous in feeling . . . so balanced in perception and judgment," Irving Howe also finds its portrait of Orwell somewhat less than complete. In his *New York Times Book Review* article, Howe concludes: "Messrs. Stansky and Abrahams have done a real service in destroying the sentimental image of Orwell as 'secular saint.' They show him as a human being, irritable, fallible, opinionated. But they reduce the scope of his humanity in behalf of an overdrawn contrast between before [his transformation to political writer] and after. . . . [The authors], for the book they have set out to write, are too much the creatures of our subdued moment. They have restored to us the irritable Eric Blair. But where is the passionate George Orwell?" The *New York Times,* critic, however, commends the authors' portrait as "so vivid that we can practically picture [Orwell] entering the room."

BIOGRAPHICAL/CRITICAL SOURCES: New York Times, June 11, 1979; *New York Times Book Review,* July 8, 1979, April 20, 1980; *Times Literary Supplement,* January 11, 1980; *Chicago Tribune Book World,* April 20, 1980; *Washington Post Book World,* May 11, 1980.

* * *

STAVE, Bruce M(artin) 1937-

PERSONAL: Born May 17, 1937, in New York, N.Y.; son of Bernard R. (an attorney) and Mildred (Silberman) Stave; married Sondra T. Astor (a regional library coordinator, food columnist, and restaurant critic), June 16, 1961; children: Channing M.L. *Education:* Columbia University, A.B., 1959, M.A., 1961; University of Pittsburgh, Ph.D., 1966. *Politics:* Democrat. *Home:* 200 Broad Way, Coventry, Conn. 06238. *Office:* Department of History, University of Connecticut, Storrs, Conn. 06268.

CAREER: Samuel Lubell Associates, New York, N.Y., and Washington, D.C., political pollster (intermittently), 1958-64; University of Bridgeport, Bridgeport, Conn., instructor, 1965-66, assistant professor of history, 1966-70; University of Connecticut, Storrs, assistant professor, 1970-71, associate professor, 1971-75, professor of history, 1975—, director of oral history project, 1979-81, director of Center for Oral History, 1981—. Fulbright professor of American history in India, 1968-69, and New Zealand, Australia, and Philippines, 1977. Guest fellow and visiting lecturer in history, Yale University, fall, 1976.

MEMBER: American Historical Association, Organization of American Historians, Oral History Association, Social Science History Association, Immigration History Society, Academy of Political Science, American Association of University Professors, New England Historical Association, New England Association of Oral History (president, 1982-83), Association for the Study of Connecticut History, Connecticut Civil Liberties Union (member of board, 1967-68 and 1978-81), Northeastern Connecticut Civil Liberties Union (founder and member of board, 1972—; president, 1975-76), Fairfield County (Conn.) Civil Liberties Union (chairman, 1967-68), Greater Hartford (Conn.) Civil Liberties Union (vice-chairman, 1971-72). *Awards, honors:* National Endowment for the Humanities fellowship, 1974; Harvey Kantor Memorial Award from New England Association of Oral History, 1977, for outstanding achievement in oral history; grant for public programs from National Endowment for the Humanities and Connecticut Humanities Council, 1980-84.

WRITINGS: The New Deal and the Last Hurrah: Pittsburgh Machine Politics, University of Pittsburgh Press, 1970; (editor) *Urban Bosses, Machines, and Progressive Reformers,* Heath, 1972, revised edition (with wife, Sondra Astor Stave), Robert E. Krieger, 1984; (editor with D. L. Ashby) *The Discontented Society,* Rand McNally, 1972; (editor and contributor) *So-*

cialism in the Cities, Kennikat, 1975; *The Making of Urban History,* Sage Publications, 1977; (editor) *Modern Industrial Cities: History, Policy, and Survival,* Sage Publications, 1981. Contributor of articles and reviews to periodicals. *Journal of Urban History,* member of editorial board, 1974-76, associate editor, 1976—.

WORK IN PROGRESS: A research project, "Running Away: A History of Urban America."

AVOCATIONAL INTERESTS: Travel, photography.

* * *

STAVENHAGEN, Rodolfo 1932-

PERSONAL: Born August 29, 1932, in Frankfurt, Germany; immigrated to Mexico in 1940, naturalized in 1951; son of Kurt (a businessman) and Lore (Gruenbaum) Stavenhagen; married Maria Eugenia Vargas (an anthropologist), December 20, 1958 (divorced, 1983); children: Marina, Andrea. *Education:* University of Chicago, B.A., 1951; University of Mexico, M.A., 1958; University of Paris, Ph.D., 1965. *Home:* Aida 8, Lomas de San Angel Inn, Mexico City 20, D.F., Mexico. *Office:* El Colegio de Mexico, Apdo. 20-671, Mexico City 20, D.F., Mexico.

CAREER: National University of Mexico, Mexico, beginning 1956, began as instructor, became professor; Latin American Center for Research in the Social Sciences, Rio de Janeiro, Brazil, general secretary, 1962-65; International Institute for Labour Studies, Geneva, Switzerland, senior staff associate, 1969-71; El Colegio de Mexico, Mexico City, director of department of sociology, 1972-77; director general for popular cultures, Ministry of Education, 1977-79; United Nations Educational, Scientific and Cultural Organization (UNESCO), Paris, France, assistant director general, 1979-81; El Colegio de Mexico, general academic coordinator, 1983—. *Member:* International Social Science Council, Latin American Social Science Council, Latin American Sociological Association, Latin American Faculty of Social Sciences (president), Society for Applied Anthropology.

WRITINGS: Classes, Colonialism and Acculturation, Social Science Institute, Washington University, 1965; (contributor) *Neolatifundismo y explotacion de Emiliano Zapata a Anderson, Clayton & Co.,* Nuestro Tiempo (Mexico), 1968; *Las Clases sociales en las sociedades agrarias,* Siglo XXI (Mexico), 1969, translation by Judy Hellman published as *Social Classes in Agrarian Societies,* Doubleday, 1975; (editor) *Agrarian Problems and Peasant Movements in Latin America,* Doubleday, 1970; *Sociologia y subdesarrollo,* Nuestro Tiempo, 1971; (coauthor) *Estructura agraria y desarrollo agricola en Mexico,* Fondo de Cultura Economica (Mexico), 1974; *Testimonios,* Universidad Nacional Autonoma de Mexico, 1978; *Problemas etuicos y campesinos,* Instituto Nacional Indigenista, 1980; *Between Underdevelopment and Revolution,* South Asia Books, 1981; *Peasant Societies and Development,* Iwanami, 1981. Contributor of articles to various scholarly journals.

WORK IN PROGRESS: A comparative study of ethnicity and social and economic development.

* * *

STEBBINS, Robert A(lan) 1938-

PERSONAL: Born June 22, 1938, in Rhinelander, Wis.; son of William N. (a business executive) and Dorothy (Guy) Stebbins; married Karin Y. Olson, January 11, 1964; children: Paul, Lisa, Christi. *Education:* Macalester College, B.A., 1961; University of Minnesota, M.A., 1962, Ph.D., 1964. *Politics:* None. *Religion:* None. *Home address:* P.O. Box 1056, Cochrane, Alberta, Canada T0L 0W0. *Office:* Department of Sociology, University of Calgary, Calgary, Alberta, Canada T2N 1N4.

CAREER: Presbyterian College, Clinton, S.C., associate professor of sociology, 1964-65; Memorial University of Newfoundland, St. John's, assistant professor, 1965-68, associate professor of sociology and chairman of department of sociology and anthropology, 1968-73; University of Texas at Arlington, professor of sociology, 1973-76; University of Calgary, Calgary, Alberta, professor of sociology and chairman of department, 1976—. President, St. John's Symphony Orchestra, 1968-69. *Military service:* Minnesota National Guard, 1956-64; became staff sergeant. *Member:* International Sociological Association, Canadian Sociology and Anthropology Association, American Sociological Association, Society for the Study of Symbolic Interaction, Society for the Study of Social Problems (member of publications committee, 1976-79), Pacific Sociological Association, International Society of Bassists (chairman of amateur division, 1974—). *Awards, honors:* Canada Council leave fellowship, 1971-72; National Endowment for the Humanities summer stipend, 1976.

WRITINGS: Commitment to Deviance: The Nonprofessional Criminal in the Community, Greenwood Press, 1971; *The Disorderly Classroom: Its Physical and Temporal Conditions,* Memorial University of Newfoundland, 1974; *Teachers and Meaning,* E. J. Brill, 1975; *Amateurs: On the Margin between Work and Leisure,* Sage Publications, 1979; (editor with William B. Shaffir and Allan Turowetz) *Fieldwork Experience: Qualitative Approaches to Social Research,* St. Martin's, 1980; (editor with Turowetz and Michael Rosenberg) *The Sociology of Deviance,* St. Martin's, 1982; *The Magician: Career, Culture, and Social Psychology in a Variety Art,* Clark, Irwin, 1984; *Sociology: The Study of Society,* F. E. Peacock, 1984.

Contributor of articles to journals in United States, Canada, and England. Member of editorial board, *Canadian Review of Sociology and Anthropology,* 1970-73; associate editor, *Journal of Jazz Studies,* 1973—.

WORK IN PROGRESS: Canadian Football as Work and Leisure: A Sociological Account of Amateur and Professional Life-Styles.

SIDELIGHTS: Robert A. Stebbins told *CA:* "The work in progress, the book on magicians, the book on amateurs, and other books to follow in the next five years or so number among the reports of my interest in amateur-professional relations in art, science, sport, and entertainment. Since early 1974, I have been investigating various kinds of amateurs and professionals in these four areas in an attempt to amass sufficient field data and interview data to write a definitive statement on the complicated interplay between and life-styles of those who pursue either a vocation or an avocation there. Among the other topics being studied are the careers of those who participate in these areas, the ways the central activity intersects with family roles and leisure or occupational roles, and the thrills and disappointments and costs and rewards connected with the activity."

* * *

STEINBERG, Erwin R(ay) 1920-

PERSONAL: Born November 15, 1920, in New Rochelle, N.Y.; son of Samuel (a women's clothes cutter) and Lea (Neumann)

Steinberg; married Beverly Mendelson, August 15, 1954; children: Marc W., Alan J. *Education:* Attended City College (now City College of the City University of New York), 1937-38, and Plattsburgh State Normal School (now State University of New York College at Plattsburgh), 1938-40; New York College for Teachers (now State University of New York at Albany), B.S., 1941, M.S., 1942; New York University, Ph.D., 1956. *Home:* 1376 Sheridan Ave., Pittsburgh, Pa. 15206. *Office:* Department of English, Carnegie-Mellon University, Pittsburgh, Pa. 15213.

CAREER: Carnegie-Mellon University, Pittsburgh, Pa., instructor, 1946-49, assistant professor, 1949-55, associate professor, 1955-61, professor of English, 1961-75, professor of English and interdisciplinary studies, 1975-81, Thomas S. Baker Professor of English and Interdisciplinary Studies, 1981—, dean, Margaret Morrison Carnegie College, 1960-73, dean, College of Humanities and Social Sciences, 1965-75, chairman of board, Carnegie-Mellon Education Center, 1968-75, director, Carnegie-Mellon Communications Design Center, 1979-81. Visiting scholar, Center for Advanced Study in Behavioral Sciences, 1970-71. Vice-chairman, Commission of Scholars, Illinois Board of Higher Education. Communications consultant to various companies in Pennsylvania, New York, Ohio, and California, and to Educational Testing Service, 1963-67, U.S. Office of Education, 1963-64, Learning Institute of North Carolina, 1965, and American Institutes for Research, 1965-66. *Military service:* U.S. Army Air Forces, 1943-46; became sergeant.

MEMBER: National Council of Teachers of English, Conference on College Composition and Communication, Modern Language Association, Kappa Delta Pi, Phi Delta Kappa, Phi Kappa Phi. *Awards, honors:* Carnegie Teaching Award, 1956; Distinguished Alumnus, State University of New York at Albany, 1969; Alumnus of the Year, State University of New York College at Plattsburgh, 1971.

WRITINGS: (With William M. Schutte) *Communication in Business and Industry,* Holt, 1960; (editor with Schutte) *Personal Integrity,* Norton, 1961; (with Schutte) *Communication Problems from Business and Industry,* Encyclopaedia Britannica Films, 1961; (editor) *The Rule of Force,* Norton, 1962; *Needed Research in the Teaching of English,* U.S. Department of Health, Education, and Welfare, Office of Education, 1963; (with others) *Curriculum Development and Evaluation in English and Social Studies,* Carnegie Institute of Technology, 1964; (editor with Lois S. Josephs and contributor) *English Education Today,* Noble, 1970; (editor with Alan M. Markman) *English Then and Now: Readings and Exercises,* Random House, 1970; *The Stream of Consciousness and Beyond in Ulysses,* University of Pittsburgh Press, 1973; (editor) *The Stream-of-Consciousness Technique in the Modern Novel,* Kennikat, 1979; (co-editor) *Cognitive Processes in Writing,* Erlbaum, 1980; (co-editor) *Exercises in the History of English,* University Press of America, 1983.

Contributor: G. Kerry Smith, editor, *Current Issues in Higher Education,* Association of Higher Education, 1963; A. J. McCaffrey, editor, *Implications of Research, Development, and Experimentation in American Education,* American Textbook Publishers Institute, 1964; M. E. Manty, editor, *New Theology—Number One,* Macmillan, 1964; Michael Shugrue, editor, *Patterns and Models for Teaching English,* National Council of Teachers of English, 1964; D. H. Russell, editor, *Research Design and the Teaching of English,* National Council of Teachers of English, 1964; Gary Tate, editor, *Reflections on High School English,* University of Tulsa, 1965; *Educationally Disadvantaged Students,* Council on Social Work Education, 1968; P. F. Neumeyer, editor, *Twentieth Century Interpretations of "The Castle,"* Prentice-Hall, 1969; (with Schutte) T. F. Stanley and B. Benstock, editors, *Approaches to "Ulysses,"* University of Pittsburgh Press, 1970; Fritz Senn, editor, *New Light on Joyce from the Dublin Symposium,* Indiana University Press, 1972.

General editor, "Insight" series, Noble, 1968-73. Contributor to numerous periodicals and journals, including *Literature and Psychology, Journal of Modern Literature, Modern Fiction Studies, James Joyce Review, Quarterly Journal of Speech, English Journal, Educational Forum, University Quarterly, PMLA,* and *American Journal of Orthopsychiatry.*

WORK IN PROGRESS: Archetype and Myth in Modernist Literature, completion expected in 1985.

SIDELIGHTS: The Stream of Consciousness Technique in the Modern Novel has been translated into Spanish.

*   *   *

STEISS, Alan Walter 1937-

PERSONAL: Born February 15, 1937, in Woodbury, N.J.; son of Walter and Martha (Schroeder) Steiss; married Patricia McClintock, June 13, 1959; children: Carol Jean, Darren Christopher, Todd Alan. *Education:* Bucknell University, A.B., 1959; University of Wisconsin, M.A., 1966, Ph.D., 1969. *Home:* 2004 Carroll Dr., Blacksburg, Va. 24060. *Office:* Office of Sponsors Programs, Virginia Polytechnic Institute and State University, Blacksburg, Va. 24061.

CAREER: State of New Jersey, Division of State and Regional Planning, Trenton, assistant planner, 1960-61, senior planner, 1961-62, principal planner, 1962-63, supervising planner, 1963-64, section chief, 1964-65; Virginia Polytechnic Institute and State University, Blacksburg, assistant professor, 1967-69, associate professor, 1969-72, professor, 1972—, assistant director, 1968-69, director of Center for Urban and Regional Studies, 1969-70, chairman of Division of Environmental and Urban Systems, 1969-75, associate dean, 1974-78, acting dean for research and graduate studies, 1978, associate dean for research in Office of the Provost, 1978-83, director of Sponsored Programs, 1982—, associate provost for research, 1983—.

Lecturer at Rider College, 1963-64, New York University, 1964, and Georgia Institute of Technology, 1968-70. Member of firm, Planning Sciences Organization, 1967-73, and Anthony J. Catanese & Associates, 1973; principal investigator, National Training and Development Service Urban Management Curriculum Development Project, 1976-78. Consultant to numerous state and industrial groups, including Trust Territory of the Pacific, 1968, State of Hawaii, 1974-77, Federal-State Land Use Planning Commission for Alaska, 1978, and Virginia Department of Health, 1978-79.

MEMBER: American Institute of Planners (chairman of committee on programs for planning students, 1960-64), Association of Collegiate Schools of Planning (member of executive committee, 1970-71; secretary, 1971-72), American Association of University Professors, National Urban Coalition, Urban America, Inc., Psi Chi, Lambda Alpha, Lambda Chi Alpha, Tau Delta Rho. *Awards, honors:* Named one of Outstanding Young Men in America by U.S. Junior Chamber of Commerce, 1970; named Outstanding Educator of America, 1972; Teaching Excellence Award, 1975.

WRITINGS: (With James Collins and George McKnight) *The Setting for Regional Planning in New Jersey*, New Jersey Department of Conservation and Economic Development, 1961; (with Collins) *An Open Space Plan for New Jersey*, New Jersey Department of Conservation and Economic Development, 1963; (with Harold F. Wise, Henry Fagin, and Edward Schten) *Planning Administration*, Wisconsin Department of Resource Development, 1966; *A Framework for Planning in State Government*, Council of State Governments, 1968.

(Contributor) James T. Murray, editor, *Dynamic Factors in Transportation*, Duke University Press, 1970; (contributor) *Handbook for Regional Research and Regional Planning*, Akademie fur Raumforschung and Landesplanung, 1970; (with Charles Burchard and F. D. Regetz) *A Public Service Option for Architectural Curricula*, Association of Collegiate Schools of Architecture, 1971; *Administracion y Presupuestos Publicos*, Editorial Diana, 1974; *Performance/Program Budgeting*, NTDS, 1978; (with Leo Herbert and Larry Killough) *Government Accounting and Control*, Brooks/Cole, 1983.

Published by Heath: (with Anthony J. Catanese) *Systemic Planning: Theory and Application*, 1970; *Public Budgeting and Management*, 1972; *Urban Systems Dynamics*, 1974; *Models for the Analysis and Planning of Urban Systems*, 1974; (with John Dickey, Michale Harvey, and Bruce Phelps) *Dynamic Change and the Urban Ghetto*, 1975; *Local Government Finance: Capital Facilities Planning and Debt Administration*, 1975; *Performance Administration*, 1980; *Management Control in Government*, 1982. Also author of other research reports on land use and urban planning. Contributor of more than fifty articles to planning and urban affairs journals in the United States and Europe.

WORK IN PROGRESS: With Leo Herbert and Larry Killough, *Fundamentals of Accounting and Control for Government Organizations*, for publication by McGraw; with Richard E. Zody, *Public Budgeting in the 80s*.

SIDELIGHTS: Alan Walter Steiss told CA: "My colleagues ask me how I find time to teach, hold down a full-time administrative post, and still find time to write a book every year or so. I tell them I teach because I enjoy the challenge of young minds who question rather than accept dogma. I work as an administrator because it affords me an opportunity to put into practice that which I teach (and to gain from such experience new insights to take back to the classroom—what some call 'war stories'). And I write books because the discipline of putting one's thoughts down in this extended format represents a culmination of the other two activities."

* * *

STENDAHL, Krister 1921-

PERSONAL: Born April 21, 1921, in Stockholm, Sweden; came to United States in 1954; son of Olof (an engineer) and Sigrid (Ljungquist) Stendahl; married Brita Johnsson, September 7, 1946; children: John, Anna, Dan. *Education:* University of Uppsala, B.D., 1944, Teol. lic., 1949, Th.D., 1954; also studied at Cambridge University and in Paris, France. *Home:* 85 Trowbridge St., Cambridge, Mass. 02138. *Office:* Harvard University Divinity School, 45 Francis Ave., Cambridge, Mass. 02138.

CAREER: Clergyman of Church of Sweden (Lutheran), and pastor of Lutheran Church of America, 1968—. Assistant priest in diocese of Stockholm, Sweden, 1944-46; University of Uppsala, Uppsala, Sweden, chaplain to students, 1948-50, instructor in New Testament and Old Testament exegesis, 1951-54; Harvard University, Divinity School, Cambridge, Mass., assistant professor, 1954-56, associate professor, 1956-58, John H. Morison Professor of New Testament Studies, 1958-63, Frothingham Professor of Biblical Studies, 1963-68, dean and John Lord O'Brian Professor, 1968-79, professor of divinity, 1979-80, Andrew W. Mellon Professor of Divinity, 1981—. *Member:* American Academy of Arts and Sciences (fellow), Studiorum Novi Testamenti Societas, Society for Religion in Higher Education, Society of Biblical Literature, Society Pro Fide Christianismo, Nathan Soederblom Saellskapet. *Awards, honors:* A.M., Harvard University, 1956; Guggenheim fellowship, 1959-60 and 1974-75; Litt.D., Uppsala College, East Orange, N.J., 1963, Thiel College, 1966; D.D., Colby College, 1970, St. Olaf College, 1971, Whittier College, 1971; S.T.D., Carthage College, 1971; L.L.D., Susquehanna University, 1973; L.H.D., Miami University, Oxford, Ohio, 1978, Hebrew Union College, 1980, Brandeis University, 1981.

WRITINGS: *Bibelns Mening* (title means "The Meaning of the Bible"), Svenska Kyrkens Diakonistyrelsens Bokforlag (Stockholm), 1952; *The School of St. Matthew and Its Use of the Old Testament*, Gleerups (Lund), 1954, 2nd edition, 1968; (editor and contributor) *The Scrolls and the New Testament*, Harper, 1957, Greenwood Press, 1975; (editor and author of introduction) *Immortality and Resurrection: Four Essays* (Ingersoll lectures), Macmillan, 1965; *The Bible and the Role of Women*, Fortress, 1966; (author of introduction) Leo Baeck, *The Pharisees and Other Essays*, Schocken, 1966; (author of foreword) Johannes Munck, *Christ and Israel: An Interpretation of Romans 9-11*, Fortress, 1967.

(Author of foreword) Merle Severy, editor, *Great Religions of the World*, National Geographic Society, 1971; (author of foreword) Anton Fridrichsen, *The Problem of Miracle in Primitive Christianity*, Augsburg, 1972; *Holy Week*, Fortress, 1974; (with Theodore A. Gill and Robert Bellah) *Religion and the Academic Scene*, edited by David Noel Freedman and A. Theodore Kachel, [Waterloo, Ontario], 1975; *Paul among Jews and Gentiles and Other Essays*, Fortress, 1976.

Contributor to *Interpreter's Dictionary of the Bible*, *Encyclopaedia Britannica*, and of over 150 articles and reviews to theological journals in the United States and abroad. †

* * *

STEPHENS, W(illiam) P(eter) 1934-

PERSONAL: Born May 16, 1934, in Penzance, Cornwall, England; son of Alfred Cyril William Joseph and Jennie Eudora (Trewavas) Stephens. *Education:* Attended Cambridge University, 1952-57, University of Lund, 1957-58, University of Strasbourg, 1965-67, and University of Muenster, 1966-67; Cambridge University, M.A., 1961, B.D., 1971; University of Strasbourg, Docteur es sciences religieuses, 1967. *Office:* The Queen's College, Somerset Rd., Birmingham B15 2QH, England.

CAREER: Hartley Victoria College, Manchester, England, assistant tutor in New Testament, 1958-61; University of Nottingham, Nottingham, England, Methodist chaplain, 1961-65; minister of Methodist church in Shirley, Croydon, England, 1967-71; Hartley Victoria College, Ranmoor Chair of Church History, 1971-73; University of Bristol, Wesley College, Bristol, England, Randles Chair of Historical and Systematic Theology, 1973-80; The Queen's College, Birmingham, England, research fellow, 1980-81, lecturer in church history, 1981—.

Fernley Hartley Lecturer, 1972, 1982; James A. Gray Lecturer at Duke University, 1976. Chairman of Shirley Group of Churches, 1969-70, Croydon Anti-Apartheid Group, 1970-72, Withington World Development Movement, 1972-73, and British Council of Churches Advisory Committees on Western Europe, 1974—, and East-West Relations, 1975—. Member of Bristol City Council, 1976-83.

MEMBER: World Methodist Council International Commission, Lutheran World Federation, Society for Study of Theology (secretary, 1963-76), Conference of European Churches (member of advisory committee), British Roman Catholic-Methodist Commission.

WRITINGS: The Holy Spirit in the Theology of Martin Bucer, Cambridge University Press, 1970; *Faith and Love* (sermons), Epworth, 1971; *Christians Conferring,* Epworth, 1978; *Our Churches,* Catholic Truth Society, 1978; *Methodism in Europe,* [Cincinnati], 1982. Also author of many articles on churches in Eastern and Western Europe.

WORK IN PROGRESS: The Theology of Ulrich Zwingli.

SIDELIGHTS: W. P. Stephens told *CA:* "My writing on the reformation is primarily for scholars and students. My other works are intended for a wider audience, frequently interpreting . . . a theology or a tradition which [is not the reader's] own."

Stephens is competent in French, German, Swedish, Hebrew, Latin, and Greek.

* * *

STERN, Karl 1906-1975

PERSONAL: Born April 8, 1906, in Cham, Bavaria, Germany; died November 7, 1975, in Montreal, Quebec, Canada; naturalized Canadian citizen; son of Adolf and Ida (Rosenbaum) Stern; married Liselotte von Baeyer, 1936; children: Anthony, Katherine Stern Skorzewska, Michael. *Education:* Attended University of Munich and University of Berlin; University of Frankfurt, M.D., 1930. *Religion:* Roman Catholic. *Home:* 3800 Grey Ave., Montreal, Quebec, Canada.

CAREER: Served medical internship and residency in Germany; trained in psychoanalysis as Rockefeller fellow at German Research Institute for Psychiatry, 1932-36; National Hospital for Nervous Diseases, London, England, work under research grant, 1936-39; McGill University, Montreal, Quebec, lecturer in neuropathology, 1940-44, assistant professor of psychiatry, 1944-52; University of Ottawa, Ottawa, Ontario, professor of psychiatry, 1952-75; University of Montreal, Montreal, associate professor of psychiatry, 1955-75; St. Mary's Hospital, Montreal, psychiatrist-in-chief, 1958-68. Canadian representative, UNESCO Institute for Education, 1951-59. *Member:* Canadian Psychiatric Association, American Psychiatric Association, American Association of Neuropathologists, P.E.N. *Awards, honors:* Christopher Award, 1951, 1954; Canadian Newman Award, 1961; honorary Ph.D., Laval University.

WRITINGS: The Pillar of Fire, Harcourt, 1951; *The Third Revolution: A Study of Psychiatry and Religion,* Harcourt, 1954; *Through Dooms of Love* (novel), Farrar, Straus, 1960; *The Flight from Woman,* Farrar, Straus, 1965; *Love and Success, and Other Essays,* Farrar, Straus, 1975. Contributor of more than sixty articles to scientific journals.

SIDELIGHTS: "There is nothing purely rational which is strong enough to bind the heart of man," wrote psychiatrist Karl Stern in his autobiographical book *The Pillar of Fire.* Though educated as a scientist, Stern recognized the needs of the emotional as well as the rational part of man. A convert from Judaism to Roman Catholicism, Stern wrote *The Pillar of Fire* as an account of his spiritual growth, of his attempt to integrate the rational, the emotional, and the spiritual elements of his own psyche.

John M. Oesterreicher stated in *Commonweal* that *The Pillar of Fire* "is a book of unusual beauty, of the modern spiritual autobiographies the best. Utterly unpretentious, it is superbly written, evoking with great clarity many levels of experience: life in a small Bavarian town, at the German universities, in Munich, London and Montreal; the storm-heavy atmosphere of post-war Germany, the political crisis of the thirties; Jewish life at home, in the synagogue, in the youth movement; friendship and courtship; medicine, psychiatry, education, music, art. And interwoven with all these, religious search."

According to Stephen R. Maloney in a *Georgia Review* article, Stern "[was] a significant member of an important twentieth-century literary phenomenon: the Christian Renaissance . . . , [which] included figures as various as [T. S.] Eliot, [W. H.] Auden, [Jacques] Maritain, Caroline Gordon, and Evelyn Waugh. . . . Yet, among all the great modern Christian writers, no one [had] been more successful than Karl Stern in fusing a mode of life and a theologically-based philosophy. Moreover, Stern's achievements [were] not limited to his literary efforts; a Renaissance man in a dark age, Stern [had] accomplishments in various fields—from musical performance . . . to brain research and from theology to psychiatry." *The Pillar of Fire,* Maloney concluded, conveys "what 'it means to experience and to get to know something by suffering,' to 'suffer a thing through with your entire being, rather than to figure it out.'"

The Flight from Woman has been translated into French.

AVOCATIONAL INTERESTS: Philosophy, music.

BIOGRAPHICAL/CRITICAL SOURCES: Karl Stern, *The Pillar of Fire,* Harcourt, 1951; *New York Times,* February 25, 1951, November 8, 1975; *Commonweal,* March 2, 1951, December 24, 1954; *New York Herald Tribune Book Review,* April 15, 1951; *Nation,* July 7, 1951; *Saturday Review,* July 17, 1965; *New York Times Book Review,* August 1, 1965; *Georgia Review,* summer, 1974.

OBITUARIES: New York Times, November 8, 1975.†

* * *

STEVENS, Carla M(cBride) 1928-

PERSONAL: Born March 26, 1928, in New York, N.Y.; daughter of Charles James (an engineer) and Marie (an opera singer; maiden name, Minon) McBride; married Leonard A. Stevens (a writer), December 18, 1954; children: Timothy, Brooke, Sara, April. *Education:* New York University, B.A., 1946, M.A., 1949. *Home:* Christian St., Bridgewater, Conn. 06752. *Office:* Human Relations Center, New School for Social Research, New York, N.Y. 10011.

CAREER: Chairman of primary school in New York City, 1946-55; Addison-Wesley Publishing Co., Inc., New York City, juvenile editor of "Young Scott Books," 1955-69; New School for Social Research, New York City, instructor, 1969-82, director of Human Relations Center, 1982—. Member of board of directors of Regional Educational Services Center, 1967-70, and Pratt Education Center, 1969-83.

WRITINGS—All for children: *Rabbit and Skunk and the Scary Rock*, Scholastic Book Services, 1962; *Catch a Cricket*, Addison-Wesley, 1964; *Rabbit and Skunk and the Big Fight*, Scholastic Book Services, 1966; *Rabbit and Skunk and Spooks*, Scholastic Book Services, 1968; *The Birth of Sunset's Kittens*, illustrated with photographs by husband, Leonard A. Stevens, Addison-Wesley, 1969.

Your First Pet and How to Take Care of It, Macmillan, 1974; *Hooray for Pig!*, Seabury, 1975; *How to Make Possum's Honey Bread*, Seabury, 1976; *Stories from a Snowy Meadow*, Seabury, 1976; *Bear's Magic and Other Stories*, Scholastic Book Services, 1976; *Insect Pets: Catching and Caring for Them*, Greenwillow Books, 1978; *Pig and the Blue Flag*, Seabury, 1977; *Trouble for Lucy*, Clarion Books, 1979.

Sara and the Pinch, Clarion Books, 1980; *Rabbit on Bear Mountain*, Clarion Books, 1980; *Anna, Grandpa, and the Big Storm*, Clarion Books, 1982. Also author of *Good Friends, Bad Friends*, 1980.

WORK IN PROGRESS: Journals and How to Keep Them.

SIDELIGHTS: About Carla M. Stevens's *The Birth of Sunset's Kittens*, a critic for the *New York Times Book Review* writes, "[The narration] is economical, pleasantly explanatory and comfortable, urging one to consider that as it was with kittens, so it was with oneself." Zena Sutherland calls the book "an excellent job of straightforward treatment" in the *Saturday Review*. *Avocational interests:* Weaving, botany, early American history (especially the westward movement).

BIOGRAPHICAL/CRITICAL SOURCES: Saturday Review, April 19, 1969; *Book World*, May 4, 1969; *New York Times Book Review*, June 15, 1969.

* * *

STEVENS, Leonard A. 1920-

PERSONAL: Born November 7, 1920, in Lisbon, N.H.; son of Lawrence A. and Margaret (Healy) Stevens; married Carla McBride (a teacher of writing, New School for Social Research, New York, N.Y.), December 18, 1954; children: Timothy, Brooke, Sara, April. *Education:* Attended St. Anselm's College (now St. Anselm College); University of Iowa, B.A., 1947, M.A., 1949. *Politics:* Democrat. *Home:* Christian St., Bridgewater, Conn. 06752. *Office address:* Box 38, New Milford, Conn. 06776.

CAREER: Writer. Executive director of Housatonic Valley Association, Conn., 1973-74; speech maker for Citizens Committee for the Hoover Report, New York, N.Y.; news editor at Radio Station WSUI, Iowa City, Iowa, for two years. Former chairman, Bridgewater Board of Education; member, Bridgewater Conservation Commission. Delegate, National Democratic Convention, 1968, 1972; chairman, Bridgewater Democratic Town Committee. *Military service:* U.S. Army Air Forces, World War II; served in Guam with 20th Air Force; became captain.

WRITINGS—For young people, except as indicated: (With Ralph G. Nichols) *Are You Listening?* (adult), McGraw, 1957; *Old Peppersass: The Locomotive that Climbed Mount Washington*, Dodd, 1959; *New York to Rome: Jet Flight 808* (adult), Harper, 1962; *On Growing Older* (adult), U.S. Government Printing Office, 1964; *The Ill-Spoken Word: The Decline of Speech in America* (adult), McGraw, 1966; *The Trucks that Haul by Night*, Crowell, 1966; *The Elizabeth: Passage of a Queen*, Knopf, 1968; *North Atlantic Jet Flight*, Crowell, 1968; (photographic illustrator) Carla M. Stevens, *The Birth of Sunset's Kittens*, Addison-Wesley, 1969.

How a Law Is Made: The Story of a Bill against Air Pollution, Crowell, 1970; *The Town that Launders Its Water: How a California Town Learned to Reclaim and Reuse Its Water*, Coward, 1971; *Explorers of the Brain* (adult), Knopf, 1971; *Salute! The Case of the Bible vs. the Flag*, Coward, 1973; *Clean Water: Nature's Way to Stop Pollution*, Dutton, 1974; *Neurons: Building Blocks of the Brain*, Crowell, 1974; *Equal! The Case of Integration vs. Jim Crow*, Coward, 1976; *Trespass!: The People's Privacy vs. the Power of the Police*, Coward, 1977; *Death Penalty: The Case of Life vs. Death in the United States*, Coward, 1978; *Returning the Platte to the People: A Story of a Unique Committee, the Platte River Development Committee*, Greenway Foundation, 1981. Author of booklets and newspapers for Citizens Committee for the Hoover Report, New York. Contributor to magazines, including *Saturday Evening Post*, *Collier's*, *Nation*, *Reader's Digest*, *Nation's Business*, and *Catholic Digest*.

* * *

STOVER, Allan C(arl) 1938-

PERSONAL: Born June 28, 1938, in Cleveland, Ohio; son of Paul James (a railway clerk) and Blanche (Scramlin) Stover; married Elizabeth Bagaporo, September 6, 1971; children: Grace, Natalie. *Education:* Pacific State University, B.S.E.E. (with highest honors), 1962; attended Florida Institute of Technology, 1964; Vanderbilt University, M.S., 1978. *Residence:* Ellicott City, Md. *Office:* Westinghouse Electric, MS T-105, Box 1897, Baltimore, Md. 21203.

CAREER: Systems project engineer, Pan American World Airways, Florida, 1963-65; engineer, Philco Ford Corporation, 1966-71; planning installation engineer, RCA Service Company, 1972-73; engineer, Planned Systems International, 1973-74; Westinghouse Electric, Baltimore, Md., senior engineer, 1975—. Registered professional engineer in California; licensed able seaman (unlimited). Contributor to symposiums. *Military service:* U.S. Coast Guard, 1953-56.

MEMBER: Precision Instruments Association (senior member and chairman of Technical Committee on Automatic Test Equipment), Institute of Electrical and Electronic Engineers (senior member), Precision Measurements Association of the Philippines (founder and first president). *Awards, honors:* Outstanding Science Book award from National Science Teachers Association, 1974, for *You and the Metric System*.

WRITINGS: You and the Metric System, Dodd, 1974; *ATE: Automatic Test Equipment*, McGraw, 1984. Contributor to technical journals in the United States, Canada, and England.

WORK IN PROGRESS: A book on electronic measurements; a book on computers.

SIDELIGHTS: Allan C. Stover writes *CA*: "I began to write late in life, at the age of thirty-two.... I write at night and on the weekends. I enjoy taking a complex subject and breaking it down so the casual reader will understand it.

"I helped the Philippine Government in their changeover to the metric system. This gave me the idea to write a book on the subject, since it was obvious the United States would soon begin to change to metric. I knew that many books on the subject would be difficult for the student and casual reader to understand. I wanted my book to be one that would be easy to understand, but still cover everything everyone should know about the metric system. I have been in many countries where metric units were used, so I had a feel for the system. I have spent nine years in the Philippines, three years in South America, two years in Greece, and two years on islands in the Pacific.

"I began working with automatic test equipment (ATE) a few years ago. I soon found that few textbooks on ATE were available. After I gained some experience, I wrote a few chapters of a book on the subject and sent it off to McGraw-Hill. I thought I might as well start with the most prestigious technical book publisher and work down. They sent me a contract and I had my second book."

AVOCATIONAL INTERESTS: Travel (has visited Mexico, Okinawa, Taiwan, Japan, West and East Germany, Hong Kong, Nicaragua, Belize, Panama, Colombia, Ecuador, Zaire, South Africa, Antigua, Bahamas, Trinidad, Cuba, Jamaica, Haiti, Puerto Rico, Virgin Islands, and the Netherlands Antilles).

* * *

STRANGER, Joyce
See WILSON, Joyce M(uriel Judson)

* * *

STRAWSON, John 1921-

PERSONAL: Born January 1, 1921, in London, England; son of Cyril Walter (a headmaster) and Nellie (Jewell) Strawson; married Baroness Wilfried von Schellersheim, December 29, 1960; children: Viola, Carolin. *Education:* Attended Christ's College, Finchley, England. *Religion:* Church of England. *Home:* The Old Rectory, Boyton, Wiltshire, England. *Office:* Westland Pl., Yeovil, Somerset, England.

CAREER: British Army, 1940—, with current rank of major general. Assigned to 4th Hussars, 1942-50, 1952-54, 1956-58, British Staff College, 1951-52, and U.S. Armored Center, Fort Knox, Ky., 1954-56; instructor at British Staff College, 1958-60; with War Office, 1960-62; commanding Queen's Royal Irish Hussars, 1963-65; commanding 39th Infantry Brigade, 1966-68; at Imperial Defence College, 1969; chief of staff, Supreme Headquarters Allied Powers in Europe (SHAPE), Casteau, Belgium, 1970-72, at headquarters of United Kingdom Land Forces, 1972-76; Westland Aircraft, Ltd., Yeovil, Somerset, England, head of Cairo office, 1976-78. Military adviser, 1978—. *Member:* Cavalry and Guards Club (London). *Awards, honors*—Military: Bronze Star Medal (United States), 1946; Order of the British Empire, 1964; Commander of the Bath, 1975.

WRITINGS: The Battle for North Africa, Scribner, 1969; *Hitler's Battles for Europe,* Scribner, 1971 (published in England as *Hitler as Military Commander,* Batsford, 1971); *The Battle for the Ardennes,* Batsford, 1972; *Battle for Berlin,* Scribner, 1974; (co-author) *The Third World War: August 1985,* Macmillan, 1978; *El Alamein: Desert Victory,* Dent, 1981; *The Third World War: The Untold Story,* Sidgwick & Jackson, 1982. Contributor to *Times* (London), *Blackwood's Magazine,* and other publications.

WORK IN PROGRESS: A book on the British Special Air Service Regiment, for Secker & Warburg, publication expected in 1984.

AVOCATIONAL INTERESTS: All forms of sport, particularly horses and hunting.

BIOGRAPHICAL/CRITICAL SOURCES: Bookseller, May 15, 1971; *Times Literary Supplement,* January 29, 1982.

* * *

STRIEBER, Whitley 1945-

PERSONAL: Born June 13, 1945, in San Antonio, Tex.; son of Karl (a lawyer) and Mary (Drought) Strieber; married Anne Mattocks (a teacher), November 20, 1970. *Education:* University of Texas, B.A., 1968; London School of Economics and Political Science, certificate, 1968. *Agent:* Clyde Taylor, Curtis Brown Ltd., 575 Madison Ave., New York, N.Y. 10022. *Office:* 496 LaGuardia Pl., Suite 188, New York, N.Y. 10012.

CAREER: Writer. Cunningham & Walsh Advertising, New York, N.Y., account supervisor and vice-president, 1973-78. *Member:* Authors Guild, Authors League of America, Writers Guild, Science Fiction Writers of America, Literary Volunteers of New York City (member of board of directors).

WRITINGS—Novels, except as indicated: *The Wolfen,* Morrow, 1978; *The Hunger,* Morrow, 1981; *Black Magic,* Morrow, 1982; *The Night Church,* Simon & Schuster, 1983; (with James Kunetka) *Warday: And the Journey Onward,* Holt, 1984. Author of screenplay "Wolfen" (based on his novel *The Wolfen*), Orion Productions, 1978; also author of screenplays "Remember Thursday," and "The Process."

SIDELIGHTS: Whitley Strieber's success grows out of a series of novels concerned with the occult and the supernatural, including his first book *The Wolfen,* a work with over a million copies in print. One measure of that success is the fact that both *The Wolfen* and Strieber's next book *The Hunger* have been adapted into major motion pictures. Although he has for the most part chosen to work within the confines of a popular genre, the author's approach to horror fiction is an individual one, characterized by assiduous research and his own theories about the role such works play in society.

The plot of *The Wolfen* builds upon the traditional legend of the werewolf as portrayed in literature and folklore. The creatures it concerns differ somewhat from the popular concept of werewolves, however. The wolfen, writes Joseph McLellan in the *Washington Post Book World,* "are not human beings who turn into wolves on nights when the moon is full, but wolves who have evolved independently up to a humanoid level." Strieber sets his tale in the South Bronx, where a pack of these creatures lives an organized but hidden existence, venturing out at night to search for the food on which they survive: human beings. When the creatures are discovered by two policemen (who have difficulty persuading the world that they exist), a battle for survival ensues. While McLellan calls *The Wolfen* "standard adventure fare," Strieber's unique contribution to the genre is captured in the critic's commentary: "The book's real interest lies in its social criticism, its comparison of lupine and human behavior in a whole spectrum that ranges from mating patterns to basic social structures. The book is a howling success."

The Hunger deals with another of horror fiction's classic characters: the vampire. A *Publishers Weekly* reviewer states that in this book "a fast-paced, intriguing plot . . . with fairly plausible scientific 'findings' skillfully ensnares the readers." The story line of *The Hunger* follows the attempts of the vampire Miriam to find a human companion with whom to share her immortality. Like Miriam, her periodic succession of lovers needs to drink the blood of humans in order to survive. Unlike her, however, their lives last a mere two hundred years, after which they suddenly age within a few days. When the vampire's present lover John Blaylock reaches the end of his two hundred years, Miriam enters into a relationship with sleep and age researcher Sarah Roberts, with disastrous results.

While supernatural themes also play a prominent part in *Black Magic* and *The Night Church,* Strieber's third and fourth novels, the former is also concerned with the possibility of nuclear war, a subject important to the author and one that pervades the pages of his recent work *Warday: And the Journey Onward.* Strieber outlined for *CA* the motivation behind what he calls "a more serious" trend in his writings: "Contemporary fiction seems to me to have divided between frenetic commercial brouhaha and arid intellectualism. I wonder if it isn't possible to provide the public with entertainment and prose of value at the same time. To do so is my constant ambition."

MEDIA ADAPTATIONS: "The Hunger" was released by Metro-Goldwyn-Mayer/United Artists. Directed by Tony Scott, the film stars David Bowie, Catherine Deneuve, and Susan Sarandon. *Warday: And the Journey Onward* is scheduled to be filmed by Keith Barish productions, under the direction of Constantin Costa-Gavras.

AVOCATIONAL INTERESTS: Strieber "has participated in archaeological projects in Central America and has been involved with the attempt to authenticate the Holy Shroud that has been undertaken by a scientific group."

CA INTERVIEW

CA interviewed Whitley Strieber on August 22, 1983, at his office in New York City.

CA: You have many interests—history, archaeology, filmmaking, computer games, the supernatural. Is writing a means of channeling some of them into one activity?

STRIEBER: Yes, very definitely. And the new book, *Warday: And the Journey Onward,* involves another interest yet. It takes the form of a picaresque journey across the United States five years after a limited nuclear war.

CA: Did it grow out of Black Magic?

STRIEBER: It's a little related to *Black Magic* in the sense that a certain amount of research that I did for *Black Magic,* primarily the research into nuclear weapons, was also germane to *Warday.* But most *Warday* research was new. My collaborator was a man named James Kunetka, who is an expert on nuclear weapons and nuclear science. He has written a biography of J. Robert Oppenheimer and a nonfiction book about Los Alamos and the development of the atomic bomb called *City of Fire.*

CA: Did you have an early interest in writing?

STRIEBER: Yes, I wrote my first short story when I was six. It was twelve words long.

CA: That is *a short story. Are you still working in advertising, or are you writing full-time now?*

STRIEBER: I've been a full-time writer since 1978.

CA: Games have been an avocation of yours. Tell me about the history games that are played by mail. How do they work?

STRIEBER: First I should say that I simply have not had time for the games for the past three or four years. But the way they work is this: In the history game I designed, for example—it was called 1480 then; it must be about 1486 now because they've been playing for six years, I think—each player takes the role of the leader of a European state in a given year, and each month he carries out all of the activities that a real ruler in that time actually would have done, only he does it on paper. This is published to all of the other players in the game. And so it proceeds on a month-to-month basis, developing in real time. There's a game called the Concert of Europe that's been going on for over twenty years. This type of gaming was developed at the University of Chicago some twenty-five years ago, and I and another designer named Constantine Xanthos took the games to a much higher level of sophistication in the mid-1970s. An intense interest in history and economics and politics is a prerequisite for being in these games. One must have at least the equivalent of a Ph.D.'s knowledge of the subjects in order to play. The rules of 1480, for example, are 175 single-spaced typed pages. These are extremely serious games.

CA: You did some work with computer games too, didn't you?

STRIEBER: A little bit, but again I just scratched the surface. I found that computer programming affected my freedom of imagination and tended to make my thinking a little bit more structured than it should be for a fiction writer, so I pretty well abandoned that.

CA: What about filmmaking?

STRIEBER: Obviously I'm very interested in filmmaking, having had movies made from two of my books. I was interested in underground filmmaking when I lived in London in 1968 and 1969. I made a couple of films there, one of which was called "Remember Thursday," which was a straight art film, and the other was called "The Process," which was a documentary about an unusual religious cult. I don't know if those films still exist. "Remember Thursday" was shown at the Institute of Contemporary Art in London—to general opprobrium, I think.

CA: Your novels have fairly complex plots. How much of them do you work out in advance?

STRIEBER: Not too much. I have undergone a tremendous change. It really started last fall and came to a climax in November and December of last year. I have become a much more serious writer than I was before. Previously, I was writing entertainment pieces. Now, however, I am writing nonfiction and serious fiction (*Warday* is the first effort in this direction) because I feel that the world we live in is, in a certain sense, coming to a climax; the amount of tension is so high on so many different levels that we face a very real prospect of an explosive and civilization-destroying war. I don't feel that anyone with communication skills should ignore the problems that we face right now.

CA: So entertainment alone is no longer enough of a reason to write?

STRIEBER: Not for me personally. It certainly would be appropriate for some other people. But that doesn't mean my books won't be fun. I guarantee you will not be able to put down *Warday.*

CA: What caused this change in your writing?

STRIEBER: It was a build-up of things. First of all, I was deeply changed by the research I did on *Black Magic*. I think *Black Magic* is a very important and ignored book, by the way. As I was doing that research, I realized a lot about the nature of the mechanism of conflict that has been built up between the Soviet Union and the United States. It's a machine that could easily self-destruct at any moment, for many different reasons that go quite beyond the cliches of nuclear accident.

There are the most dangerous subtleties in the relationship between the Soviet Union and the United States that have not been plumbed. For example, I've heard rumors that the president will announce that the United States may be deploying, or is attempting to develop, satellite-based particle-beam weapons that will have the effect of making America invulnerable to attack by nuclear missiles. The next stage would then be that the United States, unilaterally, would disarm or greatly reduce its nuclear armaments once this system was deployed.

However, the danger is that the Soviet Union could view this as a highly provocative act and see the promise to disarm simply as a smokescreen. It could happen that if the Soviet Union is unable to simultaneously deploy a similar system of its own, it would end up with no choice but to attack before our system was deployed. And because of highly sophisticated targeting techniques, a nuclear war would by no means be the end of the world. Neither side is going to destroy everything in a fit of pique. What would happen in a nuclear war would be a series of surgical assaults back and forth between the two sides that would last over a period of however many days they dared to continue. It would be an awful experience and one that would lead, even if it was the most limited conceivable nuclear war, to such profound changes in life and in the liveability of the planet that our civilization could not continue as it is now. These things are *not* being considered by the planners. All they're considering is the level of immediate destruction that any given exchange may result in. We're very much closer to a nuclear war than we realize.

CA: And you wrote Warday *to get this message across?*

STRIEBER: Yes. And the reason I insisted on half a million dollars for the hardcover rights (and I could get it because it's a good book) was to make certain that the publisher would view it as the single most important thing they were doing at the time.

CA: Who are your literary heroes?

STRIEBER: The people who have influenced me most in horror novels have been, of the older ones, Algernon Blackwood and Sheridan Le Fanu; of more recent writers, Peter Straub and Ramsey Campbell. In terms of serious fiction I have been influenced heavily by Evelyn Waugh. I have been influenced by Anthony Powell. In nonfiction writing, Michael Grant's work has been very exciting to me because it's so accessible. There are so many writers running through my mind, because I really like reading; I read a tremendous amount. John Fowles I think has begun to influence me from a stylistic standpoint. **It's hard to say with a book like *Warday* exactly who the influences are. Certainly Studs Terkel is an influence on *Warday* because of the structure of the book.**

Influences can be really difficult to pinpoint. Sometimes writers influence you at levels you're not aware of. Another one who comes to mind is Edith Wharton. I've read her work with an avid interest and I have a tremendous amount of respect for it, but I can't tell you where in my own work Edith Wharton comes in except perhaps in a certain intricacy of plotting. I don't think I have ever written anything as good as her works—or John Fowles's either.

CA: Your earlier books are wonderfully scary. Do you have any thoughts about why thrillers have such a large popular appeal?

STRIEBER: I've changed my theories about this in the past couple of years. I believe that people who are happy not only enjoy being frightened but *need* to be frightened from time to time in order to relieve a certain amount of guilt that builds up in any kind of happy situation. I'll give you an example of what I mean. India has got a very active publishing industry, but they have absolutely no market for horror books. It is not a country of people who feel guilty, for example, about consuming a great deal. In the United States, up until 1979 horror stories were very popular. From 1979 through 1982 that popularity dropped off. That's because people were suffering; there was a recession on. They didn't need horror stories. Horror stories can play a rather healthy role in a happy society.

It can even be a civilizing role as long as they don't exploit aggressive or hostile emotions, and I hope mine never do. The only one I've ever written that had an element of bitterness in it was *The Night Church*. After I wrote that book I read it over—I mean actually when it was in galleys—and I said, this book is really too violent. This book is bitter. You're tired of these things. This is the last one you're going to write. It was the only really straight horror story I ever wrote and it certainly is the last one. The others all have an element of humanity in them. There's something wonderful about the ethical dilemma of the Wolfen. They aren't bad; it's just that they have to do something we consider bad in order to live. And it's the same thing with Miriam in *The Hunger*. She is simply a creature fulfilling her destiny in her place in nature—which incidentally is terribly unfortunate for everybody she meets!

CA: You must have done a lot of research for those novels.

STRIEBER: I do an enormous amount of research for everything I touch. I am an obsessive researcher. I am fascinated by the hidden.

CA: Will you do more supernatural thrillers?

STRIEBER: Not horror stories. I will probably do a sequel to *Warday* and then a novel about my home state of Texas.

CA: What kind of writing schedule do you keep? Do you write daily?

STRIEBER: I work like a maniac. I work from nine o'clock in the morning until six o'clock at night, with half an hour off for lunch. And I work six or seven days a week. I've worked as long as six months without taking a day off.

CA: You must enjoy the writing process itself.

STRIEBER: I'm enjoying it much more now than I was before I started writing more seriously.

CA: Do you get a lot of fan mail?

STRIEBER: I get at least ten or twelve letters a week, I would say. And when a book or a movie is out I get more than that.

I'm about six or seven months behind now, but I try to answer it all—the hostiles and the friendlies. I would say the friendlies are ninety-nine percent, the hostiles one percent; and the hostiles are all from people whose religious scruples have been offended in some way. I don't know why. *The Hunger* was involved in a book burning in Pennsylvania, along with some of Stephen King's and a lot of other well-known authors' works, and some rock'n'roll records. It makes me feel terrible. When I read the Bible, I can't seem to square it very well with what some of these people do in the name of Christ.

CA: Are you planning to do any commercial screenplays?

STRIEBER: I don't want to do screenplays. I'll spend a certain amount of time trying to make a movie project work, but not much. Film is a transitory medium. Books last, and they can make a difference in people's lives. Movies come and go very quickly.

CA: You seem to be quite happy with the course of your writing.

STRIEBER: I think that I have come to a new and important departure in my career, and I'm very excited about it.

BIOGRAPHICAL/CRITICAL SOURCES: Washington Post Book World, October 5, 1978; *Publishers Weekly*, December 12, 1980; *Los Angeles Times*, May 31, 1982; *Village Voice Literary Supplement*, June, 1982; *Times* (London), June 6, 1983; *Los Angeles Times Book Review*, July 31, 1983; *New York Times*, November 14, 1983.

—Interview by Jean W. Ross

* * *

STRONG, Susan
See REES, Joan

* * *

STUART, Alex
See STUART, (Violet) Vivian (Finlay)

* * *

STUART, V. A.
See STUART, (Violet) Vivian (Finlay)

* * *

STUART, (Violet) Vivian (Finlay) 1914-
(Barbara Allen, Fiona Finlay, William Stuart Long, Alex Stuart, V. A. Stuart)

PERSONAL: Indexed in some bibliographical sources under name Violet Vivian Mann; born January 2, 1914, in Rangoon, Burma; daughter of Sir Campbell Kirkman (director of Burma Oil Co.) and Lady Alice (Norton) Finlay; married third husband, Cyril William Mann (a banker), October 24, 1958; children: (previous marriages) Gillian Rushton, Jennifer Gooch, Vary and Valerie Stuart (twins). *Education:* Attended University of London; University of Budapest, pathologist qualification, 1938; Technical Institute, Newcastle, Australia, diploma in industrial chemistry and laboratory technique, 1942. *Politics:* Conservative. *Religion:* Church of England. *Home and office:* Hop Grove Farm Cottage, 461 Malton Rd., York, Yorkshire YO3 9TH, England.

CAREER: Historical novelist. Writers' Summer School, London, England, committee member, 1961-63, 1972—, vice-chairman, 1964, 1983, 1984, chairman, 1964-65, 1966-67, and 1969-71. *Military service:* Served on noncombat duty with Australian Forces, 1942-43, and as member of Women's Auxiliary Service with British Fourteenth Army in Burma, 1944-45; became lieutenant; received Burma Star and Pacific Star.

MEMBER: Romantic Novelists Association (co-founder; chairman, 1960-63), Society of Authors, Institute of Journalists, Crime Writers' Association, Society of Women Writers and Journalists, Military Historical Society, Society for Nautical Research, Navy Records Society, Association of Yorkshire Bookmen (vice-president, 1960-74), Burma Star Association (president of York and North-Eastern Area branch, 1958—). *Awards, honors: Star of Oudh* was chosen runner-up as best romantic novel of 1960, and *Like Victors and Lords* best historical romantic novel of 1964, by Romantic Novelists Association; Porgie Gold Medal, *West Coast Writers Review*, 1983, for *The Explorers*.

WRITINGS: Proud Heart, Jenkins, 1953; *Along Came Ann*, Jenkins, 1953; *Eyes of the Night*, Jenkins, 1954; *Unlit Heart*, Jenkins, 1954; *Pilgrim Heart*, Jenkins, 1955; *Lover Betrayed*, Jenkins, 1955; *No Single Star*, R. Hale, 1956; *Life Is the Destiny*, R. Hale, 1958.

The Summer's Flower, R. Hale, 1961; *Like Victors and Lords*, R. Hale, 1964, published under pseudonym V. A. Stuart as *Victors and Lords*, Pinnacle Books, 1972; *The Valiant Sailors*, R. Hale, 1964, published under pseudonym V. A. Stuart, Pinnacle Books, 1971; *The Beloved Little Admiral: The Life and Times of Admiral of the Fleet, the Honorable Sir Henry Keppel*, R. Hale, 1967, published under pseudonym V. A. Stuart, Pinnacle Books, 1968; *Black Sea Frigate*, R. Hale, 1971, published under pseudonym V. A. Stuart as *Hazard's Command*, Pinnacle Books, 1972.

(With George T. Eggleston) *His Majesty's Sloop-of-War "Diamond Rock,"* R. Hale, 1978.

Under pseudonym Barbara Allen: *Serenade on a Spanish Guitar*, Mills & Boon, 1956; *Doctor Lucy*, Mills & Boon, 1956; *Someone Else's Heart*, Mills & Boon, 1958; *The Gay Gordons*, Mills & Boon, 1961; *The Scottish Soldier*, R. Hale, 1965.

Under pseudonym Fiona Finlay: *Moon over Madrid*, Mills & Boon, 1957.

Under pseudonym William Stuart Long: "The Australians" series; published by Dell: *The Exiles*, 1979; *The Settlers*, 1980; *The Traitors*, 1981; *The Explorers*, 1982; *The Adventurers*, 1983; *The Colonists*, 1984.

Under pseudonym Alex Stuart; published by Mills & Boon, except as indicated: *The Captain's Table*, 1953; *Ship's Nurse*, 1954; *Soldier's Daughter*, 1954; *Island for Sale*, 1955; *Gay Cavalier*, 1955; *Huntsman's Folly*, 1956; *A Cruise for Cinderella*, 1956; *Bachelor of Medicine*, 1956; *The Last of the Logans*, 1957; *Queen's Counsel*, 1957; *Master of Guise*, 1957; *Garrison Hospital*, 1957, Arcadia House, 1958; *Daughters of the Governor*, 1958; *Master of Surgery*, 1958; *Castle in the Mist*, 1959; *The Peacock Pagoda*, 1959.

Star of Oudh, 1960; *Spencer's Hospital*, 1961; *Sister Margarita*, 1961; *Doctor Mary Courage*, 1961; *Doctor on Horseback*, 1962; *The Dedicated*, 1962; *The Piper of Laide*, 1963; *Maiden Voyage*, 1964; *Samaritan's Hospital*, 1965; *There but for Fortune*, 1966; *Strangers When We Meet*, 1968; *Random Island*, 1968.

Young Doctor Mason, 1970; *Research Fellow*, 1971; *The Bikers*, New English Library, 1971; *A Sunset Touch*, 1972; *On Her Majesty's Orders*, 1977.

Under pseudonym V. A. Stuart, except as indicated; all originally published by Pinnacle Books: *Brave Captains*, 1972; *Hazard of Huntress*, 1972; *Hazard in Circassia*, 1973; *Massacre at Cawnpore*, 1973; *Victory at Sebastopol*, 1973; *The Sepoy Mutiny*, 1973; *Cannons of Lucknow*, 1974; *Hazard to the Rescue*, 1974; *The Heroic Garrison*, 1975; *Guns to the Far East*, 1975; *Escape from Hell*, 1976, published under name Vivian Stuart as *Sailors on Horseback*, R. Hale, 1977. Unlisted books by V. A. Stuart may have originally been published under name Vivian Stuart (see above).

Also editor and publisher of a three-part series, "A Modern Writer's Guide."

WORK IN PROGRESS: Another volume in "The Australians" series, *The Goldseekers*.

SIDELIGHTS: Vivian Stuart told *CA:* "Having had the pen name I had used since 1953 purloined by another author—who published five novels in the [United States] as 'Vivian Stuart'—and being unable to elicit even a reply from either the offender or his agent, I was compelled to adopt a new pen name myself, that of William Stuart Long. This, however, turned out to be the best move I ever made. I signed a contract with the now famous book producer Lyle Kenyon Engel of Book Creations, Inc. and, working under his auspices, have enjoyed million copy sales for each of the titles in 'The Australians' series.

"As a Book Creations author, I now work with a highly trained and extremely efficient editorial staff; copy typing, proofreading, jacket designing, sales and promotion are all handled by BCI. All I am required to do is write the novels which, when you come to think of it, is really all an author ought to be required to do. Lyle Engel has transformed me into a bestselling writer, earning more than I did in well over twenty years as a professional novelist. . . . My only regret is that I did not sign up with Book Creations years ago."

BIOGRAPHICAL/CRITICAL SOURCES: El Paso Times, July 20, 1980, July 27, 1980; *Los Angeles Times*, October 16, 1983.

*   *   *

SULLIVAN, Mary W(ilson) 1907-

PERSONAL: Born December 25, 1907, in Grants Pass, Ore.; daughter of Roy Stanley (a "pioneer in the auto industry") and Adelia (Harth) Wilson; married Paul D. Sullivan (a machinery executive), April 15, 1931 (died June 6, 1979); children: Mary Anne, Molly, Denis Philip, Francis James, Margaret Catherine. *Education:* Attended University of Oregon, 1926-28, and Pasadena City College, 1967-77. *Politics:* Democrat. *Home:* 8811 Pacific Coast Highway, No. 118, Laguna Beach, Calif. 92651.

CAREER: Writer. McCormick Steamship Co., Portland, Ore., statistician, 1928-30; *Masonic Analyst* (magazine), Portland, Ore., member of staff, 1930-31. *Member:* P.E.N. (delegate from Los Angeles to international Congresses, 1976, 1977, and 1981; vice-president of Los Angeles chapter, 1978), Society of Children's Book Writers, Southern California Council on Literature for Children and Young People, Quill Pen Lunch Bunch Workshop, Alpha Phi. *Awards, honors:* P.E.N. Los Angeles Literary Award for Writing for Young People, 1983, for *Earthquake 2099*.

WRITINGS—Young adult novels; published by Thomas Nelson, except as indicated: *The Indestructible Old Time String Band*, 1975; *Bluegrass Iggy*, 1975; *Bluegrass Iggy* (different text; Arrow Book Club selection), Scholastic Book Services, 1976; *What's This About Pete?*, 1976; *Brian-Foot-In-the-Mouth*, 1978; *The VW Connection*, 1981; *Earthquake 2099*, Dutton, 1982.

"Happenings" series (remedial readers with teachers' manuals); published by Field Educational Publications, 1970: *Pancho Villa Rebels; Chili Peppers; Rattrap; Jokers Wild*.

WORK IN PROGRESS: Brenda's People, a book about a battered mother and daughter.

SIDELIGHTS: Mary W. Sullivan told *CA:* "As a volunteer librarian in the Catholic Boys School my sons attended, I saw the need for books on subjects other than sports. My first six books are about boys who are into teenage music, the seventh is about a boy who sews, likes it, and questions his masculinity. My next book is about a boy with a disastrous propensity for saying the wrong thing. The one after that focuses on a boy's love for Volkswagens and how he makes use of this love in finding a girl for his lonesome brother. Then comes the book I worked on for about ten years. It has to do with survival on the beach where I live after the expected earthquake. It pushes hard for an understanding of the importance of the adjustment of technology to nature, one of my deeply held convictions."

Two of Sullivan's remedial readers have been translated into Danish.

AVOCATIONAL INTERESTS: International travel (especially the British Isles).

*   *   *

SULLIVAN, Peggy (Anne) 1929-

PERSONAL: Born August 12, 1929, in Kansas City, Mo.; daughter of Michael C. (a florist) and Ella (O'Donnell) Sullivan. *Education:* Clarke College, Dubuque, Iowa, A.B., 1950; Catholic University of America, M.S. in L.S., 1953; University of Chicago, Ph.D., 1972. *Politics:* Independent. *Religion:* Roman Catholic. *Home:* 1508 Kennicott Court, Sycamore, Ill. 60178.

CAREER: Kansas City (Mo.) Public Library, assistant children's librarian, 1952-53; Enoch Pratt Free Library, Baltimore, Md., children's librarian and school services specialist, 1953-59; Arlington County (Va.) Public Library, children's work supervisor, 1959-61; Montgomery County Schools, Rockville, Md., library specialist, 1961-63; American Library Association, Chicago, Ill., project director, 1963-69; University of Pittsburgh, Graduate School of Library and Information Sciences, Pittsburgh, Pa., assistant professor, 1971-73; director, Office for Library Personnel Resources, American Library Association, 1973-74; University of Chicago, Graduate Library School, Chicago, associate professor and dean of students, 1974-77; Chicago Public Library, Chicago, assistant commissioner for extension services, 1977-81; Northern Illinois University, College of Professional Studies, DeKalb, dean, 1981—. Instructor at Catholic University of America, 1958, 1962-63, Drexel Institute, 1961, University of Maryland, 1961-62, Rutgers University, 1967, Syracuse University, 1968, University of Chicago, 1969, and Rosary College, 1969-70. Consultant to nineteen NDEA and Higher Education Act institutes. *Member:* American Library Association, Illinois Library Association, Chicago Library Club, Beta Phi Mu. *Awards, honors:* Tangley Oaks Fellowship, 1968.

WRITINGS: *The O'Donnells* (juvenile), Follett, 1956; *Impact: The School Library and the Instructional Program,* American Library Association, 1967; (editor) *Realization: The Final Report of the Knapp School Libraries Project,* American Library Association, 1968; *Many Names for Eileen* (juvenile), Follett, 1969; *Problems in School Media Management,* Bowker, 1971; *Carl H. Milam and the American Library Association,* H. W. Wilson, 1976; *Opportunities in Librarianship and Information Science,* Vocational Guidance Manuals, 1977; (with William H. Ptacek) *Public Libraries: Smart Practices in Personnel,* Libraries Unlimited, 1982. Regular reviewer for journals, including *School Library Journal,* 1958-79.

SIDELIGHTS: Peggy Sullivan told *CA:* "Many professional activities have distracted me from writing for children, but . . . I have several ideas perking. As a sometime storyteller in schools and libraries, I know what children enjoy most, and I realize how important stories—in all their many forms—are for them. I intend to contribute some more!"

* * *

SUMMERS, Gene F(ranklin) 1936-

PERSONAL: Born December 28, 1936, in Whitewater, Mo.; son of Glenn W. and Lara (Weisenstein) Summers; children: Teresa Lee, James, Jon, Robert. *Education:* Attended Southeast Missouri State College (now University), 1954-55; University of Tennessee, B.S., 1959, Ph.D., 1962. *Politics:* Democrat. *Religion:* Methodist. *Home:* 4660 Old Indian Trail, Black Earth, Wis. 53515. *Office:* Department of Rural Sociology, University of Wisconsin, Madison, Wis. 53706.

CAREER: Indiana State University, Terre Haute, instructor, 1962-63, assistant professor of sociology, 1963-64; University of Illinois at Urbana-Champaign, assistant professor of sociology, 1965-70; University of Wisconsin—Madison, associate professor, 1970-75, professor of sociology, 1976—. Visiting professor, Vanderbilt University, summers, 1963, 1964. *Member:* International Sociological Association, American Sociological Association, Community Development Society of America, Rural Sociological Society, Midwest Sociological Society, Southern Sociological Society. *Awards, honors:* National Institute of Mental Health postdoctoral fellowship at University of Wisconsin, 1964-65; Fulbright fellowship in Norway, 1978.

WRITINGS: (With C. L. Folse, R. L. Hough, and J. T. Scott) *Before Industrialization,* University of Illinois Press, 1970; (editor) *Attitude Measurement,* Rand McNally, 1970; *Industrial Invasion of Nonmetropolitan America,* Praeger, 1976; (editor with Arne Selvik) *Nonmetropolitan Growth and Community Change,* Heath, 1979; (editor with Selvik) *Energy Resource Communities,* MJM Publishing Co., 1982; (editor) *Technology and Social Change in Rural Areas,* Westview, 1983. Contributor to *Annals of the American Academy of Political and Social Science, American Sociological Review, Annual Review of Sociology, Social Forces, Rural Sociology, Sociological Quarterly, Multivariate Behavioral Research,* and numerous other periodicals.

* * *

SWANN, Lois 1944-

PERSONAL: Born November 17, 1944, in New York, N.Y.; married, August 15, 1964 (divorced, December 24, 1979); children: Peter, Polly. *Education:* Marquette University, B.A., 1966. *Home:* 12 West 72nd St., New York, N.Y. 10023.

CAREER: Writer. Manufacturers Hanover Trust, New York, N.Y., assistant secretary and publications consultant, 1983—. *Member:* Authors Guild, Authors League of America.

WRITINGS—Published by Scribner: *The Mists of Manittoo* (first novel in trilogy), 1976; *Torn Covenants* (second novel in trilogy), 1981.

WORK IN PROGRESS: Last book in American Revolutionary period trilogy, for Scribner.

BIOGRAPHICAL/CRITICAL SOURCES: *Cincinnati Enquirer,* August 22, 1976.

* * *

SWEENEY, James B(artholomew) 1910-

PERSONAL: Born July 7, 1910, in Philadelphia, Pa.; son of Anthony J. (a hotel owner) and Bertha (Collins) Sweeney; married Helen Ver (a lieutenant in U.S. Navy), December 2, 1944; children: Frank James. *Education:* Villanova University, B.S., 1932; attended University of Pennsylvania, School of Industrial Art, Philadelphia, University of Oklahoma, and University of Florida. *Home:* 4917 Ravenswood Dr., Apt. 255, San Antonio, Tex. 78227.

CAREER: Served four years with U.S. Merchant Marine before enlisting in Pennsylvania National Guard, 1940; U.S. Army, 1941-50, became regimental sergeant major, 1941, commissioned second lieutenant, Infantry, 1942, later transferred to staff of *Yank* (Army weekly); U.S. Air Force, officer, 1950-65, with duty as combat reporter during Korean War. *Member:* Authors Guild, Authors League of America, Armed Forces Writers League. *Awards, honors*—Military: Bronze Star (received as combat reporter in Korea), and sixteen other military medals. Civilian: Various medals and awards from Japanese government, Georgia Sheriff's Association, and for organizing, coaching, and managing youth marksmanship rifle teams.

WRITINGS: *Pictorial History of Oceanographic Submersibles,* Crown, 1970; *Pictorial History of Sea Monsters and Other Dangerous Marine Life,* Crown, 1972; *Vessels for Underwater Exploration,* Crown, 1973; (with Peter R. Limburg) *102 Questions and Answers about the Sea,* Messner, 1975; *Sea Monsters: A Collection of Eyewitness Accounts,* McKay, 1977; *Ghosts: Eyewitness Accounts,* McKay, 1979; *A Combat Reporter's Report,* F. Watts, 1980; *Disaster,* McKay, 1981; *True Spy Stories,* F. Watts, 1981; *A Pictorial Guide to Forts, Museums, and Historical Sites,* Crown, 1982. Contributor of articles and stories to periodicals.

SIDELIGHTS: James B. Sweeney lived in many parts of the world during his career in the military, including Japan, Germany, North Africa, England, Greece, and Turkey.

* * *

SWIDLER, Arlene (Anderson) 1929-

PERSONAL: Born March 6, 1929, in Milwaukee, Wis.; daughter of Perry H. (an engineer) and Marie (a teacher; maiden name, Wittman) Anderson; married Leonard J. Swidler (a teacher), May 11, 1957; children: Carmel, Eva-Maria. *Education:* Marquette University, A.B., 1950; University of Wisconsin, M.A., 1952; Villanova University, M.A., 1976. *Religion:* Roman Catholic. *Home:* 7501 Woodcrest Ave., Philadelphia, Pa. 19151. *Office:* Villanova University, Villanova, Pa. 19085.

CAREER: Valparaiso University, Valparaiso, Ind., instructor in English, 1953-55; University of Maryland, Munich, Germany, lecturer in English, 1958-60; Duquesne University, Pittsburgh, Pa., lecturer in English, 1960-64; National Council of Catholic Women, Washington, D.C., director of Ecumenical and Liturgical Affairs, 1967-71, editor, 1970-71; Villanova University, Villanova, Pa., lecturer in English, 1977-78, lecturer in religious studies, 1979—. Member of National Core Commission, Women's Ordination Conference, 1981—. *Member:* Sigma Tau Delta, Phi Kappa Phi. *Awards, honors:* Institute for Ecumenical and Cultural Research resident fellow in Collegeville, Minn., 1968-69; LL.D., La Salle College, 1977; Distinguished Graduate Award, Villanova University, 1982.

WRITINGS: Concern: World Religions, Silver Burdett, 1970; *Woman in a Man's Church,* Paulist/Newman, 1972; (editor) *Sistercelebrations* (collection of feminist liturgies), Fortress, 1974; (editor with husband, Leonard J. Swidler, and contributor) *Women Priests: A Catholic Commentary on the Vatican Declaration,* Paulist/Newman, 1977.

Translator from the German; published by Herder & Herder, except as indicated: Richard Gutzwiller, *The Parables of the Lord,* 1964; Heinrich Kahlefeld, *Parables and Instructions in the Gospels,* 1966; Bernard Haering, *This Time of Salvation,* 1966; Haering, *Christian Maturity,* 1967; (and editor with L. Swidler) *Bishops and People,* Westminster, 1970; (with L. Swidler) Haye van der Meer, *Women Priests in the Catholic Church?,* Temple University Press, 1973.

Contributor of regular column to *National Catholic Reporter,* 1971-74. Contributor to periodicals, including *Concilium, America, American Benedictine Review, Commonweal,* and *Liturgy. Journal of Ecumenical Studies,* co-founder and managing editor, 1964-71, education editor, 1972-81.

WORK IN PROGRESS: Research on American Catholic Church history.

AVOCATIONAL INTERESTS: Music, ballet, camping, traveling.

SYRED, Celia 1911-

PERSONAL: First syllable of surname rhymes with "my"; born April 10, 1911, in Westbury-on-Severn, Gloucestershire, England; daughter of Charles (an actor) and Georgina (an actress; maiden name, France) Whitlock; married Errol Syred (a farmer), April 20, 1952 (deceased). *Education:* Royal College of Art, A.R.C.A., 1934; additional study at Cheltenham School of Art. *Politics:* None. *Religion:* Church of England. *Home:* 19 Old South Rd., Bowral, New South Wales 2576, Australia.

CAREER: Taught art at colleges and art schools in England and Wales, 1934-55; author of children's books. *Member:* Australian Society of Authors. *Awards, honors:* Highly commended by Children's Book Council of Australia, 1967, for *Cocky's Castle,* and 1977, for *Hebe's Daughter.*

WRITINGS—Youth books: *Cocky's Castle,* Angus & Robertson, 1966; *Baker's Dozen,* Angus & Robertson, 1969; *An Innkeeper,* Oxford University Press, 1970; *A Printer,* Oxford University Press, 1971; *Hebe's Daughter,* Hodder & Stoughton, 1976; (contributor of short story) Barbara Ker Wilson, editor, *A Handful of Ghosts,* Hodder & Stoughton, 1976; (contributor of short story) Leon Garfield, editor, *A Swag of Stories,* Ward Lock, 1977; *Melissa Woodruff,* Hodder & Stoughton (Australia), 1981; *The Shop in Woolloomooloo,* Hodder & Stoughton, 1983.

WORK IN PROGRESS: Revising a youth book about eighteenth-century Scotland, particularly the Jacobite rising; other books based in England about subjects including eighteenth-century Lord Mayor's show and strolling players; research into cheese-making in the southern highlands of New South Wales.

SIDELIGHTS: Baker's Dozen was translated into Spanish. *Avocational interests:* Modern embroidery.

BIOGRAPHICAL/CRITICAL SOURCES: Times Literary Supplement, June 26, 1969.

T

TALMON, Shemaryahu 1920-

PERSONAL: Surname is pronounced Tal-*mon;* born May 28, 1920, in Poland; son of Litmann and Hella (Ell) Zelmanowicz; married Yonina Garber (a professor), November 17, 1948 (deceased); married Penina Moraq (a lecturer), March 18, 1969; children: (first marriage) Efrath, Tamar; (second marriage) Nogah, Tammy. *Education:* Hebrew University of Jerusalem, M.A., 1945, Ph.D., 1955. *Religion:* Jewish. *Home:* 5 Smuts St., Jerusalem, Israel. *Office:* Faculty of Humanities, Hebrew University, Jerusalem, Israel.

CAREER: University of Leeds, Leeds, England, lecturer in Semitic studies, 1950-51; University of Tel-Aviv, Tel-Aviv, Israel, lecturer in Bible studies, 1953-55; Hebrew University of Jerusalem, Jerusalem, Israel, instructor, 1955-57, lecturer in Bible studies, 1958-61; Brandeis University, Waltham, Mass., professor of Near Eastern studies, 1961-63; Hebrew University of Jerusalem, senior lecturer, 1963-66, associate professor, 1966-74, Magnes Professor of Bible Studies, 1974—, rector of University College, Haifa, 1968-69, dean of faculty of the humanities, 1975-78. Rector, Hochschule fur Judische Studien, Heidelberg, Germany, 1981—. Visiting professor, Harvard University, 1970-71, University of California, Berkeley, 1978-79, and Theologische Fakultat Luzern, 1980-81; Foster Visiting Professor of Bible Studies, Brandeis University, 1971-72. *Military service:* Israeli Defence Army, Infantry, 1948-49; became captain.

MEMBER: World Association of Jewish Studies, Israel Exploration Society, Israel Historical Society, Israel Society of Bible Research, Society of Old Testament Study (Great Britain), Society of Biblical Literature (United States), American Oriental Society, American Schools of Oriental Research.

WRITINGS: (Editor) *Selections from the Pentateuch in the Samaritan Version,* Hebrew University, 1957; (editor with M. Avi-Yonah and A. Malamat) *Views of the Bible World* (in English and Hebrew), International Publishers, Volume II, 1959, Volume III, 1960; (editor) *Textus: Annual of the Hebrew University Bible Project,* Magnes Press of Hebrew University, Volume IV, 1964, Volume V, 1966, Volume VI, 1967, Volume VII, 1969, Volume VIII, 1973, Volume IX, 1981, Volume X, 1982; *Darkhe hasipur ba-Mikra* (on the Bible as literature), Akademon, Hebrew University, 1965; (editor) *Toldot nosah ha-Mikra bamehkar he-hadish* (readings on the history of the Bible text in recent literature; chiefly in English), Akademon, Hebrew University, 1966; (author of introduction) Roman-Francois Butin, *The Ten Nequdoth of the Torah,* Ktav Publishing, 1969.

The Old Testament Text: The Cambridge History of the Bible, Volume I, edited by P. R. Akroyd and C. F. Evans, Cambridge University Press, 1970; (editor with F. M. Cross) *Qumran and the History of the Biblical Text,* Harvard University Press, 1975; (editor with G. Siefer) *Religion und Politik,* [Bonn], 1978; (editor with K. Yaron and J. Emanuel) *Kaan we'ahshav: Iyunim behaguto hahevratit wehadatit shel M. Buber,* [Jerusalem], 1982; (editor with A. Falaturi and W. Strolz) *Zukunftshoffnung und Heilserwartwng in den momotheistischen Religionen,* Herder (Freiburg), 1983.

Also contributor to *Encyclopaedia Biblica, Hebrew Bible Dictionary, Enciclopedia de la Biblica, Interpreter's Dictionary of the Bible,* and *Theologisches Woerterbuch zum Alten Testament.* Contributor of more than one hundred articles and a number of reviews to journals in Israel, United States, England, Netherlands, Italy, Spain, and Germany.

WORK IN PROGRESS: The Covenanters from the Judean Desert, a sociological analysis; *The Biblical Narrative,* an introduction to biblical prose literature; a critical edition of the Book of Jeremiah; a commentary on the Books of Ezra and Nehemiah.

* * *

TAYLOR, Robert Brown 1936-

PERSONAL: Born May 31, 1936, in Elmira, N.Y.; son of Olaf C. (a book salesman) and Elizabeth (Brown) Taylor; married Anita Dopico (a clinical counselor), July 30, 1959; children: Diana Marie, Sharon Jean. *Education:* Attended Bucknell University, 1957; Temple University, M.D., 1961. *Religion:* Protestant. *Home:* 2301 Buena Vista Rd., Winston-Salem, N.C. 27104. *Office:* Department of Family and Community Medicine, Bowman Gray School of Medicine, 300 South Hawthorne Rd., Winston-Salem, N.C. 27103.

CAREER: In private practice of medicine in New Paltz, N.Y., 1964-78; Kingston City Hospital, Kingston, N.Y., attending staff member, 1964-78; Benedictine Hospital, Kingston, staff physician, 1964-78; Bowman Gray School of Medicine, Department of Family and Community Medicine, Winston-Salem, N.C., professor, 1978—. Diplomate from American Board of Family Practice, 1971. *Wartime service:* U.S. Public Health Service, 1961-64. *Member:* American Academy of Family Physicians (charter fellow), Society of Teachers of Family Medicine, North Carolina Medical Society, North Carolina Academy of Family Physicians, Alpha Omega Alpha.

WRITINGS: Common Problems in Office Practice, Harper, 1972; *The Practical Art of Medicine,* Harper, 1972; *A Primer of Clinical Symptoms,* Harper, 1972; *Feeling Alive after Sixty-Five,* Arlington House, 1973; *Doctor Taylor's Guide to Healthy Skin for All Ages,* Arlington House, 1974; (editor) Jean Valnet, *Organic Garden Medicine,* Erbonia Books, 1975; *Welcome to the Middle Years: A Doctor's Guide,* Acropolis Books, 1976; *Doctor Taylor's Self-Help Medical Guide,* Arlington House, 1977; (editor with John L. Buckingham and others) *Family Medicine: Principles and Practice,* Springer-Verlag, 1978, 2nd edition, 1983; (with wife, Anita Taylor) *Couples: The Art of Staying Together,* Acropolis Books, 1978; *Health after Forty,* Acropolis Books, 1982; (editor with John R. Ureda and John W. Denham) *Health Promotion: Principles and Clinical Applications,* Appleton-Century-Crofts, 1982; (editor) *Difficult Diagnosis,* Saunders, 1984. Contributing editor, *Physician's Management Magazine, Female Patient Magazine,* and *Family Practice Research Journal.*

WORK IN PROGRESS: For ages nine to twelve, *A Shot in Time: The Story of Immunization.*

SIDELIGHTS: Robert Brown Taylor told *CA:* "Doctor comes from the Latin word for teacher, and . . . the modern physician must not only heal but also teach—both patients and young physicians. My patient education books are written for patients in my office, while my medical textbooks emphasize both the science and the art of medical practice."

* * *

TEGNER, Henry (Stuart) 1901-
(The Northumbrian Gentleman, The Ruffle)

PERSONAL: Born August 15, 1901, in Yokohama, Japan; son of Frederik May (a merchant) and Beatrix (Eldridge) Tegner; married Helen Elizabeth Henderson, February 25, 1924; children: Ann, Veronica, Alison, John. *Education:* Cambridge University, M.A., 1923. *Politics:* Conservative. *Religion:* Church of England. *Home:* Seven Stars, Whalton, Northumberland, England.

CAREER: Affiliated with Anglo-American Oil Co. Ltd., 1924-34, and with Scott & Turner Ltd. (pharmacists), 1934-59; Sherlock & Edmenson (stockbrokers), Newcastle upon Tyne, England, partner, 1964—. *Military service:* Royal Air Force, 1939-45; became wing commander; created Chevalier of the Belgian Crown, 1957. *Member:* Mammal Society of the British Isles, Fauna Preservation Society, Natural History Society of Northumberland, Durham and Newcastle upon Tyne (vice-president).

WRITINGS: (Under pseudonym The Ruffle) *Sporting Respite,* Lincoln Williams, 1935; *The Sporting Rifle in Britain,* Batchworth Press, 1951; *The Roe Deer,* Batchworth Press, 1951; *The White Foxes of Gorfenletch,* Hollis & Carter, 1954; *The Buck of Lordenshaw,* Batchworth Press, 1955; *A Border County,* R. Hale, 1955; *The Tale of a Deer Forest,* Bles, 1957; (under pseudonym The Northumbrian Gentleman) *The Old Man Hunts,* Hutchinson, 1959.

(Under pseudonym The Northumbrian Gentleman) *Across the Hills and Faraway,* Hutchinson, 1961; *Beasts of the North Country,* Galley Press, 1961; *The Sporting Rifle,* Jenkins, 1962; *Wild Cheviot,* Kimber & Co., 1962; *Game for the Sporting Rifle,* Jenkins, 1963; *Rhymeside,* Kimber & Co., 1964; *The Molecatcher Says,* Phoenix Press, 1964; *The Buck of the Saughs,* Kimber & Co., 1965; *The Long Bay of Druridge,* Frank Graham, 1968; *The Magic of Holy Island,* Frank Graham, 1969; *The Story of a Regiment: Being a Short History of the Northumberland Hussers Yeomanry, 1918-1969,* Frank Graham, 1969; *Wild Hares,* John Baker, 1969.

The Charm of the Cheviots, Frank Graham, 1970; *Naturalist on Speyside,* Bles, 1971; *Natural History in Northumberland and Durham,* Frank Graham, 1972; *Ghosts of the North Country: Being an Account of Some of the Folklore and Ghost Stories of the Northern Counties of Northumberland and Durham and Their Adjacent Lands,* Frank Graham, 1974.

Contributor to *Times* and *Sunday Times* (London), *Punch, Field, Country Life,* and other outdoor and popular magazines.†

* * *

TENENBAUM, Frances 1919-

PERSONAL: Born September 16, 1919, in New York, N.Y.; daughter of Emanuel (a businessman) and Regina (Musken) Mendelson; married Frank Tenenbaum, May 22, 1943 (deceased); children: Jane, David. *Education:* Attended Skidmore College, 1936-38; University of Michigan, B.A., 1941; Columbia University, M.S., 1942. *Residence:* Cambridge, Mass. *Office:* Houghton Mifflin Co., 2 Park St., Boston, Mass. 02107.

CAREER: New York Herald Tribune, New York, N.Y., reporter, 1942-45; free-lance magazine writer, 1945-54; reporter and columnist for *Great Neck Reporter,* 1954-62; worked in editorial and publicity departments at Channel Press, 1962-64; educational columnist for *Great Neck News,* 1964-67; assistant editor for Better Homes and Gardens Book Clubs, 1971-72; Houghton Mifflin Co., Boston, Mass., editor, 1973—.

WRITINGS: Gardening with Wild Flowers, Scribner, 1973; *Nothing Grows for You?,* Scribner, 1975; *Plants from Nine to Five,* Scribner, 1977; *Over 55 Is Not Illegal: A Resource Book for Active Older People,* Houghton, 1979; (co-author) *Diet against Disease,* Houghton, 1980; *Carry-Out Cuisine,* Houghton, 1982; *Field Guide to Wildflowers Coloring Book,* Houghton, 1982.

BIOGRAPHICAL/CRITICAL SOURCES: Washington Post Book World, August 26, 1979.

* * *

TEPPER, Michael 1941-

PERSONAL: Born September 4, 1941, in Baltimore, Md.; son of Jack and Betty (Chodak) Tepper; married Veronica Schofield, November 15, 1972; children: Alexander, Megan, Sarah. *Education:* University of Maryland, B.A. (special honors), 1963; New York University, M.A., 1965, Ph.D., 1970. *Office:* Genealogical Publishing Co., 1001 North Calvert St., Baltimore, Md. 21202.

CAREER: Mills College of Education, New York, N.Y., instructor in English, 1967-68; Genealogical Publishing Co., Baltimore, Md., managing editor, 1970—. *Member:* Baltimore Bibliophiles.

WRITINGS—Published by Genealogical Publishing: (Editor) *Emigrants to Pennsylvania, 1641-1819,* 1975; (editor) *Passengers to America,* 1977; *Immigrants to the Middle Colonies,* 1978; *New World Immigrants,* 1979; *Passenger Arrivals at the Port of Baltimore, 1820-1834,* 1982; (with Ira A. Glazier) *The Famine Immigrants, 1846-1851,* 1984. Contributor to journals.

* * *

TERRIS, Susan 1937-

PERSONAL: Born May 6, 1937, in St. Louis, Mo.; daughter of Harold W. (a realtor) and Myra (Friedman) Dubinsky; married David Warren Terris (a stockbroker), August 31, 1958; children: Daniel, Michael, Amy. *Education:* Wellesley College, A.B., 1959; San Francisco State College (now University), M.A., 1966. *Politics:* Democrat. *Religion:* Jewish. *Home:* 11 Jordan Ave., San Francisco, Calif. 94118. *Agent:* Marilyn Marlow, Curtis Brown, Ltd., 575 Madison Ave., New York, N.Y. 10022.

CAREER: Teacher of "Writing for Children" course and of writing workshops at University of California Extension, San Francisco. Has done tutoring, library work, and research. Lecturer on children's books to schools and libraries.

WRITINGS—Juveniles; published by Doubleday: *The Upstairs Witch and the Downstairs Witch,* 1970; *The Backwards Boots,* 1971; *On Fire,* 1972; *The Drowning Boy,* 1972; *Plague of Frogs,* 1973; *Whirling Rainbows,* 1974; *Amanda, the Panda, and the Redhead,* 1975; *No Boys Allowed,* 1976.

Other publishers: *Pickle,* Four Winds Press, 1973; *The Pencil Families,* Greenwillow, 1975; *The Chicken Pox Papers,* F. Watts, 1976; *Two Ps in a Pod,* Greenwillow, 1977; *Tucker and the Horse Thief,* Four Winds Press, 1979; *Stage Brat,* Four Winds Press, 1980; *No Scarlet Ribbons,* Farrar, Straus, 1981; *Wings and Roots,* Farrar, Straus, 1982; *Octopus Pie,* Farrar, Straus, 1983; *Baby-Snatcher,* Farrar, Straus, 1984.

Also contributor to a series of elementary school texts. Contributor of stories and articles to magazines, and of book reviews to *New York Times.*

AVOCATIONAL INTERESTS: Sewing, knitting, needlepoint work, fancy cooking, hiking.

BIOGRAPHICAL/CRITICAL SOURCES: Washington Post Book World, November 6, 1983.

* * *

THAYER, Frederick C(lifton), Jr. 1924-
(Jack Walker)

PERSONAL: Born September 6, 1924, in Baltimore, Md.; son of Frederick Clifton (a photographer) and Marian (Walter) Thayer; married Phyllis Dirksen, May 14, 1949 (divorced, 1950); married Carolyn Easley, October 31, 1952; children: Jeffrey, Sarah. *Education:* U.S. Military Academy, B.S., 1945; Ohio State University, M.A., 1954; University of Denver, Ph.D., 1963. *Residence:* Pittsburgh, Pa. *Office:* Graduate School of Public and International Affairs, University of Pittsburgh, Pittsburgh, Pa. 15260.

CAREER: U.S. Air Force, career officer, 1945-69, worked in Aerospace Policies Division, 1963-66, visiting military fellow at Council on Foreign Relations, 1966-67, assistant deputy chief of staff in operations at Military Airlift Command, 1968-69, retiring as colonel; currently professor of public and international affairs at University of Pittsburgh, Pittsburgh, Pa. Visiting lecturer at American University, 1971, George Washington University, 1975, University of North Carolina and York University, 1976, and Pennsylvania State University and California State College, Stanislaus, 1977; visiting associate professor at Syracuse University, spring, 1973, University of Southern California, 1973, 1975, 1976, 1977, 1983-84, West Virginia University, 1976, and University of Calgary, 1981. Consultant to MITRE Corp. *Member:* American Political Science Association, American Society of Public Administration, Academy of Management.

WRITINGS: Air Transport Policy and National Security, University of North Carolina Press, 1965; *Citizen Participation and Liberal Democratic Government,* Queen's Printer (Canada), 1971; *An End to Hierarchy! An End to Competition!: Organizing the Politics and Economics of Survival,* F. Watts, 1973, 2nd revised edition published as *An End to Hierarchy and Competition: Administration in the Post-Affluent World,* 1981; (contributor) Frank Trager and Philip Kronenberg, editors, *National Security and American Society,* University Press of Kansas, 1973; (contributor) Bach and Sulzner, editors, *Perspectives on the Presidency,* Heath, 1974; *Organization Theory and the New Public Administration,* Allyn & Bacon, 1980; *Rebuilding America: The Case for Economic Regulation,* Praeger, 1984. Contributor of about forty articles to professional journals, including *Worldview* (sometimes under pseudonym Jack Walker). Member of board of editors of *Public Administration Review,* 1971-76, and *Administration and Society,* 1974—.

WORK IN PROGRESS: Research on contradictions in political, economics, and organization theories.

SIDELIGHTS: Frederick C. Thayer, Jr. writes: "Assuming natural resources to be finite, the world can survive only if a profound social transformation occurs, the first such change since the shift from hunting to agricultural societies some four to five thousand years ago.

"Through an accident of history (the manner in which I had to pursue graduate studies), I was compelled to become interdisciplinary, beginning with studies of air transport policy. I concluded then that competition among airlines was essentially unworkable and inherently wasteful. I now conclude that if resources are finite, and that if we must recognize and act soon on that assumption, we must search for an alternative to the only organized systems with which we are familiar. Neither centralized planning systems (monopoly capitalism, state socialism) nor competitive market systems (capitalist, socialist, or mixed) can possibly work; the former because nobody can possibly command the knowledge required, the latter because it relies upon the absence of planning (except by the individual organization or nation-state). We must search for a global system which combines the total absence of authority and comprehensive planning. Resources simply must be shared, and the agreement on sharing must be arrived at without coercion. Among other things, this must lead to the end of private property as we know it, the end of all superior-subordinate relationships, and the separation of work from income. If we do not do this, the world inevitably faces nuclear holocaust, as we enter the global struggle for possession of the resources that are left. The time is short, perhaps less than a decade.

"Because the fundamental purpose of nation-states is to fight and win wars, they cannot be the agents for the needed change."

THEOHARIS, Athan G(eorge) 1936-

PERSONAL: Born August 3, 1936, in Milwaukee, Wis.; son of George A. and Adeline (Konop) Theoharis; married Nancy Artinian, August 21, 1966; children: Jeanne Frances, George Thomas, Elizabeth Armen. *Education:* University of Chicago, A.B., 1956, A.B., 1957, A.M., 1959, Ph.D., 1965. *Politics:* Democrat. *Religion:* Greek Orthodox. *Home:* 8527 North Manor Lane, Fox Point, Wis. *Office:* Department of History, Marquette University, Milwaukee, Wis. 53233.

CAREER: Texas A&M University, College Station, instructor in history, 1962-64; Wayne State University, Detroit, Mich., assistant professor of history, 1964-68; Staten Island Community College of the City University of New York, Staten Island, N.Y., associate professor of history, 1968-69; Marquette University, Milwaukee, Wis., associate professor, 1969-76, professor of American history, 1976—. State University of New York at Buffalo, Thomas B. Lockwood Professor of History, 1982-83. *Member:* American Historical Association, Organization of American Historians, Academy of Political Science, American Civil Liberties Union, National Committee for a Sane Nuclear Policy (member of board), University of Chicago Alumni (member of board, 1968-70). *Awards, honors:* Grants from Truman Institute for National and International Affairs, 1965, 1966, Wayne State University, 1967, Marquette University, 1970, 1979, Institute for Humane Studies, 1971, Field Foundation, 1980, Warsh-Mott Funds, 1980, Fund for Investigative Journalism, 1980, and the C. S. Fund, 1981; American Bar Association Gavel awards; National Endowment for the Humanities Summer Fellowship, 1976; Binkley-Stephenson Award, 1979; Albert Beveridge research grant, 1980.

WRITINGS: Anatomy of Anti-Communism, Hill & Wang, 1969; *The Yalta Myths: An Issue in U.S. Politics, 1945-1955,* University of Missouri Press, 1970; *Seeds of Repression: Harry S Truman and the Origins of McCarthyism,* Quadrangle, 1971; (editor with Robert Griffith) *The Specter: Original Essays on the Cold War and the Origins of McCarthyism,* New Viewpoints, 1974; (co-author) *Twentieth Century United States,* Prentice-Hall, 1978; *Spying on Americans: Political Surveillance from Hoover to the Huston Plan,* Temple University Press, 1978; (editor) *The Truman Presidency: The Origins of the Imperial Presidency and the National Security State,* Earl M. Coleman, 1979; (with Melvyn Dubofsky) *Imperial Democracy: The United States Since 1945;* Prentice-Hall, 1982; (editor) *Beyond the Hiss Case: The FBI, Congress, and the Cold War,* Temple University Press, 1982.

Contributor: B. J. Bernstein, editor, *Politics and Policies of the Truman Administration,* Quadrangle, 1970; M. Small, editor, *Public Opinion and Historians,* Wayne State University Press, 1970; Howard H. Quint and Milton Cantor, editors, *Men, Women, and Issues in American History,* Dorsey, 1975. Contributor to journals, including *New University Thought.*

WORK IN PROGRESS: Research on internal security policy since 1936; compiling and editing files of important FBI internal security cases and federal surveillance policy, to be issued on microfilm by Scholarly Resources; compiling and editing collection of original essays to be entitled *Liberty and Security: The Intelligence Community in a Democratic Society.*

SIDELIGHTS: Athan G. Theoharis's *The Yalta Myths: An Issue in U.S. Politics, 1945-1955* explores the history of the Cold War policies that developed from the notion that Franklin Delano Roosevelt and Winston Churchill compromised the West in their dealings with Stalin at the Yalta Conference in 1945. "Although Republicans raised the issue primarily in order to discredit Truman," Allen Weinstein writes in the *New York Times Book Review,* "Theoharis considers the President almost as culpable as his Congressional opponents in perpetuating 'the Yalta myths.'"

Theoharis examines the domestic effects of Truman's policies in *Seeds of Repression: Harry S Truman and the Origins of McCarthyism.* In that report, *New York Review of Books* critic Murray Kempton concludes, "our desire to have the period's characters rendered in their proper proportions could hardly be better satisfied. McCarthy is relegated in this composition to the place and comparative dimensions of one of Veronese's dwarfs, since it is Mr. Theoharis's judgement that Mr. Truman set the tone of the national possession by fear of the Communist danger and that McCarthyism was only Trumanism carried to its logical conclusion." According to Kempton, Theoharis's "argument is not without weaknesses; but none of them seriously affects its essential strength. He has successfully, if not always gracefully, closed the question of major blame."

AVOCATIONAL INTERESTS: Sports.

BIOGRAPHICAL/CRITICAL SOURCES: New York Times Book Review, March 7, 1971; *New York Review of Books,* March 11, 1971, September 2, 1971; *American Political Science Review,* spring, 1976.

* * *

THIELE, Colin (Milton) 1920-

PERSONAL: Surname is pronounced Tee-lee; born November 16, 1920, in Eudunda, South Australia; son of Carl Wilhelm (a farmer) and Anna (Wittwer) Thiele; married Rhonda Gill (a teacher and artist), March 17, 1945; children: Janne Louise (Mrs. Geoffrey Minge), Sandra Gwenyth (Mrs. Ron Paterson). *Education:* University of Adelaide, B.A., 1941, Diploma of Education, 1947; Adelaide Teachers College, Diploma of Teaching, 1942. *Home:* 24 Woodhouse Crescent, Wattle Park, South Australia 5066, Australia.

CAREER: South Australian Education Department, English teacher and senior master at high school in Port Lincoln, 1946-55, senior master at high school in Brighton, 1956; Wattle Park Teachers College, Wattle Park, South Australia, lecturer, 1957-61, senior lecturer in English, 1962-63, vice-principal, 1964, principal, 1965-73; director, Murray Park College of Advanced Education, 1973; Wattle Park Teachers Centre, Wattle Park, principal, 1973-80. Common Wealth Literary Fund lecturer on Australian literature; speaker at conferences on literature and education in Australia and United States. *Military service:* Royal Australian Air Force, 1942-45.

MEMBER: Australian College of Education (fellow), Australian Society of Authors (council member, 1965—), English Teachers Association (president, 1957), South Australian Fellowship of Writers (president, 1961). *Awards, honors:* W. J. Miles Poetry Prize, 1944, for *Progress to Denial;* Commonwealth Jubilee Literary Competitions, first prize in radio play section, for "Edge of Ice," and first prize in radio feature section, both 1951; South Australian winner in World Short Story Quest, 1952; Fulbright scholar in United States and Canada, 1959-60; Grace Leven Poetry Prize, 1961, for *Man in a Landscape;* Commonwealth Literary Fund fellowship, 1967-68; *Blue Fin* was placed on the Honours List, Hans Andersen Award, 1972; Visual Arts Board award, 1975, for *Magpie Island;* Austrian State Prize for Children's Books, 1979, for

The SKNUKS; Book of the Year Award, Children's Book Council of Australia, 1982, for *The Valley Between;* Mystery Writers of America citation for *The Fire in the Stone;* numerous commendations in Australian Children's Book Council awards.

WRITINGS—Published by Rigby, except as indicated: *Progress to Denial* (poems), Jindyworobak, 1945; *Splinters and Shards* (poems), Jindyworobak, 1945; *The Golden Lightning* (poems), Jindyworobak, 1951; (editor) *Jindyworobak Anthology* (verse), Jindyworobak, 1953; *Man in a Landscape* (poems), 1960; (editor with Ian Mudie) *Australian Poets Speak,* 1961; (editor) *Favourite Australian Stories,* 1963; (editor, and author of commentary and notes) *Handbook to Favourite Australian Stories,* 1964; *In Charcoal and Conte* (poems), 1966; *Heysen of Hahndorf* (biography), 1968, Tri-Ocean, 1969; *Barossa Valley Sketchbook,* illustrations by Jeanette McLeod, Tri-Ocean, 1968; *Labourers in the Vineyard* (novel), 1970; *Selected Verse (1940-1970),* 1970; *Coorong,* photographs by Mike McKelvey, 1972; *Range without Man: The North Flinders,* 1974; *The Little Desert,* photographs by Jocelyn Burt, 1975; *Grains of Mustard Seed,* South Australia Education Department, 1975; *Heysen's Early Hahndorf,* 1976; *The Bight,* photographs by McKelvey, 1976; *Lincoln's Place,* 1978; *Maneater Man,* 1979.

Children's books and school texts; published by Rigby, except as indicated: *The State of Our State,* 1952.

(Editor and annotator) *Looking at Poetry,* Longmans, Green, 1960; *The Sun on the Stubble* (children's novel), 1961; *Gloop the Gloomy Bunyip* (children's story in verse; also see below), Jacaranda, 1962; (editor with Greg Branson) *One-Act Plays for Secondary Schools,* Books 1-2, 1962, one-volume edition of Books 1-2, 1963, Book 3, 1964, revised edition of Book 1 published as *Setting the Stage,* 1969, revised edition of Book 2 published as *The Living Stage, 1970; Storm Boy,* 1963, Rand McNally, 1966, new edition, with illustrations by Robert Ingpen, 1974; (editor with Branson) *Beginners, Please* (anthology), 1964; *February Dragon* (children's novel), 1965, Harper, 1976; *The Rim of the Morning* (short stories), 1966; *Mrs. Munch and Puffing Billy,* 1967, Tri-Ocean, 1968; *Yellow-Jacket Jock,* illustrations by Clifton Pugh, F. W. Cheshire, 1969; *Blue Fin* (children's novel), 1969, Harper, 1974.

Flash Flood, 1970; *Flip Flop and Tiger Snake,* 1970; *Gloop the Bunyip* (children's story in verse; contains material from *Gloop the Gloomy Bunyip),* 1970; (editor with Branson) *Plays for Young Players* (for primary schools), 1970; *The Fire in the Stone,* 1973, Harper, 1974; *Albatross Two,* 1974, published as *Fight against Albatross Two,* Harper, 1976; *Uncle Gustav's Ghosts,* 1974; *Magpie Island,* 1974; *The Hammerhead Light,* 1976, Harper, 1977; *Storm Boy Picture Book,* 1976; *The Shadow on the Hills,* 1977, Harper, 1978; *The SKNUKS,* 1977; *River Murray Mary,* 1979; *Ballander Boy,* 1979.

Chadwick's Chimney, Metheun, 1980; *The Best of Colin Thiele,* 1980; *Tanya and Trixie,* 1980; *Thiele Tales,* 1980; *The Valley Between,* 1981; *Little Tom Little,* 1981; *Songs for My Thongs,* 1982; *The Undercover Secret,* 1982; *Patch Comes Home,* 1983; *Pinquo,* 1983.

Plays: "Burke and Wills" (verse, first performed at Adelaide Radio Drama Festival, 1949), published in full in *On the Air,* edited by P. R. Smith, Angus & Robertson, 1959; "Edge of Ice" (verse), first performed on radio, 1952; "The Shark Fishers" (prose), first performed, 1954; "Edward John Eyre" (verse), first performed at Adelaide Radio Drama Festival, 1962.

Author of other verse plays for radio, and radio and television features, documentaries, children's serials, and schools broadcast programs; national book reviewer for Australian Broadcasting Commission. Thiele's poetry and short stories have appeared in many anthologies and journals; also contributor of articles and reviews to periodicals.

SIDELIGHTS: Colin Thiele told *CA:* "One of the tasks of the writer is indeed to 'hold the mirror up to Nature,' to reveal humanity to humanity, to comment on the variousness of the human condition. And although society and the environment in which people live have changed beyond recognition, and will continue to do so, human beings are still human beings. They still show human strengths and human weaknesses—kindness, cruelty, love, hatred, wisdom, stupidity, and all the rest. They still suffer loneliness and rejection, still respond to love and compassion, still rise to heights of altruism and nobility, still stoop to depths of pettiness, perfidy, and meanness.

"In exploring these themes, it doesn't much matter whether the writer uses settings in Sleepy Hollow or at the Crossroads of the World—wherever they are. The universal verities of life can be revealed anywhere because they reside in the hearts of human beings, not in facades of city streets or ephemeral houses.

"It is to reflect these convictions that I hold up my particular mirror—unpolished and inadequate as it may be."

Thiele's children's books have been translated into numerous foreign languages, including German, Russian, French, Italian, Chinese, Japanese, Afrikaans, Swedish, Finnish, and Greek.

MEDIA ADAPTATIONS: "Storm Boy" and "Blue Fin" were made into feature films by the South Australian Film Corp. in 1976 and 1978; "The Fire in the Stone" was made into a television feature by the South Australian Film Corp. in 1983.

BIOGRAPHICAL/CRITICAL SOURCES: Australian Book Review, Children's Supplement, 1964, 1967, 1969; *Kirkus,* January 1, 1966; *New York Times Book Review,* May 1, 1966, February 23, 1975; *Young Readers Review,* September, 1966; *Bulletin of the Center for Children's Books,* Volume XX, November, 1966; *Childhood Education,* December, 1966, April, 1967; *Books and Bookmen,* July, 1968; *Contemporary Literary Criticism,* Volume XVII, Gale, 1981.

* * *

THIERAUF, Robert J(ames) 1933-

PERSONAL: Born July 25, 1933, in Covington, Ky. *Education:* Xavier University, Cincinnati, Ohio, B.S.B.A., 1958, M.B.A., 1960; Ohio State University, Ph.D., 1966. *Home:* 535 Fairway Lane, Cincinnati, Ohio 45228. *Office:* Department of Management and Information Systems, Xavier University, Cincinnati, Ohio 45207.

CAREER: Lybrand, Ross Brothers & Montgomery, public accountant in Cincinnati, Ohio, 1958-60, consultant to New York office, 1960-63; certified public accountant, state of Ohio, 1963; Xavier University, Cincinnati, chairman of department of management and information systems, 1965-80, D. J. O'Conor Endowed Chair of Business Administration, beginning 1973. *Member:* American Institute of Certified Public Accountants, American Institute of Decision Sciences, Institute of Management Science, Academy of Management, Association for Computing Machinery.

WRITINGS: Richard A. Grosse, editor, *Decision Making through Operations Research,* Wiley, 1970, 2nd edition, 1975; *Data Processing for Business and Management,* Wiley, 1973; *Systems Analysis and Design of Real-Time Management Infor-*

mation Systems, Prentice-Hall, 1975; (with others) *Management Principles and Practices: A Contingency and Questionnaire Approach,* Wiley, 1977; *An Introductory Approach to Operations Research,* Wiley, 1978; *Distributed Processing Systems,* Prentice-Hall, 1978.

(With John F. Niehaus) *An Introduction to Data Processing for Business,* Wiley, 1980; *Management Auditing: A Questionnaire Approach,* AMACOM, 1980; (with George W. Reynolds) *Systems Analysis and Design: A Case Study Approach,* C. E. Merrill, 1980; *Effective Information Systems Management,* C. E. Merrill, 1982; *Decision Support Systems for Effective Planning and Control: A Case Study Approach,* Prentice-Hall, 1982; *A Manager's Complete Guide to Effective Information Systems,* Macmillan, 1983; *Effective Management Information Systems: Accent on Current Practices,* C. E. Merrill, 1984.

* * *

THOMPSON, W(illard) Scott 1942-

PERSONAL: Born January 1, 1942, in Providence, R.I.; son of Francis Willard (an educator) and Loretta (Long) Thompson; married Phyllis Anina Nitze, December 28, 1968; children: Phyllis Elizabeth Pratt, Nicholas Edwin Scott, Heidi Alexandra. *Education:* Stanford University, B.A., 1963; Balliol College, Oxford, D.Phil., 1969. *Politics:* Neo-conservative. *Home:* 1729 Que St. N.W., Washington, D.C. 20009. *Office:* United States Information Agency, 400 C St. S.W., Washington, D.C. 20547.

CAREER: Tufts University, Fletcher School of Law and Diplomacy, Medford, Mass., research associate in international development studies, beginning 1967, associate professor of politics, beginning 1967, on leave for research, 1969-71; United States Information Agency, Washington, D.C., associate director, 1982-84. White House fellow, Office of the Secretary of Defense, 1975-76. *Awards, honors:* Rhodes scholarship, 1963-66; Woodrow Wilson fellowship; Danforth fellowship; Rockefeller Foundation grant.

WRITINGS: Ghana's Foreign Policy 1957-1966: Diplomacy, Ideology, and the New State, Princeton University Press, 1969; *Unequal Partners: Philippine and Thai Relations with the United States, 1965-75,* Heath, 1975; (editor with D. D. Frizell) *Lessons of the Vietnamese War,* Crane, Russak, 1976; *Power Projection,* National Strategy Information Center, 1978; *The Third World,* Institute for Contemporary Studies, 1979, 2nd edition, 1983; (editor) *From Weakness to Strength: National Strategy for the 1980s,* Institute for Contemporary Studies, 1981. Contributor to professional journals.

WORK IN PROGRESS: A study of national strategy; a novel.

AVOCATIONAL INTERESTS: Tree farming, chamber music.

* * *

THOMSON, Derick S(mith) 1921-
(Ruaraidh MacThomais)

PERSONAL: Ruaraidh MacThomais is his name in Gaelic; born August 5, 1921, in Stornoway, Scotland; son of James (a schoolmaster) and Christina (Smith) Thomson; married Carol Galbraith (a schoolteacher), 1952; children: Domhnall Ruaraidh, Daniel James, Christina Margaret, Ranald, Roderick, Calum. *Education:* University of Aberdeen, M.A., 1947; Cambridge University, B.A., 1948. *Politics:* Scottish Nationalist.

Home: Saint Margaret's, Taybridge Road, Aberfeldy, Scotland. *Office:* University of Glasgow, Glasgow G12, Scotland.

CAREER: University of Edinburgh, Edinburgh, Scotland, assistant in Celtic, 1948-49; University of Glasgow, Glasgow, Scotland, lecturer in Welsh, 1949-56; University of Aberdeen, Aberdeen, Scotland, reader in Celtic, 1956-63; University of Glasgow, professor of Celtic, 1963—. Lecturer at conferences in Ireland, Wales, England, Finland, Germany, and elsewhere. *Military service:* Royal Air Force, World War II; became leading aircraftman. *Member:* Scottish Gaelic Texts Society (president, 1964—), Gaelic Books Council (chairman, 1968—), Gaelic Society of Inverness (chief, 1969-70), Royal Society of Edinburgh (fellow). *Awards, honors:* Festival of Britain award for group of Gaelic lyrics, 1951; Scottish Arts Council Book Award, 1971, for *An Rathad Cian;* Ossian Prize from F.V.S. Foundation, Hamburg, 1974.

WRITINGS: An Dealbh Briste (Gaelic poems), Serif Books, 1951; *The Gaelic Sources of Macpherson's "Ossian,"* Oliver & Boyd, 1952; (editor) *Branwen Uerch Lyr,* Dublin Institute for Advanced Studies, 1961, revised edition, 1968; (with J. L. Campbell) *Edward Lhuyd in the Scottish Highlands, 1699-1700,* Clarendon Press, 1963; *Eadar Samhradh Is Foghar* (Gaelic poems), Gairm Publications, 1967; (with Ian Grimble) *The Future of the Highlands,* Routledge & Kegan Paul, 1968.

An Rathad Cian (Gaelic poems), Gairm Publications, 1970; *The Far Road,* New Rivers Press, 1971; *An Introduction to Gaelic Poetry,* St. Martin's, 1974; *The New Verse in Scottish Gaelic: A Structural Analysis,* Gollancz, 1974; (translator into Gaelic) Ronald MacLeod, *Bith-eolas* (biology textbook), Gairm Publications, 1976; (editor and contributor) *Gaelic in Scotland,* Gairm Publications, 1976; *Saorsa agus an Iolaire* (Gaelic poems with English translations), Gairm Publications, 1977; (editor with A. J. Aitken and M. P. McDiarmid, and contributor) *Bards and Malears,* University of Glasgow Press, 1977.

(Editor with E. Haugen and J. D. McClure, and contributor) *Minority Languages Today,* Edinburgh University Press, 1981; *The New English-Gaelic Dictionary,* Gairm Publications, 1981; *Creachadh na Clarsaich* (collected Gaelic poems with English translations, 1940-80), Macdonald (Edinburgh), 1982; *The Companion to Gaelic Scotland,* Basil Blackwell, 1983. Editor of *Gairm* (Celtic quarterly), 1952—, and of *Scottish Gaelic Studies,* 1961-76.

WORK IN PROGRESS: History of Scottish Gaelic Literature; editions of Gaelic poetry.

SIDELIGHTS: Derick S. Thomson told *CA:* "My creative writing is almost invariably in Gaelic, and mainly in verse, but much of this verse has subsequently been translated into English and I am sometimes assured that part of this turns out to be poetry also. The themes of the verse are the Gaelic past and present, alienation, Scotland and its politics, love, people and other human concerns. The verse techniques are sometimes traditional, more often free. Some of this poetry has been translated into Welsh, Italian, and Swedish, and I have read it widely in Scotland and occasionally in England, Wales, Ireland, and Canada.

"Donning a black gown, I have written on Gaelic literature from medieval times to the present, on Welsh medieval topics, and on language and language development, especially on the problems of Gaelic as a minority language and culture. . . . As editor of *Gairm,* I am never quite free of journalistic responsibilities, and much of my spare time is given over to publishing Gaelic books. My younger sons think that as a result of all this my golf has suffered seriously."

AVOCATIONAL INTERESTS: Publishing, folksong, politics, conversation, gardening, woodworking.

BIOGRAPHICAL/CRITICAL SOURCES: *Punch,* April 10, 1968; *Lines Review,* Number 39, 1971; Maurice Lindsay, editor, *As I Remember,* R. Hale, 1979; D. Daiches, editor, *A Companion to Scottish Culture,* Edward Arnold, 1981; *PN Review,* Number 34, 1983.

* * *

THUBRON, Colin (Gerald Dryden) 1939-

PERSONAL: Surname is pronounced *Thoo*-bron; born June 14, 1939, in London, England; son of Gerald Ernest (a brigadier in the British Army) and Evelyn (Dryden) Thubron. *Education:* Attended Eton College. *Home:* Garden Cottage, 27 St. Ann's Villas, London W11 4RT, England.

CAREER: Hutchinson & Co. Ltd., London, England, member of editorial staff, 1959-62; British Broadcasting Corp. Television, London, free-lance filmmaker, 1963-64; Macmillan Co., New York, N.Y., member of editorial staff, 1964-65; writer. Member of board of directors, Dacelet Ltd. (building company). *Member:* Royal Society of Literature (fellow).

WRITINGS: *Mirror to Damascus* (Book Society alternate selection in England), Heinemann, 1967, Little, Brown, 1968; *The Hills of Adonis: A Quest in Lebanon,* Little, Brown, 1968; *Jerusalem,* Little, Brown, 1969; *Journey into Cyprus,* Heinemann, 1975; *The God in the Mountain* (novel), Heinemann, 1977, Norton, 1978; (with the editors of Time-Life Books) *The Venetians,* Time-Life, 1980; (with the editors of Time-Life Books) *The Ancient Mariners,* Time-Life, 1981; *The Royal Opera House Covent Garden,* Hamish Hamilton, 1982; *Among the Russians,* Random House, 1983. Also wrote scripts for and filmed three documentary motion pictures on Turkey, Morocco, and Japan, that have been televised in the United States and Great Britain.

WORK IN PROGRESS: A novel.

SIDELIGHTS: A frequent visitor to countries of the Near East, Colin Thubron has written of his sojourns in a series of books that several critics rank above those of most other travel writers. The typical Thubron book is a blend of history, description, and personal observation, an obviously affectionate account that, according to a *Choice* reviewer, goes "beyond the facade of the monuments and events" to evoke a "beautifully poetic but not romantic" portrait of places and people the author has come to know. In a *Times Literary Supplement* review of *Journey into Cyprus,* for instance, David Hunt states: "The book is mainly about people. . . . [It] is full of the most fascinating conversations. . . . [But] for all its concentration on personalities and on village life [*Journey into Cyprus*] will also serve very well as a guide-book. The principal antiquities are poetically but accurately described, and history is so subtly interwoven into the narrative that by the end the reader has learnt painlessly all he needs to know of it."

Another *Times Literary Supplement* critic has a similar opinion on *Mirror to Damascus.* Observes the reviewer: "[Thubron's] narrative [exhibits] one great quality often missing from modern books of travel: its continual reference to the reality of another society and its actual people. His hosts and their relatives and friends emerge as individuals, not as stereotypes. . . . All this provides a pungent counterpoint of personal involvement and adventure to a solid account of the city's present flavour and past development, and the way Mr. Thubron has woven these elements together is a lesson for anyone who tries to combine entertainment with instruction."

BIOGRAPHICAL/CRITICAL SOURCES: *Times Literary Supplement,* December 21, 1967, October 31, 1968, June 6, 1975, December 30, 1977; *Choice,* December, 1968; *New York Times Book Review,* May 18, 1969, December 7, 1969; *Listener,* September 22, 1977; *Times* (London), December 15, 1983.

* * *

THURBER, Walter A(rthur) 1908-

PERSONAL: Born November 27, 1908, in East Worcester, N.Y.; son of Louis A. (a storekeeper) and Anna (Lape) Thurber; children: David L., Robert N. *Education:* Union College, Schenectady, N.Y., B.S. in E.E., 1933; New York College for Teachers (now State University of New York at Albany), M.S., 1938; Cornell University, Ph.D., 1940. *Politics:* Republican. *Religion:* Methodist. *Office:* 6708 Jennifer Dr., Temple Terrace, Fla. 33617.

CAREER: Teacher in New York public schools, 1926-29, and 1933-38; Cortland State Teachers College (now State University of New York College at Cortland), Cortland, N.Y., instructor, 1940-43, assistant professor of physics, physical science, and earth science, 1943-48, professor of science, 1948-59; Syracuse University, Syracuse, N.Y., visiting professor of science education, 1959-64, adjunct professor, 1964-69; Cornell University, Laboratory of Ornithology, Ithaca, N.Y., field collaborator, 1970—. Visiting professor, National University of El Salvador, 1973-80; affiliated with Ministry of Education of El Salvador; advisor to National Park Service of El Salvador. President of Cortland (N.Y.) Civic Association for Education, 1950-51. Consultant in science education to New York State Education Department, Florida State Education Department, and Organization of Central American States.

MEMBER: American Association for the Advancement of Science (fellow), American Ornithological Union, Wilson Ornithological Society, Cooper Ornithological Society, Sigma Xi.

WRITINGS—Published by Allyn & Bacon, except as indicated: *Exploring Science,* Books 1-6, 1955, 4th edition (with Mary Durkee), 1965, Books 7-9 (with Robert Kilburn), 1965-66; (with A. T. Collette) *Teaching Science in Today's Secondary Schools,* 1959, 3rd edition, 1968; (with Kilburn) *Exploring Earth Science,* 1965, 3rd edition (with Kilburn and Peter Howell), 1975; (with Kilburn) *Exploring Life Science,* 1965, 3rd edition (with Kilburn and Howell), 1975; (with Kilburn) *Exploring Physical Science,* 1966, 3rd edition (with Kilburn and Howell), 1977; *Cien Aves de El Salvador* (title means "One Hundred Birds of El Salvador"), Ministry of Education of El Salvador, 1978. Contributor of tapes to two-record album *Beautiful Bird Songs of the World,* National Audubon Society and Cornell Laboratory of Ornithology, 1977.

WORK IN PROGRESS: Life histories and distribution of Salvadoran birds; North American migrant birds in El Salvador.

SIDELIGHTS: Walter A. Thurber's books have been published in Canada, Great Britain, and Asia. He was active in promoting the conservation of plants and animals in El Salvador from 1966 to 1980, and told *CA* he speaks "some Spanish."

AVOCATIONAL INTERESTS: Mountain climbing, travel.

TICE, George A(ndrew) 1938-

PERSONAL: Born October 13, 1938, in Newark, N.J.; son of William S. and Margaret T. (Robertson) Tice; divorced; children: Christopher, Loretta, Lisa, Lynn, Jennifer. *Education:* Attended high school in Newark, N.J. *Home:* 323 Gill Lane, No. 9B, Iselin, N.J. 08830.

CAREER: New School for Social Research, New York, N.Y., instructor in photography, 1970—. *Military service:* U.S. Navy, 1956-59. *Awards, honors:* Grand Prix du Festival d'Arles, 1973, for *Paterson;* National Endowment for the Arts fellowship and Guggenheim fellowship, both 1973.

WRITINGS: (Illustrator) Millen Brand, *Fields of Peace: A Pennsylvania German Album,* Doubleday, 1970; (illustrator) George Mendoza, *Goodbye, River, Goodbye* (juvenile), Doubleday, 1971; *Paterson,* Rutgers University Press, 1972; (illustrator) Martin Dibner, *Seacoast Maine: The People and Places,* Doubleday, 1973; *George A. Tice: Photographs, 1953-1973,* Rutgers University Press, 1975; *Urban Landscapes: A New Jersey Portrait,* Rutgers University Press, 1975.

Artie Van Blarcum, Addison House, 1977; *Urban Romantic: The Photographs of George Tice,* David R. Godine, 1982.

WORK IN PROGRESS: Photography book on Abraham Lincoln's legacy in America.

SIDELIGHTS: George A. Tice told *CA* that "photography is whatever we want it to be."

* * *

TODD, Herbert Eatton 1908-

PERSONAL: Born February 22, 1908, in London, England; son of Henry Graves (a headmaster) and Minnie Elizabeth Todd; married Bertha Joyce Hughes, 1932 (died, 1968); children: Jonathan (died, 1964), Mark, Stephen. *Education:* Attended Christ's Hospital, Horsham, England, 1919-25. *Politics:* Conservative. *Religion:* Church of England. *Home:* St. Nicholas, 2 Brownlow Rd., Berkhamsted, Hertfordshire, England.

CAREER: Writer. Houlder Brothers Ltd., London, England, shipping clerk, 1925-27; British Foreign and Colonial Corp., London, investment clerk, 1927-29; Bourne & Hollingsworth Ltd., London, hosiery underbuyer, 1929-31; F. G. Wigley & Co. Ltd., London, 1931-69, began as traveler, became director. Broadcaster of "Bobby Brewster" stories and children's musical programs on radio and television; performer in local operatic productions, 1945-62. *Military service:* Royal Air Force, 1940-45; became squadron leader. *Member:* Berkhamsted Amateur Operatic and Dramatic Society (choir master, 1948-52; chairman, 1956-60; president, 1961-71). *Awards, honors:* White Rose Award, 1971, for *Bobby Brewster and the Ghost.*

WRITINGS: The Sick Cow, Brockhampton Press, 1974, 5th edition, 1982; *George the Fire Engine,* Hodder & Stoughton Children's Books, 1976, 2nd edition, 1979; *Changing of the Guard,* Hodder & Stoughton Children's Books, 1978; *The Roundabout Horse,* Hodder & Stoughton Children's Books, 1978; *The Very Very Very Long Dog,* Carousel, 1978, 4th edition, 1981; (with Val Biro) *The King of Beasts,* Hodder & Stoughton Children's Books, 1979; *Here Comes Wordman!,* Carousel, 1980; *The Big Sneeze,* Hodder & Stoughton Children's Books, 1980, 3rd edition, 1982; *Jungle Silver,* Hodder & Stoughton Children's Books, 1981; *The Crawly Crawly Caterpillar,* Carousel, 1981; *The Dial-a-Story Book,* Puffin, 1981; *The Tiny Tiny Tadpole,* Carousel, 1982; *The Scruffy Scruffy Dog,* Carousel, 1983.

"Bobby Brewster" series; published by Brockhampton Press prior to 1975, and by Hodder & Stoughton Children's Books after 1975, except as indicated: *Bobby Brewster and the Winker's Club,* Edmund Ward, 1949; *Bobby Brewster,* 1954, 8th edition, 1981; *Bobby Brewster, Bus Conductor,* 1955, 8th edition, 1981; *Bobby Brewster's Shadow,* 1956, 7th edition, 1979; *Bobby Brewster's Bicycle,* 1957, 8th edition, 1983; *Bobby Brewster's Camera,* 1959, 7th edition, 1982.

Bobby Brewster's Wallpaper, 1961, 6th edition, 1975; *Bobby Brewster's Conker,* 1963, 5th edition, 1973; *Bobby Brewster, Detective,* 1964, 3rd edition, 1970; *Bobby Brewster's Potato,* 1964, 5th edition, 1973; *Bobby Brewster and the Ghost,* 1966, 7th edition, 1971; *Bobby Brewster's Kite,* 1967, 5th edition, 1981; *Bobby Brewster's Scarecrow,* 1967, 5th edition, 1980; *Bobby Brewster's Torch,* 1968, 3rd edition, 1971.

Bobby Brewster's Balloon Race, 1970, 5th edition, 1979; *Bobby Brewster's First Magic,* 1970; *Bobby Brewster's Typewriter,* 1971, 2nd edition, 1972; *Bobby Brewster's Bee,* 1972, 3rd edition, 1983; *Bobby Brewster's Wishbone,* 1974, 2nd edition, 1977; *Bobby Brewster's Bookmark,* 1975, 3rd edition, 1982; *Bobby Brewster's Tealeaves,* 1979, 3rd edition, 1983; *Bobby Brewster's First Fun,* 1974; *Bobby Brewster's Lamp Post,* 1982.

Author, with Capel Annand, of *Blackbird Pie,* a musical play for children, Boosey & Hawkes, 1956; also author of five adult musical revues and ten children's musical programs, produced by British Broadcasting Corp., 1949-57.

SIDELIGHTS: Herbert Eatton Todd comments: "I write very simple short stories, and insist that each has a plot with a beginning, a middle, and an end. I started as a story*teller,* firstly to my own sons—and from then on I have told stories and talked about writing in over 5000 schools and libraries throughout Britain and in several other English-speaking countries. I have also broadcast and televised my stories on British radio and TV stations and in other countries, many times. I write purely for fun—both for my listeners and readers (I hope) and myself—and only sit down to write a story when I have the urge and when I have formed in my mind the complete plot—most particularly the end." Several of Todd's books have been translated into foreign languages.

* * *

TOMPKINS, Peter 1919-

PERSONAL: Born April 29, 1919; son of Laurence (a sculptor) and Mary (Arthur) Tompkins; married Jerree Lee Talbot Smith, April 3, 1945 (divorced); married Elizabeth B. Vreeland; children: (first marriage) Elektra Robin, Timothy Christopher, Ptolemy Christian. *Education:* Attended Stowe School, Buckinghamshire, England, and Harvard University; additional study at Sorbonne, University of Paris. *Home:* 8900 Gallant Green Dr., McLean, Va. 22102. *Agent:* Carl Brandt, Brandt & Brandt Literary Agents, Inc., 1501 Broadway, New York, N.Y. 10036.

CAREER: Writer. Left Harvard University to become war correspondent, 1939-41; worked for *New York Herald Tribune* Rome Bureau; was Mutual Broadcasting System's representative for Italy, and National Broadcasting Co. correspondent in Greece. *Wartime service:* U.S. Office of Strategic Services. *Member:* National Press Club (Washington, D.C.).

WRITINGS: (Editor and author of introduction) George Bernard Shaw, *To a Young Actress: The Letters of Bernard Shaw to Molly Tompkins,* C. N. Potter, 1960; (editor) *Shaw and Molly Tompkins in Their Own Words,* Anthony Blond, 1961, C. N. Potter, 1962; *A Spy in Rome,* Simon & Schuster, 1962; *The Eunuch and the Virgin: A Study of Curious Customs,* C. N. Potter, 1963; *The Murder of Admiral Darlan: A Study in Conspiracy,* Simon & Schuster, 1965; *Italy Betrayed,* Simon & Schuster, 1966; *Secrets of the Great Pyramid,* Harper, 1971; (with Christopher Bird) *The Secret Life of Plants,* Harper, 1973; *Mysteries of the Mexican Pyramids,* Harper, 1976; *The Magic of Obelisks,* Harper, 1981. Author of over twenty film and television scripts. Contributor to *New Yorker, New Republic, Esquire, Sunday Times* (London), *Times of India,* and *Associated Press.*

SIDELIGHTS: Peter Tompkins, "co-author of 'The Secret Life of Plants' and sole progenitor of 'Secrets of the Great Pyramid,' has evidently decided," notes Raymond A. Sokolov about *Mysteries of the Mexican Pyramids* in a *New York Times Book Review* article, "that the way to success is to tempt the public with secret information. I am hard pressed to name a single piece of hitherto stifled information that he has actually revealed. But I am very happy to have the book that Tompkins in fact wrote, a lively history of the Pyramids of Teotihuacan outside Mexico City."

Richard Severo similarly comments in a *New York Times* review of *Mysteries of the Mexican Pyramids* that Tompkins' book "isn't exactly new evidence [of the advanced civilization of the Mayas] but more a skillful presentation of ideas that have been around for a while. It is a healthy if not overrich mixture of fact, lore, romantic history, supposition and imagination. Although Mr. Tompkins is writing about the Mexican pyramids, he is really presenting us with an exercise in erudition, always engrossing if not always successful, in his effort to give the lay reader a perspective on cosmic knowledge as it existed in ancient times."

BIOGRAPHICAL/CRITICAL SOURCES: *New York Times,* December 12, 1973, December 16, 1976; *New York Times Book Review,* December 30, 1973, March 13, 1977; *Times Literary Supplement,* February 8, 1974.

* * *

TOWNLEY, Rod 1942-

PERSONAL: Born June 7, 1942, in Orange, N.J.; son of William Richard (a businessman) and Elise (Fredman) Townley; married Libby Blackman (a reference librarian), April 4, 1970 (divorced, 1980); children: Jesse Blackman. *Education:* Attended Hamilton College, 1960-61, and University of Chicago, 1961-62; Bard College, A.B., 1965; Rutgers University, M.A., 1970, Ph.D., 1972. *Home:* 7 West 14th St., New York, N.Y. 10011. *Office: TV Guide,* 1290 Avenue of the Americas, New York, N.Y. 10104.

CAREER: Passaic County Community College, Paterson, N.J., associate professor of world literature, 1972-73; free-lance writer in Philadelphia, Pa., 1973-80; *TV Guide,* New York, N.Y., editorial writer, 1980—. Fulbright professor of English at University of Concepcion, Chile, 1978-79.

WRITINGS: *Blue Angels Black Angels* (poetry), privately printed, 1972; (contributor) Daniel Hoffman, editor, *University and College Poetry Prizes: 1967-1972,* Academy of American Poets, 1974; (contributor) Ray Boxer, editor, *Eleven Young Poets: The Smith Seventeen* (poetry anthology), The Smith, 1975; *The Early Poetry of William Carlos Williams* (criticism), Cornell University Press, 1975; *Summer Street* (chapbook), The Smith, 1975; *Minor Gods* (novel), St. Martin's, 1976; *Three Musicians* (poetry), The Smith, 1978; (contributor) Carroll F. Terrell, editor, *William Carlos Williams: Man and Poet,* National Poetry Foundation, 1983; *The Year in Soaps: 1983,* Crown, 1984. Regular contributor to *Today,* 1974-78. Contributor to *Studies in Short Fiction, Philadelphia, TV Guide, Village Voice, Detroit Free Press,* and other publications.

WORK IN PROGRESS: Another novel; another volume of poetry.

SIDELIGHTS: Rod Townley told *CA:* "I've found that earning a living by writing entails compromise, but that compromise has a positive side. It pulls down one's vanity, and it leads one in unexpected directions. My books are in four genres, and I hope to explore others."

* * *

TREAHEARNE, Elizabeth
See MAXWELL, Patricia

* * *

TREBACH, Arnold S. 1928-

PERSONAL: Born May 15, 1928, in Lowell, Mass.; son of Morris (a merchant) and Vina (Sandler) Trebach; married Shirley Zuckerman, February 6, 1954 (died, 1976); children: David, Paul. *Education:* Calvin Coolidge College, A.A., 1948; Portia Law School, LL.B., 1951; Princeton University, M.A., 1956, Ph.D., 1958. *Politics:* Independent Democrat. *Religion:* Hebrew. *Office:* School of Justice, American University, Massachusetts and Nebraska Aves. N.W., Washington, D.C. 20016.

CAREER: Admitted to Massachusetts Bar, 1951; practicing attorney in Boston, Mass., 1951-52; University of Tennessee, Knoxville, assistant professor of political science, 1957-60; U.S. Commission on Civil Rights, Washington, D.C., chief of Administration of Justice Section, 1960-63; National Legal Aid and Defender Association, American Bar Center, Chicago, Ill., administrator of National Defender Project, supported by Ford Foundation grant, 1963-64; Howard University, Washington, D.C., director of Law and Human Rights Program, beginning 1964; currently professor of law at American University, Washington, D.C. Investigator, Administrative Office of the Courts of New Jersey, 1955; director, Institute on Drugs, Crime, and Justice, England. *Military service:* U.S. Army, 1952-54; became sergeant. *Member:* International Political Science Association, American Bar Association (member of committee on defense of indigent persons), American Political Science Association.

WRITINGS: (Contributor) *Equal Justice for the Accused* (report of Special Committee to Study Defender Systems), Doubleday, 1959; *The Rationing of Justice: Constitutional Rights and the Criminal Process,* Rutgers University Press, 1964; (with Evelyn M. Idelson) *Jobs, Race, and Justice: Strategies for Change,* University Research Corp., 1970; (with Idelson) *New Careers in Justice: A Status Report,* National Institute for New Careers, 1970; (editor) *Drugs, Crime, and Politics,* Praeger, 1978; *The Heroin Solution,* Yale University Press, 1982.

SIDELIGHTS: Arnold Trebach's aim in writing *The Heroin Solution,* says Gina Bari Kolata in a *Washington Post Book World* article, "is to trace the history of attempts to control the drug in this country and in England and to argue for more humility and more humaneness in our approaches to heroin addicts. He largely succeeds in this goal, writing a readable and fascinating book about a drug whose emotional connotation as 'evil incarnate' complicates any attempts to deal rationally with it."

"The virtue of *The Heroin Solution*," comments David H. Rosenthal in the *Village Voice*, "is that it painstakingly reviews all available information, carefully and thoughtfully constructs its arguments, and offers such a mass of evidence that its points seem virtually irrefutable in their own practical terms. In a nation struggling to accept personal preferences it previously labeled 'vices,' surely the time is approaching when we have to stop stigmatizing people who depend on a given drug, for we do so at great cost to ourselves and our peace of mind. Those who wish to step back and reconsider the matter could find no better starting point than this book, which attempts to clear away the accumulated misinformation, hysteria, fire and brimstone, and wishful thinking of sixty years of disastrous social policy."

BIOGRAPHICAL/CRITICAL SOURCES: *New Republic*, October 25, 1982; *Washington Post Book World*, November 2, 1982; *Village Voice*, March 22, 1983; *Times Literary Supplement*, June 10, 1983.†

* * *

TREE, Christina 1944-

PERSONAL: Born September 1, 1944, in Honolulu, Hawaii; daughter of Alfred E. (an international banker) and Martha (a nurse; maiden name, Rudneski) Tree; married William A. Davis (a travel editor), September 2, 1971; children: Liam, Timothy, Christopher. *Education:* Mount Holyoke College, B.A., 1965. *Politics:* Liberal. *Religion:* "Liberal Roman Catholic." *Home:* 15 Whittier St., Cambridge, Mass. 02140. *Agent:* Herbert Kenny, 804 Summer St., Manchester, Mass. 01944. *Office:* Boston Globe, Boston, Mass. 02140.

CAREER: *Columbia College Today*, New York City, editorial assistant, 1965-66; *Jubilee*, New York City, staff writer, 1966-67; *Boston Globe*, Boston, Mass., assistant travel editor, 1962-72, contributor, 1977—. *Member:* Society of American Travel Writers.

WRITINGS: *How New England Happened*, Little, Brown, 1976, new edition, 1981; *Massachusetts: An Explorer's Guide*, Countryman Press, 1979; *Maine: An Explorer's Guide*, Countryman Press, 1982; *Vermont: An Explorer's Guide*, Countryman Press, 1983. Contributor to magazines.

SIDELIGHTS: Christina Tree writes: "Before my children were born, I traveled abroad constantly, but at present am content writing about New England, which I do regularly and with ever-increasing enjoyment." *Avocational interests:* "For relaxation I sketch and I collect islands without electricity which our family can retreat to."

* * *

TRIPODI, Tony 1932-

PERSONAL: Born November 30, 1932, in Sacramento, Calif.; son of Nicholas and Christina (Grandinetti) Tripodi; married Roni Ann Roberts (a social worker); children: Lee Anna, Anthony Carroll, David Elliot, Stephen Joseph, Rachel Ann Newman (stepdaughter). *Education:* University of California, Berkeley, A.B., 1954, M.S.W., 1958; Columbia University, D.S.W., 1963. *Politics:* Independent. *Religion:* No preference. *Home:* 330 Hazelwood, Ann Arbor, Mich. 48103. *Office:* School of Social Work, University of Michigan, Ann Arbor, Mich. 48104.

CAREER: California Department of Mental Hygiene, Sacramento, research technician, 1958-59; California Youth Authority, Sacramento, research analyst, 1959-60; Brooklyn College (now Brooklyn College of the City University of New York), Brooklyn, N.Y., research associate in department of psychology, 1963-65; Columbia University, School of Social Work, New York, N.Y., assistant professor of social research, 1963-65; University of California, School of Social Welfare, Berkeley, assistant professor of social welfare, 1965-66; University of Michigan, School of Social Work, Ann Arbor, professor of social work, 1966—.

Evaluation consultant, San Francisco State College (now University), Institute of Social Sciences, 1965-66; evaluation consultant, monitor, and technical assistant specialist, U.S. Office of Economic Opportunity, 1966-68; associate director and research consultant, Family and School Consultation Project, Ann Arbor, 1969-74. *Military service:* U.S. Naval Reserve, 1954-62. *Member:* Academy of Certified Social Workers, National Association of Social Workers, American Psychological Association, California Scholarship Organization (life member), Phi Theta Kappa (life member).

WRITINGS: (With James Bieri, Alvin Atkins, Scott Briar, Robin Lehman, and Henry Miller) *Clinical and Social Judgment*, Wiley, 1966; (with Phillip Fellin and Meyer) *The Assessment of Social Research*, F. E. Peacock, 1969, 2nd edition, 1983; (editor with Fellin and Meyer) *Exemplars of Social Research*, F. E. Peacock, 1969.

(Contributor) P. B. Warr, editor, *Thought and Personality: A Book of Readings*, Penguin, 1970; (with Fellin and Irwin Epstein) *Social Program Evaluation*, F. E. Peacock, 1971; (with Fellin, Epstein, and Roger Lind) *Social Workers at Work*, F. E. Peacock, 1972, 2nd edition, 1976; *Uses and Abuses of Social Research in Social Work*, Columbia University Press, 1974; (with Epstein) *Research Techniques for Program Planning, Monitoring, and Evaluation*, Columbia University Press, 1980; *Evaluation Research for Social Workers*, Prentice-Hall, 1983. Contributor of articles and reviews to professional journals. Editor of *Social Work Research and Abstracts*, 1980-84.

* * *

TRIPP, Miles (Barton) 1923-
(John Michael Brett, Michael Brett)

PERSONAL: Born May 5, 1923, in Ganwick Corner, near Barnet, England; son of Cecil Lewis and Brena Mary (Yells) Tripp. *Education:* Attended county school in Hertfordshire. *Address:* c/o Macmillan Publishers Ltd., Little Essex St., London WC2R 3LF, England.

CAREER: Free-lance writer. *Member:* Society of Authors (England), Crime Writers Association (England; chairman, 1968-69).

WRITINGS—Published by Macmillan (London), except as indicated: *Faith Is a Windsock*, P. Davies, 1952; *The Image of Man*, Darwen Finlayson, 1955; *A Glass of Red Wine*, Macdonald & Co., 1960; *Kilo Forty*, 1963, Holt, 1964; (under pseudonym Michael Brett) *Diecast*, Fawcett, 1963, published under pseudonym John Michael Brett, Pan Books, 1966; *The Skin Dealer*, Holt, 1964; (under pseudonym Michael Brett) *A*

Plague of Dragons, Arthur Barker, 1965, published under pseudonym John Michael Brett, Pan Books, 1966; *A Quartet of Three,* 1965; *The Chicken,* 1966; (under pseudonym John Michael Brett) *A Cargo of Spent Evil,* Arthur Barker, 1966; *The Fifth Point of the Compass,* 1967; *One Is One,* 1968; *The Chicken* [and] *Zilla,* Pan Books, 1968; *Malice and the Maternal Instinct,* 1969; *The Eighth Passenger,* Heinemann, 1969.

A Man without Friends, 1970; *Five Minutes with a Stranger,* 1971; *The Claws of God,* 1972; *Obsession,* 1973; *Woman at Risk,* 1974; *A Woman in Bed,* 1976; *The Once a Year Man,* 1977; *The Wife-Smuggler,* 1978; *Cruel Victim,* 1979; *High Heels,* 1980; *Going Solo,* 1981. Also author of television adaptation "A Man without Friends" based on his novel, broadcast in England, 1972.

* * *

TRUEBLOOD, Paul Graham 1905-

PERSONAL: Born October 21, 1905, in Macksburg, Iowa; son of Charles Elmer and Adele (Graham) Trueblood; married Helen Churchill, August 19, 1931; children: Anne Brodzky, Susan (Mrs. Larry A. Stuart). *Education:* Willamette University, B.A., 1928; Duke University, M.A., 1930, Ph.D., 1935. *Politics:* Independent. *Religion:* Quaker and Methodist. *Home and office:* 2635 Bolton Ter. South, Salem, Ore. 97302.

CAREER: Friends University, Wichita, Kan., instructor, 1931-34; Mohonk School for Boys, Lake Mohonk, N.Y., head of English studies, 1935-37; University of Idaho, Moscow, instructor in English, 1937-40; Stockton College, Stockton, Calif., associate professor of English, 1940-46; Rollins College, Winter Park, Fla., interim assistant professor, 1946-47; University of Washington, Seattle, assistant professor of English, 1947-52; University of Oregon, Eugene, visiting professor of English, 1954-55; Willamette University, Salem, Ore., professor of English, and chairman of department, 1955-70, professor emeritus, 1971—. Visiting lecturer, University of British Columbia, 1963. Participant in First International Byron Seminar, Cambridge University, 1974, Third International Byron Seminar, Missolonghi, Greece, 1976, and Sixth International Byron Seminar, University of Delaware, 1979.

MEMBER: International P.E.N., Modern Language Association of America, Keats-Shelley Association of America, Byron Society (founding member of American committee; member of board of directors, 1975), American Association of University Professors, Philological Association of the Pacific Coast (member of executive committee, 1964). *Awards, honors:* Pendle Hill fellow, 1934-35; American Council of Learned Societies scholar, 1952-53; Willamette University Distinguished Alumni citation, 1975.

WRITINGS: The Flowering of Byron's Genius: Studies in Byron's Don Juan, Stanford University Press, 1945, revised edition, Russell, 1962; *Lord Byron,* Twayne, 1969, 2nd revised edition, G. K. Hall, 1977; (editor) *Byron's Political and Cultural Influence in Nineteenth Century Europe,* Humanities, 1981. Contributor to *Saturday Review, Keats-Shelley Journal, Byron Journal,* and other periodicals.

WORK IN PROGRESS: The Applegate Trail, a historical novel of pioneer Oregon in 1846.

SIDELIGHTS: Paul Graham Trueblood spent sabbatical year, 1964-65, following Byron's trail from England to Greece and traveled and wrote in Europe (chiefly Greece), 1971-72. Trueblood was the first American invited to address the Byron Society in Parliament's House of Lords, 1975. *Avocational interests:* Vocal and piano music, swimming, mountain climbing, dramatics.

* * *

TRUNGPA, Chogyam 1939-

PERSONAL: Born February, 1939, in Geje, Kham, Tibet; son of Yeshe (a farmer) and Bo-chung Dargye. *Education:* Received the highest initiations of the Nyingma and Kagyu orders of Tibetan Buddhism; holds the Khenpo degree, the equivalent of a Doctor of Divinity degree; attended Oxford University, 1963-67. *Politics:* None. *Religion:* Buddhist. *Office:* 1345 Spruce St., Boulder, Colo. 80302.

CAREER: Trungpa is the eleventh Trungpa Tulku, considered to be the tenth successive reincarnation of a great Tibetan teacher; in 1959, forced to escape Tibet, he fled to India where, by appointment of His Holiness the Dalai Lama, he served as spiritual advisor to the Young Lamas' Home School in Dalhousie; he then chose Scotland as a retreat, where he founded Samye Ling, a Buddhist meditation center, in 1967; Trungpa moved to the United States in 1970 and is Vajracarya the Venerable (president) of Vajradhatu, a nationwide association of Tibetan Buddhist meditation communities and centers which he founded, based in Boulder, Colo.; he also founded the Nalanda Foundation, also located in Boulder, which includes Shambhala Training, Naropa Institute, and the Mudra Theatre Group. *Awards, honors:* Spaulding fellow, Oxford University, 1963-67.

WRITINGS—Published by Shambhala, except as indicated: (As told to Esme Cramer Roberts) *Born in Tibet,* Allen & Unwin, 1966, Harcourt, 1968, revised edition, Great Eastern Book Co., 1981; *Meditation in Action,* 1969; *Mudra,* 1972; *Cutting through Spiritual Materialism,* 1973; *Glimpses of Abhidharma,* Prajna Press, 1975; *Visual Dharma,* 1975; (with Herbert Guenther) *The Dawn of Tantra,* 1975; (translator with Francesca Fremantle, and author of commentary) *The Tibetan Book of the Dead,* 1975; *The Myth of Freedom and the Way of Meditation,* 1976; *Empowerment,* Vajradhatu Publications, 1976.

(Translator, and author of foreword) *The Rain of Wisdom,* 1980; *Journey without Goal: The Tantric Wisdom of the Buddha,* Prajna Press, 1981; (contributor) Deborah E. Klimburg-Salter, editor, *The Silk Route and the Diamond Path,* University of California, Los Angeles, Art Council, 1982; (translator, and author of preface) *The Life of Marpa,* Prajna Press, 1982; (author of foreword) Osel Tendzin, *Buddha in the Palm of Your Hand,* 1982; *First Thought, Best Thought,* 1983; *Shambhala: The Sacred Path of the Warrior,* 1984; *The Teachings of the Theravadin Tradition,* 1984; *Exchanging Self for Others: The Mahayana Teachings of Compassion,* Prajna Press, 1984.

Contributor to *Naropa Institute Journal of Psychology, Loka,* and *Loka 2* (journals of the Naropa Institute). Editor, with his students, of an occasional journal, *Garuda.*

WORK IN PROGRESS: The Complete Teachings of Mahayana, for publication by Shambhala; a translation, with the Nalanda Translation Group, of *Biographies of the Mahasiddhas,* for publication by Prajna Press.

SIDELIGHTS: Chogyam Trungpa has dedicated his life to spiritual learning and Buddhist teachings. At the age of one, he was taken to a monastery where he studied until the Chinese invaded Tibet. When he was thirteen months old, he was enthroned as the supreme abbot of the Surmang group of monasteries. There he completed his scholastic and meditative training before the 1959 Communist assumption of power in Tibet. He continued his spiritual education in India after fleeing Tibet; he then founded a Buddhist meditation center, Samye Ling, in Scotland, saying that he felt the need to preserve the immense amount of teaching he had received. He has settled in Boulder, Colorado, where he founded Vajradhatu, an association of Tibetan Buddhist meditation centers, and serves as its Vajracarya the Venerable, or president. There he also founded the Nalanda Foundation, which includes other Buddhist groups and organizations.

* * *

TRUSSLER, Simon 1942-

PERSONAL: Born June 11, 1942, in Tenterden, Kent, England; son of John and Joan (Ovenden) Trussler; married Glenda Leeming (a lecturer), August 23, 1966 (divorced, 1983); children: two. *Education:* University College, London, B.A., 1963, M.A., 1966. *Politics:* Radical. *Home:* Great Robhurst, Woodchurch, Ashford, Kent, England. *Office:* Goldsmith's College, University of London, Lewisham Way, New Cross, London SE14 6NW, England.

CAREER: Lecturer in English at Hammersmith College of Art, London, England, 1963-65, and Enfield College of Technology, London, 1965-67; London drama critic, *Drama Review,* 1963-70; *Tribune,* London, drama critic, 1965-73; Tufts University, London programme, London, lecturer in drama, 1973-81; University of London, Goldsmith's College, London, lecturer in drama, 1981—. Lecturer in drama, Oxford University Delegacy for Extra-Mural Studies. Founding member, Board of Management, British Theatre Institute, 1975; associate director, British Centre of the International Theatre Institute, 1979.

WRITINGS: (Editor with Charles Marowitz) *Theatre at Work,* Methuen, 1967, Hill & Wang, 1968; (editor) *New English Dramatists XIII,* Penguin, 1968; (editor) *Burlesque Plays of the Eighteenth Century,* Oxford University Press, 1969; (author of an introduction and notes) William Duncan Taylor, compiler, *Eighteenth Century Comedy,* Oxford University Press, 1969; *The Plays of John Osborne: An Assessment,* Gollancz, 1969.

(With Glenda Leeming) *The Plays of Arnold Wesker: An Assessment,* Gollancz, 1971; *The Plays of John Whiting: An Assessment,* Gollancz, 1972; *John Arden,* Columbia University Press, 1973; *The Plays of Harold Pinter: An Assessment,* Gollancz, 1973; *A Classification for the Performing Arts,* British Theatre Institute, 1974; *Edward Bond,* Longman, 1976; (compiler) *Royal Shakespeare Company, 1978,* Royal Shakespeare Company, 1979.

(Editor) *New Theatre Voices of the Seventies,* Eyre Methuen, 1981; (editor with others) *Oxford Companion to the Theatre,* 4th edition, Oxford University Press, 1983. Contributor to periodicals, including *Plays and Players, Times, Teacher, London Magazine, Flourish,* and *Listener.* Founding editor, *Prompt,* 1962, *Theatre Quarterly,* 1971, and *Theatre International,* 1981; editor, *Encore,* 1965, *Theatrefacts,* 1974.

WORK IN PROGRESS: Editing "Methuen Theatre Checklists" series; a research project on the history of popular entertainments.

TUCCILLE, Jerome 1937-

PERSONAL: Surname pronounced too-*chilly;* born May 30, 1937, in New York, N.Y.; son of Salvatore J. (a taxi owner) and Virginia (Marano) Tuccille; married Marie Winkler, January 23, 1965; children: Jerome, Christine. *Education:* Manhattan College, B.S., 1959. *Politics:* "Anarchist-Libertarian." *Religion:* None. *Residence:* Cos Cob, Conn. *Agent:* Collier Associates, 875 Ave. of the Americas, Suite 1003, New York, N.Y. 10001.

CAREER: Writer. Investment broker, 1975—. *Military service:* U.S. Marine Corps, 1957-63; became sergeant.

WRITINGS: Radical Libertarianism: A Right Wing Alternative, Bobbs-Merrill, 1970; *It Usually Begins with Ayn Rand: A Libertarian Odyssey* (novel), Stein & Day, 1971; *Here Comes Immortality,* Stein & Day, 1973; *Who's Afraid of 1984,* Arlington House, 1975; *Everything the Beginner Needs to Invest Wisely,* Arlington House, 1977; *The Optimist's Guide to Making Money in the 1980's: A Complete Program for Investing in the American Economic Miracle of the Next Decade,* Morrow, 1978; *Dynamic Investing: The System for Automatic Profits, No Matter Which Way the Market Goes,* New American Library, 1981, revised edition published as *Dynamic Investing,* New American Library, 1982; *Inside the Underground Economy,* New American Library, 1982; *How to Profit from the Wall Street Mergers: Riding the Takeover Wave,* New American Library, 1983; *Kingdom: The Story of the Hunt Family of Texas,* Jameson Books, 1984. Also author of *The New Tax Law and You,* New American Library. Contributor of articles to newspapers and periodicals, including *New York Times, Libertarian Forum, Nation,* and *National Review.*

WORK IN PROGRESS: A novel.

AVOCATIONAL INTERESTS: Travel (Australia, Europe), tennis, squash, and skiing.

BIOGRAPHICAL/CRITICAL SOURCES: National Review, October 6, 1970; *Nation,* November 16, 1970.

* * *

TUCKER, Michael R(ay) 1941-

PERSONAL: Born April 3, 1941, in Dallas, Tex.; son of Raymond E. (an administrator) and Irene (an artist; maiden name, Wallace) Tucker; married Nancy E. Shull, August 26, 1961; children: Mark David, Haddon Criswell, Shannon Noel. *Education:* Western Baptist Bible College, B.A., 1963; Dallas Theological Seminary, Th.M., 1967; Denver Theological Seminary, D.Min., 1979. *Home:* 9127 South Juniper St., Tempe, Ariz. 85284. *Office:* Bethany Community Church, 6240 South Price Rd., Tempe, Ariz. 85283.

CAREER: Ordained Baptist minister, 1970; pastor of Baptist church in Birmingham, Ala., 1967-70; Southeastern Bible College, Birmingham, teacher, 1968-70; Colorado Springs Christian School, Colorado Springs, Colo., president of board of directors, 1971-81; currently affiliated with Bethany Community Church, Tempe, Ariz. Chaplain for Civil Air Patrol, 1971-73. *Member:* National Association of Evangelicals, Conservative Baptist Association of America (board member, 1975-78), Rocky Mountain Conservative Baptist Association (board member, 1973-78), Arizona Association of Evangelicals (board member, 1982—).

WRITINGS: The Church That Dared to Change, Tyndale, 1975; *Live Confidently: How to Know God's Will,* Tyndale, 1976;

The Church: Change or Decay, Tyndale, 1978. Contributor to church periodicals.

SIDELIGHTS: Michael R. Tucker writes: "I believe the evangelical church has gained a new place in American life. Presidents, well-known athletes, movie stars, senators, and other spotlight people are publicly acknowledging their faith in Jesus Christ. People are looking for an anchor and a guide. Evangelical Christianity provides both, and Christian books are part of what God is doing in the last quarter of the twentieth century."

* * *

TULLY, John (Kimberley) 1923-

PERSONAL: Born July 7, 1923, in Sutton Coldfield, England; son of John (an actor) and Ruby (an actress; maiden name, Kimberley) Tully; married Margaret Else; children: Richard, David, Katharine, Diana. *Education:* Attended school in North Wales. *Home:* 209 Jersey Rd., Isleworth, Middlesex TW7 4RE, England.

CAREER: Began writing for newspapers, later turned to film, television, and books. *Military service:* Royal Air Force, 1940-45; became flight sergeant. *Member:* Writers Guild of Great Britain (vice-chairman, 1976-77; joint chairman, 1977-78).

WRITINGS—Plays: *Woman Alive,* Evans Brothers, 1958.

Juveniles, except as indicated: *The Crocodile* (also see below), BBC Publications, 1972; *The Raven and the Cross* (also see below), BBC Publications, 1974; *The Glass Knife,* Methuen, 1974; *The White Cat,* Methuen, 1975; *Johnny Goodlooks,* Methuen, 1977; *Johnny and the Yank,* Methuen, 1978; *Muhammed Ali: King of the Ring,* Collins, 1978; *Natfact 7* (young adult), Methuen, 1984.

Published by Collins English Library: *Inspector Holt and the Fur Van,* 1977; *Inspector Holt Gets His Man,* 1977; *Where Is Bill Ojo?,* 1978; *The Bridge,* 1979; *Cats in the Dark,* 1980.

Film scripts: "The Man from Nowhere," Children's Film Foundation, 1976; "One Hour to Zero," Children's Film Foundation, 1976. Also author of documentary films for Shell Oil Co., British Gas Council, Midland Bank, Mobil Oil Co., Amoco Oil Co., British Electricity Council, British Central Electricity Generating Board, and British Aerospace.

Also author of television serials, including "The Viaduct," 1972, "Thursday's Child," 1973, "Tom's Midnight Garden," 1974, "Kizzy," 1976, and "The Phoenix and the Carpet," 1977. Writer of television plays, including "The Crocodile," "The Raven and the Cross," "The King of Argos," "A Choice of Friends," "The Jo-Jo Tree," and "The Silver Fish." Also contributor to television documentaries, including "Going to Work," "Exploring Science," "Merry-Go-Round," "Countdown," and "Maths Counts."

WORK IN PROGRESS: A series of books entitled "Starpol" for slow readers, for Ginn.

SIDELIGHTS: John Tully told *CA:* "The BBC commissioned me to dramatise a children's novel. Broadcasting dates were fixed. The studio facilities were lined up. All that was lacking was a suitable book to dramatise.

"There are many good novels written for children but few fit the precise demands of time, budget, scope, and aims of a particular TV series. Everyone in the department was reading books furiously, to no avail. At last the producer, in desperation, suggested to me, 'Why don't you write an original television play, and then write the novel to go with it?'

"I snapped up the idea and wrote *The Crocodile.* While the play was in production I started writing the book, with a traumatic realisation that if children were being advised to read it, this had better be good! Not just a 'book of the film' but something worth reading in its own right. I hope I succeeded.

"By the time I had completed a second, similar exercise, *The Raven and the Cross* I had caught the book-writing bug. What tales I could tell if I were not restricted by the mechanics of television! So why not write a book for its own sake, with no holds barred? The result was *The Glass Knife.*

"Drama was and is, I suppose, my first love because I was brought up in the theatre, both sides of my family being up to their hairlines in greasepaint. My grandmother was writing popular melodramas and touring them round England before I was born. My childhood memories are of plays, revues, variety bills, and backstreet digs.

"I have written for a number of adult TV series as well as many children's programmes and I have learned a curious fact, that popular 'adult' material is often the most 'childish.' It's the kids who want to know the truth about the world in terms more thoughtful and sincere." Tully's books have been published in Germany, Sweden, Denmark, South Africa, Holland, and France.

* * *

TURNER, Frederick 1943-

PERSONAL: Born November 19, 1943, in England; came to the United States in 1967; son of Victor Witter (an anthropologist) and Edith (a writer; maiden name, Davis) Turner; married Mei Lin Chang, June 25, 1966; children: Daniel, Benjamin. *Education:* Christ Church, Oxford, B.A., 1965, M.A., 1967, B.Litt., 1967. *Home:* 205 East Woodside Dr., Gambier, Ohio 43022. *Agent:* Virginia Kidd, Box 278, Milford, Pa. 18337. *Office:* Department of English, Kenyon College, Gambier, Ohio 43022.

CAREER: University of California, Santa Barbara, assistant professor of English, 1967-72; Kenyon College, Gambier, Ohio, associate professor of English, 1972—. Has given poetry readings on various radio shows, including "At the Arabica," a nationally syndicated program. *Member:* International Society for the Study of Time, Modern Language Association of America. *Awards, honors:* Levinson Poetry Prize.

WRITINGS: *Deep Sea Fish* (poetry), Unicorn, 1968; *Birth of a First Son* (poetry), Christopher's Books, 1969; *The Water World* (poetry), Christopher's Books, 1970; *Shakespeare and the Nature of Time,* Oxford University Press, 1971; *Between Two Lives* (poetry), Wesleyan University Press, 1972; (editor) William Shakespeare, *Romeo and Juliet,* University of London Press, 1974; (translator) *Three Poems from the German,* Pothanger Press, 1974; *A Double Shadow* (science fiction), Berkley/Putnam, 1978; *Counter-Terra* (poetry), Christopher's Books, 1978; *The Return* (poetry), Countryman Press, 1981.

Contributor to *Chaucer Review, Missouri Review, Kenyon Review, Poetry, Bennington Review, Cumberland Poetry Review,* and numerous other magazines and periodicals. Editor, *Kenyon Review,* 1978-82.

WORK IN PROGRESS: *The Garden,* poems and aphorisms; *The New World,* epic poem; *The Sunstone,* novel; a new collection of poems; various essays.

SIDELIGHTS: Frederick Turner comments that his commitment is "to the essential unity of nature and history; a belief in creative evolution. I oppose the distinction between science and the humanities; I believe that language is coterminous with the world." He adds that major influences have been Shakespeare, Eliot, Yeats, Milton, Homer, and Pasternak.

A Double Shadow has been translated into French and Japanese.

AVOCATIONAL INTERESTS: Natural science, philosophy, anthropology, brain science.

* * *

TURNER, William W. 1927-

PERSONAL: Born April 14, 1927, in Buffalo, N.Y.; son of William Peter (a printing executive) and Magdalen (Weyand) Turner; married Margaret Peiffer (a registered nurse), September 12, 1964; children: Mark Peter, Lori Ann. *Education:* Canisius College, B.S., 1949. *Politics:* Democrat. *Religion:* Roman Catholic. *Home:* 163 Mark Twain Ave., San Rafael, Calif. 94903. *Agent:* Barbara Lowenstein, 250 West 57th St., New York, N.Y. 10019.

CAREER: Federal Bureau of Investigation, special agent in various field offices, 1951-61; free-lance writer in California, 1963—; *Ramparts* (magazine), San Francisco, Calif., senior editor, beginning 1967. Investigator and consultant, National Wiretap Commission, 1975. *Military service:* U.S. Navy, 1945-46; served in Pacific Theater. *Member:* Authors Guild, Authors League of America, International Platform Association, Press Club of San Francisco.

WRITINGS: *The Police Establishment*, Putnam, 1968; *Invisible Witness: The Use and Abuse of the New Technology of Crime Investigation*, Bobbs-Merrill, 1968; *Hoover's F.B.I.: The Men and the Myth*, Sherbourne, 1970; (with E. Asinof and W. Hinckle) *The Ten Second Jailbreak*, Holt, 1973; (contributor) *Investigating the FBI*, Doubleday, 1973; (with John Christian) *The Assassination of Robert F. Kennedy*, Random House, 1978; (with Hinckle) *The Fish Is Red: The Story of the Secret War against Castro*, Harper, 1981.

Author and editor of police science material for "Police Evidence Library," Bancroft-Whitney Co. Contributor to *Nation, Cosmopolitan, Saga,* and *Cavalier.*

SIDELIGHTS: William W. Turner told *CA* that he "became interested in writing as a career when I was sent to Dallas as an ex-FBI man by *Saga* to cover the aftermath of the John F. Kennedy assassination. I gradually became convinced that Kennedy was the victim of a political conspiracy. . . . Am recognized as one of the established critics of the Warren Report." Turner ran as an "assassination conspiracy" candidate in the Democratic primaries in California's Sixth Congressional District. He says he polled "an unexpectedly large number of votes."

In his book, *Hoover's F.B.I.: The Men and the Myth*, Turner offers readers an insider's view of the agency and its former director, revealing "a highly political and totally corrupt institution built around the political ambitions of one man, and despite its reputation, extraordinarily inept," according to Andy Truskier in *Ramparts*. Frank J. Donner writes in the *Nation* that "Turner's book is especially valuable because he examines aspects of the FBI's functioning which have never been adequately aired before: the agency's bureaucratic solidarity, minimizing the risk of defections; the organization of former agents which zealously promotes a climate of reverence for the agency; the tireless official efforts to suppress or neutralize criticism; the obsessive concern with image, frequently at the expense of the public interest; Hoover's maneuvers to influence local law enforcement by remote control and without taking responsibility for its failures."

MEDIA ADAPTATIONS: *The Ten Second Jailbreak* was made into the film "Breakout."

BIOGRAPHICAL/CRITICAL SOURCES: *Time,* June 17, 1968; *Book World,* June 23, 1968; *Ramparts,* August, 1970; *Nation,* February 8, 1971; *New York Times Book Review,* September 13, 1981; *Washington Post Book World,* October 18, 1981; *Los Angeles Times Book Review,* October 18, 1981.

* * *

TYLER, Ron(nie) C(urtis) 1941-

PERSONAL: Born December 29, 1941, in Temple, Tex.; son of Jasper J. and Melba (James) Tyler; married. *Education:* Temple Junior College, A.A., 1962; Abilene Christian College, B.S.E., 1964; Texas Christian University, M.A., 1966, Ph.D., 1968. *Home:* 3216 Odessa Ave., Fort Worth, Tex. 76109. *Office address:* Amon Carter Museum of Western Art, P.O. Box 2365, Fort Worth, Tex. 76113.

CAREER: Austin College, Sherman, Tex., assistant professor of history, 1967-69; Amon Carter Museum of Western Art, Fort Worth, Tex., assistant director for collections and programs, 1969—. *Member:* American Association of Museums, Conference on Latin American History, Latin American Studies Association, Western History Association, Southwestern Council on Latin American Studies, Texas State Historical Association. *Awards, honors:* Carroll Award, for *The Mexican War: A Lithographic Record;* Tullis Award, for *The Big Bend.*

WRITINGS: *Joseph Wade Hampton, Editor and Individualist,* Texas Western Press, 1969; *Vision, Destiny—War!: Manifest Destiny and the Mexican War,* Steck, 1970; (editor with Lawrence R. Murphy) *Slave Narratives of Texas,* Encino Press, 1971; *Santiago Vidaurri and the Confederacy,* Texas State Historical Association, 1973; *The Mexican War: A Lithographic Record,* Texas State Historical Association, 1973; *The Cowboy,* Ridge Press, 1975; *The Big Bend: The Last Texas Frontier,* National Park Service, 1975; *The Image of America in Caricature and Cartoon,* Amon Carter Museum, 1975; *The Rodeo Photographs of John Addison Stryker,* Encino Press, 1977; (editor) *Posada's Mexico,* Library of Congress, 1979.

(Editor) *Alfred Jacob Miller: Artist on the Oregon Trail,* Amon Carter Museum, 1982; *Visions of America: Pioneer Artists in a New World,* Thames & Hudson, 1983; (editor) *Prints of the American West,* Amon Carter Museum, 1983; (editor with Paula Eyrich Tyler) *Texas Museums: A Guidebook,* University of Texas Press, 1983.

Contributor to history journals.

* * *

TYLER, Zeke
See MARSHALL, Mel(vin D.)

U

UDOFF, Yale M(aurice) 1935-

PERSONAL: Born March 29, 1935, in Brooklyn, N.Y.; son of Julius I. (a businessman) and Martha (Schneider) Udoff. *Education:* Michigan State University, B.A., 1957; Georgetown Law School, law study, 1958-59. *Home:* 3383 North Knoll Dr., Hollywood, Calif. 90068. *Agent:* Douglas Rae, 28 Charing Cross Rd., London NC2H ODB, England; and Marty Shapiro, Shapiro/Lichtman, 1800 Avenue of the Stars, Los Angeles, Calif. 90067.

CAREER: National Broadcasting Co., New York City, trainee, 1961-62; American Broadcasting Co., New York City, director of prime time program development, 1962-66; playwright, television and film writer, 1966—. *Military service:* U.S. Army, 1958-59; became first lieutenant. *Member:* Dramatists Guild, Writers Guild of America. *Awards, honors:* Stanley Drama Award, 1969, for "The Club" and "The Little Gentleman"; Charles MacArthur Playwriting Award (honorable mention), 1974, for "Magritte Skies"; "Bad Timing/A Sensual Obsession" was named best film at the Toronto Film Festival, 1980, and was selected for the Berlin Film Festival and the New York Film Festival, both in 1980; "Vera" won first prize for short feature at the Houston Film Festival, 1983.

WRITINGS—Plays: *A Gun Play* (full-length; first produced in Hartford, Conn. by Hartford Stage Co., January, 1971; produced Off-Broadway at Cherry Lane Theatre, October, 1971), Samuel French, 1972; "Magritte Skies" (full-length), first produced as staged reading at Eugene O'Neill Theatre Conference, July, 1973, produced in New York City at Playwrights Horizons, 1975; "Shade" (one-act; published in *Mademoiselle*, April, 1972), first produced in Paris, France, December, 1972; "The Academy of Desire" (one-act), first produced in San Francisco, Calif. at American Conservatory Theatre, March, 1973; "Fault Line" (full-length), first produced at Squaw Valley Writers Conference, 1976; "The Example" (full-length), first produced in Los Angeles, Calif. at the Melrose Theatre, 1979; "First Draft" (full-length), first produced at Eugene O'Neill Theatre Conference, 1982. Also author of plays, "The Little Gentleman" (one-act), published in *Best Short Plays of 1971*, Chilton, 1972, and in *Nine Modern Short Plays*, Bantam, 1977; "The Club" (one-act); "His Master's Voice" (one-act); "The Rose Critic" (one-act); "Dust to Dust" (one-act).

Filmscripts: "No One to Blame," 1965; "Systems," 1966; (with Lev Mailer) "On the Walls of the Subway," 1972; "The Artist Type" (adapted from novel of the same name by Brian Glanville), 1973; "The Velvet Vampire," New World, 1973; "Scream, Blacula, Scream," American International Pictures, 1975; "Stops Along the Way," 1975; "Out of Hand," 1976; "Wives and Other Women," 1977; "Bad Timing/A Sensual Obsession," F. Arthur Rork, 1977, World Northal, 1980; "The Quest," 1978; "The Catcher," 1979; "The Reluctant Assassin," 1980; "Mirror Image," 1982; "Vera," 1983; "The Investigator," 1983.

Television filmscripts: "Hitchhike," telecast on ABC, 1974; "The Doorstep War," Larry Gordon/Columbia; "Sound of Distant Thunder," Mace Neufeld/CBS; "Jealousy," Fries Co./ABC.

Also author of television scripts for "The Survivors," "Man from U.N.C.L.E.," "Toma," "Baretta," "McNaughton's Daughter," "Batman," and "Nightmare Anthology." Author of two television pilots, "The Generation," and "Doctor Rembrandt," and of one television special, "The Beach House," for CBS Playhouse.

Contributor of film criticism to *Film Quarterly*, *Film Comment*, *7th Art*, and *Kulchur*.

WORK IN PROGRESS: A full-length play; a screenplay.

SIDELIGHTS: Yale M. Udoff told *CA*: "The sounds words produce, the rhythms of sentences, the music of pauses often say more than the words themselves actually mean. Music is what theatre aims for—at least what I'm interested in. Film is, naturally, another 'story'."

BIOGRAPHICAL/CRITICAL SOURCES: New York Times, February 3, 1971, September 21, 1980; *Saturday Review*, February 20, 1971; *Sight and Sound*, spring, 1980; *Observer* (London), April 13, 1980; *Los Angeles Times*, October 12, 1980; *Chicago Tribune*, February 9, 1981.

* * *

**UNADA
See GLIEWE, Unada (Grace)**

USHER, Dan 1934-

PERSONAL: Born May 15, 1934, in Montreal, Quebec, Canada; son of Abe and Rose (Leventhal) Usher; married Samphan Chayarahs, June 27, 1962; children: Ann, David. *Education:* McGill University, B.A., 1955; University of Chicago, Ph.D., 1960. *Religion:* Jewish. *Home:* 168 Churchill Crescent, Kingston, Ontario, Canada. *Office:* Department of Economics, Queen's University, Kingston, Ontario, Canada.

CAREER: United Nations Economic Commission for Asia and the Far East, assistant economic affairs officer in Bangkok, Thailand, 1960-61; University of Manchester, Manchester, England, research fellow, 1961-63; Oxford University, Nuffield College, Oxford, England, research fellow, 1963-66; Columbia University, Graduate School of Business, New York, N.Y., assistant professor of economics, 1966-67; Queen's University at Kingston, Kingston, Ontario, associate professor, 1967-69, professor of economics, 1969—. Consultant, Canadian International Development Agency, 1969; consultant in Malaysia, Harvard Development Advisory Service, 1974. *Member:* International Association for Research in Income and Wealth, Canadian Economic Association, American Economic Association.

WRITINGS: The Price Mechanism and the Meaning of National Income Statistics, Clarendon Press, 1968; *The Measurement of Economic Growth,* Blackwell & Mott, 1980; *The Measurement of Capital,* University of Chicago Press, 1980; *The Economic Prerequisite to Democracy,* Blackwell & Mott, 1981. Contributor to economic journals.

WORK IN PROGRESS: Research in economic theory and public finance.

V

VAIL, Robert William 1921-

PERSONAL: Born October 29, 1921, in Columbus, Ohio; son of Robert David (an artist) and Dorothy (Mosier) Vail; married Martha Henderson (a banker), April 7, 1939; children: William N., Veronica (Mrs. David Fish), David A., Ashley M., Victor, Lorelei (Mrs. Dennis Meade), Hilary W. *Education:* Attended Ohio State University, 1938-39. *Politics:* Republican. *Religion:* Presbyterian. *Home:* 1701 East 12th St., Apt. 20-T, Cleveland, Ohio 44114.

CAREER: Barnebey-Cheney Engineering Co., Columbus, Ohio, research chemist, 1941-44; Koppers Co., Petrolia, Pa., senior chemist, 1944-49; insurance agent in Butler, Pa., 1949-51; Carborundum Co., Niagara Falls, N.Y., research and development engineer, 1951-55; Allied Chemical Corp., New York, N.Y., in technical sales, 1955-60; U.S. Ceramic Tile Co., Canton, Ohio, research laboratory director, 1960-62; Ferro Corp., Cleveland, Ohio, sales manager of Ferro Chemical Division, 1962-70; R. William Vail, Inc., Cleveland, president, 1970-72; Manpower Inc., Cleveland, manager of technical services, 1972-74; Vail, Shaker Heights, Ohio, owner and manager, 1974-78; Hayden, Hemen, Smith & Associates, Cleveland, senior consultant, 1978-82, vice president, 1982-83, management consultant, 1983—. *Military service:* U.S. Naval Reserve, 1944. *Member:* Masonic Blue Lodge (member of chapter and council), Al Koran Shrine.

WRITINGS: Teardrops Falling (poetry), Golden Quill, 1963; *Voice of the Old Frontier*, Octagon, 1970; *Knickerbocker Birthday: A Sesquicentennial History of the New York Historical Society*, University Press of Virginia, 1975. Contributor to *Encyclopedia of Basic Materials for Plastics*, 1967; contributor of articles to *Profitable Hobbies, Ford Times, Church Management;* contributor to poetry journals.

WORK IN PROGRESS: In the Beginning, the story of one of the first amateur radio operators and his early misadventures and exploits.

SIDELIGHTS: Robert William Vail speaks French, Spanish, and German. *Avocational interests:* Operating amateur radio station K8AQS, handball, magic, hypnotism, contesting, chess, acting and directing in little theater, fishing, hunting, computers.

VALE, Eugene 1916-

PERSONAL: Born April 11, 1916, in Zurich, Switzerland. *Education:* Attended schools in Switzerland. *Home:* 9000 Cynthia St., Los Angeles, Calif. 90069.

CAREER: Novelist, playwright, and writer for television and films. *Member:* Academy of Motion Picture Arts and Sciences, Dramatists Guild, Writers Guild of America. *Awards, honors:* Arts of the Theatre Prize, for "Of Shadows Cast by Men"; commendation from City of Los Angeles, 1959, Christopher Gold Medal, Rupert Hughes Award of Authors' Club of Southern California, California Writers Guild Award, Commonwealth Gold Medal for best work of fiction by a California author, 1960, and Annual Book Award of National Secondary Education Board, all for *The Thirteenth Apostle;* nominations for television and film script awards from Writers Guild of America West, Screen Writers Guild, and Academy of Motion Picture Arts and Sciences.

WRITINGS: The Technique of Screenplay Writing, Crown, 1944, revised and enlarged edition published as *The Technique of Screen and Television Writing*, Prentice-Hall, 1983; (contributor) L. G. Yoakem, editor, *TV and Screen Writing*, University of California Press, 1958; *The Thirteenth Apostle* (novel), Scribner, 1959, new edition, Jubilee Press, 1983; *Chaos below Heaven* (novel), Doubleday, 1966; *Some State of Affairs* (satire), W. H. Allen, 1972; *The Children's Crusade* (novel), Bertelsmann, 1977; *Passion Play* (novel), Jubilee Press, 1984.

Also author of plays "Devils Galore," "The Buffoon," and "Of Shadows Cast by Men," and of screenplays "A Global Affair," "Francis of Assisi," "The Second Face," "The Bridge of San Luis Rey," "The Dark Wave," and others for Twentieth Century-Fox, United Artists, and Paramount; author of about sixty television dramas, including scripts for Four Star Playhouse, Fireside Theatre, Hallmark Hall of Fame, and Lux Video Theatre. Contributor of short stories, poems, and novelettes to *Esquire* and other periodicals in the United States and Europe.

WORK IN PROGRESS: A novel.

SIDELIGHTS: The original manuscript of *The Thirteenth Apostle* was acquired by the American Literature Collection of University of Southern California.

VALERIANI, Richard (Gerard) 1932-

PERSONAL: Born August 29, 1932, in Camden, N.J.; son of Nicholas (a foundry foreman) and Christina (Camerota) Valeriani; married Coralee Hall, January 22, 1965 (divorced). Education: Yale University, B.A., 1953; graduate study at University of Pavia, 1953-54. Home: 3025 Arizona Ave. N.W., Washington, D.C. 20016. Office: NBC News, 4001 Nebraska Ave. N.W., Washington, D.C. 20016.

CAREER: Trentonian, Trenton, N.J., reporter, 1957; Associated Press, writer in New York City, 1957-59, in Havana, Cuba, 1959-61; National Broadcasting Company, Inc., NBC News, reporter, 1961-64, correspondent in Washington, D.C., 1964—. Notable assignments include the Bay of Pigs invasion, 1961, civil rights movement throughout the United States, 1962-65, presidential campaigns, 1964, 1968, and 1972, civil war in Dominican Republic, 1965, the White House, 1972-73, and travels of Henry Kissinger, 1973-76. Presidential Debate panelist, 1976. Lecturer in American foreign policy. Military service: U.S. Army, 1955-56. Member: Overseas Writers, State Department Correspondents' Association (president, 1976-77), Elihu Society, Yale Club (Washington, D.C.). Awards, honors: Overseas Press Club Award for best radio reporting abroad, 1965, for work in Dominican Republic; Peabody Award, 1965, for civil rights television special.

WRITINGS: Travels with Henry, Houghton, 1979. Author of scripts for television broadcast, including news and documentaries. Contributor to periodicals, including TV Guide, Ladies' Home Journal, Good Housekeeping, and Penthouse.

SIDELIGHTS: A well-known reporter and correspondent for the National Broadcasting Company (NBC), Richard Valeriani has covered presidential campaigns, the White House, the State Department, and other government agencies and events of national interest. From 1973 to 1976, he was one of several newsmen who logged over half a million miles accompanying Henry Kissinger on his diplomatic missions around the world. Valeriani's book, Travels with Henry, is "a humorous, generally friendly account of Kissinger's road show," writes John Maclean in the Chicago Tribune Book World, "that shows Kissinger's jokiness as a negotiating tool, loosening up government officials at key moments."

John Kenneth Galbraith, reviewing the book in the Washington Post Book World, says that Valeriani demonstrates Kissinger's ability to ingratiate himself with foreign leaders, members of the press, and American dignitaries through his wit. But Galbraith believes Valeriani unintentionally deals the former secretary of state "a heavy blow" by presenting a plethora of examples: "I share the view that Kissinger can be very amusing; his rumbled self-deprecating asides are both easy and apt. But no one, not Bob Hope, not Mark Twain, not even Harry Lauder, can or could stand having all his funny lines stacked, one on top of another, for several pages, with no regard for context. That is what Valeriani does to Kissinger, although, to be fair, he does intersperse a few lines of his own."

Maclean, nevertheless, states: "Valeriani accomplished what he set out to do. He put together all those pithy remarks and scintillating vignettes that used to make it special to be around Kissinger." The critic adds, moreover, that Valeriani "doesn't ignore Kissinger's warts. The former super-diplomat's penchant for pettiness, secrecy, and deviousness are well documented. . . . As one of the boys who rode the plane, I can attest that Valeriani's reporting rings true. Future biographers will use [Travels with Henry] as a handy compendium of the 'vit and visdom' of Kissinger."

BIOGRAPHICAL/CRITICAL SOURCES: Washington Post Book World, May 6, 1979; Chicago Tribune Book World, June 17, 1979; Saturday Review, August 1, 1979; Annals of the American Academy of Political and Social Science, November, 1979.

* * *

Van De VALL, Mark 1923-

PERSONAL: Born January 20, 1923, in Heiloo, Netherlands; married Anneke Korthals; children: (previous marriage) Renee, Monique. Education: Municipal University of Amsterdam, B.A., 1950, M.A., 1955, Ph.D., 1963. Office: Department of Sociology, University of Leyden, 242 Stationsplein, 2312 AR Leyden, Netherlands.

CAREER: State University of New York at Buffalo, professor, 1963-77, adjunct professor of sociology, 1978—; University of Leyden, Leyden, Netherlands, professor of social research, 1977—. Director, Leyden Institute for Social Policy Research, 1980—. Special research fellow, Department of Health, Education and Welfare, Washington, D.C., 1969-71; fellow, Netherlands Institute for Advanced Study in the Humanities and Social Sciences. Member: International Sociological Association (vice-president, Sociotechnics section, 1982—).

WRITINGS: De Vakbeweging in de Welvaartsstaat, J. A. Boom (Meppel), 1963, translation published as Labor Organizations: A Macro-and Micro-Sociological Analysis on a Comparative Basis, Cambridge University Press, 1970; (with Charles D. King) Models of Industrial Democracy: Consultation, Co-Determination and Workers' Management, Mouton, 1978; Sociaal Beleidsonderzoek, Samsom (Alphen a/d Rijn), 1980.

Contributor: H. Matthes, editor, Soziologie und Gesellschaft in den Niederlanden, Luchterhand Verlag (Neuwied/Rhein), 1965; Milton Albrecht, editor, Studies in Sociology, Buffalo Studies, 1965; Desmond Graves, editor, Management Research: A Cross-Cultural Perspective, Jossey Bass, 1973; Frank Baker and H. C. Schulberg, editors, Program Evaluation in the Health Fields, Behavioral Publications, 1977; D. Horowitz, editor, Policy Studies Review Annual, Sage Publications, 1981; P. J. Taylor and B. Cronin, editors, Information Management Research in Europe, ASLIB, 1982.

Contributor to Proceedings of 17th and 22nd annual meetings of Industrial Relations Research Association. Contributor of over fifty articles and reports on sociological and political science subjects, in Dutch, German, French, and English, to periodicals.

WORK IN PROGRESS: With Cheryl Bolas, Theory and Methods of Social Policy Research; with Herb J. Ulrich, A Model of Social Policy Research.

* * *

Van ZANDT, E. F.
See CUDLIPP, Edythe

* * *

VERCORS
See BRULLER, Jean (Marcel)

* * *

VERCORS, J. Bruller
See BRULLER, Jean (Marcel)

VERNON, Philip Ewart 1905-

PERSONAL: Born June 6, 1905, in Oxford, England; son of Horace Middleton and Katherine Dorothea (Ewart) Vernon; married Annie Gray, 1939 (died, 1947); married Dorothy Fairly Lawson (a teacher of backward children), September 22, 1947; children: Philip Anthony. *Education:* St. John's College, Cambridge, B.A., 1927, M.A., 1930, Ph.D., 1931; additional study at Yale University, 1929-30 and Harvard University, 1930-31. *Religion:* Church of England. *Home:* 3719 49th St. N.W., Apt. 402B, Calgary, Alberta, Canada T3A 2E3. *Office:* Department of Educational Psychology, University of Calgary, Calgary, Alberta, Canada.

CAREER: Cambridge University, St. John's College, Cambridge, England, fellow, 1931-33; London County Council, London, England, psychologist at Maudsley Hospital, 1933-35; Jordanhill Training Center, Glasgow, Scotland, head of psychology department, 1935-38; Glasgow University, Glasgow, head of psychology department, 1938-47; University of London, Institute of Education, London, professor of educational psychology, 1949-68, professor emeritus, 1968—; University of Calgary, Calgary, Alberta, professor of educational psychology, 1968—. Lecturer in Australia and New Zealand, 1953; visiting professor at Princeton University, Universities of Minnesota, British Columbia, and Alberta, 1957, 1962, and American University of Beirut, 1963. Psychological research adviser, British Army and Navy, 1942-49; psychological research consultant, British Admiralty, 1949-61; chief examiner, East Sussex County Council.

MEMBER: British Psychological Society (president, 1954-55), American Psychological Association. *Awards, honors:* D.Sc., University of London, 1953; fellow, Center for Advanced Study in the Behavioral Sciences, Stanford, Calif., 1961-62; LL.D., University of Calgary, 1980.

WRITINGS: (With Gordon Allport) *Studies in Expressive Movement,* Macmillan, 1933, reprinted, Hafner, 1967; *The Measurement of Abilities,* University of London Press, 1940, 2nd edition, 1956, reprinted, 1972; (with J. B. Parry) *Personnel Selection in the British Forces,* University of London Press, 1947; *The Structure of Human Abilities,* Methuen, 1950, 2nd edition, 1961, reprinted, Greenwood Press, 1979; *Personality Tests and Assessments,* Methuen, 1953, revised edition, 1969; (editor with C. A. Mace) *Current Trends in British Psychology,* Methuen, 1956; (editor) *Secondary School Selection,* Methuen, 1957, revised edition, 1964.

Intelligence and Attainment Tests, University of London Press, 1960; *Selection for Secondary Education in Jamaica,* Government of Kingston, 1961; *Personality Assessment: A Critical Survey,* Methuen, 1963; *Intelligence and Cultural Environment,* Methuen, 1969.

(With Allport) *Study of Values: A Scale for Measuring the Dominant Interests in Personality,* 3rd edition (Vernon was not associated with previous editions), Houghton, 1970; (editor) *Creativity: Selected Readings,* Penguin, 1970; *Advances in Educational Psychology,* University of London Press, 1972; (with wife, Dorothy F. Vernon, and Georgina Adamson) *The Psychology and Education of Gifted Children,* Westview, 1977; *Intelligence: Heredity and Environment,* W. H. Freeman, 1979; *Intelligence Testing, 1928-1978: What Next?,* Scottish Council for Research in Education, 1979; *Abilities and Achievements of Orientals in North America,* Academic Press, 1982.

Contributor of many articles to numerous psychological journals. Editor of *British Journal of Educational Psychology,* 1956-61.

SIDELIGHTS: Discussing Philip Ewart Vernon's *The Psychology and Education of Gifted Children,* J. C. Dancy writes in *Times Literary Supplement* that this book offers "a sensible introduction to the problem of giftedness. 'Gifted' is here used to designate the top 2 per cent of the population—in IQ terms, 130-plus. The book surveys the problems and the proposed solutions in a balanced way. . . . It is written at a fairly non-technical level and could be useful to any interested teacher or parent."

BIOGRAPHICAL/CRITICAL SOURCES: Times Literary Supplement, October 14, 1977.

* * *

VERNON, Walter N(ewton), Jr. 1907-

PERSONAL: Born March 24, 1907, in Verden, Okla.; son of Walter Newton (a minister) and Fannie (Dodd) Vernon; married Ruth Mason (a public school teacher), December 17, 1931; children: Walter N. III, Kathleen Frances (Mrs. Stanley P. Clark). *Education:* Southern Methodist University, B.A., 1928, B.D., 1931, M.A., 1934. *Politics:* Democrat. *Home and office:* 4013 Dorcas Dr., Nashville, Tenn. 37215.

CAREER: Ordained to Methodist ministry, 1931; pastor in Dallas, Tex., 1931-38; The Methodist Church Board of Education, Editorial Division, Nashville, Tenn., administrative associate and editor, general publications, 1938-72. National Council of Churches, member of audio-visual team to Africa, 1953, delegate to World Convention on Christian Education, Tokyo, 1958, chairman of editors section, Division of Christian Education. Chairman of history commission of South Central Jurisdiction, United Methodist Church, 1972-80. *Member:* Western Writers of America (Nashville corral), Texas United Methodist Historical Society (organizer and president, 1976-80), North Texas United Methodist Conference (conference historian), Sigma Delta Chi. *Awards, honors:* D.Litt. from West Virginia Wesleyan College, 1963; received commemorative plaque from College of Bishops, South Central Jurisdiction of the United Methodist Church, 1981, for ministerial and journalistic achievements; inducted into United Methodist Communicators Hall of Fame, 1983.

WRITINGS: Methodist Profile, Methodist Publishing House, 1959; (compiler) *Living with Your Children,* Graded Press, 1961; *William Stevenson, Riding Preacher,* Southern Methodist University Press, 1964; *Methodism Moves across North Texas,* North Texas Conference, 1967; *United Methodist Profile,* Graded Press, 1968, 3rd edition, 1983; (editor) Theodore L. Agnew, *The South Central Jurisdiction, 1939-1972,* United Methodist Church, 1972; *Forever Building: The Life and Ministry of Paul E. Martin,* Southern Methodist University Press, 1973; (contributor) Walter Prescott Webb, editor, *The Handbook of Texas,* Volume III, Texas State Historical Association, 1976; *Methodism in Arkansas, 1816-1976,* Joint Committee for the History of Arkansas Methodism, 1976; (editor and contributor) *One in the Lord: A History of Ethnic Minorities in the South Central Jurisdiction, the United Methodist Church,* Commission on Archives and History, South Central Jurisdiction, United Methodist Church, 1977; (contributor) Archie P. McDonald, editor, *Eastern Texas History: Selections from the East Texas Historical Journal,* Jenkins Publishing, 1978; *Jubilee: Two Hundred Years of American Methodism,* Graded

Press, 1982; (editor and contributor) *The Methodist Excitement in Texas*, Texas United Methodist Historical Society, 1984.

Wrote words for hymn, "God of All, Who Art Our Father," published by Hymn Society of America, 1961. Contributor to *Westminster Dictionary of Christian Education*. Also contributor to newspapers and Methodist periodicals and to *Christian Century, Chronicles of Oklahoma, Tennessee Historical Quarterly, Arkansas Historical Quarterly, Red River Valley Historical Review, Methodist History,* and *East Texas Historical Journal*. Associate editor, *Encyclopedia of World Methodism*, 1974.

WORK IN PROGRESS: The Methodist Publishing House: A History, Volume II; a history of Methodism in Louisiana.

* * *

VILLA, Jose Garcia 1914-
(Doveglion)

PERSONAL: Surname is pronounced *Vil-ah*; born August 5, 1914, in Manila, Philippines; son of a doctor who was Army chief of staff in the Philippine revolution against Spain; came to the United States in 1930; married Rosemarie Lamb, 1946 (divorced, 1954); children: Randall, Lance. *Education:* Attended University of the Philippines, 1929; University of New Mexico, B.A., 1933; graduate study at Columbia University, 1942. *Home:* 780 Greenwich St., New York, N.Y. 10014.

CAREER: Poet. Began writing short stories as an undergraduate at University of New Mexico, receiving almost instant recognition (Edward J. O'Brien's *Best American Short Stories of 1932* was dedicated to Villa); began writing poetry, and wrote and studied its forms for a long period before his first collection was published in the Philippines; associate editor with New Directions Publishing Corp., New York City, 1949-51; director of poetry workshop at City College of the City University of New York, New York City, 1952-60; lecturer at New School for Social Research, New York City, 1964-73. Cultural attache to Philippine Mission to the United Nations, 1952-63; adviser on cultural affairs to the President of the Philippines, 1968—.

AWARDS, HONORS: American Academy of Arts and Letters grant, 1942; Guggenheim fellowship in poetry, 1943; Bollingen Foundation fellowship, 1951-52; Shelley Memorial Award, Poetry Society of America, 1959; D.Litt., Far Eastern University, Manila, 1959; Pro Patria Award, 1961; Philippine Cultural Heritage Award, 1962; Rockefeller Foundation grant, 1964; elected Philippines National Artist, 1973; D.H.L., University of the Philippines, 1973.

WRITINGS: (Editor) *Philippine Short Stories*, Philippines Free Press, 1929; *Footnote to Youth* (short stories), introduction by Edward J. O'Brien, Scribner, 1933; *Many Voices* (poems), Philippine Book Guild, 1939; (under pseudonym Doveglion) *Poems by Doveglion*, Philippine Writers' League, 1941; *Have Come, Am Here* (poems), Viking, 1942; (editor) *A Celebration for Edith Sitwell*, New Directions, 1946, reprinted, Books for Libraries, 1972; *Volume Two* (poems), New Directions, 1949; *Selected Poems and New*, Obolensky, 1958; *Selected Stories*, A. S. Florentino (Manila), 1962; *Poems in Praise of Love*, A. S. Florentino, 1962; (editor under pseudonym Doveglion) *A Doveglion Book of Philippine Poetry*, Arguilla Salas (Manila), 1962; *Poems 55: The Best Poems of Jose Garcia Villa as Chosen by Himself*, A. S. Florentino, 1962; *The Portable Villa* (includes *Poems 55, Selected Stories, Poems in Praise of Love*, with comments by Mark Van Doren, and critical essays by David Daiches and others), A. S. Florentino, 1962; *The Essential Villa* (includes *Poems 55* and *Selected Stories*), A. S. Florentino, 1965; (editor under pseudonym Doveglion) *The New Doveglion Book of Philippine Poetry*, Caliraya Foundation (Manila), 1975; *Apassionata*, King & Cowan, 1979.

Contributor: Justine Van Gundy, R. Husband, and Caroline Shrodes, editors, *Psychology through Literature*, Oxford University Press, 1943; William R. Benet and Conrad Aiken, editors, *Anthology of Famous English and American Poetry*, Modern Library, 1945; Selden Rodman, editor, *New Anthology of Modern Poetry*, Modern Library, 1946; James Laughlin, editor, *Spearhead: Ten Years' Experimental Writing in America*, New Directions, 1947; C. Stroven and A. G. Day, editors, *The Spell of the Pacific*, introduction by James A. Michener, Macmillan, 1949; Edith Sitwell, editor, *A Book of the Winter*, Macmillan, 1950; H. M. Husted, editor, *Love Poems of Six Centuries*, Coward, 1950; Balachandra Rajan, editor, *Modern American Poetry*, Dobson, 1950; Sitwell, editor, *The American Genius*, Lehmann, 1951; W. H. Auden, editor, *Criterion Book of Modern American Verse*, Criterion, 1956.

Aiken, editor, *Twentieth Century American Poetry*, Modern Library, 1963; C. H. Carver and H. G. Sliker, editors, *Literature of the World Around Us*, 2nd edition, Prentice-Hall, 1963; J. H. Middendorf, R. S. Loomis, and D. L. Clark, editors, *Modern English Readings*, 8th edition, Holt, 1963; G. J. Firmage, editor, *A Garland for Dylan Thomas*, Clark & Way, 1966; H. Gregory and M. Zaturenska, editors, *Mentor Book of Religious Verse*, Mentor Books, 1968; M. R. Martin and Sheilah Beckett, editors, *The World's Love Poetry*, Bantam, 1968; L. F. Faderman and B. Bradshaw, editors, *Speaking for Ourselves*, Scott, Foresman, 1969; K. D. Newman, editor, *The American Equation*, Allyn & Bacon, 1971; Grove Day, editor, *The Art of Narration: The Short Story*, McGraw, 1971; Jerome Rothenberg and George Quasha, editors, *America: A Prophecy*, Random House, 1974; Jean Garrigue, editor, *Love's Aspects: The World's Great Love Poems*, Doubleday, 1975; Cline, Delan, and others, editors, *New Voices: Literature, Language, and Composition*, Ginn, 1978, 2nd edition published as *New Voices*, 1984.

Hodgins, editor, *Adventures in American Literature*, Heritage edition, Harcourt, 1980; Kennedy, editor, *Knock at a Star: A Child's Introduction to Poetry*, Little, Brown, 1982. Also contributor to numerous other anthologies, including *Poems of Our Time*, Everyman's Library, *New Philippine Writing*, Cornell University Press, *A Nation of Nations*, Free Press, *Asian-Pacific Literature*, University of Hawaii, and *Literature*, Macdougal, Little.

Also contributor to periodicals. Editor of E. E. Cummings issue, *Harvard Wake*, 1945, and of Marianne Moore issue, *Quarterly Review*, 1947. Editor, *Bravo: The Poet's Magazine*, 1981—.

SIDELIGHTS: Jose Garcia Villa is a highly talented and innovative poet whose talent has been lauded and whose innovations have been met with mixed reactions. The short story was the first literary form Villa used, but he soon realized that poetry was more suitable for what he wished to accomplish in his writing. He has stated: "I am not at all interested in description or outward appearance, nor in the contemporary scene, but in *essence*. A single motive underlies all my work and defines my intention as a serious artist: the search for the metaphysical meaning of man's life in the Universe—the finding of man's selfhood and identity in the mystery of Creation. I use the term *metaphysical* to denote the ethic-philosophic force behind all essential living. The development and unification of the human personality I consider the highest achievement [possible]." His first book of poetry to be published in the United States, *Have Come, Am Here,* appeared in 1942, and it was highly praised. In this volume he introduced a new method of rhyming which he terms "reversed consonance." In *Volume Two* he introduced "comma poems." In the preface to the volume he explains: "The commas are an integral and essential part of the medium: regulating the poem's verbal density and time movement: enabling each word to attain a fuller tonal value, and the line movement to become more measured." With this volume he met with disapproval for what was considered by many to be typographical games. David Daiches was one who criticized this volume, and yet he had highest praise for Villa's clarity and precision with words and his ability to transmit the innocence and indignant anger which characterizes much of his writing.

Edith Sitwell, in the preface to *The American Genius,* writes: "Mr. Villa's poems are of great beauty. Poem 68 springs straight from the heart of Being. I hold it to be one of the most wonderful short poems of our time, and reading it, I knew that I was seeing for the first time the work of a poet with a great and perfectly original gift. This poetry springs with a wild force, straight from the poet's being, from his blood, from his spirit, as a fire breaks from wood, or as a flower grows from its soil.

"All his poems are short. But as Blake said, 'A little flower is the labour of ages.' These strange, passionate, and beautiful poems are equally the labour of ages, growing from the poet's earth. Some of [his] poems are born from a religious ardour and fire, some are love poems. In some of [his] poems of the religious kind, the soul of Man is engaged, not only in adoration, but also, at times, in a glorifying and joyous combat with his God. 'All absolute sensation is religious,' wrote Novalis. And this absolute sensation is known by Mr. Villa. It shines and burns in his love poems, as in his poems about God. All have a strange luminosity (as if they came from the very heart of light) alternating with an equally strange darkness; and this luminosity, this darkness, bears a resemblance to that in the work of Blake and of Boehme. 'Sir, there's a tower of fire in me' cries the poet . . . and . . . 'O the brightness of my dark.' These lines, with the poem which includes the lines 'Ferocious and beautiful Leopard that thrives / On the rose-imagination' seem to epitomize the spirit of this poet."

BIOGRAPHICAL/CRITICAL SOURCES: Henry Willis Wells, *Introduction to Emily Dickinson,* Hendricks House, 1947; Edith Sitwell, editor, *The American Genius,* Lehmann, 1951; Sona Raiziss, *The Metaphysical Passion,* University of Pennsylvania, 1952; Mark Van Doren, *Autobiography,* Harcourt, 1958; Babette Deutsch, *Poetry in Our Time,* 2nd edition, Doubleday, 1963; Earle Birney, *The Creative Writer,* Canadian Broadcasting Corporation (Toronto), 1966.

* * *

VINCENT, Claire
See ALLEN, Charlotte Vale

* * *

VIRGINES, George E. 1920-

PERSONAL: Born February 11, 1920, in Chicago, Ill.; son of Nickolas (a chef) and Mary (Drogush) Virgines; married Loraine Dunlap, February 11, 1941; children: Valerie Virgines Judge, Linda Virgines Neiman. *Education:* Attended technical high school in Chicago. *Home:* 1224 LaCharles Dr. N.E., Albuquerque, N.M. 87112.

CAREER: Worked as chauffeur, florist, baker, salesman, handyman, and truck driver prior to 1942; Super Electric Construction Co., Chicago, Ill., 1945-80, held various positions, including truck driver and machinery operator; full-time writer and consultant, 1980—. Toured country for many years as a fancy gun handling expert and exhibition shooter with the Roving Gunslingers Western Variety and Wild West Show. Deputy sheriff in Lincoln County, N.M., 1962-69, and DuPage County, Ill., 1967-69. Former book reviewer of Western nonfiction and fiction for American Library Association. Speaker on western lore. Technical advisor on the sport of fast draw to *Guns* (magazine) and Colt Firearms Co.; consultant to Franklin Mint. *Military service:* U.S. Army, 1942-45; served in Africa and Italy; became staff sergeant; received two battle stars. *Member:* Western Writers of America, Westerners (deputy marshall of Chicago Posse, 1965-73; sheriff of Chicago corral, 1973-75).

AWARDS, HONORS: Awarded honorary commissions as law officer from several states, including Illinois, Alabama, Oregon, Texas, and South Dakota, and from Arizona Rangers chapters in seven states; recipient of presentation gun from the Colt Firearms Co. and handcrafted silver replica of the Arizona Rangers' badge from A. A. White Co., for work on the Arizona Rangers Commemorative Gun; also recipient of presentations from the Westerners and several fast draw clubs and associations.

WRITINGS: Saga of the Colt Six-Shooter and the Famous Men Who Used It, Fell, 1969; *Famous Guns and Gunners,* Pine Mountain Press, 1980; *Police Relics,* Collector Books, 1982.

Also author of booklet *History of the Arizona Rangers* for Colt Firearms Co., 1972; contributor of chapters to books on firearms. Contributor of over one hundred articles on western lore, lawmen, outlaws, firearms, badges, and police relics to *Guns, Gunworld, Frontier Times, True West, Relics, Rarities, New Mexico Magazine, Western Horseman, Real West,* and other publications.

WORK IN PROGRESS: Articles and books.

BIOGRAPHICAL/CRITICAL SOURCES: Newsweek, December 1, 1958; *Guns,* August, 1961, June, 1975; *New Mexico Magazine,* August, 1963; *Westerners Brand Book,* November, 1965, March, 1974, March, 1975; *Buckskin Bulletin* (publication of Westerners International), winter/spring, 1978.

* * *

VITAL, David 1927-

PERSONAL: Surname originally Grossman; adopted surname is pronounced Vee-*tal;* born April 10, 1927, in London, England; son of Meir (a journalist) and Barbara (DePorte) Grossman; married Alisa Waxman (a musician), May 1, 1957; children: Tamar, Adam Elie, Ruth. *Education:* Oxford University, B.A., 1951, M.A., 1956, D.Phil., 1966. *Religion:* Jewish. *Home:* 75 Rehov Hazorea, Kfar Shmaryahu, Israel. *Office:* Department of Political Science, Tel-Aviv University, Ramat-Aviv, Tel-Aviv, Israel.

CAREER: Journalist in Israel, 1952-54; government service in Israel, 1954-66; University of Sussex, Brighton, England, lecturer in international relations, 1966-68; Bar-Ilan University, Ramat-Gan, Israel, associate professor of political studies, 1968-71, Winston Churchill Professor of International Relations, 1969-71, professor of political studies, 1971-72; University of

Haifa, Haifa, Israel, professor of political science, 1972-77; Tel-Aviv University, Ramat-Aviv, Tel-Aviv, Israel, professor of political science, 1977—, member of academic advisory committee of Center for Strategic Studies.

Visiting professor at University of California, Los Angeles, 1969, University of Jerusalem, 1969-70, and Dartmouth College, 1981; visiting fellow at Australian National University, 1974, Wolfson College, Oxford University, 1974-75, and Institute for Advanced Studies, Jerusalem, 1981-82. Member of Senate Standing Committee and Board of Governors, University of Haifa, 1972-74. *Military service:* British Army, 1945-48. Israel Defense Forces, Reserves, 1953-82. *Member:* Political Studies Association (United Kingdom), Institute for Strategic Studies (London). *Awards, honors:* Harold H. Wingate Literary Prize, *Jewish Chronicle*, and Kenneth B. Smilen Literary Prize for History, *Present Tense*, both for *Zionism: The Formative Years*.

WRITINGS: The Inequality of States: A Study of the Small Power in International Relations, Oxford University Press, 1967; *The Making of British Foreign Policy*, Praeger, 1968; *The Survival of Small States; Studies in Small Power/Great Power Conflict*, Oxford University Press, 1971; *The Origins of Zionism*, Oxford University Press, 1975; *Zionism: The Formative Years*, Oxford University Press, 1982. Contributor to numerous periodicals, including *International Affairs, International Journal, Economist, Jerusalem Post, Journal of Contemporary History, Political Science Quarterly*, and *Times Literary Supplement*.

WORK IN PROGRESS: A history of the Zionist movement; foreign policy analysis.

SIDELIGHTS: The Inequality of States and *The Making of British Foreign Policy* have been translated into Spanish, *The Origins of Zionism* and *Zionism: The Formative Years* have been translated into Hebrew, and *The Survival of Small States* has been translated into both Spanish and Hebrew.

W

WADDINGTON, Miriam 1917-
(E. B. Merritt)

PERSONAL: Born December 23, 1917, in Winnipeg, Manitoba, Canada; daughter of Isidore (a small manufacturer) and Musha (Dobrushin) Dworkin; married Patrick Donald Waddington, July 5, 1939 (divorced, 1965); children: Marcus Frushard, Jonathan John. *Education:* University of Toronto, B.A., 1939, Diploma in Social Work, 1942, M.A., 1968; University of Pennsylvania, M.S.W., 1945. *Home:* 32 Yewfield Crescent, Don Mills, Toronto, Ontario, Canada M3B 2Y6. *Office:* Department of English, York University, Toronto, Ontario, Canada.

CAREER: Jewish Child Welfare Bureau, Montreal, Quebec, assistant director, 1945-46; McGill University, School of Social Work, Montreal, field instructor, 1946-49; Montreal Children's Hospital, Montreal, staff member, 1952-54; John Howard Society, Montreal, staff member, 1955-57; Jewish Family Bureau, Montreal, caseworker, 1957-60; North York Family Service, Toronto, Ontario, casework supervisor, 1960-62; York University, Toronto, 1964—, began as assistant professor, currently professor of English and Canadian literature. Writer-in-residence, University of Ottawa, 1974, and Windsor Public Library, 1983; Canada Council exchange poet to Wales, 1980; has given poetry readings or lectured at International Poetry Evenings, Struga, Yugoslavia, 1980, Yaddo Artists Colony, and most Universities across Canada; annual drama awards judge, Association of Canadian Television and Radio Artists.

MEMBER: International P.E.N., Modern Language Association of America, Otto Rank Association. *Awards, honors:* Canada Council senior fellowship in creative writing, 1962-63; Canada Council academic grant, 1968-69; Senior Arts fellowship, 1971-72 and 1979-80; J. I. Segal award, 1972, for *Driving Home;* D.Litt., Lakehead University, 1975; Association of Quebec and Canadian Literatures Citation, 1979, for her contribution to Canadian literature.

WRITINGS: Green World, First Statement Press, 1945; *The Second Silence,* Ryerson, 1955; *The Season's Lovers,* Ryerson, 1958; *The Glass Trumpet,* Oxford University Press, 1966; (author of poems accompanying the photographs) *Call Them Canadians,* Queen's Printer, 1968; *Say Yes* (poetry), Oxford University Press, 1969; *A. M. Klein* (criticism), Copp, 1970, 2nd edition, 1974; *Driving Home: Poems New and Selected,* Oxford University Press, 1972; *The Dream Telescope* (poetry), Routledge & Kegan Paul, 1973; (editor) *John Sutherland: Essays, Controversies, Poems,* New Canadian Library, 1973; (editor) *The Collected Poems of A. M. Klein,* McGraw, 1974; *The Price of Gold,* Oxford University Press, 1976; *Mister Never,* Turnstone (Winnipeg), 1978; *The Visitants,* Oxford University Press, 1981; *Summer at Lonely Beach and Other Stories,* Mosaic Valley Editions, 1982.

Contributor: C. Klinck and R. Walters, editors, *Canadian Anthology,* revised edition, Gage, 1974.

Contributor of translations: Irving Howe and Eliezer Greenberg, editors, *A Treasury of Yiddish Poetry,* Holt, 1969; Howe and Greenberg, editors, *Yiddish Stories New and Old,* Horizon (New York), 1974; Howe and R. Wisse, editors, *The Best of Sholom Aleichem,* [New York], 1980; S. Mayne, editor, *Generations,* Mosaic Valley Editions, 1982. Also contributor of translations to *The Ark,* edited by H. Schwartz and others, 1980.

Writer of radio scripts on Chekhov and Poe. Contributor to *Borestone Mountain Best Poems in English,* 1963, 1966, and 1967, and to other anthologies. Contributor of reviews, stories, and articles to magazines and newspapers, including *Canadian Literature, Tamarak Review, Queen's Quarterly, Canadian Forum,* and *Saturday Night.* Poetry editor, *Poetry Toronto,* 1981-82.

WORK IN PROGRESS: Collected Criticism of Miriam Waddington; collected poems; new poems.

SIDELIGHTS: Miriam Waddington's poems have been incorporated into a number of recent works and exhibitions of Canadian artists Helen Duffy, Jo Manning, Tobie Steinhouse, and Sarah Jackson, and about a dozen of her songs have been set to music by various Canadian and American composers. Her poems have also been broadcast in Canada, New Zealand, and Australia. In 1979, Waddington was honored at the annual meeting of the Association of Quebec and Canadian Literatures for her contributions to Canadian literature.

Waddington told *CA:* "I began writing poetry when I was ten and never really stopped. I don't know or care what motivates me—maybe it's belief in life itself. To me writing is one aspect of living and being human, of being connected to others. After a lifetime of writing the process is still a mystery to me.

"Why do I write? I suppose I hope to express the feeling of living in my time and place—not just in my own life but in the lives of other people who seem ordinary but never are. It makes me feel less lonesome in the world to believe that I'm part of a huge company of writers—living and dead—who express the continuity of human feeling, making, and learning in a world that is exhausted and violated, but nevertheless inexhaustible.

"The contemporary scene? It is so terrible that it's wonderful that so many authentic writers are still able and willing to write. [George] Gissing's *New Grub Street* was prophetic re the commodification of art and artists in our society. There are too many cookbooks. They tell us how to make and package everything—politics, art, sex, and personality. There is so much individualism in North American art that individuality is (paradoxically) lost. But there are always some authentic artists everywhere at every time, and their work is a refuge, a shelter, and a source of renewal."

Some of her work has been translated and published in the Soviet Union, Hungary, Japan, Romania, and South America.

BIOGRAPHICAL/CRITICAL SOURCES: *Poetry*, February, 1968; *Essays in Canadian Writing*, fall, 1978; John Pearce, *Twelve Voices*, Borealis Press, 1980; *Books in Canada*, May, 1982.

* * *

WAHL, Jan 1933-

PERSONAL: Born April 1, 1933, in Columbus, Ohio; son of Russell Rothenburger (a physician) and Nina Marie (Boyer) Wahl. *Education:* Cornell University, B.A., 1953; University of Copenhagen, graduate study, 1953-54; University of Michigan, M.A., 1958. *Religion:* Presbyterian. *Home:* 2116 Potomac Dr., Toledo, Ohio 43607; and Apartado Postal 33, San Miguel de Allende, Guanajuato, Mexico. *Agent:* Pat White, Deborah Rogers Ltd., 49 Blenheim Crescent, London W11 2EF, England.

CAREER: Worked with Danish film director Carl T. Dreyer during the making of Dreyer's prize-winning "Ordet," 1954-55; returned to Denmark to be secretary to Isak Dinesen, the writer, 1957-58; later worked with illustrator Garth Williams in Mexico, and with Erik Blegvad in England, 1966-67; writer for young people. *Awards, honors:* Fulbright scholar in Copenhagen, 1953-54; Avery and Jule Hopwood Award in fiction, 1955, for a group of short stories collectively entitled "Seven Old Maids" (the stories appeared in various magazines); Young Critics' award at International Children's Book Fair, Bologna, Italy, 1969, for *Pocahontas in London;* Ohioana Book Award winner, 1970, for *The Norman Rockwell Storybook;* Parents' Choice for Literature award, 1982, for *Tiger Watch.*

WRITINGS—All juveniles: *Pleasant Fieldmouse*, Harper, 1964; *The Howards Go Sledding*, Holt, 1964; *The Beast Book*, Harper, 1964; *Hello Elephant*, Holt, 1964; *Cabbage Moon*, Holt, 1965; *The Muffletumps: A Story of Four Dolls*, Holt, 1966; *Christmas in the Forest*, Macmillan, 1967; *A Wolf of My Own*, Macmillan, 1967; *Pocahontas in London*, Delacorte, 1967; *Runaway Jonah, and Other Tales*, Macmillan, 1968; *Push Kitty*, Harper, 1968; *Rickety Rackety Rooster*, Simon & Schuster, 1968; *The Furious Flycycle*, Delacorte, 1968; *Cobweb Castle*, Holt, 1968; *How the Children Stopped the Wars* (fable), Farrar, Straus, 1969; *The Fisherman*, Norton, 1969; *May Horses*, Delacorte, 1969; *The Norman Rockwell Storybook*, Windmill Books, 1969.

The Mulberry Tree, Norton, 1970; *The Animals' Peace Day*, Crown, 1970; *Doctor Rabbit*, Delacorte, 1970; *The Prince Who Was a Fish*, Simon & Schuster, 1970; *The Six Voyages of Pleasant Fieldmouse*, Delacorte, 1971; *The Wonderful Kite*, Delacorte, 1971; *Anna Help Ginger*, Putnam, 1971; *Crabapple Night*, Holt, 1971; *Margaret's Birthday*, Four Winds Press, 1971; *Lorenzo Bear and Co.*, Putnam, 1971; *Abe Lincoln's Beard*, Delacorte, 1971; *Grandmother Told Me*, Little, Brown, 1972; *Cristobal and the Witch*, Putnam, 1972; *Magic Heart*, Seabury, 1972; *The Very Peculiar Tunnel*, Putnam, 1972; *Crazy Brobobalou*, Putnam, 1973; *S.O.S. Bobomobile!*, Delacorte, 1973; *Pleasant Fieldmouse's Halloween Party*, Putnam, 1974; *Jeremiah Knucklebones*, Holt, 1974; *Woman with the Eggs*, Crown, 1974; *Juan Diego and the Lady*, Putnam, 1974; *Five in the Forest* (picture book), Follett, 1974; *Mooga Mega Mekki*, O'Hara Publications, 1974.

Bear, Wolf and Mouse, Follett, 1975; *Clumpets Go Sailing*, Parents' Magazine Press, 1975; *Screeching Door*, Four Winds Press, 1975; *The Muffletump Storybook*, Follett, 1975; *Muffletumps' Christmas Party*, Follett, 1975; *Follow Me Cried Bee*, Crown, 1976; *Great-Grandmother Cat Tales*, Pantheon, 1976; (with Joanne Scribner) *Grandpa's Indian Summer*, Prentice-Hall, 1976; *The Pleasant Fieldmouse Storybook*, Prentice-Hall, 1977; *Doctor Rabbit's Foundling*, Pantheon, 1977; *Carrot Nose*, Farrar, Straus, 1977; *Muffletumps' Halloween Scare*, Follett, 1977; *Frankenstein's Dog*, Prentice-Hall, 1977; *Pleasant Fieldmouse's Valentine Trick*, Dutton, 1977; *Jamie's Tiger*, Harcourt, 1978; *Dracula's Cat*, Prentice-Hall, 1978; *Youth's Magic Horn*, Elsevier/Nelson, 1978; *Drakestail*, Greenwillow, 1978; *Who Will Believe Tim Kitten?*, Pantheon, 1978; *Carrot Nose*, Farrar, Straus, 1978; *The Teeny Tiny Witches*, Putnam, 1979; *Sylvester Bear Overslept*, Parents Magazine Press, 1979; *Needle and Noodle*, Pantheon, 1979; *Doctor Rabbit's Lost Scout*, Pantheon, 1979.

Old Hippo's Easter Egg, Harcourt, 1980; *The Cucumber Princess*, Stemmer House, 1981; *The Little Blind Goat*, Stemmer House, 1981; *Grandpa Gus's Birthday Cake*, Prentice-Hall, 1981; *Tiger Watch*, Harcourt, 1982; *The Pipkins Go Camping*, Prentice-Hall, 1982; *Peter and the Troll Baby*, Golden Press, 1984.

Also author of *Button Eye's Orange*, 1980, and *More Room for the Pipkins*, 1983. Author of play, "Paradiso! Paradiso!," produced at Cornell University, 1954. Contributor of short stories to a number of literary magazines, including *Transatlantic Review*, *Prairie Schooner*, and *Epoch*. Poetry and articles on films have appeared in periodicals in America and abroad.

WORK IN PROGRESS: Material for the Muppet Press and a book for Green Tiger Press on animated cartoons, tentatively entitled *Happy Harmonies: The Art of Hugh Harman and Rudolph Ising*.

SIDELIGHTS: Jan Wahl wrote CA: "Almost twenty years ago, when I acted as amanuensis to the late Isak Dinesen in Rungsted, Denmark, she discovered my wish was to be a professional writer too, and her advice was: 'Don't write!' I understood what she meant; that it is a difficult life; but happily my fables and fairytales have been well received by children in the United States and abroad; besides, it is life's blood to me and I have no wish to do anything else!! When my first children's book, *Pleasant Fieldmouse*, won reviews such as 'belongs on the same high shelf as Beatrix Potter' and 'not since *Wind in the Willows*' and 'if you buy only one book this year, make it this one,' all my own childhood dreams seemed to come true.

Today, in [the] German edition, under the title *Fidel Feldmaus*, this book is in a series entitled 'Children's Classics.' This makes me feel very old—yet writing for children is the best means by which to stay young, and I am lucky I did not follow Isak Dinesen's advice.

"Although I may seem prolific, actually I usually write slowly, rather like corals building up a coral reef—piece by piece by piece until the structure is complete and appearing effortless. I used to feel it was necessary to write every day; but perhaps living in Mexico has taught me the virtues of writing less but ultimately (I hope) better. I still love *Fieldmouse* most of all my creations yet strive to let this be a standard or model for me. Writing for children is not easy; it must be done in a state of real 'grace' but given the world we now live in I believe it is more important than ever to write out of conviction in the great virtues, the positive qualities, of Life and living. Most novels of today seem pessimistic or without hope, unlike those of Willa Cather or Charles Dickens or even Isak Dinesen whose sense of the lyrical and the beautiful renders her view on the side of Optimism. My own advice to a young writer would be: 'WRITE.'"

AVOCATIONAL INTERESTS: Collecting old films ("[I] believe these have helped me think visually, since a number of my books have been picture books"), particularly animated films by Lotte Reiniger, Ladislas Starevitch, Max Fleisher, Walt Disney, Hugh Harman, and Rudolph Ising; and gathering "an extensive collection of old toys including Felix the Cat, Mickey Mouse, and Betty Boop"; traveling from the Sahara Desert to Lapland to the Yucatan.

BIOGRAPHICAL/CRITICAL SOURCES: New York Times Book Review, December 3, 1967; *Book World*, December 10, 1967; *National Observer*, December 11, 1967; *Newsweek*, December 6, 1982.

* * *

WALKER, Edward Joseph 1934-
(Ted Walker)

PERSONAL: Born November 18, 1934, in Lancing, England; son of Edward Joseph (a carpenter) and Winifred (Schofield) Walker; married Lorna Benfell, August 11, 1956; children: Edward, Susan, Margaret, William. *Education:* St. John's College, Cambridge, B.A. (with honours), 1956. *Politics:* "Leftish." *Religion:* "Apprehensive agnostic." *Home:* Argyll House, The Square, Eastergate, Chichester, West Sussex, England.

CAREER: Poet. High School for Boys, Chichester, Sussex, schoolmaster and teacher of French and Spanish, 1953-67; fulltime author and broadcaster, 1967-71; New England College, Arundel, Sussex, poet-in-residence, 1971—. *Member:* Society of Authors, Royal Society of Literature (fellow). *Awards, honors:* Eric Gregory award, 1964; Cholmondeley Award, 1966, for *The Solitaries;* Alice Hunt Bartlett Award, 1967, for *The Solitaries;* Major Arts Council of Great Britain award, 1978; J. R. Ackerley Prize, 1982, for *The High Path*.

WRITINGS—Under name Ted Walker; poetry, except as indicated: *Those Other Growths*, Northern House, 1964; *Fox on a Barn Door*, J. Cape, 1965, Braziller, 1966; *The Solitaries*, Braziller, 1967; *The Night Bathers*, J. Cape, 1970; *Gloves to the Hangman*, J. Cape, 1973; *Burning the Ivy*, J. Cape, 1979; *The Lion's Cavalcade*, J. Cape, 1980; *The High Path* (autobiography), Routledge & Kegan Paul, 1982. Regular contributor of poems to *New Yorker;* contributor of short stories to other periodicals. Founding editor, with John Cotton, *Priapus*.

SIDELIGHTS: A British writer, editor, and translator, Ted Walker is best known for his carefully crafted poems, many of which follow the tradition of English Nature poetry. In his precise observation of animals, fish, and birds, Walker detects a natural harmony that is missing in civilized life. He describes his works as "in the main a poetry of fear and loss which looks for the beauty that remains among the ruins of lost faith, lost innocence and lost animal strength," according to the *Library Journal*.

"His best poems are the ones in which he dramatizes segments of being that have been crushed or suppressed by the conditions of civilized life, 'wants kept caged on roofs / of the mind's tenements,'" writes Laurence Lieberman in the *Yale Review*. "In weaker poems, the shifts from description to message—statement of human analogy—are abrupt and unaccountable, and jar in the reader's ear. In the best poems, these two movements are carried on simultaneously, joined and jointed, seamlessly, in the poem's drama."

Though Walker turned to prose for his autobiography *The High Path*, this work exhibits many of the strengths of his poems. There is the same respect for language—reflecting what *Times Literary Supplement* reviewer Edward Blishen calls "the poet's habit of not allowing words to report for duty half-asleep"—and the same carefully delineated, emotionally charged detail. In describing, for example, his father's eating habits and his mother's sewing drawer, Walker makes clear how these seemingly pedestrian things influenced his perceptions. "If the source of my tendency towards woozy romanticism may be traced to the exuberant chaos of my mother's sewing drawer," he writes, "then my regard for orderly techniques and craftsmanship of form stems from observing my father eat." Blishen commends Walker's powers of observation and his ability to make "sense of the brimming nonsense of a life." The critic concludes by relating that Walker's father "had a term for anything beautifully done: *umpity poo*. There seems no better term for *The High Path*."

BIOGRAPHICAL/CRITICAL SOURCES: Library Journal, July, 1966; *New York Times Book Review*, November 20, 1966; *Kenyon Review*, January, 1967; *Poetry,* March, 1967, May, 1967; *Observer*, March 26, 1967; *Books and Bookmen*, May, 1967; *New Statesman*, May 12, 1967; *Yale Review*, winter, 1968; *Times Literary Supplement*, June 18, 1970, June 8, 1973, January 14, 1983; *Contemporary Literary Criticism,* Volume XIII, Gale, 1980; Ted Walker, *The High Path*, Routledge & Kegan Paul, 1982.

* * *

WALKER, Jack
See THAYER, Frederick C(lifton), Jr.

* * *

WALKER, Ted
See WALKER, Edward Joseph

* * *

WALLACE, Helen M(argaret) 1913-

PERSONAL: Born February 18, 1913, in Hoosick Falls, N.Y.; daughter of Jonas and Ray (Schweizer) Wallace. *Education:* Wellesley College, A.B., 1933; Columbia University, M.D., 1937; Harvard University, M.P.H. (cum laude), 1943. *Home:* 1515 Oxford St., Berkeley, Calif. 94709. *Office:* Division of

Maternal and Child Health, Graduate School of Public Health, San Diego State University, San Diego, Calif. 92182.

CAREER: New York City Department of Health, New York City, began as junior health officer, became director of Bureau for Handicapped Children, 1943-55; New York Medical College, New York City, professor of preventive medicine and chairman of department, 1955-56; University of Minnesota, Minneapolis, professor of maternal and child health, 1956-59; U.S. Children's Bureau, Washington, D.C., chief of professional training, 1959-60, chief of child health research, 1961-62; University of California, Berkeley, professor of maternal, child, and family health, 1962-80, chairman of program, 1962-80, director of Makerere Medical School, 1968-73; San Diego State University, San Diego, Calif., professor and head of Division of Maternal and Child Health at the Graduate School of Public Health, 1980—. Visiting professor of Makerere Medical School, 1969, 1971. Consultant to World Health Organization and California State Department of Developmental Services.

MEMBER: American Public Health Association (fellow; member of governing council), American Academy of Pediatrics (fellow), American Medical Association (fellow), American School Health Association (fellow), American College of Preventive Medicine (fellow), American Academy of Cerebral Palsy (fellow), American College of Obstetricians and Gynecologists, Association of Teachers of Maternal and Child Health (president), Alameda-Contra Costa County Medical Society.

AWARDS, HONORS: World Health Organization traveling fellowship to South America, summer, 1957, and to Soviet Union, 1979; National Institutes of Health and Ford Foundation grants to England and Sweden, 1973; Martha May Eliot Award, American Public Health Association; Job Smith Award, American Academy of Pediatrics; Alumnae Achievement Award, Wellesley College; various awards from United Cerebral Palsy of New York City, United Cerebral Palsy of Minnesota, New York Philanthropic League, and Muscular Dystrophy Association of New York City.

WRITINGS: The Child with Cardiac Limitations, Board of Education (New York, N.Y.), 1953; *The Child with Orthopedic Limitations,* Board of Education (New York, N.Y.), 1954; *Standards for General Convalescent Homes Caring for Cardiac Children,* Public Health Committee, New York Heart Association, 1954; *Standards and Recommendations for Hospital Care of New Born Infants,* Committee on Fetus and Newborn, American Academy of Pediatrics, 1954.

Health Supervision of Young Children, Child Health Committee, American Public Health Association, 1955; *Services for Handicapped Children,* Committee on Child Health, American Public Health Association, 1955; *Services for Children with Cleft Lip and Cleft Palate,* Committee on Child Health, American Public Health Association, 1955; *Services for Children with Cerebral Palsy,* Committee on Child Health, American Public Health Association, 1955; *Services for Children with Cerebral Palsy,* Committee on Child Health, American Public Health Associaton, 1955; *Services for Children with Dento-Facial Handicaps,* Committee on Child Health, American Public Health Association, 1955.

(With C. Meinert and P. J. Englund) *A Study of Cerebral Palsy,* United Cerebral Palsy of Minnesota, 1962; (with others) *Services for Children with Orthopedic Handicaps,* American Public Health Association, 1962; *Health Services for Mothers and Children,* Saunders, 1962; (with others) *Maternal and Newborn Care in Fallout Shelters,* U.S. Children's Bureau, 1963; (with others) *The Care of Infants and Children in Community Fallout Shelters,* U.S. Children's Bureau, 1963.

Maternal and Child Health Practices, C. C Thomas, 1973; *Health Care of Mothers and Children under National Health Services,* Ballenger Publishing, 1975; (editor) *Infant Mortality Around the World,* Ross Laboratories, 1975.

Maternal and Child Health Around the World, Macmillan, 1981.

Contributor: Frampton and Gall, editors, *Special Education for the Exceptional,* Volume II, Sargent, 1955; H. Michal-Smith, editor, *Management of the Handicapped Child,* Grune, 1957; Fred Delli Quadri, editor, *Helping the Family in Urban Society,* Columbia University Press, 1963; *Rural Youth in Crisis,* U.S. Government Printing Office, 1965; Green and Hagerty, editors, *Textbook on Ambulatory Pediatrics,* Saunders, 1968; John G. Howells, editor, *Modern Perspectives in Psycho-Obstetrics,* Oliver & Boyd, 1972.

Contributor to *Encyclopedia of Educational Research.* Contributor of about two hundred and thirty articles and reviews to medical journals. Guest editor of *Woman Physician,* October, 1971.

* * *

WALLERSTEIN, Robert S(olomon) 1921-

PERSONAL: Born January 28, 1921, in Berlin, Germany; came to United States in 1923, naturalized in 1928; son of Lazar (a physician) and Sara (Guensberg) Wallerstein; married Judith Saretsky (a university instructor), January 26, 1947; children: Michael, Nina, Amy. *Education:* Columbia University, B.A., 1941, M.D., 1944. *Home:* 290 Beach Rd., Belvedere, Calif. 94920. *Office:* Langley-Porter Psychiatric Institute, University of California, 401 Parnassus, San Francisco, Calif. 94143.

CAREER: Certified by American Board of Psychiatry and Neurology, 1953, and by Topeka Institute for Psychoanalysis, 1958; Mount Sinai Hospital, New York, N.Y., intern, 1944-45, assistant resident, 1945-46, resident, 1948-49; Winter VA Hospital, Topeka, Kan., resident, 1949-51, chief of psychosomatic section and staff psychiatrist, 1951-53; Menninger Foundation, Topeka, senior psychiatrist and associate director of department of research, 1954-65, director of department of research, 1965-66; Topeka Institute for Psychoanalysis, Topeka, training and supervising analyst, 1965-66; Mount Zion Hospital, San Francisco, Calif., chief of psychiatry, 1966-78; San Francisco Psychoanalytic Institute, San Francisco, training and supervising analyst, 1966—; University of California, San Francisco, clinical professor, 1967-75, professor of psychiatry, chairman of department, and director of Langley-Porter Psychiatric Institute, 1975—. Lecturer at Menninger School of Psychiatry, 1951-66, and Topeka Institute of Psychoanalysis, 1959-66; fellow, Center for Advanced Study in the Behavioral Sciences, 1964-65, 1981-82. Research Scientist Career Development Committee, National Institute of Mental Health, member, 1966-70, chairman, 1968-70. Consultant to psychosomatic section, Winter VA Hospital, 1954-66, and to psychiatric staff, Topeka State Hospital, 1957-66. *Military service:* U.S. Army, medical officer, 1946-48; became captain.

MEMBER: International Psychoanalytic Association (vice-president, 1977—), American Psychoanalytic Association (member of executive committee, 1970-72; president, 1971-72), American Psychiatric Association (fellow), American College of Physicians (fellow), American Orthopsychiatric Association (fellow), American Medical Association, American Association for the Advancement of Science, Center for Advanced Psychoanalytic Studies, Group for the Advancement of Psychiatry (chairman of committee on research, 1960-66), California Medical Association, San Francisco Psychoanalytic Society, San Francisco Medical Society. *Awards, honors:* Heinz Hartmann Award, New York Psychoanalytic Institute, 1968; Arthur Marshall Distinguished Alumnus Award, Menninger Foundation, 1972; J. Elliott Royer Award, University of California, San Francisco, 1973.

WRITINGS: (With others) *Hospital Treatment of Alcoholism: A Comparative, Experimental Study,* Basic Books, 1957; (with Rudolf Ekstein) *The Teaching and Learning of Psychotherapy,* Basic Books, 1958, reprinted, International Universities Press, 1972; (with others) *Prediction in Psychotherapy Research: A Method for the Transformation of Clinical Judgments in Testable Hypotheses,* International Universities Press, 1968; *Psychotherapy and Psychoanalysis: Theory, Practice, Research,* International Universities Press, 1975; (editor) *Becoming a Psychoanalyst: A Study of Psychoanalytic Supervision,* International Universities Press, 1981; (co-editor) *Psychotherapy: Impact on Psychoanalytic Training,* International Universities Press, 1982; *42 Lives in Treatment: A Study of Psychoanalysis and Psychotherapy,* Guilford Press, 1984.

Contributor: Eli A. Rubinstein and Morris B. Parloff, editors, *Research in Psychotherapy,* American Psychological Association, 1959; Mary R. Haworth, editor, *Child Psychotherapy,* Basic Books, 1964; Louis A. Gottschalk and Arthur H. Auerbach, editors, *Methods of Research in Psychotherapy,* Appleton, 1966; John M. Schlien, editor, *Research in Psychotherapy,* Volume III, American Psychological Association, 1968.

Irwin M. Marcus, editor, *Currents in Psychoanalysis,* International Universities Press, 1971; Robert R. Holt, editor, *New Horizon for Psychotherapy,* International Universities Press, 1971; Louise Diamant, editor, *Case Studies in Psychopathology,* C. E. Merrill, 1971; Daniel Offer and Daniel Freedman, editors, *Modern Psychiatry and Clinical Research: Essays in Honor of Roy R. Grinker, Sr.,* Basic Books, 1972; Jack Citrin and Paul M. Sniderman, editors, *Handbook of Research on Personality and Politics,* Aldine, 1972; Albert Cain, editor, *Survivors of Suicide,* C. C Thomas, 1972; Bergin, Frank, Lang, Marks, Matarazzo, and Strupp, editors, *Psychotherapy,* 1971, Aldine, 1972; Bergin, Lang, Marks, Matarazzo, Patterson, and Strupp, editors, *Psychotherapy and Behavior Change,* 1973, Aldine, 1974; Gill and Holzman, editors, *Psychology versus Metapsychology: Psychoanalytic Essays in Memory of George S. Klein,* International Universities Press, 1976; Stanley Goodman, editor, *Psychoanalytic Education and Research: The Current Situation and Future Possibilities,* International Universities Press, 1977; Peter Ostwald, editor, *Communication and Social Interaction,* Grune & Stratton, 1977; Arnold Goldberg, editor, *The Future of Psychoanalysis,* International Universities Press, 1983; Kaplan and Lichtenberg, editors, *Reflections on Self Psychology,* Analytic Press, 1983.

Contributor to more than 25 professional journals, including *American Journal of Tropical Medicine, American Practitioner, Psychiatry,* and *International Journal of Psychoanalysis.* Member of editorial boards of several professional journals, including *Psychological Issues,* 1959—, *Journal of Psychiatric Research,* 1963-64, *International Review of Psychoanalysis,* 1974—, *Psychiatric Journal of the University of Ottawa,* 1976—, and *Review of Psychoanalytic Books,* 1980—.

WARD, Benedicta 1933-

PERSONAL: Born February 4, 1933, in Durham, England; daughter of Oswald Alleyn (a minister) and Florence Susannah (Linnet) Ward. *Education:* University of Manchester, B.A. (honors), 1955; St. Anne's College, Oxford, D.Phil., 1977. *Home:* Convent of the Incarnation, Fairacres, Oxford, England.

CAREER: Member of a contemplative enclosed order of women religious in the Church of England. Lecturer in England and the United States. Tutor in medieval history, Centre for Medieval and Renaissance Studies, Oxford University.

WRITINGS: *Prayers and Meditations of St. Anselm,* Penguin, 1973; *The Sayings of the Desert Fathers,* Mowbrays, 1975; *The Wisdom of the Desert Fathers,* SLG Press, 1975; (editor and contributor) *The Influence of St. Bernard,* SLG Press, 1976; *Lives of the Desert Fathers,* Mowbrays, 1978; *Miracles and the Medieval Mind,* Scolar Press, 1981.

Contributor: M. Basil Pennington, editor, *Contemplative Community,* Cistercian Publication, 1972; Pennington, editor, *Bernard of Clairvaux,* Cistercian Publications, 1973; Pennington, editor, *One Yet Two,* Cistercian Publications, 1976; *Dictionary of Spirituality,* Society for Promoting Christian Knowledge, 1983; *Study of Spirituality,* Oxford University Press, 1984. Also contributor to *Famulus Christi,* edited by G. Bonner, 1976.

WORK IN PROGRESS: Translations for Cistercian Publications; translating William of Malmesbury's *Gesta Pontificum* and John Cassian's *Institutes: Exordium Magnum Cisterciense.*

* * *

WARD, Philip 1938-
(Darby Greenfield)

PERSONAL: Born February 10, 1938, in Harrow, England; son of Albert Edwin (a company secretary) and Mildred (Elsey) Ward; married Audrey Joan Monk, April 4, 1964; children: Carolyn, Angela. *Education:* Northwestern Polytechnic, London, A.L.A.; studied at universities in Perugia, Italy, Lebanon, and in Coimbra, Portugal. *Politics:* None. *Religion:* Scientific humanism. *Office:* Oleander Press, 17 Stansgate Ave., Cambridge CB2 2QZ, England.

CAREER: Chief cataloger at National Central Library, Holborn (now Camden) Public Libraries, Middlesex County Library, and Wimbledon Public Libraries, England, 1962-63; Oasis Oil Co. of Libya, Inc., Tripoli, co-ordinator of library services, 1963-70; UNESCO library consultant in Shibin al-Kum, Egypt, 1973; UNESCO/Indonesia Development of National Library Service Project, Jakarta, Indonesia, UNESCO project manager, 1973-74; editor, *Oxford Companion to Spanish Literature,* 1974-76; Oleander Press, Cambridge, England, managing director, 1976—. *Member:* Private Libraries Association (London; founding secretary), Royal Society of Arts (fellow).

WRITINGS—Published by Oleander Press, except as indicated: (With Roderick Cave) *Simplified Cataloguing Rules for Private Libraries,* Private Libraries Association, 1959; *Collected Poems,* 1960; *Periodicals in Libya,* Oasis Oil Co. of Libya, 1963; *A Survey of Libyan Bibliographical Resources,* [Tripoli], 1964, 2nd edition, 1965; (editor) Evenyn Quell, *The Quell-Finger Dialogues,* [North Harrow, England], 1965; *Poems for Par-*

ticipants: A Work-Book, Labris, 1967; *Seldom Rains: Libyan Poems,* 1967; *Ambigamus; or, The Logic Box,* Wattle Grove Press (Tasmania), 1967; *Drama Workshop,* 1967; *Loakrime: Idol of the Shattered Pyramid,* Openings Press, 1967; *The Theory and Practice of Library Classification,* Oasis Oil Co. of Libya, 1968; *A Musical Breakfast* (one-act play), Brewhouse Private Press (Wymondham, England), 1968; *At the Best of Times: Libyan Poems,* 1968; *The Poet and the Microscope,* 1968; *Apuleius on Trial at Sabratha* (essay), 1968; *Spanish Literary Appreciation* (textbook), University of London Press, 1969; *A Lizard and Other Distractions* (stories), Magpie Press, 1969; *Fiction List of Murdoch Lenz* (story), 1969; *Okefani: Song of Nij Zitru,* Magpie Press, 1969.

Garrity and Other Plays, 1970; *Maps on the Ceiling: Libyan Poems,* 1970; (editor) *The Libyan Civil Code,* 1970; *The Libyan Research Library Catalog,* Oasis Oil Co. of Libya, 1970; *Planning and the Future: A Reading List,* Oasis Oil Co. of Libya, 1971; (contributor) Norbert E. Chantz, *Just Pick a Murricane?,* 1971; *The Libyan Revolution,* 1971; *Pincers* (play), 1973; *Planning a National Library Service,* Indonesian Library Association, 1973; *A House on Fire: Selected Poems,* 1973; (editor) *Indonesian Traditional Poetry* (anthology), 1975; *Television Plays,* 1976; *Indonesia: The Development of a National Library Service,* three volumes, UNESCO (Paris), 1976; *Maltese Boyhood: Stories,* 1976; (editor) *Oxford Companion to Spanish Literature,* Oxford University Press, 1977; *Imposters and Their Imitators: Poems,* 1977; *The Keymakers* (poems), Interim Press, 1978; *A Dictionary of Common Fallacies,* Volume I, 1978, Volume II, 1980; *Cambridge Street Literature,* 1978; (with wife, Audrey J. Ward) *The Small Publisher,* 1979; (editor) Richard F. Burton, *The Gold-Mines of Midian,* 1979.

Lost Songs and Other Political Poems, 1981; *A Lifetime's Reading,* 1982.

Translator; published by Oleander Press: Lope de Rueda, *Las Aceitunas,* 1962; Miguel Torga, *Jesus,* 1963; Angelo Pesce, *Colours of the Arab Fatherland,* 1972; *The Scandalous Life of Cesar Moro in His Own Words: Peruvian Surrealist Poetry,* 1976; Ramon Gomez de la Serna, *Greguerias,* 1982.

Travel guides; Published by Oleander Press, except as indicated: *Touring Libya: The Western Provinces,* Faber, 1967; *Touring Libya: The Southern Provinces,* Faber, 1968; *Touring Libya: The Eastern Provinces,* Faber, 1969; *Tripoli: Portrait of a City,* 1969; *Touring Iran,* Faber, 1970; (with Pesce) *Motoring to Nalut,* 1970; *Sabratha: A Guide for Visitors,* 1970; (with Ed van Weerd) *The Way to Wadi al-Khail,* 1970; *Touring Lebanon,* Faber, 1971; *Come with Me to Ireland,* 1972; *Touring Cyprus,* 1972; *The Aeolian Islands,* 1974; *Bangkok: Portrait of a City,* 1974; (under pseudonym Darby Greenfield) *Indonesia: A Traveler's Guide,* Volume I: *Java and Sumatra,* 1975, Volume II: *Bali and East Indonesia,* 1976; *Across Arabia,* Saudi Arabian Airlines, 1976; *Albania,* 1982; *Ha'il: Oasis City of Saudi Arabia,* 1983.

Contributor to *Labris* (Belgium), *Libyan Review, Transatlantic Review, Quest, Maelstrom, The Private Library,* and other periodicals.

WORK IN PROGRESS: A novel, *Forgotten Games,* and a travel book, *Central Asian Cities.*

SIDELIGHTS: "Assembling a private library of world civilisation and living in a close loving family are my twin delights," Philip Ward told *CA.* "I write to fill in gaps in the literature (the first modern English-language guidebook to Albania, for instance, or a corrective reference book on fallacies to expose the superstitious and ignorant theories of cults such as the Bermuda Triangle, Scientology, spoonbending and time regression) and, creatively, to explore tensions such as a poet under totalitarianism *(Lost Songs)* or the conflict between Cortes and Montezuma *(Forgotten Games).*

"As a poet, I pervert the courtly love tradition to encompass eulogy for my own wife. As a playwright, I revert to the tradition before the Greeks invented a third character (and prefer for the same reason plainchant to polyphony). As a novelist, I take the keenest pleasure in persuading the reader to guess which of the words are truths and which fictions. As a travel writer, I erect a scaffolding of images on which the reader may embroider his own canvas—for no country can be perceived alike by two visitors, and a reader is simply a visitor at one remove. As a translator, I seek to restore Spanish literature to the key role it possessed in English at the time of the first Elizabeth. As a reader, I learn languages to take full advantage of publishers' bilingual editions, or to read in the original wherever possible, a model being *The Penguin Book of Russian Verse.* My guide to the greatest world literature, *A Lifetime's Reading* (1982) was published at the age of forty-four, leaving me another lifetime's reading to enjoy.

"I am privileged to be alive at a time of great Renaissance in literature, with Latin American and Eastern European writers dominating the scene, and more important writers creating now than ever before. The task is to struggle free of one's fetters of bias—race, religion, language, class, political indoctrination—and see the world pristine and prelapsarian. A writer should be fresh, alert, but at the same time aware of all the greatest writings—from Tu Fu to Cervantes, from Abu Il-'Ala al-Ma'arri to Chekhov. In other words, a powerful original talent has no right arrogantly to ignore past and present masters. Our lives are too short for ignorance, fear, or hatred."

BIOGRAPHICAL/CRITICAL SOURCES: Books and Bookmen, May, 1970, September, 1982; *Times Literary Supplement,* January 13, 1978, May 9, 1980, June 13, 1980; *Britain Book News,* July, 1981; *Daily Telegraph,* August 15, 1981; *Library Association Record,* January, 1982; *Guardian,* May 17, 1982; *Bookseller,* June 12, 1982.

* * *

WARREN, Mary Bondurant 1930-

PERSONAL: Born February 5, 1930, in Athens, Ga.; daughter of John Parnell (a lumber dealer) and Mary Claire (a personnel director; maiden name, Brannon) Bondurant; married James Randolph Warren (a farm equipment dealer), November 27, 1953; children: Eve Bondurant (Mrs. James Corbin Weeks), Mark Standard, Amy Moss (Mrs. Edward Victor Sanders), Stuart Heard, Lisa Brannon. *Education:* University of Georgia, B.S., 1950; Oak Ridge Institute of Nuclear Studies, D.R.I.P., 1953. *Religion:* Methodist. *Home address:* Pocataligo, Route 2, Box 65, Danielsville, Ga. 30633. *Office:* Heritage Papers, Danielsville, Ga. 30633.

CAREER: Union Carbide, Oak Ridge, Tenn., staff member, 1950-51; Oak Ridge Institute of Nuclear Studies, Medical Division, Oak Ridge, conducted radio biophysics research, 1951-52; Emory University, School of Medicine, Atlanta, Ga., conducted radioisotope research, 1952-53; Georgia Institute of Technology, Atlanta, technical editor for engineering experiment station, 1954; Veterans Administration Hospital, Atlanta, radioassay consultant, 1956-57; Heritage Papers, Danielsville, Ga., owner, 1964—. Chairman of Clarke County (Ga.) Civil

War Centennial Commission, 1961-65. *Member:* South Carolina Historical Society, South Caroliniana Society (life member), North Carolina Genealogical Society, Georgia Genealogical Society, Athens Historical Society (charter member; member of board of directors; president, 1962-63), Augusta Genealogical Society.

WRITINGS—Published by Heritage Papers, except as indicated: (Contributor) John Stegeman, *These Men She Gave*, University of Georgia Press, 1964; *Jackson Street Cemetery, Athens, Ga.*, 1966; *Mars Hill Baptist Church, Oconee County, Ga.*, 1966; *Marriage Book "A", Clarke County, Ga.*, 1966; *Georgia Genealogical Bibliography, 1963-67*, 1968; *Marriages and Deaths, 1763 to 1820, Abstracted from Extant Georgia Newspapers*, 1968.

Family Puzzlers, 1964-1967, 1969; *Family Puzzlers, 1968*, 1970; *Family Puzzlers, 1969*, 1970; (editor and author of revision) L. M. Hill, *Hills of Wilkes County, Ga., and Allied Families*, 1972; *Marriages and Deaths, 1820 to 1830, Abstracted from Extant Georgia Newspapers*, 1972; *South Carolina Jury Lists, 1718 Through 1783*, 1977; *Citizens and Immigrants: South Carolina, 1768*, 1978; (editor) Bowen, *Chronicles of Wilke's County, Georgia*, 1978; (editor) A. L. Hull, *Annals of Athens, Georgia*, 2nd edition (Warren was not associated with the 1st edition), 1978.

South Carolina Wills, 1981; (editor) A. B. Stroud, *The Strouds*, 2nd edition (Warren was not associated with the 1st edition), 1983; (compiler) *Georgia Marriages, 1811-1820*, 1984; (compiler) *Georgia Memorials, 1755-1775*, 1984; (annotator and indexer) Reverand Morgan Edwards, *Materials towards a Baptist History, 1770-1772*, Volume I: *Pennsylvania, Rhode Island, New Jersey, Delaware*, 1984, Volume II: *Maryland, Virginia, North Carolina, South Carolina, Georgia*, 1984.

Author of "Athens Lives and Legends," a column in *Athens Daily News*, and "Family Puzzlers," a column in *Athens Banner Herald*, *Oglethorpe Echo*, and *Athens Daily News*, 1964-67. Editor of *Family Puzzlers*, 1964—, *Carolina Genealogist*, 1970—, and *Georgia Genealogist*, 1970—.

SIDELIGHTS: Mary Bondurant Warren writes: "My interest is *research*—discovering, codifying, and publishing source records of historical and genealogical value. It has been satisfying to locate, recognize, and publish significant federal and state documents in a form useful to researchers. *Family Puzzlers*, our weekly genealogical magazine, now completing its twentieth year, strives to increase the research skills of its readers."

* * *

WATSON, Alan
   See WATSON, William Alexander Jardine

* * *

WATSON, William Alexander Jardine 1933-
   (Alan Watson)

PERSONAL: Born October 27, 1933, in Hamilton, Scotland; son of James Walker and Janet (Jardine) Watson; married Cynthia Balls (a university teacher), July 5, 1958 (divorced, 1982); children: David Jardine, Eleanor Ann Jardine. *Education:* University of Glasgow, M.A., 1954, LL.B., 1957; Oxford University, M.A., 1958, D.Phil., 1961. *Office:* Law School, University of Pennsylvania, Philadelphia, Pa. 19104.

CAREER: Oxford University, Oxford, England, lecturer in law at Wadham College, 1957-59, lecturer in law at Oriel College, 1959-60, university lecturer in law, 1959-65, fellow of Oriel College, 1960-65; University of Glasgow, Glasgow, Scotland, Douglas Professor of Civil Law, 1965-68; University of Edinburgh, Edinburgh, Scotland, professor of civil law, 1968-69; University of Pennsylvania, Philadelphia, professor of law, history, and classics, 1979—. *Member:* Society of Public Teachers of Law, Societe Internationale de l'Histoire des Droits de l'Antiquite, Stair Society. *Awards, honors:* D.C.L., Oxford University, 1973.

WRITINGS—All under pseudonym Alan Watson: *Contract of Mandate in Roman Law*, Clarendon Press, 1961; *The Law of Obligations in the Later Roman Republic*, Clarendon Press, 1965; *The Law of Persons in the Later Roman Republic*, Clarendon Press, 1967; *The Law of Property in the Later Roman Republic*, Clarendon Press, 1968.

The Law of the Ancient Romans, Southern Methodist University Press, 1970; *The Law of Succession in the Later Roman Republic*, Clarendon Press, 1971; *Roman Private Law around 200 B.C.*, Edinburgh University Press, 1971; *Law Making in the Later Roman Republic*, Clarendon Press, 1974; *Legal Transplants: An Approach to Comparative Law*, University Press of Virginia, 1974; (editor) *Daube Noster: Essays in Legal History for David Daube*, Scottish Academic Press, 1974: *Rome of the Twelve Tables: Persons and Property*, Princeton University Press, 1975; *Society and Legal Change*, Scottish Academic Press, 1977; *The Nature of Law*, Edinburgh University Press, 1978.

The Making of the Civil Law, Harvard University Press, 1981. Contributor to British, Continental, and American law journals.

AVOCATIONAL INTERESTS: Literature, the theater.

* * *

WATTS, Elizabeth (Bailey) Smithgall 1941-
   (Elizabeth Smithgall)

PERSONAL: Born May 27, 1941, in Atlanta, Ga.; daughter of Charles Augustus (a newspaper publisher) and Lessie (a journalist; maiden name, Bailey) Smithgall; married John Robert Watts, Jr. (a dentist), June 15, 1968. *Education:* Attended L'Institute d'Ethnologie and Sorbonne, University of Paris, 1961-62, and Medical College of South Carolina (now Medical University of South Carolina), summer, 1964; Tulane University, A.B., 1963; University of Pennsylvania, Ph.D., 1971. *Office:* Department of Anthropology, Tulane University, New Orleans, La. 70118.

CAREER: Tulane University, New Orleans, La., visiting instructor, spring, 1968, instructor, 1968-70, assistant professor, 1971-73, associate professor of anthropology, 1974—, chairman of department, 1978-81. *Member:* International Association of Human Biologists, International Primatological Society, American Anthropological Association, American Association of Physical Anthropologists (member of executive committee, 1977-80), American Society of Primatologists, Society for the Study of Human Biology (secretary-treasurer, 1972—; member of executive committee, 1979—), Human Biology Council, Southern Anthropological Society.

WRITINGS: (Contributor) G. H. Bourne, editor, *The Rhesus Monkey*, Volume II, Academic Press, 1975; *Biology of the Living Primates*, W. C. Brown, 1975; (editor with F. E. Johnston and G. W. Lasker) *Biosocial Interrelations in Population*

Adaptation, Mouton, 1975; (contributor) H. Rothschild, editor, *Biocultural Aspects of Disease*, Academic Press, 1981; (editor and contributor) *Nonhuman Primate Models for Human Growth and Development*, Alan R. Liss, 1984; (contributor) F. Falkner and J. M. Tanner, editors, *Human Growth*, Volume I, 2nd edition, Plenum, 1984; (contributor) C. Susanne, editor, *Genetical and Environmental Factors During the Growth Period*, Plenum, in press; (contributor) W. R. DuKelow, editor, *Comparative Primate Biology: Endocrinology, Reproduction and Development*, Volume V, Alan R. Liss, in press. Contributor of articles and reviews, some under name Elizabeth Smithgall, to scientific journals. Consulting editor of *American Journal of Primatology*, 1980—; member of editorial board of *Human Biology*, 1982—.

WORK IN PROGRESS: Research on hand-wrist ossification centers in two laboratory colonies of rhesus monkeys; research in adolescent growth and sexual dimorphism in chimpanzees and rhesus monkeys.

* * *

WATTS, Peter Christopher 1919-
(Matt Chisholm, Cy James, Duncan Mackinlock, Tom Owen)

PERSONAL: Born December 25, 1919, in London, England; son of Frank (a telegraphist) and Lillian (a musician; maiden name, Thayers) Watts; married Sonia Chism; children: Matthew, Jeremy. *Education:* Educated in England. *Home:* 15 Nower Hill, Pinner, Middlesex HA5 5QR, England. *Agent:* A. D. Peters & Co. Ltd., 10 Buckingham St., London WC2N 6BU, England; and Peter Matson, Harold Matson Co., Inc., 276 Fifth Ave., New York, N.Y. 10001.

CAREER: Writer. *Military service:* British Army, 1940-46; served in North Africa, Syria, and Burma. *Member:* EAV Society of Britain and Ireland (founder and secretary), Western Writers of America.

WRITINGS—Fiction, except as indicated: *Out of Yesterday*, Hodder & Stoughton, 1950; *Scream and Shout*, Transworld Publications, 1965; *A Dictionary of the Old West, 1850-1900* (nonfiction), Knopf, 1977; *The True Book of the Wild West* (juvenile nonfiction), Mitchell Beazley, 1978.

Translated from original English manuscript into Norwegian; published by Bladkompaniet: *Blodig Snoe*, 1982; *Doedens Land*, 1982; *Leiemorder*, 1983; *En Texaners Doed*, 1983; *Hestetyvene*, 1983.

Under pseudonym Matt Chisholm; published by Panther Books, except as indicated: *Halfbreed*, 1958; *Hodge*, 1958; *Riders at the Ford*, 1958; *Hang a Man High*, 1959; *Sutter's Strike*, 1959; *The Saga of Trench Godden*, 1959; *Blood on the Land*, 1959; *Joe Blade*, 1959; *Never Give Ground*, 1959; *Wild Mustanger*, 1959; *The Law of Ben Hodge*, 1959.

A Posse of Violent Men, 1960; *Fury at Tombstone*, 1960; *Pursuit in the Sun*, 1960; *Prayer for a Gunman*, 1960; *Hangrope for a Gunman*, 1960; *Advance to Death*, 1961; *A Rage of Guns*, 1961; *Bitter Range*, 1962; *Three for Vengeance*, Mayflower Books, 1963; *The Proud Horseman*, Mayflower Books, 1963.

Indians!, Odhams, 1965; *The Last Gun*, 1966; *Cash McCord*, 1966; *Spur to Death*, 1966; *Hunted*, 1966; *Gun Marshall*, 1967; *Range War*, 1967; *Indian Scout*, 1967; *A Gun for Bragg's Woman*, 1967; *Apache Kill*, 1967; *Gun Lust*, 1968; *A Bullet for Brody*, 1968; *High Peak*, 1968; *Spur*, 1968; *Three Canyons to Death*, Mayflower Books, 1968; *The Trail of Fear*, 1968.

"Blade Western" series; published by Hamlyn: *The Laredo Assignment*, 1978; *The Indian Incident*, 1978; *The Tucson Conspiracy*, 1978; *The Pecos Manhunt*, 1978; *The Colorado Virgins*, 1979; *The Mexican Proposition*, 1979; *The Arizona Climax*, 1979; *The Nevada Mustang*, 1980; *The Montana Deadlock*, 1980; *The Cheyenne Trap*, 1980; *The Navaho Trail*, 1981; *The Last Act*, 1981.

"McAllister" series; published by Panther Books, except as indicated: *The Hard Men*, Mayflower Books, 1963; *Death at Noon*, Mayflower Books, 1963; *The Hangman Rides Tall*, Mayflower Books, 1963; *McAllister*, Mayflower Books, 1963, Beagle Books, 1971.

Kiowa, 1967; *Death Trail*, 1967; *Tough to Kill*, 1968; *McAllister Justice*, 1969, Beagle Books, 1971; *Rage of McAllister*, 1969, Beagle Books, 1971; *Hell for McAllister*, 1969, Beagle Books, 1970; *McAllister Strikes*, 1969, Beagle Books, 1971; *Kill McAllister*, 1969, Beagle Books, 1972; *McAllister Rides*, 1969, Beagle Books, 1971; *McAllister Makes War*, 1969, Beagle Books, 1971; *McAllister's Fury*, 1969, Beagle Books, 1971; *McAllister Fights*, 1969, Beagle Books, 1971; *Gunsmoke for McAllister*, 1969, Beagle Books, 1970; *Blood on McAllister*, 1969, Beagle Books, 1970.

McAllister Says No, 1970, Beagle Books, 1971; *Danger for McAllister*, 1970; *McAllister Gambles*, 1970, Beagle Books, 1971; *Hang McAllister*, Beagle Books, 1970; *Shoot McAllister*, 1970, Beagle Books, 1971; *Trail of McAllister*, 1970, Beagle Books, 1971; *McAllister Runs Wild*, Mayflower Books, 1972; *Brand McAllister*, Mayflower Books, 1972; *Battle of McAllister*, Mayflower Books, 1972; *McAllister Trapped*, Mayflower Books, 1973; *McAllister Must Die*, Mayflower Books, 1974; *Vengeance of McAllister*, Mayflower Books, 1974; *The McAllister Legend*, Mayflower Books, 1974.

McAllister and the Comanche Crossing, Hamlyn, 1981; *McAllister and the Spanish Gold*, Hamlyn, 1981; *McAllister: Quarry*, Hamlyn, 1981; *McAllister Never Surrenders*, Hamlyn, 1982; *McAllister and the Cheyenne Death*, Hamlyn, 1982; *McAllister: Die-Hard*, Hamlyn, 1983; *McAllister: Wolf-Bait*, Hamlyn, 1983; *McAllister: Firebrand*, Hamlyn, 1983.

"The Storm" series; published by Mayflower Books, except as indicated: *Stampede*, Panther Books, 1971; *Hard Texas Trail*, Panther Books, 1971; *Riders West*, 1971; *One Notch to Death*, 1972; *One Man, One Gun*, 1972; *A Breed of Men*, 1973; *Thunder in the West*, 1973; *Battle Fury*, 1973; *Blood on the Hills*, 1973.

Under pseudonym Cy James; published by Panther Books, except as indicated: *The Brasada Guns*, 1961; *The Gun Is My Brother*, 1961; *The Violent Hills*, 1961; *Death Rides Fast*, 1964; *The Battle of Red Rock*, 1964; *Ride the Far Country*, 1964; *Hellion*, 1964; *Hangrope Posse*, 1965; *Gun-Rage*, 1965; *Blood Creek*, 1965; *Gun Hand*, 1965; *Savage Horseman*, 1966; *Man in the Saddle*, 1966; *The Running Gun*, 1966; *My Gun Is Justice*, 1966.

"The Spur" series; published by Mayflower Books: *The Cimmaron Kid*, 1969; *Longhorn*, 1970; *Gun*, 1971; *The Brave Ride Tall*, 1971; *Blood at Sunset*, 1972.

Under pseudonym Duncan Mackinlock: *Island of Hell*, Panther Books, 1961.

Under pseudonym Tom Owen: *The Dread and the Glory*, Panther Books, 1959; *Circus of Horror*, Panther Books, 1960; *The Corgi Sports Almanac* (nonfiction), Corgi, 1965.

Also author of four novels published in Norwegian by Bladkompaniet, 1978-83, and of over forty short stories and novelettes under pseudonyms Matt Chisolm and Cy James, including the "McCool" and the "Robin Hood" series.

WORK IN PROGRESS: "A number of 'serious' books," including a bibliography of the literature of the American West.

SIDELIGHTS: Peter Christopher Watts told *CA* he believes "reading and writing are habits to be indulged each day for the sake of health and sanity. Neither presents a problem; both are pure pleasure." Having slowed his output of western novels, Watts is now dedicated to working for the EAV Society of Britain and Ireland, which he founded "as a debt to that system of electro-acupuncture." Among his works, which have been translated into German, Norwegian, Swedish, Finnish, Dutch, Serbo-Croat, and Italian, *A Dictionary of the Old West, 1850-1900* is his favorite, and it represents "the culmination of years of fascination for the language of the Old American West."

* * *

WEATHERBY, W(illiam) J(ohn)

PERSONAL: Born in Heaton Moor, England; son of William (an artist) and Kathleen (Glancy) Weatherby. *Politics:* "democrat (with a small 'd')." *Religion:* "Christian of no color." *Residence:* New York, N.Y. *Office:* Simon & Schuster, Inc., 1230 Avenue of the Americas, New York, N.Y. 10020.

CAREER: Former journalist in England and the United States, and editor for Penguin Books, Inc., New York City; Simon & Schuster, Inc., New York City, editor, beginning 1972.

WRITINGS: Breaking the Silence: The Negro Struggle in the U.S.A. (also see below), Penguin, 1965, published as *Love in the Shadows*, Stein & Day, 1966; *Out of Hiding* (fiction), Hart-Davis, 1966, Doubleday, 1967; (editor with Roi Ottley) *The Negro in New York: An Informal Social History*, New York Public Library and Oceana, 1967; *One of Our Priests Is Missing* (novel), Doubleday, 1968; "Breaking the Silence" (play; based on his nonfiction work of the same title), produced at Liverpool Playhouse, winter, 1969; *Conversations with Marilyn*, Mason/Charter, 1976; *Squaring Off: Mailer versus Baldwin*, Mason/Charter, 1977; *Death of an Informer*, Robson Books, 1977; *Murder at the UN*, Robson Books, 1977. Book reviewer and essayist for *Times Literary Supplement* and *Manchester Guardian*.

SIDELIGHTS: W. J. Weatherby has traveled throughout Europe and the United States.

BIOGRAPHICAL/CRITICAL SOURCES: New York Times Book Review, March 5, 1967; *Best Sellers*, March 15, 1967.†

* * *

WEIL, Gordon L(ee) 1937-

PERSONAL: Surname is pronounced "wile"; born March 12, 1937, in Mineola, N.Y.; son of Irving (in insurance) and Sadye (in public health; maiden name, Gordon) Weil; married Roberta Meserve (executive director of Maine State Retirement Fund), April 6, 1962; children: Anne Inger, Richard Clement. *Education:* Bowdoin College, A.B. (magna cum laude), 1958; College of Europe, diploma (with distinction), 1959; Columbia University, Ph.D., 1961. *Politics:* Democrat. *Home and office address:* R.F.D. 1, Box 359, South Harpswell, Maine 04079.

CAREER: Rutgers University, New Brunswick, N.J., lecturer in American government, 1962; Drew University, Madison, N.J., assistant professor of political science, 1962-63; Commission of the European Economic Community, Brussels, Belgium, deputy official spokesman, 1963-66; *Washington Post*, Washington, D.C., economic correspondent from Europe, 1966-68; Twentieth Century Fund, New York City, research associate in public affairs, 1968-70; executive assistant to Senator George McGovern in Washington, D.C., 1970-72; WNET-Television, New York City, producer and correspondent, 1973-75; Political Intelligence, Inc., Washington, D.C., president and publisher of *Political Intelligence*, 1974-79; State of Maine, Augusta, commissioner of Business Regulation, 1979-80, director of Office of Energy Resources, 1980-82, public advocate, 1981-82; Weil & Firth, Inc., Augusta, president, 1982—.

Professorial lecturer at American University, 1963-64; faculty member at College of Europe, 1966-67; lecturer at Bernard M. Baruch College of the City University of New York, 1969-70, and Colby College, 1977; visiting professor at Bowdoin College, 1973-74. *Military service:* U.S. Army, Adjutant General's Corps, personnel officer, 1961-62; became first lieutenant. *Member:* Phi Beta Kappa.

AWARDS, HONORS: Rockefeller Foundation grant, 1966-68; nominated for New York area Emmy Award by Academy of Television Arts and Sciences, 1974-75, for "The Round Table."

WRITINGS: The European Convention on Human Rights, Sijthoff, 1963; (editor) *A Handbook on the European Economic Community*, Praeger, 1965; *Trade Policy in the Seventies*, Twentieth Century Fund, 1969; *The Benelux Nations*, Holt, 1970; *A Foreign Policy for Europe*, College of Europe, 1970; (with Ian Davidson) *The Gold War: The Story of the World's Monetary Crisis*, Holt, 1970; *The Long Shot: George McGovern Runs for President*, Norton, 1973; *American Trade Policy: A New Round*, Twentieth Century Fund, 1975; *The Consumers Guide to Banks*, Stein & Day, 1975, revised edition, 1977; *Election '76: A Complete Guide to the Campaign*, Political Intelligence, Inc., 1976; *Sears, Roebuck U.S.A.: The Great American Catalog Store and How It Grew*, Stein & Day, 1977; *The Welfare Debate of 1978*, Institute for Socioeconomic Studies, 1978.

Contributor to *Encyclopedia Americana* and *Grolier's Encyclopedia*. Contributor to American and foreign journals and newspapers, including *New Times, Nation, Newsweek* and *Politicks*.

WORK IN PROGRESS: A book on energy emergency readiness and one on political liberalism; a television series "on important state and local stories that don't usually receive national attention."

SIDELIGHTS: Gordon L. Weil told *CA:* "I am most interested in writing about economic subjects in ways which make them appealing to nonexperts. All too often these important and intriguing stories are not accessible because they are regarded as being too technical or complicated." Weil adds that he hopes to write corporate biographies that will interest general readers.

* * *

WEINIG, Jean Maria 1920-
(Mother Mary Anthony, Sister Mary Anthony Weinig)

PERSONAL: Born May 19, 1920, in New York, N.Y.; daughter of Anthony Joseph (a businessman) and Elizabeth L. (O'Brian) Weinig. *Education:* Rosemont College, B.A., 1942; Fordham University, M.A., 1951, Ph.D., 1957. *Home and office:* Rosemont College, Rosemont, Pa. 19010.

CAREER: Entered Society of the Holy Child Jesus (congregation of teaching religious), 1940, and took her vows as Mother Mary Anthony, 1942 (in 1968 the order changed the form of name used by its members and she became Sister Mary Anthony Weinig); teacher at Catholic high school in Suffern, N.Y., 1943-56; Rosemont College, Rosemont, Pa., 1956—, began as instructor, professor of English, 1970—. *Member:* Modern Language Association, College English Association, English Institute, Research Society for Victorian Periodicals, Poetry Society of America. *Awards, honors:* American Philosophical Society research grants, 1965, 1982; Danforth associate, 1968.

WRITINGS—Under name Sister Mary Anthony Weinig, except as indicated: (Under name Mother Mary Anthony) *Fire in the Well* (poems), published as special (entire) issue of *South and West,* summer, 1966; *Rain in the Chimney,* Twayne, 1972; *Coventry Patmore,* G. K. Hall, 1981; *Verbal Pattern in Four Quartets: A Close Reading of T. S. Eliot's Poem,* International Book Centre, 1982; (contributor) Joseph Tylenda, editor, *Portraits in American Sanctity,* Franciscan Herald, 1983. Contributor of articles to literary journals and of poetry to about twenty periodicals; regular abstracter, *Abstracts of English Studies;* regular reviewer, *Choice.*

WORK IN PROGRESS: Articles for a book, *British Literary Magazines,* edited by Alvin Sullivan; articles on "minor Victorians, including F. G. Stephens, Thomas Woolner, Basil Champneys, and William Allingham."

SIDELIGHTS: Jean Maria Weinig told *CA:* "Teaching, scholarship, and poetry are good companions. I welcome the opportunity to share insights, facilitate research, and work toward a richer understanding of the aesthetic and spiritual aspects of our experience."

BIOGRAPHICAL/CRITICAL SOURCES: Poetry Review, summer, 1967; *Choice,* February, 1982, July-August, 1983; *Cithara,* November, 1982.

* * *

WEINIG, Sister Mary Anthony
See WEINIG, Jean Maria

* * *

WEIR, Molly 1920-

PERSONAL: Born March 17, 1920, in Glasgow, Scotland; daughter of Thomas (an engineer) and Jeannie (Clark) Weir; married Alexander Hamilton (a shipbroker). *Education:* Attended University of Glasgow. *Politics:* Conservative. *Religion:* Protestant. *Residence:* Pinner, Middlesex, England.

CAREER: Actress and writer. Has appeared in revues and plays in the theatre, in films, and on radio and television, including roles in "Scrooge," starring Albert Finney, Sir Alec Guinness, and Dame Edith Evans, released in America, 1970, and in "One of Our Dinosaurs Is Missing," starring Helen Hayes and Peter Ustinov, for Walt Disney Productions, 1975; currently appearing as Hazel the McWitch in British Broadcasting Corp. television program "Rentaghost." Speaker with Associated Speakers, London, 1970—. Member of National Trust, 1960—. *Member:* National Film Society (actress member), B.B.C. Club (actress member). *Awards, honors:* Voted "Scotswoman of the year," 1977.

WRITINGS—Published by Hutchinson, except as indicated: *Molly Weir's Recipes,* Collins, 1960; *Shoes Were for Sunday* (early autobiography), 1970; *Best Foot Forward,* 1972; *A Toe on the Ladder,* 1973; *Stepping into the Spotlight,* 1975; *Walking into the Lyon's Den,* 1977; *One Small Footprint,* 1980; *Spinning Like a Peerie,* Gordon Wright, 1983. Contributor, *Woman's Hour Anthology,* 1971. Columnist in *People's Journal* (Scottish weekly), 1960—; contributor to newspapers, magazines, and to British Broadcasting Corp. radio and television (as writer as well as actress).

SIDELIGHTS: Molly Weir told *CA*, "My books have practically all derived from people urging me to write them! When I spoke to the Women's Press Club in London, the top journalists of the capital immediately urged me to get my childhood memories between hard covers. And that's how all those autobiographies began. I've just finished the seventh, for I write in great detail of the people and circumstances around me everywhere. They're not just about me, they're about life and times wherein I moved and worked.

"It's an enormous relief when a book is finished, and I turn joyfully to articles and short pieces, and live the life of a 'literary butterfly' for a while until the urge to get on with another book gives me no peace until I sit down and tackle it. And almost before I am aware of it, I'm on the treadmill once more."

* * *

WEISS, David 1909-

PERSONAL: Born June 12, 1909, in Philadelphia, Pa.; son of Hyman (a painter) and Rebecca (a writer; maiden name, Goldberg) Weiss; married Stymean Karlen (a poet), November 25, 1945. *Education:* Temple University, B.Sc., 1933; attended New School for Social Research, 1942-45. *Politics:* Liberal. *Home:* 8110 El Paseo Grande, Apt. 104, La Jolla, Calif. 92037. *Agent:* William Morris Agency, 1350 Avenue of the Americas, New York, N.Y. 10019.

CAREER: Full-time writer. Has worked at more than fifty jobs, including stevedore, story editor for David O. Selznick, meatloader, actor, welfare worker, ghost writer, store clerk, and basketball and swimming instructor; also has held editorial posts with other major Hollywood studios, including Paramount, Twentieth Century-Fox, RKO, and Columbia Pictures. *Awards, honors:* Frieder Literary Award for best novel on a Jewish theme published in America, 1953, for *The Guilt Makers;* certificate of honor, General Alumni Association of Temple University School of Business Administration, 1981.

WRITINGS: The Guilt Makers, Rinehart, 1953; *The Spirit and the Flesh* (novel based on the life of Isadora Duncan), Doubleday, 1959; *Naked Came I: A Novel of Rodin* (Literary Guild selection), Morrow, 1963; *Justin Moyan,* Morrow, 1965; *The Great Fire of London,* Crown, 1968; *Sacred and Profane: A Novel of the Life and Times of Mozart,* Morrow, 1968; *The Assassination of Mozart,* Morrow, 1970; *No Number Is Greater than One,* Coward, 1972; *Myself, Christopher Wren,* Coward, 1974; *Physician Extraordinary,* Delacorte, 1975; *The Venetian,* Morrow, 1976; *I, Rembrandt,* St. Martin's, 1979.

WORK IN PROGRESS: A novel.

SIDELIGHTS: David Weiss bases many of his novels on the lives of historical figures such as Isadora Duncan, Auguste Rodin, Wolfgang Amadeus Mozart, and Rembrandt. Weiss's books—which are often popular if not always critical successes—attempt to capture the feel and flavor of the times in which his protagonists lived, as well as to depict a segment of his heroes' lives. "I have a deep interest in history, particularly creative history," Weiss once told CA.

Although *Naked Came I: A Novel of Rodin* has been Weiss's most popularly successful book—distributed by major book clubs and translated into twenty-five languages—*Sacred and Profane: A Novel of the Life and Times of Mozart* is his greatest critical success. As with many of his other works, *Sacred and Profane* is cited for its skillful blending of biographical detail and fictional dramatization. "Mr. Weiss has put down every harrowing detail from birth to death in his lengthy book, which is a 'novel' only to the extent that it dramatizes biographical material with a generous recreation of some rather poignant scenes and 'imagines' others where there are gaps in Mozart's known affairs," writes one *Publishers Weekly* reviewer. "There are no new insights into what made Mozart the superbly natural artist he was, but this is still a welcome addition to Mozartiana and a sincere tribute which will be read by many." A *Choice* critic comments that "particularly for a novelist, Weiss understands Mozart's life and music excellently.... Weiss consulted all the major Mozart specialists and sources for both the spirit and substance of this very easily read and absorbing book. It will rest only infrequently on the shelves of public libraries." Peter Wolfe in the *New York Times Book Review* praises *Sacred and Profane* for capturing "both the glitter and gloom of late 18th-century Europe [and showing] the effects of nonmusical events upon the musical climate of the time.... The book is a web of dualisms, interweaving life and death, loss and gain, from the start."

In 1980, Temple University established a David Weiss Collection at its library.

BIOGRAPHICAL/CRITICAL SOURCES: *New York Times Book Review*, November 15, 1959, November 24, 1963, December 8, 1968, April 4, 1971; *Newsweek*, November 25, 1963; *Book Week*, December 15, 1963; *Critic*, December, 1963-January, 1964; *America*, January 11, 1964; *Publishers Weekly*, July, 1968; *Library Journal*, July, 1968; *Choice*, June, 1969; *Los Angeles Times Book Review*, June 17, 1979; *West Coast Review of Books*, September, 1979; *New York Review of Books*, September 27, 1979.

* * *

WELLS, Lisa
See RACINA, Thom

* * *

WELLS, Robert Vale 1943-

PERSONAL: Born July 14, 1943, in Bridgeport, Conn.; son of Ronald Vale (a clergyman) and Patricia (Woodburne) Wells; married Cathie Marie Andersen, September 5, 1964; children: Lisa, Vanessa. Education: Denison University, B.A., 1965; Princeton University, Ph.D., 1969. Home: 1769 Randolph Rd., Schenectady, N.Y. 12308. Office: Department of History, Union College and University, Schenectady, N.Y. 12308.

CAREER: Union College and University, Schenectady, N.Y., instructor, 1969, assistant professor, 1969-74, associate professor, 1974-80, professor of history, 1980—. Member: American Historical Association, Organization of American Historians, Population Association of America. Awards, honors: American Philosophical Society grant, 1971; U.S. Department of Health, Education and Welfare grant, 1972; fellow of Charles Warren Center at Harvard University, 1974-75; Guggenheim fellowship, 1977-78.

WRITINGS: *The Population of the British Colonies in America before 1776: A Survey of Census Data*, Princeton University Press, 1975; *Revolutions in Americans' Lives: A Demographic Perspective on the History of Americans, Their Families, and Their Society*, Greenwood Press, 1982; (editor with Manfred Jonas) *New Opportunities in a New Nation: The Development of New York after the Revolution*, Union College Press, 1982.

Contributor: T. K. Rabb and R. I. Rotberg, editors, *The Family in History*, Harper, 1973; Michael Gordon, editor, *The American Family in Social Historical Perspective*, St. Martin's, 1978; W. M. Fowler and W. Coyler, editors, *The American Revolution: Changing Perspective*, Northeastern University Press, 1979; Mary Beth Norton and Carol Berkin, editors, *Women of America: A History*, Houghton, 1979; Maris Vinovskis, editor, *Studies in American Historical Demography*, Academic Press, 1979; Peter Laslett and others, editors, *Bastardy and Its Comparative History*, Harvard University Press, 1980; V. Fox and M. Quitt, editors, *Loving, Parenting and Dying*, Atlantic Institute, 1981.

Also contributor of book reviews and articles to numerous journals, including *American Historical Review*, *Journal of Interdisciplinary History*, and *Journal of American History*.

WORK IN PROGRESS: *Current Issues in American Demographic History*, for State University of New York Press; *A Bibliographic Guide to American Demographic History*, for Greenwood Press.

SIDELIGHTS: Robert Vale Wells wrote CA: "My main interest is to establish the importance of birth, death, marriage, and migration in people's lives, and to trace the major historical changes which have occurred with regard to these matters during the past two centuries. The history of the family is also important to my work."

* * *

WETHERBEE, Winthrop (III) 1938-

PERSONAL: Born July 10, 1938, in Boston, Mass.; son of Winthrop, Jr. (a physician) and Carolyn (Hall) Wetherbee; married Andrea Kempf, March 25, 1962; children: Peter, Jonathan. Education: Harvard University, B.A., 1960; University of Leeds, M.A., 1962; University of California, Berkeley, Ph.D., 1967. Home: 6011 South Ingleside Ave., Chicago, Ill. 60637. Office: Department of English, University of Chicago, Chicago, Ill. 60637.

CAREER: Cornell University, Ithaca, N.Y., assistant professor, 1967-72, associate professor, 1972-74, professor of English, 1974-80; University of Chicago, Chicago, Ill., professor of English, 1980—. Member: Mediaeval Academy of America. Awards, honors: American Council of Learned Societies fellowship, 1970-71; Guggenheim fellowship, 1974-75.

WRITINGS: *Platonism and Poetry in the Twelfth Century*, Princeton University Press, 1972; *The Cosmographia of Bernardus Silvestris*, Columbia University Press, 1973; *Chaucer and the Poets*, Cornell University Press, 1984.

WORK IN PROGRESS: A textbook on medieval Latin; a study of the poetry of John Gower.

* * *

WETHERILL, Peter Michael 1932-

PERSONAL: Born October 18, 1932, in Leeds, England; son of Sydney (an electrician) and Agnes (Sowden) Wetherill; married Francine Hatchuel (a university professor), January 25, 1958; children: Katherine Anne, Isabelle Jean. *Education:* University of Birmingham, B.A., 1954, M.A., 1956; University of Strasbourg, Docteur de l'Universite, 1962. *Home:* 14 Alma Rd., Stockport SK4 4PU, England. *Office:* Department of French, University of Manchester, Manchester M13 9PL, England.

CAREER: University of New England, Armidale, New South Wales, Australia, lecturer in French, 1958-60; University of Leeds, Leeds, England, lecturer in French, 1961-68; University of Manchester, Manchester, England, senior lecturer, 1968-75, reader in French, 1975—. *Military service:* British Army, Signal Corps, 1956-58; became second lieutenant. *Member:* Society for French Studies, Association of University Teachers.

WRITINGS: Baudelaire et la poesie d'E.A. Poe (title means "Baudelaire and the Poetry of E. A. Poe"), Nizet, 1962; *Flaubert et la creation litteraire* (title means "Flaubert and Literary Creation"), Nizet, 1963; *The Literary Text: An Examination of Critical Methods*, University of California Press, 1974; (contributor) R. Debray-Genette, *Flaubert a l'oeuvre*, Flammarion, 1980; (editor and contributor) *Flaubert, la dimension du texte*, Manchester University Press, 1982; (editor) Gustave Flaubert, *L'Education sentimentale*, Garnier, 1983. Contributor to language and literature journals.

WORK IN PROGRESS: A study of the way in which novels are written, with particular reference to manuscript material; historical discourse in the novel.

AVOCATIONAL INTERESTS: Music, travel (Europe and Southeast Asia).

* * *

WHIFFEN, Marcus 1916-

PERSONAL: Born March 4, 1916, near Ross, England; son of Harold Alfred and Joyce (Thomas) Whiffen; married Jean le Fleming Burrow (a physical therapist), March 1, 1941; children: Paul, Godfrey, Pamela. *Education:* Cambridge University, B.A., 1937, M.A., 1945. *Home:* 4703 East Exeter Blvd., Phoenix, Ariz. 85018. *Office:* College of Architecture, Arizona State University, Tempe, Ariz. 85281.

CAREER: Architect and Building News, London, England, editorial assistant, 1938-39; *Architectural Review,* London, England, assistant editor, 1946-52; Massachusetts Institute of Technology, Cambridge, lecturer in architectural history, 1952-53; University of Texas, Main University (now University of Texas at Austin), visiting lecturer in architectural history, 1953-54; Colonial Williamsburg, Williamsburg, Va., architectural historian, 1954-59; Vassar College, Poughkeepsie, N.Y., lecturer in architectural history, 1959-60; Arizona State University, Tempe, associate professor, 1960-65, professor of architecture, 1966—. Visiting professor at University of British Columbia, 1971.

MEMBER: College Art Association of America, Society of Architectural Historians (director, 1967-69, 1975—), Architectural Association (England), Association of Collegiate Schools of Architecture (director, 1962-67). *Awards, honors:* Annual book award and Alice Hitchcock Medallion from Society of Architectural Historians, 1958, for *The Public Buildings of Williamsburg.*

WRITINGS: Stuart and Georgian Churches, Batsford, 1948; *Thomas Archer: Architect of the English Baroque,* Art and Technics, 1950, revised edition, Hennessey, 1973; *An Introduction to Elizabethan and Jacobean Architecture,* Art and Technics, 1952; *The Public Buildings of Williamsburg,* Colonial Williamsburg, 1958; *The Eighteenth-Century Houses of Williamsburg,* Holt for Colonial Williamsburg, 1960; (editor) *The Teaching of Architecture,* American Institute of Architects, 1964; (editor) *The History, Theory, and Criticism of Architecture,* M.I.T. Press, 1965; (editor) *The Architect and the City,* M.I.T. Press, 1966; *American Architecture since 1780: A Guide to Styles,* M.I.T. Press, 1969; (with Frederick Koeper) *American Architecture, 1607-1976,* M.I.T. Press, 1981; (with Carla Breeze) *Pueblo Deco: The Art Deco Architecture of the Southwest,* University of New Mexico Press, 1983.

Contributor to art, architecture, education, and literary journals, and to *Listener, Burlington Magazine, Times Literary Supplement, New Statesman,* and *Nation.* Editor of *Journal of Architectural Education,* 1962-68.

SIDELIGHTS: Architectural historian Marcus Whiffen specializes in making architectural concepts accessible to the general reader. For instance, in *American Architecture since 1780: A Guide to Styles,* he delineates thirty-nine basic building styles in an easy-to-follow guidebook format. Writing about that book in *London Magazine,* Lionel Brett comments, "This book is a portent. It is not written for architects but for 'building watchers' and it is modelled on a Bird Book." While noting that many aspects of Whiffen's book are "fun," Brett also comments that "the important thing about this book is that it is serious [as well]. . . . Yet here is this ex-English professor, in his impressive and scholarly manner, just looking at outsides, oblivious of plan, function, social context, relevance. . . . I commend his ingeniously illustrated handbook unreservedly."

Although Brett finds Whiffen's approach to architecture—merely looking at and classifying styles without regard to function or meaning—useful and enjoyable, *New Republic* contributor William Hubbard believes it does a disservice to readers by ignoring the use of "ideology—that is, the concepts we use to make sense of the world" of architecture. In his review of *American Architecture, 1607-1976,* Hubbard explains that the book presents a view of architecture in America "that leaves us with a picture in which we see things change but can't make out what's causing them to change. The authors characterize the nature of the change as an oscillation between an impulse toward tastefulness—toward the fashionable 'new' (whatever that may be at the moment)—and an impulse toward tradition, the 'familiar.' But that oscillation, though true, does not in itself provide any explanation, any agency of stylistic change. Just from the slice of history we have lived through, we know that style constantly changes, and for a variety of reasons. But in a history of such shifts we want . . . at least some individual explanations of the more important shifts."

Still, Hubbard praises *American Architecture, 1607-1976* for its "scrupulousness about biases. For example, [the authors] avoid the East Coast bias that traditionally has infected histories of American architecture. Thus they pay as much attention to the Spanish mission churches as to the early architecture of

New England and Virginia, and they provide welcome insight into the early French architecture of the Midwest. They also avoid the elitist slant of stressing only the name of the architectural firm and neglecting the actual creator of the work. But the most important bias they avoid is the view that modernism represents the inevitable course of architectural history."

According to some critics the lightheartedness apparent in *American Architecture since 1780* seems to be missing in *American Architecture, 1607-1976*. "The book is eminently serious and respectable, rather boring and dull, and certainly designed to become a standard textbook in architectural history courses," says Richard Guy Wilson in *Virginia Quarterly Review*. Notes John Dreyfuss in *Los Angeles Times Book Review:* "The book won't keep you up all night. But it will inform you on who's who and what's what in American architecture."

BIOGRAPHICAL/CRITICAL SOURCES: *London Magazine,* January, 1970; *Observer,* January 19, 1981; *Los Angeles Times Book Review,* May 24, 1981; *New Republic,* November 18, 1981; *Times Educational Supplement,* January 22, 1982; *Virginia Quarterly Review,* summer, 1982.

* * *

WHITE, Anthony Gene 1946-

PERSONAL: Born November 8, 1946, in Eugene, Ore.; son of Wallace Eugene (a city manager) and Vivian Arlene (a sales manager; maiden name, Thomson) White; married Carole Ann Price (a life insurance service manager), May 17, 1969. *Education:* Oregon State University, B.S., 1967; Portland State University, M.S., 1971, M.P.A., 1977. *Politics:* Independent. *Religion:* Christian. *Home:* 3270 Forest Court, West Linn, Ore. 97068.

CAREER: City-County Charter Commission, Portland, Ore., research associate, 1971-74; Multnomah County Administrative Services, Portland, property control officer, 1974-75; Portland Area Boundary Commission, Portland, administrative assistant, 1975-76; District Attorney's Office, Portland, program evaluator, 1976-77; Marylhurst College, Marylhurst, Oregon, assistant administrator for public administration, 1977-79; Oregon Public Utilities Commissioner's Office, Salem, economic analyst, 1979—. Consultant on local government matters. *Military service:* U.S. Army, 1969-72.

MEMBER: American Association for the Advancement of Science, American Mathematical Society, National Municipal League, World Future Society, Futures Information Network, Western Political Science Association, Western Governmental Research Association.

WRITINGS: *Reforming Metropolitan Governments,* Garland Publishing, 1975; *Municipal Bonding and Taxation,* Garland Publishing, 1979. Author of bibliographic monographs for Council of Planning Librarians, and Vance Bibliographies. Contributor to planning and civic affairs journals.

WORK IN PROGRESS: Research on public administration, urban problems, architecture, and futures studies.

SIDELIGHTS: Anthony Gene White comments: "In many forms of writing, it is useful and/or essential that the author be well-versed in the subject before beginning. Certainly this is true of the journal articles I've prepared. At the same time, however, it is possible to use the writing experience as a learning experience, in expansion of breadth and depth across fields of study. The many bibliographic monographs I've prepared for Vance Bibliographies have taken me into realms of public administration, urban problems, and architecture that, ten years ago, I would never have dreamed would hold fascination for me.

"New writers should also know that it is acceptable to 'run dry,' to block after an initial success, to be unable to kindle a creative flame. With so many writers in the world today, competing for a few subjects and story-lines, it can be very discouraging. With patience, observation, and reflection new topics and expressions are forthcoming. Writing is work—sometimes not rewarding work—and in which an effort *must* be made. Even if only for an audience of one, each piece deserves the best one can do."

* * *

WHITE, G(eorge) Edward 1941-

PERSONAL: Born March 19, 1941, in Northampton, Mass.; son of George L. (a book publisher) and Frances D. (a teacher; maiden name, McCafferty) White; married Susan Valre Davis (a lawyer), December 31, 1966; children: Alexandra Valre, Elisabeth McCafferty Davis. *Education:* Amherst College, B.A., 1963; Yale University, M.A., 1964, Ph.D., 1967; Harvard University, J.D., 1970. *Residence:* Charlottesville, Va. *Office:* School of Law, University of Virginia, Charlottesville, Va. 22903.

CAREER: American Bar Foundation, Chicago, Ill., visiting scholar, 1970-71; U.S. Supreme Court, Washington, D.C., law clerk to Chief Justice Earl Warren, 1971-72; University of Virginia, Charlottesville, assistant professor, 1972-74, associate professor, 1974-76, professor of law, 1977—. *Member:* American Society for Legal History, Phi Beta Kappa. *Awards, honors:* American Bar Association, Gavel Award Certificates of Merit, 1979, for *Patterns of American Legal Thought,* and 1981, for *Tort Law in America: An Intellectual History,* Silver Gavel Award, 1983, for *Earl Warren: A Public Life.*

WRITINGS: *The Eastern Establishment and the Western Experience,* Yale University Press, 1968; *The American Judicial Tradition,* Oxford University Press, 1976; *Patterns of American Legal Thought,* Bobbs-Merrill, 1978; *Tort Law in America: An Intellectual History,* Oxford University Press, 1980; *Earl Warren: A Public Life,* Oxford University Press, 1982. Editor of "Studies in Legal History" series, University of North Carolina Press. Contributor to law journals.

WORK IN PROGRESS: *The Marshall Court, 1815-1835,* for Macmillan.

SIDELIGHTS: In *Earl Warren: A Public Life,* G. Edward White presents readers with an in-depth study of how various events in the life of the late Supreme Court chief justice may have shaped his legal philosophy and approach to the responsibilities of the Court. White takes upon himself the job of reconciling some of the circumstances of Warren's early career (such as his support for the wartime confinement of Japanese-Americans in internment camps) with his later status as one of America's most liberal Supreme Court justices. In the process the author traces the changing role of the Supreme Court in American society, "throwing fresh light on an amazing period in the . . . Court's history," according to Anthony Lewis in the *New York Times Book Review.*

Earl Warren: A Public Life is first and foremost the story of Warren himself, however, and "it is in the analysis of Warren's philosophy that White excels," writes James E. Clayton in the *Washington Post Book World.* White's portrait of Warren is that of a man for whom ethical considerations and timely interpretation carried more weight than legal precedent and scholarly abstraction. In Clayton's words, "it is a view that Warren reverted to the 19th-century practice of letting a personal sense of right and wrong determine the outcome of cases, supporting the result with any convenient legal rationale." Jerry Pacht, writing in the *Los Angeles Times Book Review,* believes that White overcomes the pitfalls associated with trying to piece together the influences that give form to the personality and ideals of a major public figure: "This is no pretentious psychobiography. White makes a serious and usually successful effort to show us the people and forces, events, ideas, plans and accidents that made Warren what he became. [His] conclusions about the genesis of Warren's attitudes, drives, and suspicions are supported by facts."

Joseph Sobran, in a *National Review* article, takes a different tack, remarking of Warren: "Liberal opinion was more than kind to him. So is White. [The author] calls Warren's premises 'broad and vague,' and so they were. White's own analysis, unfortunately, is also broad and vague." Sobran's comments are testimony to the fact that Warren remains a politically controversial figure, and Pacht asserts as much in the opening lines of his review, insisting that the book's value lies in its historical rather than political point of view: "[Warren] has been praised and vilified; simplistic explanations have been offered for his conduct. Broad and largely inapt labels have been placed on his work, his personality and his attitudes. . . . White has gone beyond the labels and given us the man."

Questions of partisan opinion aside, the real strength of *Earl Warren: A Public Life* lies not in whether, as Lewis claims, "one finishes this book with a renewed respect for Warren," but in the fact that, as Joseph L. Rauh points out in the *New Republic,* White furnishes "both Warren's supporters and detractors with a wealth of material for the continuing debate over Warren's role." Sobran identifies the immediate value of White's achievement, stating that "We haven't had a full biography until now." But it is Clayton who singles out the long-term impact of the book: "[White develops] a thesis of Warren's decision-making process with which every future Warren biographer or Supreme Court historian will have to cope."

BIOGRAPHICAL/CRITICAL SOURCES: *New York Times Book Review,* January 16, 1977, July 4, 1982; *Washington Post Book World,* August 1, 1982; *Los Angeles Times Book Review,* August 1, 1982; *New Yorker,* August 2, 1982; *New Republic,* August 9, 1982; *Wall Street Journal,* August 26, 1982; *National Review,* October 29, 1982.

* * *

WHITE, K(enneth) D(ouglas) 1908-

PERSONAL: Born November 22, 1908, in Liverpool, England; son of James (a veterinary surgeon) and Gladys (Eveline) White; married Isobel Helen MacKay (an occupational psychologist), June 6, 1936; children: James, Caroline, Catherine. *Education:* University of Liverpool (with honors in classics), B.A., 1929; University of Cambridge, B.A., 1931, M.A., 1936. *Politics:* Liberal. *Religion:* Anglican. *Home:* Garden Flat, 6 Alexander St., London W2, England. *Office:* Department of Ancient History, University College, University of London, London, England.

CAREER: University of Edinburgh, Edinburgh, Scotland, assistant in Greek, 1931-33; University of Leeds, Leeds, England, assistant lecturer in classics, 1933-38; Rhodes University, Grahamstown, South Africa, professor of classics and head of department, 1938-58; University of Natal, Pietermaritzburg, South Africa, professor of classics, 1958-62; University of Ibadan, Ibadan, Nigeria, professor of ancient history, 1962-65; University of Reading, Reading, England, professor of classics, 1965-74, currently professor emeritus in ancient history; University of Jos, Jos, Nigeria, visiting professor in humanities, 1975-79; University of London, University College, London, England, honorary research fellow, 1981—. City of Grahamstown, South Africa, city councillor, 1954-58, deputy mayor, 1956-58. Commonwealth fellow, St. John's College, Cambridge University, 1960-61; visiting professor of classics, University of Toronto, 1971-72; senior research fellow, Leverhulme Trust, 1975-77; Balsdan senior research fellow, British School at Rome, 1980. *Member:* Society for Roman Studies (member of council, 1970-71), South African Association of University Teachers (president, 1955-56), Classical Association of Nigeria (president, 1964-65).

WRITINGS: *Agricultural Implements of the Roman World,* Cambridge University Press, 1967; *Roman Farming,* Cornell University Press, 1970; *A Bibliography of Roman Agriculture,* Reading University Press, 1970; *Farm Equipment of the Roman World,* Cambridge University Press, 1975; *Country Life in Classical Times,* Cornell University Press, 1977; *Greek and Roman Technology,* Cornell University Press, 1983. Contributor of articles to *Journal of Roman Studies, Antiquity, Classical Review, Latomus,* and other periodicals.

WORK IN PROGRESS: *Studies in Roman Agrarian History; Social and Economic History of the Roman Empire; Resources, Technology and Power in the Roman World; Food, Diet, and Health in the Classical World.*

SIDELIGHTS: K. D. White told *CA:* "My research interests have been concentrated in recent years on the infrastructure of the Roman Empire, more particularly on the environmental factors and constraints, the sources of power, the raw materials (sources of supply and methods of extraction, etc.), and the technological achievements and limitations. I have travelled extensively in the Mediterranean area in search of material in libraries and museums, as well as on the ground, with the aim of finding correlations between field archaeology, air photography and written sources, in the hope that I might discover the patterns of land settlement and their vicissitudes in the passage of time.

"I have, during a teaching career of 50 years, and in seven different universities, had the opportunity of teaching traditional classics in its literary and linguistical aspects as well as in the historical areas of study where I am specially qualified, and at all levels from pass degree to doctorate. Most recently, I have worked in a new Third World University, where "humanities" represent a broader approach, and where it has been my task to justify the study of ancient history as providing a much-needed perspective for men and women destined for leadership in a rapidly developing society, in an age of swift transition from traditional cultures and values into those of the late twentieth century."

* * *

WHITE, Ted
See WHITE, Theodore Edwin

WHITE, Theodore Edwin 1938-
(Ted White; pseudonym: Ron Archer; joint pseudonym: Norman Edwards)

PERSONAL: Born February 4, 1938, in Washington, D.C.; son of Edwin Paul (a photographer) and Dorothea (Belz) White; married Sylvia Dees, November 30, 1958; married second wife, Robin Postal, February 26, 1966 (divorced); children: Arielle. *Education:* Attended public schools in Falls Church, Va. *Politics:* "Nominally Democrat; iconoclastic." *Religion:* "Agnostic; personal theism." *Home:* 1014 North Tuckahoe St., Falls Church, Va. 22046.

CAREER: Writer, with a work background of "every job every would-be novelist has held, save that of shoe salesman." Editor of *Void* (fan magazine), 1959-68; Scott Meredith Literary Agency, Inc., New York City, head of foreign department, 1963; *Magazine of Fantasy and Science Fiction,* New York City, assistant editor, 1963-67, associate editor, 1967-68; *Amazing Stories* and *Fantastic,* managing editor, 1969, editor, 1970-78; *Heavy Metal,* New York City, editor, 1979-80; president of New Decade Productions, Inc., 1980—. Associate editor, Lancer Books, 1966. Chairman of Twenty-fifth World Science Fiction Convention. *Member:* Fantasy Amateur Press Association (president, 1957), Washington (D.C.) Science Fiction Association (president, 1955), New York Futurians, New York Fanoclasts (founder), Falls Church Fanoclasts (founder). *Awards, honors:* Hugo Award for best fan writer, 1968.

WRITINGS—Under name Ted White, except as indicated: (With Terry Carr under joint pseudonym Norman Edwards) *Invasion from 2500,* Monarch, 1964; *Android Avenger,* Ace Books, 1965; *Phoenix Prime,* Lancer Books, 1966, reprinted, Starblaze, 1982; *The Sorceress of Qar,* Lancer Books, 1966, reprinted, Starblaze, 1983; *The Jewels of Elsewhen,* Belmont Books, 1967; *Secret of the Marauder Satellite,* Westminster, 1967; (under pseudonym Ron Archer; with Dave Van Arnam) *Lost in Space* (novelization of television series "Lost in Space"), Pyramid Publications, 1967; *Captain America: The Great Gold Steal,* Bantam, 1968; (with Van Arnam) *Sideslip,* Pyramid Publications, 1968; *Spawn of the Death Machine,* Paperback Library, 1968; *No Time Like Tomorrow* (juvenile), Crown, 1969.

By Furies Possessed, Signet, 1970; *Trouble on Project Ceres* (juvenile), Westminster, 1971; *Starwolf,* Lancer Books, 1971; (editor) *The Best from "Amazing Stories,"* Manor, 1973; (editor) *The Best from "Fantastic,"* Manor, 1973; (with Dave Bischoff) *Forbidden World,* Popular Library, 1978. Contributor of articles and stories to periodicals, including *Rogue, Gamma, Startling Mystery, If,* and *Magazine of Fantasy and Science Fiction;* contributor of record reviews and musical criticism to *Metronome, Jazz Guide, 33 Guide, Unicorn Times,* and *Trouser Press.*

WORK IN PROGRESS: Further books.

SIDELIGHTS: Theodore Edwin White told *CA:* "The creative urge finds many avenues of expression. I have been writing and editing for more than twenty-five years, and at times I chafe at the solitude required—the need to be alone with my typewriter—and the absence of any immediate feedback. To that end I began teaching myself to play an alto saxophone in the sixties and began performing in public on both the alto and tenor sax in the seventies. In many respects, making music is directly complementary to writing: it can be done before an audience which will respond immediately and spontaneously. I continue to write, but I write less and I write less often. Music fills the gaps."

WHITMAN, Ruth (Bashein) 1922-

PERSONAL: Born May 28, 1922, in New York, N.Y.; daughter of Meyer D. (a lawyer) and Martha (Sherman) Bashein; married Cedric Whitman, October 13, 1941 (divorced, 1958); married Firman Houghton, July 23, 1959 (divorced, 1964); married Morton Sacks (a painter), October 6, 1966; children: (first marriage) Rachel Whitman, Leda Whitman; (second marriage) David Houghton. *Education:* Radcliffe College, B.A. (magna cum laude), 1944; Harvard University, M.A., 1947. *Politics:* Liberal. *Religion:* "Secular Jewish." *Home:* 40 Tuckerman Ave., Middletown, R.I. 02840. *Office:* 1559 Beacon St., Brookline, Mass. 02146.

CAREER: Poet and translator. Houghton Mifflin Co., Boston, Mass., editorial assistant, 1941-42, educational editor, 1944-45; Harvard University Press, Cambridge, Mass., free-lance editor, 1945-60; *Audience* (magazine), Cambridge, poetry editor, 1958-63; Cambridge Center for Adult Education, Cambridge, teacher of poetry workshop, 1965-68; lecturer in poetry at Radcliffe College, Cambridge, 1970—, and Harvard University, Cambridge, 1982—. Poet-in-residence, Hamden-Sydney College, 1974, Mishkenot Sha'ananim, 1977, 1979, 1981, Holy Cross College, 1978, Centre College of Kentucky, 1980, and Kentucky Arts Commission, 1981; visiting lecturer at Trinity College, Hartford, 1975, University of Denver, 1976, Massachusetts Institute of Technology, 1979, and University of Massachusetts—Boston, 1980. Director of Poetry in the Schools Program, Massachusetts Council on the Arts, 1970-73. Has read her poetry on television and at numerous universities and cultural centers, including Harvard University, Tufts University, Brown University, Massachusetts Institute of Technology, Brandeis University, Wheaton College, Northwestern University, Folger Shakespeare Library, Tel Aviv University, and New School for Social Research. Member of board of directors, New Poet's Theater, Cambridge, and Cambridge School of Ballet.

MEMBER: P.E.N., Authors Guild, Authors League of America, Poetry Society of America (member of executive board, 1962—; regional vice-president, 1978—), New England Poetry Club, Phi Beta Kappa, Signet Club (Harvard).

AWARDS, HONORS: Reynolds Lyric Award, 1962, Alice Fay di Castagnola Award, 1968, for manuscript of *The Marriage Wig, and Other Poems,* William Marion Reedy Award, 1974, Consuelo Ford Award, 1975, and John Masefield Award, 1976, all from Poetry Society of America; MacDowell Colony fellowships, 1962, 1964, 1972-74, 1979, and 1982; Jennie Tane Award of *Massachusetts Review,* 1962; Radcliffe Institute for Independent Study fellowship, 1968-70; grants from National Foundation for Jewish Culture, 1968, National Endowment for the Arts, 1974-75, Martin Tananbaum Foundation, 1979, 1980, and Rhode Island State Council on the Arts, 1981; Kovner Award, Jewish Book Council of America, 1969; Chanin Foundation Award for translation, 1972; Guiness International Poetry Award, 1973; finalist in Virginia Commonwealth University manuscript competition, 1977.

WRITINGS: Blood and Milk Poems, Clarke & Way, 1963; (translator with Samuel Beckett and others) Alain Bosquet, *Selected Poems,* New Directions, 1963; (co-translator) Isaac Bashevis Singer, *Short Friday,* Farrar, Straus, 1966; (editor and translator) *An Anthology of Modern Yiddish Poetry,* bilingual edition, October House, 1966, 2nd edition, Workmen's Circle Education Department, 1979; (translator with others)

Singer, *The Seance*, Farrar, Straus, 1968; *The Marriage Wig, and Other Poems*, Harcourt, 1968.

(Editor and translator) *The Selected Poems of Jacob Glatstein*, October House, 1972; *The Passion of Lizzy Borden: New and Selected Poems*, October House, 1973; (editor) *Poemmaking: Poets in Classrooms*, Massachusetts Council of Teachers of English, 1975; *Tamsen Donner: A Woman's Journey*, Alice James Books, 1975; *Permanent Address: New Poems, 1973-1980*, Alice James Books, 1980; (contributor) Hedges and Wendt, editors, *In Her Own Image: Women Working in the Arts*, Feminist Press, 1980; *Becoming a Poet: Source, Process, and Practice*, Writer, Inc., 1982.

Work represented in anthologies, including: *The "New Yorker" Anthology*, Viking, 1969; *The "New York Times" Anthology*, Macmillan, 1970; *The Berkshire Anthology*, Bookstore Press, 1972; *Messages*, edited by X. J. Kennedy, Little, Brown, 1972; *Rising Tides*, Washington Square Press, 1973; *Search the Silence: Poems of Self-Discovery*, Scholastic Book Services, 1974; *To See the World Afresh*, Athenaeum, 1974; *Another Way Out*, Holt, 1974; *Images of Women in Literature*, Houghton, 1977.

Also translator of modern French and Greek poetry. Author and narrator of television documentary "Sachuest Point," 1977. Contributor to periodicals, including *Writer, Radcliffe Quarterly, Massachusetts Review, Jewish Quarterly, American Poetry Review, Antioch Review*, and *Boston Public Library Quarterly*.

WORK IN PROGRESS: A book-length novella in prose and poetry, *The Testing of Hannah Senech*, and a new collection of poems, *Waiting for You*.

SIDELIGHTS: Ruth Whitman recorded her work for the Library of Congress in 1974 and 1981.

BIOGRAPHICAL/CRITICAL SOURCES: Poetry, May, 1964, March, 1970.

* * *

WILEY, David Sherman 1935-

PERSONAL: Born November 9, 1935, in Eldorado, Ill.; son of Kenneth L. (an auto dealer) and Martha Louise (Summers) Wiley; married Marylee Crofts (a curriculum consultant), June 20, 1959; children: Stephen B., Thomas M. C. *Education:* Wabash College, B.A., 1957; Yale University, M.Div., 1961; Princeton University, Ph.D., 1971. *Religion:* Protestant. *Home:* 729 Sunset Lane, East Lansing, Mich. 48823. *Office:* African Studies Center, Michigan State University, East Lansing, Mich. 48824.

CAREER: University of Zambia, instructor, 1966-67; University of Wisconsin—Madison, assistant professor of sociology, 1968-76, chairman of African studies program, 1972-77; Michigan State University, East Lansing, assistant professor of sociology and director of African Studies Center, 1977—. Co-chairperson of task force on elementary, secondary, and undergraduate education, National Council on Foreign Language and International Studies, 1980—. Worked with the Madison Area Committee on Southern Africa, 1969. *Member:* American Sociological Association, Society for Scientific Study of Religion, African Studies Association.

WRITINGS: (With wife Marylee C. Wiley) *The Third World: Africa*, Pendulum Press, 1972; (co-editor) *Southern Africa: Society, Economy, and Liberation*, African Studies Center, Michigan State University, 1982. Guest editor and editorial advisor for *Issue*, 1973—.

WORK IN PROGRESS: A study of housing, health, education, and the labor force in Zambia; a book on urban society in Zambia.

SIDELIGHTS: David Sherman Wiley told *CA* that he is "deeply concerned with United States policy concerning Southern Africa and Africa in general; involved in extension of information and interest concerning Africa into schools and universities in the Midwest; working actively in policy-related research for the development of independent African nations."

* * *

WILLIAMS, Herbert (Lloyd) 1932-

PERSONAL: Born September 8, 1932, in Aberystwyth, Wales; son of Richard David (a painter and decorator) and Minnie Esther (Jones) Williams; married Dorothy Maud Edwards, November 13, 1954; children: Peter, David, Alan, Mary, John. *Education:* Attended public schools in Aberystwyth, Wales. *Home:* 107 Pantbach Rd., Rhiwbina, Cardiff, Wales.

CAREER: Welsh Gazette, Aberystwyth, Wales, reporter, 1951-53; *Reading Standard*, Reading, England, reporter, 1953; *Cambrian News*, Aberystwyth, reporter and sub-editor, 1953-56; *South Wales Echo*, Cardiff, reporter, industrial correspondent, then sub-editor, 1956-60; *Scottish Daily Mail*, Edinburgh, Scotland, sub-editor, 1960-61; *South Wales Echo*, chief feature writer, 1961-72; *Birmingham Evening Mail*, Birmingham, England, features sub-editor, 1972-73; general programmes producer, British Broadcasting Corp., Wales, 1973-79; free-lance writer and producer, 1979—.

WRITINGS: Too Wet for the Devil (poems), Outpost, 1962; *The Dinosaurs* (poems), Triskel Press, 1966; *The Trophy* (poems), Christopher Davies, 1967; *A Lethal Kind of Love* (verse play), John Jones, 1968; *Battles in Wales*, John Jones, 1975; *Come Out Wherever You Are*, Quartet, 1977; *Stage Coaches in Wales*, Stewart Williams, 1977; *Railways in Wales*, Christopher Davies, 1981; *Sharing* (short stories), Alun Books, 1984.

Contributor of poetry to anthologies: Bryn Griffiths, editor, *Welsh Voices*, Dent, 1967; J. Stuart Williams and M. Stephens, editors, *The Lilting House: An Anthology of Anglo-Welsh Poetry, 1917-67*, Dent, 1969; Dannie Abse, editor, *Corgi Poets I*, Corgi, 1971; Sam Adams and Gwilym Rees Hughes, editors, *Dragon's Hoard*, Gomer Press, 1976; E. L. Black, editor, *Topics in Modern Poetry*, John Murray, 1982; Abse, editor, *Wales in Verse*, Secker & Warburg, 1983.

Also author of television scripts, including seven episodes of "Taff Acre," produced by HTV for ITV (United Kingdom), 1981, "A Welsh Rarebit," produced by BBC-Wales, 1983, and "A Solitary Mister," produced by BBC-2, 1983.

* * *

WILLIAMS, Kate
See FLYNN, Donald R(obert)

* * *

WILLIS, Maud
See LOTTMAN, Eileen

* * *

WILSON, A(lfred) Jeyaratnam 1928-

PERSONAL: Born October 4, 1928, in Colombo, Ceylon (now

Sri Lanka); son of Kanagasabai Rajaratnam (a businessman) and Elizabeth (Dutton) Wilson; married Susilavati Chelvanayakam (a librarian), April 10, 1953; children: Mallihai (daughter), Maithili (daughter), Kumanan (son). *Education:* University of Ceylon (now University of Peradeniya), B.A., 1950; London School of Economics and Political Science, Ph.D., 1956, D.Sc. (economics). *Politics:* "Suffer from a social conscience." *Religion:* Methodist. *Home:* 79 Colonial Heights St., Fredericton, New Brunswick, Canada. *Office:* Department of Political Science, University of New Brunswick, Fredericton, New Brunswick, Canada.

CAREER: University of Leicester, Leicester, England, research fellow in politics, 1964-65; University of Ceylon (now University of Peradeniya), Peradeniya, Sri Lanka, professor of political science and head of department of economics and political science, 1970-72; University of New Brunswick, Fredericton, professor of political science and chairman of department, 1972—. Vice-chairman of Presidential Commission on Development Councils, Sri Lanka, 1979-80. *Awards, honors:* Leverhulme research scholar at London School of Economics and Political Science, University of London, 1955; research associate at McGill University, 1970-71; Simon senior fellow at University of Manchester, 1971-72; senior associate member, St. Antony's College, Oxford University, 1977, and Columbia University, 1978.

WRITINGS: Politics in Sri Lanka, 1947-1973, Macmillan (London), 1974, 2nd edition published as *Politics in Sri Lanka, 1947-1979,* 1979; *Electoral Politics in an Emergent State: The Ceylon General Election of May, 1970,* Cambridge University Press, 1975; *The Gaullist System in Asia,* Macmillan (London), 1980; (editor with Dennis Dalton) *The States of South Asia: Problems of National Integration,* Hurst & Co., 1980, University Press of Hawaii, 1983. Contributor to journals in his field. Member of editorial board of *Round Table, Journal of Commonwealth and Comparative Politics,* and *Ceylon Journal of Historical and Social Studies.*

WORK IN PROGRESS: "The Framework of Secession," a monograph.

AVOCATIONAL INTERESTS: Reading, writing, traveling, "marginally interested in Sri Lankan political problems."

* * *

WILSON, Jeanne (Patricia Pauline) 1920-

PERSONAL: Given name is pronounced Zhan; born May 31, 1920, in London, England; daughter of Francis Arthur and Emily Grace (Williams) Staples; married Wilbert Jeffrey-Smith Wilson (a physician; chief medical officer of Jamaica), July 12, 1943; children: Roger Francis Jeffrey-Smith. *Education:* Educated in private schools and drama school in London, England. *Home and office:* 19 Waterloo Rd., No. 19K, Kingston 10, Jamaica, West Indies.

CAREER: Westminster Hospital, London, England, nurse, 1940-42; Wolmer's Girls School, Kingston, Jamaica, teacher of speech and drama, 1960-67; writer, 1968—. Has performed in more than one hundred radio and stage plays; producer of plays for adults. Member of nominating committee for Nobel Prize in literature, 1980-83. *Member:* P.E.N. (Jamaica center), Authors Guild, Authors League of America, Society of Authors.

AWARDS, HONORS: Awards of high commendation from Jamaica Independence Festival, 1965, for radio plays "No Medicine for Murder" and "Reality Is Relevant," and 1966, for radio play "No Truth at All"; Centennial Medal, Institute of Jamaica, 1979; American Biographical Research Institute life fellow; awarded Key to International Biographical Centre, Cambridge, England.

WRITINGS: No Medicine for Murder (based on her radio play of the same title; also see below), Ward, Lock, 1967; *Model for Murder,* Ward, Lock, 1968, reprinted, Kingston Publishers, 1984; *Weep in the Sun,* M. Evans, 1976 (published in England as *Weep in the Sun: An Island Chronicle,* Macmillan [London], 1976); *Troubled Heritage,* M. Evans, 1977 (published in England as *Troubled Heritage: An Island Chronicle,* Macmillan [London], 1977); *Holiday with Guns: An Adventure Story for Young People,* Macmillan, 1978; *Flight from the Islands: Two Stories,* Macmillan, 1978; *The House That Liked to Travel, and Other Stories,* Macmillan, 1978; *Mulatto,* M. Evans, 1978; (editor) *West Indian Plays for Schools,* Jamaican Publishing House, 1979; *The Golden Harlot,* Macmillan (London), 1979, St. Martin's, 1980; *Take Time for Murder,* Kingston Publishing, 1984; *Ad Lib for Murder,* Kingston Publishing, in press; *Program for Murder,* Kingston Publishing, in press.

Plays: *No Justice in October* (one-act; first produced in Kingston, Jamaica, March, 1961), Evans Brothers, 1967; *A Legacy for Isabel* (one-act; first produced in Kingston at Little Theatre, March, 1962), Evans Brothers, 1967. Also author of radio plays "No Medicine for Murder," 1959, "Reality Is Relevant," and "No Truth at All."

Contributor to *Daily Gleaner.*

WORK IN PROGRESS: A revised edition of *No Medicine for Murder; Find Me a Victim; The Spanish Widow; Fettered Freedom; Dark Valley,* a historical novel about the effects of the 1865 uprising on three Jamaican families; *Rim of Power,* the story "of the *real* Macbeth—Maelbeatha, Mormaer of Moray—set in eleventh-century Scotland."

SIDELIGHTS: Jeanne Wilson writes: "The motivation for writing historical fiction is that I have always been extremely interested in history. The history of the West Indies has been written—by West Indians—quite recently . . . , and there is very little historical fiction written about Jamaica, or the West Indies as a whole. I feel that accuracy is very important in writing historical fiction, and that comprehensive research must be done. I took three years before I began *Weep in the Sun,* and my research covered West Indian history, European history, the histories of law, architecture, money, the Navy, the cost of living, costumes, and social histories. I am well aware that some writers feel that absolute accuracy is not important. I disagree, and I am also well aware that I will be pounced upon if I am caught out in a historical error!

"My working habits are that I set myself a minimum of two thousand words a day for the first draft, which I write in long hand. For the second and third drafts, which I type, I set a minimum of five pages a day but quite often accomplish ten to twelve. My son, who is a manager at IBM's Jamaica branch, has acquired a personal computer; he says that in the future I must type my final draft on it. I'm rather looking forward to that.

"To give advice to aspiring writers is treading on rocky ground. I can only say that if you want to write then *write.* Never give up whatever the setbacks. I don't believe that anyone can be *taught* to write—they can be helped, but writing comes from within and from experience. That is my view; others will no doubt differ. Every writer has his own method. One cannot lay down rules except for one: *discipline*. Write no matter what you feel like!''

AVOCATIONAL INTERESTS: Old buildings, reading dictionaries, reference books, and novels, cooking, swimming, travel (Scotland, Wales, Norway, Sweden, the United States, Surinam, Trinidad), cats, the theatre.

* * *

WILSON, Joyce M(uriel Judson) (Joyce Stranger)

PERSONAL: Born in London, England; daughter of Ralph (an advertising manager) and Beryl Judson; married Kenneth Wilson (patents manager with Imperial Chemicals Industry), February 28, 1944; children: Andrew Bruce, Anne Patricia and Nicholas David (twins). *Education:* University College, London, B.Sc., 1942. *Religion:* Church of England. *Agent:* Hughes Massie Ltd., 31 Southhampton Row, London WC1B 4HL, England.

CAREER: Writer. Imperial Chemicals Industry, Manchester, England, research chemist, 1942-46. *Member:* Society of Authors, Society of Women Journalists and Writers, Council for Wild Life, Institute of Journalists.

WRITINGS—All under pseudonym Joyce Stranger: *Wild Cat Island* (juvenile), Methuen, 1961; *Circus All Alone* (juvenile), Harrap, 1965; *The Running Foxes* (novel), Hammond, Hammond, 1965, Viking, 1966; *Breed of Giants* (novel), Hammond, Hammond, 1966, Viking, 1967; *Rex* (novel), Harvill, 1967, Viking, 1968; *Jason* (juvenile), Dent, 1967; *Casey* (novel), Harvill, 1968, published as *Born to Trouble,* Viking, 1969; *Rusty* (novel), Harvill, 1969, published as *The Wind on the Dragon,* Viking, 1970; *The Honeywell Badger* (juvenile), Dent, 1969; *One for Sorrow* (novel), Corgi, 1969.

Zara (novel), Harvill, 1970, Viking, 1971; *Chia: The Wildcat* (novel), Harvill, 1971; *Paddy Joe* (juvenile), Collins, 1972; *The Hare at Dark Hollow* (juvenile), Dent, 1972; (contributor) Noel Streatfeild, editor, *Summer Holiday Book,* Dent, 1972; *Lakeland Vet* (novel), Harvill, 1972, Viking, 1973; (contributor) Streatfeild, editor, *Christmas Holiday Book,* Dent, 1973; *Walk a Lonely Road* (novel), Harvill, 1973; *Never Count Apples* (novel), Harvill, 1974; *Trouble for Paddy Joe* (juvenile), Collins, 1974; *A Dog Called Gelert, and Other Stories,* Dent, 1974; *The Secret Herds* (juvenile), Dent, 1974; *Paddy Joe at Deep Hollow Farm* (juvenile), Collins, 1975; *Never Tell a Secret* (novel), Harvill, 1975; *Joyce Stranger's Book of Hanak Animals* (verse), Dent, 1976; *The Fox at Drummers' Darkness* (juvenile), Dent, 1976; *Flash* (novel), Harvill, 1976, Reader's Digest Press, 1982; *The Wild Ponies* (juvenile), Kaye & Ward, 1976; *Khazan* (novel), Harvill, 1976; *Kym: The True Story of a Siamese Cat,* M. Joseph, 1976, Coward, 1977; *Two's Company* (autobiography), M. Joseph, 1977; *A Walk in the Dark* (novel), M. Joseph, 1978; *The Curse of Seal Valley* (juvenile), Dent, 1979; *The January Queen* (novel), M. Joseph, 1979.

Three's a Pack (autobiography), M. Joseph, 1980; *All about Your Pet Puppy,* Pelham, 1980; *The Stallion* (novel), M. Joseph, 1981; *How to Own a Sensible Dog,* Corgi, 1981; *Vet on Call,* Carousel, 1981; *Double Trouble,* Carousel, 1981; *Vet Riding High,* Carousel, 1982; *No More Horses,* Carousel, 1982; *Dial V.E.T.,* Carousel, 1982; *Marooned* (juvenile), Kaye & Ward, 1982; *Two for Joy* (autobiography), M. Joseph, 1982; *The Monastery Cat and Other Stories,* Corgi, 1982; *The Hound of Darkness,* Dent, 1983; *Josse,* M. Joseph, 1983.

Former author of "The World about Us" column in *Annabel.* Contributor of short stories to *Woman's Journal, Woman's Own,* and other periodicals; contributor of articles to *Gamekeeper and Countryside, Dog World, Alsatian League Magazine,* and *Dog Training Weekly.*

SIDELIGHTS: Joyce M. Wilson told *CA:* "I trained as a biologist. My main interest was animal behavior and this I furthered for many years by field study. When I began writing in 1949, I found most fields well covered, but discovered a lack of knowledge among ordinary people about the animal world and the relationship of man and animal. . . . [So] I began to write about [this] relationship.

"My animal books work because I watched the animals and studied animal behavior. I knew where the foxes laired and bred their cubs; where the hare hid, and watched her as she moved around and when she was caught by a fox or dog; I listened to a goose on an island as it died when the fox caught it. . . . I hid in trees to watch badgers; I ride [horses] and I am in daily contact with many dogs. Farm animals are all around me—I can see sheep and cattle as I write.

"The world beyond the human is vastly exciting; [it] has much to reveal to us.''

MEDIA ADAPTATIONS: Jason has been filmed by Walt Disney Productions; *The Fox at Drummers' Darkness* has been filmed as "The Wild Dog"; *The Honeywell Badger* and *The Hare at Dark Hollow* have both been adapted for television by British Broadcasting Corp.

BIOGRAPHICAL/CRITICAL SOURCES: Joyce Stranger, *Two's Company,* M. Joseph, 1977; Stranger, *Three's a Pack,* M. Joseph, 1980; Stranger, *Two for Joy,* M. Joseph, 1982.

* * *

WILSON, Pat 1910-

PERSONAL: Born October 25, 1910; daughter of Alfred Lakin (a member of RQMS 13th Gloucesters); married Oliver Godfrey Wilson, 1934; children: Mike, Robin, Briony (Mrs. Richard Jenkins), Bridget (Mrs. Stuart Carter). *Education:* Attended secondary school in England. *Politics:* "Usually vote Tory." *Religion:* None. *Home:* 66 Marwood Dr., Great Ayton, Middlesborough, Cleveland TS9 6PD, England.

CAREER: Secretary in a tuberculosis dispensary, 1927-33; director of a small foundry, 1949—; part-time lecturer at Longlands College of Further Education, Middlesborough, England. *Awards, honors:* Co-winner of prize for play, "3 Sheep, 2½ Kangaroos"; Dublin Theatre Festival Award, 1970, for "Thy Kingdom Come."

WRITINGS—Plays; published by Hub Publications, except as indicated: *Four for a Boy,* 1970; *Enchanted Pantomime,* 1970; *Funeral Tea* (also see below), 1971, Performance Publishing, 1973; *The Little Miracle,* 1972; *The Adventures of Pinocchio,* 1973; *The Snow Queen,* 1973; *Christmas Eve at the Mortuary,* 1973; *Rectory Return,* 1973; *The Reunion* (also see below), 1974; *Send Us Victorias,* 1974; *New Broom,* 1974; *Christmas Cake and Chipatees,* 1975; *The Tektite,* 1975; *Thy Kingdom Come,* 1975.

Published by Performance Publishing: *Ballet Who?,* 1972; *One More Time,* 1972; *Get It All Together,* 1973; *Mix-Up at the Mortuary,* 1973; *Mixed Bag,* 1973; *Hairy Holiday,* 1973; *Rummage Rip-Off,* 1974; *Heavenly High-Rise,* 1975; *Queen Bee,* 1975; *Wedding Picture Mixture,* 1976; *Ashes to Ashes, Crumbs to Crumbs* (also see below), 1976.

Published by Pat Wilson's Plays: *Jan Adamant*, 1971; *A Prince for Cinderella, a Curtain Raiser*, 1971; *Fairies at the Bottom of the Garden*, 1974; *You Too Can Be a Glamourous Gran*, 1978; *I Wish I'd Never Asked Them to Come*, 1978; *I Was Here before You So Shove Up!*, 1978; *What Shall We Call the Baby?*, 1978; *Things That Go Bump in the Night*, 1979; *There Is a Fairy Upstairs in Our Attic*, 1979; *Hi Jiminy*, 1979.

Medium Rare, 1980; *Anybody Seen My Body?*, 1980; *No, My Darling Daughter*, 1980; *Midsummer Nightmare*, 1981; *Look Both Ways*, 1981; *The Wok*, 1982; *Nymphs and Shepherds*, 1983.

Other writings: *A Summer's Tale* (three-act play), Evans, 1968; *Funeral Tea* (novel; also see above; story of three one-act plays: *Funeral Tea*, *The Reunion*, and *Ashes to Ashes, Crumbs to Crumbs*), Pat Wilson's Plays, 1983. Also author of four monologues, seven duologues, other one-act plays, a television series, a passion play, and two booklets of poems.

SIDELIGHTS: Pat Wilson told *CA*: "Having had a hard and curious life, I write mostly comedy and farce, as I believe that people always try to carry on normally whatever hits them, and the idiotic 'keep to the norm' can be priceless. My father, Alfred Lakin, RQMS 13th Gloucesters, died when I was eighteen as a result of the First World War. My mother, having had a stroke, was brain damaged; however in spite of dire poverty, my brother Arthur Lakin served in Bomber Command, was shot down over Germany and taken POW, suffered much, but returned home and recovered to become a Ph.D., and as Dr. Lakin was Head of Maths at Sandhurst."

BIOGRAPHICAL/CRITICAL SOURCES: *Drama*, spring, 1969.

* * *

WILT, Judith 1941-

PERSONAL: Born September 17, 1941, in Pittsburgh, Pa.; daughter of Thomas B. and Katherine Wilt. *Education:* Duquesne University, B.A., 1967; Indiana University, Ph.D., 1972. *Politics:* Democrat. *Religion:* Roman Catholic. *Home:* 11 Charlesbank Rd., Newton, Mass. 02158. *Office:* Department of English, Boston College, Chestnut Hill, Mass. 02167.

CAREER: Feature and editorial writer for weekly newspapers in Pittsburgh, Pa., 1959-67; Princeton University, Princeton, N.J., assistant professor of English, 1972-78; Boston College, Chestnut Hill, Mass., associate professor of English, 1978—. Hospital volunteer worker and adult education teacher.

WRITINGS: *The Readable People of George Meredith*, Princeton University Press, 1975; *Ghosts of the Gothic: Austen, Eliot, and Lawrence*, Princeton University Press, 1980.

WORK IN PROGRESS: Gothic fiction; popular literature; science fiction; detective historical romances; feminist literature; a book length study on the novels of Walter Scott.

BIOGRAPHICAL/CRITICAL SOURCES: *Times Literary Supplement*, January 2, 1981; *Modern Fiction Studies*, summer, 1981.

* * *

WINANS, A(llan) D(avis, Jr.) 1936-

PERSONAL: Born January 12, 1936, in San Francisco, Calif.; son of Allan Davis and Claire Edith (Grierson) Winans. *Education:* City College of San Francisco, A.A., 1960; San Francisco State College (now University), A.B., 1962. *Politics:* Independent. *Religion:* Protestant. *Home:* 118 Laidley St., San Francisco, Calif. 94131. *Office address:* Second Coming, Inc., P.O. Box 31249, San Francisco, Calif. 94131.

CAREER: Poet and writer. Second Coming Press, San Francisco, Calif., publisher and editor, 1971—. Office of Naval Intelligence, San Francisco, special agent, 1965-72; free-lance writer, 1973-75; San Francisco Arts Commission Neighborhood Arts Program, San Francisco, editor and writer, 1975-80. Founder of Western Independent Publishers, 1977. Member of board of directors, Committee of Small Magazine Editors and Publishers (COSMEP), 1974—, and South of Market Cultural Center, 1979; member of Coordinating Council of Literary Magazines, 1974-83. *Military service:* U.S. Air Force, 1954-58. *Member:* P.E.N., Poetry Society of America. *Awards, honors:* P.E.N. writing award, 1974, 1980, 1982; Coordinating Council of Literary Magazines small magazine grant, 1974-80; National Endowment for the Arts small press grant, 1975, 1977, 1980; California Arts Council small press grant, 1976, 1978, 1982.

WRITINGS: *Carmel Clowns*, Atom Mind Publications, 1970; *Crazy John Poems*, Grande Ronde Press, 1972; *Tales of Crazy John*, Second Coming Press, 1975; *Straws of Sanity*, Thorp Springs Press, 1975; *Org Minus One*, Scarecrow, 1977; *All the Graffiti on All the Bathroom Walls in the World Can't Hide These Scars of Mine*, Fallen Angel, 1977; *North Beach Poems*, Second Coming Press, 1977; *Further Adventures of Crazy John*, Second Coming Press, 1980.

Work represented in anthologies. Contributor of poetry, prose, articles, and book reviews to over three hundred literary and commercial magazines in the United States, Canada, Australia, New Zealand, Germany, Italy, England, Brazil, and Spain. Editor of *Second Coming* (magazine).

WORK IN PROGRESS: *Screams and Busted Dreams*, a collection of prose and short stories dealing with the post-beat generation life of North Beach; *Collected Poems, 1958-1983*; *The Reagan Psalms*.

SIDELIGHTS: A. D. Winans told *CA*: "I began seriously writing poetry at the age of thirty-four. My poetry is largely autobiographical, telling the story of my life and the people who have entered and departed it. Like Charles Bukowski, I don't strictly consider myself a poet in the traditional sense. . . . I write poetry because I have to—like the late poet, William Wantling: 'I would carry a lunchbox just like the rest of them if only these strange words inside my head would let me be.' My work is influenced by the likes of . . . Bukowski and . . . Wantling and D. A. Levy. Poetry is not a way of life for me, but is my life. There is no distinguishing between the two."

* * *

WINER, Richard 1929-

PERSONAL: Born May 14, 1929, in South Dakota; married wife, Peggy (divorced); children: Lee, Frederick, Sharon. *Education:* University of Minnesota, B.S., 1951. *Home:* 712 Southwest Fourth Pl., Fort Lauderdale, Fla. 33312. *Office address:* P.O. Box 1673, Fort Lauderdale, Fla. 33302.

CAREER: Worked as reporter and photographer, 1951-59, as a missile photographer at Cape Canaveral, 1959-65, as a television network newsreel cameraman, 1965-71, and as a documentary film maker, 1971-75; writer, 1974—. Member of Fort Lauderdale Marine Advisory Board, 1974-75. *Military service:* U.S. Navy. *Member:* Sierra Club, Greenpeace Foundation, Authors League, Classic Car Club of America, Antique Automobile Club of America, American Association of Private Railroad Car Owners. *Awards, honors:* Golden Eagle Documentary Film Award, Council on International Nontheatrical Events (CINE), 1971, for "The Devil's Triangle."

WRITINGS—All published by Bantam: *The Devil's Triangle,* 1974; *The Devil's Triangle II,* 1975; *From the Devil's Triangle to the Devil's Jaw,* 1977; *Haunted Houses,* 1979; *More Haunted Houses,* 1981; *Houses of Horror,* 1983; *Trilogy of Terror,* in press. Also author of documentary film, "The Devil's Triangle," 1971. Contributor of articles to periodicals.

WORK IN PROGRESS: God in a Black Robe, an "expose about erratic judges"; *Red Water,* "a twentieth-century *Moby Dick*," about modern whale-hunting; *Super Eight.*

SIDELIGHTS: Richard Winer told *CA:* "Being a full-time author, I write about what my publisher wants. When I become rich and famous, I shall write for the love of the art. I am also a staunch environmentalist, 'sailor of fortune,' and adventurer."

He adds: "I am hoping to make the transition from nonfiction to factual fiction (novels based on fact). *Trilogy of Terror* is to be my first published attempt.

"I feel that writing books is the loneliest of all the arts. As Leon Uris once said, 'When a writer begins a new book, he enters the deep, dark pit of loneliness.'"

Winer also told *CA* that his all-time favorite author is Jack London, and his favorite contemporary author is William Manchester. His book, *The Devil's Triangle,* spent twelve weeks on the bestseller list and has been printed in fourteen languages.

* * *

WITT, Hubert 1935-

PERSONAL: Born June 20, 1935, in Breslau, Germany (now Wroclaw, Poland); son of August (a railroad employee) and Berta (Werner) Witt; married Sina Heins (a manuscript reader), March 5, 1960; children: Ines, Jan. *Education:* Attended University of Leipzig, 1953-57. *Home:* Fechnerstrasse 5, 7022 Leipzig, German Democratic Republic.

CAREER: Editor, writer, and translator. Reclam Verlag, Leipzig, German Democratic Republic, manuscript reader of German philology, philosophy, and twentieth-century literature, 1959-75, 1978—. *Member:* Schriftstellerverband der Deutschen Demokratischen Republik.

WRITINGS—Editor, except as indicated: *Erinnerungen an Brecht* (anthology), Reclam, 1964, revised edition, 1966, translation of revised edition by John Peet published as *Brecht as They Knew Him,* International Book Publishers, 1974; (and translator from the Yiddish) *Der Fiedler vom Getto* (poetry from Poland), Reclam, 1966, abridged edition published as *Meine juedischen Augen,* Claassen, 1969; (and translator) Oswald von Wolkenstein, *Um dieser Welten Lust* (poetry), Insel, 1968; Bertolt Brecht, *Von der Freundlichkeit der Welt* (poetry), Insel, 1971; (translator) Langston Hughes, editor, *Gedichte aus Afrika* (poetry), Reclam, 1972; (with Annie Voigtlaender) *Denkzettel* (anthology of political lyrics from West Germany and West Berlin), Roederberg, 1974.

Thinking It Over (short stories from the German Democratic Republic), Seven Seas Publishers, 1977; (and translator from the Yiddish) Mendele Mojcher Sforim, *Fischke der Lahme* (novel), Reclam and Hanser, 1978; Heinrich Boell, *Mein trauriges Gesicht: Humoresken und Satiren,* Reclam, 1979; Brecht, *Der Staedtebauer* (short stories), Insel, 1979; (and translator) Walther von der Vogelweide, *Frau Welt, ich hab von dir getrunken* (poetry), Ruetten & Loening, 1979; (and translator from the Yiddish) Rajzel Zychlinski, *Vogelbrot* (poetry), Insel, 1981.

Translator with others for Reclam of the poetry of Carl Michael Bellman, 1965—, Ossip Mandelstam, 1975, Jannis Ritsos, 1979, and Louis Aragon, 1984. Author of afterwords to books by Bertolt Brecht, Johann Peter Hebel, Joseph Roth, Stephan Hermlin, Guenter Kunert, and Arno Schmidt.

WORK IN PROGRESS: Editing and translating the medieval lyrics of Neihart von Reuenthal, *Der ackermann und der tod* by Johann von Tepl, the novel *Stempenju* by Scholem Alejchem, and the poetry of Itzik Manger; editing an anthology of West German lyrics from 1945-1980; writing poetry, short stories, and plays.

* * *

WITTREICH, Joseph Anthony, Jr. 1939-

PERSONAL: Surname is pronounced *Wit*-trick; born July 23, 1939, in Cleveland, Ohio; son of Joseph Anthony (a supervisor) and Mamie (Pucel) Wittreich. *Education:* University of Louisville, B.A., 1961, M.A., 1962; Western Reserve University (now Case Western Reserve University), Ph.D., 1966. *Home:* 320 South 16th St., Philadelphia, Pa. 19102. *Office:* Department of English, University of Maryland, College Park, Md. 20742.

CAREER: University of Wisconsin—Madison, assistant professor, 1966-70, associate professor, 1970-74, professor of English, 1974-76; University of Maryland, College Park, professor of English, 1977—. Guest lecturer at California State University, Los Angeles, summer, 1970, and fall, 1972. *Member:* Modern Language Association of America, Milton Society of America (member of executive committee), Blake Foundation of America (member of board of directors), Renaissance Society.

AWARDS, HONORS: American Philosophical Society fellow, 1967; Henry E. Huntington fellow, 1968, 1976; Folger fellow, 1971, 1974; National Endowment for the Humanities fellow, 1974, 1976; Newberry Library fellow, 1974; Wisconsin Institute for Research in the Humanities fellow, 1975.

WRITINGS: (Author of introduction) William Hayley, *Life of Milton,* facsimile edition, Scholars' Facsimiles & Reprints, 1970; (contributor) John T. Shawcross and Michael Lieb, editors, *Achievements of the Left Hand: Essays on John Milton's Prose Work,* University of Massachusetts Press, 1974; *Angel of Apocalypse: Blake's Idea of Milton,* University of Wisconsin Press, 1975; (contributor) Shawcross and others, editors, *Milton Encyclopedia,* Bucknell University Press, 1976; (contributor) Balachandra Raja, editor, *Homage to Milton,* University of Georgia Press, 1976; *Visionary Poetics: Milton's Tradition and His Legacy,* Huntington Library, 1979; *"Image of That Horror": History, Prophecy, and Apocalypse in "King Lear,"* Huntington Library, 1984.

Editor: (And author of introduction and notes) *The Romantics on Milton: Formal Essays and Critical Asides,* Press of Case Western Reserve University, 1970; (and author of introduction) *Early Lives of William Blake, 1806-1910,* Scholars' Facsimiles & Reprints, 1970; (and author of introduction and notes) *Nineteenth-Century Accounts of William Blake,* Scholars' Facsimiles & Reprints, 1970; Richard Meadowcourt, *Milton's "Paradise Regained": Two Eighteenth-Century Critiques*, facsimile edition, Scholars' Facsimiles & Reprints, 1971; *Calm of Mind: Tercentenary Essays on "Paradise Regained" and "Samson Agonistes,"* Press of Case Western Reserve University, 1971; (with Stuart Curran and contributor) *Blake's Sublime Allegory: Essays on "The Four Zoas," "Milton," and "Jerusalem,"* University of Wisconsin Press, 1973.

(With Eric Rothstein) *Literary Monographs*, University of Wisconsin Press, Volume VI: *Medieval and Renaissance Literature*, 1975, Volume VII: *Thackeray, Hawthorne, Melville, and Dreiser*, 1975, Volume VIII: *Mid-Nineteenth-Century Writers: Eliot, De Quincy, Emerson*, 1976; (and contributor) *Milton and the Line of Vision*, University of Wisconsin Press, 1975.

Contributor of numerous articles, essays, and reviews to periodicals, including *PMLA, Blake Studies, Studies in Philology, English Language Notes, Milton Quarterly, Milton Studies, Bucknell Review, Keats-Shelley Journal, Huntington Library Quarterly, Genre, Renaissance Quarterly, Seventeenth-Century News, Blake Newsletter*, and *Journal of English and Germanic Philology. Blake Studies*, member of editorial advisory board, 1968—, guest editor, 1972; member of editorial advisory board, *Literary Monographs*, 1971—, *Genre*, 1973—, and *Milton and the Romantics*.

WORK IN PROGRESS: Milton: Revolutionary Artist.

* * *

WOLDENDORP, R(ichard) 1927-

PERSONAL: Born January 1, 1927; son of Gerad (a hotelier) and Marie (Spijkerman) Woldendorp; married Lynette Dockery, October 19, 1962; children: Yolanta, Gemma, Eva (all daughters). *Education:* Attended a technical school in the Netherlands for five years. *Religion:* Roman Catholic. *Home:* 2 Binbrook Pl., Darlington, Western Australia 6070, Australia. *Agent:* (Photographs) Photo Index, 80 Churchill Ave., Subiaco, Western Australia 6008, Australia.

CAREER: Free-lance photographer in Australia and Southeast Asia. Has had exhibitions at Macquarie Galleries, Sydney, New South Wales, and at Australia and Photographers Gallery, London, England. *Awards, honors:* Transfield Book of the Year Award, 1970; Australian Professional Photographer of the Year Award, 1982-83.

WRITINGS: (With Peter Slater) *The Hidden Face of Australia*, Thomas Nelson, 1968; (illustrator) Thomas A. G. Hungerford, *A Million Square: Western Australia*, Thomas Nelson, 1969; (with Tony Johns) *Indonesia*, Thomas Nelson, 1972; *Walkabout*, Day Dawn Press, 1974; *Looking West*, Day Dawn Press, 1977; *Australia's West*, Day Dawn Press, 1983. Contributor of photographs to *Reader's Digest*.

WORK IN PROGRESS: Photography for *On the Sheep's Back*, for publication by Five Mile Press.

* * *

WOLOCH, Isser 1937-

PERSONAL: Born October 16, 1937, in New York, N.Y.; son of Nathan M. and Edith (Kramer) Woloch; married Nancy Spelman (an historian), July, 1962; children: David, Alexander. *Education:* Columbia University, A.B., 1959; Princeton University, M.A., 1961, Ph.D., 1965. *Home:* 50 West 97th St., New York, N.Y. 10025. *Office:* Department of History, Columbia University, New York, N.Y. 10027.

CAREER: Indiana University at Bloomington, lecturer, 1963-64, assistant professor of history, 1964-66; University of California, Los Angeles, assistant professor of history, 1966-69; Columbia University, New York, N.Y., associate professor, 1969-75, professor of history, 1975—. Member, Institute for Advanced Studies, Princeton University, 1973-74. *Member:* American Historical Association, Society for French Historical Studies, Phi Beta Kappa. *Awards, honors:* Woodrow Wilson fellowship, 1959-60; American Council of Learned Societies fellowship, 1973-74; National Endowment for the Humanities fellowship, 1980-81; Guggenheim fellowship, 1981-82.

WRITINGS: Jacobin Legacy: The Democrat Movement under the Directory, Princeton University Press, 1970; (editor) *The Peasantry in the Old Regime: Conditions and Protests*, Holt, 1970; (co-author) *The Western Experience*, Knopf, 1974, 3rd edition, 1983; *The French Veteran from the Revolution to the Restoration*, University of North Carolina Press, 1979; *Eighteenth-Century Europe: Tradition and Progress, 1715-1789*, Norton, 1982. Contributor to *Worldbook Encyclopedia* and *Encyclopedia Americana*; contributor of articles to *Journal of Modern History, Journal of Interdisciplinary History*, and *Reviews in European History*.

WORK IN PROGRESS: The New Regime: The Transformation of the French Civic Order, 1789-1830.

* * *

WOOD, James E(dward), Jr. 1922-

PERSONAL: Born July 29, 1922, in Portsmouth, Va.; son of James Edward and Elsie Elizabeth (Bryant) Wood; married Alma Leacy McKenzie, August 12, 1943; children: James Edward III. *Education:* Carson-Newman College, B.A., 1943; Southern Baptist Theological Seminary, B.D., 1947, Th.M., 1948, Ph.D., 1957; Columbia University, M.A., 1949; Yale University, Chinese certificate; Naganuma School of Japanese Studies, Tokyo, diploma; attended University of Tennessee, 1943-44, and Oxford University, 1983. *Politics:* Democrat. *Home:* 3306 Lake Heights, Waco, Tex. 76708. *Office address:* Box 380, Baylor University, Waco, Tex. 76798.

CAREER: Baptist clergyman and educator, 1942—. Pastor in Baptist churches in Tennessee and Kentucky, 1942-48; Seinan Gakuin University, Fukuoka, Japan, professor of religion and literature, 1950-55; Baylor University, Waco, Tex., assistant professor, 1955-57, associate professor, 1957-59, professor of history of religions and director of J. M. Dawson Institute of Church and State Studies, 1959-73, Simon and Ethel Bunn Professor of Church-State Studies, 1980—, chairman of church-state studies, 1962-73, 1980—, chairman, Far Eastern educational exchange program committee. Visiting lecturer, Ashland Theological Seminary, 1971; visiting professor, Southern Baptist Theological Seminary, 1974, Oklahoma Baptist University, 1977, and North American Baptist Theological Seminary, 1979. Executive director, Baptist Joint Committee on Public Affairs, 1972-80; member of several commissions for Baptist World Alliance, including Commission on Religious Liberty and Human Rights 1965-75, Commission on Freedom, Justice, and Peace, 1975-80, and Commission on Human Rights, 1980-85. Participant in numerous interfaith organizations; has lectured and presented papers at professional meetings. Editor-in-chief, Markham Press, Baylor University, 1970-72. Advisor, *First Freedom*, 1981—; consultant, World Council of Churches, 1963-65.

MEMBER: American Academy of Religion, American Society of Church History, National Council on Religion and Public Education (president), National Council of Churches (member of religious liberty committee), Public Education and Religious Liberty (member of executive committee), American Society of International Law, American Civil Liberties Union (president of Waco, Tex. chapter, 1969-72), Planned Parenthood (president of Waco, Tex. chapter, 1971-72), American Association of University Professors, Texas Civil Liberties Union (member of board, 1969-72), Washington Council (member of executive committee), Phi Eta Sigma, Pi Kappa Delta, Alpha Psi Omega, Rotary International.

AWARDS, HONORS: Named a colonel, State of Texas, 1969; distinguished alumnus award, Carson-Newman College, 1974; Religious Liberty Award, Alliance for the Preservation of Religious Liberty, 1980; Henrietta Szold Award, Hadassah (Texas region), 1981.

WRITINGS—Published by Baylor University Press, except as indicated: *A History of American Literature: An Anthology,* Kenkyusha (Japan), 1952; (with E. Bruce Thompson and Robert T. Miller) *Church and State in Scripture, History, and Constitutional Law,* 1958; (editor and contributor) *Church and State,* Scottish Rite, 1960; (editor and contributor) Joseph Martin Dawson, *A Thousand Months to Remember: An Autobiography,* 1964; *The Problem of Nationalism in Church-State Relationships,* Herald Press, 1969; (editor and contributor) *Jewish-Christian Relations in Today's World,* 1971; (editor and contributor) *Religion and Public Education,* 1972; (editor and contributor) *Baptists and the American Experience,* Judson Press, 1976; *Nationhood and the Kingdom,* Broadman Press, 1977; (editor and contributor) *Religion and Politics,* 1983; (editor and contributor) *Religion, the State, and Education,* 1984; (editor and contributor) *Religion and the State: Essays in Honor of Leo Pfeffer,* 1984.

Contributor: *We Hold These Truths,* Americans United, 1964; *The Teacher's Yoke: Essays Honoring Henry Trantham,* 1964; *The Best of Church and State, 1948-1975,* Americans United for Separation of Church and State, 1975; *Taxation and the Free Exercise of Religion,* Baptist Joint Committee, 1978; *The Church, the State, and Human Rights,* Baptist Joint Committee, 1980; *The Bible Vote,* Pilgrim, 1981; *Government Intervention in Religious Affairs,* Pilgrim, 1982; *Freedom of Religion in America: Historical Roots, Philosophical Concepts, and Contemporary Problems,* Transaction Books, 1982; *The Minister's Manual for 1983,* Harper, 1982.

Also contributor to *The Encyclopedia of Modern Christian Missions,* 1967, *Encyclopedia of Southern Baptists,* Volume IV, 1982, and *Dictionary of Theology,* 1983. Contributor of more than one hundred articles and reviews to professional journals.

Founder and editor, *Journal of Church and State,* 1959-73, 1980—, member of editorial board, 1973-80; editor, *Report from the Capital,* 1975-80; member of editorial board, National Council on Religion and Public Education *Bulletin,* 1982—; member of board of advisors, *Religious Freedom Reporter,* 1982—.

WORK IN PROGRESS: Religious Liberty.

* * *

WORMLEY, Stanton Lawrence 1909-

PERSONAL: Born February 7, 1909, in Washington, D.C.; son of Lawrence Riggs (an engineer) and Mary (a registered nurse; maiden name, Burruss) Wormley; married Freida Hare, August 12, 1950; children: Stanton Lawrence, Jr. *Education:* Howard University, A.B., 1930, A.M., 1931; University of Hamburg, diploma, 1932; Cornell University, Ph.D., 1939. *Politics:* Independent. *Religion:* Episcopalian. *Home and office:* 5735 Kansas Ave. N.W., Washington, D.C. 20011.

CAREER: Writer. Virginia State College, Petersburg, instructor, 1932-33, assistant professor, 1933-36, associate professor of English, 1936-38, chairman of department of foreign languages, 1933-38, chairman of graduate program in English, 1936-38; Howard University, Washington, D.C., assistant professor, 1938-44, associate professor, 1944-45, professor of German, 1945-71, head of department of German and Russian, 1945-64, director of summer school, 1950-64, acting dean of graduate school, 1952-55, 1960-64, academic vice-president, 1964-69, acting president, 1965-67. Visiting professor at City College (now of the City University of New York), summer, 1948.

Member of executive committee of Washington Center for Metropolitan Studies (also member of board of trustees), 1965-69, and Consortium of Washington Universities (also vice-chairman), 1965-69; vice-chairman of District of Columbia Police Complaint Review Board, 1965-71; member of Coordinating Council on Education for the Disadvantaged, 1967; member of Health and Welfare Council of the National Capital Area, 1971. Member of board of directors of Center for Community Action Education, 1965-67, WETA-TV, 1966-68, 1969-71, National Harmony Memorial Park (also member of executive committee), 1960—, and national capital area National Conference of Christians and Jews, 1966-73; member of board of trustees of Nathaniel Hawthorne College, 1968-80, and Washington Hospital Center, 1973—; member of administrative committee and board of trustees of Meriwether Home for Dependent Children, 1965-69, member of advisory council, 1968. Member of advisory board of WDCA-TV, 1965, and Washington Planetarium and Space Center, 1966; member of interim committee of Central Atlantic Regional Educational Laboratory, 1966. Member of Rock Creek Foundation, 1971 (past president); chairman of board of governors of Rock Creek Cemetery, 1972—. Consultant to U.S. State Department.

MEMBER: Modern Language Association of America, American Association of Teachers of German, College Language Association, Goethe Society of America, American Bible Society (honorary member), Columbian Harmony Society (president, 1964—). *Awards, honors:* Julius Rosenwald Foundation fellowship, 1939-43; named honorary member of Accion Civica Istmena (Panama), 1955; American International Academy fellowship, 1961, Order of the Star and Cross, 1961; Ed.D. from Nathaniel Hawthorne College, 1969; distinguished service award from U.S. Air Force, 1969; Bradford Cross from Rock Creek Parish, 1977.

WRITINGS: Heine in England, University of North Carolina Press, 1943; (editor with L. H. Fenderson) *Many Shades of Black,* Morrow, 1969; (with Paul E. Sluby, Sr.) *Civil War Cemeteries of the District of Columbia Metropolitan Area,* Columbian Harmony Society, 1982; (with Sluby) *The Diary of Charles Fisher,* Columbian Harmony Society, 1983; (with Sluby) *The Narrative of Billy Tilghman,* Columbian Harmony Society, 1983; (with Sluby) *Appo-Fisher-Hawkins,* Columbian Harmony Society, 1983. Contributor of articles and reviews to journals. Editor of *Virginia State College Gazette* and *Research Journal,* both 1937-38; translator and reviewer for monthly periodical *Hamburg-Amerika Post,* 1931-32.

WORSTER, Donald E(ugene) 1941-

PERSONAL: Born November 14, 1941, in Needles, Calif.; son of Winfred Delbert (a bookkeeper) and Bonnie Pauline (Ball) Worster; married Beverly Marshall, August 23, 1964; children: William Thomas, Catherine Anne. *Education:* University of Kansas, B.A., 1963, M.A., 1964; Yale University, M.Phil., 1970, Ph.D., 1971. *Office:* Department of American Studies, Brandeis University, Waltham, Mass. 02154.

CAREER: University of Maine, Orono, instructor in speech and drama, 1964-66; Brandeis University, Waltham, Mass., assistant professor of American studies, 1971-74; University of Hawaii at Manoa, Honolulu, associate professor, 1975-80, professor of American studies, 1980-83; Brandeis University, Waltham, professor of history and American studies, 1984—. Mellon fellow at Aspen Institute for Humanistic Studies, summer, 1974; fellow, Humanities Research Centre, Australian National University, 1984. *Member:* Organization of American Historians, Forest History Society, Friends of the Earth, Wilderness Society, Sierra Club. *Awards, honors:* National Endowment for the Humanities fellowship, 1974-75; American Council of Learned Societies fellow, 1977-78; Bancroft Prize, 1980, for *Dust Bowl: The Southern Plains in the 1930s;* Guggenheim fellow, 1981-82.

WRITINGS: (Editor) *American Environmentalism: The Formative Period, 1860-1915,* Wiley, 1973; *Nature's Economy: The Roots of Ecology,* Sierra Club Books, 1977, 2nd edition, Cambridge University Press, 1984; *Dust Bowl: The Southern Plains in the 1930s,* Oxford University Press, 1979.

WORK IN PROGRESS: The Rivers of Empire: Water and Society in the American West, Pantheon Books.

SIDELIGHTS: Reflecting on the scope of his research, Donald E. Worster once told *CA:* "I am interested in finding ways for myself, family, and others to live on this fragile planet with the least impact, the fullest humanity, and the greatest amount of personal freedom compatible with ecological integrity." Worster's concern for environmental issues, evident in this statement, is an important part of the thesis of his Bancroft Prize-winning book, *Dust Bowl: The Southern Plains in the 1930s.*

According to historian Gilbert C. Fite, the main theme of Worster's book is that the inhabitants of the southern Great Plains area of the United States, rather than natural weather conditions, were the direct cause of the disastrous dust storms and droughts that caused that area to become known as the "Dust Bowl." In *American Historical Review,* Fite explains that Worster believes "man's relationship to the land was exploitative and that he paid the price for foolishly destroying the ecological balance of the Plains." Specifically, Worster blames the U.S. political-economic system for the Dust Bowl catastrophe. James W. Ware notes in the *Journal of American History:* "Worster argues that more than prolonged drought and high winds created the Dust Bowl. He maintains that the aggressive greed inherent in capitalism was responsible for the problems of southern plains farmers during the 1930s."

While Fite and Ware do not completely agree with Worster's theory, both critics praise Worster's book. Fite, for example, remarks: "While I disagree with many of the positions taken in this book, I found it an exciting, provocative, and stimulating study." Ware adds: "Worster . . . is a little too critical of the people of the plains. The Dust Bowl's farmers were . . . no more or less foolish and greedy than any other Americans. . . . Despite [this fault], Worster has contributed a major work to the historiography of the United States in the twentieth century."

Hugh Brogan is another critic who admires Worster's writing. In the *Times Literary Supplement* he observes: "It is perhaps the most convincing demonstration of Worster's skill, that, without losing his sense of proportion . . . he manages to make the southern plains as fascinating a subject as others have the South, New England, and California." *Dust Bowl,* he concludes, "is . . . a lucid, succinct, intelligent and informative history of the Great Plains."

BIOGRAPHICAL/CRITICAL SOURCES: Journal of American History, June, 1980; *American Historical Review,* June, 1980; *Times Literary Supplement,* September 12, 1980; *Reviews in American History,* December, 1980; *Pacific Historical Review,* May, 1981.

* * *

WORTIS, Avi 1937-
(Avi)

PERSONAL: Given name is pronounced Ah-vee; born December 23, 1937, in New York, N.Y.; son of Joseph (a psychiatrist) and Helen (a social worker; maiden name, Zunser) Wortis; married Joan Gabriner (a weaver), November 1, 1963; children: Shaun, Kevin. *Education:* University of Wisconsin—Madison, B.A., 1959, M.A., 1962; Columbia University, M.S.L.S., 1964. *Home:* 89 West Bridge St., New Hope, Pa. 18938. *Agent:* Dorothy Markinko, McIntosh & Otis, Inc., 475 Fifth Ave., New York, N.Y. 10017. *Office:* Roscoe L. West Library, Trenton State College, Trenton, N.J. 08625.

CAREER: New York Public Library, Performing Arts Research Center, New York, N.Y., librarian for Theatre Collection, 1962-70; Trenton State College, Trenton, N.J., assistant professor and humanities librarian, 1970—. *Member:* Authors Guild, Authors League of America.

AWARDS, HONORS: Snail Tale: The Adventures of a Rather Small Snail was named one of the best books of the year by British Book Council, 1973; grants from New Jersey State Council on the Arts, 1974, 1976, 1978, and from Trenton State College, 1978; runner-up for Best Mystery of the Year, Mystery Writers of America, 1975, for *No More Magic,* and 1978, for *Emily Upham's Revenge;* nominations for William Allen White Award, Dorothy Canfield Fisher Award, Mark Twain Award, and Young Hoosier Book Award, 1979, all for *Night Journeys;* Christopher Book Award, 1980, for *Encounter at Easton;* Children's Choice Award, International Reading Association, 1980, for *Man from the Sky.*

WRITINGS: (Contributor) Ted Perry, editor, *Performing Arts Resources, 1974,* Drama Books, 1975.

Juveniles; all under name Avi; published by Pantheon, except as indicated: *Things That Sometimes Happen,* Doubleday, 1970; *Snail Tale: The Adventures of a Rather Small Snail,* 1972; *No More Magic,* 1975; *Captain Grey,* 1977; *Emily Upham's Revenge,* 1978; *Night Journeys,* 1979; *Encounter at Easton,* 1980; *Man from the Sky,* Knopf, 1980; *History of Helpless Harry,* 1980; *A Place Called Ugly,* 1981; *Sometimes I Think I Hear My Name,* 1982; *Shadrach's Crossing,* 1983; *The Fighting Ground,* Lippincott, 1984.

Contributor to periodicals, including *New York Public Library Bulletin, Top of the News, Children's Literature in Education,* and *Writer.* Book reviewer for *Library Journal, School Library Journal,* and *Perviews,* 1965-73.

WORK IN PROGRESS: Another novel, *St. Anthony's Wilderness.*

SIDELIGHTS: "I was born into a family with a writing tradition," Avi Wortis told *CA.* "Two great-grandfathers had been writers. My grandmother wrote. My parents aspired to become writers, too. . . . The idea that writing was a splendid thing to do could hardly fail to make its mark on me.

"Not surprisingly I was a big reader, reading all sorts of things—children's books, adult books, and not the least, comic books. Beyond reading, my grandparents were excellent storytellers, and my mother read to me and my twin sister, the poet Emily Leider, nightly. I can even recall telling my own tales of adventure to a slightly younger cousin when quite young. I do believe that if you want to be a writer you have to read a lot.

"Despite this background, my first desire was to become an airplane designer, then a biologist. After my junior year in high school, my parents were informed that I was in desperate need of a tutor, for somehow I had never taken the time to learn to write or to spell. That summer I met every day with a wonderful teacher who not only taught me writing basics, but also instilled in me the conviction that I wanted to be a writer myself. Perhaps it was stubbornness. It was generally agreed that was one thing I could not possibly do.

"My journey to children's literature was not direct. First it was the theatre, playwriting. Then it was writing novels for adult readers. In the meantime I had all kinds of jobs: sign printer (sometimes with spelling mistakes), carpenter, theatre coach, a whole host of jobs I never did with much satisfaction or success.

"At last I found an opportunity to work in a library; I was home at last. There I found no conflict between my desire to write and the demands of good librarianship. Quickly, I enrolled in library school, attending night classes. I still work as a librarian as well as write, so I am surrounded by books morning, noon, and night.

"Even then it was only when I had children of my own and had begun to invent stories for them that I thought of writing children's books. Once begun, I soon left other writing interests and concentrated on books for young people.

"While I am a fast writer and never at a loss for ideas, I do a very great deal of re-writing, over and over again. I'm never convinced I can't improve a book, be it only a word or two. After writing my books a number of times, I try them out on my children. Their reactions are always useful. More re-writing and my wife is asked to criticize. More re-writing and then visits to local schoolrooms. More re-writing, then to my agent. More re-writing, then to the publisher. Actually, I do my least re-writing then.

"The history of children's literature fascinates me, and from time to time I teach college courses or speak to groups about it. When I have the time, I visit flea markets and used book stores, for I am building up a collection of children's books. It makes me proud to put my own books in the midst of them all!"

BIOGRAPHICAL/CRITICAL SOURCES: New York Times Book Review, March 1, 1981.

WRIGHT, Beatrice A(nn)   1917-

PERSONAL: Born December 16, 1917, in New York, N.Y.; daughter of Jerome and Sonia (Gillen) Posner; married M. Erik Wright (a university professor and psychiatrist), September 7, 1940 (died May 11, 1981); children: Colleen (Mrs. Kenneth Rand), Erik, Woody. *Education:* Brooklyn College (now Brooklyn College of the City University of New York), B.A., 1938; University of Iowa, M.A., 1940, Ph.D., 1942. *Office:* Department of Psychology, University of Kansas, Lawrence, Kan. 66044.

CAREER: Swarthmore College, Swarthmore, Pa., instructor in psychology, 1942-43; counselor, U.S. Employment Service, 1944-46; Stanford University, Stanford, Calif., research associate, 1946-48; San Francisco State College (now University), San Francisco, Calif., assistant professor of psychology, 1948-49; employed in parent education programs, California State Board of Education, Adult Education Division, 1950-51; researcher and writer, 1951-59; University of Western Australia, Perth, visiting lecturer, 1960-61; University of Kansas, Lawrence, research associate in psychology, 1961-62; Menninger Foundation, Topeka, Kan., rehabilitation research and clinical fellow, 1962-64; University of Kansas, associate professor, 1964-67, professor of psychology, 1967—.

Lecturer at numerous conferences and symposia. Visiting professor at University of Oregon, summer, 1962, University of Hawaii, summer, 1965, California State College (now University), Dominguez Hills, 1968-69, and St. Edwards University, 1975; distinguished professor, Department of Exceptional Children, University of Southern California, summer, 1967. Member of United Cerebral Palsy Association task force on staff training and professional education, 1968-73; member of professional advisory council, National Easter Seal Society, 1973-81; member of advisory board, The Healing Community, 1974—, and Institut fur Soziale Rehabilitation, Switzerland, 1974—; member of advisory council, Kansas Rehabilitation Continuing Education Project, 1975—, and National Academy, Gallaudet College, 1979-81. Consultant to numerous institutions, including Kansas Neurological Institute, 1964-73, Institute of Logopedics, 1966, and New York State Rehabilitation Hospital, 1969.

MEMBER: Rehabilitation International (member of World Commission on Social Aspects of Disability, 1969—), National Rehabilitation Association, American Association of University Professors, American Psychological Association (fellow; president of division on psychological aspects of disability, 1962-63; member of council, 1966—), American Orthopsychiatric Association (fellow), Kansas Psychological Association (fellow), Sigma Xi.

AWARDS, HONORS: Kansas Book Award (shared with F. Heider), 1958, for *Interpersonal Relations;* research award of division of rehabilitation counseling, American Personnel and Guidance Association, 1959, for co-authored report, "Adjustment to Misfortune"; Child Study Association of America Book Award, 1960, for *Physical Disability: A Psychological Approach;* research grants from National Society for Crippled Children and Adults, Vocational Rehabilitation Administration, and various foundations.

WRITINGS: (With Roger G. Barker, Lee Meyerson, and Mollie R. Gonick) *Adjustment to Physical Handicap and Illness: A Survey of the Social Psychology of Physique and Disability,* Social Science Research Council, 1946, revised edition, 1953; (with F. Heider) *Interpersonal Relations,* Wiley, 1958; *Psy-*

chology and Rehabilitation, American Psychological Association, 1959; *Physical Disability: A Psychological Approach,* Harper, 1960, revised edition published as *Physical Disability: A Psychosocial Approach,* 1983.

Contributor: M. R. Harrower-Erickson and M. E. Steiner, *Large Scale Rorschach Techniques,* C. C Thomas, 1945; Eric Wittkower and R. A. Cleghorn, editors, *Recent Developments in Psychosomatic Medicine,* Lippincott, 1954; M. Harrower, editor, *Medical and Psychological Teamwork in the Care of the Chronically Ill,* C. C Thomas, 1955.

B. J. Biddle and E. J. Thomas, editors, *Role Theory,* Wiley, 1966; D. Malikin and H. Rusalem, editors, *The Vocational Rehabilitation of the Disabled,* New York University Press, 1969; M. H. Goldberg, editor, *Blindness Research: The Expanding Frontiers,* Pennsylvania State University Press, 1969.

Selected Articles from Artificial Limbs, Robert E. Krieger, 1970; L. A. Faas, editor, *The Emotionally Disturbed Child,* C. C Thomas, 1970; M. Schreiber, editor, *Social Work and Mental Retardation,* John Day, 1970; C. H. Patterson and H. A. Moses, editors, *Readings in Rehabilitation Counseling,* Stipes Publishing, 1971; A. Sales, editor, *Supervision of Rehabilitation Contacts: Selected Psychological Considerations,* Kansas State Teachers College, 1971; E. P. Trapp and P. Himelstein, editors, *Readings on the Exceptional Child,* revised edition, Appleton-Century-Crofts, 1972; Sales, editor, *Rehabilitation of Federal Target Groups: Psychological Considerations,* Kansas State Teachers College, 1973; Moses and Patterson, editors, *Research Readings in Rehabilitation Counseling,* Stipes Publishing, 1973; R. P. Marinelli and A. Dell Orto, editors, *The Psychological and Social Impact of Physical Disability,* Springer Publishing Co., 1977; J. Stubbins, editor, *Social and Psychological Aspects of Disability,* University Park Press, 1977; E. Chigier, editor, *New Dimensions in Rehabilitation,* Ben-Noon Press (Tel Aviv), 1978; B. Bolton and M. Jaques, editors, *The Rehabilitation Client,* University Park Press, 1979.

Co-author of book-length monograph "Adjustment to Misfortune: A Problem of Social Psychological Rehabilitation," published in *Artificial Limbs,* 1956. Contributor to *Exceptional Children, Journal of Abnormal and Social Psychology,* and numerous other professional journals. *Bulletin* (publication of American Psychological Association), editor, 1956-59, associate editor, 1959-69; contributing editor of *Rehabilitation Psychology,* 1970—; *Rehabilitation Literature,* editorial consultant, 1974-79, member of editorial board, 1980—; member of board of editors of *International Journal of Rehabilitation Research,* 1978—.

SIDELIGHTS: *Psychology and Rehabilitation* has been translated into Japanese; *Physical Disability* has been translated into Dutch and Polish.

* * *

WU, Yuan-li

EDUCATION: University of Berlin, language certificate, 1939, London School of Economics and Political Science, B.Sc., 1942, Ph.D., 1946. *Office:* Hoover Institution on War, Revolution, and Peace, Stanford, Calif. 94305.

CAREER: United Nations, New York, N.Y., member of Chinese delegation to Economic and Social Council, 1946, expert consultant, Economic Affairs Department, 1949-50; Stanford University, Stanford, Calif., lecturer in economics, 1952, coordinator of research, Human Relations Area Files Project, 1955-56; Marquette University, Milwaukee, Wis., associate professor of economics, 1956-58, director of Institute for Asian Studies, 1958-60; Hoover Institution on War, Revolution, and Peace, Stanford, consultant, beginning 1960; University of San Francisco, San Francisco, Calif., professor of economics, beginning 1960. Deputy Assistant Secretary of Defense, 1969-70; visiting fellow at Australian National University, summer, 1977. Member of advisory board to Asian Studies Center, Heritage Foundation, 1983. Consultant, Stanford Research Institute, 1960-63, 1965.

MEMBER: American Economic Association, Association for Asian Studies, Royal Economic Society (fellow), Mont Pelerin Society. *Awards, honors:* Social Science Research Council and American Council of Learned Societies research grant, 1961; Ford Foundation faculty research fellowship, 1961-62; Social Science Research Council research grant, 1962-63; Earhart Foundation research grants, 1970s.

WRITINGS: *Economic Warfare,* Prentice-Hall, 1952; *An Economic Survey of Communist China,* Bookman Associates, 1956, reprinted, Octagon, 1977; *Economic Development and the Use of Energy Resources in Communist China,* Praeger, 1963; *The Economy of Communist China: An Introduction,* Praeger, 1965; *The Steel Industry in Communist China,* Praeger, 1965; *Food and Agriculture in Communist China,* Praeger, 1966; (with H. C. Ling and Grace Hsiao Wu) *The Spatial Economy of Communist China: A Study on Industrial Location and Transportation,* Praeger, 1967; (editor) *Arms Control Arrangements for the Far East,* Hoover Institution Press, 1967; (editor) *Communist China and Arms Control: A Contingency Study,* Hoover Institution Press, 1968; *As Peking Sees Us: People's War in the United States and Communist China's America Policy,* Hoover Institution Press, 1969.

(With Robert B. Sheeks and others) *The Organization and Support of Scientific Research and Development in Mainland China,* Praeger, 1970; (editor) *China: A Handbook,* Praeger, 1973; *Raw Material Supply in a Multipolar World,* Crane, Russak, 1973; *The Strategic Land Ridge: Peking's Relations with Thailand, Malaysia, Singapore, and Indonesia,* Hoover Institution Press, 1975; *U.S. Policy and Strategic Interests in the Western Pacific,* Crane, Russak, 1975; *Japan's Search for Oil: A Case Study on Economic Nationalism and International Security,* Hoover Institution Press, 1977; (editor with Kung-Chia Yeh) *Growth, Distribution, and Social Change: Essays on the Economy of the Republic of China,* School of Law, University of Maryland, 1978; (editor) *The Economic Condition of Chinese Americans,* Pacific/Asian Mental Health Research Center, 1980; (with Chun-hsi Wu) *Economic Development in Southeast Asia: The Chinese Dimension,* Hoover Institution Press, 1980; (co-editor) *The Taiwan Experience,* Praeger, 1981; *Adversaries, Allies and Foreign Economic Policy,* American Enterprise Institute for Public Policy Research, 1984.

Author of papers on Communist China for Hoover Institution and U.S. Army. Articles on China have appeared in *Current History, Orbis, Contemporary China,* and other journals. Member of editorial board of *Asian Affairs* and *Sino-American Relations.*

WORK IN PROGRESS: Collaborating on *Mathematical Programming and the Theory of the Firm.*

SIDELIGHTS: Yuan-li Wu is competent in Japanese, Russian, German, Italian, French, and English.

WYLDER, Delbert E(ugene) 1923-

PERSONAL: Born October 5, 1923, in Jerseyville, Ill.; son of Robert Maines (a banker) and Blanche (Coulthard) Wylder; married Jean Williams, June 5, 1948; married second wife, Edith Perry Stamm (a professor of literature), July 15, 1965; children: (first marriage) Stephen John, William Creighton; (stepchildren) Paul Stamm. *Education:* Attended Coe College, 1941-42, and University of Illinois, 1942; National University of Mexico, summer study, 1946, 1947; University of Iowa, B.A., 1948, M.F.A., 1950, Ph.D., 1968. *Religion:* None. *Home address:* Route 7, Box 583, Murray, Ky. 42071. *Office:* Department of English, Murray State University, Murray, Ky. 42071.

CAREER: Bradley University, Peoria, Ill., instructor in English, 1950-52; University of Iowa, Iowa City, instructor in communication skills, 1952-58; Sandia Corp., Albuquerque, N.M., technical writer, 1958-61, consultant, 1963-65; University of New Mexico, Albuquerque, instructor and director of freshman English, 1961-65; Utah State University, Logan, Utah, assistant professor of American literature, 1965-66; Colorado State University, Fort Collins, assistant professor of American literature, 1966-68; Bemidji State College, Bemidji, Minn., associate professor of American literature, 1968-69; Southwest State University, Marshall, Minn., professor of literature and American language, 1969-77; Murray State University, Murray, Ky., professor of English and chairman of department, 1977—. *Military service:* U.S. Army Air Forces, 1942-45; fighter pilot in Italy; became second lieutenant; received Air Medal with three oak-leaf clusters. *Member:* Modern Language Association of America, American Studies Association, Western Literature Association (president, 1967; member of executive council, 1969-72), Rocky Mountain Modern Language Association, Midwest Modern Language Association, Kentucky Philological Association.

WRITINGS: (With W. L. Garner and D. G. Pugh) *Reading Factual Prose,* Scott, 1956; (with John C. Gerber and Jeffrey Fleece) *Toward Better Writing,* Prentice-Hall, 1958; *Hemingway's Heroes,* University of New Mexico Press, 1969; (contributor) Astro and Benson, editors, *Hemingway in Our Time,* Oregon State University Press, 1974; *Emerson Hough,* G. K. Hall, 1981; (contributor) Erisman and Etulain, editors, *Fifty Western Writers,* Greenwood Press, 1982. Also author of pamphlet on Emerson Hough in Steck-Vaughn Southwest Writer's Series. Contributor to literary periodicals. Associate editor, *Western American Literature,* 1966-68, member of editorial advisory board, 1968—; managing editor, *Crazy Horse,* 1979-81; editor, *Kentucky Philological Bulletin,* 1983.

WORK IN PROGRESS: Contributing to *History of Western American Literature;* with Etulain, editing a collection of Western short stories; continuing research in Western American literature; writing short stories.

Y

YAFFE, James 1927-

PERSONAL: Born March 31, 1927, in Chicago, Ill.; son of Samuel (a manufacturer) and Florence (Scheinman) Yaffe; married Elaine Gordon (a journalist), March 1, 1964; children: Deborah Anne, Rebecca Elizabeth, Gideon Daniel. *Education:* Yale University, B.A. (with highest honors), 1948. *Religion:* Jewish. *Home:* 1215 North Cascade, Colorado Springs, Colo. 80903. *Office:* Department of English, Colorado College, Colorado Springs, Colo. 80903.

CAREER: Free-lance writer; Colorado College, Colorado Springs, 1968—, began as writer-in-residence, currently professor of English. *Military service:* U.S. Navy, 1945-46. *Member:* American Association of University Professors, Writers Guild East, P.E.N., Phi Beta Kappa. *Awards, honors:* National Arts Foundation Award, 1967, for *Ivory Tower*.

WRITINGS: Poor Cousin Evelyn, Little, Brown, 1951; *The Good-for-Nothing*, Little, Brown, 1954; *What's the Big Hurry?*, Little, Brown, 1956; *Nothing but the Night*, Little, Brown, 1959; *Mister Margolies*, Random House, 1962; *Nobody Does You Any Favors*, Putnam, 1965; *The American Jews*, Random House, 1968; *The Voyage of the "Franz Joseph,"* Putnam, 1970; *So Sue Me!*, Saturday Review Press, 1972; *Saul and Morris, Worlds Apart*, Holt, 1982.

Plays: *The Deadly Game* (two-act; based on the novel *Trapps*, by Frederick Duerrenmatt; produced on Broadway at Longacre Theatre, February 2, 1960), Dramatists Play Service, 1960; (with Jerome Weidman) *Ivory Tower*, Dramatists Play Service, 1967; "Immorality Play," produced in Atlanta at Alliance Theatre, 1983.

Also author of *My Mother, the Detective*, a collection of short stories published in Japan. Author of television plays for "U.S. Steel Hour," "Studio One," "GE Theater," "Frontiers of Faith," "The Defenders," "Breaking Point," "Alfred Hitchcock Presents," "The Doctors and the Nurses," and other programs. Contributor of short stories to magazines, including *Esquire, Atlantic, Ladies Home Journal, Commentary*, and *Ellery Queen's Mystery Magazine*.

SIDELIGHTS: James Yaffe told *CA*: "My life has become divided between teaching literature and writing. I write nonfiction, but think of myself primarily as a novelist. The creation of character—that is, the act of empathizing and imagining other lives and bringing them to being in prose—absorbs, delights, frustrates, and obsesses me. It also absorbs me as a teacher; my chief purpose is to make students, in this age of impersonality and technology, understand the peculiar grandeur and moral importance of fiction."

F. Yorick Blumenfeld comments on Yaffe's book *The American Jews* in a *Newsweek* article: "One of the phenomena which mark off American Jews from other ethnic groups is the number of novels, plays and sociological studies they write about themselves. This self-preoccupation is developing into something of an obsession and James Yaffe's book is a gossipy, informative addition to this mushrooming shelf."

"James Yaffe's study of American Jews," writes Meyer Levin in the *New York Times Book Review*, "starts from scratch, defines everything from the American Jewish Committee around to the American Jewish Congress, but is by no means a dry statistical study. Yaffe is a gifted novelist with a wry (Jewish?) sense of humor."

BIOGRAPHICAL/CRITICAL SOURCES: Newsweek, November 11, 1968; *Commentary*, December, 1968; *Saturday Review*, December 7, 1968; *New York Times Book Review*, January 26, 1969; *The New Republic*, March 15, 1969.

* * *

YAMAMOTO, Kaoru 1932-

PERSONAL: Born March 18, 1932, in Tokyo, Japan; married Etsuko Hamazaki, April 6, 1959. *Education:* University of Tokyo, B.S., 1953; University of Minnesota, M.A., 1960, Ph.D., 1962. *Home:* 2042 East Aspen Dr., Tempe, Ariz. 85282. *Office:* College of Education, Arizona State University, Tempe, Ariz. 85287.

CAREER: Worked as an engineer and chemist for two industrial firms in Tokyo, Japan, 1953-57, and 1958-59; Kent State University, Kent, Ohio, assistant professor of education, 1962-65; University of Iowa, Iowa City, 1965-68, began as assistant professor, became associate professor of education; Pennsylvania State University, University Park, professor of education, 1968-72; Arizona State University, Tempe, professor of education, 1972—. *Member:* American Psychological Association (fellow), American Sociological Association, American Orthopsychiatric Association, Society for Psychological Anthropology, Society for Applied Anthropology, Society for Research in Child Development.

WRITINGS: (Editor) *College Student and His Culture: An Analysis*, Houghton, 1968; (editor and contributor) *Teaching: Essays and Readings*, Houghton, 1969; (contributor) *The Elementary School*, National Education Association, 1971; (editor and contributor) *The Child and His Image*, Houghton, 1972; (contributor) Edwin L. Herr, editor, *Vocational Guidance and Human Development*, Houghton, 1974; *Individuality*, C. E. Merrill, 1975; (contributor) Louise M. Berman and Jessie A. Roderick, editors, *Feeling, Valuing, and the Art of Growing: Insights into the Affective*, Association for Supervision and Curriculum Development, 1977; (editor and contributor) *Death in the Life of Children*, Kappa Delta Pi Press, 1978; (editor and contributor) *Children in Time and Space*, Teachers College Press, 1979. Author of experimental scoring manuals for "Minnesota Tests of Creative Thinking and Writing," 1964. Contributor of over 100 articles to professional journals. Editor, *American Educational Research Journal*, 1973-75.

WORK IN PROGRESS: *Myths, Symbols, and Children*; research in mental health and human development.

AVOCATIONAL INTERESTS: Winter sports.

* * *

YOUNG, Donald (Richard) 1933-

PERSONAL: Born June 29, 1933, in Indianapolis, Ind.; son of Thomas F. and Lucile (Boston) Young. *Education:* Indiana University, B.A., 1955; Butler University, M.A., 1964. *Home:* 166 East 61st St., Apt. 3-C, New York, N.Y. 10021.

CAREER: *Indianapolis Star*, Indianapolis, Ind., copy editor, 1955-63; *Encyclopedia Americana*, New York City, member of editorial staff, 1963-66; American Heritage Publishing Co., New York City, member of editorial staff, 1966-67; *Encyclopedia Americana*, senior editor in American history and political science, 1967-77; free-lance writer, photographer, and owner of rare coin business, 1978—. Photographs have been exhibited at Soho Photo Gallery, New York City, in group exhibitions of the Sierra Club, and on "Today" Show, NBC. *Military service:* U.S. Army, 1956-58. *Member:* American Society of Picture Professionals. *Awards, honors:* Indiana University Author Award, 1965; Award of Merit, State Historical Society of Wisconsin, 1971.

WRITINGS: *American Roulette: The History and Dilemma of the Vice-Presidency*, Holt, 1965, 2nd revised edition, Viking, 1974; (contributor) Kenneth W. Leish, editor, *The American Heritage Pictorial History of the Presidents of the United States*, Simon & Schuster, 1968; (editor and contributor) *Adventure in Politics: The Memoirs of Philip La Follette*, Holt, 1970; (author and photographer) *The Great American Desert* (juvenile), Messner, 1980.

Also contributor of photography to textbooks. Assistant editor, "Smithsonian Library" series, American Heritage, 1967—. Also contributor to *Encyclopedia Americana* yearbooks. Contributor of articles and photographs to periodicals, including *Saturday Review*, *Popular Photography*, *Utah Holiday*, and *Backpacking Journal*.

SIDELIGHTS: Donald Young told *CA*: "During the 1970s, I began, in a serious way, to explore the Southwest, especially the geologically-fascinating region of eastern and southern Utah known as the canyonlands. I have photographed this area extensively. Subjects of particular interest include the deep river canyons, Indian rock art (pictographs and petroglyphs), and unusual geological formations, such as natural arches and bridges. In addition to the book and articles cited above, twenty-one of my photographs appeared in an exhibition at the Soho Photo Gallery (New York), and I have been represented in several group exhibitions presented by the Sierra Club."

* * *

YOUNG, Elaine L.
See SCHULTE, Elaine L(ouise)

* * *

YOUNG, Rose
See HARRIS, Marion Rose (Young)

* * *

YUDKIN, Leon Israel 1939-

PERSONAL: Born September 9, 1939, in Northampton, England; son of Solomon and Ada (Mankin) Yudkin; married Meirah L. Goss (a lecturer), August 29, 1967. *Education:* University College, London, B.A., 1960, M.A. (with distinction), 1963. *Politics:* Non-party. *Religion:* Jewish. *Home:* 51 Hillside Ct., 409 Finchley Rd., London NW3 6HQ, England. *Office:* Department of Hebrew, University of Manchester, Manchester, Lancashire, England.

CAREER: University of London, London, England, lecturer in modern Hebrew, 1964-65; University of South Africa, Pretoria, lecturer in Judaica, 1965-66; University of Manchester, Manchester, England, lecturer in modern Hebrew, 1966—.

WRITINGS: *Isaac Lamdan: A Study in Twentieth Century Hebrew Poetry*, Cornell University Press, 1970; (editor with B. Tammuz) *Meetings with the Angel*, Deutsch, 1973; *Escape into Siege*, Routledge & Kegan Paul, 1974; *U. Z. Greenberg: On the Anvil of Hebrew Poetry*, Hebrew Publishing, 1975; *Jewish Writing and Identity in the Twentieth Century*, Croom Helm, 1982; *1948 and After: Aspects of Israeli Fiction*, Journal of Semitic Studies, 1984. Contributor of articles and columns to periodicals, including *Zionist Record*, *Jewish Chronicle*, *European Judaism*, *Jewish Quarterly*, *Federation Chronicle* (South Africa), *Moz ayim* (Israel), *Modern Hebrew Literature* (Israel), *Books Abroad* (United States), and *Jewish Spectator* (United States).

WORK IN PROGRESS: A study of Jewish fiction in England and France.

* * *

YUNKEL, Ramar
See MARTIN, Jose L(uis)

Z

ZAINU'DDIN, Ailsa
See ZAINU'DDIN, Ailsa G(wennyth) Thomson

* * *

ZAINU'DDIN, Ailsa G(wennyth) Thomson 1927-
(Ailsa Zainu'ddin)

PERSONAL: Surname is pronounced Zine-*oo*-din; born April 8, 1927, in Melbourne, Australia; daughter of Boyd Kyle (a teacher) and Thelma Beryl (a teacher; maiden name, Roberts) Thomson; married, December 10, 1954; husband's name Zainu'ddin (a teacher and translator); children: Nurel Zainila, Lisa Zafrina (both daughters). *Education:* Attended Methodist Ladies College, Melbourne; Melbourne University, B.A. (with honors), 1948, M.A., 1954, B.Ed., 1964; Monash University, Ph.D., 1983. *Office:* Education Faculty, Monash University, Clayton, Victoria, 3168 Australia.

CAREER: Melbourne University, Melbourne, Australia, history tutor, 1948-51, 1961-64; Canberra University College, Canberra, Australia, research assistant in history department, 1951-54; Ministry of Education, English Language Inspectorate, Jakarta, Indonesia, teacher, 1954-56; Monash University, Melbourne, Australia, lecturer in education, 1965—. *Member:* Australian and New Zealand History of Education Society, Australian Indonesian Association (Victoria), Australian Society of Authors, Victoria Historical Association, Immigration Reform Group, Victorian Women Graduates Association.

WRITINGS—Under name Ailsa Zainu'ddin, except as indicated: *How to Cook Indonesian Food,* Australian Indonesian Association, 1964, 3rd revised edition (under name Ailsa G. Thomson Zainu'ddin), 1982; *A Short History of Indonesia,* Cassell (Melbourne), 1968, Praeger, 1970, revised edition (under name Ailsa G. Thomson Zainu'ddin), Cassell, 1980; (author and translator) *Songs of Indonesia,* music by Helen McMahon, Heinemann (Melbourne), 1969; (contributor) D. Johnson, editor, *The Making of the Modern World,* Volume I, Benn, 1971; (with husband, Zainu'ddin) *Indonesia,* Angus & Robertson, 1973, McGraw, 1975; *Indonesia,* Longman (Australia), 1975.

Under name Ailsa G. Thomson Zainu'ddin: (Editor and contributor) *Kartini Centenary: Indonesian Women Then and Now,* Monash University, 1980; *They Dreamt of a School: A Centenary History of M.L.C. Kew, 1882-1982,* Hyland House (Melbourne), 1982; (contributor) Farley Kelly and Marilyn Lake, editors, *Very Different Lives,* Penguin, 1984; (contributor) R.J.W. Selleck and M. Sullivan, editors, *Not So Eminent Victorians,* Melbourne University Press, 1984.

Contributor of articles to *Melbourne Studies in Education;* editor of newsletters for Volunteer Graduate Association, 1956-62, and Australian Indonesian Association, 1964-66.

WORK IN PROGRESS: A history of Geelong Ladies' College, 1849-1906, with Marjorie R. Theobald; a study of the teaching of Japanese at Melbourne University; a study of education for girls in Victoria, Australia, 1872-1912; a comparison of the role of the Methodist Church in the higher education of women in Ontario, Great Britain and Australia.

SIDELIGHTS: Ailsa G. Thomson Zainu'ddin told *CA:* "My writing on Indonesia has been motivated by a desire to introduce Indonesia and Indonesians to their next-door neighbours in Australia. It is less an attempt to see ourselves as others see us than to see others as they see themselves. . . . Now I am moving away from my concern with Indonesia to a concern with the role of women in society, as I see considerable parallels between racism, colonialism and sexism." Zainu'ddin has traveled in Indonesia, Malaysia, the Philippines, Japan, Canada, the United States, England, and the Netherlands.

BIOGRAPHICAL/CRITICAL SOURCES: Ivan Southall, *Indonesia Face to Face,* Lansdowne, 1964.

* * *

ZEITLIN, Patty 1936-

PERSONAL: First syllable of surname rhymes with "rate"; born June 25, 1936, in Council Bluffs, Iowa; daughter of Henri Arthur (an acrobat, vaudeville actor, and musician) and Dorothea Pattison; married David Zeitlin, June 15, 1961 (divorced). *Education:* Studied at Los Angeles City College two years and at Center for Early Education, Los Angeles, one year; Antioch College, B.A., 1972; graduate study at Pacific Oaks College. *Religion:* "Emissary." *Address:* c/o Dorothea Kelsey, 1601 Glen View Rd., Apt. 64J, Seal Beach, Calif. 90740.

CAREER: Writer, composer, and performer. Teacher and director at cooperative nursery schools in Compton, Calif., 1957-

58, and Los Angeles, Calif., 1958-61; John Tracy Clinic, Los Angeles, teacher of the handicapped, 1960; Center for Early Education, Los Angeles, training teacher and music teacher, 1960-64; Little Village Nursery School, Los Angeles, teacher and music specialist, 1966-78; musical director and composer for Troubadour Puppeteers, seven years. Consultant on Head Start teacher training, San Fernando Valley State College (now California State University, Northridge), 1966-67; consultant to reading readiness workshop and extension classes, University of California, Los Angeles. *Awards, honors:* William A. Oliver Award, for "Flowers in This Land," and again for "Ballade of the Great Bullfrog"; awards from Woody Guthrie Festival of Songs, 1974, and Festival of New Music, 1976; grants from California Arts Council, 1979, for ecology songs.

WRITINGS: Castle in My City (nursery school songs; also see below), illustrated by children from Watts, Golden Gate, 1968; (also director) "Flesh-Colored Crayons" (musical), first produced in Los Angeles at Provisional Theatre, 1978; *A Song Is a Rainbow: Body Movement, Music, and Rhythm Instruments in the Nursery School and Kindergarten,* Scott, Foresman, 1982.

Record albums; produced by Educational Activities: *Won't You Be My Friend?*, 1972; *I'm Not Small,* 1973; *Spin, Spider, Spin,* 1974; *Everybody Cries, Sometimes,* 1974; *Rainy Day Dances, Rainy Day Songs,* 1975; *My Mommy Is a Doctor,* 1977; *Castle in My City,* 1978.

Arranger of a song in *Boll Weevil* and one in *Casey Jones,* both books published by Golden Gate, and of the musical score for a film adaptation of Mark Taylor's *Henry the Explorer.* Author with Marvin Harrison of and performer in KFRE-TV series using songs, puppets, and stories.

WORK IN PROGRESS: A musical play for children and adults; a television show for young children.

SIDELIGHTS: "The motivation for most of what I've written," Patty Zeitlin told *CA,* "has been the desire to open the lines of communication with children about how they feel and perceive their inner and outer worlds, and then to nourish the strong, life-enhancing force inside them as much as possible. Since I've worked directly with the very young for many years, I've had a chance to observe firsthand the powerful effect of stories and songs on their thinking, feelings, and behavior. I've discovered that these mediums can be a means to either encourage or disrupt the natural inclinations children have towards true friendship with one another, and a caring and respectful attitude towards the earth and all living things.

"I always acknowledge (without judgment) in what I write the fact that people aren't always loving and friendly and do at times feel scared, lonely, angry or sad. But I offer songs, stories, and movement activities as creative outlets that will allow children to be victorious in handling these strong feelings, instead of being victimized by them.

"In my opinion, however, nothing is more important than opening a child's heart to the truth that each of us is unique and beautiful and is here for a specific life-enhancing purpose. We have important work to do together as one body of humanity, but if we are ever to have a peaceful world, it must begin with the peace known by each of us. We must learn to live harmoniously with those closest, in our own households and neighborhoods. I think those of us who write, teach, or perform for children have a great opportunity and a responsibility, because we have a power that is almost magical when it comes to affecting and even transforming their lives.

"We must also remain conscious of the fact that we are living models of whatever we write about or teach, so writing can't really be separate from living. Children feel terribly let down by adults who proclaim one thing and do another. Even if we are unseen authors, who we are comes through in what we write. So it's up to us to do and live by what we know is the truth."

AVOCATIONAL INTERESTS: Acting.

* * *

ZIJDERVELD, Anton C(ornelis) 1937-

PERSONAL: Surname is pronounced *Zy-*der-veld; born November 21, 1937, in Malang, Indonesia; son of Jacobus Hendrik and Charlotte (Moulijn) Zijderveld; married Angelika Dissmann, May 25, 1967; children: Gabriele Maria, Susanne Micheline, Christiaan Robert, Thomas Tassilo. *Education:* University of Utrecht, B.D., 1960, M.Th., 1963; Hartford Seminary Foundation, Hartford, Conn., S.T.M., 1964; University of Leiden, Ph.D., 1966. *Home:* 52 Goirleseweg, Tilburg, Netherlands. *Office:* Faculty of Social Science, Tilburg University, 225 Hogeschoollaan, Tilburg, Netherlands.

CAREER: Wagner College, Staten Island, N.Y., assistant professor of sociology, 1966-68; Sir George Williams University, Montreal, Quebec, associate professor of sociology, 1968-70; Tilburg University, Tilburg, Netherlands, professor of sociology, 1971—.

WRITINGS: Institutionalisering: Een studie over het methodologisch dilemma der sociale wetenschappen, Hilversum, 1966, second edition, 1976; *The Abstract Society: A Cultural Analysis of Our Time,* Doubleday, 1970; *Sociologie van de zotheid: De humor als sociaal verschijnsel* (title means "Sociology of Folly: Humor as Social Phenomenon"), Meppel, 1971; *De Theorie van het symbolisch interactionisme* (title means "The Theory of Symbolic Interactionism"), Meppel, 1973, second edition, 1975; *De relativiteit van kennis en werkelijkheid: Inleiding tot de kennis-sociologie* (title means "The Relativity of Knowledge and Reality: Introduction to the Sociology of Knowledge"), Meppel, 1974; *On Cliches: The Supersedure of Meaning by Function in Modernity,* Routledge & Kegan Paul, 1979.

(With H. Adriaansens) *Vrijwillig initiatief en de verzorgingsstaat* (title means "Voluntary Initiative and the Welfare State"), Van Loghum Slaterus, 1981; *Reality in a Looking-Glass,* Routledge & Kegan Paul, 1982; *Steden zonder stedelijkheid* (title means "Cities without Urbanity"), Van Loghum Slaterus, 1982; *De culturele factor* (title means "The Cultural Factor"), Vuga, 1983; *Sociologie als cultuurwetenschap* (title means "Sociology as a Cultural Science"), Vuga, 1983.

AVOCATIONAL INTERESTS: Music (pianist), literature, the theater.

BIOGRAPHICAL/CRITICAL SOURCES: Times Literary Supplement, March 14, 1980.

* * *

ZIMMERMAN, Franklin B(ershir) 1923-

PERSONAL: Born June 20, 1923, in Wauneta, Kan.; son of Tony H. (a teacher, lumberman, and entrepreneur) and Asenith (Dungan) Zimmerman; married Rachel M. Phillip (divorced); married Mary Jane Fitch, 1976; children: (first marriage) Eve, Guy, Claire, Grace; (second marriage) Amy, Emily. *Education:* University of Southern California, B.A., 1949, M.A.,

1952, Ph.D., 1958; Oxford University, B.Litt., 1956. *Religion:* Protestant. *Home:* 225 South 42nd St., Philadelphia, Pa. 19104. *Office:* Department of Music, University of Pennsylvania, Philadelphia, Pa. 19104.

CAREER: State University of New York College at Potsdam, assistant professor of music, 1958-59; University of Southern California, Los Angeles, visiting associate professor, 1960, associate professor of music and chairman of department of music history and literature, 1961-64; Dartmouth College, Hanover, N.H., professor of music, 1964-68; University of Pennsylvania, Philadelphia, professor of music and chairman of department, 1968—. Visiting professor at University of Kentucky, 1967-68; senior fellow at University of California, Los Angeles, 1967, 1968; lecturer at Merton College, Oxford University, summer, 1969. French horn player with Tucson (Ariz.) Symphony Orchestra, 1938-40, 1945-46, with Sinfonia Nacional de Panama, 1941-42; conductor of Oxford University Repertory Orchestra, 1953-56; associate conductor of London Senior Orchestra, London Junior Orchestra, and Ernest Read Children's Concerts, all 1955-58; conductor of concerts at Dartmouth College, and in Los Angeles, Oxford, Philadelphia, New York, and London; lecturer on music in United States, England, Germany, and Austria. Founder and director of Pennsylvania Pro Musica, 1968—. *Military service:* U.S. Army, 1940-44; director of regimental band; served in New Guinea; became technical sergeant.

MEMBER: International Musicological Society, International Handel Society, American Musicological Society, Royal Music Society (London), Renaissance Society of America, College Music Society, Plainsong and Medieval Music Society (London), Gesellschaft fuer Musikforschung. *Awards, honors:* Fulbright scholar, 1953-55; American Council of Learned Societies fellowship, 1959-60, grant, 1963, 1971; International Gold Medal for Musicology, Arnold Bax Foundation, 1960.

WRITINGS: (Contributor) *Henry Purcell: Essays on His Music,* Oxford University Press, 1959; (editor) Henry Purcell, *I Will Love Thee, O Lord* (edition of anthem), University of Pittsburgh Press, 1961; *Henry Purcell, 1659-1695: An Analytical Catalogue of His Music,* Macmillan (London), 1963; (contributor) *Festschrift for O. E. Deutsch,* Baerenreiter, 1963; *Henry Purcell, 1659-1695: His Life and Times,* Volume I, Macmillan, 1967, revised edition, University of Pennsylvania Press, 1983; *Sound and Sense in Purcell's Single Songs,* University of California, 1968.

The Anthems of Henry Purcell (monograph), American Choral Foundation, 1972; (editor) *John Playford's Introduction to the Skill of Music* (facsimile edition), DeCapo Press, 1973; *Henry Purcell, 1659-1695: Melodic and Intervallic Indexes to His Complete Works,* Smith-Edwards-Dunlap, 1975; (contributor) *Louis Grabu's "Albion and Albanius": The Works of John Dryden,* Volume XV, University of California Press, 1975; (editor) *A Facsimile Edition of the William Kennedy Gostling Manuscript,* University of Texas Press, 1976; (contributor) *Festschrift for Charles Cudworth,* University of Cambridge Press, 1981; (editor) George Frederick Handel, *There in Blissful Shade,* Oxford University Press, 1983; (editor and author of introduction) *The Symphonies of C. F. Abel's Opus I,* Garland Publishing, 1983.

Contributor to *Hinrichsen's Yearbook,* 1958, 1959, *Anuario Musical,* Instituto de Musicologia (Barcelona), 1959, *Harvard Dictionary, Honegger's Dictionary,* and other reference works on music. Contributor of articles and reviews to music journals,

including *Musical Quarterly, Music and Letters, Journal of the American Musicological Society,* and *Musical Times.*

WORK IN PROGRESS: Revised edition of *Henry Purcell, 1659-1695: An Analytical Catalogue of His Music; Henry Purcell, 1659-1695: Analytical Essays on His Music; Juan del Encina: A Concordance of His Poetry and Music; G. F. Handel: A First-Line and Thematic Index to His Complete Works;* various essays and analytical studies of Handel's major works.

SIDELIGHTS: Franklin B. Zimmerman told *CA:* "Although the disputations continue as to what a musicologist really *should* do, and although no one has as yet created a definition of musicology satisfactory even to a majority of contending parties, my feeling has been that there is much room in the field for variety, and that all 'musicologists' should communicate as fully and as variously as they can with as many audiences as possible. While scholarly discipline must by no means be relaxed, I believe that the musicologist must from time to time venture forth from his narrow special field, perhaps laying aside rigorous methodologies and technical jargon momentarily so that he may address a broad, even a somewhat untutored public.

"I do not believe that musicologists fulfill their total responsibility through ever more specialized and technical discussions addressed only to their professional colleagues. My convictions in this regard lead even to the area of musical performance—a form of communication which almost anyone can understand, no matter how deep or technically complicated the research behind the performance may have been."

Zimmerman's musical activities as director of the Pennsylvania Pro Musica, an organization that specializes in musicological research and authentic revivals of masterworks of the past, have been well received by Philadelphia's music critics.

Max de Schauensee, for example, reviews a performance by Pro Musica in the *Sunday Bulletin,* writing that it "was one of which Philadelphia might well be proud. This was due to Dr. Frank Zimmerman's devotion to authenticity and his desire to present the work as closely to the composer's intentions and with [as much] fidelity to his period as was possible. The result of this research and integrity was that we realized the genius of Handel anew."

BIOGRAPHICAL/CRITICAL SOURCES: Sunday Bulletin, December 13, 1970.

* * *

ZINSSER, William (Knowlton) 1922-

PERSONAL: Surname is pronounced *Zin-*zer; born October 7, 1922, in New York, N.Y.; son of William H. and Joyce (Knowlton) Zinsser; married Caroline Fraser, October 10, 1954; children: Amy, John William. *Education:* Princeton University, A.B., 1944. *Politics:* Democrat. *Religion:* Presbyterian. *Home:* 45 East 62nd St., New York, N.Y., 10021. *Office:* Book-of-the-Month Club, 485 Lexington Ave., New York, N.Y. 10017.

CAREER: New York Herald Tribune, New York City, feature writer, 1946-49, drama editor, 1949-54, film critic, 1955-58, editorial writer, 1958-59; free-lance writer, 1959—; Yale University, New Haven, Conn., member of English faculty, 1970-79, master of Branford College, 1973-79; Book-of-the-Month Club, New York City, executive editor, 1979—. Entertainment critic on "Sunday," National Broadcasting Co. television program, 1963-64. Member of board of governors, Brooklyn Museum, 1965-72. *Military service:* U.S. Army, 1943-45;

in North Africa and Italy; became sergeant. *Member:* Century Association, Coffee House (both New York).

WRITINGS: Any Old Place with You, Simon and Schuster, 1957; *Seen Any Good Movies Lately?,* Doubleday, 1958; *Search and Research,* New York Public Library, 1961; *The City Dwellers,* Harper, 1962; (author with Howard Lindsay, Harry Golden, Walt Kelly, and John Updike) *Five Boyhoods,* Doubleday, 1962; *Weekend Guests,* Harper, 1963; *The Haircurl Papers,* Harper, 1964; *Pop Goes America,* Harper, 1966; *The Paradise Bit* (novel), Little, Brown, 1967; *The Lunacy Boom,* Harper, 1970; *On Writing Well: An Informal Guide to Writing Nonfiction,* Harper, 1976; 2nd edition, 1980; *Writing with a Word Processor,* Harper, 1983; *Willie and Dwike: An American Profile,* Harper, 1984.

Columnist for *Look,* 1967, *Life,* 1968-72, and *New York Times,* 1977. Contributor to magazines, including *New Yorker.*

SIDELIGHTS: "Remember, then, that words are the only tools that you will be given," William Zinsser advises in *On Writing Well: An Informal Guide to Writing Nonfiction.* "Learn to use them with originality and care. Value them for their strength and their infinite diversity." While in this book Zinsser draws on his thirteen-year experience as writer, critic, and drama editor for the *New York Herald Tribune* to explain the rudiments of good writing to beginners, in his *Writing with a Word Processor* Zinsser himself is the beginner and he writes about his initiation into the world of writing with computers. Despite this difference, both books contain what a *New York Times* reviewer calls "a discussion and an exhortation on good writing."

The advice contained in *On Writing Well* originally was part of a course in writing nonfiction that Zinsser started at Yale University in the seventies. The course proved so popular that Zinsser decided to expand it into a book. It, too, has been a success; currently in its second edition, the volume has sold more than 225,000 copies and is used as a textbook by writing teachers in colleges and universities throughout the United States.

The emphasis of Zinsser's book, according to Joseph Barbato in the *Chronicle of Higher Education,* is "the need for humanity and warmth in all forms of nonfiction writing." Zinsser stresses a similar point in *Writing with a Word Processor.* The use of a word processor, he notes, helps the writer "to achieve three cardinal goals of good writing—clarity, simplicity, and humanity." However, while a word processor can aid a good writer, the machine will not improve a writer's style. To do this, Zinsser recommends simply to write. "A professional writer must establish a daily schedule and stick to it," he observes in *On Writing Well.*

And, during this time spent writing, the writer should follow the tenets of good nonfiction writing which Zinsser summarizes for Barbato: "Simplify. Be clear. Get rid of pomposity in your writing. Above all, be yourself."

BIOGRAPHICAL/CRITICAL SOURCES: William Zinsser, *On Writing Well: An Informal Guide to Writing Nonfiction,* Harper, 1976, 2nd edition, 1980; *Washington Post Book World,* February 24, 1980; *Chronicle of Higher Education,* September 23, 1981; Zinsser, *Writing with a Word Processor,* Harper, 1983; *New York Times,* March 20, 1983, March 31, 1983; *Chicago Tribune Book World,* September 25, 1983.

* * *

ZIOLKOWSKI, Theodore (Joseph) 1932-

PERSONAL: Born September 30, 1932, in Birmingham, Ala.; son of Miecislaw (a pianist) and Cecilia (Jankowski) Ziolkowski; married Yetta Goldstein, March 26, 1951; children: Margaret Cecilia, Jan Michael, Eric Joseph. *Education:* Duke University, A.B., 1951, A.M., 1952; graduate study at University of Innsbruck, 1952-53; Yale University, Ph.D., 1957. *Politics:* Democrat. *Home:* Wyman House, 50 Springdale Rd., Princeton, N.J. 08540. *Office:* Office of the Graduate School, 205 Nassau Hall, Princeton University, Princeton, N.J. 08544.

CAREER: Yale University, New Haven, Conn., instructor, 1956-60, assistant professor of German, 1960-62; Columbia University, New York, N.Y., associate professor, 1962-64; Princeton University, Princeton, N.J., professor of German, 1964-69, Class of 1900 Professor of Modern Languages, 1969—, professor of comparative literature, 1975, chairman of German department, 1973-79, dean of Graduate School, 1979—. Visiting professor at Rutgers University, 1966, Yale University, 1968, 1975, and City College of the City University of New York, 1971; visiting lecturer at University Center in Virginia, 1971, and Piedmont University Center of North Carolina, 1971; Dancy Memorial Lecturer at University of Montevallo, 1973; Christopher Longest Lecturer at University of Mississippi, 1979; Patten Foundation Lecturer at Indiana University, 1980. Chairman of New York State doctoral evaluation program in German, 1975-80.

MEMBER: Internationale Vereingung der Germanisten, Modern Language Association of America, American Association of Teachers of German, American Comparative Literature Association, Authors Guild, Authors League of America, American Academy of Arts and Sciences.

AWARDS, HONORS: Fulbright research fellow in Germany, 1958-59; American Philosophical Society grant, 1959; Guggenheim fellow, 1964-65; American Council of Learned Societies fellow, 1972-73, 1976; James Russell Lowell Prize in Criticism, Modern Language Association of America, 1973, and National Book Award nomination in philosophy and religion, both for *Fictional Transfigurations of Jesus;* National Endowment for the Humanities fellow, 1978; Howard T. Behrman Award for distinguished achievement in humanities, 1978; Lucius Wilbur Cross Medal for distinguished achievement.

WRITINGS: Hermann Broch, Columbia University Press, 1964; *Hermann Hesse,* Columbia University Press, 1966; (editor) Hermann Hesse, *Autobiographical Writings,* Farrar, Straus, 1972; (editor) Hesse, *Stories of Five Decades,* Farrar, Straus, 1972; (editor) *Hesse: A Collection of Critical Essays,* Prentice-Hall, 1973; (editor and author of introduction) Hesse, *My Belief: Essays on Life and Art,* Farrar, Straus, 1974; (editor) Hesse, *Tales of Student Life,* Farrar, Straus, 1976; (with Stanley A. Corngold and Michael Curschmann) *Aspekte der Goethezeit,* Vandenhoeck & Ruprecht, 1977; *Der Schriftsteller Hermann Hesse,* Suhrkamp Verlag, 1979; (editor and author of introduction) Hesse, *Pictor's Metamorphoses, and Other Fantasies,* Farrar, Straus, 1982.

Published by Princeton University Press: *The Novels of Hermann Hesse: A Study in Theme and Structure,* 1965; (translator with wife, Yetta Ziolkowski) Herman Meyer, *The Poetics of Quotation in the European Novel,* 1968; *Dimensions of the Modern Novel: German Texts and European Contexts,* 1969; *Fictional Transfigurations of Jesus,* 1972; *Disenchanted Images: A Literary Iconology,* 1977; *The Classical German Elegy, 1795-1950,* 1980; *Varieties of Literary Thematics,* 1983.

Contributor of articles to literary journals in the United States and Germany. Former member of editorial board of *Germanic*

Review, Dimension, and *PMLA.* Princeton University Press, former member of editorial board, member of board of trustees, 1982-85.

WORK IN PROGRESS: Romanticism and Its Institutions.

SIDELIGHTS: Theodore Ziolkowski is convinced that literature cannot be studied from a national point of view alone, and that criticism is by its very nature essentially comparative literature. This conviction is apparent in his work, particularly in *The Novels of Hermann Hesse: A Study in Theme and Structure.* Concentrating on Hesse's six major novels, the book begins with an analysis of Hesse's attitudes toward such thinkers as Nietzsche, Dostoevsky, and Jung, as well as his interest in German Romanticism and Oriental philosophy. "For Ziolkowski," writes Joseph Mileck in *Modern Philology,* "Hesse is a writer and not just a German writer. His study addresses itself not to the Germanist but to the serious and sensitive student of literature. Hesse's major works are carefully analyzed and meaningfully related thematically and structurally to the present and the past. Shortcomings notwithstanding, this is a brilliant, informative, and delightfully provocative book employing a methodology well worth emulating."

In *Modern Language Journal,* K. W. Jonas calls *The Novels of Hermann Hesse* "a real contribution to the field of comparative literature." Pointing out that the book is written for the general reader, Jonas adds that the specialist too "will be richly rewarded for the time spent in working his way through this book. . . . There are few books which a reviewer can recommend so wholeheartedly and without reservations as this one, and [Ziolkowski] is to be congratulated on a job well done. It is a must not only for every student of modern German literature but for anyone seriously interested in the contemporary novel."

Nominated for a National Book Award in philosophy and religion, Ziolkowski's *Fictional Transfigurations of Jesus* surveys a wide range of nineteenth- and twentieth-century novels that incorporate some element of the original Gospel story. From the works of such writers as Hermann Hesse, Carlo Coccioli, Guenter Grass, Graham Greene, and William Faulkner, Ziolkowski concludes that Jesus Christ "has become a 'mythic figure,' a 'culture hero,'" notes Thomas Molnar in the *Georgia Review,* "and as such, responding quite well to the novelist's probing, no matter to what school the latter belongs. Thus there has been the Christian-socialist Jesus, the comrade Jesus, the Freudian, the mythical, the rock Jesus—and Ziolkowski's own 'scholar-critic's Jesus,' as he calls him at the end of his book with a touch of regret."

"Ziolkowski positively establishes the validity of his 'transfigurational' categories," says Michael Cooke in the *Yale Review,* "and . . . [distinguishes them] from one another by an enriching use of the prism of biography, cultural bias, and political and psychological investigation of the several authors. In terms of sheer critical explication, the discussion of authorial perspective . . . proves very fruitful, and on the whole the pages on Benito Perez Galdos, Gerhart Hauptmann, and above all Guenter Grass abound with keen insight and lucid reflection."

Both Cooke and Molnar, however, question Ziolkowski's thesis that Jesus has become a mythic figure. Molnar, who argues Jesus "may still be a haven for novelists and other truth-seekers," maintains that the Jesus story "is not a myth; it is an event in time, in everybody's time, the writer's and the reader's. This is so true that although Judas in 'Jesus Christ Superstar' warns Jesus not to believe the myth grown up around him . . . , the public at the musical sees in the whole thing a religious message."

Cooke concludes that Ziolkowski, "perhaps too idealistically devoted to the secular and pragmatic setting of his subject, in a sense explains rather than understands the dynamics of transfiguration; by making us see how, he forces us to ask why Jesus as it were keeps coming back, and this crucial question goes largely unacknowledged. . . . [Thus,] it is the intrinsic power of the story of Jesus that, at some cost, *Fictional Transfigurations* neglects. Conceivably, of course, it has all drained away, and we are dealing with incidental allusions. . . . But this is unrealistic; it appears rather that the transfigurations work because the story somehow matters, and that, even where parody or blasphemy is involved, an original force is being confessed."

Molnar, nevertheless, commends Ziolkowski's methodology, for "it is almost invariably an opportunity to bring out latent themes, cross-influences, symptoms of this or that orientation of our culture. Ziolkowski remarks, for example, that Jesus-novels around the turn of the century—by Galdos, Fogazzaro, Hauptmann, etc.—show their author's emotional commitment to Christ (whether a positive or negative one) but that the present generation, Lars Goerling, Guenter Grass or Gore Vidal, regard him with genuine indifference, as a mere sight of the cultural panorama, fictionally useful." For this reason, a *Times Literary Supplement* critic believes *Fictional Transfigurations of Jesus* will "do much to bridge the two worlds of a vulnerable religious tradition and its literary progeny."

BIOGRAPHICAL/CRITICAL SOURCES: Modern Language Journal, March, 1966, April, 1978; *Modern Philology,* February, 1967; *Yale Review,* spring, 1973, autumn, 1977; *Commonweal,* April 20, 1973; *Times Literary Supplement,* August 17, 1973, November 18, 1977, October 3, 1980; *Georgia Review,* spring, 1974; *Sewanee Review,* spring, 1978.

—Sketch by James G. Lesniak

* * *

ZWEIFEL, Frances W. 1931-

PERSONAL: Born May 26, 1931, in Hampton, Va.; daughter of Robert William (an air force officer) and Helen (Huber) Wimsatt; married Richard Zweifel (a museum curator and herpetologist), July 30, 1956; children: Matthew, Kenneth, Ellen. *Education:* Trinity College, B.A., 1952; University of Arizona, M.A., 1956. *Politics:* "Ambiguous." *Religion:* Roman Catholic. *Home:* 412 Glendale Rd., Northvale, N.J. 07647.

CAREER: Free-lance biological illustrator. American Museum of Natural History, New York, N.Y., scientific illustrator, 1956-58.

WRITINGS: (Self-illustrated) *A Handbook of Biological Illustration,* University of Chicago Press, 1961; (illustrator) Evelyn Shaw, *Alligator,* Harper, 1972; *Bony,* Harper, 1977; (self-illustrated) *Pickle in the Middle and Other Easy Snacks* (juvenile), Harper, 1979; *Animal Baby-Sitters* (juvenile; Junior Literary Guild selection), Morrow, 1981; (contributor of illustrations) Samuel Luoma, *Introduction to Environmental Biology,* Macmillan, in press.